Specially for the Allens

"Merry Christmas"

Love,
Nick & N
Dec 2012.

EXPLORE
AUSTRALIA

EXPLORE
AUSTRALIA
2013

CONTENTS

INTRODUCTION	iv

NEW SOUTH WALES	**viii**
Sydney	4
Regions	22
Towns from A to Z	24

AUSTRALIAN CAPITAL TERRITORY	**106**
Canberra	108

VICTORIA	**120**
Melbourne	124
Regions	140
Towns from A to Z	142

SOUTH AUSTRALIA	**206**
Adelaide	210
Regions	222
Towns from A to Z	224

WESTERN AUSTRALIA	**268**
Perth	272
Regions	286
Towns from A to Z	288

NORTHERN TERRITORY	**340**
Darwin	344
Regions	354
Towns from A to Z	356

QUEENSLAND	370
Brisbane	374
Regions	388
Towns from A to Z	390

TASMANIA	452
Hobart	456
Regions	468
Towns from A to Z	470

ROAD ATLAS	500
Inter-city Route Maps	504
New South Wales and ACT	507
Victoria	530
South Australia	552
Western Australia	569
Northern Territory	587
Queensland	598
Tasmania	620

INDEX	631

EXPLORE AUSTRALIA

Australia is breathtaking in beauty, daunting in size and rich in diversity. There is so much to explore as you travel the length and breadth of this extraordinary country. For centuries 'The Great South Land' remained undiscovered and unexplored by Europeans, and it is this relative 'newness' that has helped protect so many of its secrets. As a visitor you have an astonishing 7 686 850 square kilometres of land to cover – so plan your trip wisely!

For more than 50 000 years before European settlement, Aboriginal people lived on the continent, occupying country across the landscape, including its driest deserts. Living in great affinity with the land on which they were dependent, they established rich, diverse and highly spiritual cultures with sacred places, Dreaming tracks and art sites. With permission, much of this can be explored by travellers who are prepared to sit, listen and learn from Indigenous Australians.

Australians live and work right across this vast continent. Graziers, farmers, jackaroos and jillaroos, and miners work the land and there are plenty of outback rural towns where the warm greeting you'll receive will be as welcome as the cold drink served at the local pub.

However, most Australians live in coastal cities. The expanding east-coast cities of Sydney, Melbourne and Brisbane are the three largest in the country and are representative of people from around the world. They have thriving arts, music, sport and dining cultures. The other capital and major cities also have unique flavours and heritage, and are worth visiting in their own right.

A visit to Australia means you must travel widely, taste boldly and be tempted to find out what's around that next corner. If you're lucky (you are travelling in the lucky country after all!), you might just uncover another of Australia's secrets.

WESTERN
AUSTRALIA

PERTH

INDIGENOUS AUSTRALIANS

For an estimated 50–65 000 years, Aboriginal people have lived in Australia. They are believed to have occupied the country from the north, reaching Tasmania about 35 000 years ago. Aboriginal people were traditionally separated into some 600 different societies, most with completely different languages from those around them. Rather than settling in one spot, they lived and moved around their 'country'.

There are close to half a million Aboriginal people in Australia today, and although much of the cultures have been destroyed or damaged by European settlement, many Aboriginal communities still proudly carry on rich traditions, and have some of the oldest surviving cultural practices in the world.

Must-see Indigenous places and experiences:

- Uluru-Kata Tjuta National Park, Northern Territory
- Kimberley rock art sites, Western Australia
- Kakadu National Park/Arnhem Land, Northern Territory
- Thursday Island, Torres Strait
- Burrup Peninsula, Western Australia
- Bunya Mountains, Queensland
- Tjapukai Aboriginal Cultural Park, Queensland

[ABORIGINAL DANCERS AT THE BARUNGA FESTIVAL, NORTHERN TERRITORY]

WORLD HERITAGE SITES

[PORT ARTHUR HISTORIC SITE, TASMANIA]

Australia has 18 listings on UNESCO's World Heritage register. Most are areas of extreme natural beauty and hold exceptional conservation value. However, the latest additions placed on the list in 2010 included 11 penal sites, such as Port Arthur in Tasmania and Fremantle Prison in Western Australia. There are two other Australian sites listed exclusively for cultural reasons: the Sydney Opera House and Melbourne's Royal Exhibition Building in Carlton Gardens.

The other listings are:

- Australian Fossil Mammal Sites: Riversleigh, Boodjamulla (Lawn Hill) National Park, Queensland and Naracoorte Caves, South Australia
- Fraser Island, Queensland
- Gondwana Rainforests, Queensland and northern NSW
- Great Barrier Reef, Queensland
- Greater Blue Mountains Area, New South Wales
- Heard and McDonald Islands, sub-Antarctic islands
- Kakadu National Park, Northern Territory
- Lord Howe Island Group, New South Wales
- Macquarie Island, sub-Antarctic island
- Purnululu National Park, Western Australia
- Shark Bay, Western Australia
- Tasmanian Wilderness
- Uluru-Kata Tjuta National Park, Northern Territory
- Wet Tropics of Queensland
- Willandra Lakes Region, New South Wales

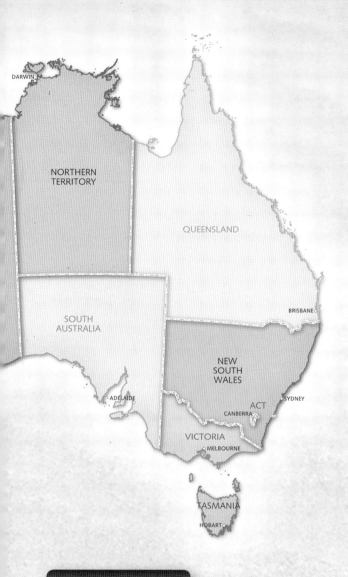

BUILDING A STYLE

[FEDERATION SQUARE, MELBOURNE, VICTORIA]

As an eclectic mix of cultures, Australia has a rich diversity of styles on which to build its architecture. From the Aboriginal humpy or shelter, to the world-famous white sails of the Sydney Opera House, architects have much to admire and ponder.

Much of suburbia is dominated by production-line 'McMansions', but occasionally hints of Australia peak through: bits of corrugated iron; large, airy verandahs; the classic 'Queenslander' up on stilts; and in historic or official buildings, the prolific use of granite or local sandstone.

Increasingly, Australian architecture is focusing on sustainability. This can mean everything from solar technology to the use of natural heating and cooling, and the return of sustainably harvested timbers – each making use of our resourceful land.

FOOD AND WINE

[VINEYARDS IN THE BAROSSA VALLEY, SOUTH AUSTRALIA]

Australia is one of the world's major food producers. Wherever you travel, food production is apparent on the landscape, from the vast inland sheep and cattle stations, to the canefields of New South Wales and Queensland. Coastal towns abound in fresh seafood, and increasingly there is an interest in other foods indigenous to Australia, such as bush plums, nuts, herbs and kangaroo. Visit the many farm gates or food trails to access this local produce, or pick up fresh bargains at farmers' markets.

Australia is consistently in the world's top ten producers of wine, making more than 1.4 billion litres a year. Australia's major wine growing regions are nearly all tourist attractions in their own right, with delightful B&Bs, historic places to explore and cellar doors galore.

Don't miss these experiences:

- Honey from Ligurian bees on Kangaroo Island, South Australia
- Margaret River's chocolate, dairy and wines, Western Australia
- Sydney Fish Markets, New South Wales
- Tasmania's pinot noir, cheese and berries
- Queensland's mangoes and other tropical fruits
- Historic wine regions such as Rutherglen, Victoria
- Barramundi and crocodile, Northern Territory

NATURAL WONDERS

One of the great attractions of travelling around Australia is the unique plant and animal life. You'll see startlingly white ghost gums set against red rocks in Central Australia, and in contrast, lime-green cushion plants in the Tasmanian highlands. Australia is exceedingly rich in diversity, in fact, south-western Australia is one of the world's major biodiversity hotspots.

Australia holds more than 18 000 flowering plant species, as well as grasses and innumerable fungi and lichens, and thousands of these species are unique to this country.

Our animal life includes the largest collection of marsupials on earth, as well as more than 860 bird species (about half of which are only found here), a similar number of reptile species, and more than 200 species of frog. In the water you can also find more than 4400 fish species, and 400 coral species on the Great Barrier Reef alone.

Australia is truly a land of natural wonders.

[SNORKELLING IN THE GREAT BARRIER REEF, QUEENSLAND]

TRAVEL THROUGH HISTORY

Although still relatively young, Australia has an interesting and rich history since European discovery, and many of the most important sites can be visited and experienced by travellers today. Wars on home soil have been mercifully limited, but there has been no end to other challenges and conflicts, including floods, droughts, fires and plagues.

Through this turbid history, the legend of the 'Australian spirit' has been forged: easygoing outdoor-loving people who will barrack for the underdog, stick by their mates, challenge authority, and do it all with a sense of humour that's as dry as the Simpson Desert.

~50 000 YEARS AGO

First people arrive in northern Australia.

1629

[THE VOYAGE OF THE *BATAVIA*]

The Dutch ship *Batavia*, one of several to have explored the Great South Land, is wrecked on the Houtman Abrolhos, WA. See timbers from the wreck at the Western Australian Maritime Museum, at Fremantle, and discover more about our early maritime explorers.

1770

[JAMES COOK]

Englishman Captain James Cook, in the *Endeavour*, sights the east coast, landing several times. Visit Botany Bay, in Sydney, and the town of Seventeen Seventy, 400 km north of Brisbane.

1788

The First Fleet arrives, establishing the first settlement at Botany Bay, then Sydney Cove.

1803

A settlement is established on the Derwent River in Tasmania – Hobart is born.

1813

Blaxland, Lawson and Wentworth find a way through the Blue Mountains, New South Wales, one of the barriers to settling further west. See the legendary tree they are believed to have blazed near Katoomba.

1824

The Moreton Bay Penal Settlement is established near what will become Brisbane.

1830s

Port Arthur in Tasmania becomes one of the prime penal colonies in Australia.

1851

[ZEALOUS GOLD DIGGERS IN BENDIGO]

Gold is discovered in New South Wales and Victoria, leading to mass gold rushes. Relive this lustrous history in Victorian towns such as Clunes, Bendigo and Ballarat.

1860–61

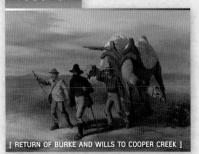

[RETURN OF BURKE AND WILLS TO COOPER CREEK]

Explorers Burke and Wills cross the continent from south to north, but then die on the return, tragic journey. See the infamous Dig Tree and death sites along Cooper Creek near Innamincka, in the far north-east corner of South Australia.

1872

The 3200 km Overland Telegraph line between Darwin and Port Augusta, South Australia, is completed, allowing fast communication between Australia and the rest of the world. The repeater station at Alice Springs has been partially restored.

1880

[PORTRAIT OF NED KELLY]

Australia's best-known bushranger, Ned Kelly, is captured at Glenrowan, in Victoria, and hung at Melbourne Gaol.

1891

Shearers across Australia go on strike for better pay and conditions. The protests are centred around Barcaldine in Queensland.

MID-1890s

Gold is discovered in remote Western Australian fields, particularly around Kalgoorlie and Coolgardie, prompting another gold rush.

1901

[MELBOURNE'S ROYAL EXHIBITION BUILDING]

The six Australian colonies form the Commonwealth of Australia in a grand celebration at the Royal Exhibition Building in Melbourne's Carlton Gardens. The building is now listed on the World Heritage register.

1908

Land at the foothills of the Australian Alps is chosen as the site of the national capital. It is later named Canberra meaning meeting place.

1914–18

World War I: Australia fights against Germany and its allies. Vessels carrying ANZAC soldiers bound for Gallipoli depart from Albany in Western Australia. Learn more of this history at the Australian War Memorial in Canberra.

1927

The former Parliament House opens in Canberra. It now houses the Museum of Australian Democracy.

1939–45

[AUSTRALIAN SOLDIERS DURING WORLD WAR II]

World War II: Australia fights in Europe and the Pacific. Darwin is bombed and Sydney attacked by Japanese submarines. There are still plenty of old WW II airstrips hidden in the dense jungles and scrub of the Top End.

1949–74

Australia's largest engineering project to date, the Snowy Mountains Hydro-Electric Scheme, is built.

1955–63

Large atomic bombs are detonated for testing at Maralinga in western South Australia. Visit the ground zero site at Emu Junction, or the museum at Woomera.

1965

Australia joins the Vietnam War, last combat troops come home in 1972.

1973

[GOUGH WHITLAM AT THE NATIONAL PRESS CLUB]

Legal end to the white Australia policy with the Whitlam government.

1974

Cyclone Tracy devastates Darwin on Christmas Eve.

1988

[CANBERRA'S NEW PARLIAMENT HOUSE]

At the bicentenary of settlement, Australia's new Parliament House opens in Canberra.

1992

Native land title is recognised after a decade of litigation. This is known as the 'Mabo' Judgement.

2000

Olympic Games held in Sydney. Tour the Olympic site at Homebush.

2008

On February 13, Prime Minister Kevin Rudd apologises for the hurt caused by decades of state-sponsored ill-treatment of Indigenous Australians.

2009

In February, Victoria suffers the most catastrophic bushfire disaster in Australian history, with the loss of 173 lives. Saturday, February 7, becomes known as Black Saturday. See towns that have rebuilt in places like Kinglake and Marysville.

2011

In January, three-quarters of Queensland is declared a disaster zone as a result of flooding. Highly affected populated areas included Toowoomba, Brisbane and Ipswich. In February severe tropical cyclone Yasi devastates Queensland again.

NEW SOUTH WALES IS...

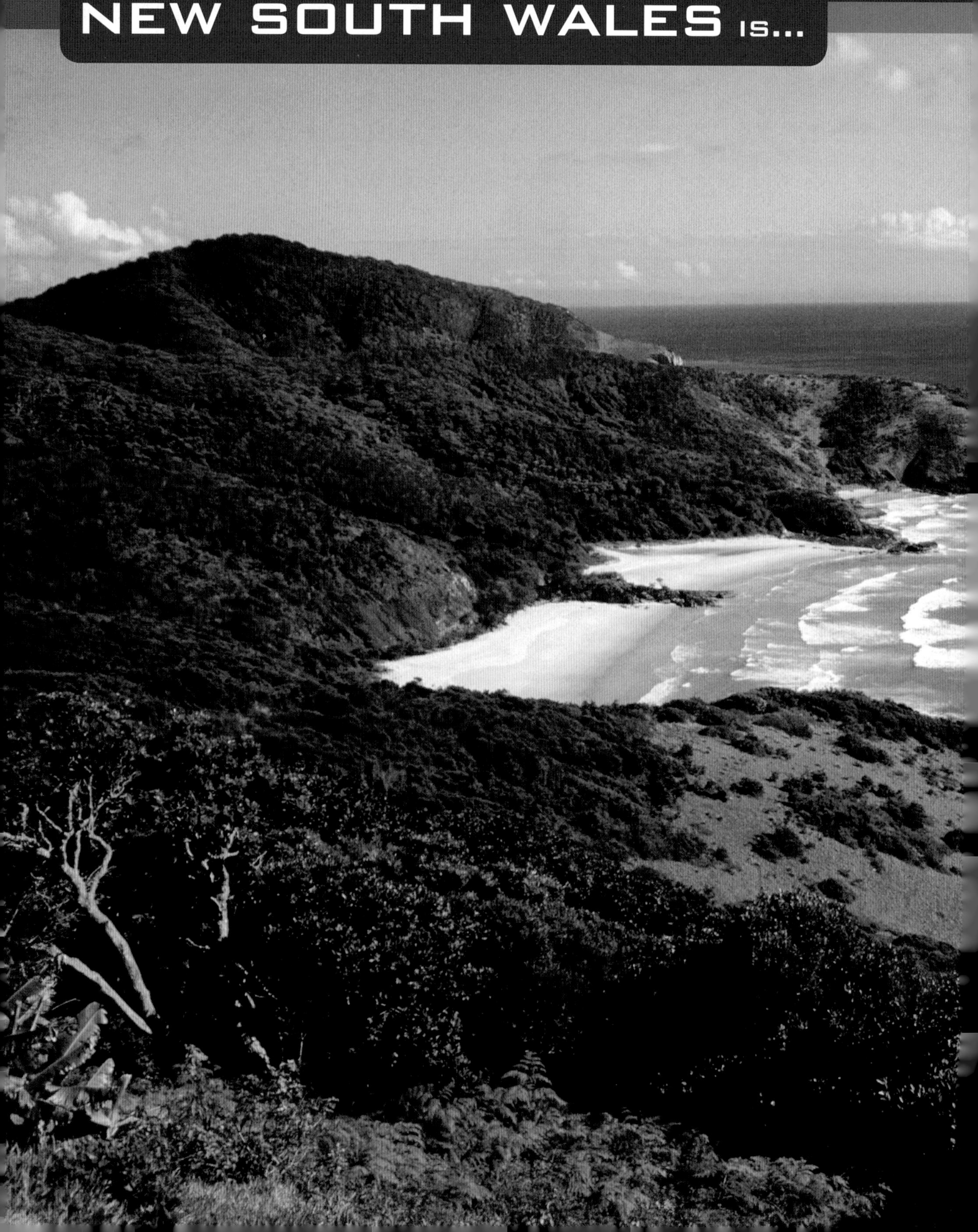

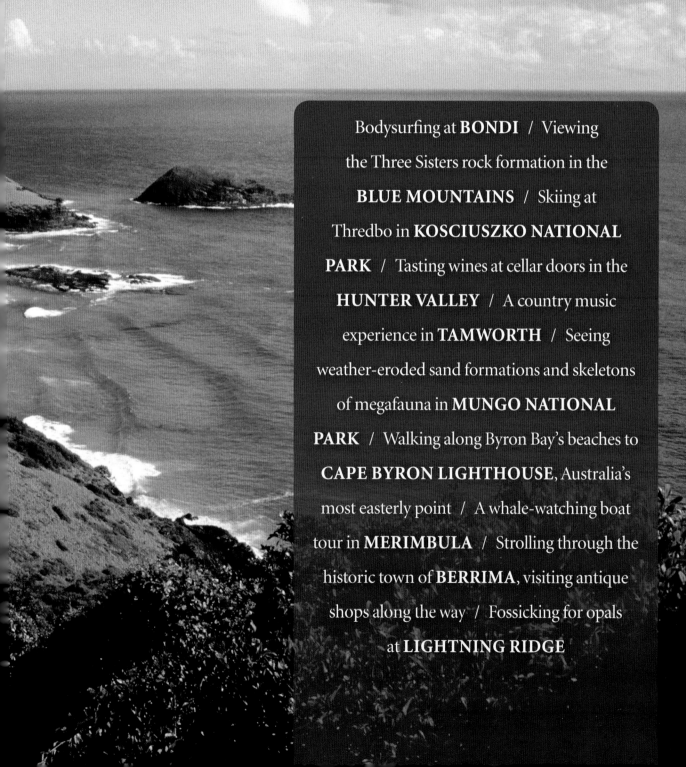

Bodysurfing at **BONDI** / Viewing the Three Sisters rock formation in the **BLUE MOUNTAINS** / Skiing at Thredbo in **KOSCIUSZKO NATIONAL PARK** / Tasting wines at cellar doors in the **HUNTER VALLEY** / A country music experience in **TAMWORTH** / Seeing weather-eroded sand formations and skeletons of megafauna in **MUNGO NATIONAL PARK** / Walking along Byron Bay's beaches to **CAPE BYRON LIGHTHOUSE**, Australia's most easterly point / A whale-watching boat tour in **MERIMBULA** / Strolling through the historic town of **BERRIMA**, visiting antique shops along the way / Fossicking for opals at **LIGHTNING RIDGE**

NEW SOUTH WALES

is a land of contrasts. Lush rainforests, pristine beaches, snowfields and the rugged beauty of the outback all vie for visitors' attention.

Beaches are a clear drawcard, with those at Bondi and Byron Bay among the most popular. Surfing, swimming and whale-watching can be enjoyed almost anywhere along the coast, but Hyams Beach in Jervis Bay National Park is home to the whitest sand in the world.

The discovery of Mungo Man and Woman, the miraculously preserved remains of two ancient Aboriginal people found in a dune over four decades ago, prove that civilisation existed here 40 000 years ago. Numerous Aboriginal nations have called the state home, and still do. Well-preserved fish traps in Brewarrina are thought by some to be the oldest man-made structures in the world.

The state's settled history began after the American War of Independence spelt the end for British penal settlements in North America, and New South Wales became the solution to overcrowded prisons. Conditions were harsh; the first inmates of Maitland Gaol, who included

[ZENITH BEACH AT SUNRISE, TOMAREE NATIONAL PARK]

many children, were forced to march the 6 kilometres from the wharf at Morpeth to the prison in shackles and chains.

Harsh conditions were not limited to the prisons. In 1845, explorer Charles Sturt lost his second-in-command, due to the pitiless terrain, and was stranded for six months in the outback near Milparinka. Today remote Silverton stands as a reminder of outback isolation, with its buildings and stark surrounds featuring in Australian films such as *Mad Max II* and *The Adventures of Priscilla, Queen of the Desert*.

[PELICANS ON WALLIS LAKE, FORSTER–TUNCURRY]

In stunning contrast, Sydney's bright lights and sophistication sit beside the sparkling waters of the largest natural harbour in the world. The iconic Harbour Bridge and Opera House, along with the successes of the 2000 Olympics and the popular Gay and Lesbian Mardi Gras, have ensured Sydney and New South Wales a place on the world stage.

fact file

Population 7 303 700
Total land area 800 628 square kilometres
People per square kilometre 8.5
Sheep per square kilometre 48
Length of coastline 2007 kilometres
Number of islands 109
Longest river Darling River (1390 kilometres)
Largest lake Lake Eucumbene, (145 square kilometres)
Highest mountain Mount Kosciuszko (2228 metres)
Highest waterfall Wollomombi Falls (220 metres), Oxley Wild Rivers National Park
Highest town Cabramurra (1488 metres)
Hottest place Bourke (average 35.6°C in summer)
Coldest place Charlotte Pass (average 2.6°C in winter)
Wettest place Dorrigo (average 2004 millimetres of rain per year)
Most remote town Tibooburra
Strangest place name Come-by-Chance
Most famous local Nicole Kidman
Quirkiest festival Stroud International Brick and Rolling Pin Throwing Competition
Number of 'big things' 49
Most scenic road Lawrence Hargrave Drive, Royal National Park
Favourite food Sydney rock oysters
Local beer Tooheys
Interesting fact The Stockton Sand Dunes, 32 kilometres long, 2 kilometres wide and up to 30 metres high, form the largest moving coastal sand mass in the Southern Hemisphere

gift ideas

Cookies, Byron Bay Cookie Company, Byron Bay Drool-worthy cookies in flavours like triple choc fudge or white choc chunk and macadamia nut. See Byron Bay p. 39

Australian country music CD, Big Golden Guitar Tourist Centre, Tamworth Bring back a music sample by one of Australia's talented country music legends. See Tamworth p. 88

Mead, Dutton's Meadery, Manilla Manilla is home to one of the few meaderies in Australia, producing this ancient alcoholic beverage from fermented local honey and water. Purchase some bottles and see the private museum. Barraba St, Manilla. See Manilla p. 69

Replica of Sydney Opera House, Sydney Opera House Shop, Sydney Take home a tiny replica of this icon in gleaming pewter or sparkling Waterford crystal. See Sydney Opera House p. 11

Sydney Harbour Bridge coathanger, Pylon Lookout Souvenir Shop, Sydney A quirky – and useful – variation on the old 'Coathanger' itself. See Sydney Harbour Bridge p. 12

Beach gear, Bondi Beach Sun hats, beach towels and unique swimwear that sport the name of this iconic beach in bold letters are available from various stores. See Bondi Beach p. 15

Arts and crafts, Paddington Markets Local artisans sell fabulous artworks, jewellery, clothing and collectibles. See Markets p. 19

Gumnut products, Nutcote, Neutral Bay The home of May Gibbs sells beautiful books, postcards, CDs, DVDs, tea towels and more, featuring the enchanting lives of Snugglepot, Cuddlepie and the Banksia Men. See Nutcote p. 16

Wool products, Big Merino, Goulburn Stylish woollen clothing, slippers lined with lambs wool and beauty products made from lanolin. See Goulburn p. 53

Wine, Hunter Valley Try the shiraz and chardonnay from one of Australia's most renowned wine-producing districts. See Cessnock p. 42

SYDNEY is...

Bodysurfing at **BONDI** / Wandering through the lanes and alleyways of **THE ROCKS** / Views from **SYDNEY TOWER** / A trip on the **MANLY FERRY** / Fish and chips at **WATSONS BAY** / Soaking up the atmosphere of **KINGS CROSS** / A picnic at **TARONGA ZOO** / Harbour views from **MRS MACQUARIES CHAIR** / A performance at the **SYDNEY OPERA HOUSE** / Climbing the **SYDNEY HARBOUR BRIDGE** / A stroll through **BALMAIN** / Bargain hunting at **PADDY'S MARKETS** / Following the Games Trail at **OLYMPIC PARK** / Visiting **ELIZABETH FARM** in Parramatta

VISITOR INFORMATION
Sydney Visitor Centre
→ Level 1, cnr Argyle and Playfair sts, The Rocks
→ 33 Wheat Rd, Darling Harbour
(02) 9240 8788 or 1800 067 676
www.sydneyvisitorcentre.com

Australia's largest city stretches from the shores of the Tasman Sea to the foot of the Blue Mountains. Along with outstanding natural assets – stunning beaches, extensive parklands and the vast expanse of the harbour – Sydney boasts an impressive list of urban attractions, including world-class shopping and a host of superb restaurants and nightclubs.

Sydney began life in 1788 as a penal colony, a fact long considered a taint on the city's character. Today, echoes of those bygone days remain in areas such as the Rocks, Macquarie Street and the western suburb of Parramatta.

Since those early days, the one-time prison settlement has become one of the world's great cities. Home to two of Australia's most famous icons, the Sydney Harbour Bridge and the Sydney Opera House, Sydney attracts more than two million international visitors a year. For a true Sydney experience, try watching a Rugby League Grand Final at ANZ Stadium with a crowd of 80 000 cheering fans. Or if good food and fine wine are more your style, sample the waterfront dining at Circular Quay or Darling Harbour, and multicultural flavours in inner-city Darlinghurst.

With a population of 4 650 000, Sydney offers a multitude of activities. Surf the breakers at Bondi Beach or jump on a Manly ferry and see the harbour sights. Whatever you do, Sydney is a great place to explore.

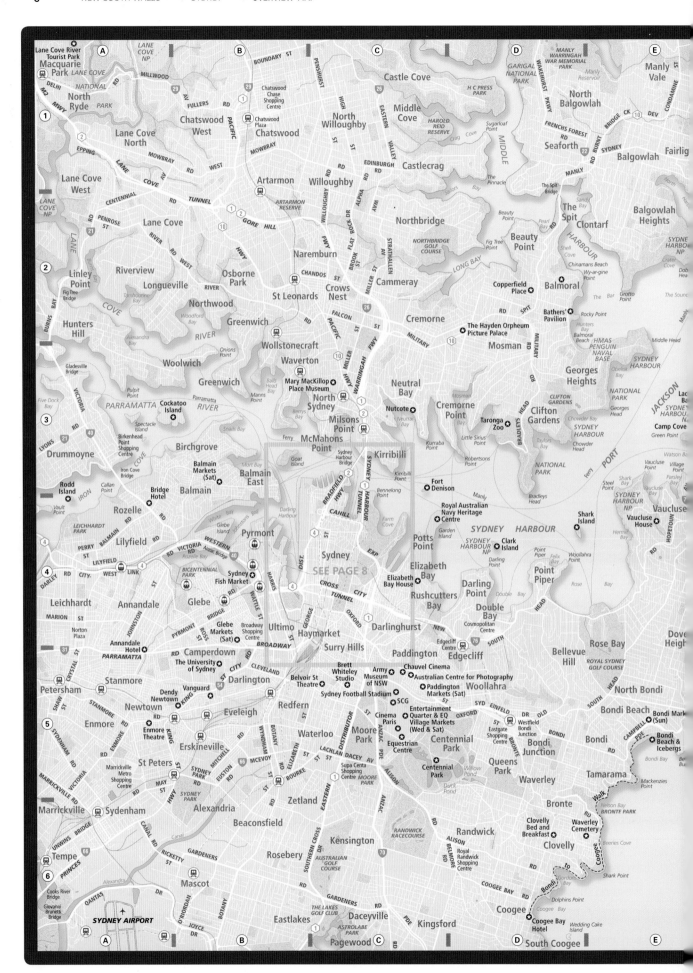

CITY CENTRE

The city centre is primarily a retail district, with shops ranging from small boutiques to big department stores. During weekdays, the area is crowded with office workers.

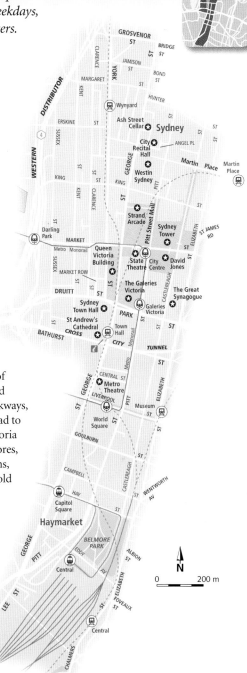

Martin Place 8 C4

High Victorian and Art Deco buildings line Martin Place all the way to Macquarie Street. Chief among them is the old **GPO**, corner of Martin Place and George Street. Designed by colonial architect James Barnet, it has been transformed into the stunning five-star hotel the **Westin Sydney**. An up-market food hall fills the lower ground floor along with a carefully preserved part of the old **Tank Stream**. Once a major source of water for the Eora people, it was also a deciding factor in the choice of Sydney Cove as a settlement site.

Pitt Street Mall 8 B4

Head south along Pitt Street from Martin Place to find the busy pedestrian precinct of the Pitt Street Mall. The heart of the CBD's retail area and home of Westfield Sydney Shopping Centre, its overhead walkways, small arcades and underground tunnels lead to David Jones and the QVB (the Queen Victoria Building). The mall houses department stores, boutiques, and music and book emporiums, as well as the lovely **Strand**, the last of the old arcades in what was once a city of arcades.

Sydney Tower 8 B4

A visit to Sydney Tower is a must. Your ticket grants you access to the 250-metre observation tower, which commands superb views of Sydney, all the way from the Blue Mountains to the Pacific Ocean. Access the tower by Westfield Sydney in Pitt Street Mall. Included in your ticket price is a 4D-movie 'flight' through Sydney. For those who like to live on the edge, there's the Skywalk, an outdoor walk on clear glass. *Level 5, 100 Market St; (02) 9333 9222; www.sydneytowereye.com.au; open 9am–10.30pm daily.*

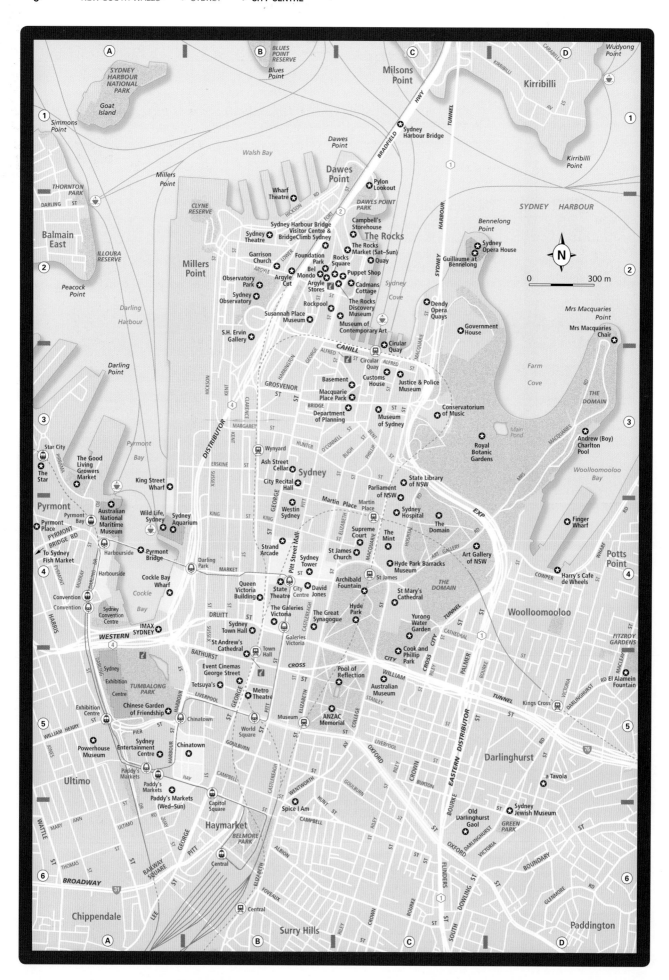

[INTERIOR OF QUEEN VICTORIA BUILDING]

State Theatre 8 B4

A mix of Art Deco, Italianate and Gothic architecture, the State Theatre embodies opulence. Built in 1929, it boasts marble columns, mosaic floors, plush furnishings, the Koh-i-Noor chandelier, and paintings by well-known Australian artists. A National Trust building, it remains a working theatre, showcasing performances by the likes of Bette Midler and Rudolf Nureyev. *49 Market St; tours Mon–Wed at 10am and 1pm, tickets through Ticketmaster, 136 100.*

Queen Victoria Building 8 B4

Built in 1898 to replace the old Sydney markets, the QVB at various times housed a concert hall and the city library before being restored in 1984 to some of its former splendour. Now one of Sydney's most cherished landmarks, it has three levels of stylish shops and cafes, with elaborate stained-glass windows, intricate tiled floors, arches, pillars, balustrades and a mighty central dome. The building's best-kept secret is the old ballroom on the third floor, now used as the elegant Tea Room function centre. *455 George St.*

Sydney Town Hall 8 B4

South of the QVB stands the Sydney Town Hall, a wildly extravagant piece of Victoriana, now the seat of city government. It was built in 1869 over a convict burial ground, recently evidenced by the accidental discovery of an old brick tomb. Since 1890 it has housed the Grand Organ. Free lunchtime concerts, lectures and other events are held occasionally. *483 George St.*

HYDE PARK AND MACQUARIE STREET

This historically significant district contains one of the oldest parks in the city, Australia's first museum, a Gothic cathedral and the beautiful old buildings of Macquarie Street, once the heart of Sydney's fashionable society.

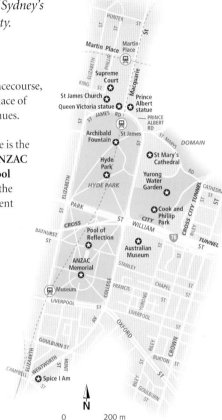

Hyde Park 8 C4

Once the city's first racecourse, Hyde Park is now a place of sunny lawns and avenues. At its quiet end, near Liverpool Street, there is the beautiful Art Deco **ANZAC Memorial** and the **Pool of Reflection.** Below the memorial is an excellent ongoing exhibition, 'Spirit of ANZAC'. At its busy end is the gorgeously kitsch **Archibald Fountain,** commemorating the association of France and Australia during World War I.

Australian Museum 8 C5

This excellent museum houses several unique natural-history collections and a superb display of Indigenous Australian culture. Established in 1827, the present complex is an intriguing mix of Victorian museum and 21st-century educational centre. On Tuesdays in summer it is open 5.30–9.30pm, with a bar, performers, DJs and artists. *6 College St; (02) 9320 6000; 9.30am–5pm daily.*

Cook and Phillip Park 8 C5

For a change of pace, go for a swim at the centre, located across from the Australian Museum at the southern end of the park. Don't miss the mural depicting the career of Australian swimming champion Annette Kellerman, which graces the western wall of the Olympic pool. Be sure to visit the **Yurong Water Garden** near the northern end of the park. (02) 9326 0444; open Mon–Fri 6am–10pm and Sat–Sun 7am–8pm.

St Mary's Cathedral 8 C4

The cathedral is located on the east side of Hyde Park North, and was designed by William Wardell in a soaring Gothic Revival style that recalls the cathedrals of medieval Europe. A particular highlight is the crypt beneath the nave, which features a stunning terrazzo mosaic floor. *College St, facing Hyde Park; (02) 9220 0400.*

St James Church 8 C4

This fine sandstone church, with its elegant tower and copper-sheathed spire, is Sydney's oldest ecclesiastical building. The commemorative tablets on the walls read like a history of early Australia, while the enchanting mural in the little children's chapel depicts the land and seascapes of Sydney Harbour. Regular lunchime concerts. *173 King St, opposite Hyde Park; (02) 8227 1300.*

Macquarie Street 8 C4

Named after one of Sydney's most dynamic governors, Macquarie Street was a thriving centre of upper-class society during the 19th century. It is home to some magnificent buildings and statues, including **Queen Victoria** and her royal consort, **Prince Albert**, near Hyde Park. Visit the **Buena Vista** cafe in the **Supreme Court** building for one of the best harbour views in Sydney, all for the price of a latte. Reservations may be needed. (02) 9230 8221.

GARDENS AND DOMAIN

This lovely area includes extensive parkland, once part of the property surrounding the first Government House. The wisdom of governors Phillip and Macquarie saved this land from 200 years of ferocious development.

Hyde Park Barracks Museum 8 C4

Every elegant line and delicate arch of Hyde Park Barracks, one of the loveliest of Sydney's older buildings, bears the stamp of its convict architect, Francis Greenway. Built in 1819, the barracks have accommodated a wide range of individuals including convicts. Various ongoing exhibitions reveal the building's rich social history. *Cnr College and Macquarie sts; (02) 8239 2311; open 9.30am–5pm daily.*

The Mint 8 C4

Once the South Wing of the old Rum Hospital, the site of the colony's first mint is now the headquarters of the Historic Houses Trust. It houses a pleasant reading room, and a cafe with balcony seating and fine views of Macquarie Street and Hyde Park. The mint artefacts are now housed in the Powerhouse Museum *(see p. 14). 10 Macquarie St; (02) 8239 2288; open 9am–5pm Mon–Fri; general admission free.*

Sydney Hospital 8 C4

Now housing both the Sydney Hospital and the Sydney Eye Hospital, these imposing sandstone buildings occupy part of the old Rum Hospital. Weekday tours of its historic buildings are available (bookings essential, *(02) 9382 7111).* Its oldest building, the Nightingale Wing, houses the **Lucy Osburn-Nightingale Foundation Museum** where you'll find the sewing basket used by Florence Nightingale in the Crimea. *Museum open 10.30am–3pm Tues; (02) 9382 7427.*

Be sure to visit '**Il Porcellino**', a favourite photo opportunity with tourists and a 'collector' of money for the hospital. Rub the statue's nose for luck, then toss a coin in the fountain and make a wish.

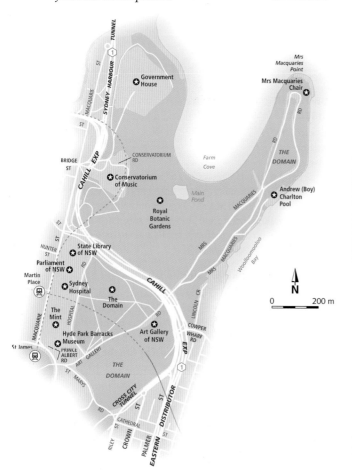

[FLOWERS IN THE DOMAIN]

Parliament of New South Wales 8 C4

Between the Sydney Hospital and the State Library stands the northern wing of the old Rum Hospital, now the seat of the Parliament of New South Wales. There is a free public tour on the first Thursday of each month at 1pm. *(02) 9230 2047.*

State Library of New South Wales 8 C3

Facing the Royal Botanic Gardens, on the corner of Macquarie Street and Shakespeare Place, the state library houses a remarkable collection of Australian books, records, personal papers, drawings, paintings and photographs. Visit the magnificent Mitchell Library Reading Room, the exquisite lobby mosaic and, outside, the statues of **Matthew Flinders** and his beloved cat **Trim**. Stolen at least four times, Trim now sits well beyond the reach of souvenir hunters. *Open 9am–8pm Mon–Thurs, 9am–5pm Fri, 10am–5pm Sat–Sun.*

Royal Botanic Gardens 8 C3

Sweeping parklands, formal gardens, including the Aboriginal garden, Cadi Jam Ora, and a stunning rose garden make up this landscaped oasis on the harbour's edge. Stroll the grounds or have a picnic, stock up on bush tucker, see botanical drawings at the Red Box Gallery, watch a film by moonlight (summer only), or even adopt a tree. Ask at the Gardens Shop for details. *Mrs Macquaries Rd; (02) 9231 8125.*

Government House 8 C2

Government House, in the north-west corner of the Botanic Gardens, was built in 1845 in the elaborate Gothic Revival style. *Free tour, Fri–Sun 10.30am–3pm (but call to check it isn't closed for an official function); (02) 9931 5222.*

The Domain 8 C4

The Domain falls into two distinct parts. To the south is parkland where soapbox orators and hecklers once gathered each Sunday. Now, this area hosts popular jazz, opera and symphony concerts in January. North of the Cahill, the Domain runs along the promontory to **Mrs Macquaries Chair**, a seat carved out of the sandstone bluff for Elizabeth Macquarie so she could watch ships arriving from England with longed-for letters from home.

The Art Gallery of New South Wales 8 C4

The gallery sits opposite the South Domain. An imposing Classical Revival-style building, it houses an impressive collection of Australian and international artworks, including a large permanent collection of Aboriginal art and a superb Asian collection. *Art Gallery Rd, The Domain; open 10am–5pm Thurs–Tues, 10am–9pm Wed; general admission free; 1800 679 278 or (02) 9225 1744.*

Andrew (Boy) Charlton Pool 8 D3

A sensational place for a quick dip, a swimming lesson or a bite at the harbourside cafe, this wonderful pool was named after Boy Charlton, a national swimming idol who competed in three Olympic Games (1924, 1928 and 1932). *Mrs Macquaries Rd; (02) 9358 6686; 6am–8pm in daylight saving, and 6am–7pm in other months of Sep–May (closed during winter).*

AROUND CIRCULAR QUAY

This area contains one of Sydney's most famous icons, the Sydney Opera House, two must-see museums and one of the few corners of the CBD that has remained unaltered for almost 200 years.

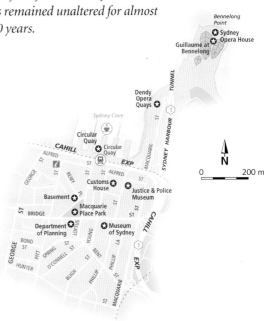

Circular Quay 8 C3

Circular Quay has been a hub of activity since Sydney was declared a settlement. Bus, train and ferry access *(see Getting around, p. 18)* make it a natural meeting place. Watch street performers on the quay, or eat at the many excellent cafes and bars offering stunning views of the harbour.

Sydney Opera House 8 C2

This icon stands at the far end of East Circular Quay, breathtaking in its beauty against the backdrop of Sydney Harbour. Its sails appear to echo those in the harbour, but it was in fact a segmented orange that inspired Jørn Utzon's design. A guided tour is recommended (bookings essential, 9am–5pm daily), or take the intimate back-stage tour. *(Tours (02) 9250 7250).* A variety of music, theatre, ballet and other performances on every day and night. *(02) 9250 7777.*

Museum of Sydney 8 C3

Built of sandstone, steel and glass, the museum retains its original foundations of the first Government House. It showcases displays, exhibitions and films that reveal the making of Sydney. *Cnr Phillip and Bridge sts; (02) 9251 5988; open 9.30am–5pm daily.*

Macquarie Place Park 8 C3

This park was once the old Government House garden. An elegant sandstone obelisk near the south-east corner marks the place from which all distances in the colony were once measured. The nearby anchor and small gun belonged to Arthur Phillip's flagship *Sirius*.

THE ROCKS

Once the haunt of pickpockets, prostitutes and sailors, the Rocks contains some of the city's most important historic sites, and is one of Sydney's most treasured attractions.

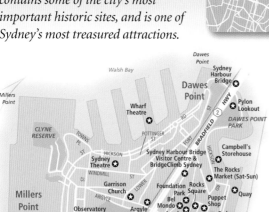

Sydney Visitor Centre 8 B2

Start a visit to the Rocks here, for accommodation, dining, shopping and sightseeing tips. Ask about the guided tours, including walking tours and a ghost tour. *Cnr Argyle and Playfair sts; (02) 9240 8788; open 9.30am–5.30pm daily.*

George Street — north 8 B2, C2

Glimpse the Rocks' previous character as a notorious seaport rookery in the winding streets and tiny lanes that run behind George Street. There are quiet courtyard cafes and some unusual shops to be found here, including the **Puppet Shop**, with its exquisitely handcrafted marionettes – a must-see, and not just for children. *77 George Street; (02) 9247 9137.*

Museum of Contemporary Art 8 C2

The museum occupies the old Maritime Services building – a brooding Art Deco structure dominating the western side of Circular Quay. A major redevelopment in 2011/2012 added a new wing. View an ever-changing display of sculptures, paintings, photographs and video installations by Australian and international artists. There are several free tours daily. *140 George St; (02) 9245 2400; open 10am–5pm daily; general admission free.*

Cadmans Cottage 8 C2

Sydney's oldest surviving residence, built in 1816, was the home of John Cadman, an ex-convict and boatman to Governor Macquarie. Today it is a national parks information centre, and the starting point for tours of the harbour islands *(see Harbour islands, p. 21). 110 George St; (02) 9253 0888; open 9.30am–4.30pm Mon–Fri and 10am–4.30pm Sat–Sun.*

Playfair Street 8 B2

This is the place to be, particularly on the weekends. There's corn-on-the-cob, street performers, and endless live entertainment. Find a seat in **Rocks Square** and soak it all up. Nearby are the boutiques of **Argyle Stores**. Enter via Argyle Street, by way of Mary Reibey's old bond stores.

Foundation Park 8 B2

Hidden behind a row of souvenir shops in Playfair Street is this quirky park. An almost-vertical site of three former dwellings that were built into the face of the sandstone escarpment, all that remains now are foundations scattered among the grassy terraces of the park, a stairway or two leading nowhere, and the occasional object from those long-vanished homes.

Susannah Place Museum 8 B2

From the top of Foundation Park, this wonderful museum is just up the Argyle Stairs and around the corner in Gloucester Street. Occupying four terrace houses, it affords a glimpse of life for working-class people in the Rocks at varying stages in its history. *58–64 Gloucester St; (02) 9241 1893; open 2–6pm Mon–Fri, 10am–6pm Sat–Sun and school holidays. Closes at 5pm in winter.*

Sydney Harbour Bridge 8 C1

Completed and opened to traffic in 1932 the bridge offers arguably the best view of Sydney from the **Pylon Lookout**, on the south-east pylon, which contains an excellent exhibition detailing the bridge's history; *(02) 9240 1100; open 10am–5pm daily.* The **Sydney Harbour Bridge Visitor Centre** also has an exhibition and cinemas showing how the bridge was built. The same entrance leads to **BridgeClimb Sydney**, offering tours to the very top of the span at dawn, twilight, during the day or at night *(see Walks and tours, p. 20). 3 Cumberland St; (02) 8274 7777; office open 8am–5pm Mon–Fri, 9am–5pm Sat–Sun.*

Argyle Cut 8 B2

Work on connecting the eastern and western sides of the Rocks commenced in 1843, with chained convicts doing most of the hard labour. Initially much narrower than it is now, it was once the haunt of 'pushes' (larrikin youths who specialised in gang warfare and rolling the lone passer-by). In the heyday of the pushes, even the police went through the Argyle Cut in pairs.

Observatory Park 8 B2

High above the Rocks stands Observatory Park with its old-world ambience and stunning views of the western harbour. For stargazers, there's the **Sydney Observatory**, offering astronomy exhibitions, talks, films and night-sky viewings (bookings essential). *Bookings (02) 9921 3485; open 10am–5pm daily, start times of night tours varies.* Nearby is the old Fort Street School for Girls, now the headquarters for the National Trust, and the site of the **S. H. Ervin Gallery**, renowned for its innovative art exhibitions. *Upper Fort St, Observatory Hill; (02) 9258 0173; open 11am–5pm Tue–Sun.*

DARLING HARBOUR

Easily accessed by ferry, light rail and monorail, Darling Harbour is the focus of much of the city's culture and entertainment. It includes the popular Powerhouse Museum, the glitz of The Star casino, and the delicacies of the Sydney Fish Market.

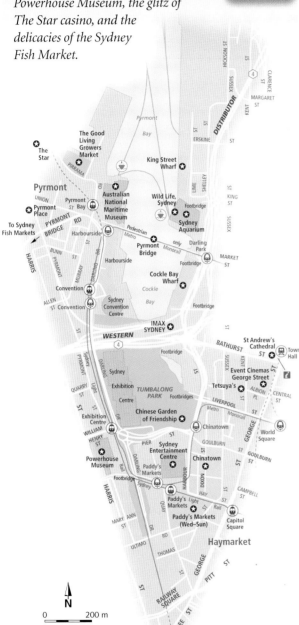

Sydney Aquarium 8 A4

The aquarium rates among the world's best for sheer spectacle-value. Underwater tunnels let you walk with the stingrays and sharks – and don't miss the Great Barrier Reef exhibition, two of only five dugongs in captivity in the world, and the Seal Sanctuary. *Aquarium Pier; (02) 8251 7800; open 9am–8pm daily.*

Wild Life, Sydney 8 A4

Next door to the aquarium, at Wild Life, Sydney, see over 250 different Australian species living within their own natural habitats and ecosystems, in bush, desert and tropical settings. *Aquarium Pier; (02) 9333 9288; open 9am–5pm daily.*

Chinese Garden of Friendship 8 A5

In the southern area, enjoy these gardens with their airy pavilions, tiny arched bridges, tranquil lakes, and elegant teahouse that serves traditional Chinese teas. In dry weather, for a small fee, you can also dress up in costumes from the Peking Opera (from 11am). *(02) 9240 8888; open 9.30am–5.30pm daily.*

Australian National Maritime Museum 8 A4

To the north of Pyrmont Bridge, this museum highlights Australia's relationship with the sea, from the days of convict transports and immigrant ships to today's beach culture. Special exhibitions include tours of the museum's fleet. *2 Murray St, Darling Harbour; (02) 9298 3777; open 9.30am–5pm daily.*

South of the harbour 8 A5, B5

Just past the **Sydney Entertainment Centre**, host to international music stars, you'll find **Paddy's Markets** *(see Markets, p. 19).* Opposite its Thomas Street entrance is Dixon Street, the main thoroughfare of **Chinatown**, where you'll find inexpensive souvenirs, beautiful Chinese items, and superb Asian cuisine.

Darling Harbour East 8 A4

Once a working harbour, Darling Harbour's maritime past remains in the structures that surround its landscaped promenades. The National Trust–classified **Pyrmont Bridge** spans the harbour from east to west, and north-east of the bridge are **King Street Wharf** and **Cockle Bay Wharf**, renowned for exclusive shopping and dining. South-east of Pyrmont Bridge, **IMAX SYDNEY** boasts the largest cinema screen in the world. *(02) 9281 3300.*

[SYDNEY SKYLINE FROM DARLING HARBOUR]

Powerhouse Museum 8 A5

South-west of Darling Harbour, the museum showcases an extraordinary collection of oddments and treasures. Highlights include the Hall of Transport, with its fleet of aeroplanes, and the tiny 1930s-style cinema with its program of old newsreels and documentaries. Tours, talks and daily activities. *500 Harris St, Ultimo; (02) 9217 0111; open 10am–5pm daily.*

The Star 8 A3

Sydney's only official casino is found to the north-west of Darling Harbour and is home to the Lyric Theatre and several restaurants that offer fine dining with views over Darling Harbour. *80 Pyrmont St, Pyrmont; (02) 9777 9000; open 24 hours.*

Sydney Fish Market 6 B4

Within walking distance of Darling Harbour, but probably best accessed by light rail, is this fast-paced, vibrant market with a bakery, deli and the freshest seafood you're ever likely to find. Guided tours enable you to watch a Dutch auction, but only for the early risers. *Bank St, Pyrmont; tours (02) 9004 1143; open 7am–4pm daily.*

INNER WEST

This area includes the historic suburbs of Glebe and Balmain. Glebe has retained many of its grand Victorian homes, Federation houses and modest workers' cottages, and has a reputation as an alternative suburb, while Balmain has an arty flair, in complete contrast to its previous population of dockland workers.

Glebe 6 B4

The leafy streets, old weatherboard houses, Victorian terraces and occasional mansion make Glebe a fabulous area to walk through. With Sydney University close by, you can find excellent bookshops, lively cafes and great weekend markets here *(see Markets, p. 19)*. At the far end of Glebe Point Road are the **Glebe foreshore parks**, which feature landscaped walks with views of Blackwattle Bay and Anzac Bridge.

Balmain 6 B3

Tucked away on its own little peninsula, Balmain is a suburb of quaint houses, stepped lanes and harbour views. Visit Darling Street, a lively area with cafes, boutiques and top-quality shops. Quickly and easily reached by ferry, this is another suburb best seen on foot.

INNER EAST

The inner-eastern suburbs begin just beyond the Domain and include suburbs that were once the haunt of some of the city's most notorious gangsters and are now home to some very trendy cafes and restaurants.

Woolloomooloo 8 D4

Get there by bus or take the stairs near the Art Gallery in Mrs Macquaries Road. The 'Loo's most recent and controversial development is the **Finger Wharf**, once known for toughness and lawlessness but now one of Sydney's most exclusive addresses. Try **Harry's Cafe de Wheels**, a piewagon and long-time Sydney icon on the eastern side of the bay.

Kings Cross 8 D5

The Cross is one of the most fascinating parts of Sydney. The strip clubs of Darlinghurst Road swing into action at night, but by daylight it retains the charm of its bohemian past, with gracious tree-lined streets and pretty sidewalk cafes. Look for the thistle-like **El Alamein Fountain**.

Elizabeth Bay House 6 C4

Designed in the early 19th century by John Verge as a home for colonial secretary Alexander Macleay, this elegant house became a shabby boarding house and artists' squat for a while, but it is now a Historic Houses Trust museum, its rooms restored to their former graciousness. *7 Onslow Ave, Elizabeth Bay; (02) 9356 3022; open 9.30am–4pm Fri–Sun.*

Paddington 6 C5

Paddington is now one of Sydney's most beautiful suburbs. Iron-lace-trimmed terraces line its backstreets, and its main thoroughfare, Oxford Street, is home to dozens of boutiques, galleries and cafes. The **Paddington Markets** *(see Markets, p. 19)* are in full swing each weekend. Easily accessed by bus – disembark on Oxford Street.

EAST

Sydney's east is dominated by the city's green lungs, Centennial Park. Stretching south of Paddington, the park is a magnet for joggers, sun-worshippers, picnickers, tai-chi exponents, horseriders and lovers of the great outdoors.

Centennial Park 6 C5, D5

South of Paddington lies Centennial Park's playing fields, bridle paths and riding tracks. Once a catchment of creeks, swamps, springs, sand dunes and ponds fed by groundwater, the 189-hectare park has picnic areas galore, historic sites and great walking and cycle paths. *(02) 9339 6699.* Bicycle hire found on Clovelly Road, on the south side of the park.

INNER SOUTH

The Moore Park precinct in the city's inner south takes in the Entertainment Quarter, one of Sydney's premier leisure playgrounds.

Entertainment Quarter 6 C5

One of Sydney's newer entertainment centres, the Entertainment Quarter sits on the old showgrounds next to the **Sydney Cricket Ground** and **Sydney Football Stadium** at Moore Park. Film studios and sound sets occupy much of the site, as well as a vast village green, the Showring, and a vibrant pedestrian precinct lined with fashion and homewares outlets, cinema complexes, restaurants, bars and weekly markets *(see Markets, p. 19)* .

Equestrian Centre 6 C5

On the corner of Lang and Cook roads in Moore Park is this centre, offering park rides for the experienced and riding lessons for those less so through five riding schools.

EASTERN BEACHSIDE

Vaucluse is one of Sydney's most exclusive suburbs, and old and new money abounds in the lavish homes gracing the harbour foreshore. Nearby Watsons Bay is recognised as Australia's oldest fishing village, established in 1788.

Vaucluse House 6 E4

Once owned by the flamboyant William Charles Wentworth, and now a Historic Houses Trust museum, this site exemplifies an early Victorian well-to-do household. *Wentworth Rd; (02) 9388 7922; open 9.30am–4pm Fri–Sun, daily during school and public holidays.*

Watsons Bay 7 E3

Here you'll find the spectacular ocean cliffs of **the Gap**, and the famous **Doyles** seafood restaurant. Nearby is **Camp Cove**, a popular family beach and the starting point of a 1.5-kilometre walking track winding past Sydney's first nude-bathing beach, **Lady Bay**, to the windswept promontory of **South Head**.

Bondi Beach 6 E5

In summer, Bondi is about as iconic as it gets – a sweep of pale sand covered with a rainbow of towels. The beach stretches 800 metres between a set of headlands, from the **Icebergs** sea baths in the south to a rockpool at the northern end. In the south is sizeable, if a little inconsistent, surf, while the more sheltered north is suitable for families.

Bondi to Coogee Walk 6 D6, E6, E5

Start at the southern end of **Bondi Beach**, known for its excellent weekend market *(see Markets, p. 19)* and its cafes. Wind south along the cliffs to **Tamarama**. In October and November, you can see the Sculpture by the Sea exhibition here *(see Walks and tours, p. 20)*. **Bronte**, a lovely beach with a natural-rock swimming pool known as the Bogey Hole, completes the track, or continue to **Waverley Cemetery** (where you can find the grave of poet and author Henry Lawson), past **Clovelly** (a popular swimming place), to **Coogee**, with the shops and cafes of Arden Street, and the lively **Coogee Bay Hotel**.

[BEACHGOERS, COOGEE]

SOUTH-EASTERN BAYSIDE

The city of Botany Bay is Australia's largest municipality. Botany Bay National Park straddles its headlands, and at its entrance is the suburb of La Perouse, home to an intriguing combination of natural and cultural heritage.

La Perouse 511 M10

On the northern head of Botany Bay, this was originally the home of the Muru-ora-dial people. Named after French navigator Jean-Francois de Galoup, the Comte de La Perouse, who arrived in Botany Bay around the same time as the First Fleet, it offers beautiful beaches, interesting walks, and an excellent museum *(see Museums and galleries, p. 19).*

Bare Island 511 M10

La Perouse was considered crucial to the defence of the colony at settlement. Governor Macquarie built the sandstone tower that stands at the highest point of the promontory, and fortifications at Bare Island were added in 1885. Guided tours are the only way to view these buildings (featured in *Mission: Impossible 2). Accessed via a footbridge from Anzac Pde; (02) 9247 5033; guided tours Sun 1.30pm, 2.30pm and 3.30pm.*

La Perouse Museum 511 M10

Occupying the old Cable Station, this museum was once an Aboriginal mission station and a Depression-era shanty town. Focusing on La Perouse himself, its galleries are devoted to the history of Pacific exploration and the voyage to Botany Bay. *Anzac Pde, La Perouse; (02) 9247 5033; open 10am–4pm Sun.*

[GIRAFFE AT TARONGA ZOO]

INNER NORTH

Sydney's inner north includes some of the city's most sought-after suburbs, including Neutral Bay, Mosman and the harbour beach suburb of Balmoral.

Nutcote 6 C3

Once home to May Gibbs, famous Australian author and illustrator of children's books, Nutcote is in the exclusive harbourside suburb of Neutral Bay. It is now a centre for children's literature, the arts and the environment. *5 Wallaringa Ave; (02) 9953 4453; open 11am–3pm Wed–Sun.*

Taronga Zoo 6 D3

Located at the end of Bradleys Head Road in Mosman, the zoo is accessible by ferry from Circular Quay. Housing about 4000 animals, it is a world leader in conservation and the care of rare and endangered species. Enjoy animal feeding, keeper talks and displays, stay overnight or have a picnic or barbecue there. In February and March, enjoy its *Twilight at Taronga* open-air concerts. *(02) 9969 2777; open 9am–5pm daily.*

Balmoral 6 D2

Balmoral, with its curving promenade, shady trees and elegant bridge, is reminiscent of Edwardian Sydney. Extremely popular in summer, it has a lovely beach with a fenced-in pool, pleasant foreshore and excellent restaurants.

NORTH-EAST

Manly 7 F2

Manly has the holiday atmosphere of a seaside village. The Manly ferry, from Circular Quay, is the most pleasant way to get there, while highlights include two beaches, an aquarium *(see next entry)*, the Old Quarantine Station *(see entry on this page)* and the carnival atmosphere of Manly Corso.

Oceanworld Manly 7 F2

To the west of the ferry terminal is this exciting bottom-of-the-sea experience, including a touch pool, an underwater tunnel, daily shark-feedings, exhibitions of some of Australia's deadliest snakes and spiders, plus the chance to dive with sharks. *West Esplanade, Manly; (02) 8251 7877; open 10am–5.30pm daily.*

Q Station 7 F2

Up the road from Manly is the Old Quarantine Station, now the Q Station, a unique resort with a restaurant, interactive tours and a theatre experience within Sydney National Park. Built to house incoming passengers and crew suspected of carrying contagious diseases from the 1830s to 1984, it contains 65 heritage buildings and fascinating 19th-century rock carvings made by those interned here. Access is via car or water taxi from the Rocks or Manly, and tour bookings are essential. *North Head Scenic Dr, Manly; (02) 9466 1551.*

parramatta

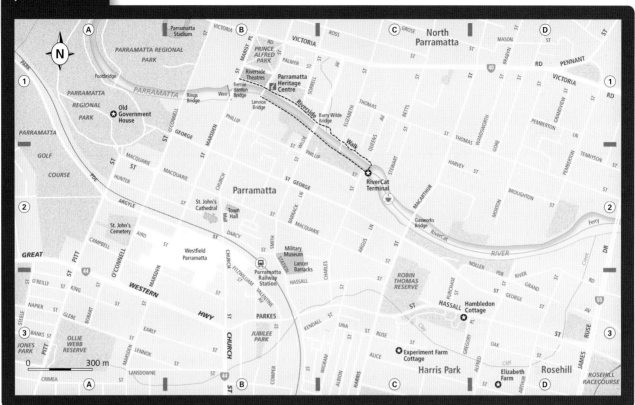

WEST

Sydney Olympic Park, Homebush Bay 511 K8

The site of the 2000 Olympic Games, this park now hosts the annual Royal Easter Show and other events. Access is by Parramatta Road, by rail or by RiverCat from Circular Quay. Take a lift to the Observation Deck on the 17th floor of the Novotel Hotel for fantastic views, and visit **Bicentennial Park**, with its extensive wetlands and bird sanctuaries, and the fabulous **Aquatic Centre**.

OUTER WEST

Elizabeth Farm, Rosehill 17 D3

Elizabeth Macarthur ran a large merino farm here while her husband was away in England, giving the wool industry an essential kickstart. The sandstone building and gardens now house a museum. Visitors can wander the rooms, touch the furniture, try the featherbeds and behave as if they are guests of the family. *Alice St; (02) 9635 9488; open 9.30am–4pm Fri–Sun.*

Hambledon Cottage, Harris Park 17 C3

This quaint cottage was built for a Miss Penelope Lucas, governess of the Macarthur children. Its style reflects the early reign of Queen Victoria. *63 Hassall St; (02) 9635 6924; open 11am–3.30pm, Thurs–Sun.*

Parramatta 17 B2

The quickest way to Parramatta is by train, but the most pleasant way is by RiverCat. The colony's first private farm was established here in November 1788, making this outer suburb almost as old as Sydney itself. Historical and lively, Parramatta is a fascinating spot to visit.

On arrival, head to the **Parramatta Heritage Centre**, alongside the Parramatta River, for historical exhibitions. *346A Church St; (02) 8839 3311; open 9am–5pm daily.*

Follow the nearby **Riverside Walk** for more insight into the history of this area and its inhabitants from the perspective of the Aboriginal people.

Close by, in the sweeping grounds of Parramatta Regional Park, stands **Old Government House,** one of the oldest public buildings in Australia. Guided tours are available and a ghost tour runs on the third Friday of each month; bookings essential. *(02) 9635 8149; open 10am–4pm Tues–Fri, 10.30am–4pm Sat–Sun.*

Don't miss the **Experiment Farm Cottage**. Built in 1798 on the site of Australia's first private farm, it is now run by the National Trust, which runs exhibitions there from time to time. *Ruse St; (02) 9635 5655; open 10.30am–3.30pm Tues–Fri, 11am–3.30pm Sat–Sun.*

FAR OUTER WEST

Featherdale Wildlife Park, Doonside 511 I7

Over 2000 animals live in the beautiful bushland setting here, and there are opportunities to cuddle koalas and handfeed kangaroos. It is also perfect for picnics and barbecues. *217 Kildare Rd; (02) 9622 1644; open 9am–5pm daily.*

CITY ESSENTIALS
SYDNEY

Climate

Sydney is blessed with a warm, sunny climate, often described as Mediterranean, making it possible to enjoy outdoor activities all year-round. The driest time of year occurs in spring, with autumn being the wettest season. Summers are hot and humid, with temperatures often in the mid-30s, while winters are cool and mostly dry, with temperatures usually around 15–17°C.

	MAX °C	MIN °C	RAIN MM	RAIN DAYS
JANUARY	25	18	102	8
FEBRUARY	25	18	116	8
MARCH	24	17	130	9
APRIL	22	14	125	8
MAY	19	11	122	8
JUNE	16	9	128	8
JULY	16	8	97	7
AUGUST	17	8	81	7
SEPTEMBER	19	11	69	7
OCTOBER	22	13	77	8
NOVEMBER	23	15	83	8
DECEMBER	25	17	77	8

Getting around

Sydney has an extensive network of rail, bus and ferry services. When negotiating the inner city, buses are probably best, with regular services on George and Elizabeth streets, between Park Street and Circular Quay, including the free 555 CBD Shuttle. The Red Explorer bus covers city attractions, and the Blue Explorer bus focuses on the eastern beach and harbourside suburbs. Trains are another option, with services every two or three minutes on the City Circle line, which runs in a loop between Central Station and Circular Quay.

The monorail, an elevated ride through the streets of Sydney, is an experience in itself. It runs in a circle that includes the north, west and south sides of Darling Harbour, and Liverpool, Pitt and Market streets.

The light-rail service runs from Central Station to the inner-west suburb of Lilyfield. As Sydney's only tram service, it is particularly useful for accessing places such as The Star casino and the Sydney Fish Market.

Ferries are also a great way to travel, with services to many locations on the inner and outer harbour (see Getting around on ferries, this page). Inquire about Travel 10, MyMulti Day Pass and weekly tickets, as these can considerably reduce the cost of your trip. On Sundays, a $2.50 ticket will give you unlimited access to Sydney trains, buses and ferries.

If you're driving, an up-to-the-minute road map is essential. There are ten tollways in Sydney, including the Harbour Bridge and the Cross-City Tunnel. Tolls can sometimes be paid on the spot, but the Cross-City Tunnel, Sydney Harbour Bridge, Sydney Harbour Tunnel, Lane Cove Tunnel, Falcon Street Gateway and M7 will only accept payment by E-tag, an electronic device that can be obtained through the Roads and Traffic Authority (RTA).

Public transport Train, bus and ferry information line 13 1500.

Tollways Roads and Traffic Authority (RTA) 13 2213.

Motoring organisation NRMA 13 1122.

Harbour cruises Sydney Harbour Ferries 13 1500; Captain Cook Cruises (02) 9206 1111.

Car rental Avis 13 6333; Bayswater Car Rental (02) 9360 3622; Budget 13 2727; Hertz 13 3039; Thrifty 1300 367 227.

Specialty trips Monorail and Metro Light Rail (02) 8584 5288.

Taxis ABC Taxis 13 2522; Legion Cabs 13 1451; Manly Warringah Cabs 13 1668; Premier Cabs 13 1017.

Airport rail service Airport Link (02) 8337 8417.

Water taxis Water Taxis Combined 1300 666 484; Yellow Water Taxis 1300 138 840.

Tourist bus City sightseeing (02) 9567 8400.

Bicycle hire Centennial Park Cycles (02) 9398 5027; Bonza Bike Tours (02) 9247 8800.

Getting around on ferries

Ferries are a great way to get about and see the harbour. Sydney Ferries and private operators run daily services from Circular Quay to more than 30 locations around the harbour and Parramatta River. Timetables, network maps and information about link tickets (combining a ferry fare with admission to various tourist attractions) can be obtained from the Sydney Ferries Information Centre at Circular Quay. Matilda Catamarans and Captain Cook Cruises are the main private ferry operators. They run ferry cruises and some express services to various points around Sydney Harbour, including some not serviced by Sydney Ferries.

Sydney Ferries from Circular Quay
Manly Ferry Departs Wharf 3.

Manly JetCat Express Service to Manly, departs Wharf 2.

Taronga Zoo Ferry Departs Wharf 2.

Watsons Bay Ferry Darling Point (Mon–Fri only), Double Bay, Rose Bay and Watsons Bay, departs Wharf 4.

Mosman Ferry Mosman and Cremorne, departs Wharf 4 (Mon–Sat) and Wharf 2 (Sun).

North Sydney Ferry Kirribilli, North Sydney, Neutral Bay and Kurraba Point, departs Wharf 4.

Woolwich Ferry North Shore, Balmain, Cockatoo Island and Drummoyne, departs Wharf 5 (Mon–Sat) and Wharf 4 (Sun).

Parramatta RiverCat Express Service to Parramatta, departs Wharf 5.

Rydalmere RiverCat North Sydney, Balmain, Darling Harbour and the Parramatta River to Rydalmere, departs Wharf 5.

Birkenhead Point Ferry North Sydney, Balmain and Birkenhead Point, departs Wharf 5.

Darling Harbour Ferry North Sydney, Balmain and Darling Harbour, departs Wharf 5.

Private services from Darling Harbour and Circular Quay
Manly Flyer Catamaran service to Manly from Circular Quay and Darling Harbour. Tickets may be purchased on board.

Matilda Catamaran City Loop Service, Darling Harbour to Circular Quay via Luna Park. Tickets may be purchased on board.

Matilda Catamaran Cruise + Attraction Combines Matilda Harbour Express ferry ticket with entry to one of the following harbourside attractions: Taronga Zoo, Shark Island or Fort Denison. Bookings on (02) 8270 5188.

Captain Cook Cruises Hop-on and hop-off cruise departs Darling Harbour, stopping at Luna Park, Circular Quay, Taronga Zoo, Shark Island, Fort Denison and Watsons Bay. Bookings on 1800 804 843.

Aboriginal Cruise An island visit, a welcome dance, and the Aboriginal names and history of the harbour. Bookings on (02) 9699 3491.

Top events

Sydney Festival A celebration of the city, this includes cultural events at Sydney's most stunning indoor and outdoor venues. January.

Sydney Mardi Gras A 2-week cultural festival celebrating diversity of sexuality and gender, including a spectacular street parade. February–March.

Royal Easter Show The country comes to the city in the Great Australian Muster. Easter.

Archibald Prize The Archibald national portrait prize and exhibition is one of Sydney's most controversial events. March–June.

Sydney Comedy Festival Three weeks of local and international comedy acts at various venues. April–May.

Vivid Sydney See Sydney's nocturnal face change in this winter festival of light, music and ideas. May–June.

Sydney Film Festival A showcase for the newest offerings in cinema. June.

City to Surf A 14-kilometre fun run, from Hyde Park to Bondi. August.

Crave Sydney International Food Festival A month-long festival of food and outdoor art, including the Sydney International Food Festival, Darling Harbour Fiesta and Art & About. October.

Rugby League Grand Final The leaders of the football competition compete for the title in the final match of the season. October.

Sydney to Hobart Yacht Race Classic blue-water sailing event. 26 December.

Museums and galleries

Army Museum of NSW Military pride in the colonial setting of Victoria Barracks, with the history of the army from 1788. Oxford St, Paddington; (02) 8335 5330; open 10am–1pm Thurs, 10am–4pm Sun; admission free.

Australian Centre for Photography Exhibitions of work by the world's best art, fashion and documentary photographers. 257 Oxford St, Paddington; open 12–7pm Tues–Fri, 10am–6pm Sat–Sun; admission free.

Brett Whiteley Studio Paintings and sculptures in the former studio and home of this great Australian artist. 2 Raper St, Surry Hills; open 10am–4pm Sat–Sun.

Justice and Police Museum Located in the old Water Police Station, with exhibitions on crime and punishment in Sydney, including the city's most notorious cases. Cnr Albert and Phillip sts, Circular Quay; open 9.30am–5pm daily.

Mary MacKillop Place Museum A tribute to this remarkable woman who brought education to the children of the bush. 7 Mount St, North Sydney; open 10am–4pm daily.

Royal Australian Navy Heritage Centre Over 100 years of navy history in the harbourside setting of Garden Island. Take Watsons Bay ferry from Circular Quay to Garden Island; 9.30am–3.30pm daily.

Sydney Jewish Museum A history of the Jewish people in Australia, along with a poignant tribute to the victims of the Holocaust. Cnr Darlinghurst Rd and Burton St, Darlinghurst; closed Sat and Jewish holidays.

Sydney Tramway Museum Historic trams from Sydney, Nagasaki, Berlin and San Francisco. Entry fee includes unlimited rides on the trams. Cnr Pitt St and Rawson Ave, Loftus; open 10am–3pm Wed, 10am–5pm Sun, daily during school holidays.

The Rocks Discovery Museum A fascinating glimpse into the chequered past of the Rocks, featuring both interactive technology and archaeological artefacts. 2–8 Kendall La, the Rocks; open 10am–5pm daily; admission free.

See also Australian Museum, p. 9, Hyde Park Barracks Museum, p. 10, Museum of Sydney, p. 11, Museum of Contemporary Art, p. 12, Susannah Place Museum, p. 12, Australian National Maritime Museum, p. 13, Powerhouse Museum, p. 14, La Perouse Museum, p. 16.

Grand old buildings

Customs House Elegant sandstone building designed by colonial architect James Barnet in the Classical Revival style. Alfred St, Circular Quay.

Department of Planning This building is particularly noteworthy for the statues of famous explorers and legislators that grace the exterior. 22–33 Bridge St.

Conservatorium of Music Much altered, but the castellated facade still recalls Macquarie's fancy Government House Stables. Macquarie St.

Cadmans Cottage Sydney's oldest surviving residence, now a NPWS office. 110 George St, the Rocks.

Campbell's Storehouse Built from bricks made by convicts, its serried roof has long been a Sydney landmark. Hickson Rd, the Rocks.

Garrison Church View the red-cedar pulpit and the beautiful stained-glass window. Lower Fort St, Millers Point.

The Great Synagogue Exotic and remarkable in its originality, with a gorgeous mix of Byzantine and Gothic architecture, and sumptuous interiors. Elizabeth St.

St Andrew's Cathedral With twin towers that recall York Minster, it is best seen in November through a cloud of purple jacaranda. Cnr Bathurst and George sts.

Old Darlinghurst Gaol Impressive early Victorian sandstone prison with an imposing entrance. Now houses the National Art School. Cnr Burton and Forbes sts.

The University of Sydney Landscaped grounds and historic sandstone buildings. Parramatta Rd, Broadway.

See also Queen Victoria Building, p. 9, Sydney Town Hall, p. 9, Hyde Park Barracks Museum, p. 10.

Shopping

Pitt Street Mall, City Sydney's major shopping area.

Castlereagh Street, City Sheer indulgence with some of the world's leading designer labels.

The Galeries Victoria, City A dazzling array of top-quality fashion and lifestyle brands.

George Street, City In recent years, several major designer labels have moved to the northern end of George Street, between Town Hall and the Rocks. This includes the Apple store, the new Louis Vuitton Maison and brands such as Burberry.

The Rocks The place to go for top-quality Australian art, jewellery and clothing.

Oxford Street, Darlinghurst Up-to-the-minute street fashion and funky, alternative clothing.

Oxford Street, Paddington Cutting-edge designers and a mecca for antique hunters.

Double Bay Sydney's most exclusive shopping suburb.

Birkenhead Point, Drummoyne Designer shopping at bargain prices in a historic venue.

Military Road, Mosman Classy shopping in a village atmosphere.

Markets

Paddy's Markets Fabulous mix of fashion, artworks, jewellery and collectibles in one of Sydney's trendiest suburbs. Sat. 8 A5

The Rocks Market Classic street market with a dedicated designers section, some superb Indigenous art, stylish homewares and exquisite jewellery for sale. Sat–Sun, Fri evening Nov–Mar, farmers market Fri–Sat. 8 C2

Paddington Markets Fabulous mix of fashion, artworks, jewellery and collectibles in one of Sydney's trendiest suburbs. Paddington Uniting Church, 395 Oxford St; (02) 9331 2923; every Sat from 10am. 6 C5

Sydney Flower Market Freshly cut flowers at wholesale prices, and breakfast at the market cafes. Flemington; Mon–Sat. 511 K9

EQ Village Markets Gourmet food, produce and coffee in the village-like atmosphere of the Showring. Moore Park; Wed and Sat, Kidz Zoo Wed, Sat–Sun. 6 C5

Balmain Markets   Jewellery and leather goods, arts and craft in the grounds of an old sandstone church. St Andrews Church; Sat. 6 B3

Bondi Beach Markets   Clothes, jewellery, a range of new and second-hand collectibles, and a lively beachside atmosphere. Sun. 6 E5

The Good Living Growers Market   The gourmet's choice, with superb breads, cheeses, fruit and vegetables, close to Darling Harbour. 7–11am, 1st Sat each month. 8 A3

Glebe Markets   Decorative homewares, arts and crafts, new and second-hand clothing, with a background of live music. Sat. 6 B4

Paddy's Swap and Sell Market   Sydney's biggest garage sale where second-hand goods are bought and sold and occasionally even swapped. Flemington; Sat. 511 K9

See also Sydney Fish Market, p. 14.

Walks and tours

The Rocks Walking Tours   The history of the Rocks and its many colourful characters are brought to life during this 90-minute tour. Bookings on (02) 9247 6678.

Harbour Circle Walk   For a comprehensive overview of Sydney's harbour, this walk covers 26 kilometres and could take you the whole day. Download a map from: planning.nsw.gov.au/harbour

BridgeClimb   Various tours of the Sydney Harbour Bridge that involve climbing to the top of the span clad in protective clothing and secured with a harness. Bookings on (02) 8274 7777.

Sculpture by the Sea   During October and November, this free outdoor exhibition on the Bondi to Tamarama coastal walk draws large crowds viewing over 100 modern-art pieces with the sea as their backdrop.

Sydney Ferry Harbour Walks   Discover some of Sydney's more out-of-the-way places on foot. Pick up a brochure at the Sydney Ferries Information Centre at Circular Quay, take a ferry to any of the listed destinations, and start walking.

Oz Jetboating Tours   Tour the harbour in a high-performance V8 jet boat. Bookings on (02) 9808 3700.

Destiny Tours   Stories of sex, scandal, murder, suicide and the supernatural. Explore Sydney's darker side on this night-time minibus tour. Bookings on (02) 9487 2895.

Harley Davidson Tours   See Sydney from the back of an East Coast Harley-Davidson. Bookings on 1300 882 065.

Gourmet Safaris   Choose from a range of foodie tours that uncover Sydney's multicultural world of gourmet food. Experienced chefs will take you to local shops and invite you to try traditional Greek, Italian, Lebanese, Portuguese, Turkish or Vietnamese cuisine. Bookings on (02) 9960 5675.

City Sightseeing Sydney and Bondi Tours   Cover the city and the eastern suburbs in a double-decker, open-topped bus, hopping on and off as often as you like. (02) 9567 8400.

Chocolate Espresso Tours   Tour the city's CBD and shopping districts, with a focus on either coffee or chocolate. Bookings on 0417 167 766.

Aboriginal Heritage Tour   Experience the Dreamtime of the Rocks with an Aboriginal guide. Bookings (02) 9240 8788.

Entertainment

Cinema   Located in George Street, between Bathurst and Liverpool streets, the 17-screen Event Cinemas George Street complex is the major cinema centre in the CBD. Arthouse cinemas include the Chauvel at Paddington Town Hall; the Dendy at Newtown and Circular Quay; and the Cinema Paris at the Entertainment Quarter. For a unique cinema experience, try the Hayden Orpheum Picture Palace in Cremorne, famous for its Art Deco interior and Wurlitzer pipe organ. See the newspapers for details of films being shown.

Live music   Sydney has always had a strong live-music scene with some excellent venues throughout the city. Apart from the larger, more formal places for live bands that include the Enmore Theatre and the Metro Theatre in George Street, the city's pubs are the main focus for live music. Try the Annandale Hotel, a popular venue for local indie bands; or the legendary Bridge Hotel in Rozelle, which specialises in blues and pub rock. For jazz lovers, there's the Vanguard in Newtown and the famous Basement at Circular Quay. Check newspaper lift-outs such as 'Metro' for what's on, or get hold of one of the free magazines such as *3D World* or *Drum Media* for details.

Classical music and performing arts   The ultimate harbourside venue for theatre, dance and classical music, the Sydney Opera House plays host to companies such as the Sydney Symphony Orchestra, the Sydney Theatre Company, Opera Australia and the Australian Ballet. It's worth checking out some of the smaller venues, such as the City Recital Hall in Angel Place or the Conservatorium of Music. Other venues for excellent live theatre include the Belvoir St Theatre in Surry Hills, and the Sydney Theatre Company, at Walsh Bay. If you are interested in dance, you can catch the Sydney Dance Company and the Bangarra Aboriginal dance group between tours at the Sydney Theatre or at the Sydney Opera House. For details, check *The Sydney Morning Herald*'s Friday lift-out, 'Metro', or *Time Out Sydney* magazine.

Sport

Sydneysiders have always been passionate about their sport. As a city that has recently hosted the Olympic Games, Sydney is now home to some of the best sporting facilities in the world.

Football, cricket and racing dominate the sporting scene. Although Sydney does have two **AFL** (Australian Football League) teams – the Sydney Swans and Greater Western Sydney Giants – Rugby League and Rugby Union hold more sway here, with the season for both codes beginning in March. Key games throughout the **Rugby League** season are played at the Sydney Football Stadium at Moore Park, with the Grand Final taking place in September at ANZ Stadium, in Olympic Park. A particular highlight is the **State of Origin** competition, which showcases the cream of Rugby League talent in a series of three matches between Queensland and New South Wales. These take place in the middle of the season, and the New South Wales matches are played at ANZ Stadium.

The Waratahs are the New South Wales side in the Super 12s, the **Rugby Union** competition in which local and overseas teams go head to head. These games are played at Sydney Football Stadium, while the **Bledisloe Cup** games (between Australia's Wallabies and the New Zealand All Blacks) are played at ANZ Stadium and attract up to 80 000 spectators.

In summer, **cricket** takes centre stage. The highlight is an international test, followed by the One-Day Internationals, all of which are played at the Sydney Cricket Ground (SCG). Sydney's official **soccer** (football) team is Sydney FC, which competes in the Hyundai A-League at Sydney Football Stadium.

Netball test series between Australia and New Zealand are always exciting, with at least one game usually held at Homebush in Sydney.

Other sporting highlights include the **Sydney Carnival**, with the world's richest horserace for two-year-olds, the Golden Slipper, being held the first Saturday in April.

Where to eat

a Tavola   Authentic Italian in an intimate dining-room setting in the heart of Sydney's trendy inner east. 348 Victoria St, Darlinghurst; (02) 9331 7871; open Fri for lunch and Mon–Sat for dinner. 8 D5

Ash Street Cellar   European-style cuisine, including Spanish tapas, in a funky atmosphere. The Ivy, 1 Ash St; (02) 9240 3000; open 8.30am–11pm Mon–Fri. 8 B3

Bathers' Pavilion   Stunning location on Balmoral Beach and sophisticated, contemporary fare to match. 4 The Esplanade, Balmoral; (02) 9969 5050; open daily for lunch and dinner. 6 D2

Bel Mondo   Contemporary Sydney cuisine served with delicious glimpses of the Harbour Bridge and Opera House. Gloucester Walk, the Rocks; (02) 9241 3700; open Fri lunch and Tues–Sat dinner. 8 B2

Guillaume at Bennelong   Lavished with awards, this impeccable eatery is almost as much of an icon as the Opera House in which it nestles.

Bennelong Point; (02) 9241 1999; open Thurs–Fri for lunch and Mon–Sat for dinner. 8 C2

Jonah's   Beautifully situated above Whale Beach, this elegant restaurant features a southern European menu, appropriately dominated by fresh seafood. 69 Bynya Rd, Whale Beach; (02) 9974 5599; open daily for breakfast, lunch and dinner. 509 C10

Quay   Right at the top of everyone's list for first-class dining. The location – directly opposite the Opera House – isn't bad either. Upper Level, Overseas Passenger Terminal, Circular Quay West; (02) 9251 5600; open Tues–Fri for lunch and daily for dinner. 8 C2

Rockpool   A hallmark of fine dining in Sydney, Rockpool offers a sumptuous menu and you can watch the chefs at work from the exclusive 10-seater 'Chef's Table'. 107 George St; (02) 9252 1888; open Tues–Sat for dinner, lunch Fri–Sat. 8 C2

Spice I Am   It might not look like much, but Spice I Am has the best Thai food in Sydney and at affordable prices. 90 Wentworth Ave, Surry Hills; (02) 9280 0928; open Tues–Sun for lunch and dinner. 8 B5

Tetsuya's   Experience a genius of Japanese–French fusion and individuality with the incredible degustation at Tetsuya's. 529 Kent St; (02) 9267 2900; open Sat for lunch and Tues–Sat for dinner. 8 B5

Where to stay

BIG4 Sydney Lakeside Holiday Park Lake Park Rd, North Narrabeen; (02) 9913 7845.

Beachhaven Bed & Breakfast 13 Bundeena Dr, Bundeena; (02) 9544 1333.

Beaufort at the Beach 8 Quinton Rd, Manly; (02) 9977 2968.

Clovelly Bed and Breakfast 2 Pacific St, Clovelly; (02) 9665 0009.

Copperfield Place 9 Killarney St, Mosman; (02) 9969 5770.

Cronulla Retreat B&B 54 Glaisher Pde, Cronulla; (02) 9527 1327.

Lane Cove River Tourist Park Plassey Rd, Macquarie Park; (02) 9888 9133.

Pyrmont Place 109 Pyrmont St, Pyrmont; (02) 9660 7433.

Scotland Island Lodge 2 Kevin Ave, Scotland Island; (02) 9979 3301.

Sheralee Caravan Park 88 Bryant St, Rockdale; (02) 9567 7161.

Sydney Tourist Park Cnr Wingello and Garnet rds, Miranda; (02) 9522 7143.

Harbour islands

Sydney Harbour is dotted with islands, but only five of them are open to the public. Four come under the authority of the National Parks & Wildlife Service, which charges a $7 landing fee per person. Visits must be prebooked and prepaid, so the information and tour-booking office located in Cadmans Cottage, George St, the Rocks, is the starting point for any tour or visit to the islands (except Cockatoo Island).

Fort Denison   Crime, punishment and the defence of Sydney Harbour are all part of Fort Denison's past. Now it plays a vital role in assessing and predicting the tides, and is the site of the One O'clock Gun. Access is by guided tour only, and there is a restaurant on the island. 6 C3

Shark Island   Sandy beaches, shaded grassy areas and superb views of the harbour make this the perfect place for a picnic. Matilda Catamarans runs a daily ferry service from Darling Harbour and Circular Quay to Shark Island, with the fare including the landing fee. 6 D4

Clark Island   Named for Ralph Clark, an officer of the First Fleet who once planted a vegetable garden here, Clark Island is now a place of unspoiled bushland and pleasant grassy areas, and is popular with picnicking families. Access by private vessel or water taxi. 6 D4

Rodd Island   Another favourite picnic place, Rodd Island has a colonial-style hall, which dates back to 1889, and 1920s summer houses that shelter long tables, making the island suitable for picnicking in all seasons. Access by private vessel or water taxi. 6 A4

Cockatoo Island   A former prison and shipyard, Cockatoo Island has abandoned workshops and wharves, a camping ground and cafe, and hosts art and concert events. Tours are available. It's free to visit and accessible by regular ferries from Circular Quay Wharf 5 or 4. 6 B3

Other suburbs

Surry Hills   Where old Sydney meets new urban chic, with 19th-century streetscapes, trendy cafes, bars and clusters of fashion warehouses close to Central Station. 8 B6

Newtown   A suburb with a funky, alternative feel, Newtown seems to sleep late and party late. It is best visited in the afternoon and early evening, when the shops and cafes of King Street come alive. 6 A5

Leichhardt   Sydney's little Italy, with some of the city's best Italian restaurants, superb shopping in Norton Street and the unique shopping and dining precinct of Italian Forum. 6 A4

Cabramatta   The heart of the Vietnamese community, with a vibrant shopping strip specialising in good-quality fabrics, fresh Asian produce and fabulous pho (rice noodle soup). 511 J9

Avalon   Pretty beachside village with a stunning backdrop of bush-clad hills, and a laid-back shopping precinct crammed with delis, cafes and some very up-market clothing and homewares stores. 511 N6

Penrith   Close to the Nepean River, this is a paradise for watersports enthusiasts, with the Cables Waterski Park and the Whitewater Stadium located here. There is a pleasant shopping precinct with some good eateries, and an excellent regional gallery. 510 H6

Camden   One of Sydney's most far-flung suburbs, with a pleasant rural atmosphere, pretty, old-world streetscapes and good cafes. 510 G11

Cronulla   With some interesting shops and cafes in the main street and a superb beach close by, this is a good starting point for trips to Royal National Park and the important historical site of Kurnell (Captain Cook's landing site and the birthplace of modern Australia). 511 L11

Day tours

Blue Mountains   Only 100 kilometres from Sydney, the brooding sandstone cliffs and deep, tree-lined gorges of the Blue Mountains provide a superb natural retreat. Aboriginal cave art, cool-climate gardens, charming mountain villages, walking trails and adventure activities are among the many attractions to be explored, along with historic towns like Katoomba.

Central Coast and Hawkesbury   The Upper Hawkesbury, north-west of Sydney, encompasses a scenic river landscape dotted with charming Georgian villages. It is Australia's most historic rural area. On the coast, on the north side of the Hawkesbury, is the scenic water playground of the Central Coast, with quiet bays in Bouddi National Park and popular surf beaches such as Terrigal, Avoca and The Entrance.

Hunter Valley   Located about 160 kilometres north-west of Sydney, the Lower Hunter area is Australia's oldest winegrowing district, with about 120 wineries radiating from the town of Cessnock. Take a tour of the wineries, starting with a visit to the wine centre in town, or book into one of the many excellent restaurants.

Ku-ring-gai Chase   North of Sydney, Ku-ring-gai Chase National Park encloses a magnificent stretch of bushland, set around the glittering waters of the Hawkesbury River and Broken Bay. Fishing, river cruises and bushwalking are popular activities here.

South along the coast   Abutting Sydney's southern suburbs, Royal National Park encloses a landscape of sandstone outcrops, wild heathland, rainforest, plunging cliffs and secluded beaches – perfect for walks, fishing, wildlife-watching and camping. Beyond the park you'll find the city of Wollongong and a magnificent stretch of surf coast dotted with pleasant resort towns.

Southern Highlands   Nestled into the folds and hills of the Great Dividing Range, the Southern Highlands offer pretty rural scenery, historic townships, such as Bowral and Berrima, with superb European-style gardens, a variety of festivals, and wonderful guesthouses and restaurants.

REGIONS
of New South Wales

Listed here are some of the top attractions and experiences in each region.

14 OUTBACK

Aboriginal rock art in Mutawintji National Park / see p. 37
Back O'Bourke Exhibition Centre, Bourke / see p. 34
Mungo National Park / see p. 27
Silverton (pictured) / see p. 37

13 MURRAY

Peppin Heritage Centre / see p. 47
Federation Museum, Corowa / see p. 44
Perry Sandhills (pictured) / see p. 99
Watersports at Lake Mulwala / see p. 73

12 RIVERINA

The Dog on the Tuckerbox, Gundagai / see p. 56
Museum of the Riverina, Wagga Wagga / see p. 96
POW Internment Camp Interpretive Centre, Hay / see p. 57
Riverina wine region (pictured) / see p. 96

9 CAPITAL COUNTRY

Big Merino, Goulburn (pictured) / see p. 53
19th-century buildings in Braidwood / see p. 35
Namadgi National Park / see p. 83
National Cherry Festival, Young / see p. 105

8 CENTRAL WEST

The Breadknife, Warrumbungle National Park / see p. 43
Siding Spring Observatory / see p. 43
V8 Supercars 1000, Bathurst / see p. 28
Taronga Western Plains Zoo, Dubbo (pictured) / see p. 49

11 SNOWY MOUNTAINS

Alpine Way / see p. 63
Skiing at Thredbo (pictured) / see p. 93
Watersports at Lake Jindabyne / see p. 61
Yarrangobilly Caves, Kosciuszko National Park / see p. 94

10 SOUTH COAST

Jervis Bay (pictured) / see p. 60
Montague Island Nature Reserve / see p. 75
National Trust–classified town of Central Tilba / see p. 75
Old goldmining town of Mogo / see p. 29

QUEENSLAND

SOUTH AUSTRALIA

14

12

13

NEW ENGLAND

Big Golden Guitar Tourist Centre, Tamworth / see p. 88
Fossicking at Lightning Ridge / see p. 66
National Trust–classified buildings in Armidale (pictured) / see p. 26
Wollomombi Falls, Oxley Wild Rivers National Park / see p. 26

TROPICAL NORTH COAST

Birdwatching in Iluka Nature Reserve / see p. 59
Cape Byron Lighthouse, Byron Bay (pictured) / see p. 39
Jacaranda trees in Grafton / see p. 54
Wollumbin National Park / see p. 74

HOLIDAY COAST

Bellingen Bat Island / see p. 30
Pet Porpoise Pool, Coffs Harbour / see p. 45
Skywalk, Dorrigo National Park / see p. 48
Timbertown, Wauchope (pictured) / see p. 98

HUNTER VALLEY AND COAST

Barrington Tops National Park / see p. 53
Bottlenose dolphins near Port Stephens / see p. 76
Hunter Valley wine region (pictured) / see p. 42
Stockton Sand Dunes / see p. 77

CENTRAL COAST AND HAWKESBURY

Ku-ring-gai Chase National Park (pictured) / see p. 53
Pelican-feeding at Memorial Park, The Entrance / see p. 91
Historic Riverboat Postman Ferry / see p. 53
Wollemi National Park / see p. 68

SOUTHERN HIGHLANDS

The International Cricket Hall of Fame, Bowral / see p. 35
Kiama Blowhole (pictured) / see p. 63
Minnamurra Rainforest Centre / see p. 60
Morton National Park / see p. 79

BLUE MOUNTAINS

Everglades Gardens / see p. 64
Jenolan Caves / see p. 80
Echo Point and Three Sisters / see p. 65
Zig Zag Railway (pictured) / see p. 68

SYDNEY

CANBERRA

ACT

VICTORIA

LEGEND

(i) VISITOR INFORMATION

RADIO STATIONS

IN TOWN

WHAT'S ON

WHERE TO EAT

WHERE TO STAY

NEARBY

[WALLAGOOT GAP, BOURNDA NATIONAL PARK]

* Distances for towns nearby are calculated as the crow flies.
* Food and accommodation listings in town are ordered alphabetically with places nearby listed at the end.

Adaminaby

Pop. 235

Map ref. 519 B6 | 520 E7 | 522 E12 | 539 D2

(i) Snowy Region Visitor Centre, Kosciuszko Rd, Jindabyne; (02) 6450 5600 or 1800 004 439; www.snowymountains.com.au

97.7 Snow FM, 1602 AM ABC Local

Over 100 buildings were moved in the 1950s to Adaminaby's current town site. The remaining town and surrounding valley were flooded to create Lake Eucumbene as part of the Snowy Mountains Hydro-Electric Scheme. The lake is regularly restocked with trout and Adaminaby is now a haven for anglers. Due to its proximity to Selwyn Snowfields, Adaminaby is also a popular base in winter for skiers.

 **The Big Trout** The world's largest fibreglass rainbow trout was erected after a local angler, attempting to drink a gallon of Guinness while fishing, was pulled into the water by a large trout and almost drowned. Legend has it the man then managed to finish the Guinness, but the 10 m high trout stands as a tribute to 'the one that got away'. Lions Club Park at town entrance.

Snowy Scheme Museum: opened late in 2011, this facility houses equipment and machinery, photographs, memorabilia and stories from the building of the Snowy Mountains Hydro-Electric Scheme; 10am–2pm, Sat–Sun; 5199 Snowy Mountains Hwy; (02) 6454 1643. *Leigh Stewart Gallery:* displays historical information including pictures and films; 3 Denison St; (02) 6454 2285. *Historic buildings:* several buildings, including 2 churches that were moved from Adaminaby's original site; details from visitor centre.

Snow Goose Hotel Motel: Diverse pub fare; Cnr Baker and Denison Sts; (02) 6454 2202

Rainbow Pines Tourist Caravan Park: Lucas St, Old Adaminaby; (02) 6454 2317.

Lake Eucumbene It is said that anyone can catch a trout in Lake Eucumbene, the largest of the Snowy Mountains artificial lakes. Its abundance of rainbow trout, brown trout and Atlantic salmon make it a popular spot for anglers. The Snowy Mountains Trout Festival draws hundreds of anglers every November. Fishing boats can be hired at Old Adaminaby, and for fly-fishing tours contact the visitor centre; access via Old Adaminaby; 9 km sw.

Selwyn Snowfields With 10 lifts spread over 45 ha, Selwyn Snowfields is a gentle, family-oriented ski resort, ideally suited to beginner skiers, snowboarders and tobogganers; Kings Cross Rd, Mt Selwyn; (02) 6454 9488; 30 km w.

Kosciuszko National Park On the road to Tumut is the historic goldmining site of Kiandra. North of the road, via Long Plain Rd, is historic Coolamine Homestead. All of NSWs' ski fields exist inside Kosciuszko National Park; the focal point is Mt Kosciuszko, Australia's highest mountain. The summit can be reached easily via the Kosciuszko Express Chairlift (operating all year), which drops you at the beginning of a 13 km return walk. Among a myriad of natural wonders in the park, the Yarrangobilly Caves are a highlight. The string of 70 limestone caves was formed from the shells and skeletons of sea animals around 40 million years ago. Six caves are open to the public, featuring underground pools, 'frozen' waterfalls, a bizarre web of limestone formations and a naturally formed thermal pool offering year-round swimming. For guided and self-guide tours, call (02) 6454 9597; more details from visitor centre.

Reynella Rides: join the long tradition of horseriding across the high country with this experienced outfit. There are homestead rides on the 1200 ha sheep and cattle property, or excellent multi-day safaris in Kosciuszko National Park; 669 Kingston Rd; (02) 6454 2386 or 1800 029 909; 5 km E. *Old Adaminaby Racetrack:* featured in the film *Phar Lap* (1984); on the road to Rosedale, Cooma side of town. *Power Stations*: tours and interactive displays; details from visitor centre.

TOWNS NEARBY: Berridale 41 km, Cooma 42 km, Jindabyne 48 km, Khancoban 63 km, Thredbo 70 km

Adelong
Pop. 827
Map ref. 519 A4 | 520 B2 | 522 D10 | 543 P2

ⓘ Tumut Region Visitor Centre, 5 Adelong Rd, Tumut; (02) 6947 7025; www.tumut.nsw.gov.au

📻 96.3 FM Sounds of the Mountain, 99.5 FM ABC Radio National

Adelong was established and thrived as a goldmining town in the late 19th century. Wilham Williams discovered gold and prospectors flocked to Adelong to seek their fortunes. Legend has it that Williams bought a mining claim for £40 000, only to sell it later the same day for £75 000. By World War I, over a million ounces of gold had been extracted from the mines, leaving little behind. The people began to disappear immediately. What is left is a charming rural village with a turn-of-the-century feel.

🏠 **Historic buildings** Many of the beautifully preserved buildings in Adelong have been classified by the National Trust. Take a stroll through Adelong's streets to discover banks, hotels and churches of the gold-rush era.

🍴 *Coat of Arms Kaffeehaus Restaurant:* authentic European; Beaufort Guest House, 77 Tumut St; (02) 6946 2273.

⊗ **Adelong Falls Reserve** Richie's Gold Battery was one of the foremost gold-processing and quartz-crushing facilities in the country. See the ruins of its reefer machine, including water wheels and a red-brick chimney. Three clearly signposted walks explore the falls, and other ruins in the reserve. 1 km N.

TOWNS NEARBY: Tumut 14 km, Batlow 24 km, Gundagai 27 km, Tumbarumba 52 km, Wagga Wagga 68 km

Albury
Pop. 43 784
Map ref. 522 A12 | 527 O12 | 543 K6 | 545 I2

ⓘ Gateway Visitor Information, Gateway Island, Hume Hwy, Wodonga; 1300 796 222; www.alburywodongaaustralia.com.au

📻 105.7 FM The River, 990 AM ABC Radio National

The twin towns of Albury–Wodonga are 7 kilometres apart on opposite sides of the Murray River, which is also the New South Wales–Victoria border. Originally inhabited by Aboriginal people, the Albury area was 'discovered' in 1824 by explorers Hume and Hovell, who carved their comments into the trunks of two trees. Hume's tree was destroyed by fire, but Hovell's still stands today in Hovell Tree Park.

🏠 **Albury Library Museum** Exhibits include a display on one of Australia's largest postwar migrant centres, which existed at nearby Bonegilla. Free wireless is also available. Cnr Kiewa and Swift sts; (02) 6023 8333.

Botanical Gardens: array of native and exotic plants and signposted rainforest and heritage walks; Cnr Wodonga Pl and Dean St. *The Parklands:* comprises Hovell Tree, Noreuil and Australia parks. Enjoy riverside walks, swimming, kiosk and picnic areas; Wodonga Pl. *Monument Hill:* spectacular views of town and alps; Dean St. *Albury Regional Art Centre:* extensive Russell Drysdale collection; Dean St; (02) 6023 8187. *Wonga Wetlands:* rehabilitated wetland along the Murray River, home to the black cormorant; Riverina Hwy.

🌸 *Rotary Community Market:* Townsend St; Sun. *Opera in the Alps:* Jan. *Kinross Country Muster:* Feb. *Albury Gold Cup Racing Carnival:* Mar/Apr. *Food and Wine Festival:* Sept/Oct. *Mungabareena Ngan-Girra (Festival of the Bogong Moth):* Nov.

🍴 *Green Zebra:* classic cafe fare; 484 Dean St; (02) 6023 1100.

🏕 *Albury Central Tourist Park:* 286 North St; (02) 6021 8420. *Albury All Seasons Tourist Park:* 481 Wagga Rd, Lavington; (02) 6025 1619. *Albury Citygate Holiday Park:* 508 Wagga Rd (via Catherine Cres), Lavington; (02) 6040 6275. *Lake Hume Tourist Park:* 37 Murray St, Lake Hume Village; (02) 6049 8100. *Wymah Valley Holiday Park – Aspen Parks:* 14 Hore Rd, Bowna; (02) 6020 3236.

⊗ *Lake Hume:* watersports, camping and spectacular dam wall; 14 km E. *Hume Weir Trout Farm:* handfeeding and fishing for rainbow trout; Lake Hume; 14 km E. *Jindera Pioneer Museum:* originally a German settlement featuring a general store, a slab hut and a wattle and daub cottage; 14 km NW. *Albury–Wodonga Trail System:* walking trails in the footsteps of Hume and Hovell; maps available from visitor centre. *Hume and Hovell Walking Track:* 23-day, 440 km trek from Albury to Yass. For a kit, including maps, contact Department of Lands, Sydney (02) 6937 2700.

TOWNS NEARBY: Wodonga (Vic.) 6 km, Yackandandah (Vic.) 28 km, Tallangatta (Vic.) 28 km, Chiltern (Vic.) 30 km, Beechworth (Vic.) 38 km

Alstonville
Pop. 5001
Map ref. 516 G5 | 525 O3 | 609 N12

ⓘ Ballina Visitor Information Centre, cnr Las Balsas Plaza and River St, Ballina; (02) 6686 3484 or 1800 777 666; www.discoverballina.com

📻 101.9 Paradise FM, 738 AM ABC Local

Alstonville is between Lismore and Ballina, surrounded by macadamia and avocado plantations. It's known for its immaculate gardens and purple tibouchina trees that blossom in March, as well as quirky antique and gift shops.

🏠 *Lumley Park:* walk-through reserve of native plants, flying fox colony and open-air pioneer transport museum; Bruxner Hwy. *Budgen Avenue:* several shops and galleries with local art and craft. *Elizabeth Ann Brown Park:* rainforest park with picnic facilities; Main St.

🍴 *E.S.P. Espresso Bar:* excellent coffee and food; Shop 1A, 76 Main St; (02) 6628 3433.

🏕 *Annie's Place Bed & Breakfast:* 465 Rous Rd, Tregeagle; (02) 6629 5285. *Pines on the Plateau:* 7 Converys La, Wollongbar; (02) 6628 1319.

⊗ **Victoria Park Nature Reserve** This remarkable rainforest reserve contains 68 species of trees in only 17.5 ha, 8 ha of which remain largely untouched. The area is also home to red-legged pademelons, potoroos, water rats and possums. There is a boardwalk, clearly marked walking trails and a spectacular lookout taking in the surrounding countryside. 8 km s.

Summerland House with No Steps: nursery, avocado and macadamia orchard, garden, crafts, fruit-processing plant, kids water park and Devonshire tea. Completely run by people with disabilities; (02) 6628 0610; 3 km s.

TOWNS NEARBY: Ballina 12 km, Lismore 16 km, Byron Bay 28 km, Evans Head 31 km, Mullumbimby 33 km

Armidale

Pop. 26 000
Map ref. 515 B1 | 525 J8

ℹ 82 Marsh St; (02) 6770 3888; www.armidaletourism.com.au

📻 92.1 2ARM FM, 720 AM ABC Radio National

Armidale is the largest town in the New England district. It has over 30 National Trust–listed buildings, and is home to New England University, the first university in Australia established outside a capital city. The transplanted birch, poplar and ash trees that line the broad streets make Armidale seem like an English village. It is one of those rare towns in Australia that enjoy four distinct seasons, with autumn turning the leaves stunning shades of crimson and gold. National parks in the area offer breathtaking forests, gorges and waterfalls.

🏛 **New England Regional Art Museum** The museum (closed Mon) has over 40 000 visitors each year and 8 gallery spaces, an audiovisual theatre, artist studio and cafe. The Howard Hinton and Chandler Coventry collections are among the most important and extensive regional collections, and include works by legendary Australian artists such as Arthur Streeton, Tom Roberts, Margaret Preston and John Coburn. There is also a separate Museum of Printing (open Thurs–Sun) featuring the F. T. Wimble & Co collection; open 10am–5pm Tue–Fri, 10am–4pm Sat–Sun; 106–114 Kentucky St; (02) 6772 5255.

Armidale Heritage Tour: includes Railway Museum, St Peter's Anglican Cathedral (built with 'Armidale blues' bricks) and University of New England; departs daily from visitor centre and is free. ***Aboriginal Cultural Centre and Keeping Place:*** includes museum, education centre and craft displays; 10am–4pm Mon–Fri, 10am–2pm Sat–Sun; 128 Kentucky St; (02) 6771 3606. ***Armidale Folk Museum:*** National Trust–classified building with comprehensive collection of pioneer artefacts from the region including toys and buggies; 1–4pm daily; Cnr Faulkner and Rusden sts; (02) 6771 4398. ***Self-guide heritage walk and heritage drive:*** 3 km walk and 25 km drive provide history and points of interest in and around the town; maps from visitor centre.

🎪 ***Armidale Markets:*** Beardy St; last Sun each month (3rd Sun in Dec). ***Armidale Show:*** Mar. ***Autumn Festival:*** Mar.

🍴 ***Archie's on the Park:*** modern Australian in historic homestead; Moore Park Inn, Uralla Rd; (02) 6772 2358. ***Caffiends in the Mall Armidale:*** great coffee and food; 192 Beardy St; (02) 6772 0277.

🛏 ***Highlander Van Village:*** 76 Glen Innes Rd; (02) 6772 4768. ***Pembroke Tourist and Leisure Park:*** 39 Waterfall Way; (02) 6772 6470.

🚶 **Oxley Wild Rivers National Park** World Heritage–listed with the largest area of dry rainforest in NSW, this park includes Dangars Falls (21 km SE), a 120 m waterfall in a spectacular gorge setting, and Wollomombi Falls (40 km E), which at 220 m is one of the highest falls in the state. Activities in the park include camping, canoeing, walking and horseriding.

University of New England: features Booloominbah Homestead, Antiquities Museum, Zoology Museum and kangaroo and deer park; Handel St; (02) 6773 3333; 5 km NW. ***Saumarez Homestead:*** National Trust–owned house offering tours; weekends and public holidays 10am–5pm, closed mid–June to end Sept; Saumarez Rd; (02) 6771 3255; 5 km s. ***Dumaresq Dam:*** walking trails, boating, swimming and trout fishing (Oct–June); Dumaresq Dam Rd; 15 km NE. ***Hillgrove:*** former mining town with Rural Life and History Museum featuring goldmining equipment (open Fri–Mon 10am–5pm, honesty box with gold-coin donation) and self-guide walk through old town site; brochure at visitor centre; 31 km E.

TOWNS NEARBY: Uralla 22 km, Guyra 32 km, Walcha 53 km, Glen Innes 86 km, Manilla 95 km

Ballina

Pop. 14 675
Map ref. 516 G5 | 525 O3 | 609 N12

ℹ Cnr River St and Las Balsas Plaza; (02) 6686 3484 or 1800 777 666; www.discoverballina.com

📻 101.9 Paradise FM, 738 AM ABC Local

Ballina sits on an island at the mouth of the Richmond River in northern New South Wales surrounded by the Pacific Ocean and nearby fields of sugarcane. The sandy beaches, clear water and warm weather make the area popular. Ballina's name comes from the Aboriginal word 'bullenah', which is said to mean 'place where oysters are plentiful'. This is still the case, with fresh seafood readily available in many seaside restaurants.

🏛 **Shelly Beach** A superb spot for the whole family. Dolphins can be seen frolicking in the waves all year round and humpback whales migrate through these waters June–July and Sept–Oct. The beach itself has rockpools, a wading pool for toddlers and a beachside cafe. Off Shelly Beach Rd.

Naval and Maritime Museum: features a restored Las Balsas Expedition raft that sailed from South America in 1973; Regatta Ave; (02) 6681 1002. ***Kerry Saxby Walkway:*** from behind the visitor centre to the river mouth with great river and ocean views. ***The Big Prawn:*** much-loved Ballina icon currently undergoing renovation; Pacific Hwy. ***Richmond Princess and Bennelong:*** river cruises; bookings at visitor centre. ***Shaws Bay:*** swimming and picnic area; off Compton Dr. ***Ballina Water Slide:*** River St.

🎪 ***Ballina Markets:*** Canal Drive; 3rd Sun each month. ***Ballina Cup:*** horserace; Sept.

🍴 ***Ballina Manor Boutique Hotel:*** modern Australian in Edwardian manor; 25 Norton St; (02) 6681 5888. ***Pelican 181:*** waterfront seafood, eat in or takeaway; 12–24 Fawcett St; (02) 6686 9181. ***Sandbar and Restaurant:*** modern European, tapas; 23 Compton Dr; (02) 6686 6602.

🛏 ***Ballina Central Holiday Park:*** 1 River St; (02) 6686 2220. ***Ballina Gardens Caravan Park:*** 126 Tamarind Dr (Old Pacific Hwy); (02) 6686 2475. ***Ballina Waterfront Village & Tourist Park:*** 586 River St; (02) 6686 2984. ***Ballina Beach Village, Dolphin Bay:*** 440 South Ballina Beach Rd, South Ballina; (02) 6686 3347. ***Ballina Headlands Leisure Park:*** 35 Skennars Head Rd, Skennars Head; (02) 6687 7450. ***Lake Ainsworth Holiday Park:*** Cnr Ross St and Pacific Pde, Lennox Head; (02) 6687 7249. ***Sandalwood Van & Leisure Park:*** 978 Pimlico Rd, Wardell; (02) 6683 4221. ***Shaws Bay Holiday Park:*** 1 Brighton St, East Ballina; (02) 6686 2326.

Lennox Head A beachside town with a good market on the 2nd and 5th Sun each month on the shores of Lake Ainsworth (also a popular spot for windsurfing). The lake has been nicknamed the Coca-Cola lake due to coloration from surrounding tea trees. Pat Morton Lookout affords excellent views along the coast, with whale-watching June–July and Sept–Oct. Below is The Point, a world-renowned surf beach. The outskirts of town offer scenic rainforest walks. 10 km N.

Thursday Plantation: tea-tree plantation with product sales and maze; (02) 6620 5150; 3 km W. *Macadamia Castle:* features macadamia products, industry displays, minigolf and children's wildlife park; (02) 6687 8432; 15 km N. *Whale-watching:* bookings at visitor centre.

TOWNS NEARBY: Alstonville 12 km, Byron Bay 25 km, Lismore 29 km, Evans Head 31 km, Mullumbimby 35 km

Balranald

Pop. 1217
Map ref. 526 H7 | 547 M9

 Heritage Park, 81 Market St; (03) 5020 1599; www.balranald.nsw.gov.au

 93.1 FM ABC Radio National, 102.1 FM ABC Local

Balranald is the oldest town on the lower part of the Murrumbidgee River. Situated on saltbush and mallee plains, the area now embraces the viticulture, horticulture and tourism industries. A string of dry lake beds stretches to the north of Balranald, the most famous of which are preserved in Mungo National Park. Recently, the oldest remaining human footprints in Australia were found in the park, estimated to be up to 23 000 years old.

Heritage Park Investigate the old gaol, the Murray pine schoolhouse, local history displays and a historical museum. There are also picnic and barbecue facilities. Market St.

Art gallery: exhibitions by local artists, housed in 1880s Masonic Lodge; Mayall St. *Balranald Weir:* barbecues, picnics, fishing. *Memorial Drive:* great views. *Frog Sculptures:* 14 throughout town. *Self-guide town walk:* historically significant buildings in the town; maps available from visitor centre.

Balranald Cup: horserace; Feb/Mar.

Balranald Caravan Park: 60 Court St; (03) 5020 1321. *Euston Riverfront Caravan Park & Cafe:* 27 Murray Tce, Euston; (03) 5026 1543.

Mungo National Park This park is the focal point of the Willandra Lakes World Heritage Area, a 240 000 ha region dotted with 17 dry lakes. These lakes display astounding evidence of ancient Aboriginal life and of creatures that existed during the last Ice Age, including Mungo Man, a full male skeleton estimated to be around 40 000 years old. The highlight is the 33 km crescent-shaped dune on the eastern edge of Lake Mungo, called the Walls of China, which you can visit on a 70 km self-guide drive through the park. The park contains some remarkable animal remains, as well as ancient fireplaces, artefacts and tools. The Mungo Visitor Centre delves into the heritage of the Willandra Lakes, and has a replica of the diprotodon, a massive wombat-like marsupial; Arumpo Rd; (03) 5021 8900 or 1300 361 967. A 70 km self-guide drive tour, suitable for conventional vehicles, takes in the Walls of China, old tanks and wells and an old homestead site. Accommodation in the park includes the old Mungo Shearers' Quarters and a campground. 100 km N.

Moulamein The oldest town in the Riverina, Moulamein has fascinating historic structures to explore including its restored courthouse (1845) and Old Wharf (1850s). There are picnic areas by the Edward River and Lake Moulamein. 99 km SE.

Yanga Lake: fishing and watersports; 7 km SE. *Homebush Hotel:* built in 1878 as a Cobb & Co station, the hotel now provides meals and accommodation; (03) 5020 6803; 25 km N. *Kyalite:* home to Australia's largest commercial pistachio nut farm and popular with campers and anglers; 36 km S. *Redbank Weir:* barbecues and picnics; Homebush–Oxley Rd; 58 km N.

TOWNS NEARBY: Robinvale (Vic.) 73 km, Swan Hill (Vic.) 78 km, Hay 119 km, Barham 121 km, Ouyen (Vic.) 123 km

Barham

Pop. 1131
Map ref. 527 I10 | 542 A2 | 549 O4

Golden Rivers Tourism, 15 Murray St; (03) 5453 3100

107.7/102.5 Mix FM, 594 AM ABC Local

Barham and its twin town, Koondrook, sit beside the Murray River and the New South Wales–Victoria border. Barham is known as the southern gateway to Golden Rivers country and is surrounded by river flats and red hills. The Murray River makes Barham a great place for anglers with Murray cod, golden perch, catfish and yabbies in abundance. Barham Bridge is one of the oldest bridges on the Murray and was lifted manually until 1997.

Barham Lakes Complex The complex is popular with locals and visitors alike. It has 4 artificial lakes stocked with fish and yabbies, grasslands with hundreds of native plants, a walking track and barbecue facilities. Murray St.

Border Flywheelers Vintage Engine Rally: Feb. *The Country Music Stampede:* Feb and Aug. *Jazz Festival:* June. *Barham Produce and Food Festival:* Aug. *Golden Rivers Red Gum Forest to Furniture Showcase:* Oct.

Barham Caravan & Tourist Park: 1 Noorong St; (03) 5453 2553. *Barham Lakes Murray View Caravan Park:* East Barham Rd; (03) 5453 2009. *Koondrook Caravan Park:* Keene St, Koondrook, Vic.; (03) 5453 2103.

Koondrook State Forest Koondrook State Forest is 31 000 ha of native bushland that is perfect for birdwatchers and nature enthusiasts. The forest has over 100 bird species, kangaroos, emus and wild pigs. Forest drives winding through the park are well signposted. 12 km NE.

Koondrook: old sawmilling town and river port with historic buildings and tramway; 5 km SW. *Murrabit:* largest country markets in the region; 1st Sat each month; Murrabit Rd; 24 km NW.

TOWNS NEARBY: Cohuna (Vic.) 22 km, Kerang (Vic.) 22 km, Pyramid Hill (Vic.) 48 km, Swan Hill (Vic.) 60 km, Deniliquin 76 km

Barraba

Pop. 1163
Map ref. 524 H7

112 Queen St; (02) 6782 1255.

99.1 FM ABC Local, 648 AM ABC Local

The tree-lined streets of Barraba lie in the valley of the Manilla River. Surrounded by the Nandewar Ranges, Horton Valley and

 RADIO STATIONS IN TOWN WHAT'S ON WHERE TO EAT WHERE TO STAY NEARBY

undulating tablelands, Barraba is a quiet and idyllic town. The area was once busy with mining and, although some mines still operate, the main industries today centre around sheep and wool.

Heritage walk The walk takes in a heritage-listed organ and historic buildings such as the courthouse, church, clock tower and the visitor centre itself. The Commercial Hotel on Queen St was once a Cobb & Co changing station.

Clay Pan and Fuller Gallery: exhibits art, craft and pottery; Queen St. *The Playhouse:* accommodation including a theatre and exhibition space; Queen St; (02) 6782 1109.

Market: 1st Sat each month; Queen St. *Australia's Smallest Country Music Festival:* Jan. *Barraba Agricultural Show and Rodeo:* Feb/Mar. *Australia's Smallest Jazz and Blues Festival:* Easter. *Frost Over Barraba:* art show; July. *BarrArbor Festival:* celebration of culture; Nov. *Horton Valley Rodeo:* Dec.

Mt Kaputar National Park This park is excellent for hiking, rising as high as 1200 m, and is the site of the now extinct Nandewar Volcano. The diverse vegetation ranges from semi-arid woodland to wet sclerophyll forest and alpine growth. Wildlife is abundant, especially bats, birds and quolls. Access to the park from Barraba is by foot only, although permission for 4WD access can be granted by the visitor centre. 48 km w.

Adams Lookout: panoramic views of the town and countryside; 5 km NE. *Millie Park Vineyard:* organic wine cellar-door tastings and sales; 5 km N. *Glen Riddle Recreation Reserve:* on Manilla River north of Split Rock Dam, for boating, fishing and picnicking; 15 km SE. *Ironbark Creek:* gold and mineral fossicking, with ruins of old village; 18 km E. *Horton River Falls:* 83 m waterfall, swimming and bushwalking; 38 km w. *Birdwatching trails:* the 165 species in the area include the rare regent honeyeater. Guides are available from the visitor centre.

TOWNS NEARBY: Manilla 42 km, Bingara 57 km, Gunnedah 74 km, Narrabri 80 km, Inverell 83 km

Bathurst

Pop. 30 748
Map ref. 522 H5

ℹ️ Kendall Ave; (02) 6332 1444 or 1800 681 000; www.visitbathurst.com.au

📻 96.7 FM ABC Radio National, 99.3 B-Rock FM

Bathurst, on the western side of the Great Dividing Range, is Australia's oldest inland city. Originally occupied by the Wiradjuri people, it was the site of enormous conflict in 1824 between its original inhabitants and the European settlers. Since then, Bathurst has become known as the birthplace of Ben Chifley, Australian prime minister 1945–49, and for its magnificent Georgian and Victorian architecture. Today it is best known for its motor racing circuit, Mount Panorama.

Miss Traill's House Ida Traill (1889–1976) was a fourth-generation descendant of pioneers William Lee and Thomas Kite who came to Bathurst in 1818. Her house, a colonial Georgian bungalow filled with artefacts and bequeathed to the National Trust, was built in 1845, making it one of the oldest houses in Bathurst. The 19th-century cottage garden is particularly charming in spring. Russell St; (02) 6332 4232.

Bathurst District Historical Museum: features notable local Aboriginal artefacts in the east wing of the Neoclassical Bathurst Courthouse; Russell St; (02) 6330 8455. *Australian Fossil and Mineral Museum:* exhibits close to 2000 fossil and mineral specimens, including rare and unique displays, housed in the 1876 public school building; Howick St; (02) 6331 5511. *Bathurst Regional Art Gallery:* focuses on Australian art after 1955, with frequently changing exibitions; Keppel St; (02) 6333 6555. *Machattie Park:* Victorian-era park in the heart of the city, with a begonia house full of blooms Feb–Apr; Keppel, William and George sts. *Self-guide historical walking tour and self-drive tour:* takes in Bathurst Gaol, the courthouse and historic homes, including Ben Chifley's house; map from visitor centre.

Gold Crown Festival: harness racing; Mar. *Autumn Colours:* variety of events celebrating autumn; Mar–May. *V8 Supercars 1000:* Oct.

Church Bar + Woodfired Pizza: gourmet pizza; 1 Ribbon Gang La; (02) 6334 2300. *Cobblestone Lane:* modern Australian; Shop 2, 173–179 George St; (02) 6331 2202.

Bathurst Heights Bed & Breakfast: 9 John Norton Pl; (02) 6331 6330. *Magnolia Manor Boutique Hotel B & B:* 209 William St; (02) 6332 3143. *Lochinvar Luxury Cottages Mt Panorama:* 448 Conrod Straight, Mt Panorama; (02) 6331 2469. *Tanwarra Lodge:* 324 Hill End Rd, Sofala; (02) 6337 7537.

Mt Panorama The inaugural Bathurst 1000 was held here in 1960 and has since become an Australian institution. The 6.2 km scenic circuit is open year-round, and while the lap record is 129.7 seconds (over 170 km/h), visitors are limited to 60 km/h. The National Motor Racing Museum at the circuit displays race cars, trophies, memorabilia and special exhibits; (02) 6332 1872. Also at Mt Panorama are the Bathurst Goldfields, a reconstruction of a historic goldmining area, and McPhillamy Park, which features the Sir Joseph Banks Nature Reserve with great views over Bathurst, especially at sunrise and sunset. 2 km S.

Abercrombie House: impressive 1870s baronial-style Gothic mansion; Ophir Rd; 6 km w. *Bathurst Sheep and Cattle Drome:* visitors can milk a cow and see shearing and sheepdog demonstrations; Limekilns Rd; 6 km NE. *Bathurst Observatory:* program varies throughout the year. The visitor centre features mineral, fossil and space displays. The complex is closed in inclement weather; 12 km NE. *Wallaby Rocks:* wall of rock rising from the Turon River and a popular spot for kangaroos and wallabies. Also an ideal swimming and picnic spot; 40 km N. *Sofala:* historic gold town and the setting for scenes from the films *The Cars That Ate Paris* (1974) and *Sirens* (1994); 42 km N. *Hill End Historic Site:* former goldfield with many original buildings. The area has inspired painters Russell Drysdale, Donald Friend, John Olsen and Brett Whiteley. There is a National Parks & Wildlife Service visitor centre in old Hill End Hospital, which has a historical display and information on panning and fossicking, with equipment for hire; (02) 6337 8206. Old gold towns nearby include Peel, Wattle Flat, Rockley, O'Connell and Trunkey; 86 km NW.

TOWNS NEARBY: Blayney 33 km, Oberon 41 km, Orange 47 km, Lithgow 52 km, Blackheath 70 km

Batlow

Pop. 997
Map ref. 519 A5 | 520 C4 | 522 D11 | 543 P3

ℹ️ Tumut Region Visitor Centre, 5 Adelong Rd, Tumut; (02) 6947 7025; www.tumut.nsw.gov.au

📻 96.3 FM Sounds of the Mountain, 675 AM ABC Local Radio

In the 19th-century gold rush prospectors converged on nearby Reedy Creek, which sparked a sudden demand for fresh produce.

continued on p. 30

BATEMANS BAY

Pop. 10 843

Map ref. 519 F6 | 521 L6 | 522 H12

ℹ️ Cnr Princes Hwy and Beach Rd; (02) 4472 6900 or 1800 802 528; www.eurobodalla.com.au

📻 103.5 FM ABC Local, 103.5 FM ABC South East, 104.3 Power FM

Batemans Bay is a popular town for holiday-makers at the mouth of the Clyde River. It has something for everyone with rolling surf beaches, quiet coves and rockpools, and wonderful views upriver to the hinterland mountains, and out to sea to the islands on the horizon. It is the home of the famous Clyde River oyster and other excellent fresh seafood.

🏠 **Birdland Animal Park:** a hands-on experience with more than 80 species of native wildlife; from 9.30am daily; 55 Beach Rd; (02) 4472 5364. **River cruises:** daily cruises at 11.30am on the *Merinda* to historic Nelligen depart from the wharf behind The Boatshed; 1 Clyde St; (02) 4472 4052. **Houseboat hire and fishing charters:** bookings at visitor centre.

🌴 **Batemans Bay Markets:** Marine Rescue Market at Corrigans Reserve, 1st Sun each month; High School Market at Corrigans Reserve, 3rd Sun each month; Beach Rd.

🍴 **Briars Restaurant:** modern Australian; Lincoln Downs, Princes Hwy; (02) 4472 9200 or 1800 789 250. **On the Pier:** waterfront seafood; 2 Old Punt Rd; (02) 4472 6405. **Starfish Deli Restaurant:** relaxed dining; shop 1, The Promenade, 2 Clyde St; (02) 4472 4880.

🛏️ **BIG4 Batemans Bay Easts Riverside Holiday Park:** Wharf Rd; (02) 4472 4048. **Shady Willows Holiday Park:** Cnr Old Princes Hwy and South St; (02) 4472 4972. **Barlings Beach Tourist Park:** 1939 George Bass Dr, Tomakin; (02) 4471 7313. **BIG4 Batemans Bay Beach Resort:** 51 Beach Rd, Batehaven; (02) 4472 4541. **BIG4 Nelligen Holiday Park:** Kings Hwy, Nelligen; (02) 4478 1076. **BIG4 South Durras Holiday Park:** 9 Beagle Bay Rd, South Durras; (02) 4478 6028. **Clyde View Caravan Park:** 107 Beach Rd, Batehaven; (02) 4472 4224. **Lakesea Park:** Durras Lake Rd, South Durras; (02) 4478 6122.

Murramarang Beachfront Nature Resort: Mill Beach Banyandah St, South Durras; (02) 4478 6355.

⚙️ **Mogo** Born in a gold rush, Mogo is alive with a quaint village atmosphere. It has antique and collectibles stores, art galleries and specialty shops. At the Original Gold Rush Colony, pan for gold and experience life in a recreated 19th-century goldmining town, with bushrangers, mine tunnels and authentic houses; 26 James St, Mogo; (02) 4474 2123; open 7 days 10am–4pm winter, 10am–5pm summer. Wildlife enthusiasts will enjoy Mogo Zoo – it specialises in raising endangered species such as tigers, white lions, snow leopards and red pandas; 22 Tomakin Rd, Mogo; (02) 4474 4930; 9am–5pm 7 days. Mogo offers fabulous village-style shopping and cafes, featuring antique and collectibles stores, art galleries and specialty shops. Mogo State Forest is popular with birdwatchers and bushwalkers, and is home to lorikeets, kookaburras, rosellas and cockatoos. Enjoy the sclerophyll forest of the 1.3 km Mogo Bushwalk. 8 km s.

Eurobodalla Native Botanic Gardens: 42 ha of native plants, walking tracks, nursery and picnic area; open Wed–Fri 9am–4pm, weekends, school and public holidays 10am–4pm; Princes Hwy; (02) 4471 2544; 5 km s. *Murramarang National Park:* undisturbed coastline and abundant kangaroos; 10 km NE. *Murramarang Aboriginal Area:* signposted walk through 12 000-year-old Aboriginal sites and the largest midden on the south coast; just north of Murramarang National Park. *Nelligen:* an important Clyde River port in pioneer days, when goods were shipped from here down to Sydney or sent into the hinterland; nowadays, holiday-makers use the historic town as a base for waterskiing, fishing and houseboat vacations; 10 km NW. *Malua Bay:* excellent surfing; 14 km SE. *Durras Lake:* fishing, kayaking and swimming; 16 km NE. *Tomakin:* coastal holiday village by the Tomaga River with miles of pristine family-friendly beaches and forested hinterland. 15 km s.

TOWNS NEARBY: Moruya 24 km, Braidwood 45 km, Ulladulla 47 km, Narooma 57 km, Bermagui 80 km

[BODY SURFERS CATCHING A WAVE AT MALUA BAY]

The resulting orchards and farms became the town of Batlow. Set in the low-lying mountains of the state's south-west slopes, Batlow is a picturesque town still surrounded by orchards of delicious apples, pears, berries, cherries and stone fruit.

Batlow Woodworks: discover a range of art, pottery, woodworks and crafts, serving morning and afternoon tea; Pioneer St; (02) 6949 1265. *Weemala Lookout:* breathtaking views of town and Snowy Mountains; H. V. Smith Dr.

Apple Blossom Festival: Oct.

Mountain View Cafe: popular cafe; 56 Pioneer St; (02) 6949 1110.

Hume and Hovell Lookout: great views over Blowering Valley and Blowering Reservoir, with picnic area at the site where explorers rested in 1824; 6 km E. *Tumut Rd:* fresh fruit along the road. Springfield Orchard, 6 km N, grows 16 apple varieties and has picnic and barbecue facilities. *Kosciuszko National Park:* this alpine park to the east includes nearby Bowering Reservoir and Buddong Falls; *for more details see Adaminaby.* *Hume and Hovell Walking Track:* access to short sections of the 440 km track via Tumut Rd. Maps available from visitor centre.

TOWNS NEARBY: Adelong 24 km, Tumut 25 km, Tumbarumba 31 km, Gundagai 50 km, Adaminaby 77 km

Bega
Pop. 4536
Map ref. 519 E9 | 521 J12 | 539 H6

ℹ️ Lagoon St; (02) 6491 7645; www.sapphirecoast.com.au

📻 102.5 Power FM, 810 AM ABC Local

It is possible to ski and surf on the same day around Bega, set in a fertile valley with the mountains of the Kosciuszko snow resorts to the west and breathtaking coastline to the east. Bega is best known for its dairy industry, particularly cheese-making.

Bega Family Museum: houses town memorabilia including silverware, ball gowns, farm machinery and photographs; open Mon–Sat Sept–May, Tues and Fri June–Aug; Cnr Bega and Auckland sts; (02) 6492 1453.

Bega Valley Art Awards: Oct.

Bega Downs Restaurant: modern Australian; Bega Downs Motor Inn, cnr Princes Hwy and High St; (02) 6492 2944. *Pepperberry Restaurant:* friendly cafe; Shop 1, Ayres Walkway; (02) 6492 0361.

Bega Caravan Park: 256 Princes Hwy; (02) 6492 2303. *Mumbulla View:* Cnr Princes Hwy and Cobargo St, Quaama; (02) 6493 8351. *Yasuragi Cabins:* 421 Blanchards Rd, Brogo; (02) 6492 7152.

Biamanga National Park Now a popular spot for swimming, bushwalking and picnics, Biamanga National Park has long been a sacred site to the Yuin people. Mumbulla Mountain was an initiation site for young men and Mumbulla Creek was used to wash off ceremonial ochre. Visitors can now enjoy the rockpools, natural water slides, boardwalks, viewing platforms and picnic sites of this culturally significant area. 19 km NE.

Bega Cheese Heritage Centre: restored cheese factory with cheese-tasting and displays of cheese-making equipment; (02) 6491 7762; 3 km N. *Lookouts:* excellent views at Bega Valley Lookout (3 km N) and Dr George Lookout (8 km NE). *Candelo:* charming and peaceful village with market on 1st Sun each month; 24 km SW. *Brogo Dam:* haven for native birdlife such as sea eagles and azure kingfishers. Also popular for bass fishing, swimming, picnicking, boating and canoeing (canoe hire on-site; (02) 6492 7328); 30 km NW.

TOWNS NEARBY: Tathra 14 km, Merimbula 25 km, Bermagui 35 km, Eden 44 km, Narooma 57 km

Bellingen
Pop. 2878
Map ref. 515 G1 | 516 D12 | 525 M8

ℹ️ Hyde St; (02) 6655 1522; www.bellingermagic.com

📻 107.3 2BBB FM, 738 AM ABC Local

Bellingen is an attractive tree-lined town on the banks of the Bellinger River, surrounded by rich pasturelands. Traditionally serving dairy farmers and timber cutters, Bellingen is now a haven for urban folk fleeing the big cities, attracted to the relaxed and alternative lifestyle on offer. City touches can be found in shops and cafes, but the town retains its laid-back feel. The area is the setting for Peter Carey's novel *Oscar and Lucinda.*

Bellingen Bat Island This 3 ha island is home to a colony of up to 40 000 grey-headed flying foxes (fruit bats). At dusk the flying foxes set off in search of food, filling the sky. The best time to visit is Sept–Mar. Access is via Bellingen Caravan Park in Dowle St (north of the river).

Horse-drawn carriage tours: guided tours of town and river picnics (operate during holidays and by appt); 0423 671 581. *Bellingen Museum:* features extensive photo collection of early pioneer life and early transportation; Hyde St; (02) 6655 1259. *Hammond and Wheatley Emporium:* the first concrete block construction in Australia, the emporium has been magnificently restored – including a grand staircase leading to a mezzanine floor – and is now home to boutiques, homewares retailers and jewellery galleries; Hyde St. *Local art and craft:* galleries thoughout the town including The Yellow Shed, cnr Hyde and Prince sts, and The Old Butter Factory, Doepel St.

Bellingen Markets: Bellingen Park, Church St; 3rd Sat each month. *Jazz Festival:* Aug. *Global Carnival:* world music; Oct.

Lodge 241 Gallery Cafe: historic riverside cafe; 117–212 Hyde St; (02) 6655 2470. *No 2 Oak Street:* modern Australian; 2 Oak St; (02) 6655 9000. *Vintage Espresso:* great coffee in charming vintage store; 62 Hyde St; (02) 6655 0015.

Rivendell Guest House: 10 Hyde St; (02) 6655 0060. *Lily Pily Country House:* 54 Sunny Corner Rd, Kalang; (02) 6655 0522.

Raleigh Vineyard and Winery: tastings available; (02) 6655 4388; 11 km E. *Walking, cycling, horseriding and canoeing:* along the Bellinger River and in forest areas; information and maps from visitor centre. *Scenic drive:* north-east through wooded valleys and farmlands, across Never Never Creek to Promised Land; map available from visitor centre.

TOWNS NEARBY: Urunga 12 km, Dorrigo 22 km, Nambucca Heads 24 km, Coffs Harbour 27 km, Macksville 28 km

Bermagui
Pop. 1298
Map ref. 519 E8 | 521 K11

ℹ️ Bunga St; (02) 6493 3054 or 1800 645 808; www.sapphirecoast.com.au

📻 102.5 Power FM, 105.9 FM 2EC, 810 AM ABC Local

Bermagui is a charming and sleepy coastal village. The continental shelf is at its closest to the mainland off Bermagui and this results in excellent fishing for marlin, tuna and shark. Zane Grey was a famous visitor in the 1930s and the town featured in two of his books. Bermagui is also the centre of a mystery involving a geologist, Lamont Young, who was sent to investigate goldfields in 1880. When he decided to head north to investigate further, he and his assistant were offered passage on a small boat with three men. All five disappeared en route. When their boat was discovered, it was found to have five bags of clothing, Young's books and papers, and a bullet in the starboard side. Despite extensive searches and media attention, no trace of the men was ever found.

 Fish Co-op: freshly caught fish and prawns; Fishermans Wharf, harbourside. *Blue Pool:* large and attractive saltwater rockpool offering an unusual swimming experience; off Scenic Dr. *Horseshoe Bay Beach:* safe swimming spot. ***Good surfing beaches:*** Beares, Mooreheads, Cuttagee and Haywards beaches; maps from visitor centre. ***Gamefishing, deep-sea fishing and reef-fishing:*** bookings at visitor centre.

 Craft Market: Dickinson Park; last Sun each month. ***Blue Water Fishing Classic:*** Jan. ***Seaside Fair:*** Mar. ***Tag and Release Gamefishing Tournament:*** Mar. ***Four Winds Festival:*** even-numbered years, Easter. ***Victorian Southern Gamefish Challenge:*** Easter.

 Bermagui Mud Works Pottery & Cafe: cafe with Balinese feel; 23 Alexander Dr; (02) 6493 4661. *Saltwater at Bermagui:* seafood cafe; 59 Lamont St; (02) 6493 4328.

 Ocean Lake Caravan Park: Wallaga Lake Rd; (02) 6493 4055. *Zane Grey Bermagui Tourist Park:* Lamont St; (02) 6493 4382. *Green Gables:* 269 Corkhill Dr, Tilba Tilba; (02) 4473 7435. *The Old Convent Cobargo:* Wandella Rd, Cobargo; (02) 6493 6419. *Regatta Point Holiday Park:* Regatta Point Rd, Wallaga Lake; (02) 6493 4253. *Wallaga Lake Park:* Wallaga Lake Rd, Wallaga Lake; (02) 6493 4655.

 Gulaga National Park The Wallaga Lakes area has an 8 km coastal walk through wetland flora and fauna reserves and remnants of the Montreal Goldfield north to Wallaga Lake. It passes Camel Rock, an unusual rock formation in the general shape of a camel. The park is hilly with steep gullies, so it is best explored by boat (available for hire from Regatta Pt and Beauty Pt). Guided tours are available through Montreal Goldfield (bookings at visitor centre). There are good walking trails, including one to the summit of Mt Dromedary. The park is excellent for boating, fishing, swimming, picnicking and bushwalking. The Yuin people run Aboriginal cultural tours from the Umballa Cultural Centre, sharing Dreamtime stories that have never been recorded on paper. Activities include ochre painting, bark-hut building and boomerang throwing. Bookings and information (02) 4473 7232; 6 km N.

Mimosa Rocks National Park: 17 km S; *see Tathra. Mystery Bay:* the site of the discovery of Lamont Young's abandoned boat and a memorial; 17 km N. *Cobargo:* historic working village with art galleries, wood and leather crafts, antiques, pottery and tearooms. A country market on 4th Sat each month at RSL hall grounds; 20 km W.

TOWNS NEARBY: Narooma 23 km, Bega 35 km, Tathra 35 km, Merimbula 54 km, Moruya 56 km

Berridale

Pop. 844
Map ref. 519 B8 | 520 E10 | 539 D4

 Snowy Region Visitor Centre, Kosciuszko Rd, Jindabyne; (02) 6450 5600 or 1800 004 439; www.snowymountains.com.au

 97.7 Snow FM, 810 AM ABC Local

This charming small town calls itself the 'Crossroads of the Snowy' and is a popular stopover point in winter between Cooma and the snowfields. In the 1860s and 1870s it was known as Gegedzerick, but later changed its name to Berridale, the name of a local property. The main street is lined with poplars that provide a striking show in autumn. The trees were planted about 100 years ago by children from Berridale School.

 Ray Killen Gallery: landscape photographs from around Australia; Jindabyne Rd. *Historic buildings:* St Mary's (1860), Mary St; Berridale School (1883), Oliver St; Berridale Inn (1863), Exchange Sq; Berridale Store (1863), Exchange Sq. *Boulders:* unique granite boulders near to the main road were formed from crystallised magma 400 million years ago.

 Snowy Vineyard Estate: charming restaurant, wine tastings; Werralong Rd; 1300 766 608.

 Sierra Villa Lodge: 56 Oliver St; (02) 6456 3878. *Buckenderra Holiday Village:* 490 Buckenderra Rd, Buckenderra; (02) 6453 7242.

 Snowy Vineyard Estate: wine-tastings and restaurant; Werralong Rd; 1300 766 608; 3 km N. *Dalgety:* small town featuring historic Buckley's Crossing Hotel, which marks the spot where cattle used to cross the Snowy River; 18 km S. *Eucumbene Trout Farm:* sales, horseriding and tours; (02) 6456 8866; 19 km N. *Snowy River Ag Barn and Fibre Centre:* museum, craft and fibre shop, animals and restaurant; 21 km S.

TOWNS NEARBY: Jindabyne 19 km, Cooma 31 km, Adaminaby 41 km, Thredbo 49 km, Khancoban 65 km

Berrima

Pop. 867
Map ref. 517 B5 | 519 G2 | 523 I8

 Berrima Courthouse, cnr Wilshire and Argyle sts; (02) 4877 1505; www.berrimavillage.com.au

 102.9 FM 2ST, 675 AM ABC Local

A superbly preserved 1830s village, Berrima is nestled in a valley next to the Wingecarribee River. The National Heritage Council declared the village a historic precinct in the 1960s. Many buildings have been restored as antique shops, restaurants and galleries.

 Berrima Courthouse The courthouse was the scene in 1841 of Australia's first trial by jury, in which Lucretia Dunkley and Martin Beech were accused of having an affair and tried for murdering Lucretia's much older husband, Henry, with an axe. They were both found guilty and hanged. The building, said to be the finest in town, now houses displays on the trial and early Berrima. Cnr Wilshire and Argyle sts; (02) 4877 1505.

Berrima District Historical Museum: displays focus on colonial settlement and the struggles of pioneer days; Market Pl; (02) 4877 1130. *Harpers Mansion:* Georgian house built in 1834, now owned by the National Trust; Wilkinson St. *Australian Alpaca Centre:* sales of knitwear and toys; Market Pl. *The Surveyor General:* built in 1835, Australia's oldest continually licensed hotel; Old Hume Hwy. *Berrima Gaol:* Bushranger Paddy Curran was the first man hanged there in 1842 and Lucretia Dunkley was the first and only woman executed there; Argyle St.

Market: 2nd Sun each month; school grounds; Oxley St.

Eschalot: modern Australian; 24 Old Hume Hwy; (02) 4877 1977. **Josh's Cafe:** popular restaurant with Middle Eastern influences; shop 2, 9 Old Hume Hwy; (02) 4877 2200.

Wineries: numerous in the area with cellar-door tastings including Southern Highland Wines in Sutton Forest (02) 4868 2300; 10 km s; and Mundrakoona Estate in Mittagong (02) 4872 1311; 10 km NE; maps from visitor centre.

TOWNS NEARBY: Bowral 8 km, Moss Vale 8 km, Bundanoon 19 km, Robertson 26 km, Picton 43 km

Berry
Pop. 1485
Map ref. 517 D8 | 519 G3 | 523 J9

i Shoalhaven Visitors Centre, cnr Princes Hwy and Pleasant Way, Nowra; (02) 4421 0778 or 1300 662 808; www.berry.org.au

94.9 Power FM, 603 AM Radio National

The local chamber of commerce named Berry 'The Town of Trees' because of the extensive stands of English oaks, elms and beech trees planted by settlers in the 1800s. Berry is a popular weekend destination for Sydneysiders searching for bargains in the antique and craft shops and looking to enjoy the laid-back atmosphere. With the Cambewarra Ranges as its backdrop, Berry is the first truly rural town south of Sydney.

Berry Historical Museum: records and photographs of early settlement; open 11am–2pm Sat, 11am–3pm Sun, daily during school holidays; Queen St; (02) 4464 3097. **Precinct Galleries:** local contemporary art, craft and design; Alexandra St. **Great Warrior Aboriginal Art Gallery:** contemporary and traditional Aboriginal art, weapons, artefacts and didgeridoos; Queen St. **Antique and craft shops:** contact visitor centre for details.

Country Fair Markets: showground, cnr Alexandra and Victoria sts, 1st Sun each month (except Feb); Great Southern Hotel, Queen St, 3rd Sun each month. **Musicale festival:** June. **Garden Festival:** Oct.

Hungry Duck: modern Asian/Australian; 85 Queen St; (02) 4464 2323. **The Posthouse:** modern Australian; 137 Queen St; (02) 4464 2444.

Broughton Mill Farm Guesthouse Berry: 78 Woodhill Mountain Rd; (02) 4464 2446. **Coastal Palms Holiday Park:** 40 Shoalhaven Heads Rd, Shoalhaven Heads; (02) 4448 7206. **Discovery Holiday Parks – Gerroa:** 107 Crooked River Rd, Gerroa; (02) 4234 1233. **Drawing Rooms of Berry:** 21 Wattamolla Rd, Woodhill; (02) 4464 3360. **Mountain View Caravan Park:** 14 Shoalhaven Heads Rd, Shoalhaven Heads; (02) 4448 7281. **Seven Mile Beach Holiday Park:** 200 Crooked River Rd, Gerroa; (02) 4234 1340. **Shoalhaven Heads Tourist Park:** Shoalhaven Heads Rd, Shoalhaven Heads; 1300 782 222. **Tall Timbers Caravan Park:** 47 Shoalhaven Heads Rd, Shoalhaven Heads; (02) 4448 7270.

Coolangatta: convict-built cottages, winery (open for tastings) and accommodation on site of first European settlement in area; 11 km SE. **Other wineries in area:** open for tastings and sales; map from visitor centre. **Mild to Wild Tours:** adventure tours including sea-kayaking with dolphins, rock climbing, moonlight canoeing and mountain-biking; bookings (02) 4464 2211.

TOWNS NEARBY: Nowra 15 km, Jamberoo 16 km, Kiama 19 km, Robertson 23 km, Shellharbour 27 km

Bingara
Pop. 1205
Map ref. 524 H6

 i Roxy Theatre Building, Maitland St; (02) 6724 0066 or 1300 659 919; www.bingara.com.au

102.9 Gem FM, 648 AM ABC Local

Located in the centre of an area known as Fossickers Way, Bingara is an old gold- and diamond-mining town in the Gwydir River Valley. Gold was discovered here in 1852. Prospectors have been attracted to the town ever since, drawn by the chance of discovering their own fortunes in gold, tourmaline, sapphires and garnets, and by the peaceful cypress-covered mountain surrounds.

Orange Tree Memorial Orange trees along Finch St and Gwydir Oval stand as a memorial to those who have fallen in war. It is a town tradition that, during the Orange Festival, Bingara's children pick the fruit and present it to hospital patients and the elderly.

All Nations Goldmine: a stamper battery is the only visible remnant; Hill St. **Bingara Historical Museum:** slab building (1860) displays gems and minerals and 19th-century furniture and photographs; Maitland St. **Visitor Information Centre:** set in the beautifully restored 1930s Art Deco Roxy Theatre complex; Maitland St. **Gwydir River Rides:** trail rides; Keera St. **Gwydir River:** walking track along the bank, and reportedly the best Murray cod fishing in NSW. **Self-guide historical/scenic town walk and drive:** contact visitor centre for maps.

Bingara Cup Race Meeting: Feb. **Bingara Fishing Competition:** Easter. **Campdraft:** Apr. **Orange Festival:** Aug.

Bingara Riverside Caravan Park: Keera Rd; (02) 6724 1209.

Three Creeks Goldmine: working mine open to the public for gold panning, crystal fossicking and bushwalking; 24 km s. **Myall Creek Memorial:** monument to 28 Aboriginal men, women and children killed in the massacre of 1838; Delungra–Bingara Rd; 27 km NE. **Rocky Creek glacial area:** unusual conglomerate rock formations; 37 km sw. **Sawn Rocks:** pipe-shaped volcanic rock formations; 70 km sw. **Birdwatching and fossicking:** maps available from visitor centre.

TOWNS NEARBY: Warialda 36 km, Inverell 53 km, Barraba 57 km, Moree 84 km, Narrabri 91 km

Blackheath
Pop. 4178
Map ref. 510 C4 | 512 F6 | 523 I6

 i Heritage Centre, Govetts Leap Rd; (02) 4787 8877; www.visitbluemountains.com.au

89.1 BLU FM, 675 AM ABC Local

This pretty resort town, the highest in the Blue Mountains, has breathtaking views. Known for its guesthouses, gardens and bushwalks, Blackheath is in an ideal location at the edge of Blue Mountains National Park. It is also known as 'Rhododendron Town' for the myriad varieties that bloom every November.

National Parks and Wildlife Heritage Centre More than just an information resource, the centre features an interactive display on the geology, wildlife, and Aboriginal and European history

[BLACKHEATH] BACCHANTE GARDENS

of the area, and offers historical tours and guided walks. It is the starting point for the Fairfax Heritage Walk, a gentle bushwalk with wheelchair access and facilities for the visually impaired. The 4 km return trail goes to Govetts Leap Lookout for views across several waterfalls and the Grose Valley. Govetts Leap Rd.

Govett statue: commemorates the bushranger known as Govett, said to have ridden his horse over a cliff rather than be captured by police; centre of town.

Markets: Growers Market, Community Hall, Great Western Hwy, 2nd Sun each month; Community Market, School Grounds, 1st Sun each month. **Blue Mountains Food and Wine Fair:** Apr. **Rhododendron Festival:** Nov.

Ashcrofts: modern Australian; 18 Govetts Leap Rd; (02) 4787 8297. **Vulcan's:** modern Australian; 33 Govetts Leap Rd; (02) 4787 6899.

Blue Mountains Tourist Park – Blackheath Glen: 67–69 Prince Edward St; (02) 4787 8101. **Chalet Blue Mountains B&B:** 46 Portland Rd, Medlow Bath; (02) 4788 1122. **Chimney Cottage, Blueberry Lodge, The Loft:** Waterfall Rd, Mount Wilson; (02) 4756 2022. **The Peak at Mt Kanimbla:** 43 Megalong Pl, Kanimbla; (02) 6355 2330. **Secret Valley Escape:** 548 Blackheath Creek Rd, Little Hartley; (02) 4787 1967. **Tomah Mountain Lodge:** 25 Skyline Rd, Mount Tomah; (02) 4567 2111.

Mount Victoria National Trust–classified Mount Victoria is the westernmost township of the Blue Mountains. There are buildings from the 1870s, including the Imperial Hotel, St Peter's Church of England and The Manor House. Also in town are craft shops, a museum at the train station and the Mount Vic Flicks historic cinema (open Thurs–Sun and school holidays). Mount Victoria has wonderful views of the mountains and many picnic spots and walking trails. 6 km NW.

Blue Mountains National Park: in the area east of Blackheath are various waterfalls and lookout points, including the much photographed Hanging Rock (around 9 km N via Ridgewell Rd). The Blue Mountains have been home to Aboriginal people for at least 22 000 years – the Gundungurra people in the north, the Dharug people in the south and the Wiradjuri people in the west. It is an area rich not only with Dreamtime stories but also with over 700 heritage sites that descendants of the original inhabitants continue to protect today. *For other parts of the park see Katoomba and Glenbrook.* **Bacchante Gardens:** rhododendrons and azaleas; 1.5 km N. **Mermaid Cave:** picturesque rock cave where parts of *Mad Max III* (1985) were filmed; Megalong Rd; 4 km S. **Shipley Gallery:** art exhibitions (open weekends); Shipley Rd; 4.6 km S. **Pulpit Rock Reserve and Lookout:** sweeping views of Mt Banks and Grose Valley; 6 km E. **Hargraves Lookout:** overlooking Megalong Valley; Panorama Point Rd; 7.4 km SW via Shipley Gallery. **Mt Blackheath Lookout:** views of Kanimbla Valley; Mount Blackheath Rd; 8.2 km N via Shipley Gallery. **Megalong Australian Heritage Centre:** horseriding, adventure tours and tourist farm; (02) 4787 8188; 9 km S. **Werriberri Trail Rides:** various trail rides on horseback; bookings (02) 4787 9171.

TOWNS NEARBY: Katoomba 9 km, Lithgow 22 km, Glenbrook 33 km, Oberon 40 km, Richmond 43 km

Blayney

Pop. 2748
Map ref. 522 G5

97 Adelaide St; (02) 6368 3534; www.blayney.nsw.gov.au

105.9 Star FM, 576 AM ABC Radio National

Blayney is a farming town in the central tablelands. National Trust–classified buildings and avenues of deciduous trees add a touch of charm to the town, particularly in autumn.

Heritage Park: small wetland area, barbecue facilities and tennis courts; Adelaide St. **Local craft shops:** contact visitor centre for details. **Self-guide heritage walk:** includes churches and the courthouse; brochure from visitor centre.

Wellfed Blayney: relaxed cafe; 129B Adelaide St; (02) 6368 3262.

Blayney Tourist Park: 18 Quamby Pl; (02) 6368 4455.

Carcoar The National Trust–classified town of Carcoar, surrounded by oak trees on the banks of the Belubula River, has a wealth of historic buildings. In early settlement days, convicts and bushrangers caused a lot of trouble in the town. Johnny Gilbert and John O'Mealy committed Australia's first daylight bank robbery in 1863 at the Commercial Bank (still standing) on Belubula St. The hold-up was unsuccessful and the robbers fled when a teller fired a shot into the ceiling. 14 km SW.

Millthorpe: National Trust–classified village with quaint shopfronts, art and craft shops, historic churches and a museum with blacksmith's shop and old-style kitchen. Also visit the Golden Memories museum for displays of life in the 19th century; 11 km NW. **Wind farm:** with 15 turbines and an interpretive centre, the largest farm of its kind in Australia; 11 km SW. **Carcoar Dam:** watersports and camping with picnic and barbecue facilities; 12 km SW. **Newbridge:** historic buildings and craft shops; 20 km E. **Abercrombie Caves:** cave system in a

220 ha reserve that features the largest natural limestone arch in the Southern Hemisphere. Carols in the Caves is held here in Dec. Various tours are available; contact visitor centre for details. 50 km se.

TOWNS NEARBY: Orange 31 km, Bathurst 33 km, Canowindra 54 km, Oberon 60 km, Cowra 61 km

Bombala

Pop. 1204
Map ref. 519 C9 | 539 F7

i Platypus Country Tourist Information Centre, Railway Park, Monaro Hwy; (02) 6458 4622; www.platypuscountry.org.au

87.6 Bombala FM, 103.7 Monaro FM, 810 AM Radio Local

Situated halfway between the Snowy Mountains and the Sapphire Coast, this charming small town has remained largely untouched by time. It is the centre for the surrounding wool, beef, lamb, vegetable and timber industries. The Bombala River is well known as a platypus habitat and for trout fishing. Bombala was considered as a site for Australia's capital city but missed out due to lack of water.

Railway Park There is much to see at Railway Park, including the historic engine shed (open by appt) and the museum of local artefacts and farm implements. The most unusual, though, is Lavender House, home to the oldest lavender association in the country. Lavender House has education facilities, displays on distillation and an array of lavender products such as lavender jams, soaps and oils. Monaro Hwy.

Endeavour Reserve: features a 2 km return walking track to a lookout with views over town; Caveat St. *Bicentennial Park:* wetlands and a pleasant river walk; Mahratta St. *Self-guide historical walk:* 1 hr walk includes courthouse (1882) and School of Art (1871); leaflet available from visitor centre.

Market: Imperial Hotel, cnr Forbes and Maybe sts; 1st Sat each month. *Wool and Wood Festival:* Jan. *Celebrate Lavender:* Jan. *Celebration of Motorcycles:* Nov. *Riverside Festival:* celebration of diversity of regional crafts and products; Nov. *Historic Engine Shed Engine Rally:* even-numbered years, Nov.

Cosmo Cafe: country-style cafe; 133 Maybe St; (02) 6458 3510. *The Heritage Guest House:* cafe in heritage house; 121 Maybe St; (02) 6458 4464.

Bombala Park Caravan Park: Monaro Hwy; (02) 6458 3817.

Platypus Sanctuary Bombala has one of the densest populations of platypus in NSW. They can be seen here in their natural environment from the Platypus Reserve Viewing Platform. The best times for viewing are at dawn and dusk, when platypus are at their most active, but they can be seen at any time of day. Off Monaro Hwy on the road to Delegate; 3 km s.

Cathcart: charming township with historical town walk and Cathcart Collectables, a fascinating collection of Monaro history; brochure from visitor centre; 14 km NE. *Myanba Gorge:* boardwalk and bushwalks through old-growth eucalypt forest with spectacular views of waterfalls, granite boulders and Towamba Valley. Enjoy a picnic or barbecue at the gorge. South East Forest National Park; 20 km SE. *Delegate:* scenic town with Early Settlers Hut, believed to be the first dwelling on the Monaro plains, and Platypus Walk and River Walk (leaflets from visitor centre); 36 km SW. *Scenic drive:* gold fossicking en route

to Bendoc Mines in Victoria; 57 km SW. *Fly-fishing and trout fishing:* maps from visitor centre. *Mountain-biking:* there are many trails in nearby state forest areas; maps from visitor centre.

TOWNS NEARBY: Bega 60 km, Merimbula 60 km, Eden 62 km, Tathra 69 km, Berridale 71 km

Bourke

Pop. 2145
Map ref. 529 M5

i Old Railway Station, Anson St; (02) 6872 1222; www.backobourke.com.au

101.1 FM ABC Radio National, 104.9 Rebel FM

The saying 'back o' Bourke' has come to mean the middle of nowhere, which is why Bourke is known as the gateway to the real outback. Bourke is a prosperous country town in the centre of thriving wool, cotton and citrus areas on the Darling River. It wasn't always so. Charles Sturt described it as 'unlikely to become the haunt of civilised man'. In 1835 Sir Thomas Mitchell came to the area and, thinking that the local Aboriginal people were a great threat, built himself a sturdy fort out of logs. Fort Bourke, as it became known, encouraged permanent settlement. Bourke quickly became a bustling major town, with Henry Lawson describing it as 'the metropolis of great scrubs'.

Back O' Bourke Exhibition Centre This fascinating modern facility is set among river red gums on the Darling River. It tells the story of the river and the outback from the Dreamtime to 100 years into the future. Visitors walk through colourful displays that re-create the past: paddleboats, early settlers and pastoralists, Afghan cameleers, Cobb & Co coaches, the history of unionism and Aboriginal heritage. The centre also looks at the sustainability of agriculture and the social structures of the outback. Kidman Way; (02) 6872 1321.

Old Railway Station: displays of Aboriginal artefacts and local history; Anson St. *Fred Hollows' Grave and Memorial:* the eye surgeon and famous humanitarian is buried in the cemetery; Cobar Rd. *Historic wharf replica:* reminder of days when Bourke was a busy paddlesteamer port. Take a paddlesteamer ride on the river; Sturt St. *Mateship Country Tours:* include historic buildings of Bourke (such as the Carriers Arms Inn, frequented by Henry Lawson) and surrounding citrus and grape farms; bookings at visitor centre.

Morralls Bakery and Cafe: sandwiches, pies; 37 Mitchell St; (02) 6872 2086.

Gundabooka National Park The park is a woodland haven for wildlife. There are over 130 species of bird, including the endangered pink cockatoo, pied honeyeater and painted honeyeater. Kangaroos, euros and endangered bats also make their homes here. Mt Gundabooka offers great walking tracks and a spectacular lookout. The Ngemba people have a history of ceremonial gatherings in the area and their art can be seen in some caves (to book tours, contact National Parks & Wildlife Service (02) 6872 2744). The park also provides excellent camping and barbecue facilities. 74 km s.

Fort Bourke Stockade replica: memorial to Sir Thomas Mitchell, who built the original fort; 20 km SW. *Mt Oxley:* home to wedge-tailed eagles and with views of plains from the summit. A key is needed for access to the mountain (collect from visitor centre); 40 km SE. *Comeroo Camel Station:* working sheep and cattle station with artesian spa and outback experiences including a camel-drawn wagon; accommodation available; (02) 6874 7735; 150 km NW.

TOWNS NEARBY: Brewarrina 89 km, Cobar 156 km, Nyngan 202 km, Walgett 209 km, Lightning Ridge 210 km

Bowral

Pop. 11 496
Map ref. 517 C5 | 519 G2 | 523 I8

ⓘ Southern Highlands Visitor Information Centre, 62–70 Main St, Mittagong; (02) 4871 2888 or 1300 657 559; www.southern-highlands.com.au

📻 102.9 2ST FM, 1431 AM ABC Radio National

Bowral is best known as the home town of 'the boy from Bowral', cricketing legend Sir Donald Bradman. There are Bradman tours, a sporting ground and a museum. Now an up-market tourist town and the commercial centre of the Southern Highlands, Bowral's close proximity to Sydney made it a popular retreat for the wealthy in earlier times. This is still evident today in the magnificent mansions and gardens around town.

🏠 **The International Cricket Hall of Fame** A comprehensive history of cricket is on display, including an oak bat from the 1750s. The Don Bradman memorabilia collection includes the bat he used to score 304 at Headingley in 1934. A cinema plays Bradman footage and newsreels. The Bradman Walk through town takes in significant sites including the Don's two family homes. A leaflet is available from the museum. Bradman Oval; St Jude St; (02) 4862 1247.

The Milk Factory Gallery: art and design exhibition centre and cafe; Station St. *Bong Bong St:* specialty shopping including books and antiques. *Historic buildings:* mostly in Wingecarribee and Bendooley sts; leaflet available from visitor centre.

🌴 *Produce Market:* Bowral Public School, Bendooley St; 2nd Sat each month. *Autumn Gardens in the Southern Highlands:* throughout region; Apr. *Tulip Time Festival:* Sept–Oct. *Bong Bong Races:* Nov.

🍴 *Centennial Vineyards Restaurant:* local produce, vineyard views; 252 Centennial Rd; (02) 4861 8701. *Hordern's Restaurant:* modern Australian; Milton Park Country House Hotel, Horderns Rd; (02) 4861 1522. *Onesta Cucina:* modern Italian; Shop 2, The Penders, cnr Station and Wingecarribee sts; (02) 4861 6620.

🛏 *Bowral Cottage Inn:* 22 Bundaroo St; (02) 4861 4157. *Mittagong Caravan Park:* 1 Old Hume Hwy, Mittagong; (02) 4871 1574. *The Croft Bed & Breakfast:* 128 Oxley Dr, Mittagong; (02) 4872 2659.

⊗ **Mittagong** This small and appealing town has historic cemeteries and buildings. Lake Alexandra in Queen St is artificial and great for birdwatching and walking. There is a market at the Uniting Church hall on the 3rd Sat each month. 8 km NE.

Southern Highlands wine region This region around Mittagong, Bowral and Moss Vale is considered the NSW equivalent of the Adelaide Hills. The elevation is high, ranging from 550 metres to 880 metres, and the climate is cool, making it perfect for chardonnay, sauvignon blanc and pinot noir. Others varieties like pinot gris, tempranillo, petit verdot and gewürztraminer are also available. Mundrakoona Estate believes that all the ingredients for good grapes and fine wine exist in the atmosphere (earth, air, fire and water), and this philosophy is evident in its natural winemaking processes and the use of wild yeasts. Try the Artemis

Pinot Noir for an indication of its success. McVitty Grove combines winery and olive grove, and Centennial Vineyards has an excellent restaurant, servings its lovely riesling.

Mt Gibraltar: bushwalking trails and lookout over Bowral and Mittagong; 2 km N. *Box Vale Mine walking track:* begins at the northern end of Welby, passes through old railway tunnel; 12 km N. *Nattai National Park:* protects landforms, geological features, catchments and biodiversity in the Sydney Basin. Only low-impact activities are encouraged and there is a 3 km exclusion zone around Lake Burragorang; via Hilltop; 19 km N.

TOWNS NEARBY: Berrima 8 km, Moss Vale 10 km, Robertson 20 km, Bundanoon 23 km, Jamberoo 38 km

Braidwood

Pop. 1108
Map ref. 519 E5 | 521 K4 | 522 H11

ⓘ National Theatre, Wallace St; (02) 4842 1144; www.visitbraidwood.com.au

📻 94.5 Braidwood FM, 103.5 FM ABC Local

Braidwood is an old gold-rush area that has been declared a historic town by the National Trust. Gold was plentiful here in the 1800s, the largest gold discovery being 170 kilograms in 1869. With the discovery of gold came bushrangers, such as the Clarke Gang and Ben Hall, and Braidwood became one of the most infamous and dangerous towns in the region. The 19th-century buildings have been carefully maintained and restored, and are still in use. The town appears to be from a bygone era, which has come in handy for film producers, who have found Braidwood a perfect setting for movies such as *Ned Kelly* (1969), *The Year My Voice Broke* (1986) and *On Our Selection* (1994).

🏠 **Braidwood Museum** Built of local granite and originally the Royal Mail Hotel, the museum houses over 2100 artefacts and 900 photographs. On display are exhibits of Aboriginal history, goldmining, the armour worn by Mick Jagger in *Ned Kelly*, a machinery shed and a library of local records, newspapers and family histories. An unusual collection is from the Namchong family, who came here from China during the gold rush and became traders in town from the 1870s to the 1990s. Open Fri–Mon, daily during school holidays; Wallace St; (02) 4842 2310.

Galleries and craft and antique shops: details from visitor centre. *Tallaganda Heritage Trail and scenic drive:* tours of historic buildings such as the Royal Mail Hotel and St Andrew's Church; leaflet from visitor centre.

🌴 *Picnic Race Meeting:* Feb. *Braidwood Heritage Festival:* May. *Music at the Creek:* Nov. *The Quilt Event:* Nov.

🍴 *Braidwood Bakery:* pies, sandwiches; 99 Wallace St; (02) 4842 2541.

⊗ **Monga National Park** This park features a boardwalk through rainforest areas dating back to the ancient Gondwana period. Penance Grove, a small pocket of rainforest, is filled with ancient plumwood trees and tree ferns. Maps at visitor centre. Access via Kings Hwy; 20 km SE.

The Big Hole and Marble Arch The Big Hole is thought to have formed when overlying sandstone collapsed into a subterranean limestone cavern creating an impressive chasm 96 m deep and 50 m wide. Wildlife in the area includes native birds, echidnas, wallabies, wombats and tiger quolls. Marble Arch is a narrow

 RADIO STATIONS   IN TOWN   WHAT'S ON   WHERE TO EAT   WHERE TO STAY   NEARBY

canyon 3–4 m wide and 25 m deep. It is over 1 km in length and bands of marble are visible along the walls. There are caves along the way, but special permission is required to enter some of them. Some are very dark and require a torch, so it is best to check with the NSW National Parks & Wildlife Service if you intend to explore. Inquiries (02) 4887 7270; near Gundillion; 45 km s.

Scenic drives: rugged countryside; brochure from visitor centre. *Fishing:* good trout fishing, especially in the Mongarlowe and Shoalhaven rivers; details from visitor centre.

TOWNS NEARBY: Batemans Bay 45 km, Queanbeyan 52 km, Moruya 58 km, Ulladulla 62 km, Goulburn 77 km

Brewarrina

Pop. 1123
Map ref. 529 05

 Bathurst St; (02) 6830 5152; www.breshire.com

 106.5 2CUZ FM, 657 AM ABC Local

This charming outback town on the banks of the Barwon River is affectionately known as Bre. It was developed in the 1860s as a river crossing for stock, but later thrived because of its position on a Cobb & Co route. Brewarrina was once a meeting place for Aboriginal tribes, with sacred sites including burial and ceremonial grounds, pointing to a culture that revolved around the river. By far the most impressive relics are the ancient stone fish traps of the Barwon River estimated to be 40 000 years old – among the oldest constructions in the world.

Aboriginal fish traps The traditional Aboriginal story states that the traps were built during a drought. Gurrungga, the water hole at Brewarrina, dried up and this opportunity was used to build the traps in the dry bed. The Ngemba people, who were facing famine, were never hungry again. Anthropologists claim the traps are impressive evidence of early engineering, river hydrology and knowledge of fish biology. Around 500 m long, these traps relied on the currents to sweep the fish inside, where they would be confined when the water level dropped. Thousands of years ago, the traps formed the centrepiece of a seasonal festival, regularly attended by up to 50 000 people from Aboriginal groups along the east coast. At night they held corroborees and shared stories around campfires in a language common to the region. The traps preserve the memory of these ancient times. Guided tours are available from visitor centre.

Aboriginal Cultural Museum: displays on aspects of Aboriginal life, from tales of the Dreamtime to the present; open Mon–Fri; Bathurst St. *Barwon Bridge:* one of two surviving examples of the first series of lift span bridges in the state (1889); Bridge Rd. *Wildlife park:* native fauna in bush setting; Doyle St. *Self-guide drive:* 19th-century buildings; brochure from visitor centre.

 Barwon River Rodeo: Easter. *Brewarrina Annual Races:* May.

Narran Lake Nature Reserve: wetlands and a breeding ground for native and migratory birds; access permits from visitor centre; 50 km NE. *Culgoa National Park:* wildlife unique to the western flood plains including falcons, striped-faced dunnat and pied bats. Information from visitor centre; 100 km N. *Fishing:* plentiful Murray cod in the Barwon River. *Start of Darling River Run:* self-drive tour; brochure from visitor centre.

TOWNS NEARBY: Bourke 89 km, Walgett 121 km, Lightning Ridge 123 km, Nyngan 180 km, Coonamble 184 km

Bulahdelah

Pop. 1092
Map ref. 514 H4 | 515 C10 | 523 N3

 Cnr Pacific Hwy and Crawford St; (02) 4997 4981 or 1800 802 692; www.bulahdelah.net.au

101.5 FM Great Lakes, 1233 AM ABC Local

Bulahdelah is a pretty town at the foot of Bulahdelah Mountain (known to locals as Alum Mountain because of the alunite that was mined here). Surrounded by rainforests and the beautiful Myall Lakes, it is a popular destination for bushwalkers and watersports enthusiasts.

Bulahdelah Mountain Park A park of contrasts, with meandering walking trails taking in tall forest, rare orchids in spring and the remains of mining machinery. There are picnic and barbecue facilities and a lookout over Bulahdelah and the Myall Lakes. Meade St.

Bulahdelah Court House: museum featuring Bulahdelah's logging past, with cells out the back; open Sat mornings or by appt; Cnr Crawford and Anne sts; bookings on (02) 6597 4838.

Market: beside visitor centre, Crawford St; 1st Sat each month. *Bulahdelah Music Festival:* Jan. *The Bass Bash:* fishing festival; Feb. *Junior Rodeo:* July. *Bulahdelah Show:* campdraft and rodeo; Sept.

Detours Cafe: homemade hamburgers; 82 Stroud St; (02) 4997 4755. *Myalla Magic:* traditional cafe fare; 84 Stroud St; (02) 4997 4900.

Billabong Cottage Bed & Breakfast: 121 Boolambayte Rd, Boolambayte; (02) 4997 4844. *Hawks Nest Holiday Park:* Booner St, Hawks Nest; (02) 4997 0239. *Lavender Grove Farm B & B:* 55 Viney Creek Rd West, Tea Gardens; (02) 4997 1411. *Whitby on Wallis Lakefront Holiday Cottage and Bed & Breakfast:* 1770 Coomba Rd, Coomba Bay; (02) 6554 2448.

Myall Lakes National Park The 'Murmuring Myalls', 10 ha of connected lakes, and 40 km of beaches make this national park one of the most visited in the state. It is ideal for all types of watersports – canoe and houseboat hire is available, and Broughton Island, 2 km offshore, is a popular spot for diving. Enjoy the bushwalks and campsites set in the rainforest, heathlands and eucalypt forest. 12 km E.

Bulahdelah State Forest: with scenic picnic area and walking trails along old mining trolley lines, and one of the tallest trees in NSW – the 84 m flooded gum (*Eucalyptus grandis*); off The Lakes Way; 14 km N. *Wootton:* charming small town with a 6 hr rainforest walk along an old timber railway; 15 km N. *Sugar Creek Toymakers:* fine wooden toys and hand-painted dolls; (02) 4997 6142; 31 km E. *Seal Rocks:* fishing village with seals sometimes resting on the offshore rocks. Grey nurse sharks breed in underwater caves and whales pass by June–Aug. Sugarloaf Point Lighthouse (1875) has a lookout tower, and there are pleasant beaches and camping areas; 40 km E. *Wallingat National Park:* walking trails and picnic facilities. Stop at Whoota Whoota Lookout for sweeping views of forest, coast and lakes; 43 km NE.

TOWNS NEARBY: Stroud 23 km, Nelson Bay 35 km, Forster–Tuncurry 38 km, Gloucester 50 km, Raymond Terrace 58 km

BROKEN HILL

Pop. 20 000
Map ref. 528 B10 | 559 P1 | 561 O8

i Cnr Blende and Bromide sts; (08) 8080 3560;
www.visitbrokenhill.com.au

106.9 Hill FM, 999 AM ABC Local

In the arid lands of far-western New South Wales, Broken Hill was first an intermittent home for the Wilyakali people. When Charles Sturt encountered the area while searching for an inland sea, he described it as some of the most barren and desolate land he had ever seen. Enthusiasm was soon generated, however, with the discovery of silver and Broken Hill was born. A syndicate of seven men quickly bought much of the land and in 1885 they discovered the world's largest silver-lead-zinc lodes. Later that same year they decided to form a company and float shares. That company was Broken Hill Proprietary (BHP), now BHP Billiton, the largest mining company in the world. Referred to as the 'Silver City', Broken Hill is also the centre of the 16-million-hectare West Darling pastoral industry, which has 1.75 million merino sheep cordoned off by a 600-kilometre 'dog-proof' fence. As you would expect of a hot, arid mining town, Broken Hill has many pubs. Note that Broken Hill operates on Central Standard Time, half an hour behind the rest of New South Wales.

Line of Lode Miners Memorial and Visitor Centre: perched on top of the mullock heap at the centre of town, and delving into Broken Hill's mining heritage. Includes restaurant; open 10am–3pm; Federation Way; (08) 8087 1318. *Railway, Mineral and Train Museum:* displays on old mining and rail services. Also incorporates the Hospital Museum and Migrant Museum; open 10am–3pm; Blende St; (08) 8088 4660. *Albert Kersten Mining and Minerals Museum:* displays of minerals, mining specimens and a silver tree; 10am–4.45pm Mon–Fri, 1–4.45pm Sat–Sun; 2 Bromide St; (08) 8080 3500. *White's Mineral Art and Mining Museum:* walk-in mine and mining models; 9am–5pm daily; 1 Allendale St; (08) 8087 2878. *Joe Keenan Lookout:* view of town and mining dumps; Marks St. *Muslim Mosque:* one of the first mosques in Australia, built by Afghan community in 1891; open 2–4pm Sun or by appt; 246 Buck St; (08) 8088 3187. *Zinc Twin Lakes:* popular picnic spot at lakes used as a water source for mines; off Wentworth Rd, South Broken Hill. *Art galleries:* over 20 in town including Pro Hart Gallery, Wyman St; Jack Absalom Gallery, Chapple St; and Broken Hill Regional Art Gallery, Argent St, the oldest regional gallery in the state. *Heroes, Larrikins and Visionaries of Broken Hill Walk and Silver Trail self-guide historical town drive:* leaflets from visitor centre.

St Patrick's Race Day: horseraces; Mar/Apr.

Bells Milk Bar: milkshakes, diner; 160 Patton St; (08) 8087 5380. *Broken Hill Musicians Club:* cafe, community club; 276 Crystal St; (08) 8088 1777.

Lake View Broken Hill Caravan Park: 1 Mann St; (08) 8088 2250. *The Miners Arms:* 82 Crystal St; (08) 8087 7830.

Silverton The National Trust–classified town of Silverton was established when silver chloride was found 27 km NW of Broken Hill in 1883. It now has less than 100 inhabitants and is surrounded by stark, arid plains, making it popular with

[CAMELS OUTSIDE THE SILVERTON HOTEL]

filmmakers wanting an outback setting. Films such as *Mad Max II* (1981), *Razorback* (1983), *Young Einstein* (1988), *The Adventures of Priscilla, Queen of the Desert* (1994) and *Dirty Deeds* (2001) have been filmed here, and the Silverton Hotel displays photographs of the film sets on its walls. Take the Silverton Heritage Walking Trail (leaflet from visitor centre) and visit the Silverton Gaol Museum; 9.30am–4pm daily; Bourke St; (08) 8088 5317. Barrier Ranges Camel Safaris offers 15 min rides around the outskirts of town and overnight safaris; Silverton Rd; (08) 8088 5316. Mundi Mundi Plain Lookout, a further 10 km N, affords views of the desolate yet awe-inspiring landscape. Daydream Mine, 13 km NE, operated in the 1880s and is now open for 1 hr surface and underground tours; 10am–3pm Easter to November, 10–11.30am November to Easter; (08) 8088 5682.

Mutawintji National Park Bushwalks lead through a rugged terrain of colourful gorges, rock pools and creek beds, while Aboriginal rock engravings and paintings tell stories of creation. The land was returned to its traditional owners in 1998, and a historic site in the centre containing a vast gallery of rock art is accessed by tour only. Tri State Safaris offers a 1 day tour of the national park from Broken Hill; (08) 8088 2389; 130 km NE.

Royal Flying Doctor Service base and visitor centre: headquarters, radio room and aircraft hangar open to visitors for guided tour, film and Mantle of Safety Museum; at airport; (08) 8080 3714; 10 km S. *Living Desert:* magnificent sandstone sculptures set on a hillside (particularly striking at sunrise and sunset) and walking trails through the mulga-dotted landscape; leaflet available from visitor centre; Nine Mile Rd; 11 km N. *Dingo Fence:* longest fence in the world at 5300 km from Jimbour in Queensland to the Great Australian Bight. Originally contructed in the 1880s to halt rabbit invasion, now maintained to keep dingoes out of sheep grazing areas; 150 NW.

TOWNS NEARBY: Menindee 102 km, White Cliffs 198 km, Wentworth 241 km

Bundanoon

Pop. 2035
Map ref. 517 A7 | 519 G3 | 523 I9

i Southern Highlands Visitor Information Centre, 62–70 Main St, Mittagong; (02) 4871 2888 or 1300 657 559; www.southern-highlands.com.au

📻 97.3 FM ABC Local, 107.1 Highlands FM

Bundanoon is a quiet village with a European feel, thanks to its green, tree-lined avenues. The first European to investigate the district was ex-convict John Wilson, who was sent by Governor Hunter to collect information on the area that would discourage Sydney convicts from trying to escape in this direction. Today the sleepy town is a popular yet unspoiled tourist destination with many delightful guesthouses and a health resort.

 Craft shops and art galleries: several featuring local work; contact visitor centre for details. *Drive and walk to several lookouts:* map from visitor centre.

Market: Memorial Hall, Railway Ave; 1st Sun each month. *Bundanoon is Brigadoon:* highland gathering; Apr. *Village Garden Ramble:* Oct.

Ye Olde Bicycle Shoppe: popular cafe and bike hire; 11 Church St; (02) 4883 6043.

Bundanoon Lodge: 10A Elmswood Crt; (02) 4883 7813.

Morton National Park, Bundanoon section This section of the park has stunning views, lookouts and walking trails. The park consists mainly of rainforest and eucalypts and is home to myriad native fauna including wallabies, potoroos and bush rats. See glow worms at night in the remarkable Glow Worm Glen. 1 km s. *For other sections of the park see Nowra, Robertson and Ulladulla.*

Exeter: quaint village with an English feel; 7 km n.

TOWNS NEARBY: Moss Vale 13 km, Berrima 19 km, Bowral 23 km, Robertson 28 km, Nowra 37 km

Camden

Pop. 3179
Map ref. 510 G11 | 517 E1 | 519 H1 | 523 J7

i John Oxley Cottage, Camden Valley Way; (02) 4658 1370; www.visitcamden.com.au

📻 C91.3 FM Campbelltown Radio, 684 AM ABC Local

Camden, in a picturesque setting on the Nepean River just south-west of Sydney, was once a hunting ground of the Gundungurra people, who called it 'Benkennie', meaning 'dry land'. Governor Macquarie sent men to kill or imprison the Aboriginal people in 1816 and, although records are poor, the brutal mission had some success. European settlement began after eight cattle wandered off four months after the First Fleet landed. They were not seen again until 1795 when it was discovered their number had grown to more than 40. The site on which they were found was named Cowpasture Plains, but was later changed to Camden. Camden was home to John and Elizabeth Macarthur, pioneers of the Australian wool industry, and the first in Australia to grow tobacco, use mechanical irrigation, produce wine of respectable quality and quantity and make brandy. The Macarthurs sent thousands of vines to the Barossa Valley and are thereby credited with helping to start South Australia's wine industry.

 Self-guide walk and scenic drive: includes historic buildings such as the Macarthur Camden Estate, St John the Evangelist Church and Kirkham Stables; brochure from visitor centre.

Produce Market: Cnr Exeter and Mitchell sts; 2nd and 4th Sat each month. *Craft and Fine Food Market:* Camden Showground; 3rd Sat each month (except Jan). *Food, Wine and Music Festival:* Sept. *Camden House Open Weekend:* Nov.

Enzo Italian Restaurant: modern Italian; 39 John St; (02) 4655 9260.

Poplar Tourist Park: 21 Macarthur Rd, Elderslie; (02) 4658 0485.

Camden Museum of Aviation This privately owned museum has the largest specialist aircraft collection in Australia. Where possible, the aircraft have been painstakingly restored (to a standard allowing them to taxi along a runway but not necessarily fly), with accurate wartime markings and camouflage colours carefully researched through service records and photographs. Open Sun and public holidays; (02) 4648 2419; 3 km NE.

Struggletown Fine Arts Complex: gallery featuring stained glass, pottery, traditional art and a restaurant; 3 km N. *Belgenny Farm:* includes Belgenny Cottage (1820) and the oldest surviving collection of farm buildings in Australia; (02) 4655 9651; 6 km SE. *Camden Aerodrome:* ballooning, gliding and scenic flights with vintage aircraft on display; (02) 4655 8064; 3 km NW. *Cobbitty:* historic rural village with market 1st Sat each month; 11 km NW. *The Oaks:* small town in open countryside featuring the slab-built St Matthew's Church and Wollondilly Heritage Centre, a social history museum; 16 km W. *Burragorang Lookout:* views over Lake Burragorang; 24 km W. *Yerranderie:* this fascinating old silver-mining town can be reached by normal vehicle in dry conditions, otherwise only by 4WD or plane; 40 km W. *Wineries:* several in the area; contact visitor centre for map; Gledswood (10 km N) features a working colonial farm.

TOWNS NEARBY: Campbelltown 11 km, Picton 13 km, Glenbrook 36 km, Wollongong 43 km, Bowral 51 km

Campbelltown

Pop. 147 460
Map ref. 510 H11 | 517 F1 | 519 H1 | 523 J7

i Quondong Cottage, 15 Old Menangle Rd; (02) 4645 4921 or 1800 655 991; www.visitmacarthur.com.au

📻 C91.3 FM Campbelltown, 603 AM ABC Radio National

Campbelltown was founded in 1820 by Governor Macquarie and named after his wife, Elizabeth Campbell. While the town is being engulfed by the urban sprawl of Sydney, it manages to combine the best of two worlds, enjoying the convenience of city living with the rustic charm of 19th-century buildings. It is also the location of the legend of Fisher's ghost. In 1826 an ex-convict, Frederick Fisher, disappeared. Another ex-convict, George Worrell, claimed that Fisher had left town, leaving him in charge of Fisher's farm. A farmer claimed to have seen the ghost of Fisher pointing at the creek bank where his body was subsequently found. Worrell was tried and hanged for Fisher's murder.

Campbelltown Arts Centre Visitors can see, explore and participate in art-creation at this interactive centre. Exhibitions are diverse and include local, regional, national and international shows of art and craft. Behind the gallery is a sculpture garden established in 2001 as a Centenary of Federation project. New permanent sculptures are added to the garden on a regular basis. Adjacent to the gallery is the Koshigaya-tei Japanese Teahouse and Garden, a bicentennial gift to the people of Campbelltown from its sister city, Koshigaya. The garden is a peaceful area with

continued on p. 40

BYRON BAY

Pop. 4978
Map ref. 516 H4 | 525 O3 | 609 N12

i 80 Jonson St; (02) 6680 8558; www.visitbyronbay.com

92.2 FM North Coast Radio, 720 AM ABC Local

Byron Bay's excellent beaches, laid-back feel and great weather have made it a long-time destination for surfers, backpackers and alternative-lifestylers. A forward-thinking council moved early to ban all drive-in takeaway food outlets and all buildings more than three storeys high. Now people from all walks of life, including celebrities, flock to Byron Bay for whale-watching, surfing, swimming and relaxing. The town centre has an array of restaurants and cafes, shops selling discount surfboards, New Age products and interesting clothing, and galleries with everything from handmade jewellery to timber furniture. Day spas, yoga centres and natural therapy parlours offer expert pampering.

Tours and activities: everything from diving and sea-kayaking to surf lessons, skydiving and gliding; contact visitor centre for details. **Beach Hotel:** well-established venue for live music and dining, with a beer garden that has ocean views; Cnr Jonson and Bay sts; (02) 6685 6402. **Beaches:** safe swimming at Main Beach (patrolled in summer school holidays and at Easter), and surfing at Clarkes Beach and the Pass; look out for 'sandologist' Steve Machell and his fabulous sand sculptures on Main or Clarkes beaches; there's more surfing at Wategos, child-friendly swimming at secluded Little Wategos, dogs are welcome at Belongil and Brunswick Heads, or go horseriding or beach-fishing at Seven Mile Beach stretching towards Lennox Head. **Health and wellbeing:** relax and unwind with a massage at Byron's numerous spas, including the tropical day spa at Buddha Gardens Balinese Spa, 15 Gordon St; (02) 6680 7844; and Relax Haven at Belongil Beachhouse, 25 Childe St; (02) 6685 7868, with massage therapy and float tanks. **Byron Bay Arts & Industry Park:** arts precinct 3 km from town with artists', jewellers' and sculptors' studios, galleries, cafes and restaurants; Artist Trail guide from visitor centre.

Farmers Market: Thurs mornings; Butler St Reserve. **East Coast Blues and Roots Festival:** Easter. **Byron Bay Writers Festival:** July/Aug. **Taste of Byron Food Fest:** Sept. **Buzz-Byron Bay Film Fest:** Oct.

The Balcony Bar & Restaurant: bohemian charm, world menu; Cnr Lawson and Jonson sts; (02) 6680 9666. **Byron Beach Cafe:** modern Australian; Clarkes Beach, Lawson St; (02) 6685 8400. **Fishmongers Cafe:** gourmet fish and chips; Bay La; (02) 6680 8080. **Italian at the Pacific:** contemporary Italian; Bay St; (02) 6680 7055. **Red Ginger:** eat dumplings in the store's front window; shop 2, 111 Jonson St; (02) 6680 9779. **Twisted Sista Cafe:** light meals and desserts; shop 1, 4 Lawson St; (02) 6685 6810.

Aarons @ Byron: 44 Shirley St; (02) 6680 7551. **Beaches of Byron:** 5 Broken Head Rd; (02) 6685 6751. **Belongil Fields:** 394 Ewingsdale Rd; (02) 6680 8999. **Clarkes Beach Holiday Park:** off Lighthouse Rd; (02) 6685 6496. **First Sun Holiday Park:** Lawson St; (02) 6685 6544. **Amber Gardens Guesthouse:** 66 Plantation Dr, Ewingsdale; (02) 6684 8215. **Broken Head Holiday Park:** Beach Rd, Broken Head; (02) 6685 3245. **Bundaleer Retreat:** 1 Bundaleer Rd, Broken Head; (02) 6687 6488. **Sojourn at Byron:** 42A Bay Vista La, Ewingsdale; (02) 6684 7083. **Suffolk Beachfront Holiday Park:** Alcorn St, Suffolk Park; (02) 6685 3353.

Cape Byron This headland forms part of the world's oldest caldera – the rim of an enormous extinct volcano (the centre is Mt Warning). It is the easternmost point on the mainland and provides breathtaking views up and down the coast. Dolphins can be seen year-round and humpback whales migrate up the coast June–July and back down Sept–Oct. Cape Byron Lighthouse, the 22 m structure completed in 1901, houses a visitor centre with displays of the area's cultural and natural history. 3 km SE.

Julian Rocks Aquatic Reserve: protects 450 underwater species and is great for diving; 3 km s. **Broken Head Nature Reserve:** rainforest, secluded beaches and dolphin-watching; (02) 6627 0200; 9 km s. **Bangalow:** rustic village with magnificent scenery, antique shops, arts and crafts, walking tracks and a popular market on the 4th Sun each month; 10 km SW.

TOWNS NEARBY: Mullumbimby 15 km, Ballina 25 km, Alstonville 28 km, Lismore 38 km, Nimbin 38 km

[BYRON BAY'S MAIN BEACH]

a waterfall, koi pond and timber bridge, perfect for picnics and tranquil contemplation. Art Gallery Rd; (02) 4645 4100.

Campbelltown Visitor Information Centre: formerly St Patrick's, the first Catholic school in Australia, displays include early world maps, desks, inkwells, canes and curriculums (1840); Old Menangle Rd. **Stables Museum:** display of historic farm equipment and household goods on 1st, 3rd and 5th Sun each month; Lithgow St. **Self-guide heritage walks:** take in numerous historic buildings including St Peter's Church (1823), Emily Cottage (1840) and Fisher's Ghost restaurant, formerly Kendall's Millhouse (1844); leaflet from visitor centre.

 Ingleburn Festival: Mar. **Autumn Harvest Food and Wine Fair:** Mar/Apr. **Festival of Fisher's Ghost:** Nov.

Mt Annan Botanic Garden Australia's largest botanic garden is a striking 400 ha garden with 20 km of walking trails. Attractions include 2 ornamental lakes with picnic areas, a nursery, an arboretum, themed gardens, the rare and endangered plants garden and the banksia garden. The botanic garden is a haven to over 160 bird species and mammals such as the wallaroo and swamp wallaby. The human sundial allows visitors to tell the time by standing in its centre and raising their arms. Guided tours are available; (02) 4648 2477; 3 km w.

Sugarloaf Horse Centre: heritage-listed site with amazing views and trail-rides for all skill levels; (02) 4625 9565; 2.2 km sw. **Macarthur Centre for Sustainable Living:** showcasing sustainable homes, gardens and lifestyles. To promote sustainable living, the centre is entirely self-sufficient. Regular workshops are also held throughout the year; (02) 4647 9828; 3 km w. **Steam and Machinery Museum:** history of Australia's working past, including interactive displays; Menangle Rd; 5 km sw. **Menangle:** small town featuring a historic homestead (1834) and The Store (1904), an old-style country store with everything from antiques to ice-creams, and the Menangle Railway Bridge (1863), the colony's first iron bridge; 9 km sw. **Eschol Park House:** grand colonial home (1820) set in landscaped gardens; 15 km N. **Appin:** historic coalmining town with a monument to Hume and Hovell (who began their 1824 expedition to Port Phillip from this district). Also weekend markets in 10 locations (leaflet available from visitor centre) and a celebration of Scottish links through the Highland Gathering and Pioneer Festival each Nov; 16 km s.

TOWNS NEARBY: Camden 11 km, Picton 21 km, Glenbrook 39 km, Wollongong 40 km, Windsor 51 km

Canowindra

Pop. 1501
Map ref. 522 F5

ⓘ Age of Fishes Museum, Gaskill St; (02) 6344 1008; www.ageoffishes.org.au

📻 104.3 FM ABC Radio National, 105.1 2GZ FM

Canowindra, meaning 'home' in the Wiradjuri language, is in the Lachlan Valley with sandstone mountains to the west and the old volcano, Mount Candobolas, to the north-east. Ben Hall and his gang struck in the town twice in 1863. During the first visit they robbed two homesteads and then forced residents and local police into Robinson's Inn (now the Royal Hotel), where they held an impromptu and compulsory two-day party. Two weeks later they returned and held a similar three-day party, reportedly at their own expense. Today Canowindra is still a genuine old-style country town with a National Trust–classified main street (Gaskill St) that follows the crooked path of an old bullock track.

It is now known for balloons, fossils and boutique cellar doors. Canowindra calls itself the 'balloon capital of Australia' because there are more hot-air balloon flights here than anywhere else in the country. In 1956, 3500 fish fossils over 360 million years old were found in the area. Another major dig took place in 1993.

Age of Fishes Museum Long before dinosaurs walked the earth bizarre fish populated local rivers, including fish with armoured shells, fish with lungs and fish with jaws like crocodiles. The museum displays many of the fossils from the Devonian era found during the 1956 and 1993 digs along with information about the digs. There are also live aquarium displays and re-creations of life in the Devonian period. Gaskill St.

Historical museum: local history displays and agricultural equipment; weekends or by appt; Gaskill St. **Hot-air balloon rides:** over picturesque Lachlan Valley; Mar–Nov (weather permitting); details at visitor centre. **Historical tourist drive and riverbank self-guide walks:** include historic buildings of Gaskill St; brochure available from visitor centre.

Springfest: wine and art; Oct.

Taste Canowindra: cakes, lunches, wine tastings; 42 Ferguson St; (02) 6344 2332. **Tom's Waterhole Winery:** ploughman's lunches; 752 Longs Corner Rd; (02) 6344 1819.

Canowindra Caravan Park: Tilga St; (02) 6344 1850. **Cudal Caravan Park:** Main St, Cudal; (02) 6364 2040.

Gondwana Dreaming Historical Fossil Digs Tours of 1–6 days can be arranged to go on real archaeological digs led by palaeontologists to learn about and possibly find fossils. The tours promote hands-on learning and focus on the area as a whole, including local flora and fauna. This program funds ongoing scientific research. Bookings on (02) 6285 1872.

Wineries and vineyards: cellar-door tastings and tours; maps from visitor centre.

TOWNS NEARBY: Cowra 30 km, Eugowra 31 km, Orange 51 km, Blayney 54 km, Grenfell 59 km

Casino

Pop. 9398
Map ref. 516 E5 | 525 N3 | 609 M12

ⓘ 86 Centre St; (02) 6662 3566; www.richmondvalley.nsw.gov.au

📻 107.9 COW FM, 738 AM ABC Local

Beside the Richmond River in the north-east of the state, Casino is a town of grand old buildings and magnificent parklands. Casino is named after the beautiful Italian town of Monte Cassino and is known as the beef capital of Australia. More than 12 000 cattle are sold each year at the Casino Livestock Selling Centre.

Jabiru Geneebeinga Wetlands These parklands have picnic facilities and are home to native bird species and wildlife including the jabiru (black-necked stork), egret and black swan. The park is circled by a mini-railway that operates each Sun. West St.

Casino Folk Museum: locally significant documents and photographs; open Mon, Wed afternoons and Sun mornings; Walker St. **Self-guide heritage and scenic walks and drives:** include Bicentennial Mural, St Mark's Church of England and Cecil Hotel; maps available from visitor centre.

Flower and Art Show: Mar. **Beef Week Festival:** May. **Gold Cup:** horseracing; May. **Primex:** primary industry exhibition; June.

 Clydesdale Motel and Steak Barn: steakhouse; Bruxner Hwy; (02) 6662 5982.

Casino Village RV Resort: 69 Light St; (02) 6662 1069.

Fossicking: gold, labradorite and quartz (both smoky and clear types); maps from visitor centre. *Freshwater fishing:* Cookes Weir and Richmond River are popular fishing spots; maps from visitor centre.

TOWNS NEARBY: Lismore 23 km, Kyogle 27 km, Nimbin 34 km, Alstonville 38 km, Evans Head 47 km

Cessnock

see inset box on next page

Cobar

Pop. 4127
Map ref. 529 L9

Great Cobar Heritage Centre, Barrier Hwy; (02) 6836 2448; www.cobar.nsw.gov.au

103.7 Zoo FM, 810 AM ABC Local

Cobar got its name from the Aboriginal word 'kubbur', meaning 'burnt earth'. The story goes that three European settlers were camping at Kubbur watering hole near where Cobar is today when they noticed the unusual colour of the water. They took samples and showed them to the publicans at the Gilgunnia Pub who identified them as copper ore. From this discovery, the Cobar mining industry was born. The mines made Cobar so prosperous that at one point the town had a population of 10 000 and its own stock exchange. Mines still operate, including the CSA Copper Mine which is the deepest in Australia. Today Cobar is a surprisingly green and picturesque outback town.

Great Cobar Outback Heritage Centre This centre has displays on the local mining of copper, gold and silver-lead-zinc, an authentic re-creation of a local woolshed and displays on Aboriginal culture. Learn about the chronic water shortages in the early days of European settlement and the bush skills the settlers needed to survive the harsh environment. The Centenary of Federation Walking Track begins here and is a 2 hr scenic walk past mines and a slag dump. Barrier Hwy; (02) 6836 2448.

Commonwealth Meteorological Station: visitors can view the radar tracking process and the launching of weather balloons at 9.15am and 3.15pm daily (Eastern Standard Time); Louth Rd; inquiries (02) 6836 2149. *Golden Walk:* tour the operating Peak Gold Mine or view from observation deck; Kidman Way; (02) 6830 2265. *Self-guide heritage walks and heritage bus tours:* historic buildings including the courthouse and the Great Western Hotel (with the longest iron-lace verandah in NSW), and mining and agricultural sites around town; brochure from visitor centre.

Festival of the Miner's Ghost: Oct.

Copper's: modern Australian; Cobar Copper City Motel, 40 Lewis St; (02) 6836 1022. *Empire Hotel:* steaks, pub food; 6 Barton St; (02) 6836 2725.

Mt Grenfell Historic Site The 5 km Ngiyambaa Walkabout leads visitors on a scenic tour with breathtaking views of the Cobar area. There are hundreds of Aboriginal stencils and paintings of great cultural significance in spectacular reds, yellows and ochres on rock overhangs along the trail. Picnic and barbecue facilities are available. Off Barrier Hwy; 67 km NW.

The Old Reservoir and Devil's Rock: Devil's Rock was a site for ceremonial rites for the Ngemba people. Good swimming and watersports at the reservoir; 3 km N. *Mount Drysdale:* deserted mining town where visitors can investigate old mine shafts and remains of the town. Features historic Aboriginal sites including rock wells; permission required (02) 6836 3462; 34 km N.

TOWNS NEARBY: Nyngan 128 km, Bourke 156 km, Brewarrina 196 km, Lake Cargelligo 206 km

Coffs Harbour

see inset box on page 45

Cooma

Pop. 6587
Map ref. 519 C7 | 520 G9 | 539 E3

119 Sharp St; (02) 6450 1742 or 1800 636 525; www.visitcooma.com.au

92.1 FM 2XL, 97.7 Snow FM, 810 AM ABC Local

The regional centre of the Snowy Mountains, Cooma was once dubbed Australia's most cosmopolitan city, thanks to the thousands of migrants who flocked to the region to work on the Snowy Mountains Hydro-Electric Scheme. It is a charming and bustling centre with visitors coming for the snow in winter and the greenery and crisp mountain air in summer. Motorists are advised to stop here to check tyres and stock up on petrol and provisions before heading into the alpine country.

Centennial Park Originally a swamp, Centennial Park was established in 1890. During WW II slit trenches were dug here in case of air attacks. The Avenue of Flags was constructed in 1959 to commemorate the 10th anniversary of the Snowy Mountains Hydro-Electric Scheme with one flag for each of the 27 nationalities of the workers. The Time Walk depicts the district's history in 40 ceramic mosaics laid below the flags. There is also a sculpture of Banjo Paterson's famous 'Man from Snowy River'. Sharp St.

Snowy Mountains Hydro-Information and Education Centre: interactive displays, photographs, models and films on the scheme. A memorial next door commemorates the 121 people killed while working on it; Monaro Hwy; inquiries 1800 623 776. *NSW Corrective Services Museum:* features unique displays of over 200 years of history, from convicts through to the modern prison system in the old Cooma Gaol; Vale Street; (02) 6452 5974. *Southern Cloud Park:* features Southern Cloud Memorial, a display of remains of the aircraft *Southern Cloud,* which crashed in the region in 1931 and was found in 1958. *Bike path:* picturesque path following Cooma Creek between Lambie St and Rotary Oval. *Historic railcar:* trips from Cooma to Bunyan on weekends; bookings at visitor centre. *Lambie Town self-guide walk:* designed in 1985, with over 5 km of easy walking. The tour incorporates 3 National Trust heritage areas including Lambie St, lined with huge oaks, pines and elms, and St Paul's Church, constructed with local alpine ash and granite and with striking stained-glass windows; brochure available from visitor centre.

Market: Centennial Park; 3rd Sun each month. *Rodeo:* Feb. *Back to Earth Festival:* Apr. *Cooma Festival:* Oct. *Cooma Street Fair:* celebrating Cooma's multicultural society; Nov. *Cooma Races and Sundowner Cup:* Dec.

The Lott Food Store, Bakery & Cafe: excellent cafe and bakery; 178–180 Sharp St; (02) 6452 1414.

continued on p. 43

 RADIO STATIONS IN TOWN WHAT'S ON WHERE TO EAT WHERE TO STAY NEARBY

CESSNOCK

Pop. 18 318

Map ref. 509 E2 | 514 A8 | 523 L4

ⓘ 455 Wine Country Dr, Pokolbin; (02) 4990 0900; www.winecountry.com.au

📻 96.5 CHR-FM Community Radio, 1044 AM ABC Local

Best known for being the hub of a region that produces some of Australia's best wines and fresh produce, Cessnock is a relaxed, large town with a range of coffee shops, galleries, craft and antique shops. It has a railway station and services including banks, grocery and hardware stores, but also serves as a centre for ballooning, sky-diving, wine-tasting tours and golf.

🏠 *Galleries and antique and craft shops:* brochures from visitor centre.

✳ *Harvest Festival:* throughout region; Mar–Apr. *Lovedale Long Lunch:* May. *Jazz in the Vines:* Oct. *Opera in the Vineyards:* Oct.

🍴 *Esca Bimbadgen:* modern Australian; Bimbadgen Estate, 790 McDonalds Rd, Pokolbin; (02) 4998 4666. *The Kurrajong Restaurant:* pub bistro; Cessnock Hotel, 234 Wollombi Rd; (02) 4991 4414. *Swill N Grill:* international; The Australia Hotel, 136 Wollombi Rd; (02) 4990 1256.

🛏 *BIG4 Valley Vineyard Tourist Park:* 137 Mt View Rd; (02) 4991 6692. *Bluebush Estate:* 196 Wilderness Rd, Rothbury; (02) 4930 7177. *The Grange on Hermitage:* 820 Hermitage Rd, Pokolbin; (02) 4998 7388. *Hunter Valley Bed & Breakfast:* 1443 Wine Country Dr, North Rothbury; (02) 4938 2193. *Hunter Valley Cooperage Bed & Breakfast:* 41 Kelman Vineyards, 2 Oakey Creek Rd, Pokolbin; (02) 4990 1232. *Sunrise Bed & Breakfast:* 59 Gills La, Brunkerville; (02) 4938 0015.

⊗ **Hunter Valley wine region** Established in 1830 near Singleton, this is Australia's oldest wine region – and one of its most recognised. The area now offers a wealth of vineyards and wineries, with around 120 cellar doors in the Lower valley between Singleton, Cessnock and Maitland. Semillon and shiraz are the signature drops, but you will also find beautiful chardonnay and cabernet sauvignon. The terroir of the valley leaves an unmistakable mark in many of the wines, which delights winemakers and drinkers alike. Labels include McWilliam's Mount Pleasant, Tyrrell's, Lake's Folly, Tulloch Wines, De Bortoli. Drayton's Family Wines and Ernest Hill Wines. Great food and accommodation is also in abundance. If you're interested in attending a 2 hr 'wine school', head to Hermitage Road Cellars & Winery, Hermitage Rd Pokolbin; (02) 4998 7777. The Upper valley has not captured the public's interest like its lower counterpart, despite embodying the same hilly scenery fanning out around the towns of Muswellbrook, Aberdeen, Scone and Denman. This may be because of the various large operations, yet there are still many fantastic wines to be discovered. The large Rosemount Estate's Roxburgh label is one of the region's most outstanding chardonnays, while its Diamond label has had success with shiraz and riesling. Other wineries to visit are Pyramid Hill Wines, James Estate and Yarraman Estate.

Watagans National Park This park features several lookout points over mountains and valleys. The lookout at Gap Creek Falls reveals rainforest gullies of magnificent red cedar and Illawarra flame trees, and the Monkey Face Lookout takes in the Martinsville Valley below. There are many scenic rainforest walks along the creek, which is ideal for swimming. Some walks lead to picnic and barbecue facilities at Heaton, Hunter and McLean's lookouts and the serene Boarding House Dam picnic area, which is set among large blackbutt and blue gum trees; 33 km SE.

Hunter Valley Zoo: hands-on zoo where many animals (native and introduced) can be patted and fed; 9am–4pm Thu–Tue; 130 Lomas Lane, Nulkaba; (02) 4990 7714; 7 km NW. *Bimbadeen Lookout:* spectacular views over Hunter Valley; 10 km E. *Hunter Valley Cheese Factory:* factory tours, tastings and sales; 9am–5.30pm daily; McGuigan Cellars Complex, McDonalds Rd, Pokolbin; (02) 4998 7744; 13 km NW. *Richmond Vale Railway Museum:* rail and mining museum with steam-train rides and John Brown's Richmond Main Colliery, once the largest shaft mine in the Southern Hemisphere; 10am–4pm 1st 3 sun of each month; Leggetts Drive, Richmond Vale; (02) 4001 0197; 17 km NE. *Wollombi:* picturesque village with a wealth of historic sandstone buildings. Tour the Aboriginal cave paintings (inquire at general store). Visit Undercliff Winery and Studio (for etchings); 29 km SW. *Galleries and Craft shops:* arts and crafts by local artists; maps from visitor centre.

TOWNS NEARBY: Maitland 22 km, Singleton 34 km, Raymond Terrace 38 km, Newcastle 41 km, Wyong 50 km

[OAK BARRELS AT ALLANDALE WINERY, LOWER HUNTER VALLEY]

Cooma Snowy Mountains Tourist Park: 286 Sharp St; (02) 6452 1828.

Tuross Falls Part of Wadbilliga National Park, the stunning Tuross Falls are a drop of 35 m. A picturesque 2 km walk from the camping area at Cascades leads visitors to the lookout platform, which affords views of the falls and the Tuross River Gorge. 30 km E.

Kosciuszko Memorial: donated in 1988 by the Polish government commemorating Tadeuz Kosciuszko, a champion of the underprivileged, after whom Australia's highest mountain is named; 2.5 km N. *Mt Gladstone Lookout:* impressive views, mountain-bike trails and Austrian teahouse; 6.5 km w. *Transylvania Winery:* cellar-door tastings of cool-climate organic wines; Monaro Hwy; 14 km N. *Whitewater Rafting:* Snowy River tours from half-day to 2 day overnight trips; pick-up from Cooma, Jindabyne or Thredbo; bookings on 1800 677 179.

TOWNS NEARBY: Berridale 31 km, Adaminaby 42 km, Jindabyne 49 km, Bombala 75 km, Thredbo 79 km

Coonabarabran
Pop. 2605
Map ref. 524 E9

Newell Hwy; (02) 6849 2144 or 1800 242 881; www.warrumbungleregion.com.au

92.9 FM Tamworth's Hit Music Station, 549 AM ABC Local

Coonabarabran is located on the Castlereagh River and is nestled in the foothills of the stunning Warrumbungle Mountain Range. It is known as the 'Astronomy Capital of Australia' as it has some of the clearest skies in the country, and is the gateway to the striking scenery of the Warrumbungles.

Information Centre The Australian Museum worked with Warrumbungle Shire Council to produce the unique Diprotodon and Megafauna Exhibition. The diprotodon is the largest marsupial that ever lived and the skeleton on show was found in a creek bed 40 km east of town in 1979; daily 9am–5pm; Newell Hwy.

Crystal Kingdom: unique collection of minerals, including zeolite crystals and fossils, from the Warrumbungle Range; 8am–5pm Oct–April, 9am–5pm May–Sep; Newell Hwy; (02) 6842 1927. *Newcastle Hats:* hat factory outlet store; 8am–4.30pm Mon–Fri; Ulan St; (02) 6842 5864.

Market: Dalgamo St; fourth Sun each month, 9am–2pm. *Bunny Bazaar:* includes markets; Easter Sat. *Festival of the Stars:* includes Coona Cup Racing Carnival; Oct.

Amber Court Restaurant: Homestyle cuisine; Amber Court Motor Inn, 512 Oxley Hwy; (02) 6842 1188; open Mon–Sat for dinner. *Blue Wren Cafe:* cafe and pottery shop; Pilliga Pottery, Dandry Rd; (02) 6842 2239.

Getaway Tourist Park: Newell Hwy; (02) 6842 1773. *John Oxley Caravan Park:* Cnr Newell Hwy and Chappell Ave; (02) 6842 1635.

Warrumbungle National Park Forested ridges, rocky spires and deep gorges coupled with excellent camping and visitor facilities have made this one of the state's most popular parks. Highlights include the Breadknife, a 90 m high rock wall, and the Grand High Tops walking trail with fabulous views of ancient volcanic remains. The park is outstanding for rock climbing, but climbing is prohibited on the Breadknife and permits are required

for other areas (contact visitor centre). The Crooked Mountain Open Air Concert takes place here in Nov. Guided nature walks are conducted during school holidays or by appt. 35 km w.

Warrumbungle Observatory: night-sky viewing of the stars through computerised telescopes; 841 Timor Rd; 0488 425 112; 10 km w. *Siding Spring Observatory:* Australia's largest optical telescope, with a hands-on exhibition, science shop and cafe. No night viewing but open during the day; 9.30am–4pm Mon–Fri, 10am–4pm Sat–Sun; Timor Rd; (02) 6842 6255; 27 km w. *Goanna Tracks Motocross and Enduro Complex:* a range of tough motocross courses; Kurrajong Rd; 18 km NW. *Pilliga Pottery:* terracotta pottery, showrooms and tearooms in an attractive bushland setting, pottery workshops, horseriding and guided birdwatching tours; Dandry Rd; (02) 6842 2239; 34 km NW. *Sandstone caves:* formed by natural erosion of sandstone, these impressive caves are not signposted, so visitors are advised to seek directions from the visitor centre; 35 km N. *Pilliga Forest:* 450 000 ha of white cypress and ironbark trees, with plains of dense heath and scrub. It is an excellent habitat for koalas, which can be spotted from signposted viewing areas. Also scenic forest drives and walking trails; maps available from the visitor centre; 44 km NW. *Sculptures in the Scrub:* 4 magnificent sculptures that overlook Dandry Gorge, with picnic and camping facilities and a walking track; via Pilliga Forest Discovery Centre, Wellington St Barradine; (02) 6843 4011; 50 km NE. *Local wineries:* open for tastings and cellar-door sales; contact visitor centre for details.

TOWNS NEARBY: Gilgandra 76 km, Coonamble 92 km, Gunnedah 99 km, Narrabri 116 km, Wee Waa 117 km

Coonamble
Pop. 2550
Map ref. 524 C8

26 Castlereagh St; (02) 6822 4532; www.coonamble.org

91.9 MTM FM, 648 AM ABC Local

Coonamble owes its existence to the discovery of artesian water in the area in the 1890s. On the Great Inland Way, the route via Coonamble provides an alternative to the more commonly taken coastal route between Queensland and the southern states. This town lost many of its buildings in the great fire of 1929. Castlereagh Street had to be rebuilt, so most constructions are relatively modern. Coonamble is also the birthplace of Sir Edward Hallstrom, the pioneer of refrigeration.

Historical Museum Housed in the old police station, the museum outlines the rich Aboriginal and pastoral history of Coonamble through photographs, household items and stables. Behind the museum is an authentic Cobb & Co coach and stables. Open by appt (02) 6822 4532; Aberford St.

Warrana Creek Weir: swimming, boating and fishing; southern outskirts of town. *Self-guide town walk:* takes in historic sites; brochure from visitor centre.

Rodeo and Campdraft: largest combined event in Southern Hemisphere; June. *Gold Cup Race Meeting:* Oct.

Sons of the Soil Hotel: bistro-style meals; 46–54 Castlereagh St; (02) 6822 5400.

Quambone Locally known as the gateway to Macquarie Marshes, Quambone also has Australia's smallest library and the Marthaguy Picnic Races in Sept. 55 km w.

Gulargambone: a small town with a restored steam train in Memorial Park; 45 km s. *Macquarie Marshes:* 80 km w; *see Nyngan.*

TOWNS NEARBY: Gilgandra 88 km, Coonabarabran 92 km, Walgett 106 km, Wee Waa 129 km, Nyngan 133 km

Cootamundra

Pop. 5565
Map ref. 519 A2 | 522 D8

 Railway station, Hovell St; (02) 6942 4212; www.cootamundra.nsw.gov.au

107.7 Star FM, 675 AM ABC Local

This prosperous rural service centre and major junction on the railway line between Sydney and Melbourne prides itself on being the birthplace of cricketing legend Sir Donald Bradman. Much reference is made to him and to cricket around the town. Cootamundra also lends its name to the famous Cootamundra wattle (*Acacia baileyana*), which blooms in the area each July and August, and Cootamundra Gold, the locally produced canola oil.

Pioneer Park This natural bushland reserve on the northern outskirts of town has a scenic 1.3 km walking trail to the top of Mt Slippery. At the summit there are panoramic views. The park also has excellent picnic sites. Backbrawlin St.

Bradman's birthplace: restored cottage where 'the greatest batsman the world has ever known' was born. Contains memorabilia from cricket and his life in the Cootamundra district; Adams St. *Arts Centre:* community arts space with exhibitions, workshops, art sales and a theatre; Wallendoon St. *Memorabilia Cottage:* displays local history memorabilia and bric-a-brac; Adams St. *Captains Walk:* bronze sculptures of Australia's past cricket captains; Jubilee Park, Wallendoon St. *Heritage Centre:* local memorabilia including an Olympic cauldron and war relics; railway station, Hovell St. *Self-guide 'Two Foot Tour':* includes Sir Donald Bradman's birthplace and the town's historic buildings; brochure from visitor centre. *Local crafts:* at visitor centre and at Art and Craft Centre, Hovell St.

Markets: Fisher Park, 2nd Sun each month; Wallendbeen, 1st Sun each month. *Wattle Time Festival:* Aug. *Rose Show:* Nov.

Country Cuisine: cafe with homemade sweet treats; 265 Parker St; (02) 6942 1788. *Helen's Coffee Lounge:* cafe-style fare or hearty mains; 248 Parker St; (02) 6942 7400.

Murrumburrah This small rural community has the Harden–Murrumburrah Historical Museum, which is open weekends and features pioneer artefacts, an old chemist shop exhibit and early Australian kitchenwares. Also in town are local craft shops and some outstanding picnic spots. 35 km NE. Stocks Native Nursery in Harden, 2 km E on Simmonds Rd, features 1.5 ha of native bush garden with a scenic walking trail and billabong. The Picnic Races are held here in Nov.

Green Tree Indigenous Food Gardens: Australian bush garden divided into different zones providing education on how Indigenous people survived on bush tucker; tours available; (02) 6943 2628; 8 km N. *Migurra Reserve:* bushland walking trail with birdwatching and 5 species of wattles; 15 km SW. *The Milestones:* cast-concrete sculptures representing the importance of wheat to the area; 19 km NE. *Bethungra:* dam ideal for canoeing and sailing. The rail spiral is an unusual engineering feat; 23 km SW. *Kamilaroi Cottage Violets:* violet farm with tours by appt; bookings (02) 6943 2207; 25 km N. *Illabo:* charming town with impressive clock museum; 33 km SW. *Cellar doors:* in the Harden area; winery brochure from visitor centre.

TOWNS NEARBY: Young 44 km, Gundagai 48 km, Temora 50 km, Adelong 74 km, Tumut 75 km

Corowa

Pop. 5628
Map ref. 527 M12 | 543 I5 | 544 F1

 88 Sanger St; (02) 6033 3221 or 1800 814 054; www.visitcorowashire.com.au

105.7 FM The River, 675 AM ABC Local

Corowa has been known for its goldmining, winemaking, timber milling and as the 'birthplace of Federation'. Traders in the 19th century had to pay taxes both in New South Wales and Victoria when taking goods over the border, which caused much agitation. It was argued that free trade would benefit everyone and the Border Federation League was formed in Corowa, which led to the 1893 Corowa Federation Conference. In 1895 the proposals put forth at the conference were acted upon and on 1 January 1901 the Commonwealth of Australia was born. In 1889 Tom Roberts completed his iconic painting *Shearing the Rams* at a sheep station nearby the town.

Federation Museum This museum focuses on the reasons behind Federation and Corowa's involvement in it. Also on display are local Aboriginal artefacts, Tommy McRae sketches, horse-drawn vehicles and saddlery, and antique agricultural implements. Open Sat and Sun afternoons; Queen St.

Murray Bank Yabby Farm: catch and cook yabbies, go canoeing and enjoy a picnic or barbecue; Federation Ave; (02) 6033 2922. *Self-guide historical town walk:* includes Sanger St, Corowa's historic main street with its century-old verandahed buildings. Guide available for groups; brochure from visitor centre.

Market: Bangerang Park; 1st Sun each month (except Feb). *Federation Festival:* Jan. *Billycart Championships:* Easter.

Easdown House Restaurant: modern Australian; 1 Sanger St; (02) 6033 4077.

Ball Park Caravan Park: Bridge Rd; (02) 6033 1426. *Corowa Caravan Park:* 84 Federation Ave; (02) 6033 1944. *John Foord Guesthouse:* 7 Braintree Ave; 0408 258 634. *Rivergum Holiday Retreat:* 386 Honour Ave (Albury Rd); (02) 6033 1990. *Howlong Caravan Park:* 55 Hume St, Howlong; (02) 6026 5304. *Kismet Riverside Lodge:* 5189 Riverina Hwy, Howlong; (02) 6026 5748. *Stableford House Bed & Breakfast:* 22 East St, Howlong; (02) 6026 8524. *The Old Post Office Bed & Breakfast:* 39 Hawkins St, Howlong; 0438 048 043.

All Saints Estate Situated in the respected Rutherglen district, All Saints is a winery like no other. Behind the hedge fence and imposing set of gates lies an enormous medieval castle built by the original owner, George Smith, based on the Castle of Mey in Scotland. Now owned and operated by Peter Brown (of the famous Brown Brothers), All Saints offers a large cellar-door operation, a renowned restaurant, The Keg Factory, Indigo Cheese and beautiful gardens. Inquiries (02) 6035 2222; 5 km SW.

Corowa Jump Shak: skydiving and gliding weekends, weather permitting; off Redlands Rd; (02) 6033 2435. *Savernake Station:* offers eco-heritage tours of their 400 ha woodland including 120 bird species, woodshed and shearers quarters (1912) and cooks museum (1930) and store; inquiries (02) 6035 9415; 50 km NW.

TOWNS NEARBY: Rutherglen (Vic.) 9 km, Chiltern (Vic.) 26 km, Mulwala 35 km, Yarrawonga (Vic.) 35 km, Wangaratta (Vic.) 40 km

COFFS HARBOUR

Pop. 47 710
Map ref. 515 H1 | 516 E12 | 525 N8

Cnr Pacific Hwy and McLean St; (02) 6648 4990 or 1300 369 070; www.coffscoast.com.au

107.9 2AIR FM, 819 AM ABC Local

Coffs Harbour, a subtropical holiday town on Coffs Coast, is known for its banana plantations (and the iconic Big Banana) and for its great fishing. The combination of great weather, stunning hinterland forests, sandy beaches and a growing cosmopolitan centre make it a popular spot for tourists seeking fun and relaxation.

Muttonbird Island Nature Reserve Visitors can get an up-close look at the life cycle of one of Australia's most interesting migratory birds. The wedge-tailed shearwaters (muttonbirds) fly thousands of kilometres from South-East Asia each August, with large numbers settling at Muttonbird Island to breed. A walking trail winds through the burrows of the birds, which can be seen Aug–Apr. Muttonbird Island is also a vantage point for whale-watching June–Nov and is a great place for fishing and picnics. Access is via a 500 m walk along the sea wall from the harbour.

Bunker Cartoon Gallery: largest private collection of cartoons in the Southern Hemisphere, housed in a WW II bunker; City Hill; (02) 6651 7343. *Legends Surf Museum:* displays of classic photography, videos and equipment; Gaudrons Rd; (02) 6653 6536. *Coffs Harbour Regional Gallery:* varied program of contemporary art exhibitions; Cnr Coff and Duke sts; (02) 6648 4863. Tue–Sat 10am–4pm. *Coffs Harbour International Marina:* departure point for fishing charters, scuba diving and whale-watching trips (June–Nov); Marina Dr; (02) 6651 4222. *North Coast Regional Botanical Gardens:* rainforest, mangrove boardwalks, herbarium and diverse birdlife; Hardacre St; (02) 6648 4188. *Pet Porpoise Pool:* performing dolphins and seals with research and nursery facilities; Orlando St; (02) 6659 1900; open 9am–4pm every day. *Self-guide walks:* include Jetty Walk and Coffs Creek Walk; maps from visitor centre.

Growers market: Harbour Dr; Thurs Nov–Mar. *Market:* jetty, Harbour Dr; Sun. *Uptown Market:* Vernon St; Sun. *Pittwater and Coffs Harbour Offshore Series:* yachting; Jan. *Sawtell Chilli Festival:* July. *International Buskers and Comedy Festival:* Sept–Oct. *Food and Wine Festival:* Oct.

Fiasco Ristorante + Bar: northern Italian; 22 Orlando St; (02) 6651 2006. *Ocean Front Brasserie:* spectacular views and seafood platters; Coffs Harbour Deep Sea Fishing Club, 1 Jordan Espl; (02) 6651 2819. *Shearwater Restaurant:* seafood; 321 Harbour Dr; (02) 6651 6053.

The Clog Barn Holiday Park: 215 Pacific Hwy; (02) 6652 4633. *Harbour City Holiday Park:* 123 Pacific Hwy; (02) 6652 1694. *Park Beach Holiday Park:* 1 Ocean Pde; (02) 6648 4888. *Creekside Inn B&B:* 59 Boronia St, Sawtell; (02) 6658 9099. *Moonee Beach Holiday Park:* 50 Moonee Beach Rd, Moonee Beach; (02) 6653 6552. *Santa Fe Luxury Bed & Breakfast:* 235 The Mountain Way, Sapphire Beach; (02) 6653 7700. *Sapphire Beach Holiday Park:* 48 Split Solitary Rd, Sapphire Beach; (02) 6653 6212. *Sawtell Beach Caravan Park:* 5 Lyons Rd, Sawtell; (02) 6653 1379.

Big Banana Large banana-shaped landmark with displays on the banana industry, giant water slides and toboggan rides; 351 Pacific Hwy; (02) 6652 4355; open 9am–4.30pm every day; 4 km N.

Bindarri National Park Not for the unseasoned bushwalker, Bindarri National Park is a largely untouched forest without facilities, but amazing views reward those who make the effort. The headwaters of the Urumbilum River form breathtaking waterfalls in a remote and rugged setting. Pockets of old-growth forest are scattered across the plateau and rich rainforest protects the steeper slopes. While there are no campgrounds, backpack camping is allowed and there are bushwalking trails to follow; (02) 6652 0900; 20 km W.

Clog Barn: Dutch village with clog-making; Pacific Hwy; (02) 6652 4633; 2 km N. *Bruxner Park Flora Reserve:* dense tropical jungle area of vines, ferns and orchids with bushwalking trails, picnic area and Sealy Lookout; Korora; Bruxner Park Rd, Korora; (02) 6652 8900; 9 km NW. *Butterfly House:* enclosed subtropical garden with live native and exotic butterflies; 5 Strouds Rd, Bonville; (02) 6653 4766; open 9am–4pm daily; 9 km S. *Adventure tours:* include whitewater rafting, canoeing, reef-fishing, diving, horseriding through rainforest, surf rafting, skydiving, helicopter flights, go-karting and surf schools; see visitor centre for brochures and bookings.

TOWNS NEARBY: Woolgoolga 22 km, Urunga 24 km, Bellingen 27 km, Dorrigo 39 km, Nambucca Heads 40 km

[COFFS HARBOUR'S HISTORIC JETTY]

Cowra

 Olympic Park, Mid Western Hwy; (02) 6342 4333; www.cowratourism.com.au

99.5 Star FM, 549 AM ABC Local

Cowra is nestled in the Lachlan Valley, where you can enjoy local food and wine. The peaceful air of this town on the Lachlan River belies its dramatic history. The Cowra Breakout was an infamous World War II incident in Australia when 1000 Japanese POWs staged a mass breakout that was the biggest in British and Australian war history. While it remains what Cowra is most famous for, the town has moved forward.

Australia's World Peace Bell Each country has only one peace bell and it is normally located in the nation's capital, but Cowra was awarded Australia's Peace Bell owing to local efforts for peace. The bell is a replica of the United Nations World Peace Bell in New York City and was made by melting down coins donated from 103 member countries of the United Nations. It is rung each year during the Festival of International Understanding. Darling St.

Japanese Garden This garden, opened in 1979, is complete with a cultural centre (with a collection of Japanese artwork and artefacts), a traditional teahouse, a bonsai house and a pottery. The garden itself represents the landscape of Japan, with mountain, river and sea re-created. From here gracious Sakura Ave, lined with cherry trees that blossom in spring, leads to the site of the POW camp and to the Australian and Japanese cemeteries. The camp includes the original foundations and replica guardtower, with photo displays and signage; audio tours available. Off Binni Creek Rd; (02) 6341 2233.

Olympic Park: information centre with a fascinating interpretive POW display and theatre. Also here is Cowra Rose Garden with over 1000 rose bushes in over 100 varieties; Mid Western Hwy. *Cowra–Italy Friendship Monument:* in recognition of Italians who died in WW II (Italian POWs interned at Cowra formed a strong friendship with the town); Kendal St. *Lachlan Valley Railway Museum:* displays and train rides; Campbell St. *Cowra Mill Winery:* winery in former flour mill (1861) with cellar-door tastings and restaurant; Vaux St; (02) 6341 4141. *Aboriginal murals:* by local artist Kym Freeman on pylons of bridge over the Lachlan River. *Cowra Heritage Walk:* Federation, colonial and Victorian buildings including the town's first hotel and oldest home; map from visitor centre.

Farmers market: showgrounds; 3rd Sat each month. *Festival of International Understanding:* Mar. *Picnic Races:* July. Cowra Wine Show: July. *Sakura Matsuri:* cherry blossom festival; Sept/Oct. *Cowra Cork and Fork:* Nov.

Neila: modern Australian; 5 Kendal St; (02) 6341 2188.

Cowra Holiday Park: 10256 Mid Western Hwy (Sydney Rd); (02) 6342 2666. *Cowra Van Park:* 2 Lachlan St (off Kendal St); (02) 6340 2110. *Grabine Lakeside State Park:* Grabine Rd, Bigga; (02) 4835 2345. *Wyangala Waters State Park:* 2891 Reg Hailstone Way, Wyangala; (02) 6345 0877.

Cowra wine region Though just next door to Orange, the Cowra region has a warmer climate, and the vines are exposed to warm winds that blow across the plains from Central Australia. These conditions best suit chardonnay, the area's main wine. The vineyards surround the towns of Cowra and Canowindra and are side-by-side with grazing properties in low river valleys.

Cowra Estate is the area's oldest winery, established in 1973, while Windowrie Estate has its cellar door in an old flour mill.

Cowra museums: war, rail and rural museums all in one complex; Sydney Rd; 5 km E. *Darby Falls Observatory:* one of the largest telescopes accessible to the public. Check opening times; (02) 6345 1900 or 0417 461 162; Observatory Rd; 25 km SE. *Conimbla National Park:* known for its wildflowers, rock ledges, waterfalls, bushwalks and picnics; 27 km W. *Lake Wyangala and Grabine Lakeside State Park:* ideal for watersports and fishing; 40 km SE. *Self-guide drives:* through countryside including a wine-lovers' drive; brochure from visitor centre.

TOWNS NEARBY: Canowindra 30 km, Grenfell 50 km, Eugowra 54 km, Blayney 61 km, Young 64 km

Crookwell

 106 Goulburn St; (02) 4832 1988; www.upperlachlantourism.com

106.1 2GN FM, 846 AM ABC Radio National

This picturesque tree-lined township is a service centre to the local agricultural and pastoral district, and enjoys a cool climate and lush gardens. Australia's first grid-connected wind farm was opened here in 1998 and is capable of supplying electricity to 3500 homes. The Country Women's Association was formed here in 1922 and has since spread nationwide.

Crookwell Wind Farm: viewing platform and information board; Goulburn Rd.

Market: Uniting Church, Goulburn St; 1st Sat each month. *Crookwell Country Festival:* traditional country festival with music, markets, sports and a parade; Mar. *Open Gardens weekends:* spring and autumn (dates from visitor centre).

Paul's Cafe: sandwiches, burgers, fish and chips; 102 Goulburn St; (02) 4832 1745.

Wombeyan Caves Caravan & Camping Reserve: Wombeyan Caves Rd, Wombeyan Caves; (02) 4843 5976.

Wombeyan Caves There are 5 caves open to the public including Figtree Cave, widely regarded as the best self-guide cave in NSW. Junction Cave has a colourful underground river; Wollondilly Cave has 5 main chambers with outstanding formations; Mulwarree Cave is intimate, with delicate formations; and Kooringa Cave is huge and majestic. Wombeyan Gorge is made of marble, providing an unusual swimming experience. There are several campgrounds and walking trails in the area. 60 km E.

Redground Lookout: excellent views of surrounding area; 8 km NW. *Willow Vale Mill:* restored flour mill with restaurant and accommodation; Laggan; (02) 4837 3319; 9 km NE. *Lake Wyangala and Grabine Lakeside State Park:* upper reaches ideal for waterskiing, picnicking, fishing, bushwalking and camping; 65 km NW. *Bike riding:* the area surrounding Crookwell is popular for bike riding; trail maps from visitor centre. *Historic villages:* associated with goldmining, coppermining and bushrangers, these villages include Tuena, Peelwood, Laggan, Bigga, Binda (all north) and Roslyn (south), the birthplace of poet Dame Mary Gilmore; maps from visitor centre. *Historical and scenic drives:* explore sites and countryside frequented by bushrangers such as Ben Hall; brochure from visitor centre.

TOWNS NEARBY: Goulburn 40 km, Yass 67 km, Bundanoon 79 km, Berrima 80 km, Moss Vale 83 km

Culcairn

Pop. 1118
Map ref. 522 B11 | 527 O11 | 543 L4

 Greater Hume Shire Visitor Information Centre, 15 Wallace St, Holbrook; (02) 6036 2422; www.greaterhume.nsw.gov.au/tourism.html

93.1 Star FM, 675 AM ABC Local

Culcairn is located at the heart of 'Morgan country' where Dan 'Mad Dog' Morgan terrorised the district between 1862 and 1865. This peaceful town owes its tree-lined streets and lush green parks to an underground water supply discovered in 1926.

Stationmaster's Residence: beautifully restored museum (1883) reflects the importance of the railway; just across railway line. *Billabong Creek:* good fishing, one of the longest creeks in the Southern Hemisphere. *National Trust–classified buildings:* includes historic Culcairn Hotel (1891), still operating; Railway Pde and Olympic Way.

Henty This historic pastoral town has the Headlie Taylor Header Memorial, a tribute to the mechanical header harvester that revolutionised the grain industry. The nearby Sergeant Smith Memorial Stone marks the spot where Morgan fatally wounded a police officer, and the adjacent Doodle Cooma Swamp is 2000 ha of breeding area for waterbirds. 24 km N.

John McLean's grave: McLean was shot by Mad Dog Morgan; 3 km E. *Premier Yabby Farm:* tours through yabby-related displays and open ponds; also fishing, picnicking and barbecue facilities; (02) 6029 8351; 6 km SW. *Round Hill Station:* where Morgan committed his first hold-up in the area; Holbrook Rd; 15 km E. *Walla Walla:* old schoolhouse (1875) and the largest Lutheran church in NSW (1924); 18 km SW. *Morgan's Lookout:* granite outcrop on otherwise flat land, allegedly used by Morgan to look for approaching victims and police; 18 km NW.

TOWNS NEARBY: Holbrook 26 km, Albury 46 km, Wodonga (Vic.) 52 km, Tallangatta (Vic.) 62 km, Chiltern (Vic.) 66 km

Deniliquin

Pop. 7433
Map ref. 527 J10 | 542 D2

 Peppin Heritage Centre, George St; (03) 5898 3120 or 1800 650 712; www.denitourism.com.au

99.3 FM ABC Radio National, 102.5 Classic Rock FM

Deniliquin, at the centre of Australia's largest irrigation system, lies on the Edward River, part of the Murray River and formed by a fault in the earth. Situated next to the world's largest red-gum forest, birdlife and wildlife remain abudant, despite the drought currently crippling the town's rice-growing industry. 'Deni' proclaims itself the 'ute capital of the world', holding the official record for most utes mustered in one place in 2007.

Peppin Heritage Centre This museum is dedicated to George Hall Peppin and his sons' development of the merino sheep industry. Dissatisfied with the quality and yield of the wool from merino sheep, they developed a new breed, the peppin, that was better adapted to the harsh Australian conditions. Peppin sheep now predominate among flocks in New Zealand, South Africa and South America. The museum is housed in the National Trust–classified Old George Street Public School (1879), which still has an intact classroom on display. There is also a lock-up gaol from Wanganella and a 1920s thatched ram shed. George St.

Island Sanctuary: features kangaroos and birdlife, and the burial site of 'Old Jack', a member of the Melville gang who visited Deniliquin in 1851; off Cressy St footbridge. *Ute on a Pole:* confirms Deniliquin's status as 'ute capital of the world'; near National Bridge. *Waring Gardens:* originally a chain of lagoons, the park was established in the 1880s; Cressy St. *Pioneer Steam Museum:* private collection of steam engines and pumps; Hay Rd. *Long Paddock River Walk:* old stock route, includes interpretive panels; from Heritage Centre to Island Sanctuary. *Self-guide walks:* historical and nature walks taking in National Trust–classified buildings and town gardens; brochure from visitor centre.

Market: Waring Gardens; 4th Sat each month. *Sun Festival:* includes gala parade and international food and entertainment; Jan. *RSL Fishing Classic:* Jan. *Play on the Plains Festival and Ute Muster:* celebration of music and cars; Sept/Oct.

Deniliquin Bakery: coffee and snacks; 69 Davidson St; (03) 5881 2278.

Deniliquin Riverside Caravan Park: 20–24 Davidson St (Cobb Hwy); (03) 5881 1284. *McLean Beach Caravan Park:* 1 Butler St; (03) 5881 2448. *Pioneer Tourist Park:* 167 Hay Rd; (03) 5881 5066. *Murraybank Caravan & Camping Park:* 80 Tarragon Rd, Mathoura; (03) 5884 3518.

 Pioneer Tourist Park A modern caravan park including charming features of the past (open to the public), with an antique steam and pump display and a blacksmith shop. 2 km N.

Irrigation works: at Lawsons Syphon (7 km E) and Stevens Weir (25 km W). *Clancy's Winery:* cellar-door tastings and sales; 18 km N. *Conargo Pub:* authentic bush pub with photo gallery depicting history of merino wool in the area; 25 km NE. *Bird Observatory Tower:* excellent vantage point for birdwatching; Mathoura; 34 km S.

TOWNS NEARBY: Finley 58 km, Tocumwal 64 km, Echuca (Vic.) 71 km, Jerilderie 72 km, Cohuna (Vic.) 74 km

Dorrigo

Pop. 970
Map ref. 515 G1 | 516 C12 | 525 M8

 Hickory St; (02) 6657 2486; www.bellingermagic.com

105.5 Star FM, 738 AM ABC Local

Dorrigo is known as 'Australia's national park capital'. It is entirely surrounded by national parks including Dorrigo and Cathedral Rock. The Dorrigo Plateau provides crisp, clean air and wonderful views in all directions. The town is small enough to be friendly, but popular enough to provide excellent facilities.

Historical museum: memorabilia, documents and photographs detailing the history of Dorrigo and surrounding national parks; Cudgery St. *Local crafts:* at Pinnata Gallery; Hickory St. *Wood-fired bakery:* produces popular products with local produce; Hickory St. *Waterfall Way Winery:* unique fruit wines and fortified wines; tastings available; Hickory St.

Market: showground, Armidale Rd; 1st Sat each month. *Arts and Crafts Exhibition:* Easter. *Bluegrass Festival:* Oct.

Lick the Spoon: cafe and provedore; Red Dirt Distillery, 51–53 Hickory St; (02) 6657 1373. *Tallawalla Teahouse:* cafe in stunning surrounds; 113 Old Coramba Rd; (02) 6657 2315.

 RADIO STATIONS   IN TOWN WHAT'S ON WHERE TO EAT WHERE TO STAY NEARBY

Dorrigo Mountain Resort: Waterfall Way; (02) 6657 2564. *Lisnagarvey Cottage:* 803 Whisky Creek Rd; (02) 6657 2536.

Dorrigo National Park This park takes in World Heritage–listed rainforest and offers plenty for visitors to see and do. Attractions include spectacular waterfalls and a variety of birds such as bowerbirds and lyrebirds. The Rainforest Centre has picnic facilities, a cafe, a video theatre and exhibitions. There is also the Skywalk, a boardwalk offering views over the canopy of the rainforest, and the Walk with the Birds boardwalk. 3 km E.

Cathedral Rock National Park Giant boulders, sculpted rock, distinctive granite hills and wedge-tailed eagles make Cathedral Rock spectacular viewing and popular among photographers. Walks include a 3 hr circuit walk to the summit of Cathedral Rock for amazing 360-degree views of the tableland. 56 km SW.

Trout fishing: in streams on the Dorrigo Plateau (between Dorrigo and Urunga); contact visitor centre for locations. *Dangar Falls:* viewing platform over beautiful 30 m waterfall; 2 km N. *Griffiths Lookout:* sweeping views of the mountains; 6 km S. *Guy Fawkes River National Park:* rugged and scenic surrounds with limited facilities, but worth the effort for experienced bushwalkers. Ebor Falls has cliff-top viewing platforms above and there is also good canoeing and fishing; 40 km W. *L. P. Dutton Trout Hatchery:* educational visitor centre and trout feeding; 63 km SW. *Point Lookout:* in New England National Park for spectacular panoramic views of Bellinger Valley and across to the ocean; 74 km SW.

TOWNS NEARBY: Bellingen 22 km, Urunga 34 km, Coffs Harbour 39 km, Nambucca Heads 44 km, Macksville 45 km

Dubbo

Pop. 34 318
Map ref. 522 F1 | 524 C12

ⓘ Cnr Newell Hwy and Macquarie St; (02) 6801 4450 or 1800 674 443; www.dubbotourism.com.au

📻 92.7 Zoo FM, 549 AM ABC Local, 1251 AM 2DU

One of Australia's fastest growing inland cities, Dubbo is most famous for its world-class open-range zoo. The city, on the banks of the Macquarie River, is thriving and prosperous with more than half a million visitors each year. Dubbo prides itself on city standards with a country smile.

Western Plains Cultural Centre The centre includes the Dubbo Regional Gallery – the Armati Bequest, Dubbo Regional Museum and the Community Arts Centre. It exhibits local and national visual arts, heritage and social history. In 2007, the gallery received a generous gift from the Armati Family including Michael Riley's celebrated 'Cloud' series of photographs. To acknowledge this, the gallery was renamed the Armati Bequest. It specialises in the theme of Animals in Art, collecting works in a broad range of media and styles by artists from all areas. The museum, housed in the original Dubbo High School building, features a permanent space devoted to the story of Dubbo entitled 'People Places Possessions' and a temporary exhibition space. Closed Tues; Wingewarra Street; (02) 6801 4444.

Old Dubbo Gaol Closed as a penal institution in 1966, Old Dubbo Gaol now offers a glimpse at convict life. See the original gallows (where 8 men were hanged for murder) and solitary confinement cells, or walk along the watchtower. An amazing animatronic robot tells historical tales. There are also holograms and theatrical enactments. Macquarie St; (02) 6801 4460.

[DUBBO] BLACK RHINOCEROS, TARONGA WESTERN PLAINS ZOO

Shoyoen Sister City Garden: Japanese garden and teahouse designed and built with the support of Dubbo's sister city, Minokamo; Coronation Dr East. *Jedda Boomerangs:* Aboriginal art and culture displays; also makes and sells boomerangs. Decorate your own, or take throwing lessons (bookings essential); closed Sat; Minore Rd; (02) 6882 3110. **The Clay Pan Gallery:** exhibits include paintings, pottery, silver jewellery, woodturning, ceramics and local craft; closed Tues; Depot Rd. *Traintasia:* detailed operating model railway display with spectator interaction; Yarrandale Road; (02) 6884 9944.

Markets: Macquarie Lions Park, 1st and 3rd Sat each month; Dubbo Showground, Wingewarra St, 2nd Sun each month. *Western Plains Country Music Championships:* Easter. *Jazz Festival:* Aug. *Red Ochre Festival:* Sept.

✗ *Rose Garden Thai Restaurant:* takeaway available; 208 Brisbane St; (02) 6882 8322. *Two Doors Tapas & Wine Bar:* Spanish; 215B Macquarie St; (02) 6885 2333.

BIG4 Dubbo Parklands: 154 Whylandra St (Newell Hwy); (02) 6884 8633. *Dubbo City Holiday Park:* Whylandra St; (02) 6882 4820. *Midstate Motor Park:* 21 Bourke St (Newell Hwy); (02) 6882 1155. *Pericoe Retreat Bed and Breakfast:* 12R Cassandra Dr; (02) 6887 2705. *Poplars Caravan Park:* Cnr Bligh and Bultje sts; (02) 6882 4067. *Walls Court Bed & Breakfast:* 11L Belgravia Heights Rd; (02) 6887 3823. *Westview Tourist Caravan Park:* Mitchell Hwy; (02) 6882 1339. *'The Abbey' Bed & Breakfast:* 24 Dandaloo St, Narromine; (02) 6889 2213. *Narromine Tourist Park & Motel:* Mitchell Hwy, Narromine; (02) 6889 2129.

Taronga Western Plains Zoo Australia's first open-range zoo, with over 1000 animals from 5 continents, is set on more than 300 ha of bushland. The zoo is renowned for its breeding programs (especially with endangered species), conservation programs and education facilities and exhibits. There are talks by the keepers and early morning walks, as well as accommodation at Zoofari Lodge. Visitors can use their own cars, hire bikes or walk along the tracks. The Tracker Riley Cycleway paves the 5 km from Dubbo to the zoo and bicycles and maps are available from the visitor centre. Inquiries (02) 9969 2777; 5 km s.

Dubbo Observatory: explore the skies via Schmidt Cassegrain telescopes. Open nightly; Camp Road; (02) 6885 3022; 5.5 km s. *Dundullimal Homestead:* an 1840s restored squatter's slab-style homestead with working saddler, blacksmith and farm animals; Obley Rd; 7 km se. *Terramungamine Rock Grooves:* the 150 rock grooves were created by the Tubbagah people; Burraway Rd via Brocklehurst; 10 km n. *Narromine:* agricultural centre well known for gliding and an outstanding aviation museum. The Air Pageant and Evolution of Flight Festival is held here each Sept/Oct; 40 km e. *Heritage drives and river cruises:* brochures from visitor centre. *Wineries:* several in region offering cellar-door tastings; brochure from visitor centre.

TOWNS NEARBY: Wellington 47 km, Gilgandra 59 km, Gulgong 88 km, Mudgee 100 km, Parkes 107 km

Eden

Pop. 3010
Map ref. 519 E10 | 539 H8

i Eden Gateway Centre, cnr Princes Hwy and Mitchell St; (02) 6496 1953; www.visiteden.com.au

 102.5 Power FM, 810 AM ABC Local

Situated on the Sapphire Coast, the aptly named Eden is an idyllic and peaceful town on Twofold Bay. The location is excellent, with national park to the north and south, water to the east and woodland to the west. The beautiful bay is rimmed with mountains. Originally settled by whalers, it is now a fishing port and a popular, but relatively undeveloped, tourist town.

Aslings Beach: surf beach with rockpools and excellent platforms for whale-watching Oct–Nov; Aslings Beach Rd. *Snug Cove:* working fishing port with plenty of restaurants and cafes. *Eden Killer Whale Museum:* fascinating displays on the history of the local whaling industry including the skeleton of 'Old Tom' the killer whale; Imlay St; (02) 6496 2094.

Market: Calle Calle St; 1st Sat each month. *Eden Seafood and Arts Festival:* Easter. *Eden Whale Festival:* Oct/Nov.

Eden Fishermen's Club: steak and seafood; 217 Imlay St; (02) 6496 1577. *Essentially Eden:* modern Australian; The Great Southern Inn, 158 Imlay St; (02) 6496 1515.

Cocora Cottage B&B: 2 Cocora St; (02) 6496 1241. *Discovery Holiday Parks – Eden:* 441 Princes Hwy; (02) 6496 1677. *Eden Tourist Park:* Aslings Beach Rd; (02) 6496 1139. *Fountain Caravan Park:* 99 Princes Hwy; (02) 6496 1798. *Garden of Eden Caravan Park:* Cnr Princes Hwy and Barclay St; (02) 6496 1172. *Boydtown Caravan & Camping Park:* 1 Boydtown Park Rd, Boydtown; 0405 447 361. *Twofold Bay Beach Resort – Aspen Parks:* 731 Princes Hwy, Boydtown; (02) 6496 1572.

 **Ben Boyd National Park** This park's scenery includes rugged stretches of coastline, unique rock formations, heaths and banksia forest. The area is excellent for fishing, swimming, wreck diving, bushwalking and camping. Boyd's Tower at Red Point, 32 km se, was originally built for whale-spotting. Cape Green Lighthouse, 45 km se, is the first cast-concrete lighthouse in Australia and the second tallest in NSW; tours by appt; bookings (02) 6495 5000. The Pinnacles, 8 km n, are an unusual earth formation with red gravel atop white sand cliffs.

Jiggamy Farm: Aboriginal cultural and bush tucker experience; 9 km n. *Boydtown:* former rival settlement on the shores of Twofold Bay with convict-built Seahorse Inn (still licensed), safe beach and good fishing; 9 km s. *Davidson Whaling Station Historic Site:* provides unique insight into the lives of 19th-century whalers; Kiah Inlet; 30 km se. *South East Fibre Exports Visitors Centre:* logging and milling displays; Jews Head; bookings essential (02) 6496 0222; 34 km se. *Nadgee Nature Reserve:* walking track, access via Wonboyn Lake; 35 km se. *Wonboyn Lake:* scenic area with good fishing and 4WD tracks; 40 km s.

TOWNS NEARBY: Merimbula 19 km, Tathra 38 km, Bega 44 km, Mallacoota (Vic.) 57 km, Bombala 62 km

Eugowra

Pop. 532
Map ref. 522 E5

i Cnr Byng and Peisley sts; (02) 6393 8226 or 1800 069 466; www.orange.nsw.gov.au

 105.9 Star FM, 549 AM ABC Local

Situated on the rich basin of the Lachlan River, Eugowra is a tiny country town known for its crafts. Nearby on the Orange–Forbes road, the famous Gold Escort Robbery took place in 1862.

Eugowra Museum and Bushranger Centre: displays on pioneer life, a pistol used in the Gold Escort Robbery, gemstones, early farm equipment, wagons and Aboriginal artefacts; open Wed–Sun; (02) 6859 2214. *Local craft shops:* leaflet from visitor centre. *Self-guide bushranging tour:* maps from visitor centre.

The Lady Bushranger: quaint cafe; Shop 2, 51 Nanima St; (02) 6859 2900.

Nangar National Park The horseshoe-shaped red cliffs of the Nangar–Murga Range stand out against the central west's plains. Nangar National Park's flowering shrubs and timbered hills provide an important wildlife refuge among mostly cleared land. Rocky slopes and pretty creeks make it a scenic site for bushwalks and popular for rock climbing. The park does not have facilities, so visitors are advised to take water and provisions with them and to give friends or family their itinerary. 10 km e.

Escort Rock: where bushranger Frank Gardiner and gang (including Ben Hall) hid before ambushing the Forbes gold escort. A plaque on the road gives details; 3 km e. *Nanami Lane Lavender Farm:* products and plants for sale and workshops on growing lavender; 19 km se.

TOWNS NEARBY: Canowindra 31 km, Forbes 34 km, Parkes 37 km, Cowra 54 km, Grenfell 55 km

Evans Head

Pop. 2629
Map ref. 516 G6 | 525 O4

 Ballina Visitor Information Centre, cnr Las Balsas Plaza and River St, Ballina; (02) 6686 3484 or 1800 777 666; www.tropicalnsw.com.au

📻 92.9 FM North Coast Radio, 738 AM ABC Local

Evans Head is located at the mouth of the Evans River. It was the first prawning port in Australia and is still predominantly a fishing village, but with 6 kilometres of safe surfing beaches, sandy river flats and coastal scenery, it is also a tourist town. There is excellent rock, beach and ocean fishing.

Goanna Headland: site of great mythical importance to the Bundjalung people and favourite spot of serious surfers. *Razorback Lookout:* views up and down the coast. On a clear day, Cape Byron Lighthouse can be seen to the north; Ocean Dr.

Market: Cnr Oak and Park sts; 4th Sat each month. *Fishing Classic:* July. *Evans Head Flower Show:* Sept. *Evans Head Longboard Invitational:* Sept.

Silver Sands Holiday Park: Park St; (02) 6682 4212. *Broadwater Stopover Tourist Park:* 1–5 Pacific Hwy, Broadwater; (02) 6682 8254. *Sunrise Caravan Park:* 74 Pacific Hwy, Broadwater; (02) 6682 8388.

New Italy A monument and remains are all that are left of this settlement that was the result of the ill-fated Marquis de Rays expedition in 1880. The Marquis tricked 340 Italians into purchasing nonexistent property in a Pacific paradise. Disaster struck several times for the emigrants, as they travelled first to Papua New Guinea and then to New Caledonia. Eventually Sir Henry Parkes arranged for their passage to Australia, where the 217 survivors built this village. Also in the New Italy Complex, Guuragai Aboriginal Arts and Crafts offers quality works and information on Aboriginal culture. 23 km sw.

Bundjalung National Park: Aboriginal relics, fishing, swimming and bushwalking; 2 km s. *Broadwater National Park:* bushwalking, birdwatching, fishing and swimming; 5 km N. *Woodburn:* friendly town on the Richmond River with great spots for picnicking, swimming, fishing and boating; flower show in Aug; 11 km NW.

TOWNS NEARBY: Alstonville 31 km, Ballina 31 km, Iluka 33 km, Yamba 36 km, Lismore 37 km

Finley

Pop. 2053
Map ref. 527 L11 | 542 F3

 Tocumwal Visitor Centre, 41 Deniliquin St; (03) 5874 2131 or 1800 677 271.

📻 102.5 FM Classic Rock, 675 AM ABC Local

This town, on the Newell Highway and close to the Victorian border, is a tidy and peaceful spot. It is the centre of the Berriquin Irrigation Area. The main street spans Mulwala Canal, the largest irrigation channel in Australia.

Mary Lawson Wayside Rest Features a log cabin that is an authentic replica of a pioneer home. It houses the Finley and District Historical Museum with displays of antique pumping equipment and machinery. Newell Hwy.

Finley Lake: popular boating, sailboarding and picnic area; Newell Hwy. *Finley Livestock Exchange:* experience a cattle sale; Fri mornings.

 Rodeo: Jan.

Berrigan Lions Club Inc. Caravan Park: Jerilderie St (Riverina Hwy), Berrigan; 0400 563 979.

Berrigan: charming historic town known for its connections to horseracing; 22 km E. *Sojourn Station Art Studio:* spacious rural property providing accommodation for visiting artists; 25 km SE via Berrigan. *Grassleigh Woodturning and Crafts:* displays of woodturning in action and wood products; 37 km NE via Berrigan.

TOWNS NEARBY: Tocumwal 18 km, Cobram (Vic.) 31 km, Jerilderie 35 km, Mulwala 54 km, Yarrawonga (Vic.) 56 km

Forbes

Pop. 6954
Map ref. 522 D4

 Railway station, Union St; (02) 6852 4155; www.forbes.nsw.gov.au

📻 97.9 Valley FM, 104.3 FM Radio National

When John Oxley passed through in 1817, he was so unimpressed by the area's clay soil, poor timber and swamps that he claimed 'it is impossible to imagine a worse country'. Today Forbes is a pleasant spot bisected by Lake Forbes, a large lagoon in the middle of town. It was the discovery of gold that caused the town to be built and the legends of old bushrangers that keep it buzzing today.

Albion Hotel The first hotel in Forbes, the Albion Hotel was so popular during the gold rush that it allegedly sold more alcohol in the 1860s than any hotel in Australia – not bad for an outback town. The hotel is a former Cobb & Co depot and now houses displays on the history of the gold strikes and the must-see Bushranger Hall of Fame. Lachlan St.

Historical Museum: features relics associated with bushranger Ben Hall, a vintage colonial kitchen and antique farm machinery; open 2–4pm; Cross St; (02) 6851 6600.

Cemetery: graves of Ben Hall, Kate Foster (Ned Kelly's sister), Rebecca Shields (Captain Cook's niece) and French author Paul Wenz; Bogan Gate Rd. *King George V Park:* memorial where 'German Harry' discovered gold in 1861, and a pleasant spot for picnics and barbecues; Lawler St. *Dowling St Park:* memorial marks the spot where John Oxley first passed through in 1817; Dowling St. *Lake Forbes:* picnic spots, barbecue facilities, fishing, and a walking and cycling track; off Gordon Duff Dr. *Historical town walk:* includes the post office (1862) and the town hall (1861) where Dame Nellie Melba performed in 1909; map from visitor centre. *Local arts and crafts:* brochure from visitor centre.

Jazz Festival: Jan.

 *Signatures Restaurant:* modern Australian; Forbes Services Memorial Club, 41–43 Templar St; (02) 6851 2022. *Wattle Cafe:* light lunches; 85 Rankin St; (02) 6852 4310.

Apex Riverside Tourist Park: 88 Reymond St; (02) 6850 2318. *BIG4 Forbes Holiday Park:* 141 Flint St; (02) 6852 1055. *Country Club Caravan Park:* 33 Sam St; (02) 6852 1957. *Forbes River Meadows Caravan Park:* Cnr Newell Hwy and River Rd; (02) 6852 2694.

Gum Swamp Sanctuary: birdlife and other fauna, best seen at sunrise or sunset; 4 km s. *Banderra Estate Vineyard:* French winemaker with cellar-door tastings; off Orange Rd; 5 km E. *Chateau Champsaur:* oldest winery in the area (1886), with cellar-door tastings; (02) 6852 3908; 5 km SE. **Ben Hall's Place:** marks the site where the bushranger was shot dead by policemen; 8 km W. **Jemalong Weir:** with parklands by the Lachan River, good spot for fishing and picnicking; 24 km S.

TOWNS NEARBY: Parkes 32 km, Eugowra 34 km, Grenfell 59 km, Canowindra 64 km, Cowra 81 km

Forster–Tuncurry

Pop. 18 374
Map ref. 515 E9 | 523 O2

 Little St, Forster; (02) 6554 8799 or 1800 802 692; www.greatlakes.org.au

95.5 FM ABC Local, 107.3 Max FM

Located in the Great Lakes district, Forster is connected to its twin town, Tuncurry, by a concrete bridge across Wallis Lake, forming one large resort town. The area has an excellent reputation for its fishing and seafood, particularly its oysters.

Forster Arts and Crafts Centre: the largest working craft centre in NSW; Breese Pde. **Tobwabba Art Studio:** specialises in urban coastal Aboriginal art; Cnr Breckenridge and Little sts, Forster. **Pebbly Beach Bicentennial Walk:** gentle and scenic 2 km walk to Bennetts Head, beginning at baths off North St, Forster. **Wallis Lake Fishermen's Co-op:** fresh and cooked oysters and ocean fish; Wharf St, Tuncurry. **Dolphin-spotting and lake cruises:** bookings at visitor centre. Dolphins can also be seen from Tuncurry Breakwall and Bennetts Head.

Forster Market: Town Park; 2nd Sun each month. **Tuncurry Market:** John Wright Park; 4th Sat each month.

Forster Beach Holiday Park: Reserve Rd, Forster; (02) 6554 6269. **Lakeside Resort Forster:** 13 Tea Tree Rd, Forster; (02) 6555 5511. **Lani's Holiday Island:** 33 The Lakes Way, Forster; (02) 6554 6273. **Smugglers' Cove Holiday Village:** 45 The Lakes Way, Forster; (02) 6554 6666. **Great Lakes Holiday Park:** 1 Baird St, Tuncurry; (02) 6554 6827. **Tokelau Guest House:** 2 Manning St, Tuncurry; (02) 6557 5157. **Tuncurry Beach Holiday Park:** Beach St, Tuncurry; (02) 6554 6440. **Twin Dolphins Holiday Park:** 134 South St, Tuncurry; (02) 6554 7015. **Beachfront Holiday Resort:** 21 Redhead Rd, Hallidays Point; (02) 6559 2630. **Diamond Beach Holiday Park:** Jubilee Pde, Diamond Beach; (02) 6559 2910. **Happy Hallidays Holiday Park:** 517 Black Head Rd, Hallidays Point; (02) 6559 2967. **Pacific Palms Caravan Park:** Mariana Ave, Elizabeth Beach; (02) 6554 0209. **Sandbar & Bushland Caravan Parks:** 3434 The Lakes Way, Pacific Palms; (02) 6554 4095. **Sundowner Tiona BIG4:** The Lakes Way, Pacific Palms; (02) 6554 0291. **Wallamba River Holiday Park – Aspen Parks:** 99 Aquatic Rd, North Tuncurry; (02) 6554 3123. **Whitby on Wallis Lakefront Holiday Cottage and Bed & Breakfast:** 1770 Coomba Rd, Coomba Bay; (02) 6554 2448.

Booti Booti National Park An ideal spot for water activities, Booti Booti National Park has beautiful beaches including Elizabeth, Boomerang and Blueys beaches, all fabulous for surfing, swimming and fishing. Elizabeth Beach is patrolled by lifesavers in season. The lookout tower on Cape Hawke offers 360-degree views over Booti Booti and Wallingat national parks, the foothills of the Barrington Tops, Seal Rocks and Crowdy Bay. The park offers a variety of walking trails. 17 km s.

Cape Hawke: steep 400 m track to summit for views of Wallis Lake, Seal Rocks and inland to Great Dividing Range; 8 km s.

The Green Cathedral: open-air church with pews and altar, sheltered by cabbage palm canopy; Tiona, on the shores of Wallis Lake; 13 km s. **Smiths Lake:** sheltered lake for safe swimming; 30 km s. **Tours of Great Lakes area:** kayak, 4WD, nature and eco-tours, including bushwalks; brochure from visitor centre.

TOWNS NEARBY: Taree 30 km, Wingham 37 km, Bulahdelah 38 km, Gloucester 55 km, Stroud 57 km

Gilgandra

Pop. 2679
Map ref. 524 C10

 Coo-ee Heritage Centre, Coo-ee March Memorial Park, Newell Hwy; (02) 6817 8700; www.gilgandra.nsw.gov.au

101.3 Star FM, 549 AM ABC Local

A historic town at the junction of three highways, 'Gil' is the centre for the surrounding wool and farming country. The 1915 Coo-ee March in which 35 men, given no support from the army, marched the 500 kilometres to Sydney to enlist for World War I left from here. Along the way they recruited over 200 men, announcing their arrival with a call of 'coo-ee!' The march sparked seven other such marches from country towns.

Coo-ee Heritage Centre Memorabilia from the 1915 Coo-ee March, and items relating to the Breelong Massacre, which took place after an Aboriginal man was insulted for marrying a white woman, and on which Thomas Keneally's *The Chant of Jimmy Blacksmith* was based. Coo-ee Memorial Park, Newell Hwy.

Rural Museum: vast collection of agricultural artefacts including antique farm machinery and early model tractors on display; Newell Hwy. **Hitchen House Museum:** the home of the Hitchen brothers, who initiated the Coo-ee March. The museum has memorabilia from WW I, WW II and Vietnam; Miller St. **Orana Cactus World:** almost 1000 different cacti on display collected over 40 years; open most weekends and by appt; Newell Hwy; bookings (02) 6847 0566. **Gilgandra Observatory:** Newtonian reflector and refractor telescopes and a sundial; open 7–10pm (8.30–10pm during daylight saving) Mon–Sat; Cnr Wamboin and Willie sts; (02) 6847 2646. **Tourist drives:** around town; brochure from visitor centre.

Rodeo: Oct. **Coo-ee Festival:** Oct.

Cafe Country Style: home-style meals; 44 Miller St; (02) 6487 1571. **Holland's Family Diner:** classic cafe; 11 Castlereagh St; (02) 6847 1199.

Barney's Caravan Park: 173 Lower Miller St (Castlereagh Hwy); (02) 6847 2636. **Gilgandra Caravan Park:** 53 Newell Hwy; (02) 6847 2423.

 Warren Its location on the Macquarie River makes Warren a popular spot with anglers. For a stroll along the riverbank take the River Red Gum Walk, for birdwatching go to Tiger Bay Wildlife Reserve, and for a day of picnicking and swimming visit Warren Weir. The racecourse is known as the 'Randwick of the west' and hosts some fantastic race days. 85 km w.

Gilgandra Flora Reserve: 8.5 ha of bushland, perfect for picnics and barbecues. Most plants flower in spring, making the park particularly spectacular Sept–Nov; 14 km NE. **Emu Farm:** raised for oil, leather and meat, guided tours; Tooraweenah; 40 km NW.

TOWNS NEARBY: Dubbo 59 km, Coonabarabran 76 km, Coonamble 88 km, Wellington 97 km, Gulgong 109 km

Glen Innes

Pop. 5944
Map ref. 525 K5

 152 Church St (New England Hwy); (02) 6730 2400;
www.gleninnestourism.com

106.7 Gem FM, 819 AM ABC Local

This beautiful town, set among rolling hills on the northern tablelands of New South Wales at an elevation of 1075 metres, is known for its fine parks, which are especially striking in autumn. It was the scene of many bushranging exploits in the 19th century, including some by the infamous Captain Thunderbolt. In the 1830s, two particularly hairy convict stockmen, Chandler and Duval, advised and guided settlers to new land where they settled stations. Because of Chandler and Duval, people came to know Glen Innes as the 'land of the beardies', a nickname that has stuck to this day. The town is undeniably proud of its Celtic beginnings (the first settlers were predominantly Scots), as illustrated by its attractions and festivals.

Centennial Parklands The site of Celtic monument 'Australian Standing Stones', which was built with 38 giant granite monoliths in recognition of the contribution made in Australia by people of Celtic origin. A full explanation of the stones can be read at Crofters Cottage, which also sells Celtic food and gifts. St Martin's Lookout provides superb views. Meade St.

Land of the Beardies History House: folk museum in the town's first hospital building; it has a reconstructed slab hut, period room settings and pioneer relics; Cnr Ferguson St and West Ave; (02) 6732 1035. *Self-guide walks:* past historic public buildings, especially on Grey St; brochure from visitor centre.

Market: Grey St; 2nd Sun each month. *Minerama Gem Festival:* world-class gems on display and guided fossicking trips to unique locations; Mar. *Australian Celtic Festival:* Apr/May. *Gourmet in the Glen:* Oct. *Land of the Beardies Festival:* Nov.

The Hereford Steakhouse: award-winning steakhouse; Rest Point Motor Inn, 72 Church St (New England Hwy); (02) 6732 2255. *Ramona's Restaurant:* modern Australian; New England Motor Lodge, 160 Church St (New England Hwy); (02) 6732 2922.

Craigieburn Cottages: New England Hwy; (02) 6732 1283. *Fossicker Caravan Park:* 94 Church St (New England Hwy); (02) 6732 4246. *Glen Rest Tourist Park:* 9807 New England Hwy; (02) 6732 2413. *Poplar Caravan Park:* 15–19 Church St (New England Hwy); (02) 6732 1514. *Tudor House Glen Innes:* 141 Church St; (02) 6732 3884.

Gibraltar Range National Park and Washpool National Park These adjoining parks were World Heritage–listed in 1986 because of their ancient and isolated remnants of rainforest and their great variety of plant and animal species. Gibraltar Range is known for its scenic creeks and cascades and its unusual granite formations, The Needles and Anvil Rock. Gibraltar Range also contains over 100 km of excellent walking trails. 70 km NE. Washpool has the largest remaining stand of coachwood trees in the world and a unique array of eucalypt woods and rainforest. It has some of the least disturbed forest in NSW. 75 km NE.

Stonehenge: unusual balancing rock formations; 18 km s. *Emmaville:* the Australian beginnings of St John Ambulance occurred here. Includes a mining museum; 39 km NW. *Deepwater:* good fishing for trout, perch and cod with regular fishing safaris; bookings at visitor centre; 40 km N. *Mann River Nature Reserve:* popular camping spot due to fantastic swimming holes; 40 km NW. *Torrington:* gem fossicking, bushwalks and unusual rock formations; 66 km NW. *Convict-carved tunnel:* road tunnel halfway between Glen Innes and Grafton; Old Grafton Rd; 72 km W. *Horse treks:* accommodation at historic pubs; bookings at visitor centre.

TOWNS NEARBY: Guyra 54 km, Inverell 61 km, Tenterfield 81 km, Armidale 86 km, Uralla 103 km

Glenbrook

Pop. 5138
Map ref. 510 G6 | 513 L10 | 523 J6

 Blue Mountains Visitor Information Centre, Great Western Hwy; 1300 653 408; www.visitbluemountains.com.au

89.1 BLU FM, 576 AM ABC Radio National

Glenbrook is a picturesque village on the edge of the Blue Mountains. It was originally known as Watertank because it was used for the storage of water for local steam trains. Today it is a charming town with a large lagoon, close to the impressive Red Hands Cave that lies in Blue Mountains National Park.

Lapstone Zig Zag Walking Track The track follows the 3 km path of the original Lapstone Zig Zag Railway. The track includes convict-built Lennox Bridge (the oldest surviving bridge on the mainland), the abandoned Lucasville Station and numerous lookouts with views of Penrith and the Cumberland Plain. Nearby there is a monument to John Whitton, a pioneer in railway development. Starts in Knapsack St.

Glenbrook Lagoon: filled with ducks, and a perfect picnic spot with walking trails.

Market: Infants School, Ross St; 3rd Sat each month. *Spring Festival:* Nov.

Mash Cafe Restaurant: modern Australian, Fair Trade; 19 Ross St; (02) 4739 5908.

Nepean River Holiday Village: Mackellar St, Emu Plains; 1300 851 820. *Storey Grange:* 105 Lalor Dr, Springwood; (02) 4751 2672.

Faulconbridge This scenic town features the Corridor of Oaks, a line of trees, each one planted by an Australian prime minister. There is also the grave of Sir Henry Parkes, 'the father of Federation', and the stone cottage where Norman Lindsay lived, now a gallery and museum dedicated to his life and work. Lindsay was the author of Australian classics such as *The Magic Pudding* and was the subject of the film *Sirens* (1994). 16 km NW.

Wascoe Siding Miniature Railway: 300 m of steam and motor railway plus picnic and barbecue facilities. Trains operate 1st Sun each month; off Great Western Hwy; 2.5 km W. *Blue Mountains National Park:* Red Hands Cave is accessed by a 6 km return walk. The cave features hand stencils (mostly red, although some are white or orange) that were created between 500 and 1600 years ago. The artists created the stencils by placing their hands against the cave wall and blowing a mixture of ochre and water from their mouths. Euroka Clearing, 4 km s, is a popular camping spot home to many kangaroos. *For other parts of the park see Katoomba and Blackheath. Springwood:* galleries and craft and antique shops. Also home to the Ivy Markets; 2nd Sat each month (except Jan); civic centre, Macquarie Rd; 12 km NW. *Linden:* impressive Kings Cave with Caleys Repulse Cairn nearby commemorating early surveyor George Caley; 20 km W.

TOWNS NEARBY: Richmond 22 km, Windsor 25 km, Katoomba 28 km, Blackheath 33 km, Camden 36 km

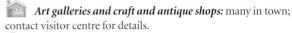

Gloucester

Pop. 2446
Map ref. 515 C8 | 523 M1 | 525 K12

 27 Denison St; (02) 6558 1408; www.gloucester.org.au

 97.7 Breeze FM, 100.9 FM ABC Local

At the foot of the impressive monolithic hills of the Bucketts Range, Gloucester calls itself the base camp to the Barrington Tops. This green and peaceful town is known for its top-quality produce including Barrington beef and perch.

Minimbah Aboriginal Native Gardens: bush-tucker gardens; Gloucester District Park. *Folk Museum:* pioneer household relics, toys, and gemstones and rocks; open 10am–2pm Thurs and Sat, 11am–3pm Sun; Church St; (02) 6558 9989. *Town heritage walk:* includes Lostrochs Cordial Factory and Gloucester Powerhouse; brochure from visitor centre. *Walking trails:* through nearby parks, brochure from visitor centre.

Shakespeare Festival: May. *Mountain Man Triathlon:* kayaking, mountain-biking and running; Sept.

Perenti: chic cafe with local produce; 69 Church St; (02) 6558 9219.

Gloucester Cottage Bed and Breakfast: 61 Denison St; (02) 6558 2658. *Gloucester on Avon Bed & Breakfast:* Cnr Jacks and Combo rds; (02) 6558 9339. *Villa Medici Bed & Breakfast:* 100 Gloucester Tops Rd; 0414 923 479.

Barrington Tops National Park This World Heritage-listed rainforest on one of the highest points of the Great Dividing Range (1600 metres) is enormous and has a great variety of landscapes, flora and fauna, and some snow in winter. There are some good walking trails, beautiful forest drives, gorges and waterfalls, and breathtaking views from Mt Allyn, 1100 m above sea level. The Barrington Tops Forest Dr from Gloucester to Scone has rainforest walks and picnic spots en route; brochure from visitor centre. 60 km w.

Copeland State Conservation Area: easily accessible dry rainforest, well known for its gold production in the 1870s and large stands of red cedar. Walking trails that utilise the old wagon and logging tracks are open to the public; 17km w. *The Bucketts Walk:* 90 min return with great views of town; Bucketts Rd; 2 km w. *Lookouts:* amazing views of the national park, town and surrounding hills at Kia-ora Lookout (4 km N), Mograni Lookout (5 km E) and Berrico Trig Station (14 km w). *Goldtown:* former site of the Mountain Maid Goldmine (1876), now mostly covered with rainforest. Also a historical museum, gold panning and underground mine tours; 16 km w.

TOWNS NEARBY: Wingham 42 km, Stroud 44 km, Taree 48 km, Bulahdelah 50 km, Forster–Tuncurry 55 km

Gosford

Pop. 166 626
Map ref. 509 D8 | 511 O3 | 523 L5

 200 Mann St; (02) 4343 4444 or 1300 132 975; www.visitcentralcoast.com.au

 92.5 FM ABC Local, 101.3 Sea FM

Part of the idyllic Central Coast region, Gosford is surrounded by national parks, steep hills and valleys, rainforest, lakes and ocean beaches. Understandably, Gosford continues to increase in popularity and has grown into a bustling city known for its high standard of tourism and its orchards and seafood.

Art galleries and craft and antique shops: many in town; contact visitor centre for details.

Gosford Country Show: May. *Springtime Flora Festival:* Sept. *CoastFest:* arts festival; Oct. *Gosford to Lord Howe Island Yacht Race:* Oct/Nov.

BodyFuel: fresh, healthy cafe meals; Shop 1, 9 William St; (02) 4323 6669. *Flair:* modern Australian; shop 1, 488 The Entrance Rd (Central Coast Hwy), Erina Heights; (02) 4365 2777. *Upper Deck:* seafood – great views; 61 Masons Pde; (02) 4324 6705.

Wombats Bed & Breakfast – Apartments: 144 Brisbane Water Dr; (02) 4325 5633.

Ku-ring-gai Chase National Park Here the Hawkesbury River meets the sea with winding creeks, attractive beaches, hidden coves and clear water. Highlights are Resolute Track, with Aboriginal rock engravings and hand stencils; Bobbin Head, with a visitor centre and marina; and West Head Lookout, with panoramic views over the water. 33 km sw.

Gosford City Arts Centre: local art and craft and Japanese garden; 3 km E. *Henry Kendall Cottage:* museum in the poet's sandstone home. Also picnic and barbecue facilities in the grounds; 3 km sw. *Australian Rainforest Sanctuary:* walking trails through peaceful rainforest. The Firefly Festival is held here Nov–Dec; 14 km NW. *Firescreek Fruit Wines:* Holgate; (02) 4365 0768; 10 km NE. *Australian Reptile Park:* snakes, spiders and Galapagos tortoises. See shows throughout the day. Somersby Falls nearby provide an ideal picnic spot; Somersby; 15 km NW. *Australian Walkabout Wildlife Park:* native forest with 2 km of walking trails. Animals extinct in the area have been re-introduced with success thanks to the fence that keeps out feral animals; Calga; 20 km NW. *Brooklyn:* access to lower Hawkesbury for houseboating, fishing and river cruises. Historic Riverboat Postman ferry leaves Brooklyn weekdays at 9.30am for cruises and postal deliveries; 32 km s.

TOWNS NEARBY: Woy Woy 7 km, Terrigal 10 km, The Entrance 17 km, Wyong 17 km, Wisemans Ferry 34 km

Goulburn

Pop. 20 131
Map ref. 519 E3 | 522 H9

 201 Sloane St; (02) 4823 4492 or 1800 353 646; www.igoulburn.com

 93.5 Eagle FM, 103.3 FM Community Radio, 1098 AM ABC Radio National

Goulburn is at the junction of the Wollondilly and Mulwaree rivers, in the centre of a wealthy farming district. It was one of Australia's first inland settlements and the last proclaimed city in the British Empire. It is now known for its merino wool industry, and displays elaborate 19th-century architecture.

Big Merino Even though it was only built in 1985, the Big Merino is an instantly recognisable landmark associated with Goulburn and its thriving merino wool industry. The 15 m high and 18 m long sculptured sheep has 3 floors, with a souvenir shop, an educational display on the history of wool in the area and a lookout. Cnr Hume and Sowerby sts; (02) 4882 8013.

Old Goulburn Brewery: tours of Australia's oldest brewery designed by colonial architect Francis Greenway. Brewing to original recipe; Bungonia Rd; (02) 4821 6071. *Goulburn and District Arts and Crafts Centre:* gallery and giftshop showcasing arts and crafts including jewellery, pottery and textiles; Blackshaw Rd; (02) 4822 7889. *Goulburn Historic Waterworks:* displays antique waterworks engines, beside attractive parkland with picnic and barbecue facilities on Marsden Weir; off Fitzroy St. *Rocky Hill War Memorial and Museum:* erected in 1925 as a tribute to the Goulburn men and women who served during WW I, it offers outstanding views across the city. Museum open weekends and holidays; Memorial Dr. *Self-guide tour:* historic buildings include Goulburn Courthouse and St Saviour's Cathedral; brochure from visitor centre.

Australian Blues Music Festival: Feb. *Celebration of Heritage and Roses:* Mar. *Lilac City Festival:* Oct.

Goulburn South Caravan Park: 149 Hume St; (02) 4821 3233. *Governors Hill Carapark:* 77 Sydney Rd; (02) 4821 7373. *Taralga's Lilac Cottage B & B:* 28 Orchard St, Taralga; (02) 4840 2295.

Bungonia State Conservation Area Popular for adventurers with perfect terrain for canyoning, caving and canoeing. Walking trails offer fantastic river and canyon views. One walk passes through the spectacular Bungonia Gorge. 35 km E.

Pelican Sheep Station: farm tours, shearing and sheepdog demonstrations by appt; bookings (02) 4821 4668. Accommodation is available; 10 km s. *Lake George:* 25 km long lake that regularly fills and empties. It has excellent picnic sites; 40 km sw. *Wombeyan Caves:* Daily guided and self-guide cave tours through ancient and spectacular limestone cave system; inquiries (02) 4843 5976; 70 km N.

TOWNS NEARBY: Crookwell 40 km, Bundanoon 54 km, Moss Vale 64 km, Berrima 64 km, Bowral 71 km

Grafton

Pop. 17 499
Map ref. 516 D9 | 525 M6

i Clarence River Visitor Information Centre, Pacific Hwy, South Grafton; (02) 6642 4677; www.clarencetourism.com

104.7 FM Clarence Coast, 738 AM ABC Local

With over 6500 trees in 24 parks, Grafton is known for its riverbank parks and jacaranda trees. Its city centre adds to the charm with wide streets, elegant Victorian buildings and the Clarence River passing through. Water lovers are spoiled for choice with everything from whitewater adventures, waterskiing and fishing.

Susan Island This rainforest recreation reserve in the Clarence River is home to a large fruit bat colony. Dusk is the time to visit to watch the bats flying off in search of food (wearing a hat is advisable if visiting at this time). During the day the island is a good spot for rainforest walks, barbecues and picnics. Access is via hired boat, skippered cruise or Clarence Islander ferry.

Grafton Regional Gallery: rated as one of the most outstanding regional galleries in Australia, the Grafton Regional Gallery inside Prentice House has permanent exhibitions such as the Jacaranda Art Society and Contemporary Australian Drawing collections; closed Mon; Fitzroy St; (02) 6642 3177. *National Trust–classified buildings:* include Schaeffer House, home of the Clarence River Historical Society, Christ Church Cathedral and the notorious Grafton Gaol; heritage trail brochure from visitor centre. *Local art and craft shops:* brochure from visitor centre.

Markets: Lawrence Rd, last Sat each month; Prince St, Grafton Showgrounds, 3rd Sat each month; Armidale Rd, South

Grafton, every Sat morning. *Autumn Artsfest:* Apr. *Grafton Cup:* horserace; July. *Grafton to Inverell Cycling Classic:* Sept. *Bridge to Bridge Ski Race:* Oct. *Jacaranda Festival:* Oct–Nov.

Georgie's: modern Australian and art gallery; Grafton Regional Gallery, 158 Fitzroy St; (02) 6642 6996. *Moos Restaurant:* steakhouse; Jacaranda Motor Lodge, Pacific Hwy; (02) 6642 2833. *Victoria's Restaurant:* international; Quality Inn Grafton, 51 Fitzroy St; (02) 6640 9100.

The Gateway Village: 598 Summerland Way; (02) 6642 4225. *Belvoir B & B Cottages:* 130 Centenary Dr, Clarenza; (02) 6642 3202. *Clarence River Bed & Breakfast:* 17 Riverstone Rd, Seelands; (02) 6644 0055. *Glenwood Tourist Park and Motel:* 71 Heber St, South Grafton; (02) 6642 3466. *Nymboida Canoe Centre:* 3520 Armidale Rd, Nymboida; (02) 6649 4155. *Old Kent Road Apartments:* 3 Coldstream St, Ulmarra; (02) 6644 4044. *Solitary Islands Marine Park Resort:* 383 North St, Wooli; (02) 6649 7519. *Sunset Caravan Park:* 302 Gwydir Hwy, South Grafton; (02) 6642 3824.

Museum of Interesting Things Australian actor Russell Crowe chose Nymboida's coaching station for the home of his amazing collection of film memorabilia (mostly from Crowe's films, like *Gladiator* and *L.A. Confidential*), vintage cars, motorcycles, a giant Cobb & Co coach and other 'interesting things'. Open 11am–3pm Mon–Fri, 10am–5pm Sat, 10am–3pm Sun; 3970 Armidale Rd, Nymboida; (02) 6649 4126. 47 km sw.

Nymboida Waters pumped by the hydro-electric power station from the Nymboida River into Goolang Creek provide a high-standard canoe course that hosts competitions throughout the year. Canoe hire and lessons are on offer and facilities range from the learners' pond for beginners to grade III rapids for the experienced, thrill-seeking canoeist. The beautiful rainforest surrounds are excellent for bushwalking, abseiling, trail rides and platypus viewing. 47 km sw.

Ulmarra Village: National Trust–classified turn-of-the-century river port with exceptional galleries, craft shops and studios where you can watch artists at work; 12 km NE. *Yuraygir National Park:* highlights include Wooli for unspoiled surf beaches and Minnie Water for walking trails, secluded beaches, camping and abundant wildlife (especially the very friendly wallabies). Minnie Lagoon is a popular swimming, picnicking and boating spot; 50 km SE. *Fishing:* river fishing for saltwater or freshwater fish, depending on time of year and rainfall; details at visitor centre.

TOWNS NEARBY: Yamba 50 km, Iluka 51 km, Woolgoolga 53 km, Coffs Harbour 69 km, Dorrigo 75 km

Grenfell

Pop. 1991
Map ref. 522 D6

i CWA Craft Shop and Visitors Centre, 68 Main St; (02) 6343 1612; www.grenfell.org.au

99.5 Star FM, 549 AM ABC Local

Nestled at the foot of the Weddin Mountains, Grenfell is best known as the birthplace of writer Henry Lawson. The wealth appropriated during the days of the gold rush is evident in the opulent original buildings on Main Street. Originally named Emu Creek, the town was renamed after Gold Commissioner John Granville Grenfell, who was gunned down by bushrangers.

Henry Lawson Obelisk: memorial on the site of the house where the poet is believed to have been born; next to Lawson Park on the road to Young. *Grenfell Museum:* local relics (and their stories) from world wars, the gold rush, Henry Lawson and bushrangers; open weekends 2–4pm; Camp St. *O'Brien's Reef Lookout:* views of the town on a gold-discovery site with walkway and picnic facilities; access from O'Brien St. *Weddin Bird Trails:* unique Grenfell birdlife; maps from visitors centre. *Historic buildings:* walk and drive tours; brochures from visitor centre.

Guinea Pig Races: Easter and June. *Henry Lawson Festival of Arts:* June. *Amateur Country Music Festival:* Sept. *Open Day:* Oct.

Grenfell Caravan Park: 12 Grafton St; (02) 6343 1194.

 Weddin Mountains National Park The park is a rugged crescent of cliffs and gullies providing superb bushwalking, camping and picnicking spots. Two of the highlights of the bushwalks are Ben Hall's Cave, where the bushranger hid from the police, and Seaton's Farm, a historic homestead set on beautiful parkland. The bush is also rich with fauna including wedge-tailed eagles, honeyeaters and wallabies. 18 km sw.

Company Dam Nature Reserve: excellent bushwalking area; 1 km NW. *Site of Ben Hall's farmhouse and stockyards:* memorial; Sandy Creek Rd, off Mid Western Hwy; 25 km w.

TOWNS NEARBY: Young 48 km, Cowra 50 km, Eugowra 55 km, Forbes 59 km, Canowindra 59 km

Griffith

Pop. 16 185
Map ref. 527 M7

i Cnr Banna and Jondaryan avenues; (02) 6962 4145 or 1800 681 141; www.griffith.com.au

99.7 Star FM, 549 AM ABC Local

Griffith is surrounded by low hills and fragrant citrus orchards in the heart of the Murrumbidgee Irrigation Area. It was designed by Walter Burley Griffin and named after Sir Arthur Griffith, the first Minister for Public Works in New South Wales. It is one of the largest vegetable-production regions and produces more than 60 per cent of the state's wine.

Hermits Cave and Sir Dudley de Chair's Lookout Hermits Cave is located down a path below the lookout. The cave is named because it was once home to Valerio Ricetti, an Italian miner from Broken Hill. After being jilted, he left his home and job and became a hermit in this cave. After many years of solitude he fell and broke his leg, and when he was hospitalised he was recognised by people who had known him in Broken Hill. In later years he became ill and local citizens collected money to send him back home to Italy, where he died three months later. Scenic Dr.

Pioneer Park Museum: the 11 ha of bushland features 40 replica and restored buildings, early 20th-century memorabilia and re-created Bagtown Village; Remembrance Dr. *Italian Museum:* exhibiting the lives of the early Italian migrants to Griffith including collections of memorabilia and stories from local families; Remembrance Dr. *Griffith Regional Art Gallery:* exhibition program of international and Australian artists that changes monthly; Banna Ave. *Griffith Cottage Gallery:* local paintings, pottery and handicrafts with exhibitions at various times throughout the year; Bridge Rd. *Two Foot Tour and self-drive tour:* feature the city's historic buildings and surrounding pastures; brochure from visitor centre.

Market: Griffith Showground; each Sun morning. *La Festa:* food and wine festival celebrating cultural diversity;

Easter. *UnWined in the Riverina:* food and wine festival; June. *Festival of Gardens:* Oct.

The Clock Restaurant & Wine Lounge: modern Australian; 239–242 Banna Ave; (02) 6962 7111. *La Scala:* traditional Italian; 455 Banna Ave; (02) 6962 4322.

Griffith Caravan Village: Mackay Ave (Leeton Rd); (02) 6962 3785. *Griffith Tourist Caravan Park:* 919 Willandra Ave; (02) 6964 2144.

 Cocoparra National Park Original Riverina forest full of wattles, orchids and ironbarks, the park is spectacular in spring, when the wildflowers bloom. The site is ideal for bushwalking, camping, birdwatching and picnicking, and the rugged terrain and vivid colours also make it popular with photographers. 25 km NE.

Altina Wildlife Park: range of exotic and native wildlife, on the banks of the Murrumbidgee River, horserides and cart rides; inquiries 0412 060 342; 35 km s. *Catania Fruit Salad Farm:* horticultural farm with tours at 1.30pm daily; Cox Rd, Hanwood; (02) 6963 0219; 8 km s. *Lake Wyangan:* good spot for variety of watersports and picnicking; 10 km NW. *Many wineries:* 14 wineries in the Riverina district, including De Bortoli and McWilliams, open for cellar-door tastings; map from visitor centre.

TOWNS NEARBY: Leeton 44 km, Narrandera 69 km, Hay 113 km, Lake Cargelligo 114 km, West Wyalong 114 km

Gulgong

Pop. 1904
Map ref. 522 H2

i 109 Herbert St; (02) 6374 1202; www.gulgong.net

93.1 Real FM, 107.1 FM ABC Local

Gulgong was named by the Wiradjuri people (the name means 'deep waterhole'.) The town did not excite European interest until gold was discovered in 1866. By 1872 there were 20 000 people living in the area. By the end of the decade 15 000 kilograms of gold had been unearthed, the prospectors had gone and almost all of the local Aboriginal people had been slaughtered. Today, the town stands visually almost unchanged from these times. The narrow, winding streets follow the paths of the original bullock tracks past iron-lace verandahs, horse troughs and hitching rails.

Henry Lawson Centre Housed in the Salvation Army Hall, which was built in 1922, the year Lawson died, the centre has the largest collection of Lawson memorabilia outside Sydney's Mitchell Library. It includes original manuscripts, artefacts, photographs, paintings and an extensive collection of rare first editions. 'A Walk Through Lawson's Life' is an exhibition that uses Lawson's words to illustrate the poverty, family disintegration, deafness and alcoholism that shaped his life, as well as the causes he was passionate about such as republicanism, unionism and votes for women. Mayne St; (02) 6374 2049.

Pioneers Museum: illustrates every era of Gulgong's history. Exhibits include a replica of a classroom from the 1880s, period clothing and rare antique crockery; Cnr Herbert and Bayly sts. *Red Hill:* site of the town's original gold strike, featuring restored stamper mill, poppet head and memorial to Henry Lawson; off White St. *Mayne Street Symbols:* inscribed in the pavement by a local artist, to depict the 'language of the road' used by diggers to advise their mates who may have followed them from

 RADIO STATIONS   IN TOWN   WHAT'S ON   WHERE TO EAT   WHERE TO STAY   NEARBY

other goldfields. *Town trail:* self-guide walking tour of historic buildings such as Prince of Wales Opera House and Ten Dollar Town Motel; brochure from visitor centre.

Folk Festival: Jan. *Henry Lawson Festival:* June.

Butcher Shop Cafe: relaxed atmosphere, delicious food; 113 Mayne St; (02) 6374 2322. *Phoebe's Licensed Restaurant:* modern Australian; Ten Dollar Town Motel, cnr Mayne and Medley sts; (02) 6374 1204.

Henry Lawson Caravan Park Gulgong: Mayne St; (02) 6374 1294. *Cunningham Caravan Park:* 38 Cunningham St, Coolah; (02) 6377 1338. *Redbank Gums Bed and Breakfast:* 41 Wargundy St, Dunedoo; (02) 6375 1218.

Goulburn River National Park The park follows approximately 90 km of the Goulburn River with sandy riverbanks making easy walking trails and beautiful camping sites. Rare and threatened plants abound here, as do wombats, eastern grey kangaroos, emus and birds. Highlights include the Drip, 50 m curtains of water dripping through the rocks alongside the Goulburn River, sandstone cliffs honeycombed with caves, and over 300 significant Aboriginal sites. 30 km NE.

Ulan: Ulan Coal Mine has viewing areas overlooking a large open-cut mine. Also here is Hands on the Rock, a prime example of Aboriginal rock art; 22 km NE. *Talbragar Fossil Fish Beds:* one of the few Jurassic-period fossil deposits in Australia; 35 km NE. *Wineries:* cellar-door tastings; brochure from visitor centre.

TOWNS NEARBY: Mudgee 27 km, Wellington 59 km, Rylstone 64 km, Merriwa 81 km, Dubbo 88 km

Gundagai

Pop. 1999
Map ref. 519 A3 | 520 C1 | 522 D9 | 543 P1

i 249 Sheridan St; (02) 6944 0250; www.gundagai.local-e.nsw.gov.au

94.3 FM Sounds of the Mountain, 549 AM ABC Local

Gundagai is a tiny town on the Murrumbidgee River at the foot of Mount Parnassus. The town and the nearby Dog on the Tuckerbox statue have been celebrated through song and verse for many years. Banjo Paterson, C. J. Dennis and Henry Lawson all included the town in their works. It was also the scene in 1852 of Australia's worst flood disaster when 89 of the 250 townsfolk died. The count could have been worse but for a local Aboriginal man, Yarri, who paddled his bark canoe throughout the night to rescue stranded victims. Gundagai was moved to higher ground soon after, and there are monuments celebrating Yarri's efforts. Near the visitor centre are statues of Dad, Dave, Mum and Mabel (characters from the writings of Steele Rudd).

Marble Masterpiece In an amazing display of patience and determination, local sculptor Frank Rusconi, who is also responsible for the Dog on the Tuckerbox statue, worked to create a cathedral in miniature. He built it in his spare time over 28 years, hand-turning and polishing the 20 948 individual pieces required to build it. Visitor centre, Sheridan St.

Gabriel Gallery: outstanding collection of photographs, letters and possessions illustrating Gundagai's unique history; Sheridan St. *Gundagai Museum:* relics include Phar Lap's saddle, Frank Rusconi's tools, and artefacts from the horse and buggy era; Homer St. *Lookouts:* excellent views of the town and surrounding green valleys from the Mt Parnassus Lookout in Hanley St and the Rotary Lookout in Luke St; South Gundagai. *Historical town*

walk: includes the National Trust–classified Prince Alfred Bridge and St John's Anglican Church; leaflet from visitor centre.

Turing Wave Festival: celebrating Irish heritage; Sept. *Spring Flower Show:* Oct. *Dog on the Tuckerbox Festival:* Nov. *Snake Gully Cup Carnival:* horserace; Nov. *Rodeo:* Dec.

The Poets' Recall Motel & Licensed Restaurant: country restaurant; Cnr Punch and West sts; (02) 6944 1777.

Church House B&B Gundagai: 91 Punch St; (02) 6944 1455. *Gundagai Historic Cottage:* 80 Sheridan St; (02) 6944 2385. *Gundagai River Caravan Park:* 1 Middleton Dr; (02) 6944 1702. *Gundagai Tourist Park:* 1 Nangus Rd; (02) 6944 4440.

The Dog on the Tuckerbox Originally mentioned in the poem 'Bill the Bullocky' by Bowyang Yorke, this monument to pioneer teamsters and their dogs is recognised throughout the nation as an Australian icon. It was celebrated in the song 'Where the Dog Sits on the Tuckerbox' by Jack O'Hagan (the songwriter responsible for 'Along the Road to Gundagai'). The dog was unveiled in 1932 by Prime Minister Joseph Lyons. 8.5 km N.

TOWNS NEARBY: Adelong 27 km, Tumut 28 km, Cootamundra 48 km, Batlow 50 km, Wagga Wagga 69 km

Gunnedah

Pop. 7541
Map ref. 524 G9

i Anzac Park, South St; (02) 6740 2230 or 1800 562 527; www.infogunnedah.com.au

97.5 FM Triple G, 1044 AM ABC Local

At the heart of the Namoi Valley, Gunnedah is instantly recognisable by the grain silos that tower over the town. The area is abundant with native wildlife, especially koalas. Gunnedah claims to be the koala capital of the world, with one of the largest koala populations in the country; they are often seen wandering around town. A large centre, Gunnedah still manages to keep a laid-back atmosphere and has been home to famous Australians such as Dorothea Mackellar and Breaker Morant.

Anzac Park The Water Tower Museum here, housed in the town's main water tower, has a mural and display of early explorers, memorabilia from several wars and schools, and an Aboriginal history display (open 2–5pm Sat and most Mon). Dorothea Mackellar, the renowned Australian poet responsible for 'My Country', has a memorial statue in the park. Memorabilia of her life and of the annual national school poetry competition in her name can be viewed at the park's visitor centre. South St.

Rural Museum: early agricultural machinery and the largest privately owned firearm collection in the country; Mullaley Rd. *Red Chief Memorial:* to Aboriginal warrior Cumbo Gunnerah, of the Gunn-e-dar people of the Kamilaroi tribe; State Office building, Abbott St. *Old Bank Gallery:* local art and craft; Conadilly St. *Bicentennial Creative Arts Centre:* art and pottery display and the watercolour series 'My Country' by Jean Isherwood; open 10am–4pm Fri–Sun; Chandos St. *Plains of Plenty:* local craft and produce; South St. *Eighth Division Memorial Avenue:* with 45 flowering gums, each with a plaque in memory of men who served in the 8th Division in WW II; Memorial Ave. *Breaker Morant Drive:* a plaque tells the story of Henry Morant, known as 'the breaker' because of his skill with horses. A 500 m path shows sites where he jumped horses; Kitchener Park. *Poets Drive:* celebration of Australian Poetry, the Poets Drive is a self-guide drive tour inspired by Gunnedah's iconic landmarks and local heroes. *Bindea walking track and town walk:* memorials, koala and kangaroo sites, lookouts and porcupine reserve; brochure from visitor centre.

 Market: Wolseley Park, Conadilly St; 3rd Sat each month. *National Tomato Competition:* search for Australia's biggest tomato, and related celebrations; Jan. *Week of Speed:* races include go-karts, cars, bikes and athletics; Mar. *Gunnedah Bird Expo and Sale:* Apr. *Ag Quip:* agricultural field days; Aug. *North-West Swap Meet:* vintage cars; Sept.

Two Rivers Brasserie: hearty bistro meals; Gunnedah Services and Bowling Club, 313 Conadilly St; (02) 6742 0400. *The Verdict:* modern cafe; shop 7, 147 Conadilly St; (02) 6742 0310.

Gunnedah Tourist Caravan Park: 51 Henry St; (02) 6742 1372.

Lake Keepit This lake is great for watersports, fishing and boating, and there is even a children's pool. If you want to stay a while longer, there is the Keepit Country Campout. The Campout provides all the facilities needed to camp without roughing it too much, including tents, a kitchen and showers and toilets, and there is a campfire amphitheatre for evening entertainment. For the daytime, there is all the equipment needed for canoeing, kayaking, rock climbing, gliding and bushwalking. 34 km NE.

Porcupine Lookout: views over town and surrounding agricultural area; 3 km SE. *Waterways Wildlife Park:* abundant with native animals such as kangaroos, koalas, wombats and emus; Mullaley Rd; 7 km W. *150° East Time Meridian:* the basis of Eastern Standard Time, crossing the Oxley Hwy; 28 km W.

TOWNS NEARBY: Manilla 51 km, Tamworth 65 km, Barraba 74 km, Narrabri 86 km, Nundle 99 km

Guyra

Pop. 1755
Map ref. 525 J7

ⓘ Rafters of Guyra Restaurant and Visitor Information Centre, New England Highway; (02) 6779 1876.

📻 100.3 FM, 720 AM ABC Radio National

Guyra is the highest town on the New England tablelands at an altitude of 1320 metres on the watershed of the Great Dividing Range. Snow is not unusual in winter and at other times the town is crisp and green.

Mother of Ducks Lagoon The reserve is a rare high-country wetland and home to hundreds of waterbirds. The migratory Japanese snipe is known to stop here and it is a nesting site for swans. There is a viewing platform with an identification board covering dozens of different birds. McKie Pde.

Blush Tomatoes: largest greenhouse growing tomatoes in the Southern Hemisphere. It has boosted Guyra's population and economy enormously over the last 3 years; Elm St. *Historical Society Museum:* themed room displaying town memorabilia and the story of the Guyra ghost; open by appt; Bradley St; bookings (02) 6779 2132. *Railway Station:* large display of antique machinery, rail train rides; Bradley St.

Lamb and Potato Festival: includes Hydrangea Festival; Jan.

Rafters of Guyra: hearty fare; New England Hwy; (02) 6779 1876.

Silent Grove Farm Stay B&B: 698 Maybole Rd, Ben Lomond; (02) 6733 2117.

Thunderbolt's Cave: picturesque and secluded cave, rumoured to be where the bushranger Captain Thunderbolt hid from police; 10 km S. *Handcraft Hall – The Pink Stop:* hand-knitted garments, paintings, pottery and Devonshire teas; 10 km N. *Chandler's Peak:* spectacular views of the tablelands from an altitude of 1471 m; 20 km E.

TOWNS NEARBY: Armidale 32 km, Uralla 50 km, Glen Innes 54 km, Inverell 73 km, Walcha 86 km

Hay

Pop. 2632
Map ref. 527 J7

ⓘ 407 Moppett St; (02) 6993 4045; www.hay.nsw.gov.au

📻 92.1 Hay FM, 100.9 FM ABC Radio National

Located in the heart of the Riverina, the most striking thing about Hay is the incredibly flat plains on which it sits. The saltbush flats afford amazing views across the land, especially at sunrise and sunset, and the terrain makes bicycles a popular and easy mode of transport for residents. American travel writer Bill Bryson described Hay as 'a modest splat' and 'extremely likeable'.

POW Internment Camp Interpretive Centre Housed in Hay's magnificent restored railway station, the centre documents the WW II internment in Hay of over 3000 prisoners of war. The first internees were known as the 'Dunera boys', Jewish intellectuals who had fled Germany and Austria. The camp established a garrison band and a newspaper and printed camp money. The Dunera boys even ran their own 'university', teaching subjects such as atomic research and classical Greek. The Dunera boys held a reunion in Hay in 1990 and there is a memorial on Showground Rd. Murray St; inquiries (02) 6993 4045.

Shear Outback Centre – The Australian Shearers Hall of Fame: interactive experiences and shearing deomonstrations with sheep dogs, historic Murray Downs Woolshed and exhibitions; Sturt Hwy; inquiries (02) 6993 4000. *Witcombe Fountain:* ornate drinking fountain presented to the people of Hay by mayor John Witcombe in 1883; Lachlan St. *Coach house:* features an 1886 Cobb & Co coach, which travelled the Deniliquin–Hay–Wilcannia route until 1901; Lachlan St. *Hay Gaol Museum:* contains memorabilia and photographs of the town, and the building's history from 1878 as a gaol, maternity hospital, hospital for the insane and POW compound; Church St; inquiries (02) 6993 4045. *War Memorial High School Museum:* built in recognition of those who served in WW I, with war memorabilia and an honour roll. The building still operates as a school, so call for opening times (02) 6993 1408; Pine St. *Bishop's Lodge:* restored 1888 iron house, now a museum and gallery with a unique and remarkable collection of heritage roses. Holds a market 3rd Sun in Oct. Open 2–4.30pm Mon–Sat; Cnr Roset St and Sturt Hwy. *Ruberto's Winery:* cellar-door tastings; Sturt Hwy. *Hay Wetlands:* especially spectacular in spring, the land is a breeding ground for over 60 inland bird species with a breeding island and tree plantation; north-western edge of town; brochure from visitor centre. *Hay Park:* pleasant picnic spot with a nature walk along the banks of the river; off Brunker St. *Murrumbidgee River:* excellent sandy river beaches and calm water, perfect for waterskiing, canoeing, swimming and picnics. Enjoy excellent freshwater fishing for Murray cod, yellow-belly perch and redfin. A licence is required; available from outlets in town, including visitor centre. *Heritage walk and scenic drive:* walk includes city structures built for the harsh outback such as the beautifully restored courthouse (1892) on Moppett St and the shire office (1877) on Lachlan St. The drive takes in the parklands, river and surrounding saltbush plains; brochure from visitor centre.

Sheep Show: June. **Rodeo:** Oct. **Hay Races:** Nov.

Jolly Jumbuck Bistro: relaxed bistro; 148 Lachlan St; (02) 6993 4718.

Hay Caravan Park: Sturt Hwy, Hay South; (02) 6993 1415. **Hay Plains Holiday Park:** 4 Nailor St, Hay South; (02) 6993 1875.

Booligal In an area known as the 'devil's claypan', this hot and dusty sheep- and cattle-town is mentioned in Banjo Paterson's poem 'Hay and Hell and Booligal'. The poem says that a visit to Booligal is a fate worse than hell with topics of complaint including heat, flies, dust, rabbits, mosquitoes and snakes. On the plus side, the atmosphere is relaxed and friendly. It is off the beaten tourist track and there is a memorial to John Oxley, the first European in the area, in the shape of a giant theodolite (surveyor's tool). 78 km N. Halfway to Booligal, look out for the lonely ruins of One Tree Hotel.

Hay Weir: on the Murrumbidgee River, excellent for picnics, barbecues and Murray cod fishing; 12 km W. **Sunset viewing area:** the vast plains provide amazingly broad and spectacular sunsets; Booligal Rd; 16 km N. **Maude Weir:** surprisingly green and lush oasis, ideal for picnics and barbecues; 53 km W. **Goonawarra Nature Reserve:** no facilities for visitors, but the flood plains with river red gum forests and black box woodlands are still worth a visit – waterfowl in the billabongs, plenty of Murray cod in the Lachlan River and kangaroos and emus on the plains; 59 km N. **Oxley:** tiny town with river red gums and prolific wildlife (best seen at dusk); 87 km NW.

TOWNS NEARBY: Griffith 113 km, Deniliquin 114 km, Balranald 119 km, Jerilderie 124 km, Barham 140 km

Holbrook

Pop. 1339

Map ref. 522 B11 | 527 O11 | 543 M4

ℹ **Greater Hume Shire Visitor Information Centre,** 15 Wallace St; (02) 6036 2422; www.holbrook.nsw.au

93.1 Star FM, 990 AM ABC Radio National

Holbrook is a well-known stock-breeding centre rich with history. Originally called The Germans because of its first European settlers, the name was later changed to Germanton. During World War I, with the allies fighting the Germans, even this name became unacceptable and a new name had to be found. British Commander Norman Holbrook was a war hero and had been awarded the Victoria Cross and the French Legion of Honour, so it was decided the town would be named after him.

Otway Submarine The 30 m vessel, once under the command of Norman Holbrook, was decommissioned in 1995. The town was given the fin of the submarine by the Royal Australian Navy, and was busily trying to raise funds to purchase the full piece of history, when a gift of $100 000 from Commander Holbrook's widow made the purchase possible. Mrs Holbrook was the guest of honour at the unveiling in 1996. The Submarine Museum next door features submariner memorabilia, including a control room with working periscope, and Commander Holbrook Room. Hume Hwy.

Bronze statue: Commander Holbrook and his submarine, a scale model of the one in which Holbrook won the VC in WW I; Holbrook Park, Hume Hwy. **Woolpack Inn Museum:** 22 rooms furnished in turn-of-the-century style, horse-drawn vehicles and

farm equipment surrounded by lovely gardens; Albury St. **Ten Mile Creek Gardens:** attractive gardens, excellent for picnics. Also features a miniature railway, operating on the 2nd and 4th Sun each month, and every Sat during holidays; behind museum. **National Museum of Australian Pottery:** extensive range of 19th- and early-20th-century domestic pottery, and photographs; closed Wed, and Aug; Albury St. **Ian Geddes Walk:** through tranquil bushland, following Ten Mile Creek. Begins behind Grimwood's Craft Shop; Hume Hwy.

Planes, Trains and Submarines Festival: Mar.

Holbrook Airfield: ultralight flights over town and surrounds available; 3 km N. **Hume and Hovell Walking Track:** access to short sections of the 440 km track from Albury to Yass via Woomargama; 15 km S. For a kit, including maps, contact Department of Lands, Sydney (02) 9228 6666.

TOWNS NEARBY: Culcairn 26 km, Albury 53 km, Tallangatta (Vic.) 56 km, Wodonga (Vic.) 59 km, Tumbarumba 63 km

Huskisson

Pop. 3391

Map ref. 517 D11 | 519 G4 | 521 O2 | 523 J10

ℹ **Lady Denman Heritage Complex, 11 Dent St;** (02) 4441 5999; www.ladydenman.asn.au

94.9 Power FM, 603 AM Radio National

Huskisson is a sleepy holiday resort and fishing port on Jervis (pronounced 'Jarvis') Bay. It was named after British politician William Huskisson, secretary for the colonies and leader of the House of Commons, who was killed by a train in 1830 while talking to the Duke of Wellington at a railway opening. The idyllic bay is renowned for its white sand and clear water, and there are usually several pods of dolphins living in the bay, making the area ideal for cruises and diving.

Lady Denman Heritage Complex Lady Denman is a wooden Sydney ferry that was built in 1910, retired in 1979, and now is the centrepiece of this heritage complex. There's a maritime museum, as well as an Aboriginal Arts and Craft centre, and it is the home of the regional Visitors Information Centre; 10am–4pm daily; 11 Dent St, (02) 4441 5675.

Market: Huskisson Sporting Ground; 2nd Sun each month. **White Sands Carnival:** stalls, music and entertainment; Easter.

Huskisson Bakery and Cafe: sandwiches, homemade pies; 11 Currambene St; (02) 4441 5015. **Locavore:** cafe – organic, Fair Trade; 2/66 Owen St; (02) 4441 5464. **Seagrass Brasserie:** seafood; 13 Currambene St; (02) 4441 6124. **The Gunyah Restaurant:** modern Australian – stunning treetop views; Paperbark Camp, 571 Woollamia Rd, Woollamia; (02) 4441 7299.

Cee Spray on Owen: 30 Owen St; (02) 4441 8726. **Huskisson Beach Tourist Resort:** Beach St; 1300 733 027. **Huskisson White Sands Tourist Park:** Cnr Beach and Nowra sts; 1300 733 028. **Sandholme Guesthouse:** 2 Jervis St; (02) 4441 8855. **Riverside Caravan Park:** 96 Sussex Rd, Sussex Inlet; (02) 4441 2163. **Riviera Caravan Park:** 158 River Rd, Sussex Inlet; (02) 4441 2112. **Seacrest Caravan Park:** 30 Sussex Rd, Sussex Inlet; (02) 4441 2333. **Sussex Palms Holiday Park:** 40 Sussex Rd, Sussex Inlet; (02) 4441 2395. **Swan Lake Tourist Village:** 4 Goonawarra Dr, Cudmirrah; 1300 555 517.

Sussex Inlet: coastal hamlet with fishing carnival in July; 34 km SW. **Booderee National Park:** see Jervis Bay.

TOWNS NEARBY: Jervis Bay 10 km, Nowra 19 km, Berry 30 km, Ulladulla 39 km, Kiama 45 km

Iluka

Pop. 1739
Map ref. 516 F7 | 525 O5

ℹ️ Lower Clarence Visitor Centre, Ferry Park, Pacific Hwy, Maclean; (02) 6645 4121; www.clarencetourism.com

📻 104.7 FM Clarence Coast's FM, 738 AM ABC Local

Located at the mouth of the Clarence River on the north coast, Iluka is a relatively uncommercial fishing and holiday village. Its attractiveness is evident in the long stretches of sandy white beaches and rare and accessible rainforest. Iluka Nature Reserve has the largest remnant of littoral rainforest (trees obtaining water via filtration through coastal sand and nutrients from airborne particles) in New South Wales.

🏠 *River cruises:* day cruises and evening barbecue cruises (Wed only); Wed, Fri and Sun; from the Boatshed. *Passenger ferry:* travelling daily to Yamba; from the Boatshed. *Iluka Fish Co-op:* fresh catches on sale from 9am; adjacent to the Boatshed. *Walking track:* picturesque coastline walk; access via Iluka Bluff to the north and Long St to the south.

🍴 *Boatshed Cafe:* waterfront cafe; 2A Charles St; (02) 6646 5212.

🛏️ *Anchorage Holiday Park:* Marandowie Dr; (02) 6646 6210. *Clarence Head Caravan Park Iluka:* 113 Charles St; (02) 6646 6163. *Iluka Riverside Tourist Park:* 4 Charles St; (02) 6646 6060. *Bimbimbi Riverside Caravan Park:* 286 Iluka Rd, Woombah; (02) 6646 4272. *Browns Rocks Caravan Park:* 391 Goodwood Island Rd, Goodwood Island; (02) 6646 4324. *Woombah Woods Caravan Park:* 54 Iluka Rd, Woombah; (02) 6646 4544.

⊗ **Iluka Nature Reserve** This area, nestled on the narrow peninsula where the Clarence River meets the ocean, was World Heritage–listed in 1986. It happens to be the largest remaining coastal rainforest in NSW. It is rich with birdlife and is a beautiful spot for activities such as fishing, swimming, surfing, canoeing, walking and camping. 1 km N.

Iluka Bluff Beach: safe swimming beach with good surf and a whale-watching lookout; brochure from visitors centre; 1 km N. *Bundjalung National Park:* protects ancient rainforest and the Esk River, the largest untouched coastal river system on the north coast. Woody Head has rare rainforest with campground, fishing and swimming; 4 km N. *Woombah Coffee Plantation:* world's southernmost coffee plantation; tours by appt; bookings (02) 6646 4121; 12 km NW.

TOWNS NEARBY: Yamba 3 km, Evans Head 33 km, Grafton 51 km, Alstonville 63 km, Ballina 64 km

Inverell

Pop. 9748
Map ref. 525 I5

ℹ️ Campbell St; (02) 6728 8161 or 1800 067 626; www.inverell-online.com.au

📻 95.1 Gem FM, 738 AM ABC Local

This town on the Macintyre River at the centre of the New England tablelands is known as the 'Sapphire City'. It is also rich in other mineral deposits, including zircons, industrial diamonds and tin. The country here has lush farm and grazing land and excellent weather conditions with cool nights and warm sunny days. A Scottish immigrant gave Inverell its name, which means 'meeting place of the swans' in Gaelic.

🏠 **Pioneer Village** This collection of homes and buildings dating from 1840 was moved from its original site to form a 'village of yesteryear'. Attractions include Grove homestead, Paddy's Pub and Mt Drummond Woolshed. Gooda Cottage has an impressive collection of gems and minerals. Tea and damper are served by prior arrangement. Tingha Rd; (02) 6722 1717.

Visitor Centre and Mining Museum: local and imported gems, a static display on the local mining industry, photographs and a video of local mines, and a working scale model of a sapphire plant; Water Towers Complex, Campbell St. *Inverell Art Centre:* paintings, pottery and craft; Evans St. *Gem Centre:* visitors can see local stones being processed; Byron St. *Transport Museum:* over 200 vehicles on display with an impressive collection of rarities; Taylor Ave. *Town Stroll:* includes sites such as the National Trust–classified courthouse and the CBC Bank building with stables at the rear; brochure from visitor centre. *Arts, crafts and wood-turning:* work by local artists; brochure from visitor centre.

🎪 *Market:* Campbell Park: 1st (except Jan) and 3rd Sun each month. *Outback Festival:* Sept. *Grafton to Inverell Cycling Classic:* Sept. *Sapphire City Festival:* Oct. *Antique Machinery Rally:* Oct. *Great Inland Fishing Festival:* Dec. *Inverell Jockey Club Boxing Day Meeting:* Dec.

🍴 *The Royal Club Hotel Motel:* international cuisine; 260 Byron St; (02) 6722 2811.

🛏️ *Fossickers Rest Tourist Park:* Lake Inverell Dr; (02) 6722 2261. *Inverell Caravan Park:* Cnr Glen Innes Rd (Gwydir Hwy) and Tingha Rd; (02) 6722 3036. *Copeton Waters State Park:* Copeton Dam Rd, Copeton Dam; (02) 6723 6269.

⊗ **Kwiambal National Park** The Macintyre River flows through gorges and plunge pools to Macintyre Falls and then leads into the Severn River. The park is rich with protected woodlands of white cypress pine, box and ironbark. Bat nurseries can be viewed with a torch in the remarkable Ashford Caves, which until the 1960s were mined for guano (bat droppings) to be used as fertiliser on local farms. The park makes a serene site for swimming, bushwalking and camping. Encounters with kangaroos, emus and koalas are common. 90 km N.

McIlveen Lookout: excellent views of town and surrounding pastures and nature reserve; 2 km W. *Lake Inverell Reserve:* 100 ha of unique aquatic sanctuary for birds and wildlife. Also an excellent site for picnics, bushwalking, birdwatching and fishing; 3 km E. *Draught Horse Centre:* 6 breeds of horse and displays of harnesses and memorabilia, horses are paraded twice daily; Fishers Rd; 4 km E. *Goonoowigall Bushland Reserve:* rough granite country rich with birdlife and marsupials, it offers superb birdwatching, remains of a Chinese settlement, bushwalking trails and picnic areas; 5 km S. *Morris' Honey Farm:* visitors can see working bees, taste honey and learn how it is produced. Ride the miniature train and explore the animal park and bottle museum; inquiries (02) 6723 6281; 8 km SW. *Copeton Dam State Recreation Area:* perfect for boating, waterskiing, swimming, fishing, bushwalking and rock climbing. It also has adventure playgrounds, water slides, and picnic and barbecue facilities. Kangaroos graze on the golf course at dusk; inquiries (02) 6723 6269; 17 km S. *DeJon Sapphire Centre:* working sapphire mine with sales; Glen Innes Rd; (02) 6723 2222; 19 km E. *Gwydir Ranch 4WD Park:* rugged and colourful gorge country ideal for canoeing, camping, fishing, bushwalking and swimming.

Also popular with photographers and artists; 28 km w. ***Green Valley Farm:*** working sheep property with zoo, accommodation, extensive gardens, playground and picnic and barbecue facilities. The highlight is Smith's Mining and Natural History Museum, with a rare collection of gems and minerals, local Aboriginal artefacts, antiques and period clothing; inquiries (02) 6723 3370; 36 km SE. ***Pindari Dam:*** fishing, swimming, camping and picnic and barbecue facilities; 58 km N. ***Gwydir River:*** one of the best whitewater rafting locations in the country during the summer months; brochure from visitor centre. ***Warm-weather wineries:*** cellar-door tastings; brochure from visitor centre. ***Fossicking sites:*** great spots for searching for tin, sapphires, quartz or even diamonds; maps at visitor centre.

TOWNS NEARBY: Bingara 53 km, Warialda 58 km, Glen Innes 61 km, Guyra 73 km, Barraba 83 km

Jamberoo
Pop. 935
Map ref. 517 E7 | 519 H3 | 523 J9

i Jamberoo Newsagency Visitor Centre, Shop 2, 18 Allowrie St; (02) 4236 0100; www.kiama.com.au

i98 FM, 603 AM ABC Radio National

One of the most picturesque areas of the New South Wales coast, Jamberoo was once tropical forest. The town is surrounded by nature reserves and national parks, but is now situated on the lush green dairy pastures that have made Jamberoo prosperous as a dairy farming region. The surrounding forests are popular with bushwalkers and birdwatchers.

Jamberoo Hotel: charming 1857 building with meals and Sun afternoon entertainment; Allowrie St.

Market: Kevin Walsh Oval; last Sun each month.

Bed and Views Kiama: 69 Riversdale Rd; (02) 4232 3662. ***Park Meadows B & B:*** 227 Tongarra Rd, Albion Park; (02) 4256 5355.

Budderoo National Park This park offers views from a plateau across sandstone country, heathlands and rainforest. There are excellent walking trails, including one that is accessible by wheelchair, and there are 3 lookouts with views of Carrington Falls. The Minnamurra Rainforest Centre is the highlight with an elevated boardwalk through rainforest and a steep paved walkway to Minnamurra Falls. 4 km w.

Jamberoo Action Park: family fun park with water slides, speedboats, racing cars and bobsleds; (02) 4236 0114; 3 km N. ***Jerrara Dam:*** a picturesque reserve on the banks of a 9 ha dam that was once the town's main water supply. Picnic area surrounded by remnant rainforest and freshwater wetland; 4 km SE. ***Saddleback Lookout:*** 180-degree views of the coast and the starting point for Hoddles Trail, a 1 hr walk with beautiful views to Barren Grounds escarpment; 7 km s. ***Barren Grounds Nature Reserve:*** this 1750 ha heathland plateau on the Illawarra Escarpment protects over 450 species of plant and 150 species of bird, including the rare ground parrot and eastern bristlebird. It has fabulous bushwalking and birdwatching; guided tours available (bookings (02) 4423 2170); park details from Fitzroy Falls Visitor Centre (02) 4887 7270; 10 km sw.

TOWNS NEARBY: Kiama 7 km, Shellharbour 12 km, Berry 16 km, Robertson 18 km, Wollongong 27 km

Jerilderie
Pop. 769
Map ref. 527 L10 | 542 G1

i The Willows Museum, 11 Powell St; (03) 5886 1666.

Classic Rock 102.5 FM, 94.1 FM ABC Radio National

Jerilderie is an important merino stud area, but is better known for its links with the Kelly Gang. In 1879 the gang captured the police, held the townspeople hostage for two days, cut the telegraph wires and robbed the bank. It was here that Kelly handed over the famous Jerilderie Letter, justifying his actions and voicing his disrespect for police, whom he called 'a parcel of big ugly fat-necked wombat-headed, big-bellied, magpie-legged, narrow-hipped, splay-footed sons of Irish bailiffs or English landlords'. The town of Jerilderie is now the gateway to the Kidman Way, an 800-kilometre outback highway.

Telegraph Office and The Willows Museum The well-preserved Telegraph Office is where the Kelly Gang cut the telegraph wires in 1879. The Willows Museum next door houses photographs, including some of the Kelly Gang, documents of local historical significance and the cell door from the old police station. Samples of local craft are also on display and Devonshire teas are available. Powell St.

St Luke Park: features Steel Wings, one of the largest windmills in the Southern Hemisphere. The park runs along the bank of Lake Jerilderie, which is popular for all watersports, especially waterskiing. ***Mini Heritage Steam Rail:*** runs along charming Billabong Creek, which also features the 1.8 km Horgans Walk. Entry behind The Willows Museum; runs 2nd and 5th Sun each month. ***Ned Kelly Heritage Trail:*** retraces the gangs' visit; brochure from visitor centre.

Fairways Bed & Breakfast at Jerilderie: Lot 124 Showground Rd; (03) 5886 9200. ***Jerilderie Motel & Caravan Park:*** 121 Jerilderie St; (03) 5886 1366. ***Urana Caravan Park & Aquatic Centre:*** Corowa Rd, Urana; (02) 6920 8192.

Coleambally Officially opened in 1968, Coleambally is NSW's newest town and is at the centre of the Coleambally Irrigation Area. It features the Wineglass Water Tower and a dragline excavator used in the irrigation scheme. The excavator is still in working order and can be viewed in the Lions Park at the town's entrance. Tours of the rice mill and of the farms are possible. The area is a haven for birdlife and kangaroos. 62 km N.

TOWNS NEARBY: Finley 35 km, Tocumwal 53 km, Cobram 63 km, Deniliquin 72 km, Mulwala 75 km

Jervis Bay
Pop. 200
Map ref. 517 D12 | 519 G4 | 521 O3 | 523 J10

i Lady Denman Heritage Complex, 11 Dent St, Huskisson; (02) 4441 5999; www.ladydenman.asn.au

92.7 Bay and Basin Community Radio

Although just a tiny village, Jervis Bay is the largest town in the Jervis Bay Territory. It is home to the HMAS *Creswell* Navy Base. With the spectacular waters of the Jervis Bay Marine Park just offshore, and the stunning Booderee National Park nearby, Jervis Bay plays host to tourists enjoying the natural beauty of this region.

Hyams Beach This famous beach has pristine sand and stunning turquoise water. While the sheltered outlook makes this a great place to swim, the beach is unpatrolled.

Jervis Bay Marine Park: the clear waters, reefs and deep-water cliffs with caves offer superb diving. Bookings are taken at the

[JERVIS BAY] WADING IN WHITING BAY, BOODEREE NATIONAL PARK

visitor centre for dolphin-watching cruises. ***Booderee Botanic Gardens:*** the gardens received heritage status in 1994 and have a large selection of native plants; Caves Beach Road, Jervis Bay; (02) 4443 0977.

Jervis Bay Triathlon Festival: Feb and Oct.

Green Patch Camping Area: Jervis Bay Rd, Booderee National Park; (02) 4443 0977. ***Jervis Bay Cabins & Hidden Creek Real Camping:*** 55 Goodlands Rd, Woollamia; (02) 4441 5809. ***Jervis Bay Caravan Park:*** 785 Woollamia Rd, Woollamia; (02) 4441 5046. ***My Place, Sanctuary Point B&B:*** Cnr Walmer Ave and Paradise Beach Rd, Sanctuary Point; (02) 4443 0505. ***Palm Beach Caravan Park:*** 105 Ethel St, Sanctuary Point; (02) 4443 0356. ***Paradise Beach Apartments:*** 119 Walmer Ave, Sanctuary Point; (02) 4443 2500. ***Sanddancers Bed & Breakfast:*** 311 Elizabeth Dr, Vincentia; (02) 4441 6857.

Booderee National Park This park used to be known as Jervis Bay National Park and was renamed by the Wreck Bay Aboriginal community. Booderee is home to some spectacular beaches, including Murrays Beach. There's a range of water-based activities available at this national park, including swimming, snorkelling and whale-watching, as well as some spectacular bushwalks.

Jervis Bay Kayak Company: kayak the pristine waters of Jervis Bay Marine Park; closed Tues, open 9.30am–5pm other weekdays, 9.30am–3pm Sat–Sun; 13 Hawke St Huskisson; (02) 4441 7157.

TOWNS NEARBY: Huskisson 10 km, Nowra 29 km, Ulladulla 33 km, Berry 39 km, Kiama 53 km

Jindabyne
Pop. 1902
Map ref. 519 B8 | 520 E10 | 539 C4

ℹ️ Snowy Region Visitor Centre, Kosciuszko Rd; (02) 6450 5600; www.snowymountains.com.au

📻 97.1 FM Radio National, 97.7 Snow FM

Jindabyne, adjacent to the south-eastern section of Kosciuszko National Park (*see Adaminaby and Thredbo*) and just below the snowline, was relocated from its original site on the banks of the Snowy River to make way for the Snowy Mountains Hydro-Electric Scheme. Some 100 000 men from 30 countries worked for 25 years on the scheme, the largest engineering project of its kind in Australia. The original town was flooded, but a few of the buildings were moved to their current site beside Lake Jindabyne. The area is popular with skiers in the winter and with anglers, bushwalkers and whitewater rafters in the summer.

Walkway and cycleway: around Lake Jindabyne's foreshore, from Banjo Paterson Park on Kosciuszko Rd to Snowline Caravan Park. ***Winter shuttle bus service:*** several operators depart from various spots in town to Bullocks Flat and Thredbo; contact visitor centre for more information.

Speed and Marathon Championships: Lake Jindabyne; Jan. ***Flowing Festival:*** music and dragon-boat races: Feb. ***Lake Light Sculpture:*** Apr. ***Snowy Mountains Trout Festival:*** fishing competition throughout region; Nov. ***Boxing Day Rodeo:*** Dec.

Mario's Mineshaft Restaurant and Bar: modern Italian; Lakeview Plaza Motel, 2 Snowy River Ave; (02) 6456 2727.

Discovery Holiday Parks – Jindabyne: Cnr Alpine Way and Kosciuszko Rd; (02) 6456 2099. ***Jindabyne Holiday Park:*** Kosciuszko Rd; (02) 6456 2249. ***Peppers Over The Lake:*** 12 Candlebark Circuit; (02) 6456 2575. ***Sages' Haus B&B:*** 28 Clyde St; 0409 800 269. ***Andrea's White House:*** 9 Post Office La (off Alpine Way), Crackenback; (02) 6456 1690. ***Bimblegumbie:*** 942 Alpine Way, Crackenback; (02) 6456 2185. ***Kosciuszko Mountain Retreat:*** 1400 Kosciuszko Rd, Kosciuszko National Park; (02) 6456 2224.

Perisher The largest ski resort in Australia with an impressive 1250 ha of skiing area, Perisher caters for all levels of skier and snowboarder. State-of-the-art equipment includes many high-quality snow guns and Australia's first 8-seater chairlifts. The resort consists of slopes, accommodation, restaurants, bars and all the facilities and equipment hire needed to enjoy winter sports at Perisher and the nearby skiing areas of Smiggin Holes, Mt Blue Cow and Guthega. 30 km w.

Lake Jindabyne: well stocked with rainbow trout and ideal for boating, waterskiing and other watersports. When the water level is low, remains of the submerged town can be seen; western edge of town. ***Kunama Gallery:*** over 200 paintings by local artists and work by acclaimed water colourist Alan Grosvenor. Also panoramic views of Lake Jindabyne; (02) 6456 1100; 7 km NE. ***Snowy Valley Lookout:*** stunning views of Lake Jindabyne;

8 km N. *Gaden Trout Hatchery:* daily tours and barbecues along Thredbo River; (02) 6451 3400; 10 km NW. *Wildbrumby Schnapps Distillery:* boutique schnapps made from seasonal fruits, with cafe and cellar door; Wollondibby Rd; (02) 6457 1447; 11 km W. *Crackenback Cottage:* local craft, maze, restaurant and guesthouse; (02) 6456 2198; 12 km SW. *Sawpit Creek:* the Kosciuszko Education Centre can be found here. The start of the Palliabo (walking) Track is at the Sawpit Creek picnic area; 14 km NW. *Bullocks Flat:* terminal for Skitube, a European-style alpine train to Perisher ski resort; operates daily during ski season; 20 km SW. *Wallace Craigie Lookout:* views of Snowy River Valley; 40 km SW. *Charlotte Pass:* highest ski resort in Australia with challenging slopes for experienced skiers. Magnificent 24 km walking track past Blue Lake in summer; 45 km W. *Scenic walks:* varying lengths; brochures from visitor centre. *Alpine Way:* 111 km road through mountains to Khancoban provides superb scenic touring in summer; chains frequently required in winter.

TOWNS NEARBY: Berridale 19 km, Thredbo 30 km, Adaminaby 48 km, Cooma 49 km, Khancoban 50 km

Katoomba

see inset box on page 64

Kempsey

Pop. 8139
Map ref. 515 G4 | 525 M10

i South Kempsey Park, Lachlan St (Pacific Hwy), South Kempsey; (02) 6563 1555 or 1800 642 480; www.macleayvalleycoast.com.au

105.1 ROX FM, 684 AM ABC Local

Kempsey is an attractive town in the Macleay River Valley on the mid-north coast, with white sandy beaches and an unspoiled hinterland. It claims two quintessential Aussies as its own: singer Slim Dusty was born here in 1927 (while he died in 2003, he remains one of the country's best-loved country singers) and the Akubra hat has been made here since 1974.

 Wigay Aboriginal Cultural Park: Aboriginal cultural experience, including introduction to bush tucker, learning about the use of plants and throwing a boomerang; Sea St. *Cultural Centre:* incorporates the Macleay River Historical Society Museum and visitor centre, a settlers cottage, displays on Akubra hats and Slim Dusty, and a working model of a timber mill; Pacific Hwy, South Kempsey. *Historical walks:* carefully restored historic buildings include the courthouse, post office and West Kempsey Hotel; brochure from visitor centre.

Markets: showground, 1st Sat each month; South West Rocks, 2nd Sat each month. *Gaol Break Swim:* 2.7 km race along Trial Bay beach to South West Rocks; Easter. *Kempsey Cup:* horserace; May. *Akubra Classic Motorcycle Championships:* June. *Truck and Ute Show:* Oct. *Kempsey Country Music Festival:* Oct/Nov.

Netherby River Cafe: tranquil cafe; Netherby House, 5 Little Rudder St; (02) 6563 1777.

Crescent Head Holiday Park: Pacific St, Crescent Head; (02) 6566 0261. *Hat Head Holiday Park:* Straight St, Hat Head; (02) 6567 7501. *Horseshoe Bay Holiday Park:* 1 Livingstone St, South West Rocks; (02) 6566 6370. *Kempsey Tourist Village:* 325 Pacific Hwy, South Kempsey; (02) 6562 7666. *Mesopotamia Lodge Deer Park:* 192 Spooners Ave, Greenhill; (02) 6563 1056. *Netherby House:* 5 Little Rudder St, East Kempsey; (02) 6563 1777.

South West Rocks Tourist Park: 39–89 Gordon Young Dr, South West Rocks; (02) 6566 6264.

 Limeburners Creek Nature Reserve Showcases a beautiful coastline of heathlands, banksia and blackbutt forests. The rare rainforest of Big Hill is home to the threatened ground parrot. The beach is popular for swimming, surfing and fishing and there are camping areas with varying levels of facilities. 33 km SE.

South West Rocks Attractions include a pristine white beach, a maritime history display at the restored Boatmans Cottage and the opportunity to handfeed fish at the Everglades Aquarium. The area is excellent for watersports, diving, camping and boating. The nearby Trial Bay Gaol (1886) was a public works prison until 1903 and reopened to hold 'enemy aliens' in WW I. Smoky Cape has a lighthouse offering tours and accommodation and clear views up and down the coast. Fish Rock Cave, just off the cape, is well known for its excellent diving. 37 km NE.

Frederickton: 'Fredo' has beautiful views of river flats, and its award-winning pie shop boasts 148 varieties; 8 km NE. *Kundabung:* tiny village with Australasian bullriding titles in Oct; 14 km S. *Gladstone:* fishing, antiques and crafts; 15 km NE. *Crescent Head:* this seaside holiday town has good surfing. There is an Aboriginal bora ring (ceremonial ground) just to the north. The Sky Show with kites, flying displays and fireworks is held each June and the Crescent Head Malibu Longboard Classic is in May (the largest longboard competition in Australia); 20 km SE. *Barnett's Rainbow Beach Oyster Barn:* direct purchases and viewing of oyster processing; 31 km NE. *Hat Head National Park:* magnificent dunes and unspoiled beaches, popular for birdwatching, snorkelling, swimming and walking. Korogoro Point is a fabulous spot for whale-watching May–July and Sept–Oct; 32 km E. *Bellbrook:* classified by the National Trust as a significant example of a turn-of-the-century hamlet; 50 km NW. *Walks and self-guide drives:* nature-reserve walks and historical and scenic drives; details from visitor centre.

TOWNS NEARBY: Port Macquarie 40 km, Macksville 42 km, Wauchope 43 km, Nambucca Heads 51 km, Laurieton 63 km

Khancoban

Pop. 279
Map ref. 519 A7 | 520 B8 | 539 A3 | 543 P7 | 545 P4

i Khancoban Visitor Centre, Scott Street; (02) 6076 9373 or (02) 6076 9382; www.snowymountains.com.au

89.7 FM ABC Local Radio

Khancoban is a pretty town on the edge of the Snowy Mountains, just a few kilometres from the Victorian border. Perhaps best known for being part of the Snowy Mountains scheme, Khancoban is set among parks and gardens, rolling farmland and impressive mountains.

Khancoban pondage: This 3 km long pondage offers plenty of water-based recreational activities, from fishing to boating, as well as plenty of amenities; open year-round. *Khancoban National Parks and Wildlife Information Centre:* has displays on both the history and natural beauty of the region; 9am–4pm every day; Cnr Scott and Mitchell sts; (02) 6076 9373.

Khancoban TroutFest: Nov.

Fairways Restaurant: Homestyle dinners; Khancoban Country Club, Mitchell Ave; (02) 6076 9468. *Shane O's Cafe:* Cafe, log fire, Wifi; Shop 4, Khancoban Shopping Centre, Scammel St; (02) 6076 9007.

Murray 1 Power Station and Visitors Centre Explore the history and mechanics of the Snowy Mountains Hydro Electric Scheme at this excellent information centre; Mon–Fri 9am–4pm; Oct–Apr, Sat–Sun 10am–4pm, May–Sept, closed weekends; Alpine Way; 1800 623 776. 10 km E.

Kosciuszko National Park: home to Mt Kosciuszko, the highest mountain on mainland Australia, this national park is famous for its skiing in winter, but also offers a range of activities, including bikeriding, bushwalks and horseriding in the warmer months. *Alpine Way:* takes a picturesque route through the Snowy Mountains en route to Jindabyne and Cooma, past the ski resort of Thredbo.

TOWNS NEARBY: **Corryong 21 km, Thredbo 35 km, Jindabyne 50 km, Tumbarumba 50 km, Adaminaby 63 km**

Kiama

Pop. 12 290
Map ref. 517 F7 | 519 H3 | 523 J9

Blowhole Point Rd; (02) 4232 3322 or 1300 654 262; www.kiama.com.au

i98 FM, 1431 AM ABC Radio National

This popular holiday town, hosting one million visitors each year, is best known as the home of the Kiama Blowhole. The rocky coastline, sandy beaches and appealing harbour provide an attractive contrast to the green rolling hills of the lush dairy pastures of the hinterland.

Kiama Blowhole The spectacular blowhole sprays to heights of 60 m and is floodlit at night. Beside the blowhole is a constructed rockpool and a cafe. Pilots Cottage Historical Museum has displays on the blowhole, early settlement, the dairy industry and shipping. Blowhole Pt; (02) 4232 1001.

Family History Centre: world-wide collection of records for compiling and tracing family history; Railway Pde; (02) 4233 1122. *Heritage walk:* includes terraced houses in Collins St and Pilots Cottage; leaflet from visitor centre. *Specialty and craft shops:* several in town showcasing local work; leaflet from visitor centre. *Beaches:* perfect for surfing, swimming and fishing.

Craft market: Black Beach; 3rd Sun each month. *Produce market:* Black Beach; 4th Sat each month. *Rotary Antique Fair:* Jan. *Jazz and Blues Festival:* Mar. *Big Fish Classic:* game-fishing competition; Apr.

Bed & Breakfast @ Kiama: 15 Riversdale Rd; (02) 4232 2844. *Easts Beach Holiday Park – Kiama:* Ocean St; (02) 4232 2124. *The Green Cottage B & B:* 126 Manning St; 0431 955 243. *Kendalls on the Beach Holiday Park:* Bonaira St; (02) 4232 1790. *Surf Beach Holiday Park:* Bourroul St; (02) 4232 1791. *Werri Beach Holiday Park:* Pacific Ave, Gerringong; (02) 4234 1285.

Gerringong A coastal town with a renowned heritage museum featuring remarkable scale models of the Illawarra coast. Gerringong's name comes from the Wodi Wodi language and is said to mean 'place of peril'. It is unclear where the peril lies, however, with safe beaches ideal for surfing, swimming and fishing. Heavy rainfall means the hinterland is lush and green. 10 km S.

Little Blowhole: smaller but more active than the Kiama Blowhole; off Tingira Cres; 2 km S. *Bombo Headland:* blue-metal quarrying in the 1880s left an eerie 'moonscape' of basalt walls and columns, which have been used in commercials and

video clips; 2.5 km N. *Cathedral Rocks:* scenic rocky outcrop best viewed at dawn; Jones Beach; 3 km N. *Kingsford Smith Memorial and Lookout:* site of Charles Kingsford Smith's 1933 take-off in the *Southern Cross*, with panoramic views; 14 km S. *Seven Mile Beach National Park:* surrounded by sand dunes, this low forest is inhabited by birds and small marsupials. It makes a pretty spot for picnics and barbecues, beach fishing and swimming; 17 km S. *Scenic drives:* in all directions to visit beaches, rock formations, cemeteries and craft shops; brochure from visitor centre.

TOWNS NEARBY: **Jamberoo 7 km, Shellharbour 10 km, Berry 19 km, Robertson 26 km, Wollongong 27 km**

Kyogle

Pop. 2730
Map ref. 516 E4 | 525 N3 | 609 M12

Summerland Way; (02) 6632 2700; www.tropicalnsw.com.au

104.3 FM 2LM, 738 AM ABC Local

Located at the upper reaches of the Richmond River and the base of the charmingly named Fairy Mountain, Kyogle is known as the 'gateway to the rainforests'. It is almost completely surrounded by the largest remaining areas of rainforest in New South Wales.

Captain Cook Memorial Lookout: at the top of Mt Fairy, the lookout provides stunning views of the town and surrounding countryside; Fairy St. *Botanical Gardens:* combination of formal gardens and revegetated creek environments on the banks of Fawcetts Creek; Summerland Way.

Campdraft: July. *Fairymount Festival – Hell on Hooves:* bullriding; July. *Gateway to the Rainforest Motorcycle Rally:* Sept. *Fairymount Festival – Remembering Yesterday, Dreaming Tomorrow:* Nov.

Ripples on the Creek: popular restaurant/cafe; 602 Gradys Creek Rd (Lions Road Tourist Dr), Gradys Creek; (02) 6636 6230.

Kyogle Gardens Caravan Park: Summerland Way; (02) 6632 1204.

Border Ranges National Park World Heritage–listed, this 30 000 ha park has walking tracks, camping, swimming, rock climbing and fantastic views of Mt Warning and the Tweed Valley. Sheepstation Creek is an attractive picnic spot. The Tweed Range Scenic Drive (64 km) is a breathtaking journey of rainforest, deep gorges and waterfalls. Brochure from visitor centre. 27 km N.

Wiangaree: rural community with rodeo in Mar; 15 km N. *Roseberry Forest Park:* picturesque picnic spot; 23 km N. *Moore Park Nature Reserve:* tiny reserve with the most important example of black bean rainforest in NSW; 26 km NW. *Toonumbar Dam:* built from earth and rocks, this offers scenic bushwalking with picnic and barbecue facilities. Nearby Bells Bay is known for its bass fishing and has a campsite; 31 km W. *Toonumbar National Park:* contains 2 World Heritage–listed rainforests and the volcanic remnants of Edinburgh Castle, Dome Mountain and Mt Lindesay; 35 km W. *Richmond Range National Park:* protected rainforest perfect for camping, birdwatching, picnics and barbecues, with good bushwalking on a 2 km or 6 km track; 40 km W. *Scenic forest drive:* via Mt Lindesay (45 km NW), offers magnificent views of both the rainforest and the countryside; brochure from visitor centre.

TOWNS NEARBY: **Nimbin 22 km, Casino 27 km, Lismore 34 km, Mullumbimby 49 km, Alstonville 49 km**

KATOOMBA

Pop. 7923
Map ref. 510 D5 | 512 F9 | 523 I6

 Echo Point Rd; 1300 653 408;
www.visitbluemountains.com.au

89.1 BLU FM, 97.3 FM ABC Local

Originally named Crushers but renamed a year later, Katoomba stands at an elevation of 1017 metres and is the region's principal tourist destination. Blue Mountains National Park lies to the north and south of town. The explanation for why these mountains look blue lies in the eucalyptus trees covering them; they disperse eucalyptus oil into the atmosphere, highlighting the sun's rays of blue light.

The Edge Cinema: daily screenings of *The Edge* (images of Blue Mountains) on a 6-storey screen; Great Western Hwy (access through Civic Pl); programs (02) 4782 8900. *The Carrington Hotel:* Katoomba's first hotel; Katoomba St.

Blue Mountains Festival of Folk, Roots and Blues: Mar. *Six Foot Track Festival:* Mar. *Winter Magic Festival:* June. *Yulefest:* throughout region; June–Aug. *Spring Gardens Festival:* throughout region; Sept–Nov.

The Conservation Hut Cafe: modern Australian; Fletcher St, Wentworth Falls; (02) 4757 3827. *Darley's Restaurant:* modern Australian; Lilianfels Blue Mountains Resort & Spa, Lilianfels Ave; (02) 4780 1200. *Echoes:* modern Australian, great location; 3 Lilianfels Ave; (02) 4782 1966. *Hominy Bakery:* best bread in the Blue Mountains; 185 Katoomba St; (02) 4782 9816. *The Rooster:* seasonal French fare; Jamison Guesthouse, 48 Merriwa St, Katoomba; (02) 4782 1206. *Seven:* Italian;

7 Station St, Wentworth Falls; (02) 4757 4997. *Silks Brasserie:* modern Australian; 128 The Mall, Leura; (02) 4784 2534. *Solitary:* French-influenced menu, great views; 90 Cliff Dr, Leura; (02) 4782 1164.

Blue Mountains Tourist Park – Katoomba Falls: 101 Katoomba Falls Rd; (02) 4782 1835. *Melba House Bed & Breakfast:* 98 Waratah St; (02) 4782 4141. *Shelton-Lea Bed & Breakfast:* 159 Lurline St; (02) 4782 9883. *Windradyne Boutique B & B:* 6 Cliff Dr; (02) 4782 9999. *Bethany Manor Bed & Breakfast:* 8 East View Ave, Leura; (02) 4782 9215. *Braeside Bed & Breakfast:* 97 Bedford Rd, Woodford; (02) 4758 6279. *Broomelea Bed & Breakfast:* 273 Leura Mall, Leura; (02) 4784 2940. *Fairway Lodge Bed and Breakfast:* 3 Sublime Point Rd, Leura; (02) 4784 3351. *The Greens of Leura:* 26 Grose St, Leura; (02) 4784 3241. *Megalong Manor:* 151 Megalong St, Leura; (02) 4784 1461. *Silvermere Guest House:* 1 Lake St, Wentworth Falls; (02) 4757 3311.

Leura Considered the most urbane and sophisticated village in the Blue Mountains, Leura has a beautiful tree-lined main street with impressive gardens, specialty shops, galleries and restaurants. Everglades Gardens (Everglades Ave) is a celebrated 1930s garden with a gallery devoted to its creator, Paul Sorensen. Leuralla (Olympian Pde) is a historic Art Deco mansion with a major collection of toys, dolls, trains and railway memorabilia. There are spectacular mountain views from Sublime Pt and Cliff Dr. The Leura Gardens Festival is held in Oct. Lyrebird Dell, near Leura, is an Aboriginal campsite estimated to be 12 000 years

[PARAGLIDING NEAR THE THREE SISTERS, BLUE MOUNTAINS NATIONAL PARK]

old. Relics can be found throughout the area, including rock engravings, axe-grinding grooves and cave paintings. All Aboriginal sites, discovered or undiscovered, are protected and are not to be disturbed by visitors. 3 km E.

Blue Mountains National Park Echo Pt is the best place to view the Three Sisters, which are floodlit at night. Aboriginal Dreamtime legend tells of 3 beautiful sisters, Meehni, Wimlah and Gunnedoo, who lived in the Jamison Valley with the Katoomba people. The girls fell in love with 3 brothers from the Nepean people, but tribal law forbade their marriages. The brothers would not accept this and attempted to capture the sisters, causing a major battle. A witchdoctor from the Katoomba people feared that the girls were in danger, so he turned them to stone to protect them, intending to return them to their true forms when the battle was over. This was not to be, however, as the witchdoctor was killed in battle and the 3 sisters, at 922 m, 918 m and 906 m high, remain trapped as a magnificent rock formation. Nearby Orphan Rock is thought to be the witchdoctor. Also at Echo Pt is the Giant Stairway: 800 steps leading to the valley floor. Near Wentworth Falls, 7 km E, is an eco-designed cafe with great views, and the Valley of the Waters picnic area. *For other parts of the park see Blackheath and Glenbrook.*

Blue Mountains Scenic World Located near Katoomba Falls, the Three Sisters and Echo Pt, Scenic World takes in some of the best scenery in the national park. Take a ride on the Scenic Railway, which was originally built to transport coal and miners and is the world's steepest railway, or on the Scenic Skyway, a 7 km ride in a cable car high up over the Jamison Valley. There is also Sceniscender, which descends into the heart of the valley, and plenty of other attractions to explore on foot; (02) 4780 0200, 1300 759 929; south of town.

Explorers Tree: blackbutt tree reportedly carved with initials of Blaxland, Wentworth and Lawson (there is some question about whether this was done by the explorers or by early tourism operators); west of town, off hwy. *Hazelbrook:* small village with Selwood Science and Puzzles featuring a puzzle room, science kits, bookshop and local artwork. Hazelbrook hosts Regatta Day in Feb on Wentworth Falls Lake; 17 km E.

TOWNS NEARBY: Blackheath 9 km, Glenbrook 28 km, Lithgow 30 km, Oberon 42 km, Richmond 43 km

Lake Cargelligo

Pop. 1149
Map ref. 522 A4 | 527 N4

ⓘ 1 Foster St; (02) 6898 1501; www.lakecargelligo.net.au

📻 99.7 Star FM, 549 AM ABC Local

Lake Cargelligo is a surprisingly attractive small town in the heart of the wide, brown Riverina plains. Built beside the lake of the same name, the town's activities revolve around the water with fishing and regular lake festivals.

Lake Cargelligo The lake dominates the town and is popular for fishing (silver perch, golden perch and redfin), boating, sailing, waterskiing and swimming. It is also appealing to birdwatchers, being home to many bird species including the rare black cockatoo. There is a historic walkway and bicycle track.

Wagon Rides and Working Horse Demonstrations: can be arranged by appt on (02) 6898 1384. *Information centre:* houses a large gem collection and carved stone butterflies; Foster St. *Kejole Koori Studio:* Aboriginal art, jewellery and didgeridoos; Grace St.

Blue Waters Art Exhibition and Competition: June. *Lake Show:* Sept. *Lake Cargelligo Fisharama*: Oct.

Lake View Caravan Park: Cnr Naradhan and Womboyn sts; (02) 6898 1077. *Riverview Caravan Park:* Diggers Ave, Condobolin; (02) 6895 2611.

Willandra National Park Once one-eighth of a huge merino sheep station, the 20 000 ha park features a restored homestead (offering accommodation), stables, a shearing complex and men's quarters. The buildings house a display of pastoral and natural history of the area. Plains, wetlands and Willandra Creek make up the rest of the park, with a walking track that is best at dawn or dusk to see the myriad waterbirds, kangaroos and emus. The creek is popular for canoeing and fishing. 163 km w.

Murrin Bridge Vineyard: Australia's first Aboriginal wine producer; 13 km N. *Cockies Shed Lavender Farm and Crafty Corner:* Tullibegeal; 13 km E. *Lake Brewster:* 1500 ha birdwatcher's paradise with fishing and picnic area. No guns, dogs or boats; 41 km W. *Nombinnie Nature Reserve:* birdwatching, bushwalking and abundant spring wildflowers Sept–Dec; 45 km N. *Hillston:* main street lined with palms, thanks to its situation on top of a large artesian basin. Hillston Lake is popular for watersports and picnics, and a swinging bridge provides access to a nature reserve and walking trail; 93 km SW.

TOWNS NEARBY: West Wyalong 104 km, Griffith 114 km, Leeton 139 km, Forbes 152 km, Narrandera 162 km

Laurieton

Pop. 2088
Map ref. 515 F7 | 523 O1 | 525 L12

ⓘ Greater Port Macquarie Tourism, cnr Gordon and Gore sts, Port Macquarie; (02) 6581 8000 or 1300 303 155; www.portmacquarieinfo.com.au

📻 100.7 2MC FM, 100.7 2MC FM, 684 AM ABC Local

Laurieton is on an attractive tidal inlet at the base of North Brother Mountain. The mountain, which was named by Captain Cook in 1770, provides Laurieton with shelter from the wind, so the weather is mild all year-round. There are spectacular views and bushwalks on the mountain and the inlet is popular for estuary fishing.

Historical museum: documents history of the town in old post office; open by appt; Laurie St; bookings (02) 6559 9096. *Armstrong Oysters:* oyster farm on the river open to the public for fresh oysters; Short St.

Riverwalk Market: Cnr Tunis and Short sts; 3rd Sun each month. *Camden Haven Music Festival:* internationally acclaimed music artists from all genres; Apr. *Watermark Literary Muster:* biennial event attracting scholars, authors and writers from around the world; odd-numbered years, Oct.

✕ *Rock Lobster & Maharaja Indian Restaurant:* cafe favourites and Indian curries; Shop 3, 80 Bold St; (02) 6559 8322.

🛏 *The Haven Caravan Park:* 2 Arnott St; (02) 6559 9584. *Laurieton Gardens Caravan Resort:* 478 Ocean Dr; (02) 6559 9256. *Beachfront Holiday Park:* 109 The Parade, North Haven; (02) 6559 9193. *Benbellen Country Retreat & Cottages:* 60 Cherry Tree La, Waitui; (02) 6556 7788. *Bonny Hills Holiday Park:* Ocean Dr, Bonny Hills; (02) 6585 5276. *Brigadoon Holiday Park:* Eames Ave, North Haven; (02) 6559 9172. *Diamond Waters Caravan Park:* 152 Diamond Head Rd, Dunbogan; (02) 6559 9334. *Dunbogan Caravan Park:* Bell St, Dunbogan; (02) 6559 9375. *Jacaranda Caravan Park:* 85 The Parade, North Haven; (02) 6559 9470. *The Watertank Bed and Breakfast:* 69 Forest Rd, Moorland; 0423 057 616.

◉ **Crowdy Bay National Park** The park is known for its prolific birdlife and magnificent ocean beach. Diamond Head is an interesting sculpted rock formation and the hut beneath is where Kylie Tennant wrote *The Man and the Headland*. A headland walking track offers stunning views and the area is also popular for fishing, birdwatching and the abundant wildlife. Campsites are at Diamond Head, Indian Head and Kylies Beach. 5 km s.

Dunbogan: this seaside village borders the river and ocean. A fisherman's co-op offers the best fish and chips in the region. River cruises and patrolled swimming beach; 2 km SE. *Kattang Nature Reserve:* in spring the Flower Bowl Circuit leads through stunning wildflowers. Enjoy good coastal views all year-round from sharp cliffs jutting into the ocean; 5 km E. *Dooragan National Park:* according to local Aboriginal legend, Dooragan (North Brother Mountain) was the youngest of 3 brothers who avenged his brothers' deaths at the hands of a witch by killing the witch and then killing himself. Blackbutt and subtropical forest is home to gliders, bats and koalas. Viewing platforms on North Brother Mountain provide some of the best views anywhere on the NSW coast; 6 km W. *North Haven:* riverside dining, boutique gift shops and patrolled swimming beach; 6 km NE. *Queens Lake Picnic Area:* a beautiful reserve with St Peter the Fisherman Church nearby. Kayak access to the river; 6 km W. *Kendall:* poets walk, art and craft galleries. Also market 1st Sun each month on Logans Crossing Rd; 10 km W. *Big Fella Gum Tree:* 67 m flooded gum tree in Middle Brother State Forest; 18 km sw. *Lorne Valley Macadamia Farm:* tours at 11am and 2pm, products for sale and cafe; open Sat–Thurs; 23 km W.

TOWNS NEARBY: Wauchope 22 km, Port Macquarie 26 km, Taree 44 km, Wingham 47 km, Kempsey 63 km

Leeton
Pop. 6829
Map ref. 527 N8

ℹ 10 Yanco Ave; (02) 6953 6481; www.leetontourism.com.au

📻 99.7 Star FM, 549 AM ABC Local

Leeton was designed by Walter Burley Griffin, the American architect who designed Canberra. Like Canberra, the town is built in a circular fashion with streets radiating from the centre. The Murrumbidgee Irrigation Area brought fertility to the dry plains of the Riverina and now Leeton has 102 hectares of public parks and reserves and a thriving primary industry.

🏛 *Visitor centre:* beautifully restored building with photographic displays, local artwork and a heritage garden; Yanco Ave. *Sunrice Centre:* product displays and tastings, with 'Paddy to Plate' video presentation at 9.30am and 2.45pm on weekdays; Calrose St. *Mick's Bakehouse:* home of award-winning pies; Pine Ave. *Art Deco streetscape:* includes Roxy Theatre and historic Hydro Motor Inn; Chelmsford Pl.

🌴 *Bidgee Classic Fishing Competition:* Mar. *Sunrice Festival:* even-numbered years, Easter. *Picnic Races:* May. *Australian Birdfair:* Nov. *Light up Leeton:* Dec.

✕ *Pages on Pine Restaurant:* modern Australian; 119B Pine Ave; (02) 6953 7300.

🛏 *Leeton Caravan Park:* Yanco Ave; (02) 6953 3323.

◉ **Yanco** This town is the site where Sir Samuel McCaughey developed the irrigation scheme that led to the establishment of the Murrumbidgee Irrigation Area. Attractions in town include McCaughey Park, the Powerhouse Museum and a miniature train that runs on market days. Village Markets are held at Yanco Hall on the last Sun each month. 8 km s.

Fivebough Wetlands: 400 ha home to over 150 species of waterbird with interpretive centre, walking trails and viewing hides; 2 km N. *Brobenah Airfield:* gliding and hot-air ballooning; 9 km N. *McCaughey's Mansion:* 1899 mansion with stained-glass windows and attractive gardens, now an agricultural high school, but drive-through inspections welcome. Yanco Agricultural Institute nearby is open to the public and provides farmer-training facilities, research and advisory services; 11 km s. *Murrumbidgee State Forest:* scenic drives; brochure from visitor centre; 12 km s. *Whitton Historical Museum:* housed in old courthouse and gaol with photographs, documents and early farming equipment; 23 km W. *Gogeldrie Weir:* pleasant spot for fishing, picnics and camping; 23 km sw. *Wineries:* cellar-door tastings and tours at Toorak and Lillypilly Estate; brochure at visitor centre.

TOWNS NEARBY: Narrandera 26 km, Griffith 44 km, West Wyalong 101 km, Temora 104 km, Wagga Wagga 108 km

Lightning Ridge
Pop. 2598
Map ref. 524 B3 | 608 E12

ℹ Lions Park, Morilla St; (02) 6829 1670; www.lightningridge.net.au

📻 91.3 NOW FM, 549 AM ABC Local

This famous opal-mining town is the only place in Australia where true black opals are found. Miners on the opal fields in most cases need to provide their own electricity and catch or cart their own water as these services are not available, making residents pretty creative and resilient. The otherwise desolate area receives 80 000 visitors each year and has modern facilities in an otherwise minimalist town. Famous finds in the region include Big Ben and the Flame Queen, which was sold for £80 because the miner who found it had not eaten properly in 3 weeks. Local Aboriginal legend explains the opals by saying that a huge wheel of fire fell to earth, spraying the land with brilliant stones. Lightning Ridge is notoriously hot in summer but boasts ideal weather in winter, and has lots of native marsupials and birdlife.

🏛 *Bottle House Museum:* collection of bottles, minerals and mining relics; originally a miner's camp; Opal St. *Big Opal:* opal-cutting demonstrations and daily underground working-mine tours; Three Mile Rd. *John Murray Art:* exclusive outlet for original paintings, limited-edition prints, postcards and posters; Opal St. *Goondee Aboriginal Keeping Place:* Aboriginal artefacts and educational tours of the premises; open by appt; Pandora St. *Chambers of the Black Hand:* unique underground sculptures and carvings in sandstone walls of an old mine; also underground shop; Three Mile Rd. **Displays of art and craft:** including beautiful displays of black opal in the many opal showrooms; several locations; leaflet from visitor centre. **Ridgelightning:** local lightning photography gallery and shop; Gem St. **Car Door Explorer Tours:** follow painted car doors to find attractions; brochure from visitor centre.

Local craft market: Morilla St; every Fri and most Sun. **Great Goat Race:** Easter. **Rodeo:** Easter. **Opal Open Pistol Shoot:** June. **Opal and Gem Festival:** July.

Chats on Opal: homemade cakes, gourmet sandwiches; shop 1, 5 Opal St; (02) 6829 4228. **Morilla's Cafe:** light meals, cakes; shop 2, 2 Morilla St; (02) 6829 0009. **Nobbies Restaurant:** bistro; Lightning Ridge Outback Resort & Caravan Park, cnr Onyx and Morilla sts; (02) 6829 0304.

Crocodile Caravan Park: 5 Morilla St; (02) 6829 0437. **Lightning Ridge Outback Resort & Caravan Park:** Onyx St; (02) 6829 0304. **Opal Caravan Park:** Pandora St; (02) 6829 4884. **Sonja's Bed & Breakfast:** 60 Butterfly Ave; (02) 6829 2010.

Walk-In Mine: working mine with easy access and tours on demand. Also a cactus nursery nearby; off Bald Hill Rd; 2 km N. **Hot artesian bore baths:** open baths with average temperature 42°C; 2 km NE. **Kangaroo Hill Tourist Complex:** displays of antiques, bottles, shells, rocks and minerals, and mining memorabilia with a fossicking area outside; 3 km S. **Opal fields:** Grawin (65 km W) and Sheepyards (76 km W); brochure from visitor centre. **Designated fossicking areas:** maps from visitor centre.

TOWNS NEARBY: Walgett 68 km, Brewarrina 123 km, St George 165 km, Wee Waa 167 km, Coonamble 174 km

Lismore

Pop. 30 088
Map ref. 516 F5 | 525 O3 | 609 N12

ℹ️ Cnr Ballina and Molesworth sts; (02) 6626 0100 or 1300 369 795; www.visitlismore.com.au

📻 92.9 FM North Coast Radio, 738 AM ABC Local

This regional centre of the Northern Rivers district is on the banks of the Wilsons River. European settlement came in 1840 when John Brown broke an axle near a small chain of ponds and stopped to have a look around. He liked what he saw and decided to settle. Called Browns Water Hole until 1853, it was changed to Lismore after a town in Ireland. The town is now known for its ecotourism.

Rotary Rainforest Reserve There are 6 ha of original tropical rainforest in the middle of the city, but this is only a small remnant of the original 'Big Scrub' that stood here before European settlement. Over 3 km of paths, including a boardwalk, lead visitors past hoop pines and giant figs, with rare species of labelled rainforest plants. Rotary Dr.

Visitor centre: indoor rainforest walk, historical displays, and local art and craft. The surrounding Heritage Park has pleasant picnic areas and a mini steam train offering rides (10am–2pm Thurs and public holidays, 10am–4pm Sat, Sun and school holidays). Cnr Ballina and Molesworth sts. **Richmond River Historical Museum:** geological specimens, Aboriginal artefacts and pioneer clothing, implements, furniture and handiwork; Molesworth St. **Lismore Regional**

Art Gallery: permanent collection of paintings, pottery and ceramics with changing exhibitions by local and touring artists; Molesworth St. **Robinson's Lookout:** views south across the river to South Lismore and north to the mountains; Robinson Ave. **Claude Riley Memorial Lookout:** views over Lismore city; New Ballina Rd. **Wilsons Park:** contains original rainforest with labelled trees; Wyrallah St, East Lismore. **Riverside Walk:** along the banks of the Wilsons River from the town centre to Spinks Park, where there are picnic and barbecue facilities. **Koala Care Centre:** looks after injured and orphaned koalas. Guided tours 10am and 2pm Mon–Fri, and 10am Sat; Rifle Range Rd. **Cafe and Culture Trail:** self-guide walk through sites of historical significance and cafes in the town centre. **Heritage walk:** historic buildings and churches; brochure from visitor centre.

Car Boot Markets: Shopping Sq, Uralba St; 1st and 3rd Sun each month. **Rainbow Region Organic Markets:** Lismore Showground, Tues morning until 11am; Alexander Pde. **Lismore Gemfest:** May. **Lantern Parade:** June. **Cup Day:** horserace; Sept.

Fire in the Belly: award-winning gourmet pizza; 109 Dawson St; (02) 6621 4899. **Paupiettes:** French; 56 Ballina St; (02) 6621 6135.

Lismore Palms Caravan Park: 42–58 Brunswick St; (02) 6621 7067. **Elindale House B&B:** 34 Second Ave, East Lismore; (02) 6622 2533. **Melville House:** 267 Ballina St, East Lismore; (02) 6621 5778.

Boatharbour Reserve: 17 ha of rainforest, wildlife sanctuary, picnic area and walking tracks; maps from visitor centre; 6 km E. **Tucki Tucki Koala Reserve:** woodland planted by local residents to protect the diminishing koala population, with walking track and Aboriginal bora ring nearby; 15 km S. **Rocky Creek Dam:** between Nightcap National Park and Whian Whian State Forest, includes spectacular views of the lake, boardwalks, walking trails, platypus-viewing platform, barbecues and a playground; 18 km N.

TOWNS NEARBY: Alstonville 16 km, Casino 23 km, Nimbin 25 km, Ballina 29 km, Kyogle 34 km

Lithgow

Pop. 11 298
Map ref. 510 B2 | 512 D2 | 523 I5

ℹ️ Great Western Hwy; 1300 760 276; www.tourism.lithgow.com

📻 107.9 2ICE FM, 1395 AM ABC Local

Lithgow promotes itself as being 'surrounded by nature'. Easy access to several of the state's finest national parks and the city's charm make it worth visiting this isolated but staggeringly beautiful region. It was isolated from the coastal cities until the revolutionary Zig Zag Railway, built with gently sloping ramps to cut through the mountains, opened it up in 1869.

Eskbank House Museum Built in 1842, this sandstone Georgian mansion houses an extensive collection of Lithgow pottery, memorabilia and photographs. The front 4 rooms are authentically furnished with Regency and Victorian furniture. In the gardens are a stone stable, coach house and picnic area. Open Wed–Sun or by appt; (02) 6351 3557; Bennett St.

Blast Furnace Park: ruins of Australia's first blast furnace complex (1886) with a pleasant walk around adjacent Lake Pillans Wetland; off Inch St. **State Mine Railway Heritage Park:** mining and railway equipment and historic mining buildings; State Mine Gully Rd. **Small Arms Museum:** established in 1912, some argue that this is the birthplace of modern manufacturing in Australia. Displays range from firearms to sewing machines. Open 9.30am–2.30pm Tues and Thurs, 10am–4pm Sat, Sun, public and school holidays; Methven St.

Ironfest: cultural festival celebrating metal; Apr. *Rally of Lithgow:* May. *Celebrate Lithgow:* Nov.

Secret Creek Cafe and Restaurant: modern/native Australian; Secret Creek Sanctuary, 35 Crane Rd; (02) 6352 1133. *Lochiel House:* modern Australian; 1259 Bells Line of Road, Kurrajong Heights; (02) 4567 7754.

Lithgow Tourist & Van Park: 58 Cooerwull Rd; (02) 6351 4350. *Seclusions Blue Mountains:* 209 Martins Rd, Rydal; (02) 6355 6300.

Wollemi National Park This is the largest wilderness area in NSW at 500 000 hectares, and is a breathtaking display of canyons, cliffs and undisturbed forest. In 1994 the discovery of a new tree species – the Wollemi pine – in a rainforest gully was compared to finding a living dinosaur. Highlights include historic ruins at Newnes, the beaches of the Colo Gorge and the glow worms in a disused rail tunnel. The park also includes Glen Davis, home to more species of birds than anywhere else in the Southern Hemisphere. Mt Wilson, surrounded by the park, is a 19th-century village with large homes and superb gardens, many open to the public. Via the town is the Cathedral of Ferns; begins16 km E.

Blue Mountains SpaRadise: Japanese bathhouse; Bowenfels; 1 km N. *Hassans Walls Lookout:* spectacular views of the Blue Mountains and Hartley Valley; via Hassans Walls Rd; 5 km S. *Lake Lyell:* stunning lake in mountain setting, popular for activities such as power-boating, waterskiing, trout fishing and picnics. Also canoe and boat hire available on-site; 9 km W. *Zig Zag Railway:* built in 1869, and later restored, it offers train trips of 1 hr 40 min return, departing 11am, 1pm and 3pm daily; via Bells Line of Road, Clarence; 10 km E. *Lake Wallace:* sailing and trout fishing; 11 km NW. *Jannei Goat Dairy:* produces cheeses, yoghurt and milk and is open to visitors, with free cheese tastings; 11 km NW. *Hartley:* became obsolete after the construction of the Great Western Railway in 1887. Explore 17 historical buildings administered by the National Parks & Wildlife Service; 14 km SE. *Portland:* charming town with a power station offering tours and interactive exhibits, a museum with much Australian memorabilia and several pleasant picnic areas; 17 km NW. *Mt Piper Power Station:* hands-on exhibits in the information centre and daily tours at 11am; 21 km NW. *Gardens of Stone National Park:* fascinating pagoda rock formations, sandstone escarpments and beehive-shaped domes caused by erosion. This is a great spot for rock climbing and picnics; 30 km N. *Mount Tomah Botanic Garden:* 5000 species of cool-climate plants at over 1000 m above sea level. Also award-winning restaurant; 35 km E.

TOWNS NEARBY: Blackheath 22 km, Katoomba 30 km, Oberon 36 km, Bathurst 52 km, Glenbrook 54 km

Lord Howe Island Settlement
Pop. 344

ℹ️ Lord Howe Island Museum, cnr Lagoon and Middle Beach rds; (02) 6563 2114 or 1800 240 937; www.lordhoweisland.info

📻 100.1 FM

Situated beside a coral lagoon on this stunning World Heritage–listed island, the Lord Howe Island settlement takes up a small area in the central-north part of the island. Many people get around by pushbike. The main street has cafes, art and craft shops, banks, a general store and post office.

 Lord Howe Island Museum and Visitors Centre Displays and reams of information on the island's history and World Heritage listing. Open 9.30am–3pm, Mon–Fri, 9.20am–2pm Sun; Lagoon Rd; 1800 240 937.

Kentia Palm Nursery: as well as learning about growing the biggest-selling indoor palm in the world, see the breeding program for the Lord Howe Island phasmid, an extremely rare insect. Enquire at Visitors Centre.

Discovery Day: Feb; *Jazz Festival:* Jun–Aug. *Gosford to Lord Howe Island Yacht Race:* Oct–Nov; *Lord Howe Island Golf Open:* Nov.

Pandanus: International cuisine; Anderson Rd; (02) 6563 2400. *Pinetrees:* International cuisine; (02) 6563 2177; lunch and dinner, 7 days.

Golf: Situated at the base of imposing Mt Lidgbird, Lord Howe Island's golf course is one of Australia's most scenic – its 9 holes incorporate lush vegetation and open fairways with superb coastal views. Visitors are welcome to tee off at any time on this World Heritage turf, and you can even participate in the annual Lord Howe Open Golf Tournament held in November; (02) 6563 2179. *Bushwalks:* the island abounds in great bushwalks along stunning coastline, among bird rookeries, through dense subtropical forest, and to the peak of the 2 towering mountains. The premier walk is to the top of 875 m Mt Gower, an all-day adventure that can only be done with a guide, and involves ropes at some points. Enquire at the visitors centre. *Snorkelling and Diving:* Lord Howe Island's coral reefs and drop-offs abound with fish, turtles and other marine life. There are 2 dive operators and numerous places to hire snorkels on the island. Snorkels and masks are also available at Neds Beach, with an honesty box system.

Macksville
Pop. 2658
Map ref. 515 G2 | 525 M9

ℹ️ Cnr Pacific Hwy and Riverside Dr, Nambucca Heads; (02) 6568 6954 or 1800 646 587; www.nambuccatourism.com

📻 105.9 FM Radio Nambucca, 738 AM ABC Local

Macksville is a fishing and oyster-farming town on the banks of the Nambucca River. There is an abundance of water-based activities, with picnic areas and riverside parks from which dolphins can often be observed. The town bustles with activities and festivals including the country's second oldest footrace, the Macksville Gift, each November.

Mary Boulton Pioneer Cottage: replica of a pioneer home and farm buildings with horse-drawn vehicles. Open by appt 2–4pm Wed–Sat; River St; (02) 6568 1280. *Hotels:* Star Hotel, River St, and Nambucca Hotel, Cooper St, both heritage buildings from late 1800s with many original features; both offer meals and accommodation. *Nambucca MacNuts Factory:* macadamia products at wholesale prices; Yarrawonga St.

Market: Scout Hall, Partridge St; 4th Sat each month. *Patchwork and Quilt Display:* Easter. *Rusty Iron Rally:* heritage machinery show; Sept. *Macksville Gift:* Nov.

Dangerous Dan's Butchery: excellent butchery; 13 Princess St; (02) 6568 1036. *Short Order Cafe:* light meals, cakes; Shop 1, 10 Princess St; (02) 6568 4550.

 Nambucca River Tourist Park: 143 Nursery Rd; (02) 6568 1850. *Grassy Head Holiday Park:* Reserve Rd, Grassy Head; (02) 6569 0742. *Scotts Head Holiday Park:* 1 Short St, Scotts Head; (02) 6569 8122. *Stuarts Point Holiday Park:* Marine

Pde, Stuarts Point; (02) 6569 0616. *Yarrahapinni Homestead:* 340 Stuarts Point Rd, Yarrahapinni; (02) 6569 0240.

Bowraville This unspoiled town has much to see with a National Trust–classified main street, the Bowra Folk Museum, Frank Partridge VC Military Museum, Bowra Art Gallery and many craft galleries. There are markets on 3rd Sun each month, regular races at the racecourse and the Bowraville Hinterland Festival each Oct. 16 km NW.

Mt Yarahappini Lookout: the highest point in Nambucca Valley with fabulous 360-degree views, in Yarriabini National Park; 10 km S. *Scotts Head:* coastal town with good beaches for surfing, swimming, fishing and dolphin-watching; 18 km SE. *Pub with No Beer:* built in 1896, this is the hotel that was made famous in Slim Dusty's song 'The Pub with No Beer', so named because it would often run out of beer before the next quota arrived. It is still largely in its original form and offers meals; 26 km SW. *Bakers Creek Station:* old cattle station, now an impressive resort offering horseriding, fishing, rainforest walking, canoeing and picnicking as well as accommodation; (02) 6564 2165; 30 km W. *Local craft:* featured in several shops and galleries in the area; leaflet from visitor centre.

TOWNS NEARBY: Nambucca Heads 11 km, Urunga 25 km, Bellingen 28 km, Kempsey 42 km, Dorrigo 45 km

Maitland

Pop. 61 431
Map ref. 509 F1 | 514 C7 | 515 A11 | 523 L3

i Ministers Park, cnr New England Hwy and High St; (02) 4931 2800; www.maitlandhuntervalley.com.au

106.9 NX FM, 549 AM ABC Local

Maitland is in the heart of the world-class Hunter Valley wine region, on the Hunter River. Built on flood plains, it has suffered 15 major floods since settlement. The city has a significant Polish community as a result of immigration after World War II.

Maitland Gaol The gaol was built in 1844 and served as a maximum security prison for 154 years. The first inmates were convicts, including some children, and were forced to march 6 km from the wharf at Morpeth in shackles and chains. It has been home to some of Australia's most notorious and dangerous criminals and is now said to be the most haunted gaol in the country. Audio tours are available or there are guided tours with ex-inmates and ex-officers. For the extremely brave, there are also overnight stays. John St, East Maitland; bookings (02) 4936 6482.

Grossman House: National Trust–classified Georgian-style house, now a museum with pioneer silverware, porcelain and handmade clothing; Church St. *Maitland Regional Gallery:* city's art collection specialising in local works; High St. *Self-guide heritage walks:* showcasing Maitland, Morpeth, Lorn and East Maitland; brochures from visitor centre.

Market: showground; 1st Sun each month (except Jan). *Hunter Valley Steamfest:* celebration of steam trains; Apr. *Garden Ramble:* Sept. *Bitter & Twisted International Boutique Beer Festival:* Nov.

The Angels Inn Restaurant: modern Australian; Molly Morgan Motor Inn, New England Hwy; (02) 4933 5422. *The Old George & Dragon Restaurant:* modern European; 48 Melbourne St; (02) 4933 7272. *Organic Feast:* excellent provedore; 10–12 William St, East Maitland; (02) 4934 7351.

CBC Bed & Breakfast: 19 King St, Paterson; (02) 4938 5767. *Clevedon Bed & Breakfast:* 2034 Gresford Rd, East Gresford; (02) 4938 9488. *Peacock Grove Biodynamic Farm & B & B:* 84 Valley St, Gosforth; 0417 292 642.

Morpeth This riverside village has been classified by the National Trust. The town can be explored on foot and features magnificent old sandstone buildings such as St James Church (1830s), and antique and craft shops. There is the Weird and Wonderful Novelty Teapot Exhibition in Aug. A self-guide heritage walk brochure is available from the visitor centre. 5 km NE.

Walka: a scenic drive from Maitland, this former pumping station, now an excellent recreation area, is popular for picnics and bushwalks; 3 km N. *Tocal Homestead:* historic Georgian homestead; open by appt; bookings (02) 4939 8888; 14 km N. *Paterson:* signposted scenic drive leads to this charming hamlet on the Paterson River; 16 km N.

TOWNS NEARBY: Raymond Terrace 18 km, Cessnock 22 km, Newcastle 30 km, Singleton 41 km, Stroud 53 km

Manilla

Pop. 2081
Map ref. 524 H8

i 197 Manilla St; (02) 6785 1207; www.manillamuseum.org.au

92.9 FM, 648 AM ABC Local

This rural town is located at the junction of the Manilla and Namoi rivers and surrounded by attractive rural countryside. Its location between Lake Keepit and Split Rock Dam has made it a popular setting for myriad outdoor activities, especially aerosports. Nearby Mount Borah hosted the world's paragliding championships in 2007. Manilla is also known for its production of mead (an alcoholic drink made from fermented honey and water). It is home to one of only two meaderies in the country.

Dutton's Meadery: tastings and sales of honey and mead; Barraba St. *Manilla Heritage Museum:* incorporates Royce Cottage Collection and exhibits pioneer items such as clothing and furniture, and a bakery. Also has displays on platypus, which are often found in the area. *Manilla St:* antique and coffee shops.

National and international paragliding competitions: Nov–Apr.

Manilla River Gums Caravan Park: 86 Strafford St; (02) 6785 1166. *Oakhampton Homestead & Country Holidays:* 1254 Oakhampton Rd; (02) 6785 6517. *Lake Keepit State Park:* 234 Lake Keepit Rd, Lake Keepit; (02) 6769 7605.

Warrabah National Park At this peaceful riverside retreat you'll find enormous granite boulders sitting above still valley pools and rapids suitable for experienced canoeists. Activities include swimming and fishing in the Namoi and Manilla rivers and rock climbing on the cliffs. 40 km NE.

Manilla Paragliding: offers tandem flights; a 2-day introduction, and a 9-day 'live in' licensing course with equipment supplied; Mt Borah; (02) 6785 6545; 12 km N. *Split Rock Dam:* watersports, boating, camping and fishing for species such as Murray cod and golden perch; turn-off 15 km N. *Manilla Ski Gardens:* area at the northern end of Lake Keepit with waterskiing, fishing and swimming; 20 km SW. *For more details on Lake Keepit see Gunnedah.*

TOWNS NEARBY: Barraba 42 km, Tamworth 43 km, Gunnedah 51 km, Uralla 76 km, Walcha 88 km

 RADIO STATIONS   IN TOWN   WHAT'S ON   WHERE TO EAT   WHERE TO STAY   NEARBY

Menindee

Pop. 331
Map ref. 528 E11

i Yartla St; (08) 8091 4274.

95.7 FM ABC Radio National, 97.3 FM ABC Western Plains

Menindee is like an oasis in the middle of a desert. Although located in the state's arid inland plains, its immediate surrounds comprise fertile land, thanks to the 20 lakes in the area fed by the Darling River and a dam constructed in the 1960s. The orchards and vegetable farms provide a stark contrast to the vast freshwater lakes full of dead trees, and surrounding saltbush and red soil, on the way into this tiny settlement.

Maiden's Menindee Hotel: Burke and Wills lodged here in 1860. Meals and accommodation are available; Yartla St. *Ah Chung's Bakehouse Gallery:* William Ah Chung established one of the first market gardens in town. His bakery (c. 1880) now houses a gallery featuring local artists. Open for groups by appt from visitor centre; Menindee St. *Heritage trail:* through town; maps from visitor centre.

Copi Hollow Caravan Park: Steve Hutton Dr, Copi Hollow; (08) 8091 4880.

Kinchega National Park When full, the lakes support waterbirds such as egrets, cormorants, black swans and spoonbills, and numerous other wildlife. There are giant river red gums growing along the banks of the Darling River, and campsites along the river in the north. Attractions include the wreck of paddlesteamer *Providence*, the old homestead and woolshed from Kinchega Station, and accommodation in the restored shearers' quarters. There is also a cemetery near the homestead. Activities include swimming, fishing and canoeing. 1 km w.

Menindee Lakes: in dry times only the upper lakes have water, making them the most reliable for fishing, swimming, birdwatching and watersports, and the best place for camping; details from visitor centre. *Menindee Lake Lookout:* good views of the lake; 10 km N. *Copi Hollow:* great spot for waterskiers, swimmers and powerboat enthusiasts, with campsites on the waterfront; 18 km N.

TOWNS NEARBY: Broken Hill 102 km, White Cliffs 182 km, Wentworth 195 km, Mildura (Vic.) 200 km, Robinvale (Vic.) 245 km

Merimbula

Pop. 3851
Map ref. 519 E9 | 539 H7

i Beach St; (02) 6495 1129; www.merimbulatourism.com.au

105.5 2EC FM, 810 AM ABC South East

Merimbula is a modern seaside town known for its surfing, fishing and oyster farming. Middens found in the area indicate that oysters were gathered here by Aboriginal people well before the arrival of Europeans. The town began as a private village belonging to the Twofold Bay Pastoral Association, who opened it as a port in 1855.

Merimbula Aquarium Twenty-seven tanks here present a wide range of sea life and an oceanarium showcases large ocean fish including sharks. Fish feeding time is 11.30am Mon, Wed and Fri (Mon–Fri in school holidays). Excellent seafood restaurant on-site. Merimbula Wharf, Lake St.

Old School Museum: town history displayed in excellent collection of photos, documents and memorabilia; Main St. *Scenic flights:* view the Sapphire Coast from the air. Bookings through Merimbula Air Services; (02) 6495 1074. *Trike Tours:* enjoy the beauty of the coast on 3 wheels; (02) 6495 2300.

Seaside Markets: Ford Oval; 3rd Sun each month. *Jazz Festival:* June. *Country Music Festival:* Nov.

Poppy's Courtyard Cafe: peaceful cafe; 15 The Plaza; (02) 6495 1110. *Zanzibar Cafe:* modern Australian; Cnr Main and Market sts; (02) 6495 3636.

NRMA Merimbula Beach Holiday Park: 2 Short Point Rd; (02) 6499 8999. *Robyns Nest Guest House:* 188 Merimbula Dr; (02) 6495 4956. *Sapphire Valley Caravan Park:* 29 Sapphire Coast Dr; (02) 6495 1746. *Discovery Holiday Parks – Pambula Beach:* 1 Pambula Beach Rd, Pambula Beach; (02) 6495 6363. *Dolphin Cove Bed & Breakfast:* 336 Pacific Way, Tura Beach; (02) 6495 9193. *Jen and Tonyx B&B:* 264 Old Mill Rd, Wolumla; (02) 6494 9301.

Pambula This historic sister village of Merimbula has excellent fishing on the Pambula River and a market 2nd Sun each month. Pambula Beach has a scenic walking track and lookout, with kangaroos and wallabies gathering on the foreshore at dawn and dusk; 7 km sw.

Magic Mountain Family Recreation Park: rollercoaster, water slides, minigolf and picnic area; Sapphire Coast Dr; 5 km N. *Tura Beach:* resort town with excellent beach for surfing; 5 km NE. *Yellow Pinch Wildlife Park:* peaceful bushland setting with array of native animals, birds and reptiles; 5 km E. *Oakland Farm Trail Rides:* scenic trail rides to the Pambula River; Princes Hwy, South Pambula; 0428 957 257; 10 km sw. *Whale-watching (Oct–Nov), boat cruises and boat hire:* bookings at visitor centre.

TOWNS NEARBY: Tathra 19 km, Eden 19 km, Bega 25 km, Bermagui 54 km, Bombala 60 km

Merriwa

Pop. 944
Map ref. 523 J1 | 524 G12

i Vennacher St; (02) 6548 2607.

101.9 FM ABC Local, 102.7 Power FM

This small town in the western Hunter region beside the Merriwa River is known for its majestic early colonial buildings. It is the centre of a vast farming district of cattle, sheep, horses, wheat and olive trees. People converge on the town each year for the Festival of the Fleeces, which includes shearing competitions, yard dog trials and a woolshed dance.

Historical Museum: in stone cottage (1857) with documented history of the region and the belongings of European pioneers; Bettington St. *Bottle Museum:* over 5000 bottles of all shapes and sizes; open Mon–Fri; visitor centre. *Self-guide historical walk:* early school buildings, Holy Trinity Anglican Church (1875) and the Fitzroy Hotel (1892); brochure from visitor centre.

Polocrosse Carnival: June. *Festival of the Fleeces:* June. *Merriwa Motorcycle River Rally:* Oct.

Merriwa Cakes and Pastries: bakery; 147 Bettington St; (02) 6548 2851.

Merriwa Caravan Park: Bettington St; (02) 6548 2109. *Sandy Hollow Tourist Park:* 1618 Merriwa Rd (Golden Hwy), Sandy Hollow; (02) 6547 4575.

Coolah Tops National Park The plateaus at high altitude in this park provide wonderful lookouts over the Liverpool plains and some spectacular waterfalls. Vegetation consists of giant grass trees and tall open forests of snow gums, providing a home for wallabies, gliders, eagles and rare owls. There are superb campsites, walking trails and picnic spots. 107 km NW.

Cassilis: tiny village with historic sandstone buildings including St Columba's Anglican Church (1899) and the courthouse/police station (1858). The main streets have been declared an urban conservation area; 25 km NW. *Flags Rd:* old convict-built road leading to Gungal; 25 km SW. *Gem-fossicking area:* open to the public; 27 km SW. *Goulburn River National Park:* mostly sandstone walking tracks along the Goulburn River, honeycombed with caves; good rafting and access for boats; 35 km S.

TOWNS NEARBY: Scone 49 km, Muswellbrook 52 km, Murrurundi 62 km, Gulgong 81 km, Rylstone 82 km

Moree

Pop. 8085
Map ref. 524 G4

ℹ️ Lyle Houlihan Park, cnr Newell and Gwydir hwys; (02) 6757 3350; www.moreetourism.com

📻 98.3 NOW FM, 819 AM ABC New England North West

Moree sits at the junction of the Mehi and Gwydir rivers and is the centre of the thriving local farming district. Thanks to its rich black-soil plains, one local claimed, 'You could put a matchstick in the ground overnight and get a walking-stick in the morning'. The town is also known for its artesian spas, with therapeutic qualities said to cure arthritis and rheumatism.

🏠 **Spa complex** These spas were discovered accidentally when settlers were searching for reliable irrigation water. A bore was sunk into the Great Artesian Basin and the water that emerged was 41°C. The complex also has an outdoor heated pool and an array of leisure activities that attract 300 000 visitors each year. Cnr Anne and Gosport sts.

Moree Plains Regional Gallery: contemporary Aboriginal art and artefacts and changing exhibitions; Frome St. *The Big Plane:* DC3 transport plane with tours available at Amaroo Tavern; Amaroo Dr. *Dhiiyaan Indigenous Centre:* located in the town's library, this was the first Aboriginal genealogy centre where Indigenous people could access historical family information and photographs; Cnr Balo and Albert sts. *Barry Roberts Historical Walk:* self-guide tour includes the courthouse and the Moree Lands Office, which was restored after a fire in 1982; brochure from visitor centre.

🌴 *Market:* Jellicoe Park; 1st Sun each month (not Jan). *Opera in the Paddock:* odd-numbered years; Mar. *Picnic Races:* May. *Moree on a Plate:* food and wine festival; May. *Australian Cotton Trade Show:* May. *Harmony on the Plains Multicultural Festival:* Aug. *Golden Grain Festival:* Nov.

🍴 *Dragon & Phoenix Palace:* Chinese; 361 Frome St; (02) 6752 4444.

🛏️ *Gwydir Carapark:* Cnr Newell Hwy and Amaroo Dr; (02) 6752 2723. *Mehi River Van Park:* 28 Oak St; (02) 6752 7188.

⊗ *Trewalla Pecan Farm:* largest orchard in the Southern Hemisphere yielding 95 per cent of Australia's pecans; tour bookings at visitor centre; 35 km E. *Cotton Gins:* inspections during harvest; Apr–July; details at visitor centre. *Birdwatching:* several excellent sites in the area; brochure from visitor centre.

TOWNS NEARBY: Warialda 72 km, Bingara 84 km, Wee Waa 93 km, Narrabri 96 km, Goondiwindi (Qld) 111 km

Moruya

Pop. 2433
Map ref. 519 F7 | 521 L7

ℹ️ Vulcan St; (02) 4474 1345 or 1800 802 528; www.eurobodalla.com.au

📻 104.3 Power FM, 105.1 FM ABC Radio National

This town on the Moruya River was once a gateway to local goldfields, but is now a riverside township. It is known for dairying and oyster farming, and also for its granite, which can be seen in some of the older buildings in town and was also used to build the pylons of the Sydney Harbour Bridge.

🏠 *Eurobodalla Historic Museum:* depicts gold discovery at Mogo and the district history of shipping, dairying and goldmining; town centre. *South Head:* beautiful views across the river mouth.

🌴 *Market:* Main St; Sat. *Jazz Festival:* Oct. *Rodeo:* New Year's Day.

🍴 *The River Moruya:* modern European, fantastic views; 16B Church St; (02) 4474 5505.

🛏️ *Riverbreeze Tourist Park:* 9 Princes Hwy; (02) 4474 2370. *BIG4 Broulee Beach Holiday Park:* 6 Lyttle St, Broulee; (02) 4471 6247. *East's Dolphin Beach Holiday Park:* South Head Rd, Moruya Heads; (02) 4474 2748. *Tuross Beach Holiday Park:* 83 Nelson Pde, Tuross Head; (02) 4473 8236. *Tuross Lakeside Tourist Park:* 211 Hector McWilliam Dr, Tuross Head; (02) 4473 8181.

⊗ **Deua National Park** A wilderness of rugged mountain ranges, plateaus, gentle and wild rivers and a magnificent limestone belt, the area is popular for canyoning and caving. The rivers are a base for most water activities, including swimming, fishing and canoeing. There are scenic walking and 4WD tracks and 4 main campsites to choose from. 20 km W.

Broulee: great surfing and swimming; 12 km NE. *Bodalla:* All Saints Church, built from local granite, is of historical significance; 24 km S. *Comans Mine:* visit the historic tramway and stamper battery used to crush ore and separate the gold; 40 km SW. *Nerrigundah:* former goldmining town with a monument to Miles O'Grady, who was killed here in a battle with the Clarke bushranging gang; 44 km SW.

TOWNS NEARBY: Batemans Bay 24 km, Narooma 35 km, Bermagui 56 km, Braidwood 58 km, Ulladulla 71 km

Moss Vale

Pop. 6725
Map ref. 517 B6 | 519 G3 | 523 I9

ℹ️ Southern Highlands Visitor Centre, 62–70 Main St, Mittagong; (02) 4871 2888 or 1300 657 559; www.southern-highlands.com.au

📻 102.9 FM 2ST, 1431 AM ABC Radio National

Moss Vale is the industrial and agricultural centre of Wingecarribee Shire and the Southern Highlands. Once it was home to the Dharawal people, but by the 1870s they had all been driven off or killed. The town stands on part of the 1000 acres (approximately 400 hectares) of land granted to explorer Charles Throsby by Governor Macquarie in 1819. For most of the last century Moss Vale was a railway town and is dominated by the architecture of the Victorian railway station.

🏠 *Leighton Gardens:* picturesque area popular for picnics; Main St. *Historical walk:* includes Aurora College (formerly

Dominican Convent) and Kalourgan, believed to have been a residence of Mary MacKillop; brochure from visitor centre.

🌴 *Southern Highlands Country Fair:* showgrounds; 4th Sun each month. *Autumn Gardens in the Southern Highlands:* throughout region; Apr. *Tulip Time Festival:* throughout region; Sept–Oct.

🍴 *Katers:* modern Australian; Peppers Manor House, Kater Rd, Sutton Forest; (02) 4860 3111.

🏨 *Heronswood House B&B:* 165 Argyle St; (02) 4869 1477. *Moss Vale Village Caravan Park:* 43–53 Willow Dr; (02) 4868 1099.

⊙ **Sutton Forest** Set among green hills, this tiny town has a shop called A Little Piece of Scotland for all things Scottish, and The Everything Store, c. 1859. Hillview House, just north, was the official residence of NSW governors 1882–1958. 6 km sw.

Throsby Park Historic Site: owned for 150 years by the Throsby family. Buildings that depict early settlement life include original stables, former barn, flour mill, Gundagai Cottage and Christ Church. Access is by tour only; bookings (02) 4887 7270; 1.5 km E. *Cecil Hoskins Nature Reserve:* tranquil wetland with over 90 bird species, one-third of which are waterfowl; 3 km NE.

TOWNS NEARBY: Berrima 8 km, Bowral 10 km, Bundanoon 13 km, Robertson 21 km, Berry 38 km

Mudgee

Pop. 8248
Map ref. 522 H2

ⓘ 84 Market St; (02) 6372 1020; www.visitmudgeeregion.com.au

📻 93.1 Real FM, 549 AM ABC Central West

Mudgee derives its name from the Wiradjuri word 'moothi', meaning 'nest in the hills'. The name is apt as the town is situated among green and blue hills in the Cudgegong River Valley. Mudgee is graced with wide streets and historic Victorian buildings and is the centre of the Mudgee Wine Region, one of the largest winegrowing regions in Australia. Local produce features heavily in town and includes fresh silver perch, yabbies, venison, lamb, asparagus, summer berries, peaches and hazelnuts.

🏛 *Colonial Inn Museum:* local history in photographs, documents, machinery, dolls and agricultural implements; check opening times (02) 6372 3365; Market St. *Honey Hive:* honey, jam and mustard tastings, and bees under glass; Church St. *Heart of Mudgee:* a gourmand's delight where you can enjoy the local produce, tastings, local art and craft; Court St. *Lawson Park:* home to possums, water rats and tortoises. Includes a playground, barbecues and duck pond; Short St. *Mandurah at the Railway:* local art and craft cooperative at the historic railway station; Cnr Inglis and Church sts. *Mudgee Brewing Company:* enjoy some pale ale at this home-grown brewery; Church St. *Roth's Wine Bar:* oldest wine bar in NSW with displays of wine history in the region and a wide selection of local wines; Market St. *Mudgee Observatory:* astronomical wonders of the NSW sky. Day and night sessions available; Old Grattai Rd. *Melrose Park Deer Farm:* deer roam in parkland setting; venison tastings and sales; Melrose Rd. *Town trail:* self-guide walk taking in National Trust buildings including St John's Church of England (1860) and the Regent Theatre; brochure available from visitor centre.

🌴 *Markets:* St John's Anglican Church, 1st Sat each month; Lawson Park, 2nd Sat each month; St Mary's Catholic Church,

3rd Sat each month; Railway Station, 4th Sat each month. *Small Farm Field Days:* July. *Mudgee Wine and Food Fair:* Aug. *Mudgee Wine Festival:* Sept. *Mudgee Cup:* Dec.

🍴 *Blue Wren Restaurant:* modern Australian, located at beautiful winery; 433 Cassilis Rd; (02) 6372 6205. *Deeb's Kitchen:* Lebanese; Cnr Buckeroo La and Cassilis Rd; (02) 6373 3133. *Eltons Brasserie:* modern Australian; 81 Market St; (02) 6372 0772.

🏨 *AJ's Mudgee Guesthouse:* 51 Henry Lawson Dr; (02) 6372 3222. *Bed & Breakfast Pottier's Mudgee:* 9 Mulgoa Way; (02) 6372 1861. *Evanslea:* 146 Market St; (02) 6372 4116. *Kurrara Guesthouse & Cottages:* Henry Lawson Dr; (02) 6373 3734. *Mudgee Riverside Caravan & Tourist Park:* 22 Short St; (02) 6372 2531. *Mudgee Tourist & Van Resort:* Lions Dr; (02) 6372 1090. *Mudgee Valley Tourist Park:* 2 Bell St; (02) 6372 1236. *Wombadah:* Tierney La (off Henry Lawson Dr); (02) 6373 3176. *Bushlands Tourist Park:* 1879 Windeyer Rd, Windeyer; (02) 6373 8252.

⊙ **Mudgee wine region** Just over the Great Dividing Range from the famous Hunter, but here the sun is brighter, the nights are colder, and there is less rainfall (what a difference a mountain range can make). These conditions are ideal for the region's specialty, cabernet sauvignon, with shiraz a close 2nd. Winemaking here began in 1858, kick-started by 3 German families. One of the original wineries continues today under the name Poet's Corner. The cellar door also represents Montrose, one of the largest wineries in the region and one of the 1st in Australia to plant Italian varieties such as sangiovese, barbera and nebbiolo. Huntington Estate makes splendid cabernet sauvignon and hosts the annual Huntington Estate Music Festival. Botobolar was one of the first organic vineyards in the country. Self-guide drives brochure from visitor centre.

Munghorn Gap Nature Reserve Over 160 bird species have been identified here, including the rare regent honeyeater. For bushwalkers, the Castle Rock walking trail is an 8 km journey with stunning views from sandstone outcrops. Camping, barbecue and picnic facilities are available; 34 km NE.

Mount Vincent Mead: one of the few places in the country producing mead (an alcoholic drink made from fermented honey and water). Tastings and sales available; 4 km sw. *Site of Old Bark School:* attended by Henry Lawson and made famous in several of his poems. Eurunderee Provisional School is nearby with historical displays of school life; 6 km N. *Fragrant Farm:* garden and craft shop with doll museum; 8 km sw. *Pick Your Own Farm:* variety of fruit and vegetables; open Oct–May; 12 km s. *Windermere Dam:* watersports, trout fishing and camping facilities; 24 km SE. *Hargraves:* old goldmining town where Kerr's Hundredweight was discovered in 1851, yielding 1272 oz of gold. Ask at general store for gold-panning tours; 39 km sw.

TOWNS NEARBY: Gulgong 27 km, Rylstone 42 km, Wellington 60 km, Orange 88 km, Merriwa 89 km

Mullumbimby

Pop. 3130
Map ref. 516 G4 | 525 O3 | 609 N12

ⓘ Byron Visitor Centre, 80 Jonson St, Byron Bay; (02) 6680 8558; www.tropicalnsw.com.au

📻 103.5 Radio 97 FM, 720 AM ABC North Coast

When Mullumbimby's economy, based on local agriculture, started to flag in the late 1960s, the town was saved by becoming

an alternative-lifestyle centre. Drawn by lush subtropical countryside and excellent weather conditions, people settled at the foot of Mount Chincogan. The town still has a delightful laid-back feel today with all the facilities of a mature tourist town.

Brunswick Valley Historical Museum The museum covers local history in detail, including timber-getters, dairy farmers, pioneers and local government. It is in a pleasant park on the banks of Saltwater Creek. Outdoor displays include horse-drawn agricultural equipment and a pioneer slab cottage. Opening times vary so check with museum; Stuart St; (02) 6685 1385.

Mullumbimby Art Gallery: changing exhibitions of paintings, sculptures and prints; Cnr Burringbar and Stuart sts. *Cedar House:* National Trust–classified building housing an antiques gallery; Dalley St. *Brunswick Valley Heritage Park:* over 200 rainforest plants, including palms, and a 2 km park and river walk; Tyagarah St.

Market: Stuart St; 3rd Sat each month. *Chincogan Fiesta:* community celebration with stalls, parade and mountain footrace; Sept.

Milk and Honey: Mediterranean/Italian; Shop 5, 59A Station St; (02) 6684 1422. *Poinciana:* funky 'global' cafe; 55 Station St; (02) 6684 4036.

Ferry Reserve Holiday Park: Riverside Cres, Brunswick Heads; (02) 6685 1872. *Massey Greene Holiday Park:* Tweed St, Brunswick Heads; (02) 6685 1329. *Terrace Reserve Holiday Park:* Fingal St, Brunswick Heads; (02) 6685 1233.

Brunswick Heads This town on the Brunswick River estuary is a charming mix of quiet holiday retreat and large commercial fishing town. Despite having some truly beautiful beaches, Brunswick Heads has managed to remain remarkably serene and unassuming. Enjoy the excellent seafood in town. Highlights during the year include a wood-chopping festival in Jan and the Kite and Bike Festival in Mar. 7 km w.

Crystal Castle: spectacular natural crystal display, jewellery and gifts; 7 km sw. *Tyagarah Airstrip:* skydiving and paragliding; Pacific Hwy; 13 km sw. *Wanganui Gorge:* scenic 4 km bushwalk through the gorge with rainforest trees, enormous strangler figs and a pretty swimming hole; 20 km w. *Crystal Creek Miniatures:* enjoy the amazing world of minature animals; 40 km nw.

TOWNS NEARBY: Byron Bay 15 km, Murwillumbah 27 km, Nimbin 27 km, Alstonville 33 km, Ballina 35 km

Mulwala
Pop. 1629
Map ref. 527 M12 | 542 H5 | 544 D1

Irvine Pde, Yarrawonga; (03) 5744 1989 or 1800 062 260; www.yarrawongamulwala.com.au

96.9 Sun FM, 675 ABC AM Riverina

Mulwala and Yarrawonga (in Victoria) are twin towns sitting astride the Murray River. Mulwala prides itself on being an 'inland aquatic paradise', with plenty of water-based activities for visitors to enjoy. It is surrounded by forests and vineyards.

Lake Mulwala This artificial lake was formed by the 1939 damming of the Murray River at Yarrawonga Weir and is now home to myriad birdlife. The eastern end has river red gums up to 600 years old. The lake is popular for yachting, sailboarding, canoeing, swimming and fishing (especially for Murray cod).

The Mulwala Water Ski Club is the largest in the world with 6000 members; it offers lessons and equipment hire for skiing, wakeboarding, and banana and tube rides. Day and evening cruises can be booked at the visitor centre.

Linley Park Animal Farm: working farm with horse and pony rides, and opportunity to handfeed native and exotic animals. Open weekends and school holidays; Corowa Rd. *Pioneer Museum:* historic farming exhibits, photographs and local artefacts; open Wed–Sun; Melbourne St. *Tunzafun Amusement Park:* minigolf, mini-train and dodgem cars; Melbourne St.

E.C. Griffiths Cup: powerboat racing; Apr.

La Porchetta: Italian; Mulwala Waterski Club, 158 Melbourne St; (03) 5744 1507. *The Border Bistro:* lively country bistro; Yarrawonga Mulwala Golf Club Resort, Gulai Rd; (03) 5744 1911.

Lakeside Holiday Park: 102 Corowa Rd; (03) 5743 2888. *Sun Country Holiday Village:* Cnr Tocumwal and Corowa rds; (03) 5743 1074.

Savenake Station Woolshed: 1930s-style woolshed in working order producing merino wool; open by appt; bookings (02) 6035 9415; 28 km N. *Everglade and swamp tours:* to waterbird rookeries and native animal habitats; bookings at visitor centre. *Local wineries:* several in area offering cellar-door tastings; brochure from visitor centre.

TOWNS NEARBY: Yarrawonga 3 km, Cobram 33 km, Corowa 35 km, Rutherglen 42 km, Tocumwal 44 km

Murrurundi
Pop. 804
Map ref. 524 H11

113 Mayne St; (02) 6546 6446.

96.6 FM ABC Upper Hunter, 1044 AM ABC Local

Murrurundi (pronounced 'Murrurund-eye') is a rural town set in the lush Pages River Valley at the foot of the Liverpool Ranges. It is a well-preserved, quiet town and any changes have been gradual, thanks to the lack of heavy industry in the region. The main street has been declared an urban conservation area.

Paradise Park This horseshoe-shaped park lies at the base of a steep hill. Behind the park take a walk through the 'Edge of the Needle', a small gap in the rocks that opens to a path leading to the top of the hill and fantastic views.

St Joseph's Catholic Church: 1000-piece Italian marble altar; Polding St. *Self-guide heritage walk:* National Trust–classified sites; brochure from visitor centre.

Murrurundi Markets: last Sun of the month; outside visitor centre. *Australia Day Carnival:* markets, parade and activities; Jan. *King of the Ranges Stockman's Challenge:* May. *Bushmans Rodeo and Campdraft Carnival:* Oct. *Murrurundi Stampede:* Dec.

Cafe Telegraph: licensed cafe; 155 Mayne St; (02) 6546 6733.

Quirindi Caravan Park: 24 Rose St, Quirindi; (02) 6746 2407.

Wallabadah Rock The 2nd largest monolith in the Southern Hemisphere, the rock is a large plug (959 m high) of an extinct volcano. There are spectacular flowering orchids in Oct. The rock is on private property, with a good view from the road.

Access is possible with the owner's permission (02) 6546 6881. 26 km NE.

Chilcotts Creek: diprotodon remains were found here (now in Australian Museum, Sydney); 15 km N. *Burning Mountain:* deep coal seam that has been smouldering for at least 5000 years; 20 km S.

TOWNS NEARBY: Scone 32 km, Nundle 43 km, Muswellbrook 56 km, Merriwa 62 km, Tamworth 75 km

Murwillumbah
Pop. 7954
Map ref. 516 G2 | 525 O2 | 600 F12 | 609 N11

ⓘ World Heritage Rainforest Centre, cnr Tweed Valley Way and Alma St; (02) 6672 1340 or 1800 674 414; www.tweedtourism.com.au

📻 101.3 Tweed Coast Country, 720 AM ABC Local

Murwillumbah is located on the banks of the Tweed River near the Queensland border. It is a centre for sugarcane, banana and cattle farms. In 1907 Murwillumbah was almost completely wiped out by fire. The town was rebuilt and many of those buildings can still be seen on the main street today.

🏛 **Tweed River Regional Art Gallery** This gallery displays a variety of paintings, portraits, glasswork, pottery, ceramics and photography. The two main themes are Australian portraits (nationwide subjects in all mediums), and depictions of the local area by regional artists. It is also home to the Doug Moran National Portrait Prize, the richest portrait prize in the world. Past winners are on display along with changing exhibitions. Mistral Rd; (02) 6670 2790.

Escape Gallery: sculpture, glass and fine arts showcasing local and regional artists, exhibitions changing constantly; Brisbane St. *World Heritage Rainforest Centre:* visitor centre with displays on local vegetation and wildlife, local Aboriginal and European history, and World Heritage regions; Cnr Pacific Hwy and Alma St. *Tweed River Regional Museum:* war memorabilia, genealogy documents, and domestic items and clothing through the ages; open Wed, Fri and 4th Sun each month, or by appt on (02) 6672 1865; Cnr Queensland Rd and Bent St.

🌿 **Market:** Knox Park, 1st and 3rd Sat each month; showground, 4th Sun each month. *Tweed Valley Banana Festival and Harvest Week:* Aug. *Speed on Tweed:* classic car rally; Sept.

🍴 **The Modern Grocer:** provedore; Shop 1, 3 Wollumbin St; (02) 6672 5007.

🛏 **BIG4 North Star Holiday Resort:** 1 Tweed Coast Rd, Hastings Point; (02) 6676 1234. *Craglands Cottage:* 19 Natural Bridge Rd, Natural Bridge, Qld; (07) 5533 6134. *Hastings Point Holiday Park:* Tweed Coast Rd, Hastings Point; (02) 6676 1049. *Mt Warning Holiday Park:* 153 Mt Warning Rd, Mount Warning; (02) 6679 5120. *Pottsville North Holiday Park:* 27 Tweed Coast Rd, Pottsville Beach; (02) 6676 1221. *Pottsville South Holiday Park:* Tweed Coast Rd, Pottsville Beach; (02) 6676 1050.

⊗ **Wollumbin National Park** World Heritage–listed Mt Warning is the rhyolite plug of a massive ancient volcano left behind after surrounding basalt eroded away. The local Bundjalung nation calls the mountain Wollumbin. It is a traditional place of cultural law, initiation and spiritual education, so visitors are requested not to climb the mountain. For those who ignore this advice, it is steep in places and the return trip takes 4–5 hours, so take plenty of water and make sure there is enough time to return before sunset. The National Parks & Wildlife Service conducts regular tours in the park; contact visitor centre for bookings. 17 km SW.

Lisnagar: historic homestead in lush surrounds; northern edge of town just past showgrounds; open Sun. *Stokers Siding:* historic village at the foot of the Burringbar Ranges, includes pottery gallery with resident potter; 8 km S. *Madura Tea Estates:* tea plantation with tastings and tours by appt; bookings (02) 6677 7215; 12 km NE. *Banana Cabana:* garden and shop with over 20 bush-tucker species and exotic fruits; Chillingham; 12 km NW. *Mooball:* small town with a cow theme that has painted almost anything that stands still in the style of a black and white cow, including buildings, cars and electricity poles; 19 km SE.

TOWNS NEARBY: Tweed Heads 22 km, Burleigh Heads (Qld) 27 km, Mullumbimby 27 km, Nimbin 34 km, Surfers Paradise (Qld) 36 km

Muswellbrook
Pop. 10 225
Map ref. 523 K2

ⓘ 87 Hill St; (02) 6541 4050; www.muswellbrook.nsw.gov.au

📻 98.1 Power FM, 1044 AM ABC Upper Hunter

Muswellbrook (the 'w' is silent) is in the Upper Hunter Valley and prides itself on being 'blue heeler country'. Here cattle farmers developed the blue heeler dog by crossing dingoes with Northumberland Blue Merles to produce a working dog that thrives in Australia's harsh conditions. The blue heeler is now in demand all over the world. There are several open-cut coal mines in the local area and the Upper Hunter Valley has many fine wineries.

🏛 **Muswellbrook Art Gallery:** in the restored town hall and School of the Arts building, its centrepiece is the Max Watters collection, which displays pieces from renowned Australian artists in paintings, drawings, ceramics and sculptures; Bridge St. *Upper Hunter Wine Centre:* displays on the local wine industry and information on Upper Hunter wineries; Loxton House, Bridge St. *Historical town walk:* 4.5 km walk featuring St Alban's Church, the police station and the town hall; map from visitor centre.

🌿 **Muswellbrook Cup:** Apr. *Spring Festival:* Aug–Nov.

🍴 **Hunter Belle Cheese:** cheese factory with licensed cafe; 75 Aberdeen St (New England Hwy); (02) 6541 5066. *Pukara Estate:* olive grove with tastings; 1440 Denman Rd; (02) 6547 1055.

🛏 **Pinaroo Leisure Park:** New England Hwy; (02) 6543 3905. *Denman Van Village:* Macauley St, Denman; (02) 6547 2590.

⊗ **Aberdeen** This small town is famous for its prize-winning beef cattle. There are markets at St Joseph's High School on the 3rd Sun each month and the famous Aberdeen Highland Games are held each July. The Scottish festivities including Scottish food and music, Highland dancing, caber tossing, a jousting tournament, a warriors competition and a kilted dash. 12 km N.

Bayswater Power Station: massive electricity source with coal-fired boilers and cooling towers; 16 km S. *Sandy Hollow:* picturesque village surrounded by horse studs and vineyards, with Bush Ride in Apr; 36 km SW. *Local wineries:* those open for cellar-door tastings include Arrowfield Wines (28 km S) and Rosemount Estate (35 km SW); brochure from visitor centre.

TOWNS NEARBY: Scone 24 km, Singleton 42 km, Merriwa 52 km, Murrurundi 56 km, Cessnock 77 km

Nambucca Heads

Pop. 5874
Map ref. 515 H2 | 525 M9

 Cnr Pacific Hwy and Riverside Dr; (02) 6568 6954 or 1800 646 587; www.nambuccatourism.com

105.9 2NVR FM, 684 AM ABC Mid North Coast

Located at the mouth of the Nambucca River, this is a beautiful coastal holiday town. The stunning long white beaches offer perfect conditions for fishing, swimming, boating and surfing.

V-Wall Breakwater Also known as the Graffiti Gallery, this rock wall gives visitors the opportunity to paint their own postcards on a rock. Mementos from all over the world are on display, including cartoons, paintings and poetry. Wellington Dr.

Headland Historical Museum: photographic history of the town and its residents, historic documents, antique farming implements and household tools; Headland Reserve. *Model Train Display:* miniature display models, including the Ghan and the Indian Pacific; Pelican Cres. *Stringer Art Gallery:* showcases local art and craft; Ridge St. *Valley Community Art:* cooperative of local artists and crafters with work for sale; Bowra St. *Mosaic sculpture:* the history of the town portrayed in a mosaic wrapped around a corner of the police station; Bowra St. *Gordon Park Rainforest:* unique walking trails through rainforest in the middle of urban development; between town centre and Inner Harbour. *Foreshore Walk:* 5 km pathway from Pacific Hwy to V-Wall with storyboards on shipbuilding yards and mills.

Market: Nambucca Plaza; 2nd Sun each month. *Country Music Jamboree:* Easter. *Breakfast by the River:* Apr. *VW Spectacular:* odd-numbered years, July–Aug. *Show 'n' Shine Hot Rod Exhibition:* Oct. *Hinterland Spring Festival:* Oct.

Matilda's: seafood and steak; 6 Wellington Dr; (02) 6568 6024.

BIG4 Nambucca Beach Holiday Park: 26 Swimming Creek Rd; (02) 6568 6120. *Foreshore Caravan Park:* 25 Riverside Dr; (02) 6568 6014. *Nambucca Headland Holiday Park:* 50 Liston St; (02) 6568 6547. *Pelican Park:* 5982 Pacific Hwy; (02) 6568 6505. *White Albatross Holiday Park:* 52 Wellington Dr; (02) 6568 6468.

Valla Beach Apart from secluded beaches and rainforest surrounds, Valla Beach is a hive of activity. Attractions include an art and craft gallery, the Valla Smokehouse (specialising in smoked products), the Australiana Workshop and the Gallery of Hidden Treasures. The Valla Beach Fair is held each Jan; 10 km N.

Swiss Toymaker: visitors can view wooden toys being crafted; closed Sun; 5 km N.

TOWNS NEARBY: Macksville 11 km, Urunga 16 km, Bellingen 24 km, Coffs Harbour 40 km, Dorrigo 44 km

Narooma

Pop. 3100
Map ref. 519 F8 | 521 L10

 Ken Rose Park, Princes Hwy; (02) 4476 2881 or 1800 240 003; www.eurobodalla.com.au

104.3 Power FM, 810 AM ABC Local

Narooma is a tranquil resort and fishing town at the mouth of Wagonga Inlet, well known for its natural beauty. The stunning beaches and waterways continue to draw people back to enjoy the excellent boating, aquatic sports and big-game fishing. Excellent fresh local seafood is a specialty in many of the restaurants.

Wagonga Princess This environmentally friendly, electronically powered boat is a converted huon pine ferry offering scenic cruises most days, taking in mangroves, forests and birdlife. The tour includes Devonshire tea. Commentary and tales (both tall and true) of local history, flora and fauna are provided by a third-generation local. Bookings (02) 4476 2665.

Walking tracks: several walking tracks incorporate places such as the Mill Bay Boardwalk, Australia Rock and lookout and numerous foreshore paths; maps from visitor centre. *Whale-watching cruises:* humpback and killer whales can be seen migrating, often with calves, Sept–Nov; bookings at visitor centre. *Scuba-diving cruises:* to shipwrecks; bookings at visitor centre.

Narooma Oyster Festival: May. *Great Southern Blues and Rockabilly Festival:* Oct.

Quarterdeck Marina & Cafe: retro cafe; Riverside Dr; (02) 4476 2723. *The Whale Restaurant:* modern Australian; Whale Motor Inn, 104 Wagonga St (Princes Hwy); (02) 4476 2411. *Anton's at Kianga:* seaside cafe; 65 Dalmeny Dr, Kianga; (02) 4476 1802.

Anchors Aweigh Bed & Breakfast: 5 Tilba St; (02) 4476 4000. *BIG4 Narooma Easts Holiday Park:* 41 Princes Hwy; (02) 4476 2046. *Island View Beach Resort:* Princes Hwy; (02) 4476 2600. *Surfbeach Holiday Park – Narooma:* 5 Ballingalla St; (02) 4476 2275. *Beachcomber Holiday Park:* Blackfellow Point Rd, Potato Point; (02) 4473 5312.

Montague Island Nature Reserve This isolated island, with access only by guided tours (bookings at visitor centre), is a major shearwater breeding site and home to little penguins and Australian and New Zealand fur seals. Whales can be viewed off the coast Sept–Nov. The tour includes historic buildings such as the Montague Lighthouse, which was first lit in 1881 but is now fully automated. Recently, stays in the lighthouse keeper's quarters were introduced. Guides also explain the history of the island (known as Barunguba) as a fertile hunting ground for the Walbanga and Djiringanj tribes. 9 km SE.

Central Tilba Classified as an 'unusual mountain village' by the National Trust, Central Tilba was founded in 1895 and has many quality arts and craft shops. It has several old buildings worth a visit, including the ABC Cheese Factory in original 19th-century condition. The Tilba Festival is held here each Easter. 17 km SW. Tilba Tilba, a further 2 km S, features Foxglove Spires, a historic cottage surrounded by a beautiful 3.5 ha garden.

Mystery Bay: popular spot with strange-looking stones, snorkelling and access to Eurobodalla National Park; 17 km S.

TOWNS NEARBY: Bermagui 23 km, Moruya 35 km, Bega 57 km, Batemans Bay 57 km, Tathra 58 km

Narrabri

Pop. 6104
Map ref. 524 F7

 Newell Hwy; (02) 6799 6760 or 1800 659 931; www.visitnarrabri.com

91.3 MAX FM, 648 ABC AM New England North West

The fledgling town of Narrabri was devastated by a flood in 1864, but was rebuilt and grew in regional importance from 1865 when the newly constructed courthouse took over local services from Wee Waa. Cotton was introduced to the area in 1962 and the region now enjoys one of Australia's largest yields. This success has brought prosperity to Narrabri and surrounding towns. The town is located between the Nandewar Range and Pilliga Scrub country in the Namoi River Valley.

Narrabri Old Gaol and Museum: historic museum with local artefacts. Night tours of the gaol on offer; Barwan St. **Riverside park:** pleasant surroundings next to the Namoi River with barbecue and picnic facilities; Tibbereena St. **Self-guide town walk:** historic buildings including the original courthouse (1865) and police residence (1879); leaflet from visitor centre.

Rodeo: Mar. **Nosh on the Namoi:** food and wine festival; Mar.

BigSky Caravan Park: 11 Tibbereena St; (02) 6792 1294. **Highway Tourist Village:** 86 Cooma Rd; (02) 6792 1438.

Paul Wild Observatory Here you'll find an impressive line of 22 m diameter antennas all facing the sky. They are connected on a rail track and are moved around to get full coverage. A 6th antenna lies 3 km away, and all 6 are sometimes connected with telescopes at Coonabarabran and Parkes. The visitor centre features a video, displays and an opportunity to view the telescope; open Mon–Fri (weekends during school holidays); 25 km w.

Yarrie Lake: birdwatching, waterskiing and windsurfing; 32 km w. **Scenic drive:** includes Mt Kaputar National Park (*see Barraba*) and cotton fields; leaflet from visitor centre.

TOWNS NEARBY: Wee Waa 35 km, Barraba 80 km, Gunnedah 86 km, Bingara 91 km, Moree 96 km

Narrandera

Pop. 3960
Map ref. 522 A8 | 527 N8

ⓘ Narrandera Park, Newell Hwy; (02) 6959 1766 or 1800 672 392; www.narrandera.com.au

📻 92.3 FM, 549 AM ABC Central West

This historic town on the Murrumbidgee River in the Riverina district is an urban conservation area with several National Trust–classified buildings. It has been home to two Australian writers: local magistrate Thomas Alexander Browne, who used the nom de plume Rolf Boldrewood to write early Australian novels such as *Robbery Under Arms* and father Patrick Hartigan, parish priest of St Mel's Catholic Church, who was better known as poet John O'Brien.

 Parkside Cottage Museum Displays include the scarlet Macarthur Opera Cloak, made from the first bale of merino wool the Macarthur family sent to England in 1816. Also on display are a snow shoe and ski from Scott's Antarctic expedition, a valuable collection of shells from around the world and a set of silver ingots commemorating 1000 years of the British monarchy. Open 2–5pm daily; Newell Hwy.

Lake Talbot: boating, waterskiing, fishing and canoeing. Also scenic walking trails around the lake; Lake Dr. **Lake Talbot Holiday Complex:** water slides, swimming and barbecue facilities. Aquatic facilities open Oct–Mar; Lake Dr. **NSW Forestry Tree Nursery:** seedlings of a huge range of native trees for sale; open Mon–Fri; Broad St. **Narrandera Park and Tiger Moth Memorial:** beautiful park that houses the restored DN82 Tiger Moth commemorating the WW II pilots who trained in the district; Cadell St. **Visitor Centre:** features a 5.8 m playable guitar; Narrandera Park. **Lavender Farm:** tours and product

sales; Bells Rd. **Two-foot town heritage tour:** sights include the Royal Mail Hotel (1868) and the former police station (c. 1870); brochure from visitor centre. **Antique Corner and Objects d'Art:** beautifully restored historic home which now houses fine antiques; Larmer St. **Bundidgerry Walking Track:** track passes through the koala regeneration reserve; best viewing time is at dawn; brochure from visitor centre. **Blue Arrow scenic drive:** historic sites, cemetery and lake; brochure from visitor centre.

Rodeo: Jan. **John O'Brien Bush Festival:** Mar. **Hot Rod Rally:** Easter. **National Cavy Show:** guinea pig show; Aug. **National Model Aeroplane Championships:** Apr. **Camellia Show:** Aug. **Narrandera Cup:** horse racing; Aug.

Narrandera Bakery: cafe and fantastic bakery; 108 East St; (02) 6959 3677.

The Doulton Luxury B&B: 53 Douglas St; 0427 533 682. **Lake Talbot Tourist Park:** Gordon St; (02) 6959 1302. **Lockhart Caravan Park:** 162 Green St, Lockhart; 0458 205 303. **Narrandera Caravan Park:** Cnr Newell and Sturt hwys, Gillenbah; (02) 6959 2955. **The Bank & Stable Bed & Breakfast:** Cnr Green and Matthews sts, Lockhart; (02) 6920 5443.

John Lake Centre: fisheries visitor centre with live exhibits, audiovisual presentations and guided tours; open Mon–Fri; 6 km SE. **Craigtop Deer Farm:** deer raised for venison and velvet with presentation on deer-farming and a tour of the deer-handling facility; 8 km NW. **Robertsons Gladioli Farm:** produces flowers for Sydney and regional markets; 8 km W. **Berembed Weir:** picnicking, fishing and boating; 40 km SE.

TOWNS NEARBY: Leeton 26 km, Griffith 69 km, Wagga Wagga 84 km, Temora 96 km, Jerilderie 101 km

Nelson Bay

Pop. 8153
Map ref. 514 G8 | 515 C12 | 523 N4

ⓘ Port Stephens Visitor Information Centre, Victoria Pde; (02) 4980 6900 or 1800 808 900; www.portstephens.org.au

📻 1233 AM ABC Newcastle

Nelson Bay is a coastal tourist centre that has remained small enough to maintain its charm. With outstanding white beaches and gentle waters, it is a superb spot for all aquatic activities and enjoys close proximity to Tomaree National Park. The attractive bay is the main anchorage of Port Stephens.

 Inner Lighthouse This 1872 lighthouse, originally lit with 4 kerosene lamps, has been restored by the National Trust and is now completely automated. The adjacent museum features a display of the area's early history, souvenirs and a teahouse. Views of Nelson Bay are stunning. Nelson Head.

Port Stephens This is a haven of calm blue waters and sandy beaches, offering excellent boating, fishing and swimming. It is also something of a wildlife haven: over 100 bottlenose dolphins are permanent residents here; migrating whales can be seen in season on a boat cruise; and koalas can be spotted at Tilligerry Habitat.

Community Art Centre: oil and watercolour paintings, pottery, china and quilting; Shoal Bay Rd. **Self-guide heritage walk:** from Dutchmans Bay to Little Beach; brochure from visitor centre. **Cruises:** dolphin-watching (all year-round) and whale-watching (May–July and Sept–Nov); on the harbour, Myall River and to Broughton Island. Also dive charters; bookings at visitor centre. **4WD tours:** along coastal dunes; bookings at visitor centre.

Craft markets: Neil Carroll Park, Shoal Bay Rd, 1st and 3rd Sun each month; Lutheran Church grounds, Anna Bay, 1st Sat each month. *Tomaree Markets:* Tomaree Sports Complex, Nelson Bay Rd, Salamander Bay; 2nd and 4th Sun each month. *Medowie market:* Bull 'n' Bush Hotel; 2nd Sat each month. *Jazz Wine and Food Festival:* Sept. *Port Stephens Whale Festival:* Sept–Oct. *Tastes of the Bay Food, Wine and Jazz Festival:* Nov.

Fishermen's Wharf Seafoods: fish and chips; 1 Teramby Rd; (02) 4984 3330. *Ritual Organics:* modern Australian; Shops 1 and 2, Austral St Shopping Village, Austral St; (02) 4981 5514. *Zest Restaurant:* modern Australian; 16 Stockton St; (02) 4984 2211.

Halifax Holiday Park: 5 Beach Rd; 1800 600 201. *Nelson Bay Bed & Breakfast:* 81 Stockton St; (02) 4984 3655. *Nelson Bay Getaway:* 31 Thurlow Ave; (02) 4984 4949. *The Anchor Light:* 1 Corlette Point Rd, Corlette; (02) 4984 3577. *Anne's Waterfront Haven Bed & Breakfast:* 44A Danalene Pde, Corlette; (02) 4984 1178. *Bays Holiday Park:* 23 Port Stephens Dr, Anna Bay; (02) 4982 1438. *BIG4 Soldiers Point Holiday Park:* 122 Soldiers Point Rd, Soldiers Point; (02) 4982 7300. *Birubi Beach Holiday Park:* 37 James Paterson St, Anna Bay; (02) 4982 1263. *Fingal Bay Holiday Park:* 52 Marine Dr, Fingal Bay; 1800 600 203. *The Mitchells Waterfront Bed & Breakfast:* 6 Mitchell St, Soldiers Point; (02) 4982 0402. *Mylinfield Bed & Breakfast:* Lot 1 McKinnon Rd, Boat Harbour; (02) 6625 1835. *Salamander Beach Accommodation:* 196 Soldiers Point Rd, Salamander Bay; (02) 4984 7270. *Sandys At The Point:* 34 Soldiers Point Rd, Soldiers Point; (02) 4984 7247. *Shoal Bay Holiday Park:* Shoal Bay Rd, Shoal Bay; 1800 600 200. *Soldiers Point Holiday Park:* Ridgeway Ave, Soldiers Point; 1800 600 204.

Tomaree National Park This park consists of bushland, sand dunes, heathland, native forest and over 20 km of rocky coastline and beaches. There is a signposted walk around the headland and another up to Fort Tomaree Lookout for breathtaking 360-degree views. Yacaaba Lookout across the bay (70 km by road) also offers great views. The park is a popular spot for bushwalking, swimming, surfing, snorkelling, fishing and picnicking. The park stretches from Shoal Bay (3 km NE) to Anna Bay (10 km SW).

Little Beach: white beach with native flora reserve behind; 1 km E. *Gan Gan Lookout:* spectacular views south to Newcastle and north to Myall Lakes; Nelson Bay Rd; 2 km S. *Shoal Bay:* popular and protected bay with spa resort; 3 km NE. *Shell Museum:* diverse display of shells, some rare; Sandy Point Rd; 3 km SW. *Toboggan Hill Park:* toboggan runs, minigolf and indoor wall-climbing; 5 km SW. *Oakvale Farm and Fauna World:* 150 species of native and farm animals, with visitor activities and feeding shows; 16 km SW. *Tomago House:* 1843 sandstone villa with family chapel and 19th-century gardens; open 11am–3pm Sun; Tomago Rd; 30 km SW. *Stockton Sand Dunes:* this 32 km dune area, the largest moving coastal land mass in the Southern Hemisphere, is popular for sand-boarding and whale-watching. Access is from Anna Bay or Williamtown by 4WD or safari (bookings at visitor centre); 38 km SW. *Port Stephens wineries:* several in area, with Stephens Winery featuring Jazz at the Winery in Mar; brochure from visitor centre.

TOWNS NEARBY: Bulahdelah 35 km, Raymond Terrace 37 km, Stroud 39 km, Newcastle 41 km, Maitland 55 km

 Newcastle   *see inset box on next page*

 Nimbin   Pop. 351
Map ref. 516 F4 | 525 O3 | 609 N12

ℹ 3/46 Cullen St; (02) 6689 1388; www.visitnimbin.com.au

📻 102.3 NIM FM, 738 AM ABC Local

Situated in a beautiful valley, Nimbin is a colourful and interesting town of artists and others trying to live an alternative lifestyle to the mainstream. It is the centre of Australian efforts to make cannabis legal and some visitors may therefore find the culture unsettling. Originally a place of healing and initiation for the Bundjalung people, the Nimbin area was cleared and used for dairy and banana farming. Nimbin hit a depression in the late 1960s when the dairy industry collapsed. It took the 1973 Aquarius Festival to establish Nimbin as the alternative-culture capital of Australia.

Nimbin Museum: dedicated to hippie culture and Aboriginal heritage; Cullen St; (02) 6689 1123. **Nimbin Candle Factory:** produces stunning, environmentally friendly candles sold throughout Australia and the world; Butter Factory, Cullen St; (02) 6686 6433. **Town hall:** features mural of Aboriginal art; Cullen St. **Rainbow Power Company:** take a tour of this alternative power supplier, now exporting power products such as solar water pumps and hydro-generators to over 20 countries; Alternative Way; (02) 6689 1430. **Local art, craft and psychedelia:** brochure from visitor centre.

Market: local craft; Nimbin Community Centre, Cullen St; 3rd and 5th Sun each month. **Rainbow Lane Markets:** next to museum, Sat mornings. **Artist Gallery Autumn Extravaganza:** Mar/Apr. **Mardi Grass Festival:** organised by the Nimbin HEMP (Help End Marijuana Prohibition) Embassy; May.

Rainbow Cafe: infamous cafe with gorgeous courtyard and colourful paintings; 64A Cullen St; (02) 6689 1997.

Nimbin Caravan & Tourist Park: 29 Sibley St; (02) 6689 1402.

Nightcap National Park This lush World Heritage–listed forest offers signposted bushwalks from easy to very difficult, requiring a map and compass. The dramatic Protestors Falls is the site of the 1979 anti-logging protest that led to the area being gazetted as a national park. Rocky Creek Dam has a platypus-viewing platform and views of Mt Warning. 5 km NE.

Nimbin Rocks: spectacular remnants of an ancient volcano overlooking the town. This is a sacred initiation site for the Bundjalung people, so viewing is from the road only; Lismore Rd; 3 km S. *The Channon:* town featuring an alternative-craft market, 2nd Sun each month; Opera at the Channon in Aug; and Music Bowl Live Band Concert in Nov. 15 km SE.

TOWNS NEARBY: Kyogle 22 km, Lismore 25 km, Mullumbimby 27 km, Murwillumbah 34 km, Casino 34 km

Nowra   Pop. 30 953
Map ref. 517 D9 | 519 G4 | 521 O1 | 523 I10

ℹ Shoalhaven Visitors Centre, cnr Princes Hwy and Pleasant Way, Nowra; (02) 4421 0778 or 1300 662 808; www.shoalhaven.nsw.gov.au

📻 94.9 Power FM, 104.5 Triple U FM, 603 AM ABC Radio National

continued on p. 79

 RADIO STATIONS   IN TOWN   WHAT'S ON   WHERE TO EAT   WHERE TO STAY   NEARBY

NEWCASTLE

Pop. 493 465

Map ref. 509 H3 | 514 D9 | 515 A12 | 523 M4

 3 Honeysuckle Dr; 1800 654 558; www.visitnewcastle.com.au

 105.3 New FM, 1233 AM ABC Local

Newcastle began as a penal settlement and coalmining town, with a shipment of coal to Bengal in 1799 noted as Australia's first export. It soon became an industrial city, known for its steel works and port. As the steel industry is phased out, Newcastle is developing a reputation for being an elegant and cosmopolitan seaside city. The spectacular harbour is the largest export harbour in the Commonwealth and the town is bordered by some of the world's finest surfing beaches.

Fort Scratchley This fascinating fort was built in 1882 amid fears of Russian attack. Soldiers' barracks and officers' residences were built in 1886. It is one of the few gun installations to have fired on the Japanese in WW II and it remains in excellent condition. Explore networks of tunnels, gun emplacements and fascinating military and maritime museums, all perched high above Newcastle Harbour. Nobbys Rd; (02) 4929 3066; open Wed–Mon, 10am–4pm.

Queens Wharf: centre point of foreshore redevelopment with restaurants, boutique brewery and observation tower linked by a walkway to Hunter Street Mall. *Newcastle Regional Art Gallery:* broad collection of Australian art including works by Arthur Streeton, Brett Whiteley, William Dobell, Sidney Nolan and Russell Drysdale, as well as changing exhibitions; closed Mon; Laman St; (02) 4974 5100. *Darby Street:* Newcastle's bohemian enclave has vibrant restaurants and cafes, giftshops, galleries and young designer boutiques. *King Edward Park:* waterfront recreation reserve since 1863 featuring sunken gardens, ocean views, band rotunda (1898), Soldiers Baths (public pool) and Bogey Hole, a hole cut in rocks by convicts; Shortland Espl. *Merewether Baths:* largest ocean baths in the Southern Hemisphere; Scenic Dr. *Blackbutt Reserve:* 182 ha of bushland with duck ponds, native animal enclosures, walking trails, and picnic and barbecue facilities; New Lambton, off Carnley Ave; (02) 4904 3344. *Hunter Wetlands Centre:* 45 ha wetlands reserve 10 min from the city centre, with bike trails, playground, treasure hunt, guided eco-tours, canoe hire, picnic areas and cafe; Sandgate Rd, Shortland; (02) 4951 6466. *Self-guide walks:* include Town Walk and Shipwreck Walk; maps from visitor centre. *Cruises:* on the river and harbour; bookings at visitor centre.

Surfest: Mar. *Newcastle Show:* Mar. *Offshore Superboat Championships:* Apr.

Bacchus: modern European; 141 King St; (02) 4927 1332. *Queens Wharf Brewery:* seafood; 150 Wharf Rd; (02) 4929 6333. *Restaurant Deux:* modern European; 8 Bolton St; (02) 4929 1233. *Silo Restaurant & Lounge:* modern Australian, harbourside; shop 18, 1 Honeysuckle Dr, The Boardwalk; (02) 4926 2828.

Bell Chapel B & B: 34 Excelsior Pde, Carey Bay; (02) 4959 8811. *Belmont Bayview Park:* 1 Gerald St, Belmont; (02) 4945 3653. *Belmont Pines Lakeside Holiday Park:* 24 Paley Cres, Belmont; (02) 4945 4750. *Blacksmiths Beachside Holiday Park:* 20 Gommera St, Blacksmiths; (02) 4971 2858. *Brezza Bella Bed & Breakfast:* 1 Rowan Cres, Merewether; (02) 4963 3812. *Chaucer Palms Boutique Bed & Breakfast:* 59 James St, Hamilton; (02) 4961 0111. *Maison De May Bed & Breakfast:* 41 Young St, Carrington; 0417 227 177. *Newcastle's Stockton Beach Tourist Park:* 3 Pitt St, Stockton; (02) 4928 1393. *Paradise Palms Carey Bay:* 42 Ambrose St, Carey Bay; (02) 4959 1271. *Redhead Beach Holiday Park:* 1A Kalaroo Rd, Redhead; (02) 4944 8944. *Spinnakers Leisure Park:* 687 Pacific Hwy, Belmont; (02) 4945 3405. *Swansea Gardens Lakeside Holiday Park:* 15 Wallarah St, Swansea; (02) 4971 2869. *Travellers Home B&B:* 51 Maud St, Cardiff South; (02) 4956 6513. *Wangi Point Lakeside Holiday Park:* Watkins Rd, Wangi Wangi; (02) 4975 1889.

Lake Macquarie The enormous saltwater lake provides a huge aquatic playground with secluded bays and coves, sandy beaches and well-maintained parks lining its foreshore. Lake cruises leave from Toronto Wharf and Belmont Public Wharf. Dobell House, on the shore at Wangi Wangi, was the home of artist Sir William Dobell and has a collection of his work and memorabilia. Open to the public Sat and Sun 1pm-4pm and public holidays; (02) 4975 4115. The Lake Macquarie Heritage Afloat Festival is held here every Apr. 20 km s.

Munmorah State Recreation Area: Munmorah State Conservation Area: coastal wilderness with great walking, picnicking, camping, swimming, surfing and fishing; 15 km w; (02) 4972 9000. *Eraring Power Station:* regular tours include access to cooling towers and a simulator used to train operators; bookings essential, phone (02) 4973 0700; 22 km s. *Swansea:* modern resort town enjoying both lake and ocean exposure. It is popular with anglers and has excellent surf beaches; 24 km s. *Surf beaches:* many with world-class breaks, including Newcastle, Merewether and Nobbys; details from visitor centre.

TOWNS NEARBY: Raymond Terrace 19 km, Maitland 30 km, Nelson Bay 41 km, Cessnock 41 km, Wyong 52 km

[EARLY SPRING EVENING AT NEWCASTLE MARINA]

Nowra is the principal town in the Shoalhaven district and is popular with tourists for its attractive river and water activities. The racehorse Archer began his famous 550-mile (880-kilometre) walk from Terara, on the outskirts of Nowra, to compete in the Melbourne Cup. He was led and ridden by his jockey, Dave Power. The two went on to be the first winners of the Melbourne Cup in 1861 and returned for a second win in 1862.

 Meroogal Said to be the most intact 19th-century home in NSW, this 1885 property was passed down through 4 generations of women. Furniture, household objects, diaries, letters, scrapbooks, photographs and even clothes have been saved so visitors can see relics from each generation of its occupation. Open Sat afternoon and Sun; Cnr Worrigee and West sts; (02) 4421 8150.

Shoalhaven Historical Museum: old police station exhibiting the history of the town in records, photographs, household items and tools; Cnr Plunkett and Kinghorne sts; (02) 4421 8150. *Shoalhaven River:* fishing, waterskiing, canoeing and sailing. *Shoalhaven River Cruises:* departing from Nowra Wharf, Riverview Rd; bookings and times 0429 981 007. *Hanging Rock:* 46 m above the river with scenic views; off Junction St. *Nowra Animal Park:* native animals, reptiles and birds plus pony rides and opportunities to pat a koala; Rockhill Rd. *Scenic walks:* include Bens Walk along the river and Bomaderry Creek Walk from Bomaderry; leaflets from visitor centre.

 Market: Nowra Greyhound Track; 4th Sun each month.

 Boatshed by the Bridge: modern Australian, beautiful setting; 10 Wharf Rd; (02) 4423 4936.

 Shoalhaven Caravan Village: 17 Terara Rd; (02) 4423 0770. *Barefoot Springs:* 155 Carrington Rd, Beaumont; (02) 4446 0509. *Coral Tree Lodge:* 142 Greens Rd, Greenwell Point; (02) 4447 1358. *Crookhaven Heads Tourist Park:* Prince Edward Ave, Culburra Beach; 1300 733 026. *Crystal Creek Meadows Luxury Cottages & Spa Retreat:* 1655 Kangaroo Valley Rd, Kangaroo Valley; (02) 4465 1406. *Currarong Beachside Tourist Park:* Nowra Rd, Currarong; 1300 555 515. *Hampden Cottage:* 2031 Mossvale Rd, Kangaroo Valley; (02) 4465 1502. *Kangaroo Valley Glenmack Caravan Park:* 215 Moss Vale Rd, Kangaroo Valley; (02) 4465 1372. *Kangaroo Valley Tourist Park:* Moss Vale Rd, Kangaroo Valley; 1300 559 977. *Myola Tourist Resort Caravan Park:* Myola Rd, Myola; (02) 4446 5534. *Treehaven Tourist Park:* 278 Princes Hwy, Bomaderry; (02) 4421 3494.

 Kangaroo Valley This town of historic buildings has the National Trust–classified Friendly Inn, a Pioneer Settlement Reserve (a reconstruction of an 1880s dairy farm) and the Hampden Bridge, built in 1898 and is the oldest suspension bridge in Australia. The scenic route leading from the highlands to the coast (from Moss Vale to Nowra) takes in the 80 m high Fitzroy Falls, crosses the suspension bridge, and passes through the historic township. Kangaroo Valley Fruit World is a working fruit farm open to visitors. Canoeing and kayaking safaris to Kangaroo River and Shoalhaven Gorge can be booked at the visitor centre. There is also beautiful rural scenery along Nowra Rd. 23 km NW.

Fleet Air Arm Museum Australia's largest aviation museum with displays and planes over 6000 sq m. The Wings Over Water exhibition tells the story of Australian naval aviation and the Royal Australian Navy's Fleet Air Arm; (02) 4424 1999; 8 km sw.

Shoalhaven Coast wine region The main cluster of wineries is around Nowra, and most rely on the tourist trade for sales. Yet, there are a few notable labels specialising in chardonnay. Coolangatta Estate employs Tyrrell's from the Hunter Valley to make its wines. Enjoy the semillon as well as the excellent chardonnay. At Cambewarra Estate, try the chardonnay and verdelho, and at Kladis Estate sample award-winning cabernet sauvignon.

Marayong Park Emu Farm: group tours include the emu incubation room, brooder area, chick-rearing shed and breeding pen. Chicks hatch Aug–Oct; bookings required (02) 4447 8505; 11 km s. *Cambewarra Lookout:* spectacular views of the Shoalhaven River and Kangaroo Valley; 12 km NW. *Greenwell Point:* fresh fish and oyster sales; 14 km E. *Bundanon:* National Estate–listed homestead donated to the nation by artist Arthur Boyd and his wife Yvonne. The Bundanon collection and Boyd's studio are open Sun; (02) 4423 5999; 21 km w. *Culburra:* nearby Lake Wollumboola and coastal beaches are good for surfing, swimming, prawning and fishing. Culburra also holds the Open Fishing Carnival each Jan; 21 km SE. *Morton National Park:* the Nowra section features the Tallowa Dam water-catchment area, a popular spot for picnics; via Kangaroo Valley; 38 km NW. *For the Ulladulla section of the park see Ulladulla. Beaches:* many beautiful beaches in the vicinity for swimming and surfing; maps at visitor centre.

TOWNS NEARBY: Berry 15 km, Huskisson 19 km, Jervis Bay 29 km, Jamberoo 31 km, Robertson 33 km

Nundle

Pop. 290
Map ref. 525 I10

 Fossickers Tourist Park, Jenkins St; (02) 6769 3355.

 92.9 2TTT FM, 648 AM ABC New England North West

A thriving gold town in the 1850s, Nundle drew prospectors from California, Jamaica, China and Europe. Today the town is a quiet place nestled between the Great Dividing Range and the Peel River, but traces of gold can still be found and it is known as 'the town in the hills of gold'. The Peel River is well known for its fishing, with yellow-belly, trout and catfish being common catches.

 Woollen Mill: Australia's famous wool mill offers a fascinating insight into one of the country's largest industries. View the inner workings of the mill from the observation deck or take the factory tour. Retail store also on site; Oakenville St. *Courthouse Museum:* built in 1880, now housing a history of Nundle and the gold-rush era; Jenkins St. *Peel Inn:* 1860s pub with meals and accommodation; Jenkins St. *Mount Misery Gold Mine:* walk back in time through a re-created goldmine evoking life on the Nundle goldfields 150 years ago; Gill St.

 Go for Gold Chinese Festival: Easter. *Nundle Dog Race:* May.

 Birches B&B at Nundle: 71 Gill St; (02) 6769 3227. *Fossickers Tourist Park Nundle:* Jenkins St; (02) 6769 3355.

 Hanging Rock The area is popular for mineral fossicking, with good samples of scheelite and an excellent site for gold panning on the Peel River. Sheba Dams Reserve is home to numerous birds and animals. Activities include picnicking, bushwalking, camping and fishing, with regular stockings of trout and salmon. 11 km w.

Chaffey Reservoir: enjoy good swimming, fishing, sailing and picnicking. Dulegal Arboretum, an attractive garden of native trees and shrubs, is on the foreshore; 11 km N. *Fossicker's Way tour:* through scenic New England countryside; brochure from visitor centre.

TOWNS NEARBY: Murrurundi 43 km, Tamworth 46 km, Scone 69 km, Walcha 69 km, Manilla 89 km

Nyngan

Pop. 1975
Map ref. 529 O10

i Nyngan Leisure and Van Park, 12 Old Warren Rd; (02) 6832 2366; www.nyngan.com

95.1 FM ABC Local, 96.7 Rebel FM, 100.7 FM Outback Radio

Nyngan is a pleasant country town on the Bogan River, on the edge of the outback. It was largely unknown to the rest of the country until 1990, when the worst floods of the century struck here, doing damage worth $50 million. A helicopter was called in to airlift 2000 people – almost the whole town – to safety. Today the town is at the centre of a sheep, wheat and wool district.

Nyngan Museum: local memorabilia, photographs, an audio room with local stories, an 1800s kitchen and remnants from the 1990 flood; at railway station, Railway Sq. *Mid-state Shearing Shed:* informative displays of the continuing importance of shearing to the region, with work of local artists in murals; Mitchell Hwy. *Historical town drive and Levee Tour:* includes historic buildings in Cobar and Pangee sts, the Bicentennial Mural Wall and the heritage-listed railway overbridge with a lookout over town. The levee was built after the 1990 floods; brochure from visitor centre.

ANZAC Day Race Meeting: horserace; Apr. *Nyngan Show:* highlights the produce of the area; May.

Beancounters House: 103 Pangee St; (02) 6832 1610. *Nyngan Leisure and Van Park:* 12 Old Warren Rd; (02) 6832 2366. *Nyngan Riverside Caravan Park:* Cnr Barrier and Mitchell hwys; (02) 6832 1729. *Macquarie Caravan Park:* Hospital Rd, Warren; (02) 6847 4706. *The State Centre Caravan Park:* Tullamore Rd, Tottenham; (02) 6892 4126. *Willie Retreat Macquarie Marshes:* 2549 Gibson Way, Macquarie Marshes; (02) 6824 4361.

Macquarie Marshes This mosaic of semi-permanent wetlands includes 2 major areas: the south marsh and the north marsh. The wetlands expand and contract, depending on recent rainfall, and provide a waterbird sanctuary and breeding ground. It is thought that the Macquarie Marshes contributed to the early myth of an inland sea, which led explorers – most notably Charles Sturt – on many ill-fated journeys. NSW National Parks & Wildlife Service has discovery rangers available to take visitors on tours of the reserve. Bookings in advance (02) 6842 1311. Marsh Meanders offers a range of activities including kayaking and bushwalking. Inquiries (02) 6824 2070. Both tours are seasonally dependant on water levels. 64 km N.

Cairn: marking the geographic centre of NSW. It is on private property but visible from the road; 65 km s. *Richard Cunningham's grave:* botanist with explorer Major Mitchell's party, Cunningham was killed by Aboriginal people in 1835 and buried here; 70 km s.

TOWNS NEARBY: Cobar 128 km, Coonamble 133 km, Gilgandra 141 km, Dubbo 154 km, Brewarrina 180 km

Oberon

Pop. 2475
Map ref. 522 H6

i 137–139 Oberon St; (02) 6336 0666; www.oberonweb.com

549 AM ABC Central West

This picturesque farming town is 1113 metres above sea level, which gives Oberon a mountain climate of cool summers, crisp winters and occasional snow. The town was named after the king in *A Midsummer Night's Dream* at the suggestion of a local Shakespeare enthusiast, after it was decided that the original name Glyndwr was unpleasant to the ear.

Oberon Museum Almost 1 ha of displays including early farming equipment, a fully furnished early settlers' house, a blacksmith shop and a functioning forge. A wide collection of artefacts and memorabilia are housed in the town's original 1920s railway station. Open 2–5pm Sat or by appt; Lowes Mount Rd.

Lake Oberon: good spot for trout fishing (both brown and rainbow). Boats and swimming are not permitted, but there are barbecue and picnic facilities; Jenolan St. *The Common:* green park with a small lake and picnic facilities; Edith Rd. *Reef Reserve:* natural bushland with access to the lake foreshore; Reef Rd. *Cobweb Craft Shop:* 8 tapestries on show depicting the town's landscape and buildings; Oberon St.

Market: Anglican Church; 1st Sat each month. *Rodeo:* Feb. *Kowmung Music Festival:* chamber music in caves; Mar. *Sheep Show:* Aug. *Daffodil Festival:* Sept.

Jenolan Caravan Park: 7 Cunynghame St; (02) 6336 0344. *McKeown's Rest Jenolan Caves:* 5194 Jenolan Caves Rd; (02) 6335 6252.

Kanangra–Boyd National Park This is a rugged and dramatic piece of Australia with vast gorges, spectacular lookouts and scenic rivers. Sandstone formations of Thurat Spires, Kanangra Walls and Mt Cloudmaker are breathtaking and the park is excellent for bushwalking, rock climbing and camping. The Jenolan Caves are just outside the park border and are justifiably the country's best-known cluster of caves. Of the 300 or so 'rooms', 9 are open to the public, by tour only. Tours of the majestic caverns feature fascinating flowstone deposits, helictites, columns and lakes. On the south-east edge of the park is Yerranderie, a restored silver-mining town with accommodation and walking trails. Inquiries (02) 6336 1972; Jenolan Caves 30 km SE; Kanangra Walls 52 km SE; Yerranderie 85 km SE.

Evans Crown Nature Reserve: bushwalking area with diverse flora and fauna and granite tors. Crown Rock was an initiation and corroboree site for the Wiradjuri people and is now popular for abseiling; 21 km N. *Abercrombie River National Park:* low eucalypt forest ideal for bushwalks, with kangaroos, wallaroos and wallabies. Abercrombie River, Retreat River and Silent Creek are havens for platypus and great for fishing, swimming and canoeing; (02) 6336 1972; 40 km s. *Driving tours:* routes taking in caves, national parks and surrounding towns; brochure from visitor centre. *Wood mushrooms:* delicacies that grow in Jenolan, Vulcan and Gurnang state forests Jan–early May. Mushrooms should be correctly identified before picking. Brochure from visitor centre.

TOWNS NEARBY: Lithgow 36 km, Blackheath 40 km, Bathurst 41 km, Katoomba 42 km, Blayney 60 km

NEW SOUTH WALES

Orange

 i Cnr Byng and Peisley sts; (02) 6393 8226 or 1800 069 466; www.orange.nsw.gov.au

105.9 Star FM, 549 AM ABC Central West

Before European occupation this area was home to the Wiradjuri people, who thrived on the plentiful bush tucker resulting from the fertile volcanic soil and the abundant kangaroos and wallabies. The town was named by explorer Sir Thomas Mitchell after the Dutch Prince of Orange – they had fought together in a war in Spain. Today the prosperous 'colour city' on the slopes of Mount Canobolas enjoys a reputation for excellent food, wine, parks and gardens. It is also known for its goldmining history and as the birthplace of renowned Australian poet A. B. (Banjo) Paterson.

Civic Square This is Orange's cultural hub and also the first stop for visitors, with the visitor centre (incorporating a wine-tasting facility), the City Library, the Civic Theatre and a monument to Banjo Paterson. The Orange Regional Gallery (open Tues–Sun) is one of the busiest in the country. It has touring exhibitions as well as permanent collections that focus on jewellery, ceramics and clothing. Cnr Byng and Peisley sts.

Cook Park: colourful in any season with a begonia house (flowers Feb–May), duck pond, fernery, native bird aviary, Cook Park Guildry (for arts and crafts) and a picnic area; Summer St. *Botanic Gardens:* 17 ha parklands with an impressive exotic and native plant collection and a signposted walk through billabongs, rose gardens, orchards and woodlands; Kearneys Dr. *Banjo Paterson Memorial Park:* remains of Narambla Homestead, Paterson's birthplace, and a memorial obelisk; Ophir Rd. *Self-guide historical walk:* 90 min stroll past historic homes and buildings; brochure from visitor centre.

Market: Kmart carpark; Sun. *Farmers market:* showgrounds; 2nd Sat each month. *Slow Food Festival:* Feb. *Orange Cup:* horseracing; Mar. *FOOD (Food of Orange District) Week:* Apr. *Music Week:* Aug. *Orange Region Winefest:* Oct.

Bistro Ceello: modern Australian; 179 Anson St; (02) 6361 1179. *Lolli Redini:* modern Australian; 48 Sale St; (02) 6361 7748. *Tonic Resaurant:* modern Australian; Cnr Pym and Victoria sts, Millthorpe; (02) 6366 3811.

Abby Lodge: 224 Strathnook La; (02) 6365 1231. *Canobolas Caravan Park:* 166 Bathurst Rd; (02) 6362 7279. *Colour City Caravan Park:* 203 Margaret St; (02) 6362 7254. *Cotehele – The Magistrates House:* 177 Anson St; (02) 6361 2520. *Ophir Gold Bed & Breakfast:* 538 Ophir Rd; (02) 6365 1040. *Molong Caravan Park:* Cnr Watson and Hill sts, Molong; (02) 6366 8328.

Ophir goldfields This was the site of the 1st discovery of payable gold in Australia (1851). The 1850s saw an influx of immigrants from Britain, Germany and China, all hoping to strike it rich. Features today include a fossicking centre, picnic area, walking trails to historic tunnels and tours of a working goldmine. There is still plenty of gold to be found in the area; the gold medals at the 2000 Sydney Olympic Games were made of Ophir gold. Brochure from visitor centre; 27 km N.

Orange wine region Orange is a cool-climate area with snow common in winter, thanks to its high altitude above 600 metres. The result is elegant chardonnay, cabernet sauvignon and shiraz. Philip Shaw, CEO of Cumulus Wines, also believes (and is trying to prove) that Orange has the potential to produce Australia's best merlot. Look out for the beautiful chardonnay by Canobolas-Smith. Cargo Road Winery produces zinfandel, and Mayfield Vineyard has a restaurant set in an old schoolhouse overlooking the vines. Belgravia at Union Bank is the cellar door for Belgravia Vineyards, also featuring a tapas and wine bar.

Campbell's Corner: cool-climate gardens and popular picnic spot; Pinnacle Rd; 8 km s. *Lake Canobolas Reserve:* recreation area with trout fishing in the lake, diving pontoons, children's playground and picnic and barbecue facilities; 9 km sw. *Lucknow:* old goldmining town and site of Australia's 2nd gold discovery, now with historic bluestone buildings and craft shops; 10 km se. *Mt Canobolas Park:* 1500 ha bird and animal sanctuary; 14 km sw. *Borenore Caves:* undeveloped caves with evidence of fossils. Outside are walking trails, and picnic and barbecue facilities. Torch required if entering the caves; brochure from visitor centre; 22 km w. *Cadia Mines:* largest goldmine and coppermine in NSW; check with visitor centre for open days; 25 km se. *Mitchell's Monument:* site of Sir Thomas Mitchell's base camp; 33 km w. *Molong:* charming rural town with Yarn Market, Craft Cottage and Coach House Gallery; 35 km nw. Grave of Yuranigh, Mitchell's Aboriginal guide, lies 2 km e of Molong.

TOWNS NEARBY: Blayney 31 km, Bathurst 47 km, Canowindra 51 km, Eugowra 70 km, Cowra 72 km

Parkes

i Kelly Reserve, cnr Newell Hwy and Thomas St; (02) 6863 8860; www.visitparkes.com.au

95.5 ROK FM, 549 AM ABC Local

Parkes is most famous for its huge telescope. It originated as a tent city, which grew into a town named Bushmans, built almost overnight when gold was found in the area in 1862. The name of the town changed following visits from New South Wales Colonial Secretary Henry Parkes in 1873. The main street, Clarinda Street, was named after Mrs Parkes the following year.

Pioneer Park Museum Set in a historic school and church, displays include early farm machinery and transport. The museum incorporates the collection of the previously separate Henry Parkes Historical Museum, which specialises in memorabilia from the gold rush, and includes the fascinating 1000-volume personal library of Sir Henry Parkes. Pioneer St, North Parkes; (02) 6862 3509.

Motor Museum: displays of vintage and veteran vehicles and local art and craft; Cnr Bogan and Dalton sts. *Memorial Hill:* excellent views of the town and surrounds; Bushman St, North Parkes. *Kelly Reserve:* playground and picnic and barbecue facilities in bush setting; Newell Hwy, North Parkes. *Bushmans Hill Reserve:* take the walking trail to a lookout, passing mining relics and a memorial to those who lost their lives in local mines; Newell Hwy, North Parkes. *Tyndalls Lavender Farm:* visitors welcome to watch distillation process; also includes shop; Wellington Rd. *Self-guide historical town walk and drive:* highlights include the police station (1875), post office (c. 1880) and Balmoral, one of the town's oldest homes, noted for its iron lace, Italian marble and stained-glass windows; brochure from visitor centre.

Elvis Festival: Jan. *Parkes National Marbles Championships:* Mar. *Parkes Astrofest:* July. *Trundle Bush Tucker Day:* Sept. *Country Music Spectacular:* Oct.

 RADIO STATIONS IN TOWN WHAT'S ON WHERE TO EAT WHERE TO STAY NEARBY

[PARKES] CSIRO RADIO TELESCOPE AT TWILIGHT

Dish Cafe: homemade lunches; Parkes Radio Telescope; (02) 6862 1566. *Parkes International Restaurant:* diverse menu; Parkes International Comfort Inn, 18–30 Newell Hwy; (02) 6862 5222. *Station Hotel:* modern Australian; 82 Peak Hill Rd (Newell Hwy); (02) 6862 8444.

Kadina Bed & Breakfast: 22 Mengarvie Rd; (02) 6862 3995. *Parkes Overnighter Caravan Park:* 48 Bushman St; (02) 6862 1707. *Rose Garden on Church BnB:* 40 Church St; 0419 250 510. *Spicer Caravan Park:* Cnr Albert and Victoria sts; (02) 6862 6162. *Welcome Cottage Bed & Breakfast:* 35 The Welcome Rd; (02) 6862 3768. *Peak Hill Caravan Park:* 2 Ween St, Peak Hill; (02) 6869 1422.

Parkes CSIRO Radio Telescope Commissioned in 1961, the telescope is the largest and oldest of the 8 antennae making up the Australian Telescope National Facility. It has been used for globally important work such as identifying the first quasar in 1963, mapping important regions of the Milky Way, and tracking the NASA Apollo moon missions. It was most famously instrumental in transmitting images of Neil Armstrong's 1st steps on the moon to the world. The story of the events on the ground at Parkes is portrayed in the film *The Dish* (2000). The visitor centre explains the uses of the telescope and has 3-D displays. Inquiries (02) 6861 1777; 23 km N.

Condobolin This country town is where the 1st *Australian Idol* runner-up, Shannon Noll, has his roots. A lookout on Reservoir Hill gives views over the town, which is at the junction of 2 rivers and surrounded by red-soil plains. Mt Tilga, 8 km N, is said to be the geographical centre of NSW, and Gum Bend Lake, 5 km w, is a good spot for fishing and watersports. 95 km w.

Macusani Alpaca Farm and Shop: includes workshops throughout the year; Tichborne, 10 km s. *Peak Hill:* working goldmine with lookout offering views of Parkes; 48 km N.

TOWNS NEARBY: **Forbes 32 km, Eugowra 37 km, Canowindra 66 km, Grenfell 84 km, Orange 88 km**

Picton

Pop. 3025
Map ref. 510 F12 | 517 D2 | 519 G1 | 523 J7

i Old Post Office, cnr Argyle and Menangle sts; (02) 4677 8313; www.visitwollondilly.com.au

C91.3 FM Campbelltown, 603 AM ABC Radio National

Located in the foothills of the Southern Highlands, Picton was once a thriving town, but since the re-routing of the Hume Highway it has become a peaceful and well-preserved village. Originally gazetted as Stonequarry, the town was renamed after Thomas Picton, one of Wellington's generals at the battle of Waterloo.

George IV Inn and Scharer's Brewery This is one of Australia's oldest operating inns. It only serves beer from its own brewery made from its own original German recipe (one of only a few pub breweries in the country) and has meals and regular entertainment. Argyle St; (02) 4677 1415.

Picton Botanical Gardens: quiet rural park with views over the farmland, barbecues and picnic facilities; Regreme Rd. *Self-guide historical walk:* includes the splendid railway viaduct (1862) over Stonequarry Creek, and St Mark's Church (1848). *Ghost tours:* local pioneer ghost tour and tales with supper or 2-course meal. Bookings essential (02) 4677 2044.

Brush with the Bush: art festival; Oct.

Mowbray Park Farm Stay: 745 Barkers Lodge Rd; (02) 4680 9243. *Avon Caravan Village:* 79 Avon Dam Rd, Bargo; (02) 4684 1026.

Thirlmere This quiet and attractive town is best known for its NSW Rail Transport Museum. The complex offers steam-train rides on the 1st and 3rd Sun of each month (except in summer when the diesel trains run). The Festival of Steam is held here in Mar, and includes market stalls and street parade. 5 km sw. Thirlmere Lakes National Park (a further 3 km sw) protects 5 reed-fringed freshwater lakes that are home to waterbirds and other wildlife. This is a great place for swimming, picnicking and canoeing, and there is a scenic walk around the lakes.

Jarvisfield Homestead: 1865 home of pioneer landowners, now the clubhouse of Antill Park Golf Club; Remembrance Dr; 2 km N. *Sydney Skydiving Centre:* catering for beginners and experienced skydivers with video-viewing facilities and a picnic and barbecue area; (02) 9791 9155; 5 km E. *Maldon Suspension Bridge:* bungee jumping; 5 km SE. *Wirrimbirra Sanctuary:* native flora and fauna including Dingo Sanctuary, with regular events and twilight tours. Overnight cabins are available. Closed Mon; inquiries (02) 4684 1112; 13 km sw.

TOWNS NEARBY: **Camden 13 km, Campbelltown 21 km, Wollongong 38 km, Bowral 38 km, Berrima 43 km**

Port Macquarie

see inset box on page 84

Queanbeyan

Pop. 38 593
Map ref. 518 F6 | 519 D5 | 520 H3 | 522 F11

i Cnr Farrer Pl and Lowe St; (02) 6299 7307; www.visitqueanbeyan.com.au

106.3 Mix FM, 549 AM ABC Local

Queanbeyan is a growing city adjoining Canberra. Even though most of the city is in New South Wales, the outskirts sprawl into the ACT. Queanbeyan takes its name from a squat ex-convict

Timothy Beard inhabited near the Molonglo River. He called it 'Quinbean' after an Aboriginal word meaning 'clear waters'.

 History Museum: documented history of the city in restored police sergeant's residence; open 1–4pm Sat and Sun; Farrer Pl. *Queanbeyan Printing Museum:* includes memorabilia from the 1st newspaper in Queanbeyan; open 2–4pm Sat and Sun; Farrer Pl. *Queanbeyan Art Society Inc:* exhibits local art and craft; Trinculo Pl. *Railway Historical Society:* steam-train rides depart from station in Henderson St; check times (02) 6284 2790. *Self-guide town walks:* include Byrne's Mill (1883), now a restaurant, and St Benedict's Convent, built in the 1800s for the Sisters of the Good Samaritan; now home to an art and bead gallery; brochure available from visitor centre.

Queanbeyan Gift: footrace; Nov.

Crestview Tourist Park: 81 Donald Rd; (02) 6297 2443. *Queanbeyan Riverside Tourist Park:* 41 Morrisett St; (02) 6297 4749. *Canberra South Motor Park:* Canberra Ave, Symonston, ACT; (02) 6280 6176.

Bungendore This historic country village is set in a picturesque valley near Lake George and still consists of old stone, brick and timber buildings that have been there since the 19th century. The town square contains charming colonial-style shops selling crafts and antiques, and there are several hobby farms in the area. There is a Country Muster in Feb and a rodeo in Oct. 26 km NE. Lark Hill Winery, 7 km N of Bungendore, has cellar-door tastings and sales.

Molonglo Gorge: scenic drive and 3 km walking trail provide spectacular views of Molonglo River; 2 km N. *Googong Dam:* fishing, bushwalking and picnicking; 10 km S. *London Bridge Woolshed and Shearers' Quarters:* visual history of turn-of-the-century farming and settlement life. Take the easy 1 km walk to a remarkable limestone arch. 24 km S. *Captains Flat:* tiny mining town, ideal for walking around, with historic buildings; 45 km S. *Namadgi National Park:* takes in much of the Brindabella Range, covering almost half of the ACT. It boasts significant Aboriginal rock art and beautiful bushland, regenerating after the 2003 bushfires. Camping and bushwalking are popular. The excellent Namadgi Visitor Centre is just south of Tharwa.

TOWNS NEARBY: Braidwood 52 km, Yass 64 km, Goulburn 80 km, Adaminaby 83 km, Tumut 92 km

Raymond Terrace

Pop. 12 700
Map ref. 509 H2 | 514 D7 | 515 A12 | 523 M4

ⓘ Communicate Port Stephens, shop 7, 42 William St; (02) 4987 5276; www.portstephens.nsw.gov.au

102.9 KO FM, 1233 AM ABC Newcastle

Situated on the banks of the Hunter and William rivers just outside Newcastle, Raymond Terrace was an important wool-shipping area in the 1840s. Many historic buildings from that era remain today. The town is in the middle of a koala corridor thanks to the vast remaining eucalypt forests in the region.

Sketchley Cottage: built in 1840 and rebuilt after being destroyed by fire in 1857. Displays include early Australian farming equipment, wine casks, furniture, handicrafts and photography; Pacific Hwy. *Self-guide historical town walk:* includes courthouse (1838) and an 1830s Anglican church built of hand-hewn sandstone; map from visitor centre.

Golden Terrace Chinese Restaurant: takeaway available; Pacific Gardens Van Village, 2231 Pacific Hwy; (02) 4983 1515.

Bellhaven Caravan Park: 206 Adelaide St (Old Pacific Hwy); (02) 4987 2423. *Australian Motor Homes Tourist Park:* 4406 Pacific Hwy, Twelve Mile Creek; (02) 4987 0171. *BIG4 Karuah Jetty:* 88 Holdom Rd, Karuah; 1800 005 552. *Discovery Holiday Parks – Port Stephens:* 2 Oyster Farm Rd, Lemon Tree Passage; (02) 4984 5573. *Larkwood of Lemon Tree Bed & Breakfast:* 1 Oyster Farm Rd, Lemon Tree Passage; (02) 4982 4656. *Tomago Village Van Park:* 819 Tomago Rd, Tomago; (02) 4964 8066.

Tanilba House Home to the first white settler in Tanilba Bay, Lieutenant Caswell, Tanilba House was convict-built in 1831. Features of the house include decorative quoins defining the building edge, door and window openings, and high ceilings, archways and large rooms. There is said to be a resident ghost, thought to be an 1830s governess; 36 km NE.

Hunter Region Botanic Gardens: over 2000 native plants and several theme gardens; Pacific Hwy; 3 km S. *Grahamstown Lake:* beautiful serene lake with picnic facilities; 12 km N. *Fighter World:* hands-on displays of old fighter planes, engines and equipment; RAAF base, Williamtown; 16 km NE. *Clarence Town:* this historic village was one of the first European settlements in Australia; 27 km NW. *Tilligerry Habitat:* ecotourism centre with art and craft and guided walks to see koalas; 34 km NE. *Koala Reserve:* boardwalk through koala colony; 40 km N.

TOWNS NEARBY: Maitland 18 km, Newcastle 19 km, Nelson Bay 37 km, Cessnock 38 km, Stroud 44 km

Richmond

Pop. 25 011
Map ref. 510 H4 | 513 N7 | 523 J6

ⓘ Hawkesbury Visitor Information Centre, Ham Common, Hawkesbury Valley Way, Clarendon; (02) 4578 0233 or 1300 362 874; www.hawkesburytourism.com.au

89.9 FM Hawkesbury Radio, 94.5 FM ABC Local

Richmond provides a peaceful country atmosphere on the Hawkesbury River, but is close enough to Sydney to enjoy the best of both worlds. Many residents commute to the city each day. The township was settled in 1794 because of the rich Hawkesbury River flats. Richmond was soon being used as a granary to supply half of Sydney's grain and is still important agriculturally. There are magnificent views of the Blue Mountains.

Bowman's Cottage: restored c. 1815 cottage, now National Parks & Wildlife office; Windsor St. *Pugh's Lagoon:* pleasant picnic spot with plentiful waterbirds; Kurrajong Rd. *Self-guide historical town walks:* features many heritage buildings including St Peter's Church (1841) and adjacent pioneer graves; brochure from visitor centre.

Bellbird Craft Markets: March St; 2nd Sat each month. *Fruits of the Hawkesbury Festival:* throughout region; Sept–Nov.

Bilpin Springs Lodge: 46 Bilpin Springs Rd, Bilpin; (02) 4567 0300.

Bilpin This tiny town is known for its apples and apple juice. It was originally named Belpin after Archibald Bell Jnr, who was the first European to cross the mountains from Richmond (Bells Line of Road is also named after him). The fact that he

continued on p. 85

 RADIO STATIONS   IN TOWN   WHAT'S ON   WHERE TO EAT   WHERE TO STAY   NEARBY

PORT MACQUARIE

Pop. 39 508
Map ref. 515 G6 | 525 M11

[SUNSET OVER PORT MACQUARIE]

i Cnr Clarence and Hay sts at the Glasshouse; (02) 6581 8000 or 1300 303 155; www.portmacquarieinfo.com.au

102.3 Star FM, 684 AM ABC Local

Port Macquarie, one of the oldest towns in the state, was established in 1821 as a self-sufficient penal settlement. Convicts chosen for their skills and good behaviour maintained the fledgling town, doing everything from farming, boatbuilding and blacksmithing to teaching, baking and clerical duties. Today the city is a major holiday resort at the mouth of the Hastings River. It provides a fascinating history and features historic buildings, nature reserves, excellent surf and fishing beaches, an outstanding museum and scenic coastal walking tracks.

Historical Society Museum This award-winning museum has over 20 000 items in its ever-increasing collection. It specialises in letters, photographs and documents covering convict and free settlement and the evolution of the town from penal colony to coastal metropolis. The museum is in one of the town's beautifully restored older buildings (c. 1836). Clarence St; (02) 6583 1108.

St Thomas' Church: 3rd oldest surviving church in Australia (1824–28), designed by convict architect Thomas Owen; Hay St. Port Macquarie Historic Courthouse: built in 1869, it served the community for 117 years; tours of the restored building by appt; closed Sun; Cnr Hay and Clarence sts; (02) 6584 1818. *Mid-north Coast Maritime Museum:* shipwreck relics, model ships and early photographs; William St; (02) 6583 1866. *Kooloonbung Creek Nature Reserve:* 50 ha of nature reserve with boardwalks and picnic area. Visit the historic cemetery nearby dating from 1842; Gordon St. *Koala Hospital:* Koala rehabilitation and adoption centre, the only one of its kind in NSW; Lord St; (02) 6584 1522; open 8am–4pm, feeding at 8am and 3pm. *Roto House and Macquarie Nature Reserve:* adjacent to the koala hospital and built in 1890, classified by the National Trust; off Lord St; (02) 6584 2180; 10am–4pm Mon–Fri, 9am–1pm Sat. *Port Macquarie Observatory:* planetarium, telescope and solar system display; call for opening times (02) 6582 2397; William St. *Billabong Koala and Wildlife Park:* wide variety of Australian and exotic wildlife with kangaroo-feeding and koala photo sessions each day; Billabong Dr; (02) 6585 1060. *Town beach:* patrolled swimming and surfing beach with sheltered coves at one end. *Cruises:* depart daily; bookings at visitor centre. *Scenic walks:* 9 km coastal walk from Westport Park in the town centre to Tacking Point Lighthouse; traverses beaches and subtropical rainforest with picnic spots, interpretative signs and viewing platforms along the trail; look out for the dolphins of Hastings River and a variety of birdlife; walk takes 3 hrs 30 min one way; brochure from visitor centre.

Market: Findlay Ave; 2nd and 4th Sun each month. *Golden Lure Tournament:* deep-sea fishing; Jan. *Australian Ironman Triathlon:* May. *Heritage Festival:* Apr. *FreshArt:* youth arts festival; June. *Australian Surfing Festival:* Aug. *Aquasculpture:* odd-numbered years, Oct. *Tastings of the Hastings:* food and wine festival; Oct. *Festival of the Sun:* music festival; Dec.

Bliss Restaurant: modern Mediterranean; Level 1, 74 Clarence St; (02) 6584 1422. *The Restaurant at Cassegrain:* modern Australian; Cassegrain Winery, 764 Fernbank Creek Rd; (02) 6582 8320.

Aquatic Caravan Park: 259 Hastings River Dr; (02) 6584 9155. *Azura Beach House Bed & Breakfast:* 109 Pacific Dr; (02) 6582 2700. *Edgewater Holiday Park:* 221 Hastings River Dr; (02) 6583 2799. *Flynns Beach Caravan Park:* 22 Ocean St; (02) 6583 5754. *Jordan's Boating Centre & Holiday Park:* 11 McInherney Close; (02) 6583 1005. *Leisure Tourist Park & Holiday Units:* 202 Hastings River Dr; (02) 6584 4555. *Lighthouse Beach Holiday Village:* 140 Matthew Flinders Dr; (02) 6582 0581. *Melaleuca Caravan Park:* 128 Hastings River Dr; (02) 6583 4498. *Sundowner Breakwall BIG4:* 1 Munster St; (02) 6583 2755. *Anchors B & B:* 52 Anderson St, Lighthouse Beach; (02) 6582 6750. *Stoney Park:* 16 Hacks Ferry Rd, Telegraph Point; (02) 6585 0080. *Telegraph Retreat:* 126 Federation Way, Telegraph Point; (02) 6585 0670.

Lake Innes Nature Reserve The picturesque reserve is home to koalas, kangaroos and bats, but was once the location of the grand Lake Innes House. Unfortunately, the house was left to decay, and the ruins are all that remain today. Guided tours are available; (02) 6588 5555. 7 km sw.

Sea Acres Rainforest Centre: elevated 1.3 km boardwalk through canopy; tours available; Pacific Dr; (02) 6582 3355; 4 km s. *Lighthouse Beach:* 16 km expanse of white sand with camel rides, dolphin-watching from shore and breathtaking views up and down the coast from the grounds of Tacking Point Lighthouse at the northern end of the beach (lighthouse not open to public);

10 km s. *Lake Cathie:* holiday town between surf beach and tidal lake for swimming and fishing; 16 km s. *Wineries:* several in the area offering cellar-door tastings including Lake Innes Vineyard (7 km w) and Cassegrain Winery (13 km w). *Skydiving, sea plane flights, trike tours, golf:* brochures at visitor centre.

TOWNS NEARBY: Wauchope 18 km, Laurieton 26 km, Kempsey 40 km, Taree 69 km, Wingham 70 km

did this with the help of local Aboriginal people, who had been doing it for thousands of years, did not seem to detract from the achievement. Bilpin now has many orchards that are part of the Hawkesbury Farm Gate Trail. Brochures are available from the visitor centre. In keeping with the Australian penchant for 'big' attractions, Bilpin has the Big Bowl of Fruit. There are markets every Sat. 31 km NW.

RAAF base: oldest Air Force establishment in Australia, used for civilian flying from 1915; Windsor–Richmond Rd; 3 km E. *Kurrajong:* quaint mountain village that's home to shops, cafes and galleries, and the Scarecrow Festival held in Oct. Just off Bells Line of Rd; 10 km NW. *Bellbird Hill Lookout:* clear views across to Sydney skyline; Kurrajong Heights; 13 km NW. *Hawkesbury Lookout:* great views of Sydney over the Cumberland plain; 15 km sw. *Avoca Lookout:* stunning views over Grose Valley; 20 km w. *Mountain Lagoon:* mountain bushland setting with walking trails leading down to the pristine Colo River; brochure from visitor centre; 40 km NW.

TOWNS NEARBY: Windsor 6 km, Glenbrook 22 km, Wisemans Ferry 32 km, Katoomba 43 km, Blackheath 43 km

Robertson

Pop. 1207
Map ref. 517 D6 | 519 G3 | 523 J9

 Southern Highlands Visitor Information Centre, 62–70 Main St, Mittagong; (02) 4871 2888 or 1300 657 559; www.southern-highlands.com.au

102.9 2ST FM, 603 AM ABC Radio National

Robertson sits high atop Macquarie Pass with some points in town enjoying spectacular views all the way across to the Pacific Ocean. The region's rich red soil has made Robertson the centre of the largest potato-growing district in New South Wales and there is a 'big potato' on the main street, although it is not signposted and visitors could be forgiven for thinking it is merely a large brown cylinder. The undulating hills create a picturesque setting and were featured in the film *Babe* (1996).

Kev Neel's Old Time Music Machines This music museum displays antique gramophones (some still in working condition) and music memorabilia from as early as the 1800s. Outside are deer, birds and views of the Illawarra Escarpment. Tour the grounds and use the picnic facilities. Illawarra Hwy.

Cockatoo Run Heritage Railway: steam train (when available) to Port Kembla. Robertson Railway Station. For running times call

1300 653 801. *Art and craft shops:* several in town featuring local work; details from visitor centre.

Market: Robertson School of Arts; 2nd Sun each month. *Springtime Festival:* Oct.

Pizzas in the Mist: Italian/modern Australian; 42 Hoddle St; (02) 4885 1799.

Rose Ella: McGuinness Dr, Mt Murray; (02) 4885 1401.

Morton National Park, Robertson section This section of the park has two attractive features: Belmore Falls (10 km sw) and Fitzroy Falls (15 km sw). Belmore Falls plunges into 2 separate rockpools, which then cascade down to the valley below. The area also features walking tracks and pleasant picnic facilities. At Fitzroy Falls is the National Parks & Wildlife Service visitor centre, which has maps and information about the entire national park and offers guided tours. The falls drop 80 m over sandstone cliffs onto black rocks and then another 40 m into the valley below. The walking trail around the falls has excellent lookouts. *For other sections of the park see Bundanoon, Nowra and Ulladulla.*

Illawarra Fly Tree Top Walk Visitors can experience the Southern Highlands' native flora and fauna from 25 m above ground. The 600 m walkway has 2 cantilevered arms stretching to the forest fall line, with expansive views of Lake Illawarra and the South Pacific Ocean. For those who want to get even higher, a spiralling tower reaches 45 m above ground. The environmentally friendly visitor centre has a cafe. Knights Hill Rd; 1300 362 881; 15 km SE.

Robertson Rainforest: 5 ha portion of what was the 2500 ha Yarrawah Brush. It is home to abundant birdlife and features an attractive bushwalk; 2 km s. *Fountaindale Grand Manor:* c. 1924 with over 80 rooms and uninterrupted views of the surrounding hills and valley. Deer and peacocks roam the immaculate, landscaped grounds. It is now a guesthouse and function centre; Illawarra Hwy; (02) 4885 1111; 3 km E. *Burrawang:* 19th-century village with an excellent historic pub; 6 km w. *Macquarie Pass National Park:* preserved section of the Illawarra Escarpment with bushwalks through eucalypt forest and picnic facilities; 10 km E. *Budderoo National Park:* Robertson section features Carrington Falls, a 50 m waterfall with adjacent walking tracks, lookouts and picnic facilities; 10 km SE. *Manning Lookout:* views over Kangaroo Valley; 16 km sw.

TOWNS NEARBY: Jamberoo 18 km, Bowral 20 km, Moss Vale 21 km, Berry 23 km, Kiama 26 km

Rylstone

Pop. 616
Map ref. 523 I3

ⓘ Council offices, Louee St; (02) 6379 4318; www.rylstone.com

📻 98.7 KRR FM, 549 AM ABC Central West

Visitors are drawn to Rylstone for its rural tranquillity. This old stone village is on the Cudgegong River and is a popular spot for birdwatching and fishing.

🏠 **Jack Tindale Park** This park is a pleasant green reserve, perfect for swimming, picnics and barbecues. Platypus are sometimes spotted in the water here and in the river below the showground. Cox St.

Olive Press: see how fresh olives are pressed, and sample or purchase some of the region's best olive oil. Open Sat and Sun Apr–Oct; Lue Rd. *Self-guide historical walk:* includes the Bridge View Inn (restaurant, formerly a bank) and the post office; brochure from visitor centre. *Art and craft outlets:* several featuring local work; details at visitor centre.

Agricultural Show: Feb. *Great Escapade Bike Ride:* Apr. *StreetFeast:* highlight is the Long Lunch, with gourmet regional food served to 350 people on long tables; Nov.

✕ *Jessie's Steakhouse:* steaks, pub bistro; Rylstone Hotel, 62 Louee St; (02) 6379 1118.

Lue Station: Walkers La (via Lue Rd), Lue; (02) 6373 6452.

Kandos: industrial town known for its cement. It features the Bicentennial Industrial Museum (open weekends) and holds the Kandos Street Machine and Hot Rod Show each Jan; 3 km s. *Fern Tree Gully:* tree ferns in subtropical forest with walking trails and lookouts; 16 km N. *Dunn's Swamp:* camping, fishing, bushwalking; 18 km E. *Windermere Dam:* watersports, fishing, camping, picnic and barbecue facilities. Also home of fishing competition each Easter; 19 km w. *Military Vehicle Museum:* vehicles from WW II and the Korean and Vietnam wars; 20 km N. *Turon Technology Museum:* power museum with restored steam engines; 20 km s. *Glen Davis:* this fascinating shale oil ghost town is at the eastern end of the Capertee Valley. The valley is almost 30 km across and is surrounded by sheer sandstone cliffs, which makes it the largest enclosed valley in the Southern Hemisphere; 56 km SE. *Wineries:* several in the area, including De Beaurepaire and Louee Winery; brochure from visitor centre.

TOWNS NEARBY: Mudgee 42 km, Gulgong 64 km, Lithgow 77 km, Bathurst 78 km, Merriwa 82 km

Scone

Pop. 4628
Map ref. 523 K1 | 524 H12

ⓘ Cnr Susan and Kelly sts; (02) 6540 1300; www.upperhuntertourism.com.au

📻 98.1 Power FM, 549 AM ABC Local

Set among rolling green hills in the Hunter Valley, Scone (rhymes with stone) is a pleasant rural town with tree-lined streets. It is known as the 'horse capital of Australia' and is the world's second largest thoroughbred and horse-breeding centre.

🏠 *Australian Stock Horse Museum:* photographs and displays on stockhorse history, and the headquarters of the Australian Stock Horse Society; open Mon–Fri; Kelly St. *Mare and Foal:* life-size sculpture by Gabriel Sterk; Kelly St. *Historical Society Museum:* large collection of local photographs and household furniture and appliances in an old lock-up (1870); open 9.30am–2.30pm Wed, 2.30–4.30pm Sun; Kingdon St.

Horse Festival: May.

✕ *Kerv Espresso Bar:* excellent coffee, light meals; 108 Liverpool St; (02) 6545 3111. *The Larda:* gourmet cafe plus homewares; 122 Kelly St; (02) 6545 9533.

Middlebrook Station Farmstay B & B: Middlebrook Rd; (02) 6545 0389. *Strathearn Park Lodge:* Lot 51 New England Hwy; (02) 6545 3200. *Craigmhor Mountain Retreat:* 2120 Upper Rouchel Rd, Upper Rouchel; (02) 6543 6393.

Moonan Flat This small town sits at the base of the Barrington Tops. It has a beautiful suspension bridge, a small post office and the Victoria Hotel (1856). The hotel was a Cobb & Co coach stop during the gold-rush era and was reputedly patronised by bushranger Captain Thunderbolt. It is small but friendly, and has accommodation and an adjoining restaurant. 50 km NE. *For Barrington Tops National Park, see Gloucester.*

Lake Glenbawn: watersports, bass fishing, picnic, barbecue and camping facilities and a rural-life museum; 15 km E. *Burning Mountain:* deep coal seam that has been smouldering for at least 5000 years. Take the 4.6 km track through the bush; 20 km N. *Wineries:* several offering cellar-door tastings; brochure from visitor centre. *Tours:* thoroughbred stud and sheep station; bookings at visitor centre. *Trail rides:* throughout area, and mustering opportunities for experienced riders; bookings at visitor centre.

TOWNS NEARBY: Muswellbrook 24 km, Murrurundi 32 km, Merriwa 49 km, Singleton 64 km, Nundle 69 km

Shellharbour

Pop. 64 296
Map ref. 517 F6 | 519 H3 | 523 J9

ⓘ Lamerton House, Lamerton Cres; (02) 4221 6169; www.tourismshellharbour.com.au

📻 97.3 FM ABC Illawarra, 99.8 Wave FM

Shellharbour was a thriving port in the 1830s when development could not keep up with demand. The first shops did not appear until the 1850s and the courthouse and gaol were erected in 1877. Prior to this the local constable had to tie felons to a tree. Today the town is an attractive holiday resort close to Lake Illawarra and one of the oldest settlements on the South Coast.

🏠 **Illawarra Light Railway Museum** The museum offers tram rides, displays of steam trains and vintage carriages and a miniature railway. The ticket office and kiosk are in an original 1890s rail terminus and the volunteer staff are knowledgeable. Open Tues, Thurs and Sat. Steam-train rides 2nd Sun each month and Sun during public holiday weekends. Russell St.

Historical walk: take in the historical buildings of the town, beginning at the Steampacket Inn, parts of which date back to 1856. Contact visitor centre for more information. *Snorkelling and scuba diving:* at Bushranger's Bay; details from visitor centre or Shellharbour Scuba Centre; (02) 4296 4266.

Craft market: Shellharbour Public School, Mary St; 2nd Sun each month. *Gamefishing Tournament:* Feb. *City Festival:* 3-day local sports extravaganza; Mar. *Festival in the Forest:* Sept.

✕ *Relish on Addison:* modern Australian; Shop 4, 6 Addison St; (02) 4295 5191.

Montclare Bed and Breakfast: 10 Baudin Ave; (02) 4295 3396. *Pelicans Rest Shellharbour:* 7 Boollwarroo Pde; (02) 4296 4571. *Shellharbour Beachside Tourist Park:* 1 John St;

(02) 4295 1123. *Lakeside Homestay B&B:* 99 Madigan Blvd, Mount Warrigal; (02) 4296 5212. *Surfrider Caravan Park:* 50 Junction Rd, Barrack Point; (02) 4295 1941. *Windang Beach Tourist Park:* Fern St, Windang; (02) 4297 3166.

 Lake Illawarra This large tidal estuary was once a valuable source of food for the Wadi Wadi people. It is home to waterbirds such as black swans, pelicans and royal spoonbills, and has picnic and barbecue areas. The lake is excellent for boating, swimming, waterskiing, windsurfing, fishing and prawning. 7 km N.

Blackbutt Forest Reserve: remnant of coastal plain forest in urban area. Walking trails offer views of Lake Illawarra and Illawarra Escarpment; 2 km w. *Killalea Recreation Park:* foreshore picnic area with an ideal beach for surfing, diving, snorkelling and fishing; 3 km s. *Bass Point Aquatic and Marine Reserve:* top spot for scuba diving, snorkelling, fishing and surfing, with a nice picnic area on the shore; 5 km SE. *Tongarra Museum:* shows area's history through photographs, maps and sketches; 11 km w. *Crooked River Wines:* specialty is Chardonnay White Port, with gorgeous restaurant also on-site; 20 km s.

TOWNS NEARBY: Kiama 10 km, Jamberoo 12 km, Wollongong 17 km, Robertson 26 km, Berry 27 km

Singleton

Pop. 13 665
Map ref. 523 K3

ℹ Singleton Visitor Information and Enterprise Centre, Townhead Park, New England Hwy; (02) 6571 5888 or 1800 449 888; www.visitsingleton.com

📻 98.1 Power FM, 1044 AM ABC Upper Hunter

Singleton is a pleasant and sleepy town set next to the Hunter River among beautiful pasturelands, mountains and national parks. It is the geographical heart of the Hunter Valley and is known for its excellent wines, with several famous vineyards.

🏠 **Singleton Mercy Convent** The Sisters of Mercy arrived from Ireland in 1875 and set up this convent. Set in manicured gardens is the prominent convent, a chapel with an impressive marble altar, and the Sisters of Mercy Museum in an old Georgian cottage. Tours are conducted by the sisters at 2pm on weekends Mar–Nov; Queen St.

James Cook Park: riverside park with picnic facilities and the largest monolithic sundial in the Southern Hemisphere; Ryan Ave. *Singleton Historical Museum:* memorabilia in Singleton's 1st courthouse and gaol from the town's pioneer days; Burdekin Park, New England Hwy. *Town walk:* enjoyable walk passing a historic Anglican church and lush parklands; brochure from visitor centre.

🎪 *Market:* Burdekin Park, New England Hwy; 4th Sun each month. *Countryfest:* includes the Australian Wife Carrying Race; Apr.

✖ *Charades Restaurant and Bar:* modern Australian; Quality Inn Charbonnier Hallmark, 44 Maitland Rd; (02) 6572 2333. *Henri's Brasserie:* modern Australian; Level 1, 85 John St; (02) 6571 3566. *Roberts:* modern Australian, in National Trust cottage; Halls Rd, Pokolbin; (02) 4998 7330. *Muse Restaurant and Cafe:* winery restaurant; Hungerford Hill, 2450 Broke Rd, Pokolbin; (02) 4990 0711.

🏨 *Country Acres Caravan Park:* Maison Dieu Rd; (02) 6572 2328. *Ferguson's Hunter Valley Getaway:* 130 Hill St,

Broke; (02) 6579 1046. *The Mews – Lavender Ridge Vineyard:* 618 Milbrodale Rd, Fordwich; 0488 881 100.

 **Yengo National Park** Mt Yengo is of cultural significance to local Aboriginal communities and there are extensive carvings and paintings in the area. The park is a rugged area of steep gorges and rocky ridges with several walking tracks and lookouts. Old Great North Rd, along the south-east boundary, is an intact example of early 19th-century convict roadbuilding. There are picnic and barbecue areas and campsites throughout the park. Inquiries (02) 6574 5555; 15 km s.

Royal Australian Military Corps Museum: traces history of the infantry corps in Australia; 5 km s. *Wollemi National Park:* Singleton section features picturesque walking trails, lookouts and campsites; (02) 6372 7199; 15 km sw. *For further details on the park see Lithgow. Hillside Orange Orchard:* pick your own oranges; Windsor–Putty Rd; 25 km sw. *Lake St Clair:* extensive recreational and waterway facilities and you can camp onshore. Nearby lookouts offer magnificent views of Mount Royal Range; 25 km N. *Broke:* tiny township with breathtaking national park views and village fair in Sept; 26 km s. *Mt Royal National Park:* rainforest area with scenic walking tracks and lookouts with spectacular 360-degree views from Mt Royal over the entire region; (02) 6574 5555; 32 km N. *Local Hunter Valley wineries:* wineries with cellar-door tastings including Wyndham Estate, Australia's oldest winery, and Cockfighters Ghost; tours available; brochure from visitor centre.

TOWNS NEARBY: Cessnock 34 km, Maitland 41 km, Muswellbrook 42 km, Raymond Terrace 59 km, Scone 64 km

Stroud

Pop. 669
Map ref. 514 F4 | 515 B10 | 523 M3

ℹ Forster Visitor Information Centre, Little St; Forster; (02) 6554 8799 or 1800 802 692; www.greatlakes.org.au

📻 93.1 Breeze FM, 1512 AM ABC Radio National

This delightful town is nestled in the green Karuah Valley and seems to be from another era. The absence of tourist facilities combined with the plethora of historic buildings gives Stroud an unaffected charm. The annual International Brick and Rolling Pin Throwing Competition sees residents competing against towns called Stroud in the United States, England and Canada.

🏠 **St John's Anglican Church** This convict-built church was made with bricks of local clay in 1833 and features beautiful stained-glass windows and original cedar furnishings. The church is noted as the place where bushranger Captain Thunderbolt married Mary Ann Bugg. Cowper St.

Underground silo: one of 8 brick-lined silos built in 1841 for grain storage, it can be inspected by descending a steel ladder; Silo Hill Reserve, off Broadway St. *Self-guide town walk:* covers 32 historic sites including Orchard Cottage (1830s) and St Columbanus Catholic Church (1857), which is still in original condition; brochure from visitor centre.

🎪 *International Brick and Rolling Pin Throwing Competition:* July. *Rodeo:* Sept/Oct.

✖ *Terra Cottage Gallery and Cafe:* great coffee and desserts; 17 Bucketts Way; (02) 4994 5338.

 **Dungog** In 1838 this town, nestled in the Williams River valley, was established as a military outpost to prevent

bushranging by local villains such as Captain Thunderbolt. North of Dungog is Chichester Dam, with its blue-gum surrounds, and east of the dam is Chichester State Forest. In the foothills of the Barrington Tops, the forest has picnic spots, camping, lookouts and walking trails. 22 km w.

TOWNS NEARBY: Bulahdelah 23 km, Nelson Bay 39 km, Gloucester 44 km, Raymond Terrace 44 km, Maitland 53 km

Tamworth

Pop. 42 496
Map ref. 524 H9

ℹ️ 561 Peel St; (02) 6755 4300; www.visittamworth.com

📻 92.9 FM Tamworth's Hit Music Station, 648 ABC AM New England North West

Tamworth is a prosperous city and the self-proclaimed country music capital of Australia, an image that has been carefully cultivated since the late 1960s. There is no question that Tamworth has increased country music's credibility and acceptance in Australia, with local events helping to launch the international careers of several stars. Thousands of fans flock to the Tamworth Country Music Festival every year.

Walk a Country Mile Interpretive Centre From the air this building is guitar-shaped, and it features various displays including one that cleverly documents the history of country music through lyrics. This is also Tamworth's visitor centre, and the first port of call for information on the festival. Peel St.

Hands of Fame Park: Country Music Hands of Fame Cornerstone features handprints of over 200 country music stars; Cnr New England Hwy and Kable Ave. *Australian Country Music Foundation:* features the Legends of Australian Country Music exhibition, a display on the Country Music Awards and a theatrette playing films and documentaries; Brisbane St. *Calala Cottage:* National Trust–classified home of Tamworth's 1st mayor with antique household items and original shepherd's slab hut; Denson St. *Tamworth Regional Gallery:* houses over 700 works including some by Hans Heysen and Will Ashton, and the National Fibre Collection; closed Mon; Peel St. *Powerhouse Motorcycle Museum:* collection of immaculate motorbikes from the 1950s through to the 1980s; Armidale Rd. *Oxley Park:* sanctuary for kangaroos and other marsupials, with picnic and barbecue facilities; off Brisbane St. *Oxley Lookout:* views of the city and beautiful Peel Valley. It is also the starting point for the Kamilaroi walking track (6.2 km); brochure from visitor centre; top of White St. *Powerstation Museum:* traces Tamworth's history as the 1st city in the Southern Hemisphere to have electric street lighting (installed in 1888); Peel St. *Joe Maguire's Pub:* features Noses of Fame, nose imprints of country music stars; Peel St. *Anzac Park:* attractive picnic and barbecue spot with playground; bordered by Brisbane, Napier, Fitzroy and Upper sts. *Bicentennial Park:* fountains, granite sculptures and period lighting; Kable Ave. *Regional Botanic Gardens:* 28 ha of native flora and exotic displays; top of Piper St. *Line dancing:* various venues; lessons offered; brochure from visitor centre. *Historical town walks:* two available of 90 min each, visiting churches, theatres and hotels; brochure from visitor centre. *Art and craft:* several shops and galleries; brochure from visitor centre.

Market: Showground Pavilion; 2nd Sun each month. *Main St Market:* Peel St Blvd; 3rd Sun each month. *Tamworth Country Music Festival:* Jan. *National Pro Rodeo:* Jan. *Gold Cup Race Meeting:* horserace; Apr/May. *Australian Line Dance Festival:* May. *Hats Off to Country Festival:* July. *Bush Poets*

[TAMWORTH] BIG GOLDEN GUITAR TOURIST CENTRE

and Balladeers: traditional Australian variety show with poets and country singers: July. *National Cutting Horse Association Futurity:* competition and entertainment; Sept–Oct. *North-West Craft Expo:* Dec.

Bellepoque Restaurante: Mediterranean; Cnr Darling and Marius sts; (02) 6766 3495. *Golden Guitar Coffee Shop:* cafe and tourist attraction; The Big Golden Guitar Tourist Centre, 2 Ringers Rd; (02) 6765 2688.

Paradise Tourist Park: 575 Peel St; (02) 6766 3120. *Austin Tourist Park:* 581 Armidale Rd, East Tamworth; (02) 6766 2380. *Kootingal Kourt Caravan Park:* 3 Churchill Dr (New England Hwy), Kootingal; (02) 6760 3103. *Minoru Bed & Breakfast:* 146 Carthage St, East Tamworth; (02) 6766 5602. *Plumes on the Green:* 25 The Ringers Rd, Hillvue; (02) 6762 1140. *The Retreat at Froog Moore Park:* 78 Bligh St, North Tamworth; (02) 6766 3353. *Tamworth North Holiday Park:* 4 Somerset Pl, Nemingha; (02) 6760 9356.

Big Golden Guitar Tourist Centre The 12 m golden guitar is a giant replica of the country music award and an Australian icon. Inside the complex is the Gallery of Stars Wax Museum, which features wax models of Australian country music legends alongside current stars. Opposite is the outdoor Country Music Roll of Renown, which is said to be Australia's highest honour in country music. There are special tributes to, among others, Tex Morton, Smoky Dawson and Slim Dusty. 6 km s.

Oxley anchor: the original anchor from John Oxley's ship marks the point where he crossed the Peel River on his expedition to the coast; 9 km NW. *Birdwatching routes:* great birdwatching walks and drives in and around Tamworth; brochure from visitor centre.

TOWNS NEARBY: Manilla 43 km, Nundle 46 km, Walcha 64 km, Gunnedah 65 km, Uralla 74 km

Taree

Pop. 16 519
Map ref. 515 E8 | 523 N1 | 525 L12

ⓘ Manning Valley Visitor Information Centre, 21 Manning River Dr, Taree North; (02) 6592 5444 or 1800 182 733; www.gtcc.nsw.gov.au

📻 107.3 MAX FM, 684 AM ABC Local

Taree is a big modern town on the Manning River and the commercial hub of the Manning River district. It is well known for its handicrafts and its beautiful parklands and nature reserves.

🏠 Fotheringham Park and Queen Elizabeth Park These parklands make an ideal riverside picnic spot to watch the boats go by. To mark the bicentenary in 1988, an unusual herb and sculpture garden was established – the herbs are available to locals for cooking. There are also several memorials throughout the park. Between Pacific Hwy and Manning River.

Taree Craft Centre: huge craft centre featuring local work and picnic facilities; Manning River Dr, Taree North; (02) 6551 5766. *Manning Regional Art Gallery:* changing exhibitions always include some local works; Macquarie St; (02) 6592 5455. *Self-guide historical walks:* through eastern and western sections of town; brochure from visitor centre. *Manning Valley River cruises:* offering a variety of cruises on the Manning River; bookings at visitor centre.

🌴 *Weekly markets:* at various venues in the region; contact visitor centre for details. *Manning River Summer Festival:* Jan. *Powerboat racing:* Easter. *Envirofair:* June. *Manning Valley Festival of the Arts:* even-numbered years, June.

🍴 *Raw Sugar Cafe:* traditional cafe favourites; 214 Victoria St; (02) 6550 0137. *Rio's Bar & Grill:* Brazilian barbecue, waterfront setting; Best Western Taree Motor Inn, 1 Commerce St; (02) 6552 3511.

🛏 *Colonial Leisure Village:* 716 Harrington Rd, Harrington; (02) 6556 3312. *Dawson River Tourist Park:* 1 Manning River Dr, Cundletown; (02) 6553 9237. *East's Ocean Shores Holiday Park:* 32 Manning St, Manning Point; (02) 6553 2624. *Lani's On The Beach:* Old Bar Rd, Old Bar; (02) 6553 7274. *Mescal's at Pampoolah B&B:* 53 Malcolms Rd, Pampoolah; (02) 6557 8578. *Weeroona Holiday Park:* 21 Main Rd, Manning Point; (02) 6553 2635.

⊗ Coorabakh National Park The park features the volcanic plug outcrops of Big Nellie, Flat Nellie and Little Nellie. The Lansdowne escarpment is made up of sandstone cliffs and also has spectacular views. From Newbys Lookout you might see sea eagles and wedge-tailed eagles. 20 km NE.

Ellenborough Falls: One of the longest single-drop waterfalls in the Southern Hemisphere at 200 m. Viewing platforms and a boardwalk to the bottom of the falls. Bulga Plateau, via Elands; 50 km NW. *Joy-flights and tandem skydiving:* flights over the Manning Valley depart from the airport on the northern outskirts of town; Lansdowne Rd; (02) 6551 7776. *Deep Water Shark Gallery:* Aboriginal art and craft; Peverill St; 8 km SW. *Ghinni Wines:* boutique winery; Pacific Hwy, Ghinni Ghinni; 10 km NE. *The Big Buzz Funpark:* toboggan run, water slides and go-karts; Lakes Way; (02) 6553 6000; 15 km S. *Beaches:* excellent surfing conditions; 16 km E. *Hallidays Point:* features a rainforest nature walk; brochure from visitor centre; 25 km SE. *Manning River:* 150 km of navigable waterway with beaches, good fishing

and holiday spots. *Art and craft galleries:* several in the area; brochure from visitor centre. *Nature reserves:* numerous in the area with abundant wildlife in rainforest settings and walking trails; map from visitor centre.

TOWNS NEARBY: Wingham 9 km, Forster–Tuncurry 30 km, Laurieton 44 km, Gloucester 48 km, Wauchope 56 km

Tathra

Pop. 1622
Map ref. 519 E9

ⓘ Andy Poole Dr; (02) 6494 1436; www.sapphirecoast.com.au

📻 87.6 Hot Country FM, 810 AM ABC South East

Tathra is an idyllic family holiday location with a 3-kilometre surf beach, frequented by dolphins, that is safe for swimming and excellent for fishing. The town started as a small jetty that served as a shipping outlet for a group of local farmers. It is now the only sea wharf on the east coast. The region is abundant with prawns from November to May.

🏠 Sea wharf Deterioration of the 1860s wharf led to a demolition order in 1973. Only strenuous local action and the intervention of the National Trust saved the wharf. It has always been a popular fishing platform and there is also a seafood cafe. Above the wharf is the Maritime Museum, which traces the history of the wharf and steam shipping in the area and has replicas of early vessels. Fur seals and little penguins can often be seen.

Tathra Beach: 3 km patrolled beach with excellent surfing conditions. *Fishing spots:* several good spots for salmon and tailor; map from visitor centre.

🌴 *Wharf to Waves Weekend:* includes 1200 m swim; Jan.

🛏 *Seabreeze Holiday Park:* 41 Andy Poole Dr; (02) 6494 1350. *Tathra Beach Motor Village:* Andy Poole Dr; (02) 6494 1577. *Tathra Beach Tourist Park:* Andy Poole Dr; (02) 6494 1302. *Countryside Caravan Park:* Old Wallagoot Rd, Kalaru; (02) 6494 1417.

⊗ Mimosa Rocks National Park This beautifully rugged coastal park features secluded campsites, surf beaches, caves, offshore rock stacks, lagoons, patches of rainforest and incredible volcanic sculptures. It is excellent for snorkelling, surfing, bushwalking, birdwatching and foreshore fossicking. The name of the park comes from the steamship *Mimosa*, which was wrecked on volcanic rock in 1863; (02) 4476 2888; 17 km N.

Kianinny Bay: known fossil site with steep cliffs and rugged rocks, and diving and deep-sea fishing charters available. The 9 km Kangarutha track follows the coast with spectacular scenery; 1 km S. *Mogareeka Inlet:* safe swimming ideal for small children; northern end of Tathra Beach; 2 km N. *Bournda National Park:* picturesque conservation area for great camping and bushwalking. Wallagoot Lake has a wetland area with birdwatching, fishing, prawning, swimming, watersports and boat hire; (02) 6495 5000; 11 km S.

TOWNS NEARBY: Bega 14 km, Merimbula 19 km, Bermagui 35 km, Eden 38 km, Narooma 58 km

Temora

Pop. 4082
Map ref. 522 C7 | 527 P7

ⓘ 294–296 Hoskins St; (02) 6977 1511; www.temora.com.au

📻 89.1 FM ABC Radio National, 549 AM ABC Local

In 1879 gold was discovered in the area and in 1880 the town site was chosen. By 1881 the Temora district was producing half of the state's gold. Of course this could not be maintained, and the population of around 20 000 dwindled quickly. What is left now is a quiet rural Riverina town with several historic buildings. It is also a harness-racing centre with numerous studs in the district.

Temora Rural Museum This award-winning museum has several impressive displays on rural life. There are fashions from the mid-1800s, ranging from baby clothes to wedding dresses, and a replica flour mill and display explaining the history of wheat since 3000 BC. Don Bradman's 1st home, a hardwood slab cottage, has been moved to the grounds from Cootamundra. There is also an impressive rock and mineral collection with an emphasis on the local gold industry. Wagga Rd; (02) 6977 1291.

Skydive Centre: instruction and adventure jumps; weekends; Aerodrome Rd. *Aviation Museum:* This claims to be the world's finest collection of flying historic aircraft. The museum is home to the country's only 2 flying spitfires, the oldest Tiger Moth still flying in Australia, a WW II Hudson, the only flying Gloster Meteor F.8 in the world and many more. The museum holds regular flying weekends throughout the year; Menzies St; (02) 6977 1088. *Heritage walk and drives:* include Edwardian and Federation buildings around town; brochure from visitor centre.

Quota Markets: Pale Face Park; last Sat each month. *Temora Rural Museum Exhibition Day:* Mar.

Waratah Cafe: takeaway/burgers; 222 Hoskins St; (02) 6977 2054.

Courthouse Cottage B&B: 158 Deboos St; 0407 009 750.

Lake Centenary: boating, swimming and picnicking; 4 km N. *Ingalba State Forest:* 10 000 ha of state forest featuring flora and fauna native to the area; 10 km W. *Paragon Goldmine:* working mine until 1996; 15 km N. *Ariah Park:* town known as 'Wowsers, Bowsers and Peppercorn Trees', with beautiful historic streetscape lined with peppercorn trees. Hosts the Mary Gilmore Country Music Festival in Oct; 35 km W.

TOWNS NEARBY: Cootamundra 50 km, West Wyalong 66 km, Young 72 km, Wagga Wagga 77 km, Grenfell 84 km

Tenterfield

Pop. 3129
Map ref. 516 A5 | 525 L4 | 609 L12

157 Rouse St; (02) 6736 1082; www.tenterfield.com

89.7 Ten FM, 738 AM ABC North Coast

Tenterfield is a town of four seasons with many deciduous trees making it particularly spectacular in autumn. It is perhaps best known from Peter Allen's song 'Tenterfield Saddler', which he wrote about his grandfather George Woolnough. But Tenterfield is also the self-proclaimed 'birthplace of the nation', as it is where Sir Henry Parkes delivered his famous Federation speech in 1889.

Sir Henry Parkes Museum Sir Henry Parkes made his Federation speech in this National Trust-classified building built in 1876. Today it stands as a monument to Parkes. Memorabilia includes a life-size portrait by Julian Ashton and Parkes' scrimshaw walking-stick made of whale ivory and baleen. Guided tours available. Cnr Manners and Rouse sts.

Centenary Cottage: 1871 home with local history collection. Open Wed–Sun; Logan St. *Railway Museum:* railway memorabilia in a beautifully restored station; Railway Ave. *Tenterfield Saddler:* handmade saddles at the place that inspired

the Peter Allen song. Still open for business, it is classified by the National Trust of Australia, and its customers have included Banjo Paterson; High St. *Stannum House:* stately mansion built in 1888 for John Holmes Reid, a tin-mining magnate. Homestay and group tours; Rouse St. *Self-guide historical town walk:* includes early residential buildings in Logan St, St Stephens Presbyterian (now Anglican) Church where Banjo Paterson married Alice Walker in 1903 and the grand National Trust–classified post office; brochure from visitor centre.

Railway Market: railway station; 1st Sat every 2nd month. *Tenterfield Show:* Feb. *Bavarian Beerfest:* odd-numbered years, Mar. *Oracles of the Bush:* Australian culture and bush poetry festival; Apr. *Food and Wine Affair:* Nov.

Kurrajong Downs Wines: international, wine tastings; Casino Rd; (02) 6736 4590.

Craigs Caravan Park: 102 Rouse St (New England Hwy); (02) 6736 1585. *Tenterfield Lodge Caravan Park:* 2 Manners St; (02) 6736 1477.

Bald Rock National Park There are excellent 360-degree views from the summit of Bald Rock, the largest granite monolith in Australia. The park is full of canyons and stone arches, and kangaroos abound. Guided tours are available daily to Bald Rock with information on the park's Aboriginal and European heritage. Bookings at visitor centre; (02) 6736 4298; 35 km N.

New England wine region Most of the vineyards in this cool, elevated area on the western slopes of the Great Dividing Range are clustered around Glen Innes, Inverell and Tenterfield, with a few also around Tamworth. Semillon, cabernet sauvignon, pinot noir and chardonnay are some of the region's best wines. Wineries with cellar doors include Kurrajong Downs, which also has a lovely restaurant; Richfield Estate and Tangaratta Estate.

Mt McKenzie Granite Drive: 30 km circuit from Molesworth St in town including Ghost Gully and Bluff Rock, an unusual granite outcrop; 10 km S. *Thunderbolt's Hideout:* reputed haunt of bushranger Captain Thunderbolt; 11 km NE. *Drake:* old goldmining town now popular for fossicking and fishing; 31 km NE. *Boonoo Boonoo National Park:* several bushwalks include an easy 30 min stroll to the spectacular 210 m Boonoo Boonoo Falls. Pleasant swimming area above the falls; (02) 6736 4298; 32 km NE.

TOWNS NEARBY: Stanthorpe (Qld) 44 km, Glen Innes 81 km, Killarney (Qld) 83 km, Texas (Qld) 86 km, Warwick (Qld) 92 km

Terrigal

Pop. 9746
Map ref. 509 E8 | 511 P3 | 523 L5

Gosford Visitor Information, 200 Mann St; Gosford; (02) 4343 4444 or 1300 130 708; www.visitcentralcoast.com.au

101.3 Sea FM, 1512 AM ABC Radio National

Terrigal is a scenic and peaceful coastal town well known for its outstanding beaches, which are popular for surfing, swimming and surf-fishing. The Norfolk pines along the beachfront add to the relaxed feel and the boutique shops and restaurants add a sophisticated touch.

Rotary Park: pleasant for picnics and barbecues, backing onto Terrigal Lagoon, a good family swimming spot; Terrigal Dr.

Artisans Market: Rotary Park; 2nd Sat each month. *Terrigal Food and Wine Festival:* July.

Onda Ristorante Italiano: Italian; 150 Terrigal Dr; (02) 4384 5554. *The Reef Restaurant:* modern Australian; The Haven; (02) 4385 3222. *Seasalt:* seafood and stunning views; Crowne Plaza Terrigal, Pine Tree La; (02) 4384 9133. *Lamiche:* modern Australian; shop 2, 80 Oceanview Dr, Wamberal; (02) 4384 2044.

Villa by the Sea: 27 Tabletop Rd; (02) 4385 1170. *Forresters Beach Bed & Breakfast:* 9 Yumbool Close, Forresters Beach; (02) 4385 3282. *The Acreage B & B:* 110 Picketts Valley Rd, Picketts Valley; (02) 4381 2881. *The Palms at Avoca:* Carolina Park Rd, Avoca Beach; (02) 4382 1227. *Terrigal Hinterland B&B:* 2/31 Lea Ave, Wamberal; (02) 4385 5354.

 Bouddi National Park This park ranges from secluded beaches beneath steep cliffs to lush pockets of rainforest, with several signposted bushwalks. Maitland Bay is at the heart of a 300 ha marine park extension to protect marine life, one of the first in NSW, and contains the wreck of the PS *Maitland*. Fishing is allowed in all other areas. Putty Beach is safe for swimming and Maitland Bay is good for snorkelling. Tallow Beach is not patrolled and is recommended for strong swimmers only. 17 km s.

The Skillion: headland offering excellent coastal views; 3 km SE. *Erina:* pretty town with St Fiacre Distillery; 4 km W. *Ken Duncan Gallery:* largest privately owned photographic collection in Australia; 8 km NW. *Several excellent beaches:* Wamberal Beach, a safe family beach with rockpools (3 km N), Avoca Beach (7.5 km s) and Shelly Beach (13 km N), both popular for surfing. *Sea-kayaking tours:* various routes available; bookings (02) 4342 2222.

TOWNS NEARBY: Gosford 10 km, Woy Woy 12 km, The Entrance 13 km, Wyong 18 km, Wisemans Ferry 43 km

The Entrance

Pop. 2632
Map ref. 509 E7 | 511 P2 | 523 L5

i Memorial Park, Marine Pde; (02) 4334 4444 or 1300 130 708; www.theentrance.org

📻 101.3 Star FM, 1233 AM ABC Local

This immaculate seaside and lakeside town is named for the narrow channel that connects Tuggerah Lake to the Pacific Ocean. Given its proximity to Sydney and Newcastle, it has become a popular aquatic playground for residents of both cities.

Memorial Park: pelican-feeding with informative commentary at 3.30pm daily; Marine Pde. *The Waterfront:* town mall with shops, pavement eateries and children's playground.

Markets: Waterfront Plaza, Sat; Bayview Ave, Sun. *Art and craft market:* Marine Pde; Sun. *Central Coast Country Music Festival:* Mar. *Tuggerah Lakes Mardi Gras Festival:* Dec.

Ocean Restaurant: seafood; 102 Ocean Pde, Blue Bay; (02) 4334 4600.

Blue Bay Camping & Caravan Park: Cnr Bay Rd and Narrawa Ave; (02) 4332 1991. *El Lago Tourist Park:* 41 The Entrance Rd; (02) 4332 3955. *Lavender House B&B:* 66 Denning St; (02) 4332 2234. *Blue Lagoon Beach Resort:* 10 Bateau Bay Rd, Bateau Bay; (02) 4332 1447. *Budgewoi Holiday Park:* Weemala St, Budgewoi; (02) 4390 9019. *Canton Beach Holiday Park:* 1 Oleander St, Canton Beach; (02) 4396 3252. *Dunleith Tourist Park:* Hutton Rd, The Entrance North; (02) 4332 2172. *Norah Head Holiday Park:* Victoria St, Norah Head; (02) 4396 3935.

Sun Valley Tourist Park: 2 Bateau Bay Rd, Bateau Bay; (02) 4332 1107. *Toowoon Bay Holiday Park:* 1 Koongara St, Toowoon Bay; (02) 4332 2834. *Toowoon Bay Van Park:* Cnr Bay Rd and Charlton Ave, Toowoon Bay; (02) 4332 5934. *Two Shores Holiday Village:* 200 Wilfred Barrett Dr, The Entrance North; 1300 653 602.

 Wyrrabalong National Park With sections lying north and south of town, this park conserves the last significant coastal rainforest on the Central Coast. Signposted walking tracks lead along rocky cliffs and beaches with lookouts and picnic spots along the way providing stunning coastal views. 5 km N and s.

Shell Museum: extensive shell collection; Dunleith Caravan Park; 1 km N. *Crabneck Point Lookout:* magnificent coastal views; 6 km s. *Nora Head Lighthouse:* attractive automated lighthouse built in 1903 after several ships were wrecked on the coast; 8 km N. *Toukley:* unspoiled coastal hamlet with breathtaking scenery. Holds markets each Sun in the shopping centre carpark and the Gathering of the Clans (Scottish festival) in Sept; 11 km N. *Munmorah State Recreation Area:* signposted bushwalking trails with magnificent coastal scenery; 21 km N. *Lakes:* 80 sq km lake system, on average less than 2 m deep and shark-free. The linked Tuggerah Lake, Budgewoi Lake and Lake Munmorah all empty into the ocean at The Entrance and are fabulous for fishing and prawning (in summer), as well as watersports.

TOWNS NEARBY: Wyong 9 km, Terrigal 13 km, Gosford 17 km, Woy Woy 23 km, Wisemans Ferry 48 km

Thredbo

see inset box on page 93

Tibooburra

Pop. 161
Map ref. 528 D2 | 618 H11

i National Parks and Wildlife Service, Briscoe St; (08) 8091 3308.

📻 999 AM ABC Local

Tibooburra is one of the hottest and most isolated towns in New South Wales. Its name means 'heaps of rocks' in the local Aboriginal language and refers to the 450-million-year-old granite tors that surround the town. In a similar tale to the creation of the Blue Mountains' Three Sisters, three brothers were turned to stone after marrying women from another tribe, creating three large rocks (only one remains today). Gold was discovered in 1881 but a poor yield, outbreaks of typhoid and dysentery and a lack of water meant the population explosion did not last.

Pioneer Park: features a replica of the whaleboat Charles Sturt carried with him on his 1844–46 expedition to find an inland sea; Briscoe St. *Courthouse Museum:* history of the region told with photographs, relics and documents in the restored 1887 courthouse; Briscoe St. *Tibooburra Aboriginal Land Council Keeping Place:* photographs and Indigenous artefacts on display include a cockatoo-feather headdress; check opening times (08) 8091 3435; Briscoe St. *School of the Air:* most remote school in NSW servicing students of Tibooburra and the Cameron Corner region. Tours during school terms; Briscoe St. *Family Hotel:* pub walls have been painted on by artists including Russell Drysdale, Clifton Pugh and Rick Amor; Briscoe St.

Gymkhana and Rodeo: Oct.

 RADIO STATIONS   IN TOWN   WHAT'S ON   WHERE TO EAT   WHERE TO STAY   NEARBY

Sturt National Park Occupying 310 000 hectares of Corner Country – the point where 3 states meet – is this semi-desert park, which begins on the edge of town. It is noted for its wildlife – wedge-tailed eagles, kangaroos and myriad reptiles. The landscape is diverse, ranging from ephemeral lakes to jump-ups, grassy plains and the rolling dunes of the Strzelecki Desert. Temperatures range from well over 40°C in summer to below 0°C at night in winter. Lake Pinaroo in the west is the site where Charles Sturt once built a fort to protect his party's supplies and sheep. There is an outdoor pastoralist museum and camping and homestead accommodation at Mt Wood, and short walking trails that lead from here and the park's 3 other campsites. Details from visitor centre.

Milparinka The Albert Hotel continues to do business in this small settlement, now almost a ghost town; (08) 8091 3863. Historic buildings include a restored courthouse, the remains of an old police station, a bank, a general store and a post office; 40 km s. Depot Glen Billabong, 14 km nw of Milparinka, is where Charles Sturt was marooned for 6 months in 1845 while searching for an inland sea. One of the worst droughts in Australia's history kept the party there due to diminishing water supplies. The grave of James Poole, Sturt's second-in-command, who died of scurvy, is 1 km further east under a grevillea tree. Poole's initials and the year of his death were carved into the tree and can still be seen. Poole's Cairn, commemorating the disastrous expedition, is located at Mt Poole, 7 km n of Depot Glen.

Cameron Corner: where Queensland, NSW and SA meet. The Dog Fence, the longest fence in the world, runs through here from Jimbour in Queensland to the Great Australian Bight; 133 km nw.

TOWNS NEARBY: White Cliffs 188 km, Innamincka (SA) 225 km

Tocumwal

Pop. 1863
Map ref. 527 L11 | 542 F4

i 41 Deniliquin St; (03) 5874 2131 or 1800 677 271; www.toconthemurray. com.au

102.5 Classic Rock FM, 675 AM ABC Riverina

This picturesque town ('Toc' to the locals) is on the northern bank of the Murray River. The region is a popular holiday spot due to its pleasant river beaches and laid-back lifestyle.

Foreshore Park: peaceful green park shaded by tall gum trees, and featuring a large fibreglass Murray cod. Foreshore markets are held 11 times during the year (dates from visitor centre); Deniliquin Rd. *River cruises, walks, drives and bike tracks:* self-guide and guided tours of town and the river; brochures from visitor centre. *Art and craft shops:* several in town featuring local work; brochure from visitor centre.

Foreshore market: Foreshore park; 3rd Sat each month (not July). *Farmers market:* 3rd Sat each month. *Tocumwal Classic:* fishing competition; Jan. *Horseraces:* Easter.

The Big Strawberry: cafe with strawberry picking; 7034 Goulburn Valley Hwy, Koonoomoo, Vic.; (03) 5871 1300.

BIG4 Tocumwal Tourist Park: 1 Bruton St; (03) 5874 2768. *Boomerang Way Tourist Park:* 65 Murray St; (03) 5874 2313.

 Blowhole and the Rocks This area is sacred to the Ulupna and Bangaragn people. The Rocks change colour according to weather conditions, and the Blowhole is a 25 m deep hole that legend says was home to a giant Murray cod that ate young

children who fell into it. One young boy escaped the cod and was chased into the crevice, only to emerge in the Murray, suggesting that the Blowhole and the river are linked. Strangely, water has been known to flow from the Blowhole in times of drought. Adjacent to it is a working granite quarry. Rocks Rd; 8.5 km NE.

Tocumwal Aerodrome: largest RAAF base in Australia during WW II, now home to international Sportavia Soaring Centre (glider joy-flights and learn-to-glide packages); 5 km NE. *Beaches:* around 25 attractive river beaches in the vicinity, some with picnic areas; map from visitor centre. *Wineries:* there are several wineries in the area; brochure from visitor centre.

TOWNS NEARBY: **Cobram** (Vic.) 14 km, **Finley** 18 km, **Mulwala** 44 km, **Yarrawonga** (Vic.) 45 km, **Jerilderie** 53 km

Tumbarumba

Pop. 1487
Map ref. 519 A6 | 520 B5 | 522 D12 | 543 P5

i 10 Bridge St; (02) 6948 3333; www.visittumbashire.com.au

107.7 FM Radio Upper Murray, 675 AM ABC Local

This former goldmining town in the foothills of the Snowy Mountains remains seemingly untouched by the modern world with old-style charm and well-preserved buildings. This has been helped by the fact that it has been bypassed by major road and rail routes. It experiences four distinct seasons and enjoys European-style vistas of snow-capped mountains, forested hills, rolling green pastures and a crystal-clear creek. Tumbarumba's name comes from the Wiradjuri language and is thought to mean 'sounding ground'. This relates to the suggestion that there are places in the region where the ground sounds hollow.

Bicentennial Botanic Gardens: mix of native and exotic trees, especially striking in autumn; Prince St. *Artists on Parade Gallery:* run by local artists, exhibitions change regularly; The Parade. *Tumbarumba Museum and Information Centre:* includes working model of a water-powered timber mill; Bridge St.

Campdraft: Jan. *Tumbafest:* food, wine and music festival; Feb. *Heritage Week:* Nov. *Christmas Street Carnival:* Dec.

Tumbarumba Creek Caravan Park: Lauder St; (02) 6948 3330.

 Site of Old Union Jack Mining Area: memorial to the students of the Union Jack school who died in WW I; 3 km N. *Henry Angel Trackhead:* starting point for a 12 km section of the Hume and Hovell Walking Track along Burra Creek. It includes waterfalls and the place where Hume and Hovell first saw the Snowy Mountains. The full walking trail is a 23-day, 440 km trek from Albury to Yass. For a kit (including maps), contact Department of Lands, Sydney (02) 6937 2700; Tooma Rd; 7 km SE. *Pioneer Women's Hut:* fascinating domestic and rural museum focusing on women's stories. The National Quilt Register was an initiative of the women who run this museum. Open Wed, Sat and Sun; Wagga Rd; (02) 6948 2635; 8 km NW. *Paddy's River Falls:* the waterfall cascades over a 60 m drop in a beautiful bush setting with a scenic walking track and picnic area. A concreted walkway is at the bottom and lookouts are at the top; 16 km S. *Tooma:* historic town with old hotel (c. 1880); 34 km SE. *Wineries:* several with cellar doors including Glenburnie Vineyard; brochure from visitor centre; (02) 6948 2570.

TOWNS NEARBY: **Batlow** 31 km, **Corryong** (Vic.) 48 km, **Khancoban** 50 km, **Adelong** 52 km, **Tumut** 56 km

THREDBO

Pop. 477
Map ref. 519 A8 | 520 C10 | 539 B4

i Thredbo Resort Centre, Friday Flat Dr; 1800 020 589; or Snowy Region Visitor Centre, Kosciuszko Rd, Jindabyne; (02) 6459 4100; www.thredbo.com.au

88.9 FM ABC Local, 97.7 Snow FM

Thredbo, a mountain village in Kosciuszko National Park (*see Adaminaby*), is a unique year-round resort, with some of Australia's best skiing and winter sports in the colder months and angling, bushwalking and mountain-biking in summer.

Ski fields Thredbo has 480 ha of skiing terrain and the longest ski runs in Australia (up to 5.9 km) with a vertical drop of 672 m. Night skiing is a feature in July and Aug. There are slopes for beginners to advanced skiers and snowboarders, with lessons and equipment hire available. Thredbo Snowsports Outdoor Adventures offers off-piste skiing, freeheeling, cross-country and snowshoeing lessons and excursions; Friday Dr; bookings (02) 6459 4044.

Thredbo Alpine bobsled: 700 m luge-style track; adjacent to ski lifts; 10am–5pm daily, closed in winter; (02) 6459 4119. *Thredbo Leisure Centre:* quality sporting facilities used by athletes for high-altitude training, with pool, squash courts, gym and climbing wall; northern end of the village; (02) 6459 4138. *Thredbo River:* excellent trout fishing. *Village walks:* include the Meadows Nature Walk through tea trees and the Thredbo Village Walk for diversity of alpine architecture; brochure from visitor centre. *Mountain-biking:* several tracks including the Village Bike Track; all bike and equipment hire available from Thredbo Service Station; 9am–5pm Nov–May; Valley Terminal; (02) 6457 6282.

Blues Festival: Jan. *Jazz Festival:* Mar. *Top to Bottom Ski Race:* Aug.

[CARVING UP THREDBO'S SLOPES]

Santé Churrasco: Brazilian barbecue, Shop 4, Squatter Run, Village Square; (02) 6457 6083. *Terrace:* modern Australian; Denman Hotel, Diggings Tce; (02) 6457 6222.

Pilot Lookout: magnificent view dominated by The Pilot (1828 m) and The Cobberas (1883 m) in Vic; 10 km SE. *Skitube:* access to Perisher and Mt Blue Cow ski fields via this European-style train from Bullocks Flat. This winter-only service passes through Australia's largest train tunnel; 15 km NE. *Mt Kosciuszko:* Australia's highest mountain, with access via chairlift from Thredbo and 13 km walk; contact visitor centre for more details.

TOWNS NEARBY: Jindabyne 30 km, Khancoban 35 km, Berridale 49 km, Corryong (Vic.) 50 km, Adaminaby 70 km

Tumut

Pop. 5926
Map ref. 519 A4 | 520 C2 | 522 D10

i 5 Adelong Rd; (02) 6947 7025; www.tumut.nsw.gov.au

96.3 FM Sounds of the Mountains, 97.9 FM ABC Riverina

Tumut (pronounced 'Tyoomut') is located in a fertile valley, surrounded by spectacular mountain scenery. The poplar and willow trees planted by early settlers make summer and autumn particularly striking. Prior to European settlement, Tumut was the seasonal meeting place for three Aboriginal tribes. Each summer the tribes would journey to the mountains to feast on Bogong moths.

Old Butter Factory Tourist Complex: local art and craft, and visitor centre; Snowy Mountains Hwy. *Millet Broom Factory:* 90 per cent of the state's broom millet comes from the region and visitors can see the factory in action; open Mon–Fri; Snowy Mountains Hwy. *Tumut Art Society Gallery:* specialises in work by local artists; open 10am–4pm Tues–Thurs and Sat; Cnr Tumut Plains Rd and Snowy Mountains Hwy. *Tumut Museum:* large collection of farm and domestic items and an excellent display of Miles Franklin memorabilia (the author was born in nearby Talbingo); open 1–4pm Sat and Sun; Cnr Capper and Merrivale sts. *River walk:* along Tumut River; from Elm Dr.

Historical and tree-identifying walks: include Alex Stockwell Memorial Gardens with European trees and a WW I memorial; brochure from visitor centre.

Tumut Show: Mar. *Festival of the Falling Leaf:* autumn celebration; Apr/May. *Boxing Day Horse Races:* Dec.

Chit Chat: cafe with homemade treats; Shop 5, Wynyard Centre, Wynyard St; (02) 6947 1187. *The Coach House:* cafe with homemade bread; Tumut Connection, Russell St; (02) 6947 9143.

Riverglade Caravan Park: Snowy Mountains Hwy; (02) 6947 2528.

Blowering Reservoir This enormous dam is an excellent centre for watersports and fishing for rainbow trout, brown trout and perch. With the dam containing the largest trout hatchery in Australia, almost everyone catches a fish. There is a spectacular lookout over the dam wall, and the Blowering Cliffs walk (19 km s) is a pleasant 5 km stroll in Kosciuszko National Park along stunning granite cliffs; 10 km s.

Air Escape: powered hang-gliding; airport, off Snowy Mountains Hwy; 6 km E. *Tumut Valley Violets:* largest African violet farm in Australia with over 1000 varieties; Tumut Plains Rd; 7 km s.

[TUMUT] GLORY ARCH, ENTRANCE TO YARRANGOBILLY CAVES, KOSCIUSZKO NATIONAL PARK

Snowy Mountains Trout Farm: NSW's largest trout farm with fresh trout sales; 10 km SE. **Talbingo Dam and Reservoir:** dam in steep, wooded country; 40 km S. **Power station:** Tumut Power 3, tours available; 45 km S. **Kosciuszko National Park:** massive alpine park to the south-east includes nearby Yarrangobilly Caves; (02) 6947 7025; 60 km S. *See Adaminaby.*

TOWNS NEARBY: Adelong 14 km, Batlow 25 km, Gundagai 28 km, Tumbarumba 56 km, Cootamundra 75 km

Tweed Heads

Pop. 84 325

Map ref. 516 H2 | 525 O1 | 600 G11 | 601 H10 | 609 N11

ⓘ Wharf St; (07) 5536 6737 or 1800 674 414; www.tweedtourism.com.au

📻 94.5 FM ABC North Coast, 96.9 FM ABC Radio National

Tweed Heads is the state's northernmost town and – along with its twin town Coolangatta over the Queensland border – is a popular holiday destination at the southern end of the Gold Coast. The region has long been celebrated for its weather, surf beaches, night-life and laid-back atmosphere.

🏠 **Point Danger** This lookout is on the Queensland–NSW border and overlooks Duranbah Beach, which is popular for surfing. It was named by Captain James Cook to warn of the dangerous coral reefs that lay under the waves off the coast. The world's 1st laser-beam lighthouse is located here. Dolphins may be seen off the coast along the pleasant cliff-edge walk. There are several picnic spots with stunning ocean views.

Tweed Maritime and Heritage Museum: 4 original buildings house maritime, heritage and photographic collections; Pioneer Park, Kennedy Dr, Tweed Heads West. **Tweed Cruise Boats:** cruises visit locations along the Tweed River; River Tce. **Fishing and diving charters and houseboat hire:** guided and self-guide river excursions; bookings at visitor centre. **Tweed Snorkelling and Whale Adventures:** whale-watching adventures and snorkelling tours to Cook Island marine reserve; bookings (07) 5536 6737. **Catch a Crab Cruises, Birds Bay Oyster Farm, deep-sea fishing:** these tours depart daily, bookings from visitor centre.

🎪 **Craft market:** Florence St; Sun. **Tweed Harbour Fireworks Challenge:** Apr. **Wintersun Carnival:** festival and music; June. **Greenback Tailor Fishing Competition:** June. **Tweed River Festival:** Oct.

🍴 **Ivory Tavern:** international; 156 Wharf St; (02) 5506 9988. **Signatures Restaurant:** seafood/modern Australian; Outrigger Twin Towns Resort, Wharf St; (02) 5536 2277.

🛏 **BIG4 Tweed Billabong Holiday Park:** Holden St, Tweed Heads South; (07) 5524 2444. **Boyds Bay Holiday Park:** 3 Dry Dock Rd, Tweed Heads South; (07) 5524 3306. **Drifters Holiday Village – Kingscliff:** 46 Wommin Bay Rd, Chinderah; (02) 6674 2505. **Chinderah Village:** 94 Chinderah Bay Dr, Chinderah; (02) 6674 1536. **Colonial Tweed Holiday & Home Park:** 158 Dry Dock Rd, Tweed Heads South; (07) 5524 2999. **Fingal Holiday Park:** Prince St, Fingal Head; (07) 5524 2208. **Homestead Holiday Park:** 200/25 Chinderah Bay Dr, Chinderah; (02) 6674 1824. **Kingscliff Beach Holiday Park:** Marine Pde, Kingscliff; (02) 6674 1311. **Kingscliff North Holiday Park:** Marine Pde, Kingscliff; (02) 6674 1071. **Kirra Beach Tourist Park:** 10 Charlotte St, Kirra, Qld; (07) 5667 2740. **Pyramid Holiday Park:** 145 Kennedy Dr, Tweed Heads West; (07) 5536 3666. **River Retreat Caravan Park:** 8 Philp Pde, Tweed Heads South; (07) 5524 2700. **Tweed River Hacienda Holiday Park:** 300/37 Chinderah Bay Dr, Chinderah; (02) 6674 1245.

🏛 **Minjungbal Aboriginal Cultural Centre** The Aboriginal Heritage Unit of the Australian Museum is dedicated to self-determination and the importance of promoting, protecting and preserving Australian Indigenous cultures. The unit runs this museum, which features displays on all aspects of Aboriginal life on the north coast. There is also a walk encompassing a ceremonial bora ring and a mangrove and rainforest area. Located just over Boyds Bay Bridge.

Currumbin Wildlife Sanctuary: home to a huge range of Australian native wildlife; night tours available; Currumbin; (07) 5534 1266; 7 km N. **Beaches:** idyllic white sandy beaches for surfing and swimming, including Fingal (3 km S) and Kingscliff (14 km S). **Melaleuca Station:** re-created 1930s railway station in a tea-tree plantation with train rides, a tea-tree oil distillation plant and an animal nursery; Chinderah; 9 km S. **Tropical Fruit World:** home to the world's largest variety of tropical fruit with plantation safari, jungle riverboat cruise, fauna park and fruit tastings; 15 km S. **John Hogan Rainforest:** spectacular palm rainforest walks and picnic areas; 17 km SW.

TOWNS NEARBY: Burleigh Heads (Qld) 13 km, Surfers Paradise (Qld) 22 km, Murwillumbah 22 km, Nerang (Qld) 29 km, Mullumbimby 42 km

Ulladulla

Pop. 10 302

Map ref. 519 G5 | 521 N4 | 523 I11

ⓘ Shoalhaven Visitors Centre, Princes Hwy; (02) 4444 8819; www.shoalhaven.nsw.gov.au

📻 94.9 Power FM, 702 AM ABC Local

This fishing town, built around a safe harbour, is surrounded by beautiful lakes, lagoons and white sandy beaches. It is a popular holiday destination, especially for surfing and fishing, and enjoys mild weather all year-round. Visitors flock here each Easter Sunday for the Blessing of the Fleet ceremony.

🏠 **Coomie Nulunga Cultural Trail** This 30 min signposted walk along the headland was created by the local Aboriginal Land Council. Along the path are hand-painted and hand-carved information posts incorporating names of local plants and animals. Dawn and dusk are the best times to experience the wildlife along the walk, but visitors are advised to stay on the path for the good of the local fauna and for their own protection (from snakes). Starts Deering St opposite Lighthouse Oval carpark.

Funland Timezone: large indoor family fun park; Princes Hwy; (02) 4454 3220. **Warden Head:** lighthouse views and walking tracks. **South Pacific Heathland Reserve:** walks among native plants and birdlife; Dowling St. **Ulladulla Wildflower Reserve:** 12 ha with walking trails and over 100 plant types including waratah and Christmas bush. Best in spring; Warden St.

 Royal Coastal Patrol Markets: harbour wharf; 2nd Sun each month. **Blessing of the Fleet:** Easter. **Gamefishing Tournament:** June.

Elizans: modern Australian; Ulladulla Guest House, 39 Burrill St; (02) 4455 1796. **Hayden's Pies:** excellent pies; shop 2, 166 Princes Hwy; (02) 4455 7798. **Rick Stein at Bannisters:** award-winning seafood; Bannisters Point Lodge, 191 Mitchell Pde, Mollymook; (02) 4455 3044.

Beach Haven Holiday Resort: 370 Princes Hwy; (02) 4455 2110. **Ulladulla Guest House:** 39 Burrill St; (02) 4455 1796. **Ulladulla Headland Tourist Park:** 14 Did-Dell St; 1300 733 021. **Ulladulla Holiday Village:** 300 Kings Point Dr; 1300 854 910. **Acacia House Bed & Breakfast:** 203 Evans La, Woodstock; (02) 4454 5652. **Bendalong Point Tourist Park:** Red Point Rd, Bendalong; 1300 733 025. **BIG4 Bungalow Park:** 123 Princes Hwy, Burrill Lake; 1800 552 944. **Burrill Lake Tourist Park:** Princess Ave, Burrill Lake; 1300 555 525. **Bushview Cottage:** 16 Tallow Wood Rd, Woodstock; (02) 4455 7060. **Conjola Lakeside Van Park:** 1 Norman St, Lake Conjola; (02) 4456 1407. **Dolphins Point Tourist Park:** Lot 12 Dolphin Point Rd, Dolphin Point; (02) 4455 1606. **Kioloa Beach Holiday Park:** 635 Murramarang Rd, Kioloa; (02) 4457 1072. **Lake Conjola Entrance Tourist Park:** Lake Conjola Entrance Rd, Lake Conjola; 1300 133 395. **Lake Tabourie Tourist Park:** Princes Hwy, Tabourie Lake; 1300 559 966. **The Long Weekend Retreat:** Narrawallee Creek Rd, Lake Conjola; 0419 489 302. **Meadowlake Lodge:** 318 Wilford La, Milton; (02) 4455 7722. **Merry Beach Caravan Resort:** 46 Merrybeach Rd, Kioloa; (02) 4457 1065. **Milton Tourist Park:** 12 Slaughterhouse Rd, Milton; (02) 4455 2028. **Mollymook Caravan Park:** Cnr Princes Hwy and Ilett St, Mollymook; (02) 4455 1939. **Mrs. Top at Milton:** 63 Wason St, Milton; (02) 4455 2099. **Racecourse Beach Tourist Park:** 381 Murramarang Rd, Bawley Point; (02) 4457 1078. **Sinclair's Country Retreat:** E1490 Princes Hwy, Conjola; (02) 4456 4291. **Times Past Bed & Breakfast:** 51 Princes Hwy, Milton; (02) 4455 5194. **Wairo Beach Tourist Park:** Princes Hwy, Tabourie Lake; (02) 4457 3035.

Pigeon House Mountain, Morton National Park The Ulladulla section of Morton National Park features this eye-catching mountain, which Captain James Cook thought looked like a square dovehouse with a dome on top, hence its name. The local Aboriginal people obviously had a different viewpoint and named it Didhol, meaning 'woman's breast'. The mountain has now been assigned a dual name by the Geographic Names Board. The area is an Aboriginal women's Dreaming area. A 5 km return walk to the summit (for the reasonably fit) provides 360-degree views taking in the ocean, Budawang Mountains and Clyde River Valley. 25 km NW. *For the Nowra section of the park see Nowra.*

Mollymook: excellent surfing and beach fishing; 2 km N. **Narrawallee Beach:** popular surf beach; nearby Narrawallee Inlet has calm shallow water ideal for children; 4 km N. **Lakes:** good

swimming, fishing and waterskiing at Burrill Lake (5 km sw) and Lake Conjola (23 km NW). **Milton:** historic town with art galleries and outdoor cafes. Village markets are held on the highway 1st Sat each month, the Scarecrow Festival in June and the Escape Arts Festival in Sept; 7 km NW. **Pointer Gap Lookout:** beautiful coastal views; 20 km NW.

TOWNS NEARBY: Jervis Bay 33 km, Huskisson 39 km, Batemans Bay 47 km, Nowra 54 km, Braidwood 62 km

Uralla

Pop. 2270
Map ref. 515 B1 | 525 J8

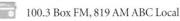

i 104 Bridge St; (02) 6778 4496; www.uralla.com

100.3 Box FM, 819 AM ABC Local

This charming New England town is famous for its connection with bushranger Captain Thunderbolt, who lived and died in the area. It is no coincidence that this was a rich goldmining district at the time. Uralla's name comes from the Anaiwan word for 'ceremonial place'. Uralla is at its most striking when the European deciduous trees change colour in autumn.

McCrossin's Mill This restored 3-storey granite and brick flour mill (1870) is now a museum of local history. The ground floor and gardens are used for functions, but the upper levels have fascinating exhibitions, including the Wool Industry, Gold Mining (featuring a replica Chinese joss house) and an Aboriginal diorama. The Thunderbolt exhibition contains a set of 9 paintings depicting the events leading up to his death, painted by Phillip Pomroy. Inquiries (02) 6778 3022; Salisbury St.

Hassett's Military Museum: large and impressive collection; features displays on military history and memorabilia, including war vehicles, uniforms and a field kitchen. Many of the displays were donated by local families; Bridge St; (02) 6778 4600. **Thunderbolt statue:** of 'gentleman' bushranger Fred Ward dominates the corner of Bridge St and Thunderbolt's Way. **Thunderbolt's grave:** he was hunted by police for over 6 years before being shot dead at nearby Kentucky Creek in 1870. His grave is clearly identified among some other magnificent Victorian monumental masonary headstones; Old Uralla Cemetery, John St. **New England Brass and Iron Lace Foundry:** beginning in 1872, it is the oldest of its kind still operating in Australia. Visitors are welcome and tours available; East St; (02) 6778 3297. **Self-guide heritage walk:** easy 2 km walk that includes 30 historic buildings, most built in the late 1800s; brochure from visitor centre.

Get off your Arts: Mar/Apr. **Thunderbolt Country Fair:** Nov.

Stoker's Restaurant and Bar: bistro, heritage building; Bushranger Motor Inn, 37 Bridge St (New England Hwy); (02) 6778 3777. **Thunderbolt Inn:** bistro-style country fare; Cnr Bridge St (New England Hwy) and Hill St; (02) 6778 4048. **White Rose Pizzeria:** pizza and salads; 82 Bridge St; (02) 6778 3008.

Country Road Caravan Park: 170 Bridge St (New England Hwy); (02) 6778 4563. **Uralla Caravan Park:** 17 Queen St; (02) 6778 4763.

Mt Yarrowyck Nature Reserve This dry eucalypt reserve has plentiful wildlife including kangaroos, wallaroos and wallabies, and is ideal for bushwalking and picnics. The highlight is the 3 km Aboriginal cultural walk – about halfway along the trail is a large overhang of granite boulders under which is a set of red-ochre paintings of circles and bird tracks. 23 km NW.

Dangars Lagoon: bird sanctuary and hide; 5 km SE. *Gold fossicking:* gold and small precious stones can still be found; map and equipment hire from visitor centre; 5 km SW. *Thunderbolt's Rock:* used by the bushranger as a lookout. Climb with care; 6 km S. *Tourist Drive 19:* signposted drive includes historic Gostwyck Church (11 km SE) and Dangars Falls and Gorge (40 km S); brochure from visitor centre.

TOWNS NEARBY: Armidale 22 km, Walcha 39 km, Guyra 50 km, Tamworth 74 km, Manilla 76 km

Urunga

Pop. 2685
Map ref. 515 H2 | 516 D12 | 525 M8

ℹ️ Pacific Hwy; (02) 6655 5711; www.bellingen.com

📻 738 AM ABC North Coast

Urunga is a sleepy, attractive town at the junction of the Bellinger and Kalang rivers and is regarded by locals as one of the best fishing spots on the north coast. Because it is bypassed by the Pacific Highway, the town has remained relatively untouched by tourism. A large percentage of the population are retirees and there are some beautiful walks around the foreshore.

 Oceanview Hotel: refurbished with original furniture. Meals and accommodation are available; Morgo St. *Urunga Museum:* in historic building with photographs, documents and paintings from the local area; Morgo St. *Anchor's Wharf:* riverside restaurant and boat hire. *The Honey Place:* huge concrete replica of an old-style straw beehive with glass beehive display, honey-tasting, gallery and gardens; Pacific Hwy. *Watersports and fishing:* both on the rivers and beach; brochures from visitor centre.

🍴 *Anchors Wharf Cafe:* seafood/steak and boat hire; 4–6 Bellingen St; (02) 6655 5588.

🛏️ *Aquarelle Bed & Breakfast:* 152 Osprey Dr; (02) 6655 3174. *The Kabana Luxury Accommodation:* 30 Shortcut Rd; (02) 6655 6582. *Urunga Heads Holiday Park:* 2 Morgo St; (02) 6655 6355. *Urunga Waters Tourist Park:* 8531 Pacific Hwy; (02) 6655 6242. *North Beach Holiday Park:* Beach Pde, Mylestom; (02) 6655 4250. *Bellinger River Tourist Park:* 96 Mylestom Dr, Repton; (02) 6655 4755.

🌳 **Bongil Bongil National Park** This stunning park is 10 km of unspoilt coastal beaches, pristine estuaries, wetlands, rainforest and magnificent views. The estuaries are perfect for canoeing and birdwatching, with abundant protected birdlife. The beaches provide outstanding fishing, surfing and swimming, as well as important nesting areas for a variety of wading birds and terns. There are signposted bushwalks and scenic picnic spots; (02) 6651 5946; 15 km N.

Hungry Head: beautiful beach for surfing and swimming; 3 km S. *Raleigh:* charming town with Prince of Peace Anglican Church (1900), winery, horseriding and a go-kart complex; 4 km N.

TOWNS NEARBY: Bellingen 12 km, Nambucca Heads 16 km, Coffs Harbour 24 km, Macksville 25 km, Dorrigo 34 km

Wagga Wagga

Pop. 52 491
Map ref. 522 B9 | 527 P9 | 543 M1

ℹ️ Tarcutta St; (02) 6926 9621 or 1300 100 122; www.waggawaggaaustralia.com.au

📻 91.3 Star FM, 102.7 FM ABC Local

Wagga Wagga ('place of many crows' in the Wiradjuri language) is the largest inland city in New South Wales and is regarded

as the capital of the Riverina. In 1864 Wagga Wagga received international attention when a man arrived claiming to be Roger Tichborne, a baronet who was believed drowned when his ship disappeared off South America. While Tichborne's mother believed him, the trustees of the estate were not so sure. What followed is believed to be the longest court case in England's history. The man was found to be Arthur Orton, a butcher, and sentenced to 14 years for perjury. Mark Twain found this story so fascinating that he insisted on visiting Wagga Wagga when he visited Australia in the 1890s.

🏛️ **Museum of the Riverina** The museum is divided into 2 locations, one at the historic Council Chambers (Baylis St) and the other at the Botanic Gardens, Wagga Wagga (Lord Baden Powell Dr). The chambers museum has a regular program of travelling exhibitions (inquiries on (02) 6926 9655). The museum at the botanic gardens focuses on the people, places and events that have been important to Wagga Wagga and incorporates the Sporting Hall of Fame, which features local stars such as former Australian cricket captain Mark Taylor.

Botanic Gardens: themed gardens, mini-zoo, free-flight aviary, miniature railway; picnic and barbecue facilities; Willans Hill. *Wagga Wagga Regional Art Gallery:* offers an extensive and changing exhibition program and includes the National Art Glass Collection; closed Mon; Cnr Baylis and Morrow sts; inquiries (02) 6926 9660. *Lake Albert:* watersports, fishing, bushwalking and birdwatching; Lake Albert Rd. *Charles Sturt University Winery and Cheese Factory:* open daily for tastings with a range of premium wines and handmade cheeses; off McKeown Dr. *Bikeways:* along Lake Albert, Wollundry Lagoon, Flowerdale Lagoon and the Murrumbidgee River.

🎪 *Farmers market:* Wollundry Lagoon; 2nd Sat each month. *Wagga Wagga Wine and Food Festival:* Mar. *Gold Cup Racing Carnival:* May. *Jazz and Blues Festival:* Sept.

🍴 *Clancy's Restaurant:* modern Australian; Carriage House Motor Inn, cnr Sturt Hwy and Eunony Bridge Rd; (02) 6922 7374. *Three Chefs Restaurant:* modern Australian; 97 Fitzmaurice St; (02) 6921 5897.

🛏️ *East's Riverview Holiday Park – Wagga Wagga:* 93 Hammond Ave (Sturt Hwy); (02) 6921 4287. *Millies Accommodation:* 199 Gurwood St; (02) 6931 7638. *Wagga Wagga Beach Caravan Park:* 2 Johnston St; (02) 6931 0603. *Coolamon Caravan Park:* Bruce St, Coolamon; (02) 6927 3013. *Dunn's B&B:* 63 Mitchelmore St, Turvey Park; (02) 6925 7771. *Forest Hill Caravan Park:* Sturt Hwy, Forest Hill; (02) 6922 7219. *Horseshoe Motor Village Caravan Park:* 23 Horseshoe Rd, Cartwrights Hill; (02) 6921 6033.

🌳 **Junee** This important railhead and commercial centre is located on Olympic Way. It has several historic buildings and museums. Monte Cristo Homestead is a restored colonial mansion with an impressive carriage collection. The Roundhouse Museum in Harold St contains an original workshop, locomotives, a model train and memorabilia. The visitor centre is located in Railway Sq in 19th-century railway refreshment rooms. 41 km NE.

Riverina wine region While the Riverina has a reputation for big business and an overall lack of atmosphere, the region produces good, great and sometimes even world-class wines. One such wine is the Noble One Botrytis Semillon produced by De Bortoli, as no other region in Australia has had the same success with this dessert wine. The Riverina also offers some of the best value for

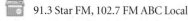

money drops in the country. Wineries to visit include De Bortoli, McWilliam's and Miranda.

Lake Albert: watersports, fishing, bushwalking and birdwatching; 7 km s. *Kapooka:* self-drive tours of the military base; brochure from visitor centre; 9 km sw. *RAAF Museum:* indoor and outdoor exhibits and barbecue facilities; open 10am–3pm; 10 km E. *The Rock:* small town noted for its unusual scenery. Walking trails through the reserve lead to the summit of the Rock; 32 km sw. *Aurora Clydesdale Stud and Pioneer Farm:* encounters with Clydesdales and other farm animals on a working farm; closed Thurs and Sun; 33 km w. *Lockhart:* historic town with National Trust–listed Green St for an impressive turn-of-the-century streetscape. Also several pleasant walking tracks in the area, and picnic races in Oct; 65 km w. *Wagga Wagga Winery:* tasting area and restaurant has an early-Australian theme; 427 Oura Rd; (02) 6922 1221. *River cruises and walking tracks:* guided and self-guide tours of the city sights; brochures from visitor centre.

TOWNS NEARBY: Holbrook 66 km, Culcairn 66 km, Adelong 68 km, Gundagai 69 km, Temora 77 km

Walcha
Pop. 1625
Map ref. 515 B3 | 525 J9

i 51W Fitzroy St; (02) 6774 2460; www.walchansw.com.au

88.5 FM ABC Local, 90.1 FM ABC Radio National

Walcha (pronounced 'Wolka') is an attractive service town to the local farming regions on the eastern slopes of the Great Dividing Range. Modern sculptures are featured throughout the town and the beautiful Apsley Falls are a must-see for visitors.

 Amaroo Museum and Cultural Centre This unique centre features Aboriginal art and craft with the artists working on-site; visitors are invited to watch them at work. The artists use traditional designs combined with contemporary flair to make original clothing, homewares, gifts, jewellery and art. Also on display is a collection of local Aboriginal artefacts. Open Mon–Fri; Derby St; (02) 6777 1111.

Open-Air Sculptures Situated throughout town, the works include street furniture created by local, national and international artisans; brochure from visitor centre. *Pioneer Cottage and Museum:* includes a blacksmith's shop and the 1st Tiger Moth used for crop dusting in Australia; Derby St.

Walcha Bushmans Carnival and Campdraft: Jan. *Timber Expo:* May. *Walcha Garden Festival:* Nov.

Cafe Graze: great food and coffee; 21N Derby St; (02) 6777 2409. *Walcha Road Hotel Restaurant:* modern Australian; Walcha Rd; (02) 6777 5829.

Walcha Caravan Park: Cnr Middle and North sts; (02) 6777 2501.

Oxley Wild Rivers National Park This national park encompasses a high plateau, deep gorges and numerous waterfalls. The Walcha section of the park features Apsley Falls (20 km E), where 7 platforms and a bridge provide access to both sides of the gorge and waterfall. Tia Falls (35 km E) has beautiful rainforest scenery. Campsites at Riverside and Youdales Hut

are accessible by 4WD. *Trout fishing:* several good locations; brochure from visitor centre.

TOWNS NEARBY: Uralla 39 km, Armidale 53 km, Tamworth 64 km, Nundle 69 km, Guyra 86 km

Walgett
Pop. 1734
Map ref. 524 B5

i 88 Fox St; (02) 6828 6139; www.walgett.nsw.gov.au

102.7 Power FM, 105.9 FM ABC Local

Walgett is the service centre to a large pastoral region. The name Walgett, which means 'the meeting of two waters', is apt, as the town is at the junction of the Barwon and Namoi rivers. The rivers provide excellent Murray cod and yellow-belly fishing. The area is rich in Aboriginal history, and archaeological digs in the shire have demonstrated that human life existed here up to 40 000 years ago.

 Norman 'Tracker' Walford Track: signposted 1.5 km scenic walk includes the first European settler's grave on the banks of the Namoi River; from levee bank at end of Warrena St. *Dharriwaa Elders Group:* Aboriginal arts and craft with local work including paintings, carved emu eggs and wooden items; Fox St. *Hot artesian springs:* relaxing and therapeutic baths at swimming pool; Montekeila St.

Campdraft and rodeo: Aug. *Bulldust to Bitumen Festival:* Sept.

Come-by-Chance This town 'came by chance' to William Colless when all of the land in the area was thought to be allocated, but it was discovered that some had been missed. Colless came to own most of the buildings, including the police station, post office, hotel, blacksmith shop and cemetery. It is now an attractive and quiet town with riverside picnic spots, bushwalks and abundant wildlife. There are picnic races in Sept. 65 km SE.

Grawin, Glengarry and Sheepyard opal fields: go fossicking, but be warned that water is scarce so an adequate supply should be carried. Brochure from visitor centre; 70 km NW. *Macquarie Marshes:* 100 km sw; *see Nyngan.*

TOWNS NEARBY: Lightning Ridge 68 km, Coonamble 106 km, Brewarrina 121 km, Wee Waa 130 km, Narrabri 164 km

Warialda
Pop. 1204
Map ref. 524 H5

i Heritage Centre, Hope St; (02) 6729 0046.

102.9 Gem FM, 648 AM ABC New England North West

Warialda is a historic town in a rich farming district. Its location on Warialda Creek gives the town a charm and contributes to its lush greenery. The origin of Warialda's name is uncertain but is thought to mean 'place of wild honey' and is presumed to be in the language of the original inhabitants, the Weraerai people.

Carinda House: historic home, now a craft shop featuring local work; Stephen St. *Pioneer Cemetery:* historic graves from as early as the 1850s in a bushland setting; Queen and Stephen sts. *Heritage Centre:* visitor centre and Well's Family Gem and Mineral collection; Hope St. *Koorilgur Nature Walk:* 3.6 km stroll through areas of wildflowers and birdlife; self-guide brochure from visitor centre. *Self-guide historical walk:* historic town buildings in Stephen and Hope sts; brochure from visitor centre.

 RADIO STATIONS IN TOWN WHAT'S ON WHERE TO EAT WHERE TO STAY   NEARBY

Agricultural Show: May. *Warialda Off-Road 200:* motor race; Sept. *Honey Festival:* Nov.

Warialda Caravan Park: Cnr Gwydir Hwy and Holden St; 0427 291 008.

Cranky Rock Nature Reserve It is rumoured that during the gold rush a 'cranky' Chinese man, after being challenged about a wrongdoing, jumped to his death from the highest of the balancing granite boulders. Today you'll find picnic spots, camping, fossicking, wildflowers and wildlife. A suspension bridge leads to an observation deck above Reedy Creek for breathtaking views. 8 km E.

TOWNS NEARBY: Bingara 36 km, Inverell 58 km, Moree 72 km, Barraba 93 km, Texas (Qld) 96 km

Wauchope

Pop. 5499
Map ref. 515 F6 | 525 L11

High St; (02) 6586 4055.

100.7 2MC FM, 684 AM ABC Local

Wauchope (pronounced 'Waw-hope') is the centre of the local dairy and cattle industries, and the gateway to over 40 000 hectares of national parks and state forests. Bursting with country hospitality, its popularity with visitors has vastly increased since the introduction of the fascinating Timbertown.

Historical town walk: self-guide walk past historic buildings such as the old courthouse and the bank; brochure from visitor centre.

Hastings Farmers Markets: Wauchope Showground; 4th Sat each month. *Community Markets:* Hastings St; 1st Sat each month. *Lasiandra Festival:* community festival; Mar. *Jazz in the Vines:* Bago Vineyards; 2nd Sun each month.

Cooking with Company: cooking classes; The Company Farm, 3470 Oxley Hwy, Gannons Creek; (02) 6585 6495.

Auntie Ann's Bed & Breakfast: 19 Bruxner Ave; (02) 6586 4420. *Blue Poles Cafe, Gallery & B&B:* 1086 Comboyne Rd, Byabarra; (02) 6587 1167.

Timbertown This re-created 1880s sawmillers' village demonstrates the struggles and achievements of early pioneers. It features steam-train rides, Cobb & Co horserides and carriage rides, blacksmith, wood turner, art gallery, farmyard patting pen, bullock demonstrations, whip cracking, boutique winery, old-fashioned lolly shop and saloon bar with bush ballads. Roast meats and damper can be enjoyed in the authentic 1880s hotel. Oxley Hwy; (02) 6586 1940; 2 km w.

Billabong Koala and Nature Park: 2.5 ha of lush parkland and waterways with exotic and native animals and birds, and koala patting 3 times daily; 10 km E. *Bellrowan Valley Horse Riding:* relaxing horserides through the Australian bush with experienced guides. Daily trail rides and overnight packages; Beechwood; 5 km NW. *Old Bottlebutt:* the largest known bloodwood tree in NSW; 6 km s. *Bago Winery:* cellar-door tastings and sales with regular Jazz in the Vines concerts; 8 km sw. *Bago Bluff National Park:* signposted bushwalks (various fitness levels) through rugged wilderness; 12 km w. *Werrikimbie National Park:* magnificent World Heritage–listed wilderness with rainforests, rivers and wildflowers (best viewed in spring). Also several excellent sites for camping and picnics; 80 km w. *4WD tours and abseiling:* bookings at visitor centre.

TOWNS NEARBY: Port Macquarie 18 km, Laurieton 22 km, Kempsey 43 km, Taree 56 km, Wingham 57 km

Wee Waa

Pop. 1692
Map ref. 524 E6

Narrabri Shire Visitor Information Centre, Newell Hwy, Narrabri; (02) 6799 6760 or 1800 659 931; www.weewaa.com

91.3 Max FM, 648 AM ABC New England North Coast

Wee Waa is a dynamic rural community near the Namoi River and also the base for the Namoi Cotton Cooperative, the largest grower-owned organisation in the country. Cotton has only been grown here since the 1960s, but the town claims to be the 'cotton capital of Australia'. Wee Waa, meaning 'fire for roasting', comes from the local Aboriginal language.

Wee Waa Museum: fascinating display of machinery, artefacts and documents pertaining to the history of the Wee Waa district. Open Wed–Sat at various times; Rose St; (02) 6796 1760.

Wee Waa Show: May. *Village Fest:* food, music and games; June. *Rodeo:* Sept. *Christmas Mardi Gras:* Dec.

Wee Waa Chinese Restaurant: traditional Chinese; Wee Waa Bowling Club, 69 Alma St; (02) 6795 4108. *Wee Waa Hot Bread Shop:* bakery/cafe with freshly baked bread; 82 Rose St; (02) 6795 4393.

Guided cotton gin and farm tour First the tour visits a local cotton farm to view the picking and pressing of cotton into modules ready for transporting to the cotton gin. At the gin the cotton is transformed from modules into bales and then goes to the classing department for sorting. Runs Mar–Aug; bookings (02) 6799 6760.

Cuttabri Wine Shanty The slab-construction shanty was built in 1882 and was once a Cobb & Co coach stop between Wee Waa and Pilliga. It was issued the 2nd liquor licence in Australia and is the only wine shanty still operating in the country. 25 km sw.

Yarrie Lake: boating, swimming and birdwatching; 24 km s. *Cubbaroo Cellars:* cellar-door tastings and sales; 48 km w. *Barren Junction:* hot artesian bore baths (over 100 years old) in a pleasant location surrounded by tamarind trees; 51 km w.

TOWNS NEARBY: Narrabri 35 km, Moree 93 km, Barraba 114 km, Gunnedah 115 km, Bingara 116 km

Wellington

Pop. 4660
Map ref. 522 F2

Cameron Park, Nanima Cr; (02) 6845 1733 or 1800 621 614; www.visitwellington.com.au

89.5 Zoo FM, 549 AM ABC Central West

Wellington is a typical Australian country town with a wide main street, numerous monuments to significant local people and attractive parklands. Sitting at the foot of Mount Arthur, it is best known for the nearby Wellington Caves.

Oxley Museum: the history of Wellington is told with photographs and artefacts; in the old bank (1883); open 1.30–4.30pm Mon–Fri, other times by appt; Cnr Percy and Warne sts. *Orana Aboriginal Corporation:* authentic Aboriginal ceramics, paintings, clothing and artefacts; open Mon–Fri; Swift St. *Cameron Park:* known for its rose gardens and suspension bridge over the Bell River, it also has picnic and barbecue facilities; Nanima Cres. *Self-guide town walk:* taking in historic buildings including hotels and churches; brochure from visitor centre.

Market: Cnr Percy St and and Nanima Cres; last Sat each month. *Vintage Fair:* with street parade and swap meet; Mar.

[WENTWORTH] OUTDOOR DUNNY, MUNGO NATIONAL PARK

The Wellington Boot: horseraces; Mar. *Wellington Show:* Apr. *Festivale:* week of celebrations; Oct. *Carols in the Cave:* Dec.

The Grange Restaurant: modern Australian; Hermitage Hill, 135 Maxwell St; (02) 6845 4469. *Keston Rose Garden Cafe:* light lunches and cakes; Mudgee Rd; (02) 6845 3508.

Carinya B&B: 111 Arthur St; (02) 6845 4320. *Wellington Caves Caravan Park:* Caves Rd; (02) 6845 2970. *Wellington Riverside Caravan Park:* 1 Federal St; (02) 6845 1370. *Wellington Valley Caravan Park:* 44 Curtis St; (02) 6845 2006. *Banderra B & B Farmstay:* Gowangreen Rd, Bakers Swamp; (02) 6846 7201. *Lake Burrendong State Park:* Fashions Mount Rd, Lake Burrendong; (02) 6846 7435.

Wellington Caves These fascinating limestone caves include Cathedral Cave, with a giant stalagmite, and Gaden Cave, with rare cave coral. For thousands of years the caves have acted as natural animal traps, and fossils of a diprotodon and a giant kangaroo have been found here. There are guided tours through the old phosphate mine (wheelchair-accessible). Nearby is an aviary, an opal shop, Japanese gardens, picnic facilities, kiosk and the bottle house, a structure made from over 9000 wine bottles. 9 km s.

Mt Arthur Reserve: walks to the lookout at the summit of Mt Binjang; maps from visitor centre; 3 km w. *Angora Tourist Farm:* demonstrations of shearing angora rabbits and alpacas; 20 km sw. *Eris Fleming Gallery:* original oil paintings and watercolours by the artist; 26 km s. *Nangara Gallery:* Aboriginal art and craft with artefacts dating back over 20 000 years; 26 km sw. *Lake Burrendong State Park:* watersports, fishing, campsites and cabins, and spectacular lake views from the main wall. Burrendong Arboretum is a beautiful spot for birdwatching and features several pleasant walking tracks. Also excellent camping, picnic and barbecue sites at Mookerawa Waters Park; 32 km se. *Stuart Town:* small gold-rush town formerly known as Ironbark, made famous by Banjo Paterson's poem 'The Man from Ironbark'; 38 km se. *Wineries:* several in the area offering cellar-door tastings and sales. Glenfinlass Wines sell exclusively through cellar door; brochure from visitor centre.

TOWNS NEARBY: Dubbo 47 km, Gulgong 59 km, Mudgee 60 km, Orange 82 km, Parkes 97 km

Wentworth
Pop. 1305
Map ref. 526 D5 | 546 F5

66 Darling St; (03) 5027 3624; www.wentworth.nsw.gov.au

90.7 Hot FM, 999 AM ABC Broken Hill

At the junction of the Murray and Darling rivers, Wentworth was once a busy and important town. With the introduction of the railways it became quieter and is now an attractive and peaceful holiday town with a rich history.

Old Wentworth Gaol The first Australian-designed gaol by colonial architect James Barnett. The bricks were made on-site from local clay, and bluestone was transported from Victoria. Construction took from 1879 to 1891. Closed as a gaol in 1927, the building is in remarkably good condition. Beverley St.

Pioneer World Museum: over 3000 historic artefacts including space junk, prehistoric animals and the country's largest collection of paddleboat photos; Beverley St. *Sturt's Tree:* tree on the riverbank marked by explorer Charles Sturt when he weighed anchor and identified the junction of the Murray and Darling rivers in 1830; Willow Bend Caravan Park, Darling St. *Fotherby Park:* PS *Ruby,* a historic paddlesteamer (1907), and statue of 'The Possum', a man who became a hermit during the Depression and lived in trees for 50 years; Wentworth St. *Lock 10:* weir and park for picnics; south-west edge of town. *Historical town walk:* self-guide walk includes the town courthouse (1870s) and Customs House (1 of 2 original customs houses still standing in Australia); brochure from visitor centre.

Market: Inland Botanic Gardens; 1st and 3rd Sat each month. *National Trust Festival Week:* Apr. *Country Music Festival:* Sept/Oct. *Wentworth Cup:* horserace; Nov.

Willow Bend Caravan Park: Darling St; (03) 5027 3213. *Buronga Riverside Caravan Park:* West Rd, Buronga; (03) 5023 3040. *Coomealla Club Accommodation Resort:* Silver City Hwy, Dareton; 1800 854 737. *Glenbar Cottage:* 512 Wentworth Rd, Yelta, Vic.; (03) 5025 1239. *Rivergardens Tourist Park:* Cnr Sturt Hwy and Punt Rd, Gol Gol; (03) 5024 8541.

Perry Sandhills These magnificent orange dunes are estimated to have originated during the last Ice Age, around 40 000 years ago. Skeletal remains of mega-fauna (kangaroos, wombats, emus and lions) have been found here. In WW II the area was used as a bombing range, but recently it has been used in film and television. The Music Under the Stars concerts are held here each Mar. Off Silver City Hwy; 5 km NW.

Mungo National Park: 157 km N; *see Balranald. Yelta:* former Aboriginal mission, now a Victorian town with model aircraft display; 12 km SE. *Australian Inland Botanic Gardens:* the desert blooms with some exotic and colourful plant life. There are tractor/train tours of the gardens and a light lunch the last Sun each month; 28 km SE. *Pooncarie:* 'outback oasis' with natural 2-tier wharf, weir, museum and craft gallery; 117 km N. *Harry Nanya Aboriginal Cultural Tours:* travel to Mungo National Park with a Barkindji guide; brochure and bookings at visitor centre. *Heritage and nature driving tours:* various sites include Mildura and Lake Victoria; brochure from visitor centre. *Houseboat hire:* short- or long-term river holidays; brochure from visitor centre.

TOWNS NEARBY: **Mildura (Vic.) 24 km, Robinvale (Vic.) 95 km, Renmark (SA) 108 km, Ouyen (Vic.) 113 km, Berri (SA) 123 km**

West Wyalong
Pop. 3189
Map ref. 522 B6 | 527 P6

 i Bland Shire Library, 6 Shire St; (02) 6979 0272; www.blandshire.nsw.gov.au

99.7 Star FM, 549 AM ABC Local

John Oxley was the first European explorer to visit West Wyalong. He disliked the region, claiming 'these desolate areas would never again be visited by civilised man'. He was proved wrong when squatters moved in, and the discovery of gold in 1893 meant the town became inundated with settlers. West Wyalong is now in one of the state's most productive agricultural regions.

 West Wyalong Local Aboriginal Land Council Arts and Crafts The craft shop features local Aboriginal work. Handcrafted items are on display and for sale and include boomerangs, didgeridoos, hand-woven baskets, clothing, and traditional beauty and skin-care products. The library features a collection of historic and contemporary titles relating to Aboriginal heritage, culture and modern issues. Open Mon–Fri; Main St; (02) 6972 3493.

Bland District Historical Museum: displays of goldmining including a scale model of a goldmine and records from mines such as the Black Snake, the Blue Jacket and the Shamrock and Thistle; Main St.

West Wyalong Campdraft: Sept.

Ace Caravan Park: Newell Hwy; (02) 6972 3061. *West Wyalong Caravan Park:* 60 Main St; (02) 6972 3133.

Lake Cowal When it is full, this is the largest natural lake in NSW and a bird and wildlife sanctuary. There are over 180 species of waterbird living in the area, with many rare or endangered. The lake is also excellent for fishing. No visitor facilities are provided. Via Clear Ridge; 48 km NE.

Barmedman: mineral-salt pool believed to help arthritis and rheumatism; 32 km SE. *Weethalle Whistlestop:* Devonshire teas, art and craft; Hay Rd; 65 km W.

TOWNS NEARBY: **Temora 66 km, Grenfell 89 km, Forbes 96 km, Leeton 101 km, Lake Cargelligo 104 km**

White Cliffs
Pop. 120
Map ref. 528 F7

 i White Cliffs General Store, Keraro Rd; (08) 8091 6611.

107.7 FM ABC Broken Hill, 1584 AM ABC Local

White Cliffs is first and foremost an opal town. The first mining lease was granted in 1890, and a boom followed with an influx of 4500 people. The area is still known for its opals, particularly the unique opal 'pineapples' and the opalised remains of a plesiosaur, a 2-metre-long 100-million-year-old fossil found in 1976. The intense heat has forced many people to build underground, often in the remains of old opal mines. The buildings left on the surface are surrounded by a pale and eerie moonscape with an estimated 50 000 abandoned opal digs.

Solar Power Station The country's 1st solar power station was established by the Australian National University in 1981 at White Cliffs because it receives the most solar radiation in NSW. The row of 14 giant mirrored dishes is a striking sight between the blue sky and red earth. Next to council depot.

Outback Treasures: opal jewellery and Aboriginal art; Smiths Hill. *Jock's Place:* dugout home and museum with an opal seam along one wall; Turleys Hill. *Wellington's Underground Art Gallery:* paintings and polished opals by local artist; The Blocks. *Otto Photography:* gallery of outback landscape photos; Smiths Hill. *Self-guide and guided historical walks and fossicking:* include the old police station (1897) and school (1900) and several fossicking sites; brochures and maps from visitor centre. *Underground accommodation:* various standards available in dugout premises. Underground temperatures come as a relief at 22°C; details from visitor centre. *Opal shops:* several in town sell local gems; details from visitor centre.

 Ironman Cliffhanger: 4WD challenge; July.

Opal Pioneer Caravan & Camping Tourist Park: Johnston St; (08) 8091 6688.

Paroo–Darling National Park: section 20 km E of town contains magnificent Peery Lake, part of the Paroo River overflow, where there is birdlife, Aboriginal cultural sites and walking trails. Southern section of park has camping along the Darling River. *Wilcannia:* small town with many fine sandstone buildings, an opening bridge across the Darling River and an old paddlesteamer wharf. Also a self-guide historical walk available; brochure from council offices in Reid St; 93 km S. *Mutawintji National Park:* 150 km SW; *see Broken Hill.*

TOWNS NEARBY: **Menindee 182 km, Tibooburra 188 km, Broken Hill 198 km**

Windsor
Pop. 1899
Map ref. 508 A2 | 511 I5 | 513 P7 | 523 J6

 i Hawkesbury Visitor Information Centre, Ham Common, Hawkesbury Valley Way, Clarendon; (02) 4578 0233 or 1300 362 874; www.hawkesburytourism.com.au

89.9 FM Hawkesbury Radio, 702 AM ABC Local

Windsor, located on a high bank of the Hawkesbury River, is the third oldest European settlement on mainland Australia, after Sydney Cove and Parramatta. There are still many old buildings standing and the surrounding national parks make for breathtaking scenery.

Hawkesbury Regional Museum Built as a home in the 1820s, the building became the Daniel O'Connell Inn in 1843.

In the late 1800s it was used to print *The Australian*, a weekly newspaper. Today it houses the history of the local area in photographs, documents and artefacts, with special displays on riverboat history and the Richmond Royal Australian Air Force base. Thompson Sq.

Hawkesbury Regional Gallery: displays contemporary and traditional works by national and international artists; George St. *St Matthew's Church:* designed by convict architect Francis Greenway and built in 1817, St Matthews is the oldest Anglican church in the country. The adjacent graveyard dates back to 1810 and contains the graves of some of the First Fleet pioneers; Moses St. *Self-guide tourist walk/drive:* historic sites include the original courthouse and doctor's house; brochure from visitor centre.

Market: Windsor Mall; Sun. *Bridge to Bridge Powerboat Classic:* May. *Bridge to Bridge Water Ski Race:* Nov. *Hawkesbury Canoe Classic:* Nov. *Hawkesbury Wine, Food and Music Affair Raceday:* Nov.

Clydesdales Horse Drawn Restaurant: modern Australian in horsedrawn carriage; 61 Hawkesbury Valley Way; (02) 4577 4544. *The Harvest Restaurant:* modern Australian/international; The Sebel Resort & Spa Hawkesbury Valley, 61 Hawkesbury Valley Way; (02) 4577 4222.

Dural House at Round Corner: 679 Old Northern Rd, Round Corner; (02) 9651 5777. *OK Caravan Corral:* 51 Terry Rd, Rouse Hill; (02) 9629 2652. *Ossian Hall:* 1928 Putty Rd, Colo; (02) 4575 5250. *Riverside Ski Park:* 307 Cattai Rd, Cattai; (02) 4572 8764. *Sydney Gateway Holiday Park:* 30 Majestic Dr, Stanhope Gardens; (02) 8814 4222. *Sydney Getaway Holiday Park & Avina Van Village:* 217 Commercial Rd, Vineyard; (02) 9627 1847. *Sydney Hills Holiday Park:* 269 New Line Rd, Dural; (02) 9651 2555. *Tizzana Winery Bed & Breakfast:* 518 Tizzana Rd, Ebenezer; (02) 4579 1150. *Town & Country Estate:* 140 Hollinsworth Rd, Marsden Park; (02) 9628 4757.

Cattai National Park First Fleet assistant surgeon Thomas Arndell was granted this land and today the park features his 1821 cottage. There are also grain silos and the ruins of a windmill believed to be the oldest industrial building in the country. The old farm features attractive picnic and barbecue areas and campsites. In a separate section nearby, Mitchell Park offers walking tracks and canoeing on Cattai Creek. 14 km NE.

Ebenezer: picturesque town with Australia's oldest church (1809), colonial graveyard and schoolhouse; 11 km N. *Wollemi National Park:* Windsor section features the spectacular Colo River and activities including abseiling, canoeing (bring your own), bushwalking and 4WD touring; via Colo; 26 km N.

TOWNS NEARBY: Richmond 6 km, Glenbrook 25 km, Wisemans Ferry 30 km, Katoomba 48 km, Blackheath 49 km

Wingham

Pop. 4813
Map ref. 515 D8 | 523 N1 | 525 K12

i Manning Valley Visitor Information Centre, 21 Manning River Dr, Taree North; (02) 6592 5444 or 1800 182 733; www.gtcc.nsw.gov.au

107.3 MAX FM, 756 AM ABC Local

Heritage-listed Wingham is the oldest town in the Manning Valley. It has many Federation buildings surrounding the enchanting town common, which was based on a traditional

English square. The wonderful Manning River and Wingham Brush bring nature to the centre of town. The Chinese Garden at the town's entrance marks the importance of the early Chinese settlers to the town's heritage. Best-selling Australian author Di Morrissey's book *The Valley* is based on the pioneering characters and places of the Manning Valley. It is largely set in and around Wingham where she was born.

Wingham Brush The unique brush is part of the last 10 ha of subtropical flood-plain rainforest in NSW. It is home to 195 species of native plants including giant Moreton Bay fig trees, a large population of endangered grey-headed flying foxes and 100 bird species. The brush includes a boardwalk, picnic and barbecue facilities and a boat-launching area on the Manning River. Farquar St.

Manning Valley Historical Museum: housed in an old general store (1880s), this has one of the most extensive collections of historical memorabilia on the north coast. Includes displays on local farming, commercial and timber history; part of an attractive square bounded by Isabella, Bent, Farquar and Wynter sts. *Manning River:* picturesque waterway with several locations for swimming, boating, fishing and waterskiing. *Self-guide historical town walk:* tour of the town's Federation buildings; brochure from museum.

Market: Wynter St; 2nd Sat each month. *Wingham Farmers Market:* Wingham Showground, Gloucester Rd; 1st Sat each month. *Summertime Rodeo:* Jan. *Wingham Beef Week and Scottish Heritage Festival:* May. *Junior Rodeo and Bute Ute Show:* July. *All Breeds Horse Spectacular and A-Koo-Stik Festival:* Oct. *Killabakh Day in the Country:* country fair; Nov.

Bent on Food: cafe and provedore; 95 Isabella St; (02) 6557 0727.

Tourist Drive 8 This enjoyable drive begins in Taree and passes through Wingham, Comboyne and Bybarra before finishing in Wauchope (36 km is unsealed; not suitable for motorists towing caravans). The highlight is Ellenborough Falls, 40 km N, one of the highest single-drop falls in NSW, with easy walking trails, lookouts and barbecue facilities. Red Tail Wines in Marlee (13 km N) has free tastings. Brochure from visitor centre.

TOWNS NEARBY: Taree 9 km, Forster–Tuncurry 37 km, Gloucester 42 km, Laurieton 47 km, Wauchope 57 km

Wisemans Ferry

Pop. 80
Map ref. 509 A7 | 511 K2 | 523 K5

i Hawkesbury River Tourist Information Centre; 5 Bridge St, Brooklyn; (02) 9985 7064; www.hawkesburyaustralia.com.au

89.9 FM Hawkesbury Radio, 702 AM ABC Local

Wisemans Ferry is a sleepy town built around what was once an important crossing on the Hawkesbury River. The mainland route from Sydney to Newcastle had always gone via this region, but when people started using the Castle Hill route, Solomon Wiseman, who had been granted a parcel of land and opened an inn, built a ferry to take people and cargo across the river. Today car ferries still cross at this point.

Wisemans Ferry Inn Before it was an inn, this was the home of Solomon Wiseman; he called it Cobham Hall. Wiseman later opened a section of the building as an inn and it is said to be haunted by his wife, whom he allegedly pushed down the front

steps to her death. The inn provides food and accommodation. Old Northern Rd; (02) 4566 4301.*Cemetery:* early settlers' graves include that of Peter Hibbs, who travelled on the HMS *Sirius* with Captain Phillip in 1788; Settlers Rd.

Riverbend Restaurant: modern Australian; Australis Retreat at Wisemans, 5564 Old Northern Rd; (02) 4560 0593. *Wiseman's Steakhouse Bistro:* steakhouse, traditional pub; Wiseman's Inn Hotel, 6 Old Northern Rd; (02) 4566 4739.

Del Rio Riverside Resort: 76 Chaseling Rd, Webbs Creek; (02) 4566 4330. *Price Morris Cottage:* 37 Upper Macdonald Rd, St Albans; (02) 4568 2121.

Dharug National Park The multicoloured sandstone provides striking scenery on this historic land. The convict-built Old Great North Road is a great example of early 19th-century roadbuilding. Convicts quarried, dressed and shifted large sandstone blocks to build walls and bridges, but the road was abandoned before it was finished because of poor planning. Signposted walking tracks lead through beautiful bushland and to Aboriginal rock engravings. The clear-water tributaries are popular for swimming, fishing and canoeing. North side of the river.

Yengo National Park and Parr State Conservation Area: rugged land of gorges, cliffs and rocky outcrops. Discovery walks, talks and 4WD tours are conducted by the National Parks & Wildlife Service; north-east side of the river (accessible by ferry); bookings (02) 4784 7301. *Marramarra National Park:* undeveloped park with wetlands and mangroves for canoeing, camping, bushwalking (experienced only) and birdwatching; 28 km s.

TOWNS NEARBY: Windsor 30 km, Richmond 32 km, Woy Woy 33 km, Gosford 34 km, Wyong 43 km

Woolgoolga

Pop. 4358
Map ref. 516 E11 | 525 N7

Cnr Beach and Boundary sts; (02) 6654 8080; www.coffscoast.com.au

105.5 Star FM, 738 AM ABC Radio National

'Woopi' (as it is affectionately known to locals) is a charming and relaxed seaside town with a significant Sikh population. Punjabi migrants who were working on the Queensland cane fields headed south for work on banana plantations, many settling in Woolgoolga. Today Indians make up between a quarter and a half of the town's population, providing a unique cultural mix. The beaches are popular for fishing, surfing and swimming.

Guru Nanak Sikh Temple: spectacular white temple with gold domes; River St. *Woolgoolga Art Gallery:* exhibits local works; Turon Pde.

Market: Beach St; 2nd Sat each month.

Solitary Islands Lodge: 3 Arthur St; (02) 6654 1335. *Sunset Caravan Park:* 64 Newman St; (02) 6654 1499. *Woolgoolga Beach Caravan Park:* 55 Beach St; (02) 6654 1373. *BIG4 Emerald Beach Holiday Park:* 73 Fishermans Dr, Emerald Beach; (02) 6656 1521. *Corindi Beach Holiday Park:* 93 Pacific St, Corindi Beach; (02) 6649 2803. *Headlands Beach Guest House:* 17 Headland Rd, Arrawarra Headland; (02) 6654 0364. *NRMA Darlington Beach Holiday Park:* 104–134 Eggins Dr, Arrawarra; (02) 6640 7444. *Red Rock Holiday Park:* 1 Lawson St, Red Rock; (02) 6649 2730. *The Lorikeet Tourist Park:* 210 Eggins Dr, Arrawarra; 1800 555 858.

Yarrawarra Aboriginal Cultural Centre The focus of this centre is to help Aboriginal and Islander peoples maintain their heritage while teaching others about it. Visitors are encouraged to browse through the rooms of locally produced art, craft, books and CDs. The Bush Tucker Cafe offers meals with an Indigenous twist. Tours offered through the local area explore middens, ochre quarries and campsites while teaching about bush tucker and natural medicines. Stone and tool workshops and accommodation are also offered. Red Rock Rd; (02) 6649 2669; 10 km N.

Yuraygir National Park: Woolgoolga section is excellent for bushwalking, canoeing, fishing, surfing, swimming, picnicking and camping on unspoiled coastline; 10 km N. *Wedding Bells State Forest:* subtropical and eucalypt forest with walking trails to Sealy Lookout and Mt Caramba Lookout; 14 km NW.

TOWNS NEARBY: Coffs Harbour 22 km, Urunga 46 km, Bellingen 47 km, Dorrigo 52 km, Grafton 53 km

Woy Woy

Pop. 9985
Map ref. 508 H1 | 509 D8 | 511 N3 | 523 K6

Shop 1, 18–22 The Boulevard; (02) 4341 2888 or 1300 130 708; www.visitcentralcoast.com.au

101.3 Sea FM, 702 AM ABC Local

Woy Woy is the largest of the numerous holiday villages clustered around Brisbane Water, a shallow but enormous inlet. Along with nearby Broken Bay, the Hawkesbury River and Pittwater, it draws visitors looking for aquatic holidays. The nearby national parks encompass breathtaking wilderness and lookouts.

Woy Woy Hotel: historic 1897 hotel offering meals and accommodation; The Boulevard. *Waterfront reserve:* picnic facilities with Brisbane Water view.

Everglades Country Club Brasserie: modern bistro; Everglades Country Club, Dunban Rd; (02) 4341 1866. *Halftide Brasserie:* international; Ettalong Beach Club, 51–52 The Esplanade, Ettalong Beach; (02) 4343 0111. *Manfredi at Bells:* modern Italian; Bells at Killcare, 107 The Scenic Rd, Killcare Heights; (02) 4360 2411. *Lizotte's:* modern Australian, with live music; Lot 3, Avoca Dr, Kincumber; (02) 4368 2017. *Pearls on the Beach:* modern Australian; 1 Tourmaline Ave, Pearl Beach; (02) 4342 4400. *Stillwaters:* modern Australian; 1 Restella Ave, Davistown; (02) 4369 1300 *Yum Yum Eatery:* modern Australian; 60 Araluen Dr, Hardys Bay; (02) 4360 2999.

Ettalong Beach Holiday Village: Fassifern St, Ettalong Beach; (02) 4344 2211. *Granny's Cottage:* 16 Putty Beach Dr, Killcare; (02) 4360 1950. *NRMA Ocean Beach Holiday Park:* Sydney Ave, Umina Beach; (02) 4379 9488.

Brisbane Water National Park A beautiful park of rugged sandstone with spring wildflowers, bushwalks and birdlife. Staples Lookout has superb coastal views. Warrah Lookout enjoys a sea of colour in spring when the wildflowers bloom. A highlight is the Bulgandry Aboriginal engravings on Woy Woy Rd. 3 km SW.

Ettalong Beach: great swimming beach with seaside markets each Sat and Sun (Mon on long weekends); 3 km s. *Milson Island:* recreation reserve once used as an asylum and then as a gaol. *HMAS Parramatta:* a WW I ship, it ran aground off the northern shore and the wreck is still there today; 5 km s. *Mt Ettalong Lookout:* stunning coastal views; 6 km s. *Pearl Beach:* chic holiday spot favoured by the rich and famous, with magnificent sunsets; 12 km s. *Boating, fishing and swimming:* excellent conditions on Brisbane Water, Broken Bay and Hawkesbury River.

TOWNS NEARBY: Gosford 7 km, Terrigal 12 km, The Entrance 23 km, Wyong 24 km, Wisemans Ferry 33 km

WOLLONGONG

Pop. 263 537
Map ref. 517 F5 | 519 H2 | 523 J8

i Southern Gateway Centre, Princes Highway, Bulli Tops;
(02) 4267 5910 or 1800 240 737;
www.tourismwollongong.com

96.5 Wave FM, 1431 AM ABC Radio National

As a major iron and steel producer, Wollongong has an undeserved reputation for being an unattractive industrial city. In fact, Wollongong enjoys some of the best coastal scenery and beaches in the state, superbly positioned with mountains to the west and ocean to the east. It has the facilities and sophistication missing in many smaller towns and has been awarded the title of 'Australia's most liveable regional city'.

Wollongong Botanic Garden The magnificent gardens encompass 27 ha of undulating land and feature a sunken rose garden, a woodland garden, rainforests, and flora representing a range of plant communities. Guided walks and bus tours are available. Various workshops including crafts and gardening throughout the year; Murphys Ave, Keiraville; (02) 4225 2636; call for opening hours. The adjacent Gleniffer Brae Manor House is a Gothic-style 1930s house now home to the Wollongong Conservatorium of Music and used for music recitals. Northfields Ave, Keiraville.

Flagstaff Point: 180-degree views of the ocean and historic light lighthouse (1872); Endeavour Dr. *Illawarra Historical Society Museum:* highlights include handicraft room and Victorian parlour; open weekends and 12–3pm Thurs; Market St; (02) 4283 2854. *Wollongong City Gallery:* collection of 19th- and 20th-century art including Aboriginal art; Cnr Burelli and Kembla sts; Tue–Fri 10am–5pm, Sat–Sun 12–4pm; (02) 4228 7500. *Mall:* soaring steel arches and water displays; Crown St. *Five Islands Brewing Company:* locally brewed beers; Crown St; (02) 4220 2854. *Wollongong Harbour:* home to a huge fishing fleet and Breakwater Lighthouse. *Surfing beaches and rockpools:* to the north and south, with excellent surfing and swimming conditions. *Foreshore parks:* several with superb coastal views and picnic facilities.

Market: Harbour St; Sat. *Illawarra Folk Festival:* Jan. *Wings over Illawarra:* Feb. *Mt Kembla Mining Heritage Festival:* July. *Viva La Gong:* street-arts festival; Oct.

Lorenzo's Diner: modern Italian; 119 Keira St; (02) 4229 5633. *Diggies:* beachside cafe; 1 Cliff Rd, Wollongong North; (02) 4226 2688. *Lagoon Seafood Restaurant:* seafood, incredible views; Stuart Park, cnr George Hanley Dr and Kembla St, North Wollongong; (02) 4226 1677.

Bulli Beach Tourist Park: 1 Farrell Rd, Bulli; (02) 4285 5677. *Corrimal Beach Tourist Park:* Lake Pde, Corrimal; (02) 4285 5688. *Southview:* 19 Southview St, Bulli; 0410 088 394. *Wollongong Surf Leisure Resort:* 201 Pioneer Rd, Fairy Meadow; (02) 4283 6999.

Royal National Park Established in 1879, this is the second-oldest national park in the world after Yellowstone in the USA. There is much natural diversity packed into a compact parkland. Highlights include walking and cycling along Lady Carrington Drive through rich forest, swimming at the beach or in the lagoon at Wattamolla, enjoying the Victorian-park atmosphere at

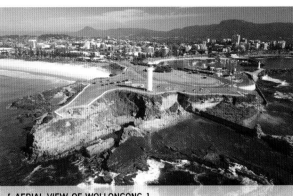

[AERIAL VIEW OF WOLLONGONG]

Audley (with causeway, picnic lawns and rowboats) and walking the magnificent 26 km Coast Track; (02) 9542 0648; 35 km N. Grand Pacific Drive, a new tourist route along the coast, links Royal National Park with Wollongong. The 70 km drive takes in spectacular scenery and the Sea Cliff Bridge.

Illawarra Escarpment: forms the western backdrop to the city and has spectacular lookouts at Stanwell Tops, Sublime Point, Mt Keira and Mt Kembla. *Wollongong Science Centre and Planetarium:* hands-on displays and activities for all ages; Squires Way, Fairy Meadow; (02) 4286 5000; open 10am–4pm every day; 2 km N. *Nan Tien Temple:* largest Buddhist temple in the Southern Hemisphere with a range of programs available; closed Mon; Berkeley Rd, Berkeley; (02) 4272 0600; 5 km SW. *Lake Illawarra:* stretching from the South Pacific Ocean to the foothills of the Illawarra Range, the lake offers good prawning, fishing and sailing. Boat hire is available; 5 km S. *Port Kembla:* up-close view of local industry and the steel works at Australia's Industry World with tours; bookings (02) 4275 7023. *Mount Kembla:* site of horrific 1902 mining disaster. Also here are several historic buildings and a historical museum featuring a pioneer kitchen, a blacksmith's shop and a reconstruction of the Mount Kembla disaster. The Mount Kembla Mining Heritage Festival is held each winter in memory of those lost; 10 km W. *Bulli Pass Scenic Reserve:* steep scenic drive with stunning coastal views. Bulli Lookout at the top of the escarpment has great views and a walking path leads to Sublime Pt Lookout, which enjoys stunning views over Wollongong and has a restaurant; 16 km N. *Symbio Wildlife Park:* koalas, eagles, wombats and reptiles, as well as Sumatran tigers; Lawrence Hargrave Drive, Helensburgh; (02) 4294 1244; 32 km N. *Just Cruisin Motorcycle Tours:* Cruise Grand Pacific Dr and the spectacular South Coast on a chauffeured Harley Davidson; (02) 4294 2598. *Lawrence Hargrave Memorial and Lookout:* on Bald Hill, this was the site of aviator Hargrave's first attempt at flight in the early 1900s. Now popular for hang-gliding; 36 km N. *Illawarra Fly Treetop Walk:* the Treetop Walk offers inspiring views; 182 Knights Hill Road, Knights Hill; (02) 4885 1010. *Heathcote National Park:* excellent for bushwalks through rugged bushland, past hidden pools and gorges; (02) 9542 0648; 40 km N. *Dolphin Watch Cruises:* see dolphins and whales at Jervis Bay; 50 Owen Street, Huskisson; (02) 4441 6311 or 1800 246 010 .

TOWNS NEARBY: Shellharbour 17 km, Jamberoo 27 km, Kiama 27 km, Robertson 33 km, Picton 38 km

Wyong

Pop. 149 382

Map ref. 509 E7 | 511 P1 | 514 A12 | 523 L5

i Rotary Park, Terrigal Dr, Terrigal; (02) 4343 4444 or 1300 130 708; www.visitcentralcoast.com.au

101.3 Sea FM, 1512 AM ABC Radio National

Wyong is an attractive holiday town surrounded by Tuggerah Lakes and the forests of Watagan, Olney and Ourimbah. After World War II it became a popular area for retirees and it retains a relaxed atmosphere today.

District Museum Features displays of local history, including early ferry services across the lakes and records of the logging era. It is situated in historic Alison Homestead, with picnic and barbecue facilities on 2 ha of rolling lawns. Cape Rd; (02) 4352 1886.

Wyong Shire Festival of the Arts: Feb–Mar.

Karinyas Restaurant and Bar: modern Australian; Kooindah Waters Residential Golf & Spa Resort, 40 Kooindah Blvd; (02) 4355 5777 or 1800 705 355.

All Comfort B & B: 34 Highland Cres, Hamlyn Terrace; 0422 056 449. *BIG4 Lake Macquarie Monterey Tourist Park:* Lot 28 Monterey Ave, Mannering Park; (02) 4359 1033. *Christina's B&B Lake Macquarie:* 10 Doree Pl, Dora Creek; (02) 4973 4088. *Kemeys Mountain Hideaway:* 410 Sauls Rd, Mandalong; (02) 4977 2525. *Lake Macquarie Village:* 1A Stockton St, Morisset; (02) 4973 1883.

Olney State Forest This native rainforest has several scenic walks. The Pines picnic area has an education shelter and Mandalong and Muirs lookouts have sensational views. 17 km NW.

Burbank Nursery: 20 ha of azaleas (flowering in Sept); 3 km s. *Fowlers Lookout:* spectacular forest views; 10 km sw. *Yarramalong Macadamia Nut Farm:* offers tours, talks and sales in beautiful Yarramalong Valley; 18 km w. *Frazer Park:* recreational park in natural bush setting; 28 km NE.

TOWNS NEARBY: The Entrance 9 km, Gosford 17 km, Terrigal 18 km, Woy Woy 24 km, Wisemans Ferry 43 km

Yamba

Pop. 5515

Map ref. 516 F8 | 525 O5

i Lower Clarence Visitor Centre, Ferry Park, Pacific Hwy, Maclean; (02) 6645 4121; www.yambansw.com.au

100.3 Yamba Radio FM, 738 AM ABC North Coast

This quiet holiday town at the mouth of the Clarence River offers excellent sea, lake and river fishing. It is the largest coastal resort in the Clarence Valley, with excellent facilities for visitors, but it manages to maintain a peaceful atmosphere. Fishing fleets from Yamba, Iluka and Maclean catch approximately 20 per cent of the state's seafood, so this is a great spot for lovers of fresh seafood.

Story House Museum This quaint museum tells the story of the development of Yamba from the time it was merely a point of entry to the Clarence River. The collection of photographs and records tells a compelling tale of early development of a typical Australian coastal town. River St.

Clarence River Lighthouse: coastal views from the base; via Pilot St. *Yamba Boat Harbour Marina:* departure point for daily ferry service to Iluka, river cruises, deep-sea fishing charters and whale-watching trips. Also houseboat hire; off Yamba Rd. *arthouse australia:* showcase of local artwork; Coldstream St. *Whiting Beach:* sandy river beach ideal for children. *Coastal*

beaches: several in town with excellent swimming and surfing conditions; map from visitor centre.

River Market: Ford Park; 4th Sun each month. *Easter Yachting Regatta:* Easter. *Family Fishing Festival:* Oct. *Hot Rod Run:* Nov.

Beachwood Cafe: Mediterranean; 22 High St; (02) 6646 9781. *Pacific Bistro:* modern Australian; Pacific Hotel, 18 Pilot St; (02) 6646 2466.

Blue Dolphin Holiday Resort: Yamba Rd; (02) 6646 2194. *Calypso Holiday Park Yamba:* 14 Harbour St; (02) 6646 8847. *Yamba Waters Holiday Park:* Golding St; (02) 6646 2930. *Ashby Cottage:* 2 Tullymorgan Rd, Ashby; (02) 6645 4686. *BIG4 Saltwater @ Yamba Holiday Park:* 286 O'Keefes La, Palmers Island; (02) 6646 0255. *Brooms Head Caravan Park:* Ocean Rd, Brooms Head; (02) 6646 7144. *Fishing Haven Holiday Park:* 35 River Rd, Palmers Island; (02) 6646 0163. *Maclean Riverside Caravan Park:* 109 River St, Maclean; (02) 6645 2987.

Maclean This quirky village is known as the 'Scottish town' because of the many Scots who first settled here. Some street signs are in Gaelic as well as English. Highlights in the town include Scottish Corner, Bicentennial Museum and a self-guide historical walk with a brochure available from the visitor centre. There is a market on the 2nd Sat each month and a Highland Gathering each Easter. A 24 hr ferry service crosses the river to Lawrence; 17 km w.

Lake Wooloweyah: fishing and prawning; 4 km s. *Yuraygir National Park:* Yamba section offers sand ridges and banksia heath, and is excellent for swimming, fishing and bushwalking; (02) 6627 0200; 5 km s. *The Blue Pool:* deep freshwater pool 50 m from the ocean, popular for swimming; 5 km s.

TOWNS NEARBY: Iluka 3 km, Evans Head 36 km, Grafton 50 km, Alstonville 66 km, Ballina 66 km

Yass

Pop. 5330

Map ref. 519 C3 | 522 F9

i Coronation Park, 259 Comur St; (02) 6226 2557 or 1300 886 014; www.yass.nsw.gov.au

100.3 Yass FM, 549 AM ABC Central West

Yass is set in rolling countryside on the Yass River. Explorers Hume and Hovell passed through on their expedition to Port Phillip Bay. Hume returned in 1839. Yass is also the end of the Hume and Hovell Walking Track, which begins in Albury.

Cooma Cottage The National Trust has restored and now maintains this former home of explorer Hamilton Hume. He lived with his wife in the riverside house from 1839 until his death in 1873. It now operates as a museum with relics and documents telling of Hume's life and explorations. Open Thurs–Sun, closed winter; Yass Valley Way.

Yass Cemetery: contains the grave of explorer Hamilton Hume; via Rossi St. *Yass and District Museum:* historical displays including a war exhibit encompassing the Boer War, WW I and WW II. Open Sat and Sun, or by appt, archive open Tues; Comur St. *Railway Museum:* history of the Yass tramway; open Sun; Lead St. *Aingeal Ridge Alpacas:* alpaca farm. *Self-guide town walk and drive:* highlight is the National Trust–listed main street; brochure from visitor centre.

Picnic races: Mar. *Yass Show and Rodeo:* Mar. *Wine Roses and all that Jazz:* food, wine and music festival in the Murrumbateman area; Oct. *Rodeo:* Nov.

Cafe Dolcetto: cakes, sandwiches; 129 Comur St; (02) 6226 1277. *Ewe'n Me:* steak, seafood; Thunderbird Motel, 264 Comur St; (02) 6226 1158. *Swaggers Restaurant:* steakhouse; Sundowner Yass Swaggers Motor Inn, cnr Laidlaw and Castor sts; (02) 6226 9900. *Smokehouse Cafe:* lovely cafe in restored farm cottage, gourmet produce available for purchase; Poachers Pantry, 431 Nanima Rd, Hall; (02) 6230 2487.

Kerrowgair Bed & Breakfast: 24 Grampian St; (02) 6226 4932. *The Globe Inn:* 70 Rossi St; (02) 6226 3680. *Yass Caravan Park:* Cnr Laidlaw and Grampian sts; (02) 6226 1173. *Burrinjuck Waters State Park:* 2373 Burrinjuck Rd, Bookham; (02) 6227 8114. *Cooradigbee Homestead:* Caves Rd, Wee Jasper; (02) 6227 9680. *Country Guesthouse Schonegg:* 381 Hillview Dr, Murrumbateman; (02) 6227 0344. *Lake Burrinjuck Leisure Resort:* 590 Woolgarlo Rd, Woolgarlo; (02) 6227 7271. *The Old School Country Retreat:* 76 Yass St, Rye Park; (02) 4845 1230. *Redbrow Garden B & B:* 1143 Nanima Rd, Murrumbateman; (02) 6226 8166.

Wee Jasper This picturesque village, where Banjo Paterson owned a holiday home, is set in a valley at the foot of the Brindabella Ranges. The Goodradigbee River is excellent for trout fishing. Carey's Caves are full of limestone formations and were the site of the 1957 discovery of the spine of a large extinct wombat. 50 km sw.

Canberra wine region Canberra has around 35 cellar doors, a few in the boundary of the ACT itself, but the majority a little further north around Murrumbateman and Lake George. The first vines in this hilly terrain were planted in 1971. Many of the original winemakers had no experience in winemaking and came from government or science jobs in the ACT. Their wine was slow to take off, but there are no such limitations now. The region produces a great range of styles, with many varieties considered excellent. Clonakilla makes good shiraz and riesling, but its shiraz viognier is the standout – it is difficult to get hold of, but worth trying at the small cellar door. Helm reaches similar heights with riesling and Lark Hill with pinot noir. Follow the signs on Barton Hwy; brochure from visitor centre.

Bookham: village with historic cemetery, markets 2nd Sun each month and Sheep Show and Country Fair in Apr; 30 km w. *Binalong:* historic town with Motor Museum, Southern Cross Glass and the grave of bushranger Johnny Gilbert; 37 km NW. *Burrinjuck Waters State Park:* bushwalking, cruises, watersports and fishing. Burrinjuck Ski Classic is held each Nov (water level permitting); off Hume Hwy; 54 km sw. *Brindabella National Park:* birdwatching, camping and bushwalking in alpine surrounds. 4WD access only; via Wee Jasper; (02) 6122 3100; 61 km sw. *Hume and Hovell Walking Track:* 23-day, 440 km trek from Albury to Yass. For a kit (including maps), contact Department of Infrastructure, Planning and Natural Resources, Sydney (02) 9762 8044.

TOWNS NEARBY: Queanbeyan 64 km, Crookwell 67 km, Goulburn 75 km, Gundagai 77 km, Tumut 81 km

Young

Pop. 7129

Map ref. 519 B1 | 522 E7

ⓘ 2 Short St; (02) 6382 3394 or 1800 628 233; www.visityoung.com.au

93.9 Star FM, 96.3 FM ABC Local

Young is an attractive town in the western foothills of the Great Dividing Range with a fascinating history of goldmining. The Lambing Flat goldfields were rushed after a discovery was announced in 1860. Within a year there were an estimated 20 000 miners in town, 2000 of whom were Chinese. A combination of lawlessness and racism boiled over in the Lambing Flat riots in 1861, which gave rise to the Chinese Immigration Restriction Act, the first legislation to herald the infamous White Australia Policy. Today the town is the peaceful centre of a cherry-farming district.

Lambing Flat Folk Museum This museum is recognised as one of the finest in the country. Meticulously maintained photographs and relics tell the story of the town during the 1800s and 1900s. The full horrific story of the Lambing Flat riots is covered. Items on display include a 'roll-up' flag carried by miners during the riots. Campbell St; (02) 6382 2248.

Burrangong Art Gallery: hosts changing exhibitions from guest and local artists; at visitor centre; Short St. *J. D.'s Jam Factory:* tours, tastings and Devonshire teas; Henry Lawson Way; (02) 6382 4060.

Hilltops Flavours of the Harvest Festival (Young): Feb. *Lambing Flat Festival:* Apr. *National Cherry Festival:* Nov/Dec.

Elevations: modern Australian; Hilltops Retreat Motor Inn, Olympic Hwy; (02) 6382 4177. *Rappjam Catering:* modern Australian; Young Services Club, Cloete St; (02) 6382 7419. *Young Cafe de Jour:* modern Australian; shop 4, 21 Lovell St; (02) 6382 1413.

Young Tourist Park: 17 Edward St; (02) 6382 2190. *Boorowa Caravan Park:* Brial St, Boorowa; (02) 6385 3658.

Young wine region Three low-key wine regions form an arc to the west of the ACT and east of Riverina. In the north is Hilltops, where a handful of wineries are clustered around Young. Barwang Vineyard is the largest and oldest, and produces consistently excellent drops. For a cellar door, head to Grove Estate, a thriving label whose wines are made by the legendary Clonakilla winemaker from the Canberra district; or Chalkers Crossing, whose French winemaker is responsible for wines of the highest quality. Look out for the Freeman label too, with interesting varieties such as tempranillo and a blend of rondinella and corvina. Beneath Hilltops is a small region around Gundagai, producing particularly good shiraz, try Paterson's. South again are the wineries around Tumbarumba, a lofty region abutting Kosciuszko National Park. Here the major varieties are pinot noir and chardonnay, both of which are put into sparkling wines. Cellar-door information at visitor centre.

Chinaman's Dam Recreation Area: scenic walks, playground, and picnic and barbecue facilities. Includes Lambing Flat Chinese Tribute Gardens with Pool of Tranquility; Pitstone Rd; 4 km SE. *Yandilla Mustard Seed Oil Enterprises:* tours by appt; bookings (02) 6943 2516; 20 km s. *Murringo:* historic buildings, a glassblower and engraver; 21 km E. *Cherries and stone fruit:* sales and pick-your-own throughout the area Nov–Dec. Cherries blossom in Sept/Oct.

TOWNS NEARBY: Cootamundra 44 km, Grenfell 48 km, Cowra 64 km, Temora 72 km, Yass 81 km

CANBERRA is...

A dawn hot-air balloon flight over a waking city / A picnic in the AUSTRALIAN NATIONAL

BOTANIC GARDENS / A bushwalk in the beautiful BRINDABELLA RANGE / A visit to

PARLIAMENT HOUSE / Fine dining in one of Canberra's many restaurants / Discovering

Australia's unique war history at the AUSTRALIAN WAR MEMORIAL / Fun science activities

at QUESTACON / City views from MOUNT AINSLIE / Watching Australia's elite athletes

train at the AUSTRALIAN INSTITUTE OF SPORT / A trip to the NATIONAL MUSEUM

OF AUSTRALIA / Counting the country's dollars at the ROYAL AUSTRALIAN MINT

VISITOR INFORMATION
Canberra and Region Visitors Centre
→ 330 Northbourne Ave, Dickson
(02) 6205 0044 or 1300 554 114
www.visitcanberra.com.au

Canberra really is the bush capital – kangaroo-dotted nature reserves are scattered throughout the city, and the Brindabella mountain range bounds the south-western edge. As the national capital, Canberra claims some of the nation's most significant institutions, including a magnificent art gallery and a remarkable war museum. Grand public buildings and monuments complement the order and beauty of the city's original design, and the landmark flagpole of Parliament House can be seen from many parts of the city.

Many visitors are attracted by Canberra's national collections or the experience of federal politics, but the city has much more to offer. The capital also boasts cool-climate wineries, top-class restaurants and bars, attractions for children and a full calendar of cultural and sporting events.

With a population of about 358 000, life in Canberra moves at a comfortable pace; and with the snow and the sea both only two hours away, the locals have the best of both worlds. The city's creation solved the debate between Sydney and Melbourne over the location of Australia's capital, and Canberra is now one of the world's few completely planned cities.

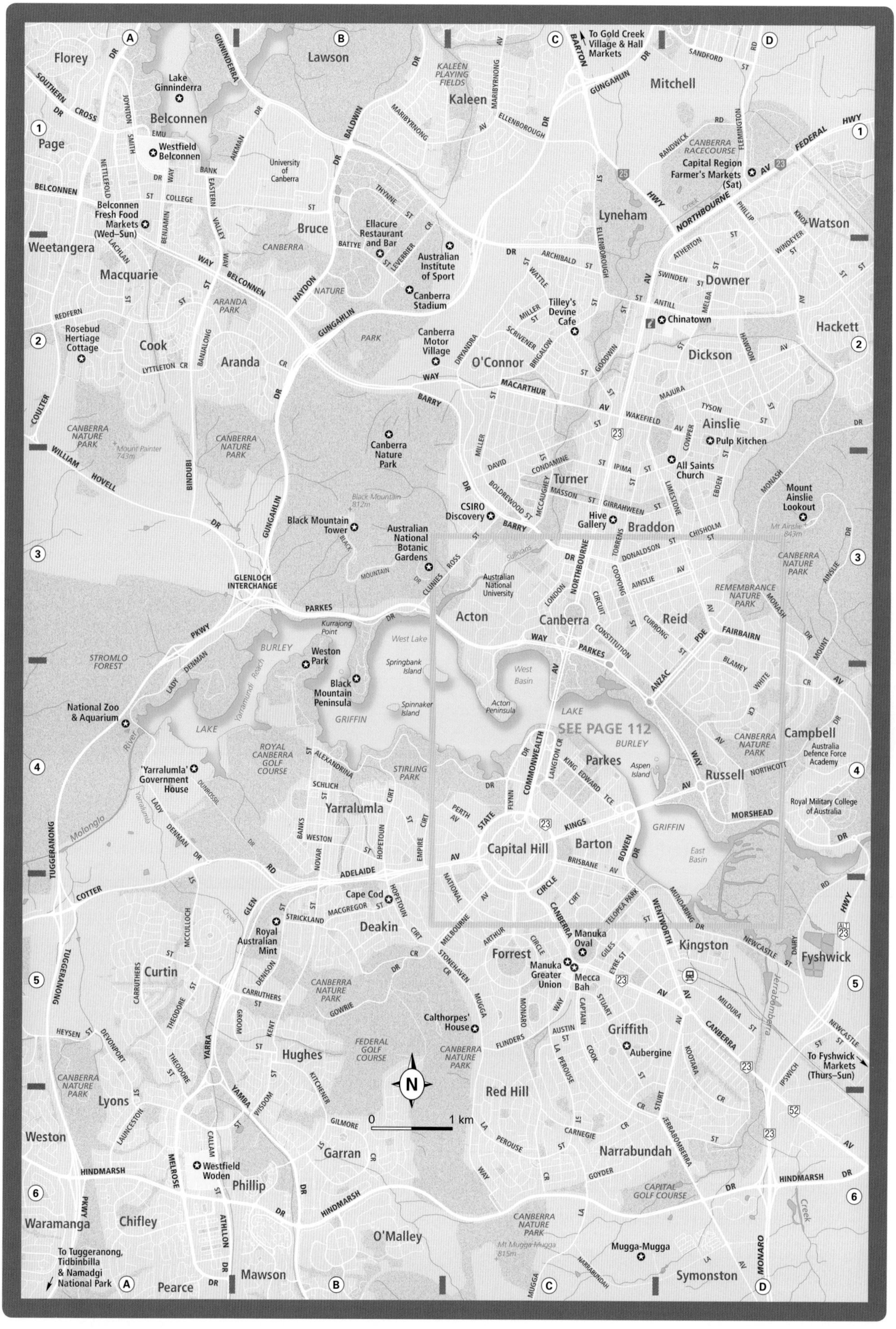
To Gold Creek Village & Hall Markets
Florey
Lawson
Lake Ginninderra
Belconnen
Kaleen
Mitchell
KALEEN PLAYING FIELDS
Page
Westfield Belconnen
University of Canberra
CANBERRA RACECOURSE
Capital Region Farmer's Markets (Sat)
Belconnen Fresh Food Markets (Wed–Sun)
Bruce
Ellacure Restaurant and Bar
Australian Institute of Sport
Canberra Stadium
Lyneham
Watson
Weetangera
Macquarie
CANBERRA NATURE PARK
ARANDA PARK
Downer
Chinatown
Tilley's Devine Cafe
Hackett
Rosebud Hertiage Cottage
Cook
Aranda
Canberra Motor Village
O'Connor
Dickson
CANBERRA NATURE PARK
Mount Painter 743m
Canberra Nature Park
Ainslie
Pulp Kitchen
All Saints Church
Turner
Mount Ainslie Lookout
Mt Ainslie 843m
Black Mountain 812m
CSIRO Discovery
Hive Gallery
Braddon
Black Mountain Tower
Australian National Botanic Gardens
Australian National University
GLENLOCH INTERCHANGE
CANBERRA NATURE PARK
REMEMBRANCE NATURE PARK
Acton
Canberra
Reid
Kurrajong Point
West Lake
STROMLO FOREST
BURLEY
Weston Park
Springbank Island
West Basin
Black Mountain Peninsula
Spinnaker Island
Acton Peninsula
National Zoo & Aquarium
LAKE
GRIFFIN
LAKE
SEE PAGE 112
BURLEY
Campbell
Australia Defence Force Academy
ROYAL CANBERRA GOLF COURSE
STIRLING PARK
CANBERRA NATURE PARK
'Yarralumla' Government House
Parkes
Aspen Island
Russell
Royal Military College of Australia
Yarralumla
GRIFFIN
Capital Hill
Barton
East Basin
Cape Cod
Royal Australian Mint
Deakin
Manuka Oval
Kingston
Fyshwick
Forrest
Manuka Greater Union
Mecca Bah
Curtin
CANBERRA NATURE PARK
Calthorpes' House
Griffith
Aubergine
Hughes
FEDERAL GOLF COURSE
CANBERRA NATURE PARK
To Fyshwick Markets (Thurs–Sun)
CANBERRA NATURE PARK
Lyons
Red Hill
0
1 km
Weston
Garran
Narrabundah
Westfield Woden
Phillip
CAPITAL GOLF COURSE
Waramanga
Chifley
O'Malley
CANBERRA NATURE PARK
Mt Mugga Mugga 815m
Mugga-Mugga
To Tuggeranong, Tidbinbilla & Namadgi National Park
Pearce
Mawson
Symonston

PARLIAMENTARY TRIANGLE AND WAR MEMORIAL

The vision of Canberra's architect, Walter Burley Griffin, can be seen in the tree-lined avenues, spectacular lake views and spacious parks of central Canberra. The focal point is Parliament House, atop Capital Hill, situated at the apex of the Parliamentary Triangle.

❶ Aboriginal Tent Embassy
❷ Commonwealth Place
❸ High Court of Australia
❹ Museum of Australian Democracy
❺ National Archives of Australia
❻ National Gallery of Australia
❼ National Library of Australia
❽ National Portrait Gallery
❾ National Rose Gardens
❿ Questacon – The National Science and Technology Centre
⓫ Reconciliation Place

National Capital Exhibition 112 B2

Interactive displays, rare photographs, a 3D sound-and-light display and various audiovisual material tell the story of Canberra. *Regatta Point, Barrine Dr, Commonwealth Park; (02) 6257 1068; open 9am–5pm Mon–Fri, 10am–4pm Sat–Sun; closed public holidays except Australia Day and Canberra Day; admission free.*

Parliament House 112 A5

Opened in 1988, both houses of Federal Parliament sit here, so you might get to see democracy in action from the public galleries (check www.aph. gov.au, for sitting dates). There are permanent displays too, including Australian art, the Great Hall Tapestry and one of only four surviving 1297 copies of the Magna Carta. Guided tours recommended. There are also landscaped gardens to walk through. *Parliament Dr, off State Circle; (02) 6277 5399; recorded information (02) 6277 2727; open 9am–5pm daily; admission free.*

Reconciliation Place 112 B3

Adjacent to Commonwealth Place on Lake Burley Griffin is this site, symbolising the journey of reconciliation between Indigenous and white Australians. Artworks, known as slivers, surround a central circular mound, while pathways link it to Commonwealth Place, national institutions and Lake Burley Griffin.

Museum of Australian Democracy at Old Parliament House 112 B4

This heritage-listed building was home to Federal Parliament from 1927 to 1988. Now it celebrates Australia's social and political history. Free guided tours are available. Outside are the **Old Parliament House Gardens**, while across the road is the **Aboriginal Tent Embassy**, established in 1972 to protest against a lack of land rights for the country's Indigenous peoples, and the **National Rose Gardens**. *18 King George Tce, Parkes; (02) 6270 8222; open 9am–5pm daily.*

[HALL OF MEMORY, AUSTRALIAN WAR MEMORIAL]

AUSTRALIAN CAPITAL TERRITORY

National Portrait Gallery 112 B4

Bounded by the High Court and National Gallery of Australia is this permanent display of over 450 portraits of those who have contributed to Australian society. Included are paintings, sculptures, photographs and multimedia works, as well as temporary exhibitions. *King Edward Tce, Parkes; (02) 6102 7000; open 10am–5pm daily; general admission free.*

National Archives of Australia 112 B4

The National Archives are housed in Canberra's first GPO building, where a permanent exhibition, Memory of a Nation, highlights a glimpse of treasures from the collection, including ASIO surveillance photos and an 1897 draft of the Constitution complete with edits. Learn here how to search for war service and migration records. *Queen Victoria Tce, Parkes; (02) 6212 3600; open 9am–5pm daily; admission free.*

National Library of Australia 112 B3

This is the country's largest reference library, with approximately 10 million items in the collection including newspapers, periodicals, photographs, music scores, websites and oral histories collected since 1901. Free behind-the-scenes tours run on alternate Thursdays and Saturdays. The Library cafe, Bookplate, is a good spot for lunch. *Parkes Pl, Parkes; (02) 6262 1111; open 9am–9pm Mon–Thurs, 9am–5pm Fri–Sat, 1.30pm–5pm Sun; admission free.*

[PARLIAMENT HOUSE]

Questacon – The National Science and Technology Centre 112 B3

Questacon makes science fun for all: experience an earthquake and a cyclone, see lightning created and free-fall 6 metres on the vertical slide. *King Edward Tce, Parkes; (02) 6270 2800; open 9am–5pm daily.*

High Court of Australia 112 C4

Visitors can explore the public gallery and timber courtrooms, and view Jan Senbergs' murals, reflecting the history and functions of the court, and the role of the states in Federation. *Parkes Pl, Parkes; (02) 6270 6811; open 9.45am–4.30pm Mon–Fri, 12–4pm Sun; admission free.*

National Gallery of Australia 112 C4

With over 140 000 works, the gallery provides a brilliant overview of Australian art and an impressive international collection. Enjoy a picnic lunch in the tranquil **Sculpture Garden,** among more the 26 sculptures. *Parkes Pl, Parkes; (02) 6240 6411; open 10am–5pm daily; general admission free.*

Blundell's Cottage 112 C3

Built in the 1860s, the cottage was part of the Campbell family's 12 800-hectare estate and home to tenant farm workers. Now a museum, it records the region's early farming history. *Wendouree Dr, off Constitution Ave, Parkes; (02) 6272 2902; open 10–11.30am, 12–4pm Thurs and Sat.*

Australian War Memorial 112 D1

Set at the foot of Mount Ainslie at the end of Anzac Parade, the memorial commemorates Australians who have served in war. Free guided tours run daily. Visitors can browse over 20 exhibition galleries or see the Hall of Memory, the Tomb of the Unknown Australian Soldier, the Pool of Reflection and the Roll of Honour, which lists the names of over 102 000 Australian servicemen and servicewomen who died in war. *Treloar Cres, Campbell; (02) 6243 4211; open 10am–5pm daily; admission free.*

National Zoo and Aquarium 110 A4

Animals ranging from big cats to bears, otters and monkeys inhabit the zoo's naturalistic enclosures. The aquarium houses a Great Barrier Reef and a Predators of the Deep exhibit. Special tours include keeper talks, handfeeding the big cats and bears and meeting a cheetah. (These tours cost extra.) *Scrivener Dam, Lady Denman Dr, Yarralumla; (02) 6287 8400; open 10am–5pm daily.*

Royal Australian Mint 110 B5

Learn how coins are made and see the production floor from an elevated gallery. There are displays of old coins, a video on coin production, and visitors can even make their own coins. *Denison St, Deakin; (02) 6202 6999; open 9am–4pm Mon–Fri, 10am–4pm Sat–Sun; admission free.*

[MINI Q AT QUESTACON]

CITY CENTRE

The modest size of Canberra's city centre, Civic, is a reminder of Canberra's small population at just over 358 000 people. It includes excellent shopping, the peaceful Glebe Park, great cafes and Casino Canberra.

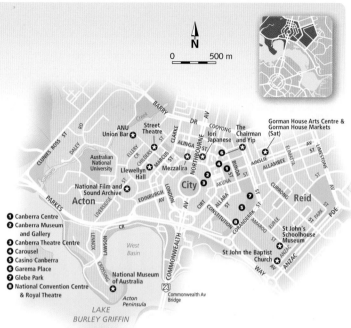

Garema Place 112 B1

At the top end of Civic, this open public space is encircled by cafes and restaurants, and features a large movie screen (movies screen at night in summer). Head south down the tree-lined City Walk towards the large Canberra Centre mall to see Civic's landmark carousel, built in 1914.

Canberra Museum and Gallery (CMAG) 112 B1

CMAG's permanent collection reflects the history, environment, culture and community of the Canberra region. Featuring dynamic exhibitions and community events, it also exhibits a changing selection of works by renowned artist Sir Sidney Nolan. *Cnr London Circuit and Civic Sq, Civic; (02) 6207 3968; open 10am–5pm Mon–Fri, 12–5pm Sat–Sun; admission free.*

National Film and Sound Archive 112 A2

Housed in the former Institute of Anatomy next to the Australian National University, the archive preserves Australia's film and sound heritage. Displays include film memorabilia, special exhibitions and interactive activities along with the screening of Australian movies in the Arc cinema. *McCoy Circuit, Acton; 1800 677 609; open 9am–5pm Mon–Fri, 10am–5pm Sat–Sun; admission free.*

National Museum of Australia 112 A3

The museum uses state-of-the-art technology and interactivity to engage with Australia's past, present, and future. Permanent displays explore Indigenous culture, Australian icons and environmental change, and children will love the virtual-reality 'KSpace'. Guided tours available. *Lawson Cres, Acton Peninsula; (02) 6208 5000; open 9am–5pm daily; general admission free.*

CSIRO Discovery 110 C3

The centre showcases Australia's scientific research and innovation. Try hands-on experiments, experience the virtual-reality theatre and find out about research breakthroughs. *Off Clunies Ross St, Acton; (02) 6246 4646; open 9am–5pm Mon–Fri, 11am–3pm Sat–Sun.*

St John the Baptist Church and St John's Schoolhouse Museum 112 C2

Canberra's oldest church and first schoolhouse was built in the 1840s. The restored buildings now form an interesting museum. The adjoining cemetery has some of Canberra's oldest headstones. *Constitution Ave, Reid; (02) 6249 6839; open 10am–12pm Wed, 2–4pm Sat–Sun and public holidays; general admission free, museum entry by donation.*

INNER NORTH

This area is an enjoyable mix of relaxed cafes, interesting attractions and nature reserves with excellent walking and mountain-bike tracks.

Mount Ainslie Lookout 110 D3

Drive to the top for a stunning view and to see the geometry of the capital's design. During autumn, you'll see the capital's amazing array of natural colours here. *Mt Ainslie Dr, off Fairbairn Ave, Campbell.*

Ainslie, Braddon and Dickson 110 C3, D2

For a good coffee, a tasty Chinese meal or a beer in the sun, head to the inner north-eastern suburbs. Traditionally populated by Canberra's students, this area offers small art galleries, interesting fashion and cafes. **Ainslie** and **Braddon** have some of Canberra's earliest houses. In Braddon, browse the Hive Gallery (on Lonsdale Street) for one-of-a-kind gifts. Ainslie is also home to the historic **All Saints Church** (on Cowper Street), while **Dickson** is a hive of activity and home to Canberra's small version of Chinatown (on Woolley Street).

NORTH-WEST

This area is a hub of activity, with the leafy suburbs of Turner, O'Connor and Lyneham particularly popular with students from the nearby Australian National University. Canberra Nature Park's Mount Ainslie and Mount Majura lie nearby, and further out is Belconnen, with a large shopping mall, a top-quality sports and aquatic centre and Lake Ginninderra, a favourite picnic spot. Further north is Gungahlin Town Centre with its shopping centre, Gungahlin Lake and Yerrabi Pond district.

Australian National Botanic Gardens 110 B3

The gardens, at the base of Black Mountain, are the largest collection of Australian native flora in the world. Take the Aboriginal Plant Use Walk to discover the species used for foods and medicines by Indigenous Australians, and enjoy evening picnics and weekend twilight concerts here in summer. *Clunies Ross St, Acton; (02) 6250 9450; open 8.30am–5pm daily, extended hours in Jan to 6pm weekdays and 8pm weekends; admission free.*

Black Mountain Tower 110 B3

The communications tower rises 195 metres above the summit of Black Mountain and offers superb views. It has two open viewing platforms, a cafe and gift shop and the revolving restaurant **Alto**. *Black Mountain Dr, Acton; (02) 6219 6111; open 9am–10pm daily.*

Australian Institute of Sport (AIS) 110 C2

The AIS is the training ground for elite athletes. Enter via the Sports Visitors Centre and view exhibitions and sporting memorabilia, then take a tour, led by athletes, for an insight into the life of an elite athlete. The tours include Sportex, where you can test your sporting skills against Olympic records and see the latest in sport technology. *Leverrier Cres, Bruce; (02) 6214 1111; open 9am–5pm Mon–Fri, 10am–4pm Sat–Sun; general admission free.*

NORTH

In Canberra's north is Gold Creek Village, a tourist attraction that takes its name from an old property established in the area in the mid-1800s, but which has no creek and no history of goldmining. It has specialty shops, galleries, cafes, historic buildings and a host of attractions, including Gold Creek Station, a large working merino property, open to visitors (groups only; bookings (02) 6230 9208).

National Dinosaur Museum 518 E3

The museum has an extensive display of fossilised dinosaur remains, full skeletons and full-size replicas. During school holidays there are plenty of activities for children as well as guided tours. *Cnr Gold Creek Rd and Barton Hwy, Gold Creek Village; (02) 6230 2655; open 10am–5pm daily.*

[SCULPTURES OUTSIDE THE AUSTRALIAN INSTITUTE OF SPORT]

Cockington Green 518 E3

Journey through a magical world of miniatures, from a Stonehenge replica to a village cricket match amid beautifully manicured gardens, or take a ride on a miniature steam train. *11 Gold Creek Rd, Gold Creek Village; 1800 627 273; open 9.30am–5pm daily.*

Canberra Reptile Sanctuary 518 E3

This is the place for all things reptilian. See Australian and exotic species, including a boa constrictor; Australia's longest snake, the scrub python; and local favourites such as the blue-tongue lizard and children's python. *O'Hanlon Pl, Gold Creek Village; (02) 6253 8533; open 10am–5pm Tues–Sat 10am–4pm Sun. canberrareptilesanctuary.org.au*

The Bird Walk 518 E3

Feed, photograph and walk among over 500 birds representing 54 species from around the world that fly free in this 1000-square-metre, 9-metre-high aviary. *Federation Sq, Gold Creek Village; (02) 6230 2044; open 10am–4.30pm daily in summer, 11am–3pm daily in winter.*

Ginninderra Village 518 E3

This old village once serviced the surrounding farming districts, including the property of Gold Creek Station. Today it is part of Gold Creek Village, and contains the old Ginninderra schoolhouse and the township's old Roman Catholic church, among gift shops, craft studios and galleries. *O'Hanlon Pl, Gold Creek Village; open daily.*

[COCKINGTON GREEN GARDENS]

INNER SOUTH

Drive around Canberra's leafy inner-south suburbs to see official residences, Art Deco bungalows, carefully tended gardens and the diplomatic precinct. The Lodge, the prime minister's Canberra residence, next to Parliament House, is noticeable by the large cream brick wall around it. It is not open to the public, but occasional open days are held along with Government House, the governor-general's residence at Yarralumla, a grand 1920s building.

Manuka and Kingston 110 C5, D5

Manuka and Kingston have vibrant shopping precincts, cafes, restaurants, nightclubs, bars and pubs. The lovely **Telopea Park** is only a few minutes away, while the Kingston Foreshore has the **Canberra Glassworks**, nestled in an old powerhouse next to the weekly Old Bus Depot Markets. The nearby suburb of **Griffith** has fabulous organic and alternative shopping, and some excellent restaurants and cafes.

Calthorpes' House 110 C5

Built in 1927 in a blend of Spanish Mission and Federal Capital styles, the house contains the original furnishings and photos, offering glimpses into what domestic life was like in the then-fledgling capital. There are guided tours during the week (group bookings only) and open house on the weekend. *24 Mugga Way, Red Hill; (02) 6295 1945; open 1–4pm Sat–Sun.*

Mugga-Mugga 110 C6

Set on 17 hectares of grazing land, Mugga-Mugga is a collection of buildings and cultural objects dating from the 1830s to the 1970s. The option of combined admission fees with Calthorpes' House and Lanyon Homestead *(see Day tours, p. 119)* offers good value. *129 Narrabundah La, Symonston; (02) 6239 5607; open 1.30–4.30pm Sat–Sun.*

SOUTH

Tuggeranong Homestead 518 D6

Sitting on 31 hectares, this historic homestead started life as an 1830s cottage and was rebuilt in 1908. A stone barn built by convicts in the 1830s is still standing. The Commonwealth government then acquired it in 1917 for military purposes. War historian Charles Bean lived here from 1919 to 1925. It is now a conference centre during the week with markets held there every second Sunday of the month. *Johnson Dr, opposite Calwell Shops, Richardson; (02) 6292 8888; open by appt.*

Lake Tuggeranong 518 D6

Lake Tuggeranong offers waterside recreation for Canberra's inhabitants, who come here to ride the cycle paths, enjoy a picnic, have a swim or go fishing, sailing or windsurfing.

CITY ESSENTIALS
CANBERRA

Climate

Canberra has a climate of extremes and seasons of beauty. Summer in the capital is hot and very dry, with temperatures sometimes reaching the mid to high 30s. Winter is cold and frosty, thanks to Canberra's altitude of roughly 600 metres, its inland location and its proximity to the Snowy Mountains. Don't let this stop you, though – Canberra winter days are breathtakingly crisp and usually fine, with cloudless, bright blue skies after the early morning fogs lift. Spring is Canberra at its most pleasant – the city is awash with colour and flowers abound – although some say that it is in autumn that Canberra is at its most beautiful.

	MAX °C	MIN °C	RAIN MM	RAIN DAYS
JANUARY	28	13	59	5
FEBRUARY	28	13	51	4
MARCH	24	11	55	4
APRIL	20	7	49	5
MAY	15	4	47	5
JUNE	12	1	37	5
JULY	11	0	52	6
AUGUST	13	1	47	7
SEPTEMBER	16	4	65	7
OCTOBER	19	6	61	7
NOVEMBER	23	9	58	7
DECEMBER	26	11	46	5

Getting around

Canberra is an easy city to get around if you have a car and a map. The road infrastructure is probably the best in Australia, with wide, well-planned roads, and visitors will find that they can cover long distances in a short time. Certainly in the central area of the city it is very easy to travel from one attraction to the next by car or public transport. Walking between the attractions in the Parliamentary Triangle is also very pleasant.

Buses are the only public transport available in Canberra, but these services can be variable at off-peak times. For a convenient way to get around the main attractions, catch one of the sightseeing buses that depart regularly from the Melbourne Building on Northbourne Avenue. Canberra is a city full of cyclists, and major roads have on-road cycling lanes, often marked with green where roads merge. Take care, as cyclists have right of way on the green lanes.

Public transport ACTION Buses 13 1710 or www.action.act.gov.au

Motoring organisation NRMA 13 1122, roadside assistance 13 1111.

Car rental ACT Car Rentals (02) 6282 7272; Avis 13 6333; Budget 13 2727; Hertz 13 3039; Rumbles (02) 6280 7444; Thrifty 1300 367 227.

Taxis Canberra Cabs 13 2227.

Bicycle hire Mr Spokes Bike Hire (02) 6257 1188.

Top events

Summernats Car Festival Canberra becomes a 'cruise city' full of street machines. January.

National Multicultural Festival A showcase of cultures in food, art and performance. February.

National Autumn Balloon Spectacular An eight-day festival with over 50 hot-air balloons launched daily from the lawns of the Museum of Australian Democracy at Old Parliament House. March.

National Folk Festival Hundreds of performers and thousands of spectators create one of Canberra's biggest parties. Easter.

Fireside Festival Warm up winter with fireside food, wine and arts. August.

Floriade A celebration of spring, flowers and fun. September–October.

Wine, Roses and All That Jazz Open weekend of the cool-climate vineyards, with music, food and much wine-tasting. November.

Monuments

Anzac Parade Memorials Eleven dramatic monuments set along the striking red gravel of Anzac Parade commemorate Australian involvement in military conflicts, and the Australians who served in the various defence forces. 112 C2, D2

Australian–American Memorial Celebrates America's World War II contribution to Australia's defence in the Pacific. 112 D4

Captain Cook Memorial Jet An impressive 150-metre water jet – hire a paddleboat to cruise under the spray. 112 B3

National Carillon The largest carillon in Australia, with 53 bells, it was a gift from the British government to celebrate Canberra's 50th anniversary. Regular recitals can be heard. 112 C4

Reconciliation Place An acknowledgement of the ongoing journey towards reconciliation. 112 B3

See also Australian War Memorial, p.113

Shopping

Canberra Centre, City Recently expanded, this stylish mall has department stores, a wide variety of smaller shops and speciality stores, in the heart of the CBD.

Kingston Old-fashioned speciality shopping and restaurants.

Manuka Up-market fashion and homewares, streets lined with cafes, and a supermarket open till midnight.

Westfield Woden One of Canberra's largest shopping malls with department stores, over 200 speciality shops, Hoyts 8 cinemas and plenty of parking.

Other suburban malls These include Westfield Shopping Centre in Belconnen, the Tuggeranong Hyperdome and two factory outlet centres in Fyshwick.

Markets

Belconnen Fresh Food Markets Fresh fruit, vegetables, produce and home to one of Australia's 'big things' – the Giant Mushroom. Wed–Sun. 110 A1

Capital Region Farmer's Markets, Exhibition Park Farmers and growers from the coast to the capital bring their food to these markets off Northbourne Ave. Sat. 110 D1

Fyshwick Markets Fresh-produce markets with a great atmosphere and excellent value. Thurs–Sun. 518 E5

Gorman House Markets, Braddon Art and craft, home-baked treats, plants, clothes and a great up-beat atmosphere, near the city centre. Sat. 112 C1

Hall Markets   Set in the historic showgrounds of Hall village on the outskirts of Canberra, with up to 500 stalls of crafts, home produce, plants and homemade stylish clothing. 1st Sun each month (closed Jan). 518 D3

Old Bus Depot Markets, Kingston   A local favourite, showcasing the creativity of the Canberra region, with handcrafted and home-produced arts, crafts and jewellery, gourmet food, New Age therapies, kids' activities and musical entertainment. Sun. 112 C5

Walks and tours

Anzac Parade Walk   Follow the war memorials set along the regal Anzac Parade on this self-guide walk (2.5 kilometres). Brochure available from the visitor centre or download a tour podcast (www.nationalcapital.gov.au).

Australians of the Year Walk   On the lake foreshore in front of the National Library, this walk honours the award's recipients, with plaques for each year of the award.

Balloon Aloft!   Experience the beauty of Canberra as you float above the city in a hot-air balloon. Bookings on (02) 6285 1540.

Burley Griffin Walk or Ride   A self-guide walk, takes in the north-eastern shores of Lake Burley Griffin, from the National Capital Exhibition to the National Carillon (4.6 kilometres). Brochure available from the visitor centre.

Canberra Tracks   Drive one, or all three, of these fascinating, signed road trips. Track 1 explores the path of Canberra's original Indigenous peoples; Track 2 takes you through the pastoral era; and Track 3 gives you an overview of Canberra's layout, via lookouts. Brochures available from the visitor centre.

Lakeside Walk   This self-guide walk begins at Commonwealth Place and passes the National Gallery, the High Court and the National Library (1.8 kilometres). Brochure available from the visitor centre.

Entertainment

Cinema   The big suburban malls of Woden and Belconnen have Hoyts multiplexes, but for arthouse and independent cinema try the Dendy Canberra Centre in the city or Limelight Cinemas in Tuggeranong. Manuka Greater Union has a wide range of interesting new releases. See the *Canberra Times* for details of current films.

Live music   Canberra has a surprisingly busy music scene and there is usually a good selection of live music around town, ranging from rock gigs at the ANU Union Bar to mellow jazz or soul at Tilley's Devine Cafe in Lyneham. Big acts play at the Canberra Theatre Centre or the Royal Theatre, both in the city centre. You will find nightclubs

aplenty in Civic, Kingston, Manuka and Braddon. For gig details pick up a copy of the *Canberra Times* on Thursday for its lift-out entertainment guide 'Fly', or its 'Panorama' on Saturday, or look for the free street magazine *BMA*.

Classical music and performing arts
The main venue for performing arts is the Canberra Theatre Centre. A couple of smaller venues around town, such as Gorman House Arts Centre in Braddon and the Street Theatre on Childers Street, cater to more eclectic tastes. Classical music concerts most often take place at Llewellyn Hall, part of the ANU's Canberra School of Music, in Acton. See the *Canberra Times* for details of what's on.

Sport

If a visit to the Australian Institute of Sport leaves you wanting more, then there is plenty of sport to see in Canberra. Watch a game of **basketball** as the two Canberra WNBL teams, the Capitals and the AIS, go head-to-head or play interstate teams. The Capitals play their home games at Southern Cross Stadium in Tuggeranong and the AIS team at the AIS.

See Canberra's **Rugby League** side, the Raiders, take on the rest of the nation at Canberra Stadium. The ACT Brumbies, the capital's **Rugby Union** team, also play at Canberra Stadium, to partisan capacity crowds. Canberra doesn't have an **AFL** (Australian Football League) team of its own, but one Melbourne team plays a couple of 'home' games a year at the picturesque Manuka Oval.

If **cricket** is more your thing, visit in summer to see the Prime Minister's XI take on one of the touring international sides at Manuka Oval.

Where to eat

Aubergine   Canberra's only two-chef-hat restaurant. It is elegant and classy with a contemporary menu that reflects strong French and European overtones. 18 Barker St, Griffith; (02) 6260 8666; open Mon–Sat for dinner. 110 C5

Cape Cod   Seafood restaurant with an Asian influence that offers a regular changing menu, accompanied with a fine wine selection. Deakin Shops, Shop 3, Duff Pl, Deakin; (02) 6282 8697; open Tues–Fri for lunch and Mon–Sat for dinner. 110 B5

Ellacure Restaurant and Bar   Great cafe with a good, casual menu in the pizza and pasta mode. Cnr Braybrook and Battye sts, Bruce; (02) 6251 0990; open Tues–Sun for lunch and Tues–Sat for dinner. 110 B2

Iori Japanese   Inner-city Japanese restaurant where the emphasis is on really exciting food. 41 East Row; (02) 6257 2334; open Mon–Fri for lunch and Mon–Sat for dinner. 112 B1

Italian and Sons   Casual-feel restaurant with regional Italian menu that uses fresh local produce. 7 Lonsdale St, Braddon; (02) 6162 4888; open Tues–Fri for lunch and Mon–Sat for dinner. 112 B1

Mecca Bah   Buzzing Middle Eastern bazaar with a fun menu and a great feel. Shop 25–29, Manuka Terrace, cnr Flinders Way and Franklin St, Manuka; (02) 6260 6700; open daily for lunch and dinner. 110 C5

Mezzalira   Top-notch Italian restaurant in the city where you'll get serious and very good food. Melbourne Building, cnr London Circuit and West Row; (02) 6230 0025; open Mon–Fri for lunch and Mon–Sat for dinner. 112 B1

Ottoman Cuisine   The ultimate Ottoman Empire experience from elegant favourites to complex sophistication. 9 Broughton St, Barton; (02) 6273 6111; open Tues–Fri for lunch and Tues–Sat for dinner. 112 C4

Pulp Kitchen   Classy, simple brasserie-style restaurant that offers some of the best, most uncluttered food in town. Shop 1, Wakefield Gardens, Ainslie shops; (02) 6257 4334; open Tues–Fri for lunch and Tues–Sat for dinner. 110 D2

The Chairman and Yip   Modern Asian offering delicate, classic dishes along with an extensive wine collection. 108 Bunda St; (02) 6248 7109; open Tues–Fri for lunch and Mon–Sat for dinner. 112 B1

Where to stay

Anzac Park Homestay   108 Anzac Park, Campbell; (02) 6161 4143.

Canberra Carotel Motel & Caravan Park   Cnr Aspinall and Zelling sts, Watson; (02) 6241 1377.

Canberra Motor Village   2 Kunzea St, O'connor; (02) 6247 5466.

Capital Country Holiday Village   47 Bidges Rd, Sutton, NSW; (02) 6230 3433.

Eaglehawk Holiday Park   1246 Federal Hwy, Sutton, NSW; (02) 6241 6411.

Last Stop Ambledown Brook   198 Brooklands Rd, Wallaroo, NSW; (02) 6230 2280.

Rosebud Heritage Cottage   16 Skinner St, Cook; (02) 6251 3159.

Waterside retreats

Black Mountain Peninsula   A picnic and barbecue spot on the edge of the lake in the shadow of Black Mountain. 110 B4

Casuarina Sands   Where the Cotter and Murrumbidgee rivers meet. 518 C5

Commonwealth Park   Formal gardens, parkland and public art on the edge of the lake. 112 C3

Commonwealth Place Promenade on the shores of the lake, with the International Flag Display and vistas of the Australian War Memorial and Parliament House. 112 B3

Jerrabomberra Wetlands A refuge for wildlife, including 77 bird species. 112 D5

Weston Park A woodland and lakeside recreation area with play equipment for children. 110 B4

Yerrabi Ponds A skating park and children's playground near Gungahlin Lakes. 518 E3

 ## Day tours

Namadgi National Park Namadgi is part of the Australian Alps and the informative visitor centre is only a 45-minute drive from the city centre. Walking the 160 kilometres of marked trails is a popular way to explore the park. Beautiful scenery can be enjoyed in the rugged Bimberi Wilderness in the western part of the park. Namadgi has a wide range of natural environments, an abundance of native wildlife and a rich Aboriginal heritage with the evidence of several rock-art sites in the park.

Lanyon Homestead South of Canberra is one of Australia's most historic grazing properties and a beautiful 19th-century homestead. On the banks of the Murrumbidgee River, the homestead and its gardens provide a glimpse of the 1850s. The homestead's outbuildings (the kitchen, dairy, storerooms and workers' barracks) were built from wood and stone — the stone was cut and quarried by convict labour. Parts of the homestead have been restored and furnished in the style of the period.

Tidbinbilla Nature Reserve South-west of Canberra is the Tidbinbilla Nature Reserve, which includes dry and wet forests, subalpine areas and wetlands. Enjoy a bushwalk or picnic, play with the kids in the Discovery Playground at Tidbinbilla, or marvel at the free-ranging wildlife at The Sanctuary. Near the reserve is the Canberra Deep Space Communication Complex, one of three facilities in the world that form NASA's Deep Space Network. Here you can view a genuine piece of moon rock that is 3.8 billion years old, astronaut suits, space food, spacecraft models and photographs. Just south of the Tidbinbilla Nature Reserve is Corin Forest, which has an 800-metre bobsled alpine slide, a flying fox, a waterslide and some great bushwalks and picnic areas. Admission fee applies to Tidbinbilla Nature Reserve.

Canberra wine district Canberra district wineries have established a sound reputation for their cool-climate wines. With numerous vineyards and wineries within 35 minutes' drive from the city centre, making a winery tour is a must. You can pick up a guide to the wineries from the visitor centre or from cellar doors around the region. In addition to cellar-door sales, some wineries offer excellent dining facilities and entertainment, with the annual Wine, Roses and all that Jazz Festival proving popular each November.

Historic towns A number of towns within easy driving distance of Canberra are noted for their heritage buildings and are filled with a sense of the area's farming and goldmining history. These towns include Captains Flat, Goulburn, Braidwood, Bungendore, Yass and Young; most are within an hour or so of the capital. Historic Bungendore, full of craft galleries and antique shops, is a great daytrip, although at only 30 minutes away it is easy enough to visit just for a fine meal or an enjoyable shopping expedition.

AUSTRALIAN CAPITAL TERRITORY

VICTORIA is...

Barracking for your team at a footy match at the **MCG** / Watching penguins waddle from the sea to their burrows on **PHILLIP ISLAND** / Taking a paddlesteamer ride on the Murray River from **ECHUCA** / Panning for gold and enjoying traditional hard-boiled lollies at **SOVEREIGN HILL** in Ballarat / Soaking in a mineral spa in **DAYLESFORD** or **HEPBURN SPRINGS** / Driving along the spectacular **GREAT OCEAN ROAD** to see the **TWELVE APOSTLES** / Bushwalking in a timeless mountain landscape in **GRAMPIANS NATIONAL PARK** / A daytrip to the **DANDENONGS**, stopping off at some cellar doors in the **YARRA VALLEY** / Hitting the slopes at **MOUNT BULLER**

VICTORIA

is possibly Australia's most diverse state. In a half-hour drive from Melbourne you could be taking in mist-laden mountain ranges and fern gullies. In an hour you could be lying on a sandy beach in a sheltered bay, or surfing in the rugged Southern Ocean. In around four hours you could be standing on the edge of the immense desert that stretches away into Australia's interior. In a country full of mind-numbing distances, nothing seems far away in Victoria.

More than five million people live in Victoria, with over four million in Melbourne. The city was only founded in 1835, as a kind of afterthought to Sydney and Hobart, but by the 1850s Victoria was off to a racing start. A deluge of people from all corners of the world fanned out across the state in response to the madness that was gold. It brought prosperity to Victoria and it also brought the certain wildness treasured in the state's history – uprisings like the Eureka Rebellion and bushrangers like Ned Kelly.

Two centuries later, Victoria has also recognised the richness of its natural landscape. To the west of Melbourne, beyond Geelong, a tract of cool-temperate rainforest unravels on its

[MOUNT HOTHAM AT SUNSET, ALPINE NATIONAL PARK]

way to the vivid green Cape Otway, where a lighthouse stands on the cliff-top. The Great Ocean Road winds past here, en route to the state's iconic limestone stacks, the Twelve Apostles.

On the other side of Melbourne, the land falls away into a series of peninsulas, islands and isthmuses. One leads to Wilsons Promontory, an untouched landscape of forested hills, tea-brown rivers and beaches strewn with enormous rust-red boulders.

The amber-hued Yarra Valley produces some of the country's finest cool-climate wines, and from here the landscape begins its gradual climb up into the High Country, which becomes a vista of snowfields in winter.

Perhaps Victoria's most cherished place is the Grampians, an offshoot of the Great Dividing Range. With a quarter of the state's flora and 80 per cent of its Aboriginal rock art, the Grampians is a living gallery and a superb place for bushwalking and camping.

[GEELONG WATERFRONT]

fact file

Population 5 624 100
Total land area 227 010 square kilometres
People per square kilometre 22.1
Sheep per square kilometre 94
Length of coastline 1868 kilometres
Number of islands 184
Longest river Goulburn River (566 kilometres)
Largest lake Lake Corangamite (209 square kilometres)
Highest mountain Mount Bogong (1986 metres), Alpine National Park
Hottest place Mildura (77 days per year above 30°C)
Wettest place Weeaproinah (1900 millimetres of rain per year), Otway Ranges
Oldest permanent settlement Portland (1834)
Most famous beach Bells Beach, Torquay
Tonnes of gold mined 2500 (2 per cent of world total)
Litres of milk produced on Victorian dairy farms per year 7 billion
Quirkiest festival Great Vanilla Slice Triumph, Ouyen
Famous locals Germaine Greer, Barry Humphries, Kylie Minogue
Original name for the Twelve Apostles The Sow and Piglets
Best invention Bionic ear
First Ned Kelly film released *The Story of the Kelly Gang*, 1906 (also believed to be the world's first feature film)
Local beer Victoria Bitter

gift ideas

Raspberry drops, Sovereign Hill, Ballarat Delicious, old-fashioned lollies from the gold-rush days are still made and sold at Charles Spencer's Confectionery Shop in Main Street and at the Sovereign Hill Gift Shop. See Ballarat p. 148

Replica of Melbourne tram, Best of Souvenirs, Melbourne Prince Christian of Denmark received a real tram on the occasion of his birth, but you can take home a smaller – and beautifully crafted – version of Melbourne's distinctive transportation. Melbourne Visitor Centre, Federation Square, cnr Flinders and Swanston sts, Melbourne. See Federation Square p. 127

Football souvenirs, MCG, Richmond Scarves, beanies and jerseys with team colours and souvenirs from the home of Australian Rules Football. See MCG p. 134

Bread, pastries and provisions, Phillippa's, Armadale, Brighton and Melbourne CBD A small business that produces delicious baked goods. Highly recommended are the chocolate brownie and caramel, date and walnut blondie. 1030 High St, Armadale; 608 Hampton St, Brighton; 15 Howey Pl, Melbourne. See Melbourne p. 124

Beach boxes souvenirs, the Esplanade Market St Kilda, Melbourne Victoria's famous beach boxes are represented on fridge magnets, key holders, coasters and prints. See Markets p. 137

Stefano's products, Mildura Dine at the acclaimed Stefano's restaurant and then take home jams, chutneys, pasta and pasta sauces. See Mildura p. 180

Wine, Yarra Valley and Mornington Peninsula Fantastic chardonnay, pinot noir and sparkling varieties from these two wine-producing regions. See Yarra Glen p. 204 and Mornington p. 179

Red Hill muesli, Red Hill Market This popular muesli comes in different varieties including roast hazelnut, tropical and Wicked (with chocolate). See Flinders p. 163

Ned Kelly memorabilia, Glenrowan Victoria's famous bushranger is remembered through everything from replicas of his head armour to belt buckles and T-shirts. See Glenrowan p. 164

Spa and skincare products, Daylesford and Hepburn Springs The heart of Victoria's Spa Country offers a range of locally made beauty, spa and skincare products from shops and spa centres. See Daylesford p. 161

MELBOURNE is...

Barracking for your team at a footy match at the MCG / Admiring architecture and art in

FEDERATION SQUARE / Shopping for produce at the QUEEN VICTORIA MARKET / A stroll

along the ST KILDA foreshore / Taking a ferry trip to WILLIAMSTOWN / Moonlight Cinema

in the ROYAL BOTANIC GARDENS during summer / Sweating it out in the crowd at the

AUSTRALIAN OPEN / Stopping for coffee in DEGRAVES STREET, one of the city's laneways /

Live music at a pub in FITZROY / Waterside dining at SOUTHGATE or NewQuay, DOCKLANDS

VISITOR INFORMATION
Melbourne Visitor Centre
→ Federation Square, cnr Flinders and Swanston sts
(03) 9658 9658
www.visitmelbourne.com

Melbourne is renowned as Australia's cultural capital. The city has a decidedly European feel, with neo-Gothic banks and cathedrals, much-loved department stores, art galleries and theatres around every corner. And hidden among these buildings is a string of vibrant laneways given over to cafe culture and boutique shopping. Yet Melbourne wouldn't be Melbourne without sport – seeing a footy match at the MCG is a must.

Melbourne was born in 1835, and quickly became a city. With the boom of Victoria's goldfields, unbelievable wealth was poured into public buildings and tramways, grand boulevards and High Victorian masterpieces.

Today Melbourne's population of around 4 077 000 still enjoys the good life, at the very centre of which is a love of good food and fine dining. You can find comfort food in a cosy corner pub or meals with a view and a waterfront setting – a trend in so many of the country's coastal cities. Southbank, the shopping and eating precinct on the Yarra River, has become an extension of the city centre, while Docklands is the city's latest waterside area.

You might come to Melbourne for the dining and the shopping; the gardens and the architecture; the arts and music; the football, cricket and tennis. The city has as much diversity as it has suburbs, and at last check these were marching right down the Mornington Peninsula.

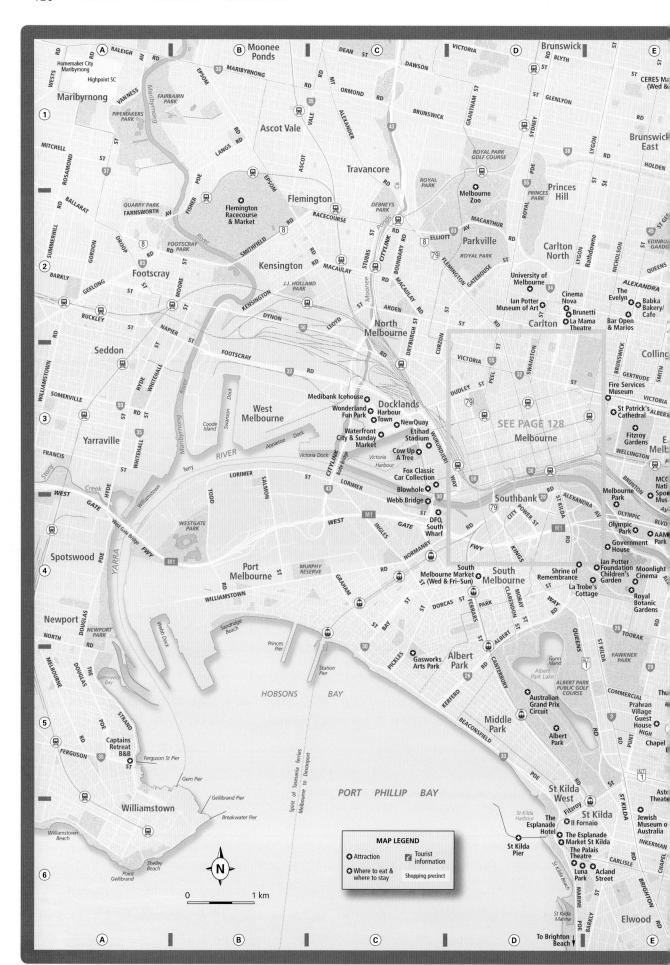

MAP LEGEND

⊕ Attraction
❂ Where to eat & where to stay
ℹ Tourist information
Shopping precinct

N

0   1 km

CBD CENTRAL

Melbourne's central business district (CBD) lies on the north bank of the Yarra River. The train system runs a ring around the CBD and trams amble up and down most of its main streets, behind which lies a charming network of arcades and backstreets.

A station, a pub and a cathedral 128 C4

Flinders Street Station is the CBD's major train station. Three other landmarks face it: Federation Square *(see next entry)*, St Paul's Cathedral and the **Young and Jackson Hotel**. Across Swanston Street is the grandiose **St Paul's Cathedral**, built in 1891. Its mosaic interior is well worth a look.

Federation Square 128 C4

Melbourne's most significant building project in decades has a central piazza paved with 7500 square metres of coloured Kimberley sandstone, surrounded by bars, cafes, restaurants and shops. Down by the river, Federation Wharf is home to Rentabike *(see Getting around, p. 136)* and a departure point for river cruises *(see Walks and tours, p. 137)*. Fed Square's must-visit attractions are the Ian Potter Centre: NGV Australia and the Australian Centre for the Moving Image *(see below)*.

Ian Potter Centre: NGV Australia 128 D4

Indigenous art – traditional and modern – as well as colonial artists, such as Tom Roberts and Arthur Streeton, fill this gallery, dedicated to Australian art. The NGV Kids Corner is outstanding for pre-schoolers. *Federation Sq; (03) 8620 2222; open 10am–5pm Tues–Sun; general admission free. The National Gallery of Victoria's international collection can be found on St Kilda Rd (see p. 132).*

Australian Centre for the Moving Image (ACMI) 128 C4

ACMI explores all guises of the moving image. Cinemas screen films and darkened galleries exhibit screen-based art and temporary exhibitions. Check the newspapers for film screenings or visit the website (www. acmi.net.au). *Federation Sq; (03) 8663 2200, bookings (03) 8663 2583; open 10am–6pm daily, open later for scheduled film screenings; general admission free.*

Swanston Street 128 C3, C4

Walk down the east side and see a grand, tree-lined boulevard, significant historic buildings *(see Grand old buildings, p. 137)* and quirky sculptures, while the west side is overcrowded with discount stores, souvenir shops and fast-food outlets. The street is closed to cars other than taxis.

Corner Swanston and Collins streets is the **Melbourne Town Hall**, hosting events including the Melbourne International Comedy Festival *(see Top events, p. 136)*. Opposite is a statue of doomed explorers **Burke and Wills**, and further north is the State Library of Victoria *(see p. 131)*.

Collins Street 128 C4, D3

This is Melbourne's most dignified street. The 'Paris end', towards the east, has a European ambience and designer boutiques. Near Elizabeth Street is **Australia on Collins**, housing Australian fashion labels and a food court. Towards Spencer Street are impressive buildings, such as the Old ANZ Bank *(see Grand old buildings, p. 137)*.

VICTORIA

North Melbourne

Carlton

QUEENSBERRY

VICTORIA

COURTNEY ST

BERKELEY ST

ELIZABETH ST

PELHAM ST

UNIVERSITY SQUARE

LINCOLN SQUARE

PIAZZA ITALIA

PELHAM

CARLTON ST

Melbourne Museum & IMAX Melbourne

Royal Exhibition Building

QUEENSBERRY

LEICESTER ST

BOUVERIE ST

SWANSTON ST

CARDIGAN ST

LYGON ST

DRUMMOND ST

RATHDOWNE ST

NICHOLSON ST

VICTORIA

PEEL ST

Queen Victoria Market (Tues & Thurs–Sun)

THERRY

CHETWYND

HOWARD ST

EADES PARK

QUEEN ST

FRANKLIN

ELIZABETH ST

City Baths

Old Melbourne Gaol

Old Melbourne Magistrates' Court

RUSSELL ST

Bennetts Lane Jazz Club

EXHIBITION ST

SPRING ST

VICTORIA PDE

ALBERT ST

DUDLEY

CAPEL ST

St James' Old Cathedral

Robinsons in the City

Flagstaff Gardens

WALSH ST

KING ST

ABECKETT ST

SWANSTON

Melbourne Central

State Library of Victoria

On3

QV Melbourne

Chinese Museum

Her Majesty's Theatre

Princess Theatre

Parliament of Victoria

Parliament

SPENCER ST

Flagstaff

LA TROBE

WILLIAM ST

QUEEN ST

Former Royal Mint

Melbourne Central

The Toff

Chinatown

Flower Drum

Pellegrini's Espresso Bar

Hotel Windsor

Koorie Heritage Trust

HARDWARE

Supreme Court of Victoria

Melbourne's GPO

Myer

David Jones

Bourke St Mall

Greater Union Cinema

Kino Cinemas

Old Treasury Building

TREASURY GARDENS

LONSDALE

ROSE ALLEY

LANGS LA

Royal Arcade

Capitol Theatre

Melbourne Town Hall

Athenaeum Theatre

Regent Theatre

Collins Place

Craft Victoria

LITTLE

BOURKE

Block Arcade

Manchester Unity Building

Burke & Wills

Anna Schwartz Gallery

Flinders Lane Gallery

The Press Club

COLLINS

Old ANZ Bank & Banking Museum

Australia on Collins

Melbourne

Centre Place

Journal Canteen

Nicholas Building

MoVida Bar de Tapas y Vino

Forum Theatre

LITTLE

WURUNDJERI WAY

Southern Cross Railway Station

Collins

Olderfleet Building

Degraves Espresso

Degraves Street

Young and Jackson Hotel

St Paul's Cathedral

ACMI

Ian Potter Centre: NGV Australia

Chocolate Buddha

BATMAN AV

Vue de Monde

FLINDERS

Immigration Museum

Flinders Street Station

Federation Square

Birrarrung Marr

YARRA RIVER

Princes Bridge

Sandridge Bridge

Hamer Hall

Victoria Police Museum

BATMAN PARK

Melbourne Aquarium

Queens Bridge

Kings Bridge

ENTERPRIZE PARK

RIVERSIDE QUAY

Eureka Tower & Eureka Skydeck 88

Southgate

Sunday Market

Arts Centre Melbourne Theatres Building

ALEXANDRA GARDENS

ALEXANDRA

QUEEN VICTORIA GARDENS

SIDDELEY

Spencer Street Bridge

Crown Entertainment Complex

Southbank

SOUTHBANK

NGV International

ST KILDA RD

To DFO South Wharf

Polly Woodside

CLARENDON RD

BRIDGE

QUEENS

CITY RD

POWER ST

MOORE ST

Melbourne Recital Centre (MRC)

Melbourne Theatre Company (MTC)

BVD

Sidney Myer Music Bowl

LINLITHGOW

BURNLEY TUNNEL

Melbourne Convention Centre

Melbourne Exhibition Centre

South Wharf

WEST

NORMANBY

HAIG ST

MORAY ST

BALSTON ST

KAVANAGH ST

KINGS WAY

CITYLINK

WADEY

Australian Centre for Contemporary Art (ACCA)

Malthouse Theatre

DOMAIN TUNNEL

Kings Domain

GATE

FWY

FERRARS ST

WHITEMAN ST

CHESSELL ST

MILES ST

STURT ST

DODDS ST

WELLS ST

COVENTRY

STURT ST RESERVE

ROYAL BOTANIC GARDENS

M1

CITY

MARKET

0   300 m

N

Laneways and arcades 128 C3, C4

From Flinders Street Station to Bourke Street Mall are narrow, darkened, bustling laneways filled with cafes, fashion boutiques and jewellers.

The section of **Degraves Street** closest to Flinders Lane is closed to cars and is full of cafes spilling onto the paved street. Across from Degraves Street is **Centre Place**, with more eateries and designer-fashion outlets.

Block Arcade runs between Collins and Little Collins streets. It boasts Italian mosaic floors, ornate glass ceilings, tearooms and exclusive boutiques. Follow the arcade to Elizabeth Street, or to the laneway that joins it to Little Collins Street, where there are yet more cafes.

Over Little Collins Street is Australia's oldest arcade, **Royal Arcade**. Above the entrance stand two giants, Gog and Magog, of the ancient British legend. You can take Royal Arcade to Bourke Street Mall or Elizabeth Street. (To get to the mall you can also take the adjacent, cafe-lined **Causeway**.)

Bourke Street Mall 128 C3

Bourke Street Mall is the heart of Melbourne's shopping district, with the big department stores **Myer** and **David Jones** and brand-name fashion outlets. Between Elizabeth and Swanston streets the mall is only open to trams and pedestrians. At the west end is **Melbourne's GPO**, once the city's post office but now a smart shopping complex showcasing a who's who of fashion labels, cafes and bars.

Art spaces 128 C4

Flinders Lane is home to an array of art galleries (*see Flinders Lane galleries, p. 130*), including the **Anna Schwartz Gallery**. Expect to be surprised and delighted, especially if you're into conceptual art. Corner Flinders Lane and Swanston Street is the **Nicholas Building**, home to numerous small, artist-run spaces. *Anna Schwartz Gallery: 185 Flinders La; (03) 9654 6131; open 12–6pm Tues–Fri, 1–5pm Sat; admission free.*

[DEGRAVES STREET]

CBD WEST

This part of Melbourne stretches from the Queen Victoria Market down to the Yarra River, taking in the city's legal district including the **Supreme Court of Victoria**. *The architecturally superb* **Southern Cross Railway Station** *is worth a visit even if you're not planning a train ride.*

Hardware Lane 128 B3

Between Bourke and Lonsdale streets, west of Bourke Street Mall, is Hardware Lane, where office workers and bar seekers crowd at lunchtime and in the evenings. The cobblestone paving, window boxes and the brightly painted old buildings add to the atmosphere.

Former Royal Mint 128 B3

Built in Renaissance Revival style and set off by a dazzling coat of arms, the building was originally constructed to mint the bounty from Victoria's goldfields. In 1968 it became home to the **Hellenic Museum**, displaying Byzantine objects and displays related to Greek migration to Australia. *280 William St; (03) 8615 9016; open 10am–4pm Mon–Fri.*

[SLIPPER STALL AT QUEEN VICTORIA MARKET]

Melbourne Aquarium 128 B5

Beside the Yarra River, journey into the depths of the ocean, past rockpool and mangrove habitats, jellyfish, and a close-up encounter with sharks and stingrays. See King and Gentoo penguins plus other Antarctic creatures in the **Antarctica** exhibition. *Cnr King and Flinders sts; (03) 9923 5999; open 9.30am–6pm daily.*

Immigration Museum 128 B4

Far from being specialist, this museum is about Australia's most relevant characteristic since settlement. It explores journeys, tumultuous new beginnings, and the various cultures brought here over the years. It also investigates our changing government policies on immigration, and how they continue to shape Australia. *400 Flinders St; (03) 9927 2700; open 10am–5pm daily.*

Koorie Heritage Trust 128 A3

Walking through this centre you will realise the drastic, violent and totally irreversible changes made to a culture over 40 000 years old. Displays take you through the traditions, lifestyle, and history of Aboriginal people of south-eastern Australia. There are also changing exhibitions by local Aboriginal artists. *295 King St; (03) 8622 2600; open 9am–4.45pm Mon–Fri, 10am–4pm Sat–Sun; entry by donation.*

Queen Victoria Market 128 B2

This famous market is spread across 7 hectares under the shelter of a massive shed. There is a meat hall, fruit, vegetable and herb stalls. On Saturdays the aisles are crammed, and the clothing and souvenir stalls make this a hot spot for tourists too. *Main entrance cnr Elizabeth and Victoria sts; (03) 9320 5822; open 6am–2pm Tues and Thurs, 6am–5pm Fri, 6am–3pm Sat, 9am–4pm Sun.* On Wednesday evenings in summer, enjoy the **Suzuki Night Market**, with live music, international food, and clothing and craft stalls.

Flagstaff Gardens 128 A2

Originally Burial Hill – where many of Melbourne's early settlers ended up – these were Melbourne's first public gardens and once served as a signalling station for ships arriving from Britain. It is now a lovely space, with lawns, established trees, sporting facilities and barbecues. *Bounded by William, Latrobe, King and Dudley sts; sports bookings (03) 9663 5888.*

CBD EAST

This is Melbourne's most distinguished quarter, taking in some fine old buildings and the government district. The Parliament of Victoria occupies a suitably prominent position on Spring Street at the top of a hill.

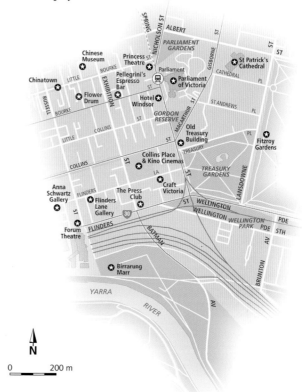

Parliament of Victoria 128 D3

From 1901 to 1927 this was the seat of federal government. Free tours run when parliament is not sitting (see parliament's website: www.parliament.vic.gov.au). *Spring St, facing Bourke St; (03) 9651 8911.* South of parliament, facing Collins St, is the **Old Treasury Building**, housing the Victorian Marriage Registry. Find the **Built on Gold** exhibition and temporary exhibitions here too. *Spring St; (03) 9651 2233; open 10am–4pm Sun–Fri; admission free.*

Flinders Lane galleries 128 C4, D3, D4

This laneway boasts the highest concentration of commercial galleries in Australia, mainly between Spring and Swanston streets. With a focus on Indigenous and contemporary art, standout galleries include **Flinders Lane Gallery** and **Anna Schwartz Gallery** *(see Art spaces, p. 129)*; and **Craft Victoria**, which fosters creativity in craft and design. *Flinders Lane Gallery: 137 Flinders La; (03) 9654 3332; open 11am–6pm Tues–Fri, 11am–4pm Sat. Craft Victoria: 31 Flinders La; (03) 9650 7775; open 10am–5pm Mon–Sat; admission free.*

CBD NORTH

This part of town is occupied mainly by office buildings, but among them are the Old Melbourne Gaol, the State Library of Victoria, Chinatown, and the QV shopping and food precinct.

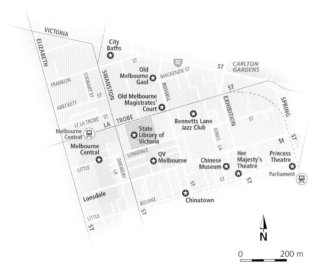

0   200 m

N

QV Melbourne 128 C3

Between Swanston, Lonsdale, Russell and Little Lonsdale streets is QV Melbourne, divided up into a series of laneways: high-end fashion stores line Albert Coates Lane, while Artemis Lane is a wonderland of homewares. You can also explore Red Cape and Jane Bell lanes. (The names relate to the site's history – it was once the site of the Queen Victoria Women's Hospital, a part of which still remains.) *(03) 9207 9200; open 10am–6pm Mon–Wed and Sat, 10am–7pm Thurs, 10am–9pm Fri, 10am–5pm Sun.*

State Library of Victoria 128 C2

Pre-Fed Square, this Roman-style building was the city centre's biggest public space and the main meeting spot for demonstrations. It houses an impressive five-storey octagonal reading room, several art galleries, and is home to the **Wheeler Centre: Books, Writing and Ideas**, the centrepiece of Melbourne's UNESCO City of Literature Initiative, hosting a year-round literary program. *Cnr Lonsdale and Swanston sts; (03) 8664 7000; open 10am–9pm Mon–Thurs, 10am–6pm Fri–Sun.*

Old Melbourne Gaol 128 C2

Many notorious early Victorian criminals were executed here. For the brave, take a Hangman's Night Tour (four times a week at 8.30pm, 7.30pm in winter) or a ghost hunt (held monthly); contact Ticketek (13 2849). *Russell St, between Victoria and Latrobe sts; (03) 8663 7228; open 9.30am–5pm daily; at 12.30pm and 2pm Sat the story of Ned Kelly, 'Such a Life', is performed (free with entry).*

Chinatown 128 C3

Chinatown has flourished since the first Chinese migrated to Victoria at the beginning of the gold rush. Decorated archways herald the entrance to the Little Bourke Street strip at the Swanston, Russell and Exhibition street ends. The **Chinese Museum**, in Cohen Place off Little Bourke Street, tells of Chinese migration during the gold rush, and houses Dai Loong (Big Dragon), which roams the streets during Chinese New Year. *22 Cohen Pl; (03) 9662 2888; open 10am–5pm daily.*

Lonsdale Street 128 C3

The section of Lonsdale Street between Russell and Swanston streets is the centre of Melbourne's Greek community. On the southern side are Greek bookshops, music stores, cafes and restaurants.

Melbourne Central 128 C3

Built above the underground railway station of the same name, the shopping and entertainment complex surrounds a historic nine-storey shot tower, preserved under a massive glass cone. *(03) 9922 1122; open 10am–6pm Mon–Thurs and Sat, 10am–9pm Fri, 10am–5pm Sun.*

VICTORIA

[PARLIAMENT HOUSE]

SOUTHBANK

This inner-city suburb takes in some of Melbourne's best leisure and dining precincts and public arts institutions. Behind Flinders Street Station is Southgate, a stylish shopping and dining area on the Yarra River.

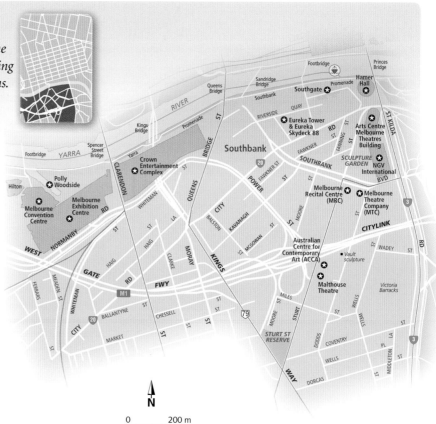

Eureka Tower 128 C5

At 300 metres, this is Melbourne's tallest building and boasts the Southern Hemisphere's highest viewing platform. The top ten levels feature 24-carat, gold-plated glass. On the 88th floor, **Eureka Skydeck 88** offers a 360-degree view of the city, bay and mountains. For a heart-stopping experience, step inside The Edge, a three-metre glass cube that projects out of the side of the building. *7 Riverside Quay, Southbank; (03) 9693 8888; open 10am–10pm daily.*

Southgate 128 C4

Southgate was an industrial site that was slowly reinvented. Apartments, office blocks, shops, restaurants and a tree-lined promenade form what is today an essential part of Melbourne, with a food court, restaurants, bars and shops that become increasingly exclusive the higher up the complex you go. *(03) 9686 1000; open 10am–7pm Mon–Thurs, 10am–8pm Fri and Sat, 10am–6pm Sun; food court breakfast–dinner.*

Crown Entertainment Complex 128 B5

This huge complex begins just over Queensbridge Street. As well as a casino, Crown contains shops, a food court, nightclubs and cinemas. Restaurants include world-class dining such as Neil Perry's Rockpool Bar and Grill, Japanese restaurant Nobu and Silks for Chinese banquets. Big names in fashion like Versace and Prada reside here too. *8 Whiteman St, Southbank; (03) 9292 8888.*

Melbourne Exhibition Centre 128 A5

Over Clarendon Street from Crown is this venue for most of Melbourne's major expos. *2 Clarendon St, South Wharf; (03) 9235 8000.*

Next to the centre in Duke's Dock is the 1885 tall ship **Polly Woodside**. Step aboard for a journey into Melbourne's maritime history. *2A Clarendon St, South Wharf; (03) 9699 9760; open 9.30am–5pm daily.*

Arts Centre Melbourne 128 C5

The Arts Centre consists of **Hamer Hall** and the **Theatres Building** beneath its distinctive lattice spire, which is intended to resemble a ballerina's tutu. The Theatres Building includes three theatres: the State Theatre, the Playhouse, and the Fairfax Studio. There is also **Gallery 1**, the main exhibition space for the **Performing Arts Collection**, which preserves a variety of Australian performing-arts memorabilia. *100 St Kilda Rd; (03) 9281 8000, bookings on 1300 182 183; open 8am–end of last performance daily; general admission free.*

NGV International 128 C5

Since 1968 this large grey building has been the home of the NGV. Its highly regarded international component has permanent and touring exhibitions. There are more than 30 galleries, the iconic water curtain at the entrance, and a magnificent stained-glass roof by Leonard French at the back. *180 St Kilda Rd; (03) 8620 2222; open 10am–5pm daily; general admission free. NGV Australia can be found at Federation Square (see p. 127).*

Sturt Street arts 128 C5, C6

The Malthouse Theatre, the Australian Centre for Contemporary Art (ACCA) and the new Melbourne Recital Centre (MRC)/Melbourne Theatre Company (MTC) complex sit on Sturt Street. Once a malt factory, the **Malthouse Theatre** is home to the contemporary Malthouse Theatre company. Next door, the **ACCA** is housed in a rusted-steel building intended to resemble Uluru against a blue sky. Contemporary exhibitions run inside. *CUB Malthouse: 113 Sturt St; bookings on (03) 9685 5111. ACCA: 111 Sturt St; (03) 9697 9999; open 10am–5pm Tues–Fri, 11am–6pm Sat–Sun and public holidays; admission free.*

Resembling a giant beehive in parts, the **Melbourne Recital Centre** comprises the Elisabeth Murdoch Hall for chamber music, the smaller Salon and a cafe-bar. Adjacent is the **Melbourne Theatre Company** in an equally cutting-edge structure. *Cnr Sturt St and Southbank Blvd, Southbank; MRC bookings on (03) 9699 3333, MTC bookings on (03) 8688 0800.*

[ETERNAL FLAME, SHRINE OF REMEMBRANCE]

CBD SOUTH-EAST

Sidney Myer Music Bowl 128 D5

Set in the Kings Domain gardens, the iconic Sidney Myer Music Bowl is a massive grassy amphitheatre. It hosts numerous summer events, including the annual Christmas extravaganza, Carols by Candlelight, and free concerts by the Melbourne Symphony Orchestra. *Linlithgow Ave, Kings Domain; (03) 9281 8000.*

Gardens 126 D4, E4; 128 D6

Bordered by the Yarra and St Kilda Road is a series of public gardens, including Kings Domain and the Royal Botanic Gardens. In **Kings Domain** are the Sidney Myer Music Bowl *(see previous entry)* and the **Shrine of Remembrance**, commemorating generations of Australian war veterans. The shrine is the centre for ANZAC Day commemorations. *Birdwood Ave, South Yarra; (03) 9661 8100; open 10am–5pm daily; admission free.*

East of the shrine is **La Trobe's Cottage**, a prefabricated house built in England and brought to Australia for Victoria's first lieutenant governor. **Government House** is located nearby. *Cnr Birdwood Ave and Dallas Brooks Drive; (03) 9656 9800; open 2–4pm Sun, Oct–May, and select days June–Sept. Tours of La Trobe's Cottage and Government House, Mon and Wed; (03) 8663 7260.*

Opposite the shrine, across Birdwood Avenue, is Observatory Gate, surrounding the **Royal Botanic Gardens**, with its cafe and the historic Melbourne Observatory. The visitor centre has information on garden walks and activities *(see Walks and tours, p. 137)*. The **Ian Potter Foundation Children's Garden** is an interactive space for kids, with a program of activities. In summer the gardens host **Moonlight Cinema**, screening new releases and classics. *Birdwood Ave; (03) 9252 2300; open 7pm–sunset daily Dec–Mar; Ian Potter Foundation Children's Garden open 10am–sunset, Wed–Sun in school term time and daily in school holidays, but closed eight weeks in winter.*

For a riverfront picnic spot, look across to Alexandra Avenue. Free gas barbecues dot the Yarra bank from Swan Street Bridge to Anderson Street.

Melbourne and Olympic parks 126 E4

Between the city and Richmond and Abbotsford are Melbourne's biggest sporting venues, scattered on either side of the rail yards. The two major ones are the **MCG** *(p. 134)* and **Melbourne Park**, incorporating the **Rod Laver** and **Hisense** arenas, and home of the Australian Open and big-ticket concerts. Heading towards Richmond, **AAMI Park** in the **Olympic Park** precinct is the home of Melbourne Rebels (Rugby Union), Melbourne Storm (Rugby League) and Melbourne Victory (soccer). *Olympic Blvd; (03) 9286 1600.*

DOCKLANDS

Until the 1960s this was a busy shipping port; now it is being transformed into a residential, business, entertainment and retail precinct, with nine mini neighbourhoods including NewQuay, Waterfront City and Victoria Harbour.

NewQuay and Waterfront City 126 C3

At the northern end of Docklands, NewQuay and Waterfront City comprise high-rise apartments, offices, shops, galleries, marinas and the bulk of Docklands' bars and restaurants. There's **Wonderland Fun Park**, with a host of rides for kids, and **Medibank Icehouse**, a world-class ice-sports and entertainment venue. *1300 756 699; open daily; session times and events www.icehouse.com.au.* There's also **Harbour Town** shopping centre, and the weekly **Sunday Market** (10am–5pm) for trash and treasure at Waterfront City Promenade.

Etihad Stadium 126 C3

This is a major venue for Australian Football League (AFL) games, other sporting events and concerts. Take a 'Behind the Scenes' tour to inspect, among other things, the AFL players' change rooms and the coaches' box. The one-hour tours leave at 11am, 1pm and 3pm Monday to Friday from the Customer Service Centre opposite Gates 2 and 3; different times on event days. *Bound by Bourke and Latrobe sts, Wurundjeri Way and Harbour Esplanade; tour bookings (03) 8625 7277.*

Art Journey 126 C3, C4

This self-guide urban art tour takes you past more than 30 superb, large-scale public artworks, including the whimsical wind-powered **Blowhole**, the sublimely sculptural **Webb Bridge**, and the amusing **Cow Up A Tree**. Barbecues, recreation areas and a children's playground line the way. Information from the Melbourne Visitor Information Centre, or the Docklands website (www.docklands.com).

Fox Classic Car Collection 126 C3

There are up to 50 vintage vehicles on display here, including Bentley, Jaguar, Rolls Royce and some ultra-cool Porsche and Mercedes Benz, in the historic Queen's Warehouse building. *Cnr Batmans Hill Dr and Collins St; (03) 9620 4086; open 10am–2pm Tues Feb–Nov.*

VICTORIA

INNER SOUTH-EAST

This area includes some of the city's most exclusive suburbs: South Yarra, Toorak, Malvern and Armadale. On Toorak Road, exclusive clothing stores, cafes and food shops abound, while nearby Chapel Street is a non-stop run of shops and cafes.

Chapel and Greville streets 126 E5

The northern end of Chapel Street, between Toorak and Commercial roads, is fashion central. Further down is the **Jam Factory**, a shopping complex, cinema and food court in the old Australian Jam Company premises.

On Commercial Road, off Chapel Street, is the **Prahran Market**, Australia's oldest continually running market. *163 Commercial Rd, South Yarra; (03) 8290 8220; open 7am–5pm Tues, Thurs and Sat, 7am–6pm Fri, 10am–3pm Sun.*

Further on, Greville Street runs off to the west, lined with cafes, bars, hip clothing shops and original occupants such as **Greville Records**.

South of Greville Street is **Chapel Street Bazaar**, a treasure trove for collectors. South of Commercial Road, Chapel Street is more down-to-earth, lined with interesting cafes, restaurants and bohemian shops.

Como House and Herring Island 126 F4

Stroll around the gardens and take a tour of this National Trust-listed mansion. You can visit the gorgeous cafe (open Wednesday to Sunday) without paying admission. Nearby take a punt from Como Landing across to Herring Island with its sculpture park and barbecue facilities. *Como House: cnr Williams Rd and Lechlade Ave, South Yarra; (03) 9827 2500; open 10am–4pm Wed, Sat–Sun, daily May–Aug. Herring Island punt: open 11am–5pm Sat–Sun Dec–Apr.*

INNER NORTH

Carlton and Fitzroy are two lively inner-city suburbs. Carlton is the heart of Victorian-terrace territory, while Fitzroy is where many young Melburnians would choose to live if they could afford it. Nearby Smith Street is blossoming with cafes and independent fashion designers.

Lygon Street, Carlton 126 D2

This is Carlton's main artery and the centre of Melbourne's Italian population, with restaurants, cafes, bookstores, clothing shops and the excellent **Cinema Nova**. Stop for authentic pasta, pizza, gelato and coffee at places such as **Brunetti**, on Faraday Street, an institution for Italian-pastry lovers. **Rathdowne Street**, parallel to Lygon Street, also has more cafes, restaurants and shops.

Brunswick Street, Fitzroy 126 E2

Brunswick Street offers an eclectic mix of cafes, pubs, live-music venues and shops, as well as leisurely breakfasts at cafes such as **Babka** and **Marios**.

Royal Exhibition Building 128 D1

This is Melbourne's most significant historic building, and Australia's first man-made structure to achieve World Heritage status. It is considered an enduring monument to the international exhibition movement, and no comparable 'great halls' survive elsewhere in the world. At dusk its lit-up vista harks back to the heady days of 1880s Melbourne. Interior tours run from the adjacent Melbourne Museum (*see next entry*) at 2pm daily when the building is not in use (bookings 13 1102). The area comes alive during the Melbourne International Flower and Garden Show (Mar–Apr). *11 Nicholson St, Carlton.*

Melbourne Museum 128 D1

Housed next to the Royal Exhibition Building is this museum, featuring dinosaur skeletons, a living rainforest and impressive science displays. It is also the resting place of Phar Lap, Australia's champion racing horse, standing proud and tall in a dimly lit room. Bunjilaka is an Aboriginal cultural centre, telling the Koorie story from the Koorie perspective. In the same building is the **IMAX Melbourne**, screening films in 2-D and 3-D. *Melbourne Museum: Nicholson St, Carlton; 13 1102 or 1300 130 152; open 10am–5pm daily.*

Melbourne Zoo 126 D1

Australia's oldest zoo is a far cry from caged zoos of the past. Elephants live in a re-creation of an Asian rainforest, complete with a plunge pool, while the Butterfly House is another wonder. From mid-January to mid-March the zoo runs evening jazz sessions called Zoo Twilights. *Elliott Ave, Parkville; (03) 9285 9300; open 9am–5pm daily, to 9.30pm for Zoo Twilights.*

INNER EAST

For both food and clothing, the combination of quality and price in Richmond and Abbotsford is hard to beat. Further out is a stretch of parkland that follows the Yarra River.

Bridge Road, Richmond 127 E3, F3

Bridge Road, between Hoddle and Church streets, is a shopper's heaven, filled with designer-clothing stores and factory outlets. Between Church and Burnley streets are restaurants of various cuisines. Swan Street, south of Bridge Road, is good for wining and dining, and features the **Corner Hotel**, staging local and international bands.

Victoria Street, Abbotsford 127 F3

Victoria Street, north of Bridge Road, is a living piece of Vietnam. From Hoddle Street to Church Street it overflows with Asian grocery stores and Vietnamese restaurants.

Melbourne Cricket Ground (MCG) 126 E3

A footy or cricket match at the 'G', as it is known, is a must-see. But if you visit in the off-season then take a tour on non-event days, 10am–3pm, from Gate 3 in the Olympic Stand. Tour prices can include entry to the MCG's interactive National Sports Museum, with artefacts including legendary cricketer Sir Don Bradman's baggy green cap. *Brunton Ave, Richmond; open 10am–5pm daily; (03) 9657 8879.*

[SUNSET AT ST KILDA PIER]

Fitzroy Gardens 126 E3

This is one of a handful of public gardens surrounding the CBD. It boasts **Cooks' Cottage**, a fairy tree and a model Tudor village. *Cook's Cottage: (03) 9419 4677; open 9am–5pm daily.*

Yarra Bend Park 127 F2

This bushland sanctuary is a few minutes' drive from the city. Enjoy walking tracks, a golf course, and boat-hire facilities and a cafe at the historic **Studley Park Boathouse**. *Off Studley Park Rd, Kew; (03) 9853 1828; boathouse and kiosk open 9am–5pm daily.*

BAYSIDE

The suburbs here sprawl down towards the Mornington Peninsula. Port Melbourne, at the top of the bay, was once an entry point for migrants and is now the docking point for Spirit of Tasmania ferries. It has a range of pubs, shops and cafes on offer, as does South Melbourne. Nearby Albert Park is the venue for the Australian Formula One Grand Prix each March, and a spot for jogging and boating. Further south again is St Kilda.

St Kilda 126 D6, E6

Once a seaside holiday destination, St Kilda is now a hub of activity.

Fitzroy Street has shoulder-to-shoulder cafes, restaurants, bars and pubs leading to a palm-lined foreshore and **St Kilda Pier** with its historic kiosk.

The foreshore path goes from Port Melbourne in the north to beyond Brighton in the south and is packed with cyclists, rollerbladers and walkers. **The Esplanade Hotel** (The Espy) is an integral part of Melbourne's live-music scene, and **The Palais Theatre**, a grand, French-style theatre, is the venue for concerts. Next door is Luna Park *(see next entry)*, and an arts and crafts market runs on The Esplanade every Sunday *(see Markets, p. 137)*.

On **Acland Street** are the famous continental cake shops, and south from St Kilda is a string of swimming beaches, including **Brighton Beach** with its trademark colourful bathing boxes.

Luna Park 126 E6

This iconic fun park retains the colour and thrill of its heyday in the early 20th century. Traditional rides like the carousel, Ferris wheel and rollercoaster now sit among the heart-racing Shock Drop, Enterprise and G Force. *Lower Esplanade, St Kilda; (03) 9525 5033; see www.lunapark.com.au for monthly operating hours.*

Rippon Lea 126 E6

The gardens of this grand Romanesque mansion yield hidden water features, paths and beautiful picnic spots. *192 Hotham St, Elsternwick; (03) 9523 6095; gardens open 10am–5pm daily; entry to house by tour, last departure 3.30pm.*

OUTER MELBOURNE

Heide Museum of Modern Art 537 J5

Surrounded by beautiful parklands and intriguing sculptures, this was home to John and Sunday Reed, patrons of the arts in the 1930s and 40s, who founded its museum of modern art. Café Vue at Heide, operated by renowned chef Shannon Bennett of Vue de Monde, offers wonderful fare. *7 Templestowe Rd, Bulleen; (03) 9850 1500; open 10am–5pm Tues–Sun; restaurant (03) 9852 2346; open 10am–5pm Tues–Fri, 9am–5pm Sat and Sun; admission free to gardens and sculpture park. 1300 336 932.*

CITY ESSENTIALS
MELBOURNE

Climate

'Four seasons in one day' is a familiar phrase to all Melburnians. It might reach 38°C in the morning then drop to 20°C in the afternoon – and the weather the next day is anyone's guess. Generally though, winter is cold – daytime temperatures of 11–12°C are not unusual – and spring is wet. January and February are hot, with temperatures anywhere between the mid 20s and high 30s. The favourite season of many locals is autumn, when the weather is usually dry and stable.

	MAX °C	MIN °C	RAIN MM	RAIN DAYS
JANUARY	25	14	48	5
FEBRUARY	25	14	47	5
MARCH	23	13	50	6
APRIL	20	10	57	8
MAY	16	8	56	9
JUNE	14	6	49	9
JULY	13	5	47	9
AUGUST	14	6	50	10
SEPTEMBER	17	7	58	10
OCTOBER	19	9	66	10
NOVEMBER	21	11	59	8
DECEMBER	24	12	59	7

Getting around

Melbourne's trams are an icon, but also a very good way of getting around the city. The City Circle tram is free and extends to Docklands. Trams depart every 12 minutes between 10am and 6pm from Sunday to Wednesday, and till 9pm from Thursday to Saturday. Other (paid) services head out into the suburbs, with especially good coverage of the eastern, south-eastern and northern suburbs. A map of the different services can be found inside most trams.

Trains are generally a faster option if there is a service that goes to your destination. Details of services can be found at each of the five stations in the CBD *(see map on p. 128)*.

Buses tend to cover the areas that trains and trams don't service. The free Melbourne City Tourist Shuttle is a hop-on, hop-off bus service stopping at 13 key city destinations. The service runs every 30 minutes between 9.30am and 4.30pm daily and includes an informative on-board commentary. Details of routes and stops can be found at www.thatsmelbourne.com.au,

or pick up a brochure from the Melbourne Visitor Information Centre at Federation Square.

Melbourne's public transport system is progressively moving from Metcard tickets to plastic myki smart cards. Initially, myki will only be available for train travel. While this is happening you will notice two types of ticketing equipment on the train, tram and bus networks. The price of your journey will depend on which of the two 'zones' you need to travel to. For an update on ticketing and an excellent journey planner facility, see www.metlinkmelbourne.com.au

For drivers, the much-talked-about feature of Melbourne's roads is the hook-turn, a process of moving to the left of the road in order to turn right, and therefore getting out of the way of trams. If you wish to use the tollways CityLink or the new EastLink, either an e-TAG or a day pass is required (there are no tollbooths, but day passes can be purchased over the phone either before or after making a journey).

Public transport Tram, train and bus information line 13 1638.

Airport shuttle bus Skybus (03) 9335 2811.

Tollways CityLink 13 2629; EastLink 13 5465.

Motoring organisation RACV 13 7228, roadside assistance 13 1111.

Car rental Avis 13 6333; Budget 1300 362 848; Hertz 13 3039; Thrifty 1300 367 227.

Taxis 13CABS 13 2227; Silver Top 13 1008; West Suburban (03) 9689 1144.

Water taxi Melbourne Water Taxis 0416 068 655.

Tourist buses AAT Kings (03) 9663 3377; Australian Pacific Tours 1300 655 965.

Bicycle hire Rentabike @ Federation Square 0417 339 203; Bike Now (South Melbourne) (03) 9696 8588; St Kilda Cycles (03) 9534 3074.

Top events

Australian Open One of the world's four major tennis Grand Slams. January.

Australian Grand Prix Elite motor racing and plenty of off-track entertainment. March.

Melbourne Food and Wine Festival Eat your way through Melbourne and regional Victoria. March.

Melbourne International Comedy Festival Just as many laughs as in Edinburgh and Montreal. April.

Melbourne International Film Festival Features, shorts and experimental pieces from around the world. July–August.

AFL Grand Final The whole city goes footy-mad. September.

Melbourne International Arts Festival Visual arts, theatre, dance and music in indoor and outdoor venues. The alternative Melbourne Fringe Festival usually overlaps. October.

Melbourne Cup The pinnacle of the Spring Racing Carnival. November.

Boxing Day Test Boxing Day in Melbourne wouldn't be the same without this cricket match. December.

Museums and galleries

ANZ Banking Museum Old money boxes, staff uniforms, historic displays and an interactive ATM exhibit in the glorious Gothic setting of the Old ANZ Bank. 380 Collins St; open 10am–3pm Mon–Fri; admission free.

Fire Services Museum Huge collection of fire brigade memorabilia, including vintage vehicles and historic photos. 39 Gisborne St, East Melbourne; (03) 9662 2907; open 9am–3pm Thurs and Fri, 10am–4pm Sun.

Ian Potter Museum of Art An extensive art collection, including cultural artefacts and contemporary artworks. University of Melbourne, Swanston St, between Faraday and Elgin sts, Parkville; (03) 8344 5148; open 10am–5pm Tue–Fri, 12pm–5pm Sat and Sun; admission free.

Jewish Museum of Australia A record of the experiences of Australia's many Jewish migrants. 26 Alma Rd, St Kilda; (03) 8534 3600; open 10am–4pm Tues–Thurs, 10am–5pm Sun.

Montsalvat An artist's colony that began in 1934; magnificent French provincial buildings and artworks for view in the gallery. 7 Hillcrest Ave, Eltham; (03) 9439 7712; open 9am–5pm daily.

Victoria Police Museum Victoria's life of crime revealed, from the capture of Ned Kelly to the Hoddle Street shootings. Mezzanine Level, World Trade Centre, 637 Flinders St; (03) 9247 5214; open 10am–4pm Mon–Fri; admission free.

See also City Museum at Old Treasury, p. 130, Immigration Museum, p. 130, Koorie Heritage Trust, p. 130, ACCA, p. 132, Heide Museum of Modern Art, p. 135, Ian Potter Centre: NGV Australia, p. 128 , NGV International, p. 132, Australian Centre for the Moving Image, p. 127.

 ## Grand old buildings

Old ANZ Bank Known as the Gothic Bank, with an incredible, gold-leafed interior and a banking museum. 380 Collins St.

Manchester Unity Building Chicago-style building with stark vertical lines, once the city's tallest skyscraper. Cnr Collins and Swanston sts.

Capitol Theatre Designed by the architects of Canberra with a ceiling that will amaze you. 109–117 Swanston St.

St Patrick's Cathedral Victoria's largest church building, built with tonnes of Footscray bluestone. Cnr Gisborne St and Cathedral Pl, East Melbourne.

Princess Theatre The dramatic exterior culminates in three domes with cast-iron tiaras. 163 Spring St.

Forum Theatre Moorish domes, and a starry night sky on the inner ceiling of the main theatre. Cnr Russell and Flinders sts.

St Paul's Cathedral Gothic cathedral made of sandstone. Cnr Flinders and Swanston sts.

Old Melbourne Magistrates' Court The rough sandstone exterior and deeply set archways make for a grim atmosphere. Cnr Russell and Latrobe sts.

Olderfleet Building An intricate Gotham City facade. Nearby is The Rialto, designed by the same architect. 477 Collins St.

Regent Theatre Melbourne's most glamorous theatre, with an interior of Spanish-style lattice and red carpet. 191 Collins St.

St James' Old Cathedral A humble relic of Melbourne's founding years. 419–435 King St.

University of Melbourne More historic buildings than you can count. Parkville.

Hotel Windsor Layered like a wedding cake and fit for a queen. 111 Spring St.

City Baths A feast of domes on the skyline, this building dates back to the days when bathrooms were a luxury few could afford. Cnr Swanston and Victoria sts.

 ## Shopping

Bourke Street Mall, City With department stores Myer and David Jones as well as the swish Melbourne GPO.

Bridge Road, Richmond Back-to-back factory outlets and designer warehouses.

Brunswick Street and Gertrude Street, Fitzroy Unique design and fashion stores.

Chapel Street, South Yarra Where shopping is an event to dress up for.

Collins Street, City Glamorous shopping strip with the big names in high-end fashion. Check out the boutique-style shopping on adjacent Flinders Lane and Little Collins Street too.

DFO, South Wharf Shopping mall of factory outlets for bargain hunters.

Melbourne Central and QV Melbourne, City These two nearby precincts are a shopper's paradise.

Southgate, Southbank A classy range of clothing, art and gifts.

 ## Markets

Camberwell Market Melbourne's best trash and treasure event. Sun. 537 J6

CERES Market Count your organic food miles as you shop at this community-run environmental park in Brunswick East. Cafe, nursery and inspiration for greening your life. Wed and Sat. 126 E1

Collingwood Children's Farm – Farmers' Market Victorian produce, from free-range eggs to fresh fruit and vegetables, in a lovely setting on the Yarra. 2nd Sat each month. 127 F3

The Esplanade Market St Kilda Melbourne's oldest art and craft market, with over 200 artisans. Sun. 126 D6

Flemington Racecourse Market Art, craft and regional produce. 3rd or 4th Sun each month. 126 B2

South Melbourne Market Produce, deli items, clothing and homewares. Wed and Fri–Sun. 126 D4

St Andrews Market Laid-back market with alternative crafts, foods, music and clothing, an hour's drive from the city. Sat. 537 K4

Sunday Market, Southbank Crafts galore, leading from the Arts Centre. 128 C5

See also Queen Victoria Market, p. 130, Prahran Market, p. 134.

 ## Walks and tours

Aboriginal Heritage Walk With an Aboriginal guide and a gum leaf for a ticket, stroll through the Royal Botanic Gardens and learn about the bushfoods, medicines and traditional lore of the Boonerwrung and Woiwurrung people, whose traditional lands meet here. Bookings on (03) 9252 2429; 11am Thurs–Fri and 1st Sun each month.

Carlton United Brewery Tours Free tastings of CUB draught beers are preceded by a tour around Abbotsford Brewery, the home of Fosters. Bookings on (03) 9420 6800; 10am, 12pm and 2pm Mon–Fri.

Chocoholic Tours A range of tours to get you drooling, taking in Melbourne's best chocolatiers,

candy-makers, ice-creameries and cafes. Bookings on (03) 9686 4655.

Foodies' Tours Get tips on picking the best fresh produce, meet the specialist traders and taste samples from the deli at Queen Victoria Market. Bookings on (03) 9320 5835; 10am Tues and Thurs–Sat.

Golden Mile Heritage Trail Walk with a guide or navigate this trail on your own. It leads from the Immigration Museum to Melbourne Museum, taking in historic buildings and heritage attractions along the way (walkers gain discounted entry to various places). Bookings 1300 780 045, or get a self-guide brochure from the Melbourne Visitor Information Centre at Federation Square. 10am daily.

Harley Rides Take the Introduction to Melbourne tour, exploring the bay and over the West Gate Bridge with the wind whistling through your hair. Bookings on 1800 182 282; tours daily.

Haunted Melbourne Ghost Tours Get the adrenalin pumping as you traipse down dark alleys and enter city buildings that the ghosts of early Melbourne are known to haunt. Bookings on (03) 9670 2585.

Hidden Secrets Tours Various tours focusing on the city's laneways, innovative fashion, design, architecture and food culture. Bookings on (03) 9663 3358.

River Cruises A trip down the Yarra or the Maribyrnong or across to Williamstown will give you new views of Melbourne. Melbourne River Cruises (03) 8610 2600, City River Cruises (03) 9650 2214, Williamstown Ferry (03) 9517 9444, Maribyrnong River Cruises (03) 9689 6431.

 ## Parks and gardens

Albert Park A great spot for exercising around the lake, and the site for the Australian Formula One Grand Prix. Albert Park. 126 D5

Birrarung Marr Melbourne's newest park, with sculptural displays, a colourful playground and a bike track leading up to Federation Square. City. 128 D4

Brimbank Park With wetlands, a children's farm, a visitor centre with a cafe and walking trails along the Maribyrnong River. Keilor. 531 C5

Eltham Lower Park Featuring the Diamond Valley Miniature Railway, which offers rides for kids on Sun 11am–5pm. Eltham. 531 F5

Gasworks Arts Park Sculptures, native gardens, barbecues, a cafe and artist studios in the former South Melbourne Gasworks. Albert Park. 126 C5

Jells Park A haven for waterbirds and a great place for a stroll through the bush. Wheelers Hill. 531 F7

Wattle Park Native bush and birds, a nine-hole golf course and accessible by tram. Surrey Hills. 531 F6

Westerfolds Park   On the Yarra and popular for canoeing and cycling, with the Mia Mia Aboriginal Art Gallery on top of the hill. Templestowe. 531 F4

Yarra Bend Park   Closest bushland to the city, with boats for hire, a golf course, great views and a strong Aboriginal heritage. Kew/Fairfield. 127 F2

See also Royal Botanic Gardens, p. 133.

Entertainment

Cinema   The major cinemas in the city are Hoyts in Melbourne Central's On3 entertainment floor and Greater Union in Russell Street. For arthouse films, try Kino Cinemas in Collins Place. Standout cinemas in the inner-city area include: Cinema Nova in Carlton for a great range of popular and arthouse films; Village Jam Factory in South Yarra or Village in the Crown Entertainment Complex for a Hollywood-style experience; the Rivoli in Camberwell for an old-world cinema experience; and the Astor in St Kilda East, where they play re-runs of the classics and recent releases. See daily newspapers for details.

Live music   Melbourne is renowned for its live-music scene. Fitzroy is one of the major centres of original music, with venues like Bar Open and the Evelyn hosting bands most nights. Further north is the Northcote Social Club, with local and international acts. On the south side of town is The Esplanade Hotel (The Espy) in St Kilda, one of Melbourne's best original rock venues, and in Richmond there's the Corner Hotel, showing many local acts. For jazz, try Bennetts Lane Jazz Club, off Little Lonsdale Street. The Toff, located in the historic Curtin House, hosts local and international music from pop to country. Bigger local and international acts play at other venues around town. Pick up one of the free street publications, *Beat* or *Inpress*, or get the 'EG' lift-out from *The Age* on Fridays.

Classical music and performing arts
The theatres building of the Arts Centre is Melbourne's premier venue for theatre, opera and ballet, and Hamer Hall, next door, is the venue for classical music concerts. The new Melbourne Recital Centre is a world-class chamber-music venue. Popular musicals and theatrical productions are held at the Regent, Her Majesty's, the Princess and the Athenaeum theatres. The Malthouse Theatre company and the Melbourne Theatre Company (MTC) host plays, and La Mama in Carlton is the venue for more experimental works. Check out the arts section of *The Age* for details. Most performances are booked through Ticketmaster and Ticketek.

Sport

Melbourne is possibly Australia's most sporting city, with hardly a gap in the calendar for the true sports enthusiast. **AFL** (Australian Football League) is indisputably at the top of the list. The season begins at the end of March and, as it nears the finals in September, footy madness eclipses the city. Victoria has ten teams in the league, and the blockbuster matches are played at the **MCG** and **Etihad Stadium**.

After the football comes the **Spring Racing Carnival**, as much a social event as a horseracing one. October and November are packed with events at racetracks across the state, with the city events held at Caulfield, Moonee Valley, Sandown and Flemington racetracks. The Melbourne Cup, 'the race that stops the nation', is held at Flemington on the first Tuesday in November, and is a local public holiday.

Cricket takes Melbourne through the heat of summer. One Day International and Test matches are usually played at the MCG, and the popular Boxing Day Test gives Christmas in Melbourne a sporting twist.

In January Melbourne hosts the Australian Open, one of the world's four major **tennis** Grand Slams. The venue is **Melbourne Park**, home to the Rod Laver Arena and the Hisense Arena, both of which host other sporting events and concerts throughout the year.

Come March and the **Australian Formula One Grand Prix** comes to town, attracting a large international crowd. The cars race around Albert Park Lake, which for the rest of the year is the setting for rather more low-key sporting pursuits such as jogging and rollerblading.

See also Melbourne Cricket Ground (MCG) and National Sports Museum, p. 134, and Melbourne and Olympic parks, p. 133.

Where to eat

Babka Bakery/Cafe   Bakery and cafe serving freshly baked loaves, pies and cakes. The short, regularly changing menu features Eastern European dishes such as borscht, potato dumplings and sweet blintzes. 358 Brunswick St, Fitzroy; (03) 9416 0091; open Tues–Sun for breakfast and lunch. 126 E2

Chocolate Buddha   Quick and delicious modern Japanese served at long communal tables overlooking Federation Square's piazza. Federation Square, cnr Flinders and Swanston sts; (03) 9654 5688; open daily for lunch and dinner. 128 C4

Degraves Espresso   Excellent coffee, breakfasts and lunches served amidst stylishly 'distressed' decor or outside at a laneway table. 23–25 Degraves St, (03) 9654 3655; open daily for breakfast and lunch and Mon–Fri for dinner. 128 C4

Flower Drum   Melbourne's iconic Cantonese restaurant, with dishes such as crayfish with ginger and their famous Peking duck. 17 Market La; (03) 9662 3655; open daily for lunch and dinner. 128 D3

Il Fornaio   Smart Italian bakery serving breakfast pastries and rustic breads, coffee and light lunch or brunch dishes. 2 Acland St, St Kilda; 9534 2922; open daily for breakfast and lunch. 126 D6

Journal Canteen   Bright and cheery with a daily changing menu of simple, rustic and unfailingly delicious Sicilian-inspired food. Level 1, 253 Flinders La; (03) 9650 4399; open weekdays for lunch and Mon–Sat for dinner. 128 C4

MoVida Bar de Tapas y Vino   Always-packed Spanish restaurant with a big-flavoured selection of tapas dishes. The sweet end of the meal is also well worth considering as the churros (Spanish doughnuts) here are among the best in town. 1 Hosier La; (03) 9663 3038; open daily for lunch and dinner. 128 C4

Pellegrini's Espresso Bar   The city's original Italian eatery, where the pasta arrives only minutes after ordering and the ice-cold granitas are always good. 66 Bourke St; (03) 9662 1885; open daily for lunch and dinner. 128 D3

The Press Club   Exciting, modern take on Greek food that includes spit-roasted lamb and cumin-roasted beetroot salad; Greek wine is a highlight of the lengthy list. 72 Flinders St; (03) 9677 9677; open daily for lunch and dinner. 128 D4

Vue de Monde   Watch super-chef Shannon Bennett prepare some of the best food in Australia in this sky-high dining room. Level 55, Rialto South Tower, 525 Collins St; (03) 9691 3888; open Tues–Fri for lunch and Mon–Sat for dinner. 128 B4

Where to stay

Adrienne's Place on the Hill   67 Craig Hill Dr, Wheelers Hill; (03) 9561 3324.

Ashley Gardens BIG4 Holiday Village – Aspen Parks   129 Ashley St, Braybrook; (03) 9318 6866.

Captains Retreat B&B   2 Ferguson St, Williamstown; (03) 9397 0352.

Carlisle Bed & Breakfast   400 Glenferrie Rd, Kooyong; (03) 9822 4847.

Carter Cottages Bed & Breakfast Inn   1 College Rd, Werribee; 0424 867 259.

Chestnut Cottage   15 Chestnut St, Surrey Hills; (03) 9808 6644.

Crystal Brook Tourist Park   182 Warrandyte Rd, Doncaster East; (03) 9844 3637.

Glenmore Homestyle Accommodation   46 Husband Rd, Forest Hill; (03) 9893 3333.

Hazelwood House   44 Holland Rd, Ringwood East; (03) 9870 9817.

Jackson's on Middle Park 404 Richardson St, Middle Park; (03) 9534 7615.

Ningana B & B 7 O'Grady St, Burwood East; (03) 9802 6902.

North Haven By The Sea B & B Merrett Dr, Williamstown; (03) 9399 8399.

Prahran Village Guest House 39 Perth St, Prahran; (03) 9533 6559.

Robinsons in the City Cnr Batman and Spencer sts, West Melbourne; (03) 9329 2552.

Staughton Bed & Breakfast Cnr Staughton Rd and Downing Ave, Glen Iris; (03) 9889 4372.

Sundowner Caravan & Cabin Park 870 Princes Hwy, Springvale; (03) 9546 9587.

Treetops Bed & Breakfast 16 Linum St, Blackburn; (03) 9877 2737.

Wantirna Park 203 Mountain Hwy, Wantirna; (03) 9887 1157.

Warrandyte Goldfields Bed & Breakfast Cnr Yarra and Whipstick Gully rds, Warrandyte; (03) 9844 0666.

Werribee South Caravan Park 39 Beach Rd, Werribee South; (03) 9742 1755.

Other suburbs

Balaclava Kosher butchers mixed with an emerging cafe culture. 127 F6

Black Rock One of many bayside suburbs shifting from a sleepy village into sought-after real estate, fronting two of Melbourne's best beaches. 537 J7

Brunswick Sydney Road is the place to come to for bargain fabrics, authentic Turkish bread and a healthy dose of Middle Eastern culture. 126 D1

Camberwell and Canterbury Melbourne's eastern money belt, with fashion outlets lining Camberwell's Burke Road, and the elegant Maling Road shopping precinct in Canterbury. 531 E6

Dandenong One of Melbourne's most diverse communities – with food stores galore and a vibrant market. 537 K7

Eltham All native trees and mud-brick architecture, this suburb feels like a piece of the country only 30 min from the city. 531 F5

Footscray A mini-Saigon that is the lesser-known version of Victoria Street, Abbotsford, now with a growing African flavour. Jam-packed with cheap eateries and one of Melbourne's best produce markets. 126 A2

Hawthorn With a strong student culture from the nearby university, and a strip of shops on Glenferrie Road offering everything from Asian groceries to smart fashion. 531 E6

Yarraville A gem tucked away in a largely industrial sweep of suburbs, with cafes and a superb Art Deco cinema. 126 A3

Day tours

Bellarine Peninsula The Bellarine Peninsula separates the waters of Port Phillip from the famously rugged coastline of Victoria's south-west. Beyond the historic buildings, streets and Geelong's waterfront are quaint coastal villages, excellent beaches, golf courses and wineries.

The Dandenongs These scenic hills at the edge of Melbourne's eastern suburbs are a popular daytrip. Native rainforests of mountain ash and giant ferns, cool-climate gardens, the popular steam train Puffing Billy, which runs through Emerald, and galleries, craft shops and cafes, many serving Devonshire tea, are among the many attractions.

Mornington Peninsula This holiday centre, including Portsea and Sorrento, features fine-food producers, around 40 cool-climate vineyards, historic holiday villages, quiet coastal national parks, 18 golf courses and many attractions for children.

Mount Macedon and Hanging Rock Country mansions and superb 19th- and 20th-century European-style gardens sit comfortably in the native bushland. Here you'll find wineries, cafes, nurseries, galleries and the mysteriously beautiful Hanging Rock near Woodend.

Phillip Island The nightly Penguin Parade on Phillip Island is one of Victoria's signature attractions. For the avid wildlife-watcher, seals and koalas are the other stars of the show, though the island also boasts magnificent coastal scenery from Cowes and great surf breaks.

Sovereign Hill Ballarat's award-winning re-creation of a 19th-century goldmining village conjures up the detail and drama of life during one of the nation's most exciting periods of history. You can even stay the night at a new accommodation complex within the village, with full period costume thrown in!

Spa country For a few hours of health-giving indulgence, visit the historic spa complex at Hepburn Springs. Explore Daylesford, enjoy a meal at one of the region's excellent eateries, or take a peaceful forest drive.

Yarra Valley and Healesville High-quality pinot noir and sparkling wines are produced across one of Australia's best-known wine areas. Pick up a brochure from the visitor centre in Healesville and map out your wine-tasting tour. Worthy of its own daytrip is Healesville Sanctuary, featuring around 200 species of native animals in a bushland setting.

REGIONS
of Victoria

Listed here are some of the top attractions and experiences in each region.

8 GRAMPIANS AND CENTRAL WEST

Brambuk – The National Park & Cultural Centre, Halls Gap / see p. 169
Desert Discovery Walk, Little Desert National Park / see p. 183
Mt Arapiles–Tooan State Park (pictured) / see p. 183
Mount Zero Olives at Laharum / see p. 170

9 MALLEE COUNTRY

Murray–Sunset National Park / see p. 182
Stefano's, Mildura / see p. 180
Swan Hill Pioneer Settlement (pictured) / see p. 194
Wyperfeld National Park / see p. 168

7 GOLDFIELDS

Begonia Festival, Ballarat / see p. 148
Buda Historic Home and Garden, Castlemaine / see p. 152
The Golden Dragon Museum, Bendigo / see p. 150
Sovereign Hill, Ballarat (pictured) / see p. 148

5 WERRIBEE AND BELLARINE

Surfing at Ocean Grove / see p. 183
Waterfront Geelong / see p. 166
Werribee Park and the Open Range Zoo (pictured) / see p. 167
You Yangs Regional Park / see p. 167

6 SOUTH-WEST COAST

Cape Bridgewater / see p. 188
Otway Fly / see p. 144
The Twelve Apostles in Port Campbell National Park (pictured) / see p. 187
Whale-watching at Warrnambool / see p. 200

4 SPA AND GARDEN COUNTRY

Hanging Rock / see p. 203
Hepburn Springs spas / see p. 161
Lavandula Swiss Italian Farm (pictured) / see p. 16▪
Organ Pipes National Park / see p. 145

10 GOULBURN AND MURRAY

Barmah National Park (pictured) / see p. 161
Paddlesteamers at Port of Echuca / see p. 160
Royal Hotel, Seymour / see p. 192
Tahbilk Winery in Nagambie wine region / see p. 183

11 HIGH COUNTRY

Lake Eildon National Park / see p. 162
Mount Buffalo National Park (pictured) / see p. 153
Kate's Cottage Museum, Glenrowan / see p. 164
Rutherglen wine region / see p. 191

12 EAST GIPPSLAND

Buchan Caves Reserve / see p. 149
Croajingolong National Park / see p. 176
Fishing around Mallacoota (pictured) / see p. 176
Snowy River National Park / see p. 186

YARRA AND DANDENONGS

Healesville Sanctuary / see p. 167
***Puffing Billy* (pictured)** / see p. 163
Yarra Valley wine region / see p. 204
William Ricketts Sanctuary / see p. 184

PHILLIP ISLAND AND GIPPSLAND

Baw Baw National Park / see p. 179
Penguin Parade on Phillip Island (pictured) / see p. 158
Walhalla Goldfields Railway / see p. 197
Wilsons Promontory National Park / see p. 164

2 MORNINGTON PENINSULA

Arthurs Seat State Park / see p. 179
Mornington Peninsula wine region (pictured) / see p. 179
Queenscliff–Sorrento car ferry / see pp. 189 and 195
Red Hill Market / see p. 163

TOWNS A–Z
Victoria

LEGEND

 VISITOR INFORMATION

📻 RADIO STATIONS

🏠 IN TOWN

🌼 WHAT'S ON

🍴 WHERE TO EAT

🛏 WHERE TO STAY

◉ NEARBY

* Distances for towns nearby are calculated as the crow flies.
* Food and accommodation listings in town are ordered alphabetically with places nearby listed at the end.

[MOUNT DIFFICULT RANGE, GRAMPIANS NATIONAL PARK]

Aireys Inlet
Pop. 754
Map ref. 536 D10 | 538 F3 | 551 N9

ⓘ **Geelong and Great Ocean Road Visitor Information Centre,** Princes Hwy, Little River; (03) 5283 1735 or 1800 620 888; www.aireysinlet.org.au

📻 94.7 The Pulse FM, 774 AM ABC Local Radio

Aireys Inlet is one of the prettiest towns on the Great Ocean Road and is famed for being home to the Split Point Lighthouse. While there are many attractions in town to entice, the lure of this town lies in its proximity to the stunning ochre cliffs and secluded beaches of the Great Ocean Road, and to some of the best national parks in Victoria.

🏠 **Split Point Lighthouse** This famous lighthouse is still operating and is visible for kilometres on the Great Ocean Road. Tours run 11am–2pm daily year-round; 1800 174 045; www.splitpointlighthouse.com.au

Eagles Nest Fine Art Gallery: a small gallery featuring the work of local artists; open 10am–5pm; 50 Great Ocean Rd; (03) 5289 7366.

🌼 *Farmers' market:* Aireys Inlet Community Hall; 2nd Sun each month. *Aireys Open Mic Music Festival:* Mar. *Cimarron Sculpture Weekend:* Apr. *Aireys Inlet Festival of Words:* Aug. *International Lighthouse Weekend:* Aug.

🍴 *a la grecque:* Greek cuisine; 60 Great Ocean Rd; (03) 5289 6922. *Willows Tea House:* regional-produce menu and tea; 7 Federal St; (03) 5289 6830.

🛏 *Aireys Inlet Holiday Park:* 19–25 Great Ocean Rd; (03) 5289 6230. *Lorneview Bed & Breakfast:* 677 Great Ocean Rd, Eastern View; (03) 5289 6430.

◉ **Great Otway National Park** This national park surrounds Aireys Inlet and is home to ancient forests and some of the most spectacular ocean scenery on the Great Ocean Rd. Highlights include Triplet Falls and Wreck Beach, where there are remains from a few shipwrecks. Contact Parks Victoria on 13 1963. *See Apollo Bay.*

Surf Coast Walk: this ocean walk continues for 66 km along the Great Ocean Road and takes you through scenery including pristine beaches and imposing cliffs; details from visitor centre. *Eagle Rock Marine Sanctuary:* found off the coast of Aireys Inlet, this marine sanctuary protects an abundance of marine life.

TOWNS NEARBY: Anglesea 9 km, Lorne 14 km, Torquay 24 km, Winchelsea 26 km, Barwon Heads 39 km

Alexandra
Pop. 2142
Map ref. 534 F1 | 537 N1 | 540 F1 | 542 F12 | 544 B10

ⓘ 36 Grant St; (03) 5772 1100 or 1800 652 298; www.alexandratourism.com

📻 102.9 FM ABC Local Radio, 106.9 UGFM Upper Goulburn Community Radio

Alexandra was apparently named after Alexandra, Princess of Wales, although, coincidentally, three men named Alexander discovered gold here in 1866. Situated in the foothills of the Great Dividing Range, Alexandra is supported primarily by agriculture. Nearby, the Goulburn River is an important trout fishery.

Alexandra Timber Tramways: museum housed in the original railway station that offers an insight into the timber industry around Alexandra; open 2nd Sun each month; Station St. *Art and craft galleries:* many outlets around town displaying and selling local art, pottery and glassware.

Bush market: Perkins St; 3rd Sat each month (excluding winter). *Picnic Races:* Jan, Mar, Oct and Nov. *Truck, Ute and Rod Show:* June. *Open Gardens Weekend:* Oct. *Rose Festival:* Nov.

Essence Coffee Lounge: good country fare; 79 Grant St; (03) 5772 2122. *Stonelea Country Estate:* excellent country-house fare; Cnr Connellys Creek Rd and Maroondah Hwy, Acheron; (03) 5772 2222. *Tea Rooms of Yarck:* regional Italian; 6585 Maroondah Hwy, Yarck; (03) 5773 4233.

Alexandra Tourist Park: 5016 Maroondah Hwy; (03) 5772 1222. *BIG4 Taggerty Holiday Park:* 3380 Maroondah Hwy, Taggerty; (03) 5774 7263. *Breakaway Twin Rivers Caravan Park:* 91 Breakaway Rd, Acheron; (03) 5772 1735. *Idlewild Park Farm Accommodation:* 5545 Maroondah Hwy, Koriella; (03) 5772 1178.

McKenzie Nature Reserve: in virgin bushland, with orchids and wildflowers during winter and spring. *Self-guide tourist drives:* the Skyline Rd from Alexandra to Eildon features lookouts along the way; information from visitor centre. *Taggerty:* home to the Willowbank Gallery and a bush market; open 4th Sat each month; 18 km s. *Trout fishing:* in the Goulburn, Acheron and Rubicon rivers. *Lake Eildon National Park:* excellent walking trails in the north-west section of the park; *for more details see Eildon. Bonnie Doon:* a good base for exploring the lake region. Activities include trail-riding, bushwalking, watersports and scenic drives; 37 km NE near Lake Eildon.

TOWNS NEARBY: Eildon 18 km, Yea 25 km, Marysville 35 km, Mansfield 37 km, Euroa 50 km

Anglesea

Pop. 2292
Map ref. 536 E10 | 538 F3 | 551 N9

Off Great Ocean Rd; or ring Torquay Information Centre, (03) 5261 4219 or 1300 614 219; www.visitgreatoceanroad.org.au

94.7 The Pulse FM, 774 AM ABC Local Radio

A pretty and sheltered part of the surf coast, Anglesea is one of the smaller holiday hamlets along the Great Ocean Road. The main beaches are patrolled from Christmas through to Easter, making it a favourite destination for both swimmers and beginner surfers.

 Coogoorah Reserve Set on the Anglesea River, the name of this park means 'swampy reed creek'. Coogoorah was established after the 1983 Ash Wednesday fires and now features a network of boardwalks weaving through the distinctive wetland vegetation. Keep an eye out for local birdlife, including the peregrine falcon.

Anglesea Golf Course: golfers share the greens with kangaroos; Golf Links Rd. *Melaleuca Gallery:* open daily 11am–5.30pm; Great Ocean Rd. *Viewing platform:* overlooks open-cut brown-coal mine and power station; behind town in Coalmine Rd. *Paddleboats:* for hire on the banks of the Anglesea River.

Markets: local crafts and produce, held over summer, Easter and Melbourne Cup weekend; by the Anglesea River. *Rock to Ramp Swim:* Jan. *Anglesea Art Show:* June. *ANGAIR Wildflower and Art Show:* Sept.

Locanda Del Mare: a slice of Italy; 5 Diggers Pde; (03) 5263 2904.

Anglesea Beachfront Family Caravan Park: 35 Cameron Rd; (03) 5263 1583.

J. E. Loveridge Lookout: 1 km w. *Pt Roadknight Beach:* a shallow, protected beach, popular with families; 2 km sw. *Ironbark Basin Reserve:* features ocean views, local birdlife and good bushwalking. The Pt Addis Koorie Cultural Walk leads through the park, highlighting sites of Indigenous significance; 7 km NW, off Pt Addis Rd. *Great Otway National Park:* the park begins near Anglesea and stretches to the south and west. The section near Anglesea features unique heathland flora and good walking trails; access via Aireys Inlet, 11 km sw. *For more details see Apollo Bay. Surf Coast Walk:* 30 km from Torquay to Moggs Creek (south of Aireys Inlet). The track passes through Anglesea. *Surf schools:* learn to surf on one of the beginner courses available at nearby beaches; details from visitor centre.

TOWNS NEARBY: Aireys Inlet 9 km, Torquay 15 km, Lorne 24 km, Winchelsea 25 km, Barwon Heads 30 km

Apollo Bay

Pop. 1373
Map ref. 536 B12 | 538 C6 | 551 L10

Great Ocean Road Visitor Information Centre, 100 Great Ocean Rd; 1300 689 297; www.visitgreatoceanroad.org.au

89.5 FM ABC Local Radio, 104.7 Otway FM

Named after a local schooner, Apollo Bay has become the resting place of many shipwrecks, yet it maintains an appeal for all lovers of the ocean. The town is situated near Great Otway National Park with a wonderful contrast between rugged coastline and tranquil green hills. The seaside town is popular with fishing enthusiasts and, like many other coastal towns, its population swells significantly over summer as visitors flock here for the holidays.

Old Cable Station Museum: features artefacts from Australia's telecommunications history and informative displays exploring the history of the region; open 2–5pm weekends and school and public holidays; Great Ocean Rd. *Bass Strait Shell Museum:* holds an impressive array of shells and provides many facts about the marine life along the Victorian south-west coast; Noel St. *Great Ocean Walk:* enjoy stunning views on this 91 km walk between Apollo Bay and Glenample Homestead, near the Twelve Apostles. Walkers must register to use campgrounds en route. Further information available at www.greatoceanwalk.com

Foreshore Market: each Sat. *Apollo Bay Music Festival:* Apr.

Bay Leaf Cafe: substantial cafe food; 131 Great Ocean Rd; (03) 5237 6470. *Chris's Beacon Point Restaurant & Villas:* Mediterranean/Greek; 280 Skenes Creek Rd; (03) 5237 6411. *Great Ocean Hotel:* modern Australian and bar menu; 29 Great Ocean Rd; (03) 5237 6240. *La Bimba Restaurant & Cafe:* modern Mediterranean; 125–127 Great Ocean Rd; (03) 5237 7411.

Apollo Bay Holiday Park: 27 Cawood St; (03) 5237 7111. *Apollo Bay Recreation Reserve Caravan & Camp Park:* 70 Great Ocean Rd; (03) 5237 6577. *Arcady Homestead:* 925 Barham River Rd; (03) 5237 6493. *Captain's at the Bay:* Cnr Pascoe and Whelan sts; (03) 5237 6771. *Casa Favilla B & B:* 18 Great Ocean Rd; (03) 5237 1199. *Marengo Holiday Park:* Marengo Cres; (03) 5237 6162. *Nelson's Perch Bed & Breakfast:* 54 Nelson St; (03) 5237 7176. *Pisces Holiday Park:* 311 Great Ocean Rd; (03) 5237 6749. *A Room with a View B&B:* 280 Sunnyside Rd, Wongarra; (03) 5237 0218. *Bimbi Park:* 90 Manna Gum Dr, Cape Otway; (03) 5237 9246.

VICTORIA

Great Otway National Park Formerly named Otway National Park, this section of the 103 000 ha park includes some of the most rugged coastline in Victoria, particularly around Cape Otway and the stretch of coast towards Princetown. It is an ideal location for a bushwalking adventure taking in sights through the park to the sea, from the scenic Elliot River down to adjacent Shelly Beach. Many species of wildlife inhabit the park, including koalas and the rare tiger quoll. Also look out for the historic Cape Otway Lighthouse, built in 1848. Another highlight is Melba Gully, where, at dusk, visitors can witness a show of twinkling lights from glow worms. The Great Ocean Rd, west of Apollo Bay, passes through the park. Contact Parks Victoria on 13 1963; 13 km sw.

Otway Fly The consistently popular Otway Fly is a steel-trussed walkway perched high among the temperate rainforest treetops of the Otway Ranges. The 'Fly' is 25 m high and stretches for 600 m. It is accessible to all ages and levels of mobility. Get a bird's-eye view of ancient myrtle beech, blackwood and mountain ash while looking out for a variety of wildlife, including pygmy possums and the raucous yellow-tailed black cockatoo. A springboard bridge takes you over Youngs Creek, where you might spot a shy platypus. Inquiries on 1800 300 477; 62 km nw via Lavers Hill.

Marriners Lookout: with views across Skenes Creek and Apollo Bay; 1.5 km nw. *Barham Paradise Scenic Reserve:* in the Barham River Valley, it is home to a variety of distinctive moisture-loving trees and ferns; 7 km nw. *Tanybryn Gallery:* displays and sells art and craft work in the magnificent surrounds of the Otway Ranges; Skenes Creek Rd; 20 km ne. *Forests and Waterfall Drive:* 109 km loop drive featuring spectacular Otway Ranges scenery. Waterfalls include Beauchamp, Triplet and Houptoun falls. Drive starts at Apollo Bay, travels west to Lavers Hill and around to Skenes Creek. Map from visitor centre. *Charter flights:* views of the Twelve Apostles, the Bay of Islands and the 'Shipwreck Coast'; details from visitor centre.

TOWNS NEARBY: Lorne 36 km, Colac 47 km, Aireys Inlet 50 km, Anglesea 60 km, Port Campbell 60 km

Ararat

Pop. 7170
Map ref. 549 I12 | 551 I2

ⓘ Ararat and Grampians Visitor Information Centre, Ararat Railway Station, 91 High St (Western Hwy); (03) 5355 0281 or 1800 657 158; www.ararat.vic.gov.au

📻 99.9 VoiceFM, 107.9 FM ABC Local Radio

Ararat is a city with a vibrant history. Once inhabited by the Tjapwurong Aboriginal people, the promising lands soon saw squatters move in, and the area really started to boom when gold was discovered in 1854. Thousands of prospectors arrived, and Ararat finally came into existence when Chinese immigrants rested on the town's site in 1857, after walking from South Australian ports in order to avoid Victorian poll taxes. One member of the party discovered alluvial gold, and Ararat was born. Today Ararat is a service centre to its agricultural surrounds.

 J Ward The town's original gaol, 'J Ward' served as an asylum for the criminally insane for many years and offers an eerie glimpse into the history of criminal confinement. Now guided tours reveal in chilling detail what life was like for the inmates. Girdlestone St; daily tours; (03) 5352 3357.

Gum San Chinese Heritage Centre Gum San means 'hill of gold', a fitting name for this impressive centre built in traditional Southern Chinese style and incorporating the principles of feng shui. The centre celebrates the contribution of the Chinese community both to Ararat, which is said to be the only goldfields town founded by Chinese prospectors, and to the surrounding Goldfields region. The experience is brought to life with interactive displays and an original Canton lead-mining tunnel, uncovered during the building of the centre. Western Hwy; (03) 5352 1078.

Alexandra Park and Botanical Gardens: an attractive formal garden featuring ornamental lakes, fountains and an orchid glasshouse; Vincent St. *Historical self-guide tours (walking or driving):* of particular note are the bluestone buildings in Barkly St, including the post office, town hall, civic square and war memorial; details from visitor centre. *Ararat Art Gallery:* a regional gallery specialising in wool and fibre pieces by local artists; Barkly St. *Langi Morgala Museum:* displays Aboriginal artefacts; Queen St.

Jailhouse Rock Festival: Mar. *Australian Orchid Festival:* Sept. *Golden Gateway Festival:* held over 10 days; Oct.

✕ *Nectar Ambrosia:* smart eatery in old pub; 157–159 Barkly St; (03) 5352 7344.

🛏 *Acacia Caravan Park:* 6 Acacia Ave; (03) 5352 2994. *Beaufort Lake Caravan Park:* 39 Park Rd (Skipton Rd), Beaufort; (03) 5349 2196.

Mt Buangor State Park The park features the Fern Tree Waterfalls and the 3 impressive peaks of Mt Buangor, Mt Sugarloaf and Cave Hill. Its diverse terrain with many varieties of eucalypts offers great sightseeing, bushwalking and picnicking. There are more than 130 species of birds, as well as eastern grey kangaroos, wallabies and echidnas. Contact Parks Victoria on 13 1963. Access to the southern section is via Ferntree Rd off the Western Hwy; 30 km e. Mt Buangor and Cave Hill can be accessed from the main Mt Cole Rd in the Mt Cole State Forest.

Garden Gully Winery: hosts a scarecrow competition each Apr, with ingenious entries from across the state scattered through the vineyard; 17 km n on Western Hwy. Many more of the region's wineries can be accessed on the Great Grape Rd, a circuit through Ballarat and St Arnaud. This region is famous for sparkling whites and traditional old shiraz varieties; brochure and map from visitor centre. *Green Hill Lake:* great for fishing and water activities; 4 km e. *McDonald Park Wildflower Reserve:* an extensive display of flora indigenous to the area, including wattles and banksias, impressive during the spring months; 5 km n on Western Hwy. *One Tree Hill Lookout:* 360-degree views across the region; 5 km nw. *Langi Ghiran State Park:* Mt Langi Ghiran and Mt Gorrin form the key features of this park. A popular walk starts at the picnic area along Easter Creek, then goes to the Old Langi Ghiran Reservoir and along the stone water race to a scenic lookout; access via Western Hwy, Kartuk Rd; 14 km e. *Mt Cole State Forest:* adjoins Mt Buangor State Park, with bushwalking, horseriding, 4WD tracks and trail-bike riding. The Ben Nevis Fire Tower offers spectacular views; 35 km e.

TOWNS NEARBY: Stawell 29 km, Halls Gap 40 km, Avoca 53 km, Dunkeld 66 km, Clunes 76 km

Avoca

Pop. 948
Map ref. 535 A6 | 549 L12 | 551 L1

ⓘ 122 High St; (03) 5465 1000 or 1800 206 622; www.pyreneestourism.com.au

📻 91.1 FM ABC Local Radio, 96.5 Radio KLFM

Avoca was built during the gold boom of the 19th century and is renowned for its wide main street, divided by a stretch of park with trees and a war memorial. Avoca is set in the picturesque Pyrenees Ranges, with the Avoca River flowing by the town.

 Historic walk: takes in the original courthouse, one of the oldest surviving courts in Victoria, as well as the powder magazine and Lalor's, one of the state's earliest pharmacies; map from visitor centre. *Cemetery:* Chinese burial ground from the goldmining period; on outskirts of town.

 Avoca Fine Wine, Arts and Craft Market: 3rd Sun each month. *Blue Pyrenees Pink Lamb and Purple Shiraz Race Meeting:* country race meeting; Mar. *Petanque Tournaments (French Bowls):* Mar and Dec. *Mt Avoca Anzac Day Races:* Apr. *Taltarni Cup Races:* Oct.

 Warrenmang Vineyard & Resort: regional food; 188 Mountain Creek Rd, Moonambel; (03) 5467 2233.

 Pyrenees Ranges State Forest Covering a large stretch of bushland, these ranges are great for bushwalking and picnics and camping. Visitors can see a variety of wildlife, including koalas, wallabies, kangaroos and goannas. Orchids and lilies can be found growing around the base of the ranges in season. An 18 km walking track starts at The Waterfall camping area and finishes at Warrenmang–Glenlofty Rd. Access via Sunraysia or Pyrenees hwys. For further information contact the Department of Sustainability and Environment Customer Sevice Centre on 13 1186.

Pyrenees wine region Shiraz is the Pyrenees' premium drop and its big names are Blue Pyrenees Estate and Taltarni. Dalwhinnie has been highly praised for its Eagle Series Shiraz. It is also doing well in a range of styles including chardonnay, cabernet sauvignon and pinot noir. Redbank Winery is known for its Sally's Paddock blend, comprising merlot, cabernet sauvignon, shiraz and cabernet franc.

Mt Lonarch Arts: displays and sells fine bone china made on the premises; Mt Lonarch; 10 km s. *Warrenmang Vineyard Resort:* with cottage-style accommodation and a restaurant specialising in regional produce. The vineyard is also the venue for A Sparkling Affair each Nov, an event celebrating the release of sparkling wines; 22 km NW.

TOWNS NEARBY: Maryborough 24 km, Dunolly 34 km, Clunes 36 km, Creswick 53 km, Ararat 53 km

Bacchus Marsh

Pop. 13 258
Map ref. 535 G11 | 536 G4 | 540 A3 | 551 O5

 Lerderderg Library, 215 Main St; (03) 5367 7488; www.visitmoorabool.com.au

 98.5 3APL Apple FM, 774 AM ABC Local Radio

Bacchus Marsh shares part of its name with the Roman god of wine, but is actually better known for the apples that grow so well in the fertile valley region between the Werribee and Lerderderg rivers. Considered a satellite town within commuting distance of Melbourne, Bacchus Marsh retains a certain charm with stunning heritage buildings and a rural atmosphere.

 Avenue of Honour Visitors to the town are greeted by the sight of the renowned Avenue of Honour, an elm-lined stretch of road built in honour of the Australian soldiers who fought in WW I. Eastern approach to town.

Big Apple Tourist Orchard: fresh-produce market; Avenue of Honour. *Historic buildings:* include The Manor, the original home of the town's founder, Captain Bacchus (now privately owned), and Border Inn, built in 1850, thought to be the state's first stop for Cobb & Co coaches travelling to the goldfields; details from visitor centre. *Local history museum:* connected to the blacksmith cottage and forge; open Sat–Sun; Main St. *Naturipe Fruits, Strawberry, Peach and Nectarine Farm:* pick-your-own fruits and roadside sales; Avenue of Honour.

 Rotary Art Show: June.

 Bacchus Marsh Caravan Park: 26 Main St; (03) 5367 2775. *Sundowner Rockbank:* 2057 Western Hwy, Rockbank; (03) 9747 1340.

 Lerderderg State Park Featuring the imposing Lerderderg Gorge, the 14 250 ha park is a great venue for picnics, bushwalking and swimming, while the Lerderderg River is ideal for trout fishing. The area was mined during the gold rush, and remnants from the water races used for washing gold can still be found upstream from O'Brien's Crossing. Late winter and spring are good times to see wildflowers and blossoming shrubs. Look out for koalas nestled in giant manna gums and for the magnificent sulphur-crested cockatoo and the wedge-tailed eagle. Contact Parks Victoria on 13 1963. Access via Western Fwy to Bacchus Marsh-Gisborne and Lerderderg Gorge rds; 10 km N.

Werribee Gorge State Park Over time the Werribee River has carved through ancient seabed sediment and lava flows to form a spectacular gorge. The name 'Werribee' comes from the Aboriginal word 'Wearibi', meaning 'swimming place' or 'backbone', perhaps in reference to the snake-like path of the river. Rock climbing is permitted at Falcons Lookout and a popular walk follows the Werribee River from the Meikles Pt picnic area, providing views of the river and the gorge cliff-faces. Contact Parks Victoria on 13 1963. Access via Western Fwy and Pentland Hills Rd to Myers Rd, or via Ironbark Rd (the Ballan-Ingliston Rd) from the Bacchus Marsh-Anakie Rd; 10 km w.

Sunbury wine region This small but historic wine region is found on the north-west doorstep of Melbourne, just beyond Tullamarine airport. Goona Warra Vineyard was established in 1863, and its winery is set in an original bluestone building. Craiglee, just over the road, was established only a year later in 1864. Shiraz is the specialty of both labels, and Craiglee's shiraz has won several trophies. Other wineries include Galli Estate, Wildwood and Witchmount.

Long Forest Flora Reserve: a great example of the distinctive mallee scrub that once covered the region; 2 km NE. *St Anne's Vineyard:* with a bluestone cellar built from the remains of the old Ballarat Gaol; Western Fwy; 6 km w. *Merrimu Reservoir:* attractive park area with picnic facilities; about 10 km NE. *Organ Pipes National Park:* lava flows have created a 20 m wall of basalt columns in this small park near Sunbury. The 'organ pipes' can be seen close-up via an easy walking trail. *Melton:* now virtually a satellite suburb of Melbourne, this town has a long and rich history of horse breeding and training. Visit the Willow Homestead to see exhibits detailing the life of early settlers (open Wed, Fri and Sun), picnic on the Werribee River at Melton Reservoir, or taste the fine wines in the nearby Sunbury Wine Region; 14 km E. *Brisbane Ranges National Park:* with good walking tracks, wildflowers during spring and the imposing,

 RADIO STATIONS   IN TOWN   WHAT'S ON   WHERE TO EAT   WHERE TO STAY   NEARBY

VICTORIA

steep-sided Anakie Gorge; 16 km sw. **Ballan:** try the refreshing mineral-spring water at Bostock Reservoir, or join in the festivities at the Vintage Machinery and Vehicle Rally in Feb, and an Autumn Festival held each Mar; 20 km nw. **Blackwood:** visit the Mineral Springs Reserve and Garden of St Erth (closed Wed and Thurs). Blackwood is also the start of the 53 km return scenic drive through the Wombat State Forest; 31 km nw.

TOWNS NEARBY: Woodend 37 km, Daylesford 45 km, Kyneton 48 km, Ballarat 52 km, Geelong 53 km

Bairnsdale

Pop. 11 284
Map ref. 541 M5

ℹ️ 240 Main St; (03) 5152 3444 or 1800 637 060; www.lakesandwilderness.com.au

📻 100.7 FM ABC Local Radio, 105.5 3REG Radio East Gippsland FM

An attractive rural centre situated on the Mitchell River Flats and considered to be the western gateway to the lakes and wilderness region of East Gippsland. The area has a rich Koorie history brought to life through local landmarks, especially in Mitchell River National Park, where a fascinating piece of Aboriginal folklore is based around the Den of Nargun.

Aboriginal culture The Krowathunkoolong Keeping Place, on Dalmahoy St, details the cultural history of the region's Kurnai Aboriginal people and provides an insight into the impact of white settlement. To explore local Aboriginal history further, visit Howitt Park, Princes Hwy – a tree here has a 4 m scar where bark has been removed to make a canoe. The Bataluk Cultural Trail from Sale to Cann River takes in these and other Indigenous sites of East Gippsland. Details of the trail from Krowathunkoolong.

Historical Museum: built in 1891, contains relics from Bairnsdale's past; Macarthur St. **Jolly Jumbuck Country Craft Centre:** wool spinning and knitting mills, plus woollen products for sale; edge of town. **Self-guide heritage walks:** take in St Mary's Church, with wall and ceiling murals by Italian artist Francesco Floreani, and the Court House, a magnificent, castle-like construction; details from visitor centre.

Howitt Park Market: 4th Sun each month. **Line Dancing Championships:** Mar. **East Gippsland Agricultural Field Days:** popular event with family entertainment; Apr. **Easter Races:** Easter. **Bairnsdale Cup:** Sept.

Paper Chase: modern bookshop cafe; Collins Booksellers, 166 Main St; (03) 5152 5181.

Dalfruin & Ballyvista B&B: 18 McCulloch St; (03) 5152 7155. **Mitchell Gardens Holiday Park:** 2 Main St (Princes Hwy); (03) 5152 4654. **Tara House Bed & Breakfast:** 37 Day St; (03) 5153 2253. **Bairnsdale Holiday Park:** 139 Princes Hwy, Bairnsdale East; (03) 5152 4066. **Dargo Bed & Breakfast:** 1 Lower Dargo Rd, Dargo; (03) 5140 1228. **Old School Bed and Breakfast:** 720 Fernbank–Glenaladale Rd, Fernbank; (03) 5157 6235. **Lakes Bushland Caravan Park:** 363 Stephenson Rd, Nicholson; (03) 5156 8422. **Nicholson River Caravan Park:** 915 Princes Hwy, Nicholson; (03) 5156 8348. **Stringybark Cottages:** 77 Howards Rd, Sarsfield; (03) 5157 5245.

Mitchell River National Park Set in the remnants of temperate rainforest, this park has its own piece of mythology. According to Koorie history, Nargun was a beast made all of stone except for his hands, arms and breast. The fierce creature would drag the unwary to his den, a shallow cave beneath a waterfall on the Woolshed Creek. This Den of Nargun can be found in the park, as can giant kanooka trees, wildflowers and over 150 species of birds. There is a circuit walk to Bluff Lookout and Mitchell River, and Billy Goat Bend is good for picnics. Contact Parks Victoria on 13 1963; Princes Hwy; 15 km w near Lindenow.

McLeods Morass Wildlife Reserve: a boardwalk extends over the freshwater marshland, allowing a close-up view of the many species of waterbirds found here; southern outskirts of town, access via Macarthur St; 2 km s. **Wineries:** include Nicholson River Winery, for tastings and sales; 10 km e. **Bruthen:** hosts a Blues Bash each Feb; 24 km nw. **Dargo:** historic township in Dargo River valley and major producer of walnuts. Dargo Valley Winery has accommodation and cellar-door sales. The road beyond Dargo offers a scenic drive through high plains to Hotham Heights, stunning in spring when wattles bloom (unsealed road, check conditions); 93 km nw.

TOWNS NEARBY: Paynesville 14 km, Lakes Entrance 34 km, Sale 57 km, Maffra 58 km, Buchan 62 km

Ballarat

see inset box on page 148

Barwon Heads

Pop. 2994
Map ref. 532 C6 | 536 G9 | 538 H2 | 540 A7 | 551 O8

ℹ️ Geelong and Great Ocean Road Visitor Information Centre, Princes Hwy, Little River; (03) 5283 1735 or 1800 620 888; www.visitgreatoceanroad.org.au

📻 94.7 The Pulse FM, 774 AM ABC Local Radio

This picturesque village, situated on the banks of the Barwon River near Bass Strait in Victoria, was established in the late 18th century and more recently received nationwide fame as the setting for the ABC's TV show *SeaChange*. Although well known for its river beaches and coastal activities, Barwon Heads is experiencing a sea change of its own as the hometown of 2011 Tour de France winner Cadel Evans, which has revived interest in the town. The population of this coastal town swells during the holiday season, as people take advantage of the range of activities on offer and the friendly village atmosphere. Apart from cycling and water activities, Barwon Heads is also home to one of the top links golf courses in Victoria.

Golf Courses: include Thirteenth Beach and the Barwon Heads Golf Club. **Barwon Heads Bridge:** the recently restored bridge is a heritage-listed structure.

Festival of the Sea: Mar.

Annie's Provedore: regional-produce menu; 2/50 Hitchcock Ave; (03) 5254 3233. **At the Heads:** Mediterranean-style menu; Jetty Rd; (03) 5254 1277.

Barwon Heads Caravan Park: Ewing Blyth Dr; (03) 5254 1115.

Barwon Bluff Marine Sanctuary: covering 17 ha of ocean, the sanctuary is home to a vast array of marine life, as well as kelp forests and a couple of shipwrecks; contact Parks Victoria on 13 1963. **Swim with dolphins:** swim with dolphins and other marine life in the beautiful waters of the Bass Strait. **Jirrahlinga Koala and Wildlife Reserve:** home to an abundance of Australian wildlife, including koalas; Taits Rd; open 9am–4.30pm; (03) 5254 2484.

TOWNS NEARBY: Ocean Grove 3 km, Drysdale 14 km, Queenscliff 15 km, Torquay 15 km, Geelong 19 km

Beechworth

Pop. 2644
Map ref. 543 J7 | 544 H4

i Ford St; (03) 5728 3233 or 1300 366 321; www.beechworth.com

📻 101.3 Oak FM, 106.5 FM ABC Local Radio

Set in the picturesque surrounds of the Australian Alps, Beechworth is one of the state's best preserved 19th-century gold towns, with over 30 buildings listed by the National Trust. The grandeur of Beechworth's buildings can be explained by the fact that during the 1850s over four million ounces of gold were mined here. There is a delightful tale about Beechworth's heyday: the story goes that Daniel Cameron, a political candidate vying for support from the Ovens Valley community, rode at the head of a procession through the town on a horse shod with golden shoes. Sceptics claim they were merely gilded, but the tale offers a glimpse into the wealth of Beechworth during the gold rush.

🏠 **Historic and cultural precinct** This fantastic precinct provides a snapshot of 19th-century Beechworth. Featuring fine, honey-coloured granite buildings, the area incorporates the telegraph station, gold office, Chinese prospectors' office, town hall and powder magazine. Of particular interest is the courthouse, site of many infamous trials including Ned Kelly's, and where Sir Isaac Isaacs began his legal career. Also in the precinct is the Robert O'Hara Burke Memorial Museum, with the interesting 'Strand of Time' exhibition where 19th-century Beechworth shops are brought to life.

Beechworth Gaol Built in 1859, the original wooden gates of this gaol were replaced with iron ones when it was feared prisoners would break out in sympathy with Ned Kelly during his trial. The gaol is located in William St but not presently open to the public.

Walking tours: Ned Kelly and Gold Rush walking tours operate daily, and Ghost Tours are available at the former Mayday Hills Asylum; bookings at visitor centre. *Carriage Museum and Australian Light Horse Exhibition:* National Trust horse-drawn carriage display and Australian Light Horse Exhibition housed at the historic Murray Breweries, which also offers turn-of-the-century gourmet cordial made to time-honoured recipes; 29 Last St. *Beechworth Honey Experience:* interpretive display on the history of honey; includes a glass-fronted live bee display. A wide range of premium Australian honey is on offer in the concept shop; Cnr Ford and Church sts. *Harry Power's Cell:* under the shire offices, where the 'gentleman bushranger' was once briefly held; Albert Rd. *The Beechworth Pantry:* gourmet cafe and centre for produce of the north-east; Ford St. *Beechworth Bakery:* famous for its pastries and cakes; Camp St.

🎪 *Country Craft Market:* Queen Victoria Park, 4 times a year; details from visitor centre. *Golden Horseshoes Festival:* a celebration of the town's past, with street parades and a variety of market stalls; Easter. *Harvest Celebration:* May; details from visitor centre. *Drive Back in Time:* vintage car rally; May. *Celtic Festival:* music festival; Nov.

🍴 *Provenance Restaurant:* contemporary regional food; 86 Ford St; (03) 5728 1786. *The Green Shed Bistro:* European-influenced; 37 Camp St; (03) 5728 2360. *The Ox and Hound:* contemporary bistro; 52 Ford St; (03) 5728 2123. *Wardens Food & Wine:* modern Italian; 32 Ford St; (03) 5728 1377.

🏨 *Barnsley House B&B:* 5 John St; (03) 5728 1037. *Country Charm Cottages:* 24 Malakoff Rd; (03) 5728 2435. *Finches of*

Beechworth Bed & Breakfast: 3 Finch St; (03) 5728 2655. *Freeman on Ford:* 97 Ford St; (03) 5728 2371. *Lake Sambell Caravan Park:* 20 Peach Dr; (03) 5728 1421. *The Old Priory:* 8 Priory La; (03) 5728 1024. *Silver Creek Caravan Park:* 151 Stanley Rd; (03) 5728 1597.

 Beechworth Cemetery This cemetery is a fascinating piece of goldfields history. More than 2000 Chinese goldminers are buried here. Twin ceremonial Chinese burning towers stand as a monument to those who died seeking their fortune far from home. Northern outskirts of town.

Beechworth wine region According to many wine writers, this boutique region is one to watch. With only small quantities being produced, and much of it quickly whisked away by a discerning clientele, Beechworth's wines can be hot property. Castagna Vineyard grows its grapes biodynamically and is known for its superb Genesis Syrah Viognier. Giaconda produces outstanding chardonnay, while Sorrenberg is a leader in gamay and does a wonderful blend of cabernet sauvignon, cabernet franc and merlot.

Beechworth Historic Park: surrounds the town and includes Woolshed Falls Historical Walk through former alluvial goldmining sites. *Gorge Scenic Drive (5 km):* starts north of town. *Beechworth Forest Drive:* takes in Fletcher Dam; 3 km SE towards Stanley. *Kellys Lookout:* at Woolshed Creek; about 4 km N. *Mt Pilot Lookout:* views of Murray Valley, plus signposted Aboriginal cave paintings nearby; 5 km N. *Stanley:* a historic goldmining settlement with fantastic views of the alps from the summit of Mt Stanley; 10 km SE.

TOWNS NEARBY: Yackandandah 15 km, Myrtleford 23 km, Chiltern 24 km, Milawa 25 km, Wodonga 32 km

Benalla
Pop. 9128
Map ref. 542 G8 | 544 D5

i 14 Mair St; (03) 5762 1749; www.benalla.vic.gov.au

📻 97.7 FM ABC Local Radio, 101.3 Oak FM

Motorists from Melbourne entering Benalla will notice the Rose Gardens positioned beside the highway a short distance before Lake Benalla – gardens for which the city has become known as the 'Rose City'. The town is Sir Edward 'Weary' Dunlop's birthplace and proudly advertises the fact with a museum display and a statue in his honour at the Benalla Botanical Gardens.

🏠 **Benalla Art Gallery** Set beside Lake Benalla, the gallery has an impressive collection including contemporary Australian art, works by Sidney Nolan, Arthur Streeton, Tom Roberts and Arthur Boyd, and a substantial collection of Indigenous art. Built in 1975, the gallery is a striking work of modern architecture. There is a permanent exhibition featuring the works of Laurie Ledger, a local resident, and examples of the Heidelberg School and early colonial art. Bridge St; (03) 5762 3027.

Benalla Ceramic Art Mural: a Gaudi-inspired community construction, this fascinating 3D mural is opposite the art gallery on Lake Benalla. *The Creators Gallery:* paintings, pottery and craft; at the information centre. *Benalla Costume and Pioneer Museum:* has period costumes, a Ned Kelly exhibit (including Kelly's cummerbund) and a feature display of Benalla's 'famous sons', in particular, Sir Edward 'Weary' Dunlop; Mair St. *Lake Benalla:* created in Broken River, it has good recreation and picnic facilities and is a haven for waterbirds. Take the self-guide

continued on p. 149

BALLARAT

Pop. 85 196
Map ref. 535 C10 | 536 D3 | 551 M4

ⓘ 43 Lydiard St North; 1800 446 633; www.visitballarat.com.au

📻 99.9 VoiceFM, 107.9 FM ABC Local Radio

Ballarat is Victoria's largest inland city and features grand old buildings and wide streets that create an air of splendour. Built on the wealth of the region's goldfields, Ballarat offers activities ranging from fine dining in the many restaurants to real-life experiences of the area's goldmining past. Lake Wendouree provides a beautiful backdrop for picnics and the many festivals that take place during the year. Ballarat was the site of the infamous Eureka Rebellion of 3 December 1854. When goldfields police attempted to quell the miners' anger over strict mining-licence laws, a bloody massacre eventuated. The Eureka Rebellion is viewed by many as a symbol of the Australian workers' struggle for equity and a 'fair go'. The best place to get a feel for this historic event is at Sovereign Hill.

🏠 **Sovereign Hill** This is the main destination for visitors to Ballarat and a good place to get a taste for what life was like on the Victorian goldfields. Spread over 60 ha, Sovereign Hill is a replica goldmining town, complete with authentically dressed townspeople. Panning for gold is a popular activity, while in the evening the Blood on the Southern Cross show re-enacts the Eureka Rebellion. Bradshaw St; (03) 5337 1100.

Eureka Centre for Australian Democracy: multimillion-dollar cultural centre with information about the famous battle; Cnr Eureka and Rodier sts; (03) 5333 1854. *Ballarat Botanic Gardens:* an impressive collection of native and exotic plants; Prime Minister Ave features busts of all of Australia's prime ministers; Wendouree Pde. *Ballarat Wildlife Park:* houses native Australian animals such as koalas, kangaroos, quokkas and crocodiles; Cnr Fussel and York sts, Ballarat East; (03) 5333 5933. *Art Gallery of Ballarat:* holds a significant collection of Australian art. The original Eureka Stockade flag is also on display; 40 Lydiard St North; (03) 5320 5791. *Gold Museum:* details the rich goldmining history of the area; opposite Sovereign Hill, Bradshaw St; (03) 5337 1107; admission free with Sovereign

Hill Ticket. *Historic buildings:* include Her Majesty's Theatre, built in 1875 and Australia's oldest intact, purpose-built theatre, and Craig's Royal and the George hotels, with classic old-world surroundings; Lydiard St. *Vintage Tramway:* via Wendouree Pde; rides weekends, and public and school holidays. *Avenue of Honour and Arch of Victory:* honours those who fought in WW I; western edge of city.

🌸 *Lakeside Farmers Market:* Lake Wendouree foreshore; 2nd and 4th Sat every month. *Organs of the Ballarat Goldfields:* music festival held in historic venues; Jan. *Begonia Festival:* popular event for garden lovers with floral displays, gardening forums, street parades, fireworks, art shows, kids' activities; Mar. *Heritage Weekend:* May. *Royal South Street Eisteddfod:* music festival; Sept–Nov. *Ballarat Cup:* Nov.

🍴 *Boatshed Restaurant:* modern Australian restaurant by the lake; 27A Lake Wendouree Foreshore; (03) 5333 5533. *Europa Cafe:* cafe with all-day breakfast; 411 Sturt St; (03) 5338 7672. *L'espresso:* Italian cafe; 417 Sturt St; (03) 5333 1789. *Masons Cafe & Foodstore:* blackboard specials; 32 Drummond St North; (03) 5333 3895.

🛏 *Shady Acres Accommodation Caravan Park:* 9435 Western Hwy; (03) 5334 7233. *Braeside Garden Cottages:* 3 Albion St, Golden Point; 0419 815 012. *Canadian Lodge:* 10 Valley Dr, Canadian; (03) 5330 1327. *Cruzin the 50's 60's Bed & Breakfast:* 7 Handford Crt, Invermay; (03) 5333 2484. *Eureka Stockade Holiday Park:* 104 Stawell St South, Ballarat East; (03) 5331 2281. *Lake Burrumbeet Caravan Park:* Avenue of Honour, Burrumbeet; (03) 5344 0583. *Wintarni Olives:* 40 Clearview Rd, Invermay; 0409 812 470.

🔘 **Enfield State Park** Great for bushwalking or horseriding, the park is home to many species of orchids and numerous animals including echidnas, koalas, bats and frogs. There is a pretty picnic ground at Remote Long Gully, and numerous walking tracks. Also featured are the remnants of early goldmining settlements, including the Berringa Mines Historic Reserve. Contact Parks Victoria on 131 963. Access via Incolls and Misery Creek rds; 25 km s.

Buninyong Buninyong features many fine art and craft galleries. The Buninyong Flora and Bird Park, home to many species of parrots, has raised walkways through the aviaries. 408 Eddy Ave, Mt Helen; (03) 5341 3843. Buninyong Good Life Festival; 3rd weekend in Oct, and in May for the Buninyong Film Festival. The Mt Buninyong Lookout east of town offers great views. 13 km SE.

Kirks and Gong Gong reserves: ideal for picnics and bushwalking, these parks include many unique, indigenous plants; on opposite sides of Daylesford Rd; 5 km NE. *Kryal Castle:* replica of a medieval castle, with daily tours and family entertainment; (03) 5334 7422; 9 km E. *Yuulong Lavender Estate:* set in scenic landscaped gardens, the estate produces and sells lavender products; closed May–Sep; Yendon Rd, Mt Egerton; (03) 5368 9453; 25km SE. *Lal Lal Falls:* plunge 30 m into the Moorabool River; 18 km SE. *Lal Lal Blast Furnace:* fascinating 19th-century archaeological remains; 18 km SE. *Lake Burrumbeet:* this 2100 ha

[GOLD NUGGET, SOVEREIGN HILL]

lake is a popular fishing spot, especially for redfin in spring and summer. Watersports and family activities are available on the lake; various boat ramps provide access. Caravan parks are set on the lakeside and are popular with holiday-makers; 22 km NW. *Skipton:* in town is an eel factory selling smoked eel and other products; 51 km SW. South of town are the Mt Widderin Caves – one has been named the Ballroom, as it was once a venue for dances and concerts. The caves are on private property; tours by appt (03) 5340 2081. *Beaufort:* a small town on the shores of Lake Beaufort, an artificial lake surrounded by gardens, providing

a picturesque location for picnics and leisurely walks; 54 km W. South of town is Lake Goldsmith, home of a major rally of steam-driven machinery and vehicles each May and Oct. *Mooramong Homestead:* built in the 1870s and then altered during the 1930s by its ex-Hollywood owners. It is surrounded by beautiful gardens and a flora and fauna reserve, and is open for tours 3rd Sun each month; 56 km NW via Skipton. *Great Grape Rd:* circuit through Avoca, St Arnaud and Stawell, visiting local wineries.

TOWNS NEARBY: Creswick 16 km, Clunes 31 km, Daylesford 35 km, Bacchus Marsh 52 km, Maryborough 59 km

---

walk around the lake. *Botanical Gardens:* features a splendid collection of roses and memorial statue of Sir Edward 'Weary' Dunlop; Bridge St. *Aeropark:* centre for the Gliding Club of Victoria, offering hot-air ballooning and glider flights; northern outskirts of town; bookings on (03) 5762 1058.

Lakeside Craft and Farmers Market: near the Civic Centre; 3rd Sat each month. *Benalla Festival:* Feb/Mar.

Benalla Gallery Cafe: contemporary local-produce menu; Benalla Art Gallery, Bridge St; (03) 5762 3777. *Georgina's:* modern Australian menu; 100 Bridge St East; (03) 5762 1334. *North Eastern Hotel:* regional contemporary dishes; 1 Nunn St; (03) 5762 7333. *Raffety's Restaurant:* homemade modern Australian dishes; 55 Nunn St; (03) 5762 4066.

Belmont Bed & Breakfast: 80 Arundel St; (03) 5762 6575. *Glen Falloch Farm Cottage:* 252 Warrenbayne West Rd, Baddaginnie; 0403 340 660. *Glenrowan Tourist Park:* 2 Old Hume Hwy, Glenrowan; (03) 5766 2288. *Melliodora Farm:* 21 Bowers Rd, Winton; (03) 5766 4320.

Reef Hills State Park Features grey box, river red gum, wildflowers in spring and wattle blossom in winter. The park offers scenic drives, bushwalks, picnics and horseriding. There are more than 100 species of birds, including gang-gang cockatoos and crimson rosellas, plus animals such as eastern grey kangaroos, sugar gliders, brush-tailed possums, echidnas and bats. Contact Parks Victoria on 13 1963; 4 km SW, western side of the Midland Hwy.

Lake Mokoan: depending on water levels, great for fishing, boating and waterskiing; 10 km NE. *1950s-style cinema:* showing classic films at Swanpool; 23 km S.

TOWNS NEARBY: Glenrowan 24 km, Wangaratta 37 km, Milawa 42 km, Euroa 43 km, Shepparton 56 km

---

Bendigo
see inset box on page 150

Bright
see inset box on page 153

Buchan
Pop. 326
Map ref. 519 A11 | 539 A10 | 541 P4

General Store, Main St; (03) 5155 9202 or 1800 637 060; www.lakesandwilderness.com.au

90.7 FM 3REG Radio East Gippsland, 828 AM ABC Local Radio

Situated in East Gippsland, Buchan is primarily an agricultural town renowned for offering some of the best caving in Victoria. Although the origin of the town's name is disputed, it is said to be derived from the Aboriginal term for either 'smoke-signal expert' or 'place of the grass bag'.

Foothills Festival: Jan. *Canni Creek Races:* Jan. *Rodeo:* Easter. *Flower Show:* Nov.

Buchan Caves Reserve: Caves Rd; (03) 5162 1900.

Buchan Caves Reserve The reserve features more than 350 limestone caves, of which the Royal and Fairy caves are the most accessible – the Fairy Cave alone is over 400 m long, with impressive stalactites. Europeans did not discover the caves until 1907, but from then on they became a popular tourist destination. Now visitors can cool off in the spring-fed swimming pool after exploring the caves. Tours of the Royal and Fairy caves run daily. Off Buchan Rd, north of town; (03) 5162 1900.

Snowy River Scenic Drive The drive takes in the Buchan and Snowy rivers junction and runs along the edge of Snowy River National Park to Gelantipy. Beyond Gelantipy is Little River Gorge, Victoria's deepest gorge. A short walking track leads to a cliff-top lookout. Near the gorge is McKillops Bridge, a safe swimming spot, a good site to launch canoes, and the starting point for 2 walking tracks. Care is required on the road beyond Gelantipy; 4WD is recommended. Details from visitor centre.

Suggan Buggan: this historic townsite, surrounded by Alpine National Park, features an 1865 schoolhouse and the Eagle Loft Gallery for local art and craft; 64 km N.

TOWNS NEARBY: Orbost 33 km, Lakes Entrance 45 km, Bairnsdale 62 km, Paynesville 62 km, Omeo 68 km

---

Camperdown
Pop. 3164
Map ref. 538 H7 | 551 J7

Old Courthouse, Manifold St; (03) 5593 3390; www.greatoceanrd.org

104.7 Otway FM, 594 AM ABC Local Radio

Located at the foot of Mount Leura, a volcanic cone, Camperdown is more famous for its natural attractions than for the town itself, being situated on the world's third largest volcanic plain. But that should not detract from Camperdown: National Trust–listed Finlay Avenue features 2 kilometres of regal elm trees, while in the town centre the Gothic-style Manifold Clock Tower proudly stands as a tribute to the region's first European pioneers.

continued on p. 151

 RADIO STATIONS IN TOWN WHAT'S ON WHERE TO EAT WHERE TO STAY NEARBY

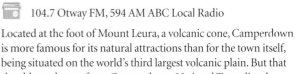
VICTORIA

BENDIGO

Pop. 81 941

Map ref. 535 F3 | 542 A9 | 549 O10

i Post Office, 51–67 Pall Mall; (03) 5434 6060 or 1800 813 153; www.bendigotourism.com

89.5 The Fresh FM, 91.1 FM ABC Local Radio, 96.5 Radio KLFM

Bendigo was the place of one of the world's most exciting gold rushes, with more gold found here between 1850 and 1900 than anywhere else in the world. Elaborate buildings and monuments from the golden past line the main streets, offering an ever-present reminder of the riches from the goldfields. Today modern life weaves itself around this legacy with a vibrant pace. The town's new wealth can be seen in many areas including art, culture, dining, wine and shopping.

The Golden Dragon Museum The museum commemorates the contribution of the Chinese community to life on the goldfields. On display are exhibitions depicting the daily life and hardships of Chinese immigrants and an impressive collection of Chinese memorabilia and processional regalia, including what is said to be the world's oldest imperial dragon, 'Loong' (which first appeared at the Bendigo Easter Fair in 1892), and the world's longest imperial dragon, 'Sun Loong'. Adjacent to the museum is the Classical Chinese Garden of Joy and newly-developed Dai Gum San precinct; 1–11 Bridge St; (03) 5441 5044.

Central Deborah Gold Mine Perhaps the best way to get a feel for life in a goldmining town is to take a trip down this mine, where you can still see traces of gold in the quartz reef 20 storeys below the ground. The Central Deborah Gold Mine was the last commercial goldmine to operate in Bendigo. From 1939 to 1954 around a tonne of gold was excavated; 76 Violet St; (03) 5443 8322 for tour details.

Bendigo Art Gallery: well-regarded for contemporary exhibitions plus an extensive permanent collection with a focus on Australian artists, including Arthur Boyd, Tom Roberts and Arthur Streeton; guided tours daily; 42 View St; (03) 5434 6088. *Self-guide heritage walk:* takes in landmarks including the Shamrock Hotel, built in 1897, cnr Pall Mall and Williamson St; Sacred Heart Cathedral, the largest outside Melbourne, Wattle St; Alexandra Fountain, built in 1881, one of the largest and most ornate fountains in regional Victoria, at Charing Cross; and the Renaissance-style post office and law courts at Pall Mall. Details on heritage walks available from visitor centre. *Bendigo Pottery:* Australia's oldest working pottery, with potters at work, a cafe and sales; 146 Midland Hwy, Epsom; (03) 5448 4404. *Dudley House:* National Trust–classified building; View St. *Pall Mall:* this tree-lined, French-style boulevard is probably country Australia's most impressive street. *Vintage Trams:* run from mine on 8 km city trip, including a stop at the Tram Depot Museum; taped commentary provided. *Chinese Joss House:* National Trust–classified temple built by Chinese miners; included on the vintage tram trip; Finn St, North Bendigo; (03) 5442 1685. *Rosalind Park:* majestic parklands that sit beautifully in the centre of Bendigo offering stately gardens for leisure and relaxation, includes a lookout tower, Cascades water feature and Conservatory Gardens; Pall Mall. *Discovery Science and Technology Centre:* features more than 100 hands-on displays;

[ROSALIND PARK]

7 Railway Pl; (03) 5444 4400. *Making of a Nation Exhibition:* permanent interpretive display providing details about Bendigo's role in Federation; at the visitor centre, Pall Mall.

Bridge Street Market: features local produce and handmade arts and crafts; 3rd Sat each month, 8am–1pm; Bridge St near Golden Dragon Museum. *Showgrounds Market:* Prince of Wales Showgrounds, Holmes St; 8.30am–3pm every Sun. *Farmers Market:* fresh regional produce; Sidney Myer Pl; 9am–1pm, 2nd Sat each month. *International Madison:* major cycling event, Mar long weekend. *Easter Festival:* first held in 1871, the festival spans 4 days and is a major event on the town's calendar, with free music and entertainment, craft markets, art exhibits, food, wine and the famous procession featuring Sun Loong. *Australian Sheep and Wool Show:* showcases everything from farming to fashion; July. *Heritage Uncorked:* wine event in the historic streets; 2nd weekend Oct. *National Swap Meet:* Australia's largest meet for vintage cars and bikes, Bendigo Showgrounds; Nov. *Bendigo Cup:* horseracing; Nov.

The Bridge: contemporary gastropub; 49 Bridge St; (03) 5443 7811. *The Dispensary Enoteca:* European menu; 9 Chancery La; (03) 5444 5885. *The Exchange Cafe Bar*

Restaurant: cafe fare and tapas; Shop 11, Bendigo Centre; (03) 5444 2060. *GPO Bendigo:* cafe and bar; 60–64 Pall Mall; (03) 5443 4343. *Whirrakee Restaurant:* contemporary French; 17 View Pt; (03) 5441 5557. *Wine Bank on View:* Mediterranean wine bar; 45 View St; (03) 5444 4655.

 Bishopscourt Bed & Breakfast: 40 Forest St; (03) 5443 9456. *A-Line Holiday Village:* 5615 Calder Hwy, Big Hill; (03) 5447 9568. *Avondel Caravan Park:* 723 Calder Hwy, Maiden Gully; (03) 5449 6265. *BIG4 Bendigo Ascot Holiday Park:* 15 Heinz St, Ascot; (03) 5448 4421. *Gold Nugget Tourist Park:* 293 Midland Hwy, Epsom; (03) 5448 4747. *Central City Caravan Park:* 362 High St (Calder Hwy), Golden Square; (03) 5443 6937. *Lynnevale Estate:* 83 Cahills Rd, Mandurang; (03) 5439 3635. *Marong Caravan & Cabin Village:* 1449 Calder Hwy, Marong; (03) 5435 2329.

 Greater Bendigo National Park The park, which extends to the north and south of town, protects some high-quality box-ironbark forest and is popular for scenic driving, cycling, walking and camping. Relics of the region's goldmining and eucalyptus-oil industries can be found within. Fauna includes over 170 species of birds including the grey shrike-thrush, a pretty songbird. In the early morning and later in the evening, look out for eastern grey kangaroos, black wallabies and echidnas. Detailed maps of the park are available at the visitor centre. Contact Parks Victoria on 13 1963; access via Loddon Valley Hwy through Eaglehawk; 8 km N.

Bendigo wine region Like neighbouring Heathcote, this area is responsible for some of the country's richest reds. Both its shiraz and cabernet sauvignon are wonderfully reliable varieties that could only be shaken by a very bad season. Wineries to visit are Pondalowie Estate, Passing Clouds, Water Wheel and the picturesque Balgownie Estate, with its lovely cafe and boutique cottages. Bress also dabbles in traditional apple cider.

One Tree Hill observation tower: panoramic views; 4 km S. *Eaglehawk:* site of the gold rush in 1852, it features remnants of goldmining days and fine examples of 19th-century architecture; details of self-guide heritage tour from visitor centre; 6.5 km NW. *Mandurang:* features historic wineries and is the exact centre of Victoria; 8 km S.

TOWNS NEARBY: Maldon 32 km, Castlemaine 35 km, Inglewood 42 km, Heathcote 42 km, Dunolly 50 km

 Manifold Clock Tower: an imposing structure built in 1896; open 1st Sun each month; Cnr Manifold and Pike sts. *Historical Society Museum:* displays Aboriginal artefacts, local historical photographs, and household and farming implements; Manifold St. *Courthouse:* built in 1886–87, described as one of the most distinctive courthouses in Australia; Manifold St. *Buggy Museum:* collection of 30 restored horse-drawn buggies; Ower St.

 Craft market: Finlay Ave or Theatre Royal; 1st Sun each month. *Heritage Festival:* Nov.

 Lakes and Craters Holiday Park: 220 Park Rd; (03) 5593 1253. *Grand Central Accommodation B&B:* 30 Victoria St, Cobden; (03) 5595 1881.

 Crater lakes Surrounding Camperdown are spectacular crater lakes that provide an interesting history of volcanic activity over the past 20 000 years, as well as opportunities for watersports and excellent fishing. Travelling west of town, take the scenic drive around the rims of lakes Bullen Merri and Gnotuk, and join in the watersports and swimming at South Beach. The lakes are regularly stocked with Chinook salmon and redfin. For a scenic picnic spot, and some of the best fishing, visit Lake Purrumbete; 15 km SE. By far one of the most impressive lakes is Lake Corangamite, the Southern Hemisphere's largest permanent salt lake. This lake lies 25 km E, but the best viewing spot is Red Rock Lookout; *see Colac.*

Derrinallum and Mt Elephant Mt Elephant rises to almost 200 m behind the small township of Derrinallum – it doesn't sound like a lot, but across the plains of the Western District you can see it from up to 60 km away. A gash in the elephant's western side is the result of decades of quarrying. The mountain is actually the scoria cone of an extinct volcano, and inside is a 90 m deep crater. Now owned by the community, there is a walking trail to the top, and the Music on the Mount festival is held here in Nov. Lake Tooliorook on the other side of town offers good fishing for trout and redfin, and watersports. 40 km N.

Camperdown–Timboon Rail Trail: walking or riding track through bush, following historic railway line. *Mt Leura:* extinct volcano close to the perfect cone of Mt Sugarloaf. A lookout offers excellent views over crater lakes and volcanoes, and north across the plains to the Grampians; 1 km S. *Camperdown Botanic Gardens:* feature rare examples of Himalayan oak and a lookout over lakes Bullen Merri and Gnotuk; 3 km W. *Cobden Miniature Trains:* operates 3rd Sun each month; Cobden; 13 km S.

TOWNS NEARBY: Terang 20 km, Colac 40 km, Port Campbell 45 km, Warrnambool 61 km, Winchelsea 73 km

Cann River

Pop. 223
Map ref. 519 C11 ; 539 E10

 Parks Victoria Cann River office, (03) 5158 6351; or East Gippsland Visitor Information Centre, 1800 637 060; www.lakesandwilderness.com.au

 101.7 FM 3MGB Wilderness Radio, 106.1 FM ABC Local Radio

Cann River is situated at the junction of the Princes and Cann Valley highways, and is notable for its proximity to several spectacular national parks. The area boasts excellent fishing, bushwalking and camping in the rugged hinterland, with nearby Point Hicks notable for being the first land on the east coast of Australia to be sighted by Europeans.

 Point Hicks Lighthouse: Point Hicks Rd; (03) 5158 4268.

 Lind National Park The park includes the Euchre Valley Nature Drive through temperate rainforest gullies. It also

VICTORIA

supports open eucalypt forests with grey gum, messmate and silvertop ash. Watch for wildlife such as the pretty masked owl and the elusive long-footed potoroo. Has picnic facilities. 15 km w.

Coopracambra National Park This park is in one of the most remote sections of Victoria. Ancient fossil footprints have been found in the red sandstone gorge of the Genoa River, and the surrounding granite peaks create a spectacular scene. The 35 000 ha area protects unique ecosystems and rare flora and fauna. Only experienced and well-equipped hikers should undertake walks in the rugged and remote parts of this park. A 'trip intentions' form needs to be lodged at the Cann River or Mallacoota office of Parks Victoria prior to departure, and parks staff must be notified upon return. 30 km N near NSW border.

Croajingolong National Park: the road travelling south of Cann River leads to Pt Hicks and its historic 1890 lighthouse (daily tours offered); *for further details on the park see Mallacoota.*

TOWNS NEARBY: Mallacoota 53 km, Orbost 63 km, Bombala (NSW) 73 km, Buchan 87 km, Eden (NSW) 87 km

Casterton

Pop. 1654
Map ref. 550 C3 | 568 H11

ⓘ Shiels Tce; (03) 5581 2070; www.castertonnow.org.au

94.1 FM ABC Local Radio, 99.3 Coastal FM

Casterton is a Roman name meaning 'walled city', given to the town because of the natural wall of hills surrounding the valley where it lies. These hills, and the Glenelg River that flows through town, create an idyllic rural atmosphere. The region is colloquially known as 'Kelpie Country' as it is the birthplace of this world-famous breed of working dog. In the mid-1800s a prized Scottish collie female pup from nearby Warrock Homestead was sold to a stockman named Jack Gleeson, who named her 'Kelpie' – she was bred out with various 'black and tan' dogs, and so began the long line of the working man's best friend.

Historical Museum: housed in the old railway station, the museum displays local artefacts; open by appt; Cnr Jackson and Clarke sts. *Alma and Judith Zaadstra Fine Art Gallery:* Henty St. *Mickle Lookout:* a great view across the town; Moodie St, off Robertson St on the eastern edge of town.

Vintage Car Rally: Mar. *Polocrosse Championships:* Mar. *Casterton Cup:* June. *Australian Kelpie Muster and Kelpie Working Dog Auction:* June/July.

Dergholm State Park The park features a great diversity of vegetation, including woodlands, open forests, heaths and swamps. An abundance of wildlife thrives, including echidnas, koalas, kangaroos, reptiles and the endangered red-tailed black cockatoo. A key attraction is Baileys Rocks, unique giant green-coloured granite boulders. Contact Parks Victoria on 13 1963; 50 km N.

Long Lead Swamp: waterbirds, kangaroos, emus and a trail-bike track; Penola Rd; 11 km w. *Geological formations:* in particular, The Hummocks, 12 km NE, and The Bluff, viewable from Dartmoor Rd, 20 km SW. Both rock formations are around 150 million years old. *Warrock Homestead:* a unique collection of 33 buildings erected by its founder, George Robertson. The homestead was built in 1843 and is National Trust–classified; open day on Easter Sun; 26 km N. *Bilston's Tree:* 50 m high and arguably the world's largest red gum; Glenmia Rd; 30 km N.

TOWNS NEARBY: Coleraine 26 km, Penola 55 km, Hamilton 58 km, Coonawarra 60 km, Mount Gambier 61 km

Castlemaine

Pop. 7250
Map ref. 535 F6 | 549 N12 | 551 N1

ⓘ Castlemaine Market Building, 44 Mostyn St; (03) 5471 1795 or 1800 171 888; www.maldoncastlemaine.com

91.1 FM ABC Local Radio, 106.3 Radio KLFM

Castlemaine is a classic goldmining town known for its grand old buildings and sprawling botanical gardens. This area was the site of the greatest alluvial gold rush that the world has ever seen. Now the town relies largely on agriculture and the manufacturing sectors, as well as being home to a thriving artistic community that takes inspiration from the area's red hills.

Castlemaine Art Gallery Housed in an elegant Art Deco building, the gallery was designed in 1931 by Peter Meldrum and is renowned for its collection of Australian art. Along with the permanent collection, many exhibitions appear here. Works by Rembrandt, Francisco Goya and Andy Warhol have all been displayed at this delightful gallery. 14 Lyttleton St; (03) 5472 2292.

Buda Historic Home and Garden Buda is considered to have one of the most significant examples of 19th-century gardens in Victoria. The house itself is furnished with period pieces and art and craft created by the Leviny family, who lived here for 118 years. Ernest Leviny was a silversmith and jeweller. Five of his 6 daughters never married, but remained at Buda and pursued woodwork, photography and embroidery. Open 12–5pm Wed–Sat, 10am–5pm Sun; 42 Hunter St; (03) 5472 1032.

Victorian Goldfields Railway This historic railway runs from Castlemaine to Maldon. The steam train journeys through box-ironbark forest in a region that saw some of the richest goldmining in the country. As well as the regular timetable, it also hosts special events throughout the year. Castlemaine Railway Station, Kennedy St; recorded information (03) 5475 2966, inquiries (03) 5470 6658.

Diggings Interpretive Centre: housed in the restored 19th-century Castlemaine Market building, the centre features interactive displays about the area's many goldmines as well as various exhibitions; Mostyn St. *Theatre Royal:* hosts live shows and films and also offers luxurious backstage accommodation; Hargraves St. *Castlemaine Botanic Gardens:* one of Victoria's oldest and most impressive 19th-century gardens; Cnr Walker and Downes rds. *Old Castlemaine Gaol:* restored gaol now offers tours; Bowden St. *Food and wine producers:* dotted throughout the area; food and wine trail brochures from visitor centre.

Castlemaine Farmers Market: 1st Sun each month. *Wesley Hill Market:* each Sat; 2.5 km E. *Castlemaine State Festival:* odd-numbered years, Apr. *Festival of Gardens:* Nov.

Bold Cafe Gallery: Asian-influenced nursery cafe; 146 Duke St; (03) 5470 6038. *The Empyre:* modern gastropub; 68 Mostyn St; (03) 5472 5166. *Saffs Cafe:* casual cafe food; 64 Mostyn St; (03) 5470 6722. *Togs Place:* popular breakfast & lunch spot; 58 Lyttleton St; (03) 5470 5090.

BIG4 Castlemaine Gardens Holiday Park: Doran Ave (off Walker St); (03) 5472 1125. *Castlemaine Central Cabin & Van Park:* 101 Barker St; (03) 5472 2160. *Clevedon Manor:* 260 Barker St; (03) 5472 5212. *Penrhos Cottage:* 3101 Calder Hwy, Harcourt; (03) 5474 2415.

Castlemaine Diggings National Heritage Park The wealth on Castlemaine's streets springs from the huge hauls of gold found on the Mt Alexander Diggings, east and south of town. Thousands of miners worked the fields. Towns such as

continued on p. 154

BRIGHT

Pop. 2113
Map ref. 543 K9 | 545 I7

 76a Gavan St; 1300 551 117; www.brightescapes.com.au

89.7 FM ABC Local Radio, 101.3 Oak FM

Bright is situated in the Ovens Valley in the foothills of the Victorian Alps. A particularly striking element of the town is the avenues of deciduous trees, at their peak during the autumn months. The Bright Autumn Festival is held annually in celebration of the spectacular seasonal changes. The Ovens River flows through the town, providing a delightful location for picnics or camping. The town also offers off-the-mountain accommodation for nearby Mt Hotham and Mt Buffalo.

Old Tobacco Sheds You could easily spend half a day here, wandering through the sheds filled with antiques and bric-a-brac and through the makeshift museums, which give an insight into the local tobacco industry and the gold rush. Also on-site is a historic hut, and the Sharefarmers Cafe serves Devonshire tea. Open 9am–5pm (Sept–May), 10am–4pm (June–Aug); 7377 Great Alpine Rd; (03) 5755 2344.

Gallery 90: local art and craft; 90 Gavan St; (03) 5755 1385. *Centenary Park:* with a deep weir, children's playground and picnic facilities; Gavan St. *Bright Art Gallery and Cultural Centre:* community-owned gallery, displays and sells fine art and handicrafts; 28 Mountbatten Ave; (03) 5750 1660. *Bright Brewery:* enjoy award-winning beers or brew your own; 121 Great Alpine Rd; (03) 5755 1301. *Bright and District Historical Museum:* in the old railway station building, with artefacts and photographs from the town's past; open by appt (contact visitor centre); Cnr Gavan and Anderson sts. *Walking tracks:* well-marked tracks around the area include Canyon Walk along the Ovens River, where remains of gold-workings can be seen; details from visitor centre. *Murray to the Mountains Rail Trail:* Bright sits at one end of this 94 km track suitable for cycling and walking; links several townships.

Craft market: 3rd Sat each month; Burke St. *Autumn Festival:* activities include craft markets and entertainment; Apr/May. *Alpine Spring Festival:* free entertainment, displays and open gardens, celebrating the beauty of Bright in spring; Oct.

Poplars: French-inspired menu; Shop 8, Star Rd; (03) 5755 1655. *Simone's of Bright:* excellent Italian cuisine; 98 Gavan St; (03) 5755 2266. *Villa Gusto:* Tuscan-style regional menu; 630 Buckland Valley Rd, Buckland; (03) 5756 2000.

Badrocks Bed & Breakfast: 21 Delany Ave; (03) 5755 1231. *BIG4 Bright:* 1 Mountbatten Ave; (03) 5755 1064. *Bright Accommodation Park:* 438 Great Alpine Rd; (03) 5750 1001. *Bright Holiday Park:* Cherry Ave; (03) 5755 1141. *Bright Pine Valley Tourist Park:* 7–15 Churchill Ave; (03) 5755 1010. *Bright Riverside Holiday Park:* 4 Toorak Ave; (03) 5755 1118. *Eucalypt Mist:* 152A Delany Ave (Great Alpine Rd); (03) 5755 1336. *Abby's Cottages – Bright:* 165 School Rd, Wandiligong; 0417 367 494. *BIG4 Porepunkah Holiday Park:* 6674 Great Alpine Rd, Porepunkah; 1800 234 798. *The Buckland Luxury Retreat:* 116 McCormacks La, Buckland Valley; 0419 133 318. *Freeburgh Cabins and Caravan Park:* 1099 Great Alpine Rd, Freeburgh; (03) 5750 1306. *Lavender Hue:* 20 Great Alpine Rd,

Harrietville; (03) 5759 2588. *Porepunkah Bridge Caravan Park:* 36 Mt Buffalo Rd, Porepunkah; (03) 5756 2380. *Porepunkah Pines Tourist Resort:* 7065 Great Alpine Rd, Porepunkah; (03) 5756 2282. *Riverview Caravan Park:* Junction Rd, Porepunkah; (03) 5756 2290.

Wandiligong A National Trust–classified hamlet, the area contains well-preserved historic buildings from the town's goldmining days. The tiny village is set in a rich green valley, with an enormous hedge maze as the dominant feature and over 2 km of walkways surrounded by lush gardens. The maze is well signposted. Open 10am–5pm Wed–Sun; 6 km s.

Mount Buffalo National Park This 31 000 ha national park is the state's oldest, declared in 1898. A plateau of boulders and tors includes The Horn, the park's highest point and a great place for views at sunrise. Walking tracks are set among streams, waterfalls, stunning wildflowers, and snow gum and mountain ash forest. There is summer camping, swimming and canoeing at Lake Catani, and rock climbing and hang-gliding are also popular. In winter, the Mount Buffalo ski area is popular with families. Contact Parks Victoria on 13 1963; 10 km NW.

Tower Hill Lookout: 4 km NW. *Boyntons/Feathertop Winery:* open for sales and tastings; at junction of Ovens and Buckland rivers, Porepunkah; 6 km NW. *The Red Stag Deer and Emu Farm:* Hughes La, Eurobin; 16 km NW. *Harrietville:* a former goldmining village located just outside the Alpine National Park. Attractions include Pioneer Park, an open-air museum and picnic area; Tavare Park, with a swing bridge and picnic and barbecue facilities; and a lavender farm; 20 km SE. *Alpine National Park: see Mount Beauty;* to the south-east of town.

TOWNS NEARBY: Mount Beauty 19 km, Myrtleford 28 km, Yackandandah 47 km, Beechworth 48 km, Milawa 57 km

[THE COLOURS OF AUTUMN CREATE A PICTURESQUE SETTING]

Fryerstown, Vaughan and Glenluce, now almost ghost towns, supported breweries, schools, churches and hotels. Today visitors can explore Chinese cemeteries, mineral springs, waterwheels and old townsites. Fossicking is popular. Details of self-guide walks and drives from visitor centre. 4 km s.

Chewton: historic buildings line the streets of this former gold town; 4 km E. *Harcourt:* this town is known for its many wineries, including Harcourt Valley Vineyard and Blackjack Vineyards, with tastings and cellar-door sales. Also at Harcourt is the Skydancers Orchid and Butterfly Gardens. The town hosts the Apple Festival in Mar and spring, and the Orchid Festival in Oct; 9 km NE. *Big Tree:* a giant red gum over 500 years old; Guildford; 14 km SW. *Koala Reserve:* Mt Alexander; 19 km NE.

TOWNS NEARBY: Maldon 15 km, Kyneton 29 km, Daylesford 31 km, Bendigo 35 km, Woodend 42 km

Chiltern

Pop. 1067
Map ref. 527 N12 | 543 J6 | 544 H2

i 30 Main St; (03) 5726 1611; www.chilternvic.com

101.3 Oak FM, 106.5 FM ABC Local Radio

Now surrounded by rich pastoral farmland, Chiltern was once at the centre of a goldmining boom and had as many as 14 suburbs. After the Indigo gold discovery in the 1850s, there was a major influx of miners and settlers, but the boom was brief and farming was soon prominent in the town's economy. Today the rich heritage of the 19th century can be seen in the streetscapes, a vision not lost on Australian filmmakers keen for that 'authentic' 1800s scene.

 Athenaeum Museum: historic building with heritage display; Conness St. *Dow's Pharmacy:* old chemist shop with original features; Conness St. *Star Theatre and Grapevine Museum:* the quaint theatre still operates and the museum, formerly the Grapevine Hotel, boasts the largest grapevine in Australia, planted in 1867 and recorded in the Guinness World Records; Main St. *Federal Standard newspaper office:* open by appt for groups; Main St. *Lakeview House:* former home of author Henry Handel Richardson; open afternoons on weekends and public and school holidays; Victoria St. *Lake Anderson:* picnic and barbecue facilities; access via Main St.

Antique Fair: Aug. *Ironbark Festival:* heritage fair with woodchopping, live music and markets; Oct.

Lake Anderson Caravan Park: Alliance St; (03) 5726 1298.

Chiltern–Mt Pilot National Park This park stretches from around Chiltern south to Beechworth and protects remnant box-ironbark forest, which once covered much of this part of Victoria. Also featured are significant goldmining relics, including the impressive Magenta Goldmine (around 2 km E). Of the park's 21 000 ha, 7000 were exposed to bushfire in Jan 2003. But its regeneration is evidence of the hardiness of the forest, and there are now upgraded visitor facilities. An introduction to the forest scenery and goldmining history is on the 25 km scenic drive signposted from Chiltern. Other activities include canoeing and rafting, fishing, and cycling and walking trips along the many marked trails. Contact Parks Victoria on 13 1963; access via Hume Hwy and the road south to Beechworth.

TOWNS NEARBY: Rutherglen 17 km, Beechworth 24 km, Wodonga 25 km, Corowa (NSW) 26 km, Yackandandah 28 km

Clunes

Pop. 1024
Map ref. 535 C8 | 536 C1 | 551 M2

i Old School Complex, 70 Bailey St; (03) 5345 3896; www.visitclunes.com.au

99.9 VoiceFM, 107.9 FM ABC Local Radio

The first registered gold strike in the state was made at Clunes on 7 July 1851. The town, north of Ballarat, is said to be one of the most intact gold towns in Victoria, featuring historic buildings throughout. Surrounding the town are a number of extinct volcanoes. A view of these can be obtained 3 kilometres to the south, on the road to Ballarat. The town was used as a location for the film *Ned Kelly*, starring Heath Ledger.

 Clunes Museum: local-history museum featuring displays on the gold-rush era; open weekends and school and public holidays; Fraser St. *Bottle Museum:* in former South Clunes State School; open Wed–Sun; Bailey St. *Queens Park:* on the banks of Creswick Creek, the park was created over 100 years ago.

Market: Fraser St; 2nd Sun each month. *Booktown:* large-scale book fair; May. *Words in Winter Celebration:* Aug.

Talbot This delightful, historic town has many 1860–70 buildings, particularly in Camp St and Scandinavian Cres. Attractions include the Arts and Historical Museum in the former Methodist Church; the Bull and Mouth Restaurant in an old bluestone building, formerly a hotel; and a market (holds the honour of being the first farmers market in the region) selling local produce, 3rd Sun each month. 18 km NW.

Mt Beckworth Scenic Reserve: popular picnic and horseriding reserve with panoramic views from the summit; 8 km W.

TOWNS NEARBY: Creswick 17 km, Maryborough 28 km, Ballarat 31 km, Daylesford 32 km, Avoca 36 km

Cobram

Pop. 5061
Map ref. 527 L12 | 542 F4

i Cnr Station St and Punt Rd; (03) 5872 2132 or 1800 607 607.

101.3 Oak FM, 106.5 FM ABC Local Radio

At Cobram and nearby Barooga (across the New South Wales border) the Murray River is bordered by sandy beaches, making it a great spot for fishing, watersports and picnics. The stretch of land between the township and the river features river red gum forests and lush wetlands, with tracks leading to various beaches, the most accessible of which is Thompsons Beach, located near the bridge off Boorin Street. The town is supported by peach, nectarine, pear and orange orchards and dairies, earning it the nickname 'peaches and cream country'. A biennial festival is held in honour of these industries.

 Historic log cabin: built in Yarrawonga in 1875, then moved piece by piece to its current location; opposite the information centre on Station St. *Station Gallery:* at the railway station, displays a collection of art by local artists.

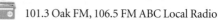 *Market:* Punt Rd; 1st Sat each month. *Peaches and Cream Festival:* free peaches and cream, a rodeo, fishing competitions and other activities; odd-numbered years, Jan. *Rotary Art Show:* May. *Antique Fair:* June. *Open Gardens Display:* Oct.

Cobram East Caravan Park: 3186 Murray Valley Hwy; (03) 5872 1207. *Cobram Oasis Tourist Park:* Cnr Koonoomoo and Racecourse rds; (03) 5871 2010. *The Cobram Willows Caravan Park:* Cnr Murray Valley Hwy and Ritchie Rd; (03) 5872 1074. *RACV Cobram Resort:* 154 Campbell Rd; (03) 5872 2467.

Cobram Barooga Golf Resort: Golf Course Rd, Barooga, NSW; (03) 5873 4523. *Numurkah Caravan Park:* 158 Melville St, Numurkah; (03) 5862 1526.

Quinn Island Flora and Fauna Reserve: home to abundant birdlife and Aboriginal artefacts, including scar trees, flint tools and middens, the island can be explored on a self-guide walk; on the Murray River, accessed via a pedestrian bridge off River Rd. *Binghi Boomerang Factory:* large manufacturer and exporter of boomerangs. Free demonstrations are offered with purchases; Tocumwal Rd, Barooga, across the river. *Scenic Drive Strawberry Farm:* strawberry-picking during warmer months; Torgannah Rd, Koonoomoo; 11 km w. *Cactus Country:* Australia's largest cacti gardens; Strathmerton; 16 km w. *Ulupna Island:* part of Barmah National Park; turn-off after Strathmerton; *see Echuca for details*. *Murray River Horse Trails:* a fantastic way to explore the Murray River beaches; (03) 5868 2221. *Cobram Barooga golf course:* across the river in NSW is this renowned 36-hole course.

TOWNS NEARBY: Tocumwal (NSW) 14 km, Finley (NSW) 31 km, Mulwala (NSW) 33 km, Yarrawonga 34 km, Shepparton 55 km

Cohuna

Pop. 1891
Map ref. 527 I11 | 542 A3 | 549 O5

i Gannawarra Shire Council, 49 Victoria St, Kerang; (03) 5450 9333; www.gannawarra.vic.gov.au

99.1 Smart FM, 594 AM ABC Local Radio

A peaceful, small service centre located on the Murray River. Cohuna's claim to fame is that its casein factory developed produce that became part of the diet of the astronauts flying the Apollo space missions. East of town is Gunbower Island, at the junction of the Murray River and Gunbower Creek. The island is home to abundant wildlife, including kangaroos and emus, plus breeding rookeries for birdlife during flood years.

Cohuna Historical Museum: housed in the former Scots Church, the museum features memorabilia relating to explorer Major Mitchell; Sampson St.

Murray River International Music Festival: Feb. *Bridge to Bridge Swim:* Mar. *Austoberfest:* Oct.

Gunbower Family Hotel: excellent steakhouse; 18 Main St (Murray Valley Hwy), Gunbower; (03) 5487 1214.

Cohuna Waterfront Holiday Park: Island Rd; (03) 5456 2562. *Gunbower Caravan Park:* 74–80 Main st, Gunbower; (03) 5487 1412.

Gunbower Island This island, surrounded by Gunbower Creek and the Murray River, is an internationally recognised wetland, with a great variety of waterbirds and stands of river red gum forest. A 5 km canoe trail flows through Safes Lagoon and bushwalking is another highlight.

Grove Patchwork Cottage and Tearooms: for local art and craft; Murray Valley Hwy; 4 km SE. *Mathers Waterwheel Museum:* features waterwheel memorabilia and outdoor aviary; Brays Rd; 9 km w. *Murray Goulburn Factory:* cheese factory; Leitchville; 16 km SE. *Kow Swamp:* bird sanctuary with picnic spots and fishing at Box Bridge; 23 km s. *Section of Major Mitchell Trail:* 1700 km trail that retraces this explorer's footsteps from Mildura to Wodonga via Portland. From Cohuna, follow the signposted trail along Gunbower Creek down to Mt Hope; 28 km s.

Torrumbarry Weir: during winter the entire weir structure is removed, while in summer waterskiing is popular; 40 km SE.

TOWNS NEARBY: Barham (NSW) 22 km, Kerang 28 km, Pyramid Hill 29 km, Echuca 61 km, Deniliquin (NSW) 74 km

Colac

Pop. 10 859
Map ref. 536 B9 | 538 B2 | 551 L8

i Cnr Murray St (Princes Hwy) and Queen St; (03) 5231 3730 or 1300 689 297; www.visitgreatoceanroad.org.au

104.7 Otway FM, 594 AM 3WV ABC Local Radio

Colac was built by the shores of Lake Colac on the volcanic plain that covers much of Victoria's Western District. The lake, once the largest freshwater body in Victoria, is gradually returning to health after having been dried out by harsh drought. Still, the town acts as the gateway to the Otways. The area was once described by novelist Rolf Boldrewood as 'a scene of surpassing beauty and rural loveliness … this Colac country was the finest, the richest as to soil and pasture that I had up to that time ever looked on'.

Colac Heritage Walk: self-guide tour of the history and architectural wonders of Colac; details from visitor centre. *Performing Arts and Cultural Centre:* incorporates the Colac Cinema, open daily; and the Historical Centre, open 2–4pm Thurs, Fri and Sun; Cnr Gellibrand and Ray sts. *Botanic Gardens:* unusual in that visitors are allowed to drive through the gardens. Picnic, barbecue and playground facilities are provided; by Lake Colac. *Barongarook Creek:* prolific birdlife, and a walking track leading from Princes Hwy to Lake Colac; on the northern outskirts of town.

Lions Club Market: Memorial Sq, Murray St; 3rd Sun each month. *Go Country Music Festival and Truck Show:* Feb. *Colac Cup:* Feb. *Kana Festival:* community festival with family entertainment, music and displays; Mar. *Garden Expo:* Colac Showgrounds; Oct.

Old Lorne Road Olives: Mediterranean-inspired cafe; 45 Old Lorne Rd, Deans Marsh; (03) 5236 3479. *Otway Estate Winery and Brewery:* tasting plates and more; 10–30 Hoveys Rd, Barongarook; (03) 5233 8400.

Central Caravan Park: 50 Bruce St; (03) 5231 3586. *Duffs Cottage Fine Accommodation:* 41 Gellibrand St; 0457 140 349. *Colac Caravan & Cabin Park:* 490 Princes Hwy, Colac West; (03) 5231 5337. *Elliminook:* 585 Warncoort Birregurra Rd, Birregurra; (03) 5236 2080. *Otways Tourist Park:* 25 Main Rd, Gellibrand River; (03) 5235 8357.

Red Rock Lookout The lookout features a reserve with picnic and barbecue facilities, plus spectacular views across 30 volcanic lakes, including Lake Corangamite, Victoria's largest saltwater lake. At the base of the lookout is the Red Rock Winery. Near Alvie; 22 km N. The Volcano Discovery Trail goes from Colac to Millicent in SA, and follows the history of volcanic activity in the region; details from visitor centre.

Old Beechy Rail Trail: 45 km trail that follows one of the state's former narrow-gauge railway lines from Colac to Beech Forest, suitable for walkers and cyclists. The trail starts at Colac railway station; details from visitor centre. *Art and craft galleries:* at Barongarook (12 km SE); details from visitor centre. *Burtons Lookout:* features Otway Estate Winery and Brewery with its well-known Prickly Moses ale range, views of the Otways;

VICTORIA

13 km s. *Tarndwarncoort Homestead:* wool displays and sales; off Warncoort Cemetery Rd; 15 km E. *Birregurra:* township located at the foot of the Otway Ranges and the edge of volcanic plains; 20 km E. *Forrest:* old timber and logging town in the Otway Ranges; 32 km SE. Attractions nearby include fishing, walking and picnics at the West Barwon Reservoir (2 km s), or spotting a platypus at Lake Elizabeth, formed by a landslide in 1952 (5 km SE).

TOWNS NEARBY: Winchelsea 36 km, Camperdown 40 km, Lorne 41 km, Apollo Bay 47 km, Aireys Inlet 47 km

Coleraine

Pop. 992
Map ref. 550 E3

 Lonsdale St, Hamilton; 1800 807 056; www.sthgrampians.vic.gov.au

94.1 FM ABC Local Radio, 99.3 Coastal FM

Situated in Victoria's Western District, Coleraine is a small, picturesque town supported by wool and beef industries. A chocolate factory, the ultimate native garden and vintage cars are just a few of the intriguing prospects that await in Coleraine.

Peter Francis Points Arboretum Two thousand species of native flora are found here, including 500 species of eucalyptus. 'The Points' sprawls up the hillside behind the town, with great views from the top, on Portland–Coleraine Rd. In town is the Eucalyptus Discovery Centre, designed to complement the arboretum and give an insight into the natural history and commercial applications of eucalypts. Whyte St.

Glenelg Fine Confectionery: immerse yourself in the rich aroma of German-style continental chocolates; tastings available; Whyte St. *Historic Railway Station:* also site of the visitor centre, it displays and sells local arts and crafts; Pilleau St. *Coleraine Classic Cars:* open by appt; Whyte St.

Tour of Southern Grampians Cycling: Apr. *Coleraine Cup:* Sept.

Coleraine Caravan Park: 4 Winter St; (03) 5575 2268.

Bochara Wines: wine-tasting available Fri–Sun; Glenelg Hwy. *Glacier Ridge Redgum:* gallery of wooden products for sale; open by appt. *Balmoral:* historic township west of the Grampians; 49 km N. Nearby features include the Glendinning Homestead, just east of town, with gardens and a wildlife sanctuary. The town is also the gateway to Rocklands Reservoir, for watersports and fishing, and Black Range State Park, for bushwalking. It also holds the Balmoral Annual Show in Mar.

TOWNS NEARBY: Casterton 26 km, Hamilton 34 km, Dunkeld 58 km, Edenhope 71 km, Penola (SA) 80 km

Corryong

Pop. 1229
Map ref. 520 A8 | 543 O7 | 545 O3

 50 Hanson St; (02) 6076 2277; www.pureuppermurrayvalleys.com

88.7 FM Radio Upper Murray, 99.7 FM ABC Local Radio

Welcome to authentic 'Man from Snowy River' country. This district offers superb mountain scenery and excellent trout fishing in the Murray River and its tributaries, with the town being known as the home and final resting place of Jack Riley, the original 'Man from Snowy River'. A life-size statue depicting 'that terrible descent' made famous by Banjo Paterson's poem sits in the town. An annual festival honours Riley's memory with a feature event called the 'Challenge' to find his modern-day

equivalent. Corryong is also the Victorian gateway to Kosciuszko National Park across the New South Wales border.

The Man from Snowy River Folk Museum Banjo Paterson's poem evoked the lives of the High Country's settlers. This charming museum proudly does the same, with local exhibits, memorabilia and photos depicting the hardships of local life, as well as a unique collection of historic skis. Hanson St.

Jack Riley's grave: Corryong cemetery. *Man from Snowy River Statue:* Hanson St. *Large wooden galleon:* Murray Valley Hwy. *Playle's Hill Lookout:* for a great view of the township; Donaldson St.

Towong Cup: Sat long weekend in Mar. *The Man from Snowy River Bush Festival:* music, art and horsemanship challenges; Apr. *Upper Murray Challenge:* 1st Sat in Oct. *Corryong Pro Rodeo:* New Year's Eve.

Corryong Bed and Breakfast: 148 Harris St; (02) 6076 1268. *The Miners Cottage:* 93 Hansen St; (02) 6076 1066. *Mother Hubbard's B & B:* 57 Donaldson St; (02) 6076 1570. *Mt Mittamatite Caravan Park:* Murray Valley Hwy; (02) 6076 1152. *Clearwater by the Murray:* 17 Tintaldra Back Rd, Tintaldra; (02) 6077 9207. *Colac Colac Caravan Park:* 1994 Murray Valley Hwy, Colac; (02) 6076 1520. *Jemba Rock B&B:* 10645 Murray River Rd, Walwa; (02) 6077 9236.

Burrowa–Pine Mountain National Park Pine Mountain is one of Australia's largest monoliths. Mt Burrowa is home to wet-forest plants and unique wildlife, including wombats and gliders. Both mountains provide excellent and diverse opportunities for bushwalkers, campers, climbers and birdwatchers. The Cudgewa Bluff Falls offer fabulous scenery and bushwalking. Contact Parks Victoria on 13 1963; main access is from the Cudgewa–Tintaldra Rd, which runs off Murray Valley Hwy; 27 km W.

Khancoban This NSW town was built by the Snowy Hydro for workers on the hydro-electric scheme. Its willow- and poplar-lined streets, historic rose garden and mountains give the town a European feel. Huge trout are caught in Khancoban Pondage. Nearby, Murray 1 Power Station Visitor Centre reveals the workings of this 10-turbine station. South, along Alpine Way through Kosciuszko National Park, is the spectacular Scammell's Spur Lookout and historic Geehi Hut. 32 km E.

Nariel: Nariel Creek is a good spot for trout fishing. The town hosts the Nariel Creek Folk Music Festival each Dec; 8 km SW. *Towong:* historic Towong Racecourse is where scenes from *Phar Lap* were filmed. Gangster Squizzy Taylor also once stole the takings; 12 km E. *Lookouts:* lookout with views over Kosciuszko National Park at Towong, 12 km NE; Embery's Lookout over Mt Mittamatite, 16 km N. *Walwa:* hire canoes and mountain bikes from Upper Murray Holiday Resort and Winery; 47 km NW. *Touring routes:* Murray River Rd, Lakeside Loop, Mitta Valley Loop; details from visitor centre.

TOWNS NEARBY: Khancoban (NSW) 21 km, Tumbarumba (NSW) 48 km, Thredbo (NSW) 50 km, Tallangatta 65 km, Jindabyne (NSW) 69 km

Cowes

see inset box on page 158

Creswick

Pop. 2487
Map ref. 535 C9 | 536 D2 | 551 M3

 1 Raglan St; (03) 5345 1114; www.creswick.net

99.9 VoiceFM, 107.9 FM ABC Local Radio

Creswick is an attractive and historic town, a symbol of the rich and heady life of the gold-rush days of the 1850s. Unfortunately, the goldmining also decimated the surrounding forests. Today the town is surrounded by pine plantations over 100 years old; they exist thanks to the initiative and foresight of local pioneer John La Gerche and – while they are no replacement for the Australian bush – they have given Creswick the title of 'the home of forestry'. Creswick was the birthplace of renowned Australian artist Norman Lindsay, many of whose paintings can be seen in the local historical museum.

 Historic walk: self-guide tour, map from visitor centre. **Giant Mullock Heaps:** indicate how deep mines went; Ullina Rd. **Creswick Museum:** photos and memorabilia from the town's goldmining past as well as an exhibition of Lindsay paintings; open Sun, public holidays or by appt; Albert St. **Gold Battery:** est. 1897; Battery Cres. **Creswick Woollen Mills:** last coloured woollen mill of its type in Australia; offers product sales, regular demonstrations and exhibitions; Railway Pde.

Makers Market: 1st Sun each month. **CALCAN Market:** 3rd Sat each month. **Forestry Fiesta:** Oct.

Harvest 383: regional produce menu; Novotel Forest Resort Creswick, 1500 Midland Hwy; (03) 5345 9600.

Creswick Regional Park After La Gerche replanted the denuded hills around Creswick in the 1890s, the state established a nursery that it continues to operate today. Further natural history can be explored on the various walking trails, including the 30 min Landcare Trail or the longer La Gerche Forest Walk. Visit St Georges Lake, once a mining dam and now popular for picnics and watersports, and Koala Park, an old breeding ground for koalas that was highly unsuccessful (they escaped over the fences). Slaty Creek is great for gold panning or picnics, with abundant birdlife. The park stretches east and south-east of town. Contact Parks Victoria on 13 1963 or the Creswick Landcare Centre, located within the park, on (03) 5345 2200.

Tangled Maze: a maze formed by climbing plants; 5 km E. **Smeaton:** pretty little town with the historic Smeaton House, the Tuki Trout Farm and Anderson's Mill; 16 km NE.

TOWNS NEARBY: Ballarat 16 km, Clunes 17 km, Daylesford 24 km, Maryborough 44 km, Castlemaine 49 km

Daylesford
see inset box on page 161

Dimboola
Pop. 1493
Map ref. 548 F8

i Dim E-Shop, 109–111 Lloyd St; (03) 5389 1588; www.hindmarsh.vic.gov.au

96.5 Triple H FM, 594 AM ABC Local Radio

Dimboola, on the Wimmera River, is a key access point to the Little Desert National Park. The area was home to the Wotjobaluk Aboriginal people until the first European settlers arrived. The district was known as 'Nine Creeks' because of the many little streams that appear when the river recedes after floods. Many of the early white settlers were German.

 Historic buildings: include the mechanics institute in Lloyd St and the Victoria Hotel, a grand 2-storey structure with grapevines hanging from the verandahs (cnr Wimmera and Victoria sts). **Walking track:** follows a scenic stretch of the

Wimmera River. The track can be followed all the way to the Horseshoe Bend camping ground in the Little Desert National Park 7 km away; details of walks from visitor centre.

Little Desert National Park This park covers 132 647 ha. The eastern block (the section nearest to Dimboola) has picnic and camping facilities and good walking tracks. The park does not resemble the typical desert – it contains extensive heathlands and, during spring, more than 600 varieties of wildflowers and over 40 types of ground orchids. The park is home to the distinctive mallee fowl, and the large ground-nests built by the male birds can be seen during breeding season. Kangaroos, possums and bearded dragons are just some of the other wildlife that inhabit the park. 6 km SW. *See also Nhill.*

Pink Lake: a salt lake that reflects a deep pinkish colour, particularly impressive at sunset, but has dried up in recent years; 9 km NW. **Ebenezer Mission Station:** founded in 1859 in an attempt to bring Christianity to the local Aboriginal people. The site contains fascinating ruins of the original buildings, a cemetery and a restored limestone church; off the Dimboola–Jeparit Rd; 15 km N. **Kiata Lowan Sanctuary:** the first part of Little Desert National Park to be reserved, in 1955. Home to the mallee fowl; Kiata; 26 km W.

TOWNS NEARBY: Horsham 32 km, Natimuk 32 km, Jeparit 35 km, Nhill 37 km, Warracknabeal 39 km

Donald
Pop. 1429
Map ref. 526 F12 | 549 J7

i Council Offices, cnr Houston and McCulloch sts; (03) 5497 1300.

96.5 Triple H FM, 99.1 FM ABC Local Radio

Donald is on the scenic Richardson River and referred to by locals as 'Home of the Duck', owing to the many waterbirds that live in the region. The town also features Bullocks Head, a tree on the riverbank with a growth that looks like its namesake. The 'bull' is also used as a flood gauge – according to how high the waters are, the 'bull' is either dipping his feet, having a drink or, when the water is really high, going for a swim.

 Bullocks Head Lookout: beside Richardson River; Byrne St. **Steam Train Park:** a restored steam locomotive, an adventure playground and barbecue facilities; Cnr Hammill and Walker sts. **Historic Police Station:** dates back to 1865; Wood St. **Shepherds hut:** built by early settlers; Wood St. **Agricultural Museum:** an impressive collection of agricultural machinery; Hammill St. **Scilleys Island:** reserve on the Richardson River featuring wildlife, walking tracks and picnic facilities; access by footbridge from Sunraysia Hwy. **Kooka's Country Cookies:** tours and sales; Sunraysia Hwy.

Scottish Dancing Country Weekend: June. **Donald Cup:** Nov.

Lake Buloke The lake is filled by the floodwaters of the Richardson River, so its size varies greatly with the seasons. This extensive wetland area is home to a variety of birdlife and is a popular venue for fishing, picnicking and bushwalking. The end of the park closest to town is a protected bird sanctuary. 10 km N.

Fishing There is good fishing for redfin and trout in the many waterways close to town. Good spots include Lake Cope Cope, 10 km S; Lake Batyo Catyo and Richardson River Weir, both

continued on p. 159

VICTORIA

COWES

Pop. 4217
Map ref. 533 L10 | 537 K11 | 540 D8

ⓘ 895 Phillip Island Tourist Rd, Newhaven; (03) 5956 7447 or 1300 366 422; www.visitphillipisland.com

89.1 3MFM South Gippsland, 774 AM ABC Local Radio

Situated on the north side of Phillip Island, Cowes is its major town. It is linked to the Mornington Peninsula by a passenger ferry service to Stony Point and by road to Melbourne via the San Remo bridge. The Cowes foreshore offers fantastic coastal walks and safe swimming beaches, with the focal point being the town's jetty. It is a popular fishing spot, as well as a departure point for several ferries. Seal-watching cruises to Seal Rocks operate from the jetty and are the best way to see the fascinating fur seals close-up. A major drawcard for the island is the International Motorcycle Grand Prix, which has been held since 1928. There is an abundance of other activities and events that attract 3.5 million visitors to Phillip Island each year. All are within easy reach of Cowes.

Seal-watching cruises: depart from the jetty to Seal Rocks; bookings on 1300 763 739.

Market: crafts and second-hand goods; Settlement Rd, Cowes; each Sun. *Farmers market:* Churchill Island; 4th Sat each month. *World Superbike Championships:* Grand Prix Circuit; Feb/Mar. *Churchill Island Heritage Farms Easter Fun:* farm show; Easter. *Australian Motorcycle Grand Prix:* Grand Prix Circuit; Oct. *V8 Supercars:* Grand Prix Circuit; Sept.

Harry's on the Esplanade: waterfront dining; Shop 5, 17 The Esplanade; (03) 5952 6226. *Hotel Phillip Island:* casual bistro dining; 11–13 The Esplanade; (03) 5952 2060. *Infused:* modern Australian; 115 Thompson Ave; (03) 5952 2655. *Foreshore Bar and Restaurant:* seafront gastropub dining; 11 Beach Rd, Rhyll; (03) 5956 9520.

A Maze 'N Things Holiday Park: 1805 Phillip Island Rd; (03) 5952 2020. *Anchor Belle Holiday Park:* 272 Church St; (03) 5952 2258. *Beach Park Tourist Caravan Park:* 2 McKenzie Rd; (03) 5952 2113. *Cowes Caravan Park:* 1654 Church St; (03) 5952 2211. *Silver Waters Bed & Breakfast:* 9 Gordon St; (03) 5952 5509. *Hill of Content:* 33 Rhyll–Newhaven Rd, Rhyll; (03) 5956 9197. *San Remo Holiday Park:* 4 Mary Gr, San Remo; (03) 5678 5220.

Penguin Parade The nightly penguin parade is Phillip Island's most popular attraction. During this world-famous event, little penguins emerge from the sea after a tiring fishing expedition and cross Summerland Beach to their homes in the dunes. Tours run at sunset each night, and the penguins can be spotted from the boardwalks and viewing platforms. The site also has an interactive visitor centre with fascinating details about these adorable creatures. Note that no cameras are allowed beyond the visitor centre. Bookings on (03) 5951 2800; 12 km sw.

The Nobbies Centre and Seal Rocks An interactive centre gives visitors an insight into local marine life, including Australia's largest colony of Australian fur seals via cameras that you can control yourself. Outside, the island features a cliff-side boardwalk with views of the fantastic natural landmark The Nobbies and out to Seal Rocks. Walk around to the Blowhole to hear the thunderous noise of huge waves and look out for the nesting sites of vast colonies of seagulls and short-tailed shearwaters that migrate to the island annually. Informative displays explain each natural attraction. Ventnor Rd; 15 km sw.

Phillip Island Wildlife Park: features native fauna, with visitors able to handfeed kangaroos and wallabies; Phillip Island Rd; (03) 5952 2038; 3 km s. *Koala Conservation Centre:* view these lovely creatures in their natural habitat from an elevated boardwalk; Phillip Island Rd; (03) 5951 2800; 5 km se. *Grand Prix Circuit:* the circuit is steeped in both old and recent history, which is detailed thoroughly in the visitor centre. You can also go go-karting on a replica of the Grand Prix track; Back Beach Rd; (03) 5952 9400; 6 km s. *A Maze 'N Things:* family fun park featuring a large timber maze, optical-illusion rooms and 'maxigolf'; Phillip Island Rd; 6 km se. *Rhyll Inlet:* wetlands of international significance, with the marshes and mangroves providing an important breeding ground for wading birds. There are various loop walks, as well as an excellent view from the Conservation Hill Observation Tower; 7 km e. *Rhyll Trout & Bush Tucker Farm:* fish for rainbow trout in the indoor Rainforest Pool, take a fishing lesson or wander around the self-guide bush tucker trail; open 10am–5pm; 36 Rhyll Newhaven Rd, Rhyll; (03) 5956 9255. *Wineries:* Philip Island Vineyard and Winery offers tastings, sales and casual dining; Berrys Beach Rd; (03) 5956 8465; 7 km sw. Purple Hen Wines also offers tastings and light meals; McFees Rd, Rhyll; (03) 5956 9244; 9 km se. *Churchill Island:* a road bridge provides access to this protected parkland, which features a historic homestead, a walking track and abundant birdlife; 16 km se. *National Vietnam Veterans Museum:* details the history of Australian involvement in the Vietnam War, displays around 6000 artefacts; 25 Veterans Dr, Newhaven; (03) 5956 6400; 16 km se. *Phillip Island Chocolate Factory:* visit Panny's Amazing World of Chocolate with information on the chocolate-making process and a model of Dame Edna made

[LITTLE PENGUINS, PHILLIP ISLAND]

from 12 000 chocolate pieces; visitors can even make their own chocolate; Newhaven; (03) 5956 6600; 16 km SE. *Pelicans:* see these unusual birds up close, with feeding time daily at 12pm; San Remo Pier (opposite the Fishing Co-op); 17 km SE. *Cape Woolamai:* the beach is renowned for its fierce and exciting surf (patrolled in season). From the beach there are a number of 2–4 hr loop walks, many to the southern end of the cape

and passing the Pinnacles rock formations on the way. South of Cape Woolamai township; 18 km SE. *Wildlife Wonderland:* centre includes the Earthworm Museum, a giant earthworm and Wombat World; (03) 5678 2222; 31 km E.

TOWNS NEARBY: Flinders 19 km, Mornington 31 km, Wonthaggi 35 km, Koo-Wee-Rup 36 km, Sorrento 45 km

20 km S; Watchem Lake, 35 km N; and the Avoca River, which runs through Charlton, 43 km NE.

Mt Jeffcott: flora, kangaroos and views over Lake Buloke; 20 km NE.

TOWNS NEARBY: St Arnaud 37 km, Wycheproof 39 km, Warracknabeal 54 km, Wedderburn 57 km, Stawell 78 km

Drysdale

Pop. 10 217
Map ref. 531 A9 | 532 D4 | 536 G8 | 540 A6 | 551 O7

i Queenscliff Visitor Information Centre, 55 Hesse St, Queenscliff; (03) 5258 4843; www.visitgreatoceanroad.org.au

94.7 The Pulse FM, 774 AM ABC Local Radio

Drysdale, situated on the Bellarine Peninsula, is primarily a service centre for the local farming community. The town is close to the beaches of Port Phillip Bay and there are a number of wineries in the area, including the delightful Spray Farm Winery. Drysdale is now considered a satellite town of Geelong, yet retains a charming, holiday-resort atmosphere.

Old Courthouse: home of the Bellarine Historical Society; High St. *Drysdale Community Crafts:* High St.

Celtic Festival: June. *Community Market:* at the reserve on Duke St; 3rd Sun each month Sept–Apr.

Loam Restaurant: local-produce menu; 650 Andersons Rd; (03) 5251 1101. *The Ol' Duke Hotel:* contemporary cuisine; 40 Newcombe St, Portarlington; (03) 5259 1250. *Port Pier Cafe:* casual Spanish; 6 Pier St, Portarlington; (03) 5259 1080.

Bellarine Bayside Holiday Parks – Anderson Reserve: The Esplanade (opposite Pigdon St), Indented Head; (03) 5259 2764. *Bellarine Bayside Holiday Parks – Batman Park:* The Esplanade (opposite Helen St), Indented Head; (03) 5259 2764. *Bellarine Bayside Holiday Parks – Portarlington:* Boat Rd (off Sproat St), Portarlington; (03) 5259 2764. *Bellarine Bayside Holiday Parks – St Leonards Area 3:* Bluff Rd, St Leonards; (03) 5259 2764. *Bellarine Bayside Holiday Parks – Taylor Reserve:* The Esplanade (opposite Batman Rd), Indented Head; (03) 5259 2764. *Bellarine Day Spa @ Portarlington Cedar Lodge:* Cnr Tower Rd and Oxley St, Portarlington; (03) 5259 1760. *Dylene Caravan Park:* 5 Mercer St, Portarlington; (03) 5259 2873. *Pelican Sands Bed & Breakfast:* 149 Pt Richards Rd, Portarlington; 0409 424 462. *St Leonards Caravan Park:* 99 Leviens Rd, St Leonards; (03) 5257 1490.

 Bellarine wine region For over 150 years vines have been grown on the Bellarine Peninsula, and most vineyards here today remain family owned and operated. Owing to the peninsula's varying soil conditions, a range of white and red wines are produced. Many wineries in the area offer cellar-door tastings and sales. These include the historic Spray Farm Winery, which runs the summer concert series each Feb and Mar, known as A Day on the Green, in a natural amphitheatre. Great views to the sea can be had from Scotchmans Hill Winery. Winery map from visitor centre.

Bellarine Peninsula Railway: steam-train rides from Queenscliff to Drysdale and return; *see Queenscliff. Lake Lorne picnic area:* 1 km SW. *Portarlington:* a popular seaside resort town with a restored flour mill featuring displays of agricultural history, a safe bay for children to swim in and fresh mussels for sale near the pier. There is a market at Parks Hall, last Sun each month; 10 km NE. *St Leonards:* a small beach resort, which includes Edwards Point Wildlife Reserve, a memorial commemorating the landing of Matthew Flinders in 1802 and of John Batman in 1835; 14 km E.

TOWNS NEARBY: Ocean Grove 11 km, Queenscliff 13 km, Barwon Heads 14 km, Geelong 19 km, Sorrento 24 km

Dunkeld

Pop. 400
Map ref. 550 G4

i Lonsdale St, Hamilton; 1800 807 056; www.sthgrampians.vic.gov.au

94.1 FM ABC Local Radio, 99.3 Coastal FM

Dunkeld is considered the southern gateway to the Grampians, and its natural beauty has long been recognised since the explorer Major Thomas Mitchell camped here in 1836. It was originally named Mount Sturgeon after the mountain that towers over the town. Both Mount Sturgeon and Mount Abrupt (to the north of town) have been renamed to recognise the ancient Aboriginal heritage of the landscape; they are now known as Mount Wuragarri and Mount Murdadjoog respectively.

Dunkeld Arboretum Exotic species from all over the world have been planted. Ideal for walking, cycling, fishing and picnics. Old Ararat Rd.

Historical Museum Housed in an old church, the museum features displays on the history of the local Aboriginal people, the wool industry and the journeys of explorer Major Mitchell. It also offers dining and accommodation. Open weekends or by appt; Templeton St.

Corea Wines: open by appt. *Varrenti Wines:* open 12–5pm; Blackwood Rd. *Sandra Kranz Art Studio:* Glass St. *Waiting Room Art Gallery:* Parker St. *Bushwalking:* walking trails include Mt Abrupt, Mt Sturgeon and the Piccaninny Walk.

 Dunkeld Cup: Nov. *Arts Festival:* biennial, Nov.

VICTORIA

Dunkeld Gourmet Pantry: cafe and provedore; 109 Parker St (Glenelg Hwy); (03) 5577 2288. *Royal Mail Hotel:* outstanding contemporary menu, exceptional wine list; 98 Parker St (Glenelg Hwy); (03) 5577 2241.

Grampians National Park The southern section of the park includes Victoria Valley Rd, a scenic drive that stops at Freshwater Lake Reserve (8 km N), popular for picnics. Also near Dunkeld are various hiking destinations and the Chimney Pots, a formation popular for rock climbing; access via Henty Hwy. *For further details on the park see Halls Gap.*

Grampians Pure Sheep Dairy: sample some of the sheep milk, yoghurts and cheeses while also watching how they are made; Glenelg Hwy.

TOWNS NEARBY: Hamilton 30 km, Coleraine 58 km, Halls Gap 59 km, Ararat 66 km, Stawell 76 km

Dunolly

Pop. 605
Map ref. 535 C4 | 549 M10

i 109 Broadway; (03) 5468 1205.

91.1 FM ABC Local Radio, 99.1 Goldfields FM

The towns of Dunolly, Wedderburn and Inglewood formed the rich goldfield region colloquially known in the 1850s as the 'Golden Triangle'. The district has produced more gold nuggets than any other goldfield in Australia, with 126 unearthed in Dunolly itself. The 'Welcome Stranger', considered to be the largest nugget ever discovered, was found 15 kilometres northwest of Dunolly, at Moliagul.

Restored courthouse: offers a display relating to gold discoveries in the area; open Sat afternoons; Market St. *Original lock-up and stables:* viewable from street only; Market St. *Gold-themed tours of the region:* include gold panning in local creeks; details from visitor centre.

Market: with local produce, crafts and second-hand goods; Market St; 3rd Sat each month. *Community Street Market:* Broadway; 4th Sat each month.

Laanecoorie Lakeside Park: 58 Brownbill Reserve Rd, Laanecoorie; (03) 5435 7303.

Moliagul: the Welcome Stranger Discovery Walk leads to a monument where the Welcome Stranger nugget was found in 1869. Moliagul is also the birthplace of Rev. John Flynn, founder of the Royal Flying Doctor Service; 15 km NW. *Laanecoorie Reservoir:* a great spot for swimming, boating and waterskiing, water levels permitting, with camping and picnic facilities; 16 km E. *Tarnagulla:* a small mining town with splendid Victorian architecture and a flora reserve nearby; 16 km NE. *Bealiba:* hosts a market 2nd Sun each month; 21 km NW.

TOWNS NEARBY: Maryborough 21 km, Maldon 33 km, Inglewood 34 km, Avoca 34 km, Clunes 48 km

Echuca

Pop. 12 361
Map ref. 527 J12 | 542 C5

i 2 Heygarth St; (03) 5480 7555 or 1800 804 446; www.echucamoama.com

91.1 FM ABC Local Radio, 104.7 Radio EMFM

Visitors to this delightful town are transported back in time by the sight of beautiful old paddleboats cruising down the Murray River. The town is at the junction of the Murray, Campaspe and Goulburn rivers. Once Australia's largest inland port, its name comes from an Aboriginal word meaning 'meeting of the waters'. A historic iron bridge joins Echuca to Moama, in New South Wales.

Port of Echuca The massive red-gum wharf has been restored to the grandeur of its heyday, with huge paddlesteamers anchored here. Cruises are available on many boats, including the paddlesteamer *Pevensey,* renamed *Philadelphia* for the TV miniseries *All the Rivers Run;* the D26 logging barge; PS *Alexander Arbuthnot;* and PS *Adelaide.* Cruises are also available on PS *Canberra, Pride of the Murray* and PS *Emmylou.* The MV *Mary Ann* also features a fine restaurant.

Historic buildings: many along Murray Espl including the Star Hotel, with an underground bar and escape tunnel, and the Bridge Hotel, built by Henry Hopwood, the founder of Echuca, who ran the original punt service. *Red Gum Works:* wood-turning demonstrations; Murray Espl. *Sharp's Magic Movie House and Penny Arcade:* award-winning attractions; Murray Espl. *Echuca Historical Society Museum:* housed in former police station; open 11am–3pm daily; High St. *Billabong Carriages:* Murray Espl. *National Holden Museum:* Warren St.

Southern 80 Ski Race: from Torrumbarry Weir to Echuca; Feb. *Riverboats, Jazz, Food and Wine Festival:* Feb. *Steam, Horse and Vintage Rally:* June. *Winter Blues Festival:* July. *Port of Echuca Steam Heritage Festival:* Oct.

Ceres: appealing modern menu; 554 High St; (03) 5482 5599. *Left Bank:* modern bistro; 551 High St; (03) 5480 3772. *Oscar W's Wharfside:* modern Australian; 101 Murray Espl; (03) 5482 5133. *PS Emmylou:* set-price three-course dinner aboard reproduction paddlesteamer; Murray River Paddlesteamers, 57 Murray Espl; (03) 5482 5244.

Cadell Bed & Breakfast: 12 Tyler St; (03) 5482 1163. *Coriander Bed & Breakfast:* 8473 Northern Hwy; (03) 5480 1254. *Echuca Holiday Park:* 52 Crofton St; (03) 5482 2157. *Steampacket Inn B&B:* 37 Murray Esp; (03) 5482 3411. *A Shady River Holiday Park – Aspen Parks:* Merool La, Moama, NSW; (03) 5482 5500. *All the Rivers Run Caravan Park:* Headworks Rd, Torrumbarry; (03) 5487 7321. *Barmah Caravan Park:* Murray St, Barmah; (03) 5869 3225. *Maiden's Inn Holiday Park – Aspen Parks:* Deniliquin St, Moama, NSW; (03) 5480 9253. *Merool On The Murray:* 131 Merool Rd, Moama, NSW; (03) 5480 9111. *Moama Riverside Caravan Park:* Cobb Hwy, Moama, NSW; (03) 5482 3241. *Morning Glory River Resort:* Gilmour Rd, Moama, NSW; (03) 5869 3357. *Murray River Holiday Park – Aspen Parks:* 2 Blair St, Moama, NSW; (03) 5480 9899. *Torrumbarry Weir Holiday Park:* 835 Weir Rd, Torrumbarry; (03) 5487 7277. *Yarraby Holiday Park – Aspen Parks:* 75 River Ave, Echuca Village; (03) 5482 1533.

 Barmah National Park This park combines with NSW's Millewa forest to form the largest river red gum forest in the world. Nearby are Barmah Lakes, a good location for fishing and swimming. Canoes and barbecue pontoons are available for hire. Walking trails take in various Aboriginal sites, and the Dharnya Centre interprets the culture of the local Yorta Yorta people. Ulupna Island, in the eastern section of the park (near Strathmerton), has river beaches, camping and a large population of koalas. Barmah Muster, a festival celebrating Barmah's drovers, is held in the park in Apr. Contact Parks Victoria on 13 1963; 39 km NE.

continued on p. 162

DAYLESFORD

Pop. 3071
Map ref. 535 E8 | 536 E1 | 551 N3

ℹ 98 Vincent St; (03) 5321 6123; www.visitdaylesford.com

99.9 VoiceFM, 107.9 FM ABC Local Radio

Daylesford is at the centre of Victoria's spa country. The area developed with the discovery of gold, which lured many Swiss–Italian settlers, but it was the discovery of natural mineral springs that proved a more lasting attraction. Of the 72 documented springs in the area, the most famous are nearby Hepburn Springs. The water is rich with minerals that dissolve into it as it flows from the crest of the Great Dividing Range through underground rocks, and it is known for its rejuvenating and healing qualities. Daylesford has grown as a destination in itself, complete with beautiful gardens, interesting shopping, great eating and a huge range of accommodation. The streets are lined with trees that blaze with colour in autumn, and inside the attractive old buildings are restaurants, cafes, galleries, bookshops, bakeries and chocolate shops. Overlooking the lake is one of regional Victoria's most highly regarded restaurants, the Lake House.

Convent Gallery A magnificent building surrounded by delightful cottage gardens, this former convent and girls school has been restored and features an impressive collection of artwork, sculptures and jewellery. A cafe serves local produce and Devonshire tea. Open 10am–5pm; Cnr Hill and Daly sts; (03) 5348 3211.

Historical Museum: features a collection of photographs from the region's past and artefacts from the local Djadja Wurrung people; open weekends and public and school holidays; Vincent St; (03) 5348 1453. *Lake Daylesford:* a lovely spot for picnics,

with paddleboats and rowboats for hire in the warmer months. The Tipperary walking track starts here and ends at the Mineral Springs Reserve. Access to lake is from Bleakly Rd. *Wombat Hill Botanical Gardens:* established in 1861, these lovely gardens are situated on the hill overlooking town; Central Springs Rd. *Daylesford Spa Country Train:* leaves railway station for Bullarto (11 km SE) each Sun; Raglan St; (03) 5348 1759.

✹ *Market:* for arts, crafts and local produce; Sun morning; Raglan St, near railway station. *Silver Streak Champagne Train:* train journey with gourmet food; 1st Sat each month; bookings 0421 780 100. *Hepburn Swiss–Italian Festival:* Apr/May. *Highland Gathering:* Dec.

✕ *The Farmers Arms Hotel:* hearty rustic dishes; 1 East St; (03) 5348 2091. *Frangos & Frangos:* city-chic European menu; 82 Vincent St; (03) 5348 2363. *Lake House:* exceptional regional dining; King St; (03) 5348 3329. *Mercato @ Daylesford:* modern Italian; 32 Raglan St; (03) 5348 4488. *Cosy Corner:* quaint eatery; 3 Tenth St, Hepburn Springs; (03) 5348 2576.

🛏 *Balconies Daylesford:* 35 Perrins St; (03) 5348 1322. *Daylesford Victoria Caravan Park:* Ballan Rd; (03) 5348 3821. *Goldmine Cottage:* 71 Duke St; (03) 5348 2171. *Jubilee Lake Holiday Park:* 151 Lake Rd; (03) 5348 2186. *Station House Daylesford:* 15 Raglan St; (03) 5348 1591. *Azidene House:* 68 Central Springs Rd; (03) 5348 1140.

⊘ **Hepburn Springs spas** The Hepburn Spa and Bathhouse Wellness Retreat offers pure mineral water spas and hydrotherapy, massage therapies and an extensive range of relaxation, health and beauty treatments. Mineral Springs Cres, Hepburn Springs; (03) 5348 8888. Dating back to 1894, the recently renovated Hepburn Bathhouse has state-of-the-art communal and private mineral bathing, spas and therapies utilising the renowned local mineral springs, plus a day spa for massage, facials and indulgent beauty treatments. Mineral Springs Reserve Rd, Hepburn Springs; (03) 5321 6000; 4 km N.

Lavandula Swiss Italian Farm A sprawling estate featuring fields of lavender, cottage gardens and sales of lavender-based products. The Lavandula Harvest Festival is a popular event with a variety of family entertainment, held in Jan. Open daily, winter months weekends only; Shepherds Flat; (03) 5476 4393; 10 km N.

Hepburn Regional Park: located around Daylesford and Hepburn Springs, this park features goldmining relics, mineral springs and the impressive Mt Franklin, an extinct volcano, with panoramic views from the summit and picnic, barbecue and camping facilities around the base. There are good walking tracks. *Waterfalls:* several in area, including Sailors Falls, 5 km S; Loddon Falls, 10 km NE; Trentham Falls, 21 km SE. *Breakneck Gorge:* early goldmining site; 5 km N. *Glenlyon:* small town that hosts the popular Glenlyon Sports Day on New Year's Day, and the Fine Food and Wine Fayre in July; 8 km NE. *Lyonville Mineral Springs:* picnic and barbecue facilities; 15 km SE. *Yandoit:* historic Swiss–Italian settlement; 18 km NW.

TOWNS NEARBY: Creswick 24 km, Kyneton 29 km, Castlemaine 31 km, Clunes 32 km, Woodend 34 km

[LAKE HOUSE RESTAURANT]

 RADIO STATIONS   IN TOWN   WHAT'S ON   WHERE TO EAT   WHERE TO STAY   NEARBY

Moama: attractions include the Silverstone Go-Kart Track and the Horseshoe Lagoon nature reserve; 2 km N. *Mathoura:* set among the mighty red gums, Mathoura is a charming Murray town over the NSW border. Fishing is popular, with sites including Gulpa Creek and the Edward and Murray rivers. To see the forest in its splendour, take the Moira Forest Walkway or, for that authentic Murray River experience, visit nearby Picnic Pt, popular for camping, picnics, waterskiing and fishing; 40 km N. *Nathalia:* a town on Broken Creek with many historic buildings. Walking tracks along the creek take in fishing spots, old homesteads and a lookout; 57 km E.

TOWNS NEARBY: Rochester 25 km, Rushworth 55 km, Pyramid Hill 58 km, Cohuna 61 km, Shepparton 64 km

Edenhope
Pop. 787
Map ref. 548 C11 | 568 H9

ⓘ 96 Elizabeth St; (03) 5585 1509; www.westwimmera.vic.gov.au

94.1 FM ABC Local Radio, 96.5 Triple H FM

Just 30 kilometres from the South Australian border, Edenhope is set on the shores of Lake Wallace, a haven for waterbirds. The town is renowned as the site where, in 1868, Australia's first all-Aboriginal cricket team trained – their coach was T. W. Wills, who went on to establish Australian Rules football. A cairn in Lake Street honours the achievements of this early cricket team.

Edenhope Antiques: offers an extensive variety of antique wares; Elizabeth St. *Bennetts Bakery:* Elizabeth St. *Lake Wallace:* walking tracks and birdwatching hides; Wimmera Hwy.

Henley-on-Lake Wallace Festival: with market and family entertainment; Feb. *Races:* Mar long weekend.

Glendara Cottage: 1484 Mooree Culla Rd, Culla; (03) 5583 1503.

Harrow One of Victoria's oldest inland towns, Harrow has many historic buildings in Main St, including the Hermitage Hotel, the police station and an early log gaol. The Johnny Mullagh Cricket Centre, a celebration of the first Australian Aboriginal cricketer to travel overseas, is also located in town. Kelly's Garage and Transport Museum in Main St is popular with car enthusiasts, and the National Bush Billycart Championship is held here in Mar. 32 km SE.

Dergholm State Park: 26 km S; *see Casterton. Naracoorte Caves National Park:* World Heritage site of fabulous caves with extensive fossil history to explore; around 50 km W over SA border. *Fishing:* redfin, trout and yabbies in many lakes and swamps nearby. Availability depends on water levels; contact visitor centre for locations.

TOWNS NEARBY: Coonawarra (SA) 50 km, Naracoorte (SA) 50 km, Penola (SA) 55 km, Casterton 62 km, Natimuk 67 km

Eildon
Pop. 742
Map ref. 534 H1 | 537 O1 | 540 G1 | 542 G12 | 544 C11

ⓘ High St; (03) 5774 2909; www.murrindinditourism.com.au

97.3 FM ABC Local Radio, 106.9 UGFM Upper Goulburn Community Radio

Eildon established itself as a town to service dam workers, and later holiday-makers, when the Goulburn River was dammed to create Lake Eildon in the 1950s. This is the state's largest constructed lake, irrigating a vast stretch of northern Victoria and providing hydro-electric power. In recent years low water levels

have revealed homesteads that were submerged when the dam was constructed. The lake and the surrounding national park are popular summer holiday destinations, especially for watersports, fishing and boating.

Lions Club Monster Market: Easter. *Opening of Fishing Season Festival:* Sep.

Bluegums Riverside Holiday Park: 746 Back Eildon Rd; (03) 5774 2567. *Jamieson Caravan Park:* Grey St, Jamieson; (03) 5777 0567.

Lake Eildon National Park Comprising the lake and surrounding woodlands, hills and wilderness areas, this national park provides a venue for many water- and land-based activities. When full, Lake Eildon has 6 times the capacity of Sydney Harbour. Hire a kayak, boat or houseboat from the outlets in Eildon to explore the waters, or enjoy the thrills of waterskiing with the picturesque foothills of the Australian Alps providing a backdrop. In the surrounding hills and woodlands there are various nature walks, scenic drives and panoramic lookout points. Many of the walks start at the campgrounds; details from visitor centre, or from Parks Victoria on 13 1963.

Lake Eildon Wall Lookout: 1 km N. *Eildon Pondage and Goulburn River:* for excellent fishing – there is no closed season for trout in Lake Eildon. *Mt Pinniger:* for views of Mt Buller, the alps and the lake; 3 km E. *Freshwater Discovery Centre:* native-fish aquariums and displays; Snobs Creek; 6 km SW. *Waterfalls:* include Snobs Creek Falls and Rubicon Falls; 18 km SW via Thornton. *Eildon Trout Farm:* towards Thornton on Back Eildon Rd.

TOWNS NEARBY: Alexandra 18 km, Mansfield 25 km, Marysville 34 km, Yea 43 km, Healesville 58 km

Emerald
Pop. 6317
Map ref. 531 H7 | 533 O1 | 534 C10 | 537 L7 | 540 E5

ⓘ Dandenong Ranges Information Centre, 1211 Burwood Hwy, Upper Ferntree Gully; (03) 9758 7522; www.dandenongrangestourism.com.au

97.1 FM 3MDR Mountain District Radio, 774 AM 3LO ABC Local Radio

Emerald is a delightful little town set in the Dandenong Ranges, which lie behind Melbourne's eastern suburbs. Over the weekend people come from the city into 'the hills' to take in the scenic forests and visit the cafes, galleries, and antique and craft stores.

Emerald Lake The lake is a lovely, tranquil spot ideal for picnics and walks. Attractions include the largest model railway display in the Southern Hemisphere, paddleboats, cafe and tearooms, fishing, free wading pool (summer months) and a variety of walking trails. Picnic shelters are available for hire throughout the year. *Puffing Billy* stops at Emerald Lake and many passengers spend a day here before returning on the train in the late afternoon. Emerald Lake Rd.

Galleries and craft shops: a wide variety, specialising in locally made products; along Main St.

PAVE (Performing and Visual Arts in Emerald) Festival: Apr. *Great Train Race:* runners attempt to race *Puffing Billy* from Belgrave to Emerald Lake Park; 1st Sun in May.

Elevation at Emerald: casual dining with views; 374 Main Rd; (03) 5968 2911.

Fernglade on Menzies B & B: 11 Caroline Cres; (03) 5968 2228. *Glenview Retreat:* 48 Fernglade Dr; (03) 5968 5399.

BIG4 Dandenong Tourist Park: 370 Frankston–Dandenong Rd, Dandenong South; (03) 9706 5492. *Yuulong Bed & Breakfast:* 574 Salisbury Rd, Beaconsfield Upper; 0418 310 524.

Puffing Billy Victoria's favourite steam train runs the 25 km between Belgrave and Gembrook, stopping at Emerald Lake. The views from the train are of tall trees and ferny gullies, and if you time your trip for the last Sat of the month you could catch the local craft and produce market at Gembrook station. Also at Gembrook is the Motorist Cafe and Museum. *Puffing Billy* operates every day of the year, except Christmas Day; 24 hr recorded timetable and fare information on 1900 937 069, all other inquiries (03) 9757 0700; Belgrave 9 km w, Gembrook 14 km e.

Menzies Creek This town is home to Cotswold House, where visitors enjoy gourmet food amid fantastic views. Nearby is Cardinia Reservoir Park, where picnic spots are shared with free-roaming kangaroos, and Lake Aura Vale, a popular spot for sailing. Belgrave–Gembrook Rd; 4 km NW.

Sherbrooke Equestrian Park: trail-rides; Wellington Rd; 3 km W. *Australian Rainbow Trout Farm:* Macclesfield; 8 km N. *Sherbrooke Art Gallery:* impressive collection of local artwork; Monbulk Rd, Belgrave; 11 km NW. *Bimbimbie Wildlife Park:* Mt Burnett; 12 km SE.

TOWNS NEARBY: Olinda 11 km, Warburton 30 km, Koo-Wee-Rup 30 km, Yarra Glen 31 km, Healesville 32 km

Euroa

Pop. 2773
Map ref. 542 F9 | 544 A7

i Strathbogie Ranges Tourism Information Service, BP Service Centre, 29–33 Tarcombe St; (03) 5795 3677; www.strathbogie.vic.gov.au

97.7 FM ABC Local Radio, 98.5 FM 98.5

Euroa was the scene of one of Ned Kelly's most infamous acts. In 1878 the notorious bushranger staged a daring robbery, rounding up some 50 hostages and making off with money and gold worth nearly £2000. The Strathbogie Ranges, once one of the Kelly Gang's hideouts, now provide a scenic backdrop to the town, and the region really comes to life in spring, when stunning wildflowers bloom. During this time and in autumn a number of private gardens are open to the public.

Farmers Arms Historical Museum The museum features displays explaining the history of Ned Kelly and Eliza Forlonge; Eliza and her sister are said to have imported the first merino sheep into Victoria. Open Fri–Mon afternoons; Kirkland Ave.

Walking trail: self-guide trail to see the rich history and architecture of the town, including the National Bank building and the post office, both in Binney St; brochure available from visitor centre. *Seven Creeks Park:* good freshwater fishing, particularly for trout; Kirkland Ave.

Miniature steam-train rides: Turnbull St; last Sun each month. *Wool Week:* Oct.

Ruffy Produce Store: excellent regional-produce store; 26 Nolans Rd, Ruffy; (03) 5790 4387.

Euroa Caravan & Cabin Park: 73–103 Kirkland Ave; (03) 5795 2160. *Forlonge Bed & Breakfast:* 76 Anderson St; (03) 5795 2460.

Faithfull Creek Waterfall: 9 km NE. *Longwood:* includes the delightful White Hart Hotel and horse-drawn carriage rides;

14 km SW. *Gooram Falls:* a scenic drive takes in the falls and parts of the Strathbogie Ranges; 20 km SE. *Locksley:* popular for gliding and parachuting; 20 km SW. *Polly McQuinns Weir:* historic river crossing and reservoir; Strathbogie Rd; 20 km SE. *Mt Wombat Lookout:* spectacular views of surrounding country and the Australian Alps; 25 km SE. *Blue Wren Lavender Farm:* lavender products and Devonshire tea; Boho South; 28 km E. *Avenel Maze:* Ned Kelly–themed maze; open Thurs–Mon, school and public holidays; 37 km SW.

TOWNS NEARBY: Nagambie 37 km, Benalla 43 km, Shepparton 45 km, Seymour 49 km, Alexandra 50 km

Flinders

Pop. 575
Map ref. 533 I10 | 537 I11 | 540 C8

i Nepean Hwy, Dromana; (03) 5987 3078 or 1800 804 009.

98.7 3RPP FM, 774 AM ABC Local Radio

Flinders is set on the south coast of the Mornington Peninsula, a region famous for its wineries. During the 1880s, it became known as a health and recreation resort and a number of guesthouses and hotels began to emerge. Today Flinders remains a popular holiday spot, with its renowned cliff-top golf course and gastropub. Heritage buildings have wide verandahs, often shading antique and curio shops or excellent cafes, giving the town an enchanting and historic air. This, combined with the view across the bay to The Nobbies and Seal Rocks, makes it easy to understand the town's perennial appeal.

Foreshore Reserve: popular for picnics and fishing from the jetty. *Studio @ Flinders:* small but unique art gallery with emphasis on ceramics, also exhibits handcrafted jewellery, glass, textiles, wood and paintings; Cook St. *Historic buildings:* 'Bimbi', built in the 1870s, is the earliest remaining dwelling in Flinders; King St. 'Wilga' is another fine Victorian-era home; King St. *Flinders Golf Links:* great views across Bass Strait; West Head, Wood St.

Peninsula Piers and Pinots: the region's winemakers showcase their pinots with local food and produce at Flinders Pier; Mar long weekend.

Foxeys Hangout: casual winery cafe; 795 White Hill Rd, Red Hill; (03) 5989 2022. *Merricks General Wine Store:* wine-friendly rustic fare; 3460 Frankston–Flinders Rd, Merricks; (03) 5989 8088. *Montalto:* slick vineyard restaurant; 33 Shoreham Rd, Red Hill South; (03) 5989 8412. *Ten Minutes by Tractor:* cellar-door bistro; 1333 Mornington–Flinders Rd, Main Ridge; (03) 5989 6080.

Between The Bays Retreat: 28 Curzon Rd, Boneo; (03) 5988 5353. *The Orchard Luxury Accommodation:* 45 Thomas Rd, Red Hill South; (03) 5989 3152. *Somers Holiday Village:* 93 Camp Hill Rd, Somers; (03) 5983 5538.

Red Hill This is fine wine country, where vineyards are interspersed with noted art galleries, farm gates, cafes and restaurants. The Red Hill Market is legendary and held on the first Sat of each month from Sept to May. It specialises in local crafts, clothing and fresh produce. The town also features a number of galleries and The Cherry Farm, where you can 'pick your own' cherries and berries in a pleasant setting (in season); Arkwells La. The Mornington Peninsula Winter Wine Fest is held annually on the Queen's Birthday weekend (June) and the Cool Climate Wine Show is in Mar.

 RADIO STATIONS IN TOWN WHAT'S ON WHERE TO EAT WHERE TO STAY NEARBY

VICTORIA

Mornington Peninsula National Park The park covers 2686 ha and features a diverse range of vegetation, from the basalt cliff-faces of Cape Schanck to banksia woodlands, coastal dune scrubs and swampland. One of the park's many attractions is the Cape Schanck Lighthouse, built in 1859, which provides accommodation in one of the lighthouse keepers' houses. Historic Pt Nepean retains its original fortifications and has information displays and soundscapes. Also available here is a 'hop-on, hop-off' tractor train with commentary, and bicycle hire. There are ocean beaches for swimming and surfing, while the Bushranger Bay Nature Walk, starting at Cape Schanck, and the Farnsworth Track at Portsea are just 2 of the many walks on offer. Contact Parks Victoria on 13 1963; access to Cape Schanck from Rosebud–Flinders Rd; 15 km w.

French Island National Park French Island once served as a prison where inmates kept themselves entertained with their own 9-hole golf course. This unique reserve features a range of environments from mangrove saltmarsh to open woodlands. During spring more than 100 varieties of orchids come into bloom. The park is home to the most significant population of koalas in Victoria. Long-nosed potoroos and majestic sea-eagles can also be spotted. There is a variety of walking tracks on the island and bicycles can be hired from the general store. There are also guesthouses, and camping and picnic facilities. Contact Parks Victoria on 13 1963; access is via a 30 min ferry trip from Stony Pt, 30 km NE of Flinders.

Ashcombe Maze and Lavender Gardens: a large hedge maze surrounded by beautifully landscaped gardens; closed Aug; Red Hill Rd, Shoreham; 6 km N. *Ace Hi Horseriding and Wildlife Park:* beach and bush trail-rides and a native-animal sanctuary; Cape Schanck; 11 km w. *Main Ridge:* Sunny Ridge Strawberry Farm – pick your own berries in season; Mornington–Flinders Rd. Also The Pig and Whistle, English-style pub, Purves Rd; 11 km NW. *Pt Leo:* great surf beach; 12 km NE via Shoreham. *Balnarring:* hosts a market specialising in handmade crafts; 3rd Sat each month Nov–May; 17 km NE. Nearby is Coolart Homestead, an impressive Victorian mansion with historical displays, gardens, wetlands and a bird-observation area.

TOWNS NEARBY: Cowes 19 km, Mornington 28 km, Sorrento 28 km, Queenscliff 39 km, Ocean Grove 49 km

Foster

Pop. 1039
Map ref. 540 G9

ⓘ Stockyard Gallery, Main St; 1800 630 704; www.visitpromcountry.com.au

📻 89.5 3MFM South Gippsland, 100.7 FM ABC Local Radio

Foster was originally a goldmining town settled in the 1870s. The town boasts close access to Wilsons Promontory – affectionately called 'the Prom' – and is a popular base for visitors. Set in the centre of a rich agricultural area, Foster is the main shopping precinct for the Prom, Corner Inlet and Waratah Bay.

Historical Museum: in old post office; Main St. *Stockyard Gallery:* Main St. *Hayes Walk:* view the site of Victory Mine, Foster's largest goldmine; starts in town behind the carpark. *Pearl Park:* picturesque picnic spot.

Tastes of Prom Country: Jan. *Great Southern Portrait Prize:* Jan. *Prom Coast Seachange Festival:* Apr. *Mt Best Art Show:* Apr. *Prom Country Challenge:* fun run; Aug. *Promontory Home Produce and Craft Market:* Nov–Apr.

📷 *Prom Central Caravan Park:* 38 Nelson St; (03) 5682 2440. *Bayview House:* 202 Soldiers Rd, Yanakie; (03) 5687 1246. *Shallow Inlet Caravan Park:* 350 Lester Rd, Yanakie; (03) 5687 1385.

Wilsons Promontory National Park The Prom is well loved across the state for its wild and untouched scenery. Its 130 km coastline is framed by granite headlands, mountains, forests and fern gullies. Bordered on all sides by sea, it hangs from Victoria by a thin, sandy isthmus. Limited road access means opportunities for walking are plentiful. The park features dozens of walking tracks, ranging from easy strolls to more challenging overnight hikes that take visitors to one of 11 campsites only accessible by foot. Hikes range from beginner to intermediate, and permits are required. Detailed information is provided at the park's own visitor centre: the remnants of a commando training camp from WW II. Contact Parks Victoria on 13 1963; 32 km s.

Toora An internationally recognised wetland site located on Corner Inlet, it is renowned for the huge variety of migratory birds that nest in the area. Toora is also home to Agnes Falls, a wind farm, a lavender farm and the Bird Hide where you can watch migratory and indigenous birdlife. 12 km E.

Foster North Lookout: 6 km NW. *Wineries:* Windy Ridge Winery; 10 km s. *Fish Creek:* A rural village, which attracts many visitors en route to the Prom. From the novelty of the giant mullet on top of the Promontory Gate Hotel to the fish-shaped seats around town, there is more to this unusually themed town than meets the eye. Galleries and vineyards are located in the area. Access the Great Southern Trail and walk, ride or cycle your way to Foster. Nearby Mt Nicol offers a lookout with spectacular views; 13 km sw. *Turtons Creek Reserve:* features mountain ash, blackwood and tree ferns, and a small waterfall. Bush camping is available; 18 km N. *Coastal towns:* popular bases during summer months; Sandy Pt, 22 km s; Waratah Bay, 34 km sw; Walkerville, 36 km sw. *Cape Liptrap:* views over rugged coastline and Bass Strait; 46 km sw.

TOWNS NEARBY: Welshpool 21 km, Leongatha 30 km, Korumburra 41 km, Inverloch 42 km, Yarram 42 km

Geelong
see inset box on page 166

Glenrowan

Pop. 324
Map ref. 542 H8 | 544 E5

ⓘ Wangaratta Visitor Information Centre, 100 Murphy St, Wangaratta; 1800 801 065; www.visitwangaratta.com.au

📻 101.3 Oak FM, 106.5 FM ABC Local Radio

Glenrowan is a town well known to most Victorians as the site of Ned Kelly's final showdown with the police in 1880. Most of the attractions in Glenrowan revolve around the legends surrounding Kelly's life – a giant statue of Kelly himself towers over shops in Gladstone Street. Almost as legendary as Ned Kelly are the numerous wineries and fruit orchards in the area.

Kate's Cottage Museum: with an extensive collection of Kelly memorabilia as well as a replica of the Kelly homestead and blacksmith shop; Gladstone St. *Cobb & Co Museum:* an underground museum featuring notorious stories of Kelly and other bushrangers; Gladstone St. *Kellyland:* a computer-animated show of Kelly's capture; Gladstone St. *Kelly Gang Siege Site Walk:* discover the sites and history that led to the famous siege on this self-guide walk (brochure available). *Wine and produce outlets:* over 22 local wines are offered for tastings and sales at the Buffalo Mountain Wine Centre; Gladstone St. Gourmet jams and fruit products are also available at Smiths Orchard and The Big Cherry; Warby Range Rd. **White Cottage Herb Garden:** herb sales; Hill St.

 Trails, Tastings and Tales wine and food event: June.

Old Block Cafe: weekend platters and grazing food; Baileys of Glenrowan, 779 Taminick Gap Rd; (03) 5766 1600.

Warby Range State Park The 'Warbys', as they are known locally, extend for 25 km north of Glenrowan. The steep ranges provide excellent viewing points, especially from Ryans Lookout. Other lookouts include the Pangarang Lookout near the Pine Gully Picnic Area and the Mt Glenrowan Lookout, the highest point of the Warbys at 513 m. There are well-marked tracks for bushwalkers and a variety of pleasant picnic spots amid open forests and woodlands, with wildflowers blossoming during the warmer months. Access from Taminick Gap Rd.

TOWNS NEARBY: Wangaratta 14 km, Milawa 19 km, Benalla 24 km, Beechworth 43 km, Myrtleford 46 km

Halls Gap

see inset box on page 169

Hamilton

Pop. 9379
Map ref. 550 F4

i Lonsdale St; (03) 5572 3746 or 1800 807 056; www.sthgrampians.vic.gov.au

94.1 FM ABC Local Radio, 99.3 Coastal FM

Hamilton is a prominent rural centre in the heart of a sheep-grazing district. This industry is such an important part of the town's economy that it has been dubbed the 'Wool Capital of the World'. It is both the geographical and business hub of the Western District. A thriving country city, Hamilton is filled with cultural experiences, whether gazing at botanical, artistic or architectural beauty, browsing through great shops or putting in a bid as part of a 50 000-head sheep sale.

Hamilton Art Gallery This gallery is said to be one of regional Australia's finest, featuring a diverse collection of fine arts and museum pieces dating back to the earliest European settlements in Australia. Many trinkets and treasures of the region's first stately homes are on display, as well as English and European glass, ceramic and silver work. There is also a good collection of colonial art from the Western District. Guided heritage tours of the gallery and district are available. Brown St.

Botanic Gardens First planted in 1870 and classified by the National Trust in 1990, these gardens have long been regarded as one of the most impressive in rural Victoria. Designed by the curator of the Melbourne Botanic Gardens, William Guilfoyle, the gardens feature his 'signature' design elements of sweeping lawns interrupted by lakes, islands, and contrasting plant and flower beds. Keep an eye out for the free-flight aviary, enormous English oaks and historic band rotunda. French St.

Lake Hamilton: attractive landscaped man-made lake used for swimming, sailing, yachting and rowing, and featuring an excellent walking/bike track; off Ballarat Rd. **Sir Reginald Ansett Transport Museum:** birthplace of Ansett Airlines, the museum tells the story of Ansett and our aviation history in one of the airline's original hangars; Ballarat Rd. **Hamilton Pastoral**

Museum: features farm equipment, tractors, engines, household items and small-town memorabilia; Ballarat Rd. **Big Wool Bales:** built in the shape of 5 giant wool bales and surrounded by native red gums, the Wool Bales tell the fascinating story of Australia's wool industry; Coleraine Rd. **Mt Baimbridge Lavender:** set on 12 acres. Wander through gardens and browse the gallery; Mt Baimbridge Rd; tours available by appt (03) 5572 4342. **Hamilton History Centre:** features the history of early Western District families and town settlement; Gray St.

Farmer's Market: last Sat each month. **Harvest Rally:** Jan. **Beef Expo:** Feb. **Hamilton Cup:** Apr. **Promenade of Sacred Music:** Apr. **Plough and Seed Rally:** May. **Sheepvention:** promotes the sheep and wool industries; Aug.

Darriwill Farm: produce/wine store and cafe; 169 Gray St; (03) 5571 2088. **The Roxburgh:** wine-bar-cum-cosy-cafe; 64 Thompson St; (03) 5572 4857. **Cafe Catalpa:** game-heavy menu; 7921 Hamilton Hwy, Tarrington; (03) 5572 1888.

Ashwick House: 88 Ballarat Rd; (03) 5572 5929. **Penshurst Caravan Park:** Cnr Cox and Martin sts, Penshurst; (03) 5576 5220.

Mt Eccles National Park The key feature of this park is a large volcanic crater lake. A range of walks let visitors explore the scoria cones and caves formed 20 000 years ago by volcanoes. The 3 main craters hold a 700 m long lake, Lake Surprise, fed by underground springs. Excellent walking trails and camping is available. Contact Parks Victoria on 13 1963; near Macarthur; 40 km s.

Grampians National Park *See Halls Gap.* 35 km NE.

Tarrington: established by German settlers and originally named Hochkirch, this area is fast becoming a well-known 'pinot noir' grape-producing area; 12 km SE. **Waterfalls:** Nigretta Falls has a viewing platform; 15 km NW. Also Wannon Falls; 19 km W. **Mt Napier State Park:** features Byaduk Caves (lava caves) near the park's western entrance, part of a giant, 24 km lava flow stretching to Mt Eccles. They are a wonderland of ropey lava, columns, stalactites and stalagmites. Only 1 cave is accessible to the public; 18 km s. **Cavendish:** a small town en route to the Grampians, notable for the 3 beautiful private gardens open during the Southern Grampians Open Gardens Festival each Oct; 25 km N. **Penshurst:** a lovely historic town at the foot of Mt Rouse. Excellent views from the top of the mountain, where there is a crater lake. Country Muster each Feb; 31 km SE.

TOWNS NEARBY: Dunkeld 30 km, Coleraine 34 km, Casterton 58 km, Port Fairy 73 km, Portland 76 km

Healesville

Pop. 7357
Map ref. 534 D6 | 537 L4 | 540 E4

i Yarra Valley Visitor Information Centre, Old Courthouse, Harker St; (03) 5962 2600; www.visityarravalley.com.au

99.1 Yarra Valley FM, 774 AM ABC Local Radio

To the west of Yarra Ranges National Park and within easy reach of Melbourne, Healesville has a charming rural atmosphere. There are good restaurants and cafes in town, all focusing on quality local produce, especially the world-class Yarra Valley wines. On top of this is a host of art and craft boutiques and two major attractions – TarraWarra Museum of Art and the famous Healesville Sanctuary, one of the best places in Victoria to experience Australia's unique wildlife close-up.

continued on p. 167

GEELONG

Pop. 160 989

Map ref. 532 B4 | 536 F8 | 538 G1 | 540 A6 | 551 O7

26 Moorabool St; (03) 5222 2900 or 1800 620 888; www.visitgreatoceanroad.org.au

94.7 The Pulse FM, 774 AM ABC Local Radio

Situated on Corio Bay, Geelong is the largest provincial city in Victoria. Geelong was traditionally a wool-processing centre, and the National Wool Museum in Moorabool Street details its early dependence upon the industry. The town was first settled by Europeans in the 1830s, but Geelong and its surrounds were originally home to the Wathaurong people, with whom the famous convict escapee William Buckley lived for many years. Buckley later described the unique culture of the Aboriginal tribes who welcomed him into their lives, and his writing is now one of the most priceless historical records of Indigenous culture in southern Australia. Geelong is a beautifully laid-out city, and a drive along the scenic Esplanade reveals magnificent old mansions built during its heyday.

Waterfront Geelong This superbly restored promenade stretches along Eastern Beach and offers a variety of attractions. Visitors can relax in the historic, 1930s-built sea-baths, enjoy fine dining in seaside restaurants and cafes or stroll along the famous Bollards Trail featuring colourful sculptures. The Waterfront district is on Eastern Beach Rd, with the beautiful old Cunningham Pier as a centrepiece.

National Wool Museum Housed in a historic bluestone wool store, the centre features audiovisual displays plus re-created shearers' quarters and a mill-worker's cottage. There is a licensed restaurant and bar in the cellar, and a souvenir shop selling locally made wool products. 26 Moorabool St; (03) 5272 4701.

Geelong Art Gallery: this regional gallery is considered one of the finest in the state. The focus is on late-19th- and early-20th-century paintings by British artists and members of the Royal Academy, such as Tom Roberts and Arthur Streeton; Little Malop St; (03) 5229 3645. *Historic buildings:* there are over 100 National Trust–classifications in Geelong, including Merchiston Hall, Osborne House and Corio Villa. 'The Heights' is a 14-room prefabricated timber mansion set in landscaped gardens; contact visitor centre for details of open days; Aphrasia St, Newtown. Christ Church, still in continuous use, is the oldest Anglican Church in Victoria; Moorabool St. *Ford Discovery Centre:* Geelong has long been a major manufacturing centre for Ford and this centre details the history of Ford cars with interactive displays; closed Tues; Cnr Brougham and Gheringhap sts; (03) 5227 8700. *Wintergarden:* a historic building housing a gallery, a nursery, antiques and a giftshop; 51 McKillop St. *Botanic Gardens:* overlooking Corio Bay and featuring a good collection of native and exotic plants; part of Eastern Park; Garden St. *Johnstone Park:* picnic and barbecue facilities; Cnr Mercer and Gheringhap sts. *Queens Park:* walks to Buckley Falls; Queens Park Rd, Newtown. *Balyang Bird Sanctuary:* 50 Marnock Rd, Newton, off Shannon Ave. *Barwon River:* extensive walking tracks and bike paths in parkland by the river. *Norlane Water World:* waterslides; Princes Hwy, Norlane. *Corio Bay beaches:* popular for swimming, fishing and sailing; boat ramps provided.

Steampacket Gardens Market: on foreshore at Eastern Beach; 1st Sun each month. *Farmers Market:* Little Malop St; 2nd Sat each month. *Audi Victoria Week:* sailing regatta; Jan. *Pako Festa:* Victoria's premier multicultural event; Pakington St; last Sat in Feb. *Highland Gathering:* Mar. *National Celtic Folk Festival:* Port Arlington, June. *Geelong Show:* Oct. *Geelong Cup:* Oct. *Christmas Carols by the Bay:* Eastern Beach; Dec. *New Year Waterfront Festival:* New Year's Eve.

[COLOURFUL BOLLARDS ALONG GEELONG'S WATERFRONT]

2 Faces: contemporary cuisine; 8 Malop St; (03) 5229 4546. *The Beach House:* contemporary beachside; Eastern Beach Reserve; (03) 5221 8322. *Fishermen's Pier:* seafood; bay end of Yarra St; (03) 5222 4100. *Fishermen's Pier:* mix and match miniature main courses; 247 Moorabool St; (03) 5229 9935.

Vailima Waterfront Apartment & B&B: 26 Eastern Beach Rd; 0417 300 877. *Ardara House B&B:* 4 Aberdeen St, Geelong West; (03) 5229 6024. *Barwon River Tourist Park:* 153 Barrabool Rd, Belmont; (03) 5243 3842. *Geelong Riverview Tourist Park – Aspen Parks:* 59 Barrabool Rd, Belmont; (03) 5243 6225. *Riverglen Holiday Park:* 75 Barrabool Rd, Belmont; (03) 5243 5505.

You Yangs Regional Park These granite outcrops that rise 352 m above Werribee's lava plains have an ancient link to the Wathaurong people as they provided a much-needed water source – rock wells were created to catch water, and many of them can still be seen at Big Rock. The park is a popular recreational area: activities include the 12 km Great Circle Drive and the climb to Flinders Peak for fantastic views of Geelong, Corio Bay, Mt Macedon and Melbourne's skyline. There is also a fairly easy walk (3.2 kilometres return) from the carpark to the top of Flinders Peak. Contact Parks Victoria on 131 963. 24 km N.

Werribee Park and the Open Range Zoo The key feature of Werribee Park is a beautifully preserved 1870s mansion with the interior painstakingly restored to its original opulence. The mansion is surrounded by 12 ha of gardens, including a grotto and a farmyard area, complete with a blacksmith. Within the grounds is the Victoria State Rose Garden with over 500 varieties of flowers. Next to the park is the Werribee Open Range Zoo, developed around the Werribee River. The zoo covers 200 ha and has a variety of animals native to the grasslands of Africa, Asia, North America and Australia, including giraffes, rhinos, meerkats, cheetahs and vervet monkeys. Guided safaris through the replicated African savannah are a must. Access from the Princes Hwy; Werribee Park: 131 963; Open Range Zoo: (03) 9731 9600; 40 km NE.

Geelong and Bellarine wine region During the 1800s, the Geelong region had a large wine industry that competed with Rutherglen for prominence. But when the devastating phylloxera disease hit, all the vines were pulled out. Today Geelong is a re-emerging district and two of its highly regarded labels are found at Bannockburn. The 30-year-old Bannockburn Vineyards and the combined By Farr and farr rising, run by a father and son team, produce shiraz, pinot noir and chardonnay of serious quality. While neither have a cellar door, look out for the wines on local menus or head to Bannockburn Cellars. Scotchmans Hill is a large winery and cellar-door complex on the Bellarine Peninsula with views over Port Phillip to Melbourne. It also owns Spray Farm Estate, which regularly hosts the popular outdoor music concerts known as A Day on the Green. The region's two other must-visit vineyards are Pettavel, home to one of the best winery restaurants in the state; and Shadowfax, part of Werribee Park where you can also visit Werribee Open Range Zoo and spend a luxurious night at Sofitel Mansion & Spa. Various cellar doors offer tastings and sales; map from visitor centre.

Fyansford: one of the oldest settlements in the region, with historic buildings including the Swan Inn, Balmoral Hotel and Fyansford Hotel. The Monash Bridge across the Moorabool River is thought to be one of earliest reinforced-concrete bridges in Victoria; outskirts of Geelong; 4 km W. *Adventure Park:* Victoria's first waterpark, with more than 20 attractions and rides; open Oct–Apr; 1251 Bellarine Hwy, Wallington; (03) 5250 2756; 15 km SE. *Avalon Airfield:* hosts the Australian International Air Show in odd-numbered years; off Princes Hwy; 20 km NE. *Serendip Sanctuary:* a wildlife research station that includes nature trails, bird hides and a visitor centre; just south of the You Yangs. *Fairy Park:* miniature houses and scenes from fairytales; 2388 Ballan Rd, Anakie; (03) 5284 1262; 29 km N. *Steiglitz:* once a gold town, now almost deserted. The restored courthouse is open on Sun; 37 km NW.

TOWNS NEARBY: **Barwon Heads 19 km, Drysdale 19 km, Ocean Grove 19 km, Torquay 20 km, Queenscliff 29 km**

Silvermist Studio Gallery: handmade gold and silver jewellery; Maroondah Hwy. *Open-air trolley rides:* from Healesville railway station; open Sun and public holidays. *Giant Steps/Innocent Bystander Winery:* thoroughly modern cellar door in the town centre with an excellent bakery, bistro serving mouth-watering pizzas, and cheese room; 336 Maroondah Hwy; (03) 5962 6111 or 1800 661 624.

Market: River St; 1st Sun each month. *Grape Grazing Festival:* events held throughout wine district to celebrate the harvest; Feb. *Australian Car Rally Championship:* Sept.

Giant Steps/Innocent Bystander: bakery, cafe, cellar door; 336 Maroondah Hwy; (03) 5962 6111 or 1800 661 624. *Healesville Hotel:* country gastropub; 256 Maroondah Hwy; (03) 5962 4002. *Mt Rael Restaurant:* contemporary with views; Mt Rael, 140 Healesville–Yarra Glen Rd; (03) 5962 1977.

Bella Vedere: bakery, cafe-cum-restaurant; 874 Maroondah Hwy, Coldstream; (03) 5962 6161.

Annabelle of Healesville: 10 Glenfern Ave; (03) 5962 6655. *Barbs B&B:* 23 Marna St; (03) 5962 5172. *Myers Creek Cascades:* 269 Myers Creek Rd; (03) 5962 3351. *Sunway Farm B&B & Tours:* 19 Bridges Rd; (03) 5962 4612. *Wide Horizons Bed & Breakfast:* 19 Juliet Cres; (03) 5962 4119. *Lyrebird Cottages:* 140 Moora Rd, Mount Toolebewong; (03) 5962 3343.

Healesville Sanctuary Australia's unique animal species are on show at this 32 ha reserve. The sanctuary is also one of the few places in the world to have successfully bred platypus in captivity. Allow at least half a day to visit and see the animal hospital or go on a behind-the-scenes keeper tour (bookings on (03) 5957 2800). Badger Creek Rd; 4 km S.

 RADIO STATIONS   IN TOWN   WHAT'S ON   WHERE TO EAT   WHERE TO STAY   NEARBY

TarraWarra Museum of Art TarraWarra Estate has been operating as a vineyard since 1983, producing a selection of fine chardonnay and pinot noir. Now there is a striking building housing an extensive private collection of modern art. The collection focuses on the 3 key themes of Australian Modernism – landscape, figuration and abstraction – and works by artists such as Howard Arkley, Arthur Boyd and Brett Whiteley can be found within. Healesville–Yarra Glen Rd; (03) 5957 3100.

Hedgend Maze: giant maze and fun park; Albert Rd; 2.5 km s. *Corranderrk Aboriginal Cemetery:* once the burial ground for an Aboriginal mission, and the final resting place of well-known Wurundjeri leader William Barak; 3 km s. *Maroondah Reservoir Park:* a magnificent park set in lush forests with walking tracks and a lookout nearby; 3 km NE. *Donnelly's Weir Park:* starting point of the 5000 km Bicentennial National Trail to Cooktown (Queensland). The park also has short walking tracks and picnic facilities; 4 km N. *Badger Weir Park:* picnic area in a natural setting; 7 km SE. *Mallesons Lookout:* views of Yarra Valley to Melbourne; 8 km s. *Mt St Leonard:* good views from the summit; 14 km N. *Toolangi:* attractions include the Singing Gardens of C. J. Dennis, a beautiful, formal garden; the Toolangi Forest Discovery Centre, for a fascinating insight into the local forests and how they were formed; and Toolangi Pottery; 20 km NW. *Yarra Valley wine region:* around 85 in the area open for tastings and sales. Tours available; details from visitor centre. *See also Yarra Glen.*

TOWNS NEARBY: Yarra Glen 13 km, Warburton 19 km, Marysville 26 km, Olinda 26 km, Emerald 32 km

Heathcote

Pop. 1572
Map ref. 542 B10 | 549 P11

ⓘ Cnr High and Barrack sts; (03) 5433 3121; www.heathcote.org.au

 91.1 FM ABC Local Radio, 100.7 Highlands FM

Heathcote is located near the outskirts of the scenic Heathcote–Graytown National Park, with the McIvor Creek flowing by the town. Heathcote was established during the gold rush, but is now known as a prominent wine region with good red wines produced from a number of new vineyards.

Courthouse Crafts: displays relating to the gold rush, plus arts and crafts; High St. *Pink Cliffs:* eroded soil from gold sluices gave the cliffs their remarkable pink colour; Pink Cliffs Rd, off Hospital Rd. *McIvor Range Reserve:* walking tracks; off Barrack St; details of walks from visitor centre. *Heathcote Winery:* this winery, in the old Thomas Craven Stores building, has an art gallery and cellar-door sales; High St.

World's Longest Lunch: Mar. *Rodeo:* Mar long weekend. *Heathcote Wine and Food Festival:* 1st weekend in Oct.

Hut on the Hill: 720 Dairy Flat Rd, Heathcote South; 0412 194 921.

Heathcote–Graytown National Park Compared with many of Victoria's national parks, Heathcote–Graytown was declared quite late as part of a statewide plan to preserve box-ironbark forest. Now protecting the largest forest of this type in the state, the park is not only an important nature reserve but also has a long history of settlement. Take one of the many walks or scenic drives to explore evidence of Aboriginal, goldmining and pioneering history, or take in scenic views from the lookouts at Mt Black, Mt Ida and Viewing Rock (just near Heathcote).

Contact Parks Victoria on 13 1963; access from Northern Hwy and Heathcote–Nagambie Rd.

Heathcote wine region Heathcote shiraz makes wine lovers go weak at the knees. Its depth is the result of the dark, red Cambrian soil and the continental climate. Jasper Hill is the most exclusive name in the area. Its elegant red wines can be hard to come by, so if you manage to find a bottle it is worth purchasing it on the spot. Other good wineries include Heathcote Winery with its cellar door located on the town's main street, Shelmerdine Vineyards, Wild Duck Creek Estate and Red Edge. To find most of the region's wines under one roof, head to Cellar and Store, which also stocks a full range of local gourmet produce.

Lake Eppalock: one of the state's largest lakes, great for fishing, watersports and picnics; 10 km w.

TOWNS NEARBY: Seymour 40 km, Bendigo 42 km, Kyneton 42 km, Nagambie 43 km, Rushworth 46 km

Hopetoun

Pop. 591
Map ref. 526 E10 | 548 H4

ⓘ Gateway Beet, 75 Lascelles St; (03) 5083 3001; www.hopetounvictoria.com.au

📻 92.9 3MBR-FM Mallee Border Radio, 594 AM ABC Local Radio

This small Mallee town, south-east of Wyperfeld National Park, was named after the first governor-general of Australia, the Earl of Hopetoun. The Earl was a friend of Edward Lascelles, who played a major role in developing the Mallee Country by eradicating vermin, developing water strategies to cope with the dry conditions, and enticing settlers to the region.

Hopetoun House: the residence of Lascelles, this majestic building is now National Trust–classified; Evelyn St. *Mallee Mural:* depicts history of the region; wall of Dr Pete's Memorial Park, cnr Lascelles and Austin sts. *Lake Lascelles:* good for boating, swimming and fishing when filled, presently dry. Camping facilities available; access from end of Austin St.

Hopetoun Bowl Club Annual Carnival: Apr. *Hopetoun A & P Society Annual Show:* Oct.

Hopetoun Caravan Park: Austin St; (03) 5083 3001.

Wyperfeld National Park Outlet Creek connects the network of lake beds that are the main highlight for visitors to this park. They fill only when Lake Albacutya overflows, which in turn fills only when Lake Hindmarsh overflows. Once a corroboree ground, the main lake bed, Wirrengren Plain, has flooded only once in the last 100 years. Eastern grey kangaroos can be seen grazing on Wirrengren and the other lake beds, and the Eastern Lookout Nature Drive is a great way to see the range of vegetation in the park – river red gums, black box, mallee and cypress pine, and wildflowers in spring. The park is home to the endangered mallee fowl, a turkey-size bird that makes nesting mounds up to 5 metres across. A variety of walking trails leave from the 2 campgrounds – Wonga Campground in the south and Casuarina Campground in the north, near the lakes. Contact Parks Victoria on 13 1963; 50 km NW.

Patchewollock: the northern gateway to the Wyperfeld National Park, and also home of the Patchewollock Outback Pub; 35 km NW.

TOWNS NEARBY: Jeparit 57 km, Warracknabeal 58 km, Ouyen 73 km, Dimboola 86 km, Wycheproof 87 km

HALLS GAP

Pop. 279
Map ref. 548 H12 | 550 H1

 Halls Gap and Grampians Visitor Information Centre; Grampians Rd; (03) 5356 4295 or 1800 065 599; www.visithallsgap.com.au

94.1 FM ABC Local Radio, 99.9 VoiceFM

The little village of Halls Gap is set in the heart of the Grampians. It was named after Charles Browing Hall, who discovered the gap and valley in 1841. The valley was later developed by cattle-station owners, but the town really took off in the early 1900s when tourists, nature-lovers and botanists caught on to the beauty and diversity of the mountain ranges that would later become Grampians National Park. The town itself has its own charm – shops, galleries and cafes lend a laid-back atmosphere that befits the location, while in the evening long-billed corellas arrive to roost opposite the shops in the main street.

Brambuk – The National Park & Cultural Centre A short drive south of the town centre, it features interactive displays and written information about the park's attractions, bringing to life the culture of the local Jardwadjali and Djab Wurrung people. 277 Grampians Rd; (03) 5361 4000.

Grampians Adventure Golf: world class mini-golf, 18-hole course set on 2 acres; 481 Grampians Rd; 4 km s near Lake Bellfield. *Halls Gap Zoo:* explore the park's nature track and view the animals, many of which are free-range; (03) 5356 4668; 7 km SE.

Grampians Jazz Festival: Feb. *Grampians Grape Escape:* wine and food festival; May. *Film Festival:* Nov.

The Balconies Restaurant: contemporary Australian cuisine; Main Rd; (03) 5356 4232. *Halls Gap Hotel:* modern gastropub; 2262 Grampians Rd; (03) 5356 4566.

DULC: 9 Thryptomene Crt; (03) 5356 4711. *Grampians Gardens Tourist Park:* 2223 Grampians Rd; (03) 5356 4244. *Halls Gap Caravan & Tourist Park:* Grampians Rd; (03) 5356 4251. *Aurora Cottages:* 300 Tunnel Rd, Pomonal; 0433 131 054. *Corella Rise – Bed & Breakfast:* 171 Lake Lonsdale Rd, Lake Lonsdale; (03) 5356 4660. *Lake Fyans Holiday Park:* 650 Mokepilly Rd, Lake Fyans; (03) 5356 6230.

Grampians National Park Aboriginal occupation of the area known as the Grampians dates back over 5000 years (some evidence suggests up to 30 000 years). To local Koorie communities, this magnificent mountain range is known as Gariwerd. Within the 168 000 ha park is a startling array of vegetation and wildlife, including 200 bird species and a quarter of Victoria's native flora species. The heathlands abound in colourful shows of wildflowers including Grampians boronia, blue pincushion lily and Grampians parrot-pea. Twenty of the park's 800 plant species are not found anywhere else in the world. Natural highlights of the Grampians include MacKenzie Falls, the largest of the park's many waterfalls; Zumsteins picnic ground, a beautiful spot with tame and friendly kangaroos; and the Balconies, a rock ledge once known as the Jaws of Death, offering views over Victoria Valley. The most popular section of the park is the Wonderland Range, true to its name with features including Elephants Hide, Grand Canyon, Venus Baths and Silent Street. There are over 90 bushwalks available in the park, all varying in length and degree of difficulty. Visitors are advised to consult a ranger before embarking on one of the longer treks. For further information, contact Brambuk – The National Park and Cultural Centre on (03) 5361 4000.

Grampians wine region Between Stawell and Ararat, the small town of Great Western encompasses some winemaking treasures and hosts the Champagne Picnic Races every Australia Day. Dating from the 1860s, Seppelt is famous for the historic underground tunnels that form its cellars. Its name goes hand in hand with sparkling white wine, although most of the grapes for this variety are actually grown elsewhere. If you're after local sparkling, try Seppelt's sparkling burgundy, made from shiraz. Best's most prized wine is its Thomson Family Shiraz. The winery has its own set of historic buildings and a small plot of unique vines possibly found nowhere else in the world. East of Ararat, Mount Langi Ghiran Vineyards produces what might be the region's best shiraz, as well as a great cabernet sauvignon.

Grampians Horse Riding Adventures: morning and afternoon rides lasting 2 hrs, also has on-site accommodation; Brimpaen; (03) 5383 9225; 44 km w. *Scenic drive:* from Halls Gap drive to Boroka Lookout, Reed Lookout and MacKenzie Falls, and break for lunch at the Zumsteins picnic area.

TOWNS NEARBY: Stawell 25 km, Ararat 40 km, Horsham 55 km, Dunkeld 59 km, Natimuk 68 km

[BOROKA LOOKOUT, GRAMPIANS NATIONAL PARK]

VICTORIA

Horsham

 20 O'Callaghan Pde; (03) 5382 1832 or 1800 633 218; www.visithorsham.com.au

96.5 Triple H FM, 594 AM ABC Local Radio

Horsham is an important centre for the Wimmera district. Prior to European settlement, Horsham and its surrounds were occupied by the Jardwa and Wotjobaluk Aboriginal people, who referred to the region as 'Wopetbungundilar'. This term is thought to have meant 'place of flowers', a reference to the flowers that grow along the banks of the Wimmera River. Flowers continue to play an important role in Horsham, which is considered to be one of the prettiest regional towns in Victoria – the town prides itself on its clean streets and picturesque gardens. Although the Wimmera is a renowned wheat-growing region, Horsham is also a centre for fine wool production.

Horsham Regional Art Gallery This is one of Victoria's key regional galleries, with an extensive collection housed in a 1930s Art Deco building. Most of the artwork is centred on the Mack Jost collection of Australian art, with contemporary Australian photography another specialty. 80 Wilson St; (03) 5362 2888.

Botanic Gardens: picturesquely set on the banks of the Wimmera River; Cnr Baker and Firebrace sts. *The Wool Factory:* produces extra-fine wool from Saxon-Merino sheep, with tours daily; Golf Course Rd. *Wimmera River:* key attraction for the town, with scenic picnic spots along the river's edges. Visit the river at dusk for spectacular sunsets.

Market: showgrounds on McPherson St; 2nd Sun each month. *Haven Recreation Market:* 1st Sat each month. *Wimmera Machinery Field Days:* Longerenong; Mar. *Art Is:* community festival; Apr. *Awakenings Festival:* largest Australian festival involving disabled patrons; Oct. *Spring Garden Festival:* Oct. *Horsham Show:* Oct. *Kannamaroo Rock 'n' Roll Festival:* Nov. *Karkana Strawberry Festival:* Nov.

Cafe Chickpea: hearty breakfasts and light lunches; 30A Pynsent St; (03) 5382 3998.

Horsham Caravan Park: 190 Firebrace St; (03) 5382 3476. *Murtoa Caravan Park:* 47 Lake St, Murtoa; 0448 511 879.

Murtoa This town lies on the edge of Lake Marma, which has dried out in recent times. The Water Tower Museum (open Sun) displays the history of the area as well as James Hill's 1885–1930 taxidermy collection of some 500 birds and animals. On the eastern side of town, among the grain silos, is an unusual relic called the Stick Shed. The roof of this now empty storage shed is held up with 640 unmilled tree trunks, and the interior is an evocative sight (open once a year in Oct); 31 km NE.

Jung: market on last Sat each month; 10 km NE. *Fishing:* redfin and trout in local lakes, depending on water levels. Reasonable levels at Taylors Lake; 18 km SE. *Mount Zero Olives:* the largest olive grove in the Southern Hemisphere, with 55 000 trees on 730 hectares. The first trees were planted in 1943, after World War II stopped olive oil imports. You can buy oil, vinegar and lentils, and stay overnight.; Laharum; 30 km S.

TOWNS NEARBY: Natimuk 23 km, Dimboola 32 km, Warracknabeal 54 km, Halls Gap 55 km, Stawell 64 km

Inglewood

 Loddon Visitor Information Centre, Wedderburn Community Centre, 24 Wilson St, Wedderburn; (03) 5494 3489; www.loddonalive.com.au

89.5 The Fresh FM, 91.1 FM ABC Local Radio

North along the Calder Highway from Bendigo is the 'Golden Triangle' town of Inglewood. Sizeable gold nuggets were found in this area during the gold rush and are still being unearthed. Inglewood is also known as Blue Eucy town, due to the once vigorous blue mallee eucalyptus oil industry. The town is also the birthplace of Australian aviator Sir Reginald Ansett.

Old eucalyptus oil distillery: not in operation but can be viewed; Calder Hwy, northern end of town. *Old courthouse:* local historical memorabilia; open by appt; Southey St. *Streetscape:* historic buildings are evidence of the town's goldmining history.

Kooyoora State Park The park sits at the northern end of the Bealiba Range and features extensive box-ironbark forests. The Eastern Walking Circuit offers a great opportunity for bushwalkers, passing through strange rock formations and giant granite slabs. The Summit Track leads to Melville Caves Lookout. The caves were once the haunt of the notorious bushranger Captain Melville. Camping is allowed around the caves. Contact Parks Victoria on 13 1963; 16 km W.

Bridgewater on Loddon: fishing and watersports, Old Loddon Vines Vineyard, Water Wheel Vineyards and horse-drawn caravans for hire; 8 km SE. *Loddon Valley wine region:* the warm climate and clay soils of this region are known for producing outstanding red varieties and award-winning chardonnays. Taste the wines at cellar doors like Pandalowie at Bridgewater on Loddon (8 km SE) and Kingower (11 km SW); winery map from visitor information centre.

TOWNS NEARBY: Wedderburn 29 km, Dunolly 34 km, Bendigo 42 km, Maldon 50 km, Maryborough 53 km

Inverloch

A'Beckett St; 1300 762 433; www.visitbasscoast.com

88.1 3MFM South Gippsland, 100.7 FM ABC Local Radio

Inverloch is a small seaside resort set on the protected waters of Anderson Inlet, east of Wonthaggi. It is characterised by long stretches of pristine beach that offer good surf and excellent fishing.

Bunurong Environment Centre: natural history displays with special focus on dinosaur diggings; also sales of natural products; The Esplanade. *Shell Museum:* The Esplanade.

Food and Wine Festival: Feb. *Annual Dinosaur Dig:* Feb/Mar. *Jazz Festival:* Mar. *Billy Cart Derby:* Nov.

Tomo's Japanese Inverloch: sophisticated Japanese; Shop 1, 23 A'Beckett St; (03) 5674 3444. *Vela 9:* modern Australian/Mediterranean; 9 A'Beckett St; (03) 5674 1188.

RACV Inverloch Resort: 70 Cape Paterson–Inverloch Rd; (03) 5674 0000. *Venus Bay Caravan Park:* 113A Jupiter Blvd, Venus Bay; (03) 5663 7728.

Bunurong Coastal Drive Stretching the 14 km of coastline between Inverloch and Cape Paterson is this spectacular coastal drive with magnificent views to Venus Bay and beyond. Carparks offer access to beaches and coastal walks along the drive. The waters offshore are protected within Bunurong Marine National Park, and offer opportunities to surf, snorkel, scuba dive or simply explore the numerous rockpools that are dotted along the coast.

Anderson Inlet: the most southerly habitat for mangroves in Australia. This calm inlet is popular for windsurfing and watersports, and nearby Townsend Bluff and Maher's Landing offer good birdwatching; adjacent to town. *Fishing:* in nearby waterways such as the Tarwin River; 20 km SE.

TOWNS NEARBY: Wonthaggi 11 km, Korumburra 23 km, Leongatha 26 km, Foster 42 km, Cowes 46 km

Jeparit
Pop. 374
Map ref. 526 D12 | 548 F6

ⓘ Wimmera–Mallee Pioneer Museum, Charles St; (03) 5397 2101.

📻 96.5 Triple H FM, 594 AM ABC Local Radio

This little town in the Wimmera is 5 kilometres south-east of Lake Hindmarsh, which was once the largest natural freshwater lake in Victoria. Sadly, it has been empty for the past several years. Former prime minister Sir Robert Menzies was born here in 1894.

🏠 **Wimmera–Mallee Pioneer Museum** This unique museum details what life was like for early settlers in the Wimmera through a collection of colonial buildings furnished in the style of the period. The buildings on display are spread over a 4 ha complex and include log cabins, a church and a blacksmith's shop. The museum also features displays of restored farm machinery. Southern entrance to town, Charles St; open weekdays 9.30am–12pm, 1–4.30pm, weekends 1–4.30pm or by request; (03) 5397 2101.

Menzies Sq: site of the dwelling where Menzies was born; Cnr Charles and Roy sts. *Wimmera River Walk:* 6 km return; starts at museum.

 Lake Hindmarsh Victoria's largest freshwater lake has seen dire water levels for the past several years. It was fed by the Wimmera River. Boating, waterskiing and fishing were all popular pastimes (Schulzes Beach has a boat ramp), with pelicans and other waterbirds existing at the lake in breeding colonies. Picnic and camping spots are available on the lake's shores. A historic fisherman's hut can also be seen. Contact the visitor centre for an update on water levels. 5 km NW.

Rainbow: a charming little Wimmera township, with Pasco's Cash Store, an original country general store, and Yurunga Homestead, a beautiful Edwardian home with a large collection of antiques and original fittings (northern edge of town, key available); 35 km N. *Pella:* former German settlement with Lutheran church and old schoolhouse; 40 km NW via Rainbow. *Lake Albacutya:* fills only when Lake Hindmarsh overflows; 44 km N. *Wyperfeld National Park:* great for bushwalking; known for its birdlife, including the endangered mallee fowl, and wildflowers in spring; 60 km NW via Rainbow; *for details see Hopetoun.*

TOWNS NEARBY: Dimboola 35 km, Nhill 37 km, Warracknabeal 38 km, Hopetoun 57 km, Horsham 66 km

Kerang

Pop. 3780
Map ref. 526 H11 | 549 N4

ⓘ Sir John Gorton Library, cnr Murray Valley Hwy and Shadforth St; (03) 5452 1546; www.gannawarra.vic.gov.au

📻 99.1 Smart FM, 102.1 FM ABC Local Radio

Kerang, situated on the Loddon River just south of the New South Wales border, lies at the southern end of the Kerang wetlands and lakes. They extend from Kerang 42 kilometres north-west to Lake Boga and offer a wonderland for watersports enthusiasts and birdwatchers; the lakes contain what are reputedly the world's largest ibis breeding grounds. The town itself is a service centre for its agricultural surrounds.

🏠 *Lester Lookout Tower:* town views; Cnr Murray Valley Hwy and Shadforth St. *Historical Museum:* focuses on cars and antique farm machinery; Riverwood Dr.

🌴 *Races:* Easter and Boxing Day. *Tour of the Murray River:* cycling race; late Aug/early Sept.

🛏️ *Ibis Caravan Park:* Murray Valley Hwy; (03) 5452 2232. *Kerang Caravan & Tourist Park:* 21 Museum Dr; (03) 5452 1161. *Pelican Waters Lake Charm Tourist Park:* Cnr Benjeroop and Boat Ramp rds, Lake Charm; (03) 5457 9318. *Quambatook Caravan Park:* Meering Rd, Quambatook; 0428 857 122.

 Reedy Lakes: a series of 3 lakes. Apex Park, a recreation reserve for swimming, picnicking and boating, is set by the 1st lake, and the 2nd features a large ibis rookery. Picnic facilities are available at the third lake; 8 km NW. *Leaghur State Park:* on the Loddon River flood plain, this peaceful park is a perfect spot for a leisurely walk through the black box woodlands and wetlands; 25 km SW. *Murrabit:* a historic timber town on the Murray surrounded by picturesque forests, with a country market 1st Sat each month; 27 km N. *Quambatook:* hosts the Australian Tractor Pull Championship each Easter; 40 km SW. *Lake Boga:* popular for watersports, with good sandy beaches; 42 km NW. *Fishing:* Meran, Kangaroo and Charm lakes all offer freshwater fishing; details from visitor centre.

TOWNS NEARBY: Barham (NSW) 22 km, Cohuna 28 km, Pyramid Hill 40 km, Swan Hill 55 km, Wycheproof 73 km

Kilmore
Pop. 4720
Map ref. 537 J1 | 540 C1 | 542 C12

ⓘ Library, 12 Sydney St; (03) 5781 1319.

📻 97.1 OKR FM, 774 AM ABC Local Radio

Kilmore is Victoria's oldest inland town, known for its historic buildings and many horseracing events. Like many towns in the central goldfields, Kilmore was the scene of a Kelly family saga. In this case, it was Ned Kelly's father who had a run-in with the law. In 1865 John 'Red' Kelly was arrested for killing a squatter's calf to feed his family, and was locked away in the Kilmore Gaol for six months. It was a crime that Ned had actually committed. Soon after Red's release, he died of dropsy and was buried in the small town of Avenel, where the Kelly family lived for some time.

🏠 **Old Kilmore Gaol** An impressive bluestone building, established in 1859, that is now a privately owned auction house; Sutherland St.

Hudson Park: picnic/barbecue facilities; Cnr Sydney and Foote sts. *Historic buildings:* Whitburgh Cottage, Piper St, and a number of 1850s shops and hotels along Sydney St; brochure from visitor centre.

 Celtic Festival: June. *Kilmore Cup:* harness racing; Oct.

Bindley House: Cnr Powlett and Piper sts; (03) 5781 1142. *Kilmore Caravan Park:* 110 Northern Hwy; (03) 5782 1508. *Daisyburn Homestead:* 540 Daisyburn Rd, Glenaroua; (03) 5793 8114.

Tramways Heritage Centre at Bylands: extensive display of cable cars and early electric trams, with tram rides available; open Sun only; just south of town. *Broadford:* a small town featuring a historic precinct on High St; 17 km NE. Mt Piper Walking Track: wildlife and wildflowers can be spotted along the way (1 hr return); near Broadford. *Strath Creek:* walks to Strath Creek Falls and a drive through the Valley of a Thousand Hills; starts at outskirts of Broadford.

TOWNS NEARBY: Seymour 34 km, Woodend 38 km, Yea 43 km, Kyneton 45 km, Heathcote 47 km

Koo-Wee-Rup

Pop. 1423
Map ref. 531 H10 | 533 O6 | 537 L9 | 540 E7

ⓘ Newsagency, 277 Rossiter Rd; (03) 5997 1456.

📻 103.1 3BBR FM West Gippsland Community Radio, 774 AM ABC Local Radio

Koo-Wee-Rup and the surrounding agricultural area exist on reclaimed and drained swampland. It has given rise to Australia's largest asparagus-growing district. The town's name derives from the Aboriginal name meaning 'blackfish swimming', a reference to the fish that were once plentiful in the swamp.

Historical Society Museum: local history; open Sun; Rossiter Rd.

Pakenham Caravan Park: Cnr Princes Hwy and Racecourse Rd, Pakenham; (03) 5941 2004.

 Swamp Observation Tower: views of remaining swampland and across to Western Port. A market with local produce operates regularly at the base; South Gippsland Hwy; 2 km SE. *Bayles Fauna Reserve:* native animals; 8 km NE. *Harewood House:* restored 1850s house with original furnishings; South Gippsland Hwy towards Tooradin. *Tooradin:* offers good boating and fishing on Sawtells Inlet; 10 km W. *Caldermeade Farm:* originally a premier beef cattle property but now a fully operational modern dairy farm focused on educating and entertaining visitors; 10 km SE. *Pakenham:* now considered a suburb of Melbourne, Pakenham is home to the Military Vehicle Museum, Army Rd, and the Berwick Pakenham Historical Society Museum, John St; 13 km N. *Tynong:* attractions include Victoria's Farm Shed, featuring farm animals and shearing, and Gumbaya Park, a family fun park; 20 km NE. *Royal Botanic Gardens Cranbourne:* renowned, wonderfully maintained native gardens; 22 km NW. *Grantville:* hosts a market 4th Sun each month; 30 km S.

TOWNS NEARBY: Emerald 30 km, Cowes 36 km, Warragul 39 km, Korumburra 39 km, Mornington 40 km

Korumburra

Pop. 3145
Map ref. 537 N11 | 540 F8

ⓘ Prom Country Information Centre, South Gippsland Hwy; (03) 5655 2233 or 1800 630 704; www.visitpromcountry.com.au

 88.1 3MFM South Gippsland, 100.7 FM ABC Local Radio

Established in 1887, Korumburra stands firmly as the heritage centre of South Gippsland. The township was a primary producer of black coal for Victoria's rail industry until the last mine closed in 1958. Korumburra is set in the rolling green hills of South Gippsland, with scenic drives found in any direction.

Coal Creek Heritage Village Coal Creek is an open-air museum that offers all the fascination of life in a 19th-century coalmining village, including history and memorabilia of the area. The village contains beautiful picnic areas, bush tramway and cafe, and community events are held throughout the year. South Gippsland Hwy; (03) 5655 1811.

Korumburra Federation Art Gallery: South Gippsland Hwy. *Whitelaw Antiques & Collectibles:* 9 Mine Rd.

Farmers Market: Railway Siding; 3rd Sat each month. *Agricultural Show:* Feb. *Rotary Club of Korumburra Art Show:* Feb.

Korumburra Tourist Park: 56 Bourke St; (03) 5655 2326.

 South Gippsland Tourist Railway This railway travels to Leongatha, Korumburra, Loch and Nyora, and provides a scenic way to view the ever-changing South Gippsland landscape. Trains operate Sun and public holidays with a Wed service during school holidays. The grand Edwardian Railway Station behind the main street is also worth a visit. (03) 5658 1111.

Loch: a thriving art and craft village with cosy eateries, antique stores and galleries; 14 km NW. *Poowong:* beautiful country town nestled among the rolling hills of South Gippsland with Poowong Pioneer Chapel, est. 1878; 18 km NW.

TOWNS NEARBY: Leongatha 12 km, Inverloch 23 km, Wonthaggi 28 km, Warragul 32 km, Koo-Wee-Rup 39 km

Kyneton

Pop. 4286
Map ref. 535 G8 | 536 G1 | 540 A1 | 542 A11 | 551 O2

ⓘ Jean Haynes Reserve, High St; (03) 5422 6110; www.visitmacedonranges.com

📻 91.1 FM ABC Local Radio, 100.7 Highlands FM

Part of Victoria's picturesque spa and garden country, Kyneton is a well-preserved town with many attractive bluestone buildings. Caroline Chisholm, who helped many migrants find their feet in this country, lived in Kyneton, where her family owned a store and her husband worked as a magistrate. While living in the town, she established a series of affordable, overnight shelters for travellers on the Mount Alexander Road (now the Calder Highway), a road frequented by gold prospectors. Remnants of the shelters can be seen at the historic township of Carlsruhe, south-east of Kyneton.

Kyneton Museum: in a former bank building, with a drop-log cottage in the grounds; open Fri–Sun; Piper St. *Wool on Piper:* features a spinning mill, with yarns and handmade garments for sale; Piper St. *Botanic Gardens:* 8 ha area scenically located above Pipers Creek. The gardens feature rare varieties of trees; Clowes St. *Historic buildings:* many in town, including mechanics institute on Mollison St and old police depot, Jenning St. *Campaspe River Walk:* scenic walk with picnic spots; access from Piper St.

Farmers market: farmgate produce; Piper St; 2nd Sat each month. *Daffodil and Arts Festival:* Sept. *Kyneton Cup:* Nov.

Annie Smithers: French Provincial; 72 Piper St; (03) 5422 2039. *Dhaba:* Indian; 18 Piper St; (03) 5422 6225. *Little Swallow Cafe:* European-style cafe; 58A Piper St; (03) 5422 6241. *Pizza Verde:* city-smart pizzeria; 62 Piper St; (03) 5422 7400. *Royal George Hotel:* contemporary dining room; 24 Piper St; (03) 5422 1390. *Star Anise Bistro:* modern bistro; 29A Piper St; (03) 5422 2777.

Airleigh – Rose Cottage: 10 Begg St; 0402 783 489.

Trentham and Wombat State Forest This picturesque spa-country town has a mixed history of gold, timber and farming. It has a charming streetscape and attractions include a historic foundry and Minifie's Berry Farm, where you can pick your own berries in season. Just north-east of town is Wombat State Forest – deep within is Victoria's largest single-drop waterfall, Trentham Falls. Cascading 32 m onto a quartz gravel base, the falls are an impressive backdrop for a picnic. 22 km sw.

Reservoirs: several offering scenic locations for walks and picnics. Upper Coliban, Lauriston and Malmsbury reservoirs all nearby. *Paramoor Farm and Winery:* a former Clydesdale horse farm, now winery and B&B; Carlsruhe; 5 km sE. *Malmsbury:* a town noted for its old bluestone buildings. It features historic Botanic Gardens and The Mill, National Trust–classified, not open to the public. Also wineries in the area; 10 km NW. *Turpins and Cascade Falls:* with picnic area and walks; near Metcalfe; 22 km N.

TOWNS NEARBY: Woodend 14 km, Castlemaine 29 km, Daylesford 29 km, Heathcote 42 km, Maldon 44 km

Lakes Entrance

see inset box on next page

Leongatha

Pop. 4501
Map ref. 537 N11 | 540 G8

Michael Place Complex; (03) 5662 2111; www.visitpromcountry.com.au

88.1 3MFM South Gippsland, 100.7 FM ABC Local Radio

Leongatha is a thriving town, considered the commercial centre of South Gippsland. Idyllically positioned as a gateway to Gippsland destinations and attractions, any major road departing Leongatha provides access to popular attractions, all within an easy one hour's drive.

Historical Society Museum: McCartin St. *Leongatha Gallery:* Cnr McCartin St and Michael Pl. *Mushroom Crafts:* craft sales and gallery; 40 Blair St. *Great Southern Rail Trail:* commencement of 50 km rail trail that winds between Leongatha and Foster.

South Gippsland Golf Classic: Feb. *Music for the People Concert:* Mossvale Park; Feb. *Mossvale Music Festival:* Mar. *Raw Vibes Youth Festival:* Mar. *Daffodil Festival:* Sept. *Garden and Lifestyle Expo:* Nov.

The Koonwarra Store: foodstore and emporium, excellent regional fare, courtyard setting; South Gippsland Hwy, Koonwarra; (03) 5664 2285.

Leongatha Apex Caravan Park: 14 Turner St; (03) 5662 2753. *Hudspeth House Bed & Breakfast:* Cnr McKitterick and Welsford sts, Meeniyan; (03) 5664 7461.

Koonwarra Situated between Leongatha and Meeniyan on the South Gippsland Hwy, Koonwarra became the first eco-wise

town in Australia. The town prides itself on its commitment to sustainable lifestyles. Drop in to the Koonwarra Fine Food & Wine Store to purchase local wines, cheese and pantry items. On the first Sat of each month, Koonwarra holds a farmers market. The town also boasts an organic cooking school, day spa, specialty shops, pottery and winery nearby. 8 km sE.

Gippsland wine region This dispersed wine region stretches from Phillip Island to Lakes Entrance, with the main cluster of wineries around Leongatha. Bass Phillip makes what is regarded as Australia's greatest pinot noir. Phillip Island Vineyard is responsible for another superb version, as well as an excellent botrytis riesling, in spite of the island's fierce winds and hungry birds. Chardonnay is Gippsland's other specialty, evident from wineries such as Narkoojee and Nicholson River. The latter makes a particularly wonderful merlot and a blend called The Nicholson (merlot and shiraz).

Meeniyan: great place to visit for the art and craft enthusiast. Places of interest include Meeniyan Art Gallery, South Gippsland Craft Merchants, Beth's Antiques and Lacy Jewellery. Meeniyan hosts an annual art and craft exhibition over the Melbourne Cup weekend; 16 km sE. *Mossvale Park:* tranquil setting for a picnic or barbecue. Music concerts and festivals are held here in Feb and Mar; 16 km NE. *Mirboo North:* situated among the picturesque Strzelecki Ranges, the township is decorated with murals depicting the history of the area. Grand Ridge Brewery, Lyre Bird Forest Walk and the Grand Ridge Rail Trail are also located here; 26 km NE.

TOWNS NEARBY: Korumburra 12 km, Inverloch 26 km, Foster 30 km, Wonthaggi 34 km, Warragul 35 km

Lorne

Pop. 971
Map ref. 536 D11 | 538 E4 | 551 M9

15 Mountjoy Pde; (03) 5289 1152; www.visitgreatoceanroad.org.au

94.7 The Pulse FM, 774 AM ABC Local Radio

Lorne is one of Victoria's most attractive and lively coastal resorts. The approach into town along the Great Ocean Road is truly spectacular, with the superb mountain scenery of the Otways on one side and the rugged Bass Strait coast on the other. The village of Lorne was established in 1871 and quickly became popular with pastoralists from inland areas, leading to its development around the picturesque Louttit Bay. When the Great Ocean Road opened in 1932 Lorne became much more accessible; however, the area has remained relatively unspoiled with good beaches, surfing, fishing and bushwalking in the hills – activities made all the more enjoyable by the area's pleasant, mild climate.

Teddys Lookout: excellent bay views; behind the town, at the end of George St. *Shipwreck Walk:* walk along the beach taking in sites of the numerous shipwrecks along this stretch of coast; details from visitor centre. *Foreshore Reserve:* great spot for a picnic, with paddleboats available for hire. *Qdos:* contemporary art gallery; Allenvale Rd. *Lorne Fisheries:* on the pier with daily supplies.

Pier to Pub Swim: Jan. *Mountain to Surf Foot Race:* Jan. *Great Ocean Road Marathon:* May. *Anaconda Adventure Race:* Dec. *Falls Festival:* Dec–Jan.

Ba Ba Lu Bar & Restaurant: Spanish-style menu; 6A Mountjoy Pde; (03) 5289 1808. *Lorne Ovenhouse:* modern

continued on p. 175

 RADIO STATIONS   IN TOWN   WHAT'S ON   WHERE TO EAT   WHERE TO STAY   NEARBY

VICTORIA

LAKES ENTRANCE

Pop. 5545
Map ref. 541 O6

ℹ️ **Lakes Entrance Visitor Information Centre, cnr The Esplanade and Marine Pde; (03) 5155 1966 or 1800 637 060; www.discovereastgippsland.com.au**

📻 90.7 FM 3REG Radio East Gippsland, 100.7 FM ABC Local Radio

Lakes Entrance is a lovely holiday town situated at the eastern end of the Gippsland Lakes, an inland network of waterways covering more than 400 square kilometres. The artificially created 'entrance' of the town's name allows the Tasman Sea and the lakes to meet, creating a safe harbour that is home to one of the largest fishing fleets in Australia. While many of the attractions in Lakes Entrance are based around the water, there is also opportunity for foodies to indulge themselves with a variety of cafes and restaurants lining The Esplanade, plus sales of fresh fish and local wines.

🏠 *Griffiths Seashell Museum:* 125 The Esplanade; (03) 5155 1538.

🎪 *Markets:* Lakes Entrance Primary School, Myer St; 3rd Sat each month. *Arts Festival:* Forest Tech Living Resource Centre; Mar long weekend. *Lakes Motor Fest:* biannual; Apr. *New Year's Eve Entertainment and Fireworks:* Dec.

🍴 *The Boathouse Restaurant:* local seafood; 201 The Esplanade; (03) 5155 3055. *Ferryman's Seafood Cafe:* local seafood; Middle Boat Harbour, The Esplanade; (03) 5155 3000. *Miriam's:* local seafood; Level 1, cnr The Esplanade and Bulmer St; (03) 5155 3999. *Bancroft Bites:* cafe with excellent homemade cakes; 2/57 Metung Rd, Metung; (03) 5156 2854. *The Metung Galley:* excellent local produce menu; 3/59 Metung Rd, Metung; (03) 5156 2330.

🛏️ *BIG4 Whiters Holiday Village:* Cnr Roadknight and Whiters sts; (03) 5155 1343. *Eastern Beach Holiday Park:* 42 Eastern Beach Rd; (03) 5155 1581. *Echo Beach Tourist Park:* 31–33 Roadknight St; (03) 5155 2238. *Golden Terrace Holiday Park:* 651 Esplanade (Princes Hwy); (03) 5155 1237. *Idleours:* 649 Esplanade; (03) 5155 1788. *Lakes Entrance Tourist Park:* 127 Princes Hwy; (03) 5155 1159. *Lakes Haven Caravan Park:* 3 Jemmeson St; (03) 5155 2254. *North Arm Tourist Park:* 76 Marine Pde; (03) 5155 2490. *Silver Sands Tourist Park:*

33 Myer St; (03) 5155 2343. *Sunnyside Caravan Park:* 60 Myer St; (03) 5155 1735. *Waters Edge Holiday Park:* 623 Esplanade; (03) 5155 1914. *Woodbine Tourist Park:* 33 Church St; (03) 5155 1718. *Lake Tyers Camp & Caravan Park:* 558 Lake Tyers Beach Rd, Lake Tyers Beach; (03) 5156 5530. *The Lakes Beachfront Holiday Retreat:* 430 Lake Tyers Beach Rd, Lake Tyers Beach; (03) 5156 5582.

🌐 **Gippsland Lakes** Five rivers end their journey to the sea here, forming a vast expanse of water tucked in behind Ninety Mile Beach. The lakes are a true playground for anyone with an interest in water activities, especially fishing and boating. Explore the lakes on a sightseeing cruise, including one to Wyanga Park Winery, or on the ever-popular houseboats that can be hired over summer. Contact visitor centre for details. At the centre, the Lakes National Park offers birdwatching, walking, swimming and camping. Access is via boat from Paynesville or road and foot from Loch Sport.

Jemmys Point: great views of the region; 1 km w. *Lake Bunga:* nature trail along foreshore; 3 km ᴇ. *Lake Tyers:* sheltered waters ideal for fishing, swimming and boating. Cruises depart from Fishermans Landing in town. Lake is 6–23 km ɴᴇ, depending on access point. Lake Tyers Forest Park is great for bushwalking, wildlife-spotting, picnicking and camping; 20 km ɴᴇ. *Nyerimilang Heritage Park:* 1920s homestead, with original farm buildings and the wonderfully maintained East Gippsland Botanic Gardens. Rose Pruning Day, with demonstrations, is held in July; 10 km ɴᴡ. *Swan Reach:* Rosewood Pottery; Malcolm Cameron Studio Gallery, open weekends; 14 km ɴᴡ. *Metung:* a scenic town on Lake King with boat hire, cruises and a marina regatta each Jan. Chainsaw Sculpture Gallery has chainsaw sculpture and a display of Annemieke Mein's embroidery art; 15 km w. *Nicholson River Winery:* 22 km ɴᴡ. *East Gippsland Carriage Co:* restored horse-drawn carriages, and tours; 30 km ᴇ. *Bataluk Cultural Trail:* driving tour taking in Aboriginal cultural sites in the East Gippsland region; self-guide brochure available from visitor centre.

ᴛᴏᴡɴꜱ ɴᴇᴀʀʙʏ: Paynesville 25 km, Bairnsdale 34 km, Buchan 45 km, Orbost 45 km, Sale 85 km

[FERRY CRUISING THROUGH LAKES ENTRANCE]

wood-fired menu; 46A Mountjoy Pde; (03) 5289 2544.
Qdos Cafe: cafe-bar; Qdos Arts, 35 Allenvale Rd; (03) 5289 1989.

 Chatby Lane: 4 Howard St; (03) 5289 1616. *Lorne Foreshore Caravan Parks:* 2 Great Ocean Rd; 1300 364 797. *BIG4 Wye River Tourist Park:* 25 Great Ocean Rd, Wye River; (03) 5289 0241.

Great Otway National Park This park covers 103 000 ha and includes a range of environments, from the timbered ridges of the eastern Otways to fern gullies, waterfalls and a coastline with tall cliffs, coves and sandy beaches. Around Lorne there are more than 100 walking tracks and the rock platforms along the coast provide ideal spots for ocean fishing. The Falls Festival, a major rock-music festival, is held over New Year's Eve at a property near the Erskine Falls, 9 km NW. These popular falls are a peaceful location and drop 30 m over moss-covered rocks. As well as driving, you can walk to the falls from Lorne along the river. The park surrounds Lorne and can be accessed from various points along the Great Ocean Rd. Contact Parks Victoria on 13 1963.

Cumberland River Valley: walking tracks and camping; 4 km sw. *Mt Defiance Lookout:* 10 km sw. *Wye River:* a small coastal village, good for rock and surf fishing, surfing and camping; 17 km sw. *Old Lorne Road Olives:* olive grove, cafe and gallery; closed Tues and Wed; Deans Marsh Rd; 22 km N. *Gentle Annie Berry Gardens:* pick your own; open Nov–Apr; 26 km NW via Deans Marsh. *Scenic drives:* west through the Otway Ranges, and south-west or north-east on the Great Ocean Rd.

TOWNS NEARBY: Aireys Inlet 14 km, Anglesea 24 km, Winchelsea 33 km, Apollo Bay 36 km, Torquay 38 km

Maffra
Pop. 4151
Map ref. 541 K6

96 Johnson St; (03) 5141 1811; www.tourismwellington.com.au

100.7 FM ABC Local Radio, 104.7 Gippsland FM

Maffra, settled in the 1840s, has the charm and old-style hospitality of another era. Named after Maffra in Portugal because many of the early Gippsland settlers had fought in that area of Europe during the Peninsula War, the town's early days were fraught with drought until a sugar beet industry established in the 1890s provided a major boost. The Glenmaggie Irrigation Scheme of 1919 also signalled a new heyday and ensured the viable and lengthy success of today's dairy industry. The sugar beet factory closed in 1948 owing to World War II's labour shortages and the competing dairy industry, but Maffra continues to support its rich agricultural surrounds. It also holds a great sense of history in its original shop verandahs and grand homesteads.

Maffra Sugar Beet Historic Museum: local history museum with special interest in the sugar beet industry; open Sun afternoon; River St. *Mineral and gemstone display:* large collection of rare gemstones and fossils at the information centre; Johnson St. *All Seasons Herb Garden:* Foster St. *Gippsland Vehicle Collection:* outstanding rotating display of interesting vehicles; located in a historic vegetable-dehydrating factory; Maffra–Sale Rd; (03) 5147 3223. *Gippsland Plains Rail Trail:* recreational trail for cycling and walking that passes through town; still under development but when complete will link

Stratford in the east to Traralgon in the west by traversing dairy country.

 Gippsland Harvest Festival: Mar. *Mardi Gras:* Mar.

Abington Bed & Breakfast: 56 Coghlans La, Heyfield; (03) 5148 2430. *Lake Glenmaggie Caravan Park:* Heyfield–Licola Rd, Glenmaggie; 0409 854 106. *Stratford On The River Tourist Park:* 16 McMillan St, Stratford; (03) 5145 6588.

Stratford: the scenic Avon River flows through town. Knobs Reserve is a site where the local Aboriginal people once sharpened axe heads on sandstone grinding stones – it is part of the Bataluk Cultural Trail, which takes in significant Indigenous sites throughout East Gippsland. Stratford hosts the Shakespeare Celebration in May; 9 km E. *Australian Wildlife Art Gallery and Sculpture:* Princes Hwy near Munro; 25 km E. *Robotic Dairy:* the first Australian dairy farm to install 4 'Astronaut Milking Robots' where the cows decide when to be milked; open on public visitor days or by appt; Toongabbie Rd, Winnindoo; (03) 5199 2212; 26 km W. *Lake Glenmaggie:* popular watersports venue; 42 km NW via Heyfield. *Alpine National Park:* sprawls from Licola, 75 km NW, to the NSW border. Near Licola is Lake Tali Karng, which lies 850 m above sea level and is a popular bushwalking destination during the warmer months. *Scenic drives:* the Traralgon to Stratford Tourist Route highlights attractions of the area. For stunning scenery, drive north along Forest Rd, through the Macalister River Valley to Licola and Mt Tamboritha in Alpine National Park; or to Jamieson (166 km NW via Heyfield), with access to snowfields or Lake Eildon.

TOWNS NEARBY: Sale 17 km, Traralgon 46 km, Walhalla 47 km, Bairnsdale 58 km, Morwell 59 km

Maldon
Pop. 1222
Map ref. 535 E5 | 549 N11 | 551 N1

High St; (03) 5475 2569; www.maldon.org.au

91.1 FM ABC Local Radio, 106.3 Radio KLFM

Maldon is one of Victoria's best-known gold towns and a popular weekend getaway for Melburnians. The town has been wonderfully preserved, with the wide, tree-lined main street featuring old buildings and shopfronts. There is also a tourist steam train. Aside from the cafes and galleries, the town seems unchanged from the gold rush days. Maldon was declared Australia's first 'notable town' by the National Trust in 1966.

Historic town walk: grab a brochure from the visitor centre and take to the wide, old footpaths to discover the historic delights of Maldon. See preserved 19th-century shopfronts and old stone cottages. Highlights include the restored Dabb's General Store in Main St, and the Maldon Hospital in Adair St. *Museum:* displays on mining as well as domestic memorabilia from Maldon's past, in heritage building; open 1.30–4pm daily; High St. *The Beehive Chimney:* southern end of Church St. *Anzac Hill:* the walk to the top is rewarded with magnificent views of the area; southern end of High St.

Fair: Easter. *Vintage Car Hill Climb:* Oct. *Folk Festival:* Oct–Nov.

Penny School Gallery/Cafe: international cuisine; 11 Church St; (03) 5475 1911. *Zen Eden Produce:* vegetarian cafe and produce store; 6 Main St; 0408 319 188.

VICTORIA

[MANSFIELD] FARMLAND WITH SNOW-CAPPED MOUNT BULLER IN THE BACKGROUND

Palm House: 2 High St; (03) 5475 2532.

Porcupine Township This award-winning tourist attraction is a reconstruction of an early 1850s goldmining town, with an array of slab, shingle and mudbrick buildings moved here from other goldfields. The village, complete with a blacksmith's, a doctor's surgery and even a bowling alley, is located in rugged bushland on the site of the original Porcupine diggings, where the first gold discovery between Castlemaine and Bendigo was made. Visitors to the township can pan for gold, handfeed emus or take a ride on the Little Toot train, which does a circuit through the diggings. Cnr Maldon–Bendigo and Allans rds; (03) 5475 1000; 3 km NE.

Mt Tarrangower Lookout Tower: town views; 2 km W. *Carman's Tunnel Mine:* guided mine tours feature relics from goldmining days; 2 km SW. *Nuggetty Ranges and Mt Moorol:* 2 km N. *Cairn Curran Reservoir:* great for watersports and fishing, water levels permitting; features picnic facilities and a sailing club near the spillway; 10 km SW. *Victorian Goldfields Railway:* historic steam trains run from Maldon Railway Station (Hornsby St) through scenic forest to Castlemaine; operates Wed, Sun and public holidays; bookings on (03) 5470 6658.

TOWNS NEARBY: **Castlemaine 15 km, Maryborough 30 km, Bendigo 32 km, Dunolly 33 km, Daylesford 39 km**

Mallacoota

Pop. 973
Map ref. 519 D11 | 539 G11

ℹ️ Visitor Information Shed, Main Wharf; (03) 5158 0800; www.visitmallacoota.com

📻 101.7 FM 3MGB Wilderness Radio, 104.9 FM ABC Local Radio

Mallacoota is a popular holiday centre in far East Gippsland, offering excellent fishing, walking, boating and swimming. It is surrounded by the scenic Croajingolong National Park, which features Point Hicks, notable for being the first land on the east coast of Australia to be sighted by Europeans, as well as remote ocean beaches and estuarine waterways. There are spectacular surf beaches near the town, with Mallacoota Inlet offering great fishing. Boats can be hired in town.

WW II bunker and museum: restored and located at the airport. *Information shed:* a mural depicting Mallacoota's history is painted on the external walls; Main Wharf. *The Spotted Dog Gold Mine:* established in 1894, this was the most successful goldmine in the Mallacoota district.

Holiday markets: Easter and Christmas. *Bream Fishing Classic:* Mar (round 1) and June (round 2). *Tour of Gippsland Cycling Event:* July/Aug. *Flora and Fauna weekend:* 1st weekend in Nov.

Lucy's Noodles: authentic noodles with home-grown produce; 64 Maurice Ave; (03) 5158 0666.

A Wangralea Caravan Park: 78 Betka Rd; (03) 5158 0222. *Mallacoota's Shady Gully Caravan Park:* Lot 5 Genoa Rd; (03) 5158 0362. *Mallacoota Foreshore Holiday Park:* Allan Dr; (03) 5158 0300. *The Wave Oasis – Luxury:* 36 Vista Dr; (03) 5158 0995.

Croajingolong National Park This park takes up a vast portion of what has been dubbed the Wilderness Coast. It protects remote beaches, tall forests, heathland, rainforest, estuaries and granite peaks, as well as creatures such as wallabies, possums, goannas and lyrebirds. Offshore, you might be lucky enough to spot dolphins, seals or southern right and humpback whales. Pt Hicks Lighthouse is a popular spot to visit, and Tamboon and Mallacoota inlets are good spots for canoeing. Access the park via a track west of town or various roads south of the Princes Hwy; contact Parks Victoria on 13 1963.

Surf beaches: Bastion Point, 2 km S; Bekta, 5 km S. *Gabo Island Lightstation Reserve:* take a scenic daytrip or stay in the Lightkeeper's Residence; 11 km E (offshore). *Gipsy Pt:* a quiet holiday retreat overlooking the Genoa River; 16 km NW.

TOWNS NEARBY: **Cann River 53 km, Eden (NSW) 57 km, Merimbula (NSW) 76 km, Bombala (NSW) 85 km, Tathra (NSW) 94 km**

Mansfield

Pop. 2846
Map ref. 542 H11 | 544 D9

ⓘ The Station Precinct, 173 Maroondah Hwy; 1800 039 049; www.mansfield-mtbuller.com.au

📻 99.7 FM Radio Mansfield, 103.7 FM ABC Local Radio

Mansfield is located in Victoria's High Country at the junction of the Midland and Maroondah highways. It is within easy reach of Lake Eildon's network of rivers, Alpine National Park and Mansfield State Forest. Activities ranging from hiking to horseriding to skiing make it an ideal destination for anyone with a love of outdoor adventure, no matter what the season.

🏠 *Troopers' Monument:* monument to police officers shot by Ned Kelly at Stringybark Creek; Cnr High St and Midland Hwy. *Mansfield Mullum Wetlands Walk:* along reclaimed railway line; starts from behind the visitor centre. *Self-guide town walk:* take in many buildings of historical significance.

🎇 *The High Country Autumn Festival and Merrijig Rodeo:* Mar long weekend. *High Country Spring Arts Festival:* 24 Oct – 4 Nov.

🍴 *Mansfield Hotel:* pizza and DIY barbecue; 86 High St; (03) 5775 2101. *Mansfield Regional Produce Store:* popular local cafe, great coffee; 68 High St; (03) 5779 1404. *The Magnolia Restaurant:* modern Australian; 190 Mt Buller Rd; (03) 5779 1444. *Jamieson Brewery:* menu complements house-crafted ales; Eildon Rd, Jamieson; (03) 5777 0515.

🛏 *High Country Holiday Park:* 1 Ultimo St; (03) 5775 2705. *Mansfield Holiday Park:* Mt Buller Rd; (03) 5775 1383. *Bluegum Ridge Cottages:* 434 Buttercup Rd, Merrijig; (03) 5777 5015. *Bonnie Doon Caravan Park:* Arnot St, Bonnie Doon; (03) 5778 7254. *Bonnie Doon's Lakeside Leisure Resort:* 240 Hutchinsons Rd, Bonnie Doon; (03) 5778 7252. *Midland Holiday Park:* 3028 Midland Hwy, Lima South; (03) 5768 2416. *Rothesay Park:* 108 Bromfield Dr, Tolmie; (03) 5776 2177. *Willowlake:* 16 Willowlake Dr, Macs Cove; (03) 5777 3814. *Wombat Hills:* 55 Lochiel Rd, Barwite; (03) 5776 9507.

⚙ **Mt Buller** Victoria's largest and best alpine skiing resort is Mt Buller, whose summit stands 1804 m above sea level. The 24 lifts, including the 6-seater Holden chairlift (first of its kind in Australia), give access to 180 ha of ski trails, from gentle 'family runs' to heart-stopping double black diamond chutes. If you are a beginner, take on the friendly Bourke Street (Green Run) to find your 'ski legs', or join one of the ski schools there. There is also a half pipe at Boggy Creek and Terrain Park, or cross-country skiing at nearby Mt Stirling. Mt Buller Village offers resort accommodation, and the ski season runs between early June and late Sept. (03) 5777 6077; 47 km E.

Craig's Hut The High Country is synonymous with courageous and hardy cattlemen, transformed into Australian legends by Banjo Paterson's iconic ballad 'The Man from Snowy River'. The men would build huts on the high plains for shelter during summer cattle drives. Craig's Hut on Mt Stirling is a replica of one such shelter, used as a set on the 1983 film *The Man from Snowy River*. It burnt down in the 2006 bushfires, but was rebuilt and reopened in January 2008. The last 2 km of the track to the hut is 4WD or 1.5 km via a fairly steep walking track. 50 km E.

Delatite Winery: Stoneys Rd; 7 km SE. *Mt Samaria State Park:* scenic drives, camping and bushwalking; 14 km N. *Lake Eildon:* houseboat hire, fishing and sailing; 15 km S; *see Eildon for further details. Lake Nillahcootie:* popular for boating, fishing and watersports; 20 km NW. *Jamieson:* an old goldmining town on the Jamieson River with historic buildings; 37 km S. *Alpine National Park:* begins around 40 km SE (*see Mount Beauty*). *Scenic drive:* take the road over the mountains to Whitfield (62 km NE), in the King River Valley, passing through spectacular scenery, including Powers Lookout (48 km NE) for views over the valley. *Lake William Hovell:* for boating and fishing; 85 km NE. *Mt Skene:* great for bushwalking, with wildflowers in summer; 85 km SE via Jamieson. *Fishing:* good spots include the Delatite, Howqua, Jamieson and Goulburn rivers. *Horse trail-riding:* a different way to explore the region, from 2 hr rides to 10-day treks; details from visitor centre. *Mountain-biking:* summer months reveal an expanding network of downhill and cross-country trails at Mt Buller and Mt Stirling.

TOWNS NEARBY: Eildon 25 km, Alexandra 37 km, Benalla 56 km, Euroa 57 km, Marysville 59 km

Maryborough

Pop. 7690
Map ref. 535 C5 | 549 M11 | 551 M1

ⓘ Cnr Alma and Nolan sts; (03) 5460 4511 or 1800 356 511; www.visitmaryborough.com.au

📻 99.1 Goldfields FM, 107.9 FM ABC Local Radio

Maryborough is a small city set on the northern slopes of the Great Dividing Range. Its historic 19th-century buildings, particularly around the civic square, are a testament to the riches brought by the gold rush of the 1850s. Stroll through the streets to enjoy the cafes, craft shops and magnificent buildings, such as the National Trust–listed courthouse, post office and town hall.

🏠 **Maryborough Railway Station** So immense and impressive is this building that Mark Twain, on his visit to the town, remarked that Maryborough was 'a station with a town attached'. Rumour has it that the building was actually intended for Maryborough in Queensland. The beautifully preserved station houses the visitor centre, the extensive Antique Emporium, the Woodworkers Gallery (open weekends only), and Twains Wood and Craft Gallery. Station St.

Pioneer Memorial Tower: Bristol Hill. *Worsley Cottage:* a historical museum featuring local relics; open Sun; Palmerston St. *Central Goldfields Art Gallery:* features an impressive collection of local artworks, housed in the old fire station; Neill St. *Phillips Gardens:* Alma St.

🎇 *Highland Gathering:* New Year's Day. *Energy Breakthrough:* energy expo; Nov.

🛏 *Maryborough Caravan Park:* 7 Holyrood St; (03) 5460 4848. *Crofter's Cottage Stay:* 376 Majorca Rd; (03) 5460 5683.

⚙ **Paddys Ranges State Park** This park offers the chance to enjoy red ironbark and grey box vegetation on a scenic walk or drive. The majority of walks start from the picnic area – see old goldmines and relics or keep an eye out for the rare painted honeyeater and other birdlife. There is also fossicking within the park, but in designated areas only. Access to the park is just south of Maryborough. Contact Parks Victoria on 13 1963.

Aboriginal wells: impressive rock wells; 4 km S. *Carisbrook:* holds a popular tourist market 1st Sun each month; 7 km E.

TOWNS NEARBY: Dunolly 21 km, Avoca 24 km, Clunes 28 km, Maldon 30 km, Castlemaine 43 km

 RADIO STATIONS   IN TOWN   WHAT'S ON   WHERE TO EAT   WHERE TO STAY   NEARBY

VICTORIA

Marysville

Pop. 516
Map ref. 534 F5 | 537 N3 | 540 F3

ℹ️ Marysville Rebuilding Advisory Centre and Community Facility, Murchison St; (03) 5963 4567; www.marysvilletourism.com; www.marysvilletourism.com

📻 98.5 UGFM Upper Goulburn Community Radio, 774 AM ABC Local Radio

For 100 years, the beautiful subalpine village of Marysville was a much-frequented holiday destination for Melburnians. Providing access to the magnificent 84-metre Steavenson Falls nearby, the town charmed visitors with its cafes, galleries and popular guesthouses. Tragically, the town was almost totally destroyed by bushfire on 7 February 2009. With the help of the community, state and federal governments, this once idyllic township is slowly being rebuilt.

🏠 *Uncle Fred & Aunty Val's Lolly Shop & Produce Store:* old-fashioned candy store; 8 Murchison St; (03) 5963 3644. *Bruno's Art & Sculpture Garden:* gardens featuring sculptures by artist Bruno Torfs; open 10am–5pm daily; 51 Falls Rd; (03) 5963 3513.

Community Market: Murchison St; 2nd Sun each month. *Farmers Market:* Murchison St; 4th Sun each month. *Taggerty 4 Seasons Market:* Taggerty Hall; Jan, Easter, June, Nov.

🍴 *Black Spur Inn:* country-style restaurant; 436 Maroondah Hwy, Narbethong; (03) 5963 7121. *Fraga's Cafe:* stop for lunch or a coffee; shop 1, 19 Murchison St; (03) 5963 3216. *Marysville Country Bakery:* country-style bakery and cafe; 17 Murchison St; (03) 5963 3477. *My Chef, Mike:* excellent pizza, light lunches, coffee and cakes; 49 Darwin St; (03) 5963 4512.

🛏️ *Delderfield Luxury B&B:* 1 Darwin St; (03) 5963 4345. *Marysville Caravan and Holiday Park:* 1130 Buxton Rd; (03) 5963 3247.

Cathedral Range State Park The word 'imposing' does not do justice to the 7 km rocky ridge that forms the backbone of this park. Challenging hikes up the ridge to lookout points offer unparalleled views to the valley below. Walks can include overnight stays at the Farmyard, so named because lyrebirds imitate the noises of the domestic animals in the farmyards below. Contact Parks Victoria on 13 1963; 15 km N.

Lake Mountain Renowned for first-rate cross-country skiing, the area is also great for tobogganing, snow tubing and sled rides. When the snow melts and the wildflowers bloom, hikers can take the Summit Walk (4 km return) over the mountain. Ski and walk brochure available from visitor centre.

Lady Talbot Forest Drive: this 46 km route begins east of town. Stop en route to enjoy picnic spots, walking tracks and lookouts. *Buxton Trout & Salmon Farm:* drop a line in one of the well-stocked ponds, purchase smoked fish or enjoy a barbecue lunch; open 9am–5pm daily; 2118 Maroondah Hwy, Buxton; (03) 5774 7370; 12 km SE. *Scenic walks:* many tracks in the area, including a short walk to Steavenson Falls, from Falls Rd; 4 km loop walk in Cumberland Memorial Scenic Reserve, 16 km E; 4 km Beeches Walk through ancient beech and mountain ash forests (accessed via Lady Talbot Forest Dr). *Big River State Forest:* camping, fishing and gold fossicking; 30 km E.

TOWNS NEARBY: Healesville 26 km, Warburton 28 km, Eildon 34 km, Alexandra 35 km, Yarra Glen 37 km

Milawa

Pop. 202
Map ref. 543 I8 | 544 F5

ℹ️ Wangaratta Visitor Information Centre, 100 Murphy St, Wangaratta; 1800 801 065; www.visitwangaratta.com.au

📻 97.7 FM ABC Local Radio, 101.3 Oak FM

Milawa is the perfect destination for lovers of fine food and wine. The Milawa gourmet region boasts over 13 wineries, including the renowned Brown Brothers vineyard. Other fresh local-produce outlets sell olives, honey, cheese, chocolates and berries.

🏠 *Milawa Mustards:* a wide range of locally produced mustards; set in attractive cottage gardens; Snow Rd. *Milawa Cheese Company:* sales and tastings of specialist, gourmet cheeses; Factory Rd. *Milawa Muse Gallery:* ever-changing collection of various art mediums complementing the fine quality of the region; Milawa Cheese Factory complex. *Brown Brothers:* cellar-door tastings and sales; Bobinawarrah Rd. *EV Olives:* working olive grove open for tastings and sales; Everton Rd, Markwood.

A Weekend Fit for a King: be treated like a king at the King Valley wineries festival; Queen's Birthday weekend, June. *Beat the Winter Blues and Jazz Festival:* July. *King Valley Shed Show:* Oct. *La Dolce Vita:* wine and food festival at the Milawa/King Valley wineries; Nov.

🍴 *The Epicurean Centre:* rustic dishes to match wines; Brown Brothers Vineyard, 239 Milawa–Bobinawarrah Rd; (03) 5720 5540. *Milawa Cheese Factory Restaurant:* French-influenced menu; Milawa Cheese Company, 17 Milawa–Bobinawarrah Rd; (03) 5727 3589. *Restaurant Merlot:* contemporary Australian; Lindenwarrah Hotel, Milawa–Bobinawarrah Rd; (03) 5720 5777.

🛏️ *Milawa Muscat Retreat B&B:* 1422 Glenrowan Myrtleford Rd; (03) 5727 3999. *Gentle Annie Caravan & Camping Reserve:* 98 Gentle Annie La, Whitfield; (03) 5729 8205. *Valley View Caravan Park:* 6 Valley View Dr, Whitfield; (03) 5729 8350.

King Valley wine region Given that this region is known for its cheese, make sure to enjoy its wines with a decadent cheese platter. Italian heritage is evident in many of the vineyards. Varieties such as sangiovese, nebbiolo and barbera rub shoulders with cabernet sauvignon, chardonnay and merlot. Brown Brothers is the biggest name with the most established cellar door – a barn-like building featuring some enormous oak barrels of ageing wine. It also incorporates the Epicurean Centre restaurant, which is perfect for long, lazy lunches. To the west, Miranda King Valley is known for its chardonnay. Its cellar door also represents Symphonia Wines, producing some of the region's more interesting varieties such as saperavi and tannat. Heading south are Pizzini, whose sangiovese is one of Australia's best, and Dal Zotto.

Oxley: home to many wineries as well as the Blue Ox Blueberry Farm and King River Cafe; 4 km W.

TOWNS NEARBY: Wangaratta 14 km, Glenrowan 19 km, Beechworth 25 km, Myrtleford 29 km, Chiltern 37 km

Mildura

see inset box on page 180

Moe

Pop. 15 581
Map ref. 537 P9 | 540 H7

i Latrobe Visitor Information Centre, The Old Church, Southside Central, Princes Hwy; 1800 621 409; www.visitlatrobevalley.com

100.7 FM ABC Local Radio, 104.7 Gippsland FM

Like many of the towns in this region, Moe is supported by the power industry, but it has managed to avoid becoming a grim industrial centre. Instead there is a small-town feel and a number of pretty gardens and public parks.

Gippsland Heritage Park Also known as Old Gippstown, this is a re-creation of a 19th-century community with over 30 restored buildings and a fine collection of fully restored horse-drawn carriages. Lloyd St; (03) 5127 8709.

Cinderella Dolls: Andrew St. *Race track:* picturesque country horse track with regular meetings; Waterloo Rd.

Old Gippstown Market: at Gippsland Heritage Park, with local crafts and produce; last Sat each month Sept–May. *Fairies in the Park:* Feb. *Jazz Festival:* Mar. *Blue Rock Classic:* cross-country horserace; Mar. *Moe Cup:* horserace; Oct.

Moe Gardens Caravan Park: 1 Mitchells Rd; (03) 5127 3072.

Baw Baw National Park The landscape of Baw Baw ranges from densely forested river valleys to alpine plateaus and the activities on offer are equally varied – from canoeing river rapids and fishing for trout to skiing, horseriding and bushwalking. Wildflowers carpet the alpine areas in spring. Baw Baw Alpine Resort is located 90 km north of Moe, while the popular Aberfeldy picnic and camping area is accessed via a track north of Walhalla. Contact Parks Victoria on 13 1963.

Edward Hunter Heritage Bush Reserve: 3 km s via Coalville St. *Trafalgar Lookout and Narracan Falls:* near Trafalgar; 10 km w. *Old Brown Coal Mine Museum:* explore the history and memorabilia of the original township known as 'Brown Coal Mine' and the establishment of the power industry in the Latrobe Valley; Cnr Third St and Latrobe River Rd, Yallourn North; 10 km e. *Blue Rock Dam:* fishing, swimming and sailing; 20 km nw. *Thorpdale:* a town renowned for its potatoes. A bakery sells potato bread and a potato festival is held each Mar; 22 km sw. *Walhalla Mountain River Trail:* leads to the picturesque old mining township of Walhalla; Tourist Route 91; details from visitor centre. *See Walhalla.*

towns nearby: Morwell 13 km, Traralgon 25 km, Warragul 29 km, Walhalla 31 km, Leongatha 43 km

Mornington

Pop. 20 821
Map ref. 531 D10 | 533 J5 | 537 J9 | 540 C7

i Mornington Peninsula Visitor Information Centre, Point Nepean Rd, Dromana; (03) 5987 3078 or 1800 804 009; www.visitmorningtonpeninsula.org

98.7 3RPP FM, 774 AM ABC Local Radio

Mornington was once the hub of the Mornington Peninsula, which is the reason this long arm of land was eventually given the same name. Today Melbourne's urban sprawl has just about reached the town, and it has virtually become a suburb. It still retains a seaside village ambience, particularly with a historic courthouse and post office museum that provide a glimpse of the past. The Rocks restaurant on the harbour provides a stunning

view over the famous yachts. In the distance, colourful bathing boxes line Mills Beach.

Historic Mornington Pier: built in the 1850s, the pier remains popular today for walks and fishing. *Mornington Peninsula Regional Gallery:* print and drawing collection, including works by Dobell, Drysdale and Nolan; open Tues–Sat; Dunns Rd. *World of Motorcycles Museum:* Tyabb Rd. *Old post office:* now home to a local history display; Cnr Main St and The Esplanade. *Mornington Tourist Railway:* 10 km journey on steam train; departs from cnr Yuilles and Watt rds; 1st, 2nd and 3rd Sun each month, with additional trips running on Thurs in Jan.

Street Market: Main St; each Wed. *Mornington Racecourse Craft Market:* 2nd Sun each month. *RACV Vintage Car Rally:* Jan. *Mornington Food and Wine Festival:* Oct.

Afghan Marcopolo: Afghan cuisine; 11 Main St; (03) 5975 5154. *Brass Razu Wine Bar:* modern European; 13 Main St; (03) 5975 0108. *The Rocks:* seafood with yachts; Mornington Yacht Club, 1 Schnapper Point Dr; (03) 5973 5599.

Mornington Bed & Breakfast: 16 Wilsons Rd; (03) 5975 6688. *Mornington Country Cottages:* 900 Moorooduc Hwy; (03) 5978 8887. *Mornington Gardens Holiday Village:* 98 Bungower Rd; (03) 5975 7373. *Arthurs Superb Views & Luxury Accommodation:* 10 Nestle Crt, Arthurs Seat; (03) 5981 8400. *BIG4 Frankston Holiday Park:* 2 Robinsons Rd, Frankston South; (03) 5971 2333. *Club Pet:* 55 Palm Beach Dr, Patterson Lakes; (03) 9773 2145. *The Courtyard Mt Eliza:* 25 Granya Gr, Mount Eliza; (03) 9787 7434. *Discovery Holiday Parks – Carrum Downs:* 1165 Frankston–Dandenong Rd, Carrum Downs; (03) 9782 1292. *Discovery Holiday Parks – Chelsea:* 100 Broadway, Bonbeach; (03) 9772 2485. *Discovery Holiday Parks – Frankston:* 1325 Frankston–Dandenong Rd, Carrum Downs; (03) 9786 8355. *Dromana Holiday & Lifestyle Village:* 131 Nepean Hwy, Dromana; (03) 5981 0333. *Kangerong Holiday Park:* 105 Point Nepean Rd, Dromana; (03) 5987 2080. *Lakeside Villas At Crittenden Estate:* 25 Harrisons Rd, Dromana; (03) 5987 3275. *Marina View Van Village:* 38 Salmon St, Hastings; (03) 5979 2322. *Mount Martha Bed & Breakfast by the Sea:* 539 Esplanade, Mount Martha; (03) 5974 1019. *Peninsula Holiday Park:* 10 Ponderosa Pl, Dromana; (03) 5987 2095. *Seahaze B&B:* 40 Seahaze St, Arthurs Seat; (03) 5987 2568. *South East Holiday Village:* 29 Wells Rd, Chelsea Heights; (03) 9772 8436. *The Studio & The Barn:* 190 Purves Rd, Arthurs Seat; (03) 5989 6267. *The TreeHouse on the Lake:* 61 Bulldog Creek Rd, Merricks North; (03) 5989 7651.

Arthurs Seat State Park At 309 m, Arthurs Seat is the highest point on the Mornington Peninsula. The summit can be reached by foot or vehicle and offers panoramic views of the bay and surrounding bushland. Picnic facilities and a restaurant are on the summit. There are many short walks, plus the historic Seawinds Park with gardens and sculptures. The Enchanted Maze Garden is set in superb gardens, with a variety of mazes and the Maize Maze Festival in Feb–Apr. Contact Parks Victoria on 13 1963; Arthurs Seat Rd, near Dromana; 16 km sw.

Mornington Peninsula wine region Featuring many boutique wineries, the peninsula's signature styles are chardonnay and pinot noir, with shiraz, pinot gris and sauvignon blanc also grown here. Paringa Estate repeatedly receives gold medals for its pinot noir, while Stonier creates beautiful chardonnay. Plenty of the wineries also have excellent restaurants, pairing food and wine

continued on p. 181

VICTORIA

MILDURA

Pop. 46 035
Map ref. 526 E6 | 546 G6

i Mildura Visitor Information and Booking Centre, 180–190 Deakin Ave; (03) 5018 8380 or 1800 039 043; www.visitmildura.com.au

104.3 FM ABC Local Radio, 106.7 HOTFM Sunraysia Community Radio

Mildura offers a Riviera lifestyle, with the Murray River flowing by the town and sunny, mild weather throughout the year. It is one of Victoria's major rural cities. Its development has been aided by the expansion of irrigation, which has allowed the city to become a premier fruit-growing region.

Mildura Arts Centre & Rio Vista The arts centre and theatre, reopening in late 2011 after a major redevelopment, houses an impressive permanent collection including Australia's largest display of Orpen paintings, works by Brangwyn, frequent temporary exhibitions and performing arts. Outside, a delightful Sculpture Trail winds through the landscape gardens surrounding the centre. 199 Cureton Ave; (03) 5018 8330.

The Alfred Deakin Centre: interactive exhibitions and displays of the region; Deakin Ave. *Harry Nanya tours:* a tour with and an Indigenous Barkindji guide to Mungo National Park in NSW; tours run 2.30–10.30pm Nov–Mar, 8.30am–5pm Apr–Oct; bookings and information (08) 8234 8324 or from visitor centre. *Mildura Brewery:* produces natural and specialty beers inside the former Art Deco Astor Theatre; view the brewing process or eat at the Brewery Pub; 20 Langtree Ave; (03) 5021 5399. *Langtree Hall:* Mildura's first public hall now contains antiques and memorabilia; open Tues–Sat; 79 Walnut Ave; (03) 5021 3090. *Mildura Wharf:* paddleboats departing here for river cruises include the steam-driven PS *Melbourne;* PV *Rothbury* for day trips to Trentham Winery on Thursday and Gol Gol Hotel on Tuesday; and PV *Mundoo* for a Thursday dinner cruise. Access from Hugh King Drive; bookings (03) 5023 2200. *Aquacoaster waterslide:* cnr Seventh St and Orange Ave.

Arts Festival: Mar. *Cup Carnival:* May. *Writers Festival:* July. *Golf Week:* July. *Country Music Festival:* Sept. *Vintage Tractor Pull:* Oct. *Jazz Food and Wine Festival:* Nov.

The Gol Gol Hotel: good pub dining; Sturt Hwy, Gol Gol, NSW; (03) 5024 8492. *The new Spanish Bar and Grill:* up-market steakhouse; Quality Hotel Mildura Grand, cnr Langtree Ave and Seventh St; (03) 5021 2377. *Stefano's:* excellent Italian in historic hotel cellar, featuring the culinary skills of TV chef Stefano de Pieri; Quality Hotel Mildura Grand, Langtree Ave; (03) 5023 0511. *Stefano's Cafe Bakery:* informal Italian-style bakery; Deakin Ave; (03) 5021 3627. *Trentham Estate Restaurant:* modern Australian vineyard restaurant; Sturt Hwy, Trentham Cliffs, NSW; (03) 5024 8888.

All Seasons Holiday Park: 818 Fifteenth St (Calder Hwy); (03) 5023 3375. *Apex RiverBeach Holiday Park:* 435 Cureton Ave (western end); (03) 5023 6879. *BIG4 Mildura Crossroads Holiday Park:* 860 Fifteenth St; 1800 675 103. *BIG4 Mildura Deakin Holiday Park:* 472 Deakin Ave (Sturt Hwy); (03) 5023 0486. *Calder Tourist Park:* 775 Fifteenth St (Calder Hwy); (03) 5023 1310. *Desert City Tourist and Holiday Park:* 832 Fifteenth

[AERIAL VIEW OF THE MURRAY RIVER]

St; (03) 5022 1533. *Golden River Holiday Park – Aspen Parks:* 199–205 Flora Ave; (03) 5021 2299. *Sun City Caravan Park:* Cnr Benetook and Cureton aves; (03) 5023 2325. *Lake Cullulleraine RSL Holiday Park:* 5302 Sturt Hwy, Cullulleraine; (03) 5028 2226. *The Palms Caravan Park:* Cnr Cureton and Cowra aves, Mildura East; (03) 5023 1774. *Red Cliffs Caravan Park:* 8760 Calder Hwy, Red Cliffs; (03) 5024 2261.

Murray Darling wine region The Mediterranean-style climate mixed with irrigated lands has contributed to making this wine region Victoria's largest. The region is well regarded for its varieties of chardonnay, cabernet sauvignon and shiraz. Among the large-scale wineries such as Lindemans Karadoc, smaller boutique wineries offer specialty wines for tastings and sales. Brochure available from visitor centre.

Orange World: tours of citrus-growing region; Silver City Hwy, Buronga; (03) 5023 5197; 6 km N. *Australian Inland Botanic Gardens:* unique semi-arid botanic gardens with tractor tour and lunch last Sat each month; open daily; River Rd, Buronga; (03) 5023 3612; 8km NE. *Ornamental Lakes Park:* farmers market held 1st and 3rd Sat each month; Hugh King Dr. *Kings Billabong Wildlife Reserve:* situated on the Murray River flood plain, home to river red gums and abundant birdlife. Attractions include Psyche Pump Station, Bruce's Bend Marina and Kings Billabong Lookout; 8 km SE. *Angus Park:* dried fruits and confectionery; 10 km SE. *Red Cliffs:* an important area for the citrus and dried fruit industries. The town features the 'Big Lizzie' steam traction engine; 15 km S. *Hattah–Kulkyne National Park:* 70 km S; *see Ouyen. Murray–Sunset National Park:* attractions near Mildura include Lindsay Island, for boating, swimming and fishing. Access from Sturt Hwy, about 100 km W of Mildura. *See Murrayville for further details on park. Mungo National Park:* 104 km NE over NSW border (*see Balranald, NSW*).

TOWNS NEARBY: Wentworth (NSW) 24 km, Robinvale 71 km, Ouyen 99 km, Renmark (SA) 131 km, Balranald (NSW) 138 km with great views. Red Hill Estate is one of the biggest wineries on the peninsula and features a much-applauded restaurant, Max's at Red Hill Estate. Salix restaurant at Willow Creek offers a cosy dining room. At Montalto, the acclaimed restaurant is set in a large, light-filled piazza with beautiful views of the vineyard and modern sculpture displays. The latest restaurant to receive rave reviews is at Ten Minutes By Tractor, where both international and the winery's own wines are matched to the wonderfully flavoursome dishes. For something different, you can tour the wineries by horseback (Spring Creek Farm, 356 Shands Rd, Main Ridge, (03) 5989 6119).

Mount Martha: here is The Briars with a significant collection of Napoleonic artefacts and furniture. The town also features many gardens, plus wetlands great for birdwatching and bushland walks; 7 km s. *Ballam Park:* historic, French-farmhouse-style homestead built in 1845; open Sun; Cranbourne Rd, Frankston; 14 km NE. *Mulberry Hill:* former home of artist Sir Daryl Lindsay and author Joan Lindsay, who wrote *Picnic at Hanging Rock*; open Sun afternoons; Golf Links Rd, Baxter; 14 km NE. *Tyabb Packing House Antique Centre:* Australia's largest collection of antiques and collectibles; Mornington–Tyabb Rd, Tyabb; 16 km E. *Hastings:* coastal town on Western Port with 2 km walking trail through wetlands and mangrove habitat; 21 km SE. *Moonlit Sanctuary Wildlife Conservation Park:* wildlife park featuring endangered native Australian animals; visit 11am–5pm or take an evening tour; night tour bookings on (03) 5978 7935; 550 Tyabb–Tooradin Rd, Pearcedale; 24 km E. *Beaches:* the stretch of coast between Mornington and Mount Martha features sheltered, sandy bays popular with holiday-makers.

TOWNS NEARBY: Flinders 28 km, Sorrento 29 km, Cowes 31 km, Queenscliff 33 km, Koo-Wee-Rup 40 km

Morwell

Pop. 13 398
Map ref. 540 H7

Latrobe Visitor Information Centre, The Old Church, Southside Central, Princes Hwy, Traralgon; 1800 621 409; www.visitlatrobevalley.com

100.7 FM ABC Local Radio, 104.7 Gippsland FM

Morwell is primarily an industrial town and Victoria's major producer of electricity. Nestled in the heart of the Latrobe Valley, it contains one of the world's largest deposits of brown coal. Among all the heavy machinery is the impressive Centenary Rose Garden, featuring over 4000 rose bushes and regarded as one of the finest rose gardens in the Southern Hemisphere.

PowerWorks: dynamic displays on the electrical industries; tours of mines and power stations daily; Ridge Rd. *Centenary Rose Garden:* off Commercial Rd. *Latrobe Regional Gallery:* hosts outstanding works of contemporary Australian art by local and national artists; Commercial Rd. *Gippsland Immigration Wall of Recognition:* acknowledges all immigrants who contributed to the development of the Gippsland region.

Market: Latrobe Rd; each Sun.

Jumbuk Cottage Bed & Breakfast: 570 Jumbuk Rd, Yinnar South; (03) 5122 3344.

Morwell National Park This park protects some of the last remnant vegetation of the Strzelecki Ranges, including pockets of rainforest and fern gullies. The area was once occupied by the Woollum Woollum people, who hunted in the ranges. In

the 1840s European settlers cleared much of the surrounding land. On the Fosters Gully Nature Walk, keep your eyes peeled for orchids (over 40 species are found here) and native animals. Contact Parks Victoria on 13 1963; 16 km s.

Hazelwood Pondage: warm water ideal for year-round watersports; 5 km s. *Arts Resource Collective:* housed in an old butter factory; Yinnar; 12 km SW. *Lake Narracan:* fishing and waterskiing; 15 km NW. *Narracan Falls:* 27 km W. *Scenic drives:* routes along the Strzelecki Ranges and Baw Baw mountains offer impressive views over the Latrobe Valley.

TOWNS NEARBY: Moe 13 km, Traralgon 14 km, Walhalla 33 km, Warragul 41 km, Yarram 44 km

Mount Beauty

Pop. 1705
Map ref. 543 L10 | 545 J7

Alpine Discovery Centre, 31 Bogong High Plains Rd; (03) 5754 1962 or 1800 111 885; www.visitalpinevictoria.com.au

92.5 Alpine Radio FM, 720 AM ABC Local Radio

At the foot of Mount Bogong, Victoria's highest mountain at 1986 metres, Mount Beauty was originally an accommodation town for workers on the Kiewa Hydro-electric Scheme. Today, the town is regarded as an adventure mecca and a focal point for a variety of adventure activities, with mountain-biking, hang-gliding and bushwalking just a few on offer. The pairing of adventure with more leisurely outdoor activities like golf, swimming and fishing makes Mount Beauty an ideal holiday destination.

Mt Beauty Pondage: for watersports and fishing; just north of Main St. *Wineries:* cool-climate vineyards at Annapurna Estate, Bogong Estate and Recline. *Scenic walks:* several scenic walking tracks; details from visitor centre.

Markets: Hollonds St; 1st Sat each month. *Bogong Cup:* Jan. *MTBA National Series:* mountain-biking championships; Jan. *Music Muster:* Apr. *Mitta Mitta to Mount Beauty Mountain Bike Challenge:* Oct.

Mongans Bridge Camping Park: 42 Bay Creek La, Mongans Bridge; (03) 5754 5226. *Tawonga Caravan Park:* 117 Mountain Creek Rd, Tawonga; (03) 5754 4428.

Alpine National Park Covering 646 000 ha in 4 sections, this is Victoria's largest park, containing the highest mountains in the state. Most of Australia's south-east rivers, including the mighty Murray, have their source here. The area is known for its outstanding snowfields during winter, and bushwalking and wildflowers in summer. Other activities include horseriding, canoeing, rafting and mountain-bike riding. 30 km SE.

Falls Creek Surrounded by Alpine National Park, Falls Creek is a winter playground for downhill and cross-country skiers. When the snow is falling, the ski resort caters for skiers and snowboarders with a variety of runs and terrain, including some to suit beginners. Novelty tours are also available, such as the Snowmobile Tours. Each Aug, Falls Creek hosts the Kangaroo Hoppet cross-country ski race. In spring and summer, take a walk on the Bogong High Plains or fly-fish in one of the lakes and rivers nearby; 30 km SE.

Tawonga Gap: features a lookout over valleys; 13 km NW. *Bogong:* scenic walks around Lake Guy and nearby Clover Arboretum for picnics; 15 km SE. *Scenic drives:* to Falls Creek and the Bogong

VICTORIA

High Plains (not accessible in winter beyond Falls Creek); details from visitor centre.

TOWNS NEARBY: Bright 19 km, Myrtleford 45 km, Omeo 55 km, Yackandandah 56 km, Tallangatta 58 km

Murrayville
Pop. 210
Map ref. 526 B9 | 546 C11 | 548 C1 | 559 O10 | 568 H4

i Ouyen Information Centre, 17 Oke St, Ouyen; (03) 5092 2006; www.visitmildura.com.au/murrayville

📻 103.5 3MBR-FM Malle Border Radio, 594 AM ABC Local Radio

Murrayville is a small town on the Mallee Highway near the South Australia border. It is near three major, remote national parks: Murray–Sunset National Park; Wyperfeld National Park; and Big Desert Wilderness Park, one of Victoria's largest wilderness zones.

🏛 **Historic buildings:** include the restored railway station and the old courthouse. **Walking tracks:** several, including the Pine Hill Walking Trail in the town.

🌲 **Murray–Sunset National Park** Millions of years ago this area was submerged beneath the sea. When the sea retreated, large sand ridges and dunes were left. Now there is a variety of vegetation including grasslands, saltbush and mallee eucalypts. In spring, wildflowers abound; look out for Victoria's largest flower, the Murray lily. Access roads to the park are off Mallee Hwy. The Pink Lakes saltwater lakes, with a distinctive, pinkish hue, are a key attraction and are especially remarkable at sunset. There are many good walking tracks near the lakes, as well as excellent camping facilities. Lakes access via Pink Lakes Rd (turn-off at Linga, 50 km E); contact Parks Victoria on 13 1963. *For north section of park see Mildura.*

Cowangie: a small, historic town with several 19th-century buildings, including Kow Plains Homestead; 19 km E. *Big Desert Wilderness Park:* a remote park with no access other than by foot. True to its name, this park has remained relatively untouched by Europeans and includes many reptile species and plants adapted to arid conditions; the track south of town takes you close to the park boundary. *Wyperfeld National Park:* access via Underbool or by 4WD track south of Murrayville; *for further details see Hopetoun.*

TOWNS NEARBY: Pinnaroo (SA) 25 km, Ouyen 106 km, Loxton (SA) 106 km, Hopetoun 119 km, Keith (SA) 119 km

Myrtleford
Pop. 2726
Map ref. 543 J8 | 544 H6

i Post Office Complex, Great Alpine Rd; (03) 5752 1044; www.visitalpinevictoria.com.au

📻 91.7 FM ABC Local Radio, 101.3 Oak FM

Myrtleford is a pretty town in Victoria's alpine High Country. Originally called Myrtle Creek Run in the early 1800s, it is a thriving agricultural district and gateway to Mount Hotham.

🏛 **The Phoenix Tree:** a sculpture created by Hans Knorr from the trunk of a red gum; Lions Park. **The Big Tree:** a huge old red gum; Smith St. **Old School:** the town's original school, now fully restored; open Thurs, Sun or by appt; Albert St. **Swing Bridge over Myrtle Creek:** Standish St. **Reform Hill Lookout:** a scenic walking track from Elgin St leads to the lookout, which has great views across town; end of Halls Rd. **Parks:** Rotary Park in Myrtle

St and Apex Park in Standish St are both delightful picnic spots. **Michelini Wines:** Great Alpine Rd. **Murray to the Mountains Rail Trail:** the cycle touring loop from Bright to Wangaratta runs through the town.

🎪 **Market:** local produce; Great Alpine Rd; each Sat Jan–Apr. **Alpine Classic Bike Ride:** to Bright; Jan. **Myrtleford Festival:** Mar. **Golden Spurs Rodeo:** Dec.

🍴 **The Butter Factory:** produce store/cafe; 15 Myrtle St (Great Alpine Rd); (03) 5752 2435.

🛏 **Arderns Caravan Park:** Willow Gr; (03) 5752 1394. **Carawah Ridge Bed & Breakfast:** 514 Buffalo Creek Rd; (03) 5752 2147. **Myrtleford Caravan Park:** 8 Lewis Ave; (03) 5752 1598.

🌲 **Mt Buffalo National Park:** 7 km S; *see Bright.* **Wineries:** several in the region, including Rosewhite Vineyards and Winery; open weekends, public holidays and throughout Jan; Happy Valley Rd; 8 km SE. **Gapsted:** home to the Victorian Alps Winery, offers tours and sales; 8 km NW. **Eurobin:** a number of farms near the town with sales of local produce, including Red Stag Deer Farm and Bright Berry Farm, offering homemade jams and berries Dec–Mar; 16 km SE. **Fishing:** in the Ovens and Buffalo rivers and Lake Buffalo (25 km S).

TOWNS NEARBY: Beechworth 23 km, Bright 28 km, Milawa 29 km, Yackandandah 29 km, Wangaratta 43 km

Nagambie
Pop. 1381
Map ref. 542 D9

i 319 High St; (03) 5794 2647 or 1800 444 647; www.nagambielakestourism.com.au

📻 97.7 FM ABC Local Radio, 98.5 FM 98.5

Nagambie is found between Seymour and Shepparton on the Goulburn Valley Highway. The town is on the shores of Lake Nagambie, which was created by the construction of the Goulburn Weir in 1891. Activities such as waterskiing, speedboating and especially rowing are popular on this man-made lake.

🏛 **The Jetty:** fine dining, lakeside apartments and spa; High St. **The Grapevine by the Lake:** sales of nuts and local produce; High St. **Nagambie Lakes Entertainment Centre:** renovated 1890s building with bars, gaming lounge and non-motorised boat hire; High St.

[NAGAMBIE] HISTORIC TAHBILK WINERY

Rowing Regatta: Jan–Mar. *Head of the River:* Mar. *Nagambie On Water Festival:* Mar long weekend. *After Vintage Festival:* May. *Shiraz Challenge:* a search for the best shiraz in the region; Nov. *Fireworks over the Lake:* New Year's Eve.

Mitchelton Restaurant: regional-produce menu; Mitchelton Wines, Mitchells Town Rd; (03) 5794 2388. *Tahbilk Cafe:* casual cafe food; Tahbilk Winery, 254 O'Neils Rd, Tabilk; (03) 5794 2555. *3one7 on High Bar + Cafe:* modern Australian; The Jetty, 317 High St; (03) 5794 1964.

Nagambie Caravan Park: 143 High St (Goulburn Valley Hwy); (03) 5794 2681.

 Nagambie wine region Tahbilk Winery has a small pocket of its original 1860 shiraz vines, which continue to produce wine that's worth its weight in gold. The winery also makes stunning marsanne and cabernet franc. It is worth spending some time at Tahbilk to explore the winery's wetland, wildlife reserve and 3-tiered chateau that is classified by the National Trust. You can then hop on a cruise along the Goulburn River to the other big name in the area, Mitchelton. This winery has excellent shiraz and shiraz viognier. Within the grounds is Mitchelton's famous tower with views of the Goulburn River, a lovely art gallery and Mitchelton Restaurant. You can also buy a picnic hamper or pack your own for a lunch outing by the river.

Goulburn Weir The construction of this weir resulted in the creation of Lake Nagambie. It is the diversion weir on the Goulburn River for the Goulburn Valley Irrigation area and feeds water by channel and pipeline to Bendigo, among other places. A walkway runs across the weir offering views of the structure and lake. Picnic and barbecue facilities are available; 12 km N.

TOWNS NEARBY: Rushworth 25 km, Seymour 27 km, Euroa 37 km, Heathcote 43 km, Shepparton 50 km

Natimuk
Pop. 445
Map ref. 548 F9

ℹ National Hotel, Main St; (03) 5387 1300.

📻 96.5 Triple H FM, 594 AM ABC Local Radio

Natimuk is popular for its proximity to Mount Arapiles, a 369-metre sandstone monolith that has been described as 'Victoria's Ayers Rock'. The mountain was first climbed by Major Mitchell in 1836, and today is a popular rock-climbing destination with over 2000 marked climbing routes.

Arapiles Historical Society Museum: housed in the old courthouse; open by appt; Main St. *Arapiles Craft Shop:* features local arts and crafts; Main St. *The Goat Gallery:* showcases works of local and regional artists; Main St. *Self-guide heritage trail:* details from visitor centre.

Nati Frinj: biennial arts festival; Oct/Nov.

Natimuk Lake Caravan Park: Lake Rd; 0407 800 753.

 Mt Arapiles–Tooan State Park This park is divided into 2 blocks, the larger Tooan block and the smaller Mt Arapiles block; Mt Arapiles offers rock climbing and is by far the most popular. Mitre Rock presents a smaller climbing challenge if required. Should you choose not to scale one of the various rock faces, great views are still available from the walking tracks, or you can drive to the summit. Nature study is another possibility – a huge 14 per cent of the state's flora is represented in the

Mt Arapiles section alone. Contact Parks Victoria on 13 1963; access is from the Wimmera Hwy; 12 km SW.

Banksia Hill Flower Farm: 10 km E. *Duffholme Museum:* 21 km W.

TOWNS NEARBY: Horsham 23 km, Dimboola 32 km, Nhill 52 km, Jeparit 66 km, Edenhope 67 km

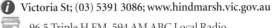
Nhill
Pop. 1919
Map ref. 526 C12 | 548 E7

ℹ Victoria St; (03) 5391 3086; www.hindmarsh.vic.gov.au

📻 96.5 Triple H FM, 594 AM ABC Local Radio

The name of this town is derived from the Aboriginal word 'nyell', meaning 'white mist on water'. Nhill is exactly halfway between Melbourne and Adelaide, and claims to have the largest single-bin silo in the Southern Hemisphere. The town is a good starting point for tours of Little Desert National Park.

Historical Society Museum: open Thurs, Fri or by appt; McPherson St. *Cottage of John Shaw Neilson (lyric poet):* open by appt; Jaypex Park, Victoria St. *Boardwalk:* scenic walk from Jaypex Park to Nhill Lake. *Lowana Craft Shop:* local crafts; Victoria St. *Self-guide historical walk:* details from visitor centre.

Boxing Day Races: Dec.

Nhill Caravan Park: 93 Victoria St; (03) 5391 1683. *Kaniva Caravan Park:* Baker St, Kaniva; 0458 687 054.

 Little Desert National Park: during spring, more than 600 varieties of wildflowers and over 40 types of ground orchids flourish in this 132 647 ha park. With nearly 600 kilometres of tracks, it is ideal for four-wheel driving, but perhaps the best way to appreciate the colourful spring display is on foot: for keen hikers, there is the 84 km Desert Discovery Walk. The Little Desert Lodge is in the central section of the park, south of Nhill, and is a departure point for day tours and a popular place to stay. There are walking trails in the central and western sections. 15 km S. See also Dimboola. *Mallee Dam:* lately dry, once offered fantastic birdwatching with bird hides provided; 20 km SW.

TOWNS NEARBY: Dimboola 37 km, Jeparit 37 km, Natimuk 52 km, Horsham 65 km, Warracknabeal 67 km

Ocean Grove
Pop. 14 351
Map ref. 532 C6 | 536 G9 | 538 H2 | 540 A7 | 551 O8

ℹ Geelong Visitor Information Centre, Stead Park, Princes Hwy, Corio; (03) 5275 5797 or 1800 620 888; www.visitgreatoceanroad.org.au

📻 94.7 The Pulse FM, 774 AM ABC Local Radio

Ocean Grove is a popular summer-holiday destination near the mouth of the Barwon River. The beaches around the town offer great surfing and safe swimming, with surf patrols operating during the summer months.

Ocean Grove Nature Reserve This reserve contains the only significant example of woodland on the Bellarine Peninsula, preserved virtually as it was prior to European settlement. A bird hide lets visitors look out for any number of the 130 different species that live here. Contact Parks Victoria on 13 1963; Grubb Rd.

Ocean Grove Holiday Park: 90 Wallington Rd; (03) 5256 2233. *Ocean Hideaway:* 12 Woodlands Dr; (03) 5255 2192.

VICTORIA

Riverview Family Caravan Park: Barwon Heads–Ocean Grove Rd; (03) 5256 1600. *Arusha B&B:* 50 Mirranda Crt, Wallington; (03) 5250 6200.

 HMAS *Canberra* **Dive Site** Opened to the public in December 2009, this purposely sunken warship is Victoria's first artificial site created specifically for diving. Divers can visit every area of the ship's 138 m length, from the captain's cabin to the galley. Bookings must be made with a charter boat operator or dive shop to be taken to the dive site. For details, call 0414 922 916. 4 km SE.

Lake Connewarre State Game Reserve: with mangrove swamps and great walks, the game reserve is home to a variety of wildlife, including wallabies; 7 km N. *Wallington:* the town is home to A Maze'N Games, a timber maze with minigolf, picnic/barbecue facilities and a cafe, Koombahla Park Equestrian Centre, Adventure Park and Bellarine Adventure Golf. A strawberry fair is held in Wallington in Nov; 8 km N.

TOWNS NEARBY: Barwon Heads 3 km, Drysdale 11 km, Queenscliff 12 km, Torquay 18 km, Geelong 19 km

Olinda

Pop. 1568
Map ref. 531 G6 | 534 B9 | 537 L6 | 540 E5

i Dandenong Ranges Information Centre, 1211 Burwood Hwy, Upper Ferntree Gully; (03) 9758 7522; www.olindavillage.com.au

97.1 FM 3MDR, 98.1 Radio Eastern FM, 774 AM ABC Local Radio

Olinda is in the centre of the Dandenong Ranges, a landscape of towering mountain ash forests, lush fern gullies, waterfalls, English gardens and picnic spots. The ranges have been a retreat for Melburnians since the 1800s. Olinda and nearby Sassafras are known for their many galleries and cafes, particularly the numerous tearooms serving traditional Devonshire teas.

Rhododendron and Daffodil Festivals: Aug–Nov.

Lady Hawke Cafe: Middle Eastern cafe; 1365–1367 Mt Dandenong Tourist Rd, Mount Dandenong; (03) 9751 1104. *Miss Marple's Tea Room:* traditional tearoom fare; 382 Mt Dandenong Tourist Rd, Sassafras; (03) 9755 1610. *Ripe – Australian Produce:* foodie cafe/produce store; 376–378 Mt Dandenong Tourist Rd, Sassafras; (03) 9755 2100. *Wild Oak Restaurant and Wine Bar:* French-influenced modern Australian menu; Cnr Ridge and Mt Dandenong Tourist rds; (03) 9751 2033.

A Country House At Winstanley: 13 Warwick Farm Rd; (03) 9755 1783. *Arcadia Cottages:* 188–190 Falls Rd; (03) 9751 1017. *Candlelight Cottages:* 7–9 Monash Ave; (03) 9751 2464. *Cambridge Cottages:* Cnr Falls and Williams rds; (03) 9751 1178. *Folly Farm Rural Retreat:* 192 Falls Rd; (03) 9751 2544. *Gracehill B&B:* 28 Chalet Rd; (03) 9751 1019. *Woolrich Retreat:* 20 Woolrich Rd; (03) 9751 0154. *Boronia on Albert:* 128 Albert Ave, Boronia; (03) 9761 0408. *Dalblair Bed & Breakfast:* 65 Ducks La, Seville; (03) 5961 9041. *Eagle Hammer Cottages:* 440 Old Emerald Rd, Monbulk; (03) 9756 7700. *Fleurbaix B & B:* 286 Mt Dandenong Tourist Rd, Sassafras; (03) 9755 1185. *Garden Heights:* 73 Lockwood Rd, Belgrave Heights; (03) 9754 5308. *Goodwood B&B Cottage:* 833 Mt Dandenong Rd, Montrose; 0419 875 699. *Holly Gate House B&B:* 1308 Mt Dandenong Tourist Rd, Kalorama; (03) 9728 3218. *Kalorama Holly Lodge:* 7 Erith La, Kalorama; (03) 9728 6064. *Lakeside Cottage:* 11 Tereddan Dr, Kilsyth South; (03) 9761 9791.

Mast Gully Gardens: 20 Dealbata Rd, Upwey; (03) 9752 5275. *Springfields:* 4 Springfield Ave, Camberwell; (03) 9809 1681. *Tavlock Retreat B & B:* Toorak Rd, Mount Dandenong; (03) 9751 2336. *Tranquillity Cottage:* 12 Eileen Ave, Kalorama; (03) 9751 1017. *Wild Cattle Creek Estate:* 473 Warburton Hwy, Seville; (03) 5964 4755.

Dandenong Ranges National Park This park offers great walking tracks and picnic facilities. Visitors may be lucky enough to spot an elusive lyrebird, a species renowned for its ability to mimic sounds – from other bird calls to human voices and even chainsaws. Most walking tracks leave from picnic grounds, such as the Thousand Steps Track from Ferntree Gully Picnic Ground (south-west via the Mt Dandenong Tourist Rd) and the walk to Sherbrooke Falls from the Sherbrooke Picnic Ground (via Sherbrooke Rd from the Mt Dandenong Tourist Rd). The park extends to the east and west of town. Contact Parks Victoria on 13 1963; 2 km NE, 6 km SW.

William Ricketts Sanctuary William Ricketts was a well-known artist and conservationist whose intricate sculptures focus on Aboriginal people and the complexities of Australia's native vegetation. Many sculptures are displayed in a bushland setting on the scenic Mt Dandenong Tourist Rd. Contact Parks Victoria on 13 1963; 3 km N.

National Rhododendron Gardens: the gardens begin just east of town and are something of a mecca for garden enthusiasts, with superb displays of rhododendrons and azaleas in season. *R. J. Hamer Arboretum:* good walking tracks through 100 ha of rare and exotic trees; Olinda–Monbulk Rd, shortly after turn-off to Rhododendron Gardens. *Cloudehill Gardens:* twilight concerts are held here in summer; south of R. J. Hamer Arboretum. *Mt Dandenong Lookout:* spectacular views over Melbourne; picnic/barbecue facilities; 3 km N. *Alfred Nicholas Gardens:* an ornamental lake with the original boathouse and the George Tindale Memorial Garden, with flowering plants beneath mountain ash trees. The original Nicholas family home (built 1920s) is here; Sherbrooke; 4 km SE. *Kawarra Australian Plant Garden:* an impressive collection of native plants; Kalorama; 4.5 km N. *Markets:* art, craft, plants and homemade goods; nearby markets include Kallista Market, 6 km S, 1st Sat each month, and Upper Ferntree Gully Market, 12 km SE, every Sat and Sun. *Burrinja Gallery:* a memorial to artist Lin Onus, with Aboriginal and Oceanic sculptures and paintings; Upwey; 10 km SW. *Silvan:* prominent flower-growing region with many tulip farms. The famous Tesselaar's Tulip Farm hosts a popular festival each Sept–Oct with sales of flowers and bulbs, and traditional Dutch music and food; Monbulk Rd; 15 km NE. *Silvan Dam:* an area to the north of this major Melbourne water supply has walking tracks and picnic/barbecue facilities; turn-off after Silvan. *Mont De Lancey:* wonderfully preserved house, built in 1882 and set in landscaped gardens; includes a museum and a chapel; open 2nd Sat each month; Wandin North; 22 km NE via Mt Evelyn.

TOWNS NEARBY: Emerald 11 km, Yarra Glen 22 km, Healesville 26 km, Warburton 31 km, Koo-Wee-Rup 40 km

Omeo

Pop. 226
Map ref. 541 M1 | 543 M12 | 545 M11

i 152 Great Alpine Rd; (03) 5159 1679; www.omeoregion.com.au

90.9 FM High Country Radio, 720 AM ABC Local Radio

Omeo is an Aboriginal word meaning mountains – appropriate for this picturesque town in the Victorian Alps. Today Omeo is a peaceful farming community, but it wasn't always so. During the 1800s gold rush, Omeo was an unruly frontier town, which early Australian novelist Rolf Boldrewood described as the roughest goldfield in Australia. Despite taking damage in the 1939 Black Friday bushfires, several historic buildings still remain.

A. M. Pearson Historical Park The park preserves a piece of Omeo's rich history in a peaceful, bushland setting. Buildings on display include the old courthouse, which now houses a museum, a log gaol, stables and a blacksmith's. Day Ave (Great Alpine Rd).

Historic buildings: many distinctive structures from the 19th century can be seen in town, including the post office, primary school and shire offices; Day Ave. *Shops:* several unique stores, including the German Cuckoo Clock Shop, Petersen's Gallery, High Country Paintings and Octagon Bookshop; Day Ave.

High Country Calf Sales: Mar. *Alpine Discovery Festival and Picnic Races:* Mar. *Rodeo, Easter Market and Easter Egg Hunt:* Easter. *Cobungra Polo Match:* Apr.

The Golden Age Hotel Motel: up-market country fare; Cnr Day Ave (Great Alpine Rd) and Tongio Rd; (03) 5159 1344.

Omeo Caravan Park: 111 Old Omeo Hwy; (03) 5159 1351.

Oriental Claims The Claims was a major goldmining area, and remains the highest alluvial goldfield in Australia. French–Canadians, Americans and Europeans all worked alongside Australians and Chinese during the gold boom. The word 'Oriental' in the mine's name may conjure an image of Chinese workers, but 'Oriental Claims' was actually the name of a European company. The Omeo Sluicing Company, however, was Chinese. There are a variety of walks around the site and visitors should look out for the flora, including wild orchids. High cliffs, left by the hydraulic sluicing process, offer impressive views across town, and signs throughout the Parks Victoria–managed site explain the history of the Claims. Contact Parks Victoria on 13 1963; 1.5 km w on Great Alpine Rd.

Mt Hotham This popular downhill ski resort is suited to both budding and experienced skiers. Skiing areas range from the beginners' Big D Playground through to the more advanced slopes around Mary's Slide and the black diamond chutes of Heavenly Valley. In summer, the mountain is a popular hiking and mountain-bike-riding destination. (03) 5759 3550; 56 km w.

Livingstone Park and Creek: walking tracks and swimming area adjacent to the Oriental Claims. *Mt Markey Winery:* on the site of the old Cassilis Hotel, on the touring loop from Omeo to Swifts Creek; Cassilis Rd, Cassilis; 15 km s. *Lake Omeo:* scenic natural landscape, dry for most parts of the year; Benambra; 21 km NE. *Benambra:* gateway to the Alpine National Park; 24 km N. *Anglers Rest:* historic Blue Duck Inn, a good base for horseriding, whitewater rafting and fly-fishing; 29 km NW. *Swifts Creek:* this town situated at the junction of Swifts Creek and Tambo River has the Great Alpine Art Gallery; 40 km s. *Taylors Crossing suspension bridge:* part of the scenic Australian Alps Walking Track and also a great base for camping and fishing the Mitta Mitta River; off Tablelands Rd; 44 km NE. *Dinner Plain:* relaxed village surrounded by the Alpine National Park that offers many activities such as skiing, walking, horseriding and Australia's 1st indoor–outdoor alpine spa; 46 km w.

Ensay: small but picturesque town that is home to the well-known Ensay Winery; 70 km s. *Great Alpine Rd:* covers over 300 km from the High Country to Gippsland Lakes and offers 6 individual self-guide touring routes with a diverse combination of scenery; details from visitor centre. Note that some drives cross state forests or alpine areas, so be alert for timber trucks and check conditions in winter. Omeo is located on this road. *Mitta Mitta and Cobungra rivers:* great trout fishing, waterskiing and whitewater rafting (only available in spring); details from visitor centre. *High Country tours:* explore the high plains around Omeo – on horseback, by 4WD or, for keen hikers, on challenging bushwalks; details from visitor centre.

TOWNS NEARBY: Mount Beauty 55 km, Buchan 68 km, Bright 70 km, Bairnsdale 81 km, Thredbo (NSW) 92 km

Orbost

Pop. 2096
Map ref. 519 A12 | 539 B11

Slab Hut, 35 Nicholson St; (03) 5154 2424; www.discovereastgippsland.com.au

90.7 FM 3REG Radio East Gippsland, 97.1 FM ABC Local Radio

Situated on the banks of the legendary Snowy River, Orbost is on the Princes Highway and surrounded by spectacular coastal and mountain territory. For those who love arts and crafts, there are many shops in the area supplying and displaying local products.

Visitor information centre: display explains complex rainforest ecology; Slab Hut, 39 Nicholson St. *Old Pump House:* behind relocated 1872 slab hut; Forest Rd. *Historical Museum:* details local history with displays of artefacts; Ruskin St. *Snowy River Country Craft:* Forest Rd. *Netherbyre Gemstone and Art Galley:* Cnr Browning and Carlyle sts. *Exhibition Centre:* equipped with 2 galleries, one dedicated to the National Collection of Australian Wood Design, the other presenting monthly exhibitions; Nicholson St. *Mirrawong Woolworks:* sells wool and felt handmade items; 295 Nicholson St. *Heritage walk:* weaves its way through town with storyboards, fingerboards and plaques explaining the historic buildings; begins at Slab Hut.

Australian Wood Design Exhibition: Jan.

A Lovely Little Lunch: local-produce cafe menu; 125A Nicholson St; (03) 5154 1303.

Orbost Caravan Park on the Snowy River: Lochiel St; (03) 5154 1097. *Cape Conran Coastal Park:* Yeerung Rd, Cape Conran; (03) 5154 8438. *Snowy River Homestead Bed & Breakfast:* 77 Grandview Rd, Newmerella; 0409 542 432.

Errinundra National Park The park is one of the largest remaining stands of cool temperate rainforest in Victoria, and features giant eucalypt forests. There is the rainforest boardwalk and for keen hikers there are walking tracks, as well as camping and picnic facilities. Enjoy superb views from Ellery View, Ocean View Lookout and the peak of Mt Morris. In winter, snow and rain can make access difficult. Errinundra Rd, off Princes Hwy; contact Parks Victoria on 13 1963; 54 km NE.

Marlo: a popular fishing spot also known for its galleries and Bush Races in Jan; 14 km; also in Marlo cruise the Snowy River on the Paddle Steamer Curlip II; book on 0411 395 903 s. *Cape Conran Coastal Park:* rugged coastal scenery and excellent walks. Turn south after Cabbage Tree Creek (26 km E) or take the coastal

VICTORIA

route from Marlo. *Cabbage Tree Palms Flora Reserve:* 27 km E. *Bemm River Scenic Reserve:* a 1 km signposted rainforest walk and picnic facilities; off Princes Hwy; 40 km E. *Snowy River National Park:* in the south of the park is Raymond Creek Falls. A 40 min return walk leads to the falls, with a further 1 hr walk leading to the Snowy River; 42 km N; 2WD access, check road conditions. McKillops Bridge, 148 km N via Deddick, is one of the most accessible parts of this park; *for more details see Buchan.* *Sydenham Inlet:* a good spot for bream fishing; 58 km E. *Tranquil Valley Tavern:* on the banks of the Delegate River near the NSW border; about 115 km NE. *Baldwin Spencer Trail:* a 262 km scenic drive following the route of this explorer, taking in old mining sites and Errinundra National Park; details from visitor centre.

TOWNS NEARBY: Buchan 33 km, Lakes Entrance 45 km, Cann River 63 km, Paynesville 69 km, Bairnsdale 76 km

Ouyen
Pop. 1058
Map ref. 526 E8 | 546 H11

i 17 Oke St; (03) 5092 2006; www.visitmildura.com.au/ouyen

92.9 3MBR-FM Mallee Border Radio, 594 AM ABC Local Radio

Ouyen was once little more than a station on the Melbourne–Mildura train route, but it has since grown to become an important service town. Ouyen is at the centre of the Mallee region, which was developed in the early 1900s – relatively late when compared with other regions of rural Victoria. This was mainly due to the difficulties in clearing the land as well as the harsh climate. The current success of agriculture in the region, in particular wheat-growing, is a testament to the hardiness of early farmers and settlers.

Roxy Theatre: newly restored and functioning tropical-style theatre, only one of its type in southern Australia; Oke St.

Great Australian Vanilla Slice Triumph: 1st Fri in Sept.

Ouyen Caravan Park: 10 Calder Hwy; (03) 5092 1426.

Hattah–Kulkyne National Park This park protects an area of 48 000 ha that includes typical mallee country with both low scrub and open native pine woodlands. The freshwater Hattah Lakes are seasonally filled by creeks connected to the Murray River, which brings the area to life with plants and waterbirds. Activities within the park include bushwalking, canoeing, fishing and scenic drives. There are picnic and camping facilities at Mournpall and Lake Hattah. Contact Parks Victoria on 13 1963; off the Calder Hwy; 35 km N.

Speed: Mallee Machinery Field Days held here in Aug; 39 km S.

TOWNS NEARBY: Robinvale 68 km, Hopetoun 73 km, Mildura 99 km, Murrayville 106 km, Wentworth (NSW) 113 km

Paynesville
Pop. 3455
Map ref. 541 N6

i Community Craft Centre, Esplanade; (03) 5156 7479; www.lakesandwilderness.com.au

90.7 FM 3REG Radio East Gippsland, 100.7 FM ABC Local Radio

Paynesville is a popular tourist resort close to the rural city of Bairnsdale, on the McMillan Straits. The town is set on the Gippsland Lakes and the beaches of the Tasman Sea, making it a favourite destination for fishing and waterskiing.

 St Peter-by-the-Lake Church: built in 1961, this unique structure incorporates seafaring images in its design; The Esplanade. *Community Craft Centre:* displays and sells local arts and crafts; The Esplanade.

 Market: Gilsenan Reserve; 2nd Sun each month. *Jazz Festival:* Feb. *Marlay Pt Paynesville Overnight Yacht Race:* Mar long weekend.

Allawah Caravan & Boat Park: 79 Slip Rd; (03) 5156 7777. *Resthaven Caravan Park:* 4–14 Gilsenan St; (03) 5156 6342. *Bayview Loft:* 2 Bay Rd, Eagle Point; (03) 5156 7132. *Lake King Waterfront Caravan Park:* 67 Bay Rd, Eagle Point; (03) 5156 6387.

Gippsland Lakes This area incorporates The Lakes National Park, Gippsland Lakes Coastal Park and the famous Ninety Mile Beach – an incredible stretch of scenic coastline offering great swimming beaches. Lake cruises, boat charters and organised scenic tours of the region are all available; details from visitor centre.

Eagle Pt: a small fishing community set by Lake King. The Mitchell River empties here, where it forms curious silt jetties that stretch out into the distance. The town hosts the annual Australian Powerboat Racing Championships at Easter; 2 km NW. *Raymond Island:* Koala Reserve and Riviera Meadows, an animal farm that specialises in miniature breeds; the island is just east of Paynesville and can be accessed by a ferry that departs from the foreshore.

TOWNS NEARBY: Bairnsdale 14 km, Lakes Entrance 25 km, Sale 61 km, Buchan 62 km, Maffra 65 km

Phillip Island
see Cowes

Port Albert
Pop. 253
Map ref. 541 I10

i Old Courthouse, 9 Rodgers St, Yarram; (03) 5182 6553.

100.7 FM ABC Local Radio, 104.7 Gippsland FM

Port Albert is a tranquil port on the south-east coast. Looking at this peaceful village now, it is hard to believe that it was the first established port in Victoria, with ships from Europe and America once docking at its jetty. Ships from China arrived here during the gold rush, bringing thousands of prospectors to the Gippsland goldfields. Still a commercial fishing port, the sheltered waters of Port Albert are popular with anglers and boat owners, which sees its population swell considerably during summer.

Port Albert Hotel This attractive old building has wide verandahs, and offers genuine country hospitality and a glimpse into the area's past. The hotel was first licensed in 1842, which makes it one of the oldest hotels in Victoria still operating. Wharf St.

Historic buildings: include original government offices and stores, and the Bank of Victoria, which now houses a maritime museum with photographs and relics from the town's past. Georgian and Victorian architectural styles are evident in over 40 buildings; Tarraville Rd. *Warren Curry Art:* a gallery featuring country-town streetscapes; Tarraville Rd.

 Fishing Contest: Mar.

 **Wildfish:** waterfront dining, freshest local seafood; 40 Wharf St; (03) 5183 2007.

Port Albert Bed & Breakfast: 27 Wharf St; (03) 5183 2525. **Port Albert Seabank Caravan Park:** 95 Old Port Rd; (03) 5183 2315.

Nooramunga Marine and Coastal Park Surrounding Port Albert and comprising the waters and sand islands offshore, this marine park is a fishing enthusiast's delight. Snapper, flathead and Australian salmon can be caught from the surf beaches or from a boat. The Aboriginal middens that dot the shorelines prove that fishing has been carried on here for many thousands of years. This park is an important reserve for migratory wading birds. Camping is allowed but permits must be obtained. Contact Parks Victoria on 13 1963.

Christ Church: built in 1856, this was the first church to be established in Gippsland; Tarraville; 5 km NE. **Beaches:** Manns, for swimming, 10 km NE; and Woodside, on Ninety Mile Beach, for good surfing, 34 km NE. Note that both beaches are patrolled during summer. **St Margaret Island:** a protected area featuring a wildlife sanctuary; 12 km E.

TOWNS NEARBY: Yarram 11 km, Welshpool 22 km, Foster 43 km, Traralgon 54 km, Morwell 54 km

Port Campbell
Pop. 258
Map ref. 538 F10 | 551 I9

i 12 Apostles Visitor Information Centre, 26 Morris St; 1300 137 255; www.visit12apostles.com.au

103.7 3WAY-FM, 774 AM ABC Local Radio

This peaceful seaside resort – the base of a small crayfishing industry – is in the centre of Port Campbell National Park on the Great Ocean Road. The Twelve Apostles, one of Victoria's most famous attractions, can be found nearby.

Historical Museum: open Wed, Thurs and Sat; Lord St. **Fishing:** good from rocks and pier; boat charters available.

Market: Lord St; each Sun in summer and Easter.

The Craypot Bistro: great-value food, seasonal crayfish; Port Campbell Hotel, 40 Lord St; (03) 5598 6320. **Room Six Cafe Restaurant:** traditional Greek fare; 28 Lord St; (03) 5598 6242. **Timboon Railway Shed Distillery:** local-produce-driven menu; The Railway Yard, Bailey St, Timboon; (03) 5598 3555.

Loch Ard Bed & Breakfast: 309 Yaruck Rd; (03) 5598 6456. **Port Campbell Holiday Park:** 1 Morris St; (03) 5598 6492. **Great Ocean Road Tourist Park:** Cnr Great Ocean Rd and Irvine St, Peterborough; (03) 5598 5477. **Apostles Camping Park & Cabins:** 32 Post Office Rd, Princetown; (03) 5598 8119.

Port Campbell National Park The park is a major attraction on the Great Ocean Rd, with magnificent rock formations jutting out into the ocean. Particularly impressive when viewed at dusk (when penguins can be seen) and dawn, the key coastal features are The Arch, 5 km w; London Bridge, 6 km w; Loch Ard Gorge, 7 km SE; and the world-famous Twelve Apostles, which begin 12 km SE of Port Campbell and stretch along the coast. These spectacular limestone stacks were part of the cliffs until wind and water left them stranded in wild surf off the shore. Other notable features are The Grotto, Bay of Islands and Bay of Martyrs. There are walking tracks throughout the park, and the

[PORT CAMPBELL] LOCH ARD GORGE, PORT CAMPBELL NATIONAL PARK

Historic Shipwreck Trail marks 25 sites along the coast between Moonlight Head and Port Fairy (sites are also popular with divers – a charter company is based in Port Campbell; details from visitor centre). For the ultimate view of this coastline, take an ever-popular scenic flight (details from visitor centre).

Mutton Bird Island: attracts short-tailed shearwaters, best viewed at dawn and dusk Sept–Apr; just off coast. **Great Ocean Walk:** between Apollo Bay and the Twelve Apostles. The 91 km walk offers stunning views; walkers must register to use campgrounds en route; information available at greatoceanwalk.com.au **Timboon:** a pretty town in the centre of a dairy district. Timboon Farmhouse Cheese offers tastings and sales of gourmet cheeses, while Timboon Railway Shed Distillery offers a variety of spirits. A scenic drive goes from Port Campbell to the town. It is also on one end of the Camperdown–Timboon (Crater to Coast) Rail Trail. Pick your own berries in season at nearby Berry World; 16 km N. **Otway Deer and Wildlife Park:** 19 km SE. **Gourmet Food and Wine Loop:** map from visitor centre.

TOWNS NEARBY: Terang 43 km, Camperdown 45 km, Warrnambool 52 km, Colac 60 km, Apollo Bay 60 km

Port Fairy
Pop. 2597
Map ref. 538 B8 | 550 F8

i Railway Place, Bank St; (03) 5568 2682; www.visitportfairy-moyneshire.com.au

103.7 3WAY-FM, 1602 AM ABC Local Radio

VICTORIA

Port Fairy was once a centre for the whaling industry and one of the largest ports in Australia. Today many visitors are attracted to it for its charming old-world feel, its legacy of historic bluestone buildings, the small fleet of fishing boats that line the old wharf, and its great beach and lively atmosphere in summer. The town truly comes alive in March, when the Port Fairy Folk Festival is held. International folk and blues acts play, and tickets are best booked well in advance.

History Centre: displays relating to local history housed in the old courthouse; Gipps St. *Battery Hill:* old fort and signal station at the river mouth; end of Griffith St. *Port Fairy Wharf:* sales of fish and crayfish when in season. *Historic buildings:* many are National Trust–classified, including the splendid timber home of Captain Mills, Gipps St; Mott's Cottage, Sackville St; Caledonian Inn, Bank St; Seacombe House, Cox St; St John's Church of England, Regent St; and the Gazette Office, Sackville St.

Folk Festival: Mar. *Spring Music Festival:* Oct. *Moyneyana Festival:* family entertainment; Dec.

L'Edera: authentic Italian; 20 Bank St; (03) 5568 3058. *Merrijig Inn:* contemporary Mediterranean; 1 Campbell St; (03) 5568 2324. *Portofino on Bank:* contemporary Mediterranean; 26 Bank St; (03) 5568 2251. *time&tide High Tea by the High Sea:* memorable high teas; 21 Thistle Pl; (03) 5568 2134.

Cherry Plum Cottages: Albert Rd; (03) 5568 2595. *Clonmara Cottages:* 106 Princes Hwy; (03) 5568 2595. *Cottages for Couples – Wytonia:* 27 Thistle Pl; (03) 5568 3425. *Gardens By East Beach Caravan Park:* 111 Griffith St; (03) 5568 1060. *Gum Tree Caravan Park:* 8 Amble La; (03) 5568 1462. *Oscars Waterfront Boutique Hotel:* 41B Gipps St; (03) 5568 3022. *Southcombe by the Sea Caravan Park:* James St; (03) 5568 2677. *Killara Bed & Breakfast:* 104 Survey La, Killarney; (03) 5568 7318. *Codrington Settlement & Gardens:* 4887 Princes Hwy, Yambuk; (03) 5568 4203.

Griffiths Island Connected to town by a causeway, this island is home to a large colony of short-tailed shearwaters. Each year they travel across the Pacific Ocean from North America to nest in the same burrows (Sept–Apr). Also on the island is a much-photographed lighthouse. *The Crags:* rugged coastal rock formations; 12 km w.

Yambuk: a small township centred on an old inn with Yambuk Lake, a popular recreation area, nearby; 17 km w. *Lady Julia Percy Island:* home to a fur seal colony; charters can be arranged from Port Fairy Wharf; 22 km off coast. *Codrington Wind Farm:* Victoria's first wind-power station; 27 km w. *Mahogany Walk to Warrnambool:* a 6–7 hr walk (one way, can return by bus) taking in a magnificent stretch of coastline; details from visitor centre. *Historic Shipwreck Trail:* between Port Fairy and Moonlight Head with 25 wreck sites signposted along the way.

TOWNS NEARBY: Warrnambool 22 km, Portland 55 km, Terang 63 km, Port Campbell 72 km, Hamilton 73 km

---

Portland	Pop. 9824
	Map ref. 550 D8

ⓘ Lee Breakwater Rd; (03) 5522 2130 or 1800 035 567; www.glenelg.vic.gov.au

📻 96.9 AM ABC Local Radio, 99.3 Coastal FM

Portland is the most westerly of Victoria's major coastal towns and the only deep-water port between Melbourne and Adelaide.

It was also the first permanent settlement in Victoria, founded in 1834 by the famous pastoralist Henty family. The township, which features many National Trust–classified buildings, overlooks Portland Bay. The Kerrup-Tjmara people, who once numbered in the thousands, were the original inhabitants of the district and referred to it as 'Pulumbete' meaning 'Little Lake' – a reference to the scenic lake now known as Fawthorp Lagoon.

Portland Maritime Discovery Centre The centre features a 13 m sperm whale skeleton, and the lifeboat used to rescue 19 survivors from the *Admella* shipwreck in 1859. Another wreck, the *Regia*, is displayed in 2 m of water. The centre shares the building with the information centre. Lee Breakwater Rd.

Botanical Gardens: established in 1857, with both native and exotic plant life. A restored 1850s bluestone worker's cottage is within the grounds and open to the public; Cliff St. *Historical buildings:* more than 200 around town, many National Trust–classified. The best way to explore buildings such as the courthouse, Steam Packet Inn and Mac's Hotel is to take either a guided or self-guide walk; details from visitor centre. *History House:* a historical museum and family research centre in the old town hall; Charles St. *Burswood:* a bluestone, regency-style mansion that was once the home of pioneer settler Edward Henty. The house is set amid 5 ha of gardens; Cape Nelson Rd. *Fawthorp Lagoon:* prolific birdlife; Glenelg St. *Powerhouse Car Museum:* Percy St. *Watertower Lookout:* displays of WW II memorabilia on the way up the 133 steps to magnificent 360-degree views across Portland and the ocean, where whales and dolphins can sometimes be spotted; Percy St. Another good spot for whale-watching is Battery Hill.

Anzac Day Floral Display: Apr. *Bay Festival:* Nov. *3 Bays Marathon:* Nov.

Bridgewater Bay Beach Cafe: views and food worthy of detour; 1661 Bridgewater Rd, Cape Bridgewater; (03) 5526 7155. *Fergie's Cafe & Wine Bar:* contemporary Australian; Cnr Cliff and Bentinck sts; (03) 5523 4777. *The Lido Larder:* contemporary cafe; 5 Julia St; (03) 5521 1741.

Clifftop Accommodation Portland: 13 Clifton Crt; (03) 5523 1126. *Dutton Way Caravan Park:* 215 Dutton Way; (03) 5523 1904. *Henty Bay Beach Front Van & Cabin Park:* 342 Dutton Way; (03) 5523 3716. *Portland Bay Holiday Park:* 184 Bentinck St; (03) 5523 1487. *Seascape Accommodation:* 271 Hanlon Pde; (03) 5523 3960. *Whalers Cottage B & B:* 12 Whalers Crt; (03) 5521 7522. *Cape Bridgewater Sea View Lodge:* 1636 Bridgewater Rd, Cape Bridgewater; (03) 5526 7276.

Cape Bridgewater This cape is home to a 650-strong colony of Australian fur seals. A 2 hr return walk leads to a viewing platform, or you can take a 45 min boat ride that leads into the mouth of a cave to see them up close (bookings essential, (03) 5526 7247). Across the cape towards Discovery Bay are the Petrified Forest and the Blowholes – spectacular during high seas. 21 km sw.

Lower Glenelg National Park The Glenelg River is a central feature of the park. It has cut an impressive 50 m deep gorge through a slab of limestone. Watch for platypus, water rats, moorhens and herons around the water's edge. Bushwalking, camping, fishing and canoeing are all popular, and Jones Lookout and the Bulley Ranges offer great views. Also in the park are the Princess Margaret Rose Caves on the north side of the river – you can drive there via Nelson or Dartmoor. Alternatively, boat tours operate from Nelson. Contact Parks Victoria on 13 1963; 44 km NW.

Cape Nelson: here a lighthouse perches on top of tall cliffs and lightstation tours are available; 11 km SW. *Narrawong State Forest:* a short walk leads to Whalers Pt, where Aboriginal people once watched for whales; 18 km NE. *Discovery Bay Coastal Park:* Cape Bridgewater is included in this park, though the majority of it is remote and relatively untouched. The Great South West Walk *(see below)* offers the best chance to take in the park's scenery. Behind Cape Bridgewater are the Bridgewater Lakes (19 km W) – popular for waterskiing and fishing. A walking track leads from here to the beach. *Mt Richmond National Park:* a 'mountain' formed by an extinct volcano. The area has abundant spring wildflowers and native fauna, including the elusive potoroo; 25 km NW. *Heywood:* home to the Bower Birds Nest Museum, and the Wood, Wine and Roses Festival in Feb. Budj Bim National Heritage Landscape, the traditional lands of the Gunditjmara people, is located here also. Visitors can experience the aquaculture system including stone eel traps, permanent stone houses and smoking trees; Budj Bim Tours (03) 5527 1699; 28 km N. *Nelson:* a charming hamlet near the mouth of the Glenelg River. There is good waterskiing in the area; 70 km NW. *Great South West Walk:* this epic 250 km walking trail takes in the full range of local scenery – the Glenelg River, Discovery and Bridgewater bays and Cape Nelson are some of the highlights. It is possible to do just small sections of the walk; maps and details from visitor centre.

TOWNS NEARBY: Port Fairy 55 km, Hamilton 76 km, Warrnambool 77 km, Coleraine 83 km, Port MacDonnell (SA) 85 km

Pyramid Hill

Pop. 467
Map ref. 527 I12 | 549 N6

ℹ️ Loddon Visitor Information Centre, Wedderburn Community Centre, 24 Wilson St, Wedderburn; (03) 5494 3489; www.pyramidhill.net.au

📻 91.1 FM ABC Local Radio, 104.7 Radio EMFM

Pyramid Hill's namesake is an unusually shaped, 187-metre-high hill. The town, which is located in a wheat-growing district about 30 kilometres from the New South Wales border, was a source of inspiration to notable Australian author Katherine Susannah Pritchard, who based a character in her book *Child of the Hurricane* on a woman she met while staying in Pyramid Hill during World War I.

 Pyramid Hill A climb to the top of this eerily symmetrical hill reveals views of the surrounding irrigation and wheat district. There are abundant wildflowers in spring.

Historical Museum: features local story displays; open Sun afternoons or by appt; McKay St.

🏨 **Boort Lakes Caravan Park:** Durham Ox Rd, Boort; (03) 5455 2064.

🟢 **Terrick Terrick National Park** The park is a large Murray pine forest reserve with granite outcrops, including Mitiamo Rock. There is a variety of good walking tracks, and the park is a key nesting area for the distinctive brolga. Contact Parks Victoria on 13 1963; access is via the Pyramid Hill–Kow Swamp Rd; 20 km SE.

Mt Hope: named by explorer Major Mitchell, who 'hoped' he would be able to spot the sea from the mountain's peak. Now

known for its wildflowers; 16 km NE. *Boort:* nearby lakes provide a habitat for swans, ibis, pelicans and other waterbirds, and a place for watersports, fishing and picnics; 40 km W.

TOWNS NEARBY: Cohuna 29 km, Kerang 40 km, Barham (NSW) 48 km, Echuca 58 km, Wedderburn 60 km

Queenscliff

Pop. 3892
Map ref. 531 A10 | 532 E6 | 536 H9 | 540 B7 | 551 P8

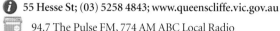

ℹ️ 55 Hesse St; (03) 5258 4843; www.queenscliffe.vic.gov.au

📻 94.7 The Pulse FM, 774 AM ABC Local Radio

Queenscliff is a charming seaside town on the Bellarine Peninsula. It began life as a resort for wealthy Victorians in the 1800s, as testified by lavish buildings such as the Queenscliff Hotel, with its ornate lattice work and plush interiors. The town's wide main street is lined with cafes and restaurants, plus an array of art galleries, and the nearby beaches become a playground for holiday-makers during summer. A ferry runs between Queenscliff and Sorrento, a resort town across Port Phillip Bay.

🏠 **Queenscliff Maritime Museum** The museum explores the town's long association with ships and the sea through a collection of maritime memorabilia. It features a re-created fisherman's cottage, a diving-technology display and an array of navigational equipment. Weeroona Pde; (03) 5258 3440.

Marine Discovery Centre This is a great family destination where visitors can learn all about the local marine life. It has a number of aquariums and touch-tanks. The centre also runs various tours, including boat cruises off Port Phillip and 'rockpool rambles'. Adjacent to the Maritime Museum, Weeroona Pde; (03) 5258 3344.

The Blues Train An incredibly popular attraction that provides a unique dining and entertainment experience on board a steam train. Round trips provide 4 carriages, each with a different blues musician. Guests can change carriages at stops on the journey and purchase drinks from the mobile bar at each station platform. Operates Sat nights Oct–May. Departs from and returns to Queenscliff Railway Station; bookings at Ticketek on 132 849, or contact visitor centre for more information.

Fort Queenscliff: built during the Crimean War, it includes the unique 'Black Lighthouse'. Tours of the fort run most days; details from visitor centre. *Queenscliff Historical Museum:* open daily 2–4pm; Hesse St. *Bellarine Peninsula Railway:* beautifully restored steam trains run between Queenscliff and Drysdale. There are many engines on display around the station. Trains run Sun, public holidays and other times during school holidays; Symonds St. *Bellarine Rail Trail:* 32.5 km track that extends from South Geelong to Queenscliff; on reaching Drysdale it runs along the Bellarine Peninsula Railway and ends in the town.

🌴 *Market:* with crafts and second-hand goods; Princes Park, Gellibrand St; last Sun each month except winter. *Music Festival:* major event attracting local and international music acts; Nov.

🍴 *Athelstane House:* contemporary Australian; 4 Hobson St; (03) 5258 1024. *Vue Grand Hotel:* classic menu, impressive dining room; 46 Hesse Street; (03) 5258 1544.

🏨 *Queenscliffe Tourist Parks:* 134 Hesse St; (03) 5258 1765. *Lonsdale Views:* 25 Gill Rd, Point Lonsdale; (03) 5258 2990.

VICTORIA

Pt Lonsdale This peaceful holiday town offers gorgeous beaches suitable for either surfing or swimming. A lookout from the cliff-top provides a great view of the treacherous entrance to Port Phillip known as 'The Rip'. A market is held here on the 2nd Sunday of each month. 6 km sw.

Lake Victoria: an important waterbird habitat; 7 km sw via Pt Lonsdale. *Harold Holt Marine Reserve:* incorporates Mud Island and coastal reserves. Guided boat tours can be arranged from the Marine Discovery Centre.

TOWNS NEARBY: Sorrento 11 km, Ocean Grove 12 km, Drysdale 13 km, Barwon Heads 15 km, Geelong 29 km

Robinvale

Pop. 2216
Map ref. 526 F7 | 547 J8

i Kyndalyn Park Information Centre, Bromley Rd; (03) 5026 1388; www.murrayriver.com.au/html/towns/robinvaleeuston.html

90.7 HOTFM Sunraysia Community Radio

Robinvale is set on the New South Wales border by a pretty stretch of the Murray River. The Robinswood Homestead, built in 1926, was home to the town's founder, Herbert Cuttle (you can find the homestead in River Road). Herbert's son, Robin, was killed during World War I, so he named both the homestead and the town in Robin's honour. As another form of remembrance, the town has a sister city in France, near where young Robin died.

Rural Life Museum: housed in the information centre, with locally grown almonds for sale; open by appt; Bromley Rd. *Murray River:* the beaches around Robinvale are popular for picnics and fishing, while in the river waterskiing and swimming are favourite summer pastimes.

Ski Race: Mar. *Tennis Tournament:* Easter. *Almond Blossom Festival:* Aug.

Robinvale Riverside Caravan Park: Riverside Dr; (03) 5026 4646. *Weir Caravan Park Robinvale:* Pethard Rd; (03) 5026 3415. *Boundary Bend General Store and Caravan Park Murray River:* 27 Murray Valley Hwy, Boundary Bend; (03) 5026 8201.

Euston Weir and Lock on Murray: created as an irrigation water store, it features a 'fish ladder' that enables fish to jump over the weir. Picnic and barbecue facilities are provided; Pethard Rd, south-west edge of town. *Robinvale Organic and Bio-dynamic Wines:* tastings and sales of these distinctive, preservative-free wines. Also a children's playground; Sea Lake Rd; 5 km s. *Olive oil:* this region is renowned for its award-winning olive oil. Robinvale Estate offers farmgate sales and tastings; Tol Tol Rd; 8 km se. There is also Boundary Bend Estate; Boundary Bend; Murray Valley Hwy; 1 km s of the Murray River. *Robinvale Indigenous Arts and Crafts:* learn about the local bush tucker; River Rd. *Hattah–Kulkyne National Park:* 66 km sw; *see Ouyen.*

TOWNS NEARBY: Ouyen 68 km, Mildura 71 km, Balranald (NSW) 73 km, Wentworth (NSW) 95 km, Swan Hill 110 km

Rochester

Pop. 2827
Map ref. 542 C7

i Council offices, 43 Mackay St; (03) 5484 4500; www.rochester.org.au

91.1 FM ABC Local Radio, 104.7 Radio EMFM

On the Campaspe River, near Echuca, Rochester is the centre of a rich dairying and tomato-growing area. There are several lakes and waterways near town, making Rochester a popular destination for freshwater fishing.

The 'Oppy' Museum The museum details the history of Sir Hubert Opperman, affectionately known as Oppy, a champion cyclist who competed in the Tour de France. There is a collection of memorabilia related to Oppy's career as a cyclist, as well as artefacts from the town's past. A statue of Oppy is opposite the museum. Moore St.

Heritage walk: take in the town's attractive old buildings. *Campaspe River Walk:* a pleasant, signposted walk by the river.

Kyabram Fauna Park This park, owned by the Kyabram community, is home to over 140 animal species – everything from wombats to waterfowl. It has been built from the ground up on a piece of degraded farmland, and is now heavily involved in breeding programs for endangered species such as the eastern barred bandicoot. There is a walk-through aviary and Australia's first energy-efficient reptile house. (03) 5852 2883; 35 km ne.

Campaspe Siphon: an impressive engineering feat, where the Waranga–Western Main irrigation channel was redirected under the Campaspe River; 5 km n. *Fishing:* nearby channels, rivers and lakes are popular with anglers for redfin and carp. Lakes include Greens Lake and Lake Cooper (14 km se), also good for picnicking and watersports. *Elmore:* here is the Campaspe Run Rural Discovery Centre, which explains Koorie and colonial history and heritage. Elmore Field Days are held each Oct; 17 km s.

TOWNS NEARBY: Echuca 25 km, Rushworth 38 km, Bendigo 58 km, Nagambie 62 km, Heathcote 62 km

Rushworth

Pop. 1041
Map ref. 542 D8

i 33 High St; (03) 5856 1117; www.campaspe.vic.gov.au/community/rushworth/main.htm

97.7 FM ABC Local Radio, 98.5 FM 98.5

Situated in central Victoria off the Goulburn Valley Highway, this delightful little town was once a goldmining settlement. The original site of the township was known as Nuggetty owing to the numerous gold nuggets found during the 19th century. Rushworth has retained much of its original character, with well-preserved early buildings lining the main street.

Historic buildings: many along High St are National Trust–classified, including the Church of England, the Band Rotunda, the former Imperial Hotel, the Glasgow Buildings and the Whistle Stop. Take the High St Heritage Walk to see these and others; map from visitor centre. *History Museum:* housed in the old mechanics institute with displays relating to the town's goldmining heritage; Cnr High and Parker sts. *Growlers Hill Lookout Tower:* views of the town, Rushworth State Forest and the surrounding Goulburn Valley; Reed St.

Lake Waranga Caravan Park & Holiday Camp: 98 Waranga Basin Rd, Waranga Shores; (03) 5856 1243.

Rushworth State Forest The largest natural ironbark forest in the world, Rushworth State Forest is also renowned for the orchids and wildflowers that blossom here in spring. Picnics and bushwalks are popular activities in this attractive reserve where over 100 species of birds, along with echidnas and kangaroos, can be seen. Access via Whroo Rd; 3 km s.

[RUTHERGLEN] HUMOROUS SIGN IN RUTHERGLEN'S TOWN CENTRE

Jones's Eucalyptus Distillery: eucalyptus oil is extracted from blue mallee gum; Parramatta Gully Rd, just south of town. *Waranga Basin:* an artificial diversion of the Goulburn weir constructed in 1916, now a haven for boating, fishing, swimming and watersports; 6 km NE. *Whroo Historic Reserve:* Balaclava Hill, an open-cut goldmine, along with camping and picnic facilities, the Whroo cemetery and an Aboriginal waterhole; 7 km S. *Murchison:* a small town picturesquely set on the Goulburn River. Town attractions include the Italian war memorial and chapel; Meteorite Park, the site of a meteorite fall in 1969; Longleat Winery; and Campbell's Bend Picnic Reserve; 19 km E. *Days Mill:* a flour mill with buildings dating from 1865; 39 km NE via Murchison. *Town ruins:* goldmining played a huge role in the development of this region, but not all towns survived the end of the gold rush. Ruins of Angustown, Bailieston and Graytown are all to the south of Rushworth.

TOWNS NEARBY: Nagambie 25 km, Rochester 38 km, Shepparton 41 km, Heathcote 46 km, Seymour 50 km

Rutherglen

Pop. 1991
Map ref. 527 N12 | 543 J6 | 544 G1

ℹ️ 57 Main St; (02) 6033 6300 or 1800 622 871; www.rutherglenvic.com

 101.3 Oak FM, 106.5 FM ABC Local Radio

Rutherglen is the centre of one of the most important winegrowing districts in Victoria, with a cluster of vineyards surrounding the town. Many of the local wineries are best known for their fortified wines. Rutherglen's main street features preserved late-19th-century architecture.

Rutherglen Wine Experience: interpretive displays of Rutherglen's wine history; visitor centre, Main St. *Common School Museum:* local history displays and a re-creation of a Victorian-era schoolroom; behind Main St. *Historic tours:* take a self-guide walk, bike ride or drive, following maps provided at the visitor centre. *Lake King:* originally constructed in 1874 as Rutherglen's water storage, it is now a wildlife sanctuary and offers a scenic walk.

Tastes of Rutherglen: celebration of the region's gourmet food and wine; Mar. *Rutherglen and District Art Society Show:* Mar. *Easter in Rutherglen:* Easter. *Winery Walkabout:* June. *Country Fair:* June. *Wine Show:* Sept. *Tour de Rutherglen:* cycling and wine event; Oct. *Young Bloods and Bloody Legends:* food and wine event; Oct.

Vintara Winery: contemporary menu matched to wines; 105 Fraser Rd; 0447 327 517. *Pickled Sisters Cafe:* local-produce cafe; Cofield Wines, Distillery Rd, Wahgunyah; (02) 6033 2377. *Terrace Restaurant:* regional vineyard menu; All Saints Estate, All Saints Rd, Wahgunyah; (02) 6035 2209.

Admurraya House: 16 Meehan St; (02) 6032 9747. *Bank on Main:* 80 Main St; (02) 6032 7000. *Carlyle House Rutherglen:* 147 High St; (02) 6032 8444. *'Cuddle Doon' Cottages B&B:* 12 Hunter St; (02) 6032 7107. *Ready Cottage:* 92 High St; (02) 6032 7407. *Rutherglen Caravan & Tourist Park:* 72 Murray St; (02) 6032 8577.

Rutherglen wine region Winemaking in Rutherglen has been more or less continuous since 1839, and many of the wineries go back well beyond 100 years. Campbells, Jones, St Leonards and Warrabilla produce the bold reds – shiraz and durif – that the region is renowned for. But Rutherglen is even better known for its world-class fortified wines, mostly muscat and tokay. In this category, Chambers Rosewood and Morris lead the way. Look out for All Saints, with its historic building, and Pfeiffer, Chambers, Gehrig Estate and Campbells. The countryside of grassy paddocks and big old gum trees is dotted with many beautiful historic buildings, and some of the wineries are located on the banks of the Murray River. A popular Winery Walkabout is held every June.

Great Northern Mine: marked by mullock heaps associated with the first alluvial goldmine in the district. Historical details are provided on-site; Great Northern Rd, 5 km E. *Lake Moodemere:* found near the winery of the same name, the lake is popular for watersports and features ancient Aboriginal canoe trees by the shores; 8 km W. *Old customs house:* a relic from the time when a tax was payable on goods from NSW; 10 km NW.

TOWNS NEARBY: Corowa (NSW) 9 km, Chiltern 17 km, Wangaratta 36 km, Wodonga 39 km, Beechworth 39 km

St Arnaud

Pop. 2274
Map ref. 549 K9

ℹ️ 4 Napier St; (03) 5495 1268 or 1800 014 455.

🖻 91.1 FM ABC Local Radio, 99.1 Goldfields FM

A former goldmining town surrounded by forests and scenic hill country, St Arnaud is a service centre for the district's farming community, yet retains a peaceful rural atmosphere. The main street is lined with well-preserved historic buildings, many of which feature impressive ornate lacework. Together, these buildings form a nationally recognised historic streetscape.

Self-guide historic tour: brochure available from visitor centre. *Queen Mary Gardens:* great spot for a picnic; Napier St. *Old Post Office:* now a B&B and restaurant; Napier St. *Police lock-up:* built in 1862; Jennings St.

Heritage Festival: Nov.

St Arnaud Caravan Park: Cnr Dundas and Alma sts; (03) 5495 1447.

St Arnaud Range National Park The park protects an oasis of dense box-ironbark forest and woodland surrounded by agricultural land. Over 270 different species of native flora have been recorded here and provide a glimpse of what the area would have looked like before the land-clearing that occurred during and after the gold rush. Within the park are the Teddington

VICTORIA

Reservoirs, popular for brown trout and redfin fishing. The rugged terrain throughout provides a great opportunity for keen bushwalkers or 4WD enthusiasts. Wedge-tailed eagles can be seen soaring above the steep, forested ranges. Contact Parks Victoria on 131 963. Sunraysia Hwy; 15 km s.

Great Grape Rd: wine-themed circuit through Stawell and Ballarat; details from visitor centre.

TOWNS NEARBY: Donald 37 km, Wedderburn 39 km, Dunolly 50 km, Inglewood 55 km, Avoca 56 km

Sale

Pop. 13 335
Map ref. 541 K7

i Wellington Visitors Information Centre, Princes Hwy; (03) 5144 1108 or 1800 677 520; www.tourismwellington.com.au

104.7 Gippsland FM, 828 AM ABC Local Radio

Situated by the Thomson River near the Latrobe River junction, Sale grew on the back of the gold rush and became Gippsland's first city in 1950. Although largely considered an industrial town, with the nearby Bass Strait oilfields providing a large part of the town's economy, Sale has a lot more to offer. The Port of Sale is being redeveloped and there are many good cafes and restaurants, and a number of fine-art galleries and craft outlets. The lakes near Sale are home to the unique Australian black swan – the bird that has become a symbol for the town.

Gippsland Arts Gallery The gallery promotes the work of artists and craftspeople in central Gippsland. Works range from traditional landscapes to visual statements on environmental and cultural issues, and may be in any medium from painting and photography to film and video. Foster St; (03) 5142 3372.

Lake Guthridge Parklands This major recreational area within Sale comprises the Lake Guthridge and Lake Guyatt precincts, the Sale Botanic Gardens and the Regional Aquatic Complex. The precinct showcases over 35 ha of historically significant botanic gardens, walking trails, Indigenous artworks and a contemporary fauna park. It also provides sensory gardens, abundant seating, an adventure playground for children and tennis courts. Foster St.

Historical Museum: local history memorabilia; Foster St. *Ramahyuck Aboriginal Corporation:* offers local arts and crafts and is part of the Bataluk Cultural Trail, which takes in sites of Aboriginal significance in the region; Foster St. *Historical buildings:* include Our Lady of Sion Convent in York St; Magistrates Court and Supreme Court, Foster St; St Paul's Anglican Cathedral featuring fine stained-glass windows, Cunninghame St; St Mary's Cathedral, Foster St. Bicentennial clock tower in the mall utilises the original bluestone base, ironwork and clock mechanisms; Raymond St. *RAAF base:* home of the famous Roulettes aerobatic team; Raglan St. *Sale Common and State Game Refuge:* protected wetland area with a boardwalk; south-east edge of town. *Textile art:* Sale is the home of internationally recognised textile artist Annemieke Mein. Her work is on permanent display in the foyer of the Port of Sale Civic Centre, ESSO BHP Billiton Wellington Entertainment Centre and St Mary's Cathedral; Foster St.

Sale Cup: Greenwattle Racecourse; Oct.

Equus Cafe Bar: contemporary menu; 100 Foster St; (03) 5144 3388. *Relish at the Gallery:* modern cafe; Gippsland Art Gallery, 68–70 Foster St; (03) 5144 5044.

Minnies Bed and Breakfast: 202 Gibsons Rd; (03) 5144 3344. *Sale Showground Caravan & Motorhome Park:* 2 Maffra–Sale Rd; (03) 5144 6432. *Sale Motor Village:* Princes Hwy; (03) 5144 1366. *90 Mile Beach Holiday Retreat:* Track 10 (via Longford–Loch Sport Rd), Loch Sport; (03) 5146 0320.

Holey Plains State Park The open eucalypt forests in this park are home to abundant wildlife, while swamps provide a habitat for many frog species. There is a good swimming lake, and a series of fascinating fossils can be seen nearby in a limestone quarry wall. Bushwalking, picnicking and camping are all popular activities, particularly around Harriers Swamp. Access from Princes Hwy; 14 km sw.

Fishing: good fishing for trout in the Avon River near Marlay Pt and also in the Macalister, Thomson and Latrobe rivers, especially at Swing Bridge; 5 km s. *Marlay Pt:* on the shores of Lake Wellington with boat-launching facilities provided. The yacht club here sponsors an overnight yacht race to Paynesville each Mar; 25 km E. *Seaspray:* a popular holiday spot on Ninety Mile Beach; offers excellent surfing and fishing; 32 km s. *Golden and Paradise beaches:* 2 more townships on Ninety Mile Beach with great surfing and fishing; 35 km SE. *Loch Sport:* set on Gippsland Lakes and popular for camping and fishing; 65 km SE. *For details on Gippsland Lakes see Lakes Entrance and Paynesville. Howitt Bike Trail:* 13-day round trip beginning and ending in Sale; details from visitor centre. *Bataluk Cultural Trail:* takes in sites of Indigenous significance from Sale to Cann River; brochure from visitor centre.

TOWNS NEARBY: Maffra 17 km, Traralgon 47 km, Walhalla 57 km, Bairnsdale 57 km, Morwell 61 km

Seymour

Pop. 6062
Map ref. 542 D10

i Old Courthouse, 47 Emily St; (03) 5799 0233; www.mitchellshire.vic.gov.au

87.6 Seymour FM, 97.7 FM ABC Local Radio

Seymour is a commercial, industrial and agricultural town on the Goulburn River. The area was recommended for a military base by Lord Kitchener during his visit in 1909. Nearby Puckapunyal became an important training place for troops during World War II, and remains a major army base today.

Royal Hotel: featured in Russell Drysdale's famous 1941 painting *Moody's Pub;* Emily St. *Old Courthouse:* built in 1864, it now houses local art; Emily St. *Fine Art Gallery:* in the old post office; Emily St. *Goulburn River:* a walking track goes by the river and the Old Goulburn Bridge has been preserved as a historic relic. *Goulburn Park:* for picnics and swimming; Cnr Progress and Guild sts. *Seymour Railway Heritage Centre:* restored steam engines and carriages; open by appt; Railway Pl. *Australian Light Horse Memorial Park:* Goulburn Valley Hwy.

Market: Kings Park; 3rd Sat each month. *Alternative Farming Expo:* Feb. *Tastes of the Goulburn:* food and wine festival; Oct. *Seymour Cup:* Oct.

Fowles Wine: local-produce-driven menu; Cnr Hume Fwy and Lambing Gully Rd, Avenel; (03) 5796 2150. *The Shed Cafe:* slick contemporary cafe; 8447 Goulburn Valley Hwy, Trawool; (03) 5799 1595.

Goulburn River Tourist Park: 30 Trevan St; (03) 5792 1530. *Highlands Caravan Park:* 33 Emily St; (03) 5792 2124.

Tallarook State Forest Tallarook is a popular destination for bushwalking, camping, rock climbing and horseriding. The key features are Mt Hickey, the highest point in the park and the location of a fire-lookout tower, and Falls Creek Reservoir, a scenic picnic spot. Warragul Rocks offers great views over the Goulburn River. 10 km s.

Travellers note: *Lookout from Warragul Rocks can only be accessed via private property. The landowner requests that any visitor contact him first to arrange access: Ron Milanovic, 0413 402 744.*

Wineries: several in the area, including Somerset Crossing Vineyards, 2 km s; Plunkett Fowles, 21 km NE; Tahbilk, 26 km N; Mitchelton, 28 km N. *RAAC Memorial and Army Tank Museum:* Puckapunyal army base; 10 km w.

TOWNS NEARBY: Nagambie 27 km, Yea 33 km, Kilmore 34 km, Heathcote 40 km, Euroa 49 km

Shepparton
Pop. 44 598
Map ref. 542 E7

Victoria Park Lake, 534 Wyndham St; (03) 5831 4400 or 1800 808 839; www.greatershepparton.com.au

97.7 FM ABC Local Radio, 98.5 FM

Shepparton has recently become a popular destination for conferences and sporting events, and so has plenty of modern accommodation and good restaurants in town. Indeed, Shepparton is a thriving city and is considered the 'capital' of the Goulburn Valley. It is home to many orchards irrigated by the Goulburn Irrigation Scheme.

Art Gallery: features Australian paintings and ceramics; Welsford St. *Bangerang Cultural Centre:* displays and dioramas on local Aboriginal culture; Parkside Dr. *Historical Museum:* in the Historical Precinct; open even-dated Sun afternoons; High St. *Emerald Bank Heritage Farm:* displays of 1930s farming methods; Goulburn Valley Hwy. *Victoria Park Lake:* scenic picnic spot; Tom Collins Dr. *Reedy Swamp Walk:* prolific birdlife; at the end of Wanganui Rd. *Moooving Art:* mobile interactive public art of life-size 3-D cow sculptures; various parks in Shepparton including Monash Park, Queens Gardens and Murchison riverbank. *Factory sales:* Pental Soaps and Campbells Soups.

Trash and treasure market: Melbourne Rd; each Sun. *Craft market:* Queens Gardens, Wyndham St; 3rd Sun each month. *International Dairy Week:* Jan. *Bush Market Day:* Feb. *Shepparton Fest:* major local arts festival with family entertainment; Mar. *Spring Car Nationals:* car competitions; Nov.

Bohjass: contemporary with tapas; Level 1, 276B Wyndham St; (03) 5822 0237. *Cellar 47 Restaurant & Wine Bar:* top regional restaurant; 170 High St; (03) 5831 1882. *Letizia's Cafe Bar & Restaurant:* contemporary cross-cultural menu; 67 Fryers St; (03) 5831 8822. *The Teller Collective:* modern Australian; 55 Fryers St; (03) 5822 4451.

Goulburn Valley Motor Village: 8049 Goulburn Valley Hwy; (03) 5823 1561. *Strayleaves Caravan Park:* Cnr Mitchell St and Old Dookie Rd; (03) 5821 1232. *Victoria Lake Holiday Park:* 536 Wyndham St (Goulburn Valley Hwy); (03) 5821 5431. *Acacia Gardens Mooroopna Caravan Park:* 6705 Midland Hwy, Mooroopna; (03) 5825 2793. *BIG4 Shepparton Parklands:* 7835 Goulburn Valley Hwy, Kialla; (03) 5823 1576. *Tatura Caravan Park:* 23 Hastie St, Tatura; (03) 5824 2155.

SPC Ardmona KidsTown: a fun attraction with a maze, flying fox, enormous playground and miniature railway, and camel rides on the weekends; Midland Hwy; (03) 5831 4213; 3 km w. *Mooroopna:* a small town in the fruit-growing district. It hosts the Fruit Salad Day in Feb. SPC Ardmona also has a factory sales supermarket here; 5 km w. *Kialla:* Ross Patterson Gallery, with displays and sales of local artwork. Also here is Belstack Strawberry Farm, where you can pick your own berries; Goulburn Valley Hwy; 9 km s. *Tatura:* a museum with displays on local WW II internment camps. Taste of Tatura is held each Mar; 17 km sw. *Wunghnu:* the town (pronounced 'one ewe') is centred on the well-known Institute Tavern in the restored mechanics institute building. A tractor-pull festival is held each Easter; 32 km N.

TOWNS NEARBY: Rushworth 41 km, Euroa 45 km, Nagambie 50 km, Cobram 55 km, Benalla 56 km

Sorrento
see inset box on page 195

Stawell
Pop. 5879
Map ref. 549 I11 | 551 I1

Stawell and Grampians Visitor Information Centre, 6 Main St; (03) 5358 2314 or 1800 330 080; www.ngshire.vic.gov.au

96.5 Triple H FM, 594 AM ABC Local Radio

Pastoral runs were established in the Stawell (rhymes with ball) region in the 1840s, but it was the discovery of gold in 1853 by a shepherd at nearby Pleasant Creek that was the catalyst for creating a town. Stawell remains a goldmining centre with Victoria's largest mine. However, it is actually better known as the home of the Stawell Gift, Australia's richest footrace, and is the gateway to the Grampians.

Stawell Gift Hall of Fame Museum In 1878 the Stawell Athletic Club was formed by local farmers and businessmen who were keen to have a sports day each Easter. The club put up the prize pool of £110, and the race was on. The annual Stawell Gift has run almost continuously since and is now one of the most prestigious races in the world. The race has been run at Central Park since 1898. Visit the museum to discover the glory and heartbreak of the race since its inception. Open 9–11am weekdays; Main St; (03) 5358 1326.

Big Hill Lookout and Stawell Gold Mine viewing area: the Pioneers Lookout at the summit of this local landmark presents magnificent 360-degree views of the surrounding area. Continue down Reefs Rd to Stawell Gold Mine viewing area to hear about the daily operations of Victoria's largest gold-producing mine. *Casper's Mini World:* miniature tourist park with working models of famous world attractions such as the Eiffel Tower and including dioramas and commentaries; London Rd. *Fraser Park:* displays of mining equipment; Main St. *Pleasant Creek Court House Museum:* local history memorabilia; Western Hwy. *Stawell Ironbark Forest:* spring wildflowers, including rare orchids; northern outskirts of town, off Newington Rd.

SES Market: Drill Hall, Sloane St; 1st Sun each month. *Farmer's Market:* Harness Racing Club, Patrick St; last Sun each month. *Stawell Gift:* Easter.

 RADIO STATIONS IN TOWN WHAT'S ON WHERE TO EAT WHERE TO STAY   NEARBY

VICTORIA

🛏 *Stawell's Grampians Gate Caravan Park:* 2 Burgh St; 1800 301 183. *Bellellen Homestead:* 17 Bellellen Rd, Black Range; (03) 5358 4800.

☼ **Bunjil's Shelter** This is Victoria's most important Aboriginal rock-art site. It depicts the creator figure, Bunjil, sitting inside a small alcove with his 2 dingoes. Bunjil created the geographical features of the land, and then created people, before disappearing into the sky to look down on the earth as a star. The site is thought to have been used for ceremonies by the local Djab Wurrung and Jardwadjali people. Off Pomonal Rd; 11 km s.

The Sisters Rocks: huge granite tors; beside Western Hwy; 3 km SE. *Great Western:* picturesque wine village with Seppelt Great Western Winery, est. 1865, featuring National Trust–classified underground tunnels of cellars and Champagne Picnic Races in Jan; 16 km SE. *Tottington Woolshed:* rare example of a 19th-century woolshed; road to St Arnaud; 55 km NE. *Great Grape Rd:* circuit through Ballarat and St Arnaud, stopping at wineries, including Best's and Garden Gully; details from visitor centre.

TOWNS NEARBY: **Halls Gap 25 km, Ararat 29 km, Avoca 62 km, Horsham 64 km, St Arnaud 65 km**

Swan Hill
Pop. 9684
Map ref. 526 G9 | 547 L12 | 549 L2

ℹ Swan Hill Region Information Centre, cnr McCrae and Curlewis sts; (03) 5032 3033 or 1800 625 373; www.swanhillonline.com

📻 99.1 Smart FM, 102.1 FM ABC Local Radio

In 1836, explorer Thomas Mitchell named this spot Swan Hill because of the black swans that kept him awake all night. The town's swans remain, but there are many other attractions in this pleasant city on the Murray Valley Highway.

🏛 **Swan Hill Pioneer Settlement** This museum re-creates the Murray and Mallee regions from the 1830s to the 1930s. There are barber shops and chemists, and rides available on the PS *Pyap* or horse-drawn carts. There is also the Sound and Light Tour; bookings required. An Aboriginal canoe tree can also be found in the park. End of Gray St on Little Murray River.

Swan Hill Regional Art Gallery: an impressive permanent collection plus touring exhibitions; opposite the Pioneer Settlement Museum.

🌴 **Market:** Curlewis St; 3rd Sun each month. *Racing Cup Carnival:* June. *Australian Inland Wine Show:* Oct.

✕ **Java Spice:** South-East Asian; 17 Beveridge St; (03) 5033 0511. *Quo Vadis:* Italian restaurant and pizza parlour; 255–259 Campbell St; (03) 5032 4408. *Yutaka Sawa:* Japanese; 107 Campbell St; (03) 5032 3515.

🛏 *BIG4 Riverside Swan Hill:* 1 Monash Dr; (03) 5032 1494. *BIG4 Swan Hill:* 186 Murray Valley Hwy; (03) 5032 4372. *Swan Hill Holiday Park:* Murray Valley Hwy; (03) 5032 4112. *Pental Island Caravan Park & Holiday Farm:* 519 Pental Island Rd; (03) 5032 2071. *Best's Riverbed & Breakfast:* 7 Kidman Reid Dr, Murray Downs; (03) 5032 2126. *Burrabliss Farms:* 169 Lakeside Dr, Lake Boga; (03) 5037 2527. *Hill Top Resort:* 659 Murray Valley Hwy, Tyntynder South; (03) 5033 1515.

☼ **Swan Hill wine region** The region, which starts around Tresco to the south-east and ends around Piangil to the north-west, takes advantage of the Murray River and the Mediterranean-style climate. The first vines were planted here in 1930, but the proliferation of vineyards really began when Sicilian immigrants arrived on the Murray after WW II. Today cellar doors offer tastings and sales of predominantly shiraz, colombard and chardonnay varieties. Winery map from visitor centre.

Lake Boga The town has an interesting history as an RAAF flying-boat repair depot during WW II. The depot serviced over 400 flying boats, one of which can be seen at the Flying Boat Museum. The underground museum is in the original communications bunker in Willakool Dr. At Lake Boga, the water mass is popular for watersports, fishing and camping, and is home to a variety of bird species that can be seen on the various walks. A yachting regatta is held here each Easter. 17 km SE.

Lakeside Nursery and Gardens: over 300 varieties of roses; 10 km NW. *Tyntyndyer Homestead:* built in 1846; open Tues and Thurs 10am–4pm or by appt; Murray Valley Hwy; 20 km NW. *Nyah:* good market with local produce; 2nd Sat each month; 27 km NW. *Tooleybuc:* situated in NSW, it has a tranquil riverside feel and good fishing, picnicking and riverside walks. The Bridgekeepers Cottage has sales and displays of dolls and crafts; 46 km N.

TOWNS NEARBY: **Kerang 55 km, Barham (NSW) 60 km, Balranald (NSW) 78 km, Cohuna 79 km, Wycheproof 87 km**

Tallangatta
Pop. 955
Map ref. 543 L7 | 545 K3

ℹ 50 Hanson St, Corryong; (02) 6076 2277; www.pureuppermurrayvalleys.com

📻 101.3 Oak FM, 106.5 FM ABC Local Radio

When the old town of Tallangatta was going to be submerged in 1956 after the level of the Hume Weir was raised, the residents simply moved the entire township 8 kilometres west. Tallangatta now has an attractive lakeside location and sits directly north of Victoria's beautiful alpine region.

🏛 *The Hub:* local art and craft, and Lord's Hut, the only remaining slab hut in the district; Towong St.

🌴 *Farm and Water Festival:* Apr. *Fifties Festival:* Oct. *Garage Sale Festival:* Oct.

🛏 *Tallangatta Lakelands Caravan Park:* Queen Elizabeth Dr; (02) 6071 2457. *Magorra Caravan Park:* Mitta North Rd, Mitta Mitta; (02) 6072 3568. *The Witches Garden – Cottage on the Creek:* 608 Dartmouth Rd, Mitta Mitta; (02) 6072 3533.

☼ **Lake Hume** Tallangatta is on the shores of this enormous and attractive lake, formed when the then largest weir in the Southern Hemisphere was constructed. It is now a picturesque spot for swimming, waterskiing, windsurfing and fishing. The foreshore reserves are perfect for barbecues.

Eskdale: craft shops, and trout fishing in the Mitta Mitta River; 33 km S. *Lake Dartmouth:* great for trout fishing and boating; hosts the Dartmouth Cup Fishing Competition over the June long weekend. Also here is The Witches Garden featuring unique medicinal plants; 58 km SE. *Mitta Mitta:* remnants of a large open-cut goldmine. Also a gallery, Butcher's Hook Antiques and Bharatralia Jungle Camp. Hosts the Mitta Muster on Sun on the long weekend in Mar; 60 km S. *Australian Alps Walking Track:* passes over Mt Wills; 108 km S via Mitta Mitta. *Scenic drives:* to Cravensville, to Mitta Mitta along Omeo Hwy and to Tawonga and Mount Beauty.

TOWNS NEARBY: **Albury (NSW) 28 km, Wodonga 28 km, Yackandandah 32 km, Beechworth 47 km, Chiltern 52 km**

SORRENTO

Pop. 1530

Map ref. 531 B11 | 532 F7 | 536 H9 | 540 B7 | 551 P8

[POINT KING]

(i) Mornington Peninsula Visitor Information Centre, Point Nepean Rd, Dromana; (03) 5987 3078 or 1800 804 009; www.virtualsorrento.com.au

98.7 3RPP FM, 774 AM ABC Local Radio

Just inside Port Phillip Heads on the Mornington Peninsula, in 1803 Sorrento was the site of Victoria's first European settlement. The town is close to historic Point Nepean and major surf and bayside beaches. Its population swells significantly over summer as visitors flock to soak up the holiday-resort atmosphere. A ferry links Sorrento to Queenscliff on the Bellarine Peninsula.

Collins Settlement Historic Site: marks the state's first European settlement and includes early graves; on Sullivan Bay; contact Parks Victoria on 13 1963. *Historic buildings:* Sorrento Hotel on Hotham Rd and Continental Hotel on Ocean Beach Rd. Both are fine examples of early Victorian architecture, with the latter reputed to be the largest limestone building in the Southern Hemisphere. The visitor centre can give details of self-guide historical walks. *Nepean Historical Society Museum and Heritage Gallery:* a collection of local artefacts and memorabilia in the National Trust–classified mechanics institute. Adjacent is Watt's Cottage and the Pioneer Memorial Garden; Melbourne Rd; (03) 5984 0255. *Day spas:* all types of relaxation therapies available at health and wellness centres; details from visitor centre.

World's Longest Lunch Sorrento: 3 courses with Mornington Peninsula wines; Sorrento foreshore; bookings and information (03) 5984 1500; Mar. *Taste of Sorrento:* week-long gastronomic journey; bookings and information 0424 000 391; June. *Sorrento Fiesta:* Oct.

Acquolina: Italian trattoria; 26 Ocean Beach Rd; (03) 5984 0811. *The Baths:* iconic beachside eatery; 3278 Point Nepean Rd; (03) 5984 1500. *Loquat Restaurant & Bar:* modern Mediterranean; 3183 Point Nepean Rd; (03) 5984 4444. *Smokehouse Sorrento:* pizza and Mediterranean fare; 182 Ocean Beach Rd; (03) 5984 1246.

Carmel of Sorrento: 142 Ocean Beach Rd; (03) 5984 3512. *Eastcliff Cottage:* 881 Melbourne Rd; (03) 5984 0668. *Amberlee Four Star Family Holidays:* 306 Jetty Rd, Rosebud; (03) 5982 2122. *Capel Sound Foreshore:* Point Nepean Rd, Rosebud West; (03) 5986 4382. *Four Winds B&B:* 29 Ford St, Rye; (03) 5985 8939. *Harmony B&B:* 45 Placadena Rd, Fingal; (03) 5988 6375. *Hilltonia Homestead:* 282 Browns Rd, Rye; (03) 5985 2654. *Plantation House Bed & Breakfast:* 33 Maori St, Rye; (03) 5985 5926. *Weeroona:* 26 Creedmore Dr, Rye; (03) 5985 3946.

Mornington Peninsula National Park The park incorporates Sorrento, Rye and Portsea back beaches and stretches south-east to Cape Schanck and beyond (*see Flinders*). Walks, picnics and swimming are the main attractions, but there is also the unique rock formation of London Bridge, at Portsea. The rugged coastline offers good surfing. Point Nepean and historic Fort Nepean can be accessed by a daily transport service departing from Point Nepean Information Centre. You can also choose to walk the paths or cycle to the tip (bike hire is available). A former Quarantine Station on Point Nepean offers tours, which include a visit to the Army Health Services Museum, on Sundays and public holidays. Contact Parks Victoria on 131 963.

Portsea: an opulent holiday town with good, safe swimming beaches. It hosts the Portsea Swim Classic each Jan; 4 km NW. *Blairgowrie:* a boutique bayside village with easy access to sailing. *Popes Eye Marine Reserve:* an artificially created horseshoe-shaped island and reef, now popular for diving. Gannets nest here. Cruises available; ask at visitor centre; 5 km offshore at Portsea. *Rye:* a beachside holiday spot; 8 km E. *Peninsula Hot Springs:* relaxing, outdoor, naturally heated pools. Private mineral pools, baths and massage therapies available; Springs La, Rye. *Moonah Links Golf Course:* two fantastic 18-hole golf courses, one designed specifically for the Australian Open; Peter Thompson Dr, Fingal. *Rosebud:* a bayside resort town with gorgeous, safe swimming beaches. Summer fishing trips depart from Rosebud pier. An international kite festival is held in Mar; 15 km E. *McCrae Homestead:* National Trust drop-slab property built in 1844; open Wed, Sat and Sun afternoons, group bookings by appt; McCrae; 17 km E.

TOWNS NEARBY: Queenscliff 11 km, Ocean Grove 21 km, Barwon Heads 23 km, Drysdale 24 km, Flinders 28 km

VICTORIA

Terang

Pop. 1830
Map ref. 538 F7 | 551 I7

i Old Courthouse, 22 High St; (03) 5592 1984.

103.7 3WAY-FM, 774 AM ABC Local Radio

Terang is in a fertile dairy-farming district. It is a well-laid-out town with grand avenues of deciduous trees, and is known throughout the state for its horseracing carnivals.

Cottage Crafts Shop: in the old courthouse on High St. *District Historical Museum:* old railway station and memorabilia; open 3rd Sun each month; Princes Hwy. *Lions Walking Track:* 4.8 km, beside dry lake beds and majestic old trees; begins behind Civic Centre on High St. *Historic buildings:* many examples of early-20th-century commercial architecture. A Gothic-style Presbyterian church is in High St.

Terang Cup: Nov.

Demo Dairy: demonstrates dairy-farming practices; Princes Hwy, 4 km w. *Lake Keilambete:* 2.5 times saltier than the sea and reputed to have therapeutic properties; must obtain permission to visit as it is surrounded by private land; 4 km NW. *Modelbarn Australia:* collection of model cars, boats and planes; open by appt; 6209 Princes Hwy; (03) 5592 1592 or 0407 052 227; 5 km E. *Noorat:* birthplace of Alan Marshall, author of *I Can Jump Puddles*. The Alan Marshall Walking Track here involves a gentle climb to the summit of Mt Noorat, an extinct volcano, with excellent views of the crater, the surrounding district and the Grampians; 6 km N.

TOWNS NEARBY: Camperdown 20 km, Warrnambool 41 km, Port Campbell 43 km, Colac 59 km, Port Fairy 63 km

Torquay

Pop. 9848
Map ref. 532 A7 | 536 F9 | 538 G2 | 551 N8

i Surfworld Australia, Surf City Plaza, cnr Surfcoast Hwy and Beach Rd; (03) 5261 4219 or 1300 614 219; www.visitgreatoceanroad.org.au

94.7 The Pulse FM, 774 AM ABC Local Radio

Torquay was one of the first resort towns on Victoria's coast, and remains one of the most popular today. It was named in honour of the famous English resort, but its heritage is very different. Not only does Torquay and its coast have some of the best surf beaches in the world, it was also the birthplace of world leaders in surfboards, wetsuits and other apparel, including Rip Curl and Quiksilver, founded here in the 1960s and 70s.

Surf City Plaza This modern plaza houses some of the biggest names in surfing retail alongside smaller outlets. The complex boasts the world's biggest surfing museum, Surfworld. See how board technology has developed over the last century, find out exactly what makes a good wave, and learn about the history of surfing at Bells Beach. A theatre here screens classic 1960s and 70s surf flicks and the latest surf videos. Beach Rd.

Fishermans Beach: good spot for fishing, with a sheltered swimming beach and a large sundial on the foreshore. *Tiger Moth World:* theme park based around the1930s Tiger Moth biplane. Joy-flights available; Blackgate Rd. *Surf schools:* programs available to suit all abilities, with many courses run during summer school holidays; details from visitor centre.

Cowrie Community Market: foreshore; 3rd Sun each month Sept–Apr. *Danger 1000 Ocean Swim:* Jan. *Surf for Life Surfing Contest:* Jan. *Kustom Jetty Surf Pro:* Jan. *Rip Curl Pro:* Easter. *Hightide Festival:* fireworks display; Dec.

Growlers: cafe/bar and restaurant; 23 The Esplanade; (03) 5264 8455. *Scorched:* modern Australian; 17 The Esplanade; (03) 5261 6142. *The Surf Rider:* modern fusion menu; 26 Bell St; (03) 5261 6477. *Sunnybrae Restaurant and Cooking School:* regionally inspired weekend lunches; Cnr Cape Otway and Lorne rds, Birregurra; (03) 5236 2276.

South Beach Haven: 1040 Horseshoe Bend Rd; (03) 5261 5669. *Torquay Foreshore Caravan Park:* 35 Bell St; (03) 5261 2496. *Whitesbeach Torquay:* 1212 Horseshoe Bend Rd; (03) 5264 8875. *Breamlea Caravan Park:* Horwood Dr, Breamlea; (03) 5264 1352. *Geelong Surfcoast Holiday Park:* 621 Torquay Rd (Surfcoast Hwy), Mount Duneed; (03) 5264 1243.

Surf coast It is no wonder the coast that runs from Torquay through to Eastern View (past Anglesea) has dubbed itself the Surf Coast. Submerged reefs cause huge waves that are a surfer's paradise. Most famous is Bells Beach, around 5 km SW of Torquay. The clay cliffs provide a natural amphitheatre for one of the best surf beaches in the world and the longest running surf competition, the Rip Curl Pro, which started in 1973 and attracts top competitors. Other good surf beaches include Jan Juc, Anglesea and Fairhaven. To see the coast on foot, take the 30 km Surf Coast Walk, starting at Torquay and travelling south to Moggs Creek.

Hinterland: delightful towns like Bellbrae, Deans Marsh and Birregurra are dotted along the vista of the Surf Coast hinterland; starts 8 km w. *Bicycle lane:* runs along Surfcoast Hwy from Grovedale to Anglesea.

TOWNS NEARBY: Anglesea 15 km, Barwon Heads 15 km, Ocean Grove 18 km, Geelong 20 km, Aireys Inlet 24 km

Traralgon

Pop. 21 960
Map ref. 541 I7

i Latrobe Visitor Information Centre, The Old Church, Southside Central, Princes Hwy; 1800 621 409; www.visitlatrobevalley.com

100.7 FM ABC Local Radio, 104.7 Gippsland FM

Traralgon is one of the Latrobe Valley's largest towns; a commerical hub located on the main Gippsland rail and road routes. Primarily a service centre for neighbouring agricultural communities, timber and electricity production, it also retains a certain village atmosphere with historic buildings in its wide streets and attractive public gardens.

Historic buildings: include the old post office and courthouse; Cnr Franklin and Kay sts. *Victory Park:* a great spot for picnics. Also here is a band rotunda and miniature railway; Princes Hwy.

Farmers market: 4th Sat each month. *International Junior Tennis Championships:* Jan. *Traralgon Cup:* Nov.

Cafe Aura Deli: cafe-deli-cum-restaurant; Shop 3, 19–25 Seymour St; (03) 5174 1517. *Iimis Cafe:* good Mediterranean/Greek; 28 Seymour St; (03) 5174 4577. *Neilsons:* contemporary Australian; 13 Seymour St; (03) 5175 0100. *Terrace Cafe:* modern fare; Century Inn, cnr Princes Hwy and Airfield Rd; (03) 5173 9400.

Walhalla Mountain Rivers Trail: this scenic drive (Tourist Route 91) winds through pretty hills to the north of town. *Loy Yang power station:* tours available; 5 km s. *Toongabbie:* a small town that hosts the Festival of Roses each Nov; 19 km NE.

[WALHALLA] POSTERS ON THE SIDE OF THE CORNER STORE

Hazelwood Cooling Pond: year-round warm water makes this a popular swimming spot; outskirts of Churchill; 20 km sw. *Tarra–Bulga National Park:* temperate rainforest; 30 km s.

TOWNS NEARBY: Morwell 14 km, Moe 25 km, Walhalla 29 km, Yarram 43 km, Maffra 46 km

Walhalla
Pop. 15
Map ref. 541 I5

 Latrobe Visitor Information Centre, The Old Church, Southside Central, Princes Hwy, Traralgon; 1800 621 409.

100.7 FM ABC Local Radio, 104.7 Gippsland FM

This tiny goldmining town is tucked away in dense mountain country in Gippsland – in a steep, narrow valley with sides so sheer that some cemetery graves were dug lengthways into the hillside. The town has a tiny population and is a relic from a long-gone era – it was only connected to electricity in 1998.

Long Tunnel Gold Mine One of the most prosperous goldmines in the state during the 19th century with over 13 tonnes of gold extracted here. Guided tours take visitors through sites such as Cohen's reef and the original machinery chamber 150 m below the ground. Tours operate daily at 1.30pm; Main St.

Historic buildings and goldmining remains: include the old post office, bakery and Windsor House, now a B&B. *Walks:* excellent walks in the town area, including one to a cricket ground on top of a 200 m hill. Another walk leads to a historic cemetery with graves of early miners; details from visitor centre. *Old Fire Station:* with hand-operated fire engines and firefighting memorabilia; open weekends and public holidays. *Museum and Corner Store:* local history displays plus goldmining artefacts; Main St. *Walhalla Goldfields Railway:* wonderfully restored old steam engine; departs from Thomson Station on Wed, Sat, Sun and public holidays. *Gold panning:* try your luck along pretty Stringers Creek, which runs through town. *Ghost tours:* spook yourself with a night-time guided ghost tour of Walhalla using old-fashioned lanterns; details from visitor centre.

Parker's Restaurant: contemporary hotel dining room; Walhalla's Star Hotel, Main Rd; (03) 5165 6262.

Deloraine Gardens: terraced gardens; just north of town. *Thomson River:* excellent fishing and canoeing; 4 km s. *Rawson:* a town built to accommodate those who helped construct the nearby Thomson Dam. Mountain trail-rides are available; 8 km sw. *Erica:* visit this small timber town to see

a timber-industry display at the Erica Hotel. The King of the Mountain Woodchop is held in town each Jan; 12 km sw. *Baw Baw National Park:* park areas accessible from Walhalla include the Aberfeldy River picnic and camping area; 12 km N. *See Moe.* *Moondarra State Park:* great for walks and picnics. Moondarra Reservoir is nearby; 30 km s. *4WD tours:* to gold-era 'suburbs' such as Coopers Creek and Erica. Tours can be organised through Mountain Top Experience, (03) 5134 6876. *Australian Alps Walking Track:* starts at Walhalla and goes for an incredible 655 km. It can be done in sections; details from visitor centre.

TOWNS NEARBY: Traralgon 29 km, Moe 31 km, Morwell 33 km, Maffra 47 km, Warragul 52 km

Wangaratta
Pop. 16 846
Map ref. 543 I7 | 544 E4

 100 Murphy St; (03) 5721 5711 or 1800 801 065; www.visitwangaratta.com.au

101.3 Oak FM, 106.5 FM ABC Local Radio

Wangaratta lies in a rich agricultural district in north-eastern Victoria that produces a diverse range of crops including kiwifruit, wine grapes, walnuts and wheat. An entry for both the Murray to the Mountains Rail Trail and the Great Alpine Road, it offers the services of a rural city while retaining a country-town warmth. A short drive in any direction will lead to world-class wineries, gourmet food and some spectacular views.

Self-guide historical walk: historic sites and buildings, such as the majestic Holy Trinity cathedral, Vine Hotel Cellar Museum and the Wangaratta Historical Museum; details from visitor centre. *Wangaratta Cemetery:* headless body of infamous bushranger Daniel 'Mad Dog' Morgan is buried here; Tone Rd. *Wangaratta Exhibitions Gallery:* changing exhibitions by national and regional artists; Ovens St. *Brucks Textile Factory:* a factory outlet for Sheridan sheets; Sicily Ave. *Australian Country Spinners:* an outlet for local wool products; Textile Ave.

Trash and Treasure Market: Olympic Swimming Pool carpark, Swan St; each Sun. *Stitched Up Festival:* textile displays; June/July. *Wangaratta Show:* agricultural show; Oct. *Festival of Jazz:* well-known jazz festival; Oct/Nov.

Atrium Restaurant: imaginative dining room; Quality Hotel Wangaratta Gateway, 29–37 Ryley St; (03) 5721 8399. *Rinaldo's Casa Cucina:* Italian; 8–10 Tone Rd; (03) 5721 8800.

Painters Island Caravan Park: 2 Pinkerton Cres; (03) 5721 3380. *Wangaratta Caravan & Tourist Park:* 79 Parfitt Rd; (03) 5721 3368. *BIG4 Wangaratta North Cedars Holiday Park:* Parfitt Rd, Wangaratta North; (03) 5721 5230. *Mount Pleasant Homestead:* 181 Wightons Rd, East Wangaratta; (03) 5722 2616.

Warby Range State Park The steep ranges of the 'Warbys', as they are known locally, provide excellent viewing points, especially from Ryan's Lookout. Other lookouts include the Pangarang Lookout, near Pine Gully Picnic Area, and Mt Glenrowan Lookout, the highest point of the Warbys at 513 m. There are well-marked tracks for bushwalkers and a variety of pleasant picnic spots amid open forests and woodlands, with wildflowers blossoming during the warmer months. 12 km w.

Eldorado Eldorado is a fascinating old goldmining township named after the mythical city of gold. The main relic of the gold

 VICTORIA

era is a huge dredge, the largest in the Southern Hemisphere, which was built in 1936. There is a walking track with information boards around the lake where the dredge now sits. The Eldorado Museum provides details of the town's mining past, alongside WW II relics and a gemstone collection. 20 km NE.

Wombi Toys: old-fashioned, handmade toys for sale; Whorouly; 25 km SE. *Reids Creek:* popular with anglers, gem fossickers and gold panners; near Beechworth; 28 km E. *Newton's Prickle Berry Farm:* pick your own blackberries and buy organic berry jams; Whitfield; 45 km S. *Scenic drives:* one goes for 307 km along the Great Alpine Rd through the alps to Bairnsdale. The road south leads through the beautiful King Valley and to Paradise Falls. A network of minor roads allows you to fully explore the area, including a number of tiny, unspoiled townships such as Whitfield, Cheshunt and Carboor. *Murray to the Mountains Rail Trail:* following historical railway lines with 94 km of bitumen sealed track, the trail ventures into pine forests, natural bushland and open valleys. It links several townships. Suitable for both cycling and walking; a gentle gradient makes the track appropriate for all ages and levels of fitness.

TOWNS NEARBY: Milawa 14 km, Glenrowan 14 km, Beechworth 33 km, Chiltern 35 km, Rutherglen 36 km

Warburton
Pop. 1949
Map ref. 534 F8 | 537 M5 | 540 F4

i Water Wheel Visitor and Information Centre, 3400 Warburton Hwy; (03) 5966 9600; www.warburtononline.com

99.1 Yarra Valley FM, 774 AM ABC Local Radio

Warburton was established when gold was discovered in the 1880s, but its picturesque location and proximity to Melbourne meant it quickly became a popular tourist town, with many guesthouses built over the years. There are fine cafes and antique and craft shops in town.

Information centre: local history display and an old-style, operating water wheel, 6 m in diameter. A wood-fire bakery is adjacent to the centre; Warburton Hwy. *River Walk:* 9 km return walk, following a pretty stretch of the Yarra River; starts at Signs Bridge on Warburton Hwy. *Upper Yarra Arts Centre:* cinema with regular screenings and a variety of live performances held during the year; Warburton Hwy. *Warburton Golf Course:* with great views across the river valley; Dammans Rd. *O'Shannassy Aqueduct Trail:* good walking and cycling track that follows the historic open channelled aqueduct; details from visitor centre.

Film Festival: Upper Yarra Arts Centre; June. *Winterfest:* wood festival; July.

Wild Thyme: bohemian cafe for music lovers; 3391 Warburton Hwy; (03) 5966 5050. *Bulong Estate Winery, Cellar Door and Restaurant:* modern French menu; 70 Summerhill Rd, Yarra Junction; (03) 5967 1358.

Charnwood Cottages at Warburton: 2 Wellington Rd; (03) 5966 2526. *Casa Valeri:* 26 Brett Rd; (03) 5966 5821. *Warburton Caravan & Camping Park:* 30 Woods Point Rd; (03) 5966 2277. *Hoddles Highland:* 380 Jameson Rd, Hoddles Creek; (03) 5967 4240. *3 Kings B&B:* 2480 Warburton Hwy, Yarra Junction; 0409 678 046.

 Yarra Ranges National Park Here, tall mountain ash trees give way to pockets of cool temperate rainforest. Mt Donna Buang, a popular daytrip destination – especially during winter,

when it is often snow-covered – is 17 km NW of Warburton. The Rainforest Gallery on the southern slopes of the mountain features a treetop viewing platform and walkway. Night-walk tours here reveal some of Victoria's unique nocturnal creatures. Acheron Way is a scenic 37 km drive north through the park to Marysville. Along the way are views of Mt Victoria and Ben Cairn. Drive starts 1 km E of town.

Yarra Centre: indoor sports and swimming; Yarra Junction, Warburton Hwy; 9 km SW. *Yarra Junction Historical Museum:* local history displays; open 1–5pm Sun or by appt; Warburton Hwy; 10 km SW. *Upper Yarra Reservoir:* picnic and camping facilities; 23 km NE. *Walk into History:* takes in the goldmining and timber region from Warburton East to Powelltown (25 km S); details from visitor centre. *Ada Tree:* a giant mountain ash over 300 years old; access from Powelltown. *Yellingbo State Fauna Reserve:* good for nature spotting. Home to the helmeted honeyeater, a state emblem; 25 km SW. *Vineyards:* several in the region, many with tastings and sales. They include the Yarra Burn Winery, the Five Oaks Vineyard and the Brahams Creek Winery. *Rail trails:* former railway tracks now used for walking, bikeriding or horseriding, the main one being the Lilydale to Warburton trail; details from visitor centre.

TOWNS NEARBY: Healesville 19 km, Marysville 28 km, Emerald 30 km, Yarra Glen 30 km, Olinda 31 km

Warracknabeal
Pop. 2491
Map ref. 526 E12 | 548 H7

i 119 Scott St; (03) 5398 1632; www.wag.wimmera.com.au

96.5 Triple H FM, 594 AM ABC Local Radio

The town's Aboriginal name means 'the place of the big red gums shading the watercourse', a name that is both beautifully descriptive and accurate, especially for the part of town around Yarriambiack Creek. Warracknabeal is a major service town at the centre of a wheat-growing district.

Historical Centre: includes a pharmaceutical collection, clocks, and antique furnishings of child's nursery; open afternoons; Scott St. *Black Arrow Tour:* a self-guide driving tour of historic buildings. *Walks:* including the Yarriambiack Creek Walk; details from visitor centre. *National Trust–classified buildings:* include the post office, the Warracknabeal Hotel and the original log-built town lock-up. *Lions Park:* by the pleasant Yarriambiack Creek with picnic spots and a flora and fauna park; Craig Ave.

Y-Fest: golf, horseracing, machinery and country music; Easter.

Warracknabeal Caravan Park: 2 Lyle St; (03) 598 1201.

North Western Agricultural Machinery Museum: displays of farm machinery from the last 100 years; Henty Hwy; 3 km S.

TOWNS NEARBY: Jeparit 38 km, Dimboola 39 km, Horsham 54 km, Donald 54 km, Hopetoun 58 km

Warragul
Pop. 11 501
Map ref. 537 N9 | 540 G7

i Gippsland Food and Wine, 123 Princes Hwy, Yarragon; 1300 133 309; www.westgippsland.com.au

99.1 Yarra Valley FM, 104.7 Gippsland FM

Warragul is a thriving rural town with a growing commuter population, being the dairying centre that supplies much of

Melbourne's milk. An excellent base to explore the delightful countryside including the Baw Baw snowfields and 'Gippsland Gourmet Country', the town itself showcases 19th-century architecture, especially in the ornate facades and arched windows of Queen St.

West Gippsland Arts Centre Part of the town's fantastic, architect-designed civic centre complex, the centre is a mecca for art lovers from across the state. It houses a good permanent collection of contemporary visual arts and is known for the variety of theatre productions and events held here throughout the year. Ask inside for a full program of events. Civic Pl; (03) 5624 2456.

Harvest of Gippsland: Mar.

The Grange Cafe & Deli: local-produce menu; 15 Palmerston St; (03) 5623 6698. *The Outpost Retreat:* modern regional fare; 38 Loch Valley Rd, Noojee; (03) 5628 9669. *Sticcado Cafe:* features local Gippsland beef; Shop 6, The Village Walk, Yarragon; (03) 5634 2101.

Southside Bed and Breakfast: 20 Korumburra Rd; (03) 5623 6885. *Warragul Gardens Holiday Park:* 44 Burke St; (03) 5623 2707. *El Paso Caravan Park:* 262 Princes Way, Drouin; (03) 5625 1710. *Glen Cromie Caravan Park:* 850 Main Neerim Rd, Drouin West; (03) 5626 8212. *Janalli:* 285 Wagner Rd, Neerim South; (03) 5628 1476. *Neerim South Caravan Park:* 410 Neerim East Rd, Neerim South; (03) 5628 1248. *Springbank Bed & Breakfast:* 240 Williamsons Rd, Nilma North; (03) 5627 8060.

Mt Worth State Park This park protects a rich variety of native flora including the silver wattle and the Victorian Christmas bush. The Giant's Circuit is a walk that takes in a massive old mountain ash that is 7 m in circumference. Other walks include the Moonlight Creek and MacDonalds tracks, both of which are easily accessible. No camping is permitted. Contact Parks Victoria on 13 1963; access via Grand Ridge Rd; 22 km SE.

Yarragon Nestled in the foothills of the Strzelecki Ranges and with views of green rolling hills, Yarragon is a wonderful destination with an abundance of delightful shops and accommodation options. It boasts one of Gippsland's leading antique stores and a unique gallery renowned for its quality original artwork, exquisite jewellery, beautiful handblown glass and much more. Sample local wines and gourmet produce, including award-winning cheeses from Tarago River and Jindi Cheese. 13 km SE.

Gippsland Gourmet Country: the renowned 'Gippsland Gourmet Country' takes in lush green pastures and state forests to reveal a diverse range of superb gourmet delights. Previously known as 'Gourmet Deli Country', Gippsland Gourmet encompasses some of the best food and wine producers in the region, including trout, venison, cheese, berries, potatoes, herbs and wine. Sure to tempt your tastebuds and tantalise the senses; details from visitor centre. *Darnum Musical Village:* a complex of buildings housing a collection of musical instruments dating back to the 1400s; Princes Hwy; 8 km E. *Oakbank Angoras and Alpacas:* sales of yarn and knitted goods; near Drouin, 8 km W. *Waterfalls:* Glen Cromie, Drouin West (10 km NW); Glen Nayook, south of Nayook; and Toorongo Falls, just north of Noojee. *Neerim South:* visit Tarago Cheese Company for tastings and sales of top-quality cheeses, or enjoy a picnic or barbecue at the

pleasant reserve near the Tarago Reservoir. Scenic drives through mountain country start from town; 17 km N. *Grand Ridge Road:* 132 km drive that starts at Seaview, 17 km S, and traverses the Strzelecki Ranges to Tarra–Bulga National Park *(see Yarram for park details). Nayook:* good fresh produce, a fruit-and-berry farm, and the Country Farm Perennials Nursery and Gardens; 29 km N. *Childers:* Sunny Creek Fruit and Berry Farm, and Windrush Cottage; 31 km SE. *Noojee:* a mountain town featuring a historic trestle bridge and the Alpine Trout Farm; 39 km N.

TOWNS NEARBY: Moe 29 km, Korumburra 32 km, Leongatha 35 km, Koo-Wee-Rup 39 km, Morwell 41 km

Warrnambool
see inset box on next page

Wedderburn
Pop. 702
Map ref. 549 L8

ℹ️ Loddon Visitor Information Centre, Wedderburn Community Centre, 24 Wilson St; (03) 5494 3489; www.loddonalive.com.au

📻 91.1 FM ABC Local Radio, 99.1 Goldfields FM

Wedderburn, part of the 'Golden Triangle', was once one of Victoria's richest goldmining towns. Many large nuggets have been unearthed here in the past and – for some lucky people – continue to be discovered today. The town's annual Detector Jamboree, with music, historical re-enactments and family entertainment, is growing every year and recognises the importance of gold in the development of so many towns.

Hard Hill Tourist Reserve Hard Hill is a fascinating former mining district with original gold diggings and Government Battery. There is a good walking track through the site, where old mining machinery can be seen. Hard Hill is in a pleasant bushland setting, and picnic facilities are provided. Nearby is a fully operational eucalyptus distillery offering tours and selling eucalyptus products. Northern outskirts of town.

Coach House Cafe and Museum: a 1910 building restored to its original appearance, with authentic, old-fashioned stock and coach-builders quarters; High St. *Bakehouse Pottery:* old bakery now used as a pottery, also home to gold pistachio nuts; High St. *Nardoo Creek Walk:* takes in the key historic buildings around town; map from visitor centre.

Detector Jamboree: gold festival; Mar long weekend. *Historic Engine Exhibition:* Sept.

Wedderburn Pioneer Caravan Park: Hospital St; (03) 5494 3301.

Mt Korong: bushwalking; 16 km SE. *Wychitella Forest Reserve:* wildlife sanctuary set in mallee forest, home to mallee fowl; 16 km N. *Kooyoora State Park: see Inglewood for details. Fossickers Drive:* takes in goldmining sites, places of Aboriginal significance, local wineries and the Melville Caves; details from visitor centre. *Dunolly:* the Goldfields Historical and Arts Society, with replicas of impressive gold finds; 75 Broadway St. *St Arnaud:* boasts the beautiful Queen Mary Gardens and a number of old pubs and verandah-fronted shops.

TOWNS NEARBY: Inglewood 29 km, St Arnaud 39 km, Dunolly 50 km, Wycheproof 51 km, Donald 57 km

 RADIO STATIONS   IN TOWN   WHAT'S ON   WHERE TO EAT   WHERE TO STAY   NEARBY

VICTORIA

WARRNAMBOOL

Pop. 30 393
Map ref. 538 C8 | 550 G8

 Flagstaff Hill Maritime Village, 89 Merri St; (03) 5559 4620 or 1800 637 725; www.visitwarrnambool.com.au

103.7 3WAY-FM, 594 AM ABC Local Radio

Warrnambool lies at the end of the Great Ocean Road on a notorious section of coastline that has seen over 80 shipwrecks. The best known was the *Loch Ard* in 1878, which claimed the lives of all but two of those on board. While the wreck site itself is closer to Port Campbell, impressive relics from the ship are held at the Flagstaff Hill Maritime Museum in town. Warrnambool, as Victoria's fifth-largest city, offers first-rate accommodation and dining as well as a fantastic swimming beach. Each year from June to September, southern right whales can be spotted from Warrnambool's Logans Beach. There's a purpose-built viewing platform at the beach (binoculars or a telescope are recommended), and the local visitor centre releases daily information on whale sightings.

Flagstaff Hill Maritime Museum This reconstructed 19th-century maritime village is complete with a bank, hotel, schoolhouse and surgery. There are also 2 operational lighthouses and an authentic keeper's cottage, now housing the Shipwreck Museum, where relics retrieved from the *Loch Ard* – including the famous earthenware Loch Ard Peacock – are kept. On display is the Flagstaff Hill tapestry, an intricate work depicting themes of Aboriginal history, sealing, whaling, exploration, immigration and settlement. At night, visitors can watch the sound-and-light show 'Shipwrecked', which details the story of the *Loch Ard*. The local history museum, History House, is also now located here. Merri St; (03) 5559 4600.

Main beach: a safe swimming beach with a walkway along the foreshore from the Breakwater to near the mouth of the Hopkins River. **Lake Pertobe Adventure Playground:** a great spot for family picnics; opposite main beach, Pertobe Rd. **Art Gallery:** local artwork, plus European and avant-garde collections;

Timor St. **Customs House Gallery:** open 11am–5pm Thurs–Sun; Gilles St; (03) 5564 8963. **Botanic Gardens:** pretty regional gardens designed by Guilfoyle (a curator of Melbourne's Royal Botanic Gardens) in 1879; Cnr Queens Rd and Cockman St. **Fletcher Jones Gardens/Mill Markets:** award-winning landscaped gardens and market in front of former Fletcher Jones factory; Cnr Flaxman St and Raglan Pde. **Portuguese Padrao:** monument to early Portuguese explorers; Cannon Hill, southern end of Liebig St. **Heritage walk:** 3 km self-guide walk taking in the many historic buildings around town; details from visitor centre. **Hopkins River:** great for fishing and boating, with Blue Hole, at the river's mouth, a popular spot for family swimming and rockpool exploration. Cruises are available; east of town. **Proudfoots Boathouse:** National Trust–classified boathouse on the Hopkins; Simpson St. **Wollaston Bridge:** an unusual bridge, built over 100 years ago; northern outskirts of town. **Tours and charters:** fishing, whale-watching and diving tours (including shipwreck sites); contact visitor centre for details.

Sunday market: showgrounds on Koroit St; each Sun. **Hillside market:** Flagstaff Hill; operates throughout summer. **Wunta Fiesta:** family entertainment, food stalls, music; Feb. **Tarerer Festival:** Indigenous culture and music; Mar. **Racing Carnival:** Grafton Rd; May. **Fun 4 Kids:** children's festival; June. **Melbourne–Warrnambool Cycling Classic:** Oct. **Flower shows:** held in spring.

Donnelly's Restaurant: contemporary regional fare; 78 Liebig St; (03) 5561 3188. **Kermond's Hamburgers:** excellent old-fashioned hamburgers; 151 Lava St; (03) 5562 4854. **Nonna Casalinga:** up-market Italian; 69 Liebig St; (03) 5562 2051. **Pippies by the Bay:** contemporary food with a view; 91 Merri St; (03) 5561 2188.

Discovery Holiday Parks – Warrnambool: 25 Pertobe Rd; (03) 5561 1514. **Fig Tree Holiday Village:** 33 Lava St;

[SOUTHERN RIGHT WHALE BREACHING OFF LOGANS BEACH]

(03) 5561 1233. *Hopkins River Caravan Park:* 125 Jubilee Park Rd; (03) 5565 1327. *Merton Manor Exclusive Bed and Breakfast:* 62 Ardlie St; (03) 5562 0720. *Surfside Holiday Park – Warrnambool:* Pertobe Rd; (03) 5559 4700. *Warrnambool Holiday Park:* Simpson St; (03) 5562 5031. *Burnbrow Manor:* 1 Hopetoun St (Princes Hwy), Allansford; (03) 5565 1380. *Manor Gums:* 170 Shadys La, Mailors Flat; (03) 5565 4410. *The Olde Courthouse Inn:* 100 Commercial Rd, Koroit; (03) 5565 8346.

Tower Hill State Game Reserve This is a beautiful piece of preserved bushland featuring an extinct volcano and a crater lake, with tiny islands. Nature walk starts at the Worn Gundidj Visitor Centre in the reserve. For further information contact (03) 5561 5315. 12 km NW, just after the turn-off to Koroit.

Logans Beach Each year in June, southern right wales return to the waters along the south coast of Australia to give birth, raise their young and start the breeding cycle again. Each female seems to have a favourite spot to give birth, which means that many familiar faces keep reappearing at Warrnambool's Logans Beach. The beach features a purpose-built viewing platform above the sand dunes (binoculars or telescopes are recommended), and the local visitor centre releases information on whale sightings daily.

Allansford Cheeseworld: for cheese tastings and sales; 10 km E. *Hopkins Falls:* scenic picnic spot, particularly spectacular in winter after heavy rain. In spring hundreds of baby eels migrate up the falls, creating a most unusual sight; 16 km NE. *Cudgee Creek Wildlife Park:* deer, crocodiles and other native fauna, plus an aviary. Picnic and barbecue facilities are provided. Cudgee; 18 km E. *Koroit:* see National Trust–classified buildings, good local arts and crafts shops, botanic gardens, and an Irish festival in Apr; 19 km NW.

TOWNS NEARBY: Port Fairy 22 km, Terang 41 km, Port Campbell 52 km, Camperdown 61 km, Portland 77 km

Welshpool
Pop. 200
Map ref. 540 H10

i Old Courthouse, 9 Rodgers St, Yarram; (03) 5182 6553.

89.5 3MFM South Gippsland, 828 AM ABC Local Radio

Welshpool is a small dairying community in South Gippsland. On the coast nearby, Port Welshpool is a deep-sea port servicing the local fishing and oil industries. Barry Beach Marine Terminal, a short distance west of Port Welshpool, services the offshore oil rigs in Bass Strait.

Port Welshpool This popular coastal town has all the natural attractions that a seaside village could want. It is frequented by families who enjoy the safe beaches and fabulous coastal walks, and has fantastic views across to Wilsons Promontory. Fishing enthusiasts should drop a line from the historic jetty, or try from a boat. The port's long link with the sea is detailed in the Port Welshpool and District Maritime Museum, which exhibits shipping relics and local history displays as well. 2 km S.

Franklin River Reserve: great bushwalking with well-marked tracks; near Toora; 11 km W. *Agnes Falls:* the highest single-span falls in the state, spectacular after heavy rain; 19 km NW. *Scenic drive:* head west to see magnificent views from Mt Fatigue; off South Gippsland Hwy. *Fishing and boating:* excellent along the coast.

TOWNS NEARBY: Foster 21 km, Port Albert 22 km, Yarram 24 km, Leongatha 48 km, Morwell 48 km

Winchelsea
Pop. 1336
Map ref. 536 D8 | 538 E1 | 551 M8

i Old Library, Willis St (Princes Hwy); open 11am–4pm Fri–Sun; 1300 614 219; www.historicwinchelsea.com.au

94.7 The Pulse FM, 774 AM ABC Local Radio

This charming little town on the Barwon River west of Geelong was first developed with cattle runs in the 1830s. Many of the historic buildings that grew from this development can still be seen around town, the most impressive being the nearby Barwon Park Homestead – a mansion built by famous settlers of the district, Thomas and Elizabeth Austin. Winchelsea soon became a key stopover for travellers taking the road from Colac to Geelong, and it still serves that purpose for travellers on the Princes Highway.

Barwon Bridge: an impressive arched bridge, built from stone in 1867; Princes Hwy. *Antiques and collectibles:* many shops in town that outline its history; Main St and Princes Hwy. *Winchelsea Historical Trail:* map available from visitor information centre, or check township information boards. *Barwon Hotel:* known locally as the 'bottom pub' of the town, offers country style; Main St. *Winchelsea Tavern:* recently renovated Art Deco 'top pub'; Princes Hwy. *Old Shire Hall:* beautifully restored bluestone building, now housing popular tearooms; Princes Hwy. *Old Library:* houses the visitor information centre; Princes Hwy. *Marjorie Lawrence Trail:* details the life of one of the world's most adored dramatic sopranos from the 1900s; details from visitor centre.

Winchelsea Festival: wool shearing, dog trials, wool classing, children's activities, local produce and market stall, plus more; Nov.

Barwon Park Homestead Only the greatest estate would satisfy Elizabeth Austin, and her husband, Thomas, acquiesced. Barwon Park, built in 1869, was the biggest mansion in the Western District. Featuring 42 rooms furnished largely with original pieces, the bluestone building is an impressive example of 19th-century design. The name Austin might be familiar: Thomas Austin reputedly imported the first of Australia's devastating rabbit population and Elizabeth Austin contributed to major charities, and established the Austin Hospital in Melbourne. Open 11am–4pm Wed and Sun; Inverleigh Rd; (03) 5267 2209; 3 km N.

Country Dahlias Gardens: beautiful gardens, best viewed during spring, with sales of dahlia plants; open Feb–Apr; Mathison Rd; 5 km s. *Killwarrie Cottage:* rose garden display, home-grown vegetables; open Nov–Mar; 7 km sw.

TOWNS NEARBY: Anglesea 25 km, Aireys Inlet 26 km, Torquay 32 km, Lorne 33 km, Geelong 34 km

Wodonga
Pop. 29 713
Map ref. 522 A12 | 527 N12 | 543 K6 | 545 I2

ⓘ Visitor Information Centre, Gateway Island, Lincoln Causeway; 1300 796 222; www.destinationalburywodonga.com.au

106.5 FM ABC Local Radio, 107.3 Ten-73 Border FM

Wodonga and its twin town, Albury *(in New South Wales)*, sit astride the Murray River. There are many attractions around the Murray and nearby Lake Hume, making the region a popular holiday destination. These twin cities blend city style and country pace, history and contemporary attractions, art and adventure.

🏠 *Gateway Village:* includes woodwork shops and cafes. Also houses the visitor centre; Lincoln Causeway. *The Bonegilla Migrant Experience:* a rare example of post-war migrant accommodation camps, the first Australian home for some 300 000 post-war migrants from over 50 countries; visitor centre is open 10am–4pm Mon–Sat; 10 km E. *The Bandiana Army Museum:* located just out of Wondonga and is one of the largest army museums in Australia. Open to the public 9.30am–5pm, daily; Anderson Rd, South Bandiana. *Arts Space Wodonga:* shows works by North East Victorian artists. Its program includes exhibitions, performances, workshops, recitals and forums. Cnr Lawrence and Hovell sts; open 9.30am–6pm, Mon–Wed, and Fri. *Huon Hill Lookout:* maps from visitor centre. *Sumsion Gardens at Belvoir Park:* a pretty lakeside park with walking track, picnic and barbecue facilities; Church St. *Tennis Centre:* the largest grass court centre of its kind in Australia; Melrose Dr.

🎭 *Craft Market:* Woodland Gr; 1st Sat each month. *Farmers market:* Gateway Village; 2nd Sat each month. *Wodonga Show:* Mar. *Todos Arte:* a 2-week art festival leading up to Carnivale Wodonga, Mar. *Carnivale Wodonga:* with live music, workshops and a street market; during the long weekend, Mar; High Street. *In My Backyard Festival:* raises environmental awareness; Mar. *Paws in the Park:* an even for pet dogs and cats, Apr. *Children's Fair:* Oct. *Wine and Food Festival:* Oct.

🍴 *O'Maille's Pub:* hearty bistro fare; 34–36 High St; (02) 6024 1335. *Steak Pit Restaurant:* upmarket steakhouse; Elgin's of Wodonga, 51–53 Elgin Boulevard; (02) 6024 1262. *Zilch Food Store:* friendly modern cafe; Shop 1, 8 Stanley St; (02) 6056 2400.

🛏 *Wodonga Caravan & Cabin Park:* 186 Melbourne Rd; (02) 6024 2598. *Boathaven Holiday Park:* 33 Boathaven Rd, Ebden; (02) 6020 6130.

⊙ **Mt Granya State Park** This landscape contrasts between steep, rocky slopes and open eucalypt forests. Bushwalking is a popular pastime and the display of wildflowers in spring is magnificent. There is a pleasant picnic spot at Cottontree Creek, and a short walk leads to the Mt Granya summit, which offers spectacular views of the alps. Murray River Rd; 56 km E.

Military Museum: Bandiana; 4 km SE. *Hume Weir:* good spot for walks and picnics; 15 km E. *Tours:* winery and fishing tours, as well as scenic drives through the Upper Murray region, the mountain valleys of north-east Victoria and the Riverina; details from visitor centre.

TOWNS NEARBY: Albury (NSW) 6 km, Yackandandah 22 km, Chiltern 25 km, Tallangatta 28 km, Beechworth 32 km

Wonthaggi
Pop. 6528
Map ref. 537 L12 | 540 E9

ⓘ Watt St; 1300 854 334; www.visitbasscoast.com

88.1 3MFM South Gippsland, 100.7 FM ABC Local Radio

Once the main supplier of coal to the Victorian Railways, Wonthaggi, near the beachside town of Cape Paterson, is South Gippsland's largest town. There are good tourist facilities in town and a number of pretty beaches nearby.

🏠 *Bass Coast Rail Trail:* 16 km trail that runs between Wonthaggi and Anderson. Suitable for walking and cycling, it is the only coastal rail trail in Victoria with landscape that varies from flat farmland and bushland to rugged coastline.

🌴 *Energy and Innovation Festival:* Mar.

🛏 *Jongebloed's Bed & Breakfast:* 27 Berry's Rd; (03) 5672 2028. *Cape Paterson Foreshore Caravan Park:* 1 Surf Beach Rd, Cape Paterson; (03) 5674 4507.

 State Coal Mine The demand for black coal created a thriving industry in Wonthaggi from 1909 until 1968, and the mine site has been retained to show visitors the lifestyle and working conditions of the miners. Daily underground tours offer close-up views of the coalface, a short walk into the East Area Mine and a cable-hauled skip ride to the surface. Above ground, visit the museum for an introduction to the history of the mine and of Wonthaggi itself, or take a walk around the historic buildings. Inquiries (03) 5672 3053 or Parks Victoria on 13 1963; Cape Paterson Rd; 1.5 km s.

Cape Paterson: waters offshore are protected by Bunurong Marine and Coastal Park and are good for surfing, swimming, snorkelling and scuba diving; 8 km s. *George Bass Coastal Walk:* starts at Kilcunda; 11 km NW. Ask at visitor centre for details of other walks. *Gippsland Gourmet Country:* takes in central Gippsland's gourmet food and wine producers; details from visitor centre.

TOWNS NEARBY: Inverloch 11 km, Korumburra 28 km, Leongatha 34 km, Cowes 35 km, Koo-Wee-Rup 46 km

Woodend
Pop. 3166
Map ref. 535 H9 | 536 G2 | 540 B2 | 542 B12 | 551 P3

ⓘ High St, beside Five Mile Creek; (03) 5427 2033 or 1800 244 711; www.visitmacedonranges.com

100.7 Highlands FM, 774 AM ABC Local Radio

During the gold rushes of the 1850s, travellers sought refuge from mud, bogs and bushrangers at the 'wood's end' around Five Mile Creek, where a town eventually grew. In the late 19th century Woodend became a resort town, and its lovely gardens and proximity to spectacular natural sights, such as Hanging Rock and Mount Macedon, still make it a popular daytrip and weekend getaway for visitors from Melbourne.

🏠 *Bluestone Bridge:* built in 1862, the bridge crosses Five Mile Creek on the northern outskirts of town. *Clock Tower:* built as a WW I memorial; Calder Hwy. *Courthouse:* historic structure built in 1870; Forest St.

Craft market: 3rd Sun each month Sept–May. *Winter Arts Festival:* June. *Macedon Ranges Budburst Festival:* held throughout the wine district; Nov.

Campaspe Country House: lovely regional dining room; 29 Goldies La; (03) 5427 2273. *Holgate Brewhouse:* modern menu; 79 High St; (03) 5427 2510.

Auberge Woodend: 40 Plants La; 0408 599 066. *Macedon Caravan Park:* Cnr Blackforest Dr and McBean Ave, Macedon; (03) 5426 1528.

Hanging Rock A massive rock formation made famous by *Picnic at Hanging Rock*, the novel by Joan Lindsay that was later made into a film. The story, about schoolgirls who mysteriously vanished while on a picnic in the reserve, became something of a legend. There is certainly something eerie about Hanging Rock with its strange rock formations, created by the erosion of solidified lava, and narrow tracks through dense bushland. Hanging Rock is renowned for the annual races held at its base, especially the New Year's Day and Australia Day races. Other events include a Vintage Car Rally and Harvest Picnic, both held in Feb. The reserve also has a discovery centre and cafe. Access from South Rock Rd, off Calder Hwy; 8 km NE.

Macedon Ranges wine region This is mainland Australia's coolest wine region and, like Tasmania, it's responsible for some very good sparkling wine. Most wineries are found east of the Calder Fwy around Romsey, Lancefield and Kyneton. Hanging Rock Winery achieves iconic status thanks to its position behind Hanging Rock, and its Non Vintage Macedon Cuvee sparkling wine is said to be one of the most complex sparkling wines in Australia. Also try the sauvignon blanc. Curly Flat is known for its excellent pinot noir and chardonnay, and Granite Hills for riesling and shiraz. Portree also produces chardonnay, and Virgin Hills is worth visiting for its blend of cabernet sauvignon, shiraz and merlot.

Macedon: a town at the foot of Mt Macedon. Home to the Church of the Resurrection, with stained-glass windows designed by Leonard French, and excellent plant nurseries; 8 km SE. *Mt Macedon:* a township located higher up the mountain, 2 km from Macedon, renowned for its beautiful gardens, many open to the public in autumn and spring. *Macedon Regional Park:* bushwalking and scenic drives. The Camels Hump marks the start of a signposted walk to the summit of the mountain where there stands a huge WW I memorial cross. Access via turn-off after Mt Macedon township. *Gisborne:* a variety of craft outlets. Gisborne Steam Park holds a steam-train rally each May; 16 km SE. *Glen Erin at Romsey/Cope-Williams Winery:* tastings and sales, surrounded by charming English-style gardens, tennis courts and a cricket green; Romsey; 19 km E. *Lancefield:* historic buildings and wineries. Mad Gallery and Bankart Gallery offer contemporary and fine art, respectively. The town is also home to a woodchopping competition in Mar and a farmers market, for local produce, 4th Sat each month; 25 km NE. *Monegeetta:* in town is the Mintaro Homestead, a smaller replica of Melbourne's Government House, but not open to the public; 27 km E via Romsey.

TOWNS NEARBY: Kyneton 14 km, Daylesford 34 km, Bacchus Marsh 37 km, Kilmore 38 km, Castlemaine 42 km

Wycheproof

Pop. 686
Map ref. 526 G12 | 549 K6

i Wycheproof Community Resource Centre, 280 Broadway; (03) 5493 7455; www.wycheproof.vic.au

99.1 Goldfields FM, 102.1 FM ABC Local Radio

Wycheproof is renowned for the long wheat trains that travel down the middle of the main street, towing up to 60 carriages behind them. There are many historic buildings in town, as well as rare, old peppercorn trees. Mount Wycheproof, at a mere 43 metres, has been named the smallest mountain in the world.

Mt Wycheproof A walking track leads up and around the mountain. Emus and kangaroos can be seen up close in a fauna park at the mountain's base.

Willandra Museum: farm machinery, old buildings and historical memorabilia; open by appt; Calder Hwy. *Centenary Park:* aviaries, 2 log cabins and barbecue facilities; Calder Hwy.

Music on the Mount: Oct. *Racing Carnival:* Oct/Nov.

Wycheproof Caravan Park: Calder Hwy; (03) 5493 7278. *Charlton Travellers Rest Ensuite Caravan Park:* 45 High St, Charlton; (03) 5491 1613.

Tchum Lakes: artificially created lakes, great for fishing and watersports dependent on water levels; 23 km W. *Birchip:* visitors to town are greeted by the town's beloved 'Big Red' mallee bull in the main street. Also in town is the Soldiers Memorial Park with large, shady Moreton Bay fig trees, a great spot for a picnic; 31 km W.

TOWNS NEARBY: Donald 39 km, Wedderburn 51 km, St Arnaud 60 km, Kerang 73 km, Warracknabeal 78 km

Yackandandah

Pop. 663
Map ref. 543 K7 | 545 I4

i The Athenaeum, High St; (02) 6027 1988; www.uniqueyackandandah.com.au

101.3 Oak FM, 106.5 FM ABC Local Radio

Yackandandah, with its avenues of English trees and traditional buildings, is so rich with history that the entire town is National Trust–classified. It is situated south of Wodonga in the heart of the north-east goldfields region. In fact, many of the town's creeks still yield alluvial gold.

Historic buildings: the post office, several banks and general stores, with the Bank of Victoria now preserved as a museum, open Sun and school holidays. Explore these and other buildings on a self-guide walk; details from visitor centre; High St. *Ray Riddington's Premier Store and Gallery:* displays and sales of local art; High St. *The Old Stone Bridge:* a beautiful old structure, built in 1857; High St. *Arts and crafts:* many outlets in town, including Yackandandah Workshop, cnr Kars and Hammond sts, and Wildon Thyme, High St. *Antiques:* Finders Bric-a-Brac and Old Wares, High St; Frankly Speaking, High St; and Vintage Sounds Restoration, specialising in antique gramophones, radios and telephones, Windham St. *Rosedale Garden and Tea Rooms:* Devonshire teas; Kars St.

Folk Festival: 3rd weekend Mar. *Spring Migration Festival:* Sept. *Flower Show:* Oct.

VICTORIA

Haig Room Restaurant: pub classics; Star Hotel, 30 High St; (02) 6027 1493. *Sticky Tarts Cafe:* charming casual cafe; 26 High St; (02) 6027 1853.

Yackandandah Holiday Park: Myrtleford–Yackandandah Rd; (02) 6027 1380.

Kars Reef Goldmine: take a tour of this fascinating old goldmine, or try your hand at gold panning (licence required); details of tours from visitor centre; Kars St. *Lavender Patch Plant Farm:* sales of plants and lavender products; Beechworth Rd; 4 km w. *Kirbys Flat Pottery and Gallery:* Kirbys Flat Rd; open weekends or by appt; 4 km s. *Indigo Valley:* a picturesque area with a scenic drive leading along the valley floor to Barnawatha; 6 km NW. *Allans Flat:* a great destination for food lovers, with The Vienna Patisserie for coffee, ice-cream and delicious Austrian cakes (closed Tues). Also here are Parks Wines and Schmidt's Strawberry Winery, both with tastings and sales; 10 km NE. *Wombat Valley Tramways:* a small-gauge railway; open Easter or by appt for groups; Leneva; 16 km NE.

TOWNS NEARBY: Beechworth 15 km, Wodonga 22 km, Albury (NSW) 28 km, Chiltern 28 km, Myrtleford 29 km

Yarra Glen

Pop. 2598

Map ref. 531 H4 | 534 C6 | 537 L4 | 540 E4

i Yarra Valley Visitor Information Centre, Old Courthouse, Harker St, Healesville; (03) 5962 2600; www.yarraglen.com.au

99.1 Yarra Valley FM, 774 AM ABC Local Radio

Yarra Glen is in the heart of the Yarra Valley wine region, nestled between the Yarra River and the Great Dividing Range. It is a gorgeous area featuring lush, vine-covered hills and fertile valleys, all within easy reach of Melbourne. Fine wines and top-quality local produce, fascinating antique, specialty gift and clothing shops, and restaurants are all in town to entice. For the more adventurous, Yarra Glen is home to hot-air ballooning, scenic helicopter flights over the valley and even skydiving at nearby Coldstream airfield. The bushfire of February 2009 came very close to the township of Yarra Glen, and some businesses and townsfolk were directly affected.

Yarra Glen Grand Hotel: imposing heritage-listed and National Trust–classified hotel, built in 1888 with a recently refurbished restaurant, stands like a sentinel in the main street; 19 Bell St; (03) 9730 1230. *Hargreaves Hill Brewing Co:* the old Colonial Bank building houses a fine-dining restaurant specialising in local produce and an extensive choice of Yarra

[YARRA GLEN] HOT-AIR BALLOON RIDE OVER THE YARRA VALLEY AT SUNRISE

Valley and European boutique beers; 25 Bell St; (03) 9730 1905. *Den of Antiquities and Yarra Valley Antique Centre:* boasts large collections of genuine antique furniture, china and glass, vintage radios and other collectibles; 25A Bell St; (03) 9730 2111. *Yarra Glen Railway Station:* old station on the 1888 Healesville–Lilydale railway line, rebuilt in 1915 and now being restored as part of the Yarra Valley Tourist Railway; King St.

Yarra Valley Farmers Market: historic barn at Yering Station; 3rd Sun each month. *Shortest Lunch:* midwinter fine food and wine at the smaller boutique wineries; June. *Yarra Valley Food & Wine:* regional produce and music throughout the year including the midsummer Twilight Cellar Door, Gumboot Season in the winter months and Shedfest in Oct; details from visitor centre.

Hargreaves Hill Brewing Company Restaurant: Mediterranean-style dishes; 25 Bell St; (03) 9730 1905. *TarraWarra Estate Wine Bar Cafe:* rustic European fare; 311 Healesville–Yarra Glen Rd; (03) 5957 3510. *Eleonore's Restaurant at Chateau Yering:* elegant dining room; Chateau Yering, 42 Melba Hwy, Yering; (03) 9237 3333. *Yering Station Wine Bar Restaurant:* modern Australian; 38 Melba Hwy, Yering; (03) 9730 0100.

Araluen Villas: 603 Steels Creek Rd; (03) 5965 2013. *Melba Lodge:* 939 Melba Hwy; (03) 9730 1511. *The Gatehouse at Villa Raedward:* 26 Melba Hwy, Yering; (03) 9739 0822.

Yarra Valley wine region With over 50 cellar-door outlets and around 100 wineries, the Yarra Valley is home to some exceptional names. De Bortoli is Australia's oldest family-owned winery and is well recognised throughout the country. Owned by the legendary Moet & Chandon, Domaine Chandon makes sophisticated sparkling wines that can be enjoyed in the glass-walled tasting room overlooking the vines. Yering Station produces excellent shiraz viognier as well as award-winning pinot noir. It is also the site of a produce store, a good restaurant, and the Yarra Valley Regional Farmers' Market held in an old barn (3rd Sun of the month). To combine wine with art, head to TarraWarra Estate, well known for its chardonnay and pinot noir, and its modern gallery that holds exhibitions of work by Australian greats from Arthur Boyd to Peter Booth *(also see Healesville)*. For a trendy wine experience, Giant Steps/ Innocent Bystander is a thoroughly modern cellar door near the town of Healesville with an excellent cafe/bakery (try their Portuguese tarts), bistro serving mouth-watering pizzas and cheese room.

Kinglake National Park Kinglake's beautiful messmate forests, fern gullies, panoramic lookouts and bushwalking tracks were devastated by the bushfire of February 2009. Park access and camping have reopened after extensive restoration works. Phone Parks Victoria on 13 1963 for further information.

Gulf Station: this National Trust–owned pastoral property, preserved as it was during pioneering days and recently restored, features old-fashioned farming implements and early animal breeds; open Wed–Sun and public holidays; 2 km NE. *Yarra Valley Dairy:* a working dairy with sales of specialty cheeses, clotted cream and local produce; 4 km s. *Ponyland Equestrian Centre:* trail rides and riding lessons; 7 km w. *Sugarloaf Reservoir Park:* sailing, fishing and walking, with barbecue and picnic facilities available; 10 km w. *Yarra Valley Regional Food Trail:* a self-guide tour, taking in the many gourmet food outlets in the region; details from visitor centre.

TOWNS NEARBY: Healesville 13 km, Olinda 22 km, Warburton 30 km, Emerald 31 km, Marysville 37 km

Yarram

Pop. 1716
Map ref. 541 I9

i Old Courthouse, 9 Rodgers St; (03) 5182 6553;
www.tourismwellington.com.au

89.5 3MFM South Gippsland, 100.7 FM ABC Local Radio

Yarram is deep in the dairy country of South Gippsland, and at the heart of some of its most beautiful locales, from the splendour of Ninety Mile Beach to the refreshingly cool atmosphere of Tarra–Bulga National Park. Yarram was originally settled on a swamp, and its name is derived from an Aboriginal word meaning 'plenty of water'. In town are some notable examples of early architecture, including the recently restored Regent Theatre and the historic courthouse.

Regent Theatre: built in 1930, this theatre has been wonderfully restored. Cinemas operate on weekends and school holidays; Commercial Rd.

Tarra Festival: Easter.

Tarra Valley Tourist Park 'Fernholme': 1906 Tarra Valley Rd, Tarra Valley; (03) 5186 1283. **Woodside Beach Caravan Park:** Woodside Beach Rd, Woodside Beach; (03) 5187 1214.

Tarra–Bulga National Park Tarra–Bulga is a tranquil park with spectacular river and mountain views. Fern Gully Walk, starting from the Bulga picnic ground, takes in the dense temperate rainforests of mountain ash, myrtle and sassafras. The walk leads across a suspension bridge high among the treetops. A walk to Cyathea or Tarra falls, surrounded by lush fern gullies, completes the rainforest experience. Keep an eye out for rosellas, lyrebirds and the occasional koala. The Tarra–Bulga Visitor Centre is on Grand Ridge Rd near Balook; from Yarram, access the park from Tarra Valley Rd; 20 km NW.

Won Wron Forest: great for walks, with wildflowers in spring; Hyland Hwy; 16 km N. **Beaches:** there are many attractive beaches in the region, including Manns, for fishing, 16 km SE; McLoughlins, 23 km E; and Woodside Beach, which is patrolled in summer; 29 km E. **Tarra Valley:** there are many great gardens, including Eilean Donan Gardens and Riverbank Nursery; located just north-west of Yarram. **Scenic drive:** a 46 km circuit goes from Yarram through Hiawatha and takes in Minnie Ha Ha Falls on Albert River, where picnic and camping facilities are provided.

TOWNS NEARBY: Port Albert 11 km, Welshpool 24 km, Foster 42 km, Traralgon 43 km, Morwell 44 km

Yarrawonga

Pop. 5726
Map ref. 527 M12 | 542 H5 | 544 D1

i Irvine Pde; (03) 5744 1989 or 1800 062 260;
www.yarrawongamulwala.com.au

101.3 Oak FM, 106.5 FM ABC Local Radio

Yarrawonga and its sister town Mulwala, across the New South Wales border, are separated by a pleasant stretch of the Murray River and the attractive Lake Mulwala. The 6000-hectare lake was created in 1939 during the building of the Yarrawonga Weir, which is central to irrigation in the Murray Valley. Yarrawonga's proximity to such great water features has made it a popular holiday resort. The sandy beaches and calm waters are ideal for watersports, and are also home to abundant wildlife.

Yarrawonga and Mulwala foreshores: great locations for walks and picnics, with shady willows, water slides, barbecue

facilities and boat ramps. **Canning A.R.T.S Gallery:** work by local artists; Belmore St. **Tudor House Clock Museum:** Lynch St. **Cruises:** daily cruises along the Murray on paddleboats *Paradise Queen* or *Lady Murray*; depart from Bank St.

Rotary Market: local crafts and second-hand goods; showgrounds; 3rd Sun each month. **Powerboat Racing:** May. **Murray Marathon:** Dec.

Paradise Queen Lake Cruises: lunch and dinner cruises on Lake Mulwala; 1 Bank St; (03) 5744 1989.

Yarrawonga Holiday Park: Piper St; (03) 5744 3420.

Fyffe Field Wines: tastings and sales; Murray Valley Hwy; 19 km W. **Fishing:** Murray River for Murray cod and yellow-belly. **Guided tours:** local wineries; book at visitor centre.

TOWNS NEARBY: Mulwala (NSW) 3 km, Cobram 34 km, Corowa (NSW) 35 km, Rutherglen 42 km, Tocumwal (NSW) 45 km

Yea

Pop. 1051
Map ref. 534 D1 | 537 L1 | 540 E1 | 542 E12

i Old Railway Station, Station St; (03) 5797 2663;
www.murrindinditourism.com.au

88.9 UGFM Upper Goulburn Community Radio, 97.7 FM ABC Local Radio

This town sits by the Yea River, a tributary of the Goulburn River. Hume and Hovell, the first explorers through the region, discovered this wonderfully fertile area – a discovery that led in part to the settlement of the rest of Victoria. Near the Yea–Tallarook Road there are beautiful gorges and fern gullies, a reminder of what Yea looked like thousands of years ago.

Historic buildings: Beaufort Manor, High St; General Store, now a restaurant, High St. **Wetlands Walk:** sightings of abundant birdlife and glider possums; eastern outskirts of town.

Market: local craft and produce; Main St; 1st Sat each month Sept–May. **Autumn Fest:** Mar.

Marmalades: hearty country food; 20 High St; (03) 5797 2999.

Yea Family Caravan Park: 1 Court St; (03) 5797 2972. **Molesworth Recreation Reserve:** Reserve Rd, Molesworth; (03) 5797 6278. **Strath Valley View B and B:** 1204 King Parrot Creek Rd, Strath Creek; (03) 5784 9209.

Murrindindi Reserve: see the impressive Murrindindi Cascades and a variety of wildlife including wombats, platypus and lyrebirds; 11 km SE. **Ibis Rookery:** Kerrisdale; 17 km W. **Flowerdale Winery:** Whittlesea–Yea Rd; 23 km SW. **Grotto:** a beautiful old church set in the hillside; Caveat; 27 km N. **Berry King Farm:** pick your own fruit; Two Hills Rd, Glenburn; 28 km S. **Wilhelmina Falls:** spectacular falls and a great spot for walks and picnics; access via Melba Hwy; 32 km S. **Kinglake National Park:** 32 km S; *see Yarra Glen*. **Mineral springs:** Dropmore, off back road to Euroa; 47 km N. **Scenic drives:** many in the region. Best time is Aug–Sept when wattles are in bloom; maps from visitor centre.

TOWNS NEARBY: Alexandra 25 km, Seymour 33 km, Eildon 43 km, Kilmore 43 km, Marysville 44 km

VICTORIA

Seeing a performance at the **ADELAIDE FESTIVAL OF ARTS** / Walking along **NORTH TERRACE** in Adelaide / Admiring the glittering, panoramic night view from **WINDY POINT** in Belair / Enjoying excellent wine and gourmet food in the **BAROSSA VALLEY** / Birdwatching in **COORONG NATIONAL PARK** / Taking a scenic flight over **WILPENA POUND** in the Flinders Ranges / Exploring **NARACOORTE CAVES** by guided tour / Visiting historic towns, wineries and galleries in the **ADELAIDE HILLS** / Sleeping underground and searching for opals in **COOBER PEDY** / Discovering native fauna on **KANGAROO ISLAND** / Driving across the **NULLARBOR**

SOUTH AUSTRALIA

SOUTH AUSTRALIA is a million square kilometres of ancient Dreamtime landscapes and wild coastal beauty. It is also a land of incredible contrasts: the endless desert of the north and the fertile vales of the south-east are a world apart.

In 1836 Colonel William Light chose the site for the capital of South Australia on Kaurna land beside the River Torrens. The settlement's early days were far from ideal as the first colonists huddled in squalid mud huts, perhaps regretting they had no convict labour to call on. But today the world's first planned city is a gracious capital of wide streets and generous public parks.

In the 1840s German Lutherans fleeing persecution in Europe settled in the Adelaide Hills and the Barossa Valley, bringing traditions of wine-growing and social liberty that have flourished here ever since. In the early 1970s the election of flamboyant rebel Don Dunstan as premier launched a decade of social reform unmatched in any other state. South Australians are proud of their history of social innovation, and their state has a well-earned reputation for tolerance and cultural diversity.

[BUNDA CLIFFS, HEAD OF BIGHT]

For travellers, South Australia is the perfect place to get off the beaten track. The state has the most centralised population in the country and the outback begins just an hour or two up the road from Adelaide.

The Flinders Ranges are one of the oldest mountain ranges on earth. At their centre is the natural amphitheatre Wilpena Pound (Ikara), a lost world of cypress pines and hidden creeks, its gorges created by Akurra the serpent as he travelled north with a grumbling belly full of salt water.

The state's Southern Ocean coastline includes the sheer cliffs of the Great Australian Bight and the sheltered wetlands of the Coorong. This refuge for native and migratory birds begs you to sit quietly with a pair of binoculars.

[STURT'S DESERT PEA, SOUTH AUSTRALIA'S FLORAL EMBLEM]

fact file

Population 1 657 000
Total land area 984 377 square kilometres
People per square kilometre 1.6
Sheep per square kilometre 13.25
Length of coastline 3816 kilometres
Number of islands 346
Longest river Murray River (650 kilometres)
Largest lake Lake Eyre (9500 square kilometres)
Highest mountain Mount Woodroffe (1440 metres), Musgrave Ranges, Pitjantjatjara Land
Lowest place Lake Eyre, 15 metres below sea level (Australia's lowest point)
Hottest place 50.7°C – Australia's hottest recorded temperature – was reached in Oodnadatta in 1960
Driest place Lake Eyre (a mere 125 millimetres of rain per year)
Longest place name Nooldoonooldoona, a waterhole in the Gammon Ranges
Best surf Cactus Beach, near Ceduna
Best discoveries and inventions Penicillin by Howard Florey (he describes the discovery as 'a terrible amount of luck'); the wine cask by Tom Angove
Most dangerous coast There are 80 shipwrecks around Kangaroo Island
Best political stunt Premier Don Dunstan wore pink hot pants into parliament to campaign for gay law reform in the 1970s
Favourite takeaway food Adelaide's pie floater (a meat pie floating in a bowl of pea soup – with or without tomato sauce)
Local beer Coopers
Interesting fact Adelaide boasts a higher ratio of restaurants to residents than any other state

gift ideas

Leather boots, R. M. Williams Outback Heritage Museum, Adelaide This iconic bushman began making saddlery and leather boots while camping in South Australia's Gammon Ranges. 5 Percy St, Prospect. See Adelaide p. 210

Beerenberg strawberry jam, Hahndorf Now world famous, but the original signature product can still be bought from the pioneer farm. Mt Barker Rd, Hahndorf. See Hahndorf p. 238

Ligurian honey, Kangaroo Island The purest organic honey of its type in the world. See Kingscote p. 243

Glass art, JamFactory, Adelaide Pick up a finely crafted, unique piece of glass or ceramic art from an emerging or established artist. See JamFactory p. 216

Wine, Barossa and Clare valleys Take home some cases of wine from two of Australia's eminent wine regions, particularly famous for shiraz and riesling. See Lyndoch p. 241 and Clare p. 231

Jewellery, Zu design, Adelaide Arcade, Adelaide Distinctive contemporary objects of adornment from Adelaide artists. See Adelaide p. 210

Shiraz-filled chocolates, David Medlow, McLaren Vale Delightfully rich shiraz liqueur encased in dark chocolate. McLarens on the Lake, Kangarilla Rd, McLaren Vale. See McLaren Vale p. 243

Premium oysters, Coffin Bay Pure from the nutrient-rich water currents of the Southern Ocean. See Coffin Bay p. 232

King George whiting, South Australian waters Sweet, delicate and always fresh from stores around the state.

Opals, Coober Pedy Although available around the country, purchase these beautiful stones directly from this mining town. See Coober Pedy p. 233

ADELAIDE is...

Coffee at Lucia's in ADELAIDE CENTRAL MARKET / A Popeye cruise along the

RIVER TORRENS / A tram trip to GLENELG / Surveying the city from LIGHT'S

VISION / A visit to the Australian Aboriginal Cultures Gallery at the SOUTH

AUSTRALIAN MUSEUM / Shopping at Adelaide's historic RUNDLE MALL /

HENLEY SQUARE on a Sunday afternoon, for lunch and a walk by the sea / A night

out in EAST END / A stroll around the JAMFACTORY craft and design gallery

VISITOR INFORMATION
South Australian Visitor and Travel Centre
→ 18–20 Grenfell St, Adelaide
1300 764 227
www.southaustralia.com

One of the best-planned cities in the world, Adelaide remains testament to the work of its first surveyor, Colonel William Light, whose statue stands on Montefiore Hill, overlooking Adelaide Oval.

Settled in 1836, Adelaide was Australia's first free settlement. Like other well-planned cities around the world, Adelaide has few skyscrapers and its architecture blends both heritage and contemporary styles, retaining a 'human scale'. Since the 1970s Adelaide has been famous for food and wine. The state is the powerhouse of the booming Australian wine industry, producing almost 60 per cent of the total output, while Adelaide Central Market is possibly the finest fresh-produce market in Australia. The city is renowned for its restaurants – from the fish cafes of Gouger Street to the many gourmet eateries dotted around the CBD and tucked away in quiet corners. Adelaide also knows how to throw a party, and with a population of 1 203 000 the city is compact enough to generate a feeling of all-over revelry. First on the calendar is the Adelaide Festival of Arts, one of the world's great arts festivals. During February and March every second year, the festival and the now annual Adelaide Fringe take over the city.

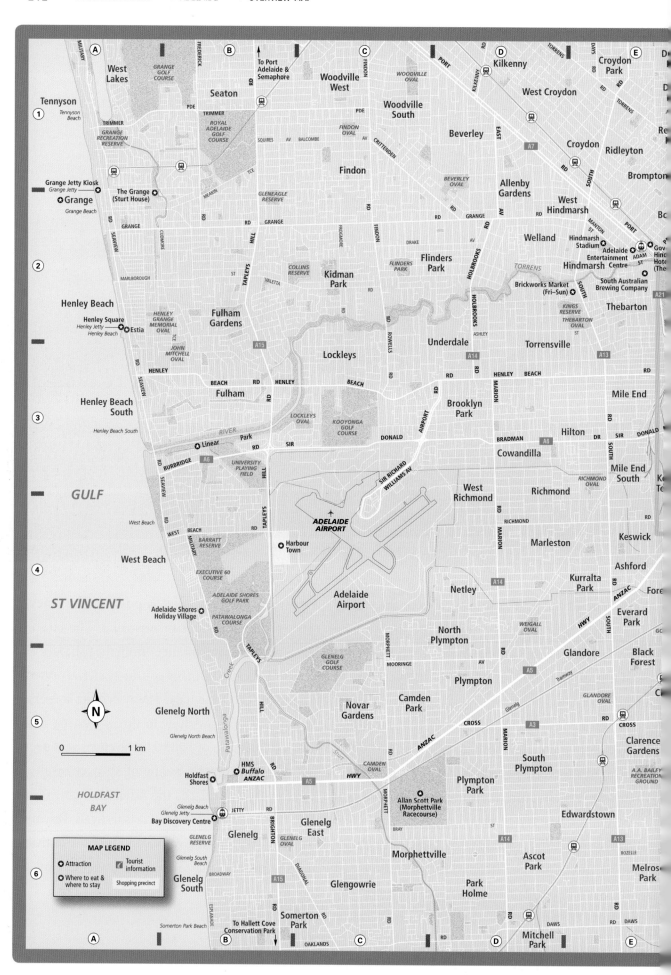

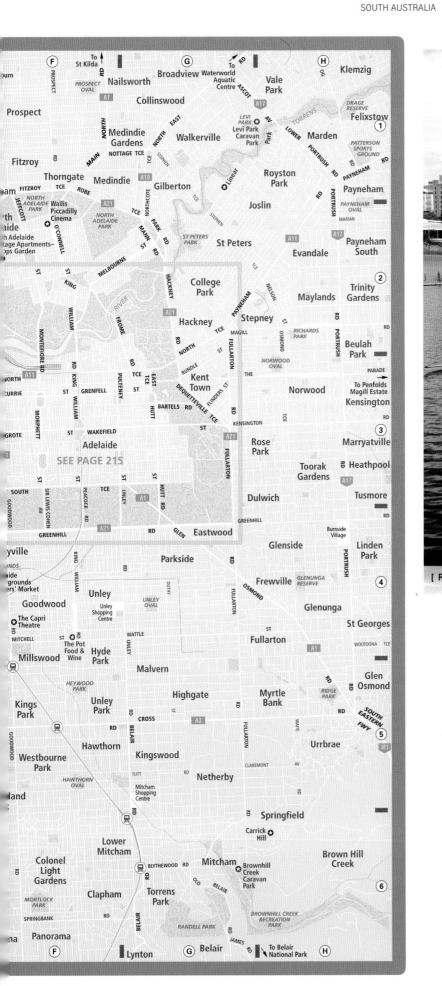

[ROWING ON THE RIVER TORRENS]

SOUTH AUSTRALIA

CBD NORTH

This part of Adelaide is based around two features: North Terrace, a tree-lined boulevard with a university at either end, the state library, the museum and the art gallery; and Rundle Mall shopping district.

Rundle Mall 215 C2

This mall, Australia's first, is the city's shopping heart, with major department stores, clothing shops, souvenir and craft stores, and eateries. Sculptures dot the mall, including two silver balls known as the 'Malls Balls'. Haigh's Chocolates on historic Beehive Corner is a must *(visit the Haigh's factory in Parkside, see p. 217)*. Rundle Mall runs parallel to Grenfell Street, and they are joined by two treasures of old Adelaide – Adelaide Arcade and Regent Arcade. The latter, opened in 1885, was the first retail establishment in the country to have electric lights.

East End 215 C2

The east end of the mall, beyond the shops, is the hub of Adelaide's nightlife. On Friday and Saturday nights the East End throbs with bars and clubs, and there are over 50 restaurants. Among the shops is **Mary Martin Bookshop**, Adelaide's oldest bookseller. On Sundays visit the craft and fashion street market. The **Rundle Lantern**, corner Rundle and Pulteney streets, delivers digital art from dusk until midnight, with extended hours for special events.

Hindley Street 215 A2, B2

Sometimes known as the West End, this is another lively part of town. The ornate Wests Coffee Palace building, constructed in 1903 as the Austral Stores, is now the home of **Arts SA**.

Parliament House and Government House 215 B2

These impressive buildings adorn the northern intersection of North Terrace and King William Road. Government House, the oldest in Australia, was where the first council of government met. As the council expanded it came to include what is now **Old Parliament House**. These buildings, and several statues and monuments, such as the **War Memorial** on Kintore Avenue, make for an interesting walk. Government House normally has two open days a year; phone (08) 8203 9800 for details. Guided tours of Parliament House run on non-sitting days (Monday and Friday) at 10am and 2pm; see the website for sitting days (www.parliament.sa.gov.au).

State Library of South Australia 215 C2

The State Library complex blends charming 19th-century buildings with modern technology. It includes the Bradman Digital Library and Trail, the ultimate research source for the career of cricketer Sir Donald Bradman, who lived in Adelaide for much of his life. *North Tce; open daily; admission free.*

Migration Museum 215 C2

This museum details immigrant life in Australia. Once Adelaide's Destitute Asylum, its 'Behind the Wall' exhibition tells the stories of former inhabitants from the 1850s to 1918. *82 Kintore Ave; open 10am–5pm Mon–Fri, 1–5pm Sat–Sun and public holidays; admission free.*

South Australian Museum 215 C2

Over 3000 objects are exhibited at **Australian Aboriginal Cultures**, the world's most comprehensive Aboriginal cultural exhibition, while the **Origin Energy Fossil Gallery** has a fascinating collection of opalised fossils. Australia's richest natural-history art exhibition, the Waterhouse Natural History Art Prize, is held each year in the **ETSA Utilities Gallery** from July to September. *North Tce; open daily.*

Art Gallery of South Australia 215 C2

A permanent collection of Australian, Asian and European works are shown here. The Australian collection includes works from Margaret Preston and Stella Bowen. The European collection features contemporary British art along with major works including those of French sculptor Auguste Rodin. The Asian collection includes delicate Japanese artworks and South-East Asian ceramics. There is also a program of changing exhibitions. *North Tce; open daily; general admission free.*

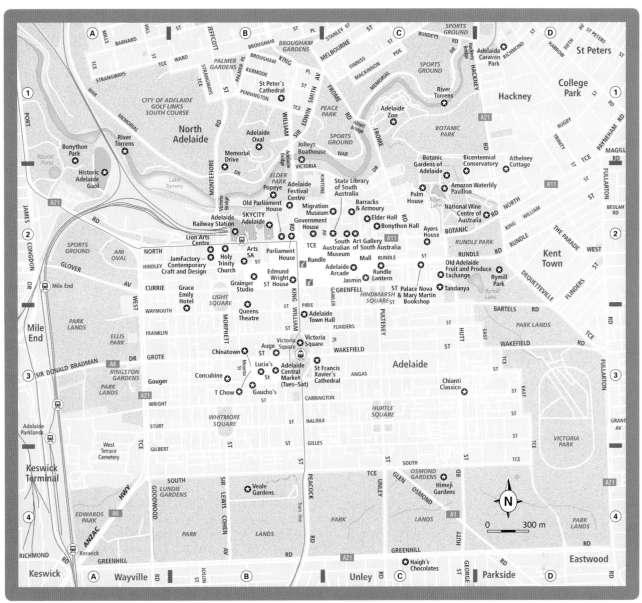

[ART GALLERY OF SOUTH AUSTRALIA]

SOUTH AUSTRALIA

[SCULPTURES IN FRONT OF THE SOUTH AUSTRALIAN MUSEUM]

Ayers House 215 C2

North Terrace was the home of wealthy and prestigious figures such as Premier Henry Ayers. After years in the hands of the Royal Adelaide Hospital, the original decorations of the building have now been painstakingly restored, and one wing has been transformed into a luxurious restaurant. *288 North Tce; open 10am–4pm Tues–Fri, 1–4pm Sat–Sun.*

Botanic Gardens of Adelaide 215 C2

These gardens were laid out in the mid-1800s. The **Palm House**, imported in 1875, is a fine example of German engineering, while the impressive **Bicentennial Conservatory** is the largest single-span conservatory in the Southern Hemisphere. Inside, walkways run through a lush rainforest environment, past endangered plant species. **Amazon Waterlily Pavilion** is the most recent addition, opened in 2007. A superb restaurant overlooks the Main Lake. *North Tce; open daily, guided walks 10.30am.*

National Wine Centre of Australia 215 D2

Take a Wine Discovery Journey through the stages of wine-production, meet winemakers and try winemaking – all through virtual technology. The centre also has its own vineyard and shop. *Cnr Botanic and Hackney rds; open daily; admission free.*

Adelaide Zoo 215 C1

The zoo's 19th-century buildings and landscaped gardens make it a very attractive place. The **Elephant House**, now classified by the National Trust, is a highlight with a design based on an Indian temple. The zoo's giant pandas, Wang Wang and Funi, are also very popular. *Frome Rd; open daily.*

The River Torrens 215 A1

A scenic setting for leisure activities, including **Popeye** cruises and motor launches. From the Elder Park Wharf, the cruises operate hourly on weekdays, and every 20 minutes on weekends. Paddleboats can be hired on weekends from **Jolleys Boathouse** under the Adelaide Bridge on King William Road. Take a romantic Venetian gondola ride from Red Ochre restaurant, or just enjoy the food and views at the boathouse restaurant.

Adelaide Festival Centre 215 B2

Overlooking Elder Park and the River Torrens, the Festival Centre consists of four theatres and is an architectural landmark. Take in a show or view the centre's artworks as well as the changing displays of the **Performing Arts Collection of South Australia**. Visit the website (www.adelaidefestivalcentre.com.au) to see what's on.

JamFactory – Contemporary Craft and Design 215 B2

The JamFactory produces some of the most innovative craft on the Australian market. Changing exhibits of international and JamFactory works show in the gallery, and one-off designs are sold in the store. Nearby is another Adelaide arts institution, the **Australia Experimental Art Foundation** at the Lion Arts Centre, with the best in new media works. *JamFactory:19 Morphett St; open daily; admission free. There is also a JamFactory outlet in Rundle Plaza, open Mon–Fri.*

Historic Adelaide Gaol 215 A2

Tour the cells and yards of this complex (a gaol from 1841 to 1988) take a night tour (bookings required) or a Ghost Tour. *Gaol Rd; tour bookings (08) 8231 4062; open 11am–4pm Mon–Fri and Sun.*

CBD SOUTH

This area is home to some stellar attractions – the Adelaide Central Market is an absolute must-see, and there is superb dining on Gouger Street.

Adelaide Central Market 215 B3

Located just off Victoria Square, the market showcases the state's fresh produce and has evolved into a significant shopping and social centre. Grab lunch at Zuma's, Malacca Corner or Lucia's, or just wander the aisles. *Open Tues–Sat.*

Gouger Street 215 A3, B3

Originally a spin-off from Central Market, Gouger Street has many restaurants, cafes, bars and clubs. It winds down earlier than East End, but has its own character and appeal, including several Chinese restaurants.

Adelaide's **Chinatown** is centred on Moonta Street between Gouger and Grote streets. Look for T Chow, an institution.

INNER SOUTH

Haigh's Chocolates 215 C4

Australia's oldest chocolate-maker is just south of the CBD. See displays of original factory machinery and a delightful old-world shop with a tempting array of chocolates, or take a tour (bookings essential). *154 Greenhill Rd, Parkside; tour bookings (08) 8372 7077; free tours 11am, 1pm and 2pm Mon–Sat.*

INNER WEST

South Australian Brewing Company 212 E2

Learn all about beer-making and tour the premises of these makers of brands including Tooheys, XXXX, Hahn, Lion Red, Steinlager and Speight's. (bookings essential; children over 12 only). *107 Port Rd, Thebarton; tour bookings (08) 8354 8888; tours 10.30am Mon–Thurs.*

SOUTHERN BAYSIDE

Glenelg 212 B6

On the sweep of Holdfast Bay is South Australia's best-known beach and most developed piece of coastal real estate. It spills over with shops, restaurants, high-rise apartments and people strolling, sunbaking, cycling and rollerblading. Since the late 1800s Adelaidians have flocked here, and the Glenelg tram still runs there from Victoria Square in the city. Other relics remain, including the 1875 town hall, housing the **Bay Discovery Centre**, exhibiting on the area's history.

A replica of the HMS *Buffalo* – which carried the first South Australian settlers – stands along the foreshore, with the addition of an onboard seafood restaurant and a museum. Nearby is **Holdfast Shores**, with restaurants, boutique shopping and a massive marina.

At The Beachouse, on the Glenelg foreshore, there's waterslides, mini-golf and fun for all ages. *(08) 8295 1511.*

Enjoy walking trails along the coast (for information, visit the Bay Discovery Centre), and swim, fish or sail in the calm waters. The iconic South Australian pier is the perfect spot for fish and chips at sunset, or swim with dolphins from the *Temptation* catamaran. *0412 811 838; www.dolphinboat.com.au*

Hallett Cove Conservation Park 554 A10

An incredible record of glaciation is found here. Take a guided geological tour to see some spectacular ochre- and sand-coloured rock formations. For the energetic, walk the Marino Rocks to Hallett Cove boardwalk and try the Marino Rocks Cafe.

WESTERN BAYSIDE

Henley Beach to Semaphore 112 A2, B1

At Henley Beach a long jetty extends into Gulf St Vincent. Set behind it is **Henley Square**, with restaurants, bars and cafes. Straight up Seaview Road is the suburb of **Grange**. Enjoy the beach or grab a bite at the Grange Jetty Kiosk. Further along is **Semaphore**, a suburb with fine heritage buildings, cafes and sea views. The Art Deco **Semaphore Palais** offers waterfront dining, while the Semaphore Waterslide Complex is great for kids. A walk and cycle track heads north to Largs Bay and North Haven Marina, or take a 40-minute tourist train to Fort Glanville, built in 1878 in response to fears of a Russian invasion. *Train operates 11am–4pm Sat–Sun (Oct–April), school and public holidays.*

NORTH-WEST

Port Adelaide 554 A8

'The Port', established in 1840, retains its historical charm, with weekend markets, pubs, cafes, galleries and antique shops. It is, however, still a working port, with a grain terminal, a tug-base, and fishing and pleasure boats on the upper reaches of the Port River, and a container terminal and wharves in the outer harbour. Drive along the Dolphin Trail to see the famed dolphins, or take a cruise. Details at the Port Adelaide Visitor Information Centre. *66 Commercial Rd; (08) 8405 6560 or 1800 629 888; open daily.*

South Australian Maritime Museum 554 B8

Behind the red-and-white lighthouse in the middle of Port Adelaide, on Queens Wharf, visitors can climb aboard a replica ketch, or learn about the state's rock-lobster industry at this first-class centre. *126 Lipson St, Port Adelaide; open daily.*

Ships' Graveyard 554 B8

Around 25 wrecks were abandoned on the south side of Garden Island, including barges, sailing ships and steamers. View this watery graveyard from the Garden Island Bridge, or on a kayak tour with Adventure Kayaking SA. *(08) 8295 8812.*

NORTH-EAST

Waterworld Aquatic Centre 213 G1

Refresh and entertain the kids here, with three waterslides and a fun Splash Ground. Open from 6am weekdays, 7am Sat, 9am Sun. *Golden Grove Road, Ridgehaven, (08) 8397 7439.*

[CARRICK HILL]

NORTH

St Kilda 554 B7

This outer suburb is a short distance (as the crow flies) from Port Adelaide and the Lefevre Peninsula. The drive passes vast salt-crystallisation pans to arrive at an idyllic little marina. Visit the **Mangrove Trail and Interpretive Centre** for insight into this unique ecosystem, and at the **Tramway Museum** (open afternoons on Sundays and public holidays) see the 20 historic trams. Then take a tram to the showcase attraction, a free adventure playground featuring a wooden ship, giant slides and a monorail.

North Adelaide 213 F2

This is one of the city's most exclusive residential addresses, rich in history with a mix of mansions and workers' cottages. From Light's Vision, walk through Lower North Adelaide, and take Palmer Place into Brougham Place to see old mansions with city views.

Down the hill on Stanley Street are stone cottages from South Australia's first subdivision. Nearby Melbourne Street is Adelaide's classiest street, with art galleries, boutiques, restaurants and the restored Lion Hotel.

Head to O'Connell Street for old pubs bedecked with Victorian iron lace, as well as restaurants and cafes. Tynte Street, which runs off O'Connell Street, has fine 19th-century buildings.

SOUTH

Carrick Hill 213 H6

Once the home of wealthy couple Edward and Ursula Hayward, this 1930s art-filled house was built in the style of a 17th-century English manor. The gardens contain a citrus orchard, a pleached pear arbour and avenues of poplars. Take the **Children's Storybook Trail** through the grounds, an enchanting walk encompassing scenes from 10 popular children's classics. *46 Carrick Hill Dr, Springfield; open Wed–Sun and public holidays.*

EAST

Penfolds Magill Estate 554 C9

This winery was Penfolds' first venture. Established in 1844, the vintage cellar is still used for making shiraz, while the Still House, once used for making brandy, has cellar-door tastings and sales. The restaurant has views over the Adelaide Plains, fine food and an incredible wine list with Grange by the glass! *78 Penfold Rd, Magill; (08) 8301 5551; tours 11am and 3pm daily, lunch Fri, dinner Tues–Sat.*

CITY ESSENTIALS
ADELAIDE

Climate

Adelaide's weather is described as temperate Mediterranean, with temperatures in summer rising to around 40°C on a number of days, and falling to a minimum near zero a couple of times in winter. The in-between seasons are near-perfect, with maximum temperatures in the mid-20s for much of March, April, September and October.

	MAX °C	MIN °C	RAIN MM	RAIN DAYS
JANUARY	28	16	20	2
FEBRUARY	28	16	20	2
MARCH	26	15	24	3
APRIL	22	12	44	6
MAY	18	10	68	10
JUNE	15	8	71	11
JULY	14	7	66	12
AUGUST	16	8	61	11
SEPTEMBER	18	9	51	9
OCTOBER	21	11	44	7
NOVEMBER	24	13	30	5
DECEMBER	26	15	26	4

Getting around

Adelaide has a wide range of public transport. First there is the city's tram service, which runs from Glenelg all the way to the city, through Victoria Square and City West, to the Adelaide Entertainment Centre on Port Road, Hindmarsh. Then there is the Adelaide O-Bahn – the longest and fastest guided bus service in the world. It travels along Currie and Grenfell streets in the city, then heads out to Westfield Tea Tree Plaza in Modbury.

The City Loop Bus and the Terrace to Terrace Tram are two free services that operate around the city centre. The City Loop bus runs every 15 minutes and takes in North Terrace and Light, Hindmarsh and Victoria squares; the Terrace to Terrace Tram runs every ten minutes and includes Victoria Square, King William Street and the railway station. Board either the Glenelg or South Terrace tram anywhere between South Terrace and North Terrace during shopping hours. Look out for the free Tindo bus, which is the first solar-powered electric bus in the world.

The Adelaide Metroticket JetBus is a daily service linking the airport to the city, Glenelg, West Beach and the north-eastern suburbs.

Four train routes operate from the CBD to Adelaide's suburbs: to Gawler in the north, Outer Harbour in the north-west, Noarlunga in the south and Belair in the Adelaide Hills. There are also plenty of bus services operating around the suburbs. All public transport in Adelaide is covered by one ticketing system, and tickets can be purchased at train stations and on buses and trams, as well as from newsagents and convenience stores displaying the Metroticket signage, and the Adelaide Metro InfoCentre, corner King William and Currie streets in the City centre.

Public transport Passenger Transport InfoLine (08) 8210 1000 or 1800 182 160.

Airport shuttle bus Skylink Airport Shuttle (08) 8413 6196.

Motoring organisation RAA (08) 8202 4600, roadside assistance 13 1111.

Car rental Avis 13 6333; Budget 13 2727; Europcar 13 1390; Hertz 13 3039; Thrifty 1300 367 227.

Taxis Independent Taxis 13 2211; Suburban Taxis 13 1008; Yellow Cabs 13 2227.

Tourist bus Adelaide Explorer (replica tram) (08) 8293 2966.

Bicycle hire Contact Bicycle SA for operators (08) 8168 9999.

Top events

Schützenfest Traditional German folk festival with music, food, and frivolity in Bonython Park. January.

Santos Tour Down Under Professional cyclists – and social riders – from all over the world descend on Adelaide for this race into the hills. January.

Adelaide Festival of Arts The city's defining event, and one of the world's highest-regarded arts festivals. February–March (even-numbered years).

Adelaide Fringe Alongside the Festival of Arts, the edgy performances of this world-renowned annual festival are great entertainment. February–March.

WOMADelaide A huge festival of world music and dance in Botanic Park. March.

Clipsal 500 Adelaide V8 supercars race on city streets in what is regularly awarded as Australia's best motorsport event. March.

Glendi Festival Greek culture, food, song and dance in Ellis Park, West Terrace. March.

Tasting Australia International event celebrating food, wine and beer as well as chefs and writers. April (even-numbered years).

Feast Festival One of the country's top gay and lesbian events, with theatre, film, dance and more. November.

Credit Union Christmas Pageant An Adelaide institution since 1933 welcomes Father Christmas to the city streets. November.

Carnevale Adelaide Italian culture, food, song and dance at the Adelaide Showgrounds. February.

Grand old buildings

Adelaide Railway Station Built in 1856, the main feature is the Great Hall, with marble floors, Corinthian columns and a domed ceiling. SKYCITY Adelaide casino now occupies much of the station's upper floors. North Tce.

Adelaide Town Hall Opened in 1866, this building is much admired for its magnificent tower and classic portico, and its equally grand interior. Free tours run on Monday at 10am; bookings essential (08) 8203 7590. Regular classical music concerts and recitals. 128 King William St.

Barracks and Armoury Built in 1855, these magnificent examples of colonial architecture were the local Australian Army headquarters from 1857 to 1870. Behind South Australian Museum.

Bonython Hall Part of the University of Adelaide, the hall has an unusual sloping floor. This was insisted upon by benefactor Langdon Bonython, a strict Methodist, to prevent dancing. North Tce.

Churches As well as St Francis Xavier's Cathedral near Victoria Square, there's St Peter's Cathedral in North Adelaide and the Holy Trinity Church on North Terrace.

Edmund Wright House Wright was the architect of some of Adelaide's grandest buildings, including Parliament House, the GPO and the Adelaide and Glenelg town halls. This elaborate Italianate creation was completed in 1878 and used as a banking chamber. 59 King William St.

Elder Hall This church-like building in the grounds of the University of Adelaide is in fact a concert venue with a spectacular pipe organ. Next to Bonython Hall.

Old Adelaide Fruit and Produce Exchange The charming facade of this old wholesale market still stands on East Terrace. The rear has been converted into apartments.

Queens Theatre For a theatre, this is a surprisingly humble affair – perhaps because it is the oldest theatre on the mainland, built in 1840. Cnr Gilles Arcade and Playhouse La.

The Grange (Sturt House) The home of Charles Sturt, the man who sailed into South Australia on a whaleboat down the Murray, which led to the settlement of the state. Many original furnishings remain. Jetty St, Grange; open Fri–Sun and public holidays.

See also Carrick Hill, p. 218.

 Shopping

Harbour Town This complex offers seconds and discount stores.

Jetty Road, Glenelg A great mix of stores, and food and drink outlets.

King William Road, Hyde Park Hip fashion outlets sprinkled among cafes, and furniture and homewares stores.

Magill Road, Stepney For antiques and second-hand treasures.

Melbourne Street, North Adelaide Adelaide's most exclusive shopping strip, with designer fashion boutiques.

Rundle Mall, City The CBD's main shopping area, with major department stores as well as individual offerings of clothing, chocolates and much more.

The Parade, Norwood Very cosmopolitan, with an array of stores and plenty of places to stop for a coffee, a meal or a drink.

See also Adelaide Central Market, p. 217, Gouger Street, p. 217.

 Markets

Adelaide Showgrounds Farmers' Market, Goodwood Great range of fresh produce and gourmet goods. 9am–1pm Sun. 213 F4

Brickworks Market, Torrensville Located in an old kiln, the market's 100 stalls offer a wide range of wares, including clothing and crafts, as well as produce. Fri–Sun, public hols. 212 E2

Fisherman's Wharf Market, Port Adelaide Fresh seafood and other produce are the main

drawcards, but other food stalls and bric-a-brac make up the mix. Sun and Mon public hols. 554 B8

Junction Markets, Kilburn Popular market offering fresh produce and specialty stores. Fri–Sun. 553 C6

Torrens Island Open Air Market, Port Adelaide Buy fish direct from the boat. Other food stalls also showcase quality local produce. Sun mornings. 554 A8

See also Adelaide Central Market, p. 217.

 Walks and tours

Adelaide Oval Tours Get an up-close view of this Adelaide icon as well as access to the Adelaide Oval Museum. Weekdays at 10am, departing from the southern gate (no bookings required). **Note:** The oval is about to undergo a major redevelopment and tour times may change, depending on construction. (08) 8300 3800.

City of Adelaide Historical Walking Trails Pick up a brochure from the City of Adelaide office or the SATC tourist centre on Grenfell Street and head out on themed walks covering everything from the grand buildings of North Adelaide to the places of interest around Rundle Mall and Adelaide's historic cinemas and theatres.

Market Adventures Follow the experts through Adelaide's famous Central Market. There are several foodie-type options, including the popular 'Grazing on Gouger' tour, giving people the chance to eat five courses at five of Gouger Street's best restaurants. Bookings (08) 8386 0888.

Port Walks Take a walk through historic Port Adelaide. Contact the Port Adelaide Visitor Centre for details. 66 Commercial Rd; (08) 8405 6560.

Wineries at your doorstep Visit McLaren Vale, one of Australia's greatest wine regions, just 40 minutes from Adelaide. Enjoy the local tasty foods too. Check out www.mclarenvale.info

Yurrebilla Trail Take in the magnificent bushland on Adelaide's doorstep on this 52-kilometre trail that links Black Hill and Morialta conservation parks in the north with Belair National Park in the south. The scenery includes unsurpassed views of the city.

The Yurrebilla Trail connects directly with the Heysen Trail for 12 kilometres, joining between Mount Lofty and Third Falls in the Morialta Conservation Park.

Yurrebilla Trail bushwalking maps are available from most national park offices and visitor centres.

 Parks and gardens

Bonython Park A park with native style. The river attracts birdlife, and there is also a children's playground and a popular picnic area. Thebarton. 215 A1

Himeji Gardens Created in conjunction with Himeji, Adelaide's sister city, this garden blends classic Japanese styles. City. 215 C4

Linear Park This park follows the curves of the Torrens all the way from West Beach to Paradise, and is great for bike riding. The sections near the city offer fantastic views, while further out the track runs through a thick corridor of bushland. 212 B3, 213 G1

Rymill Park The centrepiece is Rymill Lake, with rowboats for hire, but there is also a large rose garden. City. 215 D2

Veale Gardens For some years the green belt around Adelaide was more paddock than parkland, but a town clerk named William Veale started beautifying the gardens in the mid-1900s. Veale Gardens were his pièce de résistance. City. 215 B4

 Entertainment

Cinema Those who want an atmospheric cinema-going experience should head for the Wallis Piccadilly Cinema in North Adelaide, which screens mainstream and arthouse films. A similar line-up is available at the Palace Nova cinemas in Rundle Street's East End. Adelaide's main alternative cinema is the Mercury at the Lion Arts Centre – it shows cult classics, foreign-language and arthouse movies, and holds short-film festivals. The Capri Theatre, in Goodwood, is notable for the live organ recitals that introduce film screenings on Tuesday, Saturday and Sunday nights. Check the *Adelaide Advertiser* for daily listings.

Live music The best live-music venue in Adelaide, without question, is the Governor Hindmarsh Hotel on Port Road, opposite the Adelaide Entertainment Centre. Offering everything from Irish fiddlers in the front bar to major international acts in the large, barn-like concert room at the back, The Gov (as it's known to the locals) has been the top venue in town for at least a decade. Plenty of other pubs also offer live music, like the Grace Emily on Waymouth Street, an intimate venue that also boasts an excellent beer garden, and the Worldsend Hotel, on Hindley Street. The best way to find out what's on is to pick up a copy of *Rip It Up*, the local contemporary-music paper.

Classical music and performing arts The Adelaide Festival Centre is the hub of mainstream performing arts activity in Adelaide, hosting the three major and highly regarded state companies: State Theatre SA, State Opera of South Australia and Adelaide Symphony Orchestra (ASO). The ASO also holds small recitals at its Grainger Studio in Hindley Street. Adelaide nurtures a diverse range of theatre companies – look out for performances by the Australian Dance Theatre (contemporary dance), Vitalstatistix (women's theatre) and Windmill Performing Arts (children's theatre). The Lion Arts Centre is the venue for two innovative companies: Nexus (cabaret) and Doppio Teatro (multicultural). Indigenous dance is also on display in daily performances at Tandanya. The *Adelaide Advertiser* publishes a listing of entertainment events each Thursday.

Sport

Adelaide has been passionate about **cricket** from its earliest beginnings. Until his death in 2001, Adelaide was the proud home of Australia's greatest cricketer, Sir Donald Bradman. The city is also home to the Adelaide Oval, regarded as one of the most beautiful sporting arenas in the world. Adelaide's cricket test is a great event. The oval is due for major renovation during 2013–14 so the famed Bradman Collection may not be open for visitors.

With two local **AFL** (Australian Football League) teams, Adelaide and Port Adelaide, football is the city's other sporting passion. Showdown is the twice-yearly match between the two teams, and the whole city stops to watch what is considered Adelaide's own grand final. AAMI Stadium at West Lakes is the city's home of AFL.

Also on the calendar is the AAPT Championships, the international **tennis** tournament held at Memorial Drive near the Adelaide Oval in early January. The Santos Tour Down Under pro-tour **cycling** race, in Jaunary, finishes off a great summer of sport in Adelaide.

In March there is a **motor race** that literally takes over the city. Sections of the Clipsal 500 Adelaide track, centring on Victoria Park Racecourse, are run on Wakefield Road and East Terrace in the southeast of the city. This V8 event was created after Adelaide lost the Australian Formula One Grand Prix to Melbourne and, interestingly, is more popular than Formula One ever was.

Adelaide's United **soccer** team matches are held at Hindmarsh Stadium, and the NBL 36ers play **basketball** on their home court at Beverley.

Each Year, on a public holiday Monday early in March, Adelaide comes alive with **horseracing** fever for the SKYCITY Adelaide Cup at Allan Scott Park, Morphettville.

Staged annually on the last Sunday in September is the Bay to Birdwood **vintage car rally**. More than 1500 vehicles drive the 70-kilometre route from Adelaide Shores, West Beach to the National Motor Museum Birdwood, watched by over 100 000 spectators.

Where to eat

Auge   Classy, contemporary Italian cuisine. Expect goat, venison, rabbit and pigeon – it's all about quality produce and authentic flavours. 22 Grote St; (08) 8410 9332; open Tues–Fri for lunch and Tues–Sat for dinner. 215 B3

The Art Gallery Restaurant   A happy blend of modern dishes and 'old masters'; inviting and stylish. North Tce; (08) 8232 4366, open daily for lunch. 215 C2

Chianti Classico   A welcoming family-run trattoria serving Italian regional fare with rustic charm. 160 Hutt St; (08) 8232 7955; open daily for breakfast, lunch and dinner. 215 C3

Concubine   Another award-winning Gouger St restaurant. For a special occasion, ask for the Secret Room; 132 Gouger St; (08) 8212 8288. Open Sun, Tues–Fri for lunch and dinner; Sat for dinner. 215 B3

Estia   A well-known Greek restaurant that is a real drawcard in the summer months. Great beach views. 255 Seaview Rd; (08) 8353 2875; open Tues–Sun for lunch and dinner. 212 A2

Gaucho's   One for the carnivores. More than a dozen steak options on the grill, plus seafood and game. 91 Gouger St; (08) 8231 2299, open daily for lunch and dinner. 215 B3

Jasmin   Perennial favourite for authentic Indian dishes brought to life by quality ingredients and spices. 31 Hindmarsh Sq; (08) 8223 7837; open Thurs–Fri for lunch and Tues–Sat for dinner. 215 C2

Jolleys Boathouse   Smart, bistro-style dining featuring contemporary flavours in a relaxing riverside setting. Jolleys La; (08) 8223 2891; open Sun–Fri for lunch, Mon–Sat for dinner. 215 B1

The Pot Food & Wine   A serious foodie destination offering a degustation menu to a more casual experience and great shared tasting plates. 160 King William Rd, Hyde Park; (08) 8373 2044. Open Tues–Sun for lunch and Tues–Sat for dinner. 213 F4

T Chow   A diverse, crowd-pleasing menu of southern Chinese fare, including famed duck dishes. 68 Moonta St; (08) 8410 1413; open daily for lunch and dinner. 215 B3

Where to stay

Adelaide Caravan Park   46 Richmond St, Hackney; (08) 8363 1566.

Adelaide Shores Caravan Park   Military Rd, West Beach; (08) 8355 7300.

Athelney Cottage   7 Athelney Ave, Hackney; (08) 8132 0069.

Belair National Park Caravan Park   Upper Sturt Rd, Belair; (08) 8278 3540.

Brighton Caravan Park & Holiday Village   Burnham Rd, Kingston Park; (08) 8377 0833.

Brownhill Creek Caravan Park   Brownhill Creek Rd, Mitcham; (08) 8271 4824.

Discovery Holiday Parks – Adelaide Beachfront   349 Military Rd, Semaphore Park; (08) 8449 7767.

'The Gums' Bed & Breakfast   6 Patricia St, Coromandel Valley; (08) 8270 6623.

Highway One Caravan & Tourist Park   925–963 Port Wakefield Rd (Princes Hwy), Bolivar; (08) 8250 3747.

Levi Park Caravan Park   1A Harris Rd, Vale Park; (08) 8344 2209.

Marion Holiday Park   323 Sturt Rd, Bedford Park; (08) 8276 6695.

North Adelaide Heritage Apartments – Bishops Garden   82 Molesworth St, North Adelaide; (08) 8267 2020.

Petts Wood Lodge   542 Glynburn Rd, Burnside; (08) 8331 9924.

Sturt River Caravan Park   Lot 51 Brookside Rd, Darlington; (08) 8296 1113.

Time and Tide Beach Apartment   8 Newman St, Semaphore; (08) 8449 7727.

Windsor Gardens Caravan Park   78 Windsor Gr, Windsor Gardens; (08) 8261 1091.

Day tours

Adelaide Hills   The hills directly east of Adelaide have long been a retreat for citysiders including, most famously, 19th-century governors. Today the attractions of this beautiful semi-rural area include the town of Hahndorf, cool-climate wineries, gourmet produce, forests and lookouts over the city.

Barossa Valley   Australia's best-known winegrowing region is a landscape of rolling yellow hills carpeted with vines. It boasts around 50 wineries, including some of the top names in the business, like The Seppelts estate, NW of Tanunda. The district owes much to its strong German heritage, which is also expressed in the local food, architecture and many cultural events.

Clare Valley   Boutique wineries, attractive 19th-century buildings and magnificent food and accommodation make the scenic Clare Valley a favourite weekend retreat. Just east of Clare is another world altogether – the old mining region of Burra, with landmarks that recall the immense copper boom.

Fleurieu Peninsula   The small seaside villages along Gulf St Vincent and the historic maritime town of Victor Harbor are irresistible seaside destinations close to the capital. En route to the peninsula, visitors can stop in at one of the cellar doors around McLaren Vale, one of the country's top wine regions. Keep an eye out for the Willunga Farmers Market every Saturday morning in the town square.

Murraylands   Before ending its long journey at Lake Alexandrina and onto the rich wetlands of the Coorong, the Murray River passes through diverse landscapes of rugged cliffs, mallee scrub, river red gum forests and pastoral lands. Visitors to Goolwa can relive the river's rich history as a bustling trade route and take a relaxing cruise from one of the ports of yesteryear.

REGIONS
of South Australia

Listed here are some of the top attractions and experiences in each region.

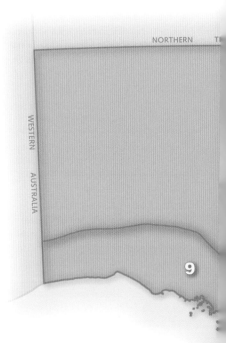

8 FLINDERS RANGES AND OUTBACK

Innamincka Regional Reserve / see p. 237
Ridgetop Tour / see p. 226
Umoona Opal Mine and Museum, Coober Pedy / see p. 233
Wilpena Pound in Flinders Ranges National Park (pictured) / see p. 266

9 EYRE PENINSULA AND NULLARBOR

Coffin Bay National Park / see p. 232
Nullarbor National Park (pictured) / see p. 231
Lincoln National Park / see p. 255
Murphy's Haystacks / see p. 260

5 YORKE PENINSULA

Diving around Edithburgh / see p. 234
Fishing around Wallaroo / see p. 262
Innes National Park (pictured) / see p. 267
Kernewek Lowender festival, Kadina / see p. 239

4 MID-NORTH

Burra Heritage Passport (pictured) / see p. 230
Clare Valley wine region / see p. 231
19th-century buildings in Mintaro / see p. 247
Sevenhill Cellars / see p. 231

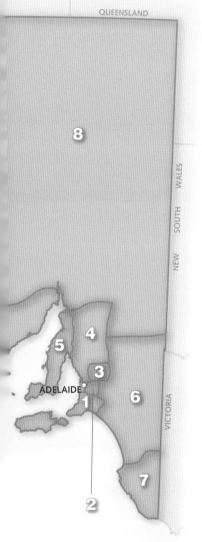

QUEENSLAND

8

NEW SOUTH WALES

5 4

3

ADELAIDE

1 6

2

VICTORIA

7

2

7 LIMESTONE COAST

Blue Lake, Mount Gambier (pictured) / see p. 250
Bool Lagoon Game Reserve / see p. 251
Coonawarra wine region / see p. 251
Naracoorte Caves National Park / see p. 249

6 MURRAY

Watersports at Murray Bridge / see p. 249
The Coorong in Coorong National Park / see p. 246
Houseboats at Long Island Marina, near Murray Bridge (pictured) / see p. 249
Riverland wine region / see p. 228

3 BAROSSA VALLEY

Barossa Valley wine region / see p. 243
Eden Valley wine region / see p. 225
Kaiserstuhl Conservation Park / see p. 225
Maggie Beer's Farm Shop (pictured) / see p. 253

2 ADELAIDE HILLS

Belair National Park / see p. 238
Cleland Conservation Park (pictured) / see p. 238
Mount Lofty Botanic Gardens / see p. 238
National Motor Museum, Birdwood / see p. 228

1 FLEURIEU PENINSULA

Horse-drawn tram, Victor Harbor / see p. 263
Southern Fleurieu wine region (pictured) / see p. 264
Mount Compass / see p. 265
Heritage-listed sand dunes at Normanville / see p. 267

TOWNS A–Z
South Australia

LEGEND

 VISITOR INFORMATION

RADIO STATIONS

IN TOWN

WHAT'S ON

WHERE TO EAT

WHERE TO STAY

NEARBY

* Distances for towns nearby are calculated as the crow flies.
* Food and accommodation listings in town are ordered alphabetically
  with places nearby listed at the end.

[CANOLA FIELD NEAR ADELAIDE]

Aldinga Beach
Pop. 5979
Map ref. 556 H9 | 559 J10 | 568 B4

i McLaren Vale and Fleurieu Visitor Centre, Main Rd,
McLaren Vale; (08) 8323 9944 or 1800 628 410;
www.mclarenvale.info

94.7 5EFM, 639 AM ABC North and West

The rolling hills of the southern Mount Lofty Ranges form the
backdrop to Aldinga Beach, a long curve of white sand facing
Gulf St Vincent. One and a half kilometres off the coast is
one of the state's best diving spots – the Aldinga Drop Off, an
underwater cliff where divers say the marine life has to be seen to
be believed. The township – to the west of the original Aldinga,
which grew as a small farming centre in the mid-1800s – is a
popular holiday spot.

Gnome Caves: 5 theme 'caves', great for kids;
Aldinga Beach Rd.

Star of Greece: stunning cliff-top seafood; 1 The Esplanade,
Port Willunga; (08) 8557 7420.

Aldinga Beach Holiday Park: 111 Cox Rd; (08) 8556 3444.
Anchor Cottage: Anchor Tce, Port Willunga; (08) 8557 8516.
Port Willunga Tourist Park: 22 Tuit Rd, Aldinga; (08) 8556 6113.

Star of Greece In 1888 the *Star of Greece* plunged to the
ocean floor in a wild storm. The ship was only a short distance
from land, but at 3am, and in gigantic swells, 17 of the 28 people
on board drowned. Today a portion of the vessel can be seen from
shore at low tide. A plaque lies on the seabed for the benefit of
divers, but for those wanting to stay dry, pictures of the wreck line
the walls of the Star of Greece Cafe. Port Willunga; 3 km N.

Aldinga Scrub Conservation Park: walk through remnant coastal
vegetation; the park is ablaze with colourful wildflowers in spring;
end of Dover St, off Aldinga Beach Rd; 1 km S. *Aldinga:* Uniting
Church cemetery has the graves of those who died in the *Star of
Greece* shipwreck. Community Market held 1st Sat each month
in Institute Hall, Old Coach Rd; 4 km NE. *Beaches:* many north
and south of Aldinga Beach including Port Willunga Beach, with
the remains of an old jetty and caves built in the cliff by anglers
(3 km N); Sellicks Beach, with boat access and good fishing
(8 km S); and Maslin Beach, Australia's first official nudist beach
(10 km N). *Lookouts:* one south of Sellicks Beach (11 km S) and
another over the Myponga Reservoir (23 km S).

TOWNS NEARBY: Willunga 9 km, McLaren Vale 10 km, Yankalilla
22 km, Victor Harbor 34 km, Port Elliot 34 km

Andamooka
Pop. 528
Map ref. 560 F3

i Dukes Bottlehouse Motel (incorporating post office), 275
Opal Creek Blvd; (08) 8672 7007; www.andamookaopal.com.au

105.9 FM ABC North and West

If Queen Elizabeth II had ever been to Andamooka, perhaps she
would have thought differently about the Andamooka Opal given
to her as a gift in 1954 on her first visit to Australia. The opal
weighed 203 carats and glistened in blues, reds and greens. It was
the result of an extensive search for the most beautiful opal in the
state, yet Andamooka itself is a misshapen collection of tin sheds,
dugouts and fibros in the middle of the desert. With constant
water shortages, no local council and an all-consuming drive to

find opals, residents have become experts in making do. The town offers old-fashioned outback hospitality to an increasing number of tourists.

Opal showrooms: showrooms in town include Andamooka Gems and Trains, attached to Dukes Bottlehouse Motel, with opals and a model railway. **Historic miners huts:** a handful of old semi-dugouts line the creek bed in the centre of town, complete with old tools and furnishings. Access is by tour, which includes a visit to an underground mine; details from post office. **Cemetery:** with miners' nicknames on the headstones.

Market and barbecue: local art and craft; Sat long weekends (Easter, June and Oct).

Fossicking: noodling in unclaimed mullock dumps surrounding town; details from post office. **Lake Torrens:** one of the state's largest salt lakes stretches away to the south-east; 4WD recommended for access.

TOWNS NEARBY: Roxby Downs 28 km, Woomera 89 km, Leigh Creek 120 km, Marree 124 km, Blinman 164 km

Angaston

Pop. 1865
Map ref. 559 K8 | 568 C2

Barossa Visitor Information Centre, 66–68 Murray St, Tanunda; (08) 8563 0600 or 1300 852 982; www.barossa.com

89.1 Triple B FM, 1062 AM ABC Riverland

Angaston takes its name from George Fife Angas who purchased the original plot of land on which the town now stands. He was a prominent figure in the South Australian Company and one of the shareholders who used his substantial buying power to get the best plots of land and dictate the terms of purchase. Many of the town's public buildings were funded by him, even before he emigrated. In a sense, the town's strong German heritage was also funded by him as he sponsored many Lutherans to make the journey to South Australia. Angaston still has strong ties with its history. In town is a German butcher shop that has been making wursts for more than 60 years, a blacksmith shop over a century old and a cafe and specialty food shop named the South Australian Company Store. Jacarandas and Moreton Bay figs line the main street.

A. H. Doddridge Blacksmith Shop This is the town's original blacksmith, started by Cornish immigrant William Doddridge. The shop closed in 1966 and 15 years later it was purchased by local townspeople. On Sat and Sun it operates as a working smithy, complete with the original bellows that Doddridge brought out from England. Murray St.

Angas Park Fruit Co: retail outlet for Angas Park dried fruits and nuts; Murray St. **The Abbey:** second-hand clothing and period pieces inside the old church; open Thurs–Sun; Murray St. **The Lego Man:** one of Australia's largest Lego collections; Jubilee Ave. **Food outlets:** include Angaston Gourmet Foods, famous for their baguettes, and the Barossa Valley Cheese Company, which makes cheese on the premises; Murray St. **Angaston Heritage Walk:** brochure from visitor centre.

Farmers market: behind Vintners Bar & Grill, Nuriootpa Rd; Sat mornings. **Angaston Show:** Feb/Mar. **Barossa Vintage Festival:** celebration of locally produced food and wine in various locations; odd-numbered years, Apr. **Barossa Gourmet Weekend:** Aug.

Blond Coffee: homemade snacks and lunches; 60 Murray St; (08) 8564 3444. **Vintners Bar & Grill:** robust Mediterranean flavours; Nuriootpa Rd; (08) 8564 2488.

Country Pleasures Bed and Breakfast: 54–56 Penrice Rd; 0438 643 477. **Marble Lodge Bed & Breakfast:** 21 Dean St; (08) 8564 2478.

Eden Valley wine region This is another history-rich region abutting the Barossa Valley to the east, but with a cooler climate that creates different wines. Henschke has a shiraz plot that dates back to the winery's inception in 1868, and the Hill of Grace label vies with PENFOLDS Grange as Australia's classic red. Pewsey Vale and Heggies Vineyard make fine examples of riesling, and share a cellar door with Yalumba.

Collingrove Homestead: the old Angas family home, now owned by the National Trust and open for tours, boutique accommodation and dining; 7 km SE. **Mengler Hill Lookout:** views over the Barossa Valley; 8 km SW. **Kaiserstuhl Conservation Park:** a small pocket of native flora and fauna, with walking trails; 10 km S. **Butcher, Baker, Winemaker Trail:** between Lyndoch and Angaston, taking in wineries and gourmet-food producers along the way. Smartcard available for purchase, which allows you VIP experiences and rewards points; details and brochure from visitor centre.

TOWNS NEARBY: Nuriootpa 6 km, Tanunda 8 km, Lyndoch 18 km, Kapunda 22 km, Gawler 30 km

Ardrossan

Pop. 1125
Map ref. 556 F5 | 559 I7 | 568 A1

Ardrossan Bakery, 39 First St, (08) 8837 3015; or Harvest Corner Visitor Information Centre, 29 Main St, Minlaton, (08) 8853 2600 or 1800 202 445; www.yorkepeninsula.com.au

89.3 Gulf FM, 639 AM ABC North and West

A cluster of bright white grain silos sit atop the red clay cliffs at Ardrossan, an industrial town on Yorke Peninsula. The town has two jetties – one for the export of grain, salt and dolomite, and the other for the benefit of local anglers. Ardrossan is well known for its blue swimmer crabs that are found under the jetty or in the shallows at low tide. The best season for crabbing is between September and April.

Stump Jump Plough A lonely stump-jump plough stands in the cliff-top park opposite East Tce. Mallee scrub once covered much of this area and caused endless grief to early farmers because it was so difficult to clear. The invention of the stump-jump plough made it possible to jump over stumps left in the ground and plough on ahead. The plough's design was perfected in Ardrossan. The original factory, on Fifth St, now houses a historical museum. Open 2.30–4.30pm Sun.

Ardrossan Caravan Park: 1 Park Tce; (08) 8837 3262. **Highview Holiday Village Caravan Park:** 15A Highview Rd; (08) 8837 3399. **Pine Point Caravan Park:** 46 Main Coast Rd, Pine Point; (08) 8838 2239. **Port Clinton Caravan Park:** The Parade, Port Clinton; (08) 8837 7003.

Zanoni wreck South Australia's most complete shipwreck is 15 km south-east of Ardrossan off Rogues Point. The wreck was lost for over 100 years, but was eventually rediscovered by some local fishermen. It lies virtually in one piece on the seabed. Some artefacts from the ship can be found at the Ardrossan historical museum, but divers wanting to see the wreck in situ need a permit from Heritage South Australia. (08) 8204 9245.

Walking trail: 3 km track along cliff-tops to Tiddy Widdy Beach; begins at the boat ramp in town. **BHP Lookout:** view of Gulf St Vincent and dolomite mines; 2 km S.

SOUTH AUSTRALIA

Clinton Conservation Park: mangrove swamps and tidal flats with an array of birdlife; begins after Port Clinton, 25 km N, and stretches around the head of Gulf St Vincent.

TOWNS NEARBY: Maitland 23 km, Port Victoria 41 km, Minlaton 49 km, Moonta 50 km, Kadina 54 km

Arkaroola
Map ref. 557 F2 | 561 K3

 Arkaroola Village reception; (08) 8648 4848 or 1800 676 042; www.arkaroola.com.au

999 AM ABC Broken Hill

Arkaroola is set in an incredible landscape of ranges laced with precious minerals, waterholes nestled inside tall gorges and places with songful names like Nooldoonooldoona and Bararranna. What's more, the Flinders Ranges are still alive, rumbling with up to 200 small earthquakes a year. It was a place that geologist Reg Sprigg found fascinating, and worth conserving. He purchased the Arkaroola property in 1968 and created a wildlife sanctuary for endangered species. Today a weather station, seismograph station and observatory (tours available) add to its significance and the spectacular four-wheel-drive tracks entice many visitors. The village has excellent facilities for such a remote outpost.

Ridgetop Tour This, the signature attraction of the northern Flinders Ranges, is a 4WD tour along an insanely steep track. The original track, built for mining exploration, wound through the creek beds, but run-off from the ridges washed the road away in just a few years. The idea was formed to create a track along the ridges themselves. A few bulldozers later, the track was complete. This is a guided tour, but Arkaroola Wilderness Sanctuary also has 100 km of self-guide 4WD tracks, including the popular Echo Camp Backtrack.

Vulkathunha–Gammon Ranges National Park This park is directly south of Arkaroola, taking in much of the distinctive scenery of the northern Flinders Ranges. The Adnyamathanha people believe that the Dreamtime serpent, Arakaroo, drank adjacent Lake Frome dry and carved out Arkaroola Gorge as he dragged his body back to his resting spot, inside Mainwater Pound. His restlessness is the cause of the earthquakes. Features include the surprisingly lush Weetootla Gorge, fed by a permanent spring, and Italowie Gorge, the unlikely spot where an impoverished R. M. Williams began making shoes. Park Headquarters at Balcanoona; (08) 8648 0048; 32 km S.

Waterholes: many picturesque waterholes along Arkaroola Creek and tributaries west and north-east of the village. *Bolla Bollana Smelter ruins:* where the ore from surrounding mines was once treated. It includes a Cornish beehive-shaped kiln; 7 km NW. *Paralana Hot Springs:* the only active geyser in Australia, where water heated by radioactive minerals bubbles through the rocks. Swimming or extended exposure is not recommended; 27 km NE. *Big Moro Gorge:* rockpools surrounded by limestone outcrops. The gorge is on Nantawarrina Aboriginal Land; obtain permit from Nepabunna Community Council, (08) 8648 3764; 59 km S. *Astronomical Tours:* boasts some of the best star-watching conditions in the Southern Hemisphere at 3 magnificent observatories; (08) 8648 4848. *Scenic flights:* over the ranges or further afield; details from village reception.

TOWNS NEARBY: Leigh Creek 95 km, Blinman 108 km, Marree 143 km, Wilpena 152 km, Hawker 195 km

Balaklava
Pop. 1627
Map ref. 556 H4 | 559 J7

 Council offices, Scotland Pl; (08) 8862 0800.

90.9 Flow FM, 1062 AM ABC Riverland

Balaklava is set on the Wakefield River in an area dominated by traditional wheat and sheep farms. It sprang up as a stopping point between the Burra copper fields and Port Wakefield, but a grain merchant from Adelaide, Charles Fisher, soon turned the focus to agriculture. He built grain stores here before there was any sign of grain. This proved a canny move, as it lured farmers to the area. The town features old sandstone buildings and a 'silent cop', a curious keep-left sign in the middle of a roundabout.

Courthouse Gallery The arts are alive and well in Balaklava, as shown by this community-run art gallery that has a changing program of local and visiting exhibitions, plus a popular art prize in July. Open 2–4pm Thurs, Fri and Sun; Edith Tce.

Balaklava Museum: old household items and local memorabilia; Old Centenary Hall, May Tce. *Urlwin Park Agricultural Museum:* old agricultural machinery, 2 old relocated banks and a working telephone exchange; open 2–4pm, 2nd and 4th Sun each month or by appt; Short Tce; (08) 8862 1854. *Walking trail:* scenic 3 km track along the riverbank.

Adelaide Plains Cup Festival: arts and crafts exhibitions, as well as golf and clay-shooting competitions; 1st Sun in Mar. *Balaklava Cup:* major regional horserace; Aug. *Balaklava Show:* Sept.

Amy's House: 6 Church St, Auburn; 0408 492 281. *Cygnets at Auburn:* Main North Rd, Auburn; (08) 8849 2030. *Dennis Cottage:* St Vincent St, Auburn; (08) 8843 0048. *Lavender Blue Country Apartments:* Main North Rd, Auburn; (08) 8849 2594. *Wild Olive Cottage:* St Vincent St, Auburn; (08) 8843 0048.

Port Wakefield Behind the highway's long line of takeaways and petrol stations is a quiet town that began life as a cargo port to carry the copper mined in Burra's Monster Mine back to Port Adelaide. It is set on the mangrove-lined Wakefield River at the top of Gulf St Vincent. The wharf, which has a floor of mud at low tide, is now used by the local fishing industry. A historical walk brochure is available from the Port Wakefield/Rivergum Information Centre. This is a popular spot for fishing, crabbing and swimming. 25 km W.

Devils Garden: a picnic spot among river box gums, once a 'devil of a place' for bullock wagons to get through as the black soil quickly turned to mud; 7 km NE. *Rocks Reserve:* walking trails and unique rock formations by the river; 10 km E. *Balaklava Gliding Club:* offers weekend 'air experience flights' with an instructor; Whitwarta Airfield; (08) 8864 5062; 10 km NW.

TOWNS NEARBY: Mintaro 38 km, Clare 39 km, Kapunda 51 km, Ardrossan 55 km, Gawler 59 km

Barmera
Pop. 1927
Map ref. 526 A6 | 559 N7 | 568 G1

 Barwell Ave; (08) 8588 2289; www.barmeratourism.com.au

93.1 MAGIC FM, 1062 AM ABC Riverland

Barmera lies in the middle of a swooping hairpin bend of the Murray River, close to the Victorian border, but it is hard to tell where the river stops and where the flood plains and tributaries begin in the area to the west of town. The wetlands eventually flow into Lake Bonney, a large body of water to the north of Barmera. Swimming, waterskiing, sailing and fishing are some of the activities popular on the lake. The town was established in 1921 as a settlement for returned World War I soldiers, who were all promised a patch of well-irrigated farmland.

Rocky's Country Music Hall of Fame Dean 'Rocky' Page established Barmera's famous country music festival and was a well-known musician in his own right. Within the centre is an array of country music memorabilia and a display of replica guitars with the handprints of the legends who used them. The pièce de résistance is Slim Dusty's hat. Open Wed–Fri; Barwell Ave; (08) 8588 1463.

Donald Campbell Obelisk: commemorates an attempt in 1964 to break the world water-speed record, but 347.5 km/h was not quite enough to make the books; Queen Elizabeth Dr. *Bonneyview Winery:* cosy atmosphere with award-winning reds and light pastries; Sturt Hwy; (08) 8588 2279.

5RM Barmera Main Street Market: 1st Sun each month Sept–Dec. *Lake Bonney Yachting Regatta:* Easter. *South Australian Country Music Festival:* June. *Riverland Field Days:* Sept. *Barmera Bonnie Sheepdog Trials:* Oct.

Banrock Station Wine & Wetland Centre: stylish eco-cafe with wine tastings; Holmes Rd, Kingston-on-Murray; (08) 8583 0299. *The Overland Corner Hotel:* historic bush pub; Old Coach Rd, Overland Corner; (08) 8588 7021.

Discovery Holiday Parks – Lake Bonney: Lakeside Ave; (08) 8588 2234. *Cobdogla Station Caravan Park:* Shueard Rd (Old Sturt Hwy), Cobdogla; (08) 8588 7164. *Kingston-on-Murray Caravan Park:* 461 Holmes Rd, Kingston-on-Murray; (08) 8583 0209.

Banrock Station Wine & Wetland Centre Fruity wines mix with a cacophony of birds and frogs at Banrock Station. In these new times of sensitive agriculture, Banrock is working with environmental organisations to breathe life back into a pocket of wetland that was ruined by irrigation (almost 70% of all Murray wetlands have been affected). The natural cycles of flooding and drying have seen the return of black swans, native fish and ibis, and a boardwalk gives visitors a close-up look. Kingston-on-Murray; (08) 8583 0299; 10 km w.

Overland Corner This was the first settlement in the area, a convenient stop en route for drovers and people travelling to the goldfields. By 1855 a police post had been established to deal with the odd bushranger and quell the problems flaring between drovers and the indigenous inhabitants. In 1859 the Overland Corner Hotel opened its doors. Its thick limestone walls and red gum floors have seen many floods. An 8 km walking track into the adjacent Herons Bend Reserve leaves from the hotel. 19 km NW.

Cobdogla Irrigation and Steam Museum: has the world's only working Humphrey Pump, used in the early days of irrigation. Also local memorabilia and steam-train rides; open Sun long weekends; 5 km W. *Highway Fern Haven:* garden centre featuring an indoor rainforest; 5 km E. *Napper's Old Accommodation House:* ruins of a hotel built in 1850 on the shores of the lake; turn east over Napper Bridge; 10 km NW. *Loch Luna Game Reserve:* linking Lake Bonney and the Murray, these wetlands form an important refuge for waterbirds and one of the few inland nesting sites for sea eagles. Chambers Creek, which loops around the reserve, is popular for canoeing; turn west over Napper Bridge; 16 km NW. *Moorook Game Reserve:* these wetlands surround Wachtels Lagoon; 16 km SW. *Loveday Internment Camps:* guided tour or self-guide drive to the camps where Japanese, Italian and German POWs were held during WW II; details from visitor centre.

TOWNS NEARBY: Berri 13 km, Loxton 24 km, Renmark 28 km, Waikerie 45 km, Morgan 78 km

Beachport

Pop. 342
Map ref. 568 E10

ℹ️ Millicent Rd; (08) 8735 8029; www.wattlerange.sa.gov.au

📻 107.7 5THE FM, 1161 AM ABC South East

Beachport started out as a whaling port. Today the crayfish industry has taken over and the town has South Australia's second-longest jetty, favoured by anglers young and old with regular catches including whiting, flathead and garfish. People flock here for summer holidays to relax on the beautiful sandy beaches and swim in the bay. The Bowman Scenic Drive provides stunning views over the Southern Ocean with access to sheltered coves and rocky headlands for the adventurous to explore. It is also a great place for whale-watching.

Old Wool and Grain Store Museum The old store contains a whaling and fishing display including harpoons and whaling pots, as well as relics from shipwrecks off the coastline. Upstairs

[BEACHPORT] SWEEPING BEND IN THE ROAD AT BEACHPORT

 RADIO STATIONS   IN TOWN   WHAT'S ON   WHERE TO EAT   WHERE TO STAY   NEARBY

SOUTH AUSTRALIA

rooms are furnished in the style of the day. Natural history display features local and migratory seabirds. Open 10am–4pm daily (holiday period), 10am–1pm Sun (other times) Railway Tce.

Lanky's Walk: a short walk through bushland to Lanky's Well, where the last full-blood member of the Boandik tribe camped while working as a police tracker; begins on Railway Tce North; details on this and other walks from visitor centre. *Pool of Siloam:* this small lake, 7 times saltier than the sea, is said to be a cure for all manner of ailments. Also a popular swimming spot; end of McCourt St. *Lighthouse:* the original lighthouse was located on Penguin Island, a breeding ground for seals and penguins offshore from Cape Martin, where the current lighthouse now stands. It offers good views of the island from the cape; south of town.

Market: Sat long weekends (Jan, Easter and Oct). *Duck Race:* Jan. *Festival by the Sea:* stalls and entertainment; odd-numbered years, Feb/Mar.

Beachport Caravan Park: Beach Rd; (08) 8735 8128. *Beachport's Southern Ocean Tourist Park:* Somerville St; (08) 8735 8153.

Beachport Conservation Park This park is a succession of white beaches, sand dunes and rugged limestone cliffs, with the southern shore of Lake George lying inland. The coast is dotted with ancient shell middens and is accessed primarily by 4WD or on foot. Five Mile Drift, a beach on Lake George, is a good base for swimming, sailing and windsurfing. Access to the coast side is via Bowman Scenic Dr, which begins at the lighthouse. Access to the Lake George side is via Railway Tce North. 4 km NW.

Woakwine Cutting: an incredible gorge, cut through Woakwine Range by one man to drain swampland and allow farming, with viewing platform, information boards and machinery exhibit; 10 km N.

TOWNS NEARBY: Millicent 32 km, Robe 41 km, Kingston S.E. 74 km, Penola 74 km, Coonawarra 76 km

Berri
Pop. 4009
Map ref. 526 A6 | 546 A6 | 559 N7 | 568 G1

ⓘ Riverview Dr; (08) 8582 5511; www.berribarmera.sa.gov.au

 93.1 MAGIC FM, 1062 AM ABC Riverland

Orange products and wine are big business in this Riverland town, which has Australia's largest winery and is one of the major growing and manufacturing centres of the country's biggest orange-juice company. The Big Orange, on the north-west outskirts of town, makes this rather clear. The name 'Berri' has nothing to do with fruit, though. It comes from the Aboriginal 'Bery Bery', thought to mean 'bend in the river'. The town was established in 1911, the year after irrigation of the Murray began.

Berri Direct: makers of Berri fruit juice and other products, with sales and a video presentation detailing production history of the Riverland; Old Sturt Hwy. *Riverlands Gallery:* local and touring art exhibitions; open Mon–Fri; Wilson St. *Gilbert Street Gallery:* artwork by local artists, including some amazing glassware and woodwork; Gilbert St. *Berri Community Mural:* enormous community-painted mural commemorating the past and present fruit industry; Old Sturt Hwy next to Berri Direct. *Berri Lookout Tower:* panoramic views of river, town and surrounds from a converted water tower; cnr Fiedler St and Vaughan Tce. *Lions Club Walking Trail:* 4 km riverfront walk from Berri Marina to Martin Bend

Reserve, a popular spot for picnics and waterskiing; an Aboriginal mural and totems are under the bridge and further along are monuments to famous Aboriginal tracker Jimmy James. *Birdwatching safaris:* to Bookmark Biosphere Reserve; tours offered by Jolly Goodfellows Birding; (08) 8583 5530. *Berri Air Tours:* offering scenic flights over the Riverland; (08) 8582 2799.

Farmers Market: Sat. *Speedboat Spectacular:* Mar (subject to river conditions). *Riverland Renaissance:* Oct. *Craft Fair:* Nov.

Berri Riverside Caravan Park: Riverview Dr; (08) 8582 3723.

Riverland wine region A booming 25 per cent of all Australian grapes are grown in Riverland. Yet, the region is slowly attempting to alter its reputation, focusing on quality as well as quantity. Banrock Station, whose inexpensive wines are some of the region's better drops, is also helping to protect the Murray environment. On the 1700-hectare property, only 240 hectares are vines, with the rest a restored wetland and sanctuary for birds, fish and frogs. Other wineries to visit are Angove's, Kingston Estate and Organic Vignerons Australia, which represents organic vineyards in Loxton and Waikerie as well as others across the state.

Murray River National Park, Katarapko section In this park, see the merging of 2 distinct vegetations – of the famous Murray River flood plains and the equally renowned Mallee region. The 6 km Mallee Drive takes the visitor into the heart of the park and to the distinctive mallee terrain. There are also walking trails to see some of the park's inhabitants, including the ever-popular kangaroo. Just south of Berri; (08) 8595 2111.

Angas Park Fruit Company: dried fruits and other products; open 8.30am–5pm Mon–Fri, 10am–12pm Sat and public holidays; Old Sturt Hwy; (08) 8561 0800; 3 km W. *Monash:* a small irrigation town best known for the free family attractions at the Monash Adventure Park on Morgan Rd. Enjoy delicate handmade chocolates at the Chocolates and More store opposite the park, or taste the wines at nearby Thachi Wines; 12 km NW.

TOWNS NEARBY: Barmera 13 km, Renmark 18 km, Loxton 19 km, Waikerie 58 km, Morgan 91 km

Birdwood
Pop. 733
Map ref. 553 H5 | 559 K9 | 568 C2

ⓘ Shannon St; (08) 8568 5577.

98.7 Power FM, 1062 AM ABC Riverland

The small town of Birdwood is set picturesquely in the Torrens Valley in the northern part of the popular Adelaide Hills district. The region's beauty would have been a welcome sight for German settlers escaping religious persecution in the 1840s. Like many of the German-settled towns in the area, Birdwood was originally named after a Prussian town, Blumberg. However, anti-German sentiment during World War I created a feeling of unrest and the town's name was changed to Birdwood after the commander of the ANZAC forces in Gallipoli, Sir William Birdwood.

National Motor Museum The largest in the Southern Hemisphere, this impressive collection of over 300 vintage cars, motorcycles and commercial vehicles is housed in the 1852 flour mill. The vehicles are lovingly restored, often from simply a shell. Visit the workshop complex to see the process of restoration as coach builders and mechanics work tirelessly on these old machines. The building's original history as a flour mill can be seen in the Mill Building. Shannon St; (08) 8568 5006.

Birdwood Wine and Cheese Centre: introduces visitors to boutique wines and cheeses of regional SA with tastings and sales; open Wed–Sun; Shannon St. *Blumberg Inn:* imposing 1865 inn harking back to German-settler days; Main St.

Rock and Roll Rendezvous: Apr. *Bay to Birdwood Run:* vintage motoring event attracting more than 1600 vehicles; even-numbered years, Sept.

Saunders Gorge Sanctuary B&B: Walkers Flat Rd, Mount Pleasant; (08) 8569 3032. *SunnyBrook Bed & Breakfast:* Mannum Rd, Tungkillo; (08) 8568 2159.

Lobethal The quaint town of Lobethal features historic German-style cottages and an 1842 Lutheran seminary. Fairyland Village takes the visitor into the world of fairytales; open weekends. The National Costume Museum houses a collection of dresses, suits and accessories dating from 1812 (closed Mon). The town lights up each Christmas in the 'Lights of Lobethal' festival. 13 km sw.

The Toy Factory: a family business manufacturing wooden toys from a shop adjacent to an 18 m giant rocking horse; Gumeracha; 7 km w. *Chain of Ponds Wine:* boutique winery with tastings, sales, viewing platform, restaurant and B&B (1880s cottage); 9 km w. *Herbig Tree:* an extraordinary insight into Friedrich Herbig and the hollow red gum tree where he raised a family in the 1850s. School museum and pioneer cemetery also on-site; Springton; group bookings only (08) 8568 2287; 15km NE. *Malcolm Creek Vineyard:* boutique winery with cellar door and friendly deer; open weekends and public holidays; Bonython Rd, Kersbrook; 20 km NW. *Roachdale Reserve:* self-guide nature trail with brochure; 23 km NW via Kersbrook. *Torrens Gorge:* spectacular cliffs and streams make this a popular spot for picnics; 25 km w. *Samphire Wines and Pottery:* a small boutique winery and handmade pottery shop; Cnr Watts Gully and Robertson rds; 27 km NW via Kersbrook. *Warren Conservation Park:* difficult trails, including part of the long-distance Heysen Trail, lead to spectacular views over countryside and Warren Gorge; adjacent to Samphire Wines and Pottery. *Mt Crawford Forest:* walkers, horseriders and cyclists will enjoy the forest tracks of this park, which is scattered in various locations north, west and south-west of Birdwood; visit the information centre on Warren Rd (signposted turn-off between Kersbrook and Williamstown) for a map.

TOWNS NEARBY: Lyndoch 25 km, Hahndorf 27 km, Gawler 31 km, Tanunda 33 km, Mannum 33 km

Blinman
Pop. 151
Map ref. 557 C7 | 561 I5

General store, Mine Rd; (08) 8648 4370; www.blinman.org.au

During the 19th century numerous mining townships dotted the northern Flinders Ranges. Blinman is the sole surviving town surveyed at the time. The discovery of copper here in 1859 was accidental; the story goes that a shepherd, Robert Blinman, used to watch his sheep from a boulder. One day he absentmindedly broke off a chunk and discovered it was copper. Historic buildings in the main street are reminders of those rich (and temporary) days.

Land Rover Jamboree: Easter. *Cook Outback:* food/wine festival with camp oven competition; Oct long weekend.

Blinman Hotel: rustic bush pub; Mine Rd; (08) 8648 4867. *Prairie Hotel:* innovative outback cuisine; Cnr High St and West Tce, Parachilna; (08) 8648 4844 or 1800 331 473.

Blinman Cottage: 201 Hancock St; 0417 084 003.

Blinman Mine Historic Site: a 1 km self-guide walk explains the history and geology of the site. Contact the caretaker on (08) 8648 4874 for a guided tour; just north-east of Blinman. *Great Wall of China:* impressive limestone ridge; Wilpena Rd; 10 km s. *Angorichina Tourist Village:* Start point for 4 km walk along creek bed to Blinman Pools, permanent spring-fed pools in scenic surrounds. Accommodation ranges from tents to cabins; (08) 8648 4842; 14 km w. *Glass and Parachilna gorges:* 10 km NW and 15 km w of town are these 2 beautiful gorges. Parachilna Gorge is the end point of the 1200 km Heysen Trail (bushwalking trail), which begins at Cape Jervis; for information contact Parks SA, (08) 8124 4792. *Flinders Ranges National Park: see Wilpena for more details;* 26 km s; *Prairie Hotel:* a historic hotel at Parachilna offering cuisine with a bush-tucker twist as well as first-rate accommodation. Hotel staff can arrange activities including 4WD tours, scenic flights and visits to nearby Nilpena Station on the edge of Lake Torrens to sample the outback life; (08) 8648 4844; 32 km w. *Scenic drive:* travel east through Eregunda Valley (around 20 km E), then north-east to Mt Chambers Gorge (around 75 km NE), with its rockpools and Aboriginal carvings; further north is Vulkathunha–Gammon Ranges National Park; *see Arkaroola. Mawson Trail:* this 900 km bike trail from Adelaide ends in Blinman. It is named after famous Australian explorer Sir Douglas Mawson and traverses the Mt Lofty and Flinders ranges; for details contact Bicycle SA, (08) 8411 0233.

TOWNS NEARBY: Wilpena 47 km, Leigh Creek 64 km, Hawker 89 km, Arkaroola 108 km, Quorn 150 km

Bordertown
Pop. 2584
Map ref. 526 A12 | 548 A7 | 568 G7

Tolmer Park, 81 North Tce; (08) 8752 0700 or 1800 520 700; www.tatiara.sa.gov.au

106.1 5TCB FM, 1062 AM ABC Riverland

In spite of its name, Bordertown is actually 18 kilometres from the South Australia–Victoria border in the fertile country of the Tatiara District. Thought to be the Aboriginal word for 'good country', Tatiara's name is justified by the region's productive wool and grain industries. For a different native-animal experience, look out for Bordertown's famous white kangaroos, Australia's only known colony. Former Australian prime minister Robert (Bob) J. L. Hawke was born here.

Robert J. L. Hawke's childhood home: includes memorabilia. Visit by appt only, contact visitor centre for details; Farquhar St. *Bordertown Wildlife Park:* native birds and animals, including pure-white kangaroos; Dukes Hwy. *Hawke Gallery:* in foyer of council chambers; Woolshed St. *Bordertown Recreation Lake:* popular spot for fishing, canoeing and walking, with artwork on display; northern outskirts of town.

Bordertown Show: Oct.

Bordertown Caravan Park: 41 Penny Tce; (08) 8752 1752. *Padthaway Caravan Park:* Beeamma–Parsons Rd, Padthaway; 0412 546 792.

SOUTH AUSTRALIA

Padthaway wine region Though Padthaway's soil is not quite as rich as that of the Coonawarra region, it is a wonder that this region is not more prominent. With vines growing in terra rossa (red earth), wineries include Padthaway Estate, where visitors can also taste the wines of Browns of Padthaway. The winery's 1882 Padthaway Homestead has a restaurant and accommodation, and is situated near the red gums and stringybarks of Padthaway Conservation Park. Stonehaven is a large, modern operation producing quality, well-priced wine including chardonnay.

Clayton Farm: incorporates the Bordertown and District Agricultural Museum and features vintage farm machinery and a National Trust–classified thatched-roof building and woolshed; 3 km s. **Mundulla:** a historic township featuring the heritage-listed Mundulla Hotel; 10 km sw. **Bangham Conservation Park:** a significant habitat for the red-tailed black cockatoo; 30 km se.

TOWNS NEARBY: Keith 44 km, Naracoorte 72 km, Nhill (Vic.) 79 km, Edenhope (Vic.) 94 km, Kingston S.E. 101 km

Burra

Pop. 976
Map ref. 559 K5

ⓘ 2 Market Sq; (08) 8892 2154; www.visitburra.com

📻 105.1 Trax FM, 1062 AM ABC Riverland

The Burra region exploded into activity when copper was found by two shepherds in 1845. Settlements were established based on the miners' country of origin: Aberdeen for the Scottish, Hampton for the English, Redruth for the Cornish and Llwchwr for the Welsh. The combined settlement grew to be the second largest in South Australia, but the miners were fickle – with riches promised on the Victorian goldfields, they did not stay for long. In 1877 the Monster Mine closed. Luckily, Burra did not turn into a ghost town. Instead, the rich heritage of its past has been carefully preserved by the community, resulting in the town being declared a State Heritage Area in 1993. Burra is in the Bald Hill Ranges, named for the 'naked' hills around the town.

Burra Heritage Passport This 'passport' allows visitors to discover the major heritage sites of Burra – armed with an unlimited-access 'key' and a brief history of each site outlined in the pamphlet *Discovering Historic Burra*. Included in the passport is the Burra Historic Mine Site (off Market St), with an ore dressing tower and powder magazine offering views of the open-cut mine and town. At the site is Morphetts Enginehouse Museum (additional entry fee), featuring an excavated 30 m entry tunnel and engine displays. Another site is the Burra Creek Miners' Dugouts (alongside Blyth St) – these dugouts cut into the creek beds housed 1800 people in the boom. Visit the Unicorn Brewery Cellars (Bridge Tce) that date back to 1873, the police lock-up and stables (Tregony St) – these were the first built outside Adelaide – and Redruth Gaol (off Tregony St), which served as a gaol, then a girls reformatory from 1856 to 1922. You can also visit the ruins of a private English township called Hampton, on the northern outskirts of town. Passports are available from the visitor centre and can be upgraded to provide access to the town's museums.

Bon Accord Mine Complex: National Trust interpretive centre with working forge and model of Burra Mine. Guided tours available; closed Mon and Fri; Railway Tce. **Market Square Museum:** an old-style general store, post office and family home returned to its heyday; opposite visitor centre. **Malowen Lowarth Cottage:** restored 1850s Cornish miners cottage; Kingston St.

Burra Regional Art Gallery: local and touring exhibitions; Market St. **Thorogoods:** enjoy some of Australia's best apple wine and cider; John Barker St. **Antique shops:** in Commercial and Market sts. **Burra Creek:** canoeing and picnicking.

Jailhouse Rock Festival: Feb. **Music in the Monster Mine:** Mar. **Antique and Decorating Fair:** May. **Burra Show:** Oct.

Burra Bakery: classic Cornish fare; 16 Commercial St; (08) 8892 2070. **Burra Hotel:** hearty country fare; 5 Market Sq; (08) 8892 2389.

Burra Caravan & Camping Park: 12 Bridge Tce; (08) 8892 2442. **Burra Heritage Cottages – Tivers Row:** 8 Truro St; (08) 8892 2461. **Morse Cottage:** 22 Chapel St; (08) 8352 4046.

Burra Trail Rides: horseriding adventures in Bald Hills Range; bookings 0427 808 402. **Burra Gorge:** picnics, camping and walking tracks around gorge and permanent springs; 23 km se. **Dares Hill Drive:** scenic 90 km drive with lookout; begins 30 km n near Hallett; map available from visitor centre.

TOWNS NEARBY: Mintaro 33 km, Clare 34 km, Jamestown 60 km, Balaklava 71 km, Kapunda 74 km

Ceduna

Pop. 2304
Map ref. 567 M8

ⓘ 58 Poynton St; (08) 8625 3343 or 1800 639 413; www.ceduna.net

📻 94.5 5CCR FM, 693 AM ABC Eyre Peninsula and West Coast

The name Ceduna is derived from the Aboriginal word 'chedoona', meaning resting place, which is apt for those who have just traversed the Nullarbor. Ceduna is also the last major town for those about to embark on the journey west – the place to check your car and stock up on food and water. The difficulty of obtaining supplies and provisions has a long history around Ceduna. Denial Bay, where the original settlement of McKenzie was situated, was where large cargo ships brought provisions for the early pioneers. Ceduna was established later, in 1896, and is situated on the shores of Murat Bay with sandy coves, sheltered bays and offshore islands. In the 1850s there was also a whaling station on St Peter Island (visible from Thevenard).

Old Schoolhouse National Trust Museum: pioneering artefacts, including those from British atomic testing at Maralinga; closed Sun; Park Tce. **Ceduna Arts Cultural Centre:** original paintings, local pottery and ceramics; open weekdays; Cnr Eyre Hwy and Kuhlmann St. **Oyster tours:** offered to Denial Bay, Thevenard and Smoky Bay; book at visitor centre. **Ceduna Oyster Bar:** fresh oysters year-round; western outskirts, on Eyre Hwy. **Local beaches:** swimming, boating, waterskiing and fishing. The foreshore is an ideal spot for walks and picnics (sharks have been known to frequent these waters – seek local advice). **Encounter Coastal Trail:** 3.8 km interpretive trail from the foreshore to Thevenard.

Oysterfest: community festival including street parade and fireworks; Oct long weekend. **Ceduna Races:** horseracing; Dec and Jan.

Ceduna Airport Caravan Park and Restaurant: Eyre Hwy; (08) 8625 2416. **Ceduna Foreshore Caravan Park:** 25 Poynton St; (08) 8625 2290. **Ceduna Shelly Beach Caravan Park:** Lot 178 Decres Bay Rd; (08) 8625 2012. **Penong Caravan Park:** 3 Stiggants Rd, Penong; (08) 8625 1111.

Great Australian Bight Marine Park The park preserves the fragile ecosystem of the Great Australian Bight. It has spectacular wildlife sights, including the breeding and calving of southern right whales from June to Oct. Spend a day observing these giant creatures from the viewing platform at Head of Bight. There are also spectacular views of the Bunda Cliffs, which begin at the head and trail all the way to the WA border. Whale-watching permits are purchased from the visitor centre on-site. Interpretive centre also on-site. 300 km w.

Nullarbor National Park Aboriginal culture is closely linked with this park's network of caves, part of the largest karst landscape in the world (Murrawijinie Caves north of Nullarbor Roadhouse are the only caves accessible to the public). Vast and mainly flat, the park's most beautiful scenery is along the coast where the cliffs stretch for 200 km overlooking the Southern Ocean. Visitors should take care along the unstable cliff edges. Rare and endangered species such as the Major Mitchell cockatoo and the peregrine falcon are often sighted. Watch out for the southern hairy-nosed wombat. 300 km w.

Thevenard: a deep-sea port that handles bulk grain, gypsum and salt, as well as a large fishing fleet noted for whiting hauls. Bill's Seafood Tours gives an insight into the commercial fishing industry; contact visitor centre for details. A 3.6 km interpretive trail, 'Tracks Along the Coast', runs from the Sailing Club to Pinky Point; 4 km sw. *Denial Bay:* visit the McKenzie ruins to see an early pioneering home and the heritage-listed landing where cargo was brought to shore. Denial Bay jetty is good for fishing and crabbing; 14 km w. *Davenport Creek:* see pure-white sandhills and swim in the sheltered creek. Beyond the sandhills is excellent surfing and waterskiing; 40 km w. *South-east towns and beaches:* Decres Bay for swimming, snorkelling and rock-fishing (10 km SE); Laura Bay with cove-swimming near the conservation park (18 km SE); Smoky Bay for safe swimming, fishing and boating (40 km SE); Point Brown for surf beaches, salmon fishing and coastal walks (56 km SE). *Penong:* more than 40 windmills draw the town's water from underground. See historical memorabilia and local crafts at the Penong Woolshed Museum. Camel day rides and safaris on offer; 73 km w. *Cactus Beach:* renowned for its 'perfect' surfing breaks; 94 km w. *Fowlers Bay:* this town, surrounded by a conservation park, offers long, sandy beaches and excellent fishing; 139 km sw. *North-east conservation parks and reserves:* comprising Yellabinna, Yumbarra, Pureba, Nunnyah and Koolgera, an extensive wilderness area of dunes and mallee country. Rare species of wildlife live here, including dunnarts and mallee fowl. 4WD is essential, and visitors must be experienced in outback travel; north of Ceduna. *Googs Track:* 4WD trek from Ceduna to the Trans-Australia railway track (154 km N) through Yumbarra Conservation Park and Yellabinna Regional Reserve; contact visitor centre for details.

TOWNS NEARBY: Streaky Bay 90 km, Wudinna 197 km, Elliston 204 km

Clare

Pop. 3061
Map ref. 556 H2 | 559 J6

ⓘ Cnr Main North and Spring Gully rds; (08) 8842 2131 or 1800 242 131; www.clarevalley.com.au

105.1 Trax FM, 639 ABC North and West

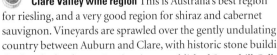

[CLARE] CELLAR AT SEVENHILL WINERY

Clare is known as the 'Garden of the North'. In the mid-1800s, Edward John Eyre reported favourably on the area and pastoral settlement followed; the town came to be known as Clare after the county in Ireland. The land has proved as favourable as Eyre claimed and Clare continues to boast a rich agricultural industry, including the famous Clare Valley wine region. The first vines were planted by Jesuit priests at Sevenhill in 1851. The Sevenhill Cellars are still operated by Jesuit brothers and the monastery buildings, including the historic St Aloysius Church, are of special interest.

Old Police Station Museum: once a prison, a casualty hospital and housing for government employees, it is now a National Trust museum with historic artefacts and photographs; open weekends and public holidays, other times by appt; Neagles Rock Rd; (08) 8842 2376. *Lookouts:* Billy Goat Hill from Wright St and Neagles Rock Lookout on Neagles Rock Rd. *Town walk:* self-guide trail; brochure from visitor centre.

Clare Races: horseraces among the vines; Easter. *Spanish Festival:* Apr. *Clare Gourmet Weekend:* May. *Clare Show:* Oct.

Artisans Table Wine Bar + Bistro: seafood and steaks; Wendouree Rd; (08) 8842 1796. *Wild Saffron Gourmet Food & Catering:* snacks and foodie treats; 288 Main North Rd; (08) 8842 4255. *Penna Lane Wines:* cellar-door platters; Penna La, Skilly Hills; (08) 8843 4033. *Sevenhill Hotel:* sturdy pub tucker and modern Australian; Main North Rd, Sevenhill; (08) 8843 4217. *Skillogalee Winery Restaurant:* stylish country fare; Trevarrick Rd, Sevenhill; (08) 8843 4311.

Brice Hill Country Lodge: 56–66 Warenda Rd; (08) 8842 2925. *Bungaree Station:* Main North Rd; (08) 8842 2677. *Clare Caravan Park:* Main North Rd; (08) 8842 2724. *Millies Cottage:* 12 Mill St; 0422 789 575. *Tree Tops at Clare:* Lot 103 White Hut Rd; (08) 8842 1846. *Wuthering Heights:* Gaelic Cemetery Rd; (08) 8842 3196. *Mundawora Mews:* Main North Rd, Stanley Flat; (08) 8842 3762. *Sevenhill Cottages Accommodation and Conference Centre:* Main North Rd, Sevenhill; 0408 850 845.

Clare Valley wine region This is Australia's best region for riesling, and a very good region for shiraz and cabernet sauvignon. Vineyards are sprawled over the gently undulating country between Auburn and Clare, with historic stone buildings dotting the landscape. Jesuit priests established Sevenhill Cellars in 1851 to ensure a steady supply of altar wine. The winemaking is still overseen by Jesuits, with riesling and shiraz the standout

SOUTH AUSTRALIA

varieties. Visit the stone cellars and St Aloysius Church. The well-known brand Annie's Lane was also established in 1851 (under a different name), and produces excellent riesling, semillon, shiraz and grenache mourvedre. Other impressive wineries include Grosset and Wendouree.

Watervale: a historic town with a self-guide walk leaflet available from the visitor centre; 12 km s. *Blyth:* a little country town overlooking the western plains. Take a short walk on the interpretive botanical trail or picnic at Brooks Lookout. Medika Gallery, originally a Lutheran church, offers an art gallery and Australian craft sales; 13 km w. *Auburn:* the birthplace in 1876 of poet C. J. Dennis. Take a self-guide walk through National Trust historic precinct in St Vincent St; 26 km s. *Scenic drive:* travel south to Spring Gully Conservation Park with its walking tracks and rare red stringybarks.

TOWNS NEARBY: Mintaro 14 km, Burra 34 km, Balaklava 39 km, Kapunda 63 km, Crystal Brook 65 km

Coffin Bay

Pop. 582
Map ref. 558 D8

ⓘ Beachcomber Agencies, The Esplanade; (08) 8685 4057; www.coffinbay.net

📻 89.9 Magic FM, 1485 AM ABC Eyre Peninsula and West Coast

A picturesque holiday town and fishing village on the shores of a beautiful estuary, Coffin Bay is popular particularly in summer, when the population quadruples. The bay offers sailing, waterskiing, swimming and fishing. The town was originally known as Oyster Town because of the abundant natural oysters in the bay, but they were dredged to extinction last century. Today the cultivated oysters are among the best in the country. The bay – in spite of what some locals will try to tell you – was named by Matthew Flinders in 1802 in honour of his friend Sir Isaac Coffin.

🏠 *Fishing:* in the bay or in game fishing areas; boat hire and charters available. *Oyster Walk:* 12 km walkway along foreshore and bushland from a lookout (excellent view of Coffin Bay) to Long Beach; brochure from visitor centre. *Coffin Bay Explorer:* catamaran offering a 3 hr cruise on Coffin Bay, visiting oyster leases and greeting dolphins and other spectacular sea life; bookings essential 0428 880 621.

🍴 *The Oysterbeds Restaurant:* bayside seafood; 61 The Esplanade; (08) 8685 4000.

🛏 *Coffin Bay Caravan Park:* 91 The Esplanade; (08) 8685 4170.

Coffin Bay National Park A mixture of rugged coastal landscapes, calm bays and waterways makes this diverse park a pleasure to wander and drive through. Conventional vehicles can access the eastern part of the park where walks through she-oak and samphire swamps reveal incredible birdlife. The beaches and lookouts provide a different perspective on this remote wilderness. 4WD vehicles and bushwalkers can access the western part, which includes Gunyah Beach, Point Sir Isaac and the Coffin Bay Peninsula. The park extends south and west of town; (08) 8688 3111.

Kellidie Bay Conservation Park: a limestone landscape popular for walking and canoeing; eastern outskirts of Coffin Bay. *Yangie Trail:* the 10 km trail starts at Coffin Bay and travels south-west via Yangie Bay Lookout, which offers magnificent views to Point Avoid and Yangie Bay. *Mt Dutton Bay:* features the restored heritage-listed jetty and woolshed, the latter now a shearing and farming museum; 40 km N. *Farm Beach:* popular swimming spot; 50 km N. *Gallipoli Beach:* location for the film *Gallipoli* (1981); 55 km N. *Scenic coastal drive:* between Mt Hope and Sheringa; 105 km N.

TOWNS NEARBY: Port Lincoln 38 km, Tumby Bay 64 km, Elliston 121 km, Cowell 169 km, Wudinna 174 km

Coonawarra

Pop. 310
Map ref. 548 A12 | 550 A2 | 568 G10

ⓘ 27 Arthur St, Penola; (08) 8737 2855; www.wattlerange.sa.gov.au

📻 96.1 Star FM, 1161 AM ABC South East

Unlike many other Australian wine regions, Coonawarra was a planned horticulture scheme – and a very successful one at that. John Riddoch, a Scottish immigrant, acquired extensive lands in South Australia's south-east in the late 1800s. He subdivided 800 hectares of his landholding specifically for orchards and vineyards. Prominent wine professionals such as Wolf Blass damned this region as a place that could never produce decent wine, and the original John Riddoch wine estate was nearly sold to the Department of Forestry and Lands (thankfully, David Wynn purchased the property and it is now Wynns Coonawarra). In the 1950s, large wine companies such as Penfolds and Yalumba finally began recognising the depth of the region's reds, and opinions began to change. Coonawarra's famed terra rossa (red earth) combined with the region's particular climate is now known to create some of the best cabernet sauvignon in the country, as well as excellent shiraz, merlot, riesling and chardonnay. Wynns Coonawarra produces world-class shiraz and cabernet sauvignon, some for purchase at reasonable prices. Other excellent wineries to visit are Balnaves of Coonawarra, Brands of Coonawarra, Majella and Zema Estate. *See Penola.*

 Coonawarra Cup: Jan. *Coonawarra After Dark:* cellar doors open in the evenings; Apr. *Penola Coonawarra Festival:* arts, food and wine; May. *Coonawarra Cellar Dwellers:* July. *Cabernet Celebrations:* Oct.

🍴 *Coonawarra Jack Cafe:* traditional cafe fare; Coonawarra Jack Winery, Riddoch Hwy; (08) 8736 3065. *Fodder:* casual dining with excellent wine list; 5 Memorial Dr; (08) 8736 3170. *Upstairs at Hollick:* elegant winery dining; Hollick Wines, cnr Riddoch Hwy and Ravenswood La; (08) 8737 2752.

TOWNS NEARBY: Penola 9 km, Naracoorte 38 km, Edenhope (Vic.) 50 km, Millicent 55 km, Casterton (Vic.) 60 km

Cowell

Pop. 883
Map ref. 556 B1 | 558 G5

ⓘ Main St; (08) 8629 2588.

📻 89.9 Magic FM, 639 AM ABC North and West

This pleasant Eyre Peninsula township is on the almost land-locked Franklin Harbour – its entrance is merely 100 metres wide. Matthew Flinders sailed past here in 1802 and, understandably, mistook the harbour for a large lagoon. The sandy beach is safe for swimming and the fishing is excellent. Oyster farming is a relatively new local industry, and fresh oysters can be purchased year-round. The world's oldest and perhaps largest jade deposit is in the district. Discovered in the Minbrie Range in 1965, the deposit is believed to have been formed around 1700 million years ago by the shifting of the earth's surface.

continued on p. 234

COOBER PEDY

Pop. 1470
Map ref. 562 A10 | 565 O10

i Coober Pedy Information Centre, Hutchison St;
(08) 8672 5298 or 1800 637 076; www.cooberpedy.sa.gov.au

104.5 Dusty Radio FM, 106.1 FM ABC Local

On 1 February 1915 a group of gold prospectors discovered opal in the area surrounding Coober Pedy. It was to become the biggest opal field in the world, which today provides around 80 per cent of the world's gem-quality opals. The name Coober Pedy is derived from the Aboriginal phrase 'Kupa Piti', loosely translating to 'white man's hole in the ground'. The town's unique underground style of living was first established by soldiers returning from World War I who were used to trench life. Today much of the population call the 'dugouts' home – as ideal places to escape the severe summer temperatures and cold winter nights. The landscape of Coober Pedy is desolate and harsh, dotted with thousands of mines. It is also home to one of the most unique golf courses in the world.

Umoona Opal Mine and Museum This award-winning underground centre provides an all-round look at Coober Pedy. A detailed town history and an Aboriginal interpretive centre comprehensively document Coober Pedy's evolution. Experience 'dugout' life in an underground home or mine life on an on-site mine tour. An excellent documentary on Coober Pedy is shown in the underground cinema. Hutchison St; (08) 8672 5228.

Old Timers Mine: museum in an original 1916 mine featuring 3 large opal seams and interpretive centre with self-guide walk; Crowders Gully Rd. *Underground churches:* St Peter and St Pauls was the first underground church in the world; Hutchison St. Other interesting churches include the Catacomb Church on Catacomb Rd and the Serbian Orthodox Church with its 'ballroom' style. *Desert Cave:* international underground hotel with shopping complex and display gallery detailing the early hardships of miners in Coober Pedy; 8am–8pm daily; Hutchison St. *Underground Art Gallery:* works of central Australian artists, including Aboriginal pieces; Hutchison St. *Opal retailers:* outlets offer jewellery and stone sales. Many demonstrate the skill required to cut and polish opals; 10am–6pm; (08) 8672 5985. *Big Winch Lookout:* monument and lookout over town; Italian Club Rd. *Outback scenic and charter flights:* local and outback tours; depart from airport; bookings (08) 8672 3067. *Mine tours:* to local mines; contact visitor centre.

Opal Festival: Easter. *Coober Pedy Greek Glendi:* celebration of Greek culture; July. *Horseracing:* Aug.

Tom & Mary's Greek Taverna: famous Greek cafe; Hutchinson St; (08) 8672 5622.

Oasis Tourist Park: Hutchison St; (08) 8672 5169. *Opal Inn Caravan Park:* Lot 1 Hutchison St; (08) 8672 5054. *Stuart Range Caravan Park:* Cnr Stuart Hwy and Hutchison St; (08) 8672 5179.

Moon Plain and the Breakaways The rocky landscape of Moon Plain (15 km NE) has been the backdrop for many movies, especially those with a science-fiction bent. Likewise, the 40 sq km reserve of the Breakaways (30 km N). The unique arid landscape of flat-topped outcrops and stony gibber desert

[THE BREAKAWAYS, NEAR COOBER PEDY]

is breathtaking, as is the wildlife that has adapted to these harsh conditions. Passes to the reserve are available from the visitor centre and other outlets in town. Return via the road past part of the Dog Fence, a 5300 km fence built to protect sheep properties in the south from wild dogs.

Coober Pedy Golf Course Play on a unique 18-hole grassless course. The only golf club in the world with reciprocal playing rights with the 'home of golf', St Andrews in Scotland. Night Golf is available by appointment, minimum of 4 people; (08) 8672 3535; 3.5 km N.

The Mail Run This overland adventure is a unique way of discovering the remote outback. Travelling with Coober Pedy's mailman, the tour travels past waterholes and through scenic landscapes on its delivery run to Oodnadatta, William Creek and the remote cattle stations in between. Travelling 600 km over outback roads and the renowned Oodnadatta Track, the mailman offers up fascinating stories and history of the landscape and people. Tours depart from the Underground Bookshop at 9am on Mon and Thurs; bookings (08) 8672 5226 or 1800 069 911.

Underground Pottery: handmade pottery depicting the colours and landscape of the desert; 2 km W. *William Creek:* the smallest town in the state. Flights offered over Lake Eyre; 166 km E. *Painted Desert:* rich colours paint the Arckaringa Hills, also noted for flora and fauna; 234 km N.

Travellers note: *Opal fields are pocked with diggings. Beware of unprotected mine shafts. Avoid entering any field area unless escorted. For safety reasons, visitors to the mines are advised to join a tour. Trespassers on claims can be fined a minimum of $1000. Coober Pedy is the last stop for petrol between Cadney Homestead (151 km N) and Glendambo (252 km S).*

TOWNS NEARBY: Oodnadatta 174 km

 RADIO STATIONS   IN TOWN   WHAT'S ON   WHERE TO EAT   WHERE TO STAY   NEARBY

 SOUTH AUSTRALIA

Franklin Harbour Historical Museum: in the old post office and its attached residence (1888), now operated by the National Trust and featuring local history displays; closed Mon and Tues; Main St; (08) 8629 2686. *Ruston Proctor Steam Tractor Museum:* open-air agricultural museum; Lincoln Hwy. *Cowell Jade Motel:* showroom and sales of local jade jewellery; Lincoln Hwy. *Turner Aquaculture:* tours of an oyster factory; Oyster Dr. *Foreshore and Mangrove Boardwalk:* ideal for a picnic, with barbecue area and adventure playground for the kids; The Esplanade. *Boat hire:* from the caravan park.

Fireworks Night: includes street party; Dec.

Cowell Foreshore Caravan Park & Holiday Units: The Esplanade; (08) 8629 2307. *Harbour View Caravan Park:* Harbour View Dr; (08) 8629 2216.

Scenic drive: 20 km drive south to Port Gibbon along a coast renowned for its history of wrecked and sunken ketches; interpretive signs detail the history at each site. *Franklin Harbour Conservation Park:* coastal peninsula park of sand dunes and mangrove habitat, popular for bush camping and fishing; 5 km s. *May Gibbs Memorial:* marks the location of children's author May Gibbs' first home; Cleve Rd; 10 km s. *The Knob:* good fishing from sheltered beach and rocks; 13 km s. *Lucky Bay:* safe swimming for children and the start of a 4WD track to Victoria Point with excellent views of the harbour. Sea SA operates a ferry from here to Wallaroo on the Yorke Peninsula 4 times a day on weekdays and twice a day on weekends; bookings (08) 8823 0777; 16 km E. *Port Gibbon:* old shipping port with remains of original jetty. Sea lions are visible from the short walk to the point; 25 km s. *Yeldulknie Weir and Reservoir:* picnics and walking; 37 km w. *Cleve:* a service town with murals depicting its early days and an observation point at Tickleberry Hill; 42 km w. *Arno Bay:* a holiday town with sandy beaches and a jetty for fishing. Regular yacht races are held on Sun in summer; 44 km sw.

TOWNS NEARBY: **Wallaroo 71 km, Moonta 75 km, Kimba 76 km, Kadina 80 km, Whyalla 94 km**

Crystal Brook
Pop. 1188
Map ref. 559 I4 | 560 H12

i Port Pirie Regional Tourism and Arts Centre, 3 Mary Elie St, Port Pirie; (08) 8633 8700 or 1800 000 424.

105.1 Trax FM, 639 AM ABC North and West

Crystal Brook serves the sheep and wheat country at the southern point of the Flinders Ranges. It once formed part of a vast sheep station, Crystal Brook Run, which extended from the current town to Port Pirie in the north-west. The country feel of the town begins on entering the tree-lined main street.

 National Trust Old Bakehouse Museum: local history collection in the town's first 2-storey building; open 2–4pm Sun and public holidays, or by appt; Brandis St; (08) 8636 2328. *Crystal Crafts:* local craft; Bowman St. *Creekside parks:* popular spots for picnics.

Crystal Brook Show: Aug.

 Crystal Brook Caravan Park: Eyre Rd; (08) 8636 2640. *Gladstone Caravan Park:* West Tce, Gladstone; (08) 8662 2522. *Laura Brewery Bed & Breakfast:* 8 West Tce, Laura; (08) 8663 2251. *Laura Caravan Park:* Mill St, Laura; (08) 8663 2296. *Stone Hut Cottages:* 1 Main North Rd, Laura; (08) 8663 2165.

The Big Goanna: we love our things big, be it fruit, rocking horses, or in this case, reptiles; 3 km N. *Bowman Fauna Park:* enjoyable walks, including part of the Heysen Trail, around ruins of the Bowman family property, Crystal Brook Run (1847); 8 km E. *Koolunga:* a small community, home to the mythical bunyip – in 1883 2 attempts to capture the beast were unsuccessful. Also craft outlets and the Bunyip River Walk on the banks of Broughton River; 10 km E. *Gladstone:* set in rich rural country in the Rocky River Valley. Heritage-listed Gladstone Gaol offers daily tours. Try traditional soft drinks, including Old Style Ginger Beer, at the Trends Drink Factory in Sixth Ave (open weekdays) or discover the town's history on foot by picking up a map from the caravan park; 21 km NE. *Redhill:* riverside walk, museum, craft shop and antique shop; 25 km s. *Laura:* boyhood home of C. J. Dennis, author of *The Songs of a Sentimental Bloke*, known for its cottage crafts, art galleries and historic buildings. Leaflet available for self-guide walking tour from Biles Art Gallery, Herbert St. The Folk Fair each Apr brings thousands of visitors to the town; 32 km N. West of town is the Beetaloo Valley and Reservoir, a pleasant picnic spot in cooler months. *Snowtown:* surrounded by large salt lakes that change colour according to weather conditions. Lake View Drive is a scenic 6 km drive around the lakes. Lochiel–Ninnes Rd Lookout provides panoramic country and lake views; 50 km s.

TOWNS NEARBY: **Port Pirie 25 km, Port Broughton 37 km, Jamestown 40 km, Melrose 58 km, Clare 65 km**

Edithburgh
Pop. 394
Map ref. 556 E8 | 558 H9

i Cnr Weaver and Towler sts, Stansbury; (08) 8852 4577; www.yorkepeninsula.com.au

98.9 Flow FM, 1044 5CS AM

Edithburgh is located on the foreshore at the south-eastern tip of Yorke Peninsula. This is an area synonymous with shipwrecks and, although reflecting tragic maritime days of old, it is a source of excitement for the diving enthusiast. Despite the construction of a lighthouse in 1856, over 26 vessels were wrecked on the coast between West Cape in Innes National Park and Troubridge Point just south of Edithburgh. Today Edithburgh is a popular coastal holiday destination overlooking Gulf St Vincent and Troubridge Island.

 Edithburgh Museum: a community museum with local history of the town and region featuring a historical maritime collection; open 2–4pm Sun and public holidays, or by appt; Edith St; (08) 8852 6187. *Native Flora Park:* walk through eucalypts and casuarinas and see a variety of birdlife; Ansty Tce. *Bakehouse Arts and Crafts:* local handcrafts and produce in a historic 1890 building; Blanche St. *Town jetty:* built in 1873 to service large shipments of salt found inland, it offers views to Troubridge Island and is popular with anglers; end of Edith St. *Natural tidal pool:* excellent for swimming; foreshore. *Nature walks:* south to Sultana Point or north to Coobowie.

Gala Day: family day of entertainment and stalls; Oct.

Edithburgh Caravan Park & Tourist Park: O'Halloran Pde; (08) 8852 6056. *Coobowie Caravan Park:* 23 Beach Rd, Coobowie; (08) 8852 8132.

Dive sites Discover the south coast of Yorke Peninsula with *The Investigator Strait Maritime Heritage Trail* brochure that includes the history and maps of 26 dive sites. By far the worst recorded shipwreck was that of the *Clan Ranald*, a huge steel steamer that, through incompetence and greed, was wrecked in 1909 just west of Troubridge Hill. The disaster claimed 40 lives – 36 bodies were later buried in the Edithburgh Cemetery.

Wattle Point Wind Farm: currently Australia's largest wind farm with 55 turbines; free viewing area 3km sw of Edithburgh. *Sultana Point:* fishing and swimming; 2 km s. *Coobowie:* a coastal town popular for swimming; 5 km N. *Troubridge Island Conservation Park:* home to penguins, black-faced shags and crested terns; tours available (30 min by boat) from town. *Scenic drive:* west along the coast to Innes National Park; *see Yorketown.*

TOWNS NEARBY: Yorketown 15 km, Stansbury 20 km, Minlaton 37 km, Port Victoria 69 km, Ardrossan 75 km

Elliston
Pop. 199
Map ref. 558 B5

 Town Hall, 6 Memorial Dr; (08) 8687 9200.

 89.5 Magic FM, 693 AM ABC Eyre Peninsula and West Coast

Nestled in a range of hills on the shores of picturesque Waterloo Bay is the small community of Elliston. The waters of the bay used to have rich abalone beds, but fierce exploitation in the 1960s decimated them. Thanks to a hatchery and rehabilitation, the abalone population is now back on the increase. The rugged and scenic coastline is spectacular and – with its excellent fishing and safe swimming beaches – Elliston is becoming a popular holiday destination. The 12-kilometre stretch of coast north of Elliston, known as Elliston's Great Ocean View, is said to rival the landscape of Victoria's Great Ocean Road, but on a smaller scale.

Town Hall Mural: the Southern Hemisphere's largest mural, which represents the history of the town and district; Main St. *Jetty:* the heritage-listed 1889 jetty has been restored and is lit by night.

Sculptures on the Cliff: Anzac Day weekend Apr. *Australian Salmon Fishing Competition:* June–Aug.

Elliston Caravan Park & Camping Area: 2 Flinders Hwy; (08) 8687 9061. *Elliston Waterloo Bay Tourist Park:* Beach Tce; (08) 8687 9076.

Elliston's Great Ocean View: scenic cliff-top drive north of town to adjacent Anxious Bay, with fabulous coastal views. Along the way is Blackfellows, reputedly one of the best surfing beaches in Australia. *Anxious Bay:* good fishing from beach and ledges for King George whiting. The boat ramp here provides access to Waldegrave Island (4 km offshore) and Flinders Island (35 km offshore), both good for fishing and seal-spotting (seek local advice about conditions before departing). *Locks Well:* a long stairwell down to a famous salmon-fishing and surf beach with coastal lookout; 12 km SE. *Walkers Rock:* good beaches for swimming and rock-fishing; 15 km N. *Lake Newland Conservation Park:* significant dunes separate the park's salt lakes and wetlands from the sea. Walk along bush tracks or try a spot of fishing; 26 km N. *Scenic drive:* to Sheringa (40 km SE). From Sheringa Beach, a popular fishing spot, see whales, dolphins and seals offshore. *Talia Caves:* spectacular scene of caves with waves crashing on edge. Another good spot for beach-fishing; 45 km N.

TOWNS NEARBY: Wudinna 85 km, Streaky Bay 113 km, Coffin Bay 121 km, Tumby Bay 138 km, Port Lincoln 150 km

Gawler
Pop. 20 002
Map ref. 553 E2 | 559 J8 | 568 C2

 2 Lyndoch Rd; (08) 8522 9260; www.gawler.sa.gov.au

89.1 BBB FM, 639 AM ABC North and West

Set in the fork of the North and South Parra rivers and surrounded by rolling hills, it is no wonder that Gawler was picked, in 1839, as the site of South Australia's first country town. The grand architecture of that era can be seen in its stately homes and buildings, especially in the Church Hill State Heritage Area. Gawler is today a major service centre to a thriving agricultural district and has a growing Adelaide commuter population.

Historical walking trail The excellent trail brochure guides the visitor past stately buildings and homes, many with original cast-iron lacework. The Church Hill State Heritage Area provides a fascinating snapshot of town planning in the 1830s, and the 2.4 km walk around it includes a look at several churches, the old school, the courthouse, and cottages of the Victorian era. Also on the way are Gawler Mill, Eagle Foundry (now a popular B&B), the Anglican Church with its pipe organ (open Sun) and Para Para Mansion (1862), a grand mansion that features a domed ballroom and has had British royalty as its guests (closed to public).

Gawler Museum: located in the Old Telegraph Station, this National Trust museum displays the history of Gawler's pioneer past; closed Sat–Mon; Murray St. *The Food Forest:* award-winning permaculture farm producing 160 varieties of organically certified food; tours available; on the Gawler River. *Fielke Cricket Bats:* the only cricket bat maker in South Australia, visit the workshop and see how the English Willow bats are meticulously handcrafted; Crown St. *Dead Man's Pass Reserve:* so named because an early pioneer was found dead in the hollow of a tree. It has picnic facilities and a walking trail; southern end of Murray St. *Community Art Gallery:* local artwork on display; 23rd St. *Adelaide Soaring Club:* glider flights over Gawler and region; Wells Rd; (08) 8522 1877.

Markets: Gawler Railway Station; Sun mornings. *Antique and Collectors Auction:* Gawler Greyhound Pavillion; 1st Sun each month. *Band Festival:* Mar. *Gawler Gourmet and Heritage Festival:* even-numbered years, Apr. *Barossa Cup:* horseracing; May. *Gawler Show:* Aug. *Christmas Street Festival:* Dec.

Eagle Foundry Bed & Breakfast: 23 King St; (08) 8522 3808. *Gawler Caravan Park:* Main North Rd; (08) 8522 3805. *Gawler Churchhill Mews Bed & Breakfast:* 19 Cowan St; (08) 8522 1244. *Oxley Farm:* Fairlie Rd, Kangaroo Flat; (08) 8522 3703.

Roseworthy Agricultural Museum: a dryland farming museum featuring vintage farm equipment, located at the Roseworthy campus of the University of Adelaide; open every Wed and 3rd Sun each month; (08) 8303 7739; 15 km N. *Freeling:* a rural town with a self-guide historical walk; 17 km NE. *Two Wells:* named for 2 Aboriginal wells found by original settlers, forgotten, then recovered in 1967. It has craft shops with local crafts; Main Rd; 24 km w. *Stockport Astronomical Facility:* run by the Astronomical Society of SA, featuring impressive observatory with public viewing nights; (08) 8338 1231; 30 km N.

TOWNS NEARBY: Lyndoch 13 km, Tanunda 21 km, Nuriootpa 27 km, Angaston 30 km, Birdwood 31 km

SOUTH AUSTRALIA

Goolwa

Pop. 5881
Map ref. 559 J11 | 568 C4

 Signal Point River Murray Interpretive Centre, Goolwa Wharf; (08) 8555 3488; www.alexandrina.sa.gov.au

87.6 Alex FM, 639 AM ABC North and West

Goolwa is a rapidly growing holiday town on the last big bend of the Murray River before it reaches open waters. In 2007 Goolwa became the first town in Australia to be declared a Cittaslow, or 'slow town', joining a network of other towns in Europe and throughout the world which aim to improve the quality of life in towns. Goolwa was originally surveyed as the capital of South Australia, but Adelaide was later thought to be a better option. Goolwa did, however, boom as a river port from the 1850s to the 1880s – in the golden days of the riverboats. The area is excellent for fishing, with freshwater fishing in the Murray and saltwater fishing in the Southern Ocean and the Coorong, as well as boating, surfing, watersports, birdwatching and photography.

Signal Point River Murray Interpretive Centre Learn about the river and district before European settlement and see the impact of later development. There is also a detailed history on Goolwa's river port, the paddlesteamers and local Aboriginal people. A highlight is the 3D model showing how the Murray River interacts with the SA landscape. The Wharf.

National Trust Museum: documents the history of Goolwa and early navigation of the Murray River; Porter St. *South Coast Regional Arts Centre:* explore the restored old court and police station and see exhibitions by local artists; Goolwa Tce. *Goolwa Barrage:* desalination point to prevent salt water from reaching the Murray River; open Mon–Fri; Barrage Rd. *Armfield Slipway:* a working exhibition of wooden boatbuilding and restoration; open Tues mornings and Fri afternoons; Barrage Rd. *Horse-Drawn Railway Carriage:* first carriages used in SA between Goolwa and Port Elliot from 1854; Cadell St. *Goolwa Beach:* popular surfing and swimming beach with large cockles to be dug up (in season); end of Beach Rd. *Cockle Train:* journey around Encounter Bay from Goolwa Wharf to Victor Harbor, stopping at Port Elliot. The train has been operating since 1887, and its name comes from the abundance of large cockles found on Goolwa's surf beach. It forms part of the longer *SteamRanger* tourist railway from Mount Barker; *see Hahndorf;* operates most weekends and public/school holidays; bookings (08) 8231 4366. *Cruises:* day tours to the mouth of the Murray, the Coorong, the Barrages and the Lower Murray; details and bookings at visitor centre. *Scenic flights:* over the region; contact visitor centre for details. *Goolwa Heritage Walk:* a self-guide tour to see the 19th-century architecture of the river port's boom days; brochure available from visitor centre.

Goolwa Wharf Markets: 1st and 3rd Sun each month. *Milang to Goolwa Freshwater Sailing Classic:* Jan. *Wooden Boat Festival:* odd-numbered years, Mar.

Aquacaf: innovative riverside fare; 94 Barrage Rd, Goolwa South; (08) 8555 1235. *Blues Restaurant:* relaxed snacks and seafood; Main Goolwa Rd, Middleton; (08) 8554 1800.

Cape House Goolwa: 17 Wildman St; 0424 469 949. *Goolwa Camping & Tourist Park:* 40 Kessell Rd; (08) 8555 2144. *Goolwa Heritage Cottages – Jackling Cottage:* 18 Oliver St; 0433 571 927. *Joseph's Cottage:* 26 Brooking St; 0433 571 927. *Rose-Eden House:* 27 Cadell St; 0448 752 012.

Hindmarsh Island: Captain Sturt located the mouth of the Murray River from here in 1830 – visit the Captain Sturt Lookout and monument. The island is now popular for both freshwater and saltwater fishing and is home to the kid-friendly Narnu farm, which offers horseriding, cottage accommodation and the opportunity to milk a cow; east of town; farm bookings (08) 8555 2002. *Currency Creek Game Reserve:* feeding grounds, breeding rookeries and hides for many waterbirds; access by boat only; 3 km E. *Currency Creek:* Lions Park is a popular picnic spot with a walking track along the creek. Near town is an Aboriginal canoe tree (a eucalypt carved to make a canoe) and also the Currency Creek Winery with a restaurant and fauna park; 7 km N.

TOWNS NEARBY: Port Elliot 10 km, Victor Harbor 15 km, Strathalbyn 29 km, Willunga 33 km, McLaren Vale 38 km

Hahndorf

see inset box on page 238

Hawker

Pop. 225
Map ref. 557 A12 | 560 H8

 Hawker Motors, cnr Wilpena and Cradock rds; (08) 8648 4022 or 1800 777 880; www.hawkersa.info

105.9 Magic FM, 639 AM ABC North and West

This small outback town was once a thriving railway centre, and historic buildings are still well preserved in its streets. Hawker was also once an agricultural region producing bumper crops of wheat. Serious drought sent the crops into decline and the industry died. Today Hawker is the place to begin exploring the fantastic natural attractions of the southern Flinders Ranges.

Fred Teague's Museum: local history displays; Hawker Motors, cnr Wilpena and Cradock rds. *Jeff Morgan Gallery:* including a 30 m painting of the view from Wilpena Pound; Cradock Rd. *Heritage walk:* self-guide walk on numbered path; brochure from visitor centre. *Scenic flights and 4WD tours:* contact visitor centre for details.

Horseracing: May. *Art Exhibition:* Sept/Oct.

Flinders Ranges Caravan Park: Hawker–Leigh Creek Rd; (08) 8648 4266. *Rawnsley Park Station:* Wilpena Rd; (08) 8648 0008.

Jarvis Hill Lookout: walking trail with views over the countryside; 7 km SW. *Yourambulla Caves:* Aboriginal rock paintings in hillside caves; 12 km SW. *Willow Waters:* popular picnic spot with a short walk to Ochre Wall; 20 km E off Cradock Rd. *Moralana Scenic Drive:* 22 km drive with superb views of Wilpena Pound and the Elder Range; leaves Hawker–Wilpena Rd 23 km N. *Cradock:* a tiny town with National Heritage–listed St Gabriel's Church (1882); 26 km SE. *Kanyaka Homestead Historic Site:* ruins of the homestead, stables and woolshed once part of a large sheep run, with informative displays explaining the history of each ruin; 28 km SW. *Kanyaka Death Rock:* once an Aboriginal ceremonial site, it overlooks a permanent waterhole; near Kanyaka Homestead ruins. *Long-distance trails:* close to Hawker you can pick up sections of the Heysen (walking) and Mawson (cycling) trails; information from visitor centre.

TOWNS NEARBY: Wilpena 43 km, Quorn 62 km, Blinman 89 km, Wilmington 90 km, Port Augusta 91 km

Innamincka

Pop. 15
Map ref. 563 N7 | 618 F8

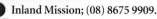 Inland Mission; (08) 8675 9909.

 1602 AM ABC North and West

This tiny settlement is built around a hotel and trading post on Cooper Creek. The first European explorer to visit the area was Charles Sturt, who discovered the Cooper in 1846 while vainly searching for an inland sea. It was also the final destination of the ill-fated Burke and Wills expedition. In 1860 all but one of Burke and Wills' party perished near the creek. John King survived owing to the outback skills of the Aboriginal people who found him. Innamincka was once a customs depot and service centre for surrounding pastoral properties, but now mainly services travellers, many of whom come from the south via the intrepid Strzelecki Track (for four-wheel-drive vehicles only).

 Australian Inland Mission Built in 1928 to service the medical needs of remote pastoral properties, this mission was attended by a rotating staff of 2 nurses on horseback. Injured workers, flood victims and even fallen jockeys from the races called on their expertise. The mission was abandoned in the early 1950s when the Royal Flying Doctor Service began providing services. The restored classic outback building now houses the national park's headquarters as well as a tribute museum to the nurses who faced the trials of this isolated region.

Boat hire and tours: fishing and cruising trips; contact hotel for details on (08) 8675 9901.

Picnic Race Meeting: Aug.

Innamincka Regional Reserve This isolated but spectacular reserve is popular with 4WD enthusiasts and nature lovers. It covers 13 800 sq km and comprises important wetland areas, the most impressive being Coongie Lakes (112 km NW). This internationally significant wetland area is a haven for wildlife, particularly waterbirds. Closer to Innamincka is Cullyamurra Waterhole, on Cooper Creek (16 km NE), for bush camping and fishing. Aboriginal rock carvings and the Cullyamurra Choke are accessible by foot at the eastern end of the waterhole. 4WD is essential in parts of the park; after heavy rains roads become impassable. A Desert Parks Pass is required; visit the Inland Mission in Innamincka or phone 1800 816 078.

Memorial plaques: to Charles Sturt and Burke and Wills; 2 km N. *Burke and Wills Dig Tree:* famous Dig Tree where supplies were buried for their expedition; 71 km across border in Qld. *Strzelecki Regional Reserve:* sand-dune desert country with birdwatching and camping at Montecollina Bore; 167 km SW.

Travellers note: *Motorists intending to travel along the Strzelecki Track should ring the Northern Roads Condition Hotline on 1300 361 033 to check conditions before departure. There are no supplies or petrol between Lyndhurst and Innamincka.*

TOWNS NEARBY: Tibooburra (NSW) 225 km, Birdsville (Qld) 247 km

Jamestown
Pop. 1408
Map ref. 559 J4 | 561 I11

(i) Country Retreat Caravan Park, 103 Ayr St; (08) 8664 0077; www. clarevalley.com.au

105.1 Trax FM, 639 AM ABC North and West

Jamestown survived the demise of wheat crops in the late 1800s to become an important service town to the thriving agricultural farmlands of the Clare Valley. John Bristow Hughes took up the first pastoral lease in 1841 and the strength of stud sheep and cattle farms, cereals, dairy produce and timber grew rapidly.

A look at the names of towns in South Australia will reveal that the governors, politicians and surveyors of the day were bent on commemorating themselves or people they liked. Jamestown followed this trend, named after Sir James Fergusson, then state governor.

 Railway Station Museum: a National Trust museum detailing local rail and Bundaleer Forest history and featuring the Both-designed iron lung (invented at Caltowie); Mannanarie Rd; (08) 8664 0522. *Heritage murals:* on town buildings. *Belalie Creek:* parks for picnics along the banks; floodlit at night. *Town and cemetery walks:* self-guide tours; brochure available from caravan park.

Producers Market: 1st Sun each month. *Bundaleer Forest Weekend:* fine music, food and wine in the autumn; Mar. *Jamestown Show:* largest 1-day show in SA; Oct. *Christmas Pageant:* Dec.

Jamestown Country Retreat Caravan Park: Cnr Ayr and Bute sts; (08) 8664 0077.

Bundaleer Forest Reserve This plantation forest, established in 1876, was the first in the world. Walking tracks start from the Arboretum, Georgetown Rd and the picnic area, and range from botanic walks to historic trails past building ruins and extensive dry-stone walls. The longer Mawson (cycling) and Heysen (walking) trails also travel through the reserve, as does a scenic drive from Jamestown, which then continues towards New Campbell Hill, Mt Remarkable and The Bluff. Each Easter Sunday the Bilby Easter Egg Hunt is held in the reserve. Spalding Rd; 9 km s.

Appila Springs: scenic picnic and camping spot; 31 km NW via Appila. *Spalding:* a town in the Broughton River valley. Picnic areas and excellent trout fishing; 34 km s.

TOWNS NEARBY: Peterborough 34 km, Crystal Brook 40 km, Port Pirie 55 km, Melrose 57 km, Burra 60 km

Kadina
Pop. 4026
Map ref. 556 E3 | 558 H6

(i) The Farm Shed Museum and Tourist Centre, 50 Moonta Rd; (08) 8821 2333 or 1800 654 991; www.yorkepeninsula.com.au

89.3 Gulf FM, 639 AM ABC North and West

Kadina exists solely as a result of the digging habits of wombats. In 1860 upturned ground from wombat diggings revealed copper. This was the starting point of coppermining on Yorke Peninsula. The wombats were commemorated by the naming of Kadina's 1862 hotel: Wombat Hotel. Kadina, along with Wallaroo and Moonta, formed part of a copper triangle colloquially named Little Cornwall because of the number of Cornish immigrants recruited to work in the mines. Kadina is now the commercial centre and largest town on Yorke Peninsula.

 The Farm Shed Museum and Tourist Centre: home to the Dry Land Farming Interpretative Centre; Matta House, former home to the mining manager's family; a 1950s style schoolroom; Kadina story, a display of the town's history; and the visitor information centre; Moonta Rd; (08) 8821 2333. *Ascot Theatre Gallery:* cultural centre exhibiting local artists' work, with sales; closed Sun; Graves St. *Victoria Square Park:* historic band rotunda and Wallaroo Mine Monument; Main St. *Heritage walk:* self-guide walk includes historic hotels such as the Wombat

continued on p. 239

 RADIO STATIONS   IN TOWN   WHAT'S ON   WHERE TO EAT   WHERE TO STAY    NEARBY

SOUTH AUSTRALIA

HAHNDORF

Pop. 1806
Map ref. 553 F9 | 559 K9 | 568 C3

ℹ️ Adelaide Hills Visitor Information Centre, 68 Main St; (08) 8388 1185; www.visitadelaidehills.com.au

📻 639 AM ABC North and West

In the heart of the Adelaide Hills is Hahndorf, Australia's oldest surviving German settlement. Prussian Lutheran refugees fleeing religious persecution in their homelands settled the area in the late 1830s. The town has retained a distinctly Germanic look and many local businesses and attractions are still operated by descendants of the original German pioneers. The surrounding countryside with its rolling hills, historic villages, vineyards, gourmet-produce farms and native bushland is renowned as a tourist destination.

Main Street: a mix of historic buildings, German-style bakeries, delis, cafes, restaurants and art and craft shops. *The Cedars:* historic paintings, gardens and home of famous landscape artist Hans Heysen; closed Sat; Heysen Rd. *Hahndorf Academy:* displays work of local artists in SA's largest regional gallery; Main St. *Clocks and Collectables:* housed in a historic butcher shop specialising in cuckoo and grandfather clocks; Mt Barker Rd. *Hahndorf Farm Barn:* interactive farm animal shows, with petting and feeding; Mt Barker Rd. *Hillstowe Wines:* wine and cheese tastings; Main St. *Hahndorf Hill Winery:* boutique cool-climate winery with tastings and the ChocoVino Experience (fine chocolates matched to wines); open weekends; Pains Rd. *Beerenberg Strawberry Farm:* balcony viewing of the farm and packing area, jam and condiment sales, and berry-picking Oct–May; Mt Barker Rd. *Historic Hahndorf:* obtain

[THE CEDARS, HOME OF ARTIST HANS HEYSEN]

A Guide to Historic Hahndorf, which lists 42 historic properties; available from visitor centre.

🎉 *Heysen Festival:* major 10-day event celebrating the life of Hans Heysen, with the Heysen Art Prize, food, wine and entertainment; Sept–Oct. *Oktoberfest:* Oct.

🍴 *The Lane Vineyard Bistro & Cellar Door:* chic menu and fine views; Ravenswood La; (08) 8388 1250. *Udder Delights Cheese Cellar:* snacks, platters and cheese tastings; 91A Main Rd; (08) 8388 1588. *The Organic Market & Cafe:* famed hills fare; 5 Druid Ave, Stirling; (08) 8339 7131. *Petaluma's Bridgewater Mill Restaurant:* sublime modern cuisine; Petaluma Wines, Mt Barker Rd, Bridgewater; (08) 8339 9200.

🛏️ *Amble At Hahndorf:* 10 Hereford Ave; 0408 105 610. *Fairview Ridge Bed & Breakfast:* Section 713, Fairview Rd; (08) 8388 1498. *The RockBare Retreat:* 102–104 Main St; (08) 8388 7155. *Adelaide Hills Bed & Breakfast Accommodation:* 35 Garrod Cres, Stirling; (08) 8339 1898. *Aldgate Lodge:* 27 Strathalbyn Rd, Aldgate; (08) 8370 9957. *Burdett's Country Retreats:* Burdetts Rd, Basket Range; (08) 8390 0296. *Dumas House:* 11 Druids Ave, Mount Barker; 0417 814 815. *Hannah's Cottage Bed & Breakfast:* 44 Jones Rd, Balhannah; 0408 838 124. *Liebelt House:* Junction Rd, Littlehampton; (08) 8391 2696. *Mt Barker Caravan & Tourist Park:* 40 Cameron Rd, Mount Barker; (08) 8391 0384. *Osteria Sanso Restaurant & Accommodation:* 14 Old Princes Hwy, Kanmantoo; (08) 8538 5008. *Thorngrove:* 2 Glenside La, Crafers; (08) 8339 6748. *Willowbank Cottage:* 65B Junction Rd, Littlehampton; (08) 8398 3364.

Cleland Conservation Park This park protects a variety of vegetation, from the stringybark forests in the highlands to the woods and grasses of the lowlands. It also includes panoramic views from the Mount Lofty Summit viewing platform. A highlight is the award-winning Cleland Wildlife Park where many native animals wander freely about. Kids will enjoy the daily animal-feeding shows and the fabulous guided night tours. Bookings (08) 8339 2444. For a rich cultural experience, take the guided Aboriginal tour on the Yurridla Trail where Dreamtime stories come alive. Mount Lofty Summit Rd; 14 km NW.

Belair National Park The oldest national park in SA was declared in 1891. There are plenty of activities, including 5 defined bushwalks ranging from the easy Wood Duck Walk to the more challenging 6.5 km Waterfall Walk, and cycling and horseriding tracks. Visitors can also visit Old Government House, built in 1859 to serve as the governor's summer residence (open Sun and public holidays); (08) 8278 5477; 19 km W.

Mount Barker: a historic town renowned for its gourmet outlets. The *SteamRanger* tourist train operates from here, including regular trips to Strathalbyn and on to the coastal section from Goolwa to Victor Harbor (this section is known as the Cockle Train; *see Goolwa*). For *SteamRanger* information and bookings contact 1300 655 991. Local events include the Highland Gathering and Heritage Festival in Feb; 6 km SE. *Bridgewater:* a historic town with excellent gardens and Petaluma's Bridgewater

Mill, which has wine-tastings, sales and an up-market restaurant for lunch in a historic flour mill; 6 km w. *Oakbank:* craft shops and historic buildings with self-guide heritage-walk brochure available from local businesses. The Oakbank Easter Racing Carnival, held each April, is the Southern Hemisphere's biggest picnic race meeting and brings thousands of visitors to the town each year; 7 km N. *Aldgate:* a historic village featuring art and craft shops and historic sites that include the Aldgate Pump and the National Trust–listed Stangate House with its extensive camellia garden; 8 km w. *Stirling:* renowned for its European gardens and architecture, including the National Estate–listed Beechworth Heritage Garden (Snows Rd). See colourful parrots in the aviaries at Stirling Parrot Farm (Milan Tce); 10 km w. *Warrawong Sanctuary:* large native animal reserve for reintroduced and endangered species, with walking trails and a boardwalk around Platypus Lakes. Guided dawn and evening tours are available; bookings (08) 8370 9197; 10 km sw via Mylor. *Jupiter Creek Goldfields:* walking trails with interpretive signs across historic fields discovered in 1852; 12 km sw. *Woodside Heritage Village:* includes Melba's Chocolate Factory (with guided tours and sales) as well as craft studios with artisans at work; Woodside; 13 km NE. *Mount Lofty Botanic Gardens:* Australia's largest botanic gardens, with walking trails past cool-climate garden species, on the eastern face of Mt Lofty; access via Summit or Piccadilly rds; 14 km NW. *Wittunga Botanic Gardens:* native plants; Shepherds Hill Rd; 21 km w at Blackwood.

TOWNS NEARBY: Strathalbyn 27 km, Birdwood 27 km, McLaren Vale 32 km, Willunga 36 km, Aldinga Beach 42 km

---

and the Royal Exchange with iron-lace balconies and shady verandahs; brochure from visitor centre.

 Kernewek Lowender: Cornish festival held with Wallaroo and Moonta; odd-numbered years, May. *Kadina Show:* Aug.

Kadina Caravan Park: Lindsay Tce; (08) 8821 2259.

Yorke Peninsula Field Days: Australia's oldest field days, started in 1884, are held each Sept (odd-numbered years); Paskeville; 19 km SE.

TOWNS NEARBY: Wallaroo 9 km, Moonta 16 km, Port Broughton 45 km, Maitland 46 km, Ardrossan 54 km

Kangaroo Island

see Kingscote

Kapunda

Pop. 2479
Map ref. 559 K7 | 568 C1

Cnr Hill and Main sts; (08) 8566 2902; www.clarevalley.com.au

99.5 Flow FM, 1062 AM ABC Riverland

Kapunda is between two wine districts – the Barossa Valley and the Clare Valley – but its history is very different. Copper was discovered here by Francis Dutton, a sheep farmer, in 1842. It was to be the highest-grade copper ore found in the world. Settlement followed, and Kapunda came into existence as Australia's first coppermining town. When the mines closed in 1878, Australia's 'cattle king' Sir Sidney Kidman moved in, eventually controlling 26 million hectares of land across Australia.

Kapunda Museum: excellent folk museum with a short Kapunda history film and displays of old agricultural machinery, an original fire engine and other vehicles in the pavilion. Detailed mining history is in Bagot's Fortune interpretive centre; open 1–4pm daily; Hill St; (08) 8566 2286. *Community Gallery:* significant regional gallery with local and touring art exhibitions; Cnr Main and Hill sts. *'Map Kernow':* 8 m bronze statue commemorating early miners, many of whom migrated from Cornwall in England; end of Main St at southern entrance of town. *High school's main building:* former residence of Sir Sidney Kidman; West Tce. *Gundry's Hill Lookout:* views over township and surrounding countryside; West Tce. *Heritage trail:* 10 km self-guide tour through town and historic Kapunda Copper Mine; *Discovering Historic Kapunda* brochure available at visitor centre.

Farm Fair: including fashion, craft and antiques; odd-numbered years, Apr/May. *Celtic Music Festival:* Sept (can vary). *Kapunda Show:* Nov.

The Wheatsheaf Pub: revamped pub, hearty food; Burra Rd, Allendale North; (08) 8566 2198.

Blue Gum Retreat: Greenock–Kapunda Rd; (08) 8563 4020. *Kapunda Tourist & Leisure Park:* Montefiore St; (08) 8566 2094. *Anlaby:* Anlaby Rd, Bagot Well; (08) 8566 2465. *Riverton Caravan Park:* Cnr Oxford Tce and Torrens Rd, Riverton; (08) 8847 2419.

Pines Reserve: nature and wildlife reserve; 6 km NW on road to Tarlee. *Anlaby Station:* historic Dutton Homestead and gardens, once a setting for large prestigious parties. Also a coach collection and historic station buildings; open 10am–4pm Wed–Sun; Anlaby Rd; 16 km NE. *Tarlee:* historic local-stone buildings; 16 km NW. *Riverton:* a historic town in the Gilbert Valley, once a stopover point for copper-hauling bullock teams. Many historic buildings remain, including the heritage-listed railway station and Scholz Park Museum, which incorporates a cottage, blacksmith and wheelwright shop; open 1–4pm weekends; 30 km NW. *Scenic drive:* 28 km drive north-east through sheep, wheat and dairy country to Eudunda.

TOWNS NEARBY: Nuriootpa 16 km, Tanunda 21 km, Angaston 22 km, Lyndoch 29 km, Gawler 33 km

Keith

Pop. 1089
Map ref. 568 F6

BP Southbound, cnr Riddock and Dukes hwys; (08) 8755 1700; www.tatiara.sa.gov.au

104.5 5TCB FM, 1062 AM ABC Riverland

Keith is a farming town in the area formerly known as the Ninety Mile Desert. Settlers found the original land unpromising, but the area has since been transformed from infertile pasture to productive farmland with the addition to the soil of missing trace elements and water piped from the Murray.

 Congregational Church: National Trust church with 11 locally made leadlight windows depicting the town's life and pioneering history; Heritage St. **Early Settler's Cottage:** limestone pioneer cottage; open by appt; Heritage St; (08) 8755 1118. **Keith Water Feature:** water sculpture; Heritage St.

Keith Show: Oct.

Ashwood Park Bed & Breakfast: 299 Park Tce; (08) 8755 3460. **Havelock House Bed & Breakfast:** Amberley, Riddoch Hwy; (08) 8755 3103. **Keith Caravan Park:** Naracoorte Rd; (08) 8755 1957. **McIntyre Cottage B&B:** 3 Tolmer Tce; (08) 8755 1126.

Ngarkat group of conservation parks Protecting 262 700 ha of sand dunes, mallee and heath are the 4 adjacent conservation parks – Ngarkat, Scorpion Springs, Mt Rescue and Mt Shaugh. The walking trails are an excellent introduction to the region's vegetation. Birdwatching is particularly good at Rabbit Island (Mt Rescue) and Comet Bore (Ngarkat). For panoramic views, try walking to the summit of Mt Rescue, Goose Hill or Mt Shaugh. Visitors can drive through the parks on the Pinaroo–Bordertown Rd. The main entrance is via Snozwells Rd near Tintinara.

Monster Conservation Park: scenic views and picnic spots; 10 km s. **Tintinara Homestead:** one of the first homesteads in the area, with woolshed, shearers quarters and pioneer cottage; caters for visitors; 38 km NW. **Mt Boothby Conservation Park:** mallee scrub, granite outcrops and wildflowers in spring; 58 km NW via Tintinara.

TOWNS NEARBY: Bordertown 44 km, Kingston S.E. 93 km, Naracoorte 101 km, Meningie 102 km, Pinnaroo 106 km

Kimba

Pop. 636
Map ref. 558 F4 | 560 D11

ⓘ Kimba Mobil Roadhouse, Eyre Hwy; (08) 8627 2040; www.kimba.sa.gov.au

📻 89.9 Magic FM, 1485 AM ABC Eyre Peninsula and West Coast

A small town on the Eyre Peninsula, Kimba is 'halfway across Australia' according to the huge sign on the Eyre Highway. It is the gateway to the outback, a fact that explorer Edward John Eyre confirmed when he traversed the harsh landscape in 1839. Early settlers thought the country too arid for settlement and it wasn't until demand for wheat production grew, and rail services were extended to the area in 1913, that the Kimba region developed. It is now major sheep- and wheat-farming country.

 Kimba and Gawler Ranges Historical Museum: a 'living' museum featuring local history and a Pioneer House (1908), a blacksmith's shop and 'Clancy' the fire truck; open 1.30–4pm Sat (closed Jan) or by appt; Eyre Hwy; (08) 8627 2349. **Halfway Across Australia Gem Shop and the Big Galah:** standing 8 m high, the Big Galah is in front of the gem shop, which offers sales of local gemstones, carved emu eggs, opal and locally mined jade, including rare black jade; Eyre Hwy. **Pine 'n' Pug Gallery:** local craft; High St. **Roora Walking Trail:** meanders through 3 km of bushland to White Knob Lookout; starts at north-eastern outskirts of town.

Kimba Show: Sept.

Lake Gilles Conservation Park: habitat for mallee fowl; 20 km NE. **Caralue Bluff:** popular for rock climbing; 20 km SW.

Carappee Hill Conservation Park: bush camping and walking; 25 km SW. **Darke Peak:** excellent views from the summit and a memorial at the base to John Charles Darke, an explorer who was speared to death in 1844; 40 km SW. **Pinkawillinie Conservation Park:** the largest mallee vegetation area on the peninsula and a habitat for small desert birds, emus and western grey kangaroos; turn-off 50 km W.

TOWNS NEARBY: Cowell 76 km, Wudinna 90 km, Whyalla 108 km, Tumby Bay 140 km, Wallaroo 143 km

Kingscote
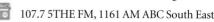 *see inset box on page 242*

Kingston S.E.
Pop. 1632
Map ref. 568 E8

ⓘ Kingston District Council Offices and Chamber, 29 Holland St; (08) 8767 2036; www.kingstondc.sa.gov.au

📻 107.7 5THE FM, 1161 AM ABC South East

Known as the 'Gateway to the South East', Kingston S.E. is at the southern end of Coorong National Park on Lacepede Bay. The area was once home to the Ngarrindjeri, river people who mastered the waterways of the Coorong and the Murray River. This famous lobster town was established in 1858 and its shallow lakes and lagoons are a haven for birdlife and a delight for photographers.

 National Trust Museum: pioneer museum; open 2–4.30pm daily during school holidays, or by appt; Cooke St; (08) 8767 2114. **Cape Jaffa Lighthouse:** built in the 1860s on the Margaret Brock Reef, it was dismantled and re-erected on its current site in the 1970s; open 2–4.30pm daily during school holidays, or by appt; Marine Pde; (08) 8767 2591. **Analematic Sundial:** an unusual sundial, 1 of only 8 in the world; on an island in the creek adjacent to Apex Park in East Tce. **Aboriginal burial ground:** Dowdy St. **Power House engine:** historic engine that produced the town's energy until 1974; Lions Park, Holland St. **The Big Lobster:** 17 m high 'Larry Lobster' has sales of cooked lobster; Princes Hwy.

Fishing Contest: Jan.

Kingston Caravan Park: 34 Marine Pde, Kingston S.E.; (08) 8767 2050.

 Butchers Gap Conservation Park: this important coastal park provides a winter refuge for bird species. Follow the walking trail from the carpark; 6 km SW. **The Granites:** rocky outcrops, a striking sight from the beach; 18 km N. **Cape Jaffa:** scenic drive south-west from Kingston S.E. leads to this small fishing village popular with anglers and divers. The Cape Jaffa Seafood and Wine Festival is held here each Jan; 18 km SW. **Mt Scott Conservation Park:** part of a former coastal dune system, with walks through stringybark forest; 20 km E. **Jip Jip Conservation Park:** features a prominent outcrop of unusually shaped granite boulders; 50 km NE.

TOWNS NEARBY: Robe 38 km, Beachport 74 km, Naracoorte 80 km, Keith 93 km, Millicent 96 km

Leigh Creek
Pop. 547
Map ref. 557 B4 | 560 H4

ⓘ 13 Black Oak Dr; (08) 8675 2723.

📻 1602 AM ABC North and West

Located in the Flinders Ranges, Leigh Creek is a modern coalmining town that services a huge open-cut mine to the north.

The original township (13 kilometres north) was unfortunately placed, as it was situated over a large coal seam. The lure of the dollar led to the town's relocation in 1982 to its current site. A tree-planting scheme has transformed the town from a barren landscape to an attractive oasis.

Copley Bush Bakery & Quandong Cafe: great pies and cakes; Railway Tce West, Copley; (08) 8675 2683.

Coal mine tours: tours to the open-cut mine each Sat from Mar to late Oct and during school holidays; contact visitor centre for details. *Aroona Dam:* in a steep-sided valley with coloured walls; picnic area near gorge; 4 km w. *Coalmine viewing area:* turn-off 14 km N (area is 3 km down road to coalmine). *Beltana:* almost a ghost town, it has a historic reserve and holds a Picnic Race Meeting and Gymkhana each Sept; 27 km s. *Lyndhurst:* starting point of the famous Strzelecki Track. It also features a unique gallery of sculptures by well-known talc-stone artist 'Talc Alf'; tours by appt (08) 8675 7781; 39 km N. *Ochre Cliffs:* here Aboriginal people used to dig for ochre. The colours range from white to reds, yellows and browns; 44 km N via Lyndhurst. *Sliding Rock Mine ruins:* access track is rough in places; 60 km SE. *Vulkathunha–Gammon Ranges National Park:* 64 km E; see Arkaroola.

Travellers note: *Care must be taken on outback roads. Check road conditions with Northern Roads Condition Hotline on 1300 361 033 before departure.*

TOWNS NEARBY: Blinman 64 km, Arkaroola 95 km, Wilpena 106 km, Marree 110 km, Andamooka 120 km

Loxton

Pop. 3432
Map ref. 526 A6 | 546 A7 | 559 N8 | 568 G2

Bookpurnong Tce; (08) 8584 7919; www.riverland.info

93.1 Magic FM, 1062 AM ABC Riverland

Although the area around Loxton was originally settled largely by German immigrants, the town's boom began when servicemen returned from World War II. The enticement of irrigated allotments brought a great number of them to town and the success of current-day industries, such as the production of citrus fruits, wine, dried fruit, wool and wheat, was due to their skill on the land. Loxton's delightful setting on the Murray River has made the town the 'Garden City of the Riverland'.

 Loxton Historical Village The Riverland's pioneering history comes to life in the 30 historic buildings, all fully furnished in the styles of late 1880s to mid-1900s. A highlight is the pine-and-pug building, Loxtons Hut, built by the town's namesake, boundary rider William Loxton. Visit on one of the Village Alive days held thrice yearly in the village. Locals dress up in period costume and the whole village steps back 100 years. Allan Hosking Dr; (08) 8584 7194.

Terrace Gallery: local art and pottery displays and sales; part of visitor centre; Bookpurnong Tce. *The Pines Historical Home:* resplendent gardens and historic home filled with antique furniture and fine china. Tours of home every Sun followed by afternoon tea; Henry St; (08) 8584 4646. *Pepper tree:* grown from a seed planted by Loxton over 110 years ago; near the historical village. *Nature trail:* along riverfront; canoes for hire. *Heritage walk:* brochure from visitor centre.

Mardi Gras: Feb. *Nippy's Loxton Gift:* SA's largest and richest footrace; Feb. *Riverland Harvest Festival & Great Grape Stomp:* Apr. *Loxton Annual Spring Show:* Oct. *Loxton Lights Up:* Christmas lights throughout town; self-guide tour map available; Nov–Dec.

Loxton Riverfront Caravan Park: Sophie Edington Dr; (08) 8584 7862. *Loxton Smiffy's B&B:* 5 Sadlier St; (08) 8584 7442. *Mill Cottage:* 2 Mill Rd; 0439 866 990.

 McGuigan Simeon Wines Loxton Cellars: wine-tasting and sales; Bookpurnong Rd, Loxton North; (08) 8584 7236; 4 km N. *Torambre Nissen Hut Wines:* boutique winery with award-winning shirazes and merlots; Balfour–Ogilvy Rd, Loxton North; (08) 8584 1530; 6 km NE. *Lock 4:* picnic/barbecue area; 14 km N on Murray River. *MV Loch Luna Eco Cruise:* relaxing 3 hr cruise around the Nockburra and Chambers creeks; departs daily from Kingston at 9am and 1.30pm; 0449 122 271. *Banrock Station Wine and Wetland Centre:* magnificently restored wetlands and mallee woodlands, with 250 ha of picturesque vineyards and a wine centre; Holmes Rd, Kingston-on-Murray; (08) 8583 0299; 35km NW.

TOWNS NEARBY: Berri 19 km, Barmera 24 km, Renmark 35 km, Waikerie 62 km, Swan Reach 90 km

Lyndoch

Pop. 1419
Map ref. 553 G2 | 559 K8 | 568 C2

Kies Family Wines, Lot 2, Barossa Valley Hwy; (08) 8524 4110; www.barossa-region.org

89.1 Triple B FM, 639 AM ABC North and West

Lyndoch is one of the oldest towns in South Australia. The first European explorers, led by Colonel Light in 1837, described the area around Lyndoch as 'a beautiful valley'. The undulating landscape and picturesque setting attracted Lutheran immigrants and English gentry, who began growing grapes here. By 1850 Johann Gramp had produced his first wine from the grapes at Jacob's Creek.

Spinifex Arts & Crafts: retail shop selling exclusive quality handcrafted goods including pottery, quilts, folk art and paintings of local scenes. All goods are locally made in the Barossa region; Barossa Valley Way. *Helicopter and balloon flights:* scenic flights over the Barossa region; contact visitor centre for details. *Historic Lyndoch Walk:* self-guide walk featuring buildings from the mid-1800s, including many built from locally quarried hard ironstone; brochure from visitor centre.

Barossa under the Stars: food, wine and music; Tanunda; Feb. *Barossa Vintage Festival:* celebration of food and wine in various locations; odd-numbered years, Apr. *Barossa Gourmet Weekend:* Aug.

Bandicoot Nest: 15 Jollytown Rd; (08) 8524 4125. *Barossa Caravan Park:* 93 Barossa Valley Hwy; (08) 8524 4262. *Barossa Country Cottages:* 55 Gilbert St; (08) 8524 4426. *Currawong Roost:* 19 Jollytown Rd; (08) 8524 4125. *Kooringal Homestead:* Cnr Yettie and Millington rds, Cockatoo Valley; (08) 8524 6196. *Queen Victoria Jubilee Park:* Springton Rd, Williamstown; (08) 8524 6363.

Para Wirra Recreation Park Para Wirra comes from the Aboriginal words for 'river with scrub'. The park has a large recreational area with extensive facilities including tennis courts,

continued on p. 243

 RADIO STATIONS   IN TOWN   WHAT'S ON   WHERE TO EAT   WHERE TO STAY   NEARBY

 SOUTH AUSTRALIA

KINGSCOTE

Pop. 1800
Map ref. 556 E10 | 558 H11

i Kangaroo Island Gateway Visitor Information Centre, Howard Dr, Penneshaw; (08) 8553 1185; www.tourkangarooisland.com.au

90.7 KIX FM

In the early days of Australia's European settlement, Kangaroo Island was a haven for some of the country's most rugged characters – escaped convicts and deserters from English and American whaleboats. These men formed gangs, hunted more than their fair share of whales, seals, kangaroos, wallabies and possums, and went on raids to the mainland to kidnap Aboriginal women. It was an island truly without law. Two centuries on, the only ruggedness to speak of is found along the island's southern coast, where the surf is Southern Ocean-style and the seals are now left in peace. The north shore is a rippling line of bays and coves, with grass-covered hills sweeping down into Investigator Strait. On the shores of the resplendent Nepean Bay is Kingscote, the island's capital and the state's first official settlement (est. 1836). Amidst the beautiful scenery and wildlife, Kingscote is also the island's main commercial and business hub.

Kangaroo Island Penguin Centre A visit to this interpretive marine centre is a must. The size and shape of the aquariums allow visitors to get up close and personal with the vast array of sea life, which includes big-bellied seahorses and giant cuttlefish. The Penguin Tour is the ultimate highlight, where you can observe the little penguins interact with each other. The penguins' breeding season is Mar–Dec, which is the best time to visit. There are two tours every night; times vary during the year. Pelican feedings and aquarium tours also on offer; the Wharf; (08) 8553 3112.

Hope Cottage Museum: this National Trust museum exhibits the town's long pioneering and maritime history through memorabilia and photographs; open 1–4pm daily; Centenary Ave; (08) 8553 3017. *St Alban's Church:* view the impressive stained-glass windows and pioneer memorials; Osmond St. *Kangaroo Island Gallery:* beautiful local artworks from ceramics and glassworks to paintings and woodcrafts; Murray St; (08) 8553 2868. *Fine Art Kangaroo Island*: traditional and contemporary artworks showcased in two renovated heritage buildings located in the main retail precinct; 10am–5pm; 80 and 91 Dauncey Street; (08) 8553 0448. *Cemetery*: SA's oldest cemetery; Seaview Rd. *Fishing:* the jetty is a hot spot for keen anglers.

Racing Carnival: Feb. *Ozone Street Party:* Feb. *KI Field Days:* Feb. *Art Exhibition:* Penneshaw; Easter. *Kangaroo Island Art Feast:* Penneshaw; Oct. *Kangaroo Island Speed Shears:* Parndana; Nov. *Kingscote Show:* Nov.

Marron Cafe: island fare; Harriet Rd, Parndana; (08) 8559 4114. *Sorrento's Restaurant:* contemporary fine dining; Kangaroo Island Seafront Resort, 49 North Tce, Penneshaw; (08) 8553 1028 or 1800 624 624. *The Rockpool Cafe:* laid-back beachfront seafood; Stokes Bay; (08) 8559 2277.

Adagio Bed & Breakfast: Lot 1 Nepean Dr, Island Beach; (08) 8553 7222. *Anchorage Apartment:* Willoughby Rd, Island Beach; (08) 8553 7184. *Bay – Ann Cottage:* 38 Bayview Tce, Brownlow; (08) 8553 2589. *Correa Corner Bed & Breakfast:* Cnr Second St and The Parade, Brownlow; (08) 8553 2498. *The Fig Tree B&B:* 107 Leander Ave, Baudin Beach; (08) 8553 1326. *Kingscote Nepean Bay Tourist Park:* Cnr First and Third sts, Brownlow; (08) 8553 2394. *The Open House Bed & Breakfast:* 70 Smith St, Parndana; (08) 8559 6113. *Seaview Lodge KI:* Lot 3 Cape Willoughby Rd, Penneshaw; (08) 8553 1132. *Stranraer Homestead Bed & Breakfast:* Wheatons/Lades Rd, Macgillivray; (08) 8553 8235. *tu EMUZ Beachfront Cottage:* 3 Rookery Rd, Emu Bay; (08) 8553 5300.

Seal Bay Conservation Park This park protects the habitat of the rare Australian sea lion, which faced extinction on the SA coast during the 1800s. Guided beach tours provide close-up

[VIVONNE BAY, POPULAR FOR SURFING AND FISHING]

encounters with the snoozing creatures. There are also views down to the beach from the 400 m boardwalk that runs through dunes to an observation deck; (08) 8559 4207; 58 km sw.

Flinders Chase National Park On the south coast of this vast park are the precariously positioned granite boulders called the Remarkable Rocks, gradually being eroded by wind and sea to form spectacular shapes. Nearby is the Cape du Couedic lighthouse, and a colony of New Zealand fur seals that can be seen from the boardwalk down to Admirals Arch, a sea cave. There are many walking trails throughout the park and a detailed map is available from the visitor centre at Rocky River. Watch for the Cape Barren geese around the visitor centre; (08) 8559 7220; 93 km sw.

Kangaroo Island wine region Make sure to take home a bottle or two of local wine. Around 10 vineyards are scattered across the eastern side of the island, although only a few have cellar doors. The most prominent establishment is The Islander Estate Vineyards, run by a well-known French winemaker. The wines come from 100 per cent estate grapes and are made and bottled on-site. There are interesting blends, such as sangiovese, cabernet franc and malbec; (08) 8553 9008. Another option is the Bay of Shoals winery, offering great wine and a view; 3 km N.

Island Pure Sheep Dairy: tasting and sales of produce, and milking demonstrations; open 1–5pm daily; (08) 8553 9110. Cygnet River; 12 km sw. *Emu Bay:* excellent swimming at the beach with fishing from the jetty; 17 km sw. *Emu Ridge Eucalyptus Oil Distillery:* sales of eucalyptus-oil products; open 9am–2pm daily; Wilsons Rd, off South Coast Rd; 20 km s. *Clifford's Honey Farm:* sales and free tasting of Kangaroo Island's unique honey produced by pure Ligurian bees; (08) 8553 8295. Hundred Line Rd; 30 km s. *Prospect Hill Lookout:* spectacular views from the spot where Matthew Flinders surveyed Kangaroo Island; on narrow neck to Dudley Peninsula; 35 km SE. *American River:* a fishing village overlooking Eastern Cove and Pelican Lagoon, havens for birdlife; 40 km SE. *Parndana:* a small town known as The Place of Little Gums, featuring the Soldier Settlement Museum; 40 km sw. *Murray Lagoon:* well-known waterbird area with tea-tree walk; 40 km sw. *Stokes Bay:* natural rock tunnel leads to a rockpool, ideal for swimming; 50 km w. *Little Sahara:* large sand dunes surrounded by bush; 55 km sw. *Penneshaw:* a small town on Dudley Peninsula where the vehicular ferry arrives from Cape Jervis. The town features a National Trust folk museum and nightly penguin tours from the Penguin Interpretive Centre at Hog Bay Beach; 60 km E. *Vivonne Bay:* popular beach for surfing and fishing (beware of strong undertow – safe swimming near the jetty, boat ramp and Harriet River); 63 km sw. *Antechamber Bay:* picturesque beach and area, excellent for bushwalking, fishing and swimming; 72 km SE. *Kelly Hill Conservation Park:* sugar gum forest walks and guided tours of limestone caves; 85 km sw. *Western River Wilderness Protection Area:* 2.5 km track to winter waterfall; 85 km E. *Scott Cove:* from here you can view the highest coastal cliffs in the state, at 263 m; near Cape Borda; 100 km w. *Cape Borda Lightstation:* historical tours offered of 1858 lighthouse. Also here is the Cape Borda Heritage Museum. Cannon is fired at 12.30pm; 105 km w.

TOWNS NEARBY: Yankalilla 68 km, Aldinga Beach 85 km, Victor Harbor 90 km, Willunga 93 km, Port Elliot 95 km

picnic and barbecue areas, and walking trails ranging from short 800 m walks to more extensive 7.5 km trails. The park consists of mostly eucalypts and is home to a large variety of native birds – including inquisitive emus that meander around the picnic areas. The historic Barossa Goldfield Trails (1.2 km or 5 km loop walks) cover the history of the old goldmines. 12 km sw.

Barossa Valley wine region The Barossa is Australia's eminent wine region, a landscape of historic villages panning out to vine-swept hills and grand buildings on old wine estates. Shiraz is the premier drop, with semillon the star of the whites. Some of the old shiraz vines date back to the 1840s, and several winemaking families, many with German backgrounds, are into their sixth generation. Senior names include Yalumba (1849), which is officially part of the Eden Valley, PENFOLDS(1844) and Seppelt (1851). You can sample the iconic PENFOLDS Grange at PENFOLDS Barossa Valley and even visit the Winemakers' Laboratory to blend your own wine to take home in a personlised bottle. Seppelt is a must-visit winery with its elegant bluestone buildings and gardens. Its range of fortified wines includes Spanish styles and classic tawnys – the jewel is Para Liqueur, a tawny released when it is 100 years old. Peter Lehmann and Wolf Blass are other well-known wineries in the area. Smaller gems include Charles Melton, known for its Nine Popes blend of shiraz, grenache and mourvedre and for the Rose of Virginia; the nearby Rockford, with fantastic wines seldom seen in other Australian states; Torbreck Vintners, offering excellent shiraz and shiraz viognier; and Langmeil. For some history on the Barossa and winemaking, the Jacob's Creek Visitor Centre has a gallery with displays next to its wine-tasting area, where you can sample some of this well-known label's varieties.

Sandy Creek Conservation Park: on undulating sand dunes, with walking trails and birdlife. See western grey kangaroos and echidnas at dusk; 5.5 km w. *Lyndoch Lavender Farm and Cafe:* wander through rows of over 60 lavender varieties. The nursery and farm shop offer lavender-product sales; open daily Sept–Feb, Mon–Fri Mar–Apr; Cnr Hoffnungsthal and Tweedies Gully rds; 6 km SE. *Barossa Reservoir and Whispering Wall:* acoustic phenomenon allowing whispered messages at one end to be audible at the other end, 140 m away; 8 km sw.

TOWNS NEARBY: Tanunda 11 km, Gawler 13 km, Nuriootpa 18 km, Angaston 18 km, Birdwood 25 km

McLaren Vale

Pop. 2907
Map ref. 553 B12 I 554 B12 I 555 E5 I 556 H9 I 559 J10 I 568 B4

McLaren Vale and Fleurieu Visitor Centre, Main Rd; (08) 8323 9944 or 1800 628 410; www.mclarenvale.info

94.7 5EFM, 639 AM ABC North and West

McLaren Vale is recognised as a region of vineyards, orchards and gourmet-produce farms. The first grape vines were planted here

SOUTH AUSTRALIA

in 1838, just two years after Adelaide was settled, and McLaren Vale has remained a prominent wine region ever since. Shiraz is the most transcendent drop and is known for its overtones of dark chocolate. Cabernet sauvignon, grenache, chardonnay and sauvignon blanc are also very respectable. Coriole makes wonderful shiraz as well as olive oil, while d'Arenberg has many interesting varieties and a good restaurant, d'Arry's Verandah. Other wineries to visit include Geoff Merrill Wines and two of the oldest and biggest names in the district: Hardys Tintara and Rosemont Estate. The best time to visit the region is late winter, when almond blossoms provide a gentle pink blush. The town is also known for its coastal vistas to the west, which provide subject matter for the artists who exhibit in the galleries.

McLaren Vale visitor centre: picturesque landscaped grounds with a vineyard and a centre that features changing art exhibitions, sales of local craft and produce, and a cafe; Main Rd; (08) 8323 9944. *The Old Bank Artel:* community cooperative of local crafts including pottery, jewellery and metalwork; Main Rd. *Almond and Olive Train:* sales of local produce, including almonds, in a restored railway carriage; Main Rd. *McLaren Valley Bakery:* produces unique 'wine pies'; Central Shopping Centre, Main Rd. *McLaren Vale Olive Grove:* grows over 26 varieties of olives and sells olive products, arts and crafts, and local gourmet produce; Warners Rd. *Medlow Confectionery and FruChocs Showcase:* tastings and sales of gourmet chocolate and other confectionery. Interactive confectionery machine for kids; Main Rd. *McLaren Vale Heritage Trail:* self-guide trail of historic sites, including wineries, with audio CD available; starts at visitor centre.

Sea and Vines Festival: music, food and wine; June. *Fiesta!:* month-long food and wine festival; Oct.

d'Arry's Verandah Restaurant: glorious cellar-door views, regional cuisine; d'Arenberg Wines, Osborn Rd; (08) 8329 4848. *Red Poles:* arty cafe; McMurtrie Rd; (08) 8323 8994. *Vale Inn Taphouse & Kitchen:* gastropub dining, craft beers on tap; Cnr McMurtrie and Main rds; (08) 8323 8769. *The Kitchen Door:* stylish rustic fare; Penny's Hill Winery, Main Rd; (08) 8557 0800.

McLaren Vale Lakeside Caravan Park: 48 Field St; (08) 8323 9255. *Rosebank B&B:* 11 Jarred St; (08) 8323 8890. *Villa Grenache Bed and Breakfast:* 323 Kangarilla Rd; (08) 8383 0204. *Wine and Roses Bed and Breakfast:* 39 Caffrey St; 0410 513 357. *Christies Beach Tourist Park:* 39 Sydney Cres, Christies Beach; (08) 8326 0311. *Moana Beach Tourist Park:* 44 Nashwauk Cres, Moana; (08) 8327 0677. *Mt Bold Estate:* Cnr Mt Bold and White rds, Kangarilla; (08) 8383 7185. *Peppercorns B&B:* 3 Baron St, Old Noarlunga; (08) 8386 3504. *Woodcroft Park Caravan Park:* Lot 1 Bains Rd, Woodcroft; (08) 8325 1233.

Onkaparinga River National Park The Onkaparinga River, SA's second longest river, travels through valleys and gorges to Gulf St Vincent. The walks in Onkaparinga Gorge are impressive, but very steep. More regulated walking trails are on the northern side of the gorge. The estuary section of the park is an altogether different environment and is best explored on the 5 km interpretive trail. Look out for the 27 species of native orchids. Access is via Main South Rd, Old Noarlunga; (08) 8278 5477; 7 km NW.

Old Noarlunga: self-guide tour of historic colonial buildings (brochure available). Walks into Onkaparinga National Park start from here; 7 km NW. *Port Noarlunga:* popular holiday destination with historic streetscapes. A marked underwater trail along the reef is provided for divers and snorkellers; 11 km NW. *Coastal beaches:* safe family beaches to the north-west include O'Sullivan, Christies and Moana.

TOWNS NEARBY: **Willunga 6 km, Aldinga Beach 10 km, Yankalilla 32 km, Strathalbyn 32 km, Hahndorf 32 km**

Maitland

Pop. 1055
Map ref. 556 E5 | 558 H7

ⓘ Council offices, 8 Elizabeth St; (08) 8832 0000; www.yorkepeninsula.com.au

89.3 Gulf FM, 639 AM ABC North and West

Maitland represents a much smaller version of the city of Adelaide, with the town layout in the same pattern of radiating squares. It is in the heart of Yorke Peninsula and is central to a rich agricultural region. In recent years tourism has grown dramatically on the peninsula, but barley and wheat industries remain strong.

 Maitland Museum: located in the former school, this National Trust museum documents local indigenous and settlement history; open 2–4pm Sun, public/school holidays, other times by appt; Cnr Gardiner and Kilkerran tces; (08) 8832 2220. *White Flint Olive Grove:* range of olive oil products produced from own trees, great food and tea on offer; appt only; South Tce; (08) 8832 2874. *St John's Anglican Church:* stained-glass windows depict biblical stories in an Australian setting; Cnr Alice and Caroline sts. *Aboriginal cultural tours:* a range of tours through Adjahdura Land (Yorke Peninsula), with an Aboriginal guide; bookings and inquiries 0429 367 121. *Heritage town walk:* interpretive walk; brochure from council in Elizabeth St.

Maitland Show: Mar. *Maitland Art/Craft Fair:* June and Nov.

Gregory's Wines: Yorke Peninsula's only commercial vineyard. Cellar-door tastings and sales 10am–5pm weekends or by appt; Lizard Rd; (08) 8834 1258; 13 km s. *Balgowan:* this town has safe, sandy beaches and is popular with anglers; 15 km w.

TOWNS NEARBY: **Port Victoria 22 km, Ardrossan 23 km, Moonta 35 km, Minlaton 45 km, Kadina 46 km**

Mannum

Pop. 2037
Map ref. 559 L9 | 568 D3

ⓘ 6 Randell St; (08) 8569 1303; www.murraylands.info

98.7 Power FM, 1062 AM ABC Riverland

Mannum is one of the oldest towns on the Murray River, at the romantic heart of the old paddlesteamer days. In 1853 the 'Father of Mannum', William Randell, built the first Murray River paddlesteamer, *Mary Ann* (named after his mother), in order to transport his flour to the Victorian goldfields. The paddlesteamer set out from Mannum in 1853 and started a boom in the river transport industry. Another first for Mannum was Australia's first steam car, built in 1894 by David Shearer.

Mannum Dock Museum This excellent museum documents the changing history of the Mannum region from ancient days through Indigenous habitation, European settlement and river history to the present day. Outside is the renowned Randell's Dry Dock, where the grand lady of the Murray, PS *Marion*, is moored. Passenger cruises on the restored paddlesteamer still operate. Randell St; (08) 8569 2733.

Mary Ann Reserve: popular recreation reserve on the riverbank with a replica of PS *Mary Ann*'s boiling engine. PS *River Murray Princess* is moored here between cruises. *Ferry service:* twin ferries operate to the eastern side of the river. *River cruises and houseboat hire:* afternoon, day and overnight cruises are available from the town wharf, including the Murray Expedition Captain's Dinner. Alternatively, hire a houseboat to discover the Murray River your own way. Contact visitor centre for details. *Town lookout:* off Purnong Rd to the east. *Scenic and historical walks:* brochures from visitor centre.

 Mannum Show: Mar. *Houseboat Hirers' Open Days:* May. *Christmas Pageant:* Dec.

Mannum Caravan Park: Purnong Rd; (08) 8569 1402. *Omaroo Bed & Breakfast:* 10 William St; (08) 8559 2282. *Riverview Rise Retreats:* 10182 Hunter Rd, Cowirra; 0400 310 380.

Mannum Falls: picnics and scenic walks, best visited in winter (after rains) when the waterfall is flowing; 6 km SE. *Kia Marina:* the largest river marina in SA; boats and houseboats for hire; 8 km NE. *Lowan Conservation Park:* mallee vegetation park with varied wildlife, including fat-tailed dunnarts, mallee fowl and western grey kangaroos; turn-off 28 km E at Bowhill. *Purnong:* scenic drive north-east, runs parallel to excellent Halidon Bird Sanctuary; 33 km E.

TOWNS NEARBY: Murray Bridge 23 km, Birdwood 33 km, Hahndorf 47 km, Swan Reach 47 km, Lyndoch 51 km

Marree

Pop. 300
Map ref. 560 H1 | 562 H12 | 618 A12

i Marree Outback Roadhouse and General Store; (08) 8675 8360.

105.7 AM ABC Local

Marree is the perfect image of a tiny outback town. It is frequented by four-wheel-drive enthusiasts taking on the legendary Birdsville and Oodnadatta tracks. The settlement was established in 1872 as a camp for the Overland Telegraph Line as it was being constructed, and also became a railhead for the Great Northern Railway (which was later known as the *Ghan*). The town soon serviced all travellers and workers heading north, including the famous Afghan traders who drove their camel trains into the desert and played a significant role in opening up the outback.

Aboriginal Heritage Museum: features artefacts and cultural history; in Arabunna Aboriginal Community Centre. *Marree Heritage Park:* includes Tom Kruse's truck that once carried out the famous outback mail run on the Birdsville Track in the 1950s. *Camel sculpture:* made out of railway sleepers. *Scenic flights:* including over Lake Eyre and the Marree Man, a 4 km long carving in a plateau of an Aboriginal hunter. The carving, visible only from the air, appeared mysteriously in 1998, and is slowly fading; contact visitor centre for details.

Australian Camel Cup: July.

Lake Eyre National Park Of international significance, Lake Eyre is dry for most of the time – it has filled to capacity on only 3 occasions in the last 150 years. When water does fill parts of the lake (usually due to heavy rains in Queensland funnelled south via creeks and rivers), birds flock to it. Avoid visiting in

[MARREE] SUNSET SILHOUETTE ALONG THE MULOORINA TRACK, LAKE EYRE NATIONAL PARK

the hotter months (Nov–Mar). Lake Eyre North is accessed via the Oodnadatta Track, 195 km W of Maree. Lake Eyre South is accessed via the 94 km track north of Marree (along this track is Muloorina Station, which offers camping alongside the Frome River). Both access routes are 4WD only. Lake Eyre South also meets the Oodnadatta Track about 90 km W of Marree, where there are good views. A Desert Parks Pass is required for the park and is available from Marree Post Office or by contacting the Desert Parks Hotline on 1800 816 078. Scenic flights are perhaps the most rewarding option, from both Marree and William Creek.

Oodnadatta Track: a 600 km 4WD track from Marree to Marla. Highlights along the track include the Dog Fence (around 40 km W) and the railway-siding ruins at Curdimurka Siding and Bore (90 km W) from the original Great Northern Railway line to Alice Springs. A short distance beyond Curdimurka is Wabma Kadarbu Mound Springs Conservation Park, with a series of springs – fed by water from the Great Artesian Basin – supporting a small ecosystem of plants and animals. Between Marree and Marla, fuel is available only at William Creek (202 km NW) and Oodnadatta (405 km NW). *Birdsville Track:* famous 4WD track from Marree to Birdsville (in Queensland) of just over 500 km, once a major cattle run. Highlights on the track include the failed date palm plantation at Lake Harry Homestead (30 km N) and the meeting of the Tirari and Strzelecki deserts at Natterannie Sandhills (140 km N, after Cooper Creek crossing). Cooper Creek may have to be bypassed if flooded (with a 48 km detour to a ferry). Between Marree and Birdsville, fuel is available only at Mungerannie Roadhouse (204 km N).

Travellers note: *Care must be taken when attempting the Birdsville and Oodnadatta tracks. These tracks are unsealed, with sandy patches. Heavy rain in the area can cut access for several days. Motorists are advised to ring the Northern Roads Condition Hotline on 1300 361 033 before departure.*

TOWNS NEARBY: Leigh Creek 110 km, Andamooka 124 km, Arkaroola 143 km, Roxby Downs 151 km, Blinman 174 km

SOUTH AUSTRALIA

Melrose

Pop. 450
Map ref. 559 I3 | 560 H10

ℹ️ Melrose Caravan and Tourist Park, Joes Rd; (08) 8666 2060; www.mountremarkable.com.au

📻 105.1 Trax FM, 639 AM ABC North and West

Melrose, a quiet settlement at the foot of Mount Remarkable, is the oldest town in the Flinders Ranges. Indigenous groups who occupied the southern Flinders Ranges around Mount Remarkable and Melrose resisted European settlement in the 1840s, but after just a few decades the population was reduced to a handful. Pastoral properties were established on the mountainous slopes of the ranges, but Melrose truly took off when copper deposits were found nearby in 1846. Bushwalking through Mount Remarkable National Park is a highlight of any visit to this area. The arid north country meets the wet conditions of southern regions to provide a diverse landscape to explore.

🏠 *National Trust Museum:* documents local history, with particular focus on early law enforcement. Original stone buildings include the courthouse and lock-up; open 2–5pm; Stuart St. *Bluey Blundstone Blacksmith Shop:* a restored shop with a cafe and B&B; closed Tues; Stuart St. *Serendipity Gallery:* Australiana arts and crafts; Stuart St. *War Memorial and Lookout Hill:* views over surrounding region. *4WD tours:* to local landmarks; contact visitor centre for operators. *Heritage walk:* self-guide walk includes ruins of Jacka's Brewery and Melrose Mine; brochure from visitor centre.

🌴 *Melrose Show:* Oct.

🍴 *The North Star Hotel:* rejuvenated landmark pub; Nott St; (08) 8666 2110. *The Old Bakery Stone Hut:* classic English-style pies; 1 Main North Rd, Stone Hut; (08) 8663 2165.

🛏️ *Melrose Caravan Park:* Joes Rd; (08) 8666 2060. *Taralee Orchards:* Forest Rd, Wirrabara; (08) 8668 4343.

⊙ **Mt Remarkable National Park** Part of the southern Flinders Ranges and popular with bushwalkers. Marked trails through the park's gorges and ranges vary in scope from short scenic walks to long 3-day hikes. Highlights include pretty Alligator Gorge and the tough but worthwhile 5 hr return walk from Melrose to the summit of Mt Remarkable (960 m), with breathtaking views from the top. Access to the park by vehicle is via Mambray Creek or Wilmington. Foot access is from carparks and Melrose. (08) 8634 7068; 2 km w.

Cathedral Rock: an impressive rock formation on Mt Remarkable Creek; just west of Melrose. *Murray Town:* a farming town with nearby scenic lookouts at Box Hill, Magnus Hill and Baroota Nob. Remarkable View Wines offers tasting and sales on weekends. Starting point for a scenic drive west through Port Germein Gorge; 14 km s. *Booleroo Centre:* this service town to a rich farming community features the Booleroo Steam Traction Preservation Society's Museum. Annual Rally Day is held in Mar/Apr; open by appt; (08) 8667 2193; 15 km SE. *Wirrabara:* you could easily lose half a day in this town's bakery-cum-antiques shop, wandering through the rooms of relics and antiques just to work up an appetite for another homemade pastry; 25 km s.

TOWNS NEARBY: Wilmington 21 km, Port Pirie 43 km, Port Augusta 54 km, Quorn 55 km, Jamestown 57 km

Meningie

Pop. 939
Map ref. 559 L11 | 568 D5

ℹ️ The Chamber, 14 Princes Hwy; (08) 8575 1770; www.coorong.sa.gov.au

📻 98.7 Power FM, 1161 AM ABC South East

Today Meningie is an attractive lakeside town, but it was once a wilderness area, home to the Ngarrindjeri people, who had a self-sufficient lifestyle on the water. They made canoes to fish on the waterways and shelters to protect themselves from the weather. However, European settlement – after Captain Charles Sturt's journey down the Murray from 1829 to 1830 – soon wiped out much of the population, largely through violence and the introduction of smallpox. Stretching south from the mouth of the Murray and located just south of Meningie, the Coorong, with its lakes, birdlife, fishing and deserted ocean beaches, attracts visitors year-round.

🏠 *The Cheese Factory Museum Restaurant:* a restaurant and separate community museum with special interest in the changing population of Meningie and the Coorong; closed Mon; Fiebig Rd. *Coorong Cottage Industries:* local craft and produce; The Chambers, Princes Hwy.

🛏️ *Coonalpyn Soldiers Memorial Caravan Park:* Richards Tce, Coonalpyn; 0427 399 089. *Gemini Downs Holiday Centre:* Princes Hwy, Salt Creek; (08) 8575 7013.

⊙ **Coorong National Park** Listed as a 'wetland of international importance', this park's waterways, islands and vast saltpans demonstrate a diverse ecological environment invaluable for the refuge and habitat of migratory and drought-stricken birds. Throughout the park are reminders of the long history of habitation by the Ngarrindjeri people. There are ancient midden heaps and burial grounds, and the Ngarrindjeri people continue to have strong links with the Coorong. There are a number of ways to see the park: take a boat, canoe or cruise on the waterways; walk one of the varied tracks offered; drive your 4WD onto the Southern Ocean beach; or simply sit and soak up the park's atmosphere. Walking is the best way to access great coastal views, birdwatching spots and historic ruins. The most comprehensive walk in the park is the Nukan Kungun Hike. This 27 km hike starts at Salt Creek and includes smaller, side trails, including the informative walk to Chinaman's Well, the ruins of a temporary settlement that sprang up en route to the goldfields. The hike ends at the 42 Mile Crossing Sand Dune Walk, which leads to the wild Southern Ocean; (08) 8575 1200; 10 km s.

Scenic drive: follows Lake Albert to the west, adjacent to Lake Alexandrina, which is the largest permanent freshwater lake in the country (50 000 ha). Ferry crossing at Narrung. *Camp Coorong:* cultural centre offering bush-tucker tours and other traditional Aboriginal experiences; (08) 8575 1557; 10 km s. *Coorong Wilderness Lodge:* operated by the Ngarrindjeri people, this accommodation lodge offers Aboriginal heritage tours of the Coorong as well as traditional bush tucker and other cultural experiences; Hacks Point; (08) 8575 6001; 25 km s. *Poltalloch Station:* a historic pastoral property established in the 1830s as a sheep station. Guided tours take in a heritage-listed farm village and museum, historic farm machinery, and past and present farm life. Cottage accommodation available; Poltalloch Rd near Narrung; (08) 8574 0043; 30 km NW.

TOWNS NEARBY: Goolwa 54 km, Port Elliot 62 km, Strathalbyn 62 km, Murray Bridge 63 km, Victor Harbor 67 km

Millicent

Pop. 4768
Map ref. 568 F11

i 1 Mt Gambier Rd; (08) 8733 0904; www.wattlerange.sa.gov.au

📻 107.7 5THE FM, 1161 AM ABC South East

Millicent, a prosperous, friendly and vibrant community located in the heart of the Limestone Coast region, is named after Millicent Glen, wife of one of the early pioneers and daughter of the first Anglican Bishop of Adelaide. In 1876 the barque *Geltwood* was wrecked off Canunda Beach, with debris, bodies and cargo littering the sands. Relics from the *Geltwood* can be found in the award-winning National Trust Living History Museum. The town's distinctive aroma can be attributed to the surrounding pine forests, which support a pulp mill, a paper mill and sawmill.

🏠 *Visitor centre and National Trust Living History Museum:* centre provides extensive information on the region and surrounding areas. Souvenirs, arts and crafts, and local produce available. History museum includes a shipwreck room, farm machinery shed, Aboriginal and natural history rooms, a T-Class locomotive and the largest collection of restored horse-drawn vehicles in SA; Mt Gambier Rd; (08) 8733 0904. *Lake McIntyre:* boardwalks and bird hides to view the lake's prolific birdlife, native fish and yabbies; northern edge of town.

🌴 *Nangula Market Days:* 2nd Sun each month (excluding Jan). *Tall Timbers Wood Work Exhibition:* pine and red-gum craft; Mar–May. *Geltwood Craft Festival:* Mar/Apr. *Pines Enduro Off-Road Championships:* Sept. *Millicent Show:* Sept.

🛏 *Millicent Hillview Caravan Park:* Dalton St; (08) 8733 2806. *Millicent Lakeside Caravan Park:* 12 Park Tce; (08) 8733 1188.

⊗ **Canunda National Park** The massive sand-dune system of the southern part of the park rises to cliffs and scrublands in the north. These 2 sections provide quite different experiences. In the north (accessed via Southend and Millicent) the walking trails pass along cliff-tops and through the scrubland. In the south (accessed via Carpenter Rocks and Millicent) the beaches and wetlands provide picturesque coastal walks. You can surf, 4WD, birdwatch, bushwalk and fish (excellent from the beaches and rocks). (08) 8735 1177; 10 km w.

Woakwine Range Wind Farms: dozens of giant turbines dominate the Woakwine Range skyline, comprising the largest wind farm development in the Southern Hemisphere. Take a drive along the Wind Farm Tourist Drive. Maps available from visitor centre; 2 km s. *Mt Muirhead Lookout:* a large viewing platform provides views of Millicent, pine plantations and Mt Burr Range. It is also the start of the Volcanoes Discovery Trail (brochure from visitor centre); 6 km NE. *Mount Burr:* a historic timber town, the first to plant pines for commercial use on the Limestone Coast; 10 km NE. *Tantanoola:* home of the famous 'Tantanoola Tiger', a Syrian wolf shot in the 1890s, now stuffed and displayed in the Tantanoola Tiger Hotel; 20 km SE. *Tantanoola Caves Conservation Park:* daily tours of an imposing dolomite cavern in an ancient limestone cliff. Also walks and picnic areas; 21 km SE. *Glencoe Woolshed:* National Trust limestone woolshed once occupied by 38 shearers; 29 km SE.

TOWNS NEARBY: Beachport 32 km, Mount Gambier 46 km, Penola 49 km, Coonawarra 55 km, Port MacDonnell 60 km

Minlaton

Pop. 772
Map ref. 556 E6 | 558 H8

i Harvest Corner Visitor Information Centre, 29 Main St; (08) 8853 2600 or 1800 202 445; www.yorkepeninsula.com.au

📻 98.9 Flow FM, 639 AM ABC North and West

This small rural centre on Yorke Peninsula was originally called Gum Flat, because of the giant eucalypts in the area, but was later changed to Minlaton – from the Aboriginal word 'minlacowrie', thought to mean 'sweet water'. Aviator Captain Harry Butler, pilot of the *Red Devil*, a 1916 Bristol monoplane, was born here.

🏠 *Butler Memorial:* in a hangar-like building stands the *Red Devil*, a fighter plane – thought to be the only one of its type left in the world – that fought in France and, less romantically, flew mail between Adelaide and Minlaton; Main St. *Minlaton Museum:* National Trust museum in the historic general store features a local history display and Harry Butler memorabilia; open 9.30am–1pm Tues–Fri, 9.30am–12pm Sat; Main St. *Harvest Corner Yorke Peninsula Visitor Information Centre:* accredited visitor centre with tourist information, craft and local produce sales, a gallery featuring local artists and tearooms; Main St. *The Creamery:* crafts, ceramics and art exhibitions in a historic building; Maitland Rd. *Gum Flat Gallery:* art workshop and gallery; open 10am–2pm Wed; Main St. *Minlaton Fauna Park:* popular spot for picnics, with kangaroos, emus and up to 43 species of birds; Maitland Rd. *Minlaton Walking Trail:* a trail to the only naturally occurring stand of river red gums in the Yorke Peninsula. See a number of historic landmarks including an old horse dip and ancient Aboriginal wells, catch a local glimpse of the birdlife at the bird hide, and learn about the area through interpretive signs; contact visitor centre for details.

🌴 *Minlaton Show:* Oct.

🍴 *Red Devil Restaurant:* smart pub dining; Minlaton Hotel, 26 Main St; (08) 8853 2014.

🛏 *Minlaton Caravan Park:* 1 Bluff Rd; (08) 8853 2435. *Port Rickaby Caravan Park:* Waimana Crt, Port Rickaby; (08) 8853 1177.

⊗ *Ramsay Park:* native flora and fauna park; between Minlaton and Port Vincent to the east. *Port Rickaby:* quiet swimming and fishing spot; 16 km NW.

TOWNS NEARBY: Stansbury 24 km, Yorketown 27 km, Port Victoria 32 km, Edithburgh 37 km, Maitland 45 km

Mintaro

Pop. 223
Map ref. 559 J6

i Cnr Main North and Spring Gully rds; (08) 8842 2131 or 1800 242 131; www.clarevalley.com.au

📻 105.1 Trax FM, 639 AM ABC North and West

Although it is in the Clare Valley region, Mintaro's prosperity is not linked with the valley's booming wine industry. Instead, its buildings date back to the 1840s and '50s, when bullock drays carried copper from the Monster Mine at Burra to Port Wakefield in the south. Many of the buildings use local slate. In 1984 Mintaro became the first town in South Australia to be classified a State Heritage Area.

🏠 *Timandra Garden:* one of the town's fine garden displays; enter via Timandra Nursery, Kingston St. *Mintaro Garden*

SOUTH AUSTRALIA

Maze: kids will love getting lost in the maze, comprising over 800 conifers; open 10am–4pm Thurs–Mon; Jacka St. *Reillys Wines:* wine-tastings, cellar-door sales and a restaurant; Burra Rd. *Mintaro Cellars:* wine-tastings and sales; Leasingham Rd. *Mintaro Slate Quarries:* fine-quality slate, produced since the quarry opened in 1854, is used world-wide for billiard tables; open 7.30am–3pm Mon–Fri; viewing platform in Kadlunga Rd. *Heritage walk:* self-guide trail includes 18 heritage-listed colonial buildings and 2 historic cemeteries; brochure available.

✕ *Reilly's Cellar Door & Restaurant:* satisfying country meals; Cnr Leasingham Rd and Hill St; (08) 8843 9013. *The Station Cafe:* weekend snacks and platters; Mount Horrocks Wines, Curling St, Auburn; (08) 8849 2202.

🛏 *Devonshire House:* Burra St; (08) 8843 9078. *Ethel's Cottage:* Main North Rd, Leasingham; (08) 8342 0406. *Granma's B&B:* Lot 201 Main North Rd, Watervale; 0408 828 459. *Quince Cottage:* Cnr South and Commercial rds, Watervale; (08) 8843 0048.

🕒 **Martindale Hall** This 1879 mansion was built for Edmund Bowman who, the story goes, commissioned it for his bride-to-be from English high society. The lady declined his offer of marriage, and Bowman lived there on his own until 1891. Today visitors can explore the National Trust, Georgian-style home with its Italian Renaissance interior. A room in the mansion was used in the 1975 film *Picnic at Hanging Rock* as a girls' dormitory. Accommodation and dining are available. Open 11am–4pm Mon–Fri, 12–4pm weekends; Manoora Rd; (08) 8843 9088; 3 km SE.

Polish Hill River Valley: a subregion of the Clare Valley wine region, with cellar doors offering tastings and sales; between Mintaro and Sevenhill. *Waterloo:* features the historic Wellington Hotel, once a Cobb & Co. staging post; 23 km SE.

TOWNS NEARBY: Clare 14 km, Burra 33 km, Balaklava 38 km, Kapunda 50 km, Nuriootpa 66 km

Moonta
Pop. 3353
Map ref. 556 E3 | 558 H6

ℹ Railway Station, Blanche Tce; (08) 8825 1891; www.yorkepeninsula.com.au

📻 89.3 Gulf FM, 639 AM ABC North and West

The towns of Moonta, Kadina and Wallaroo form the 'Copper Coast' or 'Little Cornwall', so called because of abundant copper finds and the significant Cornish population. Like so many other copper discoveries in South Australia, Moonta's was made by a local shepherd – in this case, Paddy Ryan in 1861. It was to prove a fortunate find: Moonta Mining Company paid over £1 million in dividends. Thousands of miners, including experienced labourers from Cornwall, flocked to the area. The mines were abandoned in the 1920s because of the slump in copper prices and rising labour costs. Moonta has survived as an agricultural service town with an increasing tourist trade.

🏠 *All Saints Church of England:* features a locally constructed copper bell; Cnr Blanche and Milne tces. *Queen Square:* park for picnics, with the imposing town hall opposite; George St. *Heritage walks and drives:* self-guide trails to see heritage stone buildings and historic mine sites; brochure from visitor centre.

🌴 *Kernewek Lowender:* prize-winning Cornish festival held with Kadina and Wallaroo; odd-numbered years, May. *Moonta Garden Fair:* Oct. *Moonta Antiques and Collectible Fair:* Nov.

🛏 *Amelia's Bed and Breakfast:* 31 Bay Rd, Moonta Bay; 0447 528 040. *Moonta Bay Caravan Park:* Tossell St, Moonta Bay; (08) 8825 2406. *Port Hughes Tourist Village:* South Tce, Port Hughes; (08) 8825 2106.

🕒 **Moonta Mines State Heritage Area** Take a historical walk or drive from Moonta to this significant heritage area. Interpretive walking trails guide the visitor to the major sites, including the Hughes Pump House, shafts, tailing heaps and ruins of mine offices. A 50 min historical railway tour runs from the museum (tours depart Wed 2pm, Sat and Sun 1–3pm on the hour, public/school holidays daily 11am–3pm on the hour). Also on the site is a historic 1880 pipe organ in the Moonta Mines Heritage Uniting Church; Cornish lifestyle history and memorabilia at the Moonta Mines Museum; and the National Trust furnished Miners Cottage and Heritage Garden. Open 1–4pm daily. Enjoy old-style sweets at the Moonta Mines Sweet Shop. Via Verran Tce; 2 km SE.

Wheal Hughes Copper Mine: underground tour of one of the modern mines; tours Wed, Sat and Sun; Wallaroo Rd; (08) 8825 1891; 3 km N. *Moonta Bay:* a popular seaside town for fishing and swimming. See native animals at the Moonta Wildlife Park; 5 km W.

TOWNS NEARBY: Wallaroo 15 km, Kadina 16 km, Maitland 35 km, Port Victoria 49 km, Ardrossan 50 km

Morgan
Pop. 425
Map ref. 559 L6

ℹ Shell Morgan Roadhouse, 14–18 Fourth St; (08) 8540 2354; www.riverland.info

📻 93.1 Magic FM; 1062 AM ABC Riverland

This Murray River town was once a thriving port and a stop on the rail trade route to Adelaide. Settlers saw the potential of the region, and Morgan boomed as soon as it was declared a town in 1878. Now it is a quiet holiday destination, but evidence of its boom days can still be seen in the streetscapes and the historic wharf and rail precinct.

🏠 **Port of Morgan Museum** This comprehensive museum is dedicated to the rail- and river-trade history of Morgan. In the old railway buildings are museum exhibits focusing on the paddlesteamers and trains that were the lifeblood of the town. The Landseer Building has vintage vehicles and a 12 m mural depicting the old Murray River lifestyle. Other highlights are the restored wharf and permanently moored PS *Mayflower*. Open 2–4pm Wed, Sat and Sun; Riverfront; (08) 8540 2085.

Houseboats: for hire; contact visitor centre for details. *Heritage walk:* self-guide trail covers 41 historic sites, including the impressive wharves (1877) standing 12 m high, the customs house and courthouse, the sunken barge and steamer, and the rail precinct; brochure from visitor centre.

🕒 *Morgan Conservation Park:* a diverse landscape of river flats, sand dunes and mallee scrub with abundant birdlife; across the Murray River from Morgan. *White Dam Conservation Park:* well known for red and western grey kangaroo populations; 9 km NW. *Cadell:* scenic 12 km drive east from Morgan via a ferry crossing (operates 24 hrs) to Cadell, a major citrus-growing region.

TOWNS NEARBY: Waikerie 34 km, Swan Reach 60 km, Kapunda 77 km, Angaston 77 km, Barmera 78 km

Mount Gambier

see inset box on next page

Murray Bridge
Pop. 14 048
Map ref. 559 K10 | 568 D3

ℹ 3 South Tce; (08) 8539 1142 or 1800 442 784; www.murraybridge.sa.gov.au

📻 98.7 Power FM, 1062 AM ABC Riverland

Murray Bridge, just as its name suggests, is all about bridges. The town was established in 1879 when a road bridge was built over the Murray River. The plan to make the river a major trade route from east to west and back had become a reality. In 1886 the construction of a railway line between Adelaide and Melbourne cemented the town's importance. Now watersports, river cruises and a relaxed river atmosphere make Murray Bridge South Australia's largest river town, a perfect holiday spot.

🏠 *Captain's Cottage Museum:* local history museum; open 10am–4pm weekends; Thomas St. *Dundee's Wildlife Park:* crocodiles, koalas and a bird sanctuary; Jervois Rd. *Murray Bridge Regional Gallery:* regular art exhibitions from local artists; closed Sat; Sixth St. *Heritage and Cultural Community Mural:* depicts significant aspects of Murray Bridge; Third St. *Sturt Reserve:* offers fishing, swimming, picnic and playground facilities, as well as the mythical Aboriginal creature, the Bunyip (coin-operated); Murray Cod Dr. *Long Island Marina:* houseboat hire and recreational facilities; Roper Rd. *Thiele Reserve:* popular for waterskiing; east of the river. *Avoca Dell:* a popular picnic spot with boating, waterskiing, minigolf and caravan facilities. *Swanport Wetlands:* recreational reserve with raised walkways and bird hides; adjacent to Swanport Bridge. *Charter and regular cruises:* on the Murray River; contact visitor centre. *Town and riverside walks:* brochure from visitor centre.

🎪 *AutoFest:* Australia Day weekend Jan. *International Pedal Prix:* novelty bikes and endurance event; Sept. *Murray Bridge Show:* Sept. *Waterski Race:* over 110 km; Nov. *Christmas Pageant and Fireworks:* Nov.

🛏 *The Bridge Retreat:* 18 Monash Tce; (08) 8531 2229. *Long Island Caravan Park:* 100 Roper Rd; (08) 8532 6900. *Princes Highway Caravan Park:* 315 Adelaide Rd (Princes Hwy); (08) 8532 2860. *Rainforest Retreat Murray Bridge:* 19A Torrens Rd; (08) 8532 6447. *Avoca Dell Caravan Park:* Avoca Dell Dr (via Mitchell Ave), Avoca Dell; (08) 8532 2095. *Wellington Caravan Park:* Main Rd, Wellington; (08) 8572 7302.

⊙ **Monarto Zoological Park** This open-range 1000 ha zoo features Australian, African and Asian animals. It also runs a breeding program for rare and endangered species. Jump on a safari bus tour to see the animals up close. On the way you might encounter the huge giraffe herd or some cheetahs, zebras or rhinoceroses. Tours depart hourly 10.30am–3.30pm. There are also walking tracks through native bushland and mallee country. Princes Hwy; (08) 8534 4100; 10 km w.

Sunnyside Reserve Lookout: views across the wetlands and Murray River; 10 km E. *Willow Point Winery:* cellar-door tastings and sales of famous ports, sherries and muscats; closed Sun; Jervois Rd; 10 km s. *Ferries–McDonald and Monarto conservation parks:* walking trails through important mallee conservation areas, prolific birdlife, and blossom in spring; 16 km w. *Tailem Bend:* a historic railway town with views across

the Murray River. A children's playground features an old steam locomotive, and over 90 historic buildings are displayed at the Old Tailem Town Pioneer Village; 25 km SE. *Wellington:* situated where Lake Alexandrina meets the Murray River. A museum is in the restored courthouse. Wellington and nearby Jervois have free 24 hr vehicle ferries; 32 km s. *Karoonda:* the heart of the Mallee, Karoonda is well known for the 1930 meteorite fall nearby (monument at RSL Park). Natural attractions include the limestone caves of Bakara Plains and walking trails in Pioneer Historical Park; 66 km E.

TOWNS NEARBY: Mannum 23 km, Strathalbyn 38 km, Hahndorf 43 km, Birdwood 44 km, Goolwa 62 km

Naracoorte
Pop. 4888
Map ref. 548 A10 | 568 G9

ℹ MacDonnell St; (08) 8762 1399 or 1800 244 421; www.naracoortelucindale.sa.gov.au

📻 89.7 5TCB FM, 963 AM, 1161 AM ABC South East

Naracoorte dates from the 1840s, but its growth has been slow. In the 1850s it was a stopover for Victorian gold escorts and miners. Since then it has developed a rich agricultural industry. Today it is renowned for its natural attractions, including the parks and gardens but more significantly the Naracoorte Caves, which are in a national park protected within South Australia's only World Heritage–listed site.

🏠 *The Sheep's Back:* a comprehensive museum in the former flour mill (1870) details the history and community of the wool industry, with a craft and souvenir shop and information centre; MacDonnell St; (08) 8762 1518. *Naracoorte Art Gallery:* local and touring exhibitions; open Tues–Fri; Ormerod St; (08) 8762 3390. *Mini Jumbuk Centre:* display gallery and sales of woollen products; Smith St; (08) 87623677. *Pioneer Park:* restored locomotive on display; MacDonnell St. *Walking trail:* starts at the town centre and winds 5 km along the Naracoorte Creek.

🎪 *Taste the Limestone Coast:* wine and gourmet food festival; Feb. *Naracoorte Horse Trials:* May. *Swap Meet:* May. *Limestone Coast Children's Expo:* Oct. *Naracoorte Show:* Oct. *Christmas Pageant:* Dec.

🍴 *Naracoorte Flowers Sweet Espresso:* florist offering coffee and sweet temptations; Smith St; (08) 8762 1522. *Settlers Cafe:* cafe with kid-friendly play area; Gordon St; (08) 8762 0700.

🛏 *Carolynne's Cottages:* Lot 6 Young Dr; (08) 8762 1762. *Limestone View (Naracoorte Cottages):* 44 Freeling St; 0408 810 645. *MacDonnell House (Naracoorte Cottages):* 38 MacDonnell St; 0408 810 645. *Pinkerton Hill (Naracoorte Cottages):* 40 Pinkerton Rd; 0408 810 645. *Smith Street Villa (Naracoorte Cottages):* 192 Smith St; 0408 810 645. *Willowbrook Cottages B&Bs:* 3–5 Jenkins Tce; (08) 8762 0259.

⊙ **Naracoorte Caves National Park** For thousands of years the 26 Naracoorte Caves – today protected by national park and World Heritage listing – have acted as a natural trap for animals, providing an environment that was just right for fossilisation. Twenty fossil deposits have been found throughout the 600 hectare park – an incredible record of Australia's evolution over the last 500 000 years. Guided walking tours take in the

continued on p. 251

MOUNT GAMBIER

Pop. 23 494
Map ref. 550 A5 | 568 G12

i The Lady Nelson Visitor and Discovery Centre, 35 Jubilee Hwy East; (08) 8724 9750 or 1800 087 187; www.mountgambiertourism.com.au

📻 5GTR FM 100.1, 96.1 Star FM, 1476 AM ABC South East

Mount Gambier is set on an extinct volcano – the area boasts a fascinating network of volcanic craters above sea level and limestone caves beneath. Lieutenant James Grant named the volcano in 1800 – he sighted it from HMS *Lady Nelson*, off the coast. The original settlement was known as Gambier Town. Today Mount Gambier is at the centre of the largest softwood pine plantation in the Commonwealth and is surrounded by farming, viticulture and dairy country.

🏠 **Blue Lake** The lakes formed in the craters of the extinct volcano have become an important recreational area for locals and visitors alike. The most spectacular is Blue Lake, so-called because the water's dull, blue-grey winter colour changes to a vibrant blue each Nov and stays that way until Mar the following year. Discover the area on the 3.6 km walking track around the shores. Aquifer Tours offers a trip in a lift down an old well shaft. The area also includes a wildlife park and an adventure playground; southern outskirts of town; (08) 8723 1199.

Old Courthouse: a National Trust dolomite building with a local history museum; open by appt; Bay Rd; (08) 8725 5284. *The Lady Nelson Visitor and Discovery Centre:* full-scale replica of HMS *Lady Nelson*, interactive displays on the region's history and geography, and free local information packs; 35 Jubilee Hwy East. *Riddoch Art Gallery:* changing exhibitions of local and touring art and sculpture; open Tues–Sun; Commercial St East. *Cave Garden:* a cave used as a water supply for early settlers, now a rose garden with a suspended viewing platform; Bay Rd.

Umpherston Sinkhole: a sunken garden on the floor of a collapsed cave; floodlit at night; Jubilee Hwy East. *Engelbrecht Cave:* guided tour of the limestone cave system under the city; contact visitor centre for details. *Centenary Tower:* views of the city, the lakes area and surrounding countryside; top of Mt Gambier, 190 m above sea level. *Heritage walk:* self-guide tour of historic buildings, many constructed of white Mt Gambier stone; brochure from visitor centre.

❋ *Mount Gambier Market:* behind Harvey Norman; Sat. *World Series Sprintcars:* Jan. *Generations in Jazz:* May. *Mount Gambier Gold Cup Carnival:* May. *Mount Gambier Show:* Oct. *Christmas Parade:* Nov.

🍴 *Sage & Muntries Restaurant:* imaginative, regional dishes; 78 Commercial St West; (08) 8724 8400. *Sorrento's Cafe:* relaxed all-day eatery; 6 Bay Rd; (08) 8723 0900. *The Barn Steakhouse:* excellent steaks and grills; Punt Rd; (08) 8726 8250.

🛏 *Blue Lake Holiday Park:* Bay Rd; (08) 8725 9856. *Clarendon Chalets:* Clarke Rd; (08) 8726 8306. *Colhurst House Bed & Breakfast:* 3 Colhurst Pl; (08) 8723 1309. *Mackenzie's on Jardine:* 9 Jardine St; 0409 420 864. *Mount Gambier Central Caravan Park:* 6 Krummel St; (08) 8725 4427. *Pine Country Caravan Park:* Cnr Bay and Kilsby rds; (08) 8725 1899.

🚗 *Haig's Vineyards:* wine-tastings and sales; 4 km SE. *Mt Schank:* excellent views of the surrounding district from the summit of an extinct volcano. Note that the 2 summit walks are very steep; 17 km S. *Nelson and Lower Glenelg National Park:* over the Victorian border; *see Portland (Vic.)*.

TOWNS NEARBY: Port MacDonnell 25 km, Millicent 46 km, Penola 51 km, Coonawarra 60 km, Casterton (Vic.) 61 km

[BLUE LAKE]

chambers, extensive stalagmite and stalactite deposits and fossil collections. The Victoria Fossil Cave Tour is an introduction to the ancient animal history of Australia, while the natural delights of the caves, including helictites and fabulous domed ceilings, are accessed on the 30 min Alexandra Cave Tour. The world of bats is celebrated on the Bat Tour, the highlight being unhindered views of the bats' activity from infra-red cameras. Adventure caving allows visitors to see the caves in their raw state, while also providing an opportunity for exciting squeezes and crawls through some very tight spaces. For caving beginners, try the Blackberry and Stick-Tomato tours. For the more experienced cavers, enjoy the crawls and sights on the Starburst Chamber Tour. The Fox Cave Tour is the ultimate caving experience, with access to the cave system by a small entrance, leading to great fossil collections, vast speleothem development and incredible scenery. You can get details on these tours from Wonambi Fossil Centre, located within the park; (08) 8762 2340; 12 km SE.

Wrattonbully wine region: a recently established wine region focusing mainly on red wine varieties; 15 km SE. *Bool Lagoon Game Reserve:* wetland area of international significance, a haven for ibis and over 100 waterbird species. It includes boardwalks and a bird hide; 17 km S. *Frances:* a historic railway town that each Mar holds the Frances Folk Gathering; 38 km NE. *Lucindale:* a small country town featuring a Historical Society Museum and Jubilee Park with a lake, island and bird haven. It holds mammoth South East Field Days each Mar; 41 km W. *Padthaway:* prominent wine region; 47 km NW; *see Bordertown.*

TOWNS NEARBY: Coonawarra 38 km, Penola 47 km, Edenhope (Vic.) 50 km, Bordertown 72 km, Millicent 79 km

Nuriootpa

see inset box on page 253

Oodnadatta

Pop. 277
Map ref. 562 B6

 Pink Roadhouse, Ikaturka Tce; (08) 8670 7822 or 1800 802 074.

 95.3 FM ABC North and West

Oodnadatta is a gutsy outback town on the legendary Oodnadatta Track. It was once a major railway town, but the line's closure in 1981 left it largely deserted. Local Aboriginal people have successfully kept the town operating since then. Today many travellers use it to refuel and gather supplies before heading out to the major desert parks to the north. It is believed that the name Oodnadatta originated from an Aboriginal term meaning 'yellow blossom of the mulga'.

 Pink Roadhouse: a town icon, and also the place to go for information on local road conditions and outback travel advice; Ikaturka Tce. *Railway Station Museum:* well-preserved sandstone station (1890), now a local museum; key available from roadhouse.

 Races and gymkhana: May. *Bronco Branding:* July.

 Witjira National Park This arid park is famous for the Dalhousie Springs. These thermal springs emerge from the Great Artesian Basin deep below the surface and are said to be therapeutic (visitors can swim in the main spring). They are also a habitat for many fish species that can adapt to the changing water conditions. A Desert Parks Pass is required; they are

available from Mt Dare Homestead (which has fuel and supplies), the Pink Roadhouse or Parks SA (1800 816 078); 180 km N.

Oodnadatta Track: runs from Marree (404 km SE) through Oodnadatta and joins the Stuart Hwy at Marla (212 km NW); *see Marree. Neales River:* swim in permanent waterholes. *The Painted Desert:* superb desert scenery of richly coloured hills; 100 km SW. *Simpson Desert Conservation Park and Regional Reserve:* 4WD tracks across enormous dune desert east of Witjira. Travellers must be totally self-sufficient; details from visitor centre.

TOWNS NEARBY: Coober Pedy 174 km

Penola

Pop. 1315
Map ref. 550 A2 | 568 G10

 The John Riddoch Centre, 27 Arthur St; (08) 8737 2855; www.wattlerange.sa.gov.au

 107.7 5THE FM, 1161 AM ABC South East

Penola is one of the oldest towns in south-east South Australia, and has some excellent wineries nearby. The town is noted for its association with Mary MacKillop, a Josephite nun who in 1866 established Australia's first school to cater for children regardless of their family's income or social class. In 2010 she was canonised by the Vatican, making her the first Australian to be declared a saint. Penola is also noted for its literary roots – several Australian poets have been inspired by the landscape and lifestyle.

 Mary MacKillop Interpretive Centre and Woods MacKillop Schoolhouse: details the lives of Mary MacKillop and Father Julian Tenison (who shared Mary's dream) through photos, memorabilia and displays in this 1860s-style schoolhouse; Portland St. *Petticoat Lane:* heritage area of original cottages, including Sharam Cottage, the first built in town; many are now retail outlets. *The John Riddoch Centre:* incorporates the Local History Exhibition and Hydrocarbon Centre, featuring hands-on and static displays on natural gas; Arthur St. *Toffee and Treats:* old-fashioned sweet sales; Church St. *Heritage walk:* details from visitor centre.

 Vigneron Cup: Jan. *Petanque Festival:* Feb. *Penola Coonawarra Arts Festival:* arts, food and wine; May. *Cellar Dwellers:* July. *Cabernet Celebrations:* Oct. *Penola Show:* Oct/Nov.

 Pipers of Penola: exquisite contemporary cuisine; 58 Riddoch St; (08) 8737 3999.

 Georgie's Cottage: 1 Riddoch St; 0427 100 767. *Merlot & Verdelho Accommodation:* 14 Arthur St; 0413 512 559. *Penola Caravan Park:* Cnr Riddoch Hwy and South Tce; (08) 8737 2381.

 Coonawarra wine region Prominent wine professionals such as Wolf Blass damned this region as a place that could never produce decent wine, and the original John Riddoch wine estate was nearly sold to the Department of Forestry and Lands (thankfully, David Wynn purchased the property and it is now Wynns Coonawarra). In the 1950s, large wine companies such as PENFOLDS and Yalumba finally began recognising the depth of the region's reds, and opinions began to change. Coonawarra's famed terra rossa (red earth) combined with the region's particular climate is now known to create some of the best cabernet sauvignon in the country, as well as excellent shiraz, merlot, riesling and chardonnay. Wynns Coonawarra produces

SOUTH AUSTRALIA

world-class shiraz and cabernet sauvignon, some for purchase at reasonable prices. Other excellent wineries to visit are Balnaves of Coonawarra, Brand's of Coonawarra, Majella and Zema Estate.

Yallam Park: a magnificent 2-storey Victorian home with original decorations; by appt (08) 8737 2435; 8 km w.
Penola Conservation Park: signposted woodland and wetland walk; 10 km w. ***Nangwarry Forestry & Logging Museum:*** features a fascinating array of mill machinery, firefighting equipment, photographs and other artefacts from a bygone era; 18 km s.
Glencoe Woolshed: built in 1863, this shed is unique as it was never converted to mechanised shearing. Now a museum with relics of the period; via Nangwarry; 50km s.

TOWNS NEARBY: Coonawarra 9 km, Naracoorte 47 km, Millicent 49 km, Mount Gambier 51 km, Casterton (Vic.) 55 km

Peterborough

Pop. 1689
Map ref. 559 K3 | 561 I11

ⓘ Main St; (08) 8651 2708; www.peterboroughsa.com.au

📻 105.1 Trax FM, 639 AM ABC North and West

Peterborough is a town obsessed with the railway. Its very existence and growth can be claimed by that industry. In 1881 the line to Jamestown was opened and over the next few years the town became a key intersection between all the major South Australian towns. Locals boast about how, in a mammoth one-day effort, 105 trains travelled the Broken Hill to Port Pirie line. The rail passion continued even after many of the lines closed, and today each town entrance has a welcoming model steam train.

🏛 **Steamtown** With a 100-year-old rail history this dynamic museum, located around the old locomotive workshops, is a collection of historic rolling stock, including a converted Morris car that rides the tracks. Also on display is Australia's only 3-gauge roundhouse and turntable. Main St; (08) 8651 3355.

Town hall: a beautiful, ornate 1927 building with its original theatre and a Federation wall hanging in the foyer; Main St. ***The Gold Battery:*** ore-crushing machine; contact visitor centre; end Tripney Ave. ***Meldonfield:*** view a world of miniature horse-drawn carriages modelled on the style used in the 1800s; Lloyd St. ***Dragons Rest Habitat Garden:*** reptiles and exotic plant life; Watkins Rd. ***Victoria Park:*** features a lake and islands with deer and kangaroo enclosure and a playground; Queen St. ***Bus tour:*** guided tour of sights and history of town; contact visitor centre. ***Town walk and drive:*** self-guide tour; brochure from visitor centre.

 Rodeo: Feb.

🏕 ***Orroroo Caravan Park:*** Second St, Orroroo; (08) 8658 1444.

◎ ***Terowie:*** an old railway town with well-preserved 19th-century main street. Self-guide drive or walk tour; brochure *A Tour of Terowie* available from tearooms; 24 km SE. ***Magnetic Hill:*** park the car, turn off the engine and watch it roll uphill; 32 km NW via Black Rock.

TOWNS NEARBY: Jamestown 34 km, Melrose 63 km, Crystal Brook 72 km, Burra 78 km, Wilmington 78 km

Pinnaroo

Pop. 587
Map ref. 526 B9 | 546 B11 | 548 B1 | 559 O10 | 568 H4

ⓘ Mallee Tourist and Heritage Centre, Railway Tce South; (08) 8577 8644.

📻 107.5 3MBR FM, 1062 AM ABC Riverland

In the 19th century the harshness of the land prevented settlers from properly establishing a farming community here. Instead, they chose the more fertile conditions south-west. The arrival of rail in 1906 and the influx of farming families allowed the community to grow. Although conditions remained tough, the now-renowned Mallee spirit of the farmers allowed the region's agricultural industry to strengthen to what it is today.

🏛 **Mallee Tourist and Heritage Centre** Established in 1999, the centre dwarfs its former home in the old railway station which is now a Pioneer Women's Museum. The new building comprises the D. A. Wurfel Grain Collection, featuring the largest cereal collection in Australia (1300 varieties); working letter presses in the Printing Museum; dioramas, interpretive displays and photos depicting local history in the Heritage Museum; and a collection of restored farm machinery in the Gum Family Collection. Open 10am–1pm or by appt; Railway Tce Sth; (08) 8577 8644.

Animal Park and Aviary: South Tce.

 Pinnaroo Show: Oct.

🏕 ***Pinnaroo Caravan Park:*** Mallee Hwy; (08) 8577 8618.

◎ ***Karte Conservation Park:*** includes a walking trail through low scrub and 40 m high sand dunes; 30 km NW.
Billiatt Conservation Park: the 1 km walk through mallee scrub and dune country ends with panoramic views from Trig Point; 37 km NW. ***Lameroo:*** Mallee town with historic 1898 Byrne pug-and-pine homestead (Yappara Rd) and railway station (Railway Tce); 40 km w. ***Ngarkat group of conservation parks:*** south-west of town; *see Keith.* ***Peebinga Conservation Park:*** important reserve for the rare western whipbird; Loxton Rd; 42 km N.

TOWNS NEARBY: Murrayville (Vic.) 25 km, Loxton 95 km, Keith 106 km, Berri 112 km, Bordertown 117 km

Port Augusta

Pop. 13 255
Map ref. 558 H2 | 560 G9

ⓘ Wadlata Outback Centre, 41 Flinders Tce; (08) 8641 9193 or 1800 633 060; www.wadlata.sa.gov.au

📻 105.9 Magic FM, 639 AM ABC North and West

Port Augusta is the most northerly port in South Australia. The difficulty of land transportation in the 1800s prompted the town's establishment in 1854. It was a major wool and wheat shipping depot until its closure in 1973 – luckily the power stations built by the State Electricity Trust were already generating the city's chief income. Fuelled by coal from the huge open-cut mines at Leigh Creek, the stations generate more than a third of the state's electricity. Port Augusta is also a supply centre for outback areas, an important link on the *Indian–Pacific* railway and a stopover for the Adelaide to Darwin *Ghan* train.

🏛 **Wadlata Outback Centre** This award-winning complex (recently upgraded) covers the natural history of the outback and Flinders Ranges, as well as the people that have called it home throughout the ages. There are hands-on interpretive displays, audiovisual presentations and artefacts. Discover the landscape of 15 million years ago in the Tunnel of Time, and hear ancient Dreamtime stories. The centre is a place in which to learn – Wadlata is an Aboriginal word for communicating. 41 Flinders Tce.

Homestead Park Pioneer Museum: picnic areas, re-creation of a blacksmith's shop, miniature steam and diesel train rides (1st and 3rd Sun each month), and the restored 130-year-old

continued on p. 254

Pop. 4415
Map ref. 559 K8 | 568 C1

ⓘ **Barossa Visitor Centre, 66–68 Murray St, Tanunda;
(08) 8563 0600 or 1300 852 982; www.barossa.com**

89.1 BBB FM, 639 AM ABC North and West

The long history of winemaking in this Barossa town is apparent when travelling down the main street. Old vines that glow red in autumn drape the verandahs of equally old buildings. Surprisingly, the town actually began life as a pub. As a trade route was being established northwards to the Kapunda coppermines, William Coulthard foresaw the demand for rest and refreshment. He built the Old Red Gum Slab Hotel in 1854 and the town developed around it. The Para River runs through Nuriootpa, its course marked by parks and picnic spots.

Coulthard Reserve: popular recreation area; off Penrice Rd. **Barossa Trike Tours:** provides chauffeured Barossa tours aboard an Oztrike Chopper 4 with seating for 3 as you take in the beauty and splendour of Australia's most famous wine region; South Tce; 0438 623 342.

Barossa Vintage Festival: celebration of food and wine in various locations; odd-numbered years, Apr. **Barossa Gourmet Weekend:** Aug. **Barossa Farmers Market:** each Sat morning, in historic Vintners Sheds, near Angaston.

Cucina Banco: hearty Italian bistro fare; 15 Murray St; (08) 8562 4561. **Maggie Beer's Farm Shop:** snacks and goodies; Pheasant Farm Rd; (08) 8562 4477.

Barossa Valley SA Tourist Park: Penrice Rd; (08) 8562 1404. **Whistler Farm:** 616 Samuel Rd; 0415 139 758.

Barossa wine region The Barossa is Australia's eminent wine region, a landscape of historic villages panning out to vine-swept hills and grand buildings on old wine estates. Shiraz is the premier drop, with semillon the star of the whites. Some of the old shiraz vines date back to the 1840s, and several winemaking families, many with German backgrounds, are into their sixth generation. Senior names include Yalumba (1849), which is officially part of the Eden Valley, PENFOLDS (1844) and Seppelt (1851). You can sample the iconic PENFOLDS Grange at PENFOLDS Barossa Valley (Tanunda Rd, Nuriootpa, (08) 8568 9408) and even visit the Winemakers' Laboratory to blend your own wine to take home in a personlised bottle. Seppelt (1 Seppeltsfield Rd, Seppeltsfield, (08) 8568 6217) is a must-visit winery with its elegant bluestone buildings and gardens. Its range of fortified wines includes Spanish styles and classic tawnys – the jewel is Para Liqueur, a tawny released when it is 100 years old. Peter Lehmann (Off Para Rd, Tanunda, (08) 8563 2100) and Wolf Blass (97 Sturt Hwy, Nuriootpa, (08) 8568 7311) are other well-known wineries in the area. Smaller gems include Charles Melton (Krondorf Rd, Tanunda, (08) 8563 3606), known for its Nine Popes blend of shiraz, grenache and mourvedre and for the Rose of Virginia; the nearby Rockford (Krondorf Rd, Tanunda, (08) 8563 2720), with fantastic wines seldom seen in other Australian states; Torbreck Vintners (Roennfeldt Rd, Marananga, (08) 8562 4155), offering excellent shiraz and shiraz viognier; and Langmeil (Cnr Para and Langmeil rds, Tanunda, (08) 8563 2595). For some history on the Barossa and winemaking, the Jacob's Creek Visitor Centre (Barossa Valley Way, Rowland Flat, (08) 8521 3000) has a gallery with displays next to its wine-tasting area, where you can sample some of this well-known label's varieties. *For more information on the region see Tanunda, Lyndoch and Angaston.*

Light Pass: a small, historic township with notable Lutheran churches and Luhrs Pioneer German Cottage, displaying German artefacts; 3 km E. **Maggie Beer's Farm Shop:** tastings and sales of gourmet farm produce from renowned chef and writer Maggie Beer, as well as Pheasant Farm and Beer Brothers wines. Enjoy a gourmet lunch (gourmet picnic-style lunch, (08) 8562 4477); Pheasant Farm Rd; 5 km SW. **Wolf Blass Visitor Centre:** an opportunity to discover your own unique and memorable Wolf Blass experience, be it through learning about one of Australia's most storied winemakers or enjoying the tasting room; Sturt Hwy; (08) 8568 7311.

TOWNS NEARBY: Angaston 6 km, Tanunda 7 km, Kapunda 16 km, Lyndoch 18 km, Gawler 27 km

[PENFOLDS WINERY, BAROSSA WINE REGION]

SOUTH AUSTRALIA

pine-log Yudnappinna homestead; Elsie St; (08) 8642 2035. *Fountain Gallery:* local and touring art and cultural exhibitions; open Mon–Fri; Flinders Tce. *Gladstone Square:* landscaped square surrounded by historic sites, including the courthouse, barracks and Presbyterian church; Cnr Jervois and Marryatt sts. *Australian Arid Lands Botanic Garden:* walks through 200 ha of arid-zone vegetation. Guided tours 10am weekdays; northern outskirts, on the Stuart Hwy; (08) 8641 1049. *McLellan Lookout:* site of Matthew Flinders' landing in 1802; Whiting Pde. *Water Tower Lookout:* spectacular views from the balcony of the 1882 tower; Mitchell Tce. *Matthew Flinders Lookout:* excellent view of Spencer Gulf and the Flinders Ranges; end of McSporran Cres. *Boat cruises and adventure tours:* contact visitor centre. *Heritage walk:* self-guide town walk includes courthouse and the magnificent stained glass in St Augustine's Church; brochure from visitor centre. *Curdnatta Art and Pottery Gallery:* high-quality painting, pottery and fabric art; Flinders Tce.

Cup Carnival: horseracing; June. *Outback Surfboat Carnival:* Nov.

Nuttbush Retreat Caravan Park: Pandurra Station, Eyre Hwy; (08) 8643 8941. *Port Augusta BIG4 Holiday Park – Aspen Parks:* Cnr Princes/Eyre Hwy and Stokes Tce, Port Augusta West; (08) 8642 2974.

Spencer Gulf: watersports, yachting and fishing for King George whiting in northern waters. *Scenic drive:* north-east to the splendid Pichi Richi Pass, historic Quorn and Warren Gorge. See the same sights by train on Pichi Richi Railway, a 33 km round trip operating from Quorn; *see Quorn.*

TOWNS NEARBY: Quorn 30 km, Wilmington 35 km, Melrose 54 km, Whyalla 63 km, Port Pirie 80 km

Port Broughton

Pop. 910
Map ref. 556 F1 | 559 I5 | 560 G12

 Bay St; (08) 8635 2261; www.yorkepeninsula.com.au

87.6 Easy FM, 639 AM ABC North and West

This Yorke Peninsula holiday town has a quiet coastal feel in winter and bustles with sun-seeking holiday-makers in summer. Set on a quiet inlet on Spencer Gulf, it has a long fishing history. In the 1900s the fishing fleets and ketches operated from the jetty. Today the town is still a major port for fishing boats and each week truckloads of blue swimmer crabs depart for city restaurants.

Heritage Centre: local history museum in the old school; Edmund St. *Sailboat hire and fishing charters:* from foreshore. *Town jetty:* popular fishing spot. *Historical walking trail:* grab a *Walk Around Port Broughton* booklet from the visitor centre and navigate the historical sights of the town, including the Heritage Plaques on the foreshore.

Winter Fun Fishing Competition: June. *Rubber Duck Race:* Oct.

Port Broughton Caravan Park: 2 Barker St; (08) 8635 2188.

Fisherman Bay: fishing, boating and holiday spot with over 400 holiday shacks; 5 km N along the coast.

TOWNS NEARBY: Crystal Brook 37 km, Kadina 45 km, Port Pirie 46 km, Wallaroo 46 km, Moonta 61 km

Port Elliot

Pop. 1750
Map ref. 556 H10 | 559 J11 | 568 B5

 Goolwa Wharf; (08) 8555 3488; www.visitalexandrina.com

89.3 5EFM, 639 AM ABC North and West

Port Elliot is a charming historic town set on scenic Horseshoe Bay. Its popularity as a holiday destination lies in the fabulous beaches and the relaxed coastal atmosphere. The town was established in 1854, the year Australia's first public (horse-drawn) railway began operating between Goolwa and the town. Port Elliot's intended purpose as an ocean port for the Murray River was, however, unsuccessful. The bay proved less protected than was first thought and the port was moved to Victor Harbor.

National Trust Historical Display: interpretive centre detailing local history in the old railway station; The Strand. *The Strand:* historic street of art and craft shops, cafes and restaurants. *Cockle Train:* stops at the railway station on Henry St on its journey from Goolwa Wharf to Victor Harbor, so you can do a section of the journey from here; *for more details see Goolwa. Freeman Nob:* spectacular views and coastal walks; end of The Strand. *Encounter Bikeway:* scenic coastal route between Goolwa and Victor Harbor. *Horseshoe Bay:* safe family beach with fishing from jetty. *Boomer Beach:* popular surfing beach; western edge of town. *Maritime Heritage Trail:* the town's story illustrated in foreshore displays. *Heritage walk:* brochure from railway station.

Market: Lakala Reserve; 1st and 3rd Sat each month. *Port Elliot Show:* Oct.

Flying Fish Cafe: popular seafood destination; 1 The Foreshore, Horseshoe Bay; (08) 8554 3504.

Brooklands Heritage B&B: Heysen Rd; (08) 8554 3808. *Tarooki B&B:* 13 Charteris St; (08) 8554 2886. *Trafalgar on the Strand:* 25 The Strand; (08) 8554 3888. *Middleton Caravan Park:* 23 Goolwa Rd, Middleton; (08) 8554 2383.

Basham Beach Regional Park: scenic coastal trails with interpretive signage and southern right whale sightings during their migration season, June–Sept; just north-east of Port Elliot. *Middleton:* coastal town with heritage bakery, the old flour mill and fabulous beaches; 3 km NE. *Crows Nest Lookout:* excellent views of the coast; 6 km N.

TOWNS NEARBY: Victor Harbor 6 km, Goolwa 10 km, Willunga 31 km, Yankalilla 31 km, Aldinga Beach 34 km

Port Lincoln

Pop. 14 245
Map ref. 558 D8

 3 Adelaide Pl; (08) 8683 3544 or 1300 788 378; www.visitportlincoln.net

89.9 Magic FM, 1485 AM ABC Eyre Peninsula and West Coast

Each January, this township on the Eyre Peninsula celebrates the life of the tuna – one of the few festivals in Australia devoted to a fish, and a fair indication of the reign tuna has over this town. Lincoln Cove, the marina, is the base for Australia's largest, and most expensive, tuna fleet and tuna-farming industry. Port Lincoln is set on attractive Boston Bay, which is three times the size of Sydney Harbour. The townsite was reached by Matthew Flinders in his expedition of 1802, and he named it in honour of his home, Lincolnshire, in England. Sheltered waters, a Mediterranean climate and scenic coastal roads make this a popular holiday spot.

Mill Cottage: National Trust museum with early pioneering artefacts and paintings; open 2–4pm Wed and Sun or by appt; Flinders Hwy. *Railway Museum:* relics of the railway past displayed in a historic 1926 stone building; open 1–4pm Wed, Sat and Sun; Railway Pl. *Axel Stenross Maritime Museum:* features original boatbuilding tools and working slipway; open 9am–4.30pm Tues, Thurs and Sun, 1–4.30pm, Sat and public hols; tours by appt; Lincoln Hwy; 1300 788 378. *Settler's Cottage:* stone cottage with early pioneer photos and documents; open 2–4.30pm Sun (closed July and Aug) or by appt; in Flinders Park, Flinders Hwy. *Kotz Stationary Engines:* museum collection of oil and petrol engines; Baltimore St. *Nautilus Theatre:* features 2 galleries of local and touring art, a gallery shop and a wine bar; Tasman Tce. *Kuju Arts and Crafts:* Aboriginal craft sales; closed Sat and Sun; Ravendale Rd. *Mayne Gallery:* local arts and crafts; open 12.30–4.30pm daily; King St. *Lincoln Cove:* includes marina, leisure centre with water slide, holiday charter boats and the base for the commercial fishing fleet (tastings of local catches available). Guided walking tours of the marina are available from the visitor centre; off Ravendale Rd. *Boston Bay:* swimming, waterskiing, yachting and excellent fishing. Try swimming with tuna; 1300 000 8862. *Yacht and boat charters:* for gamefishing, diving, day fishing and for viewing sea lions, dolphins and birdlife around Sir Joseph Banks Group Conservation Park and Dangerous Reef; contact visitor centre for details. *Aquaculture Cruise:* offers you a chance to view the working tuna farms (when in season) and to taste some mouth-watering local sashimi; a sea lion colony can also be visted; contact visitor centre for details. *Boston Island boat tours:* cruises around bay and island; contact visitor centre for details. *Adventure tours and safaris:* offshore and land adventure offered, including close-up tuna tours, shark expeditions and 4WD safaris; contact visitor centre for details. *Old Mill Lookout:* panoramic views of town and bay; Dorset Pl. *Parnkalla Walking Trail:* 14 km trail with coastal views and abundant wildlife. It forms part of the longer Investigator Walking Trail from North Shields to Lincoln National Park; brochure from visitor centre.

Tunarama Festival: Jan. *Adelaide to Lincoln Yacht Race and Lincoln Week Regatta:* Feb/Mar. *Port Lincoln Show:* Aug.

Del Giorno's Cafe Restaurant: wonderful Italian-inspired seafood; 80 Tasman Tce; (08) 8683 0577. *The Marina Bistro:* seafood and grills; The Marina Hotel, 13 Jubilee Dr; (08) 8682 6141. *Sarins:* great seafood and views; 1 Lincoln Hwy; 1300 766 100.

Pitstop on Telford Port Lincoln: 9 Telford Ave; (08) 8682 5353. *Port Lincoln Tourist Park:* 11 Hindmarsh St; (08) 8621 4444. *The Yardarm B&B Holiday Unit:* 14 Telford Ave; (08) 8683 0984.

Lincoln National Park This spectacular coastal park has a network of walking trails through rugged wilderness areas to fantastic coastal scenery. The park is an important sanctuary for migrating birds. To see the park from a height, take the 1.1 km return hike up Stamford Hill. At the top is the Flinders Monument and panoramic views of the coast. For a true, uninterrupted wilderness experience, grab a key and permit from the visitor centre and head on to Memory Cove, a calm bay with a fantastic beach. There is also a replica of the plaque placed by Matthew Flinders in 1802 in memory of 8 crew members lost in

seas nearby. 4WD enthusiasts would enjoy the challenges of the Sleaford Bay coast. (08) 8688 3111; 20 km s.

Delacolline Estate Wines: well known for blended variety of sauvignon blanc/semillon; tastings and sales; alfresco cafe open 11am–4pm Wed–Sun and public hols; Whillas Rd; 08 8682 4000; 1 km w. *Winters Hill Lookout:* views to Boston Bay, Boston Island and Port Lincoln; Flinders Hwy; 5 km NW. *Boston Bay Winery:* tastings and sales; open daily; Lincoln Hwy; (08) 8684 3600 6 km N. *Roseview Emu Park and Rose Gardens:* picturesque gardens in bush setting, with sales of emu produce; Little Swamp La; 10 km NW. *Glen-Forest Tourist Park:* native animals, bird-feeding and miniature golf course; Greenpatch; 15 km NW. *Poonindie Church:* quaint old church built in 1850 with the unique feature of 2 chimneys; 20 km N. *Mikkira Station and Koala Park:* historic 1842 homestead, with bushwalks to see native wildlife. Permit required, available from visitor centre; off Fishery Bay Rd; 26 km sw. *Constantia Designer Craftsmen:* guided tours of world-class furniture factory and showroom; open Mon–Fri; on road to Whalers Way. *Whalers Way:* cliff-top drive through privately owned sanctuary inhabited by seals, ospreys, kangaroos and emus. Permit from visitor centre; 32 km s.

TOWNS NEARBY: Coffin Bay 38 km, Tumby Bay 44 km, Port Victoria 150 km, Elliston 150 km, Cowell 151 km

Port MacDonnell

Pop. 624
Map ref. 550 A6 | 568 G12

7 Charles St; (08) 8738 2576; www.thelimestonecoast.com.au

96.1 Star FM, 1476 AM ABC South East

Port MacDonnell is a quiet fishing town that was once a thriving port. The establishment of the breakwater in 1975 has ensured the southern rock lobster trade many more years of fruitful operation. The fleet is now the largest in Australia. While fishing is the main focus of the area, the rich maritime history, fascinating crystal pools and coastal scenery attract visitors year-round.

Port MacDonnell and District Maritime Museum The long maritime history of this stretch of coast is littered with stories of shipwrecks and bravery. Here photos and salvaged artefacts bring the old days to life. A particularly tragic story is the crash of the *Admella* on an off-coast reef in 1859. Only 24 of the 113 people aboard survived. There is also a focus on community history and on the rock lobster industry. Open 12.30–4.30pm Wed, Fri and Sun; Meylin St; (08) 8738 7259.

Clarke's Park: popular picnic spot with natural spring; northern outskirts. *Fishing:* anglers will enjoy fishing from the jetty and landing. Boat charters available for deep-sea catches of tuna; details from visitor centre. *Heritage walk:* includes historic cemetery with hidden headstones; contact visitor centre.

Bayside Festival: Jan.

Port MacDonnell Foreshore Tourist Park: Eight Mile Creek Rd; (08) 8738 2095. *Kywong Caravan Park:* North Nelson Rd, Nelson, Vic.; (08) 8738 4174.

Ewens Ponds and Piccaninnie Ponds conservation parks For a unique snorkelling or diving experience, visit the crystal-clear waters of these parks. At Ewens Ponds (7 km E) there are 3 ponds, connected via channels. Snorkel on the surface to see the amazing plant life underwater, or go diving for the ultimate

SOUTH AUSTRALIA

[PORT MACDONNELL] **RUGGED COASTLINE**

experience. The deep caverns in Piccaninnie Ponds (20 km E) offer visitors an insight into the underwater world. Snorkellers can gaze into the depths of the Chasm, while divers can explore the limestone-filtered waters of the Cathedral, so named because of its regal white walls. While no experience is necessary for snorkelling, divers require qualifications. Inquiries and bookings to SA Parks and Wildlife, (08) 8735 1177.

Cape Northumberland Heritage and Nature Park: a coastal park famous for sunrises and sunsets. Other highlights include a historic lighthouse, a penguin colony and unusual rock formations; just west of town. ***Dingley Dell Conservation Park:*** the historic 1862 restored cottage that is located here was once the home of Australian poet Adam Lindsay Gordon and features displays on his life and work; tours 10am–4pm daily; 2 km w. ***Germein Reserve:*** 8 km boardwalk (loop track) through wetlands; opposite Dingley Dell. ***Southern Ocean Shipwreck Trail:*** over 89 vessels came to grief on the section of coast from the Victorian border to the Murray River mouth. The drive trail includes 10 interpretive sites; brochure from visitor centre.

TOWNS NEARBY: Mount Gambier 25 km, Millicent 60 km, Penola 76 km, Casterton (Vic.) 81 km, Coonawarra 85 km

Port Pirie

Pop. 13 204
Map ref. 559 I4 | 560 H11

ⓘ Regional Tourism and Arts Centre, 3 Mary Elie St; (08) 8633 8700 or 1800 000 424; www.piriehasitall.com.au

 105.1 Trax FM, 639 ABC North and West

Industry in its splendour greets the visitor at this major industrial and commercial centre. The oil tanks, grain silos and 250-metre-high smokestack all tower over the city, while on the waterfront huge local and overseas vessels are loaded and discharged. Broken Hill Proprietary Company (BHP) began mining lead in 1889 and various South Australian ports at that time vied for BHP's smelting business. Port Pirie eventually won, and created what is today the largest lead smelter in the world. Wheat and barley from the mid-north are also exported from here. Port Pirie shows great character in its old buildings and attractive main street, and Spencer Gulf and the Port Pirie River offer swimming, waterskiing, fishing and yachting.

Regional Tourism and Arts Centre This award-winning centre comprises an eclectic mix of exhibitions, art and information. A lifelike fibreglass model of the largest white pointer shark taken from SA's waters is on display. Local and regional history is presented through a series of art pieces and on the miniature railway, Pirie Rail Express, which replicates the journey from Port Pirie to Broken Hill (runs 1st and 3rd Sun each month). There are local and touring art exhibitions in the art gallery and the centre runs tours to the Pasminco smelter. Mary Elie St; (08) 8633 8700.

National Trust Museum: located in historic town buildings, including the old customs house (1882) and the Victorian pavilion-style railway station, the museum houses a local history display and rooms furnished in early-1900s style; Ellen St. ***Memorial Park:*** features the John Pirie anchor, memorials, and the Northern Festival Centre; Memorial Dr. ***Fishing:*** good local spots include the main wharf. ***Self-guide walks:*** including National Trust Walking Tours and The Journey Landscape, a 1.6 km nature trail representing changes in vegetation from Broken Hill to Port Pirie; brochures from visitor centre.

State Masters Games: even-numbered years, Apr. ***Blessing of the Fleet:*** celebrates the role of Italians in establishing the local fishing industry; Sept. ***Festival of Country Music:*** Oct.

Port Pirie Beach Caravan Park: Beach Rd; (08) 8632 4275. ***Range View Caravan and Cabin Park:*** Lot 513 Port Wakefield Rd (Princes Hwy); (08) 8634 4221. ***Port Germein Caravan Park:*** The Esplanade, Port Germein; (08) 8634 5266.

Weeroona Island: good fishing and holiday area accessible by car; 13 km N. ***Port Germein:*** a quiet beachside town with a tidal beach safe for swimming. At 1.7 km, the town's jetty is one of the longest in Australia; 23 km N. ***Telowie Gorge Conservation Park:*** follow the marked Nukunu Trail from the park's entrance to the breathtaking Telowie Gorge on the south-west edge of the Flinders Ranges. Care should be taken on less-formal tracks in the park; 24 km NE.

TOWNS NEARBY: Crystal Brook 25 km, Melrose 43 km, Whyalla 46 km, Port Broughton 46 km, Jamestown 55 km

Port Victoria

Pop. 344
Map ref. 556 D5 | 558 H8

ⓘ Port Victoria Kiosk, Esplanade; or The Farm Shed Museum and Tourist Centre, 50 Moonta Rd, Kadina; (08) 8821 2333 or 1800 654 991; www.yorkepeninsula.com.au

 89.3 Gulf FM, 639 AM ABC North and West

A tiny township on the west coast of Yorke Peninsula, Port Victoria was tipped to be a thriving port town after James Hughes travelled up the coast in 1840. Hughes, a land surveyor, studied the coastline from his schooner, *Victoria*, and reported favourably on the region. It became an important port for grain exports, with windjammers transporting wheat from here to Europe. The town still proudly proclaims that it is the 'last of the windjammer ports'.

 *Maritime Museum:* displays, relics and artefacts of the great era of the windjammer; open 2–4pm weekends and public holidays; Main St. *Jetty:* original 1888 jetty with good swimming and fishing; end of Main St. *Geology trail:* 4 km interpretive track along the foreshore explains the coast's ancient volcanic history; brochure from visitor centre.

Gulfhaven Caravan Park: Davies Tce; (08) 8834 2012.

Goose Island Conservation Park: important breeding area for several bird species and the Australian sea lion; 13 km offshore; access by private boat. *Wardang Island:* this large island is an Aboriginal reserve, and permission for access is required from Goreta (Point Pearce) Aboriginal Community Council; (08) 8836 7205; near Goose Island. *Wardang Island Maritime Heritage Trail:* this scuba-diving and overland trail includes 8 shipwreck sites with underwater plaques around Wardang Island and 6 interpretive signs at Port Victoria; waterproof self-guide leaflet available from visitor centre.

TOWNS NEARBY: Maitland 22 km, Minlaton 32 km, Ardrossan 41 km, Moonta 49 km, Stansbury 54 km

Quorn

Pop. 1073
Map ref. 559 I1 | 560 H9

3 Seventh St; (08) 8648 6419; www.flindersranges.com

89.1 5UMA FM, 1242 5CS AM

Nestled in a valley in the Flinders Ranges, Quorn was established as a town on the Great Northern Railway line in 1878. The line was built by Chinese and British workers and operated for over 45 years (it closed in 1957). Part of the line through Pichi Richi Pass has been restored as a tourist railway, taking passengers on a scenic 33-kilometre round trip via Port Augusta. The town's old charm has not been lost on movie producers – the historic streetscapes and surrounding landscapes have been used in many films.

Railway Workshop Tours: guided tours of the workshop where locomotives travelling on the Pichi Richi line are maintained and restored. Tours by appt; book at visitor centre. *Junction Art Gallery:* local art exhibition; Railway Tce. *Outback Colours Art Gallery:* Seventh St. *Town walks:* the Walking Tour of Quorn and the Quorn Historic Buildings walk; brochures from visitor centre.

Flinders Ranges Bush Festival: Apr. *Taste of the Outback:* Apr. *Race Meeting:* June. *Pichi Richi Marathon:* July. *Quorn Show:* Sept. *Spring Craft Fair:* Oct. *Christmas Pageant and Party:* Dec.

Quandong Cafe: heritage cafe; 31 First St; (08) 8648 6155.

Quorn Caravan Park: 8 Silo Rd; (08) 8648 6206.

Pichi Richi Railway: historical tourist train travels through dramatic countryside from Quorn to Port Augusta and back; tours by arrangement; bookings 1800 440 101 or through visitor centre. *Quorn Native Flora Reserve:* stone reserve, once the

town's quarry, with informative brochure available that details the reserve's flora; Quarry Rd; 2 km NW. *Pichi Richi Camel Tours:* award-winning camel tours through the gorgeous native bushland, with candlelit dinners and moonlight rides on offer; Devils Peak Rd; (08) 8648 6640; 6 km SE. *The Dutchmans Stern Conservation Park:* colourful rocky outcrops observed on 2 trails through the park. The Ridge Top Trail (8.2 km return) offers spectacular views of the Flinders Ranges and Spencer Gulf; 8 km W. *Devil's Peak Walking Trail:* panoramic views up steep climb to the summit; closed Nov–Apr (fire season); 10 km S. *Mt Brown Conservation Park:* mixed landscape of ridges and woodland. The loop trail, starting at Waukarie Falls, offers a side climb to the Mt Brown summit; Richman Valley Rd; 15 km S. *Warren Gorge:* imposing red cliffs popular with climbers. Also the habitat of the rare yellow-footed rock wallaby; 23 km N. *Buckaringa Gorge Scenic Drive:* drive past Buckaringa Sanctuary and Proby's Grave (he was the first settler at Kanyaka Station) to a lookout accessed via a short walk; begins 35 km N.

TOWNS NEARBY: Port Augusta 30 km, Wilmington 34 km, Melrose 55 km, Hawker 62 km, Whyalla 88 km

Renmark

see inset box on next page

Robe

Pop. 1249
Map ref. 568 E9

The Robe Institute, Mundy Tce; (08) 8768 2465 or 1300 367 144; www.council.robe.sa.gov.au

107.7 5THE FM, 1161 AM ABC South East

Guichen Bay and Robe's coastline would have been a welcome sight to the Chinese immigrants arriving in the mid-1800s. During the Victorian gold rush, around 16 500 Chinese disembarked here and travelled overland to the goldfields to avoid the Poll Tax enforced at Victorian ports. Robe had a thriving export trade before rail was introduced, which has left a legacy of historic buildings, from quaint stone cottages to the Caledonian Inn, with internal doors salvaged from shipwrecks. Today Robe is one of the state's most significant historic towns, but also a fishing port and holiday centre, famous for its crayfish and its secluded beaches.

The Robe Institute: incorporates the visitor centre, library and Historic Interpretation Centre with photographic and audiovisual displays on Robe's history; Mundy Tce. *Robe Customs House:* historic 1863 building, once the hub of Robe's export trade, now a museum featuring Chinese artefacts and displays; open 2–4pm Tues, Sat and daily in Jan; Royal Circus. *Art and craft galleries:* throughout town, especially in Smillie and Victoria sts. *Deep Sea Fishing charter:* sightseeing cruise also on offer; bookings (08) 8768 1807. *Crayfish fleet:* anchors in Lake Butler (Robe's harbour); sells fresh crayfish and fish Oct–Apr. *Walk and scenic drive tours:* self-guide tours available. Take the town walk past 81 historic buildings and sites; brochures from visitor centre.

Robe Easter Surfing Classic: Easter. *Blessing of the Fleet:* celebrates the role of Italians in establishing the local fishing industry; Sept. *Robe Village Fair:* last full weekend in Nov.

Caledonian Inn: historic pub, smart food; 1 Victoria St; (08) 8768 2029.

continued on p. 259

 RADIO STATIONS IN TOWN WHAT'S ON WHERE TO EAT WHERE TO STAY NEARBY

 SOUTH AUSTRALIA

RENMARK

Pop. 4342
Map ref. 526 A5 | 546 B5 | 559 O7 | 568 G1

[ERODED RED CLIFFS ALONG THE MURRAY RIVER]

ⓘ 84 Murray Ave; (08) 8586 6704; www.visitrenmark.com

93.1 Magic FM, 1062 AM ABC Riverland

It is hard to imagine that the lush lands around Renmark, thriving with orchards and vineyards, were once a veritable wasteland. In 1887 the Canadian-born Chaffey brothers were granted 30 000 acres (12 000 hectares) by the South Australian government to test their irrigation scheme. Theirs was the first of its type to succeed in Australia and today the farmlands are still irrigated with water piped from the Murray River.

Olivewood: National Trust historic building, formerly the Chaffey homestead, dressed in period furnishings, with famous olive trees in the orchard; closed Wed; Cnr Renmark Ave and Twenty-first St. *PS Industry:* 1911 grand lady of the river still operates on steam when taking visitors on her monthly cruises; 90 min tours run at 11am and 1.30pm first Sun each month; bookings at visitor centre. *Renmark Hotel:* historic community-owned and -run hotel; Murray Ave. *Nuts About Fruit:* sales of local dried fruit, nuts and other produce; closed Sun; Renmark Ave. *Renmark Riverfront walk:* wander along and take in great views of town along the Murray River. *Murray River cruises:* houseboat hire or paddlesteamer tours to cruise the mighty Murray; contact visitor centre for details.

Dash for Cash: Feb. *Riverland Dingy Derby:* Feb. *Riverland Balloon Fiesta:* June. *Rose Festival:* Oct. *Renmark Show:* Oct. *World Future Cycle Challenge:* Nov.

Renmark Club: traditional Australian bistro fare; 160 Murray Ave; (08) 8586 6611.

Riverbend Caravan Park: Sturt Hwy; (08) 8595 5131.

Bookmark Biosphere Reserve This reserve incorporates the mallee country and arid outback landscapes of Chowilla Regional Reserve and Danggali Conservation Park. In Chowilla (50 km N) are stretches of flood plains interspersed with native woodland and scrubland. Fishing, canoeing and birdwatching are popular and the history of the flood plains is explained on the Old Coach Road Vehicle Trail. Danggali (90 km N) is a vast wilderness area with interesting trails to explore. The 2 drive tours, Nanya's Pad Interpretive Drive (100 km circuit, 2WD accessible) and Tipperary Drive (100 km circuit, 4WD only), are both excellent introductions to the mallee scrub region, while the 10 km Target Mark Walking Trail passes through native vegetation to the dam.

Lock and Weir No. 5: picnic in surrounding parklands; 2 km SE. *Paringa:* small farming community featuring a historic suspension bridge (1927), Bert Dix Memorial Park and nearby Headings Cliffs Lookout; 4 km E. *Angove's:* producers of St Agnes Brandy as well as wine, with cellar-door tastings and sales; Bookmark Ave; 5 km SW. *Bredl's Wonder World of Wildlife:* unique fauna, particularly reptiles. Handling and feeding times between 11am and 3pm; (08) 8595 1431; 7 km SW. *Ruston's Rose Garden:* the Southern Hemisphere's largest rose garden with over 50 000 bushes and 4000 varieties; open Oct–May; Moorna St, off Sturt Hwy; (08) 8586 6191; 7 km SW. *Dunlop Big Tyre:* spans the Sturt Hwy at Yamba Roadhouse and marks the fruit-fly inspection point (no fruit allowed between Victoria and SA); 16 km SE. *Murray River National Park, Bulyong Island section:* popular park for water-based activities, fishing and birdwatching; just upstream from Renmark on the Murray River.

TOWNS NEARBY: Berri 18 km, Barmera 28 km, Loxton 35 km, Waikerie 70 km, Morgan 101 km

Ann's Place Bed & Breakfast: 2 Royal Circus; (08) 8768 2262. *Discovery Holiday Parks – Robe:* 70–80 Esplanade; (08) 8768 2237. *Lakeside Tourist Park:* 24 Main Rd; (08) 8768 2193. *Number 13 on the Beach:* 13 Seafarers Cres; (08) 8768 2116. *Robe Heritage Accommodation:* 1A Hagen St; (08) 8768 2770. *Sea Vu Caravan Park:* 1 Squire Dr; (08) 8768 2273.

Mt Benson wine region Mt Benson is the only sub-wine region actually located on the coast. The first vines were planted less than two decades ago, and the region is still revealing its true colours. The large venture of Norfolk Rise, established by an international company, indicates the area's promise. Make sure to try its shiraz. Other wineries to visit are Wehl's Mt Benson Vineyard, Cape Jaffa Wines and Ralph Fowler Wines, which is also the cellar door for Frog Island, inland from Robe.

Lake Fellmongery: popular spot for waterskiing; 1 km SE. *Long Beach:* 17 km pristine beach for surfing and swimming. Cars are allowed on the sand; 2 km N. *Little Dip Conservation Park:* features a complex, moving sand-dune system, salt lakes, freshwater lakes and abundant wildlife. Drive or walk through native bush to beaches for surfing and beach-fishing; some areas 4WD only; 2 km S. *Beacon Hill:* panoramic views of Robe, lakes and coast from lookout tower; Beacon Hill Rd; 2 km SE. *The Obelisk:* navigational marker at Cape Dombey. Scenic access via cliff walk from the Old Gaol at Robe; 2 km W.

TOWNS NEARBY: Kingston S.E. 38 km, Beachport 41 km, Millicent 70 km, Naracoorte 90 km, Coonawarra 97 km

Roxby Downs
Pop. 3848
Map ref. 560 E4

i Roxby Downs Cultural Precinct; (08) 8671 2001; www.roxbydowns.com

102.7 AM ABC Local, 105.5 ROX FM

In 1975 Roxby Downs station was a hard-working property on the red sand dunes of central South Australia. That was until a body of copper and uranium, the largest in the world, was discovered near a dam. Roxby Downs, the township, was built to accommodate the employees of the Olympic Dam mining project and has many modern facilities.

Cultural Precinct: incorporates the visitor centre, cinema, cafe, art gallery with local and touring exhibitions, and interpretive display on town and dam history; Richardson Pl. *Arid Discovery:* area of native landscape with sunset tours to see reintroduced native animals, including bilbies and burrowing bettongs. A highlight is the close viewing of animals in the observation hide; contact visitor centre for tour details. *Emu Walk:* self-guide flora walk through town; contact visitor centre.

Market: Richardson Pl; closest Sat to the 15th each month. *Outback Fringe Festival:* Apr.

Myall Grove Holiday Park – Aspen Parks: 56 Burgoyne St; (08) 8671 1991.

Olympic Dam Mining Complex: an extensive underground system of roadways and trains services the mine that produces refined copper, uranium oxide, gold and silver. The mine is 9 km N, but limited views are available at the site. Olympic Dam Tours run surface tours 3 days a week; times and bookings through the visitor centre.

TOWNS NEARBY: Andamooka 28 km, Woomera 72 km, Leigh Creek 145 km, Marree 151 km, Blinman 183 km

Stansbury
Pop. 521
Map ref. 556 E7 I 558 H9

i Cnr Weaver and Towler sts; (08) 8852 4577; www.stansburysa.com

98.9 Flow FM, 639 AM ABC North and West

Situated on the lower east coast of Yorke Peninsula and with views of Gulf St Vincent, Stansbury was originally known as Oyster Bay because of its claim to the best oyster beds in the state. The town has always serviced the farms inland, but its mainstay today is tourism. The bay is excellent for fishing and watersports, including diving and waterskiing.

Schoolhouse Museum: this local history museum in Stansbury's first school features cultural and environmental displays as well as the headmaster's rooms furnished in early-1900s style; open 2–4pm Wed and Sun, daily in Jan; North Tce. *Oyster farms:* see daily operations of local oyster farms and try fresh oysters. *Fishing:* popular spots include the jetty, rocks and beach. *Mills' Gully Lookout:* popular picnic spot with panoramic views of bay, town and Gulf St Vincent; northern outskirts of town. *Coastal trails:* walking and cycling trails past reserves, lookouts and a historic cemetery; start at foreshore caravan park; brochure from visitor centre.

Stansbury Seaside Markets: monthly Oct–May; check dates with visitor centre. *Stansbury and Port Vincent Wooden and Classic Boat Regatta:* even-numbered years, Apr. *Sheepdog Trials:* odd-numbered years, May.

Stansbury Progress Assoc Foreshore Caravan Park: Anzac Pde; (08) 8852 4171. *Port Vincent Caravan Park & Seaside Cabins:* 12 Minlacowie Rd, Port Vincent; (08) 8853 7011. *Port Vincent Foreshore Caravan Park:* Marine Pde, Port Vincent; (08) 8853 7073.

Kleines Point Quarry: SA's largest limestone quarry; 5 km S. *Lake Sundown:* one of the many salt lakes in the area and a photographer's delight at sunset; 15 km NW. *Port Vincent:* popular holiday destination with good swimming, yachting and waterskiing; 17 km N.

TOWNS NEARBY: Edithburgh 20 km, Yorketown 21 km, Minlaton 24 km, Port Victoria 54 km, Ardrossan 55 km

Strathalbyn
Pop. 3894
Map ref. 559 K10 I 568 C4

i Old Railway Station, South Tce; (08) 8536 3212; www.visitalexandrina.com

94.7 5EFM, 639 AM ABC North and West

This heritage town has some of the most picturesque and historic streetscapes in country South Australia. It has a predominantly Scottish heritage, first settled by Dr John Rankine, who emigrated with 105 other Scotsmen in the late 1830s. The town is set on the Angas River, with the Soldiers Memorial Gardens following the watercourse through the town. Strathalbyn is renowned for its antique and craft shops.

National Trust Museum: history display in the courtroom, Victorian-era relics in the courthouse, and a historical room and photographic displays in the Old Police Station; open 2–5pm Wed, Thurs, Sat and Sun; Rankine St. *Old Railway Station:* complex includes the visitor centre, the Station Master's Gallery with local and touring art exhibitions (open Wed–Sun), and

SOUTH AUSTRALIA

the station for the tourist railway from Mount Barker, the *SteamRanger* (*see Hahndorf*); South Tce. *St Andrew's Church:* impressive church with castle-like tower; Alfred Pl. *Original Lolly Shop:* old-fashioned lollies and fudge; High St. *Antiques, art and craft shops:* outlets in High St. *Heritage walk:* self-guide trail featuring over 30 heritage buildings and the architectural delights of Albyn Tce; brochure available from visitor centre.

Collectors, Hobbies and Antique Fair: Aug. *Strathalbyn Show:* Oct. *Glenbarr Highland Gathering:* Oct. *Rotary Duck Race:* plastic ducks; Nov.

Victoria Hotel: creative pub meals; 16 Albyn Tce; (08) 8536 2202.

Clayton Bay Caravan Park: Island View Dr, Clayton Bay; (08) 8537 0372. *Longview Vineyard:* Pound Rd, Macclesfield; (08) 8388 9694. *Milang Lakeside Caravan Park:* 1 Woodrow Dr, Milang; (08) 8537 0282. *The Old Oak Bed & Breakfast:* Cnr Bald Hill and Goolwa rds, Bull Creek; (08) 8536 6069. *The Stumps B&B:* Hill Top Rd, Macclesfield; (08) 8388 9513.

Milang This old riverboat town is now a popular holiday destination on the shores of Lake Alexandrina, Australia's largest freshwater lake. The lake offers fishing, sailing and windsurfing. In town, visit the Port Milang Railway for its local history display and pick up a Heritage Trail brochure for a self-guide walk. Each Australia Day weekend the Milang–Goolwa Freshwater Classic fills the town with visitors who come to watch hundreds of yachts begin the race. 20 km SE.

Langhorne Creek wine region This highly productive area lies to the east of McLaren Vale on the flood plains of the Bremer and Angas rivers. The flat terrain and access to water for irrigation have made it the target of large-scale operations, but the wines produced, particularly shiraz and cabernet sauvignon, have an endearing softness as well as depth of flavour. Bleasdale Vineyards dates back to 1850 and its wines are the classic Langhorne Creek label sold at reasonable prices. Zonte's Footstep also has good, value-for-money wines. Other wineries to visit in the area include Lake Breeze Wines and Temple Bruer, which is certified organic.

Lookout: views over town and district; 7 km SW. *Ashbourne:* buy local produce at roadside stalls and at the country market held 3rd Sun each month; 14 km W. *Meadows:* features Pottery at Paris Creek and Iris Gardens (open Oct–Mar) nearby. The Country Fair is held each Oct; 15 km NW.

TOWNS NEARBY: Hahndorf 27 km, Goolwa 29 km, Willunga 31 km, McLaren Vale 32 km, Port Elliot 36 km

Streaky Bay

Pop. 1059
Map ref. 558 A3 | 567 N10

ⓘ Rural Transaction and Visitor Information Centre, 21 Bay Rd; (08) 8626 7033; www.streakybay.sa.gov.au

99.3 Flow FM, 693 AM ABC Eyre Peninsula and West Coast

A holiday town, fishing port and agricultural centre for the cereal-growing hinterland. The bay was first sighted in 1627 by Dutch explorer Peter Nuyts, but it wasn't fully explored until 1802 by Matthew Flinders. Flinders named the bay after the 'streaky' colour of the water, caused by seaweed oils. While this town is pretty, it is the surrounding bays and coves, sandy beaches and towering cliffs that bring the visitors.

National Trust Museum: early pioneer history displays in the old school, as well as a restored pioneer cottage and a doctor's surgery; open 2–4pm Tues and Fri, or by appt; Montgomerie Tce;

(08) 8626 1443. *Powerhouse Restored Engine Centre:* display of old working engines; open 2–5pm Tues and Fri; Alfred Tce. *Shell Roadhouse:* Great White Shark replica (original caught with rod and reel); Alfred Tce. *Fishing:* for King George whiting, southern rock lobster, salmon, mullaway, garfish, abalone and shark (check with PIRSA & Fisheries centre).

Perlubie Sports Day: Jan. *Streaky Bay Cup:* horseracing; Apr.

Mocean Cafe: innovative seafront dining; 34B Alfred Tce; (08) 8626 1775.

Streaky Bay Foreshore Tourist Park: 82 Wells St; (08) 8626 1666. *Coodlie Park Farm Retreat:* Coodlie Park (via Flinders Hwy), Port Kenny; (08) 8687 0411.

Scenic drives: include Westall Way Scenic Drive, which starts 9 km S, taking in rock formations, high cliffs, quiet pools and the Yanerbie Sand Dunes. Also the drive west of town to Cape Bauer and the Blowhole (20 km NW), for views across the Bight. *Calpatanna Waterhole Conservation Park:* bushwalking in coastal park to an important Aboriginal waterhole; excellent birdwatching; 28 km SE. *Murphy's Haystacks:* a much-photographed cluster of pink granite boulders, with interpretive signage and paths; 40 km SE. *Baird Bay:* a small coastal town with an attractive beach for swimming, boating and fishing. Baird Bay Charters and Ocean Ecotours offer swims with sea lions and dolphins; (08) 8626 5017; 45 km SE. *Point Labatt Conservation Park:* from the cliff-top viewing platform, see the rare and endangered Australian sea lions sleeping on the beach (this colony is the only permanent one on the Australian mainland). Parts of access road unsealed; 50 km SE. *Venus Bay Conservation Park:* important reserve for breeding and reintroduction of native species. The park includes the peninsula and 7 islands with beach-fishing and swimming. Peninsula access is 4WD only; turn-off 50 km SE. *Acraman Creek Conservation Park:* this mangrove and mallee park is an important refuge for coastal birds. Popular activities include canoeing and fishing. 2WD access to beach, 4WD to Point Lindsay; turn-off 53 km N. *Port Kenny:* this small township on Venus Bay offers excellent fishing, boating and swimming, with sea lion and dolphin tours available; 62 km SE. *Venus Bay:* fishing village renowned for catches of King George whiting, trevally, garfish and many more. Its waters are safe for swimming and watersports, and nearby beaches are good for surfing. Needle Eye Lookout close by provides fantastic views, with southern right whale sightings June–Oct; 76 km S.

TOWNS NEARBY: Ceduna 90 km, Elliston 113 km, Wudinna 120 km, Kimba 210 km, Coffin Bay 234 km

Swan Reach

Pop. 237
Map ref. 559 L8 | 568 E2

ⓘ General Store, 47 Anzac Ave; (08) 8570 2036 or 1800 442 784; www.murraylands.info

93.1 Magic FM, 1062 AM ABC Riverland

This quiet little township on the Murray River was once one of five large sheep stations; the original homestead is now the Swan Reach Hotel. Established as one of the first river ports for Murray River trade, the introduction of rail, and Morgan's rise as one of the state's busiest ports, saw the era of paddlesteamers in Swan Reach decline. Today the picturesque river scenery and excellent fishing make the town a popular holiday destination.

Swan Reach Museum: local history displays with special interest in Swan Reach's flood history, the waters having devastated the town in the early 1900s; Nildottie Rd.

Yookamurra Sanctuary This sanctuary represents an initiative to restore 1100 ha of land to its original state. Fittingly, the sanctuary is named Yookamurra after the Aboriginal word for 'yesterday'. The mallee vegetation that was found here before European habitation has been replanted; keep an eye out for the rare and endangered numbat or the bilby and woylie. Walking tours and overnight stays are available. Bookings are essential, (08) 8562 5011; Pipeline Rd, Sedan; 21 km w.

Murray Aquaculture Yabby Farm: catch your own yabbies; 1.5 km E. *Ridley and Swan Reach conservation parks:* both parks represent typical western Murray vegetation and protect the habitat of the hairy-nosed wombat; 7.5 km s and 10 km w respectively. *Ngaut Ngaut Boardwalk:* guided tours of archaeological site, established when an ancient skeleton was discovered; Nildottie; 14 km s. *Big Bend:* imposing Murray cliffs, the tallest found on the river, home to diverse flora and fauna. Spectacular nightly tours are available; inquiries (08) 8570 1097; 20 km downstream. *Bakara Conservation Park:* mallee-covered plains and sand dunes, important habitat for the mallee fowl; 32 km E. *Brookfield Conservation Park:* bushwalking in limestone country to see hairy-nosed wombats, red kangaroos and a variety of bird species; 40 km NW.

TOWNS NEARBY: Mannum 47 km, Angaston 51 km, Waikerie 56 km, Nuriootpa 56 km, Tanunda 59 km

Tanunda

Pop. 4683
Map ref. 559 K8 | 568 C2

i **Barossa Visitor Information Centre, Murray St;** (08) 8563 0600 or 1300 852 982; www.barossa.com

89.1 BBB FM, 639 AM ABC North and West

Tanunda is at the heart of the Barossa and surrounded by vineyards. The modern-day township grew out of the village of Langmeil, which was the focal point for early German settlement. The German Lutherans found it only natural to plant vines, as it was a basic part of their lifestyle. Many of the Barossa's shiraz vines date back to those early days. Tanunda has a boisterous German spirit, good eateries and fine examples of Lutheran churches.

Barossa Historical Museum: situated in the former post and telegraph office (1865), its collections specialise in German heritage; Murray St. *Gourmet produce:* specialty stores include Tanunda Bakery for German breads (Murray St), Tanunda's Nice Ice for homemade ice-cream (Kavel Arcade) and Apex Bakery for traditional pastries (Elizabeth St). *Heritage walk:* includes many historic Lutheran churches; more details available from visitor centre in Murray St.

Barossa Under the Stars: Mar. *Tanunda Show:* Mar. *Barossa Vintage Festival:* celebration of locally produced food and wine in various locations; odd-numbered years, Apr. *Barossa Gourmet Weekend:* Aug. *Barossa Band Festival:* Oct.

1918 Bistro & Grill: modern Australian; 94 Murray St; (08) 8563 0405. *Apex Bakery:* traditional German bakery; 1A Elizabeth St, (08) 8563 2483. *Krondorf Road Cafe:* authentic German recipes; Krondorf Rd; (08) 8563 0889. *Appellation:* benchmark regional fine dining; The Louise, cnr Seppeltsfield and Stonewall rds, Marananga; (08) 8562 2722. *Jacob's Restaurant:* sleek cellar-door dining; Jacob's Creek Visitor Centre, Barossa Valley Way, Rowland Flat; (08) 8521 3000.

Barossa House Bed & Breakfast: Barossa Valley Way; (08) 8562 4022. *Barossa Vista:* 1B Murray St; 0423 019 353. *Blickinstal Barossa Valley Retreat:* Rifle Range Rd; (08) 8563 2716. *Clara's Cottage:* 13 John St; (08) 8563 0004. *The Dove Cote:* 13 Edward St; (08) 8563 2716. *Frieda's Cottage:* 17 Young St; (08) 8563 0004. *Goat Square Cottages:* 33 John St; (08) 8524 5353. *Jewel of the Valley:* 1 Elizabeth St; (08) 8524 5353. *Lochnagar Barossa:* 22 Paradale Dr; (08) 8524 5353. *Tanunda Caravan & Tourist Park:* Barossa Valley Way; (08) 8563 2784. *Tanunda Cottages:* 157 Murray St; 0418 831 955. *Barossa Vineyard Cottages:* Lot 575 Bethany Rd, Bethany; 0419 556 449. *Treetops Bed & Breakfast:* Seppeltsfield Rd, Marananga; (08) 8562 2522.

 Barossa wine region The Mediterranean-style climate, varying soils, specialised winemakers and long history (dating back to the 1840s) have created a world-renowned wine region in the Barossa Valley. Nearly all outfits offer cellar-door tastings and sales. Close to Tanunda is the Barossa Small Winemakers Centre, housed in the cellar door at Chateau Tanunda, Basedow Rd, and showcasing the rare and handmade varieties of the Barossa's small producers. At the Chateau Dorrien Winery Tourism Centre in Barossa Valley Way there is an interesting mural depicting Barossa heritage. Winery map available from visitor centre. *For more information see Angaston, Lyndoch and Nuriootpa.*

Norm's Coolies: see performances by a unique breed of sheepdog, Norm's coolie; 2pm Mon, Wed and Sat; just south on Barossa Valley Way; (08) 8563 2198. *Bethany:* this pretty village was the first German settlement in the Barossa, and it has a great winery sitting on a hilltop. The creekside picnic area, pioneer cemetery, attractive streetscapes and walking trail along Rifle Range Rd make it well worth a visit; 3 km SE. *The Keg Factory:* makers of American and French oak kegs, as well as barrel furniture and wine racks; (08) 8563 3012. St Halletts Rd; 4 km sw.

TOWNS NEARBY: Nuriootpa 7 km, Angaston 8 km, Lyndoch 11 km, Kapunda 21 km, Gawler 21 km

Tumby Bay

Pop. 1348
Map ref. 558 E7

i **Hales MiniMart, 1 Bratten Way; (08) 8688 2584;** www.tumbybay.sa.gov.au

89.9 Magic FM, 1485 AM ABC Eyre Peninsula and West Coast

Tumby Bay is a pretty coastal town on the east coast of Eyre Peninsula. Its development was slow – Matthew Flinders discovered the bay in 1802, settlers arrived in the 1840s and the jetty was built in 1874 to ship the grain produce, but still there was no town. It took until the early 1900s for any official settlement to be established. Now the famous long, crescent beach, white sand and blue water attract holiday-makers.

C. L. Alexander National Trust Museum: depicts early pioneer history in an old timber schoolroom; open 10–11am Wed, 2.30–4.30pm Sun or by appt; West Tce; (08) 8688 2760. *Rotunda Art Gallery:* local art display and a fantastic mural on the outside of the rotunda; open 10am–12pm Mon and Wed or by appt; Tumby Tce; (08) 8688 2678. *Excell Blacksmith and Engineering Workshop Museum:* original workshop and equipment dating from the early 1900s; open 1.30–4.30pm 4th Sun each month, or by appt; Barraud St; (08) 8688 2101.

 SOUTH AUSTRALIA

Mangrove boardwalk: 70 m walkway with interpretive signs explaining ecology of mangroves; Berryman St. *Fishing:* from the recreational jetty, beach, rocks or boats (hire and charters available).

Tumby Bay Caravan Park: Tumby Tce; (08) 8688 2208. *Cummins Community Caravan Park:* 62 Bruce Tce, Cummins; (08) 8676 2011.

Koppio Smithy Museum The early 1900s come to life in this extensive National Trust museum in the Koppio Hills. Consisting of the restored Blacksmith's Shop (1903), historic log cottage 'Glenleigh' (1893) and schoolrooms, the museum houses an eclectic collection of Aboriginal artefacts, early pioneer furniture, firearms and early machinery. Closed Mon; 30 km sw.

Trinity Haven Scenic Drive: travels south from town along the coast and offers scenic coastal views and secluded beaches and bays. *Island Lookout Tower and Reserve:* views of town, coast and islands. Enjoy a picnic in the reserve; Harvey Dr; 3 km s. *Lipson Cove:* popular spot for anglers. Walk to the coastal sanctuary on Lipson Island at low tide; 10 km NE. *Ponta and Cowleys beaches:* fishing catches include snapper and bream; 15 km NE. *Moody Tanks:* State Heritage–listed water-storage tanks once used to service passing steam trains; 30 km w. *Cummins:* rich rail heritage celebrated each Apr at the World Championship Kalamazoo Classic; 37 km NW. *Port Neill:* an old port town with a safe beach for fishing and watersports. Also Ramsay Bicentennial Gardens, and vintage vehicles at Vic and Jill Fauser's Living Museum. Port Neill Lookout, nearby, provides fantastic views of the coast; 42 km NE. *Sir Joseph Banks Group Conservation Park:* comprising around 20 islands and reefs, this park is a breeding area for migrating coastal birds and the Australian sea lion colony at Dangerous Reef; boat access is from Tumby Bay, Port Lincoln and 250 m north of Lipson Cove.

TOWNS NEARBY: **Port Lincoln 44 km, Coffin Bay 64 km, Cowell 108 km, Port Victoria 128 km, Elliston 138 km**

Waikerie
Pop. 1744
Map ref. 559 M7 | 568 F1

ⓘ Orange Tree Giftmania, 12911 Sturt Hwy; (08) 8541 2332; www.waikerietourism.com.au

93.1 Magic FM, 1062 AM ABC Riverland

Waikerie, the citrus centre of Australia, is surrounded by an oasis of irrigated orchards and vineyards in the midst of the mallee-scrub country of the Riverland. Owing to its position on cliff-tops, the area around Waikerie was not a promising settlement. However, in an experiment by the South Australian government in 1894 that attempted to alleviate unemployment and decentralise capital, 281 people were relocated from Adelaide. It was an instant town. Waikerie has beautiful views of the river gums and sandstone cliffs along the Murray River, which is a popular spot for fishing, boating and waterskiing – and the skies above are a glider's paradise due to the fantastic thermals and flat landscape.

Rain Moth Gallery: local art exhibitions; open 10.30am–2.30pm Mon–Fri, 10am–1pm Sat; Peake Tce. *Waikerie Murray River Queen:* unique floating motel, restaurant and cafe; moored near the ferry. *Harts Lagoon:* wetland area with bird hide; Ramco Rd. *Houseboat hire:* scenic trips along the Murray; contact visitor centre for details. *Bush Safari:* camel or 4WD tours to the river and outback country north-east of Waikerie; bookings (08) 8543 2280. *Scenic walk:* along cliff-top to lookout; northern outskirts of town.

Rotary Food Fair: Mar. *Horse and Pony Club Easter Horse Show:* Easter. *Music on the Murray:* odd-numbered years, Apr. *Riverland Rock 'n' Roll Festival:* May. *Hit n Miss Tractor Pull:* odd-numbered years, Sept.

Waikerie Caravan Park: 49 Peake Tce; (08) 8541 2651. *Salters Station:* 72 Paisley Rd, Blanchetown; (08) 8540 5023.

Orange Tree Giftmania: local produce sales – including citrus and dried fruits – and souvenirs. Enjoy Murray River views from the viewing platform; Sturt Hwy. *Waikerie Gliding Club:* offers recreational flights, beginner courses and cross-country training; Waikerie Aerodrome, off Sturt Hwy, east side of town; inquiries (08) 8541 2644. *Maize Island Conservation Park:* this waterbird reserve has fantastic cliffs and lagoons. Beware of strong currents when swimming; 2 km N. *Pooginook Conservation Park:* both dense and open mallee country, home to kangaroos, hairy-nosed wombats and the ever-busy mallee fowl; 12 km NE. *Stockyard Plain Disposal Basin Reserve:* varied plant and birdlife – over 130 bird species identified; key available from visitor centre; 12 km sw. *Broken Cliffs:* popular fishing spot; Taylorville Rd; 15 km NE. *Birds Australia Gluepot Reserve:* important mallee area that forms part of the Bookmark Biosphere Reserve (*see Renmark*). Also significant bird refuge, with over 17 threatened Australian species to be seen on the 14 walking trails; access key from Shell Service Station in Waikerie; 64 km N.

TOWNS NEARBY: **Morgan 34 km, Barmera 45 km, Swan Reach 56 km, Berri 58 km, Loxton 62 km**

Wallaroo
Pop. 3050
Map ref. 556 E3 | 558 H6

ⓘ The Farm Shed Museum and Tourist Centre, 50 Moonta Rd, Kadina; (08) 8821 2333 or 1800 654 991; www.yorkepeninsula.com.au

89.3 Gulf FM, 639 AM ABC North and West

Vast grain silos greet visitors to Wallaroo, a coastal town and shipping port on the west coast of Yorke Peninsula. The town is an interesting mix of tourism and industry. The safe beaches and excellent fishing prove popular with holiday-makers, while the commercial port controls exports of barley and wheat. Wallaroo exists thanks to a lucky shepherd's discovery of copper in 1859. Vast deposits were uncovered and soon thousands of Cornish miners arrived. The area boomed until the 1920s, when copper prices dropped and the industry slowly died out. Wallaroo's buildings and old Cornish-style cottages are a reminder of its colourful past. Wallaroo and nearby towns Moonta and Kadina are part of the 'Copper Coast' or 'Little Cornwall'.

Wallaroo Heritage and Nautical Museum This National Trust museum in Wallaroo's original 1865 post office features shipwreck displays, maps, charts, model ships and records, as well as local cultural and religious history. Meet George, the unlucky giant squid eaten then recovered from a whale's belly 30 years ago. Open 10.30am–4pm Mon–Fri, 2–4pm Sat–Sun; Jetty Rd; (08) 8823 3015.

Yorke Peninsula Railway: historical diesel-train journey from Wallaroo to Bute; runs 2nd Sun each month and school holidays; contact visitor centre for details. *Ausbulk:* informative drive through grain-handling facility; Lydia Tce. *Boat hire and charters:* for the ultimate gulf-fishing experience. *Self-guide historical walk:* highlight is the 1865 Hughes chimney stack, which contains over 300 000 bricks and measures more than 7 sq m at its base; brochure available from museum or town hall.

continued on p. 264

VICTOR HARBOR

Pop. 10 377

Map ref. 556 H10 | 559 J11 | 568 B5

i Causeway Building, Esplanade; (08) 8551 0777; www.tourismvictorharbor.com.au

89.3 5EFM, 639 AM ABC North and West

In the 1830s the crystal waters of Encounter Bay – and the Southern Ocean beyond – throbbed with the whalers and sealers of the south. Granite Island housed a whaling station, Victor Harbor was its port, and life revolved around the ocean slaughters. Today the whalers and sealers are gone, Granite Island is a recreation park and Victor Harbor is a holiday town. The naming of Encounter Bay comes from the unexpected meeting in the bay between explorers Matthew Flinders and Nicolas Baudin.

South Australian Whale Centre This unique centre focuses on the 25 species of whale and dolphin, and other marine life found in the southern Australian waters, with an aim to educate and conserve these species. Past atrocities are displayed alongside interactive displays and presentations that reveal the wonders of the amazing creatures. Between May and Oct, southern right whales mate and breed in Encounter Bay. The centre offers whale cruises and sighing information, as well as a Whale Information Hotline for the latest sightings (in season) 1900 WHALES (1900 942 537). Open 9.30am–5pm daily (exc Christmas Day); Railway Tce; (08) 8551 0750.

Encounter Coast Discovery Centre: National Trust museum that covers Aboriginal, whaling, settler and recent local history. A museum walk finishes at the Old Customs House, which has period furnishings; open 1–4pm daily; Flinders Pde. *Cockle Train:* departs from Railway Tce for return journey to Goolwa; bookings 1300 655 991; *for more details see Goolwa. Horse-drawn tram:* operates daily; (08) 8551 0720; www.horsedrawntram.com.au. *Amusement Park:* family fun fair on the beach with the state's historic Ferris wheel, dodgem cars and an inflatable slide; open long weekends and school holidays; the Causeway; 0418 845 540. *SteamRanger Heritage Railway:* heritage steam and diesel tourist trains run to Port Elliot, Goolwa, Strathalbyn and Mount Barker; phone 1300 655 991; www.steamranger.org.au. *Scenic flights:* helicopter joy-flights over Victor Harbor, Granite Island, local vineyards and the mouth of the Murray; (08) 8552 8196.

Rotary Art Show: Jan. *Coast to Coast Bike Ride and Victor Harbor Triathlon:* Mar. *Whale Season Opening:* June. *Whaletime Playtime Festival:* July. *Rock n Roll Festival:* Sept. *New Year's Eve Celebration:* Dec.

Anchorage Cafe Restaurant Wine Bar: steaks and seafood; Anchorage Seafront Hotel, 21 Flinders Pde; (08) 8552 5970. *eat at whalers:* contemporary bayside dining; Whalers Inn Resort, 121 Franklin Pde, Encounter Bay; (08) 8552 4400.

Morgan Park Bed & Breakfast: 1 Shetland Crt; (08) 8552 8781. *Victor Harbor Beachfront Holiday Park:* 114 Victoria St; (08) 8552 1111. *Victor Harbor Holiday and Cabin Park:* Bay Rd; (08) 8552 1949. *Adare Caravan Park & Holiday Units:* 18-38 Wattle Dr, McCracken; (08) 8552 1657. *Close Encounters Bed & Breakfast:* 69 Whalers Rd, Encounter Bay; (08) 8552 4850. *Encounter Lakes Bed & Breakfast:* 45 Matthew Flinders Dr, Encounter Bay; (08) 8552 7758. *Scenic Encounter Bed & Breakfast:* 27 Bolger Way, Encounter Bay; (08) 8552 2043.

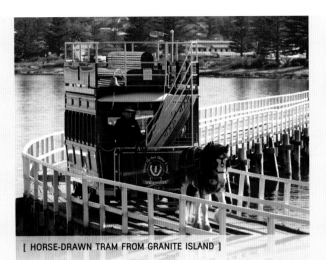

[HORSE-DRAWN TRAM FROM GRANITE ISLAND]

Granite Island Recreation Park Granite Island has a long and varied history. It has significance in the Ramindjeri people's Dreamtime; in 1837 a whaling station was established; and today the island is a recreation park. This history is detailed on the Kaiki Trail, a 1.5 km walk around the island. A highlight is the Below Decks Oceanarium, just off the Screwpile Jetty, with close-up views of marine life and tours daily; at dusk, take a guided Penguin Discovery Tour to see the penguins scuttle in and out of their burrows (all tour bookings (08) 8552 7555). The island is linked to the mainland by a 630 m causeway. Walk or take the horse-drawn tram, the last one remaining in the Southern Hemisphere; tram departs from entrance to Causeway at 10am daily. Tickets available at visitor centre or on the tram.

Hindmarsh River Estuary: peaceful picnic and fishing spot with boardwalk through coastal scrub; 1 km NE. *Greenhills Adventure Park:* family-fun activities including go-karts, jumping castle and water slide; Waggon Rd; 3.5 km N. *Victor Harbor Winery:* cellar-door tastings and sales of cool-climate reds, whites and fortified wines; open Wed–Sun; Hindmarsh Valley; 4 km N. *Urimbirra Wildlife Park:* popular fauna park with a wetland bird sanctuary, crocodile-feeding and children's farmyard; Adelaide Rd; 5 km N. *Big Duck Boat Tours:* Spectacular half hour and 1 hour tours taking in Encounter Bay and coastal parts of Victor Harbor. Leaves from Granite Island causeway; 0405 125 312. *Nangawooka Flora Reserve:* tranquil walks through native bushlands with over 1250 native plant varieties on show; opposite Urimbirra Wildlife Park. *The Bluff (Rosetta Head):* 500-million-year-old mass of granite, well worth the 100 m climb for the views; 5 km SW. *Newland Head Conservation Park:* known for its wild surf and coastal vegetation, this park protects the headland and Waitpinga and Parsons beaches, which offer surf-fishing opportunities and beach walks; turn-off 15 km SW. *Hindmarsh Falls:* pleasant walks and spectacular waterfall (during winter); 15 km NW. *Mt Billy Conservation Park:* mallee and forest park renowned for its rare orchid species; 18 km NW. *Inman Valley:* features Glacier Rock, said to be the first recorded discovery of glaciation in Australia; 19 km NW.

TOWNS NEARBY: Port Elliot 6 km, Goolwa 15 km, Yankalilla 27 km, Willunga 32 km, Aldinga Beach 34 km

SOUTH AUSTRALIA

Kernewek Lowender: Cornish festival held in conjunction with Moonta and Kadina; odd-numbered years, May.

The Boatshed Restaurant: waterfront seafood specialists; 1 Jetty Rd; (08) 8823 3455.

Office Beach Caravan Park: 11 Jetty Rd; (08) 8823 2722. *Wallaroo North Beach Tourist Park:* 1 Pamir Crt; (08) 8823 2531.

Bird Island: crabbing; 10 km s.

Travellers note: *To avoid the extra driving distance to the Eyre Peninsula, Sea SA runs a ferry service between Wallaroo and Lucky Bay 4 times a day on weekdays, and twice a day on weekends. Bookings (08) 8823 0777.*

TOWNS NEARBY: Kadina 9 km, Moonta 15 km, Port Broughton 46 km, Maitland 49 km, Ardrossan 61 km

Whyalla
Pop. 21 122
Map ref. 558 H3 | 560 G11

i Lincoln Hwy; (08) 8645 7900 or 1800 088 589; www.whyalla.com

107.7 5YYY FM, 639 AM ABC North and West

Whyalla, northern gateway to Eyre Peninsula, has grown from the small settlement of Hummock Hill to the largest provincial city in South Australia. It has become known for its heavy industry since iron ore was found in the 1890s around Iron Knob and the steel works opened in 1964. Whyalla also has an interesting natural attraction. Each year, from May to August, an incredible number of cuttlefish spawn on the rocky coast just north – a must-see for diving and snorkelling enthusiasts. The city is modern and offers safe beaches, excellent fishing and boating.

 Whyalla Maritime Museum The central attraction is HMAS *Whyalla*, a 650-tonne corvette, the largest permanently land-locked ship in Australia. It was the first ship built in the BHP shipyards. Guided tours of the ship are included in the entry price and run on the hour 11am–3pm Apr–Oct, 10am–2pm Nov–Mar. The lives of the 4 wartime corvettes built by BHP are documented, as are histories of the shipbuilding industry and maritime heritage of Spencer Gulf; Lincoln Hwy; (08) 8645 8900.

Mt Laura Homestead Museum: National Trust museum featuring the original homestead with progressive city-history displays, period furnishings in the 1914 Gay St Cottage, and the Telecommunications Museum; (08) 8645 7644; open 10am–12pm Mon–Fri, 2–4pm Sun; Ekblom St. *Tanderra Craft Village:* art and craft shops, market and tearooms; open 10am–4pm last weekend each month; next to Maritime Museum; (08) 8644 0105. *Whyalla Wetlands:* park and wetlands area with walking trails and a picnic/barbecue area; Lincoln Hwy. *Foreshore and marina:* safe beach, jetty for recreational fishing, picnic/barbecue area, access to Ada Ryan Gardens, and a marina with boatlaunching facilities. *Ada Ryan Gardens:* mini-zoo with picnic facilities under shady trees; Cudmore Tce. *Murray Cod Tour:* see a fully operational inland freshwater aquaculture venture, and learn about recycling water and the various growth stages of the Murray cod. Closed footwear required; book at visitor centre. *Steelworks Tour:* 2 hr guided tour explains steelmaking process; departs 9.30am Mon, Wed and Fri; book at visitor centre. *Hummock Hill Lookout:* views of city, gulf, steel works and coast from WW II observation post; Queen Elizabeth Dr. *Flinders and Freycinet Lookout:* Farrel St; *Whyalla Visitor Guide* from visitor centre; (08) 8648 0048.

Australian Snapper Championship: Easter. *Whyalla Show:* family activities, rides and stalls; Aug.

Sunset Bistro: relaxed family dining, with a reputation for serving the 'Big Mans 1 kg steak'; Lincoln Hwy; (08) 8645 7688. *Watersedge Restaurant:* offering top quality local produce; Watson Tce; (08) 8645 8877.

Discovery Holiday Parks – Whyalla Foreshore: Broadbent Tce; (08) 8645 7474. *Whyalla Caravan Park:* Cnr Mullaquana and Horseshoe rds, Mullaquana; (08) 8645 9357.

Whyalla Conservation Park: 30 min walking trail through typical semi-arid flora and over Wild Dog Hill; 10 km N off Lincoln Hwy. *Port Bonython and Point Lowly:* this area of coast offers beautiful views of Spencer Gulf, fishing from rocks, and dolphin sightings. Lowly Beach is a popular swimming beach and the Freycinet Trail is a scenic drive from just before Port Bonython along Fitzgerald Bay to Point Douglas (parts are gravel); 34 km E. *Iron Knob:* a mining town with museum and mine lookout tours (depart from the museum at 10am and 2pm Mon–Fri); (08) 8646 2129; 53 km NW.

TOWNS NEARBY: Port Pirie 46 km, Melrose 63 km, Port Augusta 63 km, Wilmington 66 km, Crystal Brook 70 km

Willunga
Pop. 2103
Map ref. 556 H9 | 559 J10 | 568 B4

i McLaren Vale Visitors Centre, Main Rd, McLaren Vale; (08) 8323 9944 or 1800 628 410; www.mclarenvale.info

94.7 5EFM, 639 AM ABC North and West

The historic town of Willunga grew rapidly around the slate quarries, which drove the town's economy until the late 1800s. Fortunately, by that time Willunga already had a thriving new industry – almonds. The town sits at the southern edge of the Fleurieu wine region and is surrounded by farmlands and olive groves. Its name is derived from the Aboriginal word 'willa-unga', meaning 'the place of green trees'.

Willunga Courthouse Museum: National Trust museum with local history displays in the original 1855 courtroom, cells and stables; guided 'Willunga Walks and Talks' tours; open 11am–4pm Tues, 1–5pm weekends; High St; (08) 8556 2195. *Quarry:* operated for 60 years (1842–1902), now a National Trust site; Delabole Rd. *Historical walk:* self-guide walk featuring historic pug cottages, colonial architecture and an Anglican church with an Elizabethan bronze bell; brochure from museum.

Willunga Farmers Market: Hill St; Sat mornings. *Willunga Quarry Market:* country market with local produce and crafts; Aldinga Rd; 2nd Sat each month. *Almond Blossom Festival:* running since 1970, celebrates the blooming of almond trees; July. *Fleurieu Folk Festival:* Oct.

Fino Restaurant: rustic regional cuisine; 8 Hill St; (08) 8556 4488. *Victory Hotel:* popular pub and cellar; Main South Rd, Sellicks Hill; (08) 8556 3083.

Blue Grape Vineyard Accommodation: Lot 6 Newman Close, Willunga South; (08) 8556 4078. *Mt Compass Caravan Park:* Heysen Blvd, Mount Compass; (08) 8556 8600.

 Fleurieu wine region With vineyards covering just about every other part of the Fleurieu Peninsula, including McLaren Vale and Langhorne Creek, it is not surprising that they eventually crept southwards. Critics believe this is a region to

watch, with a climate conducive to vines and some high-quality wines already being produced. Two eco-sensitive wineries have cellar doors located near Mt Compass: Minko Wines makes wonderful merlot rose, and Parri Estate produces quality white wines such as viognier chardonnay.

Mt Magnificent Conservation Park: explore virtually untouched rocky landscapes and vegetation popular for picnics and scenic walks. The highlight is the walk to the Mt Magnificent summit for coastal views; 12 km SE. *Mt Compass:* a small farming town featuring the Wetlands Boardwalk and many farms open for viewing and sales, offering both primary products and gourmet food. Australia's only Cow Race is held here each Jan/Feb; 14 km S. *Fleurieu Big Shed:* local produce, art and craft sales; 15 km S. *Kyeema Conservation Park:* completely burnt out in the 1983 Ash Wednesday fires and then again in the fires of 1994 and 2001, this park is evidence of nature's ability to constantly regenerate. It is home to over 70 species of birdlife and offers good hiking and camping. Part of the Heysen Trail passes through it; 14 km NE.

TOWNS NEARBY: McLaren Vale 6 km, Aldinga Beach 9 km, Yankalilla 28 km, Strathalbyn 31 km, Port Elliot 31 km

Wilmington
Pop. 217
Map ref. 559 I2 | 560 H10

Wilmington General Store, Main North Rd; (08) 8667 5155.

105.9 Magic FM, 639 AM ABC North and West

Robert Blinman had the foresight to build an inn, called the Roundwood Hotel, at the base of Horrocks Pass in 1861, and soon the Cobb & Co coaches were stopping there on their passenger routes. The town was built around the first hotel, and before long the farming community was thriving. Originally named Beautiful Valley by European explorers, the name was changed to Wilmington in 1876, although the original name still persists in many local establishments. Today the town retains much of its old-time feel and is renowned for its stone buildings.

Wilmington Hotel: built around 1876, the hotel is one of the town's oldest buildings and was first called The Globe Hotel. Original Cobb & Co coach stables are at the rear of the building; Main North Rd. *Mt Maria Walking Trail:* 2 km walking trail starting from town leads to vantage point over Wilmington; brochure available from general store.

Night Rodeo: Jan. *Wilmington Show:* Sept.

Spring Creek Mine Drive: 24 km scenic loop beginning south of town, passing mountain and farm scenery and an old copper mine, now the town's water supply; brochure from general store. *Horrocks Pass and Hancocks Lookout:* this historic pass was named after explorer John Horrocks who traversed the pass in 1846. Hancocks Lookout, at the highest point of the pass, offers magnificent views to Spencer Gulf; 8 km w off road to Port Augusta. *Mt Remarkable National Park:* 13 km S; *see Melrose. Winninowie Conservation Park:* coastal park of creeks and samphire flats, home to abundant birdlife; 26 km SW. *Hammond:* historic ghost town; 26 km NE. *Bruce:* historic railway town featuring 1880s architecture; 35 km N. *Carrieton:* historic buildings and Yanyarrie Whim Well in town. A rodeo is held here each Dec; 56 km NE. See Aboriginal carvings a further 9 km along Belton Rd.

TOWNS NEARBY: Melrose 21 km, Quorn 34 km, Port Augusta 35 km, Port Pirie 61 km, Whyalla 66 km

Wilpena
see inset box on next page

Woomera
Pop. 294
Map ref. 560 E5

Dewrang Ave; (08) 8673 7042 or 1300 761 620; www.woomerasa.com.au

101.7 Flow FM, 1584 AM ABC North and West

Woomera and its testing range were established in 1947 as a site for launching British experimental rockets during the Cold War era. The town was a restricted area until 1982. The Woomera Prohibited Area remains in force today and is still one of the largest land-based rocket ranges in the world. Until 2003, Woomera was the site of a controversial detention centre for refugees. The detainees are now held at the Baxter Detention Centre near Port Augusta.

Woomera Heritage and Visitor Information Centre: provides a detailed history of the area through videos, exhibitions, rocket relics and photographic displays. It also includes a bowling alley. Tours of the Rocket Range can be booked and depart here; Dewrang Ave. *Missile Park:* open-air defence display of rockets, aircraft and weapons; Cnr Banool and Dewrang aves. *Baker Observatory:* viewing the night sky through a computer-controlled telescope; contact visitor centre for details.

TOWNS NEARBY: Roxby Downs 72 km, Andamooka 89 km, Leigh Creek 165 km, Hawker 169 km, Port Augusta 169 km

Wudinna
Pop. 517
Map ref. 558 D3 | 560 B11

44 Eyre Hwy; (08) 8680 2969; www.lehunte.sa.gov.au

89.5 Magic FM, 693 AM ABC Eyre Peninsula and West Coast

The enormous silos in Wudinna are indicative of the town's major grain industry, predominantly wheat and barley, grown here since the first pastoral lease was granted in 1861. Wudinna was proclaimed a town in 1916 and has since grown as a service centre to the Eyre Peninsula. A little travelling in the surrounding countryside will reveal unusually shaped granite outcrops – the area is known as granite country.

Gawler Ranges Cultural Centre: dedicated to the exhibition of artwork with a ranges theme; Ballantyne St.

Wudinna Show: Sept.

Gawler Ranges Caravan Park: 72 Eyre Hwy; (08) 8680 2090.

Gawler Ranges National Park This rugged national park offers fantastic gorge and rocky-outcrop scenery, spectacular when the spring wildflowers are in bloom. There are no marked trails, but highlights of drive tours include the Organ Pipes, a large and unique formation of volcanic rhyolite, the Kolay Mirica Falls and Yandinga Gorge. Some areas are accessible by 2WD, but 4WD is generally recommended. Roads may be impassable after rain. Guided tours into the ranges are offered by 2 operators: Gawler Ranges Wilderness Safaris (1800 243 343) and Nullarbor Traveller (1800 816 858). 40 km N.

Wudinna Granite Trail: signposted 25 km tourist drive to all major rock formations in the area. *Mt Polda Rock Recreation Reserve:* walking trail for excellent birdwatching with views from the top of Polda Rock; 7 km NE. *Mt Wudinna Recreation Reserve:* the mountain is thought to be the second-largest granite outcrop

continued on p. 267

 RADIO STATIONS   IN TOWN   WHAT'S ON   WHERE TO EAT   WHERE TO STAY   NEARBY

WILPENA   Map ref. 557 B10 | 561 I6

 Wilpena Rd, via Hawker; (08) 8648 0048;
www.wilpenapound.com.au

ABC North and West 639 AM

Wilpena consists of a resort and caravan/camping park on the edge of Wilpena Pound, in Flinders Ranges National Park. In 1902 the Hill family, wheat farmers, built a homestead inside the pound, but abandoned it after a flood washed away the access road in 1914. The pound is a vast natural amphitheatre surrounded by peaks that change colour with the light, and is a fantastic destination for bushwalking.

Wilpena Pound Resort: partly powered by the largest solar-power system in the Southern Hemisphere (viewing area accessed by a walking trail). The visitor centre at the resort has extensive information on 4WD and organised tours, self-guide drives, scenic flights, bushwalking and hiking; (08) 8648 0004.

Wilpena Under the Stars: black-tie dinner and dance to raise funds for the Royal Flying Doctor Service; Mar. *Tastes of the Outback:* Apr. *Flinders Ranges Event Program:* events run in autumn and spring, including guided walks, tours and cultural activities; details from visitor centre.

The Woolshed Restaurant: rustic outback theme; Rawnsley Park; (08) 8648 0126.

Flinders Ranges National Park For thousands of years the ancient landscapes of the Flinders Ranges were home to the Adnyamathanha people – the 'people of the rocks'. Their Muda (Dreamtime) stories tell of the creation of the slopes and gorges that ripple across the landscape for over 400 km, from south-east of Port Augusta to north of Arkaroola. In the 1850s stock runs were established at Arkaba, Wilpena and Aroona. Foreign plant and animal species were introduced and the natural balance of the ranges was altered. Within 50 years of European settlement many endemic animals had been pushed to extinction. Today conservationists are trying to recover the natural balance of the area, and have had success in the recovery of yellow-footed rock wallabies. The central ranges are a fabulous place for hikers. There are 17 walks and hikes to choose from and the choice is difficult. All provide a different historical, geological or scenic look at the ranges. For a look into early European settlement take the 5.4 km return Hills Homestead Walk into the extraordinary natural rock formation of Wilpena Pound. Impressive rock paintings depicting the creation of the ranges can be seen on the Arkaroo Rock Hike (3 km loop track). And for nature lovers there is the Bunyeroo Gorge Hike, a 7.5 km return trail that follows the gorge and reveals fantastic wildlife and rock formations. There are also driving tours that reveal some of the park's most spectacular scenery. The popular Brachina Gorge Geological Trail is a 20 km drive that details the long physical history of the ranges, from when the hills were layers of sediment beneath an ocean, to when they were compressed and pushed up into the shape of mountains. Look out for the yellow-footed rock wallaby in the rocky upper slopes of this beautiful gorge. All the roads north of Wilpena are unsealed, but are generally 2WD accessible. Among all of this, at Wilpena, is some of the best accommodation and facilities north of Adelaide. Drop into the Wilpena Pound Visitor Information Centre for a park guide, or to book scenic flights and other tours; (08) 8648 0048.

Sacred Canyon: Aboriginal rock carvings and paintings; 19 km E. *Rawnsley Park Station:* camping and holiday-unit accommodation, scenic flights, horseriding and 4WD tours; (08) 8648 0030; 20 km s on Hawker Rd. *Moralana Scenic Drive:* 22 km route between Elder Range and south-west wall of Wilpena Pound with lookouts and picnic spots en route; drive starts 25 km s.

TOWNS NEARBY: Hawker 43 km, Blinman 47 km, Quorn 105 km, Leigh Creek 106 km, Port Augusta 133 km

[WILPENA POUND, FLINDERS RANGES NATIONAL PARK]

in the Southern Hemisphere. At its base is a picnic area, a 30 min return interpretive walking trail, and original stone walls used as water catchments. Enjoy scenic views at the mountain's summit. On the road to the reserve look out for Turtle Rock; 10 km NE. *Ucontitchie Hill:* isolated and unique granite formations, similar to Kangaroo Island's Remarkable Rocks; 32 km s. *Minnipa:* home to the Agricultural Centre, which provides invaluable research into sustainable dryland farming. Nearby are granite formations of geological significance, including Yarwondutta Rock (2 km N), Tcharkuldu Rock (4 km E) and the wave-like formation of Pildappa Rock (15 km N); 37 km NW. *Koongawa:* memorial to explorer John Charles Darke; 50 km E.

TOWNS NEARBY: Elliston 85 km, Kimba 90 km, Streaky Bay 120 km, Cowell 153 km, Tumby Bay 158 km

Yankalilla

Pop. 552
Map ref. 556 G10 | 559 J10 | 568 B4

i 104 Main South Rd; (08) 8558 2999; www.yankalilla.sa.gov.au

89.3 5EFM, 639 AM ABC North and West

Since the first land grant in 1842, Yankalilla has been the centre of a thriving farming industry. It is a growing settlement just inland from the west coast of the Fleurieu Peninsula, but it still retains its old country flavour. It has even adopted the slogan 'Yankalilla Bay – you'll love what we haven't done to the place'. In recent times it has seen an influx of visitors keen to see the apparition at Our Lady of Yankalilla Shrine. The Blessed Virgin Mary was first sighted here in 1996.

Yankalilla District Historical Museum: local history and interpretive trail; open 1–4pm Sun; Main South Rd. *Anglican Church:* historic and known for apparition of Mary; Main St.

Leafy Sea Dragon Festival: arts and cultural festival; odd-numbered years, Apr. *Yankalilla Show:* Oct long weekend.

Lilla's Cafe: creative cafe fare; 117 Main South Rd; (08) 8558 2525.

Beachside Caravan Park: Cape Jervis Rd, Normanville; (08) 8558 2458. *Corinium Roman Villa:* 2 Nosworthy Rd, Inman Valley; 0415 694 013. *Jetty Caravan Park Normanville:* Jetty Rd, Normanville; (08) 8558 2038. *Second Valley Caravan Park:* 2 Park Ave, Second Valley; (08) 8598 4054. *Yankalilla Bay Homestead B&B:* 39 Jetty Rd, Normanville; 0417 583 222.

Deep Creek Conservation Park Take one of the many walks along rugged coastal cliffs, tranquil creeks, majestic forests and scenic waterfalls. Walks range from easy and short to more challenging long-distance hikes. Keep an eye out for the western grey kangaroos at dusk on the Aaron Creek Hiking Trail or drop a line at Blowhole Creek and Boat Harbour beaches. Permits are required in the park (self-registration). 26 km sw.

Normanville: a seaside town with beach and heritage-listed sand dunes. Shipwrecks are popular with divers; 3 km w. *Myponga Conservation Park:* popular bushwalking and birdwatching park; 9 km NE. *Myponga:* a historic town with fantastic views from the Myponga Reservoir; 14 km NE. *Second Valley:* a peaceful picnic spot with a jetty for fishing; 17 km sw. *Rapid Bay:* this seaside town offers excellent fishing and diving opportunities. Sightings of the endangered leafy sea dragon in the bay make diving a must for any enthusiast; 27 km sw. *Talisker Conservation Park:* an interpretive trail explains the old silver-mine workings in the

park; 30 km sw. *Cape Jervis:* breathtaking sea and coastal views on entering town. Vehicular ferries to Kangaroo Island depart from here, and it is also the starting point of the 1200 km Heysen Trail (bushwalking trail) to the Flinders Ranges. Morgan's and Fishery beaches nearby have good fishing; 35 km s.

TOWNS NEARBY: Aldinga Beach 22 km, Victor Harbor 27 km, Willunga 28 km, Port Elliot 31 km, McLaren Vale 32 km

Yorketown

Pop. 687
Map ref. 556 E8 | 558 H9

i SYP Telecentre, Yorketown or Harvest Corner Visitor Information Centre, 29 Main St; (08) 8853 2600 or 1800 202 445; www.yorkepeninsula.com.au

98.9 Flow FM, 639 AM ABC North and West

Yorketown is a small rural community at the southern end of Yorke Peninsula. The surrounding landscape is dotted with many inland salt lakes, some of which are still mined. In the late 1840s farmers were eager to take up land here as it was prime crop-producing land. The town was settled in 1872 and has remained an important service centre on the peninsula since.

Courthouse Photographic Display: photographs of the area's pioneering days; open Fri mornings or by appt.

Marion Bay Tavern: relaxed beachside meals; 1 Stenhouse Bay Rd, Marion Bay; (08) 8854 4141.

Yorketown Caravan Park: Memorial Dr; (08) 8852 1731. *Marion Bay Caravan Park:* 17 Willyama Dr, Marion Bay; (08) 8854 4094. *Point Turton Caravan Park:* Bayview Rd, Point Turton; (08) 8854 5222.

Innes National Park In summer, soak up the sun at beaches or bays with excellent (but challenging) surf breaks at Chinamans Reef, Pondalowie Bay and West Cape. In winter, keep an eye out at Stenhouse Bay and Cape Spencer for migrating southern right whales. Diving is popular, especially near the Gap, an eroded gap in a 60 m high cliff. Other activities include beach and jetty fishing, and walking on coastal and inland tracks. Accommodation is something special in this park – enjoy fabulous coastal camping in the mallee scrub or stay at the heritage lodge in the old mining township of Inneston. The annual Yorke Surfing Classic is held here each Oct. (08) 8854 3200; 81 km sw.

Ballywire Farm and Tearooms: Experience a fully working farm by joining in farming activities. Tearooms and a licensed restaurant on-site, as well as farm produce for sale, interactive displays and a games area for kids; open 10am–5pm Wed–Sun (daily school holidays); (08) 8852 1053; 11km s. *Bublacowie Military Museum:* personal stories, memorabilia and documents, and also a craft centre; closed Mon; 25 km N. *Corny Point:* coastal town featuring a lighthouse and lookout, and fishing and camping; 69 km NW. *Daly Head:* great surfing spot with nearby blowhole; 75 km w. *Marion Bay:* popular with surfers and visitors to nearby Innes National Park; 79 km sw.

TOWNS NEARBY: Edithburgh 15 km, Stansbury 21 km, Minlaton 27 km, Port Victoria 59 km, Maitland 72 km

WESTERN AUSTRALIA is...

Spending a day at Perth's beaches, including **COTTESLOE** / Eating fish and chips on **FREMANTLE'S WHARF** / Seeing magnificent beaches and searching for quokkas on **ROTTNEST ISLAND** / Taking a camel ride along **CABLE BEACH**, Broome / Sampling wines at cellar doors in **MARGARET RIVER** / Feeding dolphins at **MONKEY MIA** / A scenic flight over the Bungle Bungles in **PURNULULU NATIONAL PARK** / Walking through giant stands of karri and tingle trees in the **VALLEY OF THE GIANTS** / A visit to **NAMBUNG NATIONAL PARK**, home to the moonscape of limestone pillars known as **THE PINNACLES** / Swimming with whale sharks in **NINGALOO REEF**

WESTERN AUSTRALIA

is defined by its size. Spanning an area of 2.5 million square kilometres, it covers one-third of the Australian continent. In dramatic contrast to its size, its population is just over two million, around one-tenth of Australia's total population. Over 72 per cent of Western Australians live in or around the capital city of Perth.

Within this great state there are incredibly diverse landscapes – an ancient terrain of rugged ranges and dramatic gorges to the north, towering forests to the south, arid deserts to the east and 12 889 kilometres of the world's most pristine coastline to the west. To match the huge variety in landscape are huge differences in climate, from the tropical humidity of the north and the dryness of the desert to the temperate Mediterranean-style climate of the south-west.

After driving for hours along empty highways, you will get a true feeling for the state's vastness. But you will be amply rewarded when you reach your destination. Western Australia boasts precious natural features, including the 350-million-year-old Bungle Bungle Range, the limestone sentinels of the Pinnacles desert and the majestic karri forests of the south-west.

[NATURE'S WINDOW, KALBARRI NATIONAL PARK]

There is the extraordinary marine life of Ningaloo Reef, the friendly dolphins of Monkey Mia and Rottnest Island's famous quokkas.

Western Australia's historic sites are also a highlight. The Aboriginal people who first inhabited the land up to 65 000 years ago left a legacy of distinctive rock art. Albany, the site of the state's first European settlement in 1826, boasts well-preserved heritage buildings, while gracious 19th-century buildings in the capital city of Perth and its nearby port of Fremantle hark back to the days of the Swan River Colony. Remnants of great gold discoveries remain around Coolgardie and Kalgoorlie from the 1890s, which transformed Western Australia into one of the world's great producers of gold, iron ore, nickel, diamonds, mineral sands and natural gas.

[SHEEP ROUND-UP, BOYUP BROOK]

 ## fact file

Population 2 346 400
Total land area 2 529 875 square kilometres
People per square kilometre 0.8
Sheep and cattle per square kilometre 9.8
Nearest interstate city Adelaide, 2700 kilometres east
Length of coastline 12 889 kilometres
Number of islands 3747
Longest river Gascoyne River (760 kilometres)
Largest constructed reservoir Lake Argyle (storage volume 10 760 million cubic metres)
Highest mountain Mount Meharry (1253 metres), Karijini National Park
Highest waterfall King George Falls (80 metres), northern Kimberley
Highest town Tom Price (747 metres)
Hottest place Marble Bar (160 days a year over 37.5°C)
Coldest place Bridgetown (33 days a year begin at below 2°C)
Most remote town Warburton
Strangest place name Walkaway
Most famous local Rolf Harris
Quirkiest festival Milk Carton Regatta, Hillarys Boat Harbour
Number of wildflowers 12 500 species
Most challenging road Gibb River Road, the Kimberley
Best beach Cable Beach, Broome
Most identifiable food Pavlova (created at Perth's Esplanade Hotel)
Local beer Swan Lager

 ## gift ideas

Gold nuggets, Kalgoorlie–Boulder Visit the Australian Prospectors and Miners Hall of Fame to find gold nuggets in presentation cases and on chains as pendants. See Kalgoorlie–Boulder p. 312

Cricket merchandise, WACA, East Perth Cricket lovers will be thrilled to receive a memento from the world-famous Western Australian Cricket Association grounds. See Museums p. 282

Ugg boots, Uggs-N-Rugs, Kenwick, Perth This iconic sheepskin footwear is available around Australia, but in January 2006, Uggs-N-Rugs won a legal battle to remove an American company's trademark for 'ugh boots' from the Australian Trademarks Registry – a major victory for Australian manufacturers. 9 Royal St, Kenwick. See Perth p. 272

Arts and crafts, Fremantle Markets, Fremantle Over 150 stalls sell everything from local arts, crafts and clothes to fresh produce. See Fremantle Markets p. 281

Argyle diamonds, Leon Baker Jewellers, Geraldton Diamonds of unique brilliance in various colours, including the world's only intense pink diamonds. See Geraldton p. 307

Freshwater pearls, Broome With its unique pearling heritage, exquisite pearl jewellery is available all over Broome. Willie Creek Pearls also has showrooms in Subiaco and Hillarys Boat Harbour, in Perth. See Broome p. 294

Wine, Margaret River There is an abundance of fine wine to choose from in this top wine-producing region. See Margaret River p. 322

Jarrah and marri woodwork, Australind Western Australia's unique woods are turned into handcrafted furniture, boxes, bowls, platters, salt and pepper grinders, to name but a few. See Australind p. 289

Wood-fired bread, biscuits and nut cake, New Norcia Made by New Norcia's Benedictine monk community. Their rich, intensely flavoured, panforte-style nut cake is also available at the New Norcia Bakeries at 163 Scarborough Beach Rd, Mount Hawthorn, and Bagot Rd, Subiaco. See New Norcia p. 326

Quokka soft toy, Rottnest Island Get a soft toy version of this small marsupial, which famously lives on 'Rotto', from the general store or gift shop. See Thomson Bay p. 333

PERTH IS...

Views across the city from **KINGS PARK** / **SWIMMING** at any of Perth's beaches

/ Eating fish and chips on **FREMANTLE'S WHARF** / Sipping a coffee on the

'cappuccino strip' of **SOUTH TERRACE**, Fremantle / Seeing black swans at **LAKE**

MONGER / A cricket match at the **WACA** / A picnic on the **MATILDA BAY**

foreshore / A visit to the **WESTERN AUSTRALIAN MUSEUM** / Eating out in

NORTHBRIDGE / Browsing the eclectic offerings at the **FREMANTLE MARKETS** /

A footy match at **SUBIACO OVAL** / Touring the forbidding **FREMANTLE PRISON**

VISITOR INFORMATION
Western Australian Visitor Centre
→ Cnr Forrest Pl and Wellington St
1300 361 351 or 1800 812 808
www.bestofwa.com.au

Perth is the most isolated capital city in the world, closer to Singapore than it is to Sydney. Its nearest neighbour, Adelaide, is 2700 kilometres away by road. Yet it is exactly this isolation that has allowed Perth to retain a feeling of space and relaxed charm.

Claimed to be the sunniest state capital in Australia, Perth has a Mediterranean climate: hot and dry in summer, cool and wet in winter. This climate, and the city's proximity to both river and ocean, fosters a relaxed lifestyle for the population of 1 705 000. One of Perth's great attributes is that its water frontages are public land, accessible to everyone. Picnicking is a popular pastime, while cafes and bars spill their tables and chairs out onto pavements to make the most of the glorious weather.

Yet for all Perth's coastal beauty, it is the Swan River that defines the city. North of the river is Kings Park and the old-money riverside suburbs with their grand homes; further on are the beaches and the newer northern beach suburbs stretching up the coast. At the mouth of the Swan is the historic port city of Fremantle, with its rich maritime history, creative community and street-cafe culture. Upstream from Perth – where the river dwindles to a meandering waterway – is the Swan Valley, the state's oldest wine district.

Trigg Retreat Bed and Breakfast

HAMERSLEY GOLF COURSE

LAKE GWELUP RESERVE

To Hillarys Boat Harbour & AQWA

To Wanneroo Markets & Yanchep NP

Nollamara Shopping Centre

Mount Yokine Reservoir

DIANELLA OPEN SPACE

Dianella

Karrinyup Shopping Centre

Gwelup

Stirling

Balcatta

Nollamara

Morley

Dianella

Karrinyup

YULUMA PARK

Centro Dianella

Trigg

South Trigg Beach

Innaloo

Brighton Beach

ROBINSON RESERVE

Tuart Hill

WESTERN AUSTRALIAN GOLF COURSE

BRECKLER PARK

Yokine

Rendezvous Observation City Hotel

Scarborough Fair Markets (Sat–Sun)

Scarborough

BIRRALEE PARK

Event Cinemas

Westfield Innaloo

Osborne Park

Joondanna

YOKINE RESERVE

MOUNT LAWLEY GOLF COURSE

Inglewood

MACAULAY PARK

Scarborough Beach

Doubleview

BENNETT PARK

BUTLERS RESERVE

Jackadder Lake

Woodlands

Glendalough

Mount Hawthorn

New Norcia Bakeries

Dog Swamp & Flinders Square Shopping Centres

Coolbinia

Above Bored Bed and Breakfast

Mount Lawley

Floreat Beach

Wembley Downs

Churchlands

MAURIE HAMER PARK

Herdsman

Herdsman Lake

Wembley

Lake Monger

Leederville

North Perth

Menora

HAMER PARK

WEMBLEY GOLF COMPLEX

BOLD PARK

West Leederville

Luna Palace

Leederville Hotel

Scitech Discovery Centre

Harbour Town

Hyde Park Hotel

Must Winebar

Nahm Thai

nib Stadium

Beaufort House

Highgate

FORREST PARK

City Beach

Mount Kenneth Reservoir

ALDERBURY PARK

Floreat

Subiaco Station St Markets (Fri–Sun)

Patersons Stadium

Northbridge

WELLINGTON

SEE PAGE 276

Perth

East Perth

Resta Amus

Queen Garden

Jolimont

Ace Cinemas Subiaco

Subiaco Pavilion Markets (Thurs–Sun)

Regal Theatre

Indigenart Mossenson Galleries

West Perth

Parliament House

City Beach

BOLD PARK

WA Basketball Centre

UWA SPORTS PARK

Challenge Stadium

Perry Lakes

UNDERWOOD

Parkside B&B

Daglish

Subiaco Arts Centre

Subiaco

Eight Nicholson

Kings Park

Fraser's Restaurant

Aspects of Kings Park

Aboriginal Art Gallery

RIVERSIDE

North Swanbourne Beach

ROCHDALE

Shenton Park

SHENTON PARK

ROSALIE PARK RD

Botanic Garden

Moonlight Cinema

Lotterywest Federation Walkway

Kings Park

The Old Brewery

Old Mill

Narrows Bridge

Perth Water

SWAN

Valley

Heirisson Islar

SIR JAMES MITCHELL PARK

INDIAN OCEAN

Mount Claremont

IRWIN BARRACKS

Quarry Point

Perth Zoo

South Perth

CAMPBELL BARRACKS

COTTESLOE GOLF CLUB

Karrakatta

Pata Negra

Somerville Auditorium

Crawley

University of Western Australia

SWAN ESTUARY MARINE PARK

Matilda Bay

RICHARDSON PARK

ANGELO PARK

ERNEST JOHNSON OVAL

Swanbourne

Lake Claremont

CRESSWELL PARK

Claremont

Windsor Cinema

Nedlands

NEDLANDS GOLF CLUB

J H ABRAHAMS RESERVE

Point Currie

Ferry

Como Beach

Cygnet Cinema

Swanbourne Beach

ALLEN PARK

Greenhill Galleries

Claremont Quarter

COLLEGE PARK

Ocean Beach Hotel

Cottesloe Beach

Indiana Cottesloe Beach Restaurant

Cottesloe Civic Centre

Claremont Museum

Peppermint Grove

Dalkeith

BEATON PARK

Melville Water

Point Heathcote

Bluewater Grill

Point Heathcote Reserve

Coffee Point

Cottesloe

SEAVIEW GOLF CLUB

Cottesloe Central

Freshwater Bay

WARATAH

POINT RESOLUTION RESERVE

JUTLAND

Point Resolution

Waylen Bay

Point Dundas

NEIL MCDOUGAL

N

0   1 km

Mosman Park

Buckland Hill Lighthouse

BUCKLAND HILL RESERVE

Mosman Bay

BAY VIEW PARK

RIVER

Point Walter

Point Walter Reserve

MOSMAN PARK GOLF CLUB

ATTADALE RESERVE

SWAN ESTUARY MARINE PARK

Lucky Bay

SHIRLEY STRICKLAND RESERVE

Applecross

DEEP WATER POINT RESERVE

Mosman Beach

North Fremantle

MINIM COVE PARK

POINT WALTER GOLF COURSE

Bicton

TROY PARK

TOMPKINS PARK

Ardross

Mount Pleasant

Leighton Beach

Preston Point

East Fremantle

Palmyra

Melville

Alfred Cove

Telecommunications Museum

Wireless Hill Park

Garden City

Blue Gum Lake

Booragoon

To Fremantle

To Fremantle

CANNING

Myaree

LEN SHEARER RESERVE

To Adventure World & Mandurah

CITY CENTRE

Perth's city centre is a compact mix of towering skyscrapers and elegant colonial buildings. It is bordered by the Swan River, with stretches of grassy parkland fringing the riverbank. Perth's central business district (CBD) harbours the city's large pedestrian-only shopping precinct, made up of a series of malls and arcades. The ultra-hip King Street is renowned for its gourmet cafes, galleries and fashion houses, while St Georges Terrace, the main commercial street, has high-rise buildings interspersed with remnants of Perth's early British heritage.

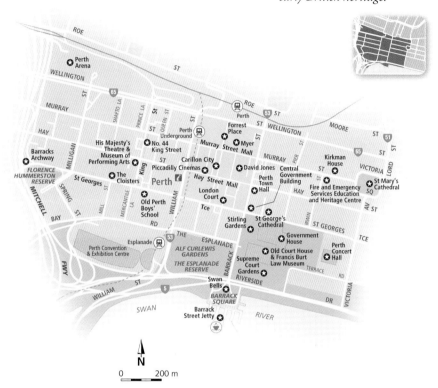

Malls, arcades and a touch of old England 276 B2

The CBD's central shopping district encompasses the **Hay Street Mall**, **Murray Street Mall** and **Forrest Place**. Fashion outlets, bookstores and homewares shops fill the malls. Myer and David Jones sit on Murray Street Mall, and the western side of Forrest Place is home to the GPO. Arcades and underground walkways run from Murray Street Mall through to Hay Street Mall and on to St Georges Terrace. **Carillon City** shopping centre sits between the malls, while **London Court**, a quaint, Elizabethan-looking arcade, runs from Hay Street Mall to St Georges Terrace. At the mall end, knights joust above a replica of Big Ben every 15 minutes, while St George and the Dragon do battle above the clock at the St Georges Terrace end.

King Street 276 B2

This historic precinct between Hay and Wellington streets dates from the 1890s gold rush. The street retains its turn-of-the-century character, and is filled with designer fashion houses, specialist bookstores, art galleries and gourmet cafes, such as **No. 44 King Street**, with its homemade bread and extensive wine list.

St Georges Terrace 276 A2, B2

Office towers and historic buildings line this main street. At the western end is the **Barracks Archway**, the only remains of the Pensioners' Barracks, which housed the retired British soldiers who guarded convicts in the mid-1800s. The **Central Government Building** on the corner of Barrack Street marks the spot where Perth was founded with a tree-felling ceremony in 1829. Around 50 years later, convicts and hired labour commenced work on the building that stands there today. Other historic buildings along the terrace include the Cloisters, the Old Perth Boys' School, the Deanery, St George's Cathedral, Government House and the Old Court House *(see Grand old buildings, p. 282)*. Commemorative plaques inlaid in the footpath celebrate over 170 notable Western Australians.

City gardens 276 C2, C3

Two delightful city gardens are located in the block bounded by St Georges Terrace, Riverside Drive, Barrack Street and Victoria Avenue. **Stirling Gardens** offer ornamental trees and well-kept lawns. Nearby within the gardens is a memorial acknowledging the state's role as one of the world's foremost producers of minerals, and hidden in the garden beds on the Barrack Street side of the gardens are small statues of May Gibbs' 'Gumnut Babies'. The gardens also house the oldest public building in Perth, now the Francis Burt Law Museum *(see Museums, p. 282)*. The **Supreme Court Gardens**, towards Riverside Drive, host concerts on summer evenings, including the annual Carols by Candlelight.

Bells and a jetty 276 B3

At Barrack Square, on the water's edge south of the city, is the Bell Tower, home of the Swan Bells, and the Barrack Street Jetty. Ferry services to Fremantle, South Perth, Rottnest Island and Carnac Island depart here, along with various leisure cruises on the Swan River and to the vineyards of the Swan Valley. Behind Jetty 6 is the Willem de Vlamingh Memorial, which features a sundial indicating Amsterdam time. The Swan Bells consist of 18 'change-ringing' bells, the largest set in the world, and you can view the bellringers in action. Head to the top of the tower for excellent views of the river and city. *Barrack Sq, cnr Barrack St and Riverside Dr; (08) 6210 0444; opening times vary seasonally (check the website, www.thebelltower.com.au); full bell ringing 12–1pm Mon, Tues, Thurs and Sat–Sun.*

[SWAN BELLS TOWER]

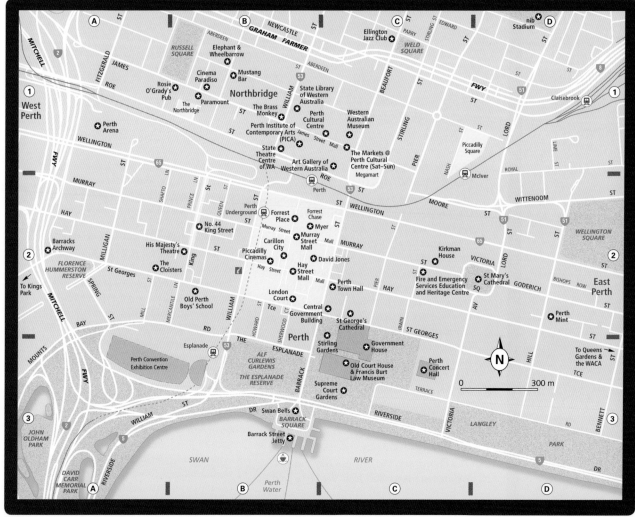

NORTHBRIDGE

Northbridge is the heart of the city's nightlife, and is connected to the city via a walkway to the Perth Cultural Centre. The centre includes the state museum, art gallery, state library and Perth's institute of contemporary arts. William Street and the streets further west are packed with restaurants and bars that offer great eating, drinking and nightclubbing.

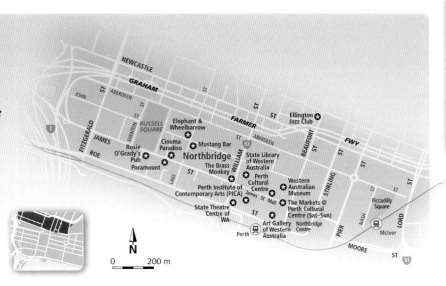

Art Gallery of Western Australia 276 C1

The state's principal public art gallery, founded in 1895, houses Australian and international paintings, sculpture, prints, craft and decorative arts. Its collection of Aboriginal art is one of Australia's finest. *Perth Cultural Centre, James St Mall; (08) 9492 6622 (24-hour information line) or (08) 9492 6600; open 10am–5pm Wed–Mon; general admission free; free guided tours available.*

Western Australian Museum 276 C1

See the 25-metre whale skeleton, the 11-tonne Mundrabilla meteorite and 'Megamouth' shark. There are exhibitions concerning the state's Aboriginal people; the origins of the universe; and dinosaur, bird, butterfly, mammal and marine galleries. The interactive Discovery Centre is great for children. Within the museum complex is the **Old Gaol**, built in 1856 and used by the Swan River Colony until 1888. *Perth Cultural Centre, James St Mall; (08) 9212 3700; open 9.30am–5pm daily; admission by donation; free guided tours available.*

Perth Institute of Contemporary Arts 276 B1

Known as PICA, this is the place to sample the latest in visual and performance art. There is an ever-changing program of exhibitions. *Perth Cultural Centre, James St Mall; (08) 9228 6300; open 11am–6pm Tues–Sun; general admission free.*

EAST PERTH

East Perth is where you'll find the Western Australian Cricket Association (WACA) oval, where cricket matches entertain the crowds over the summer months. Gloucester Park Raceway, with night harness horseracing on Friday nights, is nearby. Once the dead end of town, East Perth is now an enclave of offices and hip inner-city apartments, and home to the Perth Mint and Queens Gardens.

Perth Mint 276 D2

With a facade built in 1899 from Rottnest Island limestone, this is a prime example of Perth's gold-boom architecture. Here at Australia's oldest operating mint is the world's largest collection of natural gold specimens, including the 'Golden Beauty', a 11.5-kilogram nugget. Hold a 400-ounce gold bar, mint a coin, take a guided tour and watch gold being poured here. *310 Hay St (cnr Hill St), East Perth; (08) 9421 7277; open 9am–5pm daily.*

Queens Gardens 274 E3

The serene, English-style Queens Gardens feature a water garden with a replica of the famous Peter Pan statue that graces London's Kensington Gardens. These gardens were originally clay pits, where bricks were kilned for use in early colonial buildings. *Cnr Hay and Plain sts.*

WACA 274 E3

Across Hale Street from Queens Gardens is the WACA, home of the state's cricket team, the Western Warriors. True lovers of the sport should visit the WACA's cricket museum *(see Museums, p. 282)*.

INNER EAST

Burswood Entertainment Complex 275 F3

Built on an artificial island on the southern banks of the Swan River, this complex includes a casino, hotel, convention centre, tennis courts, golf course and Burswood Dome indoor stadium. Burswood Park, surrounding the complex, offers paths for walkers and cyclists, a heritage trail and a children's playground. *Great Eastern Hwy, Burswood; (08) 9362 7777.*

INNER NORTH

Tranby House 275 F3

Just beyond East Perth in Maylands is one of the oldest surviving buildings from the early settlement of the Swan River Colony, and a unique example of colonial farmhouse architecture. Built in 1889, the house has been beautifully restored by the National Trust. *Johnson Rd, Maylands; (08) 9272 2630; open 10am–4pm Wed–Sun (closed 24 Dec – 6 Feb).* Next door is the Peninsula Tea Gardens, where you can enjoy a traditional high tea. *(08) 9272 8894; open 10am–5pm daily.*

INNER WEST

Just minutes from the city centre, Kings Park is visited by millions of people each year. Nearby is Subiaco, with its popular shopping, cafe and market precinct. Below Kings Park, the river leads to the suburb of Crawley, passing the Old Swan Brewery site, now up-market offices, apartments and restaurants. Across from the university is the grassy Matilda Bay shoreline, with shady spots and views back up the river towards the city.

Kings Park and Botanic Garden 274 D4

From Mount Eliza in Kings Park, enjoy sweeping views of the city and the Swan River, with the Darling Range in the distance. This 400-hectare natural bushland reserve has landscaped gardens and walkways, lakes, playgrounds, a restaurant and cafes.

Lemon-scented gums honouring those who perished in war line Fraser Avenue, the main road into the park, and a clock tower and bronze bust memorialise Edith Cowan, the first woman elected to an Australian parliament.

The Lotterywest Federation Walkway, including a spectacular steel-and-glass bridge, extends 620 metres through the gardens. It offers a snapshot of Western Australia's famed flora: boabs, boronias and tuart trees on the ground and karri, marri, tingle and jarrah trees on the treetop walkway.

The Botanic Garden itself covers 17 hectares, and contains over 1700 native species, including a giant boab tree, weighing 36 tonnes and estimated to be 750 years old, which in 2008 was transported 3200 kilometres from the Kimberley town of Warnum. Other attractions are the State War Memorial precinct; the Pioneer Women's Memorial; the nearby DNA Tower; the fantastic dinosaur and fossil creations at Synergy Parkland; and the child-friendly Lotterywest Family Area. The park's newest attraction is Naturescape, where children can climb rocks and ropes, wade through creeks, build cubbies and enjoy a real 'bush' experience in the middle of the city. In spring the Kings Park Festival showcases the best of the state's wildflowers, and the park comes alive in summer with outdoor entertainment and moonlight movies (www.bgpa.wa.gov.au). *Fraser Ave; (08) 9480 3600; open daily; free guided walks from the visitor centre at 10am and 2pm daily, plus 12pm Sept–June.*

University of Western Australia 274 C4

The university is renowned for its distinctive Mediterranean-style architecture and beautiful landscaped gardens. **Winthrop Hall**, with its majestic clock tower and reflection pond, and the **Sunken Garden** are especially picturesque. The **Lawrence Wilson Art Gallery** has an extensive collection of Australian art, including works by Sidney Nolan, Arthur Boyd, Fred Williams and Rupert Bunny. *35 Stirling Hwy, Crawley; (08) 6488 3707; open 11am–5pm Tues–Fri, 12–5pm Sun; admission free.* The **Berndt Museum of Anthropology** houses an internationally renowned collection of Aboriginal art and artefacts. The collection is temporarily housed in the Lawrence Wilson Art Gallery until a new museum can be funded. *See www.berndt.uwa.edu.au*

Foreshore suburbs 274 C4, C5

From Matilda Bay towards the ocean is a series of exclusive waterfront suburbs with charming village-style shopping areas, fashionable galleries and restaurants. **Nedlands** is the suburb closest to the University of Western Australia. **Dalkeith's** Jutland Parade takes you to Point Resolution, with magnificent views of the river. Walk down the hillside to White Beach, a popular recreational spot.

Subiaco 274 C3

Beyond West Perth is the popular shopping, cafe and market precinct of Subiaco, with its village-style main street, Rokeby Road (pronounced 'Rock-a-bee'). One of Perth's oldest suburbs, it has some fine old homes in the back streets behind Rokeby Road. Here too is WA's home of AFL football, **Patersons Stadium**, formerly Subiaco Oval.

Parliament House 274 D3

Enter the corridors of power on a free, hour-long guided tour. *Harvest Tce, West Perth; (08) 9222 7259; tours 10.30am Mon and Thurs.*

Scitech Discovery Centre 274 D3

This interactive science and technology centre has more than 160 hands-on exhibits. **Horizon**, a state-of- the-art planetarium, screens extraordinary journeys into space on the largest dome screen in the Southern Hemisphere. *City West, cnr Sutherland and Railway sts, West Perth; (08) 9215 0700; open 9.30am–4pm Mon–Fri, 10am–5pm Sat–Sun, school holidays and public holidays.*

INNER NORTH-WEST

Lake Monger 274 C3

This urban wetland 5 kilometres north of Perth's CBD in the suburb of Wembley is the best place in Perth to see Western Australia's famous black swans, the official State Bird Emblem of Western Australia.

SOUTH-WESTERN BEACHSIDE

Several stunning beaches, including Cottlesoe, are close to the city, and swimming and surfing are a way of life in Perth. Scattered along these beach-fronts are lovely cafes, restaurants and bars.

Cottesloe 274 A5

Cottesloe is distinguished by its towering Norfolk Island pines and the **Indiana Cottesloe Beach Restaurant**, a neo-colonial beach-front building. *99 Marine Pde, Cottesloe; (08) 9385 5005.* The Spanish-style **Cottesloe Civic Centre** boasts magnificent gardens and ocean views. *109 Broome St; (08) 9285 5000; gardens open daily; admission free.*

Claremont 274 B4

This up-market suburb is home to Perth's swankiest shopping area, centred around Bay View Terrace. The **Claremont Museum**, on Victoria Avenue, was built in 1862 by convicts and the Pensioner Guards as the Freshwater Bay School. It now offers an interesting social-history display of more than 9000 items related to the district, including a carefully preserved schoolhouse. Nearby is a children's playground and picnic area. *66 Victoria Ave, Claremont; (08) 9340 6983; open 12–4pm Mon–Fri; admission free.*

Peppermint Grove 274 B5

Here are some of Perth's grandest homes. A drive along The Esplanade takes you past grass-backed riverside beaches, bushland and shady picnic areas. Drive around to Bay View Park – another great place for picnicking – in Mosman Park, and up the hill for sweeping views of Mosman Bay, the Swan River and Perth city skyline.

NORTH-WESTERN BEACHSIDE

Scarborough 274 A2

Renowned for its beachside cafe society, this is a top spot for surfers and sailboarders. The five-star Rendezvous Observation City Hotel dominates the landscape, reminiscent of the Gold Coast resorts. On weekends the Scarborough Fair Markets run opposite the hotel *(see Markets, p. 283)*. *Cnr Scarborough Beach Rd and West Coast Hwy; open 9am–5.30pm Sat–Sun.*

Hillarys Boat Harbour 571 B4

This ocean-side complex houses a marina, a world-class aquarium *(see next entry)*, and Sorrento Quay, a 'village' of shops, cafes, restaurants and resort apartments. The Great Escape leisure park will entertain the kids with water slides, miniature golf and trampolines. Ferries to Rottnest Island run from Hillarys, and there are whale-watching cruises from September to November. *Southside Dr, Hillarys; Boat Harbour, (08) 9448 7544; Sorrento Quay, (08) 9246 9788.*

Aquarium of Western Australia (AQWA) 571 B4

Among its five aquariums is an incredible 98-metre underwater-tunnel aquarium, surrounded by approximately 3 million litres of the Indian Ocean. See thousands of marine creatures here, and you can snorkel or swim with sharks. *Hillarys Boat Harbour, 91 Southside Dr, Hillarys; (08) 9447 7500; open 10am–5pm daily.*

INNER SOUTH

Perth Zoo 274 D4

Perth Zoo is just a short ferry ride across the river from the city. Visit the Australian Walkabout with native animals, the Penguin Plunge, African Savannah, Reptile Encounter and Rainforest Retreat. *20 Labouchere Rd, South Perth; (08) 9474 0444 or (08) 9474 3551 (recorded information line); open 9am–5pm daily.*

Old Mill 274 D4

This picturesque whitewashed windmill is at the southern end of the Narrows Bridge. Its foundation stone was laid by Captain James Stirling, the first governor, in 1835. The mill, a miller's cottage and an Education Centre provide a history of colonial flour milling. *Mill Point Rd, South Perth; (08) 9367 5788; open 10am–4pm Tues–Fri, 1–4pm Sat–Sun.*

SOUTH

Wireless Hill Park 274 D6

This natural bushland area boasts a magnificent springtime wildflower display. Three lookout towers provide views of the Swan River and the city skyline. A **Telecommunications Museum** is housed in the original Wireless Station and is open by appointment only. *Almondbury Rd, Ardross; (08) 9364 0158.*

Point Walter Reserve 274 B6

Pick a shady peppermint tree to sit under by the water's edge or enjoy a paddle in the water. A kiosk, cafe, free barbecue facilities and children's playground area are nearby. *Honour Ave, Bicton.*

Point Heathcote Reserve 274 D5

This hilltop playground and parkland area, which includes a local museum, art gallery, restaurant, kiosk and free barbecue facilities, is the best spot south of the Swan for sweeping views of the river and city.

OUTER SOUTH

Adventure World 571 C5

The state's biggest amusement park offers over 30 thrill rides and water slides. Nearby Bibra Lake is a great place to see black swans and other waterbirds. *179 Progress Dr, Bibra Lake; (08) 9417 9666; open 10am–5pm Thurs–Mon, daily in Jan and school holidays.*

FREMANTLE

Although now linked to Perth by a sprawl of suburbs, Fremantle ('Freo' to the locals) has a feel that is quite different in both architecture and atmosphere. Today it is a major boat and fishing centre at the mouth of the Swan River, but it also has the streetscape of a 19th-century port. It is a place to stay, unwind and watch the world go by. You can shop at the famous Fremantle Markets, or rest at a cafe on **South Terrace** *and wait for the arrival of 'the Fremantle Doctor', the refreshing afternoon wind that blows in off the Indian Ocean.*

European settlers arrived at Fremantle in 1829. The settlement developed gradually, its existence dependent on whaling and fishing. The population was boosted with the arrival in 1850 of British convicts, who constructed the forbidding Fremantle Prison (now open to the public) and the imposing lunatic asylum, now the Fremantle Arts Centre. Many heritage houses and terraces with cast-iron balconies from this period have survived.

Fremantle was at the centre of the world stage in 1987 when it hosted the America's Cup series of yacht races, following the win by Australia II – *a Fremantle yacht – in 1983. Preparations for this huge event included the restoration of many old buildings in Fremantle, and the boost to its tourist economy has lasted to the present day.*

VISITOR INFORMATION

Fremantle Visitor Centre
→ Town Hall, Kings Square, High St
(08) 9431 7878
www.fremantlewa.com.au

Shipwreck Galleries 280

These galleries, part of the Western Australian Maritime Museum, showcase those ships doomed to a watery grave by the state's treacherous coastline. See the reconstructed stern of the *Batavia*, wrecked in 1629. *Cliff St; (08) 9431 8469; open 9.30am–5pm daily; admission by donation.*

Grand old buildings 280

Fremantle has a compact cluster of lovely old buildings, beginning with the Georgian-style **Elder's Building** at 11 Cliff Street, once the hub of Fremantle's overseas trade. At 31–35 Cliff Street, the **Lionel Samson Building**'s rich facade epitomises the opulent style of gold-rush architecture. The **Esplanade Hotel**, on the corner of Marine Terrace and Essex Street, dates from the 1890s. Now the Challenger TAFE e-Tech,

[NATURAL SOAPS STALL AT FREMANTLE MARKETS]

the **Fremantle Technical College**, corner South Terrace and Essex Street, displays Art Nouveau decorative features. Corner Ellen and Ord streets, the grand old **Samson House** dates from 1900. Finally, there's the stone bell-tower and large stained-glass window of **St John's Anglican Church**, on the corner of Adelaide and Queen streets, and Henderson Street's **Warders' Quarters**, a row of convict-built cottages from 1851. *(See also the Round House and Fremantle Prison, on this page.)*

Fremantle Markets 280

One of the city's most popular attractions are these National Trust–classified markets, opened in 1897. Fresh produce, food, books, clothes, bric-a-brac, pottery and crafts are for sale, and buskers perform at a great tavern bar. *Cnr South Tce and Henderson St; (08) 9335 2515; open 9am–8pm Fri, 9am–6pm Sat–Sun.*

Round House 280

In fact a dodecahedron, this building was constructed in 1831 as a prison, and is the oldest public building in the state. At 1pm each day, a signal station fires a cannon that activates a time ball (an instrument once used to give accurate time readings to vessels out at sea). *10 Arthur Head; (08) 9336 6897; open 10.30am–3.30pm daily; admission by gold-coin donation.*

Western Australian Maritime Museum 280

This stunning, nautically inspired building perched on the waterfront has six galleries, each exploring a different theme in the state's maritime history. Highlights of the collection include the yacht that won the America's Cup – *Australia II* – and the *Parry Endeavour*, in which Western Australian Jon Sanders circumnavigated the world three times. Next door you can tour the submarine HMAS *Ovens*, which was in service during World War II. *Victoria Quay; (08) 9431 8334; open 9.30am–5pm daily.*

Leeuwin Ocean Adventure 280

The *Leeuwin II* – a 55-metre, three-masted barquentine – is the largest ocean-going tall ship in Australia. It is available for half-day or twilight sails and for longer voyages along the coast of Western Australia and the Northern Territory. When in Fremantle, it is open to the public. *B Berth, Victoria Quay; (08) 9430 4105.*

Fremantle Prison 280

This complex, built by convicts, was initially a barracks and became a prison in 1867, in use until 1991. Experience the forbidding atmosphere on a guided tour, running every half-hour. Enter via steps and a walkway around Fremantle Oval from Parry Street. *1 The Terrace; (08) 9336 9200; open 10am–5pm daily; Tunnels Tours daily and Torchlight Tours Wed and Fri (bookings essential).*

Fremantle Arts Centre 280

This magnificent limestone building was also built by convicts. The colony's first lunatic asylum, it now offers an interesting display on the history of Fremantle, contemporary art exhibitions, a craft shop, a ghost walk and a garden area with a cafe. *1 Finnerty St; (08) 9432 9555; open 10am–5pm daily; admission free.*

Fishing Boat Harbour 280

This popular restaurant strip overlooks the boats of local fishermen. Restaurants such as **Cicerello's** offer the catch of the day. Across the railway line is the **Esplanade Reserve**, an ideal spot to relax under the giant Norfolk Pines.

CITY ESSENTIALS
PERTH

Climate

Perth is Australia's sunniest capital, with an annual average of eight hours of sunshine per day. All this sunshine gives Perth a Mediterranean climate of hot, dry summers and mild, wet winters. The average maximum temperature in summer is 31°C; however, heat waves of temperatures in the high 30s and low 40s are not unusual. Fortunately, an afternoon sea breeze affectionately known as 'the Fremantle Doctor' eases the heat of summer.

	MAX °C	MIN °C	RAIN MM	RAIN DAYS
JANUARY	30	17	8	3
FEBRUARY	31	17	12	3
MARCH	29	16	19	4
APRIL	25	13	45	8
MAY	22	10	123	14
JUNE	19	8	184	17
JULY	18	7	173	18
AUGUST	18	8	136	17
SEPTEMBER	20	9	80	14
OCTOBER	22	11	54	11
NOVEMBER	26	14	21	6
DECEMBER	28	16	14	4

Getting around

The city is compact and easy to explore. A free bus service known as CATS (Central Area Transit Service) operates regular services, every five to ten minutes, around central Perth. The blue CAT runs in a north–south loop, the red CAT operates in an east–west loop, and the yellow CAT travels from East Perth to West Perth. (CAT bus services also operate in Fremantle and Joondalup.) You can also travel free on Transperth buses or trains within the Free Transit Zone in the city centre, but only on trips that start and finish within the zone.

Trains run from the city out to the northern suburbs and down to Fremantle while the Southern Suburbs Railway links Perth to Mandurah. Ferries and cruise boats depart regularly from Barrack Street Jetty to various destinations, including Fremantle, South Perth, Rottnest Island and the Swan Valley wine region. (Transperth runs the ferry to South Perth, while private operators travel further afield.) Perth, with its largely flat landscape, is also excellent for cycling; maps of the city's 700-kilometre

bike network are available at bike shops or online at the Department of Transport website, www.transport.wa.gov.au

Public transport Transperth Infoline (bus, train and ferry) 13 6213.

Airport shuttle bus Airport–city shuttle 1300 666 806.

Swan River Cruises Captain Cook Cruises (08) 9325 3341.

Motoring organisation RAC of WA 13 1703.

Car rental Avis 13 6333; Budget 13 2727; Hertz 13 3039; Thrifty 13 6139.

Taxis Black and White Taxis 13 1008; Swan Taxis 13 1330.

Bicycle hire About Bike Hire (08) 9221 2665.

Top events

Hopman Cup Prestigious international tennis event. January.

Perth Cup Western Australia's premier horseracing event. January.

Australia Day Skyworks A day-long party of events, culminating in a spectacular fireworks display. January.

Perth International Arts Festival Music, theatre, opera, dance, visual arts and film. February.

City of Perth Winter Arts Festival A three-month program of locally created arts and culture. June–August.

Kings Park Wildflower Festival Australia's premier native plant and wildflower exhibition. September.

Perth Royal Show Showcases the state's primary and secondary resources. September–October.

Red Bull Air Race A weekend of jaw-dropping, low-level aerial racing over the Swan River. November.

Museums

Fire and Emergency Services Education and Heritage Centre Refurbished in 2009, this limestone building dating from 1900 houses exhibitions on the history of the Perth fire brigade,

including fire rescue and old Big Red engines. Cnr Murray and Irwin sts; (08) 9323 9353; 10am–4pm Tues–Thurs; admission free.

Francis Burt Law Museum The history of the state's legal system is housed in the Old Court House. Stirling Gardens, cnr St Georges Tce and Barrack St; (08) 9325 4787; open 10am–2.30pm Wed–Fri; admission free.

Museum of Performing Arts Entertainment history brought to life through exhibitions of costumes and memorabilia taken from backstage archives. His Majesty's Theatre, 825 Hay St; (08) 9265 0900; open 10am–4pm Mon–Fri; admission by gold-coin donation.

WACA Museum Offers cricket memorabilia for fans of the sport. Gate 2, Nelson Cres, East Perth; (08) 9265 7222; open 10am–3pm Mon–Fri except match days; tours of ground and museum 10am and 1pm Mon–Thurs.

Army Museum of Western Australia Houses WA army memorabilia dating from colonial times to the present day. Artillery Barracks, Burt St, Fremantle; (08) 9430 2535; open 11am–4pm Wed–Sun.

See also See also Perth Mint, p. 277, Western Australian Museum, p. 277, Shipwreck Galleries p. 280, Fremantle Arts Centre and History Museum, p. 281.

Galleries

Aspects of Kings Park Contemporary Australian craft and design, with a focus on local artists. Fraser Ave, Kings Park and Botanic Garden, West Perth; (08) 9480 3900; open 9am–5pm daily.

Aboriginal Art Gallery A variety of innovative, contemporary and traditional Aboriginal art and artefacts. Under the lookout on Fraser Ave, Kings Park; West Perth; (08) 9481 7082; 10.30am–4.30pm Mon–Fri, 11am–4pm Sat–Sun.

Greenhill Galleries New York–style gallery features works of leading Australian artists. 16 Gugeri St, Claremont; (08) 9383 4433; open 10am–5pm Tues–Fri, 10am–4pm Sat.

Indigenart Mossenson Galleries One of Australia's foremost Aboriginal art galleries. 115 Hay St, Subiaco; (08) 9388 2899; open 10am–5pm Mon–Fri, 11am–4pm Sat.

Kailis Australian Pearls Perfectly matched strands and handcrafted pieces made from exquisite cultured and seedless pearls. 29 King St, Perth; (08) 9422 3888; cnr Marine Tce and Collie St, Fremantle; (08) 9239 9330.

See also Art Gallery of Western Australia, p. 276, Perth Institute of Contemporary Arts, p. 276.

 Grand old buildings

Government House Gothic arches and turrets reminiscent of the Tower of London. St Georges Tce (opposite Pier St).

His Majesty's Theatre The 'Maj', built in 1904, features an opulent Edwardian exterior. 825 Hay St; foyer tours 10am–4pm Mon–Fri; gold-coin donation.

Kirkman House In front of this gracious edifice is an immense Moreton Bay fig tree, planted in the 1890s and now classified by the National Trust. 10 Murray St.

Old Court House Perth's oldest surviving building (1836), now home to the Francis Burt Law Museum. Cnr St Georges Tce and Barrack St.

Old Perth Boys' School Perth's first purpose-built school was made from sandstone ferried up the Swan River by convict labour. 139 St Georges Tce.

Perth Town Hall Built by convict labour (1867–70) in the style of an English Jacobean market hall. Cnr Hay and Barrack sts.

St George's Cathedral This 1879 Anglican church features an impressive jarrah ceiling. 38 St Georges Tce.

St Mary's Cathedral Grand Gothic-style cathedral, one end of which was built in 1865. Victoria Sq.

The Cloisters Check out the decorative brickwork of this 1858 building, originally a boys' school. The old banyan tree adjoining it is something special too. 200 St Georges Tce.

 Shopping

Claremont Quarter, Claremont Perth's up-market fashion hot spot. 274 B5

Hay Street Mall, Murray Street Mall and Forrest Place, City The CBD's main shopping precinct with brand-name fashion outlets and major department stores Myer and David Jones. 276 B2

King Street, City High fashion, galleries and cafes with style. 276 B2

London Court, City Mock-Tudor arcade with souvenir, jewellery and antique stores. 276 B2

Napoleon Street, Cottesloe Cafes, boutiques and designer homewares. 274 B5

Rokeby Road, Subiaco Funky local designers sit alongside more established labels. 274 C3

 Markets

Canning Vale Markets Huge undercover flea markets, and the primary fruit and vegetable wholesale market for the state. Cnr South St and Bannister Rd; 7am–2pm Sun. 571 C6

The Markets @ Perth Cultural Centre The only regular weekend market in the city with produce, flowers and arts and crafts. 8.30am–5pm Sat–Sun. 276 C1

Scarborough Fair Markets Speciality stalls and a food hall on Scarborough Beach. Cnr Scarborough Beach Rd and West Coast Hwy; 9am–5.30pm Sat–Sun. 274 A1

Subiaco Pavilion Markets Art and craft stalls with large food hall in restored warehouse adjacent to station. Cnr Rokeby and Roberts rds, Subiaco; 10am–9pm Thurs–Fri, 10am–5pm Sat–Sun. 274 C3

Subiaco Station Street Markets A colourful outdoor and undercover market with an eclectic array of goods and live entertainment. 41 Station St, Subiaco; (08) 9382 2832; 9am–5.30pm Fri–Sun. 274 C3

Wanneroo Markets Huge undercover markets with food court selling everything from locally grown fruit and vegetables to footwear and jewellery. 33 Prindiville Dr, Wangara; (08) 9409 8397; 9am–5pm Fri–Sun. 571 B4

 Walks and tours

Fremantle Prison Tours Choose from a range of tours including the fascinating 'Doing Time Tour', every 30 minutes between 10am and 5pm, and the spooky 'Torchlight Tour' on Wednesdays and Fridays at 7pm. 1 The Terrace, Fremantle; (08) 9336 9200.

His Majesty's Theatre Tour Discover the colourful show-business history of 'The Maj' on the two-hour Grand Historical tour with theatre historian Ivan King, Tues–Thurs 10.30am. There's also a Behind the Scenes tour and foyer tours. (08) 9265 0900.

Kings Park Indigenous Heritage Tour Learn about bush medicines, bush tucker and Indigenous history in this 1.5-hour tour. (08) 9480 3600; 1.30pm daily.

Kings Park Walks Free guided walks, including the Botanic Garden Discovery, Bushland Nature Trail and the Memorials Walk, among others. (08) 9480 3600; 10am and 2pm daily, plus 12pm Sept–June.

Perth Walking Tours Take a free city orientation tour at 11am Monday to Saturday and noon on Sunday, or learn about Perth's history and culture on a free guided tour at 2pm weekdays. City of Perth Information Kiosk, Murray St Mall (near Forrest Pl).

Swan River Cruises Choose from full- or half-day cruises up the Swan River to the Swan Valley, with wine tastings included. Captain Cook Cruises, bookings on (08) 9325 3341.

The Rock 'n' Roll Mountain Biking Tours Enjoy a scenic tour of the bushlands of Western Australia on a safe, controlled mountain-biking experience. 0410 949 182 or 0428 263 668; www.rockandrollmountainbiking.com.au.

Two Feet & A Heartbeat Walking Tours Combining Perth's history with quirky tales and emerging culture, these walks include the Perth Urban Adventure and Eat/Drink/Walk Perth. There's even a Perth Shopping Tour; www.twofeet.com.au

 Entertainment

Cinema To catch a movie in the city, go to the Piccadilly Cinema in Piccadilly Arcade in the Hay Street Mall, which screens new-release films in Perth's only surviving grand old Art Deco cinema, or Cinema Paradiso, just across the railway line in Northbridge. The most easily accessible Hoyts cinemas are in Fremantle at the Queensgate on William Street and the Millennium on Collie Street. The closest Event cinema to the city is in Innaloo. Subiaco has an independent cinema, the Ace at 500 Hay St on the corner of Alvan. There's also the Luna Palace in Leederville, the Windsor in Nedlands, the Cygnet in Como and the Luna on SX (Essex Street) in Fremantle. In summer, there are a number of outdoor cinemas that operate; favourites are the Moonlight Cinema in Kings Park and the Somerville Auditorium at the University of Western Australia. The latter, which screens films for the Perth International Arts Festival from December through March, is defined by a cathedral of Norfolk pine trees and patrons sit on deckchair style seats under the stars. Programs and session times, including those for the open-air cinemas over summer, are listed daily in *The West Australian.*

Live music Northbridge, Leederville and Subiaco are the places to go for live music, as a healthy pub scene supports local musicians. In Northbridge popular venues include the Brass Monkey, the Mustang Bar, the Paramount, the Elephant & Wheelbarrow and Rosie O'Grady's. The Leederville Hotel on Oxford Street has a legendary Sunday afternoon session; the Ocean Beach Hotel in Cottesloe (known locally as the 'OBH') adds sunset views from the bar. In Fremantle, the premier live-music venues are the Fly by Night Musicians Club on Parry Street, Kulcha on South Terrace and Mojos in North Freo. Pick up the free street publication *Xpress* for gig guides or visit www.xpressmag.com.au. Jazz venues include the Hyde Park Hotel in Bulwer Street, North Perth; the Navy Club in High Street, Fremantle; and the Ellington Jazz Club at 191 Beaufort Street, Perth.

Classical music and performing arts

His Majesty's Theatre, Australia's only remaining Edwardian theatre, is Perth's premier venue for high-end theatre, opera and ballet. The State Theatre Centre of WA, opened in 2011 in Northbridge, is home to both WA's flagship theatre company, Black Swan State Theatre Company, and the Perth Theatre Company. The Regal Theatre in Subiaco stages local and imported productions; nearby, the Subiaco Arts Centre is home to Barking Gecko Theatre Company, which produces theatre for young people. Fremantle is home to Deckchair Theatre in High Street and Spare Parts Puppet Theatre in Short Street. The Perth Concert Hall in St Georges Terrace is the fine music venue for concerts by local and international musicians. Perth Arena, opened in 2012, draws crowds to Wellington Street in the city for concerts; the Burswood Entertainment Complex hosts touring shows and musicals; and NIB Stadium in East Perth is the venue for big international acts. In the warmer months, particularly in February when the Perth International Arts Festival is on, outdoor concerts are held in the Supreme Court and Queens Gardens, and in Kings Park. Check *The West Australian* for details.

 ## Sport

AFL (Australian Football League) is the most popular spectator sport in Perth, with crowds flocking to Patersons Stadium in Subiaco from April through September to support their local teams, the West Coast Eagles and the Fremantle Dockers. The **cricket** season takes up where the footy leaves off, with the famous WACA grounds in East Perth hosting both interstate and international test matches over the summer months.

Perth's **soccer** club, the Perth Glory, and WA's **Rugby Union** team, the Western Force, are both based at NIB Stadium in East Perth.

Basketball fans can catch the popular Perth Wildcats from September to February at Challenge Stadium in Mount Claremont, while their female counterparts, the West Coast Waves, play nearby at the WA Basketball Centre.

After years of being held at the Burswood Dome every January, the Hopman Cup, a prestigious international **tennis** event, moved in January 2013 to its new home at the Perth Arena in Wellington Street in the city.

Horseracing is a year-round event, split between two venues: Ascot racecourse in summer and Belmont Park in winter. Events such as the Perth Cup (held on New Year's Day), the Easter Racing Carnival and the Opening Day at Ascot draw huge crowds. Night harness racing can be seen at Gloucester Park every Friday night.

 ## Where to eat

No. 44 King Street Situated in a historic inner-city Victorian warehouse on one of Perth's most fashionable streetscapes, this all-day brasserie offers weekly menu changes, an in-house bakery, good coffee and an extensive wine list. 44 King St, Perth; (08) 9321 4476; open daily for breakfast, lunch and dinner. 276 B2

Fraser's Restaurant Boasts contemporary cuisine and spectacular views of the city. Fraser Ave, Kings Park, West Perth; (08) 9482 0100; lunch and dinner daily. 274 D3

Ha-Lu Relatively new and already an award finalist offering Japanese cuisine served in the Japanese pub style. Shop 4/401 Oxford St, Mt Hawthorn; (08) 9444 0577; open Wed–Sun for dinner. 274 D2

Must Winebar Bistro-style French Provincial cuisine with impressive wine list and always busy. 519 Beaufort St, Highgate; (08) 9328 8255; open daily for lunch and dinner. 274 E3

Nahm Thai Self-taught chef Kevin Pham creates high-end Thai food that shows superb finesse with the Asian sweet-hot-sour-salty quartet of flavour balance. 223 Bulwer St, Perth; (08) 9328 7500; open Mon–Sat for dinner. 274 D3

New Norcia Bakeries Authentic sourdough and yeasted breads baked in a traditional wood-fired oven; also many other tempting delights. 163 Scarborough Beach Rd, Mt Hawthorn; (08) 9443 4114; open daily for breakfast and lunch. 274 D2

Pata Negra The best tapas bar in Perth offers seriously tasty food that might have its heart in Spain but its innovative twists are pure Oz. 26 Stirling Highway, Nedlands; (08) 9389 5517; open Fri for lunch, Tues–Sat for dinner. 274 C4

Restaurant Amuse Innovative, award-winning chef Hadleigh Troy uses his brilliant technique and eclectic food artistry to create a dining experience like no other in Perth. 64 Bronte St, East Perth; (08) 9325 4900; open Tues–Sat for dinner. 274 E3

Rockpool Bar & Grill Voted the WA *Good Food Guide*'s 2012 Restaurant of the Year, Neil Perry's western outpost of his famous restaurant offers the best steaks in town. Burswood Entertainment Complex; (08) 6252 1900; open daily for lunch and dinner. 275 F3

The Old Brewery This premier steakhouse boasts some of the best waterside views in Perth and superb food – and it's just minutes from the CBD. 173 Mounts Bay Rd, Perth; (08) 9211 8999; open daily for lunch and dinner. 570 E6

 ## Where to stay

Beaufort House 237 Beaufort St, Perth; (08) 9227 8316.

Above Bored Bed and Breakfast 14 Norham St, North Perth; (08) 9444 5455.

Armadale Cottage Bed & Breakfast 3161 Albany Hwy, Armadale; (08) 9497 1663.

Banksia Tourist Park 219 Midland Rd, Hazelmere; (08) 9250 2398.

Cherokee Village Mobile Home & Tourist Park 10 Hocking Rd, Kingsley; (08) 9409 9039.

Discovery Holiday Parks – Perth 186 Hale Rd, Forrestfield; (08) 9453 6677.

Durham Lodge 165 Shepperton Rd, Victoria Park; (08) 9361 8000.

Eight Nicholson 8 Nicholson Rd, Subiaco; (08) 9382 1881.

Karrinyup Waters Resort 467 North Beach Rd, Gwelup; (08) 9447 6665.

Kingsway Tourist and Caravan Park Cnr Kingsway and Wanneroo Rd, Madeley; (08) 9409 9267.

Palms Bed & Breakfast 24 Dorchester Ave, Warwick; (08) 9246 9499.

Parkside B&B 21 Woolnough St, Daglish; (08) 9388 6075.

Perth Vineyards Holiday Park – Aspen Parks 91 Benara Rd, Caversham; (08) 9279 6700.

Swan Valley Tourist Park 6581 West Swan Rd, West Swan; (08) 9274 2828.

Trigg Retreat Bed and Breakfast 59 Kitchener St, Trigg; (08) 9447 6726.

 ## Day tours

Rottnest Island Just off the coast of Perth, in Thomson Bay, the low-key island resort of Rottnest makes for a perfect day tour. Access is via ferry from Fremantle, Perth or Hillarys Boat Harbour. No private cars are permitted: island transport is by foot, bicycle or bus. Visitors to Rottnest can divide their time between the beach and the scenic and historic attractions of the island.

Darling Range Follow the Great Eastern Highway for a tour of the Darling Range and its 80 000 hectares of escarpment and jarrah forest in the Hills Forest area. Highlights include a scenic drive through John Forrest National Park and a visit to the huge, forest-fringed Mundaring Weir.

Swan Valley A premier wine-growing district, with vineyards along the scenic Swan River. Other attractions include the historic town of Guildford; Woodbridge House, a Victorian mansion in West Midland; Walyunga National Park; and Whiteman Park, a 2500-hectare area that includes Caversham Wildlife Park.

Yanchep National Park On the coast north of Perth, Yanchep has long been one of the city's favourite recreation areas. Have your photo taken with a koala; see didgeridoo and dance performances; or take a guided tour of Crystal Cave, where stalactites hang above the inky waters of an underground pool.

FREMANTLE

Top events

St Patrick's Day Parade and Concert
Celebrates the Irish national holiday with much
gusto. March.

Fremantle Street Arts Festival   Local, national
and international buskers perform on the streets.
Easter.

Freo's West Coast Blues 'n Roots Festival
Day-long celebration of blues, roots, reggae and
rock, with many big-name acts. April.

Blessing of the Fleet   Traditional Italian
blessing of the fishing fleet. October.

Fremantle Festival   Performing arts and
community activities culminating in a street
parade and dance party. November.

Grand old buildings

Elder's Building   Georgian-style building, made
of brick and Donnybrook stone, once the hub of
Fremantle's overseas trade. 11 Cliff St. 280

Esplanade Hotel   This 1890s hotel has been
extended to blend in with the original facade.
Cnr Marine Tce and Essex St. 280

Fremantle Technical College   Now the
Challenger TAFE e-Tech, this building boasts
Donnybrook stone facings and plinth with Art
Nouveau decorative influences. Cnr South Tce
and Essex St. 280

Lionel Samson Building   A rich facade
epitomises the optimistic style of gold-rush
architecture. 31–35 Cliff St. 280

Samson House   Grand old 1900 house,
originally built for Michael Samson, who later
became mayor of Fremantle. Cnr Ellen and
Ord sts; 1–5pm Sun. 280

St John's Anglican Church   Features a stone
belltower and large stained-glass window.
Cnr Adelaide and Queen sts. 280

Warders' Quarters   A row of convict-built
cottages built in 1851, used until recently to
house warders from the Fremantle Prison.
Henderson St. 280

See also The Round House and Fremantle Prison,
p. 281.

Where to eat

Bluewater Grill   One of Perth's best dining
establishments, right on the Swan River, with
uninterrupted city views and an emphasis on
seafood. Heathcote Court, 56 Duncraig St;
(08) 9315 7700; open daily for breakfast, lunch
and dinner. 274 D5

Capri   Rustic, Italian comfort food at its best
at this local establishment. The osso-bucco and
pastas are deliciously more-ish, and the free soup
and bread has become a tradition. Cash only.
21 South Tce; (08) 9335 1399; open daily for lunch
and dinner. 280

Cicerello's   The epitome of fish-and-chip dining
on Fremantle's Fishing Boat Harbour. 2/1 Howard
St; (08) 9335 9811; open daily for lunch and
dinner. 280

Little Creatures   Harbour-side brewery, bar
and restaurant serves hearty fare to its enormous
following. 40 Mews Rd; (08) 9339 9500; open
Mon–Fri 10am until late, Sat–Sun 9am until
late. 280

Maya   Widely considered to be the best Indian
food in town. 75 Market St; (08) 9335 2796; open
Fri for lunch; Tues–Sun for dinner. 280

The Red Herring   Up-market seafood
restaurant boasts a magical setting right on the
river. 26 Riverside Rd, East Fremantle; (08) 9339
1611; open daily for lunch and dinner, and Sun
for breakfast.

Sandrino Cafe and Pizzeria   Rated 'the
best pizzas in town' in the 2012 *Good Food
Guide*. 95 Market St; (08) 9335 4487; open
11am–9.30pm daily. 280

Sala Thai   A local favourite, serves Thai cuisine
comparable to its country of origin. 22 Norfolk St;
(08) 9335 7749; open daily for dinner. 280

Where to stay

Fothergills of Fremantle   18–22 Ord St;
(08) 9335 6784.

Terrace Central B&B Hotel   79 South Tce;
(08) 9335 6600.

Fremantle Village   25 Cockburn Rd,
South Fremantle; (08) 9430 4866.

Heritage Cottage Bed & Breakfast
273 South Tce, South Fremantle; (08) 9433 5946.

REGIONS
of Western Australia

Listed here are some of the top attractions and experiences in each region.

8 PILBARA
Karijini National Park (pictured) / see p. 334
Marble Bar / see p. 319
Millstream–Chichester National Park / see p. 311
Dampier Archipelago and Montebello Islands / see p. 314

7 OUTBACK COAST AND MID-WEST
Dolphins at Monkey Mia (pictured) / see p. 301
Kalbarri National Park / see p. 311
Ningaloo Marine Park / see p. 299
St Francis Xavier Cathedral, Geraldton / see p. 307

1 DARLING AND SWAN
Araluen Botanic Park / see p. 325
John Forrest National Park (pictured) / see p. 325
Mundaring Weir / see p. 324
Swan Valley wine region / see p. 324

2 THE SOUTH-WEST
Busselton Jetty (pictured) / see p. 293
Mammoth and Lake caves, Leeuwin–Naturaliste National Park / see p. 323
Margaret River wine region / see p. 322
Valley of the Giants / see p. 336

3 HEARTLANDS
Avon Valley National Park / see p. 335
Spanish colonial architecture in New Norcia / see p. 326
The Pinnacles Desert in Nambung National Park (pictured) / see p. 296
Wave Rock / see p. 310

8

7

1

PERTH

3

2   4

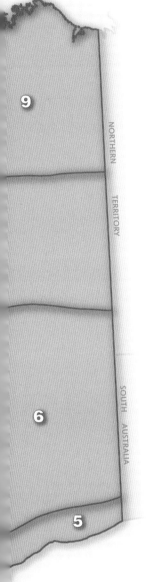

9 THE KIMBERLEY

Driving along the Gibb River Rd / see p. 303
Lake Argyle, Kununurra / see p. 315
Purnululu National Park (pictured) / see p. 309
Wolfe Creek Crater National Park / see p. 309

6 GOLDFIELDS

Ghost town of Gwalia (pictured) / see p. 313
Goldfields Exhibition Museum, Coolgardie / see p. 299
Peak Charles National Park / see p. 327
Superpit Lookout, Kalgoorlie–Boulder / see p. 312

5 ESPERANCE AND NULLARBOR

Recherche Archipelago / see p. 305
Cape Le Grand National Park (pictured) / see p. 305
Great Ocean Drive / see p. 305
90-Mile Straight / see p. 291

4 GREAT SOUTHERN

Whale World / see p. 291
Old Farm at Strawberry Hill, Albany / see p. 290
Stirling Range National Park (pictured) / see p. 300
Torndirrup National Park / see p. 291

NORTHERN TERRITORY

SOUTH AUSTRALIA

TOWNS A-Z
Western Australia

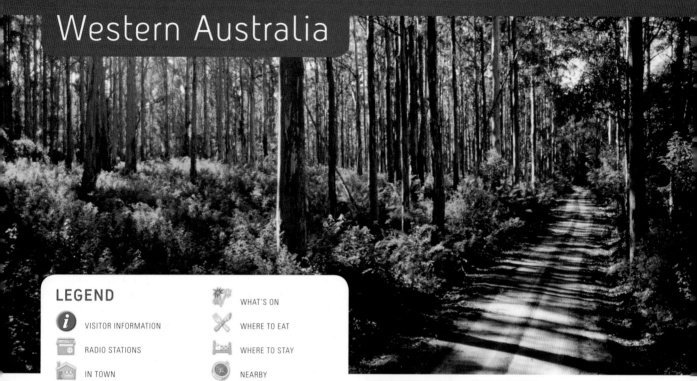

[KARRI TREES, NEAR MARGARET RIVER]

LEGEND

ⓘ VISITOR INFORMATION

🕮 RADIO STATIONS

🏠 IN TOWN

🌴 WHAT'S ON

🍴 WHERE TO EAT

🛏 WHERE TO STAY

◉ NEARBY

* Distances for towns nearby are calculated as the crow flies.
* Food and accommodation listings in town are ordered alphabetically
  with places nearby listed at the end.

Albany

see inset box on page 290

Augusta

Pop. 1072
Map ref. 572 C11 | 574 B10 | 576 B11

ⓘ Blackwood Ave; (08) 9758 0166; www.margaretriver.com

🕮 98.3 FM ABC South West Radio, 99.1 FM ABC Radio National

The town of Augusta lies in the south-west corner of Western Australia. The state's third-oldest settlement sits high on the slopes of the Hardy Inlet, overlooking the mouth of the Blackwood River and the waters of Flinders Bay. Just beyond it lies Cape Leeuwin with its unforgettable signpost dividing the oceans: the Southern Ocean to the south and the Indian Ocean to the west.

 Augusta Historical Museum Augusta's difficult beginning in 1830 is documented in this collection of artefacts and photographs. An exhibit details the 1986 rescue of whales that beached themselves near the town. Blackwood Ave; (08) 9758 0465.

Crafters Croft: locally made handcrafts, jams, emu-oil products; Ellis St.

🌴 *Augusta River Festival:* Mar. *Spring Flower Show:* Sept/Oct.

🍴 *The Colourpatch Take Away Cafe & Restaurant:* fish and chips, homemade cafe treats; 98 Albany Tce; (08) 9758 1295.

🛏 *Flinders Bay Caravan Park:* 10 Albany Tce; (08) 9758 1380. *Turner Caravan Park:* 1 Blackwood Ave; (08) 9758 1593.

◉ **Leeuwin–Naturaliste National Park** This park extends 120 km from Cape Naturaliste in the north to Cape Leeuwin in the south. Close to Augusta are 3 major attractions: Cape Leeuwin, Jewel Cave and Hamelin Bay. Cape Leeuwin (8 km sw) marks the most south-westerly point of Australia. Climb 176 steps to the top of the limestone lighthouse, mainland Australia's tallest. Nearby is the Old Water Wheel, built in 1895 from timber that has since calcified, giving it the appearance of stone. Jewel Cave (8 km nw on Caves Rd) is renowned for its limestone formations, including the longest straw stalactite found in any tourist cave. At Hamelin Bay (18 km nw) a windswept beach and the skeleton of an old jetty give little indication of the massive amounts of jarrah and karri that were once transported from here. In the heyday of the local timber industry, the port's exposure to the treacherous north-west winds resulted in 11 wrecks. These now form the state's most unusual Heritage Trail: the Hamelin Bay Wreck Trail, for experienced divers. *See also Margaret River and Dunsborough.*

The Landing Place: where the first European settlers landed in 1830; 3 km s. *Whale Rescue Memorial:* commemorates the 1986 rescue of beached pilot whales; 4 km s. *Matthew Flinders Memorial:* Flinders began mapping the Australian coastline from Cape Leeuwin in December 1801; 5 km s. *Alexandra Bridge:* picnic and camping spot with towering jarrah trees and beautiful wildflowers in season; 10 km n. *Boranup Maze and Lookout:* the maze offers a short walking track under trellis, while the lookout provides a picnic area with panoramic views towards the coast; 18 km n. *Augusta–Busselton Heritage Trail:* 100 km trail traces the history of the area through the pioneering Bussell and Molloy

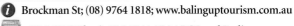
families, who settled in Augusta only to move further up the coast looking for suitable agricultural land; contact visitor centre for map. *Blackwood River:* meanders 500 km through wheatbelt plains and forested valleys to its broad estuary at Augusta. Secluded spots between Nannup and Alexandra Bridge offer tranquil camping, fishing, swimming and canoeing. *Cruises:* Blackwood River and Hardy Inlet. *Marron in season:* fishing licence required and available at the post office; Blackwood Ave. *Whale-watching:* charter boats and coastal vantage points offer sightings of migrating humpback whales (June–Aug) and southern right whales (June–Oct), plus pods of dolphins and fur seals; contact visitor centre for details.

TOWNS NEARBY: Margaret River 41 km, Nannup 67 km, Yallingup 75 km, Busselton 76 km, Dunsborough 77 km

Australind

Pop. 8716
Map ref. 572 E3 | 574 C8 | 576 C9

ⓘ Henton Cottage, cnr Old Coast and Paris rds; (08) 9796 0122.

📻 95.7 Hot FM, 1224 AM ABC Radio National

Lying on the Leschenault Estuary and bordered by the Collie River, Australind offers a multitude of aquatic pleasures including fishing, crabbing, prawning, swimming, boating, sailing and windsurfing. The town's unusual name is a contraction of Australia and India, coined by its founders in the hope of a prosperous trade in horses between the two countries.

St Nicholas Church: built in 1840, reputedly the smallest church in Australia at only 3.6 m wide and 8.2 m long; Paris Rd. *Henton Cottage:* early 1840s heritage building now houses the visitor centre and an art and craft gallery; Cnr Old Coast and Paris rds. *Featured Wood Gallery:* fine furniture and craft made from the local timbers of jarrah, she-oak, marri, banksia and blackbutt. Also includes a museum of Australian and American West history; Piggott Dr; (08) 9797 2411. *Pioneer Memorial:* site of the first settlers' landing in 1840; Old Coast Rd. *Cathedral Ave:* scenic 2 km drive through arching paperbark trees with sightings of kangaroos and black swans, especially at sunset; off Old Coast Rd.

Carols in the Park: Dec.

Australind Tourist Park: Lot 9 Old Coast Rd; (08) 9725 1206.

Leschenault Inlet Offers recreational attractions from the simple pleasure of fishing from the Leschenault Inlet Fishing Groyne to picnicking, camping and bushwalking in the Peninsula Conservation Park. The park is a haven for native wildlife with over 60 species of birds recorded. Only walking or cycling is permitted in the park except for 4WD beach access from Buffalo Rd (1 km s). The Leschenault Waterway Discovery Centre has an interpretive gazebo with information on the estuary environment. Old Coast Rd; 2 km s.

Pioneer Cemetery: graves dating back to 1842 and beautiful wildflowers in season; Old Coast Rd; 2 km N. *Binningup and Myalup:* pleasant beach towns north of Leschenault. *Australind–Bunbury Tourist Drive:* coastal scenery, excellent crabbing and picnic spots; contact visitor centre for brochure.

TOWNS NEARBY: Bunbury 9 km, Harvey 28 km, Donnybrook 34 km, Collie 42 km, Busselton 54 km

Balingup

Pop. 443
Map ref. 572 G6 | 574 C9 | 576 C10

ⓘ Brockman St; (08) 9764 1818; www.balinguptourism.com.au

📻 93.3 ABC Classic FM, 1044 AM ABC Local Radio

This small town, nestled in the Blackwood River Valley, is surrounded by rolling hills, forests and orchards. Balingup is renowned for its glowing summer sunsets, amazing autumn colours and misty winter mornings.

Birdwood Park Fruit Winery: unique award-winning fruit wines, chutneys, jams and fruits; Brockman St; (08) 9764 1172. *Tinderbox:* herbal and natural products; South Western Hwy. *Old Cheese Factory Craft Centre:* the largest art and craft centre in WA, including pottery and timber products; Balingup–Nannup Rd; (08) 9764 1018.

Opera in the Valley: Jan. *Small Farm Field Day:* festival and roadside scarecrows; Apr. *Medieval Carnivale:* Aug. *Festival of Country Gardens:* Oct/Nov. *Balingup Jalbrook Concert:* Nov.

Balingup Bronze Gallery and Cafe: healthy and tasty; Cnr South Western Hwy and Forrest St; (08) 9764 1843. *Fre-Jac French Bakery:* authentic patisserie, light lunches; The Packing Shed, South Western Hwy; (08) 9764 1983. *Fre-Jac French Restaurant:* traditional French cuisine; Forrest St; (08) 9764 1883. *Taste of Balingup:* gourmet local produce and cafe; Shop 1, 63 South Western Hwy; (08) 9764 1344.

Oakfield Country House Bed & Breakfast: 77 Bailey Heights; (08) 9764 1641.

Golden Valley Tree Park This 60 ha arboretum boasts a superb collection of exotic and native trees. Other attractions include a tree information gazebo, walk trails, lookout and the historic Golden Valley Homestead. Old Padbury Rd; 2 km s.

Jalbrook Alpacas and Knitwear Gallery: alpacas to feed and alpaca knitwear; accommodation also available; (08) 9764 1190; 2 km E. *Lavender Farm:* oil-producing lavender farm with open gardens, picnic area, art gallery and giftshop. Take a distillation tour; open Sept–Apr, Balingup–Nannup Rd; (08) 9764 1436; 2.5 km w. *Balingup Heights Scenic Lookout:* stunning views of town and orchards; off Balingup–Nannup Rd; 2.5 km w. *Greenbushes:* boasts WA's first metal-producing mine (1888), still in production and now the world's largest tantalum producer. The Discovery Centre has interactive displays and walking trails, and there is an excellent lookout at the mine; 10 km w. *Heritage Country Cheese:* cheese-producing factory with viewing window and tastings; 16 km w. *Wineries:* several in area; contact visitor centre for details. *Balingup–Nannup Rd:* enjoy wonderful scenery, interesting and historic landmarks and great marroning, fishing and picnic sites. *Bibbulmun Track:* sections of this trail pass through Balingup; *see Albany.*

TOWNS NEARBY: Bridgetown 24 km, Donnybrook 28 km, Nannup 29 km, Boyup Brook 38 km, Collie 50 km

Balladonia

Pop. 20
Map ref. 577 K7

ⓘ Balladonia Roadhouse, Eyre Hwy; (08) 9039 3453; www.dundas.wa.gov.au

Balladonia lies on the Eyre Highway on the western edge of the Nullarbor Plain. Its closest towns are Norseman, 174 kilometres to the west, and Caiguna, 176 kilometres to the east. This arid desert shrubland is one of the world's oldest landscapes, containing seashells millions of years old from when the area

continued on p. 291

ALBANY

Pop. 25 197

Map ref. 573 D11 | 574 G11 | 576 E11

i Old Railway Station, Proudlove Pde; (08) 9841 9290 or 1800 644 088; www.albanytourist.com.au

100.9 FM Albany Community Radio, 630 AM ABC Local Radio

Albany, a picturesque city on Western Australia's south coast, is the site of the state's first European settlement. On Boxing Day 1826, Major Edmund Lockyer, with a party of soldiers and convicts from New South Wales, came ashore to establish a military and penal outpost. Ninety years later, Albany was the embarkation point for Australian troops during World War I and, for many, their last view of the continent. A whaling industry, which began in the 1940s, defined the town until the Cheynes Beach Whaling Company closed in 1978. Nowadays, whale-watching has taken its place. Lying within the protected shelter of the Princess Royal Harbour on the edge of King George Sound, Albany is one of the state's most popular tourist destinations.

Historic buildings As WA's oldest town, Albany boasts more than 50 buildings of historical significance dating back to the early years of the settlement. Two of the oldest were built in the 1830s: Patrick Taylor Cottage on Duke St, which houses an extensive collection of period costumes and household goods, and the Old Farm at Strawberry Hill on Middleton Rd, site of the first government farm in WA. Other heritage buildings include the Old Gaol (1851), with its collection of social history artefacts, and the Residency Museum (1850s), a showcase of historical and environmental exhibits, both in Residency Rd. There are self-guide walks available, including the Colonial Buildings Historical Walk; contact visitor centre for brochures.

The Amity: full-scale replica of the brig that brought Albany's first settlers from Sydney in 1826; Princess Royal Dr. *St. John's Church:* 1848 Anglican church is the oldest in the state; York St. *Albany Entertainment Centre:* architecturally stunning new performing arts centre on foreshore with breathtaking harbour

views; Toll Place. *Vancouver Arts Centre:* gallery, craft shop, studio and workshop complex, originally the Albany Cottage Hospital (1887); Vancouver St. *House of Gems:* extensive range of gemstones and jewellery; Cnr York St and Stirling Tce. *Dog Rock:* granite outcrop resembling the head of an enormous labrador is a photo opportunity not to be missed; Middleton Rd. *Princess Royal Fortress:* Albany's first federal fortress, commissioned in 1893 and fully operational until the 1950s, now houses military museums and war memorials; off Forts Rd. *The White Star Hotel:* charming historic hotel with microbrewery; Stirling Tce. *Spectacular views:* lookouts at the peaks of Mt Clarence and Mt Melville have 360-degree views. Near the top of Mt Clarence is the Desert Mounted Corps Memorial statue, a recast of the original statue erected at Suez in 1932; Apex Dr. John Barnesby Memorial Lookout at the top of Mt Melville is 23 m high, with observation decks; Melville Dr. *Mt Clarence Downhill:* new downhill mountain bike trail adjacent to the peak; Apex Dr. *Bibbulmun Track:* 963 km walking track to Perth begins at Albany's Old Railway Station in Proudlove Pde; *see below. Whale-watching:* cruises daily from town jetty to see southern rights; June–Oct.

Albany Farmers Market: Collie St; 8am–12pm Sat. *Albany Boatshed Markets:* Princess Royal Dr; 10am–1pm Sun. *Vintage Blues Festival:* Jan. *Taste Great Southern Food and Food and Wine Festival:* Feb–Mar.

The Earl of Spencer Historic Inn: pub fare in historic tavern; Cnr Earl and Spencer sts; (08) 9847 4262. *Lime 303:* contemporary, creative restaurant; The Dog Rock Motel, 303 Middleton Rd; (08) 9845 7298. *The Naked Bean Coffee Roasters:* delicious snacks for coffee addicts; 21 Sanford Rd; (08) 9841 4225. *Wild Duck Restaurant:* sophisticated dining; Shop 5, 112 York St; (08) 9842 2554.

Norman House: 28 Stirling Tce; (08) 9841 5995. *Albany Happy Days Caravan Park:* 1584 Millbrook Rd, King River; (08) 9844 3267. *Albany Holiday Park:* 550 Albany Hwy, Milpara; (08) 9841 7800. *Albany's Emu Beach Holiday Park:* 8 Medcalf Pde, Emu Point; (08) 9844 1147. *Chalet Arunga:* 250 Hunwick Rd, Torbay; (08) 9845 1025. *Cheynes Beach Caravan Park:* 12 Bald Island Rd, Cheynes; (08) 9846 1247. *Kalgan River Chalets & Caravan Park:* 247 Nanarup Rd, Kalgan; (08) 9844 7937. *Middleton Beach Holiday Park:* 28 Flinders Pde, Middleton Beach; (08) 9841 3593. *Rose Gardens Beachside Holiday Park:* 45 Mermaid Ave, Emu Point; (08) 9844 1868. *Saltair B&B:* 56 Wylie Cres, Middleton Beach; (08) 9841 1663.

Bibbulmun Track At 963 km, this is WA's only long-distance walking trail and one of the longest continuously marked trails in Australia. It stretches from Kalamunda, a suburb on the outskirts of Perth, to Albany. On the way it passes through some of the state's most picturesque southern towns including Dwellingup, Collie, Balingup, Pemberton, Northcliffe, Walpole and Denmark. Named after a local Aboriginal language group, the track is marked by a stylised image of the 'Waugal' (rainbow serpent), a spirit being from the Aboriginal Dreaming. Whether taking a short walk or a 5-day hike, easy access points enable walkers of all ages and fitness levels to experience the Bibbulmun Track. Walk

[ALBANY'S TOWN HALL]

the track in springtime and see the bush at its best with WA's amazing array of wildflowers. Near Walpole you'll encounter the massive red tingle trees of the Valley of the Giants. Other well-known natural attractions on the track include Mt Cook, the highest point in the Darling Range, Beedelup Falls and the Gloucester Tree lookout. For maps and more information contact the Bibbulmun Track Office of DEC on (08) 9334 0265 or visit www.bibbulmuntrack.org.au

Torndirrup National Park Torndirrup is one of the most visited parks in the state, featuring abundant wildflowers, wildlife and bushwalking trails. Granite outcrops and cliffs alternate with dunes, and sandy heath supports peppermint, banksia and karri. The park is renowned for its rugged coastal scenery, including such features as the Gap, a chasm with a 24 m drop to the sea, and the Natural Bridge, a span of granite eroded by huge seas to form a giant arch. Exercise extreme caution on this dangerous coastline; king waves can rush in unexpectedly. 17 km s.

Whale World Even before the Cheynes Beach Whaling Company closed in 1978, Albany's oldest industry was a major tourist attraction. In its heyday, the company's chasers took up to 850 whales a season. View the restored whale-chaser *Cheynes IV*, whale skeletons, the old processing factory, an aircraft display and the world's largest collection of marine mammal paintings. This is the only whaling museum in the world created from a working whaling station. A 3D theatrette occupies one of the old whale-oil storage tanks. Free guided tours are available on (08) 9844 4021. 25 km SE.

Albany Bird Park: undercover walk-in aviary with over 250 native and exotic birds; Frenchman Bay Rd; 3.5 km SW. *Deer-O-Dome:* showcases the Australian deer industry; 6 km N. *Mount Romance Sandalwood Factory:* skincare products, perfumes, therapeutics and free guided tours; (08) 9845 6888; 12 km N. *Albany Wind Farm:* 12 giant turbines, each 100 m high; 12 km SW. *Point Possession Heritage Trail:* views and interpretive plaques; Vancouver Peninsula; 20 km SE. *Fishing:* Emu Point (8 km NE), Oyster Harbour (15 km NE), Jimmy Newhill's Harbour (20 km S), Frenchman Bay (25 km SE). *Diving:* former HMAS *Perth* was scuttled in 2001 as an artificial dive reef; Frenchman Bay; 25 km SE. *West Cape Howe National Park:* walking, fishing, swimming and hang-gliding; 30 km W. *Two Peoples Bay Nature Reserve:* sanctuary for the noisy scrub bird, thought to be extinct but rediscovered in 1961; 40 km E. *Tours:* include sailing, wineries, eco-tours, 4WDriving, and national parks tours; contact visitor centre for more details.

TOWNS NEARBY: Mount Barker 45 km, Denmark 47 km, Cranbrook 83 km, Walpole 104 km, Kojonup 145 km

---

was ocean floor. Balladonia made world headlines in 1979 when space debris from NASA's *Skylab* landed 40 kilometres east on Woorlba Station.

 Cultural Heritage Museum Learn about the crash-landing of *Skylab*, local indigenous culture, early explorers, Afghan cameleers and other chapters in the area's history. Balladonia Roadhouse, Eyre Hwy.

 Balladonia Hotel Motel: light meals and hearty fare; Eyre Hwy; (08) 9039 3453.

 90-Mile Straight Have your photo taken beside the signpost marking the western end of the longest straight stretch of road in Australia, which runs for 90 miles (146.6 km) between Balladonia and Caiguna. Begins 35 km E.

Newman Rocks: superb views from rocky outcrop, with picnic and camping areas on-site; 50 km W. *Cape Arid National Park and Israelite Bay:* great birdwatching and fishing; access via 4WD track, south of town; check track conditions at roadhouse.

TOWNS NEARBY: Norseman 174 km, Caiguna 176 km, Esperance 233 km, Cocklebiddy 236 km

Beverley

Pop. 850
Map ref. 574 E5 | 576 D7

 Aeronautical Museum, 139 Vincent St; (08) 9646 1555; www.beverleywa.com

 99.7 FM ABC News Radio, 531 AM ABC Local Radio

Beverley is a small town set on the banks of the Avon River 130 kilometres east of Perth. Its main street boasts some beautifully preserved buildings, representing Federation to Art Deco architectural styles. This farming community, while having long been associated with wheat and wool, also produces grapes, olives, emus, deer and yabbies.

 Aeronautical Museum This museum presents a comprehensive display of early aviation in WA. The museum's star attraction is the Silver Centenary, a biplane built between 1928 and 1930 by local man Selby Ford and his cousin Tom Shackles. Ford designed the plane in chalk on the floor where he worked. The plane first flew in July 1930, but was never licensed because of the lack of design blueprints. Vincent St.

Station Gallery: art exhibitions and sales in the Tudor-style (1889) railway station; Vincent St. *Dead Finish Museum:* the oldest building in town (1872) houses memorabilia and historic items from wooden cotton wheels to washing boards; open 11am–3pm Sun Mar–Nov or by appt through visitor centre; Hunt Rd.

 Yabbie Races: Apr. *Annual Quick Shear:* Aug.

 Freemasons Tavern: classic Australian pub; Cnr Vincent and Forrest sts; (08) 9646 1094.

 Beverley Bed & Breakfast: 131 Forrest St; (08) 9646 0073.

 Avondale Discovery Farm Avondale is an agricultural research station with displays of historic farming machinery and tools. The 1850s homestead is furnished in period style and set in traditional gardens. There is also an animal nursery, Clydesdale horses and a picnic area with barbecues and a children's playground. A land-care education centre houses interactive

---

 RADIO STATIONS   IN TOWN   WHAT'S ON   WHERE TO EAT   WHERE TO STAY   NEARBY

displays. The farm hosts the Clydesdale and Vintage Day in June. Waterhatch Rd; (08) 9646 1004; 6 km W.

Brookton: attractions of this nearby town include the Old Police Station Museum and the Brookton Pioneer Heritage Trail, which highlights places significant to the local Aboriginal people; 32 km S. *County Peak Lookout:* spectacular views from the summit; 35 km SE. *The Avon Ascent:* take a self-drive tour of the Avon Valley; contact visitor centre for map.

TOWNS NEARBY: York 29 km, Pingelly 49 km, Northam 56 km, Mundaring 75 km, Toodyay 76 km

Boyup Brook
Pop. 531
Map ref. 574 D9 | 576 C10

i Cnr Bridge and Abel sts; (08) 9765 1444; www.bbvisitor.mysouthwest.com.au

100.5 Hot FM, 1044 AM ABC Local Radio

Boyup Brook is on the tranquil Blackwood River in the heart of Western Australia's grass-tree country. The town's name is thought to derive from the Aboriginal word 'booyup', meaning 'place of big stones' or 'place of much smoke', which was given to the nearby Boyup Pool. Seasonal wildflowers are abundant during September and October.

 Carnaby Beetle and Butterfly Collection Keith Carnaby was such a leading light in the field of entomology that beetles have been named after him. His collection of Jewel beetles, part of which is on display at the Boyup Brook Tourist Information Centre, is regarded as the best outside the British Museum of Natural History. Cnr Bridge and Abel sts.

Pioneers' Museum: displays of historic agricultural, commercial and domestic equipment; open 2–5pm Mon, Wed, Fri or by appt; Jayes Rd. *Sandakan War Memorial:* honours 1500 Australian POWs sent to Sandakan to build an airfield for the Japanese; Sandakan Park. *The Flax Mill:* built during WW II for processing flax needed for war materials. At its peak it operated 24 hrs a day and employed over 400 people. A scale model of the mill can be viewed on-site, which is now the caravan park; off Barron St. *Heritage walk:* follows 23 plaques around town centre; self-guide pamphlet available from visitor centre. *Bicentennial Walking Trail:* pleasant walk around town and beside the Blackwood River.

Country Music Festival and Ute Muster: Feb. *Blackwood Marathon:* running, canoeing, horseriding, cycling and swimming a 58 km course to Bridgetown; Oct.

Chudacud Estate: versatile vineyard restaurant; Wade Rd; (08) 9764 4053.

Harvey Dickson's Country Music Centre This entertainment shed is decorated wall-to-wall and floor-to-rafter with music memorabilia spanning 100 years. The 'record room' containing hundreds of records also has Elvis memorabilia. There is a music show in Sept and a rodeo in Oct, with basic bush camping facilities. Open by appt; Arthur River Rd; (08) 9765 1125; 5 km N.

Roo Gully Wildlife Sanctuary: for injured and orphaned Australian wildlife, with a special focus on raising unfurred marsupial young; 1 km N. *Gregory Tree:* remaining stump of a tree blazed by explorer Augustus Gregory in 1845; Gibbs Rd; 15 km NE. *Norlup Homestead:* built in 1874, this is one of the district's first farms; to view contact (08) 9767 3034; off Norlup Rd; 27 km SE. *Wineries:* Scotts Brook Winery (20 km SE) and Blackwood Crest Winery (at Kilikup, 40 km E); both open daily.

Haddleton Flora Reserve: displays of brown and pink boronia in season. Not suitable for campers or caravans; 50 km NE. *Boyup Brook flora drives:* self-guide maps available from visitor centre.

TOWNS NEARBY: Bridgetown 27 km, Balingup 38 km, Manjimup 50 km, Collie 57 km, Donnybrook 60 km

Bremer Bay
Pop. 239
Map ref. 576 G10

i Community Resource Centre and Library, Mary St; (08) 9837 4171; www.bremerbay.com

103.5 WA FM, 531 AM ABC Local Radio

Bremer Bay on the south coast is a wide expanse of crystal-clear blue water and striking white sand. The main beach, only a ten-minute walk from the town, has a sheltered cove for swimming and fishing. Just north of Bremer Bay is the magnificent Fitzgerald River National Park with its four rivers, dramatic gorges, wide sand plains, rugged cliffs, pebbly beaches and spectacular displays of wildflowers between August and October.

 Watersports: fishing, boating, swimming, surfing, waterskiing, scuba diving, bay cruises and seasonal whale-watching are the town's main attractions. *Rammed-earth buildings:* the Bremer Bay Hotel/Motel on Frantom Way and Catholic Church on Mary St are excellent examples of rammed-earth construction.

Mount Barren Restaurant: local produce; Bremer Bay Resort, 1 Frantom Way; (08) 9837 4133.

Fitzgerald River National Park This huge 242 739 ha park, lying between Bremer Bay and Hopetoun to the east, is renowned for its scenery and flora. A staggering 1800 species of flowering plants have been recorded. Royal hakea, endemic to this region, is one of the most striking. Quaalup Homestead (1858), restored as a museum, offers meals and accommodation in the park. Point Ann has a viewing platform for whale-watching (southern rights, June–Oct). Campgrounds, barbecues and picnic areas available. 17 km N.

Wellstead Homestead Museum: the first residence in the area, now incorporating a gallery and museum with family heirlooms, historic farm equipment and vintage cars; Peppermint Grove, Wellstead Rd; (08) 9837 4448; 9 km SW. *Surfing:* nearby beaches include Native Dog Beach, Dillon Bay, Fosters Beach and Trigelow Beach; ask at visitor centre for directions.

TOWNS NEARBY: Ravensthorpe 109 km, Lake King 148 km, Albany 154 km, Mount Barker 160 km, Lake Grace 166 km

Bridgetown
Pop. 2321
Map ref. 572 H8 | 574 D9 | 576 C10

i 154 Hampton St; (08) 9761 1740 or 1800 777 140; www.bridgetown.com.au

100.5 Hot FM, 1044 AM ABC Local Radio

Bridgetown is a picturesque timber town nestled among rolling hills on the banks of the Blackwood River. Crossing the river, Bridgetown boasts the longest wooden bridge in the state, made of the area's famous jarrah. In addition to tourism, timber milling and mining (lithium, tantalum and tin) are now the largest industries in the area.

 Brierley Jigsaw Gallery The only public jigsaw gallery in the Southern Hemisphere, Brierley has over 170 jigsaws ranging from the world's smallest wooden puzzle to a huge 9000-piece

jigsaw. A highlight is an 8000-piece jigsaw of the Sistine Chapel. Back of visitor centre, Hampton St.

Bridgedale: historic house owned by John Blechynden, one of the area's first European settlers, constructed in 1862 of local timber and bricks made from riverbank clay; South Western Hwy. **Memorial Park:** picnic area with a giant chessboard, 3 ft high pieces for hire from visitor centre; South Western Hwy.

 Blackwood River Park Markets: Sun mornings each fortnight. **State Downriver Kayaking Championships:** Aug. **Blackwood Classic Powerboat Race:** Sept. **Blackwood Marathon:** between Boyup Brook and Bridgetown; Oct. **Blues at Bridgetown Festival:** Nov. **Festival of Country Gardens:** Nov.

 The Bridgetown Hotel: pub grub; 157 Hampton St; (08) 9761 1034. **Bridgetown Pottery Tearooms & Gallery:** home-style cooking; 81 Hampton St; (08) 9761 1038. **Emporium Bistro:** contemporary Australian; 145–151 Hampton St; (08) 9761 2018. **Nelson's of Bridgetown:** country charm; 38 Hampton St; (08) 9761 1641 or 1800 635 565.

 Break of Day Homestay: Lot 751 Walter Rd; (08) 9761 1284. **Ford House Retreat:** Eedle Tce; (08) 9761 1816. **Tweed Valley Lodge:** 171 Tweed Rd; (08) 9761 2828. **Woodlands of Bridgetown:** South Western Hwy; (08) 9761 2125.

 The Cidery Discover the history of Bridgetown's apple industry and sample fresh juice, cider or award-winning beers. The orchard contains over 80 varieties of apple. Closed Tues; Cnr Forrest St and Gifford Rd; (08) 9761 2204; 2 km N.

Geegelup Heritage Trail: 52 km walk retraces history of agriculture, mining and timber in the region. It starts at Blackwood River Park. **Scenic drives:** choose from 8 scenic drives in the district through green hills, orchards and valleys into karri and jarrah timber country; self-guide maps available at visitor centre. **Excellent views:** Sutton's Lookout, off Phillips St and Hester Hill, 5 km N. **Bridgetown Jarrah Park:** ideal place for a picnic or bushwalk. The Tree Fallers and Shield Tree trails commemorate the early timber history of the town; Brockman Hwy; 20 km w. **Karri Gully:** bushwalking and picnicking; 20 km w.

towns nearby: **Balingup 24 km, Boyup Brook 27 km, Manjimup 31 km, Nannup 34 km, Donnybrook 52 km**

Broome

see inset box on next page

Bunbury

see inset box on page 297

Busselton

Pop. 15 385
Map ref. 572 C6 | 574 B9 | 576 B10

 38 Peel Tce; (08) 9752 1288; www.geographebay.com

 96.5 FM Western Tourist Radio, 684 AM ABC Local Radio

First settled by Europeans in 1834, Busselton is one of the oldest towns in Western Australia. It is situated on the shores of Geographe Bay and the picturesque Vasse River. Sheltered from most prevailing winds, the tranquil waters of the bay are an aquatic playground edged with 30 kilometres of white sand beaches. Over the past three decades, the traditional industries of timber, dairying, cattle and sheep have been joined by grape-growing and winemaking. Fishing is also important, particularly crayfish and salmon in season. In spring, the wildflowers are magnificent.

 Busselton Jetty The longest timber jetty in the Southern Hemisphere was built over a 95-year period, beginning in 1865, principally for the export of timber. Over 5000 ships from all over the world docked here through the ages of sail, steam and diesel, before the port closed in 1972. The jetty stretches a graceful 1.8 km into Geographe Bay and has always been a popular spot for fishing, snorkelling and scuba diving because of the variety of marine life. Today you can take a small tourist train from one end to the other. An Interpretive Centre at the base of the jetty displays historical and environmental exhibits. At the seaward end is an Underwater Observatory featuring an observation chamber with viewing windows 8 m beneath the surface revealing vividly coloured corals, sponges and fish. Tours are available, bookings essential. End of Queen St.

Ballarat Engine: first steam locomotive in WA; Pries Ave. **St Mary's Anglican Church:** built in 1844 of limestone and jarrah, with a she-oak shingle roof. The churchyard has many pioneer graves, including John Garrett Bussell's, after whom Busselton was named; Peel Tce. **Nautical Lady Entertainment World:** family fun park with giant water slide, flying fox, minigolf, skate park, racing cars, lookout tower and nautical museum; on beachfront at end of Queen St; (08) 9752 3473. **Old Courthouse:** restored gaol cells and arts complex; Queen St. **Busselton Historical Museum:** originally a creamery, now houses historic domestic equipment; closed Tues; Peel Tce. **Vasse River Parkland:** barbecue facilities; Peel Tce.

 Markets: Barnard Park, 1st and 3rd Sat each month; Railway Building Park, Causeway Rd, 2nd and 4th Sun each month. **Southbound:** music festival; Jan. **Festival of Busselton:** Jan. **Beach Festival:** Jan. **Busselton Jetty Swim:** Feb. **Geographe Bay Race Week:** yachting; Feb. **Bluewater Fishing Classic:** Mar. **Great Escapade:** cycling; Mar. **Busselton Agricultural Show:** one of the oldest and largest country shows in WA; Oct/Nov. **Smell the Roses, Taste the Wine:** Nov. **Ironman Western Australia Triathlon:** Dec.

 Newtown House Restaurant & Accomodation: fine dining; 737 Bussell Hwy; (08) 9755 4485. **The Equinox:** beachside dining; Queen St; (08) 9752 4641. **The Goose:** jetty-side longtime favourite; Geographe Bay Rd; (08) 9754 7700. **Vasse Bar Cafe:** funky Mediterranean; 44 Queen St; (08) 9754 8560.

 Amblin Caravan & Camping Park: 583 Bussell Hwy; (08) 9755 4079. **Baudins of Busselton B&B:** 87 Bussell Hwy; (08) 9751 5576. **Four Seasons Holiday Resort:** 585 Caves Rd; (08) 9755 4082. **Inn the Tuarts Guest Lodge:** 19 Rushleigh Rd; (08) 9754 1444. **Kookaburra Caravan Park:** 66 Marine Tce; (08) 9752 1516. **Sojourn on Gale:** 59 Gale St; (08) 9751 3381. **Geographe Bay Holiday Park:** 525 Bussell Hwy, Broadwater; (08) 9752 4396. **Mandalay Holiday Resort and Tourist Park:** Mandalay Entrance (off Bussell Hwy at Lockhart St), Broadwater; (08) 9752 1328. **Peppermint Park Eco Village:** 97 Caves Rd, Abbey; (08) 9755 4241.

 Tuart Forest National Park The majestic tuart tree grows only on coastal limestone 200 km either side of Perth. Known locally as the Ludlow Tuart Forest, this 2049 ha park protects the largest natural tuart forest in the world. It also has the tallest and largest specimens of tuart trees on the Swan Coastal Plain, up to 33 m high and 10 m wide. Enjoy scenic drives, forest walks and picnics in a magnificent setting. 12 km SE.

continued on p. 295

 RADIO STATIONS   IN TOWN   WHAT'S ON   WHERE TO EAT   WHERE TO STAY   NEARBY

BROOME

Pop. 11 547

Map ref. 580 H8 I 584 A11

ℹ️ **Cnr Short and Hamersley sts; (08) 9195 2200 or 1800 883 777; www.broomevisitorcentre.com.au**

📻 Spirit 102.9FM, 101.3 WA FM, 675 AM ABC Local Radio

Broome is distinguished by its pearling history, cosmopolitan character and startling natural assets including white sandy beaches, turquoise water and red soils. The discovery of pearling grounds off the coast in the 1880s led to the foundation of the Broome township in 1883. A melting pot of nationalities flocked to its shores in the hope of making a fortune. Japanese, Malays and Koepangers joined the Aboriginal pearl divers, while the Chinese became the shopkeepers in town. By 1910 Broome was the world's leading pearling centre. In those early, heady days, over 400 pearling luggers operated out of Broome. The industry suffered when world markets collapsed in 1914, but stabilised in the 1970s as cultured-pearl farming developed. Today remnants of Broome's exotic past are everywhere, with the town's multicultural society ensuring a dynamic array of cultural influences. Broome's beaches are ideal for swimming and there is good fishing year-round.

🏚️ **Pearl Luggers** Experience Broome's pearling heritage by visiting 2 restored pearling luggers in Chinatown. Tours daily. Dampier Tce; (08) 9192 2059.

Japanese Cemetery The largest Japanese cemetery in Australia contains the graves of over 900 Japanese pearl divers, dating back to 1896. This is a sobering reminder of the perils of the early pearling days when the bends, cyclones and sharks claimed many lives. Cnr Port Dr and Savannah Way.

Staircase to the Moon This beautiful optical illusion is caused by a full moon reflecting off the exposed mudflats of Roebuck Bay at extremely low tides. Town Beach; 3 nights monthly from Mar–Oct; check dates and times at visitor centre.

Chinatown: an extraordinary mix of colonial and Asian influences, Chinatown was once the bustling hub of Broome where pearl sheds, billiard saloons and Chinese eateries flourished; now it is home to some of the world's finest pearl showrooms. *Buildings on Hamersley St:* distinctive Broome-style architecture including the courthouse, made of teak inside and corrugated iron outside; Captain Gregory's House, a classic old pearling master's house, built in 1915, now an art gallery; and Matso's Cafe, once the Union Bank Building. *Historical Museum:* pearling display and collection of photographs and literature on Broome's past; Robinson St. *Bedford Park:* war memorial, replica of explorer William Dampier's sea chest and an old train coach; Hamersley St. *Shell House:* one of the largest shell collections in Australia; Dampier Tce. *Sun Pictures:* the world's oldest operating outdoor cinema, opened in 1916; Carnarvon St. *Sisters of St John of God Convent:* built in 1926 by a Japanese shipbuilder using traditional methods that emphasise the external framing of the building; Cnr Barker and Weld sts. *Deep Water Jetty:* good for fishing; Port Dr. *Heritage trail:* 2 km walk introduces places of interest; contact visitor centre for self-guide pamphlet.

🌼 *Courthouse Markets:* Hamersley St; Sat and Sun mornings Apr–Oct, Sat only Nov–Mar. *Town Beach Markets:* Robinson St; 1st 2 nights of the Staircase to the Moon; check with visitor centre for dates and times. *Race Round:* horseracing; June–Aug. *Opera Under the Stars:* Aug. *Shinju Matsuri:* Festival of the Pearl, recalls Broome's heyday and includes Dragon Boat Regatta; Aug/Sept. *Mango Festival:* Nov.

🍴 *Club Restaurant:* fine dining; Cable Beach Club Resort & Spa, Cable Beach Rd, Cable Beach; (08) 9192 0400 or 1800 199 099. *Matso's Broome Brewery:* laid-back brewery; 60 Hamersley St; (08) 9193 5811. *The Old Zoo Cafe:* alfresco cafe; 2 Challenor Dr, Cable Beach; (08) 9193 6200. *Wharf Restaurant:* casual seafood; Port of Pearls House, 401 Port Dr; (08) 9192 5800.

🛏️ *Broome Vacation Village:* 122 Port Dr; (08) 9192 1057. *Broome Town B&B Boutique Accommodation:* 15 Stewart St; (08) 9192 2006. *Ochre Moon B&B:* 13 Godwit Cres;

[CAMEL RIDE ON CABLE BEACH]

(08) 9192 7109. *Reflections B&B:* 69 Demco Dr; (08) 9192 6610. *Roebuck Bay Caravan Park:* 91 Walcott St; (08) 9192 1366. *Cable Beach Caravan Park:* 8 Millington Rd, Cable Beach; (08) 9192 2066. *Palm Grove Caravan Resort:* Cnr Murray and Cable Beach rds, Cable Beach; (08) 9192 3336.

Cable Beach With its 22 km of pristine white sands fringing the turquoise waters of the Indian Ocean, Cable Beach is one of the most stunning beaches in the world. Every day the beach is washed clean by high tides ranging from 4 m to 10 m. It takes its name from the telegraph cable laid between Broome and Java in 1889. The $55 million Cable Beach Resort, which fronts onto the beach, is a popular tourist destination. While you're here, why not do that quintessential Broome activity and ride a camel along this famous beach? Contact visitor centre for details. 7 km NW.

Gantheaume Point Dinosaur footprints believed to be 130 million years old can be seen at very low tide. A plaster cast of the tracks has been embedded at the top of the cliff. Nearby, view the almost-perfectly round Anastasia's Pool, built by a lighthouse keeper for his wife. 5 km NE.

Crocodile Park: home to some of Australia's biggest crocodiles; Cable Beach Rd; 7 km NW. *Reddell Beach:* enjoy the dramatic sight of Broome's distinctive red soils, known as 'pindan', meeting white sands and brilliant blue water; 7 km SW. *Buccaneer Rock:* at entrance to Dampier Creek, this landmark commemorates Captain William Dampier and HMAS *Roebuck*; 15 km E.

Broome Bird Observatory: see some of the 310 species of migratory wader birds that arrive each year from Siberia; 17 km E. *Willie Creek Pearl Farm:* the Kimberley's only pearl farm open to the public, with daily tours; (08) 9192 0000; 35 km N. *Dampier Peninsula:* this remote area north of Broome boasts unspoiled coastline (4WD access only). Record-breaking game fish have been caught in the surrounding waters. Charters and tours leave from Dampier. The Sacred Heart Church at Beagle Bay (118 km NE) was built by Pallotine monks in 1917 and boasts a magnificent pearl-shell altar. Lombadina (200 km NE) is a former mission now home to an Aboriginal community that offers sightseeing, fishing and mudcrabbing tours; contact (08) 9192 4936. On the eastern side of the peninsula is Cygnet Bay Pearl Farm, the oldest Australian and family-owned pearl farm, which offers 1-hour and 1-day tours; contact (08) 9192 4283. Cape Leveque, at the north of the peninsula, is well known for its pristine beaches and rugged pindan cliffs (220 km NE). *Buccaneer Archipelago:* in Broome you can arrange scenic flights over this magnificent landscape that stretches north-east of the Dampier Peninsula. Also known as the Thousand Islands, this is a dramatic coastal area of rugged red cliffs, spectacular waterfalls and secluded white sandy beaches. Here you'll find whirlpools created by massive 11 m tides and the amazing horizontal two-way waterfall of Talbot Bay. *Hovercraft Spirit of Broome:* tours of Roebuck Bay; details from visitor centre.

TOWNS NEARBY: Derby 165 km

Wonnerup House: built in 1859, now a National Trust museum and fine example of colonial architecture, furnished in period style; 10 km N. *Bunyip Craft Centre:* Ludlow; 15 km E. *Wineries:* numerous vineyards and wineries in the area. Many are open for cellar-door tastings; contact visitor centre for map. *Augusta–Busselton Heritage Trail:* contact visitor centre for map.

TOWNS NEARBY: Dunsborough 22 km, Yallingup 29 km, Margaret River 42 km, Donnybrook 45 km, Bunbury 45 km

Caiguna
Pop. 10
Map ref. 577 M7

i Caiguna Roadhouse, Eyre Hwy; (08) 9039 3459; www.dundas.wa.gov.au

The small community of Caiguna, on the Nullarbor Plain, consists of a 24-hour roadhouse, caravan park, motel, restaurant and service station. The nearest towns are Balladonia, 182 kilometres west, and Cocklebiddy, 65 kilometres east. To the south is the coastal wilderness of Nuytsland Nature Reserve. From immediately east of Caiguna until Border Village, locals operate on Central Western Time, 45 minutes ahead of the rest of Western Australia.

John Baxter Memorial In 1841, the explorer John Baxter, together with an Aboriginal guide known as Wylie and 2 other unnamed Aboriginal men, accompanied Edward John Eyre on his epic journey across the Nullarbor Plain. The party left Fowlers Bay in SA on 25 Feb and reached the site of modern-day Eucla on 12 Mar. Later, the 2 unnamed Aboriginal men killed Baxter and,

taking most of the supplies, fled into the desert. Eyre and Wylie walked for another month and eventually reached Thistle Cove (near Esperance), where they were rescued by a French whaler. The Baxter memorial is on the Baxter Cliffs overlooking the Great Australian Bight; 4WD access only. 38 km S.

90-Mile Straight: have your photo taken beside the signpost marking the eastern end of the longest straight stretch of road in Australia, which runs for 90 miles (146.6 km) between Caiguna and a point east of Balladonia; 4 km W. *Caiguna Blowhole:* a hole in the flat limestone landscape where the earth seemingly breathes in and out; 5 km W.

TOWNS NEARBY: Cocklebiddy 64 km, Madura 151 km, Balladonia 176 km

Carnamah
Pop. 358
Map ref. 576 B4

i Council offices, Macpherson St; (08) 9951 7000; www.carnamah.wa.gov.au

101.9 WA FM, 612 AM ABC Radio National

Carnamah is a typical wheat-belt town servicing the surrounding wheat and sheep properties. From late July through to December the shire of Carnamah and the rest of the wheat belt blossoms into a wildflower wonderland. This is one of Western Australia's richest areas of flowering plants, with more than 600 species.

Historical Society Museum: displays historic domestic equipment and old farm machinery; Macpherson St.

North Midlands Agricultural Show, Rodeo and Ute Parade: Sept.

Tathra National Park This park, with its diverse range of spring wildflowers, is named after the Nyungar word for 'beautiful place'. 25 km sw.

Macpherson's Homestead: an excellent example of pioneering architecture (1869), once the home of Duncan Macpherson, the first settler in the area; open by appt; Bunjil Rd; (08) 9951 1690; 1 km E. *Yarra Yarra Lake:* this salt lake changes from pink in summer to deep blue in winter. View it from the Lakes Lookout; 16 km s. *Eneabba:* spectacular wildflowers surround this mining town; 74 km w. *Lake Indoon:* a freshwater lake popular for sailing, boating, camping, picnics and barbecues (swimming is forbidden due to poor water quality); 85 km w.

TOWNS NEARBY: Morawa 54 km, Dongara–Denison 104 km, Moora 106 km, Jurien Bay 107 km, Cervantes 119 km

Carnarvon

see inset box on page 298

Cervantes

Pop. 506
Map ref. 574 A2 | 576 A5

Pinnacles Visitor Centre, Cadiz St; (08) 9652 7672 or 1800 610 660; www.visitpinnaclescountry.com.au

99.9 WA FM, 612 AM ABC Radio National

This small but thriving fishing town was established in 1962 and named after the American whaling ship *Cervantes*, which sank off the coast in 1844. The town's fishing fleet nearly doubles in rock lobster season, and in spring the town is surrounded by spectacular displays of wildflowers with vistas of wattles stretching from horizon to horizon. Not far from Cervantes is one of Australia's best-known landscapes, the Pinnacles Desert, lying at the heart of Nambung National Park.

 Pinnacle Wildflowers: displays of native WA flora, dried flower arrangements, souvenirs. Flowers are visible year-round, but at their peak in Aug and Sept; Bradley Loop. *Thirsty Point:* lookout has superb views of the bay and Cervantes islands. A trail connects the lookouts between Thirsty Point and Hansen Bay. Popular in wildflower season; off Seville St.

The Europa Anchor Restaurant: local seafood; Cervantes Pinnacles Motel, 7 Aragon St; (08) 9652 7145. *Ronsard Bay Tavern:* bistro dining; 219 Cadiz St; (08) 9652 7009.

Cervantes Pinnacles Beachfront Caravan Park: 35 Aragon St; (08) 9652 7060.

Nambung National Park In the Pinnacles Desert, thousands of limestone pillars rise out of a stark landscape of yellow sand, reaching over 3 m in places. They are the eroded remnants of a bed of limestone, created from sea-shells breaking down into lime-rich sands. See formations like the Indian Chief, Garden Wall and Milk Bottles. The loop drive is one-way and not suitable for caravans. The park allows day visits only; tours departing morning and sunset can be arranged at the visitor centre. 17 km s.

Lake Thetis Stromatolites: one of WA's 6 known locations of stromatolites, the oldest living organism on earth; 5 km s. *Kangaroo Point:* good picnic spot; 9 km s. *Hangover Bay:* a stunning white sandy beach ideal for swimming, snorkelling, windsurfing and surfing; 13 km s.

TOWNS NEARBY: Jurien Bay 21 km, Moora 91 km, Carnamah 119 km, New Norcia 122 km, Gingin 124 km

Cocklebiddy

Pop. 75
Map ref. 577 M6

Cocklebiddy Roadhouse; (08) 9039 3462.

107.3 FM ABC Radio National, 648 AM ABC Local Radio

This tiny settlement, comprising a roadhouse with motel units, caravan sites and camping facilities, lies between Madura and Caiguna on the Nullarbor Plain. Nuytsland Nature Reserve extends southwards, a 400 000-hectare strip running along the Great Australian Bight. Locals operate on Central Western Time, 45 minutes ahead of the rest of the state.

Eyre Bird Observatory Housed in the fully restored 1897 Eyre Telegraph Station, Australia's first bird observatory offers birdwatching, bushwalking and beachcombing in Nuytsland Nature Reserve. Over 240 species of birds have been recorded at Eyre, including Major Mitchell cockatoos, brush bronzewings, honeyeaters and mallee fowl. It is near the site where Edward John Eyre found water and rested during his Nullarbor journey in February 1841. Courses, tours and whale-watching (June–Oct) as well as accommodation can be arranged on (08) 9039 3450. 4WD access only. 50 km SE.

Chapel Rock: picnic area; 4 km E. *Twilight Cove:* fishing and whale-watching spot with views of 70 m high limestone cliffs overlooking the Great Australian Bight; 4WD access only; 32 km s.

TOWNS NEARBY: Caiguna 64 km, Madura 89 km, Balladonia 236 km

Collie

Pop. 7084
Map ref. 572 G3 | 574 D8 | 576 C9

Old Collie Post Office, 63 Throssell St; (08) 9734 2051; www.collierivervalley.org.au

95.7 Hot FM, 684 AM ABC Local Radio

Collie is Western Australia's only coalmining town. The surrounding area was first explored in 1829 when Captain James Stirling led a reconnaissance party to the land south of Perth. The region was originally considered ideal for timber production and as pasturelands. However, the discovery of coal along the Collie River in 1883 changed the region's fortunes. In dense jarrah forest, near the winding Collie River, the town has many parks and gardens. The drive into Collie on the Coalfields Highway along the top of the Darling Scarp offers spectacular views of the surrounding forests, rolling hills and farms.

Tourist Coal Mine Step back in time and gain an insight into the mining industry and the working conditions in underground mines. This replica mine was constructed in 1983 to commemorate the 100-year anniversary of coal discovery. Tours by appt only; contact visitor centre for details. Throssell St.

Coalfields Museum: displays of historic photographs, coalmining equipment, rocks and minerals, woodwork by local miner Fred Kohler, a doll house and art housed in the historic Roads Board building; Throssell St. *Collie Railway Station:* the rebuilt station houses railway memorabilia, a scale model of the Collie township with model trains, tearooms and a giftshop; Throssell St. *Soldiers' Park:* bordering the Collie River, features include a war memorial, rose garden, gazebo and childrens' playground; Steere St. *All Saints Anglican Church:* impressive Norman-style church distinctive for its unusual stained-glass windows, extensive use of jarrah timbers and elaborate mural, which in 1922 took renowned stage artist Philip Goatcher 8 months to complete. Tours by appt; contact visitor centre; Venn St. *Old Collie Goods*

continued on p. 299

BUNBURY

Pop. 67 643
Map ref. 572 D4 | 574 C8 | 576 C9

i Old Railway Station, Carmody Pl; (08) 9792 7205 or 1800 286 287; www.visitbunbury.com.au

95.7 Radio West Hot FM, 684 AM ABC Local Radio

Bunbury is known as the 'city of three waters', surrounded by the Indian Ocean, Koombana Bay and the Leschenault Inlet. This is a water-lover's paradise with fishing, crabbing, diving, white sandy beaches, sailing and kayaking. Bunbury is also known for its wild dolphins that come close to the beach at Koombana Bay. Bunbury was settled by Europeans in 1838 and the Koombana Bay whalers were a source of initial prosperity. Today the port is the main outlet for the timber and mining industries.

Dolphin Discovery Centre Wild bottlenose dolphins regularly visit Koombana Bay. The centre has interpretative displays on dolphins and other marine life and offers visitors the chance to swim with dolphins under ranger guidance. A 360-degree Dolphinarium, opened in 2011, is the first of its kind in Australia. Dolphin visits usually occur in the mornings; however, times and days of visits are unpredictable. If you prefer not to get wet, take a dolphin-spotting cruise on the bay. Open daily 8am–4pm Oct–May, 9am–2pm June–Sept; 447 Koombana Dr; (08) 9791 3088.

Historic buildings: many date back to the early decades of the settlement, including the 1865 Rose Hotel; Cnr Victoria and Stephen sts; contact visitor centre for details. *King Cottage:* built in 1880 and one of the oldest buildings in Bunbury, this cottage was built by Henry King using homemade bricks. It now displays items of domestic life from the early 20th century; open daily 2–4pm; 77 Forrest Ave; (08) 9721 7546. *Sir John Forrest Monument:* born in Picton on the outskirts of Bunbury in 1847, Sir John Forrest was elected the first Premier of WA in 1890 and entered Federal Parliament in 1901; Cnr Victoria and Stephen sts. *Victoria St:* a 'cappuccino strip' of sidewalk cafes and restaurants. *Bunbury Regional Art Galleries:* built in 1887, formerly a convent for the Sisters of Mercy and now the largest art gallery in the South-West; 64 Wittenoom St; (08) 9721 8616; open 10am–4pm daily. *Miniature Railway Track:* take a ride on this 800 m track through the trees at Forest Park; 3rd Sun of each month; Blair St. *Lookouts:* Boulter's Heights, Haig Cres and Marlston Hill; Apex Dr. *Lighthouse:* painted in black-and-white check, this striking landmark has a lookout at the base; end of Ocean Dr. *Basaltic rock:* formed by volcanic lava flow 150 million years ago; foreshore at end of Clifton St, off Ocean Dr. *Mangrove boardwalk:* 200 m elevated boardwalk lets you view the southern-most mangrove colony in WA, estimated to be 20 000 years old; Koombana Dr. *Big Swamp Wildlife Park:* handfeed kangaroos, see bettongs, wombats, swamp wallabies and more, and enjoy the South-West's largest walk-through aviary with 60 species of native birds; Prince Phillip Dr; (08) 9721 8380; open 10am–5pm daily. *Kayak tours:* take to the waters of Koombana Bay, the Leschenault Estuary or the Collie River; contact Dekked Out Adventures, (08) 9796 1000. *Heritage trail:* 12 km walk from the Old Railway Station; contact visitor centre for brochure.

Viva Bunbury: Latin-themed street party as part of racing carnival; Mar. *Groovin The Moo:* music festival; May.

The Funtabulous Bunbury Kidsfest: Sept/Oct. *Geographe Crush:* food and wine festival; Nov.

Alexanders Restaurant: well-priced cuisine using local produce; Qualify Hotel Lord Forrest, 20 Symmons St; (08) 9726 5777. *Aristos Waterfront:* casual seafood; 2/15 Bonnefoi Blvd; (08) 9791 6477. *Boardwalk Bar & Bistro:* local seafood; The Parade Hotel, 1 Austral Pde; (08) 9721 2933. *Mojo's Restaurant:* contemporary Australian; Grand Cinema Complex, Victoria St; (08) 9792 5900. *Vat 2:* harbour-side dining; 2 Jetty Rd; (08) 9791 8833. *Carlaminda Wines Bistro:* French fare; Carlaminda Wines, Richards Rd, Ferguson Valley; (08) 9728 3002. *Hackersley:* seasonal menu; Ferguson Rd, Ferguson Valley; (08) 9728 3033. *Casellas:* award-winning tapas in a waterfront setting; 1 Bonnefoi Blvd; (08) 9721 6075. *L'amour De La Femme:* top-notch French cuisine; 18 Wittenoom St; (08) 9791 5504. *Danny's Restaurant:* overlooking Guppy Park; 10 Victoria St; (08) 9721 3866.

Discovery Holiday Parks – Bunbury: Cnr Bussell Hwy and Washington Ave; (08) 9795 7100. *Bunbury Glade Caravan Park:* Timperley Rd, South Bunbury; (08) 9721 3800. *Discovery Holiday Parks – Koombana Bay:* Koombana Dr; (08) 9791 3900.

St Marks Anglican Church: built in 1842, this is the second oldest church in WA. The churchyard contains the graves of many early Bunbury settlers; 5 km SE at Picton. *Featured Wood Gallery:* craft and furniture made by local artisans; 12 Piggott Dr, Australind; (08) 9797 2411; 10 km N. *Lena Dive Wreck:* apprehended by the navy in 2002 for illegal fishing, the *Lena* was sunk 3 nautical miles from Bunbury as a dive wreck; suitable for snorkelling and diving for all levels of experience; dive tours include Octopus Garden Marine Charters and Coastal Water Dive; contact visitor centre for details. *South West Gemstone Museum:* over 2000 gemstones; Lot 5 Bussell Hwy, Gelorup; (08) 9795 7143; 12 km S. *Wineries:* at the heart of the Geographe Wine Region, many in the area offer cellar-door tastings, including Willow Bridge Estate (20 km E) in the picturesque Ferguson Valley and Capel Vale Wines (27 km S); contact visitor centre for details. *Abseiling tours:* on the quarry face of the Wellington Dam; contact visitor centre for details. *Scenic flights:* over Bunbury and surrounds.

TOWNS NEARBY: Australind 9 km, Donnybrook 32 km, Harvey 36 km, Busselton 45 km, Collie 48 km

[VIEW OF BUNBURY FROM LESCHENAULT INLET]

 RADIO STATIONS   IN TOWN   WHAT'S ON   WHERE TO EAT   WHERE TO STAY   NEARBY

CARNARVON

Pop. 5283
Map ref. 575 B7 | 586 C2

 Civic Centre, 21 Robinson St; (08) 9941 1146; www.carnarvon.org.au

99.7 Hot Hits FM, 846 AM ABC Local Radio

Carnarvon is a large coastal town at the mouth of the Gascoyne River. The river and the fertile red earth surrounding it are crucial to the town's thriving agricultural industry. Plantations stretching for 15 kilometres along the riverbanks draw water from the aquifer of the river basin to grow a host of tropical fruits such as bananas, mangoes, avocados, pineapples, pawpaws and melons. Carnarvon gained national prominence when a NASA tracking station operated nearby at Browns Range from 1964 to 1974.

Robinson St In 1876 the region's founding fathers, Aubrey Brown, John Monger and C. S. Brockman, overlanded 4000 sheep from York. Carnarvon was gazetted in 1883 and developed into the centre of an efficient wool-producing area. Camel teams, driven by Afghan camel drivers, brought the wool to Carnarvon from the outlying sheep stations. This is the reason for the extraordinary width of the town's main street, which, at 40 m, gave the camel teams enough room to turn around.

Pioneer Park: good picnic spot; Olivia Tce. *Murals:* up to 15 buildings in the town, including the Civic Centre, are adorned with murals painted by local artists. *Heritage walking trail:* 20 historic landmarks around the town; contact visitor centre for map. *Gwoonwardu Mia* The Gascoyne Aboriginal Heritage and Cultural Centre celebrates the history and culture of the 5 indigenous language groups of the Gascoyne region. It houses an exhibition gallery, local indigenous art and crafts for sale, and a cafe that serves lunches with a regional bush tucker flavour. *Gascoyne Food Trail* Follow this self-drive tour of the plantations, orchards and fresh produce outlets in Carnarvon; contact visitor centre for brochure. *Bumbak's Plantation Tours* Learn just what it takes to grow bananas, grapes, and mangoes at one of the oldest family-run plantations in Carnarvon. The shop sells delicious homemade preserves, jams, fruit ice-creams and other treats. 449 North River Rd, tours at 10am daily.

Gascoyne Growers Markets and Courtyard Markets: Civic Centre; Sat mornings May–Oct. *Fremantle–Carnarvon Bluewater Classic:* odd-numbered years; Apr. *Carnafin:* fishing competition, May/June. *Taste the Gascoyne:* Aug/Sept. *Carnarvon Festival:* Aug/Sept. *Carnarvon Cup:* Sept. *Kickstarters Gascoyne Dash:* Oct.

Pickles Point Seafood & Boatyard: the freshest seafood lunch in town; Harbour Rd, South Carnarvon; (08) 9941 4078. *Sails Restaurant:* international menu with alfresco dining option; Best Western Hospitality Inn, 6 West St; (08) 9941 1600. *Water's Edge Restaurant:* à la carte menu overlooking the Fascine; The Carnarvon Hotel, 121 Olivia Tce; (08) 9941 1181.

Coral Coast Tourist Park: 108 Robinson St; (08) 9941 1438. *Carnarvon Capricorn Holiday Park:* 1042 North West Coastal Hwy, Brown Range; (08) 9941 8153. *Outback Oasis Caravan Park:* 49 Wise St, East Carnarvon; (08) 9941 1439. *Wintersun Caravan and Tourist Park:* 546 Robinson St, Kingsford; (08) 9941 8150.

Carnarvon Heritage Precinct On Babbage Island, and connected to the township by a causeway, this heritage precinct incorporates the One Mile Jetty. Built in 1897, this is the longest jetty in WA's north, stretching for 1493 m into the Indian Ocean. It offers excellent fishing and a jetty train runs its length. Other attractions include the Lighthouse Keeper's Cottage museum, prawning factory at the old whaling station (tours in season, check times at visitor centre) and Pelican Point, for picnics, swimming and fishing.

Blowholes Jets of water shoot up to 20 m in the air after being forced through holes in the coastal rock. When you arrive at the Blowholes, you are greeted by a huge sign declaring 'KING WAVES KILL' – a cautionary reminder that this picturesque coastline has claimed the lives of over 30 people in freak waves. 73 km N. Nearby, a sheltered lagoon provides good swimming and snorkeling (1 km s). A further 7 km north of the blowholes is a cairn commemorating the loss of HMAS *Sydney* in 1941.

'The Big Dish': a huge 29 m wide reflector, part of the old NASA station, with views of town and plantations from the base; 8 km E. *Bibbawarra Artesian Bore:* hot water surfaces at 65° C and picnic area nearby; 16 km N. *Bibbawarra Trough:* 180 m long, believed to be the longest in the Southern Hemisphere; adjacent to bore; 16 km N. *Miaboolya Beach:* good fishing, crabbing and swimming; 22 km N. *Rocky Pool:* picnic area and deep billabong ideal for swimming (after rains) and wildlife watching; Gascoyne Rd; 55 km E. *Red Bluff:* world-renowned surfing spot with waves 1–6 m, depending on the time of the year; 143 km N. *Mt Augustus:* considered the biggest rock in the world, twice the size of Uluru. It is known as Burringurrah to the local Aboriginal people. This 'monocline' is over 1750 million years old, cloaked in thick scrub, and offers many interesting rock formations, caves and Indigenous rock art. Camping and powered sites are available at Mt Augustus Outback Tourist Resort; (08) 9943 0527; road conditions vary; 450 km E; *see also Gascoyne Junction*. *Fishing:* excellent fishing for snapper or groper and game fishing for marlin or sailfish; charter boats available from Williams St. Also excellent fishing off One Mile Jetty.

TOWNS NEARBY: Denham 116 km, Gascoyne Junction 158 km, Coral Bay 193 km

[POINT QUOBBA]

Shed: restoration of rolling stock; Forrest St. *Central Precinct Historic Walk:* self-guide walk of historic buildings; contact visitor centre for map. *Collie River Walk:* pleasant walk along riverbank; contact visitor centre for map.

Market: Old Goods Shed, Forrest St; 1st and 3rd Sun each month (except winter). *Collie Rock and Coal Music Festival:* Mar. *Collie–Donnybrook Cycle Race:* Aug. *Collie River Valley Marathon:* Sept. *Griffin Festival:* Sept.

The Ridge: contemporary menu; Collie Ridge Motel, 185 Throssell St; (08) 9734 5000.

Wellington National Park Covering 4000 ha, this park is characterised by jarrah forest. Picnic, swim, canoe or camp at Honeymoon Pool or Potters Gorge, or go rafting in winter on the rapids below the Wellington Dam wall (note that work is being carried out on the wall until 2010, when the Quarry picnic area will reopen). 18 km w.

Minninup Pool: where the Collie River is at its widest, ideal for swimming, canoeing or picnicking; off Mungalup Rd; 3 km s. *Stockton Lake:* camping and waterskiing; 8 km E. *Brew 42:* microbrewery producing 6 different beers, especially traditional Irish and English ales. Tastings and sales Thurs–Sun or by arrangement; Allanson; (08) 97344784; 8km w. *Harris Dam:* beautiful picnic area; 14 km N. *Collie River Scenic Drive:* views of jarrah forest and wildflowers in season; contact visitor centre for map. *Munda Biddi Trail:* starting in the hills near Perth, this bike trail winds through scenic river valleys and forests south to Collie; details from visitor centre. *Bibbulmun Track:* sections of this trail pass through Collie; *see Albany.*

TOWNS NEARBY: Donnybrook 39 km, Harvey 40 km, Australind 42 km, Bunbury 48 km, Balingup 50 km

Coolgardie

Pop. 801
Map ref. 576 H5

ⓘ Goldfields Exhibition Building, Bayley St; (08) 9026 6090; www.coolgardie.wa.gov.au

📻 97.9 Hot FM, 648 AM ABC Local Radio

This town was the first settlement in the eastern goldfields. After alluvial gold was found in 1892, Coolgardie grew in ten years to a town of 15 000 people, 23 hotels, six banks and two stock exchanges. The main street, lined with some magnificent buildings, was made wide enough for camel trains to turn around in. As in many outback towns, the heat and the isolation led to innovation, in this case that of the Coolgardie safe, which used water and a breeze to keep food cool before the days of electricity.

Historic buildings There are 23 buildings in the town centre that have been listed on the National Estate register, many of them on the main street, Bayley St. Over 100 markers are positioned at buildings and historic sites across the town, using stories and photographs to recapture the gold-rush days. The index to markers is in Bayley St next to the visitor centre.

Goldfields Exhibition Museum Local photographs and displays inside the old Warden's Court including a display on the famous Varischetti mine rescue. In 1907 Modesto Varischetti was trapped underground in a flooded mine for 9 days. Varischetti survived in an air pocket until divers eventually found him. The dramatic rescue captured world attention. Bayley St.

Ben Prior's Open-Air Museum: unusual collection of machinery and memorabilia; Cnr Bayley and Hunt sts. *Warden Finnerty's House:* striking 1895 example of early Australian architecture and furnishings; open 11am–4pm daily except Wed; McKenzie St. *C. Y. O'Connor Dedication:* fountain and water course in memory of O'Connor, who masterminded the Goldfields Water Supply Scheme; McKenzie St. *Gaol tree:* used for prisoners in early gold-rush days, before a gaol was built; Hunt St. *Lindsay's Pit Lookout:* over open-cut goldmine; Ford St.

Coolgardie Day: Sept. *Metal Detecting Championships:* odd-numbered years, Sept/Oct.

Coolgardie Cemetery The town cemetery gives you an inkling of the harshness of the early gold-rush years. The register of burials records that of the first 32 burials, the names of 15 were unknown, and many entries for 'male child' and 'female child' note 'fever' as the cause of death. One of the most significant graves is that of Ernest Giles, an Englishman whose name is associated with the exploration of inland Australia. 1 km w.

Coolgardie Camel Farm: offers rides on the 'ships of the desert'; (08) 9026 6159; 4 km w. *Gnarlbine Rock:* originally an Aboriginal well, then one of the few water sources for the early prospectors; 30 km sw. *Kunanalling Hotel:* once a town of over 800 people, the ruins of the hotel are all that remain; 32 km N. *Victoria Rock:* camping, and spectacular views from the summit; 55 km sw. *Burra Rock:* popular camping and picnic area (55 km s). Cave Hill, a similar destination, lies a further 40 km s (4WD only). *Rowles Lagoon Conservation Park:* picnicking and camping spots available although recently there has been no water; 65 km N. *Wallaroo Rocks:* 3 dams with scenic views and good bushwalking; 90 km w. *Golden Quest Discovery Trail:* Coolgardie forms part of this 965 km self-guide drive trail of the goldfields; book, map and CD available at visitor centre.

TOWNS NEARBY: Kalgoorlie–Boulder 37 km, Norseman 150 km, Southern Cross 178 km, Leonora 230 km

Coral Bay

Pop. 192
Map ref. 575 B5

ⓘ Coastal Adventure Tours, Coral Bay Arcade, Robinson St; (08) 9948 5190; www.coralbaytours.com.au

📻 91.7 FM ABC Radio National, 104.9 FM ABC Local Radio

Coral Bay is famous for one thing: its proximity to Ningaloo Marine Park. Ningaloo Reef boasts an incredible diversity of marine life and beautiful coral formations. At Coral Bay the coral gardens lie close to the shore, which makes access to the reef as easy as a gentle swim. Lying at the southern end of Ningaloo Marine Park, Coral Bay has pristine beaches and a near-perfect climate: it is warm and dry regardless of the season, and the water temperature only varies from 18°C to 28°C degrees. Swimming, snorkelling, scuba diving, and beach, reef and deep-sea fishing (outside sanctuary areas) are available year-round.

Fins Cafe: beachside cafe; People's Park Shopping Village; (08) 9942 5900. *The Ningaloo Reef Cafe:* Italian and seafood; 16 Robinson St; (08) 9942 5882. *Shades:* casual dining; Ningaloo Reef Resort, 1 Robinson St; (08) 9942 5934 or 1800 795 522.

Bayview Coral Bay: Robinson St; (08) 9942 5932.

Ningaloo Marine Park This park protects the 260 km long Ningaloo Reef, the longest fringing coral reef in Australia. It is the only large reef in the world found so close to a continental land mass: about 100 m offshore at its nearest point and less than 7 km at its furthest. This means that even novice snorkellers and children can access the coral gardens. The reef is home to over 500 species of fish, 250 species of coral, manta rays, turtles and a variety of other marine creatures, with seasonal visits from humpback whales, dolphins and whale sharks. Ningaloo Reef is famous for the latter, and from Apr to June visitors from around the world visit the reef to swim with these gentle giants. Tours can be arranged in Exmouth.

Point Cloates: the wrecks of the *Zvir*, *Fin*, *Perth* and *Rapid* lie on the reef just off the point; 4WD access only; 8 km N. *Tours:* glass-bottomed boat cruises, snorkel and dive tours, kayak tours, fishing charters, scenic flights and marine wildlife-watching tours to see whale sharks (Apr–June), humpback whales (June–Nov) and manta rays (all year); contact visitor centre for details.

TOWNS NEARBY: **Exmouth 138 km, Carnarvon 193 km, Onslow 216 km**

Corrigin
Pop. 687
Map ref. 574 F5 | 576 E8

ℹ️ **Corrigin Resource Centre, Larke Cres; (08) 9063 2778; www.corrigin.wa.gov.au**

📻 92.5 ABC Classic FM, 100.5 Hot FM

Corrigin was established in the early 1900s and was one of the last wheat-belt towns to be settled. Today the town has a healthy obsession with dogs, as demonstrated by its Dog Cemetery and its national record for lining up 1527 utes with dogs in the back.

🏠 **Corrigin Pioneer Museum** Superb collection of old agricultural equipment including an original Sunshine harvester and some early steam-driven farm machinery. A small working steam train carries passengers on a short circuit around the museum and local rest area. Open Sun and by appt; Kunjin St.

RSL Monument: a Turkish mountain gun from Gallipoli; McAndrew Ave.

 Dog in a Ute event: held in varying years in Apr; contact visitor centre for dates.

🛖 *Corrigin Caravan Park:* Kirkwood St; 0427 632 515.

🐾 **Dog Cemetery** Loving dog owners have gone to the considerable expense of having elaborate headstones placed over the remains of their faithful four-footed friends. There are over 80 dogs buried in the cemetery, with gravestones dedicated to Dusty, Rover, Spot et al. There is even one statue of a dog almost 2 m high. Brookton Hwy; 7 km W.

Wildflower scenic drive: signposted with lookout; 3 km W.
Gorge Rock: large granite outcrop with picnic area; 20 km SE.

TOWNS NEARBY: **Kulin 46 km, Wickepin 61 km, Pingelly 77 km, Kellerberrin 79 km, Beverley 93 km**

Cranbrook
Pop. 279
Map ref. 574 F10 | 576 E10

ℹ️ **Council offices, Gathorne St; (08) 9826 1008; www.cranbrook.wa.gov.au**

📻 95.3 Hot FM, 630 AM ABC Local Radio

The small town of Cranbrook greets travellers with a large sign announcing that it is the 'Gateway to the Stirlings'. A mere 10 kilometres away is Stirling Range National Park, a mecca for

bushwalkers and climbers. The nearby Frankland area has gained a national reputation for its premium-quality wines.

🏠 **Station House Museum:** restored and furnished 1930s-style; Gathorne St. *Wildflower walk:* 300 m walk to Stirling Gateway with displays of orchids in spring; Salt River Rd.

 Cranbrook Shire on Show: Apr. *Wildflower Display:* Sept. *Art trail and Photographic Competition:* Oct.

🌐 **Stirling Range National Park** Surrounded by a flat, sandy plain, the Stirling Range rises abruptly to over 1000 m, its jagged peaks veiled in swirling mists. The cool, humid environment created by these low clouds supports 1500 flowering plant species, many unique to the area, earning the park recognition as one of the top-10 biodiversity hot spots in the world. This National Heritage–listed park is one of WA's premier destinations for bushwalking. Bluff Knoll, at 1073 metres, is one of the state's premier hiking challenges. Best time to visit is Oct–Dec.10 km SE.

Sukey Hill Lookout: expansive views of farmland, salt lakes and Stirling Range; off Salt River Rd; 5 km E. *Lake Poorrarecup:* swimming and waterskiing; 40 km SW. *Wineries:* the nearby Frankland River region boasts several wineries, including Alkoomi, Frankland Estate and Ferngrove; 50 km W. *Wildflower drive and heritage trail:* contact visitor centre for brochure.

TOWNS NEARBY: **Mount Barker 38 km, Kojonup 63 km, Katanning 68 km, Denmark 76 km, Albany 83 km**

Cue
Pop. 273
Map ref. 575 H10 | 576 D1 | 578 D11

ℹ️ **Golden Art Shop and Tourist Information Centre, Austin St; (08) 9963 1936; www.cue.wa.gov.au**

📻 102.9 WA FM, 106.1 FM ABC Local Radio

This town was once known as the 'Queen of the Murchison'. In 1891 Mick Fitzgerald and Ed Heffernan found large nuggets of gold not far from what was to become the main street. It was their prospecting mate, Tom Cue, who registered the claim on their behalf and when the town was officially proclaimed in 1894, it bore his name. Within ten years the population of this boom town had exploded to about 10 000 people. While Cue's population has dwindled, the legacy of those heady gold-rush days is evident in the town's remarkably grandiose buildings.

🏠 **Heritage buildings** Many early buildings still stand and are classified by the National Trust. A stroll up the main street takes in the elegant band rotunda, the former Gentleman's Club (now the shire offices, housing a photographic display of the region's history), the Old Gaol, the courthouse, the post office and the police station. One block west in Dowley St is the former Masonic Lodge built in 1899 and reputed to be the largest corrugated-iron structure in the Southern Hemisphere.

🌐 **Walga Rock** This monolith is 1.5 km long and 5 km around the base. It has several Aboriginal rock paintings. One of the most extraordinary paintings, considering that Cue is over 300 km from the sea, is of a white, square-rigged sailing ship. It is believed to depict one of the Dutch ships that visited WA's mid-west shores in the 17th century. 50 km W.

Day Dawn: once Cue's twin town, thanks to the fabulous wealth of the Great Fingall Mine. The mine office, a magnificent century-old stone building now perched precariously on the edge of a new open-cut mine, is all that remains of the town; 5 km W.
Milly Soak: popular picnic spot for early Cue residents. A tent

hospital was set up nearby during the typhoid epidemic; 3 lone graves are the only reminder of the thousands who died; 16km N. *Heritage trail:* includes the abandoned towns Big Bell and Day Dawn; contact visitor centre for brochure. *Fossicking:* areas surrounding the town; contact visitor centre for details.

TOWNS NEARBY: Mount Magnet 71 km, Meekatharra 109 km, Yalgoo 157 km

Denham
Pop. 609
Map ref. 575 B9 | 586 D7

 Knight Tce; (08) 9948 1590 or 1300 135 887; www.sharkbaywa.com.au

105.3 Hot Hits FM, 107.5 FM ABC Radio National

On the middle peninsula of Shark Bay, Denham is the most westerly town in Australia. Dirk Hartog, the Dutch navigator, landed on an island at the bay's entrance in 1616, the first known European to land on the continent. Centuries later, in 1858, Captain H. M. Denham surveyed the area and a town bearing his name was established. The Shark Bay region was once known for its pearling and fishing, and the streets of Denham were literally paved with pearl shells. In the 1960s, however, the local roads board poured bitumen over the pearl shells, and so destroyed what could have been a unique tourist attraction. Fortunately, several buildings made from coquina shell block still stand in the town. Today Shark Bay is renowned for the wild dolphins that come inshore at Monkey Mia (pronounced 'my-a'). As a World Heritage area, it also protects dugongs, humpback whales, green and loggerhead turtles, important seagrass feeding grounds and a colony of stromatolites, the world's oldest living fossils.

Shell block buildings: St Andrews Anglican Church, cnr Hughes and Brockman sts, and the Old Pearlers Restaurant, cnr Knight Tce and Durlacher St, were both built from coquina shell block. *Town Bluff:* popular walk for beachcombers; from town along beach to bluff. *Pioneer Park:* contains the stone on which Captain Denham carved his name in 1858; Hughes St.

The Old Pearler Restaurant: maritime-themed seafood restaurant; Cnr Durlacher St and Knight Tce; (08) 9948 1373. *The Boughshed Restaurant:* international cuisine; Monkey Mia Dolphin Resort, Monkey Mia; (08) 9948 1320 or 1800 653 611.

Blue Dolphin Caravan Park & Holiday Village: Lot 5 Hamelin Rd; (08) 9948 1385. *Denham Seaside Tourist Village:* 1 Stella Rowley Dr; (08) 9948 1242. *Shark Bay Caravan Park:* 6 Spaven Way; (08) 9948 1387. *Monkey Mia Dolphin Resort:* Monkey Mia Rd, Monkey Mia; (08) 9948 1320.

Monkey Mia The daily shore visits by the wild bottlenose dolphins at Monkey Mia are a world-famous phenomenon. The dolphins swim into the shallows, providing a unique opportunity for humans to make contact with them. It began in the 1960s when a local woman started feeding the dolphins that followed her husband's fishing boat to the shoreline. Feeding still occurs, although now it is carefully monitored by rangers to ensure that the dolphins maintain their hunting and survival skills. Visiting times, and the number of dolphins, vary. For a total marine encounter, dugong-watching cruises can also be arranged from here. 26 km NE.

Dirk Hartog Island The state's largest and most historically significant island, named after Dutchman Dirk Hartog who landed here in 1616 – 154 years before Captain Cook. Hartog left behind an inscribed pewter plate, which was removed in 1697 by his countryman Willem de Vlamingh and replaced with another plate. The original was returned to Holland; Vlamingh's plate is now housed in the Maritime Museum in Fremantle. Flights and cruises depart daily; bookings at visitor centre. 30 km W.

Hamelin Pool stromatolites The shores of Hamelin Pool are dotted with stromatolites, the world's largest and oldest living fossils. These colonies of micro-organisms resemble the oldest and simplest forms of life on earth, dated at around 3.5 million years old. The Hamelin Pool stromatolites are relatively new colonies however, about 3000 years old. They thrive here because of the extreme salinity of the water, the occurrence of calcium bicarbonate and the limited water circulation. Visitors can view these extraordinary life forms from a boardwalk. Close by is the Flint Cliff Telegraph Station and Post Office Museum (1884) with a history of the region. 88 km SE.

Dugongs The Shark Bay World Heritage Area has the largest seagrass meadows in the world, covering about 4000 sq km. These meadows are home to around 10 000 dugongs, 10% of the world's remaining population. An endangered species, the dugong is nature's only vegetarian sea mammal. Also known as a sea cow, the dugong can live for up to 70 years and grow up to 3 m long. Tours are available offering visitors a unique opportunity to see dugongs in the wild. Contact visitor centre for details.

Little Lagoon: ideal fishing and picnic spot; 3 km N. *Francois Peron National Park:* Peron Homestead with its 'hot tub' of artesian water; 4WD access only; 7 km N. *Ocean Park:* marine park with aquarium and touch pool; 9 km S. *Eagle Bluff:* habitat of sea eagle and a good viewing spot for sharks and stingrays; 20 km S. *Blue Lagoon Pearl Farm:* working platform where black pearls are harvested; Monkey Mia; 26 km NE. *Shell Beach:* 120 km of unique coastline comprising countless tiny coquina shells; 45 km SE. *Steep Point:* western-most point on mainland with spectacular scenery; 4WD access only; 260 km W. *Zuytdorp Cliffs:* extend from beneath Shark Bay region south to Kalbarri; 4WD access only. *Tours:* boat trips and charter flights to historic Dirk Hartog Island, catamaran cruises, safaris and coach tours; contact visitor centre for details.

TOWNS NEARBY: Carnarvon 116 km, Gascoyne Junction 194 km, Kalbarri 208 km

Denmark
Pop. 2735
Map ref. 573 A11 | 574 F11 | 576 E11

73 South Coast Hwy; (08) 9848 2055; www.denmark.com.au

92.1 FM ABC News Radio, 630 AM ABC Local Radio

Denmark lies at the foot of Mt Shadforth, overlooking the tranquil Denmark River and Wilson Inlet. It is surrounded by forests of towering karri trees that sweep down to meet the Southern Ocean. The Aboriginal name for the Denmark River is 'koorabup', meaning 'place of the black swan'. Originally a timber town, Denmark's economy is today sustained by a combination of dairying, beef cattle, fishing, timber and tourism. The town is close to some of the most beautiful coastline in the state.

Historical Museum: in old police station; Mitchell St. *Bandstand:* located on the riverbank with seating for the audience on the other side of the river; Holling Rd. *Arts and crafts:* galleries abound, including the Old Butter Factory

 RADIO STATIONS IN TOWN WHAT'S ON WHERE TO EAT WHERE TO STAY NEARBY

in North St; contact visitor centre for details. *Mt Shadforth Lookout:* magnificent views; Mohr Dr. *Berridge and Thornton parks:* shaded picnic areas; along riverbank in Holling Rd.

 Craft Market: Berridge Park; Jan, Easter and Dec. *Pantomime:* Civic Centre; Jan. *Brave New Works:* new performance art; Easter.

Pepper & Salt Restaurant: fresh contemporary Australian; Matilda's Estate, 18 Hamilton Rd; (08) 9848 3053. *Southern End Restaurant + Function Centre:* local produce; 427 Mt Shadforth Rd; (08) 9848 2600.

Denmark Rivermouth Caravan Park: Inlet Dr; (08) 9848 1262. *Mt Lindesay View Bed & Breakfast:* Cnr Mt Shadforth Tourist Dr and McNabb Rd; (08) 9848 1933. *Sensational Heights Bed & Breakfast:* 159 Suttons Rd; (08) 9840 9000. *Denmark Ocean Beach Holiday Park:* 770 Ocean Beach Rd, Ocean Beach; (08) 9848 1105.

William Bay National Park This relatively small 1867 ha park protects stunning coastline and forest between Walpole and Denmark on WA's south coast. It is renowned for its primeval windswept granite tors. Green's Pool, a natural rockpool in the park, remains calm and safe for swimming and snorkelling all year-round. Nearby are the Elephant Rocks, massive rounded boulders resembling elephants; Madfish Bay, a good fishing spot; and Waterfall Beach for swimming. 17 km sw.

Ocean Beach: one of the finest surfing beaches in WA; 8 km s. *Monkey Rock:* lookout with panoramic views; 10 km sw. *Bartholomew's Meadery:* honey, honey wines, gourmet honey ice-cream and other bee products, as well as a live beehive display; 20 km w. *Pentland Alpaca Stud and Tourist Farm:* diverse collection of animals, including alpacas, koalas, kangaroos, bison, water buffalo, llamas and many more; Cnr McLeod and Scotsdale rds; (08) 9840 9262; 20 km w. *Eden Gate Blueberry Farm:* spray-free fruit, a range of blueberry products and blueberry wines; open Thurs–Mon Dec–Apr; 25 km E. *Whale-watching:* viewing platform above Lowlands Beach (southern rights June–Oct); 28 km E. *Fishing:* at Wilson Inlet, Ocean Beach (8 km s) and Parry Beach (25 km w). *West Cape Howe National Park:* Torbay Head, WA's most southerly point, and Cosy Corner, a protected beach perfect for swimming; 30 km sw. *Wineries:* many wineries open for cellar-door tastings, including Howard Park Winery, West Cape Howe and Tinglewood Wines; contact visitor centre for map. *Scenic drives:* the 25 km Mt Shadforth Scenic Drive and the 34 km Scotsdale Tourist Drive both feature lush forests, ocean views, wineries and galleries; contact visitor centre for maps. *Heritage trails:* 3 km Mokare trail, 5 km Karri Walk or 9 km Wilson Inlet trail; contact visitor centre for maps. *Bibbulmun Track:* a section of this world-class 963 km long-distance trail passes through Denmark; *see Albany. Valley of the Giants Tree Top Walk: see Walpole;* 65 km w.

TOWNS NEARBY: Mount Barker 46 km, Albany 47 km, Walpole 57 km, Cranbrook 76 km, Northcliffe 119 km

Derby

Pop. 3091
Map ref. 581 I7 | 584 D9

2 Clarendon St; (08) 9191 1426 or 1800 621 426; www.derbytourism.com.au

102.7 WA FM, 873 AM ABC Local Radio

It is said that Derby, known as the 'Gateway to the Gorges', is where the real Kimberley region begins. The first town settled in

[DERBY] ABORIGINAL ROCK ART, THE KIMBERLEY

the Kimberley, it features some spectacular natural attractions nearby: the Devonian Reef Gorges of Windjana and Tunnel Creek are only a few hours' drive along the Gibb River Road, and the magnificent islands of the Buccaneer Archipelago are just a short cruise away. Although King Sound was first explored in 1688, it wasn't until the early 1880s that the Port of Derby was established as a landing point for wool shipments and Derby was proclaimed a townsite. The first jetty was built in 1885, the same year that gold was discovered at Halls Creek. Miners and prospectors poured into the port on their way to the goldfields but by the 1890s, as gold fever died, the port was used almost exclusively for the export of live cattle and sheep. In 1951 iron-ore mining began at Cockatoo Island, which revitalised the town. Derby is now a service centre for the region's rich pastoral and mining industries. Rain closes some roads in the area from November to March, so check conditions before setting out on any excursion.

Old Derby Gaol: built in 1906, this is the oldest building in town; Loch St. *Wharfinger House Museum:* built in the 1920s for the local harbourmaster, the design is typical of the tropics. Now houses an extensive collection of historical memorabilia and Aboriginal artefacts. Key from visitor centre; Loch St. *Derby Jetty:* some of the highest tides in Australia, up to 12 m, can be seen from the jetty. Now used to export ore from various local mines.

Market: Clarendon St; each Sat May–Sept. *King Tide Day:* festival celebrating highest tide in Australia; Apr/May. *Moonrise Rock Festival:* June. *Derby Races:* June/July. *Mowanjum Festival:* Indigenous art and culture; July. *Boab Festival:* Mardi Gras, mud football, mud crab races and bush poets; July. *Derby Rodeo:* Aug. *Boxing Day Sports:* Dec.

Lalgardi Restaurant: international cuisine; Derby Boab Inn, 98–100 Loch St; (08) 9191 1044. *Oasis Bistro:* contemporary bistro dining; King Sound Resort Hotel, 112 Loch St; (08) 9193 1044.

Windjana Gorge National Park A 350-million-year-old Devonian reef rises majestically above the surrounding plains. An easy walking trail winds through the gorge, taking in primeval life forms fossilised within the gorge walls. 145 km E.

Tunnel Creek National Park Wear sandshoes, carry a torch and be prepared to get wet as you explore the 750 m long cave that runs through the Napier Range. Nearby Pigeon's Cave was the hideout of an 1890s Aboriginal outlaw, Jandamarra, also known as 'Pigeon'. Contact visitor centre for tour details. 184 km E.

Prison tree: 1000-year-old boab tree formerly used as a prison; 7 km s. *Myall's Bore:* beside the bore stands a 120 m long cattle trough reputed to be the longest in the Southern Hemisphere; 7 km s. *Gorges:* Lennard Gorge (190 km E), Bell Gorge (214 km E), Manning Gorge (306 km E), Barnett River Gorge (340 km NE) and Sir John Gorge (350 km E); 4WD access only. *Mitchell Plateau:* highlights include the Wandjina rock art and spectacular Mitchell Falls, King Edward River and Surveyor's Pool. In this remote region, visitors must be entirely self-sufficient; via Gibb River Rd and Kalumburu Rd; 580 km NE. Scenic flights can also be arranged from Drysdale River Station and Kununurra. *Pigeon Heritage Trail:* follow the story of the Aboriginal outlaw Jandamarra, nicknamed Pigeon, and his people, the Bunuba; contact visitor centre for map. *Gibb River Rd:* 4WD road between Derby and Wyndham traverses some of the most spectacular gorge country of the Kimberley; contact visitor centre for guidebook and current road conditions. *Buccaneer Archipelago:* in Derby you can arrange a scenic flight or cruise around this archipelago which begins north of King Sound; *see Broome*.

TOWNS NEARBY: Broome 165 km, Fitzroy Crossing 227 km

Dongara–Denison

Pop. 3052
Map ref. 576 A4

ⓘ 9 Waldeck St; (08) 9927 1404; www.irwin.wa.gov.au

📻 96.5 WA FM, 828 AM ABC Local Radio

Dongara and its nearby twin town of Port Denison lie on the coast 359 kilometres north of Perth. Dongara–Denison is the self-proclaimed 'Lobster Capital' of the state, with its offshore reefs supporting a profitable industry. Dongara's main street is lined with magnificent Moreton Bay fig trees while Port Denison provides local anglers with a large marina and harbour.

🏠 **Irwin District Museum** Housed in Dongara's Old Police Station, Courthouse and Gaol (1870), the museum features exhibits on the history of the buildings, the invasion of rabbits into WA and the Irwin Coast shipwrecks. Open 10am–4pm Mon–Fri; Waldeck St; (08) 9927 1323.

Russ Cottage: a beautifully restored farm-worker's cottage (1870). The hard-packed material of the kitchen floor was made from scores of anthills, and the flood-level marker near the front door indicates how high the nearby Irwin River rose during the record flood of 1971; open 10am–12pm Sun or by appt; St Dominics Rd, Dongara. *The Priory Hotel:* this 1881 building has been an inn, a priory and a boarding college for girls and is now once again a hotel; St Dominics Rd, Dongara. *Church of St John the Baptist:* (1884) its pews were made from the driftwood of shipwrecks and its church bell is said to have come from Fremantle Gaol; Cnr Waldeck and Church sts, Dongara. *The Royal Steam Flour Mill:* (1894) it served the local wheat-growing community until its closure in 1935; northern end of Waldeck St, Dongara. *Cemetery:* headstones dating from 1874 and a wall of remembrance to Dominican sisters; brochure from visitor centre; Dodd St, Dongara. *Town heritage trail:* 1.6 km walk that features 28 historic Dongara sites; contact visitor centre for map. *Fisherman's Lookout:* 1 remaining of 2 obelisks built in 1869, with panoramic views of Port Denison; Point Leander Dr, Port Denison.

🌴 *Monthly Market:* Priory Gardens; 1st Sat each month. *Craft Market:* old police station, Dongara; Easter and Christmas.

Dongara Races: Easter. *Larry Lobster Community Festival and Blessing of the Fleet:* at the start of each rock lobster season; Nov.

✗ *The Season Tree:* cafe food with an Asian twist; 8 Moreton Tce; (08) 9927 1400.

🛏 *Seaspray Beach Holiday Park:* 79 Church St, Dongara; (08) 9927 1165. *Dongara Denison Beach Holiday Park:* 250 Ocean Dr, Port Denison; (08) 9927 1131. *Dongara Tourist Park:* 8 George St, Port Denison; (08) 9927 1210. *Western Flora Caravan Park:* Brand Hwy, 22 km N of Eneabba; (08) 9955 2030.

⊗ *Silverdale Olive Orchards:* olive oil products and tastings; open Sat Apr–Nov or by appt; 10 km N. *Mingenew:* small town in agricultural surrounds. Nearby is Fossil Cliff, filled with marine fossils over 250 million years old; 47 km E.

TOWNS NEARBY: Greenough 39 km, Geraldton 61 km, Mullewa 98 km, Carnamah 104 km, Morawa 105 km

Donnybrook

Pop. 1932
Map ref. 572 F5 | 574 C9 | 576 C10

ⓘ Old Railway Station, South Western Hwy; (08) 9731 1720; www.donnybrook-balingup.wa.gov.au

📻 95.7 Hot FM, 1224 AM ABC Radio National

Donnybrook is the centre of the oldest and largest apple-growing area in Western Australia. This is the home of the Granny Smith apple and where Lady William apples were developed. Gold was found here in 1897 but mined for only four years. Donnybrook is famous for its sandstone, which has been used in construction statewide since the early 1900s. In Perth, the GPO, St Mary's Cathedral and the University of Western Australia buildings have all been faced with Donnybrook stone. The quarry can be seen from the Upper Capel Road out of town.

🏠 *Memorial Hall:* built of Donnybrook stone; Bentley St. *Anchor and Hope Inn:* (1862) the oldest homestead in the district, now a private property; view outside from South Western Hwy. *Trigwell Place:* picnic and barbecue facilities, and canoeing on nearby Preston River; South Western Hwy.

🌴 *Gourmet Wine and Food Fest:* Feb. *Apple Festival Ball:* even-numbered years, Easter. *Marathon Relay:* Nov.

✗ *The Real River Company:* country cosiness and international cuisine; 75 Goldfields Rd; (08) 9731 0311.

⊗ **Old Goldfields Orchard and Cider Factory** Combines goldfield history with a working orchard and restaurant. Climb the reconstructed poppet head over the mine, study the history of gold on the property and try your hand at gold prospecting. The orchard provides seasonal fruit for sale and you can enjoy tastings of cider, fruit juice and wines. Open 9.30am–4.30pm Wed–Sun and public/school holidays; Goldfields Rd; (08) 9731 0322; 6 km s.

Boyanup: features a transport museum; 12 km NW. *Ironstone Gully Falls:* barbecue area en route to Capel; 19 km W. *Gnomesville:* surprising roadside collection of garden gnomes; by the side of the Wellington Mills roundabout on the road between Dardanup and Lowden; 25 km SE.

TOWNS NEARBY: Balingup 28 km, Bunbury 32 km, Australind 34 km, Collie 39 km, Busselton 45 km

Dunsborough

Pop. 3373
Map ref. 572 B6 | 574 B9 | 576 B10

ⓘ Seymour Blvd; (08) 9752 1288; www.geographebay.com

📻 98.4 FM Western Tourist Radio, 1224 AM ABC Radio National

Dunsborough is a picturesque coastal town on the south-western tip of Geographe Bay. Just west of the town is Leeuwin–Naturaliste National Park with its dramatic coastline and seasonal wildflower displays. Many of the wineries of the South-West region are only a short drive from the town.

Market: Dunsborough Hall, cnr Gibney St and Gifford Rd; 1st Sat each month. *Margaret River Wine Festival:* throughout region; Apr/May.

Dunsborough Bakery: renowned bakery; 243 Naturaliste Tce; (08) 9755 3137. *Other Side of the Moon Restaurant:* swanky fine dining; Quay West Resort Bunker Bay, Bunker Bay Rd, Naturaliste; (08) 9756 9159. *Wise Vineyard Restaurant:* seasonal international cuisine; Wise Wines, Eagle Bay Rd; (08) 9755 3331.

Leeuwin–Naturaliste National Park Close to Dunsborough at the northern end of the park is Cape Naturaliste, with its lighthouse, museum and whale-watching platform (humpback whales linger offshore Sept–Nov). Walking tracks offer spectacular views of the coastline. Sugarloaf Rock is a dramatic formation just south of the lighthouse – it is also a habitat of the endangered red-tailed tropic bird. 13 km NW. *See also Margaret River and Augusta.*

Blackwood Valley wine region This is a low-key region between Margaret River and Great Southern, which began producing wine in 1976. The climate is perfect for the full ripening of cabernet sauvignon grapes, while chardonnay and shiraz are also good performers. With over 50 wineries in the area, a few to visit include Beulah and Blackwood Crest wines.

Country Life Farm: animals galore, plus merry-go-round, giant slide and bouncing castles; Caves Rd; (08) 9755 3707; 1 km W. *Simmo's Icecreamery:* 39 flavours of homemade ice-cream made fresh daily; Commonage Rd; 5 km SE. *Quindalup Fauna Park:* specialises in birds, fish, tropical butterflies and baby animals; (08) 9755 3933; 5 km E. *Wreck of HMAS* Swan: the largest accessible dive-wreck site in the Southern Hemisphere; tour bookings and permits at visitor centre; off Point Picquet, just south of Eagle Bay; 8 km NW. *Beaches:* to the north-west, popular for fishing, swimming and snorkelling, include Meelup (5 km), Eagle Bay (8 km) and Bunker Bay (12 km). *Tours and activities:* whale-watching charters (Sept–Nov); deep-sea fishing charters; scuba diving, snorkelling and canoeing; wildflower displays in season.

TOWNS NEARBY: Yallingup 8 km, Busselton 22 km, Margaret River 37 km, Bunbury 59 km, Donnybrook 67 km

Dwellingup

Pop. 344
Map ref. 571 E10 | 574 C7 | 576 C8

ⓘ Marrinup St; (08) 9538 1108; www.murray.wa.gov.au

📻 97.3 Coast FM, 684 AM ABC Local Radio

Set among pristine jarrah forest, this is a thriving timber town that was virtually destroyed in 1961 when lightning started a bushfire that lasted for five days, burnt 140 000 hectares of forest and destroyed several nearby towns. Dwellingup was the only town to be rebuilt, and is now a forest-management centre. The Hotham Valley Tourist Railway operates here.

Forest Heritage Centre This centre records WA's jarrah forest heritage and promotes fine wood design, training and education. The building is formed from rammed earth, and designed to represent 3 jarrah leaves on a bough. It includes an Interpretive Centre, a School of Wood and a Forest Heritage Gallery. Learn about conservation and walk among the treetops on an 11 m high canopy walkway. Acacia Rd; (08) 9538 1395.

Historical Centre: includes a photographic display depicting early 1900s life in the mill towns. Also a 1939 Mack Fire Truck, the only one in WA; visitor centre, Marrinup St. *Community Hotel:* last community hotel in WA; Marrinup St.

Log Chop and Community Fair: Feb. *Giant Pumpkin Competition:* Apr.

Dwellingup Community Hotel: counter meals; 8 Marrinup St; (08) 9538 1056. *Newbliss Winery and Cafe:* rustic lunches; 101 Irwin Rd; (08) 9538 1665.

🛏 *Dwellingup Chalets & Caravan Park:* 23 Delpark Rd; (08) 9538 1157.

Lane–Poole Reserve Provides opportunities for picnicking, swimming, canoeing, rafting, fishing, camping and walking. Walk trails include sections of the Bibbulmun Track, the 18 km King Jarrah Track from Nanga Mill, the 17 km Nanga Circuit and a 1.5 km loop from Island Pool. 10 km S.

Marrinup Forest Tour: unique 16 km vehicle and walk tour that features many aspects of the Darling Scarp including the Marrinup POW camp and remnants of old mills and towns of days gone by; contact visitor centre for map. *Hotham Valley Tourist Railway:* travel from Perth via Pinjarra to Dwellingup by train, taking in lush green dairy country before climbing the Darling Range, WA's steepest and most spectacular section of railway, and finishing in the heart of the jarrah forest; steam-hauled May–Oct, diesel-hauled Nov–Apr; bookings (08) 9221 4444; Dwellingup Railway Station. *Etmilyn Forest Tramway:* takes visitors 8 km through farms and old-growth jarrah forest to the pioneer settlement of Etmilyn. *Bibbulmun Track:* long-distance walk trail runs through the middle of the town; *see Albany. Munda Biddi Trail:* WA's first long-distance off-road bike track begins in Mundaring near Perth and winds 182 km through native forest to Dwellingup. It will eventually be extended to Albany; contact visitor centre for details.

TOWNS NEARBY: Pinjarra 20 km, Mandurah 38 km, Harvey 43 km, Rockingham 58 km, Australind 71 km

Esperance

Pop. 9536
Map ref. 577 I9

ⓘ Museum Village, Dempster St; (08) 9083 1555 or 1300 664 455; www.visitesperance.com

📻 102.3 Hot FM, 837 AM ABC Local Radio

Esperance was a sleepy backwater until, in the 1950s, it was found that adding trace elements to the sandy soil made farming feasible. The town became a port and service centre for the agricultural and pastoral hinterland. However, it is the magnificent scenery, the pristine beaches and the proximity of many national parks that draw visitors to this town. Take the Great Ocean Drive, 38 kilometres of postcard-perfect scenery, and you'll understand why Esperance is a popular holiday spot.

Municipal Museum Visit one of WA's outstanding regional museums. See exhibits about shipwrecks, including the famous

Sanko Harvest, and learn of Australia's only recorded pirate, the bloodthirsty Black Jack Anderson, who roamed the Recherche Archipelago. There is also a comprehensive display about *Skylab*, which crashed and spread debris through the area in 1979. Open 1.30–4.30pm daily; James St; (08) 9071 1579.

Museum Village: collection of historic buildings housing craft shops, pottery shops, art gallery, cafe and visitor centre; Dempster St. *Cannery Arts Centre:* local exhibitions with wind garden and views behind; Norseman Rd. *Mermaid Leather:* unique range of leather products made from fish and shark skins; Wood St. *Aquarium:* 14 aquariums and touch pool; The Esplanade.

 Market: Dempster St; Sun mornings. *Wildflower Show:* Sept. *Agricultural Show:* Oct.

Bonapartes Bar and Restaurant: modern Australian; 51 The Esplanade; (08) 9071 7727. *Loose Goose:* vibrant modern restaurant; 9A Andrews St; (08) 9071 2320. *Ocean Blues Restaurant:* simple seaside fare; 19 The Esplanade; (08) 9071 7107. *Taylor Street Jetty Cafe Restaurant:* beach-side cafe; Taylor St Jetty; (08) 9071 4317. *The Deck:* a favourite for ice-creams; Cnr Clarke and Veal sts, Hopetoun; (08) 9838 3303.

Esperance Bay Holiday Park: 162 Dempster St; (08) 9071 2237. *Esperance Seafront Caravan Park:* Cnr Goldfields and Norseman rds; (08) 9071 1251. *Acclaim Pine Grove Holiday Park:* 817 Harbour Rd, Chadwick; (08) 9071 4100. *Pink Lake Tourist Park:* 113 Pink Lake Rd, Sinclair; (08) 9071 2424.

Great Ocean Drive One of Australia's most spectacular scenic drives, this 38 km loop road passes wind farms, which supply 30% of the town's electricity, and some of the region's best-known natural attractions, including sheltered swimming at Twilight Cove, and Pink Lake, rendered lipstick-colour by algae. There are coastal lookouts, and sightings of southern right whales from June to October. Contact visitor centre for map.

Cape Le Grand National Park This spectacular coastline is lined with pristine beaches, including Hellfire Bay and Thistle Cove. At Lucky Bay, kangaroos can often be spotted lying on the beach. Visit Whistling Rock, which 'whistles' under certain wind conditions, and climb Frenchman's Peak for breathtaking views. There are magnificent displays of wildflowers in spring, and many bushwalks. Camping at Cape Le Grand and Lucky Bay. 56 km E.

Recherche Archipelago The Esperance region is known as the Bay of Isles because of this collection of 110 islands dotted 250 km along the coast that provide a haven for seals and sea lions. Cruises (3 hrs 30 min, subject to numbers and weather) take you around Cull, Button, Charlie, Woody and other islands; landing is permitted only on Woody Island. If you are lucky, you might see fur seals, sea lions, dolphins and, in season, southern right whales. For an extraordinary camping experience, try a safari hut on Woody Island (open Sept–Apr). These canvas huts set high on timber decking overlook an idyllic turquoise bay framed by eucalyptus trees. Woody Island also has an interpretive centre to provide information to visitors.

Rotary Lookout: views of bay, town and archipelago; Wireless Hill; 2 km w. *Pink Lake:* a pink saltwater lake; 5 km w. *Twilight Cove:* sheltered swimming; 12 km w. *Observatory Point and Lookout:* dramatic views of bay and islands; 17 km w. *Monjingup Lake Nature Reserve:* walk trails, birdwatching and wildflowers in spring; 20 km w. *Dalyup River Wines:* the most isolated winery in WA; open weekends in summer; (08) 9076 5027;

42 km w. *Stokes National Park:* beautiful coastal and inlet scenery; 80 km w. *Cape Arid National Park:* birdwatching, fishing, camping and 4WD routes; 120 km E. *Whale-watching:* southern right whales visit bays and protected waters to calve (June–Oct); along the Great Ocean Drive and at Cape Arid. *Great Country Drive:* takes visitors 92 km inland; maps from visitor centre.

TOWNS NEARBY: Ravensthorpe 173 km, Norseman 185 km, Lake King 221 km, Balladonia 233 km, Bremer Bay 238 km

Eucla
Pop. 50
Map ref. 566 C7 | 577 P6

i Eucla Motel, Eyre Hwy; (08) 9039 3468; www.dundas.wa.gov.au

97.1 FM ABC Radio National, 531 AM ABC Local Radio

Eucla is the largest settlement on the Nullarbor Plain, located just near the South Australian border. The ruins of a telegraph station exist at the original townsite and beyond the ruins are the remains of a jetty, a reminder of pioneering days when supplies were transported by boat. Eucla is today located on the Hampton Tableland and operates on Central Western Time, 45 minutes ahead of the rest of Western Australia.

Telegraph station ruins Opened in 1877 (just 33 years after Samuel Morse invented the telegraph), the Eucla Telegraph Station helped link WA with the rest of Australia and the world, often sending over 20 000 messages a year. The first message, sent to Perth in December 1877, stated simply, 'Eucla line opened. Hurrah.' 4 km s.

Eucla Museum: local history, including exhibits of the telegraph station, told through newspaper clippings and old photographs; Eucla Motel. *Travellers' Cross:* dedicated to travellers and illuminated at night; on the escarpment, west of town. *Bureau of Meteorology:* visitors welcome; east of town; (08) 9039 3444. *9-hole golf course:* site of the Golf Classic in May; north of town.

Eucla Motor Hotel: counter meals; Eyre Hwy; (08) 9039 3468.

Eucla Caravan Park: Eyre Hwy; (08) 9039 3468.

Eucla National Park This small park extends between Eucla and Border Village. On the coast near the SA border is Wilsons Bluff Lookout, with views to the east following the Bunda Cliffs into the distance. Closer to Eucla are the enormous sculptural shapes of the Delisser Sandhills. Mark your footprints in the dunes.

Border Village: quarantine checkpoint for people entering WA (travellers should ensure they are not carrying fruit, vegetables, honey, used fruit and produce containers, plants or seeds). The Border Dash starts here every Oct; 13 km E.

TOWNS NEARBY: Madura 178 km

Exmouth
Pop. 1845
Map ref. 575 B3

i Murat Rd; (08) 9949 1176 or 1800 287 328; www.exmouthwa.com.au

107.7 ABC Radio National, 1188 AM ABC Local Radio

One of the newest towns in Australia, Exmouth was founded in 1967 as a support town for the Harold E. Holt US Naval

[EXMOUTH] SHORT-BEAKED ECHIDNA, CAPE RANGE NATIONAL PARK

Communications Station, the main source of local employment. Excellent year-round fishing and proximity to Cape Range National Park and Ningaloo Reef have since made Exmouth a major tourist destination. The town is the nearest point in Australia to the continental shelf.

Mall Market: each Sun Apr–Sept. *Gamex:* world-class game-fishing competition; Mar. *Whale Shark Festival:* Apr/May. *Art Quest:* July. *Bill Fish Bonanza:* Oct/Nov.

Mantaray's Restaurant: modern brasserie; Novotel Ningaloo Resort, Madaffari Dr; (08) 9949 0000. *Potshot Hotel Resort:* relaxed dining; 1 Murat Rd; (08) 9949 1200. *Whalers Restaurant:* local seafood; 5 Kennedy St; (08) 9949 2416.

Exmouth Cape Holiday Park – Aspen Parks: 3 Truscott Cres; (08) 9949 1101. *Ningaloo Caravan & Holiday Resort:* Lot 1112 Murat Rd; (08) 9949 2377.

Cape Range National Park This rugged landscape of arid rocky gorges is edged by the stunning coastline of Ningaloo Marine Park. Wildlife is abundant, with emus, euros, rock wallabies and red kangaroos often sighted. In late winter there is a beautiful array of wildflowers including the Sturt's desert pea and the superb bird flower. Attractions within the park include Shothole Canyon, an impressive gorge; Mangrove Bay, a sanctuary zone with a bird hide overlooking a lagoon; and Mandu Mandu Gorge where you can walk along an ancient river bed. Yardie Creek is the only gorge with permanent water. Turquoise Bay is a popular beach for swimming and snorkelling (watch for currents). The Milyering Visitor Centre (54 km SW), made of rammed earth and run by solar power, is 52 km from Exmouth on the western side of the park and offers information on both Cape Range and Ningaloo. Contact (08) 9949 2808.

Ningaloo Marine Park: see Coral Bay. *Naval Communication Station:* the centre tower in its antenna field, at 388 m, is one of the tallest structures in the Southern Hemisphere; not open to public; 5 km N. *Vlamingh Head Lighthouse and Lookout:* built in 1912, Australia's only kerosene-burning lighthouse served as

a beacon to mariners until 1967. The lookout offers panoramic 360-degree views; 19 km N. *Learmonth Jetty:* popular fishing spot, rebuilt after Cyclone Vance; 33 km S. *Wildlife-watching:* turtle-nesting (Nov–Jan); coral-spawning (Mar–Apr); boat cruises and air flights to see whale sharks (Mar–June); humpback whales (Aug–Nov) from lighthouse (17 km N) and from whale-watching boat tours. Snorkellers can swim with whale sharks and manta rays located by cruise boats. Coral-viewing boat cruises also available; contact visitor centre for details.

TOWNS NEARBY: Onslow 107 km, Coral Bay 138 km

Fitzroy Crossing

Pop. 925
Map ref. 581 K8 | 584 H11

ℹ️ Cnr Great Northern Hwy and Flynn Dr; (08) 9191 5355; www.sdwk.wa.gov.au

📻 102.9 WA FM, 106.1 FM ABC Local Radio

Fitzroy Crossing is in the heart of the Kimberley region. As its name suggests, the original townsite was chosen as the best place to ford the mighty Fitzroy River. In the wet season, the river can rise over 20 metres and spread out up to 15 kilometres from its banks. Fitzroy Crossing's main attraction is its proximity to the magnificent 30-metre-deep Geikie Gorge with its sheer yellow, orange and grey walls. Check road conditions before any excursions from December to March, as this area is prone to flooding.

Crossing Inn First established in the 1890s as a shanty inn and trade store for passing stockmen, prospectors and drovers, it has operated on the same site ever since, and is one of the very few hotels in the state to retain a true outback atmosphere. A stop-off and drink are a must for all travellers passing by. Skuthorp Rd; (08) 9191 5080.

Rodeo: July. *Garnduwa Festival:* sporting events; Oct.

Riverside Restaurant: traditional Australian fare; Fitzroy River Lodge, Great Northern Hwy; (08) 9191 5141.

Fitzroy River Lodge: 277 Great Northern Hwy; (08) 9191 5141. *Tarunda Caravan Park:* 272 Forrest Rd; (08) 9191 5330.

Geikie Gorge National Park Geikie Gorge has cliffs and sculptured rock formations carved by water through an ancient limestone reef. The Fitzroy River is home to sharks, sawfish and stingrays that have, over centuries, adapted to the fresh water. Freshwater crocodiles up to 3 m long and barramundi are plentiful, best seen on a guided boat tour. Aboriginal heritage and cultural tours are run by guides from the local Bunuba tribe; bookings essential. DEC rangers run tours on the geology, wildlife and history of the area. Entry to park is restricted during wet season (Dec–Mar). Contact visitor centre for details. 18 km NE.

Causeway Crossing: concrete crossing that was the only way across the river until the new bridge was built in the 1970s; Geikie Gorge Rd; 4 km NE. *Tunnel Creek National Park:* unique formation created by waters from the creek cutting a 750 m tunnel through the ancient reef; 4WD access only; 110 km NW. *Windjana Gorge National Park:* 350-million-year-old Devonian reef rising majestically above the surrounding plains. An easy walking trail takes you past primeval life forms fossilised within the gorge walls; 4WD access only; 145 km NW. *4WD tours:* to Tunnel Creek and Windjana Gorge; bookings essential, contact visitor centre for details.

TOWNS NEARBY: Halls Creek 222 km, Derby 227 km

Gascoyne Junction

Pop. 46
Map ref. 575 D7 | 578 A8

i Shire offices, 4 Scott St; (08) 9943 0988; www.uppergascoyne.wa.gov.au

Lying at the junction of the Lyons and Gascoyne rivers, Gascoyne Junction is a small administration centre for the pastoral industry. Sheep stations in the area, ranging in size from around 36 000 to 400 000 hectares, produce a wool clip exceeding 1.5 million kilograms annually. Devastating floods destroyed much of the town in December 2010, and the town still lacks many facilities as it slowly rebuilds.

Bush Races: Aug and Sept. **Gascoyne Dash:** cross-country endurance; Oct.

Kennedy Range National Park Along with spectacular scenery, the park is home to fossils of the earliest known species of banksia in Australia, and marine fossils that reflect the history of the region as an ocean bed. Ideal for sightseeing, hiking and bush camping, trails start from the camping area and pass through gorges where you can see honeycomb-like rock formations. 60 km N.

Mt Augustus National Park Mt Augustus is the world's largest monolith, twice the size of Uluru. It is also known as Burringurrah, named after a boy who, in Aboriginal legend, broke tribal law by running away from his initiation. On capture, he was speared in the upper right leg. The spear broke as the boy fell to the ground, leaving a section protruding from his leg. It is said that, as you look at Mt Augustus, you can see the shape of the boy's body with the stump of the spear being the small peak at the eastern end called Edney's Lookout. There are several walking and driving trails; maps available from visitor centre. 294 km NE; *see Carnarvon.*

TOWNS NEARBY: Carnarvon 158 km, Denham 194 km

Geraldton

Pop. 37 000
Map ref. 575 D12 | 576 A3

i Bill Sewell Complex, cnr Chapman Rd and Bayley St; (08) 9921 3999 or 1800 818 881; www.geraldtontourist.com.au

 94.9 ABC Classic FM, 96.5 WA FM

Situated on the spectacular Batavia Coast, Geraldton is the largest town in the mid-west region. As a port city, it is the major centre for the wheat belt and is renowned for its rock lobster industry. Geraldton is also regarded as one of the best windsurfing locations in the world, and has superb swimming and surfing beaches. The nearby Houtman Abrolhos Islands are the site of 16 known shipwrecks. The most infamous is that of the Dutch ship *Batavia*, which foundered on a reef in 1629.

HMAS *Sydney II* Memorial Built on Mt Scott overlooking the town to commemorate the loss of 645 men from HMAS *Sydney II* on 19 November 1941. The ship sank after an encounter with the German raider HSK *Kormoran*. The wrecks of both ships were found in March 2008. Seven pillars representing the 7 seas hold aloft a 9 m high domed roof formed of 645 interlocking figures of seagulls. At night an eternal flame lights the cupola. Near the memorial is the bronze sculpture of a woman looking out to sea, representing the women left behind waiting for those who would not return. The fifth and final element of the memorial, completed in 2011, is a remembrance pool, its black granite walls engraved with 644 seagulls and the remaining

2 m seagull sculpture in the centre of the pool indicating the coordinates of the sunken vessel. Tours conducted daily at 10.30am. Gummer Ave.

WA Museum Geraldton Exhibits focus on the cultural and natural heritage of the Geraldton region. Maritime displays include finds from Australia's oldest shipwrecks, notably the original stone portico destined to adorn the castle gateway in the city of Batavia and lost to the sea when the *Batavia* sank in 1629. Museum Pl, Batavia Coast Marina; (08) 9921 5080; open 9.30am–4pm daily. Adjacent in the Geraldton Marina is a replica of the *Batavia* longboat; the public is invited on harbour sailings most Sundays; check with visitor centre for details.

Historic buildings: explore the town's historic architecture dating back to the mid-1800s, with works by noted architect Monsignor John Cyril Hawes a highlight. Many of the buildings have been restored and are open to the public, including the Old Geraldton Gaol (1858), which is now a craft centre, and the Bill Sewell Complex (1884), which was built as a hospital and subsequently became a prison. In Cathedral Ave, St Francis Xavier Cathedral offers tours (10am Mon and Fri, 4pm Wed), and the Cathedral of the Holy Cross has one of the largest areas of stained glass in Australia. Brochures for Historic Walk Trails available from visitor centre. *Geraldton Regional Art Gallery:* the original Geraldton Town Hall (1907) converted to house art exhibitions and workshops; closed Mon; 24 Chapman Rd; (08) 9964 7170; 10am–4pm Tues–Sat, 1–4pm Sun. *Leon Baker Jewellers:* international jeweller works with Abrolhos pearls and Argyle diamonds. Workshop tours available; 133 Marine Tce; (08) 9921 5451. *Rock Lobster Factory:* take a tour with the Geraldton Fishermen's Co-operative and follow the journey of the town's most famous export, the western rock lobster, from processor to plate; covered shoes required; tours 9.30am Mon–Fri Nov–July; Connell Rd, Fisherman's Wharf; (08) 9965 9000. *Point Moore Lighthouse:* assembled in 1878 from steel sections prefabricated in England, and standing 34 m tall, this is the only lighthouse of its kind in Australia; information on nearby pillar; Marine Tce.

Wind on Water Festival: Jan. **Sunshine Festival:** Oct. **Markets:** 8am–12pm every Sat at Maitland Park and Sun at old Railway Station.

Boatshed Restaurant: modern Australian and seafood; 359 Marine Tce; (08) 9921 5500. **The Freemason's Hotel:** brasserie style; Cnr Durlacher St and Marine Terrace Mall; (08) 9964 3457. **Tides of Geraldton:** contemporary dining with harbour views; 103 Marine Tce; (08) 9965 4999. **Chapman Valley Wines Restaurant:** vineyard platters; Chapman Valley Wines, Lot 14 Howatharra Rd, Nanson; (08) 9920 5148.

Belair Gardens Caravan Park: 463 Marine Tce, West End; (08) 9921 1997. **Sunset Beach Holiday Park:** 4 Bosley St, Sunset Beach; (08) 9938 1655.

Houtman Abrolhos Islands These 122 reef islands with a fascinating history span 100 km of ocean and are the main source of rock lobster for the local lobster fishing industry. There are 16 known shipwrecks in the Abrolhos Islands, the most infamous of which is that of the Dutch ship *Batavia* from 1629. Captain Pelsaert and 47 of the survivors sailed north to Batavia (modern-day Jakarta) for help. When they returned 3 and a half months later, they discovered that a mutiny had taken place and 125 of the remaining survivors had been massacred. All of the mutineers were hanged, except for 2 who were marooned on the mainland, becoming Australia's first white inhabitants. There is no record of their subsequent fate. The wreck was discovered in 1963 and some skeletons of victims of the mutiny have been found on Beacon Island. The islands now offer diving, snorkelling, surfing, windsurfing, fishing and birdwatching. Access is via boat or plane; tours and charters are available. Contact visitor centre for details and bookings. 65 km w.

Fishing: good fishing spots at Sunset Beach (6 km N) and Drummond Cove (10 km N). *Mill's Park Lookout:* excellent views over Moresby Range and coastal plain; 10 km NE. *Chapman Valley:* picturesque farmlands and fields of springtime wildflowers on display July–Oct. Lavender Valley Farm offers natural body products; 1852 Chapman Valley Rd, Yetna; (08) 9920 5469; 20 km NE. Chapman Valley Wines is the northernmost winery in WA; 14 Howatharra Rd, Nanson; (08) 9920 5148; 30 km NE. *Greenough:* historic 1860s hamlet famous for its 'leaning trees', bent 90 degrees due to the coastal winds; 24 km s. *Oakabella Homestead:* one of the region's oldest pioneering homesteads with a rare buttressed barn; tours available; North West Coastal Hwy; (08) 9925 1033; 30 km N. *Scenic flights:* tours over nearby Abrolhos Islands, Murchison Gorges or the coastal cliffs of Kalbarri; contact visitor centre. *Scenic drive:* Indian Ocean Drive, with its coastal views, is a beautiful alternate route for travelling between Geraldton and Perth via Dongarra, bypassing much of the Brand Highway.

TOWNS NEARBY: Greenough 22 km, Northampton 47 km, Dongara–Denison 61 km, Mullewa 92 km, Kalbarri 126 km

Gingin

Pop. 527
Map ref. 571 C1 | 574 B3 | 576 C7

 Council offices, Brockman St; (08) 9575 2211; www.gingin.wa.gov.au

720 AM ABC Local Radio, 810 AM ABC Radio National

Gingin is one of the oldest towns in Western Australia, having been settled in 1832, only 2 years after the establishment of the Swan River Colony. For tourists, it has the charm of old original stone buildings within a picturesque natural setting. Situated 84 kilometres north of Perth, it is an ideal destination for a daytrip from the city.

Historic buildings Enjoy a pleasant self-guide stroll around the town on the Gingin Walkabout Trail, which features many fine examples of early architecture including Philbey's Cottage and St Luke's Anglican Church, both made from local stone. Contact visitor centre for map.

Granville Park: in the heart of the town with free barbecue facilities, playground and picnic area. *Self-guide walks:* stroll along the Gingin Brook on the Jim Gordon VC Trail or try the Three Bridges Recreation Trail, rebuilt after being destroyed by fire in Dec 2002; contact visitor centre for maps.

Horticultural Expo: Apr. *British Car Club Day:* May. *Market Day Festival:* Sept.

Amirage Restaurant: European fare; Cnr Gingin Brook and Military rds, Gingin West; (08) 9575 7646. *Gingin Hotel:* bistro fare; 5 Jones St; (08) 9575 2214. *Kyotmunga Estate:* platter lunches; 287 Chittering Valley Rd, Lower Chittering; (08) 9571 8001. *Stringybark Winery, Restaurant & Function Centre:* international cuisine; 2060 Chittering Rd, Chittering; (08) 9571 8069. *Willowbrook Farm Tearooms & Caravan Park:* country tearooms; 1679 Gingin Brook Rd, West Gingin.

 Gravity Discovery Centre Opened in 2003, this $4 million centre offers hands-on and static scientific displays on gravity, magnetism and electricity. It includes the biggest public astronomy centre in the Southern Hemisphere and the largest telescope in WA. Visitors can take a high-tech look at heavenly bodies in an evening presentation (bookings essential) and see a number of WA inventions relating to physics. Military Rd; (08) 9575 7577; 15 km SW.

Cemetery: with a spectacular display of kangaroo paws in early spring; northern outskirts of town. *Jylland Winery:* open to public, wine-tastings and cellar-door sales; 2 km s. *West Coast Honey:* live bee display, honey extraction, tastings, sales of honey and bee products; open 9am–4pm Wed–Sun, or Mon and Tues by appt; Gingin Brook Rd; 3 km w. *Moore River National Park:* special area for conservation featuring banksia woodlands and wildflower displays in spring; 20 km NW.

TOWNS NEARBY: Yanchep 34 km, New Norcia 51 km, Toodyay 58 km, Mundaring 66 km, Moora 79 km

Greenough

Pop. 15 394
Map ref. 576 A3

ⓘ Cnr Chapman Rd and Bayly St, Geraldton; (08) 9921 3999 or 1800 818 881; www.cgg.wa.gov.au

96.5 WA FM, 99.7 FM ABC Radio National

Lying 24 kilometres south of Geraldton, the Greenough Flats form a flood plain close to the mouth of the Greenough River. At its peak in the 1860s and '70s, Greenough (pronounced 'Grennuff') was a highly successful wheat-growing area. However, the combined effects of drought, crop disease and floods led to the area's decline and from 1900 the population dropped dramatically. The historic hamlet that was once the centre of this farming community has been extensively restored and is classified by the National Trust.

Central Greenough Historic Settlement Precinct of 11 restored stone buildings dating from the 1860s including a school, police station, courthouse, gaol and churches. Fully re-created interior furnishings. Self-guide maps are available, or tours by appt. Cnr Brand Hwy and McCartney Rd; (08) 9926 1084.

Pioneer Museum: folk display located in an original limestone cottage; tours available; Brand Hwy. *Leaning trees:* these trees are a unique sight, having grown sideways in response to the harsh salt-laden winds that blow from the Indian Ocean; seen from Brand Hwy on the Greenough Flats. *Hampton Arms Inn:* fully restored historic inn (1863); Company Rd.

Rock of Ages Cottage B&B: 18 Phillips Rd; (08) 9926 1154.

Walkaway Railway Station: built in the style of a traditional British railway station, now housing a railway and heritage museum; closed Mon; Evans Rd; 10 km E. *Greenough River mouth:* ideal for swimming, canoeing, beach and rock fishing, birdwatching and photography; 14 km N. *Flat Rocks:* surfing, swimming and rock-fishing. A round of the State Surfing Championships is held here in June every year; 10 km s. *Ellendale Pool:* this deep, freshwater swimming hole beneath spectacular sandstone cliffs is an ideal picnic area; 23 km E. *Greenough River Nature Trail:* self-guide walk; contact visitor centre for brochure. *The Greenough/Walkaway Heritage Trail:* 57 km self-drive tour of the area; contact visitor centre for map.

TOWNS NEARBY: Geraldton 22 km, Dongara-Denison 39 km, Northampton 67 km, Mullewa 87 km, Morawa 127 km

Halls Creek

Pop. 1209
Map ref. 581 N7 | 585 L11

 Cnr Great Northern Hwy and Hall St; (08) 9168 6262 or 1800 877 423; www.hallscreektourism.com.au

102.9 WA FM, 106.1 FM ABC Local Radio

In the heart of the Kimberley region and on the edge of the Great Sandy Desert, Halls Creek is the site of the first payable gold discovery in Western Australia. In 1885 Jack Slattery and Charlie Hall (after whom the town is named) discovered gold, thereby sparking a gold rush that brought over 15 000 people to the area. In 1917 a seriously injured stockman named James 'Jimmy' Darcy was taken into Halls Creek. With neither doctor nor hospital in the town, the local postmaster carried out an emergency operation using a penknife as instructions were telegraphed by morse code from Perth. The Perth doctor then set out on the ten-day journey to Halls Creek via cattle boat, model-T Ford, horse-drawn sulky and, finally, on foot, only to discover that the patient had died the day before his arrival. The event inspired Reverend John Flynn to establish the Royal Flying Doctor Service in 1928, a development that helped to encourage settlement throughout the outback.

 Russian Jack Memorial: tribute to a prospector who pushed his sick friend in a wheelbarrow to Wyndham for medical help; Thomas St. *Trackers Hut:* restored original hut of Aboriginal trackers; Robert St, behind police station.

Rodeo: July. *Picnic Races:* Oct.

Russian Jack's Restaurant: hearty fare; Best Western Halls Creek Motel, 194 Great Northern Hwy; (08) 9168 9600.

Wolfe Creek Crater National Park Wolfe Creek Crater is the second-largest meteorite crater in the world. Named after Robert Wolfe, a Halls Creek prospector, it is 870–950 m across and was probably formed by a meteorite weighing at least several thousand tonnes crashing to earth a million years ago. In Aboriginal legend, it is said to be the site of the emergence of a powerful rainbow serpent from the earth. Scenic flights afford magnificent views; contact visitor centre for details. 148 km s.

Purnululu National Park This World Heritage Area in the outback of the east Kimberley is home to the Bungle Bungle Range, a remarkable landscape of tiger-striped, beehive-shaped rock domes intersected by narrow, palm-lined gorges where pools reflect sunlight off sheer walls. A scenic flight is the best way to gain a perspective of the Bungle Bungles' massive size and spectacular scenery (details from visitor centre). The most visited site in Purnululu is Cathedral Gorge, a fairly easy walk. A couple of days and a backpack allow you to explore nearby Piccaninny Creek and Gorge, camping overnight. On the northern side of the park is Echidna Chasm, a narrow gorge totally different from those on the southern side. Purnululu is also rich in Aboriginal art, and there are many traditional burial sites within its boundaries. Purnululu is open to visitors (Apr–Dec) and is accessible by 4WD. There are few facilities and no accommodation; visitors must carry in all food and water and notify a ranger. 160 km e.

China Wall: white quartz formation said to resemble Great Wall of China; 6 km e. **Caroline's Pool:** deep pool ideal for swimming (in wet season) and picnicking; 15 km e. **Old Halls Creek:** remnants of original town including graveyard where James Darcy is buried; prospecting available; 16 km e.

[HALLS CREEK] BUNGLE BUNGLE RANGE, PURNULULU NATIONAL PARK

Palm Springs: fishing, swimming and picnicking; 45 km e. *Sawpit Gorge:* fishing, swimming, picnicking; 52 km e. *Billiluna Aboriginal Community:* fishing, swimming, camping, birdwatching and bushwalking, and bush tucker and cultural tours; 180 km s.

TOWNS NEARBY: Fitzroy Crossing 222 km

Harvey

Pop. 2602
Map ref. 572 F2 | 574 C7 | 576 C9

 James Stirling Pl; (08) 9729 1122; www.harveytourism.com

96.5 FM Harvey Community Radio, 810 AM ABC Radio National

On the Harvey River, 18 kilometres from the coast, the thriving town of Harvey is surrounded by fertile, irrigated plains. Beef production, citrus orchards and viticulture flourish in the region and intensive dairy farming provides the bulk of Western Australia's milk supply. Bordered by the Darling Range, Harvey offers a wealth of natural attractions, from the magnificent scenic drives through the escarpment to the pristine white beaches with excellent sunsets and fishing on the coast.

Tourist and Interpretive Centre: tourist information and display of local industries and May Gibbs characters; James Stirling Pl. *Big Orange:* lookout, one of Australia's big icons; Third St. *Harvey Museum:* memorabilia housed in renovated railway station; open 2–4pm Sun or by appt; Harper St. *Stirling Cottage:* replica of the home of Governor Stirling, which later became the home of May Gibbs, author of *Snugglepot and Cuddlepie*; James Stirling Pl tourist precinct. **Heritage Gardens:** picturesque country gardens on the banks of the Harvey River; James Stirling Pl tourist precinct. **Internment Camp Memorial Shrine:** the only roadside shrine of its type in the world, built by prisoners of war in the 1940s; collect key from visitor centre; South Western Hwy. **Heritage trail:** 6.2 km self-guide walk includes historic buildings and sights of town; map available at visitor centre. **Mosaics and murals:** unique collection throughout the region. See Uduc Rd, South Western Hwy, and entrances to Myalup and Binningup.

  Summer Series Concerts: Jan–Mar. **Harvest Festival:** Mar. **Spring Fair:** Sept.

Old Coast Road Brewery: tasting plates and pub fare; West Break Rd, Myalup; 1300 792 106.

Harvey Rainbow Caravan Park: 199 Kennedy St; (08) 9729 2239.

Harvey Dam: landscaped park with viewing platform, amphitheatre, barbecues and playground. Fishing is allowed in season with permit; 3 km E. **HaVe Cheese:** tours and gourmet cheese tasting; (08) 9729 3949; 3 km S. **White Rocks Museum and Dairy:** founded in 1887. Compare current technology with display of machinery from the past; open 2–4pm or by appt for groups; 15 km S. **Beaches:** Myalup Beach provides good swimming, surfing and beach fishing; 21 km W. Binningup Beach is protected by a reef that runs parallel to shore and is ideal for sheltered swimming, snorkelling, beach fishing and boating; 25 km SW. **Wineries:** more than 10 wineries open to the public, only a short distance from town; contact visitor centre for details.

TOWNS NEARBY: Australind 28 km, Bunbury 36 km, Collie 40 km, Dwellingup 43 km, Pinjarra 50 km

Hyden

Pop. 281
Map ref. 574 H5 | 576 F8

i Wave Rock; (08) 9880 5182; www.waverock.com.au

648 AM ABC Local Radio, 1296 AM ABC Radio National

The small wheat-belt town of Hyden is synonymous with its famous nearby attraction, Wave Rock, originally known as Hyde's Rock in honour of a sandalwood cutter who lived in the area. A typing error by the Lands Department made it Hyden Rock, and the emerging town soon became known as Hyden. The area around the town boasts beautiful wildflowers in spring, including a wide variety of native orchids.

Wave Rock Weekender: music festival; Sept/Oct.

Wave Rock Motel: 3 restaurants on-site; 2 Lynch St; (08) 9880 5052.

Wave Rock Caravan Park and Resort: Wave Rock Rd; (08) 9880 5022. **Tressie's Museum and Caravan Park:** 4313 Kondinin–Hyden Hwy, Karlgarin; (08) 9889 5043.

Wave Rock Resembling a breaking wave, this 100 m long and 15 m high granite cliff owes its shape to wind action over the past 2.7 billion years. Vertical bands of colour are caused by streaks of algae and chemical staining from run-off waters (4 km E). At Wave Rock Visitor Centre see the largest lace collection in the Southern Hemisphere with fine examples of antique lace, including lace worn by Queen Victoria. There are local wildflower species on display, an Australiana collection at

the Pioneer Town, fauna in a natural bush environment and a walking trail.

Hippo's Yawn: rock formation; 5 km E via Wave Rock. **The Humps and Mulka's Cave:** Aboriginal wall paintings; 22 km N via Wave Rock. **Rabbit-Proof Fence:** see the fence where it meets the road; 56 km E.

TOWNS NEARBY: Kulin 70 km, Lake Grace 81 km, Corrigin 94 km, Lake King 105 km, Merredin 121 km

Jurien Bay

Pop. 1175
Map ref. 576 A5

i Council offices, 110 Bashford St; (08) 9652 1020; www.dandaragan.wa.gov.au

103.1 WA FM, 107.9 FM ABC Radio National

Jurien Bay, settled in the mid-1850s, is the centre of a lobster fishing industry. The jetty was constructed in 1885 to enable a more efficient route to markets for locally produced wool and hides. Located within a sheltered bay protected by reefs and islands, the town has wide beaches and sparkling waters ideal for swimming, waterskiing, windsurfing, snorkelling, diving and surfing. The Jurien Bay boat harbour services the fishing fleet and has facilities for holiday boating and fishing. Anglers can fish from boat, jetty and beach.

Jurien Bay Charters: boat and fishing charters, scuba diving, sea lion tours; bookings at dive shop; Carmella St. **Old jetty site:** plaque commemorates site of original jetty. Remains of the jetty's timber piles have been discovered 65 m inland from high-water mark, which indicates the gradual build-up of coastline over time; Hastings St.

  Market: Bashford St; usually last Sat each month. **Blessing of the Fleet:** Nov.

Leuseur's Gallery Cafe: relaxed cafe; 36 Bashford St; (08) 9652 2113. **Sandpiper Bar & Grill:** bistro fare; Cnr Roberts and Sandpiper sts; (08) 9652 1229.

Jurien Bay Tourist Park: Roberts St; (08) 9652 1595.

Jurien Bay Marine Park Established in August 2003, this marine park extends from Wedge Island to Green Head and encompasses major sea lion and seabird breeding areas. The reefs within the park are populated by a wide range of plants and animals including the rare Australian sea lion, and the seagrass meadows are a breeding ground for western rock lobsters.

Lions Lookout: spectacular views of town and surrounds; 5 km E. **Drovers Cave National Park:** rough limestone country with numerous caves, all of which have secured entrances limiting public access; 4WD access only; 7 km E. **Grigsons Lookout:** panoramic views of ocean and hinterland. Also wildflowers July–Nov; 15 km N. **Lesueur National Park:** with over 900 species of flora, representing 10% of the state's known flora, Lesueur is an important area for flora conservation. Enjoy coastal views from a lookout; 23 km E. **Stockyard Gully National Park:** walk through 300 m Stockyard Gully Tunnel along winding underground creek; 4WD access only; 50 km N.

TOWNS NEARBY: Cervantes 21 km, Moora 100 km, Carnamah 107 km, Dongara–Denison 117 km, New Norcia 135 km

Kalbarri

Pop. 1329
Map ref. 575 C11

i Grey St; (08) 9937 1104 or 1800 639 468;
www.australiascoralcoast.com

102.9 WA FM, 106.1 FM ABC Local Radio

Kalbarri lies at the mouth of the Murchison River, flanked by Kalbarri National Park. Established in 1951, the town is a popular holiday resort, famous for the magnificent gorges up to 130 metres deep along the river. Just south of the township a cairn marks the spot where in 1629 Captain Pelsaert of the Dutch East India Company marooned two crew members implicated in the *Batavia* shipwreck and massacre. These were the first, albeit unwilling, white inhabitants of Australia.

Pelican feeding: daily feeding from late Apr until the end of Feb by volunteers on the river foreshore; starts 8.45am; off Grey St. *Family Entertainment Centre:* trampolines, minigolf, bicycle hire; Magee Cres; (08) 9937 1105.

Sport Fishing Classic: Mar. *Canoe and Cray Carnival:* June.

Black Rock Cafe: cafe with emphasis on seafood; 80 Grey St; (08) 9937 1062. *The Grasstree Cafe and Restaurant:* seafood with an Asian twist; 94–96 Grey St; (08) 9937 2288. *The Jetty Seafood Shack:* seafood restaurant with marina views; Shop 1, Marina Shopping Centre, 365 Grey St; (08) 9937 1067. *Zuytdorp Restaurant:* international cuisine; Kalbarri Beach Resort, 2 Clotworthy St; (08) 9937 2222.

Gecko Lodge: 9 Glass St; (08) 9937 1900. *Kalbarri Tudor Caravan Park:* 10 Porter St; (08) 9937 1077.

Kalbarri National Park Gazetted in 1963, this park has dramatic coastal cliffs along its western boundary, towering river gorges and seasonal wildflowers, many of which are unique to the park. The Murchison River has carved a gorge through sedimentary rock known as Tumblagooda sandstone, creating a striking contrast of brownish red and purple against white bands of stone. Embedded in these layers are some of the earliest signs of animal life on earth. There are many lookouts including Nature's Window at the Loop, which overlooks the Murchison Gorge, and the breathtaking scenery at Z Bend Lookout. Along the 20 km coastal section of the park, lookouts such as Mushroom Rock, Pot Alley and Eagle Gorge offer panoramic views and whale-watching sites. Dolphins, whale sharks and whales frequent the coastal waters, and the fishing is excellent. Bushwalking, rock climbing, abseiling, canoeing tours, rafting, cruises, camping safaris, coach and wilderness tours, and barbecue facilities are all available. Contact visitor centre for details. 57 km E.

Rainbow Jungle: breeding centre for rare and endangered species of parrots, cockatoos and exotic birds set in landscaped tropical gardens. Also here is the largest walk-in parrot free-flight area in Australia and an outdoor cinema featuring the latest movies; Red Bluff Rd; 3 km s. *Wildflower Centre:* view over 200 species on display along a 1.8 km walking trail. Visit the plant nursery and herbarium, where you can purchase seeds and souvenirs; open July–Nov; Ajana–Kalbarri Rd; 3km E. *Murchison House Station:* tours available of one of the oldest and largest stations in WA, which includes historic buildings and cemetery, display of local arts and crafts, and wildflowers; seasonal, check with visitor centre; Ajana–Kalbarri Rd; 4 km E. *Big River Ranch:* enjoy horseriding through the spectacular countryside; Ajana–

Kalbarri Rd; 4 km E. *Wittecarra Creek:* cairn marking the site where 2 of the mutineers from the Dutch ship *Batavia* were left as punishment for their participation in the murders of 125 survivors of the wreck; 4 km s. *Hutt River Province:* independent sovereign state founded in 1970; 50 km SE; *see Northampton.*

TOWNS NEARBY: Northampton 84 km, Geraldton 126 km, Greenough 148 km, Mullewa 161 km, Dongara–Denison 187 km

Kalgoorlie–Boulder

see inset box on next page

Karratha

Pop. 11 727
Map ref. 575 E1 | 578 B2 | 580 B12 | 582 D5

i 4548 Karratha Rd; (08) 9144 4600.

104.1 FM ABC News Radio, 106.5 WA FM

Karratha is the Aboriginal word for 'good country'. Founded in 1968 as a result of expansion of the iron-ore industry, Karratha was originally established for workers on the huge industrial projects nearby. For visitors, Karratha is an ideal centre from which to explore the fascinating Pilbara region.

TV Hill Lookout: excellent views over town centre and beyond; off Millstream Rd. *Jaburara Heritage Trail:* 3 hr walk features Aboriginal rock carvings; pamphlet available at visitor centre.

FeNaClNG Festival: this celebration takes its name from the town's mining roots (Fe is the chemical symbol for iron ore, NaCl is the symbol for salt, and NG is an abbreviation for natural gas); Aug. *Gamefishing Classic:* Aug.

Etcetera Brasserie: fine dining, Pilbara-style; Karratha International Hotel, cnr Hillview and Millstream rds; (08) 9187 3333. *Hearson's Bistro:* poolside fine dining; All Seasons Karratha, 35–45 Searipple Rd; (08) 9159 1000.

Pilbara Holiday Park: Rosemary Rd; (08) 9185 1855.

Millstream–Chichester National Park Rolling hills, spectacular escarpments and tree-lined watercourses with hidden rockpools characterise this park. The spring-fed Chinderwarriner Pool has an almost mirage-like quality. The remarkable oasis of Millstream is an area of tropical palm-fringed freshwater springs, well known to the Afghan cameleers of Pilbara's past. Other notably scenic spots are Python, Deepreach and Circular pools, and Cliff Lookout. The Millstream Homestead Visitor Centre, housed in the Gordon family homestead (1919), has displays dedicated to the local Aboriginal people, early settlers and the natural environment. Popular activities include bushwalking, picnicking, camping, fishing, swimming and boating. Tours are available; contact visitor centre for details. 124 km s.

Salt Harvest Ponds: Australia's largest evaporative salt fields. Tours are available; details at visitor centre; 15 km N. *Dampier:* port facility servicing the iron-ore operations at Tom Price and Paraburdoo, home of the famous Red Dog; 22 km N. *Hamersley Iron Port Facilities:* 3 hr tour and audiovisual presentation daily; bookings essential through visitor centre; 22 km N. *Cleaverville Beach:* scenic spot ideal for camping, boating, fishing and swimming; 26 km NE. *North-West Shelf Gas Project Visitor Centre:* displays on the history and technology of Australia's largest natural resource development, with panoramic views over the massive onshore gas plant; open 10am–4pm Mon–Fri

continued on p. 314

 RADIO STATIONS IN TOWN WHAT'S ON WHERE TO EAT WHERE TO STAY NEARBY

KALGOORLIE–BOULDER

Pop. 28 243
Map ref. 576 H5

ⓘ Cnr Hannan and Wilson sts; 1800 004 653 or (08) 9021 1966.; www.kalgoorlietourism.com

97.9 Hot FM, 648 AM ABC Local Radio

Kalgoorlie is the centre of Western Australia's goldmining industry. It was once known as Hannan's Find in honour of Paddy Hannan, the first prospector to discover gold in the area. In June 1893 Hannan was among a party of about 150 men who set out from Coolgardie to search for some lost prospectors near Yerilla. After a stop at Mount Charlotte, the main party continued on, leaving Hannan and two others behind as one of their horses had lost a shoe. Some idle 'specking' (looking on the ground for nuggets) led them to stumble on the richest goldfield the world had known – it soon grew to encompass the 'Golden Mile', which is reputedly the world's richest square mile of gold-bearing ore. Rapid development of Kalgoorlie and nearby Boulder followed, with thousands of men travelling to the field from all over the world, reaching a maximum population of about 30 000 in 1903. The shortage of water was always a problem, but in 1903 the genius of engineer C. Y. O'Connor enabled a pipeline to be opened that pumped water 560 kilometres from Perth. In its heyday Kalgoorlie and Boulder boasted eight breweries and 93 hotels. The two towns amalgamated in 1989 to form Kalgoorlie–Boulder, and today the population is again close to peak levels due to the region's second gold boom.

Historic buildings Although only a few kilometres apart, Kalgoorlie and Boulder developed independently for many years. The amalgamated towns now form a city with 2 main streets, each lined with impressive hotels and civic buildings. Built at the turn of the century, when people were flocking to the area, many of these buildings display ornamentation and fittings that reflect the confidence and wealth of the mining interests and are fine examples of early Australian architecture. The Kalgoorlie Town Hall (1908), on the corner of Hannan and Wilson sts, has hosted many a famous performer on its stage, including Dame Nellie Melba and Percy Grainger. It now displays a collection of memorabilia; tours 1.30pm Wed. The offices of newspapers the *Kalgoorlie Miner* and *Western Argus* was the first 3-storey building in town. Burt St in Boulder is regarded as one of the most significant streetscapes in WA. Buildings to see include the Grand Hotel (1897), the Old Chemist (1900), which now houses a pharmaceutical museum, and the post office (1899), which was once so busy it employed 49 staff. The Boulder Town Hall, built in 1902, is currently closed due to extensive damage caused by a 5.2 magnitude earthquake which struck Kalgoorlie–Boulder in Apr 2010. The Town Hall is home to one of the world's last remaining Goatcher stage curtains. Phillip Goatcher was one of the greatest scenic painters of Victorian times and his hand-painted drop curtains graced theatres in London, Paris and New York. Another building damaged in the earthquake was the Goldfields War Museum; a small part of the exhibition has been moved to the Kalgoorlie Town Hall (open 9am–4pm Mon–Fri). The self-guided Kalgoorlie Inner City Trail will take you on a tour of 40 historic buildings; contact the visitor centre for brochure.

Paddy Hannan's Statue: a monument to the first man to discover gold in Kalgoorlie; Hannan St. *St Mary's Church:* built in 1902 of Coolgardie pressed bricks, many of which are believed to contain gold; Cnr Brookman and Porter sts, Kalgoorlie. *WA School of Mines Mineral Museum:* displays include over 3000 mineral and ore specimens and many gold nuggets; open 8.30am–12.30pm Mon–Fri, closed on school holidays; Egan St, Kalgoorlie. *WA Museum Kalgoorlie–Boulder:* panoramic views of the city from the massive mining headframe at the entrance. Known locally as the Museum of the Goldfields, displays include a million-dollar gold collection, nuggets and jewellery. See the narrowest pub in the Southern Hemisphere, a re-created 1930s miner's cottage and other heritage buildings. Guided tours available; open 10am–4.30pm daily; 17 Hannan St, Kalgoorlie. *Goldfields Arts Centre:* art gallery and theatre; Cassidy St, Kalgoorlie. *Goldfields Aboriginal Art Gallery:* examples of local Aboriginal art and artefacts for sale; open 9am–5pm Mon–Fri or by appt; Dugan St, Kalgoorlie; (08) 9021 8533. *Paddy Hannan's Tree:* a plaque marks the spot where Paddy Hannan first discovered gold; Outridge Tce, Kalgoorlie. *Red-light district:* view the few remaining 'starting stalls', in which women once posed as prospective clients walked by, and visit the only working brothel in the world that visitors can tour. Langtrees; tours by appt; (08) 9026 2181; Hay St, Kalgoorlie. *Superpit Lookout:* underground mining on the Golden Mile became singly owned in the 1980s and '90s and was converted into an open-cut operation – what is now known as the Superpit. Peer into its depths from the lookout off Goldfields Hwy, Boulder (can coincide visit with blasting; check times at visitor centre); daily tours (free on market day) and scenic flights are also available. *Mt Charlotte:* the reservoir holds water pumped from the Mundaring Weir in Perth via the pipeline of C. Y. O'Connor. A lookout provides good views of the city; off Goldfields Hwy, Kalgoorlie. *Hammond Park:* miniature Bavarian castle made from thousands of local gemstones. There is also a sanctuary for kangaroos and emus, and aviaries for a variety of birdlife; Lyall St, Kalgoorlie. *Arboretum:* a living museum of species of the semi-arid zone and adjacent desert areas, this 26.5 ha parkland has interpretive walking trails and recreation facilities; Hawkins St, adjacent Hammond Park. *Miners' Monument:* tribute to mine workers; Burt St, Boulder. *WMC Nickel Pots:* massive nickel pots and interpretive panels describe the story of the development of the nickel industry in the region; Goldfields Hwy. *Loopline Railway Museum:* celebrates what was once one of the busiest railways in Australia, which connected Kalgoorlie and Boulder to outlying towns in the region; Boulder City Railway Station, cnr Burt and Hamilton sts; open 9am–1pm daily. *Royal Flying Doctor Visitor Centre:* climb on board an authentic RFDS plane; 45-minute tours available, on the hour; open 10am–3pm Mon–Fri; Airport, Hart Kerspien Dr. *Karlkurla Bushland:* pronounced 'gullgirla', this natural regrowth area of bushland offers a 4 km signposted walk trail, picnic areas and lookout over the city and nearby mining areas; Riverina Way. *Walks:* guided and self-guide heritage walks; details and maps at visitor centre.

Kalgoorlie Market Day: St Barbara Sq; 1st Sun each month. *Boulder Market Day:* Burt St; 3rd Sun each month. *Community Fair:* Apr. *Menzies to Kalgoorlie Cycle Race:* June. *Diggers and Dealers Mining Forum:* Aug. *Kalgoorlie Cup and*

[EXTERIOR OF THE EXCHANGE HOTEL]

Boulder Cup: Sept. *Back to Boulder Festival:* Oct. *Balzano Barrow Race:* Oct. *St Barbara's Mining and Community Festival:* Dec.

Danny's Bar & Grill: up-market steak house; 14 Wilson St, Kalgoorlie; (08) 9022 7614. *The Exchange Hotel:* traditional Irish and Australian food; 135 Hannan St, Kalgoorlie; (08) 9021 2833. *Judd's:* hearty pub fare; 319 Hannan St, Kalgoorlie; (08) 9021 3046. *Salt:* Italian restaurant; 90 Egan St, Kalgoorlie; (08) 9022 8028. *Sheffield's Bar & Grill:* all-you-can-eat bistro, woodfired pizza; The Recreation Hotel, cnr Lionel and Burt sts, Boulder; (08) 9093 3467.

Discovery Holiday Parks – Kalgoorlie: 286 Burt St, Boulder; (08) 9039 4800. *Discovery Holiday Parks – Boulder:* 201 Lane St, South Boulder; (08) 9093 1266. *Goldminer Tourist Caravan Park:* Cnr Great Eastern Hwy and Atbara St, Somerville; (08) 9021 3713. *Prospector Holiday Park:* 9 Ochiltree St, Somerville; (08) 9021 2524.

Australian Prospectors and Miners Hall of Fame Tour a historic underground mine, watch a gold pour or visit the Exploration Zone, which is designed specifically for young people. You will find interactive exhibits on exploration, mineral discoveries and surface and underground mining, including panning for gold. The Environmental Garden details the stages and techniques involved in mine-site rehabilitation. At Hannan's North Tourist Mine, historic buildings re-create an early gold-rush town and visitors can take a first-hand look at the cramped and difficult working conditions of the miners. Eastern Bypass Rd; (08) 9026 2700; 7 km N.

Bush 2-Up: visit the original corrugated-iron shack and bush ring where Australia's only legal bush 2-up school used to operate; off Goldfields Hwy; 8 km E. *Kanowna Belle Gold Mine lookouts:* wander the ghost town remains of Kanowna and see day-to-day mining activities from 2 lookouts over a previously mined open pit and processing plant; 20 km E. *Broad Arrow:* see the pub where scenes from the Googie Withers movie *Nickel Queen* were shot in the 1970s. Every wall is autographed by visitors; 38 km N. *Ora Banda:* recently restored inn; 54 km NW.

Kambalda: nickel-mining town on Lake Lefroy (salt). Head to Red Hill Lookout for views across the expanse; 55 km s. *Prospecting:* visitors to the area may obtain a miner's right from the Dept of Mineral and Petroleum Resources in Brookman St; strict conditions apply; details from the visitor centre. *Lake Ballard:* a collection of 51 black steel sculptures created by world-renowned artist Antony Gormley are scattered through the vast 10 sq km white salt plain of Lake Ballard. Made using scans of locals from the nearby town of Menzies, these taut, stick-like body-forms are best seen at sunrise and sunset; 80 km NW. *Gwalia:* almost a ghost town, it has a museum, the restored State Hotel and tin houses preserved in their lived-in state; *see Leonora; 233 km N.* *Laverton:* has historic buildings saved by the nickel industry; 100 km E. *Golden Quest Discovery Trail:* 965 km drive that traces the gold rushes of the 1890s through Coolgardie, Kalgoorlie–Boulder, Menzies, Kookynie, Gwalia, Leonora and Laverton; pick up the map, book and CD at the visitor centre. *Golden Pipeline Heritage Trail:* follow the course of the pipeline from Mundaring Weir to Mt Charlotte. Finding a reliable water supply to support the eastern goldfields' booming population became imperative after the 1890s gold rush. C. Y. O'Connor's solution was radically brilliant: the construction of a reservoir at Mundaring in the hills outside Perth and a 556 km water pipeline to Kalgoorlie. His project was criticised relentlessly by the press and public, which affected O'Connor deeply. On 19 Mar 1902 he went for his usual morning ride along the beach in Fremantle. As he neared Robb Jetty, he rode his horse into the sea and shot himself. The pipeline was a success, delivering as promised 22 million litres of water a day to Kalgoorlie, and continues to operate today. On the coast just south of Fremantle, a half-submerged statue of a man on a horse is a poignant tribute to this man of genius; guidebook available at visitor centre. *Tours:* self-drive or guided 4WD tours available to many attractions. Also fossicking, prospecting, camping and museum tours, and self-guide wildflower tours; details at visitor centre. *Scenic flights:* flights over Coolgardie, the Superpit, Lake Lefroy; details at visitor centre.

TOWNS NEARBY: Coolgardie 37 km, Norseman 164 km, Leonora 207 km, Southern Cross 212 km

Apr–Oct, 10am–1pm Mon–Fri Nov–Mar; Burrup Peninsula; 30 km N. *Aboriginal rock carvings:* there are more than 10 000 engravings on the Burrup Peninsula alone, including some of the earliest examples of art in Australia. A debate is currently raging over the damage being done to this magnificent outdoor gallery by the adjacent gas project; check with visitor centre for locations. *Dampier Archipelago:* 42 islands and islets ideal for swimming, snorkelling, boating, whale-watching and fishing; take a boat tour from Dampier. *Montebello Islands:* site of Australia's first shipwreck, the *Tryal*, which ran aground and sank in 1622. It is now a good spot for snorkelling, beachcombing, fishing and diving; beyond Dampier Archipelago. *Scenic flights:* over the Pilbara outback; details at visitor centre.

TOWNS NEARBY: Roebourne 32 km, Port Hedland 190 km, Onslow 205 km, Tom Price 238 km

Katanning
Pop. 3806
Map ref. 574 F8 | 576 E9

i Old Mill, cnr Austral Tce and Clive St; (08) 9821 4390; www.katanningwa.com

94.9 Hot FM, 612 AM ABC Radio National

Katanning lies in the middle of a prosperous grain-growing and pastoral area. A significant development in the town's history was the 1889 completion of the Great Southern Railway, which linked Perth and Albany. Construction was undertaken at both ends, and a cairn north of town marks the spot where the lines were joined.

Old Mill Museum: built in 1889, it features an outstanding display of vintage roller flour-milling processes; Cnr Clive St and Austral Tce. *All Ages Playground and Miniature Steam Railway:* scenic grounds with playground equipment for all ages. Covered shoes required to ride the train, which runs on the 2nd and 4th Sun of each month; Cnr Great Southern Hwy and Clive St. *Kobeelya:* a majestic residence (1902) with 7 bedrooms, ballroom, billiard room, tennis courts and croquet lawn, now a conference centre; Brownie St. *Old Winery Ruins:* inspect the ruins of the original turreted distillery and brick vats, with old ploughs and machinery on display; Andrews Rd. *Historical Museum:* the original school building has been converted into a museum of local memorabilia; open 2–4pm Sun, or by appt; Taylor St. *Sale Yards:* one of the biggest yards in Australia, sheep sales every Wed at 8am; viewing platform for visitors; Daping St. *Heritage Rose Garden:* with roses dating from 1830; Austral Tce. *Piesse Memorial Statue:* unveiled in 1916, this statue of Frederick H. Piesse, the founder of Katanning, was sculpted by P. C. Porcelli, a well-known artist in the early days of WA; Austral Tce. *Art Gallery:* a changing display and local collection; closed Sun; Austral Tce.

Farmers markets: Pemble St; 3rd Sat each month. *Spring Lamb Festival:* Oct.

Kimberley Restaurant: intimate dining; New Lodge Motel and Function Centre, 172 Clive St; (08) 9821 1788. *Loretta @ Feddy:* family-friendly restaurant; Federal Hotel, 111 Clive St; (08) 9821 7128.

Woodchester Bed & Breakfast: 19 Clive St; (08) 9821 7007.

Police Pools (Twonkwillingup): site of the original camp for the district's first police officers. Enjoy swimming, picnicking, birdwatching and bushwalking; 3 km S. *Lake Ewlyamartup:* picturesque freshwater lake ideal for picnicking, swimming,

boating and waterskiing, particularly in early summer when the water level is high; 22 km E. *Katanning-Piesse Heritage Trail:* 20 km self-drive/walk trail; map at visitor centre. *Watersports:* the lakes surrounding the town are excellent for recreational boating, waterskiing and swimming; details at visitor centre.

TOWNS NEARBY: Kojonup 40 km, Wagin 47 km, Cranbrook 68 km, Narrogin 91 km, Wickepin 101 km

Kellerberrin
Pop. 868
Map ref. 574 F4 | 576 D7

i Shire offices, 110 Massingham St; (08) 9045 4006; www.kellerberrin.wa.gov.au

107.3 FM ABC Radio National, 1215 AM ABC Local Radio

Centrally located in the wheat belt, Kellerberrin is 200 kilometres east of Perth. In springtime, magnificent displays of wildflowers adorn the roadsides, hills and plains around the town.

International Art Space Kellerberrin Australia This art gallery, built in 1998, is home to an ambitious art project. International artists are given the opportunity to live and work within the local community for a 3-month period. Workshops and mentoring programs provide collaboration between these established artists and emerging Australian talent. Many of the exhibitions created are then displayed in larger venues throughout Australia and the world. Massingham St; (08) 9045 4739.

Pioneer Park and Folk Museum: located in the old Agricultural Hall, displays include local artefacts, farming machinery and photographic records. Pick up the key from tourist information or Dryandra building next door; Cnr Leake and Bedford sts. *Centenary Park:* children's playground, in-line skate and BMX track, maze, heritage walkway and barbecue facilities all in the centre of town; Leake St. *Golden Pipeline Lookout:* interpretive information at viewing platform with views of the countryside and pipeline; via Moore St. *Heritage trail:* self-guide town walk that includes historic buildings and churches; brochure available.

Keela Dreaming Cultural Festival: odd-numbered years, Mar. *Central Wheatbelt Harness Racing Cup:* May.

Kellerberrin Motor Hotel: hearty counter meals; 108 Massingham St; (08) 9045 5000.

Durokoppin Reserve: take a self-guide scenic drive through this woodland area, which is beautiful in the wildflower season; contact visitor centre for map; 27 km N. *Kokerbin Wave Rock:* the third largest monolith in WA. The Devil's Marbles and a historic well are also at the site. Restricted vehicle access to the summit, but the walk will reward with panoramic views; 30 km S. *Cunderdin:* museum housed in the No 3 pumping station has displays on the pipeline, wheat-belt farming and the Meckering earthquake; 45 km W. *Golden Pipeline Heritage Trail:* one of the main stops along the trail, which follows the water pipeline of C. Y. O'Connor from Mundaring Weir to the goldfields; guidebook available at visitor centre. *See Kalgoorlie–Boulder.*

TOWNS NEARBY: Merredin 55 km, Corrigin 79 km, Beverley 92 km, York 94 km, Northam 99 km

Kojonup
Pop. 1124
Map ref. 574 F9 | 576 D10

i 143 Albany Hwy; (08) 9831 0500; www.kojonupvisitors.com

558 AM ABC Local Radio, 612 AM ABC Radio National

A freshwater spring first attracted white settlement of the town now known as Kojonup. In 1837 Alfred Hillman arrived in the area after being sent by Governor Stirling to survey a road between Albany and the Swan River Colony. He was guided to the freshwater spring by local Aboriginal people and his promising report back to Governor Stirling resulted in a military outpost being established. The Shire of Kojonup was the first shire in Western Australia to have a million sheep within its boundaries.

 Kodja Place Visitor and Interpretative Centre: fascinating and fun displays about the land and its people, with stories of Aboriginal heritage and white settlement. It also includes the Australian Rose Maze, the only rose garden in the world growing exclusively Australian roses; 143 Albany Hwy. **Kojonup Museum:** in historic schoolhouse building with displays of local memorabilia; open by appt; Spring St. **A. W. Potts Kokoda Track Memorial:** a life-size statue of the brigadier facing towards his beloved farm 'Barrule'; Albany Hwy. **Centenary of Federation Wool Wagon:** commemorates the significance of the sheep industry to the Kojonup community; Albany Hwy. **Kojonup Spring:** grassy picnic area; Spring St. **Military Barracks:** built in 1845, this is one of the oldest surviving military buildings in WA and features historical information about the building; open by appt; Spring St. **Elverd's Cottage:** display of pioneer tools and farm machinery; open by appt; Soldier Rd. **Kodja Place Bush Tucker Walk:** follows the old railway line east where 3000 trees and shrubs indigenous to the area have been planted; map from visitor centre. **Town walk trail:** self-guide signposted walk of historic sights; map from visitor centre.

 Wildflower Week: Sept. **Kojonup Show:** Oct.

 Commercial Hotel: homely pub; 118 Albany Hwy; (08) 9831 1044.

 Kojonup Caravan Park: 75 Newstead Rd; (08) 9831 1127.

 Myrtle Benn Memorial Flora and Fauna Sanctuary: walk one of the numerous trails among local flora and fauna including many protected species; Tunney Rd; 1 km w. **Farrar Reserve:** scenic bushland and spectacular wildflower display in season; Blackwood Rd; 8 km w. **Australian Bush Heritage Block:** natural woodland featuring wandoo and species unique to the South–West; 16 km N. **Lake Towerinning:** boating, waterskiing, horseriding, camping; 40 km NW. **Aboriginal guided tours:** tours of Aboriginal heritage sites; details and bookings at visitor centre.

TOWNS NEARBY: Katanning 40 km, Wagin 60 km, Cranbrook 63 km, Boyup Brook 71 km, Bridgetown 96 km

Kulin

Pop. 354
Map ref. 574 G6 | 576 E8

 Resource Centre, Johnston St; (08) 9880 1021; www.kulin.wa.gov.au

 720 AM ABC Local Radio

The sheep- and grain-farming districts surrounding Kulin provide spectacular wildflower displays in season. The flowering gum, *Eucalyptus macrocarpa*, is the town's floral emblem. A stand of jarrah trees, not native to the area and not known to occur elsewhere in the wheat belt, grows near the town. According to Aboriginal legend, two tribal groups met at the site and, as a sign of friendship, drove their spears into the ground. From these spears, the jarrah trees grew. The Kulin Bush Races event

has expanded from horseracing to a major attraction including a weekend of live music, an art and craft show, foot races and Clydesdale horserides. In the months prior to the Kulin Races, tin horses appear in the paddocks lining the road on the way to the racetrack. These, along with the tin horses from past years, create an unusual spectacle.

 Tin Horse Highway: starting in town and heading to the Jilakin racetrack, the highway is lined with horses made from a wide variety of materials. **Kulin Herbarium:** specialising in local flora; open by appt; Johnston St. **Butlers Garage:** built in the 1930s, this restored garage houses a museum of cars and machinery; open by appt; Cnr Johnston and Stewart sts. **Memorial Slide and Swimming Pool:** the longest water slide in regional WA; pool open 12–7pm Tues–Fri, 10am–7pm weekends/public holidays, summer months; check for opening hours of water slide; Holt Rock Rd; (08) 9880 1222.

 Charity Car Rally: Sept. **Kulin Bush Races:** Oct. **Longneck Roughneck Des Cook Memorial Quick Shears Shearing Competition:** Oct.

 Kulin Hotel: Australian pub; Johnston St; (08) 9880 1201.

 Macrocarpa Walk Trail: 1 km self-guide signposted walk trail through natural bush; brochure available at visitor centre; 1 km w. **Jilakin Rock and Lake:** granite monolith overlooking a 1214 ha lake; 16 km E. **Hopkins Nature Reserve:** important flora conservation area; 20 km E. **Buckley's Breakaways:** unusual pink and white rock formations; 70 km E. **Dragon Rocks Nature Reserve:** wildflower reserve with orchids and wildlife; 75 km E.

TOWNS NEARBY: Corrigin 46 km, Lake Grace 56 km, Wickepin 63 km, Hyden 70 km, Narrogin 96 km

Kununurra

Pop. 85 814
Map ref. 581 O4 | 585 M5 | 590 A11 | 592 A2

 75 Coolibah Dr; (08) 9168 1177 or 1800 586 868; www.visitkununurra.com

 102.5 WA FM, 819 AM ABC Local Radio

Kununurra lies in the East Kimberley region not far from the Northern Territory border. It was established in the 1960s alongside Lake Kununurra on the Ord River at the centre of the massive Ord River Irrigation Scheme. It has transformed a dusty, million-acre cattle station into a habitat for waterbirds, fish and crocodiles; the hills and ridges of the former station have become islands. Adjacent is the magnificent Mirima National Park. Lake Argyle to the south, in the Carr Boyd Range, was created by the damming of the Ord River and is the largest body of fresh water in Australia. The word 'Kununurra' means 'meeting of big waters' in the language of the local Aboriginal people. The climate in Kununurra and the East Kimberley is divided into two seasons, the Dry and the Wet. The Dry extends from April to October and is characterised by blue skies, clear days and cool nights. The Wet, from November to March, is a time of hot, humid days, when frequent thunderstorms deliver most of the annual rainfall to the region.

 Historical Society Museum: artefacts and photos provide a historical overview of the town; 72 Coolibah Dr; (08) 9169 3331; 11am–5pm Mon–Fri April–Nov or on request; (08) 9169 1600. **Lovell Gallery:** art gallery exhibiting Kimberley artworks for sale; seasonal opening times, check with visitor centre;

[KUNUNURRA] VIEW FROM KELLY'S KNOB LOOKOUT

144 Konkerberry Dr; (08) 9168 1781. *Waringarri Aboriginal Arts:* large and varied display of Aboriginal art and artefacts for sale; open daily, weekends by appt; 16 Speargrass Rd; (08) 9168 2212. *Red Rock Art:* gallery and studio for Indigenous painters from across the Kimberley; 50 Coolibah Dr; (08) 9169 3000. *Birdland Functional Art:* outstanding pottery and ceramics; 22 Poincettia Way; (08) 9168 1616. *Kelly's Knob Lookout:* panoramic view of town and Ord Valley; off Speargrass Rd. *Celebrity Tree Park:* arboretum on the shore of Lake Kununurra where celebrities, including John Farnham, HRH Princess Anne, Harry Butler and Rolf Harris, have planted trees. Lily Creek Lagoon at the edge of the park is a good spot for birdwatching. The boat ramp was once part of the road to Darwin; off Victoria Hwy. *Historical Society walk:* brochure available at visitor centre.

Lake Argyle Swim: May. *Ord Valley Muster:* May/June. *Kimberley Moon Experience:* June. *Kununurra Races:* Aug/Sept. *Dam to Dam Dinghy Dash:* Sept.

Gulliver's Tavern: typical pub fare; 186 Cottontree Ave; (08) 9168 1666. *Ivanhoes Gallery Restaurant:* international cuisine; All Seasons Kununurra, Messmate Way; (08) 9168 4000. *Kelly's Bar & Grill:* relaxed dining; Kununurra Country Club Resort, 47 Coolibah Dr; (08) 9168 1024 or 1800 808 999. *PumpHouse Restaurant:* stylish casual restaurant overlooking the Ord River; 3005 Lakeview Dr; (08) 9169 3222.

Discovery Holiday Parks – Lake Kununurra: Lakeview Dr; (08) 9168 1031. *Hidden Valley Caravan Park:* Weaber Plains Rd; (08) 9168 1790. *Ivanhoe Village Caravan Resort:* Cnr Ivanhoe Rd and Coolibah Dr; (08) 9169 1995. *Kimberleyland Holiday Park:* 1519 Victoria Hwy; (08) 9168 1280. *Kununurra Lakeside Resort – Caravan Park:* 50 Casuarina Way; (08) 9169 1092. *Town Caravan Park:* 40 Bloodwood Dr; (08) 9168 1763.

Mirima National Park Known by locals as the 'mini-Bungle Bungles', a striking feature of this park is the boab trees that grow on the rock faces, the seeds having been carried there by rock wallabies and left in their dung. There are walking trails within the park, and between May and Aug guided walks are available. Details at visitor centre; 2 km E.

Ivanhoe Farms: tastings and sales of melons and other local produce; open Apr–Sept; Ivanhoe Rd; (08) 9168 1774; 1 km N. *Lake Kununurra:* formed after the completion of the Diversion Dam as part of the Ord River Scheme, the lake is home to a large variety of flora and fauna and is ideal for sailing, rowing, waterskiing and boat tours; details at visitor centre; 2 km S. *City of Ruins:* unusual sandstone formation of pinnacles and outcrops that resemble the ruins of an ancient city; off Weaber

Plains Rd; 6 km N. *Ord River and Diversion Dam:* abundance of wildlife and spectacular scenery and a variety of watersports and cruises available; details at visitor centre; 7 km W. *Ivanhoe Crossing:* permanently flooded causeway is an ideal fishing spot; Ivanhoe Rd; 12 km N. *Hoochery Distillery:* visit a traditional old Country and Western Saloon Bar or take a tour of the only licensed distillery in WA; open daily May–Sept; 9am–4pm Tues–Fri, 9am–12pm Sat Oct–Apr; 300 Weaber Plains Rd; (08) 9168 2467; 15 km N. *Zebra Rock Gallery:* view the amazing display of zebra rock, nearly 600 million years old and believed to be unique to the Kimberley, or feed fish from the lakeside jetty; Packsaddle Rd; 16 km S. *Middle Springs:* picturesque spot with diverse birdlife; 4WD access only; 30 km N. *Black Rock Falls:* spectacular waterfall during the wet season that spills over rocks stained by the minerals in the water; 4WD access only; Apr–Oct (subject to road conditions); 32 km N. *Parry Lagoons Nature Reserve:* enjoy birdwatching from a shaded bird hide at Marlgu Billabong or scan the wide vistas of the flood plain and distant hills afforded from the lookout at Telegraph Hill; 65 km NW. *The Grotto:* ideal swimming hole (in the wet season) at the base of 140 stone steps; 70 km NW. *Argyle Downs Homestead Museum:* built in 1884 and relocated when the lake was formed, the building is a fine example of an early station homestead; open 7am–4pm dry season, wet season by appt; Parker Rd; (08) 9168 1177; 70 km S. *Lake Argyle:* the view of the hills that pop out of the main body of water is said to resemble a crocodile basking in the sun and is known locally as Crocodile Ridge. Fishing, birdwatching, camping, bushwalking, sailing, canoeing and lake cruises are all available; 72 km S. *Argyle Diamond Mine:* the largest producing diamond mine in the world. Access is via tour only; details at visitor centre; 120 km S. *Purnululu National Park:* scenic flights available in town; 375 km S; *see Halls Creek.* *Mitchell River National Park:* one of the Kimberley's newest national parks protects this scenic and biologically important area. Mitchell Falls and Surveyor's Pool are the 2 main attractions for visitors. The area is remote with 4WD access to the park only, and is about a 16 hr drive from Kununurra; 680 km NW. *Scenic flights:* flights from town take visitors over the remarkable Bungle Bungles, Argyle Diamond Mine, Mitchell Plateau or Kalumburu; details and bookings at visitor centre. *Tours:* bushwalks, safaris, camping, canoeing, 4WD or coach; details at visitor centre.

TOWNS NEARBY: Wyndham 74 km, Timber Creek (NT) 186 km

Lake Grace

Pop. 503
Map ref. 574 H7 | 576 E9

i Stationmaster's house, Stubbs St; (08) 9865 2140; www.lakegrace.wa.gov.au

91.7 WA FM, 531 AM ABC Local Radio

The area around Lake Grace is a major grain-growing region for the state, producing wheat, canola, oats, barley, lupins and legumes. Sandy plains nearby are transformed into a sea of colour at the height of the wildflower season in September and October.

Inland Mission Hospital Museum: the only remaining inland mission hospital in WA, this fully restored building (est. 1926) is now a fascinating medical museum. Approach the building via Apex Park along the interpretive walkway; open daily by appt; Stubbs St. *Mural:* artwork depicting pioneering women was begun in 1912; Stubbs St. *Memorial Swimming Pool:* includes water playground for children; open 11am–6pm daily Oct–Apr; Bishop St.

Market: visitor centre; every Sat Oct–Mar.
Art Exhibition: Oct.

 Lake Grace Hotel: pub fare; Stubbs St; (08) 9865 1219.

Wildflower walk: easy walk through natural bushland with informative signage; details at visitor centre; 3 km E. **Lake Grace:** combination of 2 shallow salt lakes that gives the town its name; 9 km w. **Lake Grace Lookout:** ideal spot to view the north and south lakes system; 12 km w. **White Cliffs:** unusual rock formation and picnic spot on private property; details at visitor centre; 17 km s. **Holland Track:** in 1893 John Holland and his partners cut a track from Broomehill through bushland to Coolgardie in the goldfields. Hundreds of prospectors and their families trudged along this track in search of fortune, and cartwheel ruts are still evident today. A plaque marks the place where the track crosses the road; Newdegate Rd; 23 km E. **Dingo Rock:** now on private property, this reservoir for water run-off was built by labourers from Fremantle Gaol. Wildflowers are beautiful in season; details at visitor centre; 25 km NE. **Newdegate:** small town with a pioneer museum in the heritage-listed Hainsworth building. One of WA's major agricultural events, the Machinery Field Days, is held here in Sept each year; 52 km E.

TOWNS NEARBY: Kulin 56 km, Hyden 81 km, Wickepin 97 km, Corrigin 102 km, Katanning 106 km

Lake King

Pop. 219
Map ref. 576 G8

ⓘ Lake's Breaks, Church Ave; (08) 9874 4007; www.lakeking.com.au

92.5 WA FM, 531 AM ABC Local Radio

This small rural town lies on the fringe of sheep- and grain-farming country. With a tavern and several stores, Lake King is a stopping place for visitors travelling across the arid country around Frank Hann National Park to Norseman (adequate preparations must be made as there are no stops en route). Outstanding wildflowers in late spring include rare and endangered species.

Self-guide walks: signposted walk trails; maps from visitor centre.

Lake King Tavern Motel: traditional meals; Varley Rd; (08) 9874 4048.

Lake King and Causeway: 9 km road across the salt lake studded with native scrub and wildflowers. Lookout at eastern end; 5 km w. **Pallarup Reserve:** pioneer well and lake with abundant wildflowers in season; 15 km s. **Mt Madden:** cairn and lookout with picnic area that forms part of the Roe Heritage Trail; 25 km SE. **Frank Hann National Park:** good example of inland sand plain heath flora with seasonal wildflowers. The rabbit-proof fence forms a boundary to the park. Access is subject to weather conditions; 32 km E. **Roe Heritage Drive Trail:** begins south of Lake King and covers natural reserves and historic sites. It offers panoramic views from the Roe Hill lookout and retraces part of J. S. Roe's explorations in 1848; map available at visitor centre.

TOWNS NEARBY: Ravensthorpe 64 km, Hyden 105 km, Lake Grace 114 km, Bremer Bay 148 km, Kulin 151 km

Laverton

Pop. 314
Map ref. 577 I2 | 579 I12

 Great Beyond Explorers Hall of Fame, Augusta St; (08) 9031 1361; www.laverton.wa.gov.au

102.1 WA FM, 106.1 FM ABC Local Radio

Surrounded by old mine workings and modern mines, Laverton is on the edge of the Great Victoria Desert. In 1900 Laverton was a booming district of gold strikes and mines, yet gold price fluctuations in the late 1950s made it almost a ghost town. In 1969 nickel was discovered at Mount Windarra, which sparked a nickel boom. Early in 1995 a cyclone blew through Laverton, leaving it flooded and isolated for three months. Mines closed down and supplies were brought in by air. During this time, locals held a 'wheelie bin' race from the pub to the sports club, which is now an annual event. Today the town has two major gold mines and one of the world's largest nickel-mining operations. Wildflowers are brilliant in season.

Historic buildings Restored buildings include the courthouse, the Old Police Station and Gaol, and the Mt Crawford Homestead. The original Police Sergeant's House is now the local museum with displays of local memorabilia. Contact visitor centre for details.

Great Beyond Explorers Hall of Fame: uses cutting-edge technology to bring to life the characters and stories of the early explorers of the region. It also houses the visitor centre; Augusta St. **Cross-Cultural Centre:** houses the Laverton Outback Gallery, a collection of art and artefacts made and sold by the local Wongi people; Augusta St.

Race Day: June. **Laverton Day and Wheelie Bin Race:** Nov.

The Desert Inn Hotel: traditional meals; 2 Laver Pl; (08) 9031 1188.

 Giles Breakaway: scenic area with interesting rock formation; 25 km E. **Lake Carey:** swimming and picnic spot exhibiting starkly contrasting scenery; 26 km w. **Windarra Heritage Trail:** walk includes rehabilitated mine site and interpretive plaques; Windarra Minesite Rd; 28 km NW. **Empress Springs:** discovered in 1896 by explorer David Carnegie and named after Queen Victoria. The spring is in limestone at the end of a tunnel that runs from the base of a 7 m deep cave. A chain ladder allows access to the cave. Enclosed shoes and torch required; 305 km NE. **Warburton:** the Tjulyuru Arts and Culture Regional Gallery showcases the art and culture of the Ngaanyatjarraku people; 565 km NE. **Golden Quest Discovery Trail:** Laverton forms part of the 965 km self-guide drive trail of the goldfields; book, map and CD available. **Outback Highway:** travel the 1200 km to Uluṟu from Laverton via the Great Central Rd. All roads are unsealed but regularly maintained.

Travellers note: *Permits are required to travel through Aboriginal reserves and communities – they can be obtained from the Dept of Indigenous Affairs in Perth, and the Central Lands Council in Alice Springs. Water is scarce. Fuel, supplies and accommodation are available at the Tjukayirla, Warburton and Warakurna roadhouses. Check road conditions before departure at the Laverton Police Station or Laverton Shire Offices; road can be closed due to heavy rain.*

TOWNS NEARBY: Leonora 108 km

Leonora

 Rural Transaction Centre, cnr Tower and Trump sts; (08) 9037 7016 ; www.leonora.wa.gov.au

102.5 WA FM, 105.7 FM ABC Local Radio

Leonora is the busy railhead for the north-eastern goldfields and the surrounding pastoral region. Mount Leonora was discovered in 1869 by John Forrest. Gold was later found in the area and, in 1896, the first claims were pegged. By 1908 Leonora boasted seven hotels and was the largest centre on the north-eastern goldfields. Many of the original buildings were constructed of corrugated iron and hessian, as these were versatile materials and light to transport. You can get a glimpse of these structures at nearby Gwalia, a town once linked to Leonora by tram.

Historic buildings: buildings from the turn of the century include the police station, courthouse, fire station and Masonic Lodge; details at visitor centre. *Tank Hill:* excellent view over town; Queen Victoria St. *Miners Cottages:* miners camps, auctioned and restored by locals; around town.

Leonora Golden Gift and Festival: May/June.

White House Hotel: traditional pub; 120 Tower St; (08) 9037 6030.

Gwalia Gwalia is a mining ghost town that has been restored to show visitors what life was like in the pioneering gold-rush days. The original mine manager's office now houses the Gwalia Historical Museum with displays of memorabilia that include the largest steam winding engine in the world and a headframe designed by Herbert Hoover, the first mine manager of the Sons of Gwalia mine and eventually the 31st President of the United States. Self-guide heritage walk available. 4 km s.

Mt Leonora: sweeping views of the surrounding plains and mining operations; 4 km s. *Malcolm Dam:* picnic spot at the dam, which was built in 1902 to provide water for the railway; 15 km e. *Kookynie:* tiny township with restored shopfronts, and historic memorabilia on display at the Grand Hotel. The nearby Niagara Dam was built in 1897 with cement carried by camel from Coolgardie; 92 km se. *Menzies:* small goldmining town with an interesting historic cemetery. View 'stick figure' sculptures, for which locals posed, about 55 km west of town on bed of Lake Ballard; 110 km s. *Golden Quest Discovery Trail:* self-guide drive trail of 965 km takes in many of the towns of the northern goldfields; maps, book and CD available at visitor centre, or visit www.goldenquesttrail.com

TOWNS NEARBY: Laverton 108 km, Kalgoorlie–Boulder 207 km, Coolgardie 230 km

Madura

 Madura Pass Oasis Motel and Roadhouse, Eyre Hwy; (08) 9039 3464; www.dundas.wa.gov.au

Madura, comprising a roadhouse, motel and caravan park on the Eyre Highway, lies midway between Adelaide and Perth on the Nullarbor Plain. It is remarkable, given the isolation of the area, that Madura Station was settled in 1876 to breed horses, which were then shipped across to India for use by the British Army. Now Madura is surrounded by private sheep stations. Locals operate on Central Western Time, 45 minutes ahead of the rest of Western Australia.

Blowholes: smaller versions of the one found at Caiguna. Look for the red marker beside the track; 1 km n. *Madura Pass Lookout:* spectacular views of the Roe Plains and Southern Ocean; 1 km w on highway.

TOWNS NEARBY: Cocklebiddy 89 km, Caiguna 151 km, Eucla 178 km

Mandurah

75 Mandurah Tce; (08) 9550 3999; www.visitmandurah.com

Local Radio 6MM (1116 AM), 97.3 Coast FM, 810 AM ABC Radio National

Mandurah, which has long been a popular holiday destination for Perth residents, is today the southernmost point of Perth's ever-expanding commuter belt. The Murray, Serpentine and Harvey rivers meet at the town to form the vast inland waterway of Peel Inlet and the Harvey Estuary. This river junction was once a meeting site for Aboriginal groups who travelled here to barter. The town's name is derived from the Aboriginal word 'mandjar', meaning trading place. The river and the Indian Ocean offer a variety of watersports and excellent fishing and prawning. But the aquatic activity for which Mandurah is perhaps best known is crabbing. It brings thousands during summer weekends, wading the shallows with scoop nets and stout shoes.

Christ's Church Built in 1870, this Anglican church has hand-worked pews believed to be the work of early settler Joseph Cooper. Many of the district's pioneers are buried in the churchyard, including Thomas Peel, the founder of Mandurah. In 1994 the church was extended and a bell-tower added to house 8 bells from England; Cnr Pinjarra Rd and Sholl St.

Australian Sailing Museum: displays and models of vessels from the 1860s to Olympic yachts; open daily; 22 Ormsby Tce; (08) 9534 7256. *Hall's Cottage:* (1832) restored home of one of the original settlers, Henry Hall; open 2–5pm Sun; Leighton Rd, Halls Head. *Mandurah Community Museum:* (1898) originally a school then a police station, now houses displays on Mandurah's social, fishing and canning histories; open 10am–4pm Tues–Fri, 11am–3pm Sat and Sun; 3 Pinjarra Rd; (08) 9550 3680. *King Carnival Amusement Park:* fun-fair attractions including Ferris wheel and mini golf; open 10am–10pm Sat, Sun and school holidays; Leighton Pl; (08) 9581 3735. *Just 4 Fun Aqua Park:* jump, slide and splash in this water-based adventure park of inflatable equipment, with a knee-deep area for toddlers; open 10.30am–5pm Sat and Sun Dec–Mar, daily during school holidays; Western Foreshore. *Estuary Drive:* scenic drive along Peel Inlet and Harvey Estuary.

Crab Fest: Mar. *Stretch Festival:* arts and cultural festival; May. *Mandurah Boat Show:* Oct. *Mandjar Markets:* off Mandurah Tce on eastern foreshore; 9am–4pm every Sun Oct–Apr.

Cafe Pronto: international cuisine; Cnr Pinjarra Rd and Mandurah Tce; (08) 9535 1004. *Red Manna Waterfront Restaurant:* waterfront seafood; upstairs, 5/9 Mandurah Tce; (08) 9581 1248. *Scusi:* fine dining; Shop 6, Lot 4 Old Coast Rd, Halls Head; (08) 9586 3479. *The Miami Bakehouse:* bakery cafe; Falcon Grove Shopping Centre, Old Coast Rd; (08) 9534 2705. *Cafe on the Dam:* innovative cafe; Serpentine Dam, Kingsbury Dr, Jarrahdale; (08) 9525 9920. *The Tap Bar:* tapas restaurant; Old Coast Rd Shopping Centre; (08) 9535 1055.

Sunbreakers: international cuisine; 110 Mandurah Tce; (08) 9581 5556. *The Oyster Bar:* seafood wine bar overlooking marina; The Palladio, Dolphin Quay; (08) 9535 1880.

Bellavista Bed & Breakfast: 22 Anniston Loop, Meadow Springs; (08) 9583 4849. *Mandurah Caravan and Tourist Park:* 522 Pinjarra Rd, Furnissdale; (08) 9535 1171. *Nautica Lodge:* 203 Culeenup Rd, North Yunderup; (08) 9537 8000.

Peel and Geographe wine regions On the way to Margaret River from Perth, you might consider visiting the Peel wine region around the town of Mandurah, or Geographe further to the south. Peel Estate produces one of Australia's best shiraz wines. In Geographe, Capel Vale is also known for shiraz that packs a punch and riesling made from grapes grown elsewhere. Hackersley and Willow Bridge Estate are other wineries to visit.

Coopers Mill: the first flour mill in the Murray region, located on Cooleenup Island near the mouth of the Serpentine River. Joseph Cooper built it by collecting limestone rocks and, every morning, sailing them across to the island. Accessible only by water; contact visitor centre for information. *Yalgorup National Park:* swamps, woodlands and coastal lakes abounding with birdlife. Lake Clifton is 1 of only 3 places in Australia where the living fossils called thrombolites survive. A boardwalk allows close-up viewing; 45 km s. *Tours:* including estuary cruises and dolphin interaction tours; contact visitor centre for details.

TOWNS NEARBY: Pinjarra 18 km, Rockingham 28 km, Dwellingup 38 km, Thomson Bay 61 km, Harvey 63 km

Manjimup
Pop. 4236
Map ref. 572 H10 | 573 B1 | 574 D10 | 576 C10

i 80 Giblett St; (08) 9771 1831; www.manjimupwa.com

100.5 Hot FM, 738 AM ABC Local Radio

Manjimup is the gateway to the South-West region's tall-timber country. Magnificent karri forests and rich farmlands surround the town. While timber is the town's main industry, Manjimup is also the centre of a thriving fruit and vegetable industry that supplies both local and Asian markets. The area is well known for its apples and is the birthplace of the delicious Pink Lady apple.

Timber and Heritage Park A must-see for any visitor to Manjimup, this 10 ha park includes the state's only timber museum, an exhibition of old steam engines, an 18 m climbable fire-lookout tower and a historic village with an early settler's cottage, blacksmith's shop, old police station and lock-up, one-teacher school and early mill house. Set in natural bush and parkland, there are many delightful spots for picnics or barbecues. Cnr Rose and Edwards sts.

Manjimup Motocross 15000: June. *Festival of Country Gardens:* Oct/Nov. *Cherry Harmony Festival:* Dec.

Blue Tiger Cafe: superb cafe fare; 31B Rose St; (08) 9777 2555. *Cabernet Restaurant:* international cuisine; Kingsley Motel, 74 Chopping St; (08) 9771 1177 or 1800 359 177. *Déjà Vu Cafe:* family-friendly cafe; 43A Giblett St; (08) 9771 2978.

Fonty's Pool & Caravan Park: 699 Seven Day Rd; (08) 9771 2105. *Warren Way Caravan Park:* Lot 11 South Western Hwy; (08) 9771 1060.

One Tree Bridge In 1904 a single enormous karri tree was felled so that it dropped across the 25 m wide Donnelly River,

forming the basis of a bridge. Winter floods in 1966 swept most of the bridge away; the 17 m piece salvaged is displayed near the original site with information boards. Nearby is Glenoran Pool, a scenic spot for catching rainbow trout and marron in season, with walking trails and picnic areas. Graphite Rd; 21 km w.

Manjimup and Pemberton wine regions These two regions are stacked on top of one another beneath the Blackwood Valley. Well before wineries were established here, Dr John Gladstones studied the climate of the wider region and claimed that Manjimup had similar conditions to Bordeaux. Just like Bordeaux, merlots are strong. Visit Chestnut Grove to taste some of the best merlot, as well as its verdelho. The much denser wine region of Pemberton has vineyards squeezed in between the marri and karri forests. Wineries include Salitage and Fonty's Pool, with styles such as semillon, viognier, merlot and chardonnay.

King Jarrah: estimated to be 600 years old, this massive tree is the centrepiece for several forest walks; Perup Rd; 3 km E. *Wine and Truffle Company:* tastings and information about truffle farming and dog training; (08) 9777 2474; 7 km sw. *Fonty's Pool:* dammed in 1925 by Archie Fontanini for the irrigation of vegetables, it is now a popular swimming pool and picnic area in landscaped grounds; Seven Day Rd; 7 km s. *Dingup Church:* built in 1896 by the pioneer Giblett family and doubling as the school, this church is one of the few remaining local soapstone buildings; Balbarrup Rd; 8 km E. *Pioneer Cemetery:* poignant descriptions on headstones testify to the hardships faced by first settlers; Perup Rd; 8 km E. *Diamond Tree Lookout:* one of 8 tree towers constructed from the late 1930s as fire lookouts. Climb to the wooden cabin atop this 51 m karri, used as a fire lookout from 1941 to 1947; 9 km s. *Fontanini's Nut Farm:* gather chestnuts, walnuts, hazelnuts and fruit in season; open Apr–June; Seven Day Rd; 10 km s. *Nyamup:* old mill town redeveloped as a tourist village; 20 km SE. *Four Aces:* 4 giant karri trees 220–250 years old and 67–79 m high stand in Indian file; Graphite Rd; 23 km w. *Great Forest Trees Drive:* self-guide drive through Shannon National Park; contact visitor centre for map; 45 km s. *Perup Forest Ecology Centre:* night spotlight walks to see rare, endangered and common native animals; contact DEC on (08) 9771 7988 for details; 50 km E. *Lake Muir Lookout/Bird Observatory:* boardwalk over salt lake to bird hide; 55 km E.

TOWNS NEARBY: Pemberton 25 km, Bridgetown 31 km, Northcliffe 44 km, Nannup 46 km, Boyup Brook 50 km

Marble Bar
Pop. 194
Map ref. 578 E2 | 580 E12 | 583 K5

i 11 Francis St; (08) 9176 1375.

102.7 WA FM, 107.5 FM ABC Radio National

Marble Bar has gained a dubious reputation as the hottest town in Australia. For 161 consecutive days in 1923–24 the temperature in Marble Bar did not drop below 100°F (37.8°C). This mining town was named after a bar of mineral deposit that crosses the nearby Coongan River and was originally mistaken for marble. It proved to be jasper, a coloured variety of quartz.

Government buildings: built of local stone in 1895, now National Trust listed; General St.

Marble Bar Races: July.

Marble Bar Travellers Stop: seafood; Halse Rd; (08) 9176 1166.

Comet Gold Mine This mine operated from 1936 to 1955. The Comet is now a museum and tourist centre with displays of gemstones, rocks, minerals and local history. Also here is a 75 m high smoke stack, reputed to be the tallest in the Southern Hemisphere. Underground mine tours occur twice daily. (08) 9176 1015; 10 km s.

Marble Bar Pool: site of the famous jasper bar (splash water on it to reveal its colours) and a popular swimming spot; 4 km w. *Corunna Downs RAAF Base:* built in 1943 as a base for long-range attacks on the Japanese-occupied islands of the Indonesian archipelago; 40 km se. *Doolena Gorge:* watch the cliff-face glow bright red as the sun sets; 45 km nw.

TOWNS NEARBY: Port Hedland 152 km, Newman 242 km

Margaret River
see inset box on page 322

Meekatharra
Pop. 799
Map ref. 575 H9 | 578 E10

i Shire offices, 54 Main St; (08) 9981 1002; www.meekashire.wa.gov.au

103.1 WA FM, 106.3 FM ABC Local Radio

The name Meekatharra is believed to be an Aboriginal word meaning 'place of little water' – an apt description for a town sitting on the edge of a desert. Meekatharra is now the centre of a vast mining and pastoral area. It came into existence in the 1880s when gold was discovered in the area. However, the gold rush was short-lived and it was only the arrival of the railway in 1910 that ensured its survival. The town became the railhead at the end of the Canning Stock Route, a series of 54 wells stretching from the East Kimberleys to the Murchison. The railway was closed in 1978, but the town continues to provide necessary links to remote outback areas through its Royal Flying Doctor Service.

Royal Flying Doctor Service: operates an important base in Meekatharra; open to public 9am–2pm daily; Main St. *Old Courthouse:* National Trust building; Darlot St. *Meekatharra Museum:* photographic display and items of memorabilia from Meekatharra's past; open 8am–4.30pm Mon–Fri; shire offices, Main St. *State Battery:* relocated to the town centre in recognition of the early prospectors and miners; Main St. *Meeka Rangelands Discovery Trail:* walk or drive this trail for insight into the town's mining past, Aboriginal heritage and landscapes; maps at visitor centre.

The Royal Mail Hotel: counter meals; Main St; (08) 9981 1148.

Peace Gorge: this area of granite formations is an ideal picnic spot; 5 km n. *Meteorological Office:* watch the launching of weather balloons twice daily at the airport; tours available on (08) 9981 1191; 5 km se. *Bilyuin Pool:* swimming (but check water level in summer); 88 km nw. *Old Police Station:* remains of the first police station in the Murchison; Mt Gould; 156 km nw.

TOWNS NEARBY: Cue 109 km, Mount Magnet 175 km

Merredin
Pop. 2556
Map ref. 574 G3 | 576 E6

 Central Wheatbelt Visitor Centre, 85 Barrack St; (08) 9041 1666; www.wheatbelttourism.com

105.1 Hot FM, 107.3 FM ABC Radio National

Merredin started as a shanty town where miners stopped on their way to the goldfields. In 1893 the railway reached the town and a water catchment was established on Merredin Peak, guaranteeing the town's importance to the surrounding region. An incredible 40 per cent of the state's wheat is grown within a 100-kilometre radius of the town.

Cummins Theatre Heritage-listed theatre that was totally recycled from Coolgardie in 1928. Used regularly for local productions, events and visiting artists. Open 9am–3pm Mon–Fri; Bates St. *Military Museum:* significant collection of restored military vehicles and equipment; closed Sat; Great Eastern Hwy. *Old Railway Station Museum:* prize exhibits are the 1897 locomotive that once hauled the Kalgoorlie Express and the old signal box with 95 switching and signal levers; open 9am–3pm daily; Great Eastern Hwy. *Pioneer Park:* picnic area adjacent to the highway including a historic water tower that once supplied the steam trains; Great Eastern Hwy. *Merredin Peak Heritage Walk:* self-guide walk that retraces the early history of Merredin and its links with the goldfields and the railway; contact visitor centre for map. *Merredin Peak Heritage Trail:* leads to great views of the countryside, and a rock catchment channel and dam from the 1890s. Adjacent to the peak is the interpretation site of a WW II field hospital that had over 600 patients in 1942; off Benson Rd. *Tamma Parkland Trail:* a 1.2 km walk around this 23 ha of bushland will give an insight into the flora and fauna of the area. Wildflowers in spring; South Ave.

Community Show: Oct.

Denzils Restaurant: international cuisine; Merredin Olympic Motel, Great Eastern Hwy; (08) 9041 1588. *Gumtree Restaurant:* international cuisine; Merredin Motel, 10 Gamenya Ave; (08) 9041 1886.

Merredin Tourist Park: Cnr Great Eastern Hwy and Oats St; (08) 9041 1535. *Mukinbudin Caravan Park:* Cruickshank Rd; (08) 9047 1103.

Pumping Station No 4: built in 1902 but closed in 1960 to make way for electrically driven stations, this fine example of early industrial architecture was designed by C. Y. O'Connor; 3 km w. *Hunt's Dam:* one of several wells sunk by convicts under the direction of Charles Hunt in 1866. It is now a good spot for picnics and bushwalking; 5 km n. *Totadgin Conservation Park:* interpretive walk, Hunt's Well and mini rock formation similar to Wave Rock. Picnic tables and wildflowers in spring; 16 km sw. *Rabbit-Proof Fence:* roadside display gives an insight into the history of this feature; 25 km e. *Mangowine Homestead:* now a restored National Trust property, in the 1880s this was a wayside stop en route to the Yilgam goldfields. Nearby is the Billyacatting Conservation Park with interpretative signage; open 1–4pm Mon–Sat, 10am–4pm Sun (closed Jan); Nungarin; 40 km nw. *Shackelton:* Australia's smallest bank; 85 km sw. *Kokerbin Rock:* superb views from summit; 90 km sw. *Koorda:* museum and several wildlife reserves in area; 140 km nw.

TOWNS NEARBY: Kellerberrin 55 km, Corrigin 102 km, Southern Cross 104 km, Hyden 121 km, Kulin 132 km

Moora
Pop. 1606
Map ref. 574 B2 | 576 B6

 34 Padbury St; (08) 9651 1401; www.moora.wa.gov.au

90.9 WA FM, 612 AM ABC Radio National

On the banks of the Moore River, Moora is the largest town between Perth and Geraldton. The area in its virgin state was a large salmon gum forest. Many of these attractive trees can still be seen.

 Historical Society Genealogical Records and Photo Display: open by appt; Clinch St. *Painted Roads Initiative:* murals by community artists on and in town buildings.

Moora Races: Oct.

Moora Hotel: traditional pub; Cnr Berkshire valley Rd and Gardiner St; (08) 9651 1177.

The Berkshire Valley Folk Museum James Clinch, who came from England in 1839, created a village in the dry countryside of WA based on his home town in Berkshire. Over a 25-year period from 1847 Clinch built a homestead, barn, manager's cottage, stables, shearing shed and bridge. The elaborate buildings were made from adobe, pise, handmade bricks and unworked stone. Open by appt; 19 km E.

Western Wildflower Farm: one of the largest exporters of dried wildflowers in WA, with dried flowers, seeds and souvenirs for sale and an interpretive education centre; open 9am–5pm daily Easter–Christmas; Midlands Rd, Coomberdale; (08) 9651 8010; 19 km N. *Watheroo National Park:* site of Jingamia Cave; 50 km N. *Moora Wildflower Drive:* from Moora to Watheroo National Park, identifying flowers on the way; contact visitor centre for map.

TOWNS NEARBY: New Norcia 42 km, Gingin 79 km, Cervantes 91 km, Jurien Bay 100 km, Carnamah 106 km

Morawa
Pop. 594
Map ref. 576 B4

i Winfield St (May–Oct), (08) 9971 1421; or council offices, cnr Dreghorn and Prater sts, (08) 9971 1204; www.morawa.wa.gov.au

103.1 WA FM, 531 AM ABC Local Radio

Morawa, a small wheat-belt town, has the distinction of being home to the first commercial iron ore to be exported from Australia. In springtime the area around Morawa is ablaze with wildflowers.

Church of the Holy Cross and Old Presbytery From 1915 to 1939, the famous WA architect-priest Monsignor John C. Hawes designed a large number of churches and church buildings in WA's mid-west region. Morawa boasts 2 of them: the Church of the Holy Cross and an unusually small stone hermitage known as the Old Presbytery. The latter, which Hawes used when visiting the town, is reputed to be the smallest presbytery in the world with only enough room for a bed, table and chair. Both buildings are part of the Monsignor Hawes Heritage Trail. Church is usually open; if not, contact council offices; Davis St.

Historical Museum: housed in the old police station and gaol with displays of farm machinery, household items and a collection of windmills; open by appt; Cnr Prater and Gill sts.

Koolanooka Mine Site and Lookout: scenic views and a delightful wildflower walk in season; 9 km E. *Perenjori:* nearby town has historic St Joseph's Church, designed by Monsignor Hawes, and the Perenjori–Rothsay Heritage Trail, a 180 km self-drive tour taking in Rothsay, a goldmining ghost town; 18 km SE.

Bilya Rock Reserve: with a large cairn, reportedly placed there by John Forrest in the 1870s as a trigonometrical survey point; 20 km N. *Koolanooka Springs Reserve:* ideal for picnics; 26 km E.

TOWNS NEARBY: Carnamah 54 km, Mullewa 89 km, Dongara–Denison 105 km, Yalgoo 117 km, Greenough 127 km

Mount Barker

Pop. 1760
Map ref. 573 C9 | 574 G11 | 576 E11

i Old Railway Station, Albany Hwy; (08) 9851 1163; www.mountbarkertourismwa.com.au

92.1 FM ABC News Radio, 95.3 Hot FM

Mount Barker lies in the Great Southern region of Western Australia, with the Stirling Range to the north and the Porongurups to the east. The area was settled by Europeans in the 1830s. Vineyards were first established here in the late 1960s. Today, Mount Barker is a major wine-producing area.

Old Police Station and Gaol: built by convicts in 1867–68, it is now a museum of memorabilia; open 10am–4pm Sat and Sun, daily during school holidays, or by appt; Albany Hwy, north of town. *Banksia Farm:* complete collection of banksia and dryandra species; guided tours daily, closed July; Pearce Rd; (08) 9851 1770.

Mount Barker D'Vine Wine Festival: Jan. *Mount Barker Wildflower Festival:* Sept/Oct.

Porongurup Village Inn, Shop & Tearooms: traditional tearooms; 1972 Porongurup Rd, Porongurup; (08) 9853 1110. *The Vineyard Cafe:* hilltop cafe; Windrush Wines, cnr St Werburghs and Hay River rds; (08) 9851 1353.

Mt Barker Caravan Park: Albany Hwy; (08) 9851 1691. *Rayanne Homestead:* 101 Oatlands Rd; (08) 9851 1562.

Porongurup National Park This is a park of dramatic contrasts, from stark granite outcrops and peaks to lush forests of magnificent karri trees. Many unusual rock formations, such as Castle Rock and Balancing Rock, make the range a fascinating place for bush rambles. The Tree in the Rock, a mature karri, extends its roots down through a crevice in a granite boulder. 24 km E.

Great Southern wine region There are several impressive strings to the Great Southerns bow: riesling, chardonnay, pinot noir, cabernet sauvignon and shiraz. In Frankland River, Alkoomi is one of the region's oldest wineries, and Ferngrove Vineyards has won several awards. In Mount Barker, Plantagenet is a large, long-standing operation excelling in a range of styles, while Gilberts makes stunning riesling with the region's hallmark hints of lime and apple. A Summer wine festival is held each Mar in Porongurup. The local Castle Rock Estate has superb riesling and pinot noir, and sweeping views of the Porongurup Range. In Denmark you'll find the big names of Howard Park, which has the MadFish brand, and West Cape Howe Wines. In Albany, Wignalls Wines is known for pinot noir. Contact visitor centre for map.

Lookout and TV tower: easily pinpointed on the summit of Mt Barker by 168 m high television tower, it offers panoramic views of the area from the Stirling Ranges to Albany; 5 km SW. *St Werburgh's Chapel:* small mud-walled chapel (1872) overlooking Hay River Valley; 12 km SW. *Kendenup:* historic town, location of WA's first gold find; 16 km E. *Porongurup:* hosts Wine Summer Festival each Mar and boasts many small wineries; 24 km E.

continued on p. 323

 RADIO STATIONS   IN TOWN   WHAT'S ON   WHERE TO EAT   WHERE TO STAY   NEARBY

MARGARET RIVER

Pop. 5581
Map ref. 572 B8 | 574 B10 | 576 B10

[CAPE MENTELLE VINEYARD]

i 100 Bussell Hwy (cnr Tunbridge St); (08) 9780 5911; www.margaretriver.com

100.3 Hot FM, 1224 AM ABC Radio National

One of the best known towns in Western Australia, Margaret River is synonymous with world-class wines, magnificent coastal scenery, excellent surf breaks and spectacular cave formations. In addition, the region boasts a thriving arts scene, boutique breweries, gourmet food outlets, and restaurants with views of sweeping vineyards or the sparkling ocean. The bustling township lies on the Margaret River near the coast, 280 kilometres south-west of Perth.

Wine Tourism Showroom Although the first grapevines were only planted in the area in 1967, Margaret River is now considered to be one of the top wine-producing regions in Australia. A huge 20% of Australia's premium wines are made here. The 'terroir' is perfect for grape-growing: cool frost-free winters, good moisture-retaining soils and low summer rainfall provide a long, slow ripening period. These conditions produce greater intensity of fruit flavour, the starting point for all great wines. There are now some 150 wine producers in the region, many of which are open to the public for tastings and cellar-door sales. Others have restaurants and tours of their premises. A good place to start a wine tour is the Margaret River Wine Tourism Showroom at the visitor centre. It provides information about the regional wineries and vineyards, an interactive wineries screen, videos, a sensory display and wine-making paraphernalia. 100 Bussell Hwy.

Rotary Park: picnic area on the riverbank with a display steam engine; Bussell Hwy. *St Thomas More Catholic Church:* one of the first modern buildings built of rammed earth; Wallcliffe Rd. *Fudge Factory:* fudge and chocolate made before your eyes; open 10am–5pm daily; 152 Bussell Hwy; (08) 9758 8881. *Arts and crafts:* many in town, including Margaret River Gallery on Bussell Hwy; contact visitor centre for details.

Town Square Markets: 9am–12.30pm Sun in summer, 2nd Sun each month rest of year. *Leeuwin Concert:* Feb. *Margaret*

River Pro: Mar/Apr. *Margaret River Wine Region Festival:* Mar/Apr. *Cape to Cape MTB:* 4-day mountain bike race; Oct. *Flourish Margaret River:* Oct. *Margaret River Classic:* Oct/Nov. *Movies in the Vineyard at Cape Mentelle:* Dec–Apr.

Leeuwin Restaurant: superb international cuisine; Leeuwin Estate Winery, Stevens Rd; (08) 9759 0000. *Must Margaret River:* the charcuterie plate is the best in WA; 107 Bussell Hwy; (08) 9758 8877. *Cullen Restaurant:* seasonal menu in a relaxed vineyard setting; Cullen Wines, Caves Rd, Cowaramup; (08) 9755 5656. *Sea Gardens Cafe:* tasty menu and ocean views; 9 Mitchell Dr, Prevelly; (08) 9757 3074. *Udderly Divine Cafe:* dairy-themed cafe; 22 Bussell Hwy, Cowaramup; (08) 9755 5519. *Voyager Estate:* comfort food with big flavour; 41 Stevens Rd; (08) 9757 6354. *Watershed Winery Restaurant:* stunning views of rolling vineyards; Cnr Bussell Hwy and Darch Rd; (08) 9758 8633. *Wino's:* relaxing wine bar with great food; 85 Bussell Hwy; (08) 9758 7155. *Xanadu:* perfect for a long lunch; Boodjidup Rd; (08) 9758 9531.

Honeymoon Hill Estate: 128 Illawarra Ave; (08) 9757 3929. *Loaring Place Bed & Breakfast:* 15 Loaring Pl; (08) 9758 7002. *Margaret River Tourist Park:* 44 Station Rd; (08) 9757 2180. *Riverview Tourist Park:* 8 Willmott Ave; (08) 9757 2270. *Rosewood Guesthouse:* 54 Wallcliffe Rd; (08) 9757 2845. *Gracetown Caravan Park:* Cowaramup Bay Rd, Gracetown; (08) 9755 5301. *Taunton Farm Holiday Park:* Bussell Hwy, Cowaramup; (08) 9755 5334.

Margaret River wine region One of Australia's top wine regions, with cabernet sauvignon and chardonnay at the core of its reputation. Heralded by Australian wine critic James Halliday as the 'golden triangle' are 3 outstanding wineries. Leeuwin Estate is considered to make Australia's most exquisite chardonnay, and sells its exclusive wines as part of the winery's 'Art Series', with labels designed by leading contemporary Australian artists. The actual artworks can be viewed at the spectacular cellar door's art gallery, which includes works by the likes of Sir Sidney Nolan. The grounds also host the popular annual Leeuwin Concert Series. The second outstanding winery is Voyager Estate, with its distinctive Dutch architecture and elegant rose garden, is a lovely place for tasting top-shelf wines; while the third in the triumvirate, Cape Mentelle offers fantastic chardonnay and semillon sauvignon blanc. Other outstanding wineries include Vasse Felix, Moss Wood, Ashbrook Estate and Cullen. The surrounding countryside is especially beautiful because of the pockets of bushland that have been left among the vines, and the abundance of environmentally sensitive buildings. Excellent restaurants and accommodation are found just about everywhere. For a one-stop centre for tastings and sales, offering in-depth information on local wines and wineries head to the Margaret River Regional Wine Centre; 9 Bussell Hwy, Cowaramup; (08) 9755 5501; 10am–7pm Mon–Sat, 12–6pm Sun.

Mammoth and Lake caves, Leeuwin–Naturaliste National Park
Lying beneath the Leeuwin–Naturaliste Ridge that separates the hinterland from the coast is one of the world's most extensive and beautiful limestone cave systems. Mammoth Cave is home to the fossil remains of prehistoric animals. An audio self-guide tour lets you travel through the cave at your own pace (21 km sw). Only a few kilometres away is Lake Cave, with its famous reflective lake and delicate formations. Book your guided tour at the adjacent interpretive centre, CaveWorks, which also features a walk-through cave model, interactive displays and a boardwalk with spectacular views of a collapsed cavern (25 km sw). Further south, also in the national park, are Jewel and Moondyne caves; *see Augusta and Dunsborough*.

Amaze'n Margaret River: family-friendly venue with giant hedge maze, ground puzzles, outdoor games and picnic area; Cnr Bussell Hwy and Gnarawary Rd; (08) 9758 7439; 4 km s. *Eagles Heritage:* the largest collection of birds of prey in Australia, with free-flight displays at 11am and 1.30pm daily; Boodjidup Rd; (08) 9757 2960; 5 km sw. *Surfer's Pt:* the centre of surfing in Margaret River and home to the Margaret River Pro; 8 km w, just north of Prevelley. *Candy Cow:* free tastings of fudge, nougat

and honeycomb, with demonstrations at 11am Wed–Sun; 3 Bottrill St, Cowaramup; (08) 9755 9155; 13 km N. *Miller's Icecream:* Operating dairy makes fresh ice-cream, 'from cow to cone'; 314 Wirring Rd, Cowaramup (08) 9755 9850; 13 km N. *Gnarabup Beach:* safe swimming beach for all the family; 13 km w. *Margaret River Dairy Company:* free tastings of cheese and yoghurt; Bussell Hwy, Cowarumup; (08) 9755 7588; 15 km N. *The Berry Farm:* jams, pickles, naturally fermented vinegars, fruit and berry wines; 43 Bessell Rd; (08) 9757 5054; 15 km SE. *Ellensbrook Homestead:* this wattle-and-daub homestead (1857) was once the home of Alfred and Ellen Bussell, the district's first pioneers; open weekends; (08) 9755 5173. Nearby is the beautiful Meekadarabee Waterfall, a place steeped in Aboriginal legend; 15 km NW. *Olio Bello:* boutique, handmade olive oil, with tastings available; Armstrong Rd, Cowaramup; (08) 9755 9771; 17 km NW, at Cowaramup. *Grove Vineyard:* Margaret River's only liqueur factory also boasts a winery, distillery, nano-brewery and cafe; tastings available; Cnr Metricup and Carter rds, Wilyabrup; (08) 9755 7458; 20 km N. *Arts and crafts:* many in area, including Boranup Galleries; 20 km s on Caves Rd; contact visitor centre for details. *Margaret River Chocolate Company:* free chocolate tastings, interactive displays and viewing windows to watch the chocolate products being made; Cnr Harmans Mill and Harmans South rds, Metricup; (08) 9755 6555; 30 km NW. *Bootleg Brewery:* enjoy naturally brewed boutique beers in a picturesque setting; Puzey Rd, Wilyabrup; (08) 9755 6300; 11am–6pm daily; 45 km NW. *Bushtucker River and Winery Tours:* experience the Margaret River region through its wine, wilderness and food; (08) 9757 9084. *Land-based activities:* abseiling, caving, canoeing, coastal treks, horseriding and hiking; contact visitor centre for details. *Heritage trails:* including the Rails-to-Trails and Margaret River heritage trails; contact visitor centre for maps.

TOWNS NEARBY: Yallingup 34 km, Dunsborough 37 km, Augusta 41 km, Busselton 42 km, Nannup 64 km

Mount Barker Heritage Trail: 30 km drive tracing the development of the Mount Barker farming district; contact visitor centre for map. *Stirling Range National Park:* 80 km NE; *see Cranbrook.*

TOWNS NEARBY: Cranbrook 38 km, Albany 45 km, Denmark 46 km, Walpole 94 km, Kojonup 100 km

Mount Magnet

Pop. 422
Map ref. 575 H11 | 576 D2 | 578 D12

ℹ **Hepburn St** (next to the Picture Theatre Garden); (08) 9963 4172; www.mtmagnet.wa.gov.au

📻 102.5 WA FM, 105.7 FM ABC Local Radio

In 1854 the hill that rises above this Murchison goldmining town was named West Mount Magnet by surveyor Robert Austin after he noticed that its magnetic ironstone was playing havoc with his compass. Now known by its Aboriginal name, Warramboo Hill affords a remarkable view over the town and mines. Located 562 kilometres north-east of Perth on the Great

Northern Highway, Mount Magnet offers visitors a rich mining history, rugged granite breakaway countryside and breathtaking wildflowers in season.

🏛 *Mining and Pastoral Museum:* collection of mining and pioneering artefacts includes a Crossley engine from the original State Battery; Hepburn St. *Heritage trail:* see the surviving historic buildings and sites of the gold-rush era on this 1.4 km walk; contact visitor centre for map.

🍴 *Mount Magnet Hotel:* traditional pub; 36 Hepburn St (Great Northern Hwy); (08) 9963 4002.

⊗ *The Granites:* rocky outcrop with picnic area and Aboriginal rock paintings; 7 km N. *Heritage drive:* 37 km drive of local historic and natural sights, including views of old open-cut goldmine. Also takes in the Granites and various ghost towns; contact visitor centre for map. *Fossicking for gemstones:* take care as there are dangerous old mine shafts in the area.

TOWNS NEARBY: Cue 71 km, Yalgoo 119 km, Meekatharra 175 km, Morawa 220 km, Mullewa 235 km

Mullewa

Pop. 419
Map ref. 575 E12 | 576 B3

i Jose St; (08) 9961 1500 ; www.mullewatourism.com.au

📻 107.5 FM ABC Radio National, 828 AM ABC Local Radio

Mullewa, 92 kilometres north-east of Geraldton, is in the heart of wildflower country. In spring, the countryside surrounding the town bursts forth with one of the finest displays of wildflowers in Western Australia. The wreath flower is the star attraction of the annual Mullewa Wildflower Show.

Our Lady of Mt Carmel Church This small church is widely considered to be the crowning achievement of noted priest-architect Monsignor John C. Hawes. Built of local stone, this gem of Romanesque design took 7 years to build with Hawes as architect, stonemason, carpenter, modeller and moulder. The adjoining Priest House is now a museum in honour of Hawes, housing his personal belongings, books, furniture and drawings (cnr Doney and Bowes sts). Both of these buildings are part of the Monsignor Hawes Heritage Trail, which also features the Pioneer Cemetery (Mullewa–Carnarvon Rd; 1 km N) and a site at the old showground just outside town, where a rock carved by Monsignor Hawes was once a simple altar where he held mass for the local Aboriginal people (Mt Magnet Rd; 1.5 km E). Details and a map of the trail are available from the visitor centre.

Mullewa Wildflower Show: Aug/Sept.

Butterabby Gravesite This gravesite is a grim reminder of the harsh pioneering days. A stone monument recalls the spearing to death in 1864 of a convict labourer and the hanging in 1865 of 5 Aboriginal people accused of the crime. Mullewa–Mingenew Rd; 18 km S.

Tenindewa Pioneer Well: example of the art of stone pitching that was common at the time of construction, reputedly built by Chinese labourers en route to the Murchison goldfields. Also walking trails; 18 km W. *Bindoo Hill:* glacial moraine where ice-smoothed rocks dropped as the face of the glacier melted around 225 million years ago; 40 km NW. *Coalseam Conservation Park:* remnants of the state's first coal shafts, now a picnic ground; 45 km SW. *Tallering Peak and Gorges:* ideal picnic spot; Mullewa–Carnarvon Rd; check accessibility at visitor centre; 59 km N. *Wooleen Homestead:* stay on a working sheep and cattle station in the central Murchison district. Visit Boodra Rock and Aboriginal sites, and experience station life; (08) 9963 7973; 194 km N.

TOWNS NEARBY: Greenough 87 km, Northampton 89 km, Morawa 89 km, Geraldton 92 km, Dongara–Denison 98 km

Mundaring

Pop. 3004
Map ref. 570 G5 | 571 E4 | 574 C5 | 576 C7

i The Old School, 7225 Great Eastern Hwy; (08) 9295 0202; www.mundaringtourism.com.au

📻 94.5 Mix FM, 720 AM ABC Local Radio

Mundaring is virtually an outer suburb of Perth, being only 34 kilometres east. Nearby, the picturesque Mundaring Weir is the water source for the goldfields 500 kilometres further east. The original dam opened in 1903. The hilly bush setting makes the weir a popular picnic spot.

Mundaring Arts Centre: contemporary WA fine art and design with comprehensive exhibition program; Great Eastern Hwy; (08) 9295 3991. *Mundaring District Museum:* displays on the diverse history of the shire; Great Eastern Hwy.

Mundaring Sculpture Park: collection of sculptures by WA artists, set in natural bush park with grassed areas for picnics and children's playground; Jacoby St.

Market: Nichol St, 2nd Sun each month. *Truffle Festival:* Aug. *Perth Hills Wine Show:* Aug. *Trek the Trail:* Sept. *Darlington Arts Festival:* Nov.

Little Caesars Pizzeria: award-winning pizzeria; Shop 7, 7125 Great Eastern Hwy; (08) 9295 6611. *The Loose Box:* French cuisine at its best; 6825 Great Eastern Hwy; (08) 9295 1787. *Alfred's Kitchen:* late-night hamburgers, Cnr Meadow and James St, Guilford; (08) 9377 1378. *Black Swan Winery & Restaurant:* upmarket international cuisine; 8600 West Swan Rd, Henley Brook; (08) 9296 6090. *Darlington Estate:* modern Australian vineyard restaurant; 1495 Nelson Rd, Darlington; (08) 9299 6268. *Dear Friends:* adventurous fine dining; 100 Benara Rd, Caversham; (08) 9279 2815. *Elmar's in the Valley:* German fare; 8731 West Swan Rd, Henley Brook; (08) 9296 6354. *Kappy's:* Italian; 120 Swan St Guilford; (08) 6278 2882. *King & I:* Thai; 147–149 James St, Guilford; (08) 6278 3999. *Little River Winery & Cafe:* provincial French fare; 2 Forest Rd, Henley Brook; (08) 9296 4462. *Riverside at Woodbridge:* charming cafe in heritage-listed building; 8254 Ford St, Woodbridge; (08) 9274 1469. *The Rose & Crown:* 3 restaurants within historic hotel; 105 Swan St, Guilford; (08) 9347 8100. *Sandalford Restaurant:* modern Australian; Sandalford Wines, 3210 West Swan Rd, Caversham; (08) 9374 9301. *Sittella Winery:* international cuisine with picturesque views; 100 Barrett St; Herne Hill; (08) 9296 2600. *Stewart's Restaurant:* award-winning European cuisine; Brookleigh Estate, 1235 Great Northern Hwy, Upper Swan; (08) 9296 6966.

 Falls Retreat Bed & Breakfast: 45 Falls Rd, Lesmurdie; (08) 9291 7609. *Lakeview Lodge:* 131 Lakeview Dr, Gidgegannup; (08) 9578 3009. *Stocks Country Retreat:* 26 Boulonnais Dr, Brigadoon; (08) 9296 1945.

Swan Valley wine region The Valley begins where the suburbs of Perth end, giving wine lovers the chance to leave their car behind and catch a ferry up the river. Dating back to 1830, this winemaking region is flat and hot. Fortified wines were once a staple, but are now made only by a few companies such as Talijancich and John Kosovich Wines. Houghton is responsible for one of the biggest white wine brands in the country, Houghton White Burgundy. This wine is considered unique among its cheaper counterparts, mostly because it ages well, but Houghton also has plenty to offer in the more expensive ranges. The other major winery of the valley is Sandalford. Contact visitor centre for map.

Mundaring Weir The Number 1 Pump Station, formerly known as the C. Y. O'Connor Museum, houses an exhibition on the mammoth project of connecting the weir to the goldfields (open 10am–4pm Mon–Sun and public holidays; Mundaring Weir Rd; 8 km S). This is also the starting point of the 560 km Golden Pipeline Heritage Trail to Kalgoorlie, which follows the route of O'Connor's water pipeline, taking in towns and heritage sites. Nearby, the Perth Hills National Park Centre includes Nearer to Nature who provide hands-on activities including bush craft, animal encounters, bush walks and information about Aboriginal culture; contact (08) 9295 2244. The Mundaring Weir Gallery, built in 1908 as a Mechanics Institute Hall, showcases the work of local craftspeople; open 10am–4pm Thurs, Sat, Sun and public holidays; Cnr Hall and Weir Village rds.

John Forrest National Park: declared a national park in 1947, this is one of the oldest and best-loved picnic spots in the Perth Hills. A drive through the park has vantage points with superb views across Perth and the coastal plain. A popular walk is the Heritage Trail on the western edge, past waterfalls and an old rail tunnel, and there is a lovely picnic spot beside a natural pool at Rocky Pool; 6 km w. *Karakamia Sanctuary:* native wildlife sanctuary with guided dusk walks; bookings essential on (08) 9572 3169; Lilydale Rd, Chidlow; 8 km NE. *Calamunnda Camel Farm:* camel rides; open Thurs–Sun; 361 Paulls Valley Rd; (08) 9293 1156; 10 km s. *Lake Leschenaultia:* swimming, canoeing, bushwalks and camping with picnic/barbecue facilities; 12 km NW. *Kalamunda National Park:* walking trails through jarrah forest, including the first section of the 963 km Bibbulmun Track; 23 km s; *see Albany. Kalamunda History Village:* collection of historic buildings; open Sat–Thurs; 23 km s. *Lesmurdie Falls National Park:* good views of Perth and Rottnest Island near spectacular falls over the Darling Escarpment; 29 km s. *Walyunga National Park:* beautiful bushland and wildflowers, and venue for the Avon Descent, a major whitewater canoeing event held each Aug; 30 km NW. *Munda Biddi Bike Trail:* passes through Mundaring; maps from visitor centre. *Araluen Botanic Park:* jarrah, eucalypt and marri trees frame the rockpools, cascades and European-style terraces of these beautiful 59-hectare gardens. With walking trails, picnic and barbecue areas and, in spring, magnificent tulip displays.

TOWNS NEARBY: Toodyay 48 km, Northam 56 km, York 57 km, Rockingham 59 km, Thomson Bay 60 km

Nannup
Pop. 503
Map ref. 572 F8 | 574 C10 | 576 C10

 4 Brockman St; (08) 9756 1211; www.nannupwa.com

98.9 FM ABC Radio National, 684 AM ABC Local Radio

Nannup is a historic mill town in the Blackwood Valley south of Perth. Known as 'The Garden Village', it has beautiful private and public gardens, tulip farms, daffodils and wildflowers. The countryside is a series of lush, rolling pastures alongside jarrah forests and pine plantations.

Old Police Station: now a visitor centre, original cell block open for viewing; Brockman St. *Town Arboretum:* fine collection of old trees planted in 1926; Brockman St. *Kealley's Gemstone Museum:* displays of rocks, shells, gemstones, bottles and stamps; closed Wed; Warren Rd. *Marinko Tomas Memorial:* memorial to the local boy who was the first serviceman from WA killed in the Vietnam War; Warren Rd. *Blackwood Wines:* beautiful winery and restaurant overlooking an artificial lake; closed Wed; Kearney St; (08) 9756 0077. *Arts, crafts and antiques:* many in town, including Crafty Creations for quality timber goods on Warren Rd (closed June). *Heritage trail:* in 2 sections, with a 2.5 km town walk highlighting historic buildings, and a 9 km scenic drive; contact visitor centre for map.

Market: Warren Rd; 2nd Sat each month. *Art and Photography Exhibition:* Jan. *Music Festival:* Feb/Mar. *Forest Car Rally:* Mar. *Nannup Cup Boat Race:* June. *Flower and Garden Festival:* tulips; Aug. *Rose Festival:* Nov.

Blackwood Bistro: modern Australian; Blackwood Wines, Kearney St; (08) 9756 0077. *Nannup Bridge Cafe:* cosy cafe;

1 Warren Rd; (08) 9756 1287. *Tathra Restaurant:* specialises in local produce; Tathra Hilltop Retreat, Balingup–Nannup Rd; (08) 9756 2040.

Kondil Park: bushwalks and wildflowers in season; 3 km w. *Barrabup Pool:* largest of several pools, ideal for swimming, fishing and camping. Also has barbecue facilities; 10 km w. *Cambray Sheep Cheese:* award-winning cheeses, visitors can watch the milking and cheese-making; samples available. There are also guest cottages; 12 km N. *Carlotta Crustaceans:* marron farm; 14 km s off Vasse Hwy. *Tathra:* fruit winery and restaurant; open 11am–4.30pm daily; 14 km NE. *Mythic Mazes:* mazes including sculptures of myths from around the world; 20 km N. *Donnelly River Wines:* open daily for cellar-door tastings; (08) 9301 5555; 45 km s. *Blackwood River:* camping, swimming, canoeing and trout fishing. *Self-guide walks:* wildflower (in spring), waterfall (in winter) and forest walks; contact visitor centre for maps. *Scenic drives:* through jarrah forest and pine plantations, including 40 km Blackwood Scenic Drive; contact visitor centre for maps.

TOWNS NEARBY: Balingup 29 km, Bridgetown 34 km, Donnybrook 46 km, Manjimup 46 km, Busselton 53 km

Narrogin
Pop. 4240
Map ref. 574 E7 | 576 D9

 Dryandra Country Visitor Centre, cnr Park and Fairway sts; (08) 9881 2064; www.dryandratourism.org.au

100.5 Hot FM, 918 AM Radio West

Narrogin, 192 kilometres south-east of Perth on the Great Southern Highway, is the commercial hub of a prosperous agricultural area. Sheep, pigs and cereal farms are the major industries. First settled in the 1870s, the town's name is derived from an Aboriginal word 'gnarojin', meaning waterhole.

Gnarojin Park This park is a national award winner for its original designs and artworks portraying local history and culture, which include the Centenary Pathway, marked with 100 locally designed commemorative tiles, Newton House Barbecue and Noongar Cultural Sites. Gordon St.

History Hall: local history collection; Egerton St. *Old Courthouse Museum:* built in 1894 as a school, it later became the district courthouse; open Mon–Sat; Egerton St. *Narrogin Art Gallery:* exhibitions; open 10am–4pm Tues–Fri, 10am–12pm Sat; Federal St. *Lions Lookout:* excellent views; Kipling St. *Heritage trail:* self-guide walk around the town's historic buildings; contact visitor centre for map.

State Gliding Championships: Jan. *Spring Festival:* Oct. *Rev Heads:* car rally; Nov/Dec.

Albert's Restaurant: international cuisine; Albert Facey Motor Inn, 78 Williams Rd; (08) 9881 1899.

Chuckem: 1481 Tarwonga Rd; (08) 9881 1188.

Dryandra Woodland One of the few remaining areas of virgin forest in the wheat belt, Dryandra is a paradise for birdwatchers and bushwalkers. The open, graceful eucalypt woodlands of white-barked wandoo, powderbark and thickets of rock she-oak support many species of flora and fauna including numbats (the state's animal emblem), woylies, tammar wallabies, brush-tailed possums and many others. Over 100 species of birds have been identified, including the mound-building mallee fowl. Tune your radio to 100 FM for 'Sounds of Dryandra', a 25 km radio drive trail with 6 stops featuring tales of the local Nyungar people, early forestry days, bush railways and Dryandra's unique wildlife. There are day-visitor facilities and accommodation, walk trails, a weekend Ecology Course (runs in autumn and spring; try your hand at radio-tracking, trapping and spotlighting) and school holiday programs. 22 km NW.

Barna Mia Animal Sanctuary The sanctuary, within the Dryandra Woodland, has guided spotlight walks at night that reveal threatened marsupials, including the bilby and boodie. Bookings essential; contact DEC on (08) 9881 9200 or visitor centre which also has maps; Narrogin–Wandering Rd; 26 km NW.

Foxes Lair Nature Reserve: 60 ha of bushland with good walking trails, wildflowers in spring and 40 species of birds; maps and brochures from visitor centre; Williams Rd; 1 km SW. *Yilliminning and Birdwhistle Rocks:* unusual rock formations; 11 km E. *District heritage trail:* contact visitor centre for map.

TOWNS NEARBY: Wickepin 35 km, Wagin 44 km, Pingelly 45 km, Katanning 91 km, Corrigin 93 km

New Norcia

Pop. 70
Map ref. 574 C2 | 576 C6

i Museum and art gallery, Great Northern Hwy; (08) 9654 8056; www.newnorcia.wa.edu.au

612 AM ABC Radio National, 720 AM ABC Local Radio

In 1846 Spanish Benedictine monks established a mission 132 kilometres north of Perth in the secluded Moore Valley in an attempt to help the local Aboriginal population. They named their mission after the Italian town of Norcia, the birthplace of the order's founder, St Benedict. The imposing Spanish-inspired buildings of New Norcia, surrounded by the gum trees and dry grasses of the wheat belt, provide a most unexpected vista. The town still operates as a monastery and is Australia's only monastic town. Visitors may join the monks at daily prayers.

Abbey Church This fine example of bush architecture was built using a combination of stones, mud plaster, rough-hewn trees and wooden shingles. It is the oldest Catholic church still in use in WA and contains the tomb of Dom Rosendo Salvado, the founder of New Norcia and its first Abbot. Hanging on a wall is the painting of Our Lady of Good Counsel, given to Salvado before he left for Australia in 1845 by Bishop (later Saint) Vincent Palotti. One of New Norcia's most famous stories relates how, in 1847, Salvado placed this revered painting in the path of a bushfire threatening the mission's crops. The wind suddenly changed direction and drove the flames back to the part already burnt, and the danger was averted.

Museum and art gallery: the museum tells the story of New Norcia's history as an Aboriginal mission, while the art gallery houses priceless religious art from Australia and Europe as well as Spanish artefacts, many of which were gifts from Queen Isabella of Spain. The museum gift shop features New Norcia's own produce including bread, nutcake, pan chocolatti, biscotti, wine, honey and olive oil. *Monastery:* daily tours of the interior. A guesthouse allows visitors to experience the monastic life for a few days. *New Norcia Hotel:* this magnificent building, featuring a massive divided central staircase and high, moulded pressed-metal ceilings, was opened in 1927 as a hostel to accommodate parents of the children who were boarding at the town's colleges. *Old Flour Mill:* the oldest surviving building in New Norcia dates

from the 1850s. *Heritage trail:* 2 km self-guide walk highlights New Norcia's historic and cultural significance and the role of the Benedictine monks in colonial history; contact visitor centre for map. *Guided tour:* 2 hr tour of the town with an experienced guide takes you inside buildings not otherwise open to the public; 11am and 1.30pm daily from museum.

New Norcia Hotel: town landmark; Great Northern Hwy; (08) 9654 8034.

Wongan Hills Caravan Park: Wongan Rd, Wongan Hills; (08) 9671 1009.

Mogumber: town with one of the state's highest timber-and-concrete bridges; 24 km SW. *Piawaning:* magnificent stand of eucalypts north of town; 31 km NE. *Bolgart:* site of historic hotel; 49 km SE. *Wyening Mission:* former mission, now a historic site; open by appt; 50 km SE.

TOWNS NEARBY: Moora 42 km, Gingin 51 km, Toodyay 69 km, Yanchep 85 km, Northam 87 km

Newman

Pop. 4247
Map ref. 578 E5 | 583 L11

i Cnr Fortescue Ave and Newman Dr; (08) 9175 2888 or 0437 811 961; www.newman-wa.org

88.9 Red FM, 567 AM ABC Local Radio

Located in the heart of the Pilbara, Newman was built in the late 1960s by the Mount Newman Mining Company to house the workforce required at nearby Mount Whaleback, the largest open-cut iron-ore mine in the world. At the same time a 426-kilometre railway was constructed between Newman and Port Hedland to transport the ore for export to Japan.

Mt Whaleback Mine Tours: the mine produces over 100 million tonnes of iron ore every year. Tours (minimum 4 people) run Mon–Sat Apr–Sept, Tues and Thurs Oct–Mar; book through visitor centre. *Mining and Pastoral Museum:* interesting display of relics from the town's short history, including the first Haulpak (giant iron-ore truck) used at Mt Whaleback and outback station life; located at visitor centre. *Radio Hill Lookout:* panoramic view of town and surrounding area; off Newman Dr.

Campdraft and Rodeo: Mar. *Fortescue Festival:* Aug.

Newman Hotel Motel: traditional pub food; 1401 Newman Dr; (08) 9175 1101.

Ophthalmia Dam: swimming, sailing, barbecues and picnics (no camping); 20 km E. *Mt Newman:* excellent views; 25 km NW. *Eagle Rock Falls:* permanent pools and picnic spots nearby; 4WD access only; 80 km NW. *Wanna Munna:* site of Aboriginal rock carvings; 74 km W. *Rockpools and waterholes:* at Kalgans Pool (65 km NE), Three Pools (75 km N) and Weeli Wolli (99 km W). *Newman Waterholes and Art Sites Tour:* maps available at the visitor centre. *Karijini National Park:* 196 km N; *see Tom Price.*

TOWNS NEARBY: Tom Price 212 km, Marble Bar 242 km

Norseman

Pop. 861
Map ref. 577 I7

i 68 Roberts St; (08) 9039 1071; www.norseman.info

105.7 FM ABC Goldfields, 107.3 FM ABC Radio National

Norseman is the last large town on the Eyre Highway for travellers heading east towards South Australia. Gold put Norseman on the

[NORSEMAN] CORRUGATED-IRON CAMEL SCULPTURES

map in the 1890s with one of the richest quartz reefs in Australia. The town is steeped in goldmining history, reflected in its colossal tailings dump. If visitors could stand atop this dump they could have up to $50 million in gold underfoot (although the rock has been processed, much residual gold remains). The story behind the town's name has become folklore. The settlement sprang up in 1894 when a horse owned by prospector Laurie Sinclair pawed the ground and unearthed a nugget of gold; the site proved to be a substantial reef. The horse's name was Norseman.

🏠 *Historical Collection:* mining tools and household items; open 10am–1pm Mon–Sat; Battery Rd. *Phoenix Park:* open-plan park with displays, stream and picnic facilities; Prinsep St. *Statue of Norseman:* bronze statue by Robert Hitchcock commemorates Norseman, the horse; Cnr Roberts and Ramsay sts. *Camel Train:* corrugated-iron sculptures represent the camel trains of the pioneer days; Prinsep St. *Gem fossicking:* gemstone permits are available from the visitor centre.

🌴 *Norseman Cup:* Mar.

✗ *Norseman Hotel:* traditional pub food; 90 Roberts St; (08) 9039 1023.

🛏 *Gateway Caravan Park:* Prinsep St; (08) 9039 1500.

⊘ *Beacon Hill Lookout:* spectacular at sunrise and sunset, this lookout offers an outstanding 360-degree panorama of the salt lakes, Mt Jimberlana, the township, tailings dump and surrounding hills and valleys; Mines Rd; 2 km E. *Mt Jimberlana:* reputed to be one of the oldest geological areas in the world. Take the walking trail to the summit for great views; 5 km E. *Dundas Rocks:* barbecue and picnic area amid granite outcrops near old Dundas townsite, where the lonely grave of a 7-month-old child is one of the only signs that the area was once inhabited. Travel here via the highway (22 km s) or along the 33 km heritage trail that follows an original Cobb & Co route (map available from visitor centre). *Buldania Rocks:* picnic area with beautiful spring wildflowers; 28 km E. *Bromus Dam:* freshwater dam with picnic area; 32 km s. *Peak Charles National Park:* good-weather track for experienced walkers and climbers to Peak Eleanora,

with a magnificent view from top of saltpans, sand plains and dry woodlands.; 50 km s, then 40 km w off hwy. *Cave Hill Nature Reserve:* a granite outcrop with a cave set in its side and a dam nearby. Popular spot for camping, picknicking and rock climbing; 4WD access only; 55 km N, then 50 km w. *Fraser Range Station:* working pastoral property that specialises in Damara sheep. The station has a range of available accommodation and opportunities to experience a remote working pastoral property; (08) 9039 3210; 100 km E.

TOWNS NEARBY: Coolgardie 150 km, Kalgoorlie–Boulder 164 km, Balladonia 174 km, Esperance 185 km, Lake King 220 km

Northam

Pop. 6007
Map ref. 571 G2 | 574 D4 | 576 C7

ⓘ 2 Grey St; (08) 9622 2100; www.visitnorthamwa.com.au

📻 96.5 Hot FM, 1215 AM ABC Local Radio

Northam lies in the heart of the fertile Avon Valley. The Avon River winds its way through the town and on its waters you'll find white swans, a most unusual sight in a state where the emblem is a black swan. White swans were brought to Northam from England in the 1900s and have flourished here. Northam is also synonymous with hot-air ballooning as it is one of the few areas in Western Australia ideally suited to this pastime. Northam is home to the famous Avon Descent, a 133-kilometre whitewater race down the Avon and Swan rivers to Perth.

🏠 *Historic buildings* Of the many historic buildings in Northam, 2 are particularly noteworthy: Morby Cottage (1836) on Avon Dr, the home of Northam's first settler, John Morrell, now a museum and open 10.30am–4pm Sun or by appt; and the National Trust–classified Sir James Mitchell House (1905), cnr Duke and Hawes sts, with its elaborate Italianate architecture. Take the 90 min self-guide walk for the full tour of the town. Contact visitor centre for map.

Old Railway Station Museum: displays include a steam engine and renovated carriages, plus numerous artefacts from the early 1900s; open 10am–4pm Sun or by appt; Fitzgerald St West.

Visitor centre: exhibition showcasing the area's significant postwar migrant history; Grey St. *Suspension bridge:* the longest pedestrian suspension bridge in Australia crosses the Avon River adjacent to the visitor centre.

Vintage Car Swap Meet: Feb. *Avon Descent:* Aug. *Northam Cup:* Oct. *Motorcycle Festival:* Nov. *Wheatbelt Cultural Festival:* Dec.

Avon Bridge Hotel: charming country pub; 322 Fitzgerald St; (08) 9622 1023. *Cafe Yasou:* Greek food; 175 Fitzgerald St; (08) 9622 3128.

Brackson House Quality Accommodation: 7 Katrine Rd; (08) 9622 5262. *Goomalling Caravan Park:* Throssell St, Goomalling; (08) 9629 1183.

Mt Ommanney Lookout: excellent views of the township and agricultural areas beyond; 1.5 km w. *Hot-air ballooning:* Northam Airfield; Mar–Nov; bookings essential; 2 km NE. *Meckering:* small town made famous in 1968 when an earthquake left a huge fault line in its wake; 35 km E. *Cunderdin Museum:* The museum housed in the No 3 pumping station has displays on the pipeline, wheat-belt farming and the Meckering earthquake; 50 km E.

TOWNS NEARBY: Toodyay 23 km, York 28 km, Mundaring 56 km, Beverley 56 km, Gingin 80 km

Northampton

Pop. 814
Map ref. 575 D12 | 576 A3

Old police station, Hampton Rd; (08) 9934 1488; www.northamptonwa.com.au

96.5 WA FM

Northampton, nestled in the valley of Nokarena Brook, 47 kilometres north of Geraldton, was awarded Historic Town status by the National Trust in 1993. It was declared a townsite in 1864 and is one of the oldest settlements in Western Australia. A former lead-mining centre, its prosperity is now based on sheep- and wheat-farming.

Chiverton House Historical Museum: unusual memorabilia housed in what was originally the home of Captain Samuel Mitchell, mine manager and geologist. Surrounding gardens include herbarium and restored farm machinery; open 10am–12pm and 2–4pm Fri–Mon; Hampton Rd. *Mary Street Railway Precinct:* railway memorabilia at the site of the town's 2nd railway station, built 1913; Eastern end. *Church of Our Lady in Ara Coeli:* designed in 1936 by Monsignor John Hawes, WA's famous architect-priest; Hampton Rd. *Gwalla Church and Cemetery:* ruins of town's first church (1864); Gwalla St. *Hampton Road Heritage Walk:* 2 km walk includes 37 buildings of historical interest including the Miners Arms Hotel (1868) and the Old Railway Station (1879); contact visitor centre for map.

 Market: Kings Park, cnr Essex St and Hampton Rd; 1st Sat each month. *Airing of the Quilts:* quilts hung in main street; Oct.

Miners Arms Hotel: counter meals; Hampton Rd; (08) 9934 1281. *The Railway Tavern:* great pizza, history displays; 71 North West Coastal Hwy; (08) 9934 1120.

Horrocks Beach Caravan Park: 1 North Crt, Horrocks; (08) 9934 3039.

Alma School House: built in 1916 as a one-teacher school; 12 km N. *Aboriginal cave paintings:* at the mouth of the Bowes River; 17 km w. *Oakabella Homestead:* one of the first farms in WA to plant canola, or rapeseed as it was then known. Take a guided tour of the historic homestead and outbuildings; open daily Mar–Nov; 18 km S. *Horrocks Beach:* beautiful bays, sandy beaches, good swimming, fishing and surfing; 20 km w. *Lynton Station:* ruins of labour-hiring depot for convicts, used in 1853–56; 35 km NW. *Lynton House:* squat building with slits for windows, probably designed as protection from hostile Aboriginal people; 35 km NW. *Principality of Hutt River:* visitors are given a tour by the royals of this 75 sq km principality. With their own government, money and postage stamps, Hutt River exists as an independent sovereign state, seceded from Australia in 1970; 35 km NW. *Hutt Lagoon:* appears pink in midday sun; 45 km NW. *Port Gregory:* beach settlement, ideal for swimming, fishing and windsurfing; 47 km NW. *Warribano Chimney:* Australia's first lead smelter; 60 km N.

TOWNS NEARBY: Geraldton 47 km, Greenough 67 km, Kalbarri 84 km, Mullewa 89 km, Dongara–Denison 105 km

Northcliffe

Pop. 299
Map ref. 572 H12 | 573 C4 | 574 D11 | 576 C11

Muirillup Rd; (08) 9776 7203; www.northcliffe.org.au

102.7 WA FM, 105.9 FM ABC Local Radio

Magnificent virgin karri forests surround the township of Northcliffe, 31 kilometres south of Pemberton in the state's South-West. Just a kilometre from the town centre is Northcliffe Forest Park, where you can see purple-crowned lorikeets, scarlet robins and, in spring, a profusion of wildflowers. Not far away is the coastal settlement of Windy Harbour, a popular swimming beach.

Pioneer Museum Northcliffe came into existence as a result of the Group Settlement Scheme, a WA government plan to resettle returned WW I soldiers and immigrants by offering them rural land to farm. The scheme was enthusiastically backed by English newspaper magnate Lord Northcliffe (hence the town's name). Unfortunately, by the 1920s, when the scheme began, all the good land in the state had already been settled. The group settlers were left to contend with inhospitable country and with only crosscut saws and axes, they were faced with the daunting task of clearing some of the world's biggest trees from their land. It is not surprising that by the mid-1930s all of the Group Settlement projects in the South-West timber country had failed. A visit to the Pioneer Museum with its excellent displays is the best way to understand the hardships the group settlers experienced. Open 10am–2pm daily Sept–May, 10am–2pm Sat, Sun and school holidays June–Aug; Wheatley Coast Rd; (08) 9775 1022.

Canoe and mountain-bike hire: contact visitor centre for details.

Great Karri Ride: Mar. *Mountain Bike Championship:* May/June. *Night-time Mountain Bike Race:* Nov.

The Dairy Lounge Cafe: dairy-inspired cafe; Bannister Downs Farm, Muirillup Rd; (08) 9776 6300.

Roundtu-It Eco Caravan Park: 190 Muirillup Rd; (08) 9776 7276.

Northcliffe Forest Park: follow the Hollow Butt Karri and Twin Karri walking trails or enjoy a picnic; Wheatley Coast Rd. *Warren River:* trout fishing and sandy beaches; 8 km N. *Mt Chudalup:* spectacular views of the surrounding

D'Entrecasteaux National Park and coastline from the summit of this giant granite outcrop; 10 km s. *Moon's Crossing:* delightful picnic spot; 13 km NW. *Lane Poole Falls and Boorara Tree:* 3 km walking trail leads to the falls, passing the Boorara Tree with 50 m high fire-lookout cabin; 18 km SE. *Point D'Entrecasteaux:* limestone cliffs, popular with rock climbers, rise 150 m above the sea where 4 viewing platforms provide superb views; 27 km s. *Windy Harbour:* swimming, snorkelling, fishing, camping and whale-watching (from platform, best times Sept–Nov); 27 km s. *Cathedral Rocks:* watch seals and dolphins; 27 km s. *Salmon Beach:* surf beach offers salmon fishing Apr–June; 27 km s. *The Great Forest Trees Drive:* 48 km self-guide scenic drive takes in the karri giants at Snake Gully Lookout, the Boardwalk and Big Tree Grove; contact visitor centre for map. *Bibbulmun Track:* section of this long-distance walking trail links the 3 national parks around Northcliffe: D'Entrecasteaux (5 km s), Warren (20 km NW) and Shannon (30 km E); *see Albany*. *Mountain-bike trails:* 4 permanent trails have been established around Northcliffe; contact visitor centre for details.

TOWNS NEARBY: Pemberton 22 km, Manjimup 44 km, Walpole 67 km, Bridgetown 74 km, Nannup 80 km

Onslow
Pop. 574
Map ref. 575 C2 | 582 A8

 Second Ave (May–Oct), (08) 9184 6644; or council offices, Second Ave, (08) 9184 6001; www.ashburton.wa.gov.au

106.7 WA FM, 107.5 FM ABC Radio National

Onslow, on the north-west coast between Exmouth and Karratha, is the supply base for offshore gas and oil fields. This part of the coast is among the north's most cyclone-prone and Onslow has often suffered severe damage. The town was originally at the Ashburton River mouth and a bustling pearling centre. In the 1890s gold was discovered nearby. In 1925 the townsite was moved to Beadon Bay after cyclones caused the river to silt up. During World War II, submarines refuelled here and the town was bombed twice. In the 1950s it was the mainland base for Britain's nuclear experiments at Montebello Islands. In 1963 Onslow was almost completely destroyed by a cyclone. It is now an attractive tree-shaded town.

Goods Shed Museum: memorabilia from the town's long history and collections of old bottles, shells and rocks; in visitor centre; Second Ave. *Beadon Creek and Groyne:* popular fishing spot. *Ian Blair Memorial Walkway:* 1 km scenic walk; starts at Beadon Point and finishes at Sunset Beach. *Heritage trail:* covers sites of interest in town; contact visitor centre for map.

Beadon Bay Hotel: counter meals; Second Ave; (08) 9184 6002. *Nikki's Licensed Restaurant:* modern Australian; 17 First Ave; (08) 9184 6121.

Termite mounds: with interpretive display; 10 km s. *Mackerel Islands:* excellent fishing destination. Charter boats are available for daytrips or extended fishing safaris; contact visitor centre for details; 22 km off the coast. *Ashburton River:* swimming, camping and picnicking; 45 km sw. *Old townsite heritage trail:* self-guide walk around original townsite including old gaol; contact visitor centre for map; 45 km sw.

TOWNS NEARBY: Exmouth 107 km, Karratha 205 km, Coral Bay 216 km, Roebourne 232 km

Pemberton
Pop. 757
Map ref. 572 H11 | 573 B3 | 574 D11 | 576 C11

 Brockman St; (08) 9776 1133 or 1800 671 133; www.pembertontourist. com.au

97.3 WA FM, 558 AM ABC Local Radio

Pemberton sits in a quiet valley surrounded by some of the tallest trees in the world and, in spring, brilliant wildflowers. This is the heart of karri country, with 4000 hectares of protected virgin karri forest in the nearby Warren and Greater Beedelup national parks. Pemberton is a centre for high-quality woodcraft and is renowned for its excellent rainbow trout and marron fishing.

Karri Forest Discovery Centre: interpretive centre includes museum with collection of historic photographs and forestry equipment; at visitor centre. *Pioneer Museum:* utensils, tools and other memorabilia from pioneer days plus a full-scale settler's hut; at visitor centre. *Craft galleries:* many in town, including the Fine Woodcraft Gallery in Dickinson St and the Peter Kovacsy Studio in Jamieson St.

Mill Hall Markets: Brockman St; 2nd Sat each month and public holidays. *CWA Markets:* Brockman St; 4th Sat each month. *Autumn Festival:* May.

Hidden River Estate Restaurant: superb international cuisine; Mullineaux Rd; (08) 9776 1437. *King Trout Restaurant and Marron Farm:* seafood; Cnr Northcliffe and Old Vasse rds; (08) 9776 1352. *The Shamrock Restaurant:* local fare; 18 Brockman St; (08) 9776 1186.

Pemberton Caravan Park: 1 Pump Hill Rd; (08) 9776 1300.

Gloucester National Park In this park is the town's most popular tourist attraction, the Gloucester Tree. With its fire lookout teetering 61 m above the ground and a spine-tingling 153 rungs spiralling upwards, this is not a climb for the faint-hearted. The Gloucester Tree is one of 8 tree towers constructed from the late 1930s as fire lookouts. As the extremely tall trees in the southern forests offered few vantage points for fire-lookout towers, it was decided to simply build a cabin high enough in one of the taller trees to serve the purpose. Also within the park are the Cascades, a scenic spot for picnicking, bushwalking and fishing. 1 km s.

Warren National Park This park boasts some of the most easily accessible virgin karri forest. The Dave Evans Bicentennial Tree has another fire lookout with picnic facilities and walking tracks nearby. 9 km sw.

Greater Beedelup National Park Here you'll find the Walk Through Tree, a 75 m, 400-year-old karri with a hole cut in it big enough for people to walk through. The Beedelup Falls, a total drop of 106 m, are rocky cascades best seen after heavy rain. Nearby are walk trails and a suspension bridge. 18 km w.

Lavender & Berry Farm: enjoy berry scones, lavender biscuits and other unusual produce; Browns Rd; 4 km N. *Big Brook Dam:* the dam has its own beach, picnic and barbecue facilities, trout and marron fishing in season, and walking trails; 7 km N. *Big Brook Arboretum:* established in 1928 to study the growth of imported trees from around the world; 7 km N. *King Trout Restaurant and Marron Farm:* catch and cook your own trout; closed Thurs; 8 km sw. *Founder's Forest:* part of the 100-Year-Old Forest, with karri regrowth trees over 120 years old; 10 km N. *Wineries:* more than 28 wineries in the area, many offering tours, tastings and sales; contact visitor centre for details. *Pemberton Tramway:* tramcars based on 1907 Fremantle trams operate daily through tall-forest country to the Warren River Bridge; (08) 9776 1322. *Fishing:* in rivers, inland fishing licence is required for trout and marron; contact post office for details and permits. *Tours:* river tours, scenic bus tours, 4WD adventure tours, self-guide forest drives, walking trails and eco-tours; contact visitor centre for details. *Drive trails:* include the Heartbreak Trail, a one-way drive through the karri forest of Warren National Park; contact visitor centre for maps. *Walk trails:* include the 1 hr return Rainbow Trail; contact visitor centre for maps. *Bibbulmun Track:* walking trail passes through Pemberton; *see Albany.*

TOWNS NEARBY: Northcliffe 22 km, Manjimup 25 km, Bridgetown 54 km, Nannup 57 km, Balingup 73 km

Pingelly

Pop. 817
Map ref. 574 E6 | 576 D8

i Council offices, 17 Queen St; (08) 9887 1066; www.pingelly.wa.gov.au

 99.7 FM ABC News Radio, 612 AM ABC Radio National

Located 158 kilometres south-east of Perth on the Great Southern Highway, Pingelly is part of the central-southern farming district. Sandalwood was once a local industry, but today sheep and wheat are the major produce.

Courthouse Museum: built in 1907, now houses historic memorabilia and photographs; Parade St. *Apex Lookout:* fine views of town and surrounding countryside; Stone St.

Autumn Country Show and Ute Muster: Mar.

 The Exchange Tavern: counter meals; 1 Pasture St; (08) 9887 0180.

Pingelly Heights Observatory: audio tour and telescope viewing of the stars and constellations; bookings essential on (08) 9887 0088; 5 km NE. *Moorumbine Heritage Trail:* walk or drive through this old townsite featuring early settlers' cottages and St Patrick's Church, built in 1873; contact council office for map; 8 km E. *Tutanning Flora and Fauna Reserve:* botanist Guy Shorteridge collected over 400 species of plants from here for the British Museum between 1903 and 1906; 22 km E. *Boyagin Nature Reserve:* widely recognised as one of the few areas of original fauna and flora left in the wheat belt, this picnic reserve has important stands of powderbark, jarrah and marri trees and is home to numbats and tammar wallabies; 26 km NW.

TOWNS NEARBY: Narrogin 45 km, Wickepin 48 km, Beverley 49 km, Corrigin 77 km, York 78 km

Pinjarra

Pop. 3295
Map ref. 571 D10 | 574 C6 | 576 C8

i Pinjarra Heritage Train Station, Fimmel La; (08) 9531 1438; www.pinjarravisitorcentre.com.au

 97.3 Coast FM, 585 AM ABC News Radio

A pleasant 84-kilometre drive south of Perth along the shaded South Western Highway brings you to Pinjarra, picturesquely set on the Murray River. Predominantly a dairying, cattle-farming and timber-producing area, Pinjarra was also once known as the horse capital of Western Australia when horses were bred for the British Army in India. Today horseracing, pacing and equestrian events are a major part of Pinjarra culture. The Alcoa Refinery north-east of town is the largest alumina refinery in Australia.

Edenvale Complex Built in 1888 with locally fired clay bricks, Edenvale was the home of Edward McLarty, member of the state's Legislative Council for 22 years. Nearby is Liveringa (1874), the original residence of the McLarty family, now an art gallery. There is a Heritage Rose Garden featuring 364 varieties of old-fashioned roses, a quilters' display in the Old School House, and a machinery museum. Cnr George and Henry sts.

Suspension bridge: across the Murray River, with picnic areas at both ends; George St. *Heritage trail:* 30 min river walk follows series of tiles explaining the heritage of the area; contact visitor centre for map.

Railway Markets: Lions Park; 2nd Sun morning each month Sept–June. *Community Markets:* Fimmel La; 4th Sat morning each month Sept–May. *Pinjarra Cup:* Mar. *Pinjarra Festival:* June. *Murray Arts and Craft Open Day:* Nov.

Raven Wines: revolving menu concept; 41 Wilson Rd; (08) 9531 2774. *Redcliffe on the Murray:* modern Australian; Murray River Country Estate, 13 Sutton St; (08) 9531 3894.

Pinjarra Caravan Park: 1716 Pinjarra Rd; (08) 9531 1374.

Fairbridge Established by Kingsley Fairbridge in 1912 as a farm school for British children, many of them orphans. Over the years more than 8000 English children were educated here. The boarding houses, which are today used as holiday cottages, have famous British names such as Clive, Shakespeare, Nightingale, Exeter, Evelyn and Raleigh. South Western Hwy; 1800 440 770; 6 km N.

Peel Zoo: set in lush native flora, includes opportunities to feed and interact with the animals and has picnic area and barbecues; (08) 9531 4322; 2 km N. *Old Blythewood:* beautiful National Trust property built in 1859 by John McLarty, who arrived in Australia in 1839; open Sat 10.30am–3.30pm, Sun 12.30–3.30pm, or by appt; 4 km S. *Alcoa Mine and Refinery Tours:* includes the mining process, and the world's biggest bulldozer. Tours are free Wed and the last Fri of each month (except during the summer school holidays); bookings essential on (08) 9531 6752; 6km NE. *Alcoa Scarp Lookout:* good views of coastal plain, surrounding farming area and Alcoa Refinery; 14 km E. *North Dandalup Dam:* recreation lake, picnic area and coastal views from lookout; 22 km NE. *South Dandalup Dam:* barbecues and picnic areas; 30 km E. *Lake Navarino:* formerly known as Waroona Dam, it is good for watersports, fishing, walking and horseriding; 33 km S. *Coopers Mill:* first flour mill in the Murray region, located on Cooleenup Island near the mouth of the Serpentine River. It is accessible only by water; contact visitor centre for details. *Hotham Valley Tourist Railway:* travel from Pinjarra to Dwellingup by train, taking in lush green dairy country before climbing the steep and spectacular Darling Range and finishing in the heart of the jarrah forest. The train is steam-hauled May–Oct and diesel-hauled Nov–Apr; check times with visitor centre. *Ravenswood Adventures:* explore the Murray River by kayak, dinghy, canoe or pedal boat; Ravenswood; (08) 9537 7173.

TOWNS NEARBY: Mandurah 18 km, Dwellingup 20 km, Rockingham 41 km, Harvey 50 km, Australind 74 km

Port Hedland

Pop. 11 557
Map ref. 578 D1 | 580 D11 | 582 H3

i 13 Wedge St; (08) 9173 1711.

 91.7 WA FM, 94.9 FM ABC News Radio

[PORT HEDLAND] RIO TINTO SALT OPERATIONS

Port Hedland was named after Captain Peter Hedland, who reached this deep-water harbour in 1863. An iron-ore boom that began in the early 1960s saw the town grow at a remarkable rate. Today, Port Hedland handles the largest iron-ore export tonnage of any Australian port. Iron ore is loaded onto huge ore carriers; the 2.6-kilometre trains operated by BHP Iron Ore are hard to miss. Salt production is another major industry with about 2 million tonnes exported per annum.

Don Rhodes Mining Museum: open-air museum with displays of historic railway and mining machinery; Wilson St. **Pioneer and Pearlers Cemetery:** used between 1912 and 1968, it has graves of early gold prospectors and Japanese pearl divers; off Stevens St. **Town tour:** visit the town's many attractions; 11am Mon, Wed and Fri June–Oct; book through visitor centre. **BHP Iron Ore Tour:** see the enormous machinery required to run this industrial giant; departs 9.30am Mon–Fri from visitor centre. **Heritage trail:** 1.8 km self-guide walk around the town; contact visitor centre for map.

Australia Day Festival: Jan. **Port Hedland Cup:** Aug. **Pilbara Music Festival:** Sept. **Welcome to Hedland Night:** every few months.

Heddy's Bar & Bistro: bistro by the sea; All Seasons Port Hedland, cnr Lukis and McGregor sts; (08) 9173 1511. **The Pilbara Room:** best dining in town; Hospitality Inn Port Hedland, Webster St; (08) 9173 1044. **Wedge Street Coffee Shop:** light meals; 12A Wedge St; (08) 9173 2128.

Cooke Point Holiday Park – Aspen Parks: 2 Taylor St; (08) 9173 1271. **Eighty Mile Beach Caravan Park:** Eighty Mile Beach Rd, Eighty Mile Beach; (08) 9176 5941.

Stairway to the Moon Like the Broome version, this beautiful illusion is created when a full moon rises over the ocean at low tide. The moon's rays hit pools of water left by the receding tide, creating the image of a stairway leading up to the moon. It lasts for about 15 minutes. Check with visitor centre for dates and times. Coastal side of Goode St; 7 km E.

Pretty Pool: picnic, fish and swim at this scenic tidal pool; 8 km NE. **Dampier Salt:** see giant cone-shaped mounds of salt awaiting export; 8 km s. **Royal Flying Doctor Service:** operates an important base in Port Hedland at the airport; open to public 8–11am weekdays; closed public/school holidays; 15 km s. **School of the Air:** experience schooling outback-style at the airport; open to public 8–11am weekdays; closed public/school holidays; 15 km s. **Turtle-watching:** flatback turtles nest in the area Oct–Mar at Pretty Pool, Cooke Point and Cemetery Beach. **Cruises:** scenic harbour and sunset cruises; contact visitor centre for details.

Travellers note: *Poisonous stonefish frequent this stretch of coast, especially Nov–Mar, so wear strong shoes when walking on rocky reef areas and make local inquiries before swimming in the sea.*

TOWNS NEARBY: Marble Bar 152 km, Roebourne 161 km, Karratha 190 km

Ravensthorpe

Pop. 438
Map ref. 576 G9

ℹ️ Morgans St; (08) 9838 1277; www.ravensthorpe.wa.gov.au

📻 101.9 WA FM, 105.9 FM ABC Local Radio

Ravensthorpe is encircled by the Ravensthorpe Range. This unspoiled bushland is home to many plants unique to the area such as the Qualup bell, warted yate and Ravensthorpe bottlebrush. Gold was discovered here in 1898 and by 1909 the population had increased to around 3000. Coppermining reached a peak in the late 1960s; the last coppermine closed in 1972. Many old mine shafts can be seen around the district and fossicking is a favourite pastime.

Historical Society Museum: local history memorabilia; in Dance Cottage near visitor centre, Morgans St. **Historic buildings:** many in town including the impressive Palace Hotel (1907) and the restored Commercial Hotel (now a community centre); both in Morgans St. **Rangeview Park:** local plant species, picnic and barbecue facilities; Morgans St.

Wildflower Show: Sept.

Ravensthorpe Palace Motor Hotel: traditional pub food; 68 Morgans St; (08) 9838 1005.

WA Time Meridian: plaque on a boulder marks the WA time meridian; at first rest bay west of town. *Eremia Camel Treks:* offers rides along the beach; open by appt Dec–Apr; Hopetoun Rd; (08) 9838 1092; 2 km SE. *Old Copper Smelter:* in operation 1906–18, now site of tailings dumps and old equipment; 2 km SE. *Archer Drive Lookout:* extensive views over farms and hills; 3 km N in Ravensthorpe Range. *Mt Desmond Lookout:* magnificent views in all directions; Ethel Daw Dr; 17 km SE in Ravensthorpe Range. *Hopetown:* seaside village with pristine beaches ideal for swimming, surfing, windsurfing, fishing and boating. Summer Festival each June. Walk on the Hopetoun Trail Head Loop (part of the Hopetoun–Ravensthorpe Heritage Walk) or visit Fitzgerald River National Park to the west; *see* Bremer Bay; 49 km S. *Scenic drives:* include the 170 km circular Hamersley Drive Heritage Trail; contact visitor centre for maps. *Rock-collecting:* check locally to avoid trespass.

TOWNS NEARBY: Lake King 64 km, Bremer Bay 109 km, Lake Grace 157 km, Hyden 168 km, Esperance 173 km

Rockingham

Pop. 108 312
Map ref. 570 C11 | 571 B7 | 574 B6 | 576 B8

i 19 Kent St; (08) 9592 3464;
www.rockinghamvisitorcentre.com.au

97.7 FM ABC Classic Radio, 720 AM ABC Local Radio

Lying on the edge of Cockburn Sound just 47 kilometres south of Perth, the coastal city of Rockingham offers sheltered waters ideal for swimming, snorkelling, sailing, windsurfing, fishing and crabbing. Established in 1872 to ship timber from Jarrahdale to England, Rockingham was the busiest port in Western Australia until the end of the 19th century, after which all port activities were shifted north to Fremantle. It was only because of the industrial area nearby at Kwinana in the 1950s and the development of the HMAS *Stirling* Naval Base on Garden Island in the 1970s that the town was revitalised. Today, its magnificent beaches and proximity to Perth are Rockingham's main attractions.

Rockingham Museum: folk museum featuring local history exhibits including displays on the Group Settlement farms, the timber industry, domestic items and antique photographic equipment; open 1–4pm Tues, Wed, Thurs, Sat and Sun; Cnr Flinders La and Kent St; (08) 9592 3455. *Art Gallery and Craft Centre:* features local artists; 43 Kent St; (08) 9592 7330. *The Granary:* museum of artefacts celebrating the history of WA's grain industry; open for tours (minimum group size 4) by appt; northern end of Rockingham Rd; (08) 9599 6333. *Mersey Pt Jetty:* departure point for cruises and island tours; Shoalwater. *Kwinana Beach:* hull of wrecked SS *Kwinana*. *Cape Peron:* the lookout was once the main observation post for a WW II coastal battery; Point Peron Rd. *Bell and Churchill Park:* family picnics and barbecues in shaded grounds; Rockingham Rd.

Musselfest: Feb. *Blues Alive Festival:* Mar. *Rockingham Community Fair:* Nov.

Bettyblue Bistro: steak and seafood; Shop 3, 1 Railway Tce; (08) 9528 4228. *Emma's on the Boardwalk:* innovative food with bay views; Shop 7–8, 1–3 Railway Tce; (08) 9592 8881. *Sunsets Cafe Bistro:* bay-side bistro; The Boardwalk, Palm Beach; (08) 9528 1910. *Y2K Cafe & Restaurant:* relaxed dining; 57B Rockingham Beach Rd; (08) 9529 1044.

Anchorage Guest House: 2 Smythe St; (08) 9527 4214. *Coogee Beach Holiday Park:* 3 Powell Rd, Coogee; (08) 9418 1810. *Rockingham Holiday Village:* 147 Dixon Rd, East Rockingham; (08) 9527 4240. *Woodman Point Holiday Park – Aspen Parks:* 132 Cockburn Rd, Munster; (08) 9434 1433.

Penguin Island Take a trip to this offshore island, which is home to a colony of little penguins. The Discovery Centre allows you to see the penguins up close in an environment similar to their natural habitat and to learn about them through daily feedings, commentaries and displays. The island also provides picnic areas, lookouts and a network of boardwalks, and you can swim, snorkel or scuba dive at any of the pristine beaches. The island is open to the public in daylight hours Sept–June. Ferries to the island leave regularly from Mersey Pt, south of Rockingham. The ferry also provides bay cruises and snorkelling tours.

Sloan's Cottage: restored pioneer cottage; open weekdays; Leda; 2 km W. *Lake Richmond:* walks, flora and fauna, and thrombolites (domed rock-like structures like the famous stromatolites of Hamelin Pool near Denham, built by ancient micro-organisms); 4 km SW. *Wineries:* in the area include Baldivis Estate (15 km SE) and Peel Estate (17 km SE); contact visitor centre for details. *Secret Harbour:* surfing, snorkelling and windsurfing; 20 km S. *Serpentine Dam:* major water storage with brilliant wildflowers in spring, bushland and the nearby Serpentine Falls; 48 km SE. *Garden Island:* home to HMAS *Stirling* Naval Base, two-thirds of the island is open to the public but is accessible only by private boat during daylight hours. *Shoalwater Bay Islands Marine Park:* extends from just south of Garden Island to Becher Pt. Cruises of the park are available; contact visitor centre for details. *Dolphin Watch Cruises:* swim with dolphins between Pt Peron and Garden Island; daily Sept–May; contact visitor centre for details. *Scenic drives:* including Old Rockingham Heritage Trail, a 30 km drive that takes in 23 points of interest in the Rockingham–Kwinana area, and Rockingham–Jarrahdale Timber Heritage Trail, a 36 km drive retracing the route of the 1872 timber railway.

TOWNS NEARBY: Mandurah 28 km, Thomson Bay 36 km, Pinjarra 41 km, Dwellingup 58 km, Mundaring 59 km

Roebourne

Pop. 853
Map ref. 575 F1 | 578 B2 | 580 B12 | 582 E5

i Old Gaol, Queens St; (08) 9182 1060;
www.roebourne.wa.gov.au

107.5 FM ABC Radio National, 702 AM ABC Local Radio

Named after John Septimus Roe, Western Australia's first surveyor-general, Roebourne was established in 1866 and is the oldest town on the north-west coast. As the centre for early mining and pastoral industries in the Pilbara, it was connected by tramway to the pearling port of Cossack and later to Point Samson. Now Cossack is a ghost town and Point Samson is known for its beachside pleasures.

Historic buildings: some original stone buildings remain, many of which have been classified by the National Trust. The Old Gaol, designed by the well-known colonial architect George Temple Poole, now operates as the visitor centre and museum; Queen St. *Mt Welcome:* offers views of the coastal plains and rugged hills surrounding town. Spot the railroad from Cape Lambert to Pannawonica, and the pipeline carrying water from Millstream to Wickham and Cape Lambert; Fisher Dr.

🌴 ***Roebourne Cup:*** July.

🍴 ***TaTa's Restaurant:*** international cuisine; Pt Samson Resort, 56 Samson Rd, Pt Samson; (08) 9187 1052.

🛏 ***The Cove Caravan Park:*** Lot 259 Macleod St, Pt Samson; (08) 9187 0199.

⊗ **Cossack** Originally named Tien Tsin after the boat that brought the first settlers there in 1863, Cossack was the first port in the north-west region. During its days as a pearling centre in the late 1800s the population increased dramatically. Although now a ghost town, the beautiful stone buildings have been restored and 9 are classified by the National Trust. The old post office houses a gallery and the courthouse has a museum, while the police barracks offer budget accommodation. Cruises are available from the wharf. 14 km N.

Wickham: the company town for Robe River Iron Ore offers a spectacular view from Tank Hill lookout; tours available; 12 km N. ***Pt Samson:*** good fishing, swimming, snorkelling and diving. Boat hire, whale-watching and fishing charters are available; 19 km N. ***Cleaverville:*** camping and fishing; 25 km N. ***Harding Dam:*** ideal picnic spot; 27 km s. ***Millstream–Chichester National Park:*** 150 km s; *see Karratha.* ***Emma Withnell Heritage Trail:*** 52 km historic self-drive trail, named after the first European woman in the north-west, takes in Roebourne, Cossack, Wickham and Pt Samson; map available at visitor centre. ***Tours:*** include historic Pearls and Past tour and trips to Jarman Island; contact visitor centre for details.

TOWNS NEARBY: Karratha 32 km, Port Hedland 161 km, Tom Price 223 km, Onslow 232 km

Rottnest Island
see Thomson Bay

Southern Cross
Pop. 709
Map ref. 576 F6

ⓘ Council offices, Antares St; (08) 9049 1001; www.yilgarn.wa.gov.au

📻 100.7 WA FM, 106.3 FM ABC Local Radio

A small, flourishing town on the Great Eastern Highway, Southern Cross is the centre of a prosperous agricultural and pastoral region. Its claim to fame is as the site of the first major gold discovery in the huge eastern goldfields and, although it never matched the fever pitch of Kalgoorlie and Coolgardie, Southern Cross remains the centre for a significant gold-producing area. The town's wide streets, like the town itself, were named after stars and constellations.

🏠 ***Yilgarn History Museum:*** originally the town courthouse and mining registrar's office, it now houses displays on mining, agriculture, water supply and military involvement; Antares St. ***Historic buildings:*** including the post office in Antares St, the Railway Tavern in Spica St and the restored Palace Hotel in Orion St.

🌴 ***King of the Cross:*** 2 days of motorcycle races; Aug.

🍴 ***The Club Hotel:*** international cuisine; 21 Antares St; (08) 9049 1202. ***Palace Hotel:*** traditional pub fare; Great Eastern Hwy; (08) 9049 1555.

⊗ ***Hunt's Soak:*** once an important water source, now a picnic area; 7 km N. ***Frog Rock:*** large rock with wave-like formations.

Popular picnic spot; 34 km s. ***Baladjie Rock:*** granite outcrop with spectacular views; 50 km NW. ***Karalee Rock and Dam:*** this dam was built to provide water for steam trains and is now popular for swimming and picnics; 52 km E.

TOWNS NEARBY: Merredin 104 km, Hyden 143 km, Kellerberrin 159 km, Coolgardie 178 km, Corrigin 184 km

Thomson Bay
Pop. 300
Map ref. 570 A7 | 571 A6

ⓘ Rottnest Island Visitor Centre; located at the end of the main jetty, Thomson Bay; (08) 9372 9730.; www.rottnestisland.com

Although only 11 kilometres long and 5 kilometres wide, Rottnest Island boasts crystal-clear waters for swimming, coral reefs for snorkelling and diving, and a range of beautiful sandy beaches and secluded coves. Thomson Bay, a protected north-easterly bay that faces the mainland, is Rottnest Island's largest and oldest settlement. As the site of the island's main jetty, it is the arrival and departure point for all ferries travelling to and from Perth, Fremantle and Hillarys. The visitor centre and accommodation office are at the end of the jetty.

🏠 **Historic buildings** Originally established in 1838 as a prison for Aboriginal people from the mainland, the Rottnest settlement has a number of convict-built buildings, including the Rottnest Island Museum, built in 1857 as a haystore and granary, which now features displays and photographs on the history of the island. The Salt Store, built in 1968 to hold the bagged salt collected from the island's salt lakes, is now an art gallery and exhibition centre. The octagonal 'Quod' (1864), which once served as a prison, is now part of the Rottnest Lodge and its prison cells have been transformed into hotel rooms. Vincent Way, overlooking Thomson Bay, is one of the oldest streetscapes in Australia. The original building of the Hotel Rottnest, built in 1864 as the summer residence for the governors of Western Australia, has now been revamped and joined by an alfresco beachside courtyard, bars and accommodation. Tours covering different aspects of Rottnest's history are run daily by the Rottnest Voluntary Guides; brochures on self-guide walk trails also available; contact visitors centre for details.

Quokka Walk The quokka is a native marsupial found primarily on Rottnest Island and is responsible for the island's unflattering name (which means rat's nest) – explorer Willem de Vlamingh mistook this semi-nocturnal and furry animal, which grows to the size of a hare, for a large rat. Look out for one of the 10 000 quokkas on the island or join a daily quokka-spotting tour around Thomson Bay.

Bike hire: as the use of vehicles is prohibited on Rottnest, except by the authorities, cycling is the usual mode of transport for visitors. Bring your own on the ferry or rent one from Rottnest Island Bike Hire, just behind the Hotel Rottnest; open daily, hours vary seasonally; (08) 9292 5105. ***Bus services:*** there are two bus services, both of which depart from the settlement's main bus stop. A free shuttle runs between the main accommodation areas on the island. The Bayseeker is an all-day jump-on, jump-off service that does a regular circuit of the island. ***Shopping precinct:*** just a short walk from the main jetty is the settlement's small pedestrian mall of shops, including a general store, surf wear shop, pharmacy, bakery and other food outlets. ***Family Fun Park:*** when you need a break from Rottnest's natural wonders, this fun park offers mini golf, trampolines, giant chess and a shed of

[THOMSON BAY] THE BASIN, WITH BATHURST LIGHTHOUSE IN THE BACKGROUND, ROTTNEST ISLAND

arcade amusements. ***Rottnest Island Picture Hall:*** catch a movie in the island's original picture hall, complete with deck chairs. ***Water-based activities***: Thomson Bay offers many water-based activities, from swimming at the sheltered beach to snorkelling and fishing; snorkelling equipment available for hire at Rottnest Island Bike Hire. ***Just 4 Fun Aqua Park***: jump, slide and splash in this water-based adventure park of inflatable equipment, with a knee-deep area for toddlers, situated just north of the main jetty; 10.30am–5pm daily, Nov–Apr.

🌴 ***Rottnest Channel Swim:*** Feb. ***Swim Thru Rottnest:*** Dec.

🍴 ***Aristos Waterfront Restaurant:*** fresh local seafood with ocean views; (08) 9292 5171. ***Dome Rottnest:*** light meals and coffee overlooking Thomson Bay; (08) 9292 5286. ***Hotel Rottnest:*** breezy open-plan bar with tasty food right on the beach; (08) 9292 5011. ***Marlins:*** fine dining by the pool or atrium; Rottnest Lodge; (08) 9292 1561. ***Rottnest Bakery:*** a Rotto institution, famous for its delicious baked goods; (08) 9292 5023.

⊚ **Wadjemup Lighthouse** The original lighthouse, built in 1849 by Aboriginal prisoners, was WA's first lighthouse. This was replaced in 1881 by a lighthouse with a rotating beam, which is still standing. The Rottnest Voluntary Guides run daily half-hour tours from 11am to 2.30pm; meet at the lighthouse.

Oliver Hill Take a scenic train ride up to Oliver Hill, where the evidence of Rottnest Island's military past, including a tunnel system, can be found. The gun battery was built in the 1930s to defend the WA coastline and Fremantle harbour. Find out more on one of the daily 'Guns and Tunnels' tours; contact visitor centre for details.

Beaches: Rottnest Island is home to over 60 beaches, the most popular of which is the Basin, only a short trip from Thomson Bay, and so named because the coral reef forms a basin-like swimming pool. ***Vlamingh's Lookout:*** this lookout boasts panoramic views of the island; on the way, stop at the old cemetery, the gravestones testifying to the hardships of the early settlers. ***Snorkelling and diving:*** with some 360 species of fish, over 20 species of coral, and 13 historic shipwrecks in its coastal waters, Rottnest is a perfect location for snorkelling and diving; a snorkel trail at Parker Pt features underwater interpretative plaques. ***Surfing and bodyboarding:*** Strickland Bay, Salmon Bay and Stark Bay are the island's best spots for waves. ***Birdwatching:*** its A-Class Reserve status and varied habitat – coastal, woodlands, heath, salt lakes and swamps – means Rottnest is home to a wide range of bird species; the osprey nest at Salmon Pt is estimated to be 70 years old. ***West End:*** the far western end of the island boasts a $300 000 boardwalk, the first stage of a 50 km Coastal Walk Trail under development; allow 1.5–2 hrs by bike to get there or take the bus on the Discovery Tour (contact visitor centre for details); 11 km w. ***Rottnest Island Marine Reserve:*** lying in the path of the warm Leeuwin ocean current, the waters around Rottnest support an unusually rich diversity of marine life, including coral reefs, tropical fish and migrating humpback whales, dolphins and sea lions. Day-long boat tours available or, if short on time, take the 90-minute Adventure Tour (Sept–June); Rottnest Express; 1300 467 688 or (08) 9432 8090.

TOWNS NEARBY: **Rockingham 36 km, Yanchep 51 km, Mundaring 60 km, Mandurah 61 km, Pinjarra 77 km**

Tom Price

Pop. 2721
Map ref. 575 G3 | 578 C5 | 582 G10

ⓘ Central Rd; (08) 9188 1112; www.tompricewa.com.au

📻 103.3 WA FM, 567 AM ABC Local Radio

The huge iron-ore deposit now known as Mount Tom Price was discovered in 1962 in the heart of the Pilbara, after which the Hamersley Iron Project was established. A mine, two towns (Dampier and Tom Price) and a railway line between them all followed. Today, the town is an oasis in a dry countryside. On the edge of the Hamersley Range at an altitude of 747 metres, this is the state's highest town, hence its nickname of 'Top Town in WA'.

🍴 ***Tom Price Hotel Motel:*** international cuisine; Central Rd; (08) 9189 1101.

 Karijini National Park Karijini was the name given to this area by the original inhabitants, the Banjima. The second largest national park in Western Australia, this park features ochre-coloured rock faces with bright-white snappy gums, bundles of spinifex dotting the red earth and chasms up to 100 m deep. The waterfalls and rockpools of Karijini offer some of the best swimming in the state. The park protects the many different wildlife habitats, plants and animals of the Pilbara. The landscape is dotted with huge termite mounds and the rock piles of the rare pebble mouse; other species include red kangaroos and rock wallabies, and reptiles from legless lizards to pythons. Kalamina Gorge and Pool is the most accessible gorge, while at Hamersley Gorge a wave of tectonic rock acts as a backdrop to a swimming hole and natural spa. Oxer Lookout reveals where the Joffre, Hancock, Weano and Red gorges meet. Mt Bruce, the second-tallest peak in the state, offers spectacular views and interpretive signs along the trail to the top. The Karijini Visitor Centre is located off the road to Dales Gorge and has information on camping. 50 km E.

Kings Lake: constructed lake with nearby park offering picnic and barbecue facilities (no swimming); 2 km w. *Mt Nameless Lookout:* stunning views of district around Tom Price; 6 km w via walking trail or 4WD track. *Aboriginal carvings:* thought to be 35 000 years old; 10 km s. *Mine tours:* marvel at the sheer enormity of Hamersley Iron's open-cut iron-ore mine; bookings essential, arrange through visitor centre. *Hamersley Iron Access Road:* this private road is the most direct route between Tom Price and Karratha via Karijini and Millstream national parks. It requires a permit to travel along it; available from visitor centre.

Travellers note: *To the north-east is Wittenoom, an old asbestos-mining town. Although the mine was closed in 1966, there is still a health risk from microscopic asbestos fibres present in the abandoned mine tailings in and around Wittenoom. If disturbed and inhaled, blue asbestos dust may cause cancer. The Ashburton Shire Council advocates avoidance of the Wittenoom area.*

TOWNS NEARBY: Newman 212 km, Roebourne 223 km, Karratha 238 km

Toodyay
Pop. 1068
Map ref. 571 F2 | 574 D4 | 576 C7

i 7 Piesse St; (08) 9574 2435; www.toodyay.com

558 AM ABC Local Radio, 612 AM ABC Radio National

This National Trust–classified town is nestled in the Avon Valley surrounded by picturesque farming country and bushland. The name originates from 'Duidgee', which means the 'place of plenty'. Founded in 1836, Toodyay was one of the first inland towns to be established in the colony. It was a favourite haunt of Western Australia's most famous bushranger, Joseph Bolitho Johns, who was more commonly known as 'Moondyne Joe'.

 Historic buildings Some original buildings from the early settlement of Toodyay still stand, including Stirling House (1908), Connor's Mill (1870s) with displays of working flour-milling equipment, the Old Newcastle Gaol (1865) built by convict labour and where Moondyne Joe was imprisoned, and the Police Stables (1870) built by convict labour from random rubblestone. Self-guide walk available; pamphlet at visitor centre.

Duidgee Park: popular picnic spot on the banks of the river has a miniature railway and a walking track; check at visitor centre for running times; Harper Rd. *Newcastle Park:* contains a unique stone monument of Charlotte Davies, the first white female to set foot on the soil of the Swan River Colony. Also has a children's playground; Stirling Tce. *Pelham Reserve and Lookout:* nature walks, a lookout with views over the town and a memorial to James Drummond, the town's first resident botanist; Duke St.

Moondyne Festival: May. *Avon Descent:* whitewater rafting; Aug. *Kombi Konnection:* Sept. *Music Festival:* Sept.

Cola Cafe and Museum: 1950s-style cafe; 128 Stirling Tce; (08) 9574 4407. *Victoria Restaurant:* home-style cooking; Victoria Hotel-Motel, 116 Stirling Tce; (08) 9574 2206.

Pecan Hill: Lot 59 Beaufort St; (08) 9574 2636. *Toodyay Holiday Park & Chalets:* 188 Racecourse Rd; (08) 9574 2534.

 **Avon Valley National Park** In the 1860s, bushranger Moondyne Joe hid in the forests, caves and wildflower fields of the lush Avon Valley. The park retains this landscape, offering spectacular scenery with abundant wildflowers in season. Being at the northern limit of the jarrah forests, the jarrah and marri trees mingle with wandoo woodland. This mix of trees creates diverse habitats for fauna, including a wide variety of birdlife. The Avon River, which in summer and autumn is a series of pools, swells to become impressive rapids during winter and spring. These rapids provide the backdrop for the Avon Descent, a well-known annual whitewater race held every Aug, which begins in Northam and passes through the park. The park is ideal for camping, bushwalking, canoeing and picnicking, although all roads are unsealed. Whitewater rafting tours are available. 25 km sw.

Pecan Hill Tearoom Museum: tearoom and museum set in a pecan nut orchard with a lookout offering spectacular views over the Avon Valley; Julimar Rd; 4 km NW. *Coorinja Winery:* dating from the 1870s; open for tastings and sales; closed Sun; 4 km sw. *Ringa Railway Bridge:* constructed in 1888, this timber bridge has 18 spans, but is not readily accessible; details from visitor centre; 6 km sw. *Windmill Hill Cutting:* the deepest railway cutting in Australia; 6 km SE. *Avonlea Park Alpaca Farm:* alpacas and other farm animals, and sales of alpaca wool products; 12 km SE. *Emu Farm:* one of the oldest in Australia. Birds range free in natural bushland. Also crafts and emu products for sale; 15 km sw. *Cartref Park Country Garden:* 2 ha park of English-style landscaped gardens and native plants, with prolific birdlife; 16 km NW. *Oliomio Farm:* olive and lavender farm offering tastings and sales; Parkland Dr; 20 km NW. *Wyening Mission:* this Benedictine farm and winery runs tours of their mission, cellars and grounds; by appt; (08) 9364 6463; 38 km N. *Toodyay Pioneer Heritage Trail:* honouring the pioneering spirit in the Avon Valley, this 20 km self-drive trail retraces the route of the first settlers; contact visitor centre for map. *Avon Valley Tourist Drive:* 95 km scenic drive includes Toodyay, Northam, York and Beverley; contact visitor centre for map. *Hotham Valley Steam Railway:* the famous steam-train service runs special trips including a monthly 'murder-mystery' night; contact visitor centre for details.

TOWNS NEARBY: Northam 23 km, York 47 km, Mundaring 48 km, Gingin 58 km, New Norcia 69 km

Wagin
Pop. 1424
Map ref. 574 F8 | 576 D9

i Historical Village, Kitchener St; (08) 9861 1232; www.wagintouristinfo.com.au

96.3 FM ABC News Radio, 558 AM ABC Local Radio

Wagin, 177 kilometres east of Bunbury, is the sheep capital of Western Australia. The importance of the wool industry to the district is celebrated in its annual Wagin Woolorama, one of the largest rural shows in the state, and its Giant Ram, an enormous structure that visitors from around the country come to photograph.

 **Wagin Historical Village** Explore 24 relocated or re-created historic buildings and machinery providing a glimpse of pioneering rural life. The buildings are furnished with original pieces, and audio commentaries are available. Open 10am–4pm daily; Kitchener St.

[WALPOLE] VALLEY OF THE GIANTS, TREE-TOP WALKWAY

Giant Ram and Ram Park: 9 m high statue provides a photo opportunity not to miss; Arthur River Rd. *Wagin Heritage Trail:* self-guide walk around the town; contact visitor centre for map.

Wagin Woolorama: Mar. *Foundation Day:* June.

The Palace Hotel: traditional pub; 57 Tudhoe St; (08) 9861 1003.

Puntapin Rock: spectacular views over the town and surrounding farmlands from the top of the rock. Enjoy the picnic and barbecue facilities nearby; Bullock Hill Rd; 4 km SE. *Mt Latham:* interesting rock formation with walk trails, a lookout and abundant wildflowers in season; Arthur River Rd; 8 km W. *Lake Norring:* swimming, sailing and waterskiing; picnic and barbecue facilities; water levels vary considerably; check conditions at visitor centre; 17 km SW. *Lake Dumbleyung:* where Donald Campbell established a world water-speed record in 1964. Swimming, boating and birdwatching are subject to water levels that vary considerably; check conditions at visitor centre; 18 km E. *Wait-jen Trail:* self-guide 10.5 km signposted walk that follows ancient Aboriginal Dreaming. The word 'wait-jen' means 'emu footprint' in the language of the local Aboriginal people; contact visitor centre for map. *Wheat Belt Wildflower Drive:* self-guide drive that includes the Tarin Rock Nature Reserve; contact visitor centre for map.

TOWNS NEARBY: Narrogin 44 km, Katanning 47 km, Kojonup 60 km, Wickepin 60 km, Pingelly 89 km

Walpole

Pop. 322
Map ref. 573 F6 | 574 E12 | 576 D11

ℹ️ Pioneer Cottage, South Coast Hwy; (08) 9840 1111; www.walpole.com.au

📻 102.9 WA FM, 106.1 FM ABC Local Radio

Walpole is entirely surrounded by national park and is the only place in the South-West where the forest meets the sea. The area is renowned for its striking ocean and forest scenery, which provides an idyllic setting for outdoor activities. The town of Walpole was established in 1930 through the Nornalup Land Settlement Scheme for city families hit by the Great Depression.

Pioneer Cottage: re-creation of a historic cottage to commemorate the district's pioneer settlers; South Coast Hwy.

Easter Markets: Apr.

The Nornalup Teahouse Restaurant: cottage cafe; 6684 South Coast Hwy, Nornalup; (08) 9840 1422. *Thurlby Herb Farm Cafe:* fresh produce; Gardiner Rd; (08) 9840 1249. *Tree Top Restaurant:* local produce; Tree Top Walk Motel, Nockolds St; (08) 9840 1444. *Slow Food Cafe:* local produce; Old Kent River Wines, South Coast Hwy, Rocky Gully; (08) 9855 1589.

Coalmine Beach Holiday Park: Coalmine Beach Rd; (08) 9840 1026.

Walpole–Nornalup National Park The many forest attractions include the Valley of the Giants, the Hilltop Drive and Lookout, Circular Pool and the Knoll. The park is probably best known for its huge, buttressed red tingle trees, some more than 400 years old, which are unique to the Walpole area. The world-class Bibbulmun Track, between Perth and Albany, passes through the park. *See Albany;* 4 km SE.

Valley of the Giants Here visitors can wander over a walkway suspended 38 m above the forest floor, the highest and longest tree-top walkway of its kind in the world. The Ancient Empire interpretive boardwalk weaves its way through the veteran tingle trees. Twilight walks are available in holiday season. Contact (08) 9840 8263; 16 km E.

Giant Red Tingle: a 25 m circumference defines this tree as one of the 10 largest living things on the planet; 2 km E. *Hilltop Lookout:* views over the Frankland River out to the Southern Ocean; 2 km W. *John Rate Lookout:* panoramic views over the mouth of the Deep River and of the nearby coastline and forests; 4 km W. *Thurlby Herb Farm:* herb garden display with sales of herbal products; Gardiner Rd; 13 km N. *Mandalay Beach:* site of the 1911 shipwreck of the Norwegian *Mandalay*. A boardwalk has descriptive notes about the wreck. Also popular for fishing; 20 km W. *Dinosaur World:* a collection of native birds and reptiles, and exotic birds; 25 km E. *Mt Frankland National Park:* noted for its exceptional variety of birdlife, it also offers breathtaking views from the top of Mt Frankland, known as 'Caldyanup' to the local Aboriginal people; 29 km N. *Peaceful Bay:* small fishing village with an excellent beach for swimming; 35 km E. *Fernhook Falls:* ideal picnic spot with boardwalk, at its best in winter when it is popular for canoeing and kayaking; 36 km NW. *Walk trails:* many trails in the area, including self-guide Horseyard Hill Walk Trail through the karri forest and the signposted Coalmine Beach Heritage Trail from the coastal heathland to the inlets; contact visitor centre for maps. *Tours:* take a guided cruise through the inlets and rivers, hire a boat or canoe, or go on a forest tour or wilderness eco-cruise; contact visitor centre for details.

TOWNS NEARBY: Denmark 57 km, Northcliffe 67 km, Pemberton 87 km, Mount Barker 94 km, Manjimup 98 km

Wickepin

Pop. 245
Map ref. 574 F6 | 576 D8

 District Resource and Telecentre, 24 Wogolin Rd; (08) 9888 1500; www.wickepin.wa.au

100.5 Hot FM, 612 AM ABC Radio National

The first settlers arrived in the Wickepin area in the 1890s. Albert Facey's internationally acclaimed autobiography, *A Fortunate Life*, details these pioneering times. However, Facey is not the only major literary figure to feature in Wickepin's history. The poet and playwright Dorothy Hewett was born in Wickepin in 1923, and much of her work deals with life in the area.

Historic buildings in Wogolin Road: excellent examples of Edwardian architecture. *Facey Homestead:* the home of author Albert Facey has been relocated and restored with its original furniture; open 10am–4pm daily Mar–Nov, 10am–4pm Fri–Sun and public holidays Dec–Feb.

Wickepin Hotel: traditional pub; 34 Wogolin Rd; (08) 9888 1192.

Tarling Well: the circular stone well marks the original intended site for the town; 8 km W. *Malyalling Rock:* unusual rock formation; 15 km NE. *Toolibin Lake Reserve:* see a wide variety of waterfowl while you enjoy a barbecue; 20 km S. *Yealering and Yealering Lake:* historic photographs on display in town, and swimming, boating, windsurfing and birdwatching at lake; 30 km NE. *Harrismith Walk Path:* self-guide trail through wildflowers in season, including orchids and some species unique to the area; contact visitor centre for brochure. *Albert Facey Heritage Trail:* 86 km self-drive trail brings to life the story of Albert Facey and the harshness of life in the early pioneering days of the wheat belt; contact visitor centre for map.

TOWNS NEARBY: Narrogin 35 km, Pingelly 48 km, Wagin 60 km, Corrigin 61 km, Kulin 63 km

Wyndham

Pop. 672
Map ref. 581 N4 | 585 L5

 Kimberley Motors, Great Northern Hwy; (08) 9161 1281; www.swek.wa.gov.au

102.9 WA FM, 1017 AM ABC Local Radio

Wyndham, in the Kimberley region, is the most northerly town and safe port in Western Australia. The entrance to the town is guarded by the 'Big Croc', a 20-metre-long concrete crocodile.

Historical Society Museum: in the old courthouse building, its displays include a photographic record of the town's history, artefacts and machinery; open Apr–Oct; O'Donnell St. *Warriu Dreamtime Park:* bronze statues representing the Aboriginal heritage of the area; Koolama St. *Zoological Gardens and Crocodile Park:* daily feeding of crocodiles and alligators; Barytes Rd; (08) 9161 1124. *Durack's Old Store:* has an informative plaque with details of its history; O'Donnell St.

Pioneer Cemetery: gravestones of some of the area's original settlers; Great Northern Hwy. *Boat charters:* scenic, fishing and camping cruises; contact visitor centre for details.

 Races: Aug. *Art and Craft Show:* Aug/Sept.

Wyndham Town Hotel: try the famous 'Barra Burger'; O'Donnell St; (08) 9161 1003.

Three Mile Valley On offer is spectacular scenery typical of the Kimberley region, with rough red gorges and pools of clear, cold water during the wet season. Walk trails lead the visitor through the brilliant displays of wildflowers in season. Three Mile Valley is the home of the 'Trial Tree', a sacred Aboriginal site into which, when a person died of unnatural causes, the body was placed. Rocks were placed around the base of the tree, each rock representing a relative of the deceased. When the body started to decompose, the first rock to be marked by the decomposition indicated the name of the person responsible for the death. This person was then banished from the tribe. 3 km N.

Afghan Cemetery: containing the graves of Afghan camel drivers who carried supplies throughout the Kimberley region. All the gravestones face towards Mecca; 1 km E. *Koolama Wreck Site:* the *Koolama* was hit by Japanese bombs near Darwin in 1942. After limping along the coast to Wyndham, it sank just 40 m from the jetty. The spot is marked by unusual swirling in the water; 5 km NW. *Five Rivers Lookout:* spectacular views of the Kimberley landscape from the highest point of the Bastion Range, particularly good for viewing the striking sunsets. Also a good picnic area with barbecue facilities; 5 km N. *Moochalabra Dam:* completed in 1971, the dam was constructed to provide an assured water supply to the Wyndham area. The construction is unique in Australia, designed to allow overflow to pass through the rock on the crest of the hill. 4WD access only; King River Rd; 18 km SW. *Aboriginal rock paintings:* 4WD access only; well signposted off the King River Rd; 18 km SW. *Parry Lagoons Nature Reserve:* visitors can enjoy birdwatching from a shaded bird hide at Marlgu Billabong or scan the wide vistas of the flood plain and distant hills afforded from the lookout at Telegraph Hill; 20 km SE. *Prison Tree:* 2000–4000-year-old boab tree once used by local police as a lock-up; King River Rd; 22 km SW. *The Grotto:* this rock-edged waterhole, estimated to be 100 m deep, is a cool, shaded oasis offering year-round swimming; 36 km E.

TOWNS NEARBY: Kununurra 74 km

Yalgoo

Pop. 164
Map ref. 575 F11 | 576 C2

 Old Railway Station, Geraldton–Mt Magnet Rd; (08) 9962 8157; www.yalgoo.wa.gov.au

104.5 WA FM, 106.1 FM ABC Local Radio

Alluvial gold was discovered in the 1890s in Yalgoo, which lies 216 kilometres east of Geraldton. Today, gold is still found in the district and visitors are encouraged to try their luck fossicking in the area. The name Yalgoo is from the Aboriginal word meaning 'blood', a rather odd fact given that in 1993 a Yalgoo resident was the first person in Australia to be the victim of a parcel bomb.

Courthouse Museum: exhibits of local artefacts; Gibbons St. *Gaol:* built in 1896 and recently relocated to the museum precinct, it has photographs illustrating the town's history; Gibbons St. *Chapel of St Hyacinth:* designed by Monsignor

Hawes and built in 1919 for the Dominican Sisters who lived in a wooden convent school near the chapel; Henty St. *Heritage walk:* self-guide town walk; pamphlet available at visitor centre.

 Cemetery: the history of Yalgoo as told through headstones; 5 km w. *Joker's Tunnel:* a tunnel carved through solid rock by early prospectors and named after the Joker's mining syndicate, it has panoramic views near the entrance; 10 km se. *Meteorite crater:* discovered in 1961, a portion of the meteorite is held at the WA Museum in Perth; 100 km n. *Gascoyne Murchison Outback Pathways:* 3 self-drive trips exploring outback history: the Wool Wagon Pathway, the Kingsford Smith Mail Run and the Miners Pathway; see visitor centre or website for maps.

TOWNS NEARBY: Morawa 117 km, Mullewa 117 km, Mount Magnet 119 km, Cue 157 km, Carnamah 168 km

Yallingup

Pop. 1060
Map ref. 572 A6 | 574 B9 | 576 B10

ⓘ Seymour Blvd, Dunsborough; (08) 9752 5800; www.geographebay.com

📻 98.4 FM Western Tourist Radio, 684 AM ABC Local Radio

Yallingup, known for its limestone caves and world-class surf breaks, is also an ideal location for swimming, fishing and beachcombing. Nearby Leeuwin–Naturaliste National Park offers spectacular scenery, interesting bushwalks and beautiful wildflowers in season. Art and craft galleries abound and many of the wineries of the South-West region are only a short drive from the town. Yallingup continues to live up to its Aboriginal meaning of 'place of love', being a favourite destination for generations of honeymooners and holiday-makers.

🏠 *Wardan Aboriginal Centre:* houses an interpretive display and a gallery that sells local Indigenous arts. Book ahead for workshops, including boomerang-throwing classes; closed 15 June – 15 Aug; Injidup Springs Rd; (08) 9756 6566. *Yallingup Caves Hotel:* formerly known as Caves House Hotel, this hotel was originally built in 1903 and then rebuilt after being damaged by fire in 1938. It has been a favourite destination for generations of honeymooners and holiday makers; 18 Yallingup Beach Rd; (08) 9750 1555. *Yallingup Maze:* fun for all the family, with a timber maze, indoor puzzles and games, cafe and playground. 3059 Caves Rd; (08) 9756 6500; open daily. *Yallingup Beach:* surfing, scuba diving, whale-watching and salmon fishing in season.

🎪 *Yallingup Surfilm Festival:* Jan. *Yallingup Malibu Surfing Classic:* Dec.

🍴 *Cape Lodge Restaurant:* superb fine dining; 3341 Caves Rd; (08) 9755 6311. *Yallingup Caves Hotel:* classic Aussie pub food; Yallingup Beach Rd; (08) 9750 1555. *Lamont's Margaret River:* modern Australian; Gunyulgup Valley Dr; (08) 9755 2434. *Flutes Restaurant:* modern Australian; Brookland Valley Winery, Caves Rd; Wilyabrup; (08) 9755 6250. *The Studio Gallery and Bistro:* arts venue adjacent to national park offers fine art with innovative continental cuisine; 7 Marrinup Dr; (08) 9756 6164.

🛏 *Yallingup Beach Holiday Park:* Valley Rd; (08) 9755 2164. *Craythorne Country House:* 180 Worgan Rd, Metricup; (08) 9755 7477.

🌐 *Leeuwin–Naturaliste National Park:* stretches north and south of town; *see Dunsborough, Margaret River and Augusta. Ngilgi Cave:* (pronounced 'Nillgee') an interpretive

area details the history of this cave, known for its stunning display of stalactite, stalagmite and shawl rock formations; daily adventure tours available; (08) 9756 6173; 2 km e. *Canal Rocks and Smith's Beach:* interesting rock formation plus fishing, surfing, swimming, snorkelling and diving; 5 km sw. *Gunyulgup Galleries:* over 120 artists and craftspeople are represented, with paintings, prints, ceramics and sculpture on display and for sale; Cnr Gunyulgup Valley and Koorabin drs; (08) 9755 2177; 9 km sw. *Yallingup Galleries:* specialises in custom-built furniture; Cnr Gunyulgup Valley Dr and Caves Rd; (08) 9755 2372; 9 km sw. *Quinninup Falls:* falls that are particularly attractive in winter and can be reached only by 4WD or on foot; 10 km s. *Yallingup Shearing Shed:* huge range of wool products for sale, and shearing demonstrations at 11am; closed Fri; Wildwood Rd; (08) 9755 2309; 10 km e. *Wineries and breweries:* many award-winning wineries and boutique breweries in the area offer tastings and sales; contact visitor centre for details.

TOWNS NEARBY: Dunsborough 8 km, Busselton 29 km, Margaret River 34 km, Bunbury 67 km, Donnybrook 74 km

Yanchep

Pop. 2481
Map ref. 570 A1 | 571 A2 | 574 B4 | 576 B7

ⓘ Information office, Yanchep National Park; (08) 9561 1004.

📻 94.5 Mix FM, 720 AM ABC Local Radio

Only 58 kilometres north of Perth, Yanchep is a rapidly developing recreational area and popular tourist destination. It provides safe, sandy beaches and good fishing areas, as well as natural attractions such as the series of caves found within Yanchep National Park. The town derives its name from the Aboriginal word 'yanjet', which means bullrushes, a feature of the area.

🏠 *Yanchep Lagoon:* good swimming and fishing beach; off Lagoon Dr.

🍴 *Chocolate Drops:* handmade chocolates, light meals; Yanchep National Park, Wanneroo Rd; (08) 9561 6699. *Lindsay's Restaurant:* international cuisine; Club Capricorn, Two Rocks Rd; (08) 9561 1106. *The Tudor Manor Restaurant:* international cuisine; Yanchep Inn, Yanchep National Park; (08) 9561 1001. *Blue Dolphin Restaurant:* bistro fare; shop 18, Two Rocks Shopping Centre, 8 Enterprise Ave, Two Rocks; (08) 9561 1469.

🛏 *Guilderton Caravan Park:* 2 Dewar St, Guilderton; (08) 9577 1021. *Ledge Point Holiday Park:* Lot 742 Ledge Point Rd, Ledge Point; (08) 9655 2870.

🌐 **Yanchep National Park** On a belt of coastal limestone, this 2842 ha park has forests of massive tuart trees, underground caves and spring wildflowers. Within the park, attractions include the historic Tudor-style Yanchep Inn; the Crystal Cave featuring magnificent limestone formations (daily tours available); a koala boardwalk; rowing-boat hire on freshwater Loch McNess; self-guide walk trails; and Aboriginal cultural tours (available on weekends and public holidays). Boomerang Gorge follows an ancient collapsed cave system and has an interpretive nature trail with access for people with disabilities. Grassy areas with barbecues and picnic tables provide a perfect setting for a family outing. 5 km e.

Marina: charter fishing boat hire; 6 km nw at Two Rocks. *Guilderton:* peaceful town at the mouth of the Moore River. Estuary provides safe swimming, and upper reaches of the river can be explored by boat or canoe (hire on river foreshore). Also good fishing; 37 km N. **Ledge Pt:** great destination for diving, with dive trail to 14 shipwrecks. Also the starting point for Lancelin Ocean Classic, a major windsurfing race each Jan; 62 km N. **Lancelin:** great base for fishing and boating because of a natural breakwater offshore. White sandy beaches provide safe swimming, and sand dunes at the edge of town have designated areas for off-road vehicles and sand-boarding; 71 km N.

TOWNS NEARBY: Gingin 34 km, Thomson Bay 51 km, Mundaring 64 km, Toodyay 79 km, Rockingham 81 km

York

Pop. 2091
Map ref. 571 H4 | 574 D4 | 576 C7

 Town Hall, 81 Avon Tce; (08) 9641 1301; www.yorkwa.org

101.3 York FM, 612 AM ABC Radio National

On the banks of the Avon River in the fertile Avon Valley, York is one of the best preserved and restored 19th-century towns in Australia. It is now classified by the National Trust as 'York Historic Town'. Settled in 1831, only two years after the establishment of the Swan River Colony, York was the first inland European settlement in Western Australia.

Historic buildings There are a significant number of carefully preserved historic buildings in York, many made from local stone and some built of mudbrick. The 3 remaining hotels are fine examples of early coaching inns, while the Romanesque-style Town Hall (1911) with its ornate facade reflects the wealth brought into the town by the gold rushes. Contact visitor centre for details.

Avon Park: picturesque park on the banks of the river with playground and barbecue facilities; Low St. **York Motor Museum:** vehicles on display represent the development of motor transport; Avon Tce. **York Mill Gallery:** At the York Mill Gallery there's lots to entertain the whole family, including shopping, a playground for the kids and the unique toilets. The York Mill was built in 1892 and is now the largest regional gallery in Western Australia. It's also home to the York Mill Weekend Markets and the fully licensed The Mill restaurant; 10 Henrietta Street York. **Residency Museum:** personal possessions, ceramics and silverware reflect aspects of civic and religious life in early York; open 1–3pm Tues–Thurs, 11am–3.30pm Sat, Sun and public holidays; Brook St. **Suspension bridge and walk trail:** built in 1906, the bridge crosses the Avon River at Avon Park. A 1.5 km nature and heritage walk starts at the bridge; Low St.

Antique Fair: Apr. **York Society Photographic Awards:** Apr. **Olive Festival:** June. **Jazz Festival:** Sept/Oct. **Spring Garden Festival:** Oct.

Cafe Bugatti: town favourite; 104 Avon Tce; (08) 9641 1583. **Castle Hotel York:** bistro, wood-fired pizza; 95–97 Avon Tce; (08) 9641 1007 **The York Mill Cafe & Restaurant:** arty cafe; 10 Henrietta St (Great Southern Hwy); (08) 9641 2447.

The Lodgings at Tipperary Church: 2092 Northam–York Rd; 0439 965 275.

Mt Brown Lookout: provides 360-degree views over town; 3 km SE. **Gwambygine Park:** picturesque picnic area overlooking the river with boardwalk and viewing platform; 10 km S. **Skydive Express:** award-winning centre; (08) 9641 2905; 10 km N.

Toapin Weir and Mt Stirling: panoramic views; 64 km E. **Self-drive trails:** 8 different routes including the Avon Ascent through Perth's scenic hinterland to a series of special places in the Avon Valley; contact visitor centre for maps.

TOWNS NEARBY: Northam 28 km, Beverley 29 km, Toodyay 47 km, Mundaring 57 km, Pingelly 78 km

Shopping at the **MINDIL BEACH SUNSET MARKETS** / Swimming in **LITCHFIELD NATIONAL PARK** / Exploring billabongs and Aboriginal rock-art galleries in **KAKADU NATIONAL PARK** / Seeing spectacular **ULURU** at sunrise and sunset / Visiting the **ARALUEN CULTURAL PRECINCT** / Fishing for barramundi in the Territory's **WEST COAST RIVERS** / Boarding an **ADELAIDE RIVER JUMPING CROCODILES CRUISE** / Learning about the Aboriginal legend behind the **DEVILS MARBLES (KARLU KARLU)** / Enjoying a drink at the historic **DALY WATERS PUB** / Climbing Kings Canyon in **WATARRKA NATIONAL PARK**

THE NORTHERN TERRITORY is Australia's least

settled state or territory, with vast tracts of desert and tropical woodlands. But to regard this country as empty is to do it a disservice; Aboriginal people have lived and travelled across the territory for thousands of years, and still do. Many non-Aboriginal Australians also see it as the last great frontier because of its remoteness, spectacular landscapes and hardy outback characters.

Desert regions lie towards central Australia, while the tropical Top End is lapped by the Timor and Arafura seas. Although the diversity of landscape and wildlife makes it one of Australia's most inspiring destinations, visitors should expect to cover a lot of distance between highlights.

The coastline and offshore islands are places of special beauty – pearly white beaches interspersed with rocky red cliffs and rich mangrove habitats. The coastal rivers are home to thousands of bird and marine species, and their flood plains carry the annual wet season deluge into the Timor and Arafura seas, and the Gulf of Carpentaria. The rivers are also spawning grounds for barramundi, which attract anglers from around the world.

[KINGS CANYON, WATARRKA NATIONAL PARK]

The north-east includes Arnhem Land, the largest Aboriginal reserve in Australia, where trade and mingling of cultures occurred between Yolngu people and Indonesian seafarers from the 1600s. Today it is home to many groups who still live a semi-traditional lifestyle. It is also the custodial land of Australia's most famous Indigenous instrument, the didgeridoo. Here visitors can explore parts of the Gove and Cobourg peninsulas, with their green vegetation, turquoise waters and great fishing.

The Red Centre is ancient and breathtaking, a land of intense as well as muted tones created by beautiful gorges, rock holes and vistas. While many travellers are drawn to Uluru and Kata Tjuta, the surrounding countryside is equally impressive – from the rolling red sandhills of the Simpson Desert to the undulating grasslands west of Glen Helen. North of Alice Springs, the Tanami Desert is incredibly remote and vastly interesting.

[SALTWATER CROCODILE]

fact file

Population 230 200
Total land area 1 335 742 square kilometres
People per square kilometre 0.15
Beef cattle per square kilometre 1.3
Length of coastline 5437 kilometres
Number of islands 887
Longest river Victoria River (560 kilometres)
Highest mountain Mount Zeil (1531 metres), West MacDonnell National Park
Highest waterfall Jim Jim Falls (160 metres), Kakadu National Park
Highest town Areyonga (700 metres), west of Hermannsburg
Hottest place Aputula (Finke), 48.3°C in 1960
Strangest place name Humpty Doo
Quirkiest festival Henley-on-Todd Regatta with boat races in the dry riverbed, Alice Springs
Longest road Stuart Highway (approximately 2000 kilometres)
Most scenic road Larapinta Drive, from Alice Springs to Hermannsburg
Most famous pub Daly Waters Pub
Most impressive gorge Katherine Gorge, Nitmiluk (Katherine Gorge) National Park
Most identifiable trees Pandanus palm and desert she-oak
Most impressive sight Electrical storms in the build-up to the wet season, Darwin
Favourite food Barramundi
Local beer NT Draught
Interesting fact Some 50 per cent of the Northern Territory is either Aboriginal land or land under claim

gift ideas

Aboriginal art and handmade baskets, Arnhem Land, Kakadu National Park and Darwin Authentic pieces are best purchased from Aboriginal craft centres in places like Maningrida and Gunbalunya, Arnhem Land. Alternatively, visit Marrawuddi Gallery, Kakadu National Park, or Framed – The Darwin Gallery, 55 Stuart Hwy, Darwin. See Nhulunbuy p. 363, Jabiru p. 364 and Darwin p. 344

Barramundi-skin wallets and shoes, Barra Shack, Humpty Doo Stop at this popular shop on the way to Kakadu National Park to pick up items that are true evidence of an outback experience. 41 Acacia Rd, Humpty Doo. See Noonamah pp. 363, 365

Didgeridoos, the Didgeridoo Hut, Humpty Doo Purchase an iconic Aboriginal item from this store owned and run by Indigenous people. 1 Arnhem Hwy, Humpty Doo. See Noonamah pp. 363, 365

Handmade whips, crocodile-skin and kangaroo-skin products, Mindil Beach Sunset Markets, Darwin A range of fantastic Top End products are on offer, from buffalo horns to necklaces with a crocodile tooth. In particular, visit Mick's Whips for various whips and handcrafted crocodile or kangaroo leather goods. See Mindil Beach Sunset Markets p. 350

Pukumani Poles, Bathurst and Melville islands Aboriginal burial poles found only on the Tiwi Islands can be purchased at several arts and crafts centres. See Tours p. 353

South Sea pearls, Paspaley Pearls, Darwin Found in Australia's northern waters, the largest pearls in the world are made into elegant jewellery pieces. Paspaley, 19 The Mall; Darwin. See Shopping p. 352

Yothu Yindi CD, Arnhem Land The most famous Indigenous band comes from the Yolngu people of Arnhem Land, and their well-known song 'Treaty' catapulted Indigenous music into the mainstream Australian music scene. The yearly Garma Festival, held during October in Gulkula, Arnhem Land, is organised by the Yothu Yindi Foundation. See Nhulunbuy p. 363

***Walkabout Chefs* book, Darwin** With recipes by renowned outback chef Steve Sunk, available from any bookshop in Darwin.

DARWIN is...

Window-shopping for pearls in SMITH STREET MALL / Watching a movie at the

DECKCHAIR CINEMA / A stroll along THE ESPLANADE / A safe encounter with

reptiles at CROCOSAURUS COVE / A picnic at FANNIE BAY / Sunset drinks at the

DARWIN SAILING CLUB / Shopping for arts and crafts at the MINDIL BEACH

SUNSET MARKETS / Handfeeding fish at AQUASCENE / Exploring ABORIGINAL ART

GALLERIES / Learning about cyclones at the MUSEUM AND ART GALLERY OF THE

NORTHERN TERRITORY / Fishing off STOKES HILL WHARF / Swimming in the wave

lagoon at the DARWIN WATERFRONT / Watching a thunderstorm in the evening sky

DO NOT DIVE

1.2m

VISITOR INFORMATION
Tourism Top End
→ 6 Bennett St
(08) 8980 6000 or 1300 138 886
www.tourismtopend.com.au

Regarded as Australia's northern outpost, Darwin's proximity to Asia and its immersion in Aboriginal culture makes it one of the world's most interesting cities. It retains a tropical, colonial feel despite having been largely rebuilt after the devastation wreaked by cyclone Tracy over 30 years ago.

The founding fathers of Darwin laid out the city centre on a small peninsula that juts into one of the finest harbours in northern Australia. Their names live on in the wide streets of the city centre, which is easy to get around and lacks the winding lanes of older Australian cities.

The Larrakia people are the Aboriginal traditional owners of the land that Darwin is built on. It is a beautiful green city with parklands and gardens of palm trees, raintrees and frangipani while the waters of the Timor Sea lap three sides of the city.

The population of 127 500 comprises over 50 ethnic groups, the diversity stretching back to the early days of Darwin's development when Aboriginal, European and Chinese people worked side by side. More recent arrivals include migrants from Greece, Timor, Indonesia and Africa.

Evidence of the early days remain, but Darwin is also a modern city. With so much natural beauty around its harbour, along the beaches and in its tropical parks, it remains one of the most fascinating cities in the world.

MAP LEGEND
- Attraction
- Where to eat & where to stay
- Tourist information
- Shopping precinct

N

0   1 km

TIMOR SEA

BEAGLE GULF

Nightcliff foreshore

Casuarina Beach

Casuarina Coastal Reserve

Casuarina

Casuarina Square

Alawa Ovals

WAGAMAN PARK

Alawa

Wagaman

Rapid Creek

Nightcliff

NIGHTCLIFF OVAL

Nightcliff Markets (Sun)

Frangipanni Bed & Breakfast

Rapid Creek Markets (Sun)

DARWIN WATER GARDENS

JINGILI PARK

MOIL PARK

Millner

Jingili

Moil

To Crocodylus Park

PROGRESS

Coconut Grove

BAGOT PARK

MCMILLANS

Marrara Stadium

Marrara

East Point

East Point Military Museum & Defence of Darwin Experience

East Point Reserve

Pee Wee's at the Point

Lake Alexander

Dudley Point

Ludmilla

BAGOT ABORIGINAL COMMUNITY

RAAF DARWIN GOLF CLUB

RAAF BASE DARWIN

DARWIN AIRPORT

Ludmilla

BUKATILLA RD

The Narrows

To Australian Aviation Heritage Centre & Palmerston

FANNIE BAY

Fannie Bay Gaol Museum

Fannie Bay

FANNIE BAY RACECOURSE

RICHARDSON PARK

Winnellie

Darwin Sailing Club

Vesteys Beach

Vesteys Lake

Parap Village Market (Sat)

Parap Shopping Village

Parap

Woolner

Darwin Ski Club

Territory Craft Darwin

Museum and Art Gallery of the Northern Territory

The Gardens

Bayview

Charles Darwin National Park

Mindil Beach Sunset Markets (Thurs & Sun dry season)

MINDIL BEACH RESERVE

George Brown Darwin Botanic Gardens

Stuart Park

SKYCITY Darwin

Amphitheatre

Framed– The Darwin Gallery

DINAH OVAL

CHARLES DARWIN NATIONAL PARK

Myilly Point

Evoo

Buzz Cafe

GARDENS PARK GOLF LINKS

Myilly Point Heritage Precinct

Dinah Beach

Sadgroves

Ferry to Mandorah & Bathurst Island

Yots Greek Restaurant

Cullen Bay Marina

Emery Point

Darwin City B&B

Small Boat Harbour

Larrakeyah

LARRAKEYAH ARMY BASE

Aquascene

Elliott Point

Patrol Boat Harbour

Lameroo Beach

Darwin
SEE PAGE 348

Darwin Harbour

FRANCES BAY

PORT DARWIN

East Point

CITY CENTRE

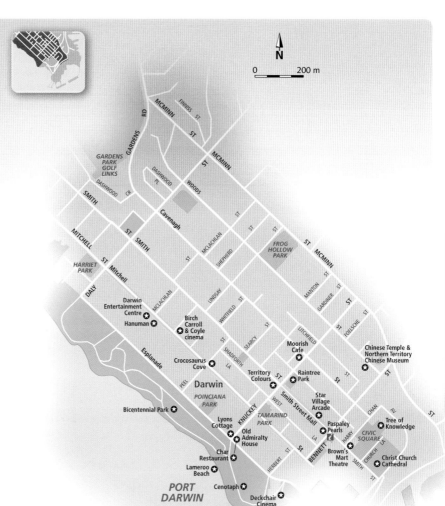

The city centre is open and vibrant with wide streets, leafy parks, a shady mall and outdoor dining. Stunning Aboriginal art and artefacts characterise the retail areas. Tall, modern buildings have replaced the old colonial-style buildings but they retain a fresh, tropical flavour.

0   200 m

Smith Street 348 B2, C2

Smith Street Mall is the retail heart of the central business district (CBD). Shady **Raintree Park** at the northern end is popular. Walk down the mall between May and the end of August and hear buskers who have travelled north to beat the southern winter. Plazas and small arcades sell Aboriginal art, locally made jewellery and tropical clothing. At the southern end of the mall are grand buildings with shops selling South Sea pearls and authentic crocodile products. Opposite is the **Star Village Arcade**, once the open-air Star Theatre. Today it houses a quirky collection of boutiques and cafes.

Smith Street continues south past **Brown's Mart Theatre,** built in 1883, home to the Darwin Theatre Company; *(08) 8981 5522.* Behind it is the Darwin City Council Chambers, with its ancient banyan tree, known as the **Tree of Knowledge**. Planted at the end of the 19th century, the tree has been a meeting place, dormitory and soapbox for generations. Nearby is the **Christ Church Cathedral**, built in 1902 and restored after damage from both Japanese bombers and cyclone Tracy.

Mitchell Street 348 A1, B2

West of Smith street is this popular dining and entertainment area. With backpacker accommodation, pubs and outdoor dining areas, cinemas and the **Darwin Entertainment Centre,** it is a bustling part of Darwin; *(08) 8980 3366.* Swim with crocodiles from the safety of a perspex cave at **Crocosaurus Cove.** *(08) 8981 7522.*

Cavenagh Street 348 B1, C1

East of Smith Street is Cavenagh Street, with commercial buildings and government departments, and a few art galleries and cafes. This street was Darwin's original Chinatown, full of ramshackle huts and the occasional opium den in the 1800s. A reminder of its Asian history is at nearby Litchfield Street where a modern **Chinese Temple** stands on the site of an older temple that was constructed in 1887. The **Northern Territory Chinese Museum** next door covers the history of Chinese people in Darwin. *Open during the dry season; admission by gold-coin donation.*

The Esplanade 348 A1, B2

Accommodation lines the Esplanade, looking out over Darwin Harbour. Many Australian and American wrecks lie at the bottom of the harbour, sunk by the Japanese bombers in February 1942. Memorial sites all around the harbour record the hundreds of bombing raids on the city during World War II, including the **Cenotaph**.

Beautiful **Bicentennial Park** runs the length of the Esplanade and a walking/cycling track goes from Doctors Gully in the north to the Wharf Precinct. Midway, a pathway leads down to **Lameroo Beach** and at the southern end steps lead to the **Deckchair Cinema**. *(08) 8941 4377.* Films screen 'under the stars' every night during the dry season.

On the corner of Knuckey Street is **Old Admiralty House**, built in 1937. It remains from before the city was devastated by cyclone Tracy in 1974, and is now part of **Char Restaurant** a beautiful outdoor dining space. *(08) 8981 4544.* Nearby is **Lyons Cottage**, the former British Australian Telegraph (BAT) headquarters for the Overland Telegraph, now housing Aboriginal Bush Traders, which promotes Indigenous tourism experiences, arts and crafts. *0448 329 933.*

STATE SQUARE

This is one of Darwin's most outstanding precincts. The thoroughly modern Parliament House and Supreme Court buildings are either loved or hated by locals, but most people agree that Government House, a reminder of the city's colonial days, is charming. The wide green lawns of Liberty Square make this an ideal picnic spot.

Palmerston Town Hall 348 C2

Darwin was initially named Palmerston, and the now-ruined Palmerston Town Hall was built in 1883. Partially destroyed by cyclone Tracy, it now stands as a memorial to the city's early colonial days and to the ferocity of the cyclone. The ruins occasionally host outdoor performances such as *A Midsummer Night's Dream*.

Parliament House, the Supreme Court and Liberty Square 348 C2

Parliament House offers one of the finest views of Darwin Harbour. Opened in 1994, it also houses the **Northern Territory Library** and **Speaker's Corner Cafe**. *(08) 8946 1439.* Look through the art and photographic exhibitions in the grand hall. Across the wide courtyard is the Supreme Court building, built in 1990 and offering an atmosphere of modern grandeur, with a spectacular mosaic floor designed by Aboriginal artist Norah Napaljarri Nelson, and a permanent exhibit of Arnhem Land burial poles. Beside Parliament House, next to the Supreme Court, are the lawns of Liberty Square. *Free guided tours are available Sat and Wed. Contact the visitor centre for times; (08) 8980 6000.*

[GOVERNMENT HOUSE]

Government House, Old Police Station and Courthouse 348 C2

Across the road from Liberty Square is Government House, an elegant, colonial-style building built in 1879, which survived both cyclones and World War II bombs. It is open to the public once a year. On the corner of Smith Street are the Old Police Station and Courthouse, now government offices. Opposite is **Survivors Lookout**, which surveys the Wharf Precinct and Darwin Harbour to East Arm Port and the terminus of the *Ghan*. It tells the story of the WWII battles that took place over the harbour.

THE WHARF PRECINCT

This precinct is the original base of the city. Stokes Hill and Fort Hill wharves date back to a century ago, when ships used to call in at Darwin to load exotic cargoes. Today the port is used for luxury liners and warships, for outdoor dining, and as the home of Darwin's convention centre and Waterfront development.

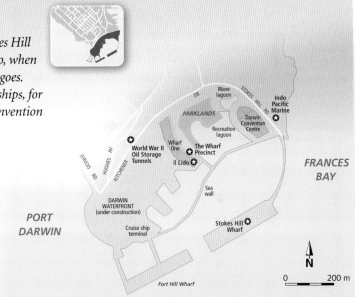

World War II Oil Storage Tunnels 348 C2

Under a set of stairs leading from Survivors Lookout to the Wharf Precinct are storage tunnels built after the above-ground tanks were bombed in early war-time raids on Darwin. One of the tunnels is open to the public along with historical displays. *Kitchener Dr; (08) 8985 6333; open daily.*

Indo Pacific Marine 348 D2

Find out what lies in Darwin Harbour, from deadly stone fish to beautiful coral. Indo Pacific Marine has been able to transfer a living ecosystem from the water into a land-based exhibition. Also on show are creatures endemic to the Top End, such as the deadly box jellyfish. *Kitchener Dr; (08) 8981 1294; open daily 10am–4pm, plus a night-time dinner tour.*

Stokes Hill Wharf 348 D3

Once northern Australia's most important port, Stokes Hill Wharf is now a place for restaurants, sunset cruises, and fishing. Watch a magnificent wet-season storm here as it gathers across the harbour. Neighbouring Fort Hill Wharf is the defence vessel facility and cruise-ship terminal. Closer to the City, The Darwin Waterfront development has transformed the Wharf Precinct into a lively recreation and commercial zone, lined with restaurants, cafes and boutiques. Swim in the lagoon or ride the waves in the wave pool. *Open daily 10am–6pm.*

INNER NORTH

The beaches of the inner north are idyllic in the dry season, but can be deadly during the build-up to the wet season when box jellyfish float in shallow waters along the shoreline.

Aquascene 346 B5

This is one of Darwin's most popular attractions, where visitors can handfeed fish that live in Darwin Harbour. Opening times depend on the high tide, but Aquascene publishes feeding times every day in the *NT News* and weekly timetables can be found at Tourism Top End. *Doctors Gully Rd; (08) 8981 7837.*

Cullen Bay Marina 346 A5

This is a popular dining and recreational area. Ferries cross Darwin Harbour to Mandorah, departing from the front of the lock at Cullen Bay, while sunset and evening charters are based within the marina. Down the road is **Myilly Point Heritage Precinct**, a small group of pre-World War II houses that survived cyclone Tracy. Devonshire tea is held every Sunday afternoon in the **Burnett House** gardens. *Confirm times with the National Trust (08) 8981 2848.*

Mindil Beach Sunset Markets 346 B5

This is arguably Darwin's most popular tourist attraction. Located off Gilruth Avenue, the markets operate on Thursday and Sunday evenings (4–9pm) from the end of April to the end of October, taking advantage of the superb dry-season weather. Stalls offer everything from international food, Aboriginal arts and Asian crafts to tarot-card readings, massages and kangaroo sausages. Theatrical and singing troupes perform alongside whip-cracking, poetry readings and bands. At sunset, walk over the sand dunes to the beach for a quintessential Darwin moment.

SKYCITY Darwin 346 B5

SKYCITY casino lies next to the market strips on Mindil Beach. There is accommodation and several restaurants in the casino, including **Evoo** (see where to eat, p. 353), one of Darwin's finest dining venues. SKYCITY is also the hub of the horseracing scene in August when a gala ball is held. *Gilruth Ave, Mindil Beach; (08) 8943 8888.*

George Brown Darwin Botanic Gardens 346 B5

The gardens, established in the 1870s, extend from the sea to a plateau providing a range of environments. Both marine and estuarine plants survive naturally here and paths wind through the large collection of native and tropical plants. There is also a self-guide Aboriginal plant-use trail. *Geranium St, The Gardens.*

Museum and Art Gallery of the Northern Territory 346 B4

This is one of Darwin's main cultural icons, housing one of the finest Aboriginal art collections in Australia, including entries to the annual Aboriginal and Torres Strait Islander Art Award. A spine-tingling gallery details the events of cyclone Tracy, and a natural history display exhibits fauna and flora of the Top End and South-East Asia. The Maritime Boatshed shows all sorts of vessels that have travelled to northern Australia over the years, from tiny jukung to large fishing vessels that carried refugees. The nearby **Territory Craft Darwin** exhibits the work of local artists and craft producers. *Conacher St, Bullocky Point; open Tues–Sun; general admission free; (08) 8999 8264.*

Sunset dining 346 B4

One of the pleasures of visiting Darwin is being able to enjoy a meal by the beach as the sun sets over Fannie Bay. A special treat is **Pee Wees**, at East Point Reserve. *(08) 8981 6868.* Also the **Darwin Ski Club** (08) 8981 6630, on the beach at Fannie Bay next to the Museum and Art Gallery of the Northern Territory, and the popular **Darwin Sailing Club**, just 200 metres further along the

[FOOD STALL AT MINDIL BEACH SUNSET MARKETS]

coast on Atkins Drive. *(08) 8981 1700.* Or pack a picnic and head up to **East Point Reserve**.

Fannie Bay Gaol Museum 346 B4

This served as Darwin's prison between 1883 and 1979, housing some of Darwin's most desperate criminals. The cells and gallows provide a sobering display for visitors, but are sometimes used as a backdrop for social events. *East Point Rd; open 10am–3pm daily; admission free; (08) 8941 2260.*

NORTH

Darwin is blessed with an attractive coastline, lush parks and excellent walking paths that meander through a beautiful urban environment. The suburbs of Fannie Bay, Nightcliff and Casuarina all front onto the Timor Sea which is flat, calm and often like liquid gold at sunset.

East Point Reserve 346 A3

The cliff-top paths through East Point Reserve are popular with joggers, rollerbladers and cyclists and the waters of Fannie Bay are enticing. However, like all beaches in Darwin, the ocean is unsafe for swimming so **Lake Alexander** is used as an alternative. **East Point Military Museum and the Defence of Darwin Experience**, in the north of the reserve, form a fascinating World War II precinct. The Defence of Darwin Experience is a highly interactive experience using high-tech touch screen technology, storyboards and olde worlde sepia photographs. Immerse yourself in the action with realistic cinerama, deafening noise and flashing gunfire. Also check out the museum, housed in the original command post bunker. *Alec Fong Lim Dr, East Point; open daily; (08) 8981 9702.*

Nightcliff foreshore 346 B1

An excellent cliff-top walkway runs from Nightcliff boat ramp to a bridge over Rapid Creek, on to Casuarina Beach. A beautiful pool, parkland, play areas and fishing spots can be found all along here.

NORTH-EAST

Australian Aviation Heritage Centre 588 D3

Darwin was the first port of call for many early aviators, including Sir Charles Kingsford Smith. Its rich aviation history is detailed here, along with superbly restored exhibits, including an American B-52 bomber and the wreckage of a Japanese Zero. *557 Stuart Hwy; (08) 8947 2145; open daily.*

Casuarina Coastal Reserve 346 C1

This reserve boasts a magnificent white sandy beach that backs on to dunes and thickets of native she-oaks. Nearby is Free Beach, Darwin's only recognised nudist bathing area.

Leanyer Recreation Park 588 D2

This popular family park offers bike-riding, skateboarding and basketball facilities; an all-abilities playground; shaded

[CROCODILE JUMPING AT CROCODYLUS PARK]

barbecues and picnic areas; paddling pools, water cannons and a water playground. *Off Vanderlin Dr; open 8am–8pm daily; admission free.*

OUTER NORTH-EAST

Holmes Jungle Nature Park 588 D3

Off Vanderlin Drive in Karama, this nature park features a monsoonal rainforest full of native fauna and flora. *Open 7am–6pm daily (check access during the Wet season).*

SOUTH-EAST

Charles Darwin National Park 346 D4

Mangroves merge with tropical woodland at this national park, off Tiger Brennan Drive. It contains a number of Aboriginal shell middens, a WWII display, a lookout, walking trails and a barbecue. *Open 8am–7pm daily.*

EAST

Crocodylus Park 588 D3

This is a research centre and tourist attraction. See the crocs at feeding times (10am, 12pm and 2pm), and well-trained guides allow children – under supervision – to handle baby crocodiles. Other animals on show include monkeys and large cats, such as tigers. *End of McMillans Rd, past the airport, near the Police Centre; open daily; (08) 8922 4500.*

CITY ESSENTIALS
DARWIN

Climate

Darwin has a constant temperature of around 30°C and the weather is always hot. Most people visit during the dry season, which extends from May to the end of September when there are clear blue skies and cool nights. The 'build-up' period (between October and December) is famous for hot, stifling weather and massive electrical storms. During the wet season (which can last until late April), the Asian monsoon drops over Darwin, either bringing days of cleansing rain or short, sharp storms. In the midst of the monsoon, the streets of the city and surrounding landscape can become waterlogged but it's only short lived. Temperatures are cooler and the although the rain may be uncomfortable, it is the time of the year when the landscape is green and lush, when native trees burst into flower and attract thousands of birds.

	MAX °C	MIN °C	RAIN MM	RAIN DAYS
JANUARY	32	25	393	15
FEBRUARY	32	25	329	15
MARCH	32	24	258	13
APRIL	33	24	102	13
MAY	32	22	14	1
JUNE	31	20	3	0
JULY	30	19	1	0
AUGUST	31	20	1	0
SEPTEMBER	33	23	12	1
OCTOBER	34	25	52	3
NOVEMBER	34	25	124	8
DECEMBER	33	25	241	11

Getting around

Darwin is easy to get around – city streets are laid out in a grid, most attractions are within walking distance, and traffic is rarely heavy.

A regular public bus service covers many of the suburbs as well as the satellite town of Palmerston (the city terminus is on Harry Chan Avenue). Taxis are available at either end of the mall but can also be hailed from the street.

The Tour Tub is an open-air bus service to the city's top sights, departing every hour from the northern end of Smith Street Mall.

Darwin's network of bicycle paths extends from the city out to the northern suburbs, and bikes can be hired from many backpacker lodges, most of which can be found on Mitchell Street.

Public transport Bus Service (08) 8924 7666.

Airport shuttle bus Darwin Airport Shuttle Bus (08) 8981 5066; Metro Minibus (08) 8983 0577.

Police road report 1800 246 199 (a good source of information for travel outside Darwin, particularly in the wet season).

Bus tours Tour Tub (08) 8985 6322.

Motoring organisation AANT (08) 8925 5901, roadside assistance 13 1111.

Car rental Avis 13 6333; Britz Campervan Rentals 1800 331 454; Budget 1300 362 848; Hertz 13 3039; Sargent's four-wheel-drive hire service 1800 077 353.

Taxis Radio Taxis 13 1008 or (08) 8981 3777.

Bicycle and scooter hire Darwin Scooter Hire (08) 8941 2434.

Top events

Darwin Beer Can Regatta Boats built from beer cans. Races held in conjunction with Mindil Beach Sunset Markets. July.

Darwin Cup Carnival The city's premier horseracing carnival. Also Darwin Turf Club Gala Ball. July/August.

Festival of Darwin A exciting programme of visual and performing arts that attracts people from around the world. August.

Royal Darwin Show Three days of rides, equestrian and agricultural displays at the Darwin Showgrounds. July.

Sky City Triple Crown V8 Supercars Championship Three days of V8 supercars at Hidden Valley Raceway. April–June (early dry season).

Telstra National Aboriginal and Torres Strait Islander Art Awards Exquisite Aboriginal and Torres Strait Islander art held at the Museum and Art Gallery of the Northern Territory. August–October.

Shopping

Casuarina Square Every popular department and chain store is under one roof here, and there is also a huge eatery with more than 30 restaurants and cafes. 346 D1

Framed – The Darwin Gallery, City One of the oldest art galleries in Darwin with some of the best Aboriginal and Islander art in northern Australia and also some of the best local craft. (08) 8981 2994. 346 B5

Parap Shopping Village With it's village atmosphere and Saturday markets, Parap is a unique shopping destination especially for Aboriginal art and crafts. 346 B4

Smith Street Mall, City Darwin's major shopping precinct with interesting shops interspersed with outdoor eateries, 5 arcades and a galleria. Paspaley Pearls is a good place to buy pearls and there are several shops near the top of the mall and in Knuckey St where you can buy Aboriginal art. Animale, in the galleria, is a terrific frock shop. 348 B2, C2

The Wharf Precinct Brand new retail and dining experience. Promenade of shops and restaurants overlooking the water. 346 C2

Markets

Nightcliff Markets These markets are focused on relaxed Sunday mornings. Offering everything from sarongs to jewellery to cosmetics. Buy pancakes, green paw paw salad, laksa or fresh fruit and vegetables. Drink coffee and read the newspapers – all in an outdoor setting. Nightcliff Shopping Centre; Sun mornings. 346 C2

Palmerston Night Markets A community event with arts and crafts for sale. Frances Mall; Fri evenings, May–Oct. 588 D3

Parap Village Market This market is about waking up to the splendours of Asia. Colourful flowers, frozen-fruit ice-cream, silk-screened sarongs, Asian food, relaxing massages and exotic blended drinks are all on offer. Parap Shopping Centre; Sat mornings. 346 B4

Rapid Creek Markets A little slice of Asia. Exotic fruits and vegetables, sticky rice parcels of sweets, Asian food stalls and live music. Rapid Creek Shopping Centre; Sun mornings. 346 C1

See also Mindil Beach Sunset Markets, on p. 350.

Walks and tours

Batji Tours Experience Darwin through the eyes of its Traditional Owners, the Larrakia people, on foot; 1300 881 186.

Darwin City Heritage Walk Organise a guided tour with Darwin Walking Tours (08) 8981 0227, or pick up a map from the visitor centre.

Ferry to Mandorah Cast a line off the Mandorah Jetty or have a meal at the Hotel. It's 130 kilometres by road, but only a 20 min ferry ride from Cullen Bay Marina. Mandorah Ferry Service. (08) 8978 5044.

Fishing Tours Darwin Fishing Charters has a huge selection of fishing adventures; see www.fishthetopend.com.

George Brown Darwin Botanic Gardens Walks Self-guide walks through different habitats; pamphlets available from the visitor centre at the Geranium Street entrance or web site. (08) 8981 1958.

Sunset Cruises Take a cruise from Cullen Bay Marina or Stokes Wharf to see the sun slip below the horizon of the Timor Sea. City of Darwin Cruises 0401 118 777; Darwin Harbour Cruises (08) 8942 3131; Anniki Pearl Lugger Cruises (08) 8941 4000.

Tour Tub Hop-on, hop-off bus. (08) 8985 6322.

 ## Entertainment

Cinema One of the first examples of entertainment infrastructure ever established in Darwin was the outdoor cinema that ran during the dry season – the nights were clear and balmy and the temperature perfect. That tradition continues to this day at the Deckchair Cinema (on the shores of Darwin Harbour just around from Lameroo Beach). There are also cinema complexes in Mitchell Street, Casuarina Shopping Square and The Hub in Palmerston. The Museum and Art Gallery of the Northern Territory also runs interesting documentaries and short films at its theatrette. Check the *Northern Territory News* for daily showings.

Live music Darwin has a young population and is a regular stopover for naval and cruise vessels from many countries. There are plenty of clubs, pubs and restaurants in the centre of the city that provide live music. SKYCITY casino has regular entertainment on its lawns during the dry season, and Stokes Hill Wharf has live music on weekends. The Amphitheatre in the Botanic Gardens is a popular venue for touring musicians especially during the Darwin Festival. Friday's edition of the *Northern Territory News* publishes a round-up of what's on in the Gig Guide, or visitors can check what's on by visiting Top End Tourism, Bennett Street.

Classical music and performing arts Darwin has a vibrant arts community that has been deeply influenced by Aboriginal and Asian cultures. Local playwrights, dancers and artists are always producing some tropical gem that can be viewed at interesting venues such as Brown's Mart, the Palmerston Town Hall ruins in Smith Street or the Darwin Performing Arts Centre (DPAC) in Mitchell Street. During the dry season the Darwin Festival is particularly stimulating. Check with Top End

Tourism for the dates of the Darwin Festival as the timing changes each year. Otherwise, see the *Northern Territory News* for weekly programs.

 ## Sport

Darwinites love their sport. **AFL** (Australian Football League) is like a second religion in Darwin and the surrounding communities, particularly for Aboriginal and Torres Strait Islander players, many of whom go on to play for big clubs. In March the NTFL grand final is held at Marrara Stadium and the Tiwi Islands Football Grand Final is held on Bathurst Island, the only time Bathurst Island is open to visitors without a permit.

Fannie Bay and Darwin Harbour are great for **sailing** or head down to the Ski Club to **water ski**.

Fishing, especially during the 'run-off' is a high priority for locals and visitors to Darwin and catching a wild barramundi is a much sought after sport. Nothing tastes better than a grilled 'barra' straight from the water.

 ## Where to eat

Opening hours based on dry season (Apr–Oct).

Buzz Cafe Modern Australian, great location overlooking the yachts at Cullen Bay Marina; (08) 8941 1141; open Mon–Sun for lunch and dinner. 346 A5

Char Restaurant Best steaks in a garden setting; Cnr The Esplanade and Knuckey St; (08) 8981 1544; open Wed–Fri for lunch; Mon–Sun for dinner. 348 B2

Darwin Sailing Club There isn't a better view in town as the sun sets across the Arafura Sea; good food, club prices. East Point Road, Fannie Bay; (08) 8981 1700; open Mon–Sun for lunch and dinner. 346 B4

Evoo Fine dining, degustation option. SKYCITY Darwin, Gilruth Ave, The Gardens; (08) 8943 8888; open Fri for lunch and Tues–Sat for dinner. 346 B5

Hanuman Special Thai dining experience. Stylish setting alongside the Holiday Inn, 93 Mitchell St; (08) 8941 3500; open Mon–Sun for lunch and dinner. 348 A1

Il Lido Magnificent waterfront setting, cocktails, tapas and full dining options, The Wharf Precinct; (08) 8941 0900; open daily for breakfast, lunch and dinner. 348 C2

Moorish Cafe Close to the centre of town serving unusual tapas with flavours inspired by Spain, the Mediterranean and Africa; 37 Knuckey St; (08) 8981 0010; open Tues–Sat for lunch and dinner. 348 B1

Pee Wee's at the Point On the beach at East Point, this stylish fine-dining establishment has one of the most magnificent views in Darwin. East Point Reserve; (08) 8981 6868; open Mon–Sun for dinner. 346 A3

Stokes Wharf Casual dining along the old jetty. Fish and chips or Thai. Great for storm

watching. The Wharf Precinct; (08) 8981 4268; open Mon–Sun for dinner. 348 D3

Yots Greek Taverna Authentic Greek dishes in a specacular waterfront setting alongside the marina at Cullen Bay; 4/54 Marina Blvd; (08) 8981 4433; open Tues–Sun for lunch and dinner. 346 A5

 ## Where to stay

Aurora Shady Glen Tourist Park 11 Farrell Cres, Winnellie; (08) 8984 3330.

Beale's Bedfish & Breakfast 2 Todd Cres, Malak; (08) 8945 0376.

Darwin City B&B 4 Zealandia Cres, Larrakeyah; (08) 8941 3636.

Darwin FreeSpirit Resort 901 Stuart Hwy, Holtze; (08) 8935 0888.

Frangipanni Bed & Breakfast 6 Waters St, Rapid Creek; (08) 8985 2797.

Hidden Valley Resort & Tourist Park 25 Hidden Valley Rd, Berrimah; (08) 8984 2888.

Palmerston Sunset Retreat 8 Renwick Crt, Gray; (08) 8932 9917.

 ## Tours

Darwin city Darwin Day Tours run ½ and 1 day tours around Darwin, including City Sights, Bombing of Darwin; (08) 8923 6523.

Kakadu National Park Preferably a 2–4 day tour to see outstanding Aboriginal rock-art galleries at Ubirr and Nourlangie and to explore the wetlands at Yellow Waters, Cooinda. xx

Katherine Gorge Further afield (a 4 hr drive) take a boat cruise up the famous Katherine Gorge.

Litchfield National Park A 2 hr drive south of Darwin, this park is a wonderful place to visit or camp, with bubbling streams, gushing waterfalls and plunge pools. This is one of the best places to swim in Darwin (pools may be closed during the Wet so check access). There are also lookouts, bush walks and plenty of scenic places for picnics and BBQs.

Territory Wildlife Park and Berry Springs Nature Park This award-winning park showcases the Top End's flora and fauna, including free-flying birds. Exhibits are connected by a 4-kilometre walk or shuttle train. Berry Springs is next door with a swimming pool and picnic facilities; (08) 8988 7200.

The Tiwi Islands Bathurst Island lies 80 kilometres north of Darwin and are the traditional homes of the Tiwi Aboriginal people. 'Tiwi' is said to mean 'the people' or 'we, the chosen people'. Tiwi Tours run a 1 day tour which includes a visit to the local communities, the art gallery to see how some of the beautiful silk-screened work is produced as well as pottery and carvings. A retail shop is available. The tour includes a return flight and necessary permits; 1300 721 365.

REGIONS
of the Northern Territory

Listed here are some of the top attractions and experiences in each region.

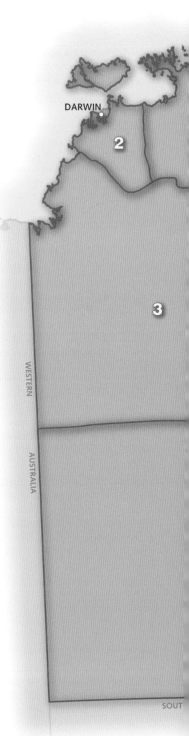

DARWIN

2

3

WESTERN

AUSTRALIA

SOUT

1 KAKADU AND ARNHEM LAND

Buku-Larrnggay Mulka / see p. 363
Jim Jim Falls and Twin Falls in Kakadu National Park / see p. 364
Nourlangie Rock in Kakadu National Park (pictured) / see p. 364
Ubirr rock in Kakadu National Park / see p. 364

2 AROUND DARWIN

Fogg Dam / see p. 365
Litchfield National Park / see p. 356
Territory Wildlife Park (pictured) / see p. 365
Window on the Wetlands / see p. 365

3 GULF TO GULF

Barramundi fishing around Daly River / see p. 356
Lost City at Cape Crawford / see p. 361
Mataranka thermal springs (pictured) / see p. 363
Nitmiluk (Katherine Gorge) National Park / see p. 366

4 RED CENTRE

Devils Marbles (Karlu Karlu) (pictured) / see p. 369
Kata Tjuṯa / see p. 368
Kings Canyon in Watarrka National Park / see p. 362
Uluṟu / see p. 368

QUEENSLAND

4

[JIM JIM FALLS, KAKADU NATIONAL PARK]

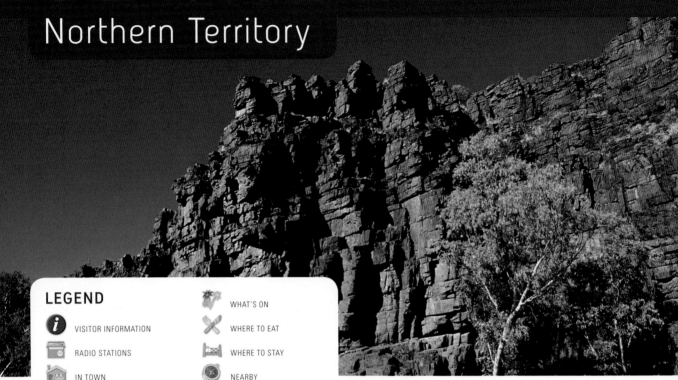

TOWNS A-Z
Northern Territory

LEGEND

(i) VISITOR INFORMATION

(radio) RADIO STATIONS

(house) IN TOWN

(flower) WHAT'S ON

(fork/knife) WHERE TO EAT

(bed) WHERE TO STAY

(x) NEARBY

* Distances for towns nearby are calculated as the crow flies.
* Food and accommodation listings in town are ordered alphabetically with places nearby listed at the end.

[TREPHINA GORGE NATURE PARK]

Adelaide River

Pop. 190
Map ref. 588 E8 | 590 D6

(i) Adelaide River Inn, 106 Stuart Hwy; (08) 8976 7047; www.adelaideriverinn.com.au

(radio) 98.9 FM ABC Territory Radio

Adelaide River is a small town located midway between Darwin and Pine Creek. A settlement was established here as a base for workers on the Overland Telegraph Line in the early 1870s and was a popular stopping place for travellers and prospectors heading south to the goldfields at Pine Creek. The building of the Northern Australia Railway, which operated from 1888 to 1976, further increased its significance on the north–south track. During World War II the still relatively sheltered town was a major military base for 30 000 Australian and US soldiers. The Adelaide River War Cemetry and historic Railway Station contain exhibits and photographic displays of these bygone days.

 Adelaide River Inn The hotel was a favourite watering hole for soldiers during WW II and still has war photographs and memorabilia adorning the walls. Hard to ignore is main attraction Charlie the Buffalo, suitably stuffed, from the film *Crocodile Dundee*. Meals and accommodation are available. Stuart Hwy.

Adelaide River Railway Station: National Trust–classified station (1888), now a museum featuring relics of local history, including the railway construction and WW II; open every day except Christmas day; Stuart Hwy; (08) 8981 2848 (National Trust Darwin). *Adelaide River War Cemetery:* a 'must-see', Australia's only war cemetery on native soil contains graves of

434 military personnel. The adjacent civil section contains the graves of 9 post-office staff killed on 19 February 1942, during the bombing of Darwin.

(flower) *Adelaide River Show inluding rodeo and Campdraft:* June. *Adelaide River Races:* June.

(fork/knife) *Diggers Bistro:* good pub food; Adelaide River Inn, 106 Stuart Hwy; (08) 8976 7047.

(x) **Daly River** Copper was discovered here in 1883 and mining began in 1884, which led to a bloody conflict between miners and Aboriginal people. Today the town, located on the banks of the river, is little more than a pub, a free caravan park and a popular destination for fishing. The Daly River is renowed for its large barramundi and there are two major fishing competitions every year, the 'Barra Nationals' and the 'Barra Classic'. The Merrepen Arts Festival is held at the nearby aboriginal community each June. 102 km sw.

Old Stuart Highway Scenic Route: runs for 61 km from Adelaide River, past Robin Falls (15 km s) and the turn off to Daly River and rejoins the Stuart Hwy just north of Hayes Creek. *Mt Bundy Station:* rural experience with 4WD tours, horseriding, fishing, walking, swimming and a wide range of accommodation; (08) 8976 7009; 3 km NE. *Robin Falls:* pleasant 15 min walk to falls that flow most of the year; 15 km s. *Grove Hill Heritage Hotel and Museum:* example of outback ingenuity made by a master blacksmith who scavenged for materials in and around the nearby mine sites. There is basic accommodation and bar meals; (08) 8078 2489; Goldfields Rd; around 70 km SE. *Litchfield National Park:* a world of waterfalls, gorges, pockets of rainforest, giant termite mounds and rock formations that resemble lost civilisations. Enjoy the scenic pools beneath the waterfalls – most offer crocodile-free swimming, but read the signs before you take the plunge; around 100 km sw. *Jumping Crocodile Cruises* Adelaide River Queen run wildlife cruises. See crocodiles in the wild; (08) 8988 8144; 111 km NE.

Travellers note: *Snake Creek, an old wartime base, is no longer accessible to visitors.*

TOWNS NEARBY: Batchelor 22 km, Noonamah 67 km, Pine Creek 102 km, Katherine 185 km, Jabiru 198 km

Aileron
Map ref. 594 H5

ⓘ Aileron Roadhouse, Stuart Hwy; (08) 8956 9703.

The highlight of the year at this popular rest stop on the Stuart Highway is the annual cricket match between local grape farmers and government officials from the Department of Primary Industries. There are even attendant seagulls, which are made by sticking parts of packing-cases onto sticks and painting them white.

 Aileron Hotel Roadhouse The roadhouse is a welcome oasis with a swimming pool, Aboriginal art, playground, and picnic and barbecue facilities. A 17 m sculpture of Charlie Portpot, a local rainmaker, stands beside the roadhouse which offers meals, including a roast for Sunday lunch, and accommodation. There is also an adjoining campsite. Stuart Hwy.

✳ *Cricket match:* dates from visitor centre.

 Ryans Well Historical Reserve The reserve is named after Ned Ryan, a 19th-century stonemason and bushman who was an expert at sinking wells. He accompanied John McKinlay on his ill-fated exploration of Arnhem Land in 1866. When they became trapped on the East Alligator River during the wet season, Ryan and another bushman fashioned a raft out of the skins of 27 pack horses to negotiate their escape. Ryans Well was hand-dug in 1889 as part of an attempt to encourage settlement in the NT. Today there is a plaque beside the well explaining the process of raising water. 7 km SE.

Glen Maggie Homestead: ruins of 1914 homestead, once used as a telegraph office but abandoned in 1934; 7 km SE. *Native Gap Conservation Reservation:* sacred Aboriginal site with picnic area surrounded by cypress pines and magnificent views of the Hahn Range; 12 km SE.

TOWNS NEARBY: Ti-Tree 57 km, Alice Springs 129 km, Glen Helen Resort 134 km, Barrow Creek 139 km, Hermannsburg 155 km

Alice Springs
see inset box on next page

Arltunga Bush Hotel
Map ref. 595 K6 | 597 N1

ⓘ Arltunga Historical Reserve Visitor Centre, (08) 8956 9770.

Arltunga was named after a subgroup of the Arrernte people who had lived in the area for at least 22 000 years before Europeans arrived.When gold was discovered in 1887, prospectors travelled 600 kilometres from the Oodnadatta railhead, often on foot, to get there. When the gold ran out, the people left, and the only remaining signs of life today are at the visitor centre. The horel is closed; ruins of the town have been well preserved by the dry climate.

 N'Dhala Gorge Nature Park The shady gorge features extensive walking tracks that provide access to a large number of rock-art sites with carvings and paintings, including more than 6000 petroglyphs. The carvings are of 2 distinct types – finely pecked and heavily pounded – and are thought to represent 2 different periods. There are also rare plants in the park such as the peach-leafed poison bush and the undoolya wattle. Access by 4WD only. 53 km SW.

Arltunga Historical Reserve: ruins of Arltunga, some of which have been restored, including police station and gaol, mines and the Government Battery and Cyanide Works (1896). The visitor centre has displays on the history of the town; behind the hotel. *Ruby Gap Nature Park:* the site of Central Australia's first mining rush, in 1886, when rubies were thought to have been found. After the stones proved to be relatively valueless garnets the boom went bust and people left. The stunning gorges are now popular sites for bushwalking and camping. Track closures are possible Nov–Apr due to wet conditions; 37 km E. *Trephina Gorge Nature Park:* known for its sheer quartzite cliffs, red river gums and sandy creek bed. Several waterholes attract native wildlife and provide a beautiful setting for bushwalking, swimming, camping and picnicking; 43 km W.

TOWNS NEARBY: Alice Springs 86 km, Aileron 165 km, Ti-Tree 196 km, Hermannsburg 202 km, Glen Helen Resort 207 km

Barrow Creek
Pop. 11
Map ref. 595 I2

ⓘ Barrow Creek Hotel; (08) 8956 9753.

📻 107.3 FM ABC Territory Radio

Although its appearance today is that of a small wayside stop on the highway, Barrow Creek was originally an important telegraph station. It was also the site of an 1874 punitive expedition against the Kaytej people by police after a telegraph station master and linesman were killed during an assault by 20 Kaytej men. This attack (thought to have been a reaction to the abuse of an Aboriginal woman) is the only known planned attack on staff of the Overland Telegraph.

Old Telegraph Station This restored stone building (1872) is set against the breathtaking backdrop of the Forster Ranges. It is 1 of 15 telegraph stations that formed the original network from Port Augusta to Port Darwin. A key is available from the hotel for those who wish to look inside. Stuart Hwy.

Barrow Creek Hotel: outback pub (1932), with original bar, cellar and tin ceilings, and memorabilia of the area on display; Stuart Hwy. *Cemetery:* graves of early settlers and local characters; information available at the hotel.

TOWNS NEARBY: Ti-Tree 86 km, Wauchope 101 km, Aileron 139 km, Tennant Creek 208 km, Arltunga Bush Hotel 231 km

Batchelor
Pop. 477
Map ref. 588 E7 | 590 D5

ⓘ Information booth, Tarkarri Rd; (08) 8976 0536.

📻 93.7 8KIN FM, 98.9 FM ABC Territory Radio

Established as a large air force base during World War II, Batchelor became prominent with the discovery of uranium at nearby Rum Jungle in 1949. Today Batchelor thrives on tourism, in particular, because of its close proximity to the increasingly popular Litchfield National Park.

continued on p. 360

NORTHERN TERRITORY

ALICE SPRINGS

Pop. 21 619

Map ref. 595 I7 | 597 J3

i Central Australian Tourism Industry Association, 60 Gregory Tce; (08) 8952 5800 or 1800 645 199; www.centralaustraliantourism.com

96.9 Sun FM, 783 AM ABC Territory Radio

Located on the Todd River in the MacDonnell Ranges, Alice Springs is almost 1500 kilometres from the nearest capital city. In 1871 Overland Telegraph Line surveyor William Whitfield Mills discovered a permanent waterhole just north of today's city. Mills named the water source after Alice Todd, wife of South Australian Superintendent of Telegraphs Sir Charles Todd. A repeater station was built on the site. In 1888 the South Australian government gazetted a town 3 kilometres to the south. It was called Stuart until 1933, when the name Alice Springs was adopted. Supplies came to the slow-growing settlement by camel train from Port Augusta. The railway line from Adelaide, known as the *Ghan* after the original Afghan camel drivers, was completed in 1929. Today 'the Alice' is an oasis of modern civilisation in the middle of a vast and largely uninhabited desert, made all the more likeable by not taking itself too seriously (as some of its annual events testify).

Alice Springs Cultural Precinct This precinct includes some of Alice Springs' best cultural attractions. At the Araluen Centre are 3 galleries of Aboriginal art, with an emphasis on work from the central desert, and a magnificent stained-glass window by local artist Wenten Rubuntja. The Museum of Central Australia offers an insight into the geological and natural history of the Red Centre, with interpretive displays and impressive fossils. Also in the precinct are the Strehlow Research Centre, Craft Central, the Central Australian Aviation Museum, several memorials and the Yeperenye Sculpture, depicting a Dreamtime caterpillar. One ticket covers the entry to each attraction. Cnr Larapinta Dr and Memorial Ave; (08) 8951 1120.

Alice Springs Desert Park David Attenborough was so impressed by this desert park that he proclaimed, 'there is no museum or wildlife park in the world that could match it.' The park invites visitors to explore the arid lands and the relationship between its plants, animals and people. A walking trail leads through 3 habitats: Desert Rivers, Sand Country and Woodland. There are films, interactive displays, free audio-guides, guided day tours, nocturnal tours (to experience the central Australian desert at night, optionally with dinner) and talks about flora, fauna and the ability of Aboriginal people to survive in such harsh conditions. The park has a spectacular desert nocturnal house with native marsupials such as the bilby and mala, and there are free-flying birds of prey in twice-daily shows. Larapinta Dr; (08) 8951 8788.

John Flynn Memorial Uniting Church: in memory of the founder of the Royal Flying Doctor Service and Australian Inland Mission; Todd Mall; (08) 8953 0826. (Flynn's grave can be found 1 km beyond the entrance to Alice Springs Desert Park.) *Adelaide House:* originally a hospital designed by Rev Flynn, now a museum displaying pedal-radio equipment he used and other artefacts and photographs; open 10am–4pm Mon–Fri and 10am–12pm Sat Mar–Nov; Todd Mall. *Sounds of Starlight Theatre:* musical journey through Central Australia; open

Apr–Nov; Todd Mall. *Alice Springs Reptile Centre:* houses the largest reptile display in Central Australia, including goannas, lizards, pythons and some of the world's most venomous snakes. There's also Terry, the saltwater crocodile, and a new Cave Room featuring a live gecko exhibit. Open daily; Stuart Tce; (08) 8952 8700. *Aboriginal Australia Art and Culture Centre:* exhibits of local Arrernte culture and an Aboriginal music museum, including the only didgeridoo university in the world. Activities include boomerang and spear throwing, and a bush tucker experience with damper and billy tea; Todd St. *Royal Flying Doctor Service Base:* operational base since 1939, with daily tours and presentations, and an interactive museum including a pedal radio; Stuart Tce; (08) 8952 1129. *National Pioneer Women's Hall of Fame:* national project dedicated to preserving women's place in Australia's history; open Feb–mid-Dec; Old Alice Springs Gaol, 2 Stuart Terrace. *Old Stuart Town Gaol:* the harsh but functional design of stone and timber reflects the community attitude to prisoners at the time of construction (1907); open 10am–12.30pm Mon–Sat; Parsons St; (08) 8952 4516. *Anzac Hill:* the most visited landmark in Alice Springs, this war memorial features panoramic views of town and the MacDonnell Ranges; Anzac Hill Rd. *Stuart Town Cemetery:* original town cemetery with graves of the earliest pioneers dating from 1889; George Cres. *Alice Springs School of the Air:* the first of its kind in Australia with a classroom size of 1.3 million sq km. See interpretive displays and hear lessons being broadcast; Head St; (08) 8951 6834. *Old Hartley Street School:* originally constructed in 1930 and closed in 1965, the school was added to several times as the population surged, reflecting the changing styles and requirements of school design through different periods; open 10am–2.30pm Mon–Fri; Hartley St; (08) 8952 4516. *Olive Pink Botanic Gardens:* named after an anthropologist who worked with Central Desert people, this is Australia's only arid-zone botanic garden. Covering 16 ha, it contains over 300 Central Australian plant species in simulated habitats such as sand dunes, woodlands and creeks; Cnr of Barrett Dr and Tuncks St; (08) 8952 2514. *The Residency:* grand home completed in 1927 and housing Central Australia's regional administrator until 1973. It has welcomed many VIPs, including Queen Elizabeth II, and now showcases local history; Cnr Parsons and Hartley sts. *Red Centre Dreaming:* authentic, traditional and modern Aboriginal dance. Australian food is served including damper, kangaroo and barramundi; North Stuart Hwy. *Aboriginal cultural experiences, art galleries and artefacts:* Alice Springs is renowned for its rich Aboriginal culture and art. Tours and galleries plus ceremonial dances and didgeridoo playing are all available. Obtain more information from the visitor centre.

Alice Springs Council Market: Todd Mall; contact city council for dates and times, (08) 8950 0505. *Heritage Festival:* Apr. *Racing Carnival:* Apr/May. *Bangtail Muster:* street parade and sports day; May. *Finke Desert Race:* car and motorbike racing; June. *Beanie Festival:* June. *Camel Cup:* July. *Show:* cooking, crafts and camels; July. *Rodeo:* Aug. *Henley-on-Todd Regatta:* boats wheeled or carried along a dry riverbed; Aug. *Masters Games:* mature-age athletics carnival, even-numbered

[BUSH TUCKER DISPLAY, ALICE SPRINGS DESERT PARK]

years; Oct. *Desert Festival:* arts festival; Sept. *Bassinthedust:* youth music festival; Oct. *Christmas Carnival:* Dec.

The Juicy Rump: impressive menu of surf and turf; Lasseters Casino, Barrett Dr; (08) 8950 7777. *Alice Vietnamese Restaurant:* authentic Vietnamese; Heffernan Rd; (08) 8952 8396. *Casa Nostra Pizza Bar & Spaghetti House:* authentic Italian; Cnr Undoolya Rd and Sturt Tce; (08) 8952 6749. *Hanuman Alice Springs:* excellent modern Asian; Crowne Plaza, 82 Barrett Dr; (08) 8953 7188. *Red Ochre Grill:* contemporary and native cuisine; Leichhardt Tce; (08) 8952 9614. *Bojangles Saloon and Dining Room:* good atmosphere, in the centre of town; Todd St; (08) 8952 2873. *Oscar's Cafe & Restaurant:* Portuguese and Spanish; Shop 1, Cinema Complex, Todd Mall; (08) 8953 0930. *Barra on Todd Restaurant and Bar:* wide choice of meat and vegetarian dishes; Chifley Alice Springs Resort, Stott Tce; (08) 8952 3523. *The Overlanders Steakhouse:* very good steaks; 72 Hartley St; (08) 8952 2159.

G'day Mate Tourist Park: Palm Circuit; (08) 8952 9589. *Heavitree Gap Outback Lodge:* Palm Circuit; (08) 8950 4444. *Heritage Caravan Park:* Lot 8483 Ragonesi Rd; (08) 8953 1418. *Kathy's Place Bed & Breakfast:* 4 Cassia Crt; (08) 8952 9791. *MacDonnell Range Holiday Park:* Palm Pl; (08) 8952 6111. *Nthaba Cottage Bed & Breakfast:* 83 Cromwell Dr; (08) 8952 9003. *Stuart Caravan & Cabin Park:* Larapinta Dr; (08) 8952 2547. *Wintersun Cabin and Caravan Park:* Cnr North Stuart Hwy and Head St; (08) 8952 4080. *A Good Rest B&B:* 51 Dixon Rd, Braitling; (08) 8952 5272.

West MacDonnell National Park The majestic MacDonnell Ranges, once higher than the Himalayas, were formed over 800 million years ago. Over time the ancient peaks have been dramatically eroded so that what remains is a spectacular environment of rugged gorges, hidden waterholes, remnant rainforest and an unexpectedly large number of animal species and flora. The jewel of the ranges is Ormiston Gorge, one of the most beautiful in Australia, while the Ochre Pits are a natural quarry once mined by Aboriginal people for ochre that they used in rock art, painting and ceremonial decoration. The Larapinta Trail is a huge 230 km walk, divided into 12 sections covering the major sites of the ranges and can be walked separately. Contact the Parks and Wildlife Service NT for maps and tour options on (08) 8951 8250; 17 km w.

Emily and Jessie Gaps Nature Park Located in the East MacDonnells, Emily Gap (13 km E) and Jessie Gap (18 km E) contain Aboriginal rock art and are important spiritual sites to the Eastern Arrernte people. The caterpillar beings of Mparntwe (Alice Springs) originated where Emily Gap lies today. They formed Emily Gap and other topographical features around Alice Springs and then spread across to the edge of the Simpson Desert. Both gaps are popular barbecue and picnic places. (08) 8951 8250.

ALICE SPRINGS *continued from previous page*

Alice Springs Telegraph Station Historical Reserve: area protecting original stone buildings and equipment, with historical display, guided tours, bushwalking and wildlife (Alice Springs waterhole is located here); 3 km N. *Old Timers Traeger Museum:* unique museum set in a retirement home and run by volunteer residents. It displays photographs and memorabilia from the early days of white settlement in Central Australia; 5 km S. *Pyndan Camel Tracks:* ride a camel through the picturesque Ilparpa Valley alongside the Western MacDonnell Ranges; 0416 170 164; 15 km. *The Date Farm:* locally grown dates and a pleasant palm garden at Australia's first commercial date farm; 7 km E. *National Road Transport Hall of Fame:* impressive collection of old trucks, cars and motorbikes; 8 km S. *Ghan Railway Museum:* re-creation of a 1930s railway siding featuring the *Old Ghan*, which runs on 8 km of private line between MacDonnell Siding and Mt Ertiva; 10 km S. *Tropic of Capricorn marker:* bicentennial project marking the Tropic of Capricorn; 30 km N. *Ewaninga Rock Carvings Conservation Reserve:* soft sandstone outcrops form natural galleries of sacred Aboriginal paintings. Custodians request that visitors do not climb on rocks or interfere with the paintings; 35 km SE. *Corroboree Rock Conservation Reserve:* significant Eastern Arrernte site for ceremonial activities with a short walk and information signs; 43 km E. *Standley Chasm:* spectacular, narrow, sheer-sided gorge that is particularly striking at midday when the sun lights up the rocks. An attractive 1 km creek walk

leads to the chasm and picnic facilities; 50 km W. *Rainbow Valley Conservation Reserve:* stunning freestanding sandstone cliffs that change colour at sunrise and sunset. Access by 4WD only; 101 km S. *Mud Tank zircon field:* prospecting for zircons, guided fossicking tours and gem-cutting at the caravan park; 135 km NE. *Henbury Meteorites Conservation Reserve:* contains 12 craters created when meteorites (comprising 90% iron) crashed to earth 4700 years ago. The largest of the meteorites was over 100 kg and is now at the Museum of Central Australia in Alice Springs; 147 km SW. *Chambers Pillar Historical Reserve:* Chambers Pillar, named by John McDouall Stuart in 1860, is a 40 m high solitary rock pillar left standing on a Simpson Desert plain after 340 million years of erosion. It served as a landmark for early pioneers and explorers and is best viewed at dawn or dusk; 149 km S. *Mereenie Loop:* this unsealed road links the West MacDonnell Ranges, Hermannsburg, Glen Helen and Palm Valley with Watarrka National Park (Kings Canyon). A permit is required because a section of the route passes through Aboriginal land; obtain a map and permit from visitor centre. *Tours:* experience scenic attractions and Aboriginal culture by foot, bus or coach, train, limousine, 4WD safari, Harley-Davidson motorcycle, camel, horse, aeroplane, helicopter or hot-air balloon; brochures at visitor centre.

TOWNS NEARBY: Arltunga Bush Hotel 86 km, Hermannsburg 116 km, Glen Helen Resort 123 km, Aileron 129 km, Ti-Tree 179 km

---

Karlstein Castle Czech immigrant Bernie Havlik worked at Rum Jungle and was a gardener there until his retirement in 1977. As a gardener he had been frustrated by a rocky outcrop that was too large to move and too difficult to keep tidy, so he decided to build over it. Havlik spent 5 years constructing a mini replica of the original Karlstein Castle that still stands in Bohemia. He added finishing touches, despite serious illness, and died just after its completion. Rum Jungle Rd.

Coomalie Cultural Centre: bush tucker garden plus display of Aboriginal works and culture; Batchelor Institute, cnr Awilla Rd and Nurudina St.

Lingalonga Festival: cultural festival; Aug/Sept.

Batchelor Butterfly Cafe: good barra and buffalo; Batchelor Butterfly and Petting Farm, 8 Meneling Rd; (08) 8976 0110. *Litchfield Cafe:* good burgers and cheesecake; Litchfield Park Rd; (08) 8978 2077.

Batchelor Resort Caravillage: 37 Rum Jungle Rd; (08) 8976 0166.

Litchfield National Park Sandstone formations and monsoon rainforest feature in this easily accessible park. There are fantastic swimming spots: plunge into the rainforest-fringed pool at Wangi Falls, swim beneath the cascading Florence Falls or relax in the waters of Buley Rockhole. Do not miss the Lost City, a series of windswept formations that eerily resemble the ruins of an ancient civilisation, and the magnetic termite mounds, so-called because they all align north–south. Access

is for experienced 4WD only, but there's always the much more civilised option of a helicopter ride from Cape Crawford. (08) 8976 0282; 20 km w.

Lake Bennett Wilderness Resort: this resort has a plethora of birdlife and native fauna that can be enjoyed in the many serene picnic areas. A range of activities are available including abseiling, swimming and barramundi fishing. Dining and accommodation are also on-site; Chinner Rd; (08) 8976 0960; 18 km NE. *Batchelor Air Charter:* scenic flights, parachuting and gliding; Batchelor Aerodrome; 1 km W. *Rum Jungle Lake:* canoeing, kayaking, diving and swimming; 10 km w.

TOWNS NEARBY: Adelaide River 22 km, Noonamah 46 km, Pine Creek 122 km, Jabiru 200 km, Katherine 206 km

---

Borroloola
Pop. 775
Map ref. 591 M11 | 593 M2

ⓘ Lot 384, Robinson Rd; (08) 8975 8799.

📻 102.9 8MAB FM, 106.1 FM ABC Territory Radio

Located beside the McArthur River, Borroloola is a small settlement with a chequered past. As a frontier town and port in the 19th century it was a base for rum smuggling from Thursday Island. It became known as the home of criminals, murderers and alcoholics, a reputation it lost only when it was virtually deserted in the 1930s. Today Borroloola's fortunes have vastly improved and it is popular with barramundi anglers and four-wheel-drive enthusiasts. Although it lies on Aboriginal land, no permit is required to enter. It also offers access to the waters around Barranyi (North Island) National Park.

 Police Station Museum: built in 1886, the museum is the oldest surviving outpost in the NT and displays memorabilia and photographs that illustrate the town's history; Robinson Rd. **Cemetery:** pioneer graves; Searcy St and other scattered sites; map from visitor centre.

 Barra Classic: Easter. **Rodeo:** Aug.

Cape Crawford This charming town is an excellent base for exploring Bukalara rocks (60 km E) and the Lost City (20 km SE). Bukalara rocks are a mass of chasms winding through ancient sandstone structures (the area is very remote and a guide is recommended). The Lost City is a collection of sandstone turrets, domes and arches formed by water seeping through cracks and eroding the sandstone. It is an important Aboriginal ceremonial site and accessible only by air or 4WD. Flights can be arranged from Cape Crawford. 110 km SW.

King Ash Bay: popular fishing spot year-round; 40 km NE. **Caranbirini Conservation Reserve:** protects weathered rock escarpments and semi-permanent waterhole rimmed by riverine vegetation and open woodland, along with many native birds. Surrounding the waterhole are 25 m sandstone spires providing a vivid contrast in colour and shape to the surrounding countryside; 46 km SW. **Barranyi (North Island) National Park:** sun-drenched wilderness with long sandy beaches and excellent angling. No permit is required, but visitors are requested to register with the Borroloola Ranger Station; Offshore; (08) 8975 8792; 70 km NE. **Lorella Springs:** campground and caravan park at thermal springs. The road is unsealed and accessible only during the dry season; 170 km NW. **Limmen Bight River Fishing Camp:** ideal conditions for barramundi and mud crabs. Accommodation is available but check road access in wet season; 250 km NW. **Fishing charters:** river and offshore fishing trips; bookings at visitor centre. **Scenic flights:** over town and the islands of the Sir Edward Pellew Group; brochures at visitor centre.

Daly Waters

Pop. 20
Map ref. 590 H12 | 592 H3

 Daly Waters Pub, Stuart St; (08) 8975 9927; www.dalywaterspub.com

106.1 FM ABC Territory Radio

The nearby springs, from which this tiny settlement takes its name, were named after the governor of South Australia by John McDouall Stuart during his south–north crossing of Australia in 1862. The town's size belies its historical importance as the first international refuelling stop for Qantas in 1935.

Daly Waters Pub Known as one of the great authentic Australian pubs with characters to match. The knickers donated by patrons and stapled to the beam above the bar have all been removed. Accommodation and meals are available with the menu including 'bumnuts on toast' and 'ambuggers'. Stuart St; (08) 8975 9927.

Campdraft: Sept.

Daly Waters Aviation Complex: display on local aviation in the oldest hangar in the NT (1930). Key available from

Daly Waters Pub; off Stuart Hwy; 1 km NE. **Tree:** marked with an 'S', reputedly by explorer John McDouall Stuart; 1 km N. **Dunmarra:** roadhouse and accommodation; 44 km S. **Historic marker:** commemorates the joining of north and south sections of the Overland Telegraph Line; 79 km S. **Larrimah:** remains of historic WW II building at Gorrie Airfield and museum with relics of the local transport industry and WW II; 92 km N.

TOWNS NEARBY: Elliott 145 km, Mataranka 151 km, Katherine 231 km

Elliott

Pop. 353
Map ref. 593 I5

ⓘ Elliott Hotel, Stuart Hwy; (08) 8969 2069.

102.9 8KIN FM, 105.3 FM ABC Territory Radio

Elliott is a shady one-street town that is used as a cattle service stop. Stock being transported from the north are given a chemical tick bath here to prevent infection of herds in the south. The town was named after Lieutenant Snow Elliott, the officer in charge of an army camp on this site during World War II.

Nature Walk: interpretive signs introduce native flora and its traditional Aboriginal uses; details from visitor centre.

Mardi Gras: Apr.

 Renner Springs This roadside stop on the Stuart Hwy is thought of as the place where the tropical Top End gives way to the dry Red Centre. It was named after Frederick Renner, doctor to workers on the Overland Telegraph Line. Dr Renner discovered the springs when he noticed flocks of birds gathering in the area. Fuel, supplies and meals are available, and there are pleasant picnic and barbecue facilities. 91 km S.

Newcastle Waters: a once-thriving old droving town featuring historic buildings and a bronze statue, The Drover; 19 km NW.

TOWNS NEARBY: Daly Waters 145 km, Tennant Creek 242 km

Glen Helen Resort

Map ref. 594 G7 | 596 C3

ⓘ Namatjira Dr; (08) 8956 7489; www.glenhelen.com.au

106.1 8ACR FM, 783 AM ABC Territory Radio

This small homestead-style resort is an excellent base for exploring the superb scenery of Glen Helen Gorge and other attractions in West MacDonnell National Park. Its facilities include accommodation, a restaurant, a bar, entertainment, tour information and an attractive natural swimming hole.

Glen Helen Gorge This breathtaking sandstone formation was created by the erosive action of the Finke River over thousands of years. There is a beautiful walk along the Finke River with towering cliffs providing a habitat for black-footed wallabies. Helicopter flights provide awe-inspiring views over Mt Sonder. 300 m E.

West MacDonnell National Park: majestic mountain range and wilderness surrounding Glen Helen Resort and featuring Ormiston Gorge (12 km NE), Ochre Pits (21 km E) and the Larapinta Trail; see *Alice Springs*. **Tnorala (Gosse Bluff) Conservation Reserve:** huge crater, 25 km in diameter, formed when a comet struck earth over 130 million years ago. Excellent views from Tylers Pass. Access permit, from visitor centre, is included with Mereenie Loop permit (Mereenie Loop links West MacDonnells with Kings Canyon Resort in the south-west); 50 km sw.

TOWNS NEARBY: Hermannsburg 30 km, Alice Springs 123 km, Kings Canyon Resort 134 km, Aileron 134 km, Ti-Tree 188 km

Hermannsburg

Pop. 555
Map ref. 594 H7 | 596 D5

ⓘ Ntaria Supermarket; (08) 8956 7480; www.hermannsburg.com.au

📻 106.1 8ACR FM, 783 AM ABC Territory Radio

This Aboriginal community lives on the site of a former mission station established by German Lutherans in 1877. During the first 14 years, they recorded the Arrernte language and culture, compiled an Arrernte dictionary and translated the New Testament into the local language. From 1894 to 1922 the mission was run by Pastor Carl Strehlow, who restored and constructed most of the extant buildings. His son, T. G. H. Strehlow, assembled a vast collection of anthropological items relating to the Arrernte way of life. Renowned artist Albert Namatjira, the first Aboriginal to paint landscapes in a European style, was born at the mission in 1902, and produced art under the acclaimed Hermannsburg School. In 1982 the mission and its land was returned to the Arrernte. Visitors are restricted to the shop, petrol station and historic precinct.

Historic precinct The National Heritage–listed mission site comprises about 13 main buildings, mostly stone, the earliest

[HERMANNSBURG] **LUTHERAN CHURCH**

dating from 1877 but generally from the period 1897–1910. They include Strehlow's House (1879), home of the pastor in charge of the mission and now Kata Anga Tea Rooms with a reputation for delicious apple strudel; old manse (1888), currently a watercolour gallery housing work by Aboriginal artists of the Hermannsburg School (guided tours available); old schoolhouse (1896); tannery (1941); and Old Colonists House (1885), now a museum displaying historic items from the missionary era.

Finke Gorge National Park For millions of years the Finke River has carved its way through the weathered ranges, creating red-hued gorges and wide valleys. There are astonishing rock formations and dry creek beds that wind through sandstone ravines, where rare flora flourishes. The park's most famous feature, Palm Valley, is a refuge for about 3000 red cabbage palms (*Livistona mariae*), which are found nowhere else in the world. The 46 000 ha area is great for bushwalking: a 1.5 km climb leads to Kalarranga Lookout for views of the amazing Amphitheatre rock; the 5 km Mpaara Walk with informative signs explains the mythology of Western Arrernte culture; and the 2 km Arankaia Walk passes through the lush oasis of Palm Valley. Park access by 4WD only. (08) 8951 8290; 20 km s.

Monument to Albert Namatjira: a 6 m red sandstone memorial to the legendary artist; Larapinta Dr; 2 km E. *Wallace Rockhole Aboriginal community:* cultural tours and camping; 46 km SE.

TOWNS NEARBY: Glen Helen Resort 30 km, Alice Springs 116 km, Kings Canyon Resort 133 km, Aileron 155 km, Arltunga Bush Hotel 202 km

Jabiru
see inset box on next page

Katherine
see inset box on page 366

Kings Canyon Resort

Map ref. 594 F8

ⓘ Luritja Rd; (08) 8956 7442; www.kingscanyonresort.com.au

Kings Canyon Resort, in Watarrka National Park, is an excellent base from which to explore the region. It has various standards of accommodation, a petrol station, supermarket, laundry, tennis courts and swimming pools.

Watarrka National Park This park's many rock holes and gorges provide refuge from the harsh conditions for many species of plants and animals. The great attraction is Kings Canyon, an enormous amphitheatre with sheer sandstone walls rising to 270 m. The 870 m Carmichael Crag is known for its majestic colours, which are particularly vibrant at sunset. There are also well-signed trails. The Rim Walk is a boardwalk through prehistoric cycads in the lush Garden of Eden and takes in unusual rock formations such as the Lost City. The Kings Creek Walk is a 1 hr return walk along the canyon floor. The 6 km (3–4 hr) Kings Canyon Walk is rough going and recommended only for experienced walkers. Tours of the park include Aboriginal tours and scenic flights. Brochures available from visitor centre; (08) 8951 8211.

Kings Creek Station: working cattle and camel station with campsites and accommodation. Quad (4-wheeled motorcycle), helicopter and camel tours of the area; 36 km SE. *Mereenie Loop:* links Alice Springs, Kings Canyon, Uluru and Kata Tjuṯa via the West MacDonnell Ranges and Glen Helen. Permit required because a section of the route passes through Aboriginal land; map and permit from visitor centre.

TOWNS NEARBY: Yulara 123 km, Hermannsburg 133 km, Glen Helen Resort 134 km, Alice Springs 249 km

Mataranka
Pop. 232
Map ref. 590 H9

 Roper Gulf Shire, Stuart Hwy; (08) 8975 4576.

 106.1 FM ABC Territory Radio

Visitors are lured to Mataranka for its thermal springs and its sense of literary history. Jeannie Gunn, author of *We of the Never Never*, lived at nearby Elsey Station in the early 20th century. The town has adopted the term 'Never Never', using it to name a museum and a festival.

Stockyard Gallery: showcases local NT artists' work and a range of territory books, leather whips, didgeridoos and souvenirs; the cafe provides light homemade snacks; Stuart Hwy; (08) 8975 4530. *Territory Manor:* restaurant and accommodation with daily feeding of barramundi at 9.30am and 1pm (open to the public); Stuart Hwy; (08) 8975 4510. *The Never Never Museum:* outdoor displays of pioneer life, railway and military history, and the Overland Telegraph; open Mon–Fri; next to the Roper Gulf Shire Offices, Stuart Hwy; (08) 8975 4576. *Giant termite mound:* sculpture with recorded information; Stuart Hwy.

Back to the Never Never Festival: celebration of the outback including a cattle muster; May. *Art show:* May. *Rodeo:* Aug.

Mataranka Homestead Tourist Resort: good food in bush setting; Homestead Rd; (08) 8975 4544. *Territory Manor Holiday Park:* barra and beef; Martin Rd, off Stuart Hwy; (08) 8975 4516.

Mataranka Cabins & Camping: 255 Martin Rd; (08) 8975 4838. *Territory Manor Caravan Park:* 51 Martin Rd; (08) 8975 4516.

Elsey National Park The park encircles the Roper River, with rainforest, paperbark woodlands, and tufa limestone formations at Mataranka Falls. The Roper River offers excellent canoeing (hire available) and barramundi fishing. There are scenic walking tracks through pockets of rainforest with wildlife observation points and camping areas. The walk from Twelve Mile Yards leads to the small but beautiful Mataranka Falls.

Elsey Cemetery: graves of outback pioneers immortalised by Jeannie Gunn, who lived on Elsey Station from 1902 to 1903; 20 km SE. *We of the Never Never:* a cairn marks the site of the original homestead near the cemetery; 20 km SE. *Bitter Springs:* set amongst palms and tropical woodlands in the Elsey National Park, these spring-fed thermal pools are an ideal place to relax and unwind; 2 km E. *Mataranka Homestead Tourist Park:* enjoy a swim in the beautiful Rainbow Springs Thermal Pool surrounded by palm trees. The 1982 movie *We of the Never Never* was filmed here, and the replica of the original homestead is still part of the attractions; (08) 8975 4544; 7 km S.

TOWNS NEARBY: Katherine 100 km, Daly Waters 151 km, Pine Creek 180 km, Jabiru 250 km

Nhulunbuy
Pop. 4111
Map ref. 591 N4

 East Arnhem Land Tourist Association; (08) 8987 2828.

 106.9 Gove FM, 990 AM ABC Territory Radio

Located on the north-eastern tip of Arnhem Land on the Gove Peninsula, Nhulunbuy and its surrounds are held freehold by the Yolngu people. The town was established to service the bauxite-mining industry and has developed as the administrative centre for the East Arnhem region. Access is by a year-round daily air service from Darwin or Cairns or, with a permit, by four-wheel drive only, through Arnhem Land.

Gayngaru Wetlands Interpretive Walk The path surrounds an attractive lagoon that is home to around 200 bird species. There are 2 viewing platforms and a bird hide, as well as signs near local flora explaining their uses in Aboriginal food and bush medicine. Visitors can take the Winter walk or Tropical Summer walk, which is shorter as a result of higher water levels. Centre of Nhulunbuy.

Garma Festival: a celebration of Aboriginal arts and crafts; August/September.

Macassans Restaurant: modern Australian; The Arnhem Club, 1 Franklyn St; (08) 8987 0600. *The Walkabout Lodge Restaurant:* modern Australian with good seafood; 12 Westal St; (08) 8987 1777. *Seagrass Restaurant:* modern Australian with Asian influence; Dugong Beach Resort, 1 Bougainvillea Dr, Alyangula; (08) 8987 7077 or 1800 877 077. *Waterfront Kitchen:* great range of seafood and steaks. Overlooking the Arafura Sea; Golf Club East Woody Rd; (08) 8987 8388.

Buku-Larrnggay Mulka This renowned community-based Aboriginal art centre was set up to educate visitors in the ways of local law and culture, and to share the art of the Yolngu people. It is located in the nearby Aboriginal community of Yirrkala. 'Buku-Larrnggay' refers to the feeling on your face as it is struck by the first rays of the sun. 'Mulka' is a sacred but public ceremony and means to hold or protect. A permit is not required to visit. Open Mon–Fri and Sat morning; (08) 8987 1701; 18 km SE.

East Woody Island and Galaru (East Woody Beach): Gove Peninsula has long sandy beaches, tropical clear-blue water and amazing sunset views; 3 km N.

Travellers note: *Visitors intending to drive to Nhulunbuy must obtain a permit from the Northern Land Council beforehand, (08) 8987 8500. It's 4WD only and conventional caravans are not allowed; conditions also apply. Allow 2 weeks for processing. A recreation permit is also required for travel outside the Nhulunbuy Town Lease, available from Dhimurru Land Management; (08) 8987 3992.*

Noonamah
Pop. 485
Map ref. 588 E4 | 590 D5

 Noonamah Tavern, Stuart Hwy; (08) 8988 1054.

 106.1 FM ABC Territory Radio

Noonamah is a tiny town outside Darwin at the centre of numerous parks and reserves. It is a great base from which to experience wildlife, native bushland and safe swimming spots (something of a rarity, considering the Northern Territory's crocodile population).

Noonamah Tourist Park: 1807 Stuart Hwy; 0407 567 899. *Berry Spring Lakes Holiday Parks:* Doris Rd, Berry Springs;

continued on p. 365

 RADIO STATIONS   IN TOWN WHAT'S ON WHERE TO EAT WHERE TO STAY   NEARBY

JABIRU

Pop. 1140
Map ref. 589 O4 | 590 G5

 6 Tasman Plaza; (08) 8979 2548.

 747 AM ABC Territory Radio

Located deep within Kakadu National Park, Jabiru was first established because of the nearby uranium mine and, although this still operates, the town is now a major centre for the thousands who come to explore Kakadu each year. Facilities include a supermarket, a bakery and a large town swimming pool. Swimming pools are the only safe place to swim in Kakadu. Note that takeaway alcohol cannot be purchased.

Gagudju Crocodile Holiday Inn This NT icon is a 250 m crocodile-shaped building that really only resembles a crocodile from the air. The entrance (the mouth of the crocodile) leads to a cool marble reception area, designed to represent a billabong, and accommodation is in the belly of the beast. The design was approved by the Gagudju people, to whom the crocodile is a totem, and was a finalist at the prestigious Quaternario Architectural Awards in Venice. Flinders St.

Aurora Kakadu Lodge & Caravan Park: accommodation laid out in traditional Aboriginal circular motif; Jabiru Dr; (08) 8979 2422.

Gunbalunya (Oenpelli) Open Day: the Aboriginal community of Gunbalunya opens its doors to visitors with sports, art and Aboriginal culture; Aug. *Mahbilil Festival:* music, dance and artistic expression celebrating Kakadu; Sept.

Escarpment Restaurant: stylish, modern Australian; Gagudju Crocodile Holiday Inn, Flinders St; (08) 8979 9000. *Jabiru Golf Club:* good, well-priced food; Jabiru Dr; (08) 8979 2575. *Jabiru Sports & Social Club:* modern Australian; Lakeside Dr; (08) 8979 2326. *Aurora Kakadu Lodge & Caravan Park:* bistro alongside pool open to non-residents; see above. *The Bark Hut Inn:* good pub fare; Arnhem Hwy, Annaburroo; (08) 8978 8988; 135 km w. *Mimi Restaurant:* relaxed, outdoor seating; Gagudji Lodge Cooinda, Kakadu Hwy, Jim Jim; (08) 8979 0145; 50 km s *The Wetlands Restaurant:* buffet breakfast and dinner; Aurora Kakadu, Arnhem Hwy, South Alligator; (08) 8979 0166; 40 km w.

Lakeview Park Kakadu: 27 Lakeside Dr; (08) 8979 3144. *Gagudju Lodge Cooinda Caravan Park & Campground:* Kakadu National Park (off Kakadu Hwy), Cooinda; (08) 8979 0145.

Kakadu National Park A World Heritage site listed for both its natural value and cultural significance, Kakadu is a place of rare beauty and grand landscapes, abundant flora and fauna, impressive rock art and ancient mythology. The largest national park in Australia, it encompasses the flood plain of the South Alligator River system and is bordered to the east by the massive escarpment of the Arnhem Land Plateau. The wide-ranging habitats, from arid sandstone hills, savannah woodlands and monsoon forests to freshwater flood plains and tidal mudflats, support an immense variety of wildlife, some rare, endangered or endemic. There are over 50 species of mammal, including kangaroos, wallabies, quolls, bandicoots, bats and dugong, as well as a plethora of reptiles and birdlife. With around 5000 rock-art sites, the park has the world's largest and possibly oldest collection of rock art, which reveals the complex culture of the

[FLOOD PLAIN OF THE SOUTH ALLIGATOR RIVER, KAKADU NATIONAL PARK]

Aboriginal people since the Creation Time, when their ancestors are believed to have created all landforms and living things. Nourlangie Rock is one of Kakadu's main Aboriginal rock-art areas. The Nourlangie Art Site walk takes visitors through a variety of rock-art styles, including prime examples of Kakadu X-ray art, which shows the anatomy of humans and animals in rich detail. The Yellow Water (Ngurrungurrudjba) wetland area is a spectacular wetland area with prolific birdlife, especially in the dry season. Boat tours give visitors a close-up view of the birdlife and the Territory's crocodiles. Other highlights of the park include Jim Jim Falls (Barrkmalam) and Twin Falls (Gungkurdul), reached via a 4WD track off the Kakadu Hwy. An incredible volume of water cascades over Jim Jim Falls in the wet season, when the falls can only be seen from the air. Not to be missed is sunset at Ubirr rock, with free ranger tours at 5pm each day from May–Nov. Aboriginal people once camped in the rock shelters here, leaving the legacy of a spectacular rock-art site. A 1 km circuit covers the main natural galleries, which feature portrayals of extinct animals and animated figures in motion. Another highlight is a shorter side track that climbs steeply to Nardab Lookout, a rocky vantage point with sensational views. Also stop in at the Warradjan Aboriginal Cultural Centre in Cooinda, which features educational displays and exhibitions.

Travellers note: *Kakadu is a special place. It is important to respect the land and its people and refrain from entering restricted areas such as sacred sites, ceremonial sites and burial grounds. For more information contact (08) 8938 1120.*

Tourist walk: a 1.5 km stroll from the town centre through bush to Bowali Visitor Centre, which features an audiovisual presentation and interpretive displays on Kakadu. *Scenic flights:* over Kakadu parklands to see inaccessible sandstone formations standing 300 m above vast flood plains, seasonal waterfalls, wetland wilderness, remote beaches and ancient Aboriginal rock-art sites; 6 km E. *Ranger Uranium Mine:* open-cut mine with educational tours available; bookings through tours office, 1800 089 113; 9 km E. *Aboriginal cultural tours:* day tours and cruises; contact Bowali Visitor Centre, (08) 8938 1120; note that a permit is required to enter Kakadu National Park; details from the visitor centre.

TOWNS NEARBY: Pine Creek 167 km, Noonamah 191 km, Adelaide River 198 km, Batchelor 200 km, Katherine 207 km

(08) 8988 6277. *Darwin Boomerang Motel & Caravan Park:* 30 Virginia Rd, Virginia; (08) 8983 1202. *Mango Meadows Homestay:* 2759 Bridgemary Cres, Humpty Doo; (08) 8988 4417. *Tumbling Waters Holiday Park:* Cox Peninsula Rd, Berry Springs; (08) 8988 6255.

Territory Wildlife Park This 400 ha bushland park provides an easy way to view native animals in their natural habitat. They can be seen from walking trails or a motorised open train. A tunnel leads through an extensive aquarium that represents a Top End river system, where visitors can come face to face with a 3.7 m crocodile. Other highlights include a bird walk, nocturnal house and daily show of birds of prey. 14 km SW.

Didgeridoo Hut: see Aboriginal craftspeople make didgeridoos and weave baskets and dilly bags. Works are for sale in the gallery and there is an emu farm on-site; 8 km N. *Lakes Resort:* great facilities for watersports including waterski and jetski hire; accommodation available; 10 km SW. *Berry Springs Nature Park:* safe swimming in spring-fed pools in a monsoon forest with pleasant walking trails and picnic areas; 13 km SW (next to Territory Wildlife Park). *Jenny's Orchid Garden:* huge and colourful collection of tropical orchids, many on sale in the nursery; 22 km NW. *Howard Springs Nature Park:* swim in the freshwater springs and see barramundi and turtles or relax with a picnic in the shade by the children's pool, 23 km NW. *Manton Dam:* safe swimming, fishing, watersports and shady picnic spots; 25 km S. *Fogg Dam:* built in the 1950s to provide irrigation to the Humpty Doo Rice Project. The agricultural scheme failed, but the dam became a dry-season refuge for an amazing range of wildlife, especially waterbirds. It's best to visit at sunrise or sunset, when there is the most activity. There are a few lovely walks through the park, such as the Monsoon Forest Walk, a 2.7 km trail that traverses a variety of fascinating habitats; also inquire about ranger-guided nocturnal walks; 41 km NE. *Window on the Wetlands:* interpretive centre offering insight into the Top End's fascinating wetland environments plus superb views over the Adelaide River flood plains. Time your visit for early morning or late afternoon, when the vistas are best; 40 km NE (7 km beyond Fogg Dam turn-off). *Adelaide River Jumping Crocodile Cruises:* see crocodiles jump out of the water with the lure of food; several tours each day; (08) 8988 8144; 41 km NE (next to wetlands centre). *Fishing:* excellent barramundi fishing at Mary River Crossing (45 km E of Fogg Dam turn-off); several 4WD tracks lead north from here to prime fishing spots in Mary River National Park such as Corroboree Billabong (houseboat hire available).

TOWNS NEARBY: Batchelor 46 km, Adelaide River 67 km, Pine Creek 155 km, Jabiru 191 km, Katherine 240 km

Pine Creek

Pop. 665
Map ref. 589 I12 | 590 F7

ℹ️ Lazy Lizard Tavern, Millar Tce; (08) 8976 1019.

📻 96.7 Mix FM, 106.1 FM ABC Territory Radio

The town was named Pine Creek by Overland Telegraph workers because of the prolific pine trees growing along the banks of the tiny creek. During the 1800s it was the centre of Chinese settlement on the Top End goldfields. Today the town benefits from an active mining industry and is a regular stop for travellers up and down the Stuart Highway.

Railway Station Museum The station (1888) is at the terminus of the uncompleted 19th-century transcontinental railway system and now houses photographs and memorabilia. Open intermittently May–Sept. The nearby historic Beyer Peacock steam train was built at Manchester in England in 1877 and used in the film *We of the Never Never* (1982). The adjacent Miners Park points to an important visible link between the railway and the mines, which depended on the railway for survival. There are interpretive signs and displays of old mining machinery that reflect life on the goldfields; Main Tce.

Water Gardens: ponds with walking trails, birdlife and picnic spots; Main Tce. *Repeater Station Museum:* once a doctor's residence, military hospital, then post office, the building now houses a historical collection, including a display on the Overland Telegraph; open 11am–5pm Mon–Fri and 11am–1pm Sat; Railway Tce. *Enterprise Pit Mine Lookout:* panoramic views of open-cut goldmine that was once Enterprise Hill but is now a water-filled pit; Enterprise Pit. *Town walk:* takes in historic buildings and mining sites; brochure from Lazy Lizard Tavern.

Races: horseracing; May. *Gold Rush Festival and Gold Panning Championships:* June. *Rodeo:* June.

Mayse's Cafe: good Australian homemade food; 38 Moule St; (08) 8976 1241.

Douglas Daly Tourist Park: Oolloo Rd, Douglas Daly; (08) 8978 2479.

Butterfly Gorge Nature Park This park is a wilderness of sheer cliff-faces, dense vegetation and scenic shady river walks. Butterfly Gorge was named for the butterflies that settle in its rock crevices and is a beautiful and safe swimming and picnic spot. Access is by 4WD only. Open only during the dry season (May–Sept); 113 km NW.

continued on p. 367

 RADIO STATIONS IN TOWN WHAT'S ON WHERE TO EAT WHERE TO STAY NEARBY

KATHERINE
Pop. 5848
Map ref. 590 F8

[BOAT TOUR ALONG KATHERINE RIVER IN NITMILUK (KATHERINE GORGE) NATIONAL PARK]

ℹ️ Cnr Katherine Tce (Stuart Hwy) and Lindsay St; (08) 8972 2650 or 1800 653 142; www.visitkatherine.com.au

📻 101.3 Katherine FM, 106.1 FM ABC Territory Radio

Katherine, on the south side of the Katherine River, has always been a busy and important area for local Aboriginal groups, who used the river and gorge as meeting places. Explorer John McDouall Stuart named the river on his way through in 1862 after the second daughter of James Chambers, one of his expedition sponsors. The town grew up around an Overland Telegraph station and was named after the river. Today its economic mainstays are pastoral, tourism and the Tindal RAAF airbase.

Katherine Museum: built as an air terminal in 1944–45, the museum houses artefacts, maps, photographs and farming displays. There is also memorabilia relating to Dr Clyde Fenton, who, as a pioneer medical aviator and Katherine's Medical Officer between 1934 and 1937, serviced an area of 8 000 000 sq km in a second-hand Gypsy Moth he bought for £500. The plane is on display. Check opening times; Gorge Rd; (08) 8972 3945. **Railway Station Museum:** displays of the area's railway history with an old steam engine in nearby Ryan Park; check at the visitor centre for opening times; Railway Tce. **School of the Air:** see displays about the history of the school and listen in on lessons; open Apr–Oct, closed on weekends; Giles St. **O'Keefe House:** built during WW II and used as the officers' mess, it became home to Sister Olive O'Keefe, whose work with the Flying Doctor and Katherine Hospital from the 1930s to the 1950s made her a NT identity. The house is one of the oldest in town and is a classic example of bush ingenuity, using local cypress pine, corrugated iron and flywire; open Mon–Fri May–Sept; Riverbank Dr. **NT Rare Rocks:** unusual rock and gem displays; Zimmin Dr; (08) 8971 0889. **Self-guided**

walks: including Pioneer Walk and Arts and Crafts Trail; brochures from visitor centre.

Tick Markets: Lindsay St; 1st Sat each month Apr–Sept. **Katherine Community Markets and Farmers' Market:** 8am–12pm every Sat Mar–Dec; Ryan Park. **Katherine Show:** rodeo, exhibitions; July. **Katherine Cup:** horseracing; May. **Katherine Festival:** community festival, theatre and music; Aug.

Katherine Country Club: traditional Australian; 40 Pearce St, off Victoria Hwy; (08) 8972 1276. **Katie's Bistro:** good cooking; Knotts Crossing Resort, cnr Giles and Cameron sts; (08) 8972 2511. **The Carriage Stonegrill Restaurant & Bar:** hot rock cooking; Paraway Motel, O'Shea Tce; (08) 8972 2644. **The Katherine Club:** value-for-money; Cnr Second St and O'Shea Tce; (08) 8972 1250. **Silver Screen Cafe:** casual dining; 20 First St; (08) 8972 3140. **Coffee Club:** cafe, bar and restaurant; 23 Katherine Tce; (08) 8972 3990.

BIG4 Katherine Holiday Park: 20 Shadforth Rd; (08) 8972 3962. **Riverview Tourist Village:** 440 Victoria Hwy; (08) 8972 1011. **Shady Lane Tourist Park:** 257 Gorge Rd; (08) 8971 0491. **Springvale Homestead Tourist Park:** Shadforth Rd; (08) 8972 1355. **Nitmiluk Tours & Accommodation:** Gorge Rd, Nitmiluk (Katherine Gorge) National Park; (08) 8971 0877.

Nitmiluk (Katherine Gorge) National Park This 292 800 ha wilderness is owned by the Jawoyn people and managed jointly with Parks and Wildlife Service NT. It is renowned for its 13 stunning gorges, carved from red sandstone over a period of 20 million years. The Katherine River flows through a broad valley that narrows dramatically between the high sandstone cliffs of the magnificent Nitmiluk Gorge. 29 km NE. High above the floodline, on the overhangs of the ancient rock walls, are Aboriginal paintings thousands of years old. The best way to explore the gorge is by flat-bottomed boat (daily cruises; bookings at visitor centre), but canoe hire is available. You can also swim in the pools or explore the 100 km network of walking tracks. Another highlight of the park is Edith Falls (Leliyn) which drops into a paperbark- and pandanus-fringed natural pool that is a popular swimming spot. 66 km NE. There are signposted bushwalks, picnic areas and campsites. Fauna in Nitmiluk includes many reptile and amphibian species, kangaroos and wallabies in higher reaches and rare birds such as the hooded parrot and Gouldian finch. The countryside is at its best Nov–Mar although the weather is hot. Magnificent scenery can be enjoyed from helicopter tours, scenic flights and boat cruises. Brochures at visitor centre; (08) 8972 2650; 29 km NE.

Knotts Crossing: site of this region's first Overland Telegraph station (1870s) around which the original township of Katherine developed. By 1888 there was a hotel, store and police station. The hotel lost its licence in 1916 and the store was given a Gallon Licence. The Gallon Licence Store (now a private residence) operated until 1942; Giles St; 2 km E. **Natural Hot Springs:** on the banks of the Katherine River with picnic facilities and pleasant walking trails; Victoria Hwy; 3 km S. **Low Level Nature Reserve:** weir built by US soldiers during WW II, now a popular waterhole for picnicking and canoeing (bring own canoe). The river is teeming with barramundi, black bream and northern snapping turtles, so fishing is a common pastime; 3 km s. *Springvale Homestead:* originally the home of Alfred Giles, this is oldest remaining homestead in the NT (1879). Accommodation, restaurant, swimming pool and camping; Shadforth Rd; 8 km w. *Cutta Cutta Caves Nature Park:* 1499 ha of the only accessible tropical limestone caves in the NT with fascinating formations 15 m underground; regular tours each day; (08) 8972 1940;

27 km se. *Manyallaluk Aboriginal Community:* camping and Aboriginal cultural tours; bookings essential, (08) 8971 0877; 100 km ne. *Flora River Nature Park:* great campsites, interesting mineral formations, pools and cascades along the river; 122 km sw, of which 46 km is unsealed.

TOWNS NEARBY: Pine Creek 85 km, Mataranka 100 km, Adelaide River 185 km, Batchelor 206 km, Jabiru 207 km

Copperfield Recreation Reserve: safe swimming in deep-water lake and picnicking on foreshore, plus a Didgeridoo Jam held each May; 6 km sw. *Bonrook Lodge and Station:* wild horse sanctuary with trail rides and overnight camps; 6 km sw. *Umbrawarra Gorge Nature Park:* good swimming, rock climbing and walking trails; 22 km sw. *Tjuwaliyn (Douglas) Hot Springs Park:* sacred place for Wagiman women with hot springs; camping available; off Stuart Hwy; 64 km nw. *The Rock Hole:* attractive secluded waterhole; 4WD access only (via Kakadu Hwy); 65 km ne. *Gold fossicking:* several locations; licence required (available along with maps from visitor centre). *Kakadu National Park:* best-known park in the Top End, this is a massive tropical savannah woodland and freshwater wetland. Highlights nearby include the spectacular views at Bukbukluk Lookout (87 km ne) and the beautiful falls and permanent waterhole at Waterfall Creek (113 km ne); see *Jabiru.*

TOWNS NEARBY: Katherine 85 km, Adelaide River 102 km, Batchelor 122 km, Noonamah 155 km, Jabiru 167 km

Tennant Creek
Pop. 2922
Map ref. 593 J9

ⓘ Battery Hill Mining Centre, Peko Rd; (08) 8962 1281 or 1800 500 879; www.barklytourism.com.au

📻 102.1 8CCC FM, 106.1 FM ABC Territory Radio

Tennant Creek is midway between Alice Springs and Katherine and according to legend, emerged when a beer truck broke down here. Gold was found in the area in the early 1930s and the town grew rapidly in the wake of Australia's last great gold rush. Gold exploration still continues in the Barkly Tableland, an area larger than Victoria.

🏠 **Nyinkka Nyunyu Cultural Centre** This centre was built near a Warumungu sacred site and its name means 'home of the spiky-tailed goanna'. Dioramas illustrate the history of the area, an Aboriginal art gallery showcases the Tennant Creek art movement, and bush tucker, dance performances and displays explain the Aboriginal people's relationship with the land. The centre is set in landscaped gardens, featuring plants used for bush tucker and medicine. Paterson St; (08) 8962 2221.

Tuxworth Fullwood Museum: housed in an old WW II army hospital (1942) and listed by the National Trust, this museum has a photographic collection and displays of early mine buildings and equipment, a 1930s police cell and a steam tractor engine; open May–Sept, check times with the visitor centre; Schmidt St. *Purkiss Reserve:* pleasant picnic area with swimming pool

nearby; Ambrose St. *Julalikari Arts:* Aboriginal art centre; (08) 8962 2163. *Winanjjikari Music Centre:* resident Aboriginal musicians; (08) 8962 3282. *Self-guided tours:* scenic drives and heritage walks including an old Australian Inland Mission built in 1934 of prefabricated corrugated iron, and the catholic church built in 1911 and relocated from Pine Creek in 1936; brochures and maps from the visitor centre.

🎪 *Drag Racing:* May. *Show:* cooking, craft, exhibitions and a big dog show; July. *Cup Day:* horseracing; May. *Desert Harmony Festival:* arts and culture; Aug/Sept. *Brunette Downs Races:* campdrafting, bronco branding and more; June; 360 km ne.

🍴 *Anna's Restaurant:* modern Australian; Bluestone Motor Inn, 1 Paterson St (Stuart Hwy); (08) 8962 2617. *Fernanda's Restaurant:* Mediterranean cuisine; Tennant Creek Squash Courts, 1 Noble St; (08) 8962 3999. *Jajjikari Cafe:* cafe food in terrific setting; Nyinkka Nyunyu Art and Culture Centre, Paterson St (Stuart Hwy); (08) 8962 2699. *Memories Restaurant:* home-style cooking; Tennant Creek Memorial Club, 48 Schmidt St; (08) 8962 2688. *Eldorado Restaurant:* indoor or outdoor dining; 1 Paterson St; (08) 8962 2617. *Wok's Up:* Chinese at the Sporties Club; Ambrose St; (08) 8962 3888.

🛏 *Outback Caravan Park:* 71 Peko Rd; (08) 8962 2459. *Threeways Road House:* Cnr Stuart and Barkly hwys, Threeways; (08) 8962 2744.

🔘 **Battery Hill** This comprises of an underground mine, a 10-head stamp battery and 2 museums. There are daily tours of the underground mine with working machinery highlighting gold extraction. Bill Allen Lookout, just past the battery, offers panoramic views, with plaques identifying significant sites. Off Peko Rd; 3.5 km e.

Tennant Creek Cemetery: pioneer graves with plaques reminding us of the hardships of pioneer life; 2 km s. *Lake Mary Ann:* man-made dam ideal for swimming, canoeing, windsurfing and picnics; 6 km ne. *Juno Bush Camp:* bush camping; contact visitor centre for details; 10 km e. *Telegraph Station:* restored stone buildings (1872), once the domain of telegraph workers, whose isolated lives are revealed by interpretive signs; key is available from Tennant Creek Visitor Centre; 11 km n. *The Pebbles:* spectacular in their quantity, these are miniature versions of the Devils Marbles (huge balancing boulders found north of Wauchope). The site is sacred to the Munga Munga women; 16 km nw (6 km of unsealed road). *Memorial Attack Creek Historical Reserve:* a memorial marks the encounter between John McDouall Stuart and local Aboriginal people; 72 km n.

continued on p. 368

NORTHERN TERRITORY

YULARA

Pop. 983
Map ref. 594 E10 | 596 D9

[ULURU]

 ⓘ Alice Springs Visitor Information Centre, Gregory Tce, (08) 8952 5800; Ayers Rock Resort, (08) 8957 7888.

📻 99.7 FM ABC Territory Radio, 100.5 8HA FM

Yulara is a resort town that was built specifically to cater for visitors coming to see Uluṟu and Kata Tjuṯa. It offers excellent visitor facilities and food and accommodation for all budgets. Advance bookings for accommodation are essential.

🏠 *Alice Springs Visitor Information Centre:* displays of geology, history, flora and fauna with a spectacular photographic collection.

🍴 *Sounds of Silence:* alfresco dining under the stars with a talk on astronomy; Ayers Rock Resort, Yulara Dr; 1300 134 044. *Pioneer BBQ and Bar:* barbecue and native meats; Outback Pioneer Hotel and Lodge, Ayers Rock Resort, Yulara Dr; 1300 134 044. *Gecko's Cafe:* gourmet pizza and pasta; Ayers Rock Resort, Yulara Dr; 1300 134 044. *Red Rock Deli:* salads and wraps; Ayers Rock Resort, Yulara Dr; 1300 134 044. *Kuniya Restaurant:* modern Australian; Sails in the Desert Hotel, Ayers Rock Resort, Yulara Dr; 1300 134 044. *Tali Wiru:* exquisite modern Australian cuisine under the stars; Ayers Rock Resort, Yulara Dr; 1300 134 044.

🛏 *Ayers Rock Campground:* Yulara Dr; (08) 8957 7002.

◎ **Uluṟu** Australia's most recognisable natural landmark and the largest monolith in the world, Uluṟu features stunning Aboriginal rock-art sites that can be viewed on guided walks and tours around the base. These sites highlight the rock's significance for Aboriginal people. The traditional owners prefer visitors not to climb Uluṟu and there are countless tales of a curse befalling those who take a piece of the rock home as a souvenir. The spectacular changing colours of Uluṟu at sunrise and sunset are not to be missed. 20 km SE.

Uluṟu-Kata Tjuṯa Cultural Centre: designed in the shape of two snakes, with displays of Aboriginal culture and sales of artwork; on approach road to Uluṟu; (08) 8956 2214; 17 km S *Kata Tjuṯa:* remarkable rock formations, with spectacular Valley of the Winds walk, fantastic views and a variety of flora and fauna; 50 km W. *Tours:* helicopter, coach and safari tours; call information centre for bookings.

TOWNS NEARBY: Kings Canyon Resort 123 km, Hermannsburg 232 km, Glen Helen Resort 243 km

---

Karlu Karlu Devils Marbles Conservation Reserve: a must-see phenomenon of huge red granite boulders; bush camping is available; 106 km S, and a 2 km sealed loop.

TOWNS NEARBY: Wauchope 110 km, Barrow Creek 208 km, Elliott 242 km

Ti-Tree

Map ref. 595 I4

 ⓘ Ti-Tree Roadhouse, Stuart Hwy; (08) 8956 9741.

 📻 105.9 8ACR FM, 107.7 FM ABC Territory Radio

This rest stop on the Stuart Highway took its name from nearby Ti Tree Wells, the source of plentiful sweet water in the 1800s.

Today the desert region supports remarkably successful fruit and vegetable industries.

 Red Sand Art Gallery: Pmara Jutunta art with exhibitions and sales; food available; Stuart Hwy. **Ti Tree Park:** picnic area and playground; Stuart Hwy.

 Central Mt Stuart Historical Reserve: the sandstone peak was noted by John McDouall Stuart as the geographical centre of Australia; no facilities, but a monument at the base; 18 km N.

TOWNS NEARBY: Aileron 57 km, Barrow Creek 86 km, Alice Springs 179 km, Wauchope 185 km, Glen Helen Resort 188 km

Timber Creek
Pop. 227
Map ref. 590 D10 | 592 D2

i Max's Victoria River Boat Tours, Victoria Hwy; (08) 8975 0850.

 106.9 FM Territory Radio

In 1855 explorer A. C. Gregory was the first European to visit this area as he followed the Victoria River south from the Timor Sea. His boat was wrecked at the site of Timber Creek, where he found the timber he needed to make repairs. The town today is growing in importance as a stop on the journey from the Kimberley in Western Australia to the major centres of the Northern Territory, and as a gateway to Gregory National Park.

 Timber Creek Police Station Museum: displays of historic artefacts in restored police station (1908); open 10am–12pm Mon–Fri; off Victoria Hwy. **Parks and Wildlife Service NT:** information for travellers to Gregory and Keep River national parks; Victoria Hwy. **Tours:** boat and fishing tours, river cruises (with abundant crocodiles) and scenic flights; brochures from visitor centre.

 Fishing competitions: Apr–May. **Rodeo:** May. **Campdraft and Gymkhana:** Sept.

 Gregory National Park This is the NT's second largest national park with 2 sections covering 13 000 sq km of ranges, gorges, sandstone escarpments, remnant rainforest, eucalypts and boab trees. There are opportunities for boating, canoeing, bushwalking, scenic flights and cruises, as well as Aboriginal and European heritage sites. Gregory's Tree (in the Victoria River section to the east) stands at Gregory's campsite with historic inscriptions and audio presentation. The tree also has special significance for the Ngarinman people and is a registered sacred site. The spectacular dolomite blocks and huge cliffs of Limestone Gorge can be found in the Bullita section to the west. Bullita station has traditional timber stockyards, an old homestead, interpretive displays and shady camping spots in summer. Check with Parks and Wildlife Service NT for current access details; (08) 8975 0888; 31 km W and 92 km E.

Jasper Gorge: scenic gorge with permanent waterhole and Aboriginal rock art; 48 km SE. **Victoria River Roadhouse:** rest stop where the Victoria Hwy crosses the Victoria River. Cruises, fishing trips and accommodation are available. There are also several scenic walks in the area including the Joe Creek Walk (10 km W); 92 km E. **Keep River National Park:** includes the traditional land of the Miriwoong and Kadjerong peoples and contains many important rock-art sites, including the accessible Nganalam site. A major attraction is the rugged sandstone formations, similar to the Bungle Bungles over the WA border. There are designated camping areas and good walking tracks. Most trails are 4WD only. Check with Parks and Wildlife Service NT for current access details; (08) 9167 8827; 180 km W.

TOWNS NEARBY: Kununurra (WA) 186 km, Katherine 232 km, Pine Creek 249 km

Wauchope
Pop. 10
Map ref. 593 J11 | 595 J1

i Wauchope Hotel, Stuart Hwy; (08) 8964 1963.

 106.1 FM ABC Territory Radio

Wauchope (pronounced 'walk-up') was established to cater for the wolfram-mining and cattle-farming communities nearby. Today it is a service town and tourist destination thanks to its proximity to the popular Devils Marbles.

 Wauchope Hotel Once catering to workers at the old Wolfram Mines, this desert oasis now offers fuel, meals (licensed restaurant and takeaway), various standards of accommodation and an adjacent campground. The walls of the pub are adorned with signed bank notes (a 'bush bank' where customers pin deposits to the wall to be retrieved on a later visit) and photographs of patrons. The landscaped beer garden features native birdlife including Bill the talking cockatoo. Stuart Hwy.

 Wycliffe Well Holiday Park: Stuart Hwy, Wycliffe Well; (08) 8964 1966.

 Wycliffe Well This roadhouse was the first in the NT to be allowed to sell water (at a penny a gallon). Once a market garden supplying troops during WW II, it now features pleasant picnic lawns surrounding Wycliffe Lake. The area is said to be at a cross-section of energy lines and has had many alleged UFO sightings (ranked 5th in the world for the number of sightings). Wycliffe Well also claims to have Australia's largest range of beers, but any connection between that and the UFO sightings is yet to be proven. Accommodation available. 17 km S.

Devils Marbles (Karlu Karlu): an iconic outback destination, where massive red and orange boulders sit precariously atop each other in a broad desert playground. Legend says that they are the eggs of the Rainbow Serpent. A network of informal tracks meanders through the rock formations; 8 km N. **Davenport Range National Park:** isolated area with important Aboriginal heritage and waterhole ecology sites; high clearance vehicles or 4WD access only; advise travel plans at the Wauchope Hotel; (08) 8962 4599; 118 km E.

TOWNS NEARBY: Barrow Creek 101 km, Tennant Creek 110 km, Ti-Tree 185 km, Aileron 240 km

NORTHERN TERRITORY

Snorkelling or scuba diving among fish and coral in the **GREAT BARRIER REEF** / A daytrip to one – or more – of the **GOLD COAST'S** many theme parks / Four-wheel driving on **FRASER ISLAND'S BEACHES** / Fossicking for gemstones around **ANAKIE, RUBYVALE, SAPPHIRE** or **WILLOWS GEMFIELDS** / Discovering tropical rainforest in **DAINTREE NATIONAL PARK** / Taking a ride on the **KURANDA SCENIC RAILWAY**, returning via the Skyrail Rainforest Cableway / Sailing in the **WHITSUNDAYS** / Walking through **NOOSA NATIONAL PARK**, followed by a coffee and shopping on **HASTINGS STREET** / Travelling on the **GULFLANDER** train between Normanton and the old goldmining town of Croydon

QUEENSLAND

QUEENSLAND is Australia's second largest state and offers numerous idyllic holiday destinations. Myriad islands, cays and atolls are scattered along its 6973-kilometre coastline. The Great Barrier Reef offers the ultimate in diving, and there are 2000 species of fish, dugongs, turtles and extensive coral gardens, all protected by World Heritage listing.

By contrast, the arid west gives visitors a chance to experience some of Australia's unique outback in towns such as Winton, established by those searching for the lost Burke and Wills expedition. Winton also has a special place in Australian folklore as the location of Dagworth woolshed where Banjo Paterson wrote the iconic 'Waltzing Matilda' in 1895.

Two-thirds of Queensland lies above the Tropic of Capricorn. In the monsoonal Far North, visitors can venture into magnificent ancient rainforests, like those of Daintree National Park, where cool respite lies in places such as the boulder-strewn Mossman Gorge.

South of Brisbane is the famous Gold Coast. With more waterways than Venice and 300 days of sunshine each year, it is the perfect place for swimming and surfing. The theme parks here will terrify and astound, while in the hinterland, an emerald-green paradise allows visitors to soak up magnificent views among waterfalls and rainforest trees.

[PANDANUS PALM, NOOSA NATIONAL PARK]

Captain James Cook and his crew were the first Europeans to unexpectedly enjoy the Queensland coast after they ran aground on a reef near Cape Tribulation in 1770. Dutch explorer Willem Jansz had sailed along the western side of Cape York 164 years earlier, but received a hostile reception from the local Aboriginal people.

European settlement of Queensland occurred quite late compared with the rest of Australia. In 1824 a convict station was built near Moreton Bay to cater for the most intractable prisoners from southern gaols, but after a year of active resistance by Aboriginal tribes it was abandoned and relocated to where Brisbane stands today.

In recent years Queensland has shaken off its reputation as a quiet backwater. This modern state is fast becoming the envy of the rest of the country with its stunning natural features, relaxed pace and languid lifestyle, all enhanced by a climate close to perfect.

[A PAIR OF RAINBOW LORIKEETS]

fact file

Population 4 580 700
Total land area 1 722 000 square kilometres
People per square kilometre 2.3
Sheep and cattle per square kilometre 12
Length of coastline 6973 kilometres
Number of islands 1955
Longest river Flinders River (840 kilometres)
Largest lake Lake Dalrymple (dam), 220 square kilometres
Highest mountain Mount Bartle Frere (1622 metres), Wooroonooran National Park
Highest waterfall Wallaman Falls (305 metres), Girringun (Lumholtz) National Park
Highest town Ravenshoe (930 metres)
Hottest place Cloncurry (average 37°C in summer)
Coldest place Stanthorpe (46 days per year begin at below 0°C)
Wettest place Tully gets 4300 millimetres of rain per year, and has a giant gumboot to prove it
Sunniest town Townsville (average 300 days of sunshine per year)
Most remote town Birdsville
Major industries Sugar and mining
Most famous local Steve Irwin, the 'Crocodile Hunter' (deceased)
Number of 'big things' 39
Best beach Whitehaven Beach, Whitsunday Island
Local beer XXXX

gift ideas

Arts and crafts, The Valley Markets, Brisbane Quirky, unusual and interesting handmade arts, crafts and fashion. See Markets p. 386

Beer glasses, XXXX Brewery, Brisbane A little something from Queensland's iconic XXXX brewery. See XXXX Brewery p. 383

Ginger products, Buderim Ginger Factory, Yandina All Queensland grown and made, including everything from ginger chocolate to ginger perfume. See Yandina p. 450

'Crocodile Hunter' souvenirs, Australia Zoo, Beerwah Choose from an incredible range of souvenirs from this internationally renowned zoo. See Landsborough p. 421

Macadamia nuts, Nutworks, Yandina Delicious and unusual produce, as well as skin products from this working nut factory. See Yandina p. 50

Great Barrier Reef mementos, Reef HQ, Townsville Beautiful photos, books and souvenirs of the Great Barrier Reef. See Townsville p. 448

Tropical fruit, Cape Tribulation Black sapote, soursop and carambola are just some of the Dr Seuss–sounding tropical fruits you can taste and purchase. Visit Cape

Trib Exotic Fruit Farm at Lot 5, Nicole Dr, Cape Tribulation, and other producers around Far North Queensland. See Daintree p. 408

Australian Arabica coffee, The Australian Coffee Centre, Mareeba The Skybury Coffee company makes pure Arabica coffee from beans grown near the Great Dividing Range. See Mareeba p. 425

Vodka and liqueurs, Tamborine Mountain Distillery, North Tamborine Award-winning vodka, schnapps and other liqueurs in hand-painted bottles from Australia's smallest pot still distillery. 87–91 Beacon Rd, North Tamborine. See North Tamborine p. 434

BRISBANE is...

A bike ride through the CITY BOTANIC GARDENS / Cocktails by the river at the

POWERHOUSE arts centre / People-watching on fashionable JAMES STREET /

City views from MOUNT COOT-THA / The latest blockbuster at the GALLERY OF

MODERN ART / Riverside dining at EAGLE STREET PIER / An adventure climb on

the STORY BRIDGE / Hugging a koala at LONE PINE KOALA SANCTUARY / A stroll

along the RAINFOREST WALK and a swim at STREETS BEACH in South Bank

VISITOR INFORMATION

**Brisbane Visitor Information &
Booking Centre**
→ Queen Street Mall
(07) 3006 6290
www.visitbrisbane.com.au

The subtropical climate may be warm, but Brisbane is decidedly cool. The population has doubled in the last two decades to almost two million people and, as a result, Brisbane has been busily reinventing itself. There is a lively young arts scene and the city has been ranked among the hottest places in the world for new music. Its young fashion designers are making a name for themselves, and the Gallery of Modern Art is bringing blockbuster exhibitions down under. But while the CBD skyline may be spiked by glittering high-rise buildings, and the river lined with big boats, thankfully, the city has lost little of its friendliness in the make-over. Life is as relaxed as ever, and firmly focused on the outdoors.

Brisbane's hilly terrain provides breathing space and a beautiful backdrop to the CBD. Step into the nearby suburbs and you will find stately Moreton Bay fig trees standing sentinel in the suburban streets and mango trees blooming in the backyards of those distinctive weatherboard houses on stilts known as 'Queenslanders'. With their shady verandahs and tin roofs just made for the patter of summer rain, you can still find them within walking distance of the CBD.

From the coast to the suburbs, the year-round warm climate means that Brisbane is ideal for a holiday; whether you want city parks or national parks, markets or museums, nightlife or wildlife, you will find it all here.

MAP LEGEND

⊕ Attraction

ℹ Tourist information

⊕ Where to eat & where to stay

Shopping precinct

SEE PAGE 378

0   1 km

CITY CENTRE

Despite being the commercial and retail heart of Brisbane, the city centre retains the buoyant holiday spirit associated with the entire Sunshine State.

Queen Street Mall 378 B4

With Queens Plaza, Myer Centre, Broadway on the Mall, the heritage-listed Brisbane Arcade and MacArthur Central (adjoining the GPO), this is the hub of the CBD. It has pedestrian access only, but a central bus station is located beneath it. Outdoor cafes and restaurants abound. At the George Street end is the Treasury Casino *(see next entry)*, the Brisbane Square Library and surrounding eateries, and the Victoria Bridge leading to the South Bank parklands. The mall leads onto ANZAC Square *(see below)* and Post Office Square, with more shopping found on Elizabeth Street, including the Elizabeth Arcade and Adelaide Street with the Brisbane City Hall *(see entry on this page)* and King George Square. Follow the plaques on the pavement to take the **Albert Street Literary Walk**.

Conrad Treasury Casino 378 B4

The spectacular Treasury Building, built between 1885 and 1928, is now the Conrad Treasury Casino. With restaurants, bars and live bands, this is a top nightspot. *George St; open 24 hours daily; admission free.*

ANZAC Square 378 C3

ANZAC Square, between Ann and Adelaide streets, is a peaceful retreat. The **Shrine of Remembrance**, built in 1930, honours Australian soldiers who died in World War I. In the pedestrian tunnel behind the square is the World War II **Shrine of Memories** (open weekdays 9am–2pm) where you can see unit plaques, honour rolls and a mosaic made from hand-cut glass enamels and soils from official World War II cemeteries. Take the steps to the walkways over Adelaide Street to reach **Post Office Square**, another of Brisbane's grassy public squares. Opposite is the **General Post Office**, built in the 1870s.

Brisbane City Hall 378 B3

The newly revamped **King George Square** contains the historic Brisbane City Hall. Built throughout the 1920s, this impressive sandstone building is topped by a soaring 92-metre clock tower. (Closed for repairs until early 2013.) *Between Ann and Adelaide sts; (07) 3403 8888.*

Museum of Brisbane 378 B3

With City Hall closed for restoration, the museum has moved, temporarily, around the corner from King George Square. Also known as MoB, it has several exhibition spaces and celebrates the history, culture and people of Brisbane. The MoB Store has fantastic things made by Brisbane's talented writers, artists and musicians. *157 Ann St; (07) 3403 8888; open daily; admission free.*

St John's Cathedral 378 C2

This striking example of Gothic-Revival architecture was designed in 1888 and constructed 17 years later. It is the last medieval construction project of its kind in the world. Next door is the **Deanery**, built in 1850 and formerly the residence of Queensland's first governor, Sir George Bowen. Free tours daily. *373 Ann St; (07) 3835 2222.*

QUEENSLAND

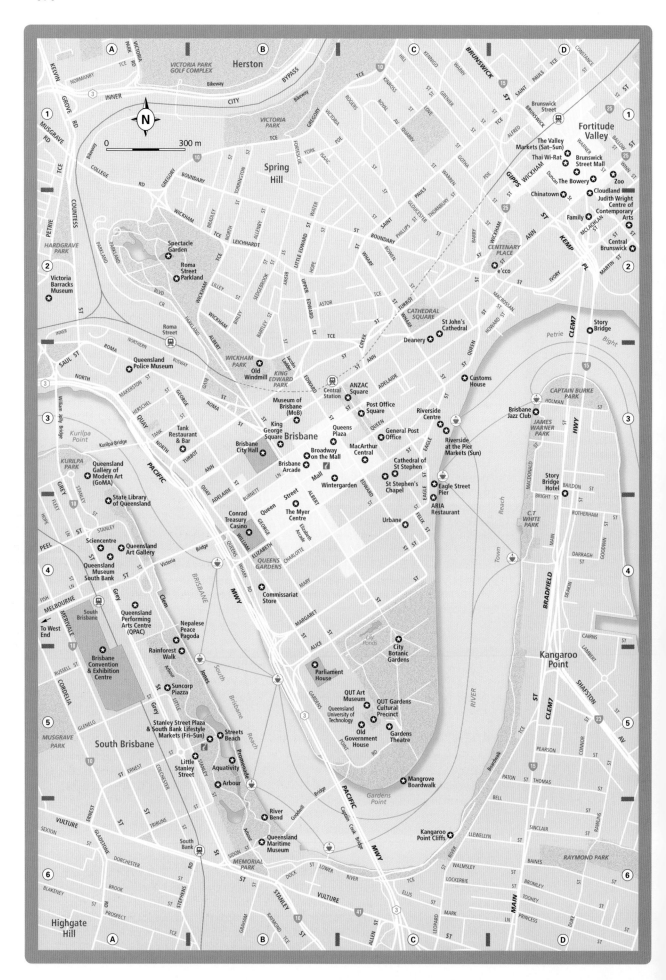

Cathedral of St Stephen 378 C3

This magnificent cathedral is a quiet place of worship amid the hustle and bustle of the city. The grounds include **St Stephen's Chapel**, the oldest surviving church in Queensland. Guided tours are available. *249 Elizabeth St; (07) 3336 9111.*

Commissariat Store 378 B4

Built by convicts in 1829 from Brisbane tuff, this is one of the oldest buildings in the city. Today it houses the offices, library and museum of the Royal Historical Society of Queensland. There is a convict display, and tours are available. *115 William St; (07) 3221 4198; open 10am–4pm Tues–Fri.*

FORESHORE

The serpentine Brisbane River curves its way through the whole city, creating cultural pockets and connecting suburbs. It is the place for award-winning restaurants, cafes and spectacular vistas. Ferries and CityCats stop at the Riverside Wharf and near the Botanic Gardens.

N
0   200 m

[CITYCAT WATER TAXI ON THE BRISBANE RIVER]

Customs House 378 C3

Built in 1889 and beautifully restored, this magnificent building on the Brisbane River served as the city's Customs House for almost a century. It is now a cultural and educational facility of the University of Queensland, and has function rooms and a waterfront brasserie. Free guided tours on sundays. *399 Queen St; (07) 3365 8999; open daily; admission free.*

Riverside Centre and Eagle Street Pier 378 C3

These two neighbouring office precincts dominate the CBD reach of the river. By day their riverside cafes, bars and restaurants are packed with professionals. At night they turn on the glamour, with some of Brisbane's best-known restaurants. On Sundays they host the popular **Riverside at the Pier Markets** *(see Markets, p. 386).* From the boardwalk, enjoy the views of **Story Bridge**, Australia's largest steel cantilever bridge.

City Botanic Gardens 378 C5

Established in 1855 in the heart of the city, these are Queensland's oldest public gardens. Majestic bunya pines and Moreton Bay figs line the avenues. Explore the rainforest glade or take the **Mangrove Boardwalk** along the river. The riverside path offers stunning views of Kangaroo Point Cliffs. Take a free guided tour, hire a bike or just sit on the grassy foreshore and relax. *Gardens Point, Alice St.*

QUT Gardens Cultural Precinct 378 C5

Next to the City Botanic Gardens, this precinct encompasses **Old Government House**, the QUT Art Museum and the Gardens Theatre. Now run by QUT, the graceful sandstone Old Government House, built in 1860, was once home to the first Queensland governor. *(07) 3138 8005; open 10am–5pm Sun–Fri; admission free.*

QUT Art Museum is housed in a 1930s neoclassical building and shows QUT's art collections, work by students and diverse contemporary exhibitions. *(07) 3138 5370; open 10am–5pm Tues–Fri, 10am–8pm Wed, 12–4pm Sat and Sun; admission free.* The cultural venue of the **Gardens Theatre** offers shows by QUT students and visiting international and Australian theatre companies.

Parliament House 378 B5

Overlooking the City Botanic Gardens, this grand old seat of government was built in 1868, with new buildings added over time. The two sandstone wings hold majestic staircases, stained-glass windows and ornate chandeliers. Watch the Queensland State Parliament in action from the visitors' gallery, or when it's not in session take one of the 30-minute tours that are run on demand. *Cnr George and Alice sts; (07) 3406 7562; open daily; admission free.*

QUEENSLAND

ROMA STREET PARKLAND

Formerly rail yards and engine sheds, this area has been transformed by the Roma Street Parkland. New pedestrian links give access from the city centre, so it's an easy stroll when you need a break from Queen Street shopping.

Old Windmill 378 B3

Brisbane's oldest convict-built structure on Wickham Terrace is also Australia's oldest extant windmill. Built in 1828 to grind flour, it was also used as a treadmill for punishment. In 1861 it became a signal station. Since then it has been used as both an observatory and a fire tower, and in 1934 the first successful experimental television transmittal was made from it. Take the Jacobs Ladder steps through the leafy King Edward Park.

Roma Street Parkland 378 A2

This huge subtropical garden is an easy walk from Queen Street through King George Square. Its 16 hectares include landscaped gardens, Queensland's largest public art collection and hundreds of unique plants. Kids will love the playground and Celebration Lawn. There is a lake precinct and a subtropical rainforest, and the **Spectacle Garden** is the parkland's horticultural heart. There are many picnic areas and cafe. Take a self-guide themed walk or a guided tour, or hop on the trackless train.

Queensland Police Museum and Victoria Barracks Museum 378 A2, A3

The museum, near Roma Street Station, has displays on police heritage, the Dog Squad and police investigative techniques. *Ground floor, Queensland Police Headquarters, 200 Roma St; (07) 3364 6432; open 9am–4pm weekdays.*

[GALLERY OF MODERN ART]

SOUTH BANK

With its large areas of parklands and major cultural institutions, this is one of Brisbane's favourite places to play and celebrate. Throughout the year thousands gather here for Christmas and New Year parties, and events such as the Brisbane Festival with its Riverfire pyrotechnic extravaganza.

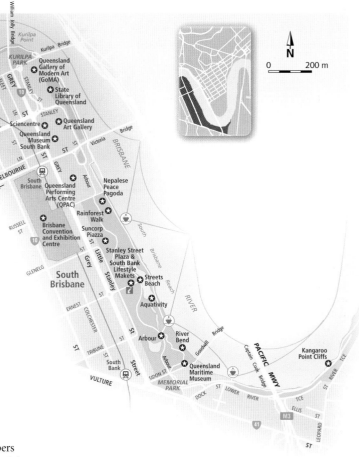

The Arbour 378 A4, A5

The beautiful kilometre-long Arbour winds through the South Bank precinct. Along the way, watch buskers, street performers or international acts in the **Suncorp Piazza**. For something more peaceful, discover the ornate **Nepalese Peace Pagoda** set among tropical rainforest trees or take a detour along the shady **Rainforest Walk**.

Kangaroo Point 378 C6, D5

Walk east along the **Cliffs Boardwalk** to watch rock climbers and abseilers on **Kangaroo Point Cliffs**, on the river beyond the Captain Cook Bridge. If you're keen, you can learn to abseil on the spot. From the Kangaroo Point Cliffs City Lookout there are great views of the city.

Streets Beach 378 B5

Streets Beach, right in the centre of Brisbane, has a lagoon patrolled by lifesavers and views across the Brisbane River to the CBD. It is popular with kids and sunbathers. Children also love South Bank's water playground, **Aquativity**, and the playground at Picnic Island Green.

Clem Jones Promenade 378 A4, B5

Walking or cycling along the riverside promenade is a great way to see the sights of South Bank. There are more than 50 cafes, restaurants and bars along here, including the **Riverbend** riverfront dining precinct. You'll also find ideal barbecue areas for picnic.

Queensland Performing Arts Centre 378 A4

This is the place for theatre, music and opera. The Cremorne Theatre is dedicated to experimental theatre; the Playhouse offers cutting-edge technology in stage design; the Lyric Theatre is the flagship of the centre, hosting everything from Opera Queensland performances to the latest blockbuster musical; and the Concert Hall has regular performances by the Queensland Orchestra as well as international classical, jazz and pop artists. The Tony Gould Gallery, an exhibition space for the **QPAC Museum**, has free exhibitions related to the performing arts, and there are cafes and a restaurant. Guided tours must be booked. *Cnr Grey and Melbourne sts; guided tours (07) 3840 7444; general admission free.*

Queensland Museum South Bank 378 A4

This excellent museum has an extensive natural history collection, including a fascinating endangered species exhibit, and displays on Queensland's Indigenous and European history. Be sure to visit the interactive **Sciencentre**. *Cnr Grey and Melbourne sts; open daily; general admission free.*

Queensland Art Gallery 378 A4

Overlooking the Brisbane River, the gallery houses the state's permanent art collection and special exhibitions. Free guided tours are available. Complementing the gallery is the **Queensland Gallery of Modern Art (GoMA)**, with cutting-edge contemporary art and the Asia-Pacific Triennial of Contemporary Art. GoMA's architecture is impressive, as are its river views. *Stanley Pl; open 10am–5pm Mon–Fri, 9am–5pm weekends; general admission free.*

State Library of Queensland 378 A4

This must rank as one of the most beautiful repositories of books, archives, manuscripts, images, prints and maps you'll find. Visit www.slq.qld.gov.au for details of events and exhibits. *(07) 3840 7666 ; open 10am–8pm Mon–Thurs, 10am–5pm Fri–Sun.*

QUEENSLAND

[COLOURFUL ARBOUR IN SOUTH BANK]

Queensland Maritime Museum 378 B6

This maritime institution has displays relics, memorabilia and exhibits. Look for displays on sailing, old diving equipment, navigation instruments used by early explorers of Queensland's coastline, historic seagoing craft, ocean-liner replicas and nautical machinery. There is also Australia's only remaining World War II frigate, HMAS *Diamantina*, and a coal-fired, steam-powered 1925 tug, the SS *Forceful*. *Sidon St at South Bank (next to Goodwill Bridge); open daily from 9.30am (last entry 3.30pm).*

Grey Street Precinct 378 A4, A5

Little Stanley Street has designer fashion stores, gourmet food shops and great cafes, bars and restaurants. Closed to traffic, **Stanley Street Plaza** also has eateries aplenty and buzzes day and night. **Grey Street**, a grand tree-lined boulevard, has shops, cafes, a hotel and a cinema complex as well as the nearby **Brisbane Convention and Exhibition Centre**.

FORTITUDE VALLEY

Known locally as 'the Valley', this cosmopolitan inner-city area is a fascinating mix of seedy history, stylish restaurants and alternative-lifestylers. First settled in 1849, it retains much of its 19th-century heritage, its old buildings housing many private art galleries and studios. The creative hub is the Judith Wright Centre of Contemporary Arts.

Brunswick Street Mall 378 D1

Dominated for almost a century by the McWhirters department-store building, now stylish apartments with shops at street level, Brunswick Street is packed with shoppers at weekends cruising through the **Valley Markets** *(see Markets, p. 386)*. Free bands play in the mall on weekends, and at night crowds flock to the restaurants and nightclubs. Further up Brunswick Street is another foodies' delight, **Central Brunswick**. For cutting-edge fashion go to Ann Street or to the TCB – formerly the TC Beirne Building – which links Chinatown with Brunswick Street Mall. Further down Ann Street there are more pubs and bars, including the GPO, in the old Fortitude Valley Post Office.

Chinatown 378 D2

Restaurants here offer excellent value and even better yum cha, supermarkets have traditional Chinese treasures and the busy Valley Markets extend into Chinatown at weekends. If you are in Brisbane in late January/early February, head to Chinatown for Chinese New Year celebrations.

James Street Precinct 376 E3

Brisbane's hottest lifestyle precinct, where fashion and furniture stores cater to the cashed-up new inner-city residents. Outdoor cafes, restaurants and bars abound, and the **James Street Market** is excellent for fresh produce. The **Centro** development includes a cinema complex, and a short walk across Ann Street is **Emporium**, with a 'village square' of outdoor cafes, restaurants, high-end fashion and gift shops.

NEW FARM AND NEWSTEAD

Adjoining Fortitude Valley, along the deep curves of the Brisbane River, are other lively suburbs well worth a visit.

New Farm Park 377 F4

Once a racecourse, this is a favourite spot for locals. Stroll through the rose garden, picnic under the trees, listen to a band in the Rotunda, contemplate the river, and let the kids loose in the much-prized playground. Settled in the 1800s, New Farm has a changing dynamic, with the strongly Italian local community being joined by young inner-urbans. A village feel remains, however, with outdoor cafes, fashion shops, art galleries and bookshops.

Newstead and Teneriffe 377 F3

Between New Farm and Breakfast Creek, these suburbs once encompassed a major industrial precinct. In 1987 development zoning was changed to high-density residential, and these days the old wool stores, warehouses, wharves and laneways provides the framework for stylish restaurants, cafes and bars, and antiques and homewares shops.

Brisbane Powerhouse 377 F4

This live arts precinct, in the restored 100-year-old New Farm Powerhouse, is the place to go for contemporary music, theatre, dance, art and comedy. Go to www.brisbanepowerhouse.org for details of upcoming shows. The landmark building itself is a great spot for a meal. Every second and fourth Saturday, Farmers Markets run *(see Markets, p. 386)*. *119 Lamington St, New Farm; (07) 3358 8622; open 9am–5pm weekdays, 10am–4pm weekends.*

Newstead House 377 F3

Brisbane's oldest surviving residence was built in 1846 by Patrick Leslie, one of the early pioneers of the city. Beautifully restored and furnished, it recreates a quintessential Australian homestead. *Newstead Park, Breakfast Creek Rd, Newstead; (07) 3216 1846; open 10am–4pm Mon–Thurs, 2–5pm Sun.*

Breakfast Creek 377 F3

Named by explorer John Oxley in 1826 when he stopped one morning to eat while charting the Brisbane River, Breakfast Creek sits on a wide, open stretch of water. The historic **Breakfast Creek Hotel**, built in 1889, but given a stunning renewal in 2003, is the ideal place for top-class steak and a cold beer. Nearby is **Breakfast Creek Wharf** with restaurants, cafes and river boat tours.

INNER NORTH-EAST

Miegunyah House Museum 377 E3

Built in 1886 in traditional Queensland fashion with long verandahs and ornate ironwork, the building is now home to the Queensland Women's Historical Association and serves as a memorial to pioneering Queensland women. Guided tours run. *35 Jordan Tce, Bowen Hills; (07) 3252 2979; open 10.30am–3pm Wed, 10.30am–4pm weekends.*

Racecourse Road and Hamilton 377 F2

Drive through Hamilton and Ascot for stunning examples of grand 19th-century Queensland homes. And if you feel like a flutter, **Eagle Farm** is the state's premier track. Racecourse Road has smart outdoor restaurants, cafes and high-end fashion shops. On Kingsford–Smith Drive, **Brett's Wharf** has an acclaimed seafood restaurant and a ferry stop. Further along the river, the newer **Portside** development is Brisbane's international cruise-ship terminal, with restaurants, shops and cinemas.

INNER EAST

Bulimba and Woolloongabba 376 E5, 377 F3

The renewal and expansion of Brisbane has seen the proliferation of cafe and shopping strips across the inner suburbs. On the southside, Oxford Street at **Bulimba** provides a pleasant break

from the city bustle. **Logan Road** is one of Brisbane's main thoroughfares, but running south from the Story Bridge through Woolloongabba there is a little dog-leg behind the **Gabba** cricket ground that's a 19th-century hideaway of antique shops, tiny cafes and top restaurants.

INNER SOUTH

West End 376 C4

This is the suburb of choice for artists, students and those seeking a low-key lifestyle. There are buildings with character, a multicultural mix of cafes and restaurants, organic provedores and alternative fashion. Davies Park runs organic markets on Saturdays *(see Markets, p. 386)*.

INNER WEST

Milton 376 D4

Dominated by the iconic XXXX Brewery *(see next entry)* and the legendary Suncorp Stadium, (formerly Lang Park), Milton is also known for bustling Park Road. Developed 20 years ago, this is a lively street of restaurants and cafes, fashion, jewellery and bookshops. There are more restaurants, cafes and delis at nearby **Baroona Road** and **Nash St, Rosalie**.

XXXX Brewery 376 D4

For beer lovers, the brewery's Ale House is a must. Bookings are recommended for tailored tours that finish with a beer sampling. *Cnr Black and Paten sts (just off Milton Rd), Milton; (07) 3361 7597; open 10am–5.30pm Mon, Tues, Thurs and Fri, 10am–8.30pm Wed, 10am–3.30pm Sat, 10am–2.30pm Sun.*

Paddington 376 C3

This distinctive, hilly inner-city suburb is lined with old timber cottages. On **Latrobe** and **Given terraces** many have been converted into small shops, including some excellent antique shops and art galleries, quirky cafes and vintage fashion shops. Given Terrace offers quality fashion, an organic provedore, top restaurants and the popular Paddington Tavern. **Caxton Street**, close to Suncorp Stadium and the Barracks, offers nightlife, bars and restaurants.

WEST

Toowong 376 C4

Toowong Cemetery has more than 100 000 graves, some dating back to 1875. Its headstones tell the story of the trials, tribulations and triumphs of Queensland's early settlers. Also built at the end of the 19th century, but very much a part of the living, the **Regatta Hotel** is a dining and drinking spot that well deserves its popularity.

Mount Coot-tha Forest 376 A4

To get a bearing on Brisbane's geography, drive up **Sir Samuel Griffith Drive** to the **Mount Coot-tha Lookout**. There are beautiful walks and picnic areas in the park, including the local favourite, **J. C. Slaughter Falls**.

QUEENSLAND

Brisbane Botanic Gardens – Mount Coot-tha 376 B4

At the foot of Mount Coot-tha, these botanic gardens are well worth a visit for the Bonsai House, Fern House, Japanese Garden, the Tropical Dome and the Australian Plant Communities section. Free guided walks are available. The **Sir Thomas Brisbane Planetarium** is on the grounds, and holds a range of events. *Mt Coot-tha Rd, Toowong; (07) 3403 2535; open daily; admission free.*

Lone Pine Koala Sanctuary 600 D5

This is the world's largest and oldest koala sanctuary. Hold koalas, handfeed kangaroos and get up close to many other species. It's an 11-kilometre drive from the city, or catch Mirimar's Koala and River Cruise *(see Walks and tours, p. 386). Jesmond Rd, Fig Tree Pocket; (07) 3378 1366; open daily.*

OUTER NORTH

Scarborough, Redcliffe, Brighton, Margate, Sandgate and Shorncliffe were popular holiday places for Brisbanites prior to World War II, and the legacy lives on in the beautiful old boarding houses, mature gardens, the rebuilt Redcliffe Jetty and Shorncliffe Pier. Together they form a pleasant coastal drive 25 to 45 minutes from Brisbane.

[ATRIUM IN BRISBANE BOTANIC GARDENS – MOUNT COOT-THA]

Northern Beaches 599 F3, F4

Eating fish and chips at Morgans Seafood, a local institution in **Scarborough**, while watching the bobbing trawlers against a background of the Glass House Mountains, is a must-do. Travel south to **Redcliffe**, the site of Queensland's first European settlement in 1824, and follow a heritage trail (ask at the information centre for brochures). Redcliffe has good beaches and little cafes. Its jetty is a popular fishing spot. **Margate** beach has shaded picnic spots with lovely bay views, and at **Woody Point** is the historic Belvedere Hotel, built in the 1890s.

Alma Park Zoo 599 E3

Set in award-winning rainforest gardens, the zoo displays native and exotic animals. You can touch koalas, and feed kangaroos and deer in the walk-through enclosures – all great for kids. Please note: the zoo was in process of relocating to Logan City in Brisbane's south at the time of publishing. *Alma Rd, Dakabin; open daily.*

EASTERN BAYSIDE

Wynnum and Manly 599 G7

Half an hour east of the city, these places offer an accessible bayside experience. The **Wynnum Mangrove Boardwalk** area abounds with fish and migrating birds, or hire a bike to ride the 1.5-kilometre **Esplanade** from Manly to Lota. At the **Manly Boat Harbour** charters and boat hire for fishing and sailing are available. Tours to the island of St Helena depart from here. This island is two-thirds national park, and served as a penal settlement between 1867 and 1932. North of Wynnum is the 19th-century **Fort Lytton**. A museum (open Sundays and public holidays) interprets Queensland's military and social history from 1879. Further north is the **Port of Brisbane**, with public tours and a visitor centre. *Wynnum–Manly Visitor Information Centre: 43A Cambridge Pde, Manly; (07) 3348 3524.*

OUTER EASTERN BAYSIDE

Cleveland 599 H8

About 40 minutes south-east of Brisbane, this is the centre of the Redland Bay district. Follow the heritage trail from the Old Courthouse to explore the rich history. Cleveland Bayside Markets run on Sundays or try the delicious counter meals at Brisbane's oldest pub, the 1851 **Grand View Hotel**. **Ormiston House**, built in 1862, is also open to visitors. *(07) 3286 1425; open Sun afternoons Mar–Nov.* From Cleveland, catch a ferry or water taxi to North Stradbroke Island *(see Day tours, p. 387).* South of Cleveland, Victoria Point and Redland Bay offer good fishing and boat hire.

CITY ESSENTIALS
BRISBANE

Climate

Queensland isn't called the 'Sunshine State' for nothing, and with an average 300 days of sunshine each year, the south-east corner has (according to many) the most liveable climate in the state and possibly the country. Summers are hot and steamy; winters are mild and dry. Summer days in Brisbane average in the high 20s or low 30s. The hot days often build up to spectacular evening thunderstorms, and Brisbane's annual rainfall of approximately 1200 mm occurs mostly in summer. In the cooler months, the average temperature is 21°C – a very pleasant 'winter' for anyone from down south!

Winter evenings can be frosty at times, so make sure you pack at least one jumper.

	MAX °C	MIN °C	RAIN MM	RAIN DAYS
JANUARY	30	21	114	8
FEBRUARY	30	21	128	11
MARCH	29	20	89	8
APRIL	27	17	56	7
MAY	25	14	64	6
JUNE	22	12	60	6
JULY	22	10	23	3
AUGUST	23	11	42	4
SEPTEMBER	26	14	33	4
OCTOBER	27	16	84	7
NOVEMBER	28	19	111	9
DECEMBER	29	20	158	10

Getting around

Brisbane has well-signed, well-maintained roads, but it's not an easy city for first-time visitors to negotiate. The region's growth has resulted in a crisscrossing network of major motorways and some significant new roadwork projects. In the city centre itself, there are many one-way streets. To make matters more confusing, the Brisbane River twists its way through the city and suburbs. An up-to-date road map and some careful route planning at the beginning of each day is a good idea. As the city has grown more crowded, cycling has become a viable and healthy option for getting around and more locals are taking to their bikes. Brisbane boasts an ever-expanding network of picturesque bikeways and pedestrian paths. Purchase a subscription to CityCycle and you can pick up and drop off hired bikes from locations around the city. The Cycle2City facility under King George Square is a first for Australia and offers showers, lockers, laundry and bike security for local city workers and visitors alike.

Trains, buses and ferries cater for all needs and a couple of bus routes are designed specifically for visitors (see below). A boat trip on the Brisbane River is a must. Plenty of tours are available to riverside tourist attractions (see Walks and tours, p. 386) and there is an excellent commuter ferry and catamaran (CityCat) service, which is again up and running after many jetties were destroyed in the 2011 flood. The Cats travel at high speed and standing on the deck and feeling the cool wind in your hair is the best way to see Brisbane. A Go Card is a cheaper alternative to buying paper tickets and can be used on all transport – ferries, trains and buses.

Public transport Translink (bus, ferry, CityCat and rail) 13 1230.

Airport shuttle bus Coachtrans Airport Service (07) 3238 4700.

Bus tours City Sights bus tours and The Loop (free buses circling the CBD and central suburbs) 13 1230.

Motoring organisation RACQ 13 1905, roadside assistance 13 1111.

Car rental Avis 13 6333; Budget 1300 362 848; Europcar 1300 131 390; Hertz 1300 132 607; Thrifty 1300 367 227.

Taxis Black and White Cabs 13 1008; Yellow Cabs 13 1924.

Airtrain Train from the airport to the city and Gold Coast 1800 119 091.

Bicycle hire Bicycle Revolution (07) 3342 7829; Valet Cycle Hire Botanic Gardens 0408 003 198; CityCycle 1800 991 529.

Top events

Brisbane Comedy Festival at the Powerhouse Some of the world's most acclaimed comedians perform stand-up routines. February–March.

Queensland Winter Racing Carnival Excitement on and off the racecourse. April–July.

Paniyiri Greek Festival Enjoy Greek food, dance, music, cooking classes and live entertainment as Musgrave Park, South Brisbane, is transformed with markets, tavernas and all things Greek. May.

Brisbane International Film Festival Superb showcase of the latest in Australian and overseas film, with an international atmosphere. July–August.

Ekka (Royal Queensland Show) A Brisbane institution where the city meets the country for ten days. Fireworks, wild rides and the iconic Ekka Strawberry Sundae. August.

Brisbane Festival Queensland's largest celebration of the performing and visual arts. Food, live music and theatre in pop-up locations around the city, kicking off with the Riverfire fireworks. September–October.

Woodford Folk Festival Huge award-winning folk festival held annually just out of Brisbane. Local, national and international musicians and artists, lots of markets and good food. December.

Shopping

Queen Street Mall, City Brisbane's premier shopping precinct, with major department stores, malls and arcades including Queens Plaza, Myer Centre, Brisbane Arcade, Elizabeth Arcade, MacArthur Central and the Wintergarden (currently undergoing renovations). 378 B4

Fortitude Valley For up-and-coming designer fashion, collectibles and books, antiques, art and trendy homewares, adventure gear and souvenirs. Markets on the weekend. 376 E3

Emporium More than 35 specialty retailers offering top-end fashion, jewellery, art, books wine and food. 376 E3

Little Stanley Street, South Bank Designer fashion, boutique homewares and gifts. 378 B5

Paddington For antiques, vintage fashion, eco and green products and homewares on Latrobe and Given terraces. 376 C3

Logan Rd, South Brisbane A quirky street with everything from antiques and vintage fashion to an artisan bakery. 376 E5

Westfield Chermside Shopping Centre Huge mall on Brisbane's north side with 350 specialty stores, all the major department stores and a 16-cinema complex including a Gold Class theatre. 599 E6

Indooroopilly Shopping Centre A mall in Brisbane's western suburbs with over 250 specialty shops, major department stores, a gym and a 16-cinema complex. Fabulous shopping. 376 B5

Direct Factory Outlet (DFO) Brisbane
Next to Brisbane Airport, this centre offers up to 120 discounted brands plus eateries. 599 F6

The Barracks A walk from Roma Street station in the old Petrie Terrace Army Barracks is this new shopping complex featuring boutique homewares, international eateries and a cinema. 378 A1

Markets

Riverside at the Pier Markets Open-air markets on the city reach of the Brisbane River at Waterfront Place, with bric-a-brac, craft, fashion, food. Sun. 378 C3

South Bank Lifestyle Markets Street performances, art and craft, jewellery and live music. Fri night and Sat–Sun. 378 B5

The Valley Markets Brisbane's alternative markets, with vintage clothing, tarot readings, gifts, old books and an exciting atmosphere. Brunswick Street Mall and Chinatown Mall. Sat–Sun. 378 D1

Farmers Markets at the Powerhouse Mix it with the locals combing the stalls for locally grown, farm-fresh produce, gourmet food, cut flowers and fresh seafood, all in the atmospheric surrounds of the Brisbane Powerhouse. New Farm, 2nd and 4th Sat each month. 377 F4

Davies Park Market West End Friendly, cosmopolitan markets on the river at Davies Park, West End, with fruit and veg, plenty of organics, bargains, art and craft, and free entertainment. Sat. 376 C4

Northey Street City Farm Organic Growers Markets Brisbane's only completely organic market, with produce and a nursery, set in a permaculture garden at Northey Street City Farm, Windsor. Sun. 376 E3

Walks and tours

Balloons Over Brisbane See the sun rise over Brisbane city at dawn – take a hot-air balloon flight, followed by a gourmet champagne breakfast. Bookings on (07) 3844 6671.

Brisbane CityWalk Explore Brisbane's green heart on this leisurely, self-guide walking tour that takes in the CBD's highlights via its three main parkland areas: the City Botanic Gardens, South Bank and Roma Street Parklands. Brochure available from the visitor centre in the Queen Street Mall.

Brisbane's Living Heritage Network Grab a copy of the Network's *Experience Guide* and take a trip back in time with these excellent self-guide tours of historic districts in the city and surrounds.

Brochures available from the visitor centre and Brisbane City Council. (07) 3403 8888.

City Sights Bus Tours Experience the cultural and historic highlights of Brisbane city in comfort. Set your own pace – you can hop off and on the clearly signed buses at any time. Brochure and tickets available from the visitor centre or call 13 1230 or (07) 3404 8888 for more information.

Ghost Tours Scare yourself silly with a variety of serious ghost tours exploring Brisbane's haunted history, or pick up a copy of the Haunted Brisbane guidebook. Bookings on (07) 3344 7265.

Gonewalking Discover Brisbane on foot with the help of experienced Brisbane City Council volunteers, or buy a copy of Great Brisbane Walks from Brisbane City Council or a good bookshop to plan your own. (07) 3403 8888.

Moreton Bay Cruises Explore beautiful Moreton Bay on one of the many cruises on offer. Details from the visitor centre.

River Tours Travel the river up to Lone Pine with Mirimar Cruises (0412 749 426) or enjoy a fine meal with stunning views on a Kookaburra River Queen cruise (07) 3221 1300).

Story Bridge Adventure Climb Take in spectacular 360-degree views of the city on this 2.5-hour climb up Brisbane's iconic Story Bridge. Bookings on 1300 254 627.

Wynnum Manly Heritage Trail Once you've explored historic Brisbane city, do the same in the nautical bayside area. Brochures available from the Wynnum Manly visitor centre.

Entertainment

Cinema Major cinemas can be found at the Myer Centre in the city (a Birch Carroll & Coyle complex) and at most of the big suburban malls. See the *Courier-Mail* for movie times. If you're in town in August you can catch the Brisbane International Film Festival (BIFF). Brisbane is a city devoted to film festivals. Look out for them throughout the year.

Live music The Valley is the centre of Brisbane's live music scene and is the home of the 'Valley Sound' – a collective name for some of Australia's best and most innovative artists. See some of the city's most famous bands immortalised in the Brunswick Street Mall's very own walk of fame. Crowded with partying people most evenings, Brunswick and Ann streets are lined with fantastic bars, pubs, nightclubs – including Family, Cloudland and The Bowery – and alternative music venues such as the Zoo, a Brisbane institution. Kangaroo Point has some good live-music venues, including the renowned Story Bridge Hotel and the Brisbane Jazz Club. For jazz you could also head to West End. Popular alternative acts play gigs at the Tivoli in the Valley; international acts play the Brisbane Entertainment Centre at Boondall. Buy a copy of

the *Courier-Mail* on Thursdays and Fridays for music listings, or pick up one of the free street papers such as *Time Off* or *Rave* for details of what's on.

Classical music and performing arts
Brisbane has a pulsing creative life with theatres of all sizes throughout the city. For high-end performing arts and music, the premier venue is the Queensland Performing Arts Centre at South Bank, which includes the Concert Hall and the Lyric Theatre. The Powerhouse, on the river at New Farm, is the place to go for world-ranking contemporary music, dance, theatre and free comedy nights. The Judith Wright Centre of Contemporary Arts in the Valley focuses on cutting-edge contemporary performance. West End is the address of the Queensland Ballet, in the Thomas Dixon Centre. The Valley has a number of smaller venues for experimental and alternative theatre, and there are often live street performances taking place in Brunswick Street Mall. The Roundhouse Theatre in the Kelvin Grove Urban Village is the venue for the La Boite Theatre Company and some brilliant productions. See the *Courier-Mail* for details of what's on.

Sport

Brisbane's weather is perfect for outdoor activities, and Brisbane's sports stadiums are state of the art. If **AFL** (Australian Football League) is your passion, you can't miss the Brisbane Lions at their home ground, the Gabba. The Gabba is also home to Queensland **cricket** – watch the Bulls defend the state's cricketing honour. You will find the Gabba (known formally as the Brisbane Cricket Ground) in the suburb of Woolloongabba, south of Kangaroo Point.

Rugby League is a way of life in Queensland, culminating in State of Origin. You can watch the Brisbane Broncos, the city's rugby league team, at the redeveloped Lang Park (also known as Suncorp Stadium), a Brisbane sporting institution in Milton. Ticket-holders enjoy free public transport on match days. Or show your true colours by supporting the Reds, Queensland's **Rugby Union** team, at their matches, which are also at Lang Park.

The Brisbane International **tennis** tournament attracts the world's leading players in the first week of January. Matches are held at the Queensland Tennis Centre in Tennyson, opened in 2009.

If you prefer the sport of thoroughbreds, head to Brisbane's **horseracing** venues at Doomben and Eagle Farm. Or for car racing at its loudest and most thrilling, head south for the **Gold Coast SuperGP** in October.

Where to eat

Anise Bistro & Wine Bar Intimate bar and equally exciting food at this tiny French treasure. 697 Brunswick St, New Farm; (07) 3358 1558; open Mon–Sat for dinner. 376 E4

ARIA Restaurant Fine dining with stunning river views, courtesy of celebrity chef Matt Moran. 1 Eagle St, Eagle Street Pier; (07) 3233 2555; open Mon–Fri for lunch and daily for dinner. 378 C4

Bretts Wharf Delicious seafood caught sustainably from local commercial fishers. 449 Kingsford Smith Dr, Hamilton; (07) 3868 1717; open daily for lunch and dinner. 377 F3

e'cco Fabulous modern Australian bistro. 100 Boundary St; (07) 3831 8344; open Tues–Fri for lunch and Tues–Sat for dinner. 378 D2

Lefkas Greek Taverna Authentic Greek fare. 170 Hardgrave Rd, West End; (07) 3844 1163; open Mon–Sat for lunch and dinner. 376 C5

Mondo Organics Fine dining using organic produce, ethically-produced beef and sustainably caught fish. 166 Hardgrave Rd, West End; (07) 3844 1132; open Tues–Fri for lunch and Tues–Sat for dinner. 376 C5

Montrachet Local pinnacle of French cuisine; fun and relaxed with superb crab souffle. 224 Given Tce, Paddington; (07) 3367 0030; open weekdays for lunch and Mon–Thurs for dinner. 376 D3

Tank Restaurant and Bar Japanese/ Australian fusion cuisine using fresh, seasonal produce. 31 Tank St, Brisbane; (07) 3003 1993; open Mon–Fri for lunch and Mon–Sat for dinner. 378 A3

Thai Wi-Rat Authentic, reasonably priced Thai street food. Chinatown Mall, 20 Duncan St, Fortitude Valley; (07) 3257 0884; open daily for lunch and dinner. 378 D1

Urbane Cutting-edge, multi-award winning contemporary cuisine. 181 Mary St, Brisbane; (07) 3229 2271; open Wed–Fri for lunch and Tues–Sat for dinner. 378 C4

Restaurant Lurleen's Fine dining featuring fresh Queensland produce matched to Sirromet's wines. Sirromet Winery, 850–938 Mt Cotton Rd, Mount Cotton; (07) 3206 2999; open daily for breakfast and lunch, and Thurs–Sat for dinner. 599 G9

Where to stay

Aynsley Bed & Breakfast 14 Glanmire St, Paddington; (07) 3368 2250.

Brisbane Bayside Village Thorneside 43 Mond St, Thorneside; (07) 3207 5086.

Brisbane Gateway Resort 200 School Rd, Rochedale; (07) 3341 6333.

Brisbane Holiday Village 10 Holmead Rd, Eight Mile Plains; (07) 3341 6133.

Fern Cottage Bed & Breakfast 89 Fernberg Rd, Paddington; (07) 3511 6685.

Leatherwood Lodge 49 Leatherwood Pl, Brookfield; (07) 3374 4122.

Nestle Inn Tourist Village 905 Manly Rd, Tingalpa; (07) 3390 4404.

Redlands Mobile Village 22–34 Collingwood Rd, Birkdale; (07) 3822 2444.

Sheldon Caravan Park 27 Holmead Rd, Eight Mile Plains; (07) 3341 6166.

Springtime Gardens Caravan Park 13 Old Chatswood Rd, Daisy Hill; (07) 3208 8184.

 ## Day tours

Mount Glorious The sleepy settlement of Mount Glorious lies to the north-west of the city in Brisbane Forest Park, a 28 500-hectare reserve of subtropical forests and hills. Mount Glorious is the base for a number of enjoyable walking tracks. Nearby Wivenhoe Lookout offers panoramic views of the surrounding country and Cedar Creek features natural falls and swimming holes.

Daisy Hill State Forest Close to Brisbane's south-eastern suburbs is Daisy Hill State Forest, best known for its large colony of koalas. The Daisy Hill Koala Centre has a variety of displays and, from a tower, you can see koalas in their favourite place – the treetops. Call 1300 130 372.

Bribie Island Connected to the mainland by a bridge at Caboolture, Bribie is the most accessible of the Moreton Bay islands. Fishing, boating and crabbing are popular activities. For a quiet picnic and walk, visit Buckleys Hole Conservation Park at the southern end.

Moreton Island This impossibly beautiful sand island is mostly national park, reached by passenger ferry from Eagle Farm or vehicular ferry from the Port of Brisbane. Vehicle access is four-wheel drive only, but guided tours are available. Walking, swimming, fishing and dolphin-watching are some of the activities on offer.

North Stradbroke Island A favourite getaway for Brisbanites, Straddie, as it's affectionately known, is the most developed of the Moreton Bay islands, with small townships at Point Lookout, Dunwich and Amity. Visit Blue Lake National Park at the centre of the island for swimming and walking (access by four-wheel drive or a 45-minute walk), or enjoy ocean views along the North Gorge Headlands Walk. The island is reached by vehicular ferry from Cleveland.

The Gold Coast An hour's drive from Brisbane, the Gold Coast is arguably Australia's most famous and busiest holiday region, with beautiful surf beaches and huge theme parks – perfect for kids of all ages. All activities on offer, from deep-sea fishing and golf to dining and shopping, are of international-resort standard.

Gold Coast hinterland Dubbed the 'green behind the gold', the region offers a peaceful retreat from the bustle of the coast. Follow the winding scenic road up to Lamington National Park, part of a World Heritage area and Queensland's most visited park. It preserves a rainforest environment and a large wildlife population with many bird species, including bowerbirds and lyrebirds.

Toowoomba Travel to Toowoomba from Brisbane and you will find yourself climbing the Great Dividing Range. This grand old lady of the Darling Downs is perched on the edge of the escarpment at 800 metres above sea level. It's not dubbed the 'Garden City' for nothing – Toowoomba is famous for its parks, gardens and tree-lined streets, and each September it celebrates the Carnival of the Flowers. The city has also long been known for its antique shops and tea parlours, and these days also offers good coffee and innovative restaurants.

REGIONS
of Queensland

Listed here are some of the top attractions and experiences in each region.

10 GULF SAVANNAH

Boodjamulla (Lawn Hill) National Park (pictured) / see p. 397
Gulflander, **Normanton** / see p. 434
Lava tubes in Undara Volcanic National Park / see p. 431
Riversleigh Fossil Centre / see p. 430

7 THE MID-TROPICS

Cape Hillsborough National Park on the Hibiscus coast / see p. 424
Ghosts of Gold Heritage Trail, Charters Towers / see p. 403
Reef HQ, Townsville (pictured) / see p. 448
Diving around the SS *Yongala* wreck / see p. 392

8 CAIRNS AND THE TROPICS

Curtain Fig Tree in Atherton Tableland / see p. 392
Daintree National Park / see p. 408
Tjapukai Aboriginal Cultural Park (pictured) / see p. 403
Whitewater rafting in Tully Gorge Alcock State Forest / see p. 446

6 CAPRICORN

Carnarvon National Park / see pp. 428, 440 and 443
Sapphire gemfields in Rubyvale, Sapphire, Anakie and Willows (pictured) / see p. 410
Mon Repos Conservation Park / see p. 398
Mount Morgan / see p. 430

11 OUTBACK

Australian Stockman's Half of Fame and Outback Heritage Centre, Longreach / see p. 423
Birdsville Cup Racing Carnival / see p. 394
Outback at Isa, Mount Isa / see p. 430
Waltzing Matilda Centre, Winton (pictured) / see p. 449

NORTHERN TERRITORY

SOUTH AUSTRALIA

9

10

11

9 CAPE YORK

Fishing tours, Weipa / see p. 449
Rinyirru (Lakefield) National Park (CYPAL) (pictured) / see p. 422
Quinkan Centre / see p. 422
Thursday Island and the Torres Strait / see p. 449

5 FRASER ISLAND AND COAST

Lake McKenzie on Fraser Island / see p. 416
Maheno **wreck on Fraser Island (pictured)** / see p. 417
Maryborough Heritage walk and Heritage drive / see p. 426
Whale-watching tours in Hervey Bay / see p. 416

3 DARLING DOWNS

Granite Belt wine region / see p. 442
Jondaryan Woolshed / see p. 435
Queen Mary Falls in Main Range National Park (pictured) / see p. 396
Japanese Garden, Toowoomba / see p. 447

2 GOLD COAST AND HINTERLAND

Currumbin Wildlife Sanctuary / see p. 399
Theme parks on the Gold Coast (pictured) / see p. 445
Lamington National Park / see p. 434
Surfing near Burleigh Heads / see p. 397

1 BRISBANE HINTERLAND

Booubyjan Homestead / see p. 432
Brisbane Forest Park / see p. 442
Bunya Mountains National Park (pictured) / see p. 420
South Burnett wine region / see p. 432

4 SUNSHINE COAST

Glass House Mountains National Park (pictured) / see p. 422
The Ginger Factory, Yandina / see p. 450
Gondolas of Noosa / see p. 437
Teewah coloured sands in Great Sandy National Park / see p. 436

8

7

6

5

1 4

3

BRISBANE

2

VALES

[SWIMMING WITH CUTTLEFISH, GREAT BARRIER REEF]

LEGEND

i VISITOR INFORMATION

RADIO STATIONS

IN TOWN

WHAT'S ON

WHERE TO EAT

WHERE TO STAY

NEARBY

* Distances for towns nearby are calculated as the crow flies.
* Food and accommodation listings in town are ordered alphabetically
with places nearby listed at the end.

Airlie Beach

Pop. 2752
Map ref. 605 F5 | 611 J3

i 277 Shute Harbour Rd; (07) 9496 6665 or 1800 819 366;
www.destinationwhitsundays.com.au

89.9 FM ABC Local Tropical North, 94.7 Hot FM

Airlie Beach is at the centre of the thriving Whitsunday coast.
This tropical holiday town offers a cosmopolitan blend of bars,
restaurants and shops just metres from the beach. From Abel
Point Marina, daytrips to the outer Great Barrier Reef and
Whitsunday islands are on offer. Watersports available include
sailing, snorkelling, diving and fishing. Nearby Shute Harbour
is one of the largest marine passenger terminals in Australia
and, along with Airlie Beach, services the majority of the
Whitsunday islands.

Airlie Beach Lagoon: safe, year-round swimming in
landscaped environment; foreshore. *Whale watching:* tours
July–Sept depart Abel Point Marina; details from visitor centre.
Sailing: be it traditional sailing, adventure or luxury crewed;
details from visitor centre. *Skydiving:* tandem skydive and take in
the stunning views from very high above; (07) 4946 9115.

Community market: Airlie Beach Esplanade; Sat
mornings. *Meridien Marinas Race Week:* sailing; Aug.
Whitsunday Fun Race: competitions for cruising yachts; Aug/
Sept. *Festival of Sport:* includes triathlon; Sept.

Déjà Vu: modern Australian; Golden Orchid Dr;
(07) 4948 4309.

Island View Bed & Breakfast: 19 Nara Ave; (07) 4946
4505. *Airlie Cove Resort & Van Park:* Cnr Ferntree and Shute
Harbour rds, Jubilee Pocket; (07) 4946 6727. *BIG4 Adventure
Whitsunday Resort:* 25 Shute Harbour Rd, Cannonvale;
(07) 4948 5400. *Island Gateway Holiday Park – Aspen Parks:*
Shute Harbour Rd, Jubilee Pocket; (07) 4946 6228.

Conway National Park Covering 35 km of coastline, this
park is renowned for its natural beauty and as the habitat of
the Proserpine rock wallaby (endangered species). Walks start
in Airlie Beach and Shute Harbour. The Mt Rooper Lookout is
a highlight, featuring a panoramic view over Hamilton, Dent,
Long and Henning islands. Access the park off the road to Shute
Harbour; (07) 4967 7355; 3 km SE.

Daydream Island A small island of volcanic rock, coral and dense
tropical foliage. Daydream has a Kids Club, tennis, outdoor
cinema, watersports centre, snorkelling, diving, and reef and
island trips. Luxurious resort (maximum 900 people); 10 km NW.

Hayman Island Close to the outer reef, with fishing, sightseeing
trips, scenic flights, diving, watersports, Kids Club and whale-
watching excursions. Big-game enthusiasts strive to catch black
marlin off the island Sept–Nov. Luxury resort (maximum
450 people); 30 km NE.

South Molle Island Numerous inlets and splendid views of
Whitsunday Passage, plus great wildflowers in spring and early
summer. There's golf, bushwalking, snorkelling, scuba diving,
windsurfing and sailing. Medium-size resort (maximum
520 people); 12 km NE.

Lindeman Island Part of Lindeman Islands National Park with bushwalking and panoramic views from Mt Oldfield. Tropical rainforest surroundings home to prolific bird and butterfly populations. Secluded beaches, crystal waters and scuba diving. Formerly the location of Club Med, at the time of going to press the resort was being sold. 39 km SE.

Whitsunday Island Entirely uninhabited national park, with a beautiful 7 km white silica beach and complex mangrove system. Camping only (maximum 40 people); details from Airlie Beach parks office; 27 km E.

Hamilton Island A large island with a wide range of facilities and activities, shops, marina and fauna park. There's windsurfing, sailing, fishing, scuba diving, parasailing, helicopter rides, tennis, squash, and reef and inter-island trips. Resort (maximum 1500 people); 27 km SE.

Hook Island: impressive waterfalls and beautiful butterflies to be seen at Butterfly Bay; 28 km NE. *Crocodile safaris and fishing trips:* to nearby coastal wetlands; details from visitor centre. *Scenic flights:* various tours over the 74 Whitsunday islands; details from visitor centre.

TOWNS NEARBY: Proserpine 21 km, Bowen 56 km, Mackay 109 km, Sarina 138 km, Ayr 157 km

Allora

Pop. 920
Map ref. 609 L10

i 49 Albion St (New England Hwy), Warwick; (07) 4661 3122; www.southerndownsholidays.com.au

89.3 Rainbow FM, 747 AM ABC Southern QLD

Allora is a charming town in the Darling Downs, central to its rich agricultural surrounds. Explored and settled with stud farms in the 1840s, Allora's main street is noted for its well-preserved historic buildings and old-time country feel.

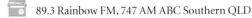 *Allora Museum:* noted for its replica of the Talgai Skull, an Aboriginal cranium dating back 15 000 years; open 1.30–4pm Sun; old courthouse, Drayton St. *St David's Anglican Church:* built in 1888 and said to be one of the finest timber churches in country Queensland; Church St. *The Gnomery:* over 100 different moveable handcrafted toys that feature in a theatre performance; New England Hwy.

Glengallan Farmers Markets: 1st Sun of each season. *Heritage Weekend:* Jan. *Allora Show:* Feb. *Allora Auction:* cars to farm machinery; June.

Goomburra Forest Retreat: 268 Forestry Reserve Rd, Goomburra; (07) 4666 6058.

Main Range National Park Located in the western foothills of the Great Dividing Range, this park has short walks around Dalrymple Creek and spectacular views from Mt Castle and Sylvesters lookouts. Take the Inverramsay Rd 40 km E to the forest. The last 6 km is unsealed and may be impassable following heavy rain. (07) 4666 1133; 49 km E.

Glengallan Homestead and Heritage Centre: restored 1867 sandstone mansion. Documents and photos chronicle its history as a pastoral station; open Thurs–Sun; New England Hwy; 11 km S.

TOWNS NEARBY: Clifton 13 km, Warwick 21 km, Killarney 46 km, Toowoomba 53 km, Gatton 60 km

Aramac

Pop. 340
Map ref. 610 D9 | 617 P9

i Post office, 22 Gordon St; (07) 4651 3147; www.aramac.qld.gov.au

540 AM ABC Western QLD

Aramac is a small service town west of the Great Dividing Range. The town was named by explorer William Landsborough; the name is an acronym for the name of Queensland premier Sir Robert Ramsay Mackenzie (RRMac). The town's sole water supply is from two bores that tap into the Great Artesian Basin.

 Harry Redford Interpretive Centre: photographic exhibition of cattle drives, also local arts and crafts; Gordon St. *White Bull replica:* commemorating Captain Starlight's arrest for cattle-stealing; Gordon St. *Tramway Museum:* with old rail motor and historical exhibits; McWhannell St.

Harry Redford Cattle Drive: May–June. *Ballyneety Rodeo:* Sept.

Lake Dunn This freshwater lake and its surrounds have greatest appeal to birdwatchers. It is also popular for swimming and fishing. Follow signs to 'The Lake'; 68 km NE.

Forest Den National Park This remote park is an important wildlife sanctuary due to its semi-permanent waterholes. Have a picnic next to Torrens Creek and go birdwatching at dusk. 4WD recommended. Torrens Creek Rd; (07) 4652 7333; 110 km N.

Gray Rock: large sandstone rock engraved with the names of hundreds of Cobb & Co. travellers. This was once the site of a hotel – a nearby cave was used as the hotel's cellar; 35 km E. *Lake Galilee:* 15 000 ha saltwater lake with large waterfowl population; some of access road unsealed; 100 km NE.

TOWNS NEARBY: Barcaldine 65 km, Muttaburra 83 km, Longreach 115 km, Blackall 163 km, Isisford 165 km

Atherton

Pop. 6249
Map ref. 606 D3 | 607 D9 | 613 L7

i Cnr Silo and Main sts; (07) 4091 4222; www.athertontableland.com

97.9 Hot FM, 720 AM ABC Far North QLD

Originally called Prior's Pocket and renamed in 1885, this town is the commercial hub of the Atherton Tableland. It is an area renowned for its volcanic crater lakes, waterfalls and fertile farmlands. Surrounding the town is dense rainforest that abounds in birdlife, and the nearby parks and forests offer a variety of watersports, bushwalking and outdoor activities.

 Chinese Interpretive Centre and Old Post Office Gallery Atherton once had a large population of Chinese working for local timber cutters. This centre exhibits photos of these days and has artefacts and works by local artists and potters. Tours of the nearby Hou Wang Temple, built in 1903 and recently restored, depart from here. Open Wed–Sun; Herberton Rd.

Hallorans Hill Conservation Park: walk to the rim of this extinct volcanic cone on the Atherton Tableland, where there is a spectacular lookout and informative displays; off Kennedy Hwy. *Crystal Caves:* explore underground tunnels and chambers lined with crystals, fossils and fluorescent minerals. The above-ground Fascinating Facets shop sells a range of jewellery and gemstones; Main St. *Birds of Prey:* interactive bird show featuring some amazing aerial predators; shows 11am and 2pm Wed–Sun (closed Feb, Mar and Nov); Herberton Rd; (07) 4091 6945.

VP60 Celebrations: military parade; Aug. *Maize Festival:* Aug.

Tolga Woodworks Cafe and Gallery: gourmet cafe food; Kennedy Hwy, Tolga; (07) 4095 4488.

Atherton Hallorans Leisure Park: 152 Robert St; 1800 885 030. *BIG4 Atherton Woodlands Tourist Park:* 141 Herberton Rd; (07) 4091 1407. *Allawah Retreat:* Marnane Rd, Tolga; (07) 4095 4900. *Discovery Holiday Parks – Lake Tinaroo:* Tinaroo Falls Dam Rd, Tinaroo Falls; (07) 4095 8232. *Tinaroo Haven Holiday Lodge:* Lot 42 Wavell Dr, Tinaroo Falls; (07) 3210 0747.

Atherton Tableland This 900-metre-high tableland is a productive farming district, thanks to the high rainfall and rich volcanic soil. Near Yungaburra is the remarkable Curtain Fig Tree, a strangler fig that has subsumed its host, sending down a curtain of roots. Volcanic lakes and spectacular waterfalls, including Millaa Millaa Falls and Zillie Falls, are among the other scenic attractions.

Lake Tinaroo With 200 km of shoreline, Lake Tinaroo is ideal for fishing, waterskiing and sailing. Walking tracks circle the lake, and dinghies and houseboats are available for hire. The Danbulla Forest Drive is a scenic 28 km drive; 15 km NE via Kairi.

Hasties Swamp National Park: local and migratory birds visit this swamp, including whistling ducks and magpie geese; (07) 4091 1844; 3 km S. *Tolga:* this town has a railway museum and craft outlets; 5 km N. *Wongabel State Forest:* important wildlife refuge in Wet Tropics World Heritage Area. An informative heritage trail gives an insight into Aboriginal culture and history; Kennedy Hwy; 8 km S.

TOWNS NEARBY: Yungaburra 12 km, Herberton 16 km, Mareeba 31 km, Millaa Millaa 31 km, Gordonvale 37 km

Ayr

Pop. 8094
Map ref. 605 B2 | 610 H2 | 613 O12

i Burdekin Visitor Information Centre, Bruce Hwy, Plantation Creek Park; (07) 4783 5988; www.burdekintourism.com.au

97.1 Sweet FM, 630 AM ABC North QLD

This busy town south-east of Townsville is surrounded by sugarcane fields – the most productive in Australia – and is the largest mango-growing area in the country. On the north side of the Burdekin River, it is linked to Home Hill to the south by the 1097-metre Silver Link Bridge, which ensures the towns are not cut off when the river floods.

Burdekin Cultural Complex: 530-seat theatre, library and activities centre. The forecourt has distinctive Living Lagoon water feature; Queen St. *Gubulla Munda:* 60 m carpet snake sculpture is the totem for the Juru Tribe, who were the original inhabitants of the area. Nearby Juru Walk passes through remnant dry tropical rainforest; Bruce Hwy, southern entrance to Ayr.

Market: Plantation Creek Park; Bruce Hwy; Sun (not 4th Sun of the month). *Barra Rush:* fishing competition; Feb. *Auto Fest:* car show; Apr. *Water Festival:* Sept.

BIG4 Ayr Silver Link Caravan Village: 34 Norham Rd; (07) 4783 3933. *Burdekin Cascades Caravan Park:* 228 Queen St; (07) 4783 1429. *Alva Beach Tourist Park:* 36 Braby St, Alva; (07) 4783 3383. *Home Hill Caravan Park:* Cnr Eighth St and Eleventh Ave, Home Hill; (07) 4782 2498.

 Home Hill This small town is just south of Ayr over the Silver Link. The towering tea trees along the main street bear plaques commemorating the town's pioneering families. The Silver Link Interpretive Centre in Eighth Ave gives a photographic history of the Burdekin River Bridge. Ashworth's Tourist Centre houses Ashworth's Jewellers, the Rock Shop and the impressive Treasures of the Earth Display, while Zaro's Cultural Gallery has original islander artworks. The Canefield Ashes cricket competition is held in Apr, the Burdekin Grower Race Day in May and the Harvest Festival in Nov; 12 km S.

SS *Yongala* **wreck** A must for divers. The world-famous wreck, which sank near Cape Bowling Green during a cyclone in 1911, lay undiscovered for half a century. Despite being under water for almost 100 years, details such as the engine room, toilets, portholes and most of the ship's name are still evident. The marine life is excellent, with beautiful corals, giant groupers and trevally, barracuda, stingrays, turtles and hundreds of other sea creatures. Access from Lynchs Beach.

Hutchings Lagoon: watersports; 5 km NW. *Brandon Heritage Precinct:* includes district's oldest church, St Patrick's (1897), now a local history museum. Ye Olde Machinery Place has an antique farm machinery display; 6 km N. *Lynchs Beach:* beach walks, birdwatching, swimming and fishing; 18 km N. *Mt Kelly:* Great views of surrounding farmlands; 18 km SW. *Charlies Hill:* WW II historic site; 24 km S. *Groper Creek:* great fishing spot with camping available; 24 km SE. *Horseshoe Lagoon:* birdwatching; 35 km N. *Mt Inkerman:* good views at top, plus picnic and barbecue facilities; 30 km S. *Burdekin Dam:* biggest dam in Queensland, holding the equivalent of 4 Sydney Harbours. Fishing and camping on offer; 180 km NW.

TOWNS NEARBY: Townsville 72 km, Ravenswood 79 km, Bowen 101 km, Charters Towers 132 km, Proserpine 153 km

Babinda

Pop. 1168
Map ref. 606 E4 | 607 G10 | 613 M7

i Cnr Bruce Hwy and Munro St; (07) 4067 1008.

94.9 Kool FM, 720 AM ABC Far North QLD

A small sugar town south of Cairns, Babinda boasts abundant wildlife, secluded swimming holes and untouched rainforest in its surrounds. In adjacent Wooroonooran National Park are the state's two highest mountains, Mount Bartle Frere (1622 metres) and Mount Bellenden Ker (1592 metres).

M&J Aboriginality: a family business specialising in traditional Aboriginal artefacts. Make your own didgeridoo or learn how to throw a boomerang; Howard Kennedy Dr; (07) 4067 1660.

Harvestfest: celebrate the start of the cane season; May.

 Wooroonooran National Park Part of the Wet Tropics World Heritage Area, the park has endemic species of plants and animals and spectacular walks through tropical rainforest. Swim in the watering hole at Josephine Falls, located at the base of Mt Bartle Frere, or see the Boulders, a large group of rocks worn smooth by tropical rains. Also visit the Mamu Canopy Rainforest Walk, which has spectacular views of the North Johnstone Gorge. Access off Bruce Hwy, west of Babinda; (07) 4061 5900.

Deeral: departure point for cruises through rainforest and saltwater crocodile haunts of the Mulgrave and Russell rivers. Deeral Cooperative makes footwear and Aboriginal artefacts; Nelson Rd; 14 km N. *Bramston Beach:* small community behind long palm-lined beach; Bruce Hwy S to Miriwinni, then 12 km E. *Russell River National Park:* small park on the coast with good birdwatching, swimming and canoeing; no facilities, 4WD access; (07) 4046 6600; 6 km N of Brampton Beach.

TOWNS NEARBY: Innisfail 23 km, Mourilyan 29 km, Gordonvale 31 km, Yungaburra 37 km, Millaa Millaa 38 km

Barcaldine
Pop. 1338
Map ref. 610 D10 | 617 P10

 Oak St; (07) 4651 1724; www.barcaldinerc.qld.gov.au

100.9 West FM, 540 AM ABC Western QLD

This pastoral and rail town is located some 100 kilometres east of Longreach. Known as the 'Garden City of the West', it was the first Australian town to tap the waters of the Great Artesian Basin, an event commemorated by the town's giant windmill. After the 1891 Shearers' Strike, the Australian Labor Party was born here.

Australian Workers Heritage Centre This centre is a tribute to the working men and women of Australia – the shearers, teachers, policemen and other workers who helped build the nation. The interpretive displays also cover the events leading to the formation of the Labor Party. Open 9am–5pm Mon–Sat, 10am–4pm Sun and public holidays; Ash St; (07) 4651 2422.

Tree of Knowledge: was a large ghost gum, which stood outside the railway station. It was fatally poisoned in 2006, but is being preserved and will be placed inside an $8 million memorial; Oak St. *Folk Museum:* display of historical memorabilia from the area; Cnr Gidyea and Beech sts. *Roses 'n' Things:* sit among over 800 roses of various varieties while enjoying Devonshire tea; Coolibah St. *National Trust–classified buildings:* Masonic lodge, Beech St; Anglican church, Elm St; shire hall, Ash St. *Murals and musical instruments:* Barcaldine is home to several murals including one painted by the late D'Arcy Doyle. There are also 2 musical instruments in the parks, which visitors are free to play; Oak St. *Between the Bougainvilleas Heritage Trail:* this award-winning heritage trail showcases Barcaldine's varied and colourful history; details from visitor centre. *Artesian Country tours:* including some to Aboriginal carvings and caves; details from visitor centre. *Bike hire:* a gold-coin donation will allow you to cycle around the town at your own leisure and take in all the sites.

Mini steam-train rides: depart Folk Museum; last Sun each month (Mar–Oct). *Easter in the Outback:* Easter. *Tree of Knowledge Festival:* festival includes the Revfest, goat races, May Day parade and markets; May.

Barcaldine Tourist Park: 51 Box St (Matilda Hwy); (07) 4651 6066. *Homestead Caravan Park:* 24 Box St (Landsborough Hwy); (07) 4651 1308.

Bicentennial Park: has botanical walk through bushland; Blackall Rd; 9 km s. *Lloyd Jones Weir:* great fishing and birdwatching venue; 15 km sw.

TOWNS NEARBY: Aramac 65 km, Blackall 98 km, Longreach 107 km, Isisford 116 km, Muttaburra 130 km

Beaudesert
Pop. 5386
Map ref. 516 F1 | 525 N1 | 600 C9 | 609 M10

 Historical Museum, 54 Brisbane St; (07) 5541 3740; www.bsc.qld.gov.au

101.5 Beau FM, 747 AM ABC Southern QLD

Beaudesert lies in the valley of the Logan River, in the Gold Coast hinterland. The town was built up around the homestead of Edward Hawkins – his property was immense, comprising land from the coast to the Logan River. Those origins continue with the area noted for its dairying, beef cattle, and fruit and vegetable produce, making the country markets a great attraction.

Centre for Arts and Culture: the region's newest attraction and hub for musicians, artists, comedians and film buffs. State-of-the-art auditorium for large performances as well as intimate spaces; Brisbane St. *Historical Museum:* displays of old machinery and tools; Brisbane St. *Community Arts Centre:* art gallery, teahouse and craft shop; Enterprise Dr.

Market: Westerman Park; 1st Sat each month. *Bikes and Bands Charity Fesitval:* food and music; Feb. *Rodeo:* May. *Equine Expo:* June. *Country and Horse Festival:* June. *Beaudesert Show:* Sept.

Country Blue Bed & Breakfast: 92 Worendo St, Veresdale; (07) 5543 1927. *Wallaby Ridge Retreat:* 88 Bambling Rd, Boyland; (07) 5543 4340.

Mt Barney National Park A remote park where the rugged peaks of Barney, Maroon, May and Lindesay mountains stand as remnants of the ancient Focal Peak Shield Volcano. The walks are not for the inexperienced, but picnicking at Yellow Pinch at the base of Mt Barney is an alternative. The challenging 10 hr ascent to Mt Barney's summit on the Logan's Ridge track rewards walkers with spectacular views; 55 km sw.

Darlington Park: recreation area with picnic/barbecue facilities; 12 km s. *Tamrookum:* has a fine example of a timber church; tours by appt; 24 km sw. *Bigriggen Park:* recreation area with picnic/barbecue facilities; 30 km sw. *Rathdowney:* great viewpoint from Captain Logan's Lookout in John St; 32 km s. *Lamington National Park:* 40 km sw; see Nerang.

TOWNS NEARBY: North Tamborine 20 km, Boonah 31 km, Nerang 33 km, Surfers Paradise 43 km, Burleigh Heads 46 km

Bedarra Island
see Mission Beach, nearby

Biggenden
Pop. 644
Map ref. 603 B5 | 604 E12 | 609 L4

 Rose's Gallery Cafe Shoppe, George St; (07) 4127 1901; www.northburnett.qld.gov.au/

102.5 Breeze FM, 855 AM ABC Wide Bay

This agricultural town south-west of the city of Bundaberg, known as the 'Rose of the Burnett', is proud of its impressive range of roses in the main street. Situated in a valley, the majestic ranges of Mount Walsh National Park tower over the town.

Historical Museum: exhibits history of shire and life of the early pioneers; open Thurs and 2nd Sat each month, or by appt; Brisbane St; (07) 4127 5137. *Blacksmith Shop:* established in 1891, this recently restored shop contains displays and relics; open by appt; George St; (07) 4127 1298.

Market: Lions Park; 3rd Sat each month. *Biggenden Show:* May. *Dallarnil Sports Day:* June. *Auto Spectacular:* Aug. *Rodeo:* Nov.

QUEENSLAND

Mountain View Caravan Park: Walsh St; (07) 4127 1399. *Paradise Dam Recreation Area:* 353 Campbells Rd, Coringa; (07) 4127 7278.

Mt Walsh National Park Featuring the impressive Bluff Range, this wilderness park commands the skyline. Walks take in rugged granite outcrops and gullies and are for the experienced bushwalker only. From the picnic area the views are still commanding; Maryborough Rd; (07) 4121 1800; 8 km s.

Mt Woowoonga: bushwalking in a forestry reserve; picnic and barbecue facilities; 10 km NW. *Coalstoun Lakes National Park:* protects 2 volcanic crater lakes. Walk up the northern crater for a view over the rim; 20 km SW. *Coongara Rock:* a volcanic core surrounded by rainforest; 4WD access only; 20 km S. *Chowey Bridge:* 1905 concrete arch railway bridge, one of 2 surviving in the country; 20 km NW. *Brooweena:* small town with Pioneer Museum; Biggenden Rd; 30 km SE. *Paradise Dam:* this 30 000-megalitre dam took 4 years to build and has a tourist centre. Walking track and fishing areas nearby; barbecue facilities; 35 km NW.

TOWNS NEARBY: Childers 38 km, Gayndah 45 km, Gin Gin 58 km, Maryborough 66 km, Mundubbera 75 km

Biloela

Pop. 5369
Map ref. 604 A8 | 609 J2

i Queensland Heritage Park, Exhibition Ave; (07) 4992 2400; www.biloela.com

96.5 Sea FM, 837 AM ABC Capricornia

This thriving town in the fertile Callide Valley is part of the Banana Shire, but do not expect to find any bananas grown here. The area was actually named after a bullock called 'Banana', whose job was to lure wild cattle into enclosures, a difficult feat that was much applauded by local stockmen.

Queensland Heritage Park Exhibition Originally an exhibition at the Expo '88 in Brisbane, the park is home to the famous silo, which stands 28 m tall. Inside are exhibitions on the history of the Callide and Dawson valleys as well as scenes of rural life. Also in the complex is Pioneer Place, home to Biloela's first church and railway station, where photographs and memorabilia document the area's past. Exhibition Ave.

Spirit of the Land Mural: amazing mural depicting the history of women in the shire; State Farm Rd. *Greycliffe Homestead:* original slab hut converted to a museum showcases the area's pioneering heritage; open by appt; Gladstone Rd; (07) 4992 1572.

 Rotary Car, Ute and Bike Show: Mar. *Biloela Rockfest:* Mar. *Callide Fishing Competition:* Mar. *Callide Valley Show:* May. *Old Wheels in Motion (Callide):* festival celebrating farm machinery and vintage cars; July. *Arts Festival (Brigalow):* Oct. *Food and Comedy Festival:* Oct. *Coal and Country Festival (Moura):* Oct.

Biloela Caravan & Tourist Park: 98 Dawson Hwy; (07) 4992 1211. *Discovery Holiday Parks – Biloela:* 1–31 Valentine Plains Rd; (07) 4992 2618.

Mt Scoria Known locally as the 'Musical Mountain' because of the basalt columns at the top that ring when hit with another rock. Walks and trails around the mountain; 14 km s.

Thangool: renowned for its race days; 10 km SE. *Callide Dam:* excellent for boating, fishing and swimming; 12 km NE. *Callide Power Station:* near Callide Dam. *Callide Mine Lookout:* view over Biloela, the mine and the dam; 18 km NE,

past dam. *Kroombit Tops National Park:* 25 km E; *see Gladstone.* *Baralaba:* historic village; watersports on the Dawson River; 100 km NW.

TOWNS NEARBY: Theodore 75 km, Monto 80 km, Mount Morgan 84 km, Gladstone 97 km, Miriam Vale 106 km

Birdsville

Pop. 115
Map ref. 563 K2 | 618 D3

i Wirrari Centre, Billabong Blvd; (07) 4656 3300.

540 AM ABC Western QLD

Birdsville is a tiny town at the northern end of the Birdsville Track, a major cattle route developed in the 1880s. In the 1870s the first European settlers arrived in the area. By 1900 the town was flourishing, boasting three hotels, several stores, a customs office and a cordial factory. When, after Federation in 1901, the toll on cattle crossing the border was abolished, the town's prosperity slowly declined. John Flynn, the famous 'Flynn of the Inland', opened an Australian Inland Mission at Birdsville in 1923. Cattle remains a major trade, as well as the tourism accompanying four-wheel-drive enthusiasts keen to take on the Birdsville Track and Simpson Desert National Park.

Working Museum: housed in 6 buildings, the museum showcases an array of old relics from tools to pottery and farming equipment. Join proprietor John Menzies for a tour and demonstration in harness making and coach building; tours daily at 9am, 11am and 3pm; Waddie Dr. *Blue Poles Gallery:* art by local painter Wolfgang John. Cafe on-site; Graham St. *Artesian bore:* water comes out at near boiling point from this 1219 m deep bore; behind the bore is a geothermal power plant; Graham St. *Adelaide Street:* ruins of Royal Hotel (1883), a reminder of Birdsville's boom days; Birdsville Hotel (1884), still an important overnight stop for travellers; cemetery, housing the grave sites of early pioneers.

Rodeo and Bronco Branding: May. *Birdsville Gift:* footrace; June. *Birdsville Cup Racing Carnival:* 1st meeting of this annual event was held in 1882 and the tradition continues on the claypan track south-east of town; held 1st Fri and Sat in Sept, when the population swells to over 6000.

[BIRDSVILLE] CAMELS IN THE SIMPSON DESERT

Simpson Desert National Park West of Birdsville, this arid national park is the largest in Queensland. The parallel windblown sand dunes are enormous – up to 90 m high, about 1 km apart, and can extend up to 200 km. A self-guide drive includes 10 sites, starting at the eastern park boundary and following the track to Poeppel's Corner. Walking any distance is not recommended and a 4WD is essential. Visit only between Apr and Oct, *see note below*; (07) 4656 3249; 65 km w.

Waddi Trees and Dingo Cave Lookout: 14 km N. *Big Red:* huge sand dune; 35 km w. *Bedourie:* Eyre Creek runs through town providing waterholes that are home to the endangered bilby and peregrine falcons; 191 km N.

Travellers note: *Travel in this area can be hazardous, especially in the hotter months (approximately Oct–Mar). Motorists are advised to check the RACQ Road Conditions Report on 1300 130 595 (or www.racq.com.au) for information before departing down the Birdsville Track and to advise police if heading west to Simpson Desert National Park. There is no hotel or fuel at Betoota, 164 km E, but fuel is available at Windorah, 375 km E.*

TOWNS NEARBY: Innamincka (SA) 247 km

Blackall

Pop. 1160
Map ref. 608 A1 | 610 D12 | 617 P12 | 619 O1

i Shamrock St; (07) 4657 4637; www.blackall.qld.gov.au

95.1 West FM, 540 AM ABC Western QLD

Blackall is west of the Great Dividing Range in sheep and cattle country, and was home to the legendary sheep-shearer Jackie Howe. In 1892 he set the record of shearing 321 sheep with blade shears in less than eight hours at Alice Downs Station.

Fossilised tree stump: preserved tree stump estimated to be possisbly 225 million years old; Shamrock St. *Major Mitchell Memorial Clock:* commemorates the founding of Blackall in 1846; Shamrock St. *The Black Stump:* the reference point used when the area was surveyed in 1886. Beautiful mural painting of the stump at the site; Thistle St. *Jackie Howe Memorial:* statue of the legendary shearer who holds the record for shearing 321 sheep in 7 hrs 40 min; Shamrock St. *Historic Ram Park:* incorporates the living history of the Blackall district, with shearing occuring all year-round; Shamrock St. *Pioneer Bore:* first artesian bore sunk in Queensland, with display of replica drilling plant; Aqua St.

Blackall Show: May. *Campdraft:* May. *Heartland Festival:* May. *Christmas in July:* July. *Flower Show:* Sept. *Springtime Affair:* celebration of the season; Sept.

Blackall Caravan Park: 53 Garden St; (07) 4657 4816.

Idalia National Park Renowned habitat of the yellow-footed rock-wallaby, which can be spotted at Emmet Pocket Lookout (which also has amazing panoramic views) or along the Bullock Gorge walking track. A self-guide drive begins at the information centre, 12 km beyond the park entrance. (07) 4652 7333; 70 km sw on Yaraka Rd; at Benlidi siding turn south.

Blackall Wool Scour: restored steam-driven wool-processing plant with demonstrations of machinery (steam operating May–Sept only); Evora Rd; 4 km N.

TOWNS NEARBY: Tambo 95 km, Barcaldine 98 km, Isisford 105 km, Aramac 163 km, Longreach 165 km

Blackwater

Pop. 5030
Map ref. 611 J11

i Central Highlands Regional Council, McKenzie St; (07) 4980 5555.

92.7 4BCB FM, 1548 AM ABC Capricornia

Blackwater is west of Rockhampton in the Capricorn region and is known as the coal capital of Queensland. The coal is transported directly from coalmines south of town to Gladstone by train. The name 'Blackwater' is not a reference to the effects of mining operations, however, but comes from the discolouration of local waterholes caused by tea trees.

Japanese Garden complex This ornate traditional Japanese garden was constructed over 8 months in 1998. It symbolises the relationship Blackwater shares with its sister town Fujisawa in Japan. The complex also houses the newly opened Blackwater International Coal Centre, which has interactive and interpretive touch-screen displays, a cinema screening films on coal mining and a cafe. There is also a craft shop and information centre that was once the town station. Capricorn Hwy.

Lions Park: displays the flags of 37 nations to commemorate the nationality of every worker on the coalmines. In terms of size and variety, the display is 2nd only to that of the United Nations' building in New York; Capricorn Hwy to the west of town. *Helicopter flights over Blackwater Coal Mine:* see the mine in action; details from visitor centre.

May Day Festival: May. *World Dingo Trap Throwing Competition:* July. *Rodeo:* Oct. *Craft Fair and Art Exhibition:* regional arts and crafts exhibit; Oct.

Blackdown Tableland National Park This national park offers spectacular scenery over mountains and lowlands, including some beautiful waterfalls. It is the traditional home of the Ghungalu people, whose stencil art can be seen on the 2.8 km Mimosa Culture Track. Walk through to Rainbow Falls Gorge and swim in rockpools. (07) 4986 1964; 30 km E to turnoff.

Bedford Weir: dam excellent for fishing; 20 km N. *Comet:* in town is the Leichhardt Dig Tree, where the explorer buried letters and marked the tree 'dig'; 30 km w.

TOWNS NEARBY: Emerald 74 km, Springsure 100 km, Clermont 153 km, Mount Morgan 154 km, Rockhampton 168 km

Boonah

Pop. 2282
Map ref. 516 D1 | 525 M1 | 600 A9 | 609 M10

i Boonah–Fassifern Rd; (07) 5463 2233; www.scenicrim.qld.gov.au

100.1 Rim FM, 747 AM ABC Southern QLD

Boonah is set in the picturesque Fassifern Valley, surrounded by hills. Once noted as a 'beautiful vale' by 19th-century explorers, a little expedition in the surrounding region will reveal the beauty and ruggedness of the area. West of town is Main Range National Park, part of the Scenic Rim.

Cultural Centre: incorporates regional art gallery; open Mon–Fri, gallery open Wed–Sun; High St. *Art and Soul:* local art and photography; Walter St. *Gliding and ultralight tours:* flights over the Scenic Rim; details from visitor centre.

Country market: Springleigh Park; 2nd and 4th Sat each month. *Rodeo:* Apr. *Country Show:* May. *SPAR Arts Festival:* Sept. *Orchid Show:* Oct.

QUEENSLAND

Lillydale Farmstay: 821 Upper Logan Rd, Mount Barney; (07) 5544 3131. *Scenic Rim View Cottages for Couples:* 357 Old Rosevale Rd, Warrill View; (07) 5464 6508.

 Main Range National Park A World Heritage–listed park of rugged mountains and landscapes with spectacular lookouts. There are walks starting at the Cunninghams Gap and Spicers Gap campsites. See the varied birdlife, including the satin bowerbird, on the 8.4 km return Box Forest track. Access park from Cunningham Hwy; (07) 4666 1133; 40 km w. In the south of the park is Queen Mary Falls; *see Killarney.*

Templin: has historical museum chronicling the history of the area; 5 km NW. *Kalbar:* historic German town with magnificent buildings including the heritage-listed Wiss Emporium; 10 km NW. *Moogerah Peaks National Park:* excellent for birdwatching, and with lookouts over the Fassifern Valley. The Frog Buttress at Mt French is one of the best rock-climbing sites in Queensland; contact EPA on 1300 130 372 for more information; 12 km w. *Lakes Maroon and Moogerah:* ideal for camping and watersports; 20 km s and sw.

TOWNS NEARBY: Beaudesert 31 km, Ipswich 43 km, Laidley 50 km, North Tamborine 50 km, Killarney 53 km

Boulia

Pop. 206
Map ref. 616 F8

i Min Min Encounter, Herbert St; (07) 4746 3386; www.outbackholidays.tq.com.au

102.5 Hot FM, 106.1 ABC FM North West QLD

Boulia is the capital of the Channel Country and is on the Burke River, named after the ill-fated explorer Robert O'Hara Burke. The town is famous for random appearances of the mysterious Min Min light, a ball of light that sometimes reveals itself to travellers at night. The isolated Diamantina National Park nearby is a haven for threatened species.

Stonehouse Museum: built in 1888, this National Trust–listed site was one of the first houses built in western Queensland. It is now a museum housing the history of the Jones family, as well as Aboriginal artefacts and photographs; Pituri St. *Min Min Encounter:* high-tech re-creation of the Min Min light, with outback characters as your guide; Herbert St. *Red Stump:* warns travellers of the dangers of the Simpson Desert; Herbert St. *Corroboree Tree:* last known of the Pitta Pitta community; near Boulia State School.

Rodeo Races and Campdraft: Easter. *Camel Race:* July. *Back to Boulia:* traditional games weekend; Sept.

Diamantina National Park This remote park south-east of Boulia is rich in colours and landscapes. Follow the 157 km Warracoota self-guide circuit drive to view the spectacular sand dunes, claypans and ranges and many rare and threatened species in their native habitat, including the greater bilby, kowari and peregrine falcon. Canoe or fish in the winding creeks and rivers. 4WD access only. Roads may become impassable after rain; check road conditions before travelling; (07) 4652 7333; 147 km SE.

Ruins of Police Barracks: 19 km NE. *Cawnpore Hills:* good views from summit; 108 km E. *Burke and Wills Tree:* on the west bank of the Burke River; 110 km NE. *Ruins of Min Min Hotel:* burned down in 1918, where the Min Min light was first sighted; 130 km E.

TOWNS NEARBY: Mount Isa 246 km

Bowen

Pop. 7483
Map ref. 605 E4 | 611 J3

i Bruce Hwy next to Big Mango, Mount Gordon; (07) 4786 4222 or (07) 4786 2208; www.tourismbowen.com.au

 88.0 Explore FM, 630 AM ABC North QLD

At the north of the Whitsundays, Bowen is positioned within 5 kilometres of eight pristine beaches and bays. Named after the state's first governor, Bowen was established in 1861 – the first settlement in north Queensland. The town and surrounding area is well known for its mangoes, the Big Mango being testimony to this fact. Bowen has more recently gained fame as the film set for Baz Luhrmann's epic movie, *Australia*.

Historical murals Around the buildings and streets of Bowen's town centre are 25 murals by local and national artists, each illustrating an aspect of the region's history. The mural by Australian artist Ken Done was displayed at Expo '88. A new mural is commissioned every 2 years.

Historical Museum: covers history of area; open 9.30am–3.30pm Mon–Fri, 10am–12pm Sun Sept–Apr, closed Feb and Mar; Gordon St. *Summergarden Theatre:* styled on the classic movie houses of Southern California. Used now to screen films and stage performances; Murroona Rd.

Bowen Show: June. *Polocrosse Carnivale:* June. *Bowen River Rodeo (Collinsville):* July. *Bowen Fest:* Aug. *Bowen Family Fishing Classic:* Sept. *Coral Coast Festival:* Oct. *Bowen Cup:* Oct.

BIG4 Bowen Coral Coast Beachfront Holiday Park: Cnr Soldiers and Horseshoe Bay rds; (07) 4785 1262. *Harbour Lights Caravan Park:* 40 Santa Barbara Pde; (07) 4786 1565. *Queens Beach Tourist Village:* 160 Mt Nutt Rd; (07) 4785 1313. *Tropical Beach Caravan Park:* Howard St; (07) 4785 1490.

Bays and beaches Choose from 8 excellent spots for swimming, snorkelling and fishing in spectacular surrounds. Rose and Horseshoe bays are connected by a walking track with panoramic views over the ocean; a sidetrack leads to Murray Bay. Impressive corals and fish can be found at Grays, Horseshoe, Murray and Rose bays. Diving enthusiasts should head to Horseshoe and Murray bays. For a more exclusive swim, visit secluded Coral Bay. Details and directions from visitor centre.

Big Mango: tribute to the local Kensington Mango, grown since the 1880s. A shop sells all things mango-related – the mango ice-cream is a highlight; Bruce Hwy, Mt Gordon; 7 km s. *Gloucester Island National Park:* group of secluded islands 23 km offshore, part of the Great Barrier Reef, boasting beaches and rainforest. Campers must be self-sufficient and obtain a permit. Access via private boat from Dingo Beach, Hideaway Bay, Bowen or Airlie Beach; (07) 4967 7355. *Cape Upstart National Park:* remote granite headland flanked with sandy beaches; self-sufficient visitors only; access by boat, ramps at Molongle Bay and Elliot River; (07) 4967 7355; 50 km NW. *Collinsville:* coalmine tours can be arranged at Bowen visitor centre; 82 km SW.

TOWNS NEARBY: Proserpine 55 km, Airlie Beach 56 km, Ayr 101 km, Ravenswood 142 km, Mackay 158 km

Brampton Island

see Mackay, nearby

Buderim

Pop. 34 454
Map ref. 602 G4 | 603 F12 | 609 N7

i Old Post Office, Burnett St; (07) 5477 0944; www.buderim.com

90.3 ABC FM Coast, 91.1 Hot 91 FM

Buderim is just inland from the Sunshine Coast, high on the fertile red soil of Buderim Mountain, a plateau overlooking the surrounding bushland and ocean. With its wide streets and abundance of small-scale art and craft galleries, it escapes the crush of nearby towns like Maroochydore and Mooloolaba.

 Pioneer Cottage This restored 1876 National Trust timber cottage is one of Buderim's earliest houses and retains many of its original furnishings. Now home to the local historical society, it has exhibits on the history of the town and its surrounds. Open 11am–3pm daily; Ballinger Cres; (07) 5450 1966.

Buderim Forest Park: subtropical rainforest reserve and a great place for a picnic or barbecue. In the south, via Quorn Close, is the Edna Walling Memorial Garden and Serenity Falls; in the north, via Lindsay Rd, is Harry's Restaurant and a boardwalk along Martins Creek. *Foote Sanctuary:* rainforest walks and more than 80 bird species; car entry via Foote St. *Arts and crafts galleries:* various shops selling locally made items; Main St. *Ginger Shoppe:* while the Buderim Ginger Factory may have relocated to Yandina, you can purchase products from the shop; Burnett St.

 Australia Day celebrations: parade and fair; Jan.

Buderim White House Grand Manor: 54 Quorn Close; (07) 5445 1961. *Parle On Buderim:* 6 Parle Cres; (07) 5450 1413. *BIG4 Forest Glen Holiday Resort:* 71 Owen Creek Rd, Forest Glen; (07) 5476 6646.

Mooloolah River National Park: 6 km SE; *see Mooloolaba.*

TOWNS NEARBY: Maroochydore 5 km, Mooloolaba 6 km, Nambour 12 km, Caloundra 15 km, Landsborough 17 km

Bundaberg

see inset box on next page

Burketown

Pop. 176
Map ref. 612 A7 | 615 D4

i Old Post Office (Apr–Sept); or council offices (Oct–Mar), Musgrave St, (07) 4745 5100; www.burkeshirecouncil.com

 567 AM ABC North West QLD

Burketown is on the edge of the Gulf of Carpentaria, on the dividing line between the wetlands to the north and the Gulf Savannah plains to the south. It was named after the ill-fated explorer Robert Burke, who was the first European (with partner William John Wills) to arrive in the area. Regularly in spring, the natural phenomenon known as Morning Glory takes over the horizon at dawn between Burketown and Sweers Island, offshore. The clouds appear as rolling tube-like formations and can extend for more than 1000 kilometres.

Museum and Information Centre: in the original post office, with displays on the history of the area plus local arts and crafts. Open Apr–Oct; Musgrave St. *Artesian bore:* operating for over 100 years and quite a sight to see due to the build up of minerals; The Great Top Rd.

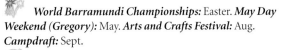

World Barramundi Championships: Easter. *May Day Weekend (Gregory):* May. *Arts and Crafts Festival:* Aug. *Campdraft:* Sept.

Boodjamulla (Lawn Hill) National Park Approximately 90 km w of the town of Gregory, this park is steeped in Aboriginal, pastoral and evolutionary history. Highlights include canoeing, swimming and walking in lush Lawn Hill Gorge, home to the Waanyi rock-art sites of Wild Dog Dreaming and Rainbow Dreaming, and the early-morning climb to Island Stack. The park's Riversleigh section contains some of the world's most significant mammalian fossils, which record the evolution of mammals over 20 million years, as the vegetation changed from rainforest to semi-arid grassland. Guided tours provide an insight into the ancient world, and there is a self-guide interpretive trail; public access is restricted to D site. Access to the park by conventional vehicle is best from Cloncurry; 4WD access from Burketown, Mount Isa and Camooweal; 200 km sw.

Original Gulf Meatworks: machinery relics of this once-thriving industry; just north of town. *Colonial Flat:* site of the Landsborough Tree. Blazed by the explorer in 1862 on his search for Burke and Wills, it became the depot camp for search parties and the resting place of Landsborough's ship Firefly – the 1st ship to enter the Albert River; 5 km E. *Nicholson River wetlands:* breeding ground for crocodiles, fish and birds; 17 km w. *Bluebush Swamp:* large wetland area ideal for birdwatchers; 30 km sw. *Sweers Island:* excellent spot for lure and fly fishing, plus golden beaches and over 100 species of birds; access by aircraft or boat, details from visitor centre; 30 km N. *Leichhardt Falls:* picturesque flowing falls in rainy months; 71 km SE. *Gregory:* small outback town that holds the Gregory River Canoe Marathon in May; 113 km s. *Fishing and boat tours:* to nearby estuaries and Wellesley Islands; details from visitor centre.

TOWNS NEARBY: Karumba 140 km, Normanton 162 km

Burleigh Heads

Pop. 7606
Map ref. 516 G1 | 525 O1 | 600 G10 | 601 F8 | 609 N11

i Shop 14B, Coolangatta Pl, Cnr Griffith and Warner sts, Coolangatta; 1300 309 440; www.verygoldcoast.com.au

89.3 4CRB FM, 91.7 FM ABC Gold Cast

Burleigh Heads is a suburb of the Gold Coast and is situated between Coolangatta and the tourist mecca Surfers Paradise. It is known for its breathtaking scenery, highlighted by the stunning Burleigh Head National Park. The famed south-easterly swells and surrounding parklands make the beaches on Burleigh Heads some of the best in the world, attracting international surfing tournaments. The relaxed charm of Burleigh Heads can be enjoyed from under the beachside pines and pandanus palms or in a nearby restaurant overlooking the stunning Pacific Ocean.

 Burleigh Head National Park: take the 2.8 km Ocean View circuit to experience the coastal vegetation, rainforest and mangroves or go to Tumgun Lookout to watch for dolphins and humpback whales (seasonal); access from Goodwin Tce; 1300 130 372. *David Fleay Wildlife Parks* displays Queensland's native animals in a natural setting with the only display of Lumholtz's tree kangaroo and mahogany gliders in the world. The park also has crocodile feeding in summer and Aboriginal-heritage programs; West Burleigh Rd. *Paramount Adventure Centre:* enjoy a rush of adrenaline and adventure at the Gold Coast's

continued on p. 399

 RADIO STATIONS IN TOWN WHAT'S ON WHERE TO EAT WHERE TO STAY NEARBY

 QUEENSLAND

BUNDABERG

Pop. 71 000

Map ref. 603 D2 | 604 F10 | 609 M3

i 271 Bourbong St; (07) 4153 8888 or 1300 722 099; www.bundabergregion.info

93.9 Hitz FM, 855 AM ABC Wide Bay

Bundaberg, the southernmost access point to the Great Barrier Reef, is proud of its parks and gardens, vineyards, breweries and scenic walks. Even more recognisable is its world-famous amber spirit, Bundaberg Rum. Fields of towering sugarcane border the town and nearby Burnett River, and when burned in harvest season (July to November) give the area a smoky haze. As the sugar industry was being developed in the 1880s and Australian labour costs were rising, South Sea Islanders were placed under 'contract' to work on the cane fields as a cheap alternative. In fact, the majority of these labourers had been lured from their island homes onto boats under the pretence of trading goods. In 1901, when Australia's Commonwealth Government was established, the Kanakas (as the labourers were known) were allowed to return home. A Kanaka-built basalt stone wall can still be seen near Bargara, a short distance north-east of town. Bundaberg proudly claims the aviator Bert Hinkler as one of its own. In 1928 Hinkler was the first to successfully fly from England to Australia on a voyage that took just over 15 days.

Bundaberg Botanical Gardens In this picturesque setting stand many buildings from Bundaberg's past. Hinkler House Memorial Museum, inside Bert Hinkler's relocated Southampton home, is a tribute to him and to aviation history. Fairymead House Sugar Museum, a restored plantation home, recalls the town's early years of sugar production, and the nearby Historical Museum chronicles the general history of the area. To see more of the grounds, take the restored Sugarcane Railway around the lakes, which runs every Sun (also Wed on school holidays); Mt Perry Rd.

Bundaberg Rum Distillery: learn about the distillation process first-hand; tours daily; Avenue St. *Schmeider's Cooperage and Craft Centre:* demonstrations of barrel making and glass-blowing, and sales of local crafts and handmade crystal jewellery; Alexandra St. *Arts Centre:* 3 galleries devoted to local and visiting art exhibitions; cnr Barolin and Quay sts. *Baldwin Swamp Conservation Park:* stroll along boardwalks and pathways through waterlily lagoons, abundant birdlife and native fauna; Steindl St. *Tropical Wines:* taste unique wines made from local fruit; Mt Perry Rd. *Alexandra Park and Zoo:* historic band rotunda, spacious picnic lawns, cactus garden, zoo (free admission); riverbank, Quay St. *Whaling Wall:* a 7-storey-high whale mural by Robert Wyland; Bourbong St. *Heritage city walk:* self-guide walking tour of 12 significant sites and buildings; starts at School of Arts Building, Bourbong St. *Bundaberg Barrel:* giant barrel building houses Bundaberg Brewed Drinks. With interactive tours, holographic 3-D adventure and free sampling; Bargara Rd.

Shalom College Markets: local crafts; Fitzgerald St; every Sun. *PCYC Markets:* Maryborough St; 2nd Sun each month. *Big House Piano:* music at Fairymead House; 1st Sun each month. *Aussie Country Muster:* music and entertainment; May. *Bundaberg Show:* Jun. *Wide Bay International Air Show:* Aug.

[LOGGERHEAD TURTLE AT MON REPOS CONSERVATION PARK]

Multicultural Food and Wine Festival: Aug. *Bundy in Bloom Festival:* spring festival and parade; Sept. *Arts Festival:* Oct. *Bundy Thunder:* power-boat spectacular; Nov. *Port2Port Yacht Rally:* Nov.

Absolute Oceanfront Tourist Park: 117 Woongarra Scenic Dr, Bargara; (07) 4159 2436. *Baffle Retreat Bed & Breakfast:* 43 Island View Dr, Winfield; (07) 4156 6299. *Bargara Beach Caravan Park:* 25 Fred Courtice Ave, Bargara; (07) 4159 2228. *Bundaberg East Cabin & Tourist Park:* 83 Princess St, Bundaberg East; (07) 4152 8899. *Burnett Heads Holiday Park:* 2 PaulMittelheuser St, Burnett Heads; (07) 4159 4313. *Dunelm House Bed & Breakfast:* 540 Bargara Rd, Bargara; (07) 4159 0909. *Elliott Heads Holiday Park:* Lihs St, Elliott Heads; (07) 4159 6193. *Finemore Holiday Park:* 33 Quay St, Bundaberg West; (07) 4151 3663. *Glenlodge Caravan Village:* 321 Goodwood Rd, Thabeban; (07) 4153 1515. *Miara Holiday Park:* 1200 Miara Rd, Miara; (07) 4156 1171. *Midtown Caravan Park:* 61 Takalvan St, Millbank; (07) 4152 2768.

Mon Repos Conservation Park This park contains the largest and most accessible mainland loggerhead turtle rookery in eastern Australia. Between Nov and Mar these giant sea turtles come ashore to lay their eggs. Hatchlings leave their nests for the sea from mid-Jan to late Mar. Access to the park is restricted during these times – guided night tours depart from the park information centre for viewing turtles up-close. When turtles are not hatching, snorkelling and exploring rockpools are popular activities; (07) 4159 1652; 15 km NE.

Burrum Coast National Park Split into 2 sections, this national park offers a variety of landscapes and activities. The northern Kinkuna section is relatively undeveloped. The vegetation along the beach is rugged and spectacular, and birdwatching in the wallum heath is a highlight. Access is via Palm Beach Road; 14 km SW; 4WD and sand-driving experience are necessary. The southern Woodgate section is more people-friendly, featuring boardwalks and established tracks that allow visitors to see abundant wildlife from every vantage. Access is via Woodgate, a small town with a magnificent ocean beach; (07) 4131 1600; 57 km s.

Lady Elliot Island A small coral cay with 19 major dive sites, bird rookeries, turtle-nesting site and whale-watching opportunities. Low-key resort (maximum 140 people), ranging from budget to island suites. Air access to Lady Elliot from Hinkler Airport. Contact visitor centre for details; 92 km NE.

Hummock Lookout: panoramic view of Bundaberg, cane fields and coast; 7 km NE. *Meadowvale Nature Park:* rainforest and walkway to Splitters Creek; 10 km W. *Sharon Nature Park:* rainforest, native fauna and walkway to Burnett River; 12 km SW. *Bargara:* coastal town with a popular surf beach and year-round fishing on man-made reef. Turtles often nest at nearby Neilson

Park, Kelly's and Rifle Range beaches; 13 km NE. *Fishing spots:* area renowned for its wide variety of fishing. Excellent spots at Burnett Heads (15 km NE), Elliott Heads (18 km SE) and Moore Park (21 km NW). *Mystery craters:* 35 small craters in sandstone slab. Their origin causes much debate, but confirmed to be over 25 million years old; 25 km SW. *Littabella National Park:* lagoons and billabongs surrounded by tea tree forest. Many sand tracks for the 4WD enthusiast can be found at nearby Norval Park Beach; (07) 4131 1600; 38 km NW. *Lady Musgrave Island:* excellent spot for snorkelling, fishing and camping. Sea access from Bundaberg Port; 107 km N.

TOWNS NEARBY: Childers 42 km, Gin Gin 42 km, Hervey Bay 71 km, Biggenden 77 km, Maryborough 83 km

---

largest adventure centre. Choose from indoor rock climbing, kayaking, mountain-biking or take part in a learn-to-surf program; Hutchinson St.

Burleigh Art and Craft Market: beachfront; last Sun each month. *Coolangatta Markets:* beachfront; 2nd Sun each month. *Burleigh Car Boot Sale:* Stocklands Shopping Centre Car Park; 2nd Sun each month. *Quiksilver Roxy Pro Surfing:* Feb/Mar. *Gold Coast Cup Outrigger Canoe Marathon:* Apr. *Wintersun Festival:* Coolangatta; May/June. *Coolangatta Gold:* famous ironman and ironwoman race; Oct.

Vecchia Roma: traditional Italian family restaurant; Cnr Gold Coast Hwy and West Burleigh Rd; (07) 5535 5988.

Burleigh Beach Tourist Park: 36 Goodwin Tce; (07) 5667 2750. *Kallora Farm Bed & Breakfast:* 823 Tomewin Mountain Rd, Currumbin Valley; (07) 5533 0361. *Mouses House:* 2807 Springbrook Rd, Springbrook; (07) 5533 5192. *Nobby Beach Holiday Village:* 2200 Gold Coast Hwy, Miami; (07) 5572 7533. *Ocean Beach Tourist Park Miami:* 22 Hythe St, Miami; (07) 5667 2710. *The Sanctuary At Springbrook Bed & Breakfast:* 2311A Springbrook Rd, Springbrook; (07) 5533 5118. *Springbrook Lyrebird Retreat:* 418 Lyrebird Ridge Rd, Springbrook; (07) 5533 5555. *Tallebudgera Creek Tourist Park:* 1544 Gold Coast Hwy, Palm Beach; (07) 5667 2700.

Currumbin Wildlife Sanctuary This 20 ha reserve is owned by the National Trust. There are free-ranging animals in open areas, the Crocodile Wetlands, with raised walkways over pools of freshwater and saltwater crocodiles, a walk-through rainforest aviary and a miniature railway. A highlight is the twice-daily feeding of wild rainbow lorikeets. The 'Wildnight Tours' are interactive tours to see the nocturnal wildlife. 8 km SE.

Springbrook National Park, Mt Cougal section This small section of the park contains a subtropical rainforest remnant and is part of the Gondwana Rainforests of Australia World Heritage Area. Mt Cougal's twin peaks and the Currumbin Valley are an interesting and diverse landscape. There is a scenic drive through the valley and a walking track through rainforest, past cascades, to the remains of an old bush sawmill. End of Currumbin Creek Rd; 27 km SW. Springbrook and Natural Bridge sections: *see Nerang.*

Palm Beach: popular golden-sands beach that has won Queensland's Cleanest Beach Award in previous years; 4 km SE. *Superbee Honeyworld:* live displays, Walks with Bees tour, honey making and sales; opposite sanctuary; 8 km SE. *Olson's Bird Gardens:* large landscaped aviaries in subtropical setting with a lilly pilly hedge maze; Currumbin Creek Rd; 16 km SW. *Greenmount and Coolangatta beaches:* sheltered white-sand beaches with beautiful views of the coast; 13 km SE. *Rainbow Bay:* sheltered beach excellent for swimming. Walk along the coast to Snapper Rocks; 15 km SE. *Snapper Rocks:* top surf area with the 'Superbank', one of the world's longest point breaks; 15 km SE. *Point Danger:* named by Captain Cook as he sailed by. It offers excellent panoramic views over the ocean and coast. Catch a glimpse of dolphins from the Captain Cook Memorial Lighthouse; 15 km SE. *Tom Beaston Outlook (Razorback Lookout):* excellent views; behind Tweed Heads; 16 km SE.

TOWNS NEARBY: Surfers Paradise 10 km, Tweed Heads (NSW) 13 km, Nerang 16 km, Murwillumbah (NSW) 27 km, North Tamborine 32 km

Caboolture

Pop. 17 739
Map ref. 599 E1 | 600 D1 | 602 F7 | 609 N8

i Bruce Hwy, Burpengary; 1800 833 100; www.moretonbay.qld.gov.au

📻 105.1 4OUR FM, 612 ABC AM Brisbane

At the northern edge of Greater Brisbane and the southern opening to the Sunshine Coast, Caboolture is surrounded by subtropical fruit farms. The town was settled in 1842 after the restricted land around Moreton Bay penal colony was opened up. The historical village north of town exhibits much of this history. Bribie Island to the east has spectacular aquatic and wildlife attractions, which bring many visitors to the region.

Trail of Reflections: self-guide trail of open-air artwork and sculptures around town that illustrate the history of the area; starts in King St; details from visitor centre.

Market: showgrounds, Beerburrum Rd; Sun mornings. *Country Music Festival:* Apr/May. *Medieval Tournament:* July. *Caboolture Show:* Aug. *Rodeo:* Nov/Dec.

QUEENSLAND

Caboolture River Caravan Park: 26 Burnett Rd; (07) 5495 1041. *Avon Lodge Bribie Island:* 132 Avon Ave, Banksia Beach; (07) 3410 7318. *Bali on Bribie:* 21 South Esplanade, Bongaree; 0417 656 693. *Bells Caravan Park:* 39 Thompson Cres, Clontarf; (07) 3284 6899. *Bongaree Caravan Park:* Welsby Pde, Bongaree; (07) 3408 1054. *Bribie Island Caravan Park:* Jacana Ave, Woorim; 1800 649 831. *D'Aguilar Mountain Retreat:* 64 Curran St, D'aguilar; (07) 5496 4848. *Donnybrook Caravan Park:* 17 Alice St, Donnybrook; (07) 5498 8219. *Silver Shores Caravan Park:* Bribie Island Rd, Sandstone Point; (07) 5497 5566. *Toorbul Caravan Park:* 109 The Esplanade, Toorbul; (07) 5498 8210.

Bribie Island This island park is separated from the mainland by Pumicestone Passage, where mangroves flourish and dugongs, dolphins, turtles and over 350 species of birds live. National park covers about a 3rd of the island and offers secluded pristine white beaches. Follow the Bicentennial Bushwalks to discover the park on foot, boat along Pumicestone Passage or 4WD along the ocean beach (permit required). Fishing and surfing are popular at Woorim Beach, just north of which are old WW II bunkers. Woorim itself is an old-fashioned resort. See migratory birds in summer at Buckleys Hole Conservation Park on the south-west tip of the island, where there are also picnic pots and walking tracks to the beach. Bridge access to island; 21 km E.

Ferryman cruises: cruise the waters of Pumicestone Passage; (07) 3408 7124. *Caboolture Historical Village:* over 50 restored buildings of historical importance house museums, with themes including maritime and transport; open 9.30am–3.30pm daily; Beerburrum Rd; 2 km N. *Airfield:* Warplane and Flight Heritage Museum with displays of WW II memorabilia and restored fighter planes. Tiger Moth and Mustang flights and gliding on offer; McNaught Rd; 2 km E. *Sheep Station Creek Conservation Park:* walks through open forest. See remains of the old bridge on original road leading from Brisbane to Gympie; 6 km SW. *Abbey Museum:* traces growth of western civilisation with displays of art and antiques; open 10am–4pm Mon–Sat; just off road to Bribie Island; 9 km E. *Woodford:* the town has one of the largest narrow-gauge steam locomotive collections in Australia; Margaret St; 22 km NW. *Mt Mee State Forest:* boardwalks through subtropical rainforest and lookouts over Neurum Valley, Moreton Bay and surrounds; 23 km W. *Donnybrook, Toorbul and Beachmere:* coastal fishing towns to the east.

TOWNS NEARBY: Strathpine 25 km, Landsborough 31 km, Caloundra 37 km, Maleny 37 km, Buderim 46 km

Cairns

see inset box on page 402

Caloundra

Pop. 87 596
Map ref. 602 H5 | 603 F12 | 609 N8

 7 Caloundra Rd; (07) 5420 6240 or 1800 644 969; www.caloundratourism.com.au

90.3 ABC FM Coast

This popular holiday spot at the southern tip of the Sunshine Coast was once a retirement haven. It now boasts a diverse population of retirees and young Brisbane commuters keen on the seaside lifestyle. The nearby beaches offer a variety of watersports – the calm waters of Golden Beach are especially popular with windsurfers. The fishing between Bribie Island and the mainland in Pumicestone Passage is excellent.

Queensland Air Museum Founded by members of the Aviation Historical Society of Australia in 1973, this museum collects important relics of Queensland's aviation heritage. Memorabilia on display includes old fighter planes and bombers. Airport, Pathfinder Dr; (07) 5492 5930.

Caloundra Regional Art Gallery: local and touring art exhibitions; open 10am–4pm Wed–Sun; Omrah Ave. *Ben Bennet Botanical Park:* easy walks through natural bushland; Queen St. *Suncoast Helicopter Flights:* over Glass House Mountains and Sunshine Coast; bookings on (07) 5499 6900. *Caloundra Cruises:* morning, lunchtime and afternoon cruises, as well as sunset charters. Scenic Pumicestone Passage cruises have spectacular views of Bribie Island and Moreton Bay; bookings on (07) 5492 8280. *Blue Water Kayak Tours:* paddle in the tranquil Moreton Bay Marine Park.

Country Market: Bulcock St; Sun. *City Show:* May. *Cairns Cup:* June. *Open Cockpit Weekend:* July. *Taste of the Coast:* food and wine festival; July. *Bowls Carnival:* July–Aug. *Classic Boat Regatta:* Aug. *Art and Craft Festival:* Oct. *Caloundra Music Festival:* Oct.

Alfie's Mooo Char and Bar: steak from paddock to plate; Cnr Otranto Tce and The Esplanade; (07) 5492 8155. *Caloundra Surf Club:* bistro fare with a modern twist; 1 Spender La, Kings Beach; (07) 5491 8418. *Cafe by the Beach:* popular surf cafe; 12 Seaview Tce, Moffat Beach; (07) 5491 9505. *The Moorings Cafe Restaurant:* masters of big breakfasts; 88 The Esplanade, Golden Beach; (07) 5492 2466.

Caloundra Waterfront Holiday Park: 44 Maloja Ave; (07) 5491 1564. *Dicky Beach Family Holiday Park:* Beerburrum St, Dicky Beach; (07) 5491 3342. *Golden Beach Holiday Park:* 1 Onslow St, Golden Beach; (07) 5492 4811.

Currimundi Lake Conservation Park This unspoiled coastal park offers quiet walks beside the lake and through to the beach. Canoe and swim in the lake or see the finches and friarbirds in the remnant wallum heath. In spring the wildflowers are spectacular. Access from Coongara Espl; 4 km N.

Opals Down Under: opal-cutting demonstrations and 'scratch patch' where visitors fossick for their own gemstones; 14 km NW. *Aussie World:* family fun-park in native garden setting, with over 30 rides and games, Side Show Alley and an Ettamogah Pub, based on Ken Maynard's cartoon; Palmview; 18 km NW. *Surrounding beaches:* include patrolled beaches of Bulcock, Kings, and Dicky with the wreck of SS *Dicky* (1893); excellent fishing at Moffat and Shelly beaches. *Scenic drives:* taking in the beaches to the north, the Blackall Range with art galleries and views of the Sunshine Coast, and the Glass House Mountains with magnificent walks and scenery; details from visitor centre.

TOWNS NEARBY: Mooloolaba 14 km, Buderim 15 km, Maroochydore 16 km, Landsborough 18 km, Nambour 26 km

Camooweal

Pop. 197
Map ref. 593 P10 | 615 A9 | 616 C1

Drovers Camp, Camooweal; (07) 4748 2022.

102.5 Hot FM, 567 AM ABC North West QLD

North-west of Mount Isa, Camooweal is the last Queensland town before the Northern Territory border. It was once the centre for enormous cattle drives travelling south. Some say that the town is a suburb of Mount Isa, which would make the 188 kilometres of Barkly Highway between Mount Isa and

Camooweal one of the longest main streets in the world. To the south of town are the incredible Camooweal Caves, a series of sinkhole caves that have evolved over millions of years.

 Historic buildings: the Drovers store; Barkly Hwy. *The Drover's Camp:* historical displays, toilets and picnic area. Guided tours May–Sept 10am–5pm daily; Barkly Hwy.

Cricket tournament: Apr. *Campdraft:* June. *Horseracing:* Aug. *Drovers Camp Festival:* Aug.

Camooweal Caves National Park On the Barkly Tableland, this national park is still evolving as water continues to filter through the soluble dolomite to create and transform the extensive cave system. The underground caves are linked by vertical shafts and only the experienced caver should attempt them. The Great Nowranie Cave is excellent to explore with an 18 m drop at the opening (climbing gear is essential). Caves may flood during wet season. If exploring the caves, inform local police or ranger beforehand. 4WD access is recommended. (07) 4722 5224; 24 km s.

Cemetery: headstones tell local history; 1 km E. *Boodjamulla (Lawn Hill) National Park:* around 300 km N via Gregory; *see Burketown.*

TOWNS NEARBY: Mount Isa 169 km

Cardwell

Pop. 1251
Map ref. 606 E7 | 613 M9

ℹ️ Rainforest and Reef Information Centre, 142 Victoria St; (07) 4066 8601; www.gspeak.com.au/cardwell

📻 91.9 Kool FM, 630 AM ABC North QLD

Cardwell is a coastal town overlooking Rockingham Bay and the nearby islands of the Great Barrier Reef. Ferries transport visitors to nearby Hinchinbrook Island, the largest island national park in Australia. Between the island and the mainland is Hinchinbrook Channel (Cardwell is at the northern edge), a popular spot for fishing and a sheltered area for houseboats.

Bush Telegraph Heritage Centre This complex comprises the old post office and telegraph station, in operation 1870–1982, and the original magistrates court and gaol cells. An informative history of communications and the region is provided through interpretive displays. Open 10am–1pm Mon–Fri, 9am–12pm Sat, other times by appt; Bruce Hwy; (07) 4066 2412.

Rainforest and Reef Information Centre: interpretive centre that acquaints visitors with landscape, flora and fauna of northern Queensland; Bruce Hwy, near jetty. *Coral Sea Battle Memorial Park:* large war memorial that commemorates the WW II battle off the coast between Australian/US forces and the Japanese; beachfront. *Boat hire and cruises:* explore the tropical waters and islands to the east at the helm of a yacht, houseboat or cruiser, or travel with an organised cruise; details from visitor centre. *Snorkelling and scuba-diving tours:* details from visitor centre.

Market: Cardwell Espl; 1st Sun each month. *Coral Sea Battle Memorial Commemoration:* May. *Seafest:* Aug. *Fishing Classic (Port Hinchinbrook):* Sept.

Cardwell Van Park: 107 Roma St; (07) 4066 8689. *Kookaburra Holiday Park:* 175 Bruce Hwy; (07) 4066 8648.

Hinchinbrook Island National Park An amazing variety of vegetation covers this island park, including rainforest, wetlands, forests and woodlands. The 32 km Thorsborne Trail on the

east coast is renowned for its spectacular scenery as it winds past waterfalls and along pristine beaches. Many people allow 4 days or more for the walk, camping on a different beach each night. Hikers must be self-sufficient and bookings are essential (limited number of walkers allowed). Shorter walks are from the camping areas at Macushla and The Haven. Small, low-key resort (maximum 45 people); Access the island via ferry from Cardwell or Lucinda; (07) 4066 8601; 26 km SE.

Scenic drive in Cardwell State Forest: this 26 km circuit from Cardwell takes in a lookout, waterfalls, swimming holes and picnic spots; begins on Braesnose St. *Girramay National Park:* boardwalk through extensive mangrove forests and variety of other vegetation to beach, with spectacular view of islands. This park is a habitat of the endangered mahogany glider; (07) 4066 8601; 4 km N. *Five Mile Swimming Hole:* attractive picnic and swimming spot safe from crocodiles, sharks and stingers; 7 km S. *Dalrymple's Gap:* original service path and stone bridge through range; 15 km S. *Brook Islands:* nesting area for Torresian imperial pigeons (Sept–Feb). Excellent snorkelling on reef of northern 3 islands. Sea access only; 30 km NE. *Murray Falls:* climb the steep 1 km path to viewing platform over falls and surrounds; 42 km NW. *Girringun National Park:* travel through World Heritage rainforest on road (dry weather only) to the 3-tier 91 m Blencoe Falls; (07) 4066 8601; 71 km W; *see Ingham for southern parts of park.*

TOWNS NEARBY: Tully 38 km, Mission Beach 44 km, Ingham 45 km, Mourilyan 76 km, Innisfail 82 km

Charleville

Pop. 3275
Map ref. 608 B5 | 619 P5

ℹ️ Matilda Hwy; (07) 4654 3057; www.murweh.qld.gov.au

📻 101.7 Triple C FM, 603 AM ABC Western QLD

Charleville is in the heart of mulga country on the banks of the Warrego River and at the centre of a rich sheep and cattle district. By the late 1890s the town had its own brewery, ten hotels and 500 registered bullock teams. Cobb & Co. recognised the value of Charleville's location on a major stock route and opened a coach-building factory in 1893. It also has strong links with aviation: the first London–Sydney flight landed here in 1919, Qantas' first fare-paying service took off in 1922 and record-setting aviator Amy Johnson landed nearby in 1930. Charleville marks the terminus of the Westlander rail service from Brisbane.

Cosmos Centre This centre explores the Australian night sky and its significance to Aboriginal culture. There are multimedia displays, nightly shows and interactive areas where the wonders of the sky are observed through powerful Meade Telescopes. The outback night sky has never looked so beautiful; Matilda Hwy; (07) 4654 7771.

Royal Flying Doctor Service Visitor Centre: museum displaying memorabilia from the past and present. View the documentary entitled *A Day in the Life of the Flying Doctor;* Old Cunnamulla Rd. *Historic House Museum:* a wonderful example of early Queensland architecture. Machinery displays including steam engine and a rail ambulance in restored Queensland National Bank building; open 9am–3pm Mon–Fri, 9am–12pm Sat, other times by appt; Alfred St. *Vortex Gun:* in 1902 this 5 m long gun was used in an unsuccessful rain-making experiment; Bicentennial Park, Matilda Hwy. *Heritage trail:* self-guide walk

continued on p. 403

QUEENSLAND

CAIRNS

Pop. 122 732
Map ref. 606 E2 | 607 F7 | 613 L6

i Cairns & Tropical North Visitor Information Centre, 51 The Esplanade; (07) 4051 3588; www.cairnsgreatbarrierreef.org.au

 102.7 Zinc, 801 AM ABC Far North QLD

This modern, colourful city is the capital of the Tropical North and the gateway to the Great Barrier Reef, but was once a service town for the sugar plantations to the south. Tourism boomed with the airport's upgrade in 1984 and the influx of visitors and commercial enterprises resulted in the unusual mix of modern architecture and original Queenslander homes that can be seen today. The Esplanade traces the bay foreshore and blends the city life with the natural attractions of the Coral Sea. With Cairns' superb location – the Great Barrier Reef to the east, mountain rainforests of the Wet Tropics and plains of the Atherton Tableland to the west, and palm-fringed beaches to the north and south – it is a good base for many activities. For fishing enthusiasts, Cairns is famous for its black marlin.

Flecker Botanic Gardens Established in 1886 as a recreational reserve, they are now the only wet tropical botanic gardens in Australia. The gardens display tropical plants from around the world, including a number of endangered species and over 200 species of palm. Follow the boardwalks through remnant lowland swamp to adjacent Centenary Lakes to see turtles and mangrove birds. Access gardens via Collins Ave; Edge Hill.

Mount Whitfield Conservation Park: 2 major walking tracks through forested mountain range to summit for views of Cairns and Coral Sea; behind botanic gardens; access via Collins Ave, Edge Hill. *McLeod Street Pioneer Cemetery:* honours local pioneers. *Tanks Art Centre:* multipurpose centre in revamped WW II oil-storage tanks, including gallery with local art; call

for event listings; 46 Collins Ave, Edge Hill; (07) 4032 6600. *Cairns Regional Gallery:* local artists exhibit in this National Trust–classified building; Mon–Sat 10am–5pm, Sun 1–5pm; Cnr Shields and Abbott Sts; (07) 4046 4800. *Cairns Museum:* displays of Aboriginal, gold-rush, timber and sugarcane history; open 10am–4pm Mon–Sat; Cnr Lake and Shields sts. *Bulk Sugar Terminal:* guided tours by arrangement during crushing season (June–Dec); Cook St; (07) 4051 3533. *Foreshore Promenade:* landscaped area with safe swimming lagoon; foreshore; pool closed Wed mornings. *Kuranda Scenic Railway:* daily trips through Barron Gorge to rainforest village of Kuranda; leaves Cairns Railway Station in Bunda St; (07) 4036 9333; *see also Kuranda. Game fishing:* contact visitor centre for details. *Dive schools:* contact visitor centre for details.

Rusty's Market: Grafton and Sheridan sts; Fri 5am–6pm, Sat 6am–3pm and Sun 6am–2pm. *Esplanade Market:* Sat 8am–5pm. *Cairns Show:* July. *Cairns Cup:* Aug. *Festival Cairns:* Aug–Sept.

Bayleaf Balinese Restaurant: Balinese with flair; Bay Village Tropical Retreat, cnr Lake and Gatton sts; (07) 4047 7955. *Blue Sky Brewery:* hearty meals and beers; 34–42 Lake St; (07) 4057 0500. *Bushfire Flame Grill:* world menu with Brazilian flame grill and Japanese barbecue; Pacific International Hotel, cnr The Esplanade and Spence St; (07) 4044 1879. *Food Trail Tours:* tastes of tropical produce; pick-ups from Cairns and northern beaches accommodation; (07) 4032 0322.

Cairns Sunland Leisure Park: 49–61 Little Pease St; (07) 4053 6888. *BIG4 Cairns Crystal Cascades Holiday Park:* The Rocks Rd, Redlynch; (07) 4039 1036. *Cairns Coconut Holiday Resort:* 23–51 Anderson Rd, Woree; (07) 4054 6644.

[SWIMMING LAGOON, CAIRNS ESPLANADE]

Cairns Holiday Park: 12–30 Little St, Manunda; (07) 4051 1467. *Cairns Villa & Leisure Park:* 28 Pease St, Manoora; (07) 4053 7133. *Cool Waters Holiday Park:* Cnr Brinsmead Rd and View St, Brinsmead; (07) 4034 1949. *First City Caravilla Caravan Park:* Kelly St, Earlville; (07) 4054 1403. *Galvins Edge Hill B&B:* 61 Walsh St, Edge Hill; (07) 4032 1308. *Kooka's Bed and Breakfast:* 40 Hutchinson St, Edge Hill; (07) 4053 3231. *Lake Placid Tourist Park:* Lake Placid Rd, Lake Placid; (07) 4039 2509.

Great Barrier Reef Take a tour, charter a boat or fly to see some of the spectacular sights just offshore. Michaelmas and Upolo cays to the north-east are important sites for ground-nesting seabirds. The surrounding waters are excellent for reef swimming. You can also take a trip to the outer Barrier Reef, which is known for its spectacular underwater scenes and huge variety of marine life. For tours contact visitor centre.

Fitzroy Island A low-key destination with a national park, white coral beaches and magnificent flora and fauna for bushwalking, diving and snorkelling. To the east are impressive snorkelling sites at Welcome and Sharkfin bays. Cabins and hostel-style accommodation (maximum 160 people) and camping (maximum 20 people) are available; 23 km E.

Green Island To the north-east is a true coral cay covered with thick, tropical vegetation. The surrounding reef is home to magnificent tropical fish; they can be seen from a glass-bottom boat, in the underwater observatory or by snorkelling or helmet diving. This popular daytrip destination has a small resort (maximum 90 people); 27 km NE.

Tjapukai Aboriginal Cultural Park The group began as an Aboriginal dance company in 1987, but the demand for more cultural information prompted the move to this large park. Four theatres, both live and film, illustrate the history and culture of the rainforest people of Tropical North Queensland. Learn skills such as bush medicine and spear throwing on a day tour or experience the theatre of an Aboriginal ceremony in the 'Tjapukai By Night' experience; open daily 9am–5pm, evening shows 7pm–10pm; Cairns Western Arterial Rd, Caravonica; (07) 4042 9999; 11 km NW.

Beaches: incredible 26 km of beaches extending from Machans Beach on north bank of Barron River, 9 km N, north to Ellis Beach. *Skyrail Rainforest Cableway*: spectacular gondola ride through rainforest to Kuranda; open daily; Cnr Cook Hwy and Cairns Western Arterial Rd, Smithfield, (07) 4038 1555; 11 km N. *Bungee jumping*: choose from a variety of jumps and other thrills in the rainforest; daily 10am–5pm; 5 McGregor Rd, Smithfield, or free transport from Cairns; (07) 4057 7188;13 km N. *Crystal Cascades*: walks by cascades and a secluded freshwater swimming hole; end of Redlynch Valley; 18 km SW. *Lake Morris and Copperlode Dam*: walking tracks; 19 km SW. *Barron and Freshwater valleys*: bushwalking, hiking, whitewater rafting and camping to the west and north-west of Cairns; contact visitor centre for details. *Safaris*: 4WD to Cape York and the Gulf Country; contact visitor centre for details.

TOWNS NEARBY: Kuranda 18 km, Gordonvale 20 km, Palm Cove 22 km, Mareeba 37 km, Yungaburra 43 km

past heritage buildings; brochure from visitor centre. *Bilby Tours:* one of Australia's most rare and endangered animals, bilbies are captively bred in Charleville. Get up-close and personal with these marsupials on the night tour; details from visitor centre.

Market: Historic House Museum; 1st Sat each month. *Charleville Show:* May. *Bilby Festival:* food, music and celebration of National Bilby Day; Sept.

Cobb & Co Caravan Park: 1 Ridgeway St; (07) 4654 1053. *Evening Star Tourist Park:* 818 Adavale Rd; (07) 4654 2430.

Tregole National Park This semi-arid national park has a vulnerable and fragile ecosystem. It is largely made up of ooline forest – rainforest species dating back to the Ice Age. Follow the 2.1 km circuit track to see the diverse vegetation and spectacular birds of the park. (07) 4654 1255; 99 km E via Morven.

Monument: marks the spot where Ross and Keith Smith landed with engine trouble on the first London–Sydney flight; 19 km NW.

TOWNS NEARBY: Tambo 169 km, Mitchell 173 km, Cunnamulla 192 km, Quilpie 198 km, Eulo 228 km

Charters Towers

Pop. 7978
Map ref. 610 F2

74 Mosman St; (07) 4761 5533; www.charterstowers.qld.gov.au

95.9 Hot FM, 630 AM ABC North QLD

Charters Towers is in the Burdekin Basin south-west of Townsville. The town's gold rush began on 25 December 1871 when Aboriginal horse-boy Jupiter discovered gold while looking for lost horses. He brought gold-laden quartz to his employer, Hugh Mosman, who rode to Ravenswood to register the claim, and the gold rush was on. Between 1872 and 1916 Charters Towers produced ore worth £25 million. At the height of the gold rush it was Queensland's second largest city and was commonly referred to as 'The World' because of its cosmopolitan population. This rich history can be seen in the preserved streetscapes of 19th- and 20th-century architecture, with many beautiful buildings including the Bank of Commerce, now restored as the New World Theatre Complex. To the north-west of Charters Towers is the 120-kilometre Great Basalt Wall, a lava wall created from the Toomba basalt flow.

Ghosts of Gold Heritage Trail This informative tour reveals the rich history of the town in the district known as 'One Square Mile'. Over 60 heritage-listed buildings are in the precinct. Of particular interest are the re-created workings of the Stock

 RADIO STATIONS IN TOWN WHAT'S ON WHERE TO EAT WHERE TO STAY NEARBY

QUEENSLAND

Exchange in Mosman St; the once heavily mined Towers Hill (1.5 km w) with interpretive walking trails and a film screening at night; and the Venus Gold Battery in Millchester Rd, an old gold-processing plant where the 'ghosts' come alive. Starts in the orientation centre behind the visitor centre.

Charters Towers Folk Museum: local historical memorabilia; Mosman St. *Civic Club:* once a gentlemen's club, this remarkable building (1900) still contains the original billiard tables; Ryan St. *Rotary Lookout:* panoramic views over region; Fraser St.

National Trust Markets: Stock Exchange Arcade; 1st and 3rd Sun each month. *Showgrounds Markets:* Cnr Mary and Show sts; 2nd Sun each month. *Goldfield Ashes Cricket Carnival:* Jan. *Rodeo:* Easter. *Ten Days in the Towers:* festival including music and bush poets; Apr–May. *Country Music Festival:* May Day weekend. *Charters Towers Show:* July.

Aussie Outback Oasis Cabin & Van Village: 76 Dr George Ellis Dr; (07) 4787 8722. *Charters Towers Tourist Park:* 37 Mt Leyshon Rd; (07) 4787 7944. *Dalrymple Tourist Van Park:* 24 Dalrymple Rd; (07) 4787 1121.

Dalrymple National Park This small national park on the Burdekin River comprises mainly woodland and is an important area for native animals including rock wallabies and sugar gliders. A highlight is the 4 million-year-old solidified lava wall, the Great Basalt Wall, parts of which are accessible from this park. The site of the old Dalrymple township is also of interest. Contact the ranger before setting out on any walks; (07) 4722 5224; 46 km N.

Greenvale: near the Gregory Development Rd with a roadhouse, caravan park, golf course and the well-known Three Rivers Hotel, made famous by Slim Dusty's song of the same name; 209 km NW. *Burdekin Falls Dam:* recreation area with barramundi fishing; 165 km SE via Ravenswood. *Blackwood National Park:* a woodland park of undulating hills and stony ridges. See the Belyando blackwood trees that give the park its name, and walk on fire trails to discover the park's interesting birdlife including squatter pigeons and speckled warblers; (07) 4722 5224; 180 km S.

TOWNS NEARBY: Ravenswood 66 km, Townsville 106 km, Ayr 132 km, Ingham 159 km, Cardwell 202 km

Childers

Pop. 1352
Map ref. 603 C4 | 604 F11 | 609 M4

i Palace Hotel (Childers Memorial), 72 Churchill St; (07) 4126 1994.

 102.5 Breeze FM, 855 AM ABC Wide Bay

Childers is a picturesque National Trust town south of Bundaberg, part of the state's sugarcane belt. With leafy streets and a lovely outlook over the surrounding valleys, the town's history has been blighted by fire. One ravaged the town in 1902 (though many of the heritage buildings survived) and another engulfed a backpacker's hostel in 2000, tragically killing 15 people and making international news. A memorial to those lost in this fire stands in Churchill Street. Thankfully life has returned to normal in Childers and the flow of backpackers on the fruit-picking trail is as strong as ever.

Pharmaceutical Museum: collection of memorabilia including leather-bound prescription books and Aboriginal wares; open 8.45am–4.30pm Mon–Fri, 8.30am–12pm Sat; Churchill St. *Historical complex:* area of historic buildings including school, cottage and locomotive; Taylor St. *Baker's Military and Memorabilia Museum:* 16 000 items on

display covering all the major wars, including uniforms and communications equipment; closed Sun (open by appt); Ashby La. *Childers Art Gallery:* Churchill St. *Snakes Downunder:* informative exhibits on native snakes; open 9am–3pm, closed Wed; Lucketts Rd. *Historic Childers:* self-guide town walk past historic buildings; highlight is the Old Butcher's Shop (1896) in Churchill St.

Village Market: historical society; 3rd Sun each month. *Festival of Cultures:* a week of celebrations also includes workshops by visiting artists and performers; July.

Mango Hill Cottages Bed & Breakfast: 8 Mango Hill Dr; (07) 4126 1311. *Burrum River Caravan Park:* 141 Old Bruce Hwy, Howard; (07) 4129 4859. *Childers Tourist Park & Camp:* 111 Stockyard Rd, North Isis; (07) 4126 1371. *R&R @ Woodgate Beach:* 7 Snapper Crt, Woodgate; (07) 4126 8767. *Woodgate Beach Tourist Park:* 88 Esplanade, Woodgate; (07) 4126 8802.

Flying High Bird Habitat The native vegetation here is home to 600 bird species. Follow the boardwalk tracks to see the many Australian parrots and finches. Cnr Bruce Hwy and Old Creek Rd, Apple Creek; 5 km N.

Buxton and Walkers Point: unspoiled fishing villages to the east. *Woodgate:* coastal town to the north-east with 16 km beach. Access to Burrum Coast National Park is from here; *see Bundaberg. Good Night Scrub National Park:* 27 km W; *see Gin Gin.*

TOWNS NEARBY: Biggenden 38 km, Bundaberg 42 km, Gin Gin 42 km, Maryborough 55 km, Hervey Bay 60 km

Chillagoe

Pop. 223
Map ref. 606 A3 | 613 J6

i The Hub, 23 Queen St; (07) 4094 7111; www.chillagoehub.com.au

 720 AM ABC Far North QLD

Chillagoe is a small outback town west of Cairns and the Atherton Tableland. Once a thriving mining town after silver and copper deposits were found in 1887, the town was practically deserted after the smelter closed in 1940. Chillagoe's history and the well-preserved Aboriginal rock art and limestone caves in the area make it a popular spot with visitors.

The Hub This major interpretive centre is constructed from local materials including marble and copper. Informative displays cover the geographical history of the local landscape (dating back 2 billion years), the town's mining and pioneering past and the region's Aboriginal heritage. Queen St; (07) 4094 7111.

Heritage Museum: displays on local history and relics of old mining days; Hill St. *Historic cemetery:* headstones from early settlement; Railway Line Rd. *Historical walks:* self-guide or guided walks taking in the old State Smelter and disused marble quarry just south of town; details from visitor centre.

Big Weekend and Rodeo: May. *Annual Wheelbarrow Race:* May. *Country Music Festival:* July.

Chillagoe–Mungana Caves National Park The impressive rugged limestone outcrops and magnificent caves of this park, south of town, are studied by scientists world-wide. The cave system was originally an ancient coral reef and is home to a wide variety of bats. Fossilised bones, including those of a giant kangaroo, have been discovered in the caves. Guided tours only;

[CHILLAGOE] OLD SMELTER

tickets from The Hub. Above ground are magnificent Aboriginal rock paintings at Balancing Rock. (07) 4046 6600; 7 km s.

Mungana: Aboriginal rock paintings at the Archways. Also a historic cemetery; 16 km w. *Almaden:* small town where cattle own the main street; 30 km SE. *4WD self-guide adventure trek:* mud maps and clues provided; details from visitor centre. *Tag-along tours:* full- and half-day tours visiting Aboriginal sites, marble quarries and other places; details from visitor centre.

TOWNS NEARBY: Herberton 95 km, Mareeba 98 km, Atherton 102 km, Mount Surprise 112 km, Yungaburra 114 km

Chinchilla

Pop. 3684
Map ref. 609 J7

 Warrego Hwy; (07) 4668 9564; www.chinchilla.org.au

97.1 Breeze FM, 747 AM ABC Southern QLD

Chinchilla is a prosperous town in the western Darling Downs. Explorer Ludwig Leichhardt named the area in 1844 after the local Aboriginal name for the native cypress pines, 'jinchilla' – there are still many in town. Today Chinchilla is known as the 'melon capital' of Australia as it produces around 25 per cent of the country's watermelons.

Historical Museum: a varied collection of memorabilia including steam engines, a replica 1910 sawmill and a slab cottage. Also an excellent display of local petrified wood known as 'Chinchilla Red'; open 9am–4pm Wed–Sun; Villiers St. *Pioneer Cemetery:* headstones tell early history. Also a monument to Ludwig Leichhardt; Warrego Hwy.

Melon Festival: odd-numbered years, Feb. *Market:* Warrego Hwy; Easter Sat. *Rotary May Day Celebrations:* May. *Chinchilla Show:* May. *Polocrosse Carnival:* Sept. *Grand Father Clock Campdraft:* Oct. *Mardi Gras:* Nov. *Chinchilla Cup:* Dec.

Chinchilla Caravan Park & Motor Inn: Wondai Rd; (07) 4662 7314.

Cactoblastis Memorial Hall: dedicated to the insect introduced from South America to eradicate the prickly pear cactus; Boonarga, 8 km E. *Fossicking:* for petrified wood at nearby properties; licences and details from visitor centre. *Fishing:* good spots include Charleys Creek and the Condamine River; details from visitor centre. *Chinchilla Weir:* popular spot for boating

and waterskiing, plus freshwater fishing for golden perch and jewfish; 10 km s.

TOWNS NEARBY: Miles 45 km, Dalby 80 km, Kingaroy 122 km, Oakey 133 km, Nanango 137 km

Clermont

Pop. 1851
Map ref. 605 B12 | 610 H9

 Cnr Herschel and Karmoo sts; (07) 4983 4755; www.isaac.qld.gov.au

102.1 4HI FM, 1548 AM ABC Capricornia

Clermont is in the central highlands south-west of Mackay. It was established over 130 years ago after the discovery of gold at Nelson's Gully. At first the settlement was at Hood's Lagoon, but was moved to higher ground after a major flood in 1916 in which 63 people died. To the east of Clermont are the prominent cone-shaped mountains of Peak Range National Park. The Wolfgang Peak between Clermont and Mackay is particularly spectacular.

Hood's Lagoon and Centenary Park Walk the boardwalks in this picturesque setting to see the colourful birdlife. The park has interesting memorials and monuments that include the Sister Mary MacKillop grotto, an Aboriginal monument and a war memorial. The tree marker at the flood memorial plaque demonstrates how high the water rose. Access via Lime St.

Railway Wagon Murals: paintings on 4 original wagons depict industries within the Belyando Shire; Hershel St. *The Stump:* memorial to the 1916 flood; Cnr Drummond and Capricorn sts.

Rodeo: Apr. *Clermont Show:* May. *Campdraft:* June. *Gold and Coal Festival:* Aug. *Country Music Festival:* Oct.

Cemetery: headstones dating back to 1860s and mass grave of 1916 flood victims; 2.5 km NE. *Clermont Museum and Heritage Park:* museum exhibits historic artefacts and machinery, including the steam engine used to shift the town after flood and historic buildings, such as the old Masonic lodge, with displays of local family histories; open daily, times vary; (07) 4983 3311; 4 km NW. *Remnants of Copperfield:* old coppermining town with museum in original Copperfield store, chimneystack, and cemetery containing 19th-century graves of coppersminers; 5 km s. *Theresa Creek Dam:* popular spot for waterskiing, sailboarding and fishing (permit required). Bushwalks nearby; off Peakvale Rd; 17 km sw. *Blair Athol open-cut mine:* free half-day tour to see the largest seam of steaming coal in the world; departs from Clermont Visitor Centre; Blair Athol; 23 km NW. *Blackwood National Park:* 187 km NW; *see Charters Towers. Fossicking for gold:* obtain licence and fossicking kit to start the search in nearby area; details from visitor centre.

TOWNS NEARBY: Emerald 94 km, Moranbah 100 km, Springsure 150 km, Blackwater 153 km, Sarina 225 km

Clifton

Pop. 1065
Map ref. 609 L10

 Council offices, 70 King St; (07) 4697 4222; www.clifton.qld.gov.au

91.9 CFM, 747 AM ABC Southern QLD

Clifton is south of Toowoomba in the fertile agricultural lands of the Darling Downs. The town's charming street facades have been a popular backdrop for many Australian movies, including

QUEENSLAND

the epic television adaptation of *The Thorn Birds*. The town is a vision of colour during the renowned annual Rose and Iris Show.

Historical Museum: in the old butter factory, with displays of early implements and farm life; open 1st and 3rd Sun each month; King St. **Alister Clark Rose Garden:** largest Queensland collection of these roses; Edward St.

Clifton Show: Apr. **Country Week:** includes the Rose and Iris Show and horseracing; Oct.

Spring Creek Caravan Park: New England Hwy; (07) 4697 3397.

Nobby This small town provided inspiration to writer Arthur Hoey Davis (Steele Rudd), author of *On Our Selection* and creator of the famous Dad and Dave characters. Rudd's Pub (1893) has a museum of pioneering memorabilia. Nearby is the burial site of Sister Kenny along with a memorial and museum dedicated to her – she was renowned for her unorthodox method of treating poliomyelitis. 8 km N.

Darling Downs Zoo Queensland's newest zoo is situated in the serene countryside where you can view native and exotic animals from Africa, South America and Asia. The zoo has a shady picnic area as well as barbecue facilities and a small kiosk. Open weekends, public and school holidays, or by appt (for large groups); Gatton–Clifton Rd; (07) 4696 4107; 10 km E.

Leyburn: holds the Historic Race Car Sprints in Aug; 30 km W.

TOWNS NEARBY: Allora 13 km, Warwick 34 km, Toowoomba 42 km, Gatton 55 km, Laidley 58 km

Cloncurry

Pop. 2385
Map ref. 615 F11 | 616 H3

ⓘ Mary Kathleen Memorial Park and Museum, McIlwraith St (Flinders Hwy); (07) 4742 1361; www.cloncurry.qld.gov.au

102.5 Hot FM, 567 AM ABC North West QLD

Cloncurry is an important mining town in the Gulf Savannah region. In 1861 John McKinlay, leading a search for Burke and Wills, reported traces of copper in the area. Six years later, pastoralist Ernest Henry discovered the first copper lodes. During World War I Cloncurry was the centre of a copper boom and the largest source of the mineral in Australia. Copper prices slumped postwar and a pastoral industry was developed. Today main industries include grazing, coppermining and goldmining. The town's interesting history extends to aviation as well. Qantas was conceived here – the original hangar can still be seen at the airport – and the town became the first base for the famous Royal Flying Doctor Service in 1928.

John Flynn Place This complex includes the RFDS Museum, with history on the service and memorabilia including the first RFDS aircraft and an original Traegar pedal wireless. There is also the Fred McKay Art Gallery, with changing exhibits of local art, the Alfred Traegar Cultural Centre and the Alan Vickers Outdoor Theatre. Open 8am–4.30pm Mon–Fri, 9am–3pm Sat–Sun (May–Sept); Cnr Daintree and King sts.

Mary Kathleen Memorial Park: with buildings from abandoned uranium mining town of Mary Kathleen including Old Police Station and Town Office – now a museum with historic items such as Robert O'Hara Burke's water bottle, local Aboriginal artefacts and a comprehensive rock, mineral and gem collection. Visitor information centre is also on-site; McIlwraith St. **Shire hall:** restored 1939 building; Scarr St. **Cemeteries:** varied cultural

background of Cloncurry can be seen in the 3 cemeteries: Cloncurry Old Cemetery, including the grave of Dame Mary Gilmore (Sir Hudson Fyshe Dr); Afghan Cemetery (part of Cloncurry Old Cemetery); and Chinese Cemetery (Flinders Hwy). **Original Qantas hangar:** airport; Sir Hudson Fyshe Dr. **Historic buildings:** including the post office, Brodie Hardware Store and the Post Office Hotel; brochure from visitor centre.

Markets: Florence Park, Scarr St; 1st Sat each month. Mary Kathleen Park, McIlwraith St; 4th Sun each month. **Cloncurry Show:** June. **Stockman's Challenge and Campdraft:** night rodeo; July. **Rockhana:** mineral and gem festival; July. **Merry Muster Rodeo:** July/Aug. **Art Show:** Sept. **Battle of the Mines:** rugby league carnival; Oct. **Cloncurry Cup:** Oct.

Cloncurry Caravan Park Oasis: Flinders Hwy; (07) 4742 1313. **Discovery Holiday Parks – Cloncurry:** Flinders Hwy; (07) 4742 2300.

Rotary Lookout: over Cloncurry and the river; Mt Isa Hwy; 2 km W. **Chinamen Creek Dam:** peaceful area with abundant birdlife; 3 km W. **Ernest Henry Copper and Gold Mine:** tours available. Departs from Mary Kathleen Park; 29 km NE. **Burke and Wills cairn:** near Corella River; 43 km W. **Kajabbi:** town holds Yabby Races in May; 77 km NW. **Kuridala:** this one-time mining town is now a ghost town. Explore the ruins including the old cemetery; 88 km S. **Fossicking:** for amethysts and other gemstones; details from visitor centre.

TOWNS NEARBY: Mount Isa 106 km, Julia Creek 128 km, Kynuna 175 km

Cooktown

Pop. 1339
Map ref. 613 L3

ⓘ Nature's Powerhouse, Cooktown Botanic Gardens, Finch Bay Rd; (07) 4069 6004 or 1800 174 895; www.cook.qld.gov.au

105.7 ABC FM Far North QLD

Cooktown is the last main town before the wilderness that is Cape York. In 1770, Captain Cook beached the *Endeavour* here for repairs after running aground on the Great Barrier Reef. Cooktown was founded more than 100 years later after gold was discovered on the Palmer River. It became the gold-rush port with 37 hotels and a transient population of some 18 000, including 6000 Chinese. Nearby are some of the most rugged and remote national parks in Australia. They form part of the Wet Tropics World Heritage Area and are a special experience for today's intrepid explorers.

James Cook Museum Housed in the old convent school (1888), this museum documents Aboriginal life prior to European settlement, Cook's voyages and the 1870s gold-rush past. Relics include the anchor from the *Endeavour*; Helen St.

Botanic Gardens: these are the oldest botanic gardens in Queensland, with native, European and exotic plants. The 'Cooktown Interpretive Centre: Nature's Powerhouse' has botanical and wildlife illustrations, and there are also walking trails to Cherry Tree and Finch bays; Walker St. **Historic cemetery:** documents the varied cultural heritage of Cooktown and includes the grave of tutor, early immigrant and heroine Mary Watson; Boundary Rd. **Chinese shrine:** to many who died on the goldfields; near cemetery. **Cooktown Wharf:** dates back to 1880s and is an excellent spot for fishing. **The Milibi Wall:** collage of traditional art by local Aboriginal people; near wharf. **Fishing:** spanish mackerel and barramundi at the wharf.

Walking trails: plenty around the town and outlying areas, including the Scenic Rim and Wharf and Foreshore Walk; details from visitor centre.

Market: Lions Park; Sat. *Discovery Festival:* re-enactment of Cook's landing with Aboriginal performances and various markets as part of the celebrations; during the Queen's Birthday long weekend, June. *Cooktown Races:* July. *Art Festival:* Aug. *Agricultural Show:* Aug. *Wallaby Creek Festival (Rossville):* music festival; Sept.

BIG4 Cooktown Holiday Park: 31–41 Charlotte St; (07) 4069 5417. *Cooktown Caravan Park:* 14 Hope St; (07) 4069 5536. *Cooktown Orchid Travellers Park:* Cnr Charlotte and Walker sts; (07) 4069 6400. *Cooktown Peninsula Caravan Park:* 64 Howard St; (07) 4069 5107.

Lizard Island National Park Comprises 6 islands to the north-east of Cooktown surrounded by the blue waters and coral reefs of the northern Great Barrier Reef. Four of the islands are important seabird nesting sites. Lizard Island is a resort island popular for sailing and fishing. Also on offer is snorkelling in the giant clam gardens of Watsons Bay. Walk to Cooks Look for a spectacular view. There are 11 species of lizard here, and green and loggerhead turtles nest in late spring. Regular flights depart from Cairns; charter flights depart from Cairns and Cooktown; charter or private boat hire is available at Cooktown; (07) 4069 5777 (use same contact number for all national parks below); 92 km NE.

Endeavour River National Park: just north of town is this park of diverse landscapes, including coastal dunes, mangrove forests and catchment areas of the Endeavour River. Most of the park is accessible only by boat (ramps at Cooktown); southern vehicle access is via Starcke St, Marton. *Black Mountain National Park:* impressive mountain range of granite boulders and a refuge for varied and threatened wildlife; Cooktown Developmental Rd; (07) 4069 5777; 25 km s. *Helenvale:* small town with historic Lions Den Hotel (est. 1875) and rodeo in June; 30 km s. *Rossville:* town with markets every 2nd Sat and Wallaby Creek Folk Festival at Home Rule Rainforest Lodge in Sept; 38 km s. *Cedar Bay National Park:* this remote coastal park is an attractive mix of rainforest, beaches and fringing reefs, with a variety of wildlife including the rare Bennett's tree kangaroo. Walk on the old donkey track once used by tin miners (remains of tin workings can be seen). Access by boat or by the walking track, which starts at Home Rule Rainforest Lodge, Rossville, 38 km s. *Elim Beach and the Coloured Sands:* spectacular beach with white silica sandhills and surrounding heathlands. The Coloured Sands are found 400 m along the beach (Aboriginal land, permit required from Hope Vale Community Centre); 65 km N. *Cape Melville National Park:* this rugged park on the Cape York Peninsula has spectacular coastal scenery. Much of the plant life is rare, including the foxtail palm. Visitors must be self-sufficient; 4WD access only in dry weather; southern access via Starcke homestead, western access via Kalpower Crossing in Rinyirru (Lakefield) National Park (CYPAL); 140 km NW. *Flinders Group National Park:* comprising 7 continental islands in Princess Charlotte Bay. There are 2 self-guide trails taking in bushfoods and Aboriginal rock-art sites on Stanley Island. Access by charter or private boat or sea plane; 195 km NW. *Sportfishing safaris:* to nearby waterways; details from visitor centre. *Guurrbi Aboriginal Tours:* full- and half-day tours of Aboriginal rock-art

sites and informative history of bush tucker and traditional medicine; details from visitor centre. *Bicentennial National Trail:* 5000 km trail that runs from Cooktown to Healesville in Victoria, for walkers, bike riders and horseriders. It is possible to do just a section of trail; details from visitor centre.

Travellers note: *Before driving to remote areas check road conditions and restrictions with Queensland Parks and Wildlife Service, 5 Webber Espl, Cooktown, (07) 4069 5777.*

TOWNS NEARBY: Daintree 87 km, Laura 87 km, Mossman 110 km, Port Douglas 115 km, Palm Cove 148 km

Crows Nest

Pop. 1443
Map ref. 609 L8

 Hampton Visitor Information Centre, 8623 New England Hwy, Hampton (12 km S); (07) 4697 9066 or 1800 009 066; www.crowsnest.info

100.7 C FM, 747 AM ABC Southern QLD

On the western slopes of the Great Dividing Range north of Toowoomba is the small town of Crows Nest. It was named after Jimmy Crow, a Kabi-Kabi Aboriginal man who made his home in a hollow tree near the present police station. He was an invaluable source of directions for passing bullock teams staying overnight in the area. A memorial to Crow can be found in Centenary Park.

Carbethon Folk Museum and Pioneer Village: many interesting old buildings and over 20 000 items of memorabilia documenting the history of the shire; open 10am–3pm Thurs–Sun; Thallon St. *Bullocky's Rest and Applegum Walk:* a 1.5 km track follows the creeks to Hartmann Park and a lookout over Pump Hole. Visit in late winter to see the beautiful wildflowers; entry from New England Hwy.

Village Markets: arts, crafts and local produce; 1st Sun each month. *Crows Nest Day:* children's worm races, crow calling competitions and battle of the band concert; Oct.

Crows Nest Caravan Park: New England Hwy; (07) 4698 1269.

Crows Nest National Park This popular park features a variety of landscapes, including granite outcrops and eucalypt forest. The wildlife is spectacular: see the platypus in the creek and the brush-tailed rock wallabies on the rocky cliffs. A steep track from the creek leads to an excellent lookout over Crows Nest Falls; follow this further to Koonin Lookout for spectacular views over the gorge, known locally as the Valley of Diamonds. (07) 4699 4333; 6 km E (look for sign to Valley of Diamonds).

Holland Wines: offers a vast collection of exquisite wines: 5 km N. *Bunnyconnellen Olive Grove and Vineyard:* perfect getaway for couples with rooms available. Enjoy the magnificent wines and gourmet food; open weekends; Swain Rd, off New England Hwy, 10 km N. *Lake Cressbrook:* set among picturesque hills is this excellent spot for windsurfing and boating. Fish the lake for silver perch; 17 km E. *Ravensbourne National Park:* a small park comprising remnant rainforest and wet eucalypt forest with over 80 species of birds, including the black-breasted button-quail that can be seen feeding on the rainforest floor on the Cedar Block track. Many bushwalks start at Blackbean picnic area; Esk–Hampton Rd; (07) 4699 4333; 25 km SE. *Beutel's Lookout:* picnic area with scenic views across the Brisbane Valley; adjacent to Ravensbourne National Park; 25 km SE. *Goombungee:* historic

QUEENSLAND

town with museum. Famous for running rural ironman and ironwoman competitions on Australia Day; 32 km w.

TOWNS NEARBY: Toowoomba 35 km, Esk 37 km, Oakey 38 km, Gatton 40 km, Laidley 53 km

Croydon
Pop. 255
Map ref. 612 F8

 Samwell St; (07) 4745 6125; www.croydon.qld.gov.au

105.9 ABC FM Far North QLD

Croydon is a small town on the grassland plains of the Gulf Savannah. It marks the eastern terminus for the Gulflander train service, which leaves each Thursday morning for Normanton. The train line was established in the late 1800s to service Croydon's booming gold industry. Many original buildings dating from 1887 to 1897, and classified by the National Trust and Australian Heritage Commission, have been restored to the splendour of the town's goldmining days.

Historical precinct: many restored buildings bring the rich history of Croydon to life. Highlights include the old courthouse with original furniture, and the old hospital featuring original hospital documents. *Outdoor Museum:* displays mining machinery from the age of steam; Samwell St. *Old Police Precinct and Gaol:* historic documents and access to gaol cells; Samwell St. *General Store and Museum:* restored store in the old ironmongers shop; Sircom St.

Poddy Dodger Festival: June.

Mining Museum: interesting display of early mining machinery including battery stamper; 1 km N. *Historic cemetery:* includes old Chinese gravestones; 2 km s. *Chinese temple site:* Heritage-listed archaeological site preserving 50 years of Chinese settlement that followed the gold discoveries of the 1880s. Take the Heritage Trail to see how the Chinese lived; on road to Lake Belmore. *Lake Belmore:* one of many sites for birdwatching, along with beautiful picnic areas and barbecue facilities. Also swimming, waterskiing and fishing (limits apply); 5 km N.

TOWNS NEARBY: Normanton 137 km, Karumba 169 km, Mount Surprise 219 km

Cunnamulla
Pop. 1218
Map ref. 608 A9 | 619 N9

 Centenary Park, Jane St; (07) 4655 8470; www.paroo.info

96.5 Triple C FM, 603 AM ABC Western QLD

Cunnamulla is on the Warrego River, north of the New South Wales border. It is the biggest wool-loading station on the Queensland railway network, with two million sheep in the area. Explorers Sir Thomas Mitchell and Edmund Kennedy were the first European visitors, arriving in 1846 and 1847 respectively, and by 1879 the town was thriving with regular Cobb & Co. services to the west. In 1880, Joseph Wells held up the local bank but could not find his escape horse. Locals bailed him up in a tree that is now known as the Robber's Tree and can be found in Stockyard Street. The wetland birdlife in the area, particularly the black swans, brolgas and pelicans, is spectacular.

Cunnamulla Fella Centre Art Gallery and Museum: gallery showcases different artist exhibitions throughout the year, while the musem displays the rich history and heritage of the town and wider Paroo shire; Jane St. *Yupunyah Tree:* planted by Princess Anne; Cnr Louise and Stockyard sts. *Outback Botanic*

Gardens and Herbarium: Matilda Hwy. *Outback Dreaming Arts and Crafts:* exhibits and sales of local Aboriginal art; Stockyard St. *The Heritage Trail:* discover the days of the late 1880s on this self-guide trail; details from visitor centre.

Cunnamulla Outback Masters Games: odd-numbered years, Apr. *Horseracing:* Aug. *Cunnamulla Festival and Bullride Championships:* Nov.

Wyandra: small town featuring Powerhouse Museum and Heritage Trail; 100 km N. *Noorama:* remote sheep station that holds picnic races each Apr; 110 km SE. *Culgoa Floodplain National Park:* 195 km SE; *see St George.*

TOWNS NEARBY: Eulo 64 km, Charleville 192 km, Quilpie 213 km, Bourke (NSW) 226 km, Brewarrina (NSW) 239 km

Daintree
Pop. 78
Map ref. 607 D2 | 613 L4

 5 Stewart St; (07) 4098 6133; www.daintreevillage.asn.au

639 AM ABC Far North QLD

The unspoiled township of Daintree lies in the tropical rainforest of Far North Queensland, at the heart of the Daintree River catchment basin surrounded by the McDowall Ranges. Daintree began as a logging town in the 1870s. Now tourism is the major industry with the Daintree River and World Heritage rainforest nearby. Saltwater crocodiles can be seen in the mangrove-lined creeks and tributaries of the Daintree River.

Daintree Timber Gallery: hand-crafted pieces from local woods exhibited and sold. Also displays showcasing local history, including logging past; Stewart St. *Eliza's Rainforest Gallery:* handmade pottery of pixies, elves and gnomes; Stewart St.

Julaymba: elegant, contemporary bush flavours; Daintree Eco Lodge & Spa, 20 Daintree Rd; (07) 4098 6100 or 1800 808 010. *Croc Eye Cafe:* try the crocodile dishes; 3–5 Stewart St; (07) 4098 6229.

Red Mill House: 11 Stewart St; (07) 4098 6233.

 Daintree National Park Arguably Australia's most beautiful and famous rainforest. The lush tangle of green protected within it is an incredible remnant from the days of Gondwana, forming part of the Wet Tropics World Heritage Area. This park, which is split into 3 distinct sections – Mossman Gorge, Cape Tribulation and Snapper Island – will dazzle visitors with its diverse landscapes, which, apart from beautiful rainforest, include canopies of sprawling fan palms, deserted mangrove-lined beaches and boulder-strewn gorges. The Mossman Gorge section takes visitors into the rainforest's green and shady heart via an easy 2.7 km walk to the Mossman River. The Cape Tribulation section is a rich mix of coastal rainforest, mangroves, swamp and heath.

Daintree Discovery Centre: informative displays for visitors; a boardwalk and aerial walkway passes through the rainforest canopy; 11 km SE. *Wonga Belle Orchid Gardens:* 3.5 ha of lush gardens; 17 km SE. *Cape Tribulation:* spectacular beaches and reefs. Reef tours and horseriding on beach can be arranged at visitor centre or Mason's Shop in Cape Tribulation; for details call (07) 4098 0070; access via Daintree River cable ferry (car ferry runs 6–12am). *River cruises:* to see the saltwater crocodiles and plentiful birdlife; details from visitor centre. *Horseriding tours:* in Cape Tribulation; (07) 4041 3244.

[DAINTREE] RAINFOREST CANOPY, DAINTREE NATIONAL PARK

Travellers note: *Beware of estuarine crocodiles that live in the sea and estuaries; never cross tidal creeks at high tide, swim in creeks, prepare food at water's edge or camp close to deep waterholes. Beware of marine stingers between Oct and Mar.*

TOWNS NEARBY: Mossman 24 km, Port Douglas 30 km, Palm Cove 66 km, Kuranda 72 km, Mareeba 83 km

Dalby

Pop. 9775
Map ref. 609 K8

i Thomas Jack Park, cnr Drayton and Condamine sts; (07) 4679 4461; www.wdrc.qld.gov.au

89.9 FM Dalby Community Radio, 747 AM ABC Southern QLD

Sitting at the crossroads of the Warrego, Moonie, Condamine and Bunya highways, Dalby is conveniently linked to all of Australia's capital cities. It was a small rural town until the soldier resettlement program after World War II in which the population influx allowed the surrounding agricultural industry to thrive. It is now a relaxed country town with uncluttered landscapes, charismatic local pubs and home-grown produce.

Thomas Jack Park: beautifully landscaped park with playground equipment and tranquil lagoon; Cnr Drayton and Condamine sts. *Cultural and Administration Centre:* regional art gallery and cinema; Drayton St. *Pioneer Park Museum:* comprises historic buildings, household and agricultural items and a craft shop; Black St. *The Crossing:* an obelisk marks the spot where explorer Henry Dennis camped in 1841; Edward St. *Historic cairn:* pays homage to the cactoblastis, the Argentinean caterpillar that controlled prickly pear in the 1920s; Myall Creek picnic area, Marble St. *Myall Creek Walk:* walk along banks of Myall Creek to see varied birdlife. *Heritage walk:* self-guide walk provides insight into town's history; brochure from visitor centre.

Cotton on to Energy Festival: 4-day festival; Mar. *Country Race Days:* Newmarket Races; Mar. *Picnic Races:* May. Saints *Race Day:* July. *Plough Inn Cup:* Aug. *Dalby Show:* Apr. *Spring Art Show:* Sept. *Spring Garden Week:* Sept.

Glasbys Caravan Park: 82 Moffatt St, Kaimkillenbun; (07) 4663 4228. *Jandowae Accommodation Park:* 104 High St, Jandowae; (07) 4668 5071.

Lake Birdwater Conservation Park The 350 ha lake is an important breeding ground for waterfowl. There are over 240 species of bird that can be seen from the short walks around the lake. Waterskiing and boating are popular on the main body of the lake when it is full (permit required); 29 km sw.

Darling Downs wine region The Darling Downs are better known for mainstream agriculture such as grains, cotton and sheep, although vineyards are beginning to pierce a few small holes in this tradition. Jimbour Wines produces red, white and fortified wines, and has a homestead dating from 1876. Rimfire Vineyards makes a unique wine called 1893 from an unidentified white grape that dates back to that year. Preston Peak is a popular tourist destination.

Historic Jimbour House: attractive French homestead, formal gardens and boutique winery; 29 km N. *Bell:* small town at the base of Bunya Mountains with traditional arts and crafts stores; 41 km NW. *Cecil Plains:* cotton town with historic murals and Cecil Plains Homestead. Also a popular spot for canoeing down Condamine River; 42 km S. *Bunya Mountains National Park:* 63 km NE; *see Kingaroy.*

TOWNS NEARBY: Oakey 53 km, Crows Nest 79 km, Chinchilla 80 km, Toowoomba 80 km, Kingaroy 91 km

Emerald

Pop. 10 999
Map ref. 611 I10

i Clermont St; (07) 4982 4142; www.emerald.qld.gov.au

96.3 4EEE FM, 1548 AM ABC Capricornia

Shady Moreton Bay fig trees line the main street in Emerald, an attractive town at the hub of the Central Highlands. Emerald was established in 1879 as a service town while the railway from Rockhampton to the west was being constructed. Several fires ravaged the town in the mid-1900s, destroying much of this early history. The largest sapphire fields in the Southern Hemisphere are nearby, where visitors can fossick for their own gems.

Pioneer Cottage Complex: historic cottage and lock-up gaol with padded cells. There is also a church and a communications museum; Morton Park, Clermont St. *Botanic Gardens:* walk around native display, herb garden and melaleuca maze. You can also visit a traditional bush chapel and ride the

QUEENSLAND

monorail; banks of Nogoa River. *Railway station:* restored 1900 National Trust–classified station with attractive lacework and pillared portico; Clermont St. *Fossilised tree:* 250 million years old; in front of town hall. *Mosaic pathway:* 21 pictures depict 100 years of Emerald history; next to visitor centre. *Van Gogh Sunflower Painting:* largest one (on an easel) in the world; Morton Park, Clermont St.

Sunflower Festival: Easter. *Gemfest:* Aug.

Discovery Holiday Parks – Lake Maraboon: Fairbairn Dam Access Rd (off Selma Rd); (07) 4982 3677. *Emerald Cabin & Caravan Village:* 64 Opal St; (07) 4982 1300. *Gem Air Village Caravan Park & Cabins:* Village Rd, Willows Gemfields; (07) 4985 5124. *Gemseekers Caravan Park:* 10 Vane–Tempest Rd, Rubyvale; (07) 4985 4175. *Rubyvale Caravan Park:* Cnr Keilambete Rd and Main St, Rubyvale; (07) 4985 4118. *Sapphire Caravan Park:* 57 Sunrise Cabins Rd, Sapphire; (07) 4985 4281.

Sapphire gemfields To the west of Emerald is the largest sapphire-producing area in the Southern Hemisphere, incorporating Rubyvale, Sapphire, Anakie and Willows gemfields. The towns feature walk-in mines, fossicking parks, gem-faceting demonstrations, jewellers and museums. Obtain a licence and map of the mining areas from local stores or the Department of Natural Resources in Emerald to start fossicking. Rubyvale offers 4WD tours of gemfields including Tomahawk Creek; 43 km w.

Lake Maraboon/Fairbairn Dam: popular spot for watersports and fishing, especially for the red claw crayfish; 18 km s. *Capella:* 1st town settled in the area. See its history at the Capella Pioneer Village. The Crafts Fair and Vintage Machinery Rally is held in Sept; 51 km NW. *Local cattle stations and farm stays:* day tours in nearby area; details from visitor centre.

TOWNS NEARBY: Springsure 66 km, Blackwater 74 km, Clermont 94 km, Moranbah 169 km, Mount Morgan 228 km

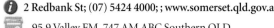

Pop. 1163
Map ref. 602 A8 | 609 M8

i 2 Redbank St; (07) 5424 4000; ; www.somerset.qld.gov.a

95.9 Valley FM, 747 AM ABC Southern QLD

Esk is a heritage town in the Upper Brisbane Valley renowned for its beautiful lakes and dams where watersports are popular. Deer roam in the grazing country north of town, progeny of a small herd presented to the state by Queen Victoria in 1873.

Antiques and local crafts: numerous shops in town.

Market: Highland St; Sat. *Multicultural Festival:* July. *Picnic Races:* July. *Rail Trail Fun Run:* July. *Esk Show:* Aug.

Esk Caravan Park: 26 Hassall St; (07) 5424 1466. *Lake Somerset Holiday Park:* Esk–Kilcoy Rd, Kilcoy; (07) 5497 1093.

Lakes and dams Known as the Valley of the Lakes, this region is popular for swimming, fishing and boating. Lake Wivenhoe (25 km E) is the source of Brisbane's main water supply. Walk to the Fig Tree Lookout for a panoramic view or ride a horse around the lake. Lake Somerset (25 km NE) is on the Stanley River and is a popular waterskiing spot. Atkinson Dam (30 km s) also attracts watersports enthusiasts.

Caboonbah Homestead: museum that houses the Brisbane Valley Historical Society, with superb views over Lake Wivenhoe; closed Thurs; 19 km NE. *Coominya:* small historic town; 22 km SE. *Ravensbourne National Park:* 33 km w; *see Crows*

Nest. Skydiving: take a tandem dive over the valley; contact visitor centre for details. *Brisbane Valley Rail Trail:* picturesque 148 km rural trail for biking enthusiasts. Trail runs between Fervale and Lowood, and Moore and Blackbutt. *Kilcoy:* small and unassuming farming town that claims to be the home of the Yowie, Australia's equivalent of the Bigfoot or Yeti. There is a large wooden statue of the supposed creature in town; 60 km N.

TOWNS NEARBY: Crows Nest 37 km, Gatton 38 km, Laidley 44 km, Ipswich 54 km, Caboolture 55 km

Eulo

Pop. 108
Map ref. 619 M9

i Centenary Park, Jane St, Cunnamulla; (07) 4655 2481; www.paroo.info

Eulo is on the banks of the Paroo River in south-west Queensland and was once a centre for opal mining. The town was originally much closer to the river but, after severe flooding, moved to where it currently stands. Eulo's population is variable as beekeepers travel from the south every winter so their bees can feed on the precious eucalypts in the area.

Eulo Queen Hotel: owes its name to Isobel Robinson who ran the hotel and reigned over the opal fields in the early 1900s; Leo St. *Eulo Date Farm:* taste the famous date wine; open Mar–Oct; western outskirts. *WW II air-raid shelter:* part of Paroo Pioneer Pathways; self-guide brochure available from visitor centre. *Destructo Cockroach Monument:* commemorates the death of a champion racing cockroach; near Paroo Track, where annual lizard races are held. *Eulo Queen Opal Centre:* opals, Aboriginal art and jewellery on display and for purchase; Leo St. *Lizard Lounge:* beautiful picnic area inspired by the frill-necked lizard; Cunnamulla Rd. *Fishing:* on the Paroo River; details from visitor centre.

Artesian Waters Caravan Park: Bluff Rd, Yowah; (07) 4655 4953. *Explorers Caravan Park:* 88 Dowling St, Thargomindah; (07) 4655 3307.

Currawinya National Park The lakes and waterholes of Paroo River form an important refuge for the abundant birdlife of this park. The 85 km circuit track for vehicles starts at the Ranger Station and is the best way to view the park. See the black swans and grebes at Lake Wyara or go canoeing at Lake Numulla. For an excellent outlook over the park, climb the Granites. 4WD necessary to reach the lakes. (07) 4655 4143; 60 km sw.

Mud springs: natural pressure valve to artesian basin that is currently inactive; 9 km w. *Yowah:* small opal-mining town where visitors can fossick for opals or take a tour of the minefields. The 'Bluff' and 'Castles' provide excellent views over the minefields. Yowah holds a craft day in June and the Opal Festival in July, which includes an international opal jewellery competition; 87 km NW. *Lake Bindegolly National Park:* walk to the lakes to see pelicans and swans. The 9.2 km lake circuit track may flood after rain. No vehicles are allowed in the park; 100 km w. *Thargomindah:* pick up a mud map at visitor centre for Burke and Wills Dig Tree site; (07) 4655 3173; 130 km w. *Noccundra Waterhole:* good fishing spot on Wilson River; 260 km w.

TOWNS NEARBY: Cunnamulla 64 km, Quilpie 188 km, Charleville 228 km, Bourke (NSW) 231 km

Fitzroy Island

see Cairns, nearby

Gatton

Pop. 6001
Map ref. 609 L9

 Lockyer Valley Cultural Centre, 34 Lake Apex Dr;
(07) 5466 3426; www.lockyervalley.qld.gov.au

100.7 C FM, 747 AM ABC Southern QLD

Located in the Lockyer Valley west of Brisbane, Gatton was founded in 1855 as one of the first rural settlements in Queensland. It is situated in the heart of the south-east's 'Salad Bowl' region and is blessed with fertile black soils, with many fruit and vegetable farms to be found in and around town. The University of Queensland's agricultural studies program is also based here. A plaque commemorating the 1974 floods can be found next to Davies Bridge, which also went under in 2011. In Gatton's town centre, the Great Dividing Range provides a scenic backdrop to historic buildings, sports and recreation facilities and quaint ale houses.

Gatton & District Historical Society Museum: complex of 11 buildings depicting the social history of the region; open 1.30–4pm or by appt; Freemans Rd. *Lake Apex:* this park and complex include a historic village with preserved heritage buildings, memorabilia and Aboriginal carvings. Follow the walking tracks to see the diverse birdlife; Old Warrego Hwy.

Markets: Rotary Park, 1st Sat each month; Showgrounds, 2nd Sat each month. *Clydesdale and Heavy Horse field days:* Apr/May. *Gatton Show:* Aug. *Multicultural Festival:* Aug.

Atkinson Dam Cabin Village & Shoreline Camping: 381 Atkinson Dam Rd, Atkinsons Dam; (07) 5426 4211. *Atkinson Dam Waterfront Caravan Park:* 545 Atkinson Dam Rd, Atkinsons Dam; (07) 5426 4151.

Agricultural College: opened in 1897. Drive through the grounds that are now part of the University of Queensland; 5 km E. *Helidon:* town noted for its sandstone – used in many Brisbane buildings – and spa water; 16 km w. *Glen Rock Regional Park:* at the head of East Haldon Valley, this park boasts rainforest gorges, creeks and excellent valley views; 40 km s. *Tourist drive:* 82 km circuit through surrounding countryside that includes farm visits; contact visitor centre for details.

TOWNS NEARBY: Laidley 14 km, Toowoomba 32 km, Esk 38 km, Crows Nest 40 km, Ipswich 48 km

Ga
Gayndah

Pop. 1820
Map ref. 609 L5

 Museum and Information Centre, 3 Simon St; (07) 4161 2226; www.northburnett.qld.gov.au/

91.5 FM Burnett River Radio, 855 AM ABC Wide Bay

Gayndah, in the Capricorn region, is one of Queensland's oldest towns. Founded in 1849, it was once competing with Brisbane and Ipswich to be the state's capital. Main Street's heritage buildings and landscaped gardens illustrate the long history of the town, which is now central to a rich citrus-growing industry.

Historical Museum An award-winning museum with several historic buildings, displays, photographs and memorabilia that illustrate the town's changing history from small settlement to thriving agricultural centre – a highlight is a restored 1864 cottage. There is also an interesting display on the lungfish and its link between sea and land animals. Simon St.

Market: Jaycees Park; 1st Sun each month. *Gayndah Show:* Apr. *Orange Festival:* odd-numbered years, June. *Triathlon:* Oct.

Riverview Caravan Park: 3 Barrow St; (07) 4161 1280.

Lookouts: several in area offering views over Burnett Valley; closest to town is Archers Lookout, atop the twin hills 'Duke and Duchess' overlooking town. *Claude Warton Weir:* excellent spot for fishing and picnics; 3 km w. *Ban Ban Springs:* natural springs and picnic area; 26 km s.

TOWNS NEARBY: Mundubbera 31 km, Biggenden 45 km, Murgon 76 km, Gin Gin 78 km, Childers 80 km

Gin Gin

Pop. 888
Map ref. 603 B2 | 604 E11 | 609 L3

 Mulgrave St; (07) 4157 3060.

93.1 Sea FM, 855 AM ABC Wide Bay

Some of Queensland's oldest cattle properties surround this pastoral town south-west of Bundaberg. The district is known as 'Wild Scotchman Country' after James McPherson, Queensland's only authentic bushranger. His antics are re-enacted every March at the Wild Scotchman Festival.

Historical Society Museum: displays memorabilia of pioneering past in 'The Residence' – a former police sergeant's house. The old sugarcane locomotive The Bunyip forms part of the historic railway display; open 8.30am–3.30pm Mon–Fri, 8.30am–12pm Sat, other times by appt; Mulgrave St. *Courthouse Gallery:* fine-arts gallery in refurbished old courthouse; Mulgrave St.

Market: Historical Museum; Sat. *Jazz and Shiraz:* Wonbah Winery; Aug. *Auto Machinery Show:* Aug. *Cane Burning and Whipcracking Festival:* Aug. *Didgeridoo Festival:* Aug/Sept. *Santa Fair:* Dec.

Lake Monduran Holiday Park: 1 Claude Wharton Dr; (07) 4157 3881. *Bungadoo Country Cottage:* 58 Bungadoo Rd, Bullyard; (07) 4157 4621. *Mingo Crossing Caravan & Recreation Area:* 2670 Gayndah–Mount Perry Rd, Mount Perry; (07) 4161 6200. *Mount Perry Caravan Park:* 54 Heusman St, Mount Perry; (07) 4156 3850.

Good Night Scrub National Park A dense remnant hoop pine rainforest in the Burnett Valley, this park is home to over 60 species of butterfly. Have a bush picnic at historic Kalliwa Hut, used during the logging days of the park. Drive up to One Tree Hill (4WD only) for a spectacular panoramic view over the area, on a clear day, all the way to Bundaberg. Turn-off is 10 km south of Gin Gin; (07) 4131 1600.

Lake Monduran: an excellent spot for watersports and fishing (permit from kiosk). Catch a barramundi or Australian bass, or walk the 6 km of tracks in the bush surrounds; 24 km NW. *Boolboonda Tunnel:* longest non-supported tunnel in the Southern Hemisphere. It forms part of a scenic tourist drive; brochure available from visitor centre; 27 km w. *Mount Perry:* small mining town, home to mountain-bike racing in June; 55 km sw.

TOWNS NEARBY: Bundaberg 42 km, Childers 42 km, Biggenden 58 km, Gayndah 78 km, Miriam Vale 83 km

QUEENSLAND

 RADIO STATIONS   IN TOWN   WHAT'S ON   WHERE TO EAT   WHERE TO STAY   NEARBY

Gladstone

Pop. 42 902
Map ref. 604 D7 | 609 K1 | 611 N12

 Marina Ferry Terminal, Bryan Jordan Dr; (07) 4972 4000; www.gladstoneregion.info

95.1 Sea FM, 837 AM ABC Capricornia

Gladstone is a modern city on the central coast of Queensland. Matthew Flinders discovered Port Curtis, Gladstone's deep-water harbour, in 1802, but the town did not truly develop until the 1960s. Today it is an outlet for central Queensland's mineral and agricultural wealth – a prosperous seaboard city with one of Australia's busiest harbours. Set among hills with natural lookouts over the harbour and southern end of the Great Barrier Reef, Gladstone is popular for swimming, surfing and fishing – especially for mud crabs and prawns.

Tondoon Botanic Gardens: displays of all-native species of the Port Curtis region with free guided tours on weekends. Also offers a recreational lake and Mt Biondello bushwalk; Glenlyon Rd. *Gladstone Regional Art Gallery and Museum:* local and regional art with history exhibitions; closed Sun; Cnr Goondoon and Bramston sts. *Maritime Museum:* artefacts and memorabilia document 200 years of port history; open Thurs and Sun; Auckland Pt. *Potters Place:* fine-art gallery and craft shop; Dawson Hwy. *Gecko Valley Winery:* tastings and sales of award-winning wines; closed Mon; Bailiff Rd. *Barney Point Beach:* historic beach including Friend Park; Barney St. *Waterfall:* spectacular at night when floodlit; Flinders Pde.

Markets: Calliope River Historical Village; selected dates (6 times a year). *Sunfest:* youth sports and arts program; Jan. *Harbour Festival:* includes the finish of the Brisbane to Gladstone Yacht Race; Mar. *Woodworker's Art and Crafts Weekend (Calliope):* July. *Multicultural Festival:* Aug. *Seafood Festival:* Sept.

Gladstone Earth & Sea Bed & Breakfast: 3 Herbert St; (07) 4972 8599. *BIG4 Barney Beach:* 10 Friend St, Barney Point; (07) 4972 1366. *Boyne River Tourist Park:* 48814 Bruce Hwy, Benaraby; (07) 4975 0769. *Kin Kora Village Tourist and Residential Home Park:* Olsen Ave, Kin Kora; (07) 4978 5461. *Lake Awoonga Caravan Park:* Awoonga Dam Rd, Benaraby; (07) 4975 0155.

Capricornia Cays National Park This park, 60–100 km offshore from Gladstone, protects the 9 coral islands and cays that form the southern end of the Great Barrier Reef. The islands are important nesting sites for seabirds and loggerhead turtles. North West Island has walking tracks through forests dominated by palms and she-oaks. The most popular activities are reef walking, diving and snorkelling in the spectacular reefs or visiting the renowned dive sites on Heron Island. The island has resort-style accommodation (maximum 250 people). Access is by private boat or charter from Gladstone; air access to Heron Island. There is seasonal closure to protect nesting wildlife. (07) 4971 6500 (same number for all national parks in the area).

Boyne Island: with beautiful foreshore parks and beaches; home to the Boyne–Tannum Hookup Fishing Competition in June. The Boyne Aluminium Smelter is Australia's largest and has an information centre and tours every Fri. The island and its twin town of Tannum Sands are linked by bridge; 25 km se. *Tannum Sands:* small community offering sandy beaches with year-round swimming, picturesque Millennium Way along the beach and 15 km of scenic walkways known as the Turtle Way. Wild Cattle Island, an uninhabited national park at the southern end of the beach, can be reached on foot at low tide; 25 km se. *Calliope:* small rural community with excellent fishing in nearby Calliope River with abundant mud crabs, salmon and flathead. The Calliope River Historical Village documents Port Curtis history in restored buildings and holds regular art and craft markets; 26 km sw. *Lake Awoonga:* a popular spot for swimming, skiing (permit required) and fishing. It has walking tracks and recreational facilities, and holds the Lions Lake Awoonga Family Fishing Festival each Sept; 30 km s. *Mt Larcom:* spectacular views from the summit; 33 km w. *Castle Tower National Park:* a rugged park of granite cliffs and the outcrops of Castle Tower and Stanley mountains. Only experienced walkers should attempt the climb to Mt Castle Tower summit, where there are superb views over the Boyne Valley and Gladstone. Access by foot or boat from Lake Awoonga; access by car from Bruce Hwy; 40 km s. *Kroombit Tops National Park:* this mountain park is on a plateau with sandstone cliffs and gorges, waterfalls and creeks. Drive the 90 min return loop road to explore the landscapes and walk to the site of a WW II bomber crash; 4WD recommended; 75 km sw via Calliope. *Curtis Island National Park:* at the north-east end of the island is this small park with a variety of vegetation and excellent spots for birdwatching. There are no walking tracks, but the 3- to 4-day hike along the east coast is worthwhile; access by boat from Gladstone or the Narrows. *Great Barrier Reef tours:* cruises depart from the Gladstone Marina; Bryan Jordan Dr.

TOWNS NEARBY: Miriam Vale 62 km, Mount Morgan 91 km, Rockhampton 92 km, Yeppoon 95 km, Biloela 97 km

Goondiwindi

Pop. 5031
Map ref. 524 H1 | 609 I11

 Cnr McLean and Bowen sts; (07) 4671 2653; www.goondiwindirc.qld.gov.au

101.9 Coast FM, 711 AM ABC Western QLD

Goondiwindi is situated beside the picturesque MacIntyre River in the western Darling Downs. Explored by Allan Cunningham in 1827 and settled by pastoralists in the 1830s, the town derives its name from the Aboriginal word 'gonnawinna', meaning 'resting place of the birds'.

Customs House Museum: explore local history in the restored 1850 customs house; closed Tues; McLean St. *Victoria Hotel:* renowned historic pub with tower; Marshall St. *Goondiwindi Cotton and Gin:* one of the largest cotton manufacturers in Australia; bus tours available, contact visitor information centre for details. *River Walk:* watch abundant birdlife and wildlife on 2 km walk along MacIntyre River; starts at Riddles Oval, Lagoon St. *'Goondiwindi Grey' Statue:* tribute to famous racehorse Gunsynd; Apex Park, MacIntyre St. *Fishing:* some of Queensland's best fishing in and around the town, Murray cod and yellow-belly in abdundance.

Market: Town Park, Marshall St; 2nd Sun each month. *Hell of the West Triathlon:* Feb. *Gourmet in Gundy:* Sept. *Spring Festival:* coincides with flowering of jacarandas and silky oaks; Oct.

Goondiwindi Tourist Park: 20 Hungerford St; (07) 4671 2566. *Gundy Star Tourist Van Park:* 36 Old Cunningham Hwy; (07) 4671 2900. *Elanbe Caravan Village:* Newell Hwy, Boggabilla, NSW; (07) 4676 2155.

Southwood National Park This brigalow–belah forest park was once known as 'Wild Horse Paradise'. Have a bush picnic and look for the black cockatoos in the belah trees, or visit at night

[GYMPIE] MARY VALLEY HERITAGE RAILWAY

and go spotlighting for feathertail gliders. 4WD is recommended. Access from Moonie Hwy; (07) 4699 4355; 125 km NW.

Botanic Gardens of Western Woodlands: 25 ha of native plants of the Darling Basin. Also here is a lake popular for swimming and canoeing; access from Brennans Rd; 1 km W. ***Toobeah:*** small town famous for its horse events; 48 km W.

TOWNS NEARBY: Texas 91 km, Moree (NSW) 111 km, Warialda (NSW) 114 km, Bingara (NSW) 149 km, Inverell (NSW) 157 km

Gordonvale
Pop. 4421
Map ref. 606 E3 | 607 F8 | 613 L6

 Cnr Bruce Hwy and Munro St, Babinda; (07) 4067 1008.

103.5 Hot FM, 801 AM ABC Far North QLD

Gordonvale is a sugar-milling town just south of Cairns with well-preserved streetscapes, historic buildings and the 922-metre-high Walsh's Pyramid that forms the backdrop to the town. People flock to the mountain in August for a race to the top. The town's less glorious claim to fame is that cane toads were released here in 1935 in an attempt to eradicate sugarcane pests.

Settlers Museum: with displays and dioramas depicting early pioneer life in the shire. Includes blacksmith's shop, old store and a Chinese display; open 10am–2pm Mon–Sat (closed Dec–Feb); Gordon St.

Barrier Reef Tourist Park: 69 Bruce Hwy, Edmonton; (07) 4055 4544. ***Fishery Falls Holiday Park:*** Bruce Hwy, Fishery Falls; (07) 4067 5283.

Goldsborough Valley State Forest The lowland rainforest along the Goldsborough Valley is protected here. Walk to the falls along the 1.6 km Kearneys Falls track and learn about the local Aboriginal culture and customs from the informative displays. The 18 km historic Goldfields Trail travels through nearby Wooroonooran National Park to the Boulders near Babinda; 25 km SW via Gillies Hwy.

Mulgrave River: runs next to Gordonvale and is popular for swimming, canoeing, kayaking and bushwalking. ***Wooroonooran National Park:*** waterfalls, walking tracks and Walsh's Pyramid; 10 km S; for the southern sections *see Babinda and Millaa Millaa.* ***Orchid Valley Nursery and Gardens:*** tours of tropical gardens; 15 km SW. ***Cairns Crocodile Farm:*** crocodiles and other

native wildlife with daily tours; around 5 min north on road to Yarrabah.

TOWNS NEARBY: Cairns 20 km, Yungaburra 28 km, Babinda 31 km, Kuranda 34 km, Atherton 37 km

Gympie
Pop. 10 933
Map ref. 603 D9 | 609 M6

 Lake Alford Visitors Information Centre, 24 Bruce Hwy, (07) 5483 6411 or 1800 444 222; or Cooloola Regional Information Centre, Matilda's Roadhouse Complex, Bruce Hwy, Kybong (15 km S), (07) 5483 5554 or 1800 444 222; www.cooloola.org.au

96.1 Zinc FM, 1566 AM ABC Wide Bay

On the banks of the Mary River on the Sunshine Coast is the major heritage town of Gympie. It was established when James Nash discovered gold in the area in 1867 and started Queensland's first gold rush to save the state from near-bankruptcy. The field proved extremely rich – four million ounces had been found by the 1920s. The gold slowed to a trickle soon after, but the dairy and agricultural industries were already well established. See the attractive jacarandas, silky oaks, cassias, poincianas and flame trees that line the streets.

Mary Valley Heritage Railway Known locally as the 'Valley Rattler', this restored 1923 steam train takes the visitor on a 40 km journey through the picturesque Mary Valley. The train departs Gympie every Wed, Sat and Sun on its way to Imbil, where it stops before returning. Special tours run each Sat. Tickets and information from visitor centre; inquiries (07) 5482 2750.

Woodworks, Forestry and Timber Museum: exhibits memorabilia from old logging days including a steam-driven sawmill; closed Sat; Fraser Rd. ***Deep Creek:*** gold-fossicking area; permits from visitor centre; Counter St. ***Public gallery:*** local and visiting art exhibitions in heritage building; Nash St. ***Heritage walk:*** self-guide walk includes the Stock Exchange and Town Hall; details from visitor centre. ***Trail rides:*** horseriding through Kiah Park and Mary Valley; details from visitor centre.

Market: Gympie South State School; 2nd and 4th Sun each month. ***Gympie Show:*** May. ***Race the Rattler:*** a race against the historic steam train; June. ***Fishing Classic:*** Rainbow Beach; July. ***Rodeo and Woodchop (Mary Valley):*** Aug.

QUEENSLAND

Country Music Muster: Amamoor State Forest; Aug. *Art Festival (Mary Valley):* Sept. *Gold Rush Festival:* Oct.

Gympie Caravan Park: 1 Jane St; (07) 5483 6800. *Amamoor Homestead B&B and Country Cottages:* 254 Kandanga–Amamoor Rd, Amamoor; (07) 5484 3760. *Amamoor Lodge:* 368 Kandanga–Amamoor Rd, Amamoor; (07) 5484 3500. *Lagoon Pocket Bed & Breakfast:* 57 Lagoon Pocket Rd, Lagoon Pocket; (07) 5483 2112.

Amamoor State Forest Over 120 native animal species find shelter in this protected forest, a remnant of the woodlands and vegetation that used to cover the Cooloola region. See the platypus in Amamoor Creek at dusk or take the Wonga walk or Cascade circuit track starting across the road from Amama. The renowned outdoor music festival, the Country Music Muster, is held in the forest on the last weekend in Aug; 30 km s.

Gold Mining and Historical Museum: delve into the area's goldmining history. It includes Andrew Fisher House (Fisher was the first Queenslander to become prime minister); 5 km s. *Mothar Mountain:* rockpools and forested area for bushwalking and excellent views; 20 km se. *Imbil:* picturesque town with excellent valley views. There is a market every Sun, and the nearby Lake Borumba offers great conditions for watersports and fishing – especially for golden perch and saratoga. Take the 14 km Imbil Forest Drive through scenic pine plantations just south of town; 36 km s. *Mary Valley Scenic Way:* enjoy this scenic route through towns of the valley, pineapple plantations and grazing farms; it runs south between Gympie and Maleny, via Kenilworth.

TOWNS NEARBY: Pomona 28 km, Kenilworth 46 km, Tin Can Bay 46 km, Noosa Heads 49 km, Yandina 51 km

Hamilton Island
see Airlie Beach, nearby

Hayman Island
see Airlie Beach, nearby

Herberton
Pop. 974
Map ref. 606 C4 | 607 C10 | 613 L7

i Herberton Mining Museum, 1 Jacks Rd; (07) 4096 3474; www.herbertonvisitorcentre.com.au

Known as the 'Village in the Hills', Herberton sits about 1000 metres above sea level on the south-west ranges of the Atherton Tableland. The first settlement on the tableland, it was established in 1880 when two prospectors discovered tin in the area. It was a thriving tin-mining town, the most important in the Herbert River field, until the mine's closure in 1978.

Mining Museum: explore local mining history in this richly informative museum, with displays of antique machinery, an array of minerals and rocks, and multimedia shows. A short walking track takes you past mining relics that made up the Great Northern Claim, now a heritage-listed site; 1 Jacks Rd. *Spy and Camera Museum:* houses some of the world's rarest, oldest and smallest cameras. See Russian spy cameras and cameras from Hitler's Germany; Grace St.

Ghost Walks: 3 times a year the ghosts of former miners and Herberton residents 'materialise' to retell their stories; dates vary, details from visitor centre.

Mt Hypipamee National Park Set on the Evelyn Tableland, this park boasts high-altitude rainforests and a climate that attracts birdlife and possums, including the green and lemuroid ringtail possums. The park is known locally as 'The Crater' because of its sheer-sided volcanic explosion crater 70 m wide. Walk to the viewing deck for the best vantage point, or see the Dinner Falls cascade down the narrow gorge. (07) 4091 1844; 25 km s.

Herberton Range State Forest: the temperate climate attracts a variety of wildlife in this rainforest park, including the attractive golden bowerbird. Walk to the summit of Mt Baldy for panoramic views over the tableland (the steep ascent should be attempted only by experienced walkers); Rifle Range Rd, between Atherton and Herberton. *Irvinebank:* many heritage-listed buildings including Mango House, Queensland National Bank Building and Loudoun House Museum; 26 km w on unsealed road. *Emuford:* small town featuring a historic stamper battery and museum; 51 km w.

TOWNS NEARBY: Atherton 16 km, Yungaburra 24 km, Ravenshoe 29 km, Millaa Millaa 29 km, Mareeba 43 km

Heron Island
see Gladstone, nearby

Hervey Bay
see inset box on page 416

Hughenden
Pop. 1154
Map ref. 610 B4 | 617 N4

i Flinders Discovery Centre, Gray St; (07) 4741 2970; www.flinders.qld.gov.au

1485 AM ABC North West QLD

Hughenden is on the banks of the Flinders River, Queensland's longest river, west of the Great Dividing Range. The first recorded Europeans to pass through here were members of Frederick Walker's 1861 expedition to search for explorers Burke and Wills. Two years later Ernest Henry selected a cattle station and Hughenden came into existence. The black volcanic soil in the region is rich with fossilised bones, particularly those of dinosaurs.

Flinders Discovery Centre Learn about the Flinders Shire history in this complex. The fossil exhibition's centrepiece is the 7 m replica skeleton of *Muttaburrasaurus langdoni*, a dinosaur found in Muttaburra (206 km s) – it was the first entire fossil skeleton found in Australia. The Historical Society also documents the shire history in their display. Gray St; (07) 4741 1021.

Historic Coolibah Tree: blazed by Walker in 1861 and again by William Landsborough in 1862 when he was also searching for Burke and Wills, and their 2 companions; east bank of Station Creek, Stansfield St East. *Flinders Poppy Art and Craft Cottage:* unique range of handmade art and craft items for sale; open 10am–2pm daily (hours can vary); Gray St.

Market: Lions Rotary Park; last Sun each month. *Country Music Festival:* Apr. *Horseracing:* Apr and Sept. *Hughenden Show:* June. *Porcupine Gorge Challenge:* fun run; June. *Arid Lands Festival:* camel endurance race; Aug. *Outback Scrap:* Aug. *Bullride:* Sept.

Hughenden Allen Terry Caravan Park: 2 Resolution St; (07) 4741 1190.

Porcupine Gorge National Park The coloured sandstone cliffs of this park are a delight and contrast with the greenery surrounding Porcupine Creek. The gorge, known locally as the 'mini Grand Canyon', has been formed over millions of years and can be seen from the lookout just off Kennedy Development Rd. Walk down into the gorge on the 1.2 km track, but be warned: the steep walk back up is strenuous. (07) 4722 5224; 61 km N.

Basalt Byways: discover the Flinders Shire landscapes on these 4WD tracks. Cross the Flinders River and see the Flinders poppy in the valleys. The longest track is 156 km; access on Hann Hwy; 7.3 km N. **Prairie:** small town with mini-museum and historic relics at Cobb & Co. yards; 44 km E. **Mt Emu Goldfields:** fossicking and bushwalking; 85 km N. **Torrens Creek:** the town, a major explosives dump during WW II, was nearly wiped out by 12 explosions when firebreaks accidentally hit the dump. Visit the Exchange Hotel, home of the 'dinosaur steaks'; 88 km E. **Kooroorinya Falls:** the small falls cascade into a natural waterhole, excellent for swimming. Walk and go birdwatching in surrounding bushland; 109 km SE via Prairie. **White Mountains National Park:** rugged park with white sandstone outcrops and varied vegetation. Burra Range Lookout on Flinders Hwy has excellent views over the park. There are no walking tracks; (07) 4722 5224; 111 km E. **Chudleigh Park Gemfields:** gem-quality peridot found in fossicking area (licence required); 155 km N. **Moorrinya National Park:** important conservation park protecting 18 different land types of the Lake Eyre Basin. The park is home to iconic Australian animals, such as koalas, kangaroos and dingoes, and includes remains of the old sheep-grazing property Shirley Station. Walking is for experienced bushwalkers only; (07) 4722 5224; 178 km SE via Torrens Creek.

TOWNS NEARBY: Richmond 111 km, Muttaburra 197 km, Winton 208 km, Charters Towers 231 km

Ingham

Pop. 4603
Map ref. 606 E8 | 613 M10

i Tyto Wetlands Information Centre, cnr Townsville Rd (Bruce Hwy) and Cooper St; (07) 4776 4792; www.tyto.com.au

91.9 FM Kool, 630 AM ABC North QLD

Ingham is a major sugar town near the Hinchinbrook Channel. Originally, Kanaka labourers were employed in the surrounding sugarcane fields, but after their repatriation at the beginning of the 20th century Italian immigrants took their place (the first Italians arrived in the 1890s). This strong Italian heritage is celebrated in the Australian Italian Festival each May. Ingham is at the centre of a splendid range of national parks. The Wallaman Falls in Girringun National Park is a highlight as the largest single-drop falls in Australia.

 Hinchinbrook Heritage Walk and Drive: displays at each historic site in Ingham and the nearby township of Halifax illustrate the dynamic history of the shire. It starts at the Shire Hall in Ingham; brochure available from visitor centre. **Memorial Gardens:** picturesque waterlily lakes and native tropical vegetation. They include Bicentennial Bush House with displays of orchids and tropical plants (open weekdays); Palm Tce.

Conroy Hall Markets: McIlwraith St; 2nd Sat each month. **Raintree Market:** Herbert St; 3rd Sat each month. **Ingham Arts Festival:** Apr. **Australian Italian Festival:** May. **Bullride:** June. **Ingham Show:** July. **Horseracing:** Aug. **Family Fishing Classic:** Sept. **Maraka Festival:** Oct.

Noorla Heritage Resort: tiffin, tapas, cakes and curry; 5–9 Warren St; (07) 4776 1100 or 1800 238 077.

Palm Tree Caravan Park: Bruce Hwy; (07) 4776 2403. **Crystal Creek Caravan Park:** Cnr Bruce Hwy and Barrilgie Rd, Mutarnee; (07) 4770 8198. **Wanderers Holiday Village – Lucinda:** 49 Bruce Pde, Lucinda; (07) 4777 8213.

Girringun National Park The Wallaman Falls section (50 km W) is in the Herbert River Valley and features waterfalls, gorges and tropical rainforest. See the crimson rosellas on the 4 km return walk from the Falls Lookout to the base of Wallaman Falls – look out for platypus and water dragons. Take a scenic drive around the Mt Fox section of the park (75 km SW) or walk the 4 km return ascent to the dormant volcano crater. There are no formal tracks and the ascent is for experienced walkers only. 4WD is recommended in both sections during the wet season; *see Cardwell for northern parts of park*; (07) 4066 8601 (same number for other national parks in area); 20 km NW.

Paluma Range National Park The Jourama Falls section of the park (24 km S) is at the foothills of the Seaview Range. Walk the 1.5 km track through rainforest and dry forest to the Jourama Falls Lookout (take care crossing the creek) to see the vibrant birdlife, including azure kingfishers and kookaburras. The Mt Spec section of the park (40 km S) features casuarina-fringed creeks in the lowlands and rainforest in the cooler mountain areas. Drive to McClelland's Lookout for a spectacular view and take the 2 short walks from there to see the varied park landscapes; 49 km S.

Orpheus Island National Park This rainforest and woodland park is a continental resort island in the Palm Islands surrounded by a marine park and fringing reefs. Snorkel and dive off the beaches or take in the wildlife on the short track from Little Pioneer Bay to Old Shepherds Hut; access is by private or charter boat from Lucinda or Taylors Beach. There's a 5-star resort (maximum 74 people) or bush camping (maximum 54 people); camping permits from Ingham parks office; 35 km E.

Tyto Wetlands: 90 ha of wetlands with birdlife and wallabies. See the rare grass owl from the viewing platform; outskirts of town. **Cemetery:** interesting Italian tile mausoleums; 5 km E. **Forrest Beach:** sandy 16 km beach overlooking Palm Islands. Stinger-net swimming enclosures are installed in summer; 20 km SE. **Taylors Beach:** popular family seaside spot for sailing with excellent fishing and crabbing in nearby Victoria Creek; 24 km E. **Hinchinbrook Island National Park:** resort island to the north-east; sea access from Lucinda; 25 km NE; *see Cardwell*. **Lucinda:** coastal village on the banks of the Herbert River at the southern end of the Hinchinbrook Channel. Take a safari or fishing tour through the channel. Stinger-net swimming enclosures are installed in summer; 27 km NE. **Broadwater State Forest:** swimming holes, walking tracks and birdwatching; 45 km W.

TOWNS NEARBY: Cardwell 45 km, Tully 83 km, Mission Beach 86 km, Townsville 97 km, Mourilyan 118 km

Innisfail

Pop. 8260
Map ref. 606 E4 | 607 G11 | 613 M7

i Cnr River Ave (Bruce Hwy) and Eslick St, Mourilyan; (07) 4061 2655; www.innisfailtourism.com.au

98.3 Kool FM, 720 AM ABC Far North QLD

Innisfail has seen destruction by cyclone more than once – most recently cyclone Larry in 2006, which destroyed homes and much of the town's banana plantations. But today Innisfail seems to have mostly recovered and travellers come to work during fruit-picking

continued on p. 417

 RADIO STATIONS IN TOWN WHAT'S ON WHERE TO EAT WHERE TO STAY  NEARBY

QUEENSLAND

HERVEY BAY

Pop. 56 427
Map ref. 603 F4 | 604 H12 | 609 N4

ⓘ **Cnr Urraween and Maryborough–Hervey Bay rds;**
(07) 4125 9855 or 1800 811 728; www.herveybaytouristinfo.com.au

📻 107.5 FM Fraser Coast Community Radio, 855 AM ABC
Wide Bay

Hervey (pronounced 'Harvey') Bay is a natural bay located
290 kilometres north of Brisbane between Maryborough and
Bundaberg. The urban centre which spreads out along the bay's
southern shore is the thriving City of Hervey Bay. The region's
climate is ideal, with hot days cooled by trade winds during the
summer. An influx of people visit during winter for a chance to
see the migrating humpback whales that frolic in the bay's warm
waters between July and November. Hervey Bay is promoted
as 'Australia's family aquatic playground' – waters are calm and
swimming is safe, even for children. Fishing is another popular
recreational activity, especially off the town's kilometre-long pier.

🏠 **Botanic Gardens:** peaceful vistas and orchid conservatory;
Elizabeth St. **Historical Village & Museum:** recalls pioneer
days in 20 historic buildings, including Acutt Cottage, the
old church and sugar machinery; open Fri–Sun; Zephyr St.
Sea Shell Museum: shell creations and displays, including
100-million-year-old shell; Esplanade. **Neptune's Reefworld:**
natural aquarium with Great Barrier Reef's coral and sea life plus
performing seals; Pulgul St. **M & K Model Railways:** award-
winning miniature village and model trains. Ride the replica
diesel train; open Tues–Fri; Old Maryborough Rd. **Thrillseekers
Amusement Park:** rides include the Bungee Rocket; Hervey
Bay Rd. **Dayman Park:** memorial commemorates landing of

[VIEWING A HUMPBACK WHALE ON A WHALE-WATCHING TOUR]

Matthew Flinders in 1799 and the Z-Force commandos who
trained there on the Krait in WW II. **Regional Gallery:** includes
rotating exhibitions of local artists plus touring exhibitions from
state and national galleries; open Mon–Sat; Old Maryborough
Rd. **Scenic walkway:** cycle or walk 15 km along the waterfront.
Whale-watching tours: half- and full-day tours to see the
migratory whales off the coast, departing from Boat Harbour;
contact visitor centre for details.

🎆 **Nikenbah Markets:** Nikenbah Animal Refuge; 1st and
3rd Sun each month. **Koala Markets:** Elizabeth St; 2nd, 4th and
5th Sun each month. **Fraser Coast Multicultural Festival:** Mar.
Fraser Coast Show: May. **World's Biggest Pub Crawl:** June. **Mary
Poppins Festival:** July **Whale Festival:** Aug. **Seafood Festival:**
Aug. **Hervey Bay Jazz and Blues Festival:** Nov.

🍴 **Bayswater Bistro & Bar:** seafood; Peppers Pier Resort,
569–571 The Esplanade, Urangan; (07) 4194 7555. **Enzo's on
the Beach:** swim between courses; 351A Charlton Esp, Scarness;
(07) 4124 6375. **Gatakers Landing Restaurant:** seafood by the
seaside; Cnr The Esplanade and Mant St, Gatakers Bay; (07) 4124
2470. **Kingfisher Bay Resort Cruises:** head to Kingfisher Bay
Resort on Fraser Island for lunch or dinner; departs from River
Heads; 1800 072 555.

🛏 **Alexander Lakeside Bed & Breakfast:** 29 Lido Pde,
Urangan; (07) 4128 9448. **Australiana Top Tourist Park:**
295 Boat Harbour Dr, Scarness; 1800 880 015. **BIG4 Point
Vernon Holiday Park:** 26 Corser St, Point Vernon; (07) 4128
1423. **Burrum Heads Beachfront Tourist Park:** Burrum St,
Burrum Heads; (07) 4129 5138. **Fraser Coast Top Tourist
Park:** 21 Denmans Camp Rd, Scarness; (07) 4124 6237. **Fraser
Lodge Holiday Park:** 20 Fraser St, Torquay; (07) 4124 9999.
Happy Wanderer Village Caravan Park: 105 Truro St, Torquay;
(07) 4125 1103. **Harbour View Caravan Park:** Jetty Rd, Urangan;
(07) 4128 9374. **Hervey Bay Caravan Park:** Cnr Margaret and
Dayman sts, Urangan; (07) 4128 9553. **Hillcrest Holiday Park:**
1 Howard St, Burrum Heads; (07) 4129 5179. **Pialba Beachfront
Tourist Park:** The Esplanade, Pialba; (07) 4128 1399. **Scarness
Beachfront Tourist Park:** The Esplanade, Scarness; (07) 4128
1274. **Sunlodge Oceanfront Tourist Park:** 26 Mant St, Point
Vernon; (07) 4128 1692. **Torquay Beachfront Caravan Park:**
Esplanade, Torquay; (07) 4125 1578. **Windmill Caravan Park:**
17 Elizabeth St, Urangan; (07) 4128 9267.

🌀 **Fraser Island** World Heritage–listed Fraser Island is the
largest sand island in the world. It is an ecological wonder with
lakes and forests existing purely on sand. Protected within Great
Sandy National Park, the island is an oasis of beaches, beautifully
coloured sand cliffs, more than 40 freshwater lakes and
spectacular rainforests. Idyllic Lake McKenzie is definitely one of
the most beautiful of these freshwater lakes – its shallow water is
dazzling aquamarine and ringed by white sandy beaches backed
by paperbark trees.The island is also home to a variety of wildlife,
including migratory birds and rare animals such as the ground
parrot and Illidge's ant-blue butterfly. Offshore, see the turtles,
dugong and dolphins soak up the warm waters and, between Aug
and Nov, look out for migrating humpback whales. There are

a variety of walks around the island, as well as swimming spots and scenic drives. The island's surf coast, on the east, takes in the beautiful Seventy Five Mile Beach; the Cathedrals, 15 m sheer cliffs composed of different-coloured sands; the wreck of the *Maheno*, a trans-Tasman luxury liner; and Eli Creek, a freshwater creek filtered through the dunes, where visitors can float beneath the pandanus trees. Care should be taken around the island's dingo population. Stay with children, walk in groups, never feed or coax the dingoes and keep all food and rubbish in vehicles or campground lockers. They are thought to be the purest strain of dingoes in eastern Australia. By the time these native dogs arrived on the mainland – they came with Asian seafarers around 5000 years ago – Fraser Island was already disconnected from the continent, and the dingoes swam across Great Sandy Strait. Unlike most mainland dingoes, they have not been hybridised by contact with domestic dogs. Vehicle and camping permits from Queensland Parks and Wildlife Service, 13 1304; 23 km E.

Great Sandy Strait: the Mary and Susan rivers to the south of Hervey Bay run into this strait where visitors can see spectacular migratory birds, including the comb-crested jacana. Look out for dugongs, the world's only plant-eating marine mammals, and fish at the mouth of the Mary River, around River Heads. Hire a houseboat to travel down the strait; contact visitor centre for details. **Toogoom:** quiet seaside resort town. Feed the pelicans on the boardwalk; 15 km W. **Burrum Heads:** pleasant holiday resort at the mouth of the Burrum River with excellent beaches and fishing. Visit at Easter for the Amateur Fishing Classic; 20 km NW. **Burrum Coast National Park:** 34 km NW; *see Bundaberg.* **Brooklyn House:** historic Queenslander pioneer house; Howard; 36 km W. **Scenic flights:** over Hervey Bay and Fraser Island in a Tiger Moth or other small plane; contact visitor centre for details.

TOWNS NEARBY: Maryborough 33 km, Childers 60 km, Tin Can Bay 71 km, Bundaberg 71 km, Biggenden 87 km

---

season. The parks and walks on the riverside, as well as the classic Art Deco buildings in the town centre, add to the charm of this town. The area is also renowned for its sugar industry and the excellent fishing in nearby rivers, beaches and estuaries.

 Innisfail and District Historical Society Museum: documents local history; Edith St. **Chinese Joss House:** reminder of Chinese presence during gold-rush days; Owen St. **Warrina Lakes and Botanical Gardens:** recreational facilities and walks; Charles St. **Historical town walk:** see classic Art Deco architecture of the town and historic Shire Hall on self-guide or guided town walk; details from visitor centre.

 Market: ANZAC Memorial Park; 3rd Sat each month. **Feast of the Senses:** March. **Innisfail Show:** July. **Game Fishing Tournament:** Sept. **Karnivale:** Oct. **Innisfail Cup:** Oct.

 August Moon Caravan Park: 64174 Bruce Hwy; (07) 4063 2211. **River Drive Van Park:** 7 River Ave (Bruce Hwy); (07) 4061 2515.

 Eubenangee Swamp National Park This important park protects the last of the remnant coastal lowland rainforest around Alice River, which is part of the Wet Tropics Region. See the rainforest birds on the walk from Alice River to the swamp where jabirus and spoonbills feed; (07) 4067 6304; 13 km NW.

Flying Fish Point: popular spot for swimming, camping and fishing; 5 km NE. **Johnstone River Crocodile Farm:** daily feeding shows at 11am and 3pm; 8 km NE. **Ella Bay National Park:** small coastal park with beach and picnic spot; (07) 4067 6304; 8 km N. **North Johnstone River Gorge:** walking tracks to several picturesque waterfalls; 18 km W via Palmerston Hwy. **Wooroonooran National Park:** 33 km W; *see Millaa Millaa.* **Crawford Lookout:** for spectacular views of North Johnstone River; 38 km W off Palmerston Hwy.

TOWNS NEARBY: Mourilyan 7 km, Babinda 23 km, Mission Beach 39 km, Millaa Millaa 44 km, Tully 47 km

---

Ipswich

Pop. 155 000
Map ref. 599 A9 | 600 B5 | 602 D12 | 609 M9

i 14 Queen Victoria Pde; (07) 3281 0555; www.ipswichtourism.com.au

94.9 FM River, 747 AM ABC Southern QLD

Ipswich is Queensland's oldest provincial city. It was first settled in 1827 on the banks of the Bremer River which burst its banks in 2011, submerging much of the city centre under water. The impressive Workshops Rail Museum honours Ipswich as the birthplace of Queensland Railways, while Australia's largest RAAF base can be found in the suburb of Amberley. The city centre, with its diverse heritage buildings, art galleries and museums, trendy cafes, and vintage and antique shops, is fast becoming one of south-east Queensland's most popular destinations.

 Workshops Rail Museum In the North Ipswich railyards, this museum offers diverse historical displays, interactive exhibitions and an impressive variety of machinery. Watch workers restore old steam trains, or look into the future of rail by taking a simulated ride in the high-speed tilt train; North St.

Global Art Links Gallery This art gallery and social history museum merges heritage and the present day at the Old Town Hall. See the local and visiting exhibitions in the Gallery, partake in the interactive displays of Ipswich history in the Hall of Time, walk through the Indigenous installation in the Return to Kabool section, or try electronic finger-painting in the Children's Gallery; D'Arcy Doyle Pl.

Queens Park Nature Centre: native flora, animals and a bird aviary; Goleby Ave. **Ipswich Heritage Model Railway Club:** miniature trains; activity days on the 1st Sat and 3rd Sun of each month, visits at other times by appt; via Workshops Rail Museum. **Pillar of Courage:** memorial to 2011's floods; Queen St. **Historical walk:** self-guide walk to see the renowned heritage buildings, churches and excellent domestic architecture of Ipswich, including the Uniting Church (1858) and Gooloowan (1864); outstanding colour brochure available from visitor centre.

Showground Market: Salisbury Rd; Sun. ***Farmers Market:*** Leichhardt Community Centre; 1st Sat each month. ***Handmade Expo:*** over 50 stalls of handmade arts and crafts; Sat. ***Rodeo:*** May. ***Ipswich Cup:*** horseracing; June. ***Circus Train:*** month-long event with circus performers and train rides; Sept–Oct. ***Model Railway Show:*** Oct. ***Jacaranda Festival (Goodna):*** Oct.

Cotton's Restaurant: modern-Australian steakhouse; Spicers Hidden Vale, 617 Grandchester–Mt Mort Rd, Grandchester; (07) 5465 5900. ***Woodlands of Marburg:*** modern Australian in heritage house; 174 Seminary Rd, Marburg; (07) 5464 4777. ***Wray Organic Market and Cafe:*** organic market and cafe; 70 Warwick Rd, Ipswich; (07) 3812 3300.

Ipswich Caravan Village: 95 Mt Crosby Rd, Tivoli; (07) 3281 7951. ***Villiers Bed & Breakfast:*** 14 Cardew St, East Ipswich; (07) 3281 7364.

Queensland Raceway: home to the Queensland 500 and host of the V8 Supercar Series. Winternationals Drag-racing Championship runs every June; 15 km w. ***Wolston House:*** historic home at Wacol; open 2nd and 4th Sun of every month; 16 km E. ***Rosewood:*** heritage town featuring St Brigid's Church, the largest wooden church in the South Pacific. The Workshops Railway Museum, with displays of the area's industrial heritage, runs Blacksmiths and Steam Shop tours daily, plus scenic steam-train rides on the first Sun of each month; museum open daily; 20 km w. ***Recreational reserves:*** popular picnic and leisure spots to the north-east of Ipswich include College's Crossing (7 km), Mt Crosby (12 km) and Lake Manchester (22 km).

TOWNS NEARBY: Laidley 36 km, Strathpine 41 km, Boonah 43 km, Beaudesert 47 km, Gatton 48 km

Isisford
Pop. 262
Map ref. 610 B11 | 617 N11

i Council offices, St Mary St; (07) 4658 8900; www.isisford.qld.gov.au

104.5 FM West, 603 AM ABC Western QLD

Isisford is a small outback community south of Longreach. In the mid-1800s large stations were established in the area. This brought hawkers, keen on trading their goods to the landowners. Two such hawkers were brothers William and James Whitman who, after their axle broke trying to cross the Alice River, decided to stay and established Isisford in 1877. First called Wittown, after the brothers, it was renamed in 1880 to recall the nearby Barcoo River ford and Isis Downs Station. The town provided inspiration to iconic Australian poet Banjo Paterson, in particular his poems 'Bush Christening' and 'Clancy of the Overflow'.

Outer Barcoo Interpretation Centre: features the world-class fossil exhibit of *Isisfordia duncani*, reported to be the ancestor of all modern crocodilians. Also local arts and crafts, town relics and theatrette; St Mary St. ***Whitman's Museum:*** photographic exhibition documents Isisford's history; St Mary St. ***Barcoo Weir:*** excellent spot for fishing and bush camping.

Sheep and Wool Show: May. ***Fishing Competition and Festival:*** July. ***Horse and Motorbike Gymkhana:*** June/July. ***Isisford Ross Cup:*** horseracing; Oct.

Oma Waterhole: popular for fishing and watersports, and home to a fishing competition and festival mid-year (subject to rains); 15 km sw. ***Idalia National Park:*** 62 km SE; *see Blackall*.

TOWNS NEARBY: Longreach 93 km, Blackall 105 km, Barcaldine 116 km, Jundah 154 km, Aramac 165 km

Julia Creek

Pop. 368
Map ref. 615 H11 | 617 J3

i Cnr Burke and Quarrell sts; (07) 4746 7690; www.mckinlay.qld.gov.au

99.5 FM Rebel, 567 AM ABC North West QLD

Julia Creek became known as 'The Gateway to the Gulf' after the road to Normanton was sealed in 1964. Pioneer Donald MacIntyre was the first to settle when he established Dalgonally Station in 1862. Julia Creek is actually named after his niece. A monument to Donald and his brother Duncan (an explorer who led a search for Leichhardt) can be seen by the grave site on the station boundary. The district's main industries are cattle, sheep and mining. It is also home to a rare and endangered marsupial, the Julia Creek dunnart, a tiny nocturnal hunter found only within a 100-kilometre radius of town.

Duncan MacIntyre Museum: local pioneering and cattle history; Burke St. ***Opera House:*** photographic display of McKinlay Shire; closed weekends; Julia St. ***Historical walk:*** stroll the 38 signposted historical sites around the town; map from visitor centre.

Dirt and Dust Festival: Apr. ***Horseracing:*** Apr–Aug. ***Campdraft and Rodeo:*** May, June and Aug. ***Cultural Capers:*** Oct.

Julia Creek Caravan Park: Old Normanton Rd; (07) 4746 7108.

WW II bunkers: remains of concrete bunkers used to assist navigation of allied aircraft; western outskirts near airport. ***Punchbowl waterhole:*** popular area for swimming and fishing on the Flinders River; 45 km NE. ***PROA Redclaw Farm:*** 12 ponds with over 16 000 redclaw; 75 km SE. ***Sedan Dip:*** popular swimming, fishing and picnicking spot; 100 km N.

TOWNS NEARBY: Kynuna 104 km, Cloncurry 128 km, Richmond 146 km, Winton 234 km, Mount Isa 234 km

Jundah
Pop. 93
Map ref. 619 J1

i Dickson St; (07) 4658 6930; www.outbackholidays.tq.com.au

101.7 FM Triple C, 540 AM ABC Western QLD

Jundah is at the centre of the Channel Country and its name comes from the Aboriginal word for women. Gazetted as a town in 1880, for 20 years the area was important for opal mining, but lack of water caused the mines to close. The waterholes and channels of the Thomson River are filled with yabbies and fish, including yellow-belly and bream. The spectacular rock holes, red sand dunes and beauty of Welford National Park are the natural attractions of this outback town.

Jundah Museum: documents area's early pioneer heritage; Perkins St. ***Post Office:*** beautiful shopfront mural; Dickson St.

Race Carnival: Oct. ***Wooly Caulfield Cup:*** sheep races; Oct.

Welford National Park This park protects mulga lands, Channel Country and Mitchell grass downs – 3 types of natural vegetation in Queensland. See the rare earth homestead (1882) that is now listed by the National Trust (not open to the public) or go wildlife-watching to see pelicans and whistling kites at the many waterholes of the Barcoo River. There are 2 self-guide drives that start at the campground: one through the mulga vegetation to the scenic Sawyers Creek; the other a desert drive past the impressive red sand dunes. 4WD is recommended. Roads are impassable in wet weather; call 000 or Jundah police station on (07) 4658 6120 in emergency. (07) 4652 7333; 20 km s.

Stonehenge: named not for the ancient English rock formation, but for the old stone hut built for visiting bullock teams. Nearby on the Thomson River are brolgas and wild budgerigars; 68 km NE. *Windorah:* holds the International Yabby Race in Sept; 95 km S.

TOWNS NEARBY: Isisford 154 km, Longreach 196 km, Quilpie 232 km, Blackall 247 km

Karumba

Pop. 522
Map ref. 612 C7 | 615 G4

 Karumba Library, Walker St, (07) 4745 9582; or call Normanton Visitor Information Centre, (07) 4745 1065; www.gulf-savannah.com.au

98.1 FM Rebel, 567 AM ABC North West QLD

Karumba is at the mouth of the Norman River in the Gulf Savannah. It is the easiest access point for the Gulf of Carpentaria, the key reason the town is the centre for the Gulf's booming prawn and barramundi industries. During the 1930s, the town was an important refuelling depot for the airships of the Empire Flying Boats, which travelled from Sydney to England. Fishing enthusiasts will enjoy the untouched waters of the gulf and nearby rivers that offer an abundance of fish.

Barramundi Discovery Centre: barramundi display and information; Riverside Dr. *Ferryman cruises:* tours include birdwatching, gulf sunset and night crocodile spotting; depart Karumba boat ramp; (07) 4745 9155. *Charters and dinghy hire:* discover the renowned fishing spots in the Gulf or on the Norman River on a charter or hire a dinghy; Karumba Port. *Heritage walk:* self-guide walk; brochure from Karumba library.

Market: Sunset Tavern; Sun. *Fishing Competition:* follows Easter event at Normanton; Apr. *Norman River Duck Race:* June.

Wetland region: extending 30 km inland from Karumba are the wetlands, habitat of the saltwater crocodile and several species of birds, including brolgas and cranes. *Cemetery:* early-settlement cemetery when Karumba was known as Norman Mouth telegraph station; 2 km N on road to Karumba Pt. *Karumba Pt:* boat hire available; note presence of saltwater crocodiles; 3 km N. *Sweers Island:* island in the Gulf with beaches, abundant birdlife, excellent fishing and caves; access is by boat or air; details from visitor centre.

TOWNS NEARBY: Normanton 32 km, Burketown 140 km, Croydon 169 km

Kenilworth

Pop. 238
Map ref. 602 E3 | 603 D11 | 609 M7

 4 Elizabeth St; (07) 5446 0122.

91.1 FM Hot, 612 AM ABC Brisbane

West of the Blackall Range in the Sunshine Coast hinterland is Kenilworth. This charming town is known for its handcrafted cheeses and excellent bushwalking. The spectacular gorges, waterfalls, creeks and scenic lookouts make Kenilworth State Forest a popular spot for bushwalking, camping and picnics.

Kenilworth Cheese Factory: tastings and sales of local cheeses; Charles St. *Historical Museum:* machinery and dairy display and audiovisual show; open 10am–3pm Sun or by appt; Alexandra St; (07) 5446 0581. *Lasting Impressions Gallery:* fine-art gallery; Elizabeth St. *Artspace Gallery:* local art on display; Elizabeth St.

Kenilworth Cheese, Wine and Food Festival: Easter. *Kenilworth Celebrates:* arts festival; Sept–Oct.

Rosevale House: 4210 Mary Valley Rd, Brooloo; (07) 5488 6770.

Kenilworth State Forest This diverse park is in the rugged Conondale Ranges. The rainforest, tall open forest and exotic pines are home to birds and wildlife, including the threatened yellow-bellied glider. There are walks signposted, but a highlight is the steep 4 km return hike from Booloumba Creek to the summit of Mt Allan, where the forest and gorge views are breathtaking. Visit Booloumba Falls from the Gorge picnic area (3 km return) or picnic in the riverine rainforest at Peters Creek. Turn-off to the park is 6 km SW.

Kenilworth wineries: tastings and sales at boutique wineries; 4 km N. *Kenilworth Bluff:* steep walking track to lookout point; 6 km N. *Conondale National Park:* this small forest reserve west of the Mary River is suitable only for experienced walkers. Take the 37 km scenic drive, starting in the adjacent Kenilworth Forest, to enjoy the rugged delights of the park; (07) 5446 0925. *Lake Borumba:* picnics and watersports, and home to a fishing competition each Mar; 32 km NW.

TOWNS NEARBY: Maleny 22 km, Yandina 23 km, Nambour 23 km, Pomona 28 km, Landsborough 33 km

Killarney

Pop. 833
Map ref. 516 C2 | 525 L1 | 609 L11

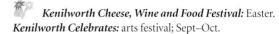 49 Albion St (New England Hwy), Warwick; (07) 4661 3122; www.southerndownsholidays.com.au

The attractive small town of Killarney is on the banks of the Condamine River close to the New South Wales border. It is

[KILLARNEY] QUEEN MARY FALLS, MAIN RANGE NATIONAL PARK

QUEENSLAND

appealingly situated at the foothills of the Great Dividing Range and is surrounded by beautiful mountain scenery.

🍴 *Spring Creek Mountain Cafe & Cottages:* local produce, great views; Spring Creek Rd; (07) 4664 7101.

🛏 *Killarney View Cabins and Caravan Park:* Cnr O'Maras and Claydon rds; (07) 4664 1522. *Oaklea Bed and Breakfast:* 1966 Condamine River Rd; (07) 4664 7161. *Queen Mary Falls Caravan Park and Cabins:* 676 Spring Creek Rd, The Falls; (07) 4664 7151. *Spring Creek Mountain Cafe & Cottages:* 1503 Spring Creek Rd, The Falls; (07) 4664 7101.

🏞 **Main Range National Park, Queen Mary Falls section** The Queen Mary Falls section of this World Heritage–listed park is right on the NSW border. Most of the vegetation is open eucalypt, but in the gorge below the falls is subtropical rainforest. Follow the 2 km Queen Mary Falls circuit to the lookout for a stunning view of the 40 m falls and continue down to the rockpools at the base. If you are lucky, the rare Albert's lyrebird might be seen on the walk or the endangered brush-tailed rock-wallaby on the cliffs; 11 km E; *see also Boonah.*

Dagg's and Brown's waterfalls: stand behind Brown's Falls and see the 38 m Dagg's Falls; 4 km s. *Cherrabah Homestead Resort:* offers horseriding and fabulous bushwalking; 7 km s.

TOWNS NEARBY: Warwick 29 km, Allora 46 km, Stanthorpe 50 km, Boonah 53 km, Clifton 59 km

Kingaroy
Pop. 7619
Map ref. 603 A10 | 609 L7

ℹ️ 128 Haly St (opposite silos); (07) 4162 6272; www.kingaroy.qld.gov.au

📻 96.3 FM Kingaroy, 747 AM ABC Southern QLD

Kingaroy is a large and prosperous town in the South Burnett region. The town's name derives from the Aboriginal word 'Kingaroori', meaning red ant. Found in the area, this unique ant has gradually adapted its colour to resemble the red soil plains of Kingaroy. The town is the centre for Queensland's peanut and navy-bean industries, and its giant peanut silos are landmarks. The region's relatively new wine industry is thriving, with excellent boutique wineries close by. Kingaroy was also the home of Sir Johannes (Joh) Bjelke-Petersen, former premier of Queensland.

🏠 *Heritage Museum:* formerly the Kingaroy Power House, the museum depicts the history of Kingaroy under the themes of people, power and peanuts. Historical displays include machinery, photos and videos on the peanut and navy-bean industries; Haly St. *Art Gallery:* local and regional artists; open 10am–3pm Mon–Fri; Civic Sq, Glendon St. *The Peanut Van:* sales of local 'jumbo' peanuts; Kingaroy St. *Apex Lookout:* panoramic views of town; Carroll Nature Reserve, Fisher St.

 Wine and Food in the Park Festival: Mar. *Peanut Festival:* includes the Strong Man Games; Aug.

🍴 *Booie Bello Vista:* modern Australian; Cnr Schellbachs and Haydens rds; (07) 4162 7632.

🛏 *BIG4 Kingaroy Holiday Park:* 48 Walter Rd (D'Aguilar Hwy); 1800 502 218. *Hillsdale Hideaway Bed & Breakfast:* 166 Hillsdale Rd; (07) 4162 4689. *Kingaroy Showgrounds Caravan Park:* 31 Youngman St; (07) 4162 5800. *Minmore Farmstay and B&B:* 583 Minmore Rd; (07) 4164 3196. *Redrock on Booie:* 45 Millers Rd; (07) 4162 4943. *Rock-Al-Roy Bed & Breakfast:* 15 Kearney St; (07) 4162 3061.

Mulanah Gardens B&B Cottages/Wedding Venue: 736 Deep Creek Rd, Inverlaw; (07) 4164 3142.

🏞 **Bunya Mountains National Park** The Bunya Mountains sit on an isolated spur of the Great Dividing Range, a cool, moist region of waterfalls, and green and scarlet king parrots. This important park the world's largest natural Bunya-pine forest, a species much depleted by early timber-getters. It is a significant Aboriginal site as many feasts were held here with the bunya nuts as the main fare. There are many walking trails for beginners and the experienced alike, including the short Bunya Bunya Track, the 8.4 km return Cherry Plain Track, or the easy 4 km Scenic Circuit from the Dandabah camping area, which winds through rainforest to Pine Gorge Lookout. Have a bush picnic and see the many butterflies or go spotlighting to glimpse owls and mountain possums. (07) 4668 3127; 58 km sw.

Aboriginal Bora Ring: preserved site; Cnr Reagan and Coolabunia rds; 17.5 km sw. *Mt Wooroolin Lookout:* excellent views over Kingaroy's farmlands; 3 km w. *Bethany:* tour the Bjelke-Petersen's property and taste the famous Bjelke-Petersen pumpkin scones; open Wed and Sat, bookings essential; (07) 4162 7046; off Goodger Rd; 9 km se. *Wooroolin:* quaint town with many heritage buildings including the Grant Hotel (1916). The Gordonbrook Dam is an excellent spot for picnics and birdwatching from the hides; 18 km n. *Scenic aeroplane flights:* over the Burnett region daily; (07) 4162 2629. *Scenic glider flights:* over surrounding area; (07) 4162 2191.

TOWNS NEARBY: Nanango 22 km, Murgon 35 km, Crows Nest 83 km, Kenilworth 89 km, Gympie 91 km

Kuranda
Pop. 1612
Map ref. 606 D2 | 607 E6 | 613 L6

ℹ️ Therwine St; (07) 4093 9311; www.kuranda.org

📻 99.5 FM Sea, 801 AM ABC Far North QLD

This small village is set in tropical rainforest on the banks of the Barron River north-west of Cairns. Its beautiful setting attracted a strong hippie culture in the 1960s and 1970s and, while it still has a bohemian feel, tourism is now the order of the day. There are many nature parks and eco-tourism experiences on offer, along with plenty of art and craft workshops, cafes and a daily market. Even transport to and from the town has been developed into an attraction – the Scenic Railway and Skyrail, both with jaw-dropping views over World Heritage–listed rainforest.

🏠 **Scenic Railway and Skyrail** The Scenic Railway is an engineering feat over 100 years old with tunnels, bridges and incredible views of Barron Falls. It begins in Cairns and ends 34 km later in the lush garden setting of Kuranda Station. Travel by rail on the way up and take the Skyrail on the way back (or vice versa), a journey via gondola across the treetops (ends at Caravonica Lakes, 11 km n of Cairns). (07) 4038 1555.

Butterfly Sanctuary: large enclosure, home to over 1500 tropical butterflies, including the blue Ulysses and the Australian birdwing, the country's largest butterfly; Rod Veivers Dr. *Birdworld:* over 50 species of birds, including the flightless cassowary and some endangered species; close to the heritage markets. *Koala Gardens:* Australian animals in a natural setting; close to the heritage markets. *The Aviary:* birds, frogs, snakes and crocodiles; Thongon St. *Arts and crafts shops:* including Kuranda Arts Cooperative, next to Butterfly Sanctuary, and Doongal Aboriginal Arts and Crafts on Coondoo St. *Emu Ridge Gallery and Museum:* unique dinosaur skeleton, fossil and gemstone museum; Therwine St. *Australian Venom Zoo:* visit the most venomous snakes and spiders in the world; Coondoo St. *World Famous Honey House:* free tastings and live bee displays; open 9am–3pm; Therwine St. *River cruises:* depart daily from the riverside landing below the railway station.

 Kuranda Heritage Markets: Rod Veivers Dr; daily. *Kuranda Original Markets:* behind the Kuranda Market Arcade; daily. *New Kuranda Markets:* 40 shops and stalls on Coondoo St; daily. *Kuranda Spring Festival:* Sept.

Cedar Park Rainforest Resort: very fine affordable food; 250 Cedar Park Rd; (07) 4093 7892.

Kuranda Rainforest Accommodation Park: 88 Kuranda Heights Rd; (07) 4093 7316.

Barron Gorge National Park Most people experience this park via the Scenic Railway or Skyrail, but those who want to get away from the crowds could set out on one of the park's bushwalking tracks leading into pockets of World Heritage wilderness. Perhaps you'll spot a Ulysses butterfly, cassowary or tree kangaroo. If you haven't already seen Barron Falls from the train or Skyrail, make your way to Barron Falls lookout 3 km from Kuranda. The falls are spectacular after rain. Access to the national park is via Cairns or Kuranda; (07) 4046 6600.

Kuranda Nature Park: wildlife, canoeing, swimming and rainforest tours aboard 4WD Hummers; 2 km w. *Rainforestation Nature Park:* rainforest tours, tropical fruit orchard, Pamagirri Aboriginal Dance troupe, Dreamtime walk, and a koala and wildlife park; 35 km E. *Carrowong Wildlife Eco-tours:* tours to see nocturnal, rare and endangered rainforest creatures; (07) 4093 7287.

TOWNS NEARBY: Palm Cove 9 km, Cairns 18 km, Mareeba 30 km, Gordonvale 34 km, Port Douglas 41 km

Kynuna

Pop. 20
Map ref. 617 J5

 Roadhouse, Matilda Hwy; (07) 4746 8683.

 95.9 FM West, 540 AM ABC Western QLD

Kynuna is a tiny outback town famous for inspiring Banjo Paterson to write his iconic tune, 'Waltzing Matilda'. It is said that Samuel Hoffmeister, at the time of the Shearers' Strike, drank his last drink at the Blue Heeler Hotel and then killed himself at Combo waterhole (south of town). This story stirred Paterson to write the now-famous ballad.

Blue Heeler Hotel: famous hotel with illuminated blue heeler statue on the roof. *Kynuna Roadhouse:* obtain a mudmap from the roadhouse to find the original Swagman's Billabong.

Surf Carnival: Apr.

Combo Waterhole Conservation Park The events described in 'Waltzing Matilda' occurred in this park, which has waterholes lined with coolibahs. On the Diamantina River, the park is an important dry-weather wildlife refuge. See the Chinese-labour-constructed historic stone causeways from the 1880s or take the 40 min return waterhole walk. The turn-off to the park is 16 km E.

McKinlay Although the town is tiny, its famous Walkabout Creek Hotel was originally known as McKinlay Hotel and is the local

watering hole in the film *Crocodile Dundee*, which starred famed Australian larrikin Paul Hogan. 74 km NW.

Swagman's Billabong: made famous in our national folk song; 2 km E.

TOWNS NEARBY: Julia Creek 104 km, Winton 146 km, Richmond 158 km, Cloncurry 175 km

Laidley

Pop. 2858
Map ref. 602 A12 | 609 M9

 Lockyer Valley Tourist Information Centre, Jumbo's Fruit Barn Complex, Warrego Hwy, Hatton Vale; (07) 5465 7642; www.laidley.qld.gov.au

100.7 FM C, 747 AM ABC Southern QLD

Located west of Brisbane in the Lockyer Valley, the township of Laidley boasts classic Queensland architecture. A landscape dominated by agricultural farmland has earned the region the nickname of 'Queensland's Country Garden'. It produces an abundance of seasonal fruit and vegetables, and farmers showcase their fresh produce at the weekly Country Market. Memorials, museums and statues commemorate Laidley's rich history as a wagon-stop route, later replaced by a rail line between Ipswich and Toowoomba.

Das Neumann Haus Restored and refurbished in 1930s style, this 1893 historic home is the oldest in the shire. It was built by a German immigrant, whose carpentry skills can be seen in the excellent detailing of the building's facade and interior. It houses a local-history museum and exhibits local art and craft; open 10am–3pm Mon–Sun; William St.

Historical walk: self-guide walk to heritage sites; contact visitor centre for details.

Street market: Patrick St; Fri. *Country market:* Ferrari Park; last Sat each month. *Rodeo:* Apr. *Heritage Day:* Apr. *Laidley Show:* July. *Spring Festival:* flower and art show, craft expo, street parade and markets; Sept. *Art Exhibition:* Oct. *Christmas Carnival:* Dec.

Laidley Caravan Park: 25 Campbell St; (07) 5465 3506.

Laidley Pioneer Village: original buildings from old township including blacksmith shop and slab hut; 1 km S. *Narda Lagoon:* flora and fauna sanctuary with picturesque suspension footbridge over lagoon; adjacent to pioneer village. *Lake Dyer:* beautiful spot for fishing, picnics and camping; 1 km w. *Lake Clarendon:* birdwatching area; 17 km NW. *Laidley Valley Scenic Drive:* attractive drive to the south of Laidley through Thornton.

TOWNS NEARBY: Gatton 14 km, Ipswich 36 km, Esk 44 km, Toowoomba 44 km, Boonah 50 km

Landsborough

Pop. 2807
Map ref. 602 F5 | 603 E12 | 609 N8

 Historical Museum, Maleny St; (07) 5494 1755; www.landsboroughtown.com.au

90.3 FM ABC Coast QLD, 91.1 FM Hot

Landsborough is just north of the magnificent Glass House Mountains in the Sunshine Coast hinterland. It was named after the explorer William Landsborough and was originally a logging town for the rich woodlands of the Blackall Ranges.

 RADIO STATIONS IN TOWN WHAT'S ON WHERE TO EAT WHERE TO STAY NEARBY

QUEENSLAND

Historical Museum: this excellent local museum documents the history of the shire through memorabilia, photographs and artefacts; open 9am–3pm Thurs–Mon; Maleny St. *De Maine Pottery:* award-winning clay pottery by Joanna de Maine; open Thurs–Mon; Maleny St.

Market: School of Arts Memorial Hall; Sat.

Landsborough Pines Caravan Park: Steve Irwin Way; (07) 5494 1207. *Eyrie Escape:* 316 Brandenburg Rd, Bald Knob; 0414 308 666.

Glass House Mountains National Park This park protects 8 rugged volcanic mountain peaks. These 20-million-year-old crags, the giant cores of extinct volcanoes, mark the southern entrance to the Sunshine Coast. Glass House Mountains Road leads to sealed and unsealed routes through the mountains, with some spectacular lookouts along the way. The open eucalypt and mountain-heath landscape is a haven for many threatened and endangered animals. Three tracks lead to mountain lookouts that provide panoramic views of the Sunshine Coast hinterland. There are picnic grounds, and challenges aplenty for rockclimbers, but only experienced walkers should attempt climbing to any of the summits. (07) 5494 3983; 13 km sw.

Australia Zoo Once a small park, this zoo was made famous by 'The Crocodile Hunter', Steve Irwin, who was tragically killed by a stingray in 2006. Originally developed by Irwin's parents, the complex is now over 20 ha and home to a wide range of animals. See the otters catching fish, the birds of prey tackling the skies, the ever-popular crocodile demonstrations or feed the kangaroos by hand in the Kids Zoo. The complex also has important breeding programs for threatened and endangered species; 4 km s.

Dularcha National Park: scenic park with excellent walks. 'Dularcha' is an Aboriginal word describing blackbutt eucalyptus country; (07) 5494 3983; 1 km NE. *Big Kart Track:* largest outdoor go-kart track in Australia, open for day and night racing and includes the 'Bungee Bullet'; 5 km N. *Beerburrum State Forest:* short walks and scenic drives to lookouts; access from Beerburrum; 11 km s.

TOWNS NEARBY: Maleny 12 km, Buderim 17 km, Caloundra 18 km, Nambour 20 km, Mooloolaba 21 km

Laura

Pop. 225
Map ref. 613 J3

i Quinkan Centre, Peninsula Development Rd; (07) 4060 3457; www.quinkancc.com.au

92.5 FM 4CA, 106.1 FM ABC Far North QLD

Laura is a tiny town in Far North Queensland that boasts only a few buildings, including the quaint old Quinkan Pub nestled in the shade of mango trees. The area to the south-east of town is known as Quinkan country after the Aboriginal spirits depicted at the incredible Split Rock and Gu Gu Yalangi rock-art sites. Every two years Laura hosts possibly the biggest Indigenous event on Australia's calendar – the Laura Dance and Cultural Festival.

 Quinkan Centre: photos and relics of Quinkan Country are on display here. Guided tours, which include rock-art sites, can also be booked from the centre; Peninsula Development Rd; (07) 4060 3457.

Laura Aboriginal Dance and Cultural Festival: around 25 Cape York and Gulf communities gather at a traditional meeting ground by the Laura River. Traditional dance, music, and art and

craft feature at the 3-day event; odd-numbered years, June. *Laura Annual Race Meeting:* race meeting on river flat that has run since 1897, and includes dances and rodeo; June.

 Split Rock and Gu Gu Yalangi rock-art sites These are Queensland's most important Aboriginal art sites. Hidden behind a tangle of trees in the chasms and crevices of the sandstone escarpment, a diorama of Aboriginal lore and culture unfolds. The Quinkan spirits – the reptile-like Imgin and stick-like Timara – can be found hiding in dark places. There are also dingoes, flying foxes, kangaroos, men, women and many hundreds of other things, both obvious and mysterious. More sites exist nearby, though only these 2 are accessible to the public. Bookings through the Quinkan Centre; 12 km s.

Rinyirru (Lakefield) National Park (CYPAL) This park is Queensland's second largest and a highlight of any visit to the Cape. The large rivers and waterholes are excellent for fishing and boating in the dry season, but become inaccessible wetlands in the wet season. In the south is the Old Laura Homestead, once en route to the Palmer River Goldfields, and in the north are plains dotted with spectacular anthills. See the threatened gold-shouldered parrot and spectacled hare-wallaby in the rainforest fringes of the Normanby and Kennedy rivers. 4WD is recommended. Access only in the dry season (Apr–Nov); (07) 4069 5777; entrance is 27 km N.

Lakeland Downs: bananas and coffee are the main fare cultivated from the area's rich volcanic soil, which is also ideal for a variety of fruit and vegetables; 62 km s.

TOWNS NEARBY: Cooktown 87 km, Daintree 121 km, Mossman 141 km, Port Douglas 150 km, Chillagoe 176 km

Lindeman Island

see Airlie Beach, nearby

Lizard Island

see Cooktown, nearby

Mackay

see inset box on page 424

Maleny

Pop. 1299
Map ref. 602 E4 | 603 E12 | 609 N7

i 25 Maple St; (07) 5499 9033; www.brbta.com

91.1 FM Hot, 612 AM ABC Brisbane

A steep road climbs from the coast to Maleny, at the southern end of the Blackall Range. The surrounding area is lush dairy country, although farmland is increasingly being sold for residential development. The town's peaceful community lifestyle and picturesque position, with views to the coast and Glass House Mountains, make it popular with artists.

Arts and crafts galleries: excellent quality galleries throughout town.

Handcraft Markets: Community Centre, Maple St; Sun. *Chainsaw to Fine Furniture Expo:* May. *Spring Fair and Flower Show:* Sept. *Scarecrow Festival:* Sept. *Fine Art Show:* Sept. *Festival of Colour:* Oct. *Christmas Show:* Nov.

Terrace of Maleny: seafood with style; Cnr Mountain View and Maleny–Landsborough rds; (07) 5494 3700. *Le Relais Bressan:* French provincial; 344 Flaxton Dr, Flaxton; (07) 5445 7157.

continued on p. 425

LONGREACH

Pop. 2976
Map ref. 610 B10 | 617 N10

 Qantas Park, Eagle St; (07) 4658 4150;
www.longreach.qld.gov.au

104.5 FM West, 540 AM ABC Western QLD

Longreach is the largest town in central-west Queensland. Lying on the Tropic of Capricorn, this 'boom and bust' country is affected by flooding rains and devastating drought. It epitomises the outback and features the renowned Australian Stockman's Hall of Fame, devoted to the outback hero. In 1922 Longreach became the operational base for Qantas and remained so until 1934. The world's first Flying Surgeon Service started from here in 1959. Longreach is bisected by the Thompson River, the vast length of which is this town's namesake.

Australian Stockman's Hall of Fame and Outback Heritage Centre Opened in 1988 by Queen Elisabeth II, this impressive centre is a tribute to the men and women who pioneered outback Australia for settlement, industry and agriculture. Its many educational and interactive displays include everything from Australia's Indigenous heritage and the challenges of outback education to the life of the modern-day stockman. Highlights include a photo gallery, an old blacksmith's shop and a 1920s kitchen; Landsborough Hwy; (07) 4658 2166.

Qantas Founders Museum This modern museum details the commercial-flight history of the 2nd oldest airline in the world. Explore the restored 1922 hangar, which features displays on early flights and a replica Avro 504K. Visit the exhibition hall to see how flying has evolved over the last century; Longreach Airport, Landsborough Hwy; (07) 4658 3737.

Powerhouse Museum: displays of old agricultural machinery, power station and local history museum; open 2–5pm Apr–Oct; Swan St. *Botanical Gardens:* walking and cycling trails; Landsborough Hwy. *Banjo's Outback Theatre and Woolshed:* bush poetry, songs and shearing; near airport. *Qantas Park:* replica of original Qantas booking office, which now houses the information centre; Eagle St. *Heritage buildings:* highlights include the courthouse (1892) in Galah St and the railway station (1916) in Sir Hudson Fysh Dr. *Kinnon and Co:* offers horse-drawn adventure tours; bookings through The Station Store; (07) 4658 2006.

Easter in the Outback: Easter. *Outback Muster and Drovers Reunion:* May. *Rodeo:* July. *Fishing Competition:* Aug. *Horseracing:* Nov.

Discovery Holiday Parks – Longreach: 12 Thrush Rd; (07) 4658 1781.

Lochern National Park Waterholes created by the Thomson River are a sanctuary for a variety of birds. Camp beside the billabong in true outback style at Broadwater Hole and watch the brolgas and pelicans. For visitors passing through, drive the 16 km Bluebush Lagoon circuit to see the natural attractions of this park and glimpse Australian favourites – the kangaroo and emu. Visitors must be self-sufficient. Check road conditions before departing – roads may be impassable in wet weather; (07) 4652 7333. Turnoff 100 km s onto Longreach–Jundah Rd, then further 40 km.

Thomson River: fishing, bushwalking and swimming; 4.6 km NW. *Ilfracombe:* once a transport nucleus for the large Wellshot Station to the south, now an interesting outdoor machinery museum runs the length of this town on the highway. Another feature is the historic Wellshot Hotel, with a wool-press bar and local memorabilia; 27 km E. *Starlight's Lookout:* said to be a resting spot of Captain Starlight. Enjoy the scenic view; 56 km NW. *Sheep and cattle station tours:* visit local stations to try mustering and shearing; contact visitor centre for details. *Thomson River cruises:* contact visitor centre for details.

TOWNS NEARBY: Isisford 93 km, Muttaburra 99 km, Barcaldine 107 km, Aramac 115 km, Blackall 165 km

[AUSTRALIAN STOCKMAN'S HALL OF FAME AND OUTBACK HERITAGE CENTRE]

 RADIO STATIONS   IN TOWN   WHAT'S ON   WHERE TO EAT   WHERE TO STAY   NEARBY

QUEENSLAND

MACKAY

Pop. 85 700

Map ref. 605 G8 | 611 K5

[SUGARCANE HARVESTING NEAR MACKAY]

ⓘ Mackay Tourism, 320 Nebo Rd (Bruce Hwy);
(07) 4944 5888 or 1300 130 001; www.mackayregion.com

101.9 FM 4MK, 630 AM ABC North QLD

The city of Mackay is an intriguing blend of 1900s and Art Deco heritage buildings mixed with modern-day architecture. It was first settled in the 1860s by explorer Captain John Mackay, the city's namesake. Sugar was first grown here in 1865. It is now known as Queensland's 'sugar city' as it produces around one-third of Australia's sugar crop and has the world's largest bulk sugar-loading terminal. Tourism is a growth industry in Mackay with the natural delights of the Great Barrier Reef just off the coast and spectacular inland national parks nearby.

Artspace Mackay This modern art gallery forms part of the Queensland Heritage Trails Network. The museum documents Mackay's history with an interesting permanent exhibition titled 'Spirit and Place: Mementos of Mackay'. The gallery section has rotating exhibits of both local and international artwork; Tues–Sat; Gordon St.

Old Town Hall: houses the Heritage Interpretive Centre with displays on Mackay's history and visitor information; Sydney St. *Regional Botanic Gardens:* follow the picturesque boardwalk over a lagoon and explore specialised gardens of central-coast flora; Lagoon St. *Queens Park:* includes the Orchid House with over 3000 orchids; Goldsmith St. *Heritage walk:* self-guide walk of 22 heritage buildings; brochure available from visitor centre. *City cemetery:* 1.5 km heritage walk; Greenmount Rd. *Horizon Mosaics:* locally-constructed mosaics of Mackay region's natural attractions; Victoria St. *Mackay Museum:* local artefacts with a research area and souvenirs for sale; open 10am–2pm every Thurs and 1st Sun each month; Casey Ave. *Great Barrier Reef tours:* snorkelling, diving, reef fishing and sailing tours; details at visitor centre.

Market: showgrounds, Milton St; Sat mornings. *Paxton's Markets:* River St; evenings 1st Fri each month. *Walkers Markets:* Harbour Rd; weekends. *Seaforth Markets:* Palm Ave; Sun mornings. *Troppo Treasure Markets:* showgrounds; 2nd Sun each month. *Seaforth Fishing Classic:* Apr. *Festival of the Arts:* July. *River to Reef Festival:* Aug. *Sugartime Festival:* Sept.

Church on Palmer: international cuisine; 15 Palmer St; (07) 4944 1466. *George's Thai on the Marina:* Thai food and harbour views; Mulherin Dr; (07) 4955 5778. *Sorbello's Italian Restaurant:* affordable Italian; 166 Victoria St; (07) 4957 8300.

Andergrove Van Park: 40–68 Beaconsfield Rd, Andergrove; (07) 4942 4922. *Cape Hillsborough Nature Resort:* 51 Risley Pde, Cape Hillsborough National Park; (07) 4959 0152. *Old Schoolhouse Mud Bath Retreat & Healing Centre:* 888 Gargett Mia Mia Rd, Septimus; (07) 4958 5760.

Eungella National Park This ecologically-diverse park is home to some unusual plants and animals including the Eungella gastric brooding frog and the Mackay tulip oak. A highlight of the visit is seeing the platypus in Broken River from a viewing deck. Visit the Finch Hatton Gorge section of the park with its breathtaking waterfalls, swimming holes and walking tracks. For the more adventurous, try sailing through the rainforest canopy on the eco-tour Forest Flying. Finch Hatton Gorge turn-off is just before Eungella. Broken River is 6 km s of Eungella; (07) 4944 7800 (same phone number for national parks below).

Hibiscus coast Comprises the quaint coastal towns of Seaforth, Ball Bay and Cape Hillsborough. Steep, rainforest-clad hills plunge to rocky headlands and white sandy beaches in this lovely and surprisingly peaceful district north of Mackay. Cape Hillsborough National Park offers the most pristine scenery, as well as tidal rockpools and walking trails. Kangaroos are often seen hopping along the deserted beaches; 43 km NW.

Northern beaches: visit fabulous beaches including Harbour (patrolled, fishing), Town, Blacks (area's longest beach), Bucasia, Illawong, Eimeo, Lamberts (excellent lookout) and Shoal Point. *Farleigh Sugar Mill:* tours during crushing season, July–Oct; 15 km N. *That Sapphire Place:* sapphire display and gem-cutting demonstrations; 20 km W. *Greenmount Homestead:* restored historic home with pioneering history museum; open 9.30am–12.30pm, closed Sat; Walkerston; 20 km W. *Homebush:* small town offers art and craft gallery, orchid farms and self-drive tour through historic area; 25 km s. *Melba House:* the home where Dame Nellie Melba spent the 1st year of her married life. Now home to Pioneer Valley Visitor Centre; Marian; 28 km W.

Mirani: small town in the Pioneer Valley with museum and Illawong Fauna and Flora Sanctuary; 33 km w. *Kinchant Dam:* popular spot for watersports and fishing; 40 km w. *Smith Islands National Park:* the largest island of this group is Goldsmith, with long sandy beaches and snorkelling in surrounding reefs; access is by private boat or water taxi; 70 km NE via Seaforth. *South Cumberland Islands National Park:* this group of islands off Mackay's coast is popular for boating and also an important rookery for flat back and green turtles; access is by private boat or water taxi. *Brampton Island:* resort island at southern end of Whitsunday Passage with pristine beaches and coral reef; sea and air access; 38 km NE. *Nebo:* historic town of Mackay region, with local artefacts and pioneering history at the Nebo Shire Museum. Nebo holds a Campdraft in Sept; 93 km sw.

TOWNS NEARBY: Sarina 30 km, Proserpine 103 km, Airlie Beach 109 km, Moranbah 150 km, Bowen 158 km

 Braeside Bed & Breakfast: 305 Maleny–Stanley River Rd; (07) 5494 3542. *Lillypilly's Country Cottages:* 584 Maleny–Montville Rd; (07) 5494 3002. *Maleny Hideaway:* 32 Sidney La (off Maleny–Kenilworth Rd); (07) 5499 9520. *Maleny Tropical Retreat:* 540 Maleny–Montville Rd; (07) 5435 2113. *Blue Summit Cottages:* 547 Maleny–Kenilworth Rd, Witta; (07) 5435 8410. *Curramore Country Cabins:* 383 Curramore Rd, Curramore; (07) 5435 8300. *Lyndon Lodge Maleny:* 3 Benecke Rd, Balmoral Ridge; (07) 5494 3307. *Monbii:* 39 Balmoral Rd, Montville; (07) 5478 5566. *Narrows Escape Rainforest Retreat:* 78 Narrows Rd, North Maleny; (07) 5478 5000. *Roseville House Bed & Breakfast:* 640 Maleny–Montville Rd, Balmoral Ridge; (07) 5494 3411. *The Spotted Chook & Amelie's Petite Maison:* 176 Western Ave, Montville; (07) 5442 9242.

Kondalilla National Park This park has scenic walks, subtropical rainforest and the spectacular Kondalilla Falls. The 4.6 km return Falls Circuit track passes rockpools to the falls, which drop 90 m; (07) 5494 3983; 21 km N via Montville.

Mary Cairncross Park: this beautiful park was donated to the community in 1941 as protected rainforest after the fierce logging days of the early 1900s. Walk through the rainforest to see superb panoramic views; 7 km SE. *Baroon Pocket Dam:* popular spot for fishing and boating. Follow the boardwalks through rainforest; North Maleny Rd; 8 km N. *Montville:* main street lined with cafes, giftshops, potteries and art and craft galleries. The town also has a growing wine industry; 16 km NE. *Flaxton:* charming tiny village surrounded by avocado orchards. Visit the local craft stores, public gardens, and miniature English village (housed in Allo Allo French Tearoom); 19 km NE. *Flaxton Barn:* antiques store with local food and wine; 21 km N via Flaxton. *Maleny–Blackall Range Tourist Drive:* this 28 km scenic drive is one of the best in south-east Queensland. Drive north-east from Maleny through to Mapleton, stopping off at museums, antique shops, fruit stalls and tearooms along the way, as well as taking in spectacular views. The drive can be extended to Nambour.

TOWNS NEARBY: Landsborough 12 km, Nambour 19 km, Kenilworth 22 km, Buderim 22 km, Yandina 24 km

Mareeba Pop. 6806

Map ref. 606 D2 | 607 D7 | 613 L6

ⓘ Heritage Museum, Centenary Park, 345 Byrnes St; (07) 4092 5674; www.mareebaheritagecentre.com.au

📻 92.3 FM Rhema, 720 AM ABC Far North QLD

Mareeba was the first town settled on the Atherton Tableland by pastoralist John Atherton in 1877. Tobacco production began in the 1950s, but was deregulated only a few years ago. Today the area produces mangoes, coffee and sugarcane. The morning balloon flights over the tableland are spectacular.

Heritage Museum: local history exhibits and information centre; Centenary Park, Byrnes St. *Art Society Gallery:* Centenary Park. *Barron River Walk:* walk along the banks to swimming hole. *Bicentennial Lakes:* park with plantings to encourage wildlife. Explore the park on the walking tracks and bridges; Rankine St. *The Coffee Works:* see the production of coffee and taste-test the results; 136 Mason St. *The Australian Coffee Centre:* this complex offers a 54-seat cinema, coffee labratory and restaurant. Daily tours take you through the coffee plantation and include tastings. Open 9am–5pm daily; 136 Ivicevic Rd.

Market: Centenary Park; 2nd and 5th Sat each month (if applicable). *Great Wheelbarrow Race:* Mareeba to Chillagoe; May. *Rodeo:* July. *Multicultural Festival:* Aug. *Walkamin Country Music Festival:* Oct.

Mareeba Tropical Savanna and Wetland Reserve This conservation reserve of over 2400 ha and 12 lagoons is home to birds, mammals, fish and freshwater crocodiles. Take a self-guide trail by hiring a timber canoe, a tour cruise or the guided 'Twilight Reserve Safari' (with cheese and wine afterwards). Open Apr–Dec (dry season); tour bookings on (07) 4093 2514; turn-off at Biboohra (7 km N).

Mako Trac International Racetrack: Australia's best track and fastest go-karts. Also 18-hole minigolf course; Springs Rd, 2 km w. *de Brueys Boutique Wines:* taste world-class tropical fruit wines, liqueurs and ports; Fichera Rd, 4 km E. *The Beck Museum:* aviation and military collection; Kennedy Hwy; 5 km s. *Warbird Adventures Adventure flights:* experience the thrill of a flight in a real Warbird; museum open Wed–Sun; Kennedy Hwy, 5 km s. *Mango Winery:* produces white wine from 'Kensington Red' mangoes; Bilwon Rd, Biboohra; 7 km N. *Granite Gorge:* impressive boulder and rock formation; 12 km sw off Chewko Rd. *Emerald Creek Falls:* walk 1.9 km and see the water as it tumbles down the mountain between massive boulders; Cobra Rd; 12 km SE. *Davies Creek National Park:* walk the 1.1 km Davies Creek Falls circuit to see the falls crashing over boulders; (07) 4091 1844; 22 km E. *Dimbulah:* small town with museum in restored railway station; 47 km w. *Tyrconnell:* historic mining town with

QUEENSLAND

 RADIO STATIONS IN TOWN WHAT'S ON WHERE TO EAT WHERE TO STAY NEARBY

tours of goldmine; 68 km NW via Dimbulah. *Scenic balloon flights:* over Atherton Tableland; details available from visitor centre.

TOWNS NEARBY: Kuranda 30 km, Atherton 31 km, Yungaburra 35 km, Cairns 37 km, Palm Cove 38 km

Maroochydore

Pop. 17 500
Map ref. 602 G4 | 603 F11 | 609 N7

 Cnr Sixth Ave and Melrose Pde; (07) 5459 9050 or 1800 882 032; www.discovermaroochy.com.au

91.9 FM Sea, 612 AM ABC Brisbane

A popular beach resort, Maroochydore is also the business centre of the Sunshine Coast. The parklands and birdlife on the Maroochy River and the excellent surf beaches began to attract a growing tourist interest in the 1960s, which has only increased since. An incredible range of watersports is available.

Maroochy River: enjoy diverse birdlife and parklands on the southern bank with safe swimming. *Endeavour Replica:* replica of Captain Cook's ship; David Low Way. *The Esplanade:* atmospheric strip of cafes, restaurants and clothing stores.

Market: Cnr Fishermans Rd and Bradman Ave; Sun mornings. *Cotton Tree Street Markets:* King St; Sun mornings.

Ebb: modern Australian, riverside location; 6 Wharf St; (07) 5452 7771. *Boat Shed:* modern Australian, great atmosphere; The Esplanade, Cotton Tree; (07) 5443 3808.

Maroochy Palms Holiday Village: 319 Bradman Ave; (07) 5443 8611. *Maroochy River Cabin Village & Caravan Park:* 1 Diura St; (07) 5443 3033. *Maroochydore Beach Holiday Park:* Melrose Pde; (07) 5443 1167. *Amytis Gardens Retreat & Spa:* 51 Malones Rd, Kiels Mountain; (07) 5450 0115. *Cotton Tree Holiday Park:* Cotton Tree Pde, Cotton Tree; (07) 5443 1253. *Mt Coolum Retreat 'A Bed & Breakfast':* 77 Mountain View Dr, Mount Coolum; (07) 5471 6532. *Mudjimba Beach Holiday Park:* Cottonwood St, Mudjimba; 1800 461 475.

Mt Coolum National Park Located above the surrounding sugarcane fields, the mountain offers cascading waterfalls after rain. The park is generally undeveloped, but take the rough 800 m trail to the summit to be rewarded with panoramic views of the coast. (07) 5447 3243; 13 km N via Marcoola.

Nostalgia Town: emphasises humour in history on a train ride through fantasy settings. Markets every Fri and Sat; Pacific Paradise; 7 km NW. *Bli Bli:* attractions include medieval Bli Bli Castle, with dungeon, torture chamber and doll museum, the 'Ski 'n Surf' waterski park and the Aussie Fishing Park. Take a cruise through Maroochy River wetlands; 9 km NW. *Marcoola:* coastal town with quiet beach; 11 km N. *Coolum Beach:* coastal resort town with long sandy beach; 17 km N. *Eco-Cruise Maroochy:* cruises to Dunethin Rock through sugarcane fields; details from visitor centre.

TOWNS NEARBY: Mooloolaba 2 km, Buderim 5 km, Nambour 14 km, Caloundra 16 km, Yandina 18 km

Maryborough

Pop. 21 499
Map ref. 603 E6 | 609 N5

 City Hall, Kent St; (07) 4190 5742 or 1800 214 789; www.visitfrasercoast.com

103.5 FM Mix, 855 AM ABC Wide Bay

Maryborough is an attractive city on the banks of the Mary River. Its fine heritage buildings and famous timber Queenslander architecture date back to the early years of settlement, when Maryborough was a village and port. Maryborough Port was an important destination in the mid-1800s as over 22 000 immigrants arrived from Europe. Today the Mary River is a popular spot for relaxed boating and some good fishing.

Bond Store Museum: located in the Portside Centre, this museum documents the history of the region from a river port to the present day; open 9am–4pm Mon–Fri, 10am–1pm Sat–Sun; Wharf St. *Customs House Museum:* also in the Portside Centre, this important cultural heritage museum depicts the area's industries and early immigration and Kanaka history; Wharf St. *Military and Colonial Museum:* fascinating look at local military and colonial history; open 9am–3pm daily; Wharf St. *Mary Poppins statue:* statue of the famed and magical nanny in honour of author Pamela Lyndon Travers, who was born in the town in 1899; Cnr Kent and Richmond sts. *Central Railway Station, Mary Ann:* replica of Queensland's first steam engine with rides in Queens Park every Thurs, market day, and last Sun each month; Lennox St. *Queens Park:* unusual domed fernery and waterfall; Cnr Lennox and Bazaar sts. *Elizabeth Park:* extensive rose gardens; Kent St. *ANZAC Park:* includes Ululah Lagoon, a scenic waterbird sanctuary where black swans, wild geese, ducks and waterhens may be handfed; Cnr Cheapside and Alice sts. *Heritage walk:* self-guide walk past 22 historic buildings, including the impressive City Hall, St Paul's bell tower (with pealing bells) and National Trust–listed Brennan and Geraghty's Store. The walk starts at City Hall, Kent St; brochure available from visitor centre. *Heritage drive:* a highlight is the original site of Maryborough (until 1885), where a series of plaques document its history. Drive starts at City Hall; brochure available from visitor centre. *Ghost tours:* discover the town's ghostly past on tours that run once a month; details from visitor centre.

Heritage markets: Cnr Adelaide and Ellena sts; Thurs. *World's Greatest Pub Crawl:* June. *Mary Poppins Festival:* July. *Technology Challenge:* Sept. *Maryborough Masters Games:* Sept/Oct.

Wallace Motel & Caravan Park: 22 Ferry St; (07) 4121 3970. *Huntsville Caravan Park:* 23 Gympie Rd, Tinana; (07) 4121 4075. *Poona Palms Caravan Park:* 101 Boronia Dr, Poona; (07) 4129 8167.

Teddington Weir: popular for watersports; 15 km S. *Tiaro:* excellent fishing for Mary River cod in surrounding waterways. See the historic Dickabram Bridge over the river, and nearby Mt Bauple National Park; 24 km SW. *Tuan Forest:* bushwalking; 24 km SE. *Fraser Island:* World Heritage–listed sand island to the east of town; *see Hervey Bay.*

TOWNS NEARBY: Hervey Bay 33 km, Tin Can Bay 51 km, Childers 55 km, Biggenden 66 km, Gympie 72 km

Miles

Pop. 1164
Map ref. 609 I7

 Historical Village, Murilla St; (07) 4627 1492; www.wdrc.qld.gov.au

94.5 FM Rebel, 747 AM ABC Southern QLD

Miles is in the Western Downs. Ludwig Leichhardt passed through this district on three expeditions and named the place

Dogwood Crossing. The town was later renamed Miles in honour of a local member of parliament. After spring rains, this pocket of the Darling Downs is ablaze with wildflowers.

Dogwood Crossing, Miles This modern cultural centre combines history and art in an innovative space. The excellent Wall of Water displays imagery and stories of the local people – a novel way of discovering the personal history of Miles. The art gallery has changing exhibitions from local and regional artists. There is an IT centre and library also on-site. Murilla St.

Historical Village: a pioneer settlement with all types of early buildings, a war museum, shell display and lapidary exhibition; Murilla St. *Wildflower excursions:* some of the most beautiful wildflowers in Australia; details from visitor centre.

St Luke's market: Dawson St; 2nd Sat each month. *Miles Show:* May. *Back to the Bush:* includes the Wildflower Festival; Sept. *Beef, Bells and Bottle Tree Festival:* massive month-long celebration including country music bash, bush poetry and fishing competition; even-numbered years, Sept.

Miles Caravan Park: 90 Murilla St; (07) 4627 1640. *Possum Park Tourist Caravan, Cabin & Camping Park:* 36865 Leichhardt Hwy; (07) 4627 1651. *Condamine River Caravan Park:* 8 Wambo St, Condamine; (07) 4627 7179.

Condamine: small town known for inventing the Condamine Bell, a bullfrog bell that, hung around bullocks, can be heard up to 4 km away. A replica and history display are in Bell Park. There is excellent fishing on the Condamine River, and the town holds a famous rodeo in Oct; 33 km s. *The Gums:* tiny settlement with historic church and nature reserve; 79 km s. *Glenmorgan:* the Myall Park Botanical Gardens; 134 km sw.

TOWNS NEARBY: Chinchilla 45 km, Taroom 119 km, Dalby 121 km, Roma 141 km, Mundubbera 162 km

Millaa Millaa
Pop. 289
Map ref. 606 D4 | 607 E11 | 613 L7

Millaa Millaa Tourist Park, Millaa Millaa–Malanda Rd; (07) 4097 2290; www.tablelands.org/millaa-millaa.html

97.9 FM Hot, 720 AM ABC Far North QLD

Millaa Millaa is at the southern edge of the Atherton Tableland, and is central to a thriving dairy industry. The 17-kilometre Waterfall Circuit and rainforest-clad Wooroonooran National Park are just two of the natural attractions that bring visitors to the mild climate of this town.

Eacham Historical Society Museum: documents history of local area, with special interest in dairy and timber industries; opening times vary, contact museum for more information; Main St; (07) 4097 2147.

Wooroonooran National Park, Palmerston section More than 500 types of rainforest trees means the landscape in this park is both diverse and breathtaking. Walks include a 5 km return track leading to spectacular gorge views at Crawford's Lookout and a short 800 m track to glimpse the Tchupala Falls. A popular activity in the park is whitewater rafting on the North Johnstone River; companies include RnR Adventures; bookings on (07) 4041 9444. Access via Palmerston Hwy; (07) 4061 5900; 25 km sw.

Waterfall Circuit This 17 km circuit road includes the Zillie, Ellinjaa and Mungalli falls, as well as the popular Millaa Millaa Falls, a great spot for swimming, with walks leading to other waterfalls. The circuit road is mostly sealed and the route leaves and rejoins Palmerston Hwy east of town.

Millaa Millaa Lookout: panoramic views of tablelands and national parks; 6 km w. *Misty Mountains walking trails:* short- and long-distance tracks through World Heritage–listed Wet Tropics, many of which follow traditional Aboriginal paths of the Jirrbal and Mamu people; details from visitor centre. *Hillside Eden Garden:* award-winning garden featured on the television program *Better Homes and Gardens*, with stunning camellias and rhododendrons; Tarzali, 20 km N.

TOWNS NEARBY: Ravenshoe 18 km, Yungaburra 27 km, Herberton 29 km, Atherton 31 km, Babinda 38 km

Miriam Vale
Pop. 362
Map ref. 604 D8 | 609 L2

Discovery Coast Information Centre, Roe St (Bruce Hwy); (07) 4974 5428; www.gladstonerc.qld.gov.au

93.5 FM Hot, 855 AM ABC Wide Bay

Miriam Vale lies south-east of Gladstone, in the hinterland of the 'Discovery Coast'. The town is renowned for its charming hospitality, its historic fig trees in the main street and its mud-crab sandwiches. The hinterland and coastal national parks are ideal places for bushwalking, four-wheel driving and horseriding.

Captain Cook Holiday Village: 384 Captain Cook Dr, Seventeen Seventy; (07) 4974 9219.

Deepwater National Park A diverse vegetation covers this coastal park, including paperbark forests, swamp mahogany, Moreton Bay ash and subtropical rainforest. Walk along the sandy beaches or enjoy the birdlife of the freshwater stream, Deepwater Creek. Bush camp at Wreck Rock, and explore the rockpools. 4WD access only; (07) 4131 1600; 63 km NE via Agnes Water.

Eurimbula National Park: rugged coastal park with walks along the beach, canoeing on Eurimbula Creek, fishing, and scenic views from Ganoonga Noonga Lookout. 4WD recommended; (07) 4131 1600; access between Miriam Vale and Agnes Water; 50 km NE. *Agnes Water:* this coastal town has the most northerly surfing beach in Queensland. A local history museum includes documents of Cook's voyage in 1770. The town holds the surfing competition 1770 Longboard Classic each Mar; 57 km NE. *Seventeen Seventy:* Captain Cook, while on his discovery voyage, made his second landing on Australian soil at the town site. Today the seaside village has the Joseph Banks Environmental Park and is the departure point for daytrips and fishing charters to the Great Barrier Reef and Lady Musgrave Island; 63 km NE.

TOWNS NEARBY: Gladstone 62 km, Monto 74 km, Gin Gin 83 km, Bundaberg 99 km, Biloela 106 km

Mission Beach
Pop. 517
Map ref. 606 E5 | 613 M8

Porter Promenade; (07) 4068 7099; www.missionbeachtourism.com

88.5 FM 4KZ, 630 AM ABC North QLD

Mission Beach is named for the Aboriginal mission established in the area in 1914. The beach that features in the town's name is a 14-kilometre-long strip of golden sand fringed by coconut palms

QUEENSLAND

and World Heritage–listed wet tropical rainforest. Artists, potters, sculptors and jewellers have settled in the area, now reliant on the strong tourism industry of the coast.

Porter Promenade: woodcarving exhibition and rainforest arboretum; next to visitor centre. *Ulysses Link Walking Trail:* this 1.2 km pathway along the foreshore features local history, sculptures and mosaics. *Great Barrier Reef tours:* cruises and day tours to islands and reefs depart from Clump Point Jetty daily. *Boat, catamaran and jetski hire:* details from visitor centre.

Market: Porter Promenade; 1st Sat and 3rd Sun each month. *Monster Markets:* Recreation Centre, Cassowary Dr; last Sun each month (Easter–Nov). *Banana Festival:* Aug. *Aquatic Festival:* Oct.

A Tropical Escape B&B: 13 Spurwood Close, Wongaling Beach; (07) 4068 9898. *Beachcomber Coconut Caravan Village:* Kennedy Esp, Mission Beach South; (07) 4068 8129. *Boutique Bungalows:* 3 Spurwood Close, Wongaling Beach; (07) 4068 9996. *Dunk Island View Caravan Park:* 21 Webb Rd, Wongaling Beach; (07) 4068 8248. *Licuala Lodge:* 11 Mission Circle, Wongaling Beach; (07) 4068 8194.

Family Islands The Family Islands National Park protects this 14 km stretch of islands. The most northerly of the group, Dunk Island, is a popular holiday destination with spectacular forest, rainforest and 14 km of walking tracks. The resort is private (maximum 360 people) but camping is available (maximum 30 people). The less-developed islands of Wheeler and Coombe are perfect for bush camping (visitors must be self-sufficient). There is an air service to Dunk Island from Cairns and Townsville or ferry from Clump Point. Islands are accessible by water taxi from Wongaling Beach.

Clump Mountain National Park: this scenic park boasts remnant lowland rainforest, an important habitat for the southern cassowary. A highlight is the 4 km Bicton Hill Track to the summit lookout over Mission Beach and coast; just north of Mission Beach on Bingil Bay Rd; (07) 4722 5224. *Bedarra Island:* this island of untouched tropical beauty is off-limits to day visitors and children under 15. There's bushwalking, snorkelling, fishing, swimming, windsurfing, sailing and tennis, and an exclusive resort (maximum 30 people); 16 km SE. *Historic cairn:* commemorates the ill-fated 1848 Cape York expedition of Edmund Kennedy; South Mission Beach Espl. *Aboriginal Midju:* display of Aboriginal culture; adjacent to cairn. *Wet Tropics walking trails:* the area around Mission Beach offers spectacular rainforest walks, including the Lacy Creek Forest circuit (1.2 km) in the major cassowary habitat of Djiru National Park, the Kennedy Trail (7 km) past lookouts and along beaches, and the trails in Licuala State Forest; brochure available from visitor centre. *Adventure activities:* include tandem parachuting, kayak trips and whitewater rafting; details from visitor centre.

TOWNS NEARBY: Tully 21 km, Mourilyan 33 km, Innisfail 39 km, Cardwell 44 km, Babinda 61 km

Mitchell

Pop. 942
Map ref. 608 E6

Great Artesian Spa Complex, 2 Cambridge St; (07) 4623 8171; www.visitmitchell.com.au

102.9 FM Outback Radio 4VL, 711 AM ABC Western QLD

Mitchell, a gateway to the outback, is on the banks of the Maranoa River at the western edge of the Darling Downs. But,

located as it is on the Great Artesian Basin, it does not suffer the dry heat or exhibit the arid landscape typical of the region. The town was named after Sir Thomas Mitchell, explorer and Surveyor-General of New South Wales, who visited the region in 1846. Its long pastoral history is shown in the fine examples of heritage buildings on the main street.

Kenniff Courthouse This courthouse was in use from 1882 to 1965. It held the murder trials for the Kenniff Brothers, infamous bushrangers who killed a policeman and station manager in 1902. The courthouse is now a museum with a bushranger exhibition, visual display, and art and craft sales. The landscaped grounds incorporate a community mosaic, an operating artesian windmill and a small billabong. Cambridge St.

Great Artesian Spa Complex: with relaxing waters in a garden setting, this is Australia's largest open-air spa; Cambridge St. *Graffiti murals:* depict the past, present and future of the Booringa Shire; around town. *Art galleries:* including the Maranoa Art Gallery and Nalingu Contemporary Indigenous Gallery. *Horse-drawn wagon tours:* in season; details from visitor centre.

Mitchell Rodeo: Mar/Apr. *Maranoa Diggers Races:* Apr. *Campdraft:* Mar. *Agricultural Show:* May. *Mitchell Show:* May. *Fire & Water Festival:* Sept/Oct. *Bushstock Contemporary Musical Festival:* Oct. *Christmas in the Park:* Dec.

Carnarvon National Park, Mt Moffatt section This section of the park is mainly for driving, with short walks to scenic spots. See the sandstone sculptures of Cathedral Rock, Marlong Arch and Lot's Wife, or visit the Tombs for the ancient stencil art of the Nuri and Bidjara people. The high-country woodlands and forest are home to a variety of wildlife, and birdwatching for raptors and lorikeets is exceptional. 4WD recommended; (07) 4984 4505; 256 km N. Gorge section: *see Roma*. Ka Ka Mundi section: *see Springsure*. Salvator Rosa section: *see Tambo*.

Neil Turner Weir: birdwatching and picnics; 3.5 km NW. *Fisherman's Rest:* good fishing spot; 6 km W. *Maranoa River Nature Walk:* informative 1.8 km circuit walk starting at Fisherman's Rest. *Kenniff Statues:* depict the story of the brothers at their last stand; 7 km S. *Major Mitchell Cruises:* cruises down Maranoa River departing from Rotary Park, Neil Turner Weir; bookings at visitor centre. *Aboriginal tours:* guided tours run by Nalingu Aboriginal Corporation; details from visitor centre.

TOWNS NEARBY: Roma 81 km, Charleville 173 km, St George 182 km, Taroom 205 km, Miles 221 km

Monto

Pop. 1155
Map ref. 604 C10 | 609 K3

Touch screen in Newton St; or council offices, 51A Newton St, (07) 4166 9999; www.northburnett.qld.gov.au

105.1 FM Rebel, 855 AM ABC Wide Bay

Monto, one of the most recent towns in the Capricorn region, was settled in 1924. It is the centre of a rich dairy and beef cattle district and is set picturesquely on a plateau surrounded by rolling hills.

Monto History Centre: local history displays and videos; closed Sat–Sun; Cnr Kelvin and Lister sts. *Historical and Cultural Complex:* variety of historic artefacts and a mineral display; Flinders St.

Country Craft Market: Mulgildie Hall; 1st Sun every month. *Campdraft:* Mar. *Fishing Classic:* Mar. *Horseracing:* Mar.

[MOOLOOLABA] WATCHING A STINGRAY AT UNDERWATER WORLD

Monto Show: Apr. *Monto Festival:* June. **Annual Cattle Drive and Trail Ride:** Aug. *Monto Garden Expo:* Oct.

Cania Gorge Caravan and Tourist Park: Phil Marshall Dr; (07) 4167 8188.

Cania Gorge National Park Part of Queensland's sandstone belt, this park has cliffs, gorges and caves of spectacular colours. The freehand Aboriginal art around the park is a reminder of the area's ancient heritage. There are over 10 walks of varying length and difficulty. See the park's goldmining history on the 1.2 km return Shamrock Mine track or experience breathtaking park views from the Giant's Chair Lookout, reached on the longer Fern Tree Pool and Giant's Chair circuit. (07) 4167 8162; 25 km NW.

Mungungo: small town with boutique Waratah Winery; 13 km N. *Lake Cania:* excellent spot for watersports, fishing (permit required) and walking to lookout. Annual Lake Cania Fishing Classic is held here every Mar; 11 km N via Cania Gorge Picnic Area. *Kalpower State Forest:* hoop pine and rainforest vegetation. 4WD or walk rugged tracks to scenic lookouts; 40 km NE. *Wuruma Dam:* swimming, sailing and waterskiing; 50 km S.

TOWNS NEARBY: Miriam Vale 74 km, Biloela 80 km, Mundubbera 83 km, Gin Gin 86 km, Gayndah 98 km

Mooloolaba
Pop. 7376
Map ref. 602 H4 | 603 F12 | 609 N7

i Cnr First Ave and Brisbane Rd; (07) 5478 2233; www.mooloolabatourism.com.au

90.3 FM ABC Sunshine Coast, 104.9 FM Sunshine

Mooloolaba is a popular holiday destination on the Sunshine Coast. Its fabulous beaches, restaurants, nightlife and resort-style shopping contribute to the constant influx of families and young people eager for the sun. Mooloolaba Harbour is one of the safest anchorages on the east coast and the base for a major prawning and fishing fleet.

UnderWater World This award-winning complex has a fantastic 80 m walkway through seawater 'ocean', with displays

of the Great Barrier Reef and underwater creatures. There are daily shows, including the seal show and crocodile feeding. Spend 15 min swimming with a seal or dive in with sharks (bookings essential). The Touch Tank is a less daunting alternative to get up-close to the animals of the sea; Wharf Complex, Parkyn Pde.

Mooloolaba Harbour: popular spot for parasailing, scuba diving and cruises; contact visitor centre for tour operators.

Triathlon: Mar. *Etchells Australian Winter Championship:* yacht race; June.

Mooloolaba Beach Holiday Park: Parkyn Pde; 1800 441 201. *Alex Beach Cabins and Tourist Park:* 21 Okinja Rd, Alexandra Headland; (07) 5443 2356.

Alexandra Headland: popular coastal town with views to the Maroochy River and Mudjimba Island. Extensive beaches and parklands on the foreshore. Surf lessons and board hire are available from Mooloolaba Wharf; just north of Mooloolaba. *Mooloolah River National Park:* take a canoe down Mooloolah River, ride along the bike trail or walk on the fire trails in this remnant wallum heath park; straddles Sunshine Motorway; (07) 5494 3983; 6 km SW. *Yachting and game fishing:* trips to nearby offshore reefs; details from visitor centre.

TOWNS NEARBY: Maroochydore 2 km, Buderim 6 km, Caloundra 14 km, Nambour 16 km, Yandina 20 km

Moranbah
Pop. 7131
Map ref. 605 C10 | 611 I7

i Library, town square; (07) 4941 4500; www.isaac.qld.gov.au

96.9 FM Rock, 104.9 FM ABC Tropical North QLD

Moranbah is a modern mining town south-west of Mackay. It was established in 1969 to support the huge open-cut coalmines of the expanding Bowen Coal Basin. Coking coal is railed to the Hay Point export terminal just south of Mackay.

Federation Walk: 1 km scenic walk starts at Grosvenor Park; Peak Downs Hwy. *Historical walk:* self-guide trail past interesting sites and heritage buildings of town; brochure from visitor centre.

Australia Day Street Party: Jan. *May Day Union Parade and Fireworks:* May.

Tours to Peak Downs Mine: leaves from town square the last Wed each month; bookings at visitor centre. *Isaacs River:* recreational area with historic monuments and a hiking trail in dry weather; 13 km S. *Lake Elphinstone:* camping, recreation activities, waterskiing, boating and fishing; 70 km N.

TOWNS NEARBY: Clermont 100 km, Sarina 138 km, Mackay 150 km, Emerald 169 km, Proserpine 186 km

Moreton Island
see Strathpine, nearby

Mossman
Pop. 1740
Map ref. 606 D1 | 607 D3 | 613 L5

i Call council offices, (07) 4099 9444; or Cairns & Tropical North Visitor Information Centre, 51 The Esplanade, Cairns, (07) 4051 3588; www.cairnsgreatbarrierreef.org.au

92.5 FM 4CA, 639 AM ABC Far North QLD

QUEENSLAND

The town of Mossman, in Far North Queensland, is set among green mountains and fields of sugarcane. Originally named after the explorer Hugh Mosman, the town changed the spelling of its name from Mosman to Mossman to avoid being confused with the Sydney suburb.

Market: Foxton Ave; Sat. **Christmas Party:** Dec.

Mossman Riverside Leisure Park: Cnr Park St and Foxton Ave; (07) 4098 2627. **Mt Carbine Caravan Park:** 6806 Mulligan Hwy, Mount Carbine; (07) 4094 3160.

Cooya Beach and Newell: coastal towns with popular beaches to the north-east. **Daintree National Park:** including the magnificent Mossman Gorge; 5 km w; *see also Daintree*. **Karnak Rainforest Sanctuary:** amphitheatre and rainforest; 8 km N. **High Falls Farm:** tropical fruit orchard, market garden and open-air restaurant in rainforest setting; 9 km N. **Wonga:** small town with an excellent beach and orchid gardens; 18 km N.

TOWNS NEARBY: Port Douglas 10 km, Daintree 24 km, Palm Cove 45 km, Kuranda 49 km, Mareeba 59 km

Mount Isa

Pop. 18 856
Map ref. 615 D11 | 616 F3

i Outback at Isa, 19 Marian St; (07) 4749 1555 or 1300 659 660; www.mountisa.qld.gov.au

102.5 Hot FM, 567 AM ABC North West QLD

The city of Mount Isa is the most important industrial, commercial and administrative centre in north-west Queensland, an oasis of civilisation in outback spinifex and cattle country. But before John Campbell Miles first discovered a rich silver-lead deposit in 1923, the area was undeveloped. Today Mount Isa Mines operates one of the world's largest silver-lead mines. Mount Isa is also one of the world leaders in rodeos, holding the third largest, which attracts rough-riders from all over Queensland and almost doubles the town's population.

Outback at Isa This modern complex shows the splendours of Queensland's outback country. Don a hard hat and take a guided tour of the 1.2 km of underground tunnels in the Hard Times Mine. The Indigenous, pioneering and mining history of Mount Isa is explored in the Sir James Foots building, and the Outback Park offers a scenic lagoon and informative walking trail. Marian St; 1300 659 660.

Riversleigh Fossil Centre This award-winning centre explores the significant discoveries of the Riversleigh Fossil Site (267 km NW). Through colourful displays, the ancient animals and landscapes come alive. The theatrette shows an excellent film on the fossil story so far and a visit to the laboratory with a working palaeontologist brings fossil discovery up-close as precious material is extracted from rocks. Adjacent to Outback at Isa.

Kalkadoon Tribal Centre and Cultural Keeping Place: preserves the heritage and culture of the Indigenous Kalkadoon people. There are displays of artefacts and guided tours by Kalkadoon descendants; open weekdays; Centenary Park, Marian St. **National Royal Flying Doctor Service Visitor Centre:** informative video, historic and modern memorabilia and photo display; open weekdays; Barkly Hwy. **Trust Tent House:** an example of the housing provided for miners in the 1930s and 1940s that was designed for good ventilation in extreme conditions; open by appt only; Fourth Ave; (07) 3229 1788. **School of the Air:** discover how distance education works in the outback; Abel Smith Pde. **City Lookout:** overview of city and

mine area; Hilary St. **Underground Hospital:** tours of hospital built in WW II; Deighton St. **Rodeo Walk of Fame:** walk the road paved with the names of Mount Isa rodeo legends; Rodeo Dr. **Mount Isa Mine:** the mine's lead smelter stack is Australia's tallest free-standing structure (265 m); informative surface tours available; details from visitor centre. **Donaldson Memorial Lookout:** lookout and walking track; off Marian St.

 Market: Library carpark, Sat. **Mining Expo:** Apr. **Mount Isa Cup:** horseracing; June. **Mount Isa Show:** June. **Isa Rodeo:** Aug. **Mardi Gras:** Aug. **Fishing Classic:** Sept.

AAOK Moondarra Accommodation Village: 2 Moondarra Dr; (07) 4743 9780. **Discovery Holiday Parks – Argylla, Mount Isa:** Barkly Hwy; (07) 4743 4733. **Discovery Holiday Parks – Mount Isa:** 185 Little West St; (07) 4743 4676. **Mt Isa Caravan Park & Tourist Village:** 112 Marian St (Barkly Hwy), Pioneer; (07) 4743 3252. **Sunset Top Tourist Park:** 14 Sunset Dr, Winston; (07) 4743 7668.

Lake Moondarra: artificial lake for picnics and barbecues, swimming, watersports and birdwatching. Home of the Fishing Classic in Sept; 20 km N. **Mt Frosty:** old limestone mine and swimming hole (not recommended for children as hole is 9 m deep with no shallow areas); 53 km E. **Lake Julius:** canoe at the lake or see the Aboriginal cave paintings and old goldmine on the nature trails; 110 km NE. **Station visits:** feel the outback spirit at one of the stations in the area; details from visitor centre. **Safari tours:** to Boodjamulla (Lawn Hill) National Park and Riversleigh Fossil Fields; details from visitor centre. **Air-charter flights:** to barramundi fishing spots on Mornington and Sweers islands in the Gulf of Carpentaria; details from visitor centre.

TOWNS NEARBY: Cloncurry 106 km, Camooweal 169 km, Julia Creek 234 km, Boulia 246 km

Mount Morgan

Pop. 2444
Map ref. 604 A6 | 611 M11

i Heritage Railway Station, 1 Railway Pde; (07) 4938 2312; www.mountmorgan.com

98.5 FM 4YOU, 837 AM ABC Capricornia

Located in the Capricorn region south-west of Rockhampton is the quaint historic mining town of Mount Morgan. Said to be the largest single mountain of gold in the world, Mount Morgan's gold supply was discovered and mined from the late 1800s. What was a big mountain is now a big crater – the largest excavation in the Southern Hemisphere. In the mine's heyday, around 1910, the town was home to about 14 000 people.

Railway Station: historic station with tearooms, rail museum and a restored 1904 Hunslett Steam Engine that operates regularly; Railway Pde. **Historical Museum:** varied collection of memorabilia traces history of this mining town; Morgan St. **Historic suspension bridge:** built in the 1890s and spans the Dee River. **Historic cemetery:** features the Chinese Heung Lew (prayer oven) and the Linda Memorial to men killed in underground mines (1894–1909); off Coronation Dr. **The Big Stack:** 76 m high 1905 brick chimney used to disperse mining fumes; at the mine site.

 Lions Club Market: Apex Park Cemetery; 3rd Sat each month. **Golden Mount Festival:** May. **Mount Morgan Show:** Aug.

Silver Wattle Caravan Park: Burnett Hwy; (07) 4938 1550.

The Big Dam: good boating and fishing; 2.7 km N via William St. **Wowan:** town featuring the Scrub Turkey Museum in old butter factory; 40 km sw. *Tours:* tour to the open-cut Mount Morgan Mine and ancient clay caves with dinosaur footprints; details available from visitor centre.

TOWNS NEARBY: Rockhampton 32 km, Yeppoon 68 km, Biloela 84 km, Gladstone 91 km, Miriam Vale 142 km

Mount Surprise

Pop. 162
Map ref. 613 J8

 Bedrock Village Caravan Park, Garnet St, (07) 4062 3193; or Mount Surprise Gems, Garland St (Savannah Way), (07) 4062 3055; www.gulf-savannah.com.au

97.9 FM Hot, 105.3 FM ABC Far North QLD

Mount Surprise is a historic rail town in the Gulf Savannah. Its name comes from the surprise the Aboriginal people felt when they were resting at the base of the mountain and the loud white people of Ezra Firth's pioneer party arrived in 1864. The region has excellent gemfields for fossicking, especially for topaz, quartz and aquamarine. The town is on the edge of the Undara lava field, formed from the craters of the McBride Plateau. The lava caves can be explored in Undara Volcanic National Park.

Savannahlander This unique train journey shows the rugged delights and beautiful landscapes between Mount Surprise and Cairns. Departing from Mount Surprise Station each Sat, the train stops at various towns in the Gulf Savannah region. There are also trips between Mount Surprise and Forsayth. Bookings on (07) 4053 6848.

Old Post Office Museum: documents the bush history of the region in a historic 1870 building; opposite railway station. *Mount Surprise Gems:* runs tours to nearby fossicking spots and provides licences; Garland St.

Campdraft: Aug.

Bedrock Village Caravan Park: Garnet St; (07) 4062 3193. *Midway Caravan Park:* North St, Georgetown; (07) 4062 1219.

Undara Volcanic National Park Undara, an Aboriginal word for long, accurately describes the tubes in Undara Volcanic National Park east of Mount Surprise. The cooling molten lava of an erupted volcano formed the 90 km of hollow underground lava tubes. At 160 kilometres, one of the lava tubes here is the longest on earth. The caves in nearby Chillagoe–Mungana Caves National Park are a feast for the senses, with bat colonies and richly decorative stalactites and stalagmites. The incredible geological history of the area is detailed at The Hub in Chillagoe. Tours are necessary to visit both the tubes and the caves; bookings on 1800 990 992; day tours also run from Bedrock Village. See the eggcup-shaped crater on the 2.5 km Kalkani Crater circuit or go birdwatching to see some of the park's 120 bird species. (07) 4046 6600; 42 km E.

O'Brien's Creek: renowned for quality topaz; obtain a licence before fossicking; 37 km NW. *Tallaroo Hot Springs:* 5 natural springs created over centuries; open Easter–Sept; 48 km NW. *Forty Mile Scrub National Park:* vine-thicket park on the McBride Plateau with informative short circuit track from day area; (07) 4046 6600; 56 km E. *Georgetown:* small town once one of many small goldmining settlements on the Etheridge Goldfields; noted for its gemstones, especially agate, and gold nuggets; 82 km W. *Forsayth:* old mining town; 132 km sw. *Cobbold Gorge:* guided boat tours through sandstone gorge;

bookings essential (07) 4062 5470. A full-day tour to Forsayth and the gorge also runs from Bedrock Village; 167 km sw via Forsayth. *Agate Creek:* fossick for gemstones; 187 km sw via Forsayth.

TOWNS NEARBY: Chillagoe 112 km, Ravenshoe 137 km, Herberton 142 km, Millaa Millaa 154 km, Atherton 157 km

Mourilyan

Pop. 423
Map ref. 606 E5 | 607 H12 | 613 M7

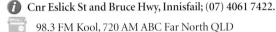 Cnr Eslick St and Bruce Hwy, Innisfail; (07) 4061 7422.

98.3 FM Kool, 720 AM ABC Far North QLD

Mourilyan is a small town in Far North Queensland. It is the bulk-sugar outlet for the Innisfail area. The history of this thriving industry can be seen at the Australian Sugar Industry Museum.

Australian Sugar Industry Museum This large museum was opened in 1977. Its permanent displays include a museum collection of photographs, books, documents and an incredible display of machinery that includes a steam engine, reputedly one of the largest ever built. See the audiovisual display on the history of Australia's sugar industry and tour the art gallery. Cnr Bruce Hwy and Peregrine St; (07) 4063 2656.

King Reef Resort Van Park: Jacobs Rd, Kurrimine Beach; (07) 4065 6144. *Paronella Park:* Japoonvale Rd (Old Bruce Hwy), Mena Creek; (07) 4065 0000.

Paronella Park This 5 ha park was the vision of immigrant sugarcane worker José Paronella. After making his fortune, he started building a mansion on the site (1930–46). Floods and other natural disasters have ruined the grand buildings, despite rebuilding efforts. Now the visitor can walk through the ruins, admire the spectacular rainforest and birdlife, swim near the falls and have Devonshire tea at the cafe. 17 km sw.

Etty Bay: quiet tropical beach with caravan and camping facilities; 9 km E.

TOWNS NEARBY: Innisfail 7 km, Babinda 29 km, Mission Beach 33 km, Tully 41 km, Millaa Millaa 46 km

Mundubbera

Pop. 1055
Map ref. 604 C12 | 609 K4

 Mundubbera Heritage and Information Centre, Bicentennial Park, Strathdee Street; or call the council (07) 4165 4746 or 1300 696 272; www.northburnett.qld.gov.au

93.1 FM Sea, 855 AM ABC Wide Bay

Mundubbera is on the banks of the Burnett River and is a major citrus-growing area in Queensland. Fruit pickers flock to the town in the cooler months. The unusual company 'Bugs for Bugs' produces a group of predatory bugs that reduces the need for pesticides. The rare Neoceratodus, or lungfish, is found in the Burnett and Mary rivers.

Historical Museum: local history; Leichhardt St. *Heritage Centre:* several displays of early settlement history; Durong Rd. *Jones Weir:* popular spot for fishing; Bauer St. *'Meeting Place of the Waters':* 360-degree town mural; Cnr Strathdee and Stuart-Russell sts. *Bugs for Bugs:* company that breeds insects; tours by appt only; Bowen St; (07) 4165 4663. *Pioneer Place:* gorgeous park with picnic facilities right in the middle of town.

QUEENSLAND

Morning Market: Uniting Church: 3rd Sat each month. *Mundubbera Show:* May.

Mundubbera Three Rivers Tourist Park: 37 Strathdee St; (07) 4165 3000. *Eidsvold Caravan Park:* 3 Esplanade St, Eidsvold; (07) 4165 1168.

Auburn River National Park In this small park the Auburn River flows through a sheer-sided gorge and over granite boulders in the riverbed. Dry rainforest grows on the upper part of the tough track that leads down the side of the gorge to the river. An easier walk is the 150 m trail to the lookout above the Auburn River. Opposite the campsite catch a glimpse of the nesting peregrine falcons. 4WD is recommended in wet weather. (07) 4165 5120; 40 km sw.

Enormous Ellendale: the big mandarin, another addition to the 'big' monuments of Queensland; outskirts of town at the Big Mandarin Caravan Park. *Golden Mile Orchard:* impressive orchard with tours; 5 km s. *Eidsvold:* town at the centre of beef cattle country featuring the Historical Museum Complex, Tolderodden Environmental Park and the R.M. Williams Australian Bush Learning Centre; 37 km nw.

TOWNS NEARBY: **Gayndah 31 km, Biggenden 75 km, Monto 83 km, Gin Gin 94 km, Murgon 96 km**

Murgon

Pop. 2133
Map ref. 603 A9 | 609 L6

ⓘ Queen Elizabeth Park; (07) 4168 3864; www.murgon.qld.gov.au

📻 90.7 FM Crow, 855 AM ABC Wide Bay

Murgon, known as 'the beef capital of the Burnett', is one of the most attractive towns in southern Queensland. Settlement dates from 1843, but the town did not really develop until after 1904, when the railway arrived and the large stations of the area were divided up. The town's name comes from a lily pond, found on Barambah Station, which was the site of the first pastoral property in the area.

Queensland Dairy Museum: static and interactive displays illustrating the history of the dairy industry, with special interest in the development of butter; Gayndah Rd.

Murgon Show: Mar. *Barambah Blowout Bull Ride:* Mar/Apr. *Kids Kapers:* fun day for the kids including a treasure hunt; May. *Dairy Heritage Festival:* June. *Rotary Arts Festival:* Sept/Oct. *Barambah Shakin' Grape Festival:* Oct. *Christmas Carnival:* Dec.

Barambah Bush Caravan Park: Cnr Borcherts Hill and Barambah rds; (07) 4168 1085. *Bjelke-Peterson Dam Visitor and Recreation Park:* Haager Dr, Moffatdale; (07) 4168 4746.

Boat Mountain Conservation Park The flat-topped crest in this park looks like an upturned boat, hence the name. The views from the top are panoramic and take in the surrounding agricultural valley. There are 2 lookout walks and an excellent 1.8 km circuit track. Watch for the bandicoot digs along the way. 20 km ne via Boat Mountain Rd.

Jack Smith Conservation Park This park comprises valuable remnant dry rainforest that used to cover the region before clearing for agriculture began. Have a picnic overlooking the South Burnett Valley before taking the 20 min return track through scrub to see the abundant birdlife of the park; 13 km n.

South Burnett wine region This is a young winemaking region, as the first vines were only planted in 1993. However, South Burnett now has more than a dozen wineries. Head to Barambah Ridge for chardonnay, Crane Winery for cabernet sauvignon, and Stuart Range for verdelho and chardonnay, at its cellar door located in an old butter factory.

Cherbourg: small Aboriginal community featuring the Ration Shed Precinct displaying a pictorial history of the area; 5 km se. *Wondai:* attractions include the Regional Art Gallery, Heritage Museum and South Burnett Timber Industry Museum. Town hosts Garden Expo in September; 13 km s. *Bjelke-Petersen Dam:* popular spot for watersports and fishing (boat hire available) with various accommodation styles at Yallakool Tourist Park. The dam is home to the Annual Fishing Competition in Oct; 15 km se. *Goomeri:* known as 'clock town' for its unique memorial clock in the town centre. It has numerous antique stores and holds the Pumpkin Festival in May; 19 km ne. *Booubyjan Homestead:* Irish brothers the Clements took up this run near Goomeri in 1847, beginning with sheep and then moving to cattle in the 1880s. The property is still in the family. Open to the public daily; 43 km n via Goomeri. *Kilkivan:* Queensland's first discovery of gold was here in 1852. Try fossicking for gold or visit the lavender farm and historical museum. The town holds the Great Horse Ride in Apr; 44 km ne. *Proston:* small community featuring Sidcup Castle and Crafts Museum (open Wed–Mon); 54 km w. *Lake Boondooma:* watersports, fishing and the Fishing Competition in Feb; 74 km nw via Proston. *Bicentennial National Trail:* a 5330 km trail for walkers, bike riders and horseriders – you can do just a part of the trail. It runs through Kilkivan. *Fossicking:* semi-precious stones in Cloyna and Windera region; details from visitor centre.

TOWNS NEARBY: **Kingaroy 35 km, Nanango 48 km, Gympie 72 km, Gayndah 76 km, Biggenden 82 km**

Muttaburra

Pop. 106
Map ref. 610 C8 | 617 O8

ⓘ Post office, Sword St; (07) 4658 7147; www.muttaburra.com

📻 104.5 FM West, 540 AM ABC Western QLD

Despite being a tiny outback community, Muttaburra has much to promote in its history. Famous cattle duffer Harry Redford (Captain Starlight) planned his daring robbery at nearby Bowen Downs Station in 1870. He stole 1000 head of cattle (thinking they wouldn't be missed) and drove them 2400 kilometres into South Australia. He was arrested and tried; the jury acquitted him, probably because his daring was so admired. These events were the basis for Rolf Boldrewood's novel *Robbery Under Arms.* More recently, a skeleton of an unknown dinosaur was found in 1963 in a creek close to the Thomson River. It was named Muttaburrasaurus. A replica can be seen in Bruford Street.

Dr Arratta Memorial Museum: this museum has medical and hospital displays with original operating theatres and wards; tours by appt; (07) 4658 7287. *Cassimatis General Store and Cottage:* restored store depicts the original family business in early 1900s. The adjacent cottage was home to the Cassimatis family; tours by appt; (07) 4658 7287.

Anzac Day Celebrations: Apr. *Landsborough Flock Ewe Show:* June. *Horseracing:* Aug. *Christmas Celebrations:* Dec.

Muttaburra Cemetery: outskirts of town; 1 km w. *Agate fossicking:* 5 km w. *Pump Hole:* swimming and fishing for golden perch and black bream; 5 km E. *Broadwater:* part of Landsborough River for fishing, birdwatching, bushwalking and camping; 6 km s.

TOWNS NEARBY: Aramac 83 km, Longreach 99 km, Barcaldine 130 km, Winton 157 km, Isisford 185 km

Nambour
Pop. 13 532
Map ref. 602 F3 | 603 E11 | 609 N7

 5 Coronation Ave; (07) 5476 1933; www.nambourtown.com.au

90.3 FM ABC Coast, 91.1 FM Hot

Nambour is a large, unpretentious service town in the Sunshine Coast hinterland. Development began in the 1860s and sugar has been the main crop since the 1890s. Small locomotives pull loads of sugarcane across the main street to Moreton Central Mill, a charming sight during the crushing season (July–October). The town's name is derived from the Aboriginal word for the local red-flowered tea tree.

Sunshine Coast Show: June. *Queensland Home Garden Expo:* July. *Australia's Greatest Rock Event:* Sept.

Chez Claude: tiny French treasure; 4 Pine Grove Rd, Woombye; (07) 5442 1511.

Palmwoods Caravan Park: 18 Landershute Rd, Palmwoods; (07) 5445 9450. *Lilyponds Holiday Park:* 26 Warruga St, Mapleton; (07) 5445 7238. *Nambour Rainforest Holiday Village:* 557 Nambour Connection Rd, Woombye; (07) 5442 1153. *Peppertree Cottage:* 10 Glen Eden Crt, Flaxton; (07) 5445 7652.

Mapleton Falls National Park Volcanic columns jut out of Pencil Creek just before the creek's water falls 120 m to the valley floor. Walk to the falls lookout or see panoramic views of the Obi Obi Valley from Peregrine Lookout. Birdwatchers will delight at the early morning and dusk flights of the park's numerous bird species. (07) 5494 3983; 3 km sw of Mapleton.

The Big Pineapple The 16 m fibreglass pineapple makes this structure hard to miss. The tourist attractions are closed for renovation, but a weekly market on Sat remains popular; 7 km s.

Mapleton: attractive arts and crafts town in the Blackall Range; holds the Yarn Festival in Oct; 15 km w; see also Maleny. *Mapleton Forest Reserve:* with excellent drive through bunya pines and blackbutt forests starting just north of Mapleton. Along the drive, walk to the top of the waterfall from Poole's Dam and take the short Piccabeen Palm Groves Walk. The drive ends with spectacular views from Point Glorious.

TOWNS NEARBY: Yandina 7 km, Buderim 12 km, Maroochydore 14 km, Mooloolaba 16 km, Maleny 19 km

Nanango
Pop. 3085
Map ref. 603 A11 | 609 L7

 Henry St; (07) 4171 6871; www.nanango.qld.gov.au

 89.1 CFM, 747 AM ABC Southern QLD

Nanango is one of the oldest towns in Queensland. Gold was mined here from 1850 to 1900 and fossickers still try their luck today. The industrial Tarong Power Station and Meandu

[NANANGO] EXTERIOR OF HISTORIC RINGSFIELD HOUSE

Coal Mine are nearby, yet Nanango still retains a welcoming country atmosphere.

Historic Ringsfield House: excellent example of colonial architecture of the 1900s. It houses the historical society and period furnishings; open weekdays, Sat–Sun by appt; Cnr Alfred and Cairns sts; (07) 4163 3345. *Tarong Power Station Display:* models and displays; adjacent to visitor centre.

Market: showgrounds; 1st Sat each month. *Nanango Show:* Apr. *Nanart:* art show; Apr/May. *Country Music Muster:* Sept. *Funfest:* Oct.

Homestead Caravan Park & Cabins: 17 Arthur St East; (07) 4163 1733. *Nanango Caravan & Motorhome Park:* 13673 D'Aguilar Hwy; (07) 4163 2322. *Wiikirri Bed and Breakfast Retreat:* 15 Bowman Rd, Blackbutt; (07) 4170 0395. *Yarraman Caravan Park:* 12121 D'Aguilar Hwy, Yarraman; (07) 4163 8185.

The Palms National Park Located at the Brisbane headwaters is this vine forest and subtropical rainforest park. Have a bush picnic and then take the 20 min Palm Circuit track through natural vegetation and along boardwalks. (07) 4699 4355; 42 km sw.

Tipperary Flat: tribute park to early pioneers with old goldmining camp, displays and walking track; 2 km E. *Seven-Mile Diggings:* gold- and gem-fossicking; currently the diggings is not open to any motorised transport – visitors are requested to park where signed and walk to the diggings; permit from visitor centre; 11 km SE. *Yarraman:* historic timber town with heritage centre and 'mud maps' for region; 21 km s. *Maidenwell:* small town with Astronomical Observatory and Coomba Falls nearby; 28 km sw. *Blackbutt:* picturesque timber town with country markets 3rd Sun each month; 41 km SE.

TOWNS NEARBY: Kingaroy 22 km, Murgon 48 km, Crows Nest 65 km, Kenilworth 73 km, Esk 75 km

Nerang
Pop. 16 066
Map ref. 516 G1 | 525 O1 | 600 F9 | 601 D6 | 609 N10

 Cavill Walk, Surfers Paradise; (07) 5538 4419.

92.1 FM Breeze, 612 AM ABC Brisbane

Nerang is in the Gold Coast hinterland. Today the town is much more similar in character to that dense urban strip of coast than to the small rural centre it started out as in the mid-1800s.

QUEENSLAND

Nerang Forest Reserve On the north-west fringe of Nerang is this hilly rainforest and open eucalypt reserve. An excellent way of exploring the landscape is on the 2.8 km return Casuarina Grove Track through rainforest and along the creek. Look out for the black cockatoos. The reserve is a popular spot for horseriders and cyclists (permit required).

Nerang River: this gorgeous river flows through town, providing a popular spot for picnics, boating, fishing and watersports.

Farmers market: Lavelle St; Sun.

Gold Coast Holiday Park: 66–88 Siganto Dr, Helensvale; 1300 789 189. *The Gold Coast Queenslander:* 26 Clarence Dr, Helensvale; (07) 5573 2241. *Jacobs Well Tourist Park:* 1161 Pimpama Jacobs Well Rd, Jacobs Well; (07) 5667 2760. *Kintail Homestay:* 59 California Dr, Oxenford; (07) 5573 7469. *The Outlook Bed & Breakfast:* 31 Macrozamia Dr, Clagiraba; (07) 5545 3989. *Riviera B&B:* 53 Evanita Dr, Gilston; (07) 5533 2499. *Rumbalara B&B:* 72 Hoop Pine Crt, Advancetown; (07) 5533 2211.

Springbrook National Park This rainforest park forms part of the Scenic Rim of mountains. The Springbrook section has an information centre, from which a short walk leads to a spectacular lookout over the Gold Coast. Access is via Springbrook (39 km sw). The Natural Bridge section features a unique rock arch over Cave Creek. Take the 1 km rainforest walk to see the natural bridge where Cave Creek plunges through an eroded hole to a cavern below. There are tours to see the glow worms or a 3 km night trail through rainforest; bookings on (07) 5533 5239. Park information (07) 5533 5147; 38 km sw. Mt Cougal section: *see Burleigh Heads.*

Lamington National Park Part of a World Heritage area, this popular park preserves a wonderland of rainforest and volcanic ridges, crisscrossed by 160 kilometres of walking tracks. The main picnic, camping and walking areas are at Binna Burra and Green Mountains, sites of the award-winning Binna Burra Mountain Lodge and O'Reilly's Rainforest Retreat. Don't miss the Tree Top Walk for an up-close look at the canopy's flora. Access to the Green Mountains section is via Canungra; (07) 5544 0634. Binna Burra is accessed via Beechmont; (07) 5533 3584.

Carrara: nearby town offers scenic balloon flights over the Gold Coast, (07) 5578 2244, and holds weekend markets; 5 km se. *Hinze Dam on Advancetown Lake:* sailing and bass-fishing; 10 km sw. *Historic River Mill:* 1910 arrowroot mill; 10 km w. *Mudgeeraba:* holds the Somerset Celebration of Literature in Mar. Nearby is the Gold Coast War Museum with militia memorabilia and skirmish paintball; 12 km s.

TOWNS NEARBY: Surfers Paradise 9 km, Burleigh Heads 16 km, North Tamborine 16 km, Tweed Heads (NSW) 29 km, Beaudesert 33 km

North Stradbroke Island
see Strathpine, nearby

Noosa Heads
see inset box on page 436

Normanton
Pop. 1098
Map ref. 612 D7 | 615 G4

Cnr Landsborough and Caroline sts; (07) 4745 1065; www.gulf-savannah.com.au

101.7 FM Rebel, 567 AM ABC North West QLD

Normanton thrived as a port town in the late 1800s when the gold rush was on in Croydon. The Normanton-to-Croydon railway line, established at that time, today runs the award-winning *Gulflander* tourist train. More recently, Australia's largest saltwater crocodile, known as Krys the Savannah King, was shot at nearby Archer's Creek in 1957. A life-size replica of his body, over 8 metres long, can be seen in the council park.

Normanton Railway Station: National Trust–listed Victorian building; Matilda St. *Original well:* settlers used it for drawing water; Landsborough St. *Giant Barramundi:* big monument to the fish; Landsborough St. *Scenic walk and drive:* self-guide tours to historic buildings including the Old Gaol in Haig St and the restored Bank of NSW building in Little Brown St; brochure available from information centre in the Burns Philip Building. *Gulflander:* this historical 152 km railway journey from Normanton to Croydon reveals the remote beauty of the Gulf Savannah; departs 8.30am Wed and returns Thurs afternoons. *Gulflander* also runs regular sunset tours with billy tea and damper, and other short trips. *'Croc Spot' Cruise:* at sunset on the Norman River; departs Norman Boat Ramp 5pm Mon–Sat. *Norman River fishing tours:* fishing trips and boat hire for barramundi and estuary fish; details from visitor centre.

Barra Classic: Easter. *Normanton Show and Rodeo:* June.

Lakes: attract jabirus, brolgas, herons and other birds; on the outskirts of Normanton. *Shady Lagoon:* bush camping, birdwatching and wildlife; 18 km se. *Fishing:* catching barramundi is very popular in the area – try the spots at Norman River in Glenore (25 km se), Walkers Creek (32 km nw) or off the bridges or banks in Normanton. *Burke and Wills cairn:* last and most northerly camp of Burke and Wills (Camp 119) before their fatal return journey; off the Savannah Hwy; 30 km sw. *Bang Bang Jump Up rock formation:* a solitary hill on the surrounding flat plains with excellent views; Matilda Hwy; 106 km sw. *Dorunda Station:* cattle station offering barramundi and saratoga fishing in lake and rivers; accommodation is available; 197 km ne. *Kowanyama Aboriginal community:* excellent barramundi fishing, guesthouse and camping; permit to visit required from Kowanyama Community Council; 359 km ne.

TOWNS NEARBY: Karumba 32 km, Croydon 137 km, Burketown 162 km

North Tamborine
Pop. 1272
Map ref. 600 E9 | 601 B4 | 609 N10

Doughty Park, Main Western Rd; (07) 5545 3200; www.tamborinemtncc.org.au

88.9 FM Breeze, 612 AM ABC Brisbane

North Tamborine is one of the towns on the Tamborine Mountain ridge in the Gold Coast hinterland. Numerous galleries, arts and crafts shops and boutique wineries make it and the nearby towns of Tamborine Village, Eagle Heights and Mount Tamborine popular weekend getaways. Tamborine National Park covers most of the mountain – the Witches Falls section was Queensland's first national park, listed in 1908.

Tamborine Mountain Distillery: award-winning distillery with a range of liqueurs, schnapps, vodkas and spirits; Beacon Rd. *Mt Tamborine Winery and Cedar Creek Estate:* tastings and sales; Hartley Rd. *Hang-gliding:* off Tamborine Mountain; Main Western Rd; (07) 5543 5631 or contact visitor centre. *Tamborine Trolley Co:* provides tours of mountain, including weekend hop-on hop-off tour to major sights; (07) 5545 2782.

Produce market: showgrounds (green shed); Sun mornings. *Tamborine Mountain Markets:* showgrounds, Main Western Rd; 2nd Sun each month. *Scarecrow Festival:* May. *Mountain Show:* Sept. *Springtime on the Mountain:* open gardens and mini-markets; Oct. *Craft Extravaganza:* Oct. *Tamborine Mountain Classic:* bike, run or walk; Nov.

Songbirds: modern Australian, lovely setting; Songbirds Rainforest Retreat, Tamborine Mountain Rd; (07) 5545 2563. *The Polish Place:* hearty Polish food and drink; 333 Main Western Rd; (07) 5545 1603. *Cork 'n Fork Winery Tours:* local wineries and lunch; Tamborine Mountain Plateau; (07) 5543 6584.

Avocado Sunset Bed & Breakfast: 186 Beacon Rd; (07) 5545 2365. *Sandiacre House:* 45 Licuala Dr; (07) 5545 3490. *Villa Della Rosa Bed & Breakfast:* 5 Platt Pl; (07) 5545 3375. *Witches Falls Cottages:* Cnr Main Western and Hartley rds; (07) 5545 4411. *Camelot Cottages:* 322 Main Western Rd, Mount Tamborine; (07) 5545 4380. *Cayambe View Bed & Breakfast:* 20 Cayambe Crt, Eagle Heights; (07) 5545 4052. *Hillside Bed & Breakfast:* 25 Leona Crt, Mount Tamborine; (07) 5545 3887. *Muscatels at Tamborine:* 161 Eagle Heights Rd, Eagle Heights; (07) 5545 3455. *Tamborine Mountain Caravan & Camping:* Cnr Tamborine Mountain and Cedar Creek Falls rds, Mount Tamborine; (07) 5545 0034.

Tamborine National Park This picturesque mountain park protects remnant subtropical rainforest. Waterfalls, cliffs and beautiful walks make it a popular spot for visitors. The scenic drive visits the major waterfalls and lookouts and there are 22 km of walks on offer. Walk highlights are the 5.4 km Jenyns Falls circuit track and the 3 km Witches Falls circuit track, both leading to spectacular waterfalls. Park access points are on Tamborine–Oxenford Rd; (07) 5576 0271.

Brisbane and surrounds wine region Wineries are scattered from the Sunshine Coast hinterland down to the Gold Coast, with the tourist trade understandably the major focus. Behind the Sunshine Coast is Settlers Rise Vineyard, where the cellar door is a historic Queenslander with panoramic views. Between Brisbane and the Gold Coast, the state-of-the-art Sirromet Wines grows the majority of its grapes in the Granite Belt and makes them into various wines here. It is also home to the popular Lurleen's restaurant. Further south is Albert River Wines, which is particularly skilled in shiraz varieties, and has some lovingly restored historic buildings and another restaurant.

Eagle Heights: pretty village to the north-east with the Gallery Walk on Long Rd featuring excellent local crafts; Botanical Gardens in Forsythia Dr are set on 9 ha of rainforest with a variety of plants; historic buildings are on show at the Heritage Centre, Wongawallen Rd. *Thunderbird Park:* wildlife sanctuary, horseriding, laser skirmish, ropes course and fossicking for 'thunder eggs'; Tamborine Mountain Rd.

TOWNS NEARBY: Nerang 16 km, Beaudesert 20 km, Surfers Paradise 26 km, Burleigh Heads 32 km, Tweed Heads (NSW) 45 km

Oakey

Pop. 3653
Map ref. 609 K9

Library, 64 Campbell St; (07) 4692 0154.

102.7 FM 4DDB, 747 AM ABC Southern QLD

Oakey is an agricultural town on the Darling Downs surrounded by beautiful rolling hills and black-soil plains. It is also the base for the aviation division of the Australian army.

Bernborough: bronze statue of famous local racehorse; Campbell St. *Oakey Historical Museum:* local memorabilia; Warrego Hwy. *Australian Army Aviation Museum:* every aircraft flown by the Australian army since WW II is represented at the museum through originals and replicas. Other aircraft can also be viewed, from the early wood Box Kite to the hi-tech Blackhawk Helicopter; at army base on Corfe Rd.

Oakridge Motel & Caravan Park: 56 Toowoomba Rd; (07) 4691 3330.

Jondaryan Woolshed Built in 1859 and still shearing under steam power, this woolshed is a memorial to pioneers of the wool industry. The complex includes the huge woolshed, historic buildings, and machinery and equipment collections. Visitors can see the shearing and sheepdog demonstrations or sit down to some billy tea and damper. Events are held throughout the year, including the Working Draft-horse Expo in June and the Australian Heritage Festival in Aug. Off Warego Hwy; 22 km NW.

TOWNS NEARBY: Toowoomba 27 km, Crows Nest 38 km, Dalby 53 km, Gatton 57 km, Clifton 58 km

Orpheus Island

see Ingham, nearby

Palm Cove

Pop. 1215
Map ref. 606 D2 | 607 F6 | 613 L5

Paradise Village Shopping Centre, Williams Espl; (07) 4055 3433; www.palmcove.net

99.5 Sea FM, 639 AM ABC Far North QLD

Serene Palm Cove, north-west of Cairns, has white, sandy beaches and streets lined with palm trees. It is essentially a resort village, with locals and tourists alike soaking up the relaxed Far North atmosphere. The lifestyle is based around the water – fishing off the jetty, horseriding along the beach and swimming in the Coral Sea's crystal-clear blue water.

Reef tours: to Green Island and the Great Barrier Reef; depart Palm Cove jetty daily. *Day tours:* to Atherton Tableland and surrounds; details from visitor centre.

Palm Cove Fiesta: Oct.

Nu Nu Restaurant: brilliant modern-Australian fusion; 123 Williams Espl; (07) 4059 1880. *Reef House Restaurant:* modern Australian; Reef House Resort & Spa, 99 Williams Espl; (07) 4055 3633. *Vivo Bar and Grill:* Italian-influenced modern Australian; 45 Williams Espl; (07) 4059 0944.

Ellis Beach Oceanfront Bungalows & Caravan Park: Captain Cook Hwy, Ellis Beach; (07) 4055 3538.

Clifton Beach: resort village with park-lined beach and attractions such as Wild World, an interactive animal zoo, and Outback Opal Mine, with simulated mine and displays of Australia's most famous stone; 3 km s. *Hartley's Crocodile Adventures:* prides itself on the range of habitats that can be seen from extensive boardwalks and river cruises. Presentations

continued on p. 437

NOOSA HEADS

Pop. 3658
Map ref. 602 H1 | 603 F10 | 609 N7

ⓘ 61 Hastings St; or Noosa Marina (Tewantin); 1300 066 672 or (07) 5430 5000; www.visitnoosa.com.au

🔲 90.3 FM ABC Sunshine Coast, 101.3 FM Noosa Community Radio

Noosa Heads, commonly known as Noosa, is a coastal resort town on Laguna Bay on the Sunshine Coast. The relaxed lifestyle, the weather and the safe year-round swimming make this a popular holiday destination. Cosmopolitan Hastings Street offers a relaxed cafe lifestyle, and within walking distance are the natural attractions of superb coastal scenery and the protected coves, surfing beaches and seascapes of Noosa National Park.

🏠 *Noosa Main Beach:* safe family swimming; beginners' surfing lessons available; 0418 787 577. *Boutique shopping:* browse clothing stores, gift shops and art galleries on stylish Hastings St. *Adventure sports:* on spectacular coastal waters of the Coral Sea and inland waterways. Activities include kite surfing, high-speed boating, surfing lessons and kayaking; book at the visitor centre. *Camel and horse safaris:* beach and bushland safari on Noosa's North Shore; book at visitor centre. *Scenic flights:* contact visitor centre for details.

🌿 *Farmers' market:* Sun 7am–12pm; AFL ground, Weyba Rd, Noosaville. *Festival of Surfing:* Mar. *Noosa Mardi Gras Recovery Week:* a week-long festival following the Sydney Gay and Lesbian Mardi Gras; Mar. *Mayfiesta:* food and wine on the Noosa River; May. *Food and Wine Festival:* May. *Winter Festival:* sporting carnival; May. *Noosa Longweekend:* arts festival; June. *Jazz Festival:* Sept. *Beach Car Classic:* Sept. *Triathlon Multi Sport Festival:* Oct/Nov.

🍴 *Berardo's Bistro on the Beach:* inspired by French bistros; 8/49 Hastings St; (07) 5448 0888. *Cafe Le Monde:* one of Noosa's longest-running eateries, with alfresco dining; 52 Hastings St; (07) 5449 2366. *Ricky's River Bar and Restaurant:* chic, modern-Australian dining; 2 Quamby Pl; (07) 5447 2455. *Sails:* delicious food, overlooking Main Beach; Cnr Park Rd and Hastings St; (07) 5447 4235. *Thomas Corner Eatery:* casual dining with first-class food, overlooking the Noosa River; 201 Gympie Tce, Noosaville; (07) 5470 2224. *Wasabi:* award-winning Japanese; 2 Quamby Pl, Noosa Sound; (07) 5449 2443.

🛏 *Noosa River Holiday Park:* 4 Russell St, Noosaville; (07) 5449 7050. *Noosa Valley Manor Luxury Bed & Breakfast:* 115 Wust Rd, Doonan; (07) 5471 0088. *Lake Weyba Cottages:* 79 Clarendon Rd, Weyba Downs; (07) 5448 2285.

🌀 **Noosa National Park, Headland section** This largely untouched rocky coastline park offers walks of varying length through rainforest and heathland. Escape the summer crowds of Noosa by taking the Tanglewood Track across the headland to Hells Gate, a popular lookout and whale-viewing spot. Return via the coastal track for scenic ocean views. Access the park via Park Rd in Noosa Heads, the coastal boardwalk from Hastings St, or Sunshine Beach; info and maps from the visitor centre.

Great Sandy National Park, Cooloola section This park has stunning coloured sands, beaches, lakes, forests and sand dunes, all of which are protected. Many rare and threatened species call it home. There are walks for all ranges of fitness and stamina from short circuit walks to overnight hikes. For the serious walker, there is the 2- to 4-day Cooloola Wilderness Trail with bush camping. For less strenuous activity, picnic in the rainforest at Bymien or see the Teewah Coloured Sands, which rise in 40 000-year-old cliffs. It is thought that oxidisation or decaying vegetation has caused the colouring; Aboriginal legend attributes it to the slaying of a rainbow serpent. The park is separated from Noosa by the Noosa River and is accessed via vehicle ferry from Tewantin. Access from the north is via Rainbow Beach; 4WD recommended. (07) 5449 7792; 14 km N. Tours combining the coastline sights with the mirrored waterways of the Noosa Everglades are operated by Noosa Everglades Discovery; (07) 5449 0393.

[JUNIOR COMPETITORS AT THE TRIATHLON MULTI SPORT FESTIVAL]

Laguna Lookout: views of Noosa River, lakes and hinterland; on Noosa Hill, access via Viewland Dr. *Sunshine Beach:* golden beach popular for surfing; 3 km SE. *Noosaville:* family-style area with Noosa River as focal point; departure point for river cruises; 5 km SW. *Peregian Beach:* beachside village with alfresco cafes, restaurants and boutique shops; 13 km S. *Lake Cooroibah:* ideal for boating, sailing and windsurfing; access by car or boat from Noosaville. *Tewantin:* Noosa Marina in Parkyn Court has restaurants, boat hire and cruises. The Big Shell and the House of Bottles are nearby; 7 km W. *Tewantin State Forest:* hilly rainforest and eucalypt forest reserve with 10 min walk to Mt Tinbeerwah Lookout offering a panoramic view over Noosa River, lakes and hinterland; 10 km W via Tewantin. *Noosa River and the*

Everglades: the river extends over 40 km north into Great Sandy National Park. Take a cruise into the mirrowed Everglades and to Harry's Hut, a relic of timber-cutting days. Kayak and canoe hire on offer, as well as camping facilities; contact visitor centre for details. *Gondolas of Noosa:* cruise the Noosa River in the style and comfort of a traditional European gondola; 3 km NW. *Eumundi:* famed markets; Wed 8am–1.30pm and Sat 6.30am–2pm (also Thurs evening Dec/Jan); see Yandina; (07) 5442 7106; 21 km SW.

TOWNS NEARBY: Yandina 23 km, Pomona 24 km, Nambour 29 km, Maroochydore 29 km, Mooloolaba 31 km

include crocodile and snake shows and koala feeding; 15 km N. *Rex Lookout:* stunning coastal views; 17 km N.

TOWNS NEARBY: Kuranda 9 km, Cairns 22 km, Port Douglas 36 km, Mareeba 38 km, Gordonvale 41 km

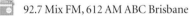
Pomona
Pop. 1003
Map ref. 602 F1 | 603 E10 | 609 N7

 Railway Station Gallery, Station St; (07) 5485 2950.

92.7 Mix FM, 612 AM ABC Brisbane

This small and relaxed farming centre is in the northern hinterland of the Sunshine Coast. Mount Cooroora rises 439 metres above the town. Each July mountain runners from around the world flock to attempt the base–summit and back again race, the winner being crowned King of the Mountain.

Majestic Theatre: authentic silent-movie theatre with cinema museum and regular screenings; Factory St. *Noosa Shire Museum:* tribute to shire's past in old council chambers; Factory St. *Railway Station Gallery:* converted station featuring local art; open Tues–Sat; Station St.

Country market: Stan Topper Park; 2nd and 4th Sat each month. *King of the Mountain:* July. *Silent Movie Festival:* at the Majestic Theatre; Nov.

Cudgerie Homestead Bed & Breakfast: 42 Cudgerie Dr, Black Mountain; (07) 5442 6681.

Boreen Point This sleepy town is on the shores of Lake Cootharba. The town features a 2.4 km walk from Teewah Land to Noosa's north shore beaches, and boardwalks into the surrounding wetlands. There are holiday cottages, and boat hire is available on Lake Cootharba. Try the many watersports on offer, including canoeing and kayaking. Windsurfing and yachting competitions are held here throughout the year. The lake is near where Mrs Eliza Fraser spent time with Aboriginal people after the wreck of *Stirling Castle* on Fraser Island in 1836; 19 km NE.

Cooroy: large residential area with excellent art gallery and cultural centre in the Old Butter Factory. The Noosa Botanical Gardens and Lake Macdonald are nearby; 10 km SE.

TOWNS NEARBY: Noosa Heads 24 km, Yandina 24 km, Gympie 28 km, Kenilworth 28 km, Nambour 31 km

Port Douglas
Pop. 951
Map ref. 606 D1 | 607 D4 | 613 L5

i Call council offices, (07) 4099 9444; or Cairns & Tropical North Visitor Information Centre, 51 The Esplanade, Cairns, (07) 4051 3588; www.cairnsgreatbarrierreef.org.au

106.3 Velvet Radio, 639 AM ABC Far North QLD

Port Douglas lies on the serene waters of a natural harbour in tropical North Queensland. Once a small village, it is now an international tourist destination. The town is surrounded by lush vegetation and pristine rainforests, and offers a village lifestyle with shops, galleries and restaurants. Its tropical mountain setting, the pristine Four Mile Beach and its proximity to the Great Barrier Reef make Port Douglas an ideal holiday destination. The drive from Cairns to Port Douglas is one of the most scenic coastal drives in Australia.

Rainforest Habitat Wildlife Sanctuary This sanctuary covers an area of 2 ha and is home to over 1600 animals. Walk along the boardwalks through the 4 habitats of North Queensland – rainforest, wetlands, woodlands and grasslands. There are regular guided tours of the sanctuary, and the special daily events of Breakfast with the Birds and Habitat After Dark (runs July–Oct); Cnr Captain Cook Hwy and Port Douglas Rd.

Flagstaff Hill: commands excellent views of Four Mile Beach and Low Isles; end of Island Point Rd. *Dive schools:* details from visitor centre. *Great Barrier Reef tours:* over 100 operators offer reef tours to outer Great Barrier Reef and Low Isles; details from visitor centre. Cane-toad racing: nightly at 8.15pm; Ironbar pub, 5 Macrossan St.

Market: Anzac Park; Sun. *Village Carnivale:* May.

Harrisons: modern Australian in tropical garden; 22 Wharf St; (07) 4099 4011. *Nautilus Restaurant:* famously modern Australian; 17 Murphy St; (07) 4099 5330. *Port O'Call Bar & Bistro:* affordable international fare; Port O'Call Eco Lodge, cnr Port St and Craven Close; (07) 4099 5422. *Salsa Bar and Grill:* excellent food in a relaxed setting; 26 Wharf St; (07) 4099 4922. *Zinc:* relaxed modern Australian; Cnr Macrossan and Davidson sts; (07) 4099 6260.

BIG4 Port Douglas Glengarry Holiday Park: 70 Mowbray River Rd; (07) 4098 5922.

QUEENSLAND

Tours: horseriding, sea-kayaking, rainforest tours, Lady Douglas paddlewheel cruises, 4WD safaris and coach tours to surrounding areas; details available from visitor centre.

TOWNS NEARBY: Mossman 10 km, Daintree 30 km, Palm Cove 36 km, Kuranda 41 km, Mareeba 57 km

Proserpine

Pop. 3314
Map ref. 605 E5 | 611 J4

i Whitsunday Information Centre, Bruce Hwy;
(07) 4945 3711 or 1300 717 407; www.tourismwhitsundays.com.au

Proserpine is the inland sugar town and service centre of the Whitsunday Shire. It was named after the Roman goddess of fertility, Proserpina, for the rich and fertile surrounding lands.

Historical Museum: local history dating back to settlement; closed weekends, open by appt; Bruce Hwy. *Cultural Centre:* displays local Aboriginal artefacts and has regular cinema screenings; Main St. *Pioneer Park and Mill Street Park:* beautiful spots with shady trees – perfect for a picnic.

Proserpine Show: June. *Harvest Festival:* includes the World Championship Cane Cutting event; Oct.

Conway Beach Tourist Park Whitsunday: 10 Daniels St, Conway Beach; (07) 4947 3147. *Midge Point Travellers Rest Caravan Park:* 29 Jackson St, Midge Point; (07) 4947 6120.

Lake Proserpine at Peter Faust Dam: boat hire, waterskiing, fishing and swimming. The Cedar Creek Falls are nearby; 20 km NW on Crystalbrook Rd. *Conway National Park:* 28 km E; *see Airlie Beach.* *Midge Point:* coastal community and an ideal spot for bushwalking, fishing, crabbing and swimming; 41 km SE. *Crocodile safaris:* take a nature tour on an open-air tractor and cruise through mangrove river system on Proserpine River; bookings on (07) 4946 5111.

TOWNS NEARBY: Airlie Beach 21 km, Bowen 55 km, Mackay 103 km, Sarina 131 km, Ayr 153 km

Quilpie

Pop. 563
Map ref. 619 L5

i Brolga St; (07) 4656 2166; www.quilpie.qld.gov.au

104.5 FM Outback Radio 4VL, 603 AM ABC Western QLD

Quilpie is on the banks of the Bullo River in the outback's famous Channel Country. The town was established as a rail centre for the area's large sheep and cattle properties. Today it is better known as an opal town and, in particular, for the 'Boulder Opal'. The world's largest concentration of this opal is found in the area surrounding Quilpie. The town takes its name from the Aboriginal word 'quilpeta', meaning 'stone curlew'.

Museum and gallery: historical and modern exhibitions; closed Sat–Sun from Oct–Mar; visitor centre, Brolga St. *St Finbarr's Catholic Church:* unique altar, font and lectern made from opal-bearing rock; Buln Buln St. *Opal sales:* various town outlets. *Lyn Barnes Gallery:* outback-inspired paintings; Brolga St.

Kangaranga Doo: Aug/Sept. *Wool and Flower Show:* includes show and rodeo; Sept.

Channel Country Tourist Park: Chipu St; (07) 4656 2087.

Mariala National Park The park was formerly used to breed Cobb & Co. horses in the early 1900s. It is remote with spectacular contrasts – the rich red earth mixed with green vegetation of mulga trees and shrubs. The threatened yellow-

footed rock wallaby and pink cockatoo find refuge in this park. There are no formal walking trails. You can bush camp, but visitors must be self-sufficient. 4WD is recommended; roads may become impassable in the wet season. (07) 4654 1255; 130 km NE.

Lake Houdraman: popular watersports and recreation area; river road to Adavale; 6 km NE. *Baldy Top:* large geological formation with spectacular views; 6 km S. *Opal fields:* guided tours (no general access); details from visitor centre; 75 km W. *Toompine:* historic hotel, cemetery and designated opal-fossicking areas nearby; 76 km S. *Eromanga:* this place is reputedly Australia's furthest town from the sea. It features the Royal Hotel, once a Cobb & Co. staging post, and holds a rodeo at Easter; 103 km W.

TOWNS NEARBY: Eulo 188 km, Charleville 198 km, Cunnamulla 213 km, Jundah 232 km

Ravenshoe

Pop. 914
Map ref. 606 D4 | 607 D12 | 613 L7

i 24 Moore St; (07) 4097 7700; www.ravenshoevisitorcentre.com.au

97.9 Hot FM, 720 AM ABC Far North QLD

At 930 metres, Ravenshoe is the highest town in Queensland. Situated on the Atherton Tableland, it is surrounded by World Heritage rainforest, with 350 species of birds, 14 species of kangaroos and 12 species of possums. Once a town with a thriving logging industry, a new, alternative-lifestlye population has now developed.

Nganyaji Interpretive Centre: showcases the lifestyle of the local Jirrbal people, including hunting techniques and community life; Moore St. *Scenic train-ride:* heritage steam-train ride to nearby Tumoulin; details available from visitor centre.

Market: railway station; 4th Sun each month. *Torimba Garden Party:* Sept. *Torimba Festival:* includes Festival of the Forest and mardi gras; Oct.

 Innot Hot Springs These natural thermal springs reputedly have healing powers. The spring water was originally bottled and sent to Europe as a healing remedy until the 1900s. 3 km E of the town is the Windy Hill Wind Farm. 32 km SW.

Millstream Falls National Park: enjoy the 1 km return walk past falls and rockpools to the Millstream Falls, the widest single-drop waterfall in Australia; (07) 4091 1844; 3 km SW. *Tully Falls:* walk 300 m to Tully Falls (in wet season) and the gorge; 25 km S. *Lake Koombooloomba:* popular spot for swimming, watersports, camping and fishing for barramundi; 34 km S. *Mount Garnet:* old tin-mining town with prospecting sites nearby; 47 km W.

TOWNS NEARBY: Millaa Millaa 18 km, Herberton 29 km, Atherton 39 km, Yungaburra 40 km, Babinda 55 km

Ravenswood

Pop. 191
Map ref. 605 A4 | 610 G3

i 74 Mosman St, Charters Towers; (07) 4761 5533; www.charterstowers.qld.gov.au

4GC 828 AM

Once a boom town in the 1860s, today Ravenswood is home to a modest population and a range of historic buildings and ruins that recall the region's goldmining past. Queensland's first major inland settlement, the area reached its peak at the turn of the century when mine manager Archibald Lawrence Wilson, 'the uncrowned king of Ravenswood', attracted investors and workers to the region to extract more than 12 000 kilograms of gold. Ravenswood is a National Trust–certified town, and a stroll down Main Street will take you past the stately Imperial Hotel to the ruins of the Mabel Mill.

Historic buildings Many have been restored or are still in use. The town was once home to more than 30 pubs, and the Imperial Hotel (c. 1902) is a beautiful Edwardian building and one of 2 bars that remain in use. Clad in multicolour brickwork, entry to the pub's lavish interior is via swinging saloon doors. The ruins of the Mabel Mill are an impressive monument to the mining past of this town, as are chimney stacks, which can be seen south of the town centre. The Railway Hotel has recently been restored and the historical school building, built in the 1870s, is still in use. Regular tours of the area are run by the local Heritage Cottage.

Courthouse Museum: displays on the town's history, people and mining industry, Wed–Mon 10am–3pm; (07) 4770 2047.

Town Markets: food and crafts; Railway Hotel; 2nd Sun each month.

White Blow Environmental Park This park is well known locally for its milky quartz outcrop, which gives White Blow its name. There is also an attractive open-woodland forest; 5 km NE.

TOWNS NEARBY: **Charters Towers 66 km, Ayr 79 km, Townsville 93 km, Bowen 142 km, Ingham 178 km**

Richmond

Pop. 554
Map ref. 617 L3

 Kronosaurus Korner, 91–93 Goldring St; (07) 4741 3429 or 1300 576 665; www.richmond.qld.gov.au

99.7 Rebel FM, 540 AM ABC Western QLD

This small town on the Flinders River in the Gulf Country serves the surrounding sheep and cattle properties. The town's main street is lined with beautiful bougainvilleas. In recent years Richmond has become the centre of attention as an area rich in marine fossils dating back around 100 million years, when outback Queensland was submerged under an inland sea.

Kronosaurus Korner This marine-fossil museum has a renowned collection of vertebrate fossils, all found in the Richmond Shire. The museum and exhibition space holds more than 200 exhibits, including the 100-million-year-old armoured dinosaur Minmi, Australia's best-preserved dinosaur. There is also an activity centre, children's discovery area and fossil preparation area where visitors can watch the palaeontologist at work. Guided museum tours, as well as tours to nearby fossicking sites with a palaeontologist, are available (groups of 10 or more, bookings essential). Goldring St; (07) 4741 3429.

Cobb & Co. coach: beautifully restored coach with informative history display; Lions Park, Goldring St. *Gidgee Wheel Arts and Crafts:* local craft; Harris St. *Lake Fred Tritton:* recreational lake for waterskiing, picnics and walks. Enjoy the Richmond Community Bush Tucker Garden, which showcases beautiful native plants and was a finalist for the Banksia Environmental Awards; eastern outskirts. *Cambridge Store:* replica of the old Cambridge Downs Homestead from the late 1800s; contains memorablia and machinery from pioneer days; Goldring St. *Heritage walk:* follow the self-guide trail with informative history

at each stop. It includes the historic flagstone and adobe building, Richmond Hotel, St John the Baptist Church and the Pioneer Cemetery; brochure available from visitor centre.

Fossil Festival: even-numbered years, Apr/May. *Richmond Great Outback Challenge:* sports carnival; odd-numbered years, Oct.

Fossicking sites: guided tours to nearby areas; details from visitor centre.

TOWNS NEARBY: **Hughenden 111 km, Julia Creek 146 km, Kynuna 158 km, Winton 183 km**

Rockhampton

Pop. 68 832
Map ref. 604 B5 | 611 M11

 Capricorn Region Tourist Information Centre, Capricorn Spire, 176 Gladstone Rd; (07) 4921 2311 or 1800 676 701; www.capricornholidays.com.au

98.5 4YOU FM, 837 AM ABC Capricornia

Rockhampton is a prosperous city that straddles the Tropic of Capricorn. It is known as the beef capital of Australia, with some 2.5 million cattle in the region. Quay Street is Australia's longest National Trust–classified streetscape, with over 20 heritage buildings set off by flowering bauhinia and brilliant bougainvilleas. Watch out for the bent-wing bat exodus in summer at Mount Etna, just north of the town, and the summer solstice light spectacular in early December to mid-January at the Capricorn Caves.

Mt Archer National Park On the north-east outskirts of Rockhampton in the Berserker Ranges, this park provides a backdrop to the city. Take a scenic drive up the mountain to Frazer Park for panoramic views. Explore the open forest and subtropical vegetation of the mountain on the 11 km walk from top to bottom. Be advised that the return trip is quite strenuous. Other, shorter walks lead to scenic lookouts. Access to the summit is via Frenchville Rd; to the base via German St; (07) 4936 0511.

Botanic Gardens Set on the Athelstane Range, these heritage-listed gardens are over 130 years old. There are tropical displays, an orchid and fern house, a Japanese-style garden and the bird haven of Murray Lagoon. The city zoo has free entry and koala and lorikeet feedings at 3pm daily. Access via Spencer and Ann sts.

Customs House: this heritage building (1901) houses the visitor centre and 'Rockhampton Discovery Centre' exhibition, which introduces the visitor to the history, culture and lifestyle of Rockhampton; Quay St. *Archer Park Station and Steam Tram Museum:* interactive displays document the history of rail transport in Rockhampton. A fully restored Purrey Steam Tram operates 10am–1pm every Sun; closed Sat; Cnr Denison and Cambridge sts. *Kershaw Gardens:* follow the Australian native flora Braille Trail; Bruce Hwy. *Rockhampton City Art Gallery:* changing exhibitions featuring various well-known Australian artists such as Sidney Nolan; Victoria Pde. *Great Western Hotel:* operates weekly rodeos at an indoor arena; Stanley St. *Fitzroy River:* a great spot for watersports, rowing and fishing. A barrage in Savage St that separates tidal salt water from upstream fresh water provides opportunities for barramundi fishing. *Capricorn Spire:* marks the line of the Tropic of Capricorn; Curtis Park, Gladstone Rd. *Heritage walk:* self-guide trail around city centre; brochure available from visitor centre.

 RADIO STATIONS IN TOWN WHAT'S ON WHERE TO EAT WHERE TO STAY NEARBY

Garden Expo: Apr. *Beef Australia:* every 3 years, May. *Rocky Swap Meet:* Aug. *Big River Jazz:* Sept. *Rocky Barra Bounty:* Oct.

Capricorn Caves: 30 Olsens Caves Rd, The Caves; (07) 4934 2883. *Discovery Holiday Parks – Rockhampton:* 394 Yaamba Rd, North Rockhampton; (07) 4926 3822. *Marlborough Motel & Caravan Park:* Bruce Hwy, Marlborough; (07) 4935 6112. *Riverside Tourist Park Rockhampton:* 2 Reaney St, North Rockhampton; (07) 4922 3779. *Southside Holiday Village:* 283 Lower Dawson Rd, Allenstown; (07) 4927 3013.

Dreamtime Cultural Centre: displays on Aboriginal and Torres Strait Islander culture set on ancient tribal site. Guided tours available; open 10am–3.30pm Mon–Fri; 7 km N on Bruce Hwy. *Old Glenmore Historic Homestead:* National Trust–classified complex of historic buildings and displays; open by appt only; 8 km N. *Rockhampton Heritage Village:* heritage buildings with unusual Time after Time clock collection and Life before Electricity exhibition; Parkhurst; 9 km N. *St Christopher's Chapel:* open-air chapel built by American servicemen; Emu Park Rd; 20 km E. *Capricorn Caves:* guided tours and wild caving adventures through limestone cave system. Visit in Dec for Carols in the Caverns; 23 km N. *Mt Hay Gemstone Tourist Park:* thunder-egg fossicking and sales; 38 km W. *Capricorn Coast Scenic Loop tourist drive:* through coast and hinterland. *Great Keppel Island:* catch the cruise boat from Rosslyn Bay to visit the beautiful white sandy beaches and clear blue waters of the island; perfect spot for snorkelling and watersports.

TOWNS NEARBY: Mount Morgan 32 km, Yeppoon 37 km, Gladstone 92 km, Biloela 113 km, Miriam Vale 151 km

Roma

Pop. 5983
Map ref. 608 G6

 Big Rig Visitor Information Centre, 2 Riggers Rd; (07) 4622 8676 or 1800 222 399; www.visitmaranoa.com.au

101.7 4RRR FM, 711 AM ABC Western QLD

Roma is in the Western Downs region and was named after the wife of Queensland's first governor. Roma boasts a few historic 'firsts' for Queensland and Australia. In 1863 Samuel Symons Bassett brought vine cuttings to Roma, and Queensland's first wine-making enterprise began – Romaville Winery is still running today. In the same year Captain Starlight faced trial in Roma for cattle stealing. Australia's first natural gas strike was at Hospital Hill in 1900. The excellent complex in town, The Big Rig, documents the oil and gas industry since this discovery.

The Big Rig This unique complex is set on an old oil derrick and features historic oil rigs and machinery displays. Photographs, memorabilia and multimedia displays provide a comprehensive history of oil and gas discovery and usage in Australia from 1900 to the present day. A highlight is the sound and light show on summer nights. Adjacent to the complex is a historic slab hut, recreational area and 1915 mini steam train that travels on a 1.4 km circuit. Open daily; 2 Riggers Rd; (07) 4622 4355.

Roma-Bungil Cultural Centre: large 3-D clay mural by a local artist depicting Roma's history; Cnr Bungil and Quintin sts, (07) 4622 1266. *Heroes Avenue:* heritage-listed street of bottle trees commemorating local soldiers who died in WW I; Wyndham and Bungil Sts. *Romavilla Winery:* Queensland's oldest winery; open Mon–Fri 8am–5pm, Sat 9am–12pm and 2–4pm; 77–83 Northern Rd, (07) 4622 1822.

RSL Market: RSL Hall; 1st Sun each month, from early morning. *Easter in the Country:* Easter. *Picnic Races:* Mar. *Polocrosse Club Annual Carnival:* Aug. *Roma Cup:* Nov. *Christmas in the Park:* Big Rig Parklands; Dec.

Roma Aussie Tourist Park: 6 Bowen St; (07) 4622 6465. *Roma Big Rig Tourist Park:* 4 McDowall St; (07) 4622 2538. *Villa Holiday Park:* 65–67 Northern Rd (Carnarvon Hwy); (07) 4622 1309.

Carnarvon National Park, gorge section The Carnarvon Creek winds through the steep-sided Carnarvon Gorge, flanked by white sandstone cliffs. There are over 21 km of walks through rainforest to waterfalls and caves, and incredible Aboriginal rock art can be found throughout the park – see rock engravings, stencils and paintings at Cathedral Cave and the Art Gallery. The turn-off to the park is 199 km N on Carnarvon Developmental Rd; (07) 4984 4505. Mt Moffatt section: *see Mitchell*. Ka Ka Mundi section: *see Springsure*. Salvator Rosa section: *see Tambo*.

Roma Salesyard: largest inland cattle market in Australia with sales on Tues and Thurs; from 8am; 4 km E. *Meadowbank Museum:* historic vehicle and machinery collection, and farm animals; by appt; (07) 4622 3836; 12 km W. *Surat:* small town featuring the Cobb & Co. Changing Station Complex with museum, art gallery and aquarium. Try fishing for Murray cod on Balonne River; 78 km SE.

TOWNS NEARBY: Mitchell 81 km, Miles 141 km, Taroom 145 km, St George 164 km, Chinchilla 185 km

St George

Pop. 2411
Map ref. 608 F9

i Cnr The Terrace and Roe St; (07) 4620 8877; www.balonne.qld.gov.au

102.9 FM 4ROM, 711 AM ABC Western QLD

On the banks of the Balonne River is the Western Downs town of St George. It is the last post in southern Queensland before the heavily populated east coast finally gives way to the sparseness of the outback. The river crossing was discovered by explorer Sir Thomas Mitchell on St George's Day, 1846, giving the town its name. St George is often referred to as the inland fishing capital of Queensland with lakes and rivers nearby, which also support the area's rich cotton, grape and grain industry.

Heritage Centre: historic buildings and a local history museum featuring Aboriginal display; Victoria St; (07) 4625 5168. *The Unique Egg:* carved, illuminated emu eggs; open Mon–Fri 9am–5pm, Sat 9am–12pm; Balonne Sports Store; Victoria St; (07) 4625 3490. *Town murals:* around town, depicting scenes of St George's history. *Riversands Vineyard:* boutique winery on the banks of the Balonne River; open daily but closed Sundays in February; Whytes Rd; (07) 4625 3643. *Jack Taylor Weir:* Sir Thomas Mitchell cairn commemorating the explorer's landmark crossing in 1846; western outskirts.

St George Show: with rodeo; May. *Boolba Wool and Craft Show:* May. *Horseracing:* St George Jockey Club; July. *Nindigully Campdraft:* Sept. *Family Fishing Competition:* Sept. *Nindigully Country Music Spectacular:* includes pig races; Nov.

Kamarooka Tourist Park: 56 Victoria St; (07) 4625 3120.

 Beardmore Dam: popular spot for watersports and picnics in surrounding parklands. It offers excellent fishing for yellow-belly and Murray cod; 21 km N. *Ancient rock well:* hand-hewn

by Aboriginal people, possibly thousands of years ago; 37 km E. *Nindigully:* town where the film *Paperback Hero* was filmed. Features Nindigully Pub, which has the oldest continual licence in Queensland, since 1864; George Rd; (07) 4625 9637; 44 km SE. *Boolba:* holds the impressive Boolba Wool and Craft Show each May; 50 km W. *Begonia Historical Homesetad:* grazing property with farmstay and museum; (07) 4625 7415; 73 km N. *Thallon:* small town with excellent swimming and fishing at Barney's Beach on the Moonie River. The nearby Bullamon homestead (1860), mentioned in Steele Rudd's *Memoirs of Corporal Keeley*, has original shingle roof and canvas ceilings; tours by appt (07) 4625 9217; 76 km SE. *Bollon:* large koala population in river red gums along Wallan Creek and a heritage and craft centre in George St; 112 km W. *Thrushton National Park:* undeveloped park of mulga scrub, sand plains and woodlands; access in dry weather only and 4WD recommended; (07) 4624 3535; 132 km NW. *Culgoa Floodplain National Park:* in the Murray–Darling basin, this park, with over 150 species of birds, is excellent for birdwatchers. There are no formal walking tracks and visitors must be self-sufficient. 4WD recommended; access via Brenda Rd, Goodooga; (07) 4654 1255; 200 km SW.

TOWNS NEARBY: Roma 164 km, Lightning Ridge (NSW) 165 km, Goondiwindi 179 km, Mitchell 182 km, Moree 200 km

St Helena Island

see Strathpine, nearby

Sarina

Pop. 3284
Map ref. 605 G8 | 611 K6

 Sarina Tourist Art and Craft Centre, Bruce Hwy; (07) 4956 2251.

📻 93.5 Kids FM

Sarina is in the hinterland of what has been dubbed the Serenity Coast, at the base of the Connor Range. It is central to the Queensland sugar belt. To the east and south are fine beaches, many of which are renowned fishing spots.

🏛 *Sarina Sugar Shed:* Australia's only fully operational miniature sugar mill and distillery. Take a tour and watch the complex process of turning sugarcanes into granules. There are also multimedia presentations and a novelty shop on-site; closed Sun; Railway Sq. *Sarina Tourist Art and Craft Centre:* excellent variety of local art and craft as well as visitor centre; Bruce Hwy. *'Field of Dreams' Historical Centre:* local industry history and memorabilia; open 10am–2pm Tues, Wed and Fri; Railway Sq.

🌴 *Market:* showgrounds; last Sun each month. *Mud Trials:* buggy racing on a mud track; May. *Scope Visual Arts Competition:* May. *Discover Sarina Festival:* May.

🛏 *Campwin Beach House Bed & Breakfast:* 37 Westcott Ave, Campwin Beach; (07) 4956 6624. *Grasstree Beach Bed & Breakfast:* 20 Wrights Rd, Grasstree Beach; (07) 4956 6428.

◎ **Cape Palmerston National Park** This remote park features rugged coastal landscapes of headlands, swamps and sand dunes. Watch for the soaring sea eagles overhead or the birdlife around the swamp. There are spots for bush camping. The park has no official walking tracks, but the outlook from the cape is spectacular. 4WD recommended. (07) 4944 7800; 46 km SE via Ilbilbie.

Beaches: including Grasstree and Half Tide beaches to the north-east (Grasstree hosts annual bike race; date depends on tidal conditions); also Sarina Beach (east), popular for boating, fishing and swimming, with a lookout over the coast, and Armstrong Beach (south), great for swimming, prawning and fishing. *Hay Point Lookout:* viewing gallery at Hay Point and Dalrymple Bay coal terminal complex – informative video and excellent views; 12 km N. *Salonika Beach:* attractive beach with amazing wildlife, including loggerhead turtles and whales in season; adjacent to Hay Point Lookout. *Lake Barfield:* picnic area and bird sanctuary; 12 km N. *Carmila:* small town with beach just to the east. Visit the nearby Flaggy Rock Exotic Fruit Garden for delicious ice-cream; 65 km S. *Clairview:* popular spot for beach fishing and crabbing; 73 km S. *St Lawrence:* once a major port, this town is now a historical tribute to past days with many historic buildings and the remains of the wharf; 110 km S.

TOWNS NEARBY: Mackay 30 km, Proserpine 131 km, Airlie Beach 138 km, Moranbah 138 km, Bowen 185 km

South Molle Island

see Airlie Beach, nearby

Springsure

Pop. 828
Map ref. 608 F1 | 611 I12

 Information shed, Rolleston Rd; or council offices; (07) 4984 1166.

📻 94.7 Hot FM, 1548 AM ABC Capricornia

Mount Zamia towers over Springsure, a small valley town in the Central Highlands, settled in the 1860s. Springsure's early history is dominated by conflicts between local Aboriginal groups and the intruding European settlers. The 1861 massacre of 19 Europeans at Cullin-la-ringo is commemorated at Old Rainworth Fort.

🏛 *Aboriginal Yumba-Burin (resting place):* in Cemetery Reserve, containing 3 bark burials (around 600 years old). *Rich Park Memorials:* includes cattleyard displays and a Dakota engine from a plane that crashed during WW II. *Historic Hospital:* heritage-listed building (1868) includes museum.

🌴 *Horseracing:* Mar. *Springsure Show:* May.

◎ **Minerva Hills National Park** The park includes the Boorambool and Zamia mountains and has unusual wildlife, such as the fawn-footed melomys, on a 2.2 km walking track to a spectacular lookout, or have a bush picnic at Fred's Gorge. (07) 4984 1716; 4 km W of Springsure, part of road unsealed.

Carnarvon National Park, Ka Ka Mundi section This remote section of the park is in Queensland's brigalow belt and features undulating plains and sandstone cliffs. See the king parrots and fig birds around the springs and creeks or the area's pastoral history at the old cattleyards near the springs. (07) 4984 1716; w on Springsure–Tambo Rd for 50 km, then s on Buckland Rd. Mt Moffatt section: *see Mitchell.* Gorge section: *see Roma.* Salvator Rosa section: *see Tambo.*

Old Rainworth Historical Complex: National Trust–listed buildings of old storehouse built after 1861 massacre; open 9am–2pm weekdays (closed Thurs), 9am–5pm Sat–Sun; 10 km S.

TOWNS NEARBY: Emerald 66 km, Blackwater 100 km, Clermont 150 km, Tambo 204 km, Theodore 221 km

QUEENSLAND

Stanthorpe

Pop. 4268
Map ref. 516 A3 | 525 L2 | 609 L11

ℹ 26 Leslie Pde; (07) 4681 2057 or 1800 060 877;
www.granitebeltwinecountry.com.au

📻 90.1 Breeze FM, 747 AM ABC Southern QLD

Stanthorpe is the main town in the Granite Belt and mountain ranges along the border between Queensland and New South Wales. The town came into being after the discovery of tin at Quartpot Creek in 1872, but the mineral boom did not last. The climate is cool, said to be the coldest in Queensland, but the numerous wineries in the vicinity offer a warm welcome. Visit in spring to see the fruit trees, wattles and wildflowers in bloom.

Heritage Museum: displays the region's past in historic buildings, such as a schoolroom, gaol and shepherd's hut; closed Mon–Tues; High St. *Regional Art Gallery:* touring and local exhibitions; open Mon–Fri, Sat–Sun afternoons; Weeroona Park, Marsh St.

Market in the Mountains: Cnr Marsh and Lock sts; 2nd and 4th Sun each month. *Apple and Grape Harvest Festival:* even-numbered years, 1st weekend in Mar. *Rodeo:* Mar. *Brass Monkey Season: winter festival;* June–Aug. *Primavera:* Sept–Nov. *Australian Small Winemakers Show:* Oct.

Vineyard Cafe: regional food and wine; 28126 New England Hwy, Ballandean; (07) 4684 1270.

Stanthorpe Top of Town Tourist Park: 10 High St; (07) 4681 4888. *Alpine Lodges:* Ridge Rd, The Summit; (07) 3256 7999. *Blue Topaz Caravan Park & Camping Ground:* 26806 New England Hwy, Severnlea; (07) 4683 5279. *Country Style Accommodation Park:* 27156 New England Hwy, Glen Aplin; (07) 4683 4358.

Granite Belt wine region This is Queensland's version of the Hunter Valley, also making successful semillon and shiraz. The region is called the Granite Belt because of the granite bed that lies beneath the northern extension of the New England Tableland. Vineyards are found at an altitude of around 800 metres and, although grapes were 1st planted in the 1960s, it is the recent vintages that have caused a stir. Ballandean Estate is known for an interesting German variety, sylvaner. Boireann is a relative newcomer growing Italian and French grapes, with a rapidly growing reputation for wines like shiraz viognier. Stop at the Stanthorpe Wine Centre for the wines of Summit Estate as well as others.

Mt Marlay: excellent views; 1 km E. *Storm King Dam:* popular spot for picnics, canoeing, waterskiing, and fishing for Murray cod and silver perch; 26 km SE. *Boonoo Boonoo National Park (NSW):* spectacular waterfall; 60 km SE. *Bald Rock National Park (NSW):* incredible granite rock formation (2nd biggest monolith in the world); 65 km SE. *Sundown National Park:* rugged national park of gorges and high peaks. Go birdwatching to see the herons and azure kingfishers along the river or take the short Red Rock Gorge Lookout Track for spectacular views; 80 km SW. *Heritage trail:* a historical drive tour of surrounding towns; brochure from visitor centre.

TOWNS NEARBY: Tenterfield (NSW) 44 km, Warwick 50 km, Killarney 50 km, Allora 69 km, Texas 78 km

Strathpine

Pop. 9534
Map ref. 599 E5 | 600 D3 | 602 F10 | 609 N9

ℹ Pine Rivers Tourism Centre, Daisy Cottage, cnr Gympie and South Pine rds; (07) 3205 4793; www.brisbanehinterland.com

📻 97.3 4BFM, 612 AM ABC Brisbane

Strathpine is north of Brisbane in the Pine Rivers region, a district that includes the forested areas and national parks closest to the capital. Taking advantage of this rural setting so close to the city are a number of art and craft industries.

Pine Rivers Festival: May.

Fishes at the Point: fish and chips by the beach; Shop 2, 15 East Coast Rd, Point Lookout, North Stradbroke Island; (07) 3415 3444. *Look Cafe and Bar:* informal Mediterranean dining; Cnr Mintee St and Mooloomba Rd, Point Lookout, North Stradbroke Island; (07) 3415 3390. *Oceanic Gelati & Coffee Bar:* delicious cakes, gelati and coffee; 19 Mooloomba Rd, Point Lookout, North Stradbroke Island; (07) 3415 3222.

BIG4 Brisbane Northside Caravan Village: Cnr Zillmere and Dorville rds, Aspley; (07) 3263 4040. *Johnstone's on Oxley Bed & Breakfast:* 585 Oxley Ave, Scarborough; (07) 3880 1001. *Kirnicama Elegant Escapes B & B:* 106 Woodward Rd, Armstrong Creek; (07) 3425 2526. *Naracoopa Bed & Breakfast:* 99 Yundah St, Shorncliffe; (07) 3269 2334. *Warrawee Bed & Breakfast:* 9 Hobbs St, Scarborough; (07) 3203 6447.

Brisbane Forest Park This natural bushland forest park has a scenic drive from the south-east corner to lookouts, mountain towns and attractive landscapes, ending at Lake Wivenhoe. It has pristine rainforest, towering trees, cascading waterfalls, deep pools, mountain streams and incredible wildlife. The small settlement of Mount Glorious is a base for forest walking tracks. Wivenhoe Lookout, 10 km further on, has superb views west to Lake Wivenhoe. There are many picnic spots – Jollys Lookout is a highlight, with views over Brisbane, the valley and north to the Glass House Mountains. A guide to the park's walks is available from the park headquarters at 60 Mt Nebo Rd, The Gap. Access via Ferny Hills.

St Helena Island This low, sandy island, 8 km from the mouth of the Brisbane River, was used as a prison from 1867 to 1932. It was dubbed 'the hell-hole of the South Pacific'. Historic ruins remain and are protected in the island's national park. Tours of the island depart from the Brisbane suburbs of Manly and Breakfast Creek; 26 km E.

North Stradbroke Island 'Straddie' is a coastal and bushland paradise, with contained pockets of development. Blue Lake National Park is an ecologically significant wetland; access is by 4WD or a 45-minute walk. Other island walking trails include the popular North Gorge Headland Walk. Travel to North Stradbroke by vehicular ferry from Cleveland. The ferry arrives at Dunwich, the site of a 19th-century quarantine and penal centre; 37 km SE.

Moreton Island Almost all of this large island is national park. It is also mainly sand, with 280 m Mt Tempest possibly the world's highest stable sandhill. On the east coast is an unbroken 36-km surf beach, with calmer beaches on the west coast. Get to the island by passenger or vehicular ferry from Scarborough or the Brisbane River. A 4WD and a permit are required for self-drive touring; 41 km E.

Lake Samsonvale: fishing, watersports and bushwalking; 8 km NW. *Old Petrie Town:* heritage park that holds markets each Sun and the popular Twilight Markets 1st Fri each month (Jan–Oct) then every Fri (Nov–Dec). Catch the free bus from

Petrie Railway Station; 9 km N. *Alma Park Zoo:* palm garden and subtropical rainforest zoo with native and exotic animals. Feed the koalas and explore the Friendship Farm for children; Alma Rd, Dakabin; 14 km N. *Australian Woolshed:* demonstrations of shearing, spinning and working sheepdogs; bush dances with bush band; Ferny Hills; 16 km sw. *Osprey House:* environmental centre; Dohles Rocks Rd; 18 km N. *Brisbane's Vineyard:* wine tastings and sales; Mt Nebo Rd, Mount Nebo; 46 km sw.

TOWNS NEARBY: Caboolture 25 km, Ipswich 41 km, Landsborough 56 km, Esk 57 km, Caloundra 59 km

Surfers Paradise

see inset box on next page

Tambo

Pop. 346
Map ref. 608 B2 | 619 P2

 Council offices, Arthur St; (07) 4654 6133; www.tambo.qld.gov.au

100.3 Outback Radio 4LG FM, 603 AM ABC Western QLD

Tambo is the oldest town in central-western Queensland. It was established in the mid-1860s to service the surrounding pastoral properties, which it continues to do today. This long history can be seen in the heritage buildings on Arthur Street.

Old Post Office Museum: display of historic photographs; Arthur St. *Tambo Teddies Workshop:* produces popular all-wool teddies; Arthur St. *Coolibah Walk:* nature walk along banks of the Barcoo River.

Tambo Stock Show: Apr. *Day/Night Rodeo:* Oct. *Market Day:* Dec.

Carnarvon National Park, Salvator Rosa section One of the more remote sections of the park, Salvator Rosa is a perfect spot to escape the crowds. The attractive Nogoa River and Louisa Creek flow through the valley. See the spectacular rock formations, Belinda Springs and other natural attractions on the self-guide trail, which starts at the Nogoa River camping area. (07) 4984 4505; 130 km E. Mt Moffatt section: *see Mitchell.* Gorge section: *see Roma.* Ka Ka Mundi section: *see Springsure.*

Wilderness Way: a 420 km self-guide drive including Aboriginal rock art, historic European settlement sites and the Salvator Rosa section of the Carnarvon National Park. Check road conditions before departing; brochure available from council office.

TOWNS NEARBY: Blackall 95 km, Charleville 169 km, Barcaldine 177 km, Isisford 196 km, Springsure 204 km

Taroom

Pop. 626
Map ref. 609 I4

 17 Kelman St; (07) 4628 6113.

102.1 Rebel FM

Taroom is on the banks of the Dawson River in the Capricorn region. Since settlers took up land in 1845, cattle raising has been the main local industry. The coolibah tree in Taroom's main street was marked 'L. L.' by explorer Ludwig Leichhardt on his 1844 trip from Jimbour House near Dalby to Port Essington, north of Darwin.

Museum: old telephone-exchange equipment, farm machinery and items of local history; open 9am–3pm Mon and Fri or by appt; Kelman St; (07) 4627 3231.

Campdraft: Apr and Oct. *Taroom Show:* May. *Rodeo:* July.

Expedition National Park This remote park features the 14 km Robinson Gorge. The 4 km return track leads to an excellent lookout. Only experienced walkers should attempt the rough track down into the gorge. The Cattle Dip Lookout overlooks a permanent waterhole reached via the 8 km return Shepherd's Peak Trail or from the carpark at the lookout. 4WD recommended; some of the road is gravel. (07) 4624 3535; 128 km NW.

Lake Palm Tree Creek: rare Livistona palms; 15 km N. *Murphy Conservation Park:* pristine lake with birdlife, and picnic and camping spots. It was the site of Leichhardt's campsite in 1844; 30 km N. *Glebe Weir:* waterskiing and fishing; 40 km NE. *Wandoan:* the local heritage trail in the town visits all the major sights, including the Waterloo Plain Environmental Park; brochure from visitor centre in Royd St; 59 km S. *Scenic and historic drives:* self-drive tours to nearby sights; brochure from visitor centre.

TOWNS NEARBY: Theodore 82 km, Miles 119 km, Roma 145 km, Chinchilla 147 km, Mundubbera 151 km

Texas

Pop. 694
Map ref. 525 J3 | 609 J12

 Newsagency, 19 High St; (07) 4653 1384; texasqld4385.com.au

90.1 Breeze FM, 711 AM ABC Western QLD

Texas lies alongside the Dumaresq River (pronounced Du-meric) and the Queensland–New South Wales border. Its name comes from the similarity between an 1850s land dispute in the area to a dispute between the Republic of Texas and Mexico. The town was originally on the river flat, 2 kilometres from its current position. Severe floods forced the move. Remains of the original town can be seen on the river off Schwenke Street.

Heritage Centre and Tobacco Museum: located in the old police building (1893), with memorabilia that shows 100 years of the tobacco industry, as well as horse-drawn vehicles, mini shearing shed and the gaol; open Sat or by appt; Fleming St; (07) 4653 1410. *Art Gallery:* local and touring art exhibitions; open Tues–Sat; High St. *Riverside Freezing and Rabbit Works:* interpretive display on the rabbit skins factory and Aboriginal artefacts; open by appt; Mingoola Rd; (07) 4653 1453.

Heritage Centre Markets: Heritage Centre; 1st Sat in June and Dec. *Texas Show:* July. *Country Music Roundup:* Sept. *Horseracing:* Dec.

Beacon Lookout: regional views; 3 km SE on Stanthorpe Rd. *Cunningham Weir:* site where Allan Cunningham crossed the Dumaresq River in 1827; 31 km w off Texas–Yelarbon Rd. *Glenlyon Dam:* excellent fishing spot; 45 km SE. *Inglewood:* Texas's twin town at the centre of Australia's olive industry. Visit Inglewood Heritage Centre for local memorabilia (open 2nd and last Sat each month or by appt). Tour the local olive groves and follow the scenic drives in area; brochure available; 55 km N. *Coolmunda Reservoir:* picnics, boating and fishing; 75 km NE via Inglewood. *Dumaresq River:* winding river popular for canoeing and fishing, and hiking through wilderness areas along its banks.

TOWNS NEARBY: Stanthorpe 78 km, Tenterfield (NSW) 86 km, Goondiwindi 91 km, Warialda (NSW) 96 km, Inverell (NSW) 102 km

QUEENSLAND

SURFERS PARADISE

Pop. 18 501

Map ref. 516 G1 | 525 O1 | 600 G10 | 601 F6 | 609 N10

ⓘ **Gold Coast Tourism, Charles Avenue; (07) 5592 2699; www.visitgoldcoast.com**

📻 89.3 4CRB FM, 91.7 FM ABC Coast

Surfers Paradise is the Gold Coast's signature settlement. The first big hotel was built here in the 1930s, among little more than a clutch of shacks. Today, high-rise apartments – including the world's tallest residential tower, Q1 Resort and Spa – front one of the state's most beautiful beaches. This area has become an international-holiday metropolis, attracting every kind of visitor from backpacker to jetsetter.

🏠 *Circle on Cavill:* exciting new-generation shopping and leisure precinct with Circle Big Screen entertainment; access via Surfers Paradise Blvd, Cavill and Ferny Aves. *Orchid Avenue:* famous strip with the best live music in town. *Ripley's Believe It or Not:* the 12 galleries of amazing feats, facts and figures will surprise and amaze. There are interactive displays and movies that bring events to life; Raptis Plaza, Cavill Ave. *Haunted House:* from the creators of Dracula's world-famous cabaret, this walk-through attraction offers 5 levels of fright and a shop of horrors; Surfers Paradise Blvd. *Q1 Observation Deck:* the tallest residential building in the world, the Q1 Observation Deck gives breathtaking panoramic views from Brisbane to Byron Bay at 230 m above sea level; Hamilton Ave. *Adventure activities and tours:* try surfing lessons or scenic flights to see Surfers Paradise in a new light or take a tour to the Gold Coast hinterland; contact visitor centre for details. *KP Go Karting:* Ferny Ave, Surfers Paradise. *Flycoaster and Bungee Rocket:* thrill rides; Cypress Ave, Surfers Paradise. *Quack'R'Duck:* take an adventure on both land and water in this amphibious vehicle; departs Surfers Paradise Blvd.

🎪 *Surfers Paradise Markets:* The Esplanade between Hanlan St and Elkhorn Ave; every Wed and Fri evening. *Broadbeach Market:* Kurrawa Park; 1st and 3rd Sun each month. *Lantern Market:* Broadbeach Mall; Fri nights, May–Sept. *Farmers Market:* Marina Mirage Shopping Centre; 1st, 3rd and 5th Sat each month. *Magic Millions Racing Carnival:* Jan. *Gold Coast Big Day Out:* Music festival; Jan. *Australian Beach Volleyball Championships:* Mar. *Blues on Broadbeach Music Festival:* May. *Sanctuary Cove International Boat Show:* May. *GC Bazaar:* month-long festival of fashion, food and fun; June. *Gold Coast Marathon:* July. *Tastes of the Gold Coast Festival:* Feb–Mar. *Broadbeach Jazz Festival:* Aug. *Gold Coast Show:* Aug–Sept. *Gold Coast Eisteddfod:* Aug–Sept. *Indy Cars Grand Prix:* Oct. *New Year's Eve fireworks:* Dec.

🍴 *Absynthe:* French and Australian; Q1 Building, Surfers Paradise Blvd; (07) 5504 6466. *Chill on Tedder:* great seafood, delicious desserts; Shop 10/26 Tedder Ave, Main Beach; (07) 5528 0388. *Kurrawa Surf Club:* modern bistro; Old Burleigh Rd, Broadbeach; (07) 5538 0806. *Moo Moo The Wine Bar and Grill:* sophisticated steakhouse; Broadbeach on the Park Resort, 2685 Gold Coast Hwy, Broadbeach; (07) 5539 9952. *Ristorante Fellini:* modern-Italian fine dining; Marina Mirage, Sea World Dr, Main Beach; (07) 5531 0300.

🛏 *Broadwater Tourist Park:* 169 Marine Pde, Southport; (07) 5667 2730. *Capri Lodge:* 59 Rapallo Ave, Isle Of Capri; (07) 5592 3086. *Main Beach Tourist Park:* 3600 Main Beach Pde, Main Beach; (07) 5667 2720. *NRMA Treasure Island Holiday Park:* 117 Brisbane Rd, Biggera Waters; (07) 5500 8666. *Southport Tourist Park:* 6 Frank St (Gold Coast Hwy), Labrador; (07) 5531 2281.

🌀 **Broadbeach** The cosmopolatin heart of the Gold Coast has sophisticated wine bars, chic cafes, sun-drenched beaches and a vibrant nightlife. Visit Pacific Fair, Australia's largest shopping centre, hit the famous Conrad Jupiters Casino and try your luck at some blackjack, or stroll down to Kurrawa Beach, home of Australia's major surf-lifesaving competition. 3 km s.

[HIGH-RISE BUILDINGS ALONG THE SURFERS PARADISE BEACHFRONT]

Main Beach This wealthy area just north of Surfers Paradise is a wash of trendy boutiques and chic eateries. The Southport Spit Jetty, or The Spit as it's commonly known, is home to Sea World and the famous Palazzo Versace Hotel, as well as many specialty shops, restaurants, outdoor cafes and weekend entertainment at Marina Mirage and Mariner's Cove. It is also a hotspot for fishing while diving can be done at the nearby wreck of the *Scottish Prince*. 3 km N.

South Stradbroke Island This resort island, separated from North Stradbroke by the popular fishing channel Jumpinpin, is a peaceful alternative to the Gold Coast. It boasts quiet coves to the west and lively ocean beaches to the east, separated by wetland and remnant rainforest. See the abundant bird and butterfly species and discover the pleasures of windsurfing and sailing on either a daytrip or longer stay. Cars are not permitted; once on the island visitors must walk or cycle. Access by ferry or private boat from Runaway Bay Marina; 13 km N.

Theme parks The Gold Coast is the theme park capital of Australia, with 4 major theme parks in the Oxenford and Coomera areas. Warner Bros Movie World is 'Hollywood on the Gold Coast' with thrilling rides, stunts and shows that will interest all ages. Just down the road is Wet 'N' Wild Water Park. Enjoy the thrill-seeking rides or relax on the man-made Calypso Beach. Further north is Dreamworld, which has a diverse range of attractions from The Giant Drop (the tallest free-fall in the world) to the famous Big Brother House. Next to Dreamworld is Whitewater World, which is the latest technology in water theme-park slides and home to the 'world's best' water slide.

Gold Coast Arts Centre: art gallery incorporating contemporary and historical Australian art. Evandale sculpture walk nearby; Bundall Rd; 2 km w. ***Miami and Nobby Beach:*** both beaches are separated by a headland known as Magic Mountain. Miami is home to many diehard surfers; 6 km s ***The Broadwater:*** sheltered waterways excellent for boating (hire available), watersports and shore walks; access from Labrador and Southport; 5 km N. ***Surfers Riverwalk:*** scenic 9 km walk from Sundale Bridge at Southport to Pacific Fair at Broadbeach. ***Sanctuary Cove:*** famous area for championship golf courses, the exclusive Pines and the immaculate Palms. Hire a houseboat or take a cruise; 23 km NW. ***High-speed racing:*** 3 professional circuit tracks to test the visitor's driving skills in V8 Supercars, Commodores and WRXs. Courses at Ormeau and Pimpama; Pacific Hwy towards Brisbane; 33 km NW.

TOWNS NEARBY: Nerang 9 km, Burleigh Heads 10 km, Tweed Heads (NSW) 22 km, North Tamborine 26 km, Murwillumbah (NSW) 36 km

---

Theodore

Pop. 442
Map ref. 609 I3

i The Boulevard; (07) 4993 1900.

📻 96.5 Sea FM, 855 AM ABC Wide Bay

Theodore, once called Castle Creek, was the site of Queensland's first irrigation project, opened in 1924. With its rich black soils, the town is surrounded by pastoral and grazing properties, with sheep, cattle, sorghum, wheat and cotton. Located on the Dawson River, irrigation has resulted in palm-lined streets and a tropical air. The town was named after Edward (Red Ted) Theodore, union leader then Queensland premier from 1919 to 1925.

🏠 ***Theodore Hotel:*** only cooperative hotel in Queensland; The Boulevard. ***Dawson Folk Museum:*** provides local history; open by appt; Second Ave; (07) 4993 1686.

🌴 ***Fishing Competition:*** Mar. ***Theodore Show:*** May.

⊗ **Isla Gorge National Park** This highland park has gorges and spectacular rock formations. The camping area overlooks the gorge and a 2 km return walk leads to the Isla Gorge Lookout. If staying overnight, watch the changing colours of the sandstone cliffs as the sun sets. (07) 4627 3358; turn-off 35 km s.

Theodore Weir: popular spot for fishing; southern outskirts of town. ***Moura:*** major cattle town that holds the annual Coal and Country Festival in Aug; 48 km NW. ***Cracow:*** where gold was produced from famous Golden Plateau mine 1932–76; 49 km SE.

TOWNS NEARBY: Biloela 75 km, Taroom 82 km, Monto 106 km, Mundubbera 143 km, Mount Morgan 148 km

---

Thursday Island

see Weipa, nearby

Tin Can Bay

Pop. 1920
Map ref. 603 F8 | 609 N6

i Cooloola Regional Information Centre, Matilda's Roadhouse Complex, Bruce Hwy, Kybong (15 km s of Gympie); (07) 5483 5554 or 1800 444 222; www.tincanbaytourism.org.au

📻 96.1 Zinc FM, 855 AM ABC Wide Bay

Tin Can Bay is a well-known fishing and prawning region north-east of Gympie. It was originally known as Tuncanbar to the local Aboriginal people. The town is a relaxing hamlet offering watersports on the quiet waters of Tin Can Bay inlet.

🏠 ***Environmental Walkway:*** a 9.5 km trail for birdwatching on the Tin Can Bay foreshore. ***Boat and yacht hire:*** cruise the inlet and Sandy Strait; Tin Can Bay Marina. ***Canoeing:*** eco-tours down estuaries; (07) 5486 4417. ***Norman Point boat ramp:*** see the dolphins up-close before 10am; access point to waterways.

🌴 ***Yacht Race:*** May. ***War Birds:*** model planes and helicopters; May. ***Seafood Festival:*** Sept.

🛏 ***Ace Caravan Park:*** Esplanade; (07) 5486 4152. ***Tin Can Bay Tourist Park:*** Trevally St; (07) 5486 4411. ***Mia Mia Bed and Breakfast:*** 13 Bobrei Crt, Wallu; (07) 5488 0461. ***Rainbow Beach Holiday Village:*** 13 Rainbow Beach Rd, Rainbow Beach; (07) 5486 3222. ***Rainbow Waters Holiday Park:*** 308 Carlo Rd, Rainbow Beach; (07) 5486 3200.

⊗ **Rainbow Beach** This relaxing coastal town to the east across the inlet offers a pristine sandy beach popular with surfers. The Family Fishing Classic is held here each July. For adventure, try paragliding from the Carlo Sand Blow; bookings on (07) 5486 3048. Tours include dolphin ferry cruises, safaris and 4WD tours. The road south (4WD) leads to the coloured sands and beaches of the Cooloola section of Great Sandy National Park; *see Noosa Heads*. Rainbow Beach is 41 km E by road.

Carlo Point: great for fishing and swimming. There is also boat access to the inlet, with houseboats and yachts available for hire; 43 km E via Rainbow Beach. *Inskip Point:* camp along the point or take the car ferry to Fraser Island; 53 km NE via Rainbow Beach.

TOWNS NEARBY: Gympie 46 km, Maryborough 51 km, Pomona 52 km, Noosa Heads 54 km, Hervey Bay 71 km

Townsville

see inset box on page 448

Tully

Pop. 2459
Map ref. 606 E6 | 613 M8

i Bruce Hwy; (07) 4068 2288; www.csc.qld.gov.au

90.3 Kool FM, 630 AM ABC North QLD

At the foot of Mount Tyson, Tully receives one of the highest annual rainfalls in Australia – around 4200 millimetres. This abundance of rain supports swift rapids on the Tully River – an attraction for any whitewater-rafting enthusiast. The river, which descends from the Atherton Tableland through rainforest gorges, is one of Queensland's three main rafting rivers (the other two are the Barron and North Johnstone), with more than 45 individual rapids up to grade 4. The area was settled in the 1870s by a family keen on growing sugarcane, and the town grew when the government decided to build a sugar mill in 1925. Sugarcane remains a major industry.

 Tully Sugar Mill: informative tours in the crushing season (approximately June–Nov); tickets from the visitor centre. *Golden Gumboot:* 7.9 m high gumboot erected to celebrate Tully as Australia's wettest town.

Tully Show: July. *Golden Gumboot Festival:* Sept.

Googarra Beach Caravan Park: 7 Tully Heads Rd, Hull Heads; (07) 4066 9325.

Tully Gorge Alcock State Forest This state forest incorporates the Tully Gorge and the raging waters of the Tully River. Visit the Frank Roberts Lookout for gorge views, take the Rainforest Butterfly Walk and visit the Cardstone Weir boardwalk in the afternoons to watch rafters negotiate the rapids. Head to the top reaches of the river for superb scenery and swimming. Visit in dry season only (May–Dec); 40 km W.

Alligator's Nest: beautiful rainforest with swimming in stream; 10 km S. *Tully Heads:* estuary and beachside fishing; separated from Hull Heads by Googarra Beach; 22 km SE. *Echo Creek Walking Trail:* take this guided trail through rainforest, walking a traditional Aboriginal trading route with Jirrba guides; turn-off after Euramo; 30 km SW. *Murray Upper State Forest:* rainforest walks to cascades, rockpools and Murray Falls; turn-off 38 km S. *Misty Mountains walking trails:* day walks or longer (up to 44 km) in Wet Tropics World Heritage Area; details from visitor centre. *Whitewater rafting:* operators run from Tully to the renowned rapids of the Tully River; details from visitor centre.

TOWNS NEARBY: Mission Beach 21 km, Cardwell 38 km, Mourilyan 41 km, Innisfail 47 km, Millaa Millaa 57 km

Warwick

Pop. 12 564
Map ref. 516 B1 | 525 L1 | 609 L10

i 49 Albion St (New England Hwy); (07) 4661 3122 or 1800 060 877; www.southerndownsholidays.com.au

89.3 Rainbow FM, 747 AM ABC Southern QLD

Warwick is an attractive city set alongside the willow-shaded Condamine River. It is known as the 'Rose and Rodeo City', as the Warwick Rodeo dates back to the 1850s, and the parks and gardens have an abundance of roses. There is even a red rose cultivated especially for Warwick – the City of Warwick Rose (or Arofuto Rose). The area was explored by Allan Cunningham in 1827, and in 1840 the Leslie brothers established a sheep station at Canning Downs. Warwick was eventually established in 1849 on the site that Patrick Leslie selected. The surrounding pastures support famous horse and cattle studs.

Australian Rodeo Heritage Centre: follow the history and relive the glory of the Australian Professional Rodeo Association's greatest champions; open 10am–3pm Mon–Sat or by appt; Alice St. *Pringle Cottage:* historic home (1870) housing large historic photo collection, vehicles and machinery; closed Mon–Tues; Dragon St. *Warwick Regional Art Gallery:* local and touring exhibitions; closed Mon; Albion St. *Jubilee Gardens:* see the displays of roses that Warwick is famous for; Cnr Palmerin and Fitzroy sts. *Lookout:* viewing platform for regional views; Glen Rd. *Historic walk or drive:* self-guide tour of historic sandstone buildings dating from the 1880s and 1890s; brochure from visitor centre.

Rock Swap Festival: Easter. *Jumpers and Jazz:* July. *Campdraft and Rodeo:* Oct.

Spicers Peak Lodge Restaurant: up-market modern Australian; Wilkinsons Rd, Maryvale; (07) 4666 1083 or 1300 253 103.

Glenrose Cottages: 138 Ogilvie Rd; (07) 4661 7476. *Guy House B&B:* 31 Guy St; (07) 4661 7669. *Harts Tourist Park:* 18 Palmer Ave; (07) 4661 8335. *Kahlers Oasis Caravan Park:* New England Hwy; (07) 4661 2874. *Pitstop Lodge Guesthouse and B&B:* 53 Canning St; (07) 4661 9393.

Leslie Dam: watersports, fishing and swimming; 15 km W. *Main Range National Park:* 61 km NE; *see Boonah and Killarney*. *Heritage drive:* 80 km cultural drive in region; brochure from visitor centre.

TOWNS NEARBY: Allora 21 km, Killarney 29 km, Clifton 34 km, Stanthorpe 50 km, Boonah 68 km

Weipa

Pop. 2832
Map ref. 614 B7

i Evans Landing; (07) 4069 7566.

100.9 KIG FM, 1044 AM ABC Far North QLD

This coastal part of Cape York was reputedly the first area in Australia to be explored by Europeans (1605). The town of Weipa was built in 1961 on the site of a mission station and Aboriginal reserve, and is now home to the world's largest bauxite mine. Although the town is remote, it offers a full range of services for travellers.

Western Cape Cultural Centre This centre was established to introduce the visitor to the culture of western Cape York. The range of artefacts and photos bring the area's Indigenous and European history alive. A highlight is the ceramic wall mural depicting sacred images of the local Aboriginal people. There

continued on p. 449

TOOWOOMBA

Pop. 159 089
Map ref. 609 L9

i Cnr James (Warrego Hwy) and Kitchener sts; (07) 4639 3797 or 1800 331 155; www.toowoombaholidays.com.au

100.7 CFM, 747 AM ABC Southern QLD

Toowoomba is a city with a distinctive charm courtesy of its wide, tree-lined streets, colonial architecture and more than 240 parks and gardens. The city is perched 700 metres above sea level on the rim of the Great Dividing Range. Established in 1849 as a small village near an important staging post, Toowoomba is now the commercial centre for the fertile Darling Downs region. The city was re-built after the devastating 2011 floods, and visitors continue to be captivated by its mild summers, leafy autumns and vibrant springs.

Cobb & Co. Museum The museum traces the history of horse-drawn vehicles in the Darling Downs region. It has been recently expanded to include the National Carriage Factory, featuring an open-plan training centre that hosts workshops for heritage skills including blacksmithing, saddlery, silversmithing and glass art, with a viewing area for visitors. There is also an interactive discovery centre for children. Open 10am–4pm daily; 27 Lindsay St; (07) 4659 4900.

Parks and gardens No trip to the 'Garden City' would be complete without a visit to some of the superb parks and gardens. Lake Annand is a popular recreation spot with boardwalks, bridges and ducks; MacKenzie St. There are imposing European trees in Queen's Park, which also includes the Botanic Gardens; Lindsay and Margaret sts. Laurel Bank Park features the unique Scented Garden, designed for the visually impaired; Cnr Herries and West sts. Birdwatchers should visit Waterbird Habitat where native birds can be watched from observation platforms and floating islands; MacKenzie and Alderley sts. The impressive Japanese Garden at the University of Southern Queensland is the largest in Australia A thousand visitors a week stroll the 3 kms of paths at Ju Raku En, opened in 1989. The garden showcases the harmony and beauty of ancient Japanese garden design with its lake, willowy beeches, islands, bridges, stream and pavilion; off West St.

Regional Art Gallery: changing exhibitions in Queensland's oldest gallery; open 10am–4pm Tues–Sat, 1–4pm Sun; 531 Ruthven St; (07) 4688 6652. *Royal Bull's Head Inn:* National Trust–listed building (1859) with small museum; open Fri–Sun 10am–4pm; Brisbane St, Drayton; (07) 4637 2278. *Empire Theatre:* live theatre in this restored Art Deco building, opened in 1911; 56 Neil St; 1300 655 299. *Picnic Point:* offers views of Lockyer Valley, mountains and waterfall. Enjoy the recreational facilities and walks through bushland. Perfect venue for Summer Tunes concerts in summer; Tourist Dr, eastern outskirts. *City tour:* Stonestreets Coaches offers a 2 hr tour of the city; book at the visitor centre or (07) 4687 5555.

PCYC Markets: 7am–12pm Sun; 219a James St; *Darling Downs Farmers Markets:* 1st and 3rd Sun each month; 7am–12pm; Victoria St. *Toowoomba Royal Show:* Mar/Apr. *Easterfest:* Music festival; Easter. *Carnival of Flowers:* Sept.

Spotted Cow Hotel: European beers and food; Cnr Ruthven and Campbell sts; (07) 4639 3264. *Veraison:* modern Australian, good wine list; 205 Margaret St;

[COBB & CO. MUSEUM]

(07) 4638 5909. *Weis:* legendary seafood smorgasbord; 2 Margaret St; (07) 4632 7666.

Beccles On Margaret B&B: 25 Margaret St, East Toowoomba; (07) 4638 5254. *BIG4 Toowoomba Garden City Holiday Park:* 34A Eiser St, Harristown; (07) 4635 1747. *ecoRidge Hideaway:* 712 Rockmount Rd, Preston; (07) 4630 9636. *Toowoomba Motor Village Caravan Park:* 821 Ruthven St, Kearneys Spring; (07) 4635 8186.

Highfields: growing town featuring Orchid Park, Danish Flower Art Centre, quaint shopping centres and historical village with vintage machinery and buildings; 12 km N. *Cabarlah:* small community that has the Black Forest Hill Cuckoo Clock Centre and holds excellent country markets on the last Sun each month; 19 km N. *Southbrook:* nearby Prestbury Farm offers accomodation and the experience of rural life; (07) 4691 0195; 34 km SW. *Lake Cooby:* fishing, walking and picnic facilities; 35 km N. *Pittsworth*: in town is the Pioneer Historical Village, featuring a single-teacher school, early farming machinery and a display commemorating Arthur Postle, or the 'Crimson Flash', once the fastest man in the world; village open Wed–Fri 10am–1pm and Sun 10am–4pm or by appt; Pioneer Way; (07) 4619 8000; 46 km SW. *Yandilla:* here you'll find the quaint, steeped All Saints Anglican Church (1877), the oldest building in the shire; 77 km SW. *Millmerran:* colourful murals illustrate the history of this industrial town, including the dairy industry mural at the Old Butter Factory, and the mural on the water reservoir showing the development of transport. The town's historical museum is open Tues–Thurs; 10am–3pm; (07) 4695 2560; 87 km SW. *Ravensbourne:* this National Park area boasts bush walks, lookouts and native wildlife; 50 km N. *Scenic drives:* take in places such as Spring Bluff, with old railway station and superb gardens (16 km N), Murphys Creek and Heifer Creek.

TOWNS NEARBY: Oakey 27 km, Gatton 32 km, Crows Nest 35 km, Clifton 42 km, Laidley 44 km

 RADIO STATIONS IN TOWN WHAT'S ON WHERE TO EAT WHERE TO STAY NEARBY

QUEENSLAND

TOWNSVILLE

Pop. 14 332

Map ref. 605 A1 | 606 G10 | 610 G1 | 613 N11

i Bruce Hwy, (07) 4778 3555 or 1800 801 902; or Flinders Mall Information Centre, 334A Flinders St, (07) 4721 3660 or 1800 801 902; www.townsvilleholidays.info

📻 106.3 FM Townsville's Best Mix, 630 AM ABC North QLD

Townsville is a bustling and vibrant tropical city boasting an enviable lifestyle, diverse landscapes, activities for all ages and a certain charm that comes with a long-standing history. Established in 1864, Townsville was set up to service a new cattle industry. The many historic buildings found around the city are a reminder of this heritage. These days, the city is better known for its cosmopolitan tastes and fast growth. Its iconic foreshore, The Strand, offers an excellent choice of cafes and restaurants, combined with tropical parks and spectacular views to Magnetic Island.

Reef HQ Home to the headquarters for the Great Barrier Reef Marine Park Authority, this underwater observatory is both informative and visually breathtaking. Its living reef is the largest 'captive' reef in the world. Get up close at the touch pools or see marine feeding and dive shows; Flinders St East; (07) 4750 0800.

Museum of Tropical Queensland: featuring artefacts from HMAS *Pandora*, a British vessel wrecked on the reef in 1791; open 9.30am–5pm daily; 70–102 Flinders St; (07) 4726 0600. *Maritime Museum:* maritime items of historical significance; open Mon–Fri 10am–4pm, Sat–Sun 12–4pm; 42–68 Palmer St; South Townsville; (07) 4721 5759. *Rock Pool Baths:* year-round swimming; The Strand. *Perc Tucker Regional Art Gallery:* local and touring exhibitions; open Mon–Fri 10am–5pm, Sat–Sun 10am–2pm; Flinders Mall; (07) 4727 9000. *Botanic Gardens:* Anderson Park, Kings Rd. *Imax Dome Theatre:* excellent viewing experience in this theatre, the 1st of its kind in the Southern Hemisphere; call for viewing times; Reef HQ Building, Flinders St East; (07) 4721 1481. *Town Common Conservation Park:* a coastline park with prolific birdlife, Aboriginal Plant Trail and forest walks; Cape Pallarenda Rd. *Castle Hill Lookout:* off Stanley St. *Jupiters Townsville Hotel and Casino:* Sir Leslie Thiess Dr; (07) 4722 2333. *Ferry Terminal:* for Magnetic Island, and daytrips and dive cruises to the Great Barrier Reef as well as extended cruises to the Whitsundays; Sir Leslie Thiess Dr. *Coral Princess:* cruise to Cairns via resort islands and reef on a luxury catamaran; contact visitor centre for details. *Adventure activities:* numerous tour operators offer scuba diving, jetskiing, waterskiing, abseiling, whitewater rafting and more; contact visitor centre for details.

Showground Market: Ingham Rd, West End; Sun 6am–2pm. *Cotters Market:* Flinders Mall; Sun 8.30am–1pm. *Horseshoe Bay Market:* Beachside Park, Magnetic Island; last Sun each month, 9am–1pm. *Opal Fashion Bash:* Apr. *Italian Festival:* May. *Townsville Show:* Jul. *Australian Festival of Chamber Music:* July/Aug. *Townsville Cup:* horseracing; July. *Magnetic Island Race Week:* sailing; Sep. *Greek Festival:* Oct.

🍴 *Michel's Cafe & Bar:* international fare; 7 Palmer St, South Townsville; (07) 4724 1460. *SugarTrain:* modern Australian; 14 Palmer St; (07) 4753 2000 *Masala:* Indian; 79 Palmer St,

[TROPICAL GARDENS OUTSIDE THE OLD QUEENS HOTEL, THE STRAND]

South Townsville; (07) 4721 3388. *Watermark:* seafood and steaks; 72 The Strand, North Ward; (07) 4724 4281.

🛏 *BIG4 Townsville Woodlands Holiday Park:* 548 Bruce Hwy, Deeragun; (07) 4751 6955. *BIG4 Walkabout Palms Townsville:* 6 University Rd, Wulguru; (07) 4778 2480. *Coral Coast Tourist Park:* 547 Ingham Rd, Garbutt; (07) 4774 5205. *Magnetic Gateway Holiday Village:* 88 Minehane St, Cluden; (07) 4778 2412. *Rollingstone Beach Caravan Resort:* 14 Hencamp Creek Rd, Rollingstone; (07) 4770 7277.

Magnetic Island More than half of this beautiful island is covered by the Magnetic Island National Park. The sandy beaches, granite headlands and hoop pine rainforest make this an attractive daytrip; or stay overnight in the private accommodation on offer, which ranges from budget to deluxe. See the natural attractions by taking some of the many walks around the island or hire a bike for a different view. Snorkel and swim at Alma Bay and see spectacular views from the old WW II forts. Access from Townsville by fast cat, passenger ferry or vehicle barge; 8 km NE.

Bowling Green Bay National Park This coastal park offers much for the self-sufficient visitor. Granite mountains blend with a variety of landscapes including saltpans and mangrove country. Walk along Alligator Creek to see cascades and waterfalls. Stay overnight at the Alligator Creek campsite and go spotlighting to glimpse brush-tail possums and sugar gliders; call 13 74 68 for camping bookings; turn-off Bruce Hwy 28 km SE; park is further 6 km.

Billabong Sanctuary: covering 10 ha of rainforest, eucalypt forest and wetlands. See koala feeding and crocodile shows. Bruce Hwy, Nome; (07) 4778 8344; 17 km SE. *Giru:* small community with waterfalls, bushwalks and swimming nearby; 50 km SE.

TOWNS NEARBY: Ayr 72 km, Ravenswood 93 km, Ingham 97 km, Charters Towers 106 km, Cardwell 138 km is also information about the landscapes and ecosystems of the Cape, and sales of local arts and crafts. Open 10am–3pm daily; Evans Landing; (07) 4069 7566.

Tours of bauxite mine: guided tours provide insight into the mining process at Weipa; details from visitor centre. *Fishing tours:* Weipa's fishing spots can be explored on tours; details from visitor centre. *Boat and houseboat hire:* details from visitor centre.

 Fishing Competition: June. *Bullride:* Aug.

 Weipa Camping Ground: Lot 172 Kerr Point Rd; (07) 4069 7871. *Seisia Holiday Park:* 6 Koraba Rd, Seisia; (07) 4069 3243.

Thursday Island and the Torres Strait Australia's only non-Aboriginal indigenous people come from this group of around 100 islands off the northern tip of Cape York. The islands stretch from the tip of Cape York Peninsula to Papua New Guinea and comprise 17 inhabited islands. The first Europeans passed through the islands in the 1600s, and by the late 1800s a pearling industry was established, which continues today along with crayfishing, prawning and trochus industries. Thursday Island is the administrative centre, reached by ferry from Seisia or Punsand Bay or by ship or plane from Cairns. The Torres Strait Islander people are of Melanesian descent and include among their number the late Eddie Mabo, famous for his successful 1992 land claim in Australia's High Court. Visit the Torres Strait Island Cultural Centre – it preserves the cultural heritage of the islands and documents their art, culture, geography and history in an excellent interpretive display. Other surrounding islands worth a visit are Friday Island where you can see pearls being cultivated at Kazu; Horn Island, which was an important posting for Australian Troops in WW II; and Badu Island, where you can enjoy traditional dances, arts and crafts and food. Getting to the Islands involves either a flight from Cairns, a trip on a cargo vessel from Cairns (through Seaswift, (07) 4035 1234), or a ferry ride from Cape York (through Peddells, (07) 4069 1551).

Jardine River National Park This remote park is on the north-east tip of Cape York Peninsula. It was known to early explorers as the 'wet desert' because of its abundant waterways but lack of food. These waters attract varied birdlife including the rare palm cockatoo. See the Fruit Bat Falls from the boardwalk or fish in restricted areas. 4WD access only. Visit between May–Oct; off Peninsula Development Rd, south of Bamaga; (07) 4069 5777.

Fishing and camping: a number of areas developed for the well-equipped visitor. *Mungkan Kandju National Park:* wilderness park of open forests, swamps and dense rainforest. There is excellent birdlife around lagoons and bushwalking along Archer River. 4WD access only; visit between May–Nov; (07) 4060 1137; turn-off 29 km N of Coen. *Mapoon:* camping and scenery; permit required; 85 km N. *Kutini–Payamu National Park:* this important lowland tropical rainforest park is a haven for wildlife. There is good fishing at Chili Beach, and bush camping for self-sufficient visitors only. 4WD recommended; visit only between Apr–Sept; (07) 4060 7170; 216 km E.

Travellers note: *Roads to the Cape may become impassable during the wet season (Nov–Apr). Motorists are advised to check the RACQ Road Conditions Report on 1300 130 595 (or www.racq.com.au) before departing. Permits for travel over Aboriginal land can be sought in Weipa; details from visitor centre. Beware of crocodiles in rivers, estuaries and coastal areas. Also beware of marine stingers in coastal areas (Oct–Apr) and swim within enclosures where possible.*

Whitsunday Island
see Airlie Beach, nearby

Winton
Pop. 983
Map ref. 617 L7

 Waltzing Matilda Centre, 50 Elderslie St; (07) 4657 1466 or 1300 665 115; www.matildacentre.com.au

95.9 West FM, 540 AM ABC Western QLD

The area surrounding Winton is known as Matilda Country, as Australia's most famous song, 'Waltzing Matilda', was written by Banjo Paterson at nearby Dagworth Station in 1895. Combo Waterhole (near Kynuna) was the setting for the ballad and the tune had its first airing in Winton. A less auspicious event in Winton's history was the declaration of martial law in the 1890s following the Shearers' Strike. In 1920 the first office of Qantas was registered here. The town's water supply comes from deep artesian bores at a temperature of 83°C. The movie *The Proposition* was filmed in the town in 2004.

Waltzing Matilda Centre Created as a tribute to the life of the swagman. The centre incorporates the 'Billabong Courtyard' with its sound and light show, the regional art gallery, interactive exhibits showcasing the swagmans life in 'Home of the Legend' hall, and the Matilda Museum that harks back to Winton's pioneering days and the first days of Qantas. Elderslie St; (07) 4657 1466.

Royal Theatre: historic open-air movie theatre and museum, one of the oldest still operating in Australia; Elderslie St. *Corfield and Fitzmaurice Store:* charming National Trust–listed store with diorama of Lark Quarry dinosaur stampede; Elderslie St. *Gift and Gem Centre:* displays and sales; the 'Opal Walk' leads to the theatre museum; Elderslie St. *Arno's Wall:* ongoing concrete-wall creation proudly containing 'every item imaginable'; Vindex St. *North Gregory Hotel:* built in 1878, this historical structure has been ravaged by 3 separate fires. Artwork and opal collection on display; Elderslie St.

Winton Show: June. *Opal Expo:* July. *Camel Races:* July. *Rodeo:* Aug. *Outback Festival:* odd-numbered years, Sept.

Lark Quarry Conservation Park This park features the preserved tracks of a dinosaur stampede from 93 million years ago – the only track of this type known in the world. The stampede occurred when a Therapod chased a group of smaller dinosaurs across the mud flats. The 'trackways' are sheltered and can be visited on a tour (details from visitor centre). The park also offers a short walk past ancient rock formations, known as the Winton Formation, to a lookout over the region. 110 km sw.

Bladensburg National Park The vast plains and ridges of this park provide an important sanctuary for a variety of wildlife, including kangaroos, dunnarts and emus. Skull Hole (40 km s) has Aboriginal paintings and bora ceremonial grounds and is believed to be the site of a late-1880s Aboriginal massacre. Walking should only be attempted by experienced bushwalkers. 'Route of the River Gums', a self-drive tour, shows the region's varied landscapes. (07) 4652 7333; drive starts 8 km s.

Carisbrooke Station: a working sheep station with Aboriginal cave paintings and scenic drives in the surrounds; day tours and accommodation available; 85 km sw. *Opalton:* see the remains of the historic town or try fossicking for opals in one of the oldest fields in Queensland; licence available from visitor centre;

QUEENSLAND

115 km s. *Air charters and ground tours:* to major regional sights; details from visitor centre.

TOWNS NEARBY: Kynuna 146 km, Muttaburra 157 km, Longreach 171 km, Richmond 183 km, Hughenden 208 km

Yandina
Pop. 1078
Map ref. 602 F3 | 603 E11 | 609 N7

 Yandina Historic House, 3 Pioneer Rd (at the roundabout); (07) 5472 7181.

90.3 AM ABC Coast FM, 91.1 Hot FM

Yandina is in the Sunshine Coast hinterland north of Nambour. The first land claims in the area were made here in 1868. It is now home to The Ginger Factory, the largest of its kind anywhere, giving rise to Yandina's title of 'Ginger Capital of the World'.

The Ginger Factory This award-winning complex is devoted to everything ginger. Visitors can see Gingertown, watch ginger-cooking demonstrations, see ginger being processed and ride on the historic Queensland Cane Train through subtropical gardens with acres of tropical plants, water features and a plant nursery – a highlight are the stunning flowering gingers. Pioneer Rd.

Yandina Historic House: local-history display, arts and crafts, art gallery and visitor centre; Pioneer Rd. *Nutworks Macadamia Processes:* see processing of macadamia nuts and taste-test the results; opposite The Ginger Factory. *Fairhill Native Plants and Botanic Gardens:* fabulous nursery and gardens – a must for any native-plant buff; also includes the excellent Elements Restaurant, with breakfast, lunch and afternoon tea in botanic garden setting; Fairhill Rd. *Heritage trail:* self-guide trail around town sights; brochure from visitor centre.

Market: town centre; Sat. *Ginger Flower Festival:* Jan.

Spirit House: superb Thai food; 20 Ninderry Rd; (07) 5446 8994.

Yandina Caravan Park: 1519 Nambour North Connection Rd; (07) 5446 7332. *Coolum Beach Holiday Park:* David Low Way, Coolum Beach; (07) 5446 1474. *Jacaranda Creek Farmstay and B&B:* 63 Eumundi Range Rd, Eumundi; (07) 5442 7037. *Musavale Lodge:* 55 Musavale Rd, Eumundi; (07) 5442 8678. *Ninderry Manor Luxury B&B:* 12 Karnu Dr, Ninderry; (07) 5472 7255.

 Eumundi This historic town has a variety of excellent galleries to visit, including some with Indigenous Australian art. Also sample exquisite handcrafted chocolates at Cocoa Chocolate, all made on-site (Etheridge St); or browse through the maze of shelves at Berkelouw Books in the main street. The impressive country markets are renowned for their size with over 600 stalls. The quality of the fresh produce, art and craft and cut flowers, along with the wonderful atmosphere, brings visitors to the town each Wed and Sat, and on Thurs night Dec–Jan; 10 km N. *Wappa Dam:* popular picnic area; west of Yandina. *Yandina Speedway:* offers a variety of motor races; call (07) 5446 7552 for details; just west on Wappa Falls Rd.

TOWNS NEARBY: Nambour 7 km, Buderim 17 km, Maroochydore 18 km, Mooloolaba 20 km, Noosa Heads 23 km

Yeppoon

Pop. 13 282
Map ref. 604 C4 | 611 M10

i Capricorn Coast Tourist Information Centre, Scenic Hwy; (07) 4939 4888 or 1800 675 785; www.capricorncoast.com.au

91.3 FM Radio Nag

The popular coastal resort of Yeppoon lies on the shores of Keppel Bay. Yeppoon and the beaches to its south – Cooee Bay, Rosslyn Bay, Causeway Lake, Emu Park and Keppel Sands – are known as the Capricorn Coast. Great Keppel Island Resort lies 13 kilometres offshore and is a popular holiday destination offering great swimming, snorkelling and diving.

The Esplanade: attractive strip of shops, galleries and cafes overlooking parkland and crystal-clear water. *Doll and Antiquity Museum:* Hidden Valley Rd.

Market: showgrounds; Sat mornings. *Fig Tree Markets:* 1st Sun each month. *Australia Day Celebrations:* Jan. *Yeppoon Show:* June. *Ozfest:* World Cooeeing Competition; July. *Village Arts Festival:* Aug. *Rodeo:* Sept. *Yeppoon Tropical Pinefest:* Sept/Oct.

While Away Bed & Breakfast: 44 Todd Ave; (07) 4939 5719. *Bell Park Caravan Park:* Pattison St, Emu Park; (07) 4939 6202. *Causeway Caravan Park:* 11 The Esplanade, Causeway Lake; (07) 4933 6356. *Coolwaters Holiday Village:* 760 Scenic Hwy, Kinka Beach; (07) 4939 6102.

Great Keppel Island Popular island-holiday destination with over 15 beaches to explore, swim and relax on. There is snorkelling and diving offshore and walks exploring the island's centre, including an interesting Aboriginal culture trail. Various styles of accommodation are offered. Access is by ferry from Keppel Bay Marina at Rosslyn Bay Harbour. 7 km s.

Byfield National Park This coastal park offers uninterrupted views of the ocean from its long beaches. Explore the open woodlands and forest or take in coastal views from the headlands at Five Rock and Stockyard Point. Fishing and boating are popular at Sandy Point at the south of the park. 4WD only; experience in sand driving is essential. (07) 4936 0511; 32 km N.

Boating: bareboat and fishing charters, sea access to Great Keppel Island and nearby underwater observatory, and water taxis to Keppel Bay islands; all from Keppel Bay Marina; 7 km s. *Wetland Tour:* Australian nature tour at Rydges Capricorn International Resort; 9 km N. *Cooberrie Park:* noted flora and fauna reserve; 15 km N. *Emu Park:* small village community with historical museum and interesting 'singing ship' memorial to Captain Cook – the sea breezes cause hidden organ pipes to make sounds. There is a Service of Remembrance to American troops each July, and Octoberfest is held each Oct; 19 km s. *Byfield State Forest:* the extremely rare Byfield fern is harvested here. Walks include the 4.3 km Stony Creek circuit track through rainforest and the boardwalk along Waterpark Creek; adjacent to Byfield National Park. *Keppel Sands:* this popular spot for fishing and crabbing is home to the excellent emerging Joskeleigh South Sea Island Museum, with the Koorana Crocodile Farm nearby; 38 km sw. *Keppel Bay Islands National Park:* this scenic group of islands is popular for walks, snorkelling, reef-walking and swimming; private boat or water taxi from Keppel Bay Marina; (07) 4933 6595. *Capricorn Coast Coffee:* Australia's largest coffee plantation; tours available; details from visitor centre. *Scenic flights:* over islands and surrounds from Hedlow Airport (between Yeppoon and Rockhampton); details from visitor centre.

TOWNS NEARBY: Rockhampton 37 km, Mount Morgan 68 km, Gladstone 95 km, Biloela 143 km, Miriam Vale 157 km

[YUNGABURRA] **CURTAIN FIG TREE**

Yungaburra

Pop. 932
Map ref. 606 D3 | 607 E9 | 613 L7

i Allumbah Pocket Cottages, Gillies Hwy, (07) 4095 3023;
or Nick's Restaurant & Yodeller's Bar, 33 Gillies Hwy,
(07) 4095 3330; www.athertontableland.com

 102.5 4KZ FM, 720 AM ABC Far North QLD

Yungaburra is a historic town on the edge of the Atherton
Tableland. Originally a resting spot for miners, it was slow to
develop. The tourism boom did not hit until the coastal road
opened from Cairns in 1926. Today the town offers craft shops,
galleries, cafes and restaurants.

Historical precinct walk: take this self-guide walk past
heritage buildings, including the popular Lake Eacham Hotel
in Cedar St; brochure available from visitor centre. *Platypus
viewing platform:* see the elusive animal at sunrise and sunset;
Peterson Creek, Gillies Hwy. *Galleries, craft and gem shops:*
various outlets in town.

Market: renowned produce and craft market; Gillies Hwy;
4th Sat each month. *Tour de Tableland:* bike race; May. *Malanda
Show:* July. *Folk Festival:* Oct.

Eden House: modern Australian; 20 Gillies Hwy; (07) 4089
7000. *Flynn's Licensed Restaurant:* European-influenced fare;
17 Eacham Rd; (07) 4095 2235. *Nick's Restaurant and Yodeller's
Bar:* Swiss–Italian; 33 Gillies Hwy; (07) 4095 3330.

Mt Quincan Crater Retreat: Peeramon Rd; (07) 4095
2255. *Williams Lodge:* 16 Cedar St; (07) 4095 3449.

Crater Lakes National Park The 2 volcanic lakes, Lake
Eacham (8 km E) and Lake Barrine (12 km NE), are surrounded by
rainforest and offer watersports, bushwalking and birdwatching.
Look for the eastern water dragons along the 3 km track around
Lake Barrine or take a wildlife cruise on the lake. There is a
children's pool at Lake Eacham, a self-guide trail through the
rainforest and a 3 km circuit shore track. Both lakes are popular
recreation areas. (07) 4091 1844.

Malanda Malanda is a small town in the middle of rich dairy-
farming country. It claims the longest milk run in the world
(to Alice Springs) and boasts the still-operating 19th-century
Majestic Theatre, and the Gourmet Food Factory, specialising in
local produce. On the southern outskirts of town is the Malanda
Falls Conservation Park, with signposted rainforest walks, and
the Malanda Environmental Centre, which has displays on local
history, vulcanology, flora and fauna. The Malanda Falls actually
flow into the local swimming pool. 20 km S.

Curtain Fig Tree: spectacular example of strangler fig with aerial
roots in curtain-like formation; 2.5 km SW. *Tinaburra:* a great
spot for swimming and watersports on Lake Tinaroo; boat ramp
provides access. Nearby Seven Sisters are 7 volcanic cinder cones;
3 km N. *Lake Tinaroo:* watersports and fishing; travel around
on a houseboat or dinghy – hire available; north of Yungaburra.
Heales Outlook: spectacular views over Gillies Range; 16 km NE.
Tinaroo Falls Dam outlet: views over lake; 23 km N.

TOWNS NEARBY: Atherton 12 km, Herberton 24 km, Millaa
Millaa 27 km, Gordonvale 28 km, Mareeba 35 km

QUEENSLAND

TASMANIA is...

Shopping for fresh produce and crafts at Hobart's **SALAMANCA MARKET** / Walking through a forest canopy at the **TAHUNE FOREST AIRWALK** / A cruise down the **GORDON RIVER** from Strahan / Bushwalking in **CRADLE MOUNTAIN–LAKE ST CLAIR NATIONAL PARK** / Learning the chilling history behind **PORT ARTHUR HISTORIC SITE** / Visiting cellar doors in the **TAMAR VALLEY WINE REGION** / Taking the one-hour walk to the lookout over **WINEGLASS BAY** in **FREYCINET NATIONAL PARK** / A chairlift ride to the top of **THE NUT**, Stanley / Discovering **CATARACT GORGE** and the nearby landscaped gardens in Launceston

TASMANIA

is bursting with wonderful surprises. A winding country road can suddenly reveal a colonial village, a boutique vineyard or a breathtaking ocean view like that of Wineglass Bay. From landscapes and history to food and culture, Australia's island state is a feast for travellers.

Although it is Australia's smallest state – only 296 kilometres from south to north and 315 kilometres east to west – Tasmania's territory also includes the Bass Strait islands and subantarctic Macquarie Island. A population of just over 510 000 is eclipsed by over half a million visitors each year, and Tasmania is famous for its friendly, welcoming and relaxed pace of life.

Tasmania's Indigenous peoples have been here for around 35 000 years, and despite the terrible impact of white settlement, they are a large and increasingly influential community today. Middens are common around the coastline, showing where generations of Aboriginal people cooked shellfish meals.

Abel Tasman sighted and named Van Diemen's Land in 1642, closely followed by French and British explorers. The British – never keen to be outdone by the French – acted in 1803 to establish a presence on the River Derwent. With the arrival of the British, white settlement

[SLEEPY BAY, FREYCINET PENINSULA]

got off to a rollicking and violent start as a penal colony for the first 50 years.

In more recent history, Tasmania is the home of the world's first 'green' political party. Local environmental politics captured international attention in the 1980s when the No Dams campaign saved the Franklin River from being flooded for a hydro-electric scheme.

The island's spirited cultural life includes the renowned Tasmanian Symphony Orchestra, David Walsh's astounding MONA museum of old and new art, and a full diary of festivals.

Although two-thirds of the land is too harsh for farming, Tasmania has a growing reputation for boutique agriculture and aquaculture. A gastronomic circumnavigation of the island offers as much diversity as the landscape and a chance to discover Tasmania's cool-climate wines, fresh seafood, fruits and fine cheeses.

[LOOKOUT ALONG ARVE ROAD FOREST DRIVE]

fact file

Population 510 600
Total land area 68 102 square kilometres
People per square kilometre 7.1
Sheep per square kilometre 49.6
Length of coastline 2833 kilometres
Number of islands 1000
Longest river South Esk River (252 kilometres)
Largest lake Lake Gordon (hydro-electric impoundment) (271 square kilometres)
Highest mountain Mount Ossa (1614 metres), Cradle Mountain–Lake St Clair National Park
Coldest place At Liawenee in August the average minimum temperature is −1.8°C
Longest place name Teebelebberrer Mennapeboneyer (Aboriginal name for Little Swanport River)
Best beach Wineglass Bay, Freycinet National Park
Biggest surfable wave Shipstern Bluff near Port Arthur
Tallest tree At 99.6 m, the Arve Valley's giant swamp gum 'Centurion' is the world's tallest eucalypt
Most famous son Ricky Ponting, former captain of the Australian cricket team
Most famous daughter Danish Crown Princess Mary Donaldson
Quirkiest festival National Penny Farthing Championships, Evandale
Most expensive gourmet produce Stigmas of *Crocus sativus*, grown on a saffron farm, which can attract a price of $30 000 per kilogram
Local beers Cascade in the south; Boags in the north

gift ideas

Arts and crafts, Salamanca Market, Hobart A range of fantastic products on offer, from Jemma Clements' hand-blown perfume bottles to handcrafted vegetable soaps. See Salamanca Place p. 461

Huon pine box, Handmark Gallery, Hobart Buttery aromatic wood endemic to Tasmania and treasured by woodworkers. 77 Salamanca Pl, Hobart. See Salamanca Place p. 461

Peter Dombrovskis poster, Wilderness Society Shop, Hobart Haunting wilderness images by the man whose photographs influenced Tasmanian conservation history, including the protection of the Franklin River against flooding. Galleria building, 33 Salamanca Pl, Hobart. See Salamanca Place p. 461

Leatherwood honey in decorative tin, Tasmanian Honey Company, Perth Full-flavoured honey from the nectar of trees found in Tasmania's rainforest wilderness. See Longford p.485

Tasmanian Devil soft toy, Tasmanian Devil Conservation Park, Taranna You can't snuggle up with the real thing, so cuddle a stuffed version of this famous marsupial. See Eaglehawk Neck p. 477

Shell necklace, Queen Victoria Museum and Art Gallery, Launceston Tasmania's Aboriginal women string traditional necklaces of iridescent blue-green maireener shells. See Launceston p. 484

750GM PRINTED METAL CAN LEATHERWOOD HONEY CANDIED

Sweets, Richmond Enter the town's old-fashioned lolly shop to find giant Tasmania-shaped freckles or uniquely Tasmanian Esmeraldas (coconut ice covered in toffee). See Richmond p. 490

Ghosts of Port Arthur book or DVD, Port Arthur Scare your friends witless with tales of strange apparitions, available from the gift shop. See Port Arthur p. 489

Oysters, Barilla Bay, Cambridge Tasmania's deep, cool and flowing waters are the key to large and juicy oysters. Barilla Bay will package them for air travel. 1388 Tasman Hwy, Cambridge. See Hobart p. 458

Cheese, King Island Dairy, King Island King Island's world-famous, handcrafted cheeses can be bought directly from the Fromagerie Tasting Room next to the factory in Loorana. The company's range covers everything from soft white cheeses to aged cheddars, yoghurts and desserts. See Currie p. 474

HOBART is...

Shopping for fresh produce and crafts at SALAMANCA MARKET / Fish and chips at

CONSTITUTION DOCK / A drive to the summit of MOUNT WELLINGTON / Exploring

Hobart's WATERFRONT / An afternoon at the ROYAL TASMANIAN BOTANICAL

GARDENS / Wandering around historic BATTERY POINT / A visit to the TASMANIAN

MUSEUM AND ART GALLERY / A counter meal in a warm colonial-era pub / Watching beer

production at CASCADE BREWERY / Coffee and a movie at North Hobart's independent

STATE CINEMA / Losing yourself in David Walsh's labyrinthine museum, MONA

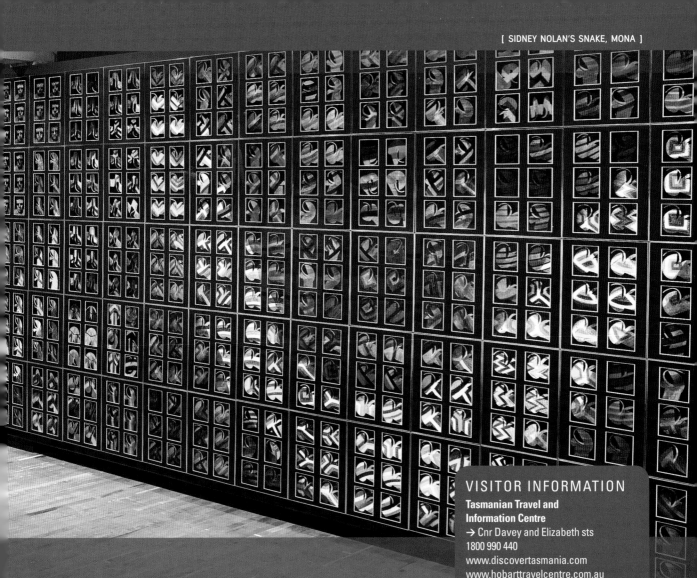

VISITOR INFORMATION
Tasmanian Travel and
Information Centre
→ Cnr Davey and Elizabeth sts
1800 990 440
www.discovertasmania.com
www.hobarttravelcentre.com.au

At the southern tip of Australia, Hobart lies nestled between the slopes of Mount Wellington and the Derwent estuary. Hobart was founded at Sullivans Cove in 1804 on land known to its Aboriginal inhabitants as Nibberloonne. It was the second city after Sydney to be established, yet today Hobart is the smallest of the capitals with just 215 000 people enjoying its glorious location and unhurried, easy-going lifestyle.

Whaling and sealing brought wealth to the town in its early years, and the dockside was soon dotted with taverns doing a brisk trade among seafarers and traders. Hobart's fortunes still centre on its picturesque deep-water harbour, but now tourist ferries, Antarctic research vessels and luxury ocean liners moor alongside freighters and fishing trawlers.

Boasting internationally recognised temperate wilderness on its doorstep, Hobart's abundance of natural beauty propelled it to the forefront of environmental politics in 1972, becoming home to the world's first 'green' political party. It also has a cosmopolitan literary and arts culture that has now been propelled onto a world stage with the opening of the MONA museum. But for all that Hobart remains a small city with a laid-back friendly vibe.

DOWNTOWN HOBART

Downtown Hobart has fashion and department stores, specialty shops, banks, cafes and restaurants in the surrounding streets and arcades. Shops are open Monday to Saturday until 5pm, and on Sundays the larger stores open 10am to 4pm.

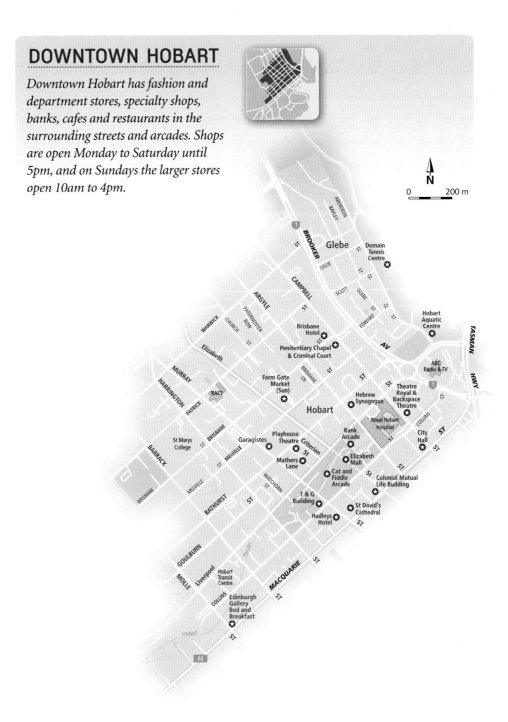

Elizabeth Mall 460 C2

Surrounded by shops and cafes, the mall is a favourite with shoppers and buskers. An information booth is open weekdays until 4pm, and from 10am until 2pm on Saturdays.

Cat and Fiddle Arcade 460 C2

Several shopping arcades are in the main retail area of Hobart, but the Cat and Fiddle Arcade's nursery rhyme musical clock lends it a certain charm. The arcade runs between the Elizabeth Mall and Murray Street.

Liverpool Street 460 B2, C2

This is Hobart's main downtown shopping strip, with interesting arcades and side streets. **Bank Arcade** (between Argyle and Elizabeth streets) will tempt you with breads, spices and tiny cafes. **Mathers Lane** and **Criterion Street** are great for coffee and all things retro.

Elizabeth Street 460 B2

Heading north from the mall, Elizabeth Street's outdoor-equipment stores give way to interesting cafes and collectibles shops.

NORTHERN WATERFRONT

The northern waterfront of Sullivans Cove is the busiest, smelliest and most fascinating part of the working dock. Along the Hunter Street waterfront contemporary apartments sit next to recycled 19th-century buildings, with Mount Wellington as the backdrop.

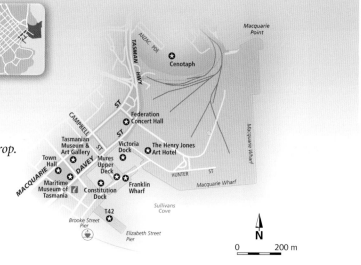

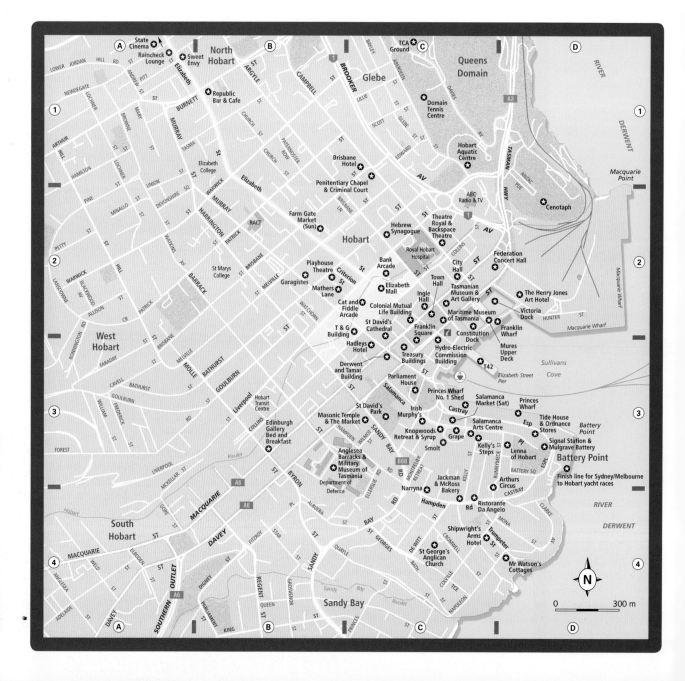

Constitution and Victoria docks 460 C2

These docks are the heart of Sullivans Cove. Excellent seafood restaurants abound and dockside punts offer outstanding takeaway fish and chips. Every New Year, Constitution Dock comes alive when the annual Sydney and Melbourne to Hobart yachts cross the finish line. Every two years **Franklin Wharf** hosts the Australian Wooden Boat Festival, the largest gathering of historic craft in the Southern Hemisphere (*see Top events p. 465*).

Federation Concert Hall 460 C2

This intimate yet grand concert hall is the home of the Tasmanian Symphony Orchestra and was designed to give priority to quality acoustics. *1 Davey St; TSO Box Office 1800 001 190.*

The Henry Jones Art Hotel 460 D2

Facing Victoria Dock, this multi-award-winning hotel complex is established in what was once the IXL jam factory. Alongside are galleries of fine Tasmanian furniture and Aboriginal art, cafes and restaurants. *25 Hunter St; (03) 6210 7700.*

Tasmanian Museum and Art Gallery 460 C2

This historic museum and gallery houses a fine collection of colonial art and Huon pine furniture. Its current redevelopment will showcase the site's remarkable Tasmanian Aboriginal and early colonial history. *Open 10am–5pm daily; tours 2.30pm Wed–Sun; admission free; 40 Macquarie St; (03) 6211 4177.*

Maritime Museum of Tasmania 460 C2

Located inside the impressive Neoclassical Carnegie Building, this museum brings to life Tasmania's rich maritime history through pictures and equipment from the whaling era, models of ships and relics from shipwrecks. *Open 9am–5pm daily, book for guided tours of the museum and port; Cnr Davey and Argyle sts; (03) 6234 1427.*

SOUTHERN WATERFRONT

The docks on the southern side of Sullivans Cove are surrounded by remarkable historic buildings. The work of the docks continues amid cafes, restaurants and pubs, contributing to the area's lively atmosphere.

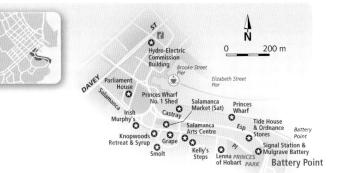

Salamanca Place 460 C3

The sandstone warehouses along Salamanca Place are Australia's finest row of Georgian dockside buildings, packed with interesting shops and galleries. Hobart's famous **Salamanca Market** runs every Saturday, offering produce, arts and crafts. *Open 8.30am–3pm Sat; (03) 6238 2843.*

For 150 years, merchants worked from the Salamanca warehouses alongside notoriously rowdy pubs and hotels. **Knopwoods Retreat** still trades and is popular for Friday night drinks. Nearby, at the **Salamanca Arts Centre**, there is a free street party every Friday evening.

Parliament House 460 C3

Designed by the colonial architect John Lee Archer and built by convicts as the first Customs House, this became the home of Tasmania's parliament in 1856. *Visitors gallery open on sitting days; tours 10am and 2pm Mon–Fri, except sitting days; between Salamanca Pl and Murray St; bookings (03) 6233 2200.*

Castray Esplanade and Princes Wharf 460 C3, D3

Built in 1870, Castray Esplanade runs behind Princes Wharf. At the city end are restaurants specialising in Tasmanian seafood and at the Battery Point end the octagonal **Tide House**, next to the **Ordnance Stores**, is the point from which all distances are measured in Tasmania.

At the far end of Princes Wharf are the CSIRO Marine Research Laboratories and for most of the year Antarctic research and supply vessels berth alongside. On the hill behind are the original **Signal Station** and **Mulgrave Battery**, built in 1818 during panic about a rumoured Russian invasion. In January **Princes Wharf No. 1 Shed** is home to the Taste of Tasmania festival.

[WOOD CRAFTS STALL AT SALAMANCA MARKET]

TASMANIA

BATTERY POINT

Battery Point, built to house the workers and merchants of the port, is on the hill behind Salamanca Place. Its compact size and village atmosphere make it perfect to explore on foot.

Kelly's Steps 460 C3

At the end of Kelly Street, historic Kelly's Steps connect Salamanca Place to Battery Point. They were built in 1839 by Captain James Kelly, an adventurer who made a comfortable living from sealing and whaling until becoming bankrupt and destitute in 1842.

Arthurs Circus 460 C4

Exploring Arthurs Circus, just off Hampden Road at the top of Runnymede Street, is like walking into an intact Georgian streetscape. The 16 cottages were built around a circular village green between 1847 and 1852, and they are still private residences.

Hampden Road 460 C4

Hampden Road winds through the heart of Battery Point from a cluster of antique shops near Sandy Bay Road downhill to Castray Esplanade and the docks. One of its earliest grand houses is **Narryna**, built in 1836 and now a heritage museum. *Open 10.30am–5pm Mon–Fri, 12.30–5pm Sat–Sun in summer, 10.30am–5pm Tues–Fri, 2–5pm Sat–Sun in winter;103 Hampden Rd; (03) 6234 2791.*

Trumpeter Street 460 C4, D4

On the top corner of Trumpeter Street is the traditional **Shipwrights Arms Hotel**, open since 1846. *29 Trumpeter St, Battery Point; (03) 6223 5551.* Down the hill, across Napoleon Street, are **Mr Watson's Cottages**, a row of simple Georgian brick dwellings built in 1850. Behind are the boat-building slip yards that date back to the 1830s.

[BATTERY POINT]

MACQUARIE STREET

Macquarie Street has always been Hobart's main thoroughfare, its classical buildings adding an air of sophistication.

Franklin Square 460 C2

This peaceful, leafy city park is a popular meeting place. A formal fountain at its centre supports a statue of Sir John Franklin, Arctic explorer and Governor of Tasmania (1837–43). Hobart's first Government House stood here until 1858 when the timber and thatch building began to collapse.

Corner of Macquarie and Murray streets 460 C3

This remarkable intersection has a historic sandstone building on every corner. Once the administrative centre of Hobart, it offers panoramic views down Macquarie Street past the Georgian **Ingle Hall**, built in 1814, and the Art Deco *Mercury* newspaper building, to the **Cenotaph**. On one corner stands **St David's Cathedral**, rebuilt several times since 1817. Across Murray Street, the **Hadleys Hotel** site dates back to the 1830s. Dating to the same era, the **Treasury Buildings** remain government offices. Nearby is the 1875 **Derwent and Tamar Building**.

St David's Park 460 C3

This formal English-style walled park on Davey Street still has old headstones displayed in the lower section – a reminder that this was the colony's first burial ground. It was made into a park in 1926. *Cnr Davey St and Sandy Bay Rd.*

Anglesea Barracks 460 B3

On the hill at the top of Davey Street is Australia's oldest military establishment still in use. Explore the **Military Museum of Tasmania,** elegant Georgian buildings and 1770s bronze cannons. *Grounds open daily; museum open 9am–1pm Tues and Thurs; tours 11am Tues; Davey St; (03) 6237 7160.*

QUEENS DOMAIN

Queens Domain is a bush reserve overlooking the Derwent River, north-east of the city centre. In Glebe there are magnificent weatherboard Federation houses built on incredibly steep streets.

Government House 458 D4

This 1857 Neo-Gothic building, one of the finest vice-regal residences in the Commonwealth, is built from local timbers and sandstone excavated on-site. *Lower Domain Rd; open to the public one Sun each year; (03) 6234 2611; admission free.*

Royal Tasmanian Botanical Gardens 458 D4

These superb gardens were established in 1818. There is a restaurant, a beautiful old-world conservatory, a subantarctic house and, of course, ABC gardener Peter Cundall's famous veggie patch. *Open daily; admission free; entry to conservatory and discovery centre by gold-coin donation; Lower Domain Rd; (03) 6236 3076.*

INNER NORTH

Elizabeth Street, North Hobart 460 B1

This cosmopolitan strip of cafes and bars is busy day and night. At the Federal Street end is the independent **State Cinema**. *375 Elizabeth St; (03) 6234 6318.* On the Burnett Street corner, the **Republic Bar & Cafe** is a popular option. *299 Elizabeth St; (03) 6234 6954.*

Cornelian Bay 458 D3

Cornelian Bay is tucked away north of the Botanical Gardens and easily accessible from the Inter-City Cycleway. It is a tranquil waterside park with barbecues, a playground, heritage boatsheds and the contemporary glass-fronted **Cornelian Bay Boathouse Restaurant**. *Queens Walk; (03) 6228 9289.* Around the bay walking trails afford nice views of the Tasman Bridge.

Runnymede 458 C3

This 1836 Georgian villa has had a number of distinguished owners including a bishop, a captain and the colony's first lawyer. It has been restored and refurbished by the National Trust. *61 Bay Rd, New Town; open 10am–4.30pm Fri, 12–4.30pm Sun, closed July and Aug; tours Tues, Wed, Thurs; bookings (03) 6278 1269.*

NORTH

Tasmanian Transport Museum 458 B2

See the restored collection of steam engines, locomotives and carriages from Tasmania's fascinating railway history, as well as old trams and trolley buses, and the relocated New Town suburban train station, a relic from a bygone era. Train rides are run at the museum on the first and third Sunday each month. *Open 1–4pm Sat–Sun and public holidays, open 11am on train-ride days; Anfield St, Glenorchy; (03) 6272 7721.*

TASMANIA

MONA (museum of old and new art) 458 B2

Embedded into riverside cliffs at Moorilla Vineyard 12 km upriver from Hobart, David Walsh's MONA houses his edgy private art collection celebrating sex and death. The vineyard's superb wines are showcased in its restaurant alongside its Moo Brew beers. Take a high-speed catamaran from Brooke St pier or a carbon-neutral leisurely pedal along the scenic Inter-City Cycleway. *MONA open 10am–6pm Wed–Mon;* **The Source** *restaurant open daily for lunch (except Tues), dinner Wed–Sat; 655 Main Rd, Berriedale; (03) 6277 9900.*

Cadbury Visitor Centre 458 B1

See chocolate being moulded, taste the raw materials and indulge in the factory shop and cafe. *100 Cadbury Rd, Claremont; open 8am–4pm (last presentation at 3pm) Mon–Fri Sept–May, 9am–3pm (last presentation at 2pm) Mon–Fri June–Aug; 1800 627 367.*

INNER SOUTH

The prosperous southern suburbs of Hobart extend from Battery Point up into the foothills of Mount Wellington. Davey Street and Sandy Bay Road are lined with impressive mansions while the hills above are dotted with contemporary houses.

Wrest Point Casino 458 D5

A Hobart landmark since 1973, the iconic Wrest Point tower houses Australia's first legal casino. A rotating top-floor restaurant offers spectacular views. **Point Revolving Restaurant**; *open daily for dinner, Fri for lunch; 410 Sandy Bay Rd; 1800 703 006.*

Sandy Bay Beach 458 D6

Lawns beside this popular swimming beach provide an ideal spot for a barbecue. There are a number of nearby eateries, from a fine-dining seafood restaurant to a tiny wood-fired pizzeria. **Prossers on the Beach**; *open Tues–Sat for lunch, Mon–Sat for dinner; Long Point Rd; (03) 6225 2276.* **Sandy Bay Beach Woodfired Pizza**; *open daily for dinner, cash only; 7A Beach Rd; (03) 6225 0019.*

Cascades Female Factory Historic Site 458 C5

Once a rum distillery, contagious-diseases hospital, home for 'imperial lunatics' and, most recently, a fudge factory, this was also a female prison for 50 years. Tour the site, watch the dramatic 'Her Story' and have an 1830s-style 'Tea with Matron'. *Tours weekdays; Her Story daily 11am; Tea with Matron Mon, Wed and Fri; 16 Degraves St, South Hobart; bookings (03) 6233 6656.*

Cascade Brewery 458 B5

This is Australia's oldest brewery. Locally grown hops, Tasmanian barley and mountain water combine to produce top beers. *Open daily for tours and tastings; 140 Cascade Rd, South Hobart; bookings (03) 6224 1117.*

Mount Nelson Signal Station 458 D6

Governor Macquarie ordered that this signal station be erected on 350-metre 'Nelson Hill' in 1811. The site affords sweeping views of the Derwent Valley and Storm Bay, and there is a

restaurant with a spectacular outlook. **The Station Cafe**; *open Tues–Sun for lunch; 700 Nelson Rd; (03) 6223 3407.*

Taroona Shot Tower 623 I6

This 58-metre-tall sandstone tower was erected to make lead shot in 1870. The tower summit is reached via hundreds of steps, and there is a tearoom to help you recover from the climb. *Open daily; 234 Channel Hwy, Taroona; (03) 6227 8885.*

INNER EAST

Over the Tasman Bridge, The 'eastern shore', as it is known, spreads along the River Derwent south to the beachside suburbs of Howrah, Rokeby and Lauderdale.

Bellerive 458 E4

This quiet suburban village, settled in the 1820s, overlooks the river and is bordered by a marina and sandy beaches. A military fort was built on **Kangaroo Bluff** in 1885 in response to sightings of Russian ships. *Open daily; admission free; (03) 6248 4053.*

The area's best-known landmark is the **Blundstone Arena**, home to the **Tasmanian Cricket Museum** and the venue for Tests, one-day cricket and Australian Rules football matches. *Museum open 10am–3pm Tues–Thurs, 10am–12pm Fri; arena tours 10am Tues, or by arrangement; Derwent St, Bellerive; tour bookings (03) 6282 0433 or (03) 6282 0400.*

EAST

The peninsula between Storm Bay and Frederick Henry Bay is a favourite haunt for surfers, with crowd-free surf breaks and deserted dune-backed beaches within an easy drive from the city.

Rokeby 621 H9

Rokeby is a 20-minute drive out of Hobart along the South Arm Highway. Settled in 1809 it grew Tasmania's first crops of wheat and apples.

St Matthew's Church houses a collection of historical items, and Tasmania's first chaplain, the notorious Reverend Robert Knopwood, was buried in a plain coffin, with no nameplate, in St Matthew's churchyard. *Cnr King St and North Pde.*

Storm Bay beaches 623 K7, L5

The beaches facing south into Storm Bay offer excellent surfing. **Clifton Beach** is a popular surfing location reached via the South Arm Highway. Eight kilometres south the **Goat Bluff** cliff-top lookout offers spectacular views. For a safe, patrolled beach, head to **Carlton**.

CITY ESSENTIALS
HOBART

Climate

Hobart's weather is changeable at any time of the year, so be prepared! Summer is mild with temperatures in the mid-20s, but sometimes the forecast highs are only reached for a short time as a cool sea breeze kicks in most afternoons. There are windless, sun-drenched days and chilly nights in autumn, but winter brings temperatures in the low teens and blustery cold conditions. Snow is rare in Hobart, but often settles on Mount Wellington's summit.

	MAX °C	MIN °C	RAIN MM	RAIN DAYS
JANUARY	23	11	44	3
FEBRUARY	22	11	39	3
MARCH	20	10	42	3
APRIL	17	8	47	4
MAY	13	6	42	4
JUNE	11	4	49	5
JULY	10	3	48	5
AUGUST	12	4	46	5
SEPTEMBER	14	6	47	5
OCTOBER	17	7	55	6
NOVEMBER	19	9	54	4
DECEMBER	21	10	51	4

Getting around

Metro buses regularly service the city and suburbs at peak times and less frequently during weekends. Timetables are displayed at most bus stops and are available from the Metro shop in the Hobart Bus Terminal at the Macquarie Street end of Elizabeth Street. A Day Rover ticket allows you to catch any number of buses after 9am Monday to Friday, and anytime on weekends. The free Hobart Hopper shuttles between Salamanca, the city centre and car parks every 10 minutes on Saturdays.

On the river you can commute between Watermans Dock and Bellerive on weekdays, and to Salamanca from Wrest Point and Bellerive on Saturdays. Water taxis operate to any safe landing and cruise boats operate from Franklin Wharf. Information is available harbourside and from the Tasmanian Travel and Information Centre, 1800 990 440.

The 15-kilometre Inter-City Cycleway runs alongside a rail track between Hobart's waterfront and the northern suburb of Claremont. With a paved surface and no hills, it's popular with commuters and recreational riders alike. Bikes of all types can be hired from the Hobart end of the cycleway.

Ferries Hobart Water Taxis 0407 036 268.

Public transport Metro bus information line 13 2201

Airport shuttle bus Airporter City Hotels Shuttle 1300 385 511; Hobart Maxi Connect 0457 900 433.

Motoring organisation RACT 13 2722, roadside assistance 13 1111.

Car rental Autorent Hertz 1800 030 222 or (03) 6237 1111; Avis 13 6333 or (03) 6234 4222; Bargain Car Rentals 1300 729 230 or (03) 6234 6959; Budget 1300 362 848 or (03) 6234 5222; Europcar 1300 131 390 or (03) 6231 1077; Lo-cost Autorent (03) 6231 0550; Thrifty 1300 972 042.

Taxis Australian Taxi Service 0411 286 780; Personal Taxi Service (03) 6224 2242; Taxi Combined Services 13 2227; United Taxis 13 1008; Yellow Cabs 13 1924.

Campervan and 4WD rental Britz 1800 331 454; Cruisin' Tasmania 1300 664 485; Tasmania Campers 1800 627 074; Tasmanian Campervan Hire 1800 807 119.

Bicycle hire Derwent Bike Hire (daily weather permitting); Cenotaph, Regatta Ground 0428 899 169.

Top events

MONA FOMA Hobart grooves with two weeks of eclectic jazz, rock, hip-hop and indie music. January.

Australian Wooden Boat Festival Biennial dockside celebration of maritime history. February (odd-numbered years).

Clarence Jazz Festival Six days and nights of good vibes around Bellerive. February.

Hobart Cup Day Join punters and picnickers for a day of racing and fashion. February.

Royal Hobart Regatta A family regatta and fireworks display since 1838. February.

Ten Days on the Island International island culture comes to Tasmania. March (odd-numbered years).

Targa Tasmania State-wide classic car rally. April.

Festival of Voices For four days winter is warmed by singers and choirs from all over Australia gathering to sing their hearts out. July.

Royal Hobart Show Four days of competitions and displays bringing country life to town. October.

Spring Community Festival Hobart's Botanical Gardens at their blooming best. October.

Sydney to Hobart and Melbourne to Hobart yacht races Gruelling races end with a dockside party, and a crowd of people to welcome the yachts no matter what time of the day or night. December.

Taste of Tasmania Hobart sparkles with fun activities and waterfront gourmet indulgence. December–January.

The Falls Festival Music lovers flock to Marion Bay to camp, swim and dance in the New Year. December–January.

Grand old buildings

City Hall Built from a competition-winning design in 1915, it is perhaps Hobart's most underrated public building. Macquarie St (between Market and Campbell sts), City.

Colonial Mutual Life Building Inter-war building with Gothic gargoyles, Moorish balconies, Art Deco chevrons and multicoloured roofing tiles. Cnr Elizabeth and Macquarie sts, City.

Hebrew Synagogue Australia's first synagogue and a rare example of Egyptian Revival architecture. Argyle St (between Liverpool and Bathurst sts), City.

Hydro-Electric Commission Building The design brief said that it should represent the new age of electricity, and its Art Deco facade suggests energy and modernity. Cnr Elizabeth and Davey sts, City.

Lenna of Hobart When Alexander McGregor made a fortune from whaling he built this rich, Italianate mansion on a cliff overlooking the cove so he could keep an eye on shipping movements. Now it's a stylish boutique hotel. 20 Runnymede St, Battery Point.

T & G Building Built for an insurance company, it has an Egyptian inspired clock tower. Cnr Collins and Murray sts, City.

Theatre Royal Classical Revival design by Henry Hunter, it stands where Hobart's founder, David Collins, pitched the first tent. Macquarie St (between Elizabeth and Argyle sts), City.

Town Hall Classical Revival design by Henry Hunter, it stands where Collins pitched the first tent in Hobart. Macquarie St (between Elizabeth and Argyle sts), City.

Penitentiary Chapel and Criminal Court Underground passages, solitary cells and an execution yard. Cnr Brisbane and Campbell sts, City *(see Walks and tours, on this page)*.

St George's Anglican Church Built by two noted colonial architects – the body in 1836–38 by John Lee Archer, and the spire in 1847 by James Blackburn – this is Australia's finest Classical Revival church. 28 Cromwell St, Battery Point.

 ## Shopping

Bathurst Street, City Fine furniture and antiques. 460 B2, C2

Cat and Fiddle Arcade, City Bargain fashion and sportswear. 460 C2

Eastlands Shopping Centre, Rosny Park Hobart's largest undercover suburban mall. 458 E4

Elizabeth Street, City Gifts, outdoor clothing and antiques. 460 B2

Liverpool Street, City Fashion and jewellery. 460 B2, C2

Salamanca Place, City Fine craft and Tasmanian art. 460 C3

Sandy Bay Road, Battery Point Antique furniture, china and art. 460 C3

Sandy Bay Road, Sandy Bay Stylish fashion stores. 460 B4

 ## Markets

Farm Gate Market Seasonal fruit and veggies plus artisan cheeses, breads and oils from local producers. 9am–1pm Sun; Melville St carpark, city. 460 B2

Hobart Showgrounds Sunday Market Trash and treasure, craft, produce and occasionally livestock. 8am–2pm Sun; Royal Hobart Showgrounds; 2 Howard Rd, Glenorchy. 458 B2

Sorell Market Produce, craft, and trash and treasure. Sorell Memorial Hall, Cole St; most Sun and public holidays. 623 K4

The Market Unique Tasmanian-designed and made jewellery, books, cards, craft and food. 10am–3pm Sun, see www.themarkethobart.com.au for dates; Masonic Temple, 3 Sandy Bay Rd. 460 C3

 ## Walks and tours

Hobart Historic Tours Choose a guided walk of Hobart or Battery Point with great stories of the early days, or a pub crawl with colourful tales thrown in. Bookings on (03) 6278 3338, (03) 6224 2556 or (03) 6238 4222.

Hobart Waterways Rivulet Tour Peek into Hobart's convict-built aqueducts while keeping your feet dry above ground. Bookings on (03) 6238 4222 or 1800 990 440.

River Cruises Combine a river cruise with delicious food and wine, step back into history aboard a square rigger, cruise to Cadbury Schweppes Chocolate Factory, MONA, Peppermint Bay or Port Arthur, or take a jet boat out into Storm Bay for a thrilling ride. For information and timetables head to the Brooke Street Pier area in Sullivans Cove, or phone Captain Fells (03) 6223 5893, Navigators (03) 6223 1914, Peppermint Bay Cruises 1300 137 919, Hobart Water Taxis 0407 036 268, Wild Thing Adventures 1800 751 229, Hobart Harbour Jet 0404 078 687 or Windeward Bound 0418 120 243 or 0409 961 321.

Kayak tours Get a sea-level perspective on Hobart's waterfront with a daytime or evening paddle around the docks. Blackaby's Sea Kayaks 0418 124 072; Freycinet Adventures (03) 6257 0500; Hobart Urban Adventures (03) 6257 0500.

Ghost Tours of Hobart and Battery Point Comfy shoes and nerves of steel are needed for this sunset tour of Hobart's spooky past. Bookings 0439 335 696.

Old Rokeby Historic Trail A self-guide tour of the outer suburb of Rokeby, one of Hobart's earliest rural districts. Brochures available at the trailhead in Hawthorn Place, Rokeby. (03) 6247 6925.

Theatre Royal Tour A guided tour backstage. Bookings on (03) 62332299; 11am Mon, Wed and Fri.

Penitentiary Chapel Historic Site Grim history of gallows, cells and tunnels illustrated by lamplight if you dare. Day-tour bookings (03) 6231 0911; ghost-tour bookings 0417 361 392.

Sullivans Cove Walks Guided evening and day walks around the waterfront unveiling Hobart's past. Bookings on (03) 6245 1208.

Louisa's Walk Follow the bleak life of convict Louisa Ryan to the Female Factory where she was imprisoned. Daily 2pm; bookings on (03) 6229 8959, 0437 276 417 or (03) 6238 4222.

Mount Wellington Walks Guided walks delving into the history, botany and ancient past of this intriguing mountain. Bookings 0439 551 197.

Mount Wellington Descent Plummet down from Mount Wellington's 1270-metre summit to sea level on a mountain bike. Gloves and ear warmers supplied. Bookings on (03) 6274 1880.

Seaplane Scenic Flights Board dockside and take off from the river. Tasmanian Air Adventures 1300 359 822.

Hobart's Historic Places Self-guide tour brings Hobart's history to life. Brochure available from the Tasmanian Travel and Information Centre.

 ## Entertainment

Cinema There are multiscreen cinemas at Glenorchy in the northern suburbs, in Bligh Street opposite Eastlands on the eastern shore and in Collins Street in the city. If your taste leans towards arthouse films, try the independent State Cinema in Elizabeth Street, North Hobart. See the *Mercury* newspaper for details of films being shown.

Live music Hobart has a small but thriving live-music scene based around a handful of pub venues. For a night of great blues you can't beat the Republic Bar & Cafe in North Hobart, for original rock and roots head to the Brisbane Hotel in the city, or to the Alley Cat Bar in North Hobart for a bit of everything. There are plenty of late-night pubs and clubs around Sullivans Cove including Syrup, Isobar, Bar Celona, Irish Murphy's, T42, Grape Bar and the Telegraph Hotel. Check out Thursday's gig guide in the *Mercury*.

Classical music and performing arts Hobart's unique Theatre Royal is the venue for visiting stage companies and local productions such as the annual University Review. Classical music is usually performed at the Federation Concert Hall, and the Derwent Entertainment Centre hosts large events. A livelier theatre scene is supported by smaller venues such as the intimate Backspace Theatre behind the Theatre Royal. The Playhouse in Bathurst Street is home to an amateur theatrical society and the Peacock Theatre specialises in contemporary works in its small space at the Salamanca Arts Centre. See the *Mercury* for details of what's on.

 ## Sport

The **Sydney to Hobart Yacht Race**, held in December, is Hobart's premier sporting event. Other twilight and weekend sailing events take place on the Derwent throughout the year.

A state-wide Australian Rules **football** league is up and running, with games played at the North Hobart Football Oval, TCA Ground on Queens Domain and at Glenorchy's KGV oval. In summer action shifts to Bellerive's Blundstone Arena – Tasmania's premier **cricket** ground *(see Bellerive, p. 464)*.

Hobart has an international-standard **hockey** centre at New Town, and national and international games attract large crowds. In January the Domain Tennis Centre hosts the Moorilla Hobart International **tennis** tournament, and Hobart's **horseracing** calendar is dominated by the Hobart Cup, run at Tattersall's Park in February.

Tasmania lays claim to Australia's very first **golf** course at Bothwell. Around Hobart there is a nine-hole course on the eastern shore at Rosny Park, while 18-hole courses are at Kingston Beach in the southern suburbs and Claremont in the north.

 ## Where to eat

Garagistes Award-winning ultra-modern communal dining and a grazing menu of seasonal dishes caught, grown and foraged locally. 103 Murray St; (03) 6231 0558; open for dinner Wed–Sat, no reservations. 460 B2

Jackman & McRoss Bakery Vibrant cafe with very good coffee and heavenly sweet and savoury pastries. 57–59 Hampden Rd, Battery Point; (03) 6223 3186; open daily for breakfast and lunch. 460 C3

Lebrina Award-winning, sophisticated dining with French style and Italian flavour in an elegant historic cottage. 155 New Town Rd, New Town; (03) 6228 7775; open Tues–Sat for dinner. 458 C4

Mures Upper Deck Perched above the dockside sights, sounds and smells, this is Hobart's best-loved seafood restaurant. Victoria Dock; (03) 6231 1999; open daily for lunch and dinner. 460 C2

Point Revolving Restaurant A Hobart favourite with exquisitely inventive versions of well-loved dishes and revolving views from the top of the casino tower. Wrest Point Casino, 410 Sandy Bay Rd, Sandy Bay; (03) 6221 1700; open Fri for lunch and daily for dinner. 458 D5

Prossers on the Beach Chef Stuart Prosser brings his passion for the sea to the table with a Mediterranean- and Asian-inspired menu at this elevated waterside pavilion. Sandy Bay Regatta Pavilion, 1 Beach Rd, Sandy Bay; (03) 6225 2276; open Wed–Fri and Sun for lunch, and Mon–Sat for dinner. 458 D6

Raincheck Lounge Hip cafe and wine bar with a 1970s vibe and great food on offer from breakfast to late night tapas. 392 Elizabeth St, North Hobart; (03) 6234 5975; open daily for breakfast and lunch, and Wed–Sat for dinner. 460 A1

Ristorante da Angelo Homemade gnocchi and Angelo and Marco's excellent fresh sauces make this as close to southern Italy as you can get in Tasmania. It's always busy, so book ahead. 47 Hampden Rd, Battery Point; (03) 6223 7011; open daily for lunch and dinner. 460 C4

Smolt Mediterranean-style dining and late-night 'small plates' with a piazza outlook and hip modern interior. 2 Salamanca Sq; (03) 6224 2554; open daily for breakfast, lunch and dinner. 460 C3

Sweet Envy A tiny cafe specialising in world-class sweet tarts, macaroons, cupcakes and wacky-flavoured ice-creams. 341 Elizabeth St, North Hobart; (03) 6234 8805; open 8.30am–6pm Tues–Fri, 8.30am–5pm Sat. 460 A1

 ## Where to stay

Edinburgh Gallery Bed and Breakfast Cnr Macquarie and Molle sts, Hobart; (03) 6224 9229.

Alexandra on Battery 3 Sonning Cres, Sandy Bay; (03) 6225 2574.

Bellerive House 89 Cambridge Rd, Bellerive; (03) 6244 7798.

Discovery Holiday Parks – Hobart 673 East Derwent Hwy, Risdon; (03) 6243 9879.

Louisa's Cottage 24 Gregory St, Sandy Bay; (03) 6224 4004.

Merre Be's Honeymoon House 17 Gregory St, Sandy Bay; (03) 6224 2900.

The Elms of Hobart 452 Elizabeth St, North Hobart; (03) 6231 3277.

Treasure Island Caravan Park 1 Alcorso Dr, Berriedale; (03) 6249 2379.

 ## Day tours

Richmond This small settlement just north of Hobart is probably Australia's best-preserved Georgian colonial village. Highlights include the convict-built Richmond Bridge, Australia's oldest bridge; the gaol, which predates Port Arthur; and galleries and cafes housed in historic shopfronts and cottages.

Tasman Peninsula The stunning setting of Port Arthur – lawns, gardens, cliffs – and the beauty of its sandstone buildings belie the site's tragic history. Other sites on the peninsula worth a look include the spectacular rock formations and blow holes around Eaglehawk Neck.

Derwent Valley The Derwent Valley, with its neat agricultural landscape and historic buildings, forms one of the loveliest rural areas of Australia, reminiscent of England. Visit the trout hatchery of Salmon Ponds, the National Trust–classified New Norfolk, and the hop museum at Oast House.

D'Entrecasteaux Channel The beauty and intricacy of Tasmania's south-eastern coastline can be experienced on a leisurely drive south from Hobart. There are stunning water views, particularly at Tinderbox (via Kingston), and Verona Sands at the Huon River entrance. At Kettering, a car ferry goes to remote Bruny Island.

Huon Valley The Huon Valley is the centre of a growing gourmet food industry. The signposted Huon Trail follows the valley between rows of apple trees, with a backdrop of forested mountains. In the far south, at Hastings, visitors can tour a dolomite cave and swim in a thermal pool.

REGIONS
of Tasmania

Listed here are some of the top attractions and experiences in each region.

King Island

1 EAST COAST

Fishing around St Helens (pictured) / see p. 491
Freycinet National Park / see p. 474
Bicheno Penguin Tours / see p. 472
Mt William National Park / see p. 480

2 SOUTH-EAST

Hastings Caves and Thermal Springs / see p. 481
Port Arthur Historic Site / see p. 489
Tahune Forest AirWalk (pictured) / see p. 479
Tasmanian Devil Conservation Park / see p. 478

4 NORTH-WEST

Cape Grim cliffs with Woolnorth tours / see p. 494
Cradle Mountain–Lake St Clair National Park (pictured) / see p. 493
The Nut, Stanley / see p. 495
Pieman River cruise / see p. 491

3 SOUTH-WEST WILDERNESS

Franklin–Gordon Wild Rivers National Park (pictured) / see p. 496
South Coast Track / see p. 496
West Coast Pioneers Memorial Museum, Zeehan / see p. 499
West Coast Wilderness Railway, Queenstown / see p. 490

5 MIDLANDS AND THE NORTH

Ben Lomond National Park / see p. 478
Ross Female Factory Site / see p. 491
Tamar Valley wine region (pictured) / see p. 485
Trout fishing in the Central Plateau Conservation Area / see p. 486

Flinders
Island

5

1

2

BART○

[COLOURFULL DISPLAY OF RICHEA SCOPARIA, WALLS OF JERUSALEM NATIONAL PARK]

TOWNS A–Z
Tasmania

LEGEND

 VISITOR INFORMATION

 RADIO STATIONS

 IN TOWN

 WHAT'S ON

 WHERE TO EAT

 WHERE TO STAY

 NEARBY

* Distances for towns nearby are calculated as the crow flies.
* Food and accommodation listings in town are ordered alphabetically
  with places nearby listed at the end.

[SUNRISE OVER WINEGLASS BAY, FREYCINET NATIONAL PARK]

Adventure Bay

Pop. 620
Map ref. 623 I11 | 625 K10

i Bruny D'Entrecasteaux Visitor Centre, 81 Ferry Rd,
Kettering; (03) 6267 4494; www.brunyisland.org.au

95.3 Huon FM, 936 AM ABC Local Radio

Adventure Bay is the primary town on largely undeveloped Bruny
Island, a peaceful retreat for many Tasmanians with its striking
landscape untainted by excessive tourism. The island is more
accurately two islands joined by a narrow isthmus. On one side
the coast is pounded by the waves of the Pacific, and on the other
it is gently lapped by the waters of the D'Entrecasteaux Channel.
After a long Aboriginal occupation, Europeans discovered the
islands. Captain Cook's interaction with the Aboriginal people
was largely amicable, but the sealers who subsequently came
to Bruny decimated the population. Of those who survived,
Truganini is the most famous. Memorials dot the island, standing
as stark reminders of the grim past amid the spectacular scenery.

 Eco-cruise Arguably one of Tasmania's greatest attractions,
this 3 hr cruise takes in the seal colonies, penguins, dolphins,
humpback whales and abundant birdlife in the area. It focuses
on the ecological and historical nature of the coastline. The tour
leaves from Adventure Bay daily; bookings on (03) 6293 1465.

Morella Island Retreat: hothouse, cafe and gum tree maze. *Bligh
Museum of Pacific Exploration:* constructed from handmade
convict bricks and housing displays of island history.

Bruny Island Cheese Co: cafe with cheese tasting;
1807 Bruny Island Main Rd, Great Bay; (03) 6260 6353.
Get Shucked Oyster Farm: fresh Pacific oysters;
1650 Bruny Island Main Rd, Great Bay; 0428 606 250.
The Hothouse Cafe: home-cooked fare in casual surrounds;
Morella Island Retreats, 46 Adventure Bay Rd; (03) 6293 1131.

Captain Cook Caravan Park: 786 Adventure Bay Rd;
(03) 6293 1128.

Bushwalking Bruny Island is a bushwalker's delight. At the
southern tip is South Bruny National Park with stunning scenery
and several tracks. Labillardiere State Reserve has a vast range of
vegetation including eucalypt woodlands, shrublands, herblands
and wildflowers. The rainforest at Mavista Falls is another
breathtaking spot, as is Cape Queen Elizabeth. Check with visitor
centre for details.

Truganini memorial: boardwalk and lookout; on isthmus
between islands; 11 km N. *Birdlife:* little penguins and short-
tailed shearwaters on Bruny's ocean beaches. *Cape Bruny
Lighthouse:* second oldest lighthouse in Australia (1836); South
Bruny National Park via Lunawanna; 29 km sw. *Beaches:* many
good swimming beaches (details from visitor centre); Dennes
Point Beach on North Bruny has picnic facilities and Cloudy Bay
(turn left at Lunawanna) is a magnificent surf beach.

TOWNS NEARBY: Dover 26 km, Kettering 26 km, Cygnet 31 km,
Hastings 33 km, Geeveston 39 km

Beaconsfield
Pop. 1055
Map ref. 627 J6 | 629 E7

 Tamar Visitor Centre, Main Rd, Exeter; (03) 6394 4454 or 1800 637 989; www.tamarvalley.com.au

91.7 FM ABC Local Radio, 103.7 FM City Park Radio

Now a modest apple-growing centre in Tasmania's north, Beaconsfield was once the wealthiest gold town in Tasmania. Gold rush–era relics include two massive Romanesque arches at the old pithead of the Tasmania Gold Mine. The Gold Festival is held each December and draws a large crowd. Tourism increased significantly in Beaconsfield following the dramatic rescue of two trapped miners in 2006.

Beaconsfield Mine and Heritage Centre This mine constantly struggled with water problems, but still managed to produce 26 tonnes of gold before it was closed in 1914. There's now a museum complex along with a miner's cottage.

Beaconsfield Walk of Gold: self-guide historical walk that starts at the Heritage Centre; 1.8 km round trip with signage; West St. *Van Diemen's Land Gallery:* art and craft; Weld St. *Gem and Stone Creations:* gallery and giftshop; Weld St.

Tamar Valley Wholefoods & Coffee Shop: cafe and organic groceries; 110B Weld St; (03) 6383 1120.

Holwell Gorge This is a fern-covered gorge with beautiful waterfalls in the Dazzler Range to the west of town. There are basic picnic facilities at the eastern entrance and a 3 hr return hiking track. Contact Parks & Wildlife Service on 1300 135 513; access is via Holwell or Greens Beach rds; 8 km w.

Auld Kirk: convict-built church (1843) at Sidmouth with views of Batman Bridge, which features a 100 m A-frame across the River Tamar; 13 km SE. *Wineries:* cellar-door tastings and sales to the east of town around Rowella, Kayena and Sidmouth; Sidmouth is 13 km E. *Lavender House:* exhibition fields of 70 varieties of lavender, plus tearooms with specialty lavender scones and giftshop with 50 health and beauty products; 15 km E.

TOWNS NEARBY: Beauty Point 5 km, George Town 11 km, Exeter 15 km, Port Sorell 23 km, Latrobe 34 km

Beauty Point
Pop. 1113
Map ref. 627 J6 | 629 E6

 Tamar Visitor Centre, Main Rd, Exeter; (03) 6394 4454 or 1800 637 989; www.tamarvalley.com.au

91.7 FM ABC Local Radio, 95.3 Tamar FM

Beauty Point is the base for the Australian Maritime College and is also a good spot for fishing and yachting. The town's main attractions are Seahorse World and Platypus House.

Seahorse World The centre acts as a breeding farm for aquariums and the Chinese medicine market, but also studies endangered species to ensure their survival. Take a guided tour to see how seahorses are bred – newborns are the size of a child's fingernail. There's also a touch pool and expo centre for local wines and craft. Inspection Head Wharf, Flinders St; (03) 6383 4111.

Platypus House This centre has 3 live displays: one with platypus and native beaver rats, another with Tasmanian butterflies, and a third with many Tasmanian leeches, blood-sucking worms and spiders. Scientists here are currently conducting research into a disease attacking the Tasmanian platypus population. Inspection Head Wharf, Flinders St; (03) 6383 4884.

Sandy Beach: safe swimming spot.

Three Peaks Race: 3-day sailing and mountain-climbing event that begins in town each Easter, heading north to Flinders Island, then south down the east coast to Hobart.

Carbones Cafe: Italian cuisine with a view; 225 Flinders St; (03) 6383 4099. **Tamar Cove Motel & Restaurant:** casual, family-friendly restaurant; 4421 West Tamar Hwy; (03) 6383 4375.

Beauty Point Cottages: 14 Flinders St; (03) 6383 4556. **Beauty Point Tourist Park:** 36 West Arm Rd; (03) 6383 4536. **Beauty Point's Pomona Spa Cottages:** 77 Flinders St; (03) 6383 4073. **BIG4 Kelso Sands Holiday Park:** 86 Paranaple Rd, Kelso; (03) 6383 9130. **Greens Beach Caravan & Holiday Park:** 1774 Greens Beach Rd, Greens Beach; (03) 6383 9222.

Narawntapu National Park This park is a popular spot for horseriding and waterskiing (conditions apply), and has excellent walks such as the 5 hr walk from Badger Head to Bakers Beach. Contact Parks & Wildlife Service on 1300 135 513; access via Greens Beach or via Badger Head or Bakers Beach rds.

York Town monument: site marks the first settlement in northern Tasmania (1804); 10 km W. *Kelso and Greens Beach:* popular holiday towns to the north-west.

TOWNS NEARBY: Beaconsfield 5 km, George Town 6 km, Exeter 19 km, Port Sorell 23 km, Lilydale 35 km

Bicheno
see inset box on next page

Bothwell
Pop. 377
Map ref. 625 J4

 Australasian Golf Museum, Market Pl; (03) 6259 4033; www.bothwell.com.au

95.7 Heart FM, 936 AM ABC Local Radio

Australia's first golf course was created in Bothwell in 1837, making golf a point of pride. There are many craft shops and art galleries in town, as well as over 50 National Trust–classified buildings.

Heritage walk Bothwell has 53 colonial cottages, churches, houses and official buildings around Queens Park. Notable are the Georgian brick Slate Cottage and St Luke's Church. The best way to appreciate the historic buildings is by a self-guide walking tour; pamphlet from visitor centre.

Australasian Golf Museum: displays of golfing memorabilia and history. The museum also sells award-winning Tasmanian Highland Cheese and local tartan; Market Pl. *Bothwell Grange:* guesthouse with tearooms and art gallery; Alexander St.

International Highland Spin-In: odd-numbered years, Feb–Mar.

Castle Hotel: great counter meals; 14 Patrick St; (03) 6259 5502.

Ratho Home to the first game of golf in Australia, Ratho was the elegant 'gentleman's residence' of Alexander Reid in the early 1800s. It is a stone house with wooden Ionic columns. The famous golf course is still intact and in use. Lake Hwy; 3 km W.

Trout fishing: some of Australia's best freshwater fishing in the region. A favourite among trout anglers is the Ouse River, which joins the Derwent north of Hamilton. Other spots include the Clyde, Jordan and Coal rivers east of the Derwent, and the

continued on p. 473

TASMANIA

BICHENO

Pop. 639
Map ref. 625 O1 | 627 O11

 Foster St; (03) 6375 1500; www.gsbc.tas.gov.au

89.7 FM ABC Local Radio, 98.5 Star FM

Bicheno (pronounced 'bish-eno') has a chequered history. It was set up as a whaling and sealing centre in 1803, predating the official settlement of Van Diemen's Land by a few months. It became a magnet for men with violent tendencies, which often found expression in the abuse of local Aboriginal women. One of these, Waubedebar, became a heroine after saving two white men from drowning in a storm. Landmarks in town bear her name, and her grave can be seen in Lions Park. After a short stint as a coal port, during which time the population increased considerably, Bicheno relaxed back into what it does best – fishing – and is known today for its abundant seafood. Situated on the east coast, the town has the mildest climate in Tasmania. It is blessed with sandy beaches and popular dive spots, and draws holiday-makers from far afield. Native rock orchids, unique to the east coast, bloom in October and November.

Bicheno Penguin Tours Join a tour at dusk to watch little penguins return home from the sea. On most nights they waddle right past you as they make their way through the coastal vegetation to their burrows. At the peak of the season, close to 600 birds inhabit the rookery. It's a popular and magical wildlife experience, run in an environmentally sensitive way. Tours depart from operator's office on Burgess St; bookings (03) 6375 1333.

Scuba diving Bicheno has some of the best diving in Tasmania and one of the best temperate dive locations in the world. The Bicheno Dive Centre runs diving tours to over 20 locations, including the main site at Governor Island Marine Reserve. In winter, divers have been known to swim among schools of dolphins or migrating whales that pass by Bicheno. Bookings (03) 6375 1138.

Bicentennial Foreshore Walk: a 3 km track with great views, it starts at Redhill Beach and continues to the blowhole. *The Gulch:*

natural harbour; foreshore. *Whalers Lookout:* off Foster St. *Sea Life Centre:* licensed restaurant and giftshop; 1 Tasman Hwy; (03) 6375 1121. *The Glass Bottom Boat:* stay warm and dry while you drift above the watery world of Bicheno's marine life in Tasmania's only glass-bottom boat; bookings on (03) 6375 1294. *Fishing tours:* rock lobster and premium gamefishing in particular; check with visitor centre.

Cyrano Restaurant: casual French homestyle cuisine; 77 Burgess St; (03) 6375 1137. *Facets Restaurant and Bar:* modern Australian; Diamond Island Resort, 69 Tasman Hwy; (03) 6375 0100. *Pasini's Cafe Bar Wine Deli:* gourmet deli, takeaway and bistro serving local wines; shop 2, 70 Burgess St; (03) 6375 1076.

Gaol House Cottages: Cnr Burgess and James sts; (03) 6375 1430. *Windows on Bicheno:* 13 James St; (03) 6375 2010.

East Coast Natureworld This park offers encounters with the region's diverse fauna. The often-misunderstood Tasmanian devil is here, as are Forester kangaroos, Cape Barren geese and Bennett's wallabies. (03) 6375 1311; 8 km N.

Douglas–Apsley National Park This national park is Tasmania's last largely undisturbed area of dry eucalypt forest. It encompasses the catchments of the Denison, Douglas and Apsley rivers and has stunning gorges and waterfalls. There is a viewing platform at Apsley Gorge Lookout and Waterhole, and safe swimming spots. Contact Parks & Wildlife Service on 1300 135 513; 14 km NW.

Freycinet National Park: begins directly south of town; *see Coles Bay. Vineyards:* to the south-west of town, including Springbrook Vineyard and adjacent Freycinet Vineyard, which hosts a jazz concert each Easter; 18 km sw on Tasman Hwy. *Scenic flights:* offered by Freycinet Air over the region; bookings (03) 6375 1694.

TOWNS NEARBY: Coles Bay 28 km, Swansea 33 km, St Marys 34 km, Fingal 38 km, St Helens 62 km

[ORANGE LICHEN–COVERED ROCKS ALONG BICHENO'S COASTLINE]

Tyenna, Styx and Plenty rivers west of the Derwent; contact visitor centre for details.

TOWNS NEARBY: Hamilton 24 km, Oatlands 31 km, Pontville 39 km, New Norfolk 44 km, Miena 51 km

Bridport

Pop. 1325
Map ref. 627 L5

 Main Rd; (03) 6356 1881; www.northeasttasmania.com.au

91.7 FM ABC Local Radio, 103.7 FM City Park Radio

Bridport is a popular seaside holiday retreat for Launceston and Scottsdale residents. It has many safe swimming beaches and fishing.

 Bridport Wildflower Reserve Best during Sept and Oct, this wildflower reserve spans 50 ha of coastal heath and woodland. There is a 2.2 km walking track that covers the length of the reserve and takes in scenic Adams Beach. Access via Main St.

Tom's Turnery: functional and souvenir woodturning; 31 Edward St.

Bridport Triathlon: Jan.

Bridport Bay Inn Bistro & Woodfired Pizza: seafood and tasty pizza; 105 Main St; (03) 6356 1238. *Bridport Cafe:* environmentally aware gourmet Mediterranean cafe; 89 Main St; (03) 6356 0057.

Tamar Valley wine region In Tasmania there is a neat division of wineries in the north stretching between Launceston and Pipers Brook, below Bridport. In all regions, white styles such as chardonnay, riesling and pinot gris are the standouts, with pinot noir holding up the reds. Pipers Brook Vineyard is one of the state's biggest names, and makes beautiful gewürztraminer and pinot noir. Its cellar also offers tastings of its Ninth Island label and Kreglinger sparkling wines. Other wineries worth visiting include Bay of Fires and Tamar Ridge. For masterpieces in sparkling, visit Clover Hill, whose picturesque cellar door is perfect for a picnic lunch, and Jansz, with its modern, architectural wine room featuring an interpretive centre.

Waterhouse Protected Area: offers 6700 ha of coastal bush camping, rockpools, sand dunes and beaches. Access via the old goldmining village, Waterhouse; 26 km E.

TOWNS NEARBY: Scottsdale 20 km, Lilydale 31 km, Derby 38 km, George Town 49 km, Exeter 50 km

Bruny Island

see Adventure Bay

Burnie

Pop. 77 408
Map ref. 626 F5

 Tasmanian Travel and Information Centre, Civic Centre Plaza, off Little Alexander St; (03) 6434 6111; www.tasmaniantravelcentre.com.au

102.5 FM ABC Local Radio, 106.1 Coast FM

The first European pioneers believed the Burnie area to be agriculturally rich, but high rainfall and dense forests covering the surrounding hills made farming virtually impossible. The deep waters in Emu Bay, however, rescued the community by providing an ideal port for the local industries of tin and timber.

Today Burnie, Tasmania's fourth largest city, is a vibrant city with beautiful parklands and charming heritage buildings.

 Burnie Park This park has lawns, shaded walkways, diverse native flora and animal enclosures with ducks, swans, wallabies, emus, peacocks and rabbits. Burnie Inn, the city's oldest building, is in the park and has been restored as a teahouse. A brochure is available from the park information centre. Bass Hwy.

Pioneer Village Museum: re-creation of old Burnie town that houses almost 20 000 items from the late 1800s and early 1900s; Civic Centre Plaza. Little Penguin Observation Centre: free guided tours Oct–Feb; Parsonage Point; 0437 436 803. *Creative Paper:* recycled-paper art with demonstrations and activities; tours available daily; Old Surrey Rd. *Walking track:* 17 km track that skirts the city; start at boardwalk. *Australian Paper:* mill tours held 2pm Mon–Fri; Bass Hwy; bookings on (03) 6430 7882. *The Cheese Tasting Centre:* dairy samples and other specialty produce; Old Surrey Rd. *Hellyers Road Distillery:* makers of single malt whisky; tours, tastings, sales and licensed eatery; open 9.30am–5.30pm daily; Old Surrey Rd, adjacent to Cheese Tasting Centre. *Burnie Regional Art Gallery:* impressive collection of Australian contemporary prints; open 10am–4.30pm Mon–Fri, 1.30–4.30pm Sat, Sun and public holidays; Wilmot St.

Burnie Farmers Market: Wivenhoe Showgrounds; 1st and 3rd Sat morning each month. *Burnie Ten:* 10 km road race; Oct. *Burnie Shines:* month-long community festival; Oct.

Bayviews Restaurant and Lounge Bar: smart seafront modern Australian bistro; Level 1, 2 North Tce; (03) 6431 7999. *Cafe Europa:* cafe favourites; Cnr Cattley and Wilson sts; (03) 6431 1897. *Rialto Gallery Restaurant:* traditional Italian; 46 Wilmot St; (03) 6431 7718.

Burnie Holiday Caravan Park: 253 Bass Hwy, Cooee; (03) 6431 1925.

Emu Valley Rhododendron Gardens Considered the city's floral emblem, the rhododendron has pride of place in Burnie. These gardens have over 9000 wild and hybrid rhododendrons on display in a natural 12 ha amphitheatre, and host the floral festival in Oct. Open Aug–Feb; off Cascade Rd; 6 km s.

Fern Glade: tranquil reserve on Emu River with walking tracks and picnic areas; off Old Surrey Rd; 5 km w. *Annsleigh Garden and Tearooms:* voted one of the 10 best gardens in Australia and comprising 2 ha of beautiful gardens and novelty buildings, plus souvenirs and food; open Sept–May; Mount Rd; 9 km s. *Upper Natone Forest Reserve:* popular picnic spot; Upper Natone Rd; 30 km s. *Lake Kara:* good trout fishing; signposted from Hampshire; 30 km s. *Bushwalks and waterfalls:* many in area, but Guide Falls (near Ridgley, 17 km s) is most accessible.

TOWNS NEARBY: Penguin 15 km, Wynyard 17 km, Ulverstone 26 km, Devonport 40 km, Latrobe 48 km

Campbell Town

Pop. 776
Map ref. 625 L1 | 627 L11

 Heritage Highway Museum and Visitor Centre, 103 High St; (03) 6381 1353; www.campbelltowntasmania.com

95.7 Heart FM, 1161 AM ABC Local Radio

This small town has been prominent in Tasmania's history: the first telephone call in the Southern Hemisphere was made from

TASMANIA

here to Launceston; the British Commonwealth's first agricultural show was held here in 1839, and the event is still held today; and it is the birthplace of Harold Gatty, the first person to fly around the world.

Heritage buildings Of the 35 heritage buildings listed on the National Estate, The Grange, an old manor house built in the centre of town in 1840, is possibly the grandest. Others include the Fox Hunter's Return, Campbell Town Inn and Red Bridge, a 3-arched structure built over the Elizabeth River by convicts in the 1830s. There is a map in Grange Park at the northern end of High Street that lists the main historic buildings.

Heritage Highway Museum: displays on local history and the first round-the-world flight navigation; 103 High St.

Market: Town Hall; 4th Sun each month. *Great Painting Race:* Jan. *Agricultural show:* Australia's oldest; June.

Campbell Town Hotel: hearty pub meals; 118 High St; (03) 6381 1158. *Zeps Cafe:* travellers cafe with city vibe; 92–94 High St (Midland Hwy); (03) 6381 1344. *St Andrews Inn:* Tasmanian country fare in historic surrounds; 12819 Midland Hwy, Cleveland; (03) 6391 5525.

Ivy on Glenelg: 9 Glenelg St; (03) 6381 1228. *Rose Cottage B&B:* 23 Barton Rd, Epping Forest; (03) 6391 5569.

Fishing: Macquarie River, just west of town, and Lake Leake, 30 km E, are 2 good trout-fishing spots in the area.

TOWNS NEARBY: Ross 12 km, Oatlands 43 km, Evandale 44 km, Longford 47 km, Fingal 51 km

Coles Bay
Pop. 473
Map ref. 625 O3

ℹ️ Freycinet National Park; (03) 6256 7000; www.freycinetcolesbay.com

📻 98.5 Star FM, 106.1 FM ABC Local Radio

Coles Bay is a tiny town with a few stores and facilities. It now has an up-market resort, and is a peaceful base from which to explore the area. It is a gateway to the spectacular scenery of The Hazards, Wineglass Bay and Freycinet Peninsula, a long, narrow paradise featuring forests, cliffs, beaches and walking trails. The beautiful Peninsula Walking Track ends at Wineglass Bay, regarded by many as one of the world's best beaches.

 Fishing competition: Southern Game Fishing Club; Mar. *Three Peaks Race:* sailing and mountain-climbing event; Easter. *Freycinet Challenge:* running, sea-kayaking, and road and mountain-bike racing at Freycinet Lodge; Oct. *Mark Webber Challenge:* Nov.

The Bay Restaurant: tranquil, intimate dining; Freycinet Lodge, Freycinet National Park; (03) 6225 7016 or 1800 420 155. *The Edge Restaurant:* fine seafood and gorgeous views; Edge of the Bay Resort, 2308 Main Rd; (03) 6257 0102. *Madge Malloys:* super fresh restaurant-caught seafood; 3 Garnet Ave; (03) 6257 0399. *Tombolo Freycinet:* gourmet takeaway cafe; 6 Garnet Ave; (03) 6257 0124.

Freycinet National Park This park is world renowned for its stunning coastal scenery, challenging rock climbs, abundant wildlife, and range of walking tracks. The park is covered in wildflowers, including 60 varieties of ground orchid. Visitors can take the 1 hr walk to the lookout over stunning Wineglass Bay, or the 2.5 hr return walk to the beach. There are many safe

swimming beaches and waterskiing, scuba diving, canoeing and sailing facilities. Check with visitor centre for details.

Freycinet Marine Farm: working oyster farm with guided tours and sampling; open 5–6pm Mon–Fri; tour bookings on (03) 6257 0140; 9 km NW. *Moulting Lagoon Game Reserve:* wetlands of international importance with many bird species; 12 km NW. *Fishing:* Great Oyster Bay is a renowned fishing spot – species include flathead and Australian salmon. Coles Bay is also a base for big-game fishing, particularly southern bluefin tuna in autumn; contact visitor centre for tour details.

TOWNS NEARBY: Swansea 18 km, Bicheno 28 km, Triabunna 52 km, Fingal 60 km, St Marys 61 km

Currie
Pop. 745
Map ref. 625 O11

ℹ️ The Trend, Edward St, Currie; (03) 6462 1355 or 1800 645 014; www.kingisland.org.au

📻 88.5 FM ABC Local Radio, 88.9 Coast FM

Located in Bass Strait, Currie is the main town on King Island. The island is well known for its gourmet produce, including superb soft cheeses and grass-fed beef. The Roaring Forties are responsible for many of the 57 shipwrecks scattered around the island. The island now has five lighthouses (to avoid any further disaster), including one at Cape Wickham, which at 48 metres is the tallest lighthouse in the Southern Hemisphere.

King Island Cultural Centre: local arts, community projects, resident artists and personal stories of King Island residents; Currie Harbour. *King Island Historical Society Museum:* memorabilia of the island; open 2–4pm daily in summer, closed in winter; Lighthouse St. *The Boathouse Gallery:* displays and sales of pottery, sculptures and paintings, plus barbecue facilities; Edward St. *Observatory:* tours when sky is clear; Rifle Range Rd. *King Island Maritime Trail:* track with interpretive signs takes in shipwreck sites; details from visitor centre. *Tours:* full- and half-day tours of the island run by King Island Coaches; bookings on (03) 6462 1138.

 King Island Imperial 20: marathon from Naracoopa to Currie; Mar. *King Island Show:* Mar. *King Island Dramatic Society Play:* Mar. *Queenscliff to Grassy Yacht Race:* Mar. *King Island Horseracing Carnival:* Nov/Dec.

Boomerang by the Sea: perfect seafood, panoramic views; Golf Club Rd; (03) 6462 1288. *King Island Bakery:* gourmet pies and breads; 5 Main St; (03) 6462 1337. *Kings Cuisine at the Bold Head Brasserie:* local-produce-driven menu; Grassy Club, 10 Main Rd, Grassy; (03) 6461 1003.

King Island Dairy Internationally recognised for its cheeses and beef, King Island Dairy has a Fromagerie Tasting Room with an excellent range of brie, camembert, cheddar, washed rind, triple cream and many others. The cows graze year-round, which makes their milk better for cheese production. Loorana; 9 km N.

Fishing: excellent salmon, flathead and whiting fishing from east-coast beaches; morwong, warehou, yellowtail kingfish and squid fishing at British Admiral Reef; 3 km S of Currie. *Penguins:* see them return to shore at dusk at Grassy in the south-east; 25 km SE. *King Island Kelp Craft:* specialising in the rare form of bull kelp handcrafts, with displays and sales; 6 Currie Rd, Grassy; 25 km SE. *Naracoopa:* seaside town with growing tourist industry; 25 km E. *Seal Rocks State Reserve:* covers 800 ha, with calcified forest and stunning cliffs at Seal Rocks; 30 km S. *Lavinia Nature*

Reserve: 6400 ha of ocean beaches, heath, dunes, wetland bird habitats, lagoons and a rare suspended lake formation. Lavinia Point has a popular surfing beach; 40 km NE. *Cape Wickham:* lighthouse on rugged cliffs; north of Egg Lagoon; 45 km NE. *Surfing:* King Island is an ideal location for surfing.

TOWNS NEARBY: Smithton 148 km, Stanley 153 km, Wynyard 200 km, Burnie 215 km, Penguin 229 km

Cygnet

Pop. 840
Map ref. 622 G8 | 625 J9

 Huon River Jet Boats and Visitor Centre, The Esplanade, Huonville; (03) 6264 1838; www.huonjet.com

98.5 Huon FM, 936 AM ABC Local Radio

Cygnet was originally named Port de Cygne Noir by French admiral Bruni D'Entrecasteaux – after the black swans in the bay. However, in 1915 two local troopers were assaulted in a pub brawl and, in an attempt to avoid eternal infamy, the town name was changed to Cygnet. Now it is a fruit-growing and alternative-lifestyle community. In spring, the surrounding area blooms with magnificent wattle, apple and pear blossom.

Living History Museum: memorabilia, historic photos; open Thurs–Sun; Mary St. *Trading Post:* antiques, second-hand treasures and collectibles; Mary St. *Town square:* Presbytery, Catholic church (with stained-glass windows dedicated to lost miners) and convent; popular photo spot. *Phoenix Creations:* turns recycled materials into one-off furniture and crafts; Mary St. *Near and Far:* handcrafts and gifts; Mary St.

Cygnet Folk Festival: music, dance and art festival; Jan.

Lotus Eaters Cafe: worldly cuisine and relaxed surrounds; 10 Mary St; (03) 6295 1996. *The Red Velvet Lounge:* popular, eclectic cafe restaurant; 24 Mary St; (03) 6295 0466.

Birdwatching: black swans and other species inhabit Port Cygnet; viewing areas off Channel Hwy. *Wineries:* many including Hartzview Wine Centre, known for pinot noir, ports and liqueurs. There are cellar-door tastings and sales; Gardners Bay; 10 km SE. *Beaches:* good boat-launching facilities and beaches at Randalls Bay (14 km s), Egg and Bacon Bay (15 km s) and Verona Sands (18 km s). *Nine Pin Point Marine Nature Reserve:* reef; near Verona Sands; 18 km s. *Fishing:* sea-run trout and brown trout from the Huon River; west and south of town. *Berry orchards:* orchards with pick-your-own sales.

TOWNS NEARBY: Geeveston 12 km, Huonville 14 km, Kettering 14 km, Dover 18 km, Kingston 27 km

Deloraine

Pop. 2242
Map ref. 627 I8 | 629 C10

 Great Western Tiers Visitor Centre, 98–100 Emu Bay Rd; (03) 6362 3471; www.greatwesterntiers.net.au

91.7 FM ABC Local Radio, 103.7 FM City Park Radio

Deloraine has become the artistic hub of northern Tasmania. Artists are inspired by the magnificent scenery, working farms and hedgerows, and the Great Western Tiers nearby. Situated on the Meander River, Deloraine is Tasmania's largest inland town and a busy regional centre that has been classified by the National Trust as a town of historical significance.

Yarns Artwork in Silk Created by more than 300 people and taking 10 000 hours to complete, Yarns is a 200 m reflection of the Great Western Tiers of Tasmania in 4 large panels. Accompanied by an audio presentation and sound and light effects, the Yarns presentation operates every half-hour. 98 Emu Bay Rd.

Jahadi Tours and Art Gallery Jahadi Indigenous Experience runs half- and full-day tours in and around Deloraine that take in the natural landscape and focus on Aboriginal sites such as caves, middens and rock shelters. Tours are organised for a maximum of 8 people to ensure a personal experience; bookings on (03) 6363 6172. The Jahadi Art Gallery exhibits artwork from local Indigenous artists; 900 Mole Creek Rd.

Deloraine Folk Museum: showcases the life of a country publican with exhibition gallery, garden, dairy, blacksmith's shop and family history room; 98 Emu Bay Rd. *Galleries:* sales and exhibits of local artwork from paintings to furniture. Venues include Gallery B on Emu Bay Rd, Artifakt on Emu Bay Rd, Artist's Garret on West Church St and Bowerbank Mill on the Bass Hwy.

Market: showgrounds, Lake Hwy; 1st Sat each month plus 3rd Sat Feb–May. *Tasmanian Craft Fair:* largest working craft fair in Australia; Nov.

Christmas Hills Raspberry Farm Cafe: 'go straight to dessert'; 9 Christmas Hills Rd (Bass Hwy), Elizabeth Town; (03)6362 2186. *etc (Elizabeth Town Bakery Cafe):* super roadside licensed cafe; 5783 Bass Hwy, Elizabeth Town; (03) 6368 1350.

Bonney's Inn Colonial B&B: 19 West Pde; (03) 6362 2974. *Drumreagh Bed & Breakfast Cabins:* 175 River Rd; (03) 6362 4492.

Liffey Falls State Reserve Liffey Falls is surrounded by cool–temperate rainforest species of sassafras, myrtle and leatherwood. There is a 45 min return nature walk from the picnic area through lush tree ferns, taking in smaller falls along the way. Contact Parks & Wildlife Service on 1300 135 513; 29 km s.

Exton: tiny township full of antique shops and charming old cottages; 5 km E. *41 Degrees South Aquaculture:* salmon farm, wetlands and ginseng nursery, with tastings and cafe; Montana Rd; 8 km w. *Ashgrove Farm Cheeses:* sales and tastings of English-style cheeses; Elizabeth Town; 10 km NW. *Lobster Falls:* 2 hr return walk from roadside through riverside forest with lookout and wide variety of local birdlife; 11 km w. *Quamby Bluff:* solitary mountain behind town, with 6 hr return walking track to summit starting near Lake Hwy; 20 km s. *Meander Falls:* stunning falls reached by 5–6 hr return trek for experienced walkers that also takes in the Tiers. Shorter walks are outlined at information booth in forest reserve carpark; 28 km s. *Fishing:* excellent trout fishing in Meander River (north and south of town) and Mersey River (around 20 km E). *Scenic drive:* through Central Highlands area via Golden Valley to Great Lake, one of the largest high-water lakes in Australia. Check road conditions with Parks & Wildlife Service; (03) 6259 8348.

TOWNS NEARBY: Westbury 16 km, Mole Creek 21 km, Sheffield 32 km, Hadspen 35 km, Exeter 35 km

TASMANIA

 RADIO STATIONS   IN TOWN   WHAT'S ON   WHERE TO EAT   WHERE TO STAY   NEARBY

Derby

Pop. 302
Map ref. 627 N6

i Derby Tin Mine Centre, Main St; (03) 6354 1062; www.northeasttasmania.com.au

91.7 FM ABC Local Radio, 94.5 Sea FM

This small north-eastern town was born when tin was discovered in 1874 and the 'Brothers Mine' opened two years later. The Cascade Dam was built and the mine prospered until 1929, when the dam flooded and swept through the town, killing 14 people. The mine closed and, although it eventually reopened, the town never fully recovered. Tourists stroll through the charming streets to view the old buildings and tin mine memorabilia.

Derby Tin Mine Centre The town's major attraction, the centre is a reconstruction of this old mining village. It includes a miner's cottage, general store, butcher's shop, huge sluice and the historic Derby gaol. The old Derby School houses a comprehensive museum with history displays, gemstones, minerals and tin-panning apparatus. Main St.

Red Door Gallerae: paintings, carvings and furniture; Main St. *Bankhouse Manor:* arts, crafts and collectibles; Main St.

Derby River Derby: raft race down Ringarooma River with markets, exhibitions and children's activities; Oct.

Berries Cafe: cute country-style cafe; 72 Main St; (03) 6354 2520. *Holy Cow Cafe:* cheesemaker's licensed cafe; Pyengana Dairy Company, St Columba Falls Rd, Pyengana; (03) 6373 6157. *Pub in the Paddock:* good-value counter meals; 250 St Columba Falls Rd, Pyengana; (03) 6373 6121.

Ralphs Falls The longest single-drop waterfall in Australia. A 20 min return walk under a myrtle rainforest canopy arrives at Norms Lookout at the top of the falls. From here views of the Ringarooma Valley, Bass Strait and the Furneaux Islands. Picnic and barbecue facilities are available. 15 km SE of Ringarooma.

Gemstone fossicking: Weld River in Moorina, where the largest sapphire in Tasmania was discovered; Tasman Hwy; 8 km NE. *Miners cemetery:* historic cemetery where early tin miners, including some Chinese, were buried; Moorina; 8 km NE. *Fishing:* excellent trout fishing along Ringarooma River north of town.

TOWNS NEARBY: Scottsdale 24 km, Gladstone 27 km, Bridport 38 km, St Helens 42 km, Lilydale 50 km

Devonport

Pop. 25 518
Map ref. 626 H6 I 628 H1 I 629 B2

i 92 Formby Rd; (03) 6424 4466; www.devonporttasmania.travel

100.5 FM ABC Local Radio, 104.7 Coast FM

Devonport, on the banks of the Mersey River, is the home port of the *Spirit of Tasmania I* and *II*. This vibrant seaport city is framed by the dramatic headland of Mersey Bluff, beautiful coastal reserves and parklands, and Bass Strait. The community is fuelled by farming, manufacturing and, of course, tourism.

Home Hill A National Trust property, once home to prime minister Joseph Lyons and Dame Enid Lyons, along with their 12 children. Houses a rich collection of personal material, giving insight into the momentous events of mid-20th century Australian. The Home Hill property comprises a beautiful old building in well-maintained gardens of wisteria and imposing trees; tours 2pm Wed–Sun, closed Jul–Aug; 77 Middle Rd; (03) 6424 8055.

Tiagarra Aboriginal Culture Centre and Museum Meaning 'keep' or 'keeping place', Tiagarra is one of the few preserved Aboriginal rock-carving sites in Tasmania. A 1 km circuit walk takes in the carvings. An adjoining art centre exhibits over 2000 artefacts. Dioramas depict the lifestyle of the original inhabitants; open Tues and Wed, 10am–2pm; Bluff Rd, Mersey Bluff; (03) 6424 8250.

Don River Railway View the largest collection of historic locomotives and passenger carriages in Tasmania and hop on an hourly train ride along Don River to Coles Beach, hauled by steam locomotives on Sundays; open daily; Forth Main Rd, Don; (03) 6424 6335.

Devonport Maritime Museum & Heritage Centre See detailed models and displays from the days of sail through the age of steam, to the present seagoing passenger ferries; open daily 10am–4pm; 6 Gloucester Ave; (03) 6424 7100.

Simon Martin Whips and Leathercraft Country leathercraft studio and expert traditional whip-maker supplying plaited kangaroo hide stockwhips to the world. Whip cracking demonstrations on request; open 8.30am–5pm Mon–Fri; 4 Formby Rd; (03) 6424 3972.

Pandemonium Discovery and Adventure Centre Something for all ages from indoor rock climbing, laser skirmish and jungle gyms to the hands-on Imaginarium Science Centre; open 10am–5.30pm Tue–Sun; 62–64 North Fenton St; (03) 6424 1333.

Devonport Regional Gallery: displays the work of contemporary Tasmanian artists in a century-old building; open 10am–5pm Mon–Fri, 12–5pm Sat and 1–5pm Sun; 45 Stewart St; (03) 6424 8296. *Australian Weaving Mills Factory Outlet:* factory seconds for Dickies and Dri-Glo products; open 9.30am–3pm Mon–Fri, 9am–12pm Sat; 45 Tasman St; (03) 6424 6345. *Devonport Lighthouse:* striking icon completed in 1899 and part of the National Estate; Mersey Bluff. *Scenic flights:* through Tasair from Devonport airport; bookings (03) 6427 9777.

Devonport Cup: Jan. *Apex Regatta:* Mar. *Taste the Harvest Festival:* Mar. *Devonport Jazz Weekend:* July. *Devonport Show:* Nov. *Athletic and Cycling Carnivals:* Dec.

Dannebrog Cafe Bar and Grill: family restaurant; 161 Rooke St; (03) 6424 4477. *Essence Food and Wine:* fine-dining licensed restaurant; 28 Forbes St; (03) 6424 6431. *Taco Villa:* popular Mexican restaurant; Shop 4, 1 Kempling St; (03) 6424 6762.

Devonport Bed & Breakfast: 27 Victoria Pde; 0439 658 503. *Birchmore of Devonport:* 8 Oldaker St; (03) 6423 1336. *Rosemount on Macfie:* 47 Macfie St; (03) 6424 7406. *Three George Street B&B:* 3 George St; 0400 637 199. *Alice Beside The Sea:* 1 Wright St, East Devonport; (03) 6427 8605. *Bay View Holiday Village:* 2 North Caroline St, East Devonport; (03) 6427 0499. *Discovery Holiday Parks – Devonport:* 13–19 Tarleton St, East Devonport; (03) 6498 6333. *Devonport Holiday Village:* 20–24 North Caroline St, East Devonport; (03) 6427 8886.

Tasmanian Arboretum Fifty-eight ha reserve of rare native and exotic plants and trees. Picnic areas, walking tracks and a lake where you can watch waterbirds and platypus; Eugenana; 10 km s.

House of Anvers Chocolate Factory The total chocolate experience – manufacturing viewing room, chocolate museum and tasting centre; Bass Hwy; 10 km sw.

Braddon's Lookout: panoramic view of coastline; near Forth; 16 km w. *Kelcey Tier Nature Walk:* 160 ha of native bushland

[EAGLEHAWK NECK] TESSELLATED PAVEMENT

and 3.6 km circuit walk with superb views of Devonport and Mersey River.

TOWNS NEARBY: Latrobe 9 km, Ulverstone 14 km, Port Sorell 17 km, Sheffield 23 km, Penguin 25 km

Dover
Pop. 461
Map ref. 622 F10 | 625 J10

 Forest and Heritage Centre, Church St, Geeveston; (03) 6297 1836; www.forestandheritagecentre.com

95.3 Huon FM, 936 AM ABC Local Radio

Dover lies beside the waters of Esperance Bay and the D'Entrecasteaux Channel, with the imposing figure of Adamson's Peak in the background. The three islands directly offshore, Faith, Hope and Charity, were named perhaps to inspire the convicts held at the original probation station. The town is a popular destination for yachting enthusiasts.

Commandant's Office: well-preserved remnant of Dover's penal history; Beach Rd.

Dover Hotel: local fare in homely pub; Main Rd (Huon Hwy); (03) 6298 1210.

Faith Island: several historic graves; access by boat. *Walking trails:* epic Tasmanian Trail to Devonport, as well as Dover Coast and Duckhole Lake tracks; details from visitor centre. *Beaches:* safe swimming beaches surround town.

TOWNS NEARBY: Hastings 13 km, Geeveston 18 km, Cygnet 18 km, Adventure Bay 26 km, Kettering 28 km

Dunalley
Pop. 310
Map ref. 623 M6 | 625 M7

 Dunalley Hotel, 210 Arthur Hwy; (03) 6253 5101.

97.7 Tasman FM, 936 AM ABC Local Radio

A quaint fishing village, Dunalley is on the isthmus separating the Forestier and Tasman peninsulas from the mainland. Nearby is

the Denison Canal, which is Australia's only purpose-built, hand-dug sea canal. The swing bridge that spans the canal has become quite a spectacle for visitors.

Tasman Monument Erected in 1942, this monument commemorates the landing of Abel Tasman and his crew. The actual landing occurred to the north-east on the Forestier Peninsula, near the fairly inaccessible Cape Paul Lamanon. Imlay St.

Dunalley Fish Market: fishmonger and cafe; 11 Fulham Rd; (03) 6253 5428. *Dunalley Hotel:* pub tucker, especially seafood; 210 Arthur Hwy; (03) 6253 5101. *Dunalley Waterfront Cafe & Gallery:* contemporary cafe and collectibles; 4 Imlay St; (03) 6253 5122. *Murdunna Store:* roadside tearoom; 4050 Arthur Hwy, Murdunna; (03) 6253 5196.

Copping Colonial and Convict Exhibition Housing a vast array of antiques and memorabilia from the convict era, it has the added highlight of containing one of only 3 cars manufactured in Australia in the 19th century. Arthur Hwy; (03) 6253 5373; 11 km N.

Marian Bay: popular swimming beach; 14 km NE.

TOWNS NEARBY: Eaglehawk Neck 17 km, Sorell 24 km, Port Arthur 29 km, Richmond 35 km, Kingston 43 km

Eaglehawk Neck
Pop. 267
Map ref. 623 N7 | 625 M8

 Port Arthur Historic Site, Arthur Hwy, Port Arthur; (03) 6251 2310 or 1800 659 101.

97.7 Tasman FM, 936 AM ABC Local Radio

Present-day Eaglehawk Neck is a pleasant fishing destination, speckled with small holiday retreats and striking scenery. Situated on the narrow isthmus between the Forestier and Tasman peninsulas, Eaglehawk Neck was the perfect natural prison gate for the convict settlement at Port Arthur. Few prisoners escaped by sea, so Eaglehawk Neck was essentially the only viable way out. The isthmus was guarded by soldiers and a line of ferocious

TASMANIA

tethered dogs. Most convicts knew not to bother, but William Hunt, convict and former strolling actor, tackled the isthmus in a kangaroo skin. As two guards took aim with their muskets, their efforts were cut short by a plaintive shout coming from the kangaroo, 'Don't shoot! It's only me – Billy Hunt!'

Bronze dog sculpture: marks the infamous dogline; access by short walking track off Arthur Hwy. **Scuba diving:** the area has a huge diversity of dive sites including the spectacular formations of Sisters Rocks, the 25 m high giant kelp forests, the seal colony at Hippolyte Rock, the SS *Nord* wreck and amazing sea-cave systems; Eaglehawk Dive Centre; bookings on (03) 6250 3566. **Surfing:** good surf beaches at Eaglehawk Neck and Pirates Bay.

The Lufra Hotel: counter meals; 380 Pirates Bay Dr; (03) 6250 3262 or 1800 639 532.

Norfolk Bayview Bed & Breakfast: RA 111 Nubeena Rd, Taranna; (03) 6250 3855.

Tasman National Park The major part of Tasman National Park is located on the Tasman Peninsula and has some of the most striking scenery in the state. Tasman Blowhole, Tasmans Arch and Devils Kitchen are the key attractions, occurring in rocks that are Permian in age (about 250 million years old). There are numerous walks throughout the park, the full track reaching from Eaglehawk Neck to Fortescue Bay, and there are fantastic shorter walks to Tasmans Arch, Waterfall Bay and Patersons Arch. Check with visitor centre for details or contact Parks & Wildlife on 1300 135 513.

Tasmanian Devil Conservation Park This animal-rescue centre features Tasmanian devils, quolls, eagles, wallabies, owls and wombats. There is a 1.5 km bird trail and free flight bird show, Kings of the Wind (11.15am and 3.30pm). The Tasmanian devil feeding time is worth waiting for (10am, 11am, 1.30pm and 5pm; 4.30pm in winter). Arthur Hwy, Taranna; (03) 6250 3230; 12 km s.

Tessellated Pavement: these rocks appear to have been neatly tiled, but their formation is entirely natural. Earth movements have fractured the pavement over the years. 1 km N. **Pirates Bay Lookout:** views across the bay, past the eastern side of Eaglehawk Neck to the massive coastal cliffs of the Tasman Peninsula; 1.5 km N. **Doo Town:** holiday town in which most of the houses bear names with variations of 'doo'; 3 km s. **Federation Chocolate:** chocolate factory with free tastings and historical museum; South St, Taranna; 10 km sw.

TOWNS NEARBY: Port Arthur 16 km, Dunalley 17 km, Sorell 40 km, Richmond 51 km, Kingston 51 km

Evandale
Pop. 1055
Map ref. 627 K9 | 629 H11

i Tourism and History Centre, 18 High St; (03) 6391 8128; www.evandaletasmania.com

91.7 FM ABC Local Radio, 103.7 FM City Park Radio

Just south of Launceston is this classified town, with beautiful buildings of historical and architectural importance. Cyclists come from as far as the Czech Republic for the annual Penny Farthing Championships, a race along the triangular circuit in the centre of the town.

Heritage walk Evandale is best appreciated with a copy of the brochure *Let's Talk About Evandale*, which lists over 35 historic buildings and sites in the town and many more in the

district. Among them are Blenheim (1832), which was once a hotel, St Andrews Uniting Church (1840) with its classic bell-tower and Doric columns, and the former Presbyterian Manse (1840). Brochure available from visitor centre.

Miniature railway: steam railway; open Sun; adjacent to market, Logan Rd.

Market: over 100 stalls; Falls Park, Russell St; Sun. **Village Fair and National Penny Farthing Championships:** largest annual event in the world devoted to racing antique bicycles; Feb. **Railex:** model railway exhibition; Mar. **Glover Prize:** Australia's second-richest art prize; Mar.

Clarendon Arms Hotel: hearty pub food; 11 Russell St; (03) 6391 8181. **Ingleside Bakery:** cafe and bakery; 4 Russell St; (03) 6391 8682. **Josef Chromy Cellar Door Cafe:** modern Australian vineyard restaurant; 370 Relbia Rd, Relbia; (03) 6335 8700.

Greg & Gills Place: 35 Collins St; (03) 6391 8248. **Hammers Bed & Breakfast:** 19 Barclay St; 0418 382 842.

Clarendon House Just north of Nile is the stunning National Trust residence, Clarendon House. It was built in 1836 by James Cox, a wealthy grazier and merchant, and has been restored by the National Trust. Clarendon's high-ceilinged rooms, extensive formal gardens and range of connected buildings (dairy, bakehouse, gardener's cottage and stable) make it one of the most impressive Georgian houses in Australia. (03) 6398 6220; 8 km s.

Ben Lomond National Park Site of Tasmania's largest alpine area and premier ski resort, this park has both downhill and cross-country skiing, with ski tows and ski hire. Ben Lomond Range is a plateau rising to over 1575 metres. The park also offers walking tracks and picnic areas in summer. Legges Tor, the second-highest point in Tasmania, has spectacular views. The area blooms with alpine wildflowers in summer. Contact Parks & Wildlife Service on 1300 135 513; 47 km E.

Symmons Plains International Raceway: venue for national V8 Supercars meeting in Nov. A track is open for conditional public use; bookings on (03) 6398 2952; 10 km s. **John Glover's grave:** burial site of prominent Tasmanian artist beside church designed by Glover; Deddington; 24 km SE. **Trout fishing:** in North Esk and South Esk rivers.

TOWNS NEARBY: Longford 11 km, Hadspen 16 km, Launceston 17 km, Westbury 34 km, Lilydale 36 km

Exeter
Pop. 339
Map ref. 627 J7 | 629 F8

i Tamar Visitor Centre, Main Rd, Exeter; (03) 6394 4454 or 1800 637 989; www.tamarvalley.com.au

91.7 FM ABC Local Radio, 95.3 Tamar FM

Exeter is a small community in Tasmania's north-east, best known for its scenic surroundings. It lies just north of Launceston, in the centre of Tamar Valley wine country, which, along with cold-climate wines, has a variety of orchards.

John Temple Gallery: beautiful, framed Tasmanian photographs.

Show: Feb.

Koukla's: home-style Greek; 285 Gravelly Beach Rd, Gravelly Beach; (03) 6394 4013.

Brady's Lookout This scenic lookout was once the hideout of bushranger Matthew Brady, who used the high vantage point to find prospective victims on the road below. Today the site is more reputable, but retains its magnificent view of the Tamar Valley and is an ideal picnic spot. 5 km SE.

Glengarry Bush Maze: excellent family venue with maze and cafe; closed in winter, except Wed; Jay Dee Rd, Glengarry; 8 km SW. *Paper Beach:* 5 km return walking track to Supply River, where there are ruins of the first water-driven flour mill in Tasmania; 9 km E. *Artisan Gallery and Wine Centre:* displays and sales of Tasmanian arts, crafts and wines from smaller, independent vineyards in the area; Robigana; 10 km N. *Tamar Valley Resort at Grindelwald:* resort in Swiss architectural style with Swiss bakery, chocolatier, crafts, souvenirs and a world-class minigolf course; 10 km SE. *Notley Fern Gorge:* 11 ha wildlife and rainforest sanctuary with giant man-ferns and moss-covered forest. A 2 hr return walk leads to Gowans Creek; Notley Hills; 11 km SW. *Tasmanian Wine Route:* a string of wineries with cellar-door tastings and sales runs on either side of the Tamar, north and south of town. Closest to Exeter are wineries around Rosevears, 10 km S; brochure available from visitor centre.

TOWNS NEARBY: Beaconsfield 15 km, Beauty Point 19 km, Launceston 22 km, Lilydale 23 km, George Town 24 km

Fingal

Pop. 340
Map ref. 627 N9

i Old Tasmanian Hotel Community Centre, Main Rd; (03) 6374 2344.

100.3 Star FM, 1161 AM ABC Local Radio

Poet James McAuley wrote of Fingal's 'blonding summer grasses', 'mauve thistledown' and the river that 'winds in silence through wide blue hours, days'. Indeed, the crags of Ben Lomond National Park and the lush valley make Fingal a quiet inspiration for many writers. The town was established in 1827 as a convict station and distinguished itself by becoming the headquarters of the state's coal industry. Just north of Fingal, at Mangana, Tasmania's first payable gold was discovered in 1852.

Historic buildings There are many heritage buildings throughout the township, particularly in Talbot St, including the Holder Brothers General Store (1859), St Peter's Church (1867) and Fingal Hotel (1840s), which claims to stock the largest collection of Scotch whiskies in the Southern Hemisphere.

Fingal Valley Festival: incorporates the World Coal Shovelling Championships and Roof Bolting Championships; Mar.

Evercreech Forest Reserve This reserve is home to the impressive White Knights, the tallest white gums in the world, including a specimen 89 m high. A 20 min circuit walk passes through a man-fern grove and blackwoods, then up a hill for a superb view. There is also a 45 min return walk to Evercreech Falls, and many picnic and barbecue spots. Contact Forestry Tasmania on 1800 367 378; on the road to Mathinna; 30 km N.

Avoca: small township with many historical buildings; 27 km SW. *Mathinna Falls:* magnificent 4-tier waterfall over a drop of 80 m, with an easy 30 min return walk to falls base; 36 km N. *Ben Lomond National Park: see Evandale; 72 km NW.*

TOWNS NEARBY: St Marys 19 km, Bicheno 38 km, St Helens 42 km, Campbell Town 51 km, Swansea 55 km

Flinders Island

see Whitemark

Geeveston

Pop. 761
Map ref. 622 F8 | 625 I9

 Forest and Heritage Centre, Church St; (03) 6297 1836; www.forestandheritagecentre.com

95.3 Huon FM, 936 AM ABC Local Radio

Geeveston, on the cusp of enormous Southwest National Park, is driven by thriving timber and forestry industries, and slow-moving timber trucks frequent the roads. Swamp Gum, the trunk of a logged eucalypt 15.8 metres in length and weighing 57 tonnes, stands on the highway as the town's mascot. The other principal industry, apple farming, is responsible for the magnificent apple blossom in late September.

Forest and Heritage Centre Comprising 4 different sections, including the Forest Room and Hartz Gallery, the centre offers a comprehensive look at forest practices with computer games, timber species exhibits and a woodturning viewing area. Church St; (03) 6297 1836.

Southern Design Centre Tasmanian timber furniture is lovingly crafted on-site here. Watch resident artisans demonstrate skills in various mediums and browse the showrooms for art and craft, exquisite giftware and home furnishings. 11 School Rd.

Geeveston Highlands Salmon and Trout Fishery: world's first catch-and-release Atlantic salmon fishery with a 1.6 ha salmon lake and 0.4 ha trout lake. Fly-fishing tuition available; bookings on (03) 6297 0030; 172 Kermandie Rd. *Bears Went Over the Mountain:* sales of teddy bears and assorted antiques; 2 Church St.

Tasmanian Forest Festival: biennial event in Mar.

Cambridge House: Cnr Huon Hwy and School Rd; (03) 6297 1561.

 Hartz Mountains National Park The Huon Valley used to be wholly glaciated and this national park displays some remarkable glacial features and morainal deposits. Lake Hartz is the largest of the glacial lakes that surround the 1255 m high Hartz Mountain. There are walking tracks through forests of Tasmanian waratah, snow gums, yellow gum and alpine heath, and Waratah Lookout affords fantastic views. Self-guide brochure and park pass are available from the visitor centre. Off Arve Rd; 23 km SW.

Tahune Forest AirWalk Opened in 2001, this is the longest and highest forest canopy walk in the world. It stretches 597 m through the treetops of the Tahune Forest Reserve and, at its highest point, is 48 m above the forest floor. It provides a bird's-eye view of wet eucalypt forest and the Huon and Picton rivers. Within the forest, visitors can go fishing, rafting and camping. Tickets from visitor centre; 28 km W.

Arve Forest Drive: scenic drive following the Arve River Valley that takes in the Look-In Lookout (an information booth and lookout perch), the Big Tree Lookout (remarkable, large swamp gum), picnic areas and the Keoghs Creek Walk (a great short streamside walk); 10 km W. *Southwest National Park:* Tasmania's largest national park offers walking tracks of varying difficulty, beautiful scenic drives and plentiful fishing. Contact Parks &

 TASMANIA

Wildlife Service in Huonville for up-to-date information on track and weather conditions; (03) 6264 8460; 60 km s.

TOWNS NEARBY: Cygnet 12 km, Huonville 18 km, Dover 18 km, Kettering 26 km, Hastings 28 km

George Town

Pop. 4265
Map ref. 627 J6 | 629 E6

 i Cnr Victoria St and Main Rd; (03) 6382 1700; www.georgetown.tas.gov.au

📻 91.7 FM ABC Local Radio, 95.3 Tamar FM

George Town is Australia's third oldest settlement, after Sydney and Hobart, and Tasmania's oldest town. European settlement can be traced back to 1804 when William Paterson camped here after running his ship, HMS *Buffalo*, aground at York Cove. Ignoring the disaster, he ran up the flag, fired three shots in the air and played the national anthem. A memorial stands at Windmill Point to honour this optimism.

🏠 *The Grove:* this classic Georgian stone house (c. 1838) was the home of Mathew Friend, the port officer and magistrate of the settlement; 25 Cimitiere St. *York Cove:* scenic cove where George Town's centre was built, with mooring and pontoon facilities, and restaurants. *Self-guide Discovery Trail:* walking route through town; brochure from visitor centre. *George Town Watch House:* community history room and female factory display; Macquarie St.

🌴 *Tamar Valley Folk Festival:* Jan.

🍴 *Cove Restaurant:* Mediterranean-influenced modern Tasmanian; Peppers York Cove, 2 Ferry Blvd; (03) 6382 9990. *The Pier Hotel Bistro:* chic bistro with pizza; 5 Elizabeth St; (03) 6382 1300.

🛏 *Nannas Cottage at The Grove:* 25 Cimitiere St; (03) 6382 1336. *Low Head Tourist Park:* 136 Low Head Rd, Low Head; (03) 6382 1573.

⊗ **Low Head** This popular holiday retreat has safe swimming and surf beaches. The Maritime Museum is housed in Australia's oldest continuously used pilot station and has fascinating displays of memorabilia discovered in nearby shipwrecks. At the Tamar River's entrance stands a 12 m high lighthouse, built in 1888, behind which lies a little penguin colony. Penguin-watching tours start around sunset; bookings on 0418 361 860; 5 km N.

Mt George Lookout: scenic views of George Town, the north coast, and south to the Western Tiers. The lookout has a replica of a Tamar Valley semaphore mast used to relay messages in the 1800s; 1 km E. *Fishing:* excellent fishing at Lake Lauriston and Curries River Dam; 13 km E. *Lefroy:* old goldmining settlement, now a ghost town, with ruins of old buildings; 16 km E. *Hillwood Strawberry Farm:* sales and pick-your-own patch, along with sampling of local fruit wines and cheeses; 24 km SE. *Seal tours:* cruises to Tenth Island fur seal colony, a short distance offshore in Bass Strait; bookings on (03) 6382 3452. *Tasmanian Wine Route:* many wineries to the east of town with cellar-door sales and tastings; brochure from visitor centre. *Beaches:* the area has many beautiful beaches including East Beach (facing Bass Strait and ideal for walking, swimming and surfing) and Lagoon Beach on the Tamar River (for family swimming).

TOWNS NEARBY: Beauty Point 6 km, Beaconsfield 11 km, Port Sorell 24 km, Exeter 24 km, Lilydale 37 km

Gladstone

Pop. 42
Map ref. 627 O5

i Gladstone Hotel, 37 Chaffey St; (03) 6357 2143.

📻 91.7 FM ABC Local Radio, 93.7 Star FM

The north-eastern district surrounding Gladstone was once a thriving mining area, yielding both tin and gold. Today many of the once-substantial townships nearby are ghost towns. Gladstone has survived, but its successful mining days have long since given way to tourism. It acts as a tiny service centre for surrounding dairy, sheep and cattle farms, as well as for visitors to Mount William National Park, and has the distinction of being Tasmania's most north-easterly town.

🏠 *Gladstone cemetery:* A historic reminder of the miners, including many Chinese, who were drawn to the area; Carr St.

⊗ **Mt William National Park** This fairly remote park, created in 1973, protects Tasmania's forester kangaroo and many bird species. The view takes in the sandy beaches and coastal heath of the state's north-east corner and extends north to the Furneaux Islands and south to St Marys. With rolling hills, rugged headlands and pristine beaches this park offers swimming, fishing, diving and bushwalking. Georges Rocks and Eddystone Pt are favoured diving spots, while Ansons Bay is well known for bream and Australian bass fishing. Walks vary in difficulty and are signposted. At Eddystone Pt, at the southern end of the park, stands a historic, pink-granite lighthouse. Contact Parks & Wildlife Service on 1300 135 513; 25 km E.

Bay of Fires Walk This 4-day guided walk takes in the best of Mt William National Park while offering first-class accommodation and catering. The highlight (along with the scenery) is kayaking in Ansons Bay and, of course, bedding down for the night in the architecturally superb Bay of Fires Lodge, surrounded by bush. (03) 6391 9339.

Blue Lake: disused tin mine filled with brilliant blue water (coloured by pyrites) and safe for swimming and waterskiing; South Mt Cameron; 8 km s. *Cube Rock:* large granite monolith on an outcrop, reached by 3 hr return climb; South Mt Cameron; 8 km s. *Beaches:* magnificent beaches to the north, including Petal Pt; 25 km N. *Geological formations:* impressive granite formations between Gladstone and South Mt Cameron. *Gem fossicking:* smoky quartz, topaz and amethyst can be found in the district; contact visitor centre for details.

TOWNS NEARBY: Derby 27 km, St Helens 45 km, Scottsdale 47 km, Bridport 52 km, St Marys 70 km

Hadspen

Pop. 1929
Map ref. 627 K8 | 629 G10

i Launceston Travel and Information Centre, Cornwall Square Transit Centre, 12–16 St John St, Launceston; (03) 6336 3133 or 1800 651 827; www.ltvtasmania.com.au

📻 93.7 FM ABC Local Radio, 103.7 FM City Park Radio

Hadspen's best-known resident, Thomas Reibey III, became premier of Tasmania after being fired as archdeacon of Launceston's Church of England. Reibey was prepared to fund construction of Hadspen's Church of the Good Shepherd, but withdrew his offer after a dispute with the bishop, who allegedly discovered Reibey's unorthodox sexual preferences and refused the 'tainted' money. As a result, the church only reached completion in 1961, more than 100 years later.

Historic buildings: Hadspen's Main Rd is lined with heritage buildings, including the Red Feather Inn (c. 1844) and Hadspen Gaol (c. 1840).

Carrick Inn: traditional pub fare; 46 Meander Valley Hwy, Carrick; (03) 6393 6143. *Rutherglen Cafe:* family dining; Rutherglen Holiday Village, Meander Valley Rd; (03) 6393 6442.

Discovery Holiday Parks – Hadspen: Cnr Main St and Meander Valley Hwy; (03) 6393 7142.

Entally House Thomas Reibey's original abode, built in 1819, is one of the most impressive heritage homes in the state. Entally has sprawling gardens (maintained by Parks & Wildlife Service), Regency furniture and other antiques, as well as a stunning riverside location on the South Esk River. 1 km w.

Carrick: neighbouring town with historical buildings. It hosts Agfest, one of Australia's biggest agricultural field days, in May; 10 km sw. *Tasmanian Copper Gallery:* sales and exhibitions of original copper artworks; 1 Church St, Carrick; 10 km sw.

TOWNS NEARBY: Launceston 9 km, Longford 12 km, Evandale 16 km, Westbury 19 km, Exeter 25 km

Hamilton

Pop. 300
Map ref. 622 F1 | 625 I5

Council offices, Tarleton St; (03) 6286 3202.

97.1 Mid FM, 936 AM ABC Local Radio

Hamilton, an unspoilt National Trust–classified town, has avoided the commercialisation found in some parts of the state. Its buildings and tranquil lifestyle just outside Hobart conjure up an image of 1830s Tasmania.

Hamilton Sheep Centre Demonstrates sheepshearing methods and the use of working farm dogs. Farm tours can be arranged, with meals provided. Bookings on (03) 6286 3332.

Glen Clyde House: convict-built c. 1840, this place now houses an award-winning craft gallery and tearooms; Grace St. *Hamilton Heritage Museum:* small museum with artefacts and memorabilia of the area; Old Warder's Cottage, Cumberland St. *Jackson's Emporium:* sells local products and wines; Lyell Hwy. *Heritage buildings:* many buildings of historical importance include the Old Schoolhouse (1856) and St Peter's Church (1837), which is notable for having just 1 door to prevent the once largely convict congregation from escaping.

The Highlander Arms: hearty pub-style meals; Tarraleah Estate, Oldina Dr, Tarraleah; (03) 6289 0111.

Hamlet Downs Country Accommodation: 50 Gully Rd, Fentonbury; (03) 6288 1212.

Lake Meadowbank: popular venue for picnics, boating, waterskiing and trout fishing; 10 km NW.

TOWNS NEARBY: Bothwell 24 km, New Norfolk 31 km, Pontville 38 km, Oatlands 52 km, Richmond 53 km

Hastings

Pop. 35
Map ref. 622 F11 | 625 I10

Hastings Caves and Thermal Springs Centre, Hastings Cave Rd; (03) 6298 3209.

95.3 Huon FM, 936 AM ABC Local Radio

Hastings lies in Tasmania's far south and is known for the stunning dolomite caves to the west of town. The caves were discovered in 1917 by a group of timber workers who, among others, flocked to the small town in more prosperous days.

Southport Hotel Bar & Restaurant: Australia's southernmost counter meals; 8777 Huon Hwy, Southport; (03) 6298 3144.

Southport Hotel & Caravan Park: 8777 Huon Hwy, Southport; (03) 6298 3144.

Hastings Caves and Thermal Springs This is the only cave system in Tasmania occurring in dolomite rather than limestone. Newdegate Cave, which began forming more than 40 million years ago, has stalactites, stalagmites, columns, shawls, flowstone and the more unusual helictites (distorted stalactites), making it – and especially Titania's Palace within it – one of Australia's most beautiful caves. There are 245 steps leading to its vast chambers of formations. Tours run throughout the day. Near Newdegate Cave is a thermal pool surrounded by native bushland. It remains at 28°C year-round and is an extremely popular swimming and picnic spot. The Sensory Trail, an easy walk through magnificent forest, starts near the pool. 8 km NW.

Ida Bay Railway: originally built to carry dolomite, the train now carries passengers to Deep Hole Bay along a scenic section of track. Train times change, so ring for details (03) 6298 3110; Lune River Rd; 5 km s. *Lunaris:* gemstone display and shop; Lune River Rd; 5 km s. *Southport:* seaside resort town and one of the oldest settlements in the area; good fishing, swimming, surfing and bushwalking; 6 km SE. *Cockle Creek:* the southernmost point of Australia that can be reached by car, the town is surrounded by beautiful beaches and mountainous terrain and is the start of the 10-day South Coast walking track; 25 km s. *Hastings Forest Tour:* this self-drive tour begins off Hastings Rd west of town, leads north to the Esperance River, then heads to Dover. Short walks and picnic spots en route; map available from visitor centre.

TOWNS NEARBY: Dover 13 km, Geeveston 28 km, Cygnet 31 km, Adventure Bay 33 km, Kettering 41 km

Huonville

Pop. 1814
Map ref. 622 G7 | 625 J8

Huon River Jet Boats and Visitor Centre; The Esplanade; (03) 6264 1838; www.huonjet.com

98.5 Huon FM, 936 AM ABC Local Radio

Huonville produces more than half of Tasmania's apples and is surrounded by blossoming fields of apples, cherries, plums, pears, berries and hops. Although relatively small, it is a prosperous community and the largest town in the Huon Valley.

Apple and Heritage Centre This centre houses 3 attractions: the museum, providing a comprehensive insight into the lives of Huon Valley's early settlers; Apple Blossom's Gifts, with a selection of gifts, souvenirs and samples of local products; and The Starving Artist, an art gallery and heritage apple orchard. 2064 Huon Hwy; (03) 6266 4345.

Huon River Jet Boats: exciting 35 min jet-boat rides along Huon River rapids; river cruises also on offer, and aqua-bikes and pedal boats for hire; bookings on (03) 6264 1838; The Esplanade.

Market: Websters Car Park, Cool Store Rd; 10am–2pm, 2nd and 4th Sun each month. *A Taste of the Huon:* festival venue

[HUONVILLE] ABUNDANT APPLE ORCHARD

changes towns yearly; check visitor centre for details; Mar. **Huon Agricultural Show:** biggest 1-day agricultural show in state; Nov.

Boat House Cafe: fish and chips on the river; The Esplanade; (03) 6264 1133. **Huon Manor:** classy seafood; 2–4 Short St; (03) 6264 1311. **Franklin Aqua Grill:** seafood and crepes; 3419 Huon Hwy, Franklin; (03) 6266 3368. **Home Hill Winery Restaurant:** dramatic award-winning vineyard restaurant; 38 Nairn St, Ranelagh; (03) 6264 1200. **Petty Sessions:** exciting Tasmanian fare; 3445 Huon Hwy, Franklin; (03) 6266 3488.

Huonville Guesthouse: 184 Main Rd; (03) 6264 1615. **Walton House B&B:** 2720 Huon Hwy; (03) 6264 1640. **Crabtree House and River Cottages:** 130 Crabtree Rd, Grove; 0429 626 640.

Ranelagh Almost an outer suburb of Huonville, Ranelagh has the atmosphere of a charming English village, complete with an old oast house to process the hops. 5 km NW.

Wooden Boat Centre – Tasmania: workshop and interpretive centre; Main St, Franklin; 8 km SW. **Glen Huon Model Village:** features doll and rock display including the 'crooked man'; open Sept–May; Glen Huon; 8 km W. **Studio Karma:** studio, gallery and home of Terry Choi-Lundberg; original paintings, quality cards and prints of the artist's work; open 10am–4pm Thurs–Sun, by appt May–Sept; Glen Huon; 8 km W. **Pelverata Falls:** stunning waterfall with medium-to-difficult walk over scree slope; 14 km SE. **Huon Bushventures:** 4WD tours of the region; bookings on (03) 6264 1838. **Fishing:** good trout fishing in Huon River and tributaries.

TOWNS NEARBY: Cygnet 14 km, Geeveston 18 km, Kettering 20 km, Kingston 22 km, New Norfolk 28 km

Kettering

Pop. 389
Map ref. 622 H8 | 625 K8

ⓘ Bruny D'Entrecasteaux Visitor Centre, 81 Ferry Rd; (03) 6267 4494; www.tasmaniaholiday.com

📻 95.3 Huon FM, 936 AM ABC Local Radio

The area around Kettering, in the state's south-east, was first explored in 1792 by Bruni D'Entrecasteaux, after whom the surrounding channel is named. The town was settled in the 1800s by timber cutters, sealers and whalers, and the community was a transient one. Kettering is now principally the launching point to Bruny Island, but is charming in its own right with a sheltered harbour full of yachts and fishing vessels.

Oyster Cove Marina: well-known marina with boats for hire, skippered cruises and fishing charters; Ferry Rd. **Ocean-kayaking:** guided day tours with Roaring 40s Ocean Kayaking company; bookings on (03) 6267 5000. **Herons Rise Vineyard:** picturesque vineyard specialising in cool-climate white and pinot noir wines; sales; 120 Saddle Rd.

Fleurtys Cafe: uniquely Tasmanian gourmet meals; 3866 Channel Hwy, Birchs Bay; (03) 6267 4078. **Mermaid Cafe:** a Tasmanian twist on traditional cafe fare; 79 Ferry Rd, (03) 6267 4494. **Peppermint Bay Dining Room:** top Tasmanian gourmet food; 3435 Channel Hwy, Woodbridge; (03) 6267 4088. **Snug Tavern:** generous serves of counter-meal fare; 2236 Channel Hwy, Snug; (03) 6267 9238.

Oyster Cove Chalet: 42 Manuka Rd, Oyster Cove; (03) 6267 5084. **Snug Beach Cabin & Caravan Park:** 35 Beach Rd, Snug; (03) 6267 9138.

Peppermint Bay This is one of Tasmania's top gastronomic experiences, with a first-class restaurant and a store full of local products. There is also an arts and crafts gallery and fine views across the waterfront. The Peppermint Bay Cruise, departing from Hobart and touring the D'Entrecasteaux Channel along the way, is another way to visit this spectacular location; bookings on 1800 751 229. 3435 Channel Hwy, Woodbridge; 5 km S.

Woodbridge Hill Handweaving Studio: weaving tuition and sales of products woven from silk, cotton, linen, wool, alpaca, mohair and collie-dog hair; Woodbridge Hill Rd; 4 km S. **Channel Historical and Folk Museum:** displays of historical memorabilia of the D'Entrecasteaux Channel region; closed Wed; 2361 Channel Hwy, Lower Snug; 5 km N. **Conningham:** good swimming and boating beaches; 6 km N. **Snug Falls:** pleasant

1.5 hr return walk to falls; 8 km N. *Grandvewe Sheep Cheesery:* 15 different types of cheese at Tasmania's only sheep cheesery; Birchs Bay; 9 km s. *Bruny Island ferry:* trips throughout the day from Ferry Rd Terminal; for information on the island, *see Adventure Bay.*

TOWNS NEARBY: Cygnet 14 km, Kingston 18 km, Huonville 20 km, Geeveston 26 km, Adventure Bay 26 km

King Island
see Currie

Kingston
Pop. 31 500
Map ref. 623 I6 | 625 K8

 Council offices, Civic Centre, 15 Channel Hwy; (03) 6211 8200; www.kingborough.tas.gov.au

 92.1 Hobart FM, 936 AM ABC Local Radio

Almost an outer suburb of Hobart, this pleasant seaside town sits just beyond the city limits. Its literary claim to fame is that Nobel Laureate Patrick White holidayed at Kingston Beach as a child.

Australian Antarctic Division Headquarters The display area houses imagery, historical items and information about Australia's science program and operations in Antarctica; 203 Channel Hwy; (03) 6232 3209.

Rotary Club Sunday Market: library carpark; Sun. *Community Market:* bric-a-brac and crafts at Brookfield, Margate; Wed. *Day on the Beach:* a celebration of Australian culture on Australia Day; Jan. *Summer Survival:* sports carnival on the beach; Feb. *Oliebollen Festival:* Dutch food and more, cnr Sophia St and Maranoa Rd; Oct. *King of the Beach:* fancy dress beach volleyball; Dec.

Beachfront 32: bistro and takeaway; 32 Osbourne Espl; (03) 6229 4891. *Citrus Moon Cafe:* wholefoods cafe; 23 Beach Rd; (03) 6229 2388. *The Beach:* popular beachside bistro; 14 Ocean Espl, Blackmans Bay; (03) 6229 7600.

Channel View B&B: 24 Rays Crt; 0410 459 350.

Shot Tower One of the state's most historic industrial buildings (with a National Trust 'A' classification), completed in 1870. There are wonderful views of the Derwent Estuary from the top of the 66 m structure and a museum and a craft shop at the base; open daily; 318 Channel Hwy, Taroona; (03) 6227 8885; 4 km NE.

Kingston Beach: popular, family-friendly beach with plenty of shade and nice cafes nearby; 3 km SE. *Kingston Beach Golf Course:* well-regarded 18-hole course with specific holes picked by international players as their favourites; 1 Channel Hwy; (03) 6229 8300; *Boronia Hill Flora Trail:* 2 km track follows ridge line between Kingston and Blackmans Bay through remnant bush; begins at end of Jindabyne Rd and finishes at Peter Murrell Reserve, renowned for its many native orchids; Kingston. *Blackmans Bay blowhole:* small blowhole at the northern end of the beach that is spectacular in stormy weather; Blowhole Rd; 7 km s. *Alum Cliffs walk:* excellent scenic 45 min return walk from Browns River area along the coastal cliffs to Taroona. *Margate Train:* 1950s passenger train (non-operational) with tearooms in the buffet car, and collectibles, lollies and book shops in other carriages. Sun market; 1567 Channel Hwy, Margate;

9 km s. *Tinderbox Marine Reserve:* follow the underwater snorkel trail; Tinderbox; 11 km s. *Scenic drives:* south through Blackmans Bay, Tinderbox and Howden, with magnificent views of Droughty Pt, South Arm Peninsula, Storm Bay and Bruny Island from Piersons Pt. *Fishing:* good bream fishing at Browns River, for sport but not for the pan. *Horseriding:* lessons and trail rides at Cheval Equitation; bookings on (03) 6229 4303.

TOWNS NEARBY: Kettering 18 km, Huonville 22 km, Cygnet 27 km, Richmond 29 km, New Norfolk 29 km

Latrobe
Pop. 2846
Map ref. 626 H6 | 628 H2 | 629 B7

 48 Gilbert St; (03) 6421 4699; www.latrobetasmania.com.au

 100.5 FM ABC Local Radio, 104.7 Coast FM

Latrobe was once Tasmania's third largest settlement with inns, hotels, a hospital and no less than three newspapers in circulation. As it was the best place to cross the Mersey River, it became the highest-profile town on the north coast. Since the early 19th century, however, Latrobe has ceded its importance as a port town and relaxed into a gentler pace.

Australian Axeman's Hall of Fame This attraction honours the region's renowned axemen and details the role of the town in the creation of woodchop competition. Also featured at the facility is the Platypus and Trout Experience, including an interactive display of Tasmanian wildlife heritage. There is also a cafe and giftshop selling local crafts and souvenirs. 1 Bells Pde.

Platypus tours: with a LandCare guide; check at visitor centre for departure times and cost; bookings on (03) 6426 1774. *Court House Museum:* located in a heritage building under the National Trust register with over 600 prints and photographs; open 1–4pm Tues–Fri, other times by appt; Gilbert St; (03) 6426 2777. *Sherwood Hall Museum:* original home of pioneering couple Thomas Johnson and Dolly Dalrymple; open 10am–4pm daily Oct–Mar, Tues and Thurs or by appt in other months; Bells Parade. *Anvers Confectionery:* factory of well-known Belgian chocolatier, this outlet has tastings and sales of premium chocolates, fudges and pralines; 9025 Bass Hwy. *Sheean Memorial Walk:* 3 km return walk commemorating local soldiers and WW II hero; Gilbert St. *Bells Parade Reserve:* beautiful picnic ground along riverbank where town's docks were once located; River Rd. *Historical walk:* starts at western end of Gilbert St and turns into Hamilton St.

Markets: Gilbert St; 7am–2pm Sun. *Henley-on-the-Mersey regatta:* Jan. *Chocolate Winterfest:* July. *Latrobe Wheel Race:* prestige cycling event; Dec. *Latrobe Gift footrace:* Dec.

House of Anvers: European cafe and chocolatier; 9025 Bass Hwy; (03) 6426 2703. *Lucas Hotel:* excellent bistro meals; 46 Gilbert St; (03) 6426 1101.

Sherwood View Accommodation: 298 Coalhill Rd; (03) 6426 2797.

Warrawee Forest Reserve An excellent place for platypus viewing, swimming, bushwalking and barbecues. A 5 km walking track winds through sclerophyll forest and a boardwalk has been installed around the lake to allow disabled access to trout fishing. Tours are run by LandCare; bookings on (03) 6426 2877; 3 km s.

continued on p. 485

 RADIO STATIONS   IN TOWN   WHAT'S ON   WHERE TO EAT   WHERE TO STAY   NEARBY

TASMANIA

LAUNCESTON

Pop. 99 676

Map ref. 627 K8 | 629 F1

ⓘ Cornwall Square Transit Centre, 12-16 St John St; (03) 6336 3133 or 1800 651 827; www.visitlauncestontamar.com.au

🔲 91.7 FM ABC Local Radio, 103.7 FM City Park Radio

Tasmania's second-largest city and a busy tourist centre, Launceston lies nestled in northern hilly country where the Tamar, North Esk and South Esk rivers meet. An elegantly laid-back place, Launceston has the highest concentration of 19th-century buildings in Australia. Yet it is also a city of contrasts, where modern marinas meet graceful Georgian and Victorian streetscapes and parks – and you're seldom without a view of the Tamar River or surrounding valley.

🏛 **Cataract Gorge** This spectacular gorge is one of Launceston's outstanding natural attractions, and at night it's lit in spectacular fashion. Historic Kings Bridge spans the Tamar River at the entrance to the gorge. Above the cliffs on the north side of the gorge is an elegant Victorian park with lawns, European trees, peacocks and a restaurant. The world's longest single-span chairlift and a suspension bridge link this area to first basin lawns on the south side, which has a swimming pool and a kiosk. Walks and self-guide nature trails run on both sides of the gorge.

Queen Victoria Museum and Art Gallery This is considered one of the best regional museums in Australia, with permanent exhibits on Aboriginal and convict history, Tasmanian flora and fauna, and many temporary exhibitions. It is also home to Australia's newest and most exciting interactive science centre, Phenomena Factory – a free, hands-on science education centre for kids of all ages. Nearby, Launceston Tramway Museum pays homage to Launceston's early tramway system. Other features include a strong collection of colonial art, a Chinese joss house, a blacksmith shop and the Launceston Planetarium. Located at 2 venues – Wellington St and Invermay Rd. (03) 6323 3777.

Boag's Brewery J Boag and Son Brewery, where James Boag commenced his brewing tradition on the banks of the Esk River in 1852. Tours include a full circuit of the brewery from the brewhouse to the packaging line and start and finish at the 'Boag's Centre for Beer Lovers'. The centre houses a museum and a retail store where merchandise is available to purchase. Tours Mon–Fri; tasting class Sat; William St; (03) 6332 6300.

City Park: magnificent 5 ha park with European deciduous trees, it features a Japanese Macaque monkey enclosure, the John Hart conservatory, annual display beds, senses garden, and monuments; Cnr Tamar and Brisbane sts. *Seaport:* new riverside complex with restaurants, shops, marina and hotel at the head of the Tamar River. *Design Centre of Tasmania:* houses Australia's only museum collection of contemporary wood design, the Design Centre runs national and international exhibitions and tours of crafts, design and art; City Park. *National Automobile Museum of Tasmania:* displays over 40 fully restored classic vehicles spanning a hundred years of style and technical achievement; Cimitiere St. *Ritchies Mill & Stillwater River Cafe & Restaurant:* a 4-storey grain mill from the 1800s, now home to one of Launceston's most renowned

[BOAG'S CENTRE FOR BEER LOVERS]

restaurants. The award-winning Stillwater restaurant opened on the ground floor of the Mill in 2000, while The Mill Providore & Gallery is located on the first and second floor of the mill, showcasing local Tasmanian produce, art and design; Paterson St. *Aurora Stadium:* the home of AFL football in Tasmania, the stadium hosts 5 rostered matches per year and a variety of other sporting and recreation events. *Walking tour:* self-guide tour takes in 25 places of historical importance in central Launceston including Morton House, Milton Hall and Princes Sq, where the fountain was changed from a half-naked nymph to a pineapple after locals objected; brochure from visitor centre. *Waverley Woollen Mills Factory Outlet Shop:* woollen products from Australia's oldest mill, with tours and showroom; open 10am–4pm Mon–Fri; 58 George St. *Old Umbrella Shop:* unique 1860s shop preserved by the National Trust and housing a giftshop and information centre; George St. *Cocobean Chocolate:* a chocolate boutique for connoisseurs of handcrafted chocolates, drinks and desserts; open Mon–Fri, 9.30am–2pm Sat, 82 George St; (03) 6331 7016. *Scenic flights:* HeliAdventures Tasmania in Launceston; bookings on (03) 6334 0444.

🎆 *Launceston Cup:* state's biggest race day; Feb. *Festivale:* food and wine; Feb. *MS Fest:* major youth music festival; Feb. *Targa Tasmania:* tarmac road rally; Apr–May. *National Trust Tasmanian Heritage Festival:* Apr. *Agfest:* Tasmnania's largest agricultural show; May. *Royal Launceston Show:* Oct. *Tamar Valley Classic:* yacht race; Nov.

🍴 *Black Cow Bistro:* beef connoisseur's heaven; Cnr George and Paterson sts; (03) 6331 9333. *Calabrisella:* traditional Italian; 56 Wellington St; (03) 6331 1958. *Flip:* creative burgers; Cnr York and Bathurst sts; (03) 6334 6844. *Smokey Joe's Creole Cafe:* Caribbean and Cajun Creole; 20 Lawrence St; (03) 6331 0530. *Stillwater River Cafe & Restaurant:* fine Asian-inspired dining: Ritchies Mill, 2 Bridge Rd; (03) 6331 4153.

🛏 *Fiona's Bed and Breakfast:* 141A George St; (03) 6334 5965. *Hillview House:* 193 George St; (03) 6331 7388. *Kilmarnock House:* 66 Elphin Rd; (03) 6334 1514.

Waratah on York: 12 York St; (03) 6331 2081. *Werona Bed & Breakfast:* 33 Trevallyn Rd; (03) 6334 2272. *Launceston Holiday Park Legana:* 711 West Tamar Hwy, Legana; (03) 6330 1714. *Quality Inn Heritage Edenholme Grange:* 14 St Andrews St, West Launceston; (03) 6334 6666. *The River House:* 39 Rostella Rd, Dilston; (03) 6328 1319. *Treasure Island Caravan Park:* 94 Glen Dhu St, South Launceston; (03) 6344 2600. *Trevallyn House B&B:* 83A Riverside Dr, Riverside; (03) 6327 3771.

Tamar Valley wine region With around 30 wineries in the area, Pipers Brook Vineyard is one of the state's biggest names, and makes beautiful gewürztraminer and pinot noir. Its cellar also offers tastings of its Ninth Island Label and Kreglinger sparkling wines. Other wineries worth visiting include Bay of Fires and Tamar Ridge. For masterpieces in sparkling, visit Clover Hill, whose picturesque cellar door is perfect for a picnic lunch, and Jansz, with its modern, architectural wine room featuring an interpretive centre. Brochures are available from the visitor centre.

Franklin House A National Trust–listed Georgian building, Franklin House was built by convicts in 1838 for a Launceston brewer. It is furnished elaborately with period pieces and is a popular historical attraction. 6 km s.

Punchbowl Reserve: spectacular park with rhododendron plantation, a small gorge and native and European fauna in natural surroundings; 5 km sw. *Trevallyn State Reserve:* neighbour to the Cataract Gorge, good picnic spot with trail rides, kayaking, walking tracks and water activities at Trevallyn Dam; 6 km w. *Hollybank Treetops Adventure:* flying fox adventure park with a kilometre of cable strung between treetop 'cloud stations'; open daily; Hollybank Rd, Underwood. *Tamar Island Wetlands:* urban wetlands reserve; a haven for birdlife, with a 3 km boardwalk to Tamar Island, pleasing views from the middle of the river and an outstanding Interpretation Centre that offers visitors the opportunity to learn about the great value of the wetlands; 9 km NW. *Tasmania Zoo:* Tasmanian devils, emus, wallabies and other native fauna. Good fly-fishing in the lakes with tuition available; 17 km w. *Grindelwald:* Swiss village with chalet-themed Tamar Valley Resort and Swiss-style shopping square selling Swiss chocolates, cakes, crafts and souvenirs; 19 km NW.

TOWNS NEARBY: Hadspen 9 km, Evandale 17 km, Longford 19 km, Exeter 22 km, Lilydale 22 km

Henry Somerset Orchid Reserve: over 40 native orchids and other rare flora; Railton Rd; 7 km s.

TOWNS NEARBY: Devonport 9 km, Port Sorell 14 km, Sheffield 18 km, Ulverstone 21 km, Penguin 32 km

Lilydale

Pop. 292
Map ref. 627 K7 | 629 H8

ⓘ Launceston Travel and Information Centre, Cornwall Square Transit Centre, 12–16 St John St, Launceston; (03) 6336 3133 or 1800 651 827; www.ltvtasmania.com.au

📻 91.7 FM ABC Local Radio, 95.3 Tamar FM

Originally called Germantown, this small north-eastern township is better known for the 'English-style' of its gardens and the almost French quality of its countryside. Yet the bushwalks through surrounding reserves and waterfalls are distinctly Australian, with native temperate rainforests lining the trails.

Painted Poles: scattered throughout the village centre are 15 hydro poles painted by professional and community artists to show the local history.

Lilydale Tavern Bakery Cafe: pies and cakes; 1983 Main Rd; (03) 6395 1230. *Pipers Brook Winery Cafe:* acclaimed vineyard cafe; 1216 Pipers Brook Rd, Pipers Brook; (03) 6382 7527.

Lilydale Falls Situated within the temperate rainforest of Lilydale Park, the waterfall is at the end of a pleasant 5 min walk through ferns and eucalypts. A picnic area and playground are on-site, as well as 2 oak trees planted in 1937 from acorns picked near Windsor Castle in England to commemorate the coronation of King George VI. 3 km N.

Tamar Valley wine region: numerous vineyards between Lilydale and Pipers Brook include Providence (4 km N), Clover Hill (12 km N) and Brook Eden (15 km N); *see also Launceston and Bridport;* brochure from visitor centre. *Walker Rhododendron Reserve:* 12 ha park reputed to have the best rhododendron display in Australia. Other species are also on display; Lalla; 4 km w. *Appleshed:* teahouse with local art and craft; Lalla; 4 km w. *Hollybank Forest Reserve:* 140 ha forest reserve with Australia's first continuous cable treetop tour, arboretum, picnic facilities and information centre with details on walking tracks; marked turn-off near Underwood; 5 km s. *Mt Arthur:* 3 hr return scenic walk to summit (1187 m); 20 km SE. *Bridestowe Estate Lavender Farm:* this is one of the world's largest single commercial lavender farms; 296 Gillespies Rd, Nabowla; 26 km N.

TOWNS NEARBY: Launceston 22 km, Exeter 23 km, Scottsdale 27 km, Hadspen 30 km, Bridport 31 km

Longford

Pop. 3030
Map ref. 627 K9 | 629 G12

ⓘ JJ's Bakery at the Old Mill Cafe, 52 Wellington St; (03) 6391 2364.

📻 91.7 FM ABC Local Radio, 103.7 FM City Park Radio

Longford was established when numerous settlers from Norfolk Island were given land grants in the area in 1813. Fittingly, the district became known as Norfolk Plains, while the settlement itself was called Latour. Today Longford is classified as a historic town and serves the rich agricultural district just south of Launceston.

Historic buildings These include the Queen's Arms (1835) in Wellington St, Longford House (1839) in Catherine St and the Racecourse Hotel (1840s) in Wellington St, which was

TASMANIA

originally built as a railway station then used as a hospital and later a pub, and in which a patron was murdered after stealing and swallowing 2 gold sovereigns from local farmhands. The Racecourse Hotel is now a guesthouse and restaurant. Also on Wellington St is Christ Church, an 1839 sandstone building with outstanding stained-glass windows, pioneer gravestones and a clock and bell presented by George VI. Path of History is the self-guide walk; brochure available from visitor centre. *Walk:* track along the South Esk River. *The Village Green:* originally the site of the town market, now a picnic and barbecue spot; Cnr Wellington and Archer sts.

Longford Picnic Day Races: held at the oldest operating racecourse in Australia; Jan. *Blessing of the Harvest Festival:* celebration of the rural tradition with parade and Sheaf Tossing Championships; Mar.

JJs Bakery and Old Mill Cafe: historic bakery cafe; 52 Wellington St; (03) 6391 2364. *The Racecourse Inn Restaurant:* elegant modern Australian; 114 Marlborough St; (03) 6391 2352.

Longford Riverside Caravan Park: 2A Archer St; (03) 6391 1470. *The Racecourse Inn:* 114 Marlborough St; (03) 6391 2352.

Woolmers Estate Woolmers was built c. 1817 by the Archer family, who lived there for 6 generations. Tours of the house, the outbuildings, the gardens and the National Rose Garden are conducted daily and the Servants Kitchen restaurant serves morning and afternoon teas. Lyell Hwy; (03) 6286 3332; 5 km s.

Brickendon: historic Georgian homestead built in 1824, now a working farm and historic farm village; open Wed–Sun June–July, Tues–Sun Sept–May; 2 km s. *Perth:* small town with historic buildings, including Eskleigh and Jolly Farmer Inn, and market on Sun mornings; 5 km NE. *Tasmanian Honey Company:* tastings and sales of excellent range of honeys including leatherwood and flavoured varieties; 25A Main Rd, Perth; 5 km NE. *Woodstock Lagoon Wildlife Sanctuary:* 150 ha sanctuary for nesting waterfowl; 9 km w. *Cressy:* good fly-fishing at Brumby's Creek, especially in Nov when mayflies hatch; 10 km s.

TOWNS NEARBY: **Evandale 11 km, Hadspen 12 km, Launceston 19 km, Westbury 25 km, Exeter 37 km**

Miena

Pop. 104
Map ref. 625 I1 | 627 I11

Great Lake Hotel, Great Lake Hwy; (03) 6259 8163.

91.7 FM ABC Local Radio, 95.7 Heart FM

Miena is on the shores of Great Lake on Tasmania's Central Plateau and has been popular with anglers since brown trout were released into the lake in 1870. The Aboriginal name (pronounced 'my-enna') translates to 'lagoon-like'. The surrounding region, known as the Lake Country, can become very cold, with snow and road closures, even in summer.

Great Lake Hotel: fireside counter meals; 3096 Marlborough Hwy; (03) 6259 8163.

Fishing The 22 km Great Lake is the second largest freshwater lake in Australia and has excellent trout fishing. But Arthurs Lake, 23 km E, is said to be even better. The Highland Dun mayflies that hatch in summer generate an abundance of speckled brown trout, drawing fly-fishing enthusiasts. West of Liawenee (about 7 km N) are more locations for fly-fishing in

isolated lakes and tarns of the Central Plateau Conservation Area (4WD recommended for several lakes, while some are accessible only to experienced bushwalkers). Lakes are closed over winter.

Bushwalking: along the shores of Great Lake. *Circle of Life:* bronze sculptures by Steven Walker, each representing an aspect of the region's history; Steppes; 27 km SE. *Waddamana Power Museum:* housed in the first station built by the Hydro-Electric Corporation, it includes history of hydro-electricity in Tasmania; 33 km s. *Lake St Clair:* a boat service from Cynthia Bay provides access to the north of the lake and to the renowned 85 km Overland Track, which passes through Cradle Mountain–Lake St Clair National Park; *see Sheffield*; 63 km w.

TOWNS NEARBY: **Bothwell 51 km, Deloraine 51 km, Westbury 52 km, Longford 53 km, Mole Creek 54 km**

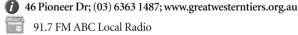

Mole Creek

Pop. 223
Map ref. 626 H8 | 628 H5 | 629 A11

46 Pioneer Dr; (03) 6363 1487; www.greatwesterntiers.org.au

91.7 FM ABC Local Radio

Mole Creek is named after the nearby creek that 'burrows' underground. Most visitors come to explore the limestone caves in Mole Creek Karst National Park. The unique honey from the leatherwood tree, which grows only in the west-coast rainforests of Tasmania, is also a drawcard. Each summer, apiarists transport hives to the nearby leatherwood forests.

Stephens Leatherwood Honey Factory At the home of Tasmania's unique aromatic honey, visitors can see clover and leatherwood honey being extracted and bottled. Tastings and sales are available. Open weekdays; 25 Pioneer Dr; (03) 6363 1170.

Mole Creek Tiger Bar: local hotel with information and memorabilia on the Tasmanian tiger; Pioneer Dr.

Mole Creek Cafe: local produce and flavours; Mole Creek Guest House, 100 Pioneer Dr; (03) 6363 1399.

Mole Creek Karst National Park Set in the forests of the Western Tiers, this national park protects the Marakoopa and King Solomons caves, spectacular caverns of calcite formations created by underground streams. Marakoopa Cave has a magnificent glow-worm display, while King Solomons Cave offers coloured stalagmites and stalactites and sparkling calcite crystals. Guided tours daily; details (03) 6363 5182; 13 km w.

Alum Cliffs Gorge: spectacular 30 min return walk; 3 km NE. *Trowunna Wildlife Park:* see Tasmanian devils and other native fauna; 4 km E. *The Honey Farm:* over 50 flavours of honey and an interactive bee display; open Sun–Fri; Chudleigh; 8 km E. *Devils Gullet State Reserve:* World Heritage area with natural lookout on a 600 m high cliff, reached by 30 min return walking track; 40 km SE. *Wild Cave Tours:* adventure tours to caves that are closed to the general public; bookings on (03) 6367 8142. *Cradle Wilderness Tours:* guided 4WD tours; bookings on (03) 6363 1173. *Walls of Jerusalem National Park:* the park is accessible on foot only, from the end of the road that turns off around 15 km w of Mole Creek and heads down to Lake Rowallan. With glacial lakes, pencil pines and dolerite peaks, it is a wonderland for self-sufficient and experienced bushwalkers.

TOWNS NEARBY: **Sheffield 20 km, Deloraine 21 km, Latrobe 36 km, Westbury 37 km, Devonport 42 km**

New Norfolk

Pop. 9000
Map ref. 622 G4 | 625 J6

i Derwent Valley Visitor Information Centre, Circle St; (03) 6261 3700; www.newnorfolk.org

📻 96.1 Hobart FM, 936 AM ABC Local Radio

This National Trust–classified town looks like a little piece of Kent in England, with colonial buildings, heritage gardens and a patchwork of riverside hop fields. Originally named for the European settlers from the abandoned Norfolk Island penal settlement who were granted land here, the district is still renowned for its hop growing, and now for its small fruits. The town is a must-see destination for antique and collectibles hunters, with a concentration of old wares and second-hand shops.

🏠 *Tynwald Willow Bend Estate:* surrounded by beautiful riverside gardens this charming 1830s mansion next to the historic Oast House offers wetland and garden walks, trout fishing, luxury accommodation and a fine-dining restaurant specialising in Tasmanian produce; 1 Tynwald Rd; (03) 6261 2667. *Old Colony Inn:* a heritage house which started life as hop cellar in 1815 now housing a folk museum, tearooms, craft shop and Australia's largest antique doll's house; 21 Montagu St; (03) 6261 2731. *Church of St Matthew:* reputedly the oldest church in Tasmania (1823). Behind the nativity scene on one of its striking stained-glass windows is the likeness of 9-year-old Nancy Hope Shoobridge, a local girl who died in 1890; Bathurst St. *Rosedown Cottage Gardens:* beautiful rose, daffodil and lilac gardens; open daily 10am–5pm, Oct–Dec; 135 Hamilton Rd; (03) 6261 2030. *Antique and collectibles outlets:* Tasmania's best collection of antique and collectibles shops, most within easy walking distance. See visitor centre for map. *Bush Inn Hotel:* longest continually licensed hotel in Tasmania; 49–51 Montagu St; (03) 6261 2256. *Jet-boat rides:* on River Derwent rapids; Tasmanian Devil Jet, The Esplanade; (03) 6261 3460. *River walk:* from Espl to Tynwald Park Wetlands Conservation Area. *Scenic lookouts:* breathtaking views from Peppermint Hill, off Blair St and Pulpit Rock, off Boyer Rd. *Self-guide historical walks:* brochure from visitor centre.

🎋 *Derwent Valley Autumn Festival:* celebrating Autumn with food, entertainment and family fun; The Esplanade; Apr.

🍴 *The Bush Inn:* generous pub meals; 49–51 Montagu St; (03) 6261 2256. *Patchwork Cafe:* cafe and quilting supplies; 15 George St; 0417 916 479. *Lachlan Food and Wine:* casual restaurant; 518 Lachlan Rd, Lachlan; (03) 6261 4545. *Possum Shed Cafe:* riverside cafe; 1654 Gordon River Rd, Westerway; (03) 6288 1364. *Tynwald:* fine Provençal food; 1 Tynwald Rd; (03) 6261 2667.

🛏 *All Saints and Sinners Colonial B&B:* 93 High St; (03) 6261 1877. *Explorers Lodge:* 105 Derwent Tce; (03) 6261 1255. *New Norfolk Caravan Park:* The Esplanade; (03) 6261 1268. *Maydena Country Cabins Accommodation & Roydon Alpaca Stud:* 46 Junee Rd, Maydena; (03) 6288 2212.

 Mt Field National Park Tasmania's first national park, Mt Field is best known for the impressive Russell and Lady Barron falls. Most walks pass through lush ferns and rainforests, while the Pandani Grove walk traverses the glaciated landscapes of the mountain country to Lake Dobson. A visitor centre on-site offers interpretive displays. Contact Parks & Wildlife Service on 1300 135 513; 40 km NW.

Norske Scog Boyer Mill: the first in the world to manufacture newsprint from hardwoods; Boyer; (03) 6261 0111; tours available Thurs, bookings advised; 5 km E. *Salmon Ponds:* first rainbow- and brown-trout hatchery in Australia, in operation since 1864. There is also a Museum of Trout Fishing, a pancake restaurant and heritage gardens; open daily; 70 Salmon Ponds Rd, Plenty; (03) 6261 5663; 11 km NW. *Possum Shed:* locally made crafts and collectibles, and riverside cafe with delectable coffee; 1654 Gordon River Rd, Westerway; 31 km NW. *Styx Big Tree Reserve:* small reserve with the tallest hardwood trees in the world, the giant swamp gums, which grow to 92 m; 73 km W via Maydena.

TOWNS NEARBY: Pontville 20 km, Huonville 28 km, Kingston 29 km, Hamilton 31 km, Richmond 31 km

Oatlands

Pop. 540
Map ref. 625 K3

i Heritage Highway Visitors Centre, 1 Mill La; (03) 6254 1212; www.heritagehighwaytasmania.com.au

📻 97.1 Mid FM, 936 AM ABC Local Radio

[NEW NORFOLK] OAST HOUSE

 RADIO STATIONS   IN TOWN   WHAT'S ON   WHERE TO EAT   WHERE TO STAY   NEARBY

Approaching Oatlands from the north, look out for the topiary and striking metal sculptures by the roadside. The topiaries are a local tradition from the 1960s, while the recently created metal sculptures depict earlier times in the district. The town is on the shores of Lake Dulverton and has the largest collection of Georgian sandstone buildings in a village environment – with much of the stone from local quarries.

 Callington Mill Built in 1836, the old mill is a feature of Oatlands that was fully operational until 1892. After being battered by the elements and gutted by fire in the early 1900s, it was finally restored as part of Australia's bicentenary. The view from the top floor takes in Lake Dulverton. The visitor centre is also located at the mill and runs tours 10am–4pm daily. 1 Mill La.

Lake Dulverton: the lake is stocked with trout and onshore is a wildlife sanctuary protecting many bird species. Popular picnic spot; Esplanade. *Fielding's Ghost Tours:* tours run by local historian Peter Fielding; bookings on (03) 6254 1135. *Historical walk:* takes in the many Georgian buildings, including the convict-built Court House (1829); 'Welcome to Historic Oatlands' brochure from visitor centre. *Scottish, Irish and Welsh Shop:* stocks over 500 tartans, clan crests, badges, pins, and arts and crafts; open Mon, Thurs, Fri and Sun; 64 High St. *Skulduggery:* mystery tour game following true crime clues around town; available from visitor centre.

Oatlands Open Day: Oct.

Casaveen: country-style lunches; 44 High St; (03) 6254 0044.

 Convict-built mud walls: 13 km s on Jericho Rd. *Fishing:* excellent trout fishing in Lake Sorell and Lake Crescent; 29 km NW.

TOWNS NEARBY: Bothwell 31 km, Ross 32 km, Pontville 43 km, Campbell Town 43 km, Richmond 48 km

Penguin
Pop. 2949
Map ref. 626 G6

i 78 Main Rd; (03) 6437 1421; www.coasttocanyon.com.au

91.7 FM ABC Local Radio, 106.1 Coast FM

This northern seaside town was named after the little penguins that shuffle up the beaches, and images of the iconic bird are peppered around town. The largest example is the much-photographed Big Penguin, which stands 3 metres tall on the beachfront and is the town's premier attraction.

Dutch Windmill The windmill was presented to the town during Australia's bicentenary to commemorate the Dutch explorers and settlers. There is also a colourful tulip display in spring and play equipment on-site. Hiscutt Park, off Crescent St.

Penguins: each evening penguins come ashore; check with visitor centre for tour details; Sept–Mar. *Johnsons Beach Reef:* popular walking spot at low tide when reef is exposed. *Penguin Roadside Gardens:* originally a labour of love for 2 town residents, now a flourishing garden beside the road; Old Coast Rd to Ulverstone. *Chocolate Lovers:* quality European and Australian chocolates of all varieties; 100 Main Rd.

Market: over 300 stalls undercover; Arnold St; Sun.

The Groovy Penguin Cafe: arty retro cafe; 74 Main Rd; (03) 6437 2101. *Neptune Grand Bistro:* beachside pub; The

Neptune Grand Hotel, 84 Main Rd; (03) 6437 2406. *Wild:* Asian-inspired fine Tasmanian fare; 87 Main Rd; (03) 6437 2000.

The Madsen Boutique Hotel: 64 Main Rd; (03) 6437 2588.

Dial Range Walks Excellent tracks include the walk up Mt Montgomery (5 km s) with magnificent views from the summit, and Ferndene Gorge (6 km s). The Ferndene Bush Walk takes in an old silver-mine shaft, Thorsby's Tunnel. Brochures on walks from visitor centre highlight more trails.

Penguin Cradle Trail This 80 km trail heads inland from the coast to the world-famous Cradle Mountain. Sections of the walk vary in difficulty. It takes 6 days to complete, but access roads mean that sections can be done as day or overnight trips.

Pioneer Park: beautiful gardens with picnic facilities and walks; Riana; 10 km sw. *Scenic drive:* along coast to Ulverstone.

TOWNS NEARBY: Ulverstone 11 km, Burnie 15 km, Devonport 25 km, Latrobe 32 km, Wynyard 32 km

Pontville
Pop. 2170
Map ref. 623 I3 | 625 K6

i Council offices, Tivoli Rd, Gagebrook; (03) 6268 7000.

96.1 Hobart FM, 936 AM ABC Local Radio

The area around Pontville (declared a town in 1830) was first explored by Europeans when Hobart experienced severe food shortages in the early 1800s. Soldiers were sent north to kill emus and kangaroos. One of them, Private Hugh Germain, is allegedly responsible for the unusual names found in the region, such as Bagdad, Jericho, Lake Tiberius and Jordan River. Legend has it that Germain carried copies of *Arabian Nights* and *The Bible* and found his inspiration within.

Historic buildings Many buildings remain from Pontville's early days, including the Romanesque St Mark's Church (1841), The Sheiling (1819) and The Row, thought to have been built in 1824 as soldiers quarters. On or adjacent to Midland Hwy.

Bonorong Wildlife Park: popular attraction showing Tasmanian devils, quolls, echidnas, koalas, wombats and Forester kangaroos; Briggs Rd, Brighton; 5 km s. *Historic towns:* Brighton (3 km s), Tea Tree (7 km E), Bagdad (8 km N), Broadmarsh (10 km w) and Kempton (19 km N).

TOWNS NEARBY: Richmond 15 km, New Norfolk 20 km, Sorell 26 km, Kingston 33 km, Hamilton 38 km

Port Sorell
Pop. 2209
Map ref. 627 I6 | 629 C6

i Latrobe Visitor Centre, River Rd, Bells Pde, Latrobe; www.latrobetasmania.com.au

100.5 FM ABC Local Radio, 104.7 Coast FM

This holiday town on the Rubicon River enjoys a mild and sunny climate nearly all year-round. It was established in the early 1820s, but sadly, many of its oldest buildings were destroyed by bushfires. The port is now a fast-developing coastal retreat for retirees and beach lovers.

 The jetty: good fishing for cocky salmon, mullet, flathead, cod and bream. There are views to Bakers Beach and Narawntapu National Park. Behind caravan park on Meredith St. *Port Sorell Conservation Area:* 70 ha of coastal reserve with much flora and fauna. Guided tours available; bookings on (03) 6428 6072; Park Espl. *Estuary:* boating and safe swimming areas.

continued on p. 490

PORT ARTHUR

Pop. 499
Map ref. 623 M9 | 625 M9

[PORT ARTHUR HISTORIC SITE]

ⓘ Port Arthur Historic Site, Arthur Hwy; (03) 6251 2300 or 1800 659 101; www.portarthur.org.au

📻 97.7 Tasman FM, 936 AM ABC Local Radio

This historic settlement on the scenic Tasman Peninsula was one of Australia's most infamous penal settlements from the 1830s to the 1870s. Over 12 000 convicts from Britain, some of whom did nothing more than steal some food to survive, were shipped to Port Arthur, dubbed 'Hell on Earth'. They lived under threat of the lash and experimental punitive measures that often drove them to madness. This grim past is offset by the stark beauty of the sandstone buildings overlooking the tranquil, often misty, waters of the bay. Port Arthur is Tasmania's number one tourist attraction.

🏠 Port Arthur Historic Site Over 30 buildings and restored ruins sit on 40 ha of land, illuminating the life of the convicts and their guards. Day entry tickets include a guided historical walking tour, access to the visitor centre, interpretation gallery and museum, and a harbour cruise. Lantern-lit historic tours depart at dusk and tours of the Isle of the Dead, the cemetery for the colony, unravel emotive stories of the convicts. The site's heritage gardens have been restored and replanted to reflect the style of the original plantings; guided and self-guide walks are available. Cruises and guided tours operate daily to the site of incarceration of juvenile male convicts at nearby Point Puer. Details at visitor centre; Arthur Hwy.

Port Arthur Memorial Garden: dedicated to the victims of the 1996 tragedy at the site in which 35 people were killed by a gunman. **Convict Trail drive:** scenic drive from Port Arthur to the Coal Mines Historic Site.

🍴 ***The Commandant's Table:*** friendly country restaurant; Comfort Inn Port Arthur, 29 Safety Cove Rd; (03) 6250 2101. ***Eucalypt:*** modern Australian cafe; 6962 Arthur Hwy; (03) 6250 2555. ***Felons Bistro:*** quality regional menu; Port Arthur Historic Site Visitor Centre; (03) 6251 2310 or 1800 659 101. ***The Fox & Hounds Inn:*** traditional fireside pub fare; 6789 Arthur Hwy; (03) 6250 2217. ***Taylor's Restaurant:*** modern Australian – book ahead; Stewarts Bay Lodge, 6955 Arthur Hwy; (03) 6250 2771.

🛏 ***Port Arthur Holiday Park:*** Garden Point Rd; (03) 6250 2340. ***White Beach Tourist Park:*** 128 White Beach Rd, White Beach; (03) 6250 2142.

⊗ **Remarkable Cave** Created by wave erosion, Remarkable Cave affords spectacular views along the coastline to Cape Raoul. It is in Tasman National Park and is the starting point of a 4–5 hr return walk to Crescent Bay. 6 km S.

Coal Mines Historic Site: Tasmania's first operational mine, with self-guide tours; 30 km NW. **Tasman Island Cruises:** 2 hr cruise exploring the beautiful coastal scenery of Tasman National Park; bookings on (03) 6250 2200.

TOWNS NEARBY: Eaglehawk Neck 16 km, Dunalley 29 km, Sorell 47 km, Kingston 48 km, Adventure Bay 48 km

TASMANIA

Market: Memorial Hall; 1st and 3rd Sat each month Sept–May. *Port Sorell Regatta:* Jan.

Hawley House: elegant candlelit dinners; Hawley Beach; (03) 6428 6221.

Moomba Holiday & Caravan Park: 24 Kermode St; (03) 6428 6140. *Tranquilles:* 9 Gumbowie Dr; (03) 6428 7555.

Shearwater: holiday town with shopping centre and good beach access; 5 km N. *Hawley Beach:* safe swimming, good fishing and historic Hawley House (1878) offering meals; 6 km N. *Walk:* 6 km return track from Port Sorell to Hawley Beach, offering excellent views of Narawntapu National Park and coastline. Starts at beach end of Rice St.

TOWNS NEARBY: Latrobe 14 km, Devonport 17 km, Beaconsfield 23 km, Beauty Point 23 km, George Town 24 km

Queenstown

Pop. 2120
Map ref. 624 D1 | 626 D11 | 628 A10

Queenstown Galley Museum, cnr Sticht and Driffield sts; (03) 6471 1483.

90.5 FM ABC Local Radio, 92.1 FM West Coast 7XS

The discovery of gold and other mineral resources in the Mount Lyell field in the 1880s led to the rapid emergence of Queenstown. Continuous mining here from 1893 to 1994 produced over 670 000 tonnes of copper, 510 000 kilograms of silver and 20 000 kilograms of gold. Operations began again in 1995, and are now owned by the Indian company Sterlite Industries. The town has modern facilities, but its wide streets and remaining historic buildings give it an old-mining-town flavour. In certain lights, multicoloured boulders on the hillsides, denuded through a combination of felling, wildfire, erosion and poisonous fumes from the smelter, reflect the sun's rays and turn to amazing shades of pink and gold. However, many Tasmanians view the place as a haunting reminder of the devastating impact humans can have on their environment.

Galley Museum The museum is housed in the Imperial (1898), Queenstown's first brick hotel, and displays over 800 photographs and general memorabilia of the history of the west coast. Cnr Sticht and Driffield sts.

West Coast Wilderness Railway This restored 1896 rack-and-pinion railway travels over 34 km of river and forest track to Strahan. It crosses 40 bridges and passes through pristine wilderness areas. Bookings on 1800 628 288.

Spion Kop Lookout: views of Queenstown and surrounding mountains; off Bowes St. *Paragon Theatre:* cinema; McNamara St. *Historical walk:* takes in 25 locations of historical importance; 'The Walkabout Queenstown' brochure from visitor centre.

Comstock Cottage: 45 McNamara St; (03) 6471 1200.

Mt Lyell Mines: guided tours of the mines north of town, either surface (1 hr) or underground (3.5 hrs); bookings on (03) 6471 1472. *Iron Blow:* original open-cut mine where gold was discovered in 1883; Gormanston; 6 km E. *Linda:* ghost town; 7 km E. *Mt Jukes Lookout:* superb panoramic views; 7 km s. *Lake Burbury:* excellent brown and rainbow trout fishing; picnic areas; 8 km E. *Nelson Falls:* short walk through temperate rainforest

leads to falls; 23 km E. *Valley views:* spectacular views from Lyell Hwy as it climbs steeply out of town.

TOWNS NEARBY: Strahan 21 km, Zeehan 29 km, Rosebery 33 km, Waratah 71 km, Mole Creek 92 km

Richmond

Pop. 879
Map ref. 623 J3 | 625 K6

 Old Hobart Town model village, 21A Bridge St, opposite Henry St; (03) 6260 2502; www.richmondvillage.com.au

97.7 Tasman FM, 936 AM ABC Local Radio

Richmond, just north of Hobart, is one of the most important historic towns in Tasmania. Richmond Bridge is the oldest surviving freestone bridge in Australia, built by convicts under appalling conditions in 1823. The situation was so bad that one convict committed suicide by throwing himself off the bridge. Other convicts beat and killed an overseer who was known for his cruelty; legend has it that his ghost still haunts the bridge.

Old Hobart Town Taking 3 years to build, this is an intricate model of Hobart in the 1820s. A remarkable feat, it is also historically accurate. Bridge St.

Richmond Gaol One of Australia's best preserved convict prisons, built in 1825 and once the abode of convict Ikey Solomon, said to be the inspiration for Dickens' Fagin. Self-guide tours. Bathurst St; (03) 6260 2127.

Richmond Maze and Tearooms: 2-stage maze with surprise ending, puzzle corner, gardens and Devonshire tea; Bridge St. *Historical walk:* many heritage buildings throughout town include Ivy Cottage, Village Store and Richmond Arms; 'Let's Talk About Richmond' brochure from visitor centre. *Art galleries:* local arts and crafts in heritage buildings include Saddlers Court (c. 1848); Bridge St. *Olde Time Portraits:* photographs of people in period costume; Bridge St. *Prospect House:* historic Georgian mansion built in 1830s, supposedly haunted by the ghost of its past owner; Richmond Rd.

Richmond Village Colonial Fair: Mar.

Abby's Restaurant: classical dining by candlelight; Prospect House, 1384 Richmond Rd; (03) 6260 2207. *Ashmore on Bridge Street:* light meals, excellent coffee; 34 Bridge St; (03) 6260 2238. *Ma Foosies:* quaint cafe in historical building; 46 Bridge St; (03) 6260 2412. *Richmond Wine Centre:* licensed modern Australian cafe; 27 Bridge St; (03) 6260 2619. *Meadowbank Estate:* fine modern European dishes; 699 Richmond Rd, Cambridge; (03) 6248 4484.

Number 3: 3 Henry St; (03) 6260 2847.

ZooDoo This Wildlife Park is on a 330 ha farm with native fauna such as Tasmanian devils, galahs, emus and the rare albino pademelon wallaby. Middle Tea Tree Rd; (03) 6260 2444; 7 km W.

Southern Tasmanian wine region: a number of wineries fan out from Hobart, with most offering cellar-door tastings. vineyards north of town include Stoney (6 km N) and Crosswinds (10 km NW); brochure from visitor centre. *Scenic drive:* north through Campania (8 km) and Colebrook (19 km).

TOWNS NEARBY: Sorell 11 km, Pontville 15 km, Kingston 29 km, New Norfolk 31 km, Dunalley 35 km

Rosebery

Pop. 1032
Map ref. 626 D9 | 628 A7

 Hay's Bus Services, 10–12 The Esplanade; (03) 6473 1247.

92.1 FM West Coast 7XS, 106.3 FM ABC Local Radio

Like the nearby towns of Queenstown, Strahan and Zeehan, Rosebery found its economic niche in mining. The region is also known for its ancient rainforests, home to unique fauna and Huon pine, one of the oldest living things on earth.

Mine tours: surface tours of the Pasminco mine; bookings on (03) 6473 1247.

Rosebery Miners, Axemen, Bush and Blarney Festival: Irish music festival; Mar.

Tullah Lakeside Lodge: pub fare beside scenic lake; Farrell St, Tullah; (03) 6473 4121.

Montezuma Falls The highest in Tasmania, the falls plummet 113 m and are accessed from Williamsford in a 3 hr return walk. The track winds through beautiful rainforest and there is a viewing platform at the falls. 11 km sw.

Pieman River cruise: daily 4-hour return trips aboard *Arcadia II*, passing lush rainforest on the way to rugged Pieman Head, where you can go ashore and explore untouched wilderness. Leaves from Corinna, a delightful spot with a goldmining heritage; bookings (03) 6446 1170; 41 km se. *Wee Georgie Wood Steam Train:* a 2 km ride along a scenic track on the fully restored steam train runs 1st Sun afternoon each month Sept–Apr; Tullah; 12 km ne. *Mt Murchison:* difficult but worthwhile 4 hr return walk rising 1275 m through ancient alpine forests; 14 km se. *Lake Johnson Reserve Tour:* alpine nature tour offering a close-up look at a stand of 10 000-year-old Huon pines; bookings on (03) 6473 1247. *Hays Trout Tours:* fishing tours of west-coast lakes and rivers, Aug–Apr; bookings on (03) 6473 1247. *Fishing:* good trout fishing in nearby lakes Rosebery, Mackintosh and Murchison; north and east of town.

TOWNS NEARBY: Zeehan 20 km, Queenstown 33 km, Waratah 37 km, Strahan 45 km, Mole Creek 77 km

Ross

Pop. 270
Map ref. 625 L2 | 627 L12

 Tasmanian Wool Centre, Church St; (03) 6381 5466; www.taswoolcentre.com.au

97.1 Mid FM, 936 AM ABC Local Radio

One of the oldest and most beautiful bridges in Australia spans the Macquarie River in Ross, a tiny village founded in 1812. Completed in 1836, the bridge was designed by colonial architect John Lee Archer and constructed by convicts, one of whom, Daniel Herbert, was given a pardon for his efforts. Herbert was responsible for 186 beautiful stone carvings along the side of the bridge, comprising images of animals, plants, Celtic gods and goddesses, and even the governor of the time, George Arthur. Ross Bridge is a point of pride in this Midlands town and it complements the many old sandstone buildings that adorn the main street. The town's central junction reveals the different aspects of Ross's history and, perhaps, its potential. The four corners are known as Temptation (hotel), Recreation (town hall), Salvation (church) and Damnation (gaol).

Tasmanian Wool Centre Regional attraction housing a museum, wool exhibition and retail area – all illustrating the national importance of the wool industry. Church St.

Ross Female Factory Site Archaeologically the most intact female convict site in Australia, this operated as a probation station for female convicts and their babies in the 19th century. The women were trained as domestic help and hired out to landowners in the area. The Overseer's Cottage has a historical display and model. Off Bond St; (03) 6223 1559.

Heritage walk: takes in 40 historic buildings in town, including Uniting Church (1885); booklet from visitor centre. *Old Ross General Store and Tearoom:* Devonshire tea and bakery, home of the famous Tassie scallop pie; Church St. *Skulduggery:* mystery tour game, following true crime clues around town; available from visitor centre. *T-Spot:* has an array of tea and coffee produce, homewares, gifts and alpaca products; Bridge St.

Bakery 31: famous scallop pies in stone-walled tearooms; 31 Church St; (03) 6381 5422. *Ross Bakery Inn:* treats from the wood-fired oven; 15 Church St; (03) 6381 5246.

Ross Caravan Park: The Esplanade; (03) 6381 5224. *Ross Village Bakery Inn:* 15 Church St; (03) 6381 5246.

Fishing There is world-class fly-fishing for brown trout in Macquarie River and some of the state's best trout-fishing lakes (Sorell, Crescent, Tooms and Leake) are within an hour's drive.

TOWNS NEARBY: Campbell Town 12 km, Oatlands 32 km, Swansea 49 km, Evandale 55 km, Bothwell 56 km

St Helens

Pop. 2049
Map ref. 627 O8

 St Helens History Room, 61 Cecilia St; (03) 6376 1744.

93.7 Star FM, 1584 AM ABC Local Radio

At the head of Georges Bay, St Helens is the largest centre on Tasmania's east coast. Excellent sport fishing, aquamarine water, pristine white-sand beaches and mild sunny weather year-round make it a very appealing and popular holiday destination. It is the base for those planning to fish the East Australian Current for tuna, marlin and shark. For land-based and inshore anglers there is the long, narrow estuary of Georges Bay.

St Helens History Room: browse memorabilia and models of local history, from a mine water wheel and a horse-drawn hearse to a vintage church organ and life-sized Tasmanian tiger; open 9am–5pm weekdays, 9am–1pm Sat and 10am–2pm Sun; 61 Cecilia St; (03) 6376 1744. *Beaches:* sheltered coves in the bay and surfable waves at nearby ocean beaches. *Fishing:* St Helens is famous for its fishing, offering everything from bream and trout in the Scamander River to blue-water gamefishing offshore. Charter boats and tours are available for deep-sea fishing and dinghy hire is available for bay fishing. Check with visitor centre for details.

St Helens Market: visitor centre carpark; Sat. *St Helens Regatta and Wood Chopping Festival:* Jan. *Tasmanian Game Fishing Classic:* Mar. *Tasmanian Sand Enduro:* Peron Dunes; Nov.

Billie T Cafe: wholefoods cafe; 67 Cecilia St; (03) 6376 2363. *Binalong Bay Cafe:* casual dining with ocean views; 64A Main Rd, Binalong Bay; (03) 6376 8116. *The Blue Shed:* provedore,

TASMANIA

takeaway and Asian-inspired seafood restaurant; Marina Pde;
(03) 6376 1170. **The Pelican Restaurant:** deckside bistro;
Tidal Waters Resort, 1 Quail St; (03) 6376 1999.

BIG4 St Helens Holiday Park: 2 Penelope St; (03) 6376
1290. **Bed in the Treetops B&B:** 701 Binalong Bay Rd, Binalong
Bay; (03) 6376 1318.

Binalong Bay This small holiday town with gorgeous beaches
is renowned for its excellent surf and rock fishing; 11 km NE.

St Helens Point: walks with stunning coastal scenery along
Maurouard Beach; brochure from visitor centre; 9 km S. **Bay of
Fires Conservation Area:** named by Captain Furneaux for the
Aboriginal campfires burning along the shore as he sailed past in
1773, this area features magnificent coastal scenery, good beach
fishing and camping. Aboriginal middens are found in the area.
A guided walk takes in the scenery to the north (*see Gladstone for
details*); begins 9 km N. *Beaumaris:* good beaches and lagoons;
12 km S. *Blue Tier Forest Reserve:* walks with wheelchair access
and interpretive sites; 27 km NW. *St Columba Falls:* dropping
nearly 90 m, the falls flow down a granite cliff-face to the
South George River. Walks through sassafras and myrtle lead
to a viewing platform; 38 km W. *Scenic flights:* flights over the
world-renowned Bay of Fires; Bay of Fires Aviation; St Helens
Aerodrome, St Helens Point Rd; 1300 391 221.

TOWNS NEARBY: St Marys 29 km, Derby 42 km, Fingal 42 km,
Gladstone 45 km, Bicheno 62 km

St Marys

Pop. 524
Map ref. 627 O9

i St Marys Coach House Restaurant, 34 Main St;
(03) 6372 2529.

100.3 Star FM, 102.7 FM ABC Local Radio

Despite being the chief centre of the Break O'Day Plains, St Marys
is a small town overshadowed by the magnificent St Patricks
Head in the eastern highlands. The roads to and from St Marys
venture through picturesque forests or down through the valley.

Rivulet Park: platypus, Tasmanian native hens and picnic
and barbecue facilities; Main St. **St Marys Railway Station:**
restored with cafe, Woodcraft Guild and Men's Shed giftshop; Esk
Main Rd. **St Marys Hotel:** iconic building; Main St.

New Year's Day Races: Jan. **Winter Solstice Festival:** June.
Car Show: June. **St Marys to Fingal Bicycle Race:** Oct.

LeBlanc: French-accented fine dining; White Sands
Estate, 21554 Tasman Hwy, Ironhouse Point; (03) 6372 2228.
Mt Elephant Pancakes: hilltop gourmet pancakes; Elephant Pass
Road (Esk Hwy), Elephant Pass; (03) 6372 2263.

Addlestone House B&B: 19 Gray Rd; (03) 6372 2783.

St Patricks Head: challenging 1 hr 40 min return walk
to top of rocky outcrop for great 360-degree views of coast and
valley; 1.5 km E. **South Sister:** an easier lookout alternative to
St Patricks Head, a 10–15 min walk leads through stringybarks
and silver wattles to spectacular views of Fingal Valley;
3 km NW. *Cornwall:* miners wall and Cornwall Collectables
shop; 6.5 km W. *Falmouth:* small coastal township with several
convict-built structures, fine beaches and good fishing; 14 km NE.
Scamander: holiday town with sea- and river-fishing, good
swimming, and walks and drives through forest plantations;
17 km N. *Douglas–Apsley National Park:* see Bicheno; 25 km SE.

TOWNS NEARBY: Fingal 19 km, St Helens 29 km, Bicheno 34 km,
Derby 58 km, Swansea 61 km

Scottsdale

Pop. 1967
Map ref. 627 M6

i Forest EcoCentre, 96 King St; (03) 6352 6520;
www.northeasttasmania.com.au

91.7 FM ABC Local Radio, 103.7 FM City Park Radio

Scottsdale, the major town in Tasmania's north-east, serves
some of the richest agricultural and forestry country in the state.
Indeed, as Government Surveyor James Scott observed in 1852, it
has 'the best soil in the island'. A visitor to the town in 1868 noted
with some surprise that the town had 'neither police station nor
public house, but the people appear to get on harmoniously
enough without them'. Present-day Scottsdale (now with both of
those establishments) still retains a sense of harmony.

Forest EcoCentre A state-of-the-art centre built to
principles of ecological sustainability, this place showcases the
story of the forests through greenhouse-style interpretive displays
and interactive features. King St.

Anabel's of Scottsdale: National Trust building now used as a
restaurant and quality motel, set in exquisite gardens; King St.
Trail of the Tin Dragon: discover the history of Chinese miners
who came to the region more than 100 years ago; brochure from
visitor centre.

The Steak Out: surf and turf meals; 15 King St;
(03) 6352 2248.

Beulah Heritage Accommodation B&B: 9 King St;
(03) 6352 3723.

Bridestowe Estate Lavender Farm One of the word's largest
lavender-oil producers, Bridestowe is renowned for growing
lavender that is not contaminated by cross-pollination. Tours
are available in the flowering season (Dec–Jan) and there are
lavender products for sale. Nabowla; (03) 6352 8182; 13 km W.

Mt Stronach: very popular 45 min climb to views of the north-
east; 4 km S. *Cuckoo Falls:* uphill 2–3 hr return walk to falls;
Tonganah; 8 km SE. *Springfield Forest Reserve:* popular picnic
spot and 20 min loop walk through Californian redwoods,
English poplars, pines and native flora; 12 km SW. *Sidling Range
Lookout:* views of town and surrounding countryside; 16 km W.
Mt Maurice Forest Reserve: walks incorporating Ralph Falls;
30 km S.

TOWNS NEARBY: Bridport 20 km, Derby 24 km, Lilydale 27 km,
Launceston 45 km, Gladstone 47 km

Sheffield

Pop. 1397
Map ref. 626 H7 | 628 H3 | 629 A8

i 5 Pioneer Cres; (03) 6491 1036;
www.sheffieldcradleinfo.com.au

91.7 FM ABC Local Radio, 104.7 Coast FM

Inspired by the Canadian town of Chemainus, Sheffield has
revitalised itself by commissioning artists to cover the town in
murals depicting local history and scenery. As a result, the town
has been transformed into Tasmania's largest outdoor gallery
and a centre for artisans creating beautiful work in wood, glass,
precious metals, stone and even chocolate.

 Story of the Sheffield Murals: audio tour that explains
how the town went from rural decline to thriving outdoor art
gallery; available from visitor centre. **Kentish Museum:** exhibits
on local history and hydro-electricity; open 10am–3pm daily;
Main St. **Blue Gum Gallery:** arts and crafts; at visitor centre.

[SHEFFIELD] WOMBAT IN CRADLE MOUNTAIN–LAKE ST CLAIR NATIONAL PARK

Steam train: Red Water Creek Steam and Heritage Society runs a train 1st weekend each month; Cnr Spring and Main sts. *Badgers Range Kimberley's Lookout:* 90 min return, with short, steep sections. Views along the walk; access from High St, Sheffield North.

Sheffield Town Hall Market: High St; 3rd Sun every 3rd month. *Friday Night Folk:* Skwiz Cafe; 63 Main St; last Fri each month. *Steam Fest:* Mar. *Mural Fest:* Apr. *Daffodil Show:* Sept.

Skwiz Cafe Gallery: part cafe, part lounge room, attracting artists and musos; 63 Main St; (03) 6425 7433. *TJ's Cafe:* daytime tearooms, evening restaurant; 60 Main St; (03) 6491 1077. *Highland Restaurant:* fine Tasmanian cuisine; Cradle Mountain Lodge, 4038 Cradle Mountain Rd, Cradle Mountain; (03) 6492 2100. *Weindorfers:* country-style restaurant; Gowrie Park Wilderness Village, 1447 Claude Rd, Gowrie Park; (03) 6491 1385.

Discovery Holiday Parks – Cradle Mountain: 3832 Cradle Mountain Rd, Cradle Mountain; (03) 6492 1395.

Cradle Mountain–Lake St Clair National Park Covering 124 942 ha, this national park has over 25 major peaks, including the state's highest, Mt Ossa, and possibly its most spectacular, Cradle Mountain. The terrain is marked by pristine waterfalls, U-shaped valleys, dolerite formations, forests of deciduous beech, Tasmanian myrtle, pandani and King Billy pine, and swathes of wildflowers. There are many tracks for all levels of experience, but visitors should always check for up-to-date information on conditions. The most famous walk is the 6-day Overland Track, a 65 km trail through spectacular alpine wilderness to Lake St Clair at the southern end of the park, and one of Australia's best-known walks for experienced, well-equipped walkers. Bookings are essential in summer and luxury guided walks are also available. Shorter trails include the Dove Lake Loop Track, a 2 hr walk circling pretty Dove Lake beneath the shadow of Cradle Mountain; the 10 min Rainforest Walk, through a patch of cool temperate rainforest behind the visitor centre; the easy 20 min Weindorfers Forest Walk, through a glade of pines and myrtles; the half-hour Enchanted Walk, beside pools and waterfalls; and the more arduous 8 hr Summit Walk to the top of Cradle Mountain. For bookings, contact Parks and Wildlife Service, Mon–Fri (03) 6233 6047; for more information, contact Cradle Mountain National Park Visitor Centre, 4057 Cradle Mountain Rd; (03) 6492 1110; 61 km sw.

Tasmazia One of the world's largest hedge mazes with 'rooms' and 'doors' leading to the Three Bears Cottage. Along with 7 other mazes, a cubby town, pancake parlour and Lower Crackpot model village there's plenty of crazy fun to keep the kids going all day; open daily; 500 Staverton Rd, Promised Land; (03) 6491 1934; 14 km sw.

devils@cradle: located near the entrance to the national park, see Tasmanian devils up close; daytime keeper tours and after-dark feeding tours are available; 3950 Cradle Mountain Rd, Cradle Mountain; (03) 6492 1491; 55 km sw. *Stoodley Forest Reserve:* experimental tree-farm forest, with a 40 min loop walk through European beech, Douglas fir, radiata pine and Tasmanian blue gum. Picnic areas; 7 km NE. *Lake Barrington Estate Vineyard:* tastings and sales; open Wed–Sun Nov–Apr; West Kentish; 10 km w. *Railton:* known as the 'Town of Topiary', Railton has over 100 living sculptures; 11 km NE. *Mt Roland:* well-marked bushwalks to the summit, which rises to 1234 m, with access from Claude Rd or Gowrie Park; 11 km sw. *Lake Barrington:* internationally recognised rowing course created by Devils Gate Dam. Picnic and barbecue facilities along the shore; 14 km sw. *Wilmot:* this 'Valley of Views' has magnificent views of the mountains of Cradle country and Bass Strait, novelty letterbox trail, and the original Coles store and family homestead; 38 km w.

TOWNS NEARBY: Latrobe 18 km, Mole Creek 20 km, Devonport 23 km, Ulverstone 27 km, Port Sorell 31 km

Smithton

Pop. 3363
Map ref. 626 C4

ⓘ Smithton Tourist Information Site; 29 Smith St, Smithton; (03) 6458 1330.

📻 88.9 Coast FM, 91.3 FM ABC Local Radio

This substantial town is renowned for its unique blackwood–swamp forests. Smithton services the most productive dairying and vegetable-growing area in the state and, with several large sawmills, is also the centre of significant forestry reserves and the gateway to The Tarkine.

Circular Head Heritage Centre: artefacts and memorabilia detailing the area's pioneering history; 8 King St. *Lookout tower:* excellent views from Tier Hill; Massey St. *Western Esplanade Community Park:* popular picnic spot overlooking the mouth of the Duck River, with fishing and walks; Western Espl. *Britton Brothers Timber Mill:* tours of the mill by appt (03) 6452 2522; Brittons Rd, southern outskirts of town.

Bridge Bistro: pub grub in modernised surrounds; Bridge Hotel/Motel, 2 Montagu St; (03) 6452 1389. *Kauri Bistro:* bistro fare in vast log cabin; Tall Timbers Hotel, Scotchtown Rd; (03) 6452 9000 or 1800 628 476. *Marrawah Tavern:* counter meals; 821 Comeback Rd, Marrawah; (03) 6457 1102.

AAA-Ye Olde Post Office Cottage–Smithton: 10 Smith St; (03) 6452 2162.

Allendale Gardens These gardens are linked to a rainforest area by 3 easy loop walks that take in the Fairy Glades, a section constructed for children, and towering 500-year-old trees. Peacocks roam the gardens, where Devonshire tea is available. Open Oct–Apr; Edith Creek; (03) 6456 4216; 13 km s.

TASMANIA

Woolnorth tours: coach tours visit spectacular Cape Grim cliffs, wind farm, and Woolnorth sheep, cattle and timber property, owned by the Van Diemen's Land Company since the 1820s; bookings on (03) 6452 1493. *River and Duck Bay:* good fishing and boating; 2 km N. *Sumac Lookout:* amazing views over Arthur River and surrounding eucalypt forest; 4 km s on Sumac Rd. *Milkshake Hills Forest Reserve:* exquisite picnic spot among eucalypts and rainforest; 10 min loop walk or 1 hr return walk to hill-top; 40 km s. *Surfing:* excellent, but turbulent surf beaches near Marrawah where Rip Curl West Coast Classic is held in Mar; 51 km sw. *Arthur River cruises:* trips into pristine wilderness of Arthur Pieman Protected Area; run Sept–June; 70 km sw. *Tarkine Forest Adventures:* take the 110 m slide into the world's only blackwood forest sinkhole; 32 km w. *Gardiner Point:* 'Edge of the World' plaque; 70 km sw.

TOWNS NEARBY: **Stanley 17 km, Wynyard 53 km, Burnie 70 km, Waratah 75 km, Penguin 85 km**

Sorell

Pop. 4179
Map ref. 623 K4 | 625 L6

i Gordon St; (03) 6269 2924.

97.7 Tasman FM, 936 AM ABC Local Radio

The south-eastern town of Sorell was founded in 1821, and was important in early colonial times for providing most of the state's grain. It was named after Governor Sorell who attempted to curb bushranging in Tasmania, but ironically the town was later targeted by bushranger Matthew Brady, who released the prisoners from gaol and left the soldiers imprisoned in their place.

Historic buildings There are 3 churches listed in the National Estate, most notably St George's Anglican Church (1826). There are also many heritage buildings including the Old Rectory (c. 1826), Old Post Office (c. 1850) and Bluebell Inn (c. 1864).

Orielton Lagoon: important habitat for migratory wading birds on western shore of town. *Pioneer Park:* popular picnic spot with barbecue facilities; Parsonage Pl.

Market: Cole St; Sun (weekly in summer, fortnightly in winter; check with visitor centre for current schedule).

Barilla Bay: oysters, seafood and … oysters; 1388 Tasman Hwy, Cambridge; (03) 6248 5454.

Barilla Holiday Park: 75 Richmond Rd, Cambridge; (03) 6248 5453. *BIG4 Hobart Airport Tourist Park:* 1 Holyman Dr, Cambridge; (03) 6248 3555.

Sorell Fruit Farm Offers pick-your-own patches as well as ready-picked. Fruits available in season include berries, apricots, cherries, pears, nashi, nectarines and peaches. Devonshire tea at the cafe. Open Oct–May; Pawleena Rd; (03) 6265 2744; 2 km E.

Southern Tasmanian wine region: many vineyards east of town include Orani (3 km E) and Bream Creek (22 km E); brochure from visitor centre. *Beaches:* around Dodges Ferry and Carlton; 18 km s.

TOWNS NEARBY: **Richmond 11 km, Dunalley 24 km, Pontville 26 km, Kingston 30 km, Eaglehawk Neck 40 km**

Strahan

see inset box on page 496

Swansea

Pop. 558
Map ref. 625 N3 | 627 N12

i Swansea Bark Mill and East Coast Museum, 96 Tasman Hwy; (03) 6257 8094.

98.5 Star FM, 106.1 FM ABC Local Radio

Perched on Great Oyster Bay, Swansea looks out to the Freycinet Peninsula. It is part of the Glamorgan/Spring Bay shire, the oldest rural municipality in the country, and many fine old buildings testify to its age. Today it is a popular holiday destination.

Swansea Bark Mill and East Coast Museum The only restored black-wattle bark mill in Australia has machinery that still processes the bark for tanning leather. The museum has comprehensive displays on life in the 1820s, and the adjoining Wine and Wool Centre has wines from over 50 Tasmanian vineyards and textiles from around the state. A cafe and tavern complete the complex. Tasman Hwy; (03) 6257 8094.

Historical walk: self-guide tour takes in charming heritage buildings including Morris' General Store (1838), run by the Morris family for over 100 years, and Community Centre (c. 1860), featuring the unusually large slate billiard table made for the 1880 World Exhibition; brochure from visitor centre. *Waterloo Point:* 1 km walking track leads to viewpoint to see short-tailed shearwaters at dusk and Aboriginal middens; Esplanade Rd.

The Banc: modern Australian fine dining; Cnr Franklin and Maria sts; (03) 6257 8896. *Kate's Berry Farm:* sinfully lavish berry desserts; 12 Addison St; (03) 6257 8428. *The Ugly Duck Out:* international fare; 2 Franklin St; (03) 6257 8850. *Kabuki by the Sea:* cliff-top Japanese restaurant; Tasman Hwy, Rocky Hills; (03) 6257 8588.

Spiky Bridge Built by convicts in 1843, the bridge was pieced together without the aid of mortar or cement. The spikes – vertical fieldstones – prevented cattle from falling over the sides. The beach nearby has a picnic area and good rock-fishing. 7.5 km s.

Coswell Beach: good spot for viewing little penguins at dusk; 1 km s along coast from Waterloo Pt. *Duncombes Lookout:* splendid views; 3 km s. *Mayfield Beach:* safe swimming beach with walking track from camping area to Three Arch Bridge. There is also great rock- and beach-fishing; 14 km s. *Vineyards:* Springvale, Coombend, Freycinet and Craigie Knowe vineyards all have cellar-door sales on weekends and holidays; 15 km N. *Lost and Meetus Falls:* bushwalks past beautiful waterfalls in dry eucalypt forest. Sheltered picnic area is nearby; 50 km NW.

TOWNS NEARBY: **Coles Bay 18 km, Bicheno 33 km, Triabunna 44 km, Ross 49 km, Campbell Town 53 km**

Triabunna

Pop. 798
Map ref. 623 N1 | 625 M5

i Cnr Charles St and Esplanade West; (03) 6257 4772.

90.5 FM ABC Local Radio, 97.7 Tasman FM

When Maria (pronounced 'mar-eye-ah') Island was a penal settlement, Triabunna (pronounced 'try-a-bunnah') was a garrison town and whaling base. After an initial boom, this small, south-east coast town settled into relative obscurity, content with its role as a centre for the scallop and abalone industries.

STANLEY

Pop. 459
Map ref. 626 D3

 45 Main Rd; 1300 138 229; www.stanley.com.au

 88.9 Coast FM, 91.3 FM ABC Local Radio

This quaint village nestles at the base of an ancient outcrop called The Nut, which rises 152 metres with sheer cliffs on three sides. Matthew Flinders, upon seeing The Nut in 1798, commented that it looked like a 'cliffy round lump resembling a Christmas cake'. Today visitors come from far and wide to see this 'lump' and the historic township beside it.

The Nut The remains of volcanic rock, The Nut looms above the surrounding sea and provides spectacular coastal views. Visitors can either walk to the summit along a steep and challenging track or take the chairlift from Browns Rd. There is a 40 min circuit walk along cliffs at the summit.

Historic buildings: many in the wharf area, including the bluestone former Van Diemen's Land (VDL) Company store in Marine Park. *Lyons Cottage:* birthplace of former prime minister J. A. Lyons, with interesting memorabilia; Alexander Tce. *Hearts and Craft:* fine Tasmanian craft; shop closes during quieter months, 12 Church St. *Discovery Centre Folk Museum:* displays of local history; Church St. *Touchwood:* quality craft and woodwork; 31 Church St. *Cemetery:* graves of colonial architect John Lee Archer and explorer Henry Hellyer; Browns Rd. *Stanley Seaquarium:* Tasmanian marine species including huge rock lobsters and giant crabs; Fishermans Dock; (03) 6458 2052. *Penguins:* evening tours to see little penguins and platypus in their natural environment Sept–Apr; bookings on 0448 916 153. *Seal cruises:* daily trips to see offshore seal colonies; bookings 0419 550 134.

Melbourne to Stanley Yacht Race: Nov.

Hursey Seafoods: freshest seafood ever; 2 Alexander Tce; (03) 6458 1103. *Moby Dicks Breakfast Bar:* famous breakfasts; 5 Church St; (03) 6458 1414. *Old Cable Station Restaurant:* intimate fine dining; 435 Green Hills Rd; (03) 6458 1312. *Stanley Hotel:* award-winning seafood bistro; 19–21 Church St;

[VIEW OF THE NUT]

(03) 6458 1161. *Stanley's on the Bay:* nautical-themed seafood; Stanley Village, 15 Wharf Rd; (03) 6458 1404.

Cable Station Restaurant & Accommodation: 435 Green Hills Rd; (03) 6458 1312. *Hanlon House Bed & Breakfast:* 6 Marshall St; (03) 6458 1149. *Stanley Cabin and Tourist Park:* 23A Wharf Rd; (03) 6458 1266. *Crayfish Creek Van & Cabin Park & Spa Tree House:* 20049 Bass Hwy, Crayfish Creek; (03) 6443 4228.

Highfield Historic Site The headquarters of VDL Co, Highfield contains a homestead with 12 rooms, a chapel, convict barracks, a schoolhouse, stables, a barn, workers' cottages and large gardens. Green Hills Rd; 2 km N.

Dip Falls: double waterfall in dense rainforest and eucalypts. There is a picnic area nearby; 40 km SE off hwy, via Mawbanna.

TOWNS NEARBY: Smithton 17 km, Wynyard 44 km, Burnie 61 km, Penguin 76 km, Waratah 78 km

---

Tasmanian Seafarers' Memorial: commemorates those who lost their lives at sea; Esplanade. *Girraween Gardens and Tearooms:* with large lily pond, day lilies, roses and agapanthus; Henry St.

Spring Bay Seafest: Easter.

Gateway Cafe: family-friendly cafe; 1 Charles St, Orford; (03) 6257 1539. *Scorchers by the River:* casual gourmet cafe; 1 Esplanade, Orford; (03) 6257 1033.

Triabunna Cabin & Caravan Park: 4 Vicary St; (03) 6257 3575.

Maria Island National Park After the convicts were moved to Port Arthur, the island was leased to Italian merchant Diego Bernacchi, who envisaged first a Mediterranean idyll and then a cement works. Both projects were short-lived. Today, bushwalks are popular. The extensive fossil deposits of the Painted Cliffs are

magnificent and the historic penal settlement of Darlington is also of interest. Daily ferry to the island from town. Contact Parks & Wildlife Service on 1300 135 513. Four-day guided walks of the island, staying in luxury accommodation, are available through Maria Island Walk; bookings (03) 6234 2999; 7 km S.

Orford: pleasant walk along Old Convict Rd following Prosser River; 7 km SW. *Thumbs Lookout:* stunning views of Maria Island; 9 km SW. *Church of St John the Baptist:* heritage church (1846) with a stained-glass window (taken from England's Battle Abbey) depicting John the Baptist's life; Buckland; 25 km SW. *Beaches:* safe swimming beaches around area; contact visitor centre for details.

TOWNS NEARBY: Sorell 43 km, Dunalley 44 km, Swansea 44 km, Richmond 47 km, Oatlands 50 km

STRAHAN

Pop. 635
Map ref. 624 C2 | 626 C12

[STRAHAN HARBOUR]

ⓘ The Esplanade; (03) 6471 7622.

92.1 FM West Coast 7XS, 107.5 FM ABC Local Radio

This pretty little port on Macquarie Harbour, on Tasmania's west coast, is the last stop before a long stretch of ocean to Patagonia. Sometimes considered the loneliest place on earth, it was dubbed 'The Best Little Town in the World' by the *Chicago Tribune* and continues to attract visitors. Strahan (pronounced 'strawn') came into being as a penal colony operating from the isolated station of Sarah Island. Known as a particularly cruel environment, the station was shut down in 1833, but not before convict Alexander Pearce had managed to escape. Pearce and seven others set off for Hobart but found the terrain too tough an adversary to overcome. Pearce, alone when discovered, was suspected of cannibalism. The following year he again escaped and again killed and ate his cohort. Pearce finally made it to Hobart, where he was executed.

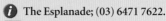 **Visitor centre** The centre has an impressive historical display on Tasmania's south-west, including Aboriginal history, European settlement, and more recent events such as the fight to save the Franklin River from being dammed in the early 1980s. In the amphitheatre there is an audiovisual slideshow and a nightly performance of 'The Ship That Never Was', about convict escapes. The Esplanade.

Morrison's Mill: one of 4 remaining Huon pine sawmills in Tasmania; tours available; The Esplanade. *Strahan Woodworks:* woodturning, arts and crafts; The Esplanade. *Tuts Whittle Wonders:* carvings from forest wood; Reid St. *Ormiston House:* built in 1899 and a fine example of Federation architecture surrounded by magnolia trees and expansive gardens. Morning and afternoon teas are served; Bay St. *Water Tower Hill Lookout:* views of township and harbour; Esk St. *West Coast Wilderness Railway: see Queenstown.*

Mount Lyell Picnic: Australia Day, Jan; West Strahan Beach.

Franklin Manor: distinguished fine dining; The Esplanade; (03) 6471 7311. *Hamers Hotel:* bistro meals; The Esplanade; (03) 6471 4335. *Risby Cove:* contemporary à la carte dining; The Esplanade; (03) 6471 7572. *Schwoch Seafoods:* excellent little seafood cafe; shop 3, 23 The Esplanade; (03) 6471 7500.

Discovery Holiday Parks – Strahan: 8 Innes St; (03) 6471 7468. *Strahan Holiday Park:* 8 West Innes St; (03) 6471 7442.

Franklin–Gordon Wild Rivers National Park This park now has World Heritage listing after an earlier state government tried to dam the Franklin River. Protests were so heated and widespread that the federal government and High Court stepped in and vetoed the proposal, saving the dense temperate rainforest and wild rivers that make up the park. Visitors can go canoeing and whitewater rafting, and there are many bush trails for experienced walkers. A 4-day walk to Frenchmans Cap takes in magnificent alpine scenery. The 40 min return walk to Donaghys Hill is easier and overlooks the Franklin and Collingwood rivers. Contact Parks & Wildlife Service on 1300 135 513. Gordon River cruises depart from Strahan. Cruises run up river to Heritage Landing, where there is a short walk to a 2000-year-old Huon pine; bookings on 1800 420 500 and (03) 6471 7174. 36 km SE.

Peoples Park: popular picnic spot in botanical gardens setting with a 45 min return walk to Hogarth Falls through marked rainforest; 2 km E. *Ocean Beach:* Tasmania's longest beach (36 km) offers horseriding, beach fishing and the opportunity to see short-tailed shearwaters in their burrows Oct–Mar; 6 km W. *Henty Sand Dunes:* vast sand dunes with sandboards and toboggans for hire; 12 km N. *Cape Sorell Lighthouse:* 40 m high lighthouse built in 1899; 23 km SW. *Sarah Island:* ruins of convict station with tours available; check with visitor centre; 29 km SE. *Scenic flights:* bird's-eye views of Gordon River, Sir John Falls and Franklin River valley; bookings (03) 6461 7718. *Strathgordon:* the place to see Tasmania's massive hydro-electricity industry at work. Along Gordon River Road are lakes Pedder and Gordon, the Gordon Dam and the underground Gordon Power Station. Bushwalkers can enter Southwest National Park via the Creepy Crawly Nature Trail; 90 km SE. *South Coast Track:* 6-to-9-day walk along the entirely uninhabited south coast for experienced trekkers. Starts at Cockle Creek and ends at Melaleuca, where you can continue walking north or take a prearranged flight out; 138 km SE.

TOWNS NEARBY: Queenstown 21 km, Zeehan 30 km, Rosebery 45 km, Waratah 81 km, Mole Creek 111 km

Ulverstone

Pop. 12 000
Map ref. 626 G6 | 628 G1

 13–15 Alexandra Rd; (03) 6425 2839; www.coasttocanyon.com.au

91.74 FM ABC Local Radio, 106.1 Coast FM

At the mouth of the Leven River on the north central coast, Ulverstone is renowned for its fine sweeping beaches and waterfront parklands. The spectacular rugged hinterland offers forest walks, caves to explore and breathtaking views into the Leven Canyon's deep ravine.

Discover the Leven Choose a 1, 2 or 5 hr fun guided cruise or walking tour of the spectacular upper Leven River in Ulverstone. Tours leave daily, on foot or in the cutest little passenger vessel in Tasmania; Tasma Pde; (03) 6425 2839.

Stories of Ulverstone Town Walk Wend your way around 6 story boards which tell the town's interesting history; start at the Shrine of Remembrance clock tower and finish in Reibey St.

Ulverstone Pedal Buggies Pedal yourself and the kids around the town's picturesque waterfront and parks; open 10am–4.30pm summer and school holidays, other times by appt; The Beach Hut; 2 Beach Rd; (03) 6425 9387.

Ulverstone Visitor Centre Gallery: crafts from local makers; open daily; 13–15 Alexandra Rd; (03) 6425 2839. *Riverside Anzac Park:* amazing children's playground, great picnic facilities and an interesting fountain. The park is named after a pine tree grown from a seed taken from Gallipoli; Beach Rd. *Fairway Park:* next to a 60 m giant waterslide; open summer and school holidays; Beach Rd; (03) 6425 3675. *Shropshire Park:* barbecues, outdoor gym equipment and underfoot the path is inscribed with the Royal Australian Navy's 75-year history; Dial St. *Legion Park:* magnificent coastal setting; The Esplanade. *Tobruk Park:* includes a memorial wall; Hobbs Pde. *Ulverstone History Museum:* pick up a guided-walk brochure and browse fascinating recreations of a general store, schoolhouse, railway station and blacksmith's foundry; open 1.30–4.30pm Mon–Sat; 50 Main St; (03) 6425 3835. *Shrine of Remembrance:* clock-tower memorial designed and built by European immigrants in 1953; Reibey St. *Ulverstone Lookout:* views over town; Upper Maud St. *Woodcraft Gallery and Workshop:* demonstrations, private tutoring and sales; open 10am–4pm Tues, Thurs and Sat; 109 Reibey St; (03) 6425 7119.

Market: The Quadrant Carpark; every 2nd Sat. *Twilight Rodeo:* Jan. *Festival in the Park:* Feb. *Forth Valley Blues Festival:* Mar. *Doll, Bear and Miniature Extravaganza:* July. *NW Woodcraft Exhibition:* Nov. *Cradle Coast Rotary Art Exhibition:* Nov. *Ulverstone Agricultural Show:* Nov. *Christmas Parade and Party in the Park:* Dec.

The Atrium: family-oriented restaurant; The Lighthouse Hotel, 33 Victoria St; (03) 6425 1197. *Furners Hotel:* good pub meals; 42 Reibey St; (03) 6425 1488. *Pedro's the Restaurant:* casual waterside seafood; Ulverstone Wharf; (03) 6425 6663.

B&B at Winterbrook: 28 Eastland Dr; (03) 6425 6324. *BIG4 Ulverstone Holiday Park:* 57 Water St; (03) 6425 2624. *Moonlight Bay B&B Guest House:* 141 Penguin Rd; (03) 6425 1074. *Love Grove Guesthouse:* 325 Masons Rd, Wilmot; (03) 6492 1165. *The Wattles:* 109 Pumping Station Rd, Forth; (03) 6428 2242.

Leven Canyon From Cruikshank's lookout down to the cantilevered Edge lookout there are 697 steps, but they're worth the effort as the views of this 275m deep ravine are breathtaking. Picnic or barbecue in a bushland setting. Loongana Rd, Loongana; 41 km s.

Gunns Plains Caves underground streams, limestone shawls and glow worms in well-lit, visitor-friendly caves. Tour daily on the hour from 10am, on the half hour from 1.30pm; Caves Rd, Gunns Plains; (03) 6429 1388; 24 km sw.

Wing's Wildlife Park Get up close to Tasmanian Devils at dinner time, let the kids explore the animal nursery and check out animals from far and wide: 137 Winduss Rd, Gunns Plains; (03) 6429 1151; tours available; open daily 10am–4pm and by appt; 24 km sw.

Bass Highway The spectacular scenery on the Ulverstone to Stanley section of this highway recalls Victoria's Great Ocean Road. The route's highlights include the little penguins at the village of Penguin, the Lactos Cheese Tasting Centre in Burnie, the colourful fields of Table Cape Tulip Farm near Wynyard, and the picturesque town of Boat Harbour.

Ulverstone Miniature railway: 1st and 3rd Sun each month Jan–Mar, 3rd Sun Apr–Dec; Maskells Rd; (03) 6425 3675; 2 km E. *Goat Island Sanctuary:* cave and good fishing, but walking access to island at low tide only; 5 km w. *Wilderness Tours:* guided forays into forests, caves and platypus habitats after dark with log cabin accommodation; Mountain Valley Wildlife Experiences; 1519 Loongana Rd, Loongana; (03) 6429 1394. *Penguins:* view little penguins at dusk; Leith; 12 km E. *Preston Falls:* easy walk to scenic views; 19 km s. *Fishing:* good fishing on beach (especially Turners Beach), river and estuary; contact visitor centre for details. *Beaches:* safe swimming beaches to east and west of town; contact visitor centre for details.

TOWNS NEARBY: Penguin 11 km, Devonport 14 km, Latrobe 21 km, Burnie 26 km, Sheffield 27 km

Waratah

Pop. 223
Map ref. 626 E7 | 628 A3

 Wynyard Visitor Centre, 8 Exhibition Link, Wynyard; (03) 6443 8330; www.wowtas.com.au

103.3 FM ABC Local Radio, 106.1 Coast FM

Waratah was the site of the first mining boom in Tasmania. Tin deposits were discovered in 1871 by James 'Philosopher' Smith, and by the late 1800s the Mount Bischoff operation was the richest tin mine in the world. The mine closed in 1947.

Waratah Museum and Giftshop: displays early photographs and artefacts of the area and provides brochure for self-drive tour of town; Smith St. *Waratah Waterfall:* in the centre of town; Smith St. *Philosopher Smith's Hut:* replica of late-19th-century miner's hut; Smith St. *St James Anglican Church:* first church in Tasmania to be lit by hydro-power; Smith St. *Lake Waratah:* pleasant picnic and barbecue area with rhododendron garden and walks to Waratah Falls; English St.

Savage River National Park The rainforest here is the largest contiguous area of cool–temperate rainforest surviving in Australia. Excellent for self-sufficient bushwalking as well as fishing, 4WD and kayaking in the adjacent regional reserve.

TASMANIA

Contact Parks & Wildlife Service on 1300 135 513; access tracks lead off the main road out of Waratah; around 20 km w.

Fishing: excellent trout fishing in rivers and lakes in the area, including Talbots Lagoon; 20 km E. *Old mines:* walks and drives to old mining sites; brochure from visitor centre.

TOWNS NEARBY: Rosebery 37 km, Zeehan 52 km, Wynyard 53 km, Burnie 53 km, Penguin 58 km

Westbury

Pop. 1357
Map ref. 627 J8 | 629 E11

ⓘ Great Western Tiers Visitor Centre, 98–100 Emu Bay Rd, Deloraine; (03) 6362 3471; www.greatwesterntiers.org.au

📻 91.7 FM ABC Local Radio, 103.7 FM City Park Radio

Westbury's village green gives the town an English air. Just west of Launceston, the town was surveyed in 1823 and laid out in 1828, the assumption being that it would be the main stop between Hobart and the north-west coast. Originally planned as a city, it never grew beyond the charming country town it is today.

🏠 **The village green** Used for parades and fairs in the 1830s, the village green is still the focal point and fairground of Westbury – with one small difference: prisoners are no longer put in the stocks for all to see. King St.

White House This collection of buildings, enclosing a courtyard, was built in 1841. Later additions include a coach depot, a bakery and a flour mill. The house has an excellent collection of 17th- and 18th-century furniture and memorabilia, and a magnificent doll's house. The outbuildings house a toy museum as well as early bicycles, vintage cars and horse-drawn vehicles. The restored bakery serves refreshments. Open Sept–June; King St.

Pearn's Steam World: said to be the largest collection of working steam traction engines in Australia; Bass Hwy. *Westbury Maze and Tearoom:* hedge maze composed of 3000 privet bushes; open Oct–June; Bass Hwy. *Culzean:* historic home with beautifully maintained temperate-climate gardens; open Sept–May; William St. *Westbury Mineral and Tractor Shed:* museum of vintage tractors and farm machinery featuring a scale-model tractor exhibition; Veterans Row.

🎋 *Maypole Festival:* Mar. *St Patrick's Day Festival:* Mar.

🍴 *Andy's Bakery Cafe:* pastries and gelato; 43–45 Meander Valley Rd; (03) 6393 1846. *Fitzpatrick's Inn:* fine European-style dishes; 56 Meander Valley Rd; (03) 6393 1153. *Hobnobs Coffee Shop & Deli:* sophisticated provincial-style food; 47 William St; (03) 6393 2007.

🛏 *Westbury Gingerbread Cottages:* 52 William St; (03) 6393 1140.

🧭 *Fishing:* good trout fishing at Four Springs Creek (15 km NE) and Brushy Lagoon (15 km NW).

TOWNS NEARBY: Deloraine 16 km, Hadspen 19 km, Longford 25 km, Launceston 26 km, Exeter 27 km

Whitemark

Pop. 598
Map ref. 624 B10

ⓘ 4 Davies St, (03) 6359 2380 or 1800 994 477; www.flindersislandonline.com.au

 91.7 FM ABC Local Radio

Flinders Island in Bass Strait is the largest of the 52 islands in the Furneaux Group, once part of a land bridge that joined Tasmania to the mainland. It's a beautiful place, but with a tragic history. In 1831 Tasmania's Aboriginal people, depleted to fewer than 160, were isolated on Flinders Island. Wybalenna ('black man's home') was set up there in 1834 to house those few survivors of Tasmania's pre-European population of over 4000. Less than a third of the people held there survived the appalling living conditions. A lack of good food and water meant that by 1847, when the settlement was finally abandoned, only 46 Aboriginal people remained. The Wybalenna Historic Site at Settlement Point stands as a reminder of the doomed community. Located near Emita, it is one of the most important historic sites in Tasmania, and includes a National Trust–restored church and cemetery. Whitemark is the island's largest town.

🏠 **Bowman History Room**: displays of memorabilia show Whitemark since the 1920s; rear of E. M. Bowman & Co, 2 Patrick St. *Diving and snorkelling:* tours to shipwreck sites, limestone reefs and granite-boulder formations including Chalky Island Caves and Port Davies Reef; bookings on (03) 6359 8429. *Fishing tours:* from Port Davies to Prime Seal Island for pike and salmon, and Wybalenna Island for couta; bookings on (03) 6359 8429.

🌴 *Three Peaks Race:* annual sailing and hiking race from Beauty Pt to Flinders Island, then down the coast to Hobart. It coincides with local produce markets and children's activities at Lady Barron; Easter. *Bass Strait Golf Classic:* June. *Flinders Island Show:* local and off-shore exhibitors; showgrounds; Oct.

🍴 *Freckles Cafe:* coffee and light meals; 7 Lagoon Rd; (03) 6359 2138. *Shearwater Restaurant:* seafood with a view; Furneaux Tavern, 11 Franklin Pde, Lady Barron; (03) 6359 3521.

🧭 **Strzelecki National Park** The only national park in the Furneaux Group, featuring the Peaks of Flinders and Mt Strzelecki, and wetlands, heathland and lagoons. A 5 hr return walk to the summit of Mt Strzelecki is steep, but affords excellent views of Franklin Sound and its islands. Trousers Pt, featuring magnificent rust-red boulders and clear waters, is located just outside the park. Contact Parks & Wildlife Service on 1300 135 513; 15 km s.

Emita Museum This museum, run by the Historical Society, has a wide range of memorabilia and houses displays on the short-tailed shearwater industry, the War Service Land Settlement and the nautical and natural histories of Flinders Island. Open 1–4pm weekends; Settlement Point Rd, Emita; 18 km NW.

Patriarchs Wildlife Sanctuary: privately owned sanctuary with a vast range of birdlife and wallabies, which can be handfed; access via Lees Rd, Memana; 30 km NE. *Logan Lagoon Wildlife Sanctuary:* houses a great diversity of birdlife in winter including the red-necked stint, common greenshank and eastern curlew; east of Lady Barron; 30 km SE. *Mt Tanner:* lookout with stunning views of the northern end of the island and Marshall Bay; off West End Rd; Killiecrankie; 40 km N. *Port Davies:* from the viewing platform see short-tailed shearwaters fly into their burrows at dusk. An enormous colony of these birds breed here between Sept and Apr and then set out on an annual migration to the Northern Hemisphere. West of Emita; 20 km NW.

Fossicking: Killiecrankie diamonds, a form of topaz released from decomposing granite, are found along the beach at Killiecrankie Bay and nearby Mines Creek. The stone is usually colourless, but sometimes pale blue or amber; brochure at visitor centre; 43 km NW. *Beachcombing:* rare paper-nautilus shells wash up along the island's western beaches.

TOWNS NEARBY: Gladstone 93 km, Bridport 111 km, Derby 116 km, Scottsdale 123 km, St Helens 135 km

Wynyard

Pop. 4810
Map ref. 626 E5

 8 Exhibition Link; (03) 6443 8330; www.wowtas.com.au

102.5 FM ABC Local Radio, 106.1 Coast FM

This small centre at the mouth of the Inglis River has charming timber buildings and is located on a stunning stretch of coastline in an extremely fertile pocket of the state.

Gutteridge Gardens: riverside gardens in the heart of town; Goldie St. *Nature walks:* include boardwalk along Inglis River; brochure at visitor centre. *Wonders of Wynyard:* an exhibition of veteran vehicles that includes one of the oldest Ford models in the world; Exhibition Link.

Wynyard Farmers' Market: 2nd and 4th Sat each month. *Bloomin' Tulips Festival:* Oct.

Buccaneers for Seafood: popular seafood eatery; 4 Inglis St; (03) 6442 4104. *Jolly Rogers on the Beach:* modern beachside bistro; 1 Port Rd, Boat Harbour Beach; (03) 6445 1710.

Alexandria: 1 Table Cape Rd; (03) 6442 4411. *Leisure Ville Holiday Centre:* 145 Old Bass Hwy; (03) 6442 2291. *Beach Retreat Tourist Park:* 30B Old Bass Hwy; (03) 6442 1998.

Boat Harbour This is a picturesque village ideal for diving and spearfishing. Boat Harbour Beach (4 km NW of town) has safe swimming, marine life in pools at low tide, fishing and waterskiing. 10 km NW.

Rocky Cape National Park With some of the best-preserved Aboriginal rock shelters and middens in Tasmania, the park incorporates the pristine Sisters Beach. Contact Parks & Wildlife Service on 1300 135 513. 29 km NW.

Fossil Bluff: scenic views from an unusual geological structure where the oldest marsupial fossil in Australia was found; 3 km N. *Table Cape Lookout:* brilliant views of the coast from 190 m above sea level. En route to lookout is Table Cape Tulip Farm, with tulips, daffodils and Dutch irises blooming Sept–Oct. From lookout a short walk leads to an old lighthouse; 5 km N. *Flowerdale Freshwater Lobster Haven:* restaurant and artificial lakes stocked with lobster; 6.5 km NW. *Fishing:* Inglis and Flowerdale rivers provide excellent trout fishing; also good sea-fishing around Table Cape. *Scenic flights:* the best way to appreciate the patchwork colours of the fields in the area; bookings at Wynyard Airport (03) 6442 1111. *Scenic walks and drives:* brochure from visitor centre.

TOWNS NEARBY: Burnie 17 km, Penguin 32 km, Ulverstone 43 km, Stanley 44 km, Waratah 53 km

Zeehan

Pop. 846
Map ref. 626 D10

 West Coast Pioneers Memorial Museum, Main St; (03) 6471 6225.

90.5 FM ABC Local Radio, 92.1 FM West Coast 7XS

After silver-lead deposits were discovered here in 1882, Zeehan boomed and between 1893 and 1908 the mine yielded ore worth $8 million, which led to its nickname, the 'Silver City of the West'. However, from 1910 the mine started to slow and Zeehan declined, threatening to become a ghost town. Fortunately, the nearby Renison Bell tin mine has drawn workers back to the area.

West Coast Pioneers Memorial Museum The old Zeehan School of Mines building (1894) has been converted into a comprehensive museum outlining the local history with extensive mineral, geological and locomotive collections. Main St.

Historic buildings: the whole town is National Trust–classified. Boom-era buildings on Main St include Gaiety Theatre, once Australia's largest theatre. Other buildings of historical interest include the post office, bank and St Luke's Church. *Scenic drives:* self-guide drives in town and nearby; brochure from visitor centre.

Treasure Island Caravan Park: Hurst St; (03) 6471 6633.

Fishing: Trial Harbour (20 km W) and Granville Harbour (35 km NW) are popular fishing spots. *Lake Pieman:* boating and good trout fishing; 42 km NW. *Cruises:* tour the Pieman River, leaving from fascinating former goldmining town, Corinna; bookings on (03) 6446 1170; 48 km NW.

TOWNS NEARBY: Rosebery 20 km, Queenstown 29 km, Strahan 30 km, Waratah 52 km, Mole Creek 96 km

ROAD ATLAS

Inter-City Route Maps

The inter-city route maps and distance charts will help you plan your route between major cities. As well, you can use the maps during your journey, since they provide information on distances between towns along the route, roadside rest areas and road conditions. The table below provides an overview of the routes mapped. The inter-city route maps can be found on pages 504–6.

INTER CITY ROUTES	DISTANCE	TIME
Sydney–Melbourne via Hume Highway/Freeway 31 M31	879 km	12 hrs
Sydney–Melbourne via Princes Highwy/Freeway 1 A1 M1	1039 km	15 hrs
Sydney–Brisbane via New England Highway 1 15	995 km	14 hrs
Melbourne–Adelaide via Western & Dukes highways M8 A8 M1	729 km	8 hrs
Melbourne–Adelaide via Princes Highway M1 A1 B1 M1	907 km	11 hrs
Melbourne–Brisbane via Newell Highway M31 A39 39 A39 A2	1676 km	20 hrs
Darwin–Adelaide via Stuart Highway 1 87 A87 A1	3026 km	31 hrs
Adelaide–Perth via Eyre & Great Eastern highways A1 1 94	2700 km	32 hrs
Adelaide–Sydney via Sturt & Hume highways A20 20 31	1415 km	19 hrs
Perth–Darwin via Great Northern Highway 95 1	4032 km	46 hrs
Sydney–Brisbane via Pacific Highway 1 1 M1	935 km	14 hrs
Brisbane–Darwin via Warrego Highway A2 66 87 1	3406 km	39 hrs
Brisbane–Cairns via Bruce Highway M1 A1	1703 km	20 hrs
Hobart–Launceston via Midland Highway 1	197 km	3 hrs
Hobart–Devonport via Midland & Bass highways 1 B52 1	279 km	4 hrs

Legend

▭▭▭▭	Freeway, with toll	**SYDNEY** ○	State capital city
M31 ▭ 31	Highway, sealed, with National Highway Route Marker	**GEELONG** ○	Major city/town
A1 ▭ 1	Highway, sealed, with National Route Marker	**Deniliquin** ○	Town
▭ 5 ▭	Highway, sealed, with Metroad Route Marker	Caldwell ○	Other population centres/localities
▭▭▭▭	Highway, unsealed	Rorruwuy ○	Aboriginal community
C141 ▭ 26	Main road, sealed, with State Route Marker	Karoonda Roadhouse ▣	Roadhouse
▭▭▭▭	Main road, unsealed	*Nullagong* ▫	Pastoral station homestead
▭▭▭▭	Connector road, on central city maps only	**ESSENDON**	Suburb, on suburbs maps only
→▭	Other road, with traffic direction, on central city maps only	**Unley**	Suburb, on central city maps only
▭	Other road, sealed	THE TWELVE APOSTLES ◉	Place of interest
▭	Other road, unsealed	✈	Airport
▭	Vehicle track	✛	Landing ground
··········	Walking track	★	Lighthouse
═══════	Mall, on central city maps only	+	Hill, mountain, peak
●───●	Railway, with station	●	Gorge, gap, pass, cave or saddle
●───●	Underground railway, with station	●	Waterhole
▼ 114 ▼	Total kilometres between two points	⚒	Mine site
▼ 45 ▼	Intermediate kilometres	▭	National park
───────	State border	▭	Other reserve
───────	World Heritage Area	▭	Marine park
▭▭▭▭	Fruit fly exclusion zone boundary	▭	Aboriginal/Torres Strait Islander land
		▭	Other named area
◠◠	River, with waterfall	✗✗	Prohibited area
◯	Lake, reservoir	⊤	Text entry in A to Z listing
◯	Intermittent lake		
◠◠	Coastline, with reefs and rocks		

Maps are in a Lamberts Conformal Conic Projection
Geocentric Datum Australia, 1994 (GDA94)

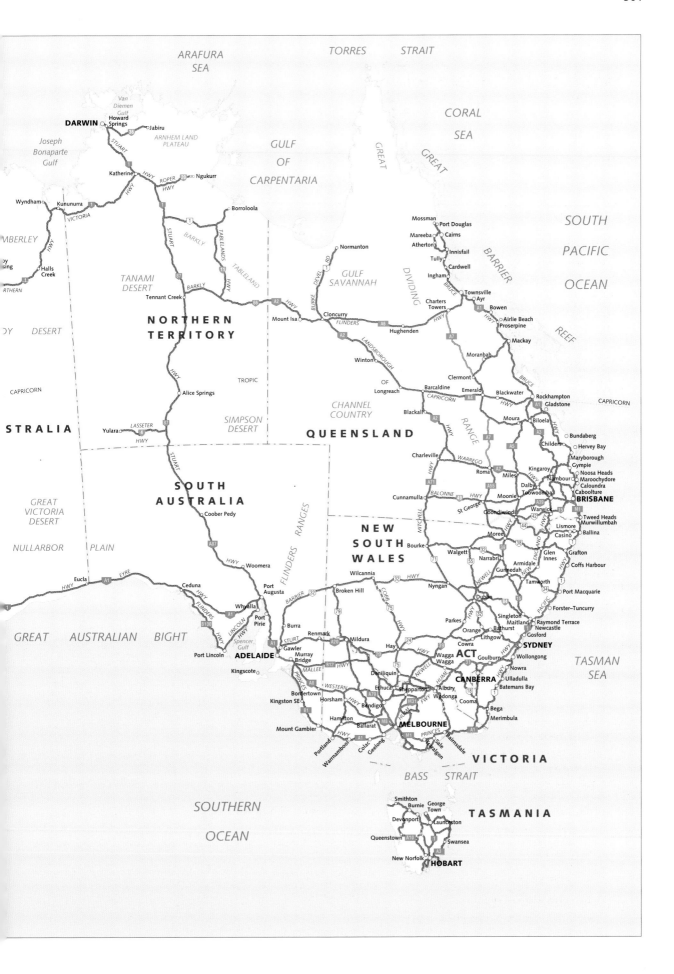

Approximate Distances AUSTRALIA

	Adelaide	Albany	Albury	Alice Springs	Ayers Rock/Yulara	Bairnsdale	Ballarat	Bathurst	Bega	Bendigo	Bordertown	Bourke	Brisbane	Broken Hill	Broome	Bunbury	Cairns	Canberra	Carnarvon	Ceduna	Charleville	Coober Pedy	Darwin	Dubbo	Esperance	Eucla	Geelong	Geraldton
Adelaide		2662	965	1537	1578	1010	625	1198	1338	640	274	1129	2048	514	4268	2887	3207	1197	3568	772	1582	847	3026	1194	2183	1267	711	3086
Albany	2662		3487	3585	3626	3672	3287	3720	4000	3302	2936	3388	4310	2773	2626	335	5466	3719	1300	1890	3841	2895	4428	3526	479	1395	3373	818
Albury	965	3487		2362	2403	336	412	466	427	313	679	779	1407	865	5093	3712	2764	348	4393	1597	1232	1672	3851	553	3008	2092	382	3911
Alice Springs	1537	3585	2362		443	2547	2162	2595	2875	2177	1811	2263	2979	1648	2731	3810	2376	2594	4114	1695	2320	690	1489	2401	3106	2190	2248	4009
Ayers Rock/Yulara	1578	3626	2403	443		2588	2203	2636	2916	2218	1852	2304	3226	1689	3174	3851	2819	2635	4532	1736	2763	731	1932	2442	3147	2231	2289	4050
Bairnsdale	1010	3672	336	2547	2588		388	802	328	423	736	1115	1743	1119	5278	3897	3100	455	4578	1782	1568	1857	4036	863	3193	2277	349	4096
Ballarat	625	3287	412	2162	2203	388		878	716	124	351	996	1747	754	4893	3512	3104	760	4193	1397	1449	1472	3651	893	2808	1892	86	3711
Bathurst	1198	3720	466	2595	2636	802	878		531	779	1180	569	1000	958	5011	3945	2416	309	4626	1830	1022	1905	3769	205	3241	2325	848	4144
Bega	1338	4000	427	2875	2916	328	716	531		751	1064	994	1399	1447	5436	4225	2910	222	4906	2110	1447	2185	4364	630	3521	2605	677	4424
Bendigo	640	3302	313	2177	2218	423	124	779	751		366	872	1623	696	4908	3527	2980	661	4208	1412	1325	1487	3666	769	2823	1907	210	3726
Bordertown	274	2936	679	1811	1852	736	351	1180	1064	366		1138	1922	788	4542	3161	3257	1071	3842	1046	1591	1121	3300	1068	2457	1541	437	3360
Bourke	1129	3388	779	2263	2304	1115	996	569	994	872	1138		922	615	4442	3613	2078	772	4294	1498	453	1573	3200	364	2909	1993	1082	3812
Brisbane	2048	4310	1407	2979	3226	1743	1747	1000	1399	1623	1922	922		1537	4648	4535	1703	1241	5216	2420	742	2495	3406	854	3831	2915	1745	4734
Broken Hill	514	2773	865	1648	1689	1119	754	958	1447	696	788	615	1537		4379	2998	2693	1097	3679	883	1068	958	3137	753	2294	1378	840	3197
Broome	4268	2626	5093	2731	3174	5278	4893	5011	5436	4908	4542	4442	4648	4379		2417	4045	5214	1451	3750	3989	3421	1870	4806	2745	3255	4979	1921
Bunbury	2887	335	3712	3810	3851	3897	3512	3945	4225	3527	3161	3613	4535	2998	2417		5691	3944	1091	2115	4066	3120	4219	3751	664	1620	3598	609
Cairns	3207	5466	2764	2376	2819	3100	3104	2416	2910	2980	3257	2078	1703	2693	4045	5691		2619	5428	3576	1625	3066	2803	2211	4987	4071	3102	5890
Canberra	1197	3719	348	2594	2635	455	760	309	222	661	1071	772	1241	1097	5214	3944	2619		4625	1829	1225	1904	3972	408	3240	2324	730	4143
Carnarvon	3568	1300	4393	4114	4532	4578	4193	4626	4906	4208	3842	4294	5216	3679	1451	1091	5428	4625		2796	4747	3801	3253	4432	1628	2301	4279	482
Ceduna	772	1890	1597	1695	1736	1782	1397	1830	2110	1412	1046	1498	2420	883	3750	2115	3576	1829	2796		1951	1005	3184	1636	1411	495	1483	2314
Charleville	1582	3841	1232	2320	2763	1568	1449	1022	1447	1325	1591	453	742	1068	3989	4066	1625	1225	4747	1951		2026	2747	817	3362	2446	1500	4265
Coober Pedy	847	2895	1672	690	731	1857	1472	1905	2185	1487	1121	1573	2495	958	3421	3120	3066	1904	3801	1005	2026		2179	1711	2416	1500	1558	3319
Darwin	3026	4428	3851	1489	1932	4036	3651	3769	4364	3666	3300	3200	3406	3137	1870	4219	2803	3972	3253	3184	2747	2179		3564	4547	3679	3737	3723
Dubbo	1194	3526	553	2401	2442	863	893	205	630	769	1068	364	854	753	4806	3751	2211	408	4432	1636	817	1711	3564		3047	2131	891	3950
Esperance	2183	479	3008	3106	3147	3193	2808	3241	3521	2823	2457	2909	3831	2294	2745	664	4987	3240	1628	1411	3362	2416	4547	3047		916	2894	1160
Eucla	1267	1395	2092	2190	2231	2277	1892	2325	2605	1907	1541	1993	2915	1378	3255	1620	4071	2324	2301	495	2446	1500	3679	2131	916		1978	1819
Geelong	711	3373	382	2248	2289	349	86	848	677	210	437	1082	1745	840	4979	3598	3102	730	4279	1483	1500	1558	3737	891	2894	1978		3797
Geraldton	3086	818	3911	4009	4050	4096	3711	4144	4424	3726	3360	3812	4734	3197	1921	609	5890	4143	482	2314	4265	3319	3723	3950	1160	1819	3797	
Grafton	1845	4177	1184	3052	3093	1397	1544	825	1069	1420	1719	808	330	1404	4975	4402	2033	911	5083	2287	1069	2362	3733	651	3698	2782	1542	4601
Horsham	433	3095	531	1970	2011	577	192	997	905	218	159	1067	1841	599	4701	3320	3145	879	4001	1205	1520	1280	3459	987	2616	1700	278	3519
Kalgoorlie–Boulder	2184	886	3009	3107	3148	3194	2809	3242	3522	2824	2458	2910	3832	2295	2338	779	4988	3241	1460	1412	3363	2417	4140	3048	407	917	2895	978
Katherine	2712	4114	3537	1175	1618	3722	3337	3455	3880	3352	2986	2886	3092	2823	1556	3905	2489	3658	2939	2870	2433	1865	314	3250	4233	3365	3423	3409
Kununurra	3224	3602	4049	1687	2130	4234	3849	3967	4392	3864	3498	3398	3604	3335	1044	3393	3001	4170	2427	3382	2945	2377	826	3762	3721	3877	3935	2897
Longreach	2098	4357	1748	1804	2247	2084	1965	1538	1963	1841	2107	969	1175	1584	3473	4582	1109	1741	4856	2467	516	2494	2231	1333	3878	2962	2016	4781
Mackay	2670	4932	2029	2451	2894	2365	2369	1681	2106	2245	2544	1544	968	2159	4120	5157	735	1884	5503	3042	1091	3141	2878	1476	4453	3537	2367	5356
Meekatharra	3055	1159	3880	3978	4019	4065	3680	4113	4393	3695	3329	3781	4703	3166	1467	950	5444	4112	627	2283	4234	3288	3269	3919	1278	1788	3766	541
Melbourne	733	3395	313	2270	2311	277	111	779	605	146	459	978	1676	842	5001	3620	3033	661	4301	1505	1431	1580	3759	822	2916	2000	72	3819
Mildura	394	2916	571	1791	1832	825	460	804	956	402	417	870	1654	294	4522	3141	2948	803	3822	1026	1323	1101	3280	800	2437	1521	546	3340
Moree	1567	3829	926	2704	2745	1262	1294	578	1003	1141	1482	441	481	1056	4608	4054	1838	781	4735	1939	702	2014	3366	373	3350	2434	1264	4253
Mount Gambier	452	3114	721	1989	2030	697	309	1187	1025	433	186	1324	2098	856	4720	3339	3402	1069	4020	1224	1777	1299	3478	1244	2635	1719	365	3538
Mount Isa	2706	4754	2383	1169	1612	2719	2600	2173	2598	2476	2742	1604	1810	2219	2838	4979	1207	2736	4221	2864	1151	1859	1596	1968	4275	3359	2651	4691
Newcastle	1553	3930	704	2805	2846	917	1116	338	589	1017	1427	768	821	1157	5111	4155	2341	431	4836	2040	1205	2115	3869	404	3451	2535	1086	4354
Perth	2700	410	3525	3623	3664	3710	3325	3758	4038	3340	2974	3426	4348	2811	2230	187	5504	3757	904	1928	3879	2933	4032	3564	738	1433	3411	422
Port Augusta	307	2355	1132	1230	1271	1317	932	1365	1645	947	581	1033	1955	418	3961	2580	3111	1364	3261	465	1486	540	2719	1171	1876	960	1018	2779
Port Hedland	3921	2025	4746	3264	3707	5100	4546	4979	5259	4561	4195	4647	5181	4032	601	1816	4578	4978	850	3149	4522	3954	2403	4785	2144	2654	4632	1320
Port Lincoln	647	2289	1472	1570	1611	1657	1272	1705	1985	1287	921	1373	2295	758	4149	2514	3451	1704	3195	399	1826	880	3059	1511	1751	894	1358	2713
Port Macquarie	1804	4136	942	3011	3052	1155	1354	565	827	1255	1665	859	584	1363	5150	4361	2287	669	5042	2246	1244	2321	3908	610	3657	2741	1324	4560
Renmark	250	2772	715	1647	1688	969	604	948	1100	546	269	1014	1798	438	4378	2997	3092	947	3678	882	1467	957	3136	944	2293	1377	690	3196
Rockhampton	2336	4598	1695	2486	2929	2031	2035	1347	1772	1911	2210	1210	634	1825	4155	4823	1069	1550	5504	2708	831	3176	2913	1142	4119	3203	2033	5022
Sydney	1414	3936	565	2811	2852	759	977	211	431	878	1288	780	966	1169	5222	4161	2479	292	4842	2046	1233	2121	3980	416	3457	2541	947	4360
Tamworth	1534	3866	893	2741	2782	1186	1233	457	858	1109	1408	589	573	1093	4880	4091	2110	700	4772	1965	974	2051	3638	340	3387	2471	1231	4290
Tennant Creek	2043	4091	2868	531	949	3053	2668	2836	3261	2683	2317	2267	2473	2154	2225	4316	1870	3039	3608	2201	1814	1196	983	2631	3612	2696	2754	4078
Toowoomba	1921	4183	1280	2852	3099	1616	1620	956	1357	1496	1795	795	127	1410	4521	4408	1705	1199	5089	2293	615	2368	3279	727	3704	2788	1618	4607
Townsville	2862	5121	2419	2061	2504	2755	2759	2071	2496	2635	2871	1733	1358	2348	3730	5346	345	2274	5113	3231	1280	2751	2488	1866	4642	3726	2757	5545
Wagga Wagga	948	3470	145	2345	2386	481	550	321	402	426	822	711	1262	848	5076	3695	2619	249	4376	1580	1164	1655	3834	408	2991	2075	527	3894
Warrnambool	649	3311	567	2186	2227	534	174	1052	862	298	383	1170	1933	829	4917	3536	3278	987	4217	1421	1623	1496	3675	1067	2832	1916	185	3735

Distances on this chart have been calculated over main roads and do not necessarily reflect the shortest route between towns.
Refer to page 630 for distance chart of Tasmania.

Approximate Distances AUSTRALIA	Grafton	Horsham	Kalgoorlie–Boulder	Katherine	Kununurra	Longreach	Mackay	Meekatharra	Melbourne	Mildura	Moree	Mount Gambier	Mount Isa	Newcastle	Perth	Port Augusta	Port Hedland	Port Lincoln	Port Macquarie	Renmark	Rockhampton	Sydney	Tamworth	Tennant Creek	Toowoomba	Townsville	Wagga Wagga	Warrnambool
Adelaide	1845	433	2184	2712	3224	2098	2670	3055	733	394	1567	452	2706	1553	2700	307	3921	647	1804	250	2336	1414	1534	2043	1921	2862	948	649
Albany	4177	3095	886	4114	3602	4357	4932	1159	3395	2916	3829	3114	4754	3930	410	2355	2025	2289	4136	2772	4598	3936	3866	4091	4183	5121	3470	3311
Albury	1184	531	3009	3537	4049	1748	2029	3880	313	571	926	721	2383	704	3525	1132	4746	1472	942	715	1695	565	893	2868	1280	2419	145	567
Alice Springs	3052	1970	3107	1175	1687	1804	2451	3978	2270	1791	2704	1989	1169	2805	3623	1230	3264	1570	3011	1647	2486	2811	2741	531	2852	2061	2345	2186
Ayers Rock/Yulara	3093	2011	3148	1618	2130	2247	2894	4019	2311	1832	2745	2030	1612	2846	3664	1271	3707	1611	3052	1688	2929	2852	2782	949	3099	2504	2386	2227
Bairnsdale	1397	577	3194	3722	4234	2084	2365	4065	277	825	1262	697	2719	917	3710	1317	5100	1657	1155	969	2031	759	1186	3053	1616	2755	481	534
Ballarat	1544	192	2809	3337	3849	1965	2369	3680	111	460	1294	309	2600	1116	3325	932	4546	1272	1354	604	2035	977	1233	2668	1620	2759	550	174
Bathurst	825	997	3242	3455	3967	1538	1681	4113	779	804	578	1187	2173	338	3758	1365	4979	1705	565	948	1347	211	457	2836	956	2071	321	1052
Bega	1069	905	3522	3880	4392	1963	2106	4393	605	956	1003	1025	2598	589	4038	1645	5259	1985	827	1100	1772	431	858	3261	1357	2496	402	862
Bendigo	1420	218	2824	3352	3864	1841	2245	3695	146	402	1141	433	2476	1017	3340	947	4561	1287	1255	546	1911	878	1109	2683	1496	2635	426	298
Bordertown	1719	159	2458	2986	3498	2107	2544	3329	459	417	1482	186	2742	1427	2974	581	4195	921	1665	269	2210	1288	1408	2317	1795	2871	822	383
Bourke	808	1067	2910	2886	3398	969	1544	3781	978	870	441	1324	1604	768	3426	1033	4647	1373	859	1014	1210	780	589	2267	795	1733	711	1170
Brisbane	330	1841	3832	3092	3604	1175	968	4703	1676	1654	481	2098	1810	821	4348	1955	5181	2295	584	1798	634	966	573	2473	127	1358	1262	1933
Broken Hill	1404	599	2295	2823	3335	1584	2159	3166	842	294	1056	856	2219	1157	2811	418	4032	758	1363	438	1825	1169	1093	2154	1410	2348	848	829
Broome	4975	4701	2338	1556	1044	3473	4120	1467	5001	4522	4608	4720	2838	5111	2230	3961	601	4149	5150	4378	4155	5222	4880	2225	4521	3730	5076	4917
Bunbury	4402	3320	779	3905	3393	4582	5157	950	3620	3141	4054	3339	4979	4155	187	2580	1816	2514	4361	2997	4823	4161	4091	4316	4408	5346	3695	3536
Cairns	2033	3145	4988	2489	3001	1109	735	5444	3033	2948	1838	3402	1207	2341	5504	3111	4578	3451	2287	3092	1069	2479	2110	1870	1705	345	2619	3278
Canberra	911	879	3241	3658	4170	1741	1884	4112	661	803	781	1069	2736	431	3757	1364	4978	1704	669	947	1550	292	700	3039	1199	2274	249	987
Carnarvon	5083	4001	1460	2939	2427	4856	5503	627	4301	3822	4735	4020	4221	4836	904	3261	850	3195	5042	3678	5504	4842	4772	3608	5089	5113	4376	4217
Ceduna	2287	1205	1412	2870	3382	2467	3042	2283	1505	1026	1939	1224	2864	2040	1928	465	3149	399	2246	882	2708	2046	1965	2201	2293	3231	1580	1421
Charleville	1069	1520	3363	2433	2945	516	1091	4234	1431	1323	702	1777	1151	1205	3879	1486	4522	1826	1244	1467	831	1233	974	1814	615	1280	1164	1623
Coober Pedy	2362	1280	2417	1865	2377	2494	3141	3288	1580	1101	2014	1299	1859	2115	2933	540	3954	880	2321	957	3176	2121	2051	1196	2368	2751	1655	1496
Darwin	3733	3459	4140	314	826	2231	2878	3269	3759	3280	3366	3478	1596	3869	4032	2719	2403	3059	3908	3136	2913	3980	3638	983	3279	2488	3834	3675
Dubbo	651	987	3048	3250	3762	1333	1476	3919	822	800	373	1244	1968	404	3564	1171	4785	1511	610	944	1142	416	340	2631	727	1866	408	1067
Esperance	3698	2616	407	4233	3721	3878	4453	1278	2916	2437	3350	2635	4275	3451	738	1876	2144	1751	3657	2293	4119	3457	3387	3612	3704	4642	2991	2832
Eucla	2782	1700	917	3365	3877	2962	3537	1788	2000	1521	2434	1719	3359	2535	1433	960	2654	894	2741	1377	3203	2541	2471	2696	2788	3726	2075	1916
Geelong	1542	278	2895	3423	3935	2016	2367	3766	72	546	1264	365	2651	1086	3411	1018	4632	1358	1324	690	2033	947	1231	2754	1618	2757	527	185
Geraldton	4601	3519	978	3409	2897	4781	5356	541	3819	3340	4253	3538	4691	4354	422	2779	1320	2713	4560	3196	5022	4360	4290	4078	4607	5545	3894	3735
Grafton		1638	3699	3419	3931	1502	1298	4570	1473	1451	367	1895	2137	491	4215	1822	5436	2162	254	1595	964	638	311	2800	431	1688	1059	1718
Horsham	1638		2451	3145	3657	2036	2463	3322	300	305	1360	257	2671	1235	3133	740	4188	1080	1462	428	2129	1096	1327	2476	1714	2800	644	230
Kalgoorlie–Boulder	3699	2451		3826	3314	3879	4454	871	2917	2438	3351	2636	4276	3452	582	1877	1737	1811	3658	2294	4120	3458	3388	3613	3705	4643	2992	2833
Katherine	3419	3145	3826		512	1917	2564	2955	3445	2966	3052	3164	1282	3556	3718	2405	2089	2745	3594	2822	2599	3666	3324	669	2965	2174	3520	3361
Kununurra	3931	3657	3314	512		2429	3076	2443	3957	3478	3564	3676	1794	4067	3206	2917	1577	3257	4106	3334	3111	4178	3836	1181	3477	2686	4032	3873
Longreach	1502	2036	3879	1917	2429		791	4750	1947	1839	1135	2293	635	1638	4395	2002	4006	2342	1677	1983	682	1749	1407	1298	1048	764	1680	2139
Mackay	1298	2463	4454	2564	3076	791		5325	2298	2276	1103	2720	1282	1606	4970	2577	4653	2917	1552	2420	334	1744	1375	1945	970	390	1884	2543
Meekatharra	4570	3322	871	2955	2443	4750	5325		3788	3309	4222	3507	4237	4323	763	2748	866	2682	4529	3165	5524	4329	4259	3624	4576	5129	3863	3704
Melbourne	1473	300	2917	3445	3957	1947	2298	3788		548	1195	420	2582	1017	3433	1040	4823	1380	1255	692	1964	878	1162	2776	1549	2688	458	257
Mildura	1451	305	2438	2966	3478	1839	2276	3309	548		1173	562	2474	1159	2954	561	4175	901	1397	144	1942	1020	1140	2297	1527	2603	554	535
Moree	367	1360	3351	3052	3564	1135	1103	4222	1195	1173		1627	1770	503	3867	1474	5088	1814	542	1317	769	641	272	2433	354	1493	781	1449
Mount Gambier	1895	257	2636	3164	3676	2293	2720	3507	420	562	1627		2928	1425	3152	759	4373	1099	1663	455	2386	1286	1584	2495	1971	3057	901	197
Mount Isa	2137	2671	4276	1282	1794	635	1282	4237	2582	2474	1770	2928		2273	4792	2399	3371	2739	2312	2618	1317	2384	2042	663	1683	892	2315	2774
Newcastle	491	1235	3452	3556	4067	1638	1606	4323	1017	1159	503	1425	2273		3968	1575	5189	1915	249	1303	1272	158	289	2936	788	1996	605	1271
Perth	4215	3133	582	3718	3206	4395	4970	763	3433	2954	3867	3152	4792	3968		2393	1629	2327	4174	2810	4636	3974	3904	4129	4221	5159	3508	3349
Port Augusta	1822	740	1877	2405	2917	2002	2577	2748	1040	561	1474	759	2399	1575	2393		3614	340	1781	417	2243	1581	1511	1736	1828	2766	1115	956
Port Hedland	5436	4188	1737	2089	1577	4006	4653	866	4823	4175	5088	4373	3371	5189	1629	3614		3548	5395	4031	4688	5195	5125	2758	5054	4263	4729	4570
Port Lincoln	2162	1080	1811	2745	3257	2342	2917	2682	1380	901	1814	1099	2739	1915	2327	340	3548		2121	757	2583	1921	1851	2076	2168	3106	1455	1296
Port Macquarie	254	1462	3658	3594	4106	1677	1552	4529	1255	1397	542	1663	2312	249	4174	1781	5395	2121		1541	1218	396	270	2975	630	1942	843	1509
Renmark	1595	428	2294	2822	3334	1983	2420	3165	692	144	1317	455	2618	1303	2810	417	4031	757	1541		2086	1164	1284	2153	1671	2747	698	652
Rockhampton	964	2129	4120	2599	3111	682	334	5524	1964	1942	769	2386	1317	1272	4636	2243	4688	2583	1218	2086		1410	1041	1980	636	724	1550	2209
Sydney	638	1096	3458	3666	4178	1749	1744	4329	878	1020	641	1286	2384	158	3974	1581	5195	1921	396	1164	1410		427	3047	926	2134	466	1132
Tamworth	311	1327	3388	3324	3836	1407	1375	4259	1162	1140	272	1584	2042	289	3904	1511	5125	1851	270	1284	1041	427		2705	499	1765	748	1407
Tennant Creek	2800	2476	3613	669	1181	1298	1945	3624	2776	2297	2433	2495	663	2936	4129	1736	2758	2076	2975	2153	1980	3047	2705		2346	1555	2851	2692
Toowoomba	431	1714	3705	2965	3477	1048	970	4576	1549	1527	354	1971	1683	788	4221	1828	5054	2168	630	1671	636	926	499	2346		1360	1135	1794
Townsville	1688	2800	4643	2174	2686	764	390	5129	2688	2603	1493	3057	892	1996	5159	2766	4263	3106	1942	2747	724	2134	1765	1555	1360		2274	2933
Wagga Wagga	1059	644	2992	3520	4032	1680	1884	3863	458	554	781	901	2315	605	3508	1115	4729	1455	843	698	1550	466	748	2851	1135	2274		724
Warrnambool	1718	230	2833	3361	3873	2139	2543	3704	257	535	1449	197	2774	1271	3349	956	4570	1296	1509	652	2209	1132	1407	2692	1794	2933	724	

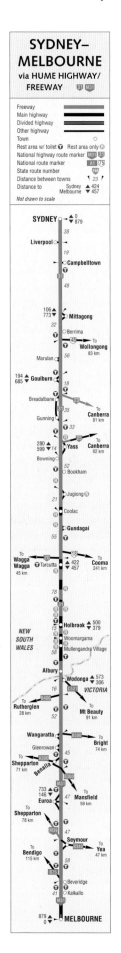

SYDNEY–MELBOURNE
via HUME HIGHWAY/ FREEWAY

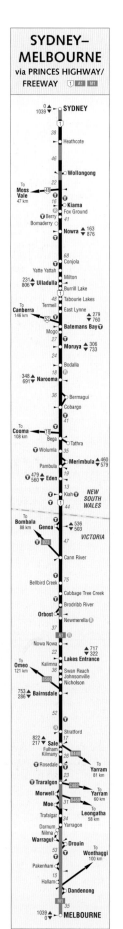

SYDNEY–MELBOURNE
via PRINCES HIGHWAY/ FREEWAY

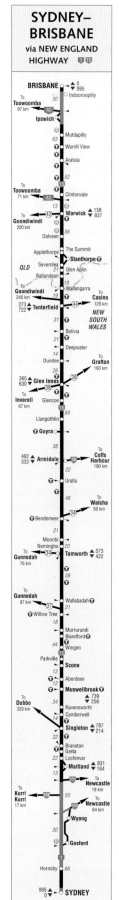

SYDNEY–BRISBANE
via NEW ENGLAND HIGHWAY

MELBOURNE –ADELAIDE
via WESTERN & DUKES HIGHWAYS

MELBOURNE –ADELAIDE
via PRINCES HIGHWAY

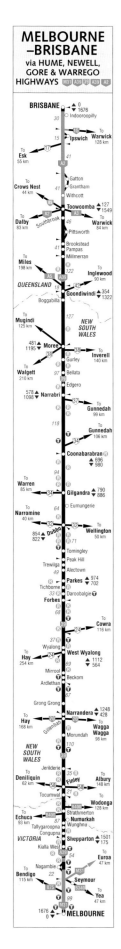

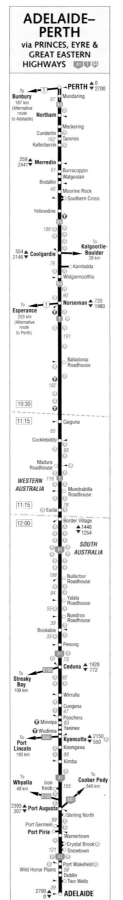

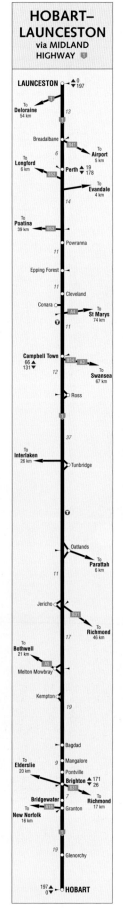

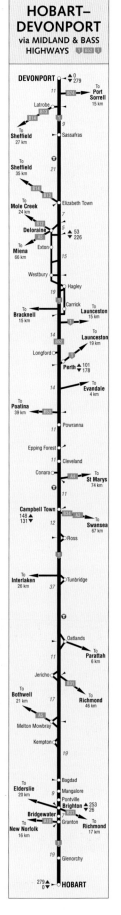

MAPS

NEW SOUTH WALES and AUSTRALIAN CAPITAL TERRITORY

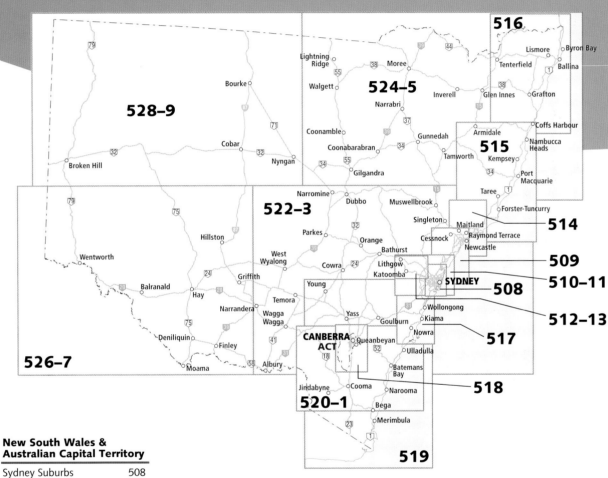

New South Wales & Australian Capital Territory

Sydney Suburbs	508
Central Coast	509
Sydney & Surrounds	510–11
Blue Mountains	512–13
Newcastle & Surrounds	514
Mid-north Coast	515
North Coast	516
Southern Highlands	517
Australian Capital Territory	518
South-eastern New South Wales	519
Snowy Mountains & The South Coast	520–1

Central-eastern New South Wales	522–3
North-eastern New South Wales	524–5
South-western New South Wales	526–7
North-western New South Wales	528–9

INTER-CITY ROUTES	DISTANCE
Sydney–Melbourne via Hume Highway/Freeway	879 km
Sydney–Melbourne via Princes Highway/Freeway	1039 km
Sydney–Brisbane via New England Highway	995 km
Sydney–Brisbane via Pacific Highway	936 km
Sydney–Adelaide via Hume & Sturt highways	1415 km

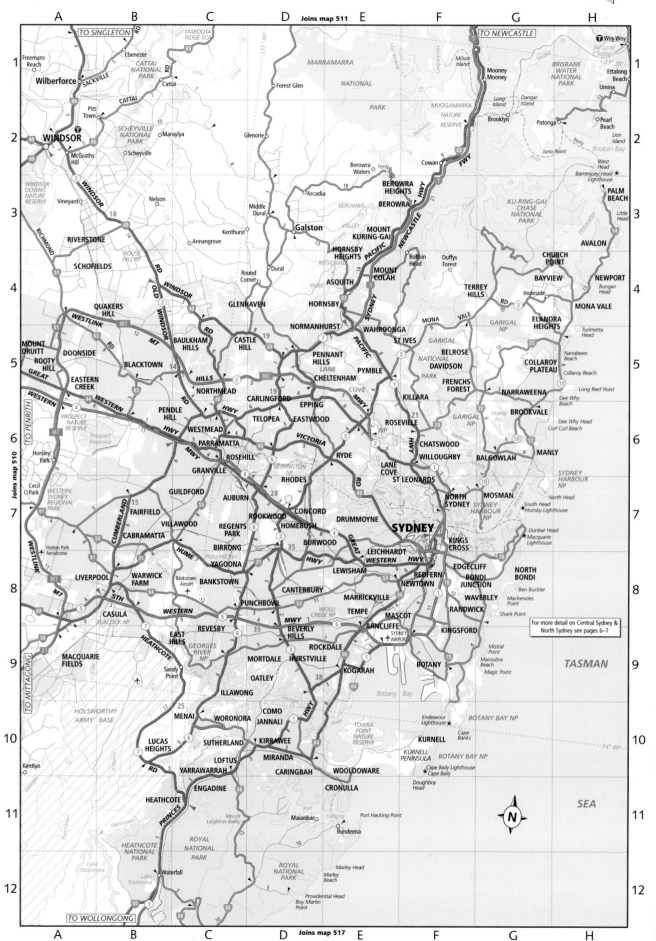

0 2 4 6 8 10 km

Joins map 511

A B C D E F G H

1

TO SINGLETON
Freemans Reach
Wilberforce
Ebenezer
Cattai
CATTAI NATIONAL PARK
MAROOTA RIDGE SCA
Forest Glen
MARRAMARRA
NATIONAL
PARK
TO NEWCASTLE
Woy Woy
Brisbane Water
BRISBANE WATER NATIONAL PARK
Ettalong Beach
Umina

2

WINDSOR
Pitt Town
McGraths Hill
SCHEYVILLE NATIONAL PARK
Maraylya
Scheyville
Nelson
Glenorie
Arcadia
Berowra Waters
Mooney Mooney
Long Island
Brooklyn
Dangar Island
Patonga
Juno Point
Pearl Beach
Lion Island
Broken Bay

3

Vineyard
WINDSOR DOWNS NATURE RESERVE
Riverstone
Schofields
ROUSE HILL RP
Annangrove
Kenthurst
Middle Dural
Round Corner
Dural
Galston
BEROWRA HEIGHTS
BEROWRA
MOUNT KURING-GAI
HORNSBY HEIGHTS
MOUNT COLAH
Bobbin Head
Cowan
Duffys Forest
MONA VALE
KU-RING-GAI CHASE NATIONAL PARK
West Head
Barrenjoey Head Lighthouse
PALM BEACH
Little Head
AVALON
CHURCH POINT
BAYVIEW
NEWPORT
Bungan Head

4

MOUNT DRUITT
ROOTY HILL
QUAKERS HILL
DOONSIDE
BLACKTOWN
BAULKHAM HILLS
CASTLE HILL
GLENHAVEN
NORMANHURST
ASQUITH
HORNSBY
WAHROONGA
ST IVES
TERREY HILLS
Ingleside
ELANORA HEIGHTS
MONA VALE
GARIGAL NP
COLLAROY PLATEAU
Narrabeen Beach
Collaroy Beach
Long Reef Point

5

EASTERN CREEK
WESTLINK
PENDLE HILL
NORTHMEAD
CARLINGFORD
PENNANT HILLS
CHELTENHAM
PYMBLE
KILLARA
BELROSE
DAVIDSON
FRENCHS FOREST
NARRAWEENA
BROOKVALE
Dee Why Beach
Dee Why Head
Curl Curl Beach

6

PROSPECT NATURE RESERVE
Prospect Reservoir
WESTMEAD
PARRAMATTA
ROSEHILL
TELOPEA
EASTWOOD
EPPING
VICTORIA
RYDE
ROSEVILLE
CHATSWOOD
WILLOUGHBY
LANE COVE
ST LEONARDS
BALGOWLAH
MANLY
SYDNEY HARBOUR NP

7

TO PENRITH
Horsley Park
Cecil Park
WESTERN SYDNEY REGIONAL PARK
GRANVILLE
GUILDFORD
AUBURN
CONCORD
DRUMMOYNE
RHODES
NORTH SYDNEY
MOSMAN
North Head
Hornby Lighthouse
SYDNEY HARBOUR NP
SYDNEY

8

WESTLINK
LIVERPOOL
WARWICK FARM
FAIRFIELD
VILLAWOOD
CABRAMATTA
REGENTS PARK
ROOKWOOD
HOMEBUSH
BURWOOD
Bankstown Airport
YAGOONA
BANKSTOWN
CANTERBURY
LEWISHAM
MARRICKVILLE
LEICHHARDT
REDFERN
NEWTOWN
EDGECLIFF
WAVERLEY
RANDWICK
KINGS CROSS
BONDI JUNCTION
NORTH BONDI
Ben Buckler
Mackenzies Point
Hoxton Park Aerodrome

9

CASULA
EAST HILLS
REVESBY
PUNCHBOWL
BEVERLY HILLS
TEMPE
MASCOT
ARNCLIFFE
ROCKDALE
KOGARAH
KINGSFORD
BOTANY
RANDWICK
SYDNEY AIRPORT
MACQUARIE FIELDS
Sandy Point
MORTDALE
HURSTVILLE
OATLEY
Mistral Point
Maroubra Beach
Magic Point
TASMAN

10

TO MITTAGONG
LUCAS HEIGHTS
HOLSWORTHY ARMY BASE
ILLAWONG
MENAI
WORONORA
COMO
JANNALI
SUTHERLAND
KIRRAWEE
MIRANDA
WOOLOOWARE
CARINGBAH
Botany Bay
Endeavour Lighthouse
Cape Banks
KURNELL
KURNELL PENINSULA
BOTANY BAY NP
Cape Baily Lighthouse
Cape Baily
TOWRA POINT NATURE RESERVE

11

Kentlyn
HEATHCOTE
ENGADINE
YARRAWARRAH
LOFTUS
CRONULLA
Maianbar
Bundeena
Port Hacking Point
Doughboy Head
Hacking
SEA
N

12

TO WOLLONGONG
HEATHCOTE NATIONAL PARK
ROYAL NATIONAL PARK
Waterfall
Lake Woronora
Lake Toolooma
Marley Head
Marley Beach
Providential Head
Boy Martin Point

A B C D E F G H

Joins map 517

For more detail on Central Sydney & North Sydney see pages 6–7

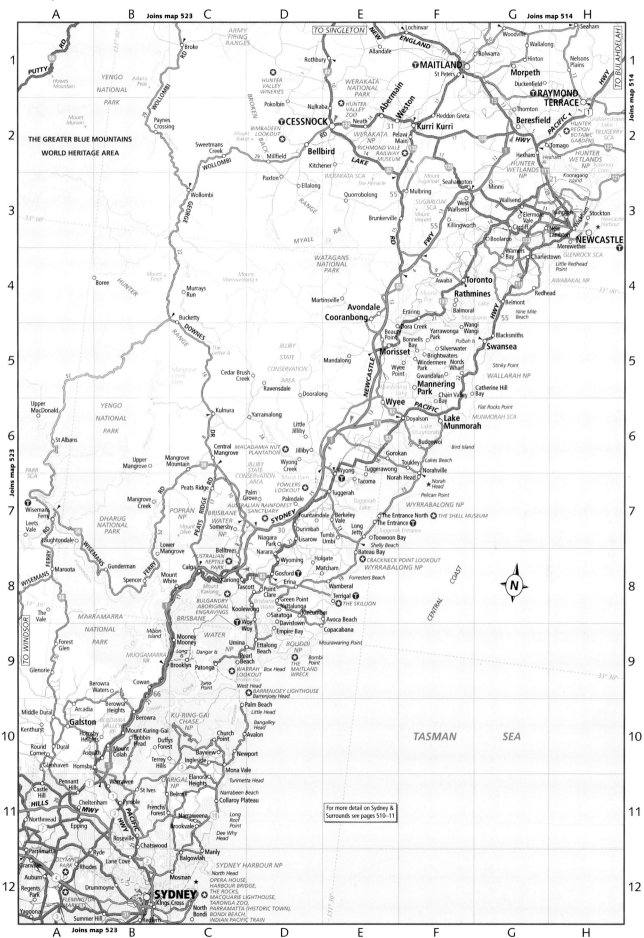

0 5 10 15 20 km

Joins map 523
Joins map 514
Joins map 523
Joins map 523
Joins map 514

THE GREATER BLUE MOUNTAINS
WORLD HERITAGE AREA

TO SINGLETON
TO BULAHDELAH
TO WINDSOR

Lochinvar
Seaham
Woodville
Wallalong
Allandale
Bolwarra
Hinton
Nelsons Plains
MAITLAND
St Peters
Morpeth
Duckenfield
RAYMOND TERRACE
Thornton
Heddon Greta
Abermain
Weston
Kurri Kurri
Beresfield
Pelaw Main
Hexham
Tomago
Broke
Rothbury
HUNTER VALLEY WINERIES
Pokolbin
Nulkaba
HUNTER VALLEY ZOO
Neath
CESSNOCK
31
WERAKATA NATIONAL PARK
WERAKATA NP
RICHMOND VALE RAILWAY MUSEUM
HUNTER REGION BOTANIC GARDENS
TILLIGERRY SCA
Paynes Crossing
Sweetmans Creek
Millfield
Bellbird
Kitchener
Paxton
Ellalong
WERAKATA SCA
The Pinnacle
Quorrobolong
Seahampton
Minmi
Mulbring
West Wallsend
Wallsend
HUNTER WETLANDS NP
Kooragang Island
Fullerton Cove
Brunkerville
SUGARLOAF SCA
Mount Vincent
Killingworth
Elermore Vale
Cardiff
New Lambton
NEWCASTLE
Merewether
Boolaroo
Warners Bay
Charlestown
GLENROCK SCA
Little Redhead Point
Boree
Murrays Run
Martinsville
Avondale
Cooranbong
Eraring
Awaba
Toronto
Balmoral
Rathmines
Belmont
Redhead
Nine Mile Beach
AWABAKAL NR
Bucketty
Beauty Point
Dora Creek
Yarrawonga Park
Wangi Wangi
Silverwater
Bonnells Bay
Pulbah Is
Blacksmiths
Swansea
Cedar Brush Creek
Ravensdale
Dooralong
Mandalong
Morisset
Brightwaters
Windermere Park
Nords Wharf
Stinky Point
WALLARAH NP
Kulnura
Yarramalong
Wyee Point
Gwandalan
Mannering Park
Chain Valley Bay
Catherine Hill Bay
Little Jilliby
Wyee
Flat Rocks Point
Upper MacDonald
St Albans
YENGO NATIONAL PARK
Central Mangrove
MACADAMIA NUT PLANTATION
Jilliby
JILLIBY STATE CONSERVATION AREA
Wyong Creek
Doyalson
Lake Munmorah
MUNMORAH SCA
Lake Munmorah
Bird Island
Upper Mangrove
Mangrove Mountain
FOWLERS LOOKOUT
Budgewoi
Gorokan
Lakes Beach
Peats Ridge
Mangrove Creek
Palm Grove
Palmdale
Wyong
Tacoma
Toukley
Norah Head
Norahville
Norah Head
WYRRABALONG NP
Lower Mangrove
POPRAN NP
AUSTRALIAN RAINFOREST SANCTUARY
Somersby
BRISBANE WATER NP
Niagara Park
Narara
Fountaindale
Ourimbah
Berkeley Vale
Tumbi Umbi
Lisarow
Tuggerawong
Tuggerah
Pelican Point
Tuggerah Lake
Long Jetty
The Entrance North
THE SHELL MUSEUM
The Entrance
Tuggerah Entrance
Toowoon Bay
Gunderman
DHARUG NATIONAL PARK
Maroota
Spencer
Mount White
BULGANDRY ABORIGINAL ENGRAVINGS
Kariong
Tascott
Wyoming
Holgate
Matcham
Gosford
Erina
Shelly Beach
Bateau Bay
CRACKNECK POINT LOOKOUT
WYRRABALONG NP
Forresters Beach
Wamberal
Terrigal
THE SKILLION
CENTRAL COAST
Wisemans Ferry
Leets Vale
Laughtondale
Koolewong
Point Clare
Green Point
Yattalunga
Saratoga
Davistown
Kincumber
Avoca Beach
Copacabana
The Vale
MARRAMARRA NATIONAL PARK
MUOGAMARRA NR
Mooney Mooney
Woy Woy
Empire Bay
BOUDDI NP
Mowararang Point
Forest Glen
Milson Island
Long Is
Dangar Is
Umina
Ettalong Beach
Pearl Beach
Patonga
WARRAH LOOKOUT
West Head
Box Head
Bombi Point
THE MAITLAND WRECK
Glenorie
Brooklyn
Juno Point
BARRENJOEY LIGHTHOUSE
Barrenjoey Head
Berowra Waters
Cowan
Palm Beach
Little Head
Bangalley Head
Middle Dural
Arcadia
Berowra Heights
Berowra
BEROWRA VALLEYS RP
KU-RING-GAI CHASE NP
Avalon
Kenthurst
Galston
Mount Kuring-Gai
Church Point
Dural
Hornsby Heights
Bobbin Head
Duffys Forest
Newport
Round Corner
Asquith
Mount Colah
Bayview
Ingleside
Mona Vale
Glenhaven
Hornsby
Terrey Hills
Elanora Heights
Turimetta Head
Pennant Hills
Warrawee
St Ives
Belrose
Narrabeen Beach
Collaroy Plateau
Long Reef Point
Northmead
Castle Hill
HILLS
Cheltenham
Pymble
Frenchs Forest
Narraweena
Brookvale
Dee Why Head
Epping
Roseville
Chatswood
Balgowlah
Manly
Parramatta
OLYMPIC PARK
Ryde
Lane Cove
Mosman
North Head
SYDNEY HARBOUR NP
Granville
Rhodes
Drummoyne
SYDNEY
Kings Cross
Auburn
FLEMINGTON MARKETS
Summer Hill
North Bondi
Regents Park
Yagoona
Redfern

OPERA HOUSE, HARBOUR BRIDGE, THE ROCKS, MACQUARIE LIGHTHOUSE, TARONGA ZOO, PARRAMATTA (HISTORIC TOWN), BONDI BEACH, INDIAN PACIFIC TRAIN

For more detail on Sydney & Surrounds see pages 510–11

TASMAN SEA

N

A | B | C | D | Joins map 523 E | F | G | H

Joins map 523

1

TO MUDGEE

Wallerawang

For more detail on the
Blue Mountains
see pages 512–13

WOLLEMI
NATIONAL
PARK

Mount
Lambie

Marrangaroo

32

PROHIBITED
AREA

BLUE
MOUNTAINS

THE GREATER BLUE MOUNTAINS
WORLD HERITAGE AREA

2

Rydal

Sodwalls

MARRANGAROO
NATIONAL
PARK

LITHGOW

Bowenfels

Clarence

Newnes
Junction

NATIONAL

PARK

Mount Irvine

Bilpin

Old Bowenfels

ZIG ZAG
RAILWAY

CATHEDRAL
OF FERNS

Lost Flat
Mountain

Mount
Tootie

Bell

Mount
Wilson

85

OF

Kurrajong
Heights

Bellbird Hill
Lookout

3

Glenroy

Hartley

WESTERN

RD

Little Hartley

32

Hartley
Vale

BELLS

BELL

LINE

EXPLORERS

BLUE MTNS
DRIVE

Mount
Tomah

Berambing

CALEY

MOUNT
TOMAH
BOTANIC
GARDEN

26

RANGE

40

PATERSON

RD

Kurrajong

Bowen
Mountain

9

Kurmond

Low
North

4

Lowther

CAVES

Hampton

Mount
Bindo

DARLING

HWY

Mount Victoria

40

MOUNT
BLACKHEATH
LOOKOUT

PULPIT ROCK
RESERVE & LOOKOUT

GOVETTS LEAP LOOKOUT

Blackheath

Mount
Banks

RANGE

MOUNT HAY RANGE

BLUE

Mount
Hay

MOUNTAINS

RANGE

Grose
Vale

AVOCA
LOOKOUT

Richmond

Agnes
Banks

5

GREAT

DIVIDING

RANGE

JENOLAN

KANANGRA-BOYD
NATIONAL
PARK

HARGRAVES
LOOKOUT

Shipley

Medlow
Bath

Megalong

EXPLORERS
TREE

KATOOMBA

Euroka

Leura

Lake
Greaves

Lake
Medlow

Cascade
Dams

Wentworth
Falls
Lake

Wentworth
Falls

ECHO POINT

SCENIC WORLD

THREE
SISTERS

Bullaburra

GREAT

Lawson

Hazelbrook

Linden

6

31

Mount
Twiss

NATIONAL

PARK

Faulconbridge

WESTERN

Woodford

Winmalee

Hawkesbury
Heights

HAWKESBURY
LOOKOUT

Hawkesbury
Heights

32

SPRINGWOOD

Valley
Heights

Warrimoo

Yellow
Rock

YELLOMUNDEE
RP

Castlereagh

Londonderry

23

6

Joins map 522

JENOLAN KARST
CONSERVATION
RESERVE

THE GREATER BLUE MOUNTAINS
WORLD HERITAGE AREA

BLACK

RANGE

BLUE

MOUNTAINS

NATIONAL

PARK

Blaxland

Glenbrook

BLUE MTNS
DRIVE

Lapstone

20

10

Emu
Plains

Penrith

MUSEUM
OF FIRE

Kingswood

HWY

WESTERN

7

MOORARA
RANGE

KANANGRA

RANGE

KANANGRA-BOYD
NATIONAL
PARK

Apple Tree
Flat

WOODFORD
RANGE

The
Ironbarks

MULGOA
NR

THE

PROHIBITED

AREA

8

Kanangra
Gorge

Mount
Cloudmaker

GANGERANG
RANGE

ERSKINE

Mount
Hall

RANGE

Mount
Erskine

Pocket
Mountain

Mulgoa

Wallacia

Warragamba
Dam

Luddenham

Warragamba

Silverdale

ELIZABETH

RD

Badgerys
Creek

37

9

KANANGRA
WALLS

34° 00'

Mount
Wallara

Mount
Colboyd

GINGRA RANGE

SCOTTS

MAIN

Kowmung

ROCK

BLUE

BROKEN

RANGE

Burragorang

MOUNTAINS

BURRAGORANG
STATE
CONSERVATION
AREA

GULGUER
NATURE
RESERVE

Werombi

45

Bringelly

Ross

Leppin

10

KANANGRA-BOYD
NATIONAL
PARK

Mount
Armour

Byrnes
Gap

NATIONAL

Mount
Hoggett

THE GREATER BLUE MOUNTAINS
WORLD HERITAGE AREA

PARK

BURRAGORANG
LOOKOUT

BURRAGORANG
STATE
CONSERVATION
AREA

Cottage
Mountain

Orangeville

Theresa
Park

Cobbitty

CAMDEN
AERODROME

Narellan

THE

NARELLAN

CAMDEN

VALLEY

11

Hub
Mountain

Mount
Colong

Yerranderie

South
Gap

YERRANDERIE

STATE

CONSERVATION

Nattai

NATTAI
STATE
CONSERVATION
AREA

Reillys
Mountain

Burragorang
Peak

BURRAGORANG
SCA

Sheehys
Mountain

Oakdale

Mount
Hunter

The
Oaks

Glenmore

Grasmere

25

Cawdor

5

Camden

Menangle Park

WILLIAM
HOWE
RP

DR

RD

12

Tomat
Creek

BLUE
MOUNTAINS
NATIONAL
PARK

Mount
Egan

AREA

Mount
Beeloon

Wollondilly

NATTAI

NATIONAL

PARK

Lakesland

Mowbray
Park

Mount
Prudhoe

Picton

Thirlmere

Maldon

REMEMBRANCE

89

56

MENANGLE

Menangle

SOUTH

APPIN

RD

69

TO MITTAGONG

A | B | C | D | Joins map 517 E | F | G | H

Joins map 517

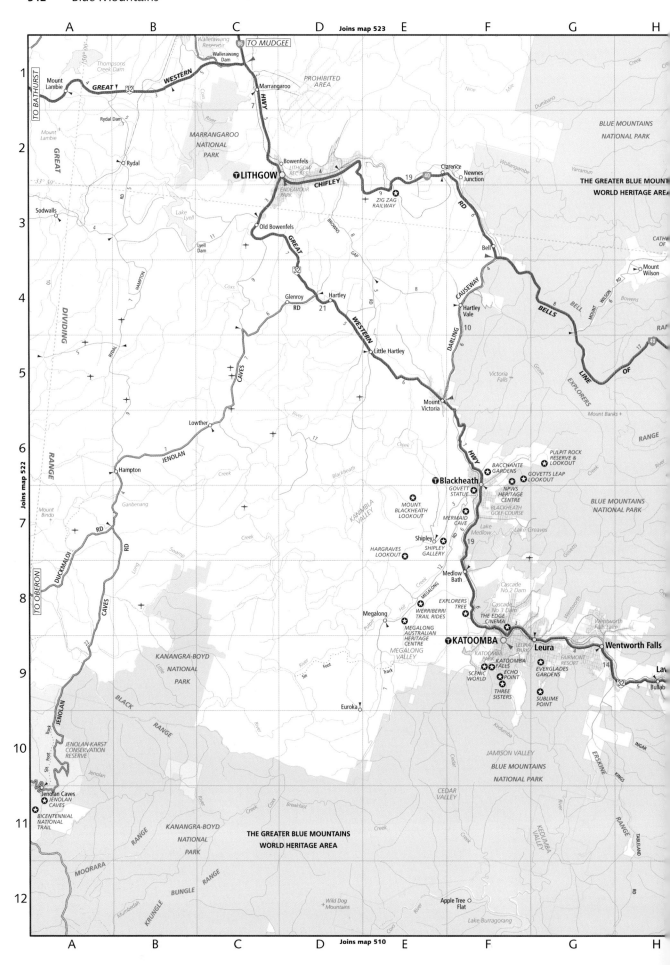

Joins map 523

Joins map 522

Joins map 510

TO MUDGEE

TO BATHURST

Mount Lambie

GREAT WESTERN HWY

Wallerawang
Reservoir

Thompsons Creek Dam

Wallerawang Dam

Marrangaroo

PROHIBITED AREA

Rydal Dam

Mount Lambie

GREAT DIVIDING RANGE

Rydal

MARRANGAROO NATIONAL PARK

Sodwalls

Lake Lyell

Bowenfels

LITHGOW

LITHGOW REC RES

ENDEAVOUR PARK

CHIFLEY

Clarence

Newnes Junction

THE GREATER BLUE MOUNT
WORLD HERITAGE ARE

Lyell Dam

Old Bowenfels

GREAT

ZIG ZAG RAILWAY

BROWNS GAP

Bell

Mount Wilson

BELLS LINE OF ROAD

Glenroy

Hartley

RD

Hartley Vale

CAUSEWAY

BELL

MOUNT WILSON RD

CAVES

WESTERN

Little Hartley

DARLING

CAUSEWAY

Victoria Falls

Mount Banks

Lowther

Mount Victoria

HWY

RANGE

JENOLAN

Hampton

Blackheath

PULPIT ROCK RESERVE & LOOKOUT

BACCHANTE GARDENS

GOVETTS LEAP LOOKOUT

Mount Bindo

Ganbenang

MOUNT BLACKHEATH LOOKOUT

GOVETT STATUE

NPWS HERITAGE CENTRE

BLACKHEATH GOLF COURSE

BLUE MOUNTAINS NATIONAL PARK

DUCKMALOI RD

KANIMBLA VALLEY

MERMAID CAVE

TO OBERON

CAVES RD

Shipley

SHIPLEY GALLERY

Lake Medlow

Lake Greaves

HARGRAVES LOOKOUT

Medlow Bath

EXPLORERS TREE

Cascade No 2 Dam

Cascade No 3 Dam

Wentworth Falls Lake

Megalong

WERRIBERRI TRAIL RIDES

THE EDGE CINEMA

KATOOMBA

Leura

Wentworth Falls

MEGALONG AUSTRALIAN HERITAGE CENTRE

MEGALONG VALLEY

LEURA PARK

FAIRMONT RESORT

KANANGRA-BOYD NATIONAL PARK

BLACK RANGE

KATOOMBA FALLS

ECHO POINT

EVERGLADES GARDENS

SCENIC WORLD

THREE SISTERS

SUBLIME POINT

JENOLAN

Euroka

JAMISON VALLEY

BLUE MOUNTAINS NATIONAL PARK

JENOLAN-KARST CONSERVATION RESERVE

Jenolan Caves

JENOLAN CAVES

CEDAR VALLEY

KEDUMBA VALLEY

ERSKINE RANGE

BICENTENNIAL NATIONAL TRAIL

KANANGRA-BOYD NATIONAL PARK

THE GREATER BLUE MOUNTAINS
WORLD HERITAGE AREA

MOORARA RANGE

KRUNGLE BUNGLE RANGE

Wild Dog Mountains

Apple Tree Flat

Lake Burragorang

TABLELAND RD

0   5   10   15 km

Joins map 523

I   J   K   L   M   N   O   P

TO SINGLETON

PUTTY

PARR STATE CONSERVATION AREA

PARR STATE CONSERVATION AREA

WOLLEMI NATIONAL PARK

THE GREATER BLUE MOUNTAINS

WORLD HERITAGE AREA

Colo Heights

PARR STATE CONSERVATION AREA

69

BLUE MOUNTAINS NATIONAL PARK

+ Bowen Hill

Upper Colo

Central Colo

Colo

WOLLEMI NATIONAL PARK

Mount Tootie

LAGOON

MOUNTAIN   LAGOON   32

FIRETRAIL

Mount Irvine

IRVINE RD   13   12

WOLLEMI NATIONAL PARK

BELLS   40   LINE

Bilpin

Berambing

CALEY RANGE

OF

BLAXLANDS   RIDGE   RD

PUTTY

36

Blaxlands Ridge

PATERSON

Kurrajong Heights

BELLBIRD HILL LOOKOUT   33

EAST   KURRAJONG

East Kurrajong

RD

Kurrajong

Kurmond

Tennyson

Glossodia

KURMOND

Bowen Mountain

RANGE

BLUE MOUNTAINS NATIONAL PARK

40

Freemans Reach

HAY RANGE

Grose Vale

AVOCA LOOKOUT

North Richmond

Lowlands

Bushells Lagoon

Wilberforce

SACKVILLE RD

WILBERFORCE RD

+ Mount Twiss

KURRAJONG   RD

Richmond

Bakers Lagoon

Pitt Town

PITT TOWN NR

HAWKESBURY

Agnes Banks

HAWKESBURY SHOWGROUNDS

Clarendon

WINDSOR

Joins map 511

73

CASTLEREAGH

AGNES BANKS NATURE RESERVE

61

PITT TOWN RD

McGraths Hill

WINDSOR RD

Hawkesbury Heights

Londonderry

GEORGE ST

9

Vineyard

40

TO SYDNEY

Faulconbridge

Winmalee

HAWKESBURY LOOKOUT

Castlereagh

THE   LONDONDERRY   RD

NORTHERN   RD

BLACKTOWN RD

WINDSOR DOWNS NR

2

Linden   WESTERN

SPRINGWOOD

WIGGINS PARK

YELLOMUNDEE RP

Valley Heights

Yellow Rock

CASTLEREAGH

CASTLEREAGH NATURE RESERVE

RICHMOND RD

Riverstone

Hazelbrook   32   18

Glenbrook

Woodford

Warrimoo

THE

HWY

CRIPPLE CREEK RESERVE

MAGURA RESERVE

Penrith Lakes

23

61   25

Schofields

Blaxland

WASCOE SIDING MINIATURE RAILWAY   20

Glenbrook   BLUE MTNS DRIVE   32

BLAXLAND PUBLIC GARDENS

Emu Plains

Nepean Rugby Park

POPONDETTA PARK

RICHMOND RD

BLUE MOUNTAINS NATIONAL PARK

Lapstone

DARKS COMMON RESERVE

RED HANDS CAVE

Penrith

PARKS MUSEUM OF FIRE

Kingswood

SHAW PARK

WHALAN RESERVE

PLUMPTON PARK

ROOTY HILL RD N

63

M7

WOODFORD RANGE

4

KINGSWOOD

COOK PARK

St Marys

GREAT   WESTERN

SOUTH CREEK PARK

MT DRUITT RD

Mount Druitt

Rooty Hill

Doonside

NURRAGINGY RESERVE

FEATHERDALE WILDLIFE PARK

FIRETRAIL

MULGOA

MULGOA NATURE RESERVE

THE   NORTHERN

9

WESTERN   14

ST CLAIR RESERVE

44

61

Eastern Creek

THE GREATER BLUE MOUNTAINS

WORLD HERITAGE AREA

Mulgoa

PROHIBITED AREA

TO PICTON

Erskine Park

HWY   RD

WALLGROVE RD

WEST LINK   MWY

TO SYDNEY

4

Prospect Reservoir

Joins map 510

I   J   K   L   M   N   O   P

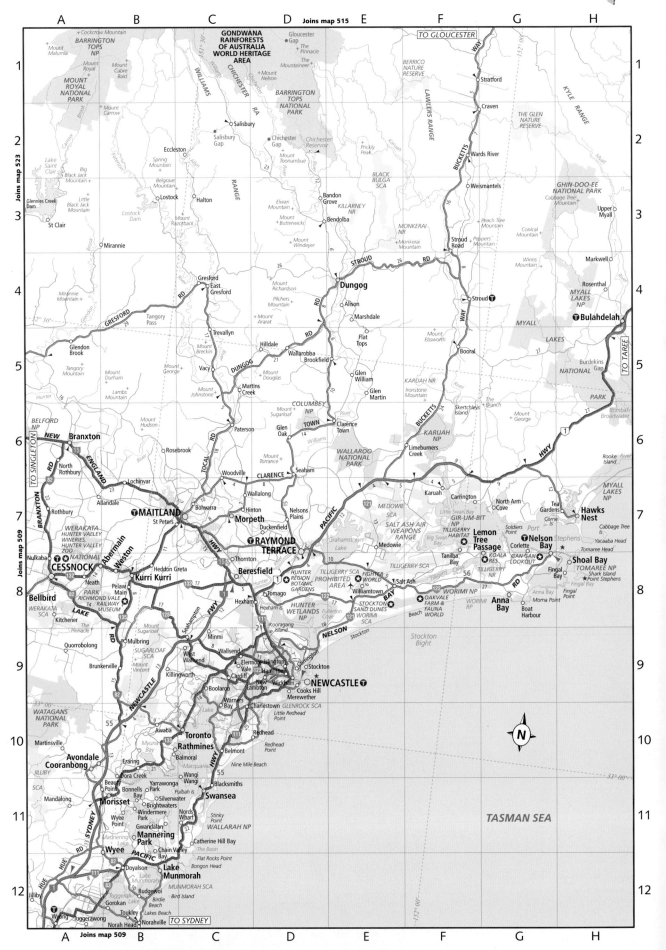

0   5   10   15   20 km

A   B   C   D   E   F   G   H

TO GLOUCESTER

GONDWANA
RAINFORESTS
OF AUSTRALIA
WORLD HERITAGE
AREA

BARRINGTON
TOPS NP

MOUNT
ROYAL NATIONAL
PARK

BARRINGTON
TOPS
NATIONAL
PARK

Joins map 523

TO SINGLETON

Joins map 509

TO SYDNEY

NEWCASTLE

MAITLAND

CESSNOCK

RAYMOND
TERRACE

Dungog

Stroud

Bulahdelah

Hawks
Nest

Nelson
Bay

Shoal Bay

Anna
Bay

TASMAN SEA

N

Morisset

Swansea

Lake
Munmorah

Wyong

Joins map 509

A   B   C   D   E   F   G   H

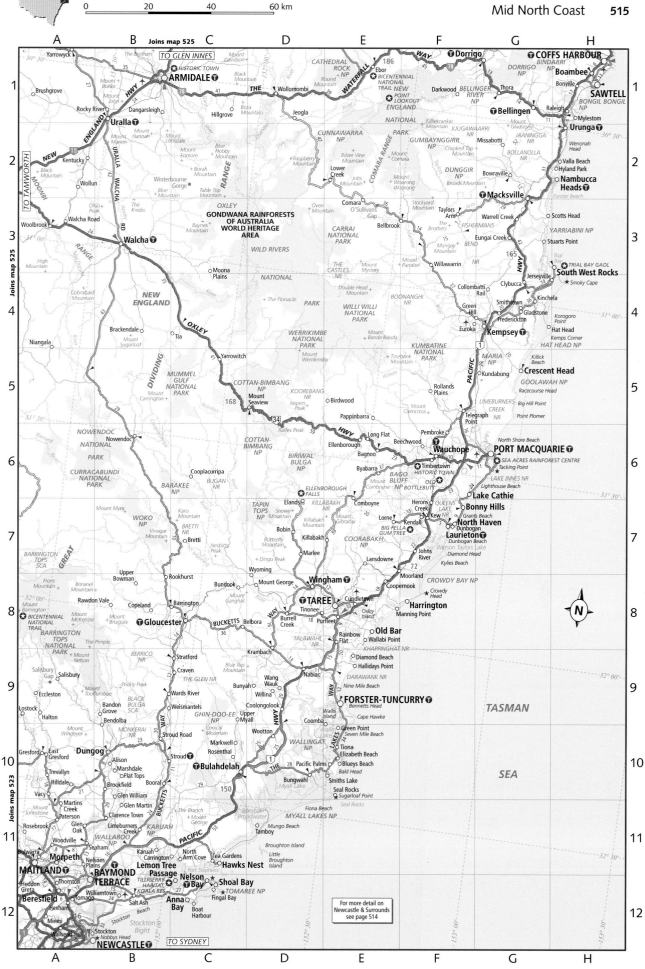

TO GLEN INNES

Joins map 525

Joins map 523

For more detail on
Newcastle & Surrounds
see page 514

TO SYDNEY

0 20 40 60 km

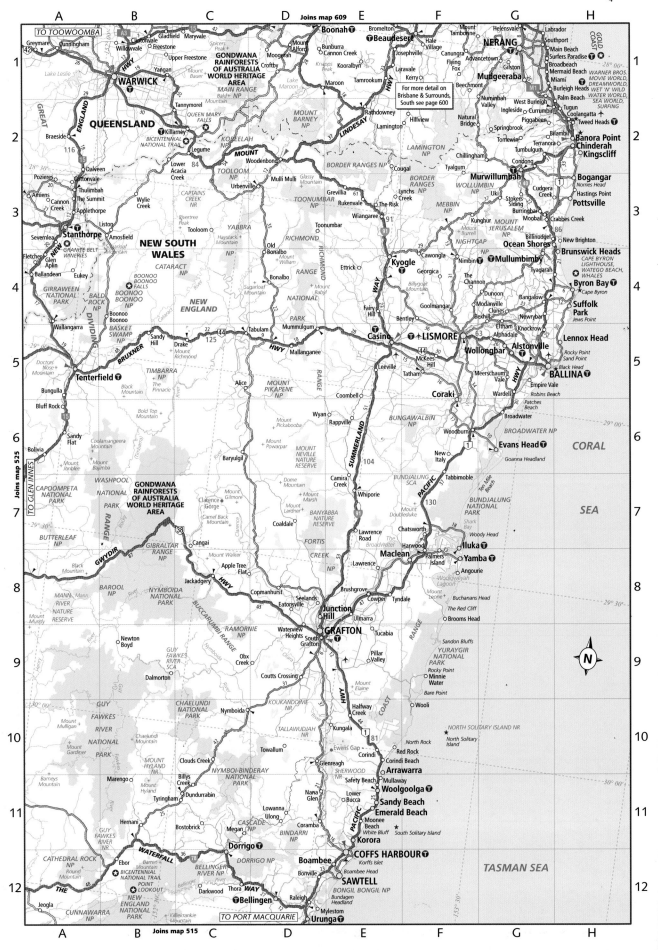

Joins map 609

Joins map 525

TO GLEN INNES

TO TOOWOOMBA

TO PORT MACQUARIE

For more detail on
Brisbane & Surrounds,
South see page 600

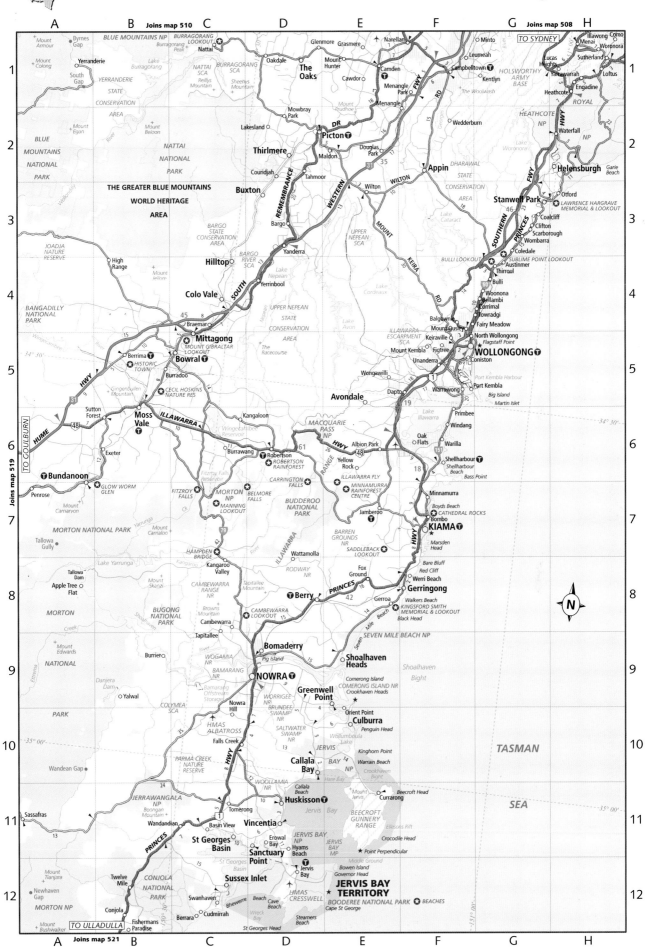

0 5 10 15 20 km

Joins map 510
Joins map 508
Joins map 519
Joins map 521

TO SYDNEY
TO GOULBURN
TO ULLADULLA

BLUE MOUNTAINS NP
Mount Armour
Byrnes Gap
Mount Coolong
Yerranderie
South Gap
YERRANDERIE STATE CONSERVATION AREA
Mount Egan
BLUE MOUNTAINS NATIONAL PARK
Mount Beloon
NATTAI NATIONAL PARK
Lake Burragorang
NATTAI SCA
Reillys Mountain
Sheehys Mountain
BURRAGORANG SCA
Burragorang Lookout
Burragorang Peak
Nattai
Oakdale
The Oaks
Glenmore
Grasmere
Narellan
Minto
Menai
Illawong
Como
Woronora
Lucas Heights
Yarrawarrah
Sutherland
Loftus
Engadine
Heathcote
ROYAL NP
HOLSWORTHY ARMY BASE
Camden
Leumeah
Campbelltown
Kentlyn
The Woolwash
Mount Hunter
Cawdor
Mowbray Park
Menangle Park
Menangle
Lakesland
Mount Prudhoe
Wedderburn
HEATHCOTE NP
Waterfall
Garie Beach
Helensburgh
Picton
DR
Thirlmere
Maldon
Douglas Park
Appin
DHARAWAL STATE CONSERVATION AREA
Stanwell Park
Otford
LAWRENCE HARGRAVE MEMORIAL & LOOKOUT
Couridjah
Tahmoor
Wilton
WILTON
Lake Cataract
Coalcliff
Clifton
Scarborough
Wombarra
Buxton
THE GREATER BLUE MOUNTAINS WORLD HERITAGE AREA
Bargo
REMEMBRANCE
WESTERN
MOUNT
KEIRA
RD
UPPER NEPEAN SCA
Coledale
Bulli Lookout
SUBLIME POINT LOOKOUT
Austinmer
Thirroul
Bulli
Woonona
Bellambi
Corrimal
Towradgi
Fairy Meadow
BARGO STATE CONSERVATION AREA
Yanderra
Bargo River SCA
Lake Nepean
JOADJA NATURE RESERVE
High Range
Mount Jellore
Hilltop
Yerrinbool
Lake Cordeaux
ILLAWARRA ESCARPMENT SCA
Balgownie
Mount Ousley
Keiraville
North Wollongong
Flagstaff Point
Colo Vale
SOUTH
Lake Avon
UPPER NEPEAN STATE CONSERVATION AREA
Mount Kembla
Figtree
WOLLONGONG
Coniston
BANGADILLY NATIONAL PARK
Braemar
Mittagong
MOUNT GIBRALTAR LOOKOUT
The Racecourse
Unanderra
Berrima
HISTORIC TOWN
Bowral
Burradoo
CECIL HOSKINS NATURE RES
Kangaloon
Wongawilli
Dapto
Warrawong
Port Kembla
Port Kembla Harbour
Big Island
Martin Islet
HUME
HWY
Sutton Forest
Gingenbullen Mountain
Moss Vale
ILLAWARRA
Avondale
Lake Illawarra
Primbee
Windang
Exeter
Burrawang
Robertson
ROBERTSON RAINFOREST
MACQUARIE PASS NP
Albion Park
Oak Flats
Warilla
Shellharbour
Shellharbour Beach
Bass Point
Bundanoon
GLOW WORM GLEN
Yellow Rock
HWY
RANGE
ILLAWARRA FLY
MINNAMURRA RAINFOREST CENTRE
Minnamurra
Penrose
Mount Carnarvon
FITZROY FALLS
BELMORE FALLS
CARRINGTON FALLS
BUDDEROO NATIONAL PARK
Jamberoo
Boyds Beach
CATHEDRAL ROCKS
Bombo
KIAMA
MORTON NATIONAL PARK
Tallowa Gully
Wingecarribee Reservoir
MORTON NP
MANNING LOOKOUT
BARREN GROUNDS NR
SADDLEBACK LOOKOUT
Marsden Head
Tallowa Dam
Apple Tree Flat
Lake Yarrunga
Mount Skanzi
HAMPDEN BRIDGE
Kangaroo Valley
Wattamolla
RODWAY NR
Fox Ground
Bare Bluff
Red Cliff
Werri Beach
Gerringong
Mount Edwards
Burrier
WOGAMIA NR
Cambewarra
CAMBEWARRA RANGE NR
Browns Mountain
CAMBEWARRA LOOKOUT
Tapitallee
PRINCES
Berry
Gerroa
Walkers Beach
KINGSFORD SMITH MEMORIAL & LOOKOUT
Black Head
MORTON
NATIONAL PARK
Danjera Dam
Yalwal
BAMARANG NR
Bomaderry
Pig Island
Shoalhaven Heads
SEVEN MILE BEACH NP
Shoalhaven Bight
Wandean Gap
COLYMEA SCA
Nowra Hill
NOWRA
WORRIGEE NR
BRUNDEE SWAMP NR
Greenwell Point
Orient Point
COMERONG ISLAND NR
Comerong Island
Crookhaven Heads
TASMAN
HMAS ALBATROSS
SALTWATER SWAMP NR
Culburra
Penguin Head
PARMA CREEK NATURE RESERVE
Falls Creek
JERVIS BAY
Kinghorn Point
Warrain Beach
Crookhaven Bight
Callala Bay
WOOLLAMIA NR
Callala Beach
Hare Bay
Wollumboula Lake
Sassafras
JERRAWANGALA NP
Boongan Mountain
Tomerong
Wandandian
Basin View
Huskisson
Mount Jervis
Currarong
Beecroft Head
BEECROFT GUNNERY RANGE
Ellsons Rift
Crocodile Head
SEA
Vincentia
JERVIS BAY NP
Twelve Mile
St Georges Basin
Erowal Bay
Hyams Beach
JERVIS BAY NP
JERVIS BAY MP
Point Perpendicular
Mount Tianjara
Newhaven Gap
Mount Bushwalker
MORTON NP
CONJOLA NATIONAL PARK
Sanctuary Point
Sussex Inlet
Jervis Bay
Middle Ground
Bowen Island
Governor Head
JERVIS BAY TERRITORY
Conjola
Fishermans Paradise
Swanhaven
Bherwerre
Cudmirrah
Berrara
Beach
Cave Beach
Wreck Bay
St Georges Basin
HMAS CRESSWELL
BOODEREE NATIONAL PARK
Cape St George
Steamers Beach
St Georges Head
BEACHES

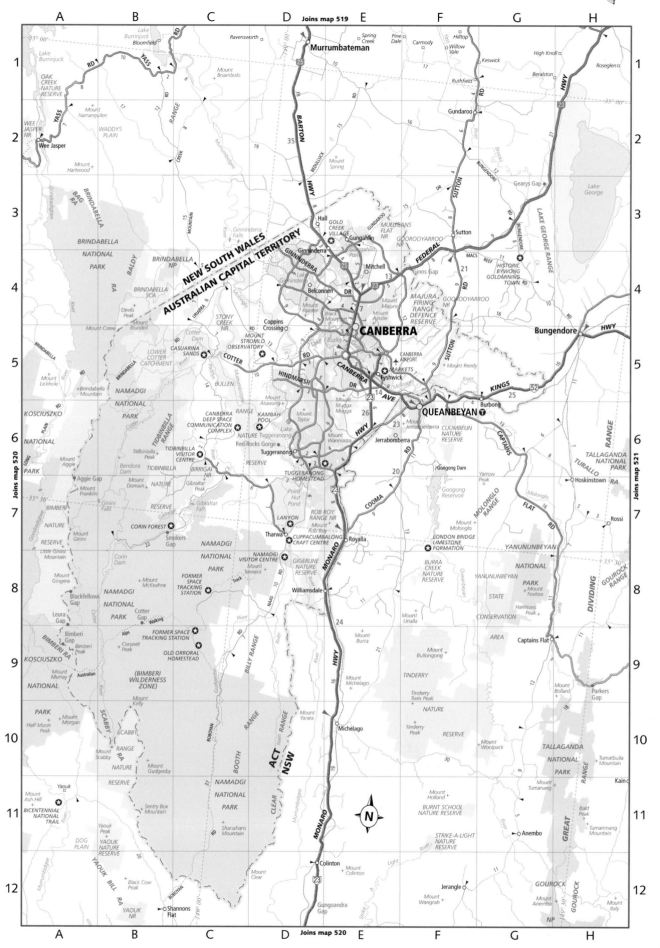

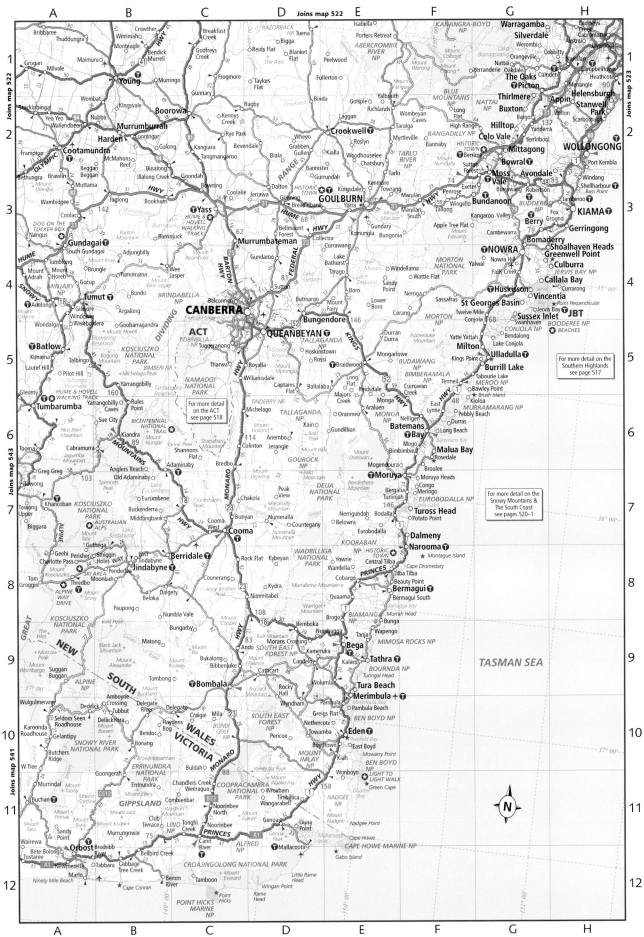

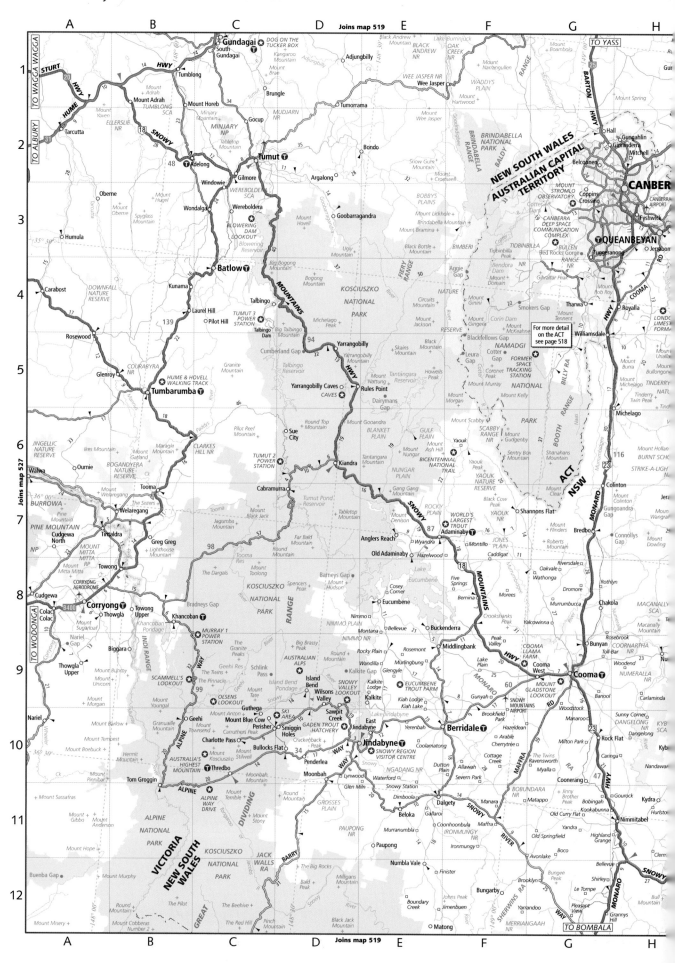

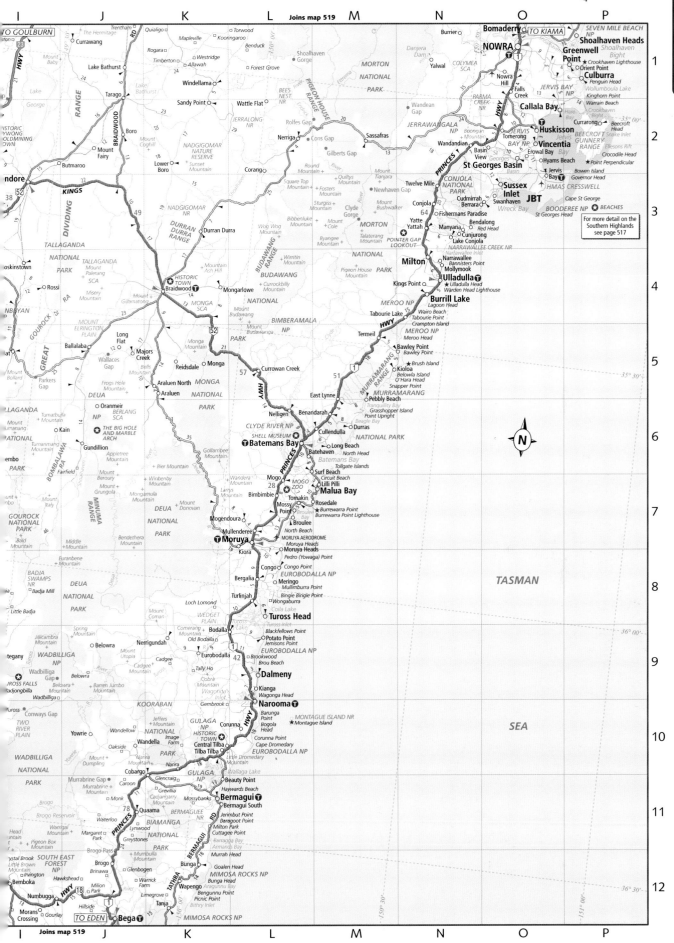

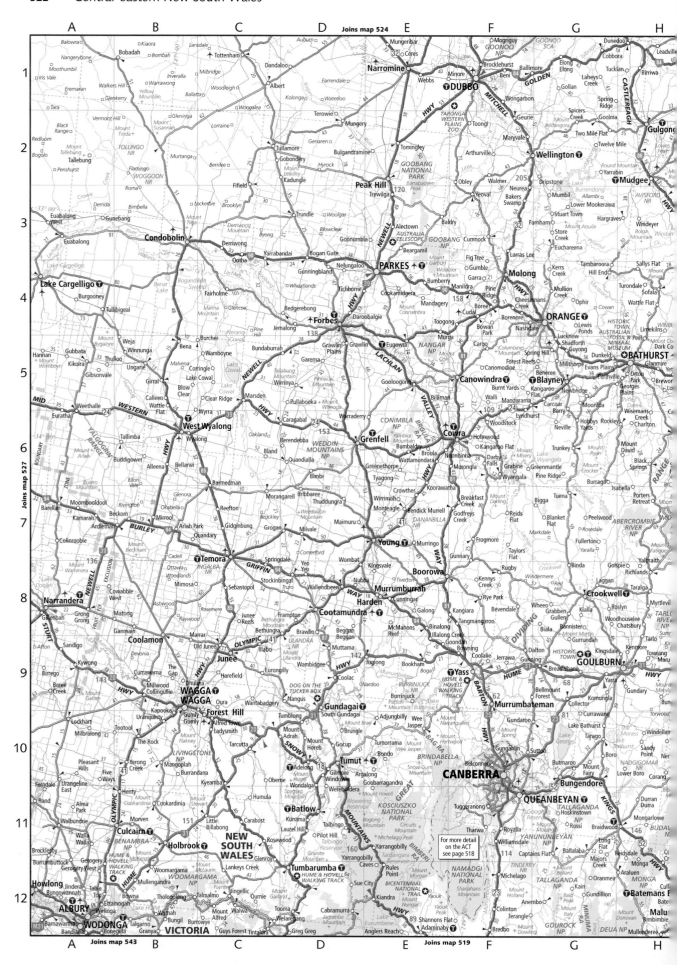

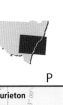

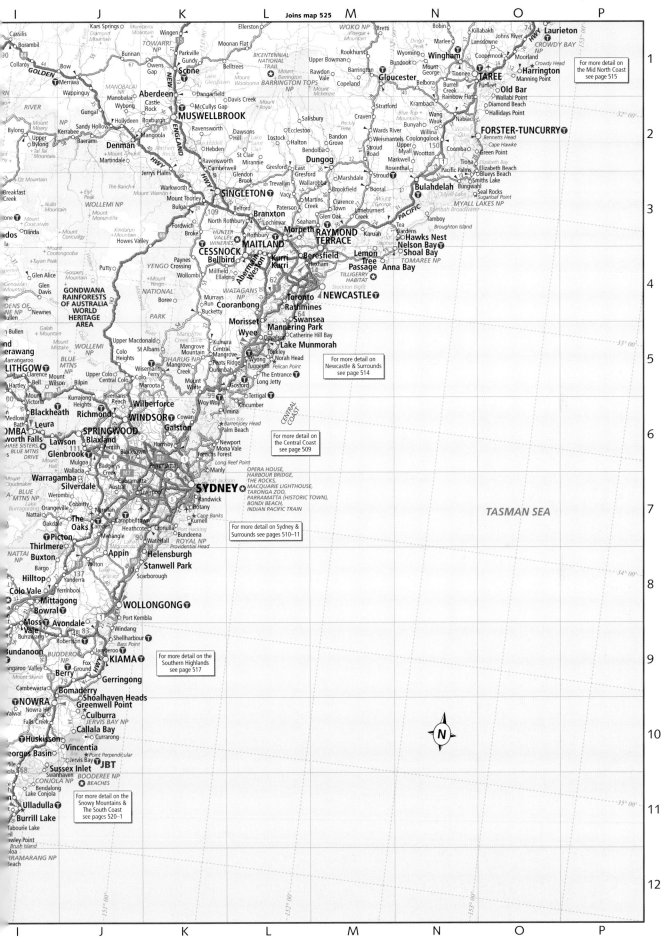

0   20   40   60   80   100 km

I   J   K   L   M   N   O   P

1

Laurieton
CROWDY BAY
Killabakh   Johns River
Bobin   Marlee   Lansdowne   Coopernook   Crowdy Head
Wyoming   Wingham   Moorland
Mount George   Tinonee   TAREE
Belbora   Manning Point
Purfleet   Old Bar
Wallabi Point
Diamond Beach
Hallidays Point

32° 00'

FORSTER-TUNCURRY
Bennetts Head
Cape Hawke
Green Point

2

MYALL LAKES NP

Bulahdelah

3

Hawks Nest
Nelson Bay
Shoal Bay
Lemon Tree Passage   Anna Bay
TOMAREE NP

NEWCASTLE

4

TASMAN SEA

7

N

10

For more detail on the Mid North Coast see page 515

For more detail on Newcastle & Surrounds see page 514

For more detail on the Central Coast see page 509

For more detail on Sydney & Surrounds see pages 510–11

For more detail on the Southern Highlands see page 517

For more detail on the Snowy Mountains & The South Coast see pages 520–1

I   J   K   L   M   N   O   P

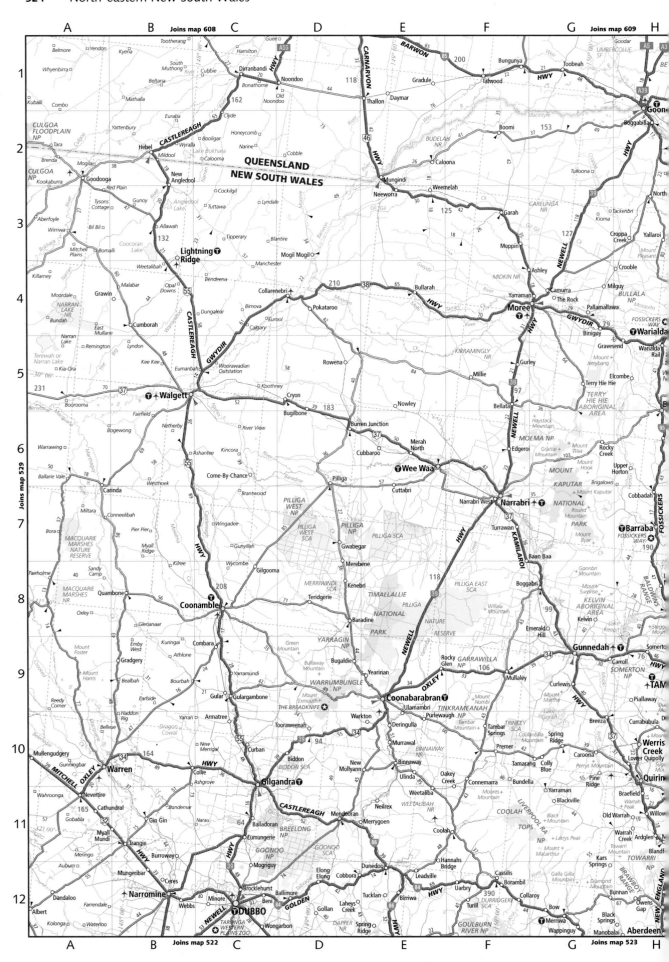

Joins map 609

Joins map 523

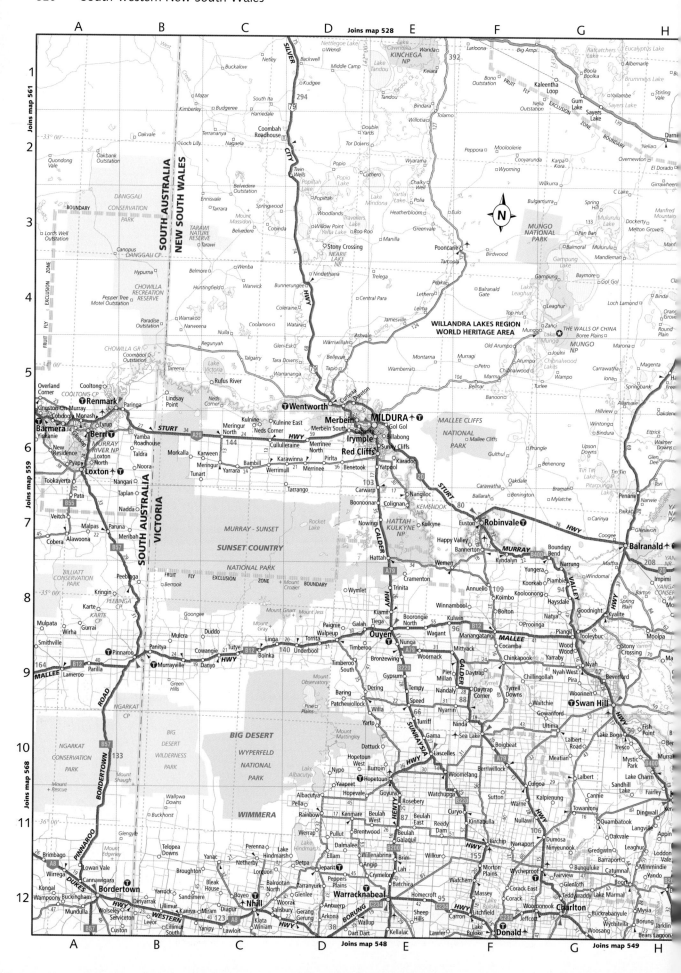

Joins map 528
Joins map 561
Joins map 559
Joins map 568
Joins map 548
Joins map 549

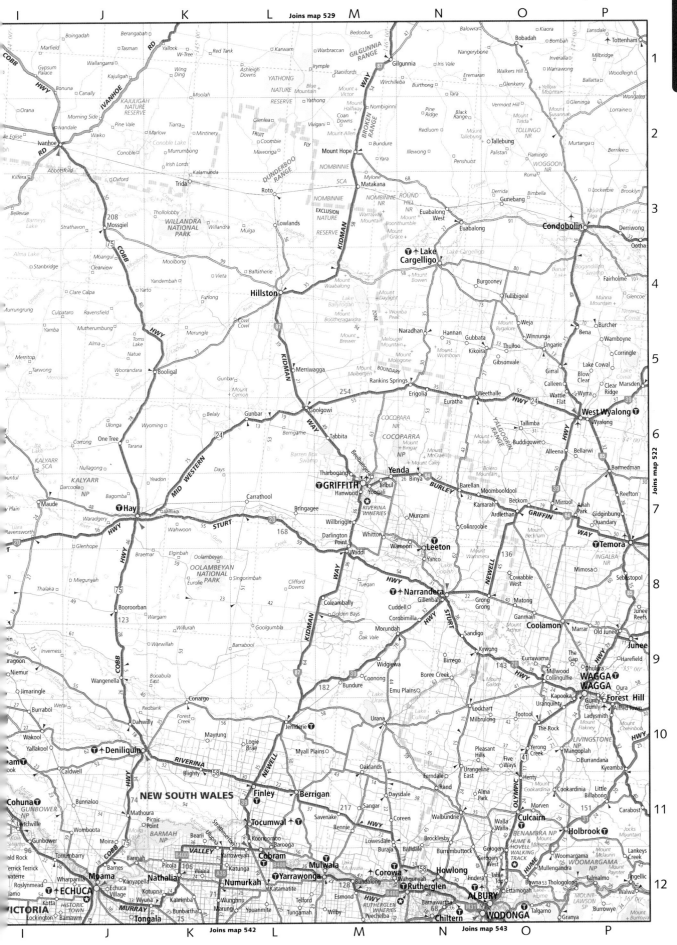

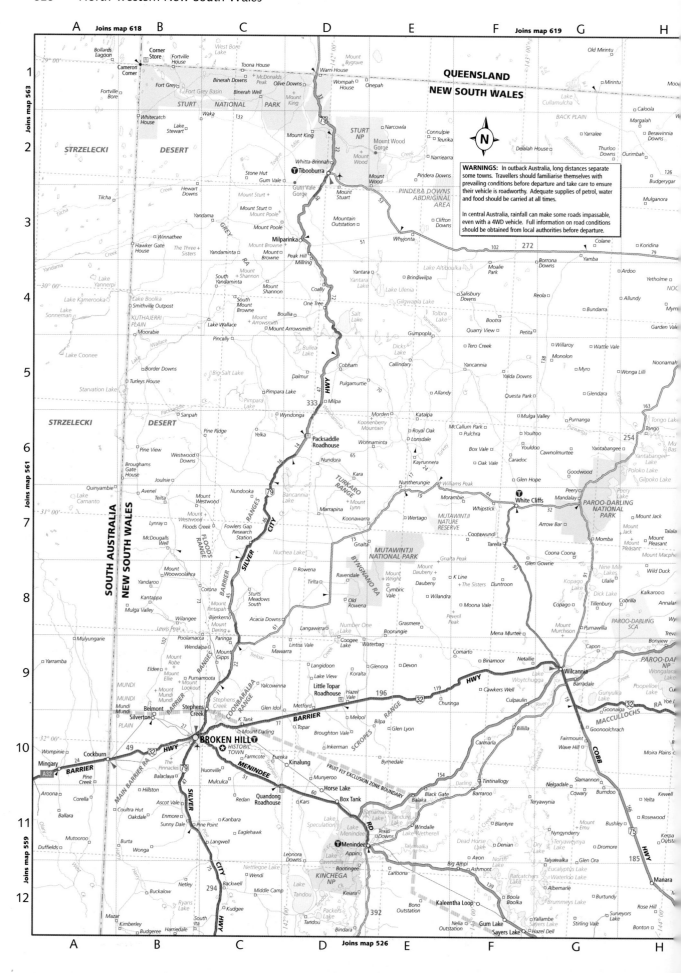

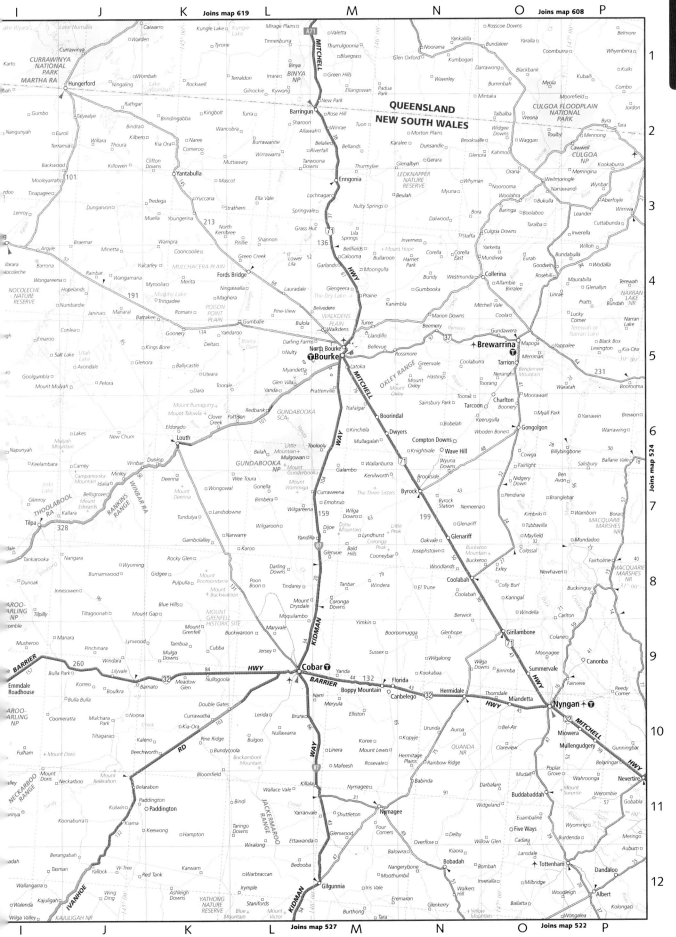

MAPS

VICTORIA

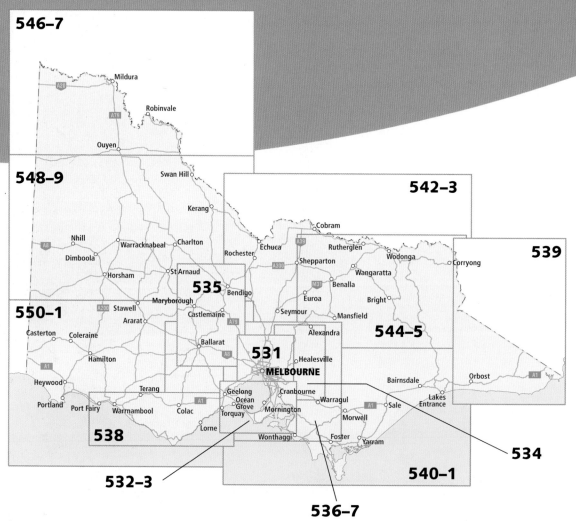

546–7

Mildura

Robinvale

Ouyen

548–9

Swan Hill

Kerang

542–3

Cobram

Nhill
Warracknabeal
Charlton

Dimboola

Horsham

Rochester
Echuca
Rutherglen
Wodonga
Corryong

539

Shepparton
Wangaratta

St Arnaud

535

Bendigo

Benalla
Bright

Maryborough

Euroa

Stawell

Castlemaine

Seymour
Mansfield

550–1

Ararat

Ballarat

Alexandra

544–5

Casterton
Coleraine

Hamilton

531

Healesville

MELBOURNE

Bairnsdale

Orbost

Heywood

Geelong
Ocean Grove
Torquay

Cranbourne
Warragul

Lakes Entrance

Portland
Port Fairy
Warrnambool
Colac

Mornington

Sale
Morwell

534

Lorne

Foster
Yarram

538

Wonthaggi

540–1

532–3

536–7

Victoria

Melbourne Suburbs	531
Mornington & Bellarine Peninsulas	532–3
Dandenong & Yarra Ranges	534
Goldfields	535
Melbourne & Surrounds	536–7
Great Ocean Road	538
Eastern Victoria	539
Southern Central Victoria	540–1
Northern Central Victoria	542–3
High Country	544–5
North-western Victoria	546–7
Central-western Victoria	548–9
South-western Victoria	550–1

INTER-CITY ROUTES		DISTANCE
Melbourne–Sydney via Hume Highway/Freeway	M31 31	879 km
Melbourne–Sydney via Princes Highway/Freeway	M1 A1 1	1039 km
Melbourne–Adelaide via Western & Dukes highways	M8 A8 M1	729 km
Melbourne–Adelaide via Princes Highway	M1 A1 B1 M1	911 km
Melbourne–Brisbane via Newell Highway	M31 A39 39 A39 A2	1676 km

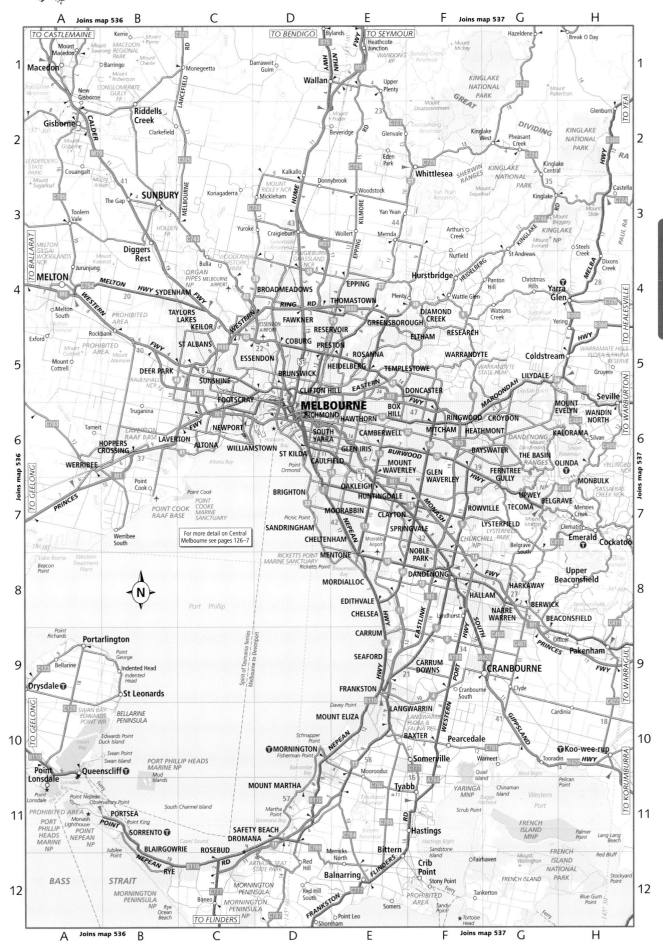

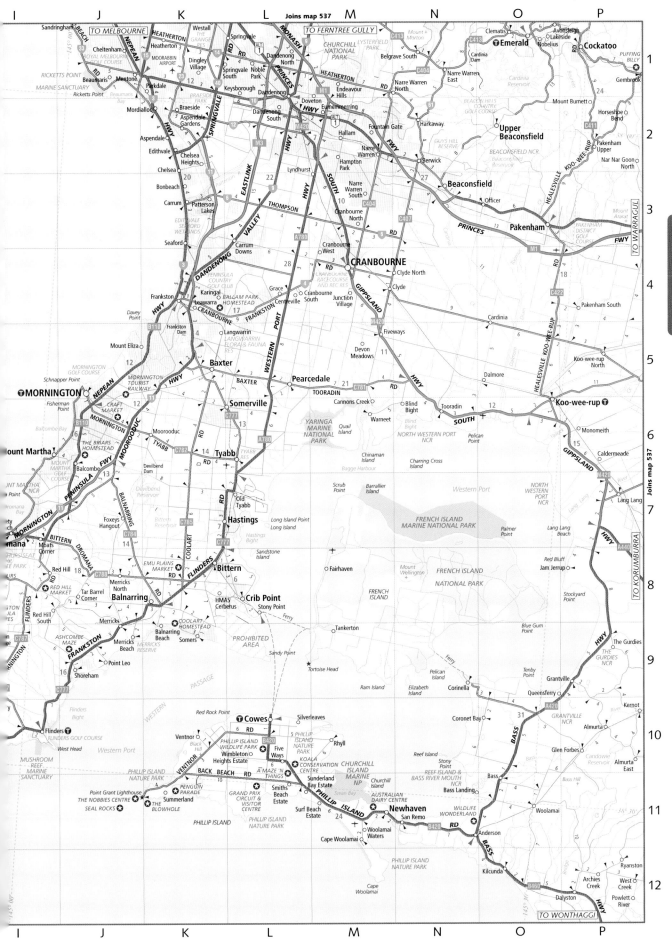

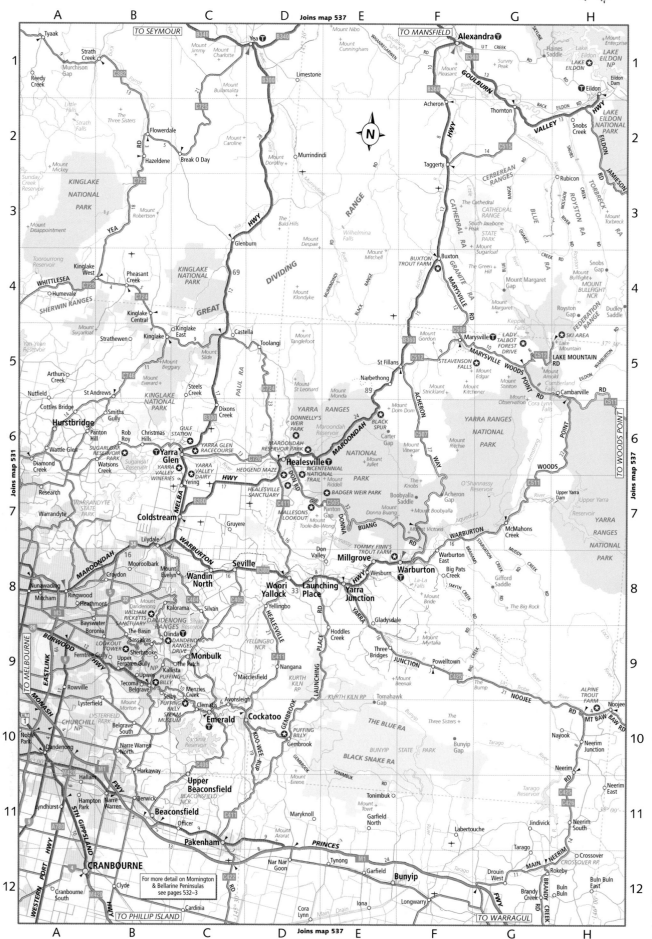

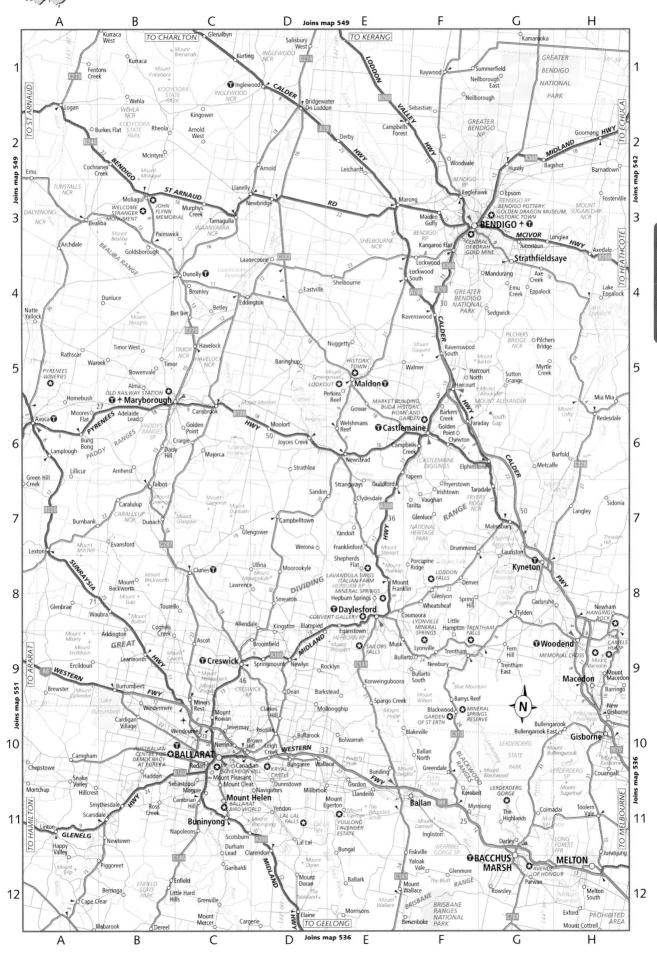

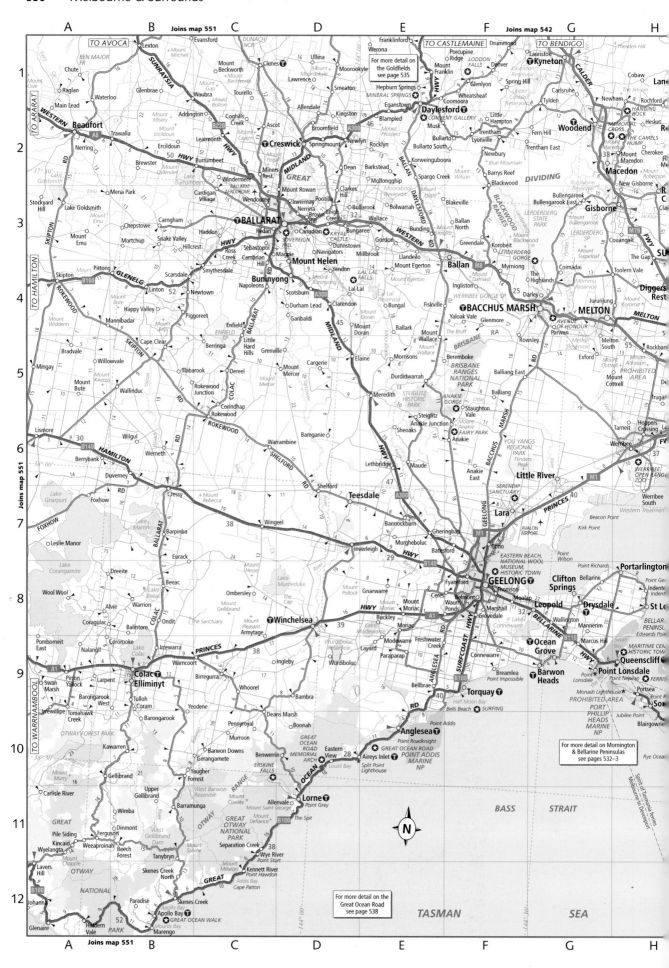

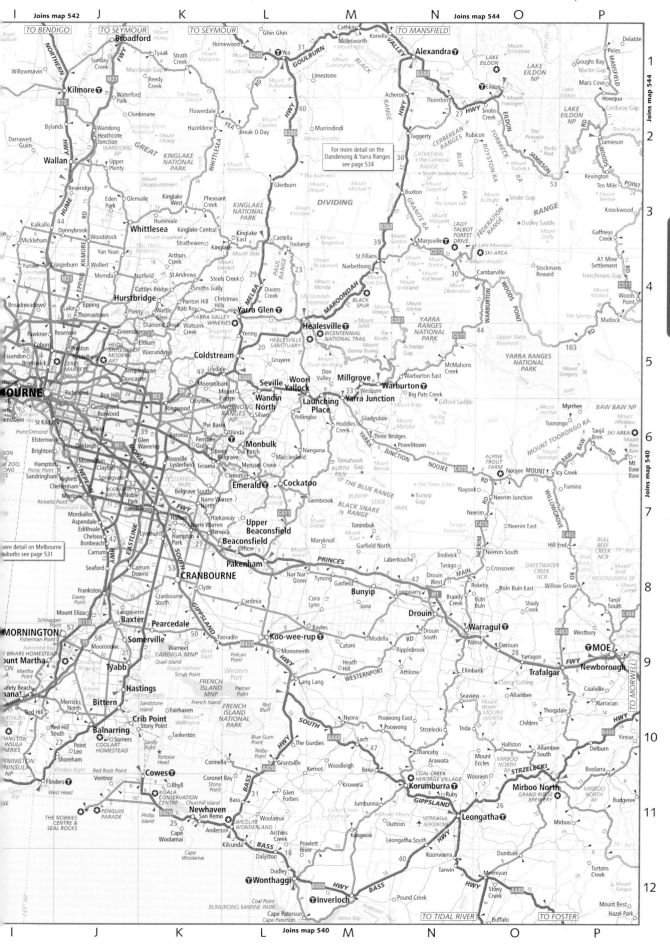

0   10   20   30   40 km

Upper map (A1–H6):

Joins map 536

TO CRESSY

Pomborneit North, Pomborneit, Pomborneit East, Stoneyford, Wool Wool, Herring Point, Vaughan Island, RED ROCK LOOKOUT, Alvie, Coragulac, Dreeite, Beeac, Lake Beeac, Warrion, C146, Ombersley, Lake Murdeduke, The Cap, Gnarwarre, Mount Pollock, BUCKLEY FALLS, Fyansford, GEELONG, HISTORIC TOWN, Ceres, Belmont, Thomson, ADVENTURE PARK, Mount Moriac, Mount Moriac, Waurn Ponds, Marshall, Moolap, Leopold, Wallington, C121, CONNEWARRE WR, Lake Connewarre, Ocean Grove

Nalangil, Balintore, Cororooke, Lake Colac, Irrewarra, Colac, Warncoort, Birregurra, Ingleby, Armytage, Winchelsea, Wurdiboluc Reservoir, Wurdiboluc, Modewarre, Freshwater Creek, Moriac, Buckley, SURFCOAST HWY, C145, C134, Connewarre, Breamlea, Barwon Heads, JIRRAHLINGA KOALA & WILDLIFE RESERVE, Barwon Head

Bungador, Swan Marsh, Pirron Yallock, Larpent, Elliminyt, Barongarook West, Tulloh, Coram, C152, Whoorel, Bambra, Bellbrae, Torquay, SURFWORLD AUSTRALIA, Half Moon Bay, TO QUEENSCLIFF

Irrewillipe, Tomahawk Creek, Barongarook, Yeodene, C155, C154, Pennyroyal, Murroon, Deans Marsh, GREAT OTWAY NATIONAL PARK, Anglesea, Bells Beach, SURFING, C163, OTWAY FOREST PARK

Carlisle River, BURTONS LOOKOUT, Kawarren, 56, Barwon Downs, Gerangamete, Yaugher, Forrest, ERSKINE FALLS, Benwerrin, Eastern View, GREAT OCEAN ROAD MEMORIAL ARCH, Aireys Inlet, Split Point Lighthouse, Eagle Nest Reef, Soapy Rock, Point Roadknight, POINT ADDIS MARINE NATIONAL PARK, Ingoldsby Reefs, Point Addis

Mount Murry, Gellibrand, Upper Gellibrand, Wimba, Dinmont, Barramunga, West Barwon Reservoir, OTWAY FOREST PARK, OTWAY RANGE, Mount Cowley, Allenvale, Mount Saint George, Point Grey, Lorne, GREAT OCEAN ROAD, C151, BASS STRAIT

Chapple Vale, Mount MacKenzie, Weeaproinah, Kincaid, Pile Siding, Ferguson, Beech Forest, GREAT OTWAY DAM, West Gellibrand Dam, Mount Sabine, GREAT OTWAY NATIONAL PARK, Mount Defiance, The Brothers, The Spit, B100, N

Wyelangta, Lavers Hill, C156, Mount Chapple, Congram Falls, Hopetoun Falls, Tanybryn, Skenes Creek North, C119, Mount Meuron, Carisbrook Falls, Separation Creek, Wye River, Point Sturt, Kennett River, Point Hawdon, Addis Bay, Cape Patton

Wangerrip, Johanna, Johanna Beach, Rotten Point, Glenaire, Hordern Vale, Paradise, MAITS REST, GREAT OTWAY NATIONAL PARK, Marengo, Mounts Bay, Cape Marengo, The Blowhole, Apollo Bay, GREAT OCEAN WALK, Skenes Creek, GREAT OCEAN RD, 96

C157, Blanket Bay, Point Lewis, Point Flinders, CAPE OTWAY LIGHTHOUSE, Cape Otway, Point Franklin, TASMAN SEA

Lower map (A7–H12):

Joins map 550

TO MORTLAKE

St Helens, Yambuk, SPENCER, Kirkstall, C178, Winslow, C175, Ballangeich, Boorcan, A1, Gnotuk, Lake Weerangourt, Camperdown, HWY

C184, Koroit, Southern Cross, Mailors Flat, Grassmere, Framlingham, Purnim, HOPKINS HWY, Terang, C156, Naroghid, Mount Leura, Weerite, Toolong, Crossley, Tower Hill, Illowa, Woodford, Bushfield, Grassmere Junction, Wangoom, Mount Warrnambool, Dixie, Cobrico, C164, Bostock Creek, Tesbury, Lake Purrumbete

Rosebrook, Killarney, Dennington, B120, Hopkins Falls, Cudgee, Panmure, Garvoc, Emu Creek, Mumblin, Tandarook, Carpendeit

Cape Reamur, Port Fairy, PORT FAIRY BEACH, Griffiths Island, WARRNAMBOOL, WHALES, Middle Island, Lady Bay, Allansford, COBDEN, Naringal, WARRNAMBOOL RD, Laang, Ecklin South, Glenfyne, 54, Cobden, Jancourt, Jancourt East, Purrumbete South, JANCOURT NATURE CONSERVATION RESERVE

Mepunga West, Mepunga East, GREAT OCEAN RD, 68, Nullawarre, Brucknell, AYRESFORD RD, Ayrford, Scotts Creek, C148, Timboon, Cowleys Creek, 73, Simpson, C163

BAY OF ISLANDS, Childers Cove, The Cove, Nirranda, Curdies, C163, Paaratte, Lower Heytesbury, Newfield, CDORIEMUNGLE CREEK FLORA RESERVE, CORADJIL NCR, C156

SOUTHERN OCEAN, Bay of Islands, Springvale, Buttress Point COASTAL, Nirranda South, Curdie Vale, Bay of Martyrs, The Spot, Newfield Bay, Peterborough, LONDON BRIDGE, THE ARCH, Sentinel Rock, Broken Head, Mutton Bird Island, LOCH ARD GORGE, THE TWELVE APOSTLES, GIBSON STEPS, Port Campbell, PORT CAMPBELL NP, PORT CAMPBELL NATIONAL PARK, GREAT OCEAN WALK, Waarre, Kennedys Creek, GREAT OTWAY NATIONAL PARK

TWELVE APOSTLES MARINE NATIONAL PARK, Princetown, Point Ronald, Pebble Point, Moonlight Beach, The Gable, Moonlight Head, Devondale, Mount Acland, Yuulong, Lower Gellibrand, Wattle Hill, Point Reginald, Cape Volney, B100, 50, 31

N, OCEAN

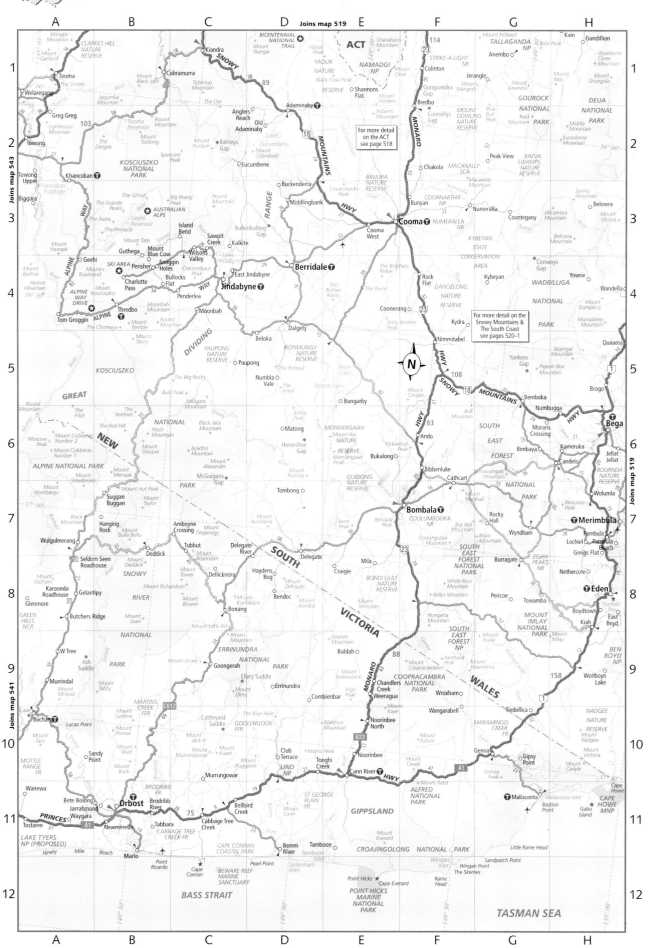

Joins map 519

Joins map 543

Joins map 541

Joins map 519

For more detail on the ACT see page 518

For more detail on the Snowy Mountains & The South Coast see pages 520–1

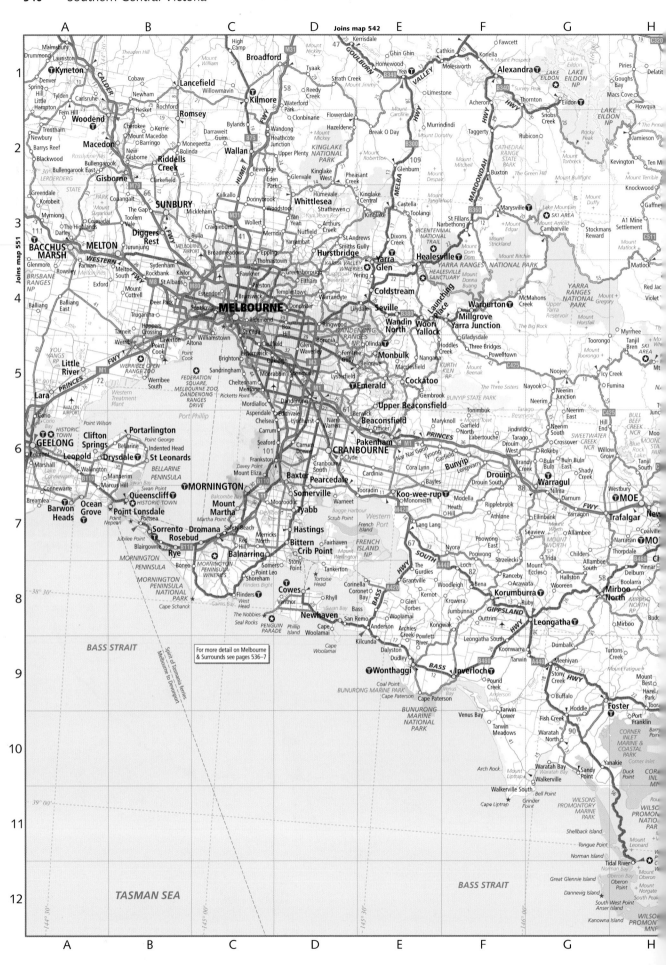

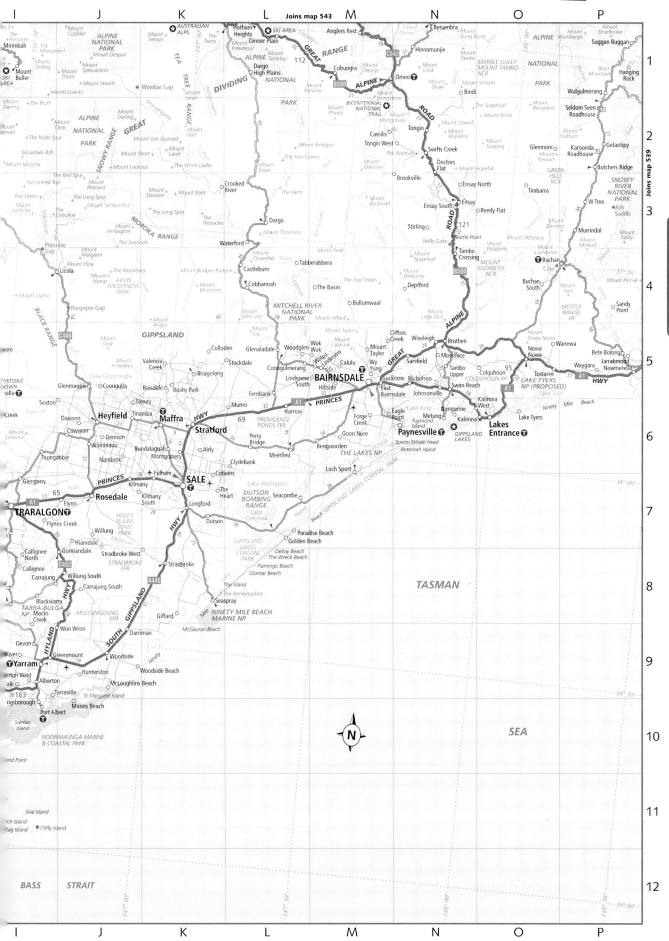

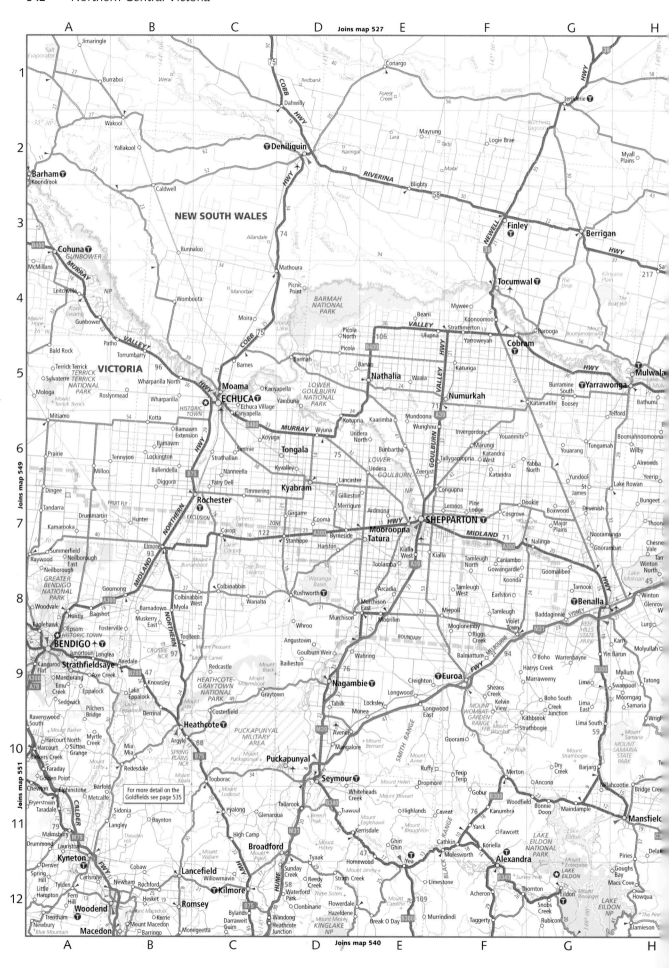

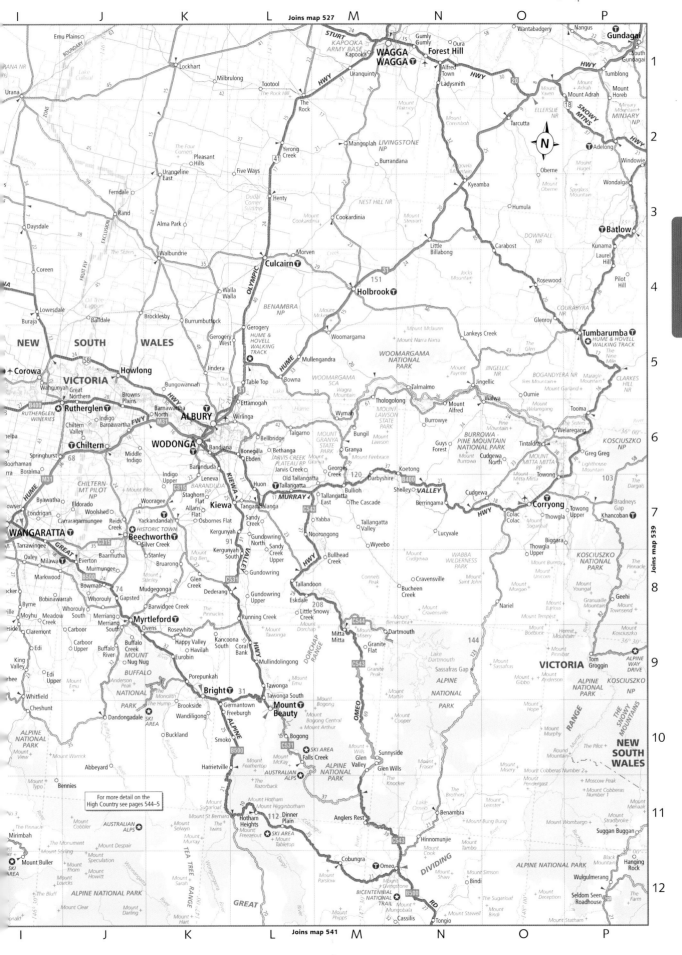

Joins map 527

Joins map 539

Joins map 541

0   10   20   30   40   50 km

For more detail on the
High Country see pages 544-5

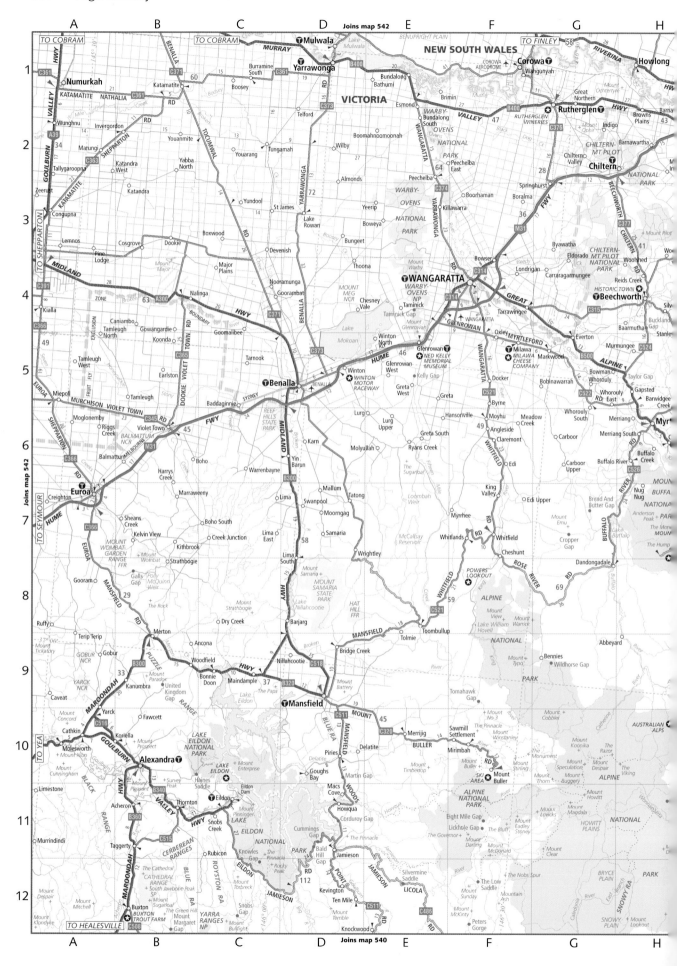

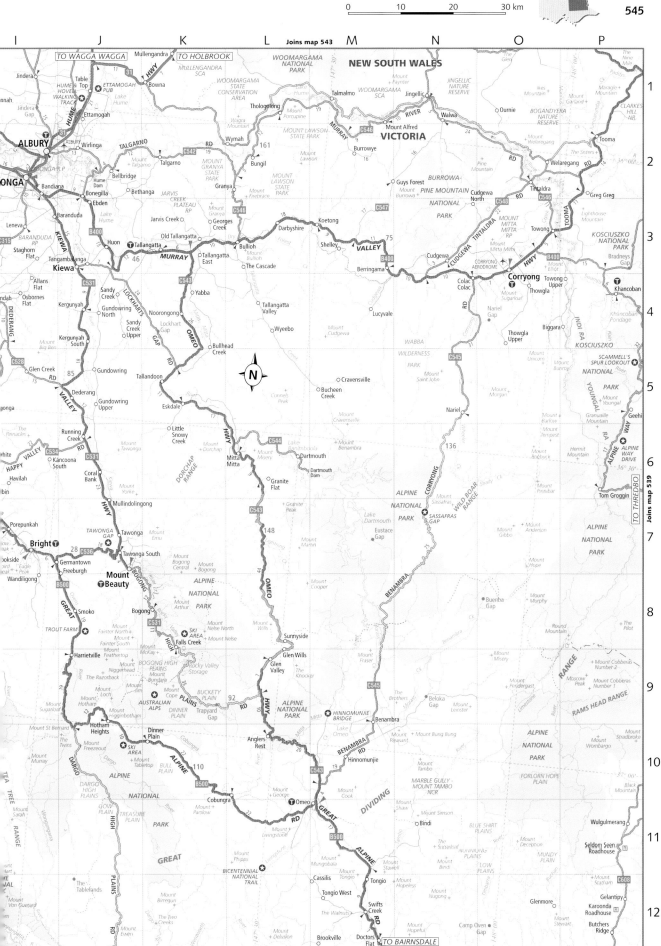

Joins map 526

A B C D E F G H

1 2 3 4 5 6 7 8 9 10 11 12

Joins map 559
Joins map 568

NEW SOUTH WALES

SOUTH AUSTRALIA

VICTORIA

DANGGALI WA

DANGGALI CP

TARAWI NATURE RESERVE

Canopus

Hypurna

CHOWILLA RR

Pepper Tree Motel Outstation

Paradise Outstation

Tarawi

Belmore

Sunshine Wenba

Huntingfield

Warwick

Springwood

Cooinda

Belvedere

Nialia Lake

Willow Point

Yelta Lake

Roo Roo

Travellers Lake

Heatherbloor

Windamingle

Stony Crossing

Wyndham

Nearie Lake

Milkengay

Lake Milkengay

Waukeroo

Trelega

Manilla

NEARIE LAKE NATURE RESERVE

Central Para

Warrakoo

Bellsgrove

Narweena

Nulla

Regunyah

Coombool Outstation

Nelwood

Bunyip Reach

Tareena

Lake Victoria

Rufus River

Talgarry

Tooperoopna

Warrananga

Coleraine

Toora

Quambi

Coolamon

Watara

Bulpunga

Lamplough

Glen-Esk

Wilton

Allanvale

Tara Downs

Milpara

Orchard Road

Bellevue

Avoca

Tapio

Garston

Balcatherine

Wamberra

Studley

Camborn

Jamesville

Burtundy

Ashvale

Warnwillah

Dunvegan

Fletchers Lake

Mourguong Saltwater Disposal Basin

Cooltong

Monash

Renmark

Paringa

COOLTONG CP

MURRAY RIVER NP

Lindsay Point

Neds Corner

Moorna

MURRAY-SUNSET NATIONAL PARK

Dareton

Wentworth

Curlwaa

Yelta

Merbein West

Merbein South

Merbein

Burunga

Gol Gol

Birdwoodton

Cabarita

MILDURA

NAT

Glossop

Lyrup

Winkie

Berri

Yamba Roadhouse

Taldra

Taparoo

MURRAY RIVER NATIONAL PARK

Pyap

Loxton North

Noora

Loxton

Nangari

Morkalla

Karween

Meringur North

Kulnine

Kulnine East

Cullulleraine

Meringur

Yarrara

Bambill

Werrimull

Karawinna

Merrinee

Sandlewood Park

Merrinee North

Pirlta

Benetook

Thurla

Koorlong

Cardross

Nichols Point

Irymple

Red Cliffs

Monak

Karadoc

Yatpool

Trentham Cliffs

Billabong

Sunny Cliffs

YARRARA FFR

Tunart

Pinemont

Redcourts

Kurnwill

Tarrango

Nangiloc

Colignan

Iraak

Carwarp

Boonoonar

Tookayerta

Pata

Taplan

Nadda

CALLACHAN PLAIN

RAAK PLAIN

Rocket Lake

HATTAH-KULKYNE NATIONAL PARK

Veitch

Malpas

Paruna

Meribah

SUNSET COUNTRY

MURRAY-SUNSET NATIONAL PARK

Alawoona

Hattah

BILLIATT WA

FRUIT FLY EXCLUSION ZONE BOUNDARY

Mount Crozier

ONE TREE PLAIN

Peebinga

Berrook

Cramenti

ANNUEL FLORA A FAUNA RESERV

Kringin

PEEBINGA CP

Wymlet

Trinita

Karte

KARTE CP

Goongee

Mount Gnarr

Mount Jess

Kiamil

Gurrai

KOONDA FR

Mount Gray

Paignie

Galah

Tiega

Ouyen

Booron North

Mulcra

Duddo

Linga

Underbool

Torrita

Walpeup

Timberoo

Boulka

Boora

Nunga

Panitya

MURRAYVILLE FR

Cowangie

Tutye

Boinka

Timberoo South

TIMBEROO FFR

Bronzewing

Pinnaroo

Murrayville

Danyo

BRONZEWING FLORA AND FAUNA RESERVE

Gypsum

Parilla

MALLEE

Green Hills

WYPERFELD NATIONAL PARK

Mount Observatory

Mount Jenkins

Dering

Patchewollock

Baring

Speed

BIG DESERT

BIG DESERT WILDERNESS PARK

NGARKAT CP

WIRRENGREN PLAIN

Pine Plains

Tempy

Joins map 548

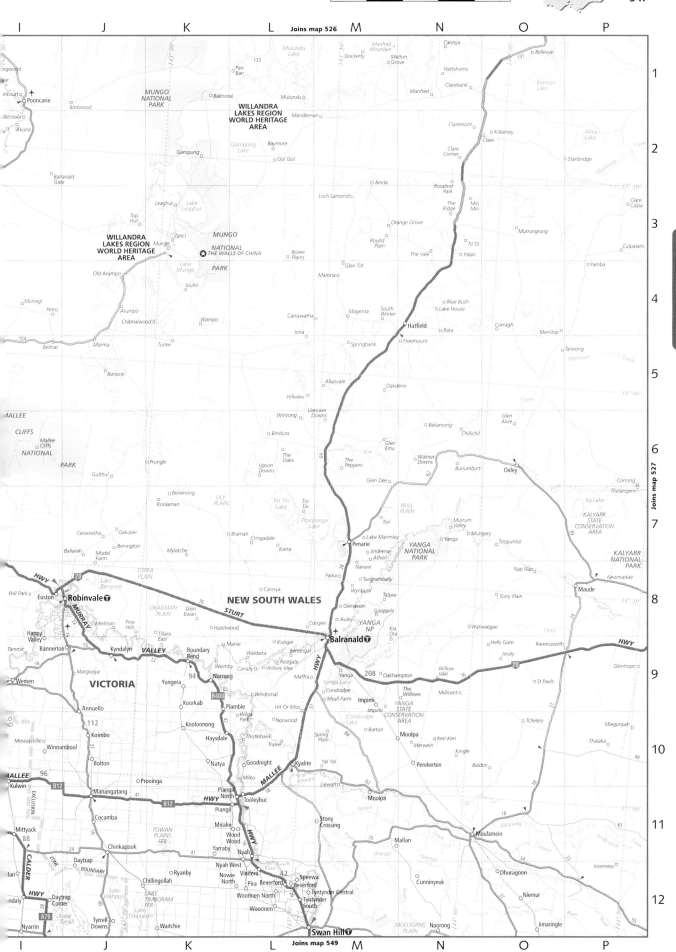

Joins map 526

Joins map 527

Joins map 549

0   10   20   30   40   50 km

I   J   K   L   M   N   O   P

1
2
3
4
5
6
7
8
9
10
11
12

MUNGO
NATIONAL
PARK

WILLANDRA
LAKES REGION
WORLD HERITAGE
AREA

WILLANDRA
LAKES REGION
WORLD HERITAGE
AREA

MUNGO

NATIONAL
THE WALLS OF CHINA

PARK

MALLEE
CLIFFS

Mallee
Cliffs

NATIONAL

PARK

NEW SOUTH WALES

YANGA
NATIONAL
PARK

KALYARR
STATE
CONSERVATION
AREA

KALYARR
NATIONAL
PARK

VICTORIA

YANGA
NP

YANGA
STATE
CONSERVATION
AREA

MALLEE

LILY
PLAIN

BULL
PLAIN

TOPRA
PLAIN

DEADMAN
PLAIN

TOWAN
PLAINS FFR

LAKE
TIMBORAM
FFR

MULLIGANS
PLAIN

Pooncarie
Birdwood
Balmoral
Mulurulu
Dockerty
Melton
Grove
Manfred
Mountain
Carinya
Bellevue
Barneys
Lake

Hartshorns

Clarebank

Tarcoola
Akuna
Pan
Ban
Manfred

Clare
Corner
Claremont
Killatney
Clare

Alma
Lake

Balranald
Gate
Garnpung
Baymore
Gol Gol
Mandleman
Binda

Rosalind
Park
The
Ridge
Min
Min

Stanbridge

Clare
Calpa

Leaghur
Lake
Leaghur
Top
Hut
Zanci
Mungo
Loch Lamond
Orange Grove

Til Til
Murrungrung
Culpataro

Old Arumpo
Lake
Mungo
Boree
Plains
Round
Plain
The Vale
Palari
Yamba

Murragi
Petro
Joulni
Glen Tilt
Marona

Arumpo
Chibnalwood
Wampo
Carrawatha
Iona
Magenta
South
Winter
Blue Bush
Lake House
Curragh
Merritop
Tarwong

Bellnar
Marma
Turlee
Springbank
Hatfield
Rata
Freemount

Banoon
Allanvale
Oakdene

Hillview
Llanover
Downs
Beliamong
Glen
Alvie

Wintong
Bindura
Glen
Emu
Chillichil

The
Oaks
The
Peppers
Walmer
Downs
Bunumburt
Oxley

Prungle
Upson
Downs
Glen Dee
Correng
Thelangerin

Gulthul
Benenong
Tin Tin
Lake
Tin
Tin
Koolaman
Pirtamonga
Lake
Tori
Murrum
Valley
Toopuntul
Ita Lake

Carawatha
Oakdale
Benington
Bramah
Cringadale
Karra
Lake Manimley
Yanga
Mungery
Nap Nap
Newmarket

Ballarah
Model
Farm
Mylatche
Penarie
Jindeena
Atheri
Narwie
Maude

HWY
Prill Park
Euston
Robinvale
Lake
Benanee
Carinya
Paika
Tangrambally
Wynburn
Talpee
Torry Plain
HWY

Happy
Valley
Bannerton
Meilman
Pine
Hills
Tillara
East
Glen
Ewan
Hazelwood
Kungie
Coogee
Auley
Glenavon
Gooparle
Kia
Ora
Warwaegae
Hells Gate
Ravensworth
Jeraly
Glenhope

Tammit
Margooya
Kyndalyn
VALLEY
Boundary
Bend
Manie
Waldaira
Bengongi
Redgate
Willow Isles
YANGA
NP
Balranald
Uara
Yanga
Oakhampton
Willow
Vale
St Pauls

Wemen
Annuello
Yungera
Koorkab
Narrung
Weimby
Canally
Maffra
Yanga Lake
Condoulpe
Myall Farm
Millicent
Tchelery
Miegunyah
Thalaka

Koimbo
Piambie
Windomal
Hit Or Miss
Norwood
Impimi
Impimi
Barton
Moolpa
Merwein
Keri Keri
Kingle
Baldon

Mowat-Ville
Winnambool
Bolton
Natya
Kooloonong
Haysdale
Wilga
Park
Thistlebank
Tralee
Spring
Plain
Condoulpe
Lake
Perekerten
Inverness

Kulwin
Manangatang
Prooinga
Goodnight
Mileu
Kyalite
Yal Yal
Liewah
Moolpa
Dhuragoon

Mittyack
Cocamba
Chinkapook
Miralie
Piangi
North
Tooleybuc
Piangil
Stony
Crossing
Mallan
Moulamein

Daytrap
Ryanby
Wood
Wood
Yarraby
Nyah
Chillingollah
Cunninyeuk
Niemur

Daytrap
Corner
Tyrrell
Downs
Nyarrin
Waitchie
Woorinen
Nyah West
Nowie
North
Pira
Vinifera
Beverford
Speewa
Beverford
Tyntynder Central
Tyntynder
South
Woorinen North
Noorong
Jimaringle

Swan Hill

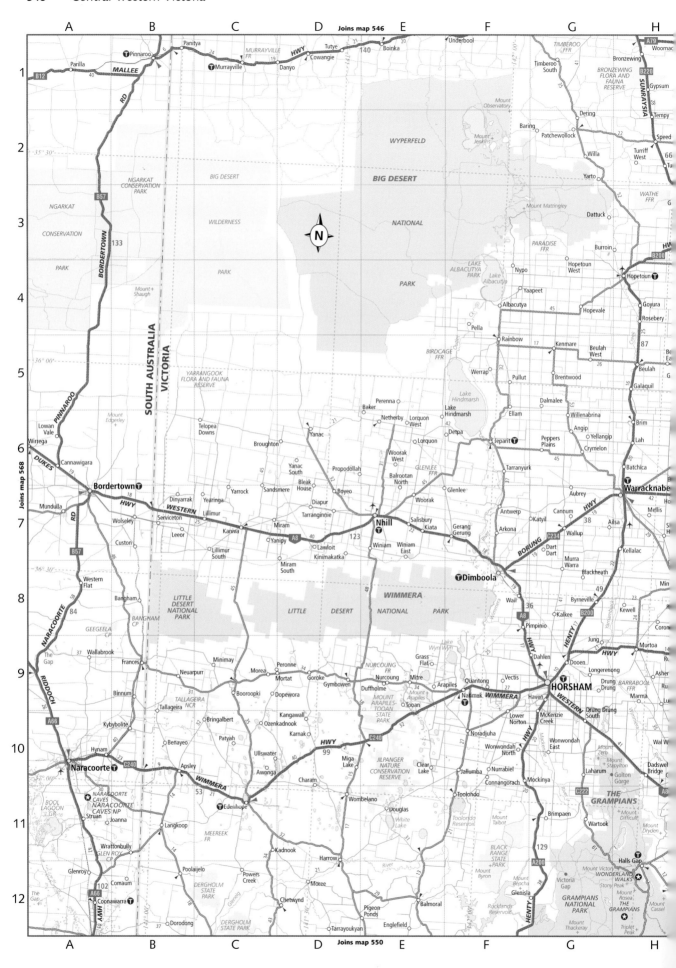

Joins map 546
Joins map 568
Joins map 550

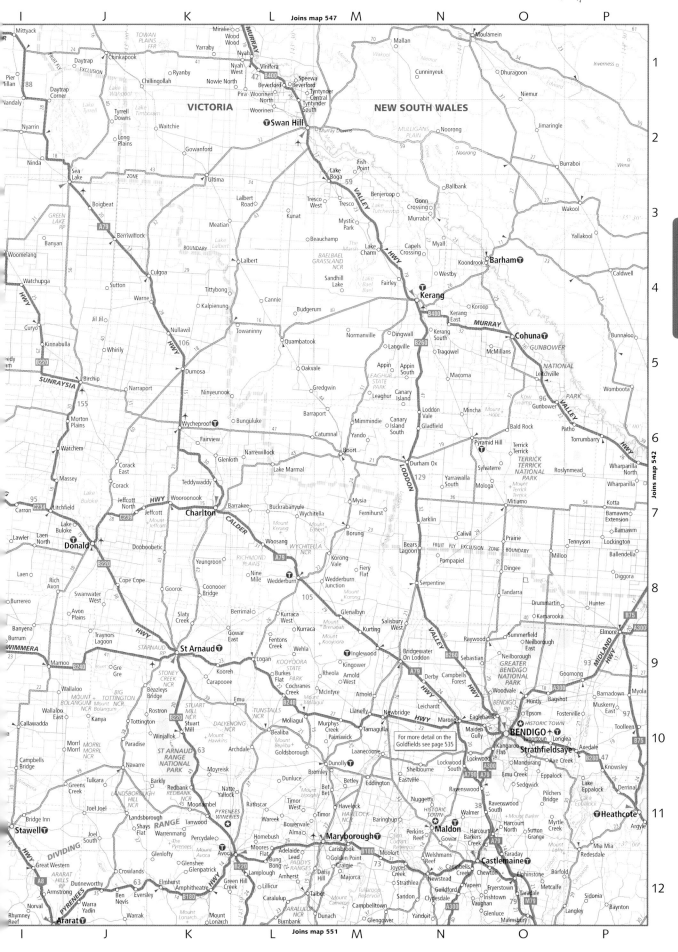

0   10   20   30   40   50 km

Joins map 547

VICTORIA

NEW SOUTH WALES

Mittyack
Pier Millan
Nandaly
Daytrap Corner
Nyarrin
Ninda
Woomelang
Watchupga
Curyo
Kinnabulla
Birchip
Narraport
Watchem
Massey
Morton Plains
Carron
Litchfield
Lake Buloke
Lawler
Laen North
Donald
Laen
Rich Avon
Burreheo
Banyena
Burrum
Marnoo
Wallaloo
Wallaloo East
Callawadda
Greens Creek
Bridge Inn
Stawell
Joel Joel
Joel South
Great Western
Norval
Rhymney Reef
Ararat
Armstrong
Warra Yadin
Warrak

Daytrap
Chinkapook
Ryanby
Chillingollah
Pira
Woorinen North
Woorinen
Waitchie
Long Plains
Gowanford
Sea Lake
Boigbeat
Banyan
Berriwillock
Sutton
Warne
Culgoa
Whirily
Nullawil
Durnosa
Ninyeunook
Fairview
Glenloth
Corack East
Corack
Teddywaddy
Jeffcott North
Jeffcott
Wooroonook
Charlton
Barrakee
Donald
Dooboobetic
Yeungroon
Cope Cope
Gooroc
Slaty Creek
Traynors Lagoon
Swanwater West
Avon Plains
Gre Gre
Kooreh
Beazleys Bridge
Carapooee
Rostron
St Arnaud
Winjallok
Tottington
Stuart Mill
Paradise
Navarre
Landsborough
Barkly
Tulkara
Shays Flat
Warrenmayne
Percydale
Glenlofty
Crowlands
Dunneworthy
Ben Nevis
Eversley
Amphitheatre
Elmhurst
Green Hill Creek

Miralie
Wood Wood
Yarraby
Nyah
Nyah West
Vinifera
Speewa
Beverford
Nowie North
Woorinen South
Tyntynder Central
Tyntynder South
Swan Hill
Murray Downs
Lake Boga
Ultima
Lalbert Road
Lalbert
Kunat
Meatian
Beauchamp
Tittybong
Cannie
Kalpienung
Budgerum
Towaninny
Quambatook
Oakvale
Gredgwin
Narrewillock
Barraport
Catumnal
Lake Marmal
Glenloth
Buckrabanyule
Wychitella
Woosang
Wedderburn
Wedderburn Junction
Kurraca West
Kurraca
Fentons Creek
Wehla
Logan
Cochranes Creek
Burkes Flat
Rheola
Emu
McIntyre
Moliagul
Bealiba
Murphys Creek
Painswick
Archdale
Moyreisk
Redbank
Moonambel
Natte Yallock
Rathscar
Timor West
Bowenvale
Homebush
Moores Flat
Adelaide Lead
Amherst
Bung Bong
Lamplough
Lillicur
Caralulup
Talbot

Tresco West
Tresco
Mystic Park
Lake Charm
Sandhill Lake
Normanville
Langville
Dingwall
Appin
Appin South
Leaghur
Canary Island
Canary Island South
Mimmindie
Yando
Boort
Mysia
Fernihurst
Borung
Jarklin
Korong Vale
Fiery Flat
Glenalbyn
Salisbury West
Kurting
Inglewood
Kingower
Arnold
Llanelly
Newbridge
Tarnagulla
Laanecoorie
Dunolly
Bromley
Betley
Eddington
Goldsborough
Bet Bet
Carisbrook
Golden Point
Moolort
Craigie
Daisy Hill
Majorca
Dunach
Campbelltown

Mallan
Cunninyeuk
Noorong
Benjeroop
Gonn Crossing
Murrabit
Capels Crossing
Myall
Westby
Fairley
Kerang
Kerang East
Kerang South
Tragowel
Macorna
Mincha
Loddon Vale
Gladfield
Durham Ox
Yarrawalla South
Mologa
Calivil
Pompapiel
Dingee
Serpentine
Tandarra
Raywood
Sebastian
Campbells Forest
Derby
Leichardt
Maldon
Marong
Eaglehawk
Maiden Gully
Huntly
Woodvale
Neilborough
Neilborough East
Summerfield
Shelbourne
Lockwood
Lockwood South
Emu Creek
Eastville
Ravenswood
Ravenswood South
Nuggetty
Baringhup
Havelock
Joyces Creek
Newstead
Welshmans Reef
Guildford
Vaughan
Yapeen
Irishtown
Fryerstown
Glenluce

Moulamein
Dhuragoon
Niemur
Jimaringle
Burraboi
Ballbank
Koondrook
Barham
Caldwell
Cohuna
McMillans
Leitchville
Gunbower
Bald Rock
Pyramid Hill
Sylvaterre
Terrick Terrick
Roslynmead
Patho
Torrumbarry
Wharparilla North
Wharparilla
Kotta
Bamawm Extension
Bamawm
Lockington
Milloo
Tennyson
Diggora
Ballendella
Drummartin
Hunter
Kamarooka
Elmore
Goornong
Barnadown
Myola
Muskerry East
Fosterville
Bagshot
Toolleen
BENDIGO
Strathfieldsaye
Axedale
Kangaroo Flat
Mandurang
Axe Creek
Eppalock
Sedgwick
Pilchers Bridge
Lake Eppalock
Derrinal
Heathcote
Argyle
Walmer
Harcourt
Harcourt North
Sutton Grange
Myrtle Creek
Mia Mia
Redesdale
Faraday
Castlemaine
Chewton
Elphinstone
Barfold
Metcalfe
Sidonia
Taradale
Langley
Baynton
Malmsbury

Inverness
Niemur
Wakool
Yallakool
Bunnaloo
Womboota

MURRAY VALLEY HWY
LODDON VALLEY HWY
CALDER HWY
SUNRAYSIA HWY
WIMMERA HWY
PYRENEES RANGE
GREAT DIVIDING RANGE
MIDLAND HWY

For more detail on the Goldfields see page 535

HISTORIC TOWN

Joins map 542
Joins map 551

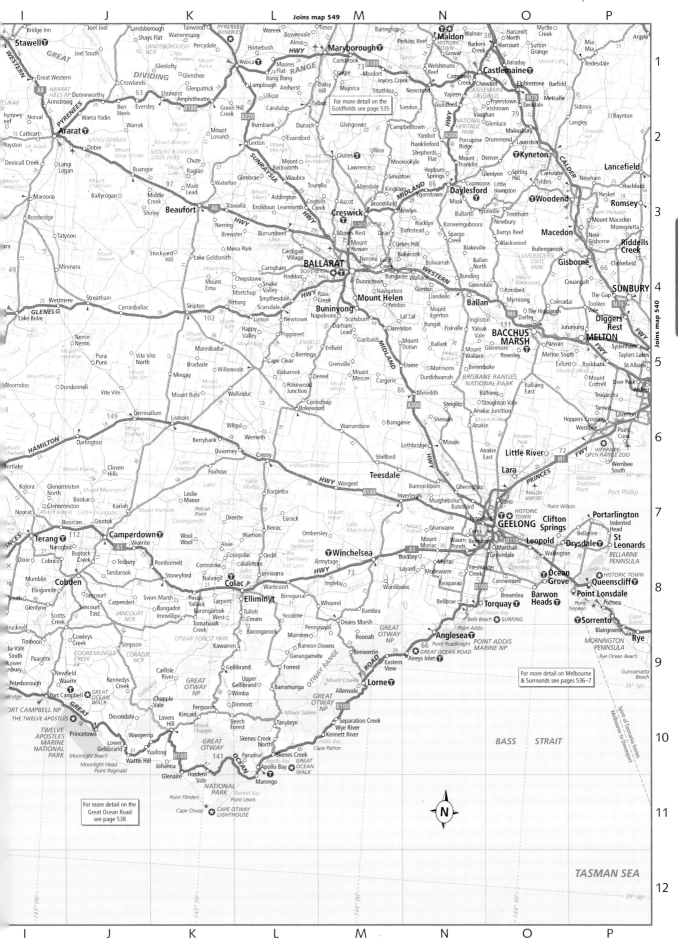

MAPS

SOUTH AUSTRALIA

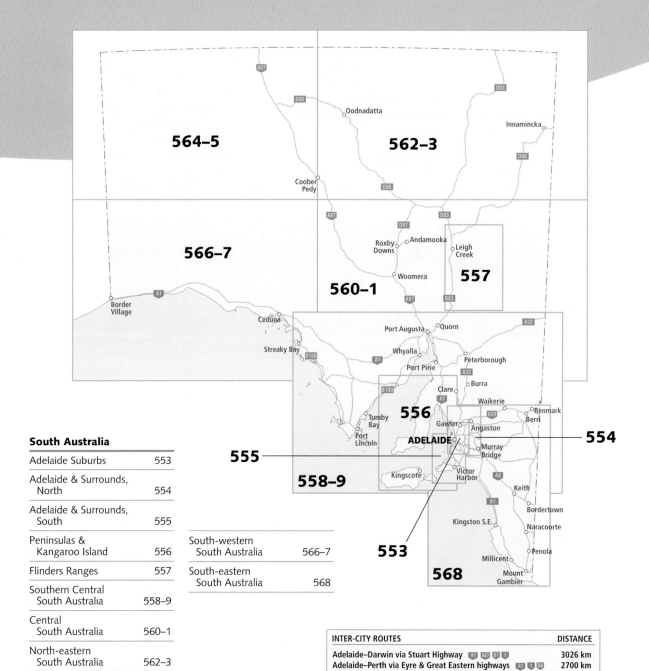

South Australia

Adelaide Suburbs	553
Adelaide & Surrounds, North	554
Adelaide & Surrounds, South	555
Peninsulas & Kangaroo Island	556
Flinders Ranges	557
Southern Central South Australia	558–9
Central South Australia	560–1
North-eastern South Australia	562–3
North-western South Australia	564–5
South-western South Australia	566–7
South-eastern South Australia	568

INTER-CITY ROUTES	DISTANCE
Adelaide–Darwin via Stuart Highway A1 A87 B7 1	3026 km
Adelaide–Perth via Eyre & Great Eastern highways A1 1 94	2700 km
Adelaide–Sydney via Sturt & Hume highways A20 20 31	1415 km
Adelaide–Melbourne via Dukes & Western highways M1 A8 M8	729 km
Adelaide–Melbourne via Princes Highway M1 B1 A1 M1	911 km

0 5 10 15 km

A B C D Joins map 554 E F G H

1

TO PORT WAKEFIELD
A1
TO BURRA A32
GAWLER RD
STURT HWY
TO NURIOOTPA
TO NURIOOTPA
WAY
Kangaroo Flat
GAWLER
Rosedale
PORT
EXP
BAROSSA
M20
Two Wells 9
24
Lewiston
GAWLER
Sandy Creek
B19
VALLEY
Rowland Flat
Lyndoch

2

WAKEFIELD
OLD PORT WAKEFIELD
Middle Beach
Angle Vale
ANGLE VALE RD
NORTHERN RD
RD
B31
South Para
SANDY CREEK CP
Pewsey Vale Peak
Williamstown
WARREN

3

Port Gawler
Virginia
RD
Bolivar
SMITHFIELD
A20
NORTH RD
PARA WIRRA RECREATION PARK
South Para Dam
HALE CP
WARREN
CRICKS MILL RD
PORT GAWLER CONSERVATION PARK
Barossa Reservoir
B34
CROMER CP RANGE

4

N
Direk
HEASLIP
EDINBURGH AERODROME
EDINBURGH RAAF BASE DEFENCE RESERVE
ELIZABETH
BLACK TOP RD
38
Little Para Reservoir
PARA
MOUNT
GOULD
WARREN
St Kilda
Point Grey
TORRENS ISLAND CP
40
WATERLOO CORNER RD
Little Para Dam
Mount Gawler
Kersbrook
Mount Gould
B34
GOULD

5

OUTER HARBOR
NORTH HAVEN
OSBORNE
TAPEROO
LARGS NORTH
Pelican Point
SALISBURY HWY
SALISBURY
PARAFIELD
Parafield Airport
GREEN FIELDS
A20
BRIDGE RD
A18
PARA HILLS
41
TEA TREE GULLY
COBBLER CREEK RP
B10
Houghton
Gumeracha
B31
Trail
Forreston
WARREN
Birdwood
RANGE
LEFEVRE PENINSULA

6

SEMAPHORE
Point Malcolm
PORT ADELAIDE
DRY CREEK
GRAND JUNCTION
ALBERTON
KILBURN
NORTHFIELD
A17
RD RD
31
A11
NORTH EAST RD
Hope Valley Reservoir
ANSTEY HILL RP
30
B31
Kangaroo Creek Reservoir
Kangaroo Creek Dam
MILLBROOK RESERVOIR
CUDLEE CREEK CP
PORTER SCRUB CP
Mount Torrens
B34
GULF
ALBERT PARK
DUDLEY PARK
MAIN NORTH RD
GORGE RD
BLACK HILL CP
RANGE

7

GRANGE
HILL RD
PORT RD
BOWDEN
NORTH ADELAIDE
ADELAIDE
MAGILL
ROSTREVOR
PORTRUSH RD
A15
River
A7
A11
MORIALTA CP
Heysen
KENNETH STIRLING CP
MONTACUTE CP
HORSNELL GULLY CP
FOREST
Lobethal
Charleston
CHARLESTON CP
TORRENS RANGE
For more detail on Central Adelaide see page 212–13

8

ST VINCENT
Holdfast Bay
GLENELG
TAPLEYS HILL RD
A6
KESWICK
ADELAIDE AIRPORT
GOODWOOD
UNLEY PARK
ANZAC HWY
A13
CROSS RD
MITCHAM
12
BELAIR
A17
A1
WATERFALL GULLY
GREENHILL RD
Summertown
Uraidla
31
BROWNHILL CREEK RP
CLELAND CP
SOUTH RD
MOUNT GEORGE CP
Oakbank
Balhannah
B34
Woodside
Brukunga
35°00'
ASCOT PARK
MARION

9

HOVE
BRIGHTON
SEACLIFF
SOUTH RD
EDEN HILLS
GLENALTA
BLACKWOOD
BELAIR NP
Upper Sturt
Mount Lofty
Stirling
Aldgate
Heathfield
Bridgewater
Hahndorf
Littlehampton
Nairne
PRINCES
EXP RD
STURT GORGE RP
Mylor
SUMMIT RESERVOIR
OLD EASTERN
MARINO CP
Marino Rocks Lighthouse
MARK OLIPHANT CP
HALLETT COVE CONSERVATION PARK
Happy Valley Reservoir
TOTNESS RP
MOUNT BARKER
M1

10

LONSDALE
REYNELLA
SOUTHERN EXP
21
MAIN RD
SCOTT CREEK CONSERVATION PARK
Mount Bold
Clarendon
33
Echunga
Wistow
FWY
TO MURRAY BRIDGE
22
Mount Bold Reservoir
Mount Bold Dam
35°00'

11

CHRISTIES BEACH
PORT NOARLUNGA
NOARLUNGA CENTRE
MORPHETT VALE
A15
A13
M2
MAIN SOUTH RD
ONKAPARINGA RIVER NATIONAL PARK
Blewitt Springs
Kangarilla
DASHWOOD GULLY RD
B34
Meadows
BATTUNGA RD
Macclesfield
B37
ONKAPARINGA RIVER RECREATION PARK
Onkaparinga River

12

SEAFORD
OLD NOARLUNGA
MOANA SANDS CP
Ochre Point
Moana
Maslin Beach
B23
TATACHILLA RD
McLaren Vale
McLaren Flat
KANGARILLA
34
Mount Wilson
BROOKMAN RD
Heysen
B34
B33
Woodchester
Hartley
Bletchley
VALLEY
LONG RD
A13
TO VICTOR HARBOR
TO VICTOR HARBOR

A B C D Joins map 555 E F G H

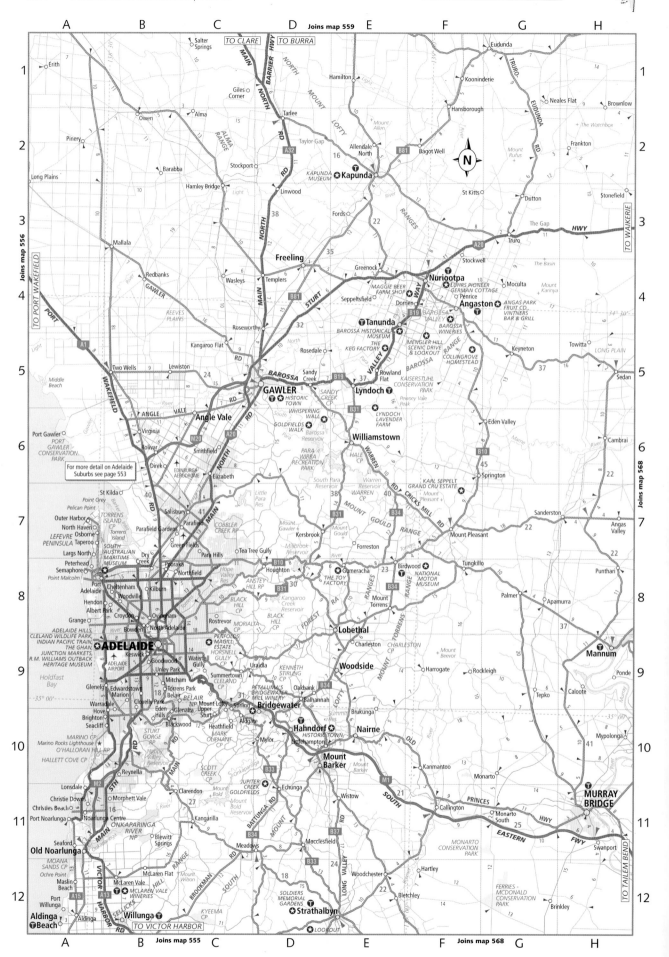

0   5   10   15   20 km

N

Joins map 554
Joins map 554
TO MURRAY BRIDGE
Joins map 568
Joins map 556

TO TWO WELLS   TO GAWLER

For more detail on Adelaide Suburbs see page 553

ADELAIDE

LEFEVRE PENINSULA
Largs North
Taperoo
Peterhead
Semaphore
Point Malcolm
Point Adelaide
Port Adelaide
MARITIME MUSEUM
Dry Creek
Pooraka
Northfield
Tea Tree Gully
Forreston
B10
Houghton
Gumeracha
THE TOY FACTORY
Cheltenham
Kilburn
Woodville
Hendon
Albert Park
Croydon
Bowden
North Adelaide
Ovingham
Rostrevor
B31
30
Kangaroo Creek Reservoir
BLACK HILL CP
MONTACUTE CP
FOREST
Lobethal
Charleston
Grange
ADELAIDE HILLS, CLELAND WILDLIFE PARK, INDIAN PACIFIC TRAIN, THE GHAN, JUNCTION MARKETS, R.M. WILLIAMS OUTBACK HERITAGE MUSEUM
Keswick
Goodwood
Unley Park
Mitcham
Waterfall Gully
Summertown
MORIALTA CP
PENFOLDS MAGILL ESTATE
HORSNELL GULLY CP
Uraidla
KENNETH STIRLING CP
Woodside
ADELAIDE AIRPORT
Holdfast Bay
Glenelg
Edwardstown
Marion
Torrens Park
Belair
BELAIR NP
Mount Lofty
Upper Sturt
CLELAND CP
Stirling
PETALUMA'S BRIDGEWATER MILL WINERY
Bridgewater
Oakbank
B34
Balhannah
Warradale
Hove
Brighton
Seacliff
Clovelly Park
Eden Hills
Glenalta
Blackwood
Heathfield
Aldgate
Mylor
Hahndorf
HISTORIC TOWN
Littlehampton
Nairne
MARINO CP
Marino Rocks Lighthouse
HALLETT COVE CP
STURT GORGE RP
MAIN RD
SCOTT CREEK CP
Mount Bold
EASTERN FWY
M1
Mount Barker
GULF
Lonsdale
M2
STH RD
Reynella
Morphett Vale
Happy Valley Reservoir
Clarendon
27
Mount Bold Reservoir
JUPITER CREEK GOLDFIELDS
B33
Echunga
Wistow
ST VINCENT
Christie Downs
Christies Beach
Port Noarlunga
Noarlunga Centre
16
11
ONKAPARINGA RIVER RP
Kangarilla
Meadows
Macclesfield
B34
B33
24
Seaford
Old Noarlunga
MOANA SANDS CP
Ochre Point
Maslin Beach
McLaren Flat
Blewitt Springs
McLaren Vale
VICTOR RD
A15
Mount Wilson
BROOKMAN RD
18
13
SOLDIERS MEMORIAL GARDENS
LONG VALLEY
Strathalbyn
Port Willunga
Aldinga
27
MCLAREN VALE WINERIES
Willunga
38
KYEEMA CP
Ashbourne
LOOKOUT
B37
Aldinga Beach
ALDINGA SCRUB CP
Silver Sands
SELLICKS HILL
MOUNT MAGNIFICENT CP
FINNISS CP
COX SCRUB CP
35
Sandergrove
Sellicks Beach
LOOKOUT
B23
B34
PAGES FLAT RD
Mount Compass
Yundi
Finniss
THE STEAM RANGER TOURIST RAILWAY
Myponga Beach
Myponga Reservoir
LOOKOUT
Myponga
STIPITURUS CP
49
Mount Compass
Nangkita
Tooperang
Gilberts
CURRENCY CREEK WINERY
Haycock Point
Carrickalinga
B23
14
YULTE CP
GUM TREE GULLY CP
Mount Cone
HARBOR
SCOTT CP
Currency Creek
CANOE TREE
Normanville
Yankalilla
RD
MYPONGA CP
29
SPRING MOUNT CP
HINDMARSH FALLS
A13
MIDDLETON WINERY
Yankalilla Bay
MOUNT
GLACIER ROCK
Hindmarsh Valley
CROWS NEST LOOKOUT
MALLEEBAA WOOLSHED
Clayton
Rapid Head
Rapid Bay
Second Valley
34
SOUTH
FLEURIEU
SOUTH
33
URIMBIRRA WILDLIFE PARK, GREENHILLS ADVENTURE PARK
GOOLWA AERODROME
Goolwa
COCKLE TRAIN
Hindmarsh Island
Rapid Bay
Mount Rapid
Delamere
RANGE
62
12
RD
B37
17
Port Elliot
Pullen Island
Middleton
SIR RICHARD PENINSULA
LOOKOUT
HEYSEN TRAIL, CAPE JERVIS LIGHTHOUSE
B23
MAIN RD
B37
16
PENINSULA
13
Victor Harbor
Granite Island
FAIRY PENGUINS
HORSE-DRAWN TRAM, S.A. WHALE CENTRE
COORONG NATIONAL PARK
Cape Jervis
Lands End
Fishery Beach
Ferry to Kangaroo Island
TALISKER CP
DEEP CREEK CONSERVATION PARK
Waitpinga
Wright Island
Rosetta Head (The Bluff)
King Head
West Island
Encounter Bay
Mundoo Island
BACKSTAIRS
PASSAGE
Tunkalilla Beach
Tunk Head
Parsons Beach
Waitpinga Beach
Newland Head
NEWLAND HEAD CONSERVATION PARK
Porpoise Head
Cuttlefish Bay
Snapper Point
THE PAGES CONSERVATION PARK
North Page
Cape Coutts
South Page
The Pages
SOUTHERN   OCEAN
LASHMAR CP
Antechamber Bay
Red House Bay
Cape St Albans
Cape Saint Alban Lighthouse
Moncrieff Bay
KANGAROO ISLAND
LESUEUR CONSERVATION PARK
Cape Willoughby Lighthouse
Cape Willoughby
Windmill Bay
SIMPSON CP
MACDONNELL (DUDLEY) PENINSULA
Cape Hart

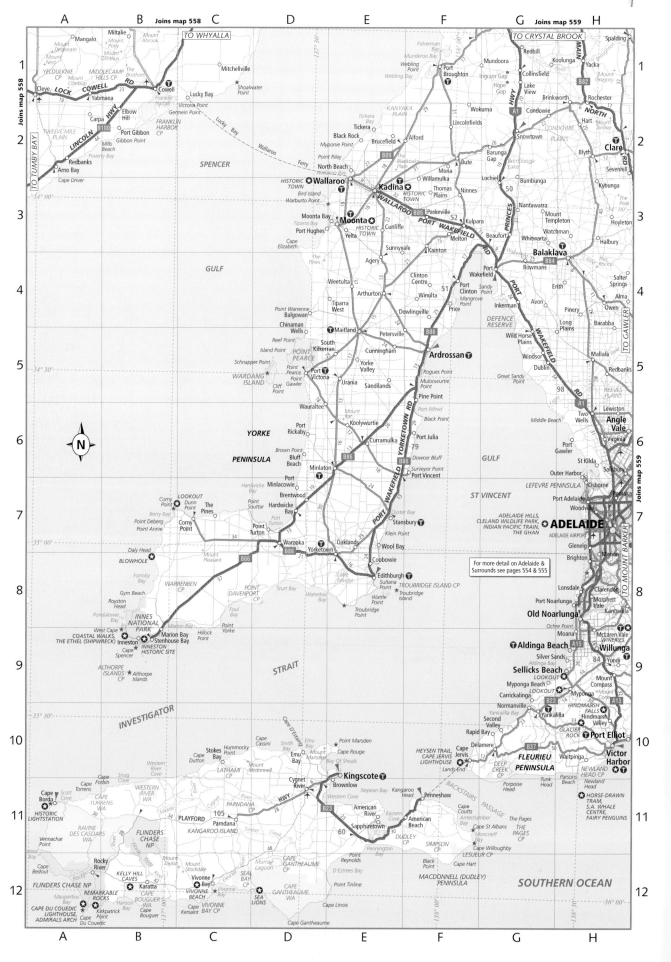

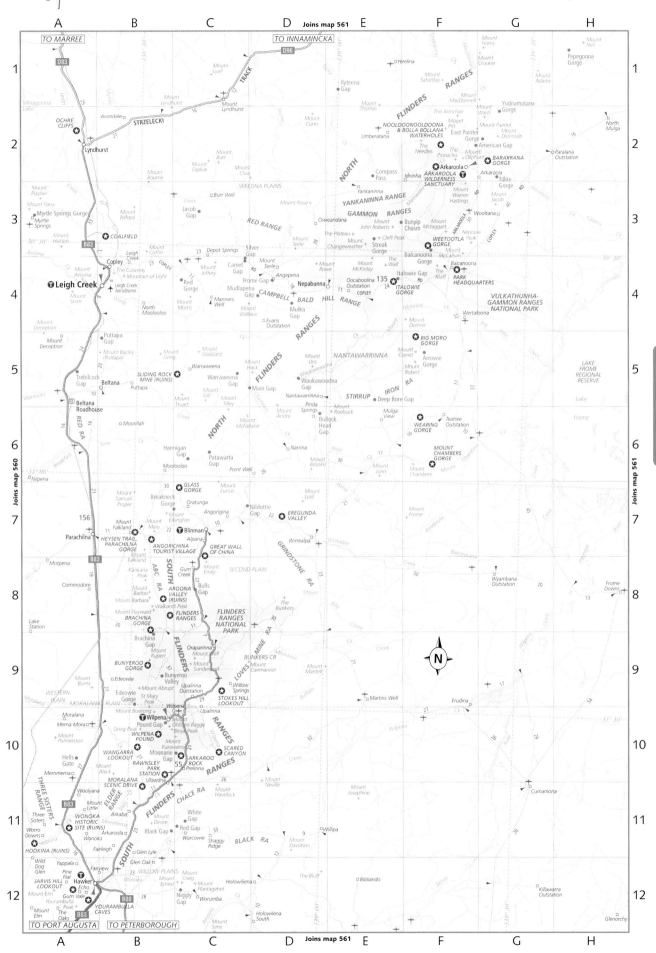

0   10   20   30   40 km

A   B   C   D   E   F   G   H

TO MARREE

TO INNAMINCKA

Mount
Harris
Mount
Crocker
Mount
Neil

Pepegoona
Gorge

Mount
Adams

Yerelina

Mount
Saturday

FLINDERS

Mount
MacDonnell

RANGES

North
Mulga

Ilyteena
Gap

Mount
Thomas

The Armchair

Mount
Ward
Mount
Dickinson

Yudnamutana
Gorge

Mount
Lyall

Mount
Lyndhurst

TRACK

Mount
Curtis

NOOLDOONOOLDOONA
& BOLLA BOLLANA
WATERHOLES

Mount
Pitt
Mount Painter

Paralana
Outstation

Avondale

STRZELECKI

Umberatana

The
Needles

The
Pinnacles

East Painter
Gorge

American Gap

Mount
Oliphant

BARARRANA
GORGE

Mount
Lyndhurst

16

Mount
Bourne

WEEDNA PLAINS

Burr Well

Mount Rose

NORTH

Compass
Pass

YANKANINNA RANGE

Arkaroola

ARKAROOLA
WILDERNESS
SANCTUARY

Arkaroola

Tillite
Gorge

Lyndhurst

Mount
Ogilvie

Mount
Clive

Jacob
Gap

Idninha

Mount
Warren
Hastings

Wooltana

Mount
Playfair

Mount
Parry

Myrtle Springs Gorge
Myrtle
Springs

OCHRE
CLIFFS

Mount
Telford

Red Range

GAMMON RANGES

Mount
Serle

Owieandana

The Plateau

John Roberts

Mount Mctaggart

Nepouie
Peak

COPLEY

Mount
Hutton

COALFIELD

Depot Springs

Silver
Gap

Changeweather

Cleft Peak

Streak
Gorge

Balcanoona

WEETOOTLA
GORGE

Mount
McCalium

Mount
Aroona

Leigh
Creek

COPLEY

Camel
Gap

Mount
Serle

Mount
Rowe

Mount
McKinlay

The
Wall

Italowie Gap

Balcanoona
Gorge

Balcanoona

The Bluff

PARK
HEADQUARTERS

Copley

The Cutaway
Mountain of Light

Mount
Jeffery

Frome Gap

Angepena

Oocaboolina
Outstation

135

Italowie
Gorge

ITALOWIE
GORGE

Leigh Creek

Leigh Creek
Aerodrome

Red
Gorge

Mudlapena
Gap

Nepabunna

24

COPLEY

VULKATHUNHA-
GAMMON RANGES
NATIONAL PARK

Mount
Scott

Manners
Well

Mount
Morris

Mount
Wallace

Mulka
Gap

CAMPBELL

BALD

HILL

RANGE

McKinlay

Wertaloona

Mount
Deception

Mount
Deception

Puttapa
Gap

Mount Bayley
(Puttapa)

Evans
Outstation

RANGES

Mount
Dorner

BIG MORO
GORGE

LAKE
FROME
REGIONAL
RESERVE

Trebilcock
Gap

Beltana

SLIDING ROCK
MINE (RUINS)

Warraweena

Warraweena

Mount
Hack

Mount
Uro

NANTAWARRINNA

Mount
Comet

Arrowie
Gorge

Mount
Robert

Puttapa

FLINDERS

Mount
Gill

Main Gap

Waukawoodna
Gap

Waukawoodna

STIRRUP

IRON

RA

Beltana
Roadhouse

Moorilla

NORTH

Mount
Stuart

Mount
Tilley

Nantawarrina

Pinda
Springs

Deep Bore Gap

Mulga
View

WEARING
GORGE

Teatree
Outstation

Nilpena

Time

Mount
McFarlane

Mount
Andre

Bullock
Head
Gap

Mount
Roebuck

MOUNT
CHAMBERS
GORGE

Hannigan
Gap

Moolooloo

Patawarta
Gap

Point Well

Narrina

Mount
Brooke

Mount
John

Mount
Chambers

GLASS
GORGE

Mount
Lucius

Mount
Lyall

Mount
Samuel
Proper

Breakneck
Gorge

Oratunga

Mount
Elkington

Nildottie
Gap

EREGUNDA
VALLEY

Mount
Frome

Parachilna

156

Mount
Falkland

Mount
Mary

Blinman

Angorigina

Alpana

Wirrealpa

Wyambana
Outstation

Motpena

HEYSEN TRAIL,
PARACHILNA
GORGE

Mount
Falkland

ANGORICHINA
TOURIST VILLAGE

GREAT WALL
OF CHINA

Gum
Creek

Mount
Emily

SECOND PLAIN

GRINDSTONE

RA

Frome
Downs

Commodore

ABC

RA

SOUTH

Kankana
Peak

Bulls
Gap

The
Bunkers

Mount
Barloo

AROONA
VALLEY
(RUINS)

Mount
Barbara

Walkandi Peak

FLINDERS
RANGES

Mount
Hayward

BRACHINA
GORGE

FLINDERS
RANGES

FLINDERS
RANGES
NATIONAL
PARK

LOVES MINE
RA

Lake
Station

Brachina
Gap

Mount
Rupert

Oraparinna
Mount Well

Mount
Sunderiest

BUNKERS CR

Mount
Caemarvon

Mount
Mantell

Martins Well

Erudina

BUNYEROO
GORGE

Bunyeroo
Valley

Edeowie

Mount
Abrupt

Upalinna
Outstation

Willow
Springs

Mount
Burns

Edeowie
Gorge

St Mary
Peak

STOKES HILL
LOOKOUT

WESTERN

PLAIN

MORALANA

PLAIN

Mount Boorong

Wilpena

Upalinna

RANGES

Moralana

Merna Mora

Pound Gap

WILPENA
POUND

Oraleen Bagge

Binya Peak

Mount
Palmerston

Greg Peak

SCARED
CANYON

Mount
Neville

Curnamona

Hells
Gate

WANGARRA
LOOKOUT

Moonarie

Mount
Karawarra

ARKAROO
ROCK

Mount
Josephine

Mernmerna

RAWNSLEY
PARK
STATION

55

Prelinna

RANGES

Mount
Aleck

MORALANA
SCENIC DRIVE

Ulowdna

CHACE RA

THREE SISTERS
RANGE

Woolyana

ELDER
RANGE

FLINDERS

Mount
Havelock

Three
Sisters

Mount
Little

WONOKA
HISTORIC
SITE (RUINS)

Arkaroola

White
Gap

Worro
Downs

Arbaba

SOUTH

Mount
Desire

Red Gap
Warcowie

BLACK RA

Willipa

Willowilena

HOOKINA (RUINS)

Black Gap

Shaggy
Ridge

Mount
Davidson

Wild
Dog
Glen

Yappala

Fairview

Glen Lyle

Glen Oak

Bibliando

JARVIS HILL
LOOKOUT

Pine
Flat

Hawker

WILLOW PLAINS

Mount
Craig

Mount
Ernest

Holowiliena

The Bluff

Killawarra
Outstation

Mount Elm

Echo

Gum Vale

Wonoka

Niggly
Gap

Mount
Plantagenet

Worumba

Holowiliena
South

Glenorchy

Mount
Elm

Yourambulla
Peak

The
Oaks

YOURAMBULLA
CAVES

Mount
Sems

TO PORT AUGUSTA   *TO PETERBOROUGH*

A   B   C   D   E   F   G   H

Joins map 560

Joins map 561

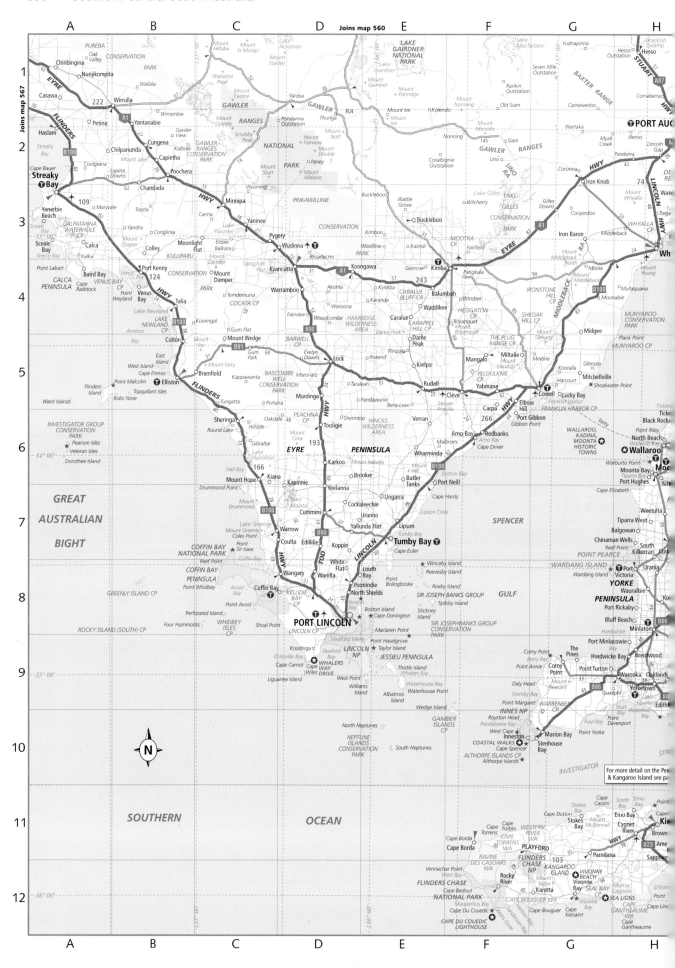

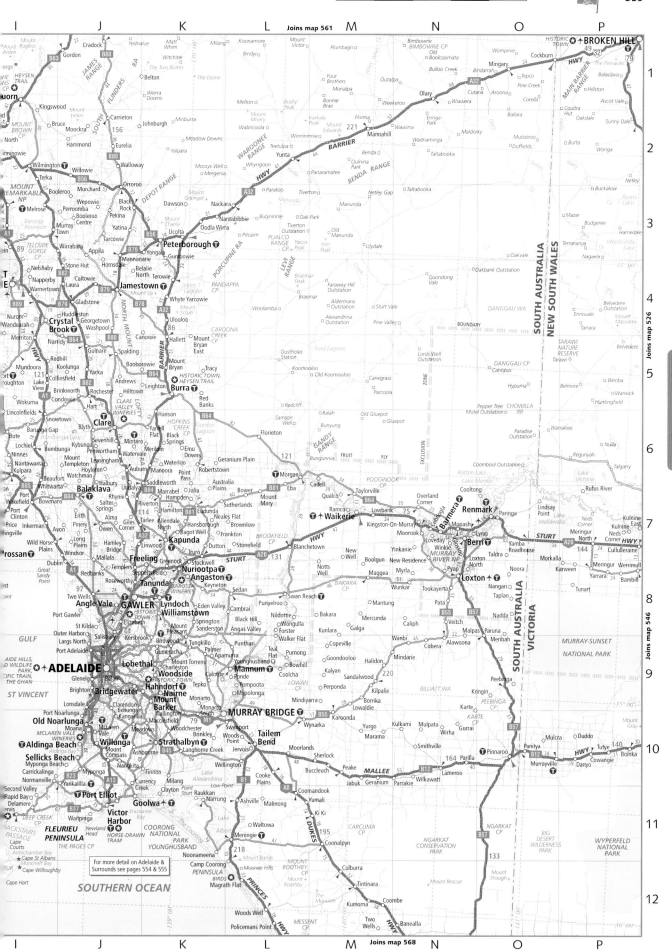

Joins map 561

Joins map 526

Joins map 546

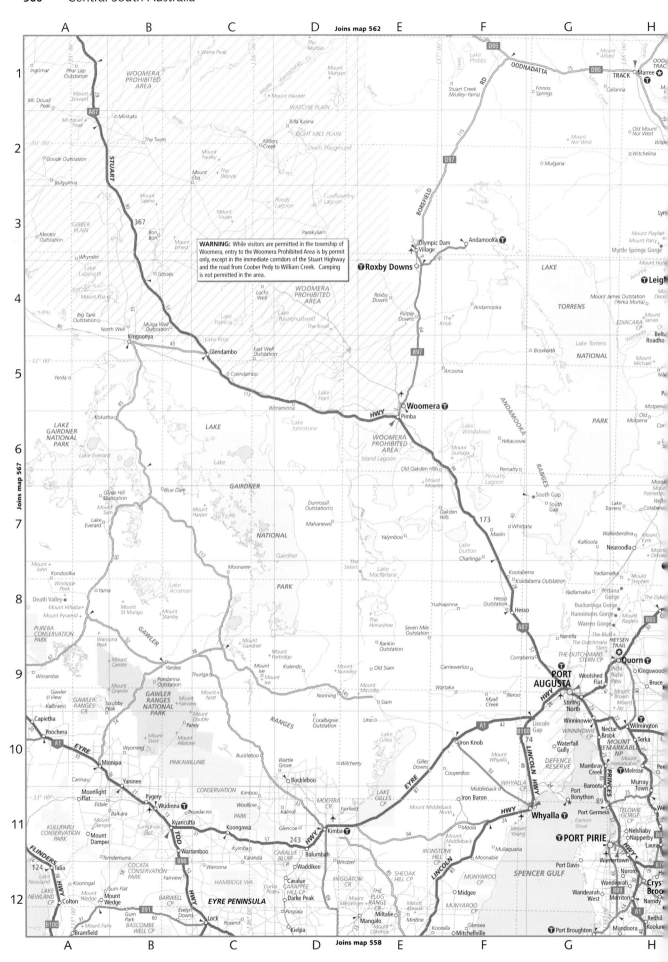

Joins map 562

Joins map 567

Joins map 558

WARNING: While visitors are permitted in the township of Woomera, entry to the Woomera Prohibited Area is by permit only, except in the immediate corridors of the Stuart Highway and the road from Coober Pedy to William Creek. Camping is not permitted in the area.

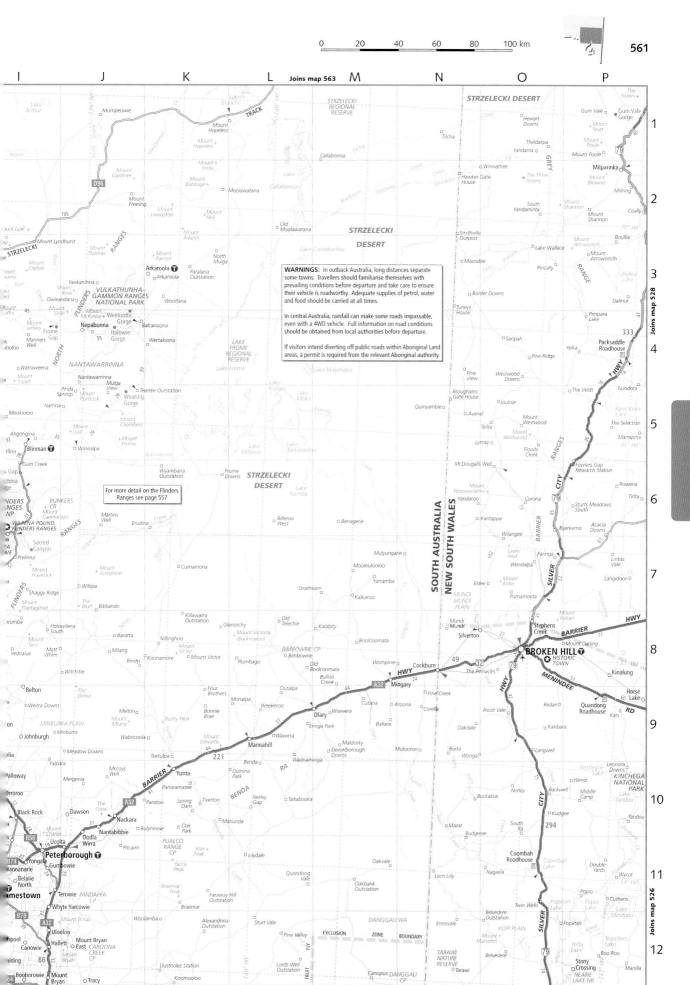

0   20   40   60   80   100 km

Joins map 563

I   J   K   L   M   N   O   P

STRZELECKI DESERT

Lake Arthur

Murnpeowie

Mount Hopeless

TRACK

STRZELECKI REGIONAL RESERVE

Gum Vale
Gum Vale Gorge

The Sisters

1

130 Hill

Mount Hopeless

Callabonna

Tilcha

Hewart Downs

Theldarpa

Mount Sturt

Mount Poole
Mount Poole

Frome

Mount Gardiner

D96

Mount Freeling

Mount Yenla

Mount Babbage

Lake Callabonna

Yandama

Winnathee

Hawker Gate House

Mount Browne

Milparinka

Milring

79

2

195

Mount Lyall

STRZELECKI

Mount Ogilvie

Mount Thomas

Mount Livingston

Mount Neil

Mount Adams

Old Moolawatana

Moolawatana

STRZELECKI DESERT

Lake Cootabarlow

South Yandaminta

Smithville Outpost

Mount Shannon

Boulla

Lake Wallace

Coally

Mount Shannon

Mount Lyndhurst

Arkaroola
Arkaroola

Mount Painter

Paralana Outstation

North Mulga

WARNINGS: In outback Australia, long distances separate some towns. Travellers should familiarise themselves with prevailing conditions before departure and take care to ensure their vehicle is roadworthy. Adequate supplies of petrol, water and food should be carried at all times.

In central Australia, rainfall can make some roads impassable, even with a 4WD vehicle. Full information on road conditions should be obtained from local authorities before departure.

If visitors intend diverting off public roads within Aboriginal Land areas, a permit is required from the relevant Aboriginal authority.

Moorabie

Pincally

Mount Arrowsmith

Mount Arrowsmith

Bullos Lake

Dalmur

RANGE

3

Joins map 528

Mount Rose

Owieandana

VULKATHUNHA–GAMMON RANGES NATIONAL PARK

Mount Selso

Mount McKinlay

Weetootla Gorge

Wooltana

Balcanoona

Border Downs

Turleys House

Pimpara Lake

Packsaddle Roadhouse

HWY

333

4

Yankaninna

Mount Jeffery

Frome Gap

Nepabunna

Italowie Gorge

Wertaloona

LAKE FROME REGIONAL RESERVE

Lake Maljanapa

Pine View

Westwood Downs

Yelka

Pine Ridge

The Veldt

Nundora

Manners Well

NANTAWARRINNA

Nantawarrinna

Mulga View

Teatree Outstation

Lake Frome

39

Lake Kuturu

Lake Moko

Broughams Gate House

Joulnie

Quinyambie

Avenel

Mount Westwood

Mount Westwood

Ban,annia Lake

The Selection

5

Mooloolo

Warraweena

Pinda Springs

Narrina

Mount Roebuck

Wearing Gorge

Eurinilla

Teilta

Lynray

Floods Creek

Marrapina

Tirlta

Angorigina

Mount Stuart

35

Mount Lyall

Wirrealpa

Mount Chambers

Lake Millyera

Lake Tarkaroolo

McDougalls Well

Corona

Sturts Meadows South

Fowlers Gap Research Station

Rowena

6

Blinman

32

Gum Creek

china

Mount Havelock

Prelinna

Mount Frome

Balcanoona

Frome Downs

STRZELECKI DESERT

Lake Namba

Mount Woowoolahra

Yandaroo

Kantappa

Bijerkerno

Wilangee

Acacia Downs

CITY

BARRIER

79

Gap

NDERS NGES NP

BUNKERS CR

Mount Caernarvon

For more detail on the Flinders Ranges see page 557

Martins Well

Erudina

Billeroo West

Benagerie

Mulyungarie

Lewis Peak

Paringa

Lintiss Vale

Langidoon

SILVER

22

7

WILPENA POUND, FLINDERS RANGES

RANGES

Willipa

Mount Josephine

Curnamona

Stratheam

Mooleulooloo

Yarramba

Kalkaroo

Mount Robe

Purnamoota

Eldee

RANGES

Sacred Canyon

Shaggy Ridge

The Bluff

Bibliando

Killawarra Outstation

Glenorchy

Mount Victoria (Buckmatool)

Old Telechie

Kalabity

Boolcoomata

BIMBOWRIE CP

Bimbowrie

Mundi Mundi

MUNDI MUNDI PLAIN

Stephens Creek

Mount Darling

BARRIER

HWY

8

FLINDERS

Mount Plantagenet

Holowilena South

Baratta

Milang

Nillinghoo

Koonamore

Mount Victor

Mount Victor

Plumbago

Old Bookcoomata

Bulloo Creek

Wompinie

HWY

Cockburn

Silverton

32

The Pinnacles

BROKEN HILL

79

HISTORIC TOWN

Kinalung

rumba

Yednalue

Matt Whim

Witchitie

Bindyi

Four Brothers

Morialpa

Outalpa

A32

Mingary

24

Pine Creek

49

Horse Lake

Kars

Redan

Quandong Roadhouse

MENINDEE

RD

60

9

Belton

Weirra Downs

The Dome

Melton

Mount Misery

Bushy Peak

Bonnie Brae

Weekeroo

Cutana

Wiawera

Olary

Eringa Park

Ballara

Aroona

Corella

Ascot Vale

Oakdale

Burta

Wonga

Kanbara

Langwell

MINBURRA PLAIN

Johnburgh

Minburra

Wabricoola

Teetulpa

Mount Edwards

221

Mannahill

37

Wawirra

Maldorky

Devonborough Downs

Mutooroo

Leonora Downs

Wendi

KINCHEGA NATIONAL PARK

Lake Tandou

10

on

Yalpara

Mergenia

Mccoys Well

Paratoo

A32

Yunta

BARRIER

41

Panaramatee

Benda

BENDA

Oulnina Park

RA

Netley Gap

Wadnaminga

Taltabooka

Buckalow

Netley

Mazar

Middle Camp

Tandou

alloway

Black Rock

Dawson

Mount Charlie

The Cone

31

Nackara

Spring Dam

Tiverton

Manunda

South Ita

Budgeree

294

Kudgee

B56

Ucolta

Oodla Wirra

Nantabibbie

Bulyninnie

Oak Park

PUALCO RANGE CP

Iron Peak

Lilydale

Oakvale

Oakbank Outstation

Coombah Roadhouse

Nagaela

Coombah Lake

Double Yards

Wycot

11

B79

Yongala

Peterborough

Gumowie

Pitcairn

Yacca Peak

Quondong Vale

Loch Lilly

Popio Lake

Cuthero

Lake Mindona

mannarie

Belalie North

mestown

Terowie

Whyte Yarcowie

PANDAPPA CP

Braemar Peak

Braemar

Faraway Hill Outstation

Alexandrina Outstation

Sturt Vale

DANGGALI WA

EXCLUSION   ZONE   BOUNDARY

Ennisvale

Belvedere Outstation

Twin Wells

KOPI PLAIN

Popitah Lake

Popio

SILVER

Travellers Lake

Roo Roo

12

B78

A32

Mount Scrub

Woolamba

Pine Valley

Lords Well Outstation

FRUIT

FLY

TARAWI NATURE RESERVE

Tarawi

Mount Massidon

Belvedere

79

Yelta Lake

Manilla

hpool

Canowie

Ulooloo

Hallett

Mount Bryan East

CAROONA CREEK CP

Dustholes Station

Koomooloo

Canopus

DANGGALI NP

NEARIE LAKE NR

Stony Crossing

86

Booborowie

Mount Bryan

Tracy

Joins map 526

Joins map 559

I   J   K   L   M   N   O   P

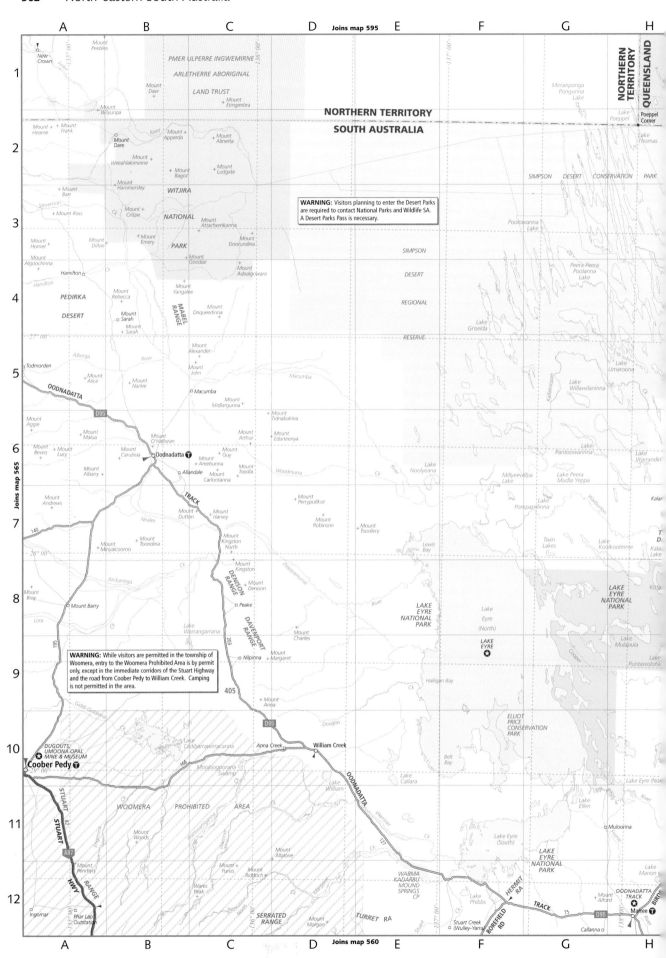

Joins map 595

Joins map 565

NORTHERN TERRITORY

SOUTH AUSTRALIA

NORTHERN TERRITORY

QUEENSLAND

Poeppel
Corner

WARNING: Visitors planning to enter the Desert Parks
are required to contact National Parks and Wildlife SA.
A Desert Parks Pass is necessary.

WARNING: While visitors are permitted in the township of
Woomera, entry to the Woomera Prohibited Area is by permit
only, except in the immediate corridors of the Stuart Highway
and the road from Coober Pedy to William Creek. Camping
is not permitted in the area.

Joins map 560

I J K L M N O P

EYRE DEV. RD

BIRDSVILLE

DEVELOPMENTAL RD

Mount Collins

Durrie

Mount Leonard

Betoota

Mount Hal

Cuddapan

Lake Cuddapan

Roseberth

Mount Lewis

Birdsville

1

QUEENSLAND

SOUTH AUSTRALIA

Shallow Lake

Moonda Lake

Mount Oakes

Haddon Corner

STURT STONY DESERT

Planet Downs Outstation

2

The West Lake

Alton Downs

Pandie Pandie

Lake Coninnie

KACHUMBA PLAIN

Curalle Tin Shed

Gilpeppee Outstation

D83

Lake Short

STURT STONY DESERT

The Sisters

SIMPSON DESERT

Lake Etamunbanie

Lake Uloowarame

Mount Howie

Nulla Outstation

Lake Yamma Yamma (MacKillop)

3

New Alton Downs

Clifton Hills Outstation

My Mountain

Mount Grow

SIMPSON DESERT REGIONAL RESERVE

TRACK

179

STURT STONY DESERT

RAINBOW PLAIN

STRZELECKI DESERT

Mount Mckinlay

RD

Cordillo Downs

Arrabury

The Gibbers

4

(OUTSIDE)

BIRDSVILLE

Lake Marroopootanie

Lake Apanburra

Lake Goyder (Coolangie)

STRZELECKI DESERT

Joes Outstation

Clifton Hills

516

133

STURT STONY DESERT

Lake Toontoowaranie

Coongie Lake

Mitkacaldratillie Lakes

Lake Pure

Lake Pure

5

Mount Gason

Lake Koolivoo

Coon Coon Tillie Lakes

COONGIE LAKES NATIONAL PARK

Old Karmona Cottage

D83

WARNINGS: In outback Australia, long distances separate some towns. Travellers should familiarise themselves with prevailing conditions before departure and take care to ensure their vehicle is roadworthy. Adequate supplies of petrol, water and food should be carried at all times.

In central Australia, rainfall can make some roads impassable, even with a 4WD vehicle. Full information on road conditions should be obtained from local authorities before departure.

If visitors intend diverting off public roads within Aboriginal Land areas, a permit is required from the relevant Aboriginal authority.

INNAMINCKA REGIONAL RESERVE

St Anne's Cottage

WAY

6

Mount Sullivan

Lake Howitt

TRACK

MONTEPIRE

CORDILLO

SOUTH AUSTRALIA
QUEENSLAND

Fly Lake

Gidgealpa

Innamincka

Innamincka

Mount McLeod

Nappa Merrie

Cooper Creek

NAPPA

MERRIE

Mount Hogarth

Mungeranie Gap

Mungerannie Roadhouse

HWY

DILLONS

47

44

ADVENTURE

7

Lake Warrakalanna

TRACK

60

TRACK

SANTOS

166

Orientos

Tennappera

8

Theare Hill

Mulka

Lake Hope (Pando)

STRZELECKI

50

INNAMINCKA REGIONAL RESERVE

Epsilon

Santos

9

TRACK

STRZELECKI DESERT

STRZELECKI

STRZELECKI

D96

STRZELECKI DESERT

Lake Killamperpunna

OLD

Merty Merty

Naryilco

Etadunna

FLOOD TRACK BYPASS

Therua Hill

Mount Wells

Lake Gregory

REGIONAL

Pigeon Lake

Old Naryilco

34

10

204

Mount Kauto

120

Omicron

kaninna

Mount Flint

Mount Jervois

Mount Way

Lake Blanche

RESERVE

STRZELECKI

127

Bollards Lagoon

Corner Store

Cameron Corner

Fortville House

Toona House

Warri House

11

The Bluff

Murnpeowie

D96

Mount Hopeless

Lake Callabonna

STRZELECKI REGIONAL RESERVE

STRZELECKI DESERT

Fortville Bore

Whitecatch House

Fort Grey

STURT NATIONAL PARK

Binerah Downs

Binerah Well

Olive Downs

Mount King

11

Mount Playford

NEW SOUTH WALES

Lake Stewart

Waka

133

Hewart Downs

Tilcha

Tilcha

Stone Hut

Gum Vale

Mount Sturt

Mount Sturt

Gum Vale Gorge

12

I J K L M N O P

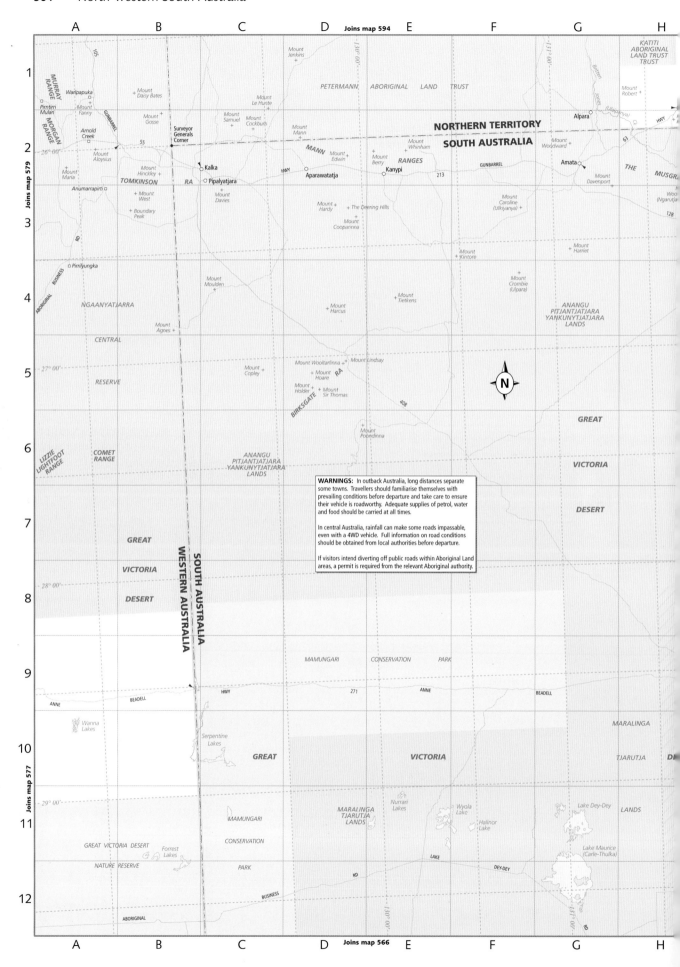

Joins map 579

Joins map 577

A   B   C   D   E   F   G   H

1   2   3   4   5   6   7   8   9   10   11   12

KATITI ABORIGINAL LAND TRUST TRUST

MURRAY RANGE

105

Warlpapuka

Pirntirri Mulan

MORGAN RANGE

Mount Fanny

Arnold Creek

Mount Aloysius

Mount Maria

Anumarrapirti

TOMKINSON RA

Mount Daisy Bates

Mount Gosse

GUNBARREL

55

Surveyor Generals Corner

Mount Hinckley

Kalka

Pipalyatjara

Mount West

Mount Agnes

Boundary Peak

Mount Davies

Mount Samuel

Mount Le Hunte

Mount Cockburn

Mount Jenkins

PETERMANN   ABORIGINAL   LAND   TRUST

Mount Mann

HWY

Aparawatatja

MANN

Mount Edwin

Mount Berry

Kanypi

RANGES

Mount Whinham

213

Mount Hardy

The Deering Hills

Mount Cooparinna

Mount Moulden

Mount Harcus

Mount Tietkens

Mount Kintore

Mount Caroline (Ulkiyanya)

Mount Crombie (Ulpara)

Mount Harriet

NORTHERN TERRITORY

SOUTH AUSTRALIA

GUNBARREL

Mount Woodward

Alpara

Amata

Mount Davenport

63

Mount Robert

THE MUSGRA

Woo (Ngarutja)

128

NGAANYATJARRA

CENTRAL

RESERVE

COMET RANGE

LIZZIE LIGHTFOOT RANGE

Pirrilyungka

ABORIGINAL BUSINESS

RD

Mount Copley

Mount Holder

BIRKSGATE RA

Mount Wooltarlinna

Mount Hoare

Mount Sir Thomas

Mount Lindsay

Mount Poondinna

408

ANANGU PITJANTJATJARA YANKUNYTJATJARA LANDS

GREAT

VICTORIA

DESERT

N

ANANGU PITJANTJATJARA YANKUNYTJATJARA LANDS

GREAT

VICTORIA

DESERT

SOUTH AUSTRALIA

WESTERN AUSTRALIA

WARNINGS: In outback Australia, long distances separate some towns. Travellers should familiarise themselves with prevailing conditions before departure and take care to ensure their vehicle is roadworthy. Adequate supplies of petrol, water and food should be carried at all times.

In central Australia, rainfall can make some roads impassable, even with a 4WD vehicle. Full information on road conditions should be obtained from local authorities before departure.

If visitors intend diverting off public roads within Aboriginal Land areas, a permit is required from the relevant Aboriginal authority.

Wanna Lakes

Serpentine Lakes

GREAT

MAMUNGARI   CONSERVATION   PARK

271

ANNE

HWY

ANNE   BEADELL

BEADELL

MARALINGA

TJARUTJA

D

VICTORIA

GREAT VICTORIA DESERT

NATURE RESERVE

Forrest Lakes

MAMUNGARI

CONSERVATION

PARK

MARALINGA TJARUTJA LANDS

Nurrari Lakes

Wyola Lake

Halinor Lake

LAKE

RD

DEY-DEY

Lake Dey-Dey

LANDS

Lake Maurice (Carle-Thulka)

BUSINESS

ABORIGINAL

130° 00'

137°

RD

26° 00'

27° 00'

28° 00'

29° 00'

130° 00'

131° 00'

137° 00'

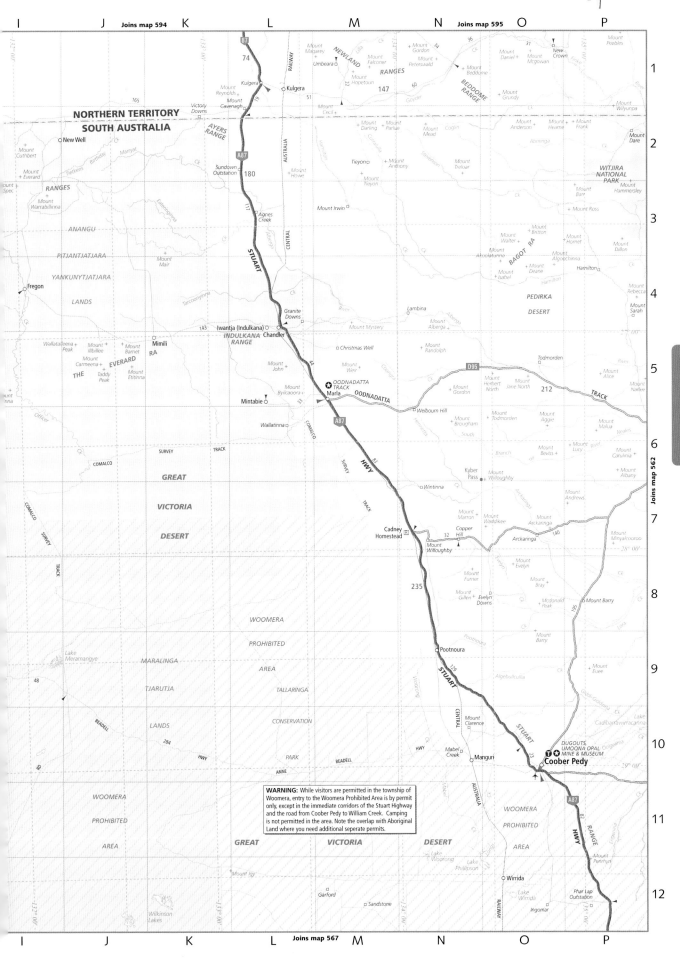

0   20   40   60   80   100 km

Joins map 594
Joins map 595
Joins map 562
Joins map 567

NORTHERN TERRITORY
SOUTH AUSTRALIA

WARNING: While visitors are permitted in the township of Woomera, entry to the Woomera Prohibited Area is by permit only, except in the immediate corridors of the Stuart Highway and the road from Coober Pedy to William Creek. Camping is not permitted in the area. Note the overlap with Aboriginal Land where you need additional seperate permits.

Coober Pedy
DUGOUTS,
UMOONA OPAL
MINE & MUSEUM

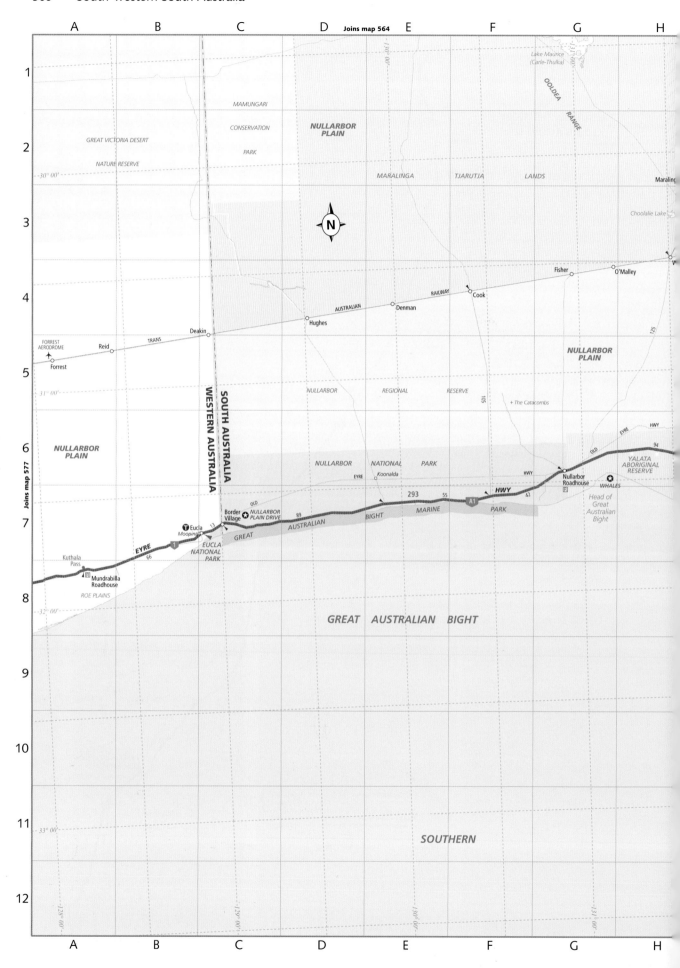

Joins map 564

Joins map 577

Joins map 565

0 20 40 60 80 100 km

WARNING: While visitors are permitted in the township of Woomera, entry to the Woomera Prohibited Area is by permit only, except in the immediate corridors of the Stuart Highway and the road from Coober Pedy to William Creek. Camping is not permitted in the area. Note the overlap with Aboriginal Land where you need additional seperate permits.

I J K L M N O P

Row 1
Wirrida
Lake Wirrida
RAILWAY
Ingomar
Phar Lap Outstation
Mount Santly
WOOMERA
Comet
McDouall Peak
Mount Soward
Mirikata
STUART

Row 2
Wilkinson Lakes
MARALINGA
Indooroopilly Outstation
Jumbuck
Commonwealth Hill
PROHIBITED
Gina Outstation
A87
367
HWY

Row 3
(ALINGA ENCE AND HIBITED REA)
TJARUTJA
Lake Anthony
Half Moon Lake
Irria Outstation
Muckanippie Outstation
Bradman Outstation
Goode Outstation
Bulgunnia
LANDS
WOOMERA
PROHIBITED
Mulgathing
AUSTRALIAN
Carne Outstation
Ooraminna Outstation
Ooldea
Bates
Lake Bring
Mount Christie
Durkin Outstation
AREA
Johns Outstation
Gibraltar Outstation
Ambrosia Outstation
CENTRAL
Ealbara Outstation
Mentor Outstation
Whymlet

Row 4
TRANS
AUSTRALIAN
Wynbring
Warrior Outstation
Carnding Road Outstation
Lake Moolkra
Tarcoola
Lake Labyrinth
Mount Ebar
ULLARBOR
REGIONAL
Lyons Camp
Malbooma Outstation
RAILWAY
Wilgena
Big Tank Outstation
North Well

Row 5
RESERVE
Lake Ifould
YELLABINNA
REGIONAL
Mount Finke
Kingoonya
Yerda
Lake Harris

Row 6
Lake Tallacootra
RESERVE
YELLABINNA WILDERNESS AREA
Kokatha
LAKE GAIRDNER NP

Row 7
Yalata
YALATA ABORIGINAL RESERVE
BOONDINA CONSERVATION PARK
Northedge
YUMBARRA CONSERVATION PARK
REGIONAL
Lake Everard
Glyde Hill Outstation
Lake Everard
Joins map 560

Row 8
AHGUNYAH ONSERVATION ARK
EYRE
55
Nundroo
Nundroo Roadhouse
202
39
Pintumba
Bookabie
Cundilippy
CHADINGA CONSERVATION PARK
Penong
35
A1
73
Koonibba
PUREBA
Mount John
Kondoolka
Mount Pollard
Yarna
EAT RALIAN GHT ARINE ARK
Wookata
Coorabie
31
Fowlers Bay
Marbra
Corrong
NULLARBOR PLAIN DRIVE
Watchbrae
CONSERVATION
Mount Wallaby
Winlippie Peak
Mount Hiltaba
Mount St Mungo
Cape Adieu
Cheetima Beach
FOWLERS BAY CP
Cape Nuyts
Fowlers Bay
Point Fowler
HWY
Ceduna
EYRE
Mudamuckla
PARK
Mount Pyramid
Wartoona Peak

Row 9
NUYTS REEF CP
Point Bell
SURFING
Cactus Beach
Point Sinclair
POINT BELL CP
Lake MacDonnell
Black Peak
Thevenard
Denial Bay
Point Peter
FLINDERS
92
Chinbingina
Oak Valley
Nunjikompita
Mount Centre
Purdie Islands
Cape D'Estrees
Smoky Bay
Kara-Pine
Carawa
222
Wirrulla
Wirrambie
GAWLER RANGES NP
Cape D'Estrees
St Peter Island
Goat Island
NUYTS ARCHIPELAGO CP
Eyre Island
Smoky Bay
30
Flagstaff
109
Petina
A1
Yantanabie
Gawler View
Mount Granite
GAWLER RANGES
Scrubby Peak

Row 10
Lacy Island
Evans Island
Franklin Islands
Point Dillon
ACRAMAN CREEK CP
Haslam
B100
Chilpanunda
Cungena
Kalbrae
Scrubby Peak
ISLES OF ST FRANCIS CP
St Francis Island
St Mary Bay
Point Brown
Gascoigne Bay
Point Collinson
Streaky Bay
HWY
Coolgrana
The Bald Hills
Mount Jane
Capietha
Poochera
74
Wyoming
Eba Island
Chandada
HWY
Minnipa
16

Row 11
OCEAN
Streaky Bay
Point Westall
Yanerbie Beach
SCEALE BAY CP
Sceale Bay
Slade Point
Searcy Bay
Cape Bauer
Corvisart Bay
Maryvale
CALPATANNA WATERHOLE CP
Calca
Mount Hall
62
Parla Peak
Yandra
Tootla
Carina
Moonlight Flat
Yaninee
Lake Yaninee
Mount Damper
Point Labatt
Baird Bay
VENUS BAY CP
Colley
Mount Misery
KULLIPARU CONSERVATION PARK
Mount Damper
COCATA CP
Cape Radstock
Port Kenny
124
FLINDERS

Row 12
Venus Bay
Talia
Conglima
B100
Talia Beach
Kooringal
Mount Wedge
Mount Wedge
Anxious Bay
Lake Newland
LAKE NEWLAND CONSERVATION PARK
HWY
Colton
B91
Mount Fairy
Bramfield

Joins map 558

0 20 40 60 80 100 km

Joins map 559

A B C D E F G H

MURRAY-SUNSET NP

Joins map 559
Joins map 546
Joins map 548
Joins map 550
Joins map 558

1

Clinton Centre Port Clinton Bowmans Erith Salter Springs Rhynie Riverton Tarnma Eudunda Sutherlands
Winulta Port Wakefield Price Inkerman Avon Pinery Giles Corner Alma Tarlee Allendale North Neales Flat Brownlow Frankton
Dowlingville Hamley Bridge Owen Mallala Wasleys Stonefield Blanchetown Ramco Waikerie Lowbank Overland Corner Renmark Paringa Lindsay Point
DEFENCE RESERVE Wild Horse Plains Long Plains Freeling Greenock Truro STURT BROOKFIELD CP Kingston-On-Murray Monash Lyrup Yamba Roadhouse
Ardrossan Windsor Dublin Redbanks Roseworthy Kapunda Stockwell Moorook Yinkanie New Residence Loxton North Pyap Taldra Morkalla Karween

YORKE Pine Point Two Wells Virginia Nuriootpa Angaston Keyneton Sedan Swan Reach Maggea Wunkar Caliph Veitch Nadda Tunart
Black Point St Kilda Lyndoch Williamstown Eden Valley Punyelroo Black Hill Bakara Galga Mercunda Paruna Meribah
Port Julia PORT GAWLER CP Port Gawler Angle Vale GAWLER Springton Angas Valley Nildottie Wongulla Mantung Alawoona Cobera Malpas

2

PENINSULA Dowcer Bluff Port Vincent Pelican Point Salisbury Elizabeth Mount Pleasant Sanderston Forster Walker Flat Copeville Wanbi Kunlara ZONE
Outer Harbor Kersbrook Birdwood Tungkillo Apamurra Punthari Purnong Goondooloo Mindarie Halidon
GULF ST VINCENT Largs North Port Adelaide Gumeracha Palmer Youngshusband Kalyan Sandalwood BILLIATT WA Peebinga
ADELAIDE HILLS CLELAND WILDLIFE PARK INDIAN PACIFIC TRAIN THE GHAN Lobethal Torrens Mannum Coolcha Perponda Mindiyarra Kringin PEEBINGA CP
ADELAIDE Woodside Mypolonga Bowhill Borrika Karte KARTE CP

3

Adelaide Airport Glenelg Hahndorf HISTORIC TOWN Monarto Lowaldie Kulkami Wirha Gurrai
Warradale Seacliff Bridgewater Nairne Tepko MURRAY BRIDGE Mypolonga Karoonda Yurgo Marama Mulpata Pinnaroo Panitya Duddo
Mount Barker Kanmantoo S.E. 79 FWY Wynarka Parilla HWY Danyo Mulcra
Old Noarlunga Macclesfield Woodchester Swanport Sherlock Buccleuch 164 Geranium Lameroo Murrayville

4

Port Noarlunga Meadows McLaren Vale Belvidere Langhorne Creek Woods Point Jervois Cooke Plains Peake Jabuk Parrakie Wilkawatt MALLEE
Moana Willunga Ashbourne Sandergrove Wellington Tailem Bend Moorlands
MCLAREN VALE WINERIES Aldinga Beach Sellicks Beach Mount Compass Finniss Milang Lake Alexandrina Raukkan Narrung Ashville Malinong Yumali Coomandook
Myponga Beach Carrickalinga Yankalilla Currency Creek Clayton Ki Ki NGARKAT CP BIG DESERT WILDERNESS PARK
Normanville Second Valley Rapid Bay Myponga Port Elliot Goolwa Waltowa Coonalpyn 195

5

Cape Jervis Delamere Waitpinga Victor Harbor Encounter Bay Murray Mouth Meningie CARCUMA CP NGARKAT CONSERVATION PARK
HEYSEN TRAIL DEEP CREEK CP FLEURIEU PENINSULA HORSE-DRAWN TRAM THE PAGES CP Noonameena Mount Boothby Culburra Mount Shaugh 133
Penneshaw Cape Coutts THE COORONG BIRDS COORONG Magrath Flat Mount Boothby Mount Rescue
KANGAROO ISLAND Cape St Albans Cape Willoughby Camp Coorong The Monolith Tintinara Coombe

6

LESUEUR CP Cape Hart Woods Well Kumorna Banealla Telopea Downs Broughton
218 MESSENT Two Wells Keith Brimbago Yarrock Sandsmere
Policemans Point Salt Creek BUNBURY CR MOUNT MONSTER CP Lowan Vale Wirrega Cannawigara Dinyarrak
NATIONAL MARTIN WASHPOOL CP GUM LAGOON CP Kongal Buckingham Bordertown Yearinga Lillimur Miram

7

Chinaman Wells PRINCES Mundulla Wolseley Serviceton Custon Leeor Kaniva Yanipy
PARK PENINSULA Willalooka Wampoony BIG DESERT Lillimur South Miram South
TILLEY SWAMP CP Mount Rough DESERT CAMP CP B57 LITTLE DESERT NATIONAL PARK

8

Long Beach B1 PEACOCK RANGE 116 Western Flat Bangham
TALAPAR Padthaway 84 Wallabrook Frances Neuarpurr Minimay Mortat
MOUNT SCOTT CP Keppoch QUARPENA PLAIN Binnum Booroopki Dopewora Morea
Kingston S.E. Wyomi FAIRVIEW Avenue Kybybolite Ozenkadnook
BUTCHER GAP CP Reedy Creek Hynam Bringalbert Patyah
Cape Jaffa Kings Camp Lucindale Naracoorte Apsley Benayeo Ullswater

9

BERNOUILLI CR Boatswain Point Mount Benson NARACOORTE CAVES Awonga Edenhope
Godfrey Islands GUICHEN BAY CP Conmurra Joanna Langkoop Kadnook
HISTORIC TOWN Robe WOAKWINE CR Struan Wrattonbully Comaum Poolaijelo Powers Creek
Cape Lannes LITTLE DIP CP Bray Junction Greenways Wattle Range Coonawarra Glenroy 102 BERGHOLM SP Chetwynd

10

Nora Creina Lake Eliza Chinaman Wells Clay Wells Penola Dorodong DERGHOLM STATE PARK
Lake St Clair Furner Comaum Dergholm Brimboal
BEACHPORT CP Lake George 155 Beachport B1 Hatherleigh Krongart Lake Mundi Wando Bridge
Cape Martin Rendelsham Nangwarry Wando Vale Dunrobin

11

SOUTHERN OCEAN B101 Southend Cape Buffon Millicent Mount Burr Kalangadoo Tarpeena Casterton
Geltwood Beach Snuggery Glencoe West B160 Sandford
CANUNDA NATIONAL PARK Tantanoola Glencoe Wandilo WILKIN FFR Strathdownie
Lake Bonney S.E. MOUNT GAMBIER Mil Lel A1 Marp

12

Cape Banks Corattum BLUE LAKE Glenburnie Puralka Winnap Lyons
Carpenter Rocks Kongorong Ob Flat Mount Schank Caroline Mumbannar Drik Drik Greenwald
Blackfellow Caves Nene Valley Allendale East Donovans Landing Wanwin Nelson Dartmoor LOWER GLENELG NP
Cape Northumberland Port MacDonnell Ewens Ponds Discovery Bay GREAT SOUTH WEST WALK CANOEING C192

For more detail on the Peninsulas & Kangaroo Island see page 556

For more detail on Adelaide & Surrounds see pages 554 & 555

SOUTH AUSTRALIA VICTORIA

MAPS

WESTERN AUSTRALIA

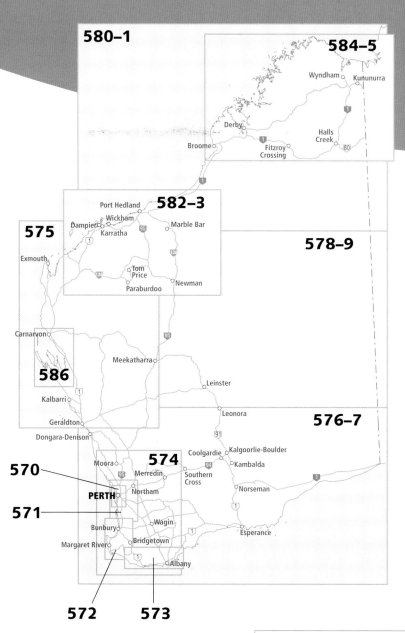

Western Australia

Perth Suburbs	570
Perth & Surrounds	571
South-west Coast	572
South Coast	573
South-western Western Australia	574
Central-western Western Australia	575
Southern Western Australia	576–7
Central Western Australia	578–9
Northern Western Australia	580–1
Pilbara	582–3
Kimberley	584–5
Shark Bay	586

INTER-CITY ROUTES		DISTANCE
Perth–Adelaide via Great Eastern & Eyre highways		2700 km
Perth–Darwin via Great Northern Highway		4032 km

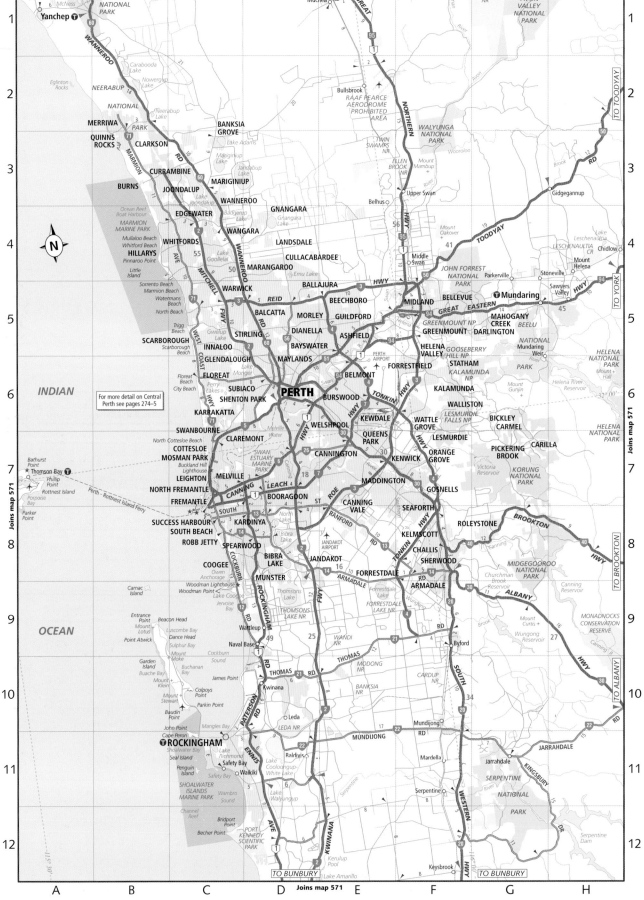

INDIAN

OCEAN

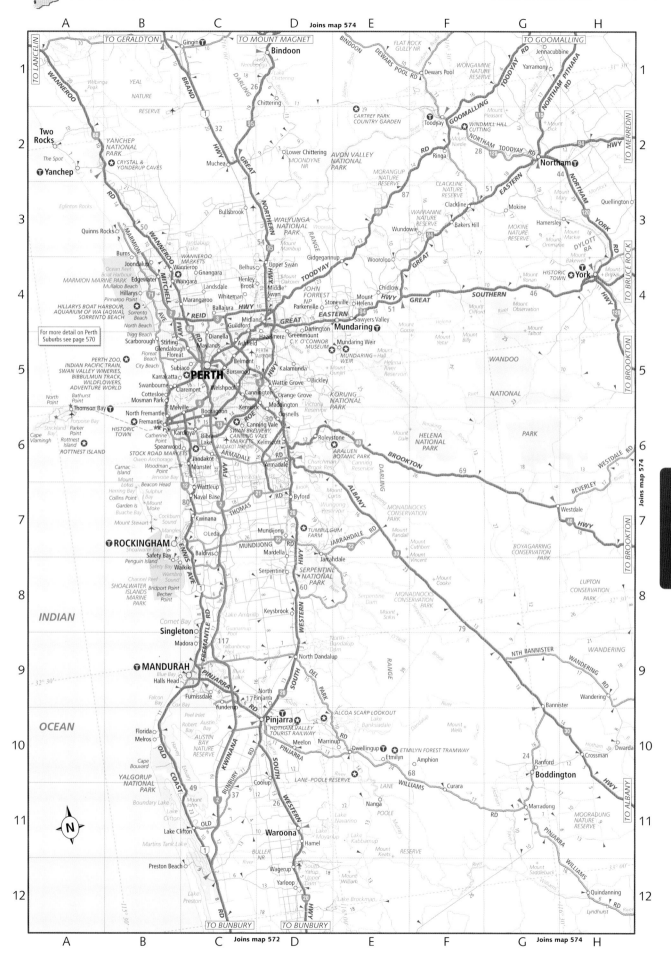

Joins map 574
Joins map 572
Joins map 574

INDIAN

OCEAN

N

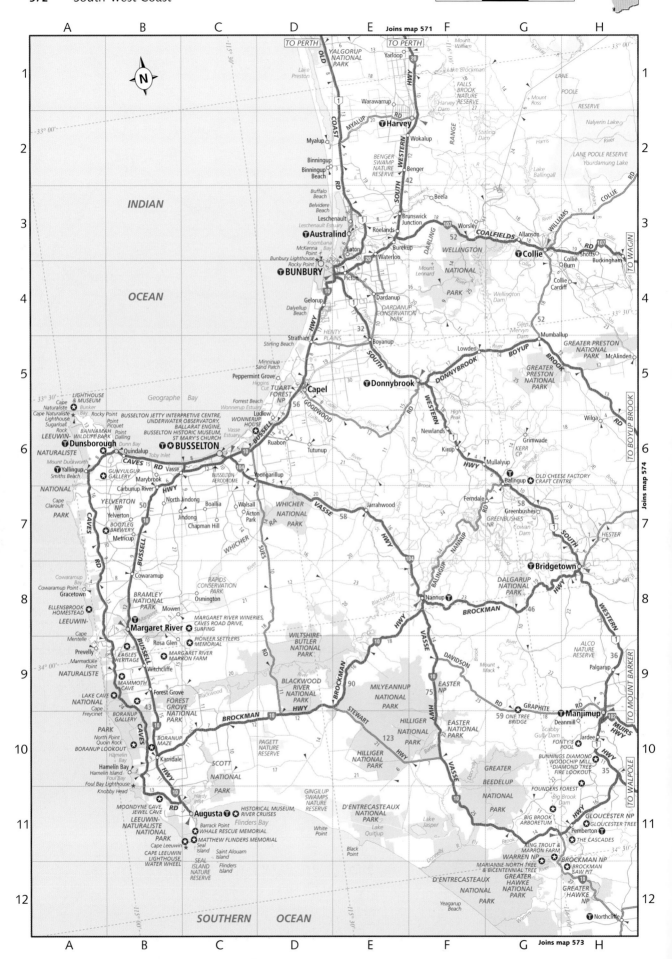

Joins map 574

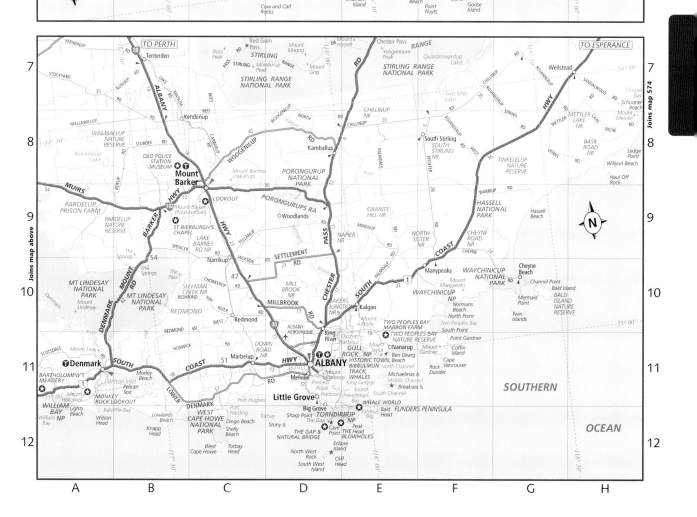

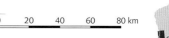

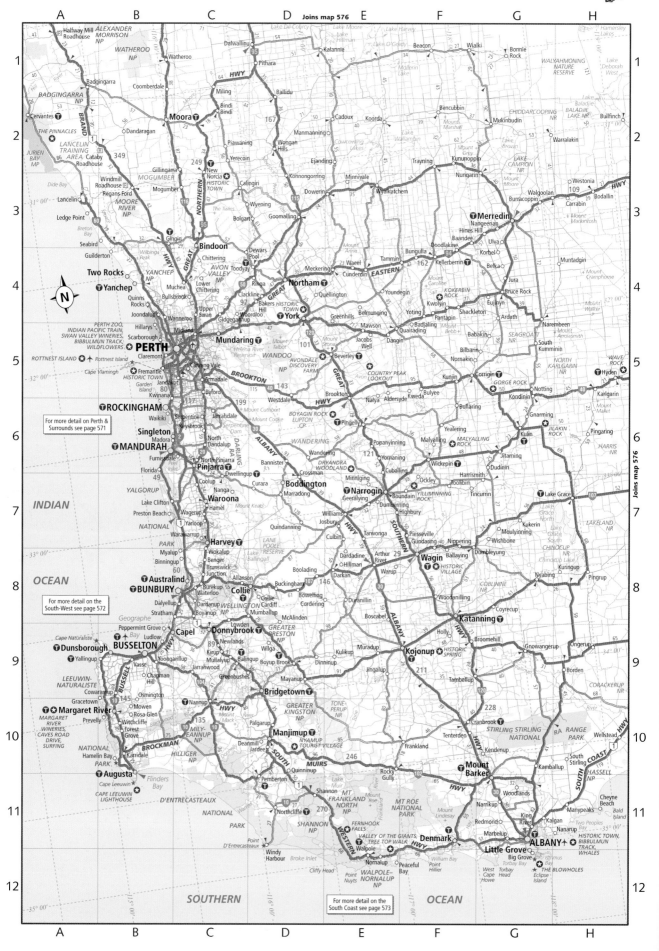

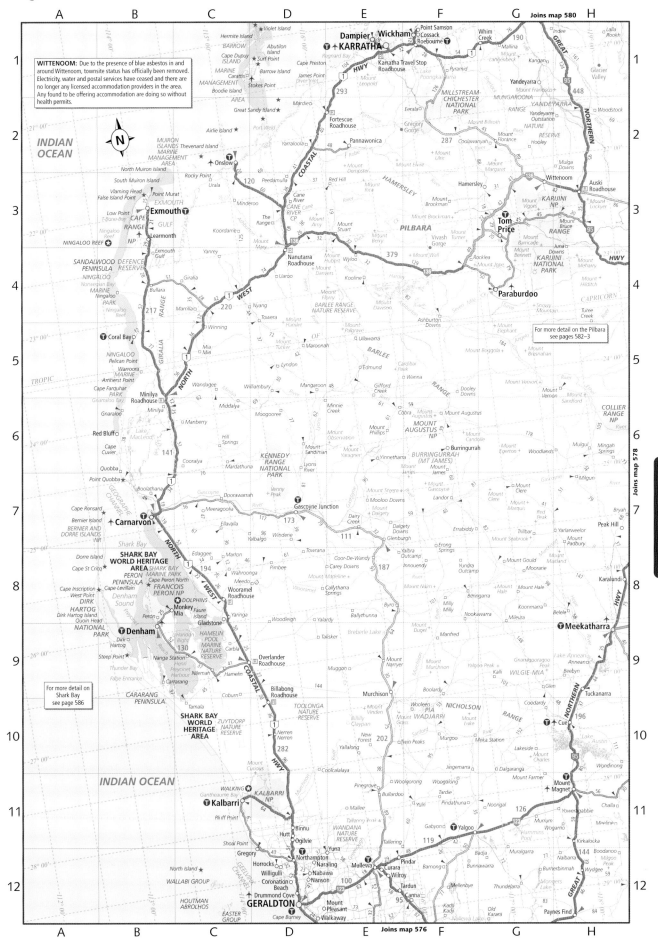

WITTENOOM: Due to the presence of blue asbestos in and around Wittenoom, townsite status has officially been removed. Electricity, water and postal services have ceased and there are no longer any licensed accommodation providers in the area. Any found to be offering accommodation are doing so without health permits.

INDIAN OCEAN

INDIAN OCEAN

For more detail on the Pilbara see pages 582–3

For more detail on Shark Bay see page 586

Joins map 578

Joins map 576

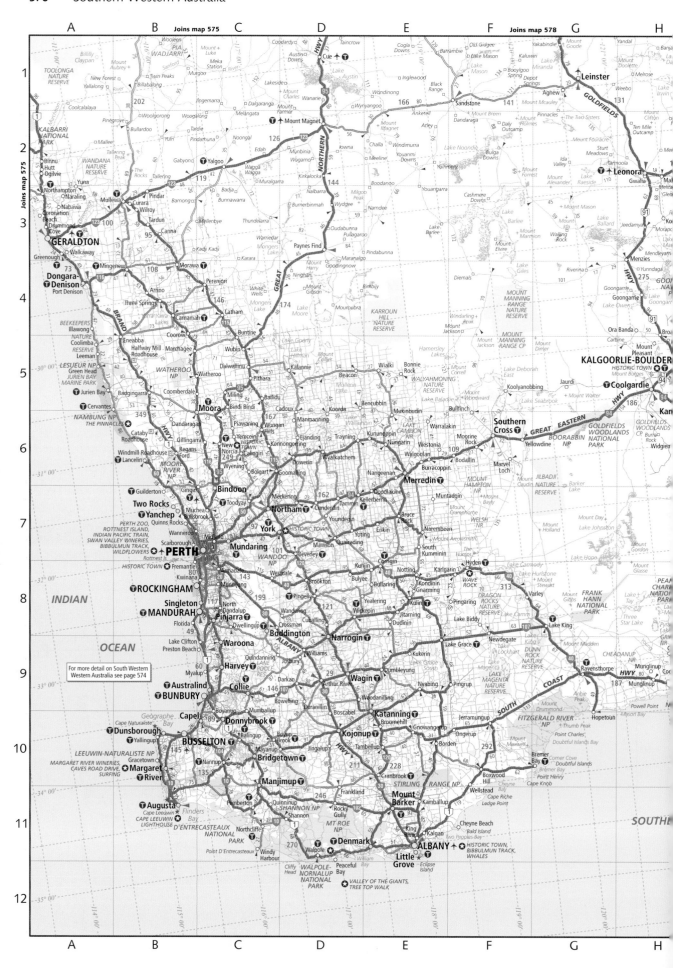

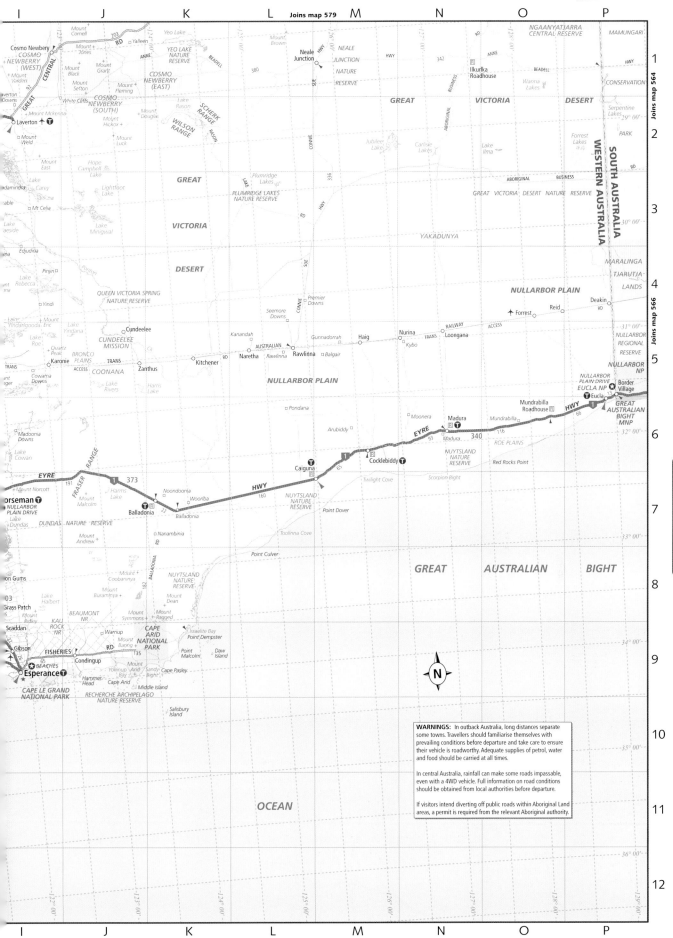

WARNINGS: In outback Australia, long distances separate some towns. Travellers should familiarise themselves with prevailing conditions before departure and take care to ensure their vehicle is roadworthy. Adequate supplies of petrol, water and food should be carried at all times.

In central Australia, rainfall can make some roads impassable, even with a 4WD vehicle. Full information on road conditions should be obtained from local authorities before departure.

If visitors intend diverting off public roads within Aboriginal Land areas, a permit is required from the relevant Aboriginal authority.

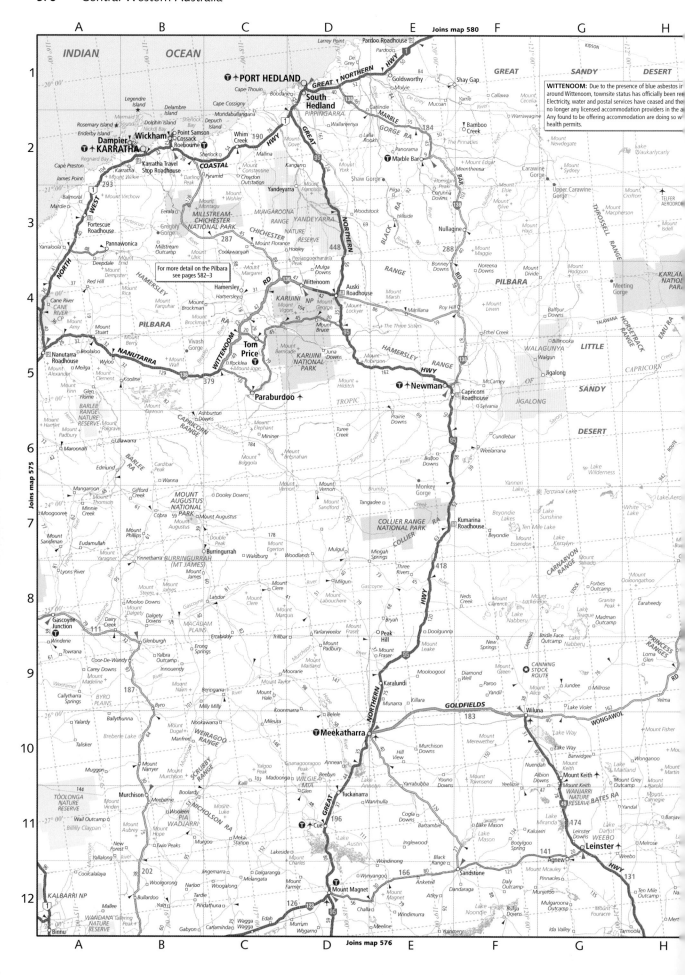

Joins map 580

Joins map 575

Joins map 576

WITTENOOM: Due to the presence of blue asbestos in and around Wittenoom, townsite status has officially been re... Electricity, water and postal services have ceased and the... no longer any licensed accommodation providers in the a... Any found to be offering accommodation are doing so w... health permits.

For more detail on the Pilbara see pages 582–3

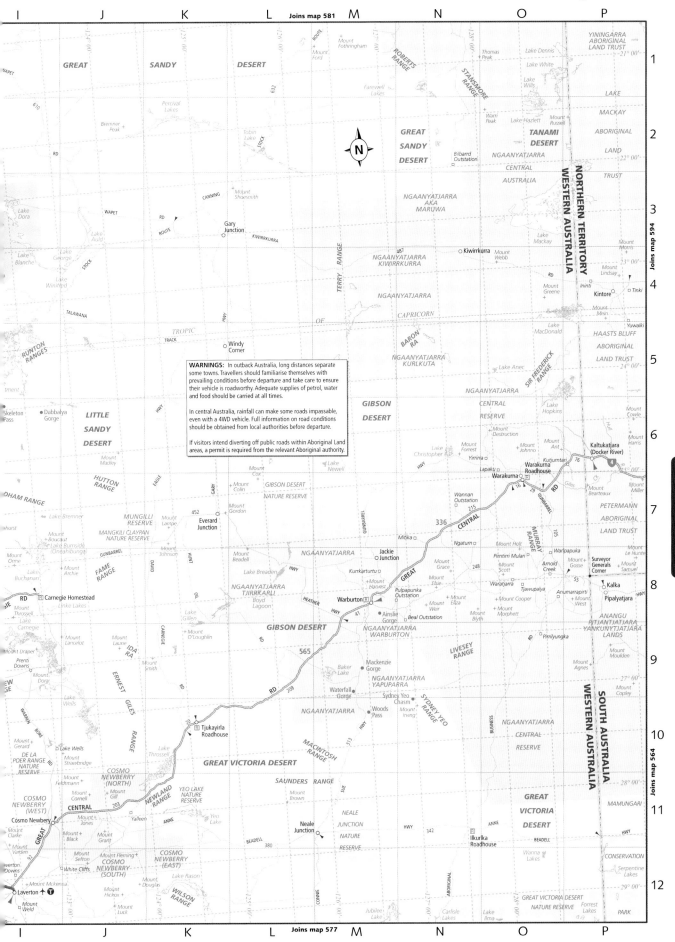

GREAT   SANDY   DESERT

Mount Fothingham

Mount Ford

ROUTE

632

ROBERTS RANGE

STANMORE RANGE

Thomas Peak

Lake Dennis

YININGARRA ABORIGINAL LAND TRUST

21° 00'

1

610

Percival Lakes

Bremner Peak

Farewell Lakes

GREAT

SANDY

DESERT

Warri Peak   *Lake Hazlett*

Lake White

Lake Wills

Mount Russell

TANAMI

DESERT

Bilbarrd Outstation

NGAANYATJARRA

LAKE

MACKAY

ABORIGINAL

LAND

22° 00'

2

RD

WAPET

Lake Dora

CANNING

Mount Shoesmith

RD ROUTE

Tobin Lake

STOCK

Gary Junction

KIWIRRKURRA

TERRY RANGE

CENTRAL

AUSTRALIA

NGAANYATJARRA AKA MARUWA

Lake Mackay

NORTHERN TERRITORY   WESTERN AUSTRALIA

3

Lake Auld

WAPET

487

Kiwirrkurra

Mount Webb

NGAANYATJARRA KIWIRRKURRA

Mount Morris

Joins map 594

4

Lake Blanche

STOCK

Lake George

HWY

OF

CAPRICORN

NGAANYATJARRA

Mount Greene

RD

Mount Lindsay

Inini

Kintore

Tinki

Lake Winifred

TALAWANA

TROPIC

TRACK

Windy Corner

BARON RA

NGAANYATJARRA KURLKUTA

Mount Mein

Yuwalki

HAASTS BLUFF

ABORIGINAL

LAND TRUST

24° 00'

5

RUNTON RANGES

Skeleton Pass

ment

Lake Anec

SIR FREDERICK RANGE

NGAANYATJARRA

GIBSON

DESERT

CENTRAL

RESERVE

Lake Hopkins

Mount Cowle

Dabbalya

LITTLE

SANDY

DESERT

Lindie Gorge

HWY

Mount Madley

Mount Destruction

Mount Forrest

Lake Christopher

Mount Ant

Mount Harris

Kaltukatjara (Docker River)

25° 00'

6

DHAM RANGE

HUTTON RANGE

EAGLE

Lake Bremner

Mount Cox

Lake Newell

Mount Colin

GIBSON DESERT NATURE RESERVE

Mount Johnno

Yirrima

Lapaku

Kutjuntari

Warakurna Roadhouse

Warakurna

76

PETERMANN

ABORIGINAL

LAND TRUST

7

MUNGILLI RESERVE

Mount Lampe

452

Mount Gordon

GARY

Everard Junction

HUNT

GUNBARREL

Wannan Outstation

215

16

29

GUNBARREL RD

Giles

Mount Bearteaux

Mount Miller

Mount Buchanan

Mount Orme

Mount Archie

MANGKILI CLAYPAN NATURE RESERVE

Lake Burnside (Oneahibunga)

GUNBARREL

Mount Johnson

DAVID

Mount Beadell

Lake Breaden

HWY

Jackie Junction

Kurrkarturtu

Mitika

336   **CENTRAL**

Ngaturn

Mount Holt

Pintirri Mulari

248

Warlpapuka

MURRAY RANGE

Arnold Creek

Mount Gosse

105

Mount Le Hunte

Mount Samuel

Surveyor Generals Corner

55

8

FAME RANGE

Carnegie Homestead

Linke Lakes

NGAANYATJARRA TJIRRKARLI

Boyd Lagoon

HEATHER

Warburton

41

Ainslie Gorge

Beal Outstation

GREAT

Warburton

Pulpapunka Outstation

Mount Harvest

Mount Grace

Mount Elsie

Mount Weir

Mount Eliza

Mount Scott

Waratjarra

Tjawupalya

Anumarrapirti

Mount West

Mount Cooper

Kalka

Pipalyatjara

ANANGU PITJANTJATJARA YANKUNYTJATJARA LANDS

Mount Throssell

Lake Carnegie

Mount Lancelot

Mount Laurie

IDA RA

Mount Smith

Mount O'Loughlin

GIBSON DESERT

565

NGAANYATJARRA WARBURTON

Mount Blyth

Mount Morphett

LIVESEY RANGE

Pirrilyungka

Mount Agnes

Mount Moulden

9

Mount Draper

Prenti Downs

Mount Dora

GE

Lake Wells

ERNEST GILES RANGE

CARNEGIE

RD

209

RD

Baker Lake

Mackenzie Gorge

Waterfall Gorge

NGAANYATJARRA YAPUPARRA

Sydney Yeo Chasm

Woods Pass

Mount Irving

SYDNEY YEO RANGE

BUSINESS

NGAANYATJARRA

CENTRAL

RESERVE

Mount Copley

27° 00'

10

New

GE

Mount Gerard

WARREN

BORE

Lake Wells

Tjukayirla Roadhouse

29

Lake Throssell

HWY

NGAANYATJARRA

MACINTOSH RANGE

313

Joins map 564

DE LA POER RANGE NATURE RESERVE

Mount Strawbridge

COSMO NEWBERRY (NORTH)

GREAT VICTORIA DESERT

SAUNDERS RANGE

Mount Brown

SUE

GREAT

VICTORIA

DESERT

MAMUNGARI

28° 00'

11

COSMO NEWBERRY (WEST)

Cosmo Newberry

Mount Feldtmann

Mount Cornell

Mount Gill

203

CENTRAL

Mount Jones

Yalleen

NEWLAND RANGE

YEO LAKE NATURE RESERVE

ANNE

Yeo Lake

NEALE JUNCTION NATURE RESERVE

Neale Junction

HWY

342

Ilkurlka Roadhouse

ANNE

BEADELL

HWY

Mount Clarke

Mount Black

Mount Grant

BEADELL

380

GREAT

Mount Varden

raverton Downs

White Cliffs

Mount Sefton

Mount Fleming

COSMO NEWBERRY (SOUTH)

COSMO NEWBERRY (EAST)

Lake Rason

CONNIE

CONSERVATION

Serpentine Lakes

12

Laverton

Mount McKenna

Mount Weld

Mount Hickox

Mount Luck

WILSON RANGE

Mount Douglas

Jubilee Lake

Carlisle Lake

Lake Ilma

GREAT VICTORIA DESERT NATURE RESERVE

Forrest Lakes

PARK

29° 00'

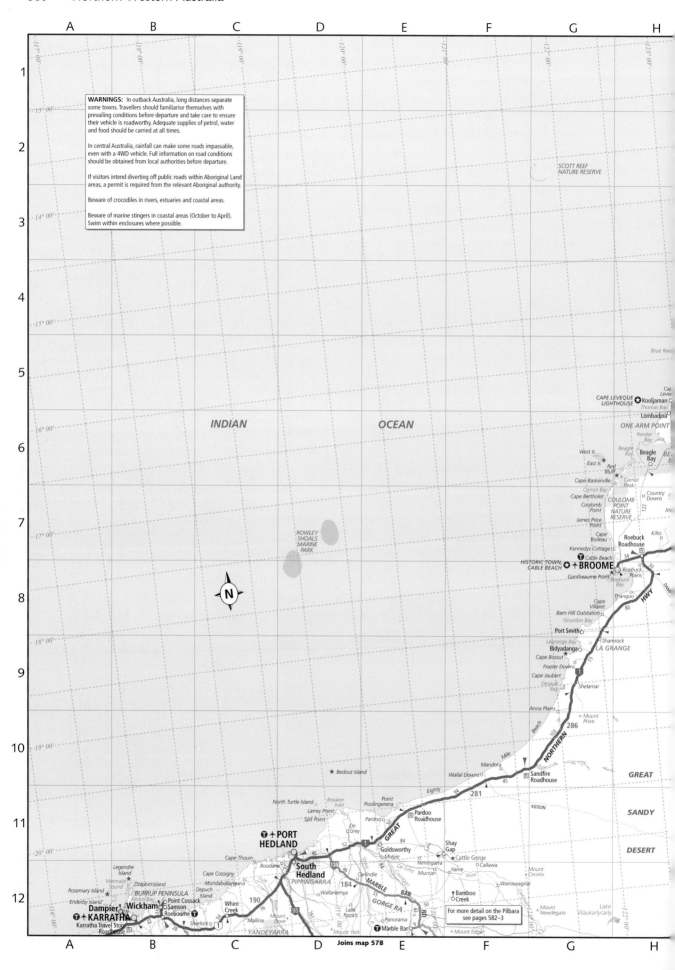

SCOTT REEF
NATURE RESERVE

INDIAN   OCEAN

Brue Reef

CAPE LEVEQUE
LIGHTHOUSE Kooljaman
Thomas Bay
Lombadina

ONE ARM POINT

West Is
East Is Red
Bluff
Cape Baskerville
Carnot
Peak
Carnot Bay
Cape Bertholet
Coulomb
Point
James Price
Point
Cape
Boileau
Kennedys Cottage
ROWLEY
SHOALS
MARINE
PARK

Beagle
Bay

Beagle
Bay

Country
Downs

COULOMB
POINT
NATURE
RESERVE

Kilto

Roebuck
Roadhouse

HISTORIC TOWN,
CABLE BEACH Cable Beach **BROOME**
Gantheaume Point Roebuck
Plains
Roebuck
Bay

Cape
Villaret
Barn Hill Outstation
Gourdon Bay
Port Smith
Lagrange Bay Shamrock
Bidyadanga LA GRANGE
Cape Bossut
Frazier Downs
Cape Jaubert
Desault
Bay Shelamar

Anna Plains Mount
Phire

N

Thangoo

HWY

Jow

Cecelia

Mandora Mile
Wallal Downs Sandfire
Roadhouse

GREAT

Bedout Island

North Turtle Island
Breaker
Inlet
Larrey Point
Spit Point

Eighty

94

281

KIDSON

SANDY

DESERT

Point
Poolingerena
Pardoo
De Grey

Pardoo
Roadhouse

Goldsworthy
Mulyie 84

Shay
Gap Cattle Gorge

Callawa

Yarrie

Mount
Cecelia

Legendre
Island
Rosemary Island
Enderby Island

Dolphin Island
Nickol Bay
Depuch
Island

Cape Thouin Boodarie

Cape Cossigny
Muridabullangana

**PORT
HEDLAND**

South
Hedland
PIPPINGARRA

52

40

138

184

Carlindie

De Grey River

Nimingarra
Muccan

Warrawagine

Bamboo
Creek

Mount
Newdegate

Lake
Waukarlycarly

Cape Cossigny

Whim
Creek

Samson
Roebourne

190

Mount
Dove

Lalla
Rookh

MARBLE

GORGE RA

BAR

50

RD

For more detail on the Pilbara
see pages 582–3

Dampier **Wickham**
KARRATHA Point Cossack
Karratha Travel Stop
Roadhouse

Mermaid
Sound

32

Sherlock

Mallina

95

181

Mount York

YANDEYARRA

Panorama

Marble Bar

Mount Edgar

0 50 100 150 200 km

I J K L M N O P

TIMOR SEA

INDIAN OCEAN

Cape Ford
Cape Scott
Dooley Point
Mount Greenwood
Cape Dombey
Hyland Bay
Cape Londonderry
Lesueur Island
Cape Rulhieres
Cape Whiskey
Cape Bernier
JOSEPH BONAPARTE GULF
Dorcherty Island
Peppimenarti
Port Keats (Wadeye)
DALY RIVER/PORT KEATS ABORIGINAL LAND TRUST
Long Reef
East-Holothuria Reef
Cape Bougainville
TROUGHTON PASSAGE
Napier Broome Bay
Cape Talbot
King
George
Cassini Island
Gibson Point
OYSTER ROCK PASSAGE
CAPE BOUGAINVILLE
Barton Plains
BARTON PLAIN
Carson River
Cape St Lambert
Mount Nicholls
Turtle Point
Quoin Island
Keeling Inlet
New Moon Inlet
Davidson Point
ADMIRALTY GULF
KALUMBURU
Kalumburu
Mount Leemrig
CAMBRIDGE GULF
BRADSHAW FIELD TRAINING AREA
Montague Sound
Bigge Island
Robroy Reefs
ADMIRALTY GULF
LAWLEY RIVER NP
Mount Reid
Wallis Peak
OOMBULGURRI
Knob Peak
Legune
Cape Pond
Kandiwal
Doongan
KIMBERLEY
DRYSDALE RIVER NATIONAL PARK
Oombulgurri
FORREST RIVER
ORD RIVER NATURE RESERVE
Marralum
Kneebone
Bullo River
York Sound
Coronation Island
MITCHELL RIVER NP
LATERITE CP
Mitchell River
Doongan
303
Mount Brookes
KEEP RIVER NP EXTENSION (PROPOSED)
Brunswick Bay
Hanover Bay
Mount York
Mount Bradshaw
Carlton Hill
Wyndham
PARRY LAGOONS NR
55
Kununurra
MIRIMA NP
102
Policemans Hole
Bulla
Champagny Islands
Jungulu Island
Mount Eyre
PRINCE REGENT NATURE RESERVE
KALUMBURU RD
Mount Hann
Drysdale River
RIVER
284
El Questro
Dunham Pilot Dam
Argyle Historic Homestead
ORD RIVER DAM
Newry
200
GREGORY NATIONAL PARK
Brecknock Harbour
Deception Bay
Prior Point
KUNMUNYA
George Water
Mount King
Pantijan
Mount Methuen
MT AGNES
BLYTHE CREEK
Mount Hickey
GIBB RIVER RD
Home Valley
Durack River
VICTORIA
HWY
151
DOON DOON
Mount Chambers
Rosewood
Mount Duncan
Amanbidji
NAGURUNGURU ABORIGINAL LAND TRUST
Macleay Island
Montgomery Reef
Doubtful Bay
Kingfisher Islands
Koolan
Collier Bay
MUNJA
MAURICE CREEK
Mount Elizabeth
GIBB
Gibb River (Ngallagunda)
Pentecost Downs (Karunjie)
Mount Sullivan
DURACK RANGE
Mount Lookout
Argyle Downs
Waterloo
MALNGIN 2 ABORIGINAL LAND TRUST
Spring Creek
Mount Wickham
Limbunya
Mount Toby
Mavis Reef
Walcott Inlet
KIMBERLEY
Mount Page
Mount Glenroyd
Kupingarri
Mt Barnett Roadhouse
Marion
Yulumbu (Tableland)
Mount John
Warmun-Turkey Creek Roadhouse
Warmun
Texas Downs
Mistake Creek
Nelson Springs
Stirling
KING LEOPOLD
YAMPI TRAINING AREA
Mount Disaster
Beverley Springs
Mount Hart
Silent Grove
Mount House
Mount Caroline
Hann
Bedford Downs
VIOLET VALLEY
HWY
Mount Buchanan
MALNGIN ABORIGINAL LAND TRUST
Mount Maiyo (Mulluya)
Kimbolton
Oobagooma
KING
LEOPOLD RANGES
CONSERVATION PARK
Imintji Store
375
Glenroy
Durack
161
BUNGLE BUNGLES
PURNULULU NATIONAL PARK
Kirkimbie
BUNTINE HWY
96
Stokes Bay
BUNGARUN
Derby
Meda
Kimberly Downs
Fairfield
Mount Percy
Blina
WINDJANA GORGE NP
TUNNEL CREEK NP
DEVONIAN REEF CP
Mount Otd
Mornington
Lansdowne
Mount Warton
KIMBERLEY
Alice Downs
Mount Coghlan
Crocodile Gorge
PURNULULU NATIONAL PARK WORLD HERITAGE AREA
Nicholson
Inverway (Mamadi)
Mount Wittenoom
YINGUALYALYA ABORIGINAL LAND TRUST
CENTRAL DESERT ABORIGINAL LAND TRUST
DERBY HWY
CURTIN AIR BASE
GIBB
DERBY
219
Ellendale
BROOKING GORGE CP
GEIKIE GORGE NP
Fossil Downs
O'Donnell
Little Gold
Sophie Downs
Marella Gorge
RD
59
Bunda
Birrindudu
Nongra Lake
Willare Bridge Roadhouse
Camballin
GREAT
KING
Fitzroy Crossing
Leopold Downs
Conical Peak
Mount Frederick
Halls Creek
Rockhole
Flora Valley
Old Flora Valley
DUNCAN
DENISON PLAINS
PURTA ABORIGINAL LAND TRUST
Looma
Myroodah
Jubilee Downs
Quanbun
Galeru Gorge
Christmas Creek
Mount Elma
Lamboo
Old Lamboo
TANAMI
Sturt
Lewis Creek
Dampier Downs
Mowla Bluff
Ardjorie
Mount Anderson
Nerrima Outcamp
Noonkanbah
Mount Gytha
NORTHERN
288
Mount Dockrell
Ruby Plains
WOLFE CREEK CRATER NATIONAL PARK
Carranya
GARDNER RANGE
Mount Frederick
Picininny Bore Outstation
Mount Jarlmai
Mount Fenton
Tilloch Peak
Cherrabun
Beefwood Park
Bulka
Bohemia Downs
Christmas
WORRAL RANGE
Mount Tuckfield
Mount Piper
Bulka Swamp
Mount Bannerman
Sturt Creek
Billiluna
CANNING STOCK ROUTE
TANAMI
MT FREDERICK (NO.2) ABORIGINAL LAND TRUST
Lake Betty
Lake Jones
Lake Lanagan
BILLILUNA
Mount Mueller
404
RD
Mount Frederick
Lake McLernon
GODFREYS TANK OR BREADEN POOL
MINNIE RANGE
LAKE GREGORY
Balgo Hills
Lake Gregory
DESERT
KEARNEY
MANGKURURRPA ABORIGINAL LAND TRUST
Tanami Downs
GON TREE SOAK TURE RESERVE
Mount Cornish
Mount Rosamund
Mount Elliott
KUNAPUNGU PLAIN
Mount Hughes
Lake Jeavons
Mount Tracey
GREAT SANDY DESERT
Mount Elgin
Mount Fothingham
Mount Ford
PANGKULANGU PLAIN
ROBERTS RANGE
Thomas Peak
Lake White
Lake Dennis
YININGARRA ABORIGINAL LAND TRUST
632
Farewell Lakes
Lake Wills
LAKE MACKAY ABORIGINAL LAND TRUST
Percival Lakes
CANNING
NGAANYATJARRA CENTRAL AUSTRALIA
Warri Peak
Mount Russell
Lake Hazlett
WILBRUNGA RANGE
Bremner Peak
610
Tobin Lake

WESTERN AUSTRALIA
NORTHERN TERRITORY

For more detail on the Kimberley see pages 584–5

I J K L M N O P

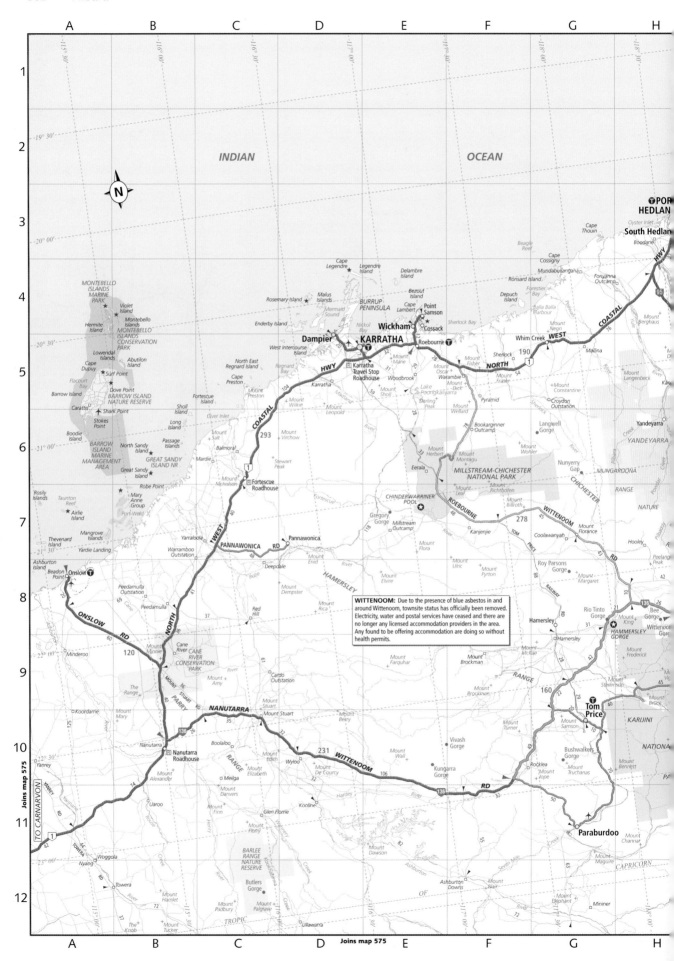

INDIAN   OCEAN

N

MONTEBELLO
ISLANDS
MARINE
PARK

Violet
Island

Montebello
Islands
MONTEBELLO
ISLANDS
CONSERVATION
PARK

Hermite
Island

Lowendal
Islands

Abutilon
Island

Cape
Dupuy

Surf Point

Dove Point
BARROW ISLAND
NATURE RESERVE

Barrow Island

Carattia

Shark Point

Stokes
Point

Boodie
Island

BARROW
ISLAND
MARINE
MANAGEMENT
AREA

North Sandy
Island

Great Sandy
Island

GREAT SANDY
ISLAND NR

Rosily
Islands

Taunton
Reef

Airlie
Island

Mary
Anne
Group

Robe Point

Port Weld

Thevenard
Island

Mangrove
Islands

Yardie Landing

Cape
Legendre

Legendre
Island

Delambre
Island

Bezout
Island

BURRUP
PENINSULA

Rosemary Island

Malus
Islands

Mermaid
Sound

Enderby Island

Cape
Lambert

Point
Samson

Wickham

Cossack

Nickol
Bay

Dampier

KARRATHA

Roebourne

West Intercourse
Island

West
Regnard
Bay

North East
Regnard Island

Cape
Preston

Karratha Travel Stop
Roadhouse

Karratha

Mount
Marie

Woodbrook

Mount
Sholl

Lake
Poongkaliyarra

Mount
Wellard

Bookarginna
Outcamp

Darling
Peak

Mount
Bick

Warambie

Mount
Fisher

Sherlock

190

Whim Creek

Sherlock

Mount
Fraser

Pyramid

Langwell
Gorge

WEST   NORTH

Mallina

Mount
Langenbeck

Mount
Constantine

Croydon
Outstation

Yandeyarra

YANDEYARRA

Nunyerry
Gap

MUNGAROONA

RANGE   NATURE

Cape
Thouin

Oyster Inlet

POR
HEDLAN

South Hedlan

Boodarie

Beagle
Reef

Cape
Cossigny

Ronsard Island

Forestier
Bay

Depuch
Island

Balla Balla
Harbour

Sherlock Bay

Mount
Negri

Forsyama
Outcamp

Mount
Berghaus

COASTAL

HWY

95

COASTAL   HWY

Fortescue
Island

Sholl
Island

Oliver Inlet

Long
Island

Passage
Islands

104

Karratha

Mount
Preston

Mount
Wilkie

Mount
Leopold

Regnard
River

Mount
Salt

Mount
Virchow

Mardie

Balmoral

Stewart
Peak

Mount
Nicholson

293

Fortescue
Roadhouse

Fortescue

Gregory
Gorge

Millstream
Outcamp

CHINDERWARRINER
POOL

Eerala

Mount
Herbert

Mount
Leal

Mount
Montagu

MILLSTREAM-CHICHESTER
NATIONAL PARK

Mount
Richthofen

ROEBOURNE

Kanjenjie

278

Coolawanyah

TOM   PRICE

CHICHESTER

Mount
Billroth

Mount
Florance

Hooley

Peelang
Peak

Mount
Wohler

WITTENOOM   RD

40

WEST

Yarraloola

PANNAWONICA   RD

Pannawonica

Warramboo
Outstation

48

Deepdale

Mount
Enid

Fortescue

River

Mount
Flora

Mount
Ulric

Mount
Pyrton

Roy Parsons
Gorge

Mount
Margaret

RAILWAY

Mount
King

Rio Tinto
Gorge

21   10   136   26

Bee
Gorge

Wittenoom
Gorge

Ashburton
Island

Beadon
Point

Onslow

Peedamulla
Outstation

Peedamulla

Cane

41

Robe

Mount
Dempster

Red
Hill

Mount
Rica

Mount
Elvire

Mount
Farquhar

Mount
Brockman

Hamersley

HAMMERSLEY
GORGE

Mount
Frederick

ONSLOW   RD

20

Minderoo

NORTH

MOUNT   STUART   RD

Mount
Minnie

Cane
River

CANE
RIVER
CONSERVATION
PARK

60

120

37

36

River

Mount
Amy

Cardo
Outstation

61

The
Range

Koordarrie

Mount
Mary

PARRY

RANGE

40

36

NANUTARRA

Nanutarra

136   26

Boolaloo

35

Mount
Stuart

Mount
Stuart

Mount
Berry

32

Mount
Wall

Vivash
Gorge

Mount
Turner

RANGE

Mount
Brockman

Mount
McRae

Hamersley

Mount
Samson

Mount
Stevenson

160

22

29

Tom
Price

KARIJINI

NATIONA

PA

Nanutarra
Roadhouse

Yanrey

74

Mount
Alexander

Uaroo

Mount
Edith

Wyloo

Meilga

Mount
Elizabeth

Mount
Danvers

Kooline

82

231

WITTENOOM

Mount
De Courcy

Mount
Finn

Hardey

106

Kungarra
Gorge

136

RD

32

Rocklea

Mount
Jope

Mount
Truchanas

50

Bushwalkers
Gorge

70

Mount
Bennett

Paraburdoo

Mount
Channar

TO CARNARVON

VANREY   RD

1

42

44

TOWERA

RD

Woggola

Nyang

Towera

River

Glen Florrie

Mount
Florry

BARLEE
RANGE
NATURE
RESERVE

Butlers
Gorge

Mount
Padbury

Mount
Palgrave

Ullawarra

Mount
Hamlet

72

The
Knob

Mount
Tucker

TROPIC

Mount
Dawson

Ashburton

Ashburton
Downs

Mount
Blair

55

OF

River

CAPRICORN

Mount
Maguire

Mount
Elephant

Mininer

Seven Mile

63

WITTENOOM: Due to the presence of blue asbestos in and around Wittenoom, townsite status has officially been removed. Electricity, water and postal services have ceased and there are no longer any licensed accommodation providers in the area. Any found to be offering accommodation are doing so without health permits.

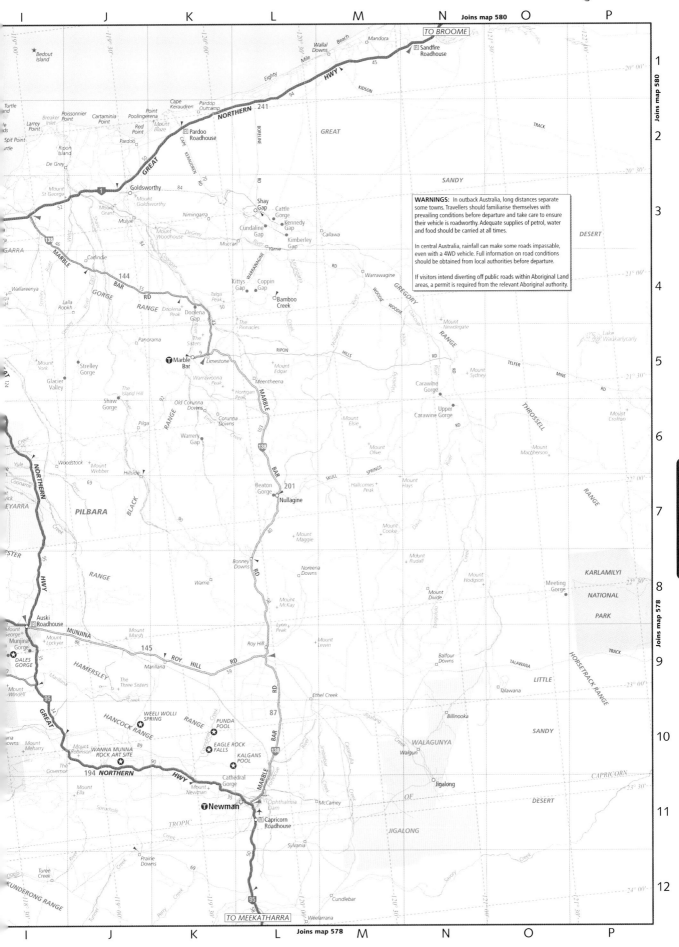

Joins map 580

TO BROOME

Joins map 580

Joins map 578

Joins map 578

WARNINGS: In outback Australia, long distances separate some towns. Travellers should familiarise themselves with prevailing conditions before departure and take care to ensure their vehicle is roadworthy. Adequate supplies of petrol, water and food should be carried at all times.

In central Australia, rainfall can make some roads impassable, even with a 4WD vehicle. Full information on road conditions should be obtained from local authorities before departure.

If visitors intend diverting off public roads within Aboriginal Land areas, a permit is required from the relevant Aboriginal authority.

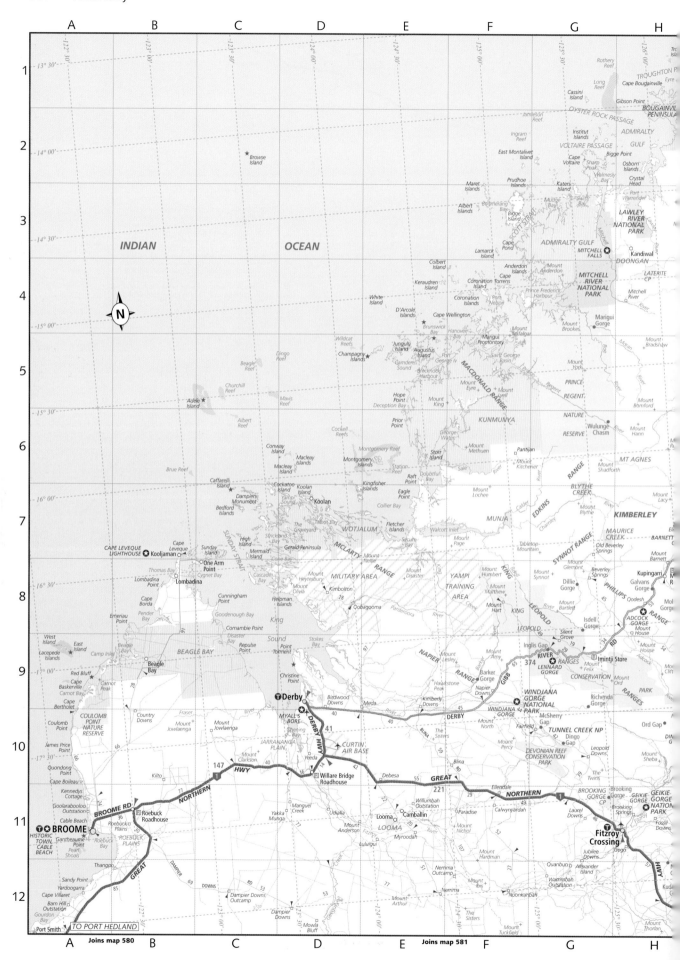

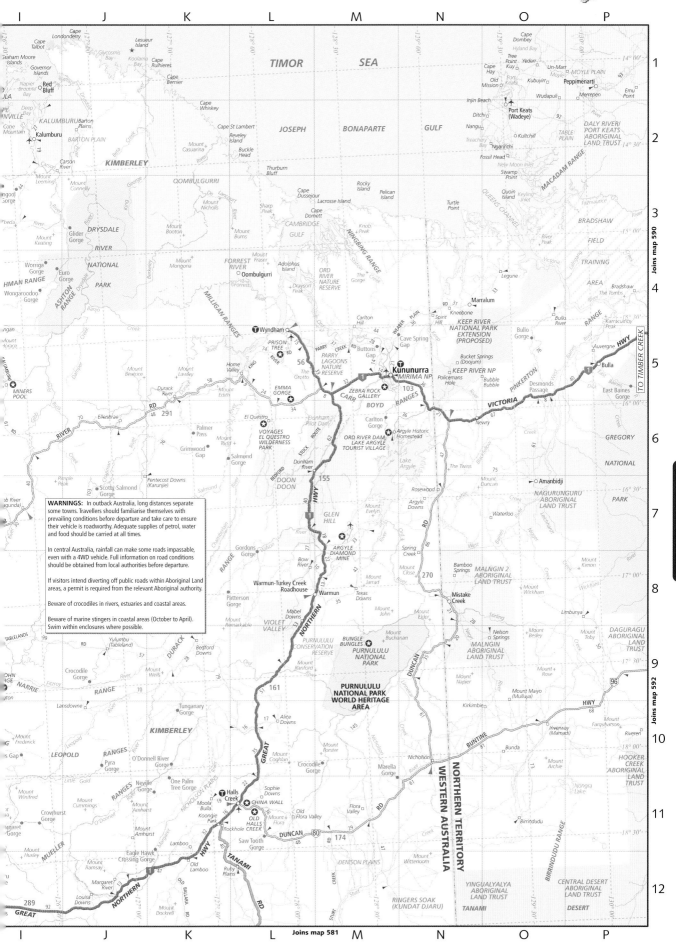

WARNINGS: In outback Australia, long distances separate some towns. Travellers should familiarise themselves with prevailing conditions before departure and take care to ensure their vehicle is roadworthy. Adequate supplies of petrol, water and food should be carried at all times.

In central Australia, rainfall can make some roads impassable, even with a 4WD vehicle. Full information on road conditions should be obtained from local authorities before departure.

If visitors intend diverting off public roads within Aboriginal Land areas, a permit is required from the relevant Aboriginal authority.

Beware of crocodiles in rivers, estuaries and coastal areas.

Beware of marine stingers in coastal areas (October to April). Swim within enclosures where possible.

Joins map 590

Joins map 592

Joins map 581

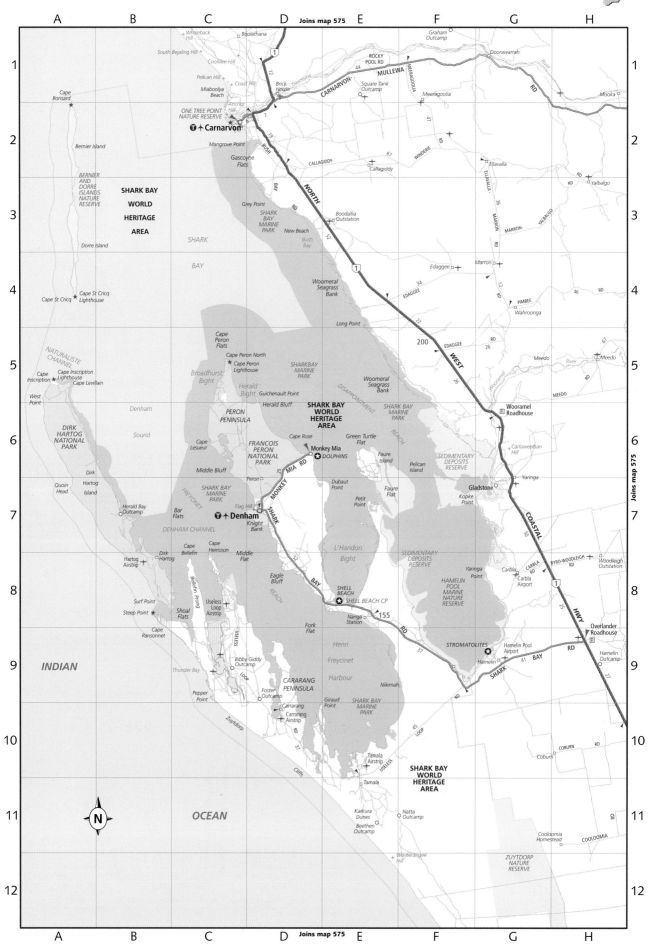

Joins map 575

0　10　20　30　40 km

Joins map 575

Joins map 575

MAPS

NORTHERN TERRITORY

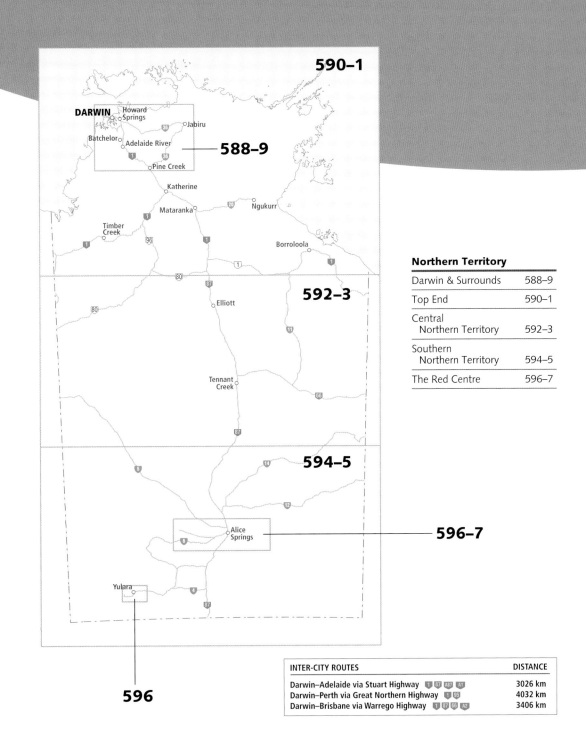

590–1

DARWIN
Howard
Springs
○Jabiru
Batchelor
○Adelaide River
588–9
○Pine Creek

Katherine
Mataranka
Ngukurr

Timber
Creek
Borroloola

Elliott

592–3

Tennant
Creek

594–5

Alice
Springs
596–7

Yulara

596

Northern Territory

Darwin & Surrounds	588–9
Top End	590–1
Central Northern Territory	592–3
Southern Northern Territory	594–5
The Red Centre	596–7

INTER-CITY ROUTES	DISTANCE
Darwin–Adelaide via Stuart Highway	3026 km
Darwin–Perth via Great Northern Highway	4032 km
Darwin–Brisbane via Warrego Highway	3406 km

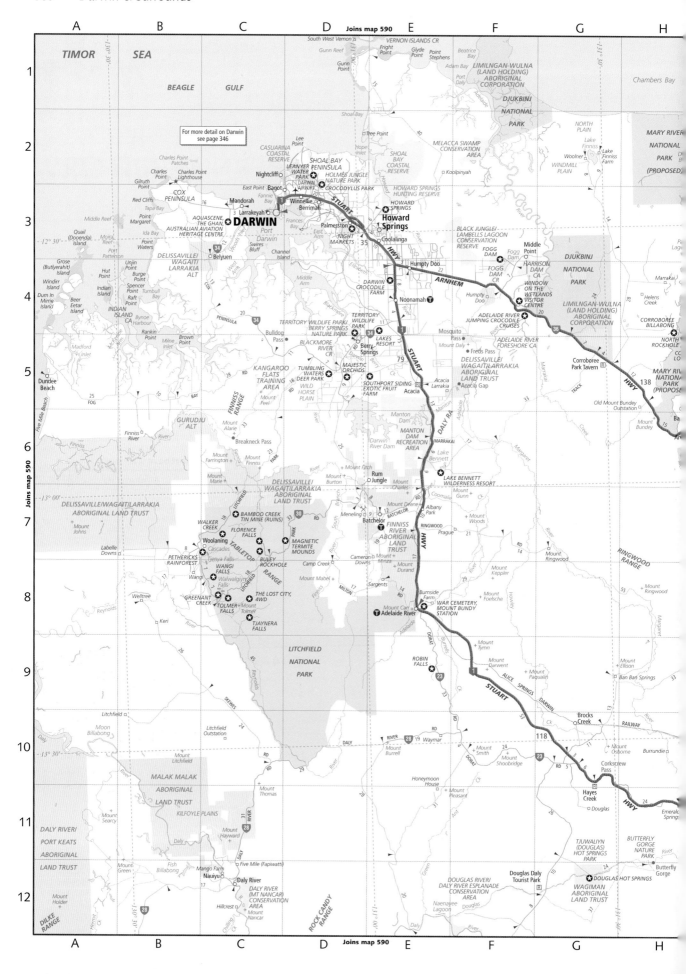

Joins map 590

For more detail on Darwin
see page 346

DARWIN

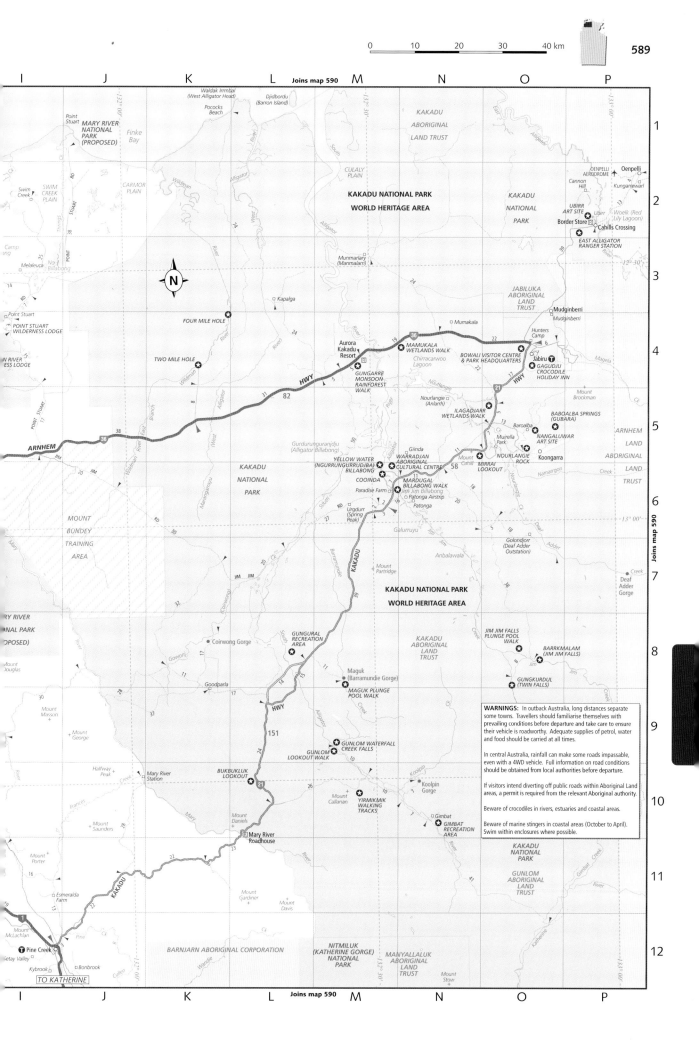

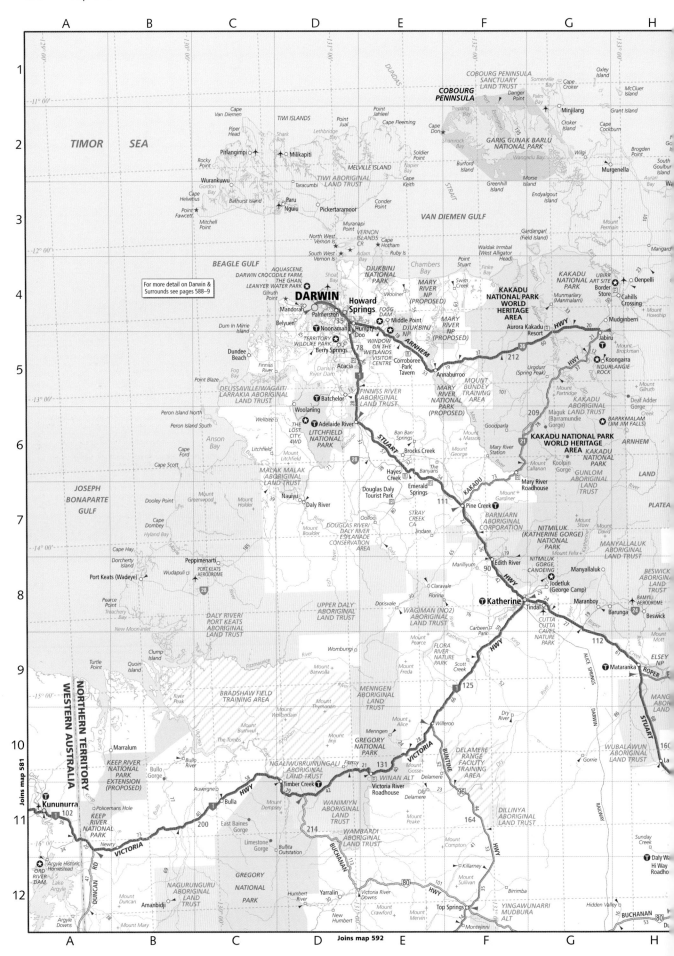

For more detail on Darwin &
Surrounds see pages 588–9

Joins map 581

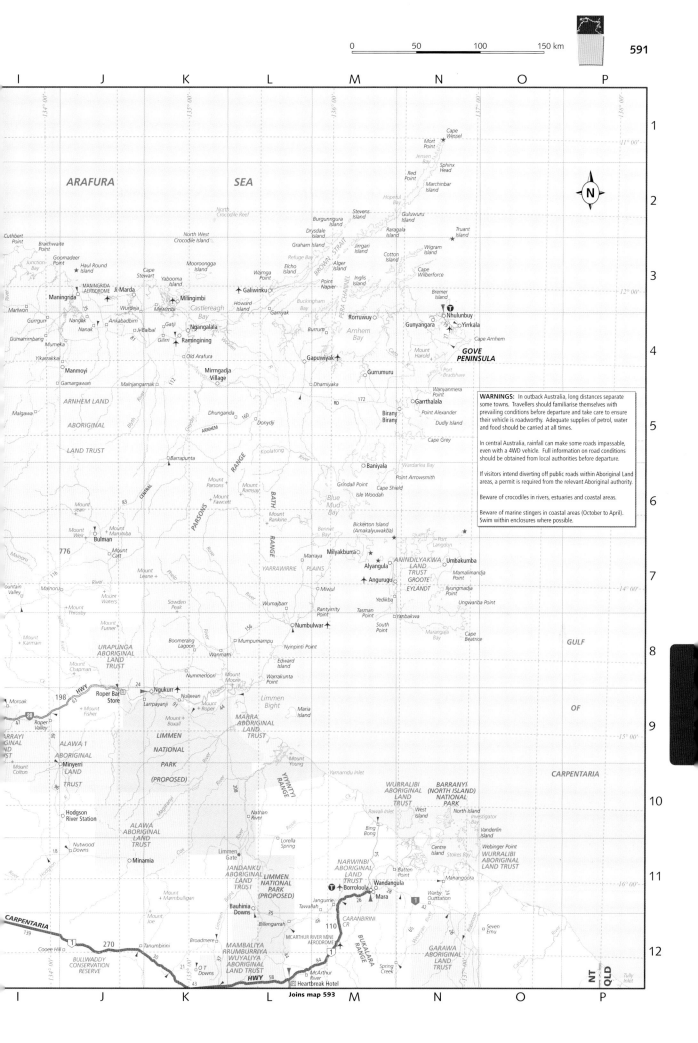

Joins map 590

A B C D E F G H

1 2 3 4 5 6 7 8 9 10 11 12

Joins map 581

WEABER PLAIN

Legune
Marralum
Kneebone
Bullo Gorge
Bullo River
Auvergne
The Tombs
Mount Bunwul
Mount Wollondain
Wymbon
BRADSHAW FIELD TRAINING AREA
Mount linji
Fitzroy
Mount Thimahan
Mount Alice
Willeroo
Dry River
GREGORY NATIONAL PARK
Menngen
Mount Gosse
Delamere
DELAMERE RANGE FACILITY TRAINING AREA
Gorrie
WUBALAWUN ABORIGINAL LAND TRUST
Lar

KEEP RIVER NATIONAL PARK EXTENSION (PROPOSED)

Kununurra
102
36
KEEP RIVER NP
Policemans Hole
Bulla
East Baines Gorge
Timber Creek
Victoria River Roadhouse
Old Delamere
131
BUNTINE
96
DILLINYA ABORIGINAL LAND TRUST
164
Sunday Creek

Newry
VICTORIA
PINKERTON RANGE
200
Limestone Gorge
Bullita Outstation
WANIMIYN ABORIGINAL LAND TRUST
Jasper Gorge
113
BUCHANAN
Mount Compton
Killarney
HWY
33
Daly Wa
Hi Way I
Roadhou

ORD RIVER DAM
Argyle Historic Homestead
Lake Argyle
The Twins
NAGURUNGURU ABORIGINAL LAND TRUST
GREGORY NATIONAL PARK
Amanbidji
Humbert River
Yarralin
214
New Humbert
30
Victoria River Downs
Mount Mervin
Top Springs
Mount Sullivan
Birrimba
YINGAWUNARRI MUDBURA ABORIGINAL LAND TRUST
Hidden Valley
53
16
Du

Rosewood
Argyle Downs
Mount Mary
Waterloo
DUNCAN
Mount Stevens
Pigeon Hole
BILINARA ABORIGINAL LAND TRUST
Mount Northcote
HWY
171
96
Montejinni
180
HWY
80
127
Murranji
MURRANJI ABORIGINAL LAND TRUST
Sp

Spring Creek
MALNGIN 2 ABORIGINAL LAND TRUST
Mount Kimon
Wickham
Mount Wickham
Mount Bajnes
Mount Sanford
Camfield
Mount Wallaston
BUNTINE
82

Mount John
Mistake Creek
Stirling
Limbunya
66

PURNULULU NATIONAL PARK
Mount Buchanan
BUNGLE BUNGLES
Nelson Springs
Mount Panton
Mount Copley
116
DAGURAGU ABORIGINAL LAND TRUST
Daguragu
Kalkarindji (Wave Hill)
Wave Hill
Mount Gordon
Cattle Creek
WAMPANA-KARLANTIJPA ABORIGINAL LAND TRUST
Newcastle (N

Kirkimbie
MALNGIN ABORIGINAL LAND TRUST
HWY
95
DAGURAGU ABORIGINAL LAND TRUST

Nicholson
96
56
Inverway (Mamadi)
Mount Farquharson
Riveren
Mount Barton
112
TANAMI DESERT

Marella Gorge
59
DUNCAN
BUNTINE
Bunda
Mount Archie
Nongra Lake
HOOKER CREEK ABORIGINAL LAND TRUST
KARLANTIJPA NORTH ABORIGINAL LAND TRUST

NORTHERN TERRITORY
WESTERN AUSTRALIA
Birrindudu
Lajamanu (Hooker Creek)

47
Mount Wittenoom
342
Mount Winnecke
Duck Ponds Outstation (Mirimnyunga)

TANAMI
YINGUALYALYA ABORIGINAL LAND TRUST
WARE RANGE
DESERT
CENTRAL

GARDNER
Lewis Creek
PURTA ABORIGINAL LAND TRUST
Supplejack Downs
DESERT

RANGE
Mount Frederick
Jiwaranpa Outstation
Lake Buck
ABORIGINAL

MOUNT FREDERICK ABORIGINAL LAND TRUST
Picininny Bore Outstation
Mount Twigg
LAND

85
79
TANAMI
RD
Mount Tanami
TRUST
Lake Surprise
KARLANTIJPA

LEWIS RANGE
MT FREDERICK (NO.2) ABORIGINAL LAND TRUST
45
Rabbit Flat Roadhouse
Mount Pilotus
SOUTH ABORIGINAL LAND TRUST

PHILLIPSON RANGE
MANGKURURRPA ABORIGINAL LAND TRUST
Mount Tracey
Tanami Downs
54
The Granites
55
Parrulyu (Mount Davidson Outstation)
Mount Solitaire
356
Mount Benner

Lake Jeavons
YININGARRA ABORIGINAL LAND TRUST
TANAMI
WIRLIYAJARRAYI ABORIGINAL LAND TRUST
Mount Windjong

Lake Dennis
Lake White
LAKE MACKAY ABORIGINAL LAND TRUST
RD
179
TANAMI DESERT
Mount Tumbull
Willowra

WARNINGS: In outback Australia, long distances separate some towns. Travellers should familiarise themselves with prevailing conditions before departure and take care to ensure their vehicle is roadworthy. Adequate supplies of petrol, water and food should be carried at all times.

In central Australia, rainfall can make some roads impassable, even with a 4WD vehicle. Full information on road conditions should be obtained from local authorities before departure.

If visitors intend diverting off public roads within Aboriginal Land areas, a permit is required from the relevant Aboriginal authority.

Beware of crocodiles in rivers, estuaries and coastal areas.

Beware of marine stingers in coastal areas (October to April). Swim within enclosures where possible.

Joins map 594

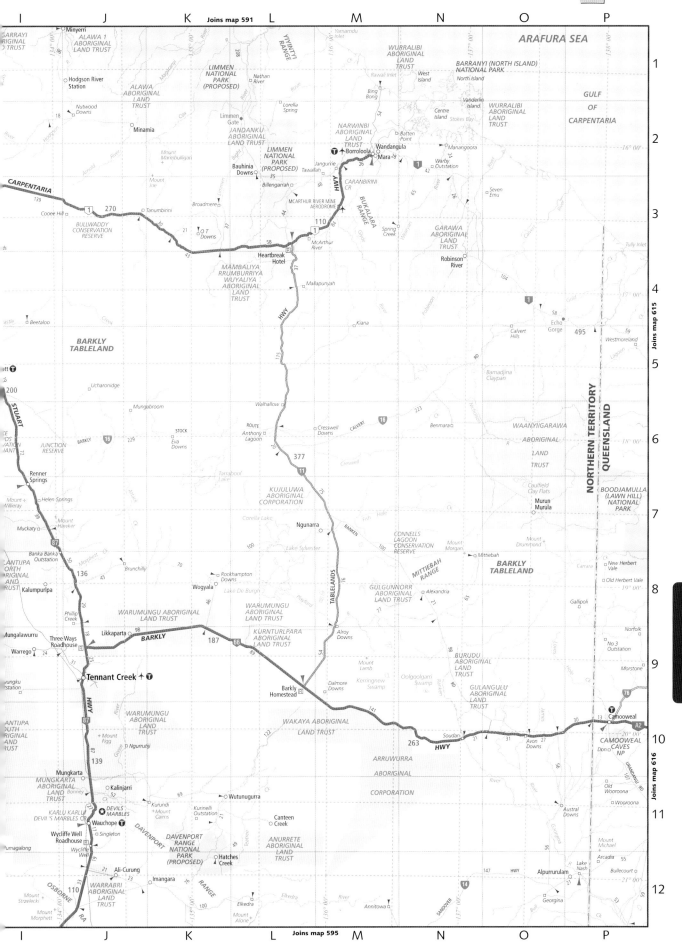

0   50   100   150 km

ARAFURA SEA

I   J   K   L   M   N   O   P

GULF
OF
CARPENTARIA

1
2
3
4
5
6
7
8
9
10
11
12

Joins map 615
Joins map 616

NORTHERN TERRITORY
QUEENSLAND

-16° 00'
-17° 00'
-18° 00'
-19° 00'
-20° 00'
-21° 00'

134° 00'   135° 00'   136° 00'   137° 00'   138° 00'

Minyerri
ALAWA 1
ABORIGINAL
LAND TRUST

Hodgson River
Station

ALAWA
ABORIGINAL
LAND
TRUST

Nutwood
Downs

Minamia

Mount
Marmbulligan

Bauhinia
Downs

Billengarrah

Broadmere

Tanumbirini

Cooee Hill

CARPENTARIA

BULLWADDY
CONSERVATION
RESERVE

O T
Downs

Heartbreak
Hotel

McArthur
River

MAMBALIYA
RRUMBURRIYA
WUYALIYA
ABORIGINAL
LAND
TRUST

Mallapunyah

Kiana

BARKLY
TABLELAND

Beetaloo

Ucharonidge

Mungabroom

STOCK
Eva
Downs

Walhallow

ROUTE
Anthony
Lagoon

Cresswell
Downs

Benmara

JUNCTION
RESERVE

Renner
Springs

Helen Springs

Mount
Willieray

Muckaty

Mount
Hawker

Tarrabool
Lake

KUJULUWA
ABORIGINAL
CORPORATION

Corella Lake

Ngunarra

Lake Sylvester

CONNELLS
LAGOON
CONSERVATION
RESERVE

Mount
Morgan

Mittiebah

BARKLY
TABLELAND

Banka Banka
Outstation

Brunchilly

Rockhampton
Downs

Lake De Burgh

WARUMUNGU ABORIGINAL
LAND TRUST

WARUMUNGU
ABORIGINAL
LAND TRUST

MITTIEBAH
RANGE

GULGUNNORR
ABORIGINAL
LAND TRUST

Alexandria

Kalumpurlpa

Phillip
Creek

Likkaparta

BARKLY

KURNTURLPARA
ABORIGINAL
LAND TRUST

Alroy
Downs

BURUDU
ABORIGINAL
LAND
TRUST

Mungalawurru

Three Ways
Roadhouse

Warrego

Tennant Creek

Barkly
Homestead

Dalmore
Downs

Mount
Lamb

Kerringnew
Swamp

Oolgoolgarri
Swamp

GULANGULU
ABORIGINAL
LAND TRUST

WARUMUNGU
ABORIGINAL
LAND TRUST

WAKAYA ABORIGINAL
LAND TRUST

Soudan

Avon
Downs

Camooweal

Mungkarta

Mount
Figg

Ngurrutji

ARRUWURRA
ABORIGINAL

CAMOOWEAL
CAVES
NP

MUNGKARTA
ABORIGINAL
LAND
TRUST

Kalinjarri

Kurundi
Mount
Cairns

Kurinelli
Outstation

Wutunugurra

ABORIGINAL

CORPORATION

Old
Wooroona

Wooroona

KARLU KARLU
DEVIL'S MARBLES CR

DEVILS
MARBLES

Wauchope

DAVENPORT

DAVENPORT
RANGE
NATIONAL
PARK
(PROPOSED)

Canteen
Creek

ANURRETE
ABORIGINAL
LAND
TRUST

Austral
Downs

Wycliffe Well
Roadhouse

Wycliffe
Well

Singleton

Hatches
Creek

Mount
Michael

STUART

Mount
Strzelecki

Ali-Curung

WARRABRI
ABORIGINAL
LAND
TRUST

Imangara

RANGE

Elkedra

Mount
Alone

Annitowa

Georgina

Alpururrulam

Lake
Nash

Arcadia

Bullecourt

OSBORNE
RA

Mount
Morphett

Yamamdu
Inlet

WURRALIBI
ABORIGINAL
LAND
TRUST

BARRANYI (NORTH ISLAND)
NATIONAL PARK

North Island

Rawali Inlet

West
Island

Bing
Bong

Batten
Point

Vanderlin
Island

Centre
Island   Stokes Bay

WURRALIBI
ABORIGINAL
LAND
TRUST

Manangoora

Seven
Emu

Tully Inlet

LIMMEN
NATIONAL
PARK
(PROPOSED)

YYINTYI
RANGE

Limmen
Gate

JANDANKU
ABORIGINAL
LAND TRUST

LIMMEN
NATIONAL
PARK
(PROPOSED)

Lorella
Spring

Nathan
River

Mount
Joe

Borroloola
Mara
Wandangula

Jangurrie

Tawallah

NARWINBI
ABORIGINAL
LAND
TRUST

CARANBIRINI
CR

Warby
Outstation

McARTHUR RIVER MINE
AERODROME

BUKALARA
RANGE

GARAWA
ABORIGINAL
LAND
TRUST

Spring
Creek

Robinson
River

Calvert
Hills

Echo
Gorge

Westmoreland

Bamadjina
Claypan

Caulfield
Clay Flats

WAANYIIGARAWA
ABORIGINAL
LAND
TRUST

Murun
Murula

BOODJAMULLA
(LAWN HILL)
NATIONAL
PARK

New Herbert
Vale

Old Herbert Vale

Cartara

Gallipoli

Norfolk

No 3
Outstation

Morstone

Don

CAMOOWEAL

URANDANGI
RD

Mount
Figg

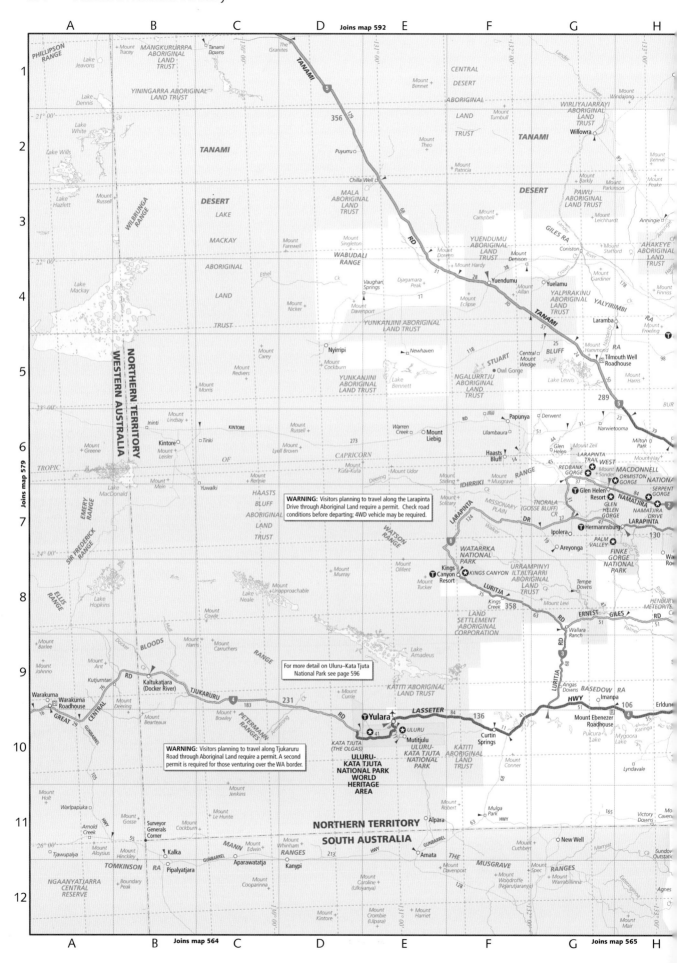

Joins map 592

Joins map 579

WARNING: Visitors planning to travel along the Larapinta Drive through Aboriginal Land require a permit. Check road conditions before departing; 4WD vehicle may be required.

For more detail on Uluru–Kata Tjuta National Park see page 596

WARNING: Visitors planning to travel along Tjukaruru Road through Aboriginal Land require a permit. A second permit is required for those venturing over the WA border.

Joins map 564

Joins map 565

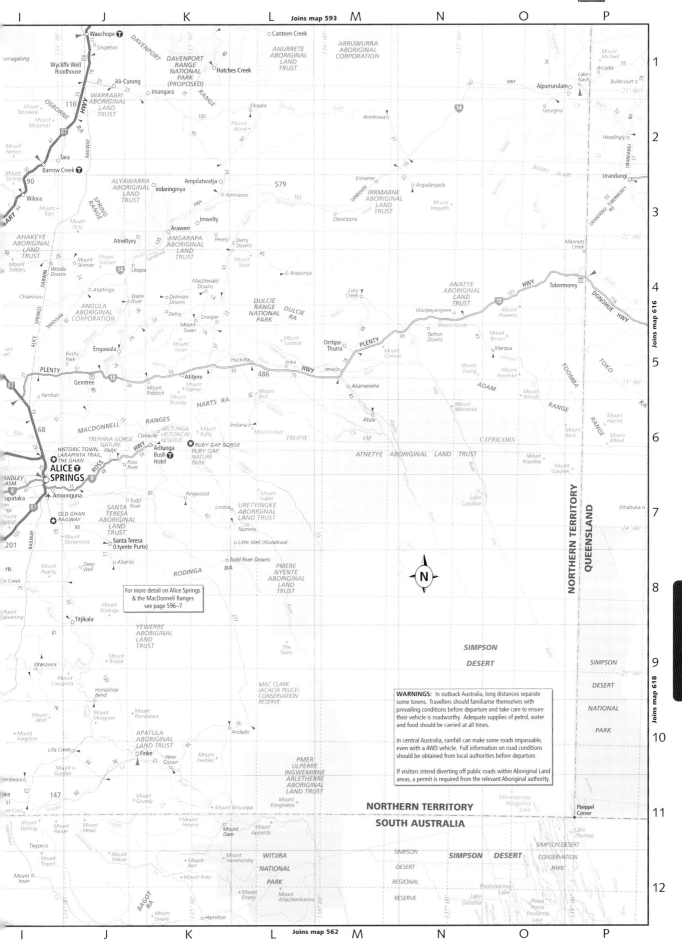

0   50   100   150 km

Joins map 593

Joins map 616

Joins map 618

Joins map 562

Wauchope

Singleton

Wycliffe Well
Roadhouse

Ali-Curung

Imangara

Canteen Creek

ANURRETE
ABORIGINAL
LAND
TRUST

ARRUWURRA
ABORIGINAL
CORPORATION

Mount
Michael

Arcadia

Bullecourt

DAVENPORT

DAVENPORT
RANGE
NATIONAL
PARK
(PROPOSED)

RANGE

Hatches Creek

Lake
Nash

Alpurrurulam

WARRABRI
ABORIGINAL
LAND
TRUST

Mount
Strzelecki

Mount
Morphett

Elkedra

Elkedra

Annitowa

HWY

Georgina

Headingly

Mount
Alone

River

Mount
Nelson

Tara

Barrow Creek

Wilora

ALYAWARRA
ABORIGINAL
LAND
TRUST

Indaringinya

Ampilatwatja

579

Ermarne

Argadargada

Mount
Hogarth

SANDOVER
IRRMARNE
ABORIGINAL
LAND
TRUST

Urandangi

SPRING

RANGE

Mount
Tops

Ammaroo

HWY

157

Sandover

River

AHAKEYE
ABORIGINAL
LAND
TRUST

Mount
Octy

Arawerr

Irrwelty

Perety

Derry
Downs

Ooratippra

Manners
Creek

Atneltyey

ANGARAPA
ABORIGINAL
LAND
TRUST

Mount
Solitary

Mount
Skinner

Mount
Skinner

Utopia

Woolla
Downs

Chianina

Atartinga

Waite
River

Delmore
Downs

Delny

MacDonald
Downs

Arapunya

Lucy
Creek

ANATYE
ABORIGINAL
LAND
TRUST

Tobermorey

DONOHUE HWY

DULCIE
RANGE
NATIONAL
PARK

DULCIE
RA

Warlpeyangrere

Mount
Pozieres

ANGULA
ABORIGINAL
CORPORATION

Dneiper

Mount
Swan

Mount
Sainthill

Orrtipa-
Thurra

PLENTY

Tarlton
Downs

Mount
Guide

Mount
Brown

Marqua

Marqua

TOKO

Engawala

Mount
Swan

Huckitta

Jinka

Mount
Cornish

Jervois

Mount
Ewing

Mount
Reinecke

RANGE

Bushy
Park

PLENTY

Gemtree

Atitjere

486

75

HWY

Akarnenehe

ADAM

Mount
Woods

RANGE

Yambah

Mount
Riddock

Mount
Palmer

Mount
Brassey

HARTS RA

Indiana

Mount
Bird

Atula

Mount
Winnecke

Mount
Harriet

Mount
Beck

Mount
Alfred

MACDONNELL   RANGES

Claraville

ARLTUNGA
HISTORICAL
RESERVE

Mount
Ruby

Mount
Lloyd

TROPIC

OF

CAPRICORN

TREPHINA GORGE
NATURE
PARK

Arltunga
Bush
Hotel

RUBY GAP GORGE
RUBY GAP
NATURE
PARK

ATNETYE ABORIGINAL LAND TRUST

Mount
Knuckey

Ethabuka

HISTORIC TOWN,
LARAPINTA TRAIL,
THE GHAN

ALICE
SPRINGS

ROSS

Ross
River

Mount
Gardner

Amoonguna

Ringwood

Mount
Isabel

Lake
Caroline

NORTHERN TERRITORY

QUEENSLAND

SANTA
TERESA
ABORIGINAL
LAND
TRUST

Todd
River

Limbla

URETYINGKE
ABORIGINAL
LAND TRUST

Numery

OLD GHAN
RAILWAY

Mount
Ooraminna

Santa Teresa
(Ltyente Purte)

Allambi

Little Well (Aluralkwa)

Mount
Peachy

Deep
Well

Todd River Downs

RODINGA

RA

PMERE
NYENTE
ABORIGINAL
LAND
TRUST

For more detail on Alice Springs
& the MacDonnell Ranges
see page 596–7

Mount
Rodinga

Titjikala

YEWERRE
ABORIGINAL
LAND
TRUST

The
Twins

SIMPSON

DESERT

SIMPSON

DESERT

Idracowra

Mount
Casuarina

Horseshoe
Bend

NATIONAL

Mount
Watt

MAC CLARK
(ACACIA PEUCE)
CONSERVATION
RESERVE

PARK

WARNINGS: In outback Australia, long distances separate
some towns. Travellers should familiarise themselves with
prevailing conditions before departure and take care to ensure
their vehicle is roadworthy. Adequate supplies of petrol, water
and food should be carried at all times.

Mount
Kingston

Mount
Musgrave

Mount
Rumbalara

Andado

APATULA
ABORIGINAL
LAND TRUST

Lilla Creek

Finke

New
Crown

Mount
Peebles

In central Australia, rainfall can make some roads impassable,
even with a 4WD vehicle. Full information on road conditions
should be obtained from local authorities before departure.

Mount
Gordon

147

Mount
Grundy

PMER
ULPERRE
INGWEMIRNE
ARLETHERRE
ABORIGINAL
LAND TRUST

If visitors intend diverting off public roads within Aboriginal Land
areas, a permit is required from the relevant Aboriginal authority.

Mirranponga
Pongunna
Lake

Poeppel
Corner

Mount
Etingimbra

Mount
Wilyunpa

NORTHERN TERRITORY

SOUTH AUSTRALIA

Lake
Thomas

Mount
Darling

Mount
Parlee

Mount
Mead

Mount
Hearne

Mount
Dare

Mount
Apperda

SIMPSON

SIMPSON   DESERT

SIMPSON DESERT

Tieyon

Mount
Tieyon

Mount
Treloar

Mount
Barr

WITJIRA

DESERT

CONSERVATION

Mount
Irwin

Mount
Ross

NATIONAL

REGIONAL

PARK

Mount
Emery

Mount
Attacherikarnna

PARK

RESERVE

Poolowanna
Lake

Lake
Griselda

Peera
Peera
Poolana
Lake

Hamilton

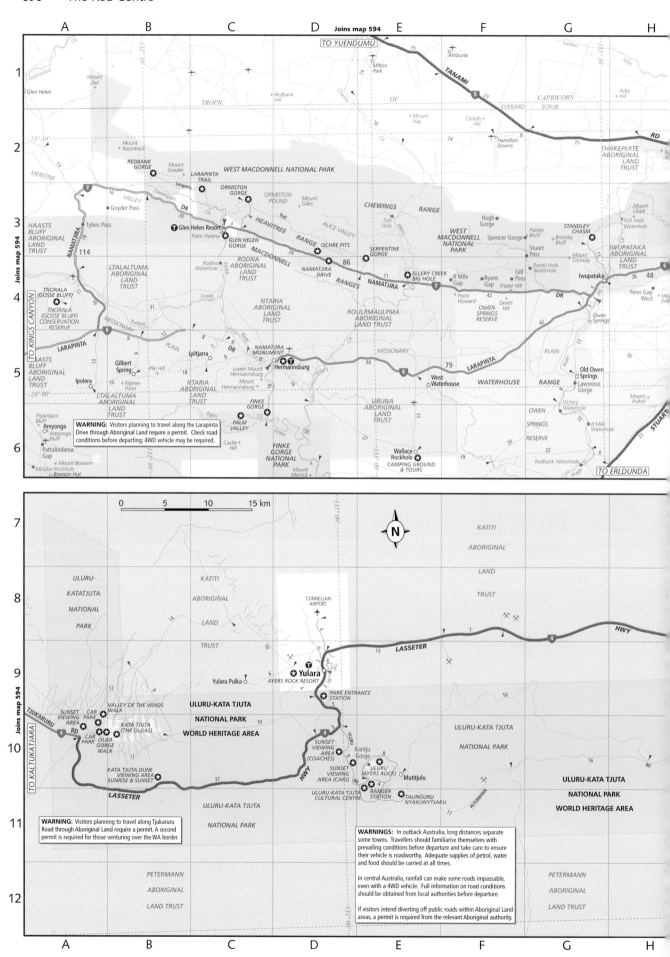

WARNING: Visitors planning to travel along the Larapinta Drive through Aboriginal Land require a permit. Check road conditions before departing; 4WD vehicle may be required.

WARNING: Visitors planning to travel along Tjukaruru Road through Aboriginal Land require a permit. A second permit is required for those venturing over the WA border.

WARNINGS: In outback Australia, long distances separate some towns. Travellers should familiarise themselves with prevailing conditions before departure and take care to ensure their vehicle is roadworthy. Adequate supplies of petrol, water and food should be carried at all times.

In central Australia, rainfall can make some roads impassable, even with a 4WD vehicle. Full information on road conditions should be obtained from local authorities before departure.

If visitors intend diverting off public roads within Aboriginal Land areas, a permit is required from the relevant Aboriginal authority.

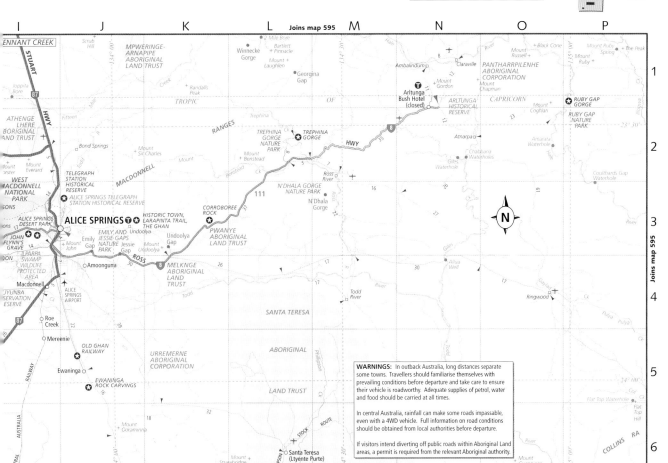

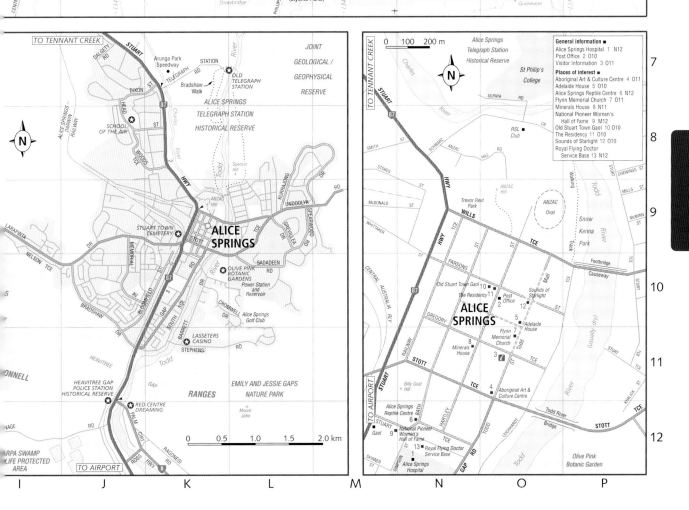

General information ■
Alice Springs Hospital 1 N12
Post Office 2 O10
Visitor Information 3 O11

Places of interest ■
Aboriginal Art & Culture Centre 4 O11
Adelaide House 5 O10
Alice Springs Reptile Centre 6 N12
Flynn Memorial Church 7 O11
Minerals House 8 N11
National Pioneer Women's
   Hall of Fame 9 M12
Old Stuart Town Gaol 10 O10
The Residency 11 O10
Sounds of Starlight 12 O10
Royal Flying Doctor
   Service Base 13 N12

WARNINGS: In outback Australia, long distances separate some towns. Travellers should familiarise themselves with prevailing conditions before departure and take care to ensure their vehicle is roadworthy. Adequate supplies of petrol, water and food should be carried at all times.

In central Australia, rainfall can make some roads impassable, even with a 4WD vehicle. Full information on road conditions should be obtained from local authorities before departure.

If visitors intend diverting off public roads within Aboriginal Land areas, a permit is required from the relevant Aboriginal authority.

MAPS

QUEENSLAND

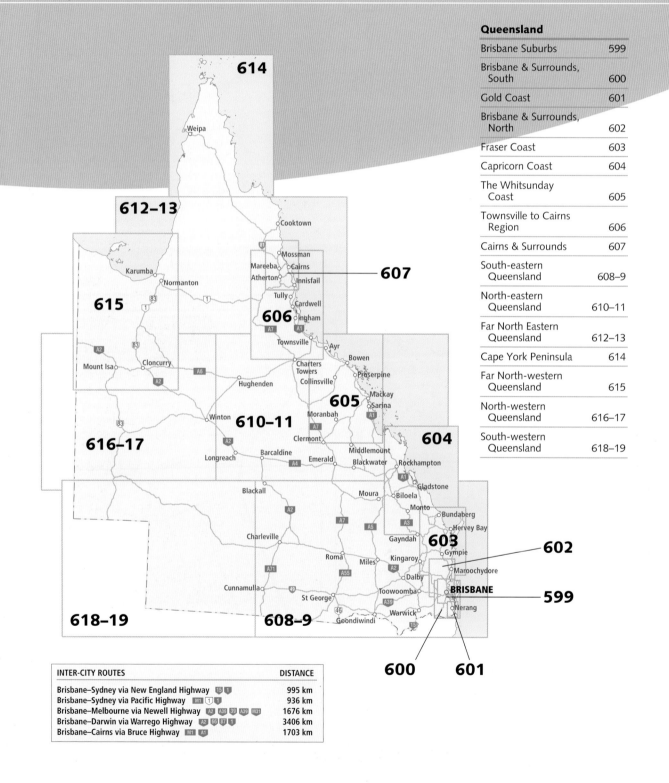

Queensland

Brisbane Suburbs	599
Brisbane & Surrounds, South	600
Gold Coast	601
Brisbane & Surrounds, North	602
Fraser Coast	603
Capricorn Coast	604
The Whitsunday Coast	605
Townsville to Cairns Region	606
Cairns & Surrounds	607
South-eastern Queensland	608–9
North-eastern Queensland	610–11
Far North Eastern Queensland	612–13
Cape York Peninsula	614
Far North-western Queensland	615
North-western Queensland	616–17
South-western Queensland	618–19

INTER-CITY ROUTES	DISTANCE
Brisbane–Sydney via New England Highway	995 km
Brisbane–Sydney via Pacific Highway	936 km
Brisbane–Melbourne via Newell Highway	1676 km
Brisbane–Darwin via Warrego Highway	3406 km
Brisbane–Cairns via Bruce Highway	1703 km

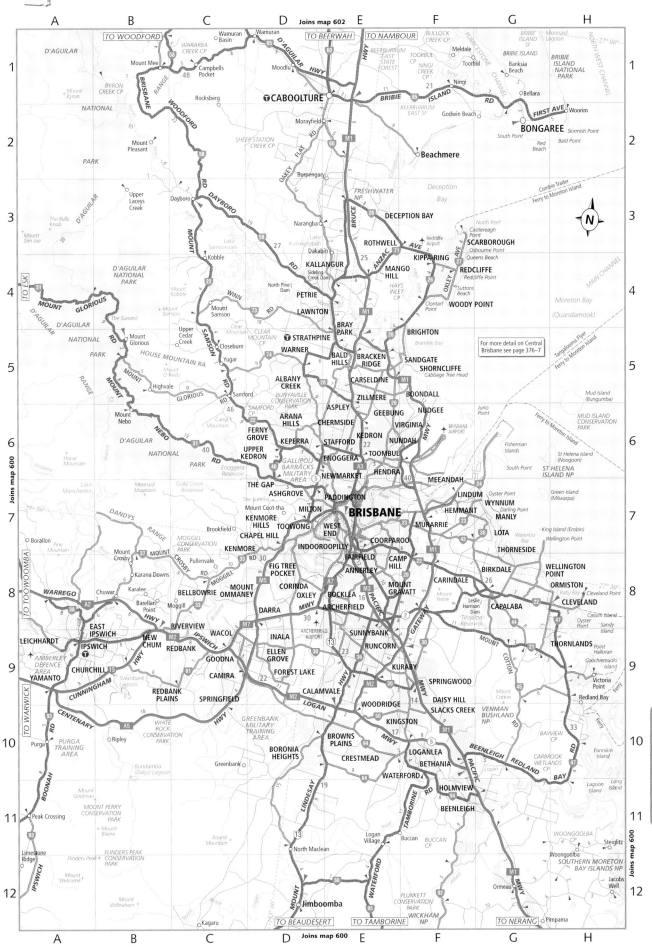

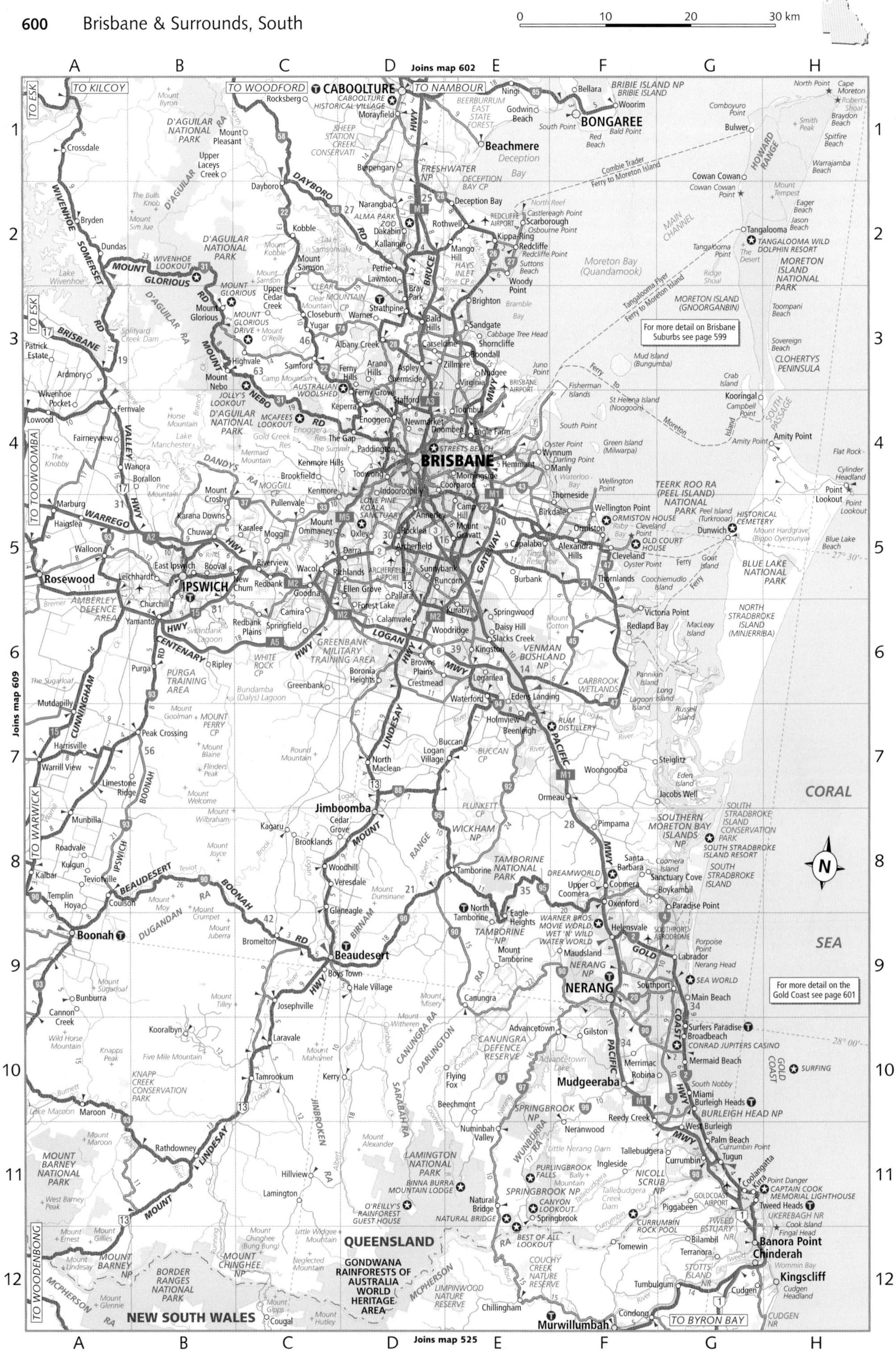

0   10   20   30 km

Joins map 602

TO KILCOY
TO WOODFORD   CABOOLTURE   TO NAMBOUR

A   B   C   D   E   F   G   H

Crossdale
Mount Byron
Rocksberg
CABOOLTURE HISTORICAL VILLAGE
Morayfield
Ningi   Bellara
BRIBIE ISLAND NP / BRIBIE ISLAND
North Point   Cape Moreton
Roberts Shoal

Upper Laceys Creek
Mount Pleasant
SHEEP STATION CREEK CONSERVATI
Godwin Beach   Woorim   BONGAREE
Bald Point
Comboyuro Point   Bulwer
Braydon Beach
Smith Peak
Spitfire Beach

D'AGUILAR NATIONAL PARK
Dayboro
BEERBURRUM EAST STATE FOREST
FRESHWATER NP
Burpengary
Beachmere
Deception Bay
Red Beach
South Point

Bryden
Dundas
WIVENHOE SOMERSET
Kobble
Narangba
Dakabin
Deception Bay
REDCLIFFE AIRPORT
Castlereagh Point
Osbourne Point
Scarborough
Cowan Cowan
Cowan Cowan Point
Mount Tempest

The Bulls Knob
Mount Sim Jue
Lake Samsonvale
WIVENHOE LOOKOUT
D'AGUILAR NATIONAL PARK
Mount Samson
Petrie
Kallangur
Rothwell
Kippa-Ring
Redcliffe
Redcliffe Point
MORETON BAY (Quandamook)
Tangalooma
The Desert
TANGALOOMA WILD DOLPHIN RESORT
MORETON ISLAND NATIONAL PARK

Patrick Estate
Ardmory
Wivenhoe Pocket
Lowood
Fairneyview
BRISBANE RD
Highvale
Samford
Arana Hills
Aspley
Zillmere
Chermside
Sandgate
Shorncliffe
BRISBANE AIRPORT
St Helena Island (Noogoon)
CLOHERTYS PENINSULA
Sovereign Beach

BRISBANE

IPSWICH

Rosewood
Churchill
Yamanto
Springfield
Forest Lake
Mount Gravatt
Capalaba
Cleveland
Victoria Point
NORTH STRADBROKE ISLAND (MINJERRIBA)
Dunwich
BLUE LAKE NATIONAL PARK
Point Lookout

Harrisville
Warrill View
Peak Crossing
Greenbank
Kingston
Loganlea
Beenleigh
SOUTHERN MORETON BAY ISLANDS NP
SOUTH STRADBROKE ISLAND

Munbilla
Roadvale
Kulgun
Kalbar
Boonah
Bromelton
Jimboomba
Tamborine
TAMBORINE NATIONAL PARK
DREAMWORLD
Coomera
Oxenford
Paradise Point
GOLD COAST

Templin
Hoya
Coulson
Beaudesert
Veresdale
Gleneagle
Mount Tamborine
WARNER BROS MOVIE WORLD
Helensvale
NERANG
Southport
SEA WORLD
Main Beach
Surfers Paradise

Bunburra
Kooralbyn
Josephville
Laravale
Canungra
Advancetown
Gilston
Mermaid Beach
Robina
Mudgeeraba
Burleigh Heads

MOUNT BARNEY NATIONAL PARK
Rathdowney
Hillview
Lamington
Beechmont
SPRINGBROOK NP
Neranwood
Ingleside
Currumbin
Tugun
Coolangatta
Kirra
Tweed Heads
Banora Point
Chinderah

BORDER RANGES NATIONAL PARK
QUEENSLAND
GONDWANA RAINFORESTS OF AUSTRALIA WORLD HERITAGE AREA
NEW SOUTH WALES
Murwillumbah
Kingscliff

CORAL SEA

Joins map 609
Joins map 525
TO BYRON BAY
TO WOODENBONG
TO WARWICK
TO TOOWOOMBA

For more detail on Brisbane Suburbs see page 599
For more detail on the Gold Coast see page 601

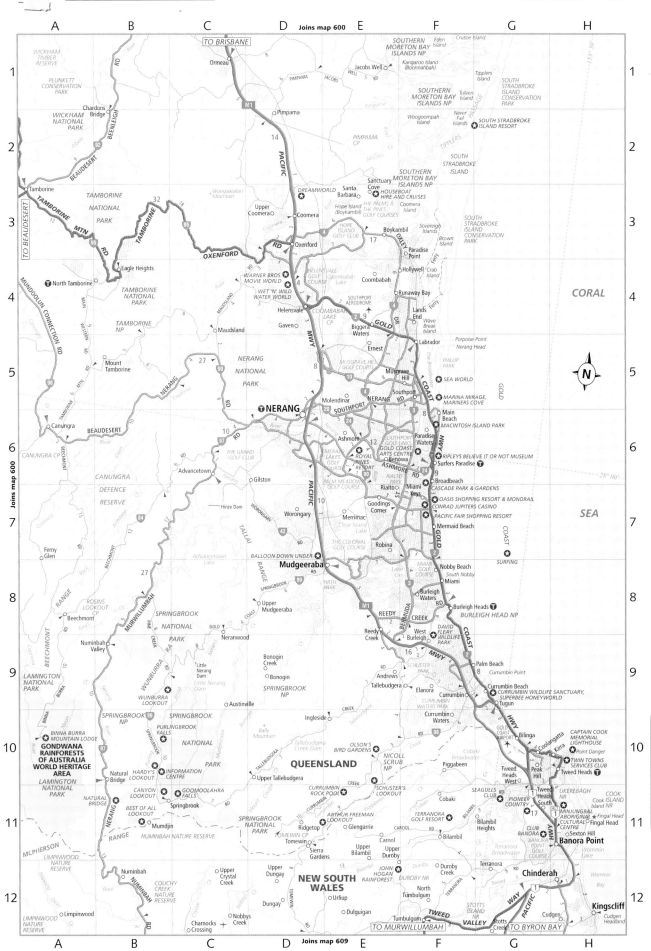

0 2 4 6 8 10 km

A B C D E F G H

0 10 20 30 km

Joins map 603
Joins map 609
Joins map 600

TO GYMPIE
TO GYMPIE
TO KINGAROY
TO TOOWOOMBA
TO WARWICK
TO BEAUDESERT
TO NERANG

GREAT SANDY NATIONAL PARK

Gallangowan
GALLANGOWAN STATE FOREST
AMAMOOR RANGE
AMAMOOR STATE FOREST
WRATTENS NATIONAL PARK
KANDANGA RANGE
ELGIN VALE STATE FOREST
WRATTENS NATIONAL PARK
Kandanga
HERITAGE RAILWAY
Imbil
Mount Kandanga
Brooloo
Mount Gibbaniee
Diaper Mountain
DIAPER STATE FOREST
YABBA STATE FOREST
CONONDALE NP
IMBIL STATE FOREST 1
Borumba Dam
Cooroy
Mount Cooroora
Pomona
Mount Cooroy
BRUCE
Tewantin
Noosa Heads
Sunshine Beach
NOOSA
Marcus Beach
Peregian Beach
NATIONAL
PARK
Eumundi
VILLAGE MARKETS
North Arm
Yandina
Coolum Beach
Mudjimba
MAROOCHYDORE
MOOLOOLABA
CORAL
SEA
Mount Pascoe
Jimna
JIMNA STATE FOREST
Yednia
CONONDALE NATIONAL PARK
MALENY NATIONAL PARK
KONDALILLA NP
Mapleton
NAMBOUR
TRIUNIA NP
Woombye
BUDERIM
Bli Bli
Marcoola
MAROOCHYDORE AERODROME
MOUNT COOLUM NATIONAL PARK
Buddina
Warana
Mount Spencer
Linville
Kenilworth
KENILWORTH
Conondale
Montville
Palmwoods
Eudlo
EUDLO CREEK NP
Mooloolah
MOOLOOLAH RIVER NP
PALMVIEW CP
SUPERBEE HONEY FACTORY
UNDERWATER WORLD
Point Cartwright
Moore
Nurinda
Harlin
D'AGUILAR RANGE
BRISBANE RANGE
Gregors Creek
Kilcoy
HWY
Maleny
Landsborough
Beerwah
AUSTRALIA ZOO
Peachester
Coochin Creek
GLASS HOUSE MOUNTAINS
Glass House Mountains
CALOUNDRA
Caloundra Head
Moffat Beach
BRIBIE ISLAND NP
Ivory Creek
Yimbun
Biarra
Toogoolawah
CRESSBROOK STATE FOREST
DEER RESERVE STATE FOREST
Woodford
Beerburrum
BEERBURRUM WEST STATE FOREST
GLASS HOUSE MOUNTAINS NATIONAL PARK
BEERBURRUM EAST STATE FOREST
BRIBIE ISLAND
BRIBIE ISLAND NATIONAL PARK
Banksia Beach
Bellara
Woorim
BONGAREE
Buaraba
The Gap
Coal Creek
Mount Beppo
Caboonbah
Somerset Dam
Delaneys Creek
Wamuran
Elimbah
CABOOLTURE HISTORICAL VILLAGE
Donnybrook
Meldale
Toorbul
Ningi
Cominya
Esk
Murrumba
Crossdale
Mount Mee
Campbells Pocket
Moodlu
CABOOLTURE
Morayfield
Beachmere
Deception Bay
Godwin Beach
South Point
Red Beach
Bald Point
Combie Trader Ferry to Moreton Island
Gallanani
Buaraba
ESK
HWY
Moombra
Bryden
Dundas
WIVENHOE LOOKOUT
D'AGUILAR NATIONAL PARK
Dayboro
Rocksberg
Mount Pleasant
Upper Laceys Creek
Burpengary
Narangba
Deception Bay
Scarborough
REDCLIFFE
Redcliffe
Kippa-Ring
Woody Point
Moreton Bay (Quandamook)
Mount Hallen
Mount Mulgowie
Buaraba
Coominya
Clarendon
Ardmory
Fernvale
Mount Nebo
Mount Glorious
Closeburn
Yugar
Albany Creek
Samford
Bray Park
Strathpine
Bald Hills
Carseldine
Zillmere
Boondall
Sandgate
Brighton
Shorncliffe
Cabbage Tree Head
Mud Island
MUD ISLAND CP
St Helena Island
ST HELENA ISLAND NP
Glenore Grove
Plainland
Prenzlau
Coolana
Minden
Marburg
Hatton Vale
Lowood
Tarampa
Fairneyview
Wanora
Borallon
Karana Downs
Mount Crosby
Kenmore
Brookfield
Pullenvale
Moggill
Riverview
BRISBANE
Indooroopilly
Toowong
Kenmore Hills
The Gap
Enoggera
Keperra
Ferny Grove
Stafford
Chermside
Aspley
Virginia
Nudgee
BRISBANE AIRPORT
Eagle Farm
Wynnum
Manly
Thorneside
Birkdale
Wellington Point
Cleveland
ORMISTON HOUSE
OLD COURT HOUSE
Ormiston
TEERK ROO RA (PEEL ISLAND) NP
Coochiemudlo Island
Victoria Point
Thornlands
Laidley
Rosewood
Forest Hill
Grandchester
Calvert
Walloon
Leichhardt
East Ipswich
Booval
New Chum
IPSWICH
Churchill
Yamanto
Redbank
Goodna
Redbank Plains
Camira
Carole Park
Wacol
Richlands
Darra
Oxley
Rocklea
Archerfield
ARCHERFIELD AIRPORT
Sunnybank
Runcorn
Burbank
Capalaba
Alexandra Hills
Birkdale
Mount Gravatt
Camp Hill
Morningside
Carina
Coorparoo
LONE PINE KOALA SANCTUARY
Ellen Grove
Pallara
For more detail on Brisbane Suburbs see page 599

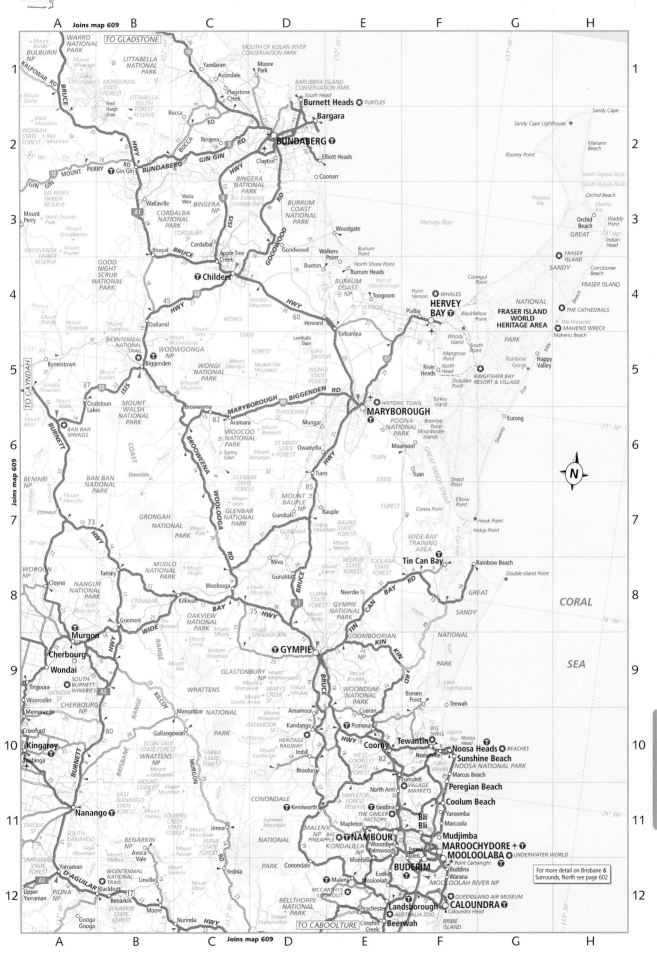

Scale: 0 10 20 30 40 50 km

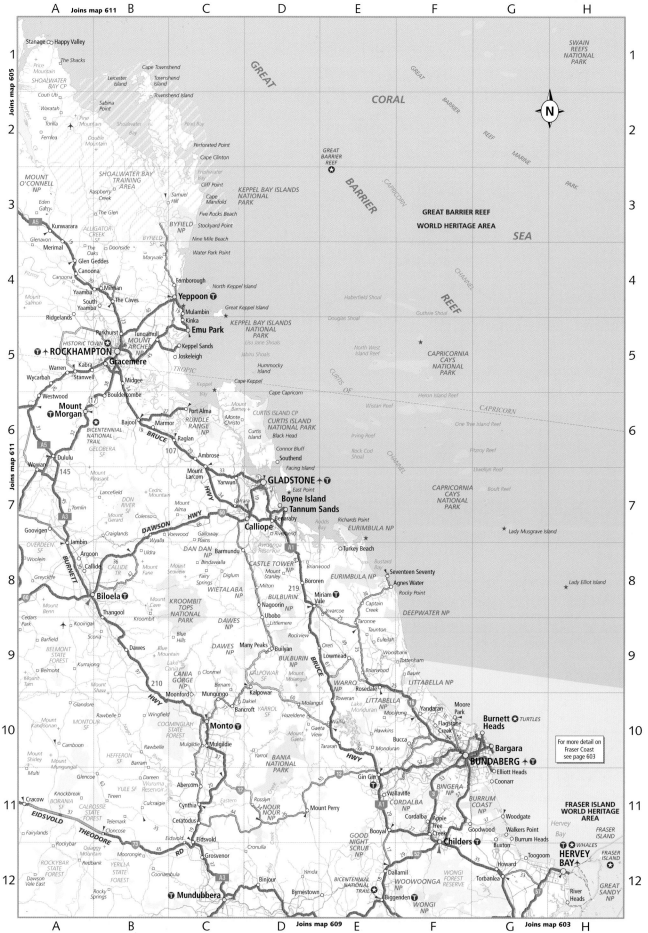

Joins map 611

A   B   C   D   E   F   G   H

SWAIN
REEFS
NATIONAL
PARK

GREAT

CORAL

BARRIER

SEA

REEF
MARINE

PARK

GREAT BARRIER REEF
WORLD HERITAGE AREA

Stanage   Happy Valley
Price
Mountain   The Shacks
Couti Uti
SHOALWATER
BAY CP
Waratah
Torilla
Fernlea
Double
Mountain

Leicester
Island
Townshend
Island
Cape Townshend
Townshend Island

Pearl Bay

MOUNT
O'CONNELL
NP
SHOALWATER BAY
TRAINING
AREA
Eden
Gatry
Raspberry
Creek
The Glen
Pine
Mountain
Samuel
Hill
Cliff Point
Cape
Manifold
Five Rocks Beach
Nine Mile Beach
Water Park Point

Perforated Point

Cape Clinton

Freshwater
Bay

GREAT
BARRIER
REEF

KEPPEL BAY ISLANDS
NATIONAL PARK

Kunwarara
Glenavon
Merimal
Glen Geddes
Canoona
Yaamba
Milman
South
Yaamba   The Caves
Ridgelands

Farnborough
North Keppel Island

Yeppoon

Mulambin
Kinka
Emu Park

Great Keppel Island

Haberfield Shoal

Douglas Shoal

Guthrie Shoal

CAPRICORNIA
CAYS
NATIONAL
PARK

HISTORIC TOWN
ROCKHAMPTON
Parkhurst
Tungamull
MOUNT
ARCHER
Kabra
Warren
Gracemere
Wycarbah
Stanwell
Midgee
Westwood
Boulcombe
Mount
Morgan
Bajool
Marmor
BICENTENNIAL
NATIONAL
TRAIL
GELOBERA
SF
Dululu
Raglan
BRUCE
107
Ambrose
Wowan
145
Mount
Pleasant
RUNDLE
RANGE
NP
Monte
Christo
Mount
Barney
CURTIS ISLAND CP
Curtis
Island
CURTIS ISLAND
NATIONAL PARK
Black Head
Connor Bluff
Southend
Facing Island
Keppel Sands
Joskeleigh
TROPIC
Keppel
Bay
Cape Keppel
Cape Capricorn
Port Alma
Mount
Larcom
Yarwun

Wistari Reef

Heron Island Reef

One Tree Island Reef

CAPRICORN

Irving Reef

Rock Cod
Shoal

Fitzroy Reef

Llewellyn Reef

Boult Reef

CAPRICORNIA
CAYS
NATIONAL
PARK

KEPPEL BAY ISLANDS
NATIONAL
PARK

North West
Island Reef

Lisa Jane Shoals
Jabiru Shoals
Hummocky
Island

GLADSTONE
East Point
Boyne Island
Tannum Sands
Benaraby
Calliope
Caffrata
Riverbend
Rodds
Bay
Richards Point
EURIMBULA NP
Turkey Beach

Lady Musgrave Island

Lady Elliot Island

Goovigen
Jambin
Argoon
Callide
DON
RIVER
SF
Cedric
Mountain
Mount
Gerard
Colenso
Craiglands
Wyalla
Voewood
Galloway
Plains
DAN DAN
NP
Barmundu
Bindawalla
Mount
Fane
Fairy
Springs
Diglum
Milton
Mount
Stanley
CASTLE TOWER
NP
219
BULBURIN
NP
Nagoorin
Ubobo
Littlemore
Miriam
Vale
Invarcoe
Briarwood
Bororen
EURIMBULA NP

Seventeen Seventy
Agnes Water
Rocky Point

Captain
Creek
Taronne
Taunton
Euleilah

DEEPWATER NP

DAWSON
HWY
Woolein
Greycliffe
BURNETT
Mount
Benn
Biloela
Thangool
CALLIDE
TR
Mount
Cave
Kroombit
KROOMBIT
TOPS
NATIONAL
PARK
WIETALABA
NP
DAWES
NP
Blue
Hills
Blue
Mountain
Lake
Cania
DAWES
NP
Many Peaks
Builyan
BULBURIN
NP
Rockview
Lowmead
Oreti
BRUCE
Mount
Molangul
WARRO
NP
Woodbank
Tottenham
Briarwood
Bauer

LITTABELLA NP

Cedars
Park
Barfield
Belmont
Mount
Tam
Kooingal
Scoria
Kurrajong
Mount
Shaw
Glandore
BELMONT
STATE
FOREST
Dawes
210
CANIA
GORGE
NP
Birnam
Moonford
Mungungo
Clonmel
Kalpower
KALPOWAR
SF
Mount
Molangul
60
Molangul
Rosedale
25
Moore
Park
Burnett
Heads
TURTLES

Mount
Kandoonan
Camboon
Mount
Shirley
Mount
Mungungal
Multi
Knockbreak
BORANIA
SF
Tireen
MONTOUR
SF
Rawbelle
HEFFERON
SF
Wingfield
Rawbelle
Barram
COOMINGLAH
STATE
FOREST
Mulgildie
Monto
Mulgildie
37
Yarrol
BANIA
NATIONAL
PARK
Dakiel
Bancroft
YARROL
SF
Hazeldene
Mount
Gaeta
Gaeta
View
Towaran
Mundurran
Hawkins
Monduran
Bucca
Flagstone
Creek
16
Moolyung
Yandaran
Bargara
BUNDABERG
Elliott Heads
Coonarr

Cracow
Fairylands
Rockybar
ROCKYBAR
STATE
FOREST
Dawson
Vale East
Rocky
Springs
EIDSVOLD
THEODORE
73
RD
A3
Moorongie
YERILLA
STATE
FOREST
Coonambula
Mundubbera
Abercorn
Cynthia
Ceratodus
Eidsvold
Grosvenor
Binjour
Byrnestown
CALROSSIE
STATE
FOREST
Telemark
Culcraigie
17
44
Rosslyn
NOUR
NOUR
NP
Mount Perry
Eastern
Cronulla
Yenda
BICENTENNIAL
NATIONAL
TRAIL
Dallarnil
Biggenden
WOOWOONGA
NP
WONGI
NP
GOOD
NIGHT
SCRUB
NP
Booyal
Gin Gin
Wallaville
A1
BINGERA
NP
CORDALBA
NP
Cordalba
Apple
Tree
Creek
Childers
Buxton
Howard
Torbanlea
WONGI
FOREST
RESERVE
Goodwood
Woodgate
Walkers Point
Burrum Heads
Toogoom
BURRUM
COAST
NP
Hervey
Bay
FRASER
ISLAND
FRASER ISLAND
WORLD HERITAGE
AREA
HERVEY
BAY
WHALES
River
Heads
GREAT
SANDY
NP
FRASER
ISLAND

For more detail on
Fraser Coast
see page 603

Joins map 609   Joins map 603

1   2   3   4   5   6   7   8   9   10   11   12

A   B   C   D   E   F   G   H

0 20 40 60 80 100 km

For more detail on Townsville
see page 606

Joins map 606
Joins map 610
Joins map 610
Joins map 611

GREAT   CORAL   SEA

GREAT   BARRIER   REEF

MARINE   PARK

HISTORIC TOWN

TOWNSVILLE
Nelly Bay
Picnic Bay
Pallarenda
Garbutt
Oonoonba
Cungulla
Cape Cleveland
Cape Ferguson
Cape Bowling Green
Bowling Green Bay
BOWLING GREEN BAY NP
Alligator Creek
Woodstock
Giru
Brandon
Gainsford
Alva
Lynchs Beach
Giffard
Grosso
Ayr
Home Hill
Inkerman
Majors Creek
Jardine
Reid River
Glendale
Clare
Inkerman
Middle Landing
Cape Upstart
CAPE UPSTART NP
Upstart Bay
Coconut Bay
Ravenswood
Plumwood
Millaroo
Dalbeg
Gumlu
Guthalungra
Rocky Ponds
Wyoming
Ness Vale
Caley Valley
Abbot Point
Abbot Bay
Euri
Merinda
Bowen
Delta
Cape Edgecumbe
Port Denison
Port of Bowen
Edingburgh Bay
Holbourne Island
HOLBOURNE ISLAND NP
GLOUCESTER ISLAND NP
Gloucester Island
Eshelby Island
George Point
Hayman Island
Dolphin Point
Pinnacle Point
Hook Island
Baird Point
Grimston Point
Hannah Point
WHITSUNDAY GROUP
WHITSUNDAY ISLANDS, WHITEHAVEN BEACH
WHITSUNDAY ISLANDS NP
Edward Island
Haslewood Island
Whitsunday Island
Craig Island
Hamilton Island
Long Island
Cannonvale **Airlie Beach**
Sugarloaf
Shute Harbour
Proserpine
CONWAY NP
Conway Beach
LINDEMAN ISLANDS NP
Lindeman Group
Mansell Island
Shaw Island
Cape Conway
ANDROMACHE CP
Burning Point
Collinsville
Scottville
Binbee
SONOMA SF
BICENTENNIAL NATIONAL TRAIL
Strathbowen
Birralee
Repulse Bay
Midge Point
Ten Mile Beach
Bloomsbury
Elaroo
Yalboroo
Calen
Seaforth
Ball Bay
Cape Hillsborough
Andrews Point
SMITH ISLANDS NP
Anchor Islands
Sir James Smith Group
Goldsmith Island
Linne Island
Carlisle Island
Brampton Island
BRAMPTON ISLANDS NP
Scawfell Island
Calder Island
Rabbit Island
St Helens Bay
Mentmore Beach
Finlaysons Point
Keswick Island
St Bees Island
SOUTH CUMBERLAND ISLANDS NP
Bailey Islet
Mount Ossa
Mount Charlton
Kuttabul
Bucasia
Eimeo
Slade Point
Eungella
EUNGELLA NP
Finch Hatton
Gargett
Marian
Farleigh
Walkerston
MACKAY
Port of Mackay
Mirani
Eton
Bakers Creek
Homebush
Hector
Half Tide
Dudgeon Point
NORTHUMBERLAND ISLANDS NP
Prudhoe Island
Coral Point
Campwin Beach
Sarina Beach
Grasstree
Sarina
Armstrong Beach
Freshwater Point
Knight Island
CAPE PALMERSTON NP
Coconut Point
Temple Island
Ridge Islet
Notch Point
Koumala
Ilbilbie
Mount Coolon
Glenden
Wollombi
Suttor North
Suttor Creek
Exvale
Hillalong
Turrawalla
Newlands Mine
HOMEVALE NP
Homevale
Carrinyah
Lake Elphinstone
Burton Gorge Dam
Kemmis Creek
St Alburns
Riverside
Ellensfield
Mulgrave
Strathfield
Nebo
Mountview
Braeside
Tootoolah
Hamilton Park
Bolingbroke
Wandoo
Yarrawonga Point
West Hill Island
WEST HILL NP
Carmila
Flaggy Rock
Avoid Island
Aquila Island
Roundhill Island
BROAD SOUND ISLANDS NP
Clairview
Clairview Bluff
GLENCOE SF
St Lawrence
Port of St Lawrence
Broad Sound
CHARON POINT CP
Moranbah
Coppabella
Annandale
Harrybrandt
Bundarra
Valkyrie
DIPPERU NP
Cockenzie
TIERAWOOMBA STATE FOREST
Quinns Gap
West Scott
Kurral Park
Coolibah
Poitrel
Olive Downs
Daunia
Devenil
Iffley
Morpeth
Saltbush Park
Cardowan
Maryland
Mount Toobier
Collaroy
MAZEPPA NP
Mooramana
Wentworth
Ellenor Downs
Coobyanga
Vicenza
Midden
Kulawin
Solferino
Wondabah
Alambe
Aroa Downs
Frankfield
Calveston
Kilcummin
Kenlogan
Coovin
Undara Downs
Tiggabon
Logan Downs
Peak Downs
Balmoral
Fletchers Awl
Cluen
Saraji
Leichhardt Downs
Bombandy
Carfax
Batheaston
Croydon
Rosedale
Killarney
Burwood
MOUNT BUFFALO SF
Tanderra
Dysart
WINCHESTER
PEAK RANGE NP
Eastern Peak
New Corry
Mount Donald
Mount Phillips
Cosmos
Norwich Park
Picardy
Warwick
Barmount
May Downs
Clermont
BLAIR ATHOL STATE FOREST
Blair Athol
Birimgan
Darrylal
Huntley
Anvil Hill
Clydevale
New Banchory
Pioneer
Monteagle
Kalang
Clunmell
Barcombe
Laurel Hills
Willesby
Durdham
Mistie Downs
Amaroo
Talki
Doorna Downs
Well Plains
Nungaroo
Myra
Wyena
Mullawa
Pretoria
Broadmeadow
Lambing Lagoon
GREGORY NP
DEVELOPMENTAL
BRUCE HWY
PEAK DOWNS HWY
FITZROY DEVELOPMENTAL RD
SARINA RD
MARLBOROUGH
DENHAM DEVELOPMENTAL RD
SUTTOR DEVELOPMENTAL RD
BOWEN DEVELOPMENTAL RD
LEICHHARDT
BURDEKIN
DALRYMPLE
HILLSBOROUGH CHANNEL
CONNORS RANGE
CLARKE RANGE
EPSOM SF
CREDITON SF
CONNORS SF
CONWAY
DRYANDER NP
PROSERPINE SF
MOUNT ABERDEEN NP
BOWLING GREEN BAY NP

TO CHARTERS TOWERS
TO EMERALD
TO ROCKHAMPTON

0 20 40 60 80 100 km

A B C Joins map 613 **D E**

TO LAKELAND
DAINTREE NP Miallo
Newell
MULLIGAN
MOSSMAN
MOSSMAN GORGE
MT LEWIS NP
Mossman
Cooya Beach
Yule Point
Port Douglas
Craiglie
Mount Carbine
Maryfarms
Rumula
Euluma
Oak Beach
CAPTAIN COOK
HIGHWAY DRIVE
FOUR MILE BEACH
Lighthouse
Mountain
Julatten
Faulty Towers
Trinity Bay
Bakers Blue
Mountain
Mount Molloy
KURANDA
MACALISTER RANGE NP
Rifle Glen
Bilwon
Palm Cove
Clifton Beach
Yorkeys Knob
Smithfield Heights
Machans Beach
Mount Mulligan
Thornborough
Kingsborough
Layland
Biboohra
Kuranda
BARRON GORGE NP
Yarrabah
Cape Grafton
Fitzroy Island
Mungana
Chillagoe
Mareeba
White Rock
CAIRNS
CHILLAGOE LIMESTONE CAVES
CHILLAGOE MUNGANA CAVES NP
Dimbulah
Tabacum
Walkamin Carbeen
Edmonton
Kamma
GREY PEAKS NP
Almaden
Petford
Mutchilba
Rocky Creek
Kairi
Tinaroo Falls
Gordonvale
Little Mulgrave
Meringa
Pyramid
Aloomba
Charringa
Meerawa
Tobias
Crystal Brook
Tolga
Tinaburra
Fishery Falls
McDonnell Creek
Atherton
Figtree Creek
Deeral
Cucania
Watsonville
Herberton
Tarzali
Yungaburra
Malanda
Bellenden Ker
Bramston Beach
Irvinebank
Kalunga
Topaz
Babinda
Three Mile Mountain
MILLAA MILLAA FALLS
Miriwinni
WOOROONOORAN NP
Evelyn
Tumoulin
Millaa Millaa
Flying Fish Point
ELLA BAY NP
Cooper Point
Howie Reef
Mount Garnet
Ravenshoe
PALMERSTON
Innisfail
Mourilyan
Innot Hot Springs
Uramo
MILLSTREAM FALLS
Blunder Creek
South Johnstone
Mena Creek
Hayter Point
Double Point
Ben Avon
WOOROONOORAN NP
Cardstone
JAPOON NP
Silkwood
Cowley Beach
KURRIMINE BEACH NP
CARDWELL RANGE
TULLY FALLS
TULLY GORGE NATIONAL PARK
El Arish
Kurrimine Beach
Bingil Bay
Mission Beach
Tully
Wongaling Beach
Dunk Island
South Mission Beach
FORTY MILE SCRUB NATIONAL PARK
TULLY GORGE WHITEWATER RAFTING
Euramo
Bedarra Island
Family Islands
UNDARA RESORT
KIRRAMA NATIONAL PARK
MURRAY FALLS
Tully Heads
GIRRAMAY NP
Leverdale
Bilyana
Rockingham Bay
Brook Island
South Island
UNDARA VOLCANIC NATIONAL PARK
Kennedy
Missionary Bay
Shepherd Island
GREAT BARRIER REEF
MOUNT ROSEY RESOURCES RES
KINRARA NATIONAL PARK
GIRRINGUN NATIONAL PARK
Cardwell
Hinchinbrook Island
HINCHINBROOK ISLAND NP
GREAT BARRIER REEF MARINE PARK
Kinrara
EMU PLAINS
Abergowrie
Bishop Peak
Hillcock Point
Mulligan Bay
George Point
Spring Creek
Conjuboy
The Gap
Wyandotte
Lannercost
Trebonne
Halifax
ORPHEUS ISLAND NP
Orpheus Island (Goolboddi)
Jervoise
WALLAMAN FALLS
MOUNT FOX FOREST RESERVE
Ingham
Toobanna
Taylors Beach
Forrest Beach
Great Palm Island
PALM ISLAND
Oasis Roadhouse
Lucky Downs
Gadara
Ryeburn
VOLCANO
Michael Creek
Bambaroo
HALIFAX BAY WETLANDS NP
Mutarnee
Great Palm Island
South West Cape
White Rock (Albino Rock)
Greenvale
JOURAMA FALLS
PALUMA RANGE NP
Paluma
Balgal Beach
Rollingstone
Acheron Island
Rattlesnake Island
MAGNETIC ISLAND NP
MCCLELLANDS LOOKOUT
Blue Range
Charlesford
Magnetic Island
Horseshoe Bay
Nelly Bay
Cape Cleveland
Blue Water Springs Roadhouse
PALUMA RANGE NATIONAL PARK
Jalloonda
Bluewater
Pallarenda
Picnic Bay
Cleveland Bay
Christmas Creek
HERVEY RANGE
Garbutt
TOWNSVILLE
Oonoonba
HISTORIC TOWN
AUSTRALIAN INSTITUTE OF MARINE SCIENCE
Bowling Green Bay
Thuringowa
Cluden
Alligator Creek
Cundalla
Giru
TOWNSVILLE TRAINING AREA
Woodstock
BOWLING GREEN BAY NATIONAL PARK
MINGELA SF
Reid River
DALRYMPLE NP
Mingela
TO AYR
GREAT BASALT WALL NATIONAL PARK
Macrossan
TO CHARTERS TOWERS
Joins map 610

TOWNSVILLE (inset)

CLEVELAND BAY
Jupiters Townsville Hotel & Casino
Marina
Anzac Memorial Park
St James Cathedral
Town Hall
FLINDERS ST
Flinders Mall
South Townsville
0 500 m
N

Accommodation
Aquarius on the Beach 1 F1
Holiday Inn Townsville 2 G3
Leisure Inn Plaza Hotel 3 G3
Reef Lodge Backpackers 4 H2
Rydges Southbank Townsville Hotel 5 G3
Note: Only a sample range of accommodation is listed; inclusion is not necessarily a recommendation.

General Information
Police Station 6 G3
Post Office 7 G2
Qantas Travel Centre 8 G2
Town Hall 9 G2
Townsville Transit Centre 10 H3

Vehicle Ferry Terminal 11 H2
Visitor Information 12 G2

Places of Interest
Perc Tucker Regional Gallery 13 G3
Flinders Mall 14 G3
Jupiters Townsville Hotel & Casino 15 H1
Maritime Museum of Townsville 16 H2
Museum of Tropical Queensland 17 H2
Reef HQ Aquarium & Imax Dome Theatre 18 H2
St James Cathedral 19 G2
Townsville Entertainment & Convention Centre 20 H1

For more detail on Cairns & Surrounds see page 607

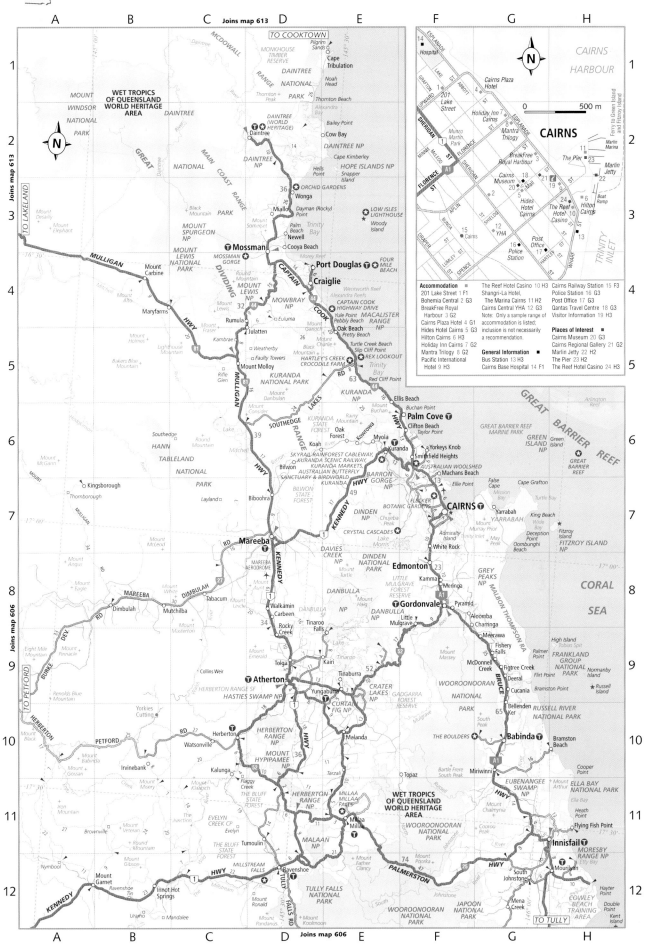

TO COOKTOWN

Joins map 613

TO LAKELAND

Joins map 606

TO PETFORD

TO TULLY

Accommodation ■
201 Lake Street 1 F1
Bohemia Central 2 G3
BreakFree Royal
  Harbour 3 G2
Cairns Plaza Hotel 4 G1
Hides Hotel Cairns 5 G3
Hilton Cairns 6 H3
Holiday Inn Cairns 7 G2
Mantra Trilogy 8 G2
Pacific International
  Hotel 9 H3

The Reef Hotel Casino 10 H3
Shangri-La Hotel,
  The Marina Cairns 11 H2
Cairns Central YHA 12 G3
Note: Only a sample range of
accommodation is listed;
inclusion is not necessarily
a recommendation.

General Information ■
Bus Station 13 H3
Cairns Base Hospital 14 F1

Cairns Railway Station 15 F3
Police Station 16 G3
Post Office 17 G3
Qantas Travel Centre 18 G3
Visitor Information 19 H3

Places of Interest ■
Cairns Museum 20 G3
Cairns Regional Gallery 21 G2
Marlin Jetty 22 H2
The Pier 23 H2
The Reef Hotel Casino 24 H3

CAIRNS

CAIRNS HARBOUR

TRINITY INLET

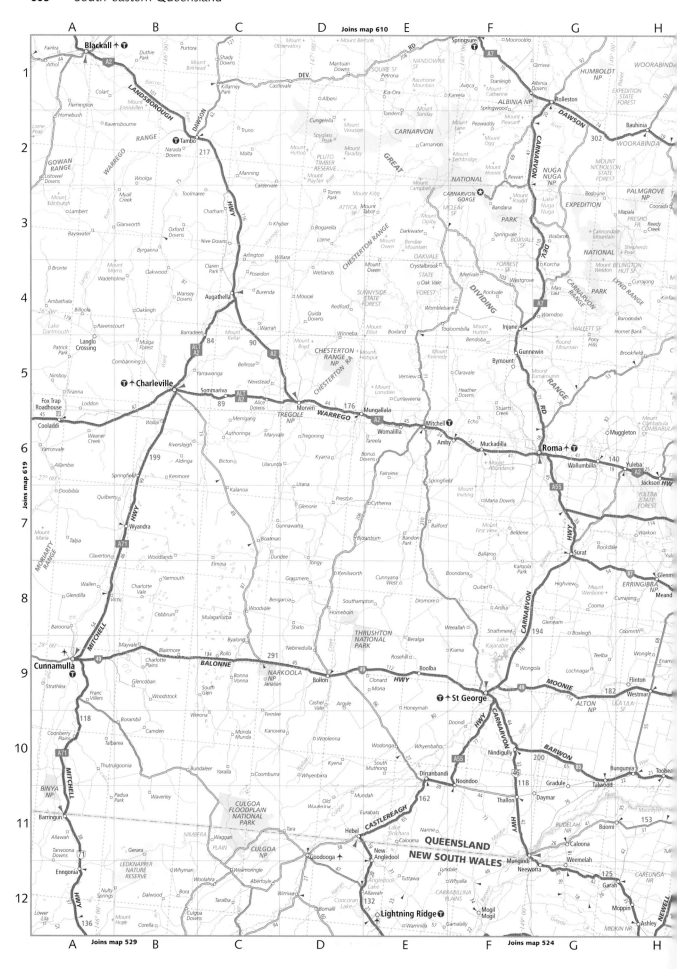

Joins map 610

Joins map 619

Joins map 524

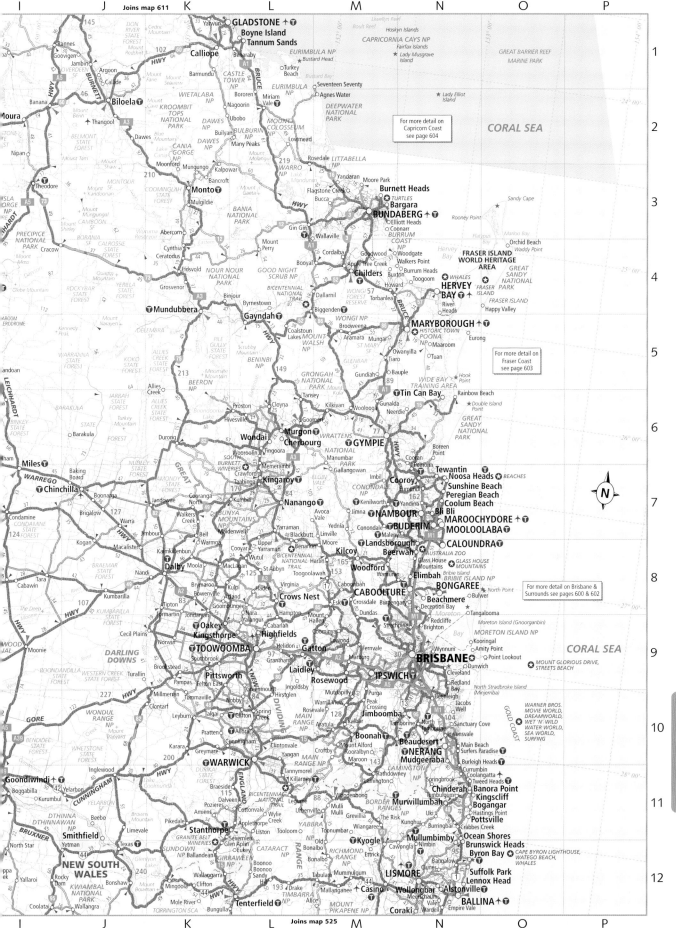

0 25 50 75 100 km

I J K L M N O P

GLADSTONE
Boyne Island
Tannum Sands
Calliope
Benaraby
Yarwun
145
102
60
Barmundu
BURNETT
HWY
Rannes
Goovigen
Jambin
OVERDEEN
A5
Argoon
Calide
46
A3
Thangool
Banana
60
Biloela
Moura
19
36
Nipan

CASTLE
TOWER
NP
EURIMBULA NP
Miriam
Vale
Turkey
Beach
BRUCE
Bustard Head
CAPRICORNIA CAYS NP
Fairfax Islands
Hoskyn Islands
Lady Musgrave
Island
GREAT BARRIER REEF
MARINE PARK

Bustard Bay
Seventeen Seventy
Agnes Water
Lady Elliot
Island
CORAL SEA

KROOMBIT
TOPS
NATIONAL
PARK
WIETALABA
NP
Bororen
Nagoorin
Ubobo
Builyan
Many Peaks
MOUNT
COLOSSEUM
NP
BULBURIN
NP
Lowmead

DAWES
NP
DAWES
NP
CANIA
GORGE
NP
Moonford
Kalpowar
Mungungo
Bancroft
210
Monto
Mulgildie

For more detail on
Capricorn Coast
see page 604

24° 00'

WARRO
NP
219
Rosedale
LITTABELLA
NP
Moore Park
Yandaran
16
Flagstone Creek
Bucca
Burnett Heads
Bargara
BUNDABERG
Elliott Heads
Coonarr
HWY
38
Gin Gin
Wallaville
A1
Cordalba
BURRUM
COAST

25° 00'

Goodwood
Woodgate
Walkers Point
Burrum Heads
Apple Tree Creek
Childers
Buxton
Toogoom
Howard
WHALES
HERVEY
BAY
River
Heads
Torbanlea
Happy Valley

FRASER ISLAND
WORLD HERITAGE
AREA
GREAT
SANDY
NATIONAL
PARK
FRASER
ISLAND
FRASER ISLAND

Orchid Beach
Waddy Point
Rooney Point
Platypus Bay
Marloo Bay
Sandy Cape

Hervey
Bay

Precipice
NATIONAL
PARK
Cracow
BORANIA
CALROSSIE
STATE
FOREST
Abercorn
Cynthia
Ceratodus
Eidsvold
Cambolon
SF
44
12
Mount
Perry
Booyal
MARYBOROUGH
HISTORIC TOWN
POONA
Maaroom

Mundubbera
Grosvenor
Binjour
Byrnestown
Dallarnil
Biggenden
Owanyilla
Tiaro
Tuan
Eurong

For more detail on
Fraser Coast
see page 603

Gayndah
Coalstoun
Lakes
MOUNT
WALSH
NP
Broweena
Aramara
Mungar
ST MARY
SF
57
Bauple
WIDE BAY
TRAINING AREA
Hook Point

NOUR NOUR
NATIONAL
PARK
GOOD NIGHT
SCRUB NP
BICENTENNIAL
NATIONAL
TRAIL
WONGI
FOREST
RESERVE
WONGI NP
BENINBI
NP
149
213
BEERON
NP
GRONGAH
NATIONAL
PARK
GLENBAR
SF
Gundiah
89
Tansey
Tin Can Bay
Rainbow Beach
Double Island
Point

Allies
Creek
ALLIES
CREEK
STATE
FOREST
Proston
Cloyna
Kilkivan
Gunalda
Neerdie
GREAT
SANDY
NATIONAL
PARK

26° 00'

Barakula
Durong
Hivesville
Goomeri
Woolooga
77
41
34
Boreen
Point

Wondai
Cherbourg
Murgon
GYMPIE
Cooran
Pomona

Miles
Chinchilla
SOUTH
BURNETT
WINERIES
Wooroolin
Memerambi
Kingaroy
Nanango
Crawford
Taabinga
Kumbia
84
Tingoora
ELGIN
VALE
SF
WRATTENS
NATIONAL
PARK
Manumbar
Gallangowan
CONONDALE
NP
Imbil
Kenilworth
Tewantin
Noosa Heads
BEACHES
Cooroy
Sunshine Beach
Peregian Beach
Coolum Beach
Eumundi
Yandina
162
Bli Bli
MAROOCHYDORE
MOOLOOLABA

Chinchilla
WARREGO
Boonara
Brigalow
127
Jandowae
Cooranga
North
Walkers
Creek
49
DUNYA
MOUNTAINS
NP
Maidenwell
Yarraman
48
Blackbutt
Benarkin
Moore
Jimna
Yednia
Condale
Malepy
NAMBOUR
BUDERIM
CALOUNDRA

Kogan
Macalister
Kaimkillenbun
Bell
Warmga
Cooyar
Upper
Yarraman
Wutul
Harlin
Kilcoy
Beerwah
Landsborough
Woodford
AUSTRALIA ZOO
GLASS HOUSE
MOUNTAINS
Glass House
Mountains
Bribie
ISLAND

Dalby
Moola
124
Tara
Cabawin
Kumbarilla
Brymaroo
Bowenville
Acland
MacLagan
125
St Aubyn
Toogoolawah
153
Elimbah
Wamuran
BONGAREE
Beachmere

The Deep
KUMBARILLA
STATE
FOREST
Moonie
Tipton
83
Jondaryan
Goombungee
Nara
Yalangur
Haden
Cabarlah
Virginia
Caboolture
CABOOLTURE
Burpengary
Deception
Bay
Redcliffe
Brighton
North Point
BRIBIE ISLAND NP
Bulwer
Tangalooma

For more detail on Brisbane &
Surrounds see pages 600 & 602

27° 00'

Cecil Plains
Formartin
Oakey
Kingsthorpe
Highfields
Hampton
Mount
Hallen
Esk
Crossdale
Dundas
Strathpine
Goominya
MORETON ISLAND NP
Moreton Island (Gnoorganbin)
Moreton
Bay

Moonie
Norwin
DARLING
DOWNS
Brookstead
TOOWOOMBA
Southbrook
Helidon
Gatton
97
Grantham
Lowood
Fernvale
Marburg
42
BRISBANE
Wynnum
Cleveland
Dunwich
Amity Point
Point Lookout
Kooringal
North Stradbroke Island
(Minjerriba)
MOUNT GLORIOUS DRIVE,
STREETS BEACH
CORAL SEA

28° 00'

Pittsworth
Felton East
Pampas
Millmerran
Tummaville
Clontarf
Nobby
Talgai
Laidley
Rosewood
Ingoldsby
Mutdapilly
Purga
IPSWICH
Warrill View
Peak
Crossing
13
Redland
Bay
Jacobs
Well
104
Sanctuary Cove
GOLD COAST
WARNER BROS.
MOVIE WORLD,
DREAMWORLD,
WET 'N' WILD
WATER WORLD,
SEA WORLD,
SURFING

227
WONDUL
RANGE
NP
Leyburn
Spring
Creek
Clifton
Pratten
Allora
MAIN
RANGE NP
128
Rosevale
Aratula
Kalbar
Boonah
Jimboomba
Tamborine
North
Helensvale
Main Beach
Surfers Paradise
Burleigh Heads

Goondiwindi
Yelarbon
42
Inglewood
Karara
Greymare
WARWICK
DUNKAI
STATE
FOREST
200
Clintonvale
Yangan
Croftby
Mount Alford
Kooralbyn
Maroon
143
NERANG
Mudgeeraba
Currumbin
Coolangatta
Tweed Heads
LAMINGTON
NP
Springbrook
Chinderah
Banora Point
Kingscliff
Bogangar
Hastings Point
Pottsville

Boggabilla
Kurumbul
YELARBON
SF
Beebo
Pikedale
Dalveen
Cottonvale
Amiens
115
Pozieres
Legume
Urbenville
Grevillia
Mulli
Mulli
The Risk
Uki
BORDER
RANGES
Murwillumbah
Burringbar
Crabbes Creek
Ocean Shores

DTHINNA
DTHINNAWAN
NP
Smithfield
Yetman
Limevale
Texas
SUNDOWN
NP
Ballandean
Glen Aplin
Eukey
Liston
Tooloom
Toonumbar
Wiangaree
Kunghur
Nimbin
Mullumbimby
Brunswick Heads
Byron Bay
CAPE BYRON LIGHTHOUSE,
WATEGO BEACH,
WHALES

NEW SOUTH
WALES
240
GRANITE BELT
WINERIES
Severnlea
Stanthorpe
GIRRAWEEN
NP
CATARACT
NP
Bonalbo
Bonalbo
Ettrick
Kyogle
Cawongla
Bangalow
Clunes
Suffolk Park
Lennox Head
BALLINA

North Star
193
Drake
TIMBARRA
NP
Mallanganee
MOUNT
PIKAPENE NP
LISMORE
Wollongbar
Alstonville
Empire Vale

Coolatai
Wallangra
Wallangarra
Mole River
Bungulla
Tenterfield
Alice
Casino
Coraki
Wardell

NEW SOUTH
WALES
KWIAMBAL
NATIONAL
PARK
Mingoola
Boonoo
Boonoo
Sandy
Hill
TORRINGTON SCA
Tabulam
Mummulgum

I J K L M N O P

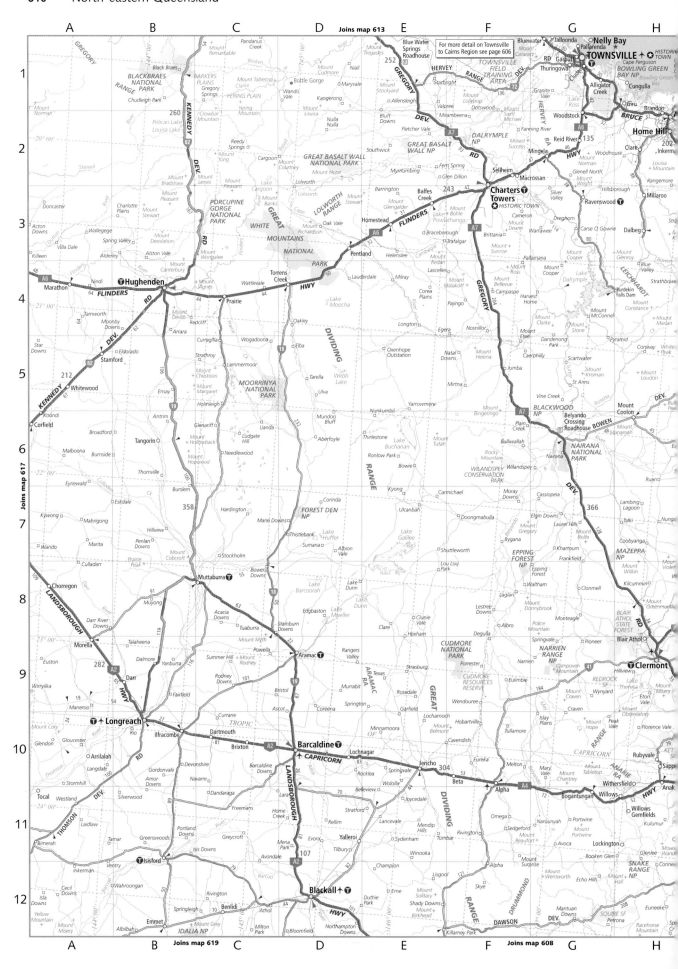

Joins map 613
Joins map 617
Joins map 619
Joins map 608

For more detail on Townsville to Cairns Region see page 606

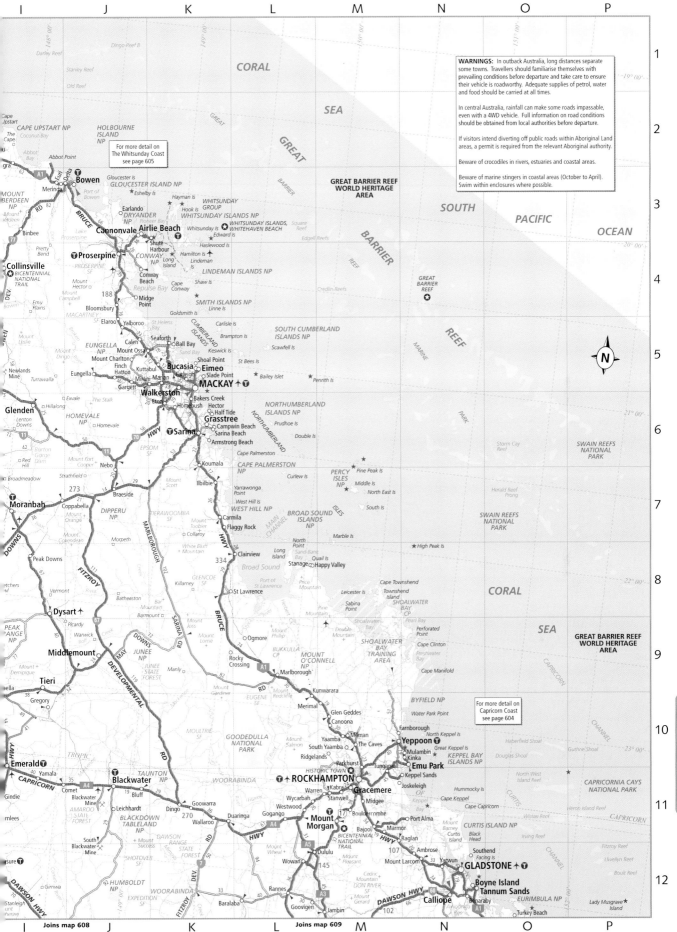

0   25   50   75   100 km

1

CORAL

SEA

GREAT

2

For more detail on The Whitsunday Coast see page 605

WARNINGS: In outback Australia, long distances separate some towns. Travellers should familiarise themselves with prevailing conditions before departure and take care to ensure their vehicle is roadworthy. Adequate supplies of petrol, water and food should be carried at all times.

In central Australia, rainfall can make some roads impassable, even with a 4WD vehicle. Full information on road conditions should be obtained from local authorities before departure.

If visitors intend diverting off public roads within Aboriginal Land areas, a permit is required from the relevant Aboriginal authority.

Beware of crocodiles in rivers, estuaries and coastal areas.

Beware of marine stingers in coastal areas (October to April). Swim within enclosures where possible.

SOUTH   PACIFIC   OCEAN

3

BARRIER

GREAT BARRIER REEF WORLD HERITAGE AREA

4

REEF

5

MARINE

6

SWAIN REEFS NATIONAL PARK

7

SWAIN REEFS NATIONAL PARK

CORAL

8

SEA

GREAT BARRIER REEF WORLD HERITAGE AREA

9

For more detail on Capricorn Coast see page 604

10

CAPRICORNIA CAYS NATIONAL PARK

11

12

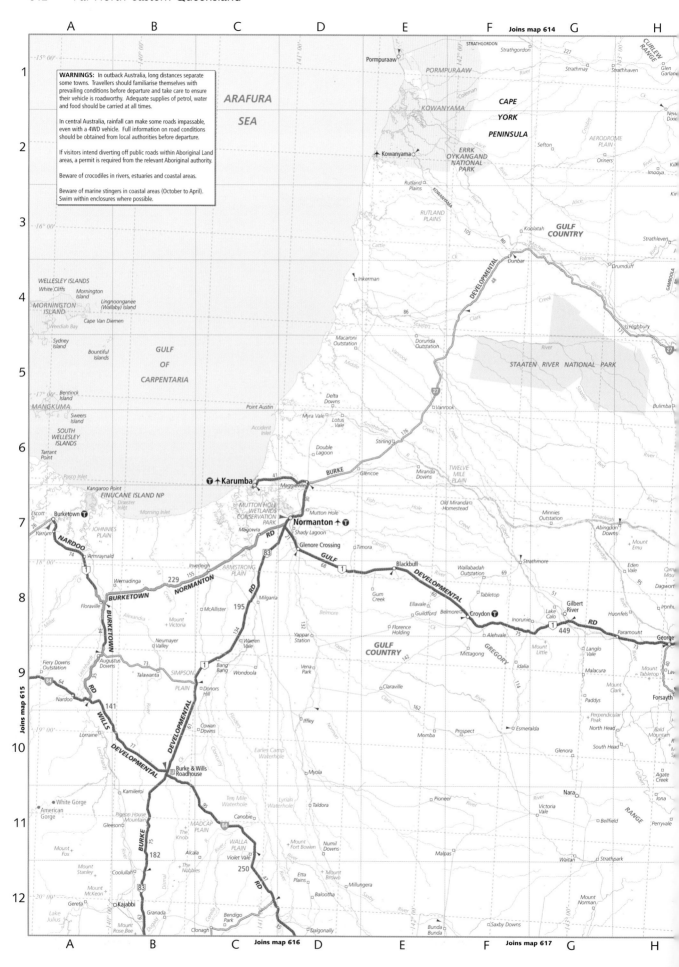

Joins map 614

WARNINGS: In outback Australia, long distances separate some towns. Travellers should familiarise themselves with prevailing conditions before departure and take care to ensure their vehicle is roadworthy. Adequate supplies of petrol, water and food should be carried at all times.

In central Australia, rainfall can make some roads impassable, even with a 4WD vehicle. Full information on road conditions should be obtained from local authorities before departure.

If visitors intend diverting off public roads within Aboriginal Land areas, a permit is required from the relevant Aboriginal authority.

Beware of crocodiles in rivers, estuaries and coastal areas.

Beware of marine stingers in coastal areas (October to April). Swim within enclosures where possible.

Joins map 615

Joins map 616

Joins map 617

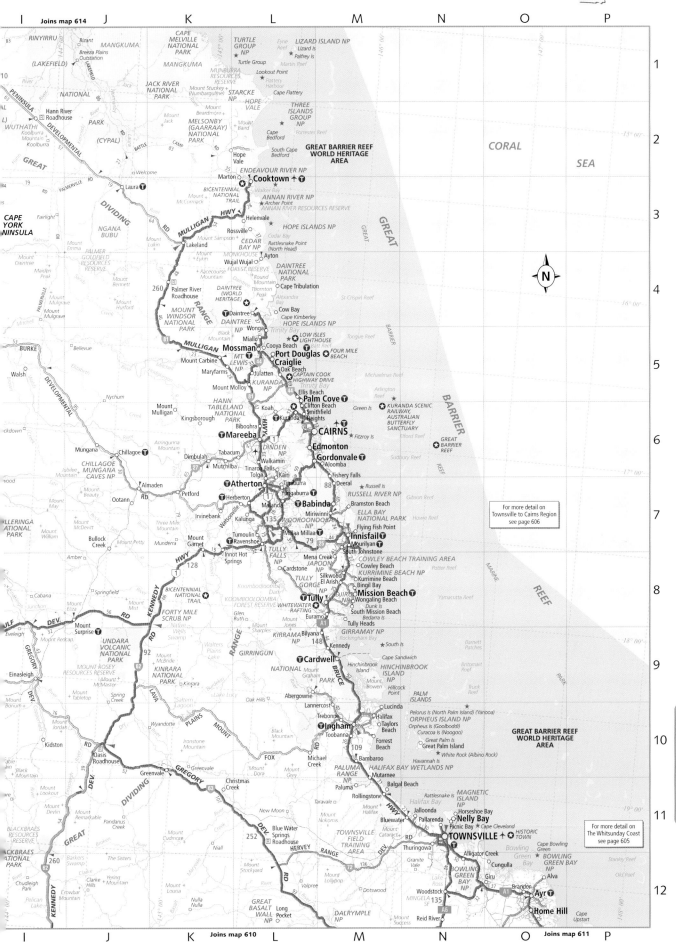

0   25   50   75   100 km

I   J   K   L   M   N   O   P

RINYIRRU
(LAKEFIELD)
Bizant
Breeza Plains
Outstation
MANGKUMA
MANGKUMA

CAPE
MELVILLE
NATIONAL
PARK

TURTLE
GROUP
Turtle Group
Eyne Reef

LIZARD ISLAND NP
Lizard Is
Palfrey Is
Martin Reef

Mount Stuckey
(Numbargulmen)
JACK RIVER
NATIONAL
PARK

MUNBURRA
RESOURCES
RESERVE
STARCKE
NP

Lookout Point
Cape Flattery

CORAL

PENINSULA
Hann River
Roadhouse
LAKEFIELD
River
NATIONAL
PARK
(CYPAL)

DIVIDING
HWY
PALMERVILLE
RD
19
Laura

MELSONBY
(GAARRAAY)
NATIONAL
PARK

CAMP

Mount
Jack

Mount
Beardmore

HOPE
VALE

Hope
Vale

South
Bedford

Cape
Bedford

ENDEAVOUR RIVER NP

THREE
ISLANDS
GROUP
Forrester Reef

GREAT BARRIER REEF
WORLD HERITAGE
AREA

SEA

WUTHATHI
Koolburra
Mountain
Koolburra

GREAT

CAPE
YORK
PENINSULA

Fairlight

NGANA
BUBU

MULLIGAN
HWY

Marton
Cooktown

ENDEAVOUR RIVER NP
Walker Bay

ANNAN RIVER NP
Archer Point
ANNAN RIVER RESOURCES RESERVE

Battery
Harbour

DIVIDING
RANGE

Mount
Emma

PALMER
GOLDFIELD
RESOURCES
RESERVE

Mount
McCormack

Helenvale

Rossville

HOPE ISLANDS NP

GREAT

Mount
Daintree
Maiden
Peak

Bellevue

260
Palmer River
Roadhouse

Lakeland

CEDAR
BAY NP
MONKHOUSE
FOREST RESERVE

Mount Sampson

Ayton
Wujal Wujal

Rattlesnake Point
(North Head)

Cedar Bay

BARRIER

BURKE

Mount
Mulgrave

MOUNT
WINDSOR
NATIONAL
PARK

Mount
Hurford

DAINTREE
(WORLD
HERITAGE)

Racecourse
Mountain

DAINTREE
NATIONAL
PARK

Cape Tribulation

St Crispin Reef

Walsh

Daintree
NP

Black
Mountain

Daintree

Wonga
Miallo

Thornton
Peak

Round
Mountain

Cow Bay
Cape Kimberley
Alexandra
Bay

HOPE ISLANDS NP

DEVELOPMENTAL

Nychum

HANN
TABLELAND
NATIONAL
PARK

Mount Carbine

Mossman

Oak Beach

LOW ISLES
LIGHTHOUSE

Trinity Bay

Mount
Mulligan

Kingsborough

Maryfarms

Mount Molloy

Julatten

KURANDA
NP

Port Douglas
Craiglie

CAPTAIN COOK
HIGHWAY DRIVE
Trinity Bay

FOUR MILE
BEACH

Michaelmas Reef

Arlington
Reef

KURANDA
SCENIC
RAILWAY,
AUSTRALIAN
BUTTERFLY
SANCTUARY

Ellis Beach

BARRIER

Mungana

Chillagoe

Dimbulah

Biboohra

Koah

Palm Cove
Clifton Beach
Smithfield
Kuranda Heights

Green Is

Fitzroy Is

GREAT
BARRIER
REEF

CHILLAGOE
MUNGANA
CAVES NP

Almaden

Tabacum

Mareeba

CAIRNS

Mount
Beauty

Ootann

Petford

Mutchilba

Walkamin

Tinaroo Falls

Tolga
Kairi

DINDEN
NP

Edmonton

Gordonvale
Aloomba

Fishery Falls

Deeral

Sudbury Reef

REEF

Mount
May

Atherton

Herberton

Tinburra
Yungaburra

Malanda

Babinda

Miriwinni

RUSSELL RIVER NP
Russell Is

Gibson Reef

Mount
McDevitt
Mount
William

Irvinebank

Watsonville

Kalunga

135

WOOROONOORAN
NP

Millaa Millaa

79

Bramston Beach

ELLA BAY
NATIONAL PARK

Howie Reef

For more detail on
Townsville to Cairns Region
see page 606

Bullock
Creek

Three Mile
Mountain

Mundera

Mount
Garnet

Tumoulin
Ravenshoe

88
Mena Creek

Flying Fish Point

Innisfail
Mourilyan
South Johnstone

44

Potter Reef

LLERINGA
ATIONAL
PARK

Amber

Mount Petty

HWY

15

Innot Hot
Springs

TULLY
FALLS
NP
JAPOON
NP

Cardstone

El Arish

Silkwood

COWLEY BEACH TRAINING AREA
Cowley Beach
KURRIMINE BEACH NP
Kurrimine Beach
Bingil Bay

MARINE

Cabana

Junction

Mount
Eliza

128

Mount
Mist

BICENTENNIAL
NATIONAL TRAIL

KOOMBOOLOOMBA
Dam

TULLY
GORGE
NP

Tully

DIRRU
NP

Mission Beach
Wongaling Beach

Dunk Is
Bedarra Is

Yamacutta Reef

REEF

Eveleigh

GULF

DEV.

Mount
Surprise

56

RD

UNDARA
VOLCANIC
NATIONAL
PARK

Mount Redcap

FORTY MILE
SCRUB NP

KOOMBOOLOOMBA
FOREST RESERVE

Native
Wells
Swamp

Glen
Ruth

WHITEWATER
RAFTING

Euramo

South Mission Beach

Tully Heads

GIRRAMAY NP
Rockingham Bay

18° 00'

Einasleigh

KINRARA
NATIONAL
PARK

92

Mount
McBride

Kinrara

Walters
Plains
Lake

KENNEDY

Saltern
Lagoon

RANGE

Mount
Jones

KIRRAMA
NP

Bilyana

148

Kennedy

South Is

Cape Sandwich

GIRRINGUN

Cardwell

Hinchinbrook
Island

HINCHINBROOK
ISLAND
NP

Barnett
Patches

Britomart Reef

GREGORY

LAVA

Spring
Creek

Wyandotte

NATIONAL

PARK

Mount
Graham

Mount
Bowen

PALM
ISLANDS

Abergowrie

Hillcock
Point

Kidston

Oasis
Roadhouse

PLAINS

Ironstone
Mountain

Lannercost

Trebonne

Lucinda
Halifax
Taylors
Beach

Pelorus Is (North Palm Island) (Yanooa)
ORPHEUS ISLAND NP
Orpheus Is (Goolboddi)
Curacoa Is (Noogoo)

MOUNT

FOX

Ingham
Toobanna

Great Palm Is
Great Palm Island

White Rock (Albino Rock)

GREAT BARRIER REEF
WORLD HERITAGE
AREA

Greenvale

DEV.

Christmas
Creek

New Moon

Michael
Creek

109

Forrest
Beach

Bambaroo

Havannah Is

260

62

DIVIDING

GREGORY

252

Blue Water
Springs
Roadhouse

HERVEY

Mount
Dora

Mount
Grey

PALUMA
RANGE
NP

Mutarnee

HALIFAX BAY WETLANDS NP

Balgal Beach

MAGNETIC
ISLAND
NP

Rattlesnake Is

Horseshoe Bay
Nelly Bay

GREAT

BLACKBRAES
RESOURCES
RESERVE

The Sisters

Mount
Stockyard

TOWNSVILLE
FIELD
TRAINING
AREA

Paluma

Rollingstone

Taravale

Mount
Halifax

Jalloonda
Bluewater
Pallarenda
Picnic Bay

Halifax Bay

Cape Cleveland

For more detail on
The Whitsunday Coast
see page 605

ACKBRAES
ATIONAL
PARK

Clarke
Hills

Mount
Lollypop

RANGE

DEV.

Thuringowa

TOWNSVILLE
HISTORIC
TOWN

19° 00'

Chudleigh
Park

Crowbar
Mountain

Nulla
Nulla

GREAT
BASALT
WALL
NP

Long
Pocket

Dotswood

Mount
Cataract

136

72

Granite
Vale

Alligator Creek

Cungulla

BOWLING
GREEN BAY
NP

Giru

Woodstock

Reid River

DALRYMPLE
NP

135

Mount
Success

A6

Brandon

Home Hill

Ayr

Stanley Reef

BOWLING
GREEN BAY
NP

Cape Upstart

I   J   K   L   M   N   O   P

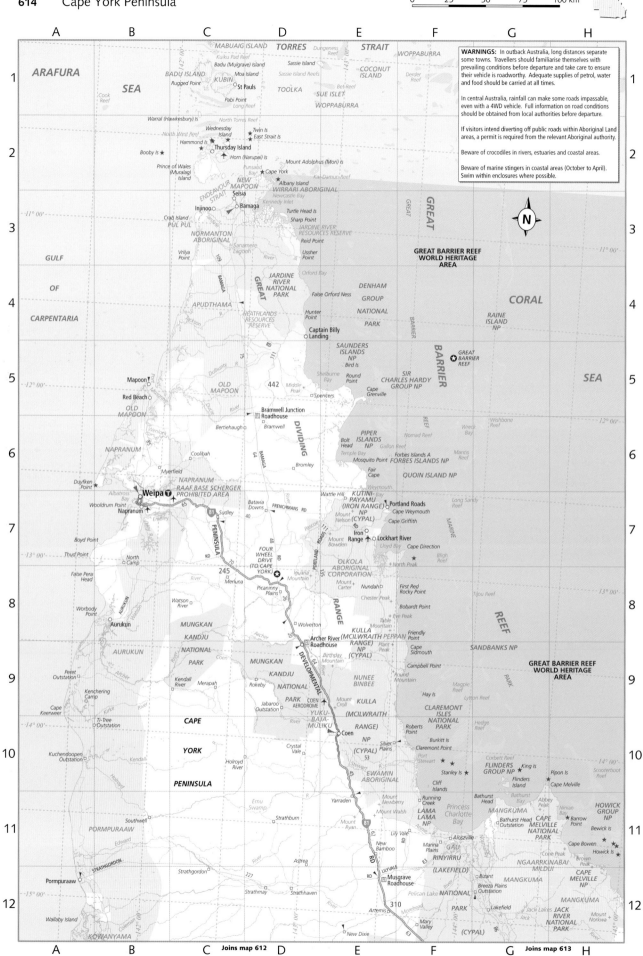

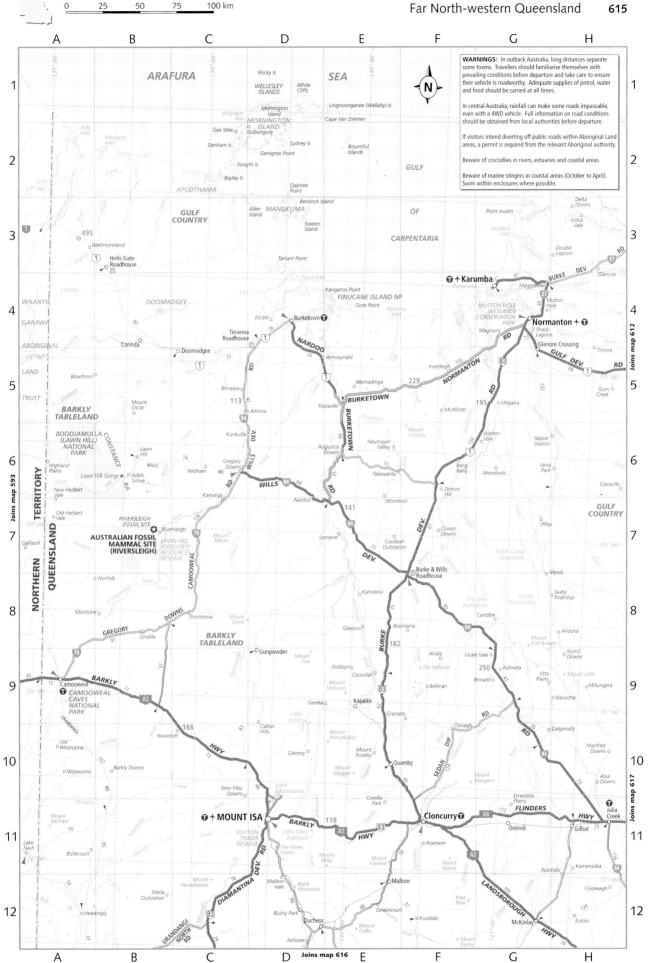

WARNINGS: In outback Australia, long distances separate some towns. Travellers should familiarise themselves with prevailing conditions before departure and take care to ensure their vehicle is roadworthy. Adequate supplies of petrol, water and food should be carried at all times.

In central Australia, rainfall can make some roads impassable, even with a 4WD vehicle. Full information on road conditions should be obtained from local authorities before departure.

If visitors intend diverting off public roads within Aboriginal Land areas, a permit is required from the relevant Aboriginal authority.

Beware of crocodiles in rivers, estuaries and coastal areas.

Beware of marine stingers in coastal areas (October to April). Swim within enclosures where possible.

0 25 50 75 100 km

ARAFURA   SEA

GULF   OF   CARPENTARIA

GULF COUNTRY

NORTHERN TERRITORY

QUEENSLAND

Joins map 593

Joins map 612

Joins map 617

Joins map 616

BARKLY TABLELAND

Mount Isa

Cloncurry

Camooweal

Normanton

Karumba

Burketown

Doomadgee

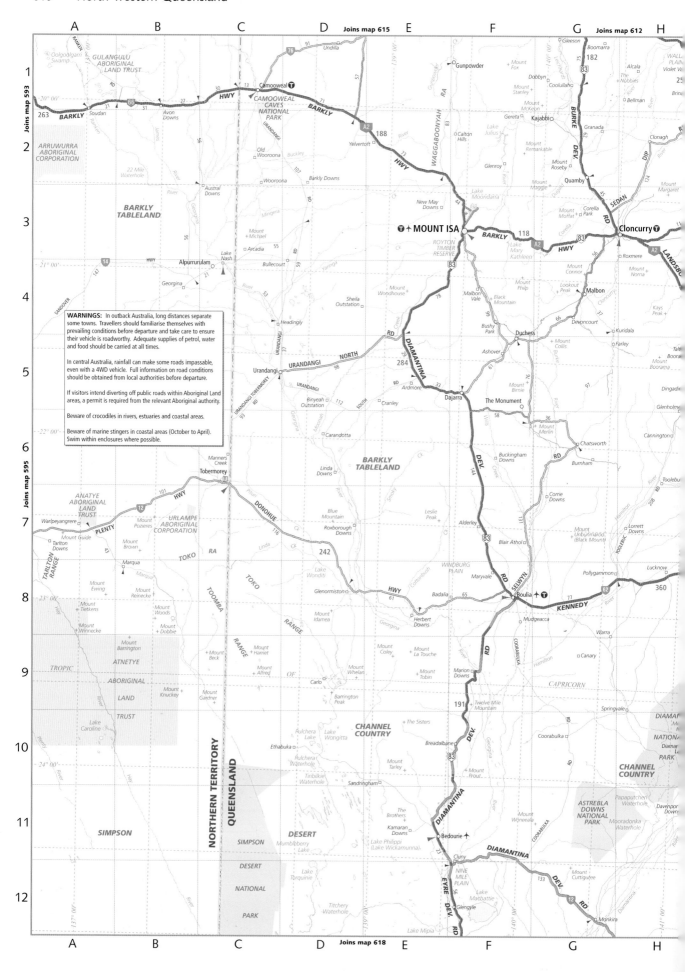

WARNINGS: In outback Australia, long distances separate some towns. Travellers should familiarise themselves with prevailing conditions before departure and take care to ensure their vehicle is roadworthy. Adequate supplies of petrol, water and food should be carried at all times.

In central Australia, rainfall can make some roads impassable, even with a 4WD vehicle. Full information on road conditions should be obtained from local authorities before departure.

If visitors intend diverting off public roads within Aboriginal Land areas, a permit is required from the relevant Aboriginal authority.

Beware of crocodiles in rivers, estuaries and coastal areas.

Beware of marine stingers in coastal areas (October to April). Swim within enclosures where possible.

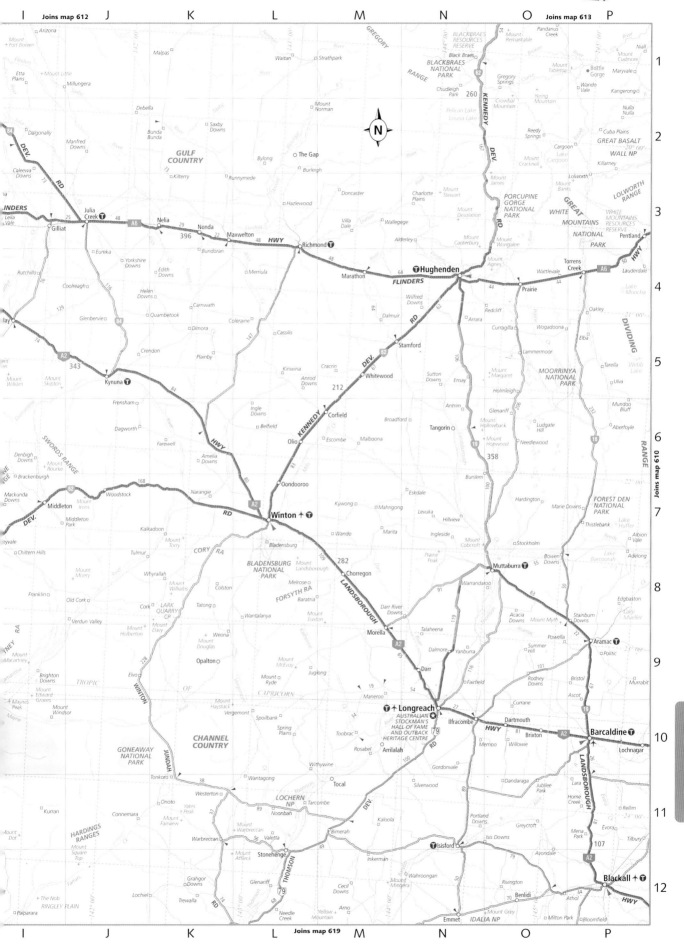

0 25 50 75 100 km

I J K L M N O P

N

1
2
3
4
5
6
7
8
9
10
11
12

I J K L M N O P

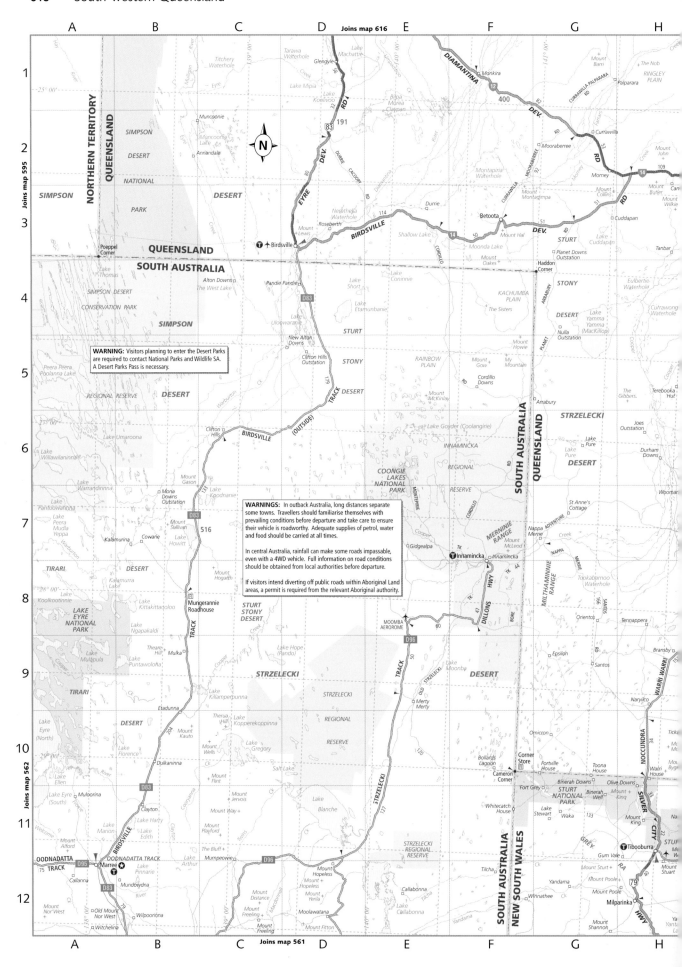

Joins map 595

Joins map 562

WARNING: Visitors planning to enter the Desert Parks are required to contact National Parks and Wildlife SA. A Desert Parks Pass is necessary.

WARNINGS: In outback Australia, long distances separate some towns. Travellers should familiarise themselves with prevailing conditions before departure and take care to ensure their vehicle is roadworthy. Adequate supplies of petrol, water and food should be carried at all times.

In central Australia, rainfall can make some roads impassable, even with a 4WD vehicle. Full information on road conditions should be obtained from local authorities before departure.

If visitors intend diverting off public roads within Aboriginal Land areas, a permit is required from the relevant Aboriginal authority.

0 25 50 75 100 km

I J K L M N O P

Joins map 617

Blackall

Grahgor Downs
Mount Jat Top
Lochiel
Trewalla
Glenariff 79
Cecil Downs
Carella
Arno
Cecil Downs
Wahroongan
Rivington
Athol
Duthie Park
Shady Downs
Killarney Park

Lina Glen
Mount Stewart
Jundah
Mount Moses
Mount Misery
Albilbah
Emmet
Benlidi
Milton Park
Flemington
Colart
Enniskillen
Barcoo
LANDSBOROUGH
101

Manilla Outstation
79 95
Galway Downs
Bonnie Doon
Ramula
Glenlock
Yaraka
Mount Ellen
Mount Grey
Mount Harden
South Terrick
Ravensbourne
Tambo
217
A2

Carranya
THOMSON
Mount Twickenham
Yellow Mountain
Mount Remarkable
Idalia
IDALIA NATIONAL PARK
GOWAN RA
Lambert
Myall Creek
Lower Lansdowne
Toolmaree
A2
116

DIAMANTINA
Windorah
Hammond Downs
CHEVIOT RA
Black Mountain
Collabara
Mount Tighe
Cory Peak
Mount Edinburgh
Bayswater
Byrganna
Cunalama
Buckeys Creek

Clifton
Tenham
Trinidad
HELL HOLE GORGE NATIONAL PARK
Milo
Wakes Lagoon
Bullecourt
Mount Morris
Oakwood
Augathella

Springfield
Bulgroo
Araluen
134
Avon Villa
Bronte
Wadeholme
Barradeen
84
A2

Keeroongooloo
DEV
14
Thylungra
Mount Canaway
Adavale
Ambathala
Oakleigh
Yarrawonga

COLEMAN RANGE
Mount Rouse
Raymore
GREY RANGE
Alaric
Milroy
Wade Hill
MARIALA NATIONAL PARK
Lake Dartmouth
Langlo Crossing
Cairns
Mulga Forest
Combanning
Charleville
Sommariva
89
ALT A2

Malagarga
Mount McCallum
Plevna Downs
Kyabra
Pinkilla
427
Gunnadorah
Mount Gunnadorah
Grenfield
Pingine
Boothulla
Tiranna
Combanning
Merrigang
Authoringa
Bicton

the Blue Hills
Eromanga
67 RD
Whynot
36
Quilpie
DIAMANTINA
Cheepie
68 45
Cooladdi
Fox Trap Roadhouse
Loddon
14
Wallal
Aldinga
Kenmore
Kalanoo

Bellalie
Mount Margaret
Nerrigundah
South Comongin
Napoleon
Fairlie
Mount Prara
Allambie
Bierbank
Yarronvale
Weaner Creek
Springfield
Quilberry
199
A71

Mount Tabbathcubbah
Tobermory
Wombin
Coparella
Wareo
Quilpeta
Mount Martin
Doobibla
Brigalow
Wyandra

Kihee
COOPER
Tindery
Ardoch
Big Creek
Buthana
Mount Bowen
Humeburn
Mount Arthur
Talpa
Claverton
Woodlands
Elmina
Yarmouth

JACKSON AERODROME
Nockatunga
BULLOO
Orinya
Yerrel Creek
Boobera
MORIARTY RANGE
Mount Young
Glendilla
MITCHELL
Victo
Cobbrum
Bendena

Noccundra
NORLEY RANGE
Karwalke
Norley
Alroy
Mount Herbert
Baroona
Tilbooroo
Yowah
BALONNE
49
Blairmore
134
HWY

Thargomindah
Lake Bullawarra
Nooyeah Downs
LAKE BINDEGOLLY NATIONAL PARK
Lake Toomaroo
Lake Bindegolly
Penaroo
Mount West
DEV
RD
Cunnamulla
Charlotte Plains
Glencoban
Woodstock
Bonna Vonna
South Glen

GREY RANGE
Mount Lucas
Mount Gay
Mount Constance
Picarilli
Urimbin
Werewilka
130
WILLIES RANGE
Mount Tunga
BULLOO
198
Eulo
Strathlea
Franc Villers
Brambil
Camden
Werona

STRZELECKI DESERT
Bulloo Downs
Kilcowera
146
Mount Koldonera
Yenloora
Mount Francis
Boorara
Mooning
Gumahah
118
A71
Talbarea
Borambil
Bundaleer
Yaralla

QUEENSLAND
NEW SOUTH WALES
Old Mirintu
Mirintu
CURRAWINYA NATIONAL PARK
Currawinya
Lake Numalla
Caiwarro
Tyrone
Pitherty
Tinnenburra
MITCHELL
Thutrulgoonia
Padua Park
Waverley
CULGOA FLOODPLAIN NATIONAL PARK

BACK PLAIN
Weebah
Hungerford
Ningaling
Lake Wombah
Rockwell
Terraldon
Turra
Barringun
CULGOA NP

Narriearra
Delalah House
Thurloo Downs
Ourimbah
Bindra
Kia Ora
Muttaway
Allawah
136
Gerara
Whyman
Woolahra

Pindera Downs
126
Killowen
Yantabulla
Ella Vale
Enngonia
71
LEDKNAPPER NATURE RESERVE
Dalwood

PINDERA DOWNS ABORIGINAL AREA
Clifton Downs
Urella Downs
Kendabooka
Nardoo
101
Tredega
Youngenina
Springvale
Mount Hope
Corella
Culgoa Downs

102
272
Colane
Yamba
79
Wanaaring
57
Minetta
213
52
HWY

I J K L M N O P

MAPS

TASMANIA

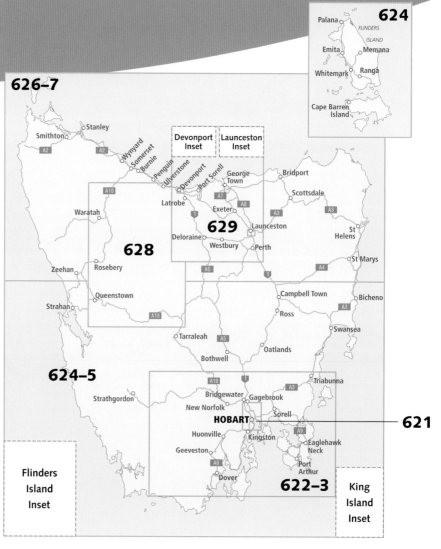

Tasmania

Hobart Suburbs	621
Hobart & Surrounds	622–3
Southern Tasmania	624–5
Northern Tasmania	626–7
Tasmanian Highlands	628
Launceston Region	629

INTER-CITY ROUTES	DISTANCE
Hobart–Launceston via Midland Highway 1	197 km
Hobart–Devonport via Midland & Bass highways 1 B52 1	279 km

0   2   4   6 km

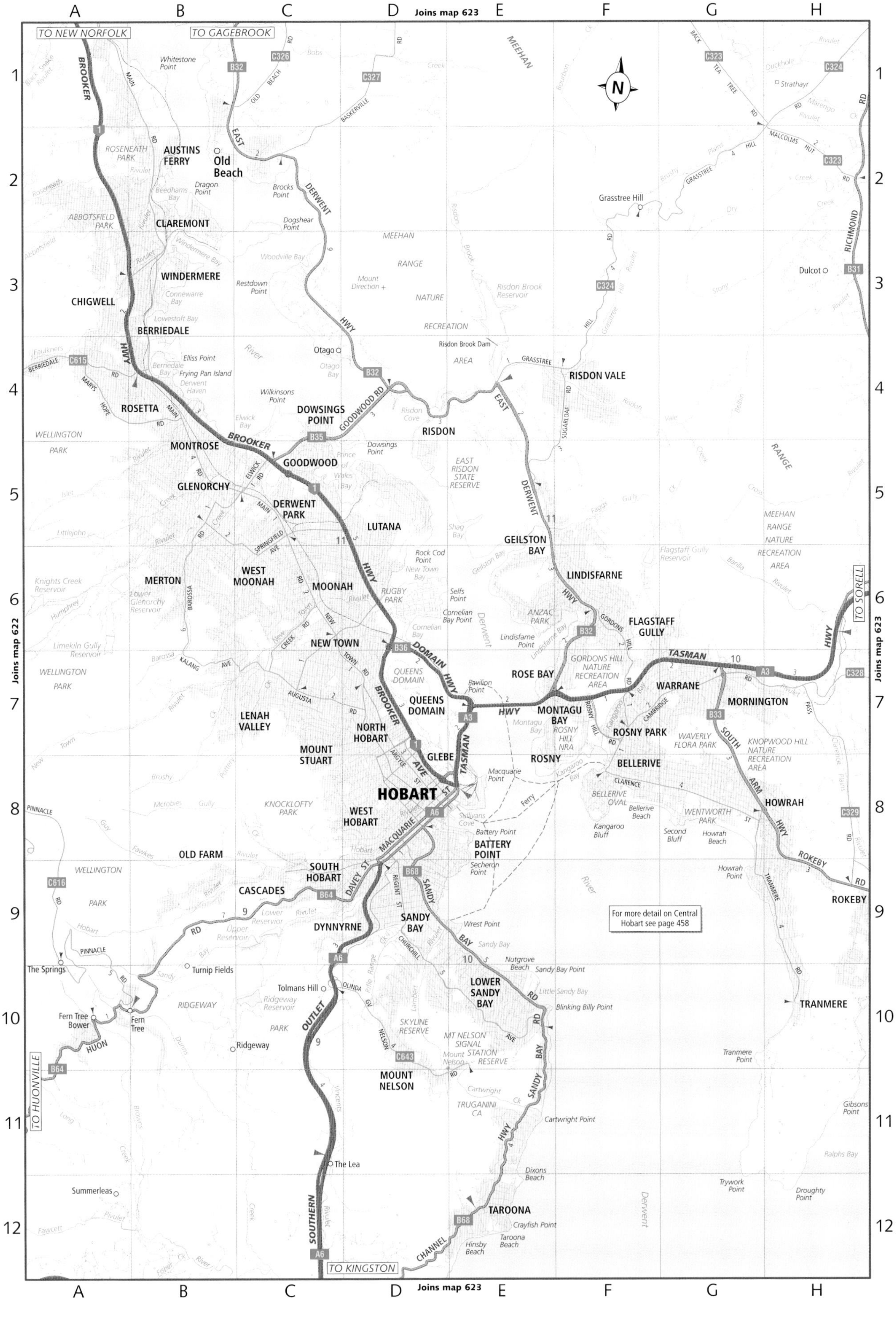

TO NEW NORFOLK
TO GAGEBROOK
Joins map 623

A B C D E F G H

N

BROOKER

Whitestone Point
ROSENEATH PARK
AUSTINS FERRY
Old Beach
Dragon Point
Beedhams Bay
ABBOTSFIELD PARK
CLAREMONT
Brocks Point
Dogshear Point
Windermere Bay
WINDERMERE
Conneware Bay
Woodville Bay
Restdown Point
Mount Direction
CHIGWELL
Lowestoft Bay
BERRIEDALE
Faulkners
BERRIEDALE
Elliss Point
Berriedale Bay
Frying Pan Island
Derwent Haven
ROSETTA
Wilkinsons Point
Otago
Otago Bay
DOWSINGS POINT
RISDON
GOODWOOD RD
Risdon Cove
MONTROSE
GOODWOOD
Prince of Wales Bay
Dowsings Point
Elwick Bay
GLENORCHY
DERWENT PARK
LUTANA

MEEHAN RANGE NATURE RECREATION AREA

Risdon Brook Dam
Risdon Brook Reservoir
GRASSTREE
RISDON VALE
Grasstree Hill
Dulcot
RICHMOND

EAST RISDON STATE RESERVE

DERWENT

Rock Cod Point
New Town Bay
Shag Bay
GEILSTON BAY
Selfs Point
LINDISFARNE
FLAGSTAFF GULLY
Flagstaff Gully Reservoir

MEEHAN RANGE NATURE RECREATION AREA

TO SORELL

MERTON
Lower Glenorchy Reservoir
WEST MOONAH
MOONAH
Rugby Park
Cornelian Bay Point
Cornelian Bay
NEW TOWN
LENAH VALLEY
AUGUSTA
QUEENS DOMAIN
Pavilion Point
ROSE BAY
Lindisfarne Point
GORDONS HILL NATURE RECREATION AREA
MONTAGU BAY
ROSNY HILL NRA
WARRANE
MORNINGTON
TASMAN
Knights Creek Reservoir
Humphreys
WELLINGTON PARK
Limekiln Gully Reservoir
Littlejohn

Knocklofty Park
MOUNT STUART
NORTH HOBART
QUEENS DOMAIN
GLEBE
HOBART
WEST HOBART
BATTERY POINT
Macquarie Point
Sullivans Cove
Battery Point
Secheron Point
ROSNY
Montagu Bay
ROSNY PARK
Waverly Flora Park
BELLERIVE
CLARENCE
BELLERIVE OVAL
Bellerive Beach
WENTWORTH PARK
Second Bluff
Howrah Beach
Howrah Point
HOWRAH
KNOPWOOD HILL NATURE RECREATION AREA
ROKEBY
ROKEBY

OLD FARM
WELLINGTON PARK
CASCADES
SOUTH HOBART
DYNNYRNE
SANDY BAY
Wrest Point
Sandy Bay
Nutgrove Beach
Sandy Bay Point
Little Sandy Bay
LOWER SANDY BAY
Blinking Billy Point
TRANMERE
Tranmere Point
Gibsons Point
Ralphs Bay

The Springs
Fern Tree Bower
Fern Tree
HUON
RIDGEWAY
Turnip Fields
Tolmans Hill
Ridgeway Reservoir
SKYLINE RESERVE
MT NELSON SIGNAL
MOUNT NELSON STATION RESERVE
Ridgeway
Cartwright
TRUGANINI CA
Cartwright Point
Dixons Beach
Trywork Point
Droughty Point

For more detail on Central Hobart see page 458

TO HUONVILLE
Summerleas
The Lea
SOUTHERN
OUTLET
CHANNEL
TO KINGSTON
TAROONA
Crayfish Point
Taroona Beach
Hinsby Beach

Joins map 622
Joins map 623

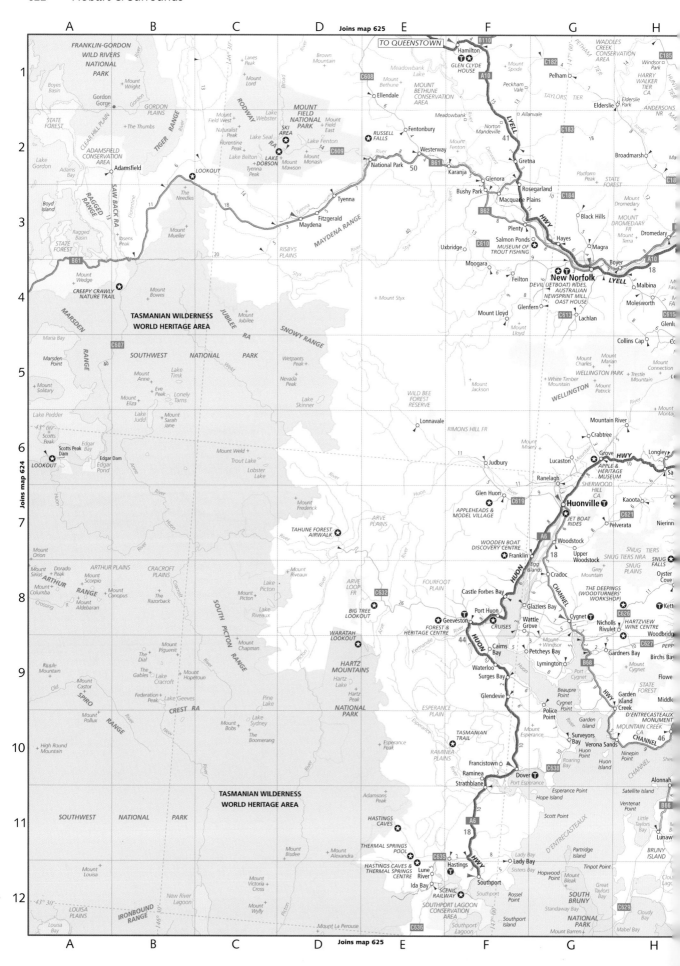

Joins map 625

Joins map 624

Joins map 625

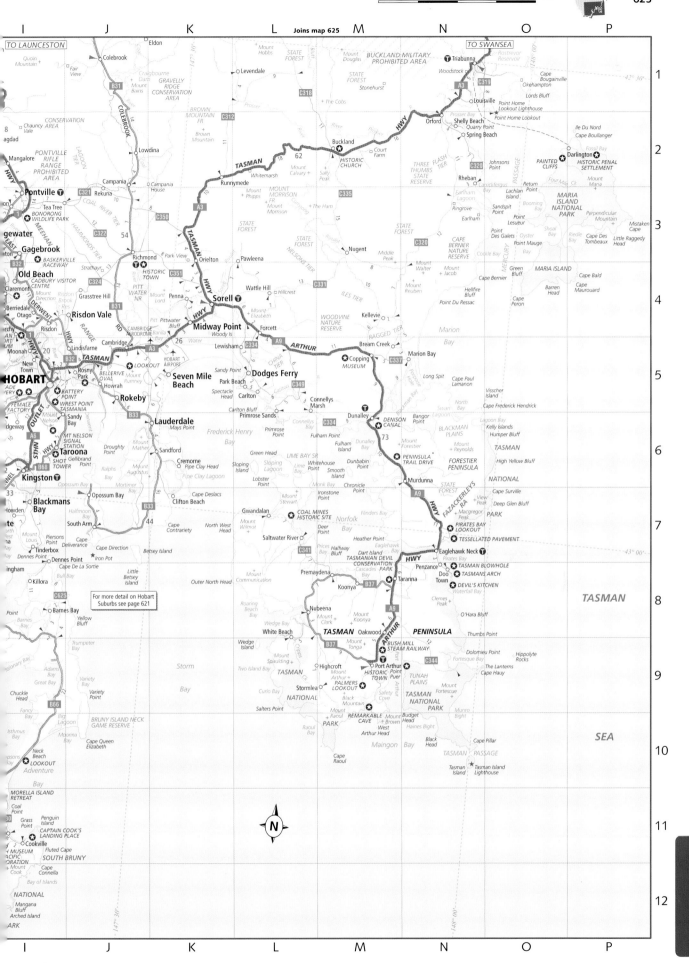

0 5 10 15 20 km

Joins map 625

TO LAUNCESTON

TO SWANSEA

For more detail on Hobart
Suburbs see page 621

N

TASMAN

SEA

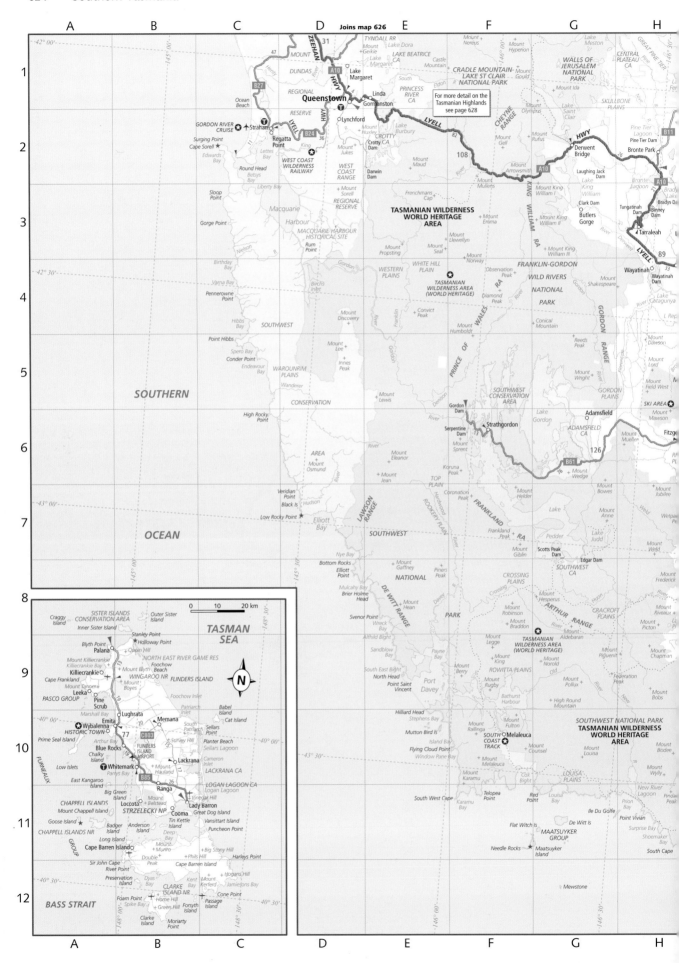

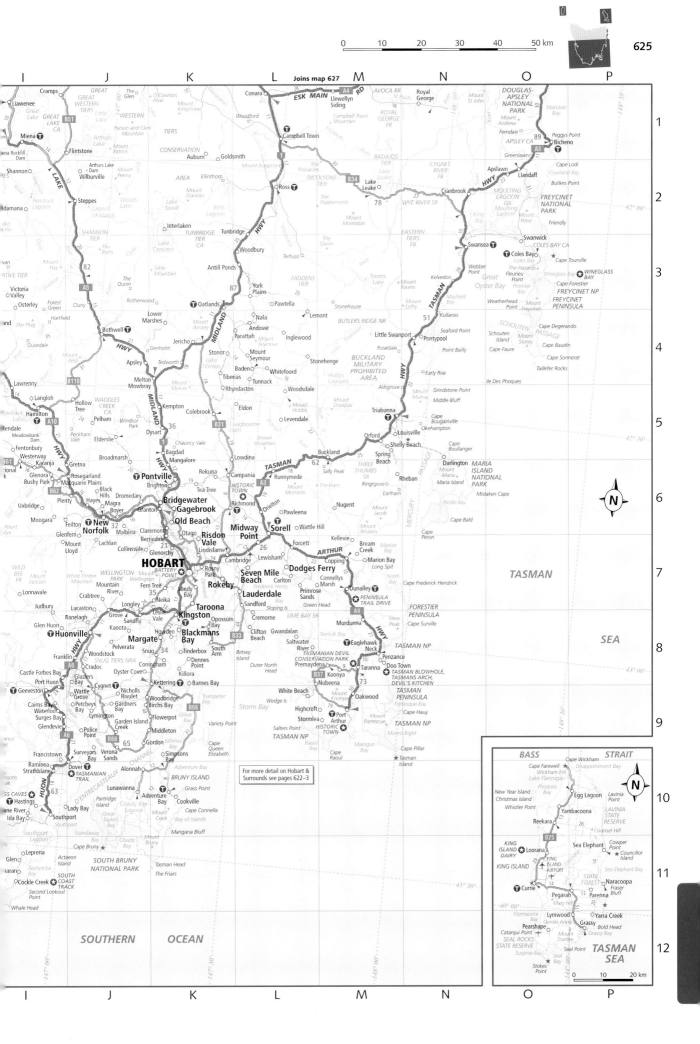

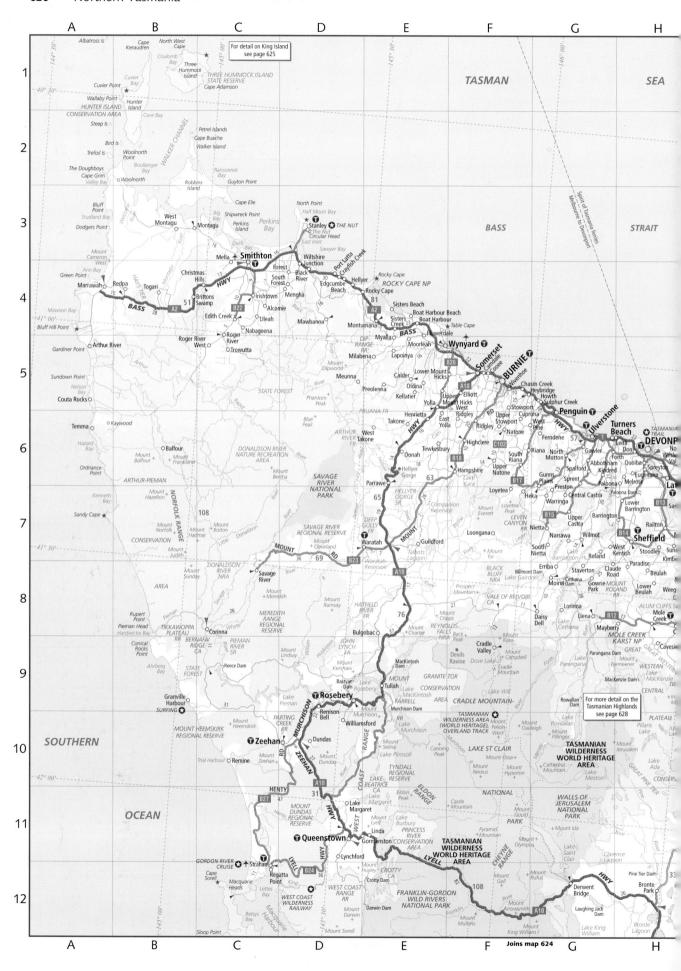

0 10 20 30 40 50 km

For more detail on Flinders Island see page 624

For more detail on Launceston Region see page 629

TASMAN SEA

BANKS STRAIT

Flinders Island

FURNEAUX GROUP

CHAPPELL ISLANDS

CHAPPELL ISLANDS NR

STRZELECKI NP

East Kangaroo Is
Big Green Is
Ranga
B85
Logan Lagoon
Loccota
Lady Barron
LOGAN LAGOON CA
Trousers Point
Mount Beestead
Mount Razorback
Great Dog Is
Goose Is
Mount Chappell Is
Anderson
Badger Island
Pigs Head Point
Tin Kettle Is
Vansittart Is
Long Is
Cape Barren Island
Mount Munro
Big Stony Hill
Boxen Is
Barretts Hill
Double Peak
Cape Barren Island
Mount Kerford Point
Sir John Cape
Neds Point
Deep Bay
Preservation Is
CLARKE ISLAND NR
Seal Point
Kent Bay
Crystal Lagoon
Rum Is
Home Hill
Forsyth Is
Passage Is
Foam Point
Clarke Island
Green Hill
Black Point Is
Lookout Head
Moriarty Point
South Head

CAMERON REGIONAL RESERVE
MUSSELROE BAY CONSERVATION AREA
MOUNT WILLIAM NATIONAL PARK

Cape Portland
Foster Islands
Lyme Regis
Swan Island
Petal Point
Cape Portland
Musselroe Point
Cape Naturaliste
Rushy Lagoon
Musselroe Bay
Stumpys Bay
Boulder Point
Waterhouse Point
Great Musselroe
Icena
Mount William
Cod Bay
Gladstone
Eddystone Point
Purdon Bay
South Mount Cameron
Ansons Bay
Ansons Bay
Winnaleah
Pioneer
Policemans Point
BAY OF FIRES
Herrick
Moorina
The Shades
The Gardens
Derby
Cascade Dam
Big Lagoon
Weldborough
BLUE TIER FR
CONSERVATION AREA
Legerwood
Lottah
Goulds Country
Binalong Bay
Grants Point
Ringarooma
Goshen
Mount Pearson
Priory
ST HELENS CA
Pyengana
Akaroa
Stieglitz
St Helens
Parnella
St Helens Island
Dianas Basin
Beaumaris
SCAMANDER CA
Scamander
Upper Scamander
Henderson Lagoon
Falmouth
NICHOLAS RANGE
Mount Nicholas
Four Mile Creek
Cornwall
St Marys
Gray
Wardlaws Point
Mangana
Fingal
Chain of Lagoons
Piccaninny Point
Thebes Throne
Long Point
DOUGLAS-APSLEY NATIONAL PARK
Seymour
TASMAN SEA
MacLean Bay
Mount Andrew
Ferndale
Peggys Point
Bicheno
APSLEY CA
Greenlawn
Cape Lodi
Llandaff
Apslawn
Butlers Bay
Cranbrook
FREYCINET NATIONAL PARK
Courtland Bay
COLES BAY
Swansea
Swanwick
Mount Stacey
Friendly Point

West Head
Low Head
STONY HEAD ARTILLERY RANGE PROHIBITED AREA
Stony Head
Lulworth
Noland Bay
DOUBLE SANDY POINT CA
Anderson Bay
Beechford
Ninth Island
Waterhouse Island
Croppies Point
St Albans Bay
East Sandy Point
WATERHOUSE CONSERVATION AREA
Waterhouse
Tomahawk
Boobyalla
Waterhouse
Bridport
West Sandy Point
RINGAROOMA BAY
Ringarooma Bay
WHITEROCK TIER
CAMERON
Greens Beach
Low Head
George Town
Weymouth
Back Creek
Leura
PENGUINS
Lefroy
Pipers River
Pipers Brook
B82
B84
North Scottsdale
Forester
Mount Horror
Badger Head
NARAWNTAPU NP
Clarence Point
BRIGGS RR
Bell Bay
The Glen
Glen
Lebrina
Golconda
B81
Lietinna
Nabowla
Scottsdale
Kamona
Telita
Branxholm
RATTLER RANGE
Beauty Point
NORTHERN TASMANIA WINERIES
Rowella
Kayena
Sidmouth
Tunnel
Wyena
West Scottsdale
Tonganah
Tulendeena
Beaconsfield
Lower Turners Marsh
Bangor
Lisle
Springfield
Cuckoo
Legerwood
Flowery Gully
Deviot
Hillwood
Robigana
Mount Direction
North Lilydale
Lilydale
South Springfield
Ringarooma
Goulds
99
TASMAN HWY
A3
Holwell
Gravelly Beach
Karoola
Lalla
MOUNT MAURICE FR
Winkleigh
Exeter
Lanena
Rosevears
Windermere
Dilston
Underwood
Myrtle Bank
Targa
Diddleum Plains
MOUNT VICTORIA FR
Mount Maurice
Talawa
Alberton
West Frankford
Glengarry
Notley Hills
Legana
Rocherlea
Patersonia
St Patricks River
Trenah
Mount Victoria
Mount Albert
Frankford
Bridgenorth
Mowbray
Nunamara
Tayene
Mount Young
Parkham
Birralee
Rosevale
Riverside
Trevallyn
Waverley
Mount Barrow
Mount Saddleback
St Helens
REEDY MARSH FR
B72
Selbourne
LAUNCESTON
HISTORIC TOWN, CATARACT GORGE
St Leonards
Burns Creek
Musselboro
Upper Esk
Reedy Marsh
Weetah
Hadspen
Kings Meadows
Corra Linn
White Hills
Roses Tier
Upper Esk
St Marys
Deloraine
Westwood
Hagley
Carrick
Relbia
Breadalbane
Blessington
Mathinna
Scamander
Exton
Westbury
Pateena
Carr Villa
Legges Tor
SKI AREA
Upper Scamander
Osmaston
Quamby Brook
Glenore
Cluan
Whitemore
Toiberry
Perth
Western Junction
Deddington
Clarendon
Nile
English Town
BEN LOMOND NATIONAL PARK
The Knuckle
Tower Hill
Beaumaris
Golden Valley
Bracknell
Bishopsbourne
Longford
Hampden
FISHERS TIER
Storys Creek
Mangana
B43
Cornwall
Four Mile Creek
Jackeys Marsh
Liffey
Cressy
Kilrae
Powranna
The Retreat
MOSS GULLY CA
Rossarden
Fingal
Gray
Blackwood Creek
B53
Esk Vale
Kelvin Grove
Ellersie
Rostrevor
Ormley
Mount Malcolm
MAIN
FINGAL TIER
Mount Punter
Breona
Poatina
Pisa
Epping Forest
Bona-Vista Estate
Brambletey
Avoca
B42
CASTLE CARY RR
A4
Royal George
Mount Foster
Cramps
Parknook
WESTERN TIERS
Cleveland
Conara
Llewellyn Siding
ST PAULS RR
AVOCA RR
St Pauls
ROYAL GEORGE
Mount St John
DOUGLAS-APSLEY NATIONAL PARK
Liawenee
Mount Blackwood
Rokeby
Woodford
Campbell Town RD
Mount Christie
Mount Henry
Mount Andrew
Ferndale
GREAT LAKE CA
Little Lake
Arthurs Lake
Mount Kingstone
Campbell Town
BADGADIS TIER
Mount Nichols
Peggys Point
Miena
Flintstone
Auburn
Goldsmith
The Pinnacles
Bicheno
Arthurs Lake Dam
Mount Patrick
Mount Penny
CONSERVATION AREA
Auburn
CYGNET RIVER FR
TASMAN HWY
Greenlawn
Shannon Lagoon Springs
Shannon
Wilburville
Ellinthorp
Ross
Lake Leake
Apslawn
St Patricks Plains
Penstock Lagoon
Mount Franklin
Bells Lagoon
Lake Leake
WYE RIVER SR
A3
Cranbrook
Mouting Lagoon
Steppes
The Peppermints
Mount Morriston
Kings Bay
FREYCINET NATIONAL PARK
A5
Woods Lake
Lake Sorell
The Quoin
PARRAMORES TIER
WINGYS TIER
COLES BAY GR
Interlaken
Lake Crescent
TUNBRIDGE TIER CA
Tunbridge
EASTERN TIERS
TASMAN HWY
A3
Swansea
Swanwick
Mount Stacey

Joins map 625

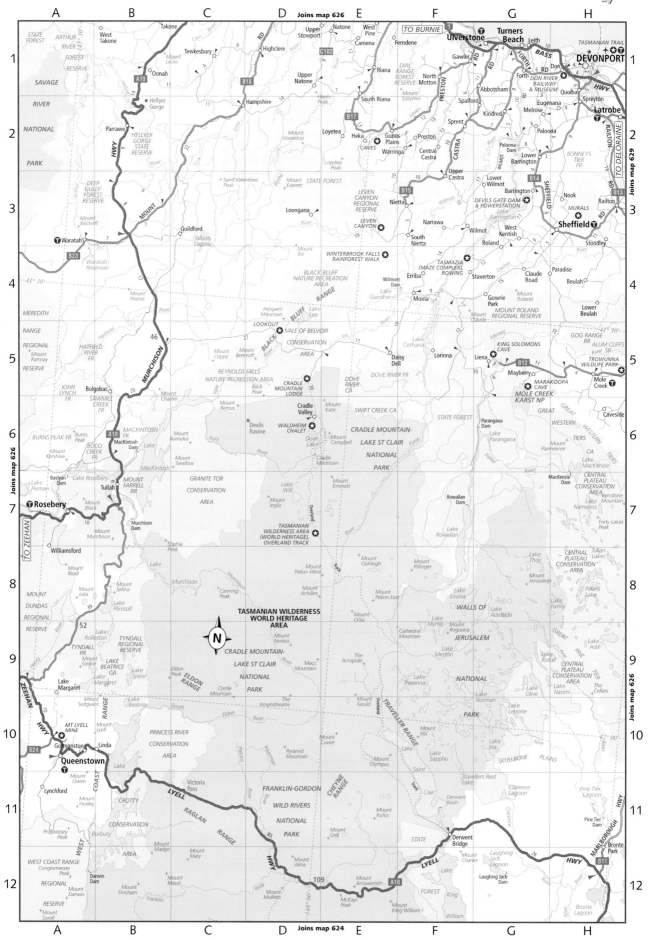

0   5   10   15   20   25 km

Inset A (Devonport)

0   0.5   1 km

Coles Beach
MERSEY BLUFF RESERVE
Mersey Bluff
Bluff Beach
Aitkenhead Spit
Don Junction
Frederick Head

BASS STRAIT

DON RES
DEVONPORT
Pardoe Beach
Pardoe Downs
PARDOE NORTHDOWN CA
TASMANIAN TRAIL
Ferry Terminal
East Devonport
Spirit of Tasmania ferries Melbourne to Devonport

TO ULVERSTONE
Highfield
Berkeley
Stony Rise
BASS
Miandetta
WIENA PARK
MIANDETTA PARK
Victoria Bridge
Rannoch
Panorama Heights
HWY
TO LAUNCESTON
N

Inset B (Launceston)

0   0.5   1 km

TO BEAUTY POINT
TO GEORGE TOWN
STATION
WEST TAMAR HWY
REATTA
DESIGN CENTRE OF TASMANIA
Trevallyn
TREVALLYN STATE RESERVE
LAUNCESTON
HISTORIC TOWN
Elphin
Killafaddy
HOBLERS BRIDGE RD
TO SCOTTSDALE
CATARACT GORGE
ZIG ZAG RESERVE
First Basin
ARBOUR PARK
East Launceston
Newstead
CATARACT GORGE RESERVE
Second Basin
West Launceston
WELLINGTON
South Launceston
Punchbowl
Norwood
LAUNCESTON GOLF COURSE
Glen Dhu
WESTBURY RD
Sandhill
CHARLTON STREET RESERVE
South Norwood
Carr Villa Cemetery
MIDLAND
Prospect
Kings Meadows
C403
COUNTRY CLUB GOLF COURSE
Summerhill
TO DEVONPORT
TO HOBART
N

Main map

TASMAN SEA

Stony Head
Tam O'Shanter Bay
Noland Bay
Pipers Head
41°00'
Spirit of Tasmania ferries Melbourne to Devonport

BASS STRAIT

West Head
Low Head
PENGUINS
MARITIME MUSEUM
Greens Beach
Badger Head
Point Sorell
Egg Island
Hawley Beach
Griffiths Point
NARAWNTAPU NATIONAL PARK
BRIGGS REGIONAL RESERVE
Port Dalrymple
Kelso
Clarence Point
GEORGE Town
Curries River Reservoir
Mount George
LEFROY FOREST RESERVE
Lefroy
STONY HEAD ARTILLERY RANGE
PROHIBITED AREA
Lulworth
Beechford
Five Mile Bluff
Weymouth
Back Creek
Bellingham
Pipers River
Pipers Brook
B82
TO BRIDPORT

TO ULVERSTONE
DEVONPORT
TASMANIAN TRAIL
Don
DON RIVER RAILWAY & MUSEUM
Spreyton
Quoiba
PORT SORELL RD
Northdown
Wesley Vale
Moriarty
Port Sorell
Squeaking Point
Thirlstane
DAZZLER RANGE
Ilfraville
Beauty Point
SEAHORSE WORLD
NORTHERN TASMANIA WINERIES
BEACONSFIELD MINE & HERITAGE CENTRE
Beaconsfield
Bell Bay
Rowella
Kayena
Middle Arm
Sidmouth
BATMAN
Deviot
TAMAR RIVER RESERVE
Paper Beach
Hillwood
Mount Direction
Lower Turners Marsh
Bangor
Tunnel
The Glen
Glen
STATE FOREST
B83
Retreat
Lebrina
LILYDALE FALLS
North Lilydale
Lilydale
Karoola
Lalla
WALKER RHODODENDRON RESERVE
Underwood
LILYDALE
B81
TO SCOTTSDALE

Eugenana
Melrose
B14
Latrobe
BONNEYS TIER FR
Lower Barrington
Nook
RAILTON
Railton
MURALS
Sheffield
B14
Stoodley
Sunnyside
Kimberley
LONG HILL FR
Merseylea
Parkham
Birralee
REEDY MARSH FOREST RESERVE
Sassafras
Sassafras East
FRANKFORD
HOLWELL GORGE SR
COPPERMINE CREEK FR
Holwell
West Frankford
Frankford
Winkleigh
Flowery Gully
Loira
A7
Exeter
Lanena
Gravelly Beach
Robigana
Glengarry
Notley Hills
NOTLEY FERN GORGE
The Tump
Bridgenorth
GRINDELWALD SWISS VILLAGE
Legana
Rosevears
Windermere
Dilston
Rocherlea
Newnham
PROSSERS FR
Mowbray
Invermay
Trevallyn
Waverley
TAMAR
Leam
WEST TAMAR HWY

BASS HWY
RAILTON RD
53
B13
Moltema
Weegena
Elizabeth Town
Dunorlan
Weetah
Reedy Marsh
Selbourne
Glenburn
Rosevale
LAUNCESTON LAKES & WILDLIFE PARK
Riverside
HISTORIC TOWN, CATARACT GORGE, DESIGN CENTRE OF TASMANIA
LAUNCESTON
FEDERAL COUNTRY CLUB CASINO
Prospect
Kings Meadows
St Leonards
Corra Linn
TASMAN HWY
A3
TO SCOTTSDALE

Lower Beulah
GOG RANGE RR
Beulah
Paradise
ALUM CLIFFS SR
TROWUNNA WILDLIFE PARK
Red Hills
Lemana
Exton
BASS
Westwood
Glenvista
Hagley
MEANDER VALLEY
Hadspen
ENTALLY HOUSE
HWY
Carrick
Relbia
Breadalbane
White Hills
FRANKLIN HOUSE
Launceston Airport
Western Junction

B12
MOLE CREEK RD
Mole Creek
Chudleigh
Needles
Deloraine
Westbury
B54
MEANDER HWY
52
Montana
Osmaston
Cluan
Glenore
Whitemore
Oaks
Bishopsbourne
Toiberry
Pateena
ILLAWARRA
B52
Perth
RELBIA RD
Evandale
HISTORIC TOWN
Longford
BRICKENDON HOMESTEAD
WOOLMERS ESTATE
Clarendon
HISTORIC HOUSE
MIDLAND HWY

GREAT WESTERN TIERS
Mount Parmeener
CONSERVATION AREA
DEVILS GULLET SR
MacKenzie Dam
Caveside
Western Creek
Meander
Golden Valley
Quamby Brook
BLACK JACK HILL FR
STOCKERS PLAINS
CLUAN TIERS
STATE FOREST
Bracknell
Liffey
Jackeys Marsh
TO MIENA
A5
CRESSY RD
Richmond Hill
SYMMONS PLAINS RACEWAY
B51

TASMANIAN WILDERNESS WORLD HERITAGE AREA
CENTRAL PLATEAU CONSERVATION AREA
Ironstone Mountain
Mother Cummings Peak

Joins map 628
Joins map 627
Joins map 627

Approximate Distances TASMANIA

	Burnie	Campbell Town	Deloraine	Devonport	Geeveston	George Town	Hobart	Launceston	New Norfolk	Oatlands	Port Arthur	Queenstown	Richmond	Rosebery	St Helens	St Marys	Scottsdale	Smithton	Sorell	Strahan	Swansea	Ulverstone
Burnie		200	101	50	391	204	333	152	328	247	432	163	304	110	300	263	222	88	318	185	267	28
Campbell Town	200		99	150	191	119	133	67	128	47	232	304	104	357	122	85	137	288	118	344	67	172
Deloraine	101	99		51	290	103	232	51	227	146	331	207	203	211	199	162	121	189	217	247	166	73
Devonport	50	150	51		341	154	283	102	278	197	382	213	254	160	250	213	172	138	268	235	217	22
Geeveston	391	191	290	341		310	58	258	95	144	157	308	85	361	313	276	328	479	84	348	197	363
George Town	204	119	103	154	310		252	52	247	166	351	310	223	314	182	182	83	292	237	350	186	176
Hobart	333	133	232	283	58	252		200	37	86	99	250	27	303	265	228	270	421	26	290	139	305
Launceston	152	67	51	102	258	52	200		195	114	299	258	171	262	167	130	70	240	185	298	134	124
New Norfolk	328	128	227	278	95	247	37	195		81	136	213	64	266	250	213	265	416	63	253	176	300
Oatlands	247	47	146	197	144	166	86	114	81		175	257	57	310	169	132	184	335	71	297	125	219
Port Arthur	432	232	331	382	157	351	99	299	136	175		349	87	402	312	275	369	520	73	389	186	404
Queenstown	163	304	207	213	308	310	250	258	213	257	349		277	53	426	389	328	253	276	40	389	191
Richmond	304	104	203	254	85	223	27	171	64	57	87	277		330	226	189	241	392	14	317	123	276
Rosebery	110	357	211	160	361	314	303	262	266	310	402	53	330		410	373	332	222	329	75	442	138
St Helens	300	122	199	250	313	182	265	167	250	169	312	426	226	410		37	99	388	240	466	126	272
St Marys	263	85	162	213	276	182	228	130	213	132	275	389	189	373	37		136	351	203	429	89	235
Scottsdale	222	137	121	172	328	83	270	70	265	184	369	328	241	332	99	136		310	255	368	204	194
Smithton	88	288	189	138	479	292	421	240	416	335	520	253	392	222	388	351	310		406	275	355	116
Sorell	318	118	217	268	84	237	26	185	63	71	73	276	14	329	240	203	255	406		316	113	290
Strahan	185	344	247	235	348	350	290	298	253	297	389	40	317	75	466	429	368	275	316		429	213
Swansea	267	67	166	217	197	186	139	134	176	125	186	389	123	442	126	89	204	355	113	429		239
Ulverstone	28	172	73	22	363	176	305	124	300	219	404	191	276	138	272	235	194	116	290	213	239	

Distances on this chart have been calculated over main roads and do not necessarily reflect the shortest route between towns.

INDEX OF PLACE NAMES

This index includes all towns, localities, roadhouses, national parks and islands shown on the maps and mentioned in the text.

Place names are followed by a map page number and grid reference, and/or the text page number on which that place is mentioned. A page number set in **bold** type indicates the main text entry for that place. For example:

Bedarra Island Qld 606 F6, 613 M8, **393**, 428

Bedarra Island	– Place name
Qld	– State
606 F6, 613 M8	– Bedarra Island appears on these map pages
393, 428	– Bedarra Island is mentioned on these pages
393	– Main entry for Bedarra Island

The alphabetical order followed in the index is that of 'word-by-word' – a space is considered to come before 'A' in the alphabet, and punctuation marks are ignored. For example:

White (Albino) Rock
White Mountains
White Rock
Whitefoord
Whiteheads Creek
Whiteman

Names beginning with Mc are indexed as Mac and those beginning with St as Saint.

The following abbreviations and contractions are used in the index:

ACT	–	Australian Capital Territory
JBT	–	Jervis Bay Territory
NSW	–	New South Wales
NP	–	National Park
NT	–	Northern Territory
Qld	–	Queensland
SA	–	South Australia
Tas.	–	Tasmania
Vic.	–	Victoria
WA	–	Western Australia

A

A1 Mine Settlement Vic. 537 P4, 540 H3
Abbeyard Vic. 543 J10, 544 H9
Abbotsham Tas. 626 G6, 628 G1
Abbott Island NT 591 L3
Abercorn Qld 604 C11, 609 K3
Abercrombie River NP NSW 519 E1, 522 H7, 80
Aberdeen NSW 523 K1, 524 H12, 74
Aberfeldy Vic. 540 H4
Abergowrie Qld 606 E7, 613 L9
Abermain NSW 509 E2, 514 A8, 523 L4
Abutilon Island WA 575 D1, 582 B5
Acacia NT 588 E5, 590 D5
Acacia Island Qld 605 F7, 611 K5
Acheron Vic. 534 F2, 537 N1, 540 F1, 542 F12, 544 B11
Acheron Island Qld 606 G9, 613 N11
Acland Qld 609 K8
Actaeon Island Tas. 625 I11
Acton Park WA 572 C7
Adaminaby NSW 519 B6, 520 E7, 522 E12, 539 D2, **24**
Adamsfield Tas. 622 A2, 624 G6
Adavale Qld 619 M4
Addington Vic. 535 B8, 536 C2, 551 L3
Adelaide SA 553 C7, 554 B9, 555 F2, 556 H7, 559 J9, 568 B3, **210**
Adelaide Lead Vic. 535 B6, 549 L12
Adelaide River NT 588 E8, 590 D6, **356**
Adele Island WA 580 H4, 584 C5
Adelong NSW 519 A4, 520 B2, 522 D10, 543 P2, **25**

Adjungbilly NSW 519 B4, 520 D1, 522 E10
Admiral Island WA 581 I5, 584 C7
Advance Island WA 581 I5, 584 D7
Advancetown Qld 516 G1, 600 F10, 601 C6
Adventure Bay Tas. 623 I11, 625 K10, **470**
Agery SA 556 E4, 558 H7
Agnes Vic. 540 H10
Agnes Banks NSW 510 H4, 513 N7
Agnes Island Qld 606 F7, 613 M9
Agnes Water Qld 604 E8, 609 M2, 427
Agnew WA 576 G1, 578 G11
Ah Chong Island WA 575 D1, 582 B5
Aileron Roadhouse NT 594 H5, **357**
Ailsa Vic. 548 G7
Aipus Island Qld 614 C1
Aireys Inlet Vic. 536 D10, 538 F3, 551 N9, **142**
Airlie Beach Qld 605 F5, 611 J3, **390**
Airlie Island WA 575 C2, 582 A7
Airly Vic. 541 K6
Akaroa Tas. 627 P8
Akens Island Qld 604 A2, 611 M8
Akone Islet Qld 614 D2
Alawoona SA 526 A7, 546 A8, 559 N9, 568 G2
Albacutya Vic. 526 D11, 548 F4
Albany WA 573 D11, 574 G11, 576 E11, **290**
Albany Creek Qld 599 D5, 600 D3, 602 F10
Albany Island Qld 614 D2
Albatross Island SA 558 E9
Albatross Island Tas. 626 A1
Albert NSW 522 C1, 524 A12, 529 P12

Albert Park SA 553 B6, 554 B8, 555 E1
Alberton SA 553 B6
Alberton Tas. 627 N7
Alberton Vic. 541 I9
Alberton West Vic. 541 I9
Albina Rock Tas. 624 C3
Albinia Island Qld 612 A5, 615 D3
Albinia NP Qld 608 F1, 611 I12
Albion Park NSW 517 E6
Albury NSW 522 A12, 527 O12, 543 K6, 545 I2, **25**
Alcomie Tas. 626 C4
Aldersyde WA 574 E5
Aldgate SA 553 E8, 554 C10, 555 G3, 239
Aldinga SA 554 A12, 555 E5, 224
Aldinga Beach SA 554 A12, 555 E6, 556 H9, 559 J10, 568 B4, **224**
Alectown NSW 522 E3
Alexander Morrison NP WA 574 A1, 576 B5
Alexandra Vic. 534 F1, 537 N1, 540 F1, 542 F12, 544 B10, 142
Alexandra Hills Qld 600 F5, 602 G12
Alford SA 556 F2, 559 I6
Alfred NP Vic. 519 C11, 539 F10
Alfred Town NSW 522 C10, 527 P10, 543 N1
Alger Island NT 591 M3
Ali-Curung NT 593 J12, 595 J1
Alice NSW 516 C5, 525 M4, 609 M12
Alice Springs NT 595 I7, 597 J3, **358**
Alison NSW 514 E4, 515 B10
Allambee Vic. 537 O9, 540 G7
Allambee South Vic. 537 O10, 540 G8
Allandale NSW 509 E1, 514 A7
Allandale Island Qld 611 M8

Allans Flat Vic. 543 K7, 545 I4, 204
Allansford Vic. 538 D8, 550 H8
Allanson WA 572 G3, 574 C8
Allaru Island NT 590 F2
Alleena NSW 522 B6, 527 P6
Allen Island Qld 615 C2
Allendale Vic. 535 D8, 536 D2, 551 M3
Allendale East SA 550 A6, 568 G12
Allendale North SA 554 E2, 559 K7, 568 C1
Allens Rivulet Tas. 622 H7
Allenvale Vic. 536 D11, 538 E4, 551 M9
Allies Creek Qld 609 K6
Alligator Creek Qld 605 G8, 606 G11, 610 G1, 613 N12
Allonby Island Qld 605 G6, 611 K5
Allora Qld 609 L10, **391**
Allora Island WA 580 H5, 584 C7
Alma SA 554 C2, 556 H4, 559 J7, 568 B1
Alma Vic. 535 B5, 549 L11, 551 L1
Alma Park NSW 522 A11, 527 N11, 543 K3
Almaden Qld 606 A3, 613 J7, 405
Almonds Vic. 542 H6, 544 D2
Almurta Vic. 533 P10
Almurta East Vic. 533 P10
Alnwick Island Qld 604 B1, 611 M8
Alonnah Tas. 622 H10, 625 J10
Aloomba Qld 606 E3, 607 F8, 613 M6
Alpara NT 564 G2, 594 E11
Alpha Qld 610 F10
Alpha Island WA 575 D1, 582 A4
Alpha Rock Qld 614 D2
Alphadale NSW 516 G5, 525 O3
Alpine NP Vic. 519 A9, 520 B11, 539 A6, 541 J2, 542 H12, 543 J12, 544 H10, 545 K8, 175, 181, 185

Alpurrurulam NT 593 P12, 595 P1, 616 C4
Alstonville NSW 516 G5, 525 O3, 609 N12, **25**
Althorpe Islands SA 556 B9, 558 F10
Alton NP Qld 608 G9
Altona Vic. 531 C6, 537 I6, 540 B5
Alva Qld 605 C2, 610 H1, 613 O12
Alvie Vic. 536 A8, 538 B1, 551 K7
Alwal NP (CYPAL) Qld 613 I2, 614 E12
Alyangula NT 591 M7
Alyinga Island NT 591 N7
Amagbirra Island NT 591 M6
Amamarrity Island NT 591 L8
Amamoor Qld 603 D10
Amamoor NP Qld 603 D9, 609 M6
Amanbidji NT 581 P5, 585 O7, 590 B12, 592 B3
Amata SA 564 G2, 594 E11
Amboyne Crossing Vic. 519 B10, 539 C7
Ambrose Qld 604 C6, 611 N12
Amby Qld 608 F6
American Beach SA 556 F11, 559 I11
American River SA 556 E11, 558 H11, 243
Amherst Vic. 535 B6, 549 L12, 551 L1
Amiens Qld 516 A3, 525 K2, 609 K11
Amity Point Qld 600 H4, 609 N9
Amoonguna NT 595 I7, 597 J4
Amosfield NSW 516 B3, 525 L2
Amphion WA 571 F10
Amphitheatre Vic. 549 K12, 551 K2
Ampilatwatja NT 595 K3
Anakie Qld 610 H10
Anakie Vic. 536 F6, 551 N6
Anakie East Vic. 536 F6, 551 O6
Anakie Junction Vic. 536 F6, 551 N6
Anchorsmith Island Qld 605 G6, 611 K4
Ancona Vic. 542 G10, 544 B9
Andamooka SA 560 F3, **224**
Anderson Vic. 533 N11, 537 L11, 540 E8
Anderson Island Tas. 624 B11, 627 O1
Anderson Islets Vic. 540 H12
Ando NSW 519 C9, 539 F6
Andover Tas. 625 L4
Andrew Island Qld 615 C2
Andrews Qld 601 E9
Andrews SA 559 J5
Anembo NSW 518 G11, 519 D6, 521 I6, 522 G12, 539 G1
Angamanja Island NT 591 M7
Angarmbulumardja Island NT 591 N6
Angas Valley SA 554 H7, 559 L8, 568 D2
Angaston SA 554 F4, 559 K8, 568 C2, **225**
Angel Island WA 575 E1, 578 B2, 580 B12, 582 D4
Angip Vic. 526 D12, 548 G6
Angle Island WA 575 D1, 578 A3, 582 B6
Angle Vale SA 553 D2, 554 C6, 556 H6, 559 J8, 568 B2

Anglers Reach NSW 519 B6, 520 E7, 522 E12, 539 D2
Anglers Rest Vic. 541 M1, 543 M11, 545 L10, 185
Anglesea Vic. 536 E10, 538 F3, 551 N9, **143**
Anglesea Island WA 572 D4, 574 C8, 576 C9
Angleside Vic. 543 I8, 544 F6
Angourie NSW 516 F8, 525 O5
Angurugu NT 591 M7
Angustown Vic. 542 D9
Ann Island Qld 605 G5, 611 K4
Anna Bay NSW 514 G8, 515 C12, 523 M4
Annaburroo NT 588 H6, 590 E5
Annan River NP Qld 613 L3
Annangrove NSW 508 C3, 511 J6
Annerley Qld 599 E8, 600 D5, 602 F11
Annie Island Qld 604 B1, 611 M8
Annuello Vic. 526 F8, 547 J9
Anser Island Vic. 540 H12
Ansons Bay Tas. 627 P6
Antill Ponds Tas. 625 L3
Antwerp Vic. 526 D12, 548 F7
Anvil Island Qld 605 G6, 611 K4
Apamurra SA 554 G8, 559 K9, 568 D3
Aparawatatja SA 564 D2, 594 C11
Apex Island WA 580 H5, 584 C7
Aplin Islet Qld 614 E3
Apollo Bay Vic. 536 B12, 538 C6, 551 L10, **143**
Appila SA 559 J3, 560 H11
Appin NSW 517 F2, 519 H2, 523 J8, 40
Appin Vic. 526 H11, 549 M5
Appin South Vic. 549 N5
Apple Tree Creek Qld 603 C4, 604 F11, 609 M4
Apple Tree Flat NSW 510 C7, 512 F12, 516 C8, 517 A8, 519 F3, 523 I9, 525 M5
Applethorpe Qld 516 A3, 525 L2, 609 L11
Apslawn Tas. 625 O2, 627 O11
Apsley Tas. 625 J4
Apsley Vic. 548 B10, 568 H9
Aquila Island Qld 605 H10, 611 L7
Arakwal NP NSW 516 H4, 525 O3, 609 N12
Araluen NSW 519 E6, 521 K5, 522 H12
Araluen North NSW 521 K5
Aramac Qld 610 D9, 617 P9
Aramara Qld 603 C6, 609 M5
Arana Hills Qld 599 D6, 600 D3, 602 E10
Arapiles Vic. 548 E9
Ararat Vic. 549 I12, 551 I2, **144**
Aratula Qld 609 M10
Arawata Vic. 537 N10, 540 F8
Arawerr NT 595 K3
Arbidej Island WA 581 I5, 584 C7
Arcadia NSW 508 D3, 509 A10, 511 K5
Arcadia Vic. 542 E8
Arch Rock Vic. 540 F10
Archdale Vic. 535 A3, 549 L10
Arched Island Tas. 623 I12, 625 K10
Archer River Roadhouse Qld 614 D9
Archerfield Qld 599 E8, 600 D5, 602 F12

Arches Marine Sanctuary, The Vic. 538 F10, 551 I10
Archies Creek Vic. 533 P12, 537 L11, 540 E9
Ardath WA 574 G4
Ardeer Vic. 537 I5, 551 P5
Ardglen NSW 524 H11
Ardlethan NSW 522 B7, 527 O7
Ardmona Vic. 542 E7
Ardmory Qld 600 A3, 602 C10
Ardrossan SA 556 F5, 559 I7, 568 A1, **225**
Areegra Vic. 549 I7
Areyonga NT 594 G7, 596 A6
Argalong NSW 519 B4, 520 D2, 522 E10
Argoon Qld 604 A8, 609 J1
Argyle Vic. 542 B10, 549 P11, 551 P1
Ariah Park NSW 522 B7, 527 P7, 90
Arid Island WA 577 J9
Arkaroola SA 557 F2, 561 K3, **226**
Arkhurst Island Qld 605 F4, 611 K3
Arkona Vic. 526 D12, 548 F7
Arltunga Bush Hotel (closed) NT 595 K6, 597 N1, **357**
Armadale WA 570 F8, 571 D6, 574 C5, 576 C8
Armatree NSW 524 C10
Armidale NSW 515 B1, 525 J8, **26**
Armit Island Qld 605 F4, 611 J3
Armstrong Vic. 549 I12, 551 I2
Armstrong Beach Qld 605 G9, 611 K6
Armytage Vic. 536 C8, 538 D1, 551 M8
Arncliffe NSW 508 E9, 511 L10
Arno Bay SA 556 A2, 558 F6, 234
Arnold Vic. 535 D2, 549 M9
Arnold Islets A Qld 614 E3
Arnold Islets B Qld 614 E3
Arnold West Vic. 535 C2, 549 M9
Arrawarra NSW 516 E10, 525 N7
Arrilalah Qld 610 A10, 617 M10
Arrino WA 576 B4
Arruwa Island NT 591 M7
Arthur River Tas. 626 A5
Arthur River WA 574 E8, 576 D9
Arthurs Creek Vic. 531 F3, 534 A5, 537 K4, 540 D3
Arthurton SA 556 E4, 558 H7
Arthurville NSW 522 F2
Ascot Vic. 535 C9, 536 C2, 551 M3
Ascot Park SA 553 C8
Ashbourne SA 555 G6, 559 J10, 568 C4, 260
Ashburton Island WA 575 C2, 582 A8
Ashens Vic. 548 H9
Ashfield WA 570 E5, 571 C5
Ashford NSW 525 I4
Ashgrove Qld 599 D7
Ashley NSW 524 F4, 608 H12
Ashmore Qld 601 E6
Ashville SA 559 L11, 568 D5
Aspatria Island Qld 605 H7, 611 L5
Aspendale Vic. 533 K2, 537 J7, 540 C5
Aspendale Gardens Vic. 533 K2
Aspley Qld 599 E5, 600 D3, 602 F10
Asquith NSW 508 E4, 509 B10, 511 L6
Astell Island NT 591 M3

Astrebla Downs NP Qld 616 G11
Atherton Qld 606 D3, 607 D9, 613 L7, **391**
Athlone Vic. 537 N9, 540 F7
Atitjere NT 595 K5
Atneltyey NT 595 J3
Attack Island WA 581 J4, 584 F6
Attunga NSW 524 H9
Aubrey Vic. 548 G7
Auburn NSW 508 D7, 509 A12, 511 K8
Auburn SA 559 J6, 232
Auburn Tas. 625 K1, 627 K11
Auburn River NP Qld 609 K5, 432
Augathella Qld 608 C4, 619 P4
Augereau Island WA 581 K3, 584 F3
Augusta WA 572 C11, 574 B10, 576 B11, **288**
Augustus Island WA 581 J4, 584 E5
Aukane Islet Qld 614 F1
Aunt Island WA 581 N2, 585 L2
Aureed Island Qld 614 E1
Aurora Kakadu Resort NT 589 M4, 590 G4
Aurukun Qld 614 B8
Auski Roadhouse WA 575 H3, 578 D4, 583 I9
Austinmer NSW 517 G4
Austins Ferry Tas. 621 B2
Austinville Qld 601 C9
Austral NSW 510 H9, 519 H1, 523 J7
Australia Plains SA 559 K7
Australind WA 572 E3, 574 C8, 576 C9, **289**
Avalon NSW 508 H3, 509 C10, 511 N6
Avalon Vic. 532 B2
Aveling Island WA 581 I5, 584 D7
Avenel Vic. 542 D10
Avenue SA 568 F9
Avoca Tas. 627 M10
Avoca Vic. 535 A6, 549 L12, 551 L1, **144**
Avoca Beach NSW 509 E8, 511 O3
Avoca Vale Qld 603 B11, 609 L7
Avoid Island Qld 605 H10, 611 L7
Avon SA 556 G4, 559 J7, 568 B1
Avon Plains Vic. 549 J8
Avon Valley NP WA 570 G1, 571 E2, 574 C4, 576 C7, 335
Avondale NSW 509 E4, 514 A10, 517 E5, 519 H3, 523 J8
Avondale Qld 603 C1
Avondale Qld 603 C1
Avonsleigh Vic. 531 H7, 533 O1, 534 C10
Awaba NSW 509 F4, 514 B10
Awonga Vic. 548 C10, 568 H9
Axe Creek Vic. 535 G4, 542 A9, 549 O10
Axedale Vic. 535 H3, 542 B9, 549 P10
Ayr Qld 605 B2, 610 H2, 613 O12, **392**
Ayrford Vic. 538 F8, 551 I8
Ayton Qld 613 L4

B

Baan Baa NSW 524 F7
Baandee WA 574 F3
Baarmutha Vic. 543 J8, 544 H4
Babakin WA 574 G5
Babbage Island WA 575 B7, 586 C2

Babel Island Tas. 624 C10
Babinda Qld 606 E4, 607 G10, 613 M7, **392**
Bacchus Marsh Vic. 535 G11, 536 G4, 540 A3, 551 O5, **145**
Back Creek Tas. 627 K5, 629 H5
Baddaginnie Vic. 542 G8, 544 C5
Baden Tas. 625 L4
Badger Island Tas. 624 A11, 627 N1
Badgerys Creek NSW 510 H8, 519 H1, 523 J7
Badgingarra WA 574 A1, 576 B5
Badgingarra NP WA 574 A1, 576 B5
Badjaling WA 574 F5
Badu (Mulgrave) Island Qld 614 C1
Baerami NSW 523 J2
Bagdad Tas. 623 I2, 625 K5
Bagnoo NSW 515 E6, 525 L11
Bago Bluff NP NSW 515 E6, 525 L11, **98**
Bagot NT 588 D3
Bagot Well SA 554 F2, 559 K7, 568 C1
Bagshot Vic. 535 G2, 542 A8, 549 O9
Bailey Islet Qld 605 H7, 611 L5
Bailieston Vic. 542 D9
Baird Bay SA 558 A4, 567 N11, **260**
Baird Island Qld 614 E6
Bairnsdale Vic. 541 M5, **146**
Bajool Qld 604 B6, 611 M11
Bakara SA 559 M8, 568 E2
Baker Vic. 548 E6
Bakers Creek Qld 605 G8, 611 K6
Bakers Hill WA 571 F3, 574 D4
Bakers Swamp NSW 522 F3
Baking Board Qld 609 J7
Balaklava SA 556 H4, 559 J7, **226**
Balcatta WA 570 D5
Balcombe Vic. 533 J6
Bald Hills Qld 599 E5, 600 D3, 602 F10
Bald Island WA 573 G10, 574 H11, 576 F11
Bald Islet Qld 605 H10, 611 L7
Bald Rock Vic. 527 I12, 542 A5, 549 O6
Bald Rock NP NSW 516 A4, 525 L3, 609 L12, **442**, **90**
Baldivis WA 570 D11, 571 C7
Baldry NSW 522 E3
Balfes Creek Qld 610 E3
Balfour Tas. 626 B6
Balgal Beach Qld 606 F9, 613 M11
Balgo Hills WA 581 N10
Balgowan SA 556 D4, 558 H7, **244**
Balgowlah NSW 508 G6, 509 C12, 511 M8
Balgownie NSW 517 F4
Balhannah SA 553 F8, 554 D9, 555 H3
Balingup WA 572 G6, 574 C9, 576 C10, **289**
Balintore Vic. 536 B8, 538 B1, 551 L8
Ball Bay Qld 605 G7, 611 K5, **424**
Balladonia WA 577 K7, **289**
Balladonia Roadhouse WA 577 K7
Balladoran NSW 524 C11
Ballajura WA 570 D5, 571 C4
Ballalaba NSW 519 E5, 521 J5, 522 G11

Ballan Vic. 535 F11, 536 F3, 551 N4
Ballan North Vic. 535 F10, 536 F3, 551 N4
Ballandean Qld 516 A4, 525 K3, 609 K12
Ballangeich Vic. 538 D7, 550 H7
Ballarat Vic. 535 C10, 536 D3, 551 M4, **148**
Ballark Vic. 535 E12, 536 E4, 551 N5
Ballaying WA 574 F8
Ballbank NSW 526 H10, 549 N3
Balldale NSW 527 N11, 543 J4
Ballendella Vic. 542 B6, 549 P8
Balliang Vic. 536 F5, 540 A4, 551 O5
Balliang East Vic. 536 F5, 540 A4, 551 O5
Ballidu WA 574 D1, 576 C5
Ballimore NSW 522 F1, 524 D12
Ballina NSW 516 G5, 525 O3, 609 N12, **26**
Ballyrogan Vic. 551 J3
Balmattum Vic. 542 F9, 544 B6
Balmoral NSW 509 F4, 514 B10, **16**
Balmoral Vic. 548 E12, 550 E2, **156**
Balnarring Vic. 531 E12, 533 K8, 537 J10, 540 C7, **164**
Balnarring Beach Vic. 533 K9
Balook Vic. 541 I8
Balranald NSW 526 H7, 547 M9, **27**
Balrootan North Vic. 526 C12, 548 E7
Balumbah SA 558 E4, 560 D11
Bamaga Qld 614 C3
Bamawm Vic. 527 I12, 542 B6, 549 P7
Bamawm Extension Vic. 542 B6, 549 P7
Bambaroo Qld 606 E9, 613 M10
Bambill Vic. 526 C6, 546 E7, 559 P8
Bamboo Creek WA 578 F2, 580 F12, 583 L4
Bamborough Island Qld 611 M7
Bambra Vic. 536 D9, 538 E2, 551 M8
Bamganie Vic. 536 D6, 551 M6
Ban Ban NP Qld 603 B7, 609 L5
Banana Qld 609 I2
Bancroft Qld 604 C10, 609 K3
Bandiana Vic. 522 A12, 543 K6, 545 I2
Bandon Grove NSW 514 D3, 515 B9, 523 M2
Banealla SA 559 N12, 568 F6
Bangadilly NP NSW 517 A4, 519 F2, 523 I8
Bangalow NSW 516 G4, 525 O3, 609 N12, **39**
Bangerang Vic. 548 H6
Bangham SA 548 B8, 568 G8
Bangor Tas. 627 K7, 629 H7
Bania NP Qld 604 D10, 609 L3
Baniyala NT 591 M6
Banksia NSW 511 L10
Banksia Beach Qld 599 G1, 602 G7
Banksia Grove WA 570 C3
Bankstown NSW 508 C8, 511 K9
Bannaby NSW 519 F2, 522 H8
Bannerton Vic. 526 F7, 547 J9
Bannister NSW 519 E2, 522 G8
Bannister WA 571 G9, 574 D6
Bannockburn Vic. 536 E7, 551 N7
Banora Point NSW 516 H2, 525 O2, 600 G12, 601 H11, 609 N11

Banyan Vic. 549 I3
Banyan Island NT 591 K4
Banyena Vic. 549 I9
Bar Island WA 572 E3, 574 C8, 576 C9
Barabba SA 554 B2, 556 H4
Baradine NSW 524 D8
Barakee NP NSW 515 B6, 525 J11
Barakula Qld 609 J6
Baralaba Qld 609 I1, 611 L12, **394**
Baranduda Vic. 543 K6, 545 I3
Barayamal NP NSW 525 I5
Barber (Boodthean) Island Qld 606 G8, 613 N10
Barcaldine Qld 610 D10, 617 P10, **393**
Bare Sand (Woolbechik) Island NT 588 A3, 590 C4
Barellan NSW 522 A7, 527 N7
Barellan Point Qld 599 B8
Barfold Vic. 535 H6, 542 A11, 549 P12, 551 P1
Bargara Qld 603 D2, 604 G10, 609 M3, **399**
Bargo NSW 517 D3, 519 G2, 523 J8
Barham NSW 527 I10, 542 A2, 549 O4, **27**
Baring Vic. 526 D9, 546 G12, 548 G2
Baringhup Vic. 535 D5, 549 N11, 551 N1
Barjarg Vic. 542 G10, 544 D8
Bark Hut Inn NT 588 H6
Barkers Creek Vic. 535 F6, 542 A10, 549 O11, 551 O1
Barkly Vic. 549 K11
Barkly Homestead NT 593 L9
Barkstead Vic. 535 E9, 536 E2, 551 N3
Barmah Vic. 527 J12, 542 D5
Barmah NP Vic. 527 K11, 542 D4, **160**
Barmedman NSW 522 C6, 527 P6, **100**
Barmera SA 526 A6, 559 N7, 568 G1, **226**
Barmundu Qld 604 C8, 609 K1
Barnadown Vic. 535 H2, 542 B8, 549 P9
Barnard Island Group NP Qld 606 F5, 607 H12, 613 M8
Barnawartha Vic. 522 A12, 527 N12, 543 J6, 544 H2
Barnawartha North Vic. 543 K6, 544 H2
Barnes NSW 527 J12, 542 C5
Barnes Bay Tas. 623 I8, 625 K8
Barnicoat Island WA 581 I5, 584 C7
Barongarook Vic. 536 B10, 538 B3, 551 L9
Barongarook West Vic. 536 B9, 538 B2, 551 K8
Barooga NSW 527 L11, 542 G4
Barool NP NSW 516 B8, 525 L5
Baroota SA 559 I3, 560 G11
Barpinba Vic. 536 B7, 551 L7
Barraba NSW 524 H7, **27**
Barrakee Vic. 549 L7
Barrallier Island Vic. 531 G11, 533 M7, 537 K9, 540 D7
Barramunga Vic. 536 B11, 538 C4, 551 L9
Barranyi (North Island) NP NT 591 N10, 593 N1, **361**

Barraport Vic. 526 H11, 549 M6
Barren Island Qld 604 A1, 611 L8
Barren Island or First Lump Qld 604 C4, 611 N10
Barrier Island WA 577 J9
Barringo Vic. 531 B1, 535 H9, 540 B2, 542 B12
Barrington NSW 515 C8, 523 M1, 525 J12
Barrington Tas. 626 H7, 628 G3
Barrington Tops NP NSW 514 D1, 515 A8, 523 L1, 525 I12, **53**
Barringun NSW 529 M2, 608 A11, 619 N11
Barron Gorge NP Qld 606 D2, 607 E6, 613 L6, **421**
Barrow Creek NT 595 I2, **357**
Barrow Island Qld 614 H11
Barrow Island WA 575 C1, 582 A6
Barrow Island Marine Management Area WA 575 C1, 582 A6
Barrow Island Marine Park WA 575 C1, 582 A6
Barry NSW 522 G5, 525 I11
Barrys Reef Vic. 535 F9, 536 F2, 540 A2, 551 O3
Barton Vic. 551 I2
Barubbra Island Qld 603 D1, 604 G10, 609 M3
Barunga NT 590 G8
Barunga Gap SA 556 G2, 559 I6
Barwidgee Creek Vic. 543 K8, 544 H5
Barwo Vic. 542 D5
Barwon Bluff Marine Sanctuary Vic. 532 C6, 536 G9, 538 H2, 540 A7, 551 O8
Barwon Downs Vic. 536 C10, 538 C3, 551 L9
Barwon Heads Vic. 532 C6, 536 G9, 538 H2, 540 A7, 551 O8, **146**
Baryulgil NSW 516 C6, 525 M4
Basin View NSW 517 C11, 521 O2
Basket Swamp NP NSW 516 B5, 525 L3, 609 L12
Bass Vic. 533 O11, 537 L11, 540 E8
Bass Landing Vic. 533 N11
Bat Island NT 591 J3
Bat Island WA 581 J3, 584 F4
Batchelor NT 588 E7, 590 D5, **357**
Batchica Vic. 526 E12, 548 H6
Bateau Bay NSW 509 E8, 511 P2
Batehaven NSW 521 L6, 522 H12
Batemans Bay NSW 519 F6, 521 L6, 522 H12, **29**
Bates SA 567 J3
Batesford Vic. 532 A2, 536 F7, 551 N7
Bathumi Vic. 542 H5, 544 E1
Bathurst NSW 522 H5, **28**
Bathurst Island NT 590 C3
Bathurst Island WA 581 I5, 584 C6
Batlow NSW 519 A5, 520 C4, 522 D11, 543 P3, **28**
Battery Point Tas. 621 E8
Baudin Island WA 575 C9, 581 K2, 584 G2, 586 E10
Bauhinia Qld 608 H2
Bauhinia Downs NT 591 L11, 593 L2
Baulkham Hills NSW 508 C5, 511 J7
Bauple Qld 603 D7, 609 M5
Baw Baw NP Vic. 537 P6, 540 H5, 541 I5, **179**, **197**

Bawley Point NSW 519 F5, 521 N5, 523 I11

Baxter Vic. 531 E10, 533 K5, 537 J9, 540 D6

Bay Island Qld 604 B2, 611 M8

Bay Rock Qld 606 G10, 613 N11

Bayles Vic. 537 M9, 540 E6

Bayley Island Qld 615 C2

Baynes Island Tas. 627 N4

Baynham Island Qld 605 G5, 611 K4

Baynton Vic. 542 B11, 549 P12, 551 P2

Bayswater Vic. 531 G6, 534 A8

Bayswater WA 570 E5

Bayview NSW 508 H4, 509 C10, 511 N6

Beachmere Qld 599 F2, 600 E1, 602 F8, 609 N8, 400

Beachport SA 568 E10, **227**

Beacon WA 574 F1, 576 D5

Beacon Island WA 575 C12

Beaconsfield Tas. 627 J6, 629 E7, **471**

Beaconsfield Vic. 531 G8, 533 N3, 534 B11, 537 K7, 540 E6

Beagle Bay WA 580 H6, 584 B9

Beagle Island Tas. 624 A11, 627 O2

Beahgoo Island Qld 612 A5, 615 D2

Bealiba Vic. 535 A3, 549 L10, 160

Beanley Island Qld 614 H11

Beardmore Vic. 541 I5

Beargamil NSW 522 E3

Bearii Vic. 527 K11, 542 E4

Bears Lagoon Vic. 526 H12, 549 N7

Beatrice (Yumunguni) Island NT 591 L9

Beatrice Islets SA 556 E10, 558 H11

Beauchamp Vic. 549 L3

Beaudesert Qld 516 F1, 525 N1, 600 C9, 609 M10, **393**

Beaufort SA 556 G3, 559 I6

Beaufort Vic. 536 A2, 551 K3

Beaumaris Tas. 627 O8, 492

Beaumaris Vic. 533 J1

Beaumont Island WA 577 J9

Beauty Point NSW 509 E5, 514 A11, 519 E8, 521 K11

Beauty Point Tas. 627 J6, 629 E6, **471**

Beazleys Bridge Vic. 549 J9

Beckom NSW 522 B7, 527 O7

Bedarra Island Qld 606 F6, 613 M8, **393**, 428

Bedgerebong NSW 522 D4

Bedourie Qld 616 E11, 395

Bedout Island WA 580 D10, 583 I1

Beeac Vic. 536 B8, 538 C1, 551 L7

Beebo Qld 525 I2, 609 J11

Beech Forest Vic. 536 B11, 538 B4, 551 K10

Beechboro WA 570 E5

Beechford Tas. 627 J5, 629 F5

Beechmont Qld 516 F1, 600 E10, 601 A8

Beechwood NSW 515 F6, 525 L11

Beechworth Vic. 543 J7, 544 H4, **147**

Beela WA 572 F3

Beelbangera NSW 527 M7

Beelu NP WA 570 G5, 571 D5, 574 C5, 576 C7

Beenleigh Qld 599 G11, 600 E7, 609 N10

Beer Eetar Island NT 588 A4, 590 C5

Beerburrum Qld 602 F6

Beeron NP Qld 609 K5

Beerwah Qld 602 F5, 603 E12, 609 N8

Beesley Island Qld 614 E6

Bega NSW 519 E9, 521 J12, 539 H6, 30

Beggan Beggan NSW 519 B2, 522 D8

Beilpajah NSW 526 H2

Belair SA 553 C8, 554 C9, 555 F3, 559 J9

Belair NP SA 553 D8, 554 C9, 555 F3, 556 H8, 559 J9, 568 B3, 238

Belalie North SA 559 J4, 561 I11

Belbora NSW 515 C8, 523 N1, 525 K12

Belconnen ACT 518 D4, 519 C4, 520 G2, 522 F10

Belford NSW 523 L3

Belford NP NSW 514 A6, 523 L3

Belgrave Vic. 531 G7, 534 B9, 537 K6, 540 E5

Belgrave South Vic. 531 G7, 533 N1, 534 B10, 537 K7

Belhus WA 570 E3, 571 D4

Belka WA 574 G4

Bell NSW 510 D2, 512 F3, 523 I5

Bell Qld 609 K7, 409

Bell Bay Tas. 627 J6, 629 E6

Bell Park Vic. 532 A3

Bellambi NSW 517 G4

Bellara Qld 599 G1, 600 F1, 602 G7

Bellarine Vic. 531 A9, 532 E3, 536 G8, 540 B6, 551 P7

Bellarwi NSW 522 B6, 527 P6

Bellata NSW 524 F5

Bellbird NSW 509 D2, 523 L4

Bellbird Creek Vic. 519 B12, 539 C11

Bellbowrie Qld 599 C8

Bellbrae Vic. 536 E9, 538 G2, 551 N8

Bellbridge Vic. 543 L6, 545 J2

Bellbrook NSW 515 F3, 525 L9, 62

Bellellen Vic. 549 I12, 551 I1

Bellenden Ker Qld 606 E3, 607 G9

Bellerive Tas. 621 F8, 464

Bellevue WA 570 F5

Bellingen NSW 515 G1, 516 D12, 525 M8, 30

Bellinger Island WA 577 K9

Bellinger River NP NSW 515 F1, 516 C12, 525 M8

Bellingham Tas. 627 K5, 629 H5

Bellmount Forest NSW 519 D3, 522 F9

Bellows Island Qld 605 G6, 611 K4

Bellthorpe NP Qld 602 D5, 603 D12, 609 M8

Belltrees NSW 509 C8, 511 N2, 523 K1, 525 I12

Belmont NSW 509 G4, 514 C10, 528 B10

Belmont Vic. 532 A4, 536 F8, 538 G1, 540 A6, 551 O7

Belmont WA 570 E6, 571 C5

Belmore NSW 511 K9

Belmunging WA 574 E4

Beloka NSW 519 B8, 520 E11, 539 D5

Belowla Island NSW 519 F6, 521 M5, 523 I12

Belowra NSW 519 E7, 521 J9, 539 H3

Belrose NSW 508 F5, 509 B11, 511 M7

Beltana SA 557 B5, 560 H4, 241

Beltana Roadhouse SA 557 A5, 560 H4

Belton SA 559 K1, 561 I9

Belvidere SA 568 C4

Belyando Crossing Roadhouse Qld 610 G6

Belyuen NT 588 C3, 590 D4

Bemboka NSW 519 D9, 521 I12, 539 G5

Bemm River Vic. 519 B12, 539 D11

Ben Boyd NP NSW 519 E10, 539 H9, 49

Ben Bullen NSW 523 I4

Ben Halls Gap NP NSW 525 I11

Ben Island WA 577 J9

Ben Lomond NSW 525 J6

Ben Lomond NP Tas. 627 M9, 478

Ben Nevis Vic. 549 J12, 551 J2

Bena NSW 522 B5, 527 P5

Bena Vic. 537 M10, 540 F8

Benalla Vic. 542 G8, 544 D5, **147**

Benambra Vic. 541 N1, 543 N11, 545 M9, 185

Benambra NP NSW 522 B11, 527 O11, 543 I4

Benandarah NSW 521 M6

Benaraby Qld 604 D7, 609 L1, 611 N12

Benarkin Qld 603 B12, 609 L8

Benarkin NP Qld 603 B11, 609 L7

Benayeo Vic. 548 B10, 568 H9

Bencubbin WA 574 F2, 576 D5

Bendalong NSW 519 G5, 521 N3, 523 I11

Bendemeer NSW 525 I9

Bendick Murrell NSW 519 B1, 522 E7

Bendidee NP Qld 524 H1, 609 I10

Bendigo Vic. 535 F3, 542 A9, 549 O10, **150**

Bendoc Vic. 519 B10, 539 D8

Bendolba NSW 514 D3, 515 B10, 523 M2

Beneree NSW 522 G5

Benetook Vic. 526 D6, 546 G7

Benger WA 572 E2, 574 C8

Bengworden Vic. 541 M6

Beni NSW 522 F1, 524 C12

Beninbi NP Qld 603 A7, 609 L5

Benjeroop Vic. 526 H10, 549 M3

Benlidi Qld 610 C12, 617 O12, 619 M1

Bennett Rock Qld 605 F6, 611 K4

Bennies Vic. 543 I11, 544 G9

Bennison Island Vic. 540 H10

Benowa Qld 601 E6

Bentinck Island Qld 612 A5, 615 D2

Bentley NSW 516 F4, 525 N3

Benwerrin Vic. 536 D10, 538 E3, 551 M9

Berambing NSW 510 E3, 513 I4

Berat Qld 525 L1

Beremboke Vic. 535 F12, 536 E5, 551 N5

Berendebba NSW 522 D6

Beresfield NSW 509 G2, 514 C8, 515 A12, 523 L4

Bergalia NSW 519 F7, 521 L8

Berkeley Tas. 629 A3

Berkeley Vale NSW 509 E7, 511 P2

Bermagui NSW 519 E8, 521 K11, **30**

Bermagui South NSW 519 E8, 521 K11

Bernier Island WA 575 B7, 586 A2

Bernouilli Island WA 581 J3, 584 F4

Berowra NSW 508 F3, 509 B10, 511 L5

Berowra Heights NSW 508 E3, 509 B10, 511 L5

Berowra Waters NSW 508 E2, 509 B9, 511 L5

Berrara NSW 517 C12, 521 O3

Berri SA 526 A6, 546 A6, 559 N7, 568 G1, **228**

Berridale NSW 519 B8, 520 E10, 539 D4, **31**

Berriedale Tas. 621 B3, 623 I4, 625 K6

Berrigan NSW 527 L11, 542 G3, 50

Berrima NSW 517 B5, 519 G2, 523 I8, **31**

Berrimah NT 588 D3

Berrimal Vic. 549 L8

Berringa Vic. 535 B12, 536 C5, 551 L5

Berringama Vic. 543 N7, 545 M3

Berriwillock Vic. 526 F10, 549 J3

Berry NSW 517 D8, 519 G3, 523 J9, **32**

Berry Springs NT 588 D5, 590 D5

Berrybank Vic. 536 A6, 551 K6

Berthier Island WA 581 J2, 584 F3

Berthoud Island WA 581 K2, 584 H2

Berwick Vic. 531 G8, 533 N2, 534 B11, 537 K7, 540 D6

Berwick Island Qld 604 C1, 611 N8

Bessie Island Qld 612 A5, 615 D2

Bessiebelle Vic. 550 E7

Bessieres (Anchor) Island WA 575 C2

Beswick NT 590 H8

Bet Bet Vic. 535 C4, 549 M11

Bet Islet Qld 614 D1

Beta Qld 610 F10

Bete Bolong Vic. 519 A12, 539 B11, 541 P5

Bethanga Vic. 543 L6, 545 J2

Bethania Qld 599 F10

Bethungra NSW 519 A3, 522 D8

Betley Vic. 535 C4, 549 M11

Betoota Qld 563 N1, 618 F3

Betsey Island Tas. 623 J7, 625 K8

Beulah Tas. 626 H8, 628 H4, 629 A9

Beulah Vic. 526 E11, 548 H5

Beulah East Vic. 526 E11, 548 H5

Beulah West Vic. 526 E11, 548 G5

Bevendale NSW 519 D2, 522 F8

Beverford Vic. 526 G9, 547 L12, 549 L1

Beveridge Vic. 531 E2, 537 J3, 540 C2

Beverlac Island Qld 611 L6

Beverley WA 574 E5, 576 D7, **291**

Beverly Hills NSW 508 D9, 511 K10

Beware Reef Marine Sanctuary Vic. 519 B12, 539 C12

Beware Rocks Qld 605 H10, 611 L7

Bewick Island Qld 614 H11

Bexhill NSW 516 G4, 525 O3

Bezout Island WA 575 F1, 578 B2, 580 B12, 582 E4

Bezout Rock WA 575 F1, 578 B2, 580 B12, 582 E4

Biala NSW 519 D2, 522 G8
Biamanga NP NSW 519 E8, 521 K11, 539 H5, 30
Biarra Qld 602 A7
Bibbenluke NSW 519 C9, 539 F6
Biboohra Qld 606 D2, 607 D7, 613 L6
Bibra Lake WA 570 D8, 571 C6
Bicheno Tas. 625 O1, 627 O11, **472**
Bickerton (Amakalyuwakba) Island NT 591 M6
Bickley WA 570 G6, 571 D5
Biddon NSW 524 D10
Bidyadanga WA 580 G9
Big Caroline Rock Tas. 624 E9
Big Green Island Tas. 624 B10, 627 O1
Big Grove WA 573 D11, 574 G12
Big Island NSW 517 G5, 519 H3, 523 J8
Big Pats Creek Vic. 534 F8, 537 N5
Big Rocky NSW 514 G8, 515 C12, 523 M4
Bigga NSW 519 D1, 522 G7
Biggara Vic. 519 A7, 520 B9, 539 A3, 543 P7, 545 P4
Bigge Island WA 581 K2, 584 F3
Biggenden Qld 603 B5, 604 E12, 609 L4, **393**
Biggera Waters Qld 601 E4
Bignell Island WA 581 L2, 584 H3
Bilambil NSW 516 G2, 600 G12, 601 F11
Bilambil Heights NSW 601 G11
Bilbarin WA 574 G5
Bilbul NSW 527 M7
Bilinga Qld 601 G10
Billabong Vic. 526 E6, 546 G6
Billabong Roadhouse WA 575 D10
Billimari NSW 522 E5
Billinudgel NSW 516 G3, 525 O2
Billys Creek NSW 516 C11, 525 M7
Biloela Qld 604 A8, 609 J2, **394**
Bilpin NSW 510 F3, 513 K4, 523 J5, 83
Bilwon Qld 606 D2, 607 D6
Bilyana Qld 606 E6, 613 M9
Bimbaya NSW 539 G6
Bimberamala NP NSW 519 F5, 521 L5, 522 H11
Bimbi NSW 522 D6
Bimbimbie NSW 519 F6, 521 L7, 522 H12
Binalong NSW 519 C2, 522 E8, 105
Binalong Bay Tas. 627 P7, 492
Binbee Qld 605 D5, 611 I3
Binda NSW 519 D2, 522 G8
Bindarri NP NSW 515 G1, 516 D11, 525 M7, 45
Bindi Vic. 541 N1, 543 N12, 545 N11
Bindi Bindi WA 574 C2, 576 C5
Bindoon WA 571 D1, 574 C3, 576 C7
Bingara NSW 524 H6, **32**
Bingera Qld 603 C2
Bingera NP Qld 603 D3, 604 F11, 609 M3
Bingil Bay Qld 606 E5, 613 M8
Binginwarri Vic. 540 H9
Biniguy NSW 524 G4
Binjour Qld 604 D12, 609 K4
Binnaway NSW 524 E10
Binningup WA 572 D2, 574 C8, 289
Binningup Beach WA 572 D2

Binnu WA 575 D11, 576 A2, 578 A12
Binnum SA 548 B9, 568 G8
Binstead Islet Qld 614 F8
Binya NSW 527 N7
Binya NP Qld 529 L1, 608 A10, 619 N11
Birany Birany NT 591 N5
Birchip Vic. 526 F11, 549 J5, 203
Birchs Bay Tas. 622 H9, 625 J9
Bird Island NSW 509 F6, 514 B12, 523 L5
Bird Island Qld 604 E7, 609 L1, 611 O12
Bird Island SA 556 D3, 558 H6, 264
Bird Island Tas. 626 B2
Bird Island WA 570 C11, 571 B7, 574 B6, 576 B8, 581 L2, 585 I1
Bird Islands Qld 614 E5
Birds Islands (South) A Qld 614 E5
Birds Islands (South) B Qld 614 E5
Birdsville Qld 563 K2, 618 D3, **394**
Birdwood NSW 515 E5, 525 L10
Birdwood SA 553 H5, 554 E8, 559 K9, 568 C2, **228**
Birdwoodton Vic. 546 G6
Biriwal Bulga NP NSW 515 D6, 525 K11
Birkdale Qld 599 G8, 600 F5, 602 G11
Birralee Tas. 627 J8, 629 E9
Birrego NSW 522 A9, 527 N9
Birregurra Vic. 536 C9, 538 D2, 551 L8, 156
Birriwa NSW 522 H1, 524 E12
Birrong NSW 508 C8, 511 K9
Bishop Island WA 581 K2, 584 G2
Bishop Rock WA 577 I10
Bishopsbourne Tas. 627 J9, 629 F12
Bittern Vic. 531 E12, 533 K8, 537 J10, 540 D7
Black Bobs Tas. 624 H4
Black Hill SA 559 L8, 568 D2
Black Hills Tas. 622 G3, 625 J6
Black Island Qld 605 F4, 611 K3
Black Island Tas. 624 D7
Black Island WA 577 I9
Black Islet NT 591 N10, 593 N1
Black Mountain NSW 525 J7
Black Mountain NP Qld 613 L3, 407
Black River Tas. 626 D4
Black Rock NSW 516 E11, 525 N7
Black Rock SA 556 E2, 558 H6, 559 J3, 561 I10
Black Rock WA 572 B10, 573 E11, 574 H11, 576 B11, 577 I9
Black Springs NSW 522 H6, 524 H12, 525 I5
Black Springs SA 559 K6
Black Swan Island Qld 604 C6, 611 N11
Blackall Qld 608 A1, 610 D12, 617 P12, 619 O1, **395**
Blackberry Corner Vic. 533 I10
Blackbraes NP Qld 610 B1, 613 I11, 617 N1
Blackbull Qld 612 E8
Blackbutt Qld 603 A12, 609 L8, 433
Blackcombe Island Qld 605 G6, 611 K4
Blackdown Tableland NP Qld 611 J11, 395

Blackfellow Caves SA 568 F12
Blackheath NSW 510 C4, 512 F6, 523 I6, **32**
Blackheath Vic. 548 G8
Blackmans Bay Tas. 623 I7, 625 K8
Blacksmith Island Qld 605 G6, 611 K4
Blacksmiths NSW 509 G5, 514 C11
Blacktown NSW 508 B5, 511 J7, 523 J6
Blackville NSW 524 G11
Blackwarry Vic. 541 I8
Blackwater Qld 611 J11, **395**
Blackwood SA 553 C9, 554 B10, 555 F3
Blackwood Vic. 535 F10, 536 F2, 540 A2, 551 O3
Blackwood Creek Tas. 627 J10
Blackwood Island Qld 614 G11
Blackwood NP Qld 610 G6, 404
Blackwood River NP WA 572 D9, 574 B10, 576 C10
Bladensburg NP Qld 617 L8, 449
Blair Athol Qld 605 B12, 610 H9
Blairgowrie Vic. 531 B12, 532 F8, 536 H10, 540 B7, 551 P9, 195
Blakeville Vic. 535 E10, 536 E3, 551 N4
Blampied Vic. 535 D9, 536 E2
Blanchetown SA 559 L7, 568 E1
Bland NSW 522 C6
Blandford NSW 524 H11
Blanket Flat NSW 519 D1, 522 G7
Blaxland NSW 510 G6, 513 K10, 523 J6
Blaxlands Ridge NSW 510 H3, 513 O4
Blayney NSW 522 G5, **33**
Bleak House Vic. 526 C12, 548 D7
Blessington Tas. 627 L9
Bletchley SA 553 H12, 554 E12
Blewitt Springs SA 553 C11, 554 B11, 555 F4
Bli Bli Qld 602 G3, 603 F11, 609 N7, 426
Blighty NSW 527 K10, 542 E3
Blind Bight Vic. 533 N6
Blinman SA 557 C7, 561 I5, **229**
Bloomsbury Qld 605 E6, 611 J4
Blow Clear NSW 522 B5, 527 P5
Blue Lake NP Qld 600 H5, 609 N9
Blue Mountains NP NSW 510 E7, 512 G7, 513 J6, 517 A2, 519 F1, 522 H7, 523 I5, 33, 52, 65
Blue Rocks Tas. 624 B10
Blue Water Springs Roadhouse Qld 606 D10, 610 E1, 613 L11
Bluebell Island WA 575 D1, 582 A4
Bluewater Qld 606 F10, 610 G1, 613 N11
Blueys Beach NSW 515 E10, 523 O3
Bluff Qld 611 J11
Bluff Beach SA 556 D6, 558 H8
Bluff Hill NP Qld 605 F7, 611 J5
Bluff (Iron Pot) Rock Qld 604 C4, 611 N10
Bluff Islet Qld 611 L7
Bluff Rock NSW 516 A6, 525 L4
Blyth SA 556 H2, 559 J6, 232
Boallia WA 572 C7
Boambee NSW 515 H1, 516 E12, 525 N8
Boat Harbour NSW 514 G8, 515 C12

Boat Harbour Tas. 626 E4
Boat Harbour Beach Tas. 626 E4
Boat Island Qld 611 M7
Boatswain Point SA 568 E9
Bobadah NSW 522 B1, 527 O1, 529 N12
Bobbin Head NSW 508 F4, 509 B10, 511 L6
Bobin NSW 515 D7, 523 N1, 525 K12
Bobinawarrah Vic. 543 I8, 544 G5
Bodalla NSW 519 E7, 521 L9, 71
Bodallin WA 574 H3, 576 F6
Boddington WA 571 G10, 574 D7, 576 C8
Bogan Gate NSW 522 D3
Bogangar NSW 516 H3, 525 O2, 609 N11
Bogantungan Qld 610 G11
Boggabilla NSW 524 H2, 609 I11
Boggabri NSW 524 G8
Bogong Vic. 543 L10, 545 K8, 181
Boho Vic. 542 G9, 544 B6
Boho South Vic. 542 G9, 544 C7
Boigbeat Vic. 526 F10, 549 J3
Boiler Rock WA 575 E1, 578 B2, 580 B12, 582 D4
Boinka Vic. 526 C9, 546 E11, 548 E1, 559 P10
Boisdale Vic. 541 K5
Bolgart WA 574 D3, 576 C6, 326
Bolinda Vic. 536 H2, 540 B2
Bolivar SA 553 C3, 554 B6
Bolivia NSW 516 A6, 525 K4
Bollon Qld 608 D9, 441
Bolton Vic. 526 F8, 547 J10
Bolwarra NSW 509 G1, 514 C7, 515 A11
Bolwarra Vic. 550 D7
Bolwarrah Vic. 535 E10, 536 E3, 551 N4
Bomaderry NSW 517 D9, 519 G4, 521 O1, 523 I9
Bombala NSW 519 C9, 539 F7, **34**
Bombo NSW 517 F7
Bonalbo NSW 516 D4, 525 M3, 609 M12
Bonang Vic. 519 B10, 539 C8
Bonaparte Island WA 581 J3, 584 F4
Bonbeach Vic. 533 K3, 537 J7
Bondi Junction NSW 508 F8, 511 M9
Bondo NSW 519 B4, 520 E2, 522 E10
Bonegilla Vic. 522 A12, 543 L6, 545 J2
Boneo Vic. 531 C12, 532 H9, 537 I10, 540 C8
Bongaree Qld 599 G2, 600 F1, 602 G8, 609 N8
Bongil Bongil NP NSW 515 H1, 516 E12, 525 N8, 96
Bonnells Bay NSW 509 F5, 514 B11
Bonnie Doon Vic. 542 G11, 544 C9, 143
Bonnie Rock WA 574 G1, 576 E5
Bonny Hills NSW 515 F7, 525 M11
Bonogin Qld 601 D9
Bonogin Creek Qld 601 D9
Bonshaw NSW 525 J3, 609 J12
Bonville NSW 515 H1, 516 D12, 525 M8
Booborowie SA 559 K5, 561 I12
Booby Island Qld 614 B2

Boobyalla Tas. 627 N5
Boodalan Island WA 571 C10,
574 C6, 576 C8
Booderee NP NSW 517 D12,
519 G5, 521 O3, 61
Boodie Island WA 575 C1, 582 A6
Boodjamulla (Lawn Hill) NP Qld
593 P7, 615 A6, 397
Boojiragi Island NT 591 K3
Bookabie SA 567 K7
Bookar Vic. 551 J7
Bookar Island Qld 603 F5, 609 N5
Bookham NSW 519 B3, 522 E9, 105
Boolading WA 574 D8
Boolaroo NSW 509 G3, 514 C9
Boolarra Vic. 537 P10, 540 H8
Boolba Qld 608 E9, 441
Booleroo SA 559 J3, 560 H10
Booleroo Centre SA 559 J3,
560 H10, 246
Boolgun SA 559 M8, 568 F1
Booligal NSW 527 K5, 58
Boomahnoomoonah Vic. 542 H6,
544 E2
Boomi NSW 524 F2, 608 H11
Boonah Qld 516 D1, 525 M1,
600 A9, 609 M10, **395**
Boonah Vic. 536 D10, 538 E3,
551 M9
Boonarga Qld 609 J7
Boondaba Island NSW 514 G7,
515 C11, 523 M3
Boondall Qld 599 F5, 600 E3,
602 F10
Boondelbah Island NSW 514 H7,
515 C12, 523 N4
Boongaree Island WA 581 K3,
584 F4
Boonoo Boonoo NSW 516 B4,
525 L3, 609 L12
Boonoo Boonoo NP NSW 516 B4,
525 L3, 609 L12, 90, 442
Boonoonar Vic. 526 E7, 546 G8
Boorabbin NP WA 576 G6
Booragoon WA 570 D7, 571 C6
Booral NSW 514 F5, 515 B10,
523 M3
Boorara–Gardner NP WA 572 H12,
573 C4, 574 D11, 576 C11
Boorcan Vic. 538 G7, 551 I7
Boorhaman Vic. 543 I6, 544 F3
Boorindal NSW 529 M6
Boorongie Vic. 546 H11
Boorongie North Vic. 526 E8,
546 H11
Booroopki Vic. 548 C9, 568 H8
Booroorban NSW 527 J8
Boorowa NSW 519 C2, 522 E8
Boort Vic. 526 H12, 549 M6, 189
Boosey Vic. 542 G5, 544 C1
Booti Booti NP NSW 515 E9,
523 N2, 51
Bootie Island Qld 614 E5
Booval Qld 600 B5, 602 D12
Booyal Qld 603 B3, 604 E11, 609 M4
Boppy Mountain NSW 529 M9
Borallon Qld 599 A7, 600 B4,
602 C11
Boralma Vic. 543 I6, 544 F3
Borambil NSW 523 I1, 524 F12
Borda Island WA 581 L2, 584 H2
Borden WA 574 H9, 576 E10
Border Island Qld 605 G4, 611 K3
Border Ranges NP NSW 516 E2,
525 N2, 600 B12, 609 M11, 63

Border Store NT 589 P2, 590 H4
Border Village SA 566 C7, 577 P5,
305
Bordertown SA 526 A12, 548 A7,
568 G7, **229**
Boree NSW 509 B4, 522 F4, 523 K4
Boree Creek NSW 522 A9, 527 N9
Boreen Point Qld 603 F9, 609 N6,
437
Borenore NSW 522 F4, 81
Boro NSW 519 E4, 521 J2, 522 G10
Boronia Vic. 534 B9, 537 K6,
540 D5
Boronia Heights Qld 599 D10,
600 D6
Bororen Qld 604 D8, 609 L2
Borrika SA 559 M9, 568 F3
Borroloola NT 591 M11, 593 M2,
360
Borung Vic. 526 H12, 549 M7
Bosanquet Island NT 591 M3
Boscabel WA 574 E8, 576 D10
Bostobrick NSW 516 C11, 525 M7
Bostock Creek Vic. 538 G7, 551 J8
Boston Island SA 558 D8
Botany NSW 508 F9, 511 L10,
523 K7
Botany Bay NP NSW 508 F10,
511 M11, 523 K7
Bothwell Tas. 625 J4, **471**
Bottom Rocks Tas. 624 D8
Boucaut Island SA 558 E8
Bouddi NP NSW 509 D9, 511 O4,
523 K6, 91
Boulder Rock Qld 614 G10
Bouldercombe Qld 604 B6,
611 M11
Boulia Qld 616 F8, **396**
Boulka Vic. 546 H11
Boullanger Island WA 576 A5
Boundain WA 574 F7
Boundary Bend Vic. 526 G7,
547 K9
Boundary Island WA 571 C9,
574 B6, 576 C8
Bountiful Islands Qld 612 A5,
615 E2
Bourke NSW 529 M5, **34**
Bourke Islet Qld 614 F1
Bournda Island NSW 519 E9
Bournda NP NSW 519 E9, 539 H7,
89
Bow NSW 523 J1, 524 G12
Bowan Park NSW 522 F4
Bowden SA 553 C7, 554 B8, 555 F2
Bowden Island Qld 606 F6, 613 M8
Bowelling WA 574 D8, 576 C9
Bowen Qld 605 E4, 611 J3, **396**
Bowen Island NSW 517 E12,
519 G4, 521 P2, 523 J10
Bowen Mountain NSW 510 G4,
513 L6
Bowenfels NSW 510 B2, 512 D2
Bowenvale Vic. 535 B5, 549 L11,
551 L1
Bowenville Qld 609 K8
Bower SA 559 L7
Boweya Vic. 542 H7, 544 E3
Bowhill SA 559 L9, 568 E3
Bowling Alley Point NSW 525 I10
Bowling Green Bay NP Qld 605 A2,
606 G11, 610 G1, 613 N12, 448
Bowman Vic. 543 J8, 544 G5
Bowmans SA 556 G4, 559 I7,
568 A1

Bowna NSW 522 B12, 527 O12,
543 L5, 545 K1
Bowning NSW 519 C3, 522 F9
Bowral NSW 517 C5, 519 G2,
523 I8, **35**
Bowraville NSW 515 G2, 525 M9,
69
Bowser Vic. 543 I7, 544 F4
Box Hill Vic. 531 E6, 537 J6, 540 D4
Box Tank NSW 528 D11
Boxen Island Tas. 624 A11, 627 N2
Boxer Island WA 577 I9
Boxwood Vic. 542 G7, 544 C3
Boxwood Hill WA 576 F10
Boyanup WA 572 E5, 574 C8,
576 C10, 303
Boydong Island Qld 614 E4
Boydtown NSW 519 E10, 539 H8,
49
Boyeo Vic. 526 C12, 548 D7
Boyer Tas. 622 H4, 625 J6
Boykambil Qld 600 F8, 601 E3
Boyndaminup NP WA 573 E3,
574 E11, 576 D11
Boyne Island Qld 604 D7, 609 L1,
611 N12, 412
Boys Town Qld 600 C9
Boyup Brook WA 574 D9, 576 C10,
292
Bracken Ridge Qld 599 E5
Brackendale NSW 515 B4, 525 J10
Bracknell Tas. 627 J9, 629 F12
Bradvale Vic. 536 A5, 551 K5
Braefield NSW 524 H11
Braemar NSW 517 C4
Braeside Qld 516 A2, 525 L2,
605 E10, 609 L11, 611 J7
Braeside Vic. 533 K2
Braidwood NSW 519 E5, 521 K4,
522 H11, **35**
Bramfield SA 558 C5, 560 A12,
567 P12
Bramley NP WA 572 B8, 574 B10,
576 B10
Brampton Island Qld 605 G6,
611 K5, **396**, 425
Brampton Islands NP Qld 605 G6,
611 K5
Bramston Beach Qld 606 E4,
607 H10, 613 M7, 392
Bramwell Junction Roadhouse Qld
614 D6
Branch Island WA 581 K2, 584 G3
Brandon Qld 605 B2, 610 H2,
613 O12
Brandy Creek Vic. 534 G12,
537 N8, 540 G6
Branxholm Tas. 627 M7
Branxholme Vic. 550 E5
Branxton NSW 514 A6, 523 L3
Brawlin NSW 519 A2, 522 D8
Bray Islet Qld 605 A1, 606 H10,
610 H1, 613 N11
Bray Junction SA 568 E10
Bray Park Qld 599 E5, 600 D3,
602 F9
Breadalbane NSW 519 E3, 522 G9
Breadalbane Tas. 627 K8, 629 H11
Break O Day Vic. 531 H1, 534 C2,
537 L2, 540 E2, 542 E12
Breakfast Creek NSW 519 C1,
522 F7, 523 I3
Breaksea Island WA 573 E11,
574 H11, 576 E11
Breaksea Islands Tas. 624 E9

Breakwater Vic. 532 B4
Bream Creek Tas. 623 M5, 625 M7
Breamlea Vic. 532 B6, 536 F9,
538 H2, 540 A7, 551 O8
Bredbo NSW 519 C6, 520 G7,
522 F12, 539 F2
Breelong NP NSW 524 C11
Breeza NSW 524 G10
Bremer Bay WA 576 G10, **292**
Bremer Island NT 591 N3
Brentwood SA 556 D7, 558 H9
Brentwood Vic. 526 D11, 548 G5
Breona Tas. 627 I10
Bresnahan Island Qld 606 F5,
607 H12, 613 M8
Bretti NSW 515 C7, 523 M1,
525 K12
Brewarrina NSW 529 O5, **36**
Brewis Island Qld 614 D3
Brewis Island WA 577 J9
Brewongle NSW 522 H5
Brewster Vic. 535 A9, 536 B2,
551 L3
Briagolong Vic. 541 K5
Bribbaree NSW 519 A1, 522 D7
Bribie Island Qld 599 G1, 600 F1,
602 G7, 603 F12, 609 N8, 387, 400
Bribie Island NP Qld 599 G1,
600 F1, 602 G7, 603 F12, 609 N8,
400
Bridge Creek Vic. 542 H10, 544 D9
Bridge Inn Vic. 549 I11, 551 I1
Bridgenorth Tas. 627 J7, 629 F9
Bridgetown WA 572 H8, 574 D9,
576 C10, **292**
Bridgewater SA 553 E8, 554 D10,
555 G3, 559 J9, 568 C3, 238
Bridgewater Tas. 623 I3, 625 K6
Bridgewater On Loddon Vic.
535 D2, 549 N9, 170
Bridgland Island NT 591 N5
Bridport Tas. 627 L5, **473**
Brigadier Island WA 578 A2,
580 A12, 582 D4
Brigalow Qld 609 J7
Bright Vic. 543 K9, 545 I7, **153**
Brighton Qld 599 F5, 600 E3,
602 F9, 609 N9
Brighton SA 553 B9, 554 B10,
555 E3, 556 H8, 559 J9
Brighton Tas. 623 I3, 625 K6
Brighton Vic. 531 D7, 537 J6,
540 C5
Brightwaters NSW 509 F5, 514 B11
Brim Vic. 526 E11, 548 H6
Brimbago SA 526 A11, 568 F7
Brimboal Vic. 550 C2, 568 H10
Brimin Vic. 543 I5, 544 E1
Brimpaen Vic. 548 G11
Brindabella NP NSW 518 A3,
519 C4, 520 F2, 522 E10, 105
Bringagee NSW 527 L7
Bringalbert Vic. 548 C10, 568 H9
Bringelly NSW 510 H9
Brinkley SA 554 G12, 559 K10
Brinkworth SA 556 H1, 559 J5
Brisbane Qld 599 E7, 600 D4,
602 F11, 609 N9, **374**
Brisbane Ranges NP Vic. 535 F12,
536 F5, 540 A4, 551 N5, 145
Brisbane Water NP NSW 508 H1,
509 C7, 511 N4, 523 K5, 102
Brisk (Culgarool) Island Qld
606 F8, 613 N10
Brit Brit Vic. 550 E3

Brittons Swamp Tas. 626 B4
Brixton Qld 610 C10, 617 O10
Broad Arrow WA 576 H4
Broad Sound Islands NP Qld
604 B1, 605 H11, 611 L7
Broadbeach Qld 516 G1, 525 O1,
600 G10, 601 F6, 444
Broadford Vic. 537 J1, 540 D1,
542 D11, 172
Broadmarsh Tas. 622 H2, 625 J6
Broadmeadows Vic. 531 D4,
537 I4, 540 C3
Broadwater NSW 516 G6, 525 O4
Broadwater Vic. 550 F6
Broadwater NP NSW 516 G6,
525 O4, 50
Brocklehurst NSW 522 F1,
524 C12
Brocklesby NSW 522 A11,
527 N11, 543 J4
Brockman NP WA 572 H12,
573 C3, 574 D11, 576 C11
Brocks Creek NT 588 G10, 590 E6
Brodies Plains NSW 525 J5
Brodribb River Vic. 519 A12,
539 B11
Brogo NSW 519 E8, 521 J12, 539 H5
Broke NSW 509 C1, 523 K3, 87
Broken Hill NSW 528 B10, 559 P1,
561 O8, **37**
Bromelton Qld 516 E1, 600 C9
Bromley Vic. 535 C4, 549 M10
Bronte Park Tas. 624 H2, 626 H12,
628 H11
Bronzewing Vic. 526 E9, 546 H11,
548 H1
Brook Islands NP Qld 606 F6,
613 M9, 401
Brooker SA 558 D6
Brookfield NSW 514 E5, 515 B10,
523 M3
Brookfield Qld 599 C7, 600 C4,
602 E11
Brooklands Qld 600 C8
Brooklyn NSW 508 G2, 509 C9,
511 M4, 53
Brookside Vic. 543 K10, 545 I7
Brookstead Qld 609 K9
Brookton WA 574 E5, 576 D8, 292
Brookvale NSW 508 G6, 509 C11,
511 M7
Brookville Vic. 541 N3, 545 M12
Brooloo Qld 602 E2, 603 D10
Broome WA 580 H8, 584 A11, **294**
Broomehill WA 574 F9, 576 E10
Broomfield Vic. 535 D9, 536 D2,
551 M3
Brooms Head NSW 516 F8, 525 N6
Brooweena Qld 603 C6, 609 M5,
394
Brothers Island Qld 605 F6, 611 K5
Broughton Vic. 526 C12, 548 D6,
568 H7
Broughton Island NSW 515 D11,
523 N3
Broughton Island WA 577 J9
Broula NSW 522 E6
Broulee NSW 519 F6, 521 L7,
522 H12, 71
Broulee Island NSW 519 F6,
521 L7, 522 H12
Brown Hill Vic. 535 C10, 536 D3
Brown Island Qld 525 O1, 600 G8,
601 F3, 609 N10
Brown Island WA 575 C3

Brown Islet NT 591 N11, 593 N2
Browne Island WA 581 J3, 584 E4
Brownlow SA 554 H1, 556 E11,
558 H11, 559 L7, 568 D1
Browns Plains Qld 599 E10, 600 D6
Browns Plains Vic. 543 J6, 544 H2
Browse Island WA 581 I2, 584 C2
Bruarong Vic. 543 K8, 545 I5
Bruce SA 559 I2, 560 H9, 265
Bruce Rock WA 574 G4, 576 E7
Brucefield SA 556 E2, 558 H6
Brucknell Vic. 538 F9, 551 I9
Bruen Island WA 581 I5, 584 C7
Brukunga SA 553 H8, 554 E9
Brungle NSW 519 A4, 520 C1,
522 D10
Brunkerville NSW 509 F3, 514 B9
Brunswick Vic. 531 D5, 537 I5,
540 C4
Brunswick Heads NSW 516 H4,
525 O3, 609 N12, 73
Brunswick Junction WA 572 E3,
574 C8
Bruny Island Tas. 622 H11,
623 I10, 625 K10, **473**
Brush Island NSW 519 F5, 521 N5,
523 I11
Brush Island Qld 605 G5, 611 K4
Brushgrove NSW 515 A1, 516 E8,
525 I8
Bruthen Vic. 541 N5
Bryden Qld 600 A2, 602 C9
Brymaroo Qld 609 K8
Buangor Vic. 551 J3
Buaraba Qld 602 A9
Bucasia Qld 605 G7, 611 K5
Bucca Qld 603 C2, 604 F10, 609 M3
Buccan Qld 599 E11, 600 E7
Buccleuch SA 559 M10, 568 E4
Buchan Vic. 519 A11, 539 A10,
541 P4, **149**
Buchan South Vic. 541 O4
**Buchanan (Yirrapurlinsay) Island
NT** 590 D3
Bucheen Creek Vic. 543 N8, 545 M5
Buckenderra NSW 519 B7, 520 E8,
539 D3
Bucketty NSW 509 C4, 523 K4
Buckingham SA 526 A12, 568 G7
Buckingham WA 572 H3, 574 D8
Buckland Tas. 623 M2, 625 M5
Buckland Vic. 543 K10, 544 H8
Buckleboo SA 558 E3, 560 D10
Buckley Vic. 536 E8, 538 F1,
551 N8
Buckrabanyule Vic. 526 G12, 549 L7
Budawang NP NSW 519 F5, 521 L4,
522 H11
Buddabaddah NSW 529 O11
Budderoo NP NSW 517 D7, 519 G3,
523 J9, 60, 85
Buddibuddi Island Qld 605 G5,
611 K3
Buddigower NSW 522 B6, 527 O6
Buddina Qld 602 H4, 603 F12
Buderim Qld 602 G4, 603 F12,
609 N7, **397**
Budgeree Vic. 537 P11, 540 H8
Budgeree East Vic. 540 H8
Budgerum Vic. 549 L4
Budgewoi NSW 509 F6, 514 B12
Buffalo Vic. 537 O12, 540 G9
Buffalo Creek Vic. 543 J9, 544 H6
Buffalo River Vic. 543 J9, 544 H6
Buffon Island WA 581 J3, 584 F4

Bugaldie NSW 524 D9
Bugilbone NSW 524 D5
Bugong NP NSW 517 B8, 519 G3,
523 I9
Builyan Qld 604 D9, 609 L2
Bukalong NSW 519 C9, 539 E6
Bukkulla NSW 525 I5
Bulahdelah NSW 514 H4, 515 C10,
523 N3, **36**
Bulart Vic. 550 F3
Bulburin NP Qld 603 A1, 604 D8,
609 L2
Buldah Vic. 519 C10, 539 E9
Bulga NSW 523 K3
Bulgandramine NSW 522 E2
Bulgobac Tas. 626 E8, 628 B5
Bulla NT 581 P4, 585 P5, 590 C11,
592 C2
Bulla Vic. 531 C4, 537 I4, 540 B3
Bullaburra NSW 510 E6, 512 H9
Bullala NP NSW 524 H4, 609 I12
Bullarah NSW 524 E4
Bullaring WA 574 F6, 576 E8
Bullarook Vic. 535 D10, 536 D3,
551 M4
Bullarto Vic. 535 F9, 536 F2,
551 N3
Bullarto South Vic. 535 F9, 536 F2
Bullengarook Vic. 535 H10,
536 G3, 540 A2, 551 O4
Bullengarook East Vic. 535 H10,
536 G3, 540 A2
Buller Island WA 574 A2, 576 B6
Bulleringa NP Qld 613 I7
Bullfinch WA 574 H2, 576 F6
Bullhead Creek Vic. 543 M8, 545 K4
Bulli NSW 517 G4
Bullioh Vic. 543 M7, 545 L3
Bullock Creek Qld 606 A5, 613 J7
Bullocks Flat NSW 520 D10,
539 B4, 62
Bulls Island NSW 514 G7, 515 C12,
523 M4
Bullsbrook WA 570 E2, 571 C3,
574 C4, 576 C7
Bullumwaal Vic. 541 M4
Bulman NT 591 J6
Buln Buln Vic. 534 H12, 537 N8,
540 G6
Buln Buln East Vic. 534 H12,
537 O8, 540 G6
Bulwer Qld 600 G1, 609 N8
Bulyee WA 574 F5, 576 D8
Bumaga Island NT 591 M3
Bumbaldry NSW 522 E6
Bumberry NSW 522 E4
Bumbunga SA 556 G2, 559 I6
Bumpus Island WA 581 J4, 584 E5
Bunbartha Vic. 527 K12, 542 E6
Bunburra Qld 516 D1, 600 A9
Bunbury WA 572 D4, 574 C8,
576 C9, **297**
Bundaberg Qld 603 D2, 604 F10,
609 M3, **398**
Bundaburrah NSW 522 D5
Bundalaguah Vic. 541 K6
Bundalong Vic. 527 M12, 542 H5,
544 E1
Bundalong South Vic. 542 H6,
544 E2
Bundanoon NSW 517 A7, 519 G3,
523 I9, **38**
Bundarra NSW 525 I7
Bundeena NSW 508 E11, 511 L12,
523 K7

Bundella NSW 524 F10
Bunding Vic. 535 E10, 536 E3,
551 N4
Bundjalung NP NSW 516 F7,
525 N5, 50, 59
Bundook NSW 515 C8, 523 N1,
525 K12
Bundure NSW 527 M9
Bung Bong Vic. 535 A6, 549 L12,
551 L1
Bunga NSW 519 E8, 521 K12
Bungador Vic. 538 A2, 551 K8
Bungal Vic. 535 E11, 536 E4,
551 N5
Bungarby NSW 519 C9, 520 F12,
539 E5
Bungaree Vic. 535 D10, 536 D3,
551 M4
Bungawalbin NP NSW 516 F6,
525 N4, 609 N12
Bungeet Vic. 542 H7, 544 D3
Bungendore NSW 518 H5, 519 D4,
521 I3, 522 G10, 83, 119
Bungil Vic. 522 B12, 543 M6,
545 L2
Bungonia NSW 519 F3, 522 H9
Bungonia NP NSW 519 F3, 522 H9
Bungowannah NSW 522 A12,
543 K5, 545 I1
Bungulla NSW 516 A5, 525 L4,
609 L12
Bungulla WA 574 F4
Bunguluke Vic. 526 G12, 549 L6
Bungunya Qld 524 F1, 608 H10
Bungwahl NSW 515 D10, 523 N3
Buninyong Vic. 535 C11, 536 D4,
551 M4, 148
Bunnaloo NSW 527 J11, 542 B3,
549 P5
Bunnan NSW 523 J1, 524 G12
Buntine WA 576 C5
Bunurong Marine NP Vic.
537 M12, 540 E9
Bunurong Marine Park Vic.
537 L12, 540 E9
Bunya Mountains NP Qld 609 K7,
420
Bunyah NSW 515 D9, 523 N2
Bunyan NSW 519 C7, 520 G9,
539 F3
Bunyip Vic. 534 E12, 537 M8,
540 F6
Buraja NSW 527 M11, 543 I4
Burbank Qld 600 E5, 602 G12
Burbong NSW 518 G5, 520 H3
Burcher NSW 522 C5, 527 P5
Burekup WA 572 E3, 574 C8
Burford Island NT 590 F2
Burgooney NSW 522 A4, 527 N4
Burgunngura Island NT 591 M2
Burke and Wills Roadhouse Qld
612 B10, 615 F8
Burke Island Qld 614 D1
Burkes Flat Vic. 535 A2, 549 L9
Burketown Qld 612 A7, 615 D4,
397
Burkitt Island Qld 614 F10
Burleigh Heads Qld 516 G1, 525 O1,
600 G10, 601 F8, 609 N11, **397**
Burleigh Head NP Qld 516 G1,
525 O1, 600 G10, 601 F8, 609 N11,
397
Burleigh Waters Qld 601 F8
Burnbank Vic. 535 A7, 549 L12,
551 L2

Burnett Heads Qld 603 D1, 604 G10, 609 M3
Burney (Malkura) Island NT 591 M6
Burnie Tas. 626 F5, **473**
Burns WA 570 B3, 571 B4
Burns Creek Tas. 627 L8
Burnside Island WA 575 C3
Burnt Yards NSW 522 F5
Buronga NSW 546 G6
Burpengary Qld 599 E2, 600 D1, 602 F8, 609 N8
Burra SA 559 K5, **230**
Burraboi NSW 527 I10, 542 A1, 549 O2
Burracoppin WA 574 G3, 576 E6
Burradoo NSW 517 B5
Burraga NSW 522 G6
Burragate NSW 539 G8
Burral Yurrul NP NSW 525 I3, 609 J12
Burramine South Vic. 542 G5, 544 C1
Burrandana NSW 522 B10, 527 P10, 543 M2
Burrawang NSW 517 C6, 519 G3, 523 I9, 85
Burrell Creek NSW 515 D8, 523 N1, 525 K12
Burren Junction NSW 524 D6
Burrereo Vic. 549 I8
Burrier NSW 517 B9, 521 N1
Burrill Lake NSW 519 G5, 521 N4, 523 I11
Burringbar NSW 516 G3, 525 O2, 609 N11
Burringurrah WA 575 F6, 578 C7
Burrinjuck NSW 519 B3, 522 E9
Burroin Vic. 526 E10, 548 H3
Burrowa–Pine Mountain NP Vic. 520 A7, 522 C12, 527 P12, 543 N6, 545 N2, 156
Burroway NSW 524 B11
Burrowye Vic. 522 C12, 527 P12, 543 N6, 545 M2
Burrum Vic. 549 I9
Burrum Coast NP Qld 603 D3, 604 G11, 609 M4, 398, 417
Burrum Heads Qld 603 E4, 604 G11, 609 N4, 417
Burrumbeet Vic. 535 B9, 536 C2, 551 L3
Burrumbuttock NSW 522 A11, 527 N11, 543 K4
Burswood WA 570 E6, 571 C5
Burton Rocks WA 577 I9
Burwood NSW 508 D7
Burwood Vic. 537 J6
Busby Islet SA 556 E10, 558 H1Í
Bush Islet Qld 611 L7, 614 D2
Bushfield Vic. 538 C7, 550 G8
Bushy Island Qld 604 D7, 609 L1, 611 N12, 614 D4
Bushy Islet (Northern) Qld 614 E5
Bushy Islet (Southern) Qld 614 E5
Bushy Park Tas. 622 F3, 625 I6
Bushy Park Vic. 541 K5
Busselton WA 572 C6, 574 B9, 576 B10, **293**
Bustard (Angwardinumanja) Island NT 591 M7
Butchers Ridge Vic. 519 A10, 539 A8, 541 P2, 545 P12
Bute SA 556 F2, 559 I6
Butler Tanks SA 558 E6

Butlers Gorge Tas. 624 G3
Butmaroo NSW 519 D4, 521 I2, 522 G10
Butterleaf NP NSW 516 A7, 525 K5
Button Island WA 577 I9
Buxton NSW 517 D3, 519 G2, 523 I8
Buxton Qld 603 D4, 604 G11, 609 M4, 404
Buxton Vic. 534 F4, 537 N3, 540 F2, 544 B12
Byabarra NSW 515 E6, 525 L11
Byaduk Vic. 550 E5
Byaduk North Vic. 550 E5
Byam Martin Island WA 581 J4, 584 E5
Byawatha Vic. 543 J7, 544 G3
Byfield NP Qld 604 C3, 611 N10, 450
Byford WA 570 F9, 571 D7, 574 C5
Bylands Vic. 531 D1, 537 J2, 540 C2, 542 C12, 172
Bylong NSW 523 I2
Bymount Qld 608 F5
Byrne Vic. 543 I8, 544 F5
Byrneside Vic. 542 D7
Byrnestown Qld 603 A5, 604 E12, 609 L4
Byrneville Vic. 548 G8
Byrock NSW 529 N7
Byron Bay NSW 516 H4, 525 O3, 609 N12, **39**
Byron Island WA 581 I5, 584 C7

C

Cabarita Vic. 526 D6, 546 G6
Cabarlah Qld 609 L9, 447
Cabawin Qld 609 I8
Cabbage Tree Creek Vic. 519 B12, 539 C11
Cabbage Tree Island NSW 514 H7, 515 C11, 523 N3
Cable Beach WA 580 H8, 584 A11, 295
Caboolture Qld 599 E1, 600 D1, 602 F7, 609 N8, **399**
Caboonbah Qld 602 B7, 609 M8
Cabramatta NSW 508 B7, 511 J9, 519 H1, 523 J7
Cabramurra NSW 519 B6, 520 D7, 522 D12, 539 B1
Cadell SA 559 M6, 248
Cadney Homestead SA 565 N7
Cadoux WA 574 E2, 576 D6
Caesar Island WA 581 I5, 584 D6
Caffarelli Island WA 581 I5, 584 C7
Cahills Crossing NT 589 P2, 590 H4
Caiguna WA 577 M7, **295**
Caiguna Roadhouse WA 577 L7
Cairncross Islets A Qld 614 D4
Cairncross Islets B Qld 614 E4
Cairncross Islets C Qld 614 E4
Cairns Qld 606 E2, 607 F7, 613 L6, **402**
Cairns Bay Tas. 622 F9, 625 I9
Calala NSW 525 I9
Calamvale Qld 599 E9, 600 D6
Calca SA 558 A3, 567 N11
Calder Tas. 626 E5
Calder Island Qld 605 H6, 611 L5
Caldermeade Vic. 533 P6
Caldwell NSW 527 I10, 542 B2, 549 P4
Calen Qld 605 F7, 611 J5

Calf Island Qld 605 F5, 611 K4
Calga NSW 509 C8, 511 M3
Calingiri WA 574 C3, 576 C6
Caliph SA 559 N8, 568 F2
Calivil Vic. 549 N7
Callala Bay NSW 517 D10, 519 G4, 521 O2, 523 J10
Callawadda Vic. 549 I10
Calleen NSW 522 B5, 527 O5
Callide Qld 604 A8, 609 J1
Callignee Vic. 541 I8
Callignee North Vic. 541 I8
Callington SA 554 F11, 559 K10, 568 C3
Calliope Qld 604 D7, 609 K1, 611 N12, 412
Calliope Island Qld 611 L7
Caloona NSW 524 E2, 608 G11
Caloote SA 554 H9, 559 K9
Caloundra Qld 602 H5, 603 F12, 609 N8, 400
Caltowie SA 559 J4, 560 H11
Calulu Vic. 541 M5
Calvert Qld 602 B12
Calvert Vic. 551 I3
Camballin WA 581 J7, 584 E11
Cambarville Vic. 534 H5, 537 O4, 540 G3
Camberwell NSW 523 K2
Camberwell Vic. 531 E6, 537 J6
Cambewarra NSW 517 C8, 519 G3, 523 I9
Cambrai SA 554 H6, 559 L8, 568 D2
Cambrian Hill Vic. 535 C11, 536 C4
Cambridge Tas. 623 J5, 625 K7
Camdale Tas. 626 F5
Camden NSW 510 G11, 517 E1, 519 H1, 523 J7, **38**
Camena Tas. 628 E1
Cameron Corner NSW 528 B1, 563 N11, 618 F10, 92
Camira Qld 599 C9, 600 C6, 602 E12
Camira Creek NSW 516 E7, 525 N4
Camooweal Qld 593 P10, 615 A9, 616 C1, **400**
Camooweal Caves NP Qld 593 P10, 615 A9, 616 C1, 401
Camp Coorong SA 559 L12, 568 D5, 246
Camp Hill Qld 599 E8, 600 E5, 602 F11
Camp Island Qld 605 D3, 611 I2
Campania Tas. 623 J2, 625 K6
Campbell Island WA 575 D1, 582 A4
Campbell Town Tas. 625 L1, 627 L11, **473**
Campbells Bridge Vic. 549 I10
Campbells Creek Vic. 535 F6, 549 N12, 551 N1
Campbells Forest Vic. 535 F2, 549 N9
Campbells Pocket Qld 599 C1, 602 E7
Campbelltown NSW 510 H11, 517 F1, 519 H1, 523 J7, **38**
Campbelltown Vic. 535 D7, 549 M12, 551 M2
Camperdown Vic. 538 H7, 551 J7, **149**
Campwin Beach Qld 605 G8, 611 K6
Camurra NSW 524 G4
Canadian Vic. 535 C10, 536 D3

Canary Island Vic. 549 N6
Canary Island South Vic. 549 M6
Canbelego NSW 529 M9
Canberra ACT 518 E5, 519 D4, 520 H3, 522 F10, 105, **108**
Candelo NSW 519 D9, 539 H6, 30
Cangai NSW 516 C7, 525 L5
Cania Gorge NP Qld 604 C9, 609 K2, 429
Caniambo Vic. 542 F8, 544 B4
Cann River Vic. 519 C11, 539 E10, **151**
Canna WA 575 F12, 576 B3
Cannawigara SA 526 A12, 548 A6, 568 G7
Cannie Vic. 526 G11, 549 L4
Canning Island WA 577 I9
Canning Vale WA 570 E8, 571 C6, 574 C5
Cannington WA 570 E7, 571 C5
Cannon Creek Qld 516 D1, 525 K2, 600 A9
Cannons Creek Vic. 533 M6
Cannonvale Qld 605 F5, 611 J3
Cannum Vic. 548 G7
Canomodine NSW 522 F5
Canonba NSW 529 P9
Canoona Qld 604 A4, 611 M10
Canowie SA 559 K4, 561 I12
Canowindra NSW 522 F5, **40**
Canteen Creek NT 593 L11, 595 L1
Canterbury NSW 508 E8, 511 L9
Canunda NP SA 568 F11, 247
Canungra Qld 516 F1, 600 E9, 601 A6
Cap Island SA 558 C6
Cap Island WA 577 J9
Capalaba Qld 599 G8, 600 E5, 602 G12
Cape Arid NP WA 577 K9, 291, 305
Cape Barren Island Tas. 624 B12, 627 O2
Cape Borda SA 556 A11, 558 F11
Cape Bridgewater Vic. 550 C8, 188
Cape Clear Vic. 535 A12, 536 B5, 551 L5
Cape Hillsborough NP Qld 605 G7, 611 K5, 424
Cape Howe Marine NP Vic. 519 E11, 539 H11
Cape Island Qld 604 B1, 611 M8
Cape Jaffa SA 568 E9
Cape Jervis SA 555 A9, 556 F10, 559 I11, 568 A5, 267
Cape Le Grand NP WA 577 I9, 305
Cape Melville NP Qld 613 K1, 614 H11, 407
Cape Palmerston NP Qld 605 H9, 611 K6, 441
Cape Paterson Vic. 537 L12, 540 E9, 202
Cape Range NP WA 575 B3, 306
Cape Rock Qld 614 G10
Cape Schanck Vic. 532 H10
Cape Tribulation Qld 607 E1, 613 L4, 408
Cape Upstart NP Qld 605 C3, 611 I2, 613 P12, 396
Cape Woolamai Vic. 533 M11, 537 K11, 540 D8, 159
Capel WA 572 D5, 574 B9, 576 C10
Capella Qld 611 I9, 410
Capels Crossing Vic. 549 N4
Capertee NSW 523 I4
Capertee NP NSW 523 I4

Capietha SA 558 B2, 560 A10, 567 O10

Capoompeta NP NSW 516 A7, 525 K5

Capps Island WA 577 I9

Capricorn Coast NP Qld 604 C4, 611 N10

Capricorn Roadhouse WA 578 E5, 583 L11

Capricornia Cays NP Qld 604 F5, 609 N1, 611 P11, 412

Capstan Island WA 581 K3, 584 G3

Captain Billy Landing Qld 614 D4

Captains Flat NSW 518 G9, 519 D5, 521 I5, 522 G11, 83

Carabost NSW 520 A4, 522 C11, 527 P11, 543 O4

Caragabal NSW 522 D6

Caralue SA 558 E4, 560 D12

Caralulup Vic. 535 B7, 549 L12, 551 L2

Caramut Vic. 550 H6

Carapooee Vic. 549 K9

Carapook Vic. 550 D3

Carawa SA 558 A1, 567 N9

Carbeen Qld 606 D3, 607 D8

Carboor Vic. 543 J9, 544 G6

Carboor Upper Vic. 543 J9, 544 G6

Carbunup River WA 572 B7

Carcoar NSW 522 G5, 33

Cardiff NSW 509 G3, 514 C9

Cardigan Village Vic. 535 B10, 536 C3, 551 L3

Cardinia Vic. 531 H10, 533 O5, 534 C12, 537 L8, 540 E6

Cardross Vic. 546 G6

Cardstone Qld 606 D5, 613 L8

Cardwell Qld 606 E7, 613 M9, **401**

Careening Island WA 581 J4, 584 E5

Carey Island WA 575 D1, 578 A2, 582 C5

Cargerie Vic. 535 D12, 536 D5, 551 M5

Cargo NSW 522 F5

Carilla WA 570 G7

Carinda NSW 524 A6

Carindale Qld 599 F8

Caringbah NSW 508 D10, 511 K11

Carisbrook Vic. 535 C6, 549 M11, 551 M1

Carlia Island WA 581 L2, 584 H2

Carlingford NSW 508 D6, 511 K7

Carlisle Island Qld 605 G6, 611 K5

Carlisle River Vic. 536 A11, 538 A4, 551 K9

Carlo Island Qld 603 F7, 609 N6

Carlsruhe Vic. 535 H8, 536 G1, 540 A1, 542 A12, 551 O3

Carlton Tas. 623 L5, 625 L7

Carlwood NSW 522 H5

Carmel WA 570 G6

Carmila Qld 605 G10, 611 K7, 441

Carnac Island WA 570 B9, 571 B6, 574 B5, 576 B8

Carnamah WA 576 B4, **295**

Carnarvon WA 575 B7, 586 C2, **298**

Carnarvon NP Qld 608 E2, 428, 440, 441, 443

Carnegie Homestead WA 579 I8

Carngham Vic. 535 A10, 536 B3, 551 L4

Caroline SA 550 A5, 568 G12

Carool NSW 601 E11

Caroona NSW 524 G10

Carpa SA 556 A2, 558 F5

Carpendeit Vic. 538 H8, 551 J8

Carpenter Rocks SA 568 F12

Carpet Snake Island Qld 605 F6, 611 K5

Carrabin WA 574 H3

Carrai NP NSW 515 E3, 525 L9

Carrajung Vic. 541 I8

Carrajung South Vic. 541 J8

Carranballac Vic. 551 J4

Carraragarmungee Vic. 543 I7, 544 G4

Carrathool NSW 527 L7

Carrick Tas. 627 J8, 629 F11, 481

Carrickalinga SA 555 C7, 556 G9, 559 I10, 568 B4

Carrieton SA 559 J2, 561 I9, 265

Carrington NSW 514 D9, 515 C11

Carroll NSW 524 G9

Carron Vic. 526 F12, 549 I7

Carronade Island WA 581 L2, 585 I1

Carrum Vic. 531 E9, 533 K3, 537 J8, 540 D6

Carrum Downs Vic. 531 F9, 533 L3, 537 J8, 540 D6

Carseldine Qld 599 E5, 600 D3, 602 F10

Carwarp Vic. 526 E7, 546 G7

Cascade WA 576 H9

Cascade NP NSW 516 C11, 525 M7

Cascades Tas. 621 C9

Cashmore Vic. 550 D7

Casino NSW 516 E5, 525 N3, 609 M12, **40**

Cassilis NSW 523 I1, 524 F12, 71

Cassilis Vic. 541 M2, 543 M12, 545 M12

Cassim Island Qld 599 H8, 600 F5, 602 H12, 609 N9

Cassini Island WA 581 K2, 584 G1

Castella Vic. 531 H3, 534 C5, 537 L3, 540 E3

Casterton Vic. 550 C3, 568 H11, **152**

Castle Forbes Bay Tas. 622 F8, 625 I8

Castle Hill NSW 508 D5, 509 A11, 511 K7

Castle Rock NSW 523 K2

Castle Tower NP Qld 604 D8, 609 L1, 412

Castleburn Vic. 541 L4

Castlemaine Vic. 535 F6, 549 N12, 551 N1, **152**

Castlemaine Diggings National Heritage Park Vic. 535 F6, 542 A10, 549 O12, 551 N1, 152

Castlereagh NSW 510 G5, 513 M8

Casuarina Islets (The Brothers) SA 556 A12, 558 F12

Casula NSW 508 B8, 511 I9

Caswell Island WA 581 K2, 584 F3

Cat Island Tas. 624 C10, 626 C12

Cataby Roadhouse WA 574 B2, 576 B6

Catamaran Tas. 625 I11

Catani Vic. 537 M9

Cataract NP NSW 516 C4, 525 L3, 609 L12

Cathcart NSW 519 D9, 539 F7, 34

Cathcart Vic. 551 I2

Cathedral Rock NP NSW 515 E1, 516 A12, 525 L8, 48

Catherine Hill Bay NSW 509 F5, 514 C11, 523 L5

Cathkin Vic. 537 M1, 540 F1, 542 F11, 544 A10

Cathundral NSW 524 A11

Cattai NSW 508 B1, 511 J4

Cattai NP NSW 508 B1, 511 J4, 523 J6, 101

Catumnal Vic. 526 G12, 549 L6

Caulfield Vic. 531 E6, 537 J6, 540 C5

Cave Island Qld 605 F6, 611 K5

Cave Island WA 577 J9

Caveat Vic. 542 E11, 544 A9

Cavendish Vic. 550 F3, 165

Caveside Tas. 626 H9, 628 H6, 629 A11

Cawdor NSW 510 G11, 517 E1

Cawongla NSW 516 F4, 525 N3, 609 N12

Cecil Park NSW 508 A7, 511 I8

Cecil Plains Qld 609 K9, 409

Cedar Bay NP Qld 613 L3, 407

Cedar Brush Creek NSW 509 D5

Cedar Grove Qld 600 D8

Ceduna SA 567 M8, **230**

Celery Top Islands Tas. 624 F10

Central Castra Tas. 626 G7, 628 F2

Central Colo NSW 511 I2, 513 P2, 523 J5

Central Mangrove NSW 509 C6, 511 N1, 523 K5

Central Tilba NSW 519 E8, 521 K10, 75

Centre Island NT 591 N10, 593 N2

Centre Rock WA 581 L2, 584 H2

Centreville Vic. 533 L4

Ceratodus Qld 604 C11, 609 K4

Ceres NSW 522 E1, 524 B12

Ceres Vic. 536 F8, 538 G1, 551 N7

Cervantes WA 574 A2, 576 A5, **296**

Cervantes Islands WA 574 A2, 576 A6

Cessnock NSW 509 E2, 514 A8, 523 L4, **42**

Chaelundi NP NSW 516 C10, 525 L6

Chain Valley Bay NSW 509 F6, 514 B11

Chakola NSW 519 C7, 520 G8, 539 F2

Chalky Island Tas. 624 A10

Challis WA 570 F8

Chambers Island WA 581 I5, 584 C7

Champagny Island WA 581 J4, 584 E5

Championet Island WA 581 K2, 584 F3

Chandada SA 558 B2, 567 O10

Chandler SA 565 L4

Chandlers Creek Vic. 519 C11, 539 E9

Channel Island NT 588 D3, 590 D4

Channel Island WA 571 C9, 574 B6, 576 C8

Channel Islet Qld 611 L7

Chapel Hill Qld 599 D7

Chapman Hill WA 572 C7, 574 B9

Chapman Island Qld 614 F7

Chapple Vale Vic. 538 A4, 551 K10

Charam Vic. 548 D10

Chardons Bridge Qld 601 B2

Charles Darwin NP NT 588 D3, 590 D4

Charleston SA 553 G7, 554 E9, 555 H2, 559 K9

Charlestown NSW 509 G4, 514 C10

Charleville Qld 608 B5, 619 P5, **401**

Charley Island WA 577 I9

Charlie Island WA 575 B9, 586 D9

Charlotte Pass NSW 519 A8, 520 C10, 539 B4, 62

Charlton NSW 522 H6, 529 O6

Charlton Vic. 526 G12, 549 K7

Charnocks Crossing NSW 601 C12

Charring Cross Island Vic. 531 G11, 533 N6, 537 K9, 540 D7

Charringa Qld 606 E3, 607 F8

Charters Towers Qld 610 F2, **403**

Chasm Creek Tas. 626 F5

Chasm Island NT 591 N6

Chatham Island WA 573 E6, 574 E12, 576 D12

Chatsbury NSW 519 E2, 522 H8

Chatswood NSW 508 F6, 509 B11, 511 L8

Chatsworth NSW 516 F7, 525 N5

Chatsworth Vic. 550 H5

Cheepie Qld 619 M6

Cheesemans Creek NSW 522 F4

Chelsea Vic. 531 E8, 533 K2, 537 J7, 540 D6

Chelsea Heights Vic. 533 K2

Cheltenham NSW 508 D5, 509 A11

Cheltenham Vic. 531 E7, 533 J1, 537 J7, 540 C5

Chepstowe Vic. 535 A10, 536 B3, 551 L4

Cherbourg Qld 603 A9, 609 L6, 432

Cherbourg NP Qld 603 A9, 609 L6

Chermside Qld 599 E6, 600 D3, 602 F10

Cherokee Vic. 536 H2, 540 B2

Cheropo Islet Qld 614 C2

Cheshunt Vic. 543 I10, 544 F7

Chesney Vale Vic. 542 H7, 544 D4

Chesterton Range NP Qld 608 D5

Chetwynd Vic. 548 D12, 550 D2, 568 H10

Cheviot Island Qld 604 C1, 611 N8

Chewton Vic. 535 F6, 542 A10, 549 O12, 551 O1, 154

Cheyne Beach WA 573 G10, 574 H11, 576 F11

Cheyne Island WA 576 F11

Chidlow WA 570 H4, 571 E4

Chigwell Tas. 621 A3

Childers Qld 603 C4, 604 F11, 609 M4, **404**

Childers Vic. 537 O10, 540 G7, 199

Chillagoe Qld 606 A3, 613 J6, **404**

Chillagoe Mungana Caves NP Qld 606 A3, 613 J6, 404

Chillingham NSW 516 G2, 600 E12

Chillingollah Vic. 526 F9, 547 J12, 549 J1

Chilpanunda SA 558 A2, 567 O10

Chiltern Vic. 527 N12, 543 J6, 544 H2, **154**

Chiltern–Mount Pilot NP Vic. 522 A12, 527 N12, 543 J7, 544 G3, 154

Chiltern Valley Vic. 543 J6, 544 G2

Chinaman Wells SA 556 D5, 558 H7, 568 E10

Chinbingina SA 558 A1, 567 N8

Chinchilla Qld 609 J7, **405**

Chinderah NSW 516 H2, 525 O2, 600 G12, 601 H12, 609 N11

Chinkapook Vic. 526 F9, 547 J11, 549 J1

Chittering WA 571 D1, 574 C4

Cholmondeley Islet Qld 614 E4

Chorregon Qld 610 A8, 617 M8

Christie Downs SA 554 A11, 555 E4

Christies Beach SA 553 A10, 554 A11, 555 E4

Christmas Creek Qld 606 C9, 613 K11

Christmas Hills Tas. 626 C4

Christmas Hills Vic. 531 G4, 534 B6, 537 K4

Christmas Island Tas. 625 O10

Chudleigh Tas. 626 H8, 629 B11

Church Point NSW 508 H4, 509 C10, 511 N6

Churchill Qld 599 A9, 600 B6, 602 D12

Churchill Vic. 540 H8

Churchill Island Vic. 533 M11, 537 K11, 540 D8, 158

Churchill Island Marine NP Vic. 533 M11, 537 K11, 540 D8

Churchill NP Vic. 531 F7, 533 M1, 534 A10, 537 K7, 540 D5

Chute Vic. 536 A1, 551 K2

Chuwar Qld 599 B8, 600 B5, 602 D12

Cid Island Qld 605 F5, 611 K3

Citadel Island Vic. 540 G12

Clack Island Qld 614 G10

Clackline WA 571 F3, 574 D4

Clairview Qld 605 H11, 611 L8, 441

Clandulla NSW 523 I3

Clara Island Qld 604 A1, 611 M8

Clare Qld 605 B3, 606 H12, 610 H2

Clare SA 556 H2, 559 J6, **231**

Claremont Tas. 621 B2, 623 I4, 625 K6

Claremont Vic. 543 I9, 544 F6

Claremont WA 570 C6, 571 B5, 574 B5, 279

Claremont Isles NP Qld 614 F10

Clarence NSW 510 C2, 512 E2, 523 I5

Clarence Point Tas. 627 J6, 629 E6

Clarence Town NSW 514 E6, 515 B11, 523 M3, 83

Clarendon NSW 511 I5, 513 O7

Clarendon Qld 602 B10

Clarendon SA 553 C10, 554 B11, 555 F4, 556 H8, 559 J9, 568 B3

Clarendon Tas. 627 K9, 629 H12

Clarendon Vic. 535 D11, 536 D4, 551 M5

Clark Island NSW 508 F7, 509 B12, 511 M9, 523 K7

Clarke Island Tas. 624 B12, 627 O3

Clarkefield Vic. 531 B2, 536 H3, 540 B2, 551 P4

Clarkes Hill Vic. 535 D10, 536 D3, 551 M3

Clarkson WA 570 B3

Claude Road Tas. 626 G8, 628 G4

Clay Wells SA 568 F10

Clayton Qld 603 D2

Clayton SA 555 H8, 559 K11, 568 C4

Clayton Vic. 531 E7, 537 J6

Clear Lake Vic. 548 E10

Clear Ridge NSW 522 C5, 527 P5

Cleft Island Vic. 540 H12

Cleft Island WA 581 I5, 584 C7

Cleghorn Island WA 581 K2, 584 G2

Clematis Vic. 531 H7, 533 O1, 534 C10, 537 L7

Clerk Island WA 581 K2, 584 G2

Clerke Island Qld 614 E5

Clermont Qld 605 B12, 610 H9, **405**

Cleve SA 556 A1, 558 F5

Cleveland Qld 599 H8, 600 F5, 602 H12, 609 N9, 384

Cleveland Tas. 627 L10

Cliff Island WA 577 I9

Cliff Island NP Qld 614 F10

Cliff Islands Qld 614 F10

Cliffy Island Vic. 541 I11

Clift Island NT 590 C2

Clifton NSW 517 G3, 525 K3, 609 K12

Clifton Qld 609 L10, **405**

Clifton Beach Qld 606 D2, 607 F6, 613 L6, 435

Clifton Beach Tas. 623 K7, 625 L8

Clifton Creek Vic. 541 M5

Clifton Hill Vic. 531 D5

Clifton Springs Vic. 532 D4, 536 G8, 540 A6, 551 O7

Clinton Centre SA 556 F4, 559 I7, 568 A1

Clintonvale Qld 516 B1, 525 L1, 609 L10

Clonbinane Vic. 537 J2, 540 D2, 542 D12

Cloncurry Qld 615 F11, 616 H3, **406**

Clonmel Island Vic. 541 I10

Clontarf Qld 609 K10

Closeburn Qld 599 C5, 600 C3, 602 E10

Cloud Island WA 577 I9

Clouds Creek NSW 516 C10, 525 M7

Clovelly Park SA 554 B9, 555 F3

Cloven Hills Vic. 551 J6

Cloyna Qld 603 A8, 609 L6

Cluan Tas. 627 J9, 629 E11

Club Terrace Vic. 519 B11, 539 D10

Cluden Qld 605 A1, 606 G10, 610 G1

Clump Island NT 581 P3, 585 O3, 590 B9

Clump Island Tas. 626 B3

Clump Mountain NP Qld 606 E5, 613 M8, 428

Clunes NSW 516 G4, 525 O3, 609 N12

Clunes Vic. 535 C8, 536 C1, 551 M2, **154**

Clybucca NSW 515 G4, 525 M9

Clyde Vic. 531 G9, 533 M4, 534 B12, 537 K8, 540 D6

Clyde North Vic. 533 N4

Clyde River NP NSW 519 F6, 521 L6, 522 H12

Clydebank Vic. 541 L6

Clydesdale Vic. 535 E7, 549 N12

Coal Creek Qld 602 B8

Coal Island Qld 611 L8

Coalcliff NSW 517 G3

Coaldale NSW 516 D7, 525 M5

Coalstoun Lakes Qld 603 A5, 609 L5

Coalstoun Lakes NP Qld 603 A5, 604 E12, 609 L5, 394

Coalville Vic. 537 P9, 540 H7

Cobains Vic. 541 K7

Cobaki NSW 601 F11

Cobar NSW 529 L9, **41**

Cobargo NSW 519 E8, 521 K10, 31

Cobaw Vic. 536 H1, 540 B1, 542 B12

Cobbadah NSW 524 H7

Cobbannah Vic. 541 L4

Cobbitty NSW 510 G10, 519 H1, 523 J7

Cobboboonee NP Vic. 550 C6, 568 H12

Cobborra NSW 522 G1, 524 D12

Cobby Cobby Island Qld 600 G7, 609 N10

Cobden Vic. 538 G8, 551 J8

Cobdogla SA 526 A6, 559 N7, 568 F1

Cobera SA 526 A7, 559 N9, 568 F2

Cobram Vic. 527 L12, 542 F4, **154**

Cobrico Vic. 538 G7, 551 I8

Cobungra Vic. 541 M1, 543 M12, 545 L10

Coburg Vic. 531 D5, 537 I5

Cocamba Vic. 526 F9, 547 J11

Cochranes Creek Vic. 535 B2, 549 L9

Cockaleechie SA 558 D7

Cockatoo Vic. 531 H7, 533 P1, 534 D10, 537 L7, 540 E5

Cockatoo Island NSW 508 E7, 509 B12, 511 L8, 523 K7

Cockatoo Island WA 581 I5, 584 D7

Cockburn SA 528 A10, 559 O1, 561 N8

Cockermouth Island Qld 605 H6, 611 L5

Cockle Creek Tas. 625 I11, 481

Cocklebiddy WA 577 M6, **296**

Cocklebiddy Roadhouse WA 577 M6

Cocoparra NP NSW 527 M6, 55

Codrington Vic. 550 E7

Coen Qld 614 E10

Coffin Bay SA 558 D8, **232**

Coffin Bay NP SA 558 C7, 232

Coffin Island WA 573 F11, 574 H11, 576 E11

Coffin Islet Qld 605 G6, 611 K5

Coffs Harbour NSW 515 H1, 516 E12, 525 N8, **45**

Coghills Creek Vic. 535 B9, 536 C2, 551 M3

Cohen Island WA 578 B2, 580 B12, 582 D4

Cohuna Vic. 527 I11, 542 A3, 549 O5, **155**

Coimadai Vic. 535 G11, 536 G4, 540 A3, 551 O4

Colac Vic. 536 B9, 538 B2, 551 L8, **155**

Colac Colac Vic. 520 A8, 543 O7, 545 N4

Colbert Island WA 581 J3, 584 E4

Colbinabbin Vic. 542 C8

Colbinabbin West Vic. 542 C8

Cole Island Qld 605 G5, 611 K4

Coleambally NSW 527 M8, 60

Colebrook Tas. 623 J1, 625 K5

Coledale NSW 517 G3

Coleraine Vic. 550 E3, **156**

Coles Bay Tas. 625 O3, **474**

Colignan Vic. 526 E7, 546 H8

Colinroobie NSW 522 A7, 527 N7

Colinton NSW 518 D12, 519 C6, 520 G7, 522 F12, 539 F1

Collarenebri NSW 524 D4

Collaroy NSW 523 I1, 524 F12

Collaroy Plateau NSW 508 H5, 509 C11, 511 N7

Collector NSW 519 D3, 522 G9

Collendina Vic. 532 D6

Collerina NSW 529 O4

Colley SA 558 B3, 567 O11

Collie NSW 524 B10

Collie WA 572 G3, 574 D8, 576 C9, **296**

Collie Burn WA 572 G4

Collie Cardiff WA 572 H4, 574 D8

Collier Range NP WA 575 H6, 578 E7

Collier Rocks WA 578 B2, 580 B12, 582 D4

Collingullie NSW 522 B9, 527 O9

Collins Cap Tas. 622 H5

Collins Island Qld 604 B1, 611 M8

Collinsfield SA 556 G1, 559 I5

Collinsvale Tas. 622 H4, 625 J7

Collinsville Qld 605 C5, 611 I4, 396

Collombatti Rail NSW 515 G4, 525 M10

Colly Blue NSW 524 G10

Colo NSW 511 I2, 513 P3, 523 J5

Colo Heights NSW 511 I1, 513 O1, 523 J5

Colo Vale NSW 517 C4, 519 G2, 523 I8

Colquhoun Vic. 541 O5

Colton SA 558 B5, 560 A12, 567 P12

Columbey NP NSW 514 D6, 515 A11, 523 M3

Comara NSW 515 E3, 525 L9

Comaum SA 548 B12, 550 B1, 568 G10

Combara NSW 524 C9

Combe Hill Island WA 581 K2, 584 G3

Combe Island WA 581 J2, 584 F3

Combe Islet Qld 614 H11

Combienbar Vic. 519 C11, 539 D9

Comboyne NSW 515 E6, 525 L11

Come-by-Chance NSW 524 C6, 97

Comet Qld 611 I11, 395

Commerson Island WA 581 J3, 584 E4

Como NSW 508 D10, 511 K10, 517 H1

Compigne Island Qld 604 D6, 611 N12

Compton Downs NSW 529 N6

Comston Island Qld 605 G5, 611 K4

Conara Tas. 625 L1, 627 L10

Conargo NSW 527 K10, 542 E1, 47

Concord NSW 508 D7, 511 K8

Condah Vic. 550 E5

Condamine Qld 609 I7, 427

Condillac Island WA 581 K2, 584 G2

Condingup WA 577 J9

Condobolin NSW 522 B3, 527 P3, **82**

Condong NSW 516 G2, 525 O2, 600 F12

Condowie SA 556 G2, 559 J5

Cone Rock WA 581 I5, 584 C7

Congo NSW 519 F7, 521 L8
Congupna Vic. 542 E7, 544 A3
Conical Rocks Qld 604 C4, 611 N10
Conilurus Island WA 581 I5, 584 C7
Conimbla NP NSW 522 E5, 46
Coningham Tas. 623 I8, 625 K8
Coniston NSW 517 F5
Conjola NSW 517 B12, 519 G5, 521 N3, 523 I11
Conjola NP NSW 517 B12, 519 G5, 521 N3, 523 I10
Conmurra SA 568 F9
Connangorach Vic. 548 F10
Connellys Marsh Tas. 623 L5, 625 L7
Connemarra NSW 524 F10
Connewarre Vic. 532 B6, 536 F9, 538 H2, 540 A7, 551 O8
Connexion (Yilikamurra) Island NT 591 M7
Connor Islet Qld 605 H10, 611 L7
Conondale Qld 602 D4, 603 D12, 609 M7
Conondale NP Qld 602 C4, 603 D11, 609 M7, 419
Conway Beach Qld 605 F5, 611 J4
Conway Island WA 581 I5, 584 D6
Conway NP Qld 605 F5, 611 J4, 390
Conzinc Island WA 575 E1, 578 B2, 580 B12, 582 D4
Coober Pedy SA 562 A10, 565 O10, **233**
Coobowie SA 556 E8, 558 H9, 235
Coochiemudlo Island Qld 599 H9, 600 F5, 602 H12, 609 N9
Coochin Creek Qld 602 F5, 603 E12
Cooee Tas. 626 F5
Coogee WA 570 C8
Coojar Vic. 550 E2
Cook SA 566 F4
Cook Island NSW 516 H2, 525 O2, 600 H11, 601 H11, 609 N11
Cookamidgera NSW 522 E4
Cookardinia NSW 522 B11, 527 O11, 543 N2
Cooke Plains SA 559 L10, 568 D4
Cooks Gap NSW 522 H2
Cooks Hill NSW 514 D9
Cooktown Qld 613 L3, 406
Cookville Tas. 623 I11, 625 K10
Cool Yal You Ma Island NT 591 M6
Coolabah NSW 529 N8
Coolac NSW 519 A3, 522 D9
Cooladdi Qld 608 A6, 619 N6
Coolah NSW 524 F11
Coolah Tops NP NSW 524 F11, 70
Coolalie NSW 519 C3, 522 F9
Coolalinga NT 588 E3
Coolamon NSW 522 B8, 527 O8
Coolana Qld 602 B11
Coolangatta Qld 516 H2, 525 O1, 600 G11, 601 G10, 609 N11, 399
Coolatai NSW 525 I4, 609 I12
Coolcha SA 559 L9, 568 D3
Coolgardie WA 576 H5, **299**
Coolimba WA 576 A5
Coolongolook NSW 515 D9, 523 N2
Cooltong SA 526 A5, 546 A5, 559 O7
Coolum Beach Qld 602 G3, 603 F11, 609 N7, 426
Coolup WA 571 D10, 574 C7

Cooma NSW 519 C7, 520 G9, 539 E3, **41**
Cooma Tas. 624 B11
Cooma Vic. 542 D7
Cooma West NSW 519 C7, 520 G9, 539 E3
Coomalbidgup WA 576 H9
Coomandook SA 559 L11, 568 E4
Coomba NSW 515 E9, 523 N2
Coombabah Qld 601 E4
Coombah Roadhouse NSW 526 C2, 561 O11
Coombe SA 559 M12, 568 F6
Coombe Island Qld 606 F6, 613 M8
Coombell NSW 516 E5, 525 N4
Coomberdale WA 574 B1, 576 C5
Coomera Qld 600 F8, 601 D3
Coominya Qld 602 B10, 609 M9, 410
Coomoora Vic. 535 E8, 536 E1, 551 N3
Coonabarabran NSW 524 E9, **43**
Coonalpyn SA 559 M11, 568 E5
Coonamble NSW 524 C8, 43
Coonarr Qld 603 D2, 604 G11, 609 M3
Coonawarra SA 548 A12, 550 A2, 568 G10, **232**, 251
Coonerang NSW 519 C8, 520 G10, 539 F4
Coongie Lakes NP SA 563 M6, 618 E6
Coongulla Vic. 541 J5
Coongulmerang Vic. 541 L5
Coonong NSW 527 M9
Coonooer Bridge Vic. 549 K8
Cooper Island WA 577 K9
Coopernook NSW 515 E8, 523 O1, 525 L12
Coopers Creek Vic. 541 I6
Cooplacurripa NSW 515 C6, 525 K11
Coopracambra NP Vic. 519 C11, 539 F9, 152
Coorabakh NP NSW 515 E7, 523 O1, 525 L12, 89
Coorabie SA 567 J8
Cooran Qld 603 E10, 609 N6
Cooranbong NSW 509 E4, 514 A10, 523 L4
Cooranga North Qld 609 K7
Coorong NP SA 555 H9, 559 K11, 568 D6, 246
Coorow WA 576 B4
Cooroy Qld 602 F1, 603 E10, 609 N7, 437
Coorparoo Qld 599 E7, 600 D4, 602 F11
Cootamundra NSW 519 A2, 522 D8, **44**
Cooya Beach Qld 606 D1, 607 D3, 613 L5, 430
Cooyal NSW 522 H2
Cooyar Qld 609 L8
Copacabana NSW 509 D9, 511 O4
Cope Cope Vic. 549 J8
Copeland NSW 515 B8, 523 M1, 525 J12
Copeland Island NT 590 G2
Copeville SA 559 M9, 568 E2
Copley SA 557 B4, 561 I4
Copmanhurst NSW 516 D8, 525 M5
Coppabella Qld 605 D10, 611 I7
Copping Tas. 623 M5, 625 M7

Coppins Crossing ACT 518 D5, 520 G3
Coquet Island Qld 611 M7, 614 H11
Cora Lynn Vic. 534 D12, 537 M8, 540 E6
Corack Vic. 526 F12, 549 J7
Corack East Vic. 526 F12, 549 J6
Coragulac Vic. 536 A8, 538 B1, 551 K8
Coraki NSW 516 F6, 525 O4, 609 N12
Coral Bank Vic. 543 L9, 545 J6
Coral Bay WA 575 B5, **299**
Coram Vic. 536 B9, 538 B2, 551 L8
Coramba NSW 516 D11, 525 M7
Corang NSW 519 F4, 521 L2, 522 H10
Corattum SA 568 F12
Corbett Island WA 577 I10
Cordalba Qld 603 C3, 604 F11, 609 M4
Cordalba NP Qld 603 B3, 604 F11, 609 M4
Cordering WA 574 E8
Coreen NSW 527 M11, 543 I4
Corfield Qld 610 A6, 617 M6
Corinda Qld 599 D8, 615 B4
Corindhap Vic. 536 C5, 551 L6
Corindi NSW 516 E10, 525 N7
Corindi Beach NSW 516 E10, 525 N7
Corinella Vic. 533 N9, 537 L10, 540 E8
Corinna Tas. 626 C8
Corio Vic. 532 B2, 536 F7, 540 A6, 551 O7
Corlette NSW 514 G7
Corneille Island WA 581 K2, 584 G2
Corner Inlet Marine and Coastal Park Vic. 540 H10
Corner Inlet Marine NP Vic. 540 H10
Corner Store Qld 528 B1, 563 N11, 618 F10
Cornwall Tas. 627 O9, 492
Cornwall Island WA 577 J9
Corny Point SA 556 C7, 558 G9, 267
Corobimilla NSW 527 N8
Coromby Vic. 548 H8
Coronation Beach WA 575 D12, 576 A3
Coronation Island WA 581 J3, 584 F4
Coronet Bay Vic. 533 O10, 537 L11, 540 E8
Corop Vic. 542 C7
Cororooke Vic. 536 A9, 538 B1, 551 K8
Corowa NSW 527 M12, 543 I5, 544 F1, **44**
Corra Linn Tas. 627 K8, 629 H10
Correebah Island NSW 514 F7, 515 B11, 523 M3
Corrie Island NSW 514 G7, 515 C11, 523 M3
Corrigin WA 574 F5, 576 E8, **300**
Corrimal NSW 517 G4
Corringle NSW 522 C5, 527 P5
Corroboree Island Qld 604 C4, 611 N10
Corroboree Park Tavern NT 588 G5, 590 E5
Corryong Vic. 520 A8, 543 O7, 545 O3, **156**

Corunna NSW 521 L10
Corvisart Island WA 581 J3, 584 F3
Cosgrove Vic. 542 F7, 544 B3
Cosmo Newbery WA 577 I1, 579 I11
Cossack WA 575 F1, 578 B2, 580 B12, 582 E4, 333
Costerfield Vic. 542 C9
Cottan–Bimbang NP NSW 515 D5, 525 K10
Cottesloe WA 570 C7, 571 B5, 279
Cottles Bridge Vic. 531 F4, 534 A6, 537 K4
Cotton Island NT 591 N3
Cottonvale Qld 516 A3, 525 L2, 609 L11
Couangalt Vic. 531 A2, 535 H10, 536 H3, 540 B3, 551 P4
Cougal NSW 516 E2, 525 N2, 600 C12
Coulson Qld 600 A8
Coulta SA 558 D7
Councillor Island Tas. 625 P11
Countegany NSW 519 D7, 521 I9, 539 G3
Couradda NP NSW 524 G6
Couran Island Qld 600 G8, 601 F1, 609 N10
Couridjah NSW 517 D2
Courts Island Tas. 625 J11
Couta Rocks Tas. 626 A5
Coutts Crossing NSW 516 D9, 525 M6
Cow and Calf Rocks WA 573 C6, 574 D12, 576 C12
Cow Bay Qld 607 E2, 613 L4
Cow Island Qld 605 F5, 611 K4
Cowabbie West NSW 522 A8, 527 O8
Cowan NSW 508 F2, 509 B9, 511 M5, 523 K6
Cowan Cowan Qld 600 G1
Cowangie Vic. 526 C9, 546 D11, 548 D1, 559 P10, 182
Cowaramup WA 572 B8, 574 B9
Cowell SA 556 B1, 558 G5, **232**
Cowes Vic. 533 L10, 537 K11, 540 D8, 158
Cowlard Island NT 590 G2
Cowle Island WA 575 D2, 578 A3, 582 B6
Cowley Beach Qld 606 F5, 613 M8
Cowleys Creek Vic. 538 G9, 551 J9
Cowper NSW 516 E8, 525 N5
Cowra NSW 522 F6, **46**
Cowrie Island Qld 605 G5, 611 K4
Cowwarr Vic. 541 J6
Coyrecup WA 574 G8
Crab Island Qld 525 O1, 600 G3, 601 F4, 609 N9, 614 C3
Crabbe Island WA 581 I5, 584 D6
Crabbes Creek NSW 516 G3, 525 O2, 609 N11
Crabtree Tas. 622 G6, 625 J7
Cracow Qld 604 A11, 609 I4, 445
Cradle Mountain–Lake St Clair NP Tas. 624 F2, 626 F9, 628 E6, 493
Cradle Valley Tas. 626 F9, 628 D6
Cradoc Tas. 622 G8, 625 J8
Cradock SA 559 J1, 561 I8, 236
Craggy Island Tas. 624 A8
Craigie NSW 519 C10, 539 E8
Craigie Vic. 535 C6, 549 M12, 551 M1

Craigieburn Vic. 531 D3, 537 I4, 540 C3
Craiglie Qld 606 D1, 607 D4, 613 L5
Cramenton Vic. 526 E8, 546 H9
Cramps Tas. 625 I1, 627 I10
Crampton Island NSW 519 G5, 521 N4, 523 I11
Cranbourne Vic. 531 G9, 533 M4, 534 A12, 537 K8, 540 D6
Cranbourne North Vic. 533 M3
Cranbourne South Vic. 531 F9, 533 L4, 534 A12, 537 K8, 540 D6
Cranbourne West Vic. 533 M4
Cranbrook Tas. 625 N2, 627 N12
Cranbrook WA 574 F10, 576 E10, **300**
Crane Island Qld 604 B2, 611 M8
Crater Lakes NP Qld 606 D3, 607 E9, 613 L7, 451
Craufurd Islet NT 591 N10, 593 N1
Craven NSW 514 G2, 515 C9, 523 M2
Cravensville Vic. 543 N8, 545 M5
Crawford Qld 603 A10, 609 L7
Crawney Pass NP NSW 525 I11
Crayfish Creek Tas. 626 D4
Creak Island WA 577 J9
Creek Junction Vic. 542 G9, 544 C7
Creery Island WA 571 C9, 574 B6, 576 C8
Creighton Vic. 542 E9, 544 A7
Cremorne Tas. 623 K6, 625 L8
Crescent Head NSW 515 G5, 525 M10, 62
Cressy Tas. 627 K9, 486
Cressy Vic. 536 B7, 551 L6
Crestmead Qld 599 E10, 600 D6
Creswick Vic. 535 C9, 536 D2, 551 M3, **156**
Crib Point Vic. 531 F12, 533 L8, 537 J10, 540 D7
Croajingolong NP Vic. 519 C12, 539 E11, 152, 176
Crocodile Island NT 588 B4, 590 D5, 591 K3
Crocus Island WA 575 D1, 582 A4
Croftby Qld 516 D1, 525 M1, 609 M10
Croker Island NT 590 G1
Cronulla NSW 508 E11, 511 L11, 523 K7
Crooble NSW 524 H4, 609 I12
Crooked River Vic. 541 K3
Crookwell NSW 519 E2, 522 G8, **46**
Croppa Creek NSW 524 H3, 609 I12
Crossdale Qld 600 A1, 602 C8, 609 M8
Crossley Vic. 538 B7, 550 G8
Crossman WA 571 H10, 574 D7, 576 C8
Crossover Vic. 534 H12, 537 O8, 540 G6
Crowdy Bay NP NSW 515 F8, 523 O1, 525 L12, 66
Crowlands Vic. 549 J12, 551 J1
Crown Rock NT 591 O11, 593 O2
Crows Nest Qld 609 L8, **407**
Crows Nest NP Qld 609 L8, 407
Crowther NSW 519 B1, 522 E7
Croxton East Vic. 550 F5
Croydon NSW 511 L9
Croydon Qld 612 F8, **408**
Croydon SA 554 B8, 555 F2
Croydon Vic. 531 G6, 534 B8, 537 K5

Crusoe Island Qld 600 G7, 601 F1, 609 N10
Crymelon Vic. 526 E12, 548 G6
Cryon NSW 524 D5
Crystal Brook SA 559 I4, 560 H12, **234**
Cuballing WA 574 E6, 576 D8
Cubbaroo NSW 524 E6
Cucania Qld 606 E3, 607 G9
Cuckoo Tas. 627 M7
Cudal NSW 522 F4
Cuddell NSW 527 N8
Cudgee Vic. 538 D8, 550 H8
Cudgen NSW 600 G12, 601 H12
Cudgera Creek NSW 516 H3
Cudgewa Vic. 520 A8, 543 O7, 545 N3
Cudgewa North Vic. 520 A7, 543 O6, 545 N3
Cudmirrah NSW 517 C12, 521 O3
Cudmore NP Qld 610 F9
Cue WA 575 H10, 576 D1, 578 D11, **300**
Culbin WA 574 E7
Culburra NSW 517 E10, 519 H4, 521 P1, 523 J10, 79
Culburra SA 559 M12, 568 E5
Culcairn NSW 522 B11, 527 O11, 543 L4, **47**
Culgoa Vic. 526 F10, 549 K4
Culgoa Floodplain NP Qld 524 A2, 529 O2, 608 C11, 619 P11, 441
Culgoa NP NSW 524 A2, 529 O2, 608 C11, 619 P11, 36
Cull Island WA 577 I9
Cullacabardee WA 570 D4
Cullen Bullen NSW 523 I5
Cullen Islet Qld 605 H9, 611 L6
Cullendulla NSW 521 M6, 522 H12
Culloden Vic. 541 K5
Cullulleraine Vic. 526 C6, 546 E6, 559 P7
Cumberland Islands Qld 611 L5
Cumberland Rock WA 572 B11, 574 B11, 576 B11
Cumborah NSW 524 B4
Cummins SA 558 D7
Cumnock NSW 522 F3
Cundeelee WA 577 J5
Cunderdin WA 574 E4, 576 D7, 314
Cundletown NSW 515 E8
Cungena SA 558 B2, 567 O9
Cungulla Qld 605 B1, 606 H11, 610 H1, 613 O12
Cunjurong NSW 521 N3
Cunliffe SA 556 E3, 558 H6
Cunnamulla Qld 608 A9, 619 N9, **408**
Cunnawarra NP NSW 515 E2, 516 A12, 525 L8
Cunningar NSW 519 B2, 522 E8
Cunningham Qld 516 A1, 525 K1, 609 K10
Cunningham SA 556 E5, 558 H7
Cunninyeuk NSW 526 H9, 547 N12, 549 N1
Cuprona Tas. 626 F6
Curacoa (Noogoo) Island Qld 606 G8, 613 N10
Curara WA 571 F11, 574 D7, 575 E12, 576 B3
Curban NSW 524 C10
Curdie Vale Vic. 538 E9, 551 I9
Curlew Island Qld 611 L7
Curlewis NSW 524 G9

Curlewis Vic. 532 C4
Curlwaa NSW 526 D5, 546 G5
Currabubula NSW 524 H10
Curracabundi NP NSW 515 A6, 525 I11
Currambine WA 570 B3
Curramulka SA 556 E6, 558 H8
Currarong NSW 517 E11, 519 H4, 521 P2, 523 J10
Currawang NSW 519 E4, 521 J1, 522 G10
Currawarna NSW 522 B9, 527 O9
Currawinya NP Qld 529 I1, 619 L10, 410
Currency Creek SA 555 G7, 559 J10, 568 C4, 236
Currie Tas. 625 O11, **474**
Currowan Creek NSW 519 F6, 521 L5, 522 H12
Currumbin Qld 516 H2, 525 O1, 600 G11, 601 F9, 609 N11
Currumbin Beach Qld 601 G9
Currumbin Waters Qld 601 F10
Curtain Fig NP Qld 606 D3, 607 E9, 613 L7
Curtin Springs NT 594 F10
Curtis Island Qld 604 C5, 609 L1, 611 N11
Curtis Island NP Qld 604 D6, 611 N11, 412
Curyo Vic. 526 F11, 549 I5
Cussen Island WA 581 I5, 584 C7
Custon SA 526 B12, 548 B7, 568 G7
Cut Feet Island NSW 514 G7, 515 C11, 523 M3
Cuttabri NSW 524 E6
Cygnet Tas. 622 G8, 625 J9, **475**
Cygnet River SA 556 D11, 558 H11
Cynthia Qld 604 C11, 609 K4

D

Dadalai (Canoe) Islet Qld 614 C1
Dadswells Bridge Vic. 548 H10
D'Aguesseau Island WA 581 J3, 584 E4
D'Aguilar NP Qld 599 B4, 600 B2, 602 D7, 609 M8
Daguragu NT 592 D5
Dahlen Vic. 548 G9
Dahwilly NSW 527 J10, 542 D1
Dailey Island WA 577 J9
Daintree Qld 607 D2, 613 L4, **408**
Daintree NP Qld 606 C1, 607 C2, 613 L4, 408, 430
Daisy Dell Tas. 626 G8, 628 E5
Daisy Hill Qld 599 F9, 600 E6
Daisy Hill Vic. 535 B6, 549 M12, 551 M1
Daisy Island WA 575 D1, 582 B4
Daisy Islet NT 591 O11, 593 O2
Dajarra Qld 616 F5
Dakabin Qld 599 E3, 600 D2, 602 F9
Dalbeg Qld 605 B4, 610 H3
Dalby Qld 609 K8, **409**
Dalby Island SA 558 E8
Dalgarup NP WA 572 G8, 574 C9, 576 C10
Dalgety NSW 519 B8, 520 E11, 539 D4, 31
Dallarnil Qld 603 B4, 604 E12, 609 M4
Dalmalee Vic. 526 D11, 548 G5
Dalmeny NSW 519 F7, 521 L9

Dalmore Vic. 533 O5
Dalmorton NSW 516 B9, 525 L6
Dalrymple NP Qld 606 E12, 610 F2, 613 M12, 404
Dalton NSW 519 D3, 522 F9
Dalveen Qld 516 A2, 525 L2, 609 L11
Dalwallinu WA 574 D1, 576 C5
Daly River NT 588 C12, 590 D7, 356
Daly Waters NT 590 H12, 592 H3, **361**
Dalyellup WA 574 C8
Dalyston Vic. 533 P12, 537 L12, 540 E9
Dalyup WA 577 I9
Dampier WA 575 E1, 578 B2, 580 B12, 582 D5
Dampiers Monument WA 581 I5, 584 C7
Dan Dan NP Qld 604 C8, 609 K1, 611 N12
Danbulla NP Qld 606 D3, 607 E8, 613 L6
Dandaloo NSW 522 D1, 524 A12, 529 P12
Dandaragan WA 574 B2, 576 B6
Dandenong Vic. 531 F8, 533 L1, 534 A10, 537 K7, 540 D5
Dandenong North Vic. 533 L1
Dandenong Ranges NP Vic. 531 G6, 534 B8, 537 L6, 540 E5, 184
Dandenong South Vic. 533 L2
Dandongadale Vic. 543 J10, 544 G8
Dangar Island NSW 508 G2, 509 C9, 511 M4, 523 K6
Dangarfield NSW 523 K1, 524 H12
Dangarsleigh NSW 515 B1, 525 J8
Danger Island Qld 611 M8
Dangin WA 574 E5
Dannevig Island Vic. 540 G12
Danyo Vic. 526 C9, 546 D11, 548 D1, 559 P10, 568 H4
Dapto NSW 517 F5
Darbada Island NT 591 K3
Darby Falls NSW 522 F6
Darbyshire Vic. 543 M6, 545 L3
Darch Island NT 590 G2
Darcy Island WA 581 J4, 584 E5
Dardadine WA 574 E8
Dardanup WA 572 E4, 574 C8
Dareton NSW 526 D5, 546 G5
Dargo Vic. 541 L3
Dargo High Plains Vic. 541 L1
Dark Corner NSW 522 H5
Darkan WA 574 E8, 576 D9
Darke Peak SA 558 E5, 560 D12
Darkwood NSW 515 F1, 516 C12, 525 M8
Darley Vic. 535 G11, 536 G4, 540 A3, 551 O4
Darlington Tas. 623 P2, 625 N5
Darlington Vic. 551 J6
Darlington WA 570 G5, 571 D4
Darlington Point NSW 527 M7
Darnick NSW 526 H2
Darnum Vic. 537 O9, 540 G7
Daroobalgie NSW 522 D4
Darr Qld 610 B9, 617 N9
Darra Qld 599 D8, 600 D5, 602 E12
Darraweit Guim Vic. 531 D1, 537 I2, 540 C2, 542 C12
Darriman Vic. 541 J9
Dart Dart Vic. 526 D12, 548 G7

Dart Island Tas. 623 M7, 625 M8
Dartmoor Vic. 550 C5, 568 H12
Dartmouth Qld 610 C10, 617 O10
Dartmouth Vic. 543 M9, 545 L6
Darwin NT 588 C3, 590 D4, **344**
Dattuck Vic. 526 E10, 548 G3
Davenport Range NP (Proposed) NT 593 K11, 595 K1, 369
David Islet NT 591 N10, 593 N1
Davidson NSW 508 F5, 511 M7
Davies Creek NP Qld 606 D3, 607 E7, 613 L6, 425
Davis Creek NSW 523 L2
Davistown NSW 509 D8, 511 O4
Davy Island WA 577 I10
Daw Island WA 577 K9
Dawes Qld 604 B9, 609 J2
Dawes NP Qld 604 C9, 609 K2
Dawson SA 559 K3, 561 J10
Dawson Vic. 541 J6
Dawsons Hill NSW 523 L2
Dawsons Islands NSW 519 F6, 521 M5, 523 I12
Dayboro Qld 599 C3, 600 C2, 602 E8
Daylesford Vic. 535 E8, 536 E1, 551 N3, 161
Daymar Qld 524 E1, 608 G11
Daysdale NSW 527 M11, 543 I3
Daytrap Vic. 526 F9, 547 J12, 549 J1
Daytrap Corner Vic. 526 F9, 547 I12, 549 I2
De Freycinet Islet WA 581 J3, 584 E4
De Witt Island Tas. 624 G11
Dead Dog Island Qld 605 G6, 611 K4
Deakin WA 566 C4, 577 P4
Dean Vic. 535 D9, 536 D2, 551 M3
Dean Island WA 581 I5, 584 C7
Deanmill WA 572 H10, 573 B1, 574 D10
Deans Marsh Vic. 536 C10, 538 D3, 551 M8
Deception Bay Qld 599 E3, 600 E2, 602 F8, 609 N8
Deddick Vic. 519 A10, 539 B7
Deddington Tas. 627 L9
Dederang Vic. 543 L8, 545 J5
Dee Lagoon Tas. 624 H3
Deep Lead Vic. 549 I11
Deepwater NSW 525 K5, 52
Deepwater NP Qld 604 F8, 609 L2, 427
Deer Park Vic. 531 B5, 536 H5, 540 B4, 551 P5
Deer Reserve NP Qld 600 A1, 602 B7, 609 M8
Deeral Qld 606 E3, 607 G9, 613 M7, 392
Defiance (Dalys) Island Qld 605 F5, 611 K4
Degerando Island WA 581 J4, 584 E5
Delambre Island WA 578 B2, 580 B12, 582 E4
Delamere SA 555 B9, 556 G10, 559 I11, 568 A5
Delaneys Creek Qld 602 E6
Delatite Vic. 537 P1, 540 H1, 542 H11, 544 D10
Delburn Vic. 537 P10, 540 H8
Delcomyn Island Qld 604 C2, 611 N9

Delegate NSW 519 C10, 539 D7, 34
Delegate River Vic. 519 B10, 539 D8
Dellicknora Vic. 519 B10, 539 C8
Deloraine Tas. 627 I8, 629 C10, **475**
Deloraine Island Qld 605 G4, 611 K3
Delta Qld 605 D4, 611 J3
Delta Island WA 575 D1, 582 A4
Delungra NSW 525 I5
Denham WA 575 B9, 586 D7, **301**
Denham Group NP Qld 614 E4
Denham Island Qld 614 G11, 615 C2
Denicull Creek Vic. 551 I2
Deniliquin NSW 527 J10, 542 D2, **47**
Denison Vic. 541 J6
Denman NSW 523 J2
Denman SA 566 E4
Denman Island Qld 605 F5, 611 K3
Denmark WA 573 A11, 574 F11, 576 E11, **301**
Dennes Point Tas. 623 I7, 625 K8
Dennington Vic. 538 C8, 550 G8
Dent Island Qld 605 G5, 611 K4
D'Entrecasteaux NP WA 572 F12, 573 A4, 574 C11, 576 C11, 329
Denver Vic. 535 F8, 536 F1, 540 A1, 542 A12, 551 O2
Deptford Vic. 541 N4
Depuch Island WA 575 F1, 578 C2, 580 C12, 582 F4
Derby Tas. 627 N6, **476**
Derby Vic. 535 E2, 549 N9
Derby WA 581 I7, 584 D9, **302**
Dereel Vic. 535 B12, 536 C5, 551 L5
Dergholm Vic. 550 C2, 568 H10
Dering Vic. 526 D9, 546 G12, 548 G2
Deringulla NSW 524 E10
Derrinal Vic. 542 B9, 549 P11
Derrinallum Vic. 551 J6, 151
Derriwong NSW 522 C3, 527 P3
Derwent Bridge Tas. 624 G2, 626 G12, 628 F11
Derwent Island Qld 611 L5
Derwent Park Tas. 621 C5
Descartes Island WA 581 K2, 584 G2
Desfontaines Island WA 581 J3, 584 F4
Detpa Vic. 526 D12, 548 F6
Deua NP NSW 519 E7, 521 K7, 522 G12, 539 H1, 71
Devenish Vic. 542 G7, 544 C3
Deviot Tas. 627 J7, 629 F7
Devon Vic. 541 I9
Devon Meadows Vic. 533 M5
Devondale Vic. 538 H11, 551 J10
Devonport Tas. 626 H6, 628 H1, 629 B2, **476**
Dewars Pool WA 571 F1, 574 C4
Dharug NP NSW 509 B7, 511 L2, 523 K5, 102
Dhulura NSW 522 B9, 527 P9
Dhuragoon NSW 527 I9, 547 O12, 549 O1
Diamantina Island Qld 604 D7, 609 K1, 611 N12
Diamantina NP Qld 616 H10, 617 I10, 396
Diamond Beach NSW 515 E9, 523 O2

Diamond Creek Vic. 531 F4, 534 A6, 537 K4
Diamond Island Tas. 625 O1, 627 O11
Dianella WA 570 D5, 571 C5
Diapur Vic. 526 C12, 548 D7
Dick Island WA 575 C12
Diddleum Plains Tas. 627 L7
Digby Vic. 550 D5
Digby Island Qld 611 L6
Diggers Rest Vic. 531 B3, 536 H4, 540 B3, 551 P4
Diggora Vic. 542 B7, 549 P8
Dilston Tas. 627 K7, 629 G8
Dimboola Vic. 548 F8, **157**
Dimbulah Qld 606 C3, 607 B8, 613 K6, 425
Dinden NP Qld 606 D3, 607 E7, 613 L6
Dingee Vic. 542 A7, 549 O8
Dingley Village Vic. 533 K1
Dingo Qld 611 K11
Dingville Island WA 575 C12
Dingwall Vic. 526 H11, 549 M5
Dinmont Vic. 536 B11, 538 B4, 551 K10
Dinner Island Qld 600 G7, 601 F1, 609 N10
Dinner Islet Qld 611 L7
Dinner Plain Vic. 541 L1, 543 L11, 545 K10, 185
Dinninup WA 574 D9
Dinoga NSW 524 H6
Dinyarrak Vic. 526 B12, 548 B7, 568 H7
Dipperu NP Qld 605 E10, 611 J7
Direction Island WA 575 C2, 582 A7
Direk SA 553 C3, 554 B6
Dirk Hartog Island WA 575 A8, 586 A5, 301
Dirk Hartog NP WA 575 A8, 586 A6
Dirranbandi Qld 524 C1, 608 E10
Disappearing Island WA 575 C12
Discovery Bay Marine NP Vic. 550 C8
Divided Island Qld 604 C5, 611 N11
Dixie Vic. 538 F7, 551 I8
Dixon Island WA 575 F1, 578 B2, 580 B12, 582 E4
Dixons Creek Vic. 531 H4, 534 C6, 537 L4, 540 E3
Djeergaree Island NT 591 M2
Djidbordu (Barron Island) NT 589 L1, 590 G4
Djiru NP Qld 606 E5, 613 M8
Djukbinj NP NT 588 F1, 590 E4
Dobie Vic. 551 J2
Docker Vic. 543 I8, 544 F5
Doctors Flat Vic. 541 N2, 545 M12
Dodges Ferry Tas. 623 L5, 625 L7
Dog Island SA 567 L9
Dog Island Vic. 541 I10
Dolphin Island WA 575 E1, 578 B2, 580 B12, 582 D4
Dome Island Qld 604 C2, 611 N9
Dome Island WA 577 K9
Don Tas. 626 H6, 628 H1, 629 A6
Don Island WA 581 K2, 584 G2
Don Junction Tas. 629 A1
Don Valley Vic. 534 E8, 537 M5
Donald Vic. 526 F12, 549 J7, **157**
Doncaster Vic. 531 E5, 537 J5, 540 D4

Dongara–Denison WA 576 A4, **303**
Donington Reef SA 558 E8
Donnybrook Qld 602 G7, **400**
Donnybrook Vic. 531 D3, 537 J3, 540 C3
Donnybrook WA 572 F5, 574 C9, 576 C10, **303**
Donovans Landing SA 550 B6, 568 G12
Doo Town Tas. 623 N8, 625 M8
Dooboobetic SA 549 K8
Doodlakine WA 574 F4, 576 E7
Dooen Vic. 548 G9
Dookie Vic. 542 F7, 544 B3
Doole Island WA 575 B4
Doomadgee Qld 615 C5
Doomben Qld 600 E4, 602 F11
Doonside NSW 508 A5, 511 I7, 513 P11
Dooragan NP NSW 515 F7, 523 O1, 525 L11, 66
Dooralong NSW 509 D5
Dopewora Vic. 548 C9, 568 H8
Dora Creek NSW 509 E5, 514 B10
Dorcherty Island NT 581 P1, 585 O1, 590 B7
Doris Island WA 581 I5, 584 C7
Dorney Island WA 581 I5, 584 C7
Dorodong Vic. 548 B12, 550 B2, 568 H10
Dorothee Island SA 558 A6
Dorothy Island WA 581 I5, 584 C7
Dorre Island WA 575 B7, 586 A3
Dorrien SA 554 F4
Dorrigo NSW 515 G1, 516 C12, 525 M8, **47**
Dorrigo NP NSW 515 G1, 516 D11, 525 M8, 48
Double Cone Island Qld 605 F4, 611 J3
Double Island Qld 606 D2, 607 F6, 611 L6, 613 L5
Double Island WA 575 B9, 586 D9
Doubtful Islands WA 576 G10
Doughboy Island Tas. 624 B11, 627 O2
Doughboy Island Vic. 540 H10
Douglas Qld 605 A1, 606 G10
Douglas Vic. 548 E11
Douglas–Apsley NP Tas. 625 O1, 627 O10, 472
Douglas Daly Tourist Park NT 588 G12, 590 E7
Douglas Island Qld 612 A5, 615 D2
Douglas Island WA 577 J9
Douglas Islet Qld 611 L7, 614 E4
Douglas Park NSW 517 E2
Dove Islet Qld 614 E1
Dover Tas. 622 F10, 625 J10, **477**
Doveton Vic. 533 M1
Dowadee Island NSW 514 G7, 515 C11, 523 M3
Dowar Islet Qld 614 G1
Dowe NP NSW 524 H8
Dowerin WA 574 E3, 576 D6
Dowlingville SA 556 F4, 559 I7, 568 A1
Downes Island WA 578 D1, 580 D11, 582 H3
Dowsings Point Tas. 621 C4
Doyalson NSW 509 F6, 514 B12, 523 L5
Drake NSW 516 C5, 525 L3, 609 L12, 90
Draper Island WA 577 J10

Dream Island Qld 603 F6, 609 N5
Dreeite Vic. 536 A8, 551 K7
Driftwood Island NT 581 P3, 585 O3, 590 B9
Drik Drik Vic. 550 C6, 568 H12
Drillham Qld 609 I6
Drillwarrina NP NSW 524 C11
Dripstone NSW 522 G2
Dromana Vic. 531 D11, 533 I7, 537 I10, 540 C7
Dromedary Tas. 622 H3, 625 J6
Dropmore Vic. 542 E11
Drouin Vic. 537 N8, 540 F6
Drouin South Vic. 537 N9, 540 F7
Drouin West Vic. 534 G12, 537 N8, 540 F6
Drovers Cave NP WA 574 A1, 576 A5, 310
Drum Island Vic. 541 I10
Drumborg Vic. 550 D6
Drumcondra Vic. 532 B3
Drummartin Vic. 542 A7, 549 O8
Drummond Vic. 535 F7, 536 F1, 540 A1, 542 A11, 551 O2
Drummond Cove WA 575 D12, 576 A3
Drummoyne NSW 508 E7, 509 B12, 511 L8
Drung Drung Vic. 548 G9
Drung Drung South Vic. 548 G10
Dry Creek SA 553 C5, 554 B8, 555 F1
Dry Creek Vic. 542 G10, 544 C8
Dryander NP Qld 605 E4, 611 J3
Drysdale Vic. 531 A9, 532 D4, 536 G8, 540 A6, 551 O7, **159**
Drysdale Island NT 591 M2
Drysdale River NP WA 581 M3, 585 J3
Dthinna Dthinnawan NP NSW 525 I3, 609 J11
Duaringa Qld 611 K11
Dubbo NSW 522 F1, 524 C12, **48**
Dublin SA 556 G5, 559 J8, 568 B1
Duchess Qld 615 D12, 616 F5
Duck Island Qld 603 F5, 604 H12, 609 N4
Duck Island Vic. 531 A10, 532 E5, 536 H9, 540 B6, 551 P8
Duckenfield NSW 509 G1, 514 D7
Duddo Vic. 526 C9, 546 D11, 559 P10, 568 H4
Dudinin WA 574 G6, 576 E8
Dudley Vic. 537 L12, 540 E9
Dudley Park SA 553 C6
Dudly Island NT 591 N5
Duffholme Vic. 548 E9
Duffield Island SA 558 E8
Duffys Forest NSW 508 F4, 509 B10, 511 M6
Dugong Islet Qld 614 E2
Duguesclin Island WA 581 J3, 584 E4
Dulacca Qld 608 H6
Dularcha NP Qld 602 F5, 603 E12, 609 N7, **422**
Dulcie Range NP NT 595 L4
Dulcot Tas. 621 H3
Dulguigan NSW 601 E12
Dululu Qld 604 A6, 611 L12
Dum In Mirrie Island NT 588 A4, 590 C5
Dumaralag Islet Qld 614 C2
Dumbalk Vic. 537 O12, 540 G9
Dumbell Island Qld 605 G4, 611 K3

Dumberning WA 574 E7
Dumbleyung WA 574 F7, 576 E9
Dumosa Vic. 526 G11, 549 K5
Dunach Vic. 535 B7, 549 M12, 551 M2
Dunalley Tas. 623 M6, 625 M7, **477**
Dunbogan NSW 515 F7, 66
Dundas Qld 600 A2, 602 C9, 609 M9
Dundas Tas. 626 D10
Dundee NSW 525 K5
Dundee Beach NT 588 A5, 590 C5
Dundonnell Vic. 551 I5
Dundurrabin NSW 516 C11, 525 L7
Dunedoo NSW 522 H1, 524 E12
Dungay NSW 601 D12
Dunggir NP NSW 515 F2, 525 L8
Dungog NSW 514 E4, 515 B10, 523 M2, 87
Dungowan NSW 525 I10
Dungurra Island Qld 605 G5, 611 K4
Dunk Island Qld 606 F6, 613 M8
Dunkeld NSW 522 G5
Dunkeld Vic. 550 G4, **159**
Dunluce Vic. 535 B4, 549 L11
Dunmarra NT 590 H12, 592 H3, 361
Dunneworthy Vic. 549 J12, 551 J2
Dunnstown Vic. 535 D10, 536 D3, 551 M4
Dunolly Vic. 535 C4, 549 M10, **160**, 199
Dunoon NSW 516 G4, 525 O3
Dunorlan Tas. 626 H8, 629 B10
Dunrobin Vic. 550 C3, 568 H11
Dunsborough WA 572 B6, 574 B9, 576 B10, **304**
Dunvert Island WA 581 I5, 584 C7
Dunwich Qld 600 G5, 609 N9
Dural NSW 508 D4, 509 A10, 511 K6
Duranillin WA 574 E8, 576 D9
Durdidwarrah Vic. 536 E5, 551 N5
Durham Lead Vic. 535 C11, 536 D4, 551 M5
Durham Ox Vic. 526 H12, 549 N6
Duri NSW 524 H10
Duroby Creek NSW 601 F12
Durong Qld 609 K6
Durran Durra NSW 519 E5, 521 K3, 522 H11
Durras NSW 519 F6, 521 M6, 523 I12
Dutson Vic. 541 K7
Dutton SA 554 G3, 559 K7, 568 D1
Duverney Vic. 536 B6, 551 L6
Dwarda WA 571 H10
Dwellingup WA 571 E10, 574 C7, 576 C8, **304**
Dwyers NSW 529 M6
Dyer Island WA 570 A7, 571 A6, 574 B5, 576 B8
Dynnyrne Tas. 621 D9
Dysart Qld 605 D12, 611 I8
Dysart Tas. 623 I1, 625 K5

E

Eagle Farm Qld 600 E4, 602 F11
Eagle Heights Qld 600 E9, 601 B4, 435
Eagle Island Qld 611 M7, 613 L1
Eagle Island WA 575 B9, 586 D8

Eagle Point Vic. 541 M6, 186
Eagle Rock Marine Sanctuary Vic. 536 D10, 538 F3, 551 N9
Eaglehawk Vic. 535 F3, 542 A8, 549 O10
Eaglehawk Island WA 575 E1, 578 A2, 580 A12, 582 D5
Eaglehawk Neck Tas. 623 N7, 625 M8, **477**
Earlando Qld 605 F4, 611 J3
Earlston Vic. 542 F8, 544 B5
East Bairnsdale Vic. 541 M5
East Boyd NSW 519 E10, 539 H8
East Bremer Islet NT 591 N3
East Devonport Tas. 629 C2
East Governor Island WA 581 L2, 585 I1
East Gresford NSW 514 C4, 515 A10, 523 L2
East Hills NSW 508 C9, 511 J10
East Intercourse Island WA 575 E1, 578 B2, 580 B12, 582 D4
East Ipswich Qld 599 A9, 600 B5, 602 D12
East Island SA 558 B5, 560 A12, 567 O12
East Island WA 575 D2, 580 G6, 582 B7, 584 A9
East Jindabyne NSW 519 B8, 520 E10, 539 C4
East Kangaroo Island Tas. 624 A10, 627 O1
East Kurrajong NSW 511 I3, 513 O5
East Launceston Tas. 629 G1
East Lewis Island WA 575 E1, 578 B2, 580 B12, 582 D4
East Lynne NSW 519 F6, 521 M5
East Mid Intercourse Island WA 575 E1, 578 B2, 580 B12, 582 D5
East Montalivet Island WA 581 K2, 584 G2
East Moore Island WA 575 F1, 578 C2, 580 C12, 582 F4
East Pyramids Tas. 624 E10
East Repulse Island Qld 605 F6, 611 K4
East Roe Island WA 581 I5, 584 C7
East Strait Island Qld 614 D2
East Sunday Island WA 581 I5, 584 C7
East Vernon Island NT 590 D3
East Wallabi Island WA 575 C12
East Woody Island NT 591 N3, 363
East Yolla Tas. 626 E6
Easter NP WA 572 F10, 573 A1, 574 C10, 576 C10
Eastern Creek NSW 508 A5, 511 I7, 513 P12
Eastern Island WA 575 C12
Eastern View Vic. 536 D10, 538 E3, 551 M9
Eastville Vic. 535 D4, 549 N10
Eastwood NSW 508 D6, 511 K7
Eaton WA 572 E3
Eatonsville NSW 516 D8, 525 M6
Eba SA 559 L6
Eba Island SA 558 A2, 567 N10
Ebden Vic. 543 L6, 545 J3
Ebenezer NSW 508 B1, 511 J4, 101
Ebor NSW 515 E1, 516 B12, 525 L8
Eborac Island Qld 614 D2
Eccleston NSW 514 C2, 515 A9, 523 L2
Echuca Vic. 527 J12, 542 C5, **160**

Echuca Village Vic. 527 J12, 542 C5
Echunga SA 553 F10, 554 D11, 555 G4, 559 J9
Ecklin South Vic. 538 F8, 551 I8
Eclipse Hill Island WA 581 L2, 584 H1
Eclipse (Garoogubbee) Island Qld 606 G8, 613 N10
Eclipse Island WA 573 D12, 574 G12, 576 E12
Eddington Vic. 535 C4, 549 M11
Eddystone Point Tas. 627 P6
Eden NSW 519 E10, 539 H8, **49**
Eden Hills SA 553 C9, 554 B10, 555 F3
Eden Island Qld 600 G7, 601 F1, 609 N10
Eden Park Vic. 531 E2, 537 J3, 540 D3
Eden Valley SA 554 G6, 559 K8, 568 C2, 225
Edenhope Vic. 548 C11, 568 H9, **162**
Edens Landing Qld 600 E6
Edgcumbe Beach Tas. 626 D4
Edgecliff NSW 508 F8, 511 M9
Edgeroi NSW 524 F6
Edgewater WA 570 C4, 571 B4
Edi Vic. 543 I9, 544 F6
Edi Upper Vic. 543 I9, 544 F7
Edillilie SA 558 D7
Edith NSW 522 H6
Edith Creek Tas. 626 C4
Edith River NT 590 F8
Edithburgh SA 556 E8, 558 H9, **234**
Edithvale Vic. 531 E8, 533 K2, 537 J7, 540 D6
Edmonton Qld 606 E3, 607 F8, 613 L6
Edward Island NT 591 L8
Edward Island Qld 604 B1, 605 G5, 611 K3
Edwards Island WA 574 A3, 576 B6
Edwardstown SA 554 B9, 555 F3
Eganstown Vic. 535 E8, 536 E2, 551 N3
Egg Island Qld 604 C6, 611 N11
Egg Island SA 567 L9
Egg Island Tas. 626 H6, 629 B6
Egg Island WA 575 B9, 586 B7
Egg Lagoon Tas. 625 P10
Egret Island WA 575 E1, 578 A2, 580 A12, 582 D5
Eidsvold Qld 604 C11, 609 K4, 432
Eildon Vic. 534 H1, 537 O1, 540 G1, 542 G12, 544 C11, 162
Eimeo Qld 605 G7, 611 K5
Einasleigh Qld 613 I9
Ejanding WA 574 E2, 576 D6
El Arish Qld 606 E5, 613 M8
Elaine Vic. 535 D12, 536 D5, 551 M5
Elamang Island Qld 605 H9, 611 L6
Elands NSW 515 D7, 525 K11
Elanora Qld 601 F9
Elanora Heights NSW 508 G4, 509 C11, 511 N6
Elaroo Qld 605 E6, 611 J5
Elbow Hill SA 556 B2, 558 F5
Elcho Island NT 591 L3
Elcombe NSW 524 H5
Elderslie Tas. 622 H1, 625 J5
Eldon Tas. 623 J1, 625 L5
Eldorado Vic. 543 J7, 544 G4, 197
Electrona Tas. 623 I7

Elermore Vale NSW 509 G3, 514 C9
Elimbah Qld 602 F7, 609 N8
Elingamite Vic. 538 G8, 551 I8
Eliza Island Qld 604 B1, 611 M8
Elizabeth SA 553 D3, 554 C6,
 559 J8, 568 B2
Elizabeth Beach NSW 515 E10,
 523 N2
Elizabeth Island Tas. 624 C2,
 626 C12
Elizabeth Island Vic. 531 G12,
 533 N9, 537 K10, 540 D8
Elizabeth Town Tas. 627 I8,
 629 C10
Ella Bay NP Qld 606 E4, 607 H11,
 613 M7, 417
Ella Rock SA 556 B8, 558 G9
Ellalong NSW 509 D3, 523 L4
Ellam Vic. 526 D11, 548 F5
Ellen Grove Qld 599 D9, 600 D5,
 602 E12
Ellenborough NSW 515 E6,
 525 L11
Ellendale Tas. 622 E1, 625 I5
Ellerslie Vic. 550 H7
Ellerston NSW 523 L1, 525 I12
Elliminyt Vic. 536 B9, 538 B2,
 551 L8
Ellinbank Vic. 537 N9, 540 G7
Elliott NT 593 I5, **361**
Elliott Tas. 626 F5
Elliott Heads Qld 603 D2, 604 G11,
 609 M3
Ellis Beach Qld 606 D2, 607 E5,
 613 L5
Ellis Island Qld 614 F8
Elliston SA 558 B5, **235**
Elmhurst Vic. 549 K12, 551 K1
Elmore Vic. 542 B7, 549 P9, 190
Elong Elong NSW 522 G1, 524 D12
Elphick Nob WA 578 A2, 580 A12,
 582 D4
Elphin Tas. 629 G1
Elphinstone Vic. 535 G6, 542 A11,
 549 O12, 551 O1
Elsey NP NT 590 H9, 363
Elsie Island WA 581 N2, 585 K2
Elsmore NSW 525 J6
Elsternwick Vic. 537 J6, 540 C5
Eltham NSW 516 G4
Eltham Vic. 531 F5, 537 J5, 540 D4
Emerald Qld 611 I10, **409**
Emerald Vic. 531 H7, 533 O1,
 534 C10, 537 L7, 540 E5, **162**
Emerald Beach NSW 516 E11,
 525 N7
Emerald Hill NSW 524 G8
Emerald Springs NT 588 H11,
 590 E7
Emita Tas. 624 B10
Emmaville NSW 525 K5, 52
Emmdale Roadhouse NSW 529 I9
Emmes Reef SA 556 B9, 558 F10
Emmet Qld 610 B12, 617 N12,
 619 M1
Empire Bay NSW 509 D9, 511 O4
Empire Vale NSW 516 G5, 525 O4,
 609 N12
Emu Vic. 535 A2, 549 L10
Emu Bay SA 556 D10, 558 H11
Emu Creek Vic. 535 G4, 542 A9,
 549 O10
Emu Downs SA 559 K6
Emu Park Qld 604 C5, 611 N10,
 450

Emu Plains NSW 510 G6, 513 M10,
 527 N9, 543 J1
Ena Island WA 581 J3, 584 F4
Endeavour Hills Vic. 533 M1
Endeavour River NP Qld 613 L2,
 407
Enderby Island WA 575 E1, 578 A2,
 580 A12, 582 D4
Endyalgout Island NT 590 G2
Eneabba WA 576 B5
Enfield Vic. 535 B12, 536 C4,
 551 M5
Engadine NSW 508 C11, 511 J11,
 517 H1
Engawala NT 595 J5
Englefield Vic. 548 E12, 550 E2
English Island SA 558 E8
English Town Tas. 627 L9
Enngonia NSW 529 M3, 608 A12,
 619 N12
Enoggera Qld 599 D6, 600 D4,
 602 F11
Ensay Vic. 541 N3, 185
Ensay North Vic. 541 N3
Ensay South Vic. 541 N3
Entrance Island NT 591 J3
Entrance Island Qld 604 C2,
 611 N9
Entrance Island SA 556 B1, 558 G5
Entrance Island WA 581 J4, 584 E5
Eppalock Vic. 535 G4, 542 A9,
 549 O10
Epping NSW 508 D5, 509 A11,
 511 K7
Epping Vic. 531 E4, 537 J4, 540 C3
Epping Forest Tas. 627 L10
Epping Forest NP Qld 610 F8
Epsom Vic. 535 G3, 542 A8,
 549 O10
Eraring NSW 509 F4, 514 B10
Ercildoun Vic. 535 A9, 536 B2,
 551 L3
Eric Island WA 581 N2, 585 K2
Erica Vic. 540 H6, 197
Erigolia NSW 527 N5
Erikin WA 576 E7
Erina NSW 509 D8, 511 O3
Erith SA 554 A1, 556 H4, 559 J7,
 568 B1
Erldunda NT 594 H9
Ernest Qld 601 E5
Eromanga Qld 619 J5, 438
Erowal Bay NSW 517 D11, 521 O2
Erriba Tas. 626 G8, 628 F4
Erringibba NP Qld 608 H8
Errinundra Vic. 519 B11, 539 D9
Errinundra NP Vic. 519 B11,
 539 D9, 185
Errk Oykangand NP Qld 612 F2
Erskine Island Qld 604 E6, 611 O11
Erskine Park NSW 510 H7,
 513 O12
Escape Island WA 576 A5
Eshelby Island Qld 605 F4, 611 J3
Esk Qld 602 A8, 609 M8, **410**
Esk Island Qld 605 G5, 611 K3
Esk (Soopun) Island Qld 606 F8,
 613 N10
Esk NP Qld 602 A9, 609 M8
Eskdale Vic. 543 L8, 545 K5, 194
Esmond Vic. 527 M12, 542 H6,
 544 E1
Esperance WA 577 I9, **304**
Essendon Vic. 531 D5, 537 I5,
 540 C4

Ethel Islet Qld 614 E5
Etisus Island WA 581 J4, 584 E5
Etmilyn WA 571 E10
Eton Qld 605 F8, 611 K6
Ettalong Beach NSW 508 H1,
 509 D9, 511 N4, 102
Ettamogah NSW 522 A12,
 527 O12, 543 L6, 545 J1
Ettrick NSW 516 E4, 525 N3,
 609 M12
Euabalong NSW 522 A3, 527 N3
Euabalong West NSW 522 A3,
 527 N3
Eubenangee Swamp NP Qld
 606 E4, 607 G11, 613 M7, 417
Euchareena NSW 522 G3
Eucla WA 566 C7, 577 P6, **305**
Eucla NP WA 566 C7, 577 P5, 305
Eucumbene NSW 519 B7, 520 E8,
 539 C2
Eudlo Qld 602 F4, 603 E12
Eudlo Creek NP Qld 602 F4,
 603 E12, 609 N7
Eudunda SA 554 G1, 559 K7,
 568 C1
Eugenana Tas. 626 H6, 628 H2,
 629 A7
Eugowra NSW 522 E5, **49**
Eujinyn WA 574 G4
Eukey Qld 516 A4, 525 L3, 609 L12
Eulo Qld 619 M9, **410**
Eumemmerring Vic. 533 M2
Eumundi Qld 602 F2, 603 E10,
 609 N7, 437, 450
Eumungerie NSW 524 C11
Eungai Creek NSW 515 G3, 525 M9
Eungella Qld 605 E7, 611 J5
Eungella NP Qld 605 E7, 611 J5,
 424
Eurack Vic. 536 B8, 551 L7
Euramo Qld 606 E6, 613 M8
Euratha NSW 522 A6, 527 N6
Eurelia SA 559 J2, 561 I9
Euri Qld 605 D4, 611 I3
Eurimbula NP Qld 604 E8, 609 L1,
 611 O12, 427
Euroa Vic. 542 F9, 544 A7, 163
Eurobin Vic. 543 K9, 545 I6, 182
Eurobodalla NSW 519 E7, 521 K9
Eurobodalla NP NSW 519 F7,
 521 L8
Euroka NSW 510 C6, 512 D9,
 515 F4
Eurong Qld 603 G6, 609 N5
Eurongilly NSW 522 C9
Euston NSW 526 F7, 547 I8
Eva Island Qld 606 F7, 613 M9
Eva Island WA 575 C3
Evandale Tas. 627 K9, 629 H11,
 478
Evans Head NSW 516 G6, 525 O4,
 50
Evans Island SA 567 L9
Evans Plains NSW 522 G5
Evansford Vic. 535 B7, 536 B1,
 551 L2
Evelyn Island WA 581 M2, 585 K1
Everard Junction WA 579 K7
Eversley Vic. 549 J12, 551 J2
Everton Vic. 543 J8, 544 G5
Ewaninga NT 597 J5
Ewens Ponds SA 550 A6, 568 G12
Exeter NSW 517 B6, 519 G3, 523 I9,
 38
Exeter Tas. 627 J7, 629 F8, **478**

Exford Vic. 531 A5, 535 H12,
 536 G5, 540 B4, 551 P5
Exmouth WA 575 B3, **305**
Expedition NP Qld 608 G3, 443
Exton Tas. 627 I8, 629 D10
Eyre Island SA 567 M9

F

Facing Island Qld 604 D6, 609 L1,
 611 N12
Fairfax Island WA 581 N3, 585 L4
Fairfax Islands Qld 604 G7, 609
 M1, 611 P12
Fairfield NSW 508 B7
Fairfield Qld 599 E8
Fairhaven Vic. 531 F12, 533 M8,
 537 K10, 540 D7
Fairholme NSW 522 C4, 527 P4
Fairley Vic. 526 H10, 549 N4
Fairlies Knob NP Qld 603 C5,
 604 F12, 609 M5
Fairneyview Qld 600 A4, 602 C11
Fairview Vic. 526 G12, 549 K6
Fairway Islands WA 581 I6, 584 C8
Fairy Dell Vic. 542 C7
Fairy Hill NSW 516 E4, 525 N3
Fairy Meadow NSW 517 F4
Falcon (Carbooroo) Island Qld
 606 F8, 613 N10
Falcon Islet Qld 611 L7
Falls Creek NSW 517 C10, 519 G4,
 521 O1, 523 I10
Falls Creek Vic. 543 L10, 545 K8,
 181
Falmouth Tas. 627 O9, 492
False Island WA 575 D2, 582 B7
Family Islands NP Qld 606 F6,
 613 M8, 428
Fantome (Eumilli) Island Qld
 606 F8, 613 N10
Faraday Vic. 535 F6, 542 A10,
 549 O12, 551 O1
Farleigh Qld 605 G7, 611 K5
Farmer Island Qld 614 E6
Farnborough Qld 604 C4, 611 M10
Farnham NSW 522 G3
Farrell Flat SA 559 K6
Farrier Island Qld 605 G6, 611 K4
Faulconbridge NSW 510 F5,
 513 K9, 53
Faure Island WA 575 C8, 586 E6
Favorite Island WA 576 A5
Fawcett Vic. 540 F1, 542 F11,
 544 B10
Fawkner Vic. 531 D5, 537 I5,
 540 C4
Feilton Tas. 622 F4, 625 I6
Felton East Qld 609 K9
Fenelon Island SA 567 L9
Fenelon Island WA 581 K2, 584 G2
Fentonbury Tas. 622 E2, 625 I5
Fentons Creek Vic. 535 A1, 549 L9
Fenwick Vic. 532 C5
Ferguson Vic. 536 A11, 538 B4,
 551 K10
Fern Hill Vic. 535 G9, 536 G2,
 540 A2, 542 A12
Fern Tree Tas. 621 A10, 623 I6,
 625 K7
Fern Tree Bower Tas. 621 A10
Fernbank Vic. 541 L5
Ferndale NSW 522 A11, 527 N11,
 543 J3
Ferndale WA 572 G7

Ferndene Tas. 626 G6, 628 E1
Fernihurst Vic. 549 M7
Fernlees Qld 611 I11
Ferntree Creek NP Qld 602 F3, 603 E11, 609 N7
Ferntree Gully Vic. 531 G7, 534 B9, 537 K6, 540 D5
Fernvale Qld 600 A4, 602 C10, 609 M9
Ferny Glen Qld 601 A7
Ferny Grove Qld 599 D6, 600 D4, 602 E10
Ferny Hills Qld 600 D3, 602 E10
Fiery Flat Vic. 549 M8
Fife Island Qld 614 F9
Fifield NSW 522 C2
Fig Tree NSW 522 F4
Fig Tree Pocket Qld 599 D8
Figtree NSW 517 F5
Figtree Creek Qld 606 E3, 607 G9
Figure of Eight Island WA 577 I9
Finch Hatton Qld 605 E7, 611 J5
Finch Island NT 591 N7
Fingal Tas. 627 N9, **479**
Fingal Vic. 532 H9
Fingal Bay NSW 514 H8, 515 C12
Fingal Head NSW 601 H11
Finger Island WA 577 I9
Finke NT 595 J10
Finke Gorge NP NT 594 H8, 596 D6, 362
Finley NSW 527 L11, 542 F3, **50**
Finniss SA 555 H7, 559 K10, 568 C4
Finucane Island NP Qld 612 A7, 615 E4
Fish Creek Vic. 540 G10, 164
Fish Point Vic. 526 H10, 549 M2
Fisher SA 566 G4
Fisher Island Qld 614 E6
Fisherman Islands Qld 599 G6, 600 E3, 602 G10, 609 N9
Fisherman Islands WA 576 A5
Fishermans Paradise NSW 517 B12, 521 N3
Fishery Falls Qld 606 E3, 607 G9, 613 M6
Fiskville Vic. 535 F11, 536 F4, 551 N5
Fitzalan Island Qld 605 G5, 611 K4
Fitzgerald Tas. 622 D3, 624 H6
Fitzgerald River NP WA 576 F10, 292
Fitzroy Crossing WA 581 K8, 584 H11, **306**
Fitzroy Island Qld 606 E2, 607 H7, 613 M6
Fitzroy Island NP Qld 606 E2, 607 H7, 613 M6
Five Rocks Qld 604 C3, 611 N9
Five Trees Cays Qld 604 B1, 611 M8
Five Ways NSW 522 A10, 527 O10, 529 O11, 543 L2
Five Ways Vic. 533 L10
Fiveways Vic. 533 M5
Flag Island WA 575 D1, 582 B4
Flaggy Rock Qld 605 G10, 611 K7
Flagstaff Gully Tas. 621 F6
Flagstone Creek Qld 603 C1, 604 F10, 609 M3
Flat Island Qld 604 C3, 611 N9
Flat Island WA 575 C2, 581 K2, 584 G2
Flat Islet Qld 614 C1
Flat Rock Qld 600 H4, 604 C5, 609 O9, 611 N11

Flat Rock Island NSW 519 F6, 521 M6, 523 I12
Flat Top Island Qld 605 G8, 611 K5
Flat Top Island Tas. 624 G11
Flat Tops NSW 514 E5, 515 B10
Flat Witch Island Tas. 624 G11
Flaxton Qld 602 F3, 425
Fletcher Qld 516 A4, 525 K3
Fletcher Island NT 591 N11, 593 N2
Flinders Vic. 533 I10, 537 I11, 540 C8, **163**
Flinders Chase NP SA 556 A12, 558 F12, 243
Flinders Group NP Qld 614 G10, 407
Flinders Island Qld 614 G10
Flinders Island SA 558 A5, 235
Flinders Island Tas. 624 B9, 627 O1, **479**, 498
Flinders Island WA 572 C12, 574 B11, 576 B11
Flinders Islet NSW 517 G5, 519 H2, 523 J8
Flinders Ranges NP SA 557 C9, 561 I6, 266
Flinton Qld 608 H9
Flintstone Tas. 625 J1, 627 J11
Flock Pigeon Island Qld 605 H11, 611 L8
Flora Island WA 581 I5, 584 C7
Floreat WA 570 C6, 571 B5
Florida NSW 529 M9
Florida WA 571 B10, 574 B6, 576 B8
Florieton SA 559 L6
Flowerdale Tas. 626 E4
Flowerdale Vic. 534 B2, 537 K2, 540 D2, 542 D12
Flowerpot Tas. 622 H9, 625 K9
Flowery Gully Tas. 627 J7, 629 E7
Fly Island Qld 606 F9, 613 N10
Fly Island WA 575 C3
Flying Fish Point Qld 606 E4, 607 H11, 613 M7, 417
Flying Fox Qld 516 F1, 600 E10
Flying Fox Island Qld 614 B5
Flynn Vic. 541 J7
Flynns Creek Vic. 541 I7
Foam Rocks WA 577 J9
Folly Island WA 581 I5, 584 C7
Fontanes Island WA 581 J3, 584 F4
Footscray Vic. 531 D5, 537 I5, 540 C4
Forbes NSW 522 D4, **50**
Forbes Islands A Qld 614 E6
Forbes Islands B Qld 614 E6
Forbes Islands C Qld 614 E6
Forbes Islands NP Qld 614 E6
Forbin Island WA 581 J3, 584 F4
Forcett Tas. 623 L4, 625 L7
Fords SA 554 E3
Fords Bridge NSW 529 L4
Fordwich NSW 523 K3
Forest Tas. 626 D4
Forest Hill NSW 522 C10, 527 P10, 543 N1
Forest Den NP Qld 610 D7, 617 P7, 391
Forest Glen NSW 508 D1, 509 A9, 511 K4
Forest Glen Qld 602 G4, 603 F12
Forest Grove WA 572 B9, 574 B10
Forest Grove NP WA 572 B9, 574 B10, 576 B10

Forest Hill Qld 602 A11
Forest Lake Qld 599 D9, 600 D6
Forest Reefs NSW 522 G5
Forester Tas. 627 M6
Forge Creek Vic. 541 M6
Formartin Qld 609 K8
Forrest Vic. 536 B10, 538 C3, 551 L9, 156
Forrest WA 566 A5, 577 O4
Forrest Beach Qld 606 F8, 613 M10, 415
Forrest Island WA 577 J9
Forrestdale WA 570 E8
Forrestfield WA 570 F6
Forreston SA 553 G5, 554 E7, 555 H1
Forsayth Qld 612 H9, 431
Forster SA 559 L8, 568 D2
Forster–Tuncurry NSW 515 E9, 523 O2, **51**
Forsyth Island Qld 615 C2
Forsyth Island Tas. 624 B12, 627 P3
Fort Denison NSW 508 F7, 509 B12, 511 M9, 523 K7
Fort Lytton NP Qld 599 F6, 600 E4, 602 G11, 609 N9
Fortescue Island WA 575 D1, 578 A2, 582 C5
Fortescue Roadhouse WA 575 E2, 578 A3, 582 C6
Fortesque River Roadhouse WA 575 E2, 578 A3, 582 C6
Forth Tas. 626 G6, 628 G1
Fortis Creek NP NSW 516 D7, 525 M5
Forty Mile Scrub NP Qld 606 B6, 613 K8, 431
Foster Vic. 540 G9, **164**
Foster Islands Tas. 627 O4
Fosterville Vic. 535 H3, 542 B8, 549 P10
Fountain Gate Vic. 533 M2
Fountaindale NSW 509 D7, 511 O2
Four Hummocks SA 558 C8
Four Mile Creek Tas. 627 O9
Fowler Island NT 591 M6
Fowler Island Qld 612 A6, 615 D3
Fowlers Bay SA 567 J8, 231
Fox Ground NSW 517 E8, 519 H3, 523 J9
Fox Trap Roadhouse Qld 608 A6, 619 N6
Foxeys Hangout Vic. 533 J7
Foxglove Island WA 575 D1, 582 A4
Foxhow Vic. 536 A7, 551 K6
Framlingham Vic. 538 E7, 550 H7
Framlingham East Vic. 550 H7
Frampton NSW 519 A2, 522 D8
Frances SA 548 B9, 568 G8, 251
Francistown Tas. 622 F10, 625 I9
Francois Peron NP WA 575 B8, 586 D6, 301
Frank Hann NP WA 576 G8, 317
Frankford Tas. 627 I7, 629 E8
Frankland WA 573 G1, 574 F10, 576 D11
Frankland Group NP Qld 606 E3, 607 H9, 613 M7
Franklin Tas. 622 G7, 625 J8
Franklin–Gordon Wild Rivers NP Tas. 622 A1, 624 E5, 626 E12, 628 D11, 496
Franklin Islands SA 567 M9
Franklinford Vic. 535 E7, 536 E1, 551 N2

Frankston Vic. 531 E9, 533 K4, 537 J8, 540 D6
Frankton SA 554 H2, 559 K7, 568 D1
Fraser Island Qld 603 G4, 604 H12, 609 O4, 416
Fraser Island WA 581 I5, 584 C7
Frazer Island WA 575 B4
Frederickton NSW 515 G4, 525 M10, 62
Fredrick Island WA 577 I9
Free Island WA 577 J9
Freeburgh Vic. 543 K10, 545 J7
Freeling SA 554 D4, 559 K8, 568 C1, 235
Freeling Island SA 567 L9
Freemans Reach NSW 508 A1, 511 I4, 513 O6, 523 J6
Freestone Qld 516 B1, 525 L1
Fregon SA 565 I4
Fremantle WA 570 C8, 571 B6, 574 B5, 576 B8, **280**, 285
French Island Vic. 531 F12, 533 M8, 537 K10, 540 D7
French Island Marine NP Vic. 531 G11, 533 M7, 537 K9, 540 D7
French Island NP Vic. 531 G12, 533 M8, 537 L10, 540 E7, 164
Frenchs Forest NSW 508 F5, 509 B11, 511 M7, 523 K6
Freshwater Creek Vic. 536 E9, 538 G2, 551 N8
Freshwater NP Qld 599 E3, 600 D1, 602 F8, 609 N8
Freycinet Island WA 575 B9, 586 D9
Freycinet NP Tas. 625 O2, 627 O12, 474
Friday Island Qld 614 C2
Friday Island WA 575 B9, 586 C8
Froggart Island WA 581 K2, 584 G2
Frogmore NSW 519 C1, 522 F7
Fryerstown Vic. 535 F7, 542 A11, 549 O12, 551 O2
Fulham Vic. 541 K7
Fulham Island Tas. 623 M6, 625 M7
Fullerton NSW 519 E1, 522 G7
Fumina Vic. 537 P7, 540 G5
Fur Rock WA 577 I9
Furner SA 568 F10
Furnissdale WA 571 C9, 574 C6
Fyansford Vic. 532 A3, 536 F8, 538 G1, 551 N7, 167
Fyshwick ACT 518 E5, 520 H3

G

Gaagal Wanggaan (South Beach) NP NSW 515 G2, 525 M9
Gabo Island Vic. 519 E11, 539 H11
Gadayim Pyramid WA 581 I5, 584 D6
Gaffneys Creek Vic. 537 P3, 540 H3
Gagebrook Tas. 623 I3, 625 K6
Gaibait (Meddler) Island Qld 614 C2
Gaibirra Island Qld 605 G5, 611 K4
Gaimard Island WA 581 K2, 584 F3
Gainaulai Island Qld 614 C1
Galah Vic. 526 D8, 546 G11
Galaquil Vic. 526 E11, 548 H5
Galaquil East Vic. 548 H5
Gale Island WA 581 J3, 584 F4
Galga SA 559 M8, 568 E2

Galiwinku NT 591 L3
Gallanani Qld 602 A8
Gallangowan Qld 602 A1, 603 C10, 609 M7
Galong NSW 519 B2, 522 E8
Galston NSW 508 D3, 509 A10, 511 K5, 523 K6
Gama Vic. 526 E10, 548 H3
Gananggarngur Island NT 591 K3
Ganmain NSW 522 B8, 527 O8
Ganumbali Island NT 591 M4
Gap Island WA 581 J4, 584 F5
Gapsted Vic. 543 J8, 544 H5, 182
Gapuwiyak NT 591 L4
Garah NSW 524 F3, 608 H12
Garalja Island NT 591 M3
Garbutt Qld 605 A1, 606 G10, 610 G1
Gardangarl (Field Island) NT 590 G3
Garden Island NSW 514 F7, 515 C11, 523 M3
Garden Island Qld 603 F6, 606 E6, 609 N5, 613 M9
Garden Island SA 558 B4, 567 O11
Garden Island Tas. 622 G10, 625 J9
Garden Island WA 570 B9, 571 B7, 574 B5, 576 B8
Garden Island Creek Tas. 622 H9, 625 J9
Gardens of Stone NP NSW 523 I4, 68
Gardners Bay Tas. 622 G9, 625 J9
Garema NSW 522 D5
Garfield Vic. 534 E12, 537 M8, 540 F6
Garfield North Vic. 534 E11, 537 M8, 540 F6
Gargett Qld 605 F7, 611 J5
Garibaldi Vic. 535 C12, 536 D4, 551 M5
Garig Gunak Barlu NP NT 590 F2
Garigal NP NSW 508 F5, 509 C11, 511 M6, 523 K6
Garra NSW 522 F4
Garrawilla NP NSW 524 F9
Garrthalala NT 591 N5
Garvoc Vic. 538 E7, 551 I8
Gary Junction WA 579 K3
Gascoyne Junction WA 575 D7, 578 A8, **307**
Gatton Qld 609 L9, **411**
Gatton NP Qld 609 L9
Gatum Vic. 550 E2
Gaven Qld 601 D4
Gawler SA 553 E2, 554 D5, 559 J8, 568 C2, 235
Gawler Tas. 626 G6, 628 F1
Gawler Ranges NP SA 558 C1, 560 B9, 567 P9, 265
Gayndah Qld 609 L5, **411**
Geebung Qld 599 E6
Geehi NSW 519 A8, 520 B10, 539 A4, 543 P8, 545 P5
Geelong Vic. 532 B4, 536 F8, 538 G1, 540 A6, 551 O7, **166**
Geelong East Vic. 532 B4
Geelong North Vic. 532 B3
Geelong South Vic. 532 A4
Geeralying WA 574 E7
Geeveston Tas. 622 F8, 625 I9
Geham NP Qld 609 L9
Geikie Gorge NP WA 581 L7, 584 H11, 306
Geilston Bay Tas. 621 F6

Gelantipy Vic. 519 A10, 539 A8, 541 P2, 545 P12
Gellibrand Vic. 536 A10, 538 B3, 551 K9
Gelliondale Vic. 541 I9
Gelorup WA 572 D4
Gembrook Vic. 534 D10, 537 M7, 540 E5
Gemtree NT 595 J5
Genoa Vic. 519 D11, 539 G10
George Island Qld 611 L7
George Island WA 577 J9
George Rocks Tas. 627 P5
George Town Tas. 627 J6, 629 E6, **480**
Georges Creek Vic. 543 M6, 545 K3
Georges Plains NSW 522 H5
Georges River NP NSW 508 C9, 511 J10, 517 H1, 519 H1, 523 K7
Georgetown Qld 612 H9, 431
Georgetown SA 559 J4, 560 H12
Georgica NSW 516 F4, 525 N3
Geraldton WA 575 D12, 576 A3, **307**
Gerang Gerung Vic. 526 D12, 548 F7
Gerangamete Vic. 536 C10, 538 C3, 551 L9
Geranium SA 559 M10, 568 F4
Geranium Islands WA 581 L1, 585 I1
Geranium Plain SA 559 K6
Germantown Vic. 543 K10, 545 I7
Germein Island SA 558 B4, 567 O11
Gerogery NSW 522 A12, 527 O12, 543 L5
Gerogery West NSW 522 A12, 527 O12, 543 L5
Gerringong NSW 517 F8, 519 H3, 523 J9, 63
Gerroa NSW 517 E8
Getullai Island Qld 614 D1
Geurie NSW 522 F2
Gheringhap Vic. 536 E7, 551 N7
Ghin-doo-ee NP NSW 514 H3, 515 C9, 523 M2
Ghin Ghin Vic. 537 L1, 540 E1, 542 E11
Giant Rocks WA 577 I10
Gibbings Island WA 581 I5, 584 C7
Gibraltar Range NP NSW 516 B7, 525 L5, 52
Gibson WA 577 I9
Gibson Island WA 581 I5, 584 C7
Gibsonvale NSW 522 A5, 527 O5
Gidgegannup WA 570 H3, 571 E4, 574 C4
Gidginbung NSW 522 C7, 527 P7
Gidley Island WA 578 B2, 580 B12, 582 D4
Giffard Vic. 541 K8
Gig Rocks WA 577 I9
Gilbert Island NT 591 N10, 593 N1
Gilbert River Qld 612 G8
Gilbert Spring NT 596 B5
Gilberts WA 555 G7
Giles Corner SA 554 C1, 559 J7, 568 C1
Gilgai NSW 525 I6
Gilgandra NSW 524 C10, **51**
Gilgooma NSW 524 C8
Gilgunnia NSW 527 M1, 529 M12
Gillenbah NSW 522 A8, 527 N8
Gilliat Qld 615 H11, 617 I3

Gillieston Vic. 542 E7
Gillingarra WA 574 C2, 576 C6
Gilmore NSW 519 A4, 520 C2, 522 D10
Gilston Qld 516 G1, 600 F10, 601 D6
Gin Gin NSW 524 B11
Gin Gin Qld 603 B2, 604 E11, 609 L3, **411**
Gindie Qld 611 I11
Gingin WA 571 C1, 574 B3, 576 C7, **308**
Ginninderra ACT 518 E3, 520 G2, 115
Gipsy Point Vic. 519 D11, 539 G10
Gir-um-bit NP NSW 514 F7, 515 B11, 523 M3
Girgarre Vic. 542 D7
Girilambone NSW 529 O9
Girral NSW 522 B5, 527 O5
Girramay NP Qld 606 E6, 613 M9, 401
Girraween NP Qld 516 A4, 525 L3, 609 K12
Girringun NP Qld 606 D7, 613 L9, 401, 415
Girt Island Qld 604 C5, 611 N11
Giru Qld 605 A2, 606 H11, 610 H1, 613 O12, 448
Gisborne Vic. 531 A2, 535 H10, 536 H3, 540 B2, 551 P4
Gladfield Qld 516 B1
Gladfield Vic. 526 H12, 549 N6
Gladstone NSW 515 G4, 525 M10, 62
Gladstone Qld 604 D7, 609 K1, 611 N12, **412**
Gladstone SA 559 J4, 560 H12, 234
Gladstone Tas. 627 O5, **480**
Gladstone WA 575 C8, 586 G7
Gladysdale Vic. 534 E8, 537 M6, 540 F5
Glanmire NSW 522 H5
Glass House Mountains Qld 602 F6, 609 N8, 400, 421, 422, 442
Glass House Mountains NP Qld 602 F6, 603 E12, 609 N8, 422
Glasse Island WA 576 G10
Glastonbury NP Qld 603 D9, 609 M6
Glauert Island WA 581 J3, 584 F4
Glaziers Bay Tas. 622 F8, 625 J8
Glebe Tas. 621 D8
Glen Tas. 627 K6, 629 G7
Glen Alice NSW 523 I4
Glen Aplin Qld 516 A4, 525 K3, 609 K12
Glen Creek Vic. 543 K8, 545 I5
Glen Davis NSW 523 I4, 86
Glen Dhu Tas. 629 F2
Glen Forbes Vic. 533 P10, 537 L11, 540 E8
Glen Geddes Qld 604 A4, 611 M10
Glen Helen Resort NT 594 G7, 596 C3, **361**
Glen Huon Tas. 622 F7, 625 I8
Glen Innes NSW 525 K5, **52**
Glen Iris Vic. 531 E6
Glen Martin NSW 514 E5, 515 B11
Glen Oak NSW 514 D6, 515 A11, 523 M3
Glen Valley Vic. 543 M10, 545 L9
Glen Waverley Vic. 531 F6, 537 J6, 540 D5
Glen William NSW 514 E5, 515 B10

Glen Wills Vic. 543 M10, 545 L9
Glenaire Vic. 536 A12, 538 A6, 551 K10
Glenaladale Vic. 541 L5
Glenalbyn Vic. 535 C1, 549 M8
Glenalta SA 553 C8, 554 B10, 555 F3
Glenariff NSW 529 N7
Glenaroua Vic. 542 C11
Glenbar NP Qld 603 C7, 609 M5
Glenbrae Vic. 535 A8, 536 B1, 551 L3
Glenbrook NSW 510 G6, 513 L10, 523 J6, **52**
Glenburn Vic. 531 H2, 534 C3, 537 L3, 540 E2
Glenburnie SA 550 A5, 568 G12
Glencoe NSW 525 K6
Glencoe SA 568 G11
Glencoe West SA 568 F11
Glendalough WA 570 D6, 571 C5
Glendambo SA 560 C5
Glenden Qld 605 D8, 611 I6
Glendevie Tas. 622 F9, 625 I9
Glendon Brook NSW 514 A5, 523 L3
Gleneagle Qld 600 C8
Glenelg SA 553 B8, 554 B9, 555 E2, 556 H7, 559 J9, 568 B3, 217
Glenfern Tas. 622 G4, 625 J6
Glenfyne Vic. 538 F8, 551 I8
Glengarrie NSW 601 E11
Glengarry Tas. 627 J7, 629 E8
Glengarry Vic. 541 I7
Glengower Vic. 535 C7, 549 M12, 551 M2
Glenhaven NSW 508 C4, 509 A10, 511 K6
Glenisla Vic. 548 G12, 550 G1
Glenlee Vic. 526 D12, 548 E7
Glenlofty Vic. 549 K12, 551 K1
Glenloth Vic. 526 G12, 549 K6
Glenluce Vic. 535 F7, 549 N12, 551 N2
Glenlusk Tas. 622 H4
Glenlyon Vic. 535 F8, 536 F1, 551 N2, 161
Glenmaggie Vic. 541 J5
Glenmore NSW 510 F11, 517 D1
Glenmore Vic. 535 F12, 536 F4, 539 A8, 540 A3, 541 O2, 545 O12, 551 O5
Glenmorgan Qld 608 H8, 427
Glennie Island WA 577 J9
Glenora Tas. 622 F2, 625 I6
Glenorchy Tas. 621 B5, 623 I4, 625 K7
Glenorchy Vic. 548 H10
Glenore Tas. 627 J9, 629 E11
Glenore Crossing Qld 612 D7, 615 G5
Glenore Grove Qld 602 A11
Glenorie NSW 508 D2, 509 A9, 511 K4
Glenormiston Vic. 551 I7
Glenormiston North Vic. 551 I7
Glenpatrick Vic. 549 K12, 551 K1
Glenreagh NSW 516 D10, 525 M7
Glenrowan Vic. 542 H8, 544 E5, **164**
Glenrowan West Vic. 542 H8, 544 E5
Glenroy NSW 510 B3, 512 D4, 519 A6, 520 B5, 522 C11, 523 I5, 543 O4

Glenroy SA 548 A12, 550 A1, 568 G10
Glenshee Vic. 549 K12, 551 K1
Glenthompson Vic. 550 H4
Glenvale Vic. 531 F2, 537 J3, 540 D2
Gliddon Reef SA 567 M9
Glossodia NSW 511 I3, 513 O5
Glossop SA 526 A6, 546 A6, 559 N7
Gloucester NSW 515 C8, 523 M1, 525 K12, **53**
Gloucester Island Qld 605 E4, 611 J3
Gloucester Island NP Qld 605 E4, 611 J3, 396
Gloucester NP WA 572 H11, 573 B2, 574 D11, 576 C11, 329
Gnandaroo Island WA 575 C3
Gnangara WA 570 D4, 571 C4
Gnarming WA 574 G6, 576 E8
Gnarwarre Vic. 536 E8, 538 F1, 551 N7
Gnotuk Vic. 538 G7, 551 J7
Gnowangerup WA 574 G9, 576 E10
Goat Island NSW 508 F7, 509 B12, 511 L8, 523 K7
Goat Island Qld 600 G5, 605 F5, 609 N9, 611 K3
Goat Island SA 567 M9
Goat Island WA 581 I5, 584 C7
Gobondery NSW 522 C2
Gobur Vic. 542 F1, 544 A9
Gocup NSW 519 A4, 520 C2, 522 D10
Godfrey Islands SA 568 E9
Godfreys Creek NSW 519 C1, 522 F7
Godsmark Island WA 581 I5, 584 C7
Godwin Beach Qld 599 G2, 600 E1, 602 G8
Gogango Qld 611 L11
Gol Gol NSW 526 E6, 546 G6
Golconda Tas. 627 L6
Golden Beach Vic. 541 L7, 192
Golden Island SA 558 C8
Golden Point Vic. 535 C6, 542 A10, 549 M12
Golden Valley Tas. 627 I9, 629 D12
Goldfields Woodlands NP WA 576 G6
Goldsborough Vic. 535 B3, 549 L10
Goldsmith Tas. 625 K1, 627 K11
Goldsmith Island Qld 605 G6, 611 K4
Goldsworthy WA 578 E1, 580 E11, 583 J3
Gollan NSW 522 G1, 524 D12
Golspie NSW 519 E2, 522 H8
Goneaway NP Qld 617 J10
Gongolgon NSW 529 O6
Gonn Crossing Vic. 549 N3
Goobang NP NSW 522 E2
Goobarragandra NSW 519 B5, 520 D3, 522 E11
Good Night Scrub NP Qld 603 B4, 604 E11, 609 L4, 411
Goodedulla NP Qld 611 L10
Goodings Corner Qld 601 E7
Goodna Qld 599 C9, 600 C5, 602 E12
Goodnight NSW 526 G8, 547 L10
Goodooga NSW 524 A2, 608 D11
Goods Island Qld 614 C2
Goodwood Qld 603 D3, 604 F11, 609 M4

Goodwood SA 553 C7, 554 B9, 555 F2
Goodwood Tas. 621 C5
Goodwyn Island WA 575 E1, 578 A2, 580 A12, 582 D4
Googa Googa Qld 603 A12
Goolawah NP NSW 515 G5, 525 M10
Goold Island Qld 606 F6, 613 M9
Goold Island NP Qld 606 F6, 613 M9
Goolgowi NSW 527 L6
Goolma NSW 522 G2
Goolmangar NSW 516 F4, 525 N3
Gooloogong NSW 522 E5
Goolwa SA 555 G8, 559 J11, 568 C4, **236**
Goomalibee Vic. 542 G8, 544 C4
Goomalling WA 574 D3, 576 C6
Goomboorian NP Qld 603 E9, 609 N6
Goombungee Qld 609 L8, 407
Goomburra Qld 609 L6, 432
Goomeri Qld 603 B8, 609 L6, 432
Goon Nure Vic. 541 M6
Goondah NSW 519 C3, 522 E9
Goondiwindi Qld 524 H1, 609 I11, **412**
Goondooloo SA 559 M9, 568 E3
Goonengerry NP NSW 516 G4, 525 O3, 609 N12
Goongarrie WA 576 H4
Goongarrie NP WA 576 H4
Goongerah Vic. 519 B11, 539 C9
Gooninnah Island NT 591 M6
Goonoo NP NSW 522 F1, 524 C11
Goonumbla NSW 522 E3
Gooram Vic. 542 F10, 544 A8
Goorambat Vic. 542 G7, 544 C4
Goornong Vic. 535 H2, 542 B8, 549 P9
Gooroc Vic. 549 K8
Goose Island SA 556 D5, 558 H7
Goose Island Tas. 624 A11, 627 N1
Goose Island WA 573 F6, 574 E12, 576 D12, 577 J9
Gooseberry Hill NP WA 570 F5, 571 D5, 574 C5, 576 C7
Goovigen Qld 604 A7, 609 J1, 611 L12
Goowarra Qld 611 K11
Gorae Vic. 550 D7
Gorae West Vic. 550 D7
Gordon SA 559 J1, 560 H8
Gordon Tas. 622 H10, 625 J9
Gordon Vic. 535 E10, 536 E3, 551 N4
Gordonvale Qld 606 E3, 607 F8, 613 L6, **413**
Gore Island Qld 614 E5
Gormandale Vic. 541 J8
Gormanston Tas. 624 E1, 626 E11, 628 A10
Gorokan NSW 509 E6, 511 P1, 514 B12
Goroke Vic. 548 D9
Gosford NSW 509 D8, 511 O3, 523 L5, **53**
Goshen Tas. 627 O7
Gosnells WA 570 F7, 571 D6
Goughs Bay Vic. 537 P1, 540 H1, 542 H12, 544 D10
Goulburn NSW 519 E3, 522 H9, **53**
Goulburn River NP NSW 523 I2, 524 F12, 56, 71

Goulburn Weir Vic. 542 D9, 183
Gould Island Qld 605 F6, 611 J4
Goulds Country Tas. 627 O7
Gourock NP NSW 518 G12, 519 D6, 521 I7, 522 G12, 539 G1
Governor Island Tas. 625 O1, 627 O11
Gowanford Vic. 526 G10, 549 K2
Gowangardie Vic. 542 F8, 544 B4
Gowar Vic. 535 E5, 549 N11, 551 N1
Gowar East Vic. 549 K9
Gowrie Park Tas. 626 G8, 628 G4
Goyura Vic. 526 E11, 548 H4
Grabben Gullen NSW 519 D2, 522 G8
Grabine NSW 522 F6
Grace Vic. 533 L4
Gracemere Qld 604 B5, 611 M11
Gracetown WA 572 A8, 574 B9, 576 B10
Gradgery NSW 524 B9
Gradule Qld 524 E1, 608 G10
Grafton NSW 516 D9, 525 M6, **54**
Graham Island NT 591 M3
Graman NSW 525 I4
Grampians NP Vic. 548 G12, 550 G2, 160, 169
Grandchester Qld 602 A12
Grange SA 553 B7, 554 A8, 555 E2
Granite Flat Vic. 543 M9, 545 L6
Granite Island SA 555 F9, 556 H10, 559 J11, 568 B5, 263
Granite Island Vic. 540 H10
Granite Island WA 581 J4, 584 E5
Granite Islands NT 591 N4
Grant Island NT 590 G1
Grantham Qld 609 L9
Grantham Island SA 558 D8
Granton Tas. 623 I3, 625 K6
Grantville Vic. 533 P9, 537 L10, 540 E8, 172
Granville NSW 508 C6, 509 A12, 511 K8
Granville Harbour Tas. 626 B9
Granya Vic. 522 B12, 527 O12, 543 M6, 545 L2
Grasmere NSW 510 G11, 517 E1
Grass Flat Vic. 548 E9
Grass Patch WA 577 I8
Grassdale Vic. 550 D5
Grasshopper Island NSW 519 F6, 521 M6, 523 I12
Grassmere Vic. 538 D7
Grassmere Junction Vic. 538 D7, 550 H8
Grasstree Qld 605 G8, 611 K6
Grasstree Hill Tas. 621 F2, 623 J4
Grassy Tas. 625 P12
Grassy Island Qld 605 F4, 611 J3
Gravelly Beach Tas. 627 J7, 629 F8
Gravesend NSW 524 H5
Grawin NSW 524 B4, 97
Grawlin NSW 522 D5
Grawlin Plains NSW 522 D5
Gray Tas. 627 O9
Graytown Vic. 542 C9
Gre Gre Vic. 549 J9
Great Australian Bight Marine Park SA 566 D7, 567 I7, 577 P6, 231
Great Barrier Reef Marine Park Qld 604 E3, 605 F2, 606 H7, 607 G6, 609 O2, 610 H1, 611 N4, 613 N7, 614 F5, 448

Great Basalt Wall NP Qld 606 B12, 610 D2, 613 L12, 617 P2
Great Dog Island Tas. 624 B11, 627 P1
Great Glennie Island Vic. 540 G12
Great Keppel Island Qld 604 C4, 611 N10, 450, 440
Great Northern Vic. 543 J6, 544 G1
Great Otway NP Vic. 536 C11, 538 B5, 551 K9, 142, 143, 144, 175
Great Palm Island Qld 606 G8, 613 N10
Great Sandy Island WA 575 D2, 578 A3, 582 B6
Great Sandy NP Qld 602 G1, 603 G4, 604 H12, 609 N6, 436
Great Western Vic. 549 I12, 551 I1, 194
Greater Beedelup NP WA 572 G10, 573 A2, 574 C10, 576 C11, 329
Greater Bendigo NP Vic. 535 F2, 542 A8, 549 O9, 151
Greater Dordagup NP WA 573 C3, 574 D11, 576 C11
Greater Hawke NP WA 572 G12, 573 B3, 574 D11, 576 C11
Greater Kingston NP WA 573 C1, 574 D10, 576 D10
Greater Preston NP WA 572 G5, 574 D8, 576 C10
Gredgwin Vic. 526 G11, 549 L5
Green Fields SA 553 C5, 554 B7
Green Head WA 576 A5
Green Hill NSW 515 G4, 525 M10
Green Hill Creek Vic. 535 A7, 549 K12, 551 K2
Green Island NSW 515 H4, 519 G5, 521 N3, 523 I11, 525 M9
Green Island Qld 605 G7, 606 E2, 607 H6, 611 K5, 613 M6, 403
Green (Milwarpa) Island Qld 599 G7, 600 F4, 602 H11, 609 N9
Green Island SA 556 D5, 558 H8
Green Island Tas. 623 I9, 625 K9
Green Island WA 581 J4, 584 E5
Green Island NP Qld 606 E2, 607 H6, 613 M6
Green Islands WA 573 D12, 574 A2, 576 E11
Green Point NSW 509 D8, 511 O3, 515 E10, 523 O2
Greenbank Qld 599 C10, 600 C6
Greenbushes WA 572 G7, 574 C9
Greendale Vic. 535 F10, 536 F3, 540 A3, 551 O4
Greenethorpe NSW 522 E6
Greenhalgh Island WA 581 I5, 584 C8
Greenhill Island NT 590 F2
Greenhills WA 574 E4
Greenmantle NSW 522 F6
Greenmount Qld 609 L9, 399
Greenmount Vic. 541 I9
Greenmount WA 570 F5, 571 D4
Greenmount NP WA 570 F5, 571 D4, 574 C5, 576 C7
Greenock SA 554 E4, 559 K8, 568 C1
Greenough WA 576 A3, **308**
Greens Beach Tas. 627 I6, 629 D5
Greens Creek Vic. 549 J11
Greensborough Vic. 531 E4, 537 J5, 540 D4
Greenvale Qld 606 B9, 613 K10

Greenwald Vic. 550 C5, 568 H12
Greenways SA 568 F10
Greenwell Point NSW 517 E9,
    519 G4, 521 P1, 523 J10, 79
Greg Greg NSW 519 A6, 520 B7,
    522 D12, 539 A2, 543 P6, 545 P2
Gregors Creek Qld 602 B6
Gregory Qld 611 I10
Gregory WA 575 D12
Gregory Island WA 581 I5, 584 C7
Gregory Islands Qld 603 E4,
    604 G11, 609 M4
Gregory NP NT 581 P4, 585 P6,
    590 C12, 592 C3, 369
Greigs Flat NSW 519 E10, 539 H7
Grenfell NSW 522 D6, **54**
Grenville Vic. 535 C12, 536 D5,
    551 M5
Gresford NSW 514 C4, 515 A10,
    523 L2
Greta Vic. 543 I8, 544 E5
Greta South Vic. 542 H9, 544 E6
Greta West Vic. 542 H8, 544 E5
Gretna Tas. 622 F2, 625 J6
Greville Island WA 581 J4, 584 F5
Grevillia NSW 516 E3, 525 N2,
    609 M11
Grey Island WA 581 J3, 584 F4
Grey Peaks NP Qld 606 E3, 607 G8,
    613 M6
Greymare Qld 516 A1, 525 K1,
    609 K10
Griffith NSW 527 M7, **54**
Griffiths Island Vic. 538 B8,
    550 F8, 188
Grimwade WA 572 G6
Grindal Island SA 558 E9
Gringegalgona Vic. 550 E2
Gritjurk Vic. 550 E3
Grogan NSW 519 A1, 522 D7
Grong Grong NSW 522 A8, 527 O8
Grongah NP Qld 603 B6, 609 L5
Groote Eylandt NT 591 N7
Groper Islet NSW 516 E11, 525 N7
Grose (Butlyerahit) Island NT
    588 A4, 590 C4
Grose Vale NSW 510 G4, 513 M6
Grosvenor Qld 604 C12, 609 K4
Grove Tas. 622 G6, 625 J7
Grovedale Vic. 532 A4, 536 F8,
    538 G1, 551 O8
Grummet Island Tas. 624 D3
Gruyere Vic. 531 H5, 534 C7, 537 L5
Gubbata NSW 522 A5, 527 N5
Guilderton WA 574 B4, 576 B7, 338
Guildford NSW 508 C7, 511 J8
Guildford Tas. 626 E7, 628 C3
Guildford Vic. 535 E7, 549 N12,
    551 N2
Guildford WA 570 E5, 571 C4
Gulaga NP NSW 519 E8, 521 K10,
    31
Gular NSW 524 C9
Gulargambone NSW 524 C9, 44
Gulch Island WA 577 J9
Gulf Creek NSW 524 H7
Gulgong NSW 522 H2, **55**
Gull Island Tas. 624 C12
Gull Rock WA 573 E11, 574 G11,
    576 E11
Gull Rock NP WA 573 E11,
    574 G11, 576 E11
Gulnare SA 559 J5, 560 H12
Guluguba Qld 609 I6
Guluwuru Island NT 591 M2

Gum Lake NSW 526 G1, 528 F12
Gumbaynggirr NP NSW 515 F2,
    516 B12, 525 L8
Gumble NSW 522 F4
Gumbowie SA 559 K3, 561 I11
Gumbrell Island Qld 605 F4, 611 J3
Gumeracha SA 553 G5, 554 E8,
    555 H1, 559 K9, 568 C2
Gumlu Qld 605 C3, 611 I2
Gumly Gumly NSW 522 C9, 527 P9,
    543 N1
Gunalda Qld 603 D8, 609 M6
Gunbar NSW 527 L6
Gunbower Vic. 527 I11, 542 A4,
    549 O6
Gunbower Island Vic 527 I11,
    542 A3, 549 O5, 155
Gunbower NP Vic. 527 I11, 542 A4,
    549 O5
Gundabooka NP NSW 529 L6, 34
Gundagai NSW 519 A3, 520 C1,
    522 D9, 543 P1, **56**
Gundaring WA 574 F7
Gundaroo NSW 518 F2, 519 D4,
    520 H1, 522 G10
Gundary NSW 519 E3, 522 H9
Gunderman NSW 509 B8, 511 L3
Gundiah Qld 603 D7, 609 M5
Gundillion NSW 519 E6, 521 J6,
    522 G12, 539 H1
Gundowring Vic. 543 L8, 545 J5
Gundowring North Vic. 543 L7,
    545 J4
Gundowring Upper Vic. 543 L8,
    545 J5
Gundy NSW 523 K1, 524 H12
Gunebang NSW 522 A3, 527 O3
Gungahlin ACT 518 E3, 520 H2,
    522 F10
Gungal NSW 523 J2
Gunjarra Island Qld 606 E3,
    607 G8, 613 M6
Gunn Island Qld 605 F5, 611 K3
Gunnary NSW 519 C2, 522 F7
Gunnedah NSW 524 G9, **56**
Gunnewin Qld 608 F5
Gunning NSW 519 D3, 522 G9
Gunningbland NSW 522 D4
Gunns Plains Tas. 626 G6, 628 E2
Gunpowder Qld 615 D9, 616 F1
Gunton Island WA 577 I9
Gunyangara NT 591 N4
Gunyerwarildi NP NSW 524 H4,
    609 I12
Gurley NSW 524 F5
Gurrai SA 526 A8, 546 A10,
    559 N10, 568 G4
Gurrumuru NT 591 M4
Gurrundah NSW 519 D3, 522 G9
Guthalungra Qld 605 D3, 611 I2
Guthega NSW 519 A8, 520 C10,
    539 B4
Guy Fawkes River NP NSW 515 E1,
    516 A10, 525 L7, 48
Guyong NSW 522 G5
Guyra NSW 525 J7, **57**
Guys Forest Vic. 522 C12, 543 N6,
    545 M2
Gwabegar NSW 524 D7
Gwakura Island NT 591 M3
Gwalia WA 576 H2, 313, 318
Gwandalan NSW 509 F5, 514 B11
Gwandalan Tas. 623 L7, 625 L8
Gwydir River NP NSW 524 H6,
    525 I6

Gymbowen Vic. 548 D9
Gympie Qld 603 D9, 609 M6, **413**
Gympie NP Qld 603 E8, 609 M6
Gypsum Vic. 526 E9, 546 H12,
    548 H1

H

Haasts Bluff NT 594 F6
Haddon Vic. 535 B10, 536 C3,
    551 L4
Haddon Corner Qld 563 O2,
    618 G4
Haden Qld 609 L8
Hadspen Tas. 627 K8, 629 G10,
    480
Haggerston Island Qld 614 E5
Hagley Tas. 627 J8, 629 E11
Hahndorf SA 553 F9, 554 D10,
    555 H3, 559 K9, 568 C3, **238**
Haig WA 577 M5
Haigslea Qld 600 A5, 602 C11
Halbury SA 556 H3, 559 J6
Hale Village Qld 516 F1, 600 D9
Hales Island Qld 614 H10
Half Tide Qld 605 G8, 611 K6
Halfway Creek NSW 516 E10,
    525 N6
Halfway Island Qld 604 C5,
    611 N10, 614 F1
Halfway Islet Qld 614 E4
Halfway Mill Roadhouse WA
    574 A1, 576 B5
Halidon SA 559 M9, 568 F3
Halifax Qld 606 F8, 613 M10
Halifax Bay Wetlands NP Qld
    606 F9, 613 M10
Hall ACT 518 D3, 520 G2
Hallam Vic. 531 F8, 533 M2,
    534 A11, 537 K7
Hallett SA 559 K5, 561 I12
Hallidays Point NSW 515 E9,
    523 O2, 89
Halls Creek WA 581 N7, 585 L11,
    309
Halls Gap Vic. 548 H12, 550 H1, **169**
Halls Head WA 571 B9
Hallston Vic. 537 O10, 540 G8
Halton NSW 514 C3, 515 A9, 523 L2
Hamel WA 571 D11, 574 C7
Hamelin Bay WA 572 B10, 574 B10
Hamelin Island WA 572 B10,
    574 B10, 576 B11
**Hamelin Pool Marine Nature
    Reserve WA** 575 C9, 586 F8, 301
Hamersley WA 571 H3, 575 G3,
    578 C4, 582 G8
Hamilton NSW 514 D9
Hamilton SA 554 E1, 559 K7,
    568 C1
Hamilton Tas. 622 F1, 625 I5, **481**
Hamilton Vic. 550 F4, **165**
Hamilton Island Qld 605 G5,
    611 K4, 391, **414**
Hamley Bridge SA 554 C3, 559 J7,
    568 B1
Hamlyn Heights Vic. 532 A3
Hammer Island Qld 605 G6,
    611 K4
Hammond SA 559 J2, 560 H9, 265
Hammond Island Qld 614 C2
Hampden SA 559 K7
Hampshire Tas. 626 F6, 628 C2
Hampton NSW 510 A4, 512 B6,
    523 I6

Hampton Qld 609 L9
Hampton Vic. 537 J6
Hampton Island Qld 614 H11
Hampton NP Qld 609 L9
Hampton Park Vic. 533 M2,
    534 A11, 537 K7
Hancock Island WA 580 H5, 584 C7
Hand Islet NT 591 M7
Hanging Rock Vic. 539 B7, 541 P1,
    543 P12, 139, 203
Hann River Roadhouse Qld 613 I2
Hann Tableland NP Qld 606 C2,
    607 B6, 613 K6
Hannah Island Qld 614 F10
Hannahs Bridge NSW 524 E11
Hannan NSW 522 A5, 527 N5
Hannibal Islets Qld 614 D4
Hansborough SA 554 F1, 559 K7
Hanson SA 559 K6
Hansonville Vic. 543 I8, 544 E6
Hanwood NSW 527 M7
Happy Valley Qld 603 G5, 604 A1,
    609 O4, 611 L8
Happy Valley Vic. 526 F7, 535 A12,
    536 B4, 543 K9, 545 I6, 547 I9,
    551 L5
Harbour Islets Tas. 626 B2
Harcourt Vic. 535 F5, 542 A10,
    549 O11, 551 O1, 154
Harcourt North Vic. 535 F5,
    542 A10, 549 O11, 551 O1
Harcus Island Tas. 626 B3
Harden NSW 519 B2, 522 E8
Hardwicke Bay SA 556 D7, 558 H9
Hardy Island NT 591 M4
Hareby Island SA 558 E8
Harefield NSW 522 C9, 527 P9
Harford Tas. 627 I6, 629 C7
Hargraves NSW 522 H3, 72
Harkaway Vic. 531 G8, 533 N2,
    534 B10, 537 K7
Harlin Qld 602 A6, 609 M8
Harney Island NT 591 N10, 593 N2
Harold Island Qld 605 G5, 611 K3
Harrietville Vic. 543 L10, 545 J9
Harrington NSW 515 F8, 523 O1,
    525 L12
Harris Island NT 590 C2
Harrismith WA 574 G7
Harrison Island Qld 604 B1,
    611 M8
Harrisville Qld 600 A7
Harrogate SA 554 F9
Harrow Vic. 541 L6, 548 D11,
    550 D1, 162
Harrys Creek Vic. 542 F9, 544 B6
Harston Vic. 542 D7
Hart SA 556 H2, 559 J6
Hart Island SA 567 L10
Hartley NSW 510 B3, 512 D4,
    523 I5, 68
Hartley SA 553 H12, 554 F12
Hartley Vale NSW 510 C3, 512 F4
Hartz Mountains NP Tas. 622 D9,
    624 H9, 625 I9, 479
Harvey WA 572 F2, 574 C7, 576 C9,
    309
Harvey Island Qld 614 E5
Harwood NSW 516 F8, 525 N5
Haslam SA 558 A2, 567 N9
Hasler Island WA 577 J9
Haslewood Island Qld 605 G5,
    611 K3
Hassell NP WA 573 F9, 574 H10,
    576 F11

Hasties Swamp NP Qld 606 D3, 607 D9, 613 L7, **392**
Hastings Tas. 622 F11, 625 I10, **481**
Hastings Vic. 531 F11, 533 K7, 537 J9, 540 D7, 181
Hastings Island WA 577 I9
Hastings Point NSW 516 H3, 525 O2, 609 N11
Hat Head NSW 515 G4, 525 M10
Hat Head NP NSW 515 G4, 525 M10, 62
Hatches Creek NT 593 K12, 595 K1
Hatfield NSW 526 H5, 547 N4
Hatherleigh SA 568 F10
Hattah Vic. 526 E7, 546 H9
Hattah–Kulkyne NP Vic. 526 E7, 546 H8, 180, 186
Hatton Vale Qld 602 A11
Haul Off Rock WA 573 H8, 576 F11
Haul Round Island NT 591 J3
Hauy Island WA 578 B2, 580 B12, 582 E4
Havannah Island Qld 606 F9, 613 N10
Havelock Vic. 535 C5, 549 M11
Haven Vic. 548 G9
Havilah Vic. 543 K9, 545 I6
Hawick Island WA 581 K2, 584 G2
Hawk Island NT 591 N6
Hawker SA 557 A12, 560 H8, **236**
Hawkesbury Heights NSW 510 G5, 513 L8
Hawkesdale Vic. 550 G6
Hawknest Island NT 591 M6
Hawks Nest NSW 514 H7, 515 C11, 523 N3
Hawley Beach Tas. 627 I6, 629 C6, 490
Hawthorn Vic. 531 E6
Hay NSW 527 J7, **57**
Hay Island Qld 614 F9
Hay Island Tas. 624 E9
Haycock Island Qld 606 E2, 607 F6, 613 M9
Haycock Island WA 575 E1, 578 B2, 580 B12, 582 D5
Haydens Bog Vic. 519 B10, 539 D8
Hayes Tas. 622 G3, 625 J6
Hayes Creek NT 588 G10, 590 E6
Hayman Island Qld 605 F4, 611 K3, 390, **414**
Haysdale Vic. 526 G8, 547 K10
Haystack Island SA 556 B9, 558 G10
Hazel Island WA 581 I5, 584 C8
Hazel Park Vic. 537 P12, 540 H9
Hazelbrook NSW 510 E6, 513 I9, 65
Hazeldene Vic. 531 G1, 534 B2, 537 K2, 540 D2, 542 D12
Hazelmere WA 571 D4
Hazelwood Vic. 540 H7
Healesville Vic. 534 D6, 537 L4, 540 E4, 139, 165
Heartbreak Hotel NT 591 L12, 593 L3
Heath Hill Vic. 537 M9, 540 F7
Heath Island Qld 600 H1, 609 N8
Heathcote NSW 508 C11, 511 J11, 517 H1, 519 H1, 523 K7
Heathcote Vic. 542 B10, 549 P11, 168
Heathcote–Graytown NP Vic. 542 C9, 549 P11, 551 P1, 168
Heathcote Junction Vic. 531 E1, 537 J2, 540 C2, 542 C12

Heathcote NP NSW 508 B11, 511 J12, 517 G2, 519 H1, 523 J7, 103
Heatherton Vic. 533 K1
Heathfield SA 553 E9, 554 C10, 555 G3
Heathmere Vic. 550 D7
Heathmont Vic. 531 F6, 534 A8
Hebden NSW 523 K2
Hebel Qld 524 B2, 608 D11
Hecla Island WA 581 L2, 584 H1
Hector Qld 605 G8, 611 K6
Heddon Greta NSW 509 F2, 514 B8, 515 A12
Hedley Vic. 541 I9
Hedley Island WA 581 J3, 584 E4
Heidelberg Vic. 531 E5, 537 J5
Heka Tas. 626 F7, 628 E2
Helby Island WA 577 J9
Helena NP WA 570 H6, 571 E5, 574 C5, 576 C7
Helena Valley WA 570 F5
Helensburgh NSW 517 H2, 519 H2, 523 K8
Helensvale Qld 516 G1, 525 O1, 600 F9, 601 D4, 609 N10
Helenvale Qld 613 L3, 407
Helidon Qld 609 L9, 411
Helipad Island WA 581 J5, 584 E7
Hell Hole Gorge NP Qld 619 L3
Hells Gate Roadhouse Qld 615 B3
Hellyer Tas. 626 D4
Helsinki Island WA 575 C12
Hemmant Qld 599 F7, 600 E4, 602 G11
Hen Island Tas. 624 H11
Henderson Island Qld 611 L6
Hendon SA 554 B8, 555 E1
Hendra Qld 599 E6
Hendy Island WA 577 I9
Heney Island WA 581 I5, 584 C8
Henley Brook WA 571 D4
Henning Island Qld 605 G5, 611 K4
Henrietta Tas. 626 E6
Hensley Park Vic. 550 F4
Henty NSW 522 B11, 527 O11, 543 L3
Henty Vic. 550 D4, 47
Hepburn Springs Vic. 535 E8, 536 E1, 551 N2, 161
Herald Island Qld 606 G9, 613 N11
Herald Islet NT 591 M3
Herberton Qld 606 C4, 607 C10, 613 L7, **414**
Herberton Range NP Qld 606 D4, 607 D10, 613 L7
Hermannsburg NT 594 H7, 596 D5, **362**
Hermidale NSW 529 N10
Hermite Island WA 575 D1, 582 A4
Hernani NSW 516 B11, 525 L7
Heron Island Qld 604 F6, 611 O11, **414**
Herons Creek NSW 515 F7, 525 L11
Herrick Tas. 627 N6
Hervey Bay Qld 603 F4, 604 H12, 609 N4, **416**
Hervey Rocks NT 591 N10, 593 N1
Hesket Vic. 536 H2, 540 B2, 542 B12, 551 P3
Hesso SA 558 H1, 560 F8
Hexham NSW 509 G2, 514 D8, 515 A12, 523 L4
Hexham Vic. 550 H6
Hexham Island Qld 604 B1, 611 M8

Heybridge Tas. 626 F5
Heyfield Vic. 541 J6
Heywood Vic. 550 D6, 189
Heywood Island WA 581 J4, 584 E5
Hi Way Inn Roadhouse NT 590 H12, 592 H3
Hiamdale Vic. 541 J7
Hiawatha Vic. 541 I9
Hibbs Pyramid Tas. 624 C5
Hicks Island Qld 614 E5
Hidden Island WA 581 I5, 584 C7
High Black Rock NT 590 F2
High Camp Vic. 540 C1, 542 C11
High Island Qld 606 E3, 607 H9, 613 M6, 614 C2
High Island WA 581 I5, 584 C7
High Islands Qld 605 F6, 611 K5
High Peak Island Qld 604 C1, 611 N8
High Range NSW 517 B4, 519 G2, 523 I8
Highbury WA 574 E7
Highclere Tas. 626 F6, 628 D1
Highcroft Tas. 623 L9, 625 M9
Highett Vic. 537 J7
Highfield Tas. 629 A3
Highfields Qld 609 L9, 447
Highlands Vic. 542 E11
Highton Vic. 532 A4
Highvale Qld 599 B5, 600 C3, 602 D10
Highwater Islet Qld 605 G8, 611 K6
Hilgay Vic. 550 D4
Hill End NSW 522 G4, 28
Hill End Vic. 537 P7, 540 H6
Hillarys WA 570 B4, 571 B4, 574 B5
Hillcrest Vic. 535 A11, 536 B3
Hilldale NSW 514 D5, 515 A10
Hillgrove NSW 515 C1, 525 K8, 26
Hilliger NP WA 572 E10, 574 C10, 576 C11
Hillman WA 574 E8
Hillside Vic. 541 M5
Hillston NSW 527 L4, 65
Hilltop NSW 517 C4, 519 G2, 523 I8
Hilltown SA 559 J5
Hillview Qld 516 F2, 525 N1, 600 C11
Hillwood Tas. 627 J7, 629 F7
Hinchinbrook Island Qld 606 F7, 613 M9
Hinchinbrook Island NP Qld 606 F7, 401, 415
Hindmarsh Island SA 555 H8, 559 K11, 568 C5, 236
Hindmarsh Valley SA 555 F8, 556 H10
Hines Hill WA 574 G3
Hinnomunjie Vic. 541 N1, 543 N11, 545 M10
Hinton NSW 509 G1, 514 C7
Hippolyte Rocks Tas. 623 O9, 625 N9
Hirst Islet Qld 611 L6
Hirstglen Qld 609 L10
Hivesville Qld 609 L6
Hixson Island Qld 611 M7
HMAS Cerberus Vic. 533 K8
Hobart Tas. 621 D8, 623 I5, 625 K7, **456**
Hobbs Island Tas. 624 E8
Hobbys Yards NSW 522 G6
Hobler Island NT 591 N11, 593 N2
Hoddle Vic. 540 G10

Hoddles Creek Vic. 534 E9, 537 M6, 540 E5
Hodgson River Station NT 591 J10, 593 J1
Holbourne Island Qld 605 E3, 611 J2
Holbourne Island NP Qld 605 E3, 611 J2
Holbrook NSW 522 B11, 527 O11, 543 M4, **58**
Holgate NSW 509 D8, 511 O2
Hollow Tree Tas. 625 J5
Holly WA 574 F9
Hollydeen NSW 523 J2
Hollywell Qld 601 F4
Holmview Qld 599 F11, 600 E7
Holmwood NSW 522 F6
Holt Island Qld 604 B1, 611 M8
Holtham Island WA 580 H5, 584 C8
Holwell Tas. 627 J7, 629 E8
Home Hill Qld 605 B2, 610 H2, 613 O12, 392
Homebush NSW 508 D7
Homebush Qld 605 G8, 611 K6, 424
Homebush Vic. 535 A5, 549 L11, 551 L1
Homecroft Vic. 526 E12, 548 H7
Homerton Vic. 550 E6
Homestead Qld 610 E3
Homevale NP Qld 605 E8, 611 J6
Homewood Vic. 537 L1, 540 E1, 542 E11
Hood Island WA 577 I10
Hook Island Qld 605 F4, 611 K3, 391
Hope Island Tas. 622 G11, 625 J10
Hope Island WA 577 I9
Hope Islands Qld 613 L3
Hope Islands NP Qld 607 E2, 613 L3
Hope Vale Qld 613 K2
Hopetoun Vic. 526 E10, 548 H4, **168**
Hopetoun WA 576 G10, 332
Hopetoun West Vic. 526 D10, 548 G3
Hopevale Vic. 526 E11, 548 G4
Hopkins Island SA 558 E9
Hoppers Crossing Vic. 531 B6, 536 H6, 540 B5, 551 P6
Horatio Island WA 576 F10
Hordern Vale Vic. 536 A12, 538 B6, 551 K10
Horn (Narupai) Island Qld 614 C2
Hornsby NSW 508 E4, 509 B10, 511 L6, 523 K6
Hornsby Heights NSW 508 E4, 509 B10, 511 L6
Hornsdale SA 559 J4, 561 I11
Horrocks WA 575 D12
Horse Lake NSW 528 D11, 561 P9
Horseshoe Bay Qld 606 G10, 613 N11
Horseshoe Bend Vic. 533 P2
Horseshoe Island Qld 615 D2
Horsham Vic. 548 G9, **170**
Horsley Park NSW 508 A6, 511 I8
Horton Falls NP NSW 524 G7
Hoskinstown NSW 518 H7, 519 D5, 521 I4, 522 G11
Hoskyn Islands Qld 604 G7, 609 M1, 611 P12
Hotham Heights Vic. 541 L1, 543 L11, 545 J9

Hotspur Vic. 550 D5
Hotspur Island Qld 611 M6
Houghton SA 553 E5, 554 D8, 555 G1
Houghton Island Qld 614 H11
Houtman Abrolhos Islands WA 575 C12, 307
Hove SA 553 B8, 554 B10, 555 E3
Howard Qld 603 D4, 604 G12, 609 M4
Howard Island NT 591 L3
Howard Island WA 580 H5, 584 C7
Howard Islet Qld 611 M7
Howard Springs NT 588 E3, 590 D4
Howden Tas. 623 I7, 625 K8
Howe Island WA 577 I10
Howes Valley NSW 523 K3
Howick Group NP Qld 614 H11
Howick Island Qld 614 H11
Howie Island Tas. 626 C3
Howlong NSW 522 A12, 527 N12, 543 J5, 544 H1
Howqua Vic. 537 P1, 540 H1, 542 H12, 544 D11
Howrah Tas. 621 G8, 623 J5
Howth Tas. 626 G5
Hoya Qld 600 A8
Hoyleton SA 556 H3, 559 J6
Huddleston SA 559 J4, 560 H12
Hudson (Bird) (Coolah) Island Qld 606 F6, 613 M8
Hughenden Qld 610 B4, 617 N4, **414**
Hughes SA 566 D4
Hugo Island WA 577 I10
Hull Island Qld 611 L6
Hull River NP Qld 606 E6, 613 M8
Humboldt NP Qld 608 G1, 611 J12
Humevale Vic. 534 A4, 537 K3, 540 D3
Hummock Hill Island Qld 604 D7, 609 L1, 611 N12
Hummock Island WA 575 C12, 581 J4, 584 E5
Hummocky Island Qld 604 D5, 611 N11
Humpty Doo NT 588 E4, 590 D4
Humpy Island Qld 604 C5, 611 N10
Humula NSW 520 A3, 522 C11, 543 O3
Hungerford Qld 529 J1, 619 L11
Hunter Vic. 542 B7, 549 P8
Hunter Island Qld 611 M7
Hunter Island Tas. 626 B2
Hunter Wetlands NP NSW 509 G2, 514 D8, 515 A12, 523 L4
Hunterston Vic. 541 J9
Huntingdale Vic. 531 E7
Huntly Vic. 535 G2, 542 A8, 549 O9
Huon Vic. 543 L7, 545 J3
Huon Island Tas. 622 G10, 625 J9
Huonville Tas. 622 G7, 625 J8, **481**
Hurstbridge Vic. 531 F4, 534 A6, 537 K4, 540 D3
Hurstville NSW 508 D9, 511 K10
Huskisson NSW 517 D11, 519 G4, 521 O2, 523 J10, **58**
Hutchinson Island Qld 606 F5, 607 H12, 613 M8
Hutchison Islands WA 575 C9, 586 G7
Hutt WA 575 D11, 576 A2
Hyams Beach NSW 517 D11, 521 O2

Hyden WA 574 H5, 576 F8, **310**
Hyland Park NSW 515 H2, 525 M9
Hynam SA 548 A10, 568 G9

I

Icy Creek Vic. 537 O6, 540 G5
Ida Bay Tas. 622 E12, 625 I10
Ida Island Qld 614 D2
Idalia NP Qld 610 B12, 617 N12, 619 M2, 395
Iem (North Possession Island) Islet Qld 614 C1
Ilbilbie Qld 605 G9, 611 K7
Ile des Phoques Tas. 625 N4
Ile du Golfe Tas. 624 G11
Ile du Nord Tas. 623 P2, 625 N5
Ilford NSW 522 H4
Ilfracombe Qld 610 B10, 617 N10, 423
Ilfraville Tas. 629 E6
Ilkurlka Roadhouse WA 577 N1, 579 N11
Illabarook Vic. 535 A12, 536 B5, 551 L5
Illabo NSW 522 C9, 44
Illalong Creek NSW 519 C3, 522 E9
Illawarra Vic. 549 I11, 551 I1
Illawong NSW 508 C9, 511 J10
Illawong WA 576 A4
Illowa Vic. 538 C7, 550 G8
Iluka NSW 516 F7, 525 O5, **59**
Imangara NT 593 K12, 595 K1
Imanpa NT 594 G9
Imbil Qld 602 D1, 603 D10, 609 M7, 414
Imintji Store WA 581 K6, 584 G9
Impimi NSW 526 H8, 547 M9
Ina Islet WA 581 N3, 585 L3
Inala Qld 599 D9
Indaringinya NT 595 K3
Indented Head Vic. 531 B9, 532 F4, 536 H8, 540 B6, 551 P7
Indian Island NT 588 A4, 590 C5
Indigo Vic. 543 J6, 544 G2
Indigo Upper Vic. 543 K7, 545 I3
Indooroopilly Qld 599 D7, 600 D4, 602 E11
Indwarra NP NSW 525 J6
Infelix Islets Qld 611 L8
Ingham Qld 606 E8, 613 M10, **415**
Ingleby Vic. 536 C9, 538 D2, 551 M8
Ingleside NSW 508 G4, 509 C10, 511 N6
Ingleside Qld 516 G2, 600 F11, 601 E10
Inglewood Qld 525 J1, 609 J11, 443
Inglewood Tas. 625 L4
Inglewood Vic. 535 D1, 549 M9, **170**
Inglis Island NT 591 M3
Ingliston Vic. 535 F11, 536 F4, 551 O4
Ingoldsby Qld 609 L9
Ingot Islets Qld 605 G6, 611 K4
Ingram Island Qld 614 H11
Injinoo Qld 614 C3
Injune Qld 608 F4
Inkerman Qld 605 C3, 610 H2
Inkerman SA 556 G4, 559 I7, 568 A1
Innaloo WA 570 C5
Innamincka SA 563 N7, 618 F8, **236**

Inner Island WA 573 F11, 574 H11, 576 E11
Inner Rock NSW 515 D11, 523 N3
Inner Sister Island Tas. 624 B8
Innes Island Qld 605 H10, 611 L7
Innes NP SA 556 B8, 558 F10, 267
Inneston SA 556 B9, 558 F10
Innisfail Qld 606 E4, 607 G11, 613 M7, **415**
Innot Hot Springs Qld 606 C5, 607 B12, 613 K7, 438
Inshore Island WA 577 J9
Intercourse Island WA 575 E1, 578 B2, 580 B12, 582 D5
Interlaken Tas. 625 K2, 627 K12
Inverell NSW 525 I5, **56**
Invergordon Vic. 542 F6, 544 B2
Inverleigh Vic. 536 D7, 551 M7
Inverloch Vic. 537 M12, 540 F9, **170**
Invermay Tas. 629 G10
Invermay Vic. 535 C10, 536 D3
Iona Vic. 534 E12, 537 M8
Ipolera NT 594 G7, 596 A5
Ipswich Qld 599 A9, 600 B5, 602 D12, 609 M9, **417**
Ireby Island Qld 605 G5, 611 K3
Irishtown Tas. 626 C4
Irishtown Vic. 535 F7, 549 N12, 551 N2
Iron Baron SA 558 G3, 560 F11
Iron Knob SA 558 G2, 560 F10, 264
Iron Pot Tas. 623 J7, 625 K8
Iron Range Qld 614 E7, 449
Irrewarra Vic. 536 B9, 538 C2, 551 L8
Irrewillipe Vic. 536 A9, 538 A2, 551 K8
Irrititu Island NT 590 D3
Irrwelty NT 595 K3
Irvine Island WA 581 I5, 584 C7
Irvinebank Qld 606 C4, 607 B10, 613 K7, 414
Irving Islet Qld 605 H9, 611 L6
Irymple Vic. 526 E6, 546 G6
Isabella NSW 519 E1, 522 H7
Isabella Island Tas. 624 B10
Isisford Qld 610 B11, 617 N11, **418**
Isla Gorge NP Qld 609 I3, 445
Islam Islets WA 575 C3
Island Bend NSW 520 D9, 539 C3
Island Head Qld 604 C2, 611 M8
Isle of the Dead Tas. 623 M9, 625 M9
Isle Woodah NT 591 M6
Islington NSW 509 H3, 514 D9
Ivanhoe NSW 527 I2
Ivis Island WA 615 C2
Ivory Creek Qld 602 A6
Ivy Island WA 575 D1, 582 B4
Iwantja (Indulkana) SA 565 L4
Iwupataka NT 595 I7, 596 G4

J

Jabiru NT 589 O4, 590 G5, **364**
Jabuk SA 559 M10, 568 F4
Jack River Vic. 541 I9
Jack River NP Qld 613 K1, 614 H12
Jackadgery NSW 516 C8, 525 M5
Jackeys Marsh Tas. 627 I9, 629 C12
Jackie Junction WA 579 M8
Jackson Qld 608 H6
Jackson Island WA 580 H5, 581 J3, 584 E4

Jacobs Well Qld 599 H12, 600 F7, 601 E1, 609 N10
Jacobs Well WA 574 E5
Jalloonda Qld 606 G10, 610 G1, 613 N11
Jallumba Vic. 548 F10
Jam Jerrup Vic. 533 P8
Jamberoo NSW 517 E7, 519 H3, 523 J9, **60**
Jambin Qld 604 A8, 609 J1, 611 M12
Jamestown SA 559 J4, 561 I11, **237**
Jamieson Vic. 537 P2, 540 H2, 542 H12, 544 D11
Jan Juc Vic. 532 A7
Jancourt Vic. 538 G8, 551 J8
Jancourt East Vic. 538 H8, 551 J8
Jandakot WA 570 D8, 571 C6, 574 C5
Jandowae Qld 609 K7
Jane NP WA 573 C3, 574 D11, 576 C11
Jannali NSW 508 D10
Japoon NP Qld 606 E5, 607 F12, 613 M8
Jar Island WA 581 L2, 584 H2
Jardee WA 572 H10, 573 B1, 574 D10
Jardine Islet Qld 614 E4
Jardine River NP Qld 614 D4, 449
Jarklin Vic. 526 H12, 549 N7
Jarman Island WA 575 F1, 578 B2, 580 B12, 582 E4
Jarra Jarra NT 592 H12, 594 H1
Jarrahdale WA 570 G11, 571 D7, 574 C6
Jarrahmond Vic. 539 B11, 541 P5
Jarrahwood WA 572 E7, 574 C9
Jarvis Creek Vic. 543 L6, 545 K3
Jaurdi WA 576 G5
Jawbone Marine Sanctuary Vic. 531 C6, 537 I6, 540 C4
Jeffcott Vic. 526 F12, 549 J7
Jeffcott North Vic. 549 J7
Jellat Jellat NSW 539 H6
Jemalong NSW 522 D4
Jennacubbine WA 571 G1
Jenolan Caves NSW 512 A11, 523 I6, 80
Jeogla NSW 515 D1, 516 A12, 525 K8
Jeparit Vic. 526 D12, 548 F6, **171**
Jerangle NSW 518 F12, 519 D6, 520 H7, 522 F12, 539 G1
Jericho Qld 610 E10
Jericho Tas. 625 K4
Jericho Vic. 540 H4
Jerilderie NSW 527 L10, 542 G1, **60**
Jerrabomberra NSW 518 E6, 520 H3
Jerramungup WA 576 F10
Jerrawa NSW 519 D3, 522 F9
Jerrawangala NP NSW 517 B11, 519 G4, 521 N2, 523 I10
Jerrys Plains NSW 523 K2
Jerseyville NSW 515 G4, 525 M9
Jervis Bay JBT 517 D12, 519 G4, 521 O3, 523 J10, **60**
Jervis Bay Marine Park NSW 517 E11, 519 G4, 521 P2, 523 J10, 60
Jervis Bay NP NSW 517 D10, 519 H4, 521 P1, 523 J10, 61
Jervois SA 559 L10, 568 D4
Jessie Island Qld 606 F5, 607 H12, 613 M8

Jetsonville Tas. 627 L6
Ji-Marda NT 591 J3
Jigalong WA 578 G5, 583 N11
Jil Jil Vic. 549 J4
Jilliby NSW 509 D6, 514 A12
Jimaringle NSW 527 I9, 542 A1, 547 O12, 549 O2
Jimboomba Qld 599 D12, 600 D8, 609 N10
Jimbour Qld 609 K7
Jimmy Islet NT 591 O11, 593 O2
Jimna Qld 602 B3, 603 C11, 609 M7
Jindabyne NSW 519 B8, 520 E10, 539 C4, **61**
Jindera NSW 522 A12, 527 O12, 543 K5, 545 I1
Jindivick Vic. 534 G11, 537 N8, 540 G6
Jindong WA 572 B7
Jingalup WA 574 E9, 576 D10
Jingellic NSW 522 C12, 527 P12, 543 N5, 545 N1
Jirke Island Qld 612 A4, 615 D2
Jirrgari Island NT 591 M3
Jitarning WA 574 G6, 576 E8
Joanna SA 548 A11, 568 G9
Joass Island NSW 514 F7, 515 B11, 523 M3
Jodetluk (George Camp) NT 590 G8
Joel Joel Vic. 549 J11, 551 J1
Joel South Vic. 549 J11, 551 J1
Johanna Vic. 536 A12, 538 A5, 551 K10
John Forrest NP WA 570 F4, 571 D4, 574 C5, 576 C7, 325
John Island WA 577 J9
Johnburgh SA 559 J2, 561 I9
Johns River NSW 515 F7, 523 O1, 525 L12
Johnson Islet Qld 614 D2
Johnsonville Vic. 541 N5
Johnston Islet NT 591 N10, 593 N1
Jolly Islet NT 591 N11, 593 N2
Jondaryan Qld 609 K8
Jones Island SA 558 A4, 567 N11
Jones Island WA 581 L1, 585 I1
Joondalup WA 570 C3, 571 B4, 574 B4
Josbury WA 574 E7, 576 D9
Josephville Qld 516 E1, 525 N1, 600 C9
Joskeleigh Qld 604 C5, 611 M11
Joyces Creek Vic. 535 D6, 549 N12, 551 N1
Judbury Tas. 622 F6, 625 I8
Jugiong NSW 519 B3, 522 E9
Julatten Qld 606 D1, 607 D5, 613 L5
Julia SA 559 K7
Julia Creek Qld 615 H11, 617 J3, **418**
Jumbuk Vic. 541 I8
Jumbunna Vic. 537 M11, 540 F8
Junction Hill NSW 516 D8, 525 M6
Junction Village Vic. 533 M4
Jundah Qld 619 J1, **418**
Junee NSW 522 C9, 527 P9, 96
Junee NP Qld 611 J9
Junee Reefs NSW 522 C8, 527 P8
Jung Vic. 548 G9, 170
Jungulu Island WA 581 J4, 584 E5
Junortoun Vic. 535 G3, 542 A9, 549 O10
Junuy Juluum NP NSW 515 G1, 516 C11, 525 M7

Jura WA 574 G4
Jurien Bay WA 576 A5, **310**
Jurien Bay Marine Park WA 574 A1, 576 A5, 310
Jurunjung Vic. 531 A4, 535 H11, 536 H4, 540 B3, 551 P5
Jussieu Island WA 581 J3, 584 F3

K

Kaarimba Vic. 527 K12, 542 E6
Kabra Qld 604 A5, 611 M11
Kadina SA 556 E3, 558 H6, **237**
Kadnook Vic. 548 C11, 550 C1, 568 H10
Kadungle NSW 522 D2
Kagaru Qld 599 C12, 600 C8
Kai-Kudulug Qld 614 C2
Kai-Yelubi (Great Woody) Island Qld 614 C2
Kaimkillenbun Qld 609 K8
Kain NSW 518 H11, 519 D6, 521 I6, 522 G12, 539 H1
Kainton SA 556 F3, 559 I7
Kairi Qld 606 D3, 607 E9, 613 L6
Kajabbi Qld 612 B12, 615 E9, 616 G2, 406
Kakadu NP NT 589 N3, 590 G4, 364, 367
Kalamunda WA 570 F6, 571 D5
Kalamunda NP WA 570 F6, 571 D5, 574 C5, 576 C7, 325
Kalangadoo SA 550 A3, 568 G11
Kalannie WA 574 D1, 576 D5
Kalaru NSW 519 E9
Kalbar Qld 600 A8, 609 M10, 396
Kalbarri WA 575 C11, **311**
Kalbarri NP WA 575 D11, 576 A2, 578 A12, 311
Kaleentha Loop NSW 526 G1, 528 F12
Kalgan WA 573 E10, 574 G11, 576 E11
Kalgoorlie–Boulder WA 576 H5, **312**
Kalimna Vic. 541 O6
Kalimna West Vic. 541 N6
Kalinjarri NT 593 J11
Kalka SA 564 C2, 579 P8, 594 B11
Kalkallo Vic. 531 D2, 537 I3, 540 C3
Kalkarindji (Wave Hill) NT 592 D5
Kalkee Vic. 548 G8
Kalkite NSW 520 E9, 539 C3
Kallangur Qld 599 E4, 600 D2, 602 F9
Kallista Vic. 534 B9
Kalorama Vic. 531 G6, 534 B8
Kalpienung Vic. 526 G11, 549 K4
Kalpowar Qld 604 D9, 609 K2
Kaltukatjara (Docker River) NT 579 P6, 594 B9
Kalumburu WA 581 L2, 585 I2
Kalumpurlpa NT 593 I8
Kalunga Qld 606 C4, 607 C10, 613 L7
Kalyan SA 559 M9, 568 E3
Kalyarr NP NSW 522 J7, 547 P7
Kamarah NSW 522 A7, 527 O7
Kamarooka Vic. 535 G1, 542 A7, 549 O8
Kambalda WA 576 H5, 313
Kamballup WA 573 D8, 574 G10, 576 E11
Kameruka NSW 519 D9, 539 H6

Kamma Qld 606 E3, 607 F8
Kamona Tas. 627 M6
Kamutnab Islet Qld 614 C1
Kanangra–Boyd NP NSW 510 A7, 512 B11, 517 A1, 519 F1, 522 H6, 523 I7, 80
Kancoona South Vic. 543 K9, 545 I6
Kandanga Qld 602 D1, 603 D10
Kandiwal WA 581 K3, 584 H3
Kandos NSW 523 I3, 86
Kangaloon NSW 517 C6
Kangarilla SA 553 D11, 554 C11, 555 F4, 556 H8, 559 J10, 568 B3
Kangaroo (Boonnahbah) Island Qld 599 H12, 600 G7, 601 E1, 609 N10
Kangaroo Flat NSW 522 F5
Kangaroo Flat SA 553 D1, 554 C5
Kangaroo Flat Vic. 535 F3, 542 A9, 549 O10
Kangaroo Island Qld 603 F5, 604 H12, 609 N4
Kangaroo Island SA 555 A10, 556 C11, 558 G12, 568 A5, **239**, 242
Kangaroo Island Tas. 626 B3
Kangaroo Island WA 575 B9, 586 D9
Kangaroo Valley NSW 517 C8, 519 G3, 523 I9, 79
Kangawall Vic. 548 D10
Kangiara NSW 519 C2, 522 F8
Kanig Island Qld 614 C1
Kaniva Vic. 526 B12, 548 C7, 568 H7
Kankanmengarri Island WA 581 K2, 584 G2
Kanmantoo SA 554 F10
Kannamatju Island WA 581 J4, 584 E5
Kanowna Island Vic. 540 H12
Kanumbra Vic. 542 F11, 544 B9
Kanya Vic. 549 J10
Kanyapella Vic. 527 J12, 542 C5
Kanypi SA 564 E2, 594 D11
Kaoota Tas. 622 H7, 625 J8
Kapinnie SA 558 D7
Kapooka NSW 522 B10, 527 P10, 543 M1, 97
Kapril (Black) Rock Qld 614 C1
Kapunda SA 554 E2, 559 K7, 568 C1, **239**
Karabeal Vic. 550 F3
Karadoc Vic. 526 E6, 546 H6
Karalee Qld 599 B8, 600 C5, 602 D12
Karalundi WA 575 H8, 578 E9
Karana Downs Qld 599 B8, 600 B5, 602 D11
Karanja Tas. 622 F2, 625 I6
Karangi Island WA 575 D1, 582 B4
Karanja Tas. 622 F2, 625 I6
Karara Qld 525 K1, 609 K10
Karatta SA 556 B12, 558 G12
Karawinna Vic. 526 D6, 546 E7
Kardinya WA 570 D8, 571 C6
Kariah Vic. 551 J7
Karijini NP WA 575 G3, 578 D5, 582 H10, 583 I10, 334
Karingal Vic. 533 K4
Kariong NSW 509 C8, 511 N3
Karkoo SA 558 D6
Karlamilyi NP WA 578 H4, 579 I3, 583 P8
Karlgarin WA 574 H5, 576 F8

Karn Vic. 542 H9, 544 D6
Karnak Vic. 548 D10
Karniga Island Qld 614 C2
Karonie WA 577 I5
Karoola Tas. 627 K7, 629 H8
Karoonda SA 559 M10, 568 E3, 249
Karoonda Roadhouse Vic. 519 A10, 539 A8, 541 P2, 545 P12
Karragarra Island Qld 600 G6, 609 N9
Karrakatta WA 570 C6, 571 B5
Karratha WA 575 E1, 578 B2, 580 B12, 582 D5, **311**
Karratha Travel Stop Roadhouse WA 575 E1, 578 B2, 580 B12, 582 D5
Karridale WA 572 B10, 574 B10
Kars Springs NSW 523 J1, 524 G12
Karslake Island NT 590 D2
Karte SA 526 A8, 546 A10, 559 N9, 568 G3
Kartja Island WA 581 K3, 584 F4
Karuah NSW 514 F7, 515 B11, 523 M3
Karuah NP NSW 514 E6, 515 B11, 523 M3
Karumba Qld 612 C7, 615 G4, **419**
Karween Vic. 526 C6, 546 C6, 559 P8, 568 H1
Katamatite Vic. 527 L12, 542 F5, 544 B1
Katandra Vic. 542 F6, 544 B3
Katandra West Vic. 542 F6, 544 A2
Katanning WA 574 F8, 576 E9, **314**
Katers Island WA 581 K2, 584 G2
Katherine NT 590 F8, **366**
Kathleen Island Tas. 624 E9
Kathleen Island WA 581 I5, 584 C7
Katoomba NSW 510 D5, 512 F9, 523 I6, **64**
Katunga Vic. 527 K12, 542 F5
Katyil Vic. 548 G7
Kawarren Vic. 536 B10, 538 B3, 551 L9
Kay Islet Qld 614 E6
Kay Reef Cay A Qld 614 E6
Kay Reef Cay B Qld 614 E6
Kayena Tas. 627 J6, 629 F7
Keast Island WA 578 B2, 580 B12, 582 D4
Kedron Qld 599 E6
Keelan Island Qld 611 L6
Keep River NP NT 581 O4, 585 N5, 590 A11, 592 A2, 369
Keep River NP Extension (Proposed) NT 581 P4, 585 N5, 590 A10, 592 B1
Keilor Vic. 531 C5, 537 I5, 540 B4
Keiraville NSW 517 F5
Keith SA 568 F6, **239**
Kellalac Vic. 526 E12, 548 H7
Kellatier Tas. 626 E5
Kellerberrin WA 574 F4, 576 D7, **314**
Kellevie Tas. 623 M4, 625 M7
Kelly Islands Tas. 623 N6, 625 M7
Kelmscott WA 570 F8, 571 D6
Kelso Tas. 627 J6, 629 E6
Kelvin NSW 524 G8
Kelvin NP Qld 605 G9, 611 K6
Kelvin View Vic. 542 F9, 544 B7
Kempsey NSW 515 G4, 525 M10, **62**
Kempton Tas. 623 I1, 625 K5
Kendall NSW 515 F7, 525 L11, 66

Kendenup WA 573 B8, 574 G10, 321
Kendrew Island WA 575 E1, 578 A2, 580 A12, 582 D4
Kenebri NSW 524 D8
Kenilworth Qld 602 E3, 603 D11, 609 M7, **419**
Kenmare Vic. 526 D11, 548 G5
Kenmore NSW 519 E3, 522 H9
Kenmore Qld 599 D7, 600 D5, 602 E11
Kenmore Hills Qld 599 D7, 600 D4, 602 E11
Kennedy Qld 606 E6, 613 M9
Kennedy Range NP WA 575 D6, 578 A8, 307
Kennedys Creek Vic. 538 H10, 551 J9
Kennett River Vic. 536 C12, 538 D5, 551 M10
Kennys Creek NSW 519 C2, 522 F8
Kent Island Qld 606 F5, 607 H12, 613 M8
Kent Island WA 581 N3, 585 L4
Kentbruck Vic. 550 C6
Kenthurst NSW 508 D3, 509 A10, 511 K5
Kentlyn NSW 508 A10, 511 I11, 517 G1
Kentucky NSW 515 A2, 525 J8
Kenwick WA 570 E7, 571 D5
Keperra Qld 599 D6, 600 D4, 602 E10
Keppel Bay Islands NP Qld 604 D5, 611 N10, 450
Keppel Rocks Qld 604 C5, 611 N11
Keppel Sands Qld 604 C5, 611 N11
Keppoch SA 568 G8
Kerang Vic. 526 H11, 549 N4
Kerang East Vic. 526 H11, 549 N4
Kerang South Vic. 526 H11, 549 N5
Keraudren Island WA 581 J3, 584 E4
Kergunyah Vic. 543 L7, 545 J4
Kergunyah South Vic. 543 L8, 545 J4
Kermadec (Wedge) Island WA 577 J9
Kernot Vic. 533 P10, 537 L10, 540 E8
Kerrabee NSW 523 J2
Kerrie Vic. 531 B1, 540 B2, 542 B12
Kerrisdale Vic. 540 D1, 542 D11
Kerrs Creek NSW 522 G4
Kerry Qld 516 F1, 525 N1, 600 D10
Kersbrook SA 553 F5, 554 D7, 559 K9, 568 C2
Keru Island WA 575 C12
Keswick SA 553 C7, 554 B9, 555 F2
Keswick Island Qld 605 H7, 611 L5
Ketchem Island Tas. 624 F10
Kettering Tas. 622 H8, 625 K8, **482**
Keverstone NP NSW 519 D1, 522 G7
Kevington Vic. 537 P2, 540 H2, 544 D12
Kew NSW 515 F7, 525 L11
Kewdale WA 570 E6
Kewell Vic. 548 H8
Keyneton SA 554 G5, 559 K8, 568 C2
Keysborough Vic. 533 L1
Keysbrook WA 570 F12, 571 D8, 574 C6
Keyser Island Qld 605 G6, 611 K4

Khancoban NSW 519 A7, 520 B8, 539 A3, 543 P7, 545 P4, **62**, 156
Ki Ki SA 559 M11, 568 E5
Kiah NSW 519 E10, 539 H8
Kialla NSW 519 E2, 522 G8
Kialla Vic. 542 E7, 544 A4, 193
Kialla West Vic. 542 E7
Kiama NSW 517 F7, 519 H3, 523 J9, **63**
Kiamil Vic. 526 E8, 546 H10
Kiana SA 558 C6
Kiandra NSW 519 B6, 520 D6, 522 E12, 539 C1
Kianga NSW 521 L9
Kiata Vic. 526 C12, 548 E7
Kid Island WA 581 J4, 584 E6
Kidney Island WA 581 L2, 584 H2
Kidston Qld 613 I10
Kielpa SA 558 E5, 560 D12
Kiewa Vic. 543 L7, 545 J3
Kikoira NSW 522 A5, 527 O5
Kilburn SA 553 C6, 554 B8, 555 F1
Kilcoy Qld 602 C6, 609 M8
Kilcunda Vic. 533 O12, 537 L11, 540 E9
Kilkivan Qld 603 C8, 609 M6, 432
Killabakh NSW 515 E7, 523 N1, 525 L12
Killafaddy Tas. 629 H1
Killara NSW 508 F5, 511 L7
Killarney Qld 516 C2, 525 L1, 609 L11, **419**
Killarney Vic. 538 B7, 550 G8
Killawarra Vic. 543 I6, 544 E3
Killiecrankie Tas. 624 A9
Killingworth NSW 509 F3, 514 B9
Killora Tas. 623 I8, 625 K8
Kilmany Vic. 541 J7
Kilmany South Vic. 541 J7
Kilmore Vic. 537 J1, 540 C1, 542 C12, **171**
Kilpalie SA 559 M9, 568 F3
Kim Island WA 581 L1, 585 I1
Kimba SA 558 F4, 560 D11, **240**
Kimberley Tas. 626 H7, 629 B9
Kinalung NSW 528 D10, 561 P8
Kincaid WA 577 K5
Kincaid Qld 536 A11, 538 B5, 551 K10
Kinchega NP NSW 526 E1, 528 D12, 561 P10, 70
Kinchela NSW 515 G4, 525 M10
Kincumber NSW 509 D8, 511 O3, 523 L6
Kindred Tas. 626 G6, 628 G2
King (Erobin) Island Qld 599 G7, 600 F4, 602 H11, 609 N9
King George Island Tas. 623 M6, 625 M8
King Hall Island WA 581 I5, 584 C7
King Island Qld 614 G10
King Island Tas. 625 O11, 474, **483**
King Island WA 581 I5, 584 D6
King River WA 573 D10, 574 G11, 576 E11
King Valley Vic. 543 I9, 544 F7, 178
Kingaroy Qld 603 A10, 609 L7, **420**
Kingfisher Islands WA 581 I5, 584 D7
Kinglake Vic. 531 G3, 534 B5, 537 L3, 540 E3
Kinglake Central Vic. 531 G2, 534 B4, 537 K3, 540 E3
Kinglake East Vic. 534 C5, 537 L3
Kinglake NP Vic. 531 F1, 534 A3, 537 K2, 540 D2, 542 D12, 204

Kinglake West Vic. 531 G2, 534 B4, 537 K3, 540 D2
Kingoonya SA 560 B5, 567 P5
Kingower Vic. 535 C2, 549 M9
Kings Camp SA 568 E9
Kings Canyon Resort NT 594 F8, **362**
Kings Cross NSW 508 F8, 509 B12, 511 M9, 14
Kings Meadows Tas. 627 K8, 629 G4
Kings Plains NP NSW 525 J5
Kings Point NSW 519 G5, 521 N4, 523 I11
Kingsborough Qld 606 C2, 607 A7, 613 K6
Kingscliff NSW 516 H2, 525 O2, 600 H12, 601 H12, 609 N11
Kingscote SA 556 E10, 558 H11, **242**
Kingsdale NSW 519 E3, 522 H9
Kingsford NSW 508 F8, 511 M10
Kingsthorpe Qld 609 L9
Kingston Qld 599 F10, 600 E6
Kingston Tas. 623 I6, 625 K8, **483**
Kingston Vic. 535 D9, 536 D2, 551 M3
Kingston-on-Murray SA 526 A6, 559 N7, 568 F1
Kingston S.E. SA 568 E8, **240**
Kingstown NSW 525 I8
Kingsvale NSW 519 B2, 522 E8
Kingswood NSW 510 H6, 513 N11
Kingswood SA 559 I2, 560 H9
Kinimakatka Vic. 548 D7
Kinka Qld 604 C5, 611 N10
Kinnabulla Vic. 526 F11, 549 I5
Kinrara NP Qld 606 B7, 613 K9
Kintore NT 579 P4, 594 B6
Kioloa NSW 519 F6, 521 M5, 523 I12
Kiora NSW 521 L7
Kippa-Ring Qld 599 F4, 600 E2, 602 G9
Kirkby Island SA 558 E8
Kirkstall Vic. 538 B7, 550 G7
Kirra Qld 600 G11, 601 H10
Kirrama NP Qld 606 D6, 613 L8
Kirrawee NSW 508 D10, 511 K11
Kirup WA 572 F6, 574 C9
Kitchener NSW 509 E2, 514 A8
Kitchener WA 577 K5
Kithbrook Vic. 542 F10, 544 B7
Kiwirrkurra WA 579 N4
Knife Island NT 588 B5, 590 D5
Knight Island Qld 605 H9, 611 L6
Knockrow NSW 516 G5, 525 O3
Knockwood Vic. 537 P3, 540 H3, 544 E12
Knowsley Vic. 542 B9, 549 P10
Koah Qld 607 D6, 613 L6
Kobble Qld 599 C4, 600 C2, 602 E9
Koetong Vic. 543 N6, 545 M3
Kogan Qld 609 J8
Kogarah NSW 508 E9, 511 L10
Koimbo Vic. 526 F8, 547 J10
Kojonup WA 574 F9, 576 D10, **314**
Koks Island WA 575 B7, 586 A1
Kolgan Island WA 580 H5, 584 C7
Koloona NSW 524 H5
Kolora Vic. 551 I7
Komungla NSW 519 E3, 522 G9
Konagaderra Vic. 531 C3, 537 I3
Kondalilla NP Qld 602 E4, 603 E11, 609 N7, 425

Kondinin WA 574 G5, 576 E8
Kongal SA 526 A12, 568 G7
Kongorong SA 568 F12
Kongwak Vic. 537 M11, 540 F8
Konnongorring WA 574 D3, 576 C6
Konong Wootong Vic. 550 E3
Konong Wootong North Vic. 550 E2
Koo-Wee-Rup Vic. 531 H10, 533 O6, 537 L9, 540 E7, **172**
Koo-Wee-Rup North Vic. 533 P5
Koojarra Shoal WA 581 L1, 585 I1
Kookynie WA 576 H3, 318
Koolan WA 581 I5, 584 D7
Koolan Island WA 581 I5, 584 D7
Koolewong NSW 509 D8, 511 N3
Kooljaman WA 580 H5, 584 B7
Kooloonong Vic. 526 G8, 547 K10
Koolunga SA 556 G1, 559 J5, 560 H12, 234
Koolyanobbing WA 576 F5
Koolywurtie SA 556 E6, 558 H8
Koonda Vic. 542 F8, 544 B5
Koondrook Vic. 527 I10, 542 A2, 549 O4, 27
Koongarra NT 589 O5, 590 G5
Koongawa SA 558 D4, 560 C11, 267
Koonibba SA 567 L7
Kooninderie SA 554 F1
Koonoomoo Vic. 527 L11, 542 F4
Koonwarra Vic. 537 N12, 540 G9, 173
Koonya Tas. 623 M8, 625 M8
Kooraban NP NSW 519 E8, 521 K10, 539 H3
Kooralbyn Qld 516 E1, 525 N1, 600 B10, 609 M10
Koorawatha NSW 522 E6
Koorda WA 574 E2, 576 D6, 320
Kooreh Vic. 549 K9
Kooringal Qld 600 G4, 609 N9
Koorkab Vic. 526 G8, 547 K9
Koorlong Vic. 546 G6
Kootingal NSW 525 I9
Koppio SA 558 D7
Korbel WA 574 G4
Koreelah NP NSW 516 C2, 525 M2, 609 L11
Korffs Islet NSW 515 H1, 516 E12, 525 N8
Koriella Vic. 537 M1, 540 F1, 542 F11, 544 B10
Korobeit Vic. 535 F11, 536 F3, 540 A3, 551 O4
Koroit Vic. 538 C7, 550 G7, 201
Korong Vale Vic. 549 M8
Koroop Vic. 549 N4
Korora NSW 516 E11, 525 N7
Korumburra Vic. 537 N11, 540 F8, **172**
Korung NP WA 570 G7, 571 E5, 574 C5, 576 C7
Korweinguboora Vic. 535 E9, 536 E2, 551 N3
Kosciuszko NP NSW 518 A9, 519 A7, 520 C8, 522 E11, 539 B2, 543 P8, 545 P5, 24, 30, 63, 94
Kotta Vic. 527 I12, 542 B6, 549 P7
Kotupna Vic. 527 L12, 542 D6
Koumala Qld 605 G9, 611 K6
Kowanyama Qld 612 E2
Kowrowa Qld 607 E6
Koyuga Vic. 542 C6
Krambach NSW 515 D8, 523 N2

Kringin SA 526 A8, 546 B10, 559 O9, 568 G3
Krongart SA 550 A3, 568 G10
Kroombit Tops NP Qld 604 C8, 609 K2, 412
Krowera Vic. 537 M11, 540 F8
Ku-ring-gai Chase NP NSW 508 G3, 509 C10, 511 M5, 523 K6, 21, 53
Kukerin WA 574 G7, 576 E9
Kulbai Kulbai (Spencer) Island Qld 614 C1
Kulbi (Portlock Island) Islets Qld 614 C1
Kulgera NT 565 L1, 595 I11
Kulgun Qld 600 A8
Kulikup WA 574 E9
Kulin WA 574 G6, 576 E8, **315**
Kulkami SA 559 N10, 568 F4
Kulkyne Vic. 526 E7, 546 H8
Kulla (McIlwraith Range) NP (CYPAL) Qld 614 E10
Kulnine Vic. 526 C6, 546 E6, 559 P7
Kulnine East Vic. 526 C6, 546 E6, 559 P7
Kulnura NSW 509 C6, 523 K5
Kulpara SA 556 F3, 559 I6
Kulpi Qld 609 K8
Kulwin Vic. 526 E8, 547 I10
Kumarina Roadhouse WA 578 E7
Kumarl WA 577 I8
Kumbarilla Qld 609 J8
Kumbatine NP NSW 515 F4, 525 L10
Kumbia Qld 609 L7
Kumboola Island Qld 606 F6, 613 M8
Kumorna SA 559 M12, 568 F6
Kunama NSW 519 A5, 520 B4, 522 D11, 543 P3
Kunat Vic. 549 L3
Kundabung NSW 515 G5, 525 M10, 62
Kungala NSW 516 E10, 525 N7
Kunghur NSW 516 F3, 525 O2, 609 N11
Kunjin WA 574 F5, 576 E8
Kunlara SA 559 M8, 568 E2
Kuntjumal Kutangari Island WA 581 K2, 584 H2
Kununoppin WA 574 F2, 576 E6
Kununurra WA 581 O4, 585 M5, 590 A11, 592 A2, **315**
Kunwarara Qld 604 A3, 611 L10
Kupingarri WA 581 L6, 584 H8
Kuraby Qld 599 E9, 600 E6
Kuranda Qld 606 D2, 607 E6, 613 L6, **420**
Kuranda NP Qld 606 D2, 607 D5, 613 L5
Kuringup WA 574 H8
Kurmond NSW 510 H4, 513 N5
Kurnell NSW 508 F10, 511 L11, 523 K7
Kurraca Vic. 535 B1, 549 L9
Kurraca West Vic. 535 B1, 549 L8
Kurrajong NSW 510 G4, 513 M5, 85
Kurrajong Heights NSW 510 G3, 513 L5, 523 J5
Kurri Kurri NSW 509 F2, 514 B8, 523 L4
Kurrimine Beach Qld 606 E5, 613 M8
Kurrimine Beach NP Qld 606 E5, 613 M8

Kurting Vic. 535 C1, 549 M9
Kurumbul Qld 524 H2, 609 I11
Kutini–Payamu (Iron Range) NP (CYPAL) Qld 614 E7, 449
Kuttabul Qld 605 F7, 611 K5
Kweda WA 574 F5
Kwiambal NP NSW 525 I3, 609 J12, 59
Kwinana WA 570 D10, 571 C7, 574 B5, 576 C8
Kwolyin WA 574 F4
Kyabram Vic. 542 D6, 190
Kyalite NSW 526 G8, 547 L10, 27
Kyancutta SA 558 D4, 560 B11
Kybeyan NSW 519 D8, 520 H10, 539 G4
Kybunga SA 556 H3, 559 J6
Kybybolite SA 548 B10, 568 G9
Kydra NSW 519 D8, 520 H11, 539 F4
Kyeamba NSW 522 C10, 527 P10, 543 N3
Kyndalyn Vic. 526 F7, 547 J9
Kyneton Vic. 535 G8, 536 G1, 540 A1, 542 A11, 551 O2, **172**
Kynuna Qld 617 J5, **421**
Kyogle NSW 516 E4, 525 N3, 609 M12, **63**
Kyup Vic. 550 F3
Kyvalley Vic. 542 D6
Kywong NSW 522 A9, 527 N9

L

Laanecoorie Vic. 535 D4, 549 M10
Laang Vic. 538 E8, 551 I8
Labertouche Vic. 534 F11, 537 N8, 540 F6
Labrador Qld 516 G1, 525 O1, 600 G9, 601 F5
Labu Islet NT 591 N11, 593 N2
Lacey Island Qld 614 D2
Lachlan Tas. 622 G4, 625 J7
Lachlan Island Tas. 623 O3, 625 N6
Lachlan Island WA 581 I6, 584 C8
Lackrana Tas. 624 B10
Lacrosse Island WA 581 N3, 585 L3
Lacy Island SA 567 L9
Lady Barron Tas. 624 B11, 627 P1
Lady Bay Tas. 622 F11, 625 I10
Lady Elliot Island Qld 604 H8, 609 N2, 399
Lady Island Qld 605 G5, 611 K3
Lady Julia Percy Island Vic. 550 E8, 188
Lady Musgrave Island Qld 604 G7, 609 M1, 611 P12, 399
Lady Nora Island WA 578 A2, 580 A12, 582 D4
Ladysmith NSW 522 C10, 527 P10, 543 N1
Ladysmith Island Qld 605 G6, 611 K4
Laen Vic. 549 I8
Laen North Vic. 549 I7
Lafontaine Island WA 581 K2, 584 G2
Laggan NSW 519 E2, 522 G8
Lagoon Island Qld 599 H10, 600 F6, 609 N10
Lagrange Island WA 581 K2, 584 G2
Lah Vic. 526 E12, 548 H6
Laharum Vic. 548 G10

Laheys Creek NSW 522 G1, 524 D12
Laidley Qld 602 A12, 609 M9, **421**
Lajamanu (Hooker Creek) NT 592 D7
Lake Bathurst NSW 519 E4, 521 J1, 522 G10
Lake Biddy WA 576 F8
Lake Bindegolly NP Qld 619 L8, 410
Lake Boga Vic. 526 H10, 549 M3, 171, 194
Lake Bolac Vic. 551 I4
Lake Buloke Vic. 526 F12, 549 J7, 157
Lake Cargelligo NSW 522 A4, 527 N4, **65**
Lake Cathie NSW 515 F6, 525 M11, 85
Lake Charm Vic. 526 H10, 549 M4
Lake Clifton WA 571 C11, 574 B7, 576 C9
Lake Condah Vic. 550 E6
Lake Conjola NSW 519 G5, 521 N3, 523 I11
Lake Cowal NSW 522 C5, 527 P5, 100
Lake Eildon NP Vic. 534 H1, 537 O1, 540 G1, 542 G11, 544 C11, 143, 162
Lake Eppalock Vic. 535 H4, 542 B9, 549 P11, 168
Lake Eyre NP SA 560 F1, 562 H8, 618 A8, 245
Lake Gairdner NP SA 558 E1, 560 C7, 567 P6
Lake Goldsmith Vic. 536 A3, 551 K4
Lake Grace WA 574 H7, 576 E9, **316**
Lake Hindmarsh Vic. 526 D11, 548 E6, 171
Lake King WA 576 G8, **317**
Lake Leake Tas. 625 M2, 627 M12
Lake Margaret Tas. 624 D1, 626 D11, 628 A9
Lake Marmal Vic. 526 G12, 549 L6
Lake Muir NP WA 573 F3, 574 E11, 576 D11
Lake Mundi Vic. 550 B3, 568 H11
Lake Munmorah NSW 509 F6, 514 B12, 523 L5
Lake Rowan Vic. 542 G7, 544 D3
Lake Torrens NP SA 560 G4
Lake Tyers Vic. 541 O6, 174
Lake Tyers NP (Proposed) Vic. 519 A12, 539 A11, 541 O5
Lake View SA 556 G1, 559 I5
Lakeland Qld 613 K3
Lakes Entrance Vic. 541 O6, **174**
Lakes NP, The Vic. 541 M6
Lakeside Vic. 533 O1
Lakesland NSW 510 E12, 517 D2
Lal Lal Vic. 535 D11, 536 D4, 551 M4
Lalbert Vic. 526 G10, 549 L4
Lalbert Road Vic. 526 G10, 549 L3
Lalla Tas. 627 K7, 629 H8
Lallat Vic. 549 I8
Lallowan Island WA 580 H5, 584 C7
Lalor Vic. 537 J4
Lama Lama NP (CYPAL) Qld 614 F11
Lamarck Island WA 581 J3, 584 F3
Lamb (Ngudooroo) Island Qld 600 G6, 609 N9

Lameroo SA 526 A9, 559 N10, 568 G4, 252
Lamington Qld 516 F2, 525 N1, 600 C11, 609 M11
Lamington NP Qld 516 F2, 525 N2, 600 D12, 601 A10, 609 N11, 434
Lamplough Vic. 535 A6, 549 L12, 551 L1
Lancaster Vic. 542 D6
Lancefield Vic. 536 H1, 540 B1, 542 B12, 551 P2, 203
Lancelin WA 574 A3, 576 B6, 339
Lancelin Island WA 574 A3, 576 B6
Lands End Qld 601 F4
Landsborough Qld 602 F5, 603 E12, 609 N8, **421**
Landsborough Vic. 549 J11, 551 J1
Landsdale WA 570 D4, 571 C4
Lane Cove NSW 508 F6, 509 B12, 511 L8
Lane Cove NP NSW 508 E5, 509 A11, 511 L7, 523 K6
Lane Island NT 591 N6
Lanena Tas. 627 J7, 629 F8
Lang Lang Vic. 533 P7, 537 L9, 540 E7
Langford Island Qld 605 F4, 611 K3
Langhorne Creek SA 559 K10, 568 C4, 260
Langi Logan Vic. 551 I2
Langkoop Vic. 548 B11, 550 B1, 568 H9
Langley Vic. 535 H7, 542 A11, 549 P12, 551 P2
Langlo Crossing Qld 608 A5, 619 O5
Langloh Tas. 625 I5
Langsborough Vic. 541 I10
Langton Island SA 558 E8
Langville Vic. 526 H11, 549 M5
Langwarrin Vic. 531 E10, 533 K5, 537 J8
Lankeys Creek NSW 522 C12, 527 P12, 543 N5
Lannercost Qld 606 E8, 613 M10
Lansdowne NSW 515 E7, 523 O1, 525 L12
Laplace Island WA 581 K2, 584 G2
Lapoinya Tas. 626 E5
Lapstone NSW 510 G7, 513 L11
Lara Vic. 532 B1, 536 F7, 540 A5, 551 O7
Lara Lake Vic. 532 B1
Laramba NT 594 H4
Laravale Qld 516 E1, 525 N1, 600 C10
Large Island WA 575 D2, 582 B7
Largs North SA 553 B5, 554 A7, 555 E1, 559 J9, 568 B2
Larpent Vic. 536 A9, 538 B2, 551 K8
Larrakeyah NT 588 C3
Larras Lee NSW 522 F3
Larrimah NT 590 H10, 592 H1
Lascelles Vic. 526 E10, 548 H3
Laseron Island WA 581 J4, 584 E4
Latham WA 576 C4
Latrobe Tas. 626 H6, 628 H2, 629 B7, **483**
Lauangi Island WA 581 K2, 584 G2
Lauderdale Tas. 623 K6, 625 L7
Laughtondale NSW 509 A7, 511 K2
Launceston Tas. 627 K8, 629 F1, **484**

Launching Place Vic. 534 D8, 537 M5, 540 E4
Laura Qld 613 J3, **422**
Laura SA 559 J4, 560 H11, 234
Laurel Hill NSW 519 A5, 520 B4, 522 D11, 543 P4
Laurieton NSW 515 F7, 523 O1, 525 L12, **65**
Lauriston Vic. 535 G8, 536 F1, 540 A1, 542 A11, 551 O2
Lavers Hill Vic. 536 A12, 538 A5, 551 K10
Laverton Vic. 531 B6, 536 H6, 540 B4, 551 P6
Laverton WA 577 I2, 579 I12, **317**
Lavoisier Island WA 581 K2, 584 G2
Law Island NT 591 N10, 593 N1
Lawler Vic. 526 E12, 549 I7
Lawley River NP WA 581 L3, 584 H3
Lawloit Vic. 526 C12, 548 D7
Lawnton Qld 599 E4, 600 D2, 602 F9
Lawrence NSW 516 E8, 525 N5
Lawrence Vic. 535 D8, 536 D1, 551 M2
Lawrence Road NSW 516 E7, 525 N5
Lawrence Rocks Vic. 550 D8
Lawrenny Tas. 625 I5
Lawson NSW 510 E6, 512 H9, 523 I6
Lawson Island NT 590 G1
Layard Vic. 536 E9, 538 F1, 551 N8
Le Roy Vic. 541 I8
Leadville NSW 522 H1, 524 E12
Leaghur Vic. 526 H11, 549 M5
Leam Tas. 629 F8
Learmonth Vic. 535 B9, 536 C2, 551 L3
Learmonth WA 575 B3
Leasingham SA 559 J6
Leawarra Vic. 533 K4
Lebrina Tas. 627 K6, 629 H7
Leda WA 570 D10, 571 C7
Ledge Islet WA 573 C5, 574 D11, 576 C11
Ledge Point WA 574 A3, 339
Leeka Tas. 624 A9
Leelinger Island Tas. 624 C5
Leeman WA 576 A5
Leeor Vic. 526 B12, 548 B7, 568 H7
Leeton NSW 527 N8, **66**
Leets Vale NSW 509 A7, 511 J2
Leeuwin–Naturaliste NP WA 572 A6, 574 A9, 576 B10, 288, 304, 323, 338
Leeville NSW 516 E5, 525 N4
Lefebre Island WA 575 B9, 586 D8
Lefroy Tas. 627 J6, 629 G6
Legana Tas. 627 K7, 629 G9
Legendre Island WA 578 B1, 580 B12, 582 D4
Legerwood Tas. 627 M7
Leggatt Island Qld 614 H11
Legume NSW 516 C2, 525 L2, 609 L11
Leicester Island Qld 604 B1, 611 M8
Leichardt Vic. 535 E2, 549 N10
Leichhardt NSW 508 E8
Leichhardt Qld 599 A9, 600 B5, 602 C12, 611 J11
Leigh Creek SA 557 B4, 560 H4, **240**

Leigh Creek Vic. 535 D10, 536 D3, 551 M4
Leighton SA 559 K5
Leighton WA 570 C7
Leila Island WA 581 I5, 584 C8
Leinster WA 576 G1, 578 G11
Leitchville Vic. 527 I11, 542 A4, 549 O5
Leith Tas. 626 H6, 628 G1
Lemana Tas. 629 C10
Lemnos Vic. 542 E7, 544 A3
Lemon Rock Tas. 625 O3
Lemon Tree Passage NSW 514 G8, 515 C12, 523 M4
Lemont Tas. 625 L4
Lenah Valley Tas. 621 C7
Leneva Vic. 543 K6, 545 I3
Lennards Island NSW 519 E10, 539 H8
Lennox Head NSW 516 H5, 525 O3, 609 N12, 27
Leo Island WA 575 C12
Leongatha Vic. 537 N11, 540 G8, **173**
Leongatha South Vic. 537 N11, 540 F9
Leonie Island WA 580 H5, 584 C7
Leonora WA 576 H2, **318**
Leopold Vic. 532 C4, 536 G8, 538 H1, 540 A6, 551 O7
Leppington NSW 510 H9
Leprena Tas. 625 I11
Leschenault WA 572 E3, 289
Leslie Manor Vic. 536 A7, 551 K7
Leslie Vale Tas. 622 H6, 625 K7
Lesmurdie WA 570 F7
Lesmurdie Falls NP WA 570 F6, 571 D5, 574 C5, 576 C7, 325
Lesueur Island WA 581 M1, 585 J1
Lesueur NP WA 574 A1, 576 A5, 310
Lethbridge Vic. 536 E6, 551 N6
Leumeah NSW 510 H11, 517 F1
Leura NSW 510 D5, 512 G9, 523 I6, 64
Levendale Tas. 623 L1, 625 L5
Leveque Island WA 580 H5, 584 B7
Lewis Island SA 558 E9
Lewis Ponds NSW 522 G4
Lewisham NSW 508 E8
Lewisham Tas. 623 L5, 625 L7
Lewiston SA 553 C1, 554 B5, 556 H6
Lexton Vic. 535 A7, 536 B1, 551 L2
Leyburn Qld 609 K10, 406
Liawenee Tas. 625 I1, 627 I11
Licola Vic. 541 J4
Lidcombe NSW 511 K8
Liena Tas. 626 G8, 628 G5
Lietinna Tas. 627 L6
Liffey Tas. 627 J9, 629 E12
Lightning Ridge NSW 524 B3, 608 E12, **66**
Liguanea Island SA 558 D9
Likkaparta NT 593 J9
Lileah Tas. 626 C4
Lilford Rock WA 573 G6, 574 E12, 576 D11
Lilli Pilli NSW 521 M7
Lillicur Vic. 535 A6, 549 L12, 551 L1
Lillimur Vic. 526 B12, 548 C7, 568 H7
Lillimur South Vic. 526 B12, 548 C7, 568 H7

Lilydale Tas. 627 K7, 629 H8, **485**
Lilydale Vic. 531 G5, 534 B7, 537 L5, 540 E4
Lima Vic. 542 G9, 544 C7
Lima East Vic. 542 G9, 544 C7
Lima South Vic. 542 G10, 544 D7
Limeburners Creek NSW 514 F6, 515 B11, 523 M3
Limekilns NSW 522 H4
Limestone Vic. 534 D1, 537 M1, 540 E1, 542 E12, 544 A11
Limestone Ridge Qld 599 A12, 600 B7
Limevale Qld 525 J2, 609 J11
Limmen NP (Proposed) NT 591 K9, 593 K1
Limpet Rock WA 577 I9
Limpinwood NSW 601 A12
Lincoln NP SA 558 D9, 255
Lincolnfields SA 556 F2, 559 I6
Lind NP Vic. 519 B11, 539 D10, 151
Linda Tas. 624 E1, 626 E11, 628 B10
Lindeman Island Qld 605 G5, 611 K4, 391, **422**
Lindeman Islands NP Qld 605 G5, 611 K4, 391
Linden NSW 510 F6, 513 J9, 52
Lindenow Vic. 541 M5
Lindenow South Vic. 541 M5
Lindisfarne Tas. 621 F6, 623 J5, 625 K7
Lindquist Island Qld 606 F5, 607 H12, 613 M8
Lindsay Point Vic. 546 C5, 559 O7, 568 H1
Lindsay Point Vic. 526 B5
Lindum Qld 599 F7
Linga SA 526 C9, 546 E11, 548 E1
Lingeleah Island Qld 612 A4, 615 D2
Lingham Island Qld 604 B1, 611 M8
Lingnoonganee (Wallaby) Island Qld 612 A4, 615 D1
Linne Island Qld 605 G6, 611 K4
Linton Vic. 535 A11, 536 B4, 551 L4
Linville Qld 602 A4, 603 B12, 609 M7
Linwood SA 554 D3, 559 J7
Lion Island NSW 508 H2, 509 C9, 511 N4, 523 K6
Lion Island WA 577 I9
Lipson SA 558 E7
Lipson Island SA 558 E7
Lisarow NSW 509 D7, 511 O2
Lisle Tas. 627 L7
Lismore NSW 516 F5, 525 O3, 609 N12, **67**
Lismore Vic. 536 A6, 551 K6
Liston NSW 516 B3, 525 L2, 609 L11
Litchfield Vic. 526 F12, 549 I7
Litchfield NP NT 588 D9, 590 D6, 356, 360
Lithgow NSW 510 B2, 512 D2, 523 I5, **67**
Littabella NP Qld 603 B1, 604 E10, 609 M2, 399
Little Adolphus Island Qld 614 D2
Little Allen Island Qld 615 C2
Little Anderson Island Tas. 624 B11, 627 O1
Little Badger Island Tas. 624 A11, 627 O1

Little Betsey Island Tas. 623 J8, 625 K8
Little Billabong NSW 522 C11, 527 P11, 543 N3
Little Boydong Islet Qld 614 E4
Little Broughton Island NSW 515 D11, 523 N3
Little Chalky Island Tas. 624 A10
Little Desert NP Vic. 526 C12, 548 B8, 568 H8, 157, 183
Little Dog Island Tas. 624 B11, 627 P1
Little Dog Island Vic. 541 I10
Little Eyre Island SA 567 M9
Little Fitzroy Island Qld 606 E2, 607 H7, 613 M6
Little Goat Island Qld 599 F1, 602 G7, 609 N8
Little Green Island Tas. 624 B11, 627 P1
Little Grove WA 573 D11, 574 G12, 576 E11
Little Hampton Vic. 535 F9, 536 F2, 540 A2, 542 A12, 551 O3
Little Hard Hills Vic. 535 B12, 536 C4
Little Hartley NSW 510 C3, 512 E5
Little Island NSW 514 H7, 515 C12, 523 N3
Little Island NT 591 N11, 593 N2
Little Island WA 570 B4, 571 B4, 574 B5, 576 B7, 577 I10
Little Islet Qld 605 H10, 611 L7
Little Jilliby NSW 509 D6
Little Lindeman Island Qld 605 G5, 611 K4
Little Mulgrave Qld 606 E3, 607 F8
Little Muttonbird Island NSW 515 H1, 516 E12, 525 N8
Little North Island WA 575 C12
Little River Vic. 536 G6, 540 A5, 551 O6
Little Rocky Island WA 575 D2, 582 B7
Little Sir Charles Hardy Islands C Qld 614 F5
Little Snake Island Vic. 540 H10, 541 I10
Little Snowy Creek Vic. 543 L8, 545 K6
Little Swan Island Tas. 627 O4
Little Swanport Tas. 625 N4
Little Topar Roadhouse NSW 528 D9
Little Turtle Islet WA 578 D1, 580 D11, 583 I2
Little Vanderlin Island NT 591 N11, 593 N2
Little Waterhouse Island Tas. 627 M4
Little Woody (Walangoora) Island Qld 603 G5, 604 H12, 609 N4
Littlehampton SA 553 G9, 554 D10, 555 H3
Liverpool NSW 508 B8, 511 J9, 519 H1, 523 J7
Livingstone Island WA 580 H5, 584 C8
Livingstone NP NSW 522 B10, 527 P10, 543 M2
Lizard Island Qld 613 L1, **422**
Lizard Island WA 581 J5, 584 E6
Lizard Island NP Qld 613 L1, 407
Llandaff Tas. 625 O2, 627 O11

Llandeilo Vic. 535 E11, 536 E3, 551 N4
Llanelly Vic. 535 D3, 549 M10
Llangothlin NSW 525 K7
Llapnab Islet Qld 614 C1
Llewellyn Siding Tas. 625 M1, 627 M10
Lloyd Islands A Qld 614 E7
Lloyd Islands B Qld 614 E7
Lloyd Islands C Qld 614 E7
Lloyd Islands D Qld 614 E7
Lobethal SA 553 G7, 554 E8, 555 H2, 559 K9, 568 C3, 229
Loccota Tas. 624 B11, 627 O1
Loch Vic. 537 M10, 540 F8, 172
Loch Sport Vic. 541 M6, 192
Lochern NP Qld 617 L11, 423
Lochiel NSW 539 H7
Lochiel SA 556 G3, 559 I6
Lochinvar NSW 509 F1, 514 B7, 523 L3
Lochnagar Qld 610 D10, 617 P10
Lock SA 558 D5, 560 C12
Locker Island WA 575 C3
Lockhart NSW 522 A10, 527 N10, 543 K1, 97
Lockhart River Qld 614 E7
Lockington Qld 610 H11
Lockington Vic. 527 I12, 542 B6, 549 P7
Locksley NSW 522 H5
Locksley Vic. 542 E9, 163
Locksmith Island Qld 605 G6, 611 K4
Lockwood Vic. 535 F4, 549 N10
Lockwood South Vic. 535 F4, 549 N10
Lockyer NP Qld 609 L9
Locust Rock Qld 612 A6, 615 D3
Loddon Vale Vic. 526 H11, 549 N6
Loftus NSW 508 C10, 511 K11, 517 H1
Logan Vic. 535 A2, 549 L9
Logan Village Qld 599 E11, 600 E7
Loganlea Qld 599 F10, 600 E6
Logie Brae NSW 527 L10, 542 F2
Loira Tas. 627 J7, 629 F8
Lombadina WA 580 H6, 584 B8
Londonderry NSW 510 H5, 513 N8
Londrigan Vic. 543 I7, 544 F4
Long Beach NSW 519 F6, 521 M6
Long Flat NSW 515 E6, 519 E5, 521 J5, 522 G11, 523 I8, 525 L11
Long Island NSW 508 G2, 509 C9, 511 M4, 523 K6
Long Island Qld 599 H10, 600 G6, 604 A1, 605 F5, 609 N10, 611 K4, 614 B8
Long Island Tas. 624 B11, 627 O2
Long Island Vic. 531 F11, 533 L7, 537 K9, 540 D7
Long Island WA 575 D1, 577 I9, 578 A3, 581 I5, 582 B6, 584 C8
Long Jetty NSW 509 E7, 511 P2, 523 L5
Long Plains SA 554 A2, 556 H5, 559 J7, 568 B1
Long Plains Vic. 549 J2
Long Pocket Qld 613 L12
Long Rock Qld 605 G6, 611 K4
Longerenong Vic. 548 G9
Longford Tas. 627 K9, 629 G12, **485**
Longford Vic. 541 K7
Longitude Island WA 581 I5, 584 C7

Longlea Vic. 535 G3, 542 A9, 549 O10
Longley Tas. 622 H6, 625 J7
Longreach Qld 610 B10, 617 N10, **423**
Longwarry Vic. 534 F12, 537 N8, 540 F6
Longwood Vic. 542 E9, 163
Longwood East Vic. 542 E9
Lonnavale Tas. 622 E6, 625 I7
Lonsdale SA 553 B10, 554 A11, 555 E4, 556 H8, 559 J9
Looking Glass Isle NSW 515 D11, 523 N3
Looma WA 581 J7, 584 E11
Loongana Tas. 626 F7, 628 D3
Loongana WA 577 N5
Loorana Tas. 625 O11
Lord Island WA 581 I5, 584 C7
Lorinna Tas. 626 G8, 628 F5
Lorne NSW 515 E7, 525 L11
Lorne Vic. 536 D11, 538 E4, 551 M9, **173**
Lorquon Vic. 526 C12, 548 E6
Lorquon West Vic. 548 E6
Lorraine Island WA 577 J9
Lostock NSW 514 B3, 515 A9, 523 L2
Lota Qld 599 G7
Lottah Tas. 627 O7
Louis Island WA 581 L2, 585 I1
Louisa Island Tas. 622 A12, 624 G11
Louisville Tas. 623 N1, 625 M5
Lound Island SA 567 L9
Lourah Island Tas. 624 E9
Louth NSW 529 K6
Louth Bay SA 558 D8
Louth Island SA 558 E8
Loveday SA 559 N7
Lovely Banks Vic. 532 A2
Low Head Tas. 627 J6, 629 E5, 480
Low Island NT 591 M4
Low Island Qld 604 A1, 605 F4, 606 D1, 607 E3, 611 J3, 613 L5
Low Island WA 575 E1, 578 A2, 580 A12, 581 L2, 582 D5, 584 H2
Low Islets Tas. 624 A10
Low Rock NT 591 L8
Low Rock WA 577 I9, 581 J3, 584 F4
Low Wooded Island Qld 613 L2
Lowaldie SA 559 M9, 568 E3
Lowan Vale SA 526 A12, 548 A6, 568 G7
Lowanna NSW 516 D11, 525 M7
Lowbank SA 559 M7, 568 F1
Lowden WA 572 F5, 574 C8
Lowdina Tas. 623 J2, 625 K5
Lower Acacia Creek NSW 516 B2, 525 L2
Lower Barrington Tas. 626 H7, 628 G2, 629 A7
Lower Beulah Tas. 626 H8, 628 H4, 629 A10
Lower Boro NSW 519 E4, 521 K2, 522 H10
Lower Bucca NSW 516 E11, 525 N7
Lower Chittering WA 571 D2, 574 C4
Lower Creek NSW 515 E2, 525 L9
Lower Gellibrand Vic. 538 H11, 551 J10
Lower Glenelg NP Vic. 550 B6, 568 H12, 188

Lower Goulburn NP Vic. 527 K12, 542 D5
Lower Heytesbury Vic. 538 F10, 551 I9
Lower Mangrove NSW 509 B8, 511 M2
Lower Marshes Tas. 625 K4
Lower Mookerawa NSW 522 G3
Lower Mount Hicks Tas. 626 F5
Lower Norton Vic. 548 F10
Lower Quipolly NSW 524 H10
Lower Sandy Bay Tas. 621 E10
Lower Turners Marsh Tas. 627 K6, 629 G7
Lower Wilmot Tas. 628 G3
Lowesdale NSW 527 M11, 543 I4
Lowlands NSW 510 H4, 513 O6, 527 L3
Lowmead Qld 604 E9, 609 L2
Lowood Qld 600 A4, 602 B10, 609 M9
Lowrie Islet Qld 614 F8
Lowry Islet Qld 614 D1
Lowther NSW 510 B4, 512 C6, 523 I6
Loxton SA 526 A6, 546 A7, 559 N8, 568 G2, **241**
Loxton North SA 526 A6, 546 A7, 559 N8, 568 G1
Loyetea Tas. 626 F7, 628 E2
Lubeck Vic. 548 H9
Lucas Heights NSW 508 B10, 511 J11, 517 H1
Lucas Island WA 581 J4, 584 E4
Lucaston Tas. 622 G6, 625 J7
Lucinda Qld 606 F8, 613 M10, 415
Lucindale SA 568 F9, 251
Lucknow NSW 522 G5, 81
Lucknow Vic. 541 M5
Lucky Bay SA 556 C1, 558 G5, 234
Lucyvale Vic. 543 N7, 545 M4
Luddenham NSW 510 G8
Ludlow WA 572 D6, 574 B9
Lue NSW 522 H3
Lughrata Tas. 624 B10
Lulim Island WA 581 J4, 584 E5
Lulworth Tas. 627 K5, 629 G5
Lunawanna Tas. 622 H11, 625 J10
Lune River Tas. 622 E12, 625 I10
Lupton Island Qld 605 G5, 611 K3
Lurg Vic. 542 H8, 544 E6
Lurg Upper Vic. 542 H8, 544 E6
Lusby Island SA 558 E8
Lutana Tas. 621 D5
Lyiltjarra NT 596 C5
Lyme Regis Tas. 627 O4
Lymington Tas. 622 G9, 625 J9
Lymwood Tas. 625 P12
Lynchford Tas. 624 D2, 626 D11, 628 A11
Lynchs Creek NSW 516 E3, 525 N2
Lyndhurst NSW 522 F5
Lyndhurst SA 557 A2, 560 H3, 241
Lyndhurst Vic. 531 F8, 533 M3, 534 A11, 537 K7, 540 D6
Lyndoch SA 552 G3, 554 E5, 559 K8, 568 C2, **241**
Lyons Vic. 550 D6, 568 H12
Lyonville Vic. 535 F9, 536 F2, 551 O3, 161
Lyrup SA 526 A6, 546 A6, 559 N7, 568 G1
Lysterfield Vic. 531 G7, 534 B9, 537 K6, 540 D5

M

Maaroom Qld 603 F6, 609 N5
Maatsuyker Island Tas. 624 F11
Mabel Island Qld 606 F3, 607 H9, 613 M7
Mabuiag Island Qld 614 C1
McAlinden WA 572 H5, 574 D8
Macalister Qld 609 J8
Macalister Range NP Qld 606 D1, 607 E5, 613 L5
Macarthur Vic. 550 F6
Macarthur Island A Qld 614 E5
Macarthur Island B Qld 614 E5
Macarthur Island C Qld 614 E5
Macarthur Island D Qld 614 E5
Macclesfield SA 553 F11, 554 D11, 555 H5, 559 K10, 568 C4
Macclesfield Vic. 531 H7, 534 C9, 537 L6, 540 E5
McCluer Island NT 590 H1
McCrae Vic. 532 H8
McCullys Gap NSW 523 K2
Macdonnell NT 597 I4
McDonnell Creek Qld 606 E3, 607 G9
Macedon Vic. 531 A1, 535 H9, 536 G2, 540 B2, 542 B12, 551 P3, 203
McEwen Island Qld 605 H11, 611 L8
McGraths Hill NSW 508 A2, 511 I5, 513 P7
Machans Beach Qld 606 E2, 607 F6
McHugh Island Vic. 540 G12
McIntyre Vic. 535 B2, 549 M9
McIntyre Island WA 581 I5, 584 C6
Mackay Qld 605 G8, 611 K5, **424**
McKees Hill NSW 516 F5
McKenzie Creek Vic. 548 G9
MacKenzie Island Qld 604 C5, 611 N11
MacKenzie (Round) Island WA 577 I10
McKinlay Qld 615 G12, 617 I4, 421
Macks Creek Vic. 541 I9
Macksville NSW 515 G2, 525 M9, **68**
Maclagan Qld 609 K8
McLaren Flat SA 553 C12, 554 B12, 555 F5
McLaren Vale SA 553 B12, 554 B12, 555 E5, 556 H9, 559 J10, 568 B4, **243**
Maclean NSW 516 F8, 525 N5, 104
Maclean Island Qld 614 G10
Maclean Island Tas. 627 N4
Macleay Island Qld 599 H9, 600 G6, 602 H12, 609 N9
Macleay Island WA 581 I5, 584 D6
McLoughlins Beach Vic. 541 J9
MacMahon Island WA 581 I5, 584 C8
McMahons Creek Vic. 534 G7, 537 N5, 540 F4
McMahons Reef NSW 519 B2, 522 E8
McMillans Vic. 542 A4, 549 O5
McNamara Island NT 591 N5
Macorna Vic. 526 H11, 549 N5
Macquarie Fields NSW 508 A9, 511 I10
Macquarie Pass NP NSW 517 D6, 519 G3, 523 J9, 85
Macquarie Plains Tas. 622 F3, 625 I6

Macrossan Qld 606 F12, 610 F2
Macs Cove Vic. 537 P1, 540 H1, 542 H12, 544 D11
Madalya Vic. 541 I9
Maddington WA 570 F7, 571 D6
Madora WA 571 C9, 574 B6
Madura WA 577 N6
Madura Roadhouse WA 577 N6
Maer Island Qld 614 G1
Mafeking Vic. 550 H2
Maffra Vic. 541 K6, **175**
Maggea SA 559 M8, 568 F2
Magistrate Rocks WA 577 I9
Magnetic Island Qld 605 A1, 606 G10, 610 G1, 613 N11, 448
Magnetic Island NP Qld 605 A1, 606 G10, 610 G1, 613 N11, 448
Magpie Vic. 535 C11, 536 C3
Magra Tas. 622 G3, 625 J6
Magra Islet Qld 614 E5
Magrath Flat SA 559 L12, 568 D6
Maher Island Qld 605 G5, 611 K4
Mahogany Creek WA 570 G5
Mai Islet Qld 614 D2
Maianbar NSW 508 D11, 511 K12
Maiden Gully Vic. 535 F3, 549 O10
Maidenwell Qld 609 L7, 433
Mailors Flat Vic. 538 C7, 550 G7
Maimuru NSW 519 B1, 522 D7
Main Beach Qld 516 G1, 525 O1, 600 G9, 601 F6, 609 N10, 445
Main Lead Vic. 536 A1, 551 K3
Main Range NP Qld 516 C1, 525 M1, 609 L10, 391, 396, 420
Main Ridge Vic. 533 I9
Maindample Vic. 542 G11, 544 C9
Maine Island NT 591 J3
Maitak Island Qld 614 C1
Maitland NSW 509 F1, 514 C7, 515 A11, 523 L3, **69**
Maitland SA 556 E5, 558 H7, **244**
Major Plains Vic. 542 G7, 544 C4
Majorca Vic. 535 C6, 549 M12, 551 M1
Majors Creek NSW 519 E5, 521 J5, 522 G11
Malaan NP Qld 606 D4, 607 D11, 613 L7
Malanda Qld 606 D4, 607 E10, 613 L7, 451
Malbina Tas. 622 H4, 625 J6
Malbon Qld 615 E12, 616 G4
Malby Island WA 581 J3, 584 F4
Malcolm WA 576 H2
Malcolm Island WA 581 L2, 584 H3
Maldon NSW 510 F12, 517 E2
Maldon Vic. 535 E5, 549 N11, 551 N1, **175**
Maleny Qld 602 E4, 603 E12, 609 N7, **422**
Maleny NP Qld 602 E3, 603 D11, 609 M7
Malinong SA 559 L11, 568 D5
Mallacoota Vic. 519 D11, 539 G11, **176**
Mallala SA 554 B3, 556 H5, 559 J7, 568 B1
Mallan NSW 526 H9, 547 M11, 549 M1
Mallanganee NSW 516 D5, 525 M3, 609 M12
Mallanganee NP NSW 516 D5, 525 M3, 609 M12
Mallee Cliffs NP NSW 526 F6, 546 H6, 547 I6

Mallison Island NT 591 M3
Mallum Vic. 542 H9, 544 D7
Malmsbury Vic. 535 G7, 540 A1, 542 A11, 549 O12, 551 O2, 173
Malpas SA 526 A7, 546 A8, 559 N9, 568 G2
Malua Bay NSW 519 F6, 521 M7, 522 H12, 29
Malyalling WA 574 F6
Mambray Creek SA 559 I3, 560 G10
Manangatang Vic. 526 F8, 547 J11
Manara NSW 527 I1, 528 H12
Mandagery NSW 522 E4
Mandalong NSW 509 E5, 514 A11
Mandorah NT 588 C3, 590 D4
Mandurah WA 571 C9, 574 B6, 576 C8, **318**
Mandurama NSW 522 F5
Mandurang Vic. 535 G4, 542 A9, 549 O10
Mangalo SA 556 A1, 558 F5, 560 E12
Mangalore Tas. 623 I2, 625 K6
Mangalore Vic. 542 D10
Mangana Tas. 627 N9
Mango Hill Qld 599 E4, 600 E2, 602 F9
Mangoola NSW 523 J2
Mangoplah NSW 522 B10, 527 O10, 543 M2
Mangrove Creek NSW 509 B7, 511 M1, 523 K5
Mangrove Islands Qld 604 A1, 611 L8
Mangrove Mountain NSW 509 C6, 511 M1, 523 K5
Manguri SA 565 N10
Manicom Island WA 577 J9
Manildra NSW 522 F4
Manilla NSW 524 H8, **69**
Maningrida NT 591 J3
Manjimup WA 572 H10, 573 B1, 574 D10, 576 C10, **319**
Manley Islet Qld 614 E5
Manly NSW 508 G6, 509 C12, 511 M8, 523 K6, 16
Manly Qld 599 G7, 600 E4, 602 G11, 384
Manmanning WA 574 E2, 576 D6
Manmoyi NT 591 J4
Mannahill SA 559 M2, 561 L9
Mannanarie SA 559 J3, 561 I11
Mannerim Vic. 532 D5, 536 G8, 540 A6
Mannering Park NSW 509 F5, 514 B11, 523 L5
Mannibadar Vic. 536 A4, 551 K5
Manning Point NSW 515 E8, 523 O1, 525 L12
Manns Beach Vic. 541 J10
Mannum SA 554 H9, 559 L9, 568 D3, **244**
Manobalai NSW 523 J1, 524 H12
Manoora SA 559 K6
Manowar Island Qld 615 D1
Mansell Island Qld 605 G5, 611 K4
Mansfield Vic. 542 H11, 544 D9, **177**
Mantung SA 559 M8, 568 F2
Manumbar Qld 603 C10, 609 M6
Many Peaks Qld 604 D9, 609 L2
Manyalluluk NT 590 G8
Manyana NSW 521 N3
Manypeaks WA 573 F10, 574 H11
Mapleton Qld 602 F3, 603 E11, 433

Mapleton Falls NP Qld 602 E3, 603 E11, 609 N7, 433
Mapoon Qld 614 B5, 449
Mara NT 591 M11, 593 M2
Maralinga SA 566 H3
Marama SA 559 M10, 568 F4
Maranboy NT 590 G8
Marangaroo WA 570 C4, 571 C4
Marathon Qld 610 A4, 617 M4
Maraylya NSW 508 B2, 511 J4
Marbelup WA 573 C11, 574 G11
Marble Bar WA 578 E2, 580 E12, 583 K5, **319**
Marble Island Qld 611 M7
Marburg Qld 600 A5, 602 B11, 609 M9
Marchagee WA 576 B5
Marchinbar Island NT 591 N1
Marcoola Qld 602 G3, 603 F11, 426
Marcus Vic. 532 D5
Marcus Beach Qld 602 H2, 603 F10
Marcus Hill Vic. 532 D5, 536 G9, 540 A7
Mardanaingura Island NT 591 K3
Mardella WA 570 F11, 571 D7
Mardie Island WA 575 D1, 578 A2, 582 C6
Mareeba Qld 606 D2, 607 D7, 613 L6, **425**
Marengo NSW 516 B11, 525 L7
Marengo Vic. 536 B12, 538 C6, 551 L11
Marengo Reefs Marine Sanctuary Vic. 536 B12, 538 C6, 551 L11
Maret Island WA 581 J2, 584 F2
Margaret Island Qld 612 A5, 615 D3
Margaret Island WA 581 I5, 584 C7
Margaret River WA 572 B8, 574 B10, 576 B10, **322**
Margate Tas. 623 I7, 625 K8
Maria Creek NP Qld 606 E5, 613 M8
Maria Island NT 591 L9
Maria Island Tas. 623 O2, 625 N6
Maria Island NP Tas. 623 O3, 625 N6, 495
Maria NP NSW 515 G5, 525 M10
Mariala NP Qld 619 N4, 438
Marian Qld 605 F7, 611 K5
Mariginiup WA 570 C3
Marion SA 553 B8, 554 B9, 555 E3, 556 H8
Marion Bay SA 556 B9, 558 G10, 267
Marion Bay Tas. 623 N5, 625 M7
Markwell NSW 514 H4, 515 C10, 523 N2
Markwood Vic. 543 I8, 544 G5
Marla SA 565 M5
Marlborough Qld 611 L9
Marlee NSW 515 D7, 523 N1, 525 K12
Marlo Vic. 519 A12, 539 B11
Marma Vic. 548 H9
Marmion Marine Park WA 570 B4, 571 B4, 574 B4, 576 B7
Marmor Qld 604 B6, 611 M11
Marndungum Island WA 581 J5, 584 E6
Marnoo Vic. 549 I9
Marong Vic. 535 E3, 549 N10
Maroochydore Qld 602 G4, 603 F11, 609 N7, **426**
Maroon Qld 516 D1, 525 N1, 600 A10, 609 M10

Maroona Vic. 551 I3
Maroota NSW 509 A8, 511 K3, 523 K5
Marp Vic. 550 C5, 568 H12
Marquis Island Qld 604 B2, 611 M8
Marrabel SA 559 K7
Marradong WA 571 G11, 574 D7
Marralum NT 581 P3, 585 N4, 590 B10, 592 B1
Marramarra NP NSW 508 E1, 509 B8, 511 K3, 523 K5, 102
Marrangaroo NSW 510 B1, 512 C1, 523 I5
Marrangaroo NP NSW 510 B1, 512 C2, 523 I5
Marrar NSW 522 B9, 527 P9
Marrawah Tas. 626 A4
Marraweeny Vic. 542 F9, 544 B7
Marree SA 560 H1, 562 H12, 618 A12, **245**
Marrickville NSW 508 E8, 511 L9
Marrinan Island NT 591 M6
Marrinup WA 571 E10
Marsden NSW 522 C5, 527 P5
Marshall Vic. 532 A4, 536 F8, 538 G1, 540 A6, 551 O7
Marshdale NSW 514 E4, 515 B10, 523 M3
Mart Islands WA 577 J9
Martin Islet NSW 517 G5, 519 H3, 523 J8
Martin Islet Qld 605 G5, 611 K3
Martindale NSW 523 J2
Martins Creek NSW 514 C5, 515 A11, 523 L3
Martinsville NSW 509 E4, 514 A10
Marton Qld 613 L3
Marulan NSW 519 F3, 522 H9
Marulan South NSW 519 F3, 522 H9
Marum Island SA 558 E8
Marungi Vic. 527 L12, 542 F6, 544 A2
Marvel Loch WA 576 F6
Mary Anne Island WA 575 C9, 582 B7, 586 E10
Mary Island WA 581 L2, 585 I1
Mary Island North WA 581 I6, 584 D9
Mary Island South WA 581 I7, 584 D9
Mary River NP (Proposed) NT 588 H2, 589 J1, 590 E4
Mary River Roadhouse NT 589 L10, 590 F6
Maryborough Qld 603 E6, 609 N5, **426**
Maryborough Vic. 535 C5, 549 M11, 551 M1, **177**
Marybrook WA 572 B6
Maryfarms Qld 606 C1, 607 B4, 613 K5
Maryknoll Vic. 534 D11, 537 M7, 540 E6
Maryland NP NSW 516 B3, 525 L2, 609 L11
Maryport Islet Qld 605 G6, 611 K5
Marysville Vic. 534 F5, 537 N3, 540 F3, **178**
Maryvale NSW 522 F2
Maryvale Qld 516 C1
Mascot NSW 508 F8, 511 L9
Masillon Island SA 567 L9
Maslin Beach SA 553 A12, 554 A12, 555 E5

Massey Vic. 526 F12, 549 I7
Masthead Island Qld 604 E6, 611 O11
Matakana NSW 527 M3
Mataranka NT 590 H9, **363**
Matcham NSW 509 D8, 511 O3
Matheson NSW 525 J5
Mathinna Tas. 627 N8
Mathoura NSW 527 J11, 542 D4
Matlock Vic. 537 P4, 540 H4
Matong NSW 519 B9, 520 E12, 522 B8, 527 O8, 539 D6
Maude NSW 527 I7, 547 P8
Maude Vic. 536 E6, 551 N6
Maudsland Qld 600 F9, 601 C4
Mausoleum Island Qld 605 F7, 611 K5
Mawbanna Tas. 626 D4
Mawby Island WA 575 E1, 578 B2, 580 B12, 582 D4
Mawson WA 574 E5, 576 D7
Maxwelton Qld 617 K3
Mayanup WA 574 D9, 576 D10
Mayberry Tas. 626 H8, 628 G5
Maydena Tas. 622 D3, 624 H6
Maylands WA 570 D6, 571 C5
Mayrung NSW 527 K10, 542 E2
Mazeppa NP Qld 605 A10, 610 G7
Meade Island WA 575 B9, 586 B8
Meadow Creek Vic. 543 I8, 544 F6
Meadowbank NSW 511 K8
Meadows SA 553 E11, 554 D11, 555 G5, 559 J10, 568 C4, 260
Meandarra Qld 608 H8
Meander Tas. 627 I9, 629 C12
Meatian Vic. 526 G10, 549 K3
Mebbin NP NSW 516 F3, 525 N2, 609 N11
Meckering WA 574 E4, 576 D7, 328
Medlow Bath NSW 510 C5, 512 F8, 523 I6
Medowie NSW 514 E7
Meeandah Qld 599 F7
Meekatharra WA 575 H9, 578 E10, **320**
Meelon WA 571 D10
Meeniyan Vic. 537 O12, 540 G9, 173
Meerawa Qld 606 E3, 607 G9
Meerlieu Vic. 541 L6
Meerschaum Vale NSW 516 G5, 525 O4, 609 N12
Megalong NSW 510 C5, 512 E8
Megan NSW 516 C11, 525 M7
Meggi-Kudulug Qld 614 C2
Meggi-Yelubi Island Qld 614 C2
Melaleuca Tas. 624 F10
Melbourne Vic. 531 D6, 537 I5, 540 C4, **124**
Meldale Qld 599 F1, 602 G7
Mella Tas. 626 C4
Mellis Vic. 548 H7
Melomys Island WA 581 I5, 584 D7
Melros WA 571 B10
Melrose SA 559 I3, 560 H10, **246**
Melrose Tas. 626 H6, 628 G2, 629 A7
Melsonby (Gaarraay) NP Qld 613 K2
Melton SA 556 F3, 559 I6
Melton Vic. 531 A4, 535 H12, 536 G4, 540 B3, 551 P5
Melton Mowbray Tas. 625 K4

Melton South Vic. 531 A4, 535 H12, 536 G4, 540 B4, 551 P5
Melville WA 570 D7, 571 C6, 573 D11
Melville Forest Vic. 550 E3
Melville Island NT 590 C2
Memana Tas. 624 B10
Memerambi Qld 603 A10, 609 L6
Mena Creek Qld 606 E5, 607 G12, 613 M8
Mena Park Vic. 536 A3, 551 K4
Menai NSW 508 C10, 511 J11, 517 H1
Menangle NSW 510 G12, 517 F2, 519 H1, 523 J7, 40
Menangle Park NSW 510 H11, 517 F1
Mendooran NSW 524 D11
Mengha Tas. 626 D4
Menindee NSW 528 E11, **70**
Meningie SA 559 L11, 568 D5, **246**
Mentone Vic. 531 E8, 533 J1, 537 J7, 540 C5
Menzies WA 576 H3, 318
Menzies Creek Vic. 531 H7, 534 C9, 537 L6, 163
Mepunga East Vic. 538 E8, 550 H8
Mepunga West Vic. 538 D8, 550 H8
Merah North NSW 524 E6
Merbein Vic. 526 D6, 546 G6
Merbein South Vic. 526 D6, 546 G6
Merbein West Vic. 546 G5
Mercunda SA 559 M8, 568 F2
Merebene NSW 524 D7
Meredith Vic. 536 E5, 551 N5
Mereenie NT 597 I5
Merewether NSW 509 H3, 514 D9
Meribah SA 526 B7, 546 B8, 559 O8, 568 G2
Merildin SA 559 K6
Merimal Qld 604 A3, 611 M10
Merimbula NSW 519 E9, 539 H7, **70**
Merinda Qld 605 D4, 611 I3
Meringa Qld 606 E3, 607 F8
Meringa Island NT 591 M6
Meringo NSW 519 F7, 521 L8
Meringur Vic. 526 C6, 546 D7, 559 P8
Meringur North Vic. 526 C6, 546 D6, 559 P7
Merino Vic. 550 D4
Mermaid Beach Qld 516 G1, 600 G10, 601 F7
Mermaid Island WA 581 I5, 584 C7
Mernda Vic. 531 E3, 537 J4, 540 D3
Meroo NP NSW 519 F5, 521 N5, 523 I11
Merredin WA 574 G3, 576 E6, **320**
Merri Marine Sanctuary Vic. 538 C8, 550 G8
Merriang Vic. 543 J8, 544 H6
Merriang South Vic. 543 J9, 544 H6
Merricks Vic. 533 J9
Merricks Beach Vic. 533 J9
Merricks North Vic. 531 E12, 533 J8, 537 J10, 540 C7
Merrigum Vic. 542 D7
Merrijig Vic. 540 H1, 542 H11, 544 E10
Merrimac Qld 600 F10, 601 E7
Merrinee Vic. 526 D6, 546 F7
Merrinee North Vic. 526 D6, 546 F6

Merriton SA 559 I5, 560 H12
Merriwa NSW 523 J1, 524 G12, **70**
Merriwa WA 570 B2
Merriwagga NSW 527 L5
Merrygoen NSW 524 D11
Merrylands NSW 511 J8
Merseylea Tas. 626 H7, 629 B8
Merton Tas. 621 B6
Merton Vic. 542 F10, 544 B9
Metcalfe Vic. 535 G6, 542 A11, 549 O12, 551 O1
Meth Islet Qld 614 C1
Metricup WA 572 B7
Metung Vic. 541 N6, 174
Meunna Tas. 626 D5
Mewstone Tas. 624 G12
Mia Mia Vic. 535 H5, 542 B10, 549 P11, 551 P1
Miall Island Qld 604 C4, 611 N10
Miallo Qld 606 D1, 607 D3, 613 L5
Miami Qld 516 G1, 600 G10, 601 F8, 445
Miami Keys Qld 601 F7
Miandetta NSW 529 O10
Miandetta Tas. 629 B3
Michael Creek Qld 606 E8, 613 L10
Michaelmas and Upolu Cays NP Qld 606 E1, 613 M5
Michaelmas Island WA 573 E11, 574 G11, 576 E11
Michelago NSW 518 E10, 519 C6, 520 H5, 522 F12
Mickleham Vic. 531 D3, 537 I3, 540 C3
Mictyis Island WA 581 J3, 584 F4
Mid Molle Island Qld 605 F5, 611 K3
Middle Brother Islet Qld 614 D2
Middle Brother NP NSW 515 F7, 523 O1, 525 L12
Middle Creek Vic. 551 K3
Middle Dural NSW 508 D3, 509 A10, 511 K5
Middle Indigo Vic. 543 J6, 544 H2
Middle Island Qld 604 C4, 605 E4, 606 F6, 611 J3, 613 M9
Middle Island Vic. 538 C8, 550 G8
Middle Island WA 575 D1, 577 J9, 578 A3, 580 G6, 582 B6, 584 C8
Middle Mary Anne Island WA 575 D2, 582 B7
Middle Osborn Island WA 581 L2, 584 H2
Middle Pasco Island Tas. 624 A9
Middle Point NT 588 F3, 590 E4
Middle Rock WA 577 I10
Middle Swan WA 570 F4, 571 D4
Middlemount Qld 611 J9
Middleton Qld 617 I7
Middleton SA 555 G8, 254
Middleton Tas. 622 H9, 625 J9
Middlingbank NSW 519 B7, 520 E9, 539 D3
Midge Island Qld 605 F6, 611 J4
Midge Point Qld 605 F6, 611 J4, 438
Midgee Qld 604 B5, 611 M11
Midgee SA 558 G4, 560 F12
Midgegooroo NP WA 570 G8, 571 D6, 574 C5, 576 C8
Midland WA 570 F5, 571 D4, 574 C5, 576 C7
Midway Island WA 581 J4, 584 F5
Midway Point Tas. 623 K4, 625 L7
Miena Tas. 625 I1, 627 I11, **486**

Miepoll Vic. 542 E8, 544 A5
Miga Lake Vic. 548 D10
Migo Island WA 573 C12, 574 G12, 576 E11
Mil Lel SA 550 A4, 568 G11
Mila NSW 519 C10, 539 E8
Milabena Tas. 626 E5
Milang SA 559 K10, 568 C4, 260
Milawa Vic. 543 I8, 544 F5, **178**
Milbrulong NSW 522 A10, 527 O10, 543 K1
Mildura Vic. 526 E6, 546 G6, **180**
Mile Island Tas. 624 A10
Miles Qld 609 I7, **426**
Miles Island NT 591 N4
Miles Island WA 577 J9
Milguy NSW 524 G4, 608 H12
Milikapiti NT 590 D2
Miling WA 574 C1, 576 C5
Milingimbi NT 591 K3
Milingimbi Island NT 591 K3
Millaa Millaa Qld 606 D4, 607 E11, 613 L7, **427**
Millaroo Qld 605 B4, 610 H3
Millbrook Vic. 535 D11, 536 E3
Millfield NSW 509 D2, 523 L4
Millgrove Vic. 534 E8, 537 M5, 540 F4
Millicent SA 568 F11, **247**
Millie NSW 524 F5
Millmerran Qld 609 K9, 447
Milloo Vic. 542 A6, 549 O8
Millstream–Chichester NP WA 575 F2, 578 C3, 582 F6, 311
Millstream Falls NP Qld 606 D4, 607 D12, 613 L7, 438
Millthorpe NSW 522 G5, 33
Milltown Vic. 550 D6
Millwood NSW 522 B9, 527 O9
Milman Qld 604 B4, 611 M10
Milman Islet Qld 614 E3
Milparinka NSW 528 D3, 561 P2, 618 H12, 92
Miltalie SA 556 B1, 558 F5, 560 E12
Milton NSW 519 G5, 521 N4, 523 I11, 95
Milton Qld 599 E7, 383
Milvale NSW 519 A1, 522 D7
Milyakburra NT 591 M7
Milyeannup NP WA 572 E9, 574 C10, 576 C10
Milyema Island NT 591 N6
Mimi Islet Qld 614 F1
Mimili SA 565 K5
Mimmindie Vic. 526 H12, 549 M6
Mimosa NSW 522 B8, 527 P8
Mimosa Rocks NP NSW 519 E9, 521 K12, 539 H6, 31, 89
Minamia NT 591 J11, 593 J2
Mincha Vic. 526 H11, 549 N6
Mindarie SA 559 M9, 568 F3
Minden Qld 602 B11
Mindiyarra SA 559 M9, 568 E3
Miners Rest Vic. 535 C9, 536 C2, 551 M3
Minerva Hills NP Qld 610 H12, 611 I12, 441
Mingary SA 528 A10, 559 O1, 561 M8
Mingay Vic. 536 A5, 551 K5
Mingela Qld 606 F12, 610 G2
Mingenew WA 576 B4, 303
Mingoola NSW 525 K3, 609 K12
Minhamite Vic. 550 G6
Minilya Roadhouse WA 575 B6

Minimay Vic. 548 C9, 568 H8
Mininera Vic. 551 I4
Minintirri Island NT 591 L8
Minjary NP NSW 519 A4, 520 C2, 522 D10, 543 P2
Minjilang NT 590 G1
Minlaton SA 556 E6, 558 H8, **247**
Minmi NSW 509 G3, 514 C9, 515 A12
Minnamurra NSW 517 F7
Minnie Water NSW 516 F9, 525 N6
Minniging WA 574 E7
Minnipa SA 558 C3, 560 A10, 567 P10, **267**
Minnivale WA 574 E3
Minore NSW 522 E1, 524 C12
Minster Island Qld 611 L6
Mintabie SA 565 L5
Mintaro SA 559 J6, **247**
Minto NSW 511 I10, 517 G1
Minyerri NT 591 J10, 593 J1
Minyip Vic. 548 H8
Miowera NSW 529 P10
Mipe Islet Qld 614 C1
Miralie Vic. 547 L11, 549 L1
Miram Vic. 526 C12, 548 C7, 568 H7
Miram South Vic. 548 D7, 568 H7
Miranda NSW 508 D10, 511 K11
Mirani Qld 605 F8, 611 K5
Mirannie NSW 514 B3, 523 L2
Mirboo Vic. 537 P11, 540 H8
Mirboo North Vic. 537 P11, 540 G8, **173**
Miriam Vale Qld 604 D8, 609 L2, **427**
Mirima NP WA 581 O4, 585 M5, 590 A11, 592 A2, 316
Mirimbah Vic. 541 I1, 543 I11, 544 F10
Miriwinni Qld 606 E4, 607 G10, 613 M7
Mirranatwa Vic. 550 G3
Mirrngadja Village NT 591 K4
Mirrool NSW 522 B7, 527 O7
Missabotti NSW 515 G2, 525 M8
Mission Beach Qld 606 E5, 613 M8, **427**
Mistake Creek NT 581 O6, 585 N8, 592 A4
Mistaken Island WA 573 E11, 574 G11, 575 E1, 576 E11, 578 B2, 580 B12, 582 D5
Mitcham SA 553 C8, 554 B9, 555 F2
Mitcham Vic. 531 F6, 534 A8
Mitchell ACT 518 E4, 520 H2
Mitchell Qld 608 E6, **428**
Mitchell River NP Vic. 541 L4, **146**
Mitchell River NP WA 581 K3, 584 G4, 316
Mitchellville SA 556 C1, 558 G5, 560 F12
Mitiamo Vic. 527 I12, 542 A6, 549 O7
Mitre Vic. 548 E9
Mitta Mitta Vic. 543 M9, 545 L6, **194**
Mittagong NSW 517 C5, 519 G2, 523 I8, **35**
Mittyack Vic. 526 F9, 547 I11, 549 I1
Miva Qld 603 D8
Moa Island Qld 614 C1
Moama NSW 527 J12, 542 C5, **162**
Moana SA 553 A12, 556 H9, 559 J10, 568 B4

Moats Corner Vic. 533 I7
Mockinya Vic. 548 F10
Moculta SA 554 G4
Modanville NSW 516 F4, 525 O3
Modella Vic. 537 M9, 540 F7
Modewarre Vic. 536 E9, 538 F1, 551 N8
Moe Vic. 537 P9, 540 H7, **179**
Moema NP NSW 524 F6
Moffat Vic. 550 H5
Mogendoura NSW 519 F6, 521 L7
Moggill Qld 599 C8, 600 C5, 602 D12
Mogil Mogil NSW 524 D3, 608 F12
Moglonemby Vic. 542 F8, 544 A6
Mogo NSW 519 F6, 521 L7, **29**
Mogogout Island NT 590 G2
Mogriguy NSW 522 F1, 524 C12
Mogriguy NP NSW 522 F1, 524 C12
Mogumber WA 574 C3, 326
Moina Tas. 626 G8, 628 F4
Moira NSW 527 J11, 542 C4
Mokepilly Vic. 548 H11, 550 H1
Mokine WA 571 G3
Mole Creek Tas. 626 H8, 628 H5, 629 A11, **486**
Mole Creek Karst NP Tas. 626 G8, 628 G5, **486**
Mole River NSW 525 K4, 609 K12
Molema Island WA 581 I5, 584 D7
Molendinar Qld 601 E5
Molesworth Tas. 622 H4
Molesworth Vic. 537 M1, 540 F1, 542 F11, 544 A10
Moliagul Vic. 535 B3, 549 L10, **160**
Moliere Island WA 581 K2, 584 H2
Molle Islands NP Qld 605 F5, 611 K3
Mollongghip Vic. 535 D9, 536 E2
Mollymook NSW 521 N4, **95**
Mologa Vic. 542 A5, 549 O7
Molong NSW 522 F4, **81**
Moltema Tas. 626 H8, 629 B10
Molyullah Vic. 542 H9, 544 E6
Mona SA 556 F2
Mona Rock Qld 614 D2
Mona Vale NSW 508 H4, 509 C10, 511 N6, 523 K6
Monak NSW 546 H6
Monarto SA 554 G10, 559 K9
Monarto South SA 554 G11, 559 K10, 568 C3
Monash SA 526 A6, 546 A6, 559 N7, 568 G1, **228**
Monbulk Vic. 531 H7, 534 C9, 537 L6, 540 E5
Mondrain Island WA 577 I9
Monea Vic. 542 E10
Monegeetta Vic. 531 C1, 536 H2, 540 B2, 542 B12, 551 P3, **203**
Monga NSW 519 E5, 521 K5, 522 H11
Monga NP NSW 519 E6, 521 K5, 522 H12, **35**
Mongarlowe NSW 519 E5, 521 K4, 522 H11
Monge Island WA 581 K2, 584 G2
Monkey Mia WA 575 B8, 586 D6, 301
Monomeith Vic. 533 P6, 537 L9, 540 E7
Montagu Tas. 626 B3
Montagu Bay Tas. 621 F7
Montagu Island Tas. 626 B3
Montague Island NSW 519 F8, 521 L10, **75**

Montana Tas. 627 I9, 629 C11
Monteagle NSW 519 B1, 522 E7
Montebello Islands Marine Park WA 575 C1, 582 A4, 314
Montgomery Vic. 541 K6
Montgomery Rocks Tas. 624 C6
Monto Qld 604 C10, 609 K3, **428**
Montrose Tas. 621 B5
Montumana Tas. 626 E4
Montville Qld 602 F4, 603 E11, 425
Mooball NSW 516 G3, 74
Mooball NP NSW 516 G3, 525 O2, 609 N11
Moockra SA 559 J2, 560 H9
Moodlu Qld 599 D1, 602 E7
Moogara Tas. 622 F4, 625 I6
Moogerah Qld 516 D1, 525 M1
Moogerah Peaks NP Qld 516 D1, 525 M1, 600 A8, 609 M10, 396
Moola Qld 609 K8
Moolap Vic. 532 B4, 536 F8, 538 H1
Mooloolaba Qld 602 H4, 603 F12, 609 N7, **429**
Mooloolah Qld 602 F5, 603 E12
Mooloolah River NP Qld 602 G4, 603 F12, 609 N7, 429
Moolort Vic. 535 D6, 549 M12, 551 M1
Moolpa NSW 526 H8, 547 M11
Moombooldool NSW 522 A7, 527 N7
Moombra Qld 602 B9
Moon Island NSW 509 G5, 514 C11, 523 L4
Moona Plains NSW 515 C3, 525 K9
Moonah Tas. 621 C6, 623 I5
Moonambel Vic. 549 K11
Moonan Flat NSW 523 L1, 525 I12, 86
Moonbah NSW 519 B8, 520 D10, 539 C4
Moonbi NSW 525 I9
Moonboom Islands Qld 603 F6, 609 N5
Moondalbee Island Qld 612 A4, 615 E1
Moondarra Vic. 540 H6
Moonee Beach NSW 516 E11, 525 N7
Mooney Mooney NSW 508 G1, 509 C9, 511 M4
Moonford Qld 604 C10, 609 K3
Moonie Qld 609 I9
Moonlight Flat SA 558 C3, 560 A11, 567 P11
Moonta SA 556 E3, 558 H6, **248**
Moonta Bay SA 556 E3, 558 H6, 248
Moora WA 574 B2, 576 B6, **320**
Moorabbin Vic. 531 E7, 537 J6, 540 C5
Moorabool Vic. 532 A2
Mooralla Vic. 550 F2
Moore Qld 602 A5, 603 B12, 609 M8
Moore Park Qld 603 D1, 604 F10, 609 M3
Moore River NP WA 574 B3, 576 B6, 308
Moores Flat Vic. 535 A6, 549 L11, 551 L1
Moorilda NSW 522 G5
Moorilim Vic. 542 E8
Moorina Tas. 627 N6
Moorine Rock WA 576 F6

Moorland NSW 515 E7, 523 O1, 525 L12
Moorlands SA 559 L10, 568 E4
Moorleah Tas. 626 E5
Moorngag Vic. 542 H9, 544 D7
Moorooduc Vic. 531 E10, 533 K6, 537 J9, 540 C7
Moorook SA 559 N7, 568 F1
Moorookyle Vic. 535 D8, 536 D1, 551 M2
Mooroolbark Vic. 534 B8, 537 K5
Mooroongga Island NT 591 K3
Mooroopna Vic. 542 E7, **193**
Moorrinya NP Qld 610 C5, 617 O5, 415
Moppin NSW 524 F3, 608 H12
Moranbah Qld 605 C10, 611 I7, **429**
Morangarell NSW 522 C7
Morans Crossing NSW 519 D9, 521 I12, 539 G6
Morawa WA 576 B4, **321**
Morchard SA 559 J2, 561 I10
Mordialloc Vic. 531 E8, 533 K2, 537 J7, 540 C5
Morea Vic. 548 C9, 568 H8
Moree NSW 524 G4, **71**
Moree Vic. 548 D12, 550 D1
Morella Qld 610 A9, 617 M9
Moresby Range NP Qld 606 E4, 607 H12, 613 M7
Moreton (Gnoorganbin) Island Qld 600 G3, 609 N9, 442
Moreton Island NP Qld 600 H2, 609 N9, 387, **429**
Morgan SA 559 L6, **248**
Morgan Island NT 591 M6
Moriac Vic. 536 E8, 538 F1, 551 N8
Moriarty Tas. 626 H6, 629 B7
Morisset NSW 509 E5, 514 B11, 523 L4
Morkalla Vic. 526 B6, 546 C6, 559 P8, 568 H1
Morkar Island Qld 611 M7
Morley WA 570 D5
Morley Island WA 575 C12
Morningside Qld 600 E4, 602 F11
Mornington Tas. 621 G7
Mornington Vic. 531 D10, 533 J5, 537 J9, 540 C7, **179**
Mornington Island Qld 612 A4, 615 C1
Mornington Peninsula NP Vic. 531 B12, 532 G9, 533 I10, 536 H10, 537 I10, 540 B8, 551 P8, 164, **195**
Morongla NSW 522 F6
Morpeth NSW 509 G1, 514 C7, 515 A11, 523 L3, 69
Morpeth Islet Qld 604 C1, 611 M8
Morphett Vale SA 553 B10, 554 B11, 555 E4, 556 H8
Morris Island Qld 614 H11
Morrisey Islet WA 581 I5, 584 C8
Morrisons Vic. 535 E12, 536 E5, 551 N5
Morrl Morrl Vic. 549 J10
Morse Island NT 590 F2
Mortat Vic. 548 D9, 568 H8
Mortchup Vic. 535 A11, 536 B3, 551 L4
Mortdale NSW 508 D9
Mortlake Vic. 551 I6

Morton NP NSW 517 A9, 519 F4, 521 M1, 522 H10, 523 I10, 38, 79, 85, 95
Morton Plains Vic. 526 F12, 549 J6
Morundah NSW 527 M9
Moruya NSW 519 F7, 521 L7, **71**
Moruya Heads NSW 519 F7, 521 L7
Morven NSW 522 B11, 527 O11, 543 L4
Morven Qld 608 D5
Morwell Vic. 540 H7, **181**
Morwell NP Vic. 540 H8, 181
Mosman NSW 508 G7, 509 C12, 511 M8
Mosman Park WA 570 C7, 571 B5
Mosquito Islands Qld 600 G7, 609 N10
Moss Glen Tas. 625 I11
Moss Vale NSW 517 B6, 519 G3, 523 I9, **71**
Mossgiel NSW 527 J3
Mossiface Vic. 541 N5
Mossman Qld 606 D1, 607 D3, 613 L5, **429**
Mossy Point NSW 521 L7
Mother Macgregor Island Qld 604 C5, 611 N11
Mouinndo Islet Qld 614 C3
Moulamein NSW 527 I9, 547 N11, 549 N1, 27
Moulyinning WA 574 G7
Mount Aberdeen NP Qld 605 D4, 611 I3
Mount Adolphus (Mori) Island Qld 614 D2
Mount Adrah NSW 519 A4, 520 B1, 522 D10, 543 P1
Mount Alford Qld 516 D1, 525 M1, 609 M10
Mount Alfred Vic. 522 C12, 543 N6, 545 M1
Mount Archer NP Qld 604 B5, 611 M11, 439
Mount Augustus NP WA 575 F6, 578 B7, 307
Mount Barker SA 553 F10, 554 D10, 555 H3, 559 K9, 568 C3, 238
Mount Barker WA 573 C9, 574 G11, 576 E11, **321**
Mount Barnett Roadhouse WA 581 L6, 584 H8
Mount Barney NP Qld 516 D2, 525 M1, 600 A12, 609 M11, 393
Mount Bauple NP Qld 603 D7, 609 M5, 426
Mount Baw Baw Vic. 537 P6, 540 H5
Mount Beauty Vic. 543 L10, 545 J7, **181**
Mount Beckworth Vic. 535 B8, 536 C1, 551 L2
Mount Benson SA 568 E9, 259
Mount Beppo Qld 602 B7
Mount Best Vic. 537 P12, 540 H9
Mount Binga NP Qld 603 A12, 609 L8
Mount Blue Cow NSW 520 C10, 539 B4
Mount Bryan SA 559 K5, 561 I12
Mount Bryan East SA 559 K5, 561 J12
Mount Buffalo NP Vic. 543 J9, 544 H7, 545 I7, 153, 182
Mount Buller Vic. 541 I1, 543 I12, 544 F10, 177

Mount Burnett Vic. 533 P2
Mount Burr SA 568 F11, 247
Mount Bute Vic. 536 A5, 551 K5
Mount Carbine Qld 606 C1, 607 B4, 613 K5
Mount Chappell Island Tas. 624 A11, 627 O1
Mount Charlton Qld 605 F7, 611 J5
Mount Chinghee NP Qld 516 E2, 525 N2, 600 C12, 609 M11
Mount Clear Vic. 535 C11
Mount Clunie NP NSW 516 C2, 525 M2, 609 M11
Mount Colah NSW 508 E4, 509 B10, 511 L6
Mount Colosseum NP Qld 604 D9, 609 L2
Mount Compass SA 555 F6, 556 H9, 559 J10, 568 B4, 265
Mount Cook NP Qld 613 L3
Mount Coolon Qld 605 B8, 610 H6
Mount Coolum NP Qld 602 G3, 603 F11, 609 N7, 426
Mount Coot-tha Qld 599 D7, 384
Mount Cottrell Vic. 531 A5, 535 H12, 536 H5, 540 B4, 551 P5
Mount Crosby Qld 599 B8, 600 B5, 602 D11
Mount Damper SA 558 C4, 560 A11, 567 P11
Mount David NSW 522 H6
Mount Direction Tas. 627 K7, 629 G7
Mount Doran Vic. 535 D12, 536 D4, 551 M5
Mount Druitt NSW 508 A5, 511 I7, 513 O11
Mount Dunned Vic. 532 A5
Mount Ebenezer NT 594 G10
Mount Eccles Vic. 537 O10, 540 G8
Mount Eccles NP Vic. 550 E6, 165
Mount Egerton Vic. 535 E11, 536 E4, 551 N4
Mount Eliza Vic. 531 E10, 533 K5, 537 J8, 540 C6
Mount Emu Vic. 536 A3, 551 K4
Mount Etna Caves NP Qld 604 B4, 611 M10
Mount Evelyn Vic. 531 H6, 534 C8, 537 L5
Mount Fairy NSW 519 E4, 521 J2, 522 G10
Mount Field NP Tas. 622 D2, 624 H5, 625 I5, 487
Mount Frankland NP WA 573 E4, 574 E11, 576 D11, 336
Mount Frankland North NP WA 573 F4, 574 E11, 576 D11
Mount Frankland South NP WA 573 E5, 574 E11, 576 D11
Mount Franklin NSW 535 E8, 536 E1, 551 N2
Mount Gambier SA 550 A5, 568 G12, **250**
Mount Garnet Qld 606 C5, 607 A12, 613 K7, 438
Mount George NSW 515 D8, 523 N1, 525 K12
Mount Glorious Qld 599 B5, 600 B3, 602 D9, 387
Mount Gravatt Qld 599 E8, 600 E5, 602 F12
Mount Hallen Qld 602 A9, 609 M9
Mount Helen Vic. 535 C11, 536 D4, 551 M4

Mount Helena WA 570 H4, 571 E4
Mount Hope NSW 527 M2
Mount Hope SA 558 C6
Mount Horeb NSW 519 A4, 520 B1, 522 D10, 543 P1
Mount Hunter NSW 510 F11, 517 E1
Mount Hypipamee NP Qld 606 D4, 607 D10, 613 L7, 414
Mount Imlay NP NSW 519 D10, 539 G8
Mount Irvine NSW 510 E2, 513 J3
Mount Isa Qld 615 D11, 616 F3, **430**
Mount Jerusalem NP NSW 516 G3, 525 O2, 609 N11
Mount Jim Crow NP Qld 604 B4, 611 M10
Mount Kaputar NP NSW 524 G6, 28
Mount Keith WA 578 G10
Mount Kembla NSW 517 F5, 103
Mount Kuring-gai NSW 508 E3, 509 B10, 511 L6
Mount Lambie NSW 510 A1, 512 A1, 523 I5
Mount Larcom Qld 604 C6, 611 N12
Mount Lewis NP Qld 606 C1, 607 C4, 613 L5
Mount Liebig NT 594 E6
Mount Lindesay NP WA 573 A10, 574 F11, 576 D11
Mount Lloyd Tas. 622 F4, 625 I7
Mount Lofty SA 553 D8, 554 C10, 555 G3
Mount Lonarch Vic. 549 K12, 551 K2
Mount Macedon Vic. 531 A1, 535 H9, 536 H2, 540 B2, 542 B12, 551 P3, 139, 203
Mount Mackay NP Qld 606 E6, 613 M8
Mount Magnet WA 575 H11, 576 D2, 578 D12, **323**
Mount Martha Vic. 531 D11, 533 I6, 537 I9, 540 C7, 181
Mount Martin NP Qld 605 F7, 611 K5
Mount Mary SA 559 L7
Mount Mee Qld 599 B1, 602 D7
Mount Mercer Vic. 535 C12, 536 D5, 551 M5
Mount Molloy Qld 606 C1, 607 C5, 613 L5
Mount Morgan Qld 604 A6, 611 M11, **430**
Mount Moriac Vic. 536 E8, 538 F1, 551 N8
Mount Mulligan Qld 606 B2, 613 K6
Mount Nebo Qld 599 B6, 600 B3, 602 D10
Mount Nelson Tas. 621 D10, 464
Mount Nothofagus NP NSW 516 D2, 525 M2, 600 A12, 609 M11
Mount O'Connell NP Qld 604 A3, 611 L9
Mount Ommaney Qld 599 D8, 600 C5, 602 E12
Mount Ossa Qld 605 F7, 611 J5
Mount Ossa NP Qld 605 F7, 611 J5
Mount Ousley NSW 517 F4
Mount Perry Qld 603 A3, 604 D11, 609 L4, 411

Mount Pikapene NP NSW 516 D5, 525 M4, 609 M12
Mount Pinbarren NP Qld 603 E10, 609 N6
Mount Pleasant Qld 599 B2, 600 C1, 602 D8
Mount Pleasant SA 554 F7, 559 K9, 568 C2
Mount Pleasant Vic. 535 C10
Mount Pleasant WA 575 D12, 576 H5
Mount Remarkable NP SA 559 I3, 560 H10, 246
Mount Richmond Vic. 550 C7
Mount Richmond NP Vic. 550 C7, 189
Mount Roe NP WA 573 G4, 574 F11, 576 D11
Mount Rowan Vic. 535 C10, 536 D3, 551 M3
Mount Royal NP NSW 514 A1, 523 L2, 87
Mount Samson Qld 599 C4, 600 C2, 602 E9
Mount Schank SA 550 A5, 568 G12
Mount Seaview NSW 515 D5, 525 K11
Mount Seymour Tas. 625 L4
Mount Spurgeon NP Qld 606 C1, 607 C3, 613 K5
Mount Stuart Tas. 621 C7
Mount Surprise Qld 613 J8, **431**
Mount Tamborine Qld 516 G1, 600 E9, 601 B5
Mount Tarampa Qld 602 B10
Mount Taylor Vic. 541 M5
Mount Templeton SA 556 G3, 559 J6
Mount Thorley NSW 523 K3
Mount Tomah NSW 510 E3, 513 I4
Mount Torrens SA 553 H6, 554 E8, 559 K9, 568 C3
Mount Victoria NSW 510 C4, 512 E5, 523 I6, 33
Mount Wallace Vic. 535 E12, 536 E5, 551 N5
Mount Walsh NP Qld 603 B5, 604 E12, 609 L5, 394
Mount Waverley Vic. 531 E6
Mount Webb NP Qld 613 L2
Mount Wedge SA 558 C5, 560 A12, 567 P12
Mount White NSW 509 C8, 511 M3, 523 K5
Mount William NP Tas. 627 P5, **480**
Mount Wilson NSW 510 D3, 512 H4, 523 I5
Mount Windsor NP Qld 607 A2, 613 K4
Mountain River Tas. 622 H6, 625 J7
Moura Qld 609 I2
Mourilyan Qld 606 E5, 607 H12, 613 M7, **431**
Moutajup Vic. 550 G4
Mowbray Tas. 627 K8, 629 G9
Mowbray NP Qld 606 D1, 607 D4, 613 L5
Mowbray Park NSW 510 E12, 517 D2
Mowen WA 572 B8, 574 B10
Moyhu Vic. 543 I8, 544 F6
Moyreisk Vic. 549 K10
Moyston Vic. 551 I2

Muchea WA 570 E1, 571 C2, 574 C4, 576 C7
Muckadilla Qld 608 F6
Mud Island NSW 514 F8, 515 B12, 523 M4
Mud Island Qld 604 C6, 609 K1, 611 N11
Mud (Bungumba) Island Qld 599 H5, 600 F3, 602 H10, 609 N9
Mud Islands Vic. 531 B10, 532 F6, 536 H9, 540 B7, 551 P8
Mudamuckla SA 567 N8
Mudgee NSW 522 H2, **72**
Mudgeeraba Qld 516 G1, 525 O1, 600 F10, 601 E8, 609 N10, 434
Mudgegonga Vic. 543 K8, 545 I5
Mudginberri NT 589 O3, 590 G4
Mudjimba Qld 602 G3, 603 F11
Mudjimba (Old Woman) Island Qld 602 H3, 603 F11, 609 N7
Mudlo NP Qld 603 B8, 609 M6
Muggleton Qld 608 G6
Muir Island WA 581 I5, 584 D6
Muiron Islands Marine Management Area WA 575 B2
Mukinbudin WA 574 G2, 576 E6
Muknab Rock Qld 614 C1
Mulambin Qld 604 C4, 611 N10
Mulbring NSW 509 F3, 514 B9
Mulcra Vic. 526 B9, 546 C11, 559 O10, 568 H4
Mulgildie Qld 604 C10, 609 K3
Mulgoa NSW 510 G8, 523 J6
Mullaley NSW 524 F9
Mullalyup WA 572 F6, 574 C9
Mullaway NSW 516 E11, 525 N7
Mullenderee NSW 521 L7, 522 H12
Mullengandra NSW 522 B12, 527 O12, 543 L5, 545 K1
Mullengudgery NSW 524 A10, 529 P10
Mullewa WA 575 E12, 576 B3, **324**
Mulli Mulli NSW 516 D3, 525 M2, 609 M11
Mullindolingong Vic. 543 L9, 545 J7
Mullion Creek NSW 522 G4
Mullumbimby NSW 516 G4, 525 O3, 609 N12, **72**
Mulpata SA 526 A8, 559 N10, 568 F4
Mulwala NSW 527 M12, 542 H5, 544 D1, 205, **73**
Mumballup WA 572 G5, 574 D8, 576 C9
Mumbannar Vic. 550 C5, 568 H12
Mumbil NSW 522 G3
Mumblin Vic. 538 F8, 551 I8
Mumdjin NSW 601 B11
Mumford Island Qld 604 B1, 611 M8
Mummel Gulf NP NSW 515 C5, 525 J10
Mummulgum NSW 516 D5, 525 M3, 609 M12
Munbilla Qld 600 A8
Mundaring WA 570 G5, 571 E4, 574 C5, 576 C7, **324**
Mundaring Weir WA 570 G6, 571 E5, 324
Mundijong WA 570 F10, 571 D7, 576 C8
Mundoona Vic. 542 E6
Mundoora SA 556 F1, 559 I5, 560 H12

Mundrabilla Roadhouse WA 566 A8, 577 O6
Mundubbera Qld 604 C12, 609 K4, **431**
Mundulla SA 526 A12, 548 A7, 568 G7, 230
Mungalawurru NT 593 I9
Mungallala Qld 608 D6
Mungana Qld 606 A3, 613 J6, 405
Mungar Qld 603 D6, 609 M5
Mungerannie Roadhouse SA 563 I8, 618 B8
Mungeribar NSW 522 E1, 524 B12
Mungery NSW 522 D2
Mungindi NSW 524 E2, 608 F11
Mungkan Kandju NP Qld 614 C9, 449
Mungkarta NT 593 J11
Munglinup WA 576 H9
Mungo NP NSW 526 F3, 547 K1, 27, 100
Mungungo Qld 604 C10, 609 K3, 429
Munro Vic. 541 L6
Munster WA 570 D9, 571 C6
Muntadgin WA 574 H4, 576 E7
Murabar (Channel Island) Islet Qld 614 C1
Muradup WA 574 E9
Murangi Islet Qld 614 D2
Murarrie Qld 599 F7
Murchison Vic. 542 D8, 191
Murchison WA 575 E9, 578 B11
Murchison East Vic. 542 E8
Murdinga SA 558 D5
Murdoch Island Qld 613 K1, 614 H11
Murdunna Tas. 623 N6, 625 M8
Murga NSW 522 E4
Murgenella NT 590 G2
Murgheboluc Vic. 536 E7, 551 N7
Murgon Qld 603 A9, 609 L6, **432**
Murmungee Vic. 543 J8, 544 H5
Murphys Creek Vic. 535 C3, 549 M10
Murra Warra Vic. 548 G8
Murrabit Vic. 526 H10, 549 N3, 27, 171
Murradoc Vic. 532 E4
Murramarang NP NSW 519 F6, 521 M5, 522 H12, 523 I12, 29
Murrami NSW 527 N7
Murrangingi Island WA 581 K2, 584 G2
Murrara Island WA 581 K3, 584 G4
Murrawal NSW 524 E10
Murray Bridge SA 554 H11, 559 K10, 568 D3, **249**
Murray River NP SA 526 A6, 546 B5, 559 N8, 568 G1, 228, 258
Murray–Sunset NP Vic. 526 C7, 546 D9, 559 P9, 568 H2, 180, 182
Murray Town SA 559 I3, 560 H11, 246
Murrays Run NSW 509 C4, 523 K4
Murrayville Vic. 526 B9, 546 C11, 548 C1, 559 O10, 568 H4, **182**
Murrindal Vic. 519 A11, 539 A9, 541 P3
Murrindindi Vic. 534 D2, 537 M2, 540 E2, 542 E12, 544 A11
Murringo NSW 519 B1, 522 E7, 105
Murroon Vic. 536 C10, 538 D3, 551 L9
Murrumba Qld 602 B8

Murrumbateman NSW 518 D1, 519 C3, 522 F9
Murrumburrah NSW 519 B2, 522 E8, 44
Murrungowar Vic. 519 B11, 539 C10
Murrurundi NSW 524 H11, **73**
Murrurundi Pass NP NSW 524 H11
Murtoa Vic. 548 H9, 170
Murun Murula NT 593 O7
Murwillumbah NSW 516 G2, 525 O2, 600 F12, 609 N11, **74**
Museums Island WA 581 J3, 584 F4
Musgrave Hill Qld 601 F5
Musgrave Roadhouse Qld 614 E12
Mushroom Reef Marine Sanctuary Vic. 533 I10, 537 I11, 540 C8
Musk Vic. 535 E9, 536 E2, 551 N3
Muskerry East Vic. 542 B8, 549 P10
Musselboro Tas. 627 L8
Musselroe Bay Tas. 627 O5
Muswellbrook NSW 523 K2, **74**
Mutarnee Qld 606 F9, 613 M10
Mutawintji NP NSW 528 E7, 37
Mutchilba Qld 606 C3, 607 B8, 613 K6
Mutdapilly Qld 600 A7, 609 M10
Mutitjulu NT 594 E10, 596 E10
Muttaburra Qld 610 C8, 617 O8, **432**
Muttama NSW 519 A3, 522 D9
Mutton Bird Island Tas. 624 E10
Mutton Bird Island Vic. 538 G10, 551 J10, 187
Muttonbird Island NSW 515 H1, 516 E12, 525 N8, 45
Myall Vic. 526 H10, 549 N3
Myall Lakes NP NSW 514 G5, 515 D11, 523 N3, 36
Myall Mundi NSW 524 B11
Myall Plains NSW 527 M10, 542 H2
Myalla Tas. 626 E5
Myalup WA 572 D2, 574 C8, 576 C9, 289
Myamyn Vic. 550 E6
Mylestom NSW 515 H1, 516 D12, 525 M8
Mylor SA 553 E9, 554 D10, 555 G3
Myola Qld 607 E6
Myola Vic. 542 B8, 549 P9
Mypolonga SA 554 H10, 559 L9, 568 D3
Myponga SA 555 E7, 556 H9, 559 J10, 568 B4, 267
Myponga Beach SA 555 D7, 556 G9, 559 J10, 568 B4
Myres Island WA 581 K2, 584 H3
Myrla SA 559 N8, 568 F2
Myrniong Vic. 535 F11, 536 F4, 540 A3, 551 O4
Myrrhee Vic. 537 P6, 540 H4, 543 I9, 544 F7
Myrtle Bank Tas. 627 L7
Myrtle Creek Vic. 535 G5, 542 A10, 549 O11, 551 O1
Myrtleford Vic. 543 J8, 544 H6, **182**
Myrtleville NSW 519 E2, 522 H8
Mysia Vic. 526 H12, 549 M7
Mystic Park Vic. 526 H10, 549 M3
Mywee Vic. 542 F4

N

Nabageena Tas. 626 C4
Nabawa WA 575 D12, 576 A3
Nabiac NSW 515 D9, 523 N2
Nabowla Tas. 627 L6
Nackara SA 559 L3, 561 J10
Nadda SA 526 B7, 546 B8, 559 O8, 568 H2
Nagambie Vic. 542 D9, **182**
Nagheer (Mount Ernest) Island Qld 614 D1
Nagoorin Qld 604 D8, 609 K2
Nairana NP Qld 610 G6
Nairne SA 553 G9, 554 E10, 555 H3, 559 K9, 568 C3
Nala Tas. 625 L4
Nalangil Vic. 536 A9, 538 B2, 551 K8
Nalinga Vic. 542 G7, 544 B4
Nalya WA 574 E5
Namadgi NP ACT 518 C8, 519 C5, 520 F5, 522 F12, 539 E1, 83, 119
Nambour Qld 602 F3, 603 E11, 609 N7, **433**
Nambrok Vic. 541 J6
Nambucca Heads NSW 515 H2, 525 M9, **75**
Nambung NP WA 574 A2, 576 B5, 296
Nana Glen NSW 516 D11, 525 M7
Nanango Qld 603 A11, 609 L7, **433**
Nanarup WA 573 E11, 574 H11
Nandaly Vic. 526 F9, 547 I12, 549 I1
Nandi Qld 609 K8
Nanga WA 571 E11, 574 C7
Nangana Vic. 534 D9, 537 L6, 540 E5
Nangar NP NSW 522 E5, 49
Nangari SA 526 B6, 546 B7, 559 O8, 568 H2
Nangeenan WA 574 G3, 576 E6
Nangiloc Vic. 526 E7, 546 H7
Nangkita SA 555 F6, 559 J10, 568 B4
Nangur NP Qld 603 A8, 609 L6
Nangus NSW 519 A3, 522 D9, 543 P1
Nangwarry SA 550 A3, 568 G11
Nanneella Vic. 542 C6
Nannup WA 572 F8, 574 C10, 576 C10, **325**
Nanson WA 575 D12
Nantabibbie SA 559 K3, 561 J10
Nantawarra SA 556 G3, 559 I6
Nanutarra Roadhouse WA 575 D4, 578 A5, 582 B10
Napoleons Vic. 535 C11, 536 C4, 551 M4
Napperby SA 559 I4, 560 H11
Napranum Qld 614 B7
Nar Nar Goon Vic. 534 D12, 537 M8, 540 E6
Nar Nar Goon North Vic. 533 P2
Nara Qld 609 L8, 612 G11
Naracoopa Tas. 625 P11
Naracoorte SA 548 A10, 568 G9, **249**
Naracoorte Caves NP SA 548 A11, 568 G9, 162, 249
Naradhan NSW 527 N5
Naraling WA 575 D12, 576 A3
Narangba Qld 599 D3, 600 D2, 602 F9
Narara NSW 509 D8, 511 O2
Narawntapu NP Tas. 627 I6, 629 D6, **471**, 490

Narbethong Vic. 534 E5, 537 M4,
540 F3
Nareen Vic. 550 D2
Narellan NSW 510 G10, 517 F1,
519 H1, 523 J7
Narembeen WA 574 G4, 576 E7
Nares Island WA 577 J9
Naretha WA 577 L5
Nariel Vic. 520 A10, 543 O8,
545 N5, 156
Naringal Vic. 538 E8, 550 H8
Narkoola NP Qld 608 C9
Naroghid Vic. 538 G7, 551 J7
Narooma NSW 519 F8, 521 L10, **75**
Narrabri NSW 524 F7, **75**
Narrabri West NSW 524 F7
Narracan Vic. 537 P10, 540 H7
Narrandera NSW 522 A8, 527 N8,
76
Narraport Vic. 526 F11, 549 J5
Narrawa Tas. 626 G7, 628 F3
Narrawallee NSW 521 N4
Narraweena NSW 508 G5,
509 C11, 511 M7
Narrawong Vic. 550 D7
Narre Warren Vic. 531 G8, 533 M2,
534 B11, 537 K7, 540 D6
Narre Warren East Vic. 533 N1
Narre Warren North Vic. 533 N1,
534 B10, 537 K7
Narre Warren South Vic. 533 M3
Narrewillock Vic. 549 L6
Narridy SA 559 J5, 560 H12
Narrien Range NP Qld 610 G9
Narrikup WA 573 C9, 574 G11
Narrogin WA 574 E7, 576 D9, **325**
Narromine NSW 522 E1, 524 B12,
49
Narrung SA 559 K11, 568 C5
Narrung Vic. 526 G8, 547 K9
Nashdale NSW 522 F4
Nathalia Vic. 527 K12, 542 E5, 162
Natimuk Vic. 548 F9, **183**
National Park Tas. 622 E2, 625 I6
Natone Tas. 626 F6, 628 E1
Nattai NSW 510 D11, 517 C1,
519 G1, 523 I7
Nattai NP NSW 510 D12, 517 C2,
519 G2, 523 I8, 35
Natte Yallock Vic. 535 A4, 549 L11
Natural Bridge Qld 516 G2,
525 O1, 600 E11, 601 B10
Natya Vic. 526 G8, 547 K10
Nauiyu NT 588 C12, 590 D7
Naval Base WA 570 D9, 571 C7
Navarre Vic. 549 J10
Navigators Vic. 535 D11, 536 D3,
551 M4
Nayook Vic. 534 H10, 537 O7,
540 G5, 199
Neale Junction WA 577 M1,
579 M11
Neales Flat SA 554 G1, 559 K7,
568 D1
Neath NSW 509 E2, 514 A8
Nebo Qld 605 E9, 611 J7, 425
Neck Island Tas. 624 C2, 626 C12
Nectar Brook SA 559 I2, 560 G10
Neds Corner Vic. 526 C6, 546 E6,
559 P7
Needle Rock WA 581 J4, 584 E5
Needle Rocks Tas. 624 F11
Needles Tas. 627 I8, 629 C11
Neerabup NP WA 570 B2, 571 B3,
574 B4, 576 B7

Neerdie Qld 603 E8, 609 N6
Neerim Vic. 534 H10, 537 O7,
540 G5
Neerim East Vic. 534 H11, 537 O7,
540 G6
Neerim Junction Vic. 534 H10,
537 O7, 540 G5
Neerim South Vic. 534 H11,
537 O7, 540 G6, 199
Neeworra NSW 524 E3, 608 G12
Neika Tas. 622 H6, 625 K7
Neilborough Vic. 535 F1, 542 A8,
549 O9
Neilborough East Vic. 535 G1,
542 A7, 549 O9
Neilrex NSW 524 E11
Nelia Qld 617 K3
Nelligen NSW 519 F6, 521 L6,
522 H12, 29
Nelly Bay Qld 605 A1, 606 G10,
610 G1, 613 N11
Nelshaby SA 559 I4, 560 H11
Nelson NSW 508 B3, 511 J5
Nelson Vic. 550 B6, 568 G12, 189
Nelson Bay NSW 514 G8, 515 C12,
523 N4, **76**
Nelson Rocks WA 578 B2, 580 B12,
582 D4
Nelsons Plains NSW 509 H1,
514 D7, 515 A11
Nelungaloo NSW 522 D4
Nemingha NSW 525 I9
Nene Valley SA 568 F12
Nepabunna SA 557 E4, 561 J4
Nerang Qld 516 G1, 525 O1,
600 F9, 601 D6, 609 N10, **433**
Nerang NP Qld 516 G1, 525 O1,
600 F9, 601 D5, 609 N10
Neranwood Qld 600 F11, 601 C8
Nerriga NSW 519 F4, 521 L2,
522 H10
Nerrigundah NSW 519 E7, 521 K9,
71
Nerrin Nerrin Vic. 551 J5
Nerrina Vic. 535 C10, 536 D3,
551 M4
Nerring Vic. 536 A2, 551 K3
Netherby Vic. 526 C11, 548 E6
Nethercote NSW 519 E10, 539 H8
Neuarpurr Vic. 548 B9, 568 H8
Neurea NSW 522 F3
Neuroodla SA 560 H7
Never Fail Islands Qld 600 G8,
601 F2, 609 N10
Nevertire NSW 524 A11, 529 P11
Neville NSW 522 G6
New Angledool NSW 524 B2,
608 E11
New Brighton NSW 516 H3
New Chum Qld 599 B9, 600 C5,
602 D12
New England NP NSW 515 E1,
516 B12, 525 L8, 48
New Gisborne Vic. 531 A2,
535 H10, 536 H3, 540 B2, 551 P3
New Island WA 577 I9
New Italy NSW 516 F6, 525 N4, 50
New Lambton NSW 509 G3, 514 D9
New Mollyann NSW 524 E10
New Norcia WA 574 C2, 576 C6,
326
New Norfolk Tas. 622 G4, 625 J6,
487
New Residence SA 526 A6, 559 N7,
568 F1

New Town Tas. 621 C7, 623 I5
New Well SA 559 M7, 565 I2,
568 E1, 594 G11
New Year Island Tas. 625 O10
New Year Island WA 577 K9
Newborough Vic. 537 P9, 540 H7
Newbridge NSW 522 G5, 33
Newbridge Vic. 535 D3, 549 M10
Newbury Vic. 535 F9, 536 F2,
540 A2, 542 A12, 551 O3
Newcastle NSW 509 H3, 514 D9,
515 A12, 523 M4, **78**
Newcastle Waters (Marlinja) NT
592 H5, 361
Newdegate WA 576 F8
Newdegate Island WA 573 F6,
574 E12, 576 D11
Newell Qld 606 D1, 607 D3, 430
Newfield Vic. 538 G10, 551 I9
Newham Vic. 535 H8, 536 H1,
540 B1, 542 B12, 551 P3
Newhaven Vic. 533 M11, 537 K11,
540 D8
Newlands WA 572 F6, 574 C9
Newlyn Vic. 535 D9, 536 D2,
551 M3
Newman WA 578 E5, 583 L11, **326**
Newmarket Qld 599 E6, 600 D4,
602 F11
Newmerella Vic. 519 A12, 539 B11,
541 P5
Newnes NSW 523 I4
Newnes Junction NSW 510 C2,
512 F2
Newnham Tas. 629 G9
Newport NSW 508 H4, 509 C10,
511 N6, 523 K6
Newport Vic. 531 C6, 537 I6
Newry Vic. 541 J6
Newry Island Qld 605 F7, 611 K5
Newry Islands NP Qld 605 F7,
611 K5
Newrybar NSW 516 G4, 525 O3
Newstead Tas. 629 G2
Newstead Vic. 535 E6, 549 N12,
551 N1
Newton Boyd NSW 516 B9, 525 L6
Newton Island Qld 614 H11
Newtown NSW 508 F8, 511 L9
Newtown Vic. 535 B11, 536 B4,
551 L4
Ngalanguru Island WA 581 J5,
584 E6
Ngangalala NT 591 K4
Nglayu Island WA 581 K2, 584 G2
Nguiu NT 590 D3
Ngukurr NT 591 K9
Ngul Island Qld 614 C1
Ngunarra NT 593 M7
Ngurtai (Quoin Rock) Islet Qld
614 C1
Nhill Vic. 526 C12, 548 E7, **183**
Nhulunbuy NT 591 N4, **363**
Niagara Park NSW
Niangala NSW 515 A4, 525 J10
Nicholls Point Vic. 546 G6
Nicholls Rivulet Tas. 622 H8,
625 J9
Nicholson Vic. 541 N5
Nicholson Island Qld 614 D2
Nicol (Lyimburrirra) Island NT
591 M6
Nicoll Scrub NP Qld 516 G2,
525 O1, 600 F11, 601 E10,
609 N11

Nicolson Island Qld 605 G5,
611 K4
Niemur NSW 527 I9, 547 O12,
549 O1
Nierinna Tas. 622 H7
Nietta Tas. 626 G7, 628 F3
Night Island Qld 614 F8
Night Island Tas. 624 B12, 627 O2
Nightcap NP NSW 516 F3, 525 O2,
609 N11, 77
Nightcliff NT 588 C2
Nildottie SA 559 L8, 568 E2
Nile Tas. 627 L9
Nillahcootie Vic. 542 G11, 544 D9
Nilma Vic. 537 O9, 540 G7
Nimaguwa Island NT 591 M6
Nimbin NSW 516 F4, 525 O3,
609 N12, **77**
Nimmitabel NSW 519 D8, 520 H11,
539 F5
Ninda Vic. 526 F10, 549 I2
Nindigully Qld 608 F10, 441
Nine Mile Vic. 549 L8
Ninety Mile Beach Marine NP Vic.
541 K8
Ningaloo Marine Park WA 575 B4,
299
Ningi Qld 599 F1, 600 E1, 602 G7
Ninnes SA 556 F3, 559 I6
Ninth Island Tas. 627 L4
Ninyeunook Vic. 526 G11, 549 L5
Nipan Qld 609 I2
Nippering WA 574 F7
Nirranda Vic. 538 E9, 550 H9
Nirranda South Vic. 538 E9, 551 I9
Nitmiluk (Katherine Gorge) NP NT
589 M12, 590 G7, 366
Noarlunga Centre SA 553 B11,
554 A11, 555 E4
Nob Island Qld 614 E5
Nobby Qld 609 L10, 406
Nobby Beach Qld 601 F8, 445
Nobby Island SA 556 C12, 558 G12
Nobbys Creek NSW 601 C12
Nobelius Vic. 533 O1
Noble Island Qld 614 H11
Noble Park Vic. 531 F7, 533 L1,
534 A10, 537 J7
Noccundra Qld 619 I8, 410
Nodlaw Island NT 590 C2
Noel Island Qld 611 L6
Nonda Qld 617 K3
Noojee Vic. 534 H10, 537 O7,
540 G5, 199
Nook Tas. 628 H3, 629 A8
Noonamah NT 588 E4, 590 D5, **363**
Noonameena SA 559 K11, 568 D5
Noonbinna NSW 522 E6
Noondoo Qld 524 D1, 608 F10
Noonga SA 526 B6, 546 B7, 559 O8,
568 H2
Nooramunga Vic. 542 G7, 544 C4
Nooramunga Marine and Coastal
Park Vic. 540 H10, 541 I10, 187
Noorat Vic. 551 I7, 196
Noorinbee Vic. 519 C11, 539 E10
Noorinbee North Vic. 519 C11,
539 E10
Noorong NSW 526 H9, 547 N12,
549 N2
Noorongong Vic. 543 L7, 545 K4
Noosa Heads Qld 602 H1, 603 F10,
609 N7, **436**
Noosa NP Qld 602 G2, 603 F10,
609 N7, 436

Noosaville Qld 602 G1, 603 F10, 437

Nora Creina SA 568 E10

Noradjuha Vic. 548 F10

Norah Head NSW 509 F7, 514 B12, 523 L5

Norahville NSW 509 F7, 514 B12

Nords Wharf NSW 509 F5, 514 C11

Norlane Vic. 532 B2

Norman Island Vic. 540 G11

Normanby Island Qld 606 F3, 607 H9, 613 M7

Normanhurst NSW 508 E5, 511 L6

Normanton Qld 612 D7, 615 G4, **434**

Normanville SA 554 E10, 555 H3, 556 G10, 559 I10, 568 B4, 267

Normanville Vic. 549 M5

Nornakin WA 574 F5

Nornalup WA 573 G6, 574 E12

Norseman WA 577 I7, **326**

North Adelaide SA 553 C7, 554 B8, 555 F2, 218

North Arm Qld 602 F2, 603 E11

North Arm Cove NSW 514 G7, 515 C11

North Beach SA 556 E2, 558 H6

North Bondi NSW 508 G8, 509 C12, 511 M9

North Bourke NSW 529 M5

North Brig Rock Tas. 625 P12

North Dandalup WA 571 D9, 574 C6, 576 C8

North East Crocodile Island NT 591 L3

North East Island Qld 611 M7

North East Regnard Island WA 575 E1, 578 A2, 580 A12, 582 C5

North East Twin Island WA 575 C2, 582 A7

North Eclipse Island WA 581 L1, 584 H1

North Fremantle WA 570 C7, 571 B6

North Goulburn Island NT 590 H2

North Guano Island WA 575 C9, 586 E10

North Haven NSW 515 F7, 525 M12, 66

North Haven SA 553 B5, 554 A7

North Hobart Tas. 621 D7

North Island NT 591 N10, 593 N1

North Island Qld 606 F6, 613 M9, 614 C1

North Island SA 556 A8, 558 F9

North Island WA 575 C12, 582 A7

North Jindong WA 572 B7

North Kangaroo Island WA 575 B9, 586 D9

North Keppel Island Qld 604 C4, 611 N10

North Lilydale Tas. 627 K7, 629 H7

North Maclean Qld 599 D11, 600 D7

North Molle Island Qld 605 F4, 611 K3

North Motton Tas. 626 G6, 628 F1

North Muiron Island WA 575 B3

North Neptunes SA 558 E10

North Page SA 555 C11, 556 G11, 559 I11, 568 A5

North Pasco Island Tas. 624 A9

North Pinjarra WA 571 D9, 574 C6

North Point Island NT 591 N6

North Repulse Island Qld 605 F6, 611 K4

North Richmond NSW 510 H4, 513 N6

North Rock NSW 515 D11, 516 F10, 523 N3, 525 N7

North Rock Qld 605 E4, 611 J3

North Rock WA 581 L2, 584 H2

North Rothbury NSW 514 A6, 523 L3

North Sandy Island WA 575 D2, 582 B6

North Scottsdale Tas. 627 M6

North Shell Island NT 588 D3, 590 D4

North Shields SA 558 D8

North Shore Vic. 532 B3

North Solitary Island NSW 516 F10, 525 N7

North Star NSW 524 H3, 609 I12

North Stradbroke (Minjerriba) Island Qld 600 G6, 609 N9, 387, **434**, 442

North Sydney NSW 508 F7, 511 M8

North Tamborine Qld 600 E9, 601 B4, 609 N10, **434**

North Tumbulgum NSW 601 F12

North Turtle Island WA 578 D1, 580 D11, 583 I2

North Twin Peak Island WA 577 J9

North West Crocodile Island NT 591 K3

North West Island Qld 604 E5, 611 O11

North West Island WA 575 D1, 582 A4

North West Islet Qld 614 C2

North West Rock NSW 516 F10, 525 N7

North West Rock WA 573 D12, 574 G12, 576 E12

North West Solitary Island NSW 516 F10, 525 N7

North West Twin Island WA 580 H5, 584 C7

North West Vernon Island NT 590 D3

North Wollongong NSW 517 F5

Northam WA 571 G2, 574 D4, 576 C7, **327**

Northampton WA 575 D12, 576 A3, **328**

Northcliffe WA 572 H12, 573 C4, 574 D11, 576 C11, **328**

Northdown Tas. 626 H6, 629 B6

Northfield SA 553 C5, 554 B8, 555 F1

Northmead NSW 508 C5, 509 A11, 511 J7

Northumberland Islands NP Qld 605 H8, 611 L6

Northumberland Isles Qld 611 L7

Norval Vic. 549 I12, 551 I2

Norwin Qld 609 K9

Norwood Tas. 629 H3

Notch Island Vic. 541 I11

Notley Hills Tas. 627 J7, 629 F9

Notting WA 574 G5, 576 E8

Notts Well SA 559 M8, 568 E1

Nour Nour NP Qld 604 D11, 609 L4

Nowa Nowa Vic. 541 O5

Nowendoc NSW 515 B6, 525 J11

Nowendoc NP NSW 515 A6, 525 J11

Nowie North Vic. 547 L12, 549 L1

Nowingi Vic. 526 E7, 546 G8

Nowley NSW 524 E5

Nowra NSW 517 D9, 519 G4, 521 O1, 523 I10, **77**

Nowra Hill NSW 517 C10, 519 G4, 521 O1, 523 I10

Nturiya NT 594 H4

Nubba NSW 519 B2, 522 D8

Nudgee Qld 599 F6, 600 E3, 602 F10

Nug Nug Vic. 543 J9, 544 H7

Nuga Nuga NP Qld 608 G2

Nugent Tas. 623 M3, 625 M6

Nuggetty Vic. 535 E5, 549 N11

Nulkaba NSW 509 E2, 514 A8

Nullagine WA 578 F3, 583 L7

Nullamanna NP NSW 525 J5

Nullan Vic. 548 H8

Nullarbor SA 566 G6

Nullarbor NP WA 566 D6, 577 P5, 231

Nullarbor Roadhouse SA 566 G7

Nullawarre Vic. 538 E9, 550 H9

Nullawil Vic. 526 G11, 549 K5

Numbla Vale NSW 519 B8, 520 E12, 539 D5

Numbugga NSW 519 D9, 521 I12, 539 H6

Numbulwar NT 591 L8

Numeralla NSW 519 D7, 520 H9, 539 F3

Numinbah NSW 601 B12

Numinbah Valley Qld 516 G1, 525 O1, 600 E11, 601 B9

Numurkah Vic. 527 K12, 542 F5, 544 A1

Nunamara Tas. 627 L8

Nunawading Vic. 534 A8

Nundah Qld 599 E6

Nundle NSW 525 I10, **79**

Nundroo Roadhouse SA 567 J7

Nunga Vic. 526 E9, 546 H11

Nunga Island Qld 605 G5, 611 K4

Nungarin WA 574 G2, 576 E6

Nungkanangka Island NT 591 L8

Nungurner Vic. 541 N6

Nunjikompita SA 558 A1, 567 N9

Nur Islet Qld 614 C1

Nurcoung Vic. 548 E9

Nurina WA 577 N5

Nurinda Qld 602 A5, 603 C12

Nuriootpa SA 554 F4, 559 K8, 568 C1, **253**

Nurom SA 559 I4, 560 H12

Nurrabiel Vic. 548 F10

Nutfield Vic. 531 F3, 534 A5, 537 K4, 540 D3

Nyabing WA 574 G8, 576 E9

Nyah Vic. 526 G9, 547 L11, 549 L1, 194

Nyah West Vic. 526 G9, 547 L11, 549 L1

Nyarrin Vic. 526 F9, 547 I12, 549 I2

Nyirripi NT 594 D5

Nymagee NSW 529 M11

Nymboi–Binderay NP NSW 516 C10, 525 M7

Nymboida NSW 516 C10, 525 M6, 54

Nymboida NP NSW 516 B8, 525 L5

Nymph Island Qld 613 L1

Nyngan NSW 529 O10, **80**

Nyora Vic. 537 M10, 540 F7

Nypo Vic. 526 D10, 548 F4

Oak Beach Qld 606 D1, 607 E5, 613 L5

Oak Flats NSW 517 F6

Oak Forest Qld 607 E6

Oakbank SA 553 F8, 554 D9, 555 H3, 239

Oakdale NSW 510 E11, 517 D1, 519 G1, 523 J7

Oakey Qld 609 K9, **435**

Oakey Creek NSW 524 F11

Oaklands NSW 527 M10, 543 I3

Oaklands SA 553 B8, 556 E7, 558 H9

Oakleigh Vic. 531 E7, 537 J6, 540 C5

Oaks Tas. 627 J9, 629 F11

Oakvale Vic. 526 G11, 549 L5

Oakview NP Qld 603 C8, 609 M6

Oakwood Tas. 623 M8, 625 M9

Oasis Roadhouse Qld 606 A8, 613 J10

Oatlands Tas. 625 K3, **487**

Oatley NSW 508 D9, 511 K10

Ob Flat SA 550 A5, 568 G12

Obelisk Islet Qld 614 C1

Oberne NSW 520 A3, 522 C10, 543 O3

Oberon NSW 522 H6, **80**

Obley NSW 522 F2

Observation Island NT 591 N10, 593 N1

Observation Island WA 575 C3

Observatory Island WA 577 I9

Obx Creek NSW 516 D9, 525 M6

Ocean Grove Vic. 532 C6, 536 G9, 538 H2, 540 A7, 551 O8, **183**

Ocean Shores NSW 516 H3, 525 O2, 609 N11

Ockley WA 574 F7

Oenpelli NT 589 P2, 590 H4

Officer Vic. 531 H9, 533 O3, 534 C11, 537 L8, 540 E6

Ogilvie WA 575 D11, 576 A2

Ogmore Qld 611 L9

O'Hara Island NSW 519 F6, 521 M5, 523 I12

Okenia Island WA 581 J4, 584 E4

Olary SA 559 N1, 561 M9

Old Adaminaby NSW 519 B7, 520 E7, 539 D2

Old Bar NSW 515 E8, 523 O1, 525 L12

Old Beach Tas. 621 B2, 623 I4, 625 K6

Old Bonalbo NSW 516 D4, 525 M3, 609 M12

Old Bowenfels NSW 510 B2, 512 C3

Old Farm Tas. 621 B9

Old Junee NSW 522 C9, 527 P9

Old Man Rock NT 588 D3, 590 D4

Old Noarlunga SA 553 B11, 554 A11, 555 E5, 556 H8, 559 J10, 568 B4, 244

Old Owen Springs NT 596 G5

Old Tallangatta Vic. 543 M7, 545 K3

Old Tyabb Vic. 533 L7

Old Warrah NSW 524 H11

Olden Island Qld 605 F4, 611 J3

Oldina Tas. 626 E5

Olinda NSW 523 I3

Olinda Vic. 531 G6, 534 B9, 537 L6, 540 E5, **184**

Olio Qld 617 L6
Olive Island SA 567 N10
Oliver Island WA 581 K2, 584 G2
Olympic Dam Village SA 560 E3, 259
O'Malley SA 566 G4
Ombersley Vic. 536 C8, 538 D1, 551 M7
Omeo Vic. 541 M1, 543 M12, 545 M11, **184**
Onad Island WA 581 J5, 584 E7
Ondit Vic. 536 B8, 538 C1, 551 L8
One Arm Point WA 580 H5, 584 C8
One Tree NSW 527 J6
One Tree Island NSW 514 G7, 515 C11, 523 M3
One Tree Island Qld 604 F6, 611 P11
Ongerup WA 574 H9, 576 F10
Onkaparinga River NP SA 553 B11, 554 A11, 555 E4, 556 H8, 559 J10, 568 B3, 244
Onslow WA 575 C2, 582 A8, **329**
Oodla Wirra SA 559 K3, 561 J10
Oodnadatta SA 562 B6, **251**
Oolambeyan NP NSW 527 K8
Ooldea SA 567 I3
Oombulgurri WA 581 N3, 585 L4
Oonah Tas. 626 E6, 628 B1
Oondooroo Qld 617 L7
Oonoonba Qld 605 A1, 606 G10
Oorindi Qld 615 G11, 617 I3
Ootann Qld 606 A4, 613 J7
Ootha NSW 522 C3, 527 P3
Opalton Qld 617 K9, 449
Ophir NSW 522 G4, 81
Opossum Bay Tas. 623 J7, 625 K8
Ora Banda WA 576 H4
Orange NSW 522 G4, **81**
Orange Grove WA 570 F7, 571 D5
Orangeville NSW 510 F10, 519 G1, 523 J7
Oranmeir NSW 519 E6, 521 J6, 522 G12
Orbost Vic. 519 A12, 539 B11, **185**
Orchard Rocks Qld 606 G10, 613 N11
Orchid Beach Qld 603 H3, 609 O4
Orford Tas. 623 N2, 625 M5, 495
Orford Vic. 550 F7
Organ Pipes NP Vic. 531 C4, 536 H4, 540 B3, 551 P5, 145
Orielton Tas. 623 K3, 625 L6
Orient Point NSW 517 E10, 521 P1
Ormeau Qld 599 G12, 600 F7, 601 C1
Ormiston Qld 599 H8, 600 F5, 602 H12
Orobillah Island NSW 514 F7, 515 B11, 523 M3
Orpheus (Goolboddi) Island Qld 606 F8, 613 N10
Orpheus Island NP Qld 606 F8, 613 N10, 415, **435**
Orroroo SA 559 J3, 561 I10
Orrtipa-Thurra NT 595 M5
Orton Island Qld 614 E5
Orton Park NSW 522 H5
Orunyah Island NT 591 M6
Osborne SA 553 B5, 554 A7, 556 H7
Osborne Island Qld 604 A1, 611 M8
Osbornes Flat Vic. 543 K7, 545 I4
Osmaston Tas. 627 I8, 629 D11
Osmington WA 572 C8, 574 B10

Osprey Island Qld 613 L1
Osprey Rock Qld 611 M7
Osterley Tas. 625 I3
Otago Tas. 621 C4, 623 I4, 625 K7
Otford NSW 517 H3
Otterbourne Island Qld 604 B1, 611 M8
Oura NSW 522 C9, 527 P9, 543 N1
Ourimbah NSW 509 D7, 511 O2, 523 L5
Ournie NSW 520 A6, 522 C12, 543 O5, 545 O1
Ouse Tas. 625 I4
Outer Harbor SA 553 B4, 554 A7, 556 H6, 559 J8, 568 B2
Outer Newry Island Qld 605 F7, 611 K5
Outer Rocks Qld 604 C4, 611 N10
Outer Sister Island Tas. 624 B8
Outtrim Vic. 537 M11, 540 F8
Ouyen Vic. 526 E8, 546 H11, **186**
Ovens Vic. 543 J9, 544 H6
Overhanging Rock WA 575 D1, 582 A5
Overland Corner SA 526 A5, 559 N7, 568 F1
Overlander Roadhouse WA 575 D9, 586 H9
Ovingham SA 554 B8, 555 F2
Owanyilla Qld 603 D6, 609 M5
Owen SA 554 B2, 556 H4, 559 J7, 568 B1
Owen Island WA 577 J9
Owens Gap NSW 523 K1, 524 H12
Oxenford Qld 600 F8, 601 D3
Oxley NSW 527 I6, 547 O6, 58
Oxley Qld 599 D8, 600 D5, 602 E12
Oxley Vic. 543 I8, 544 F5, 178
Oxley Island NT 590 G1
Oxley Wild Rivers NP NSW 515 D3, 516 A12, 525 K9, 26, 97
Oyster Cove Tas. 622 H8, 625 J8
Oyster Rocks Tas. 624 B11, 627 O1
Ozenkadnook Vic. 548 C10, 568 H9

P

Paaratte Vic. 538 F9, 551 I9
Pacific Palms NSW 515 E10, 523 N3
Packsaddle Roadhouse NSW 528 D6, 561 P4
Paddington NSW 529 K11, 14
Paddington Qld 599 E7, 600 D4, 602 F11, 383
Paddys Island Tas. 627 P8
Padthaway SA 568 F8, 230
Paignie Vic. 526 D8, 546 G11
Pains Island Qld 615 C2
Painswick Vic. 535 C3, 549 M10
Pakenham Vic. 531 H9, 533 O3, 534 C11, 537 L8, 540 E6, 172
Pakenham South Vic. 533 P4
Pakenham Upper Vic. 533 P2
Palana Tas. 624 A9
Palfrey Island Qld 613 L1
Palgarup WA 572 H9, 573 B1, 574 D10
Pallamallawa NSW 524 G4
Pallara Qld 600 D5, 602 F12
Pallarenda Qld 605 A1, 606 G10, 610 G1, 613 N11
Palm Beach NSW 508 H3, 509 C10, 511 N5, 523 K6

Palm Beach Qld 516 H2, 525 O1, 600 G11, 601 F9, 399
Palm Cove Qld 606 D2, 607 F6, 613 L5, **435**
Palm Dale NSW 511 O1
Palm Grove NSW 509 D7, 511 N1
Palmdale NSW 509 D7
Palmer SA 554 G8, 559 K9, 568 D3
Palmer River Roadhouse Qld 613 K4
Palmers Island NSW 516 F8, 525 N5
Palmers Oakey NSW 522 H4
Palmerston NT 588 D3, 590 D4
Palmerston Rocks NP Qld 606 E4, 607 G12, 613 M7
Palmgrove NP (Scientific) Qld 608 H3
Palms NP, The, Qld 603 A12, 609 L8, **433**
Palmwoods Qld 602 F4, 603 E11
Paloona Tas. 626 H6, 628 G2
Paluma Qld 606 E9, 613 M11
Paluma Range NP Qld 606 E9, 610 F1, 613 M10, 415
Pambula NSW 519 E10, 539 H7, 71
Pambula Beach NSW 519 E10, 539 H7, 71
Pampas Qld 609 K9
Pandora Reef Qld 606 F9, 613 M10
Panitya Vic. 526 B9, 546 B11, 548 B1, 559 O10, 568 H4
Panmure Vic. 538 E7, 550 H8
Pannawonica WA 575 E2, 578 A3, 582 D7
Pannikin Island Qld 599 H10, 600 F6, 603 F7, 609 N9
Panorama Heights Tas. 629 C4
Pantapin WA 574 F4
Panton Hill Vic. 531 G4, 534 A6, 537 K4
Paper Beach Tas. 629 F8
Pappinbarra NSW 515 E5
Papunya NT 594 F6
Para Hills SA 553 D5, 554 C7
Paraburdoo WA 575 G4, 578 C5, 582 G11
Parachilna SA 557 A7, 560 H5
Paradise Tas. 626 H8, 628 G4, 629 A9
Paradise Vic. 536 B12, 538 B5, 549 J10, 551 L10
Paradise Beach Vic. 541 L7, 192
Paradise Point Qld 525 O1, 600 G8, 601 F3
Paradise Waters Qld 601 F6
Parafield SA 553 D5, 554 C7
Parafield Gardens SA 554 B7
Parakeelya Island WA 575 D1, 582 A5
Paraparap Vic. 536 E9, 538 F2, 551 N8
Parattah Tas. 625 L4
Parau Island Qld 614 C3
Pardoe Downs Tas. 629 D2
Pardoo Roadhouse WA 578 E1, 580 E11, 583 K2
Parenna Tas. 625 P11
Parilla SA 526 A9, 546 A11, 548 A1, 559 N10, 568 G4
Paringa SA 526 B5, 546 B5, 559 O7, 568 G1, 258
Park Beach Tas. 623 L5
Parkdale Vic. 533 K1
Parkers Corner Vic. 540 H6

Parkerville WA 570 G4, 571 D4
Parkes NSW 522 E4, **81**
Parkham Tas. 627 I7, 629 C9
Parkhurst Qld 604 B5, 611 M10
Parkville NSW 523 K1, 524 H12
Parndana SA 556 C11, 558 G11, 241
Parnella Tas. 627 P8
Paroo–Darling NP NSW 528 G7, 529 I8, 100
Parrakie SA 559 N10, 568 F4
Parramatta NSW 508 C6, 509 A12, 511 J8, 523 K6, 17
Parrawe Tas. 626 E6, 628 B2
Parry Island WA 581 K2, 584 G2
Partney Island SA 558 E8
Partridge Island Tas. 622 G11, 625 J10
Paru NT 590 D3
Paruna SA 526 A7, 546 A8, 559 O8, 568 G2
Parwan Vic. 535 G12, 536 G4, 540 A4, 551 O5
Pascal Island WA 581 K2, 584 G2
Paschendale Vic. 550 D4
Pasco Island WA 575 C1, 577 I9, 581 I5, 582 A6, 584 C8
Paskeville SA 556 F3, 559 I6
Pasley Island WA 577 K9
Passage Island Qld 614 C1
Passage Island Tas. 624 C12, 627 P3
Passage Island WA 575 D2, 578 A3, 582 B6
Passage Islands Qld 604 D6, 611 N12
Passage Islet Qld 605 E4, 611 J3
Pata SA 526 A7, 546 A7, 559 N8, 568 G2
Patchewollock Vic. 526 D9, 546 G12, 548 G2, 168
Pateena Tas. 627 K9, 629 G11
Paterson NSW 514 C6, 515 A11, 523 L3
Patersonia Tas. 627 L7
Patho Vic. 542 B5, 549 P6
Patonga NSW 508 H2, 509 C9, 511 N4
Patricia Island WA 581 K2, 584 G2
Patrick Estate Qld 600 A3, 602 B10
Patterson Lakes Vic. 533 K3
Patyah Vic. 548 C10, 568 H9
Paupong NSW 519 B8, 520 E11, 539 C5
Pawleena Tas. 623 L3, 625 L6
Pawtella Tas. 625 L3
Paxton NSW 509 D3
Payne Island NT 591 N11, 593 N2
Paynes Crossing NSW 509 B2, 523 K4
Paynes Find WA 575 H12, 576 D3
Paynesville Vic. 541 N6, **186**
Peaceful Bay WA 573 G6, 574 E12, 576 D11
Peachester Qld 602 F5, 603 E12
Peacock Island NT 590 G1
Peak Charles NP WA 576 H8, 327
Peak Crossing Qld 599 A11, 600 B7, 609 M10
Peak Downs Qld 605 D11, 611 I8
Peak Hill NSW 522 E2, 601 G10, 82
Peak Hill WA 575 H7, 578 E8
Peak Island Qld 604 C5, 611 N11
Peak Island WA 575 C2

Peak (Perforated) Island Qld 604 C3, 611 N9
Peak Range NP Qld 605 C12, 611 I9
Peak View NSW 519 D7, 520 H8, 539 G2
Peake SA 559 M10, 568 E4
Pearce Islet NT 591 N10, 593 N1
Pearcedale Vic. 531 F10, 533 L5, 537 K9, 540 D7
Pearl Beach NSW 508 H2, 509 C9, 511 N4, 102
Pearshape Tas. 625 O12
Pearson Islands WA 577 J10
Pearson Isles SA 558 A6
Peats Ridge NSW 509 C7, 511 N1, 523 K5
Pebbly Beach NSW 519 F6, 521 M6, 523 I12
Pecked Island WA 581 I5, 584 C8
Peebinga SA 526 B8, 546 B9, 559 O9, 568 H3
Peechelba Vic. 527 M12, 543 I6, 544 E2
Peechelba East Vic. 543 I6, 544 E2
Peel NSW 522 H5
Peel (Turkrooar) Island Qld 600 G5, 602 H12, 609 N9
Peelwood NSW 519 E1, 522 G7
Peenacar Islet Qld 614 D1
Pegarah Tas. 625 P11
Pekina SA 559 J3, 561 I10
Pelaw Main NSW 509 F2, 514 B8
Pelham Tas. 622 G1, 625 J5
Pelican Island Qld 604 C5, 605 F5, 611 N10, 614 F10
Pelican Island Tas. 624 C11, 627 P2
Pelican Island Vic. 531 G12, 533 N9, 537 K10, 540 E8
Pelican Island WA 575 C8, 581 O3, 585 M3, 586 F6, 590 A9
Pelican Rock Qld 604 C5, 611 M8
Pelican Rocks WA 575 F1, 578 B2, 580 B12, 582 E4
Pella Vic. 526 D11, 548 F4, 171
Pelorus (North Palm) (Yanooa) Island Qld 606 F8, 613 N10
Pelverata Tas. 622 G7, 625 J8
Pemberton WA 572 H11, 573 B3, 574 D11, 576 C11, **329**
Pemberton Island WA 575 E1, 578 B2, 580 B12, 582 E4
Pembroke NSW 515 F5, 525 L11
Penarie NSW 526 H7, 547 M7
Penderlea NSW 519 B8, 520 D10, 539 C4
Pendle Hill NSW 508 B6, 511 J7
Penguin Tas. 626 G6, **488**
Penguin Island SA 568 E10
Penguin Island Tas. 623 I11, 625 K10
Penguin Island WA 570 C11, 571 B8, 574 B6, 576 B8, 332
Penguin Islet Tas. 626 B2
Penna Tas. 623 K4
Pennant Hills NSW 508 D5, 509 A11, 511 K7
Penneshaw SA 556 F11, 559 I11, 568 A5, 243
Pennyroyal Vic. 536 C10, 538 D3, 551 M9
Penola SA 550 A2, 568 G10, **251**
Penong SA 567 K8, 231
Penrice SA 554 F4
Penrith NSW 510 H6, 513 M11, 523 J6

Penrith Island Qld 611 L5
Penrose NSW 517 A7, 519 F3, 523 I9
Penshurst NSW 511 K10
Penshurst Vic. 550 G5, 165
Pentecost Island Qld 605 G5, 611 K4
Pentland Qld 610 D3, 617 P3
Penwortham SA 559 J6
Penzance Tas. 623 N8, 625 M8
Peppermint Grove WA 572 D5, 574 B9, 279
Peppers Plains Vic. 526 D12, 548 G6
Peppimenarti NT 581 P2, 585 P1, 590 C8
Percy Isles NP Qld 611 M7
Percydale Vic. 549 K11, 551 K1
Peregian Beach Qld 602 H2, 603 F10, 609 N7, 437
Perekerten NSW 526 H8, 547 N10
Perenjori WA 576 C4, 321
Perenna Vic. 526 C11, 548 E5
Perforated Island SA 558 C8
Pericoe NSW 519 D10, 539 G8
Perisher NSW 519 A8, 520 C10, 539 B4, 61
Perkins Island Tas. 626 C3
Perkins Reef Vic. 535 E5, 549 N11, 551 N1
Peron Island North NT 590 C6
Peron Island South NT 590 C6
Peronne Vic. 548 C9
Perponda SA 559 M9, 568 E3
Perroomba SA 559 J3, 560 H10
Perry Bridge Vic. 541 L6
Perry Island Qld 614 E5
Perseverance Island Qld 605 G5, 611 K4
Perth Tas. 627 K9, 629 H11, 486
Perth WA 570 D6, 571 C5, 574 C5, 576 C7, **272**
Perthville NSW 522 H5
Petcheys Bay Tas. 622 F9, 625 J9
Peterborough SA 559 K3, 561 I11, **252**
Peterborough Vic. 538 F10, 551 I9
Peterhead SA 554 A8, 555 E1
Petersville SA 556 F5, 559 I7
Petford Qld 606 B3, 613 K7
Pethebridge Islets Qld 613 L1
Petina SA 558 A2, 567 N9
Petrel Islands Tas. 626 B2
Petrel Islet Qld 605 G5, 611 K3
Petrie Qld 599 D4, 600 D2, 602 F9
Pheasant Creek Vic. 531 G2, 534 B4, 537 K3, 540 D3
Philips Island Tas. 624 D3
Phillip Island Vic. 533 K10, 537 J10, 540 C8, 139, 158, **186**
Pialba Qld 603 D4
Piallaway NSW 524 H9
Piambie Vic. 526 G8, 547 K9
Piangil Vic. 526 G8, 547 L11
Piangil North Vic. 547 L11
Piawaning WA 574 C2, 576 C6, 326
Picard Island WA 575 F1, 578 B2, 580 B12, 582 E4
Pickard Island Qld 614 E6
Pickering Brook WA 570 G7
Pickersgill Islet Qld 614 E5
Pickertaramoor NT 590 D3
Picnic Bay Qld 605 A1, 606 G10, 613 N11
Picnic Island Qld 603 F5, 604 H12, 609 N4, 611 N12

Picnic Point NSW 527 J11, 542 D4
Picola Vic. 527 K12, 542 D5
Picola North Vic. 542 D5
Picton NSW 510 F12, 517 D2, 519 G1, 523 J7, **82**
Picton WA 572 E4
Pidna NP Qld 603 A12, 609 L7
Pier Millan Vic. 526 F9, 547 I12, 549 I1
Piesseville WA 574 F7
Pig Island Qld 604 D7, 609 L1, 611 N12, 614 E5
Pigeon Hole NT 592 E4
Pigeon Island Qld 605 F5, 611 J3, 614 E7
Pigeon Island WA 575 C12
Pigeon Ponds Vic. 548 E12, 550 E2
Pigface Island SA 558 A2, 567 N10
Piggabeen NSW 516 G2, 600 G11, 601 F10
Piggoreet Vic. 535 A12, 536 B4, 551 L5
Pikedale Qld 525 K2, 609 K11
Pilchers Bridge Vic. 535 G5, 542 A10, 549 O11
Pile Siding Vic. 536 A11, 538 B4
Pillar Valley NSW 516 E9, 525 N6
Pilliga NSW 524 D6, 43
Pilliga NP NSW 524 D7
Pilliga West NP NSW 524 D7
Pilot Hill NSW 519 A5, 520 C4, 522 D11, 543 P4
Pimba SA 560 E6
Pimpama Qld 599 G12, 600 F8, 601 D2
Pimpinio Vic. 548 F8
Pincer Island Qld 605 G6, 611 K4
Pindar WA 575 E12, 576 B3
Pine Creek NT 589 I12, 590 F7, **365**
Pine Gap NT 597 I4
Pine Island Qld 605 F5, 611 K4
Pine Islets Qld 611 M7
Pine Lodge Vic. 542 F7, 544 A3
Pine Peak Island Qld 611 M6
Pine Point SA 556 F5, 559 I8, 568 A2
Pine Ridge NSW 522 F4, 524 G10
Pine Scrub Tas. 624 A9
Pinery SA 554 A2, 556 H4, 559 J7, 568 B1
Pingaring WA 574 H6, 576 F8
Pingelly WA 574 E6, 576 D8, **330**
Pingrup WA 574 H8, 576 F9
Pinjarra WA 571 D10, 574 C6, 576 C8, **330**
Pinnaroo SA 526 B9, 546 B11, 548 B1, 559 O10, 568 H4
Pioneer Tas. 627 N6
Pioneer Peaks NP Qld 605 F7, 611 K5
Pipa Islet Qld 614 C2
Pipalyatjara SA 564 C2, 579 P8, 594 B12
Pipeclay NP Qld 603 F8, 609 N6
Piper Islands NP Qld 614 E6
Pipers Brook Tas. 627 K6, 629 H6
Pipers River Tas. 627 K6, 629 G6
Pipon Island Qld 614 H10
Pira Vic. 526 G9, 547 L12, 549 L1
Pirie Islet Qld 614 D4
Piries Vic. 537 P1, 540 H1, 542 H11, 544 D10
Pirlangimpi NT 590 C2
Pirlta Vic. 526 D6, 546 F7

Pirron Yallock Vic. 536 A9, 538 A2, 551 K8
Pisonia Island Qld 612 A4, 615 E1
Pithara WA 574 D1, 576 C5
Pitt Town NSW 508 B2, 511 I4, 513 P7
Pittong Vic. 536 B4, 551 K4
Pittsworth Qld 609 K9, 447
Plainland Qld 602 A11
Planton Island Qld 605 F5, 611 K3
Pleasant Hills NSW 522 A10, 527 N10, 543 K2
Pleasant Island Qld 604 C4, 611 N10
Plenty Tas. 622 F3, 625 J6
Plenty Vic. 531 F4, 537 J4
Plum Pudding Island Qld 605 G5, 611 K4
Pmara Jutunta NT 595 I4
Poatina Tas. 627 J10
Pobassoo Island NT 591 M3
Poeppel Corner NT 562 H2, 595 P11, 618 A3
Point Addis Marine NP Vic. 536 E10, 538 G3, 551 N8
Point Clare NSW 509 D8, 511 N3
Point Cook Vic. 531 B7, 536 H6, 540 B5, 551 P6
Point Cooke Marine Sanctuary Vic. 531 C7, 536 H6, 540 B5, 551 P6
Point Danger Marine Sanctuary Vic. 532 A7, 536 F9, 538 G2, 551 N8
Point Hicks Marine NP Vic. 519 C12, 539 E12
Point Leo Vic. 531 E12, 533 J9, 537 J10, 540 C8, 164
Point Lonsdale Vic. 531 A11, 532 E6, 536 G9, 540 B7, 551 P8, 190
Point Lookout Qld 600 H4, 609 O9
Point Nepean NP Vic. 531 A11, 532 E7, 536 H9, 540 B7, 551 P8
Point Pass SA 559 K6
Point Samson WA 575 F1, 578 B2, 580 B12, 582 E4, 333
Point Turton SA 556 D7, 558 G9
Pokataroo NSW 524 D4
Pokolbin NSW 509 D2
Police Point Tas. 622 G9, 625 J9
Policemans Point SA 559 L12, 568 D6
Poll Islet Qld 614 D1
Pomborneit Vic. 538 A1, 551 K8
Pomborneit East Vic. 536 A9, 538 A1
Pomborneit North Vic. 538 A1
Pomona Qld 602 F1, 603 E10, 609 N7, **437**
Pomonal Vic. 548 H12, 550 H1
Pompapiel Vic. 549 N8
Pompoota SA 559 L9
Ponde SA 554 H9, 559 L9
Pontville Tas. 623 I3, 625 K6, **488**
Pontypool Tas. 625 N4
Poochera SA 558 B2, 560 A10, 567 O10
Poolaijelo Vic. 548 B12, 550 B1, 568 H10
Poole Island Qld 605 E4, 611 J3
Poolngin Island WA 580 H5, 584 C7
Poona NP Qld 603 E6, 609 N5
Pooncarie NSW 526 F3, 547 I1, 100
Poonindie SA 558 D8
Pooraka SA 554 B8, 555 F1, 556 H7

Pootilla Vic. 535 D10, 536 D3
Pootnoura SA 565 N9
Poowong Vic. 537 M10, 540 F7, 172
Poowong East Vic. 537 N10, 540 F7
Popanyinning WA 574 E6
Pope Island WA 581 I5, 584 C7
Popran NP NSW 508 F1, 509 C7, 511 M2, 523 K5
Porcupine Gorge NP Qld 610 C3, 617 O3, 414
Porcupine Ridge Vic. 535 F8, 536 F1, 551 N2
Porepunkah Vic. 543 K9, 545 I7
Pormpuraaw Qld 612 E1, 614 A12
Porongurup NP WA 573 D9, 574 G11, 576 E11, 321
Port Adelaide SA 553 B6, 554 A8, 555 E1, 556 H7, 559 J9, 568 B3, 218
Port Albert Vic. 541 I10, **186**
Port Alma Qld 604 C6, 611 N11
Port Arthur Tas. 623 M9, 625 M9, **489**
Port Augusta SA 558 H2, 560 G9, **252**
Port Bellarine Vic. 532 E3
Port Bonython SA 558 H3, 560 G11, 264
Port Broughton SA 556 F1, 559 I5, 560 G12, **254**
Port Campbell Vic. 538 F10, 551 I9, **187**
Port Campbell NP Vic. 538 G10, 551 J10, 187
Port Clinton SA 556 F4, 559 I7, 568 A1
Port Davis SA 559 I4, 560 G11
Port Denison WA 576 A4
Port Douglas Qld 606 D1, 607 D4, 613 L5, **437**
Port Elliot SA 555 F8, 556 H10, 559 J11, 568 B5, **254**
Port Fairy Vic. 538 B8, 550 F8, **187**
Port Franklin Vic. 540 H10
Port Gawler SA 553 A3, 554 A6, 556 H6, 559 J8, 568 B2
Port Germein SA 559 I3, 560 G11, 256
Port Gibbon SA 556 B2, 558 F6, 234
Port Hedland WA 578 D1, 580 D11, 582 H3, **330**
Port Hughes SA 556 D3, 558 H6
Port Huon Tas. 622 F8, 625 I9
Port Julia SA 556 F6, 559 I8, 568 A2
Port Keats (Wadeye) NT 581 P2, 585 O2, 590 B8
Port Kembla NSW 517 F5, 519 H2, 523 J8, 103
Port Kenny SA 558 B4, 567 O11, 260
Port Latta Tas. 626 D4
Port Lincoln SA 558 D8, **254**
Port MacDonnell SA 550 A6, 568 G12, **255**
Port Macquarie NSW 515 G6, 525 M11, **84**
Port Minlacowie SA 556 D7, 558 H9
Port Neill SA 558 E6, 262
Port Noarlunga SA 553 A11, 554 A11, 555 E4, 556 H8, 559 J10, 568 B3, 244
Port Phillip Heads Marine NP Vic. 531 A11, 532 E7, 536 G9, 540 B7, 551 P8
Port Pirie SA 559 I4, 560 H11, **256**

Port Rickaby SA 556 D6, 558 H8, 247
Port Smith WA 580 G8, 584 A12
Port Sorell Tas. 627 I6, 629 C6, **488**
Port Victoria SA 556 D5, 558 H8, **256**
Port Vincent SA 556 F6, 559 I8, 568 A2, 259
Port Wakefield SA 556 G4, 559 I7, 568 A1, 226
Port Welshpool Vic. 540 H10, 201
Port Willunga SA 554 A12, 555 E5
Portarlington Vic. 531 A9, 532 E3, 536 H8, 540 B6, 551 P7, 159
Porters Retreat NSW 519 E1, 522 H7
Portland NSW 523 I5, 68
Portland Vic. 550 D8, **188**
Portland Roads Qld 614 E7
Portsea Vic. 531 B11, 532 F7, 536 H9, 540 B7, 551 P8, 195
Poruma Qld 614 E1
Possession Island Qld 614 C2
Possession Island NP Qld 614 C2
Potato Point NSW 519 F7, 521 L9
Potter Island WA 575 D1, 578 A2, 582 C5
Pottsville NSW 516 H3, 525 O2, 609 N11
Pound Creek Vic. 537 N12, 540 F9
Powelltown Vic. 534 F9, 537 N6, 540 F5
Powerful Island WA 581 I5, 584 C7
Powers Creek Vic. 548 C12, 550 C1, 568 H10
Powlett River Vic. 533 P12, 537 L12, 540 E9
Powranna Tas. 627 K9
Poynter Island Qld 605 H10, 611 L7
Pozieres Qld 516 A3, 525 K2, 609 K11
Prairie Qld 610 C4, 617 O4
Prairie Vic. 527 I12, 542 A6, 549 O7
Pratten Qld 525 K1, 609 K10
Precipice NP Qld 609 I3
Premaydena Tas. 623 M8, 625 M8
Premer NSW 524 F10
Prenzlau Qld 602 B11
Preolenna Tas. 626 E5
Preservation Island Tas. 624 B12, 627 O2
Preston Tas. 626 G7, 628 F2
Preston Vic. 531 D5, 537 J5, 540 C4
Preston Beach WA 571 C12, 574 B7, 576 C9
Preston Island WA 575 D1, 578 A2, 582 C5
Prevelly WA 572 A9, 574 B10
Price SA 556 F4, 559 I7, 568 A1
Price Island SA 558 C8
Primbee NSW 517 F6
Prime Seal Island Tas. 624 A10
Primrose Sands Tas. 623 L5, 625 L7
Prince of Wales (Muralag) Island Qld 614 C2
Princetown Vic. 538 G11, 551 J10
Priory Tas. 627 O7
Probable Island NT 591 M3
Prooinga Vic. 526 F8, 547 J10
Propodollah Vic. 548 D6
Proserpine Qld 605 E5, 611 J4, **438**
Prospect Tas. 629 G10
Proston Qld 609 L6, 432

Prudhoe Island Qld 605 H8, 611 L6
Prudhoe Island WA 581 K2, 584 F2
Puckapunyal Vic. 542 D10
Pullabooka NSW 522 D5
Pullen Island SA 555 F8, 556 H10, 559 J11, 568 B5
Pullenvale Qld 599 C8, 600 C5, 602 E11
Pullut Vic. 526 D11, 548 F5
Pulu Islet Qld 614 C1
Pumicestone NP Qld 602 G6, 609 N8
Pumpkin Island Qld 604 C4, 611 N10
Punchbowl NSW 508 D8
Punchbowl Tas. 629 G3
Puncheon Island Tas. 624 C11, 627 P2
Punthari SA 554 H8, 559 L9, 568 D3
Punyelroo SA 559 L8, 568 E2
Pup Island WA 575 D2, 578 A3, 582 B6
Pura Pura Vic. 551 J5
Puralka Vic. 550 B5, 568 H12
Purdie Islands SA 567 L9
Purfleet NSW 515 E8, 523 N1, 525 L12
Purga Qld 599 A10, 600 B6, 609 M9
Purlewaugh NSW 524 E10
Purnim Vic. 538 D7, 550 H7
Purnong SA 559 L9, 568 E3, 245
Purnululu NP WA 581 O6, 585 M9, 592 A5, 309, 316
Purrumbete South Vic. 538 H8
Purrungku Island WA 581 K3, 584 F3
Putty NSW 523 J4
Pyalong Vic. 542 C11
Pyap SA 526 A6, 546 A7, 559 N8, 568 G1
Pyengana Tas. 627 N7
Pygery SA 558 C3, 560 B11
Pymble NSW 508 E5, 509 B11, 511 L7
Pyramid Qld 606 E3, 607 F8
Pyramid Hill Vic. 527 I12, 549 N6, **189**

Quaama NSW 519 E8, 521 J11, 539 H5
Quagering Island WA 573 B5, 574 D11, 576 C11
Quail (Dooenda) Island NT 588 A3, 590 C4
Quail Island Qld 604 A1, 611 L8
Quairading WA 574 E5, 576 D7
Quakers Hill NSW 508 B4, 511 I6
Qualco SA 559 M7
Quambatook Vic. 526 G11, 549 L5, 171
Quambone NSW 524 B8, 43
Quamby Qld 615 E10, 616 G2
Quamby Brook Tas. 627 I9, 629 D11
Quandary NSW 522 B7, 527 P7
Quandialla NSW 522 D6
Quandong Roadhouse NSW 528 C11, 561 P9
Quantong Vic. 548 F9
Queanbeyan NSW 518 F6, 519 D5, 520 H3, 522 F11, **82**

Queen Island WA 581 K3, 584 F3
Queens Domain Tas. 621 D7
Queens Park WA 570 E7
Queenscliff Vic. 531 A10, 532 E6, 536 H9, 540 B7, 551 P8, **189**
Queensferry Vic. 533 O9
Queenstown Tas. 624 D1, 626 D11, 628 A10, **490**
Quellington WA 571 H3, 574 D4
Quilpie Qld 619 L5, **438**
Quince Islet NT 591 N10, 593 N1
Quindalup WA 572 B6
Quindanning WA 571 H12, 574 D7, 576 C9
Quinninup WA 573 C2, 574 D10, 576 C11
Quinns Rocks WA 570 B3, 571 B3, 574 B4, 576 B7
Quirindi NSW 524 H10
Quoiba Tas. 626 H6, 628 H1, 629 A6
Quoin Island NT 581 P3, 585 O3, 590 B9
Quoin Island Qld 604 D7, 609 L1, 611 N12, 614 F6
Quoin Island NP Qld 614 F6
Quoin Islet Qld 614 C2
Quoin Rock WA 572 B10, 574 B10, 576 B11
Quorn SA 559 I1, 560 H9, **257**
Quorrobolong NSW 509 E3, 514 A9
Quoy Island WA 581 K2, 584 F2

R

Rabbit Flat Roadhouse NT 592 C10
Rabbit Island Qld 605 F6, 611 K5
Rabbit Island SA 558 C8
Rabbit Island Vic. 541 I11
Rabbit Island WA 577 I9
Rabbit Rock Vic. 540 H11
Racine Island WA 581 K2, 584 H2
Rag Island Vic. 541 I11
Raglan Qld 604 C6, 611 M11
Raglan Vic. 536 A1, 551 K3
Railton Tas. 626 H7, 628 H3, 629 B8, 493
Rainbow Vic. 526 D11, 548 F5, 171
Rainbow Beach Qld 603 F8, 609 N6, 445
Rainbow Flat NSW 515 E8, 523 N2
Raine Island NP Qld 614 G4
Raleigh NSW 515 H1, 516 D12, 525 M8, 96
Ram Island Vic. 533 M9, 537 K10, 540 D8
Ram Island WA 577 I9
Ramco SA 559 M7, 568 E1
Raminea Tas. 622 F10, 625 I10
Ramingining NT 591 K4
Ramornie NP NSW 516 C9, 525 M6
Ramsbotham Rocks Vic. 540 G12
Ranceby Vic. 537 N10, 540 F8
Rand NSW 522 A11, 527 N11, 543 J3
Randall Island WA 581 K2, 584 G2
Randwick NSW 508 F8, 511 M9, 523 K7
Ranelagh Tas. 622 G6, 625 J8, 482
Ranford WA 571 G10
Ranga Tas. 624 B10, 627 O1
Ranken Islet Qld 604 C2, 611 N9
Rankin Island WA 581 J5, 584 E7
Rankins Springs NSW 527 N5

Rannes Qld 609 I1, 611 L12
Rannoch Tas. 629 C3
Rapid Bay SA 555 B8, 556 G10,
559 I11, 568 A5, 267
Rappville NSW 516 E6, 525 N4
Raragala Island NT 591 M2
Rat Island Qld 604 D6, 611 N12
Rat Island WA 575 C12, 580 H5,
584 C7
Rathdowney Qld 516 E2, 525 N1,
600 B11, 609 M11, 393
Rathmines NSW 509 F4, 514 B10,
523 L4
Rathscar Vic. 535 A5, 549 L11
Rattlesnake Island Qld 606 G9,
613 N11
Raukkan SA 568 C5
Ravensbourne NP Qld 609 L9,
407, 447
Ravensdale NSW 509 D5
Ravenshoe Qld 606 D4, 607 D12,
613 L7, **438**
Ravensthorpe WA 576 G9, **331**
Ravenswood Qld 605 A4, 610 G3,
438
Ravenswood Vic. 535 F4, 549 N11
Ravenswood South Vic. 535 F5,
542 A10, 549 O11
Ravensworth NSW 523 K2
Rawdon Vale NSW 515 B8, 523 M1,
525 J12
Rawlinna WA 577 L5
Raymond Island Vic 541 N6, 186
Raymond Terrace NSW 509 H2,
514 D7, 515 A12, 523 M4, **83**
Raynham Island Qld 604 B1,
611 M8
Raywood Vic. 535 F1, 542 A7,
549 O9
Red Banks SA 559 K5
Red Beach Qld 614 B5
Red Bluff WA 575 B6, 585 I1
Red Clay Island Qld 605 H10,
611 L7
Red Cliff Islands Qld 605 F7,
611 K5
Red Cliffs Vic. 526 E6, 546 G6,
180
Red Hill Vic. 531 D12, 533 I8,
537 I10, 540 C7, 163
Red Hill South Vic. 531 D12,
533 I8, 537 I10
Red Hills Tas. 627 I8, 629 C10
Red Island Qld 614 C3
Red Island WA 576 G10, 581 J4,
584 E4
Red Islet NT 591 N10, 593 N1
Red Islet WA 580 G9
Red Jacket Vic. 540 H4
Red Range NSW 525 K6
Red Rock NSW 516 E10, 525 N7
Red Wallis Islet Qld 614 C3
Redan Vic. 535 C10, 536 C3
Redbank Qld 599 C9, 600 C5,
602 D12
Redbank Vic. 549 K11
Redbank Plains Qld 599 B9,
600 C6, 602 D12
Redbanks SA 554 B4, 556 A2,
558 F6, 559 J8, 568 B1
Redbill Island Qld 599 H11, 600 F7,
609 N10
Redcastle Vic. 542 C9
Redcliffe Qld 599 F4, 600 E2,
602 G9, 609 N9

Redesdale Vic. 535 H6, 542 B10,
549 P11, 551 P1
Redfern NSW 508 F8, 509 B12,
511 L9
Redhead NSW 509 G4, 514 D10
Redhill SA 556 G1, 559 I5, 560 H12,
234
Redland Bay Qld 599 H9, 600 F6,
609 N9
Redmond WA 573 C10, 574 G11
Redpa Tas. 626 B4
Reedy Creek Qld 600 F10, 601 E8
Reedy Creek SA 568 E9
Reedy Creek Vic. 534 A1, 537 K1,
540 D1, 542 D12
Reedy Dam Vic. 526 E11, 549 I5
Reedy Flat Vic. 541 O3
Reedy Marsh Tas. 627 I8, 629 D10
Reef Island Vic. 533 N10, 537 K11,
540 D8
Reef Islet Qld 605 H10, 611 L7
Reefs Island WA 578 C1, 580 C12,
582 G4
Reefton NSW 522 C7, 527 P7
Reekara Tas. 625 O10
Reevesby Island SA 558 E8
Refuge Island Tas. 625 O3
Regans Ford WA 574 B3, 576 B6
Regatta Point Tas. 624 C2, 626 C12
Regents Park NSW 508 C7,
509 A12, 511 K9
Reid WA 566 A5, 577 O4
Reid Islet Qld 605 H8, 611 L6
Reid River Qld 605 A3, 606 G12,
610 G2, 613 N12
Reids Creek Vic. 543 J7, 544 H4, 198
Reids Flat NSW 519 D1, 522 F7
Reidsdale NSW 519 E5, 521 K5,
522 H11
Rekala Island NT 591 M4
Rekuna Tas. 623 J3, 625 K6
Relbia Tas. 627 K8, 629 H11
Reliance Creek NP Qld 605 G7,
611 K5
Remark Island WA 577 I9
Remine Tas. 626 C10
Rendelsham SA 568 F11
Renison Bell Tas. 626 D9
Renmark SA 526 A5, 546 B5,
559 O7, 568 G1, **258**
Renner Springs NT 593 I7, 361
Rennie NSW 527 M11, 542 H4
Renou Islet Qld 611 L6
Repair Island Qld 605 F5, 611 K3
Repulse Islands NP Qld 605 F6,
611 K4
Research Vic. 531 F5, 534 A7
Reservoir Vic. 531 E5, 537 J5
Restoration Island Qld 614 E7
Restoration Island NP Qld 614 E7
Restoration Rock Qld 614 E7
Retreat Tas. 627 K6, 629 H6
Reveley Island WA 581 N2, 585 K2
Revesby NSW 508 C9, 511 J10
Reynella SA 553 B10, 554 B10,
555 E4
Rheban Tas. 623 N2, 625 M6
Rheola Tas. 535 B2, 549 M9
Rhodes NSW 508 D7, 509 A12,
511 K8
Rhyll Vic. 533 M10, 537 K11,
540 D8, 158
Rhymney Reef Vic. 549 I12, 551 I2
Rhyndaston Tas. 625 K5
Rhynie SA 559 J7, 568 B1

Riachella Vic. 549 I10
Rialto Qld 601 E7
Riana Tas. 626 F6, 628 E1
Rich Avon Vic. 549 I8
Richards Island WA 573 C12,
574 G12, 576 E11
Richlands NSW 519 E2, 522 H8
Richlands Qld 600 D5, 602 E12
Richmond NSW 510 H4, 513 N7,
523 J6, **83**
Richmond Qld 617 L3, **439**
Richmond Tas. 623 J3, 625 K6,
467, **490**
Richmond Vic. 531 D6, 537 J5,
540 C4, 134
Richmond Range NP NSW 516 D4,
525 M2, 609 M12, 63
**Ricketts Point Marine Sanctuary
Vic.** 531 D8, 533 J1, 537 J7, 540 C5
Riddells Creek Vic. 531 B2, 536 H3,
540 B2, 551 P3
Ridge Islet Qld 605 H9, 611 L7
Ridgelands Qld 604 A4, 611 M10
Ridgetop Qld 601 D11
Ridgeway Tas. 621 B10, 623 I6
Ridgley Tas. 626 F6
Ridgwah Island Qld 614 B8
Riggs Creek Vic. 542 F8, 544 A6
Rimbija Island NT 591 N1
Ringa WA 571 F2, 574 D4
Ringarooma Tas. 627 M7
Ringwood Vic. 531 F6, 534 A8,
537 K6, 540 D4
**Rinyirru (Lakefield) NP (CYPAL)
Qld** 613 I1, 614 F12, 422
Ripley Qld 599 B10, 600 B6
Ripple Islands Qld 604 B1,
611 M8
Ripplebrook Vic. 537 N9, 540 F7
Rippleside Vic. 532 B3
Risdon Tas. 621 D4, 623 I4
Risdon Vale Tas. 621 F4, 623 J4,
625 K7
River Heads Qld 603 F5, 604 H12,
609 N4
Riverside Tas. 627 K8, 629 G9
Riverstone NSW 508 A3, 511 I6,
513 P9
Riverton SA 559 J7, 568 C1, 239
Riverview Qld 599 B9, 600 C5,
602 D12
Riverwood NSW 511 K10
Roadvale Qld 600 A8
Rob Island WA 577 I9
Rob Roy Vic. 534 B6, 537 K4
Robb Jetty WA 570 C8
Robbins Island Tas. 626 B2
Robe SA 568 E9, **257**
Roberts Island WA 575 B4, 581 I5,
584 D7
Roberts Islet Qld 614 E1
Robertson NSW 517 D6, 519 G3,
523 J9, **85**
Robertstown SA 559 K6
Robigana Tas. 627 J7, 629 F8
Robina Qld 600 G10, 601 E7
Robinson River NT 593 N4
Robinvale Vic. 526 F7, 547 J8, **190**
Rocherlea Tas. 627 K8, 629 G9
Rochester SA 556 H1, 559 J5
Rochester Vic. 542 C7, **190**
Rochford Vic. 536 H1, 540 B1,
542 B12, 551 P3
Rock Dunder WA 573 F11,
574 H11, 576 E11

Rock Flat NSW 519 C8, 520 G10,
539 F4
Rockbank Vic. 531 B5, 536 H5,
540 B4, 551 P5
Rockdale NSW 508 E9
Rockhampton Qld 604 B5,
611 M11, **439**
Rockingham WA 570 C11, 571 B7,
574 B6, 576 B8, **332**
Rocklea Qld 599 E8, 600 D5, 602 F12
Rockleigh SA 554 F9
Rockley NSW 522 H6
Rocklyn Vic. 535 D9, 536 E2, 551 N3
Rocksberg Qld 599 C2, 600 C1,
602 E7
Rocky Cape Tas. 626 D4
Rocky Cape NP Tas. 626 E4, 499
Rocky Creek NSW 524 G6
Rocky Creek Qld 606 D3, 607 D9
Rocky Crossing Qld 611 K9
Rocky Dam NSW 525 I3, 609 I12
Rocky Glen NSW 524 E9
Rocky Gully WA 573 G2, 574 E10,
576 D11
Rocky Hall NSW 519 D10, 539 G7
Rocky Island NT 591 N10, 593 N1
Rocky Island Qld 605 F7, 606 E2,
607 G7, 611 K5, 613 L3, 614 E7,
615 D1
Rocky Island SA 556 D5, 558 H8
Rocky Island WA 581 M2, 585 M3
Rocky Island (West) A Qld 614 F7
Rocky Island (East) B Qld 614 F7
Rocky Islands WA 581 J3, 584 E4
Rocky Islets Qld 613 L1, 614 G11
Rocky Point Island Qld 614 H11
Rocky River NSW 515 B1, 525 J8
Rocky River SA 556 A12, 558 F12
Rodney Island Qld 614 E5
Rodona Island WA 577 K9
Roe Creek NT 597 I4
Roe Rocks WA 576 F10
Roebourne WA 575 F1, 578 B2,
580 B12, 582 E5, **332**
Roebuck Roadhouse WA 580 H7,
584 B11
Roelands WA 572 E3
Roger River Tas. 626 C4
Roger River West Tas. 626 C5
Rokeby Tas. 621 H9, 623 J5,
625 K7, 464
Rokeby Vic. 534 G12, 537 N8,
540 G6
Rokewood Vic. 536 C6, 551 L6
Rokewood Junction Vic. 536 B5,
551 L5
Roko Island Qld 614 C2
Roland Tas. 626 G7, 628 G4
Roleystone WA 570 G8, 571 D6
Rollands Plains NSW 515 F5,
525 L10
Rolleston Qld 608 G1
Rollingstone Qld 606 F9, 613 M11
Roly Rock WA 575 E1, 578 A2,
580 A12, 582 D4
Roma Qld 608 G6, **440**
Romsey Vic. 536 H2, 540 B2,
542 B12, 551 P3
Ronsard Island WA 578 C2,
580 C12, 582 G4
Rookhurst NSW 515 B8, 523 M1,
525 J12
Rookwood NSW 508 D7
Rooty Hill NSW 508 A5, 511 I7,
513 P11

Roper Bar Store NT 591 J9
Rorruwuy NT 591 M4
Rosa Glen WA 572 B9, 574 B10
Rosanna Vic. 531 E5
Rose Bay Tas. 621 F7
Rosebery Tas. 626 D9, 628 A7, **491**
Rosebery Vic. 526 E11
Rosebrook NSW 514 B6, 515 A11
Rosebrook Vic. 538 B7, 550 G8
Rosebud Vic. 531 C12, 532 H8,
537 I10, 540 C7, 195
Rosebud West Vic. 532 H8
Rosedale NSW 519 F6, 521 L7
Rosedale Qld 604 E9, 609 L2
Rosedale SA 553 G1, 554 D5
Rosedale Vic. 541 J7
Rosegarland Tas. 622 F2, 625 J6
Rosehill NSW 508 C6
Rosemary Island WA 575 E1,
578 A2, 580 A12, 582 D4
Rosenthal NSW 514 H4, 515 C10,
523 N2
Roses Tier Tas. 627 M8
Rosetta Tas. 621 B4
Rosevale Qld 609 M10
Rosevale Tas. 627 J8, 629 F9
Rosevears Tas. 627 J7, 629 F8
Roseville NSW 508 F6, 509 B11
Rosewall Vic. 532 B2
Rosewhite Vic. 543 K9, 545 I6
Rosewood NSW 520 A5, 522 C11,
543 O4
Rosewood Qld 600 A5, 602 B12,
609 M9, 418
Roseworthy SA 554 D4, 559 J8,
568 C2
Rosily Islands WA 575 C2, 582 A7
Roslyn NSW 519 E2, 522 G8
Roslynmead Vic. 527 I12, 542 B5,
549 P6
Rosny Tas. 621 E8
Rosny Park Tas. 621 F7, 623 J5,
625 K7
Ross Tas. 625 L2, 627 L12, **491**
Ross Creek Vic. 535 B11, 536 C4,
551 L4
Rossarden Tas. 627 M10
Rossbridge Vic. 551 I3
Rossi NSW 518 H7, 519 D5, 521 I4,
522 G11
Rossmore NSW 510 H9
Rossville Qld 613 L3, 407
Rostrevor SA 553 D6, 554 C8,
555 G1
Rostron Vic. 549 J10
Rothbury NSW 509 E1, 514 A7,
523 L3
Rothbury Island NSW 604 C1,
611 N8
Rothwell Qld 599 F3, 600 E2, 602 F9
Rothwell Vic. 532 C1
Roto NSW 527 L3
Rottnest Island WA 570 A7,
571 A6, 574 B5, 576 B7, 284,
332, 333
Round Corner NSW 508 D4,
509 A10, 511 K6
Round Hill Island NT 591 M6
Round Island Qld 603 F4, 604 C2,
606 F3, 607 H9, 609 N4, 611 N9,
613 M7
Round Island Vic. 533 J11, 537 J11,
540 C8
Round Island WA 575 D1, 577 K9,
578 A3, 581 I5, 582 B6, 584 D7

Round Islet Qld 614 C1
Round Rock Qld 604 B2, 611 M8
Round Top Island Qld 605 G8,
611 K6
Round Top Island Tas. 624 G11
Round Top Island NP Qld 605 G8,
611 K6
Roundbush Island Qld 603 F6,
609 N5
Roundish Island Qld 605 H11,
611 L8
Rowella Tas. 627 J6, 629 F7
Rowena NSW 524 D5
Rowland Flat SA 553 H1, 554 E5
Rowley Shoals Marine Park 580 D7
Rowsley Vic. 535 G12, 536 F4,
540 A4, 551 O5
Rowville Vic. 531 F7, 534 A9,
537 K6
Roxburgh NSW 523 K2
Roxby Downs SA 560 E4, **259**
Roxby Island SA 558 E8
Roy Island WA 577 I9
Royal George Tas. 625 N1, 627 N11
Royal NP NSW 508 D12, 511 J12,
517 H1, 519 H1, 523 K7, 103
Royalla NSW 518 E7, 519 D5,
520 H4, 522 F11
Roydon Island Tas. 624 A9
Ruabon WA 572 D6
Rubicon Vic. 534 H3, 537 N2,
540 G2, 542 G12, 544 C11
Ruby Vic. 537 N11, 540 F8
Ruby Island NT 590 E3
Ruby Island WA 577 J9
Rubyvale Qld 610 H10
Rudall SA 558 E5
Ruffy Vic. 542 E10, 544 A8
Rufus River NSW 526 C5, 546 D5,
559 P7
Rug Rock WA 577 I9
Rugby NSW 519 C2, 522 F8
Rukenvale NSW 516 E3, 525 N2
Rules Point NSW 519 B6, 520 D5,
522 E12
Rum Island Tas. 624 B12, 627 O3
Rum Jungle NT 588 E6
Rumula Qld 606 D1, 607 D4
Runaway Bay Qld 601 E4
Runcorn Qld 599 E9, 600 D5,
602 F12
Rundle Island Qld 604 D6, 611 N11
Rundle Range NP Qld 604 C6,
611 N11
Running Creek Vic. 543 L8, 545 J6
Running Stream NSW 522 H4
Runnymede Tas. 623 K2, 625 L6
Rupanyup Vic. 548 H9
Rupanyup North Vic. 548 H9
Rupanyup South Vic. 548 H9
Rushworth Vic. 542 D8, **190**
Russell Island Qld 600 G6, 606 F3,
607 H9, 609 N9, 613 M7
Russell Island WA 581 N3, 585 L4
Russell River NP Qld 606 E4,
607 G10, 613 M7, 392
Russell Rock WA 577 J9
Rutherglen Vic. 527 N12, 543 J6,
544 G1, **191**
Ryanby Vic. 547 K12, 549 K1
Ryans Creek Vic. 542 H9, 544 E6
Ryanston Vic. 533 P12
Rydal NSW 510 A2, 512 B2
Ryde NSW 508 E6, 509 A12,
511 L8

Rye Vic. 531 B12, 532 G8, 536 H10,
540 B7, 551 P9, 195
Rye Park NSW 519 C2, 522 F8
Rylstone NSW 523 I3, **86**
Ryton Vic. 540 H9

S

Sable Island WA 578 C2, 580 C12,
582 F4
Sackville North NSW 511 J3
Saddle Island Qld 614 D1
Saddle Island WA 573 F6, 574 E12,
576 D12
Saddleback Island Qld 605 E4,
611 J3
Saddleworth SA 559 K6
Safety Bay WA 570 C11, 571 B8
Safety Beach NSW 516 E11, 525 N7
Safety Beach Vic. 531 D11, 533 I7,
537 I9, 540 C7
Sail Rock WA 577 J9
St Albans NSW 509 A6, 523 K5
St Albans Vic. 531 C5, 537 I5,
540 B4, 551 P5
St Albans Park Vic. 532 B4
Saint Alouarn Island WA 572 C11,
574 B11, 576 B11
Saint Andrew Island WA 581 K4,
584 F5
St Andrews Vic. 531 G3, 534 B5,
537 K4, 540 D3
Saint Andrews Beach Vic. 532 G9
St Arnaud Vic. 549 K9, **191**, 199
St Arnaud Range NP Vic. 549 K10,
191
St Aubyn Qld 609 L8
St Bees Island Qld 605 H7, 611 L5
St Clair NSW 514 A3, 523 L2
St Fillans Vic. 534 F5, 537 M4,
540 F3
St Francis Island SA 567 L9
St George Qld 608 F9, **440**
St Georges Basin NSW 517 C11,
519 G4, 521 O2, 523 I10
St Helena Island NP Qld 599 G6,
600 F4, 602 H10, 609 N9
St Helena (Noogoon) Island Qld
599 G6, 600 F4, 602 H10, 609 N9,
441, 442
St Helens Tas. 627 O8, **491**
St Helens Vic. 538 A7, 550 F7
St Helens Island Tas. 627 P8
St Ives NSW 508 F5, 509 B11,
511 L7
St James Vic. 542 G7, 544 C3
St Kilda SA 553 B4, 554 B7, 556 H6,
559 J8, 568 B2, 218
St Kilda Vic. 531 D6, 537 I6, 540 C5,
135
St Kitts SA 554 F3
St Lawrence Qld 605 H11, 611 K8,
441
St Leonards NSW 508 F7, 511 L8
St Leonards Tas. 627 K8, 629 H10
St Leonards Vic. 531 B9, 532 F4,
536 H8, 540 B6, 551 P7, 159
Saint Margaret Island Vic. 541 J9,
187
St Marys NSW 510 H7, 513 O11
St Marys Tas. 627 O9, **492**
Saint Patrick Island WA 581 J4,
584 F5
St Patricks River Tas. 627 L7
St Pauls Qld 614 C1

St Peter Island SA 567 M9
St Peters NSW 509 F1, 514 B7
Sale Vic. 541 K7, **192**
Salisbury NSW 514 C2, 515 A9,
523 L2
Salisbury SA 553 D4, 554 C7,
556 H6, 559 J8, 568 B2
Salisbury Vic. 526 C12, 548 E7
Salisbury Island WA 577 K10
Salisbury West Vic. 535 D1, 549 N8
Sallys Flat NSW 522 H4
Salmon Gums WA 577 I8
Salmon Ponds Tas. 622 G3, 487
Salt Ash NSW 514 E8, 515 B12
Salt Creek SA 568 E6
Salter Islet Qld 614 D2
Salter Springs SA 554 C1, 556 H4,
559 J7, 568 B1
Saltwater NP NSW 515 E8, 523 O2
Saltwater River Tas. 623 L7, 625 L8
Salural Island WA 580 H5, 584 C7
Salutation Island WA 575 C9,
586 E10
Samaria Vic. 542 H9, 544 D7
Samford Qld 599 C5, 600 C3,
602 E10
San Remo Vic. 533 N11, 537 K11,
540 D8
Sanctuary Cove Qld 600 F8,
601 E3, 609 N10, 445
Sanctuary Point NSW 517 D11
Sand Bank No. 7 Qld 614 F9
Sand Bank No. 8 Qld 614 F9
Sand Island WA 581 K1, 584 G1
Sand Islet Qld 614 H11
Sandalwood SA 559 M9, 568 F3
Sandbanks NP Qld 614 F9
Sandergrove SA 555 H6, 568 C4
Sanderston SA 554 H7, 559 K8,
568 D2
Sandfire Roadhouse WA 580 F10,
583 N1
Sandfly Tas. 622 H6, 625 J8
Sandford Tas. 623 K6, 625 L7
Sandford Vic. 550 D3, 568 H11
Sandgate Qld 599 F5, 600 E3,
602 F10
Sandhill Tas. 629 G3
Sandhill Lake Vic. 526 H11,
549 M4
Sandigo NSW 522 A9, 527 N9
Sandilands SA 556 E5, 558 H8
Sandland Island WA 576 A5
Sandon Vic. 535 E7, 549 N12,
551 N2
Sandringham Vic. 531 D7, 533 J1,
537 J6, 540 C5
Sandsmere Vic. 526 B12, 548 C7,
568 H7
Sandstone WA 576 F1, 578 F12
Sandstone Island Vic. 531 F12,
533 L8, 537 J10, 540 D7
Sandy Bay Tas. 621 D9, 623 I6,
625 K7, 464
Sandy Beach NSW 516 E11, 525 N7
Sandy Creek SA 553 F2, 554 D5
Sandy Creek Vic. 543 L7, 545 J4
Sandy Creek Upper Vic. 543 L7,
545 J4
Sandy Flat NSW 516 A6, 525 L4
Sandy Hill NSW 516 B5, 525 L3,
609 L12
Sandy Hollow NSW 523 J2, 74
Sandy Hook Island WA 577 I9
Sandy Island NT 591 L8

Sandy Island Qld 599 H8, 600 F5, 602 H12, 609 N9
Sandy Island WA 573 B5, 574 D12, 575 E1, 576 C11, 578 A2, 580 A12, 581 M1, 582 D5, 584 A9, 585 I1
Sandy Island No. 1 NT 590 F1
Sandy Island No. 2 NT 590 F1
Sandy Islet Qld 614 F7
Sandy Point NSW 508 C9, 511 J10, 519 E4, 521 K2, 522 H10
Sandy Point Vic. 519 A11, 539 A10, 540 G10, 541 P4
Sangar NSW 527 M11, 542 H3
Santa Barbara Qld 600 F8, 601 E3
Santa Teresa (Ltyente Purte) NT 595 J7, 597 L6
Sapphire NSW 525 J5
Sapphire Qld 610 H10, 410
Sapphiretown SA 556 E11, 558 H11
Sarabah NP Qld 516 F1, 525 N1, 600 D10, 609 N10
Sarah Island Tas. 624 D3, 496
Saratoga NSW 509 D8, 511 O3
Sarbai (Bond Island) Islet Qld 614 C1
Sarina Qld 605 G8, 611 K6, **441**
Sarina Beach Qld 605 G8, 611 K6
Sarsfield Vic. 541 N5
Sassafras NSW 517 A11, 519 F4, 521 M2, 523 I10
Sassafras Tas. 626 H7, 629 B7
Sassafras Vic. 534 B9
Sassafras East Tas. 627 I7, 629 C7
Sassie Island Qld 614 D1
Satellite Island Tas. 622 H10, 625 J10
Saunders Islands NP Qld 614 E5
Saunders Islet Qld 614 E5
Savage River Tas. 626 C8
Savage River NP Tas. 626 D7, 628 A1, 497
Savenake NSW 527 M11, 542 H4
Saville Island WA 581 N3, 585 L4
Sawmill Settlement Vic. 541 I1, 543 I11, 544 F10
Sawpit Creek NSW 520 D9, 539 C3, 62
Sawtell NSW 515 H1, 516 E12, 525 N8
Sawyers Valley WA 570 H5, 571 E4
Sayers Lake NSW 526 G1, 528 F12
Scaddan WA 577 I9
Scaddan Island WA 581 I5, 584 D7
Scamander Tas. 627 O8, 492
Scarborough NSW 517 G3, 519 H2, 523 J8
Scarborough Qld 599 F3, 600 E2, 602 G9
Scarborough WA 570 C5, 571 B5, 574 B5, 576 B7, 279
Scarsdale Vic. 535 B11, 536 B4, 551 L4
Scawfell Island Qld 605 H7, 611 L5
Sceale Bay SA 558 A3, 567 N11
Scheyville NSW 508 B2, 511 J5
Scheyville NP NSW 508 B2, 511 J4, 523 J6
Schnapper Island NSW 514 F7, 515 B11, 523 M3
Schofields NSW 508 A4, 511 I6, 513 P10
School Hill Vic. 533 I9
Schouten Island Tas. 625 O4
Scone NSW 523 K1, 524 H12, **86**

Scone Mountain NP NSW 523 K1, 524 H12
Scorpion Island WA 581 L1, 585 I1
Scotsburn Vic. 535 C11, 536 D4, 551 M4
Scott Island WA 581 I5, 584 C8
Scott NP WA 572 C10, 574 B10, 576 B11
Scotts Creek Vic. 538 G9, 551 J9
Scotts Head NSW 515 G3, 525 M9, 69
Scottsdale Tas. 627 M6, **492**
Scottville Qld 605 C5, 611 I4
Sea Elephant Tas. 625 P11
Sea Lake Vic. 526 F10, 549 J3
Seabird WA 574 B3
Seabird Islet Qld 613 L1
Seacliff SA 553 B9, 554 B10, 555 E3, 568 B3
Seacombe Vic. 541 L7
Seaford SA 553 A11, 554 A11, 555 E5
Seaford Vic. 531 E9, 533 K3, 537 J8, 540 D6
Seaforth Qld 605 F7, 611 K5, 424
Seaforth WA 570 F8
Seaforth Island Qld 605 G5, 611 K4
Seagull Island NSW 515 E10, 523 N3
Seagull Island WA 573 C12, 574 G12, 575 C12, 576 E11
Seaham NSW 509 H1, 514 D6, 515 A11, 523 M3
Seahampton NSW 509 F3, 514 C9
Seal Island SA 555 F9, 556 B9, 558 G10, 559 J11, 568 B5
Seal Island Vic. 541 I11
Seal Island WA 570 C11, 571 B7, 572 C11, 573 E11, 574 B11, 575 C12, 576 B8
Seal Rock Tas. 625 O12
Seal Rock WA 577 I9
Seal Rocks NSW 515 E10, 523 N3
Seal Rocks Vic. 533 J11, 537 J11, 540 C8, 158
Seaspray Vic. 541 K8, 192
Seaton Vic. 541 J6
Seaview Vic. 537 N10, 540 G7
Seawinds Vic. 532 H8
Sebastian Vic. 535 F2, 549 O9
Sebastopol NSW 522 C8, 527 P8
Sebastopol Vic. 535 C10, 536 C3
Second Valley SA 555 B8, 556 G10, 559 I11, 568 A4
Sedan SA 554 H5, 559 L8, 568 D2
Sedgwick Vic. 535 G4, 542 A9, 549 O11
Seelands NSW 516 D8, 525 M5
Seisia Qld 614 C3
Selbourne Tas. 627 J8, 629 E10
Selby Vic. 534 B9
Seldom Seen Roadhouse Vic. 519 A10, 539 A8, 541 P2, 543 P12, 545 P11
Sellheim Qld 606 F12, 610 F2
Sellicks Beach SA 555 D6, 556 H9, 559 J10, 568 B4
Semaphore SA 553 B5, 554 A8, 555 E1
Sentinel Island Tas. 624 A9
Separation Creek Vic. 536 C11, 538 D5, 551 M10
Seppeltsfield SA 554 E4, 559 K8
Serpentine Vic. 549 N8

Serpentine WA 570 F11, 571 D8, 574 C6
Serpentine NP WA 570 G11, 571 D8, 574 C6, 576 C8
Serrurier (Long) Island WA 575 C2
Serviceton Vic. 526 B12, 548 B7, 568 H7
Seven Mile Beach Tas. 623 K5, 625 L7
Seven Mile Beach NP NSW 517 E9, 519 G3, 521 P1, 523 J9, 63
Sevenhill SA 556 H2, 559 J6
Seventeen Seventy Qld 604 E8, 609 M1, 427
Severnlea Qld 516 A3, 525 K2, 609 K11
Seville Vic. 531 H6, 534 C8, 537 L5, 540 E4
Sexton Hill NSW 601 H11
Seymour Tas. 627 O10
Seymour Vic. 542 D10, **192**
Shackleton WA 574 F4, 320
Shadforth NSW 522 G5
Shady Creek Vic. 537 O8, 540 G6
Shag Island NSW 514 G7, 515 C11, 523 M3
Shag Island SA 556 F1, 559 I5, 560 G12
Shale Island WA 581 J5, 584 E7
Shallow Inlet Marine and Coastal Park Vic. 540 G11
Shanks Islands Tas. 624 E9
Shannon Tas. 625 I2, 627 I11
Shannon WA 573 D3, 574 D11, 576 D11
Shannon NP WA 573 D3, 574 D11, 576 D11
Shannons Flat NSW 518 B12, 519 C6, 520 F7, 522 F12, 539 E1
Shark Bay Marine Park WA 575 B8, 586 D5, 301
Shark Island NSW 508 G7, 509 C12, 511 M9, 514 H8, 515 C12, 523 N4
Shaw Island Qld 605 G5, 611 K4
Shay Gap WA 578 E1, 580 E11, 583 L3
Shays Flat Vic. 549 J11, 551 J1
She Oak Island Qld 604 D7, 609 L1, 611 N12
Sheans Creek Vic. 542 F9, 544 B7
Shearwater Tas. 629 C6, 490
Sheep Hills Vic. 526 E12, 548 H7
Sheep Island WA 581 J4, 584 E5
Sheffield Tas. 626 H7, 628 H3, 629 A8, **492**
Shelbourne Vic. 535 E4, 549 N10
Shelford Vic. 536 D7, 551 M6
Shellback Island WA 540 G11
Shelley Vic. 543 N7, 545 M3
Shellharbour NSW 517 F6, 519 H3, 523 J9, **86**
Shelly Beach Tas. 623 N2, 625 M5
Shelter Island Qld 600 G7, 601 G1, 609 N10
Shelter Island WA 573 C11, 574 G12, 576 E11
Shenton Park WA 570 D6
Sheoaks Vic. 536 E6, 551 N6
Shepherds Flat Vic. 535 E8, 536 E1, 551 N2
Shepparton Vic. 542 E7, **193**
Sherbrooke Vic. 534 B9
Sheringa SA 558 C6
Sherlock SA 559 M10, 568 E4

Sherrard Island (East) B Qld 614 F8
Sherrard Island (West) A Qld 614 F8
Sherwood WA 570 F8
Shields Island Qld 604 B1, 611 M8
Shipley NSW 510 C5, 512 E7
Shirley Vic. 551 J3
Shirley Island WA 581 I5, 584 C7
Shoal Bay NSW 514 H8, 515 C12, 523 N4, 77
Shoal Point Qld 605 G7, 611 K5
Shoalhaven Heads NSW 517 E9, 519 H4, 521 P1, 523 J10
Shoalwater Islands Marine Park WA 570 C11, 571 B8, 574 B6, 576 B8, 332
Sholl Island WA 575 D1, 578 A2, 582 B6
Shooters Hill NSW 522 H6
Shoreham Vic. 531 D12, 533 J9, 537 J10, 540 C8
Shorncliffe Qld 599 F5, 600 E3, 602 F10
Short Island Qld 600 G7, 609 N10
Short Island Tas. 626 B3
Shotts WA 572 H3
Shute Harbour Qld 605 F5, 611 K3
Shute Island Qld 605 F5, 611 K3
Sibsey Island SA 558 E8
Sidmouth Tas. 627 J6, 629 F7
Sidney Island Qld 605 G5, 611 K4
Sidonia Vic. 535 H7, 542 B11, 549 P12, 551 P2
Sierra Gardens NSW 601 D11
Silkwood Qld 606 E5, 613 M8
Sillago Island Qld 605 G5, 611 K3
Silloth Rocks Qld 605 H6, 611 L5
Silvan Vic. 531 H6, 534 C8, 537 L6, 184
Silver Creek Vic. 543 J7, 544 H4
Silver Sands SA 555 D6, 556 H9
Silverdale NSW 510 F8, 519 H1, 523 J7
Silverleaves Vic. 533 L10
Silversmith Island Qld 605 G6, 611 K4
Silverton NSW 528 B10, 561 N8, 37
Silverwater NSW 509 F5, 514 B11
Simmie Vic. 542 C6
Simpson Vic. 538 H9, 551 J9
Simpson Desert NP Qld 562 H1, 563 I1, 595 P9, 616 C12, 618 B1, 395
Simpson Island WA 575 C3
Simpsons Bay Tas. 623 I10, 625 K9
Sims Island NT 590 H2
Sinclair Island Qld 614 H11
Sinclair Island SA 567 K8
Sinclair Islet Qld 614 E3
Single NP NSW 525 J6
Singleton NSW 523 K3, **87**
Singleton WA 571 C8, 574 B6, 576 C8
Sir Charles Hardy Group NP Qld 614 F5
Sir Charles Hardy Islands A Qld 614 F5
Sir Charles Hardy Islands B Qld 614 F5
Sir Frederick Island WA 581 I5, 584 C7
Sir Graham Moore Island WA 581 L1, 585 I1
Sir James Mitchell NP WA 572 H10, 573 B2, 574 D10, 576 C11

Sir Richard Island WA 581 I5, 584 C7
Sisters Beach Tas. 626 E4
Sisters Creek Tas. 626 E4
Sisters Island Qld 606 F5, 613 M8
Sisters Island Tas. 626 E4
Skenes Creek Vic. 536 B12, 538 C5, 551 L10
Skenes Creek North Vic. 536 B12, 538 C5, 551 L10
Skipton Vic. 536 A4, 551 K4
Skull Island NT 591 N10, 593 N1
Slacks Creek Qld 599 F10, 600 E6
Slade Island WA 581 J4, 584 E5
Slade Point Qld 605 G7, 611 K5
Slaty Creek Vic. 549 K8
Slipper Island WA 577 J9
Sloop Rocks Tas. 624 C3, 626 C12
Slope Island WA 575 B9, 586 C8
Sloping Island Qld 604 C4, 611 N10
Sloping Island Tas. 623 L6, 625 L8
Small Islet NT 591 N11, 593 N2
Smeaton Vic. 535 D8, 536 D1, 551 M3
Smiggin Holes NSW 519 B8, 520 D10, 539 B4
Smith (Kurrambah) Island Qld 606 F6, 613 M8
Smith Island SA 558 E9
Smith Islands WA 575 C9, 586 E10
Smith Islands NP Qld 605 G6, 611 K4, 425
Smith Rock WA 577 I9
Smithfield Qld 525 I2, 609 J11
Smithfield SA 553 D3, 554 C6
Smithfield Heights Qld 606 D2, 607 F6, 613 L6
Smiths Beach Estate Vic. 533 L11
Smiths Gully Vic. 531 G4, 534 B6, 537 K4, 540 D3
Smiths Lake NSW 515 E10, 523 N3
Smithton Tas. 626 C4, **493**
Smithtown NSW 515 G4, 525 M10
Smithville SA 526 A9, 559 N10, 568 F4
Smoko Vic. 543 L10, 545 J8
Smoky Bay SA 567 M9
Smooth Island SA 567 L9
Smooth Island Tas. 623 M6, 625 M8
Smooth Rocks WA 576 F10
Smythesdale Vic. 535 B11, 536 C4, 551 L4
Snake Island Vic. 540 H10, 541 I10
Snake Range NP Qld 610 H12
Snake Valley Vic. 535 A11, 536 B3, 551 L4
Snapper Island NSW 519 F6, 521 M6, 522 H12
Snapper Island Qld 607 E2, 613 L4
Snare Peak Island Qld 611 L6
Snipe Island Qld 599 H9, 600 F6, 609 N9
Snobs Creek Vic. 534 H2, 537 O2, 540 G2, 542 G12, 544 C11
Snowtown SA 556 G2, 559 I6, 234
Snowy River NP Vic. 519 A10, 539 B8, 541 P3, 543 P12, 545 P11, 186
Snug Tas. 623 I7, 625 K8
Snuggery SA 568 F11
Sodwalls NSW 510 A2, 512 A3
Sofala NSW 522 H4, 28
Solder Island Qld 605 G6, 611 K4
Soldiers Island Tas. 624 D3

Solitary Island WA 575 D2, 578 A3, 580 E11, 582 B6, 583 K1
Somers Vic. 531 E12, 533 K9, 537 J10, 540 D8
Somersby NSW 509 C7, 511 N2
Somerset Tas. 626 F5
Somerset Dam Qld 602 C7
Somerton NSW 524 H9
Somerton NP NSW 524 H9
Somerville Vic. 531 F10, 533 L6, 537 J9, 540 D7
Somerville Island WA 575 C3
Sommariva Qld 608 C5, 619 P5
Sorell Tas. 623 K4, 625 L6, **494**
Sorrento Vic. 531 B11, 532 F7, 536 H9, 540 B7, 551 P8, **195**
South Arm Tas. 623 J7, 625 K8
South Barren Island Qld 604 A1, 611 L8
South Beach WA 570 C8
South Brig Rock Tas. 625 P12
South Bruny NP Tas. 622 G12, 623 I12, 625 J11,
South Channel Island Vic. 531 B11, 532 G7, 536 H9, 540 B7, 551 P8
South Cumberland Islands NP Qld 605 H7, 611 L5, 425
South East Forest NP NSW 519 D10, 520 H12, 521 I12, 539 F8
South East Island WA 575 D1, 582 B4
South East Twin Island WA 580 H5, 584 C7
South Forest Tas. 626 D4
South Goulburn Island NT 590 H2
South Grafton NSW 516 D9
South Guano Island WA 575 C9, 586 E10
South Gundagai NSW 519 A4, 520 C1, 522 D9, 543 P1
South Hedland WA 578 D1, 580 D12, 582 H3
South Hobart Tas. 621 D9
South Island Qld 606 F6, 611 M7, 613 M9
South Island WA 575 D2, 582 A7
South Johnstone Qld 606 E5, 607 G12, 613 M7
South Kilkerran SA 556 E5, 558 H7
South Kumminin WA 574 G5, 576 E7
South Launceston Tas. 629 G2
South Maret Island WA 581 J2, 584 F3
South Mission Beach Qld 606 E6, 613 M8
South Molle Island Qld 605 F5, 611 K3, 390, 441
South Mount Cameron Tas. 627 N6
South Muiron Island WA 575 B3
South Neptunes SA 558 E10
South Nietta Tas. 626 G7, 628 F3
South Norwood Tas. 629 H3
South Page SA 555 C11, 556 G11, 559 I11, 568 A5
South Pasco Island Tas. 624 A9
South Passage Island WA 575 D2, 578 A3, 582 B6
South Repulse Island Qld 605 F6, 611 K4
South Riana Tas. 626 F6, 628 E1
South Solitary Island NSW 516 E11, 525 N7
South Springfield Tas. 627 L7

South Stirling WA 573 F8, 574 H10
South Stradbroke Island Qld 516 G1, 525 O1, 600 G8, 601 F4, 609 N10, 445
South Trees Island Qld 604 D7, 609 L1, 611 N12
South Twin Peak Island WA 577 J9
South Wailgwin Island WA 581 J4, 584 E5
South West Island NT 591 N10, 593 N2
South West Island WA 573 D12, 574 G12, 576 E12
South West Osborn Island WA 581 L2, 584 H2
South West Regnard Island WA 575 E1, 578 A2, 580 A12, 582 C5
South West Rocks NSW 515 H3, 525 M9, 62
South West Twin Island WA 575 C2, 582 A7
South West Vernon Island NT 588 D7, 590 D3
South Yaamba Qld 604 B4, 611 M10
South Yarra Vic. 531 D6, 134
Southbrook Qld 609 K9, 447
Southend Qld 604 D6, 611 N12
Southend SA 568 E11
Southern Cross Vic. 538 C7, 550 G7
Southern Cross WA 576 F6, **333**
Southern Moreton Bay Islands NP Qld 599 H12, 600 G8, 601 F1, 609 N10
Southport Qld 516 G1, 600 G9, 601 F5
Southport Tas. 622 F12, 625 I10
Southport Island Tas. 622 F12, 625 I10
Southwest NP Tas. 622 B5, 624 E8, 625 I10, 479
Southwood NP Qld 608 H9, 609 I9, 412
Sovereign Islands Qld 525 O1, 600 G8, 601 F3, 609 N10
Spalding SA 556 H1, 559 J5, 561 I12, 237
Spalford Tas. 626 G6, 628 G2
Spar Island WA 575 D1, 582 B4
Spargo Creek Vic. 535 E9, 536 E2, 551 N3
Sparkling Island WA 576 G10
Spearwood WA 570 D8, 571 C6
Spectacle Island NSW 508 E7, 509 B12, 511 L8, 523 K7
Speed Vic. 526 E9, 546 H12, 548 H2, 186
Speewa Vic. 547 L12, 549 L1
Spencer NSW 509 B8, 511 L3
Sphinx Islet Qld 611 M6
Spicers Creek NSW 522 G2
Spilsby Island SA 558 E8
Split Island Qld 604 C2, 611 N9
Split Solitary Island NSW 516 E11, 525 N7
Spotswood Vic. 537 I6
Sprent Tas. 626 G6, 628 F2
Spreyton Tas. 626 H6, 628 H2, 629 A7
Spring Beach Tas. 623 N2, 625 M5
Spring Creek Qld 609 L10
Spring Hill NSW 522 G5
Spring Hill Vic. 535 F8, 536 F1, 540 A1, 542 A12, 551 O2

Spring Ridge NSW 522 G1, 524 G10
Springbrook Qld 516 G2, 525 O1, 600 E11, 601 B11, 609 N11
Springbrook NP Qld 516 G2, 525 O1, 600 E11, 601 C10, 609 N11, 399, 434
Springdale NSW 522 C8
Springfield Qld 599 C9, 600 C6
Springfield Tas. 627 L7
Springhurst Vic. 543 I6, 544 G3
Springmount Vic. 535 D9, 536 D2
Springsure Qld 608 F1, 611 I12, **441**
Springton SA 554 F6, 559 K8, 568 C2
Springvale Vic. 531 F7, 533 L1, 537 J7, 538 E9, 540 D5, 550 H9
Springvale South Vic. 533 L1
Springwood NSW 510 F5, 513 K9, 523 J6, 52
Springwood Qld 599 F9, 600 E6
Square Rock WA 577 I9
Squeaking Point Tas. 629 C6
Staaten River NP Qld 612 G5
Stack Island Tas. 626 B2
Stafford Qld 599 E6, 600 D4, 602 F10
Staghorn Flat Vic. 543 K7, 545 I3
Stainer Islet Qld 614 F10
Stamford Qld 610 A5, 617 M5
Stanage Qld 604 A1, 611 L8
Stanborough NSW 525 I6
Stanhope Vic. 542 D7
Stanley Tas. 626 D3, **495**
Stanley Vic. 543 K8, 544 H4
Stanley Island Qld 614 G10
Stanley Island WA 573 H6, 574 F12, 576 D11, 577 J9
Stannifer NSW 525 J6
Stannum NSW 525 K4
Stansbury SA 556 E7, 558 H9, **259**
Stanthorpe Qld 516 A3, 525 L2, 609 L11, **442**
Stanwell Qld 604 A5, 611 M11
Stanwell Park NSW 517 G3, 519 H2, 523 J8
Stapleton Islet Qld 614 H11
Starcke NP Qld 613 K1, 614 H12
Statham WA 570 F6
Station Island WA 577 J9
Statis Rock NSW 515 E10, 523 N3
Staughton Vale Vic. 536 F5, 551 N6
Stavely Vic. 550 H4
Staverton Tas. 626 G8, 628 F4
Stawell Vic. 549 I11, 551 I1, **193**
Steamboat Island WA 575 D1, 578 A2, 582 C5
Steels Creek Vic. 531 H3, 534 C5, 537 L4
Steep Head Island WA 581 L2, 584 H2
Steep Island Qld 604 B1, 611 M8
Steep Island Tas. 626 A2
Steep Island WA 581 J5, 584 E6
Steep Rocks WA 577 I9
Steepcut Rock NT 591 N11, 593 N2
Steiglitz Qld 599 H11, 600 F7
Steiglitz Vic. 536 E6, 551 N6, 167
Stenhouse Bay SA 556 B9, 558 G10
Stephens Creek NSW 528 C9, 561 O8
Stephens Island Qld 606 F5, 613 M8
Steppes Tas. 625 J2, 627 J12
Sterile Island Tas. 625 I11

Stevens Island NT 591 M2
Stewart Island Qld 603 F6, 609 N5
Stickney Island SA 558 E8
Stieglitz Tas. 627 P8
Stirling SA 553 E8, 554 C9, 555 G3, 239
Stirling Vic. 541 N3
Stirling WA 570 C5, 571 B5
Stirling North SA 559 I2, 560 G9
Stirling Range NP WA 573 C7, 574 G10, 576 E10, 300
Stockdale Vic. 541 L5
Stockinbingal NSW 519 A2, 522 D8
Stockmans Reward Vic. 537 O4, 540 G3
Stockport SA 554 D2
Stockton NSW 509 H3, 514 D9, 515 A12
Stockwell SA 554 F3, 559 K8, 568 C1
Stockyard Gully NP WA 576 A5, 310
Stockyard Hill Vic. 536 A3, 551 K4
Stokers Siding NSW 516 G3, 525 O2, 74
Stokes Bay SA 556 C10, 558 G11, 243
Stokes NP WA 576 H9, 305
Stone Hut SA 559 J4, 560 H11
Stone Island Qld 605 F7, 611 K5
Stonefield SA 554 H3, 559 L7, 568 D1
Stonehenge NSW 525 K6, 52
Stonehenge Qld 617 L12, 419
Stonehenge Tas. 625 L4
Stoneville WA 570 G4, 571 E4, 577 I5
Stoneyford Vic. 538 A2, 551 K8
Stonor Tas. 625 K4
Stony Creek Vic. 537 O12, 540 G9
Stony Crossing NSW 526 H9, 546 F1, 547 M11, 561 P12
Stony Island WA 573 D12, 574 G12, 576 E11
Stony Point Vic. 531 F12, 533 L8, 537 J10, 540 D7
Stony Rise Tas. 629 A3
Stoodley Tas. 626 H7, 628 H3, 629 A9
Store Creek NSW 522 G3
Storehouse Island Tas. 624 C10
Stormlea Tas. 623 M9, 625 M9
Storr Island WA 581 J4, 584 E6
Storys Creek Tas. 627 M9
Stotts Creek NSW 601 G12
Stowport Tas. 626 F5
Stradbroke Vic. 541 K8
Stradbroke West Vic. 541 K8
Strahan Tas. 624 C2, 626 C12, **496**
Strangways Vic. 535 E7
Stratford NSW 514 F1, 515 C9, 523 M2
Stratford Vic. 541 K6, 175
Strath Creek Vic. 534 B1, 537 K1, 540 D1, 542 D12, 172
Strath Island NT 591 N4
Strathalbyn SA 554 E12, 555 H5, 559 K10, 568 C4, **259**
Strathallan Vic. 542 C6
Stratham WA 572 D5, 574 C8
Strathblane Tas. 622 F11, 625 I10
Strathbogie Vic. 542 F10, 544 B8
Strathdownie Vic. 550 B4, 568 H11
Strathewen Vic. 534 B5, 537 K3, 540 D3

Strathfieldsaye Vic. 535 G4, 542 A9, 549 O10
Strathgordon Tas. 624 F6, 496
Strathkellar Vic. 550 F4
Strathlea Vic. 535 D6, 549 M12, 551 M1
Strathmerton Vic. 527 K11, 542 F4
Strathpine Qld 599 E5, 600 D3, 602 F10, 609 N9, **442**
Streaky Bay SA 558 A3, 567 N10, **260**
Streatham Vic. 551 J4
Strickland Tas. 625 I4
Stroud NSW 514 F4, 515 B10, 523 M3, **87**
Stroud Road NSW 514 F3, 515 B10, 523 M2
Struan SA 548 A11, 568 G9
Struck Island Qld 607 D1, 613 L4
Strzelecki Vic. 537 N10, 540 F7
Strzelecki NP Tas. 624 B11, 627 O1, 498
Stuart Mill Vic. 549 K10
Stuart Town NSW 522 G3, 99
Stuarts Island NSW 514 F8, 515 B12, 523 M4
Stuarts Point NSW 515 G3, 525 M9
Stuarts Well NT 595 I8
Sturt NP NSW 528 B1, 561 P1, 563 O11, 618 G11, 92
Subiaco WA 570 D6, 571 C5, 278
Subur Islet Qld 614 C1
Success Harbour WA 570 C8
Sue City NSW 519 B6, 520 D6, 522 D12
Suffolk Park NSW 516 H4, 525 O3, 609 N12
Suffren Island WA 581 J3, 584 F3
Sugarloaf Qld 605 F5
Sugarloaf Rock Tas. 624 E10
Sugarloaf Rock WA 572 A6, 574 A9, 576 B10
Suggan Buggan Vic. 519 A9, 539 B7, 541 P1, 543 P11
Sulphur Creek Tas. 626 G5
Summer Hill NSW 509 B12, 511 L9
Summerfield Vic. 535 F1, 542 A7, 549 O9
Summerhill Tas. 629 E4
Summerland Vic. 533 K11
Summerleas Tas. 621 A12
Summertown SA 553 E8, 554 C9, 555 G2
Summervale NSW 529 O9
Sun Island Qld 604 A1, 611 M8
Sunbury Vic. 531 B3, 536 H3, 540 B3, 551 P4, 145
Sunday Creek Vic. 537 J1, 542 D12
Sunday Island Vic. 541 I10
Sunday Island WA 575 B3, 580 H5, 581 I5, 584 C7, 586 C8
Sunday Islet Qld 614 E5
Sunderland Bay Estate Vic. 533 L11
Sundown NP Qld 525 K3, 609 K12, 442
Sunny Cliffs Vic. 526 E6, 546 G6
Sunnybank Qld 599 E9, 600 D5, 602 F12
Sunnyside Tas. 626 H7, 629 B9
Sunnyside Vic. 543 M10, 545 L8
Sunnyvale SA 556 E3
Sunshine Vic. 531 C5, 537 I5
Sunshine Beach Qld 602 H1, 603 F10, 609 N7, 437

Sunter Island Qld 614 E7
Suomi Island WA 575 C12
Surat Qld 608 G7, 440
Surf Beach NSW 521 L6
Surf Beach Estate Vic. 533 M11
Surfers Paradise Qld 516 G1, 525 O1, 600 G10, 601 F6, 609 N10, **444**
Surges Bay Tas. 622 F9, 625 I9
Surveyor Generals Corner WA 564 B2, 579 P8, 594 B11
Surveyors Bay Tas. 622 G10, 625 J9
Sussex Inlet NSW 517 C12, 519 G4, 521 O3, 523 I10, 58
Sutherland NSW 508 D10, 511 K11, 517 H1
Sutherlands SA 559 K7, 568 D1
Sutton NSW 518 F3, 519 D4, 520 H2, 522 F10
Sutton Vic. 526 F11, 549 J4
Sutton Forest NSW 517 B6, 519 G3, 523 I9, 72
Sutton Grange Vic. 535 G5, 542 A10, 549 O11, 551 O1
Swain Reefs NP Qld 604 H1, 611 O7
Swainson Island Tas. 624 E9
Swan Estuary Marine Park WA 570 D7, 571 C5, 574 B5, 576 C7
Swan Hill Vic. 526 G9, 547 L12, 549 L2, **194**
Swan Island NSW 514 F7, 515 B11, 523 M3
Swan Island Qld 604 A1, 611 M8
Swan Island Tas. 627 O4
Swan Island Vic. 531 A10, 532 E5, 536 H9, 540 B7, 551 P8
Swan Island WA 580 H5, 584 C7
Swan Marsh Vic. 536 A9, 538 A2, 551 K8
Swan Reach SA 559 L8, 568 E2, **260**
Swan Reach Vic. 541 N5, 174
Swanbourne WA 570 C7, 571 B5
Swanhaven NSW 517 C12, 519 G4, 521 O3, 523 I10
Swanpool Vic. 542 G9, 544 D7
Swanport SA 554 H11, 559 L10, 568 D4
Swansea NSW 509 G5, 514 C11, 523 L4, 78
Swansea Tas. 625 N3, 627 N12, **494**
Swanwater West Vic. 549 J8
Swanwick Tas. 625 O3, 627 O12
Sweers Island Qld 612 A5, 615 D3, 397, 419
Sweetmans Creek NSW 509 C2
Swell Rocks WA 577 I9
Swifts Creek Vic. 541 N2, 545 M12, 185
Sydenham Vic. 531 C4, 536 H4, 540 B4, 551 P5
Sydney NSW 508 F7, 509 B12, 511 L9, 523 K7, **4**
Sydney Harbour NP NSW 508 G7, 509 C12, 511 M8, 523 K7
Sydney Island Qld 612 A5, 615 D2
Sylvaterre Vic. 527 I12, 542 A5, 549 O6

T

Taabinga Qld 603 A10, 609 L7
Tabacum Qld 606 C3, 607 C8, 613 L6

Tabbara Vic. 519 A12, 539 B11
Tabberabbera Vic. 541 L4
Tabbimoble NSW 516 F6, 525 N4
Tabbita NSW 527 M6
Tabby Tabby Island Qld 599 H12, 600 G7, 609 N10
Tabilk Vic. 542 D9
Table Top NSW 522 A12, 527 O12, 543 L5, 545 J1
Tabor Vic. 550 F5
Tabourie Lake NSW 519 F5, 521 N4, 523 I11
Tabulam NSW 516 C5, 525 M3, 609 M12
Tacoma NSW 509 E7, 511 P1
Taffy Islet Qld 605 G9, 611 K6
Taggerty Vic. 534 F2, 537 N2, 540 F2, 542 F12, 544 B11, 143
Tahara Vic. 550 E4
Tahara Bridge Vic. 550 D4
Tahmoor NSW 517 D2
Tailem Bend SA 559 L10, 568 D4, 249
Taillefer Rocks Tas. 625 O4
Takone Tas. 626 E6, 628 B1
Talab Island Qld 614 C1
Talawa Tas. 627 M7
Talbingo NSW 519 A5, 520 C4, 522 D11
Talbot Vic. 535 B7, 549 L12, 551 L2, 154
Talboys Island WA 580 H5, 584 C7
Taldra SA 526 B6, 546 B6, 559 O7, 568 G1
Talgai Qld 609 K10
Talgarno Vic. 522 B12, 527 O12, 543 L6, 545 K2
Talia SA 558 B4, 560 A12, 567 O12
Tallaganda NP NSW 518 H10, 519 D5, 521 J4, 522 G11, 539 G1
Tallageira Vic. 548 B10, 568 H9
Tallandoon Vic. 543 L8, 545 K5
Tallangatta Vic. 543 L7, 545 K3, **194**
Tallangatta East Vic. 543 M7, 545 K3
Tallangatta Valley Vic. 543 M7, 545 L4
Tallarook Vic. 542 D11
Tallebudgera Qld 600 G11, 601 F9
Tallebung NSW 522 A2, 527 O2
Tallimba NSW 522 B6, 527 O6
Tallon Island WA 580 H5, 584 C7
Tallong NSW 519 F3, 522 H9
Tallygaroopna Vic. 542 E6, 544 A2
Talmalmo NSW 522 B12, 527 P12, 543 N5, 545 M1
Talwood Qld 524 F1, 608 G10
Tamarang NSW 524 G10
Tambar Springs NSW 524 F10
Tambaroora NSW 522 G4
Tambellup WA 574 F9, 576 E10
Tambo Qld 608 B2, 619 P2, **443**
Tambo Crossing Vic. 541 N4
Tambo Upper Vic. 541 N5
Tamboon Vic. 519 C12, 539 E11
Tamborine Qld 600 E8, 601 A3, 609 N10
Tamborine NP Qld 516 G1, 525 O1, 600 E8, 601 B2, 609 N10, 435
Tamboy NSW 515 D11, 523 N3
Taminick Vic. 542 H7, 544 E4
Tamleugh Vic. 542 F8, 544 B5
Tamleugh North Vic. 542 F8, 544 A5

Tamleugh West Vic. 542 F8, 544 A5
Tammin WA 574 F4, 576 D7
Tampanmirri Island WA 581 K3, 584 G4
Tamrookum Qld 516 E1, 525 N1, 600 C10, 393
Tamworth NSW 524 H9, **88**
Tancred Island Qld 605 F5, 611 K3
Tancred Island WA 581 K2, 584 G2
Tandarook Vic. 538 H8, 551 J8
Tandarra Vic. 542 A7, 549 O8
Tangalooma Qld 600 G2, 609 N8
Tangambalanga Vic. 543 L7, 545 J3
Tangmangaroo NSW 519 C2, 522 F8
Tangorin Qld 610 B6, 617 N6
Tanilba Bay NSW 514 F7
Tanja NSW 519 E9, 521 K12
Tanjil Bren Vic. 537 P6, 540 H5
Tanjil South Vic. 537 P8, 540 H6
Tank Island SA 558 B4, 567 O11
Tankerton Vic. 531 F12, 533 M9, 537 K10, 540 D8
Tanner Island WA 581 I5, 584 C7
Tannum Sands Qld 604 D7, 609 L1, 611 N12, 412
Tannymorel Qld 516 C2, 525 L1, 609 L11
Tansey Qld 603 B8, 609 L6
Tantanoola SA 568 F11, 247
Tanunda SA 554 E4, 559 K8, 568 C2, **261**
Tanwood Vic. 549 K11, 551 K1
Tanybryn Vic. 536 B11, 538 C5, 551 L10
Taperoo SA 553 B5, 554 A7, 555 E1
Tapin Tops NP NSW 515 D7, 523 N1, 525 K11
Tapitallee NSW 517 C8
Taplan SA 526 B7, 546 B7, 559 O8, 568 H2
Tar Barrel Corner Vic. 533 J8
Tara NT 595 I2
Tara Qld 609 I8
Taradale Vic. 535 G7, 542 A11, 549 O12, 551 O2
Tarago NSW 519 E4, 521 J1, 522 G10
Tarago Vic. 534 G12, 537 N8, 540 G6
Taralga NSW 519 E2, 522 H8
Tarampa Qld 602 B11
Tarana NSW 522 H5
Taranna Tas. 623 M8, 625 M8
Tarcoola SA 567 O4
Tarcoon NSW 529 O6
Tarcowie SA 559 J3, 561 I11
Tarcutta NSW 520 A2, 522 C10, 543 O2
Tardun WA 575 E12, 576 B3
Taree NSW 515 E8, 523 N1, 525 L12, **89**
Targa Tas. 627 L7
Tarilag Island Qld 614 C2
Tarilta Vic. 535 F7
Tarlee SA 554 D2, 559 J7, 568 C1, 239
Tarlo NSW 519 E3, 522 H8
Tarlo River NP NSW 519 F2, 522 H8
Tarnagulla Vic. 535 C3, 549 M10, 160
Tarneit Vic. 531 A6, 536 H6, 540 B4, 551 P6
Tarnma SA 568 C1

Tarnook Vic. 542 G8, 544 C5
Tarong NP Qld 603 A11, 609 L7
Taroom Qld 609 I4, **443**
Taroona Tas. 621 E12, 623 I6, 625 K7
Tarpeena SA 550 A3, 568 G11
Tarra–Bulga NP Vic. 541 I8, 197, 205
Tarragal Vic. 550 C7
Tarraleah Tas. 624 H3
Tarranginnie Vic. 548 D7
Tarrango Vic. 526 D6, 546 E7
Tarrant Island WA 581 I5, 584 D7
Tarranyurk Vic. 526 D12, 548 F6
Tarraville Vic. 541 I9
Tarrawingee Vic. 543 I7, 544 F4
Tarrayoukyan Vic. 548 D12, 550 D2
Tarrington Vic. 550 F4, 165
Tarrion NSW 529 O5
Tarwin Vic. 537 N12, 540 G9
Tarwin Lower Vic. 540 F10
Tarwin Meadows Vic. 540 F10
Tarwonga WA 574 E7
Tascott NSW 509 D8, 511 N3
Tasman Island Tas. 623 N10, 625 M9
Tasman NP Tas. 623 L9, 625 M8, 478, 489
Tatham NSW 516 F5, 525 N4
Tathra NSW 519 E9, **89**
Tathra NP WA 576 B4, 296
Tatong Vic. 542 H9, 544 D7
Tatura Vic. 542 E7, 193
Tatyoon Vic. 551 I3
Taunton NP Qld 611 K11
Tawonga Vic. 543 L9, 545 J7
Tawonga South Vic. 543 L9, 545 J7
Tayene Tas. 627 L8
Taylor Island SA 558 E9
Taylor Island WA 577 J9
Taylor Rock WA 577 I9
Taylors Arm NSW 515 F3, 525 M9
Taylors Beach Qld 606 F8, 613 M10, 415
Taylors Flat NSW 519 D1, 522 F7
Taylors Lakes Vic. 531 C4, 537 I4, 551 P5
Taylorville SA 559 M7
Tea Gardens NSW 514 H7, 515 C11, 523 N3
Tea Tree Tas. 623 I3, 625 K6
Tea Tree Gully SA 553 E5, 554 C7, 555 G1
Teague Island Qld 605 G5, 611 K4
Teal Flat SA 559 L9, 568 D3
Tecoma Vic. 531 G7, 534 B9, 537 K6
Teddywaddy Vic. 526 G12, 549 K7
Teerk Roo Ra (Peel Island) NP Qld 600 G5, 602 H12, 609 N9
Teesdale Vic. 536 D7, 551 M6
Teewah Qld 603 F9
Telegraph Point NSW 515 F5, 525 M11
Telford Vic. 527 L12, 542 G6, 544 D2
Telita Tas. 627 N6
Telopea NSW 508 D6
Telopea Downs Vic. 526 B11, 548 C6, 568 H7
Temma Tas. 626 A6
Temora NSW 522 C7, 527 P7, **89**
Tempe NSW 508 E8, 511 L9
Temple Island Qld 605 H9, 611 L6
Temple Islets Qld 605 H9, 611 L7

Templer Island NT 590 G2
Templers SA 554 D4, 559 J8, 568 C1
Templestowe Vic. 531 F5, 537 J5, 540 D4
Templin Qld 600 A8, 396
Tempy Vic. 526 E9, 546 H12, 548 H2
Ten Mile Vic. 537 P3, 540 H2, 544 D12
Tennant Creek NT 593 J9, **367**
Tennyson NSW 510 H3, 513 N5
Tennyson Vic. 542 B6, 549 P7
Tent Island WA 575 C3
Tenterden WA 573 B7, 574 F10
Tenterfield NSW 516 A5, 525 L4, 609 L12, **90**
Tenth Island Tas. 627 K5, 629 G4
Tepko SA 554 G9, 559 K9, 568 D3
Terang Vic. 538 F7, 551 I7, **196**
Terau (Dayman) Island Qld 614 C2
Teridgerie NSW 524 D8
Terip Terip Vic. 542 F10, 544 A9
Terka SA 559 I2, 560 H10
Termeil NSW 519 F5, 521 M5, 523 I11
Termination Island WA 577 I10
Tern Islet Qld 614 D3
Terowie NSW 522 D2
Terowie SA 559 K4, 561 I11, 252
Terranora NSW 516 H2, 525 O2, 600 G12, 601 G12
Terrey Hills NSW 508 F4, 509 B10, 511 M6
Terrick Terrick Vic. 527 I12, 542 A5, 549 O6
Terrick Terrick NP Vic. 527 I12, 542 A5, 549 O6, 189
Terrigal NSW 509 E8, 511 P3, 523 L5, 90
Terry Hie Hie NSW 524 G5
Tesbury Vic. 538 H7, 551 J8
Teviotville Qld 600 A8
Tewantin Qld 602 G1, 603 F10, 609 N7, 437
Tewantin NP Qld 603 F10
Tewkesbury Tas. 626 E6, 628 C1
Texas Qld 525 J3, 609 J12, 443
Thallon Qld 524 E1, 608 F11, 441
Thanes Creek Qld 525 K1
Thangool Qld 604 B9, 609 J2, 394
Tharbogang NSW 527 M7
Thargomindah Qld 619 K8, 410
Tharwa ACT 518 D7, 519 C5, 520 G4, 522 F11
The Arches Marine Sanctuary Vic. 538 F10, 551 I10
The Basin Vic. 531 G6, 534 B9, 537 K6, 541 M4
The Brothers SA 558 C8
The Carbuncle Tas. 627 I6, 629 C6
The Cascade Vic. 543 M7, 545 L3
The Caves Qld 604 B4, 611 M10
The Channon NSW 516 F4, 525 O3, 77
The Child Qld 604 D4, 611 N10
The Cove Vic. 538 E9, 550 H9
The Doughboys Tas. 626 A2
The Entrance NSW 509 E7, 511 P2, 523 L5, **91**
The Entrance North NSW 509 E7, 511 P2
The Friars Tas. 625 K11
The Gap NSW 522 B9, 527 P9
The Gap Qld 599 D6, 600 D4, 602 E11, 617 L2

The Gap Vic. 531 B3, 536 H3, 540 B3, 551 P4
The Gardens Tas. 627 P7
The Glen Tas. 627 K6, 629 G7
The Gulf NSW 525 J4
The Gums Qld 609 I8, 427
The Gurdies Vic. 533 P9, 537 L10, 540 E8
The Heart Vic. 541 K7
The Highlands Vic. 535 G11, 536 F4, 540 A3, 551 O4
The Images Tas. 625 I11
The Lakes NP Vic. 541 M6
The Lanterns Tas. 623 N9, 625 M9
The Lea Tas. 621 C11
The Monument Qld 616 F5
The Nobbies Vic. 533 J11, 537 J11, 540 C8, 158
The Nuggets Tas. 625 O3
The Oaks NSW 510 F11, 517 D1, 519 G1, 523 J7, 38
The Pages SA 555 C11, 556 G11, 559 I11, 568 A5
The Palms NP Qld 603 A12, 609 L8, 433
The Patch Vic. 534 C9, 537 L6
The Pines SA 556 C7, 558 G9
The Risk NSW 516 E3, 525 N2, 609 M11
The Rock NSW 522 B10, 524 G4, 527 O10, 543 L1, 97
The Sisters Vic. 551 I7
The Skerries Vic. 519 D12, 539 F12
The Springs Tas. 621 A9
The Summit Qld 516 A3, 525 L2
The Vale NSW 509 A8
The Watchers SA 558 B5, 567 O12
Theodore Qld 609 I3, **445**
Theresa Park NSW 510 G10
Thevenard SA 567 M8, 231
Thevenard Island WA 575 C2, 582 A7
Thirlmere NSW 510 F12, 517 D2, 519 G2, 523 J7, 82
Thirlmere Lakes NP NSW 517 D2, 519 G2, 523 I8
Thirlstane Tas. 627 I6, 629 B7
Thirroul NSW 517 G4
Thistle Island SA 558 E9
Thologolong Vic. 522 B12, 527 P12, 543 M5, 545 L1
Thomas Island Qld 603 F6, 605 G6, 609 N5, 611 J3
Thomas Island WA 577 I9
Thomas Plains SA 556 F3, 559 I6
Thomastown Vic. 531 E4, 537 J4, 540 C4
Thomson Vic. 532 B4, 536 F8, 538 H1, 541 I6
Thomson Bay WA 570 A7, 571 A6, **333**
Thomson Islet Qld 614 D3
Thoona Vic. 542 H7, 544 D4
Thora NSW 515 G1, 516 C12, 525 M8
Thorneside Qld 599 G8, 600 F5, 602 G11
Thornlands Qld 599 H9, 600 F5, 602 H12
Thornton NSW 509 G2, 514 C8, 515 A12
Thornton Vic. 534 G2, 537 N1, 540 F1, 542 F12, 544 B11
Thorpdale Vic. 537 P10, 540 H7, 179

Thowgla Vic. 520 A8, 543 O7, 545 O4
Thowgla Upper Vic. 520 A9, 543 O8, 545 O4
Thredbo NSW 519 A8, 520 C10, 539 B4, **93**
Three Bays Island WA 575 C9, 586 E10
Three Bridges Vic. 534 E9, 537 M6, 540 F5
Three Hummock Island Tas. 626 B1
Three Hummocks NT 591 N5
Three Islands Qld 613 L2
Three Islands Group NP Qld 613 L2
Three Rocks Qld 611 L5
Three Springs WA 576 B4
Three Ways Roadhouse NT 593 J9
Thringa Island WA 575 D2, 578 A3, 582 B7
Thrushton NP Qld 608 D8, 441
Thuddungra NSW 519 A1, 522 D7
Thulimbah Qld 516 A3, 525 L2
Thulloo NSW 522 A5, 527 O5
Thuringowa Qld 606 G10, 610 G1, 613 N11
Thurla Vic. 546 G6
Thursday (Waiben) Island Qld 614 C2, **445**, 449
Ti-Tree NT 595 I4, **368**
Tia NSW 515 C4, 525 J10
Tiakan Islet Qld 614 D2
Tiaro Qld 603 D6, 609 M5, 426
Tiberias Tas. 625 K4
Tibooburra NSW 528 D2, 618 H11, **91**
Tichborne NSW 522 D4
Tickera SA 556 E2, 558 H6
Tidal River Vic. 540 H12
Tide Island Qld 604 D7, 609 K1, 611 L8
Tiega Vic. 526 E8, 546 G11
Tieri Qld 611 I9
Tilba Tilba NSW 519 E8, 521 K10
Tilligerry NP NSW 514 F8, 515 B12, 523 M4
Tilmouth Well Roadhouse NT 594 G5
Tilpa NSW 529 I7
Timallallie NP NSW 524 E8
Timanal (Thorpe) Island Qld 606 F6, 613 M8
Timbarra Vic. 541 O3
Timbarra NP NSW 516 B5, 525 L4, 609 L12
Timber Creek NT 590 D10, 592 D2, **369**
Timberoo Vic. 526 D9, 546 G11
Timberoo South Vic. 526 D9, 546 G11, 548 G1
Timbertown NSW 515 F6, 98
Timbillica NSW 519 D11, 539 G10
Timboon Vic. 538 F9, 551 I9, 187
Timmering Vic. 542 C7
Timor Vic. 535 B5, 549 M11, 551 M1
Timor West Vic. 535 B5, 549 L11
Tin Can Bay Qld 603 F8, 609 N6, **445**
Tin Kettle Island Tas. 624 B11, 627 O1
Tinaburra Qld 606 D3, 607 E9, 613 L7, 451
Tinamba Vic. 541 J6
Tinaroo Falls Qld 606 D3, 607 E9, 613 L6

Tincurrin WA 574 F7
Tindal NT 590 G8
Tindappah (Garden) Island Qld 599 H9, 600 F6, 609 N9
Tinderbox Tas. 623 I7, 625 K8
Tingha NSW 525 I6
Tingoora Qld 603 A9, 609 L6
Tinkrameanah NP NSW 524 F10
Tinonee NSW 515 D8, 523 N1, 525 L12
Tinonee Peak Island Qld 611 L7
Tinsmith Island Qld 605 G6, 611 K4
Tintaldra Vic. 520 A7, 522 C12, 543 O6, 545 O2
Tintinara SA 559 M12, 568 E6
Tiona NSW 515 E10, 523 N2
Tiparra West SA 556 E4, 558 H7
Tipplers Island Qld 600 G8, 601 G1, 609 N10
Tipton Qld 609 K8
Tirranna Roadhouse Qld 615 D4
Titjikala NT 595 J8
Tittybong Vic. 549 K4
Tizard Island WA 577 J9
Tjaulingari Island WA 581 K3, 584 F3
Tjukayirla Roadhouse WA 579 K10
Tjungkurakutangari Island WA 581 K3, 584 F3
Tobermorey NT 595 P4, 616 C6
Tocal Qld 610 A11, 617 M11
Tocumwal NSW 527 L11, 542 F4, **92**
Togari Tas. 626 B4
Toiberry Tas. 627 J9, 629 F12
Tolga Qld 606 D3, 607 D9, 613 L7, 392
Tollgate Islands NSW 519 F6, 521 M6, 522 H12
Tolmans Hill Tas. 621 C10
Tolmie Vic. 542 H10, 544 E8
Tom Groggin NSW 519 A8, 520 B11, 539 A4, 543 P9, 545 P6
Tom Price WA 575 G3, 578 C5, 582 G10, **334**
Tomago NSW 509 G2, 514 D8, 515 A12
Tomahawk Tas. 627 N5
Tomahawk Creek Vic. 536 A9, 538 A2, 551 K8
Tomahawk Island Tas. 627 N5
Tomakin NSW 521 L7, 29
Tomaree NP NSW 514 H8, 515 C12, 523 N4, 77
Tombong NSW 519 C9, 539 D7
Tomerong NSW 517 C11, 521 O2
Tomewin Qld 516 G2, 600 F12, 601 D11
Tomingley NSW 522 E2
Tongala Vic. 527 J12, 542 D6
Tonganah Tas. 627 M7
Tonghi Creek Vic. 519 C11, 539 D10
Tongio Vic. 541 N2, 543 N12, 545 M12
Tongio West Vic. 541 N2, 545 M12
Tonimbuk Vic. 534 E11, 537 M7, 540 F6
Tooan Vic. 548 E9
Toobanna Qld 606 E8, 613 M10
Toobeah Qld 524 G1, 608 H10, 413
Tooborac Vic. 542 C10
Toodyay WA 571 F2, 574 D4, 576 C7, **335**

Toogong NSW 522 F4
Toogoolawah Qld 602 A7, 609 M8
Toogoom Qld 603 E4, 604 G12, 609 N4, 417
Tookayerta SA 526 A6, 546 A7, 559 N8, 568 G2
Toolamba Vic. 542 E8
Toolangi Vic. 534 D5, 537 L4, 540 E3, 168
Toolern Vale Vic. 531 A3, 535 H11, 536 G4, 540 B3, 551 P4
Tooleybuc NSW 526 G8, 547 L11, 194
Toolibin WA 574 F7
Tooligie SA 558 D6
Toolleen Vic. 542 B9, 549 P10
Toolondo Vic. 548 F11
Toolong Vic. 538 B7, 550 F8
Tooloom NSW 516 C3, 525 M2, 609 L11
Tooloom NP NSW 516 C3, 525 M2, 609 L11
Tooma NSW 519 A6, 520 B7, 522 D12, 539 A1, 543 P6, 545 P2, 92
Toombul Qld 599 E6, 600 E4, 602 F10
Toombullup Vic. 542 H10, 544 E8
Toompine Roadhouse Qld 619 L7, 438
Toongabbie Vic. 541 I6, 196
Toongi NSW 522 F2
Toonumbar NSW 516 D3, 525 M2, 609 M11
Toonumbar NP NSW 516 D3, 525 M2, 609 M11, 63
Tooperang SA 555 G7
Toora Vic. 540 H9, 164
Tooradin Vic. 531 G10, 533 N6, 537 K9, 540 E7, 172
Tooraweenah NSW 524 D10
Toorbul Qld 599 F1, 602 G7, 400
Toorongo Vic. 537 P6, 540 H5
Tootgarook Vic. 532 G8
Tootool NSW 522 B10, 527 O10, 543 L1
Toowong Qld 599 D7, 600 D4, 602 F11, 383
Toowoomba Qld 609 L9, 387, **447**
Toowoon Bay NSW 509 E7, 511 P2
Top Rocks Tas. 624 D7
Top Springs NT 590 F12, 592 F3
Topaz Qld 606 D4, 607 F10
Topaz Road NP Qld 606 D4, 607 E10, 613 L7
Topgallant Isles SA 558 B5
Torbanlea Qld 603 E4, 604 G12, 609 M4
Torndirrup NP WA 573 D12, 574 G12, 576 E11, 291
Toronto NSW 509 F4, 514 C10, 523 L4
Torquay Vic. 532 A7, 536 F9, 538 G2, 551 N8, **196**
Torrens Creek Qld 610 D4, 617 P4, 415
Torrens Island SA 553 B4, 554 B7, 555 E1, 556 H6, 559 J8, 568 B2
Torrens Park SA 554 B9, 555 F2
Torrington NSW 525 K4, 52
Torrita Vic. 526 D9, 546 F11
Torrumbarry Vic. 527 I12, 542 B5, 549 P6
Tortoise Island WA 575 C2
Tory Islands WA 577 I9

Tostaree Vic. 519 A12, 539 A11, 541 O5
Tottenham NSW 522 C1, 527 P1, 529 P12
Tottington Vic. 549 J10
Toukley NSW 509 F6, 514 B12, 523 L5, 91
Tourello Vic. 535 C8, 536 C1, 551 M3
Tournefort Island WA 581 J3, 584 F3
Towallum NSW 516 D10, 525 M7
Towamba NSW 519 D10, 539 G8
Towaninny Vic. 526 G11, 549 L5
Towarri NP NSW 523 K1, 524 H12
Tower Hill Tas. 627 N9
Tower Hill Vic. 538 B7, 550 G8
Towitta SA 554 H5
Townshend Island Qld 604 B1, 611 M8
Townsville Qld 605 A1, 606 G10, 610 G1, 613 N11, **448**
Towong Vic. 519 A7, 520 B8, 539 A2, 543 O7, 545 O3, 156
Towong Upper Vic. 519 A7, 520 B8, 539 A2, 543 P7, 545 P4
Towradgi NSW 517 G4
Towrang NSW 519 E3, 522 H9
Tozer Island WA 578 B2, 580 B12, 582 D4
Tracy SA 559 K5, 561 J12
Trafalgar Vic. 537 P9, 540 G7
Tragowel Vic. 549 N5
Trangie NSW 524 B11
Tranmere Tas. 621 H10
Traralgon Vic. 541 I7, **196**
Traralgon South Vic. 541 I7
Travers Island Qld 614 C2
Traverse Island WA 581 J5, 584 E7
Trawalla Vic. 536 B2, 551 K3
Trawool Vic. 542 D11
Trayning WA 574 F2, 576 D6
Traynors Lagoon Vic. 549 J9
Treble Islet Qld 611 L7
Trebonne Qld 606 E8, 613 M10
Tree Island WA 581 I5, 584 C7
Tree Islet Qld 614 D2
Trefoil Island Tas. 626 A2
Tregole NP Qld 608 D6, 403
Trenah Tas. 627 M7
Trentham Vic. 535 F9, 536 F2, 540 A2, 542 A12, 551 O3
Trentham Cliffs NSW 546 H6
Trentham East Vic. 535 G9, 536 F2
Tresco Vic. 526 H10, 549 M3
Tresco West Vic. 549 M3
Trevallyn NSW 514 C5, 515 A10, 523 L3
Trevallyn Tas. 627 K8, 629 G10
Trewalla Vic. 550 D8
Trewilga NSW 522 E3
Triabunna Tas. 623 N1, 625 M5, **494**
Triangle Island Qld 605 G5, 611 K4
Triangular Island Qld 604 B2, 611 M8
Trida NSW 527 K3
Trida Vic. 537 N10, 540 G7
Trimouille Island WA 575 D1, 582 A4
Trinita Vic. 526 E8, 546 H10
Triunia NP Qld 602 F3, 603 E11, 609 N7
Trochus Island Qld 614 D3
Trochus Island WA 581 K2, 584 G3

Troubridge Island SA 556 E8, 558 H9
Troughton Island WA 581 L1, 584 H1
Trowutta Tas. 626 C5
Truant Island NT 591 N2
Truganina Vic. 531 B6, 536 H5, 540 B4, 551 P6
Trumpeter Islets Tas. 624 E9
Trundle NSW 522 D3
Trunkey NSW 522 G6
Truro SA 554 G3, 559 K7, 568 C1
Tryon Island Qld 604 E5, 611 O11
Tuan Qld 603 F6, 609 N5
Tuart Forest NP WA 572 D5, 574 B9, 576 B10, 293
Tubbut Vic. 519 B10, 539 C7
Tucabia NSW 516 E9, 525 N6
Tuchekoi NP Qld 602 F1, 603 E10, 609 N7
Tuckanarra WA 575 H9, 578 D11
Tucklan NSW 522 H1, 524 E12
Tuena NSW 519 D1, 522 G7
Tuft Rock Qld 614 C1
Tuggerah NSW 509 E7, 511 P1, 523 L5
Tuggeranong ACT 518 D6, 519 C5, 520 G3, 522 F11
Tuggerawong NSW 509 E7, 511 P1, 514 A12
Tugun Qld 516 H2, 600 G11, 601 G9
Tuin (Barney) Island Qld 614 C1
Tukupai Island Qld 614 C1
Tulburrerr Island Qld 615 D2
Tuleen Island Qld 600 G8, 601 F1, 609 N10
Tulendeena Tas. 627 M7
Tulkara Vic. 549 J11
Tullaberga Island Vic. 519 D12, 539 H11
Tullah Tas. 626 E9, 628 B7
Tullamore NSW 522 C2
Tullibigeal NSW 522 A4, 527 O4
Tulloh Vic. 536 B9, 538 B2, 551 L8
Tully Qld 606 E6, 613 M8, **446**
Tully Falls NP Qld 606 D5, 607 E12, 613 L8
Tully Gorge NP Qld 606 D6, 607 D12, 613 L8
Tully Heads Qld 606 E6, 613 M8, 446
Tumbarumba NSW 519 A6, 520 B5, 522 D12, 543 P5, **92**
Tumbi Umbi NSW 509 E7, 511 P2
Tumblong NSW 519 A4, 520 B1, 522 D10, 543 P1
Tumbulgum NSW 516 G2, 525 O2, 600 G12, 601 F12, 609 N11
Tumby Bay SA 558 E7, **261**
Tumby Island SA 558 E7
Tummaville Qld 609 K10
Tumorrama NSW 519 B4, 520 D1, 522 E10
Tumoulin Qld 606 D4, 607 D11, 613 L7
Tumut NSW 519 A4, 520 C2, 522 D10, **93**
Tunart Vic. 526 B6, 546 C7, 559 P8, 568 H2
Tunbridge Tas. 625 L2, 627 L12
Tungamah Vic. 527 L12, 542 G6, 544 C2
Tungamull Qld 604 B5, 611 M11
Tungkillo SA 554 F8, 559 K9, 568 C3
Tunnack Tas. 625 L4

Tunnel Tas. 627 K6, 629 H7
Tunnel Creek NP WA 581 K7, 584 G10, 302
Tura Beach NSW 519 E9, 70
Turallin Qld 609 J9
Turbin Island WA 581 J2, 584 F3
Turill NSW 523 I1, 524 F12
Turkey Beach Qld 604 E8, 609 L1, 611 O12
Turkey Island Qld 603 F5, 609 N5
Turlinjah NSW 519 F7, 521 L8
Turn Island Qld 605 H10, 611 L7
Turners Beach Tas. 626 G6, 628 G1
Turners Marsh Tas. 627 K7, 629 H8
Turnip Fields Tas. 621 B10
Turon NP NSW 522 H4, 523 I4
Turondale NSW 522 H4
Tuross Head NSW 519 F7, 521 L8
Turrawan NSW 524 F7
Turriff Vic. 526 E10, 548 H2
Turriff East Vic. 549 I2
Turriff West Vic. 548 H2
Turtle Group NP Qld 613 L1
Turtle Head Island Qld 614 D3
Turtle Island NT 588 A4, 590 C5
Turtle Island Qld 604 D7, 605 H12, 609 L1, 611 L8, 614 D3
Turtle Islet NT 591 N10, 593 N1
Turtons Creek Vic. 537 P12, 540 H9
Tutunup WA 572 D6
Tutye Vic. 526 C9, 546 D11, 548 D1, 559 P10
Tweed Heads NSW 516 H2, 525 O1, 600 G11, 601 H10, 609 N11, **94**
Tweed Heads South NSW 601 G11
Tweed Heads West NSW 601 G10
Tweed Island Qld 604 C1, 611 N8
Twelve Apostles Marine NP Vic. 538 G11, 551 J10
Twelve Mile NSW 517 B12, 519 G4, 521 N3, 522 G2, 523 I10
Twin Island Qld 614 D2
Twin Islands WA 573 G10, 574 H11, 576 F11
Twin Rocks WA 577 I10
Two Islands Qld 613 L2
Two Mile Flat NSW 522 G2
Two Rocks WA 571 A2, 574 B4, 576 B7
Two Round Rocks No. 1 Qld 604 A1, 611 M8
Two Round Rocks No. 2 Qld 604 A1, 611 M8
Two Sisters WA 573 E11, 574 G11, 576 E11
Two Wells SA 553 B1, 554 B5, 556 H6, 559 M12, 568 F6, 235
Tyaak Vic. 534 A1, 537 K1, 540 D1, 542 D12
Tyabb Vic. 531 F11, 533 L6, 537 J9, 540 D7, 181
Tyagarah NSW 516 H4, 525 O3
Tyagong NSW 522 E6
Tyalgum NSW 516 F2, 525 O2
Tyenna Tas. 622 D3, 624 H6
Tyers Vic. 541 I7
Tyers Junction Vic. 540 H6
Tylden Vic. 535 G8, 536 G1, 540 A1, 542 A12, 551 O3
Tyndale NSW 516 E8, 525 N5
Tynemouth Island Qld 611 M8
Tynong Vic. 534 E12, 537 M8, 540 E6, 172

Tyntynder Central Vic. 547 L12, 549 L1
Tyntynder South Vic. 547 L12, 549 L2
Tyra Island WA 580 H5, 584 C8
Tyrendarra Vic. 550 E7
Tyrendarra East Vic. 550 E7
Tyringham NSW 516 C11, 525 L7
Tyrrell Downs Vic. 526 F9, 547 J12, 549 J2

U

Uarbry NSW 522 H1, 524 F12
Ubobo Qld 604 D8, 609 K2
Ucolta SA 559 K3, 561 J11
Uki NSW 516 G3, 525 O2, 609 N11
Ulamambri NSW 524 E10
Ulan NSW 522 H2, 56
Ulidarra NP NSW 515 H1, 516 E11, 525 N7
Ulinda NSW 524 E10
Ulladulla NSW 519 G5, 521 N4, 523 I11, **94**
Ullina Vic. 535 D8, 536 D1, 551 M2
Ullswater Vic. 548 C10, 568 H9
Ulmarra NSW 516 E8, 525 N6, 54
Ulong NSW 516 D11, 525 M7
Ulooloo SA 559 K4, 561 I12
Ultima Vic. 526 G10, 549 K3
Ului (West) Island Qld 614 C1
Ulupna Vic. 527 K11, 542 E4
Uluru–Kata Tjuta NP NT 594 E10, 596 F10, 368
Ulva WA 574 G3
Ulverstone Tas. 626 G6, 628 G1, **497**
Umbakumba NT 591 N7
Umbanganan Island WA 581 J4, 584 E5
Umina NSW 508 H1, 509 D9, 511 N4, 523 K6
Unanderra NSW 517 F5
Uncle Island WA 581 N2, 585 L2
Undalya SA 559 J6
Undara Volcanic NP Qld 606 A6, 613 J9, 431
Undera Vic. 542 E6
Undera North Vic. 542 E6
Underbool Vic. 526 D9, 546 F11, 548 F1
Underwood Tas. 627 K7, 629 H8
Ungarie NSW 522 B5, 527 O5
Ungarra SA 558 E7
Unley Park SA 553 C8, 554 B9, 555 F2
Upper Natone Tas. 626 F6
Upper Beaconsfield Vic. 531 H8, 533 O2, 534 C10, 537 L7, 540 E5
Upper Bilambil NSW 601 E11
Upper Bingara NSW 524 H6
Upper Blessington Tas. 627 M8
Upper Bowman NSW 515 B8, 523 M1, 525 J12
Upper Bylong NSW 523 I2
Upper Castra Tas. 626 G7, 628 F3
Upper Cedar Creek Qld 599 C5, 600 C3, 602 D10
Upper Colo NSW 510 H2, 513 O2, 523 J5
Upper Coomera Qld 600 F8, 601 D3
Upper Crystal Creek NSW 601 C12
Upper Dungay NSW 601 D12
Upper Duroby NSW 601 E12
Upper Esk Tas. 627 M8
Upper Ferntree Gully Vic. 534 B9

Upper Freestone Qld 516 B1
Upper Gellibrand Vic. 536 B11, 538 C4, 551 L9
Upper Horton NSW 524 H6
Upper Kedron Qld 599 D6
Upper Laceys Creek Qld 599 B3, 600 B1, 602 D8
Upper Macdonald NSW 509 A6, 523 K5
Upper Mangrove NSW 509 B6, 511 M1
Upper Manilla NSW 524 H8
Upper Mount Hicks Tas. 626 E5
Upper Mudgeeraba Qld 601 D8
Upper Myall NSW 514 H3, 515 C9, 523 N2
Upper Natone Tas. 628 D1
Upper Plenty Vic. 531 E1, 537 J2, 540 D2
Upper Scamander Tas. 627 O8
Upper Stowport Tas. 626 F6, 628 E1
Upper Sturt SA 553 D8, 554 C10, 555 G3
Upper Swan WA 570 F3, 571 D4, 574 C4
Upper Tallebudgera Qld 601 D10
Upper Woodstock Tas. 622 G7
Upper Yarraman Qld 603 A12, 609 L7
Upwey Vic. 531 G7, 534 B9, 537 K6
Uraidla SA 553 E8, 554 C9, 555 G2
Uralla NSW 515 B1, 525 J8, **95**
Urana NSW 527 M10, 543 I1
Urandangi Qld 595 P3, 616 C5
Urangeline East NSW 522 A10, 527 N10, 543 K2
Urania SA 556 E5, 558 H8
Uranno SA 558 D7
Uranquinty NSW 522 B10, 527 O10, 543 M1
Urbenville NSW 516 D3, 525 M2, 609 M11
Urliup NSW 601 E12
Urquhart Islet NT 591 N10, 593 N1
Urunga NSW 515 H2, 516 D12, 525 M8, **96**
Usborne Island WA 581 I5, 584 D7
Uwins Island WA 581 J4, 584 F4
Uxbridge Tas. 622 F3, 625 I6

V

Vacy NSW 514 C5, 515 A10, 523 L3
Valencia Creek Vic. 541 K5
Valencia Island NT 590 G2
Valentine Island WA 581 I6, 584 C9
Valla Beach NSW 515 H2, 525 M8, 75
Valley Heights NSW 510 F6, 513 K9
Vancouver Rock WA 573 E12, 574 G12, 576 E11
Vanderlin Island NT 591 N10, 593 N2
Vansittart Island Tas. 624 B11, 627 P1
Varanus Island WA 575 D1, 582 B5
Varley WA 576 F8
Vasey Vic. 550 E2
Vasse WA 572 B6, 574 B9
Vaughan Vic. 535 F7, 549 N12, 551 N2
Vectis Vic. 548 F9
Veitch SA 526 A7, 546 A8, 559 N8, 568 G2

Venman Bushland NP Qld
599 G10, 600 E6, 609 N9
Ventnor Vic. 533 K10, 537 J11,
540 D8
Venus Bay SA 558 B4, 567 O11, 260
Venus Bay Vic. 540 F9
Veresdale Qld 600 C8
Verona Sands Tas. 622 H10, 625 J9
Veronica Island NT 591 N3
Verran SA 558 E6
Veteran Isles SA 558 A6
Vickery Island WA 581 I5, 584 C8
Victor Harbor SA 555 F9, 556 H10,
559 J11, 568 B5, **263**
Victor Islet Qld 605 G8, 611 K6
Victoria Point Qld 599 H9, 600 F6,
602 H12
Victoria River Roadhouse NT
590 E10, 592 E1
Victoria Valley Tas. 625 I3
Villawood NSW 508 C7, 511 J9
Vin Islet Qld 614 E1
Vincentia NSW 517 D11, 519 G4,
521 O2, 523 J10
Viney Island WA 581 I5, 584 D6
Vineyard NSW 508 A3, 511 I5,
513 P8
Vinifera Vic. 547 L12, 549 L1
Violet Island WA 575 D1, 582 B4
Violet Town Vic. 540 H4, 542 F8,
544 B6
Virginia Qld 599 E6, 600 E3,
602 F10, 609 L8
Virginia SA 553 C3, 554 B6, 556 H6,
568 B2
Visscher Island Tas. 623 O5, 625 N7
Vite Vite Vic. 551 J5
Vite Vite North Vic. 551 J5
Vivonne Bay SA 556 C12, 558 G12,
243
Volskow Island Qld 605 G6,
611 K4
Vulcan Island WA 581 J4, 584 E5
**Vulkathunha–Gammon Ranges
NP SA** 557 E2, 561 J3, 226

W

W Tree Vic. 519 A10, 539 A9,
541 P3
Waaia Vic. 527 K12, 542 E5
Waarre Vic. 538 G10, 551 I9
Wacol Qld 599 C9, 600 C5, 602 E12
Wadbilliga NP NSW 519 D8,
520 H11, 521 I10, 539 G4, 43
Waddamana Tas. 625 I2, 627 I12
Waddi NSW 527 M8
Waddikee SA 558 E4, 560 D12
Waeel WA 574 E4
Wagant Vic. 526 E8, 546 H11
Wagerup WA 571 D12, 574 C7
Wagga Wagga NSW 522 B9, 527 P9,
543 M1, **96**
Wagin WA 574 F8, 576 D9, **335**
Wahgunyah Vic. 527 M12, 543 I5,
544 F1
Wahring Vic. 542 D9
Wahroonga NSW 508 E5
Waikerie SA 559 M7, 568 F1, **262**
Waikiki WA 570 C11, 571 B8,
574 B6
Wail Vic. 548 F8
Wailgwin Island WA 581 J4, 584 E5
Wairewa Vic. 519 A11, 539 A11,
541 O5

Waitchie Vic. 526 F9, 547 K12,
549 K2
Waitpinga SA 555 E9, 556 H10,
559 J11, 568 B5
Wakool NSW 527 I10, 542 B2,
549 P3
Wal Wal Vic. 548 H10
Walbundrie NSW 522 A11,
527 N11, 543 K4
Walcha NSW 515 B3, 525 J9, **97**
Walcha Road NSW 515 A3, 525 J9
Walcott Island WA 575 E1, 578 B2,
580 B12, 582 E4
Walgett NSW 524 B5, **97**
Walgoolan WA 574 G3, 576 E6
Walhalla Vic. 541 I5, **197**
Walkamin Qld 606 D3, 607 D8,
613 L6
Walkaway WA 575 D12, 576 A3
Walker Flat SA 559 L9, 568 D2
Walker Island Tas. 624 F11, 626 B2
Walker Island WA 581 K2, 584 G2
Walkers Creek Qld 609 K7
Walkers Point Qld 603 E4,
604 G11, 609 M4, 404
Walkers Rock SA 558 B5, 560 A12,
567 O12
Walkerston Qld 605 G8, 611 K5
Walkerville Vic. 540 G10
Walkerville South Vic. 540 G10
Wall Island WA 581 I5, 584 C7
Walla Walla NSW 522 A11,
527 O11, 543 K4, 47
Wallabadah NSW 524 H11
Wallabi Point NSW 515 E8, 523 O1
Wallabrook SA 548 A9, 568 G8
Wallaby Island Qld 614 B8
Wallaby Island Tas. 626 B3
Wallace Vic. 535 D10, 536 E3,
551 N4
Wallace Island WA 570 A7, 571 A6,
574 B5, 576 B7
Wallace Islet Qld 611 L7, 614 E4
Wallace Rockhole NT 594 H7,
596 E6
Wallacedale Vic. 550 E5
Wallacia NSW 510 G8, 523 J7
Wallalong NSW 509 G1, 514 C7
Wallaloo Vic. 549 I9
Wallaloo East Vic. 549 J10
Wallan Vic. 531 E1, 537 J2, 540 C2
Wallangarra Qld 516 A4, 525 K3,
609 K12
Wallangra NSW 525 I4, 609 J12
Wallarah NP NSW 509 G5,
514 C11, 523 L5
Wallarobba NSW 514 D5, 523 M3
Wallaroo Qld 611 K11
Wallaroo SA 556 E3, 558 H6, **262**
Wallaroo NP NSW 509 H1, 514 E6,
515 B11, 523 M3
Wallaville Qld 603 B3, 604 E11,
609 L3
Wallendbeen NSW 519 A2,
522 D8
Wallerawang NSW 510 A1, 523 I5
Walli NSW 522 F5
Wallinduc Vic. 536 B5, 551 K5
Wallingat NP NSW 515 D10,
523 N2, 36
Wallington Vic. 532 C5, 536 G8,
538 H1, 540 A6, 551 O8, 184
Walliston WA 570 F6
Walloon Qld 600 A5, 602 C12
Walloway SA 559 J2, 561 I10

Walls of Jerusalem NP Tas. 624 G1,
626 G11, 628 G9, 486
Wallsend NSW 509 G3, 514 C9,
515 A12
Wallumbilla Qld 608 G6
Wallup Vic. 526 D12, 548 G7
Walmer NSW 522 F2
Walmer Vic. 535 F5, 549 N11,
551 N1
Walpa Vic. 541 M5
Walpeup Vic. 526 D9, 546 F11
Walpole WA 573 F6, 574 E12,
576 D11, **336**
**Walpole–Nornalup Inlets Marine
Park WA** 573 F6, 574 E12,
576 D11
Walpole–Nornalup NP WA 573 G6,
574 E12, 576 D12, 336
Walsall WA 572 C7
Walsh Qld 613 I5
Walsh Island Qld 603 F5, 604 H12,
609 N5
Walter Island Qld 611 M7
Waltowa SA 559 L11, 568 D5
Walwa Vic. 520 A6, 522 C12,
527 P12, 543 O6, 545 N1, 156
Walyunga NP WA 570 F2, 571 D3,
574 C4, 576 C7, 325
Wamberal NSW 509 E8, 511 P3
Wambidgee NSW 519 A3, 522 D9
Wamboyne NSW 522 C5, 527 P5
Wamoon NSW 527 N7
Wampoony SA 526 A12, 568 G7
Wamuran Qld 599 D1, 602 E7,
609 N8
Wamuran Basin Qld 599 C1,
602 E7
Wanaaring NSW 529 I3, 619 L12
Wanalta Vic. 542 C8
Wanbi SA 559 N9, 568 F2
Wandana Heights Vic. 532 A4
Wandandian NSW 517 C11,
521 N2
Wandangula NT 591 M11, 593 M2
Wandearah SA 559 I4, 560 H12
Wandearah West SA 559 I4,
560 G12
Wandella NSW 519 E8, 521 J10,
539 H4
Wandering WA 571 H9, 574 D6,
576 D8
Wandiligong Vic. 543 K10, 545 I8,
153
Wandilo SA 550 A4, 568 G11
Wandin North Vic. 531 H6, 534 C8,
537 L5, 540 E4
Wando Bridge Vic. 550 D3,
568 H11
Wando Vale Vic. 550 D3, 568 H11
Wandoan Qld 609 I5, 443
Wandong Vic. 531 E1, 537 J2,
540 C2, 542 C12
Wandoo NP WA 571 G5, 574 D5,
576 C7
Wandsworth NSW 525 J6
Wang Wauk NSW 515 D9, 523 N2
Wangania Island WA 581 I5,
584 C6
Wangara WA 570 C4, 571 B4
Wangarabell Vic. 519 D11, 539 F10
Wangaratta Vic. 543 I7, 544 E4, **197**
Wangary SA 558 D8
Wangenella NSW 527 J9
Wangerrip Vic. 538 A5, 551 K10
Wangi Wangi NSW 509 F5, 514 C10

Wangoindjung Island NT 590 F2
Wangoom Vic. 538 D7, 550 H8
Wanilla SA 558 D8
Wanneroo WA 570 C3, 571 B4,
574 B4, 576 B7
Wannon Vic. 550 H3
Wanora Qld 600 A4, 602 C11
Wantabadgery NSW 522 C9,
543 O1
Wanwin Vic. 550 B6, 568 H12
Wapengo NSW 519 E9, 521 K12
Wappinguy NSW 523 J1, 524 G12
Warakuiku Tabab Island Qld
614 C1
Warakurna WA 579 O7, 594 A9
Warakurna Roadhouse WA
579 O7, 594 A9
Warana Qld 602 H4, 603 F12
Waratah Tas. 626 E7, 628 A3, **497**
Waratah Bay Vic. 540 G10
Waratah Island Qld 605 H9, 611 L6
Waratah North Vic. 540 G10
Warawarrup WA 572 E1, 574 C7
Warburton Vic. 534 F8, 537 M5,
540 F4, **198**
Warburton WA 579 M8, 317
Warburton East Vic. 534 F8,
537 N5
Warburton Roadhouse WA 579 M8
Warby–Ovens NP Vic. 527 M12,
542 H7, 543 I6, 544 E3
Ward Islands SA 558 A5
Wardang Island SA 556 D5,
558 G8, 257
Wardell NSW 516 G5, 525 O4,
609 N12
Wards River NSW 514 F2, 515 B9,
523 M2
Wareek Vic. 535 B5, 549 L11,
551 L1
Warialda NSW 524 H5, **97**
Warialda NP NSW 524 H5
Warialda Rail NSW 524 H5
Warilla NSW 517 F6
Warkton NSW 524 E10
Warkworth NSW 523 K3
Warla Island NT 590 F2
Warldagawaji Island NT 590 F2
Warmga Qld 609 K8
Warmun WA 581 N6, 585 M8
**Warmun–Turkey Creek
Roadhouse WA** 581 N6
Warn Island WA 581 K2, 584 G2
Warnawi Island NT 591 M3
Warncoort Vic. 536 C9, 538 C2,
551 L8
Warne Vic. 526 F11, 549 K4
Warneet Vic. 531 G10, 533 M6,
537 K9, 540 D7
Warner Qld 599 D5, 600 D3,
602 E10
Warners Bay NSW 509 G4, 514 C10
Warnertown SA 559 I4, 560 H11
Warooka SA 556 D7, 558 H9
Waroona WA 571 D11, 574 C7,
576 C9
Warra Qld 609 J7
Warra NP NSW 516 A9, 525 K6
Warra Yadin SA 549 J12, 551 J2
Warrabah NP NSW 525 I8, 69
Warraber Qld 614 D1
Warracknabeal Vic. 526 E12,
548 H7, **198**
Warradale SA 554 B10, 555 E3,
568 B3

Warraderry NSW 522 E6
Warragamba NSW 510 F8, 519 H1, 523 J7
Warragul Vic. 537 N9, 540 G7, **198**
Warrah Creek NSW 524 H11
Warrak Vic. 549 J12, 551 J2
Warral (Hawkesbury) Island Qld 614 C1
Warralakin WA 574 G2, 576 E6
Warrambine Vic. 536 C6, 551 M6
Warramboo SA 558 D4, 560 B11
Warrandyte Vic. 531 F5, 534 A7, 537 K5, 540 D4
Warrane Tas. 621 G7
Warrawee NSW 509 B11, 511 L7
Warrawong NSW 517 F5
Warrayure Vic. 550 G4
Warrego NT 593 I9
Warrell Creek NSW 515 G3, 525 M9
Warren NSW 524 A10, 51
Warren Qld 604 A5, 611 M11
Warren NP WA 572 G11, 573 A3, 574 C11, 576 C11, 329
Warrenbayne Vic. 542 G9, 544 C6
Warrenmang Vic. 549 K11, 551 K1
Warrentinna Tas. 627 M6
Warrill View Qld 600 A7, 609 M10
Warrimoo NSW 510 G6, 513 K10
Warringa Tas. 626 G7, 628 F2
Warrion Vic. 536 B8, 538 B1, 551 L7
Warrmali Island NT 588 A4, 590 C5
Warrnambool Vic. 538 C8, 550 G8, **200**
Warro NP Qld 603 A1, 604 E9, 609 L2
Warrong Vic. 550 G7
Warrow SA 558 C7
Warrumbungle NP NSW 524 D9, 43
Warruwi NT 590 H2
Wartook Vic. 548 G11
Warup WA 574 E8
Warwick Qld 516 B1, 525 L1, 609 L10, **446**
Warwick WA 570 C5
Warwick Farm NSW 508 B8, 511 J9
Washpool SA 559 J4, 561 I12
Washpool NP NSW 516 B7, 525 L4, 52
Wasleys SA 554 C4, 568 B1
Wasp Island NSW 519 F6, 521 M6, 523 I12
Watagans NP NSW 509 E4, 514 A10, 523 L4, 42
Watarrka NP NT 594 F8, 362
Watchem Vic. 526 F12, 549 I6
Watchman SA 556 H3, 559 J6
Watchupga Vic. 526 F11, 549 I4
Water Island WA 581 K2, 584 G2
Waterfall NSW 508 B12, 511 J12, 517 H2, 523 K7
Waterfall Gully SA 553 D7, 558 H3, 560 G10
Waterford Qld 599 F10, 600 E6
Waterford Vic. 541 L3
Waterford Park Vic. 537 J2, 540 D1, 542 D12
Waterhouse Tas. 627 M5
Waterhouse Island Tas. 627 M4
Waterloo SA 559 K6, 248
Waterloo Tas. 622 F9, 625 I9
Waterloo Vic. 536 A1, 551 K3

Waterloo WA 572 E3, 574 C8
Watervale SA 559 J6, 232
Waterview Heights NSW 516 D9, 525 M6
Watheroo WA 574 B1, 576 B5
Watheroo NP WA 574 B1, 576 B5, 321
Watson SA 566 H3
Watson Island NT 591 N10, 593 N1
Watson Island Qld 614 H11
Watsons Creek NSW 525 I8
Watsons Creek Vic. 531 G4, 534 B6, 537 K4
Watsonville Qld 606 C4, 607 C10, 613 L7
Wattamolla NSW 517 D8
Wattamondara NSW 522 E6
Wattle Flat NSW 519 F4, 521 L2, 522 H10, 527 P5
Wattle Glen Vic. 531 F4, 534 A6, 537 K4
Wattle Grove Tas. 622 F8, 625 J9
Wattle Grove WA 570 F7, 571 D5
Wattle Hill Tas. 623 L4, 625 L6
Wattle Hill Vic. 538 H11, 551 J10
Wattle Island Vic. 540 H12
Wattle Range SA 568 F10
Wattleup WA 570 D9, 571 C7
Waubra Vic. 535 B8, 536 B1, 551 L3
Wauchope NSW 515 F6, 525 L11, **98**
Wauchope NT 593 J11, 595 J1, **369**
Wauraltee SA 556 D6, 558 H8
Waurn Ponds Vic. 536 F8, 538 G1, 551 N8
Wave Break Island Qld 516 G1, 525 O1, 600 G9, 601 F4, 609 N10
Wave Hill NSW 529 N6
Waverley NSW 508 G8, 511 M9
Waverley Tas. 627 K8, 629 H10
Wayatinah Tas. 624 H4
Waychinicup NP WA 573 F10, 574 H11, 576 E11
Waygara Vic. 539 A11, 541 P5
Webbs NSW 522 E1, 524 B12
Webbs Creek NSW 511 J1
Wedderburn NSW 510 H12, 517 F2
Wedderburn Vic. 549 L8, **199**
Wedderburn Junction Vic. 549 M8
Weddin Mountains NP NSW 522 D6, 55
Wedge Island Qld 604 C5, 605 G7, 611 N11
Wedge Island SA 556 A8, 558 F9
Wedge Island Tas. 623 L9, 625 L9
Wedge Island WA 574 A2, 576 B6
Wedge Rock NT 591 M6
Wedge Rocks Qld 614 G10
Wednesday Island Qld 614 C2
Wee Jasper NSW 518 A2, 519 B4, 520 F1, 522 E10, 105
Wee Waa NSW 524 E6, **98**
Weeaproinah Vic. 536 A11, 538 B4
Weegena Tas. 626 H8, 629 B10
Weemelah NSW 524 E3, 608 G12
Weeragua Vic. 519 C11, 539 E9
Weerdee Island WA 578 D1, 580 D11, 582 H3
Weerite Vic. 538 H7, 551 J7
Weeroona Island SA 559 I4, 560 H11, 256
Weetah Tas. 627 I8, 629 C10
Weetaliba NSW 524 E11
Weethalle NSW 522 A6, 527 N6
Weetulta SA 556 E4, 558 H7

Wehla Vic. 535 B1, 549 L9
Weipa Qld 614 B7, **446**
Weismantels NSW 514 F3, 515 B9, 523 M2
Weja NSW 522 B5, 527 O5
Welaregang NSW 520 B7, 522 C12, 539 A1, 543 O6, 545 O2
Weld Island WA 575 D2, 582 B7
Weldborough Tas. 627 N7
Welford NP Qld 617 L12, 619 K2, 418
Wellingrove NSW 525 J5
Wellington NSW 522 F2, **98**
Wellington SA 559 L10, 568 D4, 249
Wellington NP WA 572 F3, 574 C8, 576 C9, 299
Wellington Point Qld 599 G8, 600 F5, 602 H11
Wellstead WA 573 H7, 574 H10, 576 F10
Welshmans Reef Vic. 535 E6, 549 N12, 551 N1
Welshpool Vic. 540 H10, **201**
Welshpool WA 570 E6, 571 C5
Wemen Vic. 526 F8, 547 I9
Wendar Island Tas. 624 E10
Wendouree Vic. 535 C10, 536 C3
Wentworth NSW 526 D5, 546 F5, **99**
Wentworth Falls NSW 510 D5, 512 G9, 523 I6
Wentworthville NSW 511 J8
Wepowie SA 559 J3, 561 I10
Werakata NP NSW 509 E1, 514 A7, 523 L3
Wereboldera NSW 519 A5, 520 C3, 522 D10
Werneth Vic. 536 B6, 551 L6
Werombi NSW 510 F9, 519 G1, 523 J7
Werona Vic. 535 D7, 536 E1
Werrap Vic. 526 D11, 548 F5
Werri Beach NSW 517 F8
Werribee Vic. 531 A6, 536 H6, 540 B5, 551 P6
Werribee South Vic. 531 B7, 532 F1, 536 H7, 540 B5, 551 P6
Werrikimbe NP NSW 515 D4, 525 K10, 98
Werrimull Vic. 526 C6, 546 E7, 559 P8
Werris Creek NSW 524 H10
Wesburn Vic. 534 E8, 537 M5
Wesley Vale Tas. 626 H6, 629 B6
West Burleigh Qld 516 G1, 600 G11, 601 F9
West Cape Howe NP WA 573 C12, 574 G12, 576 E11, 291, 302
West Creek Vic. 533 P12
West End Qld 599 E7, 383
West Frankford Tas. 627 I7, 629 D8
West Governor Island WA 581 L2, 585 I1
West Hill Island Qld 605 H10, 611 K7
West Hill NP Qld 605 G10, 611 K7
West Hobart Tas. 621 D8
West Intercourse Island WA 575 E1, 578 A2, 580 A12, 582 D5
West Island NT 591 N10, 593 N1
West Island SA 555 F9, 556 H10, 558 B5, 559 J11, 560 A12, 567 O12, 568 B5
West Island WA 575 D2, 580 G6, 582 B7, 584 A9

West Kentish Tas. 626 G7, 628 G3
West Launceston Tas. 629 F2
West Lewis Island WA 575 E1, 578 A2, 580 A12, 582 D4
West MacDonnell NP NT 594 H6, 595 I7, 596 D2, 597 I3, 359, 361
West Mid Intercourse Island WA 575 E1, 578 B2, 580 B12, 582 D5
West Molle (Daydream) Island Qld 605 F5, 611 K3, 390
West Montagu Tas. 626 B3
West Montalivet Island WA 581 K2, 584 F2
West Moonah Tas. 621 C6
West Moore Island WA 575 F1, 578 C2, 580 C12, 582 F4
West Pine Tas. 626 F6, 628 E1
West Pyramid Tas. 624 E9
West Ridgley Tas. 626 F6
West Rock WA 581 L2, 584 H2
West Roe Island WA 580 H5, 584 C7
West Scottsdale Tas. 627 L6
West Side Island Qld 611 L8
West Takone Tas. 626 E6, 628 B1
West Wallabi Island WA 575 C12
West Wallsend NSW 509 F3, 514 C9
West Waterhouse NT 596 E5
West Woody Island NT 591 N4
West Wyalong NSW 522 B6, 527 P6, **100**
Westall (Combe) Island WA 577 J9
Westbury Tas. 627 J8, 629 E11, **498**
Westbury Vic. 537 P9, 540 H6
Westby Vic. 526 H10, 549 N4
Westdale NSW 524 H9
Westdale WA 571 G7, 574 D5, 576 C8
Western Creek Tas. 626 H9, 629 E3
Western Flat SA 548 A8, 568 G8
Western Junction Tas. 627 K9, 629 H11
Western Rocks Tas. 624 F11
Westerway Tas. 622 E2, 625 I6
Westmar Qld 608 H9
Westmead NSW 508 C6
Westmere Vic. 551 I4
Weston NSW 509 E2, 514 B8, 523 L4
Westonia WA 574 H3, 576 E6
Westwood Qld 604 A6, 611 L11
Westwood Tas. 627 J8, 629 F10
Weymouth Tas. 627 K5, 629 H5
Whale Rock WA 577 I9
Whalebone Island WA 575 C3
Wharminda SA 558 E6
Wharparilla Vic. 527 J12, 542 B5, 549 P7
Wharparilla North Vic. 542 B5, 549 P6
Wharton Island WA 577 J9
Wheatley Islet NT 591 N10, 593 N1
Wheatsheaf Vic. 535 F8, 536 F1
Wheeler (Toolgbar) Island Qld 606 F6, 613 M8
Wheeo NSW 519 D2, 522 G8
Whicher NP WA 572 D7, 574 B9, 576 B10
Whim Creek WA 575 G1, 578 C2, 580 C12, 582 G5
Whiporie NSW 516 E7, 525 N5
Whirily Vic. 549 J5
White (Albino) Rock Qld 606 G8, 613 N10

White Beach Tas. 623 L8, 625 L9
White Cliffs NSW 528 F7, **100**
White Flat SA 558 D8
White Hills Tas. 627 K8, 629 H11
White Island WA 575 C9, 581 J3, 584 H2, 586 E9
White Islet NT 591 N10, 593 N1
White Mountains NP Qld 610 C3, 617 P3, 415
White Rock Qld 605 F5, 606 E3, 607 F7, 611 K3
Whitefoord Tas. 625 L4
Whiteheads Creek Vic. 542 D10
Whiteman WA 571 C4
Whitemark Tas. 624 B10, **498**
Whitemore Tas. 627 J9, 629 F11
Whitewood Qld 610 A5, 617 M5
Whitfield Vic. 543 I9, 544 F7
Whitfords WA 570 C4
Whitlands Vic. 543 I9, 544 F7
Whitley Island WA 581 J3, 584 E4
Whitlock Island WA 576 A5
Whitmore Island WA 575 B4
Whitsunday Group Qld 611 K3
Whitsunday Island Qld 605 G4, 611 K3, 391, **449**
Whitsunday Islands NP Qld 605 G5, 611 K3
Whittell Island WA 574 A2, 576 B6
Whittlesea Vic. 531 F2, 537 J3, 540 D3
Whitton NSW 527 M7
Whitwarta SA 556 G3, 559 J7
Whoorel Vic. 536 C9, 538 D2, 551 M8
Whorouly Vic. 543 J8, 544 G5
Whorouly East Vic. 543 J8, 544 G5
Whorouly South Vic. 543 J8, 544 G5
Whroo Vic. 542 D8
Whyalla SA 558 H3, 560 G11, **264**
Whyte Yarcowie SA 559 K4, 561 I11
Wia Island Qld 614 C1
Wialki WA 574 F1, 576 E5
Wiangaree NSW 516 E3, 525 N2, 609 M11, 63
Wickepin WA 574 F6, 576 D8, **337**
Wickham NSW 509 H3, 514 D9
Wickham WA 575 F1, 578 B2, 580 B12, 582 E4, 333
Wickham NP Qld 599 F12, 600 E8, 601 A2, 609 N10
Wickliffe Vic. 550 H4
Widgiemooltha WA 576 H6
Widgiewa NSW 527 M9
Widul Island Qld 614 C1
Wietalaba NP Qld 604 C8, 609 K2
Wiggins Islands Qld 604 D7, 609 K1, 611 N12
Wigram Island NT 591 N3
Wigton Island Qld 605 H6, 611 L5
Wiiluntju Island WA 581 K2, 584 G2
Wilberforce NSW 508 A1, 511 I4, 513 P6, 523 J6
Wilburville Tas. 625 J2, 627 J11
Wilby Vic. 527 M12, 542 H6, 544 D2
Wilcannia NSW 528 G9, 100
Wild Cattle Island NP Qld 604 D7, 609 L1, 611 N12, 412
Wild Duck Island Qld 611 L7
Wild Horse Plains SA 556 G5, 559 I7, 568 B1
Wilds Island WA 575 B9, 586 D9
Wiley Park NSW 511 K9

Wilga WA 572 H6, 574 D9
Wilgul Vic. 536 B6, 551 L6
Wilipili Island NT 591 L8
Wilkawatt SA 559 N10, 568 F4
Wilkie Island Qld 614 F9
Wilkur Vic. 526 E11, 549 I6
Willa Vic. 526 E10, 548 G2
Willalooka SA 568 F7
Willamulka SA 556 F3
Willandra NP NSW 527 K3, 65
Willare Bridge Roadhouse WA 581 I7, 584 D10
Willatook Vic. 550 G7
Willaura Vic. 551 I3
Willawarrin NSW 515 F3, 525 L9
Willbriggie NSW 527 M7
Willenabrina Vic. 526 D11, 548 G6
Willes Island Qld 600 G6, 609 N10
Willi Willi NP NSW 515 E4, 525 L10
William Bay NP WA 573 A12, 574 F12, 576 D11, 302
William Creek SA 562 D10, 233
Williams WA 574 E7, 576 D9
Williams Island SA 558 E9
Williamsdale ACT 518 E8, 519 C5, 520 G5, 522 F11
Williamsford Tas. 626 D10, 628 A7
Williamstown SA 553 G3, 554 C4, 559 K8, 568 C2
Williamstown Vic. 531 C6, 537 I6, 540 C4
Williamtown NSW 514 E8, 515 B12
Willigulli WA 575 D12
Willina NSW 515 D9, 523 N2
Willoughby NSW 508 F6
Willow Grove Vic. 537 P8, 540 H6
Willow Tree NSW 524 H11
Willowie SA 559 J2, 560 H10
Willowmavin Vic. 537 I1, 540 C1, 542 C12
Willowra NT 592 G12, 594 G2
Willows Qld 610 H11
Willows Gemfields Qld 610 H11
Willowvale Qld 516 B1, 525 L1
Willowvale Vic. 536 A5, 551 K5
Willung Vic. 541 J7
Willung South Vic. 541 J8
Willunga SA 554 B12, 555 E6, 556 H9, 559 J10, 568 B4, **264**
Willy Islet NT 591 N10, 593 N2
Wilmington SA 559 I2, 560 H10, **265**
Wilmot Tas. 626 G7, 628 F3, 493
Wilora NT 595 I3
Wilpena SA 557 B10, 561 I6, **266**
Wilroy WA 575 E12, 576 B3
Wilson Island Qld 604 F5, 611 O11
Wilson Island WA 577 I10
Wilsons Promontory Marine NP Vic. 540 H12
Wilsons Promontory Marine Park Vic. 540 G11, 541 I11
Wilsons Promontory Marine Reserve Vic. 540 H12
Wilsons Promontory NP Vic. 540 H11, 541 I11, 164
Wilsons Valley NSW 520 D9, 539 C3
Wilton NSW 517 E3, 519 H2, 523 J8
Wiltshire–Butler NP WA 572 D9, 574 B10, 576 B10
Wiltshire Junction Tas. 626 D4
Wiluna WA 578 F10
Wimba Vic. 536 B11, 538 B4, 551 K9

Wimbleton Heights Estate Vic. 533 L10
Winceby Island SA 558 E8
Winchelsea Vic. 536 D8, 538 E1, 551 M8, **201**
Winchelsea (Akwamburkba) Island NT 591 N7
Windang NSW 517 F6, 519 H3, 523 J9
Windarra WA 577 I2, 579 I12
Windellama NSW 519 E4, 521 K1, 522 H10
Windermere Tas. 621 B3, 627 J7, 629 F8
Windermere Vic. 535 B9, 536 C2
Windermere Park NSW 509 F5, 514 B11
Windeyer NSW 522 H3
Windirr Island NT 588 A4, 590 C4
Windjana Gorge NP WA 581 K7, 584 F9, 302
Windmill Roadhouse WA 574 B3, 576 B6
Windorah Qld 619 I3, 419
Windowie NSW 519 A4, 520 C3, 522 D10, 543 P2
Windsor NSW 508 A2, 511 I5, 513 P7, 523 J6, **100**
Windsor SA 556 G5, 559 J7, 568 B1
Windy Corner WA 579 K5
Windy Harbour WA 573 B5, 574 D11, 576 C11
Wingeel Vic. 536 C7, 551 M7
Wingello NSW 519 F3, 523 I9
Wingen NSW 523 K1, 524 H12
Wingham NSW 515 D8, 523 N1, 525 K12, **101**
Winiam Vic. 526 C12, 548 E7
Winiam East Vic. 548 E7
Winjallok Vic. 549 K10
Winkie SA 546 A6, 559 N7
Winkleigh Tas. 627 J7, 629 E8
Winmalee NSW 510 G5, 513 L8
Winnaleah Tas. 627 N6
Winnambool Vic. 526 F8, 547 I10
Winnap Vic. 550 C5, 568 H12
Winnellie NT 588 D3
Winnindoo Vic. 541 J6
Winninowie SA 559 I2, 560 G10
Winnunga NSW 522 B5, 527 O5
Winslow Vic. 538 C7, 550 G7
Winton Qld 617 L7, **449**
Winton Vic. 542 H8, 544 D5
Winton North Vic. 542 H8, 544 E5
Winulta SA 556 F4, 559 I7, 568 A1
Winyalkan Island WA 581 K2, 584 G3
Wirha SA 526 A8, 559 N10, 568 G4
Wirlinga NSW 522 A12, 543 L6, 545 J2
Wirrabara SA 559 J3, 560 H11, 246
Wirrainbeia Island Qld 605 G5, 611 K3
Wirrega SA 526 A12, 548 A6, 568 G7
Wirrida SA 565 O12, 567 O1
Wirrimah NSW 519 B1, 522 E7
Wirrinya NSW 522 D5
Wirrulla SA 558 B1, 567 O9
Wirrung Island NSW 514 F7, 515 B11, 523 M3
Wiseleigh Vic. 541 N5
Wisemans Creek NSW 522 H6
Wisemans Ferry NSW 509 A7, 511 K2, 523 K5, **101**

Wishbone WA 574 G7
Wistow SA 553 G10, 554 E11, 555 H4
Witchcliffe WA 572 B9, 574 B10
Withersfield Qld 610 H10
Witjira NP SA 562 C2, 565 P2, 595 L12, 251
Witt Island Qld 604 D7, 609 K1, 611 N12
Wittenoom WA 575 G3, 578 D4, 582 H8, 335
Wivenhoe Tas. 626 F5
Wivenhoe Pocket Qld 600 A4, 602 C10
Wodonga Vic. 522 A12, 527 N12, 543 K6, 545 I2, **202**
Wogyala NT 593 K8
Wokalup WA 572 E2, 574 C8
Woko NP NSW 515 B7, 523 M1, 525 J11
Wokurna SA 556 F2, 559 I5
Wolfe Creek Crater NP WA 581 N9, 309
Wollar NSW 523 I2
Wollaston Island WA 581 K2, 584 G3
Wollemi NP NSW 509 A1, 510 G1, 511 I2, 513 L1, 523 J3, 68, 87, 101
Wollert Vic. 531 E3, 537 J4, 540 C3
Wollombi NSW 509 C3, 523 K4, 42
Wollomombi NSW 515 D1, 525 K8
Wollongbar NSW 516 G5, 525 O3, 609 N12
Wollongong NSW 517 F5, 519 H2, 523 J8, **103**
Wollumbin NP NSW 516 F3, 525 O2, 609 N11, 74
Wollun NSW 515 A2, 525 J9
Wolseley SA 526 B12, 548 B7, 568 G7
Wolumla NSW 519 E9, 539 H7
Womalilla Qld 608 E6
Wombarra NSW 517 G3
Wombat NSW 519 B2, 522 D8
Wombelano Vic. 548 D11
Wombeyan Caves NSW 519 F2, 522 H8, 46, 54
Womboota NSW 527 J11, 542 B4, 549 P5
Won Wron Vic. 541 I9
Wonboyn NSW 519 E11
Wonboyn Lake NSW 539 H9
Wondai Qld 603 A9, 609 L6
Wondalga NSW 519 A5, 520 C3, 522 D10, 543 P3
Wondul Range NP Qld 609 J10
Wonga Qld 607 D3, 613 L5
Wongaling Beach Qld 606 E6, 613 M8
Wongan Hills WA 574 D2, 576 C6
Wongarbon NSW 522 F1, 524 C12
Wongawilli NSW 517 E5
Wongi NP Qld 603 C5, 604 F12, 609 M5
Wongulla SA 559 L8, 568 D2
Wonthaggi Vic. 537 L12, 540 E9, **202**
Wonwondah East Vic. 548 G10
Wonwondah North Vic. 548 F10
Wonyip Vic. 540 H9
Woocoo NP Qld 603 C6, 609 M5
Wood Wood Vic. 526 G9, 547 L11, 549 L1
Woodanilling WA 574 F8, 576 D9
Woodbridge Tas. 622 H9, 625 J9

Woodburn NSW 516 F6, 525 O4, 50
Woodbury Tas. 625 L3
Woodchester SA 553 H12, 554 E12, 559 K10, 568 C4
Wooded Island WA 575 C12
Woodenbong NSW 516 D2, 525 M2, 609 M11
Woodend Vic. 535 H9, 536 G2, 540 B2, 542 B12, 551 P3, 202
Woodfield Vic. 542 G11, 544 B9
Woodford NSW 510 E6, 513 I9
Woodford Qld 602 E6, 609 M8, 400
Woodford Vic. 538 C7, 550 G8
Woodgate Qld 603 E3, 604 G11, 609 M4, 404
Woodglen Vic. 541 L5
Woodhill Qld 600 C8
Woodhouse Rocks NT 591 N6
Woodhouselee NSW 519 E2, 522 G8
Woodlands WA 573 D9, 574 G11
Woodleigh Vic. 537 M10, 540 E8
Woodridge Qld 599 E10, 600 E6
Woods Point SA 559 L10, 568 D4
Woods Point Vic. 537 P4, 540 H3
Woods Reef NSW 524 H7
Woods Well SA 559 L12, 568 D6
Woodsdale Tas. 625 L5
Woodside SA 553 G8, 554 E9, 555 H2, 559 K9, 568 C3
Woodside Vic. 541 J9
Woodside Beach Vic. 541 J9
Woodstock NSW 522 F6
Woodstock Qld 605 A2, 606 G11, 610 G2, 613 N12
Woodstock Tas. 622 G7, 625 J8
Woodstock Vic. 531 E3, 537 J3, 540 C3
Woodvale Vic. 535 F2, 542 A8, 549 O9
Woodville NSW 509 G1, 514 C7, 515 A11, 525 J5
Woodville SA 554 B8, 555 E1, 556 H7
Woody Island NT 591 M7
Woody Island Qld 603 F4, 604 H12, 606 D1, 607 E3, 609 N4, 613 L5
Woody Island Tas. 623 K4, 625 L7
Woody Island WA 577 I9, 305
Woody Point Qld 599 F4, 600 E2, 602 G9
Woody Wallis Island Qld 614 C3
Wool Bay SA 556 E7, 558 H9
Wool Wool Vic. 536 A8, 538 A1, 551 K7
Woolamai Vic. 533 O11, 537 L11, 540 E8
Woolamai Waters Vic. 533 M11
Woolaning NT 588 C7, 590 D5
Woolbrook NSW 515 A3, 525 I9
Woolgoolga NSW 516 E11, 525 N7, **102**
Wooli NSW 516 F10, 525 N6
Woolomin NSW 525 I10
Woolooga Qld 603 C8, 609 M6
Woolooma NP NSW 523 L1, 525 I12
Woolooware NSW 508 E11, 511 L11
Woolshed Vic. 543 J7, 544 H4
Woolshed Flat SA 559 I2, 560 G9
Woolsthorpe Vic. 550 G7
Woomargama NSW 522 B12, 527 O12, 543 M5
Woomargama NP NSW 522 B12, 527 P12, 543 M5, 545 L1

Woombye Qld 602 F4, 603 E11
Woomelang Vic. 526 E10, 549 I4
Woomera SA 560 E5, **265**
Woondum NP Qld 603 E9, 609 N6
Woongoolba Qld 599 H11, 600 F7
Woonona NSW 517 G4
Wooragee Vic. 543 J7, 544 H3
Woorak Vic. 526 C12, 548 E7
Woorak West Vic. 548 E6
Wooramel Roadhouse WA 575 C8, 586 G6
Woorarra Vic. 540 H9
Wooreen Vic. 537 O11, 540 G8
Woori Yallock Vic. 534 D8, 537 M5, 540 E4
Woorim Qld 599 H2, 600 F1, 602 H8
Woorinen Vic. 526 G9, 547 L12, 549 L2
Woorinen North Vic. 547 L12, 549 L1
Woornack Vic. 526 E9, 546 H11, 548 H1
Woorndoo Vic. 551 I5
Wooroloo WA 571 E4, 574 C4
Wooroolin Qld 603 A9, 609 L6, 420
Wooroonook Vic. 526 G12, 549 K7
Wooroonooran NP Qld 606 E4, 607 F10, 613 L7, 392, 427
Woosang Vic. 526 G12, 549 L7
Wootong Vale Vic. 550 E3
Wootton NSW 515 D10, 523 N2
Woowoonga NP Qld 603 B5, 604 E12, 609 M4
Worimi NP NSW 514 E8, 515 B12, 523 M4
Workington Island Qld 605 G5, 611 K3
Worongary Qld 601 D7
Woronora NSW 508 C10, 511 K11, 517 H1
Woroon NP Qld 603 A8, 609 L6
Worsley WA 572 F3
Worthington Island Qld 604 C6, 611 N12
Wowan Qld 604 A7, 611 L12
Woy Woy NSW 508 H1, 509 D8, 511 N3, 523 K6, **102**
Wrattens NP Qld 602 B1, 603 B10, 609 M6
Wrattonbully SA 548 B11, 550 B1, 568 G10, 251
Wreck Island Qld 604 F5, 611 P11
Wright Island SA 555 F9, 556 H10, 559 J11, 568 B5
Wrightley Vic. 542 H10, 544 D7
Wroxham Vic. 519 D11, 539 F9
Wubin WA 576 C5
Wudinna SA 558 D3, 560 B11, **265**
Wujal Wujal Qld 613 L4
Wuk Wuk Vic. 541 M5
Wulajarlu Island WA 581 J5, 584 E6
Wulalam Island WA 581 J5, 584 E7
Wulgulmerang Vic. 519 A10, 539 A7, 541 P1, 543 P12, 545 P11
Wundowie WA 571 F3
Wunghnu Vic. 527 K12, 542 E6, 544 A2, 193
Wunkar SA 559 N8, 568 F2
Wunmiyi Island NT 590 F2
Wurankuwu NT 590 C3
Wurauwulla Island WA 581 K3, 584 F3
Wurdiboluc Vic. 536 D9, 538 E2, 551 M8

Wutul Qld 609 L8
Wutunugurra NT 593 K11
Wuwirriya Island WA 581 K3, 584 G3
Wy Yung Vic. 541 M5
Wyalkatchem WA 574 E3, 576 D6
Wyalong NSW 522 B6, 527 P6
Wyan NSW 516 E6, 525 N4
Wyandra Qld 608 B7, 619 O7, 408
Wyangala NSW 522 F6
Wybalenna Tas. 624 A10
Wybalenna Island Tas. 624 A10
Wybong NSW 523 J2
Wycarbah Qld 604 A5, 611 L11
Wycheproof Vic. 526 G12, 549 K6, 203
Wychitella Vic. 526 G12, 549 L7
Wycliffe Well Roadhouse NT 593 J11, 595 J1, 369
Wye River Vic. 536 C11, 538 D5, 551 M10
Wyee NSW 509 E6, 514 B11, 523 L5
Wyee Point NSW 509 F5, 514 B11
Wyeebo Vic. 543 M7, 545 L4
Wyelangta Vic. 536 A11, 538 A5
Wyena Tas. 627 L6
Wyening WA 574 C3, 576 C6, 326
Wyer Islet Qld 614 G1
Wylie Creek NSW 516 B3, 525 L2, 609 L11
Wymah NSW 522 B12, 543 M6, 545 L2
Wymlet Vic. 526 D8, 546 G10
Wynarka SA 559 L10, 568 E3
Wynbring SA 567 M4
Wyndham NSW 519 D10, 539 G7
Wyndham WA 581 N4, 585 L5, **337**
Wynnum Qld 599 G7, 600 E4, 602 G11, 609 N9, 384
Wynyard Tas. 626 E5, **499**
Wyomi SA 568 E9
Wyoming NSW 509 D8, 511 O2, 515 D8, 523 N1, 525 K12
Wyong NSW 509 E7, 511 P1, 514 A12, 523 L5, **104**
Wyong Creek NSW 509 D6, 511 O1
Wyperfeld NP Vic. 526 C10, 546 E12, 548 E2, 559 P11, 568 H5, 168, 171
Wyrra NSW 522 B5, 527 P5
Wyrrabalong NP NSW 509 F7, 511 P3, 523 L5, 91
Wyuna Vic. 527 K12, 542 D6

Y

Y Island WA 575 C3
Yaamba Qld 604 B4, 611 M10
Yaapeet Vic. 526 D10, 548 F4
Yabba Vic. 543 L7, 545 K4
Yabba North Vic. 542 F6, 544 B2
Yabbra NP NSW 516 C3, 525 M2, 609 L11
Yabmana SA 556 A1, 558 F5
Yabooma Island NT 591 K3
Yacka SA 556 H1, 559 J5, 560 H12
Yackandandah Vic. 543 K7, 545 I4, 203
Yagoona NSW 508 C8, 509 A12
Yahl SA 550 A5, 568 G12
Yalangur Qld 609 L9
Yalata SA 567 I6
Yalata Roadhouse SA 567 I6
Yalboroo Qld 605 F6, 611 J5
Yalbraith NSW 519 E2, 522 H8

Yalgoo WA 575 F11, 576 C2, **337**
Yalgorup NP WA 571 B11, 572 D1, 574 B7, 576 C9, 319
Yallakool NSW 527 I10, 542 B2, 549 P3
Yallaroi NSW 524 H3, 609 I12
Yalleroi Qld 610 D11
Yallingup WA 572 A6, 574 B9, 576 B10, **338**
Yallourn North Vic. 540 H7
Yallunda Flat SA 558 D7
Yaloak Vale Vic. 535 F12, 536 F4, 551 N5
Yalwal NSW 517 B9, 519 G4, 521 N1, 523 I10
Yam Island Qld 614 D1
Yamala Qld 611 I11
Yamanto Qld 599 A9, 600 B6, 602 C12
Yamba NSW 516 F8, 525 O5, **104**
Yamba Roadhouse SA 526 B6, 546 B6, 559 O7, 568 G1
Yambacoona Tas. 625 O10
Yambuk Vic. 538 A7, 550 F8, 188
Yambuna Vic. 542 D5
Yammadery Island WA 575 D2, 582 B7
Yan Yean Vic. 531 E3, 537 J4, 540 D3
Yanac Vic. 526 C12, 548 D6
Yanac South Vic. 548 D6
Yanakie Vic. 540 G10
Yanchep WA 570 A1, 571 A2, 574 B4, 576 B7, **338**
Yanchep NP WA 570 B1, 571 B2, 574 B4, 576 B7, 284, 338
Yanco NSW 527 N8, 66
Yandaran Qld 603 C1, 604 F10, 609 M3
Yanderra NSW 517 D3, 519 G2, 523 J8
Yandeyarra WA 575 G1, 578 D3, 582 H6
Yandina Qld 602 F3, 603 E11, 609 N7, **450**
Yando Vic. 526 H12, 549 M6
Yandoit Vic. 535 E7, 549 N12, 551 N2, 161
Yanerbie Beach SA 558 A3, 567 N10
Yanga NP NSW 526 H6, 547 N7
Yangan Qld 516 B1, 525 L1, 609 L10
Yaninee SA 558 C3, 560 B10, 567 P10
Yanipy Vic. 526 B12, 548 C7, 568 H7
Yankalilla SA 555 D7, 556 G10, 559 J10, 568 B4, **267**
Yankakingarri Island WA 581 K2, 584 G2
Yantabulla NSW 529 K3, 619 M12
Yantanabie SA 558 B2, 567 O9
Yanununbeyan NP NSW 518 G8, 519 D5, 521 I4, 522 G11
Yapeen Vic. 535 E6, 549 N12, 551 N1
Yaraka Qld 619 L2
Yarck Vic. 542 F11, 544 A9
Yargara Island NT 591 M2
Yaringa Marine NP Vic. 531 F10, 533 M5, 537 K9, 540 D7
Yarloop WA 571 D12, 572 E1, 574 C7
Yaroomba Qld 602 G3, 603 F11

Yarra NSW 519 E3, 522 G9
Yarra Creek Tas. 625 P12
Yarra Glen Vic. 531 H4, 534 C6, 537 L4, 540 E4, **204**
Yarra Junction Vic. 534 E8, 537 M5, 540 F4
Yarra Ranges NP Vic. 534 E6, 537 N4, 540 F4, 544 C12, 198
Yarrabah Qld 606 E2, 607 G7
Yarrabandai NSW 522 C3
Yarrabin NSW 522 G2
Yarraby Vic. 526 G9, 547 K11, 549 K1
Yarragin NP NSW 524 D8
Yarragon Vic. 537 O9, 540 G7, 199
Yarrahapinni Wetlands NP NSW 515 G3, 525 M9
Yarralin NT 590 D12, 592 D3
Yarram Vic. 541 I9, **205**
Yarramalong NSW 509 D6
Yarraman NSW 524 G4
Yarraman Qld 603 A12, 609 L7, 433
Yarrambat Vic. 540 D3
Yarramony WA 571 G1
Yarrangobilly NSW 519 B5, 520 D5, 522 E11
Yarrangobilly Caves NSW 519 B6, 520 D5, 522 E12
Yarranya Island NT 591 N7
Yarrara Vic. 526 C6, 546 D7, 559 P8
Yarrawalla South Vic. 549 N7
Yarrawarrah NSW 508 C11, 511 J11, 517 H1
Yarrawonga Vic. 527 M12, 542 H5, 544 D1, **205**
Yarrawonga Park NSW 509 F5, 514 B11
Yarriabini NP NSW 515 G3, 525 M9
Yarrobil NP NSW 522 G1, 524 E12
Yarrock Vic. 526 B12, 548 C7, 568 H7
Yarroweyah Vic. 527 L12, 542 F4
Yarrowitch NSW 515 C5, 525 K10
Yarrowyck NSW 515 A1, 525 J8
Yarto Vic. 526 E10, 548 G2
Yarwun Qld 604 C7, 609 K1, 611 N12
Yass NSW 519 C3, 522 F9, **104**
Yatchaw Vic. 550 F5
Yatina SA 559 J3, 561 I11
Yatpool Vic. 526 E6, 546 G7
Yattalunga NSW 509 D8, 511 O3
Yatte Yattah NSW 519 G5, 521 N3, 523 I11
Yaugher Vic. 536 B10, 538 C3
Yea Vic. 534 D1, 537 L1, 540 E1, 542 E12, **205**
Yealering WA 574 F6, 576 D8
Yearinan NSW 524 E9
Yearinga Vic. 548 C7, 568 H7
Yednia Qld 602 B4, 603 C12, 609 M7
Yee To Wappah Island NT 591 M6
Yeelanna SA 558 D7
Yeerip Vic. 542 H6, 544 E3
Yelarbon Qld 525 I2, 609 J11
Yellangip Vic. 548 G6
Yellingbo Vic. 534 D8, 537 L6
Yellow Rock NSW 510 G6, 513 L9, 517 E6
Yellowdine WA 576 F6
Yelta SA 556 E3, 558 H6
Yelta Vic. 546 G5
Yelverton WA 572 B7

Yelverton NP WA 572 B7, 574 B9, 576 B10
Yenda NSW 527 M7
Yendon Vic. 535 D11, 536 D4, 551 M4
Yengo NP NSW 509 A5, 511 L1, 523 K4, 87, 102
Yennora NSW 511 J8
Yeo Yeo NSW 519 A2, 522 D8
Yeodene Vic. 536 B10, 538 C3, 551 L8
Yeoval NSW 522 F3
Yeppoon Qld 604 C4, 611 M10, **450**
Yerecoin WA 574 C2, 576 C6
Yering Vic. 531 H5, 534 C7, 537 L5, 540 E4
Yerong Creek NSW 522 B10, 527 O10, 543 L2
Yerranderie NSW 510 B11, 517 A1, 519 F1, 523 I7, 38
Yerrinbool NSW 517 D4, 519 G2, 523 I8
Yetholme NSW 522 H5
Yetman NSW 525 I3, 609 J12
Yeungroon Vic. 549 K8
Yilikukunyiyanga Islet NT 591 L8
Yimbun Qld 602 A6
Yin Barun Vic. 542 G9, 544 D6
Yinkanie SA 526 A6, 559 N7, 568 F1
Yinnar Vic. 537 P10, 540 H8
Yirrkala NT 591 N4
Yiundalla Island Qld 605 G5, 611 K3
Yolla Tas. 626 E5
Yongala SA 559 K3, 561 I11
Yoogali NSW 527 M7
Yoongarillup WA 572 C6, 574 B9
York WA 571 H4, 574 D4, 576 C7, **339**
York Islands WA 577 J9
York Plains Tas. 625 L3
York (Wamilug) Island Qld 614 D2
Yorke Valley SA 556 E5, 558 H7
Yorketown SA 556 E8, 558 H9, **267**
Yorkeys Knob Qld 606 E2, 607 F6
Yornaning WA 574 E6
Yoting WA 574 F4, 576 D7
Youanmite Vic. 527 L12, 542 F6, 544 B2
Youarang Vic. 542 G6, 544 C2
Youndegin WA 574 E4, 576 D7
Young NSW 519 B1, 522 E7, 105
Younghusband SA 559 L9, 568 D3
Yowah Qld 619 M8, 410
Yowrie NSW 519 E8, 521 J10, 539 H4
Yuelamu NT 594 G4
Yuendumu NT 594 F4
Yugar Qld 599 C5, 600 C3, 602 E10
Yulara NT 594 E10, 596 D9, **368**
Yulara Pulka NT 596 C9
Yuleba Qld 608 H6
Yulecart Vic. 550 E4
Yumali SA 559 L11, 568 E5
Yuna WA 575 D12, 576 A3
Yunderup WA 571 C9
Yundi SA 555 F6, 556 H9
Yundool Vic. 542 G6, 544 C3
Yungaburra Qld 606 D3, 607 E9, 613 L7, **451**
Yungaburra NP Qld 606 D3, 607 E9, 613 L7
Yungera Vic. 526 G8, 547 K9
Yunta SA 559 L2, 561 K10

Yuraygir NP NSW 516 F9, 525 N6, 54, 102, 104
Yurgo SA 559 M10, 568 F4
Yuroke Vic. 531 D3, 537 I4
Yuulong Vic. 538 H11, 551 J10

Z

Zagarsum (Tobin Island) Islet Qld 614 C1
Zanthus WA 577 J5
Zeehan Tas. 626 D10, **499**
Zeerust Vic. 542 E6, 544 A3
Zillmere Qld 599 E5, 600 D3, 602 F10
Zuna (Entrance) Island Qld 614 C2
Zurat (Phipps) Island Qld 614 C1

Acknowledgements

The publisher would like to acknowledge the following individuals and organisations:

Publications manager
Astrid Browne

Project manager
Melissa Krafchek

Editors
Janet Austin, Juliette Elfick, Elizabeth Watson, Emma Adams, Melissa Krafchek, Tracy O'Shaughnessy, Stephanie Pearson, Louise McGregor, Nicola Redhouse, Alison Proietto

Writers and researchers
Carolyn Tate, Ruth Ward, Jill Varley, Nick Dent, Frances Bruce, Alexandra Payne, Natasha Rudra, Kirsten Lawson, Rachel Pitts, Melissa Krafchek, Michelle Bennett, Heidi Marfurt, Karina Biggs, Antonia Semler, Paul Harding, Tricia Welsh, Terry Plane, Ingrid Ohlsson, Peter Dyson, Janice Finlayson, Quentin Chester, Carmen Jenner, David Hancock, Gillian Hutchison, Helen Duffy, Pamela Robson, Rowan Roebig, Lee Mylne, Jane E. Fraser, Liz Johnston, Emma Schwarcz, Anthony Roberts, Emily Hewitt, Eddie Pavuna, Ken Eastwood, Margaret Wade, Emma Adams, Jenny Turner, Heather Pearson, Sue Moffitt, Emily Lush, Sue Medlock, Chad Parkhill

Design
Erika Budiman

Layout
Megan Ellis

Cartographers
Bruce McGurty, Paul de Leur, Emily Maffei, Claire Johnston

Index
Max McMaster

Photo selection
Melissa Krafchek, Alison Proietto

Pre-press
PageSet Digital Print & Pre-press, Megan Ellis

Explore Australia Publishing Pty Ltd
Ground Floor, Building 1, 658 Church Street, Richmond, VIC 3121

Explore Australia Publishing Pty Ltd is a division of Hardie Grant Publishing Pty Ltd

hardie grant publishing

This thirty-first edition published by Explore Australia Publishing Pty Ltd, 2012

First published by George Phillip & O'Neil Pty Ltd, 1980
Second edition 1981
Third edition 1983
Reprinted 1984
Fourth edition 1985
Fifth edition 1986
Sixth edition published by Penguin Books Australia Ltd, 1987
Seventh edition 1988
Eighth edition 1989
Ninth edition 1990
Tenth edition 1991
Eleventh edition 1992
Twelfth edition 1993
Thirteenth edition 1994
Fourteenth edition 1995
Fifteenth edition 1996
Sixteenth edition 1997
Seventeenth edition 1998
Eighteenth edition 1999
Nineteenth edition 2000
Twentieth edition 2001
Twenty-first edition 2002
Twenty-second edition published by Explore Australia Publishing Pty Ltd, 2003
Twenty-third edition 2004
Twenty-fourth edition 2005
Twenty-fifth edition 2006
Twenty-sixth edition 2007
Twenty-seventh edition 2008
Twenty-eighth edition 2009
Twenty-ninth edition 2010
Thirtieth edition 2011

Copyright © Explore Australia Publishing Pty Ltd, 2012

The maps in this publication incorporate data copyright © Commonwealth of Australia (Geoscience Australia), 2006. Geoscience Australia has not evaluated the data as altered and incorporated within this publication, and therefore gives no warranty regarding accuracy, completeness, currency or suitability for any particular purpose.

Copyright Imprint and currency – VAR Product and PSMA Data

"Copyright. Based on data provided under licence from PSMA Australia Limited (www.psma.com.au)".

Hydrography Data (May 2006)
Parks & Reserves Data (May 2006)
Transport Data (November 2011)

Disclaimer
While every care is taken to ensure the accuracy of the data within this product, the owners of the data (including the state, territory and Commonwealth governments of Australia) do not make any representations or warranties about its accuracy, reliability, completeness or suitability for any particular purpose and, to the extent permitted by law, the owners of the data disclaim all responsibility and all liability (including without limitation, liability in negligence) for all expenses, losses, damages, (including indirect or consequential damages) and costs which might be incurred as a result of the data being inaccurate or incomplete in any way and for any reason.

Maps contain Aboriginal Land data (2010), which is owned and copyright of the relevant Queensland, Northern Territory, South Australia and Western Australia state government authorities. The authorities give no warranty in relation to the data (including accuracy, reliability, completeness or suitability) and accept no liability (including without limitation, liability in negligence) for any loss, damage or costs (including consequential damage) relating to any use of the data.

ISBN 9781741173789

10 9 8 7 6 5 4 3 2 1

All rights reserved. Without limiting the rights under copyright reserved above, no part of this publication may be reproduced, stored in or introduced into a retrieval system, or transmitted in any form or by any means (electronic, mechanical, photocopying, recording or otherwise) without the prior written permission of both the copyright owner and the above publisher of this book.

Printed and bound in China by 1010 Printing International Ltd

Publisher's Note: Every effort has been made to ensure that the information in this book is accurate at the time of going to press. The publisher welcomes information and suggestions for correction or improvement. Write to the Publications Manager, Explore Australia Publishing, Ground Floor, Building 1, 658 Church Street, Richmond, VIC 3121, Australia, or email info@exploreaustralia.net.au

Disclaimers: The publisher cannot accept responsibility for any errors or omissions. The representation on the maps of any road or track is not necessarily evidence of public right of way or safe travelling conditions.

Accommodation listings have been sourced from AAA Tourism. Email info@aaatourism.com.au for queries or updates.

www.exploreaustralia.net.au
Follow us on Twitter: @ExploreAus
Find us on Facebook: www.facebook.com/exploreaustralia

Assistance with research

The publisher would like to thank the following organisations for assistance with data and information:

Australian Bureau of Statistics
Bureau of Meteorology
National Road Transport Commission
Tristate Fruit Fly Committee

New South Wales
Roads and Traffic Authority
NSW Department of Environment Climate Change and Water
Destination New South Wales

Australian Capital Territory
ACT Planning and Land Authority
Australian Capital Tourism Corporation

Victoria
VicRoads
Department of Sustainability and Environment, Victoria
Tourism Victoria

South Australia
Transport SA
Primary Industries and Resources South Australia
Department of Environment and Natural Resources
South Australian Tourism Commission

Western Australia
Main Roads Western Australia
Department of Indigenous Affairs Western Australia
Aboriginal Lands Trust
Department of Environment and Conservation
Western Australia Tourism Commission

Northern Territory
Department of Transport and Infrastructure
Northern and Central land councils
Department of Natural Resources, Environment, The Arts and Sport
Parks Australia
Northern Territory Tourist Commission

Queensland
Department of Main Roads
Department of Environment & Resource Management
Queensland Parks & Wildlife Service
Tourism Queensland

Tasmania
Department of Infrastructure, Energy & Resources
Parks and Wildlife Service
Tourism Tasmania

Photography credits

Cover
All images sourced from Shutterstock.com and ©iStockphoto.com

Front endpaper
Lush Australian rainforest (leungchopan/Shutterstock.com)

Title page
Devils Marbles (Karlu Karlu), Devils Marbles Conservation Reserve, Northern Territory (Martin Horsky/Shutterstock.com)

Contents
Heart Reef, Great Barrier Reef, Queensland (deb22/Shutterstock.com)

Other images (left to right, top to bottom where more than one image appears on a page):
Pages iv–v (a) TNT (b) Joe Shemesh/Port Arthur Historic Site Management Authority (c) Darren Jew/TQ (d) TV (e) © photolibrary. All rights reserved; vi–vii (a) Francisco Pelsaert or Jan Jansz from The Voyage of the *Batavia*/Wikimedia Commons (b) Ignaz Sebastian Klauber/NLA (c) Samuel Thomas Gill/NLA (d) Nicholas Chevalier/NLA (e) John Meredith/NLA (f) TV (g) John Flynn/NLA (h) NLA (i) DNSW; viii–1 Regis Martin/LPI; 2 JD; 3 (a) CK (b) ©iStockphoto.com/titelio; 4–5 Michelangelo Gratton/Digital Vision/GI; 9 courtesy DNSW; 10 Richard Cummins/LPI; 13 Richard Cummins/LPI; 15 Jean-Paul Ferrero/AUS; 16 Andrew Watson/LPI; 22 (a)–(c) courtesy DNSW (d) JB/EAP (e) & (f) courtesy DNSW (g) ©iStockphoto.com/timstarkey; 23 (a) courtesy DNSW (b) ©iStockphoto.com/eeqmcc (c) EAP (d)–(e) courtesy DNSW; (f) NR/EAP (g) NR/courtesy DNSW; 24 Andrew Bain/LPI; 29 AS; 33 Brett Gregory/AUS; 37 JLR/AUS; 39 Andrew Gregory; 42 JD; 45 JB; 48 Wayne Lawler/AUS; 61 Suzanne Long/AUS; 64 Dallas & John Heaton/AUS; 78 tigheshillphotography.com/Flickr/GI; 82 Dr Seth Shostak/Science Photo Library/GI; 84 JB; 88 CC/Photolibrary/GI; 93 courtesy of Thredbo Media; 94 Ross Dunstan/AusGeo; 99 RL/LPI; 103 Dee Kramer; 106–107 & 108–109 RLA/LPI; 111 AC; 113 (a) BP (b) Steve Keough, Australian Capital Tourism; 115 Simon Foale/LPI; 116 RLA/LPI; 120–121 Cheryl Forbes/LPI; 122 AusGeo; 123 (a) AC (b) ©iStockphoto.com/Kolbz; 124–125 RL/LPI; 129 Glenn Beanland/LPI; 130 John Sones/LPI; 131 Tom Cockrem/Age Fotostock/GI; 133 Bill Belson/LT; 135 JBAN/Photographer's Choice RF/GI; 140 (a) Jon Nash/TV (b) Robert Blackburn/TV (c)–(d) TV (e) Dropu/Shutterstock.com (f) James Lauritz/TV; 141 (a) Robert Blackburn/TV (b) ©iStockphoto.com/photosbyash (c) Gavin Hansford/TV (d) TV (e) Gary Lewis/EAP (f) David Hannah/TV; 142 Andrew Bain/LPI; 148 Holger Leue/LPI; 150 JD; 153 JLR/AUS; 158 Chris Mellor/LPI; 161 Simon Griffiths; 166 Jon Barter/AUS; 169 AusGeo; 174 JBAN/LPI; 176 PWP/Photolibrary/GI; 180 AC; 182 CC/Photolibrary/GI; 187 GD/LPI; 191 OS/LPI; 195 AS; 197 Patrick Horton/LPI; 200 D. Parer & E. Parer-Cook/AUS; 204 Chris Putnam/OzStock Images Pty Ltd; 206–207 Ross Barnett/LPI; 208 JD; 209 (a) JL/LT (b) ©iStockphoto.com/Wilshire Images (c) ©iStockphoto.com/alicat; 210–211 Shannon Rogers/Flickr/GI; 213 & 215 SATC; 216 David Messent/Photolibrary/GI; 218 SATC; 222 (a) SATC (b) ©iStockphoto.com/travellinglight (c) Ian Woolcock/Shutterstock.com (d) SATC; 223 (a)–(d) SATC (e) Michael Major/Shutterstock.com; 224 Shayne Hill/LPI; 227 PWP/Photolibrary/GI; 231 Diana Mayfield/LPI; 233 RL; 238 AusGeo; 242 GD; 245 Julie Fletcher/Flickr/GI; 250 SATC; 253 JB; 256 NR; 258 JLR/AUS; 263 City of Victor Harbor; 266 Jocelyn Burt, OzStock Images Pty Ltd; 268–269 Manfred Gottschalk/LPI; 270 JL/LT; 271 (a) CK (b) courtesy of Cape Mentelle; 272–273 CC/Photolibrary/GI; 276 Louise Heusinkveld/Photolibrary/GI; 281 RLA/LPI; 286 (a) ©iStockphoto.com/CUHRIG (b) GMH/EAP (c) Mark Ditcham/Shutterstock.com (d) ©iStockphoto.com/GordonBellPhotography (e) JB/EAP; 287 (a) NR/EAP (b) DS/LT (c) ©iStockphoto.com/PaulMorton (d) Janelle Lugge/Shutterstock.com; 288 Peter Ptschelinzew/LPI; 290 JL/LT; 294 JD; 297 DS/LT; 298 AS; 302 Kerry Lorimer/LPI; 306 Steven David Miller/AUS; 309 NR/AusGeo; 313 CC/Photolibrary/GI; 316 John Clutterbuck/Digital Vision/GI; 322 courtesy of Margaret River Visitor Centre; 327 CC/Photolibrary/GI; 331 Fred Kamphues/AUS; 334 Paul Kennedy/LPI; 336 Andrew Watson/Photolibrary/GI; 340–341 JBAN/LPI; 342 Geoff Murray; 343 AusGeo; 344–345 John Borthwick/LPI; 349 TNT; 350 David Wall/LPI; 351 Andrew Watson/LPI; 354 (a) & (b) TNT (c) GMH/EAP (d) TNT; 355 TNT; 356 JBAN/LPI; 359 Davo Blair/AUS; 362 TNT; 364 Stuart Grant; 366 RLA/LPI; 368 AS; 370–371 RLA/LPI; 372 AS; 373 (a) BP (b) TQ; 374–375 Manfred Gottschalk/LPI; 379 TQ; 380 OS/LPI; 382 JB; 384 Christopher Groenhout/LPI; 388 (a)–(e) TQ; 389 (a) TQ (b) ©iStockphoto.com/holgs (c)–(f)TQ; 390 Bob Halstead/LPI; 394 NR/AusGeo; 398 BP; 402 TQ; 405 Sara-Jane Cleland/LPI; 409 JM; 413 TQ; 416 John Carnemolla/AUS; 419 PWP/Photolibrary/GI; 423 TQ; 424 AS; 429 Cathy Finch/LPI; 433 TQ; 436 Rose Price/OzStock Images Pty Ltd; 444 John Fisher/OzStock Images Pty Ltd; 447 TQ; 448 NR; 451 David Wall/LPI; 452–453 RB/LPI; 454 JM; 455 (a) Len Stewart/LT (b) Sue Medlock; 456–457 RLA/LPI; 461 Nick Osborne/TT; 462 Tara Downey/TT; 468 (a) Glenn Gibson/TT (b) Nick Osborne/TT (c) ©iStockphoto.com/keiichihiki (d) Glenn Gibson/TT (e) George Apostolidis/TT; 469 GD/LPI; 470 RB/LPI; 472 JB; 477 Michael Walters Photography/TT; 482 OS/LPI; 484 JB; 487 GD/LPI; 489 AusGeo; 493 Stuart Crossett/TT; 495 courtesy of Stanley Information Centre; 496 David Messent/Photolibrary/GI

Abbreviations

AC Andrew Chapman
AS Australian Scenics
AUS Auscape International
AusGeo Australian Geographic
BP Bruce Postle
CC Claver Carroll
CK Colin Kerr
DNSW Destination New South Wales
DS Dennis Sarson
EAP Explore Australia Publishing
GD Grant Dixon
GI Getty Images
GMH Graeme & Margaret Herald
JB John Baker
JBAN John Banagan
JD Jeff Drewitz
JL Jiri Lochman
JM John Meier
JLR Jean-Marc La Roque
LPI Lonely Planet Images
LT Lochman Transparencies
NLA National Library of Australia
NR Nick Rains
OS Oliver Strewe
PWP Peter Walton Photography
RB Rob Blakers
RL Rachel Lewis
RLA Richard l'Anson
SATC South Australian Tourism Commission
TNT Tourism NT
TQ Tourism Queensland
TT Tourism Tasmania
TV Tourism Victoria

USEFUL INFORMATION

STATE TOURIST BUREAUS

New South Wales
Sydney Visitor Centres
Level 1, cnr Argyle and Playfair sts,
The Rocks
(02) 9240 8788 or 1800 067 676

33 Wheat Rd, Darling Harbour
(02) 9240 8788; 1800 067 676
www.sydneyvisitorcentre.com

Canberra
Canberra and Region Visitors Centre
330 Northbourne Ave, Dickson
(02) 6205 0044 or 1300 554 114
www.visitcanberra.com.au

Victoria
Melbourne Visitor Centre
Federation Square,
Cnr Flinders and Swanston sts,
Melbourne
(03) 9658 9658
www.visitmelbourne.com

South Australia
South Australia Visitor and Travel
Centre
18–20 Grenfell St, Adelaide
1300 764 227
www.southaustralia.com

Western Australia
Western Australian Visitor Centre
Cnr Forrest Pl and Wellington St,
Perth
1300 361 351 or 1800 812 808
www.bestofwa.com.au

Northern Territory
Tourism Top End
6 Bennett St, Darwin
(08) 8980 6000 or 1300 138 886
www.tourismtopend.com.au

Queensland
Brisbane Visitor Information &
Booking Centre
Queen Street Mall, Brisbane
(07) 3006 6290
www.visitbrisbane.com.au

Tasmania
Tasmanian Travel and Information
Centre
Cnr Davey and Elizabeth sts, Hobart
1800 990 440
www.discovertasmania.com.au
www.hobarttravelcentre.com.au

MOTORING ORGANISATIONS

Roadside assistance is one of the
most valued services of Australia's
state-based motoring organisations.
The countrywide network of these
organisations gives members access
to virtually the same services in every
state and territory.

Roadside assistance (countrywide)
13 1111

New South Wales
National Roads and Motorists'
Association (NRMA)
13 1122
www.mynrma.com.au

Australian Capital Territory
National Roads and Motorists'
Association (NRMA)
13 1122
www.mynrma.com.au

Victoria
Royal Automobile Club of Victoria
(RACV)
13 1329
www.racv.com.au

South Australia
Royal Automobile Association (RAA)
(08) 8202 4600
www.raa.com.au

Western Australia
Royal Automobile Club of Western
Australia (RACWA)
13 1703
www.rac.com.au

Northern Territory
Automobile Association of the
Northern Territory (AANT)
(08) 8925 5901
www.aant.com.au

Queensland
Royal Automobile Club of
Queensland (RACQ)
13 1905
www.racq.com.au

Tasmania
Royal Automobile Club of Tasmania
(RACT)
13 2722
www.ract.com.au

For Motorcyclists
Motorcycle Riders Association
Australia
www.mraa.org.au

ROADS AND TRAFFIC AUTHORITIES

For licensing and registration,
information on vehicle standards,
and road condition reports.

New South Wales
Roads & Maritime Services
101 Miller St, North Sydney
13 2213
www.rta.nsw.gov.au

Australian Capital Territory
Road Transport Authority
Dickson Motor Registry
13–15 Challis St, Dickson
13 2281
www.rego.act.gov.au

Victoria
VicRoads Customer Service Centre
459 Lygon St, Carlton
13 1171
www.vicroads.vic.gov.au

South Australia
Service SA
EDS Centre
108 North Tce, Adelaide
13 1084
www.sa.gov.au

Western Australia
Main Roads Western Australia
Don Aitkin Centre
Waterloo Cres, East Perth
13 8138
www.mainroads.wa.gov.au

Northern Territory
Northern Territory Transport Group
Motor Vehicle Registry Parap
18 Goyder Rd, Parap
1300 654 628
www.transport.nt.gov.au

Queensland
Transport and Main Roads
229 Elizabeth St, Brisbane
13 2380
www.tmr.qld.gov.au

Tasmania
Transport Division
Department of Infrastructure, Energy
& Resources
10 Murray St, Hobart
1300 135 513
www.transport.tas.gov.au

ACCOMMODATION

General
State-based motoring organisations
are a good point of contact for
information on accommodation in
motels, apartments and caravan
parks. All share a comprehensive
accommodation database that can
be accessed from their websites (see
listings on this page).

Caravan Parks
Top Tourist Parks
(08) 8363 1901
www.toptouristparks.com.au

BIG4 Holiday Parks
1300 738 044
www.big4.com.au

Family Parks
1300 855 707
www.familyparks.com.au

Bed and Breakfasts
Bed and Breakfast Australia
www.bedandbreakfast.com.au

Backpackers
VIP Backpackers Lounge
(02) 9211 0766
www.vipbackpackers.com

YHA Australia
www.yha.com.au

EMERGENCY

**DIAL 000 FOR POLICE,
AMBULANCE & FIRE BRIGADE**

Approximate Distances AUSTRALIA

	Adelaide	Albany	Albury	Alice Springs	Ayers Rock/Yulara	Bairnsdale	Ballarat	Bathurst	Bega	Bendigo	Bordertown	Bourke	Brisbane	Broken Hill	Broome	Bunbury	Cairns	Canberra	Carnarvon	Ceduna	Charleville	Coober Pedy	Darwin	Dubbo	Esperance	Eucla	Geelong	Geraldton
Adelaide		2662	965	1537	1578	1010	625	1198	1338	640	274	1129	2048	514	4268	2887	3207	1197	3568	772	1582	847	3026	1194	2183	1267	711	3086
Albany	2662		3487	3585	3626	3672	3287	3720	4000	3302	2936	3388	4310	2773	2626	335	5466	3719	1300	1890	3841	2895	4428	3526	479	1395	3373	818
Albury	965	3487		2362	2403	336	412	466	427	313	679	779	1407	865	5093	3712	2764	348	4393	1597	1232	1672	3851	553	3008	2092	382	3911
Alice Springs	1537	3585	2362		443	2547	2162	2595	2875	2177	1811	2263	2979	1648	2731	3810	2376	2594	4114	1695	2320	690	1489	2401	3106	2190	2248	4009
Ayers Rock/Yulara	1578	3626	2403	443		2588	2203	2636	2916	2218	1852	2304	3226	1689	3174	3851	2819	2635	4532	1736	2763	731	1932	2442	3147	2231	2289	4050
Bairnsdale	1010	3672	336	2547	2588		388	802	328	423	736	1115	1743	1119	5278	3897	3100	455	4578	1782	1568	1857	4036	863	3193	2277	349	4096
Ballarat	625	3287	412	2162	2203	388		878	716	124	351	996	1747	754	4893	3512	3104	760	4193	1397	1449	1472	3651	893	2808	1892	86	3711
Bathurst	1198	3720	466	2595	2636	802	878		531	779	1180	569	1000	958	5011	3945	2416	309	4626	1830	1022	1905	3769	205	3241	2325	848	4144
Bega	1338	4000	427	2875	2916	328	716	531		751	1064	994	1399	1447	5436	4225	2910	222	4906	2110	1447	2185	4364	630	3521	2605	677	4424
Bendigo	640	3302	313	2177	2218	423	124	779	751		366	872	1623	696	4908	3527	2980	661	4208	1412	1325	1487	3666	769	2823	1907	210	3726
Bordertown	274	2936	679	1811	1852	736	351	1180	1064	366		1138	1922	788	4542	3161	3257	1071	3842	1046	1591	1121	3300	1068	2457	1541	437	3360
Bourke	1129	3388	779	2263	2304	1115	996	569	994	872	1138		922	615	4442	3613	2078	772	4294	1498	453	1573	3200	364	2909	1993	1082	3812
Brisbane	2048	4310	1407	2979	3226	1743	1747	1000	1399	1623	1922	922		1537	4648	4535	1703	1241	5216	2420	742	2495	3406	854	3831	2915	1745	4734
Broken Hill	514	2773	865	1648	1689	1119	754	958	1447	696	788	615	1537		4379	2998	2693	1097	3679	883	1068	958	3137	753	2294	1378	840	3197
Broome	4268	2626	5093	2731	3174	5278	4893	5011	5436	4908	4542	4442	4648	4379		2417	4045	5214	1451	3750	3989	3421	1870	4806	2745	3255	4979	1921
Bunbury	2887	335	3712	3810	3851	3897	3512	3945	4225	3527	3161	3613	4535	2998	2417		5691	3944	1091	2115	4066	3120	4219	3751	664	1620	3598	609
Cairns	3207	5466	2764	2376	2819	3100	3104	2416	2910	2980	3257	2078	1703	2693	4045	5691		2619	5428	3576	1625	3066	2803	2211	4987	4071	3102	5890
Canberra	1197	3719	348	2594	2635	455	760	309	222	661	1071	772	1241	1097	5214	3944	2619		4625	1829	1225	1904	3972	408	3240	2324	730	4143
Carnarvon	3568	1300	4393	4114	4532	4578	4193	4626	4906	4208	3842	4294	5216	3679	1451	1091	5428	4625		2796	4747	3801	3253	4432	1628	2301	4279	482
Ceduna	772	1890	1597	1695	1736	1782	1397	1830	2110	1412	1046	1498	2420	883	3750	2115	3576	1829	2796		1951	1005	3184	1636	1411	495	1483	2314
Charleville	1582	3841	1232	2320	2763	1568	1449	1022	1447	1325	1591	453	742	1068	3989	4066	1625	1225	4747	1951		2026	2747	817	3362	2446	1500	4265
Coober Pedy	847	2895	1672	690	731	1857	1472	1905	2185	1487	1121	1573	2495	958	3421	3120	3066	1904	3801	1005	2026		2179	1711	2416	1500	1558	3319
Darwin	3026	4428	3851	1489	1932	4036	3651	3769	4364	3666	3300	3200	3406	3137	1870	4219	2803	3972	3253	3184	2747	2179		3564	4547	3679	3737	3723
Dubbo	1194	3526	553	2401	2442	863	893	205	630	769	1068	364	854	753	4806	3751	2211	408	4432	1636	817	1711	3564		3047	2131	891	3950
Esperance	2183	479	3008	3106	3147	3193	2808	3241	3521	2823	2457	2909	3831	2294	2745	664	4987	3240	1628	1411	3362	2416	4547	3047		916	2894	1160
Eucla	1267	1395	2092	2190	2231	2277	1892	2325	2605	1907	1541	1993	2915	1378	3255	1620	4071	2324	2301	495	2446	1500	3679	2131	916		1978	1819
Geelong	711	3373	382	2248	2289	349	86	848	677	210	437	1082	1745	840	4979	3598	3102	730	4279	1483	1500	1558	3737	891	2894	1978		3797
Geraldton	3086	818	3911	4009	4050	4096	3711	4144	4424	3726	3360	3812	4734	3197	1921	609	5890	4143	482	2314	4265	3319	3723	3950	1160	1819	3797	
Grafton	1845	4177	1184	3052	3093	1397	1544	825	1069	1420	1719	808	330	1404	4975	4402	2033	911	5083	2287	1069	2362	3733	651	3698	2782	1542	4601
Horsham	433	3095	531	1970	2011	577	192	997	905	218	159	1067	1841	599	4701	3320	3145	879	4001	1205	1520	1280	3459	987	2616	1700	278	3519
Kalgoorlie–Boulder	2184	886	3009	3107	3148	3194	2809	3242	3522	2824	2458	2910	3832	2295	2338	779	4988	3241	1460	1412	3363	2417	4140	3048	407	917	2895	978
Katherine	2712	4114	3537	1175	1618	3722	3337	3455	3880	3352	2986	2886	3092	2823	1556	3905	2489	3658	2939	2870	2433	1865	314	3250	4233	3365	3423	3409
Kununurra	3224	3602	4049	1687	2130	4234	3849	3967	4392	3864	3498	3398	3604	3335	1044	3393	3001	4170	2427	3382	2945	2377	826	3762	3721	3877	3935	2897
Longreach	2098	4357	1748	1804	2247	2084	1965	1538	1963	1841	2107	969	1175	1584	3473	4582	1109	1741	4856	2467	516	2494	2231	1333	3878	2962	2016	4781
Mackay	2670	4932	2029	2451	2894	2365	2369	1681	2106	2245	2544	1544	968	2159	4120	5157	735	1884	5503	3042	1091	3141	2878	1476	4453	3537	2367	5356
Meekatharra	3055	1159	3880	3978	4019	4065	3680	4113	4393	3695	3329	3781	4703	3166	1467	950	5444	4112	627	2283	4234	3288	3269	3919	1278	1788	3766	541
Melbourne	733	3395	313	2270	2311	277	111	779	605	146	459	978	1676	842	5001	3620	3033	661	4301	1505	1431	1580	3759	822	2916	2000	72	3819
Mildura	394	2916	571	1791	1832	825	460	804	956	402	417	870	1654	294	4522	3141	2948	803	3822	1026	1323	1101	3280	800	2437	1521	546	3340
Moree	1567	3829	926	2704	2745	1262	1294	578	1003	1141	1482	441	481	1056	4608	4054	1838	781	4735	1939	702	2014	3366	373	3350	2434	1264	4253
Mount Gambier	452	3114	721	1989	2030	697	309	1187	1025	433	186	1324	2098	856	4720	3339	3402	1069	4020	1224	1777	1299	3478	1244	2635	1719	365	3538
Mount Isa	2706	4754	2383	1169	1612	2719	2600	2173	2598	2476	2742	1604	1810	2219	2838	4979	1207	2736	4221	2864	1151	1859	1596	1968	4275	3359	2651	4691
Newcastle	1553	3930	704	2805	2846	917	1116	338	589	1017	1427	768	821	1157	5111	4155	2341	431	4836	2040	1205	2115	3869	404	3451	2535	1086	4354
Perth	2700	410	3525	3623	3664	3710	3325	3758	4038	3340	2974	3426	4348	2811	2230	187	5504	3757	904	1928	3879	2933	4032	3564	738	1433	3411	422
Port Augusta	307	2355	1132	1230	1271	1317	932	1365	1645	947	581	1033	1955	418	3961	2580	3111	1364	3261	465	1486	540	2719	1171	1876	960	1018	2779
Port Hedland	3921	2025	4746	3264	3707	5100	4546	4979	5259	4561	4195	4647	5181	4032	601	1816	4578	4978	850	3149	4522	3954	2403	4785	2144	2654	4632	1320
Port Lincoln	647	2289	1472	1570	1611	1657	1272	1705	1985	1287	921	1373	2295	758	4149	2514	3451	1704	3195	399	1826	880	3059	1511	1751	894	1358	2713
Port Macquarie	1804	4136	942	3011	3052	1155	1354	565	827	1255	1665	859	584	1363	5150	4361	2287	669	5042	2246	1244	2321	3908	610	3657	2741	1324	4560
Renmark	250	2772	715	1647	1688	969	604	948	1100	546	269	1014	1798	438	4378	2997	3092	947	3678	882	1467	957	3136	944	2293	1377	690	3196
Rockhampton	2336	4598	1695	2486	2929	2031	2035	1347	1772	1911	2210	1210	634	1825	4155	4823	1069	1550	5504	2708	831	3176	2913	1142	4119	3203	2033	5022
Sydney	1414	3936	565	2811	2852	759	977	211	431	878	1288	780	966	1169	5222	4161	2479	292	4842	2046	1233	2121	3980	416	3457	2541	947	4360
Tamworth	1534	3866	893	2741	2782	1186	1233	457	858	1109	1408	589	573	1093	4880	4091	2110	700	4772	1965	974	2051	3638	340	3387	2471	1231	4290
Tennant Creek	2043	4091	2868	531	949	3053	2668	2836	3261	2683	2317	2267	2473	2154	2225	4316	1870	3039	3608	2201	1814	1196	983	2631	3612	2696	2754	4078
Toowoomba	1921	4183	1280	2852	3099	1616	1620	956	1357	1496	1795	795	127	1410	4521	4408	1705	1199	5089	2293	615	2368	3279	727	3704	2788	1618	4607
Townsville	2862	5121	2419	2061	2504	2755	2759	2071	2496	2635	2871	1733	1358	2348	3730	5346	345	2274	5113	3231	1280	2751	2488	1866	4642	3726	2757	5545
Wagga Wagga	948	3470	145	2345	2386	481	550	321	402	426	822	711	1262	848	5076	3695	2619	249	4376	1580	1164	1655	3834	408	2991	2075	527	3894
Warrnambool	649	3311	567	2186	2227	534	174	1052	862	298	383	1170	1933	829	4917	3536	3278	987	4217	1421	1623	1496	3675	1067	2832	1916	185	3735

Distances on this chart have been calculated over main roads and do not necessarily reflect the shortest route between towns.
Refer to page 630 for distance chart of Tasmania.